The ARRL Handbook for Radio Amateurs

Published by the
AMERICAN RADIO RELAY LEAGUE
Newington, CT 06111 USA

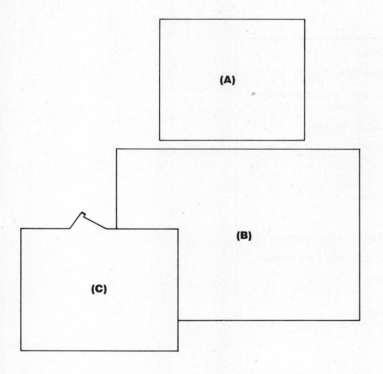

Cover photos

A—NU0X in contest mode.

B—WS1O discovers the ideal way to do tower work—with feet firmly planted on a hard surface (in this case the roof of the ARRL HQ building). *(photo by Kirk Kleinschmidt, NT0Z)*

C—A low-power transceiver for all seasons (and three bands). KH6CP designed it to be both useful and easy to build—all parts fit on one circuit board. For those who prefer to work from a kit, one is available. Details are in the HF Radio Equipment chapter.

Editors

Charles L. Hutchinson, K8CH
Joel P. Kleinman, N1BKE

Assistant Editors

Robert Schetgen, KU7G
Jim Kearman, KR1S
Gerald L. Hall, K1TD
Jon Bloom, KE3Z

Production

Deb Strzeszkowski
Joe Shea
Dianna Roy
David Pingree
Steffie Nelson, KA1IFB
Jodi Morin, KA1JPA
Seth Green
Sue Fagan, Cover
Michelle Chrisjohn, WB1ENT

Contributors

Gary Breed, K9AY
Rick Campbell, KK7B
Mike Crisler, N4IFD
Doug DeMaw, W1FB
Eric Grabowski, WA8HEB
John Grebenkemper, KI6WX
Roger Hayward, KA7EXM
Wes Hayward, W7ZOI
Dick Jansson, WD4FAB
Zack Lau, KH6CP
Roy Lewallen, W7EL
Paul Newland, AD7I
Bill Olson, W3HQT
Wayne Overbeck, N6NB
Steve Powlishen, K1FO
John J. Reh, K7KGP
Jeff Russell, KC0Q
Bud Southard, N0II
Dick Stevens, W1QWJ
Bob Zavrel, W7SX

1992
Sixty-Ninth Edition

Foreword

This 1992 edition of *The ARRL Handbook* represents the work of many people, some of whom are listed on the title page. The authors and editors have added informative theory discussions as well as practical projects, and have updated the reference sections, making the book even more valuable to all hams (regardless of areas of interest), technicians and engineers.

The complete list of new and revised items in this year's *Handbook* is too long to publish here, but they include:

- new material on radioteletype and AMTOR
- new material on operational amplifiers
- new material on the biological effects of RF energy
- 1500-W HF linear amplifier using inexpensive 3-500Z tubes
- an HF noise bridge
- VHF/UHF ¼-wavelength mobile and ground-plane antennas
- a portable CW transceiver for 20 and 30 meters
- a transverter and power amplifier for 23 cm
- updated parts-supplier, copper wire and lamp tables

This is the 69th edition of *The ARRL Handbook*. We'd like to think it's the best ever. You can help us make future editions even more useful by providing your comments and suggestions on the Feedback Form at the back of the book.

David Sumner, K1ZZ
Executive Vice President

Newington, Connecticut
October 1991

Contents

Schematic Symbols Used in Circuit Diagrams
U.S. Customary—Metric Conversion Factors
The Amateur's Code

INTRODUCTION
1 Amateur Radio
2 Electrical Fundamentals
3 Radio Design Technique and Language
4 Solid-State Basics
5 Vacuum-Tube Principles

RADIO PRINCIPLES
6 Power Supplies
7 Audio and Video
8 Digital Basics
9 Modulation and Demodulation
10 Radio-Frequency Oscillators and Synthesizers
11 Radio Transmitting Principles
12 Radio Receiving Principles
13 Radio Transceivers
14 Repeaters
15 RF Power Amplifiers
16 Transmission Lines
17 Antenna Fundamentals

MODULATION METHODS
18 Voice Communications
19 Digital Communications
20 Image Communications
21 Special Modulation Techniques

TRANSMISSION
22 Radio Frequencies and Propagation
23 Space Communications

CONSTRUCTION and MAINTENANCE
24 Construction Techniques
25 Test Equipment and Measurements
26 Troubleshooting and Repair
27 Power Supply Projects
28 Audio and Video Equipment
29 Digital Equipment
30 HF Radio Equipment
31 VHF Radio Equipment
32 UHF and Microwave Equipment
33 Antenna Projects
34 Station Accessories
35 Component Data

ON THE AIR
36 Assembling a Station
37 Operating Aids
38 Monitoring and Direction Finding
39 Interference

Printed-Circuit Board Etching Patterns
Abbreviations List
Index

Schematic Symbols Used in Circuit Diagrams

U.S. Customary — Metric Conversion Factors

International System of Units (SI) — Metric Units

Prefix	Symbol		Multiplication Factor
exa	E	10^{18} =	1,000,000,000,000,000,000
peta	P	10^{15} =	1,000,000,000,000,000
tera	T	10^{12} =	1,000,000,000,000
giga	G	10^{9} =	1,000,000,000
mega	M	10^{6} =	1,000,000
kilo	k	10^{3} =	1,000
hecto	h	10^{2} =	100
deca	da	10^{1} =	10
(unit)		10^{0} =	1
deci	d	10^{-1} =	0.1
centi	c	10^{-2} =	0.01
milli	m	10^{-3} =	0.001
micro	μ	10^{-6} =	0.000001
nano	n	10^{-9} =	0.000000001
pico	p	10^{-12} =	0.000000000001
femto	f	10^{-15} =	0.000000000000001
atto	a	10^{-18} =	0.000000000000000001

Linear
1 meter (m) = 100 centimeters (cm) = 1000 millimeters (mm)

Area
$1 \ m^2 = 1 \times 10^4 \ cm^2 = 1 \times 10^6 \ mm^2$

Volume
$1 \ m^3 = 1 \times 10^6 \ cm^3 = 1 \times 10^9 \ mm^3$
1 liter (l) = 1000 cm^3 = $1 \times 10^6 \ mm^3$

Mass
1 kilogram (kg) = 1000 grams (g)
(Approximately the mass of 1 liter of water)
1 metric ton (or tonne) = 1000 kg

U.S. Customary Units

Linear Units

12 inches (in) = 1 foot (ft)
36 inches = 3 feet = 1 yard (yd)
1 rod = 5½ yards = 16½ feet
1 statute mile = 1760 yards = 5280 feet
1 nautical mile = 6076.11549 feet

Area
$1 \ ft^2 = 144 \ in^2$
$1 \ yd^2 = 9 \ ft^2 = 1296 \ in^2$
$1 \ rod^2 = 30¼ \ yd^2$
$1 \ acre = 4840 \ yd^2 = 43,560 \ ft^2$
$1 \ acre = 160 \ rod^2$
$1 \ mile^2 = 640 \ acres$

Volume
$1 \ ft^3 = 1728 \ in^3$
$1 \ yd^3 = 27 \ ft^3$

Liquid Volume Measure
1 fluid ounce (fl oz) = 8 fluidrams = 1.804 in^3
1 pint (pt) = 16 fl oz
1 quart (qt) = 2 pt = 32 fl oz = 57¾ in^3
1 gallon (gal) = 4 qt = 231 in^3
1 barrel = 31½ gal

Dry Volume Measure
1 quart (qt) = 2 pints (pt) = 67.2 in^3
1 peck = 8 qt

1 bushel = 4 pecks = 2150.42 in^3

Avoirdupois Weight
1 dram (dr) = 27.343 grains (gr) or (gr a)
1 ounce (oz) = 437.5 gr
1 pound (lb) = 16 oz = 7000 gr
1 short ton = 2000 lb, 1 long ton = 2240 lb

Troy Weight
1 grain troy (gr t) = 1 grain avoirdupois
1 pennyweight (dwt) or (pwt) = 24 gr t
1 ounce troy (oz t) = 480 grains
1 lb t = 12 oz t = 5760 grains

Apothecaries' Weight
1 grain apothecaries' (gr ap) = 1 gr t = 1 gr a
1 dram ap (dr ap) = 60 gr
1 oz ap = 1 oz t = 8 dr ap = 480 gr
1 lb ap = 1 lb t = 12 oz ap = 5760 gr

Multiply ⟶

Metric Unit = Conversion Factor × U.S. Customary Unit

⟵ **Divide**

Metric Unit ÷ Conversion Factor = U.S. Customary Unit

Metric Unit	Conversion Factor	U.S. Unit		Metric Unit	Conversion Factor	U.S. Unit
(Length)				(Volume)		
mm	25.4	inch		mm^3	16387.064	in^3
cm	2.54	inch		cm^3	16.387	in^3
cm	30.48	foot		m^3	0.028316	ft^3
m	0.3048	foot		m^3	0.764555	yd^3
m	0.9144	yard		ml	16.387	in^3
km	1.609	mile		ml	29.57	fl oz
km	1.852	nautical mile		ml	473	pint
(Area)				ml	946.333	quart
mm^2	645.16	$inch^2$		l	28.32	ft^3
cm^2	6.4516	in^2		l	0.9463	quart
cm^2	929.03	ft^2		l	3.785	gallon
m^2	0.0929	ft^2		l	1.101	dry quart
cm^2	8361.3	yd^2		l	8.809	peck
m^2	0.83613	yd^2		l	35.238	bushel
m^2	4047	acre		(Mass)	(Troy Weight)	
km^2	2.59	mi^2		g	31.103	oz t
(Mass)	(Avoirdupois Weight)			g	373.248	lb t
grams	0.0648	grains		(Mass)	(Apothecaries' Weight)	
g	28.349	oz		g	3.387	dr ap
g	453.59	lb		g	31.103	oz ap
kg	0.45359	lb		g	373.248	lb ap
tonne	0.907	short ton				
tonne	1.016	long ton				

The Amateur's Code

The Radio Amateur is:

CONSIDERATE...never knowingly operates in such a way as to lessen the pleasure of others.

LOYAL...offers loyalty, encouragement and support to other amateurs, local clubs, and the American Radio Relay League, through which Amateur Radio in the United States is represented nationally and internationally.

PROGRESSIVE...with knowledge abreast of science, a well-built and efficient station and operation above reproach.

FRIENDLY...slow and patient operating when requested; friendly advice and counsel to the beginner; kindly assistance, cooperation and consideration for the interests of others. These are the hallmarks of the amateur spirit.

BALANCED...radio is an avocation, never interfering with duties owed to family, job, school, or community.

PATRIOTIC...station and skill always ready for service to country and community.

—The original Amateur's Code was written by Paul M. Segal, W9EEA, in 1928.—

Chapter 1

Amateur Radio

Amateur Radio. You've heard of it. You probably know that Amateur Radio operators are also called "hams." (Nobody knows quite why!) Perhaps you have seen amateur call signs (station identifiers) like W3ABC, KB6ZV, WA2DHF or K1ZZ on auto license plates. But who are these people and what do they do?

Most hams are different from non-hams in just one way—their circle of friends is not limited by distance or social class. While the broadcast media brings our world into each home, that world is still distant—you can't converse with images on the TV news. Hams, however, can have daily contact with friends anywhere in the world. As a ham, you might sit down to a conversation with one friend in Trenton —and another in Taiwan. Casual conversation with a ham in another country *really* shrinks the world. Amateur Radio enhances international relations as does no other hobby. As you read this, radio amateurs all over the world are communicating with each other. On the airwaves, there is always a friendly ear —someone to talk with.

Who might you meet at the other end of a radio? On the glamorous side, it may be an astronaut (sometimes while in space), a

homesteader in Alaska, a US legislator, a missionary, a monarch, a camper in a Canadian national park, a student at a Wyoming high school radio club, or a sailor on board a ship in the middle of the Pacific—all without leaving home! Or, you may choose to seek others with common

interests in "nets" (regular on-the-air meetings). There are nets centered on vocations, interests in different languages or different hobbies—from the Armenian Amateur Radio and Traffic Net to the Zenith National Net. *The ARRL Net Directory* lists many special-interest, maritime and

Fig 2—Bardstown (Kentucky) Middle School student and new Novice LaToya Keene, KC4IZM, is all smiles while making her first ham contact. *(Terry Boyd photo,* The Kentucky Standard*)*

Fig 4—Lizzy Gardner, KA1TOK, loves to talk. Behind her we see a typical modern ham station—complete with a world map and QSLs (colorful postcards hams exchange to confirm radio contact) on the wall. *(photo courtesy of Christine Gardner)*

Fig 3—You may meet foreign hams in space, too! Musa Manarov, U2MIR, made over 1000 contacts from the Soviet space station *Mir* (Peace). Here we see Musa on the cover of the January 1989 issue of *Radio*, the Soviet equivalent of *QST*.

Fig 1—Emmie Patience, KA4LRM, served as net control of the South Carolina SSB Emergency Net during the Hurricane Hugo crisis. *(W4DRF photo)*

Fig 5—Aekaterini Panagea, SV1VH, is Greece's pride. Kate is an accomplished gymnast, as well as an experienced radio amateur. *(photo courtesy of SV1VH)*

Fig 6—Chinese amateurs use directional antennas to search for a hidden transmitter during a "fox hunt."

Fig 7—AMSAT volunteer Jeff Zerr assembles the Weber State College Microsat. Each Microsat is assembled from a stack of subsystem modules. (N4HY photo)

Fig 8—Chuck Joseph, N5JED, had contacted over 120 countries by the end of 1989 with this small station and a 54-inch antenna. There are numerous awards and QSL cards on the wall behind Chuck. (N5JED photo)

computer nets along with information about net operation.

Public service is a large part of the Amateur Radio Service. Hams sponsor and provide radio support for various activities in their community. Field Day is the largest ham activity related to public service. One weekend each June, amateurs take their equipment into the great outdoors to simulate operation during a disaster. The challenge is to establish temporary stations and contact as many other participants as possible. A typical two-transmitter Field Day station averages about 900 contacts in a 24-hour period. Although it is practice for serious situations, you can't help but have a lot of fun when 100,000 people go camping together.

If you have a competitive nature, there are many avenues to explore in Amateur Radio. Numerous contests and awards recognize achievements in distance, number or style of radio contacts. Contests generally reward the most contacts with the greatest variety of stations, while there are awards for contacting all US states (WAS), Canadian provinces (WAVE), 100 countries (DXCC) and many others. "Fox" or "bunny" hunters track and locate moving transmitters (the "fox" or "bunny") by car or on foot. "QRP" enthusiasts strive to make radio contact using low-power transmitters.

Many hams like QRP operation because they can easily build the simple, inexpensive equipment used. Self-reliance has always been a trademark of radio amateurs; many hams want to know how their equipment works and how to fix it. Repair shops aren't always open during hurricanes or floods, and you can't call the repair service from a forest fire, chemical spill or blizzard.

If you are technically inclined, the mode of communication can be as interesting as the people you meet. Most amateurs use Morse code and voice, but they can also use teletype, facsimile (fax) and various forms of television. If computers interest you, they can be an important facet of Amateur Radio. Some hams operate wireless computer bulletin boards—both on earth and aboard orbiting satellites.

Essentially, radio signals travel in straight lines. Worldwide communication is possible because those signals can be refracted (bent), reflected or repeated (retransmitted). Refraction takes place in the earth's atmosphere. Hams use the moon, and sometimes aircraft or meteor trails, as signal reflectors. Amateur repeating stations are found on mountaintops, balloons and amateur-built satellites.

The OSCAR (Orbiting Satellite Carrying Amateur Radio) satellites are orbiting repeater stations. VHF (very-high frequency) and UHF (ultra-high frequency) signals normally do not travel much beyond the horizon, but satellites make global VHF/UHF communication possible. Amateur experiments with satellites that store messages for later delivery may lead to low-orbit global communication capabilities for third-world countries that cannot afford expensive channels on geostationary satellites.

Rest easy though; you needn't know a lot about technology to use and enjoy it.

HOW TO GET STARTED

What do you need to get started in Amateur Radio? You will need a license and a station—radio and antenna. The Federal Communications Commission (FCC) issues several classes, or levels, of Amateur Radio license. Each higher class gives the amateur more privileges in return for the skills learned to pass the examination. This license system encourages hams to improve their radio abilities.

There are several ways to prepare for the examinations, and help is available. The American Radio Relay League (ARRL or the League) publishes complete study materials for all license classes. Contact the Educational Activities Department at ARRL HQ (the address and phone number appear at the end of this chapter) for a package of information about clubs, classes and Registered Amateur Radio Instructors near your location. Amateur Radio is often taught by a buddy system. An experienced ham, or "Elmer" (who may or may not be a Registered Instructor) personally teaches one or more newcomers about Amateur Radio. This personalized teaching has brought many thousands of hams into the hobby.

Assembling a station need not be expensive. Many hams continually upgrade their stations, so there is a ready supply of used

Fig 9—Amateur Radio is person-to-person communication spanning miles and continents.

Fig 10—A QSL card from the joint Soviet/Canadian polar ski expedition shows the route taken.

Amateur Radio equipment (gear). It is still possible to assemble a 1950s/60s-vintage CW (radio telegraph) station with a separate transmitter and receiver for well under $200, but most beginners find a used transceiver ($300-$600) more cost effective in the long term. For detailed information about choosing equipment, see the ARRL beginner's licensing materials.

The HANDI-HAM System

Many people with disabilities, especially those who don't get around as much as they'd like to, find the world of Amateur Radio a rewarding way to make friends—around the block or around the world. Amateur Radio is unmatched as both a valuable therapeutic tool and as a beneficial means of person-to-person contact.

The Courage HANDI-HAM System is an international service organization of radio amateurs, with and without disabilities, working together to bring ham radio to individuals with physical handicaps. There are HANDI-HAM members ready to help in every state and in 20 other countries. If you have a disability, they can provide appropriate study materials and aids. Local HANDI-HAMs will assist you with studies at home. Once you receive your license, the Courage HANDI-HAM system may lend you basic radio equipment to get you started on the air. For information, contact the Courage HANDI-HAM System at 3916 Golden Valley Rd, Golden Valley, MN 55422, tel 612-588-0811.

LOOKING BACK

How did Amateur Radio become the almost unlimited hobby it is today? The beginnings are slightly obscure, but electrical experimenters around the turn of the century began duplicating the work of Marconi and others. In attempting to communicate among themselves (with no regulatory agencies) they interfered with other stations. Eventually, governments the world over stepped in and established licensing, laws and regulations to control the problems involved in this new technology. "Amateur" experimenter stations were then restricted to the "useless" wavelengths of 200 meters and shorter (wavelength shortens as frequency in-

creases). Amateurs soon found that they could communicate over longer distances than commercial stations on longer wavelengths. Even so, range was short, and intermediate relay stations were used to cover large distances. Thus, the American Radio Relay League was organized to establish routes of Amateur Radio communication and serve the public interest through Amateur Radio. Still, the dream of transcontinental and even transoceanic contact burned hot in the minds of Amateur Radio experimenters.

World War I brought a suspension of Amateur Radio that nearly became permanent. Although many former amateurs distinguished themselves as military radio operators, the government was reluctant to again grant amateur frequencies after the war ended. Hiram Percy Maxim, one of the founders of the League, gathered support from prewar League members and traveled to Washington, DC, for the cause. After considerable effort, Amateur Radio was reinstated on October 1, 1919.

As amateurs found that distance covered increased with frequency, commercial stations moved to the shorter wavelengths. Battles raged over the right to transmit in this new area. National and international conferences were called in the 1920s to straighten out the tangle of wavelength allocations. Through the efforts of ARRL officials, amateurs obtained frequencies on various bands from 160 through 6 meters. When amateur operators moved to 20 meters, the dream of direct nationwide and transoceanic communication was finally realized. (For a more detailed history of early Amateur Radio, see the ARRL publication *Two Hundred Meters and Down* by Clinton B. DeSoto.)

Public Service

Amateur Radio is a wonderful hobby, but this fact alone hardly justifies the wholehearted support given by nearly all world governments at international conferences. There are other reasons. One is a thorough appreciation of amateurs as skilled radio personnel. Another is best described as "public service."

The public-service record of Amateur Radio is a brilliant tribute to the work of countless hams. These activities can be roughly divided into three classes: expeditions, emergencies and community projects.

Amateur cooperation with expeditions began in 1923, when a League member, Don Mix, 1TS, accompanied Donald B. MacMillan to the Arctic on the schooner *Bowdoin* with an amateur station. During subsequent years Amateur Radio assisted perhaps 200 voyages and expeditions. This work continues: In 1978 Japanese explorer Naomi Uemura, JG1QFW, became the first person to travel, alone, to the North Pole. In 1988, a joint Soviet/Canadian expedition crossed the North Pole on skis. Amateur Radio provided daily communications, and the OSCAR 11 "talking" computer relayed position information to the expedition every 100 minutes.

Hams serve in a wide range of emergencies. Commercial communications services are often disrupted by power failures or damage that accompany natural disasters such as earthquakes, floods and hurricanes. Many amateur stations can operate from a car battery, and Field Day practice keeps hams ready to make and install antennas "on the spot" from available materials and supports. When disaster strikes, amateurs are ready to carry on communications for police, fire departments and relief organizations. In local emergencies such as auto accidents, lost persons, air crashes, blizzards and chemical spills, ham volunteers provide added manpower and communications between agencies whose normal radios are incompatible. The ability of radio amateurs to help the public in emergencies is one big reason Amateur Radio has survived and prospered.

Community projects include communications to aid the public at athletic events ("walkathons," road races), parades and so on. "Santa Claus" nets let children speak to St Nick by radio at Christmas, while more serious medical nets aid doctors in remote locations.

Technical Developments

When Amateur Radio began, hams used sparks across small air gaps to generate wide-band radio signals (much as lightning does). Since then, there has been a steady progression of operating modes (telegraph, radioteletype, data transmissions; voice and television) and hardware (spark gaps, vacuum tubes, transistors, integrated circuits) because amateurs stay at the forefront of technology. One reason for this is incessant curiosity and eagerness to try new techniques. Another is competition; certain portions of some bands are very popular, and technology is constantly driven to support more users.

Ideas from amateur "shacks" (stations) have yielded surprising results in industry. Early technical progress by amateurs provided the keystone for the development of modern military communications equipment.

In the 1950s, the Air Force was to convert its long-range communications from Morse to voice; jet bombers had no room for skilled radio operators. At the time, amateurs were communicating by voice at great distances with both homemade and commercially built single-sideband (SSB) equipment. Generals LeMay and Griswold, both radio amateurs, hatched an experiment that used ham equipment at Strategic Air Command headquarters in Omaha and an airplane traveling around the world. The system worked well; the equipment needed only slight modification to meet Air Force needs, and the expense and time of normal research and development was saved.

Many hams build an interest in Amateur Radio into a fascinating career. Later, as professionals, they may still try out their new ideas first in ham radio. The first OSCAR satellites were made at home by

Fig 12—During the 1980s, Amateur Radio flew two missions aboard Space Shuttles. Tony England, WØORE, sent this amateur slow-scan television image (and many others) to earth-bound hams from the *Challenger* during its August 1985 mission.

amateurs who worked in the aerospace industry. US amateur satellite development proceeds under the guidance of the Radio Amateur Satellite Corporation (AMSAT) with the assistance of Project OSCAR, Inc, the original nonprofit group (both affiliated with ARRL). Sister organizations in other countries aid in satellite construction and have placed amateur satellites in space.

Late in 1983, a ham first operated from space. Radio amateur Owen Garriott, W5LFL, made history by communicating with fellow hams from the Space Shuttle *Columbia*. On that mission, Owen took along a hand-held amateur station. Amateurs throughout the world got the thrill of "working" (communicating with) an astronaut aboard an orbiting spacecraft. Tony England, WØORE, transmitted slow-scan television (SSTV) from a subsequent

shuttle mission (see Fig 12), and planning is underway for a ham station on board a future manned space station.

THE ARRL

Thanks to the hard work of a few visionaries, a national Amateur Radio organization came into being in 1914. Since then, the continued hard work of dedicated ham radio operators has made the American Radio Relay League what it is today. The ARRL is headquartered near Hartford, Connecticut. Its operations are, however, national and international in scope. Through its vast network of volunteers and a professional staff, the ARRL promotes the advancement of the Amateur Radio Service.

The League operates strictly as a nonprofit, educational and scientific organization dedicated to the promotion and protection of the privileges ham operators enjoy.

Of, by and for the radio amateur, ARRL numbers within its ranks the vast majority of active amateurs in North America. Approximately 150,000 licensed US amateurs are full members of the League. An additional 11,000 foreign amateurs and unlicensed individuals are associate members. There is a place in the League for everyone who has an interest in Amateur Radio.

League Leadership

Full membership (available only to licensed radio amateurs) in ARRL gives one a voice in how the affairs of the organization are governed. League policy is set by a Board of Directors (one from each of 15 Divisions). Each year, half of the ARRL Board of Directors stands for election by

Fig 11—1989 was the 75th anniversary of the League. The motto "From Spark to Space" and the celebration logo accurately express the history of Amateur Radio and ARRL.

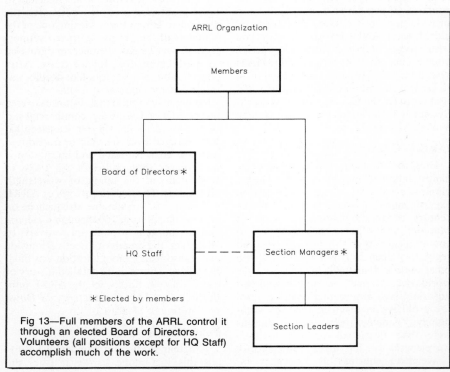

Fig 13—Full members of the ARRL control it through an elected Board of Directors. Volunteers (all positions except for HQ Staff) accomplish much of the work.

the full members they represent. The day-to-day operation of ARRL HQ is managed by an Executive Vice President and a Business Manager.

The ARRL volunteer corps is known as the Field Organization. It is headed by Section Managers (SM), who are elected by the membership in each of 69 ARRL Sections. Each SM appoints volunteers to posts that promote Amateur Radio within the Section. Some such posts enhance public service or technical growth, while others foster communication among amateurs, government agencies and the general public. The extent of involvement depends on your interests and available time, but even if you don't have spare time to volunteer, you can make a positive contribution by joining the ARRL.

ARRL Publications

A well-informed Amateur Radio community is crucial for ham radio to continue as a trained and self-disciplined volunteer service worthy of respect from federal, state and local government officials. At ARRL HQ, the staff produces *QST*, a monthly journal that keeps the membership up to date on the technical and regulatory developments that impact Amateur Radio. *QST* is *the* magazine devoted entirely to Amateur Radio, and it is included with ARRL membership. Each month, its pages report:

- News of ARRL activities.
- Pertinent Federal Communications Commission actions.

- Operating and technical tips.
- Reviews of new equipment and technology.
- Construction articles.

The staff also produces several books (one of which you are reading) about technical subjects, operating technique, license preparation, FCC Rules governing Amateur Radio and specialized communications. *The ARRL Satellite Experimenter's Handbook* is a good example of the latter. Experimentation with new or exotic modes of communications is fostered by the monthly periodical *QEX, The ARRL Experimenters' Exchange*. Certain leadership volunteers in the ARRL Field Organization can receive the *Field Forum* newsletter to support them in their role.

Membership Services

Membership in ARRL means much more than receiving *QST* each month. In addition to general representation before government agencies and administrative support to the Field Organization, ARRL offers membership services on a personal level. The ARRL DX QSL Bureau system is a good example. Radio amateurs, as a general rule, exchange postcards called "QSL cards" to confirm two-way radio contacts. For US and Canadian amateurs and shortwave listeners (SWLs), the most convenient way of sending cards to overseas stations is the ARRL Outgoing QSL Bureau System. For a minimal fee, ARRL HQ will forward members' cards to overseas QSL bureaus, where they are sorted

Fig 15—Incoming QSLs *tovarich*! Joe Carcia, NJ1Q, of the HQ staff stands next to a shipment of cards from the USSR. *(N1EOZ photo)*

for delivery to hams in those countries. (Details of the system are available from HQ for an SASE.)

"Incoming" cards, sent to amateurs in the US and Canada by overseas amateurs, are handled by a network of hard-working volunteers organized as call-area QSL bureaus. While out-of-pocket expenses for the incoming bureaus are borne by ARRL, volunteered time is crucial to incoming-bureau success. This service is available to both members and nonmembers.

The ARRL Volunteer Examiner Coordinator program plays a crucial role in

(A)

(B)

Fig 14—Some of the books (A) and periodicals (B) published by the ARRL.

Fig 16—The American Radio Relay League station, W1AW, in Newington, Connecticut, transmits Morse code practice and bulletins of interest to radio amateurs that are heard throughout the world. *(W2ABE photo)*

coordinating the scheduling, printing and administration of amateur license exams, which are given by volunteers. Do you plan on visiting a foreign country? HQ can provide you with information about how to apply for a reciprocal license from many foreign countries. ARRL also makes available low-cost equipment insurance, assists with radio-frequency-interference problems and with local government restrictions on antennas, and compiles information useful to amateurs with disabilities.

International Involvement

ARRL HQ serves as the International Secretariat of a worldwide federation of national Amateur Radio societies known as the International Amateur Radio Union (IARU). The IARU is comprised of societies like the League in over 100 countries.

The IARU has official "observer" status at the International Telecommunication Union (ITU), which is the United Nations branch in charge of world conferences and agreements concerning the radio spectrum. At the most recent World Administrative Radio Conference (WARC '79—Geneva, Switzerland), the IARU successfully defended Amateur Radio interests against many challenges. At that conference, the societies of the IARU, after many years of careful planning and coordination, stunned the communications community by accomplishing what was earlier thought impossible —the acquisition of three new high-frequency bands for the use of radio amateurs. Another WARC is planned for 1992, and the IARU member societies are hard at work preparing for that conference.

Are You a Member?

No matter what particular aspect of Amateur Radio attracts you, ARRL membership is relevant and important. There would be no Amateur Radio as we know it today were it not for the ARRL. Today, the ARRL needs broad-based support from radio amateurs and others interested in the continued existence of the Amateur Radio Service. We would be happy to welcome you as a member! (An Amateur Radio license is not required for associate membership.) For more information about the American Radio Relay League and answers to any questions you may have about Amateur Radio, write or call:

ARRL Headquarters
225 Main Street
Newington, CT 06111
Tel 203-666-1541.

Chapter 2

Electrical Fundamentals

Electricity and magnetism are familiar to everyone. The effects of static electricity on a dry, wintry day, the attraction of a compass needle to the Earth's magnetic poles, and the propagation and reception of radio waves are all examples of electromagnetic phenomena. Even the radiation of light and radiant heat from a stove are forms of electromagnetic radiation, governed by many of the same physical laws that apply to the simplest electronic circuit. Knowledge of these laws is fundamental to understanding almost every subject in Amateur Radio, and electronics in general.

Electromagnetic energy exists in the form of fields, a spatial and time-dependent pattern of energy. The analysis of electromagnetic fields, their interrelationships and their interaction with matter forms the basis of all electrical laws. Once a field problem is analyzed in a specific case, it is often possible to use the results over and over again for more general purposes. The field solution can be used to derive numerical formulas for such electrical properties as resistance, inductance and capacitance. These elements in turn form the building blocks for more complex configurations called networks or circuits.

ELECTROSTATIC FIELD AND POTENTIALS

Matter is made up of complex structures called atoms. Each atom is primarily composed of three fundamental particles called electrons, protons and neutrons. At the center of the atom is the nucleus formed by the combination of protons, particles with a positive charge, and neutrons, particles with no intrinsic charge themselves. Orbiting around the nucleus are the electrons, particles that have a negative charge. The unique combinations of these three atomic building blocks determine the chemical and electrical properties of the atom.

One of the fundamental laws of physics is the concept of electrostatic attraction and repulsion. Simply stated, particles with opposite charge (positive and negative) tend to attract, while particles with like charge (both positive or both negative) tend to repel. If charged particles are considered to exist at points in space, the force of attraction (or repulsion if the charges have like signs) is given by Coulomb's law

$$F = \frac{k_0 Q_1 Q_2}{r^2}$$

where Q_1 is the numerical value of one charge, Q_2 is the other charge value, r is the distance between particles, and F is the force charge Q_1 exerts on charge Q_2. The value of the proportionality constant, k_0, depends on the units used in specifying F, Q and r. In the metric system of units (SI — Systeme International d'Unites) the basic unit of charge is the coulomb, the unit of force is the Newton, and the unit of space is the meter. In the metric system, k_0 is then equal to

$$k_0 = \frac{1}{4\pi\epsilon_0}$$

where ϵ_0 has a value of

$$\frac{8.854 \times 10^{-12} \text{coul.}^2}{\text{Newton m}^2}$$

(usually referred to as "the permittivity of free space"). If a number of charged particles are present, the force on any one particle is a function of the positions and magnitudes of the other charges.

The fundamental forces inside an atom can be described by Coulomb's law. In the case of a complex atom, one having a number of protons in the nucleus, the repulsive forces between protons within the nucleus tend to force the protons apart. Balancing this is the attractive force between the electrons held in orbit about the nucleus and the protons in the nucleus. Although this description is highly simplistic, it does portray the actions within an atom to a surprisingly high degree of accuracy. The electron and the proton both have charges of equal magnitude — about 1.6×10^{-19} coulombs. The charge on the electron is negative, while the charge on the proton is positive. These values of charge may seem too minute to account for atomic particle interaction, but consider the distances (r) involved. Almost all atoms have an outer diameter of approximately 10^{-10} meter. It is evident that substantial forces exist within the atom.

Analyzing the forces exhibited by multiple charges is overwhelmingly cumbersome, so the concept of electrostatic or electric field strength is a useful one to introduce. If a single charged particle is moved slowly around a fixed charged particle, everywhere the moving particle moves, a force is exerted on the moving particle. The force exerted on the moving particle displays the existence of a force field. If the moving particle is assigned a value Q_t for its charge, then by Coulomb's law, the force (F_t) on the moving particle is

$$F_t = \frac{Q_1 Q_2}{4 \pi \epsilon_0 r^2}$$

Writing this as a force per unit charge gives

$$\frac{F_t}{Q_t} = \frac{Q_1}{4 \pi \epsilon_0 r^2}$$

This expression describes the force on the moving particle totally as a function of the distance from Q_1 and the magnitude of Q_1; this is called the electric field intensity. For example, if a force of 1 newton existed on a test charge of 2 coulombs, the field intensity would be 0.5 newton/coulomb.

As described by Isaac Newton, whenever a force exists on an object, an expenditure of energy is needed to move the object against that force. In some instances, mechanical energy may be recovered (such as in a compressed spring) or the energy may be converted to another form of energy (such as heat produced by friction). In electrostatics, the energy is described in terms of potential. Potential is defined as the work required from some energy source in moving a unit positive charge between two points in an electric field. For example, if an energy expenditure of 5 newton-meters (5 joules) is needed to move a charge of 2 coulombs from a point of zero energy

Fig. 1 — Field lines (solid) and potential lines (dashed) surrounding a charged sphere.

Fig. 2 — Variation of potential with distance for the charged sphere of Fig. 1.

Fig. 3 — Variation of field strength with distance around a sphere charged to 5 volts for spheres of different radii.

to a given point, the potential at that point would be 2.5 joules/coulomb. The unit joules/coulomb is rather unwieldy, so another name is given to electrical potential: the volt. One joule per coulomb is equal to 1 volt. Notice that if the voltage is divided by length (meters), the dimensions of field intensity are obtained and a field strength of 1 newton/coulomb becomes 1 volt/meter.

The relationship between field intensity and potential is illustrated by the example shown in Fig. 1. A conductive sphere is gradually charged until its surface is at a potential of 5 volts. As charges arrive on the surface of a conductor, they tend to spread out into a uniform distribution; the outside of the sphere is said to constitute an equipotential surface. Since every point on the sphere has the same charge, and the charge spreads uniformly over the sphere's surface even as charge is added or removed, the same amount of energy is needed to bring a given amount of charge from a zero reference point to any one point on the sphere as would be required to bring the same amount of charge to any other point on the sphere. The amount of energy expended also is independent of the path traveled to get to the surface. For this particular sphere, it would require 5 joules of energy to bring a charge of 1 coulomb from a point of 0 voltage to any point on the sphere (as indicated by the dotted lines in Fig. 1).

The electromotive force applied to a charged particle at the surface of the sphere must be applied perpendicular to the surface for maximum potential to be realized. Any force applied from a direction other than normal to the surface will have two components: one is performing real work by moving the charge away from the sphere, and the other tends to pull the charge along the surface. Since the charges are free to move about the charged surface already, the energy source does no work in moving charges along the surface, only away from it; the potential difference between points on the sphere is zero. Once the charges are equally distributed along the sphere's surface, an equilibrium condition will be reached and any initial field component parallel to the surface becomes zero. The motion of charge under the influence of an electric field is a very important concept in electricity. The rate at which charge flows past a reference point is defined as the current. A rate of 1 coulomb per second is defined as 1 ampere.

In the case of the symmetrical sphere, the direction of the electromotive force and the electric field can be represented by the solid straight lines in Fig. 1. The arrows indicate the direction of the force for a positive charge. At points farther away from the sphere, less energy is required to move a charged particle from the zero reference. A series of concentric spherical shells, indicated by the dashed lines, can be used to define the equipotential surfaces around the

sphere. From the definition of potential difference, it can be shown through the use of integral calculus that the potential varies inversely to the distance from the center of the sphere. This relationship is indicated by the numbers in Fig. 1 and by the graph in Fig. 2.

The electric field defines the direction and magnitude of a force on a charged object. The field intensity is equal to the negative value of the slope of the curve in Fig. 2. The slope of a curve is the rate of change of some variable with distance; in this case the variable is the potential. This is why the electric field is sometimes called the potential gradient (gradient being equivalent to slope). In the case of a curve that varies as the inverse of the distance, the slope at any point is squared.

An examination of Fig. 1 suggests that the potential variation is dependent only on the shape of the conductor, and not its actual physical size. That is, once the value of the radius, a, of the sphere in Fig. 1 is specified, the potential at any other point a given distance from the sphere is also known. Thus, Fig. 1 can be used for any number of spheres with different radii. When it is changed by a certain percentage, all the other values would change by the same percentage, too. However, the amount of charge required to produce a given voltage, or voltage change, does depend on the size of the conductor, its shape, and its position in relation to other conductors and insulators. For a given conductor configuration, the voltage is related to the required charge by the formula

$$V = \frac{Q}{C}$$

where the entity C is defined as the capacitance. Capacitance will be discussed in more detail in a later section.

Since the electric field intensity is only related to the change in potential with distance, the rate at which it changes is unaffected by the absolute physical size of the conductor configuration. However, the exact numerical potential value at any point does depend on the dimensions of the configuration. This is illustrated in Fig. 3 for spheres with different radii. Note that for larger radii, the numerical value of the field strength at the surface of the sphere (distance equal to a) is less than it is for smaller radii. This effect is important in the design of transmission lines and capacitors. (A capacitor is a device for storing charge. In older terminology, it was sometimes called a condenser.)

Even when identical voltages are applied across the terminals of two different sized transmission lines or capacitors, the field strength between the conductors is higher for configurations of small physical size than for larger physical sizes. When the field strength becomes too high for a particular insulating material, the material (including air) can break down, allowing a conductive arc to pass through the insulation. This

Fig. 4 — Spark gaps with sharp points break down at lower voltages than ones with blunt surfaces, even though the separation is the same.

Fig. 5 — Potential and field strength along a current-carrying conductor.

effect is the basis for spark plugs in internal combustion engines. The gap between electrodes in the spark plug is adjusted to provide a calibrated breakdown of the insulator (the air-gas mixture) at a particular voltage. The arc is hot enough to ignite the fuel-air mixture.

Another example of high electric field breakdown is found in lightning arrestors. These are devices used to protect radio equipment connected to an antenna that might be subjected to high levels of atmospheric electricity. "Spark-gap" conductors are connected between the antenna transmission line and ground. The spark-gap conductors or electrodes are filed to sharp points. These needlepoints appear as conductors of very small radii, so the field strength between them is higher for the same applied potential than it would be for blunt electrodes (Fig. 4). For a given potential, this allows the separation between conductors to be relatively large so the radio frequency effects of the spark gap have minimal effect on normal circuit operation.

Increasing the size of a conductor reduces the electric field strength, thereby reducing the potential for insulation breakdown. A relatively common effect in high-strength electric fields is corona. Here the air insulation breaks down and actually glows. The effect is often seen on sharp tips of high power transmitting antennas. In order to reduce the localized field strength (and reduce the unwanted corona), a blunt electrode such as a sphere is often used on the sharp tip of a whip antenna.

Examination of Fig. 3 reveals that the field strength is zero for distances less than a (the sphere radius), which includes points actually inside the sphere. The implication here is that the effect of fields and charges cannot penetrate the conducting surface and disturb conditions inside the enclosure. The conducting sphere is said to form an electrostatic shield around the contents of the enclosure. The converse is not true, however. That is, charges inside the sphere do cause or induce a field on the outside surface. This is why it is very important

that enclosures designed to confine the effects of charges be connected to a point of zero potential. Such a point is often called a ground.

Fields and Currents

In the previous section, the motion of charged particles in the presence of an electric field was described in connection with charges placed on a conducting sphere, and the concept of current was introduced. In that example, it was assumed that charges could move around unimpeded on the surface of the sphere. In the real world using obtainable materials, this is not true. The movement of charge is dependent upon the transfer of energy between adjacent atoms in the conductor. Charges appear to collide with the constituent atoms as they move through the conductor while under the influence of the electric field of the conductor. The number of "collisions" depends on the chemical characteristics of the material used. Silver acts as a very good conductor with minimal opposition to the movement of charge; carbon and certain alloys of iron are rather poor conductors of charge flow. A measure of how easily charge can flow through a conductor is defined as the conductivity, and is denoted by σ.

The current density in a conductor, J, is the rate of charge flow or current through a given cross-sectional area. It is related to the electric field and conductivity by the formula

$$J = \sigma E$$

In general, the conductivity and electric field in a conductor do not remain constant over a large cross-sectional area. However, in order to simplify understanding of the following theoretical case, both are assumed to remain constant (Fig. 5).

A cylinder of a material with conductivity σ is inserted between two end caps of infinite conductivity. The end caps are connected to a voltage source, such as a bat-

tery or generator. (A battery consists of a number of cells that convert chemical energy to electrical energy, and a generator converts mechanical energy of motion to electrical energy.) The electric field is also considered to be constant along the length, ℓ, of the cylinder. As a consequence, the slope of the potential variation along the cylinder is also a constant. This is indicated by the dashed lines in Fig. 5B. Since the electric field is constant, the current density is also constant; the total current entering the end caps is the product of the current density and the cross-sectional area. The value of the electric field is the quotient of the total voltage and the length of the cylinder. Combining these results and introducing two new entities gives the following set of equations:

$$J = \sigma \frac{V}{\ell} \text{ since } J = \sigma E \text{ and } E = \frac{V}{\ell}$$

$$I = J(A) = \frac{\sigma A V}{\ell}$$

$$\rho = \frac{1}{\sigma} \text{ and } V = I\left(\frac{\rho \ell}{A}\right)$$

$$R = \frac{\rho \ell}{A} \text{ and } V = IR$$

where
ρ = the resistivity of the conducting material
R = the resistance

The final equation, called Ohm's Law, is a very basic one in circuit theory. Configurations similar to the one shown in Fig. 5 are very common in electrical circuits and are called resistors.

It will be shown in a later section that the power dissipated in a resistor is equal to the product of the resistance and the square of the current. Resistance is often an undesirable effect (such as in a wire carrying current from one location to another one), and in these situations must be reduced as much as possible. This can be accomplished by using a conductor with a low resistivity such as silver or copper (which is close to silver in resistivity, but is not as expensive) with a large cross-sectional area and as short a length as possible. The current-carrying capability decreases as the diameter of a conductor gets smaller.

Potential Drop and Electromotive Force

The application of the relationships between fields, potential and concepts similar to the physical configuration shown in Fig. 5 permitted the derivation of the formula that eliminated further consideration of the field problem. The idea of an electrical energy source was also introduced. A similar analysis involving mechanics and field theory would be required to determine the characteristics of an electrical generator, and an application of chemistry would be involved in designing a chemical cell. However, it will be assumed that this problem has been solved and that the energy source can be replaced with a symbol such as that used in Fig. 5.

The term electromotive force (EMF) is applied to describe a source of electrical energy, and potential drop (or voltage drop) is used for a device that consumes electrical energy. A combination of sources and resistances (or other elements) that are connected in some way is called a network or circuit.

Charge Polarity and Electron Flow

The "+" and "−" symbols assigned to electromotive forces and potential drops are important in that they define the polarity of voltage and direction of current flow. These plus and minus symbols (representing positive and negative) were first used in the 18th century by Benjamin Franklin to describe two types of electric charge. Charged atoms (called ions) having more than the usual number of electrons have a negative charge, and those having less than the usual number are said to be positively charged. If a polarizing force is applied to some matter and then removed, the atoms will tend to revert to their natural states. This means that atoms deficient in electrons will attract the needed particles from those atoms having excess electrons. Thus, the transfer of electrons is from negative ions to positive ions. When the path for electrons is an electrical circuit, the current flows from negative to positive around the potential generator.

The direction of electron flow is important in applications of thermionic and semiconductor devices. The cathode of a vacuum tube is heated so that it will boil off electrons. Current will flow in the tube if and only if the anode is biased positive with respect to the cathode. This is known as the Edison effect.

Most modern circuits employ a chassis or ground plane or bus as a common conductor. This practice reduces the wiring or printed circuitry required and simplifies the schematic diagram. When the negative terminal of the power source is connected to this "ground" system, electrons flow from the negative terminal through the ground system and through the circuit elements to the positive terminal. While this is certainly a correct description of the action, it is more convenient to think of the common conductor as the return leg for all circuits. To accommodate this reasoning, electrical engineers have adopted a positive-to-negative convention. This convention is adhered to in most of the technical literature. The arrows in semiconductor schematic symbols point in the direction of this conventional current and away from actual electron flow.

In discussing network elements having one terminal connected to the "common," "ground" or "return" leg of the circuit, engineers use the terms source and sink to describe the current flow. A device is a current source if current flows away from the ungrounded terminal, and a current sink if current flows into the ungrounded terminal.

Alternating Currents

In considering current flow, it is natural to think of a single, constant force causing the electrons to move. When this is so, the electrons always move in the same direction through a path or circuit made up of conductors connected together in a continuous chain. Such a current is called a direct current, abbreviated dc. It is the type of current furnished by batteries and by certain types of generators.

It is also possible to have an EMF that periodically reverses. With this kind of EMF the current flows first in one direction through the circuit and then in the other. Such an EMF is called an alternating EMF, and the current is called an alternating current (abbreviated ac). The reversals (alternations) may occur at any rate from a few per second up to several billion per second. Two reversals make a cycle; in one cycle the force acts first in one direction, then in the other and then returns to the first direction to begin the next cycle. The number of cycles that occur in one second is called the frequency of the alternating current. The inverse of frequency, or the time duration of one cycle, is the period of the current.

The difference between direct current and alternating current is shown in Fig. 6. In these graphs, the horizontal axis indicates time, increasing toward the right. The vertical axis represents the amplitude or strength of the current, increasing in either the up or down direction away from the horizontal axis. If the graph is above the horizontal axis, the current is flowing in one direction through the circuit (indicated by the + sign). If it is below the horizontal axis the current is flowing in the

Fig. 6 — Three types of current flow. A — direct current; B — intermittent direct current; C — alternating current.

reverse direction through the circuit (indicated by the − sign). In Fig. 6A, assume that we close the circuit or make the path for the current complete at the time indicated by X. The current instantly takes the amplitude indicated by the height A. After that, the current continues at the same amplitude as time goes on. This is an ordinary direct current.

In Fig. 6B, the current starts flowing with the amplitude A at time X, continues at that amplitude until time Y and then instantly ceases. After an interval YZ the current again begins to flow and the same sort of start-and-stop performance is repeated. This is an intermittent direct current. We could get it by alternately closing and opening a switch in the circuit. It is a direct current because the direction of current flow does not change; the amplitude is always on the + side of the horizontal axis. The intermittent direct current illustrated has an ac component, however, that can be isolated by an electrical circuit called a filter. Filtering is discussed in greater detail in later sections.

In Fig. 6C the current starts at zero, increases in amplitude as time goes on until it reaches the amplitude A_1 while flowing in the + direction, then decreases until it drops to zero amplitude once more. At that time (X) the direction of the current flow reverses; this is indicated by showing the next part of the graph below the axis. As time goes on the amplitude increases, with the current now flowing in the − direction, until it reaches amplitude A_2. Then the amplitude decreases until finally it drops to zero (Y) and the direction reverses once more. This is an alternating current.

Waveforms

The type of alternating current shown in Fig. 6C is known as a sine wave. An electrodynamic machine called an alternator generates this waveshape because the current induced in the stator winding is pro-

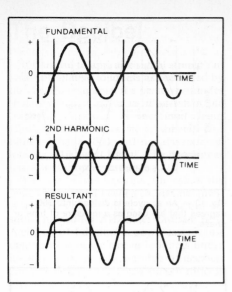

Fig. 7 — A complex waveform. A fundamental (top) and second harmonic (center) added together, point by point at each instant, result in the waveform shown at the bottom. When the two components have the same polarity at a selected instant, the resultant is the simple sum of the two. When they have opposite polarities, the resultant is the difference; if the negative-polarity component is larger, the resultant is negative at the instant.

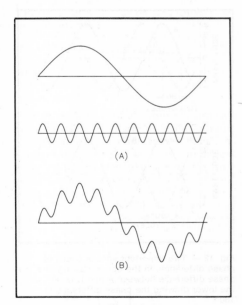

Fig. 8 — Two tones of dissimilar frequency and amplitude (A) are easily recognizable in the composite waveform (B).

portional to the sine of the angle that the winding makes with the magnetic flux lines produced by the rotating field. It is also possible to generate a sine wave electronically.

The variations in many ac waves are not so smooth, nor is one half cycle necessari-ly just like the preceding one in shape. However, these complex waves can be shown to be the sum of two or more sine waves of frequencies that are exact integral (whole-number) multiples of some lower frequency. The lowest frequency is called the fundamental, and the higher frequencies are called harmonics.

Fig. 7 shows how a fundamental and a second harmonic (twice the fundamental) might add to form a complex wave. Simply by changing the relative amplitudes of the two waves, as well as the times at which they pass through zero amplitude, an infinite number of waveshapes can be constructed from just a fundamental and second harmonic. More complex waveforms can be constructed if more harmonics are used.

When two or more sinusoidal or complex signals that are not necessarily harmonically related are applied to a common load resistor, the resultant waveform is the sum of the instantaneous voltages. If the two signals have significantly different frequencies and amplitudes, they are easily distinguishable as components of a composite wave.

The illustration in Fig. 8 is an example of this phenomenon. Two signals having equal amplitudes and nearly equal frequencies combine to produce a composite wave that is not so simply analyzed. Shown in Fig. 9 are two signals having a frequency relationship of 1.5:1. When the positive peaks coincide, the resultant amplitude is twice that of either tone. Similarly, when the maximum negative excursion of one signal corresponds with the maximum positive excursion of the other, the resultant amplitude is the algebraic sum, or zero. The negative peaks never coincide; therefore this composite waveform is not symmetrical about the zero axis. Notice the periodic variation in the amplitude or envelope of the composite waveform. This variation has a frequency equal to the difference or beat between the two tones.

FREQUENCY AND WAVELENGTH

Frequencies ranging from about 20 to 20,000 cycles per second or hertz are called audio frequencies, because the vibrations of air particles that our ears recognize as sounds occur at a similar rate. Audio frequencies (abbreviated AF) are used to actuate loudspeakers and thus create sound waves.

Frequencies above about 20,000 hertz (Hz) are called radio frequencies (RF) because they are useful in radio transmission. Frequencies all the way up to and beyond 100,000,000,000 Hz have been used for radio purposes. At radio frequencies it becomes convenient to use a unit larger than the hertz. Three such units are the kilohertz, which is equal to 1000 Hz and is abbreviated kHz, the megahertz, equal to 1,000,000 hertz or 1000 kilohertz, and is abbreviated MHz, and the gigahertz, equal to 1,000,000,000 hertz or 1000 MHz

Fig. 9 — The graphic addition of equal-amplitude signals fairly close in frequency illustrates the phenomenon of beats. The beat-note frequency is 1.5f − f = 0.5f, and is visible in the resultant waveform.

Table 1

Conversion Factors for Fractional and Multiple Units

Change From	To	Divide By	Multiply By
Units	picounits		10^{12}
	nanounits		10^9
	microunits		10^6
	milliunits		10^3
	kilounits	10^3	
	megaunits	10^6	
	gigaunits	10^9	
Picounits	nanounits	10^3	
	microunits	10^6	
	milliunits	10^9	
	units	10^{12}	
Nanounits	picounits		10^3
	microunits	10^3	
	milliunits	10^6	
	units	10^9	
Microunits	picounits		10^6
	nanounits		10^3
	milliunits	10^3	
	units	10^6	
Milliunits	picounits		10^9
	nanounits		10^6
	microunits		10^3
	units	10^3	
Kilounits	units		10^3
	megaunits	10^3	
	gigaunits	10^6	
Megaunits	units		10^6
	kilounits		10^3
	gigaunits	10^3	
Gigaunits	units		10^9
	kilounits		10^6
	megaunits		10^3

and is abbreviated GHz. Table 1 shows how to convert between the various units in common use. The prefixes attached to the basic-unit name indicate the nature of the unit. These prefixes are

pico — one trillionth (abbreviated p)
nano — one billionth (abbreviated n)
micro — one millionth (abbreviated μ)
milli — one thousandth (abbreviated m)
kilo — one thousand (abbreviated k)
mega — one million (abbreviated M)
giga — one billion (abbreviated G)

Various radio frequencies are divided into classifications. These classifications constitute the frequency spectrum as far as

Table 2
Relative Resistivity of Metals

Material	Resistivity Compared to Copper
Aluminum (pure)	1.60
Brass	3.7-4.90
Cadmium	4.40
Chromium	1.80
Copper (hard-drawn)	1.03
Copper (annealed)	1.00
Gold	1.40
Iron (pure)	5.68
Lead	12.80
Nickel	5.10
Phosphor bronze	2.8-5.40
Silver	0.94
Steel	7.6-12.70
Tin	6.70
Zinc	3.40

tions it is frequently convenient to compare the resistance of the material under consideration with that of a copper conductor of the same size and shape. Table 2 gives the ratio of the resistivity of various conductors to that of copper.

The longer the physical path, the higher the resistance of that conductor. For direct current and low-frequency alternating currents (up to a few thousand hertz) the resistance is inversely proportional to the cross-sectional area of the path the current must travel; that is, given two conductors of the same material and having the same length, but differing in cross-sectional area, the one with the larger area will have the lower resistance.

RESISTANCE OF WIRES

The problem of determining the resistance of a round wire of given diameter and length — or its converse, finding a suitable size and length of wire to provide a desired amount of resistance — can be solved easily with the help of the copper wire table given in Chapter 35. This table gives the resistance, in ohms per thousand feet, of each standard wire size.

Example: Suppose a resistance of 3.5 ohms is needed and some no. 28 wire is on hand. The wire table in Chapter 35 shows that no. 28 wire has a resistance of 66.17 ohms per thousand feet. Since the desired resistance is 3.5 ohms, the length of wire required is

$$\frac{3.5}{66.17} \times 1000 = 52.89 \text{ ft}$$

Suppose that the resistance of wire in a circuit must not exceed 0.05 ohm and that the length of wire required for making the connections totals 14 feet. Then

$$\frac{14}{1000} \times R = 0.05 \text{ ohm}$$

where R is the maximum allowable resistance in ohms per thousand feet. Rearranging the equation gives

$$R = \frac{0.05 \times 1000}{14} = 3.57 \text{ ohms/1000 ft}$$

The wire table shows that no. 15 is the smallest size having a resistance less than this value.

When the wire in question is not made of copper, the resistance values given in the wire table should be multiplied by the ratios given in Table 2 to obtain the resulting resistance.

Example: If the wire in the first example were made from nickel instead of copper, the length required for 3.5 ohms would be

$$\frac{3.5}{66.17 \times 5.1} \times 1000 = 10.37 \text{ ft}$$

Temperature Effects

The resistance of a conductor changes with its temperature. The resistance of practically every metallic conductor increases with increasing temperature. Carbon, however, acts in the opposite way; its resistance decreases when its temperature rises. It is seldom necessary to consider temperature in making resistance calculations for amateur work. The temperature effect is important when it is necessary to maintain a constant resistance under all conditions. Special materials that have little or no change in resistance over a wide temperature range are used in that case.

Resistors

A package of material exhibiting a certain amount of resistance made up into a single unit is called a resistor. Different resistors having the same resistance value may be considerably different in physical size and construction (Fig. 14). Current flowing through a resistance causes the conductor to become heated; the higher the resistance and the larger the current, the greater the amount of heat developed. Resistors intended for carrying large currents must be physically large so the heat can be radiated quickly to the surrounding air. If the resistor does not dissipate the heat quickly it may get hot enough to melt or burn.

Skin Effect

A conductor's effective resistance is not the same for alternating current as it is for direct current. With alternating current, other effects tend to force the current to flow mostly in the outer parts of the conductor. This decreases the effective cross-sectional area of the conductor, with the result that the resistance increases.

At low audio frequencies the increase in resistance is insignificant, but at radio frequencies above about 1 MHz, this "skin effect" is so pronounced that practically all the current flows within a few thousandths of an inch of a copper conductor surface. Above 10 MHz, only about the outer 0.0008 inch of the surface is used, and above 100 MHz the depth is less than 0.0003 inch. The RF resistance is consequently many times the dc resistance, and increases with frequency. In the RF range

Fig. 14 — Examples of various resistors. In the right foreground are ¼-, ½- and 1-watt composition resistors. The three larger cylindrical components at the center are wirewound power resistors. The remaining two parts are variable resistors, PC-board mount at the lower left and panel mount at the upper center.

a conductor of thin tubing will have just as low resistance as a solid conductor of the same diameter, because material not close to the surface carries practically no current.

Conductance

The reciprocal of resistance (1/R) is conductance. It is usually represented by the symbol G. A circuit having high conductance has low resistance, and vice versa. In radio work the term is used chiefly in connection with electron-tube and field-effect-transistor characteristics. The unit of conductance is the siemens, abbreviated S. A resistance of 1 ohm has a conductance of 1 siemens, a resistance of 1000 ohms has a conductance of 0.001 siemens, and so on. A unit frequently used in connection with electron devices is the microsiemens or one-millionth of a siemens. It is the conductance of a 1-million-ohm resistance.

OHM'S LAW

One of the simplest forms of electric circuit is a battery with a resistance connected to its terminals, as shown by the symbols in Fig. 15. A complete circuit must have an unbroken path so current can flow out of the battery, through the apparatus connected to it, and back into the battery. If a connection is removed at any point, the

Fig. 15 — A simple circuit consisting of a battery and resistor.

circuit is broken, or open. A switch is a device for making and breaking connections and thereby closing or opening the circuit, either allowing current to flow or preventing it from flowing.

The values of current, voltage and resistance in a circuit are by no means independent of each other. The relationship between them is known as Ohm's Law. It can be stated as follows: The current flowing in a circuit is directly proportional to the applied EMF and inversely proportional to the resistance. Expressed as an equation, it is

$$I \text{ (amperes)} = \frac{E \text{ (volts)}}{R \text{ (ohms)}}$$

The equation gives the value of current when the voltage and resistance are known. It may be transposed so that each of the three quantities may be found when the other two are known:

$$E = IR$$

(that is, the voltage is equal to the current in amperes multiplied by the resistance in ohms) and

$$R = \frac{E}{I}$$

(or the resistance of the circuit is equal to the applied voltage divided by the current).

All three forms of the equation are used often in radio work. It must be remembered that the quantities are in volts, ohms and amperes; other units cannot be used in the equations without first being converted. For example, if the current is in milliamperes it must be changed to the equivalent fraction of an ampere before the value can be substituted in the equations.

The following examples illustrate the use of Ohm's Law:

The current flowing through a resistance of 20,000 ohms is 150 milliamperes. What is the voltage? Since the voltage is to be found, the equation to use is $E = IR$. The current must first be converted from milliamperes to amperes, and reference to Table 1 shows that to do so it is necessary to divide by 1000. Therefore,

$$E = \frac{150}{1000} \times 20,000 = 3000 \text{ volts}$$

When a voltage of 150 is applied to a circuit, the current is measured at 2.5 amperes. What is the resistance of the circuit? In this case R is the unknown, so

$$R = \frac{E}{I} = \frac{150}{2.5} = 60 \text{ ohms}$$

No conversion was necessary because the voltage and current were given in volts and amperes.

How much current will flow if 250 volts is applied to a 5000-ohm resistor? Since I is unknown

$$I = \frac{E}{R} = \frac{250}{5000} = 0.05 \text{ ampere}$$

Milliampere units would be more con-

Fig. 16 — Resistors connected in series, A, and in parallel, B.

venient for the current, and 0.05 ampere × 1000 = 50 milliamperes.

SERIES AND PARALLEL RESISTANCES

Very few actual electric circuits are as simple as Fig. 15. Commonly, resistances are found connected in a variety of ways. The two fundamental methods of connecting resistances are shown in Fig. 16. In the upper drawing, the current flows from the source of EMF (in the direction shown by the arrow, let us say) down through the first resistance, R1, then through the second, R2, and then back to the source. These resistors are connected in series. The current everywhere in the circuit has the same value.

In the lower drawing, the current flows to the common connection point at the top of the two resistors and then divides, one part of it flowing through R1 and the other through R2. At the lower connection point these two currents again combine; the total is the same as the current that flowed into the upper common connection. In this case the two resistors are connected in parallel.

Resistors in Parallel

In a circuit with resistances in parallel, the total resistance is less than that of the lowest value of resistance present. This is because the total current is always greater than the current in any individual resistor. The formula for finding the total resistance of resistances in parallel is

$$R = \frac{1}{\dfrac{1}{R1} + \dfrac{1}{R2} + \dfrac{1}{R3} + \dfrac{1}{R4} + \ldots}$$

where the dots again indicate that any number of resistors can be combined by the same method. For only two resistances in parallel (a very common case), the formula becomes

$$R = \frac{R1 \times R2}{R1 + R2}$$

Fig. 17 — An example of resistors in parallel. The solution is worked out in the text.

Example: If a 500-ohm resistor is paralleled with one of 1200 ohms, the total resistance is

$$R = \frac{R1 \times R2}{R1 + R2} = \frac{500 \times 1200}{500 + 1200}$$

$$R = \frac{600,000}{1700} = 353 \text{ ohms}$$

Kirchhoff's First Law

There is another solution to the problem. Suppose the three resistors of the previous example are connected in parallel as shown in Fig. 17. The same EMF, 250 volts, is applied to all three of the resistors. The current in each can be found from Ohm's Law as shown below, I1 being the current through R1, I2 the current through R2 and I3 the current through R3.

For convenience, the resistance will be expressed in kilohms so the current will be in milliamperes.

$$I1 = \frac{E}{R1} = \frac{250}{5} = 50 \text{ mA}$$

$$I2 = \frac{E}{R2} = \frac{250}{20} = 12.5 \text{ mA}$$

$$I3 = \frac{E}{R3} = \frac{250}{8} = 31.25 \text{ mA}$$

The total current is

$$I = I1 + I2 + I3$$
$$I = 50 + 12.5 + 31.25$$
$$I = 93.75 \text{ mA}$$

This example illustrates Kirchhoff's current law: The current flowing into a node or branching point is equal to the sum of the individual currents leaving the node or branching point. The total resistance of the circuit is therefore

$$R = \frac{E}{I} = \frac{250}{93.75} = 2.667 \text{ kilohms}$$

$$R = 2667 \text{ ohms}$$

Resistors in Series

When a circuit has a number of resistances connected in series, the total resistance of the circuit is the sum of the individual resistances. If these are numbered R1, R2, R3 and so on, then

$$R \text{ (total)} = R1 + R2 + R3 + R4 + \ldots$$

where the dots indicate that as many

resistors as necessary may be added.

Example: Suppose that three resistors are connected to a source of EMF as shown in Fig. 18. The EMF is 250 volts. R1 is 5000 ohms, R2 is 20 kilohms (20,000 ohms) and R3 is 8000 ohms. The total resistance is then

R = R1 + R2 + R3
R = 5000 + 20,000 + 8000
R = 33,000 ohms.

The current flowing in the circuit is then

$$I = \frac{E}{R} = \frac{250}{33,000} = 0.00758 \text{ ampere}$$

I = 7.58 mA.

(We need not carry calculations beyond three significant figures; often, two will suffice because the accuracy of measurements is seldom better than a few percent.)

Kirchhoff's Second Law

Ohm's Law applies in any portion of a circuit as well as to the circuit as a whole. Although the current is the same in all three of the resistances in the example of Fig. 18, the total voltage divides among them. The voltage appearing across each resistor (the voltage drop) can be found from Ohm's Law.

Example: If the voltage across R1 is called E1, that across R2 is called E2, and that across R3 is called E3, then

E1 = IR1 = 0.00758 × 5000 = 37.9 volts
E2 = IR2 = 0.00758 × 20,000
    = 151.5 volts
E3 = IR3 = 0.00758 × 8000
    = 60.6 volts

Kirchhoff's second law accurately describes the situation in the circuit: The sum of the voltages in a closed current loop is equal to zero. The resistors are sinks of power, while the battery is a source of power, so the sign conversion described earlier causes the voltage potentials across the resistors to be opposite in sign from the battery voltage. Adding all the voltages yields zero. In the simple case of a single voltage source, simple algebraic manipulation implies that the sum of the individual voltage drops in the circuit must be equal to the applied voltage.

Fig. 18 — An example of resistors in series. The solution of the circuit is worked out in the text.

Fig. 19 — At A, an example of resistors in series-parallel. The equivalent circuit is shown at B. The solution is worked out in the text.

E = E1 + E2 + E3
E = 37.9 + 151.5 + 60.6
E = 250 volts

In problems such as this, when the current is small enough to be expressed in milliamperes, considerable time and trouble can be saved if the resistance is expressed in kilohms rather than in ohms. When the resistance in kilohms is substituted directly in Ohm's Law, the current will be milliamperes if the EMF is in volts.

Resistors in Series-Parallel

A circuit may have resistances both in parallel and in series, as shown in Fig. 19A. The method for analyzing such a circuit is as follows: Consider R2 and R3 to be the equivalent of a single resistor, R_{eq}, whose value is equal to R2 and R3 in parallel.

$$R_{eq} = \frac{R2 \times R3}{R2 + R3} = \frac{20,000 \times 8000}{20,000 + 8000}$$

$R_{eq} = 5.71 \text{ k}\Omega$

This resistance in series with R1 forms a simple series circuit, as shown in Fig. 19B. The total resistance in the circuit is then

R = R1 + R_{eq} = 5 kΩ + 5.71 kΩ
R = 10.71 kΩ

The current is

$$I = \frac{E}{R} = \frac{250 \text{ V}}{10.71 \text{ k}\Omega} = 23.3 \text{ mA}$$

The voltage drops across R1 and R_{eq} are

E1 = I × R1 = 23.3 × 5 = 117 volts
E2 = I × R_{eq} = 23.3 mA × 5.71 kΩ
E2 = 133 volts

with sufficient accuracy. These two voltage drops total 250 volts, as described by

Kirchhoff's first law. E2 appears across both R2 and R3 so,

$$I2 = \frac{E2}{R2} = \frac{133 \text{ V}}{20 \text{ k}\Omega} = 6.67 \text{ mA}$$

$$I3 = \frac{E2}{R3} = \frac{133 \text{ V}}{8 \text{ k}\Omega} = 16.67 \text{ mA}$$

where

I2 = current through R2
I3 = current through R3.

The sum of I2 and I3 is equal to 23.3 mA, conforming to Kirchhoff's second law.

Thevenin's Theorem

A useful tool for simplifying electrical networks is Thevenin's Theorem, which states that any two-terminal network of resistors and voltage or current sources can be replaced by a single voltage source and a series resistor. Such a transformation can simplify the calculation of current through a parallel branch. Thevenin's Theorem can be readily applied to the circuit of Fig. 19A, to find the current through R3.

In this example, R1 and R2 form a voltage divider circuit, with R3 as the load (Fig. 20A). The current drawn by the load (R3) is simply the voltage potential across R3, divided by its resistance. Unfortunately, the value of R2 affects the voltage potential across R3, just as the presence of R3 affects the potential appearing across R2. Some means of separating the two is needed; hence the Thevenin-equivalent circuit.

The voltage of the Thevenin-equivalent battery is the open circuit voltage as measured when no current is flowing from either terminal A or B. Without a load connected between A and B, the total current through the circuit is (from Ohm's Law)

$$I = \frac{E}{R1 + R2}$$

and the voltage between terminals A and B (E_{ab}) is

E_{ab} = I × R2

By substituting the first equation into the second, a simplified expression for E_{ab} can be found to be

$$E_{ab} = \frac{R2}{R1 + R2} \times E$$

Using the actual values, this becomes

$$E_{ab} = \frac{20,000}{5,000 + 20,000} \times 250 = 200 \text{ volts}$$

when nothing is connected to terminals A or B. With no current drawn, E then is equal to E_{ab}.

The Thevenin-equivalent resistance is the total net resistance between terminals A and B. The ideal voltage source, by definition, has zero internal resistance. As-

Fig. 20 — Thevenin-equivalent circuit for the circuit in Fig. 19.

Assuming the battery to be a close approximation of an ideal source, put a short between points X and Y in the circuit of Fig. 20A. R1 and R2 are then effectively placed in parallel, as viewed from terminals A and B. The Thevenin-equivalent resistance is then

$$R_{thev} = \frac{R1 \times R2}{R1 + R2} = 4000 \text{ ohms}$$

This gives the Thevenin-equivalent circuit as shown in Fig. 20B. The circuits of Figs. 19A and 19B as far as R3 is concerned are equivalent.

Once R3 is connected to terminals A and B, current will flow through R_{thev}, causing a voltage drop across R_{thev}, and reducing E_{ab}. However, the current through R3 is equal to

$$I = \frac{E_{thev}}{R_{total}} = \frac{E_{thev}}{R_{thev} + R3}$$

Substituting actual values gives

$$I = \frac{200}{4000 + 8000} = 16.67 \text{ mA}$$

This agrees with the value calculated earlier.

Norton's Theorem

Another tool for analyzing electrical networks is Norton's Theorem, which states that any two-terminal network of resistors and current or voltage sources can be replaced by a single current source and a parallel resistor. Norton's Theorem is to current sources what Thevenin's Theorem is to voltage sources. In fact, the Thevenin resistance as calculated previously is used as the equivalent resistance when using Norton's Theorem.

The circuit just analyzed by means of Thevenin's Theorem can be analyzed just as easily by Norton's Theorem. The equivalent Norton circuit is shown in Fig. 20C. The current I_{sc} of the equivalent current source is the short circuit current through terminals A and B. In the case of the voltage divider shown in Fig. 20A, the short circuit current is

$$I_{sc} = \frac{E}{R1} = \frac{250}{5000} = 50 \text{ mA}$$

The resulting Norton-equivalent circuit consists of a 50-mA current source placed in parallel with a 4000-ohm resistor. When R3 is connected to terminals A and B, by Kirchhoff's second law one third of the supply current flows through R3 and the remainder through R_{thev}. This gives a current through R3 of 16.67 mA, again agreeing with previous conclusions.

A Norton-equivalent circuit can be transformed into a Thevenin-equivalent circuit and vice versa. The equivalent resistor stays the same in both cases; it is placed in series with the voltage source in the case of a Thevenin-equivalent circuit, and in parallel with the current source in the case of a Norton-equivalent circuit. The voltage for a Thevenin-equivalent source is equal to the no load voltage appearing across the resistor in the Norton-equivalent circuit. The current for a Norton-equivalent source is equal to the short circuit current provided by the Thevenin source.

POWER AND ENERGY

Power, the rate of doing work, is equal to voltage multiplied by current. The unit of electrical power, called the watt, is equal to 1 volt multiplied by 1 ampere. The equation for power therefore is

$$P = EI$$

where

P = power in watts
E = EMF in volts
I = current in amperes.

Common fractional and multiple units for power are the milliwatt, one thousandth of a watt, and the kilowatt, or 1000 watts.

Example: The plate voltage on a transmitting vacuum tube is 2000 volts and the plate current is 350 milliamperes. (The current must be changed to amperes before substitution in the formula, and so is 0.35 ampere.) Then

$$P = EI = 2000 \times 0.35 = 700 \text{ watts}$$

By substituting the Ohm's Law equivalent for E and I, the following formulas are obtained for power:

$$P = \frac{E^2}{R}$$

$$P = I^2R$$

These formulas are useful in power calculations when the resistance and either the current or voltage (but not both) are known.

Example: How much power will be used up in a 4000-ohm resistor if the potential applied to it is 200 volts? From the equation

$$P = \frac{E^2}{R} = \frac{200^2}{4000} = \frac{40,000}{4000}$$

$$P = 10 \text{ watts}$$

Now, suppose a current of 20 milliamperes flows through a 300-ohm resistor. Then

$$P = I^2R = 0.02^2 \times 300$$
$$P = 0.0004 \times 300$$
$$P = 0.12 \text{ watt}$$

Note that the current was changed from milliamperes to amperes before substitution in the formula.

Electrical power in a resistance is turned into heat. The greater the power, the more rapidly the heat is generated. Resistors for radio work are made in many sizes, the smallest being rated to dissipate (or carry safely) about 1/10 watt. The largest resistors commonly used in amateur equipment will dissipate about 100 watts.

When electrical energy is converted into mechanical energy, and vice versa, the following relationship holds: 1 horsepower = 746 watts. This formula assumes lossless transformation; practical efficiency is taken up shortly.

GENERALIZED DEFINITION OF RESISTANCE

Electrical power is not always turned into heat. The power used in running a motor, for example, is converted to mechanical motion. The power supplied to a radio transmitter is largely converted into radio waves. Power applied to a loudspeaker is changed into sound waves. But in every case of this kind, the power is completely used up — it cannot be recovered. Also, for proper operation of the device the power must be supplied at a definite ratio of voltage to current. Both of these features are characteristics of resistance, so it can be said that any device that dissipates power has a definite value of resistance.

This concept of resistance as something that absorbs power at a definite voltage-to-current ratio is very useful; it permits substituting a simple resistance for the load or power-consuming part of the device receiving power, often with considerable simplification of calculations. Of course, every electrical device has some resistance of its own in the more narrow sense, so a part of the power supplied to it is dissipated in that resistance and hence appears as heat even though the major part of the power may be converted to another form.

Efficiency

In devices such as motors and vacuum tubes, the objective is to obtain power in some form other than heat. Therefore power used in heating is considered to be a loss, because it is not useful power. The efficiency of a device is the useful power output (in its converted form) divided by the power input to the device. In a vacuum-tube transmitter, for example, the objective is to convert power from a dc source into ac power at some radio frequency. The ratio of the RF power output to the dc input is the efficiency of the tube. That is,

$$\text{Eff.} = \frac{P_o}{P_i}$$

where

Eff. = efficiency (as a decimal)
P_o = power output (watts)
P_i = power input (watts).

Example: If the dc input to the tube is 100 watts, and the RF power output is 60 watts, the efficiency is

$$\text{Eff.} = \frac{P_o}{P_i} = \frac{60}{100} = 0.6$$

Efficiency is usually expressed as a percentage; that is, it tells what percent of the input power will be available as useful output. The efficiency in the above example is 60%.

Suppose a mobile transmitter has an RF power output of 100 W at an efficiency of 52 percent at 13.8 V. The vehicular alternator system charges the battery at a 5-A rate at this voltage. Assuming an alternator efficiency of 68 percent, how much horsepower must the engine produce to operate the transmitter and charge the battery? Solution: To charge the battery, the alternator must produce 13.8 V × 5 A = 69 W. The transmitter dc input power is 100 W/0.52 = 192.3 W. Therefore, the total electrical power required from the alternator is 192.3 + 69 = 261.3 W. The engine load then is

$$\frac{261.3}{746 \times 0.68} = 0.515 \text{ horsepower}$$

Energy

In residences, the power company's bill is for electrical energy, not for power. What you pay for is the work that electricity does for you, not the rate at which that work is done. Electrical work is equal to power multiplied by time; the common unit is the watt-hour, which means that a power

of 1 watt has been used for one hour. That is,

$$W = PT$$

where

W = energy in watt-hours
P = power in watts
T = time in hours.

Other energy units are the kilowatt-hour and the watt-second (joule). These units are self-explanatory.

Energy units are seldom used in amateur practice, but it is obvious that a small amount of power used for a long time can eventually result in a power bill that is just as large as though a large amount of power had been used for a very short time.

AC Waveform Measurements

The time dependence of alternating current raises questions about defining and measuring values of voltage, current and power. Because these parameters change from one instant to the next, one might wonder, for example, which point on the cycle characterizes the voltage or current for the entire cycle. When you are viewing a single-tone signal (that is, a pure sine wave) on an oscilloscope, the easiest dimension to measure is the total vertical displacement, or peak-to-peak voltage.

This value, abbreviated P-P, is important in evaluating the signal-handling capability of a linear processing device such as an electronic amplifier or ferromagnetic transformer. If the steepest part of the waveform has a potential of zero, the signal has equal positive and negative excursions and no dc bias. The oscilloscope measurement of the maximum positive or negative excursion, or maximum instantaneous potential, is called the peak voltage, and in a symmetrical waveform it has half the value of the peak-to-peak amplitude. Insulators, air gaps and capacitor dielectrics must withstand the peak value of an ac voltage. In a well-designed ac-to-dc power supply the rectified dc output voltage will be nearly equal to the peak ac voltage.

When an ac voltage is applied to a resistor, the resistor will dissipate energy in the form of heat, just as if the voltage were dc. The dc voltage that would cause identical heating in the ac-excited resistor is the root-mean-square (RMS) value of the ac voltage. The RMS voltage of any waveform can be determined with the use of integral calculus, but for a pure sine wave the following relationships hold:

$$V_{peak} = V_{RMS} \times \sqrt{2} \approx V_{RMS} \times 1.414$$

and

$$V_{RMS} = \frac{V_{peak}}{\sqrt{2}} \approx V_{peak} \times 0.707$$

Unless otherwise specified or obvious from context, ac voltage is rendered as an RMS value. For example, the household

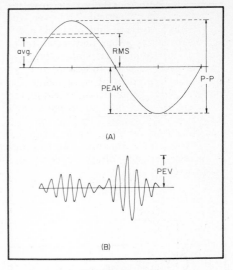

Fig. 21 — Ac voltage and current measurements. The sine-wave parameters are illustrated at A, while B shows the peak envelope voltage (PEV) for a composite waveform.

117-V ac outlet provides 117 V_{RMS}, 165.5 V_{peak} and 331 V_{P-P}.

An electrodynamic instrument such as a meter movement responds to the average value of an ac waveform. Again, integral calculus is required for computation of the average value of the general (complex) wave, but for a sinusoidal signal the peak, RMS and average voltages are related by the formulas:

$$V_{avg} = V_{peak} \times \frac{2}{\pi} \approx 0.63662 \, V_{peak}$$
$$\approx 0.9003 \, V_{RMS}$$

and

$$V_{peak} = \frac{V_{avg}}{0.636} = 1.5708 \, V_{avg}$$

Thus, our 117-V ac outlet provides an average voltage of 105.2.

Fig. 21A illustrates the four voltage parameters of a sine wave. The most accurate way to determine the RMS voltage of a complex wave is to measure the heat produced by applying the complex voltage to a known resistance and measure the dc voltage required to produce the same heat. However, some modern electronic voltmeters provide accurate RMS readings by performing mathematical operations on the waveform. The ratio of peak voltage to RMS voltage of an ac signal is called the crest factor. From the relationships presented earlier, the crest factor of a sine wave is the square root of 2.

The significant dimension of a multitone signal is the peak envelope voltage, shown in Fig. 21B. PEV is important in calculating the power in a modulated signal, such as that from an amateur SSB voice transmitter.

All that has been said about voltage measurements applies also to current (provided the load is resistive) because the waveshapes are identical. However, the terms RMS, average and peak have different meanings when they refer to ac power. The reason is that while voltage and current are sinusoidal functions of time, power is the product of voltage and current, and this product is a sine squared function. The mathematical operations that define RMS, average, and so on will naturally yield different results when applied to this new function. The relationships between ac voltage, current and power follow:

RMS voltage × RMS current = average power ≠ RMS power. The average power used to heat a resistor is equal to the dc power required to produce the same heat. RMS power is a mathematical curiosity only and has no physical significance.

Peak voltage × peak current = 2 × average power. Unfortunately, the definition given above for peak power conflicts with the meaning of the term when it is used in radio work. The peak power output of a radio transmitter is the power averaged over the RF cycle having the greatest amplitude. Modulated signals are

not purely sinusoidal because they are composites of two or more tones. However, the cycle-to-cycle variation is small enough that sine-wave measurement techniques produce accurate results. In the context of radio signals, then, peak power means maximum average power. Peak envelope power (PEP) is the parameter most often used to express the maximum signal-handling capability of a linear amplifier. To compute the PEP of a waveform such as that sketched in Fig. 21B, multiply the PEV by 0.707 to obtain the RMS value, square the result and divide by the load resistance.

Peak Power = 2 × P_avg

Avg Power = Irms Vrms

$$PEP = \frac{(0.707\ PEV)^2}{R_L}$$

Capacitance

Suppose two flat metal plates are placed close to each other (but not touching) and are connected to a battery through a switch, as illustrated in Fig. 22. At the instant the switch is closed, electrons are attracted from the upper plate to the positive terminal of the battery, and the same number are repelled into the lower plate from the negative battery terminal. Enough electrons move into one plate and out of the other to make the EMF between them the same as the EMF of the battery.

If the switch is opened after the plates have been charged in this way, the top plate is left with a deficiency of electrons and the bottom plate with an excess. Since there is no current path between the two, the plates remain charged despite the fact that the battery no longer is connected. If a wire is touched between the two plates (short-circuiting them), the excess electrons on the bottom plate flow through the wire to the upper plate, restoring electrical neutrality. The plates are discharged.

These two plates are representative of an electrical capacitor, a device possessing the property of storing electricity in the electric field between its plates. During the time the electrons are moving — that is, while the capacitor is being charged or discharged — a current flows in the circuit even though the circuit apparently is broken by the gap between the capacitor plates. However, the current flows only during the time of charge and discharge, and this time is usually very short. There can be no continuous flow of direct current through a capacitor. However, alternating current can "pass through" a capacitor. As fast as one plate is charged positively by the positive excursion of the alternating current, the other plate is being charged negatively. Positive current flowing into one plate causes a current to flow out of the other plate during one half of the cycle, while the reverse occurs during the other half of the cycle.

Fig. 22 — A simple capacitor.

The charge or quantity of electricity that can be held in the electric field between the capacitor plates is proportional to the applied voltage and to the capacitance of the capacitor:

$$Q = CV$$

where
Q = charge in coulombs
C = capacitance in farads
V = potential in volts

The energy stored in a capacitor is also a function of potential and capacitance:

$$W = \frac{V^2C}{2}$$

where
W = energy in joules (watt-seconds)
V = potential in volts
C = capacitance in farads

The numerator of this expression can be derived easily from the definitions given earlier for charge, capacitance, current, power and energy. However, the denominator is not so obvious. It arises because the voltage across a capacitor is not constant, but is a function of time; the average voltage over the time interval determines the energy stored. The time dependence of the capacitor voltage is

Table 3

Dielectric Constants and Breakdown Voltages

Material	Dielectric Constant*	Puncture Voltage**
Air	1.0	21
Alsimag 196	5.7	240
Bakelite	4.4-5.4	300
Bakelite, mica filled	4.7	325-375
Cellulose acetate	3.3-3.9	250-600
Fiber	5-7.5	150-180
Formica	4.6-4.9	450
Glass, window	7.6-8	200-250
Glass, Pyrex	4.8	335
Mica, ruby	5.4	3800-5600
Mycalex	7.4	250
Paper, Royalgrey	3.0	200
Plexiglas	2.8	990
Polyethylene	2.3	1200
Polystyrene	2.6	500-700
Porcelain	5.1-5.9	40-100
Quartz, fused	3.8	1000
Steatite, low loss	5.8	150-315
Teflon	2.1	1000-2000

*At 1 MHz   **In volts per mil (0.001 inch)

discussed in the section on time constant.

The larger the plate area and the smaller the spacing between the plates, the greater the capacitance. The capacitance also depends on the kind of insulating material between the plates; it is smallest with air insulation, and substitution of other insulating materials for air may increase the capacitance many times. The ratio of the capacitance with some material other than air between the plates to the capacitance of the same capacitor with air insulation is called the dielectric constant of that particular insulating material. The material itself is called a dielectric. The dielectric constants of a number of materials commonly used as dielectrics in capacitors are given in Table 3. If a sheet of polystyrene is substituted for air between the plates of

Fig. 23 — A multiple-plate capacitor. Alternate plates are connected together.

a capacitor, for example, the capacitance will be increased 2.6 times.

Units of Capacitance

The basic unit of capacitance is the farad, but this unit is much too large for practical work. Capacitance is usually measured in microfarads (abbreviated μF) or picofarads (pF). The microfarad is one millionth of a farad (10^{-6} F), and the picofarad is one millionth of a microfarad (10^{-12} F). Capacitors nearly always have more than two plates, the alternate plates being connected together to form two sets, as shown in Fig. 23. This makes it possible to attain a fairly large capacitance in a small space, since several plates of smaller individual area can be stacked to form the equivalent of a single large plate of the same total area. Also, all plates except the two on the ends are exposed to plates of the other group on both sides, and so are twice as effective in increasing the capacitance.

The formula for calculating capacitance is

$$C = \frac{0.224 \ KA}{d} \ (n - 1)$$

where

   C = capacitance in pF

K = dielectric constant of material between plates

A = area of one side of one plate in square inches

d = separation of plate surfaces in inches

n = number of plates

If the plates in one group do not have the same area as the plates in the other, use the area of the smaller plates.

Capacitors in Radio

The types of capacitors used in radio work differ considerably in physical size, construction and capacitance. Representative types are shown in Fig. 24. In variable capacitors (almost always constructed with air for the dielectric) one set of plates is made movable with respect to the other set so the capacitance can be varied. Fixed capacitors (those having a single, nonadjustable value of capacitance) can also be made with metal plates and with air as the dielectric. However, fixed capacitors usually are constructed from plates of metal foil with a thin solid or liquid dielectric sandwiched between, so that a relatively large capacitance can be obtained in a small unit. The solid dielectrics commonly used are mica, paper and special ceramics. An example of a liquid dielectric is mineral oil. The electrolytic capacitor uses aluminum-foil plates with a semiliquid conducting chemical compound between them. The actual dielectric is a very thin film of insulating material that forms on one set of plates through electrochemical action when a dc voltage is applied to the capacitor. The capacitance obtained with a given plate area in an electrolytic capacitor is very large, compared with capacitors having other dielectrics, because the film is so thin — much less than any thickness practical with a solid dielectric.

The use of electrolytic and oil-filled capacitors is confined to power-supply filtering and audio-bypass applications because their dielectrics have high losses at the higher frequencies. Mica and ceramic capacitors are used throughout the frequency range from audio to several hundred megahertz.

Voltage Breakdown

When high voltage is applied to the plates of a capacitor, considerable force is exerted on the electrons and nuclei of the dielectric. The dielectric is an insulator; the electrons do not become detached from atoms the way they do in conductors. If the force is great enough the dielectric will break down. Usually failed dielectrics will puncture and offer a low resistance current path between the two plates.

The breakdown voltage a dielectric can withstand depends on the chemical composition and thickness of the dielectric, as shown in Table 3. Breakdown voltage is not directly proportional to the thickness; doubling the thickness does not quite double the breakdown voltage. Gas dielectrics break down, as evidenced by a spark or arc between the plates. Once the voltage is removed, the arc ceases and the capacitor is ready for use again. Solid dielectrics are permanently damaged by dielectric breakdown, and often will totally short out and melt or explode. Breakdown occurs at a lower voltage between pointed or sharp-edged surfaces than between rounded and polished surfaces; consequently, the breakdown voltage between metal plates of given spacing in air can be increased by buffing the edges of the plates.

A thick dielectric must be used to withstand high voltages, and since the capacitance is inversely proportional to dielectric thickness (plate spacing) for a given plate area, a high-voltage capacitor must have more plate area than a low-voltage one of the same capacitance. High-voltage, high-

(A)

(B)

Fig. 24 — Fixed-value capacitors are shown at A. A large computer-grade unit is at the upper left. This 40-μF unit is an electrolytic capacitor. The smaller pieces are silver-mica, disc-ceramic, tantalum, polystrene and ceramic-chip capacitors. The small black unit (cylindrical) is a PC board-mount electrolytic. Variable capacitors are shown at B. A vacuum variable is at the upper left.

capacitance capacitors are physically large.

Capacitors in Series and Parallel

The terms parallel and series when applied to capacitance have a similar meaning as with resistances. When a number of capacitors are connected in parallel, as in Fig. 25A, the total capacitance of the group is equal to the sum of the individual capacitances:

$$C_{total} = C1 + C2 + C3 + C4 + \ldots$$

When two or more capacitors are connected in series, as in Fig. 25B, the total capacitance is less than that of the smallest capacitor in the group. The rule for finding the capacitance of a number of series-connected capacitors is the same as that for finding the resistance of a number of parallel-connected resistors. That is,

$$C_{total} = \cfrac{1}{\dfrac{1}{C1} + \dfrac{1}{C2} + \dfrac{1}{C3} + \dfrac{1}{C4} + \dfrac{1}{C5} + \ldots}$$

and, for only two capacitors in series,

$$C_{total} = \frac{C1 \times C2}{C1 + C2}$$

The same units must be used throughout; that is, all capacitances must be expressed in either μF or pF; both kinds of units cannot be used in the same equation.

Capacitors are usually connected in parallel to obtain a larger total capacitance than is available in one unit. The largest voltage that can be applied safely to a group of capacitors in parallel is the voltage that can be applied safely to the one having the lowest voltage rating.

When capacitors are connected in series, the applied voltage is divided up among them according to Kirchhoff's first law, and the situation is much the same as when resistors are in series and there is a voltage drop across each. The voltage that appears across each capacitor of a group connected in series is in inverse proportion to its capacitance, as compared with the capacitance of the whole group.

Example: Three capacitors having capacitances of 1, 2 and 4 μF, respectively, are connected in series as shown in Fig. 26. The total capacitance is

$$C =$$

$$\cfrac{1}{\dfrac{1}{C1} + \dfrac{1}{C2} + \dfrac{1}{C3}} = \cfrac{1}{\dfrac{1}{1} + \dfrac{1}{2} + \dfrac{1}{4}}$$

$$C = \frac{1}{7/4} = \frac{4}{7} = 0.571 \ \mu F$$

The voltage across each capacitor is proportional to the total capacitance divided by the capacitance of the capacitor in question, so the voltage across C1 is

$$E1 = \frac{0.571}{1} \times 2000 = 1143 \text{ volts}$$

Fig. 25 — Capacitors in parallel, A, and in series, B.

Similarly, the voltages across C2 and C3 are

$$E2 = \frac{0.571}{2} \times 2000 = 571 \text{ volts}$$

$$E3 = \frac{0.571}{4} \times 2000 = 286$$

The sum of these three voltages equals 2000 volts, the applied voltage.

Capacitors are frequently connected in series to enable the group to withstand a larger voltage (at the expense of decreased total capacitance) than any individual capacitor is rated to stand. As shown by the previous example, the applied voltage does not divide equally among the capacitors (except when all the capacitances are precisely the same) and care must be taken to ensure that the voltage rating of no capacitor in the group is exceeded.

RC TIME CONSTANT

Connecting a source of EMF directly to the terminal of a capacitor charges the capacitor to the full EMF almost instantaneously. Any resistance added to the circuit as in Fig. 27A limits the amount of current flow, lengthening the time required for the EMF between the capacitor plates to build up to the same value as the EMF of the source. During this charging period, the current flowing from the source into the capacitor gradually decreases from its initial value; the increasing EMF stored in the capacitor's electric field offers increasing opposition to the steady EMF of the source.

The voltage potential between the terminals of the capacitor while being charged is an exponential function of time, and is given by

$$V_{(t)} = E\left(1 - e^{\frac{-t}{RC}}\right)$$

where

$V_{(t)}$ = capacitor EMF in volts at t
E = potential of charging source in volts
t = time in seconds after initiation of charging current
e = natural logarithmic base = 2.718
R = circuit resistance in ohms
C = capacitance in farads

Theoretically, the charging process is never really finished, but eventually the charging current drops to an unmeasurable value. When t = RC, the above equation becomes

$$V_{(RC)} = E(1 - e^{-1}) \approx 0.632E$$

Fig. 26 — An example of capacitors connected in series. Finding the voltage drops, E1 through E3, is worked out in the text.

Fig. 27 — Illustrating the time constant of an RC circuit.

Fig. 28 — At A, how the voltage across a capacitor rises, with time, when charged through a resistor. The curve at B shows the way in which the voltage decreases across the capacitor terminals on discharging through the same value of resistance. From a practical standpoint, a capacitor may be considered as charged (or discharged) after 5RC times.

The product of R in ohms times C in farads is called the time constant of the circuit and is the time in seconds required to charge the capacitor to 63.2% of the supply voltage. After two time constants (t = 2RC) the capacitor charges another 63.2% of the difference between the capacitor voltage at one time constant and the supply voltage, for a total charge of 86.5%. After three time constants the capacitor reaches 95% of the supply voltage, and so on, as illustrated in the curve of Fig. 28A.

The time-constant equation can also be expressed as a natural logarithmic function by solving the equation for the

$$e^{\frac{-t}{RC}}$$

term and taking the natural log (ln) of both sides.

$$\frac{V(t)}{E} = 1 - e^{\frac{-t}{RC}}$$

$$e^{\frac{-t}{RC}} = 1 - \frac{V(t)}{E}$$

$$\ln\left(e^{\frac{-t}{RC}}\right) = \ln\left(1 - \frac{V(t)}{E}\right)$$

$$-\frac{t}{RC} = \ln\left(1 - \frac{V(t)}{E}\right)$$

$$\frac{t}{RC} = -\ln\left(1 - \frac{V(t)}{E}\right)$$

If a charged capacitor is discharged through a resistor, as indicated in Fig. 27B, the same time constant applies for the decay of the capacitor voltage. A direct short circuit applied between the capacitor's terminals would discharge instantly. R limits the current flow, so the capacitor voltage decreases only as rapidly as the capacitor can discharge itself through R. A capacitor discharging through a resistance exhibits the same time constant characteristics (calculated in the same way as above) as a charging capacitor. The voltage as a function of time while the capacitor is being discharged is given by

$$V_{(t)} = E\left(e^{\frac{-t}{RC}}\right)$$

where t = time in seconds after initiation of discharge. This equation can also be expressed as a natural logarithmic function, as shown above.

Alternating Current in Capacitance

In Fig. 29 a sine-wave ac voltage having a maximum value of 100 is applied to a capacitor. In the period 0A, the applied voltage increases from 0 to 38; at the end of this period the capacitor is charged to that voltage. In interval AB the voltage increases to 71; that is, 33 volts additional. In this interval a smaller quantity of charge has been added than in 0A, because the voltage rise during interval AB is smaller. Consequently the average current during

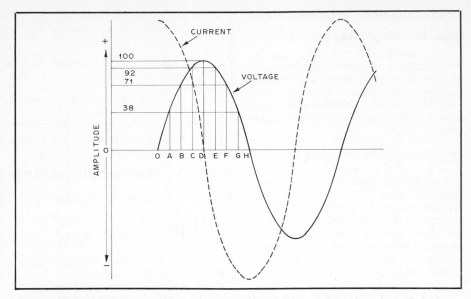

Fig. 29 — Voltage and current phase relationships when an alternating voltage is applied to a capacitor.

AB is smaller than during 0A. In the third interval, BC, the voltage rises from 71 to 92, an increase of 21 volts. This is less than the voltage increase during AB, so the quantity of electricity added is less; in other words, the average current during interval BC is still smaller. In the fourth interval, CD, the voltage increases only 8 volts; the charge added is smaller than in any preceding interval and therefore the current also is smaller.

By dividing the first quarter cycle into a very large number of intervals, it could be shown that the current charging the capacitor has the shape of a sine wave, just as the applied voltage does. The current is largest at the beginning of the cycle and becomes zero at the maximum value of the voltage, so there is a phase difference of 90° between the voltage and the current. During the first quarter cycle the current is flowing in the normal direction through the circuit, since the capacitor is being charged. Hence the current is positive, as indicated by the dashed line in Fig. 29.

In the second quarter cycle — that is, in the time from D to H — the voltage applied to the capacitor decreases. During this time the capacitor loses its charge. Applying the same reasoning, it is evident that the current is small in interval DE and continues to increase during each succeeding interval. However, the current is flowing against the applied voltage because the capacitor is discharging into the circuit. The current flows in the negative direction during this quarter cycle.

The third and fourth quarter cycles repeat the events of the first and second, respectively, with this difference — the polarity of the applied voltage has reversed, and the current changes to correspond. In other words, an alternating current flows in the circuit because of the alternate charging and discharging of the capacitance. As shown in Fig. 29, the current starts its cycle 90° before the voltage, so

the current in a capacitor leads the applied voltage by 90°.

Capacitive Reactance

The quantity of electric charge that can be placed on a capacitor is proportional to the applied EMF and the capacitance. This amount of charge moves back and forth in the circuit once each cycle, and so the rate of movement of charge (the current) is proportional to voltage, capacitance and frequency. When the effects of capacitance and frequency are considered together, they form a quantity that plays a part similar to that of resistance in Ohm's Law. This quantity is called reactance. The unit for reactance is the ohm, just as in the case of resistance. The formula for reactance is

$$X_C = \frac{1}{2\pi fC}$$

where

X_C = capacitive reactance in ohms
f = frequency in hertz
C = capacitance in farads
π = 3.1416

Although the unit of reactance is the ohm, there is no power dissipation in reactance. The energy stored in the capacitor in one portion of the cycle is simply returned to the circuit in the next.

The fundamental units for frequency and capacitance (hertz and farads) are too cumbersome for practical use in radio circuits. However, if the capacitance is specified in microfarads (μF) and the frequency is in megahertz (MHz), the reactance calculated from the previous formula retains the unit ohms.

Example: The reactance of a capacitor of 470 pF (0.00047 μF) at a frequency of 7.15 MHz is

$$X = \frac{1}{2\pi fc} = \frac{1}{2\pi \times 7.15 \times 0.00047}$$

$$X = 47.4 \text{ ohms}$$

Inductance

It is possible to show that the flow of current through a conductor is accompanied by magnetic effects; a compass needle brought near the conductor will deflect from its normal north-south position. The current sets up a magnetic field.

The transfer of energy to a magnetic field represents work performed by the source of EMF. Power is required for doing work, and since power is equal to current multiplied by voltage, there must be a voltage drop in the circuit while energy is being stored in the field. This voltage drop, exclusive of any voltage drop caused by resistance in the circuit, is the result of an opposing voltage induced in the circuit while the field is building up to its final value. Once the field becomes constant the induced EMF or back EMF disappears, since no further energy is being stored. The induced EMF opposes the EMF of the source and tends to prevent the current from rising rapidly when the circuit is closed. The amplitude of the induced EMF is proportional to the rate at which the current changes and to a constant associated with the circuit itself; the inductance of the circuit.

Inductance depends on the physical configuration of the conductor. If a conductor is formed into a coil, its inductance is increased. A coil of many turns will have more inductance than one of few turns, if both coils are otherwise physically similar. Furthermore, if a coil is placed around an iron core its inductance will be greater than it was without the magnetic core.

The polarity of an induced EMF is always such as to oppose any change in the current in the circuit. This means that when the current in the circuit is increasing, work is being done against the induced EMF by storing energy in the magnetic field. If the current in the circuit tends to decrease, the stored energy of the field returns to the circuit, and thus adds to the energy being supplied by the source of EMF. This tends to keep the current flowing even though the applied EMF may be decreasing or be removed entirely. The energy stored in the magnetic field of an inductor is given by

$$W = \frac{I^2L}{2}$$

where

W = energy in joules
I = current in amperes
L = inductance in henrys

The unit of inductance is the henry. Values of inductance used in radio equipment vary over a wide range. In radio-frequency circuits, the inductance values used will be measured in millihenrys (a mH is one thousandth of a henry) at low frequencies, and in microhenrys (μH, one millionth of a henry) at medium frequencies and higher. Although coils for radio

frequencies may be wound on special iron cores (ordinary iron is not suitable), many RF coils made and used by amateurs are of the air-core type, that is, wound on an insulating support consisting of nonmagnetic material (Fig. 30).

Every conductor passing current has a magnetic field associated with it, and therefore inductance, even though the conductor is not formed into a coil. The inductance of a short length of straight wire is small, but it may not be negligible — if the current through it changes rapidly, the induced voltage may be appreciable. This is the case in even a few inches of wire when an alternating current having a frequency of the order of 100 MHz or higher is flowing. At much lower frequencies the inductance of the same wire could be ignored because the induced voltage would be negligible.

Calculating Inductance

The approximate inductance of a single-layer air-core coil may be calculated from the simplified formula

$$L\ (\mu H) = \frac{d^2n^2}{18d + 40\ell}$$

where
L = inductance in microhenrys
d = coil diameter in inches
ℓ = coil length in inches
n = number of turns

The notation is explained in Fig. 31. This formula is a close approximation for coils having a length equal to or greater than 0.4d.

Example: Assume a coil has 48 turns wound at 32 turns per inch and a diameter of ¾ inch. Thus, d = 0.75 , ℓ = 48/32 = 1.5, and n = 48. Substituting,

$$L = \frac{0.75^2 \times 48^2}{18 \times 0.75 + 40 \times 1.5}$$

$$L = \frac{1296}{73.5} = 17.6\ \mu H$$

To calculate the number of turns of a single-layer coil for a required value of inductance

$$n = \frac{\sqrt{L\ (18d + 40\ell)}}{d}$$

Example: Suppose an inductance of 10 μH is required. The form on which the coil is to be wound has a diameter of one inch and is long enough to accommodate a coil of 1¼ inches. Then d = 1, ℓ = 1.25 and L = 10. Substituting,

$$n = \frac{\sqrt{10\ [(18 \times 1) + (40 \times 1.25)]}}{1}$$

$$n = \sqrt{680} = 26.1\ turns$$

A 26-turn coil would be close enough in practical work. Since the coil will be 1.25 inches long, the number of turns per inch

Fig. 30 — Assorted inductors. A rotary (continuously variable) coil is shown at the upper left. Slug-tuned inductors are visible in the lower foreground. An RF choke (three pi windings) is visible at the lower right.

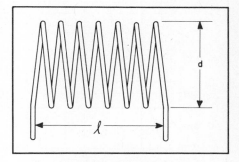

Fig. 31 — Coil dimensions used in the inductance formula. The wire diameter does not enter into the formula. The spacing has been exaggerated in this illustration for clarity. The formula is for closewound coils.

will be 26.1 / 1.25 = 20.9. Consulting the wire table in Chapter 35, we find that no. 17 enameled wire (or anything smaller) can be used. The proper inductance is obtained by winding the required number of turns on the form and then adjusting the spacing between the turns to make a uniformly spaced coil 1.25 inches long.

Inductance Charts

Most inductance formulas lose accuracy when applied to small coils (such as are used in VHF work and in low-pass filters built for reducing harmonic interference to television) because the conductor thickness is no longer negligible in comparison with the size of the coil. Fig. 32 shows the measured inductance of VHF coils, and may be used as a basis for circuit design. Two curves are given; curve A is for coils wound to an inside diameter of ½ inch; curve B is for coils of ¾ inch inside diameter. In both curves the wire size is no. 12, winding pitch is eight turns to the inch (1/8 inch center-to-center turn spacing). The inductance values given include leads ½ inch long.

Machine-wound coils with the diameters and turns per inch given in Tables 4 and 5 are available in many radio stores, under the trade names of B&W Miniductor, Airdux and Polycoil. Figs. 33 and 34 are used with Tables 4 and 5.

Fig. 32 — Measured inductance of coils wound with no. 12 bare wire, eight turns to the inch. The values include half-inch leads.

Table 4		
Machine-Wound Coil Specifications		
Coil Dia Inches	Turns Per Inch	Inductance in μH
1¼	4	2.75
	6	6.3
	8	11.2
	10	17.5
	16	42.5
1½	4	3.9
	6	8.8
	8	15.6
	10	24.5
	16	63
1¾	4	5.2
	6	11.8
	8	21
	10	33
	16	85
2	4	6.6
	6	15
	8	26.5
	10	42
	16	108
2½	4	10.2
	6	23
	8	41
	10	64
3	4	14
	6	31.5
	8	56
	10	89

Fig. 33 — Factor to be applied to the inductance of coils listed in Table 4 for coil lengths up to 5 inches.

Fig. 34 — Factor to be applied to the inductance of coils listed in Table 5, as a function of coil length. Use curve A for coils marked A, and curve B for coils marked B.

Table 5		
Machine-Wound Coil Specifications		
Coil Dia Inches	Turns Per Inch	Inductance in μH
½ (A)	4	0.18
	6	0.40
	8	0.72
	10	1.12
	16	2.9
	32	12
5/8 (A)	4	0.28
	6	0.62
	8	1.1
	10	1.7
	16	4.4
	32	18
¾ (B)	4	0.6
	6	1.35
	8	2.4
	10	3.8
	16	9.9
	32	40
1 (B)	4	1.0
	6	2.3
	8	4.2
	10	6.6
	16	16.9
	32	68

Forming a wire into a solenoid increases its inductance, and also introduces distributed capacitance. Since each turn is at a slightly different ac potential, each pair of turns effectively forms a parasitic capacitor. At some frequency the effective capacitance will have a reactance equal to that of the inductance, and the inductor will show self-resonance. (Reactance and resonance are treated later in this chapter.) Above the self-resonant frequency, a coil takes on the reactive properties of a capacitor instead of an inductor. The behavior of a coil with respect to frequency is illustrated in Fig. 35.

At low frequencies the inductance of a straight, round, nonmagnetic wire in free space is given by

$$L = 0.0002b \left[\left(\ln \frac{2b}{a} \right) - 0.75 \right]$$

where

L = inductance in μH
a = wire radius in mm
b = wire length in mm
ln = natural logarithm = 2.303 × common logarithm (base 10)

If the dimensions are expressed in inches instead of mm, the equation may still be

used, except replace the 0.0002 value with 0.00508. Skin effect reduces the inductance at VHF and above. As the frequency approaches infinity, the 0.75 constant within the brackets approaches unity. As a practical matter, the skin effect doesn't reduce the inductance by more than a few percent.

As an example, find the inductance of

a wire that is 4 mm in diameter and 100 mm long. For the calculations, a = 2 mm (radius) and b = 100. Using the natural logarithm function, the problem is formulated as follows:

$$L = 0.0002 \ (100) \left[\ln\left(\frac{2 \times 100}{2}\right) - 0.75 \right]$$

$$L = 0.02 \ [\ln (100) - 0.75]$$
$$L = 0.02 \ (4.605 - 0.75)$$
$$L = (0.02) \ (3.855) = 0.077 \ \mu H$$

Fig. 36 is a graph of the inductance for wires of various radii as a function of length.

A VHF or UHF tank circuit can be fabricated from a wire parallel to a ground plane, with one end grounded. A formula for the inductance of such an arrangement is given in Fig. 37.

Suppose it is desired to find the inductance of a wire 100 mm long and 2 mm in radius, suspended 40 mm above a ground plane. (The inductance is measured between the free end and the ground plane, and the formula includes the inductance of the 40-mm grounding link.) A person skilled in the use of a sophisticated calculator could produce the answer with only a few keystrokes, but to demonstrate the use of the formula, begin by evaluating these quantities:

$$b + \sqrt{b^2 + a^2} = 100 + \sqrt{100^2 + 2^2}$$
$$= 100 + 100.02 = 200.02$$

$$b + \sqrt{b^2 + 4h^2}$$
$$= 100 + \sqrt{100^2 + 4 \times 40^2}$$
$$= 100 + 128.06$$
$$= 228.06$$

$$\frac{2h}{a} = \frac{2 \times 40}{2} = 40$$

$$\frac{b}{4} = \frac{100}{4} = 25$$

Substituting these figures into the formula yields:

$$L = 0.0004605 \times 100 \times$$

$$\log\left(\frac{2 \times 40}{2} \times \frac{200.02}{228.06}\right)$$

$$+ \ 0.0002 \ (128.06 - 100.02 + 25 - 80 + 2) = 0.066 \ \mu H$$

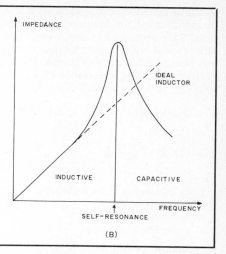

Fig. 35 — The proximity of the turns on a solenoid forms parasitic capacitors, as sketched in A. The net effect of the capacitors is called the distributed capacitance, and causes the coil to exhibit a self-resonance, illustrated in B.

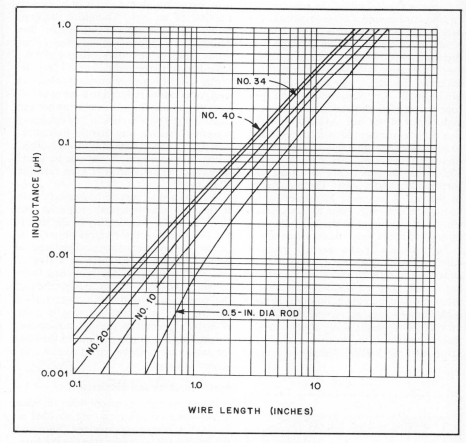

Fig. 36 — Inductance of various conductor sizes as straight wires.

$$L = 0.0004605b \left\{ \log_{10}\left[\frac{2h}{a} \left(\frac{b + \sqrt{b^2 + a^2}}{b + \sqrt{b^2 + 4h^2}} \right) \right] \right\} + 0.0002 \left(\sqrt{b^2 + 4h^2} - \sqrt{b^2 + a^2} + \frac{b}{4} - 2h + a \right)$$

where
 L = inductance in μH
 a = wire radius in mm
 b = wire length parallel to ground plane in mm
 h = wire height above ground plane in mm

Fig. 37 — Equation for determining the inductance of a wire parallel to a ground plane, with one end grounded. If the dimensions are in inches, the numerical coefficients become 0.0117 for the first term and 0.0508 for the second term.

Another conductor configuration that is frequently used for inductors is the flat strip. This arrangement has lower skin-effect loss at high frequencies than round wire because it has a higher surface-area to volume ratio. The inductance of such a strip can be found from

$$L = 0.00508b \left(\ln \frac{2b}{w + h} + 0.5 + 0.2235 \frac{w + h}{b} \right)$$

where

L = inductance in microhenrys
b = length in inches
w = width in inches
h = thickness in inches

Permeability of Iron-Core Coils

Suppose the coil in Fig. 38 is wound on an iron core having a cross-sectional area of 2 square inches. When a certain current is sent through the coil, it is found that there are 80,000 lines of force in the core. Since the area is 2 square inches, the magnetic flux density is 40,000 lines per square inch. Now suppose that the iron core is removed and the same current is maintained in the coil. Also suppose the flux density without the iron core is found to be 50 lines per square inch. The ratio of these flux densities, iron core to air, is 40,000/50 or 800. This is called the permeability of the core. The inductance of the coil is increased 800 times by inserting the iron core, since the inductance will be proportional to the magnetic flux through the coils, other things being equal.

The permeability of a magnetic material varies with the flux density. At low flux densities (or with an air core), increasing the current through the coil will cause a proportionate increase in flux. But at very high flux densities, increasing the current may cause no appreciable change in the flux. When this is so, the iron is said to be saturated. Saturation causes a rapid

Fig. 38 — Typical construction of an iron-core inductor. The small air gap prevents magnetic saturation of the iron and thus maintains the inductance at high currents.

decrease in permeability, because it decreases the ratio of flux lines to those obtainable with the same current and an air core. Obviously, the inductance of an iron-core inductor is highly dependent on the current flowing in the coil. In an air-core coil, the inductance is independent of current because air does not saturate.

Iron-core coils such as the one sketched in Fig. 38 are used chiefly in power supply equipment. They usually have direct current flowing through the winding, and the variation in inductance with current is usually undesirable. It may be overcome by keeping the flux density below the saturation point of the iron. This is done by opening the core so there is a small air gap, indicated by the dashed lines in Fig. 38. The magnetic resistance introduced by such a gap is very large compared with that of the iron, even though the gap is only a small fraction of an inch. Therefore the gap, rather than the iron, controls the flux density. This reduces the inductance, but holds the value practically constant regardless of the magnitude of the current.

For radio-frequency work, the losses in iron cores can be reduced to a more useful level by grinding the iron into a powder and then mixing it with a "binder" of insulating material in such a way that the individual iron particles are insulated from each other. Using this approach, cores can be made that function satisfactorily even into the VHF range.

Because a large part of the magnetic path is through a nonmagnetic material (the "binder"), the permeability of the iron is low compared with the values obtained at power supply frequencies. The core is usually shaped in the form of a slug or cylinder for fit inside the insulating form on which the coil is wound. Despite the fact that the major portion of the magnetic path for the flux is in air, the slug is quite effective in increasing the coil inductance. By pushing the slug in and out of the coil, the inductance can be varied over a considerable range.

Eddy Currents and Hysteresis

When alternating current flows through a coil wound on an iron core an EMF is induced, as previously explained. Since iron is a conductor, a current flows in the core. Such currents are called eddy currents. Eddy currents represent lost power because they flow through the resistance of the iron and generate heat. Losses caused by eddy currents can be reduced by laminating the core (cutting the core into thin strips). These strips or laminations are then insulated from each other by painting them with some insulating material such as varnish or shellac.

Another type of energy loss is found in loaded inductors. Iron tends to resist any change in its magnetic state, so a rapidly changing current such as ac is continually forced to supply energy to the iron in order to overcome this "inertia." Losses caused

Fig. 39 — Inductances in series and parallel.

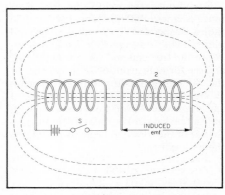

Fig. 40 — Mutual inductance. When S is closed, current flows through coil no. 1, setting up a magnetic field that induces an EMF in the turns of coil no. 2.

by this effect are referred to as hysteresis losses.

Eddy-current and hysteresis losses in iron increase rapidly as the frequency of the alternating current is increased. For this reason, ordinary iron cores can be used only at power-line and audio frequencies — up to approximately 15,000 hertz. Even then, a very good grade of iron or steel is necessary for the core to perform well at the higher audio frequencies. Iron cores of this type become completely useless at radio frequencies.

Inductances in Series and Parallel

When two or more inductors are connected in series (Fig. 39A), the total inductance is equal to the sum of the individual inductances, provided the coils are sufficiently separated so that coils are not in the magnetic field of one another. That is,

$$L_{total} = L1 + L2 + L3 + \ldots$$

If inductors are connected in parallel (Fig. 39B), and if the coils are separated sufficiently, the total inductance is given by

$$L_{total} = \frac{1}{\frac{1}{L1} + \frac{1}{L2} + \frac{1}{L3} + \ldots}$$

and for two inductances in parallel,

$$L = \frac{L1 \times L2}{L1 + L2}$$

Thus, the rules for combining inductances in series and parallel are the same for resistances, assuming the coils are far enough apart so that each is unaffected by another's magnetic field. When this is not so, the formulas given above cannot be used.

Mutual Inductance

When two coils are arranged with their axes on the same line, as shown in Fig. 40, current sent through coil 1 creates a magnetic field that cuts coil 2. Consequently, an EMF will be induced in coil 2 whenever the field strength is changing. This induced EMF is similar to the EMF of self-induction, but since it appears in the second coil because of current flowing in the first, it is a mutual effect and results from the mutual inductance between the two coils.

When all the flux set up by one coil cuts all the turns of the other coil, the mutual inductance has its maximum possible value. If only a small part of the flux set up by one coil cuts the turns of the other, the mutual inductance is relatively small. Two coils having mutual inductance are said to be coupled.

The ratio of actual mutual inductance to the maximum possible value that could theoretically be obtained with two given coils is called the coefficient of coupling between the coils. It is frequently expressed as a percentage. Coils that have nearly the maximum possible mutual inductance (coefficient = 1 or 100 percent) are said to be closely, or tightly, coupled. If the mutual inductance is relatively small the coils are said to be loosely coupled. The degree of coupling depends upon the physical spacing between the coils and how they are placed with respect to each other. Maximum coupling exists when they have a common axis and are as close together as possible (one wound over the other). The coupling is least when the coils are far apart or are placed so their axes are at right angles.

The maximum possible coefficient of coupling is closely approached when the two coils are wound on a closed iron core. The coefficient with air-core coils may run as high as 0.6 or 0.7 if one coil is wound over the other, but will be much less if the two coils are separated. Although unity coupling is suggested by Fig. 40, such coupling is possible only when the coils are wound on a closed magnetic core.

RL TIME CONSTANT

A comparable situation to an RC circuit exists when resistance and inductance are connected in series. In Fig. 41, first consider L to have no resistance and also assume that R is zero. Closing S sends a current through the circuit. The instantaneous transition from no current to a finite value, however small, represents a very rapid change in current, and a back

Fig. 41 — Time constant of an RL circuit.

Fig. 42 — Instantaneously placing the switch in position B will discharge the inductor as shown in the graph. This is a theoretical model only; a mechanical switch cannot change state instantaneously.

EMF is developed by the self-inductance of L that is almost equal and opposite to the applied EMF. The resulting initial current is very small.

The back EMF depends on the change in current and would cease to offer opposition if the current did not continue to increase. With no resistance in the circuit (which would lead to an infinitely large current, by Ohm's Law) the current would increase forever, always growing just fast enough to keep the EMF of self-induction equal to the applied EMF.

When resistance in the circuit limits the current, Ohm's Law defines the value that the current can reach. The back EMF generated in L must only equal the difference between E and the drop across R, because the difference is the voltage actually applied to L. This difference becomes smaller as the current approaches the final Ohm's Law value. Theoretically, the back EMF never quite disappears and

so the current never quite reaches the Ohm's Law value, but practically the differences become unmeasurable after a time.

The current at any time after the switch in Fig. 41 has been closed can be found from

$$I_{(t)} = \frac{E}{R}\left(1 - e^{\frac{-tR}{L}}\right)$$

where

I_t = current in amperes at time t
E = power supply potential in volts
t = time in seconds after initiation of current
e = natural logarithmic base = 2.718
R = circuit resistance in ohms
L = inductance in henrys

The time in seconds required for the current to build up to 63.2% of the maximum value is called the time constant, and is equal to L/R, where L is in henrys and R is in ohms. After each time interval equal to this constant the circuit conducts an additional 63.2% of the remaining current. This behavior is graphed in Fig. 41.

An inductor cannot be discharged in the simple circuit of Fig. 41 because the magnetic field disappears as soon as current flow ceases. Opening S does not leave the inductor charged. The energy stored in the magnetic field returns instantly to the circuit when S is opened. The rapid disappearance of the field causes a very large voltage to be induced in the coil. Usually the induced voltage is many times larger than the voltage applied, because induced voltage is proportional to the rate that the field changes. The common result of opening the switch in such a circuit is that a spark or arc forms at the switch contacts at the instant of opening. When the inductance is large and the current in the circuit is high, large amounts of energy are released in a very short time. It is not at all unusual for the switch contacts to burn or melt under such circumstances. The spark or arc at the opened switch can be reduced or suppressed by connecting a suitable capacitor and resistor in series across the contacts. Such an RC combination is called a snubber network.

If the excitation is removed without breaking the circuit, as diagrammed in Fig. 42, the current will decay according to the formula

$$I_{(t)} = \frac{E}{R}\left[1 - \left(1 - e^{\frac{-tR}{L}}\right)\right]$$

or

$$I_{(t)} = \frac{E}{R}\left(e^{\frac{-tR}{L}}\right)$$

where t = time in seconds after removal of EMF.

After one time constant the current will lose 63.2% of its steady-state value (decay to 36.8% of the steady-state value). The graph in Fig. 42 shows the current decay waveform to be identical to the voltage discharge waveform of a capacitor. However, one should be careful about applying the terms charge and discharge to an inductive circuit. These terms refer to energy storage in an electric field. An inductor stores energy in a magnetic field.

Inductive Reactance

When an alternating voltage is applied to a pure inductance (one with no resistance — all practical inductors have some resistance) the current is 90° out of phase with the applied voltage. In this case the current lags 90° behind the voltage; the opposite of the capacitor current-voltage relationship (Fig. 43.)

The primary cause for current lag in an inductor is the back EMF generated in the inductance. The amplitude of the back EMF is proportional to the rate at which the current changes. This in turn is proportional to the frequency, so the amplitude of the current is inversely proportional to the applied frequency. Since the back EMF is proportional to inductance for a given rate of current change, the current is inversely proportional to inductance for a given applied voltage and frequency. (Another way of saying this is that just enough current flows to generate an induced EMF that equals and opposes the applied voltage.)

The combined effect of inductance and frequency is called inductive reactance, also expressed in ohms. The formula for it is

$$X_L = 2\pi fL$$

wnere
X_L = inductive reactance
f = frequency in hertz
L = inductance in henrys
π = 3.1416

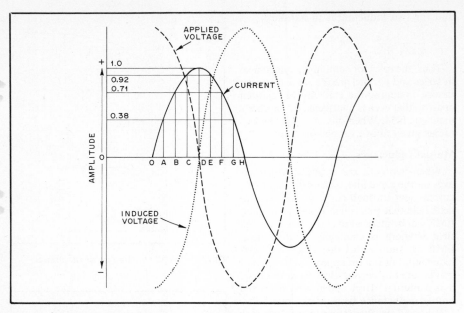

Fig. 43 — Phase relationships between voltage and current when an alternating voltage is applied to an inductance.

Example: The reactance of a coil having an inductance of 8 henrys, at a frequency of 120 hertz, is

$$X_L = 2\pi fL = 6.2832 \times 120 \times 8$$
$$X_L = 6032 \text{ ohms}$$

In radio-frequency circuits the inductance values usually are small and the frequencies are large. When the inductance is expressed in millihenrys and the frequency in kilohertz, the conversion factors for the two units cancel, and the formula for reactance may be used without first converting to fundamental units. Similarly, no conversion is necessary if the inductance is expressed in microhenrys and the frequency in megahertz.

Example: The reactance of a 15-microhenry coil at a frequency of 14 MHz is

$$X_L = 2\pi fL = 6.2832 \times 14 \times 15$$
$$X_L = 1319 \text{ ohms}$$

The resistance of the wire used to wind the coil has no effect on the reactance, but simply acts as a separate resistor connected in series with the coil.

Reactance and Impedance

Ohm's Law for Reactance

Ohm's Law equations for an ac circuit containing only reactance are

$$I = \frac{E}{X}, \qquad E = IX, \qquad X = \frac{E}{I}$$

where
E = EMF in volts
I = current in amperes
X = reactance in ohms

The reactance in the circuit may, of course, be either inductive or capacitive.

Example: If a current of 2 amperes is flowing through the capacitor of the earlier example (reactance = 47.4 ohms) at 7.15 MHz, the voltage drop across the capacitor is E = IX = 2 × 47.4 = 94.8 volts.

If 420 V at 120 hertz is applied to the 8-henry inductor of the earlier example, the current through the coil will be

$$I = \frac{E}{X} = \frac{420}{6032} = 0.0696A$$
$$= 69.6 \text{ mA}$$

Reactance Chart

The accompanying chart, Fig. 44, shows the reactance of capacitances from 1 pF to 100 μF, and the reactance of inductances from 0.1 μH to 10 henrys, for frequencies between 100 hertz and 100 megahertz. The approximate value of reactance can be read from the chart. More exact values can be calculated from the formulas.

Reactances in Series and Parallel

When reactances of the same kind are connected in series or parallel the resultant reactance is that of the resultant inductance or capacitance. This leads to the same rules that are used when determining the resistance when resistors are combined. That is, for series reactances of the same kind the resultant reactance is

$$X = X1 + X2 + X3 + X4 + \ldots$$

For reactances of the same kind in parallel the resultant is

$$X = \cfrac{1}{\frac{1}{X1} + \frac{1}{X2} + \frac{1}{X3} + \frac{1}{X4} + \ldots}$$

or for two in parallel,

$$X = \frac{X1 \times X2}{X1 + X2}$$

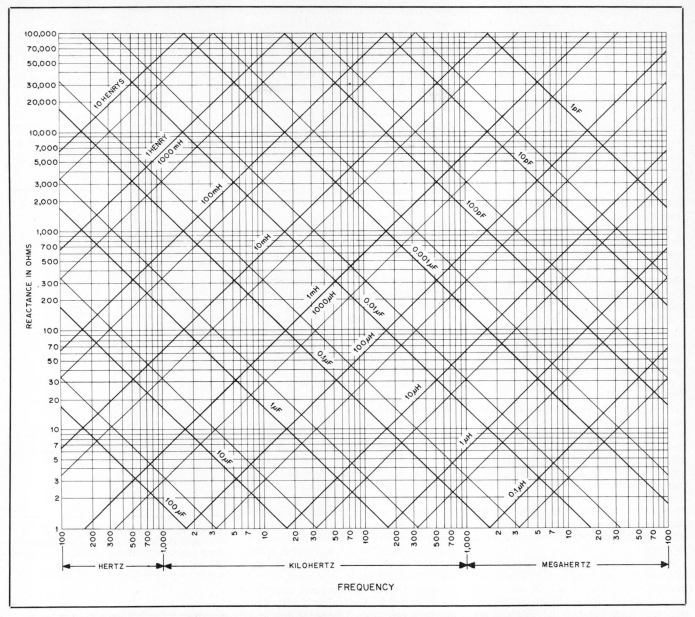

Fig. 44 — Inductive and capacitive reactance vs. frequency. Heavy lines represent multiples of 10, intermediate light lines multiples of five. For example, the light line between 10 μH and 100 μH represents 50 μH; the light line between 0.1 μF and 1 μF represents 0.5 μF, and so on. Intermediate values can be values within the chart range. For example, the reactance of 10 henrys at 60 Hz can be found by taking the reactance of 10 henrys at 600 Hz and dividing by 10 for the 10× times decrease in frequency.

The situation is different when reactances of opposite kinds are combined. Since the current in a capacitance leads the applied voltage by 90° and the current in an inductance lags the applied voltage by 90°, the voltage at the terminals of opposite types of reactance are 180° out of phase in a series circuit. (In a series circuit the current has to be the same through all elements.)

In a parallel circuit (in which the same voltage is applied to all elements), the currents in reactances of opposite types are 180° out of phase. The 180° phase relationship means the currents or voltages are of opposite polarity, so in the series circuit of Fig. 45A the voltage E_L across the inductive reactance X_L is of opposite polarity to the voltage E_C across the capacitive reactance X_C. Thus if we call X_L "positive" and X_C "negative" (a common convention) the applied voltage E_{AC} is $E_L - E_C$. In the parallel circuit at B the total current, I, is equal to $I_L - I_C$, since the currents are 180° out of phase. In the series case, therefore, the resultant reactance of X_L and X_C is $X = X_L - X_C$ and in the parallel case (Fig. 45B),

$$X = \frac{-X_L X_C}{X_L - X_C}$$

Note that in the series circuit the total reactance is negative if X_C is larger than X_L; this indicates that the total reactance

Fig. 45 — Series and parallel circuits containing opposite kinds of reactance.

is capacitive in such a case. The resultant reactance in a series circuit is always smaller

Fig. 46 — Series and parallel circuit containing resistance and reactance.

than the larger of the two individual reactances.

In the parallel circuit, the resultant reactance is positive (that is, inductive) if X_C is larger than X_L. This is just the opposite of the situation for reactances in series. In every case the resultant reactance is larger than the smaller of the two individual reactances.

There is one special case where $X_L = X_C$. The total reactance in this case is zero in the series circuit and infinitely large in the parallel circuit. In this case the circuit is said to be resonant.

Reactive Power

In Fig. 45A the voltage drop across the inductor is larger than the voltage applied to the circuit. This might seem to be an impossible condition, but it is not; the explanation is that while energy is being stored in the inductor's magnetic field, energy is being returned to the circuit from the capacitor's electric field, and vice versa. This stored energy is responsible for the fact that the voltages across reactances in series can be larger than the voltage applied to them.

In a resistance the current causes heating and a power loss equal to I^2R. The power in a reactance is equal to I^2X, but is not a loss; it is simply power that is transferred back and forth between the field and the circuit but not used up in heating anything. To distinguish this nondissipated power from the power actually consumed, the unit of reactive power is called the volt-ampere-reactive, or VAR, instead of watt. Reactive power is sometimes called wattless power.

Impedance

When a circuit contains both resistance and reactance the combined effect of the two is called impedance, symbolized by the letter Z. Impedance is thus a more general term than either resistance or reactance. The term is frequently used even for circuits that have only resistance or reactance, although usually with a qualification such as "resistive impedance" to indicate that the circuit has only resistance, for example.

The reactance and resistance comprising an impedance may be connected either in series or parallel, as shown in Fig. 46. In these circuits the reactance is shown as a

box to indicate that it may be either inductive or capacitive. In the series circuit at A the current is the same in both elements, with (generally) different voltages appearing across the resistance and reactance. In the parallel circuit at B the same voltage is applied to both elements, but different currents may flow in the two branches.

In a resistance the current is in phase with the applied voltage, while in a reactance it is 90° out of phase with the voltage. Thus, the phase relationship between current and voltage in the circuit as a whole may be anything between zero and 90°, depending on the relative amount of resistance and reactance.

The Complex Impedance Plane

The use of complex numbers in the analysis of ac circuits allows quicker solution without guess work. A complex number treats not only real numbers, but also "imaginary" numbers. An imaginary number is a number that cannot be plotted on the real axis of a graph such as shown in Fig. 47. On this graph the real axis is the horizontal axis, with positive values increasing to the right and negative values increasing to the left. Imaginary numbers are plotted on the Y axis with positive values rising from the origin and negative values descending from the origin.

In mathematical terms an imaginary number is an even root of a negative number. Since there is no real number when squared that will give a negative quantity, the imaginary system is used. Mathematicians define the value i as the square root of negative 1. In electronics, the symbol i is already used as a designation for current, so the symbol j is substituted; $j \times j$ is equal to negative 1.

The graph of Fig. 47, when used in electrical circuit analysis, is known as the complex impedance plane. The resistive components of the circuit have real values and are plotted along the real or X axis. Reactive values are plotted along the imaginary or Y axis. Inductive reactances, X_L, take on positive imaginary values because the voltage across an inductor leads the current through the inductor by 90 degrees. Capacitive reactances, X_C, take on negative imaginary values because the capacitive voltage lags the current by 90 degrees.

The familiar form, $R \pm jX$ is the rectangular coordinate form for a complex impedance as might be plotted on the complex impedance plane. For example, the value $27 - j8$ is plotted in Fig. 48A. The resistive value is 27 ohms and the capacitive reactance value is 8 ohms. So, 27 ohms positive and 8 imaginary ohms negative gives point A.

Fig. 48B shows another impedance value, where the resistance is 0.61 ohm and the inductive reactance is 1.15 ohms. The same impedance can be described in a secondary form called polar coordinate form. Here, instead of the point being

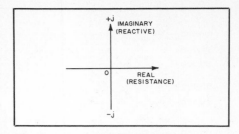

Fig. 47 — Real numbers are plotted on the X axis of the complex impedance plane; imaginary numbers are plotted on the Y axis.

Fig. 48 — At A, the complex impedance $27 - j8$ is plotted graphically in rectangular coordinate form. At B, the complex impedance $0.61 + j 1.15$ is plotted in rectangular coordinate form and is also shown in polar coordinate form.

described by its X-Y values, its position is described by the magnitude of the distance from the origin and the angle in degrees rotated counterclockwise from the positive X-axis. This is shown in Fig. 48B. The impedance now is described in the form of some magnitude times a phase angle. For example, $1.3 \underline{/62°}$.

The values $0.61 + j1.15$ and $1.3 \underline{/62°}$ both describe the same impedance, only in different forms. The values are identical and each form can be easily converted to the other. There are advantages to each form. In rectangular form, complex numbers are easily added or subtracted. In polar form, complex numbers are easily multiplied and divided. The form used is largely dependent on the mathematical process to be performed on the complex number.

Addition and Subtraction of Complex Numbers

The rule for adding and subtracting com-

Fig. 49 — Converting from rectangular to polar form.

Fig. 50 — Converting from polar to rectangular form.

plex numbers in rectangular form is very simple: add or subtract the real and imaginary terms separately.

For example: $(15 + j32) + (10 - j8) = 25 + j24$

Multiplication and Division of Complex Numbers

The rule for multiplying complex numbers in the polar form is: multiply the magnitudes and add the angles.

For example: $(8 \angle 27°) \times (2 \angle 3°) = 16 \angle 30°$

The rule for dividing complex numbers in polar form is: divide the magnitudes, but subtract the angle of denominator from the angle of the numerator.

For example: $(8 \angle 27°) / (2 \angle 3°) = 4 \angle 24°$

Converting from Rectangular to Polar Form

The easiest way to perform multiplication or division on a complex number is the use of polar form. Although it is possible to multiply complex numbers in their rectangular form, it is actually easier to first convert rectangular form to polar form and then perform the operations necessary. The magnitude of an impedance in polar form is equal to the distance the plotted impedance is from the origin. The

Pythagorean Theorem provides a simple means of calculating this distance. The magnitude is equal to

$$Z = \sqrt{R^2 + X^2}$$

This also is the formula for finding ac impedance.

The phase angle referenced to the positive real axis can also be found through simple trigonometry.

$$\theta = \arctan \frac{X}{R}$$

or

$$\theta = \arcsin \frac{X}{Z}$$

or

$$\theta = \arccos \frac{R}{Z}$$

For example: $10 - j10 = 14.14 \angle -45°$ as shown in Fig. 49.

Converting from Polar to Rectangular Form

As shown in Fig. 50, the real term of an impedance plotted in polar form is equal to $Z \cos \theta$, and the imaginary term is equal to $Z \sin \theta$. Multiplying the magnitude of the impedance in polar form by the cosine of the phase angle gives the real term. Multiplying the magnitude of the impedance in polar form by the sine of the angle gives the reactive term.

For example: $12 \angle 42°$
$R = 12 \times \cos(42°) = 8.92$
$X = j \times 12 (\sin 42°) = j8.03$
$12 \angle 42° = 8.92 + j8.03$

Series Circuits

When resistance and reactance are in series, the impedance of the circuit is

$$Z = \sqrt{R^2 + X^2}$$

where

Z = impedance in ohms
R = resistance in ohms
X = reactance in ohms

The reactance may be either capacitive or inductive. If there are two or more reactances in the circuit they may be combined into a resultant by the rules previously given before substitution into the formula above; similarly for resistances.

Parallel Circuits

With resistance and reactance in parallel, as in Fig. 46B, the impedance is

$$Z = \frac{RX}{\sqrt{R^2 + X^2}}$$

where the symbols have the same meaning as for series circuits.

Just as in the case of series circuits, a number of reactances in parallel should be combined to find the resultant reactance before substitution in the formula above;

similarly for a number of resistances in parallel.

Equivalent Series and Parallel Circuits

The two circuits shown in Fig. 46 are equivalent if the same current flows when a given voltage of the same frequency is applied, and if the phase angle between voltage and current is the same in both cases. It is in fact possible to transform any given series circuit into an equivalent parallel circuit, and vice versa.

Transformations of this type often lead to simplification in the solution of complicated circuits. However, from the standpoint of practical work the usefulness of such transformations lies in the fact that the impedance of a circuit may be modified by the addition of either series or parallel elements, depending on which happens to be more convenient in the particular case. Typical applications are considered later in connection with tuned circuits and transmission lines.

A series RX circuit can be converted into its parallel equivalent by means of the formula

$$R_p = \frac{R_s^2 + X_s^2}{R_s}$$

$$X_p = \frac{R_s^2 + X_s^2}{X_s}$$

where the subscripts p and s represent the parallel- and series-equivalent values, respectively. If the parallel values are known, the equivalent series circuit can be found from

$$R_s = \frac{R_p}{1 + \left(\frac{R_p}{X_p}\right)^2}$$

and

$$X_s = \frac{R_s R_p}{X_p}$$

Ohm's Law for Impedance

Ohm's Law can be applied to circuits containing impedance just as readily as to circuits having resistance or reactance only. The formulas are

$$I = \frac{E}{Z}$$

$$E = IZ$$

$$Z = \frac{E}{I}$$

where

E = EMF in volts
I = current in amperes
Z = impedance in ohms

Fig. 51 shows a simple circuit consisting of a resistance of 75 ohms and a reactance of 100 ohms in series. From the formula previously given, the impedance is

$$Z = \sqrt{R^2 + Z_L^2} = \sqrt{75^2 + 100^2} = 125$$

If the applied voltage is 250, then

$$I = \frac{E}{Z} = \frac{250}{125} = 2 \text{ amperes}$$

This current flows through both the resistance and reactance, so the voltage drops are

$$E_R = IR = 2 \times 75 = 150 \text{ volts}$$

$$EX_L = IX_L = 2 \times 100 = 200 \text{ volts}$$

The simple arithmetical sum of these two drops, 350 V, is greater than the applied voltage because the two voltages are 90° out of phase. Their actual resultant, when phase is taken into account, is

$$\sqrt{150^2 + 200^2} = 250 \text{ volts}$$

Power Factor

In the circuit of Fig. 51 an applied EMF of 250 V results in a current of 2 amperes, giving an apparent power of $250 \times 2 = 500$ watts. However, only the resistance actually consumes power. The power in the resistance is

$$P = I^2R = 2^2 \times 75 = 300 \text{ watts}$$

The ratio of the power consumed to the apparent power is called the power factor of the circuit. In this example the power factor would be 300/500 = 0.6. Power factor is frequently expressed as a percentage; in this case, it is 60 percent.

Real or dissipated power is measured in watts; apparent power, to distinguish it

Fig. 51 — Circuit used as an example for impedance calculations.

Fig. 52 — A series circuit containing L, C and R is resonant at the applied frequency when the reactance of C is equal to the reactance of L. The I in the circle is the schematic symbol for an ammeter.

from real power, is measured in volt-amperes (VA). It is simply the product of volts and amperes and has no direct relationship to the power actually used up unless the power factor of the circuit is known. The power factor of a purely resistive circuit is 100% or 1, while the power factor of a pure reactance is zero. In this illustration, the reactive power is

$$VAR = I^2X = 2^2 \times 100$$

$$VAR = 400 \text{ volt-amperes}$$

An equivalent definition of power factor is

$$PF = \frac{R}{Z} = \cos \theta$$

Since power factor is always rendered as a positive number, the value must be followed by the words leading or lagging to identify the phase of the voltage with respect to the current. Specifying the numerical power factor is not always sufficient. For example, many dc-to-ac power inverters can safely operate loads having a large net reactance of one sign but only a small reactance of the opposite sign.

Reactance and Complex Waves

It was pointed out earlier in this chapter that a complex wave (a nonsinusoidal wave) can be resolved into a fundamental frequency and a series of harmonic frequencies. When such a complex voltage wave is applied to a circuit containing reactance, the current through the circuit will not have the same wave shape as the applied voltage. This is because the reactance of an inductor and capacitor depend on the applied frequency. For the second-harmonic component of a complex wave, the reactance of the inductor is twice and the reactance of the capacitor is half their respective values at the fundamental frequency; for the third harmonic the inductive reactance is three times and the capacitive reactance is a third, and so on. Thus, the circuit impedance is different for each harmonic component.

Just what happens to the current wave shape depends on the values of resistance and reactance involved and how the circuit is arranged. In a simple circuit with resistance and inductive reactance in series, the amplitudes of the harmonic currents will be reduced because the inductive reactance increases in proportion to frequency. When capacitance and resistance are in series, the harmonic current is likely to be accentuated because the capacitive reactance becomes lower as the frequency is raised. When both inductive and capacitive reactance are present, the shape of the current wave can be altered in a variety of ways. The shape will depend on the circuit and the constants, or the relative values of L, C and R that are selected.

This property of nonuniform behavior with respect to fundamental and harmonics is an extremely useful one. It is the basis

of filtering, or the suppression of undesired frequencies in favor of a single desired frequency or group of such frequencies.

Resonance in Series Circuits

Fig. 52 shows a resistor, capacitor and inductor connected in series with a source of alternating current, the frequency of which can be varied over a wide range. At some low frequency the capacitive reactance will be much larger than the resistance of R, and the inductive reactance will be small compared with either the reactance of C or the resistance of R. (R is assumed to be the same at all frequencies.) On the other hand, at some very high frequency the reactance of C will be very small and the reactance of L will be very large. In either case the current will be small, because the net reactance is large.

At some intermediate frequency, the reactances of C and L will be equal. At this frequency the voltage drops across the coil and capacitor will be equal and 180° out of phase. Therefore, they cancel each other completely and the current flow is determined wholly by the resistance, R. At that frequency the current has its largest possible value, assuming the source voltage to be constant regardless of frequency. A series circuit in which the inductive and capacitive reactances are equal is said to be resonant.

The principle of resonance finds its most extensive application in radio-frequency circuits. The reactive effects associated with even small inductances and capacitances would place drastic limitations on RF circuit operation if it were not possible to cancel them out by supplying the right amount of reactance of the opposite kind — in other words, tuning the circuit to resonance.

Resonant Frequency

The frequency at which a series circuit is resonant is that at which $X_L = X_C$. Substituting the formulas for inductive and capacitance reactance gives

$$X_L = 2\pi fL = X_C = \frac{1}{2\pi fC}$$

$$2\pi fL = \frac{1}{2\pi fC}$$

$$f^2 = \frac{1}{4\pi^2 LC}$$

$$f = \frac{1}{2\pi \sqrt{LC}}$$

where
   f = frequency in hertz
   L = inductance in henrys
   C = capacitance in farads
   π = 3.14

These units are inconveniently large for radio-frequency circuits. A formula using

more appropriate units is

$$f = \frac{10^6}{2\pi \sqrt{LC}}$$

where

f = frequency in kilohertz (kHz)
L = inductance in microhenrys (μH)
C = capacitance in picofarads (pF)
π = 3.14

Example: The resonant frequency of a series circuit containing a 5-μH inductor and a 35-pF capacitor is

$$f = \frac{10^6}{2\pi \sqrt{LC}} = \frac{10^6}{6.28 \times \sqrt{5 \times 35}}$$

$$f = \frac{10^6}{6.28 \times 13.23} = 12,037 \text{ kHz}$$

The resonant frequency is not affected by resistance in the circuit.

Resonance Curves

When a plot is drawn of the current in the circuit of Fig. 52 as the frequency is varied (the applied voltage being constant), it looks like one of the curves in Fig. 53. The shape of the resonance curve is determined by the ratio of reactance to resistance.

When the reactance of either the coil or capacitor is of the same order of magnitude as the resistance, the current decreases rather slowly as the frequency is moved in either direction away from resonance. Such a curve is said to be broad. Conversely, when the reactance is considerably larger than the resistance the current decreases rapidly as the frequency moves away from resonance and the circuit is said to be sharp. A sharp circuit will respond a great deal more readily to the resonant frequency than to frequencies quite close to resonance; a broad circuit will respond almost equally well to a group or band of frequencies centered around the resonant frequency.

Both types of resonance curves are useful. A sharp circuit gives good selectivity — the ability to respond strongly (in terms of current amplitude) at one desired frequency, and to discriminate against others. A broad circuit is used when the apparatus must give about the same response over a band of frequencies, rather than at a single frequency alone.

Q

Most diagrams of resonant circuits show only inductance and capacitance; no resistance is indicated. Nevertheless, resistance is always present. At frequencies up to perhaps 30 MHz this resistance is mostly in the wire of the coil. At higher frequencies energy loss in the capacitor (principally in the solid dielectric that must be used to form an insulating support for the capacitor plates) also becomes a factor. This energy loss is equivalent to resistance. When maximum sharpness or selectivity is needed, the objective of design is to reduce the inherent resistance to the lowest possible value.

The value of the reactance of either the inductor or capacitor at the resonant frequency of a series-resonant circuit, divided by the series resistance in the circuit, is called the Q (quality factor) of the circuit, or

$$Q = \frac{X}{R}$$

where

Q = quality factor
X = reactance of either coil or capacitor in ohms
R = series resistance in ohms

Example: The inductor and capacitor in a series circuit each has a reactance of 350 ohms at the resonant frequency. The resistance is 5 ohms. The Q is

$$Q = \frac{X}{R} = \frac{350}{5} = 70$$

The effect of Q on the sharpness of resonance of a circuit is shown by the curves of Fig. 54. In these curves the frequency change is shown in percentage above and below the resonant frequency. Q values of 10, 20, 50 and 100 are shown; these values cover much of the range commonly used in radio work. The unloaded Q of a circuit is determined by the inherent resistances associated with the components.

Another way to think of Q is to define it as:

$$Q = \frac{2\pi \text{ (Energy stored per cycle)}}{\text{(Energy dissipated per cycle)}}$$

This tells us that in a high-Q circuit, much more energy is stored in the reactive component than is dissipated.

Voltage Rise at Resonance

When a voltage of the resonant frequency is inserted in series in a resonant circuit, the voltage that appears across either the inductor or capacitor is considerably higher than the applied voltage. The current in the circuit is limited only by the resistance and may have a relatively high value. However, the same current flows through the high reactances of the inductor and capacitor and causes large voltage drops.

The ratio of the reactive voltage to the applied voltage is equal to the ratio of reactance to resistance. This ratio is also the Q of the circuit. Therefore, the voltage across either the inductor or capacitor is equal to QE, where E is the voltage being applied to the series circuit. This fact accounts for the high voltages developed across the components of series-tuned antenna couplers.

Resonance in Parallel Circuits

When a variable-frequency source of constant voltage is applied to a parallel circuit of the type shown in Fig. 55, there is a resonance effect similar to that in a series circuit. In this case the line current (measured at the point indicated by the ammeter) is smallest at the frequency for which the inductive and capacitive reactances are equal. At that frequency the

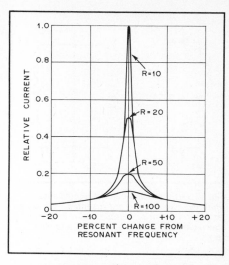

Fig. 53 — Current in a series-resonant circuit with various values of series resistance. The values are arbitrary and would not apply for all circuits, but represent a typical case. It is assumed that the reactances (at the resonant frequency) are 1000 ohms. Note that the current is substantially unaffected by the resistance in the circuit at frequencies more than plus or minus 10% away from the resonant frequency.

Fig. 54 — Current in series-resonant circuits having different Q values. In this graph the current at resonance is assumed to be the same in all cases. The lower the Q, the more slowly the current decreases as the applied frequency is moved away from resonance.

Fig. 55 — Circuit illustrating parallel resonance.

current through L is exactly canceled by the out-of-phase current through C, and only the current taken by R flows in the line. At frequencies below resonance the current

Fig. 56 — Series and parallel equivalents when the two circuits are resonant. The series resistance, R1 in A, is replaced in B by the equivalent parallel resistance R2, and vice versa.

$$R2 = \frac{X_L^2}{R1} = \frac{X_C^2}{R1}$$

Fig. 57 — Relative impedance of parallel-resonant circuits with different Q values. These curves are similar to those in Fig. 54 for current in a series-resonant circuit. The effect of Q on impedance is most marked near the resonant frequency.

through L is larger than that through C, because the reactance of L is smaller and that of C is larger than at resonance.

There is only partial cancellation of the two reactive currents, and the line current therefore is larger than the current taken by R alone. At frequencies above resonance the situation is reversed and more current flows through C than through L, so the line current again increases. The current at resonance, being determined wholly by R, will be small if R is large, and large if R is small.

The R shown in Fig. 55 is not necessarily an actual resistor. In many cases it will be the series resistance of the coil transformed to an equivalent parallel resistance (see below). It may be antenna or other load resistance coupled into the tuned circuit. In all cases it represents the total effective resistance in the circuit.

Parallel and series resonant circuits are quite alike in some respects. For instance, when an external voltage is applied the circuits given at A and B in Fig. 56 will behave

identically, if (1) L and C are the same in both cases, and (2) R1 multiplied by R2, equals the square of the reactance (at resonance) of either L or C. When these conditions are met the two circuits will have the same Q. (These statements are approximate, but are quite accurate if the Q is 10 or more.) The circuit at A is a series circuit if it is viewed from within — that is, going around the loop formed by L, C and R1 — so its Q can be found from the ratio of X to R1.

Thus, a circuit like that of Fig. 56A has an equivalent parallel resistance (at resonance) of

$$R2 = \frac{X^2}{R1}$$

where X is the reactance of either the inductor or the capacitor. Although R2 is not an actual resistor, to the source of voltage the parallel-resonant circuit looks like a pure resistance of that value. It is pure resistance because the inductive and capacitive currents are 180° out of phase and are equal; thus there is no reactive current in the line. In a practical circuit with a high-Q capacitor, the parallel impedance at the resonant frequency is

$$Z_R = QX$$

where

Z_R = resistive impedance at resonance
Q = quality factor of inductor
X = reactance (in ohms) of either the inductor or capacitor

Example: The parallel impedance of a circuit with a coil Q of 50 and having inductive and capacitive reactance of 300 ohms will be

$$Z_R = QX = 50 \times 300 = 15,000 \text{ ohms}$$

At frequencies off resonance the impedance is no longer purely resistive because the inductive and capacitive currents are not equal. The off-resonant impedance therefore is complex, and is lower than the resonant impedance for the reasons previously outlined.

The higher the circuit Q, the higher the parallel impedance. Curves showing the variation of impedance (with frequency) of a parallel circuit have the same shape as the curves showing the variation of current with frequency in a series circuit. Fig. 57 is a set of such curves. A set of curves showing the relative response as a function of the departure from the resonant frequency would be similar to Fig. 54. The −3 dB bandwidth (bandwidth at 0.707 relative response) is given by

$$\text{Bandwidth} -3 \text{ dB} = \frac{f_o}{Q}$$

where

f_o = the resonant frequency
Q = the circuit Q

It is also called the half-power bandwidth.

Parallel Resonance in Low-Q Circuits

The preceding discussion is accurate for Q values of 10 or more. When the Q is below 10, resonance in a parallel circuit having resistance in series with the coil, as in Fig. 56A, is not so easily defined. There is a set of values for L and C that will make the parallel impedance a pure resistance, but with these values the impedance does not have its maximum possible value. Another set of values for L and C will make the parallel impedance a maximum, but this maximum value is not a pure resistance.

Either condition could be called resonance, so with low-Q circuits it is necessary to distinguish between maximum impedance and resistive impedance when discussing parallel resonance. The difference between these L and C values and the equal reactances of a series-resonant circuit is appreciable when the Q is in the vicinity of 5, and becomes more marked with still lower Q values.

Q of Loaded Circuits

In many applications of resonant circuits the only power lost is that dissipated in the resistance of the circuit itself. At frequencies below 30 MHz most of this resistance is in the coil. Within limits, increasing the number of turns in the coil increases the reactance faster than it raises the resistance, so coils for circuits in which the Q must be high are made with relatively large inductance for the frequency.

However, when the circuit delivers energy to a load (as in the case of the resonant circuits used in transmitters) the energy consumed in the circuit itself is usually negligible compared with that consumed by the load. The equivalent of such a circuit is shown in Fig. 58A, where the parallel resistor represents the load to which power is delivered. If the power dissipated in the load is at least 10 times as great as the power lost in the inductor and capacitor, the parallel impedance of the resonant circuit itself will be so high compared with the resistance of the load that for all practical purposes the impedance of

Fig. 58 — Equivalent diagram of a resonant circuit delivering power to a load. This resistor R represents the load resistance. At B the load is tapped across part of L, by which transformer action is equivalent to using a higher load resistance across the whole circuit.

the combined circuit is equal to the load resistance. Under these conditions the Q of a parallel resonant circuit loaded by a resistive impedance is

$$Q = \frac{R}{X}$$

where

R = parallel load resistance (ohms)
X = reactance (ohms)

Example: A resistive load of 3000 ohms is connected across a resonant circuit in which the inductive and capacitive reactances are each 250 ohms. The circuit Q is then

$$Q = \frac{R}{X} = \frac{3000}{250} = 12$$

The effective Q of a circuit loaded by a parallel resistance increases when the reactances are decreased. A circuit loaded with a relatively low resistance (a few thousand ohms) must have low-reactance elements (large capacitance and small inductance) to have reasonably high Q.

Impedance Transformation

An important application of the parallel-resonant circuit is as an impedance-matching device in the output circuit of an RF power amplifier. There is an optimum value of load resistance for each type of tube or transistor and set of operating conditions. However, the resistance of the load to which the active device is to deliver power usually is considerably lower than the value required for proper device operation.

To transform the actual load resistance to the desired value, the load may be tapped across part of the coil, as shown in Fig. 58B. This is equivalent to connecting a higher value of load resistance across the whole circuit, and is similar in principle to impedance transformation with an iron-core transformer. In high-frequency resonant circuits the impedance ratio does not vary exactly as the square of the turns ratio, because all the magnetic flux lines do not cut every turn of the coil. A desired reflected impedance usually must be obtained by experimental adjustment.

When the load resistance has a very low value (say below 100 ohms) it may be connected in series in the resonant circuit (as in Fig. 56A, for example), in which case it is transformed to an equivalent parallel impedance as previously described. If the Q is at least 10, the equivalent parallel impedance is

$$Z_R = \frac{X^2}{R}$$

where

Z_R = resistive parallel impedance at resonance
X = reactance (in ohms) of either the coil or the capacitor
R = load resistance inserted in series

If the Q is lower than 10 the reactance will have to be adjusted somewhat, for the reasons given in the discussion of low-Q circuits, to obtain a resistive impedance of the desired value.

While the circuit shown in Fig. 58B will usually provide an impedance step-up as with an iron-core transformer, the network has some serious disadvantages for some applications. For instance, the common connection provides no dc isolation, and the common ground is sometimes troublesome with regard to ground-loop currents. Consequently, a network with only mutual magnetic coupling is usually preferable. No impedance step-up will result unless the two coils are coupled tightly enough. The equivalent resistance seen at the input of the network will always be lower regardless of the turns ratio employed. However, such networks are still useful in impedance-transformation applications if the appropriate capacitive elements are used. A more detailed treatment of matching networks will be presented in a later section.

Unfortunately, networks involving reactive elements are usually narrowband in nature; it would be desirable if such elements could be eliminated in order to increase the bandwidth. With the advent of ferrites, this has become possible, and it is now relatively easy to construct actual impedance transformers that are both broadband and permit operation well up into the VHF portion of the spectrum. This is also accomplished in part by tightly coupling the two (or more) coils that make up the transformer, either by twisting the conductors together or winding them in a parallel fashion. The latter configuration is sometimes called a bifilar winding, as discussed in the section on ferromagnetic transformers.

Transformers

Two coils having mutual inductance constitute a transformer. The coil connected to the source of energy is called the primary coil, and the other is called the secondary coil.

The usefulness of the transformer lies in the fact that electrical energy can be transferred from one circuit to another without direct connection, and in the process can be readily changed from one voltage level to another. Thus, if a device to be operated requires, for example, 7-V ac and only a 440-V source is available, a transformer can be used to change the source voltage to that required. A transformer can be used only with ac, since no voltage will be induced in the secondary if the magnetic field is not changing. If dc is applied to the primary of a transformer, a voltage will be induced in the secondary only at the instant of closing or opening the primary circuit, since it is only at these

Fig. 59 — The transformer. A is a pictorial diagram. Power is transferred from the primary coil to the secondary by means of the magnetic field. B is a schematic diagram for an iron-core transformer, and C is for an air-core transformer.

times that the field is changing.

The Iron-Core Transformer

As shown in Fig. 59, the primary and secondary coils of a transformer may be wound on a core of magnetic material. This increases the inductance of the coils so that

a relatively small number of turns may be used to induce a given value of voltage with a small current. A closed core (one having a continuous magnetic path) such as that shown in Fig. 59 also tends to ensure that practically all of the field set up by the current in the primary coil will cut the turns of the secondary coil. However, the core introduces a power loss because of hysteresis and eddy currents, so this type of construction is normally practicable only at power and audio frequencies. The discussion in this section is confined to transformers operating at such frequencies.

Fig. 60 — The equivalent circuit of a transformer includes the effects of leakage inductance and resistance of both primary and secondary windings. The resistance R_c is an equivalent resistance representing the core losses. Since these are comparatively small, their effect may be neglected in many approximate calculations.

Voltage and Turns Ratio

For a given varying magnetic field, the voltage induced in a coil in the field is proportional to the number of turns in the coil. When the two coils of a transformer are in the same field (which is the case when both are wound on the same closed core) it follows that the induced voltages will be proportional to the number of turns in each coil. In the primary the induced voltage practically equals and opposes, the applied voltage, as described earlier. Hence,

$$E_s = E_p \left(\frac{n_s}{n_p} \right)$$

where
E_s = secondary voltage
E_p = primary applied voltage
n_s = number of turns on secondary
n_p = number of turns on primary

Example: A transformer has a primary of 400 turns and a secondary of 2800 turns, and an EMF of 117 V is applied to the primary.

$$E_s = 117 \left(\frac{2800}{400} \right) = 117 \times 7$$

$$E_s = 819 \text{ volts}$$

Also, if an EMF of 819 V is applied to the 2800-turn winding (which then becomes the primary) the output voltage from the 400-turn winding will be 117 V.

Either winding of a transformer can be used as the primary, provided the winding has enough turns (enough inductance) to induce a voltage equal to the applied voltage without requiring an excessive current flow.

Secondary Current

The current that flows in the primary when no current is taken from the secondary is called the magnetizing current of the transformer. In any properly designed transformer the primary inductance is quite small. The power consumed by the transformer when the secondary is open (not delivering power) is only the amount necessary to overcome the losses in the iron core and in the resistance of the wire with which the primary is wound.

When power is taken from the secondary winding, the secondary current sets up a magnetic field that opposes the field set up by the primary current. For the induced voltage in the primary to equal the applied voltage, the original field must be maintained. The primary must draw enough additional current to set up a field exactly equal and opposite to the field set up by the secondary current.

In practical calculations on transformers it may be assumed that the entire primary current is caused by the secondary load. This is justifiable because the magnetizing current should be very small in comparison with the primary load current at rated power output.

If the magnetic fields set up by the primary and secondary currents are to be equal, the primary current multiplied by the primary turns must equal the secondary current multiplied by the secondary turns. From this it follows that

$$I_p = I_s \left(\frac{n_s}{n_p} \right)$$

where
I_p = primary current
I_s = secondary current
n_p = number of turns on primary
n_s = number of turns on secondary

Example: Suppose the secondary of the transformer in the previous example is delivering a current of 0.2 ampere to a load. Then the primary current will be

$$I_p = I_s \left(\frac{n_s}{n_p} \right) = 0.2 \left(\frac{2800}{400} \right) = 0.2 \times 7$$

$$I_p = 1.4 \text{ amperes}$$

Although the secondary voltage is higher than the primary voltage, the secondary current is lower than the primary current, and by the same ratio.

Power Relationships and Efficiency

A transformer cannot create power; it can only transfer it and change the EMF. Hence, the power taken from the secondary cannot exceed that taken by the primary from the source of applied EMF. There is always some power loss in the resistance of the coils and in the iron core, so in all practical cases the power taken from the source will exceed that taken from the secondary. Thus,

$$P_o = nP_i$$

where
P_o = power output from secondary
P_i = power input to primary
n = efficiency factor

The efficiency, n, is always less than 1. It is usually expressed as a percentage; if n is 0.65, for instance, the efficiency is 65%.

Example: A transformer has an efficiency of 85% at its full-load output of 150 watts. The power input to the primary at full secondary load will be

$$P_i = \frac{P_o}{n} = \frac{150}{0.85} = 176.5 \text{ watts}$$

A transformer is usually designed to have the highest efficiency at the power output for which it is rated. The efficiency decreases with either lower or higher outputs. On the other hand, the losses in the transformer are relatively small at low output but increase as more power is taken. The amount of power that the transformer can handle is determined by its own losses, because these losses heat the wire and core. There is a limit to the temperature rise that can be tolerated, because too high a temperature can either melt the wire or cause the insulation to break down. A transformer can be operated at reduced output, even though the efficiency is low, because the actual loss will be low under such conditions. The full-load efficiency of small power transformers such as are used in radio receivers and transmitters usually lies between about 60 and 90 percent, depending on the size and design.

Leakage Reactance

In a practical transformer not all of the magnetic flux is common to both windings, although in well designed transformers the amount of flux that cuts one coil and not the other is only a small percentage of the total flux. This leakage flux causes an EMF of self-induction; consequently, there are small amounts of leakage inductance associated with both windings of the transformer. Leakage inductance acts in exactly the same way as an equivalent amount of ordinary inductance inserted in series with the circuit. It has, therefore, a certain reactance, depending on the amount of leakage inductance and the frequency. This reactance is called leakage reactance.

Current flowing through the leakage reactance causes a voltage drop. This voltage drop increases with increasing current, hence it increases as more power is taken from the secondary. Thus, the greater the secondary current, the smaller the secondary terminal voltage becomes. The resistances of the transformer windings also cause voltage drops when current is flowing; although these voltage drops are not in phase with those caused by leakage reactance, together they result in a lower secondary voltage under load than is indicated by the turns ratio of the transformer.

At power frequencies (60 Hz) the voltage at the secondary, with a reasonably well designed transformer, should not drop more than about 10% from open-circuit conditions to full load. The drop in voltage may be considerably more than this in a transformer operating at audio frequencies because the leakage reactance increases directly with the frequency. The various transformer losses are modeled in Fig. 60.

Impedance Ratio

In an ideal transformer — one without losses or leakage reactance — the following relationship is true:

$$Z_p = Z_s \left(\frac{n_p}{n_s} \right)^2$$

where

Z_p = impedance looking into primary terminals from source of power

Z_s = impedance of load connected to secondary

n_p/n_s = turns ratio, primary to secondary

That is, a load of any given impedance connected to the secondary of the transformer will be transformed to a different value looking into the primary from the source of power. The impedance transformation is proportional to the square of the primary-to-secondary turns ratio.

Example: A transformer has a primary-to-secondary turns ratio of 0.6 (primary has 6/10 as many turns as the secondary) and a load of 3000 ohms is connected to the secondary. The impedance at the primary then will be

$$Z_p = Z_s \left(\frac{n_p}{n_s} \right)^2 = 3000 \times (0.6)^2$$

$$Z_p = 3000 \times 0.36 = 1080 \text{ ohms}$$

By choosing the proper turns ratio, the impedance of a fixed load can be transformed to any desired value, within practical limits. If transformer losses can be neglected, the transformed (reflected) impedance has the same phase angle as the actual load impedance. Thus, if the load is a pure resistance, the load presented by the primary to the source of power will also be a pure resistance. The above relationship may be used in practical work even though it is based on an ideal transformer. Aside from the normal design requirements of reasonably low internal losses and low leakage reactance, the only requirement is

that the primary have enough inductance to operate with low magnetizing current at the voltage applied to the primary.

The primary terminal impedance of a transformer is determined wholly by the load connected to the secondary and by the turns ratio. If the characteristics of the transformer have an appreciable effect on the impedance presented to the power source, the transformer is either poorly designed or is not suited to the voltage and frequency at which it is being used. Most transformers will operate quite well at voltages from slightly above to well below the design figure.

Impedance Matching

Many devices require a specific value of load resistance (or impedance) for optimum operation. The impedance of the actual load that is to dissipate the power may differ widely from this value, so a transformer is used to change the actual load into an impedance of the desired value. This is called impedance matching. From the preceding,

$$\frac{n_p}{n_s} = \sqrt{\frac{Z_p}{Z_s}}$$

where

n_p/n_s = required turns ratio, primary to secondary

Z_p = primary impedance required

Z_s = impedance of load connected to secondary

Example: A transistor AF amplifier requires a load of 150 ohms for optimum performance, and is to be connected to a loudspeaker having an impedance of 4 ohms. The turns ratio, primary to secondary, required in the coupling transformer is

$$\frac{n_p}{n_s} = \sqrt{\frac{Z_p}{Z_s}} = \sqrt{\frac{150}{4}} = \sqrt{37.5} = 6.1$$

The primary therefore must have 6.1 times as many turns as the secondary.

Impedance matching implies adjusting the load impedance, by means of a transformer or otherwise, to a desired value. However, there is also another meaning. It is possible to show that any source of power will deliver its maximum possible output when the impedance of the load is equal to the internal impedance of the source. The impedance of the source is said to be matched under this condition. The efficiency is only 50% in such a case; just as much power is used up in the source as is delivered to the load. Because of the poor efficiency, this type of impedance matching is limited to cases where only a small amount of power is available and heating from power loss in the source is not important.

TRANSFORMER CONSTRUCTION

Transformers usually are designed so that the magnetic path around the core is

Fig. 61 — Two common types of transformer construction. Core pieces are interleaved to provide a continuous magnetic path.

as short as possible. A short magnetic path means that the transformer will operate with fewer turns, for a given applied voltage, than if the path were long. A short path also helps to reduce flux leakage and therefore minimizes leakage reactance.

Two core shapes are in common use, as shown in Fig. 61. In the shell type, both windings are placed on the inner leg, while in the core type the primary and secondary windings may be placed on separate legs, if desired. This is sometimes done when it is necessary to minimize capacitive effects between the primary and secondary, or when one of the windings must operate at very high voltage.

Core material for small transformers is usually silicon steel, called transformer iron. The core is built up of laminations, insulated from each other (by a thin coating of shellac, for example) to prevent eddy currents. The laminations are interleaved at the ends to make the magnetic path as continuous as possible and thus reduce leakage.

The number of turns required in the primary for a given applied EMF is determined by the size, shape and type of core material used, and the frequency. The number of turns required is inversely proportional to the cross-sectional area of the core. As a rough indication, windings of small power transformers frequently have about six to eight turns per volt on a core of 1-square-inch cross section and have a magnetic path 10 or 12 inches in length. A longer path or smaller cross section requires more turns per volt, and vice versa.

In most transformers the coils are wound

Fig. 62 — The autotransformer is based on the transformer principle, but uses only one winding. The line and load currents in the common winding (A) flow in opposite directions, so the resultant current is the difference between them. The voltage across A is proportional to the ratio of total turns to turns in A.

Fig. 63 — An assortment of toroid cores. A ferrite rod is placed at the top of the picture for comparison. The two light-colored, plastic-encased toroids at the upper left are tape-wound types (Hypersil steel), and are suitable for audio and dc-to-dc converter transformers. The wound toroid at the right center contains two toroid cores that have been stacked atop one another to increase the power capability.

in layers, with a thin sheet of treated-paper insulation between each layer. Thicker insulation is used between adjacent coils and between the first coil and the core.

Autotransformers

The transformer principle can be used with only one winding instead of two, as shown in Fig. 62; the principles just discussed apply equally well. A one-winding transformer is called an autotransformer. The current in the common section (A) of the winding is the difference between the line (primary) and the load (secondary) currents, since these currents are out of phase. Hence, if the line and load currents are

nearly equal, the common section of the winding may be wound with comparatively small wire. The line and load currents will be equal only when the primary (line) and secondary (load) voltages are not very different.

The autotransformer is used chiefly for boosting or reducing the power-line voltage by relatively small amounts. Continuously variable autotransformers are commercially available under a variety of trade names; Variac and Powerstat are typical examples.

Ferromagnetic Transformers and Inductors

The design concepts and general theory of transformers presented earlier in this chapter apply also to transformers wound on ferromagnetic-core materials (ferrite and powdered iron). As is the case with stacked cores made of laminations in the classic I and E shapes, the core material has a specific permeability factor that determines the inductance of the windings versus the number of wire turns used.

Both ferrite and powdered-iron materials are manufactured with a wide range of μ_i (initial permeability) characteristics. The value chosen by the designer depends on the intended operating frequency and the desired bandwidth of a given broadband transformer.

Core Types in Use at RF

For use in radio-frequency circuits especially, a suitable core type must be chosen to provide the Q required by the designer. The wrong core material destroys the Q of an inductor at RF.

Toroid cores are useful from a few hundred hertz well into the UHF spectrum. Tape-wound steel cores are employed in some types of power supplies — notably dc-to-dc converters. The toroid core is doughnut shaped, as shown in Fig. 63.

The principal advantage of this type of core is the self-shielding characteristic. Another feature is the compactness of a transformer or inductor. Therefore, toroids are excellent not only in dc-to-dc converters, but at audio and radio frequencies up to at least 1000 MHz, assuming the proper core material is selected for the range of operating frequencies. Toroid cores are available from microminiature sizes to several inches in diameter. The latter can be used, as one example, to build a 20-kW balun for use in antenna systems.

Another form taken in ferromagnetic transformers and inductors is the pot-core or cup-core device. Unlike the toroid, which has the winding over the outer surface of the core material, the pot-core winding is inside the ferromagnetic material (Fig. 64). There are two cup-shaped halves to the assembly, both made of ferrite or powdered iron, which are connected tightly together by means of a screw that is passed through a center hole. The wire for the assembly is wound on an insulating bobbin that fits inside the

Fig. 64 — View of a disassembled pot core (left) and an assembled pot core (right).

Fig. 65 — A BC-band ferrite-rod loop antenna is shown at the top of the picture (J. W. Miller Co.). A blank ferrite rod is visible at the center, and a flat BC-band ferrite loop antenna in the lower foreground.

two halves of the pot-core unit.

The advantage to this type of construction is that the core permeability can be chosen to ensure a minimum number of wire turns for a given value of inductance. This reduces the wire resistance and increases the Q as opposed to an equivalent inductance wound on a core that has relatively low permeability. By virtue of the winding being contained inside the ferrite or powdered-iron pot core, shielding is excellent.

Still another kind of ferromagnetic-core inductor is the solenoidal type (Fig. 65). Transformers and inductors fabricated in this manner consist of a cylindrical, oval or rectangular rod of material over which the wire winding is placed. This variety of device does not have a self-shielding trait. Therefore, it must be treated in the same manner as any solenoidal-wound inductor (using external shield devices). An example of a ferrite-rod inductor is the built-in loop antennas found in portable radios and direction finders.

Core Size

The cross-sectional area of a ferromagnetic core should be chosen to prevent saturation from the load seen by the transformer. This means that the proper thickness and diameter are essential parameters to consider. For a specific core the maximum operational ac excitation can be determined by

$$B = \frac{E_{RMS} \times 10^8}{4.44 \, f \, n_p \, A_e}$$

Fig. 66 — Schematic and pictorial representations of one type of conventional transformer. This style is used frequently at the input and output ports of RF power amplifiers that use transistors. The magnetic material consists of two rows of 950-μ toroid cores for use from 1.8 to 30 MHz. The primary and secondary windings are passed through the center holes of the toroid-stack rows as shown.

where

A_e = equivalent area of the magnetic path in sq. cm.
E_{RMS} = applied voltage
n_p = number of core turns
f = operating frequency in hertz
B = flux density in gauss

This equation is applicable to inductors that do not have dc flowing in the winding along with ac. When both ac and dc flow

$$B = \frac{E_{RMS} \times 10^8}{4.44 \, f \, n_p \, A_e} + \frac{N_p \, I_{dc} \, A_L}{10 A_e}$$

where

I_{dc} = the dc current through the winding
A_L = the manufacturer's index for the core being used, which can be obtained by consulting the manufacturer's data sheet.

Types of Transformers

The most common ferromagnetic transformers used in Amateur Radio work are the narrow-band, conventional, broadband and transmission-line varieties. Narrow-band transformers are used when selectivity is desired in a tuned circuit, such as an audio peaking or notching circuit, a resonator in an RF filter, or a tuned circuit associated with an RF amplifier. Broadband transformers are employed in circuits which must have a uniform response over a substantial spread of frequency, as in a 2- to 30-MHz broadband amplifier. In such an example the reactance of the windings should be at least four

times the impedance the winding is designed to look into. Therefore, a transformer that has a 300-ohm primary and a 50-ohm secondary load should have winding reactances (X_L) of at least 1200 ohms and 200 ohms, respectively. The windings, for all practical purposes, can be graded as RF chokes, and the same rules apply.

The permeability of the core material plays a vital role in designing a good broadband transformer. The performance of the transformer at the low-frequency end of the operating range depends on the permeability. That is, the μ_e (effective permeability) must be high enough in value to provide ample winding reactance at the low end of the operating range. As the operating frequency is increased, the effects of the core tend to disappear until there are scarcely any core effects at the upper limit of the operating range. For this reason it is common to find very low frequency core materials in transformers that are used in broadband circuits operating into the upper HF region, or even into the VHF spectrum. By way of simple explanation, at high frequencies the low-frequency core material becomes inefficient and tends to vanish electrically. This desirable trait makes possible the use of ferromagnetics in broadband applications.

Conventional transformers are those that are wound in the same manner as a power transformer. That is, each winding is made from a separate length of wire, with one winding being placed over the previous one with suitable insulation between (Figs. 66 and 67). A transmission-line transformer is, conversely, one that uses windings that are arranged to simulate a piece of transmission line of a specific impedance. This can be done by twisting the wires together a given number of times per inch, or by laying the wires on the core (adjacent to one another) at a distance apart which provides a two-wire line impedance of a particular value. In some applications these windings are called bifilar. A three-wire winding is known as a trifilar one, and so forth (Fig. 68).

In a general comparison, the transmission-line transformer enjoys the advantage of higher efficiency, greater bandwidth and simpler construction than a conventional one. The conventional transformer, however, is capable of dc isolation. An interesting technical paper on the subject of toroidal broadband transformers was published by Sevick, W2FMI.[1] The classic reference work on the subject is by Ruthroff.[2]

Ferrite Beads

Another form of toroidal inductor is the ferrite bead. This component is available in various μ_i values and sizes, but most beads are less than 0.25 inch in diameter.

[1]J. Sevick, "Simple Broadband Matching Networks," QST, January 1976.
[2]Ruthroff, "Some Broadband Transformers," Proc. IRE, Vol. 47, August 1959, p. 137.

Fig. 67 — Another conventional transformer. Primary and secondary windings are wound over the outer surface of a toroid core.

Fig. 68 — Schematic and pictorial presentations of a transmission-line transformer in which the windings need to be arranged for a specific impedance.

Ferrite beads are used principally as VHF and UHF parasitic suppressors at the input and output terminals of amplifiers. Another practical application is in decoupling networks that are used to prevent unwanted migration of RF energy from one section of a circuit to another. They are used also in suppressing RFI and TVI in hi-fi and television sets.

In some circuits it is necessary only to

Table 6

Powdered-Iron Toroidal Cores—A_L Values (μH per 100 turns)

Core Size	41-Mix Green $\mu = 75$	3-Mix Grey $\mu = 35$ 0.05-5 MHz	15-Mix Rd & Wh $\mu = 25$ 0.1-2 MHz	1-Mix Blue $\mu = 20$ 0.5-5 MHz	2-Mix Red $\mu = 10$ 2-30 MHz	6-Mix Yellow $\mu = 8$ 10-50 MHz	10-Mix Black $\mu = 6$ 30-100 MHz	12-Mix Gn & Wh $\mu = 3$ 50-200 MHz	0-Mix Tan $\mu = 1$ 100-300 MHz
T-200	755	425	NA	250	120	100	NA	NA	NA
T-184	1640	720	NA	500	240	195	NA	NA	NA
T-157	970	420	360	320	140	115	NA	NA	NA
T-130	785	350	250	200	110	96	NA	NA	15.0
T-106	900	450	345	325	135	116	NA	NA	19.0
T-94	590	248	200	160	84	70	58	32	10.6
T-80	450	180	170	115	55	45	32	22	8.5
T-68	420	195	180	115	57	47	32	21	7.5
T-50	320	175	135	100	49	46	31	18	6.4
T-44	229	180	160	105	52	42	33	18.5	6.5
T-37	308	120	90	80	40	30	25	15	4.9
T-30	375	140	93	85	43	36	25	16	6.0
T-25	225	100	85	70	34	27	19	12	4.5
T-20	175	76	65	52	25	22	16	10	3.5
T-16	130	61	55	44	22	19	13	8	3.0
T-12	112	60	50	48	20	17	12	7.5	3.0

NA—Not available in that size.

Turns = $100 \sqrt{L_\mu H \div A_L}$ value (above)

All frequency figures optimum.

Number of Turns vs. Wire Size and Core Size

Approximate maximum of turns—single-layer-wound enameled wire

Wire Size	T-200	T-130	T-106	T-94	T-80	T-68	T-50	T-37	T-25	T-12
10	31	17	10	10	8	7	5	1	1	0
12	41	23	14	14	12	9	6	3	1	0
14	53	30	20	20	17	12	8	5	1	0
16	68	40	27	27	23	15	11	7	3	1
18	86	51	35	35	30	21	16	9	4	1
20	109	66	45	45	39	28	21	12	5	1
22	139	83	58	58	51	36	28	17	7	2
24	176	107	75	75	66	47	37	23	11	4
26	223	137	96	96	84	61	49	31	15	5
28	282	173	123	123	108	79	63	41	21	8
30	357	220	156	156	137	101	81	53	28	11
32	445	275	195	195	172	127	103	67	37	15
34	562	348	248	248	219	162	131	87	48	21
36	707	439	313	313	276	205	166	110	62	29
38	886	550	393	393	347	257	210	140	79	37
40	1115	693	496	496	438	325	265	177	101	47

Physical Dimensions

Core Size	Outer Dia (in)	Inner Dia (in)	Height (in)	Cross Sect. Area (cm²)	Mean Length (cm)	Core Size	Outer Dia (in)	Inner Dia (in)	Height (in)	Cross Sect. Area (cm²)	Mean Length (cm)
T-200	2.000	1.250	0.550	1.330	12.97	T-50	0.500	0.303	0.190	0.121	3.20
T-184	1.840	0.950	0.710	2.040	11.12	T-44	0.440	0.229	0.159	0.107	2.67
T-157	1.570	0.950	0.570	1.140	10.05	T-37	0.375	0.205	0.128	0.070	2.32
T-130	1.300	0.780	0.437	0.733	8.29	T-30	0.307	0.151	0.128	0.065	1.83
T-106	1.060	0.570	0.437	0.690	6.50	T-25	0.255	0.120	0.096	0.042	1.50
T-94	0.942	0.560	0.312	0.385	6.00	T-20	0.200	0.088	0.070	0.025	1.15
T-80	0.795	0.495	0.250	0.242	5.15	T-16	0.160	0.078	0.060	0.016	0.95
T-68	0.690	0.370	0.190	0.196	4.24	T-12	0.125	0.062	0.050	0.010	0.75

Courtesy of Amidon Assoc., N. Hollywood, CA 91607 and Micrometals, Inc.

---

place one or more beads over a short length of wire to obtain ample inductive reactance for creating an RF choke. A few turns of small-diameter enameled wire can be looped through the larger beads to increase the effective inductance. Ferrite beads are suitable as low-Q base impedances in solid-state VHF and UHF amplifiers. The low-Q characteristic prevents self-oscillation that might occur if a high-Q solenoidal RF choke were used in place of one made from beads. Miniature broadband transformers are sometimes fashioned from ferrite beads. For the most part, ferrite beads can be regarded as small toroid cores.

Number of Turns

The number of wire turns used on a toroid core can be calculated by knowing the A_L of the core and the desired inductance. The A_L is simply the inductance index for the core size and permeability being used. Table 6 provides information of interest concerning a popular assortment of powdered-iron toroid cores. The complete number for a given core is composed of the core-size designator in the upper left column, plus the corresponding mix number. For example, a half-inch diameter core with a no. 2 mix would be designated as a T-50-2 unit. The A_L would be 49 and the suggested operating frequency would be from 1 to 30 MHz. The μ_i for that core is 10.

The required number of wire turns for a specified inductance on a given type of core can be determined by

$$\text{Turns} = 100 \sqrt{\text{desired L} (\mu\text{H}) \div A_L}$$

Table 7

Ferrite Toroids—A_L Chart (mH per 1000 turns) Enameled Wire

Core Size	63/67-Mix $\mu = 40$	61-Mix $\mu = 125$	43-Mix $\mu = 850$	77 (72) Mix $\mu = 2000$	J (75) Mix $\mu = 5000$
FT-23	7.9	24.8	188.0	396	980
FT-37	19.7	55.3	420.0	884	2196
FT-50	22.0	68.0	523.0	1100	2715
FT-82	22.4	73.3	557.0	1170	NA
FT-114	25.4	79.3	603.0	1270	3170

Number turns = 1000 $\sqrt{\text{desired L (mH)} \div A_L \text{ value (above)}}$

Ferrite Magnetic Properties

Property	Unit	63/67-Mix	61-Mix	43-Mix	77 (72) Mix	J (75)-Mix
Initial perm (μ_i)		40	125	850	2000	5000
Maximum perm.		125	450	3000	6000	8000
Saturation flux density @ 10 oer	Gauss	1850	2350	2750	4600	3900
Residual flux density	Gauss	750	1200	1200	1150	1250
Curie temp.	°C	450	350	130	200	140
Vol. resistivity	ohm/cm	1×10^8	1×10^8	1×10^5	1×10^2	5×10^2
Resonant circuit frequency	MHz	15-25	0.2-10	0.01-1	0.001-1	0.001-1
Specific gravity		4.7	4.7	4.5	4.8	4.8
Loss factor	$\dfrac{1}{\mu_i Q}$	110×10^{-6} @25 MHz	32×10^{-6} @2.5 MHz	120×10^{-6} @1 MHz	4.5×10^{-6} @0.1 MHz	15×10^{-6} @0.1 MHz
Coercive force	Oer	2.40	1.60	0.30	0.22	0.16
Temp. Coef. of initial perm.	%/°C (20-70°C)	0.10	0.15	1.0	0.60	0.90

Ferrite Toroids—Physical Properties

Core Size	OD	ID	Height	A_e	I_e	V_e	A_S	A_W
FT-23	0.230	0.120	0.060	0.00330	0.529	0.00174	0.1264	0.01121
FT-37	0.375	0.187	0.125	0.01175	0.846	0.00994	0.3860	0.02750
FT-50	0.500	0.281	0.188	0.02060	1.190	0.02450	0.7300	0.06200
FT-82	0.825	0.520	0.250	0.03810	2.070	0.07890	1.7000	0.21200
FT-114	1.142	0.750	0.295	0.05810	2.920	0.16950	2.9200	0.43900

OD—Outer diameter (inches)
ID—Inner diameter (inches)
Hgt—Height (inches)
A_W—Total window area (in)^2

A_e—Effective magnetic cross-sectional area (in)^2
I_e—Effective magnetic path length (inches)
V_e—Effective magnetic volume (in)^3
A_S—Surface area exposed for cooling (in)^2

Courtesy of Amidon Assoc., N. Hollywood, CA 91607

Fig. 69 — Method for checking the inductance of a toroid winding by means of a dip meter, known capacitance value and a calibrated receiver. The self-shielding properties of a toroidal inductor prevent dip meter readings when the instrument is coupled directly to the toroid. Sampling is done by means of a coupling link as illustrated.

means of an RCL bridge or an RX meter. If these instruments are not available, close approximations can be had by using a dip meter, standard capacitor (known value, stable type, such as a silver mica) and a calibrated receiver against which to check the dipper frequency.

Fig. 69 shows how to couple a dip meter to a completed toroid for testing. The coupling link in the illustration is necessary because the toroid has a self-shielding characteristic. That characteristic makes it difficult, and often impossible, to obtain a dip in the meter reading when coupling the instrument directly to the toroidal inductor or transformer. The inductance can be determined by X_L since $X_L = X_C$ at resonance. Therefore,

$$X_C = \frac{1}{2\pi f C} \text{ and } L_{(\mu H)} = \frac{X_L}{2\pi f}$$

where
X_C = the reactance of the known capacitor value
f = frequency in MHz
C = capacitance in μF

Using an example, where f is 3.5 MHz (as noted on a dip meter) and C is 100 pF, L is determined by

$$X_C = \frac{1}{6.28 \times 3.5 \times 0.0001} = 454.7 \text{ ohms}$$

Since $X_L = X_C$ at resonance,

$$L_{(\mu H)} = \frac{454.7}{6.28 \times 3.5} = 20.7 \ \mu H$$

It is assumed, for the purpose of accuracy, that the dip-meter signal is checked for precise frequency by means of a calibrated receiver.

Practical Considerations

Amateurs who work with toroidal inductors and transformers are sometimes confused by the winding instructions given in construction articles. For the most part, winding a toroid core with wire is less complicated than winding a cylindrical single-layer coil.

When many turns of wire are required,

where A_L is obtained from Table 6. The table also indicates how many turns of a particular wire gauge can be close wound to fill a specified core. For example, a T-68 core will contain 49 turns of no. 24 enameled wire, 101 turns of no. 30 enameled wire, and so on. Generally speaking, the larger the wire gauge the higher the unloaded Q of the toroidal inductor. The inductance values are based on the winding covering the entire circumference of the core. When there is space between the turns of wire, some control over the net inductance can be effected by compressing the turns or spreading them. The inductance will increase if compression is used and will decrease when the turns are spread farther apart.

Table 7 contains data for ferrite cores. The number of turns for a specified inductance in mH versus the A_L can be determined by

$$\text{Turns} = 1000 \sqrt{\text{desired L (mH)} \div A_L}$$

where the A_L for a specific core can be taken from Table 7. Thus, if you required

a 1-mH inductor and chose a no. FT-82-43 toroid core, the number of turns would be

$$\begin{aligned} \text{Turns} &= 1000 \sqrt{1 \div 557} \\ &= 1000 \sqrt{0.001795} \\ &= 1000 \times 0.0424 = 42.4 \text{ turns} \end{aligned}$$

For an FT-82 size core, no. 22 enameled wire would be suitable as indicated in Table 6 (using the T-80 core size as the nearest one to an FT-82). If the toroid core has rough edges (untumbled), it is suggested that insulating tape (3M glass epoxy tape or Mylar tape) be wrapped through the core before the wire is added. This will prevent the rough edges of the core from abrading the enameled wire.

Checking RF Toroidal Devices

The equations given previously will provide the number of wire turns needed for a particular inductance, plus or minus 10%. However, slight variations in core permeability may exist from one production run to another. Therefore, for circuits that require exact values of inductance, it is necessary to check the toroid winding by

Table 8
Ferrite Toroid Cores — Size (Inches) Cross-Reference

OD	ID	Thickness	Amidon	Fair-Rite	Indiana General	Ferroxcube	Magnetics, Inc
0.100	0.050	0.050	—	—	—	—	40200TC
0.100	0.070	0.030	—	701	F426-1	—	—
0.155	0.088	—	—	801	F2062-1	—	40502
0.190	0.090	0.050	—	—	—	213T050	—
0.230	0.120	0.060	FT-23	101	F303-1	1041T060	40601
0.230	0.120	0.120	—	901	—	—	—
0.300	0.125	0.188	—	—	F867-1	—	40705
0.375	0.187	0.125	FT-37	201	F625-9	266T125	41003
0.500	0.281	0.188	FT-50	301	—	768T188	—
0.500	0.312	0.250	—	1101	F627-8	—	41306
0.500	0.312	0.500	—	1901	—	—	—
0.825	0.520	0.250	FT-82	601	—	—	—
0.825	0.520	0.468	—	501	—	—	—
0.870	0.500	0.250	—	401	—	—	—
0.870	0.540	0.250	—	1801	F624-19	846T250	42206
1.000	0.500	0.250	—	1501	F2070-1	—	42507
1.000	0.610	0.250	—	1301	—	—	—
1.142	0.748	0.295	FT-114	1001	—	K300502	42908
1.225	0.750	0.312	—	1601	—	—	—
1.250	0.750	0.375	—	1701	F626-12	—	—
1.417	0.905	0.591	—	—	—	K300501	—
1.417	0.905	0.394	—	—	—	K300500	—
1.500	0.750	0.500	—	—	—	528T500	43813
2.000	1.250	0.750	—	—	—	400T750	—
2.900	1.530	0.500	—	—	—	144T500	—
3.375	1.925	0.500	—	—	F1707-15	—	—
3.500	2.000	0.500	—	—	F1707-1	—	—
5.835	2.50	0.625	—	—	F1824-1	—	—

Table 9
Ferrite Toroid Cores — Permeability Cross-Reference

μ_o	Amidon	Fair-Rite	Indiana General	Ferroxcube	Magnetics, Inc.
16	—	—	Q3	—	—
20	—	68	—	—	—
40	FT-63	63, 67	Q2	—	—
100	—	65	—	—	—
125	FT-61	61	Q1	4C4	—
175	—	62	—	—	—
250	FT-64	64	—	—	—
300	—	83	—	—	—
375	—	31	—	—	—
400	—	—	G	—	—
750	—	—	—	3D3	A
800	—	33	—	—	—
850	FT-43	43	H	—	—
950	—	—	TC-3	—	—
1200	—	34	—	—	—
1400	—	—	—	—	C
1500	—	—	TC-7	—	—
1800	FT-77	77	—	3B9	—
2000	FT-72	72	TC-9	—	S, V, D
2200	—	—	05	—	—
2300	—	—	—	3B7	G
2500	FT-73	73	TC-12	—	—
2700	—	—	—	3E (3C8)	—
3000	—	—	05P	3C5	F
4700	—	—	06	—	—
5000	FT-75	75	—	3E2A	J
10,000	—	—	—	—	W
12,500	—	—	—	3E3	—

Fig. 70 — (A) Illustration of a homemade winding shuttle for toroids. The wire is stored on the shuttle and the shuttle is passed through the center hole of the toroid, again and again, until the required number of turns is in place. (B) It is best to leave a 30° gap between the ends of the toroid winding. This will reduce the distributed capacitance considerably. (C) Edgewise view of a toroid core, illustrating the method for counting the turns accurately. (D) The low-impedance winding of a toroidal transformer is usually wound over the large winding, as shown. For narrow-band applications the link should be wound over the cold end of the main winding (see text).

or a transformer winding depends in part on the distributed capacitance between the coil turns and between the ends of the winding. When a large number of turns are used (for example, 500 or 1000), the distributed capacitance can be as great as 100 pF. Ideally, there would be no distributed or parasitic capacitance, but this is not possible. Therefore, the unwanted capacitance must be kept as low as possible in order to take proper advantage of the A_L factors discussed earlier in this section. The greater the distributed capacitance, the more restrictive the transformer or inductor becomes when applied in a broadband circuit. In the case of a narrow-band application, the Q can be affected by the distributed capacitance.

The pictorial illustration at Fig. 70B shows the inductor turns distributed uniformly around the toroid core, but a gap of approximately 30° is maintained between the ends of the winding. This method is recommended to reduce the distributed capacitance of the winding. The closer the ends of the winding are to one another, the greater the unwanted capacitance. Also, in order to closely approximate the desired toroid inductance when using the A_L formula, the winding should be spread over

a homemade winding shuttle can be used to simplify the task. Fig. 70A illustrates this method. The shuttle can be fashioned from a piece of circuit-board material. A stiff piece of plastic works as well. The wire is wound on the shuttle after determining how many inches are required to provide the desired number of toroid turns. (A sample turn around the toroid core will reveal the wire length per turn.) Once the shuttle is loaded, it is passed through the toroid center again and again until the winding is completed. The edges of the shuttle should be kept smooth to prevent abrasion of the wire insulation.

How to Wind Toroids

The effective inductance of a toroid coil

Fig. 77 — Network configuration of a Butterworth high-pass filter. The low-pass prototype can be transformed as described in the text.

Fig. 78 — A Butterworth band-pass filter. Capacitance values are in picofarads.

in Fig. 77A and B, which correspond to Fig. 76A and B in Table 10. The equations for the actual high-pass circuit values in terms of the low-pass prototype are given by

$$C = \frac{1}{R2\pi f_c C_{prot.}}$$

$$L = \frac{R}{2\pi f_c L_{prot.}}$$

and the frequency response curve can be obtained from

$$A = 10 \log \left[1 + \left(\frac{f_c}{f} \right)^{2k} \right]$$

For instance, a high-pass filter with three elements, a 3.01-dB f_c of 6 MHz and a load resistance of 52 ohms, has a C1 and C3 of 510 pF and an L2 of 0.6897 μH. The insertion loss at 3.5 and 7 MHz would be 14.21 and 1.45 dB, respectively.

Butterworth Band-Pass Filters

Band-pass filters can also be designed through the use of Table 10. Unfortunately the process is not as straightforward as it is for low- and high-pass filters if a practical design is to be obtained. In essence, a low-pass filter is resonated to some center frequency with the 3.01-dB cutoff frequency being replaced by the filter bandwidth. The ratio of the bandwidth to center frequency must be relatively large; otherwise component values tend to become unmanageable.

While there are many variations of specifying such filters, a most useful approach is to determine an upper and lower frequency for a given attenuation. The center frequency and bandwidth are then given by

$$f_o = \sqrt{f_1 f_2}$$

$$BW = f_2 - f_1$$

If the bandwidth specified is not the 3.01-dB bandwidth (BW_c) this bandwidth can be determined from

$$BW_c = \frac{BW}{(10^{0.1A} - 1)^{\frac{1}{2k}}}$$

in the case of a Butterworth response or from tables of curves. A is the required attenuation at the cutoff frequencies. The upper and lower cutoff frequencies (f_{cu} and f_{cl} are then given by

$$f_{cl} = \frac{-BW_c + \sqrt{(BW_c)^2 + 4f_o^2}}{2}$$

and

$$f_{cu} = f_{cl} + BW_c$$

A somewhat more convenient method is to pick a 3.01-dB bandwidth (the wider the better) around some center frequency and compute the attenuation at other frequencies of interest by using the transformation:

$$\frac{f}{f_c} = \left| \left(\frac{f}{f_o} - \frac{f_o}{f} \right) \frac{f_o}{BW_c} \right|$$

which can be substituted into the insertion-loss formula or table of curves.

As an example, suppose you want to build a band-pass filter for the 15-meter Novice band in order to eliminate the possibility of radiation on the 14- and 28-MHz bands. For a starting choice, 16 and 25 MHz will be selected as the 3.01-dB points, giving a 3-dB bandwidth of 9 MHz. For these two points, f_o will be 20 MHz. It is common practice to equate the number of branch elements or filter resonators to certain mathematical entities called poles, and the number of poles is just the value of k for purposes of discussion here. For a three-pole filter (k of 3) the insertion loss will be 12.79 and 11.3 dB at 14 and 28 MHz, respectively.

C1, C3 and L2 are then calculated for a 9-MHz low-pass filter and the elements for this filter are resonated to 20 MHz as shown in Fig. 78A. The response shape is plotted in Fig. 78B, and it appears to be unsymmetrical about f_o. In spite of this fact, such filters are called symmetrical band-pass filters and f_o is the center frequency. If the response is plotted with a

logarithmic frequency scale, the symmetry will become apparent. Consequently, using a logarithmic plot is helpful in designing filters of this type.

Examination of the component values reveals that while the filter is practical, it is a bit untidy from a construction standpoint. Rather than using a single 340.1-pF capacitor, paralleling a number of smaller value units would be advisable. Encountering difficulty of this sort is typical of most filter designs; consequently, some tradeoffs among performance, complexity and ease of construction are usually required.

Additional Modern Filters

Butterworth filters are used where a flat passband response, well-behaved phase shift characteristics and exact impedance matching are important. They are subject to two limitations, however. For a given number of elements, the rate of attenuation (roll-off) in the transition band is not as great as can be obtained with some other designs of the same complexity. In addition, the ratio of capacitances is fixed at a number that may not result in standard component values. The values can be synthesized by connecting several capacitors in parallel, but this practice may set up parasitic resonances that greatly distort the band-pass and band-stop characteristics.

In applications requiring sharper cutoff or where some response ripple and passband impedance mismatch can be tolerated, a Chebyshev design should be considered. A variety of capacitance ratios is possible, depending on the allowable ripple. Many of these ratios result in standard-value capacitors, which greatly simplifies and economizes the circuit.

Another type of modern filter, the elliptic filter, is used in situations requiring extremely sharp cutoff with one or more infinitely deep notches in the stopband. Like the Chebyshev filter, the design parameters can be manipulated to produce circuits having at least some standard-value capacitors.

PASSIVE LC FILTER DESIGN

The following text by Ed Wetherhold, W3NQN, is adapted from a paper entitled "Simplified Passive LC Filter Design for the EMC Engineer." That work first appeared in the record of the 1985 IEEE International Symposium on Electromagnetic Compatibility, held August 20-22, 1985, in Wakefield, MA, pp. 575-584. © 1985 IEEE.

The filter design procedure presented here uses eight computer-calculated tables of performance parameters and component values for 5- and 7-branch Chebyshev and 5-branch elliptic 50-ohm filters. The tables permit the quick and easy selection of an equally-terminated passive LC filter for applications where the attenuation response is of primary interest. All of the capacitors in the Chebyshev designs and the three non-resonating capacitors in the elliptic designs have standard, off-the-shelf values to simplify construction. Although the tables cover only the 1- to 10-MHz frequency range, a simple scaling procedure gives standard-value capacitor (SVC) designs for any impedance level and virtually any cutoff frequency.

Introduction

The radio amateur frequently needs an equally-terminated inductor-capacitor (LC) filter for nonstringent applications such as harmonic attenuation or wideband preamplifier preselection where the amplitude response of sinusoidal signals is of primary concern. Suitable designs are usually obtained by scaling normalized low-pass designs for the desired frequency and impedance. These designs are published in several well-known references by Geffe, White and others.[1,2,3,4,5] The normalized tables in the first two references are based on specific levels of maximum passband ripple attenuation, while tables in the last three references are based on regular increments of reflection coefficient. Although the scaling and transformation procedures used with the normalized low-pass tables are relatively straightforward, the transformation and scaling calculations provide undesired opportunities for error. The calculated capacitor values will invariably be nonstandard, thus complicating the construction.

For most nonstringent filtering applications, it is not necessary that the actual cutoff frequency exactly match the desired cutoff frequency, and a deviation of 5% or so between the actual and desired cutoff frequencies is acceptable. In this case, it is feasible and more convenient to use design tables based on standard capacitor values instead of passband ripple attenuation or reflection coefficient.

Standard Values Used in Filter Design Calculations

Capacitors are commercially available in special series of preferred values having designations of E12 (10% tolerance) and E24 (5% tolerance).[6] The reciprocal of the E-number is the power to which 10 is raised to give the step multiplier for that particular series. By calculating normalized Chebyshev and elliptic component values based on many ratios of standard capacitor

values, and by using a 50-ohm impedance level, the parameters of a large number of designs can be calculated and tabulated to span the 1-10 MHz decade. Because of the large number of standard-value capacitor (SVC) designs in this decade, the increment in cutoff frequency from one design to the next is sufficiently small so that virtually any cutoff frequency requirement can be satisfied. Using such a table, the selection of an appropriate design consists of merely scanning the cutoff frequency column to find a design having a cutoff frequency that most closely matches the desired cutoff frequency.

Chebyshev and Elliptic SVC Design Tables

Low-pass and high-pass 5- and 7-element Chebyshev and 5-branch elliptic designs were selected for tabulation because they are easy to construct and will satisfy the majority of nonstringent filtering requirements where the amplitude response is of primary interest. The precalculated 50-ohm designs are presented in eight tables of five low-pass types (Tables 11-15) and three high-pass types (Tables 16-18) with cutoff frequencies covering the 1-10 MHz decade. The applicable filter configuration and attenuation response curve accompany each table. In addition to the component values, attenuation versus frequency data and SWR are also included in the table. The passband attenuation ripples are so low in amplitude that they are swamped by the filter losses and are not measurable. For this reason, they are not shown in the response curves.

Low-pass Tables

Tables 11 and 12 are for the low-pass 5- and 7-element Chebyshev capacitor input/output configuration. This configuration is generally preferred to the alternate inductor input/output configuration to minimize the number of inductors, and where a decreasing input impedance with increasing frequency in the stopband presents no problems. Tables 13 and 14 are also for low-pass applications, but with an inductor input/output configuration. This configuration is useful when the filter input impedance in the stopband must rise with increasing frequency. For example, some RF transistor amplifiers may become unstable when terminated in a low-pass filter having a stopband response with a decreasing input impedance. In this case, the inductor-input configuration may eliminate the instability.[7] Because only one capacitor value is required in the designs of Table 13, it was feasible to have the inductor value of L1 and L5 also be a standard value. Table 15 is for the low-pass 5-branch elliptic filter with the capacitor input/output configuration in which the nonresonating capacitors (C1, C3 and C5) are standard values. The alternate inductor input/output elliptic configuration is seldom used, and therefore it is not included.

High-pass Tables

Tables 16, 17 and 18 are for the high-pass 5- and 7-element Chebyshev and the 5-branch elliptic capacitor input/output configurations, respectively. Because the inductor input/output configuration is seldom used, it was not included. As with the low-pass elliptic filter, only capacitors C1, C3 and C5 in the high-pass elliptic filter have standard values.

Scaling the Tables to Other Frequencies and Impedances

The tables shown are for the 1-10 MHz decade and for a 50-ohm equally terminated impedance. The designs are easily scaled to other frequency decades and to other equally terminated impedance levels, however, making the tables a universal design aid for these specific filter types.

Frequency Scaling

To scale the frequency and the component values to the 10-100 or 100-1000 MHz decades, multiply all tabulated frequencies by 10 or 100, respectively, and divide all C and L values by the same number. The A_s and SWR data remain unchanged. To scale the filter tables to the 1-10 kHz, 10-100 kHz or the 0.1-1 MHz decades, divide the tabulated frequencies by 1000, 100 or 10, respectively, and multiply the component values by the same number. By changing the "MHz" frequency headings to "kHz" and the "pF" and "μH" headings to "nF" and "mH," the tables are easily changed from the 1-10 MHz decade to the 1-10 kHz decade, and the table values may be read directly. Because the impedance level is still at 50 ohms, the component values may be awkward, but this can be corrected by increasing the impedance level by ten times using the impedance scaling procedure described below.

Impedance Scaling

All the tabulated designs are easily scaled to impedance levels other than 50 ohms while keeping the convenience of standard-value capacitors and the "scan mode" of design selection. If the desired new impedance level differs from 50 ohms by a factor of 0.1, 10 or 100, the 50-ohm designs are scaled by inspection by shifting the decimal points of the component values. The other data remain unchanged. For example, if the impedance level is increased by ten or one hundred times (to 500 or 5000 ohms), the decimal point of the capacitor is shifted to the left one or two places and the decimal point of the inductor is shifted to the right one or two places. With increasing impedance the capacitor values become smaller and the inductor values become larger. The opposite is true if the impedance decreases.

When the desired impedance level differs from the standard 50-ohm value by a factor such as 1.2, 1.5 or 1.86, the following scaling procedure is used:

1. Calculate the impedance scaling ratio: $R = Z_x/50$, where Z_x is the desired new impedance level in ohms.

2. Calculate the cutoff frequency (F_{50co}) of a "trial" 50-ohm filter, where $F_{50co} = R \times F_{xco}$. R is the impedance scaling ratio and F_{xco} is the desired cutoff frequency of the filter at the new impedance level.

3. From the appropriate SVC table select a design having its cutoff frequency closest to the calculated F_{50co} value. The tabulated capacitor values of this design are taken directly, but the frequency and inductor values must be scaled to the new impedance level.

4. Calculate the exact F_{xco} values, where

$$F_{xco} = \frac{F'_{50co}}{R}$$

and F'_{50co} is the tabulated cutoff frequency of the selected design. Calculate the other frequencies of the design in the same way.

5. Calculate the inductor values for the new filter by multiplying the tabulated inductor values of the selected design by the square of the scaling ratio, R.

For example, assume a 600-ohm elliptic low-pass filter is desired with a cutoff frequency of 1.0 kHz. The elliptic low-pass table is frequency scaled to the 1-10 kHz decade by changing the table headings to kHz, nF and mH. A suitable design is then selected for scaling to 60 ohms. The 60-ohm design is then scaled to 600 ohms by shifting the decimal point to complete the scaling procedure. The calculations for this example follow, using the five steps outlined above:

1. $R = Z_x / 50 = 60/50 = 1.2$
2. $F_{50co} = 1.2 \times 1.0$ kHz = 1.2 kHz
3. From the elliptic low-pass table (Table 15), designs 5 and 10 have cutoff frequencies closest to the F_{50co} of 1.2 kHz, and either design is suitable. Design 5 is selected because of its better selectivity. The tabulated capacitor values of 2200 nF, 3900 nF, 1800 nF, 271 nf and 779 nF are copied directly.

4. All frequencies of the final design are calculated by dividing the tabulated frequencies (in kHz) of design 5 by the impedance scaling ratio of 1.2:

$F_{co} = 1.27/1.2 = 1.06$
$F_{3\,dB} = 1.45/1.2 = 1.21$
$F_{As} = 2.17/1.2 = 1.88$

Note that a cutoff frequency of 1.0 kHz was desired, but a 1.06 kHz cutoff frequency will be accepted in exchange for the convenience of using an SVC design.

5. The L2 and L4 inductor values of design 5 are scaled to 60 ohms by multiplying them by the square of the impedance ratio where $R = 1.2$ and $R^2 = 1.44$:

$L2 = 1.44 \times 7.85$ mH = 11.3 mH
$L4 = 1.44 \times 6.39$ mH = 9.20 mH

The 60-ohm design is now impedance scaled to 600 ohms by shifting the decimal points of the capacitor values to the left and the decimal points of the inductor values to the right. The final scaled component values for the 600-ohm filter are:

C1 = 0.22 μF	C4 = 77.9 nF
C3 = 0.39 μF	L2 = 113 mH
C5 = 0.18 μF	L4 = 92.0 mH
C2 = 27.1 nF	

How to Use the Filter Tables

50-ohm impedance level: Before selecting a filter design, the important parameters of the filter must be known, such as type (low-pass or high-pass), cutoff frequency, impedance level, preferred input element (for low-pass only), and an approximation of the required stopband attenuation. It is obvious which tables to use for low-pass or high-pass applications, but it is not so obvious which one design of the many possible choices is optimum for the intended application. Generally, the Chebyshev will be preferred over the elliptic because the Chebyshev does not require tuning of the inductors; if the relatively gradual attenuation rise of the Chebyshev is not satisfactory, however, then the elliptic should be considered. For audio filtering, the elliptic designs with high values of SWR are preferred because these designs have a much more abrupt attenuation rise than the Chebyshev. For RF applications, SWR values less than 1.2 are recommended to minimize undesired reflections. Low SWR is also important when cascading high-pass and low-pass filters to achieve a band-pass response more than two octaves wide. Each filter will operate as expected if it is correctly terminated, but this will occur only if both designs have the relatively constant terminal impedance that is associated with low SWR.

Knowing the filter type and the response needed, select the table of designs most appropriate for the application on a trial basis. From the chosen table, scale the 1-10 MHz data to the desired frequency decade, and search the cutoff frequency column for a value nearest the desired cutoff frequency. After finding a possible design, check the stopband attenuation levels to see if they are satisfactory. Then check the SWR to see if it is appropriate for the application. Finally, check the component values to see if they are convenient. For example, in the audio-frequency range, the capacitor values probably will be in the microfarad range, and capacitors in this size are available only in the E12 series of standard values. Then connect them in accordance with the diagram shown in the table from which the design was selected.

Impedance levels other than 50 ohms: First calculate a "trial" filter design using the impedance scaling procedure previously explained. Then search the appropriate table for the best match to the trial filter and scale the selected design to the desired impedance level. In this way, the convenient scan mode of filter selection is used regardless of the desired impedance level.

References

[1] P. Geffe, *Simplified Modern Filter Design* (New York: John F. Rider, a division of Hayden Publishing Co., 1963).

[2] *A Handbook on Electrical Filters* (Rockville, Maryland: White Electromagnetics, 1963).

[3] R. Saal, *The Design of Filters Using the Catalog of Normalized Lowpass Filters* (Western Germany: Telfunken, 1966).

[4] A. Zverev, *Handbook of Filter Synthesis* (New York: John Wiley & Sons, 1967).

[5] A. B. Williams, *Electronic Filter Design Handbook* (New York: McGraw-Hill, 1981).

[6] *Reference Data for Radio Engineers,* Sixth edition, Table 2, p. 5-3. (Indianapolis, Indiana: Howard W. Sams & Co., 1981).

[7] R. Frost, "Large-scale S Parameters Help Analyze Stability," *Electronic Design,* May 24, 1980.

Selected Filter Bibliography

The following texts and articles are recommended for more in-depth study of filter theory and application.

Allen, W. H. "Modern Filter Design for the Radio Amateur." *Radio Communication*, August 1971.

Anderson, L. H. "Top-Coupled Bandpass Filter, A Chebyshev Design." *Ham Radio*, June 1977.

Blinchikoff, H. and A. Zverev. *Filtering in the Time and Frequency Domains*. New York: John Wiley and Sons, 1976.

Christian, E. *L-C-Filters: Design, Testing, and Manufacturing*. New York: John Wiley and Sons, 1983.

Drentea, C., and L. R. Watkins. "Automatically Switched Half-Octave Filters, Parts 1 and 2." *Ham Radio*, February and March, 1988.

Geffe, P. *Simplified Modern Filter Design*. Rochelle Park, NJ: Hayden Publishing Co, 1963.

Hayward, W. "Bandpass Filters for Receiver Preselectors." *Ham Radio*, February 1975.

Hayward, W. *Introduction to Radio Frequency Design*, Chapters 2 and 3. Englewood Cliffs, NJ: Prentice Hall, Inc, 1982.

Hayward, W. "The Peaked Lowpass: A Look at the Ultraspherical Filter." *Ham Radio*, June 1984.

Jansson, D., and E. Wetherhold. "High-Pass Filters to Combat TVI." *QEX*, February 1987.

Niewiadomski, S. *Filter Handbook, A Practical Design Guide*. Boca Raton, FL: CRC Press, Inc, 1989.

Webb, J. "High-Pass Filters for Receiving Applications." *QST*, October 1983.

Wetherhold, E. "Design 7-element Low-Pass Filters Using Standard-Value Capacitors." *EDN*, Vol 26, No. 1, January 7, 1981.

Wetherhold, E. "Elliptic Lowpass Filters for Transistor Amplifiers." *Ham Radio*, January 1981.

Wetherhold, E. "Practical 75- and 300-Ohm High-Pass Filters." *QST*, February 1982.

Table 11

5-Element Chebyshev Low-pass Filter Designs
50-ohm Impedance, C-In/Out
For Standard E24 Capacitor Values

Filter No.	Fco	3 dB	20 dB	40 dB	Max. SWR	C1,5 (pF)	L2,4 (µH)	C3 (pF)	Filter No.	Fco	3 dB	20 dB	40 dB	Max. SWR	C1,5 (pF)	L2,4 (µH)	C3 (pF)
1	1.01	1.15	1.53	2.25	1.355	3600	10.8	6200	71	3.96	5.76	8.38	12.8	1.041	470	2.35	1100
2	1.02	1.21	1.65	2.45	1.212	3000	10.7	5600	72	4.39	5.84	8.31	12.6	1.079	510	2.31	1100
3	1.15	1.29	1.71	2.51	1.391	3300	9.49	5600	73	4.88	6.01	8.33	12.5	1.152	560	2.20	1100
4	1.10	1.32	1.81	2.69	1.196	2700	9.88	5100	74	5.50	6.34	8.54	12.6	1.293	620	1.99	1100
5	1.25	1.41	1.88	2.75	1.386	3000	8.67	5100	75	4.40	6.34	9.20	14.1	1.043	430	2.13	1000
6	1.04	1.37	1.94	2.94	1.085	2200	9.82	4700	76	4.91	6.45	9.13	13.8	1.087	470	2.09	1000
7	1.15	1.41	1.95	2.92	1.155	2400	9.37	4700	77	5.38	6.62	9.17	13.7	1.154	510	2.00	1000
8	1.32	1.50	2.01	2.96	1.332	2700	8.29	4700	78	6.00	6.95	9.37	13.8	1.282	560	1.83	1000
9	1.13	1.50	2.12	3.22	1.081	2000	9.00	4300	79	4.81	6.97	10.1	15.5	1.042	390	1.94	910
10	1.26	1.54	2.13	3.19	1.157	2200	8.56	4300	80	5.43	7.09	10.0	15.2	1.091	430	1.89	910
11	1.39	1.61	2.18	3.21	1.276	2400	7.88	4300	81	6.00	7.31	10.1	15.1	1.167	470	1.80	910
12	1.05	1.62	2.38	3.66	1.028	1600	8.35	3900	82	6.60	7.64	10.3	15.2	1.283	510	1.66	910
13	1.23	1.65	2.34	3.55	1.076	1800	8.19	3900	83	4.86	7.69	11.4	17.5	1.023	330	1.76	820
14	1.39	1.70	2.35	3.51	1.159	2000	7.75	3900	84	5.51	7.76	11.2	17.1	1.052	360	1.74	820
15	1.55	1.79	2.41	3.55	1.295	2200	7.05	3900	85	6.07	7.89	11.1	16.8	1.095	390	1.70	820
16	1.17	1.76	2.57	3.94	1.033	1500	7.70	3600	86	6.77	8.17	11.2	16.7	1.184	430	1.60	820
17	1.27	1.77	2.55	3.88	1.057	1600	7.64	3600	87	7.54	8.61	11.5	17.0	1.327	470	1.45	820
18	1.46	1.82	2.54	3.81	1.135	1800	7.28	3600	88	5.26	8.40	12.4	19.2	1.022	300	1.61	750
19	1.65	1.92	2.59	3.83	1.268	2000	6.64	3600	89	6.04	8.49	12.2	18.7	1.052	330	1.59	750
20	1.88	2.08	2.73	3.97	1.497	2200	5.70	3600	90	6.70	8.64	12.2	18.4	1.101	360	1.55	750
21	1.43	1.94	2.77	4.21	1.068	1500	6.96	3300	91	7.33	8.89	12.3	18.3	1.175	390	1.48	750
22	1.54	1.97	2.77	4.17	1.109	1600	6.79	3300	92	8.24	9.42	12.6	18.5	1.327	430	1.33	750
23	1.76	2.07	2.81	4.17	1.238	1800	6.21	3300	93	6.69	9.36	13.5	20.6	1.054	300	1.44	680
24	2.02	2.25	2.96	4.31	1.470	2000	5.31	3300	94	7.48	9.56	13.4	20.2	1.110	330	1.40	680
25	1.31	2.10	3.11	4.79	1.022	1200	6.43	3000	95	8.25	9.89	13.6	20.2	1.196	360	1.32	680
26	1.48	2.12	3.06	4.68	1.046	1300	6.39	3000	96	9.10	10.4	13.9	20.4	1.328	390	1.20	680
27	1.75	2.19	3.05	4.57	1.135	1500	6.07	3000	97	7.21	10.2	14.8	22.6	1.048	270	1.32	620
28	1.89	2.25	3.08	4.57	1.206	1600	5.77	3000	98	8.18	10.5	14.7	22.2	1.107	300	1.28	620
29	2.19	2.45	3.23	4.71	1.440	1800	4.92	3000	99	9.11	10.9	14.9	22.1	1.203	330	1.19	620
30	1.51	2.34	3.44	5.29	1.026	1100	5.78	2700	100	10.1	11.5	15.3	22.5	1.355	360	1.08	620
31	1.70	2.36	3.40	5.17	1.057	1200	5.73	2700	101	7.82	11.3	16.4	25.1	1.042	240	1.19	560
32	1.87	2.40	3.38	5.10	1.104	1300	5.57	2700	102	9.02	11.6	16.3	24.6	1.105	270	1.16	560
33	2.20	2.56	3.46	5.11	1.268	1500	4.98	2700	103	8.66	12.4	18.0	27.6	1.044	220	1.09	510
34	2.39	2.69	3.56	5.21	1.406	1600	4.53	2700	104	9.64	12.6	17.9	27.1	1.088	240	1.06	510
35	1.75	2.63	3.85	5.91	1.033	1000	5.14	2400	105	9.22	13.5	19.6	30.0	1.039	200	1.00	470
36	1.99	2.67	3.81	5.78	1.072	1100	5.05	2400	106	9.85	14.7	21.5	33.0	1.034	180	0.919	430
37	2.19	2.74	3.81	5.71	1.135	1200	4.85	2400									
38	2.40	2.84	3.86	5.73	1.227	1300	4.55	2400									
39	1.89	2.87	4.21	6.47	1.030	910	4.71	2200									
40	2.14	2.91	4.16	6.31	1.068	1000	4.64	2200									
41	2.39	2.99	4.16	6.23	1.135	1100	4.45	2200									
42	2.64	3.11	4.22	6.25	1.238	1200	4.14	2200									
43	2.93	3.29	4.36	6.39	1.398	1300	3.71	2200									
44	2.05	3.16	4.64	7.13	1.028	820	4.28	2000									
45	2.36	3.20	4.57	6.94	1.068	910	4.22	2000									
46	2.63	3.28	4.57	6.86	1.135	1000	4.05	2000									
47	2.93	3.43	4.65	6.89	1.251	1100	3.73	2000									
48	3.29	3.67	4.85	7.07	1.440	1200	3.28	2000									
49	2.34	3.51	5.14	7.88	1.033	750	3.85	1800									
50	2.63	3.56	5.08	7.71	1.069	820	3.79	1800									
51	2.96	3.66	5.09	7.62	1.145	910	3.61	1800									
52	3.30	3.84	5.19	7.67	1.268	1000	3.32	1800									
53	3.76	4.15	5.45	7.93	1.497	1100	2.85	1800									
54	2.70	3.96	5.76	8.82	1.039	680	3.42	1600									
55	3.06	4.03	5.71	8.63	1.086	750	3.34	1600									
56	3.38	4.14	5.73	8.57	1.159	820	3.18	1600									
57	3.82	4.39	5.89	8.67	1.311	910	2.86	1600									
58	2.77	4.21	6.18	9.48	1.030	620	3.21	1500									
59	3.14	4.26	6.10	9.26	1.067	680	3.17	1500									
60	3.51	4.38	6.10	9.14	1.135	750	3.03	1500									
61	3.88	4.56	6.20	9.17	1.241	820	2.82	1500									
62	4.46	4.95	6.51	9.48	1.473	910	2.41	1500									
63	3.39	4.88	7.08	10.8	1.044	560	2.77	1300									
64	3.84	4.98	7.02	10.6	1.097	620	2.70	1300									
65	4.26	5.14	7.08	10.5	1.181	680	2.55	1300									
66	4.79	5.46	7.29	10.7	1.341	750	2.28	1300									
67	3.61	5.28	7.68	11.8	1.039	510	2.56	1200									
68	4.06	5.36	7.61	11.5	1.083	560	2.51	1200									
69	4.55	5.54	7.65	11.4	1.167	620	2.37	1200									
70	5.07	5.84	7.84	11.5	1.304	680	2.16	1200									

C1 = C5   L2 = L4

(A)

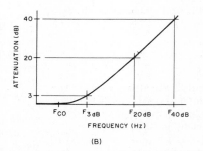

(B)

The schematic for a 5-element capacitor input/output Chebyshev low-pass filter is shown at A. At B is the typical attenuation response curve.

Table 12
7-Element Chebyshev Low-pass Filter Designs
50-ohm Impedance, C-In/Out
For Standard E24 Capacitor Values

Filter No.	F_{co}	3 dB	20 dB	40 dB	Max. SWR	C1,7 (pF)	L2,6 (µH)	C3,5 (pF)	L4 (µH)
1	1.02	1.10	1.31	1.65	1.254	3300	11.2	6200	12.6
2	1.04	1.16	1.40	1.79	1.142	2700	10.9	5600	12.6
3	1.13	1.23	1.45	1.84	1.264	3000	10.1	5600	11.3
4	1.05	1.23	1.51	1.96	1.071	2200	10.3	5100	12.3
5	1.12	1.26	1.53	1.96	1.123	2400	10.0	5100	11.7
6	1.23	1.34	1.59	2.01	1.247	2700	9.29	5100	10.4
7	1.03	1.30	1.63	2.15	1.030	1800	9.52	4700	11.9
8	1.12	1.33	1.64	2.13	1.064	2000	9.50	4700	11.4
9	1.21	1.37	1.66	2.13	1.119	2200	9.27	4700	10.8
10	1.29	1.42	1.70	2.16	1.200	2400	8.82	4700	10.0
11	1.10	1.41	1.79	2.36	1.023	1600	8.68	4300	11.0
12	1.21	1.45	1.79	2.33	1.058	1800	8.71	4300	10.5
13	1.31	1.49	1.81	2.33	1.114	2000	8.50	4300	9.91
14	1.42	1.56	1.86	2.36	1.202	2200	8.06	4300	9.14
15	1.54	1.65	1.93	2.43	1.336	2400	7.39	4300	8.18
16	1.25	1.57	1.97	2.59	1.031	1500	7.90	3900	9.85
17	1.32	1.59	1.97	2.57	1.050	1600	7.91	3900	9.62
18	1.44	1.64	1.99	2.56	1.109	1800	7.73	3900	9.04
19	1.57	1.72	2.05	2.60	1.205	2000	7.30	3900	8.27
20	1.44	1.73	2.14	2.78	1.056	1500	7.29	3600	8.82
21	1.52	1.76	2.15	2.78	1.086	1600	7.22	3600	8.54
22	1.66	1.84	2.20	2.81	1.176	1800	6.86	3600	7.83
23	1.83	1.96	2.30	2.90	1.327	2000	6.22	3600	6.90
24	1.51	1.86	2.32	3.05	1.037	1300	6.70	3300	8.27
25	1.68	1.93	2.35	3.03	1.099	1500	6.58	3300	7.72
26	1.77	1.98	2.38	3.05	1.147	1600	6.40	3300	7.37
27	1.96	2.11	2.49	3.14	1.294	1800	5.83	3300	6.50
28	1.56	2.02	2.56	3.38	1.021	1100	6.04	3000	7.68
29	1.68	2.05	2.56	3.35	1.042	1200	6.09	3000	7.47
30	1.79	2.09	2.57	3.33	1.073	1300	6.05	3000	7.21
31	1.99	2.20	2.64	3.37	1.176	1500	5.72	3000	6.52
32	2.11	2.28	2.70	3.42	1.257	1600	5.42	3000	6.08
33	1.75	2.25	2.84	3.75	1.023	1000	5.45	2700	6.89
34	1.89	2.29	2.84	3.71	1.048	1100	5.48	2700	6.68
35	2.02	2.34	2.86	3.70	1.086	1200	5.41	2700	6.40
36	2.15	2.41	2.90	3.72	1.141	1300	5.26	2700	6.06
37	2.44	2.61	3.07	3.86	1.327	1500	4.66	2700	5.18
38	2.01	2.54	3.20	4.21	1.027	910	4.86	2400	6.09
39	2.17	2.59	3.20	4.17	1.056	1000	4.86	2400	5.88
40	2.33	2.66	3.24	4.17	1.104	1100	4.77	2400	5.59
41	2.49	2.76	3.30	4.21	1.176	1200	4.57	2400	5.22
42	2.67	2.88	3.41	4.30	1.282	1300	4.27	2400	4.77
43	2.15	2.76	3.49	4.60	1.024	820	4.44	2200	5.61
44	2.35	2.82	3.49	4.55	1.053	910	4.46	2200	5.41
45	2.52	2.89	3.52	4.54	1.099	1000	4.38	2200	5.15
46	2.72	3.01	3.60	4.59	1.176	1100	4.19	2200	4.78
47	2.94	3.16	3.73	4.70	1.294	1200	3.88	2200	4.33
48	2.38	3.04	3.84	5.06	1.025	750	4.04	2000	5.09
49	2.57	3.09	3.84	5.01	1.050	820	4.06	2000	4.93
50	2.78	3.18	3.88	5.00	1.100	910	3.98	2000	4.68
51	2.99	3.31	3.96	5.05	1.176	1000	3.81	2000	4.35
52	3.26	3.50	4.12	5.19	1.308	1100	3.50	2000	3.89
53	2.67	3.38	4.26	5.61	1.027	680	3.64	1800	4.57
54	2.89	3.45	4.27	5.56	1.056	750	3.65	1800	4.41
55	3.09	3.54	4.31	5.55	1.100	820	3.59	1800	4.21
56	3.35	3.69	4.42	5.62	1.188	910	3.40	1800	3.87
57	3.65	3.92	4.60	5.80	1.327	1000	3.11	1800	3.45
58	3.07	3.82	4.80	6.30	1.033	620	3.24	1600	4.03
59	3.30	3.90	4.81	6.25	1.064	680	3.24	1600	3.88
60	3.55	4.02	4.87	6.26	1.120	750	3.15	1600	3.67
61	3.81	4.18	4.99	6.34	1.204	820	3.00	1600	3.39
62	3.16	4.05	5.12	6.75	1.024	560	3.03	1500	3.82
63	3.45	4.13	5.12	6.68	1.053	620	3.04	1500	3.69
64	3.69	4.24	5.17	6.66	1.097	680	2.99	1500	3.51
65	3.99	4.41	5.28	6.73	1.176	750	2.86	1500	3.26
66	4.31	4.64	5.48	6.91	1.297	820	2.64	1500	2.94
67	3.81	4.72	5.90	7.74	1.036	510	2.64	1300	3.26
68	4.10	4.82	5.93	7.69	1.070	560	2.62	1300	3.14
69	4.43	4.98	6.02	7.72	1.133	620	2.54	1300	2.94
70	4.78	5.21	6.19	7.85	1.230	680	2.39	1300	2.70
71	4.13	5.11	6.39	8.38	1.035	470	2.43	1200	3.01
72	4.40	5.20	6.41	8.33	1.064	510	2.43	1200	2.91
73	4.72	5.35	6.49	8.34	1.116	560	2.37	1200	2.76
74	5.12	5.60	6.67	8.48	1.214	620	2.23	1200	2.52
75	4.49	5.57	6.97	9.15	1.035	430	2.23	1100	2.76
76	4.82	5.68	7.00	9.09	1.066	470	2.22	1100	2.66
77	5.12	5.83	7.07	9.10	1.112	510	2.18	1100	2.54
78	5.52	6.07	7.24	9.21	1.196	560	2.07	1100	2.35
79	4.93	6.12	7.67	10.1	1.034	390	2.03	1000	2.51
80	5.33	6.26	7.70	10.0	1.069	430	2.02	1000	2.41
81	5.69	6.44	7.80	10.0	1.122	470	1.97	1000	2.29
82	6.08	6.68	7.97	10.1	1.198	510	1.88	1000	2.13
83	6.63	7.09	8.32	10.5	1.343	560	1.71	1000	1.89
84	5.48	6.75	8.43	11.0	1.038	360	1.85	910	2.28
85	5.84	6.87	8.46	11.0	1.068	390	1.84	910	2.20
86	6.28	7.09	8.58	11.0	1.126	430	1.79	910	2.07
87	6.75	7.39	8.80	11.2	1.213	470	1.69	910	1.91
88	5.68	7.39	9.37	12.4	1.020	300	1.65	820	2.10
89	6.17	7.52	9.36	12.2	1.043	330	1.66	820	2.04
90	6.60	7.68	9.41	12.2	1.079	360	1.65	820	1.96
91	7.01	7.89	9.53	12.2	1.131	390	1.61	820	1.86
92	7.59	8.27	9.82	12.5	1.233	430	1.51	820	1.70
93	6.72	8.21	10.2	13.4	1.042	300	1.52	750	1.87
94	7.23	8.40	10.3	13.3	1.080	330	1.51	750	1.79
95	7.72	8.66	10.4	13.4	1.138	360	1.46	750	1.69
96	8.24	9.00	10.7	13.6	1.222	390	1.39	750	1.57
97	7.36	9.04	11.3	14.8	1.039	270	1.38	680	1.70
98	7.98	9.27	11.4	14.7	1.082	300	1.37	680	1.62
99	8.58	9.59	11.6	14.8	1.148	330	1.32	680	1.52
100	9.23	10.0	11.9	15.1	1.247	360	1.24	680	1.39
101	7.91	9.86	12.4	16.2	1.032	240	1.26	620	1.56
102	8.67	10.1	12.4	16.1	1.075	270	1.25	620	1.49
103	9.39	10.5	12.7	16.2	1.145	300	1.20	620	1.39
104	8.86	11.0	13.7	18.0	1.036	220	1.14	560	1.40
105	9.49	11.2	13.8	17.8	1.068	240	1.13	560	1.35
106	9.72	12.0	15.0	19.7	1.036	200	1.03	510	1.28

The schematic for a 7-element Chebyshev low-pass filter. See Table 11 for the attenuation response curve.

Table 13
5-Element Chebyshev Low-pass Filter Designs
50-ohm Impedance, L-In/Out
For Standard-Value L and C

Filter No.	F_{co}	3 dB	20 dB	40 dB	Max. SWR	L1,5 (µH)	C2,4 (pF)	L3 (µH)
1	0.744	1.15	1.69	2.60	1.027	5.60	4700	13.7
2	0.901	1.26	1.81	2.76	1.055	5.60	4300	12.7
3	1.06	1.38	1.94	2.93	1.096	5.60	3900	11.8
4	1.19	1.47	2.05	3.07	1.138	5.60	3600	11.2
5	1.32	1.58	2.17	3.23	1.192	5.60	3300	10.6
6	0.911	1.39	2.03	3.12	1.030	4.70	3900	11.4
7	1.08	1.50	2.16	3.29	1.056	4.70	3600	10.6
8	1.25	1.63	2.30	3.48	1.092	4.70	3300	9.92
9	1.42	1.77	2.46	3.68	1.142	4.70	3000	9.32
10	1.61	1.92	2.63	3.90	1.209	4.70	2700	8.79
11	1.05	1.64	2.41	3.72	1.025	3.90	3300	9.63
12	1.29	1.80	2.60	3.96	1.054	3.90	3000	8.83
13	1.54	1.99	2.80	4.22	1.099	3.90	2700	8.15
14	1.80	2.19	3.03	4.53	1.164	3.90	2400	7.57
15	1.99	2.35	3.20	4.75	1.222	3.90	2200	7.23
16	1.34	2.00	2.93	4.49	1.034	3.30	2700	7.89
17	1.68	2.25	3.20	4.84	1.077	3.30	2400	7.15
18	1.92	2.43	3.40	5.11	1.118	3.30	2200	6.73
19	2.16	2.63	3.62	5.40	1.174	3.30	2000	6.35
20	1.65	2.46	3.59	5.51	1.035	2.70	2200	6.43
21	1.99	2.70	3.86	5.85	1.069	2.70	2000	5.93
22	2.34	2.97	4.15	6.24	1.118	2.70	1800	5.50
23	2.71	3.27	4.49	6.68	1.188	2.70	1600	5.13
24	2.92	3.43	4.67	6.92	1.233	2.70	1500	4.97
25	2.01	3.01	4.39	6.74	1.034	2.20	1800	5.26
26	2.52	3.37	4.80	7.27	1.077	2.20	1600	4.76
27	2.78	3.57	5.02	7.56	1.107	2.20	1500	4.55
28	3.34	4.02	5.52	8.21	1.190	2.20	1300	4.18
29	2.36	3.61	5.29	8.14	1.029	1.80	1500	4.38
30	3.12	4.14	5.89	8.92	1.080	1.80	1300	3.88
31	3.51	4.45	6.23	9.36	1.118	1.80	1200	3.67
32	3.93	4.78	6.60	9.85	1.169	1.80	1100	3.48
33	4.37	5.15	7.01	10.4	1.233	1.80	1000	3.31
34	3.10	4.51	6.56	10.0	1.041	1.50	1200	3.51
35	3.65	4.90	6.99	10.6	1.073	1.50	1100	3.27
36	4.21	5.34	7.47	11.2	1.118	1.50	1000	3.06
37	4.75	5.77	7.95	11.9	1.173	1.50	910	2.89
38	3.53	5.41	7.94	12.2	1.029	1.20	1000	2.92
39	4.30	5.94	8.53	13.0	1.060	1.20	910	2.69
40	5.09	6.53	9.18	13.8	1.106	1.20	820	2.49
41	5.73	7.04	9.73	14.6	1.155	1.20	750	2.35
42	6.42	7.61	10.4	15.4	1.219	1.20	680	2.23
43	4.40	6.60	9.65	14.8	1.033	1.00	820	2.40
44	5.27	7.20	10.3	15.7	1.064	1.00	750	2.22
45	6.15	7.87	11.1	16.7	1.108	1.00	680	2.07
46	6.95	8.51	11.8	17.6	1.160	1.00	620	1.95
47	7.80	9.22	12.6	18.6	1.227	1.00	560	1.85
48	5.23	7.96	11.7	17.9	1.030	0.82	680	1.99
49	6.33	8.72	12.5	19.0	1.061	0.82	620	1.83
50	7.45	9.56	13.4	20.3	1.106	0.82	560	1.70
51	8.44	10.3	14.3	21.4	1.158	0.82	510	1.60
52	9.28	11.0	15.1	22.4	1.211	0.82	470	1.53
53	6.41	9.66	14.1	21.7	1.032	0.68	560	1.64
54	7.75	10.6	15.2	23.1	1.064	0.68	510	1.51
55	8.83	11.4	16.1	24.3	1.100	0.68	470	1.42
56	9.97	12.3	17.1	25.6	1.148	0.68	430	1.34

Table 14
7-Element Chebyshev Low-pass Filter Designs
50-ohm Impedance, L-In/Out
For Standard-Value Capacitors

Filter No.	F_{co}	3 dB	20 dB	40 dB	Max. SWR	L1,7 (µH)	C2,6 (pF)	L3,5 (µH)	C4 (pF)
1	1.01	1.18	1.44	1.87	1.081	5.89	4300	13.4	5100
2	1.09	1.29	1.60	2.08	1.059	5.06	3900	12.0	4700
3	1.03	1.09	1.26	1.58	1.480	10.1	4300	17.1	4700
4	1.20	1.40	1.73	2.24	1.071	4.81	3600	11.2	4300
5	1.16	1.23	1.44	1.81	1.383	8.34	3900	14.6	4300
6	1.33	1.54	1.88	2.43	1.087	4.58	3300	10.3	3900
7	1.42	1.68	2.07	2.70	1.064	3.95	3000	9.27	3600
8	1.34	1.41	1.63	2.04	1.506	7.98	3300	13.4	3600
9	1.53	1.85	2.31	3.02	1.045	3.36	2700	8.32	3300
10	1.50	1.59	1.86	2.33	1.406	6.57	3000	11.4	3300
11	1.63	2.06	2.59	3.41	1.029	2.83	2400	7.41	3000
12	1.69	1.81	2.13	2.68	1.317	5.36	2700	9.70	3000
13	1.86	2.27	2.83	3.70	1.042	2.71	2200	6.78	2700
14	1.91	2.07	2.46	3.12	1.238	4.31	2400	8.19	2700
15	2.14	2.52	3.11	4.04	1.064	2.63	2000	6.18	2400
16	2.01	2.11	2.45	3.06	1.506	5.32	2200	8.91	2400
17	2.29	2.78	3.46	4.52	1.045	2.24	1800	5.54	2200
18	2.25	2.39	2.79	3.49	1.406	4.38	2000	7.61	2200
19	2.45	3.09	3.88	5.11	1.029	1.89	1600	4.94	2000
20	2.53	2.71	3.19	4.02	1.317	3.57	1800	6.47	2000
21	2.85	3.37	4.15	5.39	1.064	1.97	1500	4.64	1800
22	2.86	3.11	3.69	4.68	1.238	2.88	1600	5.46	1800
23	3.13	3.84	4.79	6.27	1.039	1.59	1300	4.00	1600
24	3.27	4.12	5.18	6.81	1.029	1.41	1200	3.70	1500
25	3.47	3.90	4.70	6.02	1.140	2.01	1300	4.17	1500
26	3.99	4.61	5.64	7.28	1.087	1.53	1100	3.43	1300
27	4.27	5.05	6.22	8.09	1.064	1.32	1000	3.09	1200
28	4.01	4.22	4.90	6.11	1.506	2.66	1100	4.45	1200
29	4.63	5.53	6.85	8.91	1.056	1.17	910	2.81	1100
30	4.49	4.77	5.57	6.98	1.406	2.19	1000	3.81	1100
31	5.05	6.11	7.60	9.92	1.047	1.03	820	2.53	1000
32	4.93	5.23	6.10	7.64	1.416	2.02	910	3.49	1000
33	5.58	6.70	8.31	10.8	1.052	0.954	750	2.31	910
34	5.54	5.94	6.99	8.80	1.326	1.65	820	2.97	910
35	6.23	7.41	9.16	11.9	1.059	0.881	680	2.10	820
36	5.92	6.24	7.26		1.476	1.76	750	2.98	820
37	6.79	8.12	10.0	13.1	1.055	0.796	620	1.91	750
38	6.64	7.07	8.27	10.4	1.379	1.45	680	2.54	750
39	7.46	8.97	11.1	14.5	1.051	0.711	560	1.73	680
40	7.21	7.63	8.89	11.1	1.438	1.40	620	2.41	680
41	8.18	9.85	12.2		1.050	0.645	510	1.57	620
42	8.10	8.66	10.2	12.8	1.345	1.15	560	2.05	620
43	9.21	10.8	13.2	17.1	1.074	0.633	470	1.46	560
44	8.78	9.31	10.9	13.6	1.425	1.14	510	1.96	560
45	10.1	11.8	14.4	18.7	1.081	0.589	430	1.34	510

The schematic for a 5-element inductor-input/output Chebyshev low-pass filter. See Table 11 for the attenuation response curve.

The schematic for a 7-element inductor input/output Chebyshev low-pass filter. See Table 11 for the attenuation response curve.

Table 15
5-Branch Elliptic Low-Pass Filter Designs
50-ohm Impedance
Standard E12 Capacitor Values for C1, C3 and C5

Filter No.	F_{co}	F_{3dB}	F_{As}	A_s	Max. SWR	C1	C3	C5	C2	C4	L2	L4	F2	F4
	---------(MHz)---------			(dB)		---------------------(pF)---------------------					------(µH)------		-----(MHz)-----	
1	0.795	0.989	1.57	47.4	1.092	2700	5600	2200	324	937	12.1	10.1	2.54	1.64
2	1.06	1.20	1.77	46.2	1.234	2700	4700	2200	341	982	9.36	7.56	2.82	1.85
3	1.47	1.57	2.15	45.4	1.586	2700	3900	2200	364	1045	6.32	4.88	3.32	2.23
4	0.929	1.18	1.91	48.0	1.077	2200	4700	1800	257	743	10.2	8.59	3.11	1.99
5	1.27	1.45	2.17	46.7	1.215	2200	3900	1800	271	779	7.85	6.39	3.45	2.26
6	1.69	1.82	2.54	45.9	1.489	2200	3300	1800	287	821	5.64	4.42	3.96	2.64
7	1.12	1.44	2.41	49.8	1.071	1800	3900	1500	192	549	8.45	7.25	3.95	2.52
8	1.49	1.73	2.70	48.8	1.183	1800	3300	1500	200	570	6.75	5.62	4.33	2.81
9	2.11	2.27	3.27	47.8	1.506	1800	2700	1500	213	604	4.55	3.64	5.12	3.40
10	1.28	1.66	2.63	46.3	1.064	1500	3300	1200	192	561	7.20	6.00	4.28	2.74
11	1.79	2.06	2.99	44.8	1.195	1500	2700	1200	204	592	5.52	4.42	4.75	3.11
12	2.52	2.70	3.63	43.8	1.525	1500	2200	1200	220	636	3.71	2.82	5.58	3.76
13	1.56	2.08	3.55	50.1	1.055	1200	2700	1000	127	363	5.88	5.07	5.83	3.71
14	2.23	2.59	4.04	48.8	1.183	1200	2200	1000	133	380	4.50	3.75	6.50	4.22
15	3.17	3.41	4.90	47.8	1.506	1200	1800	1000	142	402	3.03	2.42	7.68	5.10
16	1.94	2.52	4.15	48.4	1.064	1000	2200	820	115	331	4.79	4.06	6.78	4.34
17	2.73	3.14	4.73	47.0	1.199	1000	1800	820	121	348	3.66	2.99	7.56	4.93
18	3.73	4.02	5.63	46.2	1.491	1000	1500	820	129	368	2.56	2.01	8.76	5.85
19	2.39	3.11	5.20	49.4	1.065	820	1800	680	89.3	256	3.91	3.35	8.51	5.44
20	3.26	3.79	5.85	48.2	1.185	820	1500	680	93.6	267	3.07	2.54	9.39	6.10
21	4.83	5.17	7.30	47.2	1.569	820	1200	680	100	286	1.95	1.54	11.4	7.58
22	2.85	3.71	6.15	48.8	1.063	680	1500	560	76.6	220	3.26	2.78	10.1	6.43
23	4.16	4.74	7.14	47.3	1.221	680	1200	560	81.3	233	2.40	1.97	11.4	7.44
24	5.72	6.13	8.58	46.5	1.547	680	1000	560	86.3	246	1.65	1.30	13.3	8.91
25	3.67	4.69	7.95	50.5	1.076	560	1200	470	57.6	164	2.59	2.23	13.0	8.31
26	5.02	5.77	9.01	49.4	1.212	560	1000	470	60.3	171	2.01	1.68	14.5	9.40
27	7.18	7.68	11.1	48.6	1.582	560	820	470	64.1	181	1.32	1.06	17.3	11.5
28	4.40	5.60	9.24	49.3	1.079	470	1000	390	51.4	147	2.16	1.84	15.1	9.66
29	6.17	7.01	10.6	48.0	1.236	470	820	390	54.2	155	1.63	1.34	17.0	11.1
30	8.63	9.20	12.9	47.3	1.604	470	680	390	57.6	164	1.09	0.857	20.1	13.4
31	5.47	6.91	11.8	51.3	1.086	390	820	330	38.5	109	1.76	1.52	19.3	12.3
32	7.55	8.59	13.5	50.2	1.242	390	680	330	40.4	114	1.34	1.12	21.7	14.1
33	10.9	11.5	16.8	49.5	1.659	390	560	330	42.8	120	0.862	0.695	26.2	17.4
34	6.59	8.17	13.0	47.7	1.096	330	680	270	39.0	112	1.46	1.22	21.1	13.6
35	9.10	10.2	15.0	46.5	1.267	330	560	270	41.2	118	1.09	0.881	23.7	15.6
36	12.4	13.2	18.1	45.8	1.635	330	470	270	43.9	125	0.741	0.573	27.9	18.8

(A)

(B)

The schematic for a 5-branch elliptic low-pass filter is shown at A. At B is the typical attenuation response curve.

Table 16
5-Element Chebyshev High-pass Filter Designs
50-ohm Impedance, C-In/Out
For Standard E24 Capacitor Values

Filter No.	F_{co}	3 dB	20 dB	40 dB	Max. SWR	C1,5 (pF)	L2,4 (µH)	C3 (pF)
1	1.04	0.726	0.501	0.328	1.044	5100	6.45	2200
2	1.04	0.788	0.554	0.366	1.081	4300	5.97	2000
3	1.17	0.800	0.550	0.359	1.039	4700	5.85	2000
4	1.07	0.857	0.615	0.410	1.135	3600	5.56	1800
5	1.17	0.877	0.616	0.406	1.076	3900	5.36	1800
6	1.33	0.890	0.609	0.397	1.034	4300	5.26	1800
7	1.12	0.938	0.686	0.461	1.206	3000	5.20	1600
8	1.25	0.974	0.693	0.461	1.109	3300	4.86	1600
9	1.38	0.994	0.691	0.454	1.057	3600	4.71	1600
10	1.54	1.00	0.683	0.444	1.028	3900	4.67	1600
11	1.14	0.978	0.723	0.490	1.268	2700	5.09	1500
12	1.28	1.03	0.738	0.492	1.135	3000	4.64	1500
13	1.43	1.06	0.738	0.486	1.068	3300	4.44	1500
14	1.61	1.07	0.730	0.476	1.033	3600	4.38	1500
15	1.21	1.08	0.812	0.555	1.398	2200	4.82	1300
16	1.35	1.14	0.841	0.567	1.227	2400	4.29	1300
17	1.55	1.20	0.853	0.566	1.104	2700	3.94	1300
18	1.75	1.23	0.848	0.555	1.046	3000	3.81	1300
19	1.28	1.15	0.871	0.597	1.440	2000	4.57	1200
20	1.45	1.24	0.909	0.614	1.238	2200	3.99	1200
21	1.60	1.29	0.923	0.616	1.135	2400	3.71	1200
22	1.84	1.32	0.921	0.605	1.057	2700	3.54	1200
23	2.14	1.34	0.906	0.588	1.022	3000	3.50	1200
24	1.57	1.34	0.989	0.669	1.251	2000	3.69	1100
25	1.75	1.40	1.01	0.672	1.135	2200	3.40	1100
26	1.93	1.44	1.01	0.664	1.072	2400	3.27	1100
27	2.27	1.46	0.992	0.645	1.026	2700	3.21	1100
28	1.71	1.47	1.08	0.734	1.268	1800	3.39	1000
29	1.93	1.54	1.11	0.739	1.135	2000	3.09	1000
30	2.15	1.58	1.11	0.730	1.068	2200	2.96	1000
31	2.41	1.60	1.10	0.714	1.033	2400	2.92	1000
32	1.66	1.50	1.14	0.783	1.473	1500	3.54	910
33	1.82	1.59	1.18	0.803	1.311	1600	3.18	910
34	2.09	1.69	1.22	0.812	1.145	1800	2.83	910
35	2.36	1.74	1.22	0.802	1.068	2000	2.70	910
36	2.68	1.76	1.20	0.783	1.030	2200	2.66	910
37	2.12	1.81	1.33	0.898	1.241	1500	2.73	820
38	2.28	1.86	1.35	0.902	1.159	1600	2.58	820
39	2.61	1.93	1.35	0.890	1.069	1800	2.43	820
40	3.01	1.96	1.33	0.866	1.028	2000	2.39	820
41	2.17	1.90	1.42	0.970	1.341	1300	2.67	750
42	2.57	2.06	1.48	0.985	1.135	1500	2.32	750
43	2.76	2.10	1.48	0.978	1.086	1600	2.25	750
44	3.21	2.14	1.46	0.952	1.033	1800	2.19	750
45	2.45	2.13	1.58	1.08	1.304	1200	2.36	680
46	2.69	2.23	1.62	1.09	1.181	1300	2.17	680
47	3.17	2.33	1.63	1.07	1.067	1500	2.01	680
48	3.44	2.35	1.62	1.06	1.039	1600	1.99	680
49	2.70	2.34	1.74	1.18	1.293	1100	2.14	620
50	2.99	2.46	1.78	1.19	1.167	1200	1.96	620
51	3.28	2.53	1.79	1.19	1.097	1300	1.87	620
52	3.93	2.59	1.76	1.15	1.030	1500	1.81	620
53	3.02	2.60	1.93	1.31	1.282	1000	1.92	560
54	3.37	2.74	1.97	1.32	1.152	1100	1.75	560
55	3.72	2.81	1.98	1.31	1.083	1200	1.67	560
56	4.10	2.85	1.97	1.29	1.044	1300	1.64	560
57	3.31	2.86	2.12	1.44	1.283	910	1.75	510
58	3.69	3.00	2.17	1.45	1.154	1000	1.60	510
59	4.11	3.09	2.17	1.44	1.079	1100	1.52	510
60	4.59	3.14	2.15	1.41	1.039	1200	1.49	510
61	3.49	3.05	2.28	1.55	1.327	820	1.66	470
62	3.95	3.24	2.35	1.57	1.167	910	1.49	470
63	4.39	3.34	2.36	1.56	1.087	1000	1.41	470
64	4.94	3.40	2.34	1.53	1.041	1100	1.38	470
65	3.81	3.34	2.49	1.70	1.327	750	1.52	430
66	4.24	3.52	2.56	1.72	1.184	820	1.38	430
67	4.77	3.65	2.58	1.71	1.091	910	1.29	430
68	5.36	3.72	2.56	1.68	1.043	1000	1.26	430
69	4.20	3.68	2.75	1.87	1.328	680	1.38	390
70	4.72	3.89	2.83	1.90	1.175	750	1.24	390
71	5.22	4.02	2.84	1.88	1.095	820	1.17	390
72	5.93	4.10	2.82	1.85	1.042	910	1.14	390
73	4.48	3.95	2.96	2.02	1.355	620	1.30	360
74	5.01	4.18	3.05	2.05	1.196	680	1.16	360
75	5.60	4.34	3.08	2.04	1.101	750	1.09	360
76	6.23	4.42	3.07	2.01	1.052	820	1.06	360
77	4.79	4.25	3.20	2.19	1.391	560	1.22	330
78	5.44	4.55	3.33	2.24	1.203	620	1.07	330
79	6.03	4.72	3.36	2.23	1.110	680	1.00	330
80	6.77	4.82	3.35	2.20	1.052	750	0.970	330
81	7.70	4.87	3.30	2.14	1.023	820	0.962	330
82	5.28	4.68	3.53	2.41	1.386	510	1.10	300
83	5.94	4.99	3.65	2.46	1.212	560	0.978	300
84	6.66	5.20	3.70	2.46	1.107	620	0.910	300
85	7.43	5.31	3.68	2.42	1.054	680	0.882	300
86	8.56	5.36	3.62	2.35	1.022	750	0.875	300
87	6.05	5.31	3.97	2.70	1.332	470	0.956	270
88	6.69	5.58	4.07	2.74	1.196	510	0.870	270
89	7.43	5.78	4.11	2.73	1.105	560	0.817	270
90	8.39	5.91	4.08	2.68	1.048	620	0.792	270
91	7.07	6.09	4.51	3.06	1.276	430	0.818	240
92	7.84	6.38	4.61	3.08	1.155	470	0.752	240
93	8.59	6.55	4.62	3.06	1.088	510	0.719	240
94	9.64	6.66	4.58	3.00	1.042	560	0.702	240
95	7.61	6.60	4.90	3.33	1.295	390	0.760	220
96	8.53	6.95	5.02	3.36	1.157	430	0.690	220
97	9.43	7.15	5.04	3.33	1.085	470	0.658	220
98	10.4	7.26	5.01	3.28	1.044	510	0.644	220
99	7.58	6.83	5.19	3.56	1.470	330	0.776	200
100	8.53	7.33	5.42	3.67	1.268	360	0.678	200
101	9.36	7.64	5.52	3.70	1.159	390	0.628	200
102	10.4	7.88	5.54	3.66	1.081	430	0.596	200
103	8.55	7.67	5.81	3.98	1.440	300	0.685	180
104	9.69	8.24	6.06	4.09	1.238	330	0.597	180
105	10.7	8.57	6.15	4.10	1.135	360	0.556	180
106	9.80	8.73	6.58	4.50	1.406	270	0.595	160

(A)

(B)

The schematic for a 5-element capacitor input/output Chebyshev high-pass filter, is shown at A. At B is the typical attenuation response curve.

Table 17

7-Element Chebyshev High-pass Filter Designs
50-ohm Impedance, C-In/Out
For Standard E24 Capacitor Values

Filter No.	Frequency (MHz) F_{co}	3 dB	20 dB	40 dB	Max. SWR	C1,7 (pF)	L2,6 (μH)	C3,5 (pF)	L4 (μH)
1	1.02	0.826	0.660	0.504	1.036	5100	6.16	2000	4.98
2	1.00	0.880	0.724	0.563	1.109	3900	5.67	1800	4.86
3	1.08	0.905	0.732	0.563	1.058	4300	5.55	1800	4.60
4	1.16	0.922	0.734	0.558	1.030	4700	5.55	1800	4.45
5	1.00	0.924	0.780	0.617	1.257	3000	5.53	1600	4.93
6	1.09	0.971	0.806	0.630	1.147	3300	5.15	1600	4.48
7	1.16	1.00	0.819	0.634	1.086	3600	4.99	1600	4.22
8	1.23	1.02	0.824	0.632	1.050	3900	4.93	1600	4.05
9	1.34	1.04	0.825	0.625	1.023	4300	4.95	1600	3.92
10	1.03	0.958	0.815	0.648	1.327	2700	5.43	1500	4.89
11	1.13	1.02	0.853	0.669	1.176	3000	4.92	1500	4.31
12	1.22	1.06	0.871	0.676	1.099	3300	4.70	1500	4.01
13	1.30	1.09	0.879	0.675	1.056	3600	4.63	1500	3.83
14	1.39	1.11	0.880	0.670	1.031	3900	4.63	1500	3.71
15	1.22	1.13	0.954	0.755	1.282	2400	4.57	1300	4.09
16	1.34	1.20	0.994	0.776	1.141	2700	4.17	1300	3.62
17	1.45	1.24	1.01	0.780	1.073	3000	4.03	1300	3.38
18	1.57	1.27	1.02	0.775	1.037	3300	4.00	1300	3.24
19	1.31	1.21	1.03	0.816	1.294	2200	4.25	1200	3.81
20	1.41	1.28	1.07	0.836	1.176	2400	3.94	1200	3.45
21	1.55	1.34	1.09	0.845	1.086	2700	3.74	1200	3.16
22	1.68	1.37	1.10	0.841	1.042	3000	3.70	1200	3.01
23	1.41	1.32	1.12	0.887	1.308	2000	3.93	1100	3.53
24	1.54	1.39	1.16	0.912	1.176	2200	3.61	1100	3.16
25	1.65	1.44	1.19	0.921	1.104	2400	3.46	1100	2.95
26	1.80	1.49	1.20	0.919	1.048	2700	3.39	1100	2.78
27	1.97	1.52	1.20	0.907	1.021	3000	3.41	1100	2.68
28	1.54	1.44	1.22	0.971	1.327	1800	3.62	1000	3.26
29	1.70	1.53	1.28	1.00	1.176	2000	3.28	1000	2.87
30	1.82	1.59	1.31	1.01	1.099	2200	3.14	1000	2.67
31	1.95	1.63	1.32	1.01	1.056	2400	3.08	1000	2.55
32	2.15	1.67	1.32	1.00	1.023	2700	3.10	1000	2.45
33	1.85	1.67	1.40	1.10	1.188	1800	3.01	910	2.64
34	2.00	1.75	1.44	1.11	1.100	2000	2.85	910	2.43
35	2.15	1.80	1.45	1.11	1.053	2200	2.81	910	2.31
36	2.31	1.83	1.45	1.10	1.027	2400	2.81	910	2.24
37	1.91	1.77	1.50	1.19	1.297	1500	2.91	820	2.61
38	2.03	1.85	1.55	1.22	1.204	1600	2.74	820	2.42
39	2.22	1.94	1.59	1.24	1.100	1800	2.57	820	2.19
40	2.41	2.00	1.61	1.23	1.050	2000	2.53	820	2.08
41	2.61	2.03	1.61	1.22	1.024	2200	2.54	820	2.01
42	2.26	2.04	1.71	1.34	1.176	1500	2.46	750	2.16
43	2.38	2.10	1.73	1.35	1.120	1600	2.38	750	2.04
44	2.60	2.17	1.76	1.35	1.056	1800	2.31	750	1.91
45	2.83	2.22	1.76	1.34	1.025	2000	2.32	750	1.84
46	2.40	2.20	1.85	1.46	1.230	1300	2.31	680	2.05
47	2.69	2.34	1.92	1.49	1.097	1500	2.13	680	1.81
48	2.82	2.39	1.94	1.49	1.064	1600	2.10	680	1.75
49	3.11	2.45	1.94	1.47	1.027	1800	2.10	680	1.67
50	2.66	2.43	2.04	1.61	1.214	1200	2.08	620	1.84
51	2.84	2.52	2.09	1.63	1.133	1300	1.98	620	1.71
52	3.16	2.64	2.13	1.63	1.053	1500	1.91	620	1.58
53	3.33	2.67	2.13	1.62	1.033	1600	1.91	620	1.54
54	2.73	2.55	2.17	1.73	1.343	1000	2.05	560	1.85
55	2.98	2.71	2.27	1.79	1.196	1100	1.86	560	1.64
56	3.19	2.82	2.32	1.81	1.116	1200	1.77	560	1.52
57	3.39	2.89	2.35	1.81	1.070	1300	1.73	560	1.45
58	3.81	2.98	2.36	1.79	1.024	1500	1.73	560	1.37
59	3.27	2.97	2.49	1.96	1.198	1000	1.70	510	1.49
60	3.53	3.10	2.55	1.99	1.112	1100	1.61	510	1.38
61	3.76	3.18	2.58	1.99	1.064	1200	1.58	510	1.31
62	4.01	3.24	2.59	1.98	1.036	1300	1.57	510	1.27
63	3.51	3.21	2.69	2.12	1.213	910	1.58	470	1.40
64	3.79	3.35	2.76	2.15	1.122	1000	1.49	470	1.28
65	4.07	3.45	2.80	2.16	1.066	1100	1.45	470	1.21
66	4.35	3.52	2.81	2.14	1.035	1200	1.45	470	1.17
67	3.79	3.47	2.93	2.31	1.233	820	1.46	430	1.30
68	4.12	3.65	3.02	2.35	1.126	910	1.37	430	1.18
69	4.42	3.76	3.06	2.36	1.069	1000	1.33	430	1.11
70	4.77	3.85	3.07	2.34	1.035	1100	1.33	430	1.07
71	4.20	3.85	3.24	2.55	1.222	750	1.32	390	1.17
72	4.52	4.02	3.32	2.59	1.131	820	1.24	390	1.07
73	4.89	4.15	3.37	2.60	1.068	910	1.21	390	1.01
74	5.27	4.24	3.39	2.58	1.034	1000	1.20	390	0.969
75	4.48	4.13	3.48	2.75	1.247	680	1.24	360	1.10
76	4.86	4.33	3.59	2.80	1.138	750	1.15	360	1.00
77	5.20	4.47	3.65	2.82	1.079	820	1.12	360	0.942
78	5.64	4.58	3.67	2.80	1.038	910	1.11	360	0.899
79	4.87	4.49	3.79	2.99	1.254	620	1.14	330	1.01
80	5.26	4.71	3.91	3.05	1.148	680	1.06	330	0.924
81	5.67	4.87	3.98	3.07	1.080	750	1.03	330	0.864
82	6.07	4.98	4.00	3.06	1.043	820	1.02	330	0.829
83	5.32	4.91	4.15	3.28	1.264	560	1.04	300	0.930
84	5.80	5.18	4.30	3.36	1.145	620	0.965	300	0.838
85	6.22	5.36	4.37	3.38	1.082	680	0.933	300	0.787
86	6.71	5.49	4.40	3.36	1.042	750	0.923	300	0.752
87	7.25	5.58	4.40	3.33	1.020	820	0.931	300	0.731
88	5.98	5.50	4.64	3.66	1.247	510	0.926	270	0.824
89	6.46	5.77	4.78	3.74	1.142	560	0.867	270	0.752
90	6.98	5.97	4.87	3.76	1.075	620	0.837	270	0.703
91	7.50	6.11	4.89	3.74	1.039	680	0.831	270	0.675
92	6.39	5.97	5.08	4.04	1.336	430	0.873	240	0.787
93	6.94	6.32	5.29	4.16	1.200	470	0.798	240	0.704
94	7.41	6.55	5.41	4.21	1.123	510	0.762	240	0.656
95	7.95	6.75	5.48	4.22	1.068	560	0.742	240	0.620
96	8.61	6.90	5.50	4.19	1.032	620	0.740	240	0.595
97	7.56	6.88	5.77	4.54	1.202	430	0.733	220	0.646
98	8.11	7.16	5.91	4.60	1.119	470	0.697	220	0.599
99	8.63	7.35	5.98	4.61	1.071	510	0.681	220	0.570
100	9.28	7.51	6.00	4.58	1.036	560	0.677	220	0.548
101	7.70	7.19	6.11	4.86	1.327	360	0.723	200	0.652
102	8.30	7.56	6.34	4.99	1.205	390	0.667	200	0.589
103	8.97	7.90	6.51	5.06	1.114	430	0.632	200	0.542
104	9.59	8.11	6.58	5.07	1.064	470	0.618	200	0.515
105	8.72	8.09	6.86	5.44	1.294	330	0.637	180	0.571
106	9.42	8.51	7.11	5.57	1.176	360	0.590	180	0.517

C1 = C7, C3 = C5, L2 = L6

The schematic for a 7-element capacitor input/output Chebyshev high-pass filter. See Table 16 for the attenuation response curve.

Table 18
5-Branch Elliptic High-Pass Filter Designs
50-ohm Impedance
Standard E12 Capacitor Values for C1, C3 and C5

Filter No.	F_{co}	F_{3dB}	F_{As}	A_s (dB)	Max. SWR	C1	C3	C5 (nF)	C2	C4	L2	L4 (μH)	F2	F4 (MHz)
1	1.01	0.936	0.670	45.9	1.489	2.7	1.8	3.3	20.7	7.24	6.58	8.40	0.431	0.646
2	1.14	0.976	0.608	50.4	1.186	3.3	1.8	3.9	32.3	11.4	5.53	6.54	0.377	0.582
3	1.30	1.01	0.604	49.4	1.071	3.9	1.8	4.7	35.8	12.5	5.19	6.07	0.369	0.578
4	1.19	1.11	0.810	45.4	1.543	2.2	1.5	2.7	16.4	5.71	5.65	7.28	0.523	0.780
5	1.38	1.20	0.797	46.8	1.199	2.7	1.5	3.3	22.0	7.66	4.61	5.65	0.499	0.765
6	1.56	1.19	0.685	51.6	1.064	3.3	1.5	3.9	33.7	11.9	4.32	4.97	0.417	0.655
7	1.51	1.40	1.01	45.9	1.489	1.8	1.2	2.2	13.8	4.82	4.39	5.60	0.646	0.968
8	1.75	1.51	1.00	46.6	1.180	2.2	1.2	2.7	17.7	6.14	3.65	4.47	0.627	0.961
9	2.02	1.52	0.920	48.3	1.055	2.7	1.2	3.3	23.4	8.09	3.44	4.04	0.562	0.880
10	1.78	1.65	1.15	47.8	1.506	1.5	1.0	1.8	12.7	4.47	3.71	4.64	0.733	1.10
11	2.07	1.80	1.20	46.8	1.199	1.8	1.0	2.2	14.7	5.11	3.07	3.77	0.749	1.15
12	2.38	1.83	1.13	47.8	1.064	2.2	1.0	2.7	18.6	6.43	2.87	3.40	0.689	1.08
13	2.22	2.08	1.55	43.7	1.531	1.2	0.82	1.5	8.19	2.83	3.05	4.02	1.01	1.49
14	2.52	2.17	1.39	48.7	1.186	1.5	0.82	1.8	13.5	4.73	2.51	3.01	0.865	1.33
15	2.89	2.23	1.36	48.2	1.065	1.8	0.82	2.2	15.5	5.37	2.36	2.78	0.833	1.30
16	2.57	2.40	1.68	47.8	1.560	1.0	0.68	1.2	8.40	2.96	2.60	3.27	1.08	1.62
17	3.05	2.68	1.85	44.7	1.215	1.2	0.68	1.5	8.77	3.02	2.10	2.64	1.17	1.78
18	3.48	2.66	1.57	49.9	1.063	1.5	0.68	1.8	14.1	4.94	1.96	2.28	0.957	1.50
19	3.17	2.96	2.13	46.1	1.554	0.82	0.56	1.0	6.31	2.21	2.13	2.72	1.37	2.05
20	3.62	3.16	2.05	48.6	1.210	1.0	0.56	1.2	8.93	3.14	1.74	2.10	1.28	1.96
21	4.19	3.30	2.11	46.1	1.076	1.2	0.56	1.5	9.30	3.19	1.61	1.94	1.30	2.02
22	4.30	3.79	2.55	46.9	1.233	0.82	0.47	1.0	6.69	2.33	1.48	1.82	1.60	2.45
23	4.89	3.84	2.31	49.7	1.079	1.0	0.47	1.2	9.34	3.27	1.36	1.59	1.41	2.21
24	5.87	3.89	2.31	47.4	1.021	1.2	0.47	1.5	9.71	3.32	1.35	1.58	1.39	2.20
25	4.44	4.17	3.01	46.5	1.618	0.56	0.39	0.68	4.37	1.53	1.54	1.97	1.94	2.90
26	5.14	4.52	2.99	48.0	1.236	0.68	0.39	0.82	5.88	2.06	1.23	1.50	1.87	2.87
27	5.88	4.67	2.90	48.0	1.085	0.82	0.39	1.0	7.05	2.45	1.13	1.34	1.78	2.78
28	5.99	5.34	3.60	47.1	1.269	0.56	0.33	0.68	4.63	1.62	1.06	1.31	2.27	3.46
29	6.81	5.48	3.37	49.0	1.096	0.68	0.33	0.82	6.15	2.15	0.961	1.13	2.07	3.22
30	8.07	5.50	3.17	49.3	1.026	0.82	0.33	1.0	7.33	2.54	0.945	1.09	1.91	3.02
31	6.38	5.99	4.26	47.3	1.609	0.39	0.27	0.47	3.18	1.12	1.06	1.34	2.74	4.10
32	7.34	6.47	4.18	49.2	1.241	0.47	0.27	0.56	4.33	1.53	0.856	1.03	2.61	4.01
33	8.39	6.73	4.17	48.4	1.092	0.56	0.27	0.68	4.90	1.71	0.784	0.930	2.57	4.00
34	7.92	7.36	4.98	49.6	1.522	0.33	0.22	0.39	3.05	1.08	0.828	1.02	3.17	4.79
35	9.21	8.05	5.27	48.1	1.217	0.39	0.22	0.47	3.40	1.19	0.686	0.832	3.30	5.06
36	10.4	8.18	4.84	50.5	1.077	0.47	0.22	0.56	4.56	1.60	0.636	0.740	2.95	4.62

The schematic for a 5-branch elliptic high-pass filter is shown at A. At B is the typical attenuation response curve.

Wetherhold, E. "Simplified Elliptic Low-pass Filter Construction using Surplus 88-mH Inductors." *Radio Communication*. April 1983.

Wetherhold, E. "Low-pass Filters for Attenuating RF Amplifier Harmonics, Parts 1 and 2." *Short Wave Magazine*, December 1983 and January 1984.

Wetherhold, E. "Elliptical Lowpass Audio Filter Design (Using Surplus Inductors)." *Ham Radio*, February 1984.

Wetherhold, E. "Practical LC Filter Design, Parts 1-6." *Practical Wireless*, July-October, December 1984 and January 1985.

Wetherhold, E. "A CW Filter for the Radio Amateur Newcomer." *Radio Communication*, January 1985.

Wetherhold, E. "BASIC Program Analyzes Simple Ladder Networks." *Ham Radio*, August 1987.

Wetherhold, E. "Calculate 5- and 7-Element (Chebyshev) Filter Components" (using a BASIC program). *QEX*, May 1987.

Wetherhold, E. "Designing LC Filters Using SVC Filter Tables." *QEX*, June 1988.

Wetherhold, E. "CW and SSB Audio Filters Using 88-mH Inductors." *QEX*, December 1988.

Wetherhold, E. "BASIC Program Designs Equally Terminated Elliptic Filters." *EMC Technology*, May-June 1988.

Wetherhold, E. *Electric Wave Filters for Communication Systems, Volume 4, Filters and Power Conditioning*, Chapter 2. Gainesville, VA: Interference Control Technologies, Inc, 1988.

Wilkinson, J. "An Introduction of Elliptic Filters for the Radio Amateur." *Radio Communication*, February 1983.

Williams, A. B., and F. J. Taylor. *Electronic Filter Design Handbook*, 2nd Edition, New York: McGraw-Hill Book Co, 1988.

Zverev, A. *Handbook of Filter Synthesis*. New York: John Wiley and Sons, 1967.

The information contained in Figs 79 through 81 and in Tables 19 through 23 will allow the builder to select an appropriate Chebyshev filter design to fulfill a particular need. Information is included for both high-pass and low-pass filters with 1, 0.1, 0.01 and 0.001 dB band-pass ripple. These figures correspond to SWRs of 2.66, 1.36, 1.10 and 1.03, respectively. Additionally, information is provided for both T and pi types of filter configurations shown in Fig 80. The number of filter circuit elements is determined by the desired stop-band frequency roll-off and the tolerable passband ripple. Steeper roll-off requires more circuit elements as does lower passband ripple. Passband ripple manifests itself by increased passband SWR.

The filters are normalized to a frequency of 1 MHz and an input and output impedance of 50 ohms. To translate the designs to other frequencies, simply divide the component values by the new frequency in megahertz. (The 1-MHz value represents a "cutoff" frequency. That is, the attenuation increases rapidly above this frequency for the low-pass filter or below this frequency for the high-pass filter. This effect should not be confused with the variations in attenuation in the passband.) For instance, if it is desired to reduce harmonics from a VFO at frequencies above 5 MHz (the new cutoff frequency), the inductance and capacitance values would be divided by 5.

Other impedance levels can also be used by multiplying the inductor values by the ratio $Z_o/50$ and the capacitor values by $50/Z_o$, where Z_o is the new impedance. This factor should be applied in addition to the ones for frequency translation.

In order to select a suitable filter design the builder must determine the amount of attenuation required at the harmonic frequencies (for the low-pass case) or sub-harmonic frequencies (for the high-pass application). Additionally, the builder must determine the maximum permissible amount of band-pass ripple and therefore the SWR of the filter. With this information the builder can refer to Table 19 to select an appropriate filter design. The attenuation values given here are theoretical and assume perfect components, no coupling between filter sections and no signal leakage around the filter. A "real life" filter should follow these values fairly close down to the 60- or 70-dB attenuation level. At this point the theoretical response will likely be degraded somewhat by the factors just mentioned. Once the filter design has been selected the builder can refer to Tables 20 through 23 to obtain the normalized component values.

In many cases the calculated capacitor values will be sufficiently close to a standard value so that the standard-value item may be used. Alternatively, a combination of fixed-value silver-mica capacitors and mica compression trimmers can be used in parallel to obtain the chart values.

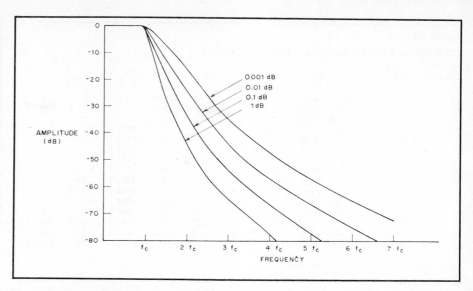

Fig 79—A representative drawing of the amplitude vs frequency response that can be expected from a 5-element low-pass filter designed from the information contained in Tables 20 or 21. The exact amount of attenuation (theoretical) can be obtained from Table 19. This drawing shows how passband ripple and roll-off slope are interrelated.

Fig 80—Shown here are the four filter types discussed in the text and Tables 19 through 23.

Table 19
Chebyshev High-Pass and Low-Pass Filters—Attenuation (dB)

No. elements	Ripple, dB	SWR	$2f_c$	$3f_c$	$4f_c$	$5f_c$	$6f_c$	$7f_c$
3	1	2.66	22.46	34.05	41.88	47.85	52.68	56.74
3	0.1	1.36	12.24	23.60	31.42	37.39	42.22	46.29
3	0.01	1.10	4.08	13.73	21.41	27.35	32.18	36.24
3	0.001	1.03	0.63	5.13	11.68	17.42	22.20	26.25
5	1	2.66	45.31	64.67	77.73	87.67	95.72	102.50
5	0.1	1.36	34.85	54.21	67.27	77.21	85.26	92.04
5	0.01	1.10	24.82	44.16	57.22	67.17	75.22	82.00
5	0.001	1.03	14.94	34.16	47.22	57.16	65.22	71.99
7	1	2.66	68.18	95.29	113.57	127.49	138.77	148.26
7	0.1	1.36	57.72	84.83	103.11	117.03	128.31	137.80
7	0.01	1.10	47.68	74.78	93.07	106.99	118.27	127.75
7	0.001	1.03	37.68	64.78	83.06	96.98	108.26	117.75
9	1	2.66	91.06	125.91	149.42	167.32	181.82	194.01
9	0.1	1.36	80.60	115.45	138.96	156.86	171.36	183.55
9	0.01	1.10	70.56	105.41	128.91	146.81	161.31	173.51
9	0.001	1.03	60.55	95.40	118.91	136.91	151.31	163.50

Note: For high-pass filter configuration $2f_c$ becomes $f_c/2$, etc.

Table 20
Chebyshev Low-Pass Filter—T Configuration

No. elements	Ripple, dB	L1	L2	L3	L4	L5	C1	C2	C3	C4
3	1	16.10	16.10				3164.3			
3	0.1	8.209	8.209				3652.3			
3	0.01	5.007	5.007				3088.5			
3	0.001	3.253	3.253				2312.6			
5	1	16.99	23.88	16.99			3473.1	3473.1		
5	0.1	9.126	15.72	9.126			4364.7	4364.7		
5	0.01	6.019	12.55	6.019			4153.7	4153.7		
5	0.001	4.318	10.43	4.318			3571.1	3571.1		
7	1	17.24	24.62	24.62	17.24		3538.0	3735.4	3538.0	
7	0.1	9.400	16.68	16.68	9.400		4528.9	5008.3	4528.9	
7	0.01	6.342	13.91	13.91	6.342		4432.2	5198.4	4432.2	
7	0.001	4.690	12.19	12.19	4.690		3951.5	4924.1	3951.5	
9	1	17.35	24.84	25.26	24.84	17.35	3562.5	3786.9	3786.9	3562.5
9	0.1	9.515	16.99	17.55	16.99	9.515	4591.9	5146.2	5146.2	4591.9
9	0.01	6.481	14.36	15.17	14.36	6.481	4542.5	5451.2	5451.2	4542.5
9	0.001	4.854	12.81	13.88	12.81	4.854	4108.2	5299.0	5299.0	4108.2

Component values normalized to 1 MHz and 50 ohms, L in µH; C in pF.

Fig 81—A photograph of a 7-element low-pass filter designed with the information contained in Table 21. The filter is housed in a small aluminum Minibox.

Table 21
Chebyshev Low-Pass Filter—Pi Configuration

No. elements	Ripple, dB	C1	C2	C3	C4	C5	L1	L2	L3	L4
3	1	6441.3	6441.3				7.911			
3	0.1	3283.6	3283.6				9.131			
3	0.01	2002.7	2002.7				7.721			
3	0.001	1301.2	1301.2				5.781			
5	1	6795.5	9552.2	6795.5			8.683	8.683		
5	0.1	3650.4	6286.6	3650.4			10.91	10.91		
5	0.01	2407.5	5020.7	2407.5			10.38	10.38		
5	0.001	1727.3	4170.5	1727.3			8.928	8.928		
7	1	6896.4	9847.4	9847.4	6896.4		8.85	9.34	8.85	
7	0.1	3759.8	6673.9	6673.9	3759.8		11.32	12.52	11.32	
7	0.01	2536.8	5564.5	5564.5	2536.8		11.08	13.00	11.08	
7	0.001	1875.7	4875.9	4875.9	1875.7		9.879	12.31	9.879	
9	1	6938.3	9935.8	10,105.	9935.8	6938.3	8.906	9.467	9.467	8.906
9	0.1	3805.9	6794.5	7019.9	6794.5	3805.9	11.48	12.87	12.87	11.48
9	0.01	2592.5	5743.5	6066.3	5743.5	2592.5	11.36	13.63	13.63	11.36
9	0.001	1941.7	5124.6	5553.2	5124.6	1941.7	10.27	13.25	13.25	10.27

Component values normalized to 1 MHz and 50 ohms, L in µH; C in pF.

Table 22
Chebyshev High-Pass Filter—T Configuration

No. elements	Ripple, dB	C1	C2	C3	C4	C5	L1	L2	L3	L4
3	1	1573.0	1573.0				8.005			
3	0.1	3085.7	3085.7				6.935			
3	0.01	5059.1	5059.1				8.201			
3	0.001	7786.9	7786.9				10.95			
5	1	1491.0	1060.7	1491.0			7.293	7.293		
5	0.1	2775.6	1661.7	2775.6			5.803	5.803		
5	0.01	4208.6	2018.1	4208.6			6.098	6.098		
5	0.001	5865.9	2429.5	5865.7			7.093	7.093		
7	1	1469.2	1028.9	1028.9	1469.2		7.160	6.781	7.160	
7	0.1	2694.9	1518.2	1518.2	2694.9		5.593	5.058	5.593	
7	0.01	3994.1	1820.9	1820.9	3994.1		5.715	4.873	5.715	
7	0.001	5401.7	2078.0	2078.0	5401.7		6.410	5.144	6.410	
9	1	1460.3	1019.8	1002.7	1019.8	1460.3	7.110	6.689	6.689	7.110
9	0.1	2662.2	1491.2	1443.3	1491.2	2662.2	5.516	4.922	4.922	5.516
9	0.01	3908.2	1764.1	1670.2	1764.1	3908.2	5.576	4.647	4.647	5.576
9	0.001	5218.3	1977.1	1824.6	1977.1	5218.3	6.657	4.780	4.780	6.657

Component values normalized to 1 MHz and 50 ohms, L in µH; C in pF.

with the information contained in Table 21. It is a 7-element, low-pass type of pi configuration. The unit is housed in a small aluminum Minibox and makes use of BNC connectors for the input and output connections.

COUPLED RESONATORS

Coupled resonators are frequently encountered in RF circuits. Applications include simple filters, oscillator tuned circuits and even antennas. The circuit shown in Fig 82A illustrates the basic principles involved. A series RLC circuit and the external terminals ab are coupled through a common capacitance, C_m. Applying the formulas for conductance and susceptance in terms of series reactance and resistance gives

$$G_{ab} = \frac{R_r}{R_r^2 + X^2}$$

$$B_{ab} = B_{cm} - \frac{X}{R_r^2 + X^2}$$

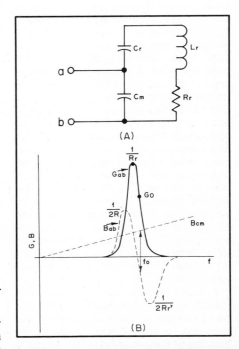

Fig 82—A capacitively coupled resonator is shown at A. See text for explanation of figure shown at B.

Toroidal inductors, because of their self-shielding properties, are ideal for use in these filters. Miniductor stock can also be used. It is much bulkier, however, and will not offer the same degree of shielding between filter sections. Disc ceramic or paper capacitors are not suitable for use in RF filters. Standard mica or silver-mica types are recommended.

Fig 81 shows a filter that was designed

Table 23

Chebyshev High-Pass Filter—Pi Configuration

No. elements	Ripple, dB	L1	L2	L3	L4	L5	C1	C2	C3	C4
3	1	3.932	3.932				3201.7			
3	0.1	7.714	7.714				2774.2			
3	0.01	12.65	12.65				3280.5			
3	0.001	19.47	19.47				4381.4			
5	1	3.727	2.652	3.727			2917.3	2917.3		
5	0.1	6.939	4.029	6.939			2321.4	2321.4		
5	0.01	10.52	5.045	10.52			2439.3	2439.3		
5	0.001	1.466	6.074	1.466			2837.3	2837.3		
7	1	7.159	5.014	5.014	7.159		1469.2	1391.6	1469.2	
7	0.1	6.737	3.795	3.795	6.737		2237.2	2023.1	2237.2	
7	0.01	9.985	4.552	4.552	9.985		2286.0	1949.2	2286.0	
7	0.001	13.50	5.195	5.195	13.50		2564.1	2057.7	2564.1	
9	1	3.651	2.549	2.507	2.549	3.651	2844.1	2675.6	2675.6	2844.1
9	0.1	6.656	3.728	3.608	3.728	6.656	2206.5	1968.9	1968.9	2206.5
9	0.01	9.772	4.410	4.176	4.410	9.772	2230.5	1858.7	1858.7	2230.5
9	0.001	13.05	4.943	4.561	4.943	13.05	2466.3	1911.8	1911.8	2466.3

Component values normalized to 1 MHz and 50 ohms, L in μH; C in pF.

Fig 83—Variation of k with input resistance for the circuit of Fig 82.

The significance of these equations can be understood with the aid of Fig 82B. At some point, the series inductive reactance will cancel the series capacitive reactance (at a point slightly below f_o where the conductance curve reaches a peak). Depending on the value of the coupling susceptance, B_m, it is possible that a point can be found where the total input susceptance is zero. The input conductance at this frequency, f_o is then G_o.

Since G_o is less than the conductance at the peak of the curve, $1/G_o$ or R_o is going to be greater than R_r. This effect can be applied when it is desired to match a low-value load resistance (such as found in a mobile whip antenna) to a more practical value. Suppose R_r and C_r in Fig 82A are 10 ohms and 21 pF, respectively, and represent the equivalent circuit of a mobile antenna. Find the value of L_r and C_m that will match this antenna to a 52-ohm feed line at a frequency of 3900 kHz. Substituting the above values into the formulas for input conductance gives

$$\frac{1}{52} = \frac{10}{10^2 + X^2}$$

Solving for X (the total series reactance) gives a value of the square root of 420 or 20.49 ohms. The reactance of a 21-pF capacitor at 3900 kHz is 1943.3 ohms so the inductive reactance must be 20.49 + 1943.3 = 1963.8 ohms. While either a positive or negative reactance will satisfy the equation for G_{ab} a positive value is required to tune out B_{cm}. If the coupling element was a shunt inductor, the total reactance would have to be capacitive or negative in value. Thus, the required inductance value for L_r will be 80.1 μH. In order to obtain a perfect match, the input susceptance must be zero. The value of B_{cm} can be found from

$$0 = B_{cm} - \frac{20.49}{10^2 + 20.49^2}$$

giving a susceptance value of 0.03941

siemens, which corresponds to a capacitance of 1608 pF.

Coefficient of Coupling

If the solution to the mobile whip antenna problem is examined, it can be seen that for given values of frequency, R_r, L_r, and C_r only one value of C_m results in an input load that appears as a pure resistance. While such a condition might be defined as resonance, the resistance value obtained is not necessarily the one required for maximum transfer of power.

A definition that is helpful in determining how to vary the circuit elements in order to obtain the desired input resistance is called the coefficient of coupling. The coefficient of coupling is defined as the ratio of the common or mutual reactance to the square root of the product of two specially defined reactances. If the mutual reactance is capacitive, one of the special reactances is the sum of the series capacitive reactances of the primary mesh (with the resonator disconnected) and the other one is the sum of the series capacitive reactances of the resonator (with the primary disconnected). Applying this definition to the circuit of Fig 82A, the coefficient of coupling, k, is given by

$$k = \sqrt{\frac{C_r}{C_r + C_m}}$$

How meaningful the coefficient of coupling will be depends on the particular circuit configuration under consideration and on which elements are being varied. For example, suppose the value of L_r in the mobile-whip antenna problem was fixed at 100 μH, and suppose C_m and C_r were allowed to vary. (Recall that C_r is 21 pF and represents the antenna capacitance. However, the total resonator capacitance could be changed by adding a series capacitor between C_m and the antenna. Thus, C_r could be varied from 21 pF to some lower value but not a higher one.)

A calculated plot of k versus input resistance, R_{in} is shown in Fig 83. Notice the rapid change in k for resistance values between 10 ohms and slightly higher resistances.

Similar networks can be designed to work with any ratio of input resistance and load resistance, but it is evident that small ratios are going to pose difficulties. For larger ratios, component tolerances are less critical. For instance, C_m might consist of switchable fixed capacitors with C_r being variable. With the given load resistance, C_m essentially sets the value of the reactance and thus the input resistance, while C_r and L_r provide the required reactance for the conductance formula. However, if L_r is varied, k varies also. Generally speaking, higher values of L_r (and consequently circuit Q) require lower values of k.

At this point, the question arises as to the significance and even the merit of such definitions as coefficient of coupling and Q. If the circuit element values are known, and if the configuration can be resolved into a ladder network, important properties such as input impedance and attenuation can be computed directly for any frequency. On the other hand, circuit information might be obscured or even lost by attempting to attach too much importance to an arbitrary definition. For example, the plot in Fig 83 merely indicates that C_m and C_r are changing with respect to each other. But it doesn't illustrate how they are changing. Such information is important in practical applications, and even a simple table of C_m and C_r vs. R_{in} for a particular R_r would be much more valuable than a plot of k.

Similar precautions must be taken with the interpretation of circuit Q. Selectivity and Q are simply related for single resonators and circuit components, but the situation rapidly changes with complex configurations. For instance, adding loss or resistance to circuit elements would seem to contradict the idea that low-loss or high-Q circuits provide the best selectivity. However, this is actually done in some filter designs to improve frequency response. In fact, the filter with the added loss has identical characteristics to one with pure elements. The method is called predistortion and is very useful in designing filters where practical considerations require the use of circuit elements with parasitic or undesired resistance.

As the frequency of operation is increased, discrete components must become physically smaller. Eventually a point is reached where other forms of networks have to be used. Here, entities such as k and Q are sometimes the only means of describing such networks. Another definition of Q that is quite useful in this instance is that it is equal to the ratio of 2π (energy stored per RF cycle)/(energy lost per RF cycle).

Mutually Coupled Inductors

A number of very useful RF networks involve coupled inductors. In a previous section, there was some discussion on iron-core transformers which represent a special case of coupled inductance. The formulas presented apply to instances where the coefficient of coupling is very close to 1.0. While it is possible to approach this condition at frequencies in the RF range, many practical circuits work at values of k that are considerably less than 1.0. A general solution is rather complex, but many practical applications can often be simplified and solved through use of the ladder-network method. In particular, the sign of the mutual inductance must be taken into account if there are a number of coupled circuits or if the phase of the voltage between two coupled circuits is important.

The phase consideration is illustrated in Fig 84. An exact circuit for the two mutually coupled coils at A is shown at B. T1 is an ideal transformer that provides the isolation between terminals *ab* and *cd*. If the polarity of the voltages between these terminals can be neglected, the transformer can be eliminated and just the circuit before the terminals *c'd'* substituted. A second circuit is shown in Fig 84C and D. Here, it is assumed that the winding sense doesn't change between L1 and L2. If so, then the circuit of Fig 84D can be substituted for the tapped coil shown in Fig 84C.

Coefficients of coupling for the circuits in Fig 84 are given by

$$k = \frac{M}{\sqrt{L1\ L2}}$$

and

$$k = \frac{L1 + M}{\sqrt{L1\ (L1 + L2 + 2M)}}$$

If L1 and L2 do not have the same value, an interesting phenomenon takes place as the coupling is increased. A point is reached where the mutual inductance exceeds the inductance of the smaller coil. The interpretation of this effect is illustrated in Fig 85. While all the flux lines (as indicated

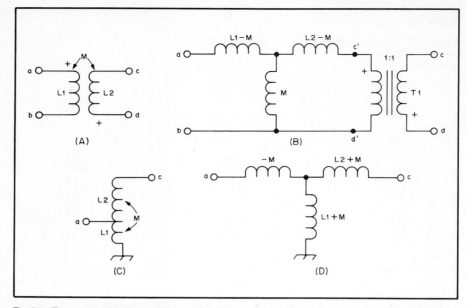

Fig 84—Two types of magnetically coupled circuits. At A, only mutual magnetic coupling exists while the circuit at C contains a common inductance also. Equivalents of both circuits at B and D permit the application of the ladder-network analysis discussed in this section. (If the sign of voltage is unimportant, T1 can be eliminated.)

by the dashed lines) associated with L1 also encircle turns of L2, there are additional ones that encircle extra turns of L2, also. Thus, there are more flux lines for M than there are for L1. Consequently, M becomes larger than L1. Normally, this condition is difficult to obtain with air-wound coils, but the addition of ferrite material greatly increases the coupling. As k increases so that M is larger than L1 (Fig 85), the network begins to behave more like a transformer. For a k of 1, the equivalent circuit of Fig 84B yields the transformer equations of a previous section. On the other hand, for small values of k, the network becomes merely three coils arranged in a T fashion. One advantage of the circuit of Fig 84A is that there is no direct connection between the two coils. This property is important from an isolation standpoint and can be used to suppress unwanted currents that are often responsible for RFI difficulties.

Piezoelectric Crystals

A somewhat different form of resonator consists of a quartz crystal between two conducting plates. If a voltage is applied to the plates, the resultant electric field causes a mechanical stress in the crystal. Depending on the size and cut of the crystal, the crystal begins to vibrate at a certain frequency. The effect of this mechanical vibration is to simulate a series RLC circuit as in Fig 82A. There is a capacitance associated with the crystal plates, which appears across the terminals (C_m in Fig 82A). Consequently, this circuit can also be analyzed with the aid of Fig 82B. At some frequency (f1 in Fig 86), the

Fig 85—Diagram illustrating how M can be larger than one of the self inductances. This represents the transition from lightly coupled circuits to conventional transformers, since an impedance step-up is possible without the addition of capacitive elements.

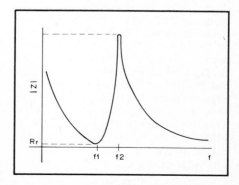

Fig 86—Frequency response of a quartz crystal resonator. The minimum value is only approximate since holder capacitance is neglected.

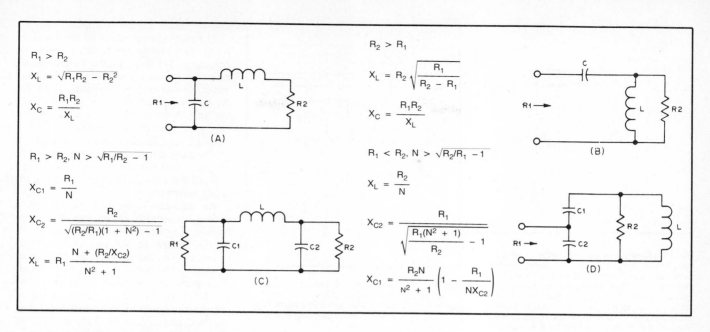

$R_1 > R_2$

$X_L = \sqrt{R_1 R_2 - R_2^2}$

$X_C = \dfrac{R_1 R_2}{X_L}$

(A)

$R_2 > R_1$

$X_L = R_2 \sqrt{\dfrac{R_1}{R_2 - R_1}}$

$X_C = \dfrac{R_1 R_2}{X_L}$

(B)

$R_1 > R_2, \; N > \sqrt{R_1/R_2 - 1}$

$X_{C1} = \dfrac{R_1}{N}$

$X_{C2} = \dfrac{R_2}{\sqrt{(R_2/R_1)(1 + N^2) - 1}}$

$X_L = R_1 \dfrac{N + (R_2/X_{C2})}{N^2 + 1}$

(C)

$R_1 < R_2, \; N > \sqrt{R_2/R_1 - 1}$

$X_L = \dfrac{R_2}{N}$

$X_{C2} = \dfrac{R_1}{\sqrt{\dfrac{R_1(N^2 + 1)}{R_2} - 1}}$

$X_{C1} = \dfrac{R_2 N}{N^2 + 1}\left(1 - \dfrac{R_1}{N X_{C2}}\right)$

(D)

Fig 87—Four matching networks that can be used to couple a source and load with different resistance values. (Although networks are drawn with R1 appearing as the source resistance, all can be applied with R2 at the source end. Also, all formulas with capacitive reactance are for the numerical or absolute value.)

series reactance is zero and G_{ab} in the preceding formula will simply be $1/R_r$. Typical values for R_r range from 10 kΩ and higher. However, the equivalent inductance of the mechanical circuit is normally extremely high (over 10,000 henrys in the case of some low-frequency units), which results in a very high circuit Q (30,000).

Above f1 the reactance is inductive, and at f2 the susceptance of the series resonator is just equal to the susceptance of the crystal holder, B_{cm}. Here the total susceptance is zero. Since B_{cm} is usually very small, the equivalent series susceptance is also small. This means the value for X in the susceptance formula will be very large, and consequently G_{ab} will be small. This corresponds to a high input resistance. A plot of the magnitude of the impedance is shown in Fig 86. The dip at f1 is called the series-resonant mode and the peak at f2 is referred to as the parallel-resonant or anti-resonant mode.

When specifying crystals for oscillator applications, the type of mode must be given along with the external capacitance across the holder or type oscillator circuit to be used. Otherwise, considerable difference in actual oscillator frequency will be observed. The effect can be used to advantage, however. The frequency of a crystal oscillator can be pulled with an external reactive element, or even frequency modulated with a device that converts voltage or current fluctuations into changes in reactance.

Matching Networks

In addition to filters, ladder networks are frequently used to match one impedance value to another one. While there are many circuits, a few of them offer such advan-

tages as simplicity of design formulas or minimum number of elements. Some of the more popular ones are shown in Fig 87. Shown at Fig 87A and 87B, are two variations of an L network. These networks are relatively simple to design. The situation is somewhat more complicated for the circuits shown at Fig 87C and 87D. For a given value of input and output resistance, there are many networks that satisfy the conditions for a perfect match. The difficulty can be resolved by introducing the dummy variable labeled N.

From a practical standpoint, N should be selected in order to optimize circuit component values. Either values of N that are too low or too high result in networks that are hard to construct.

The reason for this complication is as follows. Only two reactive elements are required to match any two resistances. Consequently, adding a third element introduces a redundancy. This means one element can be assigned a value arbitrarily and the other two components can then be found. For instance, suppose C2 in Fig 87C is set to some particular value. The parallel combination of C2 and R2 may then be transformed to a series equivalent (see Fig 88). Then, L may be found by breaking it down into two components, L' and L". One component (L") would tune out the remaining capacitive reactance of the output series equivalent circuit. The network is then reduced to the one shown in Fig 87A and the other component of L (L') along with the value of C1, could be determined from formulas (Fig 87A). Adding the two inductive components gives the actual inductive reactance required for a match in the circuit of Fig 87C.

As mentioned before, it is evident that

$X_L'' = X_{Ceq} = \dfrac{X_{C2}}{1 + (X_{C2}/R_2)^2}$

$\dfrac{R_2}{1 + (R_2/X_C)^2}$

$\dfrac{R_2}{1 + (R_2/X_{C2})^2}$

Fig 88—Illustration of the manner in which the network of Fig 87C can be reduced to the one of Fig 87A, assuming C2 is assigned some arbitrary value. (The formulas shown are for numerical reactance values.)

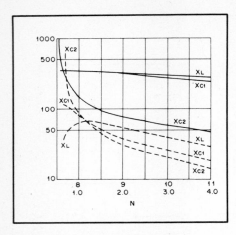

Fig 89—Network reactance variation as a function of dummy variable N. Solid curves and values of N from 8 to 11 are for an input resistance of 3000 ohms and an output resistance of 52 ohms. The dashed curves are for a similar network with an input and output resistance of 75 and 52 ohms, respectively. Values of N from 1 to 4 are for the dashed curves.

Fig 90—Input resistance vs. output reactance for an output resistance of 52 ohms. The curve is for a fixed inductor of 219 ohms (Fig 87C). X_c varies from 196 to 206 ohms.

and transistor matching applications.

The plots shown in Fig 89 are for fixed input and output resistances with the reactances variable. Similar figures can be plotted for other combinations of fixed and variable elements. An interesting case is for X_L and R1 fixed with R2, X_{C1} and X_{C2} variable. A lower limit for N also exists for this plot, except that instead of an L network, the limiting circuit is a network of three equal reactances. A feature of this circuit is that the output resistance is the ratio of the square of the reactance and the input resistance.

An analogous situation exists with a quarter-wavelength transmission-line transformer. The output resistance is the ratio of the square of the characteristic impedance of the line and the input resistance. Consequently, the special case in which all the reactances are equal in the circuit of Fig 87C is the lumped-constant analog of the quarter-wavelength transformer. It has identical phase shift (90°) along with the same impedance-transforming properties.

Frequency Response

In many instances, a matching network performs a dual role in transforming a resistance value while providing frequency rejection. Usually the most important considerations are matching versatility, component values and the number of elements. But a matching network might also

an infinite number of networks of the form shown in Fig 87C exist since C2 can be assigned any value. Either a set of tables or a family of curves for C1 and L in terms of C2 could then be determined from the method discussed earlier and illustrated in Fig 90. However, similar data along with other information can be obtained by approaching the problem somewhat differently. Instead of setting one of the element values arbitrarily and finding the other two, a third variable is contrived, and in the case of Figs 87C and 87D is labeled N. All three reactances are then expressed in terms of the variable N.

The manner in which the reactances change with variation in N for two representative circuits of the type shown in Fig 87C is shown in Fig 89. The solid curves are for an R1 of 3000 ohms and R2 equal to 52 ohms. The dashed curves are for the same R2 (52 ohms) but with R1 equal to 75 ohms. For values of N very close to the minimum specified by the inequality (Fig 87C), X_{C2} becomes infinite, which means C2 approaches zero. As might be expected, the values of X_L and X_{C1} at this point are approximately those of an L network (Fig 87A) and could be determined by means of the formulas in Fig 87A for the corresponding values of R1 and R2.

The plots shown in Fig 89 give a general idea of the optimum range of component values. The region close to the left-hand portion should be avoided since there is little advantage to be gained over an L network, while an extra component is required. For very high values of N, the capacitance values become large without producing any particular advantage either. A good design choice is an N a few percent above the minimum specified by the inequality.

Often, one of the elements is fixed, with either or both of the remaining two elements variable. In many amateur transmitters, it is the inductor that remains fixed (at least for a given band), while C1 and C2 (Fig 87C) are made variable. While this system limits the bandwidth and matching capability somewhat, it is still a very useful approach. For instance, the plot shown in Fig 90 indicates the range of input resistance values that can be matched for an R2 of 52 ohms. The graph is for an inductive reactance of 219 ohms. X_{C1} varies from 196 to 206 ohms over the entire range of R1 (or approximately 20 percent). However, X_{C2} varies from 15 to almost 100 ohms, as indicated in the graph.

Since C2 more or less sets the transformed resistance, it is often referred to as the loading control on transmitters using the network of Fig 87C, with C1 usually labeled TUNE. While the meaning of the latter term should be clear, the idea of loading in a matching application perhaps needs some explanation. For small values of X_{C2} (very large C2), the transformed resistance is very high. Consequently, a source that was designed for a much lower resistance would deliver relatively little power. However, as the resistance is lowered, increased amounts of current will flow, resulting in more power output. Then the source is said to be loaded more heavily.

Similar considerations such as those discussed for the network of Fig 87C also exist for the circuit of Fig 87D. Only the limiting L network for the latter is the one shown in Fig 87B. The circuit of Fig 87C is usually called a pi network and, as pointed out, it is used extensively in the output stage of transmitters. The circuit of Fig 87D has never been given any special name, but is quite popular in both antenna

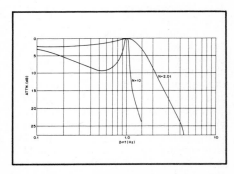

Fig 91—Frequency response of the network of Fig 87C for two values of N.

be able to provide sufficient selectivity for some application, thus eliminating the need for a separate circuit such as a filter.

Recall that Q and selectivity are closely related for simple RLC series and parallel circuits. Bandwidth and the parameter N of Fig 87 are approximately related in this manner. For values of N much greater than the minimum specified by the inequality, N and Q can be considered to mean the same thing for all practical purposes. However, the frequency response of networks that are more complex than simple RLC types is usually more complicated. Consequently, some care is required in the interpretation of N or Q in regard to frequency rejection. For instance, a simple circuit has a frequency response that results in increasing attenuation for increasing excursions from resonance.

That is not true for the pi network, as can be seen from Fig 91. For slight frequency changes below resonance, the attenuation increases as in the case of a simple RLC network. At lower frequencies, the attenuation decreases and approaches 2.55 dB. This plot is for a resistance ratio of 5:1, and the low-frequency loss is caused only by the mismatch in source and load resistance. Thus, while increasing N improves

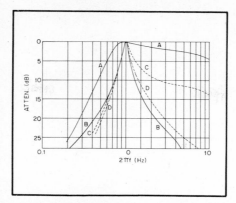

Fig 92—Frequency response of the circuit of Fig 87D (see text).

the selectivity near resonance, it has little effect on response for frequencies much farther away.

A somewhat different situation exists for the circuit of Fig 87D. At frequencies far from resonance, either a series capacitance provides decoupling at the lower frequencies or a shunt capacitance causes additional mismatch at the higher ones. This circuit, then, has a response resembling those of simple circuits unlike the pi network. Curves A and B of Fig 92 are for a resistance ratio of 5:1, with N equal to 2.01 for curve A. Curve B is for an N of 10. Curves C and D are for a resistance ratio of 50:1, with N equal to 7.04 and 10, respectively.

Chapter 3

Radio Design Technique and Language

Many amateurs desire to construct their own radio equipment, and some knowledge of design procedures becomes important. Even when some commercially manufactured equipment is used, these techniques may still be required in setting up peripheral equipment. Also, an applicant for an Amateur Radio license might be tested on material in this area.

"Pure" vs. "Impure" Components

In the chapter on electrical laws and circuits, it is assumed that the components in an electrical circuit consist solely of elements that can be reduced to a resistance, capacitance or inductance. However, such elements do not exist in nature. An inductor always has some resistance associated with its windings and a carbon-composition resistor becomes a complicated circuit as the frequency of operation is increased. Even conductor resistance must be taken into account if long runs of cable are required.

In many instances, the effects of these "parasitic" components can be neglected and the actual device can be approximated by a "pure" element such as a resistor, capacitor, inductor or a short circuit in the case of an interconnecting conductor. In other cases, the unwanted component must be taken into account. However, it may be possible to break the element down into a simple circuit consisting of single elements alone. Then the actual circuit may be analyzed by means of the basic laws discussed in the previous chapter. It may also be possible to make a selection so the effects of the residual element are negligible.

There are times when unwanted effects may not only be difficult to remove but will affect circuit operation adversely as well. In fact, such considerations often set a limit on how stringent a design criterion can be tolerated. For instance, it is a common practice to connect small-value capacitors in various parts of a complex circuit, such as a transmitter or receiver, for bypassing purposes. A bypass capacitor permits energy below some specified frequency to

Fig. 1 — Equivalent circuit of a capacitor.

pass a given point while providing rejection to energy at higher frequencies. In essence, the capacitor is used in a single form of filter. In more complicated filter designs, capacitors may be required for complex functions (such as matching) in addition to providing a low reactance to ground.

An equivalent circuit of a capacitor is shown in Fig. 1. Normally, the series resistance, R_s, can be neglected. On the other hand, the upper frequency limit of the capacitor is limited by the series inductance, L_s. In fact, above the point where L_s and C_p form a resonant circuit, the capacitor actually appears as an inductor at the external terminals. This is why it is common practice to use two capacitors in parallel for bypassing, as shown in Fig. 2. At first inspection, this might appear as superfluous duplication. But the self-resonant frequency of a capacitor is lower for high-capacitance units than it is for smaller value ones. Thus, C1 in Fig. 2 provides a low reactance for low frequencies such as those in the audio range while C2 acts as a bypass for frequencies above the self-resonant frequency of C1.

RF Leakage

Although the capacitor combination shown in Fig. 2 provides a low-impedance path to ground, it may not be very effective in preventing RF energy that travels along the conductor at point 1 from reaching point 2. At dc and low-frequency applications, a circuit must always form a closed path for a current to flow. Consequently, two conductors are required if power is to be delivered from a source to a load. In many instances, one of the conductors may be common to several other circuits and constitutes a local ground.

As the frequency of operation is increased, however, a second type of coupling mechanism is possible. Power may be transmitted along a single conductor. (Although the same effect is possible at low frequencies, unless circuit dimensions are extremely large, such transmission effects can be neglected.) The conductor acts as

Fig. 2 — A bypassing arrangement that affords some measure of isolation (with the equivalent circuit shown.) Dashed lines indicate a mode of wave travel that permits RF energy to leak past the bypass circuit and that should be taken into account when more stringent suppression requirements are necessary. (L_s and R_s in the equivalent circuit represent the ferrite bead.)

a waveguide in much the same manner that a large conducting surface, such as the earth, will permit propagation of a radio wave close to its boundary with the air. A mode similar to ground-wave propagation that can travel along the boundary of a single conductor is illustrated by the dashed lines in Fig. 2. As with the wave traveling close to the earth, a poor conducting boundary will cause attenuation. This is why a ferrite bead is often inserted over the exit point of a conductor from an area where RF energy is to be contained or excluded. In addition to loss (particularly in the VHF range), the high permeability of the ferrite introduces a series-inductive reactance as well. Finally, the shield wall provides further isolation.

While the techniques shown in Fig. 2 get around some of the deficiencies of capacitors that are used for bypass purposes, the resulting suppression is inadequate for a number of applications. Examples would be protection of a VFO to surrounding RF energy, a low-frequency receiver with a digital display, and suppression of radiated harmonic energy from a transmitter. In each of these cases, a very high degree of isolation is required. For instance, a VFO is sensitive to voltages that appear on dc power supply lines and a transmitter output with a note that sounds "fuzzy" or rough may result.

Digital displays usually generate copious RF energy in the low-frequency spectrum. Consequently, a receiver designed for this range presents a situation where a strong source of emission is in close proximity to very sensitive receiving circuits. A similar case exists with transmitters operating on a frequency that is a submultiple of a fringe-area TV station. In the latter two instances, the problem is not so severe if the desired signal is strong enough to override the unwanted energy. Unfortunately, this is not the case normally and stringent measures are required to isolate the sensitive circuits from the strong source.

A different type of bypass-capacitor configuration is often used with associated shielding for such applications, as shown in Fig. 3. To reduce the series inductance of the capacitor, and to provide better isolation between points 1 and 2, either a disc type (Fig. 3A) or a coaxial configuration (Fig. 3B) is employed. The circuit diagram for either configuration is shown in the inset. While such "feedthrough" capacitors are always connected to ground through the shield, this connection is often omitted on drawings. Only a connection to ground is shown, as in Fig. 3C.

Dielectric Loss

Even though capacitors are usually high-Q devices, the effect of internal loss can be more severe than in the case of a coil. This is because good insulators of electricity are also usually good insulators of heat. Therefore, heat generated in a capacitor must be conducted to the outside via the

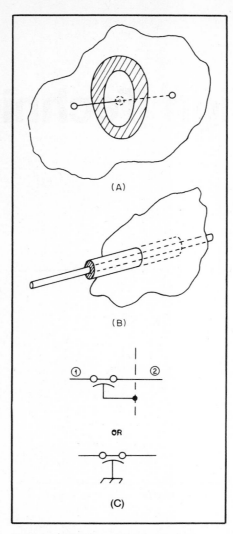

(A)

(B)

OR

(C)

Fig. 3 — A superior type of bypassing arrangement to that shown in Fig. 2. Concentric conductors provide a low-inductance path to ground and better rejection of unwanted single-wire wave modes.

conducting plates to the capacitor leads. In addition, most capacitors are covered with an insulating coating that further impedes heat conduction. The problem is less severe with capacitors using air as a dielectric for two reasons. The first advantage of air over other dielectrics is that the loss in the presence of an alternating electric field is extremely small. Second, any heat generated by currents on the surface of the conducting plates is either drawn away by air currents or through the mass of the metal.

The dielectric loss in a capacitor can be represented by R_p, as shown in Fig. 1. However, if a dc ohmmeter were placed across the terminals of the capacitor, the reading would be infinite. This is because dielectric loss is an ac effect. Whenever an alternating electric field is applied to an insulator, there is a local motion of the electrons in the individual atoms that make up the material. Even though the electrons are not displaced as they would be in a con-

Fig. 4 — Consideration of capacitor voltage and current ratings should be kept in mind in moderate power applications.

Fig. 5 — Equivalent circuit of an inductor.

ductor, this local motion requires the expenditure of energy and results in a power loss.

Consequently, some care is required in the application of capacitors in moderate to high-power circuits. The applied voltage should be such that RF current ratings are not exceeded for the particular frequency of operation. This is illustrated in Fig. 4. A parallel-resonant circuit consisting of L_p, C_p and R1 is connected to a voltage source, V_s, through a coupling capacitor, C_c. It is also assumed the Rl is much greater than either the inductive or capacitive reactance taken alone. This condition would be typical of that found in most RF power amplifier circuits using vacuum tubes.

Since the inductive and capacitive reactance of L_p and C_p cancel at resonance, the load presented to the source would be just Rl. This would mean the current through C_c would be much less than the current through either C_p or L_p. The effect of such current rise is similar to the voltage rise at resonance discussed in the previous chapter. Even though the current at the input of the parallel-resonant circuit is small, the currents that flow in the elements that make up the circuit can be quite large.

The requirements for C_c, then, would be rather easy to satisfy with regard to current rating and power dissipation. On the other hand, C_p would ordinarily be restricted to air-variable types, although

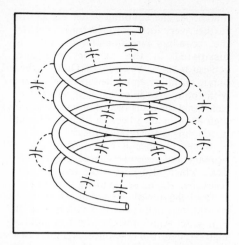

Fig. 6 — Distributed capacitance (indicated by dashed lines) affects the operation of a coil at high frequencies.

some experiments have been successful using Teflon as a dielectric. Generally speaking, the coupling capacitor should have a low reactance (at the lowest frequency of operation) in comparison to the load presented by the tuned circuit. The effect of the coupling-capacitor reactance could then be compensated by slightly retuning the parallel-resonant circuit.

Inductors

Similar considerations to those discussed in the previous sections exist with inductors also, as shown in Fig. 5. Since an inductor usually consists of a coil of wire, there will be a resistance associated with the wire material and this component is represented by R_s. In addition, there is always a capacitance associated with conductors in proximity as illustrated in Fig. 6. While such capacitance is distributed through the coil, it is a convenient approximation to consider that an equivalent capacitance, C_p, exists between the terminals (Fig. 5). Inductors are often wound on materials that have high permeability in order to increase the inductance. Thus, it is possible to build an inductor with fewer turns and that is smaller in size than an equivalent coil with an air core.

Unfortunately, high-permeability materials presently available have considerable loss in the presence of an RF field. It will be recalled that a similar condition existed with the dielectric in a capacitor. Consequently, in addition to the wire resistance, a loss resistance is associated with the core and represented by R_p in Fig. 5. Since this loss is more or less independent of the current through the coil but dependent on the applied voltage, it is represented by a parallel resistance.

RF Transformer

Although the term "transformer" might be applied to any network that transforms a voltage or an impedance from one level to another one, the term is usually reserved

for circuits incorporating mutual magnetic coupling. Examples would be IF transformers, baluns, broadband transformers and certain antenna matching networks (see Chapter 2). Of course, many devices used at audio and power frequencies are also transformers in the sense used here and have been covered in a previous chapter.

Networks that use mutual magnetic coupling exclusively have attractive advantages over other types in many common applications. A principal advantage is that there is no direct connection between the input and output terminals. Consequently, dc and ac components are separated easily, thus eliminating the need for coupling capacitors. Even more importantly, it is also possible to isolate RF currents because of the lack of a common conductor. Often, an HF receiver in an area where strong local broadcast stations are present will suffer from "broadcast harmonics" and possibly even rectified audio signals getting into sensitive AF circuits. In such cases, complicated filters sometimes prove ineffective, while a simple tuned RF transformer will clear up the problem completely. This is because the unwanted BC components are prevented from flowing on the receiver chassis, along with being rejected by the tuned transformer filter characteristic.

A second advantage of circuits using mutual magnetic coupling exclusively is that analysis is relatively simple compared to other forms of coupling, although exact synthesis is complicated. That is, finding a network with some desired frequency response would be difficult in the general case.

However, circuits using mutual magnetic coupling usually have very good out-of-band rejection characteristics when compared to networks incorporating other forms. (A term sometimes applied to transformer or mutual magnetic coupling is indirect coupling. Circuits with a single resistive or reactive element for the common impedance are called direct-coupled networks. Two or more elements in the common impedance are said to comprise complex coupling.) For instance, relatively simple band-pass filters are possible with mutual magnetic coupling and are highly recommended for VHF transmitter-multiplier chains. For receiving, such filters are often the main source of selectivity. Standard AM and FM broadcast receivers would be examples where intermediate-frequency (IF) transformers derive their band-pass characteristics from mutually coupled inductors.

A third advantage of mutually coupled networks is that practical circuits with great flexibility are possible particularly in regard to matching capabilities. For this reason, variable-coupling matching networks or those using link coupling have been popular for many years. In addition to matching flexibility, these circuits are good band-pass filters and can also provide isolation be-

Fig. 7 — Basic magnetically coupled circuit.

Fig. 8 — Equivalent single-mesh network of the two-mesh circuit of Fig. 7.

tween antenna circuits and those of the transmitter.

Design Formulas

A basic two-mesh circuit with mutual magnetic coupling is shown in Fig. 7. The reactance, X, is arbitrary and could be either inductive or capacitive. However, it is convenient to combine it with the secondary reactance (X_{LS}) since this makes the equations more compact. Hence, the total secondary reactance is defined by

$$X_s = 2\pi f L_s + X$$

The primary reactance and mutual reactance are also defined respectively as

$$X_p = 2\pi f L_p$$
$$X_m = 2\pi f M$$

A set of equations for the input resistance and reactance is given by

$$R_{in} = \frac{R_s X_m^2}{R_s^2 + X_s^2}$$

$$X_{in} = X_p - \frac{X_m^2 X_s}{R_s^2 + X_s^2}$$

This permits reducing the two-mesh circuit of Fig. 7 to the single-mesh circuit of Fig. 8.

Double-Tuned Circuits

A special case occurs if the value of X_s is zero. This could be accomplished easily by tuning out the inductive reactance of the secondary with an appropriate capacitor or by varying the frequency until a fixed capacitor and the secondary inductance resonated. Under these conditions, the input resistance and reactance would be

$$R_{in} = \frac{X_m^2}{R_s}$$

$$X_{in} = X_p$$

Then, in order to make the input impedance purely resistive, a second series capacitor could be used to cancel the reactance of X_p. The completed network is shown in Fig. 9 with C1 and C2 being the primary and secondary series capacitors.

If X_m could be varied, it is evident that the secondary resistance could be transformed to almost any value of input resistance. Usually, the desired resistance would be made equal to the generator resistance, R_g, for maximum power transfer. It might also be selected to satisfy some design goal, not necessarily related to maximum power transfer. This brings up a minor point but one that can cause considerable confusion. Normally, in transmitter circuits, the unloaded Q of the reactive components would be very high and the series parasitic resistances (discussed in a previous section) could be neglected. However, if it is not desired to do so, how should these resistances be taken into account? If maximum power transfer is the goal, the series resistance of the primary coil would be added to the generator resistance, R_g, and the transformed secondary resistance would be made equal to this sum.

On the other hand, a more common case requires the total input resistance to be equal to some desired value. For instance, an amplifier might provide optimum efficiency or harmonic suppression when terminated in a particular load resistance. Transmission lines also require a given load resistance in order to be matched. In such cases, the series resistance of the primary coil would be subtracted from the actual resistance desired and the transformed resistance made equal to this difference. As an example, suppose an amplifier required a load resistance of 3000 ohms, and the primary-coil resistance was 100 ohms. Then the transformed resistance must be equal

to 2900 ohms, (In either case, the secondary coil resistance is merely added to the secondary load resistance and the sum substituted for R_s.)

Coefficient of Coupling

Although the equations for the input impedance can be solved in terms of the mutual reactance, the transforming mechanism involved becomes clearer if the coefficient of coupling is used instead. The coefficient of coupling, k, in terms of the corresponding reactances of inductances is

$$k = \frac{X_m}{\sqrt{X_p X_s}} = \frac{L_m}{\sqrt{L_p L_s}}$$

Then, the input resistance becomes

$$R_{in} = \frac{k^2 X_p X_s}{R_s}$$

The primary and secondary Q values are defined as

$$Q_p = \frac{X_p}{R_g}$$

$$Q_s = \frac{X_s}{R_s}$$

where a loaded Q is assumed. This would mean R_s includes any secondary-coil loss. For maximum power transfer, R_g would be the total primary resistance, which consists of the generator and coil resistance.

The coefficient of coupling under these conditions reduces to a simple formula

$$k_c = \frac{1}{\sqrt{Q_p Q_s}}$$

However, if it is desired to make the input resistance some particular value (as in the case of the previous example), the coefficient of coupling is then

$$k_c = \sqrt{\frac{R_{in} - R_p}{X_p Q_s}}$$

If the primary "loss" resistance is zero, both formulas are identical.

At values of k less than k_c, the input resistance is lower than either the prescribed value or for conditions of maximum power transfer. Higher values of k result in a higher input resistance. For this reason, k_c is called the critical coefficient of coupling. If k is less than k_c the circuit is said to be undercoupled, and for k greater than k_c an overcoupled condition results. A plot of attenuation vs. frequency for the three cases is shown in Fig. 10. Critical coupling gives the flattest response, although greater bandwidth can be obtained by increasing k to approximately 1.5 k_c. At higher values, a pronounced dip occurs at the center or resonant frequency.

In the undercoupled case, a peak occurs at the resonant frequency of the primary and secondary circuit but the transformed resistance is too low and results in a mis-

match. As the coupling is decreased still further, very little power is transferred to the secondary circuit and most of it is dissipated in the primary-loss and generator-source resistances. On the other hand, an interesting phenomenon occurs with the overcoupled case. It will be recalled that the transformed resistance is too high at resonance because the coefficient of coupling is greater than the critical value. However, a special case occurs if the primary and secondary circuits are identical, which also means the transformed resistance R_{in} must equal R_s.

The behavior of the circuit under these conditions can be analyzed with the aid of Fig. 8. Assuming the Q of both circuits is high enough, the reactance, X_s, increases very rapidly on either side of resonance. If this variation is much greater than the variation of X_m with frequency, a frequency exists on each side of resonance where the ratio of X_m^2 to $R_s^2 + X_s^2$ is 1.0. Consequently, R_{in} is equal to R_s and the transformed reactance is $-X_s$. Since the primary and secondary resonators are identical, the reactances cancel because of the minus sign. The frequency plot for a k of 0.2 (k_c is 0.1) is shown in Fig. 10. If the primary and secondary circuits are not identical, a double-humped response still occurs, but at the points where the transformed resistance is equal to the desired

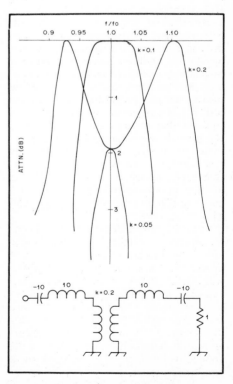

Fig. 10 — Response curves for various degrees of coupling coefficient, k. The critical coefficient of coupling for the network shown in the circuit diagram is 0.1. Lower values give a single response peak (but less than maximum power transfer) while "tighter" coupling results in a double-peak response.

Fig. 9 — Double-tuned series circuits with magnetic coupling.

value, the reactances are not the same numerically. Consequently, there is attenuation at peaks, unlike the curve of Fig. 10.

Other Circuit Forms

While the coupled network shown in Fig. 9 is the easiest to analyze, it is not commonly encountered in actual circuits. As the resistance levels are increased, the corresponding reactances become very large also. In transmitter circuits, extremely high voltages are then developed across the coils and capacitors. For high-impedance circuits, the circuit shown in Fig. 11 is often used.

Although the frequency response for the circuit of Fig. 11 is somewhat different than the circuit of Fig. 9 (in fact, the out-of-band rejection is greater), a matching network can be designed based upon the previous analysis for the series circuit. This is accomplished by changing the parallel primary and secondary circuits to series equivalents. (It should be emphasized that this transformation is good at one frequency only.) The equivalent circuit of the one shown in Fig. 11 is illustrated in Fig. 12, where the new resistance and reactance of the secondary are given by

$$R_{eq}(S) = \frac{R_s}{1 + \gamma^2}$$

$$X_{eq}(C_s) = \frac{-R_s\gamma}{1 + \gamma^2}$$

$$\gamma = R_s / X_c$$

A similar set of transformations exists for the primary circuit also. In most instances, where one high-impedance load is matched to another, R_s in Fig. 11 is much greater than the reactance of C_s and C_p. This simplifies the transformations, and approximate relations are given by

$$R_{eq}(S) \approx \frac{X_c^2}{R_s}$$

$$X_{eq}(C_s) \approx X_c$$

As an example, suppose it was desired to match a 3000-ohm load to a 5000-ohm source using a coupled inductor with a 250-ohm (reactance) primary and secondary coil. Assume the coupling can be varied. Determine the circuit configuration and the critical coefficient of coupling.

Since the load and source resistance have a much higher numerical value than the reactance of the inductors, a parallel-tuned configuration must be used. In order to tune out the inductive reactance, the equivalent series capacitive reactance must be − 250 ohms. Since both R_s and R_p are known, the exact formulas could be solved for γ and R_{eq}. However, because the respective resistances are much greater than the reactance, the simplified approximate formulas can be used. This means the primary and secondary equivalent

capacitive reactances are − 250 ohms. The equivalent secondary resistance is $250^2/3000$ or 20.83 ohms, resulting in a secondary Q of 250/20.83 or 12. (A formula could be derived directly for the Q from the approximate equations.) The equivalent primary resistance and Q are 12.5 ohms and 20, respectively. Substituting the values for Q into the formula for the critical coefficient of coupling gives $1/\sqrt{(20)(12)}$ or 0.065.

Double-tuned coupled circuits of the type shown in Fig. 11 are used widely in radio circuits. Perhaps the most common example is the IF transformer found in AM and FM BC sets. Many communications receivers have similar transformers, although the trend has been toward somewhat different circuits. Instead of obtaining selectivity by means of IF transformers (which may require a number of stages), a single filter with quartz-crystal resonators is used instead. The subject of receivers is treated in a later chapter.

Single-Tuned Circuits

In the case of double-tuned circuits, separate capacitors are used to tune out the inductive components of the primary and secondary windings. However, examination of the equivalent circuit of the coupled coil shown in Fig. 8 suggests an alternative. Instead of a separate capacitor, why not detune a resonant circuit slightly and reflect a reactance of the proper sign into the primary in order to tune out the primary inductance. Since the transformation function (shown in the box in Fig. 8) reverses the sign of the secondary reactance, it is evident that X_s must be *inductive* in order to tune out the primary inductance.

This might seem to be a strange result but it can be explained with the following reasoning. From a mathematical point of view, the choice of the algebraic sign of the transformed reactance is perfectly arbitrary. That is, a set of solutions to the equations governing the coupled circuit is possible, assuming either a positive or negative sign for the transformed reactance. However, if the positive sign is chosen, the transformed resistance would be negative. But from a physical point of view, this is a violation of the law of conservation of energy since it would imply the secondary resistance acts as a source of energy rather than an energy sink. Consequently, the solution with the negative resistance does not result in a physically realizable network.

This phenomenon has implications for circuits one might not normally expect to be related to coupled networks. For instance, consider coil 1 (Fig. 13) in proximity to the one-turn shorted coil 2. A time-varying current in coil 1 will induce a current in coil 2. In turn, the induced current will set up a magnetic field of its own. The question is, will the induced field aid or oppose the primary field. Since the energy in

Fig. 11 — Coupled network with parallel-tuned circuits of IF transformer.

Fig. 12 — Equivalent series circuit of the parallel network shown in Fig. 11. This transformation is valid only at a single frequency and must be revalued if the frequency is changed.

Fig. 13 — A coil coupled magnetically to a shorted turn provides insight to coils near solid shield walls.

a magnetic field is proportional to the square of the flux, the induced field must oppose the primary field. Otherwise the principle of the conservation of energy would be violated as it was with the "negative" resistance. Consequently, the induced current must always be in a direction such that the induced field opposes changes in the generating field. This result is often referred to as Lenz's Law.

If, instead of a one-turn loop, a solid shield wall was substituted, a similar phenomenon would occur. Since the total flux (for a given current) would be less with the shield present than it would in the absence of the shield, the equivalent coil inductance is decreased. That is why it is important to use a shield around a coil that is big enough to reduce the effect of such coupling. Also, a shield made from a metal with high conductivity such as copper or aluminum is advisable; otherwise a loss resistance will be coupled into the coil as well.

Link Coupling

An example of a very important class of

Fig. 14 — Link coupling can be used to analyze a number of important circuits.

Fig. 15 — A VHF/UHF circuit which can be approximated by a link-coupled network using conventional components.

Fig. 16 — Equivalent low-frequency analog of the circuit shown in Fig. 15.

Fig. 17 — The network of Fig. 16 can be reduced with the transformation shown in Fig. 8.

single-tuned circuits is shown in Fig. 14. The primary inductor consists of a small coil either in close proximity to or wound over one end of a large coil. Two resonators can be coupled in this manner, although there may be considerable separation (and no mutual coupling between the larger coils). Hence the term, link coupling. While this particular method is seldom used nowadays, the term is still applied to the basic configuration shown in Fig. 14. Applications would be antenna-matching networks, output stages for amplifiers, and especially important, many circuits used at VHF that have no direct HF equivalent.

The cavity resonators used in repeater duplexers are one form of VHF circuit that uses link coupling. A cross-sectional view of a representative type is shown in Fig. 15. Instead of ordinary coils and capacitors, a section of coaxial transmission line comprises the resonant circuit. The frequency of the resonator may be varied by adjusting the tuning screw that changes the value of the capacitor. Energy is coupled into and out of the resonator by means of two small, one-turn loops. Current in the input loop causes a magnetic field (shown by dashed lines). If the frequency of the generating field is near one of the resonant modes of the configuration, an electric field will also be generated (shown by solid lines). Finally, energy may then be coupled out of the resonator by means of a second loop.

A low-frequency equivalent circuit of the resonator is shown in Fig. 16. However, the circuit can be used only to give an approximate idea of the actual frequency response of the cavity. At frequencies not close to the resonant frequency, the mathematical laws governing resonant circuits are different from those of discrete components used at HF. Over a limited frequency range, the resonator can be approximated by the series LC circuit shown in Fig. 16.

By applying the formulas for coupled networks shown in Fig. 8 to the two-link circuit of Fig. 16, the output link and load can be transformed to an equivalent series resistance and reactance. This is shown in Fig. 17. In most instances the reactance, X_s in the formula, is just the reactance of the output link. Since the two-link network has been reduced to a single coupled circuit, the formulas can be applied again to find the input resistance and reactance.

Analysis of Single-Tuned Circuits

Single-tuned circuits are very easy to construct and adjust experimentally. The tuned circuit consisting of L_s, C_s, and perhaps the load, R_s, can be constructed first and tuned to the natural resonant frequency

$$f_o = \frac{1}{2\pi \sqrt{L_s C_s}}$$

Then the primary inductor, which may be a link or a larger coil, is brought into proximity of the resonant circuit. The resonant frequency will usually shift upward. For instance, a coil and capacitor combination was tuned to resonance by means of a dip oscillator (see the chapter on measurements) at a frequency of 1.8 MHz. When a two-turn link was wound over the coil and coupled to the dip oscillator, the resonant frequency had increased to 1.9 MHz. A three-turn link caused a change to 2 MHz.

Often an actual load may be an unknown quantity, such as an antenna, and insight into the effects of the various elements is helpful in predicting single-tuned circuit operation. Usually, as in the case of most matching networks, R_s (Fig. 8) and the input resistance are specified with the reactive components being the variables. Unfortunately, the variables in the case of mutually coupled networks are not independent of each other, which complicates matters.

Examination of the equivalent circuit shown in Fig. 8 would indicate the first condition is that the reactance reflected from the secondary into the primary be sufficient to tune out the primary reactance. Otherwise, even though the proper resistance transformation is obtainable, a reactive component would always be present. A plot of the reflected reactance as a function of X_s is shown in Fig. 18. From mathematical considerations it can be shown that the maximum and minimum of the curve have a value equal to $X_m^2/2R_s$. Consequently, this value must be greater than or equal to X_p so a value of X_s may exist such that the reflected reactance will cancel X_p. In the usual case where $X_m^2/2R_s$ is greater than X_p, it is interesting to note that two values of X_s exist where X_p and the reflected reactance cancel. This means there are two cases where the input impedance is purely resistive, and R_s could be matched to either one of two source resistances if so desired. The value of X_s at these points is designated as X_{s1} and X_{s2}.

On the other hand, a high value of R_s requires X_m to be large also. This could be accomplished by increasing the coefficient of coupling or by increasing the turns on the secondary coil. Increasing the turns on the primary also will cause X_m to be higher, but X_p will increase also. This is self-defeating, since X_{m2} is proportional to X_p.

An alternative approach is to use the parallel configuration of Fig. 19. The approximate equivalent series resistance of the parallel combination is then $X(C_s)^2/R_s$ and the reactance is approximately $X(C_s)$. (See diagram and text for Fig. 12.) This approach is often used in multiband antenna systems. On some frequencies the impedance at the input of the feed line is high, so the circuit of Fig. 18 is employed. This is referred to as parallel tuning. If the impedance is very low, the circuit of Fig. 14 is used and is called series tuning.

As an example, suppose a single-tuned circuit is to be used to match a 1-ohm load to a 50-ohm source, as shown in Fig. 20. It might be pointed out here that networks using mutual magnetic coupling can be scaled in the same manner that filter networks are scaled (as discussed in Chapter 2). For instance, the circuit of Fig. 20 could be scaled in order to match a 50-ohm load to a 2500-ohm source merely by multiplying all the reactances by a factor of 50.

The input resistance and reactance of the

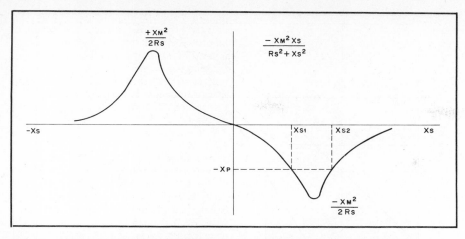

Fig. 18 — Reflected reactance into the primary of a single-tuned circuit places restraints on resistances that can be matched. This gives rise to a general rule that high-Q secondary circuits require a lower coefficient of coupling than low-Q ones.

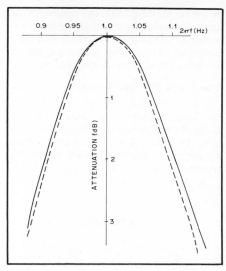

Fig. 23 — Response of the circuit shown in Fig. 20.

Fig. 19 — Single-tuned circuit with a parallel RC secondary.

Fig. 20 — Example of a single-tuned circuit.

Fig. 21 — Input resistance of the circuit of Fig. 20 as a function of frequency.

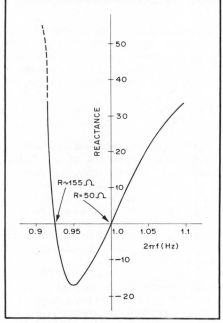

Fig. 22 — Input reactance of the network of Fig. 20. Note two resonant frequencies (where reactance is zero).

Fig. 24 — The transformation of Fig. 8 applied to the primary side of the circuit of Fig. 20.

circuit of Fig. 20 are plotted in Figs. 21 and 22, respectively. As pointed out earlier, there are two possible points where the reactance is zero, and this circuit could be used to match the 1-ohm load to either a 50-ohm or 155-ohm source. Assuming a 50-ohm source is being used, the attenuation plot as a function of frequency is given

by the solid curve of Fig. 23.

With slight modification to include the effect of the source, the transformation of Fig. 8 can be applied to the primary side of the coupled circuit shown in Fig. 20. This is illustrated in Fig. 24. The complete circuit is shown at Fig. 24A and the network with the transformed primary resistance and reactance is shown in Fig. 24B.

In a lossless transformer, the maximum available power at the secondary must be the same as that of the original source on the primary side, neglecting the effects of reactance. That is, the power delivered to a 1-ohm resistance (shown as a dashed line in Fig. 24B) must be the same as that delivered to a 50-ohm load in Fig. 24A.

This assumes that the rest of the circuit has been disconnected in either case. In order to fulfill this requirement, the original source voltage must be multiplied by the square root of the ratio of the new and old source resistance.

The single-mesh transformed network is shown in Fig. 24C. It is interesting to compare the response of an RLC series circuit that actually possesses these element values at resonance with the circuit of Fig. 20. For comparison, the response of such a circuit is shown in Fig. 23 as a dashed curve; this curve differs only slightly from the coupled-circuit curve (solid line). The reason for the similarity is that even though the transformation of the primary resistance and reactance also changes with frequency, the effect is not that great in the present case.

Broadband RF Transformers

The sensitivity of the frequency characteristic of the transformation shown in Fig. 8 depends mostly on the ratio of X_s to R_s. However, if X_s is much greater than R_s, the transformed reactance can be approximated by

$$\frac{-X_m^2 X_s}{R_s^2 + X_s^2} \approx \frac{-X_m^2}{X_s}$$

and the resistance becomes

$$\frac{R_s X_m^2}{R_s^2 + X_s^2} \approx R_s \frac{X_m^2}{X_s^2}$$

Applying this approximation to the general coupled circuit shown in Fig. 25A results in the transformed network of Fig. 25B. The coefficient of coupling for the circuit of Fig. 25A is

$$k = \frac{X_m}{\sqrt{X_1 X_2}}$$

and the network shown in Fig. 25B in terms of the coefficient of coupling is illustrated in Fig. 25C. If k equals 1.0, the input reactance is zero and the input resistance is given by

$$R_{in} = \left(\frac{X_1}{X_2}\right) R_2 = \left(\frac{L_1}{L_2}\right) R_2 \approx \left(\frac{N_1}{N_2}\right) R_2$$

Fig. 25 — Equivalent-circuit approximation of two coupled coils.

Fig. 26 — Input resistance and reactance as a function of output load resistance for X_1, and X_2 equal to 100 ohms and 10 ohms, respectively (Fig. 25).

where N_1 and N_2 are the number of turns on coil 1 and 2, respectively. From maximum-power transfer considerations such as those discussed for the circuit of Fig. 24, the voltage transfer ratio becomes

$$e_2 = \left(\frac{N_2}{N_1}\right) e_1$$

It will be recalled the above equations occurred in the discussion of the "ideal transformer" approximation in Chapter 2. It was assumed then that the leakage reactance and magnetizing current were negligible. The effects on circuit operation of these variables are shown in Fig. 26. The curves were computed for various load resistances (R_s) using the exact equations shown in Fig. 8.

X_1 and X_2 are assumed to be 100 and 10 ohms, respectively, with the solid curves for a k of 1.0 and the dashed reactance curve for k equal to 0.99 (the resistance curve for the latter values is the same as the one for k equal to 1.0). The ideal-transformer representation can be modified slightly to approximate the curve of Fig. 26 as shown in Fig. 27. The shunt reactance, X_{mag}, is called the magnetizing reactance and X_L is referred to as the leakage reactance.

Unfortunately, the two reactances are not independent of each other. That is, attempts to change one reactance so that its effect is suppressed causes difficulties in eliminating the effects of the other reactance. For instance, increasing X_1, X_m, and X_2 will increase X_{mag}, which is desirable. However, examination of Fig. 25C reveals that the coefficient of coupling, k, will have to be made closer to 1.0. Otherwise, the leakage reactance increases since it is proportional to X_1.

High-Permeability Cores

As a consequence of the interaction between the leakage reactance and the magnetizing reactance, transformers that approach ideal conditions are extremely difficult (if not impossible) to build using techniques common in air-wound or low-permeability construction. In order to build a network that will match one resistance level to another one over a wide range of frequencies, ideal transformer conditions have to be approached quite closely. Otherwise, considerable inductive reactance will exist along with the resistance component, as shown in Fig. 26.

One approach is to use a core with a higher permeability than air. Familiar examples would be power transformers and similar types common to the AF range. However, when an inductor configuration contains materials of more than one permeability, the analysis relating to Fig. 25C has to be modified somewhat. The manner in which the core affects the circuit is a bit complicated although even a qualitative idea of how such transformers work is very useful.

First, consider the coupled coils shown in Fig. 28. For a given current, I_1 a number of flux lines are generated that link both coil 1 and coil 2. Note that in coil 1, not all of the flux lines are enclosed by all the turns. The inductance of a coil is equal to the ratio of the sum of flux lines linking each turn and the generating current or

$$L_1 = \frac{\Lambda_{TOTAL}}{I_1}$$

where for the example shown in Fig. 28, Λ_{TOTAL} is given by

$$\Lambda_{TOTAL} = \Lambda_1 + \Lambda_2 + \Lambda_3 + \Lambda_4 + \Lambda_5$$

Counting up the number of flux linkages in coil 1 gives

$$\Lambda_{TOTAL} = 5 + 5 + 7 + 7 + 5 = 29$$

If all the flux lines linked all the turns,

Fig. 27 — Approximate network for the curves of Fig. 26.

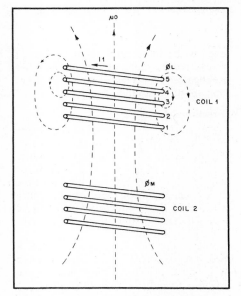

Fig. 28 — Coupled coils showing magnetic flux lines.

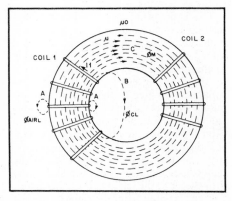

Fig. 29 — Toroidal transformer.

Λ_{TOTAL} would be 35 so L_1 is 29 / 35 or 83 percent of its maximum possible value. Likewise, if all the flux (7 lines) generated in coil one linked all the turns of coil 2, the maximum number of flux linkages would be the number of turns on coil 2 times 7 or 28. Since only three lines link coil 2, the mutual inductance is $3 \times 4/28$ or 43 percent of maximum.

Assuming both coils are perfect, if a current I_1 produced 7 flux lines in a five-turn coil, then the same current in a four-turn coil would produce (4/5)(7) flux lines, since the flux is proportional to the magnetizing current times the number of turns. Consequently, the maximum flux linkages in coil 1 from a current of the same value as I_1 but in coil 2 instead would be (4/5)(7)(5) or 28. Therefore, it can be seen that the mutual inductance is independent of the choice of coil used for the primary or secondary. That is, a voltage produced in one coil by a current in the other one would be the same if the coils were merely interchanged. (This result has been used implicitly on a number of previous occasions without proof.) In addition, the maximum flux linkages in coil 2 produced by a current, I_1, would be (4/5)(7)(4). As an exercise, substitute the maximum inductance values into the formula for the coefficient of coupling and show that k is 1.0.

The next step is to consider the effect of winding coils on a form with a magnetic permeability much higher than that of air. An example is illustrated in Fig. 29, and the configuration shown is called a toroidal transformer. Since the flux is proportional to the product of the permeability and the magnetizing current, the flux in the core shown in Fig. 29 will be much greater than the coil configuration of Fig. 28. However, not all of the flux is confined to the core. As can be seen in Fig. 29, some of the flux lines never penetrate the core (see lines marked A in Fig. 29) while others enclose all the windings of coil 1 but not coil 2 (see line marked B). The significance of these effects is as follows. The total flux linkage produced by the current, I_1, is

$$\Lambda_{\text{TOTAL}} = \Lambda_{\text{air}} + \Lambda_{\text{core}}$$

and dividing both sides of the equation by I_1 gives

$$L_T = L_{\text{air}} + L_{\text{core}}$$

Consequently, the circuit of Fig. 25 can be represented as shown in Fig. 30A. For values of X_2 much greater than the load resistance, the approximate network of Fig. 30B can replace the one of Fig. 30A.

At first sight, it might seem as though little advantage has been gained by introducing the core since the formulas are much the same as those of Fig. 25C. However, the reactances associated with the core can be made very high by using a material with a high permeability. Also, even though there may be some leakage from the core as indicated by line B in Fig. 29, it is ordinarily low and the coefficient of coupling in the core can be considered 1.0 for all practical purposes. This is especially true at AF and power frequencies with transformers using iron cores where the permeability is extremely high. This means the magnetizing reactance can be made very high without increasing the leakage reactance accordingly as is the case with the circuit in Fig. 25C. Therefore, ideal transformer conditions are considered to exist in the core, and the final circuit can be approximated by the one shown in Fig. 30C.

Bifilar and Twisted-Pair Windings

Although the core helps alleviate some of the problems with leakage and magnetizing reactance, the residual parasitic elements must still be made as low as possible. This is especially important in matching applications, as the following example illustrates. A transformer has a primary and secondary leakage reactance of 1 ohm and 0.1 ohm, respectively, with a coefficient of coupling of 1.0 in the core. X_1 and X_2 are 1000 ohms and 100 ohms.

A plot similar to the one of Fig. 26 is shown in Fig. 31, along with a curve for voltage standing wave ratio (VSWR). These results are based on the exact equations and it can be seen that the approximate relations shown in Fig. 30C are valid up to 1 ohm or so. Curve A (Fig. 31) includes only the effect of the secondary reactance and illustrates the manner in which the reactance is transformed. Curve B shows the total input reactance, which merely requires the addition of 1 ohm. The VSWR curve includes the effect of the input reactance. The useful range of the transformer is between 1 and 10 ohms, with rapid deterioration in VSWR outside of these values. (The VSWR curve is for a characteristic impedance equal to 10 times the secondary resistance. For instance, the transformer would be useful in matching a 5-ohm load to a 50-ohm line.)

Fig. 30 — Effect of a high-permeability core on transformer equivalent circuit.

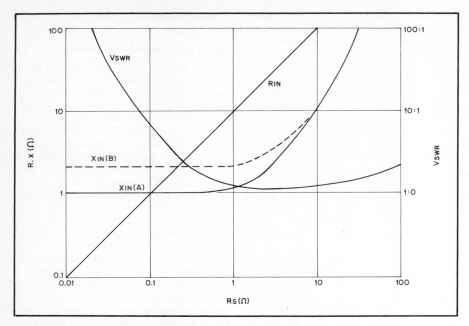

Fig 31 — Curve for transformer problem discussed in the text.

Fig. 32 — Bifilar-wound transformer on toroidal core.

Fig. 33 — Effect of distributed capacitance on transformer action.

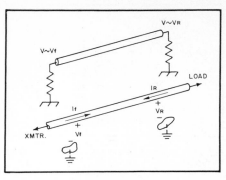

Fig. 34 — Basic configuration for a directional-coupler type of VSWR detector.

As mentioned previously, these difficulties are less pronounced at audio frequencies since the permeabilities normally encountered in iron-core transformers are so high. The actual inductance of the winding itself is therefore small in comparison to the component represented by the core. That is, a small number of turns of wire wound on a core may actually be the equivalent of a very large coil. However, materials suitable for RF applications have much lower permeabilities, and a narrower range of matching values is likely to be the result (such as in the example of Fig. 31). Therefore, other means are required in keeping the parasitic elements as low as possible. Either that, or less conventional transformer designs are used.

One approach is shown in Fig. 32. Instead of separating the windings on the core as shown in Fig. 29, they are wound in parallel fashion. This is called a bifilar winding, although a more common approach to achieve the same purpose is to twist the wires together. Either way, there are a number of advantages to be gained (and some disadvantages). With reference to Fig. 28, the fact that not all the flux lines linked all of the turns of a particular coil meant the self inductance was lower than if all the turns were linked. Since the separation between turns of a particular coil is quite large in the configuration of Fig 32, the flux linkage between turns is quite low. This means the corresponding leakage inductance is reduced accordingly. However, the coupling between both coils is increased because of the bifilar winding (flux line A) in Fig. 32 which also tends to reduce the leakage inductance of either coil.

On the other hand the capacitance between windings is increased considerably as indicated by B in Fig. 32. As a result, the coupling between windings is both electrical and magnetic in nature. Generally speaking, analysis of the problem is complicated. However, a phenomenon usually associated with such coupling is that it tends to be directional. That is, energy transferred from one winding to the other propagates in a preferred direction rather than splitting equally.

Directional Coupling

Two conductors are oriented side by side over a conducting plane as shown in Fig. 33. The current I in conductor 1 will induce a current I_m in conductor 2 because of magnetic coupling. The actual value of the current will depend on the external circuitry attached to the conductors but it will be assumed that the two of them extend to infinity in both directions.

Since capacitive coupling exists also, a second set of current components denoted by I_c will flow. The result is that a wave traveling toward the right in conductor 1 will produce a wave traveling toward the left in conductor 2. Such coupling is called contradirectional coupling, since the induced wave travels in the opposite direction to the generating wave.

This is the principle behind many practical devices and ones that are quite common in amateur applications. In adjusting a load such as an antenna, it is desirable to ensure that energy is not reflected back to the transmitter. Otherwise, the impedance presented to the transmitter output may not be within range of permissible values. A directional coupler is useful in determining how much power is reflected, as indicated in Fig. 34. Energy originating from the transmitter and flowing to the right causes a voltage to be produced across the resistor at the left. On the other hand, a wave traveling from the right to the left produces a voltage across the right-hand resistor. If both of these voltages are sampled, some idea of the amount of power reflected can be determined. (The subject of reflected power is taken up in more detail in the chapter on transmission lines.)

It some situations, the coupling described can be very undesirable. For instance, the lines shown in Fig. 34 might be conductors on a circuit board in a piece of equipment. As a result, the coupling between lines can cause feedback and, because of its directional nature, can be very difficult to sup-

Fig. 35 — Directional-coupler hybrid combiner.

Fig. 36 — Transmission-line transformer with ferrite cores.

Fig. 37 — Equivalent circuit of transmission-line transformer in the presence of the core. Dots indicate winding sense of coils. A positive current into a dotted end of one coil will produce a voltage in the other coil because of mutual coupling. The polarity of this voltage will be such that dotted end of the "secondary" coil will be positive. The crossed-arrows symbol in the middle of the parallel lines is the standard symbol for a directional coupler.

press with conventional methods. Therefore, it is good design practice to use double-sided board (board with conductive foil on both sides) so a ground plane of metal is in close proximity to the conductors. This tends to confine the fields to the region in the immediate vicinity of the wires.

Transmission-Line Transformers

In effect, sections of transmission line in close proximity act as transformers with the unique feature that the coupling is directional. For instance, if only magnetic coupling were present in the configuration of Fig. 34, power would be divided equally between the resistors at either end of the secondary section of transmission line. As another example of directional effects, the network shown in Fig. 35 can be used to couple two sources to a common load without cross-coupling of power from one

source to the other one. (This assumes the sources have the same frequency and phase. Otherwise, a resistance of value 2R must be connected from point a to d.) Such a configuration is called a hybrid combiner and is often used to combine the outputs of two solid-state amplifiers in order to increase the power-handling capability. This permits the use of less expensive low-power devices rather than very expensive high-power ones. Even though more devices are required, it is still simpler since the difficulties in producing a high-power transistor increase in a greater proportion as the power level is raised.

The manner in which the circuit shown in Fig. 35 operates is as follows. A wave from the generator on the left end of line 1 travels toward the right and induces a wave in line 2 that travels toward the left and on into the load. No wave is induced in line 2 that travels toward the right except for a small fraction of power.

A similar situation exists with the second generator connected at the right end of line 2. A wave is induced in line 1 that travels toward the right. Since the load is also connected to the right end of line 1, power in the induced wave will be dissipated here with little energy reaching the generator at the left end of line 1. In order to simulate a single load (since there are two generators involved), the value of the load resistance must be half of the generator resistance. Assuming that two separate resistors of value R were connected to the ends of the line, it would be possible to connect them together without affecting circuit operation. This is because the voltage across both resistors is of the same phase and amplitude. Consequently, no additional current would flow if the two resistors were paralleled or combined into a single resistor of R/2.

Extending the Low-Frequency Range

As might be expected, the coupling

mechanism illustrated in Figs. 32 through 34 is highly dependent on dimensions such as conductor spacing and line length. For instance, maximum coupling of power from the primary wave to the induced wave occurs when the secondary line is a quarter-wavelength long[1] or some odd multiple of a quarter-wavelength. This would normally make such couplers impractical for frequencies in the HF range. However, by running the leads through a ferrite core as shown in Fig. 36, lower frequency operation is possible. Although the transformer of Fig. 36A is seldom used, it illustrates the manner in which the conductors are employed electrically in the more complicated configurations of Fig. 32 and 36B. Also, the relationship between the parallel-line coupler in Fig. 35 and the loaded version of Fig. 36A is easier to visualize.

As covered in an earlier problem discussion (Fig. 29), a set of coupled coils wound on a high-permeability core can be broken down into combinations of two series inductances. One inductance represents the path in air while the other includes the effects of the flux in the core. As before, it is assumed that the coefficient of coupling in the core is 1.0.

If the hybrid combiner of Fig. 35 is wound on a core (such as those of Fig. 32 or Fig. 36), the low-frequency range of the entire system is increased considerably. The equivalent circuit showing the effect of the core on the air-wound coupler is illustrated in Fig. 37. (The symbol in the middle of the parallel lines is the standard for a directional coupler.) At the higher frequencies, most core materials decrease in permeability. The operation approaches that of the original air-wound coupler, and

[1]Oliver, "Directional Electromagnetic Couplers," *Proceedings of the I.R.E.*, Vol. 42, pp. 1686-1692, November 1954.

Fig. 38 — Low-frequency equivalent circuit of hybrid combiner showing isolation of sources.

Fig. 39 — Desired coupling mode of hybrid combiner.

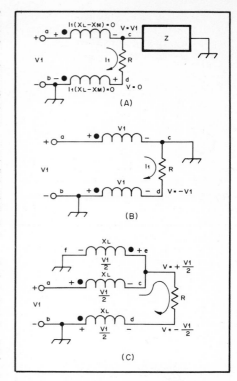

Fig. 40 — Applications of transmission-line transformers. See text.

the inductance produced by the core can be neglected. At the low end of the frequency range, the line lengths are usually too short to provide much coupling or isolation. Therefore, the circuit can be represented by the set of coupled coils shown in Figs. 38 and 39.

For a current I_{12} flowing from a source 1 over to the mesh that includes source 2, the mutual-reactance components add to the self-inductance of each coil. Consequently, a large reactance appears in series between the two sources, which effectively isolates them. On the other hand, currents from both sources that flow through the load resistor, R/2, produce fluxes that cancel, and the voltages produced by the self- and mutual-reactance terms subtract. If both sources have the same amplitude and phase, currents I_1 and I_2 must be identical because of the symmetry involved. However, if the coefficient of coupling is 1.0, the self- and mutual-reactance must be equal. Therefore the voltage across either coil is zero, since the terms subtract, and a low-impedance path exists between both sources and the load.

Other Transformer Types

The hybrid combiner is only one application of a combination transmission-line or directional-coupler transformer and conventional coupled-coil arrangement. With other variations, the low-frequency isolation is accomplished in the same manner. Mutual-reactance terms add to the self-reactance to provide isolation for some purpose with cancellation of reactive components in the path for the desired coupling. Very good bandwidth is possible

with a range from BC frequencies to UHF in the more esoteric designs. Models that cover all the amateur HF bands can be constructed easily.[2]

Unfortunately, there is also a tendency to expect too much from such devices. Misapplication or poor design often results in inferior performance. For instance, as indicated in an earlier example (Fig. 31), actual impedance levels are important, along with the desired transforming ratio. Using a transformer for an impedance level that was not intended results in undesirable reactive components and an improper transforming ratio. However, when applied properly, the transformers discussed in the previous sections can provide bandwidth characteristics that are obtainable in no other way.

Another transformer type is shown in Fig. 40A. The windings of the coils are such that the voltages across the inductors caused by the desired current are zero. This is because the induced voltages produced by the current in the mutual-reactance terms just cancel the voltage drop caused by the current flowing in the self-reactances of either coil, (assuming the coefficient of coupling is 1.0) However, an impedance connected to ground at point c would be in series with the self-reactance (X_L) of the coil connected between points a and c. But there would be no induced voltage to counter the voltage drop across this coil. Therefore, if X_L is large, very little current would flow in the impedance Z and it would be isolated effectively from the source.

In fact, terminal c could be grounded as shown in Fig. 40B. The voltage drop across the coil from a to c would then be equal to V_1. However, the induced voltage in the coil connected between points b and d would also be V_1, assuming unity coupling (k equal to 1.0). Although the voltage drop produced by the inductors around the mesh through which I_1 flows is still zero, point d is now at potential $-V1$ and a phase reversal has taken place. For this reason, the configuration shown in Fig. 40B is called a phase-reversal transformer.

Baluns

The circuit shown in Fig. 40A is useful in isolating a load from a grounded source. This is required in many applications, and the device that accomplishes this goal is called a balun (balanced to unbalanced) transformer. Baluns may also be used to transform impedances and to provide isolation. A 1:1 balun such as the one shown in Fig. 40A means the impedance at the input terminals ab will be the same as the load connected across terminals cd. Other transforming ratios, such as 4:1, are possible with the appropriate circuit connections.

[2]Ruthroff, "Some Broad-Band Transformers," *Proceedings of the I.R.E.,* Vol. 97, pp. 1337-1342, August 1959.

One disadvantage of the network of Fig. 40A is that although the load is isolated from the source, the voltages at the output are not balanced. This is important in some applications such as diode-ring mixers, where a push-pull input is required, and so the circuit of Fig. 40C is used. A third coil connected between points e and f is wound on the same core as the original transformer (Fig. 40A). This coil is connected so a voltage across it produces a flux that adds to that produced by the coil between a and c. Assuming both coils are identical, the voltage drop across either one must be the same, or half the applied voltage. However, since the coil between b and d is also coupled to this combination (and is an identical coil), the induced voltage must also be $-V_1/2$. Consequently, the end of the load connected to points c and e is at a potential of $+V_1/2$ with respect to ground, while point d is $-V_1/2$ with respect to ground when the input voltage has the polarity shown. Therefore, this circuit not only isolates the load from the source but provides a balanced voltage.

Either the circuit of Fig. 40A or Fig. 40C can be used if only isolation is desired. However, the network shown in Fig. 40C is more difficult to design and construct since the reactance of the coils between points a and f must be very high throughout the frequency range of the transformer. With both transformers, the coefficient of coupling must also be very close to 1.0 in order to prevent undesirable reactance in series with the load. This problem can be offset somewhat by reducing X_L slightly (by fewer turns) but this is counter to the requirement of a large X_L in the circuit of Fig. 40C. Isolation is reduced in both cases, although no detrimental effect on input impedance results in the transformer of Fig. 40A by reducing X_L.

Twisted Pairs — Impedance and Attenuation

Twisted pairs of wire are often used in the construction of broadband RF transformers. The question often arises as to what size conductors and what number of twists per inch should be used. To help answer these questions the information contained in Tables 1 and 2 was developed. Table 1 illustrates the approximate impedance for various size conductors with different numbers of twists per inch. These values are based on measurements in the ARRL laboratory, and should be accurate to within an ohm or two. Enameled copper wire was used for each pair. The information shown in Table 2 is the attenuation per foot for the same twisted pairs of wire. Information is not included for twists per inch greater than 7½ for the no. 20 wire

Table 1

Impedance of Various Two-Conductor Lines

Wire Size	Twists per Inch				
	2½	5	7½	10	12½
no. 20	43	39	35		
no. 22	46	41	39	37	32
no. 24	60	45	44	43	41
no. 26	65	57	54	48	47
no. 28	74	53	51	49	47
no. 30			49	46	47

Measured in ohms at 14.0 MHz

This chart illustrates the impedance of various two-conductor lines as a function of the wire size and number of twists per inch.

Table 2

Attenuation per Foot for Lines in Table 1

Wire Size	Twists per Inch				
	2½	5	7½	10	12½
no. 20	0.11	0.11	0.12		
no. 22	0.11	0.12	0.12	0.12	0.12
no. 24	0.11	0.12	0.12	0.13	0.13
no. 26	0.11	0.13	0.13	0.13	0.13
no. 28	0.11	0.13	0.13	0.16	0.16
no. 30			0.25	0.27	0.27

Measured in decibels at 14.0 MHz

Attenuation in dB per foot for the same lines as shown in Table 1.

since this results in an unusable tight pair. Likewise, the information for twists per inch less than 7½ for no. 30 wire is omitted since these pairs are extremely loose.

As a general rule the wire size can be selected based on the core size to be used and the required number of turns. The number of twists per inch can be selected according to the impedance level of transmission line that is needed. For applications where moderate levels of power are to be handled (such as in the low- and medium-level stages of a solid-state transmitter), smaller wire sizes should be avoided. For receiver applications, very small wire can be used. It is not uncommon to find transformers wound with pairs of no. 32 wire and smaller.

Nonlinear and Active Networks

Almost all the theory in previous sections has dealt with so-called passive components. Passive networks and components can be represented solely by combinations of resistors, capacitors and inductors. As a consequence, the power output at one set of terminals in a passive network cannot exceed the total power input from sources connected to other terminals in the circuit. This assumes all the sources are at one frequency. Similar considerations hold true for any network, but, it is possible for energy to be converted from one frequency (including dc) to other ones. While the total power input must still be equal to the total power output, it is convenient to consider certain elements as controllable sources of power. Such devices are called amplifiers and are part of a more general class of circuits called active networks. An active network generally possesses characteristics that are different from those of simple RLC circuits, although the goal in many instances is to attempt to represent them in terms of passive elements and generators.

Nonlinearity

Two other important attributes of passive RLC elements are that they are linear and bilateral. A two-terminal element such as a resistor is said to be bilateral since it doesn't matter which way it is connected in a circuit. Semiconductor and vacuum-tube devices such as triodes, diodes, transistors and integrated circuits (ICs) are all examples where the concept of a bilateral element no longer holds true. The manner in which the device is connected in a circuit and the polarity of the voltages involved are very important.

An implication of the failure to satisfy the bilateral requirements is that such devices are nonlinear in the strictest sense. Linearity means that the amplitude of a voltage or current is related to other voltages and currents in a circuit by a single proportionality constant. For instance, if all the voltages and currents in a circuit were doubled, a single remaining voltage or current would be doubled also. That is, it couldn't change by a factor of one half, or three, no matter how complex the network might be. Likewise, if all the polarities of the currents and voltages in a circuit are reversed, the polarity of a remaining voltage or current must be reversed also. Finally, if all the generators or sources in a linear network are sine waves at a single frequency, any voltage or current produced by these sources must also be a sine wave at the same frequency.

Consequently, if a device is sensitive to the polarity of the voltage applied to its terminals, it doesn't meet the requirements of either a bilateral element or a linear one. Because of the extreme simplicity of the mathematics of linear circuits as compared to the general nonlinear case, however, there is tremendous motivation in being able to represent a nonlinear circuit by a linear approximation. Many devices exhibit linear properties over part of their operating range or may satisfy some but not all of the requirement of linear circuits. Such devices in these categories are sometimes termed piece-wise linear (or; simply, as linear). For instance, a linear mixer doesn't satisfy the rule that a voltage or current must be at the same frequency as the generating source(s). Since the desired output voltage (or current) varies in direct proportion to the input voltage (or current), however, the term linear is applied to distinguish the mixer from types without this quasi-linear property.

Harmonic Frequency Generation

In a circuit with nothing but linear components, the only frequencies present are those generated by the sources themselves. This is not true with nonlinear elements. One of the properties of nonlinear networks mentioned earlier is that energy at one frequency (including dc) may become converted to other frequencies. In effect, this is how devices such as transistors and vacuum tubes are able to amplify radio signals. Energy from the dc power supply is converted to energy at the desired signal

Fig. 41 — Nonlinear transfer charcteristic (see text discussion).

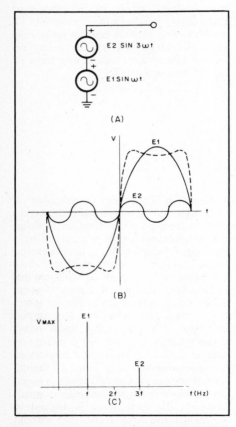

Fig. 42 — Harmonic analysis and spectrum.

frequency. Therefore, a greater amount of signal power is available at the output of the network of an active device than at the input.

On the other hand, such frequency generation may be undesirable. For instance, the output of a transmitter may have energy at frequencies that could cause interference to nearby receiving equipment. Filters and similar devices must be used to suppress this energy as much as possible.

The manner in which this energy is produced is shown in Fig. 41. A sine wave at the input of a nonlinear network (V_{in}) is "transformed" into the output voltage waveform (V_{out}) illustrated. If the actual device characteristic is known, the waveform could be constructed graphically. It could also be tabulated, if the output voltage as a function of input voltage was available in either tabular or equation form. (Only one-half of the period of a sine wave is shown in Fig. 41 for clarity.)

Although the new waveform retains many of the characteristics of the original sine wave, some transformations have taken place. It has zero value when t is either 0 or T/2, and attains a maximum at T/4. However, the fact that the curve is flattened somewhat means energy at the original sine-wave frequency has been converted to other frequencies. It will be recalled that the sum of a number of sine waves at one frequency result in another sine wave at the same frequency. Therefore, the waveform of Fig. 41 must have more than one frequency component present since it is no longer a sine wave.

One possible model for the new waveform is shown in Fig. 42A. Instead of one sine wave at a single frequency, there are two generators at three times the "fundamental" frequency ω, where ω is 2πf(Hz). If the two sine waves are plotted point by point, the dashed curve of Fig. 42B results. While this curve doesn't resemble the one of Fig. 41 very closely, the general symmetry is the same. It would take an infinite number of generators to represent the desired curve exactly, but it is evident that all the frequencies must be odd multiples of the fundamental. Even multiples would produce a lopsided curve that might be useful for representing other types of waveforms.

In either case, the multiples have a specific name and are called harmonics. There is no first harmonic. By definition, the second, third and fourth multiples are designated as the second, third and fourth harmonics. Thus the dashed curve of Fig. 42 is the sum of the fundamental and third harmonic.

Analyzing waveforms such as those of Fig. 41 is a very important procedure. A plot of harmonic amplitude such as that shown in Fig. 42C is called the spectrum of the waveform and can be displayed on an instrument called a spectrum analyzer. If the mathematical equation or other data for the curve is known, the harmonics can also be determined by means of a mathematical process called Fourier analysis.

Linear Approximations of Nonlinear Devices

Nonlinear circuits may have to be analyzed graphically as in the previous example. There are many other instances where only a graphical method may be practical, such as in power-amplifier prob-

lems. However, a wide variety of applications permit a different approach. A model is derived from the nonlinear characteristics using linear elements to approximate the more difficult nonlinear problem. This model is then used in more complicated networks instead of the nonlinear characteristics, which simplifies analysis considerably.

The following example illustrates how this is accomplished. Although a vacuum-tube application is considered, a similar process is employed in solving semiconductor problems as well. However, there are some additional factors involved in semiconductor design that do not apply to vacuum tubes. In fact, much of the analysis required with vacuum tubes is unnecessary with modern solid-state components since many of the problems have already been "solved" before the device leaves the counter at the radio store. That is, amplifiers such as those in integrated circuits have the peripheral elements built in, and there is no need to determine the gain or other parameters such as the values of bias resistors.

The Triode Amplifier

A simple network using a triode vacuum tube is shown in Fig. 43A, and a typical set of characteristic curves is illustrated in Fig. 44A. The first chore in finding a suitable linear approximation for the triode is to determine an optimum operating point. Generally speaking, a point in the center of the set of curves is desirable and is indicated by point Q in Fig. 44A. (Other areas are aften picked for power-amplifier operation, but the goal here is to find a point where the maximum voltage swing is possible without entering regions where the nonlinearities affect the linear approximation.)

In the particular operating point chosen, the cathode to grid voltage is −3, the cathode to plate voltage is 280, and the plate current is 10 mA. It is assumed that the input signal source in Fig. 43A is a short-circuit at dc, and a 3-V battery connected as shown results in a dc voltage of −3 being applied to the grid at all times. Such a battery is called a bias battery or bias supply.

The next step is to determine how the plate voltage varies with grid voltage (e_g) for a constant plate current. Assuming that the characteristic curves were completely linear, this would permit evaluation of an equivalent ac voltage generator as shown in Fig. 43B. For a constant plate current of 10 mA, the plate voltage changes from 325 (point b) to 230 (point a) when the grid voltage is changed from −4 to −2 (Fig. 44A).

These numbers can be used to compute the amplification factor (μ) of the triode which is

$$\mu = \frac{325 - 230}{(-4) - (-2)} = -47.5$$

Fig. 43 — Basic triode amplifier and equivalent circuit.

Fig. 44 — Triode characteristics and derivations of small-signal parameters.

Quite often a set of characteristics will not be published for a triode, and only the

amplification factor will be given along with a typical operating point. However, note that the amplification factor is negative. This means that for an increase in the signal voltage (e_{in}), the controlled generator decreases in voltage. Consequently, there is a 180° phase shift between the input voltage and the controlled source. (Note the polarity of the generator shown in Fig. 43B.)

In order to complete the equivalent generator circuit, the source impedance must be computed. This is accomplished by determining how the plate voltage varies with plate current at constant grid voltage as shown in Fig. 44B. The plate resistance is then

$$r_p = \frac{325 - 240}{(15 - 5) \times 10^{-3}} = 8500 \text{ ohms}$$

which must be considered to be in series with the controlled source of Fig. 43B.

It should be pointed out that the reasoning why this procedure is valid has not been presented. That is, why was the amplification factor defined as the ratio of a change in plate voltage to change in grid voltage at constant current? Unfortunately, the calculations involved, although not difficult, are somewhat sophisticated. Some knowledge of the subject of partial differential equations is required for the theoretical derivation of these parameters. However, an intuitive idea can be obtained from the following.

If the characteristics were completely linear, instead of being nonlinear as shown, the equivalent generator would not be affected by changes in plate current, but only by changes in grid voltage. For instance, if the plate current was increased from 10 to 17 mA (Fig. 44A), the amplification factor would be the equivalent of the change in voltage represented by the line cd divided by − 2. However, since the length of cd is almost the same as that of ab (the difference in plate voltage for a − 2-V change at 10 mA), it can be concluded μ doesn't change very much — at least not in the center region of the characteristics.

Similar considerations hold for the plate resistance, r_p. It wouldn't matter if the curve for − 4 or − 2 V was picked (Fig. 44B), since the change in plate voltage vs. plate current would be approximately the same. Entities such as μ and r_p are often called incremental or small-signal parameters. This means they are valid for small ac voltages or currents around some operating point, but less so for large variations in signal or for regions removed from the specified operating point. Also, such parameters are not closely related to dc voltage characteristics. For instance, a static plate resistance could be defined as the ratio of plate voltage to plate current. For the − 3-V operating point chosen, the static plate resistance would be 280 divided by 10 × 10^{-2} or 28 kΩ. This is considerably different from the small-signal

plate resistance determined previously, which was 8500 ohms.

Amplifier Gain

The ratio of the variation in voltage across the load resistance to change in input voltage is defined as the gain of the amplifier. For the equivalent circuit shown in Fig. 43B, this ratio would be

$$A = \frac{e_o}{e_{in}}$$

To solve for the gain, the first step is to determine the incremental plate current. This is just the source voltage divided by the total resistance of the circuit mesh or

$$i_p = \frac{47.5 e_{in}}{10 + 8.5} \text{mA}$$

The output voltage is then

$$e_o = i_p 10.$$

Combining these two equations gives

$$A = \frac{e_o}{e_{in}} = \frac{(47.5)(10)}{10 + 8.5} = 25.67$$

It is inconvenient to have the input and output voltages defined with opposite polarities as shown in Fig. 43B. Therefore, the gain becomes negative as illustrated in the triangle in Fig. 43C. A triangle is the standard way of representing an amplifier stage in block diagram form. The amplifier gain depends on the load resistance, Rl. A general formula for the gain of the circuit of Fig. 43B is

$$A = \frac{-\mu R_L}{r_p + R_L}$$

Feedback

Being able to eliminate the equivalent circuit and use only one parameter such as the gain permits analysis of more complicated networks. A very important application occurs when part of the output energy of an amplifier is returned to the input circuit and gets amplified again. Since energy is being fed back into the input, the general phenomenon is called feedback. The manner in which feedback problems are analyzed is illustrated in Fig. 45. The output voltage is sampled by a network in the box marked beta and is multiplied by this term. This transformed voltage then appears in series with the input voltage, e_{in} which is applied to the input terminals of the amplifier (triangle with A_o). A_o is defined as the open-loop gain. It is the ratio of the voltage that appears between terminals 3 and 4 when a voltage is applied to terminals 1 and 2. The circuit of Fig. 45 is an example of voltage feedback; a similar analysis holds for networks incorporating current feedback.

The closed-loop gain, A_c, can then be found by inspection of Fig. 45. From the

diagram, the output voltage must be

$$e_o = A_o(e_{in} + \beta e_o)$$

Rearranging terms gives

$$e_o(1 - \beta A_o) = A_o e_{in}$$

The closed-loop gain is defined by

$$A_c = \frac{A_o}{1 - \beta A_o} = \frac{e_o}{e_{in}}$$

Cathode Bias

As an application of the feedback concept, consider the amplifier circuit shown in Fig. 46. It will be recalled that a bias battery was required in the previous example. A method of eliminating this extra source is to insert a small-value resistor in series with the cathode lead to ground (Fig. 46A). In terms of the amplifier block diagram, the circuit of Fig. 46B results. The next task is to evaluate the open-loop gain and the value of β.

With the exception of the cathode resistor, the circuit of Fig. 46 is the same as that of Fig. 43. Consequently, the ac plate current must be

$$i_p = \frac{-\mu e_{12}}{r_p + R_L + R_c}$$

The open-loop gain can then be determined from

$$\frac{e_o}{e_{12}} = A_o = \frac{-\mu R_L}{r_p + R_L + R_c}$$

Next, β is determined from the expression for output voltage

$$e_o = i_p R_L$$

and the feedback voltage, which is

$$e_f = i_p R_c$$

Then β is

$$\beta = \frac{e_f}{e_o} = \frac{i_p R_c}{i_p R_L} = \frac{R_c}{R_L}$$

Note that β is positive since if the path 1 to 2 is considered, the feedback voltage is added to the input signal. Substituting the values of β and A_o into the feedback equation gives

$$A_c = \frac{A_o}{1 - \frac{R_c}{R_L} A_o}$$

which after some manipulation becomes

$$A_c = \frac{-\mu R_L}{r_p + R_L + (1 + \mu)R_c}$$

Comparison of this equation with the one for the previous circuit with no cathode resistor reveals that the gain has decreased

because of the term $(1 + \mu)R_c$ in the denominator. Such an effect is called negative or degenerative feedback.

On the other hand, if the feedback was such that the gain increased, regenerative or positive feedback would result. Positive feedback can be either beneficial or detrimental in nature, and the study of feedback is an important one in electronics. For instance, frequency generation is possible in a circuit called an oscillator. But on the other hand, unwanted oscillation or instability in an amplifier is very undesirable.

Oscillators

A special case of feedback occurs if the term $1 - \beta A_o$ becomes zero. This would mean the closed-loop gain would become infinite. An implication of this effect is that a very small input signal would be amplified and fed back and amplified again until the output voltage became infinite. Either that, or amplifier output would exist with no signal input. Random noise would trigger the input into producing output.

Of course, an infinite output voltage is a physical impossibility and circuit limitations such as the nonlinearities of the active device would alter the feedback equation. For instance, at high output voltage swings, the amplifier would either saturate (be unable to supply more current) or limit (be cut off because the grid was too negative), and A_o would decrease.

It should be stressed that it is the product of βA_o that must be 1.0 for oscillations to occur. In the general case, both β and A_o may be complex numbers unlike those of the cathode-bias problem just discussed. That is, there is a phase shift associated with A_o and β with the phase shift of the product being equal to the sum of the individual phase shifts associated with each entity.

Therefore, if the total phase shift is 180° and if the amplitude of the product is 1.0, oscillations will occur. At low frequencies, these conditions normally are the result of the effect of reactive components. A typical example is shown in Fig. 47; the configuration is called a tuned-plate tuned-grid oscillator. If the input circuit consisting of L1 and C1 is tuned to a frequency f_o, with the output circuit (L2, C2) tuned to the same frequency, a high impedance to ground will exist at the input and output of the amplifier. Consequently, a small capacitance value represented by C_f is capable of supplying sufficient voltage feedback from the plate to the grid.

At other frequencies, or if either circuit is detuned, oscillations may not occur. For instance, off-resonant conditions in the output tank will reduce the output voltage and in effect, reduce the open-loop gain to the point where oscillations will cease. On the other hand, if the input circuit is detuned far from f_o, it will present a low impedance in series with the relatively high reactance of C_f. The voltage divider thus formed will result in a small value for β and

Fig. 45 — Network illustrating voltage feedback.

Fig. 46 — Feedback example of an amplifier with cathode bias.

Fig. 47 — Tuned-plate tuned-grid oscillator.

the conditions for oscillations will not be fulfilled. However, for conditions near f_o, both the amplitude and phase of the βA_o product will be correct for oscillations to occur.

Under some conditions, the voltage across the tank circuit may be sufficient to cause the grid to be driven positive with respect to the cathode, and grid current will flow through C_g. During the rest of the RF cycle, C_g will discharge through R_g, causing a negative bias voltage to be ap-

Fig. 48 — Hartley and Colpitts oscillators.

plied to the grid. This bias voltage sets the operating point of the oscillator and prevents excessive current flow.

Two other common type of oscillators are shown in Fig. 48. In Fig. 48A, feedback voltage is applied across a tapped inductor while in Fig. 48B, the voltage is applied across a capacitor instead. Quite often, a tuned plate circuit is not employed and an RF choke coil provides a high impedance load instead.

Classes of Amplifier Service

The amplifiers discussed so far have been described mostly in terms of ideal linear gain blocks. Class-A amplifiers, with or without negative feedback, reproduce the input signal with the greatest fidelity or least distortion. They accomplish this at the expense of poor power efficiency, meaning the signal power delivered to the load is usually only a small fraction of the dc power taken from the power supply. The remainder must be dissipated as heat. The maximum theoretical efficiency for a class-A amplifier is 50 percent, with 25 percent being a more typical figure. One factor preventing the theoretical maximum efficiency from being realized is that a practical amplifying device cannot be a perfect conductor — it will have a finite minimum voltage drop that prevents the full power supply potential from being impressed across the load. The operating point for a class-A amplifier is chosen to permit power supply current to flow over the entire 360° of the input signal cycle, and the average supply current does not vary with the signal level.

An advantage of a class-A amplifier, aside from nearly perfect input waveform reproduction (linearity), is that it requires minimal energy from the signal source. So while the power efficiency is poor, the power gain can be extremely high. The amplifier described in Figs. 43 and 44 operates in class-A.

An amplifier operating in class-B is biased so that no power supply current flows without an input signal applied. Current is taken from the supply over exactly 180° of the input signal cycle. A single-ended class-B amplifier that works only into a resistor for a load is, in effect, a half-wave rectifier (see Chapter 6), because one half of the input cycle is duplicated in the output and the other half is absent. This type of circuit finds some application as a rectifier or detector in radio work, but the distortion would be intolerable if it were used as an audio amplifier.

Class-B amplifiers can be used in low-distortion applications, however. Two class-B devices can be combined in a push-pull circuit. The two input terminals are driven 180° out of phase, so the amplifying devices conduct on opposite half cycles of the input signal. The output terminals are similarly coupled out of phase (usually by means of a transformer) to reproduce the input waveform faithfully.

A single-ended class-B stage is suitable for linear RF amplification if the load is a tuned circuit having a Q of five or better. The flywheel (ringing) effect of the tank circuit supplies the missing half of the output cycle. The efficiency of this type of amplifier is typically 60 percent.

An amplifier that is biased so as to conduct over the entire cycle for small input signals but at a reduced angle for large signals is a class-AB amplifier. The operating point is adjusted for the desired compromise among efficiency, power gain and linearity.

The output terminal of a single-device class-A, AB or B amplifier operated without negative feedback acts as a current source. This means that the instantaneous power supply current is essentially independent of the supply potential and is determined by the input signal amplitude. When an amplifying device is driven into saturation, that is, increasing the input amplitude causes no further increase in output, the output terminal no longer approximates a current source. Instead, the output terminal becomes "ohmic," meaning that the supply current varies approximately linearly with the supply voltage

The signal output voltage also varies linearly with the supply voltage. This effect is highly useful in an important mode of radiotelephony. The saturated amplifier just described is called class-C. Its operating point is selected to allow power supply current to flow only in narrow pulses corresponding to the peaks of the input signal. Class-C amplifiers are extremely

nonlinear, and the harmonics produced in the wave form distortion process make the class-C amplifier useful as a frequency multiplier. High-Q tank circuits are required to suppress unwanted frequency components generated by a class-C stage.

Apart from its utility as an amplitude modulated amplifier or a frequency multiplier, the principal asset of a class-C amplifier is high power efficiency. The practical efficiency in straight amplifier service can run as high as 85 percent, but considerable drive power is required from the signal source, so the power gain is not as high as can be obtained in class-A or B. In multiplier service the maximum theoretical efficiency is the reciprocal of the harmonic number.

Still higher efficiency can be obtained from class-D and class-E amplifiers. In these circuits the active devices act as saturated switches that are controlled by the input signal. The class-E RF circuit is a recent development (1970s) by WA1HQC that yields high efficiency in an interesting way: The single active device switches the supply current through the load at critical points of the waveform. The output waveform is such that the electronic switch does not conduct current and withstand voltage simultaneously, resulting in very little energy waste. As in the class-C case, this output waveform is rich in harmonics, which must be filtered carefully.

Glossary of Radio Terms

active — As used in active filter or active device: A device or circuit that requires an operating voltage. (See passive.)

analog — A term used in computer work, meaning a system which operates with numbers represented by directly measurable quantities (analog readout mechanical dial system. See digital).

attenuator — A passive network that reduces the power level of a signal without introducing appreciable distortion.

balun — Balanced to unbalanced-line transformer.

bank wound — Pertaining to a coil (inductor) that has two or more layers of wire, each being wound over the top of the preceding one. (See solenoid.)

bandpass — A circuit or component characteristic that permits the passage of a single band of frequencies while attenuating those frequencies above and below that frequency band.

band-reject — A circuit or device that rejects a specified frequency band while passing those frequencies that lie above and below the rejected band (opposite of band-pass). Sometimes called band-rejection, as applied to a filter.

bandwidth — The frequency width of circuit or component, such as a band-pass filter or tuned circuit. Usually measured at the half-power points of the response curve (−3 dB points).

base loading — Applies to vertical antennas for mobile and fixed-location use; an inductance placed near the ground end of a vertical radiator to change the electrical length. With variations the inductor aids in impedance matching.

bifilar — Two conducting elements used in parallel; for example, two parallel wires wound on a coil form.

bilateral — Having two symmetrical sides or terminals; a filter (as one example) that has a 50-ohm characteristic at each port, with either port suitable as the input or output one.

bias — To influence current to flow in a specified direction by means of dc voltage; forward bias on a transistor stage, or grid bias on a tube type of amplifier.

blanker — A circuit or device that momentarily removes a pulse or signal so it is not passed to the next part of a circuit; a noise blanker. Not to be confused with clipper, which clips part of a pulse or waveform.

bridge — An electrical instrument used for measuring or comparing inductance, impedance, capacitance or resistance by comparing the ratio of two opposing voltages to a known ratio; to place one component in parallel with another; to join to conductors or components by electrical means.

broadband — A device or circuit that is broadband has the capability of being operated over a broad range of frequencies. A broadband antenna is one example.

cascade — One device or circuit that directly follows another; two or more similar devices or circuits in which the output of one is fed to the input of the succeeding one (tandem).

cascode — Two-stage amplifier having a grid-driven (or common-emitter or source) input circuit and a grounded-grid (or common base or gate) output circuit.

chip — Slang term for an integrated circuit, meaning a chip of semiconductor material upon which an IC is formed.

clamp — A circuit that holds or maintains each occurrence of a predetermined characteristic of a waveform at some specified level.

clipper — A device or circuit that limits the instantaneous value of a wave form to some specified maximum value. The clipper establishes a value boundary that the applied waveform is not allowed to exceed.

closed loop — A signal path that includes a forward route, a feedback path, and a summing point which provides a closed circuit. In broad terms, an amplifying circuit providing voltage or power gain while being terminated correctly at the input and output ports, inclusive of feedback.

cold end — The circuit end of a component that is connected to ground or is bypassed for ac or RF voltage (the grounded end of a coil or capacitor).

common-mode signal — The instantaneous algebraic average of two signals applied to a balanced circuit, both signals being referred to a common reference.

composite — Made of a collection of distinct components; a complete (composite) circuit rather than a discrete part of an overall circuit.

conversion loss/gain — Relating to a mixer circuit from which less output energy is taken than is supplied at the input-signal port (loss); when a mixer delivers greater signal output than is supplied to the input-signal port (gain).

converter — A circuit used to convert one frequency to another. In a receiver the converter stage converts the incoming signals to the intermediate frequency.

core — An element made of magnetic material, serving as part of a path for magnetic flux.

damping — A progressive reduction in amplitude of a wave with respect to time (usually referenced to microseconds or milliseconds); a device or network added to a circuit to damp unwanted oscillations.

decay time — The period of time during which the stored energy or information decays to a specified value less than its initial value, such as the discharge time of a timing network.

decibel (dB) — A logarithmic expression of power ratio; also used as an expression of voltage ratios, provided the voltages appear across identical values of resistance or impedance. A decibel is 1/10 of a bel, and represents the smallest change in the power level of an audio tone that the human ear can detect.

decoder — A device or circuit that translates a combination of signals into a single signal representing that combination. One such circuit is that used for decoding the output signal of a DTMF pad.

differential amplifier — An amplifier with an output signal that is proportional to the algebraic difference between two input signals (sometimes called a difference amplifier).

digital — Refers to signals having or circuits that work with a finite number of discrete levels or states, as opposed to an analog signal which may have an infinite number of levels.

diplexing — The simultaneous transmission or reception of two signals while using a common antenna, made possible by using a device called a diplexer. Used in TV broadcasting to transmit visual and aural carriers by means of a single antenna.

discrete — A single device or circuit (a transistor as opposed to an IC). (See composite.)

dish — An antenna reflector for use at VHF and higher that has a concave shape. For example, a part of a sphere or paraboloid.

Doppler — The phenomenon evidenced by the change in the observed frequency of a wave in a transmission system caused by a time rate of change in the effective length of the path of travel between source and the point of observation.

drift — A change in component or circuit operation over time.

drive — RF energy applied at the input of an RF amplifier (RF driving power or voltage).

DTMF — Dual-tone multifrequency, such as a DTMF pad, which is sometimes called a Touch-Tone® pad.

duplex — Simultaneous two-way independent transmission and reception in both directions.

duplexer — A device that permits simultaneous transmission and reception of related signal energy while using a common antenna (see diplexing).

dynamic range — Difference in decibels between the overload level and minimum discernible signal level (MDS) in a system, such as a receiver. Parameters include desensitization point and distortion products as referenced to the receiver noise floor.

EME — Earth-moon-earth. Communications carried on by bouncing signals off the lunar surface. Commonly referred to as moonbounce.

empirical — Not based on mathematical procedures; experimental endeavor during design or modification of a circuit. Founded on case-history experience or intuition.

enabling — The preparation of a circuit for a subsequent function (enabling pulse or signal).

encoder — A circuit or device which changes discrete inputs into coded combinations of outputs. A DTMF pad is an encoder.

excitation — Signal energy used to drive a transmitter stage (see drive). Voltage applied to a component to actuate it, such as the field coil or a relay.

Faraday rotation — Rotation of the plane of polarization of an electromagnetic wave when traveling through a magnetic field. In space communications this effect occurs when signals traverse the ionosphere.

feedback — A portion of the output voltage being fed back to the input of an amplifier. Description includes ac and dc voltage which can be used separately or together, depending on the particular circuit.

feedthrough — Energy passing through a circuit or component, but not usually desired. A type of capacitor which can be mounted on a chassis or panel wall to permit feeding through a dc voltage while bypassing ac or RF to ground. Sometimes called a coaxial capacitor.

ferromagnetic — Material that has a relative permeability greater than unity and requires a magnetizing force. (Ferrite and powdered-iron rods and toroids).

finite — Having a definable quantity; a

finite value of resistance or other electrical measure.

flip-flop — An active circuit or device that can assume either of two stable stages at a given time, as dictated by the nature of the input signal.

floating — A circuit or conductor that is above ac or dc ground for a particular reason. Example: A floating ground bus which is not common to the circuit chassis.

gate — A circuit or device, depending on the nature of the input signal, which can permit the passage or blockage of a signal or dc voltage.

GDO — Abbreviation for a grid-dip or gate-dip oscillator (test instrument).

ground loop — A circuit-element condition (PC board conductor, metal chassis or metal cabinet wall) that permits the unwanted flow of ac from one circuit point to another.

half-power point — The two points on a response curve that are 3 dB lower in level than the peak power. Sometimes called the 3dB bandwidth.

Hall effect — The change of the electric conduction caused by the component of the magnetic field vector normal to the current density vector, which instead of being parallel to the electric field, forms an angle with it.

high end — Refers generally to the hot (RF or dc) end of a component or circuit; the end opposite the grounded or bypassed end (see cold end).

high level — The part of a circuit which is relatively high in power output and consumption as compared to the small signal end of a circuit. Example: A transmitter PA stage is the high-level amplifier, as might be the driver also.

high pass — Related mainly to filters or networks which are designed to pass energy above a specified frequency, but attenuate or block the passage of energy below that frequency.

high-Z — The high-impedance part of a circuit; a high-impedance microphone; a high-impedance transformer winding.

hot end — see high end.

hybrid — A combination of two generally unlike things; a circuit that contains transistors and tubes, for example.

ideal — A theoretically perfect circuit or component; a lossless transformer or device that functions without any faults.

insertion loss — That portion of a signal current or voltage that is lost as it passes through a circuit or device. The loss of power through a filter or other passive network.

interpolate — To estimate a value between two known values.

leakage — The flow of signal energy beyond a point at which it should not be present. Example: Signal leakage across a filter because of poor layout (stray coupling) or inadequate shielding.

linear amplification — The process by which a signal is amplified without altering the characteristic of the input waveform. Class-A, AB and B amplifiers are generally used for linear amplification.

load — A circuit or component that receives power; the power delivered to such a circuit or component. Example: A properly matched antenna is a load for a transmitter.

loaded — A circuit is said to be loaded when the desired power is being delivered to a load.

logic — Decision-making circuitry of the type found in computers.

long wire — A horizontal wire antenna that is one wavelength or greater in size. A long piece of wire (less than one wavelength) does not qualify as a long wire.

low end — see cold end.

low level — Low-power stage or stages of a circuit as referenced to the higher-power stages (see high level).

low pass — A circuit property that permits the passage of frequencies below a specified frequency but attenuates or blocks those frequencies above that frequency (see high pass).

low-Z — Low impedance (see high-Z).

mean — A value between two specified values; an intermediate value.

master oscillator — The primary oscillator for controlling a transmitter or receiver frequency. Can be a VFO (variable-frequency oscillator), VXO (variable crystal oscillator), PTO (permeability-tuned oscillator), PLL (phase-locked loop), LMO (linear master oscillator) or frequency synthesizer.

microwaves — AC signals having frequencies greater than about 1000 MHz.

modulation index — The ratio of the frequency deviation of the modulated wave to the frequency of the modulating signal.

narrowband — A device or circuit that can be operated only over a narrow range of frequencies. Low-percentage bandwidth.

network — A group of components connected together to form a circuit that will conduct power, and in most examples effect an impedance match. Examples: An LC matching network between stages of a transistorized transmitter.

noise figure — Of a two-port transducer the decibel ratio of the total noise power to the input noise power, when the input termination is at the standard temperature of 290 K.

nominal — A theoretical or designated quantity that may not represent the actual value. Sometimes referred to as the ball-park value.

op amp — Operational amplifier. A high-gain, feedback-controlled amplifier. Performance is controlled by external circuit elements.

open loop — A signal path that does not contain feedback (see closed loop).

parameter — The characteristic behavior of a device or circuit, such as the current gain of a 2N5109 transistor.

parametric amplifier — Synonym for reactance amplifier. An inverting parametric device for amplifying a signal without frequency translation from input to output. Used for low-noise UHF and microwave amplification.

parasitic — Unwanted condition or quantity, such as parasitic oscillations or parasitic capacitance; additional to the desired characteristic.

passive — Operating without an operating voltage. Example: An LC filter that contains no amplifier, or a diode mixer.

PEP — Peak envelope power; maximum amplitude that can be obtained with any combination of signals.

permeability — A term used to express relationships between magnetic induction and magnetic force.

pill — Slang expression for a transistor or an IC.

PL — Private Line, such as a repeater accessed by means of a specified tone.

PLL — Phase-locked loop.

port — The input or output terminal of a circuit or device.

prototype — A first full-scale working version of a circuit design.

Q_L — Loaded Q of a circuit.

Q_u — Unloaded Q of a circuit.

quagi — An antenna consisting of both full-wavelength loops (quad) and Yagi elements.

resonator — A general term for a high-Q resonant circuit, such as an element of a filter.

return — That portion of a circuit which permits the completion of current flow, usually to ground; a ground return.

ringing — The generation of an audible or visual signal by means of oscillation or pulsating current; the annoying sound developed in some audio filters when the Q is extremely high.

ripple — Pulsating current. Also, the gain depressions that exist in the flat portion of a band-pass response curve (above the −3 dB points on the curve). Example: Passband ripple in the nose of an IF filter response curve.

rise time — The time required for a pulse or waveform to reach a specified value from some smaller specified value. The specified values are typically 10 and 90 percent of the peak amplitude.

RMS — Root mean square. The square root of the mean of the square of the voltage or current during a complete cycle.

rotor — A moving rotary component within a rotation-control device. Examples include the moving plates of a variable capacitor and the armature of an alternator. Not to be confused with an antenna rotator, which is the total assembly.

saturation — A condition that exists when a further change in input produces no additional output (a saturated amplifier).

selectivity — A measure of circuit capability to separate the desired signal from those at other frequencies.

shunt — A device placed in parallel with or across part of another device. Examples: meter shunts, shunt-fed vertical antennas and a capacitor placed (shunted) across another capacitor.

solenoidal — A single-layer coil of wire wound to form a long cylinder.

spectral purity — The relative freedom of an emission from harmonics, spurious signals and noise.

standing-wave ratio — The ratio of the maximum to minimum voltage or current on a transmission line at least a quarter-wavelength long.

strip — General term for two or more stages of a circuit that in combination perform a particular function. Examples: a local-oscillator strip, an audio strip or an IF strip.

subharmonic — A frequency that is an integral submultiple of a frequency to which it is referred. A misleading term that implies that subharmonic energy can be created along with harmonic energy (not true). More aptly, a 3.5-MHz VFO driving a 40-meter transmitter, with 3.5-MHz leakage at the output, qualifying as a subharmonic.

tank — A circuit consisting of inductance and capacitance, capable of storing electrical energy over a band of frequencies continuously distributed about a single frequency at which the circuit is said to be resonant, or tuned.

toroidal — Doughnut-shaped physical format, such as a toroid core.

transducer — A device which is used to transport energy from one system (electrical, mechanical or acoustical) to another. Example: A loudspeaker or phonograph pickup.

transceiver — A combination transmitter and receiver that uses some parts of the circuit for both functions.

Transmatch — An LC network used to effect an impedance match between a transmitter and a feed line to an antenna.

transmission line — One or more conductors used to convey ac energy from one point to another, as from a radio station to its antenna.

transverter — A converter that permits transmitting and receiving at a specified frequency apart from the capability of the transceiver to which it is connected as a basic signal source. Example: a 2-meter transverter used in combination with an HF-band transceiver.

trap — A device consisting of L and C components that permits the blockage of a specified frequency while allowing the passage of other frequencies. Example: a wave trap or an antenna trap.

trifilar — Same as bifilar, but with three parallel conductors.

trigger — To initiate action in a circuit by introducing an energy stimulus from an external source, such as a scope trigger.

U — Symbol for unrepairable assembly, such as an integrated circuit (U1, U2, etc.).

unloaded — The opposite condition of loaded.

varactor — A two-terminal semiconductor device (diode) which exhibits a voltage-dependent capacitance. Used primarily as a tuning device or frequency multiplier at VHF and UHF.

VCO — Voltage-controlled oscillator. Uses tuning diodes that have variable dc applied to change their junction capacitances.

VSWR — Voltage standing-wave ratio. (See standing-wave ratio).

VU — Volume unit.

VXO — Variable crystal oscillator.

wave — A periodically varying electromagnetic field radiated from a conductor.

waveguide — A hollow conducting tube used to convey microwave energy.

wavelength — The distance between the two points of corresponding phase of two consecutive cycles of an electromagnetic signal.

X — The symbol for reactance.

Zener diode — A diode used to regulate voltage or function as a clamp or clipper. Named after the inventor.

Z — Symbol for a device or circuit that contains two or more components. Example: A parasitic suppressor that contains a resistor and an inductor in parallel (Z1, Z2, etc.). Z is also the symbol for impedance.

Chapter 4

Solid-State Basics

Solid-state devices are also called semi-conductors. The prefix semi means half. They have electrical properties between those of conductors and those of insulators.

The conductivity of a material is proportional to the number of free electrons in the material. Pure germanium and pure silicon crystals have relatively few free electrons. If, however, carefully controlled amounts of impurities (materials having a different atomic structure, such as arsenic or antimony) are added, the number of free electrons, and consequently the conductivity, is increased. When certain other impurities are introduced (such as aluminum, gallium or indium), an electron deficiency, or hole, is produced. As in the case of free electrons, the presence of holes encourages the flow of electrons in the semiconductor material, and the conductivity is increased. Semiconductor material that conducts by virtue of the free electrons is called N-type material; material that conducts by virtue of an electron deficiency is called P-type.

Electron and Hole Conduction

If a piece of P-type material is joined to a piece of N-type material as at A in Fig. 1 and a voltage is applied to the pair as at B, current will flow across the boundary or junction between the two (and also in the external circuit) when the battery has the polarity indicated. Electrons, indicated by the minus symbol, are attracted across the junction from the N material through the P material to the positive terminal of the battery. Holes, indicated by the plus symbol, are attracted in the opposite direction across the junction by the negative potential of the battery. Thus, current flows through the circuit by means of electrons moving one way and holes the other.

If the battery polarity is reversed, as at C, the excess electrons in the N material are attracted away from the junction and the holes in the P material are attracted by the negative potential of the battery away from the junction. This leaves the junction region without any current carriers; consequently, there is no conduction.

In other words, a junction of P- and N-type materials constitutes a rectifier. It differs from the vacuum-tube diode rectifier

in that there is a measurable, although comparatively very small, reverse current. The reverse current results from the presence of some carriers of the type opposite to those that principally characterize the material.

With the two plates separated by practically zero spacing, the junction forms a capacitor of relatively high capacitance. This places a limit on the upper frequency at which semiconductor devices of this construction will operate, as compared with vacuum tubes. Also, the number of excess electrons and holes in the material depends on temperature, and since the conductivity in turn depends on the number of excess holes and electrons, the device is more temperature sensitive than is a vacuum tube.

Capacitance may be reduced by making the contact area very small. This is done by means of a point contact, a tiny P-type region being formed under the contact point during manufacture when N-type material is used for the main body of the device.

SEMICONDUCTOR DIODES

The vacuum-tube diode has been replaced in modern equipment designs. Semiconductor diodes are more efficient because they do not consume filament power. They are much smaller than tube diodes. In low-level applications they operate cooler than tubes do. Solid-state diodes are superior to tube types in that solid-state diodes operate into the microwave region, while most vacuum-tube diodes are not practical at frequencies above 50 MHz.

Semiconductor diodes fall into two main categories, structurally. Although they can be made from silicon or germanium crystals, they are usually classified as PN junction diodes or point-contact diodes. These formats are illustrated in Fig. 2. Junction diodes are used from dc to the microwave region, but point-contact diodes are intended primarily for RF applications. The internal capacitance of a point-contact diode is considerably less than that of a junction diode designed for the same circuit application. As the operating frequency is increased the unwanted internal and external capacitance of a diode becomes

Fig. 1 — A PN junction (A) and its behavior when conducting (B) and nonconducting (C).

Fig. 2 — A point-contact type of diode is shown at A. A junction diode is depicted at B and the diode symbol is at C. The cathode end is usually indicated by a band on the body of the device.

more troublesome to the designer. Where a given junction type of diode may exhibit a capacitance of several picofarads, the point-contact device will have an internal capacitance of 1 pF or less.

Selenium Diodes

Power rectifiers made from selenium were in common use in ac power supplies before 1965. Selenium diodes are characterized by high forward voltage drop (which increases with diode age) and high reverse leakage current. The voltage drop causes the device to dissipate power, and a typical rectifier stack has large cooling fins. An additional shortcoming of selenium rectifiers is that they sometimes emit toxic fumes when they burn out. When replacing selenium diodes with silicon units, be certain that the filter capacitors (and the entire equipment) can withstand the higher output voltage. Some early solar cells were made of selenium, but silicon devices have taken over this area, too.

Germanium Diodes

The germanium diode is characterized by a relatively large current flow when small amounts of voltage are applied in the forward direction (Fig. 1). Small currents will flow in the reverse (back) direction for much larger applied voltages. A representative curve is shown in Fig. 3. The dynamic resistance in either the forward or back direction is determined by the change in current that occurs, at any given point on the curve, when the applied voltage is changed by a small amount. The forward resistance will vary somewhat in the region of very small applied voltages. However, the curve is mostly straight, indicating a relatively constant dynamic resistance. For small applied voltages the resistance is on the order of 200 ohms or less.

The back resistance exhibits considerable variation and depends on the specific applied voltage during the test. It may vary from a few thousand ohms to well over a megohm. The back resistance of a germanium diode is considerably lower than that of a silicon diode. The back resistance for silicon is greater than a megohm in most instances, but the germanium diode is normally less than a megohm.

Common Silicon Diodes

Apart from the fact that silicon P and N materials are used in the formation of a silicon junction diode, the characteristics of these devices are similar to those of germanium diodes. The voltage/current curves of Fig. 3 are representative.

The junction barrier voltage for silicon diodes is somewhat higher (approximately 0.7 volt) than that of a germanium diode (about 0.3 volt). The majority of the diodes in use today fall into the silicon class. They are rugged and reliable from RF small-signal applications to dc power use.

Silicon diodes are available in ratings of 1000 volts (PIV) or greater. Many of these diodes can accommodate dc in excess of 100 amperes. The primary rule in pre-venting damage to any diode is to operate the device within the maximum ratings specified by the manufacturer. The device temperature is one of the important parameters. Heat sinks are used with diodes that must handle large amounts of power, thereby holding the diode junction temperature at a safe level.

The behavior of junction diodes under varying temperatures is of interest to designers of circuits that must perform over some temperature range. The relationship between forward bias current, forward bias voltage and temperature is defined by the classic diode equation:

$$I_f = I_s \left(e^{\frac{qV}{kt}} - 1 \right)$$

where q is the fundamental electronic charge (1.6×10^{-19} coulombs), V is the bias potential, k is Boltzmann's constant (1.38×10^{-23} joules/kelvin), kelvin = °Celsius + 273), t is the junction temperature in kelvins, I_s is the reverse-bias saturation current, I_f is the forward-bias current and e is the natural logarithmic base (2.718). The ratio q/k is approximately 11,600, so the diode equation can be written:

$$I_f = I_s \left(e^{\frac{11,600V}{t}} - 1 \right) \quad \text{(Eq. 1)}$$

It is useful to have an expression for the voltage developed across the junction when the forward current is held constant. To obtain such an expression we must solve the diode equation for V. Expanding the right side of Eq. 1 yields:

$$I_f = I_s e^{\frac{11,600V}{t}} - I_s \quad \text{(Eq. 2)}$$

Adding I_s to both sides gives:

$$I_f + I_s = I_s e^{\frac{11,600V}{t}} \quad \text{(Eq. 3)}$$

Dividing through by I_s produces:

$$\frac{I_f}{I_s} + 1 = e^{\frac{11,600V}{t}} \quad \text{(Eq. 4)}$$

which implies

$$\frac{11,600V}{t} = \ln \left(\frac{I_f}{I_s} + 1 \right) \quad \text{(Eq. 5)}$$

Multiplying each term by $\frac{t}{11,600}$

leaves:

$$V = \frac{t}{11,600} \ln \left(\frac{I_f}{I_s} + 1 \right) \quad \text{(Eq. 6)}$$

The undetermined quantity in Eq. 6 is I_s, the reverse saturation current. In ordinary silicon signal diodes this current approximately doubles with each 4.5 kelvin-temperature increase. A mathematical ex-

Fig. 3 — Typical point-contact diode (germanium) characteristic curve. Because the back current is much smaller than the forward current, a different scale is used for back voltage and current.

pression for this behavior as a function of temperature is:

$$I_{s(t)} = 2I_{s(t-4.5)} \quad \text{(Eq. 7)}$$

At room temperature (300 kelvins), the reverse saturation current is on the order of 10^{-13} amperes. Eq. 7 describes a phenomenon similar to radioactive decay, where the 4.5-kelvin current-doubling interval is analogous to the half-life of a radioactive substance. This equation with the given initial condition sets up an initial-value problem, the solution of which is:

$$I_{s(t)} = 10^{-13} e^{\frac{(t-300)\ln 2}{4.5}} \quad \text{(Eq. 8)}$$

Substituting this expression for I_s into Eq. 6 produces the diode voltage drop as a function of temperature for a constant current:

$$V_{(t)} = \frac{t}{11,600} \times$$

$$\ln \left[\frac{I_f}{10^{-13} e^{\frac{(t-300)\ln 2}{4.5}}} + 1 \right] \quad \text{(Eq. 9)}$$

The temperature coefficient of the junction potential can be obtained from the partial derivative of V with respect to t, but it's a simple matter (with the aid of a pocket calculator) to extract the information directly from Eq. 9. If the forward current is fixed at 1 milliampere, the diode drop at room temperature is 0.5955 volts. This potential decreases at an initial rate of 2 millivolts per kelvin. The temperature coefficient gradually increases to 3 millivolts per kelvin at 340 kelvins. While the temperature curve isn't linear, it is gradual enough to be considered linear over small intervals. When the bias current is increased to 100 milliamperes, the room temperature junction potential increases to 0.7146 volts as might be expected, but the temperature coefficient stays well-behaved. The initial potential decrease is 1.6 millivolts per kelvin, and this value increases to 2.5 millivolts per kelvin at 340 kelvins.

The significance of the very minor dependence of temperature coefficient on bias current is that it isn't necessary to use an elaborate current regulator to bias diodes used in temperature-compensation applications. The equations defining the behavior of junction diodes are approximations. Some of the voltages were expressed to five significant figures so the reader can verify his calculations, but this much precision exceeds the accuracy of the approximations.

Diodes as Switches

Solid-state switching is accomplished easily by using diodes or transistors in place of mechanical switches or relays. The technique is not a complicated one at dc and audio frequencies when large amounts of power are being turned on and off, or transferred from one circuit point to another.

Examples of shunt and series diode switching are given in Fig. 4. The illustration at A shows a 1N914 RF-switching diode as a shunt on-off element between C1 and ground. When + 12 volts is applied to D1 through R1, the diode saturates and effectively adds C1 to the oscillator tank circuit. R1 should be no less than 2200 ohms in value to prevent excessive current flow through the diode junction (I_{max} = 12 V / 2200 Ω).

Series diode switching is shown in Fig. 4B. In this example the diode, D1, is inserted in the audio signal path. When S1 is in the ON position the diode current path is to ground through R2, and the diode saturates to become a closed switch. When S1 is in the OFF state R1 is grounded and + 12 volts is applied to the diode cathode. In this mode D1 is back biased (cut off) to prevent audio voltage from reaching the transistor amplifier. This technique is useful when several stages in a circuit are controlled by a single mechanical switch or relay. RF circuits can also be controlled by means of series diode switching.

A significant advantage to the use of diode switching is that long signal leads are eliminated. The diode switch can be placed directly at the circuit point of interest. The dc voltage that operates it can be at some convenient remote point. The diode recovery time (switching speed) must be chosen for the frequency of operation. In other words, the higher the operating frequency the faster the switching speed required. For dc and audio applications one can use ordinary silicon power-supply rectifier diodes.

Diodes as Gates

Diodes can be placed in series with dc leads to function as gates. Specifically, they can be used to allow current to flow in one direction only. An example of this technique is given in Fig. 5A.

A protective circuit for the solid-state transmitter is effected by the addition of

Fig. 4 — A silicon-switching diode, D1, is used at A to place C1 in the circuit. At B is shown a series switch with D1 in the signal path.

D1 in the 13.6-volt dc line to the equipment. The diode allows the flow of positive current, but there will be a drop of approximately 0.7 volt across the diode, requiring a supply voltage of 14.3. Should the operator mistakenly connect the supply leads in reverse, current will not flow through D1 to the transmitter. In this application the diode acts as a gate. D1 must be capable of passing the current taken by the transmitter without overheating.

A power type of diode can be used in shunt with the supply line to the transmitter for protective purposes. This method is illustrated in Fig. 5B. If the supply polarity is crossed accidentally, D1 will draw high current and cause F1 to open. This is sometimes referred to as a crowbar protection circuit. The primary advantage of circuit B over circuit A is that there is no voltage drop between the supply and the transmitter.

Diodes as Voltage References

Zener diodes are discussed later in this chapter. They are used as voltage references or regulators. Conventional junction diodes can be used for the same purposes by taking advantage of their barrier-voltage characteristics. The greater the voltage needed, the higher the number of diodes

Fig. 5 — D1 at A protects the equipment if the supply leads are cross-polarized in error. At B the fuse will blow if the power supply is connected for the wrong polarity.

used in series. Some examples of this technique are given in Fig. 6. At A the diode (D1) establishes a fixed value of forward bias (0.7 V) for the transistor, thereby functioning as a regulator. R1 is chosen to permit a safe amount of current to flow through the diode junction while it is conducting at the barrier voltage.

Fig. 6 — D1 establishes a 0.7-volt bias reference at A. Approximately 1.4 volts of emitter bias is established by connecting D1 and D2 in series at illustration B.

Fig. 7 — High-speed switching diodes of the 1N914 variety can be connected back to back and used as tuning diodes. As the reverse voltage is varied by means of R1, the internal capacitance of the diodes will change.

The circuit of Fig. 6B shows two diodes inserted in the emitter return of a relay-driver transistor. D1 and D2 set up a cutoff voltage of approximately 1.4. This reduces the static current of the transistor when for-ward bias is not provided at the transistor base. If too much static current flows, the relay may not drop out when the forward bias decays across the timing network. The more sensitive the relay the greater the

chance for such a problem. D1 and D2 prevent relay dropout problems of this variety. D3 is used as a transient suppressor. A spike will occur when the relay coil field collapses. If the amplitude of the spike is great enough, the transient, while following the dc bus in a piece of equipment, can destroy transistors and diodes elsewhere in the circuit. In this application the diode (D3) can be regarded as a clamp, since it clamps the spike at approximately 0.7 volt.

Using Diodes as Capacitors

Later in this chapter there is a discussion about VVC (voltage-variable capacitor) diodes. They are known also as tuning diodes and Varicap diodes. It is possible, however, to use ordinary silicon diodes as voltage-variable capacitors. This is ac-complished by taking advantage of the in-herent changes in diode junction capaci-tance as the reverse bias applied to them is changed. The primary limitation in using high-speed switching diodes of the 1N914 variety is a relatively low maximum capaci-tance. At a sacrifice to low minimum capacitance, diodes can be used in parallel to step up the maximum available capacitance.

An example of two 1N914 silicon diodes in a diode tuning circuit is given in Fig. 7. As R1 is adjusted to change the back bias on D1 and D2, there will be a variation in the junction capacitance. That change will alter the VFO operating frequency. The junction capacitance increases as the back bias is lowered. In the circuit shown here the capacitance will vary from roughly 5 pF to 15 pF as R1 is adjusted. The diodes used in circuits of this kind should have a high Q and excellent high-frequency characteristics. Generally, tuning diodes are less stable than mechanical variable capacitors are. This is because the diode junction capacitance will change as the ambient temperature varies. This circuit is not well suited to mobile applications because of its lack of stability.

Diode Clippers and Clamps

The previous mention of diode clamping action (D3 in Fig. 6) suggests that advan-tage can be taken of the characteristic bar-rier voltage of diodes to clip or limit the amplitude of a sine-wave. Although there are numerous applications in this general category, diode clippers are more familiar to the amateur in noise limiter, audio limiter and audio compressor circuits. Fig. 8 illustrates some typical circuits that use small-signal diodes as clamps and clippers. D1 in Fig. 8A functions as a bias clamp at the gate of the FET. It limits the positive sine-wave swing at approximately 0.7 V. Not only does the diode tend to regulate the bias voltage, it limits the transconduc-tance of the FET during the positive half of the cycle. This action restricts changes in transistor junction capacitance. As a result, frequency stability of the oscillator is enhanced and the generation of harmonic

Fig. 8 — D1 serves as a bias stabilization device at A (see text). At B, D1 and D2 are employed as clippers to flatten the positive and negative AF peaks. Clipping will occur at roughly 0.7 volt if silicon diodes are used. Audio filtering is required after the clipper to remove the harmonic currents caused by the diode action.

Fig. 9 — A simple diode frequency multiplier is shown at A. A balanced diode frequency doubler is at B. T1 is a trifilar-wound broadband toroid transformer.

currents is greatly minimized.

The circuit of Fig. 8B shows how a pair of diodes can be connected in back-to-back fashion for the purpose of clipping the negative and positive sine-wave peaks in an audio amplifier. If germanium diodes are used at D1 and D2 (1N34As or similar) the audio will limit at roughly 0.3 V. With silicon diodes (1N914 or rectifier types) the voltage will not exceed 0.7 V. R1 serves as the clipping-level control. An audio gain control is normally used after the clipper filter, along with some additional gain stages. The output of the clipper must be filtered to restore the sine wave if distortion is to be avoided. Diode clippers generate considerable harmonic currents, thereby requiring an RC or LC type of audio filter.

Diode Frequency Multipliers

Designers of RF circuits use small-signal diodes as frequency multipliers when they want to minimize the number of active devices (tubes or transistors) in a circuit. The primary disadvantage of diode multipliers is a loss of signal compared to that available from an active multiplier. Fig. 9 contains examples of diode frequency multipliers. The circuit at A is useful for obtaining odd or even multiples of the driving voltage. The efficiency of this circuit is not high, requiring that an amplifier

Fig. 10 — D1 at A is used as a simple AM detector. Two versions of diode product detectors are illustrated at B and C. BFO injection for B and C should be approximately 19 volts P-P for best detector performance.

be used after the diode multiplier in most applications. Resonator L1/C1 must be tuned to the desired output frequency.

A diode frequency doubler is shown at B in Fig. 9. It functions like a full-wave power-supply rectifier, where 60-Hz energy is transformed to 120-Hz by virtue of the diode action. This circuit will cause a loss of approximately 8 dB. Therefore, it is shown with a succeeding amplifier stage. If reasonable circuit balance is maintained, the 7-MHz energy will be down some 40 dB at the output of D1 and D2 — prior to the addition of L1 and C1. Additional suppression of the driving energy is realized by the addition of resonator L1/C1. T1 is a trifilar-wound toroidal transformer. At this frequency (7 MHz) a 0.5-inch-diameter ferrite core (permeability of 125) will suffice if the trifilar winding contains approximately 10 turns. Additional information on this subject is given in the ARRL publication, *Solid State Design for the Radio Amateur*.

Diode Detectors and Mixers

Diodes are effective as detectors and mixers when circuit simplicity and strong-signal-handling capability are desired. Impedance matching is an important design objective when diodes are used as detectors and mixers. The circuits are lossy, just as is the case with diode frequency multipliers. A diode detector or mixer will exhibit a conversion loss of 7 dB or more in a typical example. Therefore, the gain before and after the detector or mixer must be chosen to provide an acceptable noise figure for the overall circuit in which the diode stage is used. This is a particularly critical factor when diode mixers are used at the front end of a receiver.

A significant advantage in the use of diode mixers and detectors is that they are broadband in nature, and they provide a wide dynamic range. Hot-carrier diodes are preferred by some designers for these circuits, but the 1N914 class of switching diodes provides good performance if they are matched for a similar resistance before being placed in the circuit.

Fig. 10 illustrates some examples of diode detectors. A basic AM detector is shown at A. The circuit at B is that of a

two-diode product detector. R1 and the two bypass capacitors serve as an RF filter to keep signal and BFO energy out of the following AF amplifier stage. A four-diode product detector is illustrated at C. T1 is a trifilar-wound broadband transformer. The characteristic input impedance of T1 is 50 ohms. An RF filter follows this detector also. BFO injection voltage for the detectors at B and C should be between 8 and 10 volts P-P for best detector performance.

Circuits for typical diode mixers are given in Fig. 11. Product detectors are also mixers except for the frequencies involved. The output energy is at audio frequencies rather than at some RF intermediate frequency. The examples at A and B can be compared to those at C and D for the purpose of illustrating the similarity between balanced modulators and mixers. It is evident that product detectors, balanced modulators and mixers are of the same family. The diodes in all examples can be hot-carrier types or matched silicon switching diodes of the 1N914 class.

C1 and C2 in Fig. 11C and D are used for balancing purposes. They can be employed in the same manner with the circuits at A and B. The transformers in each illustration are trifilar-wound toroidal types. They provide a broadband circuit characteristic.

Hot-Carrier Diodes

One of the more recent developments in the semiconductor field is the hot-carrier diode, or HCD. It is a metal-to-semiconductor, majority-carrier conducting device with a single rectifying junction. The carriers are typically high-mobility electrons in an N type of semiconductor material. The HCD is particularly useful in mixers and detectors at VHF and higher. Notable among the good features of this type of diode are its higher operating frequency and lower conduction voltage compared to a PN junction diode such as the 1N914.

When compared to a point-contact diode, the HCD is mechanically and electrically superior. It has lower noise, greater conversion efficiency, larger square-law capability, higher breakdown voltage and lower reverse current. The internal capacitance of the HCD is markedly lower than that of a PN junction diode and it is less subject to temperature variations.

Fig. 12 shows how the diode is structured internally. A typical set of curves for an HCD and a PN junction diode is given in Fig. 13. The curves show the forward and reverse characteristics of both diode types.

Fig. 14 illustrates the noise figure and conversion loss of an HCD with no bias applied. When forward bias is applied to the diode, the noise figure will change from that shown in Fig. 14. Curves for various bias amounts are given in Fig. 15. The numbers at the ends of the curves signify the amount of current (in milliamperes) flowing into the test circuit at point A.

Fig. 11 — The circuits at A and B are for use in balanced modulators. The similarity between these and balanced mixers is shown at C and D.

Fig. 12 — Cross-sectional representation of a hot-carrier diode (HCD).

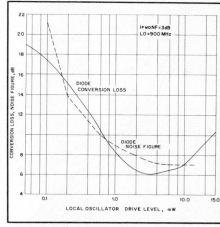

Fig. 13 — Forward and reverse characteristics of a hot-carrier diode as compared to a PN junction diode.

Fig. 14 — Noise figure and the conversion loss of a typical HCD that has no bias applied.

A set of curves showing conversion loss versus LO drive for an HCD mixer are given in Fig. 16. The test circuit used for the curve of Fig. 15 applies. The curve numbers indicate milliamperes measured at point A.

Varactor Diodes

Mention was made earlier in this chapter of diodes being used as voltage-variable capacitors, wherein the diode junction capacitance can be changed by varying the reverse bias applied to the diode. Manufacturers have designed certain diodes for this application. They are called Varicaps (variable capacitor diodes) or varactor diodes (variable reactance diodes). These diodes depend on the change in capacitance that occurs across their depletion layers. They are not used as rectifiers.

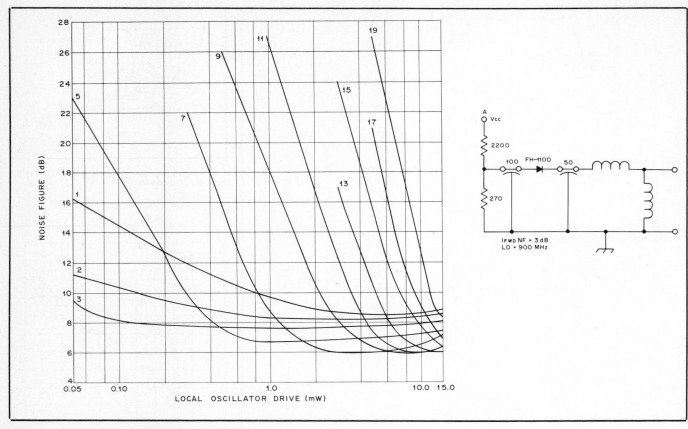

Fig. 15 — Curves for hot-carrier diode noise figure versus local-oscillator drive power. The bias currents are in milliamperes as measured at point A in the representative test circuit.

Fig. 16 — Local-oscillator drive power versus conversion loss for a specified bias amount. Bias currents are in milliamperes as measured at point A of the circuit in Fig. 15.

Varactors are designed to provide various capacitance ranges from a few picofarads to more than 100 pF. Each one has a specific minimum and maximum capacitance, and the higher the maximum amount the greater the minimum value. Therefore, the amateur finds it necessary to tailor circuits for the midrange of the capacitance curve. Ideally, he will choose the most linear portion of the curve. Fig. 17A shows typical capacitance-voltage curves for three varactor diodes.

A representative circuit of a varactor diode is presented in Fig. 18. In this equivalent circuit the diode junction consists of C_j (junction capacitance) and R_j (junction resistance). The bulk resistance is shown as R_s. For the most part R_j can be neglected. The performance of the diode junction at a particular frequency is determined mainly by C_j and R_s. As the operating frequency is increased, the diode performance degrades, owing to the transit time established by C_j and R_s.

An important characteristic of the varactor diode is the Q, or figure of merit. The Q of a varactor diode is determined by the ratio of its capacitive reactance (X_j) and its bulk resistance, R_s, just as is true of other circuit elements such as coils and capacitors, where $Q = X/R_s$ at a specified frequency. Fig. 17B characterizes the Q of three Motorola varactor diodes (versus reverse bias) at 50 MHz.

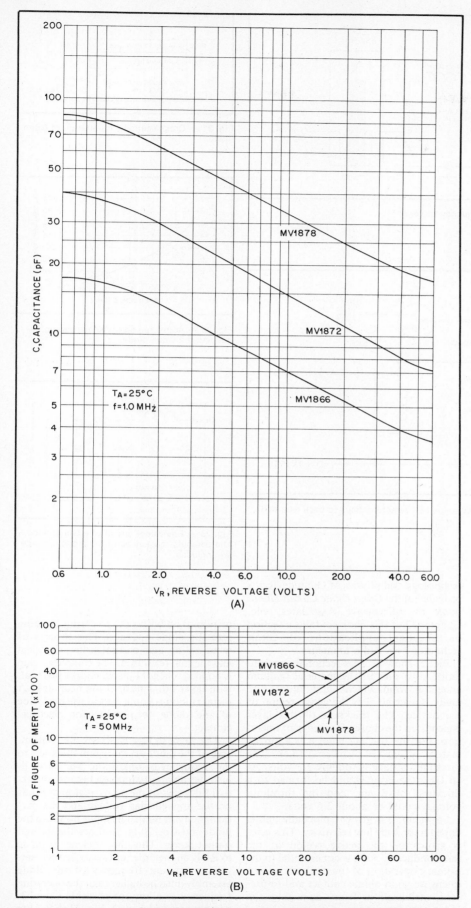

Fig. 17 — Reverse voltage respective to diode capacitance of three Motorola varactor diodes (A). Reverse voltage versus diode Q for the varactors at A are shown at B.

Fig. 18 — Representative circuit of a varactor diode showing case resistance, junction resistance and junction capacitance.

Present-day varactor diodes operate into the microwave part of the spectrum. They are quite efficient as frequency multipliers at power levels as great as 25 watts. The efficiency of a correctly designed varactor multiplier exceeds 50 percent in most instances. Fig. 19 illustrates the basic circuit of a frequency multiplier that contains a varactor diode. D1 is a single-junction device that serves as a frequency tripler in this example. FL1 is required to ensure reasonable purity of the output energy. It is a high-Q strip-line resonator. Without FL1 in the circuit there would be considerable output energy at 144, 288 and 864 MHz. Similar circuits are used as doublers, quadruplers and higher.

A Motorola MV104 tuning diode is used in the circuit of Fig. 20. It contains two varactor diodes in a back-to-back arrangement. The advantage in using two diodes is reduced signal distortion, as compared to a one-diode version of the same circuit. Reverse bias is applied equally to the two diodes in the three-terminal device. R1 functions as an RF isolator for the tuned circuit. The reverse bias is varied by means of R2 to shift the operating frequency. Regulated voltage is as important to the varactor as it is to the FET oscillator if reasonable frequency stability is to be ensured. Varactor diodes are often used to tune two or more circuits at the same time (receiver RF amplifier, mixer and oscillator), using a single potentiometer to control the capacitance of the diodes.

It is worth mentioning that some Zener diodes and selected silicon power-supply rectifier diodes will work effectively as varactors at frequencies as high as 144 MHz. If a Zener diode is used in this manner it must be operated below its reverse breakdown voltage point. The stud-mount variety of power supply diodes (with glass headers) are reported to be the best candidates as varactors, but not all diodes of this type will work effectively; experimentation is necessary.

Gunn Diodes

Gunn diodes are named after the developer, J. B. Gunn, who was studying carrier behavior at IBM Corp. in 1963. Basically, the Gunn effect is a microwave oscillation that occurs when heavy current is passed through bulk semiconductor material. A Gunn device is a diode only in

Fig. 19 — Typical circuit for a varactor-diode frequency tripler.

Fig. 20 — Example of a varactor-tuned VFO. D1 contains two varactors, back to back (see text).

Fig. 21 — Cross-sectional illustration of Gunn diode.

Fig. 22 — Active region thickness versus frequency of a Gunn diode.

Fig. 23 — Equivalent circuit of a Gunn diode. The parasitic reactances of the diode package are included.

the sense that it has two electrodes; it has no rectifying properties.

Amateurs have been using Gunn oscillators at 10 and 24 GHz, but these devices are employed commercially from 4 to 100 GHz and beyond. In high-power (>100 mW) or relatively narrow-bandwidth applications, a varactor diode is used to adjust the oscillation frequency. Gunn oscillators in octave-bandwidth systems such as laboratory sweep generators use YIG tuning. In this method, the volume of a resonant cavity is varied by the magnetic expansion of an yttrium iron garnet sphere. The magnetic force for tuning is generated by a coil external to the cavity, and the oscillation frequency is very nearly a linear function of the coil current.

YIG tuning produces a much cleaner harmonic and close-in oscillation spectrum than that obtainable with varactor tuning, because of the higher Q. The output power of YIG-tuned oscillators must be limited to about 100 mW. This is because the YIG sphere becomes a nonlinear circuit element at higher powers and can cause spurious emissions. An in-depth treatment of the technology and physics of Gunn devices is provided in the *Gunn Diode Circuit Handbook* by Microwave Associates, Inc. Chapter 32 of this book contains a section on practical applications of Gunn technology for radio amateurs.

Fig. 21 shows a cross-sectional representation of a slice of the material (gallium arsenide) from which Gunn diodes are made. Layer no. 1 is the active region of the device. The thickness of this layer depends on the chosen frequency of operation. For the 10-GHz band it is approximately 10 μm (10^{-5} meters) thick. The threshold voltage is roughly 3.3 volts. At 16 GHz the layer would be formed to a thickness of 8 μm, and the threshold voltage would be about 2.6 volts.

Layer no. 2 is grown epitaxially and is doped to provide low resistivity. This layer is grown on the active region of the semiconductor, but it is not essential to the primary operation of the diode. It is used to ensure good ohmic contact and to prevent metalization from damaging the N layer of the diode.

The composite wafer of Fig. 21 is metalized on both sides to permit bonding into the diode package. This process of metalization also ensures a low electrical and thermal resistance. The completed chip is bonded to a gold-plated copper pedestal, with layer no. 2 next to the heat sink. A metal ribbon is connected to the back side of the diode to provide for electrical contact.

The curve in Fig. 22 shows the relationship of the diode active-region thickness to the frequency of operation. The curve illustrates an approximation because the actual thickness of the active region depends on the applied bias voltage and the particular circuit used. The input power to the diode must be 20 to 50 times the desired output power. Thus the efficiency from dc to RF is on the order of two to five percent.

The resonant frequency of the diode assembly must be higher than the operating frequency to allow for parasitic C and L components which exist. Fig. 23 shows the equivalent circuit of a packaged Gunn

Fig. 24 — Illustration of a packaged Gunn diode as presented in literature from Microwave Associates.

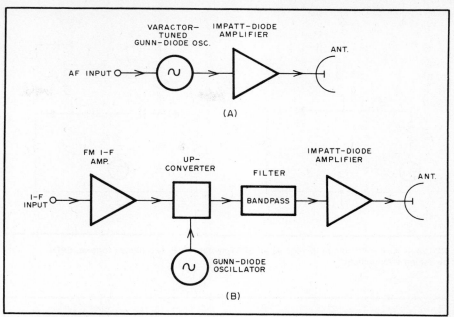

Fig. 25 — Block diagram of a simple Gunn-diode transmitter for FM (A) and an up-converter Gunn-diode transmitter (B).

diode. Assuming a diode natural resonant frequency of 17 GHz, the following approximate values result: $L_p = 0.25$ nH, $C_a = 0.15$ pF and $C_b = 0.15$ pF. Additional components exist within the diode chip. They are represented by C_d (capacitance) and $-R_d$ (negative resistance). These quantities, plus the stray resonances in the diode holder and bias leads in the microwave cavity, have a direct bearing on the electrical behavior of the Gunn oscillator. A cross-sectional representation of a packaged Gunn diode is shown at Fig. 24.

Presently, Gunn diodes are useful for generating powers between 0.1 and 1 watt. As the technology advances these power limits will increase. IMPATT (impact-avalanche transit time) diodes are useful as microwave amplifiers after a Gunn diode signal source. IMPATT diodes are also capable of providing power output in the 0.1- to 1-watt class.

Fig. 25 shows block diagrams of two Gunn-diode systems. In each example an IMPATT diode is used as an amplifier. Fig. 25A shows a direct FM transmitter which employs a varactor-deviated Gunn-diode oscillator as a signal source. FM is provided by applying audio to the bias lead of the varactor diode. The latter is coupled to the Gunn-diode cavity. Fig. 25B illustrates a microwave relay system in which a Gunn diode is used as an LO source. Essentially, the equipment is set up as a heterodyne up-converter transmitter. The upper sideband from the mixer is amplified at microwave frequency by means of an IMPATT diode.

PIN Diodes

A PIN diode is formed by diffusing heavily doped P+ and N+ regions into an almost intrinsically pure silicon layer, as illustrated in Fig. 26. In practice it is impossi-

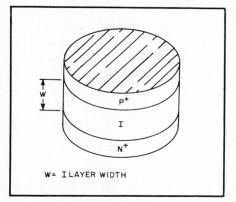

Fig. 26 — The PIN diode is constructed by diffusing P+ and N+ regions into an almost intrinsically pure silicon layer. Thus the name PIN diode.

ble to obtain intrinsically pure material, and the I layer can be considered to be a lightly doped N region. Characteristics of the PIN diode are primarily determined by the thickness, area and semiconductor nature of the chip, especially that of the I region. Manufacturers design for controlled-thickness I regions having long carrier lifetime and high resistivity. Carrier lifetime is basically a measure of the delay before an average electron and hole recombine. In a pure silicon crystal the theoretical delay is on the order of several milliseconds, although impurity doping can reduce the effective carrier lifetime to microseconds or nanoseconds.

When forward bias is applied to a PIN diode, holes and electrons are injected from the P+ and N+ regions into the I region. These charges do not immediately recom-

Fig. 27 — At A is a graph comparing diode resistance to forward-bias current for a PIN diode intended for low-level receiver applications. At B is a similar graph for a diode capable of handling over 100 watts of RF.

bine. Rather, a finite quantity of charge always remains stored and results in a lowering of the I-region resistivity. The amount of stored charge depends on the

Fig. 28 — At A a PIN diode is used as an SPST switch. At B, two diodes form an SPDT switching arrangement.

Fig. 29 — PIN diodes are used to transfer a common antenna to either a transmitter or receiver. A voltage applied to the bias terminal will switch the system to the transmit mode, connecting the output of the transmitter to the antenna. At the same time the diode across the receiver input is forward biased to a low-resistance state to protect the input stage of the receiver. The quarter-wave line isolates the low resistance of the receiver diode from the common antenna connection. At B the quarter-wave line is replaced with a lumped-element equivalent.

recombination time (carrier lifetime) and the level of the forward-bias current. The resistance of the I region under forward-bias conditions is inversely proportional to the charge and depends on the I-region width and mobility of the holes and electrons of the particular semiconductor material. Representative graphs of resistance vs. forward bias level are shown in Fig. 27A and B for low-level receiving and high-power transmitting PIN diodes.

When a PIN diode is at zero or reverse bias, there is essentially no charge, and the intrinsic region can be considered as a low-loss dielectric. As with an ordinary PN junction there is a reverse breakdown or Zener region where the diode current increases rapidly as the reverse voltage increases. For the intrinsic region to remain in a low-loss state, the maximum instantaneous reverse or negative voltage must not exceed the breakdown voltage. Also, the positive voltage excursion must not cause thermal losses to exceed the diode dissipation rating.

At high radio frequencies, when a PIN diode is at zero or reverse bias, the diode appears as a parallel plate capacitor, essentially independent of reverse voltage. It is the value of this capacitance that limits the effective isolation the diode can provide. PIN diodes intended for high isolation and not power-handling capability are designed with as small a geometry as possible to minimize the capacitance.

Manufacturers of PIN diodes supply data sheets with all necessary design data and performance specifications. Key parameters are diode resistance (when forward biased), diode capacitance, carrier lifetime, harmonic distortion, reverse voltage breakdown and reverse leakage.

PIN diodes are used in many applications, such as RF switches, attenuators and various types of phase-shifting devices. Our discussion will be confined to switch and attenuator applications since these are the most likely to be encountered by the amateur. The simplest type of switch that can be created with a PIN diode is the series SPST type. The circuit is shown in Fig. 28A. C1 functions as a dc blocking capacitor and C2 is a bypass capacitor. In order to have the signal from the generator flow to the load, a forward bias must be applied to the bias terminal. The amount of insertion loss caused by the diode is determined primarily by the diode bias current.

Fig. 28B illustrates an SPDT switch arrangement that uses essentially two SPST switches with a common connection. For a generator current to flow into the load resistor at the left, a bias voltage is applied to bias terminal 1. For signal to flow into the load at the right a bias must be applied to terminal 2. In practice it is usually difficult to achieve more than 40 dB isolation with a single diode switch at UHF and microwaves. Better performance, in excess of 100 dB, is achievable using compound switches. Compound switches are made up of two or more diodes in a series/shunt arrangement. Since not all diodes are biased for the same state, some increase in bias-circuit complexity results.

One general class of switches used in connection with transceive applications requires that a common antenna be connected to either the receiver or transmitter during the appropriate receive or transmit states. When PIN diodes are used as switching elements in these applications, higher reliability, better mechanical ruggedness and faster switching speeds are achieved relative to the electromechanical relay.

Fig. 30 — Two types of PIN diode attenuator circuits. The circuit at A is called a bridged T and the circuit at B is a pi type. Both exhibit very broadband characteristics.

Fig. 31 — A solar-energy diode cell. Electrons flow when light strikes the upper surface. The bottom of the cell is coated with foil to collect current for the load, or for the succeeding cell in series-connected arrays of cells.

A basic approach is shown in Fig. 29A and B where a PIN diode is used in series with the transmit line and another diode in shunt with the receive line. A single bias supply is used to turn on the series diode during transmit while also turning on the shunt diode to protect the receiver. The quarter-wave line between the two diodes is necessary to isolate the low resistance of the receiver diode from the antenna connection. During receive periods both diodes are effectively open circuited, allowing signal energy to be applied to the receiver. At B is the same basic circuit, although the quarter-wave line has been replaced with a lumped element section.

Two of the more common types of attenuators using PIN diodes are shown in Fig. 30. The type at A is referred to as a bridged T, while the circuit at B is the com-mon pi type. Both are useful as very broad-band devices. It is interesting to note that the useful upper frequency of these attenuators often depends on the bias circuit isolation rather than the PIN diode characteristics.

Light-Emitting Diodes (LEDs)

The primary component in optoelectronics is the LED. This diode contains a PN junction of crystal material that produces luminescence around the junction when forward bias current is applied. LED junctions are made from gallium arsenide (GaAs), gallium phosphide (GaP), or a combination of both materials (GaAsP). The latter depends on the color and light intensity desired. The available LED colors are red, green, yellow and blue.

Some LEDs are housed in plastic affixed to the base header of a transistor package. Other LEDs are contained entirely in plastic packages that have a dome-shaped head at the light-emitting end. Two wires protrude from the opposite end (positive and negative leads) for applying forward bias to the device.

There are countless advantages to the use of LEDs. Notable among them are the low current drain, long life (sometimes 50 years, as predicted) and small size. They are useful as visual indicators in place of incandescent panel lamps. One of their most common applications is in digital display units, where arrays of tiny LEDs are arranged to provide illuminated segments in numeric-display assemblies.

The forward bias current for a typical LED ranges between 10 and 20 mA for maximum brilliance. An applied voltage of 1½ to 2 is also typical. A 1000-ohm resistor in series with a 12-volt source will permit the LED to operate with a forward current of approximately 10 mA (IR drop = 10 V). In the interest of longevity for the device, do not exceed the rated maximum current.

LEDs are also useful as reference diodes, however unique the applications may seem. They will regulate dc at approximately 1.5 V.

The following are definitions and terms used in optics to characterize the properties of an LED.

Incident flux density is defined as the amount of radiation per unit area (expressed as lumens/cm² in photometry; watts/cm² in radiometry). This is a measure of the amount of flux received by a detector measuring the LED output.

Emitted flux density is also defined as radiation per unit area and is used to describe light reflected from a surface. This measure of reflectance determines the total radiant luminous emittance.

Source intensity defines the flux density that will appear at a distant surface and is expressed as lumens/steradian (photometry) or watts/steradian (radiometry).

Luminance is a measure of photometric brightness and is obtained by dividing the luminous intensity at a given point by the projected area of the source at the same point. Luminance is a very important rating in the evaluation of visible LEDs.

While luminance is equated with photometric brightness, it is inaccurate to equate luminance as a figure of merit for brightness. The only case in which this rating is acceptable is when comparing physically identical LEDs. Different LEDs are subject to more stringent examination. Manufacturers do not use a set of consistent ratings for LEDs (such as optical flux, brightness and intensity). This is because of the dramatic differences in optical measurements between point- and area-source diodes. Point-source diodes are packaged in a clear epoxy or set within a transparent glass lens. Area-source diodes must employ a diffusing lens to spread the flux over a wider viewing area and hence have much less point intensity (luminance) than the point-source diodes.

Solar-Electric Diodes

Sunlight can be converted directly into electricity by a process known as photovoltaic conversion. A solar cell is used for this purpose. It relies on the photoelectric properties of a semiconductor. Practically, the solar cell is a large-area PN junction diode. The greater the area of the cell, the higher the output current will be. A dc voltage output of approximately 0.5 is obtained from a single cell. Numerous cells can be connected in series to provide 6, 9, 12, 24 or whatever low voltage is required. In a like manner, cells can be connected in parallel to provide higher output current, overall.

The solar diode cell is built so that light can penetrate into the region of the PN junction, Fig. 31. Most modern solar cells use silicon material. Impurities (doping) are introduced into the silicon material to establish excess positive or negative charges which carry electric currents. Phosphorous is used to produce N-type silicon. Boron is used as the dopant to produce P-type material.

Light is absorbed into the silicon to generate excess holes and electrons (one hole/electron pair for each photon absorbed). When this occurs near the PN junction, the electric fields in that region will separate the holes from the electrons. This causes the holes to increase in the P-type material. At the same time the electrons will build up in the N-type material. By making direct connection to the P and N regions by means of wires, these excess charges generated by light (and separated by the junction) will flow into an external load to provide power.

Approximately 0.16 A can be obtained from each square inch of solar-cell material exposed to bright sunlight. A 3½-inch-diameter cell can provide 1.5 A of output current. The efficiency of a solar cell (maximum power delivered to a load versus total solar energy incident on the cell) is typically 11 to 12 percent.

Fig. 32 — Voltage/current/temperature curve for a Solar Power Corp. array that contains 36 solar-electric cells in series. The curves are for a model E12-01369-1.5 solar panel.

Fig. 34 — Typical characteristics of a Zener diode (30 V).

Arrays of solar cells are manufactured for all manner of practical applications. A storage battery is used as a buffer between the solar panel and the load. A PN junction diode should be used between the solar-array output and the storage battery to prevent the battery from discharging back into the panel during dark periods. An article on the subject of solar cells and their amateur applications (DeMaw "Solar Power for the Radio Amateur," August 1977 *QST)* should be of interest to those who wish to utilize solar power. *Solar Electric Generator Systems,* an application pamphlet by Solar Power Corp. of N. Billerica, MA 01862, contains valuable information on this subject.

Fig. 32 shows the voltage/current curves to a Model E12-01369-1.5 solar array manufactured by Solar Power Corp. It can be seen that temperature has an effect on the array performance.

Tunnel Diodes

One type of semiconductor diode having no rectifying properties is called a tunnel diode. The bidirectional conduction of the device is a result of heavily doped P and N regions with a very narrow junction. The Fermi level lies within the conduction band for the N side and within the valence band for the P side. A typical current-vs.-voltage curve for a tunnel diode is sketched in Fig. 33. When the forward bias potential exceeds about 30 mV, increasing the voltage causes the current to decrease, resulting in a negative resistance characteristic. This effect makes the tunnel diode capable of amplification and oscillation.

At one time tunnel diodes were expected to dominate in microwave applications, but other devices soon surpassed tunnel diodes in performance. The two-terminal oscillator concept had great fad appeal, and some amateurs built low-power transmitters based on tunnel diodes. In the 1960s the Heath Company marketed a dip meter that used a tunnel diode oscillator. Tunnel diodes are not widely used in new designs;

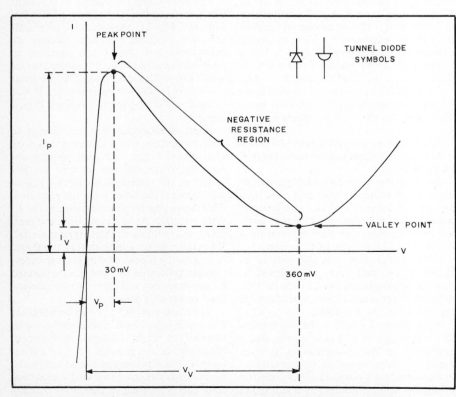

Fig. 33 — Schematic symbol and current-vs.-voltage characteristic for a tunnel diode.

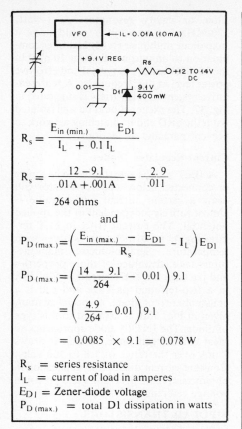

$$R_s = \frac{E_{in\,(min.)} - E_{D1}}{I_L + 0.1\,I_L}$$

$$R_s = \frac{12 - 9.1}{.01A + .001A} = \frac{2.9}{.011}$$

$$= 264 \text{ ohms}$$

and

$$P_{D\,(max.)} = \left(\frac{E_{in\,(max.)} - E_{D1}}{R_s} - I_L\right) E_{D1}$$

$$P_{D\,(max.)} = \left(\frac{14 - 9.1}{264} - 0.01\right) 9.1$$

$$= \left(\frac{4.9}{264} - 0.01\right) 9.1$$

$$= 0.0085 \times 9.1 = 0.078 \text{ W}$$

R_s = series resistance
I_L = current of load in amperes
E_{D1} = Zener-diode voltage
$P_{D\,(max.)}$ = total D1 dissipation in watts

Fig. 35 — Example of how a shunt type of Zener diode regulator is used. The equations show how to calculate the value of the series resistor and the diode power dissipation. In this example a 400-mW Zener diode will suffice (D1).

this material is included only for completeness.

Zener Diodes

Zener diodes have, for the most part, replaced the gaseous regulator tube. They have been proved more reliable than tube types of voltage regulators, are less expensive and far smaller in size.

These diodes fall into two primary classifications: voltage regulators and voltage-reference diodes. When they are used in power supplies as regulators, they provide a nearly constant dc output voltage even though there may be large changes in load resistance or input voltage. As a reference element the Zener diode utilizes the voltage drop across its junction when a specified current passes through it in the reverse-breakdown direction (sometimes called the Zener direction). This "Zener voltage" is the value established as a reference. Therefore, if a 6.8-volt Zener diode was set up in this manner, the resultant reference voltage would be 6.8.

At the present time it is possible to purchase Zener diodes rated for various voltages between 2.4 and 200. The power ratings range from ¼ to 50 watts. Fig. 34 shows the characteristics of a Zener diode designed for 30-volt operation.

Fig. 35 shows how to calculate the series

Fig. 36 — Practical examples of Zener diode applications. The circuit at A is useful for stabilizing the filament voltage of oscillators. Zener diodes can be used in series to obtain various levels of regulated voltage (B). Fixed-value bias for transmitter stages can be obtained by inserting a Zener diode in the cathode return (C). At D an 18-volt Zener diode prevents voltage spikes from harming a mobile transceiver. A Zener-diode series regulator (20-V drop) is shown at E and an RF clamp is shown at F. D1 in the latter circuit will clamp at 36 volts to protect the PA transistor from dc voltage spikes and extreme sine-wave excursions at RF. This circuit is useful in protecting output stages during no-load or short-circuit conditions.

Fig. 37 — Step-recovery-diode frequency multiplier for 10 GHz. The matching network elements are represented as lumped components but would take the form of a microstripline in an actual design.

Fig. 38 — At A, an N-channel JFET connected as a constant-current source. At B, the schematic symbol for the circuit in A when it is packaged as a two-terminal device.

resistance needed in a simple shunt regulator which employs a Zener diode. An equation is included for determining the wattage rating of the series resistor. Additional data on this subject is given in Chapter 7 of *Solid State Design for the Radio Amateur*.

Some practical applications for Zener diodes are illustrated in Fig. 36. In addition to the shunt applications given in the diagram, Zener diodes can be used as series elements when it is desired to provide a gate that conducts at a given voltage. These diodes can be used in ac as well as dc circuits. When they are used in an ac type of application they will conduct at the peak voltage value or below, depending on the voltage swing and the voltage rating of the Zener diode. For this reason they are useful as audio and RF clippers. In RF work the reactance of the diode may be the controlling factor above approximately 10 MHz with respect to the performance of the RF circuit and the diode.

Most Zener diodes which are rated higher than 1 watt in dissipation are contained in stud-mount packages. They should be affixed to a suitable heat sink to prevent damage from excessive junction temperatures. The mounting techniques are the same as for power rectifiers and high-wattage transistors.

Reference Diodes

While ordinary Zener diodes are useful as voltage regulators, they don't exhibit the thermal stability required in precision reference applications. A reverse-biased semiconductor junction has a positive temperature coefficient of barrier potential. A forward-biased junction has a negative coefficient. The way to temperature-compensate a Zener diode is to connect one or more common silicon diodes in series with it. When this is done as part of the manufacturing process, the resulting component is termed a reference diode. A 1N3499 6.2-volt reference diode will maintain a temperature coefficient of 0.0005 percent per degree over the range of 0 to 75° C. Reference diodes work best when operated at a few milliamperes of current from a high-impedance or constant-current bias source.

As the name implies, these diodes aren't suited for circuits where power is taken directly from the device. Reference diodes can't be tested with an ohmmeter because two junctions are back-to-back — the instrument can't supply enough voltage to overcome the Zener barrier potential.

Step-Recovery Diodes

One device characterized by extremely low capacitance and short storage time is the step-recovery diode (SRD), sometimes called a "snap" diode. These diodes are used as frequency multipliers well into the microwave spectrum. Switching the device in and out of forward conduction is the multiplication mechanism, and the power efficiency is inversely proportional to the frequency multiple. Very high orders of multiplication are possible with step-recovery diodes. One use for this feature is in a comb generator, an instrument used to calibrate the frequency axis of a spectrum analyzer.

A single harmonic of the excitation frequency can be selected by an interdigital

filter or cavity resonator. A 1-watt, 220-MHz FM transmitter could drive a snap diode multiplier (×46) and filter combination to an output of about 10 mW in the 10-GHz band — a typical and effective power level at that frequency. A representative system of this variety is suggested in Fig. 37. The exciter should be well isolated from the SRD and its matching network to prevent parasitic oscillations.

Current-Regulator Diodes

A JFET with its gate shorted to its source or connected below a source resistor will draw a certain current whose value is almost entirely independent of the applied potential. The current (I_{DSS} in FET terminology) is also quite stable with temperature. Semiconductor manufacturers take advantage of those properties and package the JFET circuit of Fig. 38A in a two-terminal package and call it a constant-current diode. A special symbol, given in Fig. 38B, is assigned to this type of diode. The 1N5305 diode approaches an ideal current generator, in that it draws 2 mA over the range of 1.8 to 100 volts. Constant-current diodes find application in ohmmeters, ramp generators and precision voltage references.

BIPOLAR TRANSISTORS

The word "transistor" was chosen to describe the function of a three-terminal PN junction device that is able to amplify signal energy (current). The inherent characteristic is one of "transferring current across a resistor." The transistor was invented by Shockley, Bardeen and Brattain at Bell Labs in 1947 and has become the standard amplifying device in electronic equipment. In RF and audio applications it is practical to obtain output power in excess of 1000 watts by using several amplifier blocks and hybrid power combiners. The primary limitation at the higher power levels is essentially a practical or economic one: Low voltage, high-current power supplies are required, and the cost can exceed that of a high-voltage moderate-current supply of the variety that would be employed with a vacuum-tube amplifier of comparable power. The primary advantages of solid-state power amplifiers are compactness and reliability.

In small-signal applications the transistor outweighs the vacuum-tube in performance. There remains in some quarters a belief that transistors are hard to tame, are noisier than tubes and are subject to damage at the flick of a switch. None of this is true. A transistorized circuit designed and operated correctly is almost always capable of outperforming an equivalent vacuum-tube circuit in all respects. An understanding of how transistors function will help to prevent poor circuit performance. The fundamentals outlined in this chapter are provided for the amateur designer so the common pitfalls can be avoided.

Fig. 39 — Illustration of a junction PNP transistor. Capacitances C_{be} and C_{bc} vary with changes in operating and signal voltage (see text).

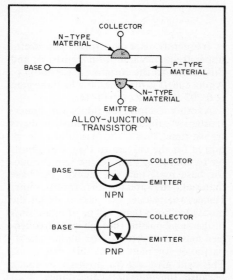

Fig. 40 — Pictorial and schematic representations of junction transistors. The base, collector and emitter can be compared to the grid, plate and cathode of a triode tube, respectively.

Fig. 39 shows a "sandwich" made from two layers of P-type semiconductor material with a thin layer of N-type between. There are in effect two PN junction diodes back-to-back. If a positive bias is applied to the P-type material at the left, current will flow through the left-hand junction, the holes moving to the right and the electrons from the N-type material moving to the left. Some of the holes moving into the N-type material will combine with the electrons there and be neutralized, but some of them also will travel to the region of the right-hand junction.

If the PN combination at the right is biased negatively, as shown, there would normally be no current flow in this circuit. However, there are now additional holes available at the junction to travel to point B and electrons can travel toward point A, so a current can flow even though this sec-

tion of the sandwich is biased to prevent conduction. Most of the current is between A and B and does not flow out through the common connection to the N-type material in the sandwich.

A semiconductor combination of this type is called a transistor, and the three sections are known as the emitter, base and collector. The amplitude of the collector current depends principally on the amplitude of the emitter current; that is, the collector current is controlled by the emitter current.

Between each PN junction exists an area known as the depletion, or transition, region. It is similar in characteristics to a dielectric layer, and its width varies in accordance with the operating voltage. The semiconductor materials either side of the depletion region constitute the plates of a capacitor. The capacitance from base to emitter is shown as C_{be} (Fig. 39), and the base-collector capacitance is represented as C_{bc}. Changes in signal and operating voltages cause a nonlinear change in these junction capacitances, which must be taken into account when designing some circuits. A base-emitter resistance, rb ', also exists. The junction capacitance, in combination with rb ', determines the useful upper frequency limit (f_T or f_a) of a transistor by establishing an RC time constant.

Power Amplification

Because the collector is biased in the back direction the collector-to-base resistance is high. On the other hand, the emitter and collector currents are substantially equal, so the power in the collector circuit is larger than the power in the emitter circuit ($P = I^2R$, so the powers are proportional to the respective resistances, if the currents are the same). In practical transistors emitter resistance is on the order of a few ohms while the collector resistance is hundreds or thousands of times higher, so power gains of 20 to 40 dB or even more are possible.

Transistor Types

The transistor may be one of the types shown in Fig. 40. The assembly of P- and N-type materials may be reversed, so that PNP and NPN transistors are both possible.

The first two letters of the NPN and PNP designations indicate the respective polarities of the voltages applied to the emitter and collector in normal operation. In a PNP transistor, for example, the emitter is made positive with respect to both the collector and the base, and the collector is made negative with respect to both the emitter and the base.

Manufacturers are constantly working to improve the performance of their transistors — greater reliability, higher power and higher frequency ratings, and improved uniformity of characteristics for any given type number. One such development provided the overlay transistor, whose

emitter structure is made up of several emitters that are joined together at a common case terminal. This process lowers the base-emitter resistance, rb ', and improves the transistor input time constant. The time constant is determined by rb ' and the junction capacitance of the device.

The overlay transistor is extremely useful in VHF and UHF applications. It is capable of high-power operation well above 1000 MHz. These transistors are useful as frequency doublers and triplers, and are able to provide an actual power gain in the process.

Another multi-emitter transistor that has been developed for use from HF through UHF should be of interest to the radio amateur. It is called a balanced-emitter transistor (BET), or "ballasted" transistor. The transistor chip contains several triode semiconductors whose bases and collectors are connected in parallel. The various emitters, however, have built-in emitter resistors (typically about 1 ohm) that provide a current-limiting safety factor during overload periods, or under conditions of significant mismatch. Since the emitters are brought out to a single case terminal the resistances are effectively in parallel, thus reducing the combined emitter resistances to a fraction of an ohm. (If a significant amount of resistance were allowed to exist it would cause degeneration in the stage and would lower the gain of the circuit.)

Most modern transistors are of the junction variety. Various names have been given to the several types, some of which are junction alloy, mesa and planar. Though their characteristics may differ slightly, they are basically of the same family and simply represent different physical properties and manufacturing techniques.

Transistor Characteristics

An important characteristic of a transistor is its beta (β), or current-amplification factor, which is sometimes expressed as H_{FE} (static forward-current transfer ratio) or h_{fe} (small-signal forward-current transfer ratio). Both symbols relate to the grounded-emitter configuration. Beta is the ratio of the collector current to the base current

$$\beta = \frac{I_c}{I_b}$$

Thus, if a base current of 1 mA causes the collector current to rise to 100 mA the beta is 100. Typical betas for junction transistors range from as low as 10 to as high as several hundred.

A transistor's alpha (α) is the ratio of the collector to the emitter current. Symbols h_{FB} (static forward-current transfer ratio) and h_{fb} (small-signal forward-current transfer ratio), common-base hookup, are frequently used in connection with gain. The smaller the base current, the closer the collector current comes to being equal to that of the emitter, and the closer alpha

Fig. 41 — Typical collector-current versus collector-voltage characteristics of a junction transistor for various emitter-current values. Because the emitter resistance is low, a current-limiting resistor (R) is placed in series with the source current. The emitter current can be set at a desired value by adjustment of this resistance.

Fig. 42 — Collector current versus collector voltage for various values of base current in a junction transistor. The illustration at A shows how the measurements are made. At B is a family of curves.

Fig. 43 — Curve-tracer display of a small-signal transistor characteristics.

Fig. 44 — Basic transistor amplifiers. Observe the input and output phase relationships for the various configurations.

comes to being 1. Alpha for a junction transistor is usually between 0.92 and 0.98.

Transistors have frequency characteristics that are important to circuit designers.

Symbol f_T is the gain bandwidth product (common-emitter) of the transistor. This is the frequency at which the gain becomes unity, or 1. The expression "alpha cutoff" is frequently used to express the useful upper-frequency limit of a transistor, and this relates to the common-base hookup. Alpha cutoff is the point at which the gain is 0.707 its value at 1000 Hz.

Another factor that limits the upper-frequency capability of a transistor is its transit time. This is the period of time required for the current to flow from emitter to collector, through the semiconductor base material. The thicker the base material, the greater the transit time. Hence, the thicker the base material the more likelihood there will be of phase shift of the signal passing through it. At frequencies near and above f_T or alpha cutoff, partial or complete phase shift can occur. This will give rise to positive feedback because the internal capacitance, C_{be}, feeds part of the in-phase collector signal back to the base. The positive feedback can cause instability and oscillation, and in most cases will interlock the input and output tuned circuits of an RF amplifier so it is almost impossible to tune them properly. This form of feedback can be corrected by using what is termed "unilateralization." Conventional positive feedback can be nullified by using neutralization, as is done with vacuum-tube amplifiers.

Characteristic Curves

The operating principles of transistors can be shown by a series of characteristic curves. One such set of curves is shown in Fig. 41. It shows the collector current vs. collector voltage for a number of fixed values of emitter current. Practically, the collector current depends almost entirely on the emitter current and is independent of the collector voltage. The separation between curves is quite uniform, indicating that almost distortionless output can be obtained over the useful operating range of the transistor.

Another type of curve is shown in Fig. 42, together with the circuit used for obtaining it. This also shows collector current vs. collector voltage, but for a number of different values of base current. In this case the emitter element is used as the common point in the circuit. The collector current is not independent of collector voltage with this type of connection, indicating that the output resistance of the device is fairly low. The base current also is quite low, which means the resistance of the base-emitter circuit is moderately high with this method of connection. This may be contrasted with the high values of emitter current shown in Fig. 41. An actual oscillograph of a characteristic family of curves for a small-signal transistor is shown in Fig. 43. It was obtained by means of a curve tracer.

Transistor Amplifiers

Amplifier circuits used with transistors fall into one of three types, known as the common-base, common-emitter and common-collector circuits. These are shown in Fig. 44 in elementary form. The three circuits correspond approximately to the grounded-grid, grounded-cathode and cathode-follower circuits, respectively, used with vacuum tubes.

The important transistor parameters in these circuits are the short-circuit current transfer ratio, the cutoff frequency, and the input and output impedances. The short-circuit current transfer ratio is the ratio of a small change in output current to the change in input current that causes it, the output circuit being short-circuited. The cutoff frequency was discussed earlier in this chapter. The input impedance is that which a signal source working into the transistor would see, and the output impedance is the internal output impedance of the transistor (corresponding to the plate resistance of a vacuum tube, for example).

Common-Base Circuit

The input circuit of a common-base amplifier must be designed for low impedance, since the emitter-to-base resistance is of the order of $26/I_e$ ohms, where I_e is the emitter current in milliamperes. The optimum output load impedance, R_L, may range from a few thousand ohms to 100,000, depending on the requirements.

In this circuit the phase of the output (collector) current is the same as that of the input (emitter) current. The parts of these currents that flow through the base resistance are likewise in phase, so the circuit tends to be regenerative and will oscillate if the current amplification factor is greater than one.

Common-Emitter Circuit

The common-emitter circuit shown in Fig. 44 corresponds to the ordinary grounded-cathode vacuum-tube amplifier. As indicated by the curves of Fig. 42, the base current is small and the input impedance is therefore fairly high — several thousand ohms in the average case. The collector resistance is some tens of thousands of ohms, depending on the

signal source impedance. The common-emitter circuit has a lower cutoff frequency than does the common-base circuit, but it gives the highest power gain of the three configurations.

In this circuit the phase of the output (collector) current is opposite to that of the input (base) current so such feedback as occurs through the small emitter resistance is negative and the amplifier is stable.

Because the common-emitter amplifier circuit illustrated in Fig. 44 is one of the most often seen applications for a bipolar transistor, a brief analysis and discussion of the design network biasing the base supplies an open-circuit potential of 1.36 V. Connecting the base has little loading effect if the transistor beta is high (a fair assumption). A beta of 100, for example, causes the 470-ohm emitter resistor to present a dc base resistance of 47 kΩ, which is a negligible shunt. The base-emitter junction drops 0.6 V, so the potential across the emitter resistor is $1.36 - 0.6 = 0.76$ V. This voltage causes 1.6 mA to flow in the emitter and the 470-ohm resistor. Since the transistor alpha is nearly unity, the collector current is also 1.6 mA, which drops 7.52 volts across the collector load resistor. The quiescent (no signal) collector voltage is therefore $15 - 7.52 = 7.48$ V. This value allows the maximum undistorted output voltage swing between cutoff and saturation.

Assuming the emitter bypass capacitor has negligible reactance at the operating frequency, the emitter is at ac ground. Because of the high alpha mentioned earlier, any emitter current variation caused by an input signal will also appear in the collector circuit. Since the current variation is the same, the voltage gain is the ratio of the collector load resistance to the (internal) emitter resistance. For small signals, this emitter resistance can be approximated by $R_e = 26/I_e$, where R_e is the emitter-to-base junction resistance, and I_e is the emitter current in milliamperes. In our example, $I_e = 1.6$, so $R_e = 16.25$ Ω. The voltage gain, then, is 289, which is 49 dB. The ac base impedance is given by R_e. Using the previous values for beta and emitter resistance results in a base impedance of 1625 Ω. The circuit input impedance is found by shunting the base impedance with the bias resistors. The result in this case is about 1189 Ω.

If the emitter bypass capacitor is omitted, the external resistor dominates the gain equation, which becomes: $A_v = R_L/R_E$, where A_v is the voltage gain, R_L is the collector load resistance as before, and R_E is the unbypassed emitter resistance. Without the bypass capacitor, the common-emitter circuit in Fig. 44 exhibits a numerical voltage gain of 10 (20 dB). The base impedance becomes βR_E, or 47 kΩ. This value is swamped by the bias network for a circuit input impedance of 3.91 kΩ. The emitter resistor has introduced 29 dB of degenerative feedback to the circuit,

Fig. 45 — Differential amplifier. This arrangement can be analyzed as a composite of the common-collector and common-base circuits.

stabilizing the gain and impedance values over a wide frequency range. A dc beta of 100 was assumed in this example, and for convenience this value was also assigned at the operating frequency. In reality, however, beta decreases with increasing frequency, as noted in the section on transistor characteristics. Degenerative feedback overcomes this effect to a large extent.

Common-Collector Circuit (Emitter-Follower)

Like the vacuum-tube cathode follower, the common-collector transistor amplifier has high input impedance and low output impedance. The latter is approximately equal to the impedance of the signal input source multiplied by $(1 - \alpha)$. The input resistance depends on the load resistance, being approximately equal to the load resistance divided by $(1 - \alpha)$. The fact that input resistance is directly related to the load resistance is a disadvantage of this type of amplifier if the load is one whose resistance or impedance varies with frequency.

The current transfer ratio with this circuit is

$$\frac{1}{1 - \alpha}$$

and the cutoff frequency is the same as in the grounded-emitter circuit. The output and input currents are in phase.

Differential Amplifier Circuit

An important variation of the fundamental amplifier types is the differential amplifier, drawn in Fig. 45. The output voltage is proportional to the difference (with respect to ground) between the

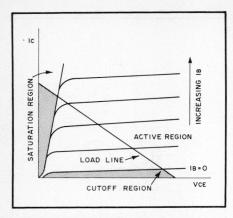

Fig. 46 — Typical characteristic for the collector of an NPN transistor that shows the three primary regions involved during switching.

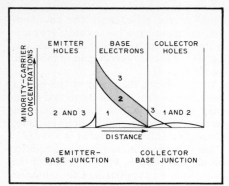

Fig. 47 — Illustration of the minority-carrier concentrations in an NPN transistor. No. 1 shows the cutoff region. No. 2 is the active region at the threshold of the saturation region. No. 3 is in the saturation region.

Fig. 48 — Circuit for a transistor switching circuit (saturated).

voltages applied to the input terminals. With the proper choice of operating conditions, several differential amplifier stages of the type shown can be cascaded directly. Fig. 45 shows the circuit in its classic balanced form, but many circuits use differential amplifiers in a single-ended configuration. When only a single input and output terminal is required, R1 could be a short circuit and the Q2 base could be grounded. Under these circumstances the differential amplifier can be understood as an emitter-follower driving a common-base stage. The output is taken between the Q2 collector and ground. R3 establishes the current in Q1 and Q2, which should be equal under static conditions.

Differential amplifiers work best when R3 is replaced by some type of constant-current source. One type of current regulator has been discussed in the diode section, and current sources made from bipolar transistors are covered later.

With a current source biasing Q1 and Q2 the input signal cannot modulate the total collector current; only the ratio of the currents varies. One beneficial result of the constant-current bias is that a higher impedance is presented to the driving signal.

Bipolar Transistor Dissipation

Apart from the characteristics mentioned earlier, it is necessary to consider the matters of collector dissipation, collector voltage and current, and emitter current. Variations in these specifications are denoted by specific parameter symbols which appear later in the chapter. The maximum dissipation ratings of transistors, as provided on the manufacturer's data sheets, tend to confuse some amateurs. An acceptable rule of thumb is to select a transistor that has a maximum dissipation rating of approximately twice the dc input power of the circuit stage. That is, if a 5-watt dc input is contemplated, choose a transistor with a 10-watt or greater rating.

When power levels in excess of a few hundred milliwatts are necessary there is a need for heat sinking. A sink is a metal device that helps keep the transistor cool by virtue of heat transfer from the transistor case to the sink. At power levels below 5 watts it is common practice to employ clip-on heat sinks of the crown variety. For powers greater than 5 watts it is necessary to use large-area heat sinks fashioned from extruded aluminum. These sinks have cooling fins on one or more of their surfaces to hasten the cooling process. Some high-power, solid-state amplifiers employ cooling fans from which the air stream is directed on the metallic heat sink. Regardless of the power level or type of heat sink used, silicone heat-transfer compound should always be used between the mating surfaces of the transistor and the heat sink. Another rule of thumb is offered: If the heat-sink-equipped transistor is too warm to touch with comfort, the heat sink is not large enough in area.

Excessive junction heat will destroy a transistor. Prior to destruction the device may go into thermal runaway. During this condition the transistor becomes hotter and its internal resistance lowers. This causes an increase in emitter/collector and emitter/base current. This increased current elevates the dissipation and further lowers the internal resistance. These effects are cumulative: Eventually the transistor will be destroyed. A heat sink of proper size will prevent this type of problem. Excessive junction temperature will eventually cause the transistor to become open. Checks with an ohmmeter will indicate this condition after a failure.

Excess collector voltage will also cause immediate device failure. The indication of this type of failure, as noted by means of an ohmmeter, is a shorted junction.

Bipolar Transistor Applications

Silicon transistors are the most common types in use today, although a few ger-

Fig. 49 — Examples of practical switching circuits. A PNP switch is used to key an oscillator at A. When R1 is grounded the switching transistor is forward biased to saturation, permitting current to flow from the dc supply line to Q2. The circuit at B shows Q1 as a relay-driver NPN switch. When +12 volts is applied to the base of Q1 it is forward biased to saturation, permitting current to flow through the field coil of K1A. D1 and D2 are included to reduce the static collector current of Q1, which in some instances could cause K1A to remain closed after forward bias was removed from Q1. D3 serves as a spike suppressor when the field of K1A collapses.

manium varieties are built for specific applications. Collector voltages as great as 1500 can be accommodated by some of the high-power silicon transistors available now. Most small-signal transistors will safely handle collector voltages of 25 or greater. Generally speaking, transistors in the small-signal class carry dissipation ratings of 500 mW or less. Power transistors are normally classed as 500-mW and higher devices.

Fig 50 — Examples of PNP and NPN amplifiers operating from a power supply with a negative ground.

Fig. 51 — RC and transformer-coupled audio amplifiers suitable for high- and low-impedance microphones.

The practical applications for all of these semiconductors range from dc to the microwave spectrum.

Bipolar Transistor Switches

Our present-day technology includes the use of solid-state switches as practical alternatives to mechanical switches. When a bipolar transistor is used in a switching application it is either in an "on" or "off" state. In the "on" state a forward bias is applied to the transistor, sufficient in level to saturate the device. The common-emitter format is used for nearly all transistor switches. Switching action is characterized by large-signal nonlinear operation of the device. Fig. 46 shows typical output characteristics for an NPN switching transistor in the common-emitter mode.

There are three regions of operation — cutoff, active and saturation. In the cutoff region the emitter-base and collector-base junctions are reverse biased. At this period the collector current is quite small and is comparable to the leakage current, I_{ceo}, I_{cev} or I_{cbo}.

Fig. 47 illustrates the minority-carrier concentration relative to an NPN transistor. During cutoff the concentration is zero at both junctions because they are reverse biased (curve 1).

The emitter-base junction is forward biased in the active region. At this time the collector-base junction is reversed biased. Fig. 46 shows a load line along which switching from the cutoff to the active region is done. The transit time (speed)

through the active region depends on the transistor frequency-response characteristics. Thus, the higher the frequency rating of the device, the faster the switching time. Curve 2 in Fig. 47 depicts the minority-carrier concentration of the active region.

In the saturation region the emitter-base and collector-base junctions are forward biased. During this period the forward voltage drop across the emitter-base junction $V_{BE(sat)}$ is larger than it is across the collector-base junction. This results in a collector-emitter voltage termed $V_{CE(sat)}$. Series resistances present in the emitter and collector legs of the circuit contribute to the determination of $V_{CE(sat)}$. Since the collector in this state is forward biased, additional carriers are injected into the base. Some also reach the collector. Curve 3 in Fig. 47 shows this minority-carrier concentration. Fig. 48 contains the circuit for a basic saturated-transistor switch.

It is extremely important to make certain that none of the transistor voltage ratings is exceeded during the "off" period. The minimum emitter-base breakdown voltage, $V_{(BR)EBO}$, must not exceed $V_{BE(off)}$. Also, the minimum collector-base breakdown voltage, $V_{(BR)CBO}$, should be no greater than $V_{cc} + V_{BE(off)}$. Finally, the minimum collector-to-emitter breakdown voltage, $V_{(BR)CERL}$, must be greater than V_{cc}. As is true in any transistor application, the junction temperature must be maintained at a safe value by whatever means necessary.

A transistor switch can be turned on by means of a pulse (Fig. 48) or by application of a dc forward bias. Typical circuits for the latter are given in Fig. 49. The circuit at A illustrates how a PNP transistor can be used as a low-power switch to turn oscillator Q2 on and off. In the "on" state R1 is grounded. This places the bipolar switch, Q1, in a saturated mode, thereby permitting current to flow to Q2. A transistor switch of the type shown at A of Fig. 49 can be used to control more than one circuit stage simultaneously. The primary criterion is that the switching transistor be

capable of passing the combined currents of the various stages under control. The method shown at A is often used in keying a transmitter.

An NPN transistor switch is shown in Fig. 49B. If desired, it can be "slaved" to the circuit of Fig. 49A by attaching R1 of circuit B to the collector of Q1 in circuit A. Because an NPN device is used at B, a positive forward bias must be applied to the base via R1 to make the transistor saturate. When in that state, current flows through the relay (K1A) field coil to actuate the contacts at K1B. D3 is connected across the relay coil to damp inductive spikes that occur when the relay-coil field collapses.

D1 and D2 may not be necessary. This will depend on the sensitivity of the relay and the leakage current of Q1 in the off state. If there is considerable leakage, K1 may not release when forward bias is removed from Q1. D1 and D2 will elevate the emitter to approximately 1.4 volts, thereby providing sufficient reverse bias to cut off Q1 in the off state. It can be seen from the illustrations in Fig. 49 that either NPN or PNP transistors can be used as electronic switches.

Transistor Audio Amplifiers

Bipolar transistors are suitable for numerous audio-amplifier applications from low-level to high power. It is common practice to use all NPN or all PNP devices, regardless of the polarity of the power supply. In other circuits a mixture of the two types may be found, especially when direct-coupled or complimentary-symmetry stages are included. Fig. 50 shows how PNP or NPN stages can be used with power supplies that have positive or negative grounds. The essential difference in the circuits concerns returning various elements to the negative or positive sides of the power supply. The illustrations show that all one needs to do to use either type of device with the same power supply is to interchange the resistor connections. The same principle applies when using NPN or PNP transistors with a power supply that has a positive ground. Knowledge of how this is done enables the designer to mix NPN and PNP devices in a single circuit. This basic technique is applicable to any type of transistor circuit — RF, audio or dc.

Some basic low-level audio amplifiers are shown in Fig. 51. These stages operate in the Class A mode. The input impedance of these circuits is low — typically between 500 and 1500 ohms. For the most part the output impedance is established by the value to the collector load resistor. A matching transformer can be used at the input of these stages (Fig. 51B) when it is necessary to use, for example, a high-impedance microphone with one of them. T1 serves as a step-down transformer.

Some direct-coupled audio amplifiers are shown in Fig. 52. The circuit at A combines PNP and NPN devices to provide a compatible interface between them. Three NPN stages are in cascade at B to provide high gain. This circuit is excellent for use in direct-conversion receivers, owing to the need for very high gain after the detector. At C is a Darlington pair, named after the person who developed the configuration. The principal advantages of this circuit are high gain, high input impedance and low output impedance.

Transistor RF Amplifiers

In most respects small-signal RF amplifiers are similar in performance to those used in audio applications. However, to effect maximum stable amplification some important design measures are necessary. Furthermore, the matter of proper impedance matching becomes more important than it is in simple audio amplifiers. Other considerations are noise figure, purity of the amplified signal and dynamic range.

Although bipolar transistors can be used as RF amplifiers for receiver front ends, they are not found there in most of the high-performance receivers: Field-effect transistors are more often the designer's choice because of their high input impedance and good dynamic-range traits. A correctly designed bipolar RF input stage can exhibit good dynamic range, however. It is necessary to operate a fairly husky low-noise transistor in Class A, using a relatively high standing collector current — 50 to 100 mA, typically.

Some RF and IF amplifier circuits that use bipolar transistors are shown in the examples of Fig. 53. When used with the appropriate L and C networks they are suitable for either application. At A in Fig. 53 the transistor base is tapped near the cold end of the input tuned circuit to provide an impedance match. The collector is tapped down on the output tuned circuit to provide a proper match. If it is desired, the base and collector taps can be moved even farther down on the tuned circuits. This will result in a deliberate mismatch. The technique is sometimes used to aid

Fig. 52 — Practical examples of direct-coupled audio amplifiers.

stability and/or lower the stage gain. The circuit at B is operated in the common-base mode. Taps are shown on the input and output coils for impedance-matching purposes.

Broadband amplifiers with heavy negative feedback are useful as small-signal RF and IF amplifiers. An example is shown at C in Fig. 53. Not only is negative feedback applied (collector to base), but degenerative feedback is obtained by virtue of the unbypassed 10-ohm emitter resistor. The use of feedback ensures an unconditionally stable stage. As the operating frequency is decreased the negative feedback increases because the feedback-network reactance becomes lower. This is important if reasonably constant gain is desired over a wide range of frequencies, say from 1.8 to 30 MHz.

This form of gain compensation is necessary because as the operating frequency of a given transistor is decreased, the gain increases. Typically, the gain will increase on the order of 6 dB per octave. Therefore, the probability of instability (self-oscillations) becomes a major consideration at low frequencies in an uncompensated RF amplifier.

The circuit of Fig. 53C operates stably and has a characteristic input and output impedance of approximately 50 ohms. The broadband 4:1 transformer in the collector circuit is required to step down the collector impedance to 50 ohms. Design information on this type of circuit is provided in the ARRL book, *Solid State Design for the Radio Amateur.* A band-pass filter is needed at the amplifier input. Another can be used at the output of the 4:1 transformer if desired. The transistor used in any of the amplifiers of Fig. 53 should have an f_T that is 5 to 10 times greater than the highest operating frequency of the stage. The 2N5179 has an f_T in excess of 1000 MHz, making it a good device up to 148 MHz for this application.

Transistor RF Power Amplifiers

RF power amplifiers that use bipolar transistors fall into two general categories — Class C and linear. The latter is used for AM and SSB signal amplification and the class of operation is A or AB. These amplifiers are designed for narrow or wideband applications, depending on the purpose for which the stage or stages will be used. Class C bipolar-transistor amplifiers are used for FM and CW work.

Most wideband amplifiers contain ferrite-loaded broadband transformers at the input and output ports. The output transformer is followed by a multipole low-pass filter for each band of operation. This is necessary to attenuate harmonic currents so they will not be radiated by the antenna system. Although this type of filtering is not always needed with a narrow-band amplifier (the networks provide reasonable selectivity), filters should be used in the interest of spectral purity. Two-section filters of the half-wave or low-pass T variety are entirely suitable for harmonic reduction at the 50-ohm output ports of amplifiers.

One of the principal difficulties encountered by amateurs who design and build their own high-power, solid-state amplifiers is instability at some point in the power range. That is, an amplifier driven to its maximum rated output may be stable when terminated properly, but when the drive level is reduced it is apt to break into self-oscillation at the operating frequency, at VHF or perhaps at very low frequencies. Part of the problem is caused by an increase in beta as the collector current is decreased. This elevates the amplifier gain to encourage instability. Also, solid-state amplifiers are designed for a specific network impedance at a specified power-output level. When the drive is reduced the

Fig. 53 — Illustrations of common-emitter and common-base RF amplifiers for narrow-band use. The circuit at C is that of a fed-back broadband amplifier that has a band-pass filter at the input.

collector and base impedances increase. This causes a mismatch. An increase in the loaded Q of the networks may also result — a situation that encourages instability. Therefore, it is best to design for a specified power output and adhere closely to that level during operation.

Solid-state power amplifiers should be operated just below their saturation points for best efficiency and stability. That is the point which occurs when no additional RF output can be obtained with increased driving power. Some designers recommend that, for example, a 28-volt transistor be used for 12-volt operation. Saturation will take place at a level where the transistors are relatively safe from damage if a significant output mismatch is present. Stability is usually better under these same conditions, although the gain of the transistors will be considerably lower than would be the case if equivalent types of 12-volt devices were used.

Fig. 54 shows two single-ended amplifiers of typical design. At A a broadband input transformer steps down the 50-ohm source to the lower base impedance of Q1. (Most power stages have a base im-

pedance of 5 ohms or less.) Although a number of suitable tuned networks can be used to effect the desired impedance match, the use of T1 eliminates components and the sometimes complex calculations required for the design of a proper network. When the actual base impedance of Q1 is unknown (it varies with respect to drive level and operating frequency), empirical adjustment of the T1 turns ratio will permit close matching. An SWR indicator can be used between T1 and the signal source to indicate a matched condition. This test should be made with the maximum intended drive applied.

To continue the discussion relating to Fig. 54A, a 10-ohm resistor (R1) is bridged across the secondary of T1 to aid stability. This measure is not always necessary. It will depend on the gain of the transistor, the layout and the loaded Q of T1. Other values of resistance can be used. A good rule of thumb is to employ only that value of resistance which cures instability. It must be remembered that R1 is in parallel with the transistor input impedance. This will have an effect on the turns ratio of T1. When excessive driving power is available, a deliberate mismatch can be introduced at the input to Q1 by reducing the number of secondary turns. If that is done, R1 can often be eliminated.

The shortcoming resulting from this technique is that the driving source will not be looking into a 50-ohm termination. T1 is normally a ferrite-loaded transformer — toroidal or solenoidal. The core material for operation from 1.8 to 30 MHz is typically the 950-μ_i (initial permeability) type. The primary winding of T1 (and other broadband transformers) should be approximately four times the terminal impedance with respect to reactance. Therefore, for a 50-ohm load characteristic the primary-winding reactance of T1 should be roughly 200 ohms.

Two RF chokes are shown in Fig. 54A. These are necessary to assure ample dc-lead decoupling along with the related bypass capacitors. The upper RF choke serves also as a collector load impedance. The reactance should be four or five times the collector impedance. Three values of bypass capacitors are used to ensure effective decoupling at VHF, HF and LF. If the decoupling is inadequate, RF from the amplifier can flow along the 12-volt bus to other parts of the transmitter, thereby causing instability of one or more of the stages. A simple low-pass T network is used for matching the collector to the 50-ohm load. It also suppresses harmonic energy. The loaded Q of this general type of matching network should be kept below 4 in the interest of amplifier stability. Information on this and other types of tuned matching networks is given in the *ARRL Electronics Data Book*. Data are also given in that volume concerning broadband transformer design.

Fig. 54B shows the same general amplifier. The difference is in the biasing. The circuit at A is set up for Class C. It is driven into the cutoff region during

Fig. 54 — Circuits for RF power amplifiers. At A is a Class C type. The circuit at B is biased for linear amplification.

operation. At B there is a small amount of forward bias applied to Q1 (approximately 0.7 volt) by means of the barrier voltage set by D1, a silicon power diode. D1 also functions as a simple bias regulator. R2 should be selected to provide fairly substantial diode current. The forward bias establishes linearity for the amplifier so

SSB and AM driving energy can be amplified by Q1 with minimum distortion.

Although some transistors are designed especially for linear amplification, any power transistor can be used for the purpose. Once the proper biasing point is found for linear amplification with a Class C type of transistor, an investigation of

Fig. 55 — Broadband transformers are employed at A for impedance matching. FL1 suppresses harmonic currents at the amplifier output. In the examples at B are feedback components C1 and R1 (see text).

Fig. 56 — Example of a fed-back, push-pull, RF power amplifier set up for broadband service from 1.8 to 30 MHz. The circuit is biased for linear amplification.

Fig. 57 — Examples of transistor oscillators that use crystal control.

linearity versus output power should be undertaken. Some Class C transistors are incapable of delivering as much power (undistorted) in Class AB as they can under Class C conditions. Most power transistors intended for linear amplification have built-in, degenerative-feedback resistors at the emitter sites. This technique aids linearity. Depending on the package style of a Class C type of transistor, an emitter-feedback resistor can be added externally. Such resistors are usually on the order of 1 ohm.

A broadband Class C amplifier is shown in Fig. 55A. T1 and T2 are 4:1 broadband transformers connected in series to provide an impedance step down of 16:1. For most applications this arrangement will provide an acceptable match between 50 ohms and the base impedance of Q1. In the example we have assumed a base impedance of approximately 3 ohms.

T3 serves as a collector load and a step-up transformer. It is useful to use a step-up transformer when the collector impedance is low (25 ohms or less). This enables the designer to work with filter-component values (FL1) that are more practical than would be the case if an attempt were made to match 10 ohms to 50 ohms with the filter network. FL1 in this example is a double pi-section low-pass type (half-wave filter). It is designed to match 40 ohms to 50 ohms and has a loaded Q of 1.

Feedback can be applied to stabilize the amplifier. This is seen in Fig. 55B. C1 and R1 are chosen to reduce the amplifier gain by whatever amount is necessary to provide stability and the broadband characteristics desired. C1 serves as a dc blocking capacitor.

A push-pull broadband linear amplifier is illustrated at Fig. 56. When additional frequency compensation is desired (beyond that available from a negative-feedback network) L1 and R1 can be added across the amplifier input. They are selected to roll off the driving power toward the low end of the amplifier operating range. As the frequency is reduced, L1 represents a lower reactance, thereby permitting some of the drive power to be dissipated in R1.

T1 is a conventional broadband transformer (not a transmission-line type) with a turns ratio set for matching 50 ohms to the base load presented by Q1 and Q2. T2, another broadband transformer, is used to provide balanced dc feed to the collectors. T3 is another broadband transformer which is wound for lowering the collector-to-collector impedance to 50 ohms. FL1 is designed for a bilateral impedance of 50 ohms in this example.

Bipolar-Transistor Oscillators

Transistors function well as crystal-controlled or LC oscillators. RC oscillators are also practical when a bipolar transistor is used as the active element. The same circuits used for tube-type oscillators apply when using transistors. The essential difference is that transistor oscillators have lower input and output impedances, operate at low voltages and deliver low output power — usually in the milliwatt range. The greater the oscillator power, the greater the heating of the transistor junction and other circuit elements. Therefore, in the interest of oscillator stability it is wise to keep the dc input power as low as practical. The power level can always be increased by means of subsequent amplifier stages at minor cost.

Some representative examples of crystal-controlled oscillators are provided in Fig. 57. At A is an oscillator that can be used to obtain output at f (the crystal frequency), or at multiples of f. The circuit at B illustrates a Pierce type of oscillator for fundamental output at 3.5 MHz. C_{fb} may be necessary with some crystals to provide ample feedback to cause oscillation. The value of C_{fb} will depend on the operating frequency and the gain of the transistor. Typically for 1.8 to 20-MHz crystals (fundamental mode) the capacitance value ranges from 25 to 100 pF. The higher values are typical at the lower end of the frequency range. In Fig. 57C is an overtone oscillator. The collector tuned circuit must be able to resonate slightly above the crystal overtone frequency in order to ensure oscillation. Low-impedance output can be had by means of the link shown. Alternatively, a capacitive divider can be placed across the inductor to provide a low-Z tap-off point. The trimmer should be retained in parallel with the inductor to permit resonating the circuit.

Some typical RF and audio oscillators are shown in Fig. 58. The circuit at A obtains feedback by means of the emitter tap on the tuned circuit. Approximately 25 percent of the oscillator RF power is used as feedback. The tap point on this type of oscillator is between 10 and 25 percent of the total coil turns. The designer should use the smallest amount of feedback that will provide reliable oscillator performance with the load connected.

Fig. 58B illustrates a series-tuned Colpitts oscillator, although this general circuit is often referred to as a "series-tuned Clapp" oscillator. It is very stable when polystyrene capacitors are used in the feedback and tuned circuits. Silver-mica capacitors can be used as substitutes at a slight sacrifice in drift stability (long term).

A twin-T audio oscillator is shown at C in Fig. 58. It is a very stable type of circuit that delivers a clean sine-wave output. Mylar or polystyrene capacitors should be used for best stability.

A simple feedback circuit is effected by means of T1 in Fig. 58D. T1 is a small transistor output transformer with a center-tapped primary and an 8-ohm secondary. This circuit is excellent for use as a code-practice or side-tone oscillator. All of the RF oscillators described in these examples should be followed by one or more buffer

Fig. 58 — The circuits at A and B are VFOs for use in transmitters or receivers. Audio oscillators are shown at C and D.

Fig. 59 — Some typical bipolar-transistor mixers. Their characteristics are discussed in the text.

mixers of Fig. 59 can be used without RF amplifier stages ahead of them for frequencies up to and including 7 MHz. The noise in that range (ambient from the antenna) will exceed that of the mixer.

The primary limitation in the performance of the mixer of Fig. 59A is that the local-oscillator voltage is injected at the base. This does not afford good LO/input-signal isolation. The unfavorable result can be oscillator "pulling" with input load changes, and/or radiation of the LO energy via the antenna if the front-end selectivity is marginal or poor. The advantage of the circuit is that it requires less injection voltage than the one at B, where emitter injection is used.

At Fig. 59B is the same basic mixer, but with LO voltage applied to the emitter. This technique requires slightly higher levels of LO energy, but affords greater isolation from the mixer input port.

A singly balanced bipolar-transistor mixer is illustrated in Fig. 59C. R1 is adjusted to effect balance. This circuit could be modified for emitter injection by changing R1 to 1000 ohms, replacing the 220-ohm resistors with 1-mH RF chokes, and injecting the LO output at the junction of the two 0.01-μF capacitors. The center tap of the input transformer (base winding) would then be bypassed by means of a 0.01-μF capacitor.

Other Uses for Bipolar Transistors

It is possible to take advantage of the junction characteristics of small-signal transistors for applications that usually employ diodes. One useful technique is using transistors as voltage-variable capacitors (varactors). This method is depicted in Fig. 60. The collector-base junction of Q1 and Q2 serve as diodes for tuning the VFO. In this example the emitters are left floating. A single transistor could be used, but by connecting the pair in a back-to-back arrangement they never conduct during any part of the RF cycle. This minimizes loading of the oscillator. The junction capacitance is varied by adjusting the tuning control, R1. In this circuit the tuning range is approximately 70 kHz.

A bipolar-transistor junction can be used as a Zener diode in the manner shown in Fig. 61. Advantage is taken of the reverse-breakdown characteristic of Q1 to establish a fixed reference level. Most transistors provide Zener-diode action between 6 and 9 volts. The exact value can be determined experimentally.

When the base and collector of a bipolar transistor are connected and a forward bias applied to the base-emitter junction, a superdiode results. If the collector were left open, the base-emitter junction would behave like an ordinary diode. With the collector tied to the base, the diode current rises much more rapidly with applied voltage because of the amplification provided by the transistor action. Two cross-

stages to prevent frequency changes resulting from load variations occurring after the oscillator chain.

Transistor Mixers

Much of the modern equipment used by amateurs contains mixers that use FETs or diode rings, both of which offer good dynamic range. However, there is no reason why a bipolar mixer can't be used to obtain satisfactory results if care is taken with the operating parameters and the gain distribution in the receiver and transmitter where they are used. The bipolar transistors used in receiver mixers should be selected

according to noise figure (low) and dynamic range (high). The signal applied to it should be kept as low as possible, consistent with low-noise operation. Most semiconductor manufacturers specify certain transistors for mixer service. Although this does not mean other types of bipolar transistors can't be used for mixing, it is wise to select a device designed for that class of service.

Fig. 59 contains examples of three basic types of transistor mixers. At A is the most common one. It is found in simple circuits such as transistor AM broadcast-band receivers. As an aid to dynamic range, the

Fig. 60 — Bipolar transistors serve as varactor tuning diodes in this circuit (Q1 and Q2).

Fig. 64 — An SCR and its discrete functional near-equivalent.

Fig. 61 — A bipolar transistor will function as a Zener diode when connected as shown here.

Fig. 62 — A peak clipper circuit using bipolar transistors connected in the superdiode configuration.

Fig. 63 — Constant-current generators made with bipolar transistors. In A, the reference voltage established by the diodes is converted to a current by the emitter resistor. A two-transistor feedback arrangement is employed at B. The functions of both circuits are explained in the text.

connected super-diodes form the basis for a highly effective peak clipper or hard limiter. Fig. 62 illustrates the application. NPN transistors are shown, but PNP units will yield identical performance.

Constant-Current Generators

The curves in Figs. 41 to 43 show that the collector current of a bipolar transistor is essentially independent of the collector-to-emitter potential when the device is biased in its active region. Fig. 63A illustrates a constant-current source (or sink, if actual electron flow is considered) using a PNP transistor. A fairly constant 1.2-volt potential drop is maintained across the diode string. The base-emitter junction introduces a diode drop, so the EMF applied to the 62-Ω resistor is a constant 0.6 volt. A constant voltage across a resistor forces a constant current. This current flows in the emitter, and the high alpha causes the collector current to be nearly the same.

The circuit of Fig. 63B works in a similar manner. R1 biases Q1 into conduction. When the EMF developed by R2 reaches 0.6 volt, Q2 begins to conduct, shunting base drive away from Q1 and limiting its collector current.

A device that passes an arbitrary current independent of the applied voltage presents an infinite dynamic impedance to the driving signal. This feature makes the constant-current generator valuable in several applications. One use for the circuits of Fig. 63 is in the bias control circuit of a differential amplifier. Either configuration can be used to establish the proper amplifier current while providing the tightest possible coupling between the emitters of the differential pair.

Another way to employ a constant-current circuit is to use it as an active load for the collector of a transistor amplifier stage. The infinite dynamic impedance of the current source causes the amplifier to exhibit very high voltage gain. When the amplifier is an NPN transistor, the current source must be a PNP device, and vice-versa.

Thyristors

Two complementary bipolar transistors connected as in Fig. 64 form the solid-state analog of the latching relay; a trigger pulse applied to the base of Q2 will initiate current flow in both devices. This current is limited only by the external circuit resistance and continues independent of the trigger signal until the main source is interrupted. Four-layer semiconductors

Fig. 65 — Schematic diagram of motor-speed control.
Q1 — Triac (silicon bidirectional thyristor), 8A, 200 V (Motorola MAC2-4 or HEP340 or equiv.).
D1 — Diac (silicon bilateral trigger), 2 A, 300 mW.

Fig. 67 — Profile and symbol for an N-channel junction field-effect transistor. In a P-channel device, all polarities are reversed and the gate arrow points away from the substrate.

Fig. 66 — A relaxation oscillator based on a unijunction transistor. The frequency of oscillation is approximately 1500 Hz.

(PNPN or NPNP) having this property are known as thyristors or silicon controlled rectifiers (SCRs). SCRs find use in power supply overvoltage protection circuits (crowbars), electronic ignition systems, alarms, solid-state commutating systems for dc motors and a host of other applications.

Two complementary SCRs fabricated in parallel, with a common gate terminal, form a triac. These are used to switch alternating currents. The most common application of the triac is in incandescent light dimmers. Triacs have sensitive gates, and prolonging the trigger signal or injecting excessive gate current can cause excessive heating. In circuits operating on 117-volt ac, a diac is used to trigger a triac. A diac is a bidirectional current-limiting diode. Structurally, it can be compared to a triac without a gate. A motor speed control illustrating the use of triacs and diacs are drawn in Fig. 65.

Unijunction Transistors

An unusual three-terminal semiconductor device is the unijunction transistor (UJT), sometimes called a double-base diode. The elements of a UJT are base 1, base 2 and emitter. The single rectifying junction is between the emitter and the silicon substrate. The base terminals are ohmic contacts, meaning the current is a linear function of the applied voltage. Current flowing between the bases sets up a voltage gradient along the substrate. In operation, the direction of flow causes the emitter junction to be reverse biased.

The relaxation oscillator circuit (the most common UJT application) of Fig. 66 illustrates the function of the UJT. When the circuit is energized, the capacitor charges through the resistor until the emitter voltage overcomes the reverse bias. As soon as current flows in the emitter, the resistance of the base 1 region decreases dramatically, discharging the capacitor. The decreased base 1 resistance alters the voltage distribution along the substrate, establishing a new bias point for the emitter junction. As more and more emitter current flows, the majority carrier injection builds a space charge in the base 1 region, which causes the emitter current to cease. Current is again available to charge the capacitor and the cycle repeats.

If the resistor were replaced by a constant-current source, the output waveform would be a linear ramp instead of a sawtooth. The UJT schematic symbol resembles that of an N-channel JFET — the angled emitter distinguishes the unijunction transistor.

Field-Effect Transistors

Field-effect transistors are assigned that name because the current flow in them is controlled by varying electric field that is brought about through the application of a voltage that controls the electrode known as the gate. By contrast, in a bipolar transistor, output current flow is controlled by the current applied to the base electrode.

There are two types of field-effect transistors (FETs) in use today — the junction FET (JFET) and the MOSFET. The JFET has no insulation between its elements. The MOSFET has a thin layer of oxide between the gate or gates and the drain-source junction. The term MOSFET is derived from metal-oxide silicon field-effect transistor. The basic characteristics of the two types are similar — high input impedance and good dynamic range. These characteristics apply to small-signal FETs. Power FETs, which will be treated later, have different characteristics.

Although some MOSFETs have but one gate, others have two gates. Single-gate FETs can be equated to a triode vacuum tube. The gate represents the grid, the anode is similar to the drain and the cathode is like the source. The input impedance of FETs is a megohm or greater. Their noise figure is quite low, making them ideal as preamplifiers for audio and RF well into the UHF region. Nearly all of the MOSFETs manufactured today have built-in gate-protective Zener diodes. Without this provision the gate insulation can be perforated easily by small static charges on the user's hands or by the application of excessive voltages. The protective diodes are connected between the gate (or gates) and the source of FET.

The Junction FET

As was stated earlier, field-effect transistors are divided into two main groups: Junction FETs and MOSFETs. The basic JFET is shown in Fig. 67.

Fig. 68 — Operation of a JFET under applied bias. A depletion region (light shading) is formed, compressing the channel and increasing the resistance to current flow.

Fig. 69 — Profile and symbol for a MOSFET.

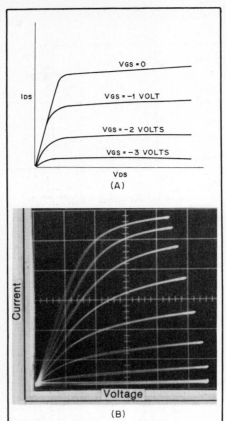

Fig. 70 — At A are typical JFET characteristic curves. The picture at B shows an actual oscillograph of the family of curves produced by a curve tracer.

Fig. 71 — Typical characteristic curves for a MOSFET.

The reason for the terminal names will become clear later. A dc operating condition is set up by starting a current flow between source and drain. This current flow is made up of free electrons since the semiconductor is N-type in the channel, so a positive voltage is applied at the drain. This positive voltage attracts the negatively charged free electrons and the current flows (Fig. 68). The next step is to apply a gate voltage of the polarity shown in Fig. 68. Note that this reverse-biases the gates

with respect to the source, channel and drain. This reverse-bias gate voltage causes a depletion layer to be formed, which takes up part of the channel. Since the electrons now have less volume in which to move, the resistance is greater and the current between source and drain is reduced. If a large gate voltage is applied, the depletion regions meet, causing pinch-off; consequently, the source-drain current is reduced nearly to zero. Since the large source-drain current changes with a relatively small gate

voltage, the device acts as an amplifier. In the operation of that JFET, the gate terminal is never forward biased, because if it were the source-drain current would all be diverted through the forward-biased gate junction diode.

The resistance between the gate terminal and the rest of the device is very high, since the gate terminal is always reverse biased, so the JFET has a very high input resistance. The source terminal is the source of current carriers, and they are drained out of the circuit at the drain. The gate opens and closes the amount of channel current that flows in the pinch-off region. The operation of an FET thus closely resembles the operation of the vacuum tube with its high grid-input impedance.

MOSFETs (Metal-Oxide Semiconductors)

The other large family that makes up field-effect transistors is the insulated-gate FET, or MOSFET, which is pictured schematically in Fig. 69. In order to set up a dc operating condition, a positive polarity is applied to the drain terminal. The substrate is connected to the source, and both are at ground potential, so the channel electrons are attracted to the positive drain. In order to regulate this source-drain current, voltage is applied to the gate contact. The gate is insulated from the rest of the device by a layer of very thin dielectric material, so this is not a PN junction between the gate and the device — thus the name insulated gate. When a negative gate polarity is applied, positive-charged holes from the P-type substrate are attracted toward the gate and the conducting channel is made more narrow; thus, the source-drain current is reduced.

When a positive gate voltage is connected, the holes in the substrate are repelled, the conducting channel is made larger and the source-drain current is increased. The MOSFET is more flexible since either a positive or negative voltage can be applied to the gate. The resistance between the gate and the rest of the device is extremely high because they are separated by a layer of thin dielectric. Thus, the MOSFET has an extremely high input impedance. In fact, since the leakage through the insulating material is generally much smaller than through the reverse-biased PN gate junction in the JFET, the MOSFET has a much higher input impedance. Typical values of R_{in} for the MOSFET are over a million megohms.

Both single-gate and dual-gate MOSFETs are available. The latter has a signal gate, gate 1, and a control gate, gate 2. The gates are effectively in series, making it an easy matter to control the dynamic range of the device by varying the bias on gate 2. Dual-gate MOSFETs are widely used as AGC-controlled RF and IF amplifiers, as mixers and product detectors and as variable attenuators. The isolation between the gates is relatively high in mixer service. This reduces oscillator "pulling"

Fig. 72 — Profile and symbol for a power FET (VMOS enhancement-mode type).

Fig. 73 — Curve showing relationship between gate-source voltage and drain current of a power FET.

Fig. 74 — Curves for 24- and 36-volt operation of a power FET.

and reduces oscillator radiation. The forward transadmittance (transconductance, or G_m) of dual-gate MOSFETs is as high as 40,000 microsiemens.

FET Characteristics

The characteristic curves for the FETs described above are shown in Figs. 70 and 71. The drain-source current is plotted against drain-source voltage for given gate voltages.

The dynamic characteristics of an FET are most heavily influenced by dynamic mutual conductance or transconductance. This parameter is defined as the ratio of drain current change to the small gate-to-source voltage change that caused it. Mathematically, the relationship is expressed $G_m = \Delta I_D / \Delta E_{GS}$, where Δ represents a small change or increment. Typical general-purpose JFETs for small-signal RF and audio work have G_m values in the neighborhood of 5000 microsiemens, while some units designed for CATV service feature transconductance over 13,000 μS. As mentioned earlier, 40,000 μS (40 mS) is the transconductance figure for the "hottest" dual-gate MOSFETs. Some JFETs intended for analog switching also have 40 mS or more of transconductance to achieve low ON resistance. The newer power FETs boast transconductance figures on the order of 1 siemen.

Transconductance is of great importance in calculating the gain and impedance values of FET circuits. In common-source and common-gate amplifiers with no degeneration, the numerical voltage gain is given by $A_v = G_m R_L$, where A_v is the gain, G_m is the transconductance in siemens and R_L is the drain load resistance

in ohms. Also, the source impedance of a common-gate or common-drain (source follower) amplifier is approximately $1/G_m$.

Classifications

Field-effect transistors are classified into two main groupings for application in circuits — enhancement mode and depletion mode. The enhancement-mode devices are those specifically constructed so they have no channel. They become useful only when a gate voltage is applied that causes a channel to be formed. IGFETs (insulated-gate FET) can be used as enhancement-mode devices since both polarities can be applied to the gate without the gate becoming forward biased and conducting.

A depletion-mode unit corresponds to Figs. 66 and 67, shown earlier, where a channel exists with no gate voltage applied. For the JFET we can apply a gate voltage and deplete the channel, causing the current to decrease. With the MOSFET we can apply a gate voltage of either polarity so the device can be depleted (current decreased) or enhanced (current increased).

To sum up, a depletion-mode FET is one that has a channel constructed; thus, it has a current flow for zero gate voltage. Enhancement-mode FETs are those that have no channel, so no current flows with zero gate voltage.

Power FETs

FETs capable of handling substantial amounts of power are available for use from dc through the VHF spectrum. They are known under more than one name — vertical FETs, MOSPOWER FETs and VMOS FETs. The power FET was introduced in 1976 by Siliconix, Inc. The device enabled designers to switch a current of 1 ampere in less than 4 nanoseconds. The transfer characteristic of the power FET is a linear one. It can be employed as a linear power amplifier or a low-noise, small-signal amplifier with high dynamic range. With

this kind of FET there is no thermal runaway, as is the case with power types of bipolar transistors. Furthermore, there is no secondary breakdown or minority-carrier storage time. This makes them excellent for use in switching amplifiers (Class D service). Of particular interest to amateurs is the immunity of power FETs to damage from a high SWR (open or short condition). These devices can be operated in Class A, AB, B or C. Zero bias results in Class C operation.

Fig. 72 illustrates the manner in which a power FET is formed. These devices operate in the enhancement mode. The current travels vertically. The source is on top of the chip but the drain is on the bottom of the chip. In this vertical structure there are four layers of material ($N+$, P, $N-$ and $N+$). This device offers high current density, high source/drain breakdown capability and low gate/drain feedback capacitance. These features make the transistor ideal for HF and VHF use.

Fig. 73 depicts the drain current as being linearly proportional to the gate-to-source voltage. The more conventional JFET exhibits a square-law response (drain current being proportional to the square of the gate-to-source voltage).

As an example, the M/A COM PHI VMP-4 power FET can provide a power just short of 20 watts (saturated) at 160 MHz. Fig. 74 shows curves for this device respective to saturated output power versus frequency. In this case both the input and output impedances of the transistor are matched conjugately. An advantage to this device over the power bipolar transistor is that these impedances are barely affected by the drive levels applied. In wideband amplifier service the power FET can be operated with complete stability. In-depth data on these devices is given in M/A COM application note AN80-2.

GaAsFETs

For low-noise amplification at UHF and

Fig. 75 — Some typical audio amplifiers that employ FETs.

A, except that a dual-gate MOSFET is used as the active device (Q1). A positive bias is supplied to gate 2 by means of a resistive divider. In the circuit of Fig. 75C, a PNP transistor is combined with a JFET to provide a direct-coupled pair. This configuration provides high gain. The amount of gain is set by the ratio of R1 and R2. Again, the input and output impedances are largely determined by the values of the input and output resistors, 1 megohm and 1000 ohms, respectively.

RF and IF Amplifiers

Small-signal RF and IF amplifiers that use FETs are capable of good dynamic range and will exhibit a low noise figure. It is for these reasons that many designers prefer them to bipolar transistors. Fig. 76 contains examples of FET RF or IF amplifiers. In the example at A the gate and drain elements of Q1 are tapped down on L2 and L3 to provide stability. This represents an intentional mismatch, which causes a slight sacrifice in stage gain. The 10-ohm drain resistor (R1) is used only if VHF parasitic oscillations occur.

Fig. 76B depicts a common-gate FET amplifier. The source is tapped well down on the input tuned circuit to effect an impedance match. This circuit is characterized by its excellent stability, provided the gate lead is returned to ground by the shortest path possible. This type of circuit will have slightly less gain capability than the common-source example at A.

In Fig. 76 at C is an illustration of a dual-gate MOSFET amplifier. Provided the input and output tuned circuits are well isolated from one another, there is less chance for self-oscillation than with a JFET. A positive bias is applied to gate 2, but AGC voltage can be used in place of a fixed-value voltage if desired. This circuit can provide up to 25 dB of gain.

Fig. 76D shows the configuration of a cascode RF amplifier in which a dual JFET (Siliconix U257) is specified. The advantage in using the dual FET is that both transistors have nearly identical characteristics, because they are fabricated on a common substrate. Two separate JFETs can be used in this circuit if the one nearest to V_{DD} has an I_{DSS} higher than its mate. This ensures proper dc bias for cascode operation. Unmatched FETs require special forward-biasing techniques and ac-coupling measures that aren't seen in this circuit.

Cascode amplifiers are noted for their high gain, good stability and low noise figure. With the circuit shown the noise figure at 28 MHz is approximately 1.5 dB. Short leads are necessary, and shielding between the tuned circuits is recommended in the interest of stability. Careful layout will permit the use of toroidal inductors at L2 and L3. These components should be spaced apart and mounted at right angles to one another in order to reduce unwanted infringing magnetic fields. AGC can be ap-

microwaves, the state of the art is defined by field-effect transistors fabricated from gallium arsenide. Also used in LEDs and microwave diodes, gallium arsenide is semiconductor compound, as opposed to silicon and germanium, which are elements. This compound exhibits greater carrier mobility (the electrons can move more freely) than silicon or germanium; hence, the transit time is reduced and high-frequency performance improved in GaAsFETs. GaAsFETs are classified as depletion-mode junction devices. The gate is made of gold or aluminum, (which is susceptible to damage from static charges).

GaAsFETs are available for both small-signal and power applications. The power devices have noise figures almost as low as those specified for the small-signal types, and naturally exhibit greater dynamic range and ruggedness. Several semiconductor manufacturers offer gallium-arsenide field-effect transistors in various noise figure, frequency and power ratings. In the U.S., Hewlett-Packard and Microwave Semiconductor Corp. feature units usable up through frequency of Ku-band. Representative type numbers are HFET-2201 and MSC H001, respectively. In Great Britain,

the Plessey GAT5 and GAT6 devices feature low-noise performance up to 14 GHz. The Nippon Electric Company of Japan is also competing strongly for leadership in the GaAsFET market. A practical GaAsFET preamplifier is featured in Chapter 32. For more background information on GaAsFETs, see Wade, "Introduction to GaAs Field-Effect Transistors," *Ham Radio,* January 1978, and Wade and Katz, "Low-Noise GaAsFET UHF preamplifiers," *QST,* June 1978.

Practical FET Circuits

Small-signal FETs can be used in the same general types of circuits given earlier for bipolar transistors. The primary obstacle in some types of amplifier circuits is instability. Certain precautions are necessary to prevent unwanted self-oscillations, but they do not differ markedly from those techniques applied when working with triode tubes.

In Fig. 75 are examples of FET audio amplifiers. The circuit at A shows a simple RC coupled stage with a gain of 10 dB or greater. The input and output impedances are set by the gate and drain resistors. The circuit at B in Fig. 75 is similar to that at plied to this amplifier by routing the control voltage to the gate of Q1B.

FET Mixers

There are three types of FET mixers in common use today — single-ended, singly balanced and doubly balanced. In all cases there is an advantage to using active devices in place of passive ones (diodes). This ensures a conversion gain that helps minimize the number of gain stages required in a given circuit.

A single-ended JFET mixer requires 0 dBm of LO injection power. It can provide several decades of bandwidth and has a good IMD characteristic. The latter is far superior to most bipolar single-ended mixers. The major shortcoming is very poor isolation between the three mixer ports (RF, LO and IF). A typical single-ended mixer using a JFET is shown in Fig. 77A. Optimum trade-off between conversion gain and IMD occurs near the point where the self-bias is 0.8 V. LO injection voltage will be on the order of 1 (P-P) to provide good mixer performance. Conversion gain with this mixer will be approximately 10 dB.

Fig. 77B illustrates a singly balanced JFET mixer. A broadband transformer (T1) provides a low-impedance source for the LO and supplies injection voltage in push-pull to the gates of Q1 and Q2. The latter should be matched FETs or a dual FET such as the U430 by Siliconix. This mixer provides between 10 and 20 dB of isolation between the mixer ports. The signal is applied in parallel across the sources of Q1 and Q2 by means of broadband transformer T2. Output at the IF is taken from a balanced tuned circuit.

A doubly balanced FET mixer is shown at C in Fig. 77. Broadband transformers are used throughout, with FL1 and FL2 providing low-pass selectivity at the mixer output. The filters also provide an impedance stepdown between the drains of Q1 and T4 (1700 ohms to 100 ohms). LO injection is supplied to the gates and signal input is to the sources. Port-to-port isolation with this mixer is on the order of 30 dB or greater. Bandwidth is one octave. In-depth information on this type of circuit is given in Siliconix application note AN-73-4.

Fig. 78 contains the circuit of a typical dual-gate MOSFET single-ended mixer. Its performance characteristics are similar to those of the mixer at Fig. 77A. The primary exception is that the port-to-port isolation is somewhat better by virtue of the gate 2 isolation from the remainder of the electrodes. This mixer and all other active FET mixers require a fairly low drain-load impedance in the interest of good IMD. If the drain tuned circuit is made high in terms of impedance (in an effort to improve conversion gain) the drain-source peak signal swing will be high. This will lead to a change in junction capacitance (varactor effect) and the generation of harmonic currents. The result is distortion.

Of primary significance is the condition called "drain-load distortion." This malady occurs when excessive signal levels overload the drain circuit. The result is degraded IMD and cross-modulation effects. R1 in Fig. 78 is used to decrease the drain-load impedance by means of swamping. A value of 10,000 ohms is suitable for a 40673 MOSFET mixer. Some JFETs require a lower drain load for optimum performance. Values as low as 5000 ohms are not unusual. This form of

Fig. 76 — Examples of FET amplifiers suitable for RF or IF applications.

Fig. 77 — Various JFET mixers. See text for data.

overloading is more pronounced at low dc drain-voltage levels, such as 6 to 8.

FET Crystal Oscillators

A group of crystal-controlled FET oscillators is presented in Figs. 79 and 80.

At Fig. 79A is an overtone type. The tuned circuit in the drain is resonated slightly higher than the crystal frequency to ensure reliable oscillation. The circuit at B is a variation of the one at A, but performs the same function. A Pierce triode oscillator is shown in Fig. 80 at A. It is suitable for use with fundamental types of crystals. A Colpitts oscillator appears at B in Fig. 80. C_{fb} in these circuits are feedback capacitors. C_{fb} in the circuit at C is chosen experimentally. Typically, it will be from

Fig. 78 — A dual-gate MOSFET single-ended mixer.

Fig. 79 — Overtone crystal oscillators using FETs.

Fig. 80 — Fundamental-mode FET crystal oscillators.

100 to 500 pF, depending on the transistor characteristics and the crystal activity.

FET VFOs

The principle of operation for FET VFOs is similar to that discussed in the section on bipolar transistor oscillators. The notable difference is the impedance level at the device input. The circuits of Fig. 81 all have high-impedance gate terminals. Furthermore, fewer parts are needed than is true of bipolar transistor equivalent circuits: There is no resistive divider for applying forward bias.

The circuits of Fig. 81A and B are identical except for the biasing of gate 2 at B. Both circuits illustrate oscillators. The source tap on L1 should be selected to provide approximately 25 percent of the oscillator power as feedback. D1 in each example is used to stabilize the gate bias. It acts as a diode clamp on positive-going excursions of the signal. This aids oscillator stability and reduces the harmonic output of the stage. The latter is reduced as a result of the positive swing of the sine-wave being limited by D1, which in turn limits the device transconductance on peaks. This action reduces changes in junction capacitance, thereby greatly restricting the varactor action that generates harmonic currents. D1 is most effective when source-bias resistors are included in the circuit (R1).

Shown in Fig. 81 at C is a series-tuned Colpitts VFO that uses a JFET. This is an exceptionally stable VFO if careful design and component choice is applied. All of the fixed-value capacitors in the RF parts of the circuit should be temperature-stable. Polystyrene capacitors are recommended, but dipped silver-mica capacitors will serve adequately as a second choice. L1 should be a rigid air-wound inductor. A slug-tuned inductor can be used if the coil Q is high. In such cases the slug should occupy the least amount of coil space possible: Temperature changes have a marked effect on ferrite or powdered-iron slugs, which can change the coil inductance markedly. Capacitors C_{fb} of Fig. 81C are on the order of 1000 pF each for 3.5-MHz operation. They are proportionally lower in capacitance as the operating frequency is increased, such as 680 pF at 7 MHz, and so on.

Power FET Examples

Fig. 82 contains examples of three amplifiers that use power FETs. The circuit at A is an audio amplifier that can deliver 4 watts of output. At 3 watts of output the distortion is approximately two percent. Feedback is employed to aid the reduction of distortion.

A Class C amplifier is shown at B in Fig. 82. The VN67AJ is capable of a saturated output near 15 watts at 30 MHz. In this circuit the power output is considerably less. A medium output power of 7 to 10 watts is suggested. The gain is approximately 8 dB over the frequency range specified (with the appropriate drain tank). If proper layout techniques are used, this amplifier is unconditionally stable.

A broadband HF linear amplifier is shown at C. A narrow-band linear VHF power amplifier is shown at D in Fig. 82. Power output is 5 watts PEP. IMD is −30 dB. It is interesting to realize that this same amplifier is suitable as a high-dynamic-range preamplifier for a VHF receiver. In this application the noise figure is on the order of 2.5 dB and the gain is 11 dB.

Other FET Uses

Fig. 83 contains illustrations of additional practical uses for JFETs. The circuit at A shows a Schmitt trigger. It is emitter-coupled and provides a comparator func-

Fig. 81 — Three examples of VFOs in which FETs are used.

tion. Q1 places very light loading on the measured input voltage. Q2 has high beta to enable the circuit to have a fast transition action and a distinct hysteresis loop. Additional applications of this type are found in *Linear Applications* by National Semiconductor Corp.

A simple FET dc voltmeter with high input impedance is shown in Fig. 83B. Multiplier resistances are given for a full-scale range of 2 or 20 volts. Meter accuracy is quite good, with a linear reading provided by M1.

A push-push frequency doubler is shown at C in Fig. 83. The input frequency (f) is applied to the gates of Q1 and Q2 in push-pull. Output from the doubler is taken with the connected drains in parallel. R1 is adjusted for best waveform purity at 2f. The efficiency of this Class C doubler is on par with that of a straight-through Class C amplifier. Careful adjustment will nearly eliminate frequency component f at the doubler output.

LINEAR INTEGRATED CIRCUITS

Introduction

There are two general types of integrated circuits (ICs): linear and digital. This section addresses linear integrated circuits (LICs); digital ICs are discussed in the Digital Basics chapter of this *Handbook*.

LICs, often called microcircuits or chips, contain many active and passive components. Some LICs have only a single type of component (diodes or transistors), while others have a combination of capacitors, diodes, resistors and transistors. Modern linear integrated circuits contain hundreds or thousands of active and passive components.

The basic IC is formed on a uniform wafer of N-type or P-type silicon. A diffusion process introduces impurities to desired depths and widths on the substrate. Depth is controlled by diffusion time and temperature, while width is controlled by masking and photoetching. The process is similar to making a printed circuit board, but on a much smaller scale. Fig 84 shows, in both pictorial and schematic form, a representative IC having three components.

Circuit designs using linear integrated circuits generally have two advantages over their counterparts made from discrete components. The first is that all similar components on the substrate have nearly identical performance characteristics—a condition impossible to realize without very closely matched discrete components. This implies that they all behave in the same, predictable way when influenced by a change in a physical property, such as temperature. This can be very important when designing balanced circuits such as balanced modulators, balanced mixers, product detectors, differential amplifiers, push-push doublers and so forth.

The second advantage is that equipment designed with linear integrated circuits does not require as much space on a printed circuit board as one using all discrete components. This leads to more compact equipment. In many instances, the IC contains most of the circuitry, and only a few discrete components will be needed to complete the design.

The linear integrated circuit family consists of distinct categories—bipolar versus metal oxide semiconductors (MOS), and array ICs versus subsystem ICs. Complementary MOS (CMOS) linear ICs consume very little power and dissipate less heat than their bipolar counterparts. Thus, CMOS linear ICs are preferred for use in battery-powered equipment.

Most of the theory for bipolar and MOS transistors, described elsewhere in this chapter, also applies to linear integrated circuits; therefore, it will not be repeated here. Rather, the remainder of this section will focus on the application of linear integrated circuits.

Practical Considerations

Linear integrated circuits are available in a variety of package styles. The most popular style is the molded plastic dual in-line package (DIP) having 8, 14, 16, 18, 20 or 22 pins. Another style is the TO-5 metal can package having 8, 10 or 12 leads. Use of this style is declining, however, because

Fig. 82 — Examples of power FETs in three amplifier circuits.

it does not provide enough leads for many modern IC designs.

Many Japanese manufacturers favor a single in-line package (SIP) having from 7 to 12 pins. Most LICs are also available in ceramic DIP packages and small outline (SO) packages suitable for surface mounting.

Rather than soldering an integrated circuit directly to the printed circuit board, it is often better to install it in an appropriate socket. Using sockets makes troubleshooting (by substitution) faster and replacement of defective ICs easier.

Be aware, however, that using a socket contributes an unknown amount of stray capacitive and inductive reactance to the circuit. This may lead to adverse effects, depending on the operating frequency. Below about 10 MHz, the effect of stray reactance is usually negligible. As the frequency rises above 10 MHz, the effect of stray reactance becomes increasingly significant.

The presence of stray reactance can cause instability. Transistors in integrated circuits are high-gain devices capable of operating at very high frequencies (typical $f_T = 250$ MHz or higher). The combination of high gain and stray reactance is an invitation for parasitic oscillation.

To some extent, the material used to manufacture the socket and the style of the socket itself have a bearing on its performance. All sockets are suitable for dc and audio applications. Low-profile sockets exhibit less stray capacitive and inductive reactance than ordinary sockets and work well into the high-frequency range. Sockets having machined pins and those made of ceramic offer better performance at higher frequencies than do any of the other styles.

Another area of concern is the accidental application of an electrostatic discharge (ESD). Walking across a carpeted room, for example, causes your body to build up a surface charge of static electricity. If you don't discharge this static electricity before touching an IC, the IC may have several thousand volts applied to it, thus destroying it.

Subjecting an IC to an ESD *may not* cause irreversible damage. Most ICs have built-in ESD protection and will survive small to moderate discharges without sustaining permanent damage. Some ICs are more susceptible to damage from a static discharge, and more care is required in handling them. To lessen the chance of damaging ICs, always discharge yourself by touching a metal object before handling them. Special handling provisions, such as wearing a grounded wrist strap, can lessen the risk of damage. (See the section on MOSFETs in the Troubleshooting and Repair chapter for information on safely handling ICs.) Such precautions are especially important in low-temperature, low-humidity environments.

Array LICs

One branch of the linear integrated

Fig. 83 — JFETs are useful in additional kinds of circuits. Here are three examples.

Fig 84—Pictorial and schematic representations of a simple IC.

every stage of communications equipment. Nearly all major semiconductor companies manufacture subsystem ICs.

The internal complexity of a subsystem IC is much greater than an array IC. It is for this reason that the internal circuitry of a subsystem IC is shown schematically using block diagram representation. The only place you are likely to find a diagram of the component-level circuitry is in the manufacturer's data sheet.

To realize a functional circuit, it is usually necessary to add only a few external components. Typically, the external components include items such as bypass and coupling capacitors, tuned circuits, filters, feedback networks and a power supply.

The following paragraphs describe only a few of the subsystem LICs available today. The discussions are organized by the service performed.

AF Amplifiers

There are a variety of linear integrated circuits available for use at audio frequencies. Depending on the particular device, AF-amplifier ICs are capable of producing maximum power outputs from 250 mW to 10 W or more.

Audio power amplifier ICs are almost always designed to drive a low-impedance load (4- to 16-Ω speaker) directly through a coupling capacitor. The reactance of the coupling capacitor must be much less than the impedance of the speaker at the lowest usable frequency. As a result, the value of this capacitor is large, ranging from 470 to 1000 μF when the lowest frequency desired is 300 Hz.

A typical example of an AF-amplifier IC is the TA7205. This is an audio subsystem that can be used as the entire AF-amplifier stage of a receiver. See Fig 86. The TA7205 has a high input impedance (50 kΩ), produces up to 5.8-W output, has a total harmonic distortion (THD) of less than 0.15% (at 1 W) and a voltage gain exceeding 50 dB. The network between pins 4 and 5 was optimized for a useful bandwidth ranging from 300 to 3000 Hz.

circuit family is the array IC. An array IC doesn't perform a specific function. Instead, it provides the circuit designer with the freedom to design a circuit using a set of closely matched components.

An array IC may contain several diodes or transistors, or both. Each component is independent from others on the substrate. The leads of each component terminate at separate pins on the IC package. The CA3019 and CA3026, two of the more popular array ICs, are shown schematically in Fig 85.

The advantage of array ICs is that all similar components (diodes, transistors, and so forth) have nearly identical characteristics. This is an important consideration when designing balanced circuits. A short course on array ICs, written by Doug DeMaw, appeared in *QST* in January, February and March 1977.

Subsystem LICs

Another branch of the linear integrated circuit family is the subsystem IC. Subsystem ICs perform one particular function or a group of related functions.

Subsystem ICs are available for nearly

Fig 85—The CA3019 and CA3026 are examples of array ICs. The electrical characteristics of each similar component on the substrate are nearly identical.

Fig 86—The TA7205 is an audio-amplifier subsystem IC. It contains both preamplifier and power-amplifier stages.

Fig 87—The LM3011 is a wide-band, small-signal amplifier IC capable of producing usable gain into the VHF region.

PIN	FUNCTION
1	Input +
2	Input −
3	AC Bypass
4	AC Bypass
5	Output
6	NC
7	NC
8	Ground
9	NC
10	V_{cc}

BALANCED RF OR IF AMPLIFIER
(A)

SINGLE-ENDED RF OR IF AMPLIFIER
(B)

PIN	FUNCTION
1	RF input
2	LO input
3	Ground
4	Bypass
5	RF input
6	IF output
7	V_{cc}
8	IF output

Fig 88—The CA3028 is a wide-band, small-signal amplifier IC that can be used with balanced or single-ended input or output, or both.

A muting feature, which permits the squelch detector output or TR switch to mute the audio output, can be added easily. The circuitry contained in the box shows one way this could be done. When the external signal turns on the transistor switch, pin 7 is pulled to dc ground level, thus muting the audio output.

Small-Signal RF and IF Amplifiers

Small-signal amplifiers used for RF or IF stages are nearly identical. The primary distinction between the two is the frequency of operation, but there is no exact dividing point. For example, 50 kHz, 100 kHz, 262 kHz, 455 kHz, 500 kHz, 9 MHz and 10.7 MHz are all commonly recognized as intermediate frequencies. HF equipment using the up-conversion technique and equipment operating at VHF/UHF also commonly use frequencies between 45 MHz and 75 MHz as intermediate frequencies, however. The distinction between RF and IF is one best left to philosophers.

Wide-band amplifier ICs can be used as small-signal amplifiers in RF and IF stages. ICs in this category are often called gain blocks, because their primary purpose is to provide a substantial amount of gain over a specified bandwidth or, for a fixed-frequency IF stage, a single frequency.

The LM3011 is a wide-band linear amplifier. See Fig 87. This gain block provides a voltage gain of about 61 dB at 10.7 MHz.

The CA3028 can be used as a differential or cascode amplifier up to 120 MHz. The circuits shown in Fig 88 are AGC-controlled amplifiers having a gain of about 40 dB. Maximum gain occurs when the AGC voltage is at its highest potential. The difference between the two configurations shown is that circuit A is balanced for both ac and dc, whereas circuit B is balanced for dc only.

The MC1350 and MC1590 wide-band amplifiers can be used as gain blocks up to 120 MHz. The circuits shown in Fig 89 are AGC-controlled amplifiers having gains of up to 62 dB. Maximum gain occurs when the AGC voltage is at its lowest potential.

The CA3076 is an amplifier-limiter intended for FM IF-amplifier service. The circuit shown in Fig 90 has a voltage gain of about 80 dB at 10.7 MHz, and −3 dB of limiting for a 50-μV input signal.

Another type of wide-band amplifier is the monolithic microwave integrated circuit (MMIC). These are bipolar ICs featuring a very large bandwidth (dc to the GHz range) and 50- or 75-Ω input and output impedances. The circuit shown in Fig 91 is a linear amplifier for use between dc and 2.5 GHz. The gain falls from about 20 dB at dc to 5 dB at 2.5 GHz. A series of comprehensive articles about MMICs, written by Al Ward, WB5LUA, appeared in *QST* in February and March 1987.

Mixers

Some of the ICs previously discussed can

U1 MC1350P	
PIN	FUNCTION
1	RF output
2	V_{cc}
3	Ground
4	RF input
5	AGC
6	RF input
7	Ground
8	RF output

Except as indicated, decimal values of capacitance are in microfarads (μF); others are in picofarads (pF); resistances are in ohms; k = 1,000, M = 1,000,000.

Fig 89—The MC1350 and MC1590 are wide-band, small-signal amplifier ICs suitable for use at 60 MHz and beyond.

U1 MC1590G	
PIN	FUNCTION
1	Output A
2	Inverting input A
3	Non−inverting input A
4	Ground
5	Non−inverting input B
6	Inverting input B
7	Output B
8	V_{cc}

(A)

(B)

Fig 90—The CA3076 is an amplifier-limiter subsystem IC for FM receivers. The value of the input and output resistors should be selected to match the characteristic impedance of the ceramic filters.

R_{FLTR} = VALUE RECOMMENDED FOR FILTER USED

Except as indicated, decimal values of capacitance are in microfarads (μF); others are in picofarads (pF).

U1 CA3076	
PIN	FUNCTION
1	IF Input
2	Bypass
3	Ground
4	IF Output
5	Ground
6	Ground
7	V_{cc}
8	IF Input

Fig 91—The MSA0204 and MSA0304 are examples of MMIC wide-band, small-signal amplifiers. The usable bandwidth of this amplifier is more than 2.5 GHz.

Except as indicated, decimal values of capacitance are in microfarads (μF); others are in picofarads (pF); resistances are in ohms.

Fig 92—Diodes in the CA3039 array IC can be used to build a doubly balanced passive mixer.

Fig 93—The CA3028 can be used as a singly balanced mixer by injecting the local-oscillator signal into pin 2 and connecting the AGC line (pin 7) to V_{cc}.

Fig 94—The MC1496 is a doubly balanced mixer. This circuit was optimized for use in a transmitter.

be used as mixers. In addition, several linear ICs were designed especially for mixer service.

For example, the diodes in an array IC such as the CA3039 can be externally configured for use as either a singly or doubly balanced passive mixer. The circuit shown in Fig 92 uses this IC as the basis for a doubly balanced passive mixer having a conversion gain (loss) of about −6 dB. The CA3028 can be used as a singly balanced active mixer. The circuit shown in Fig 93 has a conversion gain of about 30 dB.

The MC1496 is a Gilbert-cell doubly balanced active mixer. The circuit shown in Fig 94 was optimized for use as a transmitting mixer by W7ZOI and KL7IAK (*Solid State Design for the Radio Amateur*, 2nd edition, page 204).

The enhanced version of the MC1496 is an enhanced version of the MC1496. Besides a Gilbert-cell doubly balanced mixer, this IC also has an oscillator and two buffers, and is about half the size of the MC1496. The circuit shown in Fig 95 requires only a few external components, since the bias resistors are on the substrate. The input and output networks can be either single-ended or balanced for ac. The input and output impedances are about 1.5 kΩ for the single-ended configuration and about 3.0 kΩ for the balanced configuration. This IC has a mixer conversion gain of 14 dB and a third-order intercept point (input) of −15 dBm.

Fig 95—The NE602 contains a doubly balanced mixer, an oscillator, buffers and a voltage regulator.

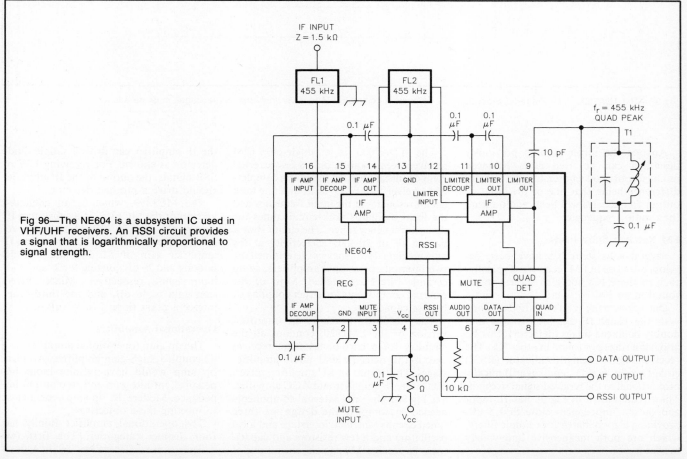

Fig 96—The NE604 is a subsystem IC used in VHF/UHF receivers. An RSSI circuit provides a signal that is logarithmically proportional to signal strength.

Fig 97—The TDA7000 is an FM-radio subsystem IC. To make a complete FM receiver, only the audio stages must be added.

Any of the mixer circuits previously described can be used as a balanced modulator or product detector, the primary difference being that one of the input or output frequencies will be at audio rather than radio frequencies.

FM Receiver Subsystems

Several subsystem ICs have been developed for use in FM receivers. Typically, each of these ICs contains several stages found in an FM receiver.

One noteworthy IC is the NE604. Along with the usual IF amplifier stages and doubly balanced mixer (detector), this IC also has a stage not found in other ICs. The received signal strength indicator (RSSI) circuit produces a dc signal logarithmically proportional to the received signal strength. The circuit shown in Fig 96 has IF input and output impedances close to 1.5 kΩ, providing a good match for ceramic filters, which are both inexpensive and widely available.

The TDA7000 is a single-chip FM receiver. Remarkably, only a few external components are needed to make a complete FM receiver. See Fig 97. The antenna tank circuit resonates at the input frequency and the local oscillator tank circuit tunes the desired frequency range. The circuit shown has an IF of 70 kHz. Selectivity at the intermediate frequency is determined by two internal operational amplifiers, so no ceramic filters are needed. Most of the external components are either coupling or bypass capacitors.

The LM3820, which is an improved version of the LM1820, contains all the circuitry for a bare-bones radio receiver except the detector and audio-amplifier stages. This IC has an RF amplifier, mixer, oscillator, IF amplifier and AGC amplifier. See Fig 98. The only external components needed to complete the design are three tuned circuits (antenna, interstage and local oscillator) and a few resistors and capacitors. To receive AM signals, the output of

the IF amplifier can drive a simple diode detector as shown. For receiving CW or SSB signals, the output of the IF amplifier should drive a product detector.

The MC3359, which is an enhanced version of the MC1357, is a subsystem IC commonly used in NBFM scanning receivers. See Fig 99. This IC features an IF amplifier gain of 51 dB, and −3 dB limiting and 20 dB quieting for 2- and 8-μV input signals, respectively. Mixer conversion gain is 46 dB, and the third-order intercept point (input) is −1 dBm.

Operational Amplifiers

The op amp (operational amplifier) is a dc-coupled, high-gain amplifier. An ideal op amp would have infinite input impedance, infinite gain and zero output impedance. Modern IC op amps come close to meeting these objectives.

The operational amplifier family has four distinct categories. The first two categories are differentiated by the type of

Fig 98—The LM3820 is a radio subsystem IC. To make a complete receiver, only audio stages and an appropriate detector must be added.

input transistor used. One uses bipolar types; the other field effect transistors (FETs). The last two categories are differentiated by their internal circuitry, and are divided into conventional (voltage) amplifiers and Norton (current) amplifiers. Within these categories, op amps are further classified by their intended function, such as general purpose, low-noise, instrumentation, wide-band, power and logarithmic.

Fig 100 shows the internal circuitry of an op amp in block diagram form. The input stage is a differential amplifier. It may consist of a matched pair of bipolar or field-effect transistors. The terminal marked "+" is the noninverting input and the one

marked "−" is the inverting input. If you apply a small positive voltage to the noninverting (+) terminal, the output of the op amp increases in the positive direction. If you apply the same voltage to the inverting (−) input, the output of the op amp increases in the negative direction. If you apply the same voltage to both terminals, the output of the op amp will be zero, theoretically.

A constant current source provides the operating bias for the differential pair. If the components making up the differential amplifier and constant current source are not precisely balanced, a small offset voltage appears at the output of the op amp. Most ICs are inherently well balanced

devices and the offset voltage is negligible. Some ICs provide a pair of terminals for connecting an external offset adjustment potentiometer. The offset control is necessary only in precise dc-coupled op amp applications where any small offset voltage would degrade circuit performance.

The differential amplifier drives a high-gain amplifier stage. This stage provides most of the voltage gain. The collector-to-base capacitance of this stage determines the overall frequency response of the op amp. Internally compensated op amps use an internal capacitor to tailor the response. Externally compensated op amps provide a pair of terminals for connecting an external compensation capacitor.

Fig 99—The MC3359 is a subsystem IC designed for VHF/UHF NBFM scanning receivers. The circuit configuration for a double-conversion receiver is shown. For a single-conversion receiver, the DBM and oscillator can be used as a frequency converter.

The high-gain amplifier drives a buffer stage. In small-signal op amps, this stage has a pair of series-connected transistors used as an emitter follower. Power op amps use a series-connected pair of Darlington transistors in the buffer stage.

Applications

Although some have useful gain to 100 MHz and beyond, op amps are used most often as linear amplifiers in the dc to 1-MHz range. As long as the op amp has sufficient open-loop gain, the response of the overall circuit depends only on the external feedback network (see Fig 101).

In Fig 102 you can see the dc-coupled amplifier configurations commonly used and the associated transfer equations. Notice that R_L does not appear in the equations, implying that the output impedance is zero; however, R_L should be at least 2 kΩ in practice.

An LH0101 power op amp can be used to drive a servo motor directly, as shown in Fig 103. The value of resistors R_{SC} depends on the maximum value of short cir-

cuit current (I_{SC}) allowable.

Fig 104 shows how a small-signal op amp, like a 741 or 1458, can be used in an ac-coupled amplifier configuration. Notice that these circuits use only a single supply.

To use an op amp with a single supply, a resistive voltage divider biases the noninverting (+) input to one-half the supply voltage. The 10-μF capacitor effectively grounds the noninverting input for ac signals.

In an ac-coupled circuit, coupling capacitors isolate the input and output of the op amp from the previous and succeeding circuits. Usually, the load resistance is the input resistance of the next stage.

An op amp can be used as an active band-pass filter, as shown in Fig 105. The noninverting input is biased to one-half the supply voltage. Additional selectivity can be realized by adding additional stages in series.

The Norton Op Amp

The Norton operational amplifier, named for the network theorem on which its operation is based, is unusual in two

respects. The input stage uses a current mirror instead of a differential pair, and the Norton op amp does not have a high impedance input. The Norton op amp is particularly well suited for dc-coupled amplifier applications where the level of dc signals is very near ground and only a single supply is available.

A simplified diagram of the input stage of a Norton amplifier appears in Fig 106. The noninverting input uses D1 and Q1 as a current mirror. When input current is applied to Q1, it "steals" base drive from Q2, the inverting input.

The Norton op amp does not a have high input impedance because it requires input current to operate. Any attempt to use a Norton op amp as a voltage follower is doomed to failure—the input stage will be destroyed by excessive current.

In the inverting amplifier configuration the numerical voltage gain is still the ratio of R_f/R_i, but the noninverting input terminal must be returned to the positive supply through a resistance of $2R_f$ to equalize the input currents.

Fig 100—Block diagram of an operational amplifier (A). The differential amplifier may consist of a pair of bipolar (B) or field-effect transistors (C).

Fig 101—Open-loop gain and closed-loop gain as a function of frequency. The vertical distance between the curves is the feedback or gain margin.

Fig 102—The four most common op amp configurations are: (A) inverting amplifier, (B) difference amplifier; (C) noninverting amplifier; and (D) voltage follower. Resistances are measured in ohms; k = 1000.

Fig 103—The LH0101 power op amp used as a dc servo amplifier. Resistors R_{SC} limit the maximum current to a safe value.

Fig 104—A typical ac-coupled, small-signal audio amplifier using a single supply.

Fig 105—A 2-pole active band-pass filter having a center frequency of 750 Hz.

Fig 106—At A, input circuit of a Norton operational amplifier. At B, Norton op amp connected as an inverting amplifier. Note the special symbol used to denote a Norton op amp.

Chapter 5

Vacuum-Tube Principles

This chapter covers the principles of vacuum-tube operation. Additional material on vacuum tubes may be found in Chapter 15. The outstanding difference between the vacuum tube and most other electrical devices is that the electric current does not flow through a conductor, but through empty space — a vacuum. This is only possible when free electrons — that is, electrons that are not attached to atoms — are somehow introduced into the vacuum. Free electrons in an evacuated space will be attracted to a positively charged object within the same space, or will be repelled by a negatively charged object. The movement of the electrons under the attraction or repulsion of such charged objects constitutes the current in the vacuum.

Thermionic Emission

The most practical way to introduce a sufficiently large number of electrons into the evacuated space is by thermionic emission. If a piece of metal is heated to incandescence in a vacuum, electrons near the surface are given enough energy of motion to fly off into the surrounding space. The higher the temperature, the greater the number of electrons emitted. In a vacuum tube, the electron-emitting material is called the cathode.

If the cathode is the only electrode in the vacuum, most of the emitted electrons stay in its immediate vicinity, forming a cloud about the cathode. The reason for this is that the electrons in the space, being negative electricity, form a negative charge (space charge) in the region of the cathode. The space charge repels those electrons nearest the cathode, tending to make them fall back on it.

Now suppose a second conductor is introduced into the vacuum, but not connected to anything else inside the tube. If this second conductor is given a positive charge by connecting a voltage source between it and the cathode, as indicated in Fig. 1, electrons emitted by the cathode are attracted to the positively charged conductor. An electric current then flows through the circuit formed by the cathode, the charged conductor and the voltage source. In Fig. 1 this voltage source is a battery (B battery); a second battery (A battery) is also indicated for heating the cathode to the

Transmitting tubes are shown in the back and center rows. Receiving tubes are in the front row (l to r): miniature, pencil, planar triode (two), Nuvistor and 1-inch-diameter cathode-ray tube.

proper operating temperature.

The positively charged conductor is usually a metal plate or cylinder (surrounding the cathode) and is called the anode or plate. Like the other working parts of a tube, the plate is a tube element or electrode. The tube shown in Fig. 1 is

Fig. 1 — Conduction by thermionic emission in a vacuum tube. The A battery is used to heat the cathode to a temperature that will cause it to emit electrons. The B battery makes the plate positive with respect to the cathode, thereby causing the emitted electrons to be attracted to the plate. Electrons captured by the plate flow back through the B battery to the cathode.

Fig. 2 — Types of cathode construction. Directly heated cathodes or filaments are shown at A, B and C. The inverted V filament is used in small receiving tubes, the M in both receiving and transmitting tubes. The spiral filament is a transmitting tube type. The indirectly heated cathodes at D and E show two types of heater construction, one a twisted loop and the other bunched heater wires. Both types tend to cancel the magnetic fields set up by the current though the heater.

Fig. 4 — Rectification in a diode. Current flows only when the plate is positive with respect to the cathode, so that only half cycles of current flow through the load resistor, R.

Fig. 3 — The diode, or two-element tube, and a typical curve showing how the plate current depends on the voltage applied to the plate.

a two-element or two-electrode tube (a diode), one element being the cathode and the other the anode or plate.

Since electrons have a negative charge, they will be attracted to the plate only when the plate is given a positive charge. If the plate is given a negative charge, the electrons will be repelled back to the cathode and no current will flow. The vacuum tube therefore can conduct only in one direction.

Cathodes

Before electron emission can occur, the cathode must be heated to a high temperature. However, it is not essential that the heating current flow through the actual material that does the emitting; the heating filament or heater can be electrically separate from the emitting cathode. Such a cathode is said to be indirectly heated, while an emitting filament is called a directly heated cathode. Fig. 2 shows both types in the forms they commonly take.

Much greater electron emission can be obtained, at relatively low temperatures, by using special cathode materials rather than pure metals. One of these is thoriated tungsten (tungsten in which thorium is dissolved). Still greater efficiency is obtained in the oxide-coated cathode, a cathode in which rare-earth oxides form a coating over a metal base.

Although the oxide-coated cathode has the highest efficiency, it can be used successfully only in tubes that operate at low plate voltages. Its use is therefore confined to receiving-type tubes and to the smaller varieties of transmitting tubes. The thoriated filament, on the other hand, will operate well in high-voltage tubes.

Plate Current

If there is only a small positive voltage on the plate, the number of electrons reaching it will be small because the space charge (which is negative) prevents those electrons nearest the cathode from being attracted to the plate. As the plate voltage is increased, the effect of the space charge is increasingly overcome and the number of electrons attracted to the plate becomes larger. That is, the plate current increases with increasing plate voltage.

Fig. 3 shows a typical plot of plate current vs. plate voltage for a two-element tube or diode. A curve of this type can be obtained with the circuit shown, if the plate voltage is increased in small steps and a current reading is taken by means of the current-indicating instrument (a milliammeter) at each voltage. The plate current is zero with no plate voltage and the curve rises until a saturation point is reached. This is where the positive charge on the plate has substantially overcome the space charge and almost all the electrons are going to the plate. At higher voltages the plate current stays at practically the same value.

The plate voltage multiplied by the plate current is the power input to the tube. In a circuit like that of Fig. 3 this power is all used in heating the plate. If the power input is large, the plate temperature may rise to a very high value (the plate may become red or even white hot). The heat developed in the plate is radiated to the bulb of the tube, and in turn to the surrounding air.

Rectification

Since current can flow through a tube in only one direction, a diode can be used to change alternating current into direct current. It does this by permitting current flow only when the anode is positive with respect to the cathode. There is no current flow when the plate is negative.

Fig. 4 shows a representative circuit. Alternating voltage from the secondary of the transformer, T, is applied to the diode tube in series with a load resistor, R. The voltage varies as is usual with ac, but current flows through the tube and R only when the plate is positive with respect to the cathode — that is, during the half cycle when the upper end of the transformer winding is positive. During the negative half cycle there is simply a gap in the current flow. This rectified alternating current therefore is an intermittent direct current.

The load resistor, R, represents the actual circuit in which the rectified alternating current does work. All tubes work with a load of one type or another; they must cause power to be developed in a load in order to serve a useful purpose. Also, to be efficient, most of the power must do useful work in the load rather than in heating the plate of the tube. Thus, the voltage drop across the load should be much higher than the drop across the diode.

With the diode connected as shown in Fig. 4, the polarity of the current through the load, R, is as indicated. If the diode were reversed, the polarity of the voltage developed across the load would be reversed.

VACUUM-TUBE AMPLIFIERS
Triodes

If a third element — called the control grid or, simply, grid — is inserted between the cathode and plate as in Fig. 5, it can be used to control the effect of the space charge. If the grid is given a positive voltage with respect to the cathode, the positive charge will tend to neutralize the negative space charge. The result is that, at any selected plate voltage, more electrons will flow to the plate than if the grid were not present. On the other hand, if the grid is made negative with respect to the cathode the negative charge on the grid will add to the space charge. This will reduce the number of electrons that can reach the plate

Fig. 5 — Construction of a basic triode vacuum tube, showing the directly heated cathode (filament), grid (with an end view of the grid wires) and plate. The relative density of the space charge is indicated roughly by the dot density.

Fig. 6 — Curves of grid voltage vs. plate current at various fixed values of plate voltage (e_b) for a typical small triode. Characteristic curves of this type can be taken by varying the battery voltages in the circuit shown.

at any selected plate voltage.

The grid is inserted in the tube to control the space charge and not to attract electrons to itself, so it is made in the form of a wire mesh or spiral. Electrons then can pass through the open spaces in the grid to reach the plate.

Characteristic Curves

For any particular tube, the effect of the grid voltage on the plate current can be shown by a set of characteristic curves. A typical set of curves is shown in Fig. 6, together with the circuit that is used for determining them. For each value of plate voltage, there is a value of negative grid voltage that will reduce the plate current to zero; that is, there is a value of negative grid voltage that will cut off the plate current.

The curves could be extended by making the grid voltage positive as well as negative. When the grid is negative, it repels electrons and therefore none of them reaches it; in other words, no current flows in the grid circuit. When the grid is positive, however, it attracts electrons and a current (grid current) flows, just as current flows to the positive plate. Whenever there is grid current there is an accompanying power loss in the grid circuit, but as long as the grid is negative no power is used.

The grid can act as a valve to control the flow of plate current. Actually, the grid has a much greater effect on plate current flow than does the plate voltage. A small change in grid voltage is just as effective in bringing about a given change in plate current as is a large change in plate voltage.

The fact that a small voltage change on the grid is equivalent to a large voltage change on the plate indicates the possibility of amplification with the triode tube. The

many uses of the electron tube are nearly all based on this amplifying characteristic. The amplified output is not obtained from the tube itself, but from the voltage source connected between its plate and cathode. The tube simply controls the power from this source, changing it to the desired form.

To utilize the controlled power, a load must be connected in the plate or output circuit, just as in the diode case. The load may be either a resistance or an impedance. The term impedance is frequently used even when the load is purely resistive.

Tube Characteristics

The physical construction of a triode determines the relative effectiveness of the grid and plate in controlling the plate current. The control of the grid increases by moving it closer to the cathode or by making the grid mesh finer.

The plate resistance of a vacuum tube is the ac resistance of the path from cathode to plate. For a given grid voltage, it is the quotient of a small change in plate voltage divided by a resultant change in plate current. Thus, if a 1-volt change in plate voltage caused a plate-current change of 0.01 mA (0.00001 or 1×10^{-5} ampere), the plate resistance would be 100,000 ohms.

The amplification factor (usually designated by the Greek letter μ) of a vacuum tube is defined as the ratio of the change in plate voltage to the change in grid voltage to effect equal changes in plate current. If, for example, an increase of 10 plate volts raised the plate current 1.0 mA, and an increase in (negative) grid voltage of 0.1 volt were required to return the plate current to its original value, the amplification factor of this triode tube would be 100. The amplification factors of triode tubes range from 2 to 100 or so. A high-μ tube

is one with an amplification of perhaps 30 or more. Medium-μ tubes have amplification factors in the approximate range 8 to 30, and low-μ tubes in the range below 7 or 8. The μ of a triode is useful in computing stage gains.

The best all-around indication of the effectiveness of a tube as an amplifier is its grid-plate transconductance — also called mutual conductance or g_m. It is the change in plate current divided by the change in grid voltage that caused the change; it can be found by dividing the amplification factor by the plate resistance. Since current divided by voltage is conductance, transconductance is measured in the unit of conductance, the siemens.

Practical values of transconductance are very small, so the microsiemens (one millionth of a siemens) is the commonly used unit. Different types of tubes have transconductance values ranging from a few hundred to several thousand. The higher the transconductance the greater the possible amplification.

Amplification

The way in which a tube amplifies is best shown by a type of graph called the dynamic characteristic. Such a graph, together with the circuit used for obtaining it, is shown in Fig. 7. The curves are taken with the plate supply voltage fixed at the desired operating value. The difference between this circuit and the one shown in Fig. 6 is that in Fig. 7 a load resistance is connected in series with the plate of the tube. Fig. 7 thus shows how the plate current will vary, with different grid voltages, when the plate current is made to flow through a load and thus do useful work.

The several curves in Fig. 7 are for various values of load resistance. When the resistance is small (as in the case of a 5-kΩ load) the plate current changes rapidly with a given change in grid voltage. If the load resistance is high (as in the 100,000-kΩ curve), the change in plate current for the same grid-voltage change is relatively small; also, the curve tends to be straighter.

Fig. 7 — Dynamic characteristics of a small triode with various load resistances from 5 kΩ to 100 kΩ.

Fig. 8 shows the same type of curve, but the circuit is arranged so that a source of alternating voltage (signal) is inserted between the grid and the grid battery (C battery in this example). The voltage of the grid battery is fixed at − 5 volts, and from the curve it may be seen that the plate current at this grid voltage is 2 milliamperes. This current flows when the load resistance is 50,000 × 0.002 = 100 volts, leaving 200 volts between the plate and cathode.

When a sine-wave signal having a peak value of 2 volts is applied in series with the bias voltage in the grid circuit, the instantaneous voltage at the grid will swing to − 3 volts when the signal reaches its positive peak, and to − 7 volts when the signal reaches its negative peak. The maximum plate current will occur at the instant the grid voltage is − 3 volts. As shown by the graph, it will have a value of 2.65 milliamperes. The minimum plate current occurs at the instant the grid voltage is − 7 volts, and has a value of 1.35 mA. At intermediate values of grid voltage, intermediate plate current values will occur.

The instantaneous voltage between the plate and cathode of the tube is also shown on the graph. When the plate current is maximum, the instantaneous voltage drop in R_p is 50,000 × 0.00265 = 132.5 volts; when the plate current is minimum the instantaneous voltage drop in R_p is 50,000 × 0.00135 = 67.5 volts. The actual voltage between plate and cathode is the difference between the plate supply potential, 300 volts, and the voltage drop in the load resistance. The plate-to-cathode voltage is therefore 167.5 volts at maximum plate current and 232.5 volts at minimum plate current.

This varying plate voltage is an ac voltage superimposed on the steady plate-cathode potential of 200 volts (as previously determined for no-signal conditions). The peak value of this ac output voltage is the difference between either the maximum or minimum plate-cathode voltage and the no-signal value of 200 volts. In the illustration this difference is 232.5 − 200 or 200 − 167.5; that is, 32.5 volts in either case. Since the grid signal voltage has a peak value of 2 volts, the voltage-amplification ratio of the amplifier is 32.5/2 or 16.25. That is, approximately 16 times as much voltage is obtained from the plate circuit as is applied to the grid circuit.

As shown by the drawings in Fig. 8, the alternating component of the plate voltage swings in the negative direction (with reference to the no-signal value of plate-cathode voltage) when the grid voltage swings in the positive direction, and vice versa. This means that the alternating component of plate voltage (that is, the amplified signal) is 180 degrees out of phase with the signal voltage on the grid.

Bias

The fixed negative grid voltage (called

Fig. 8 — Amplifier operation. When the plate current varies in response to the signal applied to the grid, a varying voltage drop appears across the load, R_p, as shown by the dashed curve, E_p. I_p is the plate current.

Fig. 9 — Distortion resulting from the choice of an operating point on the curved part of the tube characteristic. The lower half cycle of plate current does not have the same shape as the upper half cycle.

Fig. 10 — An elementary power amplifier circuit in which the power-consuming load is coupled to the plate circuit through an impedance-matching transformer.

grid bias) in Fig. 8 serves a very useful purpose. One purpose of the type of amplification shown in this drawing is to obtain, from the plate circuit, an alternating voltage that has the same wave shape as the signal voltage applied to the grid. To do so, an operating point on the straight part of

the curve must be selected. The curve must be straight in both directions from the operating point at least far enough to accommodate the maximum value of the signal applied to the grid. If the grid signal swings the plate current back and forth over a part of the curve that is not straight as shown in Fig. 9, the shape of the ac wave in the plate circuit will not be the same as the shape of the grid-signal wave. In such a case the output wave shape will be distorted.

A second reason for using negative grid bias is that any signal whose peak positive voltage does not exceed the fixed voltage on the grid cannot cause grid current to flow. With no current flow there is no power consumption, so the tube will amplify without taking any power from the signal source. (However, if the positive peak of the signal does exceed the negative bias, current will flow in the grid circuit during the time the grid is positive.)

Distortion of the output wave shape that results from working over a part of the curve that is not straight (that is, a nonlinear part of the curve) has the effect of transforming a sine-wave grid signal into a more complex waveform. As explained in an earlier chapter, a complex wave can be resolved into a fundamental frequency and a series of harmonics. In other words, distortion from nonlinearity causes the generation of harmonic frequencies — frequencies that are not present in the signal applied to the grid. Harmonic distortion is undesirable in most amplifiers, although there are occasions when harmonics are deliberately generated and used.

Class-A Amplifiers

An amplifier in which voltage gain is the primary consideration is called a voltage amplifier. Maximum voltage gain is obtained when the load resistance or impedance is made as high as possible in comparison with the plate resistances of the tube. In such a case, the major portion of the voltage generated will appear across the load.

Voltage amplifiers belong to a group called class-A amplifiers. A class-A amplifier is one operated so that the wave shape of the output voltage is the same as that of the signal voltage applied to the grid. If a class-A amplifier is biased so that the grid is always negative, even with the largest signal to be handled by the grid, it is called a class-A_1 amplifier. Voltage amplifiers are always class-A_1 amplifiers.

Power Amplifiers

Fig. 10 shows an elementary power-amplifier circuit. It is simply a transformer-coupled amplifier with the load connected to the secondary. Although the load is shown as a resistor, it actually would be some device, such as an antenna, that employs the power usefully. Every power tube requires a specific value of load resistance from plate to cathode, usually some thousands of ohms, for optimum operation. The resistance of the actual load is rarely the right value for matching this optimum load resistance, so the turns ratio of the transformer is chosen to reflect the power value of resistance into the primary. The transformer may be either step up or step down, depending on whether the actual load resistance is higher or lower than the tube wants.

The power amplification ratio of an amplifier is the ratio of the power output obtained from the plate circuit to the power required from the ac signal in the grid circuit. There is no power lost in the grid circuit of a class-A_1 amplifier, so such an amplifier has an infinitely large power amplification ratio. However, it is quite possible to operate a class-A amplifier in such a way that current flows in the grid circuit during at least part of the cycle. In such a case, power is used up in the grid circuit and the power amplification ratio is not infinite. A tube operated in this fashion is known as a class-A_2 amplifier. It is necessary to use a power amplifier to drive a class-A_2 amplifier, because a voltage amplifier cannot deliver power without serious distortion of the wave shape.

Another term used in connection with power amplifiers is power sensitivity. In the case of a class-A_1 amplifier, the term means the ratio of power output to the grid signal voltage. If grid current flows, the term usually means the ratio of plate power output to grid power input.

The ac power that is delivered to a load by an amplifier tube has to be paid for in power taken from the source of plate voltage and current. In fact, there is always more power going into the plate circuit of the tube than is coming out as useful output. The difference between the input and output power is used up in heating the plate of the tube, as explained previously. The ratio of useful power output to dc plate input is called the plate efficiency. The higher the plate efficiency, the greater the amount of power that can be taken from a tube having a given plate dissipation rating.

Parallel and Push-Pull Amplifiers

When it is necessary to obtain more power output than one tube is capable of giving, two or more similar tubes may be connected in parallel. In this case the similar elements in all tubes are connected together. This method is shown in Fig. 11 for a transformer-coupled amplifier. The power output is in proportion to the number of tubes used; the grid signal or exciting voltage required, however, is the same as for one tube. If the amplifier operates in such a way as to consume power in the grid circuit, the grid power required is in proportion to the number of tubes used.

An increase in power output also can be had by connecting two tubes in push-pull.

Fig. 11 — Parallel and push-pull AF amplifier circuits.

Fig. 12 — Class-B amplifier operation.

In this case the grids and plates of the two tubes are connected to opposite ends of a balanced circuit, as shown in Fig. 11. At any instant the ends of the secondary winding of the input transformer, T1, will be at opposite polarity with respect to the cathode connection, so the grid of one tube is swung positive at the same instant that the grid of the other is swung negative. Hence, in any push-pull connected amplifier the voltages and currents of one tube are out of phase with those of the other tube.

In push-pull operation the even-harmonic distortion (second, fourth, etc.) is balanced out in the plate circuit. This means that for the same power output the distortion will be less than with parallel operation.

The excitation voltage measured between the two grids must be twice that required for one tube. If the grids consume power, the driving power for the push-pull amplifier is twice that taken by either tube alone.

Cascade Amplifiers

It is readily possible to take the output of one amplifier and apply it as a signal to the grid of a second amplifier, then take the second amplifier's output and apply it to a third, and so on. Each amplifier is called a stage, and stages used successively are said to be in cascade.

Class-B Amplifiers

Fig. 12 shows two tubes connected in a push-pull circuit. If the grid bias is set at the point where the plate current is just cut off (when no signal is applied) then a signal can cause plate current to flow in either tube only when the signal voltage applied to that particular tube is positive with respect to the cathode. Since in the balanced grid circuit the signal voltages on the grids of the two tubes always have opposite polarities, plate current flows only in one tube at a time.

The graphs show the operation of such an amplifier. The plate current of tube B is drawn inverted to show that it flows in the opposite direction, through the primary of the output transformer, to the plate current of tube A. Thus each half of the output-transformer primary works alternately to induce a half cycle of voltage in the secondary. In the secondary of T2, the original waveform is restored. This type of operation is called class-B amplification.

The class-B amplifier has considerably higher plate efficiency than the class-A amplifier. Furthermore, the dc plate current of a class-B amplifier is proportional to the signal voltage on the grids, so the power input is small with small signals. The dc plate power input to a class-A amplifier is the same whether the signal is large, small or absent altogether; therefore the maximum dc plate input that can be applied to a class-A amplifier is equal to the rated plate dissipation of the tube or tubes. Two tubes in a class-B amplifier can deliver approximately 12 times as much audio power as the same two tubes in a class-A amplifier.

A class-B amplifier usually is operated in such a way as to provide the maximum possible power output. This requires large values of plate current. To obtain these currents, the signal voltage must completely overcome the grid bias during at least part of the cycle, so grid current flows and the grid circuit consumes power. While the power requirements are fairly low (as compared with the power output), the fact that the grids are positive during only part of the cycle means the load on the preceding amplifier or driver stage varies in magnitude during the cycle. The effective load resistance is high when the grids are not drawing current, and is relatively low when they do take current. This must be allowed for when designing the driver.

Certain types of tubes have been designed specifically for class-B service and can be operated without fixed or other form of grid bias (zero-bias tubes). The amplification factor is so high that the plate current is small without signal. Because there is no fixed bias, the grids start drawing current immediately whenever a signal is applied, so the grid-current flow is continuous throughout the cycle. This makes the load on the driver much more constant than is the case with tubes of lower μ biased to plate-current cutoff.

Class-B amplifiers used at radio frequencies are known as linear amplifiers, because they are adjusted to operate in such a way that the power output is proportional to the square of the RF excitation voltage. This permits amplification of a modulated RF signal without distortion. Push-pull is not required in this type of operation; a single tube can be used equally well.

Class-AB Amplifiers

Class-AB audio amplifiers are push-pull amplifiers with higher bias than would be normal for pure class-A operation, but less than the cutoff bias required for class-B. At low signal levels the tubes operate as class-A amplifiers, and the plate current is the same with or without signal. At higher signal levels, the plate current of one tube is cut off during part of the negative cycle of the signal applied to its grid, and the plate current of the other tube rises with the signal. The total plate current for the amplifier also rises above the no-signal level when a large signal is applied.

In a properly designed class-AB amplifier the distortion is as low as with a class-A stage, but the efficiency and power output are considerably higher than with pure class-A operation. A class-AB amplifier can be operated either with or without driving the grids into the positive region. A class-AB$_1$ amplifier is one in which the grids are never positive with respect to the cathode; therefore no driving power is required — only voltage. A class-AB$_2$ amplifier is one that has grid-current flow during part of the cycle if the applied signal is large; it takes a small amount of driving power. The class-AB$_2$ amplifier will deliver somewhat more power (using the same tubes), but the class-AB$_1$ amplifier avoids the problem of designing a driver that will deliver power without distortion into a load of highly variable resistance.

Conduction Angle

Inspection of Fig. 12 shows that either of the two vacuum tubes is working for only half the ac cycle and idling during the other half. It is convenient to describe the amount of time during which plate current flows in terms of electrical degrees. In Fig. 12 each tube has 180-degree excitation, a half cycle being equal to 180 degrees. The number of degrees during which plate current flows is called the conduction angle of the amplifier. From the description given above, it should be clear that a class-A amplifier has 360-degree excitation, because plate current flows during the whole cycle. In a class-AB amplifier the conduction angle is between 180 and 360 degrees (in each tube), depending on the particular operating conditions chosen. The

greater the amount of negative grid bias, the smaller the conduction angle becomes.

A conduction angle of less than 180 degrees leads to a considerable amount of distortion, because there is no way for the tube to reproduce even a half cycle of the signal on its grid. Using two tubes in push-pull, as in Fig. 12, would merely put together two distorted half cycles. A conduction angle of less than 180 degrees therefore cannot be used if distortionless output is wanted.

Class-C Amplifiers

In power amplifiers operating at radio frequencies, distortion of the RF waveform is relatively unimportant. Tuned circuits are usually used to filter out the RF harmonics resulting from distortion.

A radio-frequency power amplifier therefore can be used with a conduction angle of less than 180 degrees. This is called class-C operation. The advantage is that the plate efficiency is increased because the loss in the plate is proportional, among other things, to the amount of time during which the plate current flows. This time is reduced by decreasing the operating angle.

Depending on the type of tube, the optimum load resistance for a class-C amplifier ranges from about 1.5 kΩ to 5 kΩ. Tuned-circuit arrangements are normally used to transform the resistance of the actual load to the value required by the tube. The grid is driven well into the positive region, so grid current flows and power is consumed in the grid circuit. The smaller the conduction angle, the greater the driving voltage and the larger the grid driving power required to develop full output in the load resistance. The best compromise between driving power, plate efficiency and power output usually results when the minimum plate voltage is just equal to the peak positive grid voltage. These conditions must exist at the peak of the driving cycle, when the plate current reaches its highest value. Under such conditions the conduction angle is usually between 120 and 150 degrees, and the plate efficiency lies in the range of 60 to 80 percent. While higher plate efficiencies are possible, attaining them requires excessive driving power and grid bias, together with higher plate voltage than is normal for the particular tube type.

Feedback

It is possible to take a part of the amplified energy in the plate circuit of an amplifier and insert it into the grid circuit. This is called feedback.

If the voltage that is inserted in the grid circuit is 180 degrees out of phase with the signal voltage acting on the grid, the feedback is called negative or degenerative. On the other hand, if voltage is fed back in phase with the grid signal, the feedback is called positive or regenerative.

Fig. 13 — Simple circuits for producing feedback.

Negative Feedback

With negative feedback the voltage that is fed back opposes the signal voltage. This decreases the amplitude of the voltage acting between the grid and cathode and thus has the effect of reducing the voltage amplification. That is, a larger exciting voltage is required for obtaining the same output voltage from the plate circuit.

The greater the amount of negative feedback (when properly applied), the more independent the amplification becomes of tube characteristics and circuit conditions. This tends to make the frequency-response characteristic of the amplifier flat — that is, the amplification tends to be the same at all frequencies within the range for which the amplifier is designed. Also, any distortion generated in the plate circuit of the tube tends to "buck itself out." Amplifiers with negative feedback therefore have lower harmonic distortion. These advantages are worthwhile if the amplifier otherwise has enough voltage gain for its intended use.

In the circuit shown at A in Fig. 13 resistor R$_c$ is in series with the regular plate resistor, R$_p$ and this is a part of the load for the tube. Therefore, part of the output voltage will appear across R$_c$. R$_c$ also is connected in series with the grid circuit, however, so the output voltage that appears across R$_c$ is in series with the signal voltage. The output voltage across R$_c$ opposes the signal voltage, so the actual ac voltage between the grid and cathode is equal to the difference between the two voltages.

The circuit shown at B in Fig. 13 can be used to give either negative or positive feedback. The secondary of a transformer is connected back into the grid circuit to insert a desired amount of feedback voltage. Reversing the terminals of either transformer winding (but not both simultaneously) will reverse the phase.

Positive Feedback

Positive feedback increases the amplification because the feedback voltage adds to the original signal voltage, and the resulting larger voltage on the grid causes a larger output voltage. The amplification tends to be greatest at one frequency (which depends on the particular circuit arrangement) and harmonic distortion is increased. If enough energy is fed back, a self-sustaining oscillation will be set up — one in which energy at essentially one frequency is generated by the tube itself. In such cases all the signal voltage on the grid can be supplied from the plate circuit. No external signal is needed because any small irregularity in the plate current (and there are always some irregularities) will be amplified and thus give the oscillation an opportunity to build up. Positive feedback finds a major application in oscillators, and in addition is used for selective amplification at both audio and radio frequencies, the feedback being kept below the value that causes self-oscillation.

Interelectrode Capacitances

Each pair of elements in a tube forms a small capacitor. There are three such capacitances in a triode — that between the grid and cathode, that between the grid and plate, and that between the plate and cathode. The capacitances are very small, only a few picofarads at most, but they frequently have a pronounced effect on the operation of an amplifier circuit.

Input Capacitance

It was explained previously that the ac grid voltage and ac plate voltage of an amplifier having a resistive load are 180 degrees out of phase, using the cathode of the tube as a reference point. However, these two voltages are in phase going around the circuit from plate to grid as shown in Fig. 14. This means that their sum is acting between the grid and plate — that is, across the grid-plate capacitance of the tube.

As a result, a capacitive current flows around the circuit, its amplitude being directly proportional to the sum of the ac grid and plate voltages and to the grid-plate capacitance. The source of the grid signal must furnish this amount of current, in addition to the capacitive current that flows in the grid-cathode capacitance. Hence the signal source sees an effective capacitance that is larger than the grid-cathode capacitance. This is known as the Miller effect.

The greater the voltage amplification, the greater the effective input capacitance. The input capacitance of a resistance-coupled amplifier is given by the formula

$$C_{input} = C_{gk} + C_{gp} (A + 1)$$

where

    C_{gk} is the grid-to-cathode capacitance
    C_{gp} is the grid-to-plate capacitance
    A is the voltage amplification.

The input capacitance may be as much as several hundred picofarads when the

Fig. 14 — The ac voltage appearing between the grid and plate of the amplifier is the sum of the signal voltage and the output voltage, as shown by this simplified circuit. Instantaneous polarities are indicated.

voltage amplification is large, even though the interelectrode capacitances are quite small.

Output Capacitance

The principal component of the output capacitance of an amplifier is the actual plate-to-cathode capacitance of the tube. The output capacitance usually need not be considered in audio amplifiers, but becomes of importance at radio frequencies.

Tube Capacitance at RF

At radio frequencies the reactances of even very small interelectrode capacitances drop to very low values. A resistance-coupled tube amplifier gives very little amplification at RF, for example, because the reactances of the interelectrode capacitors are so low that they practically short circuit the input and output circuits, and thus the tube is unable to amplify. This is overcome at radio frequencies by using tuned circuits for the grid and plate, making the tube capacitances part of the tuning capacitances. In this way the circuits can have the high resistive impedances necessary for satisfactory amplification.

The grid-plate capacitance is important at radio frequencies because its reactance, relatively low at RF, offers a path over which energy can be fed back from the plate to the grid. In practically every case the feedback is in the right phase and of sufficient amplitude to cause self-oscillation, so the circuit becomes useless as an amplifier.

Special neutralizing circuits can be used to prevent feedback but they are, in general, not too satisfactory when used in radio receivers. They are used in transmitters, however.

Tetrodes

The grid-plate capacitance can be greatly reduced by inserting a second grid between the control grid and the plate, as indicated in Fig. 15. The second grid, called the screen grid, acts as an electrostatic shield to reduce capacitive coupling between the control grid and plate. It is made in the form of a grid or coarse screen so electrons can pass through it. A tube having a

Fig. 15 — Representative arrangement of elements in a screen-grid tetrode, with part of plate and screen cut away. This shows single-ended construction with a button base, typical of miniature receiving tubes. To reduce capacitance between control grid and plate, the leads from these elements are brought out at opposite sides. Actual tubes probably would have additional shielding between these leads.

cathode, control grid, screen grid and plate (four elements) is called a tetrode.

Because of the shielding action of the screen grid, the positively charged plate cannot easily attract electrons from the cathode as it does in a triode. In order to enhance electron flow to the plate, it is necessary to apply a positive voltage to the screen (with respect to the cathode). The screen then attracts electrons much as does the plate in a triode tube. In traveling toward the screen the electrons acquire such velocity that most of them shoot between the screen wires and then are attracted to the plate. A small proportion does strike the screen, however, with the result that some current also flows in the screen-grid circuit.

To be a good shield, the screen grid must be connected to the cathode through a circuit that has low impedance at the frequency being amplified. A bypass capacitor from screen grid to cathode, having a reactance of not more than a few hundred ohms, is generally used.

Pentodes

When an electron traveling at appreciable velocity through a tube strikes the plate, it dislodges other electrons, which splash from the plate into the interelement space. This is called secondary emission. In a triode the negative grid repels the secondary electrons back into the plate and they cause no disturbance. In the screen-grid tube, however, the positively charged screen attracts the secondary electrons, causing a reverse current to flow between screen and plate.

To overcome the effects of secondary emission, a third grid, called the suppressor grid, may be inserted between the screen and plate. This grid, negatively changed with respect to the screen and plate, acts as a shield between the screen grid and plate so the secondary electrons cannot be attracted by the screen grid. They are hence attracted back to the plate without appreciably obstructing the regular plate-current flow. A five-element tube of this type is called a pentode.

Although the screen grid in either the tetrode or pentode greatly reduces the influence of the plate voltage on plate-current flow, the control grid still can control the plate current in essentially the same way that it does in a triode. Consequently, the grid-plate transconductance (or mutual conductance) of a tetrode or pentode will be of the same order of value as in a triode of corresponding structure. On the other hand, since a change in plate voltage has very little effect on the plate-current flow, both the amplification factor and plate resistance of a pentode or tetrode are very high. Because of the high plate resistance, the actual voltage amplification possible with a pentode is very much less than the large amplification factor might indicate. A voltage gain in the vicinity of 50 to 200 is typical of a pentode stage.

In practical screen-grid tubes, the grid-plate capacitance is only a small fraction of a picofarad. This capacitance is too small to cause an appreciable increase in input capacitance by means of the Miller effect, so the input capacitance of a screen-grid tube is equal to the capacitance between the plate and screen.

The chief function of the screen grid is to serve as an accelerator of electrons, so that large values of plate current can be drawn at relatively low plate voltages. Tetrodes and pentodes have high power sensitivity compared with triodes of the same power output, although harmonic distortion is somewhat greater.

Beam Tubes

A beam tetrode is a four-element screen-grid tube constructed in such a way that the electrons are formed into concentrated beams on their way to the plate. Additional design features overcome the effects of secondary emission so that a suppressor grid is not needed. The beam construction makes it possible to draw large plate currents at relatively low plate voltages, and increases the power sensitivity of the tube.

For power amplification at radio frequencies, beam tetrodes have largely supplanted the nonbeam types. This is because large power outputs can be secured with very small amounts of grid driving power.

Input and Output Impedances

The input impedance of a vacuum-tube amplifier is the impedance seen by the signal source when connected to the input terminals of the amplifier. In the types of amplifiers previously discussed, the input impedance is the impedance measured between the grid and cathode of the tube with operating voltages applied. At audio frequencies the input impedance of a class-A1 amplifier is for all practical purposes the input impedance of the stage. If the tube

Fig. 16 — In each circuit shown, R represents the load. In the upper circuit, the grid is the junction point between the input and output circuits. In the lower drawing, the plate is the junction. In either case the output is developed in the load resistor, and may be coupled to a following amplifier by the usual methods.

is driven into the grid-current region, there is in addition a resistance component in the input impedance. The resistance has an average value equal to E^2/P, where E is the RMS driving voltage and P is the power in watts consumed in the grid. The resistance usually will vary during the ac cycle, because grid current may flow only during part of the cycle. Also, the grid-voltage/grid-current characteristic is seldom linear.

The output impedance of amplifiers of this type consists of the plate resistance of the tube shunted by the output capacitance.

At radio frequencies, when tuned circuits are employed, the input and output impedances are usually pure resistances; any reactive components are tuned out in the process of adjusting the circuits to resonance at the operating frequency.

Other Types of Amplifiers

In the amplifier circuits discussed so far, the signal has been applied between the grid and cathode, and the amplified output has been taken from the plate-to-cathode circuit. That is, the cathode has been the meeting point for the input and output circuits. However, it is possible to use any one of the three principal elements as the common point. This leads to two additional kinds of amplifiers, commonly called the grounded-grid amplifier and the cathode follower.

These two circuits are shown in simplified form in Fig. 16. In both circuits, R represents the load into which the amplifier works. The actual load may be resistance-capacitance coupled, transformer coupled, or may be a tuned circuit if the amplifier operates at radio frequencies. Also, in both circuits the batteries that supply grid bias and plate power are assumed to have such negligible impedance that they do not enter into the operation of the circuits.

Grounded-Grid Amplifier

In the grounded-grid amplifier the input signal is applied between the cathode and grid, and the output is taken between the plate and grid. The grid is thus the common element. The ac component of the plate current has to flow through the signal source to reach the cathode. The source of signal is in series with the load through the plate-to-cathode resistance of the tube, so some of the power in the load is supplied by the signal source. In transmitting applications this fed-through power is of the order of 10 percent of the total power output, using tubes suitable for grounded-grid service.

The input impedance of the grounded-grid amplifier consists of a capacitance in parallel with an equivalent resistance that would absorb the power furnished by the driving source to the grid and to the load. This resistance is of the order of a few hundred ohms. The output impedance, neglecting the interelectrode capacitances, is equal to the plate resistance of the tube. This is the same as in the case of the grounded-cathode amplifier.

The grounded-grid amplifier is widely used at radio frequencies. With a triode tube designed for this type of operation, an RF amplifier can be built that is free from the type of feedback that causes oscillation. This requires that the grid act as a shield between the cathode and plate, reducing the plate-cathode capacitance to a very low value.

Cathode Follower

The cathode follower uses the plate of the tube as the common element. The input signal is applied between the grid and plate (assuming negligible impedance in the batteries) and the output is taken between cathode and plate. This circuit is degenerative; in fact, all of the output voltage is fed back into the input circuit out of phase with the grid signal. The input signal therefore has to be larger than the output voltage; that is, the cathode follower gives a loss in voltage, although it gives the same power gain as other circuits under equivalent operating conditions.

An important feature of the cathode follower is its low output impedance, which is given by the formula (neglecting interelectrode capacitances)

$$Z_{out} = \frac{r_p}{1 + \mu}$$

where
r_p is the tube plate resistance
μ is the amplification factor.

Low output impedance is a valuable characteristic in an amplifier designed to cover a wide band of frequencies. In addition, the input capacitance is only a fraction of the grid-to-cathode capacitance of the tube, a feature of further benefit in a wide-band amplifier. The cathode follower is useful as a step-down impedance transformer, since the input impedance is high and the output impedance is low.

Cathode Circuits and Grid Bias

Most of the equipment used by amateurs is powered by the ac line. This includes the filaments or heaters of vacuum tubes. Supplies for the plate (and sometimes the grid) are usually ac that is rectified and filtered to give pure dc — that is, direct current that is constant and without a superimposed ac component. The relatively large currents required by filaments and heaters however, usually make a rectifier-type dc supply impractical. Therefore, alternating current is almost always used to heat the tube cathode.

Filament Hum

Alternating current is just as good as direct current from the heating standpoint, but some of the ac voltage is likely to be coupled to the grid and cause ac hum to be superimposed on the output. Hum troubles are worst with directly heated cathodes (filaments), because with such

Fig. 17 — Filament center-tapping methods for use with directly heated tubes.

Fig. 18 — Cathode biasing. R is the cathode resistor and C is the cathode bypass capacitor.

cathodes there has to be a direct connection between the source of heating power and the rest of the circuit.

Hum can be minimized by either of the connections shown in Fig. 17. In both cases the grid- and plate-return circuits are connected to the electrical midpoint (center tap) of the filament supply. Thus, as far as the grid and plate are concerned, the voltage and current on one side of the filament are balanced by an equal and opposite voltage and current on the other side. The balance is never quite perfect, however, so filament-type tubes are never completely hum free. For this reason directly heated filaments are employed for the most part in power tubes, where the hum introduced is extremely small in comparison with the power-output level.

With indirectly heated cathodes the chief problem is the magnetic field set up by the heater. Occasionally, also, there is leakage between the heater and cathode, allowing a small ac voltage to reach to the grid. If hum appears, grounding one side of the heater supply usually will help to reduce it, although sometimes better results are obtained if the heater supply is center-tapped and the center-tap grounded, as shown in Fig. 17.

Cathode Bias

In the simplified amplifier circuits discussed in this chapter, grid bias has been supplied by a battery. In equipment that operates from the power line, however, cathode bias is almost universally used for tubes that are operated in class-A (constant dc input).

The cathode-bias method uses a resistor (cathode resistor) connected in series with the cathode, R in Fig. 18. The direction of plate-current flow is such that the end of the resistor nearest the cathode is positive. The voltage drop across R therefore places a negative voltage on the grid with respect to the cathode. This negative bias is obtained from the steady dc plate current.

If the alternating component of plate current flows through R when the tube is

Fig. 19 — Screen-voltage supply for a pentode tube through a dropping resistor, R. The screen bypass capacitor, C, must have low enough reactance to bring the screen to ground potential for the frequency or frequencies being amplified.

amplifying, the voltage drop caused by the ac will be degenerative (note the similarity between this circuit and that of Fig. 13A). To prevent this, the resistor is bypassed by the capacitor, C, that has very low reactance compared with the resistance of R. Depending on the type of tube and the particular kind of operation, R may be between about 100 and 3000 ohms. For good bypassing at radio frequencies, capacitances of about 100 pF to 0.1 μF are used; the small values are sufficient at very high frequencies and the largest at low and medium frequencies. In the range 3 to 30 megahertz a capacitance of 0.01 μF is satisfactory.

The value of cathode resistor for an amplifier having negligible dc resistance in its plate circuit (transformer or impedance coupled) can be calculated from the known operating conditions of the tube.

Screen Supply

In practical circuits using tetrodes and pentodes, the voltage for the screen frequently is taken from the plate supply through a resistor. A typical circuit for an RF amplifier is shown in Fig. 19. R is the screen dropping resistor, and C is the screen bypass capacitor. In flowing through R, the screen current causes a voltage drop in R that reduces the plate-supply voltage to the proper value for the screen. When the plate-supply voltage and the screen current are known, the value of R can be calculated from Ohm's Law.

The reactance of the screen bypass capacitor, C, should be low compared with the screen-to-cathode impedance. For radio-frequency applications between 3 and 30 MHz, a capacitance in the vicinity of 0.01 μF is amply large.

In some vacuum-tube circuits the screen voltage is obtained from a voltage divider connected across the plate supply. The design of voltage dividers is discussed in Chapter 6.

Fig. 20 — Simplified diagram of a klystron amplifier. Not shown is the focusing magnet used to keep the electron beam from striking the cavities or body of the tube.

Fig. 21 — Simplified diagram of a traveling-wave-tube (TWT) amplifier. Like the klystron, this tube requires a focusing magnet.

Tubes for UHF and Microwaves

Earlier discussions in this chapter have assumed that the time it takes for the electrons to travel from the cathode to the plate does not affect the performance of vacuum-tube operation. As the frequency of operation is raised, this time becomes increasingly important. Called the transit time, this time depends on the voltage from the cathode to the plate and the spacing between them. The higher the voltage and the smaller the spacing, the shorter the transit time. This is why tubes designed for VHF and UHF work have very small interelectrode spacings. The power handling capabilities also get smaller as the spacing decreases, however, so there is a frequency limit above which ordinary triode and pentode tubes cannot be operated efficiently.

Many different tubes have been developed which actually use transit-time effects to an advantage. Velocity modulation of the electron stream in a klystron is one example. A small voltage applied across the gap in a reentrant cavity resonator either retards or accelerates an electron stream by means of the resultant electric field. Initially, all the electrons are traveling at the same velocity, and the current in the beam is uniform. After the velocity fluctuations are impressed on the beam, the current is still uniform for a while, but then the electrons that were accelerated begin to catch up with the slower ones that passed through when the field was zero. These faster electrons are also catching up with ones that passed through the gap earlier but were retarded. The result is that the current in the beam is no longer uniform, but consists of a series of pulses.

If the beam now passes through another cavity gap, a current will be induced in the cavity walls and an electric field also will be set up across the gap. If the phase of the electric field is right, the electron pulses or bunches pass through the gap and are retarded, thus giving up energy to the electric field. When the electric field reverses, it would normally accelerate the same number of electrons and give back the

Fig. 22 — Cross-sectional view of a typical reflex klystron. The frequency of the cavity resonator is changed by varying the spacing between the grids using a tuning mechanism and a flexible bellows.

energy, but fewer electrons now pass through the gap and the energy is from the beam to the cavity. If the voltage produced across the output cavity is greater than that across the input cavity, amplification results (assuming the two cavity impedances are the same).

A four-cavity klystron is shown in Fig. 20. In this example, a pair of intermediate cavities has been added. These additional cavities reinforce the bunching of electrons within the electron beam, which in turn increases the gain.

Not shown in Fig. 20 is the magnet that must be used to keep the electron beam focused down the center of the tube. Beam electrons must be returned through the collector and not by way of the cavities or body of the tube.

Traveling Wave Tube

As you can see in Fig. 21, a helix

Table 1
Comparison of Klystrons and TWTs

Type	Gain (dB)	Efficiency (%)	Bandwidth (%)
Klystron	40-60	30-70	1-5
Helix TWT	30-50	20-40	30-120
Cavity TWT	30-50	20-40	5-40

traveling wave tube (TWT) looks much like a klystron. The major difference is that the klystron cavities have been replaced with a helix.

A signal traveling along the helix moves more slowly than the electrons in the beam. The signal on the helix tends to retard beam electrons. As beam electrons slow down they give up energy to the signal on the helix.

Another type of TWT uses a series of coupled cavities instead of a helix. Table 1 compares TWTs and klystrons.

Microwave Oscillator Tubes

Another type of klystron is the reflex klystron oscillator, shown in Fig. 22. Here the input and output cavity are the same. The electron stream makes one pass through, becomes velocity modulated, and is turned around by the negative charge on an element called the repeller. During the second pass through, the stream is now bunched and delivers some of its energy to the cavity. The dissipated beam is then picked up by the cavity walls and the circuit is completed.

Other microwave oscillator wave tubes are the back wave oscillator (BWO) and the magnetron. The BWO works on the same principle as the TWT. The magnetron uses a magnetic field in conjunction with an electric field in its operation. Home microwave ovens use magnetrons to produce RF energy for cooking.

Chapter 6

Power Supplies

In most residential systems, three wires are brought in from the outside to the house distribution panel, although there are only two wires in older systems. In the three-wire system, the third wire is neutral and is grounded. The voltage between the two wires normally is 234. Half of this voltage appears between each of these wires and neutral, as indicated in Fig. 1A.

In systems of this type, the 117-volt household load is divided as evenly as possible between the two sides of the circuit. Half of the load is connected between one wire and neutral, and the other half of the load is connected between the other wire and neutral. Heavy appliances, such as electric stoves and heaters, are designed for 234-volt operation and are connected across the two ungrounded wires.

While both ungrounded wires should be fused, a fuse or switch should never be used in the neutral wire. The reason for this is that opening the neutral wire does not disconnect the equipment. It simply leaves the equipment on one side of the 234-volt circuit in series with whatever load may be across the other side of the circuit. Furthermore, with the neutral open, the voltage will then be divided between the two sides in inverse proportion to the load resistance. The voltage will drop below normal on one side and soar on the other side, unless the loads happen to be equal. More information on 117- and 234-V ac wiring for amateur stations may be found in Chapter 36.

The electrical power required to operate Amateur Radio equipment is usually taken from the alternating current (ac) lines when the equipment is operated where power is available. For mobile operation, the source of power is almost always the car storage battery.

Direct current (dc) voltages used in transmitters, receivers and other related equipment are derived from the commercial ac lines by using a transformer-rectifier-filter system. The transformer changes the ac voltage to a suitable value, and the rectifier converts the ac to pulsating dc. A filter is used to smooth out these pulsations to an acceptably low level. Essentially pure dc is required to prevent 60- or 120-Hz hum in most amateur equipment. If a constant voltage is required under conditions of changing load or ac

line voltage, a regulator is used following the filter.

Fusing

All transformer primary circuits should be fused properly. To determine the approximate current rating of the fuse or circuit breaker to be used, multiply each current being drawn from the supply in amperes by the voltage at which the current is being drawn. Include the current taken by bleeder resistors and voltage dividers. In the case of series resistors, use the source voltage, not the voltage at the equipment end of the resistor. Include filament power if the transformer is supplying filaments.

After multiplying the various voltages and currents, add the individual products. Then divide by the line voltage and add 10 or 20 percent. Use a fuse or circuit breaker with the nearest larger current rating.

When selecting fuses and circuit breakers for use in motor circuits (for example, blower lines) a slow-blow type should be used. When the motor is started, it can draw up to 10 times its normal operating current until the shaft reaches its normal operating speed. This can take up to 30 seconds on a large blower. Such an overload will usually open a fast- or normal-blow fuse.

For low-power semiconductor circuits, use fast-blow fuses. As the name implies, such fuses open very quickly once the cur-

rent rating is exceeded by more than 10%.

TRANSFORMERS
Volt-Ampere Rating

The number of volt-amperes (VA) delivered by a transformer depends on the type of filter used (capacitor or choke input), and on the type of rectifier used (full-wave center tap or full-wave bridge). With a capacitive-input filter, the heating effect in the secondary is higher because of the high ratio of peak-to-average current. The volt-amperes handled by the transformer may be several times the watts delivered to the load. The primary volt-amperes will be somewhat higher because of transformer losses.

Broadcast and Television Replacement Transformers

Small power transformers sold for replacement in broadcast and television receivers are usually designed for service in terms of use for several hours continuously with capacitor-input filters. In the usual type of amateur transmitter service, where most of the power is drawn intermittently for periods of several minutes with equivalent intervals in between, the published ratings can be exceeded without excessive transformer heating.

With a capacitor-input filter, it should be safe to draw 20 to 30 percent more current than the rated value. With a choke-input filter, an increase in current of about

Fig. 1 — Three-wire power-line circuits. At A, normal three-wire-line termination. No fuse should be used in the grounded (neutral) line. At B, a switch in the neutral line would not remove voltage from either side of the line; C, connections for both 117- and 234-volt transformers; D, operating a 117-volt plate transformer from the 234-volt line to avoid light blinking. T1 is a 2:1 step-down transformer.

Fig. 2 — One method of equalizing two transformers connected in parallel.

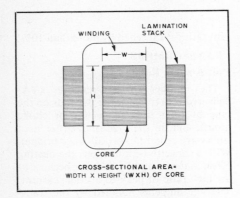

Fig. 3 — Cross-sectional drawings of a typical power transformer. Multiplying the height (or thickness of the laminations) by the width of the central core area in inches gives the value to be applied to Fig. 4.

Fig. 4 — Power-handling capability of a transformer versus cross-sectional area of core.

50 percent is permissible. If a bridge rectifier is used, the output voltage will be approximately doubled. In this case, it should be possible in amateur transmitter service to draw the rated current, thus obtaining about twice the rated output power from the transformer. This does not apply, of course, to amateur transmitter plate transformers, which usually are rated for intermittent service.

Transformers in Parallel

The secondary windings of power transformers can be connected in parallel to obtain a greater current rating than can be had with a single transformer. A common application might be a high-current, 12-V supply for a transceiver. One potential problem is equalizing the current between the two transformers.

A timeless scheme for paralleling nominally-equal transformers is shown in Fig. 2. An inductor, in this case the center-tapped secondary winding of a low-voltage filament transformer, is used to equalize the current. This winding will only see the difference between voltages E1 and E2.

In the ideal case (E1 = E2), the currents are equal but opposite in the center-tapped winding. There is no net flux, and therefore no inductive voltage drop. Ideally, there is no loss.

When E1 is not equal to E2, the open-circuit voltage at the center tap is E2 + 1/2(E1 − E2). If the difference between E1 and E2 is very small, the currents will be approximately equal, and there will be essentially only the normal transformer losses.

Rewinding Power Transformers

Although the home winding of power transformers is a task that few amateurs undertake, the rewinding of a transformer secondary to give some desired voltage is not difficult. It involves a matter of only a small number of turns, and the wire is large enough to be handled easily. Often a receiver power transformer with a burned-out high-voltage winding or the power transformer from a discarded TV set can be converted into an entirely satisfactory transformer without great effort and with little expense.

The average TV power transformer for a 17-inch or larger vacuum-tube set is capable of delivering from 350 to 450 watts, continuous duty. If an amateur transmitter is being powered, the service is not continuous, so the ratings can be increased by 40 or 50 percent without danger of overloading the transformer.

The primary volt-ampere rating of the transformer to be rewound, if known, can be used to determine its power-handling capability. The secondary volt-ampere rating will be 10 to 20 percent less than the primary rating. The power rating may also be determined approximately from the cross-sectional area of the core that is inside the windings. Fig. 3 shows the method of determining the area, and Fig. 4 may be used to convert this information into a power rating.

Before disconnecting the winding leads from their terminals, each should be marked for identification. In removing the core laminations, care should be taken to note how the core is assembled, so the reassembling will be done in the same manner. Most transformers have secondaries wound over the primary, while in some the order is reversed. In case the secondaries are on the inside, the turns can be pulled out from the center after slitting and removing the fiber core.

The turns removed from one of the original filament windings of known voltage should be carefully counted as the winding is removed. This will give the number of turns per volt; the same figure should be used in determining the number of turns for the new secondary. For instance, if the old filament winding was rated at 5 volts and had 15 turns, this is 15/5 = 3 turns per volt. If the new secondary is to deliver 18 volts, the required number of turns on the new winding will be 18 × 3 = 54 turns.

In winding a transformer, the size of wire is an important factor in the heat developed in operation. A cross-sectional area of 1000 circular mils per ampere (cmil/A) is conservative. A value commonly used in amateur-service transformers is 700 cmil/A. The larger the cmil/A figure, the cooler the transformer will run. The current rating in amperes of various wire sizes is shown in the copper-wire table in Chapter 35. If the transformer being rewound is a filament transformer, it may be necessary to choose the wire size carefully to fit the small available space. On the other hand, if the transformer is a power unit with the high-voltage winding removed, there should be plenty of room for a size of wire that will conservatively handle the required current.

After the first layer of turns is put on during rewinding, secure the ends with cellulose tape. Each layer should be insulated from the next. Ordinary household waxed paper can be used; a single layer is adequate. Sheets cut to size beforehand may be secured over each layer with tape. Be sure to bring all leads out the same side of the core so the covers will go in place when the unit is completed. When the last layer of the winding is put on, use two sheets of waxed paper, and then cover those with vinyl electrical tape, keeping the tape as taut as possible. This will add mechanical strength to the assembly.

The laminations and housing are assembled in just the opposite sequence to that followed in disassembly. Use a light coating of shellac between each lamination. During reassembly, the lamination stack may be compressed by clamping in a vise. If the last few lamination strips cannot be replaced, it is better to omit them than to force the unit together.

RECTIFIERS

Half-Wave Rectifier

Fig. 5 shows a simple half-wave rectifier circuit. As explained in Chapter 4, a rectifier (in this case a semiconductor diode) will conduct current in one direction but not the other. During one half of the ac cycle, the rectifier will conduct and current will flow through the rectifier to the load (indicated by the solid line in Fig. 5B). During the other half cycle, the rectifier is reverse biased and no current will flow (indicated by the broken line in Fig. 5B) to the load. As shown, the output is in the form of pulsed dc, and current always flows in the same direction. A filter can be used to smooth out these variations and provide a higher average dc voltage from the circuit. This idea will be covered in the section on filters.

The average output voltage — the voltage read by a dc voltmeter — with this circuit (no filter connected) is 0.45 times the RMS value of the ac voltage delivered by the transformer secondary. Because the frequency of the pulses is low (one pulsation per cycle), considerable filtering is required to provide adequately smooth dc output. For this reason the circuit is usually limited to applications where the current required is small, as in a transmitter bias supply.

The peak inverse voltage (PIV), the voltage that the rectifier must withstand when it isn't conducting, varies with the load. With a resistive load, it is the peak ac voltage ($1.4\ E_{RMS}$). With a capacitor filter and a load drawing little or no current, it can rise to $2.8\ E_{RMS}$. The reason for this is shown in Figs. 5C and 5D. With a resistive load as shown at C, the amount of voltage applied to the diode is that voltage on the lower side of the zero-axis line, or $1.4\ E_{RMS}$. A capacitor connected to the circuit (shown at D) will store the peak positive voltage when the diode conducts on the positive pulse. If the circuit is not supplying any current, the voltage across the capacitor will remain at that

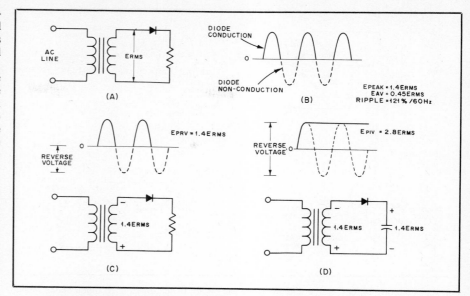

Fig. 5 — Half-wave rectifier circuit. A illustrates the basic circuit, and B displays the diode conduction and nonconduction periods. The peak-inverse voltage impressed across the diode is shown at C and D with a simple resistor load at C and a capacitor load at D. E_{PIV} is 1.4 E_{RMS} for the resistor load and 2.8 E_{RMS} for the capacitor load.

Fig. 6 — Full-wave center-tap rectifier circuit. A illustrates the basic circuit. Diode conduction is shown at B with diodes A and B alternately conducting. The peak-inverse voltage for each diode is 2.8 E_{RMS} as depicted at C.

same level. The peak inverse voltage impressed across the diode is now the sum of the voltage stored in the capacitor plus the peak negative swing of voltage from the transformer secondary. In this case the PIV is $2.8\ E_{RMS}$.

Full-Wave Center-Tap Rectifier

A commonly-used rectifier circuit is shown in Fig. 6. Essentially an arrangement in which the outputs of two half-wave rectifiers are combined, it makes use of both halves of the ac cycle. A transformer with a center-tapped secondary is required with the circuit.

The average output voltage is 0.9 times the RMS voltage of half the transformer secondary; this is the maximum that can be obtained with a suitable choke-input filter. The peak output voltage is 1.4 times

the RMS voltage of half the transformer secondary; this the maximum voltage that can be obtained from a capacitor-input filter.

As can be seen in Fig. 6C, the PIV impressed on each diode is independent of the type of load at the output. This is because the peak inverse voltage condition occurs when diode A conducts and diode B does not conduct. The positive and negative voltage peaks occur at precisely the same time, a condition different from that in the half-wave circuit. As the cathodes of diodes A and B reach a positive peak ($1.4\ E_{RMS}$), the anode of diode B is at a negative peak, also $1.4\ E_{RMS}$, but in the opposite direction. The total peak inverse voltage is therefore $2.8\ E_{RMS}$.

Fig. 6B shows that the frequency of the output pulses is twice that of the half-wave

Fig. 7 — Full-wave bridge rectifier circuit. The basic circuit is illustrated at A. Diode conduction and nonconduction times are shown at B. Diodes A and C conduct on one half of the input cycle while diodes B and D conduct on the other. C displays the peak inverse voltage for one-half cycle. Since this circuit reverse-biases two diodes essentially in parallel, 1.4 E_{RMS} is applied across each diode.

Fig. 8 — The circuit shown at A is a simple half-wave rectifier with a resistive load. The waveform shown to the right is that of output voltage and diode current. B illustrates how the diode current is modified by the addition of a capacitor filter. The diode conducts only when the rectified voltage is greater than stored capacitor voltage. Since this time period is usually only a short portion of a cycle, the peak current will be quite high. C shows an even higher peak current. This is caused by the larger capacitor, which effectively shortens the conduction period of the diode.

rectifier. Comparatively less filtering is required. Since the rectifiers work alternately, each handles half of the load current. The current rating of each rectifier need be only half the total current drawn from the supply.

Full-Wave Bridge Rectifier

Another commonly used rectifier circuit is illustrated in Fig. 7. In this arrangement, two rectifiers operate in series on each half of the cycle, one rectifier being in the lead

to the load, the other being the return lead. As shown in Fig. 7A and B, when the top lead of the transformer secondary is positive with respect to the bottom lead, diodes A and C will conduct while diodes B and D are reverse biased. On the next half cycle, when the top lead of the transformer is negative with respect to the bottom, diodes B and D will conduct while diodes A and C are reverse biased.

The output wave shape is the same as that from the simple full-wave center-tap

rectifier circuit. The maximum output voltage into a resistive load or choke-input filter is 0.9 times the RMS voltage delivered by the transformer secondary; with a capacitor filter and a light load, the output voltage is 1.4 times the secondary RMS voltage.

Fig. 7C shows the inverse voltage to be 1.4 E_{RMS} for each diode. When an alternate pair of diodes (such as D_A and D_C) is conducting, the other diodes are essentially connected in parallel in a reverse-biased direction. The reverse stress is then 1.4 E_{RMS}. Each pair of diodes conducts together on alternate half cycles with the full load current flowing through each diode during its conducting half cycle. Since each diode is not conducting during the other half cycle the average current is one half the total load current drawn from the supply.

Comparing the full-wave center-tap rectifier circuit and the full-wave bridge-rectifier circuit, it can be seen that both circuits have almost the same rectifier requirement since the center tap has half the number of rectifiers as the bridge, but these rectifiers have twice the inverse voltage rating requirement of the bridge diodes. The diode current ratings are identical for the two circuits. The bridge makes better use of the transformer's secondary than the center tap, since the transformer's full winding supplies power during both half cycles, while each half of the center tap's secondary provides power only during its positive half-cycle. The bridge rectifier often takes second place to the full-wave center tap rectifiers in high-current low-voltage applications, however, since the two forward-conducting series-diode drops in the bridge introduce an additional volt or more of voltage loss, and thus more heat to be dissipated, than does the single diode drop of the center tap.

Semiconductor Rectifier Ratings

Silicon rectifiers are being used almost exclusively in power supplies designed for amateur equipment. They are available in a wide range of voltage and current ratings. In peak inverse voltage (PIV) ratings of 600 or less, silicon rectifiers carry current ratings as high as 400 amperes. At 1000 PIV, the current ratings may be several amperes. The extreme compactness of silicon rectifiers makes feasible the stacking of several units in series for higher voltages. Stacks are available commercially that will handle up to 10,000 PIV at a dc load current of 1 A or more.

Protection of Silicon Power Diodes

The important specifications of a silicon diode are:
1) PIV, the peak inverse voltage.
2) I_O, the average dc current rating.
3) I_{REP}, the peak repetitive forward current.
4) I_{SURGE}, a nonrepetitive, peak half-sine wave of 8.3 ms duration (one-half cycle

of 60 Hz line frequency).

The first two specifications appear in most catalogs. The last two often do not, but they are very important.

Because the rectifier never allows current to flow more than half the time, when it does conduct it has to pass at least twice the average direct current. With a capacitor-input filter, the rectifier conducts much less than half the time, so that when it does conduct, it may pass as much as 10 to 20 times the average dc current, under certain conditions. This is shown in Fig. 8. At A is a simple half-wave rectifier with a resistive load. The waveform to the right of the drawing shows the output voltage along with the diode current. At B and C there are two periods of operation to consider. After the capacitor is charged to the peak-rectified voltage, a period of diode nonconduction elapses while the output voltage discharges through the load. As the voltage begins to rise on the next positive pulse, a point is reached where the rectified voltage equals the stored voltage in the capacitor. As the voltage rises beyond that point, the diode begins to supply current. The diode will continue to conduct until the waveform reaches the crest, as shown. Since the diode must pass a current equal to that of the load over a short period of a cycle, the current will be high. The larger the capacitor for a given load, the shorter the diode conduction time and the higher the peak repetitive current (I_{REP}).

When the supply is first turned on, the discharged input capacitor looks like a dead short, and the rectifier passes a very heavy current. This is I_{SURGE}. The maximum I_{SURGE} rating is usually for a duration of one-half cycle (at 60 Hz), or about 8.3 milliseconds.

If a manufacturer's data sheet is not available, an educated guess about a diode's capability can be made by using these rules of thumb for silicon diodes of the type commonly used in amateur power supplies:

Rule 1) The maximum I_{REP} rating can be assumed to be approximately four times the maximum I_o rating.

Rule 2) The maximum I_{SURGE} rating can be assumed to be approximately 12 times the maximum I_o rating. (This figure should provide a reasonable safety factor. Silicon rectifiers with 750-mA dc ratings, for example, seldom have 1-cycle surge ratings of less than 15 amperes; some are rated up to 35 amperes or more.) From this it can be seen that the rectifier should be selected on the basis of I_{SURGE} and not on I_o ratings.

Thermal Protection

The junction of a diode is quite small; hence it must operate at a high current density. The heat-handling capability is, therefore, quite small. Normally, this is not a prime consideration in high-voltage, low-current supplies. Use of high-current rectifiers at or near their maximum ratings

Fig. 9 — The primary circuit of T1 at A shows how a 117-volt ac relay and a series-dropping resistor, R_S, can provide surge protection while C charges. At B is an alternative primary circuit using an RC time delay. When silicon rectifiers are connected in series for high-voltage operation, the inverse voltage does not divide equally. The inverse voltage drops can be equalized with resistors, as shown in the secondary circuit. To protect against voltage spikes that may damage an individual rectifier, each rectifier should be bypassed by a 0.01-μF capacitor. Connected as shown, two 400-PIV silicon rectifiers can be used as an 800-PIV rectifier, although it is preferable to include a safety factor and call it a 750-PIV rectifier. The rectifiers, D1 through D4, should be of the same type number and ratings.

(usually 2-ampere or larger stud-mount rectifiers) requires some form of heat sinking. Frequently, mounting the rectifier on the main chassis — directly, or with thin mica insulating washers — will suffice. If insulated from the chassis, a thin layer of silicone grease should be used between the diode and the insulator, and between the insulator and the chassis, to assure good heat conduction. Large, high-current rectifiers often require special heat sinks to maintain a safe operating temperature. Forced-air cooling is sometimes used as a further aid. Safe case temperatures are usually given in the manufacturer's data sheets and should be observed if the maxi-

mum capabilities of the diode are to be realized. See the thermal design section presented later in this chapter for more information.

Surge Protection

Each time the power supply is activated, assuming the input filter capacitor has been discharged, the rectifiers must look into what represents a dead short. Some form of surge protection is usually necessary to protect the diodes until the input capacitor becomes nearly charged, unless the diodes used have a very high surge-current rating (several hundred amperes). Although the dc resistance of the transformer secondary can sometimes be relied on to provide ample surge-current limiting, this is seldom true on high-voltage power supplies. Series resistors can be installed between the secondary and the rectifier strings, but are a deterrent to good voltage regulation.

The best method of protecting the rectifiers is to apply low primary voltage to the transformer for a short period (typically 0.5 to 1 second) until the capacitors charge. After the capacitors have charged, full primary voltage may be applied. A variable autotransformer (Variac or Powerstat are common trade names) may be used to increase the voltage gradually. Some transformers are wound with multiple primaries, and a relay-switching scheme may be employed to step the primary up to full potential.

Fig. 9 illustrates several ways to limit inrush current automatically at turn-on. In each case, R_S is a 25-watt resistor with a resistance of between 15 and 50 ohms, depending on power-supply characteristics. At power supply turn-on, R_S introduces a voltage drop into the primary feed to T1 until the coil of K1 is energized, closing the contacts and shorting out R_S for normal operation.

In the circuit shown in Fig. 9A, K1 has an ac coil rated for the same voltage as the primary of T1. As C becomes nearly charged, the voltage drop across R_S lessens, allowing K1 to pull in. At Fig. 9B, an RC time constant determines the time between application of primary voltage and closure of K1. In this circuit, K1 has a dc coil. The delay time may be calculated using the equation

$$\tau = R_{TH}C$$

where
t = time in seconds

$$R_{TH} = \frac{R_A\,R_C}{R_A + R_C}$$

R_A = resistance of R_A in ohms
R_C = coil resistance of K1 in ohms
C = capacitance of C1 in farads

A third method of energizing K1 is with a fixed time-delay relay having appropriate ratings.

Transient Problems

A common cause of trouble is transient voltages on the ac power line. These are short spikes, mostly, that can temporarily increase the voltage seen by the rectifier to values much higher than the normal transformer voltage. They come from distant lightning strokes, electric motors turning on and off, and so on. Transients cause unexpected, and often unexplained, failure of silicon rectifiers.

It's always wise to suppress line transients, and it can be done easily. Fig. 10A shows one way. C1 looks like 280 kΩ at 60 Hz, but to a sharp transient (which has only high-frequency components), it is an

Fig. 10 — Methods of suppressing line transients. See text.

effective bypass. C2 provides additional protection on the secondary side of the transformer. It should be 0.01 μF for transformer voltages of 100 or less, and 0.001 μF for high-voltage transformers.

Fig. 10B shows another transient-suppression method using metal-oxide varistor (MOV) suppressors. The MOVs do not conduct unless the peak voltage becomes abnormally high. Then they clip the transient peaks.

Transient voltages can go as high as twice the normal line voltage before the suppressor diodes clip the peaks. Capacitors cannot give perfect suppression either. Thus, it is a good idea to use power supply rectifiers rated at about twice the expected PIV.

Diodes in Series

When the PIV rating of a single diode is not sufficient for the application, similar diodes may be used in series. (Two 500-PIV diodes in series will withstand 1000 PIV, and so on.) When this is done, a resistor and a capacitor should be placed across each diode in the string to equalize the PIV drops and to guard against transient voltage spikes, as shown in Fig. 11A. Even though the diodes are of the same type and have the same PIV rating, they may have widely different back resistances when they are cut off. The inverse voltage divides according to Ohm's Law, and the diode with the higher back resistance will have the higher voltage developed across it. The diode may break down.

If we put a swamping resistor across each diode, R as shown in Fig. 11A, the resultant resistance across each diode will be almost the same, and the back voltage will divide almost equally. A good rule of thumb for resistor size is this: Multiply the PIV rating of the diode by 500 ohms. For

Fig. 11 — (A) Diodes connected in series should be shunted with equalizing resistors and spike-suppressing capacitors. (B) Diodes connected in parallel should have series current equalizing resistors.

example, a 500-PIV diode should be shunted by 500 × 500, or 250,000 ohms. Metal film resistors are generally rated for working voltage as follows: ¼ W — 250 V (RMS); ½ W — 350 V; 1 W — 500 V; 2 W — 750 V.

The shift from forward conduction to high back resistance does not take place instantly in a silicon diode. Some diodes take longer than others to develop high back resistance. To protect the fast-switching diodes in a series string until all the diodes are properly cut off, a 0.01-μF capacitor should be placed across each diode. Fig. 11A shows the complete series-diode circuit. The capacitors should be noninductive (ceramic disc, for example) and should be well matched. Use 10-percent-tolerance capacitors if possible.

Diodes in Parallel

Diodes can be placed in parallel to

increase current-handling capability. Equalizing resistors should be added as shown in Fig. 11B. Without the resistors, one diode may take most of the current. The resistors should be selected to have about a 1-volt drop at the expected peak current.

FILTERING

The pulsating dc waves from the rectifiers are not sufficiently constant in amplitude to prevent hum corresponding to the pulsations. Filters are required between the rectifier and the load to smooth out the pulsations into an essentially constant dc voltage. The design of the filter depends to a large extent on the dc voltage output, the voltage regulation of the power supply and the maximum load current rating of the rectifier. Power-supply filters are low-pass devices using series inductors and shunt capacitors.

Load Resistance

In discussing the performance of power-supply filters, it is sometimes convenient to express the load connected to the output terminals of the supply in terms of resistance. The load resistance is equal to the output voltage divided by the total current drawn, including the current drawn by the bleeder resistor.

Voltage Regulation

The output voltage of a power supply always decreases as more current is drawn, not only because of increased voltage drops in the transformer and filter chokes, but also because the output voltage at light loads tends to soar to the peak value of the transformer voltage as a result of charging the first capacitor. Proper filter design can eliminate the soaring effect. The change in output voltage with load is called voltage regulation, and is expressed as a percentage.

$$\text{Percent regulation} = \frac{100\,(E_1 - E_2)}{E_2}$$

where

E_1 = the no-load voltage
E_2 = the full-load voltage

A steady load, such as that represented by a receiver, speech amplifier or unkeyed stages of a transmitter, does not require good (low) regulation as long as the proper voltage is obtained under load conditions. However, the filter capacitors must have a voltage rating safe for the highest value to which the voltage will soar when the external load is removed.

A power supply will show more (higher) regulation with long-term changes in load resistance than with short temporary changes. The regulation with long-term changes is often called the static regulation, to distinguish it from the dynamic regulation (short temporary load changes). A load that varies at a syllabic or keyed rate, as represented by some audio and RF

amplifiers, usually requires good dynamic regulation (15 percent or less) if distortion products are to be held to a low level. The dynamic regulation of a power supply can be improved by increasing the value of the output capacitor.

When essentially constant voltage regardless of current variation is required (for stabilizing an oscillator, for example), special voltage-regulating circuits described later in this chapter are used.

Bleeder

A bleeder resistor is a resistance connected across the output terminals of the power supply. Its functions are to discharge the filter capacitors as a safety measure when the power is turned off and to improve voltage regulation by providing a minimum load resistance. When voltage regulation is not of importance, the resistance may be as high as 100 ohms per volt. The resistance value to be used for voltage-regulating purposes is discussed in later sections. From the consideration of safety, the power rating of the resistor should be as conservative as possible, since a burned-out bleeder resistor is dangerous!

Ripple Frequency and Voltage

Pulsations at the output of the rectifier can be considered to be the result of an alternating current superimposed on a steady direct current. From this viewpoint, the filter may be considered to consist of shunt capacitors that short circuit the ac component while not interfering with the flow of the dc component. Series chokes will readily pass dc but will impede the flow of the ac component.

The alternating component is called ripple. The effectiveness of the filter can be expressed in terms of percent ripple, which is the ratio of the RMS value of the ripple to the dc value in terms of percentage.

$$\text{Percent ripple (RMS)} = \frac{100\,E_1}{E_2}$$

where

E_1 = the RMS value of ripple voltage
E_2 = the steady dc voltage

Any multiplier or amplifier supply in a CW transmitter should have less than five percent ripple. A linear amplifier can tolerate about three percent ripple on the plate voltage. Bias supplies for linear amplifiers should have less than one-percent ripple. VFOs, speech amplifiers and receivers may require a ripple reduction to 0.01 percent.

Ripple frequency is the frequency of the pulsations in the rectifier output wave — the number of pulsations per second. The frequency of the ripple with half-wave rectifiers is the same as the frequency of the line supply — 60 Hz with 60-Hz supply. Since the output pulses are doubled with a full-wave rectifier, the ripple frequency is doubled — to 120 Hz with a 60-Hz supply.

The amount of filtering (values of inductance and capacitance) required to give adequate smoothing depends on the ripple frequency. More filtering is required as the ripple frequency is lowered.

TYPES OF FILTER

Power supply filters fall into two classifications: capacitor input and choke input. Capacitor-input filters are characterized by relatively high output voltage with respect to the transformer voltage. Capacitor-input filters are especially useful with silicon rectifiers.

The output voltage of a properly de-

Fig. 12 — Capacitor-input filter circuits. At A is a simple capacitor filter. B and C are single- and double-section filters, respectively.

(A)

(B)

Fig. 13 — Dc output voltages from a half- and full-wave rectifier circuit as a function of the filter capacitance and load resistance (half-wave shown at A and full-wave shown at B). R_s includes transformer winding resistance and rectifier forward resistance. For the ratio R_s/R, both resistances are in ohms; for the RC product, R is in ohms and C is in microfarads. These curves are adapted from those published by Otto H. Schade in "Analysis of Rectifier Operation," *Proceedings of the I.R.E.*, July 1943.

signed choke-input power supply is less than would be obtained with a capacitor-input filter from the same transformer. Generally speaking, a choke-input filter will permit a higher load current to be drawn from a thermionic rectifier without exceeding the peak rating of the rectifier. This is a result of the greatly reduced peak current that the rectifier is subjected to.

Capacitor-Input Filters

Capacitor-input filter systems are shown in Fig. 12. Disregarding voltage drops in the chokes, all have the same characteristics except with respect to ripple. Better ripple reduction will be obtained when LC sections are added as shown in Figs. 12B and C.

Output Voltage

To determine the approximate dc voltage output when a capacitor-input filter is used, the graphs shown in Fig. 13 will be helpful. An example of how to use the graph is given below.

Example:
Full-wave rectifier (use graph at B)
Transformer RMS voltage = 350
Load resistance = 2000 ohms
Series resistance = 200 ohms
Input capacitance = 20 μF

$$\frac{R_s}{R} = \frac{200}{2000} = 0.1$$

$$\frac{377\ RC}{1,000,000} = \frac{377 \times 2000 \times 20}{1,000,000} = 15.08$$

From curve 0.1 and 377 RC/1,000,000 = 15, the dc voltage is (350 × 1.04) = 364.

In many cases it is desirable to know the amount of capacitance required for a power supply, given certain performance criteria. This is especially true when designing a power supply for an application such as a solid-state transceiver. The following example shows the builder how to arrive at circuit values for a power supply using a single capacitor filter.

Fig. 14 is the circuit diagram of the power supply to be used.

Requirements:
Output voltage = 12.6
Output current = 1 ampere
Maximum ripple = 2 percent
Load regulation = 5 percent

The RMS secondary voltage of T1 must be the desired output voltage plus the voltage drops across D2 and D4 divided by 1.41.

$$E_{SEC} = \frac{12.6 + 1.4}{1.41} = 9.93$$

In practice, the nearest standard transformer (10 V) would work fine. Alternatively, the builder could wind his own transformer, or remove secondary turns from a 12-volt transformer to obtain the desired RMS secondary voltage.

A two-percent ripple referenced to 12.6 volts is 0.25 V RMS. The peak-to-peak value is therefore 0.25 × 2.8 = 0.7 V. This value is necessary to calculate the required capacitance for C1.

Also needed for determining the value of C1 is the time interval (t) between the full-wave rectifier pulses, which is calculated as follows:

$$t = \frac{1}{f_{(Hz)}} = \frac{1}{120} = 8.3 \times 10^{-3}$$

where

t = the time between pulses
f = the ripple frequency in Hz

Since the circuit makes use of a full-wave rectifier, a pulse occurs twice during each cycle. With half-wave rectification, a pulse would occur only once a cycle. Thus 120 Hz is used as the frequency for this calculation.

C1 is calculated from

$$C_{(\mu F)} = \left[\frac{I_L t}{E_{rip(P-P)}}\right] 10^6$$

$$= \left[\frac{1\,A \times 8.3 \times 10^{-3}}{0.7}\right] 10^6$$

$$= 11,857\ \mu F$$

where I_L is the current taken by the load. The nearest standard capacitor value is 12,000 μF. This value is acceptable, although the tolerance of electrolytic capacitors is rather loose, so the builder may elect to use the next larger standard value.

Diodes D1-D4, inclusive, should have a PIV rating of at least two times the transformer secondary peak voltage. Assuming a transformer secondary RMS value of 10 volts, the PIV should be at least 28 volts. Four diodes rated at 50 volts will provide a margin of safety. Although the minimum current rating needed is one-half the load current, the forward current rating of the diodes should be at least twice the load current for safety. For a 1-A load, the diodes should be rated for at least 2 A.

The load resistance, R_L, is determined by E_o/I_L, which in this example is 12.6/1 = 12.6 ohms. This factor must be known in order to find the necessary series resistance for five-percent regulation. Calculate as follows:

$$R_{s(max)} = \text{load regulation} \times R_L$$

$$= 0.05 \times 12.6 = 0.63\ \text{ohm}$$

Therefore, the transformer secondary dc resistance should be no greater than 0.63 ohm. The secondary current rating should be equal to or greater than the I_L = 1 ampere. C1 should have a minimum working voltage of 1.4 times the output voltage. In this power supply the capacitor should be rated for at least 18 volts.

Choke-Input Filters

Better voltage regulation results when a choke-input filter, as shown in Fig. 15, is

Fig. 14 — This figure illustrates how to design a simple unregulated power supply. See text for a thorough discussion.

Fig. 15 — Diagram showing various voltage drops that must be taken into consideration in determining the required transformer voltage to deliver the desired output voltage.

used. Choke input permits better utilization of thermionic rectifiers, because a higher load current can be drawn without exceeding the peak current rating. Choke-input filters are generally not used with silicon rectifiers.

Minimum Choke Inductance

A choke-input filter will tend to act as a capacitor-input filter unless the input choke has at least a certain minimum value of inductance called the critical value. For full-wave 60-Hz supplies, this critical value is given by

$$L_{crit} \text{ (henrys)} = \frac{E \text{ (volts)}}{I \text{ (mA)}}$$

where

E = the supply output voltage
I = the current being drawn through the filter

If the choke has at least the critical value, the output voltage will be limited to the average value of the rectified wave at the input to the choke when the current drawn from the supply is small. This is in contrast to the capacitor-input filter in which the output voltage tends to soar toward the peak value of the rectified wave at light loads.

Minimum-Load — Bleeder Resistance

From the above formula for critical inductance, it is obvious that if no current is drawn from the supply, the critical inductance will be infinite. So that a practical value of inductance may be used, some current must be drawn from the supply at all times the supply is in use. From the formula we find that this minimum value of current is

$$I(mA) = \frac{E(\text{volts})}{L_{crit}}$$

In the majority of cases, it will be most convenient to adjust the bleeder resistance so that the bleeder will draw the required minimum current. From the formula, it may be seen that the value of critical inductance becomes smaller as the load current increases.

Swinging Chokes

Less costly chokes are available that will maintain at least the critical value of inductance over the range of current likely to be drawn from practical supplies. These chokes are called swinging chokes. As an example, a swinging choke may have an inductance rating of 5/25 H and a current rating of 200 mA. If the supply delivers 1000 volts, the minimum load current should be 1000/25 = 40 mA. When the full load current of 200 mA is drawn from the supply, the inductance will drop to 5 H. The critical inductance for 200 mA at 1000 volts is 1000/200 = 5 H. Therefore the 5/25-H choke maintains the critical inductance at the full current rating of 200 mA. At all load currents between 40 mA and 200 mA, the choke will adjust its inductance to the approximate critical value.

Output Voltage

Provided the input-choke inductance is at least the critical value, the output voltage

may be calculated quite closely by

$$E_o = 0.9E_t - (I_B + I_L) \times (R1 + R2) - E_r$$

where

E_o = output voltage
E_t = RMS voltage applied to the rectifier (RMS voltage between center-tap and one end of the secondary in the case of the center-tap rectifier)
I_B = bleeder current (A)
I_L = load current (A)
R1 = first filter choke resistance
R2 = second filter choke resistance
E_r = voltage drop across the rectifier

The various voltage drops are shown in Fig. 15. At no load, I_L is zero; hence the no-load voltage may be calculated on the basis of bleeder current only. The voltage regulation may be determined from the no-load and full-load voltages using the formulas previously given.

Output Capacitance

Whether the supply has a choke- or capacitor-input filter, the reactance of the output capacitor should be low for the lowest audio frequency if it is intended for use with a class-A AF amplifier. For vacuum-tube loads, 16 μF or more is usually adequate. When the supply is used with a class-B amplifier (for modulation or for SSB amplification) or a CW transmitter, increasing the output capacitance will result in improved dynamic regulation of the supply. However, a region of diminishing returns can be reached, and 20 to 30 μF will usually suffice for any supply subjected to large changes at a syllabic (or keying) rate.

Resonance

Resonance effects in the series circuit across the output of the rectifier, formed by the first choke and first filter capacitor, must be avoided, because the ripple voltage would build up to large values. This not only is the opposite action to that for which the filter is intended, but also may cause excessive rectifier peak currents and abnormally high peak-inverse voltages. For full-wave rectification, the ripple frequency will be 120 Hz for a 60-Hz supply; resonance will occur when the product of choke inductance in henrys times capacitor capacitance in microfarads is equal to 1.77. At least twice this product of inductance and capacitance should be used to ensure against resonance effects. With a swinging choke, the minimum rated inductance of the choke should be used. If too high an LC filter product is used, the resonance may occur at the radio-telegraph keying or voice syllabic rate, and large voltage excursions (filter bounce) may be experienced at that rate.

Ratings of Filter Components

In a power supply using a choke-input filter and properly designed choke and bleeder resistor, the no-load voltage across the filter capacitors will be about nine-tenths of the ac RMS voltage. Nevertheless, it is advisable to use capacitors rated for the peak transformer voltage. This large safety factor is suggested because the voltage across the capacitors can reach this peak value if the bleeder should burn out and there is no load on the supply.

In a capacitor-input filter, the capacitors should have a working-voltage rating at least as high, and preferably somewhat higher, than the peak voltage from the transformer. Thus, in the case of a center-tap rectifier having a transformer delivering 550 volts each side of the center tap, the minimum safe capacitor voltage rating will be 550 × 1.41, or 775 volts. An 800-volt capacitor should be used, or preferably a 1000-volt unit.

Filter Capacitors in Series

Filter capacitors are made in several different types. Electrolytic capacitors, which are available for peak voltages up to about 800, combine high capacitance with small size. This is possible because the dielectric is an extremely thin film of oxide on aluminum foil. Capacitors of this type may be connected in series for higher voltages, although the filtering capacitance will be reduced to the resultant of the two capacitances in series.

If this arrangement is used, it is important that each capacitor be shunted with a resistor of about 100 ohms per volt of supply voltage applied to the individual capacitors, with an adequate power rating.

These resistors may serve as all or part of the bleeder resistance. Capacitors with higher voltage ratings are usually made with a dielectric of thin paper impregnated with oil. The working voltage of a capacitor is the voltage that it will withstand continuously.

Filter Chokes

Filter chokes or inductances are wound on iron cores, with a small gap in the core to prevent magnetic saturation of the iron at high currents. When the iron becomes saturated, its permeability decreases, and consequently the inductance also decreases. Despite the air gap, the inductance of a choke usually varies to some extent with the direct current flowing in the winding; hence it is necessary to specify the inductance at the current which the choke is intended to carry. Its inductance with little or no direct current flowing in the winding will usually be considerably higher than the value when full load current is flowing.

Negative-Lead Filtering

For many years it has been almost universal practice to place filter chokes in the positive leads of plate power supplies. This means that the insulation between the choke winding and its core (which should be grounded to chassis as a safety measure) must be adequate to withstand the output voltage of the supply. This voltage requirement is removed if the choke is placed in the negative lead, as shown in Fig. 16. With this connection, the capacitance of the

Fig. 16 — In most applications, the filter choke may be placed in the negative instead of the positive side of the circuit. This reduces the danger of a voltage breakdown between the choke winding and core. The ripple voltage developed across the choke can be rectified to provide a free negative bias supply.

Fig. 17 — The "economy" power-supply circuit is a combination of the full-wave and bridge-rectifier circuits.

transformer secondary to ground appears in parallel with the filter chokes, tending to bypass the chokes. However, this effect will be negligible in practical application except in cases where the output ripple must be reduced to a very low figure. Choke terminals, negative capacitor terminals and the transformer center-tap terminal should be well protected against accidental contact, since these will assume full supply voltage to chassis should a choke burn out or the chassis connection fail.

A free negative supply of about 60% of the plate potential can be obtained by rectifying the ripple voltage developed across the filter choke. The voltage across the choke has an effective value of the peak secondary voltage (measured with respect to the center tap) minus the main dc output voltage. Rectification multiplies the choke voltage by 1.4.

The Economy Power Supply

In many transmitters of the 100-watt class, an excellent method for obtaining plate and screen voltages without wasting power in voltage-dropping resistors is use of the economy power supply circuit. Shown in Fig. 17, it is a combination of the full-wave and bridge-rectifier circuits. The voltage at B2 is the normal voltage obtained with the full-wave circuit, and the voltage at B1 is that obtained with the bridge circuit. The total dc power obtained from the transformer is, of course, the sum of the power used at each voltage. In CW and SSB applications, additional power can usually be drawn without excessive heating, especially if the transformer has a rectifier filament winding that isn't being used. When negative-lead choke filtering is used, the free negative bias supply scheme described above can be incorporated, making all of a transmitting tube's operating potentials available from a single transformer. The entire peak secondary voltage is used to calculate the resulting bias voltage.

VOLTAGE MULTIPLICATION

Half-Wave Voltage Doubler

Fig. 18 shows the circuit of a half-wave voltage doubler. B, C and D of Fig. 18 illustrate the circuit operation. For clarity, assume the transformer voltage polarity at the moment the circuit is activated is that shown at B. During the first negative half cycle, D_A conducts (D_B is in a nonconductive state), charging C1 to the peak rectified voltage ($1.4 E_{RMS}$). C1 is charged with the polarity shown at B. During the positive half cycle of the secondary voltage, D_A is cut off and D_B conducts, charging capacitor C2. The amount of voltage delivered to C2 is the sum of peak secondary voltage of the transformer plus the voltage stored in C1 ($1.4 E_{RMS}$). On the next negative half cycle, D_B is nonconducting and C2 will discharge into the load. If no load is connected across C2, the

Fig. 18 — Illustrated at A is a half-wave voltage-doubler circuit. B displays how the first half cycle of input voltage charges C1. During the next half cycle (shown at C), capacitor C2 is charged with the transformer secondary voltage plus that voltage stored in C1 from the previous half cycle. D illustrates the levels to which each capacitor is charged throughout the cycle.

Fig. 19 — A full-wave voltage doubler is displayed at A. One half cycle is shown at B and the next half cycle at C. Each capacitor receives a charge during every cycle of input voltage. D illustrates how each capacitor is charged alternately.

capacitors will remain charged — C1 to $1.4 E_{RMS}$ and C2 to $2.8 E_{RMS}$. When a load is connected to the output of the doubler, the voltage across C2 drops during the negative half cycle and is recharged up to $2.8 E_{RMS}$ during the positive half cycle.

The output waveform across C2 resembles that of a half-wave rectifier circuit in that C2 is pulsed once every cycle. Fig. 18D illustrates the levels to which the two capacitors are charged throughout the cycle. In actual operation, the capacitors will not discharge all the way to zero as shown.

Full-Wave Voltage Doubler

Shown in Fig. 19 is the circuit of a full-wave voltage doubler. The circuit operation

can best be understood by following B, C and D of Fig. 19. During the positive half cycle of transformer secondary voltage, as shown at B, D_A conducts charging capacitor C1 to $1.4 E_{RMS}$. D_B is not conducting at this time.

During the negative half cycle, as shown at C, D_B conducts, charging capacitor C2 to $1.4 E_{RMS}$, while D_A is nonconducting. The output voltage is the sum of the two capacitor voltages, which will be $2.8 E_{RMS}$ under no-load conditions. Fig. 19D illustrates that each capacitor alternately receives a charge once per cycle. The effective filter capacitance is that of C1 and C2 in series, which is less than the capacitance of either C1 or C2 alone.

Resistors R in Fig. 19A are used to limit

Fig. 20 — Dc output voltages from a full-wave voltage-doubling circuit as a function of the filter capacitances and load resistance. For the ratio R_s/R and for the RC product, resistances are in ohms and capacitance is in microfarads. Equal resistance values for R_s and equal capacitance values for C are assumed. These curves are adapted from those published by Otto H. Schade in "Analysis of Rectifier Operation," *Proceedings of the I.R.E.,* July 1943.

Fig. 21 — Voltage-multiplying circuits with one side of the transformer secondary used as common. A, voltage tripler; B, voltage quadrupler. Capacitances are typically 20 to 50 μF depending on output current demand. Dc ratings of capacitors are related to E_{peak} (1.4 E_{ac}).

C1 — Greater than E_{peak}
C2 — Greater than $2E_{peak}$
C3 — Greater than $3E_{peak}$
C4 — Greater than $2E_{peak}$

the surge current through the rectifiers. Their values are based on the transformer voltage and the rectifier surge-current rating, since at the instant the power supply is turned on the filter capacitors look like a short-circuited load. Provided the limiting resistors can withstand the surge current, their current-handling capacity is based on the maximum load current from the supply. Output voltages approaching twice the peak voltage of the transformer can be obtained with the voltage doubling circuit shown in Fig. 19. Fig. 20 shows how the voltage depends upon the ratio of the series resistance to the load resistance, and the load resistance times the filter capacitance. The peak inverse voltage across each diode is 2.8 E_{RMS}.

Voltage Tripling and Quadrupling

A voltage-tripling circuit is shown in Fig. 21A. On one half of the ac cycle, C1 and C3 are charged to the source voltage through D1, D2 and D3. On the opposite half of the cycle, D2 conducts and C2 is charged to twice the source voltage, because it sees the transformer plus the charge in C1 as its source (D1 is cut off during this half cycle.) At the same time, D3 conducts, and with the transformer and the charge in C2 as the source, C3 is charged to three times the transformer voltage.

The voltage-quadrupling circuit of Fig. 21B works in substantially similar fashion. In either of the circuits of Fig. 21, the output voltage will approach an exact multiple of the peak ac voltage when the output current drain is low and the capacitance values are high.

In the circuits shown, the negative leg of the supply is common to one side of the transformer. The positive leg can be made common to one side of the transformer by reversing the diodes and capacitors.

VOLTAGE STABILIZATION

Zener Diode Regulation

A Zener diode (named after Dr. Carl Zener) can be used to maintain the voltage applied to a circuit at a practically constant value, regardless of the voltage regulation of the power supply or variations in load current. The typical circuit is shown in Fig. 22A. Note that the cathode side of the diode is connected to the positive side of the supply. The electrical characteristics of a Zener diode under conditions of forward and reverse voltage are given in Chapter 4.

Zener diodes are available in a wide variety of voltages and power ratings. The voltages range from less than two to a few hundred, while the power ratings (power the diode can dissipate) run from less than 0.25 watt to 50 watts. The ability of the Zener diode to stabilize a voltage depends on the conducting impedance of the diode. This can be as low as one ohm or less in a low-voltage, high-power diode or as high

as a thousand ohms in a high-voltage, low-power diode.

Diode Power Dissipation

Zener diodes of a particular voltage rating have varied maximum current capabilities, depending on the power ratings of each of the diodes. The power dissipated in a diode is the product of the voltage across it and the current through it. Conversely, the maximum current a particular diode may safely conduct is equal to its power rating divided by its voltage rating. Thus, a 10-V, 50-W Zener diode, if operated at its maximum dissipation rating, would conduct 5 amperes. A 10-V, 1-W diode, on the other hand, could safely conduct no more than 0.1 A, or 100 mA. The conducting impedance of a diode is its voltage rating divided by the current flowing through it. In the above examples, the conducting impedance would be 2 ohms for the 50-W diode, and 100 ohms for the 1-W diode. Disregarding small voltage changes which may occur, the conducting impedance of a given diode is a function of the current flowing through it, varying in inverse proportion.

The power-handling capability of most Zener diodes is rated at 25°C, or approximately room temperature. If the diode is operated in a higher ambient temperature, its power capability must be derated. A typical 1-watt diode can safely dissipate only ½ watt at 100°C.

Part C of Fig. 22 illustrates a method for multiplying the effective power-handling capability of a small Zener diode. When the diode conducts, it supplies base current to a power transistor. This causes collector

Fig. 22 — Zener-diode voltage regulation. The voltage from a negative supply may be regulated by reversing the power-supply connections and the diode and transistor polarities. The operation of these circuits is discussed in the text.

Fig. 23 — Voltage stabilization circuit using a VR tube. A negative-supply output may be regulated by reversing the polarity of the power-supply connections and the VR-tube connections from those shown here.

current to be drawn through the series-limiting resistance (see next section). This current drops the diode voltage ($V_Z + V_{be}$) to the conduction threshold. When load current is drawn through R_S, the output voltage tends to drop below the conduction threshold. But when the diode ceases to conduct, the transistor collector ceases to draw current. This negative feedback, or servo action, stabilizes the current in the limiting resistor and regulates the output voltage at $V_Z + V_{be}$. With this approach, the conducting impedance of the Zener diode is divided by the transistor beta.

When high load current is required, a Zener diode shunt regulator is grossly inefficient because of the voltage dropped and power dissipated by the current-limiting resistor. This deficiency can be overcome by using the emitter follower arrangement of Fig. 22D. A Zener diode establishes a reference voltage for the transistor base, and the load current flows in the collector-emitter circuit. The limiting resistor is selected to provide the maximum load current divided by the minimum transistor beta, plus the desired Zener current. As with the shunt current boosting circuit described above, the output impedance of this voltage regulator will be the Zener impedance divided by the transistor beta. The output voltage is $V_Z - V_{be}$.

Limiting Resistance

The value of R_S in Fig. 22 is determined by the load requirements. If R_S is too large, the diode will be unable to regulate at large values of I_L (the current through R_L). If R_S is too small, the diode dissipation rating may be exceeded at low values of I_L. The optimum value for R_S can be calculated by

$$R_S = \frac{E_{dc(min)} - E_Z}{1.1\ I_{L(max)}}$$

When R_S is known, the maximum dissipation of the diode, P_D, may be determined by

$$P_D = \left[\frac{E_{dc(max)} - E_Z}{R_S} - I_{L(min)}\right]E_Z$$

In the first equation, conditions are set up for the Zener diode to draw 1/10 the maximum load current. This assures diode regulation under maximum load.

Example: A 12-volt source is to supply a circuit requiring 9 volts. The load current varies between 200 and 350 mA.

$E_Z = 9.1$ V (nearest available value)

$$R_S = \frac{12 - 9.1}{1.1 \times 0.35} = \frac{2.9}{0.385} = 7.5\ \text{ohms}$$

$$P_D = \left[\frac{12 - 9.1}{7.5} - 0.2\right]9.1$$

$$= 0.185 \times 9.1 = 1.7\ \text{W}$$

The nearest available dissipation rating above 1.7 W is 5; therefore, a 9.1-V, 5-W Zener diode should be used. Such a rating, it may be noted, will cause the diode to be in the safe dissipation range even though the load is completely disconnected [I_L (min) = 0].

Obtaining Other Voltages

Fig. 22B shows how two Zener diodes may be used in series to obtain regulated voltages not normally obtainable from a single Zener diode, and also to give two values of regulated voltage. The diodes need not have equal breakdown voltages, because the arrangement is self equalizing. However, the current-handling capability of each diode should be taken into account. The limiting resistor may be calculated as above, taking the sum of the diode voltages as E_Z, and the sum of the load currents as I_L.

Gaseous Regulator Tubes

Although at first glance it may seem inappropriate to discuss gaseous voltage-regulator tubes (commonly called VR tubes) in a modern Handbook, they do offer advantages over their solid-state counterparts in some applications. Tube-type amplifier screen supplies often call for regulated voltages between 200 and 400. To obtain these voltages with Zener diodes, series combinations of four to six devices are often required. The cost can add up quickly. In addition to being far less expensive than solid-state devices, gaseous regulator tubes are much more forgiving of line transients, application of overvoltage and reverse screen current.

Gaseous regulator tubes (0A2/VR150, 0B2/VR105, etc.) can be used to good advantage. The voltage drop across such tubes is constant over a moderately wide current range. Tubes are available for regulated voltages near 150, 105, 90 and 75 volts.

The fundamental circuit for a gaseous regulator is shown in Fig. 23. The tube is connected in series with a limiting resistor, R1, across a source of voltage that must be higher than the starting voltage. The starting voltage is about 30 to 40 percent higher than the operating voltage. The load is connected in parallel with the tube. For stable operation, a minimum tube current of 5 to 10 mA is required. The maximum permissible current with most types is 40 mA; consequently, the load current cannot exceed 30 to 35 mA if the voltage is to be stabilized over a range from zero to maximum load. A single VR tube may also be used to regulate the voltage to a load current of almost any value as long as the variation in the current does not exceed 30 to 35 mA. If, for example, the average load current is 100 mA, a VR tube may be used to hold the voltage constant provided the current does not fall below 85 mA or rise above 115 mA.

The value of the limiting resistor must lie between that which just permits minimum tube current to flow and that which just passes the maximum permissible tube current when there is no load current. The latter value is generally used. It is given by the equation

$$R = \frac{E_s - E_r}{I}$$

where

    R = limiting resistance in ohms
    E_s = voltage of the source across which the tube and resistor are connected
    E_r = rated voltage drop across the regulator tube
    I = maximum tube current in amperes (usually 40 mA, or 0.04 A)

Two tubes may be used in series to give a higher regulated voltage than is obtainable with one, and also to give two values of regulated voltage. Regulation of the order of one percent can be obtained with these regulator tubes when they are operated within their proper current range. The capacitance in shunt with a VR tube should be limited to 0.1 μF or less. Larger values may cause the tube drop to oscillate between the operating and starting voltages.

Do not use any of the unconnected tube-socket pins as circuit tie points even though such pins are unconnected. They penetrate the tube envelope and terminate abruptly. Depending on the voltage applied to the pin, intermittent breakdown may be experienced.

ELECTRONIC VOLTAGE REGULATION

When extremely low ripple is required, or when the supply voltage must be constant with large fluctuations of load current and line voltage, a closed-loop amplifier is used to regulate the supply. There are two main categories of electronic regulators: linear regulators, in which the condition of a control element is varied in direct proportion to the line voltage or load current; and switching regulators, in which the control device is switched on and off, with the duty cycle proportional to the line or load conditions. Each system has relative advantages and disadvantages, and there are applications for both types in Amateur Radio equipment.

Linear Regulators

The two basic forms of linear regulators are sketched in Fig. 24. A series regulator, shown at A, is used in applications requiring efficient use of the primary power source. A stable reference voltage is established by a Zener diode. In critical applications a temperature-compensated reference diode (discussed in Chapter 4) would be used. The output voltage is sampled by the error amplifier, which compares the output (usually attenuated by a voltage divider) to the reference. If the scaled-down output voltage is higher than

the reference voltage, the error amplifier reduces the drive current to the pass transistor. Conversely, if the load pulls the output voltage below the value called for, the amplifier drives the pass transistor into increased conduction. The series pass transistor forms a voltage divider with the load resistance. In a series regulator, the power dissipation of the pass transistor is directly proportional to the load current and input-output voltage differential. The series-pass element can be located in either leg of the supply. Either NPN or PNP

devices can be used, depending on the ground polarity of the unregulated input.

Fig. 24B shows a simple shunt regulator circuit. Such a system would be used when the load on the unregulated voltage source must be kept constant. The operation is similar to that of the series regulator, except that the control element is in parallel with the output load. As the load current varies, the control transistor changes resistance in opposition to the load such that the resistance of the parallel combination remains constant, drawing a constant

Fig. 24 — Linear electronic voltage regulator circuits. In these diagrams batteries represent the unregulated input voltage source. A transformer, rectifier and filter would serve this function in most applications. (A) Series regulator. (B) Shunt regulator. (C) Remote sensing overcomes poor load regulation caused by IR drop in the connecting wires by bringing them inside the feedback loop.

current through R_S. Note that the input polarity of the error amplifier is reversed with respect to the series regulator configuration. This is a result of the inversion caused by the common-emitter control transistor. The power dissipation in the control transistor is greatest when the output is unloaded.

The "stiffness" or tightness of regulation of a linear regulator depends on the gain of the error amplifier and the ratio of the output scaling resistors. The resistor scaling is usually the most significant because high-gain IC op amps can be used in the error amplifier. If the reference potential is 1 volt and the scaling resistors are selected to produce an output of 10 volts, the loop gain is reduced (hence output impedance increased) by a factor of 10. Increasing the reference potential to 5 volts and rescaling the sampling divider for the same 10-volt output will improve the regulation by a factor of five compared to the previous example. Thus, if the 10-volt supply using a 1-volt reference produced an output change of 5 mV for a certain load variation, the supply having the 5-volt reference will produce only a 1-mV change. The same rule applies to output ripple. However, this characteristic can be controlled independently of the load regulation by shunting R1 in Fig. 24 (A and B) with a capacitor. This allows the regulator to function at maximum loop gain for the ac component of the output.

The above discussion leads to the conclusion that the reference voltage in a linear regulator should be as high as possible. However, solid-state physics and fabrication technology dictate that the best temperature stability is obtained with reference diodes having operating potentials in the 6-volt region.

In any regulator, the output is cleanest and regulation stiffest at the point where the sampling network or error amplifier is connected. If heavy load current is drawn through long leads, the voltage drop can degrade the regulation at the load. To combat this effect, the feedback connection to the error amplifier can be made directly to the load. This technique, called remote sensing, moves the point of best regulation to the load by bringing the connecting loads inside the feedback loop. This is shown in Fig. 24C.

Linear voltage regulators are called for in applications requiring tight regulation with very low output noise and ripple. The trade-offs for these traits are bulk, weight and heat dissipation. Several examples of linear regulator design are given in Chapter 27.

Safe Operating Area

In choosing a suitable transistor for use as the series pass device in a linear regulator, care must be taken to ensure that the transistor chosen will survive any possible combination of voltage and current stress that may occur during normal or

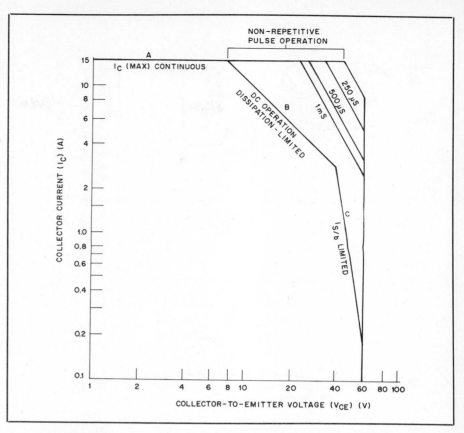

Fig. 25 — Graph of the safe operating area of a 2N3055 transistor. See text for details. This graph is based on material presented in RCA *Power Devices Data Book* SSD-220C.

short-circuit operation. Although the transistor's listed wattage rating is an indicator of its power-handling capability, it must be understood that this rating usually applies only to low forward voltage drops and high collector currents. As the collector-to-emitter voltage is increased, the power-handling capability of the transistor can decrease. This decrease, known as the forward-biased second-breakdown limit, depends greatly upon the processes used in the manufacture of the transistor.

To assist the circuit designer in choosing a transistor that will meet power ratings, transistor manufacturers provide curves relating collector current and voltage limits. These curves are referred to as safe-operating-area (SOAR) curves.

A typical SOAR curve (for a 2N3055 transistor) is shown in Fig. 25. Line A is maximum emitter current that can be handled by the device without damage to the emitter lead. Line B shows the constant power region of operation, which is the transistor's maximum power rating. Finally, line C is the second breakdown limit. Also shown are plots that represent short-term or pulsed-power limitations for various pulse widths.

The power-supply designer should consult the data sheets for his choice of transistor and check to make sure that the safe operating area limits will not be exceeded during normal and short-circuit operation

of the power supply. The addition of a current limiter or foldback limiter will help to protect the pass transistor against destruction during overload conditions.

Current Limiting for Discrete-Component Regulators

Damage to a pass transistor can occur when the load current exceeds the safe amount. Fig. 26 illustrates a simple current-limiter circuit that will protect Q1. All of the load current is routed through R1. A voltage difference will exist across R1; the value will depend on the exact load current at a given time. When the load current exceeds a predetermined safe value, the voltage drop across R1 will forward bias Q2 and cause it to conduct. Because Q2 is a silicon transistor, the voltage drop across R1 must exceed 0.6 V to turn Q2 on. This being the case, R1 is chosen for a value that provides a drop of 0.6 V when the maximum safe load current is drawn. In this instance, 0.6 volts will be seen when IL reaches 0.5 A. R2 protects the base-emitter junction of Q2 from current spikes, or from destruction in the event of failure of Q1 under short-circuit conditions.

When Q2 turns on, some of the current through R_S flows through Q2, thereby depriving Q1 of some of its base current. This action, depending upon the amount of Q1 base current at a precise moment, cuts off Q1 conduction to some degree,

(A)

(B)

Fig. 26 — Overload protection for a regulated supply can be implemented by addition of a current-overload protective circuit, as shown at A. At B, the circuit has been modified to employ current foldback limiting.

Fig. 27 — The 1-A regulator shown in Fig. 26B will fold back to 0.5 A under short-circuit conditions. See text.

Fig. 28 — At A, a Darlington-connected pair for use as the pass element in a series-regulating circuit. At B, the method of connecting two or more transistors in parallel for high current output. Resistances are in ohms. The circuit at A may be used for load currents from 100 mA to 5 A, at B for currents from 6 to 10 A.
Q1 — Motorola MJE 340 or equiv.
Q2-Q4 — Power transistor such as 2N3055 or 2N3772.

thus limiting the flow of current through it.

Foldback Limiting

Under short-circuit conditions, the previously described current limiter must withstand the full source voltage and short-circuit current simultaneously, which can impose a very high power dissipation or second breakdown stress on the series pass transistor. For example, a 12-volt regulator with current limiting set for 10 amperes and having a source of 16 volts will have a dissipation of 40 watts [(16 V – 12 V) × 10 A] at the point of current limiting (knee). But its dissipation will rise to 160 watts under short-circuit conditions (16 volts × 10 amps).

A modification of the limiter circuit can cause the regulator's output current to decrease with decreasing load resistance after the knee. With the output shorted, the output current is only a fraction of the knee current value, which protects the series pass transistor from excessive dissipation and possible failure. Using the previous example of the 12-volt, 10-amp regulator, if the short-circuit current is designed to be 3 amperes (knee is still 10 amps), the tran-

sistor dissipation with short circuit will be only 16 V × 3 A = 48 watts.

Fig. 26B shows how the current limiter example given in the previous section would be modified to incorporate foldback limiting. The divider string formed by R2 and R3 provides a negative bias to the base of Q2, which prevents Q2 from turning on until this bias is overcome by the drop in R1 caused by load current. Since this hold-off bias decreases as the output voltage drops, Q2 becomes more sensitive to current through R1 with decreasing output voltage. See Fig. 27.

The circuit is designed by first calculating the value of R1 for short-circuit current. For example, if 0.5 ampere is chosen, the value for R1 is simply 0.6 volts/0.5 amp = 1.2 ohms (with the output shorted, the amount of hold-off bias supplied by R2 and R3 is very small and can be neglected). The knee current is then chosen. For this example, the selected value will be 1.0 ampere. The divider string is then proportioned to provide a base voltage at the knee that is just sufficient to turn on Q2 (a value of 13.6 volts for 13.0 volts output). With 1.0 ampere flowing through

R1, the voltage across the divider will be 14.2 V. The voltage dropped by R2 must then be 14.2 V – 13.6 V, or 0.6 volt. Choosing a divider current of 2 milliamperes, the value of R2 is then 0.6 V/0.002 A = 300 ohms. R3 is calculated to be 13.6 V/0.002 A = 6800 ohms.

High-Current-Output Regulators

A simple Zener diode reference or IC op-amp error amplifier may not be able to source enough current to a pass transistor that must conduct heavy load current. The Darlington configuration of Fig. 28A multiplies the pass transistor beta, thereby extending the control range of the error amplifier. If the Darlington arrangement is implemented with discrete transistors, resistors across the base-emitter junctions may be necessary to prevent collector-to-base leakage currents in Q1 from being amplified and turning on the transistor pair. These resistors are contained in the envelope of a monolithic Darlington device.

When a single pass transistor is not available to handle the current required from a regulator, the current-handling capability may be increased by connecting two or more pass transistors in parallel. The circuit at B of Fig. 28 shows the method of connection. The resistances in the emitter leads of each transistor are necessary to equalize the currents.

IC Voltage Regulators

The modern trend in regulators is toward the use of three-terminal devices commonly referred to as three-terminal regulators. Inside each regulator is a reference, a high-gain error amplifier, temperature-compensated voltage-sensing resistors and transistors and a pass element. Many currently available units have thermal shutdown, overvoltage protection and current foldback, making them virtually destruction-proof. Several supplies using these ICs are featured in Chapter 27.

Three-terminal regulators (a connection for unregulated dc input, regulated dc output and ground) are available in a wide range of voltage and current ratings. Fairchild, National and Motorola are perhaps the three largest suppliers of these regulators at present. It is easy to see why regulators of this sort are so popular when one considers the low price and the number of individual components they can replace. The regulators are available in several different package styles, depending on current ratings. Low-current (100 mA) devices frequently use the plastic TO-92 and DIP-style cases. TO-220 packages are popular in the 1.5-A range, and TO-3 cases house the larger 3-A and 5-A devices.

Three-terminal regulators are available as positive or negative types. In most cases, a positive regulator is used to regulate a positive voltage and a negative regulator a negative voltage. However, depending on the systems ground requirements, each regulator type may be used to regulate the "opposite" voltage.

Fig. 29A and B illustrate how the regulators are used in the conventional mode. Several regulators can be used with a common-input supply to deliver several voltages with a common ground. Negative regulators may be used in the same manner. If no other common supplies operate off the input supply to the regulator, the circuits of Figs. 29C and D may be used to regulate positive voltages with a negative

regulator and vice versa. In these configurations the input supply is floated; neither side of the input is tied to the system ground.

Manufacturers have adopted a system of family numbers to classify three-terminal regulators in terms of supply polarity, output current and regulated voltage. For example, National Semiconductor uses the number LM7805C to describe a positive 5-V, 1.5-A regulator; the comparable unit from Texas Instruments is a UA7805KC. LM7812C describes a 12-V regulator of similar characteristics. LM7905C denotes a negative 5-V, 1.5-A device. There are many such families with widely varied ratings available from manufacturers. Fixed-voltage regulators are available with output ratings in most common values between 5 and 28 V. Other families include devices that can be adjusted from 1.25 to 50 V.

Regulator Specifications

When choosing a three-terminal regulator for a given application, the most important specifications to consider are device output voltage, output current, input-to-output differential voltage, line regulation, load regulation and power dissipation. Output voltage and current requirements will be determined by the load the supply will ultimately be used with.

Input-to-output differential voltage is one of the most important three-terminal regulator specifications to consider when designing a supply. The differential value (the difference between the voltage applied to the input terminal and the voltage on the output terminal) must be within a specified range. The minimum differential value, usually about 2.5 V, is called the dropout voltage. If the differential value is less than the dropout voltage, no regulation will take place. At the other end of the scale, maximum input-output differential voltage is generally about 40 V. If this differential value is exceeded, maximum device dissipation may be reached.

Increases in either output current or differential voltage produce proportional increases in device power consumption. By employing a safety feature called current foldback, some manufacturers have ensured that maximum dissipation will never be exceeded in normal operation. Fig. 30 shows the relationship between output current, input-output differential and current limiting for a three-terminal regulator nominally rated for 1.5-A output current. Maximum output current is available with differential voltages ranging from about 2.5 V (dropout voltage) to 12 V. Above 12 V, the output current decreases, limiting the device dissipation to a safe value. If the output terminals are accidentally short circuited, the input-output differential will rise, causing current foldback, and thus preventing the power-supply components from being over-stressed. This protective feature makes three-terminal regulators

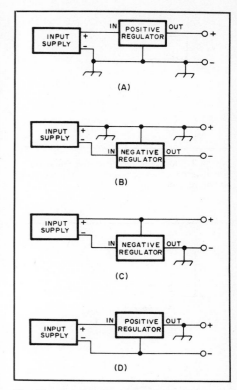

Fig. 29 — A and B illustrate the conventional manner in which three-terminal regulators are used. C and D show how one polarity regulator can be used to regulate the opposite polarity voltage.

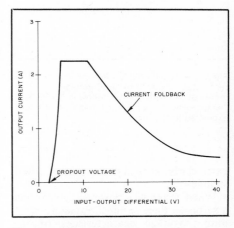

Fig. 30 — Effects of input-output differential voltage on three-terminal regulator output current.

Fig. 31 — By varying the ratio of R2 to R1 in this simple LM317 schematic diagram, a wide range of output voltages is possible. See text for details.

Fig. 32 — The basic LM317 voltage regulator is converted into a constant-current source by adding only one resistor.

$$I_{OUT} = \frac{1.2}{R} \; , \; 12 \leq R \leq 240 \; \Omega$$

$$V_{OUT} = V_{IN} - 1.25 \; V$$

Fig. 33 — Two methods for boosting the current output capacity of an IC voltage regulator. (A) NPN emitter follower. (B) PNP "wraparound." Operation of these circuits is explained in the text.

particularly attractive in simple power supplies.

When designing a power supply around a particular three-terminal regulator, input-output voltage characteristics of the regulator should play a major role in selecting the transformer secondary and filter capacitor component values. The unregulated voltage applied to the input of the three-terminal device should be higher than the dropout voltage, yet low enough that the regulator does not go into current limiting caused by an excessive differential voltage. If, for example, the regulated output voltage of the device shown in Fig. 30 was 12, then unregulated input voltages of between 14.5 and 24 would be acceptable if maximum output current is desired.

In use, all but the lowest current regulators generally require an adequate external heat sink because they may be called on to dissipate a fair amount of power.

Also, because the regulator chip contains a high-gain error amplifier, bypassing of the input and output leads is essential for stable operation.

Most manufacturers recommend bypassing the input and output directly at the leads where they protrude through the heat sink. Tantalum capacitors are usually recommended because of their excellent bypass capabilities into the VHF range.

In addition to fixed-output-voltage ICs, high-current, adjustable voltage regulators are available. These ICs require little more than an external potentiometer for an adjustable output range from 5 to 24 V at up to 5 A. The unit price on these items is only a few dollars, making them ideal for test-bench power supplies. A very popular low-current, adjustable-output-voltage three-terminal regulator, the LM317, is shown in Fig. 31. It develops a steady 1.25-V reference, V_{ref}, between the output and adjustment terminals. By installing R1 between these terminals, a constant current, I1, is developed, governed by the equation $I1 = V_{ref}/R1$. Both I1 and a 100-μA error current, I2, flow through R2, resulting in output voltage V_o. Vo can be calculated using the equation

$$V_o = V_{ref} \left(1 + \frac{R2}{R1} \right) + I_2 R_2$$

Any voltage between 1.2 and 37 volts may be obtained with a 40-volt input by changing the ratio of R2 to R1.

Fig. 32 shows one of many flexible applications for the LM317. By adding only one resistor, the voltage regulator can be changed into a constant current source, capable of charging NiCd batteries, for example. Design equations are given in the figure. The same precautions should be taken with adjustable regulators as with the fixed-voltage units. Proper heat sinking and lead bypassing are essential for proper circuit operation.

When the maximum current output from an IC voltage regulator is insufficient to operate the load, discrete power transistors may be connected to increase the current capability. Fig. 33 shows two methods for boosting the current output of a positive regulator, although the same techniques can be applied to negative regulators.

In A, an NPN transistor is connected as an emitter follower, multiplying the output current capacity by the transistor beta. The shortcoming of this approach is that the base-emitter junction is not inside the feedback loop. The result is that the output voltage is reduced by the base-emitter drop, and the load regulation is degraded by variations in this drop.

The circuit at B has a PNP transistor "wrapped around" the regulator. The regulator draws current through the base-emitter junction, causing the transistor to conduct. The IC output voltage is un-

changed by the transistor because the collector is connected directly to the IC output (sense point). Any increase in output voltage is detected by the IC regulator, which shuts off its internal pass transistor, and this stops the boost-transistor base current.

Most IC regulators are internally configured as linear series regulators. However, the manufacturer's applications literature shows how to use these devices in shunt regulators and even in switching regulators.

Thermal Design

Just as important as power-supply electrical design is power-supply thermal design. Linear power supplies are inefficient. Rectifiers, regulators and pass transistors all dissipate heat, and this heat must be safely carried away to avoid device damage. Although the black-magic rule of thumb "bigger is better" applies to heat sinks, this section will show you how to calculate heat-sink requirements and choose the right cooler for any power supply. This material was prepared by ARRL TA Dick Jansson, WD4FAB.

Creating the thermal design for a properly cooled power supply is a very well-defined process. To some amateurs experienced only in the electronic arts, heat transfer is a subject shrouded with mystery. The following information will remove these veils and show what is needed to make a good electronic design behave properly in the thermal world. An outline of the steps to be taken will show the logic to be applied:

1) Determine the expected power dissipation.
2) Identify the requirements for the dissipating elements.
3) Estimate heat-sinking requirements.
4) Rework the electronic device to meet the thermal requirements.
5) Select the heat exchanger.

To illustrate this discussion, a 28-V, 10-A power supply will be used as an example. Construction details of this supply may be found in Chapter 27. The steps described here were actually followed during the design of that supply.

The first step is to estimate the filtered, unregulated supply voltage under full load. A schematic diagram of this supply is shown in Fig. 34. The transformer has a secondary output of 32-V ac. Since this is the input to a full-wave bridge rectifier, the filtered dc output from C1 will follow those output characteristics shown in Fig. 7, presented earlier in this chapter. As a first guess, estimate 40 V as the filtered dc output at a 10-A load. The filter capacitor is 22,000 μF, so the output is reasonably well filtered. We do not know the value of the series resistance/load resistance, R_s/R, but if the power supply is going to be worth its salt, that value needs to be low! Bracketing the series resistance, R_s, would

Fig. 34 — Schematic diagram of the 28-V, 10-A power supply used to illustrate the thermal-design section.

Fig. 35 — Thermal network for air cooling a power transistor.

place the dc output of the filter between 34 V and 44 V. The estimate of 40 V output still looks good, so continue to use that value as the filtered dc value that will feed the regulator stage at a 10-A load.

The next step is to estimate the total pass-transistor power dissipation under full load. Allowing for some small voltage drops in the power-transistor emitter circuitry, the output of the series pass transistors (Q2-Q5) is about 29 V for a delivered 28 V under a 10-A load. With an unregulated voltage of 40-V, the total pass-transistor dissipation, in the form of heat, is (40 V − 29 V) × 10 A, or 110 W. The heat sink for this power supply must be able to handle that amount of dissipation and still keep the transistor junctions below the specified safe operating temperature limits.

The next consideration is the ratings of the pass transistors to be used. This supply calls for four 2N3055 pass transistors, even though a data sheet for that transistor shows that each 2N3055 is rated for 15-A service and 115-W dissipation. Why so many 2N3055s? Here we need to get past the big, bold type at the top of the specification data sheet, and on to such subtle characteristics as the junction-to-case thermal resistance, θ_{jc}, and the maximum allowable junction temperature, T_j. Unfortunately, some of these characteristics are not contained in most elementary listings of transistor properties. Don't be

deluded by the specified maximum continous device dissipation, P_d, as that value is the computed maximum dissipation at a case temperature of 25 °C. It is not practical to try to keep the case of a power transistor at 25 °C when room temperature can easily exceed that.

The Greek letter θ is used to express values of thermal resistance, while R is used to express values of electrical resistance. Thermal resistance can be equated to electrical resistance, and thermal networks that look like electrical networks can be constructed. In fact, the basic equations are the same. Heat, measured in watts, flows in the network as does electrical current, measured in amperes. Temperature differences, in degrees Celsius, are equivalent to electrical potential in volts. Resistance to heat flow is expressed in °C/W, and is equivalent to resistance measured in ohms.

The concept of thermal resistance can be understood by reviewing basic heat-flow phenomena. A thermal network that describes the flow of heat from a transistor junction to the ambient air is shown in Fig. 35. The ambient air is considered here as the ultimate heat sink. θ_{jc} describes the thermal resistance from the transistor junction to its case. θ_{cs} is the resistance of the mounting interface between the transistor case and the heat sink. θ_{sa} is the resistance of the heat sink to the ambient air.

Checking the specification sheet for

the 2N3055 shows that it is rated for $\theta_{jc} = 1.52$ °C/W, and a maximum case (and junction) temperature of 220 °C. Industry experience has shown that silicon transistor reliability suffers substantially when junctions are operated at those elevated temperatures. Most commercial and military specifications will not permit design junction temperatures to exceed 125 °C, and in some cases 110 °C. A transistor operated above 125 °C does not "go away" instantly, but will degrade slowly because of excessive thermal migration in the silicon material.

At some point, you need to decide how the power supply is going to be used. Thermal requirements (as well as other design requirements) vary significantly, depending on expected duty cycle. Continuous commercial service (CCS) is exactly what it sounds like: "Brick-on-the-key" operation, such as FM, Baudot RTTY or ATV. Amateur equipment designed primarily for CW and SSB operation is often designed for Intermittent Commercial and Amateur Service (ICAS), nominally considered to be a duty cycle of 33% of the CCS. To provide a power supply capable of performing any chore within its power output capability, the designer of the example supply has chosen to design for CCS operation, even though many amateur operators may never stress the supply to that extent. This philosophy is conservative and safe.

Other considerations in how the supply will be used include the maximum air temperature that the unit will see in service and the maximum junction temperature to be allowed for the design. A lot of deliberation of these subjects was done, with the conclusion that an ambient air temperature (T_a) of 35 °C (95 °F), $T_j = 125$ °C for ICAS operation and $T_j = 150$ °C for CCS operation were safe assumptions. These assumptions allow design flexibilities, as will be shown later.

The electrical design for this supply originally called for two 2N3055 transistors in the regulator pass stage. This design was based on electrical characteristics only, and did not take thermal considerations into account. The equivalent thermal network for a two-transistor supply is shown in Fig. 36. Each of the 2N3055s would have to dissipate 55 W.

The total thermal resistance between the junction and the heat sink is equal to the junction-to-case thermal resistance (θ_{jc}), plus the thermal resistance associated with mounting of the transistor to the heat sink (θ_{cs}).

Proper mounting of most TO-3 power transistors requires that they have an electrical insulator between the transistor case and the heat sink. This electrical insulator must, however, provide for very good thermal contact between the two. To achieve a quality mounting, you should use thin polyimid or mica formed washers and a suitable thermal compound to exclude air from the interstitial space. "Thermal greases" are commonly available for this function. Silicone grease may be used, but

Fig. 38 — Graph of thermal resistance vs. heat-sink volume for natural-convection cooling of a heat sink with a 50 °C temperature rise. This graph is based on engineering data from EG&G Wakefield.

filled silicone oils made specifically for this purpose are better.

A good starting value for mounting thermal resistance is $\theta_{cs} = 0.50$ °C/W. Lower values of θ_{cs} are possible, but the techniques needed to achieve them are expensive and not generally available to the average amateur. Furthermore, serious work on lowering θ_{cs} is not warranted in light of the somewhat higher value of θ_{jc}, which cannot be lowered without going to a somewhat more exotic pass transistor.

The total value of the junction-to-sink resistances in this example is $\theta_{js} = 2.02$ °C/W ($\theta_{jc} = 1.52 + \theta_{cs} = 0.5$). At a power dissipation (P_d) of 55 W, the transistor junction can be expected to operate 111 °C (55 W × 2.02 °C/W) above the heat-sink temperature (T_s). If the maximum value for T_j is 150 °C, then the heat-sink temperature could rise no higher than $T_s = 39$ °C. With a ambient air temperature (T_a) estimated at 35 °C (worst case), it would require an impossibly large heat sink to keep T_s within 4 °C of T_a to keep the two 2N3055s cool. The conclusion to be drawn from this analysis is that use of two 2N3055s is not feasible from a thermal standpoint, although from an electrical standpoint two transistors are more than adequate.

At this point, the power-supply design was modified to use four 2N3055 pass transistors. This change divides the dissipation load by four, making $P_d = 27.5$ W for each transistor. The equivalent thermal network for four devices is shown in Fig. 37. Going through the steps described earlier, the junction-to-sink temperature difference is now $T_j - T_s = 55.6$ °C. Initially, it was hoped to keep the target maximum junc-

tion temperature below 125 °C. At 27.5 W per transistor, that means a sink temperature of $T_s = 69$ °C. This temperature is possible to achieve with two large heat sinks (two devices per sink), or forced-air cooling of a single large heat sink.

Forced air cooling of a heat sink requires the use of a fan or blower to move the air. That means a "moving" part and thus a potential reduction in supply reliability. Also, blowers are noisy. If at all possible, the power-supply design should make use of natural-convection cooling and not rely on a blower. By reasoning that most operation would not be CCS, and that during occasional CCS operation junction temperatures of $T_j = 150$ °C are tolerable, a design is possible that offers heat-sink temperatures of $T_s = 94$ °C and a sink-to-air temperature difference $T_s - T_a = 59$ °C. It is possible to implement these parameters with a single heat sink of the "right" design. Please note that a heat-sink temperature of 94 °C is substantially hotter than the allowable "finger-touch thermometer" temperature of 52 °C. Do *not* attempt to use the finger thermometer with this design.

Now comes the big question: What is the "right" heat sink to use? We have established its requirements. It must be capable of dissipating 110 W, and it must allow a temperature rise no greater than 59 °C, or $\theta_{sa} = 0.54$ °C/W (59 °C divided by 110 W).

From Fig. 38, the relationship of heat-sink volume and thermal resistance for a natural-convection operation can be seen. This relationship presumes the use of suitably spaced fins (0.35 inch or greater)

Fig. 36 — Thermal network for a power supply with two pass transistors.

Fig. 37 — Thermal network for a power supply with four pass transistors.

(A)

(B)

Fig. 39 — Graph of the natural convection characteristics under load of the EG&G Wakefield model no. 441 heat sink. This graph is based on actual testing performed by ARRL TA Dick Jansson, WD4FAB.

Fig. 40 — The EG&G Wakefield 441 heat sink is a "three-dimensional" design that makes excellent use of space. The photo at A shows the heat sink with four 2N3055 transistors in place. At B, the wiring to the transistors is visible.

and provides a "rough order-of-magnitude" value for sizing a heat sink. The needs of the supply used for this example could be met with a heat-sink volume of approximately 120 in³, which is within the range of available heat sinks, although it certainly is not small. Unlike a heat sink for use on an RF amplifier, this application can use a heat sink where only "wire access" to the transistor connections is available. A heat sink with a "three-dimensional shape" can be used, allowing the selection of a more efficient design. Most RF designs require the transistor mounting surface to be completely exposed so that the PC board can be mounted close to the transistors.

A quick consultation with several manufacturer's catalogs reveals that Wakefield Engineering Co. model nos. 441 and 435 heat sinks meet the needs of this application.[1] A Thermalloy model no. 6441 is suitable as well. Data published in the catalogs of these manufacturers show that in natural-convection service, the expected temperature rise for 100 W dissipation would be just under 60°C, an almost perfect fit for this application. See Fig. 39. Moreover, the no. 441 heat sink can easily mount four TO-3-style 2N3055 transistors, as shown in Fig. 40.

[1]There are numerous manufacturers of excellent heat sinks. References to any one manufacturer are not intended to exclude the use of products of any others, nor to indicate any particular predisposition to one manufacturer. The catalogs and products referred to here are from: EG&G Wakefield Engineering, 60 Audubon Rd., Wakefield, MA 01880; and Thermalloy, Inc., 2021 West Valley View La., Dallas, TX 75234.

Thermal power-loading tests of a no. 441 heat sink showed a very close agreement with the manufacturer's data — a 58°C temperature rise for 110-W power dissipation. It is not necessary to test heat sinks used for every application. The tests were done just to illustrate that the data of reliable suppliers of heat sinks for transistor cooling can be believed. Once you determine the heat-sink requirements for your application, you can make use of the manufacturer's data to select the right cooler. Remember: heat sinks should be mounted with the fins and transistor mounting area vertical to promote convection cooling.

Another point here is that very satisfactory results can be obtained through the good application of "handbook and catalog engineering." There is absolutely no need for you to conduct a lengthy, detailed computer thermal analysis of individual heat sinks. Such analysis is not needed if you use existing heat-sink designs.

Switching Regulators

Just as the transistor has replaced the inefficient vacuum tube, the linear voltage regulator is rapidly being replaced by the switching regulator. This transition is being assisted by the availability of components made especially for switching supplies, such as high-speed switching transistors and diodes, capacitors, transformer cores, and so on. The introduction of switching-regulator integrated circuits has also lowered the complexity of switchers to a degree that rivals linear regulators, and new circuit design techniques have reduced regulator noise and ripple to acceptable levels for communications equipment.

The switching regulator (also known as a switching-mode regulator, or SMR) offers several advantages over the linear type:

1) Much higher efficiency resulting from minimal regulator dissipation. Very desirable for battery-powered applications.

2) Lighter in weight as a result of less heat sink material.

3) Smaller in size.

These advantages are offset, however, by slower response to load transients, increased circuit complexity and higher cost.

The simplest type of SMR somewhat resembles a linear regulator in form and is known as the voltage-bucking (buck) con-

Fig. 41 — Schematic diagram of a simple switching regulator.

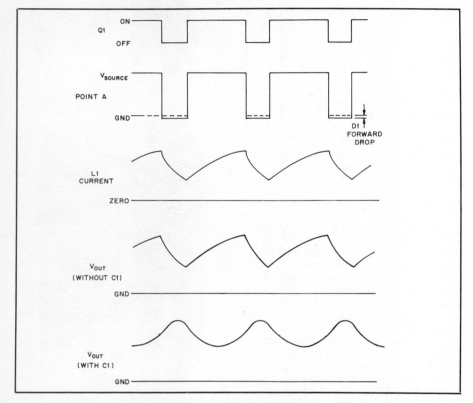

Fig. 42 — Waveforms seen at various points in the switching regulator shown in Fig. 41.

figuration. The circuit reduces (or "bucks") the input voltage to produce a lower value of output voltage. By rearrangement of circuit components, the reverse can be made to occur; the output voltage can actually be higher than the input voltage. This is known as a boost configuration.

The basic elements of the buck regulator are shown in Fig. 41. They are switch transistor Q1, inductor L1, capacitor C1 and diode D1. A positive source voltage is applied to the collector of Q1, and the load is connected as shown. Some control circuitry for applying base drive to Q1 is also needed; for the present, assume that we can turn Q1 fully on and off at will.

Initially, ignore the presence of C1. As Q1 is turned on, all of the source voltage instantaneously appears across L1 since the initial current in L1 is zero. With time, the current in L1 begins to increase and V_{OUT} begins to rise; V_{OUT} is allowed to continue to rise until it reaches the desired output voltage. When V_{OUT} exceeds the desired voltage, switch Q1 is turned off and point A in Fig. 41 immediately goes negative in an effort to maintain the current flowing in L1, thereby causing D1 to conduct. As the energy which has become stored in L1 dissipates into the load through D1, the current in L1 decreases, as does the output voltage. When V_{OUT} drops to slightly less than the desired value, Q1 is turned on again, bringing point A to the source voltage level, and the cycle repeats.

Obviously, in this circuit, Q1 must switch on and off at an extremely fast rate to minimize the swing in output voltage around the desired value, since this voltage variation is directly related to the on and off times of Q1. This situation can be improved by adding C1, which supports the output voltage while the current decreases in L1, and reduces overshoot by absorbing the excess current in L1 while Q1 is on. See

Fig. 43 — Two methods of implementing a pulse-width modulator. The circuit at A uses the ripple modulation technique, while the circuit at B employs fixed-frequency (duty-cycle) modulation.

Fig. 44 — Block diagram of the Silicon General SG3524 regulating pulse-width modulator IC. This drawing is based on information presented in the *Silicon General Product Catalog.*

the waveforms in Fig. 42. The transistor can then be switched at a slower speed, and the inductance of L1 reduced because of the smoothing effect of C1.

In this example, power is only transmitted from the source when Q1 is on, but this power is distributed to the load continuously during the entire cycle. The power delivered to the load is $V_{OUT} \times I_{LOAD}$, which must equal the power obtained from the source while Q1 conducts. Since Q1 conducts for only a portion of the cycle at an average current during conduction of I_{LOAD}, the output voltage is then equal to the duty cycle $\times V_{SOURCE}$ or

$$V_{OUT} = \frac{t_{ON}}{t_{CYCLE}} \times V_{SOURCE}$$

In actual practice, the losses in D1, forward drop in Q1, resistance in L1, and various other factors combine to affect the above formula, but except for very-low-output-voltage, high-current regulators, these losses can be neglected since the control circuits will automatically compensate for them.

The control circuit that must be added to the basic circuit in Fig. 41 has to be capable of turning the switch transistor on and off quickly and providing the proper ratio of on-time to off-time to maintain regulation. This portion of a switching regulator is referred to as a pulse-width modulator (PWM).

The simplest PWM is a comparator that has the dc output of the regulator applied through a divider to one input and a reference voltage applied to the alternate input. See Fig. 43A. A small amount of the comparator's output voltage is fed back to its non-inverting input to provide hysteresis, thereby ensuring that the comparator's output is either high or low. With the ripple-modulated PWM, there must be sufficient output ripple to overcome the hysteresis, which is why the term "ripple modulation" is used.

By forcing the regulator to switch at a fixed frequency that is much higher than the ripple modulator would produce, the output LC filter can become much more efficient. This can be done by injecting a fixed-frequency sawtooth waveform to the comparator, as shown in Fig. 43B. The output voltage is now compared to the reference at the input to an op amp. Op-amp response is slowed by a capacitor between its output and inverting terminals so that it will not respond to switching ripple. As the output of the op amp rises and falls with output voltage variations, the comparator "chops off" more or less of the sawtooth that varies the duty cycle of the drive to the switching transistor's base.

Integrated circuits are now available that provide the op amp, comparator, reference and drive circuits all in one package. A block diagram of one of these ICs, a Silicon General SG3524, is shown in Fig. 44.

Dc-to-Dc Conversion

Dc-to-dc conversion is probably the oldest form of switching technology in the power-supply field, dating back to the vibrator supplies used in automobile radios and low-power surplus gear. The noisy and unreliable mechanical vibrators were eventually replaced by transistors or SCRs.

Fig. 45 — Schematic diagram of a basic dc-to-dc converter.

The dc-to-dc converter works on the principle of chopping the dc power source to produce an ac component and then using a transformer to obtain a different voltage level. The new voltage can then be rectified to produce a dc output voltage higher or lower than the source. In the case of the old vibrator supplies, the 6-volt or 12-volt car battery voltage was chopped, transformed up to several hundred volts ac, and rectified to provide plate voltage for the equipment. Another example, still used today, eliminated the output rectifiers and used a transformer wound to produce 120-V ac to power ac equipment. This type of circuit is often referred to as a dc-to-ac inverter, although nothing is really "inverted."

The operation of a dc-dc converter is as follows. Refer to Fig. 45. Q1 and Q2 are initially biased on by R3. One transistor (assume Q1), draws slightly more current than its mate (Q2). Because of the autotransformer effect of the transformer primary, the collector of Q1 goes toward ground, while the collector of Q2 goes more positive. This primary voltage swing is reflected into the base drive winding, which applies increased base drive to the heavily-conducting transistor (Q1) while removing bias from Q2. When Q1 is saturated, the voltage across the drive winding is equal to the ratio of drive winding turns to primary turns, multiplied by the source voltage.

$$V_{\text{DRIVE WINDING} \atop \text{(END TO CENTER TAP)}} = \frac{N_D}{N_P} \times V_S$$

Since the base of Q1 does not permit the forward-biased base voltage to be more than about 1 volt, the center tap of the drive winding is pushed negative until D1 conducts, again at less than 1 volt (negative). The remainder of the winding voltage across N_D is dropped across R1, and it is the current resulting from that drop across R1 that determines the drive current

$$I_B = \frac{V_{ND} - V_{BE}(Q1) - V_{FD}(D1)}{R1}$$

Usually V_{BE} and V_{FD} are about 0.8 volts, therefore

$$I_B \approx \frac{V_{ND} - 1.6}{R1}$$

Also, V_{ND} is usually designed to be 5 volts or less in order to prevent reverse conduction of the base-emitter junction of Q2.

Q1 remains in conduction, producing output power, until the core of the transformer saturates. At that point, it is incapable of transferring power, and the base drive to Q1 reduces. The collector current rises abruptly, pulling Q1 out of saturation, since the saturated transformer's primary looks like a short circuit to Q1.

As the base drive winding swings through zero volts, the base of Q2 is turned on and collector current in Q2 begins to flow. This helps Q1 to turn off and swings the excitation in the transformer primary in the opposite direction. Q2 saturates, with Q1 off, and remains in saturation until the transformer core once again saturates, initiating another cycle.

Power is delivered to the load during each half-cycle. Neglecting diode drops and transistor saturation voltages, the output voltage is

$$V_{OUT} = \frac{N_S}{N_P} \times V_S$$

This type of self-excited, single-transformer converter design is known as a Royer Oscillator. The frequency of oscillation is dependent upon the time required to saturate the core with the applied voltage and is given by the formula

$$F_{(Hz)} = \frac{V_S \times 10^8}{4 \times N_P \times B_M \times A_C}$$

where

V_S = voltage applied at the primary center tap
N_P = no. of turns from primary center tap to one end
B_M = saturation flux density of the core in gauss
A_C = cross-sectional area of the core in cm^2

The best cores for the Royer oscillator are tape-wound toroids using orthonol or square permalloy-type alloys. Some ferrite cores are also specifically made for this application.

Since the tape-wound toroids used for self-excited dc-dc converters become very lossy at frequencies above the audible range, the self-excited configuration is rarely used above about 15 to 20 kHz. For higher frequency use, an electronically driven type is usually employed. This consists of an electronic square-wave oscillator operating at the desired frequency to drive the bases of the switching transistors. The output transformer is made with a core material that does not have sharp saturation characteristics and is designed to be operated well within the maximum flux density rating to avoid saturation. High-flux-density ferrite is usually chosen for the core.

Push-Pull Converter/Regulator

By reducing the width of the drive pulses applied to the transistor to less than 50% duty cycle, the push-pull converter just described can be made to regulate. Integrated circuits that contain most of the components necessary for the construction of a push-pull regulator are now available from several manufacturers (Silicon General, Unitrode, Texas Instruments). The popular Silicon General type SG3524 is one example.

These integrated circuits work on the basis of a constant switching frequency with variable duty cycle, and can also be used for making a much improved version of the single transistor buck regulator described earlier.

One of the big advantages of the regulating converter is the transformer isolation that it provides between the primary and secondary circuits. Since the transformer is operating at high frequency, its size and weight can be much less than a 60-Hz transformer handling the same power. To take advantage of this, the 117-V ac line is bridge rectified and capacitive-input filtered to produce about 170-V dc. This voltage is then applied to a regulating converter to produce the desired regulated and isolated dc output voltage. This application is usually referred to as off-line conversion.

Switched-Mode Power Supplies

This section, written by Frank Meyer, describes the basic operation of switched-mode power supplies. The switched-mode power supply (SMPS) evolved in the 1970s under three influences. The US Military needed to reduce the volume of its electronics and increase reliability, the energy crisis made linear power supplies less economical to operate than SMPS, and general technological advancement revitalized power conversion.

A block diagram shows little difference between a linear power supply and an SMPS. (See Fig 46.) The difference resides in the operation of its semiconductor: an SMPS operates a transistor non-linearly (it is either open or closed), and a linear supply operates its semiconductor as a variable impedance (it is neither fully open nor fully closed). A linear supply provides the dc output voltage by reducing a dc input voltage with static dissipation across a series pass element. A (buck) switched-mode supply drops the input voltage from V_{in} to V_o by first chopping the dc input voltage into a square wave and then recovering the dc voltage at the output with a low-pass filter.

In an SMPS, efficiency is typically 75%, and for a linear power supply it is usually 30%. Efficiency in a linear supply depends on input voltage and output load, but for an SMPS it is much less dependent; an SMPS can be used where the input line voltage and the output load vary widely. The efficiency of a power supply dictates its size, since the lost power must be dissipated; the heat-sinks for a linear supply are much larger than those of an SMPS for the same output power, P_o.

Switched-mode power supplies maintain regulation with very poorly filtered input voltages, unlike linear supplies. This reduces the need for input filters. The frequencies of operation are orders of magnitude different between linear and switched-mode power supplies. A 60-Hz transformer is heavier and larger than a 50-kHz SMPS transformer. All this bulk reduces volumetric efficiency: a linear power supply has an output power density of between 0.3 and 0.8 W/in.[3] and an SMPS has a density between 1 and 7 W/in.[3]; some dc-dc SMPS have densities in excess of 30 W/in.[3].

There are disadvantages to using an SMPS. A linear supply operates at 60 Hz and its radiated and conducted emissions aren't as much of a problem as for an SMPS, with its pulsating currents. Linear supplies have a simple control loop; an SMPS is non-linear and its operation is hard to analyze and control. At low output power, a linear supply has a lower output impedance than an SMPS. This means the output filtering requirements of an SMPS are higher than for a linear supply. These disadvantages translate into a cost advantage for linear power supplies up to about 75 W. There are also noise-sensitive applications for which an SMPS may never be used. The SMPS will never fully replace the linear power supply, for although they perform the same function, they do it very differently.

BASIC POWER-STAGE CIRCUIT TOPOLOGIES

Many terms in power conversion technology, such as power supply, converter, inverter, dc-dc power supply, regulator, and so on, should be used carefully. *Converter* refers to a circuit that changes input voltage or current to a different output voltage or current level without changing its output function. A dc-dc converter changes an input dc voltage level to another output dc level. An inverter changes the function of an input; an inverter would change a dc input to provide an ac output. Both inversion and conversion functions imply active circuit operation and both have been called switched-mode power supplies and converters interchangeably.

A regulator is either an inverter or a converter with a feedback loop that regulates the output to typically provide constant dc voltage or current. This is equivalent to a regulator in a linear power supply, such as a Zener regulator, which statically provides a constant output voltage from a varying input. All of these are sub-circuits of a power supply that contain additional sub-circuits such as a rectifying input stage, a control stage, a protection stage and a filter stage.

The dc-dc converter is the staple of switched-mode power supply design and is derived from three basic topologies or operating modes: the buck, the boost, and the buck-boost. The buck-boost topology has both an inductive and a capacitive type. Once the operation of these three is mastered, all converters can be understood, because any converter must be related to one of these three. The three will be illustrated in a switch form and in a "hardware" implementation as we discuss each type.

Buck Converters

Fig 47A shows the buck topology in switch form and D shows a hardware implementation. A Buck converter operates as follows: with S1 in position A (S1$_A$ is on, S1$_B$ is off) a voltage is impressed across the inductor, L. See Fig 47B. Current through the inductor rises and it supplies current to the load resistance, R$_L$, and filter capacitor, C. Next, S1 moves to position B (S1$_B$ is on, S1$_A$ is off), which interrupts the inductor current. See Fig 47C. The inductor back EMF works to maintain the current, causing S1$_B$ to

Fig 46—A shows the block diagram of a linear power supply and B shows the block diagram of a switched-mode power supply.

Fig 47—The operation of a buck converter. A through C illustrate the basic operation of this topology. D shows a typical hardware implementation of the design and E shows various circuit waveforms. F shows the output voltage calculations.

conduct ($S1_B$ is called the free-wheeling diode). Current out of the inductor decreases (but still flows out of the inductor). The additional current required by the load resistance is now supplied by the output filter capacitor, C. This cycle repeats when S1 moves back to position A, by turning $S1_A$ back on, so that inductor L reverse biases diode switch $S1_B$ off as its current increases.

Buck converters are also called choppers, down-converters, step-down converters, and down-choppers. Converters that derive from the buck topology are the most popular in switched-mode power supplies. They are more familiar when an isolation transformer is introduced and they become the forward, push-pull, half-bridge and full-bridge converters. The buck converter is a simple converter and will be used to illustrate key principles used to understand the operation of other converters.

The on- and off-times for switch $S1_A$ are determined by the control circuitry in the power supply (shown by the square wave at the base of transistor $S1_A$ in Fig 47D), while diode $S1_B$ is commutated by natural circuit action. Switch times are defined as the ratio of the switch on-time divided by the entire period of operation, T. $T = 1 / f_s$, where f_s is the frequency of operation. When an SMPS is referred to as a 100-kHz converter, it means that its period $T = 1 / f_s = 10$ μs, though the switches are only on for some fraction of that period. The switch on-time is shown as t1 in Fig 48 and the switch off-time is t2. The on-time, or duty cycle, is given as a fraction of the period.

$$D = t1 / T$$

The duty cycle is important for calculating the supply output voltage, as shown in Fig 47F.

The load resistance, R_L, is not a simple resistor but is an equivalent dc output resistance calculated by dividing the dc output voltage, V_o, by the dc output current, I_o.

$$R_L = V_o / I_o$$

It doesn't matter if the "real" load is another piece of electronic equipment as long as its requirements can be characterized at dc. A load can be modeled as other impedances, such as a capacitor or an inductor in series/parallel combination with a resistor, which is more realistic, but it would needlessly complicate this analysis.

There must be a low-pass filter located before the output of an SMPS, and the cutoff frequency, f_c must be much lower than the switching frequency, f_s. The low-pass filter generally takes the form of an LC filter. This means the output voltage is as smooth as possible because the square-wave voltage, and all its harmonics, is completely removed.

A buck converter has this LC filter built into its output stage, although it could operate without an output capacitor. The ripple would then be much larger, because the filter would be a one-pole type instead

Fig 48—The square-wave signal applied to the switch transistor controls the operation of the converter. The switch on- and off-times are represented by t1 and t2. They need not be equal.

Fig 49—The volt-second balance is shown. The product of voltage and time must be equal for the switch on- and off-times.

Fig 50—The operation of a boost converter. A through C illustrate the basic operation of this topology. D shows a typical hardware implementation of the design and E shows various circuit waveforms. F shows the output voltage calculations.

of a two-pole type. If the switching frequency, f_s, were 10 times the filter cutoff frequency, an LC low-pass filter would provide 20 dB additional filtering for the output voltage. This would reduce a 1 V P-P ripple to 100 mV P-P.

If f_s is greater than f_c, other linear assumptions can be made about the converter operation to make analysis easier. DC voltage gains are calculated by a technique called the volt-second balance. Current through a filter inductor must be constant from cycle to cycle to provide a dc output. If the output current is constant from cycle to cycle, then the voltages impressed on the inductive element must balance over a cycle. Fig 49 illustrates the volt-second balance by showing that the area on the positive side must equal the area on the negative side. Using t1 as the on-time and t2 as the off-time, we have:

$$V_{on} t1 = V_{off} t2$$

If the volt-seconds don't balance for the on- and off-time of one converter cycle there will be a flux build-up in the inductor. This will result in core saturation over a number of cycles, and would violate the assumption of linear operation.

Boost Converters

Fig 50 (Parts A through C) shows the boost topology in switch form and D shows a hardware implementation. With S1 in position A (S1$_A$ is on, S1$_B$ is off), a voltage is impressed across the inductor, L. Current through L rises, but the load resistance is not connected, so the load current is supplied by the output capacitor, C, during this period. S1$_B$ is off because it is reverse biased by the positive output voltage on the output capacitor. Energy is stored in the inductor during this period.

S1 then moves to position B (S1$_B$ is on, S1$_A$ is off). The inductor back EMF tries to maintain the current with the load resistance added to the circuit. The inductor voltage adds to the input voltage, V_{in} and causes S1$_B$ to conduct. The inductor supplies current to both the load resistance and the output capacitor. The cycle repeats itself with S1 moving to position A by turning S1$_A$ back on so that S1$_B$ naturally commutates off. Note that the low-pass filter for a boost topology is explicit with the switch in position B.

The dc voltage gain calculated by the volt-second technique for a boost converter is a paradox: gain is infinite when D is 1, but you cannot create energy; gain must be finite. Energy *is* finite and the efficiency of the converter degrades the output gain at a high duty cycle, D, since the inductor spends less time connected to the output and it delivers less energy to the output because of internal resistance in the inductor. This effect works to reduce the voltage output to zero when D = 1. (This makes sense, because the output would be disconnected if S1$_A$ were always on.)

Boost converters are also called up-converters. Their pulsating output current and high voltage stress on the switches have limited their popularity to low-voltage/low-

power applications, and are rarely used otherwise.

Buck-Boost Converters

The inductive buck-boost converter combines one operation from the buck and one from the boost converter. Fig 51 (Parts A through C) shows the buck-boost topology in switch form and D shows a hardware implementation.

When S1 is in position A, it is configured like position A of a boost converter, and when S1 is in position B it is configured like position B of a buck converter. In the inductive buck-boost converter, the inductor is charged by the input voltage and discharged by the output circuit so energy is sequentially transferred from the input to the output.

The output voltage can be greater or less than the input voltage, but the polarity of the output voltage is always inverted. This voltage inversion is the product of the reset voltage of the storage inductor when it is connected to the output. The input and output are never directly connected in the circuit.

The pulsating input current requires that a filter be placed between the converter and the input-voltage source. The pulsating output current requires stiff output capacitors.

The capacitive buck-boost converter (also called the C'uk or "optimum topology" converter) solves the problem of pulsating input and output currents by inductively feeding a capacitor, which operates as the energy storage element.

Fig 51—The operation of an inductive buck-boost converter. A through C illustrate the basic operation of this topology. D shows a typical hardware implementation of the design and E shows various circuit waveforms. F shows the output voltage calculations.

Fig 52—The operation of a capacitive buck-boost converter. A through C illustrate the basic operation of this topology. D shows a typical hardware implementation of the design and E shows various circuit waveforms. F shows the output voltage calculations.

Fig 53—The operation of a discontinuous-mode buck converter. A through D illustrate the basic operation of this topology. E shows various circuit waveforms.

Fig 52 shows the operation of the C'uk converter. Assume a dc voltage exists across C1, which is the storage element. With S1 in position A (S1$_A$ on and S1$_B$ off), V$_{in}$ is impressed across L1 and the inductor current increases. C1 is connected to L2 and supplies energy to the output capacitor C2 and the load, R$_L$, as the current through L2 increases. When S1 moves to position B (S1$_A$ off and S1$_B$ on), S1$_A$ opens and the decreasing current through L1 recharges C1 through the forward-biased S1$_B$. L2 now has one end grounded because S1$_B$ is forward-biased (on) since the back EMF across L2 tries to maintain the current into the load resistance and output capacitor. With inductors connected to the input and the output, currents at both of these terminals are non-pulsating, though operation results in a voltage inversion on the output, just as in the inductive buck-boost converter.

This converter offers significant advantages with reduced ripple voltage and current at the output; a version of this converter further reduces ripple by winding the inductors on a single core. This is called a "zero-ripple" converter. The C'uk reduces EMI problems caused by continuous inductor currents. Efficiency is increased because capacitive energy storage is less dissipative than inductive storage. The C'uk is not used very often because of two practical problems: C1 needs to have a large RMS current capability when output power exceeds 200 W, and the converter is patented, which curtails commercial use.

MODES OF CONVERTER OPERATION

The previous converter descriptions apply to continuous-mode operation; the inductor current is never zero. If the inductor current does become zero during a cycle it is called discontinuous-mode operation, which adds a third interval to each of the circuit descriptions. During that third interval, the output/storage inductor is disconnected and all of the load current is supported by the output capacitor. The third interval of the discontinuous-mode is illustrated in the discontinuous-mode buck converter of Fig 53.

This mode of operation has also been called "run-dry," which simply explains what happens to the energy in the inductor: it runs out. This *can* be an advantage in a power supply. When the output inductance has zero stored energy at the start of a switch period, the control circuitry can obtain a wide range of output power levels on nearly a cycle-by-cycle operation. This also simplifies the small-signal response of the converter because the effect of the inductor disappears and its usual contribution of 90° phase lag is removed from frequencies of interest. This makes for easier control-loop design.

Discontinuous-mode operation can be advantageous for the transient response of a converter, but the peak currents for switches and inductors are higher in this mode of operation because the average currents delivered to the output must be the same. Output capacitance is larger, and its effective series resistance requirements are more stringent since it must supply more current to the load resistance over a longer period. These larger peak currents can cause failure in a converter designed to run in continuous-mode operation.

When a converter changes modes, its dc voltage gain changes. In discontinuous-mode operation, the dc gain is strongly dependent upon the load resistance, R$_L$. Small-signal responses between continuous and discontinuous modes are also very different and changing modes may make a converter oscillate unless the control loop is designed to cope with vastly different gains. If the converter does not have a control loop, its dc gain will change with load, and the regulation will be very poor. Converters nearly always operate in one mode. Operation in one mode can be forced by "pre-loading" the output(s) with a resistor, so that the inductor stays in continuous-mode operation. This is inefficient, however, because power is wasted. Other approaches involve lossless circuit methods for ensuring operation in one mode, but they increase circuit complexity and size.

You can determine which mode a converter will operate in by looking at the component values. A dimensionless ratio,

K, is used to express the mode of operation:

$$K = \frac{2 L}{R T_s}$$

Table 1 summarizes the ideal gain values and boundary conditions for the various converter topologies.

ISOLATED POWER-STAGE CIRCUIT TOPOLOGIES

The need for input-to-output isolation is obvious for power supplies. An input line (from the ac mains) can be at several hundred volts above ground, so electronic equipment must have isolation that allows for chassis grounding to ensure operator safety. This isolation is provided by the power transformer, and it introduces another element of freedom into the three basic SMPS topologies. It allows the buck converter to become the forward, the half-bridge, the full-bridge, and the push-pull configurations. There are few boost-derived converters with or without isolation

Table 1
Ideal Converter Conditions

Topology	Ideal Continuous Mode Gain	Ideal Discontinuous Mode Gain	Boundary Condition for Continuous Mode
Buck	D	$\dfrac{2}{1 + \sqrt{1 + \dfrac{4K}{D^2}}}$	$K > (1 - D)$
Boost	$\dfrac{1}{1 - D}$	$\dfrac{1 + \sqrt{1 + 4\dfrac{D^2}{K}}}{2}$	$K > D(1 - D)^2$
Inductive Buck-Boost	$\dfrac{D}{1 - D}$	$\dfrac{D}{\sqrt{K}}$	$K > 1$

Fig 55—The operation of a one-switch forward converter. A shows the basic operation of this converter. B shows a typical hardware implementation of the design.

introduced; most designers chose flyback operation instead. An inductive buck-boost converter is called a flyback converter with or without isolation.

A forward converter comes in two types: one-switch and two-switch. This refers to the number of primary switches, but it also reflects how transformer reset is handled.

Fig 55A shows the one-switch forward converter in switch form and B shows the hardware implementation. This converter operates as follows: When S1 and S2 are in position A, the transformer is providing current to the output inductor, L, through S2, and the inductor is supplying current to the load and the output capacitor. When S1 and S2 move to position B, the inductor keeps current flowing by forward-biasing $S2_B$; $S2_A$ is reverse-biased. There is a complication that forces a forward converter to deviate from exactly duplicating a buck converter operation by simply moving both switches back to position A.

Fig 56—The basic hardware implementation of a two-switch forward converter.

Fig 57—A shows a simple diagram of a push-pull converter and B shows the typical hardware implementation of the circuit.

The flux density increases in a forward converter transformer because the impressed voltage always has the same polarity. The transformer core can saturate quickly if it isn't allowed to return to zero flux after each cycle. This limits the operating duty cycle to less than 0.5 for most forward converters. The flux reset is accomplished in the one-switch forward converter by diode D1, which allows leakage energy to be dissipated in the series resistance, R1. It is important to note that the core reset function is not part of the inherent averaging function of a switch-mode converter, but is an intrusion of the non-idealities of the transformer and its leakage inductances.

The two-switch forward converter can return leakage current to the input voltage source with a more efficient method that uses two diodes to "steer" reset current back to the input as Fig 56 shows. This converter requires two primary switches.

The push-pull converter of Fig 57 is actually two one-switch forward converters with their primary switches S1 and S2 working 180° out of phase. Either primary switch turns on and forward biases an output diode, dropping voltage across the inductor, L, which allows it to supply current to the load and output capacitor. The primary switch then opens and the output inductor must keep current flowing so its EMF reverse biases either rectifier S3A or S3B to provide "free-wheeling" current. The other primary switch is then closed, applying voltage to the transformer primary with the opposite polarity and the cycle repeats itself because the other output diode is forward-biased.

The flux in the transformer core of a push-pull converter alternates direction with each cycle. So, unlike a forward converter, which must have a circuit that provides a reset function, you may think a push-pull converter would not suffer from accidental saturation. Unfortunately, this isn't the case because the switches are never on for exactly the same time and their saturation voltages are never exactly equal. A flux imbalance will then exist in the core over one cycle, and over a number of cycles the transformer will saturate. After that it will saturate every cycle and force large current and voltage spikes in the primary switches. If the switches aren't appropriately

sized they will be destroyed. There are ways to prevent this, or at least reduce the effects, but other topologies exist that do not suffer this problem.

Another buck-derived converter, specifically push-pull derived, is the half-bridge converter shown in Fig 58. A capacitive voltage divider, C1 and C2, reduces primary switch voltage stress, since each switch sees only ½ V_{in} across the junction. The primary switches are operated 180° out of phase, as in a push-pull converter. The output inductor, L, bucks the chopped input voltage in the same manner as a push-pull circuit. The difference is in the transformer core reset circuit. A half-bridge converter uses 2 diodes, D1 and D2, known as commutating diodes to steer leakage current back to the input. A half-bridge converter also has a transformer flux that alternates direction with each cycle.

It also suffers from saturation, like a push-pull converter, unless preventative steps are taken. The common method is to insert a blocking capacitor, C_S, in series with the transformer primary. If the switch on-times or the voltage impressed on the primary are not equivalent, C_S will have a

Fig 58—A shows a simple diagram of a half-bridge converter and B shows the typical hardware implementation of the circuit.

Fig 59—A shows a simple diagram of a full-bridge converter and B shows the typical hardware implementation of the circuit.

net voltage charged to it. Another method to prevent half-bridge saturation is current-mode control, which doesn't require C_S. Current-mode control simply turns a switch off when a peak current is sensed. If a transformer core is about to saturate and currents rise, the current-mode control scheme will reduce the on-time of the switch and balance will return to the transformer. Current-mode control does have additional requirements to maintain stability in a half-bridge, adding to the circuit complexity.

A full-bridge converter (Fig 59) replaces the voltage-divider capacitors, C1 and C2, with switches S4 and S5. The 4 primary switches are now operated 180° out of phase and in pairs to provide a square wave to the output inductor, L. The considerations for transformer reset are the same for the full as for the half-bridge, so there are two more commutating diodes along with switches S4 and S5. The flux-balancing schemes are the same as for a half-bridge, although the current-mode control approach doesn't have the additional requirements for stability.

The chief advantage of a full-bridge converter is increased power-handling capability. The voltage for each of the primary switches is the same for the full- and half-bridges. The difference is in the primary currents since the full-bridge circuit sees about 1/2 that of a half-bridge; at larger output power levels this gives the full-bridge a substantial advantage. The lack of a capacitive divider is another advantage at high power levels, since the capacitors must support a large RMS current and are therefore large and expensive.

The flyback converter is an inductive buck-boost circuit with an isolation transformer added. This magnetic structure is not a conventional transformer, but is instead a coupled inductor; transformer action never occurs.

Fig 60 shows a flyback converter. When S1 is on and S2 is off, the primary inductor,

L_P, is storing energy in its core. The phasing of the inductor winding is such that S2 is reverse-biased (open) so there is no transformer action. The output capacitor, C, supplies current to the load resistance, R_L. When S1 is on, the EMF across the primary inductor tries to maintain the current. Inductor L_S is coupled to the same structure and its EMF also inverts and forward-biases D1. After the leakage energy is dissipated in the snubber resistance, R1, the bulk of the energy stored in the magnetic structure is delivered by inductor L_S to the load and the output capacitor, C. The input and output circuits are entirely decoupled.

The flyback converter is very popular for applications at low power levels (< 200 W) with multiple outputs because it has many advantages. There is no discrete output inductor, since the coupled inductor performs the function of transformer and inductor. Multiple outputs are easily derived by adding more windings to the core, and cross-regulation is good. A single output diode provides each voltage as opposed to two for buck-derived converters. The continuous-mode flyback

converter is harder to stabilize than the discontinuous-mode flyback converter.

The common switched-mode power supply topologies have been described in this section. The selection of a particular topology is a matter of design trade-offs. Each topology has characteristics that make it better suited to certain situations. Table 2 summarizes the major advantages and disadvantages of the converters. Typical application power levels (based on common uses) are also listed.

SWITCHES

The "switch" used in these converters is a device that will pass or block current when properly controlled. Bipolar transistors are used in an SMPS when switching frequencies are less than 50 kHz. They aren't normally used at higher switching frequencies because they are minority-carrier devices, and it can take many microseconds to switch a bipolar transistor on or off. The bipolar transistor requires a stiff current source to drive it at high speeds and this increases circuit cost and size. More importantly, long rise and fall times significantly increase power dissipa-

Fig 60—A shows a simple diagram of a one-switch flyback converter and B shows the typical hardware implementation of the circuit.

Table 2

Characteristics of Common Switched-Mode Power Supply Topologies

Converter	Typical Power Range	Advantages	Disadvantages
Flyback (Two-Switch)	<250 W	1. No output inductor 2. One diode per output 3. Multiple outputs easy 4. Simple control/good transient response (in discontinuous-mode)	1. Larger transformer than a bridge 2. Larger output capacitor than forward 3. Larger peak current than forward
Forward (Two-Switch)	<500 W	1. Larger output power than a flyback 2. Better output ripple than a flyback	1. Larger transformer than a bridge 2. Harder to stabilize than a discontinuous flyback (2-pole small-signal response)
Half-Bridge	<1000 W	1. Smaller transformer than a forward 2. Primary switches stressed to ½ V_{in}	1. Large RMS-current primary capacitors 2. 2-pole small-signal response
Full-Bridge	<2000 W	1. Twice P_{out} of half-bridge with same switches 2. Smaller transformer than a forward 3. No large RMS capacitors 4. Primary switches stressed to ½ V_{in}	1. Complex switch drive 2. 2-pole small-signal response
Push-Pull	<100 W	1. Very simple switch drive	1. Flux symmetry problems 2. Oversized transformer 3. Switches have 2 V_{in} rating 4. 2-pole small-signal response

Fig 61—The basic diagram of a forward converter with direct duty cycle control is shown at A. The current source and S3 provide the ramp voltage input to the comparator. Circuit waveforms are shown at B.

tion in the switch, so heat-management problems increase. Large storage times may also cause transformer flux asymmetry, leading to core saturation.

It takes some special circuitry to switch any transistor quickly. There are several techniques that reduce the switching times for bipolar transistors. Field-effect transistors have shorter switching times (nanoseconds) so they can be used in an SMPS operating in the megahertz range. At low frequencies, FETs act as voltage-controlled switches, but at frequencies above 100 kHz they require significant current to turn them on quickly.

Diodes are passive switches. They are either open or closed depending on the circuit voltage. In linear power supplies, diode transition times could be in the 100s of microseconds without problem. The SMPS requires transition times of less than a microsecond. If the diode (switch) doesn't recover (open) in time, new connections are made, and this may result in destructive currents. Forward voltage drop is also a consideration in diodes. In some applications the output voltage of a power supply is on the order of 2 V, and the forward voltage drop of a silicon diode (0.7 V) reduces efficiency significantly. Schottky diodes are often used because they have a lower forward voltage drop (0.5 V) than standard silicon and they also have very fast transition times (in the ns range). The shortcoming of a Schottky diode is its reverse-voltage breakdown rating.

MAGNETICS

Proper design of the magnetics for a switched-mode power supply is crucial. Over-sized magnetics make the power supply large, heavy, expensive and harder to cool; an under-sized ferrite core means

Fig 62—The basic diagram of a forward converter with current-mode control is shown at A. Notice that the switch current is monitored and fed to the comparator as part of the control loop. Circuit waveforms are shown at B.

source; the output voltage remains constant over a wider range of loads. The primary switch on-time relates directly to the current through it. Fig 62 shows a forward converter with current-mode control. Current-mode controllers are also available in IC packages. The UC3846 IC is an example of a high-performance current-mode control IC.

There are many advantages to current-mode control. The switch current determines switch on-time, so there is an inherent peak-by-peak current limit. Current-mode control also provides input feed-forward control, so if V_{in} increases, the current in the switch will also rise faster, decreasing on-times. The advantage of this feed-forward and peak-current balancing is flux balancing in bipolar (bridge) converters. Finally, the control-loop response is simpler because the effect of the inductor disappears; the converter (power stage) feeds a fixed current to the inductor, so its voltage response is minimal and the output filter becomes simply an output capacitor in series with the load.

There are always trade-offs, and one disadvantage of current-mode control is increased compensation complexity. Switch duty cycle cannot exceed 50% without special compensation to the current-ramp input. The current-ramp signal is often low voltage that has poor noise immunity. This means the designer must properly model all of the small-signal responses of the converter.

The circuits of Figs 61 and 62 are missing one element of a practical SMPS. The primary and secondary sides of the supply must be isolated in the feedback and control portion of the circuit. One approach is to isolate the control circuitry from the primary side by driving the primary switches through a transformer. Another approach is to use an opto-isolator in the feedback and control loop.

Soft-Start

Soft-start refers to a control circuit

more stress on the switches and primary windings, which may lead to failure. In the design of a power transformer or an inductor, there must be a starting point to estimate approximate core size. There are several approaches to estimating core size for magnetic devices. The area product (AP) approach estimates a core size that is the product of the cross-sectional area of the ferrite core, A_{fe}, and its bobbin winding area, A_{cu}. $AP = A_{cu} \times A_{fe}$ where A_{cu} and A_{fe} are found in a manufacturer's data sheet.

FEEDBACK AND CONTROL

The operation of any SMPS depends on the proper operation of the switches. These require some circuitry to sense the power supply operating conditions and use that information to control the switches. The switch on-times regulate the output voltage and current, so the control circuit is critical to the proper operation of the supply.

The two most common methods of controlling the switches in an SMPS converter are direct duty cycle control (often called voltage-mode control) and current-mode control. The direct duty cycle scheme was the first common control scheme to be

packaged as an IC. A 1524 control chip has all the necessary functions to drive and control a switched-mode converter operating in direct duty cycle control. The IC also includes provisions for protective functions such as current limiting and over-voltage shutdown.

Fig 61 shows a forward converter with direct duty cycle control. There are some trade-offs with direct duty cycle control. It doesn't monitor the input voltage, which can change dramatically if the converter is off-line, and it doesn't monitor switch currents. Some IC controller chips have added circuitry to limit switch current in order to protect the primary switches, the load, or the input, but true direct duty cycle control uses only the output voltage as the control parameter.

Current-mode control provides better control because it regulates the inductor current in addition to the voltage; this is done by "nesting" an inner control loop. The inductor current is usually monitored as switch current, since it is reflected (in a buck converter) back through the power transformer. Current-mode control is a more optimal control scheme because it makes the power supply seem like a stiffer

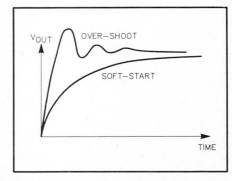

Fig 63—This graph shows the result of over-shoot of the output voltage when the power supply begins operation. If the control loop includes a soft-start feature the output voltage is brought up to the regulated level more slowly.

action that damps the output response so that it doesn't overshoot and damage the output load, or cause internal transformer saturation. Soft-start simply limits the on-times of the primary switches so that the power available to the output slowly increases to allow the control loop to regulate the output. A common method limits the error amplifier output with an RC network. See Fig 63.

Battery Power

The availability of solid-state equipment makes practical the use of battery power under portable or emergency conditions. Hand-held transceivers and instruments are obvious applications, but even fairly powerful transceivers (100 W or so output) may be practical users of battery power. Solid-state kilowatt mobile amplifiers exist, but these are intended for operation from an auxiliary battery that is constantly charged. The lower-power equipment can be powered from two types of batteries. The primary battery is intended for one-time use; the storage (or secondary) battery may be recharged many times.

A battery is a group of chemical cells, usually series-connected to give some desired multiple of the cell voltage. Each assortment of chemicals used in the cell gives a particular nominal voltage; this must be taken into account to make up a particular battery voltage.

Primary Batteries

The most common primary cell is the carbon-zinc flashlight type, in which chemical oxidation converts the zinc into salts and electricity. When there is no current flow, the oxidation stops until the next time current is required. Some chemical action does continue, so stored batteries eventually will degrade or dry out to the point where the battery will no longer supply the desired current. The time taken for degradation without battery use is called shelf life.

The carbon-zinc battery has a nominal voltage of 1.5 volts, as does its heavy-duty or industrial brother. These latter types are capable (for a given size) of producing more milliampere hours and less voltage drop than a carbon-zinc battery of the same size. They also have longer shelf life. Alkaline primary batteries have even better characteristics and will retain more capacity at low temperatures. Nominal voltage is 1.5 volts.

Lithium primary batteries have a nominal voltage of about 3 volts per cell and by far the best capacity, discharge, shelf-life and temperature characteristics. Their disadvantages are high cost and the fact that they cannot be readily replaced by other types in an emergency.

The lithium-thionyl-chloride battery is a primary cell, and should not be recharged under any circumstances. The charging process vents hydrogen, and a catastrophic hydrogen explosion can result. Even accidental charging caused by wiring errors or a short circuit should be avoided. (A rechargeable lithium battery using molybdenum disulfide was described by C. Dollard and N. Bowker, "The Magic of MOLI," *QST*, June 1987, pp 22-25.)

Silver oxide (1.5 V) and mercury (1.4 V) batteries are very good where nearly constant voltage is desired at low currents for long periods. Their main use (in subminiature versions) is in hearing aids, though they may be found in other mass-produced devices such as household smoke alarms.

Rechargeable or Storage Batteries

Many of the chemical reactions in primary batteries are theoretically reversible if current is passed through the battery in the reverse direction. For instance, zinc may be plated back onto the negative electrode of a zinc-carbon battery. Recharging of primary batteries should not be done for two reasons: It may be dangerous because of heat generated within sealed cells, and even in cases where there may be some success, both the charge and life are limited. In the zinc-carbon example, the zinc may not replate in the locations that had been oxidized. Pinholes in the case result, with consequent fluid leakage that will damage the equipment powered by the batteries.

One type of alkaline battery is rechargeable, and is so marked. If the recommended charging rate is not marked on such a battery, the manufacturer's advice should be asked. In a number of cases, the manufacturer markets chargers and recommends that only those should be used.

The most common small-storage battery is the nickel-cadmium (NiCd) type, with a nominal voltage of 1.2 V per cell. Carefully used, these are capable of 500 or more charge and discharge cycles, compared to 50 or so for alkaline types. The NiCd battery must not be fully discharged for best life. Where there is more than one cell in the battery, the most-discharged cell may suffer polarity reversal, resulting in a short circuit, or seal rupture. All storage batteries have discharge limits, and nickel-cadmium types should not be discharged to less than 1.0 V per cell.

The most widely used storage battery is the lead-acid type. In automotive service, the battery is usually expected to discharge partially at a very high rate, and then to be recharged promptly while the alternator is also carrying the electrical load. If the conventional auto battery is allowed to discharge fully from its nominal 2 V per cell to 1.75 V per cell, only about 50 cycles of charge and discharge may be expected, with reduced storage capacity.

The most attractive battery for extended high-power electronic applications is the so-called "deep-cycle" battery (intended for such use as powering electrical fishing motors and the accessories in recreational vehicles). The size 24 and 27 batteries furnish a nominal 12 volts and are about the size of small and medium automotive batteries. These batteries may furnish between 1000 and 1200 watt-hours per charge at room temperature. When properly cared for, they may be expected to last more than 200 cycles. They often have lifting handles and screw terminals, as well as the conventional truncated-cone automotive terminals. They may also be fitted with accessories such as plastic carrying cases, with or without built-in chargers.

Lead-acid batteries are also available with gelled electrolyte. Commonly called gel cells, these types may be mounted in any position if sealed, but some vented types are position sensitive.

Lead-acid batteries with liquid electrolyte usually fall into one of three classes — conventional with filling holes and vents, permitting the addition of distilled water lost from evaporation or during high-rate charge or discharge; maintenance-free, from which gas may escape but water cannot be added; and sealed. Generally, the deep-cycle batteries have filling holes and vents.

Battery Capacity

The common rating of battery capacity is ampere hours (Ah), the product of current drain and time. The symbol "C" is commonly used; C/10, for example, would be the current available for 10 hours continuously. The value of C changes with the discharge rate and might be 110 at 2 amperes but only 80 at 20 amperes. Fig 64 gives capacity-to-discharge rate for two standard-size lead-acid batteries. Capacity may vary from 35 mA hours for some of the small hearing-aid batteries to more than 100 ampere hours for a size 28 deep-cycle storage battery.

The primary cells, being sealed, usually benefit from intermittent (rather than continuous) use. The resting period allows completion of chemical reactions needed to dispose of by-products of the discharge.

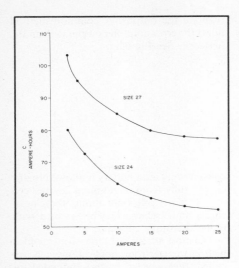

Fig 64 — Output capacity as a function of discharge rate for two sizes of lead-acid batteries.

All batteries will fall in output voltage as discharge proceeds. "Discharged" condition for a 12-V lead-acid battery, for instance, should not be less than 10.5 volts. It is also good to keep a running record of hydrometer readings, but the conventional readings of 1.265 charged and 1.100 discharged apply only to a long, low-rate discharge. Heavy loads may discharge the battery with little reduction in the hydrometer reading.

Batteries that become cold have less of their charge available, and some attempt to keep a battery warm before use is worthwhile. A battery may lose 70% or more of its capacity at cold extremes, but it will recover with warmth. All batteries have some tendency to freeze, but those with full charges are less susceptible. A full-charged lead-acid battery is safe to −30 °F (−26 °C) or colder. Storage batteries may be warmed somewhat by charging. Blow-torches or other flame should never be used to heat any type of battery.

A practical limit of discharge occurs when the load will no longer operate satisfactorily on the lower output voltage near the "discharged" point. Much gear intended for "mobile" use may be designed for an average of 13.6 V and a peak of perhaps 15 V, but will not operate well below 12 V. For full use of battery charge, the gear should operate well (if not at full power) on as little as 10.5 V with a nominal 12 to 13.6-V rating.

Somewhat the same condition may be seen in the replacement of carbon-zinc cells by nickel-cadmium storage cells. Eight of the former will give 12 V, while 10 of the same size nickel-cadmium units are required for the same voltage. If a 10-cell battery holder is used, the equipment should be designed for 15 V in case the carbon-zinc units are plugged in.

Deep-cycle and nickel-cadmium storage batteries will tolerate a light continual charge (trickle). The sealed nickel-cadmium types tolerate a near-full charging rate continuously.

Discharge Planning

Transceivers usually drain a battery at two or three rates: one for receiving, one for transmit standby and one key-down or average voice transmit. Considering just the first and last of these (assuming the transmit standby equal to receive), average two-way CW communication would require the low rate ¾ of the time and the high rate ¼ of the time. The ratio may vary somewhat with voice. The user may calculate the percentage of battery charge used in an hour by the combination (sum) of rates. If, for example, 20% of the battery capacity is used, the battery will provide five hours of communications per charge. In most actual traffic and DX-chasing situations the time spent listening should be much greater than that spent transmitting.

Caring for Storage Batteries

In addition to the precautions given above, the following are recommended. (Your manufacturer's advice will probably be more applicable.)

Gas escaping from storage batteries may be explosive. Keep flame away.

Dry-charged storage batteries should be given electrolyte and allowed to soak for at least half an hour. They then should be charged at perhaps a 15 A rate for 15 minutes or so. The capacity of the battery will build up slightly for the first few cycles of charge and discharge, and then have fairly constant capacity for many cycles. Slow capacity decrease may then be noticed.

No battery should be subjected to unnecessary heat, vibration or physical shock. The battery should be kept clean. Frequent inspection for leaks is a good idea. Leaking or spraying electrolyte should be cleaned from the battery and surroundings. The electrolyte is chemically active and electrically conductive, and may ruin electrical equipment. Acid may be neutralized with sodium bicarbonate (baking soda), and alkalies may be neutralized with a weak acid such as vinegar. Both neutralizers will dissolve in water, and should be quickly washed off. Do not let any of the neutralizer enter the battery.

Keep a record of the battery usage, and include the last output voltage and (for lead-acid storage batteries) the hydrometer reading. This allows prediction of useful charge remaining, and the recharging or procuring of extra batteries, thus minimizing failure of battery power during an excursion or emergency.

Charging Rechargeable Batteries

The rated full charge of a battery, C, is expressed in ampere-hours. No battery is perfect, so more charge than this must be offered to the battery for a full-charge. If,

for instance, the charge rate is 0.1 C (the 10-hour rate), 12 or more hours may be needed for the charge.

Basically nickel-cadmium batteries differ from the lead-acid types in the methods of charging. It is important to note these differences, since improper charging can drastically shorten the life of a battery.

Nickel-cadmium cells have a flat voltage-vs.-charge characteristic until full charge is reached; at this point the charge voltage rises abruptly. With further charging, the electrolyte begins to break down and oxygen gas is generated at the positive (nickel) electrode and hydrogen at the negative (cadmium) electrode.

Since the cell should be made capable of accepting an overcharge, battery manufacturers typically prevent the generation of hydrogen by increasing the capacity of the cadmium electrode. This allows the oxygen formed at the positive electrode to reach the metallic cadmium of the negative electrode and reoxidize it. During overcharge, therefore, the cell is in equilibrium. The positive electrode is fully charged and the negative electrode less than fully charged, so oxygen evolution and recombination "wastes" the charging power being supplied.

In order to ensure that all cells in a NiCd battery reach a fully charged condition, NiCd batteries should be charged by a constant current at about a 0.1 C current level. This level is about 50 mA for the AA-size cells used in most hand-held radios. This is the optimum rate for most NiCds since 0.1 C is high enough to provide a full charge, yet it is low enough to prevent overcharge damage and provide good charge efficiency.

Although fast-charge-rate (3 to 5 hours typically) chargers are available for hand-held transceivers, they should be used with care. The current delivered by these units is capable of causing the generation of large quantities of oxygen in a fully-charged cell. If the generation rate is greater than the oxygen recombination rate, pressure will build in the cell, forcing the vent to open and the oxygen to escape. This can eventually cause drying of the electrolyte, and then cell failure. The cell temperature can also rise, which can shorten cell life. To prevent overcharge from occurring, fast-rate chargers should have automatic charge-limiting circuitry which will switch or taper the charging current to a safe rate as the battery reaches a fully-charged state.

By contrast, the gelled-electrolyte lead-acid battery cannot tolerate overcharging, even at very low charge rates. For this reason, constant current or trickle charging should not be used for charging gel cells unless the battery voltage is monitored and charging is terminated when full charge is reached. Voltage-limited charging is best for these batteries. The proper charger would charge the battery at a safe current (C/10 or C/20) until a per-cell voltage of about 2.3 volts is reached (13.8 V for a 12-V

Fig 65 — Solar-electric arrays are excellent for short- or long-term field and emergency use to power amateur stations. A 14-volt, 1.5-A solar panel and two automobile batteries in parallel can provide many after-dark hours of operation with typical 100-watt HF-band transceivers of the solid-state variety.

battery). At this point, the charge current will taper to only enough to maintain the full-charge voltage. This makes the gel cell the optimum choice for "floating" across a regulated 13.8 volt power system to provide battery backup in the event of power failure.

Deep-cycle lead-acid cells are best charged at a slow rate, while automotive and some nickel-cadmium types may safely be given quick charges. This depends on the amount of heat generated within each cell, and cell venting to prevent pressure build-up. Some batteries have built-in temperature sensing, used to stop or reduce

Fig 66 — Schematic diagram of a solar power supply. Note that the battery-charging circuit does not employ a regulator or switch to shut off charging current once the storage battery reaches full charge state. Because the output of the solar panels is, at most, 1½ A and the storage batteries are full-size automobile batteries, the danger of damage from overcharging is not great. Anyone contemplating higher current solar panels or smaller storage batteries should give serious consideration to a regulator and/or an automatic cutoff switch for the charging circuit. (See Fig 67.)

BT1, BT2, BT3 — 20-V, ½-A solar panels by Spectrolab.
BT4, BT5 — 12-V lead-acid automobile batteries.
D1 — 1N5401 or any diode with at least 2-A capacity and with at least 50 PIV.
Q1 — NPN silicon 90-W transistor, power switching, TIP31, Radio Shack 276-2020 or equiv.

Q2 — NPN silicon 115 W transistor, power switching, 2N3055 or equiv.
R1 — 0.27 Ω, 1 W.
R2 — 220 Ω, 1 W.
R3 — 2.2 Ω, 1 W.
S1, S3, S4 — SPST, momentary-contact switch.
S2 — DPDT knife switch.

Fig 67 — Schematic diagram of the electronic switch. Resistances are in ohms; k = 1000; capacitance values are in microfarads (μF).

BT1 — Automotive storage battery, lead-acid type.
C1 — 1000-μF, 35-V electrolytic.
C2 — 0.33-μF, 35-V.
D3 — Silicon diode, PIV of 50 or more, current

rating sufficient to pass full output of the solar panel.
D6 — Light-emitting diode, any type.
Q2 — Low-frequency power transistor; 2N3055, or equiv. Use heat sink of 9 in²

or more.
R7 — 10 kΩ, ½ W, carbon control, linear taper, PC mount.
U1 — 3-terminal, 5-volt regulator.
U2 — Op amp, any of the 741 family usable.

charging before the heat rise becomes a danger. Quick and fast charges do not usually allow gas recombination, so some of the battery water will escape in the form of gas. If the water level falls below a certain point, acid hydrometer readings are no longer reliable. If the water level falls to plate level, permanent battery damage may result.

Overcharging in moderation causes little loss of battery life. However, continuous overcharge may generate a voltage depression when the cells are later discharged. For best results, charging of NiCd cells should be terminated after 15 hours at the slow rate. Better yet, circuitry may be included in the charger to stop charging, or reduce the current to about 0.02 C when the 1.43-V-per-cell terminal voltage is reached. For lead-acid batteries, a timer may be used to run the charger to make up for the recorded discharge, plus perhaps 20%. Some chargers will switch over automatically to an acceptable standby charge.

SOLAR-ELECTRIC POWER

Although solar-electric arrays are quite expensive when purchased new, surplus individual cells and groups of cells (arrays) can be bought inexpensively on occasion. Photons from the sun strike the PN junctions of the cells to generate 0.5 volt per cell (see Chapter 4). The current rating of an individual cell is dependent upon the diameter of the cell. Typical production units deliver 100 mA, 600 mA, 1 A or 1.5 A. Cells with higher current ratings are manufactured, but are quite costly.

A solar-electric panel generally contains 36 cells wired in series. This provides approximately 18 volts dc under no-load conditions at peak sunlight. The current capability of the panel is determined by the diameter of the cells. Greater amounts of current output can be had by paralleling like panels. That is, two 1.5-A panels can be operated in parallel to deliver 3 amperes of current, and so on.

The usual operating system has the array output routed through a regulator to a storage battery. The regulator prevents overcharging of the battery. The station equipment takes its power from the battery. Most automotive 12-volt batteries are suitable for use with solar-electric panels. NiCd batteries are also satisfactory. Fig 65 shows a solar array in a frame. The cells are wired in series.

Fig 66 shows a solar-electric system suitable for low- or high-power operation. If the current drain is less than the capacity of the solar bank (1.5 A in this case), the load can be powered from the solar cells through the regulator circuit. For heavier loads, the current is taken from the storage batteries, which are charged by the solar array. The circuit of Fig 66 was designed by John Akiyama, W6PQZ, and was described by John Halliday, W5PIZ in August 1980 *QST*. In the same issue, Doug Blakeslee, N1RM, described an electronic switch to automatically disconnect storage batteries from a solar system when full charge (13.5 V) is reached. The circuit is shown in Fig 67. U1, D4 and D5 establish a 6.2-V reference for comparator U2. A voltage divider composed of R1, R3 and R7 scales the battery voltage down to the reference value, while R4 provides hysteresis to prevent oscillation. When the battery potential exceeds the comparator threshold, U2 goes high, turning off Q1 and Q2. The LED, D6, indicates that the battery is being charged.

Chapter 7

Audio and Video

Of the five senses we humans possess — sight, smell, taste, hearing and feeling — three are used for communication. We communicate visually, through actions and through body language such as facial expressions. We communicate aurally, through speech. On occasion we may communicate through feeling by touching; a tap on the shoulder, for example. Aural and visual communications can be transmitted electronically, and are therefore pertinent to Amateur Radio. This chapter deals with the fundamentals involved.

SPEECH

Human speech consists predominantly of two types of sounds — voiced and unvoiced. Voiced sounds originate when air passes from the speaker's lungs through the larynx (voice box), a passage in the human throat with the opening obstructed by vocal cords. As air travels past these cords they vibrate, causing puffs of air to escape into the oral cavity, which consists of the throat, nasal cavity and mouth. Studies indicate that the acoustic waveform produced by the vocal cords has many harmonics of the fundamental vibration. Because of the irregular shape of the oral cavity, the spectral-amplitude distribution of the harmonics tends to show peaks at distinct points. As speech is produced, changes occur in the oral cavity shape, thus changing the spectral location of these peaks.

Fig. 1 shows a spectrogram or voice print of the utterance, "digital communications." The darkness of the bands indicates amplitude or voice strength. The fine structure of amplitude peaks very close together in the horizontal dimension is a measurement of vocal-cord vibration frequency or fundamental.

Notice the rather strong amplitude concentrations below 4000 Hz. These are the spectral peaks referred to above. They are called *formants*. The first three formants are shown in Fig. 1 at the beginning of the utterance. Fig. 1 also indicates a range of frequencies between the first and second formants, from approximately 600 to 1500 Hz, where little energy is present. This is identified in the figure as a spectral gap.

Unvoiced sounds in speech occur when there is no vocal track excitation. They are caused by the speaker using his or her tongue, lips and teeth to cause clicks, hisses and popping sounds. These sounds, or evidence of their occurrence by formant extensions into or from an unvoiced sound, are very important in the intelligibility of speech. The spectral amplitude distribution of unvoiced sounds is generally above 1500 Hz and is "noise-like" in that very little periodic structure is present.

One other important aspect of speech is

Fig. 1 — A speech spectrogram of the utterance, "digital communications." The vertical axis represents frequency (80-8000 Hz) and the horizontal axis represents time (0-1.5 seconds).

Fig. 2 — Long-time audio spectrum of speech. The horizontal scale is 1000 Hz per division or 0 to 5000 Hz. The vertical scale is 10 dB per division.

the pause between acoustic sounds. Juncture pauses carry meaning and cannot be eliminated without impairing intelligibility. Some long pauses can, however, be shortened and thereby reduce message length. Briefly, then, speech is the continuous production of voiced and unvoiced sounds with appropriate pauses to add clarity and distinctness.

Frequency and Amplitude Considerations

Measurements of the voices of different persons indicate that the first three formants, identified in Fig. 1, lie predominantly below 2500 Hz. Speech consisting of these three formants is of good quality both from an intelligibility and listenability standpoint. Sufficient information as to the existence of some unvoiced sounds appears to lie in this range also. For example, to produce s or hissing sounds the frequency range must extend to about 4000 Hz. This is not usually required for intelligibility, however, since contextual clues provide sufficient evidence for the listener to "hear" an s.

Fig. 2 shows a long-time amplitude spectrum of speech. Note the presence of the first three formants, appearing as peaks in the pattern. Note also that speech components above 2500 Hz (mid-scale on the horizontal axis) are 20 to 25 dB lower than those below 2500 Hz. From a frequency point of view, evidence from theory and practice indicates that a bandwidth of 300 to 2500 Hz is adequate for good-quality speech. This is a bandwidth of 2.2 kHz.

From an amplitude standpoint, tests conducted with single coherent tone interference indicate that a dynamic range of 40 dB is quite adequate for good-quality speech. This is reinforced by the information displayed in Fig. 2. Many communications channels allow only 10 to 30 dB of signal-to-noise ratio, so equipment designed to preserve more than 40 dB of dynamic range is not warranted.

SOUND WAVES

Sound waves travel through the air at the speed of approximately 1190 feet per second. They propagate as pressure waves, or alternating condensations and rarefactions of the air. The amplitudes of the pressure changes that make up sound waves from human speech are quite small. Sound power is measured in microjoules, a metric unit. One microjoule equals 10 ergs. When a sentence of a few words is spoken by a typical voice, the potential energy in the resultant sound wave is approximately 30 or 40 microjoules. Compare this to the 10^8 microjoules per second required to power a 100-watt lamp. It has been calculated that it would take 500 people talking continuously for a year to produce enough energy to heat a cup of tea. Because of the extremely low level of human speech, sensitive microphones and speech amplifiers are required in equipment intended for radio communications.

Sound intensity levels are ordinarily expressed in decibels. The reference level in power units for these decibel figures, established by the American Standards Association, is 10^{-16} watt per square centimeter. This equates approximately to 0.0002 dyne per square centimeter in pressure units, a figure that is more commonly used. (There is variation in the precise relationship between power and pressure units because of temperature and atmospheric pressure changes. However, agreement between the above values will be within 1 dB under most conditions.) The sound intensity level in decibels is calculated from the usual equation, 10 times the common logarithm of the power ratio, while using 10^{-16} watt per square centimeter as the reference. This is the same relationship as 20 times the logarithm of the pressure ratio.

Instruments are available to read sound pressure levels. These are calibrated in decibels, and are called sound level meters. Typical sound levels are 35 dB in a hospital, 40 dB in a classroom, 45 dB in offices, and 50 dB in banks, stores and restaurants. Intensity levels in factories may be as high as 80 dB.

Human speech intensities vary from one talker to another, and also vary for the same talker depending on the environment and distance between the talker and the listener. The average intensity level for talkers, both men and women, is 66 dB. Softer talkers speaking in conversational tones were measured to be as low as 54 dB, while loud talkers were as high as 75 dB. When one whispers the level is about 26 dB, while a loud shout produces an intensity level of about 86 dB. Thus, the human voice has a dynamic range of approximately 60 dB. These figures are for intensity levels averaged over a period of time. In actual speech, the instantaneous power varies from zero during pauses and intervals between words to peak values as high as 100 times the average value. Men tend to speak with greater intensity levels than women. There are other differences, too.

The pitch of a woman's voice is about one octave higher than that of a man, and a woman's voice is richer in frequencies above 3000 Hz.

HEARING

Pressure variations in the sound wave produce mechanical vibrations in the eardrum. These vibrations are transmitted to the inner ear, where nerve endings are excited. The ear consists of three parts: the outer ear, the middle ear and the inner ear. The outer ear is the external portion and the auditory canal. The middle ear consists of the ear drum and three small bones that are linked mechanically to the cochlea in the inner ear. In the cochlea are the nerves that give us the sense of hearing. The inner ear also contains parts that have no function in the mechanism of hearing, but do serve as an organ of balance or equilibrium.

Every person has a threshold of hearing, a level below which he or she cannot detect any sound, and that threshold level is quite dependent on frequency. If the sound is a single-frequency tone, as is commonly used for acuity measurements, an intermittent tone can be heard at levels 10 to 20 dB below that for a continuous tone. Frequencies of 20 Hz and 20 kHz represent the probable limits of human hearing, although not many persons can hear sounds at these extremes. A person with acute hearing has a threshold of approximately 20 dB in the mid-frequency range, 2 to 3 kHz.

As a person becomes older, hearing acuity decreases, particularly for the high frequencies. The loss below 1 kHz is usually less than 10 dB, but the losses with age run from 10 dB at 40 years to 40 dB at 60 years. (These decibel losses are referenced to normal hearing.) Hearing losses also occur with continued exposure to very loud sounds. The loss is usually permanent with continued exposure to intensities in excess of 85 dB. Men hear low frequencies better than women at comparable ages, and women hear high frequencies better, with the range from 1.5 to 2 kHz being heard about equally well.

MICROPHONES

A microphone is the transducer that converts sound waves into electrical energy. All voice transmissions begin with a microphone. Mics, as they are commonly called, have a number of basic characteristics including distortion, frequency response, impedance, output level, mechanical design, and directional or noise-canceling ability.

Distortion in a microphone refers to a nonlinear response to sound pressure waves. Distortion is not usually a problem in mics of modern design, except the carbon type.

Frequency Response

The frequency response of a mic is the bandwidth over which it responds to sound waves. In amateur transmissions, only the portion of the speech band from about 200 to 3500 Hz needs to be transmitted for good intelligibility. Mics usually have bandwidths greater than this, so the speech amplifiers in transmitters are often designed to limit the audio bandwidth to the minimum necessary.

A microphone should have a response that is as uniform as possible over the desired speech range, but this is the most difficult microphone characteristic to achieve. The inexpensive types often have peaks and valleys in their response as much as 20 dB above and below the nominal output level. This peaky response will increase the peak-to-average ratio of the speech waveform, which reduces the average level of audio power transmitted. In addition, this peaky response may overdrive the final amplifier, which can cause ALC limiting, or TVI and RFI.

Microphones are generally omnidirectional, responding to sound from all directions, or unidirectional, picking up sound from one direction. If a microphone is to be used close to the operator's mouth, an omnidirectional microphone is ideal. If, however, speech is generated a foot or more from the microphone, a unidirectional microphone will reduce reverberation by a factor of 1.7:1. Some types of unidirectional microphones have a proximity effect in that low frequencies are accentuated when the microphone is too close to the mouth.

Impedance

A microphone is a voltage generator that has an optimum load impedance. Mics are available in two broad categories of impedance, high and low. The high-Z mics are used within a short distance of the transmitter, as the connecting cable cannot be made very long without compensation or matching transformers. Shielding of the microphone cable is necessary to prevent hum and noise pickup. The actual impedance of a "high-Z" mic will vary with manufacturer and type, but values between 100 kΩ and 500 kΩ are typical.

Low-Z microphones are sold in three popular impedances, 50, 150 and 600 ohms. The 50-ohm types are used by the commercial communications services, while the 150- and 600-ohm mics are usually found in broadcast, telephone and public address applications. The amateur's choice of mic impedance is usually dictated by the requirements of the transmitter, unless an impedance-matching transformer is used.

Output Level

Related to impedance, output level varies widely with different types of microphones. There are several systems of specifying microphone output level in use, so direct comparison of various manufacturers' specifications can lead to erroneous conclusions. In addition, the test level, the reference level and the load impedances used in the specification of high-Z and low-Z mics are different, so the two cannot be compared directly.

Fig. 3 — Simplified center chamber of a noise-canceling microphone.

The popular rating for high-Z microphones is the output voltage, expressed in decibels below 1 volt, measured across an open circuit with 1 dyne per square centimeter test signal at 1000 Hz applied to the microphone. Low-Z mics use a different system with the rating in output power, expressed in decibels below 1 milliwatt, measured across a 600-ohm load and using a test tone of 10 dynes per square centimeter at 1000 Hz. Several other test procedures are in use, so direct comparison of manufacturers' specifications will be valid only if the same measurement standards have been used.

Noise Cancellation

Noise cancellation is the ability to cancel or reject noise while not attenuating the desired voice signal. A noise-canceling mic can be used to advantage in a noisy environment. The principle of noise cancellation (perhaps more properly called noise attenuation, as it is impossible to get rid of all noise) is quite simple.

See Fig. 3. The noise originating at some distant point enters the mic through two ports and is applied to both sides of the diaphragm. If the sound pressure is equal on both sides, the diaphragm will not move and the mic has no output. Speech is allowed to enter through only one port; the diaphragm moves in response to this sound pressure and output is produced. The shape of the diaphragm, the material it is made from, and the mounting are all important design considerations. A problem area is the tendency of the diaphragm to "lock up" under heavy noise pressure, distorting the desired speech signal. Considerable progress has been made in this area, and a good design will take very heavy noise without producing appreciable speech distortion.

The measurement of a mic's ability to attenuate noise is not standard, and most microphones or elements are sold simply with the label, "noise canceling," with no information on how well the mic actually cancels background noise. A good mic should attenuate noise by at least 20 dB across the speech band.

In noise-canceling mics designed for hand-held operation, the mic element itself must be physically small and light. This means the two sampling ports cannot be spaced very far apart. If the voice is allowed to enter both ports, it too will be at-

tenuated. For this reason, noise-canceling mics are inherently close-talk devices. They should be held within ½ inch of the lips for best results.

TYPES OF MICROPHONES

Microphones are available in many types. Those commonly available or popular for amateur use are discussed in the sections that follow.

Carbon Microphones

The carbon microphone consists of a metal diaphragm placed against a cup of loosely packed carbon granules. As the diaphragm is actuated by the sound pressure, it alternately compresses and decompresses the granules. When current is flowing through the element, a variable direct current corresponds to the movement of the diaphragm. The carbon mic is used almost universally by the telephone company, and until quite recently was quite popular with the military. Carbon elements are low impedance (usually between 30 and 80 ohms), and have very high output — 0.2 V or more, depending on the dc voltage across the element. They differ from most other popular types in that the transmitter (or some other source) must provide an operating voltage for the element. Practically, the voltage requirement limits the use of the element to transmitters designed for carbon mics.

The carbon mic has two principal disadvantages, a high level of distortion compared to other types and a problem when the element is exposed to moisture for long periods. Moisture in the element will pack the carbon granules together, reducing the output and increasing distortion. In some instances the element stops working altogether. The mic can sometimes be restored by heating it for several hours in the oven or with a sun lamp, and then tapping it lightly to loosen the granules.

Piezoelectric Microphones

Piezoelectric microphones make use of the phenomenon by which certain materials produce a voltage by mechanical stress or distortion of the material. A diaphragm is coupled to a small bar of material such as Rochelle salt or ceramic made of barium titanate or lead zirconium titanate. The diaphragm motion is thus translated into electrical energy. These microphones are of high impedance. The Rochelle salt or crystal mic is of a fragile nature, and is susceptible to high temperatures, high humidity and extreme dryness. For this reason is is not suitable for mobile or portable work. A crystal mic has high output and a wide frequency response.

The ceramic type is impervious to temperature and humidity. This type has become very popular with manufacturers who supply mics with their amateur and CB transceivers. The reason is that the ceramics sell for low prices when mass produced. The impedance is high, and the output of

Fig. 4 — Speech circuits for use with standard-type microphones. Typical parts values are shown.

Fig. 5 — A speech amplifier suitable for microphone or interstage use. The input and output impedances can be tailored to match a wide range of loads. Maximum gain of this circuit is 40 dB.

a modern ceramic microphone is generally enough to drive most popular rigs. However, a ceramic mic is a low-output device, and operation can be marginal with a transmitter that is lacking gain in the speech amplifier. An interesting characteristic of the ceramic microphone is that if it is terminated in a lower-than-optimum resistance (optimum being 100 kΩ to 250 kΩ), the low-frequency output is attenuated — a simple way to eliminate the unwanted frequencies below 200 Hz. This frequency characteristic is also true of microphones made with Rochelle salts, another piezoelectric material.

Many of the inexpensive ceramic mics show the effects of mass production — excessive peaks in their frequency response. Manufacturers rate the nominal frequency response for these mics, but never mention the limits of deviation from the nominal output level. It is generally true that the cost of materials for all types of microphones is quite low unless put into a very fancy housing. The yield, testing, rework and retesting that a manufacturer goes through to ensure that a microphone meets a specified frequency response within specified limits is what adds up to the price of a ''good'' microphone.

Dynamic Microphones

The dynamic microphone resembles a dynamic loudspeaker. A lightweight coil, usually made of aluminum wire, is attached to a diaphragm. This coil is suspended in a magnetic field. When sound pressure impinges on the diaphragm, it moves the coil through the magnetic field, generating an alternating voltage. Dynamic mics are one of the most popular types for radio service. Dynamic elements are low impedance; matching transformers are built in if a high-Z output is desired.

Dynamics range all the way in price until they rival the cost of a communications receiver. The very expensive types are generally intended for recording and broadcast work. The dynamic element can be made noise canceling or directional. The mounting of the diaphragm is such that sound can easily be applied to both the front and the rear of the diaphragm to produce a desired pattern or effect. Because of its excellent speech quality and reliability, the military services have been changing over to this type of mic for use on field radio sets.

Electret Microphones

The electret microphone has recently appeared as a feasible alternative to the carbon, piezoelectric or dynamic microphone. An electret is an insulator that has a quasi-permanent static electric charge trapped in or on it. The electret operates in a condenser fashion, using a set of biased plates. Motion caused by air pressure variations creates a changing capacitance and an accompanying change in voltage. The electret acts as the plates would, and being charged, it requires no bias voltage. A low voltage provided by a battery used for an FET impedance converter is the only power required to produce an audio signal.

Electrets traditionally have been suscep-

tible to damage from high temperatures and high humidity. New materials and different charging techniques have lowered the chances of damage, however. Only in extreme conditions (such as 120 °F at 49% humidity) are problems present. The output level of a typical electret is higher than that of a standard dynamic microphone.

SPEECH AMPLIFIERS

The purpose of a speech amplifier is to raise the level of audio output from a microphone to that required by the modulator of a transmitter. In SSB and FM transmitters the modulation process takes place at low levels, so only a few volts of audio is necessary. One or two simple voltage-amplifier stages will suffice. AM transmitters often use high-level plate modulation requiring considerable audio power, compared to SSB and FM. The microphone-input and audio voltage-amplifier circuits are similar in all three types of phone transmitters, however.

When designing speech equipment it is necessary to know (1) the amount of audio power the modulation system must furnish, and (2) the output voltage developed by the microphone when it is spoken into from a normal distance with ordinary loudness. It then becomes possible to choose the number and type of amplifier stages needed to generate the required audio power without overloading or undue distortion anywhere in the system.

The circuit immediately following the audio input establishes the signal-to-noise ratio of the transmitter. General-purpose ICs such as 741 op amps are widely used in speech amplifiers, but they are fairly noisy, so it is best to precede them with a lower noise discrete device (FET or bipolar transistor). The circuits

Fig. 6 — A dc voltage controls the gain of this IC, eliminating the need for shielded leads to the gain control.

Fig. 7 — Phase splitter circuits using (A) a JFET and (B) a dual operational amplifier.

in Fig. 4 fulfill this requirement.

Voltage Amplifiers

The important characteristics of a voltage amplifier are its voltage gain, maximum undistorted output voltage and its frequency response. The voltage gain is the voltage-amplification ratio of the stage. The output voltage is the maximum AF voltage that can be obtained from the stage without distortion. The amplifier frequency response should be adequate for voice reproduction; this requirement is easily satisfied.

The voltage gain and maximum undistorted output voltage depend on the operating conditions of the amplifier. The output voltage is in terms of *peak* voltage, rather than RMS; this makes the rating independent of the waveform. Exceeding the peak value causes the amplifier to distort, so it is more useful to consider only peak values in working with amplifiers.

A circuit suitable for use as a microphone preamplifier or the major gain block of a speech system is shown in Fig. 5. The response rolls off below 200 Hz to reduce hum pickup. Ordinary 741 op amps can be used in stages following the preamp, provided the voltage gain is held to about 20 (26 dB).

Gain Control

A means for varying the overall gain of the amplifier is necessary for keeping the final output at the proper level for modulating the transmitter. The common method of controlling the gain is to adjust the value of ac voltage applied to the input of one of the amplifiers by means of a voltage divider or potentiometer.

The gain-control potentiometer should be near the input end of the amplifier, at a point where the signal voltage level is so low there is no danger that the stages ahead of the gain control will be overloaded by the full microphone output. In a high-gain amplifier it is best to operate the first stage at maximum gain, since this gives the best signal-to-hum ratio. The control is usually placed in the input circuit of the second stage.

Remote gain control can be accomplished with an electronic attenuator IC, such as the Motorola MC3340P. A dc voltage varies the gain of the IC from +6 to −85 dB, eliminating the need for shielded leads to a remotely located volume control. A typical circuit is shown in Fig. 6.

Phase Inversion

Some balanced modulators and phase shifters require push-pull audio input. The obvious way to obtain push-pull output from a single-ended stage is to use a transformer with a center-tapped secondary. Phase-inverter or phase-splitter circuits can accomplish the same task electronically. A differential amplifier can be used to convert a single-ended input to a push-pull output. Two additional phase-splitter circuits are shown in Fig. 7.

Speech-Amplifier Construction

Once a suitable circuit has been selected for a speech amplifier, the construction problem resolves itself into avoiding two difficulties — excessive hum and unwanted feedback. For reasonably humless operation, the hum voltage should not exceed about one percent of the maximum audio output voltage — that is, the hum and noise should be at least 40 dB below the output level.

Unwanted feedback, if negative, will reduce the gain below the calculated value. If positive, feedback is likely to cause self-oscillation or howls. Feedback can be minimized by isolating each stage with decoupling resistors and capacitors, by avoiding layouts that bring the first and last stages near each other, and by shielding of "hot" points in the circuit, such as high-impedance leads in low-level stages.

If circuit-board construction is used, high-impedance leads should be kept as short as possible. All ground returns should be made to a common point. A good ground between the circuit board and the metal chassis is necessary. Complete shielding from RF energy is always required for low-level solid-state audio circuits. The microphone input should be decoupled for RF with a filter, as shown in Fig. 8. At A, an RF choke with a high impedance over the frequency range of the transmitter is used. For high-impedance inputs, a resistor may be used in place of the choke, shown in Fig. 8B.

When using paper capacitors as by-

Fig. 8 — RF filters using LC components, A, and RC components, B. These filters are used to prevent feedback caused by RF pickup on the microphone lead.

Fig. 9 — Typical solid-state compressor circuits. The circuit at A works on the AGC principle, while that at B is a forward-acting compressor.

passes, be sure the terminal marked "outside foil," often indicated with a black band, is connected to ground. This utilizes the outside foil of the capacitor as a shield around the "hot" foil. When paper or Mylar capacitors are used for coupling between stages, always connect the outside foil terminal to the side of the circuit having the lower impedance to ground.

Driver and Output Stages

Commonly used balanced modulators and transmitting mixers have power outputs too low for consistently effective communications. Most modern grounded-grid linear amplifiers require 30 to 100 watts of exciter output power to drive them to their rated power output. An exciter output amplifier serves to boost the output power to a useful level while providing additional selectivity to reject spurious mixing products.

Two stages are usually required to obtain the necessary power. The stage preceding the output amplifier is called the driver. Some tubes that work well as drivers are the 6CL6, 12BY7, 6EH7 and 6GK6. Since all of these tubes are capable of high gain, instability is sometimes encountered in their use. Parasitic suppression should be included as a matter of course. Some form of neutralization is recommended. Driver stages should be operated in Class A or AB1 to minimize distortion. The higher quiescent dissipation can be handled easily at these power levels. VMOS power FETs are also well suited to SSB driver circuits.

SPEECH PROCESSING

Four basic systems, or a combination thereof, can be used to reduce the peak-to-average ratio, and thus raise the average power level of an SSB signal. They are compression or clipping of the AF wave before it reaches the balanced modulator, and compression or clipping of the RF waveform after the SSB signal has been generated. One form of RF compression, commonly called automatic level control or ALC, is used almost universally in amateur SSB transmitters. Audio processing is also

used to increase the level of audio power contained in the sidebands of an AM transmitter and to maintain constant deviation in an FM transmitter. Both compression and clipping are used in AM systems, while most FM transmitters employ only clipping.

Volume Compression

Although it is obviously desirable to keep the voice level as high as possible, it is difficult to maintain constant voice intensity when speaking into the microphone. To overcome this variable output level, it is possible to use automatic gain control that follows the *average* (not instantaneous) variations in speech amplitude. This can be done by rectifying and filtering some of the audio output and applying the resultant dc to a control electrode in an early stage in the amplifier.

The circuit of Fig. 9A works on this AGC principle. One section of a Signetics NE571N IC is used. The other section can be connected as an expander to restore the dynamic range of received signals that have been compressed in transmission. Operational transconductance amplifier ICs such

as the CA3080 are also well suited for speech-compression service.

When an audio AGC circuit derives control voltage from the output signal, the system is a closed loop. If short attack time is necessary, the rectifier-filter bandwidth must be opened up to allow syllabic modulation of the control voltage. This allows some of the voice-frequency signal to enter the control terminal, causing distortion and instability. Because the syllabic frequency and speech-tone frequencies have relatively small separation, the simpler feedback AGC systems compromise fidelity for fast response.

Problems with loop dynamics in audio AGC systems can be sidestepped by eliminating the loop and using a forward-acting system. The control voltage is derived from the *input* of the amplifier, rather than from the output. Eliminating the feedback loop allows unconditional stability, but the trade-off between response time and fidelity remains. Care must be taken to avoid excessive gain between the signal input and control voltage output. Otherwise, the transfer characteristic can reverse; that is, an increase in input level can cause a

Fig. 10 — This diagram illustrates the use of JFETs or silicon diodes to clip positive and negative voice peaks.

decrease in output. A simple forward-acting compressor is shown in Fig. 9B.

To test or adjust a speech compressor, one would apply a single steady tone to the input and measure the input and output signal levels over the dynamic range of the instrument. The single-tone test may indicate gross distortion, but one cannot judge the speech performance by this result. Provided the release time is longer than the time between syllables, the compressor will generate distortion only during brief signal peaks.

Speech Clipping and Filtering

In speech waveforms the average power content is considerably less than in a sine wave of the same peak amplitude. If the high amplitude peaks are clipped off, the remaining waveform will have a considerably higher ratio of average power to peak amplitude. Although clipping distorts the waveform and the result therefore does not sound exactly like the original, it is possible to obtain a worthwhile increase in audio power without sacrificing intelligibility. Once the system is properly adjusted *it will be impossible to overdrive* the modulator stage of the transmitter because the maximum output amplitude is fixed.

By itself, clipping generates high-order harmonics and therefore will cause splatter. To prevent this, the audio frequencies above those needed for intelligible speech must be filtered out *after* clipping and *before* modulation. The filter required for this purpose should have relatively little attenuation below about 2500 Hz, but high attenuation for all frequencies above 3000 Hz.

There is a loss in naturalness with "deep" clipping, even though the voice is highly intelligible. With moderate clipping levels (6 to 12 dB) there is almost no change in "quality" but the voice power is increased considerably.

Before drastic clipping can be used, the speech signal must be amplified several times more than is necessary for normal modulation. Also the hum and noise must be much lower than the tolerable level in ordinary amplification, because the noise in the output of the amplifier increases in proportion to the gain.

In the circuit of Fig. 10B a simple diode clipper is shown following a two-transistor preamplifier section. The 1N3754s conduct at approximately 0.7 volt of audio and provide positive- and negative-peak clipping of the speech waveform. A 47-kΩ resistor and a 0.02-μF capacitor follow the clipper to form a simple RC filter for attenuating the high-frequency components generated by the clipping action, as discussed earlier. Any silicon diodes may be used in place of the 1N3754s. Germanium diodes (type 1N34A) can also be used, but will clip at a slightly lower peak audio level.

SSB Speech Processing

Compression and clipping are related, as both have fast attack times. And when the compressor release is made quite short, the effect on the waveform approaches that of clipping. Speech processing is most effective when accomplished at radio frequencies, although a combination of AF clipping and compression can produce worthwhile results. The advantage of an outboard audio speech processor is that no in-

ternal modifications are necessary to the SSB transmitter with which it will be used.

To understand the effect of SSB speech processing, consider that basic RF waveforms without processing have high peaks but low average power. With proper processing, the amount of average power is raised considerably. Fig. 11 shows a comparison of received signal-to-noise ratio with different forms of signal processing. An advantage of several decibels for RF clipping (for 20 dB of processing) is shown over any other type of processing.

Investigations by W6JES, reported in January 1969 *QST,* showed that, for a transmitted signal using 15 dB of audio clipping from a remote receiver, the intelligibility threshold was improved nearly 4 dB over a signal with no clipping. Increasing the AF clipping level to 25 dB gave an additional 1.5 dB improvement in intelligibility. Audio compression was found to be valuable for maintaining relatively con-

Fig. 11 — The improvement in received signal-to-noise ratio obtained by the simple forms of signal processing.

(A)

(C)

(B)

(D)

Fig. 12 — Two-tone envelope patterns with various degrees of RF clipping. All envelope patterns are formed using tones of 600 and 1000 Hz. At A, clipping threshold; B, 5 dB of clipping; C, 10 dB of clipping; D, 15 dB of clipping.

stant average-volume speech, but such a compressor added little to the intelligibility threshold at the receiver — only about 1 to 2 dB.

Evaluation of RF clipping from the receive side with constant-level speech, and filtering to restore the original bandwidth, resulted in an improved intelligibility threshold of 4.5 dB with 10 dB of clipping. Raising the clipping level to 18 dB gave an additional 4 dB improvement at the receiver, or 8.5 dB total increase. The improvement of the intelligibility of a weak SSB signal at a distant receiver can thus be substantially improved by RF clipping. The effect of such clipping on a two-tone test pattern is shown in Fig. 12.

Automatic level control, although a form of RF speech processing, has found its primary application in maintaining the

Fig. 13 — At A, control voltage obtained by sampling the RF output voltage of the final amplifier. The diode back bias, 40 volts or so maximum, may be taken from any convenient positive voltage source in the transmitter. R may be a linear control having a maximum resistance on the order of 50 kΩ. D1 may be a 1N34A or similar germanium diode.

At B, control voltage obtained from the grid circuit of a Class AB1 tetrode amplifier. T1 is an interstage audio transformer having a turns ratio, secondary to primary, of 2 or 3 to 1. An inexpensive transformer may be used, since the primary and secondary currents are negligible. D1 may be a 1N34A or similar type. Time constant R2-C3 is discussed in the text.

At C, control voltage is obtained from the grid of a Class AB1 tetrode amplifier and amplified by a triode audio stage.

At D, ALC system used in the Collins 32S-3 transmitter. At E, applying control voltage to the tube or, at F, to the linear IC-controlled amplifier.

peak RF output of an SSB transmitter at a relatively constant level, desirably below the point at which the final amplifier is overdriven during peaks in the audio input. These typical ALC systems, shown in Fig. 13, by the nature of their design time constants offer a limited increase in the ratio of transmitted average power to peak envelope power. A value in the region of 2 to 5 dB is typical. An ALC circuit with shorter time constants will function as an RF syllabic compressor, producing up to 6 dB improvement in the intelligibility threshold at a distant receiver. The Collins Radio Company used an ALC system with dual time constants (Fig. 13D) in their S/Line transmitters, and this has proved to be quite effective.

Heat is an extremely important consideration in the use of any speech processor that increases the ratio of average to peak power. Many transmitters, in particular those using television sweep tubes, simply are not built to withstand the effects of increased average input, either in the final-amplifier tube(s) or in the power supply. If heating in the final tube is the limiting factor, adding a cooling fan may be a satisfactory answer.

Compandoring

Compressing the audio signal prior to modulation for more efficient use of the transmitter power has been widely used by amateurs. However, by compressing only the amplitude peaks, background noise increases relative to the peaks. A significant advantage can be obtained by expanding the compressed audio at the receiver. The term "compandor" is a fusion of the terms "compressor" and "expandor." The positive effects of compandoring are illustrated in Fig. 14. A short segment of the speech time waveform is shown in Fig. 14A. When compressed and transmitted, this waveform becomes noisy because of compression, and also from the added circuit and radio channel noise. This is shown in Fig. 14B. Notice the increased noise between the two passages of speech. After the waveform is processed by an amplitude expander (the receiving portion of an amplitude compandor), the waveform appears as shown in Fig. 14C. The noise during the quiet passage has been reduced relative to the high-level passages. Although the S/N ratio during the loud passage is not as good as the input waveform, the ratio for the overall passage is much better than it would be without expansion. Noise during loud passages is not nearly as objectionable as noise between passages of speech.

Using a two-to-one amplitude compandor* (Signetics NE571N), tests performed for the FCC indicated a measurable 12- to 15-dB improvement with a full amplitude compandor (compression on

*A two-to-one amplitude compandor yields a compression of 1 dB out for every 2 dB in and an expansion of 2 dB out for every 1 dB in.

transmit and expansion on receive). When only compression was used, significant S/N ratio reduction resulted, even though a higher average transmitter power was being used.

An amplitude expander circuit is shown in Fig. 15. It is important to realize that the amplitude compandor will improve the S/N ratio, but only when sufficient signal is present for use as a reference. Thus, it has a thresholding effect. As long as the received signal is a few decibels above the noise, the expander can expand on the basis of the reference to provide a communications channel with a cleaner signal over a wider dynamic range. However, when the signal level drops into the noise, the expander will not operate properly. The S/N improvement is limited, but the improvement over the useful range is worthwhile. If we consider that a certain S/N ratio and corresponding voice quality were required, use of an amplitude compandor would allow the achievement of this goal with less transmitter power. In this respect the amplitude compandor can achieve the same quality S/N ratio with 12-15 dB less transmitted power. This is a significant power savings and can have a definite impact on the quality of communications per watt of transmitter power.

Amplitude-Compandored Single Sideband

Amplitude-compandored single-sideband (ACSSB) was developed to serve the land-mobile industry. Its purpose was to reduce the spectrum requirements per channel from that presently required for FM. Ordinary SSB operation was found to be unsatisfactory for operators accustomed to noise-free FM and who were not trained communicators. The fine tuning required for SSB was a nuisance, as was signal fading. ACSSB was introduced as a way of achieving the spectrum savings of SSB over FM, and provide mobile users everything they were accustomed to with FM, including signaling.

A conventional SSB transmission has a suppressed carrier. In order to demodulate the signal at the receiver, the missing carrier must be replaced. At the higher frequencies this becomes difficult. In ACSSB, a pilot tone is added to the audio, sufficiently separated in frequency and filtered so the two do not interfere. Although there is some variation among manufacturers, the pilot tone is usually 3 or 3.1 kHz. The pilot power level is about 10 dB below the voice peak power. Thus, with no voice modulation the transmitter has an output power of approximately 1/10th that when there is voice modulation.

At the receiver, the pilot tone is compared with an internal reference oscillator in a phase-locked loop circuit. The difference voltage thus produced is used to shift the receiver local oscillator until the frequency error is eliminated. The time constant of the phase-locked loop is short enough to be ignored by the user and to be compatible with tone decoders used for signal purposes.

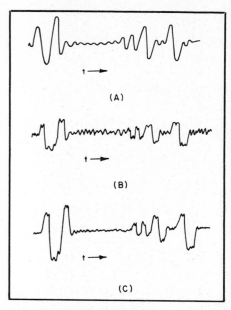

Fig. 14 — Speech waveforms for the amplitude compandor, showing amplitude (vertical axis) vs. time, t. At A is the input waveform, at B the compressed waveform with additional circuit noise as might be received, and at C the expanded waveform. Note the improvement in signal-to-noise ratio upon expansion after reception.

Fig. 15 — Amplitude expander circuit.

The compandor thresholding effect provides an operator with a sensation similar to the capture effect in FM. Thus, when the signal strengths are high, FM and ACSSB give comparable results with noticeably less flutter on ACSSB than on FM.

In non-cellular applications, ACSSB can pack nearly twice as many signals into a given band than NBFM. The pilot tones compensate for some of the shortcomings of SSB, but with additional complexity. In a channelized, cellular environment such as the land-mobile service, however, narrowband FM, with its superior adjacent-channel protection and capture effect, offers better spectrum efficiency and much greater frequency re-use capability.

ACSSB is a prime candidate for Amateur Radio experimentation. One possible application is in satellite work. ACSSB, with its pilot-tone system, may provide a reliable, automatic way to compensate for the Doppler shift inherent in most amateur satellite links.

MORSE CODE

Previous sections have been concerned

RC ACTIVE
BANDPASS FILTER

1 — Select value for C1, C2
C1 = C2
2 — Select Q
3 — Select A_v
4 — Choose f_o
then

$$R1 = \frac{Q}{A_v \omega_o C1}$$

$$R2 = \frac{Q}{(2Q^2 - A_v) \omega_o C1}$$

$$R3 = \frac{2Q}{\omega_o C1}$$

$$R4 = R5 \text{ for } V_{REF} = \frac{V_{cc}}{2}$$

$$R4, R5 \approx .02 \times R3$$

Fig. 16 — Basic circuit for an RC active band-pass filter. One pole is shown along with the fundamental equations for finding the resistance values needed.

$f_o = 900 \text{ Hz}$ $A_v = 1$ $\omega_o = 2\pi f_{o(Hz)}$

$Q = 5$ C1, C2 = 0.00068 μF

$$R1 = \frac{5}{(1)\,(6.28 \times 900)\,(0.00068 \times 10^{-6})}$$

$$= 1,300,948 \text{ ohms}$$

$$R2 = \frac{5}{[2(25) - 1]\,[6.28 \times 900\,(0.00068 \times 10^{-6})]} = 26,550 \text{ ohms}$$

$$R3 = \frac{10}{(6.28 \times 900)\,(0.00068 \times 10^{-6})} = 2,601,896 \text{ ohms}$$

$$R4, R5 \approx 2,601,896 \times 0.02 = 52,018 \text{ ohms}$$

Fig. 17 — A design example based on the circuit of Fig. 16.

primarily with voice communications, but Morse code is equally important in Amateur Radio. With computers or other logic circuits, Morse code can be copied by machine to present a visual display of the text being received, but by far the majority of operators copy code "by ear." To do this, of course, it is necessary to *hear* the received code.

Most operators prefer to receive code signals in a frequency range from 500 to 800 Hz. The ear is better able to distinguish two tones of fixed frequency separation at low pitch rather than at higher pitches. In other words, if an undesired signal is present at a frequency 200 Hz removed from a desired signal, the ear can better distinguish the desired signal if the tones are 500 Hz and 700 Hz, instead of 1100 and 1300 Hz. Thus, the ear is its own form of selective filter. For this reason, some operators prefer to adjust the receiver tuning for lower pitches yet, in the order of 200 to 300 Hz for the desired signal.

Morse code signals occupy significantly less bandwidth than do voice signals. Therefore, a much narrower filter may be used for code reception than is possible for receiving voice transmissions. Decreasing the received bandwidth improves the signal-to-noise ratio under a given set of conditions, as well as improving the selectivity.

If a receiver lacks IF selectivity, an outboard filter may be used ahead of the speaker or headphones.

Op Amps as Audio Filters

One of the more common uses to which operational amplifiers (op amps) are put can be seen in the RC active audio-filter field. Op amps have the distinct advantage of providing gain and variable parameters when used as audio filters. Passive filters that contain L and C elements are generally committed to some fixed frequency, and they exhibit an insertion loss. Finally, op amps contribute to the attainment of miniaturization that is seldom possible with bulky inductors in a passive type of audio filter.

Although RC active filters can be built with bipolar transistors, the modern approach is to use operational amplifiers. The use of an op-amp IC, such as a type 741, results in a compact filter pole that will provide stable operation. Only five connections are made to the IC, and the gain of the filter section, plus the frequency characteristic, is determined by the choice of components external to the IC.

Although there are numerous applications for RC active filters, their principal use in amateur work is that of establishing selectivity at audio frequencies. One or two poles may be used as a band-pass or low-pass section for improving the passband characteristics during SSB or AM reception. Up to four filter poles are frequently used to acquire selectivity for CW or RTTY reception. The greater the number of poles, up to a practical limit, the sharper the skirt response of the filter. Not only does a well-designed RC filter help to reduce QRM, but it improves the signal-to-noise ratio in some receiving systems.

Considerable design data is found in the National Semiconductor Corp. application note. A thorough treatment of Norton amplifiers is given, centering on the LM3900 current-differencing type of op amp. Design information is included for high-, low- and band-pass types of RC active audio filters. The simplified design data

presented here are based on the technique used in AN72-15.

Fig. 16 shows a single band-pass filter pole and gives the equations for obtaining the desired values for the resistors if the gain, Q, f_o and C1-C2 values are chosen. C1 and C2 are equal in value and should be high-Q, temperature-stable components. Polystyrene capacitors are excellent for use in this part of the circuit. Disc-ceramic capacitors *are not recommended*. R4 and R5 are equal in value and are used to establish the op-amp reference voltage. This is $V_{cc}/2$.

C1 and C2 should be standard values of capacitance. The filter design is less complicated when C1 and C2 serve as the starting point for the equations. Otherwise some awkward values for C1 and C2 might result. The resistance values can be "fudged" to the nearest standard value after the equations have been worked. The important consideration is that matched values must be used when more than one filter pole is employed. For most amateur work it will be satisfactory to use five percent, ½-watt, composition resistors. If the resistor and capacitor values are not held reasonably tight in tolerance for a multipole filter, the f_o for each pole may be different, however slight. The result is a wide nose for the response, or even some objectionable passband ripple.

Fig. 17 illustrates the design of a single-pole band-pass filter. An arbitrary f_o of 900 Hz has been specified, but for CW reception the operator may prefer something much lower — 200 to 700 Hz. An A_V (gain) of 1 (unity) and a Q of 5 are stated. Both the gain and the Q can be increased for a single-section filter if desired, but for a multisection RC active filter it is best to restrict the gain to 1 or 2 and use a maximum Q of 5. This will help prevent unwanted filter "ringing" and audio instability.

C1 and C2 are 680-pF polystyrene capacitors. Other standard values can be used from, say, 500 to 2000 pF. The limiting factor will be the resultant resistor values. For certain design parameters and

C1-C2 values, unwieldy resistance values may result from the equations. If this happens, select a new value for C1 and C2.

The resistance values assigned to R1 through R5, inclusive, are the nearest standard values to those obtained from the equations. The principal effect from this is a slight alteration of f_o and A_V.

In a practical application the RC active filter should be inserted in the low-level audio stages. This will prevent overloading the filter during the reception of strong signals. The receiver AF gain control should be used between the audio preamplifier and the input of the RC active filter for best results. If audio-derived AGC is used in the receiver, the RC active filter will give best performance when it is contained within the AGC loop. Information on other types of active filters is given by Bloom in July 1980 *QST*.

LOUDSPEAKERS AND HEADPHONES

The counterpart for the microphone at the transmitter is the loudspeaker or headphones at the receiver. These devices are transducers that convert electrical energy into vibrations of a diaphragm, thereby setting up sound waves.

Dynamic loudspeakers, or simply speakers, use a diaphragm of heavy paper or other thin material. This diaphragm is formed in the shape of a shallow cone, with its rim attached to the speaker frame. At the apex of the cone is a small core on which a coil of fine wire is wound. The core and the coil are free to move, and are suspended in the field of a permanent magnet. When a direct current is passed through the coil, the apex of the cone or diaphragm is deflected in one direction. When the current is removed, the diaphragm returns to its resting position. A direct current of the opposite polarity will deflect the diaphragm in the opposite direction. An alternating current causes the diaphragm to move back and forth at the frequency of the current and thereby set up sound waves, assuming the frequency is not too high for the diaphragm to follow.

Speakers are available from an inch or less to many inches in diameter. The larger speakers are more efficient at reproducing lower frequencies. For the best audio quality, a speaker should be mounted in a cabinet or some form of baffle. Even a good quality speaker, if operated in open air, will have a "tinny" sound — reproducing only intermediate frequencies. Low frequencies will be conspicuously absent. A baffle or cabinet serves to reinforce or enhance the low frequencies. Small speakers mounted at the bottom of a small chassis leave something to be desired also when it comes to audio fidelity.

Commonly available loudspeakers are designed with an impedance in the range of 4 to 16 Ω. Another impedance range available is 45 Ω; speakers in this range are often used in intercommunication stations. In this application the speaker doubles as a microphone for talking — sound pressure waves move the diaphragm and the attached coil in the magnetic field, thereby inducing a voltage into the coil.

Headphones operate on the same general principle as dynamic speakers. In fact, some high-quality headsets for hi-fi or stereo listening use small dynamic speakers. A thin, flat, metal diaphragm is used in most headsets. In operation the diaphragm is set in motion by a varying magnetic field caused by current flowing through the headset coils, which are wound on a magnetic core. Headphone impedances of 4 to 8 Ω are the most popular because a reasonable amount of power can be coupled to the phones with relatively low audio voltages. Headphones are also available in an impedance range of 500 to 600 Ω, and in the 2000-Ω range. Those in the 2000-Ω range are referred to as high-impedance headphones. They may be operated with relatively low currents, but do require a higher voltage amplitude than phones of lower impedance.

Video

For the sighted, much human communication is visual. In personal communication we watch faces, hands and bodies for visual cues and clues. Your grandparents used to listen to the radio — today the family watches television. Several hours a day is average. Visual communication is a part of Amateur Radio.

QST began carrying articles on TV in 1925. Those early experiments used crude mechanical methods. Nevertheless, radio amateurs were transmitting pictures. As early as 1928 a *QST* author pointed out the possibility of electronic television. The days of the motor-driven scanning disc were numbered. Introduction of the moderately priced iconoscope in 1940 made electronic television a practical reality for the amateur. By 1960, amateurs were transmitting color-TV signals.

Vision

Light is physical energy in the form of electromagnetic radiation. The visible light range falls between microwaves and X rays, as shown in Fig. 18. The human eye is sensitive to only a relatively narrow band of electromagnetic radiation. That band falls between the wavelengths of 400 and 720 nanometers, approximately.

Solar radiation contains all the visible wavelengths. Other light sources have different wavelength distributions. Incandescent sources tend to have more orange or yellow light; fluorescent light tends to be more bluish.

Physical objects selectively absorb light energy. Reflected light, therefore, has a different energy distribution than that of the original light. It is that difference that makes vision possible. Differences in reflected light account for the perception of brightness, texture and color.

Light enters the eye, and is focused by the lens onto the retina. The amount of light entering the eye is controlled by the iris. See Fig. 19. Two types of light sensors make up the retina — rods and cones.

Rods are sensitive only to black, white and shades of gray. Cones allow us to perceive color. Rods are more sensitive than cones — that is they work at lower light levels. That is why we can see color in the sky at twilight or dawn, but we can only perceive black, white and gray for the objects on the ground about us. The rela-

Fig. 18 — The electromagnetic spectrum from VHF to gamma rays.

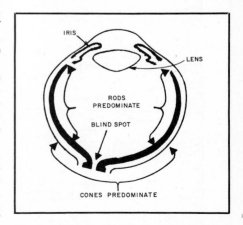

Fig. 19 — Cross-sectional view of the human eye. The retina contains rods and cones (see text). There are neither rods nor cones in the blind spot — that is where the optic nerve enters the eye.

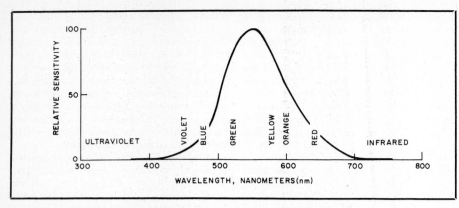

Fig. 20 — Relative sensitivity of the human eye to light at various wavelengths.

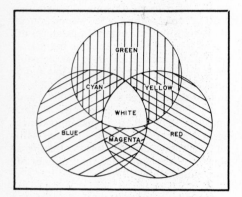

Fig. 21 — The three primary colors are red, green and blue. The primaries combine, two at a time, to form the secondary colors, yellow, cyan and magenta. White is a combination of red, green and blue.

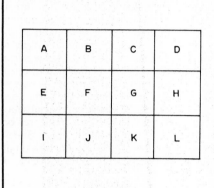

Fig. 22 — A picture can be described by dividing it into parts and then describing the parts.

tive sensitivity of the human eye to light varies with wavelength. See Fig. 20.

Color

Impulses from the rods and cones in the retina travel along the optic nerve to the central nervous system. There the impulses are "seen" as light and color. Any number of different energy distribution combinations may be perceived as the same color. The eyes do not sort out wavelengths like a prism. Cones are of three "kinds"; each kind being more sensitive to light in a particular portion of the visible spectrum. The areas of senstivity are known as red, blue and green light. Color is not a property of the electromagnetic energy that we call light. Rather, color is a psychological experience and a perceptual response to that energy.

It is possible to reproduce any color by combining in proper proportions three primary colors. The primaries are red, green and blue, as shown in Fig. 21. Combinations of equal amounts of two of the primaries form the secondary colors: yellow, cyan and magenta. White is a combination of all three primaries in the proper proportions.

Combining light is an additive process. A green light and a red light falling on a white wall make a yellow glow. This should not be confused with paints or pigments — they combine in a subtractive process.

This trichromatic system of color perception makes the transmission of color TV pictures possible. Light from the scene being transmitted is separated into red, green and blue components. These are transmitted to the receiver where they are simultaneously displayed on a screen. Through the eye and the central nervous system, the color picture is "reassembled" by the viewer.

Flicker

A flickering light can appear to be continuous. When light reaches the eye for a brief instant, the eye responds, sending the information to the brain. However, when the light stops, the eye continues to send to the brain for an additional fraction of a second. If you have ever experimented with a strobe light or viewed a motion picture, you should know that light does not have to be continuous for the eye to perceive it as such. The fact that the eye "retains" an image for a fraction of a second after it has gone makes television possible. This retention of an image is called persistence. For high-intensity light, a rate of 50 to 60 flashes per second results in no visible flicker.

PICTURE TRANSMISSION

If you wish to transmit a picture to another location, it is neither practical nor necessary to send all the information in that picture all at one time. Television and facsimile transmission systems send pictures "a piece at a time." In Fig. 22 an area has

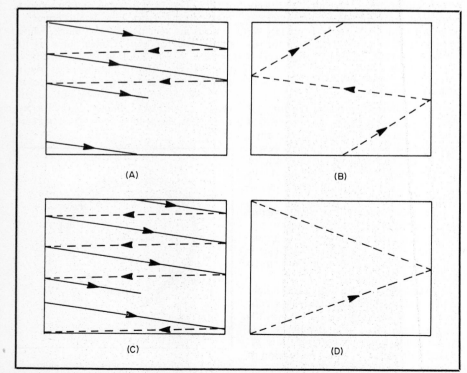

Fig. 23 — Interlaced scanning as used in TV. In field one, 262½ lines are scanned (A). At the end of field one, the electron scanning beam is returned to the top of the picture area (B). Scanning lines in field two (C) fall between the lines of field one. At the end of field two, the scanning beam is again returned to the top where scanning continues with field one (D).

been divided into a mosaic of 12 squares. If the total area contained a picture, the scene could be described by detailing the contents of the individual squares in sequence (such as A through L). That is the concept behind television. Television (and facsimile) systems ''divide'' a picture in many more than 12 portions. In a workable system, each portion would be so small that it would contain only a single value of brightness (and color). Each tiny portion becomes a picture element or pixel, as it is commonly called.

The number of horizontal lines and the number of ''pieces'' along a line varies. There are three standards used worldwide for television broadcasting. Amateurs may use commercial transmission standards for TV. They are not limited to commercial standards, however. Amateurs use slow-scan TV and many experiment with other standards and systems. See Chapter 20 for information on Amateur TV and facsimile transmission.

This chapter will cover the theory of television. Discussion details are based on U.S. commercial standards — fast-scan TV (FSTV).

The Scanning Process

Scanning is the way a picture is divided sequentially into pieces for transmission or presentation (viewing). A total of 525 scan lines comprise a frame (complete picture) in the U.S. television system. Thirty frames are generated each second. Each frame consists of two fields, each field containing 262-½ lines. Sixty fields are generated each second. Scan lines from one field fall between (interlace) lines from the other field. The scanned area is called the television raster.

Fig. 23 illustrates the principle involved in scanning an electron beam (in the pickup or receiving device) across and down to produce the television raster. Scanning of field one begins in the upper left of the picture area. The electron beam is swept across the picture to the right side. At the end of the line, the beam is ''turned off'' or blanked and returned to the left side where the process repeats. In the meantime, the beam has also been moved slightly downward. At the end of 262½ horizontal scans (lines), the beam is blanked and rapidly returned to the top of the picture area. At that point, scanning of field two begins. Notice that this time the beam starts scanning from the top in the middle of the picture. For that reason, the scanning lines of field two will fall half way between the lines of field one. At the end of 262½ lines the beam is rapidly returned to the top of the picture area again. Scanning continues — this time field one of the next frame.

Because the picture area is scanned top to bottom 60 times each second, there is no flicker. Because the entire picture area is scanned only 30 times each second, bandwidth is reduced.

It should be obvious that the horizontal

Fig. 24 — Electron beam deflection in TV cameras and receivers is usually accomplished by using two sets of coils. This is called electromagnetic deflection.

Fig. 25 — Current waveform used in electromagnetic deflection coils for deflection of the electron scanning beam.

Fig. 26 — Cross-sectional view of a vidicon.

and vertical oscillators that control the electron beam movement must be ''locked together'' for the two fields to interlace properly. If the frequencies of these oscillators are not locked, proper interlace will be lost and vertical resolution or detail will be degraded.

Deflection

In most TV applications, the electron beam is scanned (deflected) by means of two pairs of coils. Because the deflection of the electron beam is accomplished magnetically, coils for horizontal deflection are located above and below the beam. Vertical deflection coils are located on either side of the beam. See Fig. 24.

The electron beam is deflected as a result of a ''sawtooth'' current passing through the deflection coils (Fig. 25). The frequency of the horizontal sawtooth current is 15,750 Hz. A similar waveform with a frequency of 60 Hz causes vertical deflection. The electron beam is turned off during beam retrace time by a process called blanking. Blanking is only associated with the electron beam and does not affect the deflection coil current or the resulting magnetic fields.

THE TELEVISION CAMERA

Most modern TV cameras use vidicon tubes or vidicon derivatives. It is in the vidicon that optical energy is converted into a video (electrical) signal. The construction of a typical vidicon can be seen in Fig. 26.

Details, such as tube size, number of grids and the type of focus and deflection used, vary among the different types.

The cathode is the source of the electrons that form the electron beam. Grid 1 is a tubular element mounted concentric to the beam that controls the quantity of beam electrons, or the beam intensity. Grid 2, another tubular element, accelerates the beam electrons toward the target. Grid 3 operates in conjunction with an external focus coil to concentrate the beam into a focused electron stream at the target. Grid 4 is a screen mesh that is used to decelerate beam electrons and ensure that the beam strikes the target perpendicularly. Grid 4 also collects any excess beam electrons that are not attracted to the target.

The photosensitive element is made up of layers that are bonded to the faceplate glass of the tube. The layer directly adjacent to the faceplate glass is a transparent coating that is a conducting material. This coating is the signal electrode of the vidicon. Deposited on top of this layer are two more layers, the three forming the vidicon target. Adjacent to the first layer is a photoresistive layer that is backed by a conductive mosaic. A positive voltage is applied to the target to attract the beam electrons.

The target acts as a ''leaky capacitor'' at each point where the electron beam strikes the target. In other words the target can be viewed as a large number of small capacitors side by side distributed over its

Fig. 27 — Vidicon operation depicted. See text.

Fig. 28 — Vidicon equivalent circuit.

surface. On one side the capacitors are all joined together with a common connection for the output signal; on the other side the capacitors are left floating where they are exposed to the electron beam. The dielectric of these capacitors is the photoresistive layer of the target. Resistance of the middle layer is reduced in proportion to the intensity of light falling on it. This creates, in effect, a "leaky" capacitance with the amount of leakage proportional to the light falling on the target.

Target operation is depicted in Fig. 27. The light image consists of a series of black, gray and white areas. Where the image is black, the resistance of the photoresistive layer is very high. Where the image is white, the resistance is low. In the white areas, the

positive potential on the target attracts many electrons from the photoconductive mosaic — that leaves an area with a high positive potential. That is shown in Fig. 27 by a large plus sign on the photoconductive mosaic. In the gray area fewer electrons are attracted across the "leaky capacitor." That leaves a less positively charged area than for white. In the black portion, the charge is essentially zero.

Any given element of the target is scanned by the electron beam once for each frame (two fields) or every 33 ms. The charge on the floating side of the target is neutralized each time the beam scans it. As electrons are added to the back of the target, other electrons are drawn off through the target connection. This causes

varying amounts of current to flow through the target connection as the scanning beam sweeps the picture area. The amount of current flow is proportional to the amount of light in a given area. In the black areas no change in resistance occurs and the actual resistance is the static resistance of the photoresistive material (Fig. 28). Some current will flow, however, and this is called the dark current of the vidicon.

Electrons flowing from the target through the load resistor create the signal voltage or video signal that corresponds to the optical image on the face of the vidicon. The signal polarity across the load resistor is positive going for low light areas and negative going for the high light areas as shown in Fig. 29. A properly adjusted vidicon will produce approximately 0.3 μA in the high light areas and as little as 0.02 μA (dark current) in the low light areas. The difference between the dark current and the maximum current is the useful signal current.

Blanking pulses are applied to the vidicon cathode to turn off the electron beam during retrace time of the scanning beam. Usually the pulse shape at the output of the vidicon is not as clean as shown in Fig. 29. The signal requires processing.

Good signal-to-noise ratio is a function of several factors. Two factors you can control are plenty of light and only enough beam current to discharge the white highlights.

It is wise to keep scene contrast to a minimum. In other words, keep the lighting flat for best results. About 100 foot candles should be enough illumination. Too little light results in noisy video. Too much light

Fig. 29 — The vidicon output is a combination of video and blanking. See text.

Fig. 30 — Waveform showing horizontal sync pulses.

Fig. 31 — Vertical sync. Field 1 is shown at A, field 2 at B.

Table 1

Standard Video Levels

	IEEE Units	%PEV	%PEP
Zero carrier	120	0	0
White	100	12.5	1.6
Black	7.5	70	50
Blanking	0	75	56
Sync tip	−40	100	100

runs up the electrical bill and can be uncomfortable — even with air conditioning.

Synchronizing Pulses

To ensure a stable picture at the receiver, the scanning process at the transmitting and receiving ends must be synchronized. Fig. 30 shows the pulses used to control the horizontal scan. They are called horizontal sync pulses, and occur once per line — a frequency of 15,750 Hz. Horizontal sync pulses occur during the horizontal blanking interval.

Vertical scanning is controlled by vertical sync pulses, which can be seen in Fig. 31. The vertical sync pulse is preceded and followed by six equalizing pulses. The vertical sync pulse has a duration of three line times and is slotted or serrated at the end of each half-line time. Blanking turns off the electron beam during vertical retrace and sync.

The equalizing pulses are twice the frequency and approximately half the duration of horizontal sync pulses (2 equalizing pulses per line). The equalizing pulses

Fig. 32 — Composite video waveform. For transmission, sync is positive and white is negative.

Fig. 33 — Field of view nomograph.

ensure that there is always a pulse to lock the horizontal sweep to at the beginning of each line. Line 1 of field 1 begins at the first equalizing pulse and vertical sync starts at line 4. In field 2, line 1 begins at the second equalizing pulse and vertical sync starts at line 3½. This creates the ½-line offset that generates the interlaced scanning pattern shown in Fig. 23.

Composite Video

Video, as it comes from the camera shown in Fig. 29 is not suitable for transmission. Horizontal and vertical sync must be added first. The composite video signal contains video, blanking and sync. See Table 1. Fig. 32 shows these three elements combined for two horizontal lines of the visual image of Fig. 27.

Compact, hand-held cameras today require only power and light to generate a composite video signal. Some older cameras and most TV studio cameras require horizontal and vertical sync signals from an external source. Those signals can be provided by a sync generator.

Camera Optics

The camera lens is used primarily to focus the scene image on the face of the pickup tube. The two basic characteristics of lenses are focal length (FL) and diameter

Fig. 34 — Cathode ray tube using electrostatic deflection and focusing.

of the lens opening (related to f-stop).

Lens FL is the distance from the optical center of the lens to the point behind the lens where the image comes into focus. For example, if an object at infinity comes into focus 1 inch behind a lens the FL is 1 in.

Focal length governs the magnification of the image and therefore the field of view of the lens. Long focal length lenses bring objects up closer and the field of view is less. The field of view of a lens used with a camera is related to the scanned area by the ratio:

$$FL/w = D/W \qquad \text{(Eq. 1)}$$

where
  FL = focal length of the lens
  w = width of the scanned area in the same units as FL
  D = distance to the subject
  W = width of the field in the same units as D

The image size of the scanned area of a typical vidicon is 0.375 in high × 0.50 in wide. If a 1-in lens is used, the width of the field of view would be:

$$W = D \times 0.5 \text{ in}/1 \text{ in}$$

If the subject were 5 ft away from the camera the field of view would be 2.5 ft wide (and 1.875 ft high).

This same equation can be used to determine the position of a given sized object to fill the screen. Example: Use Eq. 1 to determine how far from the camera with the 1-inch lens a 2-ft wide card should be placed to fill the screen. The answer is 4 ft.

By rearranging Eq. 1, you can determine the focal length of the lens required to view a scene of a given width at a given distance. For example, if you wish to view a scene 10 ft wide at a distance of 10 feet the lens must have a FL of 0.5 in.

$$FL = w \times D/W = 0.5 \times 10/10 = 0.5$$

Fig. 33 is a nomograph that can be used to determine these relationships easily.

F Stops

The lens iris of a TV camera operates like the iris of the human eye. If you suddenly look into a bright light, the iris of your eye closes down to admit less light. Since camera tubes operate over a limited light level range, the camera lens iris must be used to control the amount of light striking the pickup tube.

The f stop of a lens is a function of the FL and lens diameter with the iris wide open:

$$f = FL/d \qquad \text{(Eq. 2)}$$

where
  f = f-stop number
  FL = focal length of the lens
  d = diameter of the iris opening in the same units as FL

Use Eq. 2 to prove that a lens with an 1-in FL and an iris opening of 0.66 in has an f-stop number of 1.5. Lenses are referred to as "fast lenses" or "slow lenses." These are expressions that refer to lens performance based on f-stop number. As the f-stop number of a lens increases, the opening size decreases and less light passes through the lens. The amount of light passing through the lens is inversely proportional to the square of the f-stop numbers. For example, the amount of light passing through an f/1.5 lens compared to an f/3 lens is:

$$(f - 3/f - 1.5)^2 = 4$$

The f/1.5 lens passes four times as much

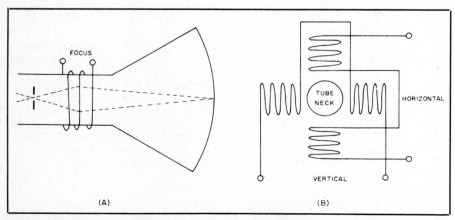

Fig. 35 — Electromagnetic focus is shown at A and deflection at B. The drawings show the physical location of the windings.

Fig. 36 — An antenna, remotely tuned converter and a black-and-white TV set comprise the major components of the ATV receiving system.

light as the f/3 lens. To put it another way, when you set an f/1.5 lens iris for f/3, light passing through the lens is reduced to one quarter of the original amount.

Depth of Field

Depth of field describes how much of the scene, from front to rear, is in focus. The larger the f-stop number used with a lens the greater is the depth of field. Also, the shorter the focal length of a lens the more depth of field it has.

There is no substitute for a good lens — beware of bargains! In choosing a lens, many other qualities should be considered. A discussion of those qualities is beyond the scope of this *Handbook*.

The TV Picture Tube

A picture or cathode-ray tube (CRT) similar to those used in oscilloscopes is shown in Fig. 34. The heater and cathode supply a stream of electrons that is controlled by the grid. Focus of the stream to a single point at the screen is realized by adjusting the voltage on the focusing anode. Voltage differences between the deflection plates control the deflection of

the electron stream. In Fig. 34 the top vertical deflection plate is positive with respect to the bottom plate. Therefore, the negatively charged electron stream is deflected upward. When the electrons strike the coating on the back of the screen there is a resulting fluorescence. Persistence and color of the fluorescence will depend on the material that coats the back of the screen.

Unlike an oscilloscope CRT, the modern TV picture tube uses electromagnetic deflection and focus. This is illustrated in Fig. 35. Notice that the top and bottom deflection coils are used to sweep the beam horizontally. That is because they are using the magnetic rather than the electric field for deflection.

Fig. 36 is a block diagram of an ATV receiving station. For best results the converter should be mounted near the antenna. Any TV set may be used after the converter. See Chapter 20 for more information on assembling and operating an ATV station.

TV Sound

In a regular TV channel, the sound is transmitted on an FM carrier 4.5 MHz

higher than the picture carrier. A separate transmitter can be used to generate the sound carrier, but that requires a hard-to-build combiner or a second antenna. It is easy to frequency-modulate the visual carrier, but that requires special circuitry for receiving. An attractive alternative to these methods is to generate an FM sound subcarrier at 4.5 MHz and combine that with the picture information at the video modulator input. Perhaps the easiest way for amateurs to transmit TV sound is to use an FM simplex channel on another band.

In many areas a 2-meter FM simplex channel is used for ATV coordination. This helps minimize interference. Another signal 50 dB weaker can cause noticeable interference to an ATV picture. When the ATV station is sending in-channel sound, the receiving station can transmit on the coordinating frequency; the result is full duplex sound — a most pleasant benefit. Most CQ calls for ATV are heard on the coordinating frequency.

COLOR TV

A color TV camera typically splits light, by means of a prism, into the three primary

Fig. 37 — Modern single-gun color picture tube. Earlier color CRTs used three guns and a shadow mask. The advantage of the single gun type of tube is that it is easier to converge. Convergence occurs when the RGB electron beams illuminate the same aperture in the slotted grill at the same time. That ensures that the constituent parts of the color image are aligned with one another.

Fig. 38 — Details of horizontal sync and blanking for color TV.

Fig. 39 — Rise time is depicted at A, bandwidth at B. See text.

colors — red, green and blue (RGB). A separate tube is used to detect each primary. The RGB outputs are combined to give a luminance (brightness) signal, which is transmitted in the normal way. In addition, difference signals are used to phase-modulate a 3.58-MHz subcarrier (actually 3,579,545 Hz) with the color, or chroma, information.

A color TV receiver is similar to the set shown in Fig. 36. The major difference is in the video detection and display. A simple envelope detector will not do for color reception; the phase-encoded chroma information must be extracted from the 3.58-MHz subcarrier. RGB plus luminance signals are detected and are then used to control three separate electron beams (one per primary) in the picture tube. A typical color picture tube can be seen in Fig. 37.

Eight to 10 cycles of color subcarrier are sent after horizontal sync. See Fig. 38. These are the color-sync burst, or color burst, as it is commonly called. Color burst is used for a subcarrier phase reference in the receiver color detector circuitry synchronous demodulator. Also given in Fig. 38 are the names for the various portions of the horizontal sync and blanking waveform.

Video Frequencies and Bandwidth

The lowest video frequency component is determined by the time rate of change of average luminance of the scene. For a picture that is uniform and unchanging, the lowest frequency component is zero — dc. It would be very difficult to pass a dc signal

Table 2

Relationship of Rise Time and Bandwidth

Rise time (µs)	Bandwidth (MHz)
0.35	1
0.18	2
0.117	3
0.087	4
0.07	5
0.058	6
0.05	7
0.044	8
0.039	9
0.035	10

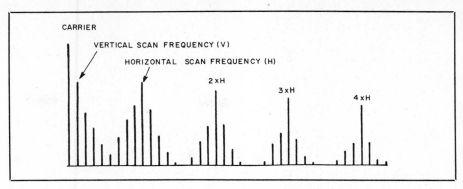

Fig. 40 — Video energy tends to "bunch" at the fundamental and harmonic frequencies of horizontal and video sync.

from the camera, through the transmitter and to the TV picture tube. The first blocking capacitor would spell and end to 0-Hz frequency response! Fortunately, that kind of response is not necessary.

A reference (dc) level can be set for each video scan line through a technique known as clamping. Clamping sets or holds a level at a reference point. Sync and blanking are present for each line of the video frame. The sync tip or the blanking level can be used to "clamp" or set a dc level at the beginning of each line time.

Maximum video frequency must be considered for three different points. First, the maximum frequency generated by the camera. Second, the maximum video frequency passed through the transmitter. Third, the maximum frequency present at the receiver picture tube.

The maximum camera frequency is determined by the size of the electron scanning beam and the bandwidth of the video amplifiers. Bandwidth limitation is based on the ability to reproduce an abrupt level change. Consider a black-to-white transition. It will take some finite amount of time for the level to shift from black to white. The time it takes for levels to shift between the 10 and 90 percent points in the level shift is called the rise time. See Fig. 39A. The bandwidth required to make that shift is depicted in Fig. 39B. The relationship of bandwidth and rise time is:

$$BW = 0.35/T \qquad \text{(Eq. 3)}$$

where

BW = bandwidth in hertz
T = rise time in seconds

The relationship between rise time and bandwidth for some specific values is given in Table 2.

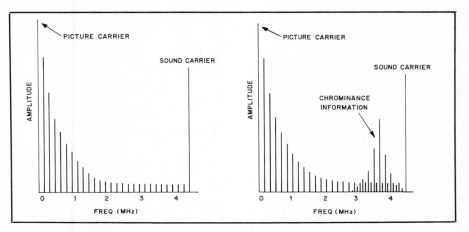

Fig. 41 — With the proper selection of sync and chrominance-subcarrier frequencies, chrominance and luminance information "bunches" fall between each other.

Video cameras typically have a bandwidth of 8 MHz or so. Simple black-and-white cameras may have less, and sophisticated color cameras have more.

The maximum video passed through a transmitter is usually limited by the transmitter circuitry. Broadcast TV transmitters are carefully designed and adjusted to pass video frequencies according to strict standards. Amateurs do not have the same restraints. A little over 4-MHz bandwidth is required to pass carrier and one sideband of a color-TV signal.

A number of factors determine the maximum video frequency to reach the TV receiver picture tube. IF bandwidth is usually the limiting factor. On-screen resolution of the CRT is also limited by the design and construction of the electron-

beam focus and deflection coils.

TV Energy Distribution

The square-wave sync pulses are transmitted at maximum power level. For that reason, power distribution in the video passband is concentrated at the fundamental and harmonics of the horizontal scanning frequency. Surrounding these are sidebands related to the vertical scanning frequency and its harmonics. That distribution is depicted in Fig. 40.

For color TV, chrominance information must be added to the luminance information. Fig. 41 shows how this is done to minimize interference between the two signal components. The chrominance subcarrier has a nonintegral relationship to the horizontal scanning frequency. The energy "bunches" from color and luminance fall between each other.

Chapter 8

Digital Basics

Digital electronics is an important aspect of Amateur Radio. Everything from simple digital circuits to sophisticated microcomputers has found application in modern Amateur Radio systems. Applications include digital communications, code conversion, signal processing, station control, frequency synthesis, amateur satellite telemetry, message handling, word processing and other information-handling operations.

The fundamental principle underlying digital electronics is that a device can have only a finite number of states. In *binary* digital systems there are two discrete states, represented in base-2 arithmetic by the numerals 0 and 1. Although binary digital systems are the most common, trinary (3 states), quaternary (4 states) and other digital systems exist. Digital systems, with their discrete states, are contrasted with analog systems, in which voltages or other quantities vary in a continuous manner. Fig 1 compares a sine wave with a digital approximation of the same waveform.

There are situations where a designer is faced with a choice between digital technology and analog technology. Some problems are best solved by digital circuits, some by analog circuits, and others by circuits using both digital and analog components. To understand Amateur Radio equipment, you will need a good working knowledge of both analog and digital circuits. This chapter examines digital electronics from the simplest digital building blocks to the complex microcomputer.

BINARY QUANTITIES

As stated above, most digital systems are binary. When discussing these systems, each binary digit, or *bit*, is represented by a 1 or a 0. The binary states described as 1 and 0 may represent on and off, a punched hole and the absence of a hole in paper tape or card, or a ''mark'' and ''space'' in a communications transmission. In most electronic digital logic systems, bits are represented by voltage levels. For example, in one common circuit family, 0 volts is a binary 0, and +5 volts is a binary 1. Because it is not always possible to achieve exact voltages in practical circuits, digital circuits consider the signal to be a 1 or 0 if the voltage comes within certain bounds, as shown in Fig 2.

In electronic circuits, changes of state do not occur instantly. The time it takes to go from a 0 to a 1 state is called *rise time*. *Fall time* is the time it takes to change from a 1 to a 0. Fig 3 shows how rise and fall times affect the shape of a binary signal, or *pulse*. Rise and fall times describe a signal at a specific point in a circuit. The distributed inductances and capacitances in a wire or PC-board trace cause rise and fall times to lengthen as a pulse gets farther from its source. Rise and fall times are typically in the microsecond or nanosecond range and vary with the logic family used.

Digital signals take a measurable amount of time to pass through a circuit. This phenomenon is called *propagation delay*, and results in an output signal being slightly delayed from an input signal, as shown in Fig 4. Propagation delay is the result of transistor switching delays, reactive element charging times and the time needed for signals to travel through wires. In complex circuits, different propagation delays through different paths can cause problems when pulses must arrive somewhere at exactly the same time.

COMBINATIONAL LOGIC

In binary digital circuits, a combination of binary inputs results in a specific binary output or combination of binary outputs.

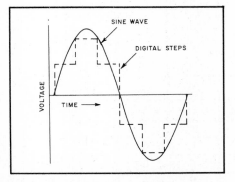

Fig 1—A sine wave and a digital approximation of that waveform. Note that the sine wave has continuously varying voltage and that the digital waveform is composed of discrete steps.

Fig 2—A typical digital logic signal is shown in A. B illustrates possible ranges of recognition for binary 1 and 0.

Fig 3—Shape of a typical digital pulse.

Fig 4—Propagation delay in a digital circuit.

These circuits are used to implement everything from simple switches to powerful computers. Some binary circuits are called *combinational logic networks*. The output of a combinational logic network is dependent only on its inputs, and its output changes immediately when its input changes. While there are more complex types of binary circuits, these circuits are usually composed of combinational logic elements. To understand complex digital circuits, one must understand combinational logic.

BOOLEAN ALGEBRA

Just as there are mathematical theories and equations used in designing analog circuits, there is a special branch of mathematics, *Boolean algebra*, that is used to describe and design binary digital circuits. In standard algebra there are several basic operations: addition, subtraction, multiplication and division. In Boolean algebra, the basic operations are *logical operations*: AND, OR and NOT. Boolean algebra is used to describe complex logical functions (often digital circuits) as combinations of these logical operators.

A logical function or operator can be defined by describing its output for all possible inputs. Such a list of inputs and outputs is called a *truth table*. In a truth table, a T represents a true or a 1 signal and an F represents a false or a 0 signal.

Boolean Operators

Figs 5 through 7 show the truth tables, circuit symbols, and Boolean algebra symbols for the three basic Boolean operations, NOT, AND and OR. All combina-

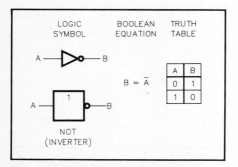

Fig 5—Inverter. The distinctive triangular symbol with a small (inversion) circle on the output is the standard inverter symbol used in ARRL and other US publications. The square symbol is used in some other countries. The other figures through Fig 13 also show the symbol with a distinctive shape used in US publications along with a square symbol used elsewhere.

Fig 6—Two-input AND gate.

tional logic functions, no matter how complex, can be described in terms of these three operators.

NOT

The NOT operation is called inversion, negation or complement. The Boolean notation for NOT is a bar over a variable or expression. As can be seen from the truth table in Fig 5, NOT 1 is 0 and NOT 0 is 1. The circuit that implements the NOT

Fig 7—Two-input OR gate.

Table 1
Useful Properties and Theorems in Boolen Algebra

Commutative Property	AB = BA
	A + B = B + A

Associative Property	A (BC) = (AB)C
	A + (B + C) = (A + B) + C

Distributive Property	A (B + C) = AB + AC
	A + (BC) = A + B (A + C)

Theorems	$A \cdot 0 = 0$
	$A \cdot 1 = A$
	$A \cdot A = A$
	$A \cdot \overline{A} = 0$
	$\overline{A} \neq A$
	$A + 0 = A$
	$A + 1 = 1$
	$A + A = A$
	$A + \overline{A} = 1$

function is called an *inverter* or *inverting buffer*.

AND

The AND operation results in a 1 only when both of its operands are 1. That is, if the inputs are called A and B, the output is 1 only if A *and* B are 1. In Boolean notation, AND is represented by a middle dot (•) between the variables, or nothing between the variables. Both of these forms are shown in Fig 6. The circuit that implements the AND function is called an AND *gate*. Gates are combinational logic elements with two or more inputs and one output state.

OR

The OR operation results in 1 if one or the other of its operands is 1 (Fig 7). This also includes the case where both operands are 1; because of this, OR is sometimes called the INCLUSIVE OR. The Boolean notation for OR is + between the two operands. The circuit that implements the OR function is called an OR gate.

Boolean Identities

Algebraic identities, such as A × B = B × A, help us solve complicated problems in mathematics. There are several identities in Boolean algebra that are useful for solving complex logic problems. These identities are shown in Table 1.

DeMORGAN'S THEOREM

One of the Boolean identities deserves special attention. This identity is called DeMorgan's Theorem. DeMorgan's theorem consists of two identities: $\overline{A \cdot B} = \overline{A} + \overline{B}$ and $\overline{A + B} = \overline{A} \cdot \overline{B}$. The truth table in Table 2 proves these identities. The important consequence of DeMorgan's theorem is that any logical function can be implemented using either inverters and AND gates or inverters and OR gates. The theorem gives the circuit designer freedom, because it allows AND gates and inverters to be substituted for OR gates, and vice

Table 2
DeMorgan's Theorem

(A) $\overline{A \cdot B} = \overline{A} + \overline{B}$

(B) $\overline{A + B} = \overline{A} \cdot \overline{B}$

	(1)	(2)	(3)	(4)	(5)	(6)	(7)	(8)	(9)	(10)
	A	B	$\overline{A}$	$\overline{B}$	$A \cdot B$	$\overline{A \cdot B}$	A + B	$\overline{A + B}$	$\overline{A} \cdot \overline{B}$	$\overline{A} + \overline{B}$
(C)	0	0	1	1	0	1	0	1	1	1
	0	1	1	0	0	1	1	0	0	1
	1	0	0	1	0	1	1	0	0	1
	1	1	0	0	1	0	1	0	0	0

(A) and (B) are statements of DeMorgan's Theorem. The truth table at (C) is proof of these statements; (A) is proven by the equivalence of columns 6 and 10; (B) is proven by the fact that columns 8 and 9 are the same.

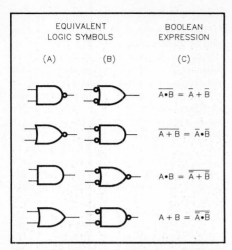

EQUIVALENT LOGIC SYMBOLS		BOOLEAN EXPRESSION
(A)	(B)	(C)

$\overline{A \cdot B} = \overline{A} + \overline{B}$

$\overline{A + B} = \overline{A} \cdot \overline{B}$

$A \cdot B = \overline{\overline{A} + \overline{B}}$

$A + B = \overline{\overline{A} \cdot \overline{B}}$

Fig 8—Each gate in column A is equivalent to the gate opposite it in column B. The Boolean expressions in column C formally state the equivalences.

versa. The gate substitutions shown in Fig 8 illustrate some uses of DeMorgan's theorem. Such substitutions can lead to simplification of design or to more efficient use of available gates.

Other Common Gates

While we have shown that any logical function can be implemented with only two logic elements (AND and NOT or OR and NOT), there are several other logic elements that are easily implemented and commonly available. Using these available gates (il-

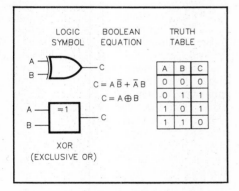

LOGIC SYMBOL	BOOLEAN EQUATION	TRUTH TABLE		
		A	B	C
	$C = A\overline{B} + \overline{A}B$	0	0	0
	$C = A \oplus B$	0	1	1
		1	0	1
		1	1	0

XOR (EXCLUSIVE OR)

Fig 9—Two-input XOR gate.

LOGIC SYMBOL	BOOLEAN EQUATION	TRUTH TABLE		
		A	B	C
	$C = \overline{A + B}$	0	0	1
		0	1	0
		1	0	0
		1	1	0

NOR

Fig 10—Two input NOR gate.

LOGIC SYMBOL	BOOLEAN EQUATION	TRUTH TABLE		
		A	B	C
	$C = \overline{A \cdot B}$	0	0	1
		0	1	1
		1	0	1
		1	1	0

NAND

Fig 11—Two-input NAND gate.

LOGIC SYMBOL	BOOLEAN EQUATION	TRUTH TABLE		
		A	B	C
	$C = \overline{A \oplus B}$	0	0	1
	$C = \overline{A} \cdot \overline{B} + A \cdot B$	0	1	0
		1	0	0
		1	1	1

XNOR (EXCLUSIVE NOR)

Fig 12—Two-input XNOR gate.

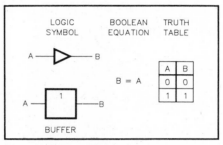

LOGIC SYMBOL	BOOLEAN EQUATION	TRUTH TABLE	
		A	B
	$B = A$	0	0
		1	1

BUFFER

Fig 13—Noninverting buffer.

lustrated in Figs 9 through 13) can simplify logic circuits.

EXCLUSIVE OR

In an EXCLUSIVE OR (XOR) gate, the output is 1 only if a single input is 1. If both inputs are 1 or both inputs are 0, the output is 0. The symbol ⊕ in a Boolean expression represents the XOR operation.

NOR

NOR means NOT OR. A NOR gate is a circuit that produces a 0 at its output if any or all of its inputs are 1.

NAND

NAND is a contraction of NOT AND. A NAND gate has a 0 output only when all of its inputs are 1.

EXCLUSIVE NOR

The EXCLUSIVE NOR (XNOR) gate produces 0 output only if a single input is 1. Note that if both of the inputs are 1, there is a 1 on the output.

Noninverting Buffer

The *noninverting buffer* does not imple-

ment a Boolean function. Its output is simply equal to its input. While not useful for logical operations, a noninverting buffer has several uses: (a) providing sufficient current to drive a number of gates, (b) interfacing between two logic families, (c) obtaining a desired pulse rise time, and (d) providing a slight delay to make pulses arrive at the proper time.

Polarity

In Boolean algebra, gates operate on the logical values 1 (true) and 0 (false). When implementing gates as electronic circuits, we need to assign voltage levels to 1 and 0. The intuitively acceptable convention is to use a higher voltage for 1 and a lower voltage for 0. This convention is called *positive logic*, and the standard logic symbols illustrated above are symbols for positive logic elements. In *negative logic*, the higher voltage represents 0 and the lower voltage represents 1. A negative logic input or output is represented by a small circle on the negative logic terminal. One can also think of these circles as representing inverted inputs or outputs. While logic polarity can be confusing, being able to think in both positive and negative logic sometimes makes circuit design easier.

SEQUENTIAL LOGIC

The previous sections discussed combinational logic, which has the outputs *immediately* dependent on *inputs only*. There is another class of logic called *sequential logic*. In sequential logic, network outputs are dependent not only on current inputs, but also on current outputs. This is a type of feedback and requires memory. The logic element that supplies memory is generally called a *flip-flop*.

A flip-flop (also known as a *bistable multivibrator* or an *Eccles-Jordan circuit*) is a binary sequential logic element with two stable states. One is the *set* state (1 state); the other is the *reset* state (0 state). The schematic symbol for a flip-flop is a rectangle with the letters FF. These letters may be omitted if there is no ambiguity.

Flip-flop inputs and outputs are normally identified by a single letter. A letter followed by a subscripted letter (such as D_C), means that the input is dependent on the input of the subscripted letter (input D_C is dependent on input C). Flip-flop outputs are labeled Q and $\overline{Q}$ (Table 3).

State Transition Tables

Conventional truth tables are difficult to apply to flip-flops, because flip-flop outputs depend on current outputs as well as on current inputs. Also, a certain input condition may not have a unique output state. The simpler sequential circuits can be defined by state tables showing input and output states as they are now, and output states as they will be after the next input pulse. These tables are called *state transition tables*. State transition tables are used for designing sequential logic networks.

Table 3

Flip-Flop Output Designations

Output	Action	Restrictions
Q (Set)	Normal output	Only two output states are
$\overline{Q}$ (Reset)	Inverted output	possible: Q = 1, $\overline{Q}$ = 0;
		and Q = 0, $\overline{Q}$ = 1.

Notes

1) $\overline{Q}$ is the complement of Q.
2) The normal output is normally marked Q or unmarked.
3) The inverted output is normally marked $\overline{Q}$. If so, if there is a 1 state at Q, there will be a 0 state at $\overline{Q}$.

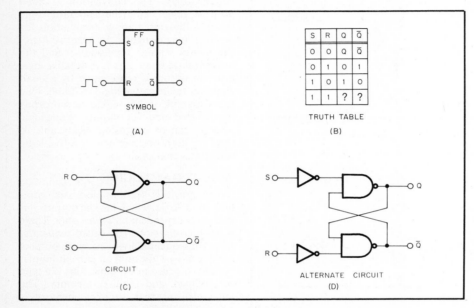

Fig 14—An unclocked R-S flip-flop. Where Q and $\overline{Q}$ are shown in the truth table, the previous states are retained. A question mark (?) indicates that the output state is unpredictable. C shows an R-S flip-flop made from two NOR gates. Circuit D is another implementation using two NAND gates and two inverters.

Fig 15—This figure illustrates the different outputs that may result when a D flip-flop is edge triggered (C) or gated (D). Notice that the short negative pulse on the input (B) is not reproduced by the edge-triggered flip-flop.

Unclocked R-S Flip-Flop

One of the simplest circuits for storing a bit of information is the R-S flip-flop. Its inputs are R (reset) and S (set). Fig 14 shows how an R-S flip-flop can be made using combinational logic elements.

When S = 0 and R = 0 the output will stay the same as it was at the last input pulse. This is indicated by the letter Q in the truth table.

If S = 1 and R = 0, Q will change to 1. If S = 0 and R = 1, Q will change to 0.

If both the R input and the S input are 1, the flip-flop output assumes an unpredictable state. This state varies from circuit to circuit, and may be Q = $\overline{Q}$ = 1 or Q = $\overline{Q}$ = 0. While Q = $\overline{Q}$ is a logical impossibility, real flip-flops may present this output state. Avoid the R = S = 1 input, and make no assumptions about the resulting output.

Synchronous Flip-Flops

The R-S flip-flop is an *asynchronous* device; its outputs change immediately to reflect changes on its inputs. *Synchronous* flip-flops change state (to reflect input conditions) only at specific times. These times are dictated by a *clock*, *toggle* or *gate* input.

Synchronizing inputs can take two forms, *static* or *dynamic*. Static, *gated*, or *level triggered* inputs allow the flip-flop to change state whenever the clock input is at a specified level (1 or 0). Dynamic or *edge triggered* inputs allow the flip-flop to change state only when the clock *changes* level. Dynamic inputs that react to a transition from 0 to 1 are called *positive-edge triggered* inputs, and are indicated by a small isosceles triangle inside the flip-flop at the clock input. Inputs that are sensitive to the transition from 1 to 0 are *negative-edge triggered*, and are indicated by the triangle and a negation symbol (a small circle outside the flip-flop rectangle). It is important to remember that input levels affect gated flip-flops whenever the clock is in a specific state, while inputs affect edge-triggered flip-flops only when the clock is in transition. Fig 15 shows how the same input to a gated and an edge-triggered flip-flop results in two different outputs.

Gated R-S Flip-Flop

The gated R-S flip-flop, or *gated latch*, has R, S and clock inputs. It is also called the R-S-T flip-flop, the "T" indicating a *toggle* input. Although not often used, the R-S-T flip-flop is important because it illustrates a step between the R-S flip-flop and the J-K flip-flop. The inputs R and S produce the same results as those on an unclocked R-S flip-flop, but no change in output will occur unless the toggle input is high. A gated R-S flip-flop is illustrated in Fig 16 along with a timing diagram to show the effect of the clock input.

Master/Slave Flip-Flop

The importance of synchronous flip-

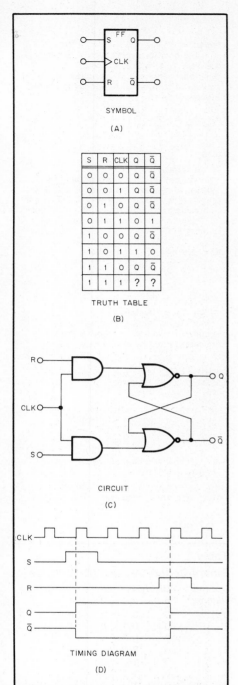

Fig 16—A gated R-S flip-flop. Where Q and $\overline{Q}$ are shown in the table, the previous states are retained. A question mark (?) indicates an unpredictable output state.

For the left figure, the labels:

SYMBOL (A)

S	R	CLK	Q	$\overline{Q}$
0	0	0	Q	$\overline{Q}$
0	0	1	Q	$\overline{Q}$
0	1	0	Q	$\overline{Q}$
0	1	1	0	1
1	0	0	Q	$\overline{Q}$
1	0	1	1	0
1	1	0	Q	$\overline{Q}$
1	1	1	?	?

TRUTH TABLE (B)

CIRCUIT (C)

TIMING DIAGRAM (D)

Fig 17—A master/slave flip-flop.

SYMBOL (A)

S	R	Q	$\overline{Q}$
0	0	Q	$\overline{Q}$
0	1	0	1
1	0	1	0
1	1	?	?

TRUTH TABLE (B)

M/S FLIP-FLOP MADE OF R-S FLIP-FLOPS AND AN INVERTER (C)

Fig 18—The D flip-flop. When T = 0, Q and $\overline{Q}$ states don't change. When T = 1, the output states change to reflect the input (D).

R-S-T FLIP-FLOP AND INVERTER (A)

PREWIRED D FLIP-FLOP (B)

T	D	Q	$\overline{Q}$
0	0	Q	$\overline{Q}$
0	1	Q	$\overline{Q}$
1	0	0	1
1	1	1	0

TRUTH TABLE (C)

R-S-T FLIP-FLOP WIRED AS T FLIP-FLOP (A)

D FLIP-FLOP WIRED AS T FLIP-FLOP (B)

TIMING DIAGRAM (C)

Fig 19—The T flip-flop. The output frequency is half of the input frequency.

flops is illustrated in the construction of the *master/slave* flip-flop. The master/slave (M/S) flip-flop solves a problem known as *race*. Race occurs when flip-flops are connected in series and triggered by the same clock pulse or when a flip-flop uses its own output as an input. When an input changes just as an output is about to change, an erroneous output may result.

This problem is solved by building a flip-flop that samples and stores its inputs before changing its outputs. Such a flip-flop

can be built by placing two gated R-S flip-flops in series. The first, or *master*, flip-flop is active when the clock is positive; it samples and stores the inputs when the clock is 1. The second, or *slave*, flip-flop takes its input from the output of the master, and acts when the clock is negative. Hence, when the clock is 1, the input is

sampled, and when the clock is 0, the output is generated. Changes in the output are now isolated from the input, and there is no race condition.

An M/S flip-flop can be made by wiring two R-S flip-flops in series and connecting an inverter between the T inputs. Thus when the T input is 1, the master (first flip-flop) is enabled. When the T input is 0, the slave (second flip-flop) is enabled and the master disabled. An R-S M/S flip-flop is shown in Fig 17.

D Flip-Flop

In a D flip-flop, the *data* input (D) is transferred to the outputs (Q and $\overline{Q}$) when the flip-flop is enabled by the T input. Fig 18 shows a typical D flip-flop and its state transition table. The logic level at D is transferred to Q when the clock is positive. The Q output will retain this logic level, regardless of any changes at D, until the next positive clock pulse.

Toggle Flip-Flop

Fig 19 shows a *toggle*, or T flip-flop. The timing diagram shows that the flip-flop output changes state with each positive clock pulse. Because of this, the T flip-flop is also called a *complementing* flip-flop. Examination of the pulses in Fig 19C shows that the output frequency of the T flip-flop is one half of the input frequency. Thus a T flip-flop is a 2:1 (also called a *modulo-2* or *radix-2*) frequency divider. Two T flip-flops connected in series form a 4:1 divider, and so on.

J-K Flip-Flop

The J-K flip-flop is a common flip-flop. It has no invalid input combinations (a disadvantage of the R-S flip-flop), and it can complement (divide by 2). The J-K flip-flop is illustrated in Fig 20.

On receipt of a clock pulse, inputs of J = 1, K = 0 sets Q = 1. J = 0, K = 1 resets Q = 0. Simultaneous J = 1, K = 1 causes Q to change state (complement). If J = 0 and K = 0, Q will not change state when the flip-flop is clocked.

Asynchronous Inputs

Most commercially available synchronous flip-flops have some asynchronous inputs. These inputs allow you to change the state of the flip-flop regardless of the state of the clock input. Asynchronous inputs usually found on flip-flops are the *direct reset*, RD, and *direct set*, SD. As their names suggest, these inputs allow the flip-flop to be set or reset asynchronously. Such inputs are used

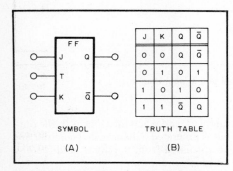

Fig 20—A J-K flip-flop. The truth table shows that if J = 0 and K = 0, the output does not change, and if J = 1 and K = 1, the output state is inverted.

Digital Number Systems

Decimal

The familiar *decimal* or *base-10* system is comprised of 10 symbols (digits or numerals): 0, 1, 2, 3, 4, 5, 6, 7, 8 and 9. The value of each depends on its position in the number. For example: In the decimal number 123, 1 = 100, 2 = 20 and 3 = 3 units.

The first position carries the greatest weight and is known as the *most significant digit (MSD)*, while right-most position is referred to as the *least significant digit (LSD)*. The positional values relative to the decimal point can be expressed in terms of *powers of 10*, also known as scientific notation.

Decimal position values of the number decimal 234.56 in powers of 10 are:

100	10	1		0.1	0.01	Decimal value
10^2	10^1	10^0		10^{-1}	10^{-2}	Power of 10 value
2	3	4	.	5	6	Decimal number
↑			↑		↑	
MSD			Decimal point		LSD	

Binary

In the *binary* or *base-2* system only two symbols are used: 0 and 1. As in the decimal system, the position of a binary digit determines its weight which is expressed in powers of 2. The left-most position is the *most significant bit (MSB)*, and the right-most position is the *least significant bit (LSB)*.

Position values of the binary number 1101011 are:

64	32	16	8	4	2	1	Decimal value
2^6	2^5	2^4	2^3	2^2	2^1	2^0	Power of 2 value
1	1	0	1	0	1	1	Binary number
↑					↑		
MSB					LSB		

Octal

In the *octal* or *base-8* system, 8 symbols are used: 0, 1, 2, 3, 4, 5, 6 and 7. Each positional value can be expressed in powers of 8. Position values for the octal number 7654 are:

512	64	8	1	Decimal value
8^3	8^2	8^1	8^0	Power of 8 value
7	6	5	4	Octal number
↑			↑	
MSD		LSD		

Hexadecimal

In the *hexadecimal (hex)* or *base-16* system 16 symbols are used: 0, 1, 2, 3, 4, 5, 6, 7, 8, 9, A, B, C, D, E and F. Each position value can be expressed in powers of 16. Position values for the hexadecimal number FF07 are:

4096	256	16	1	Decimal value
16^3	16^2	16^1	16^0	Power of 16 values
F	F	0	7	Hexadecimal number
↑		↑		
MSD		LSD		

Binary-Coded Decimal

In the *binary-coded decimal (BCD)* system the decimal numbers 0 through 9 are represented by 4-bit binary patterns:

BCD	Decimal	BCD	Decimal
0000	0	1000	8
0001	1	1001	9
0010	2	1010	
0011	3	1011	Not
0100	4	1100	Used
0101	5	1101	
0110	6	1110	
0111	7	1111	

The decimal number 789 would be expressed in BCD as:

7	8	9	Decimal number
0111	1000	1001	BCD code

to establish known conditions in a circuit or to interrupt an ongoing process.

COUNTERS

A *counter*, *divider* or *divide-by-n* counter is a circuit that stores pulses and produces an output pulse when a specified number, n, of pulses are stored. In a counter consisting of flip-flops connected in series, a change of state of the first stage affects the second stage and so on.

A *ripple*, *ripple-carry* or *asynchronous* counter passes the count from stage to stage; each stage is clocked by the preceding stage. In a *synchronous* counter, each stage is controlled by a common clock.

Weighting is the count value assigned to each counter output. In a four-stage binary ripple counter, the output of the first stage has a weight of 1, the second 2, the third 4 and the fourth 8. Base 10 (decade) counters consist of a divide-by-2 and divide-by-5 counters (encoded in binary-coded decimal or BCD code), as shown in Table 4. A base 12 counter has a divide-by-2 and a divide-by-6 counter.

Most counters have the ability to *clear* the count to 0. Some counters can be *preset* to a desired count.

Counters may either count up (increment)

Table 4
Binary-Coded Decimal (BCD) Code

Decimal Number	Binary Weights			
	8	4	2	1
0	0	0	0	0
1	0	0	0	1
2	0	0	1	0
3	0	0	1	1
4	0	1	0	0
5	0	1	0	1
6	0	1	1	0
7	0	1	1	1
8	1	0	0	0
9	1	0	0	1

Note: BCD does not use hexadecimal (base 16) numbers A (1010), B (1011), C (1100), D (1101), E (1110) or F (1111).

or down (decrement). *Up* counters count in increasing weighted values (for example: 0000, 0001, 0010, ..., 1111). *Down* counters work in the reverse order. There are also *up/down* counters that can be commanded to count either up or down.

REGISTERS

Groups of flip-flops may be used to temporarily store data. Such a data-storage

Table 5
Number Conversion

Decimal	Binary	Octal	Hexa-decimal	BCD
0	0	0	0	0000
1	1	1	1	0001
2	10	2	2	0010
3	11	3	3	0011
4	100	4	4	0100
5	101	5	5	0101
6	110	6	6	0110
7	111	7	7	0111
8	1000	10	8	1000
9	1001	11	9	1001
10	1010	12	A	0001 0000
11	1011	13	B	0001 0001
12	1100	14	C	0001 0010
13	1101	15	D	0001 0011
14	1110	16	E	0001 0100
15	1111	17	F	0001 0101
16	10000	20	10	0001 0110
17	10001	21	11	0001 0111
18	10010	22	12	0001 1000
19	10011	23	13	0001 1001
20	10100	24	14	0010 0000
21	10101	25	15	0010 0001
22	10110	26	16	0010 0010
23	10111	27	17	0010 0011
24	11000	30	18	0010 0100
25	11001	31	19	0010 0101
26	11010	32	1A	0010 0110
27	11011	33	1B	0010 0111
28	11100	34	1C	0010 1000
29	11101	35	1D	0010 1001
30	11110	36	1E	0011 0000
31	11111	37	1F	0011 0001
32	100000	40	20	0011 0010
33	100001	41	21	0011 0011
34	100010	42	22	0011 0100
35	100011	43	23	0011 0101
36	100100	44	24	0011 0110
37	100101	45	25	0011 0111
38	100110	46	26	0011 1000
39	100111	47	27	0011 1001
40	101000	50	28	0100 0000
41	101001	51	29	0100 0001
42	101010	52	2A	0100 0010
43	101011	53	2B	0100 0011
44	101100	54	2C	0100 0100
45	101101	55	2D	0100 0101
46	101110	56	2E	0100 0110
47	101111	57	2F	0100 0111
48	110000	60	30	0100 1000
49	110001	61	31	0100 1001
50	110010	62	32	0101 0000
51	110011	63	33	0101 0001
52	110100	64	34	0101 0010
53	110101	65	35	0101 0011
54	110110	66	36	0101 0100
55	110111	67	37	0101 0101
56	111000	70	38	0101 0110
57	111001	71	39	0101 0111
58	111010	72	3A	0101 1000
59	111011	73	3B	0101 1001
60	111100	74	3C	0110 0000
61	111101	75	3D	0110 0001
62	111110	76	3E	0110 0010
63	111111	77	3F	0110 0011
64	1000000	100	40	0110 0100
65	1000001	101	41	0110 0101
66	1000010	102	42	0110 0110
67	1000011	103	43	0110 0111
68	1000100	104	44	0110 1000
69	1000101	105	45	0110 1001
70	1000110	106	46	0111 0000
71	1000111	107	47	0111 0001
72	1001000	110	48	0111 0010
73	1001001	111	49	0111 0011
74	1001010	112	4A	0111 0100
75	1001011	113	4B	0111 0101
76	1001100	114	4C	0111 0110
77	1001101	115	4D	0111 0111
78	1001110	116	4E	0111 1000
79	1001111	117	4F	0111 1001
80	1010000	120	50	1000 0000
81	1010001	121	51	1000 0001
82	1010010	122	52	1000 0010
83	1010011	123	53	1000 0011
84	1010100	124	54	1000 0100
85	1010101	125	55	1000 0101
86	1010110	126	56	1000 0110
87	1010111	127	57	1000 0111
88	1011000	130	58	1000 1000
89	1011001	131	59	1000 1001
90	1011010	132	5A	1001 0000
91	1011011	133	5B	1001 0001
92	1011100	134	5C	1001 0010
93	1011101	135	5D	1001 0011

Decimal	Binary	Octal	Hexa-decimal	BCD
94	1011110	136	5E	1001 0100
95	1011111	137	5F	1001 0101
96	1100000	140	60	1001 0110
97	1100001	141	61	1001 0111
98	1100010	142	62	1001 1000
99	1100011	143	63	1001 1001
100	1100100	144	64	0001 0000 0000
101	1100101	145	65	0001 0000 0001
102	1100110	146	66	0001 0000 0010
103	1100111	147	67	0001 0000 0011
104	1101000	150	68	0001 0000 0100
105	1101001	151	69	0001 0000 0101
106	1101010	152	6A	0001 0000 0110
107	1101011	153	6B	0001 0000 0111
108	1101100	154	6C	0001 0000 1000
109	1101101	155	6D	0001 0000 1001
110	1101110	156	6E	0001 0001 0000
111	1101111	157	6F	0001 0001 0001
112	1110000	160	70	0001 0001 0010
113	1110001	161	71	0001 0001 0011
114	1110010	162	72	0001 0001 0100
115	1110011	163	73	0001 0001 0101
116	1110100	164	74	0001 0001 0110
117	1110101	165	75	0001 0001 0111
118	1110110	166	76	0001 0001 1000
119	1110111	167	77	0001 0001 1001
120	1111000	170	78	0001 0010 0000
121	1111001	171	79	0001 0010 0001
122	1111010	172	7A	0001 0010 0010
123	1111011	173	7B	0001 0010 0011
124	1111100	174	7C	0001 0010 0100
125	1111101	175	7D	0001 0010 0101
126	1111110	176	7E	0001 0010 0110
127	1111111	177	7F	0001 0010 0111
128	10000000	200	80	0001 0010 1000
129	10000001	201	81	0001 0010 1001
130	10000010	202	82	0001 0011 0000
131	10000011	203	83	0001 0011 0001
132	10000100	204	84	0001 0011 0010
133	10000101	205	85	0001 0011 0011
134	10000110	206	86	0001 0011 0100
135	10000111	207	87	0001 0011 0101
136	10001000	210	88	0001 0011 0110
137	10001001	211	89	0001 0011 0111
138	10001010	212	8A	0001 0011 1000
139	10001011	213	8B	0001 0011 1001
140	10001100	214	8C	0001 0100 0000
141	10001101	215	8D	0001 0100 0001
142	10001110	216	8E	0001 0100 0010
143	10001111	217	8F	0001 0100 0011
144	10010000	220	90	0001 0100 0100
145	10010001	221	91	0001 0100 0101
146	10010010	222	92	0001 0100 0110
147	10010011	223	93	0001 0100 0111
148	10010100	224	94	0001 0100 1000
149	10010101	225	95	0001 0100 1001
150	10010110	226	96	0001 0101 0000
151	10010111	227	97	0001 0101 0001
152	10011000	230	98	0001 0101 0010
153	10011001	231	99	0001 0101 0011
154	10011010	232	9A	0001 0101 0100
155	10011011	233	9B	0001 0101 0101
156	10011100	234	9C	0001 0101 0110
157	10011101	235	9D	0001 0101 0111
158	10011110	236	9E	0001 0101 1000
159	10011111	237	9F	0001 0101 1001
160	10100000	240	A0	0001 0110 0000
161	10100001	241	A1	0001 0110 0001
162	10100010	242	A2	0001 0110 0010
163	10100011	243	A3	0001 0110 0011
164	10100100	244	A4	0001 0110 0100
165	10100101	245	A5	0001 0110 0101
166	10100110	246	A6	0001 0110 0110
167	10100111	247	A7	0001 0110 0111
168	10101000	250	A8	0001 0110 1000
169	10101001	251	A9	0001 0110 1001
170	10101010	252	AA	0001 0111 0000
171	10101011	253	AB	0001 0111 0001
172	10101100	254	AC	0001 0111 0010
173	10101101	255	AD	0001 0111 0011
174	10101110	256	AE	0001 0111 0100
175	10101111	257	AF	0001 0111 0101
176	10110000	260	B0	0001 0111 0110
177	10110001	261	B1	0001 0111 0111
178	10110010	262	B2	0001 0111 1000
179	10110011	263	B3	0001 0111 1001
180	10110100	264	B4	0001 1000 0000
181	10110101	265	B5	0001 1000 0001
182	10110110	266	B6	0001 1000 0010
183	10110111	267	B7	0001 1000 0011
184	10111000	270	B8	0001 1000 0100
185	10111001	271	B9	0001 1000 0101
186	10111010	272	BA	0001 1000 0110
187	10111011	273	BB	0001 1000 0111

Decimal	Binary	Octal	Hexa-decimal	BCD
188	10111100	274	BC	0001 1000 1000
189	10111101	275	BD	0001 1000 1001
190	10111110	276	BE	0001 1001 0000
191	10111111	277	BF	0001 1001 0001
192	11000000	300	C0	0001 1001 0010
193	11000001	301	C1	0001 1001 0011
194	11000010	302	C2	0001 1001 0100
195	11000011	303	C3	0001 1001 0101
196	11000100	304	C4	0001 1001 0110
197	11000101	305	C5	0001 1001 0111
198	11000110	306	C6	0001 1001 1000
199	11000111	307	C7	0001 1001 1001
200	11001000	310	C8	0010 0000 0000
201	11001001	311	C9	0010 0000 0001
202	11001010	312	CA	0010 0000 0010
203	11001011	313	CB	0010 0000 0011
204	11001100	314	CC	0010 0000 0100
205	11001101	315	CD	0010 0000 0101
206	11001110	316	CE	0010 0000 0110
207	11001111	317	CF	0010 0000 0111
208	11010000	320	D0	0010 0000 1000
209	11010001	321	D1	0010 0000 1001
210	11010010	322	D2	0010 0001 0000
211	11010011	323	D3	0010 0001 0001
212	11010100	324	D4	0010 0001 0010
213	11010101	325	D5	0010 0001 0011
214	11010110	326	D6	0010 0001 0100
215	11010111	327	D7	0010 0001 0101
216	11011000	330	D8	0010 0001 0110
217	11011001	331	D9	0010 0001 0111
218	11011010	332	DA	0010 0001 1000
219	11011011	333	DB	0010 0001 1001
220	11011100	334	DC	0010 0010 0000
221	11011101	335	DD	0010 0010 0001
222	11011110	336	DE	0010 0010 0010
223	11011111	337	DF	0010 0010 0011
224	11100000	340	E0	0010 0010 0100
225	11100001	341	E1	0010 0010 0101
226	11100010	342	E2	0010 0010 0110
227	11100011	343	E3	0010 0010 0111
228	11100100	344	E4	0010 0010 1000
229	11100101	345	E5	0010 0010 1001
230	11100110	346	E6	0010 0011 0000
231	11100111	347	E7	0010 0011 0001
232	11101000	350	E8	0010 0011 0010
233	11101001	351	E9	0010 0011 0011
234	11101010	352	EA	0010 0011 0100
235	11101011	353	EB	0010 0011 0101
236	11101100	354	EC	0010 0011 0110
237	11101101	355	ED	0010 0011 0111
238	11101110	356	EE	0010 0011 1000
239	11101111	357	EF	0010 0011 1001
240	11110000	360	F0	0010 0100 0000
241	11110001	361	F1	0010 0100 0001
242	11110010	362	F2	0010 0100 0010
243	11110011	363	F3	0010 0100 0011
244	11110100	364	F4	0010 0100 0100
245	11110101	365	F5	0010 0100 0101
246	11110110	366	F6	0010 0100 0110
247	11110111	367	F7	0010 0100 0111
248	11111000	370	F8	0010 0100 1000
249	11111001	371	F9	0010 0100 1001
250	11111010	372	FA	0010 0101 0000
251	11111011	373	FB	0010 0101 0001
252	11111100	374	FC	0010 0101 0010
253	11111101	375	FD	0010 0101 0011
254	11111110	376	FE	0010 0101 0100
255	11111111	377	FF	0010 0101 0101

Decimal	Power of 2	Binary	Octal	Hexa-decimal
256	2^8	100000000	400	100
512	2^9	1000000000	1000	200
1024	2^{10}	10000000000	2000	400
2048	2^{11}	100000000000	4000	800
4096	2^{12}	1000000000000	10000	1000
8192	2^{13}	10000000000000	20000	2000
16384	2^{14}	100000000000000	40000	4000
32768	2^{15}	1000000000000000	100000	8000
65536	2^{16}	10000000000000000	200000	10000

device is called a *register*. There are two classes of registers: *shift registers* and *word* or *byte registers*. Registers are used in counters, data-storage devices, and sequence generators.

Shift Registers

A shift register is a group of flip-flops connected so that when a clock pulse occurs, each flip-flop assumes the state of the preceding flip-flop. The first flip-flop of the group usually receives its input from an external logic signal. Shift registers may provide parallel outputs (an output from each flip-flop), and they may provide a means to directly set the state of each flip-flop (parallel loading) synchronously or asynchronously. Fig 21A illustrates four D flip-flops connected as a shift register.

Shift registers can be used to delay or synchronize data. In this application, the register is constructed so that a desired bit is at the output of the register during a specified clock pulse. Any output of a shift register can be fed back to its input to produce an almost infinite array of possibilities. The *ring counter* (Fig 21B) is a shift register with its output fed back to its input. When a clock pulse is applied to a ring counter, the bit pattern stored in the register is rotated either left or right. Shift registers with several feedback paths can be used as *pseudorandom-number generators* (Fig 21C). The output of such a generator is a sequence of bits that meets one or more criteria of true randomness. Pseudorandom-number generators have applications in noise generators and spread-spectrum key generators.

Byte and Word Registers

A byte register or a word register is simply a group of flip-flops that is thought of as a single register. Such registers are used in computers for temporary data storage. The number of flip-flops in a word register depends on the word length of the computer. Word length and computer architecture will be more thoroughly discussed in later sections of this chapter.

ONE-SHOT MULTIVIBRATOR

A *one-shot* or *monostable* multivibrator is a circuit that has one stable state and an unstable state. When the one-shot is *triggered* by a clock pulse, it assumes its unstable state for a period of time determined by circuit components. Thus, the one-shot multivibrator puts out a pulse of some predetermined duration (T). If a one-shot multivibrator is triggered while it is in the unstable state, two things may happen. A *non-retriggerable* multivibrator is not affected by the second trigger pulse. A *retriggerable* multivibrator will start "counting" its pulse duration (T) from the most recent trigger pulse. Both types of one-shots are common.

Fig 22 shows a 555 timer IC connected as a one-shot multivibrator. The one-shot is activated by a negative-going pulse

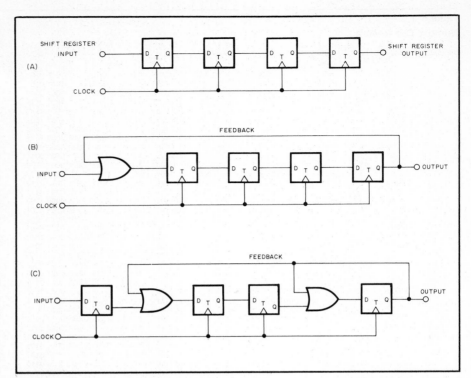

Fig 21—Shift registers. Four D flip-flops connected as a simple shift register are shown at A. B shows the same flip-flops used as a ring counter. Notice that the feedback is ORed with the input. In C, the feedback is ORed with the inputs to the second and fourth flip-flops, creating a pseudorandom number generator.

Fig 22—Part A shows a 555 timer connected as a one-shot multivibrator. B shows the equation to calculate values of R (in ohms) and C (in farads).

between the trigger input and ground. The trigger pulse causes the output (Q) to go positive and capacitor C to charge through resistor R. When the voltage across C reaches two-thirds of V_{CC}, the capacitor is quickly discharged to ground and the output returns to 0. The output remains at logic 1 for a time determined by

$$T = 1.1\ RC \qquad\qquad (Eq\ 1)$$

where

R = resistance in ohms
C = capacitance in farads

ASTABLE MULTIVIBRATOR

An *astable* or *free-running* multivibrator is a circuit that alternates between two unstable states. It can be synchronized by an input signal of a frequency that is slightly higher than the astable multivibrator free-running frequency. An astable multivibrator creates a sequence of pulses at a desired frequency and width.

Fig 23 shows an astable multivibrator circuit using the 555 timer. The capacitor C charges to two-thirds V_{CC} through R1

Fig 23—Part A shows a 555 timer connected as an astable multivibrator. B shows the equation to calculate values of R1, R2 (in ohms) and C (in farads).

$$(B) \quad f = \frac{1.46}{(R1 + 2 \times R2)\ C}$$

Fig 24—Pulse sequences showing 50% (A), 80% (B) and 20% (C) duty cycles.

and R2 and discharges to one-third V_{CC} through R2. The ratio of R1:R2 sets the *duty cycle* of the pulses. The duty cycle is the ratio of the time that the output is high to the total period of the output cycle (Fig 24). The output frequency is determined by

$$f = \frac{1.46}{(R1 + 2\ R2)\ C} \qquad (Eq\ 2)$$

where

R1, R2 = resistances in ohms
C = capacitance in farads

It may be difficult to produce a 50% duty cycle because of variations in the values of R1 and R2. One way to ensure a 50% duty cycle is to run the astable multivibrator at 2f and then divide by 2.

SUMMARY

Digital logic is playing an increasingly important role in Amateur Radio. Most of this logic is binary and can be described and designed using Boolean algebra. Using the NOT, AND, and OR gates of combinational logic, designers can build sequential logic circuits that have memory and feedback. The simplest memory circuit is called a flip-flop, or latch, and these latches can be combined to form such useful circuits as counters, shift registers, and byte registers.

Digital Integrated Circuits

Integrated circuits are the cornerstone of digital logic devices. An integrated circuit is a miniature electronic module of components and conductors manufactured as a single unit. Today's complex digital equipment would be impossible with vacuum tubes or even discrete transistors as active elements.

As one generation of ICs surpassed the previous one, it became necessary to classify them according to the number of gates on a single chip. These classifications are defined below.

Small-scale integration (SSI)—10 or fewer gates on a chip.
Medium-scale integration (MSI)—10-100 gates.
Large-scale integration (LSI)—100-1000 gates.
Very-large-scale integration (VLSI)—1000 or more gates.

COMPARING LOGIC FAMILIES

When selecting logic devices for a circuit, a designer is faced with the choice between many families and subfamilies of logic ICs. Which subfamily is right for the application at hand is often a function of several parameters. The characteristics that are usually important are *logic speed*, *power consumption* and *fan-out*.

Impedance

Gate impedance is one parameter discussed in the following sections. An ideal gate would have low output impedance, enabling it to deliver high current without dropping considerable voltage in its output stages. An ideal gate would also have infinite input impedance and would, therefore, draw no current. Unfortunately, such a gate does not exist, and the designer must compromise on input and output impedances.

Speed

Logic device families operate at widely varying clock speeds. Standard TTL devices can only operate up to a few MHz, while some ECL ICs can operate at several GHz. Gate propagation delay determines the maximum clock speed at which an IC can operate; the clock period must be long enough for all signals within the IC to propagate to their destinations. ICs with capacitively coupled inputs have minimum, as well as maximum, clock rates. While the designer might want to use the fastest available ICs, higher speed usually results in higher power consumption.

Power Consumption

In some applications, power consumption by logic gates is a critical design consideration. This power consumption can be divided into two parts: *static power* and *dynamic power*. Gates are either holding a state (high or low), or they are changing states, and each of these conditions has different power requirements. The power that is consumed when a gate changes state is called dynamic power. The power consumed when a gate is holding a state is called static power. Calculating the total power that will be required by an IC with several gates performing diverse functions is a complex task. Nominal power requirements, however, can be used to compare logic subfamilies.

Fan-out

A gate output can supply only a limited amount of current. Therefore, a single output can only drive a limited number of inputs. The measure of driving ability is called *fan-out*. Fan-out is expressed as the number of inputs (of the same subfamily) that can be driven by a single output. If a logic family that is otherwise desirable does not have sufficient fan-out, consider using noninverting buffers to increase fan-out (Fig 25).

Fig 25—Gate A (fan-out = 2) is connected to the two buffers (B and C), each with a fan-out of 2, to achieve total fan-out of 4.

Other Considerations

The parameters mentioned above are the basic considerations that influence the selection of a logic subfamily for a specific application. These considerations have complex interactions that come into play in demanding low-current, high-speed or high-complexity circuits. If you are designing a circuit, consult the application notes for the logic devices that you plan to use. Application notes contain speed, power-consumption and fan-out specifications, as well as other useful information.

DIGITAL-LOGIC IC FAMILIES

A number of families of digital logic ICs fall under the two broad categories of *bipolar* and *metal-oxide semiconductor (MOS)*. Numerous manufacturing techniques have been developed using both bipolar and MOS technologies. Each family has its own inherent advantages and disadvantages, and each of the surviving families has found its special niche in the market.

BIPOLAR LOGIC FAMILIES

Bipolar semiconductor ICs employ NPN and PNP junction transistors. While early bipolar logic was faster and had higher power consumption than MOS logic, these distinctions have blurred as manufacturing technology has developed. There are

Table 6

TTL Subfamily Performance Characteristics

Subfamily	Propagation Delay	Per-Gate Power Consumption	Flip-Flop Clock Input Maximum Frequency
Standard	10 ns	10 mW	35 MHz
L	33 ns	1 mW	3 MHz
S	3 ns	19 mW	125 MHz
LS	9.5 ns	2 mW	45 MHz
AS	1.5 ns	10 mW	175 MHz
ALS	4 ns	1 mW	50 MHz

several families of bipolar logic devices, and within some of these families there are subfamilies. The two most-used families are discussed here: *Transistor-Transistor Logic* and *Emitter-Coupled Logic*.

Transistor-Transistor Logic (TTL)

TTL (also known as T²L) has seen widespread acceptance because it is fast and has good noise immunity. The TTL family is divided into standard TTL and variations. The transistors in standard TTL circuits saturate, thus reducing operating speed. The variations cure this by clamping the transistors with *Schottky diodes* to prevent saturation or by using gold "dope" to reduce transistor recovery time. Both manufacturing processes are used, but Schottky-clamped TTL is faster.

Most TTL ICs are identified by numbers beginning with 54 or 74. The 54 prefix denotes a military temperature range of −55 to 125 °C, while 74 indicates a commercial temperature range of 0 to 70 °C.

One or two letters in the middle of a TTL device ID number indicate the special TTL subfamily, and the subfamily designation is then followed by a 2, 3 or 4-digit device-identification number. For example, a 7400 is a standard-TTL NAND gate, and a 74LS00 is a low-power Schottky NAND gate. The following TTL subfamilies are available:

74xx—*standard TTL*
L: (74Lxx)—*low-power*
S: (74Sxx)—*Schottky*
LS: (74LSxx)—*low-power Schottky*
AS: (74ASxx)—*advanced Schottky*
ALS: (74ALSxx)—*advanced low-power Schottky*

Each of the logic families is a compromise between speed and power consumption. Because the speed/power product is approximately constant, a decrease in the power consumption results in the trade-off of a slower device. For the amateur, another trade-off is cost. The advanced Schottky devices offer increased speed and reduced power consumption, but at a higher cost.

TTL Device Characteristics

Each TTL subfamily has particular characteristics that make it suitable or unsuitable for a specific design. Table 6

shows some of these parameters. The actual parameters may vary slightly from manufacturer to manufacturer. For complete information about a TTL subfamily, you should consult the manufacturer's Data Book on that subfamily.

TTL Circuits

One section of a 7404 hex inverter is represented schematically in Fig 26A. A low signal level applied to the input will cause Q1 to conduct. This will cause Q2 to be near cutoff, in turn biasing Q3 into saturation and Q4 near cutoff. As a result, the output will be high, about 1 V below V_{CC}. If the signal at the input is high, the conduction state of each transistor reverses, and the output drops nearly to ground potential (low). The input diode protects the circuitry by clamping any negative potential to approximately −0.7 V, limiting the current in Q1 to a safe value. The output diode at the emitter of Q3 is required to ensure that Q3 is cut off when the output is low.

The circuit in Fig 26B, one section of a 7400 gate, is very similar to that of A. The difference is that Q5 is a multiple-emitter transistor with one input to each emitter. A low at either input will turn on Q5, causing the output to go high. Both inputs must be high to produce a low output. This is a NAND gate.

TTL Outputs

In the TTL circuit of Fig 26A, transistors Q3 and Q4 are arranged in a *totem-pole* configuration. This output circuit has a low source impedance, allowing the gate to supply or sink substantial output current. The 130-ohm resistor between the collector of Q3 and +V_{CC} limits the current through Q3, protecting Q3 if the gate output is short-circuited.

Some TTL gates employ *open-collector* outputs, as shown in Fig 26C. Open-collector outputs have an advantage over totem-pole outputs: they can be *wire-ANDed*. In a wire-AND circuit, several open-collector outputs can be connected to a single *pull-up* resistor. When all of the outputs are high, the point where they are connected will be high. If any of the outputs are low, the connection will be low. This circuit implements the logical AND function, as shown in Fig 27. Open-collector outputs are also useful for interfacing

Fig 27—The outputs of two open-collector-output AND gates are shorted together (wire ANDed) to produce an output the same as would be obtained from a four-input AND gate.

Fig 26—TTL circuits and their equivalent logic symbols. The circuits in A and B have totem-pole outputs, while C has an open-collector output. Indicated resistor values are typical. Identification of transistors is for text reference only; these are *not* discrete components.

TTL gates to gates from other logic families. TTL outputs have a minimum high level of 2.4 V and a maximum low level of 0.4 V. A pull-up resistor, typically 2.2 kΩ, can be used to raise the high voltage level to 5 V, which may be needed to drive a non-TTL circuit. Although +5 is the recommended power-supply voltage for TTL, the pull-up resistor on an open-collector output can be connected to a different voltage, providing a high logic level that is not 5 V.

Three-State Outputs

There is another type of output that is available in TTL and other logic families. This output is called the *three-state output*. Three-state output devices are used to connect two or more outputs to a single input in such a way that *only one* of the outputs affects the input. To accomplish this, each output can take on a third, high-impedance, state (as well as the standard high and low states). When the output is in the third state, it is essentially disconnected from the circuit. Outputs in the high-impedance state do not affect the input to which they are connected; only the output that is in a normal high or low state will affect the input. Care must be taken to ensure that all of the outputs but one are in the high-impedance state. Three-state devices are used in computers to allow several devices to share a common set of wires (called a *bus*).

TTL Device Fan-Out

Each output from a TTL device can drive a certain number of inputs. Device fan-out varies from family to family, and also depends on the inputs being driven. Table 7 shows TTL device fan-out for each subfamily. Again, this information is intended to be general advice; consult the manufacturer's data sheets for more specific information.

Unused TTL Inputs

Unused inputs on TTL devices float at anywhere from 1.1 to 1.5 V, depending on the device and its subfamily. While this usually simulates a "high," many application problems can be traced to open inputs. Floating inputs are very susceptible to induced noise and can easily switch the state of the device. Unused inputs should

Table 7

TTL Subfamily Fan-Out Characteristics

Subfamily	Maximum Number of Inputs Driven					
	Standard	L	S	LS	AS	ALS
Standard	10	40	8	20	20	20
L	2	9	1	4	4	4
S	12	50	10	25	25	25
LS	5	20	4	10	10	10
AS	12	50	10	25	25	25
ALS	5	20	4	10	10	10

be tied to a solid logic level. A good design rule is to tie unused inputs to V_{CC} through a 1 kΩ to 5 kΩ resistor, because the input "high" current is usually less than the input "low" current. A single 1 kΩ resistor can handle up to 10 inputs.

Decoupling

When a TTL gate changes state, the amount of current that it draws changes rapidly. These changes in current, called *switching transients*, appear on the power supply line and can cause false triggering of other devices. For this reason, the power bus should be adequately decoupled.

For proper decoupling, connect a 0.01 to 0.1 μF capacitor from V_{CC} to ground near each device to minimize the transient currents caused by device switching and magnetic coupling. These capacitors must be high-frequency RF capacitors (disk ceramic capacitors are suitable). In addition, a large-value (50 to 100 μF) capacitor should be connected from V_{CC} to ground somewhere on the board to accommodate the continually changing I_{CC} requirements of the total V_{CC} bus line.

Emitter-Coupled Logic (ECL)

ECL, also called current-mode logic (CML), has exceptionally high speed, high input impedance and low output impedance. Some ECL devices can operate at frequencies higher than 1.2 GHz. This family is different from the other bipolar-logic families; the transistors operate in a nonsaturated mode that is analogous to that of some linear devices. ECL devices are used in UHF frequency counters, UHF frequency synthesizers and high-speed computers.

A significant feature of ECL gates is that complementary output functions are available from each circuit. For example, the circuit of Fig 28 provides both an OR output and a NOR output. Q1 or Q2, together with Q3 form a differential amplifier. When the Q2 collector goes high, the Q3 collector goes low. These levels then appear at the emitters of the output buffers, Q5 and Q6. Q4, D1, D2 and associated circuitry form a bias generator. The reference voltage at the base of Q3 determines the input switching threshold.

The typical logic swing for ECL devices is only 800 mV. ECL devices are characterized for use with a −5.2-V power supply, but operation from other supplies is possible. If the V_{CC} terminal is connected to +2.0 V and the V_{EE} terminal connected to −3.2 V, the device can drive a 50-ohm load. The power output obtained this way is about 1 mW. Heat sinking is sometimes necessary because ECL ICs dissipate a great deal of power.

There are several ECL subfamilies. High speed and low power dissipation are largely conflicting goals, so different subfamilies allow the designer to choose between the various trade-offs. ECL subfamilies are compatible, but only over a limited

Fig 28—Circuit topology of the ECL family. The functions of the various components are explained in the text. The availability of the complementary output is indicated by the modified logic symbol.

temperature range. The subfamilies differ mostly in resistance values and the presence or absence of input and output pull-down resistors.

METAL-OXIDE SEMICONDUCTOR (MOS) LOGIC FAMILIES

While bipolar devices use PNP and NPN junction transistors, MOS devices are composed of N-channel or P-channel field-effect transistors (FETs). MOS is characterized by simple device structure, small size (high density), and ease of LSI fabrication. MOS families are used extensively in microprocessors, digital watches and calculators.

P-Channel MOS (PMOS)

PMOS, in which P-type dopant is used for the source and drain, is the oldest and simplest MOS process. Electrical current in a PMOS device is conducted by the flow of positive charges (holes). PMOS power consumption is lower than that of bipolar logic, but its operating speed is slower. The only extensive use of PMOS is in calculators and watches, where low speed is acceptable and low power consumption and cost are desirable.

N-Channel MOS (NMOS)

In NMOS, N-type material is used for FET sources and drains, and electrons carry current. Since electrons flow faster than holes, NMOS has at least twice the speed of PMOS. NMOS also has greater gain than PMOS and supports greater packaging density through the use of smaller transistors.

Complementary MOS (CMOS)

CMOS uses both P-channel and N-channel devices on the same substrate to achieve high noise immunity and low power consumption (less than 1 mW per gate and negligible power during standby). This accounts for the widespread use of CMOS in battery-operated equipment.

A notable feature of CMOS devices is that the logic levels swing to within a few millivolts of the supply voltages. The input switching threshold is approximately one half the supply voltage ($V_{DD} - V_{SS}$). This characteristic contributes to high noise immunity on the input signal or power supply lines. CMOS input-current drive requirements are miniscule, so the fan-out is great, at least in low-speed systems. (For high-speed systems, the input capacitance increases the dynamic power dissipation and limits the fan-out.) There are now a number of CMOS logic IC subfamilies in production.

The original family of CMOS devices uses a 4000-series numbering system. Devices in this family have the numbers 40 or 45 followed by two or three numbers indicating the specific device. For example, a 4001 is a quad NOR gate. Other CMOS subfamilies have been developed and have been given numbers similar to the TTL numbering system. Parts in these series have the numbers 54 or 74, following by 1, 2 or 3 letters indicating the subfamily, and as many as 5 numbers indicating the specific device.

The following CMOS device families are available:

4000—(4017B)—*standard CMOS*.

C—(74Cxx)—*low-power TTL pin equivalents*. Devices in this family are pin and functional equivalents of many of the most popular parts in the 7400 TTL family. It may be possible to replace all TTL ICs in a particular circuit with 74C-series CMOS, but this family should *not* be mixed with TTL in a circuit without careful design considerations. Devices in the C series are typically 50% faster than the 4000 series.

HC—(74HCxx)—*low-power TTL compatible*. Devices in this family have speed and drive capabilities similar to LS TTL devices, but with better noise immunity and greatly reduced power consumption. This family can usually be mixed with TTL in a circuit.

HCT—(74HCTxx)—*CMOS-to-TTL interface*. Devices in this series were designed to interface TTL to CMOS systems. HCT inputs are TTL and NMOS compatible, while HCT outputs are CMOS compatible. HCT can be used to interface TTL to CMOS without adding a buffer gate. HCT devices can also be used as plug-in replacements in existing TTL circuits, although HCT propagation delays will be different from the TTL equivalents.

AC—(74ACxxxxx)—*advanced CMOS*. Devices in this family have reduced propagation delays, increased drive capability and can operate at higher speeds than standard CMOS parts.

ACT—74ACTxxxxx—*advanced TTL-compatible CMOS*. This family combines the improved performance of the AC series with TTL-compatible inputs.

As with TTL, each CMOS subfamily has characteristics that make it suitable or unsuitable for a particular design. You should consult the manufacturer's data books for complete information on each subfamily you are considering.

Special Considerations

A simplified diagram for a CMOS logic inverter is given in Fig 29. Some of the diodes in the input- and output-protection circuits are an inherent part of the manufacturing process. Even with the protection circuits, CMOS ICs are susceptible to damage from static charges. To protect against damage from static, the pins should not be inserted in Styrofoam® as is commonly done with TTL ICs. Instead a spongy conductive material is available for this purpose. Before removing a CMOS IC from its protective material, make certain that your body is grounded. Touching nearly any large metal object before handling the ICs is probably adequate to drain any static charge off your body. Some people may prefer to touch a *grounded* metal object or to use a conductive bracelet connected to the *ground*

Fig 29—Internal structure of a CMOS inverter.

terminal of a 3-wire ac outlet through a 10-megohm resistor.

All CMOS inputs should be tied to an input signal, positive supply voltage or ground. Unterminated CMOS inputs, even on unused gates, may cause gate outputs to oscillate. Oscillating gates draw high current and overheat.

The low power consumption of CMOS ICs made them attractive for satellite applications, but standard CMOS devices have proven to be sensitive to low levels of radiation—cosmic rays, gamma rays and X rays. Now, radiation-hardened CMOS ICs are able to tolerate 10^6 rads, making them suitable for space applications. (A rad is a unit of measurement for absorbed dose of ionizing radiation.)

Silicon-on-Sapphire (SOS)

SOS is a fabrication technique that takes its name from depositing a thin silicon film on an insulating sapphire substrate. This minimizes the parasitic capacitance normally found between the source, drain and a silicon substrate. SOS technology has been used to produce CMOS ICs with greatly reduced gate propagation times.

SUMMARY

There are many types of logic ICs, each with its own advantages and disadvantages. If you want low power consumption, you should probably use CMOS. If you want ultra-high-speed logic, you will have to use ECL. Whatever the application, consult up-to-date literature when designing logic circuits. IC data books and applications notes are usually available from IC manufacturers and distributors.

NOISE PRECAUTIONS

Noise is an important consideration in designing digital circuits. Noise on a signal or power line may cause logic circuits to perform erratically. Wires and printed-circuit traces may act as antennas that radiate RF noise. These same "antennas" can receive energy, especially when immersed in strong RF fields near a radio

transmitter.

Pulse rise and fall times determine the frequency of some of the electromagnetic interference radiated or conducted from a digital circuit. You can find the approximate upper frequency of the interference by dividing the constant 0.34 by the time the pulse takes to rise from 10% to 90% of its full value. For example, a rise time of 15×10^{-19} seconds between 10% and 90% levels would yield RF outputs up to 22.6 MHz. High-speed logic devices may be appealing for certain digital applications but can cause needless RFI because of fast rise and fall times. This can be avoided by using logic that is no faster than necessary.

Digital circuits also produce energy at the repetition rates of the pulses. For example, in digital equipment using a 3.579545-MHz clock, there will be RF energy at that frequency and its harmonics. Whether that energy emanates from the digital equipment and causes interference to radio reception depends largely on the design and construction of the digital equipment.

Computing devices sold in the US must comply with Part 15 of the FCC rules. A computing device, in the FCC definition, is any electronic system that generates pulses in excess of 10 kHz and uses digital techniques. Class A devices are for commercial or industrial use. Amateurs should be most concerned with Class B devices, which are for use in a residential environment. The restrictions specified in Part 15 are sufficient to minimize RFI to neighbors but inadequate to prevent interference to nearby Amateur Radio receivers. Clearly, digital equipment for the shack must be designed to meet more stringent requirements than those of Part 15 of the FCC rules!

Shielding of digital equipment is often neglected. Nonmetallic enclosures may save money initially but can allow unnecessary interference to nearby radio and television receivers. Whenever possible, use a metal enclosure that has solid electrical contact among all of its parts. Paint should be removed where parts meet. To ensure that the entire surface makes contact, you may also need to add some sheet-metal screws or sandwich some copper wire braid between the mating surfaces. Copper or aluminum screen may be used to cover holes without blocking ventilation. If a plastic or wooden enclosure cannot be avoided, it may be possible to add internal shielding using heavy-duty aluminum foil. Otherwise, consider an electrically conductive coating such as nickel-filled acrylic. Coating materials are available in spray cans or may be applied commercially.

Line filters should be used at the ac input of power supplies for digital circuits to minimize interference conducted on the power lines. Three-wire ac-power receptacles of the standard CEE-22 type with built-in line filters are recommended.

All signal and dc-power lines leaving enclosures should be bypassed or filtered. Connectors can be purchased with built-in bypass capacitors on every contact, but they are expensive. The use of individual bypass capacitors (with the shortest possible leads) on all lines capable of causing interference is an economical approach.

Large ferrite toroids can be used to decouple cables, and individual wires can be decoupled with ferrite beads.

The wires in cables that carry digital signals between enclosures may act as antennas. One solution to this problem is to avoid unnecessary external cabling by mounting different digital components in one shielded enclosure. You can also avoid the problem by using optical fibers to transmit digital signals between enclosures. Commercial fiber-optic cabling systems are expensive, but prices are expected to come down. Innovative amateurs may be able to design inexpensive fiber-optic systems.

All external wire cabling should be shielded. Each conductor may be separately shielded to minimize coupling between signal lines. In long shielded cables with a radiation problem, toroids can be added along the cable to break up the resonances. Just wind a few turns of the cable around the toroid core.

A low-impedance RF ground is as important for digital equipment as it is for radio equipment. Ensure that all digital equipment enclosures, frames, mother boards and cable shields are properly grounded. Use any space left on a PC board for an adequate ground plane.

Take design precautions to avoid power-supply noise from current spikes. Power-supply wiring should be as thick as practical, and wide PC-board power traces should be used to keep the line impedance low. This is particularly true for high-current lines. Ground traces should also be as large as possible, since they often carry as much (or more) current as individual power-supply traces. Different voltage traces should be arranged for minimum mutual coupling by separating them as much as possible. Where they cross, try to arrange them at right angles. On-board voltage regulators help isolate noise to and from the rest of the system. Be generous with decoupling capacitors—that's good engineering practice. Typical decoupling practice for +5-V lines includes: a 20-μF electrolytic capacitor at the input to the board, a 6.8-μF electrolytic capacitor in parallel with a 0.1- to 1.5-μF tantalum capacitor near every 1 to 8 devices and a 0.01- to 0.5-μF ceramic capacitor for every 1 or 2 adjacent devices.

Digital Interfacing

The term *interface* is used to describe a boundary between, or a physical or logical interconnection of, two devices, circuits or systems. *Physical interfaces* may be electrical and/or mechanical. *Electrical interfaces* must match such parameters as signal level and circuit impedance. *Mechanical interfaces* involve the mating of connectors and specific pin assignments within those connectors. *Logical interfaces* provide communication between different software modules.

Different interfacing tasks call for different levels of formality and standardization. Designers are free to define their own interfaces between logic families on a circuit board or circuit boards within a piece of equipment. When interfacing between two computers or between a terminal and a modem, however, follow existing interface standards.

INTERFACING LOGIC FAMILIES

Each semiconductor logic family has its own advantages in particular applications. For example, the highest frequency stages in a UHF counter or a frequency synthesizer would use ECL. After the frequency has been divided down to less than 25 MHz, the speed of ECL is unnecessary, and its expense and power dissipation are unjustified. TTL or CMOS are better choices at lower frequencies.

Each logic family has its own input voltage and current requirements, so they can't be mixed with satisfactory results. *Interface* can also mean the point at which one logic family ends and another begins.

A knowledge of the internal circuits of integrated circuits and their input/output (I/O) characteristics allows the designer to devise reliable digital interfaces. Typical internal structures have been illustrated for each common logic family.

The following section discusses some specific logic conversions. Often more than one conversion scheme is possible, depending on whether the designer wishes to optimize power consumption or speed. Usually one quality must be traded off for the other. Where an electrical connection between two logic systems isn't possible, an optoisolator can sometimes be used.

TTL Driving CMOS

TTL and low-power TTL can drive 74C series CMOS directly over the commercial temperature range without external pull-up resistors. TTL and low-power TTL cannot drive 4000-series CMOS directly, however, and a pull-up resistor is recommended for HC-series devices. The pull-up resistor is connected between the output of the TTL gate and V_{CC}, as shown in Fig 30A. The maximum usable value for this resistor is 15 kΩ, but the circuit capacitance, coupled with this large resistance, reduces the maximum possible speed of the CMOS gate. Lower resistance values generate a more favorable RC product at the expense of increased power dissipation. A standard TTL gate can drive a pull-up resistor of 330 Ω, but a low-power version needs a 1.2 kΩ minimum.

HCT-series CMOS devices were specifically designed to interface non-CMOS devices to a CMOS system. An HCT device is simply used as a buffer between the non-CMOS (usually TTL) and CMOS devices. The buffering may be combined with a logic function if a suitable HCT device is available. For example, an HCT flip-flop IC can have its inputs connected directly to a TTL device and its outputs connected directly to a CMOS device.

When the CMOS device is operating from a power supply other than +5 V, the TTL interface is more complex. One fairly simple technique uses a TTL open-collector output connected to the CMOS input and a pull-up resistor. The other end of the resistor is connected to the CMOS supply. Although this method works in many applications, the common-base level shifter of Fig 30B will translate a TTL output signal to a +15-V CMOS signal while preserving the full noise immunity of both gates. An operational amplifier configured as a comparator, as in Fig 30C, makes an excellent converter from TTL to CMOS using dual power supplies. An FET op amp is shown because its output voltage can usually swing closer to the rails (+ and − supply voltages) than a bipolar unit. Where the clock frequency is below 10 kHz or so, a 741 op amp may be used.

CMOS Driving TTL

CMOS devices can drive TTL loads with no additional interfacing required. The output voltages of CMOS devices are compatible with the input requirements of TTL devices. The input current requirements of the TTL devices place a strict limitation on the number of TTL loads that a CMOS device can drive from a single output (the fan-out).

Interfacing CMOS to TTL is a bit more complicated when the CMOS is operating at a voltage other than +5 V. One technique is shown in Fig 31A. The diode blocks the high voltage from the CMOS gate when it is in the high output state. A germanium diode is used because its lower forward-voltage drop provides higher noise immunity for the TTL device in the low state. The 68-kΩ resistor pulls the input high when the diode is back biased.

There are two CMOS devices that are specifically designed to interface CMOS to TTL using a lower supply voltage. The CD4050 is a non-inverting buffer that allows its input high voltage to exceed the supply voltage. This capability allows the CD4050 to be connected directly between the CMOS and TTL devices, as shown in Fig 31B. The CD4049 is an inverting buffer that has the same capabilities as the CD4050.

Summary

Most logic families and subfamilies can be interconnected. As the schematics in the preceding sections show, interface circuits are not complex. As in the initial logic family selection, high speed and low power consumption must be juggled when designing interface circuits. To construct successful interfaces, remember to stay within the current and voltage limits for gate inputs and do not draw excessive current from gate outputs.

OPTOCOUPLERS

An *optocoupler*, or *optoisolator*, is an LED and a phototransistor in a single IC package. Because they use light instead of an electrical connection, optoisolators provide a clean interface between circuits using widely differing voltages. Most LEDs in optocouplers are infrared emitters, although some operate in the visible light spectrum.

Fig 32A shows the schematic diagram of

Fig 30—Methods for driving CMOS loads from TTL sources. The circuit complexity depends on the power-supply voltages. The operation of these circuits is discussed in the text.

a typical optocoupler. In this case, the base of the phototransistor is brought outside the package. Access to the base lead is useful for controlling the transistor when the LED is not energized.

The figure of merit for an optocoupler is the current transfer ratio (CTR), the ratio of I_E to I_F, where I_E is the phototransistor emitter current and I_F is the forward current through the LED. A Darlington phototransistor is used in some devices to establish a more favorable transfer characteristic. The schematic of an optocoupler with a Darlington phototransistor is shown in Fig 32B.

In optocouplers with an internal light path, the light is transmitted from the LED to the phototransistor detector by means of a plastic light pipe or air gap. There are other configurations such as an external reflective light path and an external light gap. An *optical shaft-encoder* is an array

of open optocouplers where the light path is chopped by a rotating wheel.

It is possible to make an optocoupler from a separate light emitter and photodetector for applications such as a punched-tape or punched-card reader. Also, separate emitters and photodetectors are used for transmission of digital pulses over considerable distances. Amateur-Radio applications of this type include the use of light pipes to connect different pieces of equipment in the presence of strong RF fields. Amateurs should consider optical coupling to minimize radio-frequency interference between digital and analog equipment such as computers and radios.

An optoisolator packaged with a triac forms a *solid-state relay* that can replace electromechanical units in many applications. The advantages of this scheme include freedom from contact bounce, arcing, mechanical wear and noise. Some

Fig 31—CMOS-to-TTL interface circuits. The diode in the circuit at A is not necessary if both devices operate with a +5-volt supply. The circuit at B uses the 4050 CMOS buffer IC. The inputs of this IC can be at a higher voltage than its supply voltage. The 4049 is the inverting version of this buffer IC.

Fig 32—Optocouplers consisting of an LED and phototransistor detector. The device shown at A uses a typical single-transistor detector, while B has a Darlington phototransistor for improved transfer ratio.

solid-state relays are capable of switching 10 A at 117 V from CMOS signals.

Optoisolators can solve problems that might otherwise require complex circuits. Using optoisolators, low-voltage logic circuits can control high-voltage "real-world" devices, such as radio transceivers. Thus, optoisolators are critical to many digital control circuits. When designing circuits with optoisolators, check the current transfer ratio, isolation voltage and switching speed specifications.

INTERFACING EXTERNAL DEVICES

There are numerous considerations in design of an interface for connection with an external device. If the external device already exists and cannot be changed, the interface design task is largely a matter of meeting the established requirements of the external device. Key questions are: What type of connector is used, and what are the pin assignments? What voltage or current levels are required? What is the data rate? What is the signaling format?

If the external device can be modified or has yet to be designed, it is prudent to investigate existing standards and conventions for interfacing such devices. To do otherwise would be not only "reinventing the wheel" but limiting the interface possibilities with other similar devices. An interface standard encountered often in Amateur Radio is the Electronic Industries Association EIA-232-D and an earlier version known as RS-232-C (the two are not identical, and are not necessarily interchangeable). The International Tele-

graph and Telephone Consultative Committee (CCITT) standards V.24 and V.28 also specify an interface standard. Details of these and other established standards are presented in the Digital Communications chapter. To understand these standards, it is necessary to know something about how the data is communicated between devices.

Parallel and Serial Signaling

Within a piece of digital equipment, it is normal to handle a number of associated bits in *parallel*—all the bits in a group (byte or word) are handled exactly at the same time. Typically, but not always, there are 8 associated bits, and 8 conductors to move the information from one circuit to another. The requirement for 8 separate conductors is not a problem within a piece of equipment. When transmitting digital information over long distances, however, providing 8 wires or 8 simultaneous communications channels may be too expensive for the application.

The solution to this problem is *serial* signaling, in which each of the bits is sent in turn, according to an agreed sequence, over a single channel or wire. Continuing with 8 bits as an example, it is convenient to name the bits b_0, b_1, b_2, b_3, b_4, b_5, b_6, and b_7. (The subscripted figures represent the binary weight or significance of each bit.) One of the things that must be speci-

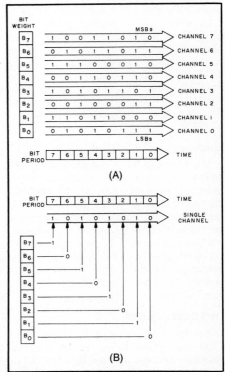

Fig 33—Parallel (A) and serial (B) signaling. Parallel signaling in this example uses 8 channels and is capable of transferring 8 bits per bit period. Serial transfer uses only one channel and can send only one bit per bit period.

fied for serial communications is whether b_0 (the least-significant bit or LSB) or b_7 (the most-significant bit or MSB) is sent first. Serial signaling makes it possible to send multi-bit binary coded data over a single digital channel.

A graphic illustration of parallel and serial signaling is given in Fig 33. In most amateur digital communications (either via radio or telephone lines), serial transmission is used to minimize cost and complexity.

Operational Mode

The number of channels needed for either serial or parallel signaling depends on the operational mode.

Simplex operation involves only one-way transmission. So only those channels needed to get the information from the sender to the receiver are necessary.

Half-duplex operation is similar to simplex except that the direction of transmission can be reversed. This permits two-way communication without the need for a separate channel each way. The penalty is that the channel must be shared and cannot provide full-time communications in both directions.

Full-duplex operation is simultaneous two-way signaling. For parallel transfer of 8 bits in both directions, 16 channels are required. Full-duplex serial communication requires two channels. This type of operation has the advantage of being able to provide communications in both directions at once.

Synchronization

In order to correctly receive data, the receiving interface must know when data bits will occur—it must be *synchronized* with the sender. There are two types of synchronization. In *asynchronous communication*, the receiver synchronizes on each incoming character. In *synchronous communication*, data is sent in long blocks, without start and stop bits or gaps between characters. Each of these schemes has its advantages and disadvantages.

Asynchronous Communications

In asynchronous communications, each character transmitted begins with a *start bit* and ends with a *stop bit*. See Fig 34A. The start bit (usually a zero) tells the receiver to begin receiving a character. The stop bit (usually a one) signals the end of a character. Between characters, the transmitting circuit sends the stop-bit state (steady one or zero). Because the receiver is always told when a character begins and ends, characters need not be sent at regular intervals. This is especially useful when there is a person typing the input characters; the typist is usually slower than the data communications equipment and may not type at an even pace.

One disadvantage of asynchronous communications is the inclusion of the start and stop bits, which are not "useful" data; if you are transmitting 8 data bits, a start bit and a stop bit, 2 of the 10 bits transmitted, or 20% of the bits, are *overhead*, used only for synchronization. On the other hand, asynchronous communications are rather simple. Because the receiver is newly synchronized at the beginning of each character, it does not need complex circuits to keep it synchronized. Because the characters need not be sent in a steady stream, no stringent demands are made on the person or process generating the characters. Amateur Baudot RTTY is usually asynchronous.

Synchronous Communications

In synchronous communications, data is sent in *blocks*, usually longer than a single

Fig 34—Serial data transmission format. In asynchronous signaling at A, a start pulse of one bit period is followed by the data bits and a stop pulse of at least one bit period. In synchronous signaling at B, the data bits are sent continuously without start or stop pulses.

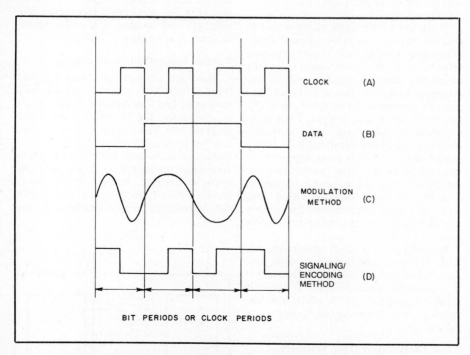

Fig 35—Recovering the clock (A) when the data (B) is transmitted allows a receiver to maintain synchronization during synchronous communication. The modulation method shown at C results in a transition of the received carrier at the beginning and end of each clock period. The encoding method shown at D results in a data transition in the middle of each clock period. Either of these methods provides enough information for clock recovery.

character. See Fig 34B. At the beginning of each block, the sender transmits a special sequence of bits that the receiver uses for initial synchronization. After becoming synchronized at the beginning of a block, the receiver must stay synchronized until the end of the block. Because the sender and receiver may be using slightly different clock frequencies, it is usually not adequate for the receiver to merely get synchronized initially and then depend on its internal clock. There are several ways for the receiver to stay synchronized. The transmitter may send the clock signal on a separate channel, but this is wasteful. The modulation technique used on the communications channel may convey clock information (Fig 35C), or the clock might be implicit in the transmitted data (Fig 35D).

One disadvantage of synchronous transmission is that the data must be sent as a continuous stream; characters must be placed in a buffer until there are enough to make a block. Also, while errors in asynchronous signaling usually only affect one character (the receiver can get resynchronized at the beginning of the next character), error recovery on synchronous channels may be a longer process involving several lost characters or an entire lost block. The major advantage of synchronous signaling is that it does not impose 20% overhead (the start and stop bits) on each character. This is an important consideration during large data transfers. AMTOR and packet radio are both synchronous systems.

Data Rate

There are limitations on how fast data can be transferred. First, the sending equipment has an upper speed at which it can produce the data in a continuous stream. Second, the receiving equipment has an upper limit on how fast it can accept and process data. Third, the signaling channel itself has a speed limit, often based on how fast data can be sent without errors. Finally, standards and the need for compatibility with other equipment may have a strong influence on the data rate used.

Data rate can be expressed in a number of ways. The terms "bauds" and "bits per second" (abbreviated bit/s) are both used to describe data-transmission rates, but the two terms are *not* interchangeable. Bauds are used to describe the *signaling* (or *symbol*) rate. This is a measure of how fast individual signal elements *could* be transmitted through a communications system. Specifically, the baud is defined as the reciprocal of the shortest element (in seconds) in the data encoding scheme. For example, in a system where the shortest element is 1 ms long, the maximum signaling rate would be 1000 elements per second. Instead of "elements per second," the term "baud" is used. This means it is *not* correct to refer to the "baud rate," because "bauds" is already a measure of speed, or rate. Continuous transmission is not re-

quired, because signaling speed is based only on the shortest signaling element.

Signaling rate in bauds says nothing about actual *information transfer rate*. The maximum information transfer rate is defined as the number of equivalent binary digits transferred per second; this is measured in *bits per second*.

So far, everything seems fairly simple. The complications arise when more sophisticated data encoding schemes are used. When binary data encoding is employed, each signaling element represents one bit. In a quadriphase shift keying (QPSK) system, a phase transition of 90 degrees represents a level shift. There are four possible states in a QPSK system; because two binary bits are required to represent four possible levels, each state can represent two binary bits. If 1000 elements per second are transmitted in a quadriphase system where each element can represent two bits, the actual information rate is 2000 bit/s.

This scheme can be extended. It is possible to transmit three bits at a time using eight different phase angles (bit/s = 3 × bauds). In addition, each angle can have more than one amplitude. A standard 9600-bit/s modem uses 12 phase angles, 4 of which have two amplitude values. This yields 16 distinct states; each state can then represent four binary bits. Using this technique, the information transfer rate is four times the signaling speed. This is what makes it possible to transfer data over a phone line at a rate that produces an unacceptable bandwidth using binary encoding. This also makes it possible to transfer data at 2400 bit/s on 10 meters, where FCC regulations allow only 1200-*baud* signals.

When are transmission speed in bauds and information rate in bit/s equal? Three conditions must be met: binary encoding must be used, all elements used to encode characters must be equal in width and synchronous transmission at a constant rate must be employed. In all other cases, the two terms are not equivalent. Each measurement is important at a different location in a communications link. Information transfer rate is most important to the communicator; how the information gets where it is going makes no difference. The link designer, however, need only worry about the signaling rate; the number of "bits per baud" is unimportant at this level.

Within a given piece of equipment, it is desirable to use the highest possible data rate. When external devices are interfaced, it is normal practice to select the highest standard signaling rate at which both the sending and receiving equipment can operate.

Error Detection in Data Transfers

Whenever data transfers are subject to errors, it is important to include some method of detecting and correcting errors. In data communications, there are numer-

ous techniques for error detection and correction. The technique employed in any specific circumstance depends on the types of errors likely to be encountered in the communications media. Some of these techniques are discussed in the Digital Communications chapter.

Parity Check

For some data transfers, *parity check* provides adequate error detection. To use the parity check, a *parity bit* is transmitted along with the data bits. In systems using *odd parity*, the parity bit is selected such that the transmitted character (data bits and parity bit) has an odd number of ones. In *even parity* systems, the parity bit is chosen to give the character an even number of ones. For example, if the data 1101001 (which has an even number of ones already) is to be transmitted in an even parity system, the parity bit should be a 0 (maintaining even parity). If the same data is to be transmitted in an odd parity system, the parity bit should be a 1, resulting in a total of 5 ones. When a character is received, the receiver checks parity by counting the ones in the character. If the parity is correct (odd in an odd system, even in an even system), the data is assumed to be correct. If the parity is wrong, an error has been detected.

Parity checking only detects a small fraction of possible errors. This can be intuitively understood by noting that a randomly chosen word has a 50% chance of having even parity and a 50% chance of having odd parity. Fortunately, on relatively error-free channels, single-bit errors are the most common, and parity checking will always detect a single bit in error. Parity checking is a simple error-detection strategy, and because it is easily implemented, it is frequently used.

Parallel Input/Output Interfacing

There are a number of parallel input/output (PIO) ICs available. Typically they have eight data lines and one or more *handshaking* lines. Fig 36 shows a simplified diagram of a PIO chip and its lines to an external device. The term "handshaking" includes a number of functions needed to coordinate the data transfer. One of these is the READY line, which, when it makes the transition from 0 to 1, indicates that data is available on all 8 data lines. If only

Fig 36—Parallel interface with READY and STROBE handshaking lines.

the READY line is used, the receiver may not be able to keep up with the data. In that case, a STROBE line is added to enable the receiver to tell the transmitter that it is ready to receive the next character. There are many other handshaking strategies that may be used during parallel signaling. The Centronics standard (Table 8) is commonly used for sending parallel data to printers.

Serial Input/Output Interfacing

Serial I/O (SIO) interfacing is more complex than parallel I/O. Fortunately there are a number of ICs available to handle the job. The advantages of serial data transfers and the general formats for asynchronous and synchronous serial transmission have been discussed earlier in this chapter. What is left to understand SIO is a discussion of the conversion process.

Within computers and other digital circuits, data is usually operated on, stored and transmitted in parallel. So, at the terminals of a serial interface, data must be converted from parallel to serial and back again. Serial-to-parallel and parallel-to-serial conversion is normally done with a shift register. The *universal asynchronous receiver/transmitter (UART)* is a shift-register device designed to handle these data conversions. The UART is capable of operating in the full-duplex communications mode. Furthermore, it can simultaneously send and receive data. UARTs can be programmed to select the number of data bits and whether the parity is odd, even, or not used. The UART transmitter accepts data in parallel form and shifts it out in asynchronous serial format. The transmitted serial format includes a start pulse, data pulse, and stop pulses of various lengths. The receiver operates by shifting the serial pulses into a register. Then, when the specified number of bits have been stored in the shift register and a stop bit is detected, the data is made available in parallel form.

The *universal synchronous receiver/transmitter (USRT)* is similar to the UART but is for synchronous operation. A more popular device is the *universal synchronous/asynchronous receiver transmitter (USART)*, which combines both a UART and a USRT on one chip.

Signaling on Lines

Inside equipment and for short runs of wire between equipment, the normal practice is to use neutral keying; that is, simply to key a voltage such as +5 V on and off. In neutral keying, the off condition is considered to be 0 V. Over longer runs of wire, the capacitance between conductors and the inductance of the conductors becomes of concern. As the capacitance increases, more time is needed to make the transition from 0 to 1 or vice versa. This decreases the maximum speed at which data can be transferred on the wire, and may also cause the 1s and 0s to be different lengths. This is known as *bias distortion*. Also, on longer

Table 8
Centronics Parallel-Printer Interface

Pin	Name	Source	Meaning
1	STROBE	Computer	Data lines are valid
2-9	D_0-D_7	Computer	Data to be printed
10	ACKNOWLEDGE	Printer	Data has been accepted
11	BUSY	Printer	Printer can't receive data
12	PAPER OUT	Printer	No paper in printer
31	INPUT PRIME	Computer	Resets printer
32	ERROR	Printer	Printer error
20-27	RETURNS	—	Grounds for D_0-D_7

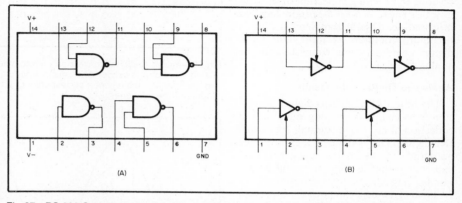

Fig 37—RS-232-C transmission-line drivers and receivers. A is a 1488 quad line driver. B is a 1489 quad line receiver. Note that pins 2, 5, 9 and 12 of the 1489 are response-control lines that are typically connected via 330-pF capacitors to ground.

lines, there is a possibility of picking up noise, which can make it difficult for the receiver to decide exactly when the transition takes place.

Because of these problems, *polar* keying (technically *bipolar* keying) is used on longer lines. Polar keying uses one polarity (for example +) for a logical 1 and the other (− in this example) for a 0. This means that the decision threshold at the receiver is 0 V for polar keying. Thus, any positive voltage can be taken as a 1, and any negative voltage becomes a 0.

Since neutral keying is usually used inside equipment, and polar keying is desirable for lines leaving the equipment, signals must be converted between polar and neutral. The old way of doing this was to use an electromechanical polar relay. Today, op amp circuits handle this conversion. Even more convenient than the op amp, however, are ICs called *line drivers* and *line receivers*. There are a number of different types available, but the most popular ones are the 1488 quad line driver and the 1489 quad line receiver. "Quad" signifies that there are four drivers or receivers in the same IC package. Diagrams of the 1488 and 1489 with their pin assignments are shown in Fig 37. The 1488 is capable of converting four data streams at

standard TTL levels to output levels that meet EIA RS-232-C or CCITT V.24 standards. The 1489 has four receivers that can convert RS-232-C or V.24 levels to TTL/DTL levels.

Summary

There are many types of digital interface, but a given interface can be categorized by answering several questions: Is it a parallel or a serial interface? Is it internal to a device, or is it between two devices? Does the interface signal asynchronously or synchronously? What recognized standards might apply to the interface? Once these broad questions have been answered, you can begin to study the interface in detail.

DIGITAL AND ANALOG INTERFACING

Until now, we have confined our discussion to digital electronics—the generation and manipulation of bits. It will come as no surprise, however, that it is an analog world. Virtually all measurable values in the physical universe are continuously variable and are thus analog. How can the many advantages of digital processing be applied to the analog world? We must employ *analog-to-digital conversion (ADC)* and *digital-to-analog conversion (DAC)*.

Why Convert?

There are many reasons for using digital techniques on analog signals. Analog signals have the undesirable characteristic that they often pick up noise, and it is difficult or impossible to remove the noise from the signal. Digital signals, on the other hand, are not likely to pick up noise (errors), and once noise has been introduced, it can often be detected and corrected. When an analog signal has been *digitized,* it is subject to the whole spectrum of logical and computerized manipulation. It can be sent from place to place in digital form. It can be stored without corruption. It can be digitally filtered. In short, anything that can be done to or with a collection of bits can now be done to or with the original analog information. Digital signal processing is becoming common as more and more digital computers are connected to the analog "real world."

Analog-to-Digital Conversion

The object of analog-to-digital conversion is to change an analog signal into a collection of bits that accurately represents that signal. This is done by measuring the amplitude of the analog signal and then expressing that amplitude as a binary number (Fig 38). As we have seen previously, binary numbers can be easily expressed and manipulated by electronic digital circuits. The process of measuring an analog signal and converting it to a binary number is called *sampling.* Correct sampling involves two things: *sampling rate* and *sampling resolution.*

Sampling Rate

Each digital sample represents the amplitude of the analog signal at a specific time. As the amplitude of the signal changes, the binary number representing the amplitude must change. The rate at which the binary number is updated is called the sampling rate. Fig 39 shows that if the sampling rate is too low, the digital amplitude values will represent a low-frequency *alias*, as well as the original analog signal. This condition is called *under sampling.* In order for the digital samples to correctly represent the analog signal, the sampling frequency must be at least two times the highest frequency component of the analog signal. This rule and its mathematical proof are the *Nyquist Sampling Theorem*, and the minimum sampling rate is called the *Nyquist rate.*

To apply the Nyquist theorem, you must know the highest frequency component in the signal that you want to sample. For example, if you want to sample a signal that has components as high as 3 kHz, the theorem specifies a minimum sampling rate of 6 kHz. In practice, it is desirable to sample above the Nyquist rate. This is because the output of an A/D converter contains not only the original signal, but "double sideband" images of the original signal, centered at multiples of the sampling frequency.

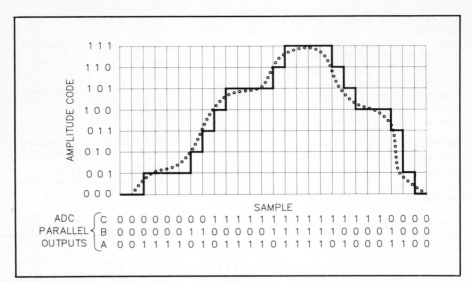

Fig 38—Analog-to-digital conversion of a complex wave. In this illustration, the voltage of the analog waveform is converted to the closest digital voltage level at the sample times. At each sample time, the digital code corresponding to the digital voltage level appears on the parallel outputs of the converter.

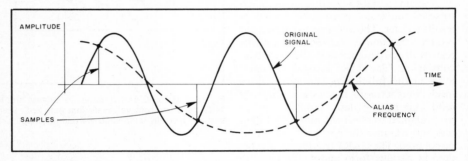

Fig 39—A sine wave sampled below the Nyquist rate. Notice that the samples specify an alias signal as well as the original sine wave.

Fig 40—The unfiltered spectral output of an A/D converter. The unshaded spectrum is that of the analog signal being sampled. F_A is the highest frequency in the analog signal. The shaded spectrum is the first set of sampling products, centered at the sampling frequency (F_S). A shows undersampling, B shows sampling at the Nyquist rate, and C shows reasonable oversampling. The dotted lines in B and C represent the filter passbands that would separate the desired signal from the sampling products.

Fig 40 shows the spectrum of an analog signal and the spectrum at the output of an analog-to-digital (A/D) converter. For clarity, only the first image spectrum (centered at the sampling frequency) is shown. The image must be eliminated if the digital sample is to correctly represent the analog signal. If the sampling frequency is below the Nyquist rate, the image overlaps the desired signal (Fig 40A). Because of the

Table 9
Signal-to-Noise Ratios for Ideal Analog-to-Digital Conversion

Number of Bits	Amplitude Levels	Signal-to-Noise Ratio (dB)
3	8	18
4	16	24
5	32	30
6	64	36
7	128	42
8	256	48
9	512	54
10	1024	60
11	2048	66
12	4096	72
13	8192	79
14	16384	84
15	32768	90
16	65536	96

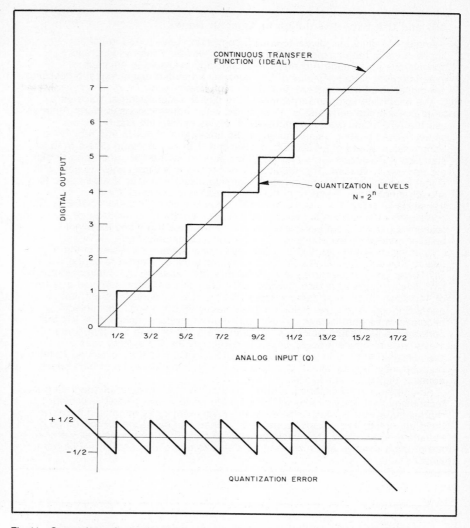

Fig 41—Comparison of a linear, analog transfer function with a quantized, digital transfer function. The difference between the two transfer functions results in quantization error, as shown at the bottom of the figure.

overlap, the image cannot be eliminated without eliminating some of the desired signal. This is called *aliasing*, and is the result of under sampling. When the sampling rate is equal to the Nyquist rate, the image is just adjacent to the desired signal (Fig 40B). In this case, an ideal filter (with vertical skirts) could eliminate the image.

Only when the sampling rate is above the Nyquist rate is there some separation between the desired signal and the image spectrum (Fig 40C). With this gap between the two spectra, real filters can filter out the image and leave the desired signal unattenuated. The higher the sampling rate with respect to the highest frequency in the analog signal, the farther the undesired image is from the desired signal.

Sampling Resolution

Analog signals are infinitely variable; they can take on an infinite number of amplitudes. An A/D converter with n output bits can only represent 2^n amplitudes (Table 9). Thus, the A/D converter cannot perfectly represent the amplitude of an analog signal. The number of bits in an A/D converter is the *resolution* of the converter. When an analog signal looks like a straight line, the output of an A/D converter has a "stair step" characteristic—it is *quantized*. Fig 41 shows the difference between an analog signal and a three-bit digital representation of that signal. At each sampling instant, there is a difference between the analog signal and the closest available digital value. This difference is called *quantization error*. Quantization error introduces noise, called *quantization noise*, to the sampled signal. The higher the resolution of the A/D converter, the lower the quantization error and the smaller the quantization noise. The relationship between resolution (in bits) and quantization noise (for an ideal A/D converter) can be expressed as

$$\frac{S}{N} = -20 \log\left(\frac{1}{2^n}\right) \qquad (\text{Eq 3})$$

where
  n = the resolution of the A/D converter in bits
  S/N = the signal-to-noise ratio in dB

This relationship can also be approximated as: $S/N = 6 \times n$.

Practical Considerations

From the preceding discussions of sampling rate and resolution, we see that large, frequent samples are ideal for A/D conversion. In practical circuits, however, these characteristics conflict with each other and with external constraints. Large samples require longer sampling times, imposing a maximum sampling rate. Samples must be transmitted to the device that is to process them, and communications channels can only handle a limited number of bits per second. Finally, the device that is processing the samples has a maximum processing speed. With all of these varying constraints and the fixed constraints of the Nyquist Theorem and S/N equations,

what is an acceptable A/D sample? Two industry standards are worth mentioning: the standard for digital telephony is 8-bit samples and an 8-kHz sampling frequency; the Compact Disk Digital Audio System takes 16-bit samples at 44.1 kHz. These systems, and their impact on amateur experimenters are explored in the sidebar.

Digital-to-Analog Conversion

Once an analog signal has been turned into a digital bit-stream and manipulated, stored or communicated, it is sometimes converted back into an analog signal. Frequency and voice synthesizers must also convert digital information into analog signals. This process is called digital-to-analog (D/A) conversion. In D/A conversion, each bit in a digital sample is converted to a voltage or current that is weighted to correspond to the bit's binary value. The resulting analog signals are summed to obtain an analog representation of the binary number. Fig 42 shows a D/A

A/D and D/A Experimentation in Amateur Radio

Analog-to-digital and digital-to-analog conversion have found important applications in the commercial and consumer worlds. These widespread applications have made A/D and D/A technology available to amateur experimenters. Two examples of this consumer-oriented digital signal processing are digital voice transmission and digital high-fidelity audio.

The telephone companies pioneered the digital transmission of voice on a large scale in the early 1960s. Most digital voice transmissions in North America use the AT&T "mu-law" standard—an 8-kHz sampling rate and 8 bits per sample. The resulting signal has an audio bandwidth of 4 kHz and requires a transmission speed of 64,000 bits per second. Mu-law encoding differs from standard A/D conversion in that the steps defined by the 256 quantizing levels are not evenly spaced. This technique causes the quantizing noise to vary with signal level, giving a nearly constant signal-to-noise ratio over a wide range of speech amplitudes. Because of the widespread use of digital speech transmission within the telephone network, mu-law coder/decoder (CODEC) ICs containing A/D and D/A converters and filters have become available at reasonable prices from several manufacturers. These ICs make excellent building blocks for experiments in digital voice communication.

Another consumer product that employs digital signal processing is the high-fidelity Compact Disk Digital Audio System, commonly referred to as the CD. A CD player uses a laser to scan a 12-cm disk that holds up to 74 minutes of very high fidelity digitized audio. The two audio channels are each sampled at a rate of 44.1 kHz, 16 bits per sample. Based on the rule of thumb 6 dB/bit, the quantizing signal-to-noise ratio is approximately 96 dB! As CD technology becomes more popular and more manufacturers produce inexpensive ICs that perform the necessary functions, experimenters will be able to adapt some of these parts to amateur applications. In particular, the CD system uses a sophisticated form of forward error correction (FEC), and ICs developed for this purpose may be very useful in improving the error performance of high speed amateur digital transmissions.

As amateurs gain experience with digital audio, the prospect of integrating this technology with packet radio will become attractive. Voice packet switching represents a way in which amateurs with diverse interests might join forces to build an "integrated voice/data network" capable of satisfying a wide range of communication needs. The basic technology needed is here today; all we need are enough creative and motivated amateurs to make this a reality.—*Phil Karn, KA9Q*

Summary

D/A and A/D conversion allows digital circuits to act on and generate analog signals. Correct A/D conversion requires sampling at or above the Nyquist rate and enough bits per sample to yield a good signal-to-noise ratio. D/A conversion produces an analog signal from a sequence of digitally encoded amplitudes.

HYBRID ANALOG AND DIGITAL ICs

There is a growing number of integrated circuits that have both analog and digital inputs and outputs. Some of these chips switch analog signals by means of digital control signals. Others are signal processors.

Analog Switches and Multiplexers

Bilateral switches are CMOS devices that act as digitally controlled, SPST, solid-state switches. The signals on the input/output ports of these switches may be either analog or digital. The switches are controlled by digital signals. The block diagram of a quad bilateral switch is shown in Fig 43.

Analog multiplexers are devices that use bilateral switches to implement single-pole multiple-throw switches. Analog multiplexers are bilateral; pins are not strictly inputs or outputs, but can be either inputs or outputs. Unlike bilateral switches, analog multiplexers do not use a single binary control for each switch. Instead, analog multiplexers use binary-coded control inputs. For example, the analog multiplexer represented in Fig 44 selects one of 8 input/output lines using three digital-control inputs.

Analog bilateral switches and multiplexers can be used to switch signals, control the gain of an amplifier, select between resistive and reactive components, and perform numerous other tasks. Typically, these devices can handle signals up

Fig 42—A D/A converter using four appropriately weighted current sources and a summing current-to-voltage converter. Notice that the MSB, representing $2^3 = 8$, generates 8 times the current generated by the LSB, which represents $2^0 = 1$.

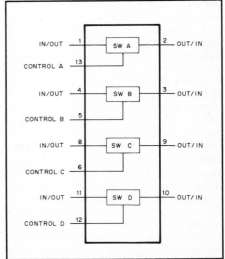

Fig 43—Block diagram of a CMOS 4066 quad bilateral switch. Each switch has its own control input.

converter using switched current sources. The output of a D/A converter is called a *digitally synthesized waveform*. Digitally synthesized waveforms are quantized, and the abrupt changes that characterize quantized signals appear on D/A converter outputs. These abrupt changes manifest themselves as unwanted high-frequency components in the output of the D/A converter. They must be removed by filtering. The correct filter for this application is a low-pass filter with cutoff frequency at or below one-half the sampling frequency.

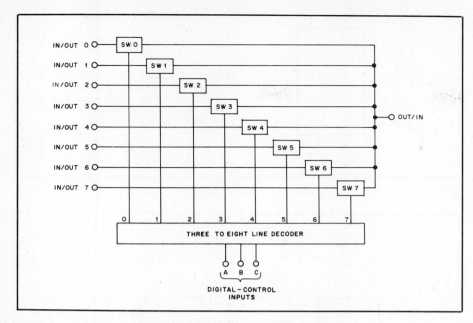

Fig 44—Block diagram of an 8-channel analog multiplexer/demultiplexer.

Fig 45—Simplified diagram of a sample-and-hold (S/H) amplifier. When the switch is in the SAMPLE position, the voltage across the capacitor is equal to the input voltage. When the switch is in the HOLD position, the capacitor retains its charge, presenting a sample of the input voltage to the S/H output.

to 15 V peak-to-peak, provided that the power supply can handle the signal excursions. Complex analog multiplexing schemes can be realized by using digital logic to control analog switches.

Sample-and-Hold Amplifiers

A *sample-and-hold (S/H)* amplifier uses a capacitor to store a sample of the input voltage. The charge on this capacitor tracks or samples the input voltage until the amplifier is put into the HOLD mode. At this time, the capacitor stops tracking and holds the input voltage (Fig 45). S/H amplifiers have numerous applications in A/D and D/A converters. They are also used in data-acquisition and synchronous-demodulation applications.

Switched-Capacitor Filters

The *switched-capacitor filter (SCF)* is an IC that can be used as a low-pass, high-pass, band-pass or notch filter with as many as five poles on a single chip. SCFs are easy to use: filter type, Q and bandwidth are determined by external resistors, and the filter center frequency is determined by an external clock signal. Furthermore, frequency and bandwidth can be digitally controlled. Currently available SCFs have dynamic ranges of around 80 dB and Qs up to 50, and they are usable at frequencies up to 250 kHz. Radio amateurs are using SCFs as CW and RTTY audio-bandpass filters and in DTMF and modem waveform generators.

SUMMARY

Interfaces take many forms. There are interfaces between IC families, interfaces between circuit boards, interfaces between digital devices and interfaces between digital and analog domains. Each type of interface places different demands on circuit designers. It is important to know what kind of interface you are designing, what its power requirements and restrictions are, what speed it will operate at, how noise is likely to be introduced into it and what standards might apply to the interface. Only when you understand these characteristics can you design and build a successful interface.

Memory Devices

Computers and other digital circuits usually rely on stored information. This stored information may be data to be acted upon or instructions to direct circuit actions. Digital information is stored in *memory devices*.

A memory device consists of a large number of *memory locations* or *words*. Each word, in turn, is composed of some number of *memory cells*, each capable of remembering one bit of binary information. The number of bits in each word, equal to the number of memory cells per memory location, is variable. Eight-, 16- and 32-bit words are common.

In order to store data in, or retrieve data from, a memory device, it is necessary to gain access to specific memory cells. The words *write* and *read* are used to signify storage and retrieval, respectively.

Memories can be divided into broad categories based on what memory cells can be accessed at a given instant. *Sequential-access memory (SAM)* must be accessed by stepping past each memory location until the desired location is reached. Magnetic tapes implement SAM; to reach information in the middle of the tape, the tape head must pass over all of the information on the beginning of the tape. Two special types of SAM are the *queue* and the *push-down stack*. In a queue, also called a *first-in, first-out (FIFO)* memory, locations must be read in the order that they were written. The queue is a "first-come, first-served" device, like a line at a ticket window. The push-down stack is also called *last-in, first-out (LIFO)* memory. In LIFO memory, the location written most recently is the next location read. LIFO can be visualized as a stack; items are added to and removed from the "top" of a push-down stack.

The second category of memory is *random-access memory (RAM)*. Random-access memory allows any memory cell to be accessed at any instant, with no time wasted stepping past "preceding" locations. Random-access memory is like a bookcase; any book can be pulled out at any time.

It is usually faster to access a desired word in random-access memory than it is to access a word in SAM. Also, all words in random-access memory have the same access time, while each word in a SAM has a different access time. Generally, the semiconductor memory devices internal to computers are random-access memories. Magnetic devices, such as tapes and disks, have at least some sequential access characteristics. We will leave tapes and disks for a later section and concentrate here on random-access, solid-state memories.

Addressing

An *address* is the identifier, or name, given to a particular location in memory. Within a memory IC, each word is given a unique address. The first word in the memory is given the address 0. To access a given word, the binary address of that word is placed on the chip's *address lines*. For example, to access the 11th word in a memory with eight address lines, the address lines would be set to 00001010. For ease of notation, programmers and circuit designers do not write addresses in binary form, but use octal (base-8) or hexadecimal (base-16) notation. In *hex*, 00001010 is written "0A".

Memory Chip Size

Internally, memory chips use binary arithmetic to specify address locations. Therefore, the number of words that a memory IC can store, and the number of bits in a word are usually powers of 2. An IC with 8 address lines has 2^8 or 256 uniquely addressable words. The size of a memory IC is usually expressed as "M × N", where M is the number of words in the IC, and N is the number of bits in each word. Memory chips are small as 16 × 4 and as large as 262,144 (256×2^{10}) × 1 are common. To understand how memory ICs are organized into large computer memory systems, one must first understand how small memory chips work. We will use a 256 × 1 IC as an example.

Memory Architecture

Memory chips, no matter how large or small, have several things in common. Each chip must have *address lines*, *data lines* and

Fig 46—Simplified 256 × 1 memory IC. The DATA line is an input during write operations and an output when data is being read from the memory. All other signals are inputs to the IC.

Fig 47—A 256 × 4 memory built with four of the ICs in Fig 46. Address and control signals are decoded by the four ICs, resulting in four bits of data (one bit from each IC) being read or written by the circuit.

control lines (Fig 46). A memory IC must have enough address lines to uniquely address each of its words. A 256 × 1 memory must, therefore, have 8 address lines. There must be as many data lines on a chip as there are bits per word in the chip, so the 256 × 1 memory has 1 data line. Data lines are both inputs to the chip (when writing) and outputs from the chip (when reading). Therefore, there must be a control line that distinguishes read operations from write operations. This line is labeled R/W in Fig 46. When R/W is 1, the chip is in the write mode.

The final control line on this simple memory is the chip select (CS). When CS is 1, the chip is selected, and it acts on the R/W, address and data information presented to it. When CS is low, the data line enters a high-impedance state, so that the deselected chip does not effect operation of devices or circuits attached to it. On actual ICs, CS and R/W may be inverted or edge-triggered inputs, and there may be other lines on a memory chip. The chip in Fig 46 does, however, provide a realistic basis for understanding memory chips.

Writing to Memory

If we want to write a 1 to the 11th word

of the 256 × 1 memory in Fig 46, we must execute the following steps:

1) Place the correct address (in this case 0A hex or 00001010 binary) on the address lines.

2) Place a 1 on the data line.

3) Set the R/W control line to 1 (write).

4) Set CS to 1. This will result in the data on the data line (1) being written to the address on the address lines (00001010). Some memory ICs use the R/W control line to activate the write cycle. Consult the manufacturer's data sheet for the IC you are using.

Reading from Memory

To read the contents of the 11th word:

1) Place the address 00001010 on the address lines.

2) Set the R/W control line to read (0).

3) Set CS to 1. When all of this has been done, the data from address 0A (hex) will be placed on the data line.

Timing

The above discussion ignores subtle timing requirements. These requirements are strict, and usually insist that data being written to the memory be present for a minimum *setup time* before and *hold time* after the CS and R/W signals. Timing specifications also define how long address lines must be stable and when data being read from the memory is valid. Consult manufacturers' data sheets and applications notes for timing information.

Larger Words

We have shown how a one-bit-wide memory works. Usually, though, we want a wider memory. Low-cost home computers use 8-bit words, and 16- and 32-bit computers are also used. One way to get wider memory is to use several 1-bit-wide memory chips, as shown in Fig 47.

The address and control lines go to each chip, and data from each chip is used as a single bit in the large word. It is easy to see that when reading from address 0A (hex), the data lines D_0 through D_3 contain the data from address 0A of chips U0 through U3. The same is true when writing to an address.

An address placed on the shared address lines (called an *address bus*) now specifies an entire word of data. Notice that one line of the address bus connects to the CS pin of each memory chip. This line is labeled ME, or *memory enable*, and sets all four ICs to read or write data at the same time.

If all four memory chips were put in a single package, they would make a 256×4 IC. This IC would look like the IC in Fig 46, except that it would have 4 data lines. It would perform like the circuit in Fig 47. In fact, ICs with 4- and 8-bit words are quite common, and even larger words are available.

More Address Space

Most tasks require more than 256 words of memory. It is not uncommon for a personal computer to address 640×2^{10} 8-bit words. To understand how such large memories are built and addressed, we will look at a 1024×8 (1-kbyte) memory built from four 256×8 memory chips (Fig 48).

Ten address lines are needed to address 1024 locations ($2^{10} = 1024$). Eight of the 10 address lines (A_0 to A_7) are used as a normal address bus for chips 0 through 3. The remaining 2 address lines (A_8 and A_9) are used to choose between the 4 memory chips. A_8 and A_9 are run through a *2-to-4-line decoder*. For each of the four combinations of A_8 and A_9, the decoder places a 1 on a different one of its outputs. When employed in this manner, the 2-to-4-line decoder is called an *address decoder*. To assert the CS input for one of the memory chips, ME must be 1 and the correct output of the 2-to-4-line decoder must also be 1. When an address is placed on A_0 through A_9, a single memory chip is selected by ME, A_8 and A_9. The other 8 address lines address a single word from that chip. The three chips that are not selected enter a high-impedance state and do not affect the data lines. This example shows how large memories are built from small memory ICs.

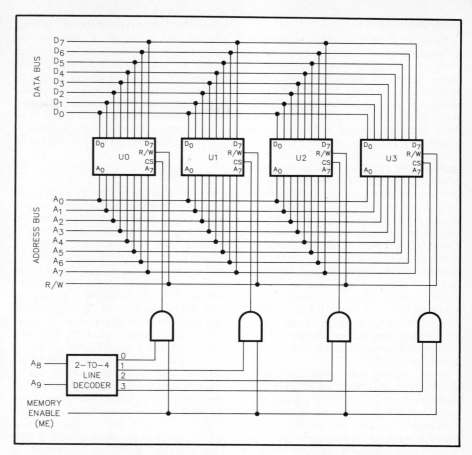

Fig 48—A 1024 × 8 memory using four 256 × 8 memory ICs. The high address bits, A_8 and A_9, select one of the memory ICs. The remaining seven address bits address a byte from the selected IC. Address and data lines shared in parallel by several chips are called a *bus*.

Summary

All memories built with more than one memory IC employ the techniques described above. Using the proper memory ICs and address decoding, any size memory with any word length can be built.

MEMORY TYPES

The concepts described above are applied to several types of random-access, semiconductor memory. Semiconductor memories are categorized by the ease and speed with which they can be written and their ability to "remember" when power is removed from the circuit.

Random-Access Memory

Random-Access Memory (RAM) is usually used for semiconductor memories that can be written to or read from with equal ease and speed. It is usually safe to assume that RAMs are "volatile," meaning that information stored in RAM will be lost if power is removed.

Two types of RAM are common: *static RAM* and *dynamic RAM*. Dynamic RAM (DRAM) stores a bit as the presence or absence of charge on MOSFET gate-substrate capacitance. Because the capacitance is not perfect, the charge leaks or degrades slowly and must be refreshed periodically (typically every few milliseconds). This memory refresh is usually performed by a *dynamic RAM controller* IC. A static RAM (SRAM) is an array of flip-flops. When a bit is stored in a flip-flop, the bit will remain until power is removed or another bit replaces it. SRAMs do not need to be refreshed. While SRAMs may seem more desirable, they are neither as simple to manufacture nor as "dense" as DRAMs. DRAMs are often 1.5 to 4 times as dense as SRAMs. Increased density and ease of manufacture make DRAMs significantly cheaper than SRAMS. There is a trade-off, however. Static RAM ICs have much faster access times than dynamic RAM ICs.

Both bipolar and MOS semiconductors are used to make RAMs. While all bipolar RAMs are SRAMs, MOS techniques can produce both static and dynamic RAMs. Cost, power consumption and access speed are the factors that help designers select static or dynamic, MOS or bipolar RAMs. Generally, MOS RAMs have lower power consumption than bipolar RAMs. Access speed varies widely within and between RAM categories. To select the best RAM for a given application, consult manufacturers' data sheets.

Read-Only Memory

Read-only memory (ROM) is nonvolatile; its contents are not lost when power is removed from the memory. Although the name "read-only memory" implies that ROMs can never be written, all ROMs can be written or *programmed* at least once. *Mask ROMs* are programmed by having ones and zeros etched into their semiconductors at manufacturing time.

Another type of ROM, called *programmable ROM (PROM)*, can be written to after manufacture. *Fusible-link PROMs* are written by electrically burning away specific diodes or transistors in a semiconductor memory array. This type of PROM can be written only once. Two types of PROMs can be erased and reprogrammed. Erasing is done by ultraviolet light for UV-erasable PROMs (EPROMS), and electronically for electronically erasable PROMs (EEPROMs). The erasure cycle for EEPROMs is long, and UV PROMs must be removed from operation for reprogramming. These requirements mean that data cannot be written as quickly and easily to ROMs as to RAMs.

What (besides their being nonvolatile) distinguishes PROMs from RAMs? Read and write times for RAMs are nearly equal, but PROMs have slow write times (in the millisecond range), and RAM-like read times (measured in nanoseconds). Two other factors make it hard to write to PROMs. First, PROMs must be erased before they can be reprogrammed. Second, PROMs often require a programming voltage higher than their operating voltage. ROMs are practical only for storing data or programs that do not change frequently and must survive when power is removed from the memory. The programs that start up a computer when it is first switched on or the memory that holds the call sign in a repeater IDer are prime candidates for ROM.

Nonvolatile RAM

For some tasks, the ideal memory would be as nonvolatile as ROM but as easy to write to as RAM. Low-power RAMs can be used in such applications if they are supplied with NiCd or lithium cells for backup power. A more elegant and durable solution to this memory problem is called a *nonvolatile RAM (NVRAM*, or Xicor NOVRAM™). A NVRAM chip includes both RAM and PROM. When power is first applied or the chip is reset, the contents of the ROM are copied into the RAM. The system using the NVRAM reads and writes to the RAM as though the ROM did not exist. When requested, perhaps before power is turned off, logic in the NVRAM copies the entire contents of the RAM into the ROM for nonvolatile storage. The RAM in an NVRAM is called *shadow RAM*, and it is standard volatile RAM. The backup ROM in NVRAM is EEPROM, and each bit in the ROM can be reversed several thousand times. Since the RAM is only copied into the ROM on command, NVRAM lasts long enough for many applications. NVRAM fills the gap between easily written memory and nonvolatile memory.

SUMMARY

With RAM, ROM and NVRAM available in many sizes and packages, you should be able to find a memory IC that meets your design requirements. By using correct address decoding, relatively small memory ICs can be used to build large memory systems. Like most IC technology, memory chips are changing quickly—getting cheaper, faster, more efficient and smaller. When designing memory systems, be sure to consult the *latest* literature.

Table 10
Comparison of Memory Chips

Type of Memory	Volatile	Frequent Writes	Erasable	Erasable in System
RAM	yes	yes	yes	yes
NVRAM	no	yes	yes	yes
ROM	no	no	no	no
PROM	no	no	no	no
EPROM	no	no	yes	no
EEPROM	no	no	yes	yes
Bubble	no	yes	yes	yes

Digital Computers

Until the early 1970s, digital computers were strictly tools of industry and education; there were no home computers or hand-held calculators as we know them. Today, only 20 years later, everything from watches to automobiles is computerized. This revolutionary increase in the availability of computers was made possible by several simultaneous changes in technology that decreased the size, increased the complexity and decreased the price of semiconductors. These advances made possible the construction of the *microprocessor* IC. This single chip performs all of the control, logical and mathematical functions necessary for computation. A microprocessor, memory and I/O circuits are all that is needed to make a *microcomputer*.

Modern Amateur Radio transceivers, scanners, digital-code converters, packet-radio controllers and television systems contain *special purpose computers*. These are dedicated microcomputers that perform specialized control tasks and are not available for other uses. Many amateurs also have *general-purpose computers* that they use for Amateur Radio applications. The obvious result of the increase in use of microcomputers by amateurs has been a substantial increase in computerized RTTY. There are many other applications of computers in Amateur Radio; CW sending and receiving, contest duping and logging, computer-aided design (CAD), computer-aided instruction (CAI), satellite tracking, propagation prediction and record keeping are just a few. Amateurs have found numerous opportunities to use microcomputers, and as pocket computers and single-chip microcomputers become less expensive, they will be found in most amateur stations.

COMPUTER ORGANIZATION

A computer consists of a number of interconnected subsystems, each of which performs some specific task. These subsystems may be spread among many chips, or they may be concentrated in a single-chip microcomputer. Fig 49 illustrates the organization of a typical computer.

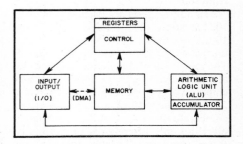

Fig 49—Major subsystems in a microcomputer. Not all of the communications paths shown on this diagram are present in every computer. DMA stands for direct memory access.

Input Devices

Input devices are used to feed the computer both *data* to work on and *programs* to tell it what to do. Some digital input devices are: switches, keyboards, magnetic disks and tapes, paper cards and tapes, demodulators and analog-to-digital converters.

Output Devices

Output devices are used to present the *results* of computer operations to the user or to some other system. Output devices also allow the computer to control external devices. Printers, video displays, LEDs, LCDs, modems, speech synthesizers, plotters, relays and magnetic disks and tapes are common output devices.

Memory

The memory subsystem usually has several thousand words of storage, both temporary (RAM) and nonvolatile (ROM). It holds computer programs as well as input, intermediate and output data.

Arithmetic Logic Unit

The *arithmetic logic unit (ALU)* performs logical operations (such as AND, OR and other operations) and arithmetic operations (addition, subtraction, multiplication and division). The ALU may depend on the control unit to supply its data and send its results to memory, or it may be able to access memory itself.

Control Unit

The *control unit* directs the operation of the computer. It takes instructions from memory and executes them. In the course of executing an instruction, the control unit may call on the ALU, perform I/O and access memory to read or write data. The control unit maintains the *program counter*, which contains the address of the next instruction that the control unit will fetch for execution. The program counter usually moves from lower addresses to higher addresses, but some instructions cause the control unit to change the contents of the program counter. This is called looping or branching. The control unit and the ALU are usually both in the microprocessor IC.

Registers

Microprocessor chips have some internal memory locations that are used by the control unit and the ALU. Because they are inside the microprocessor IC, these *registers* can be accessed much more quickly than other memory locations. Some registers are purely internal and cannot be directly accessed by programs. Others can be accessed directly. The registers that can be programmed are divided into *general-purpose* and *special-purpose registers*. General-purpose registers can be used as though they were RAM locations, although they are referred to by name rather than by address. The special-purpose registers usually include the *program counter*, the *accumulator*, the *stack pointer* and a *flag register*. The program counter, as discussed

before, contains the address of the next instruction that the computer will execute. The accumulator contains the result of the latest ALU operation. For program control, the microprocessor uses a section of RAM as a push-down stack. The stack pointer contains the address of the "top" of this stack. The flag register holds status and flag bits that indicate, among other things, whether the result of the latest ALU operation was zero, positive or negative.

Timing

The computer understands a few, relatively simple instructions: add A to B, move the contents of X to Y, send C to the output device, and so on. For the execution of these simple instructions to result in meaningful operations, thousands of instructions must be executed each second. The rate at which instructions are executed and the synchronization of the systems in a microcomputer are controlled by a single *clock*. Usually, an oscillator controlled by a quartz crystal generates the clock signal. The output of this clock goes to the microprocessor and to any other ICs that need to be synchronized with the microprocessor.

Summary

The subsystems discussed above may exist in several ICs or a single-chip microcomputer. At the least, a microprocessor *central processing unit (CPU)* contains the control subsystem and the ALU.

SELECTING A MICROPROCESSOR

Microprocessors can be classified by the number of bits their accumulators will handle at one time. Four-, 8-, 12-, 16- or 32-bit microprocessors are available. Amateurs usually use 8- or 16-bit microprocessors. Some microcomputers now have both an 8-bit and a 16-bit processor on the same PC board, permitting operation of either processor or simultaneous operation of the two.

One important consideration when selecting a microprocessor is the availability of desirable software for that processor. Familiarity of the designer with programming the microprocessor, or an earlier model with a similar instruction set, may also be an important consideration. Some microprocessors are *upwardly compatible* with older microprocessors of the same family. Upward compatibility means that programs written for the older microprocessor will run on the newer microprocessor. Upward compatibility eases the transition from one processor to another, and allows a designer to gain the advantages of a new microprocessor without having to replace a complete software library.

Speed is another important consideration in selecting a microprocessor. Clock rates typically run from 1 to over 30 MHz, with the 4- to 10-MHz range being suitable for most Amateur Radio applications. The

clock frequency defines the duration of the *machine cycle*—the basic unit of time for a microprocessor. In one machine cycle, the microprocessor can perform one basic operation. For example, it might take one machine cycle for the control unit to fetch a number from memory. Each instruction that the microprocessor can execute is made up of several basic operations and will take several machine cycles to execute. Manufacturers' data sheets may refer only to average instruction execution times. For this reason, designers wishing to select the fastest microprocessor for a given job may develop a *benchmark* program to test how fast different microprocessors execute a desired task.

When selecting a microprocessor, it is important to know whether it will be supported by the manufacturer and/or other sources. Microprocessor manufacturers usually offer an entire family of support chips, such as a parallel I/O, serial I/O (UART), direct memory access (DMA) controller and counter/timer. It is best to consider the entire chip set before making the decision to select a particular processor.

Documentation is also vital to the designer. Manufacturers may offer an array of data sheets, application notes, programmer's guides and references and other design aids. It will be helpful to know whether the manufacturer will answer technical questions over the phone. Manufacturers may avoid documenting idiosyncrasies that could be design hurdles in particular applications. There are quite a few books on how to work with specific microprocessors. Maintaining contact with other designers, either directly or via users' groups, is another way of finding design information and learning about undocumented features.

Power requirements are important in some applications and may be the primary reason for selecting a given microprocessor. Early microprocessors used as many as four voltages, complicating power-supply design. Most designers prefer chip sets that use one voltage, usually +5 V. CMOS microprocessors are normally chosen for satellites and other battery-operated equipment where power is at a premium. If supply voltage varies widely, the voltage range over which a microcomputer will operate is also important.

Future cost and availability of a microprocessor are difficult to estimate. Nevertheless, there are numerous indicators such as reputation of the manufacturer, the amount of support available and *second sourcing* (arrangements made with other manufacturers to produce the same chip). When a chip is first introduced, its cost may be high, perhaps $50 or more. If it is used in large-quantity products, the unit price will drop, probably less than $10. Many amateurs are simply concerned with the current price of the chips they use. Manufacturers pay less attention to the current cost of a chip and more to their estimate of what it will cost when they have to order production quantities. If you are designing equipment for other amateurs to build (for example, if you plan to write an article for *QST*), try to project cost and availability ahead to the probable publication date. The chips that are cheapest at the moment may be phased out by the time people want to duplicate your circuit.

MICROCOMPUTER BUSES

Most microprocessors have a single set of data, address and control pins; most of the rest of the microcomputer must be connected, in parallel, to these pins. The address, control and data circuits that connect the subsystems to a microcomputer are called a *bus*. The bus usually also carries power throughout the computer. One popular mechanism for routing the bus to various parts of the microcomputer is to print the bus as a set of parallel traces on a printed-circuit board called the *mother board*. Multi-conductor connectors, placed at intervals along these traces, are used to connect individual memory, I/O or microprocessor circuit boards to the bus (Fig 50). Common home computers like the Apple® II series and the IBM® PC have the microprocessor and some memory on the mother board and several bus connectors, called slots, available for system expansion.

One popular bus was introduced with the Altair 8800 computer in 1975. Because it was a 100-wire bus, it became known as the *S-100 bus*. The S-100 bus accommodates circuit boards measuring 5 by 10 inches.

Another bus worthy of note is the IEEE-488-1978 standard. The 488 bus was originated by Hewlett-Packard under the name HPIB and has also been called GPIB. Its main use is for computer control of electronic test equipment, but it can also be used as a microcomputer peripheral bus. Most professional test equipment can be controlled by the 488 bus.

As mentioned earlier, the IBM PC and PC/XT use plug-in cards that connect to the computer bus on the mother board. The popularity of the IBM PC and PC/XT quickly made the *PC bus* a standard for manufacturers of PC-compatible cards and computers. The PC bus is a relatively simple synchronous 8-bit bus that uses parity protection and edge-triggered interrupts. This means that each interrupt line can be used by only one adapter card. The PC bus also has no provision for an external *bus master* (a specialized bus controller)—the bus is always under the control of either the CPU or the DMA controller on the mother board.

When the IBM PC/AT was introduced in 1984, IBM expanded the *AT bus* to accommodate plug-in cards using a 16-bit bus. The AT bus remained compatible with cards using an 8-bit bus by simply adding a new connector while retaining the old 8-bit PC bus connector. IBM AT computers can use either older 8-bit cards or newer, faster, 16-bit cards. Special signal

Fig 50—The backplane of a popular personal computer has several sockets for accessory PC boards such as video adapters, serial and parallel interface cards, or disk-drive controllers.

lines on the bus connectors let the cards tell the computer how to address them. This combined *PC XT/AT bus* came to be known as the *Industry Standard Architecture (ISA) bus*. The ISA bus allows a plug-in card to take complete control of the computer bus (the card becomes a bus master).

Now that 32-bit computers (using the Intel 80386 and 80486 microprocessors) are available, manufacturers have again expanded the ISA bus to accommodate 32-bit cards. The new bus is known as the *Extended Industry Standard Architecture (EISA) bus*. The EISA bus allows bus mastering, and allows EISA cards to share interrupt lines, but only with other EISA cards—while ISA cards can be plugged into an EISA bus, ISA cards cannot share interrupts.

IBM uses a different 32-bit bus in its PS/2 computers. This bus, called the *Microchannel Architecture (MCA) bus* also allows full 32-bit data transfers at high speeds (but at slightly slower speeds than EISA).

I/O TRANSFERS

The microcomputer would be useless without I/O. Input and output allow the computer to react to and affect the outside world. Microcomputers transfer data to and from peripheral devices using several techniques.

Program-Controlled I/O

Under *program-controlled* or *polled I/O*, all input and output events are initiated by the program that is running on the microcomputer. The program must wait until the I/O device is ready to accept or deliver data and then execute the instruction that actually sends or receives the data. An example of program-controlled I/O might be a program waiting for a keyboard entry:

Has a key been pressed?

If not, then check again.

If yes, then find out what key was pressed and continue.

One of the disadvantages of program-controlled I/O is that the program must spend its time checking the status of the I/O device. If the program must perform the I/O before it can continue anyway, time spent checking I/O status is not wasted. If, on the other hand, the program could be performing other tasks while waiting for I/O to be available, time spent checking status is wasted. Program-controlled I/O is easily written and debugged. In home computers using the BASIC language, program-controlled I/O is often the only kind of I/O used.

Interrupt-Driven I/O

Program-controlled I/O might be understood by imagining a cook returning to the oven every few minutes to see if a meal is ready to be served. In *interrupt-driven I/O*, the cook would go do something else, and the meal would interrupt him when it was ready to come out of the oven. An *interrupt* is a temporary break in the normal execution of a program. Under interrupt-driven I/O, external devices that are ready to accept output or generate input interrupt the program that is executing. When the microprocessor is interrupted, it suspends whatever program it was processing, branches to an *interrupt-service program*, takes care of the device that generated the interrupt and then resumes execution of the interrupted program. The major disadvantage of interrupt-driven I/O is that program flow can get very confusing; what if an interrupt-service program gets interrupted? If a program does not work, is there a problem with the program itself, or is there a problem in an interrupt-service program? These problems are not impossible to solve, and interrupt-driven I/O is common, especially in communications programs. Programs that rely on interrupt-driven I/O do not have to constantly check the status of I/O devices. Also, each interrupting device can be given a priority, so that I/O events get serviced in order of importance. Interrupt-driven I/O, despite its complexity, is often necessary or desirable in control and communications programs.

Memory-Mapped I/O

In *memory-mapped I/O*, addresses that are treated like RAM by the microprocessor are actually I/O devices. Thus, a command that would usually be used to read or write to a memory location might actually result in an I/O operation. Memory mapping is an addressing technique and might be used with interrupt-driven or program-controlled I/O.

Direct Memory Access (DMA)

DMA is used with I/O devices that need rapid transfer of data, such as magnetic disk drives or high-speed data-communications equipment. When a device that uses DMA is ready to transfer data (either to or from memory), a DMA controller makes the transfer directly between memory and the I/O device without interrupting or using the main control unit. Thus, DMA can perform I/O while another program is running, without interrupting that program. Although some microprocessors have built-in DMA controllers, DMA usually requires a special controller IC.

PERIPHERAL DEVICES

Peripherals are devices separate from the central-processing unit that provide additional facilities such as outside communication. Tape recorders, disk drives, printers, video-display terminals, keyboards and modems are common peripherals.

Moving Media

The term *moving media* refers to the mechanical motion of the storage medium past a read or write transducer (often called a *head*). The earliest forms of moving memory used hole patterns punched in paper cards or tapes. Punched cards (also known as IBM® cards), once widely used in the computer industry, have had virtually no application in Amateur Radio. On the other hand, punched tapes have seen Amateur Radio use. The tape format that gained the most popularity among amateur radioteletype operators was the 5-level punched tape, using the Baudot code. The tapes were prepared on a perforator (or reperforator) and read on a transmitter-distributor (TD).

Magnetic Media

Magnetic tape is widely used for storing digital information. Inexpensive audio cassettes, designed primarily for analog recording, were used for digital storage on many of the early home computers. Many low-cost microcomputers used cassettes as an inexpensive magnetic storage medium.

Unfortunately, for proprietary reasons, there was little standardization of the tones and data formats used by different microcomputer manufacturers. The Kansas City standard, developed in the mid-70s was an attempt to get all manufacturers to agree on a data rate of 1200 bits per second and the tones 1200 and 2400 Hz. Although it met with little commercial success, the Kansas City standard is now used for data transmission from the UoSAT amateur satellites and by the Radio Netherlands BASICODE project.

Small tape drives using special removable tape cartridges are now available for microcomputers. These tape drives are very

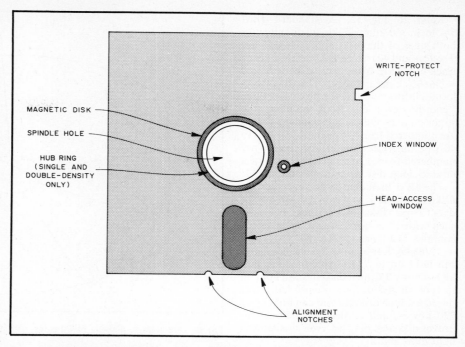

Fig 51—A typical 5¼-inch floppy diskette. The disk-drive head can be positioned anywhere within the head-access window, and the desired data then read or written when the correct spot on the disk spins under the head.

useful for backing up a large amount of information from a hard-disk drive.

The main problem with magnetic tape is that it is a *sequential access* storage medium. Data that is not near the tape-read head will take much longer to load than data that is near the head.

The *floppy disk* (also called a *diskette*) is the peripheral most widely used in microcomputers to store data. The diskette itself is a paper-thin Mylar® disk with a thin layer of magnetic material deposited on it. This disk, which is like a sheet of magnetic tape, is usually 3½, 5¼ or 8 inches in diameter. It is enclosed in an envelope that protects the magnetic coating while allowing a read/write head access to the disk. Floppy disks are read from and written to by a *disk drive*. The drive spins the disk (within its envelope) much like a record player spins a record. The read/write head may access any spot on the disk by moving to the correct point in the *head-access window* and waiting for the data to spin "into view." See Fig 51. Because the disk makes several revolutions per second, data on a diskette can be accessed much more quickly than data on magnetic tape.

Disks and disk drives may be either *single-sided (SS)* or *double-sided (DS)*. Double-sided disks are prepared for reading and writing on both sides, and double-sided drives have read/write heads for both sides of the disk. Depending on the *disk controller* used to access the disk drive, the

density of the data on the disk may vary. High data density allows more data to be written to the disk, but requires a higher-quality diskette. Common disk formats include single-sided, single-density (SSSD), single-sided, double-density (SSDD), double-sided, double-density (DSDD) and double-sided, high-density (DSHD). The DSHD format is also known as double-sided, quad-density (DSQD).

Data is stored on a disk in a number of concentric bands, called tracks. Some disks have a track density of 48 tracks per inch (tpi), while others use 96 tpi. Each track is divided into sectors—the smallest addressable unit of information on a disk. A photoelectric sensor in the disk drive may be used in conjunction with the index hole in the disk envelope to sense the radial position of the disk. Hard-sectored disks have holes in the disk for each sector. More common soft-sectored disks have only one hole. Depending on the number of tracks, sectors, bytes per sector and sides used, a floppy disk can store anywhere from 80 kilobytes to several megabytes.

Different computers use different disk formats. This is why it is not possible to exchange disks from one computer to another of a different type. Because the IBM PC is such a popular computer, that disk format has become a standard for other manufacturers who want their computers to be compatible with the PC, and it is convenient for us to use it as an example here.

Refer to Fig 52. A standard IBM 5¼-inch, 360-kilobyte (kbyte) diskette uses both sides of the disk, and each side has 9 sectors and 40 tracks. Each sector of each track holds 512 bytes (512 × 40 × 9 × 2 = 368640 bytes per disk). The IBM BIOS locates information on the disk using three "coordinates": the track number, the sector number and the side number. Tracks are numbered from 0 (the outside track) to 40 (the innermost track) and sectors are numbered from 1 to 9. The two sides of a double-sided disk are numbered 0 and 1.

The IBM high-density format allows a diskette to hold 1.2 megabytes (Mbytes) of data. These disks use 80 tracks per side, each with 15 sectors. Again, each sector contains 512 bytes (512 × 80 × 15 × 2 = 1228800). Low-density 3½-inch diskettes can hold up to 730 kbytes of data, and high-density 3½-inch diskettes can hold up to 1.44 Mbytes of data. Zenith has introduced a 2-inch diskette that can hold up to 720 kbytes, and as disk technology improves diskettes may get even smaller and hold more data.

It is important to remember that the read/write head is in contact with the surface of the floppy disk, and the disk is rotating at several revolutions per second. Dust and dirt on the disk and the imperfections in the disk surface gradually damage both the disk and the head. This means that disks eventually wear out. When a disk wears out, the data stored on that disk will probably be lost. It is prudent, therefore, to make back-up copies of your disks. Back-up disks, stored in a clean, dry, cool place, will help you avoid disaster when your disks wear out.

In *hard disk* systems, the disk is rigid, and the read/write head does not contact the disk. The absence of friction between the head and the disk allows finer head positioning and higher disk speeds. Most hard-disk systems contain more than one disk (called *platters*). Each platter has its own set of heads. For these reasons, hard disks hold more data and are accessed more quickly than floppy disks.

Hard disks currently used for microcomputers have 3½ or 5¼-inch platters and can store from 10 to several hundred megabytes of data. Hard disk systems are high-precision mechanical devices, and while they do not fail frequently, even one failure can result in the loss of megabytes of data. To avoid this, you should frequently make backup copies of your hard disk. Using floppy disks for hard-disk backup can take a lot of diskettes, but backup utilities are available that compress the data to a more manageable size, and tape drives (mentioned earlier) can easily back up a large hard disk.

Optical memory systems use lasers to read digital data from spinning platters. The first optical memory systems for computers became available in 1983. These were 12-inch WORM (write once, read many times) systems. Twelve-inch WORM

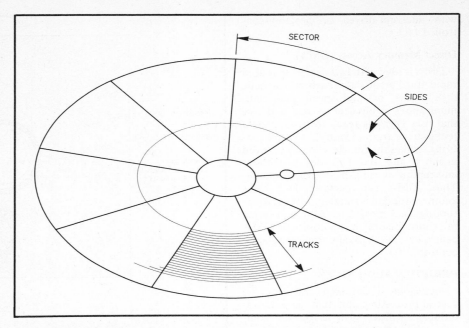

Fig 52—A 360-kbyte diskette has 2 sides, with 40 tracks and 9 sectors on both sides.

drives are still too expensive for personal-computer use, but more affordable 5¼-inch WORM systems are now available.

The audio CD (compact disk) formed the basis of the computer CD-ROM (compact disk read-only memory). A single CD-ROM disk can store up to 550 megabytes of data, but as the name implies, this data is read-only. The CD-ROM is ideal for database and software-distribution applications. Libraries use magazine indexes on CD-ROM, and software manufacturers are distributing complete libraries of application software for various markets on CD-ROM. Some CD-ROM drives will play audio CDs as well as reading CD-ROMs.

Summary

Some type of moving media is usually included in a general-purpose computer system. Inexpensive home computers may use cassette tapes, but floppy disks are more convenient. Advancing technology has been pushing the storage capacity of floppy disks up, while bringing prices down. High-capacity hard disks are within the reach of the amateur budget. Remember, whatever moving medium you use, always make backup copies of your important data.

Keyboards

A *keyboard* is an input device consisting of numerous key switches that, when pressed, cause the generation of a particular bit pattern. Most computer keyboards have keys arranged in the QWERTY order, similar to a typewriter keyboard layout. The similarity ends with the location of the 26 letters of the Latin alphabet and the 10 Arabic numerals, however. The placement of punctuation, other printable symbols and *control keys* varies. One computer-terminal keyboard layout is shown in Fig 53.

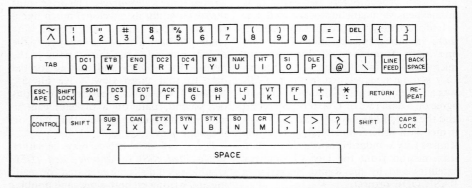

Fig 53—One computer-terminal keyboard layout. Two- and three-letter abbreviations shown at the top of letter and underline keys designate control functions. The CONTROL key must be pressed at the same time as the other keys to enter a control code. The complete ASCII-coded character set is listed in the Digital Communications chapter.

Computer keyboards have keys not traditionally found on typewriters. While typewriters have one RETURN key that issues both a carriage return (CR) and a line feed (LF) for a new line, some older computer keyboards have separate CR and LF keys. The CAPS LOCK key on a computer keyboard puts all letters in upper case but preserves the action of the SHIFT key over keys with numerals, punctuation and other symbols. Some keyboards include a special numeric keypad separate from the main keyboard. This keypad makes it easy for operators familiar with calculators or adding machines to enter lists of numbers into the computer. Other special keys often found on computer keyboards include a CONTROL (or CTRL) key, an ESCAPE (or ESC) key and perhaps some *function* keys.

Most computer keyboards will generate the entire 128-character ASCII set. (Chapter 19 examines the ASCII characters and their meanings.) Ninety-six of the ASCII characters are numerals, alphabetics and printable punctuation marks. These characters are usually generated by single keys or shifted keys. The other 32 characters are *control characters*, and are generated by pressing alphabetic and numeric keys while holding down the CONTROL key. Because control characters are nonprinting, various authors have adopted many different styles to tell the reader to enter a control character. For example, variations on how to hit the BEL character include CONTROL-G, CTRL-G, <control G>, [G], or ^G. Some control characters can be generated by single keystrokes. In particular, the CR character is generated by a key marked RETURN, ENTER or NEW LINE.

Some keyboards can generate 8-bit *extended ASCII* characters. These characters are generated by a process similar to that used for control keys, except that another special key (sometimes marked ALT, for "alternate") is held down instead of the CONTROL key. Using the CONTROL and the ALT keys, a keyboard with a reasonable number of keys can generate the complete 256-character extended ASCII character set.

Software, in conjunction with keys that generate control characters, can create special keyboard effects. When a function key is typed it can be recognized by a special program and expanded to have the effect of several keystrokes. *Escape sequences*, initiated by the ESC character, open up further possibilities. Typing the ESC key alerts software that the next character typed has a special meaning. Unlike the CONTROL key, the ESC key is not held down while the second key is typed. There has been an attempt to standardize the meanings of escape sequences, but there is still a wide variation between manufacturers.

There are many different types of key switches in use. Many provide the travel, acoustic feedback and "feel" of a type-writer keyboard. Some *membrane* keyboards are deficient in this respect but have other special features such as compactness and protection against moisture and dust. With few exceptions, individual keys simply make and break a single electrical contact. Unfortunately, the make is usually not just one clean pulse but a series of disorderly pulses resulting from mechanical contact bounce. Key bounce was a serious problem with some early keyboards. To *debounce* a keyboard, circuits that verify intended key closures and ignore key bounces and noise are added.

Computer keyboards vary from one model of computer to the next. Key placement, the meaning of escape sequences and control characters, and even the availability of specific characters may change if you change computers. The method of entering control characters and escape sequences, however, remains the same.

Screen Displays

A *video display terminal (VDT)* consists of a keyboard, as discussed above, and a *monitor*. Most monitors use a *cathode-ray tube (CRT)*. They may be either video monitors with no RF circuits or standard TV sets. Portable computers often use a flat-screen, *liquid-crystal display (LCD)*.

Whether CRT or LCD, the monitor is usually treated as a dot-matrix display with some number of picture elements *(pixels)* or dots horizontally and some number of pixels vertically. Characters are formed on the display by turning on specific pixels in a *character matrix*. Most CRTs employ *raster scanning*, a method of covering the screen by writing one row of pixels at a time. The electron beam in the CRT writes the top row of pixels first and then continues line-by-line to the bottom of the screen. Then, a *vertical retrace* brings the beam back to the top of the screen to begin again. To display characters on a raster-scanned screen, the electron beam must be turned on and off at precisely the times needed to illuminate the pixels that form the characters.

Like any other signal, the signal that turns the electron beam on and off occupies bandwidth within the monitor circuits. To calculate the bandwidth needed for a specific display, we must consider the worst-case characteristics of the electron-beam control signal. This worst case is when all of the pixels on the screen are set such that adjacent pixels have different states. The ideal control signal for such a display is shown in Fig 54A. The frequency (F) of this pulse train can be calculated by

$$F \text{ (in Hz)} = \frac{(N/2)}{T} \qquad \text{(Eq 4)}$$

where
  N = the number of pixels on the screen
  T = the time taken to complete a whole-screen scan

Fig 54—Control signals for turning on every-other pixel on a CRT. A shows the ideal square-wave control signal. The signal at B is a sine-wave approximation of the signal at A.

If the control signal were approximated by a sine wave (Fig 54B), the bandwidth needed to pass the signal would be equal to the frequency of the sine wave. Unfortunately, the sine wave does not turn the beam on and off abruptly and would produce blurred pixels. To get good definition, components up to the 3rd harmonic of the fundamental square-wave frequency (F) must be accommodated. Thus, a minimum bandwidth of 3 × F (in Hz) is necessary to scan N pixels in T seconds, where F is calculated by Eq 4. Example 1 shows how to calculate the bandwidth needed to display 25 lines, with 80 characters/line and a 10 × 7-pixel matrix used for each character.

Example 1:

(10 × 7 matrix) = 70 pixels/character
Characters/line = 80
Lines/screen = 25
Pixels/screen (N) = 70 × 80 × 25 = 140,000

$$\text{Scan time (T)} = \frac{1}{60} \text{ second}$$

Worst case frequency, F (in Hz) =

$$\frac{140,000 \, / \, 2}{1 \, / \, 60} = 4,200,000 \text{ Hz}$$

Bandwidth required = 3 × 4.2 MHz = 12.6 MHz

Raster scanning is used in television receivers (see the Audio and Video chapter for more details). These may also be used for displaying computer text. Television receivers have limited IF bandwidth—on the order of 3.5 MHz for color, 3 MHz or less for black and white. The example above shows that such bandwidth results in a poor display if 25 lines of 80 characters are desired. Computer monitors used to display 80 × 25 screens have a video bandwidth up to 25 MHz. What can be displayed on a TV receiver? Example 2 calculates the bandwidth needed for 16 lines with 40 characters on each line, with each

Fig 55—Portion of a raster-scanned video display.

Fig 56—Various character display formats.

Fig 57—Segment identification and layout for a seven-segment display.

character represented in a 9×7 pixel matrix.

Example 2:
Pixels/character = 9×7 = 63
Characters/line = 40
Lines/screen = 16
Pixels/screen (N) = $63 \times 40 \times 16$ = 40,320

Scan time (T) = $\frac{1}{60}$ second

Worst case frequency, F (in Hz) =

$\frac{40,320 / 2}{1 / 60}$ = 1,209,600 Hz

Necessary bandwidth = 3×1.2 MHz = 3.6 MHz

Thus, this example shows about as much text as can be displayed on a normal TV screen. This screen format (40×16) is used by some microcomputers to permit use of a TV receiver as an inexpensive display. The individual characters are formed as shown in Fig 55.

An alternative to raster scanning of a CRT is the *vector mode*. In this mode, the user can draw a straight line by specifying only two points. Vector-mode displays are primarily used for graphics.

Character Displays

Rather than having a full screen display, individual characters can be presented on single-character displays. Some of the formats available are shown in Fig 56. A popular display is the seven-segment version, as shown in Fig 57, which is an excellent choice for displaying numbers.

Character displays are built using several different manufacturing technologies. LEDs are common because they are easy to read when there is low ambient light. LCDs are now coming into use and are especially useful in low-current-drain battery operation. Unlike the LEDs, LCDs are visible in bright ambient light. However, since LCDs do not emit light, but reflect it, they are not visible in low-light environments. LCDs are also sluggish at low temperatures. LED and LCD characters are available in 0.3-, 0.6-inch and larger sizes.

Fig 58—A 7447 decoder/driver converts BCD data into the appropriate driving signals for a common-anode seven-segment LED display. A 7448 IC will drive a common-cathode LED display.

A numeral to be displayed on a seven-segment display is usually encoded in BCD form, and a combinational logic circuit activates the proper segments of the display. This logic circuit is called a *decoder*. Various seven-segment decoders are manufactured to drive common-cathode and common-anode displays. One decoder chip available to hobbyists is the 7447. This is an open-collector TTL device designed to pull down common-anode displays through external current-limiting resistors. Fig 58 shows how a 7447 is connected to the LED display. The 7448 is designed to drive common-cathode displays.

The dc illumination method shown in Fig 58 is the easiest to implement, but higher light output with lower energy consumption can be obtained by pulsing the display voltage. A pulse rate of 100 Hz is imperceptible because of the persistence of human vision. As more digits are added to a display, using a decoder/driver for each digit becomes unfeasible from an economic and PC-board real-estate point of view. A technique called *multiplexing* (Fig 59) allows a single decoder/driver IC to be shared by several digits. The digits are wired in parallel; that is, all of the "a" segments are connected together and so on. The multiplexer logic sends input data for a digit into the decoder and enables the common element of the correct digit. This process is repeated for each digit. Only when both a segment and its associated

Fig 59—Multiplexed character displays. BCD data for a particular display is placed at the input of the decoder/driver, and the desired display is selected by placing its "address" on the inputs to the display-select multiplexer.

common lead are selected will that segment be energized. With this system, only one digit is energized at any instant, a factor that greatly reduces power-supply requirements. To maintain the brightness of each digit, the current to each display segment must be increased. When implementing a multiplexed display, be sure not to exceed the peak- and average-currrent specifications for the display.

Printers

It is often necessary to have a printed copy or "hard copy" of communications, programs or data that are stored in a computer. Printers are used to produce such hard copy. Some printers produce *letter quality* text, with characters that look like they were typed on a typewriter. Other printers produce *data-processing* quality type, used mostly for program listings or draft copies of documents. Printers are categorized by their printing speed and the quality of type that they produce.

In the mid 1970s, a number of amateurs used ITA2 (Baudot) teleprinters as a computer output device. Since these teleprinters had a 5-bit code, they did not print all the ASCII characters. Certain characters were either ignored or converted to substitutes. These machines operated at speeds in the 45- to 75-baud range (or 6 to 10 char/s)—quite slow by computer standards. ASCII teleprinters, such as the Teletype Corporation Model 33, were only slightly better. These teleprinters operated at 110 bauds or 10 char/s.

Most printers currently used with microcomputers have the full ASCII coded character set. They are called *character printers* because they print only one character at a time, not a whole line at once as *line printers* do. Printers used with personal computers are described below.

Fully formed character printers are usually *impact printers*; they print by striking a character-shaped hammer against a ribbon. These printers may use interchangeable type elements (called daisy wheels or thimbles). Many character fonts are available. The characters are fully formed and match those of a typewriter. While characters are printed slowly (less than 80 characters/second), they can be sent to the printer at a much higher rate. The characters are stored in a FIFO buffer, and hardware or software *flow control (handshaking)* between the printer input and the computer output port keeps the computer from overfilling the buffer.

Dot-matrix printers print each character as a matrix of dots, much the same way characters are displayed on a raster-scanned monitor. Dot-matrix printers are usually referred to by the number of pins in their print heads. These pins are placed in a straight vertical line in the print head and are pushed against the ribbon as the head moves across the paper. A 7-pin printer, printing each letter as a 5-by-7 matrix (measured 5 dots wide by 7 dots high) is just adequate for the standard ASCII character set. Such a matrix makes the normal Latin letters look ragged, however. A 9-pin printer can print better-looking 7-by-9 characters, and some 9-pin printers can print *near-letter quality (NLQ)* characters (but more slowly than "draft" quality characters). Some newer dot-matrix printers have a 24-pin print head. These can print characters that are almost indistinguishable from impact printers.

While dot-matrix printers do not form perfect letters, they are fast (greater than 100 chars/sec), they can print graphics, and they can be used as plotters. Some can print multicolor graphics. Also, dot-matrix printers are generally less expensive than impact printers.

Most printers used on home computers are either dot-matrix or impact printers. Several other types of printers are also available. Like a dot-matrix printer, an *ink-jet* printer forms characters from a matrix of dots, but the printer actually sprays ink onto the paper. Ink-jet printers are faster and quieter than dot-matrix printers, but they are also more expensive. Color ink-jet printers can print full-color text and graphics.

Laser printers use a process similar to the process used in a photocopy machine, where a dye is deposited onto electrically charged paper. A laser printer uses a bit image (similar to a raster image used in a video display) to transfer the image of a printed page to a light-sensitive drum. The drum holds a positive electrical charge when it is rotated. As the laser scans the rotating drum, it transfers the bit image to the drum by neutralizing the charge on the drum everywhere there should be black on the printed page.

Next, the drum rolls though *toner* powder. The toner also has a positive charge, and it will only stick to the drum where the laser has neutralized the charge on the drum. After it rotates through the toner, the drum contains an image of the printed page in patterns of positively charged toner. The laser printer then applies a negative charge to a sheet of paper as it enters the printer. The positively charged toner is attracted to the paper, and the page image is transferred from the drum to the paper. The paper finally passes through heated rollers to "fix" the toner and fuse it to the paper. This entire process takes only a few seconds.

Laser printers are available for home computers, but they are fairly expensive. They are very fast (only several seconds per page), and can produce both graphics and letter-quality text.

Summary

Peripherals allow computers to interact with the outside world. General-purpose computers need both a monitor, to present results to the operator, and a keyboard, to accept commands and data from the operator. Mass storage devices, usually cassette tapes or floppy disks, are used to store programs and data. Printers are used to make hard copies of computer outputs. Peripherals often cost more than the microcomputer to which they are attached; when selecting a microcomputer, pay attention to the availability and price of necessary peripherals.

COMPUTER LANGUAGES

There are two broad classifications of computer languages: *low level* and *high level*. Generally, a low-level language is one that is designed to communicate with a computer in its "native tongue," while a high-level language is intended to be more like a widely used human language.

Low-Level Languages

Programmers who wish to converse with a microprocessor directly must do so in *machine language*. The symbols used in machine language are 1s and 0s. Every

Glossary of Digital Terms

Access—To read or write to memory or an I/O device.

Accumulator (ACC)—The register in a computer that holds the result of ALU operations.

Address—An expression, either numeric or symbolic, that specifies a memory location.

Algorithm—A set of directions describing a way to perform a certain task.

Architecture—Organizational structure of a system.

Arithmetic Logic Unit (ALU)—The part of a computer that performs mathematical operations.

Assemble—To convert a symbolic assembly-language program into machine language.

Assembly Language—A symbolic language representing machine language in mnemonic form.

Asynchronous—Communication in which data characters are individually synchronized and may be sent at any time.

Baud—The reciprocal (in seconds) of the shortest element in the encoding scheme.

Benchmark—A program used to compare the performance of two or more computer systems.

Binary—The base-two number system, using the numerals 0 and 1.

Bipolar—A broad category of semi-conductors based on PNP or NPN junction transistors. See MOS.

Bit—The basic element of binary information, usually represented by 0 and 1; a contraction of "binary digit."

Bug—An error that causes hardware or software to malfunction.

Byte—A group of bits, usually 8.

Central Processing Unit (CPU)—The part of a computer that interprets and executes instructions.

Chip—An integrated circuit.

Clear—To make a value or state equal to 0.

CMOS—Complementary metal-oxide semiconductor, an integrated-circuit logic subfamily employing both n-channel and p-channel FETs; noted for its low power consumption.

Compiler—Software that converts a high-level-language program into a machine- or assembly-language program.

Complex Instruction Set Computing (CISC)—CISC microprocessors improve performance by offering a large, complex instruction set. Assembly-language programs are easier to write for CISC microprocessors because of the capabilities of the instruction set.

Cross Assembler—An assembler that translates code from one machine language to another.

Debug—To remove errors from hardware or software.

Decimal—The base-ten number system, using the numerals 0 through 9.

Display—Presentation of information in a form to be sensed by humans, usually visual.

Documentation—Reference material detailing specifications and technical information on systems, hardware or software.

ECL—Emitter-coupled logic, an integrated circuit logic family capable of operating at frequencies above 1.2 GHz.

Edge-triggered—A circuit that responds to data or clock transitions, rather than responding to data or clock levels.

Execute—To interpret instructions and perform the indicated operations.

Fan out—The number of parallel loads of a given family that can be driven by one output of that family.

Flip-Flop—A circuit with two stable states, usually 0 and 1, capable of storing a single bit of information.

Floppy disk—A flexible magnetic recording medium for data storage. Also called a diskette.

Flowchart—A graphic representation of the structure of a program or process.

Handshaking—Exchange of prearranged signals between devices to determine their readiness to establish or maintain communications.

Hard disk—A rigid magnetic recording medium for data storage.

Hardware—Physical equipment.

Hexadecimal—The base-16 number system, using the numerals 0 through 9 and A through F.

Instruction—A statement that specifies a computer operation.

Instruction set—The repertoire of machine-language instructions for a microprocessor.

Interface—The common boundary between two devices or software modules.

Integrated circuit (IC)—A miniature electronic module of components and conductors manufactured as a single unit.

Interpreter—A program that translates and then immediately executes statements in a high-level language.

I/O—Input/output.

Keyboard—A set of key-switches used to enter data or commands.

Label—One or more characters used to identify a memory location or a statement or an item of data in a computer program.

Latch—A flip-flop capable of storing one bit of information. Also used as a verb meaning to hold state.

LSI—Large-scale integration; ICs with 100 to 1000 devices per chip.

---

microprocessor has a built-in instruction set, and each instruction in that set can be represented by a binary word. Few programmers actually write machine language. When they do, they express machine instructions as octal or hexadecimal numbers rather than as binary numbers. The instruction to move the contents of register B into register A, understood by the microprocessor as "01111000," would be written as "78" in hexadecimal (hex).

Most programmers cannot remember what all the numerical machine-language instructions stand for, so *assembly language* is used to substitute a mnemonic abbreviation for each instruction. In the above example, "78" would become "MOV A,B" in assembly language. Once you get a program written in assembly language, it must be *assembled* to convert it to machine language. This is done with an assembler program that converts commands from mnemonics to binary words,

"MOV A,B" would be converted to the byte "01111000." A single assembly-language instruction generates a single machine-language instruction; programming in assembly language creates programs that are as fast and efficient as if they were written in machine language.

Assembly-language programs and programs in high-level languages are usually stored as text. Such text is called *source code*, while binary files of machine-language instructions are called *object code*. A single source code instruction, such as "MOV A,B", is called a *statement*.

Both machine and assembly languages are usually different for each microprocessor. Once you learn assembly-language programming on a particular chip, however, you can usually work with others in the same family. Even when switching families, you will get the hang of the new instructions in no time. Sometimes old habits are hard to break, and you will yearn for your favorite special feature that is not

in the new instruction set. In general, you end up doing the same operations but have to learn new instructions and mnemonics. A programmer's reference guide or card can help you remember all the mnemonics until they become second nature through repetition.

Many experienced programmers prefer to work in assembly language because it gives them step-by-step control of the processing of data. Programming in assembly language usually results in smaller object code and faster execution than can be achieved with higher-level languages. This is especially useful in high-speed code-conversion (such as for Morse code and RTTY operations) and other signal-processing applications.

High-Level Languages

High-level languages are oriented toward the user or a specific task rather than toward the microprocessor. In order to appear familiar, some high-level languages

Machine—A computer.

Machine Language—The numeric form of specifying instructions used by a computer.

Microcomputer (μC)—A computer having a microprocessor CPU.

Microprocessor (μP)—One or a small set of chips capable of performing the functions of a CPU.

Mnemonic—A symbol chosen to assist the human memory. The symbolic name used to represent instructions, registers and memory locations.

Monitor—A display device, usually a cathode-ray tube. A permanent program resident in a computer to perform basic operations.

MOS—Metal-oxide semiconductor. Semiconductors based on field-effect transistors (FETs), rather than bipolar-junction transistors. See bipolar.

MSI—Medium-scale integration; ICs with 10 to 100 devices per chip.

Nyquist rate—In analog-to-digital conversion, the lowest sampling rate that will result in correct reproduction of the analog signal. This rate is twice that of the highest frequency component in the original analog signal.

Object program—A machine-language program.

Octal—The base-eight number system, using numerals 0 through 7.

Open collector—A TTL output that is not internally pulled up through a resistor or transistor.

Operating system—A group of programs that supervise I/O and the execution of other programs in a computer.

Parallel—Simultaneous handling of several bits, with a separate channel for each bit. See serial.

Port—A set of I/O connections.

Printer—An output device that produces a paper copy.

Program—A collection of instructions that perform a certain task.

Program counter (PC)—A register that specifies the address of the next instruction to be executed.

Pull-down resistor—A resistor connected from the input or output of a logic element to ground.

Pull-up resistor—A resistor used to connect the input or output of a logic element to a supply voltage.

Rails—The positive and negative supply voltages.

Random-Access Memory (RAM)—Volatile storage. Storage in which any address can be accessed as easily and quickly as any other.

Read—To copy the contents of a memory location or peripheral storage medium.

Read-Only Memory (ROM)—Storage that can be easily read but not easily written to; usually nonvolatile.

Reduced Instruction Set Computing (RISC)—RISC microprocessors improve performance by offering a small number of very fast instructions. Assembly-language programs and compilers are more difficult to write for RISC microprocessors.

RTL—Resistor-transistor logic, an early bipolar integrated-circuit logic family.

Schottky—A TTL manufacturing process that provides high speed by eliminating transistor saturation.

Sequential-access memory—Memory in which the first n addresses must be accessed in order to access address n + 1.

Serial—A process in which a group of bits are handled one at a time over a single channel.

Software—Computer programs.

SSI—Small-scale integration; ICs with 10 or fewer devices on a chip.

Start bit—The bit transmitted to indicate the beginning of an asynchronous character. See stop bit.

State—A mode or condition of a circuit or program.

State diagram—A chart showing all states in a device or process and the events leading to and resulting from each state.

Stop bit—The bit transmitted at the end of an asynchronous character and between such characters. See start bit.

Subroutine—A section of a program used to divide the work of a large program into small segments.

Synchronous—A method of communication in which data is sent as a continuous, exactly timed stream, with special synchronization information sent only at the beginning of long data blocks.

Totem pole—A TTL output circuit in which a transistor is used to pull up the collector of another transistor. See open collector.

TTL—Transistor-transistor logic, a widely used bipolar IC logic family.

UART—Universal asynchronous receiver/transmitter; an IC that converts parallel data into asynchronous serial data, or vice versa.

USART—Universal synchronous/asynchronous receiver/transmitter; an integrated circuit that converts parallel data into either synchronous or asynchronous serial data, or vice versa.

VLSI—Very-large-scale integration; ICs with 1000 or more devices on a chip.

Volatile memory—Storage that does not retain its contents when its power is removed.

Write—To place data in memory or peripheral storage.

---

are designed to look like a subset of English. Plain-English programming is not yet possible, because English has ambiguities and numerous shades of meaning and subtleties. We must be content with high-level computer languages in which words have specific meanings (strict *semantics*) and must be used according to rigid rules (*syntax*).

Many high-level languages are extensions of the assembly-language concept—that of substituting something easy to remember for something that is easy to forget. Instead of simply having a few mnemonic letters represent a few numbers, though, high-level languages set up more complex relationships. A single word (instruction or statement) in a high-level language can cause the generation and execution of several machine-language instructions. Thus, high-level languages provide a way of expressing complex computing processes in notation that is easy to understand and remember.

Like assembly-language source statements, high-level-language statements must be converted to machine language. Conversion is performed by an *interpreter* or a *compiler*. An interpreter translates a statement to machine code and then executes the code immediately. It does not create an object program. A compiler takes an entire high-level source program and translates it into a machine-language object program. The object program may be executed immediately or saved for later execution. If a particular statement is executed several times, an interpreter will translate that statement over and over, while a compiler translates it only once. Thus, compiled programs usually run faster than interpreted programs.

During program development, it is time consuming to recompile a program after every small change is made. In this case, the immediate execution offered by an interpreter can be convenient. Interpreters and compilers each have their advantages

and disadvantages. Most home computers are provided with a built-in interpreter for the BASIC computer language, and BASIC compilers can be purchased for some of these computers.

There are hundreds of high-level computer languages. Some are used for specific tasks, some for a wide range of tasks. The languages described below are common or of some specific interest to radio amateurs.

BASIC

The *B*eginner's *A*ll-purpose *S*ymbolic *I*nstruction *C*ode *(BASIC)* was developed at Dartmouth College as a simple, easy-to-learn computer language. BASIC is by far the most common high-level language in use by radio amateurs and other personal-computer users. Numerous dialects of BASIC exploit the special features of different computers. Many of these dialects implement a common set of BASIC instructions and then add *extensions* that provide new features. Fortunately, many

BASIC dialects for different computers were written by the same software company, which has had the effect of minimizing unnecessary variations.

Although there is a common core of BASIC that is *transportable* from one computer to another, do not expect to type in a BASIC program listing written for one computer and run it on another without modification. Books like *The Basic Handbook* by David A. Lien discuss translating BASIC from one dialect to another (Compusoft™ Publishing, San Diego, CA, 1978).

Here are a few common *commands* and *statements* in BASIC:

END: Stops execution of the program.
LET: Assigns values to variables. LET is often optional; "LET X = 1" and "X = 1" usually mean the same thing.
LIST: Displays the program.
PRINT: Means to display whatever follows, such as a variable (X in the line 40 below) or anything enclosed in quotes.
REM: Remarks or comments. A computer will ignore lines beginning with REM.

Example:
20 PRINT "Join the computer revolution."
30 LET X = 1
40 PRINT X
50 END

Pascal

Pascal is a structured programming language; structured programs are written as systems of interacting subroutines. Large programming tasks can be broken into many small tasks, and each of these small tasks can be translated into a Pascal subroutine. (Although BASIC can be used to write structured programs, it was not designed for easy, efficient structured programming.) Pascal is taught in many computer science courses because it provides a good basis for understanding other programming languages. Pascal software is available to amateurs for most microcomputers at modest cost.

Modula-2

Modula-2 was developed by Niklaus Wirth, the inventor of Pascal. The name Modula-2 refers to the way programs are based on modules. Modula-2 is similar to Pascal, but while Pascal is used mainly for education, Modula-2 can be used for serious systems software development. Unlike Pascal, where an entire program must be kept together and compiled as a whole, Modula-2 programs can be compiled and linked separately so that several small programs can be combined into one large program.

C

C is a very flexible and powerful structured language that, like assembly language, generates compact, fast object programs. Unlike Pascal and many other high-level languages, C allows programs to interact freely with computer hardware. In addition, it is easy to extend the capabilities of the language by adding functions to a library; these library functions can then be used in all future programs. C is a very standardized language. This makes C programs very *portable*—programs written in C for one computer will usually compile and run on any other computer using a standard C compiler.

Because of these advantages, C is used by many professional programmers and many Amateur Radio applications are now being written in C. C compilers are available for most microcomputer systems.

Lisp

Lisp (for *List Processing*) is widely used in *artificial intelligence (AI)* applications. AI is a branch of computer science where attempts are made to design computer systems that simulate the reasoning power of humans. Lisp is very effective at dealing with data structures, lists and recursive problems. Lisp is an interpreted and interactive language, so lines of code are inspected and translated as they are entered. The entire Lisp language is based on functions; many of the commands built into the language are "primitive" functions. (Primitive functions are basic math functions such as add, subtract, multiply and divide, along with trig functions and other common mathematical relationships.)

Prolog

Prolog is another language designed for artificial intelligence programming. Prolog is concerned mainly with defining objects and the relationship between them. This makes Prolog ideal for the design of *expert systems*. An expert system is an intelligent computer program that can simulate the reasoning and technical knowledge of a human expert. Medical diagnosis is an area where expert systems are being developed. The vast amount of information and interrelationships that must be considered to make an accurate diagnosis are ideal for an artificial intelligence application.

Forth

Forth is an unusual programming language. Forth programs can be visualized as a pyramid of instructions, with basic core instructions at the bottom of the pyramid and additional instructions defined at each higher level as some combination of lower-level instructions. Executing a single high-level instruction may cause countless lower-level instructions to be executed, as instructions flow down through the pyramid. This type of program structure is known as *threaded code*, and Forth programs execute very quickly and efficiently.

Forth is very powerful, fast and compact. In many cases, it runs as fast as assembly language and takes up only a small amount of memory space. These attributes make Forth ideal for real-time control applications, where memory space in a microcon-troller is at a premium. Forth's short commands and symbols make programs difficult to read and debug, however.

IPS

The *Interpreter for Process Structure (IPS)* is a derivative of Forth. IPS was written by Karl Meinzer, DJ4ZC, to control the 1802-based integrated housekeeping unit (IHU) computer in the AMSAT-OSCAR Phase III satellites.

EngLan

EngLan is a computer programming language that allows you to write simple applications on an IBM® PC or compatible computer. Syntax errors are virtually eliminated because the programmer selects commands from a series of menus. EngLan, written by Jerry Gentry, WA0H, is not as powerful as languages like BASIC or Pascal. It isn't intended for large business applications or complex programming tasks, but may be helpful for beginners interested in writing their own programs.

OPERATING SYSTEMS

An operating system is a group of computer programs that supervises the sequencing and processing of other computer programs. The operating system sits between the program you are running and the actual computer hardware. The programs supervised by an operating system are usually called applications programs. Operating systems are also responsible for I/O management—the creation and assignment of files, the maintenance of file directories, and so on. The operating system allows applications programs to use I/O devices without knowing the precise characteristics of those devices. In computers that have disk drives, the operating system is usually called the *disk operating system (DOS)*.

Multitasking operating systems allow several applications programs to share a single CPU. A good operating system will provide simple but powerful I/O services to applications programs and an understandable, complete set of commands for human users. Many operating systems today provide a graphical user interface. With a graphical user interface, the user does not have to remember a complex set of commands for a task. Instead, most tasks can be executed quickly by "pointing" and "clicking" a mouse or other similar non-keyboard input device.

CP/M

One of the first widely used microcomputer operating systems was CP/M (control program for microcomputers), written by Gary Kildall and marketed by Digital Research Inc. CP/M-80 runs on the 8080/Z80 family of microprocessors, and CP/M-86 runs on the 8086 family. CP/M has many limitations, but many amateurs are still using computers running CP/M, and some software is still available.

MS DOS

MS DOS, written by Microsoft, became popular along with the IBM® PC. A version of this DOS written specifically for the IBM PC is called PC DOS. All IBM PC clones and compatibles run some "flavor" of MS DOS. Because of the prestige of IBM, MS DOS quickly became a popular operating system. By far the greatest percentage of Amateur Radio software today is available for computers running MS DOS.

UNIX

Written by AT&T, UNIX is a multiuser, multitasking operating system. This means that it can handle more than one user at a time, and it can execute more than one program at a time. The original version of UNIX was written in assembly language for the DEC (Digital Equipment Corporation) PDP-7 computer. UNIX was later re-written in C for the DEC PDP-11 family of computers. Once UNIX was rewritten in C, it was easy to *port* (adapt) the operating system to other computers. UNIX is a very popular operating system for minicomputers and mainframes, and now that powerful 32-bit microcomputers are available, some people are using UNIX on their home or business personal computers.

OS/2

Microsoft's most recent introduction into the operating system arena is Microsoft Operating System/2, or MS OS/2. MS OS/2 is also a multitasking operating system, but it supports only a single user at a time. MS OS/2 runs only on microcomputers using Intel's 80286, 80386 or 80486 family of microprocessors. MS OS/2 allows programmers to access many of the features of these more-powerful microprocessors, including the ability to address large amounts of memory.

Other Operating Systems

There are nearly as many microcomputer operating systems as there are microcomputer manufacturers. Some manufacturers supply a proprietary operating system with specific computer models. These operating systems are intended to make the best use of hardware features or limitations. When you choose a particular personal computer, you will usually not have many operating systems to choose from. You may, however, decide to select a certain computer because it uses an operating system that you are familiar with.

Chapter 9

Modulation and Demodulation

Modulation is the process of varying some characteristic of a *carrier* wave in accordance with a signal to be conveyed. A carrier is a wave having at least one characteristic that can be varied from a known reference by modulation. That known reference is typically a steady sine wave but could be a recurring series of pulses in which no signal is present between pulses. A *modulator* is a circuit or device in which the carrier and modulating signal come together to produce a modulated carrier, or one that processes the modulating signal and presents it to the circuit or device to be modulated. That is, modulation may or may not occur in the modulator, depending how the term is applied in practice. Modulation is normally associated with transmitters. The modulator may be built into the transmitter or exist as a separate unit.

Demodulation is the process of deriving the original modulation signal from a modulated carrier wave. But that's not the whole story. The received signal usually contains noise and distortion picked up along the way. For the original modulating signal to be reproduced faithfully, the effects of noise and distortion need to be dealt with effectively during reception and demodulation. Demodulation is part of the receiving process and is performed in a *demodulator*. While a demodulator is a normal part of a radio receiver, external demodulators are used for some types of communications.

The *baseband* is the range of frequencies occupied by the signal before it modulates the carrier wave. The signal in the baseband is usually at frequencies that are substantially lower than that of the carrier. On the low end, the baseband may approach or include dc (0 Hz). The high end depends on the rate at which information occurs as well as the presence of subcarriers or other special signals within the baseband. There is a baseband for all types of signals, whether analog or digital. Also, it should be realized that the term baseband is relative to the specific modulation being considered. There can be more than one baseband in a complete modulation process. For example, to a transmitter, a keyed tone going into the microphone input is its (analog) baseband; to the tone keyer, the keying pulses are its (digital) baseband.

This chapter presents the fundamentals of the modulation and demodulation processes. Subsequent chapters provide details concerning the generation of modulated signals and demodulation circuitry for types of modulation used in the Amateur Radio Service.

DESIGNATION OF EMISSIONS

One result of the World Administrative Radio Conference held in 1979 (WARC '79) was the adoption of a new system of designating emissions according to their necessary bandwidth and their classification. These new designations are used throughout this chapter with secondary reference to the pre-WARC '79 designations.

The new designations are not without problems. The new designations take into account the method of generating a signal rather than simply what the signal looks like when transmitted. Thus, the new system would have you use one designation for direct modulation of the main carrier and a different one if you modulate a subcarrier of a single-sideband suppressed-carrier transmitter. Also, if you key a radioteletype modem with a direct-printing teletypewriter then switch to using a computer to do the same thing, the modulation designation changes under the new system.

On November 27, 1984, the FCC released the Third Report and Order for General Docket No. 80-739 to implement the new emission designators in all radio services, effective January 3, 1985. The appendix amended the Amateur Radio Service rules by deleting the old designations and replacing them with new designations. Current FCC rules also refer to *emission types,* which simplify the task of describing various emissions and the conditions under which they are permissible. These emission types are based on the emission designators, which are still frequently needed to more completely and specifically refer to a particular emission. (Refer to the Emission Designators and Emission Types tables for more details.)

Bandwidth

Whenever a carrier is modulated, *sidebands* are produced. Sidebands are the frequency bands on both sides of a carrier resulting from the baseband signal varying some characteristic of the carrier. The modulation process creates two sidebands: the *upper* sideband (USB) and the *lower* sideband (LSB). The width of each sideband is generally equal to the highest frequency component in the baseband signal. In some modulation systems, the width of the sidebands may greatly exceed the highest baseband frequency component. The USB and LSB are mirror images of each other and carry identical information.

Some modulation systems transmit only one sideband and partially or completely suppress the other in order to conserve bandwidth.

Occupied bandwidth is that between lower and upper limits of the signal where the mean power is 0.5% (−23 dB) of the total mean power. In some cases a different relative power level may be specified; for example, −26 dB (0.25%) is used in section 97.69 of the FCC rules governing digital communications. Occupied bandwidth is not always easy for the amateur to determine. It can be measured on a spectrum analyzer — a piece of test equipment that is not generally available to most amateurs. Occupied bandwidth can also be calculated, but these calculations require an understanding of the mathematics of information theory and are not covered in this chapter.

Necessary bandwidth is that part of the occupied bandwidth sufficient to ensure transmission of the information at the rate and with the quality required. Formulas used by the International Radio Consultative Committee (CCIR) and the FCC for calculation of necessary bandwidths are included in this chapter's discussion of specific modulation systems.

Assigned frequency band is the necessary bandwidth plus twice the absolute frequency tolerance. *Frequency tolerance* (expressed in parts per 10^6, percentage, or in hertz) is the maximum permissible departure by a frequency from its correct frequency.

Prior to WARC '79, the CCIR and FCC expressed necessary bandwidth in terms of kilohertz. As examples, 0.1 was used to mean 100 Hz, and 6000 for 6 MHz. Spectrum managers had no taste for ragged computer-generated columns with different numbers of places, so a more elegant technique was clearly needed. The WARC '79 delegates agreed on a new system of expressing necessary bandwidth by three numerals and one letter. The letter occupies the position of the decimal point and represents the unit of bandwidth. The letters H (Hz), K (kHz), M (MHz) and G (GHz) are used, but neither 0 nor K, M nor G may appear in the first character. Numerical values of more than three significant places are rounded off to three places. Some examples taken from the CCIR Radio Regulations are listed in the accompanying table.

MAJOR MODULATION SYSTEMS

The broadest category of modulation systems is how the main carrier is modulated. The major types are amplitude modulation, angle modulation and pulse modulation.

Amplitude Modulation

Amplitude modulation (AM) covers a class of modulation systems in which the amplitude is the characteristic that is varied. It is possible to amplitude modulate a main carrier or subcarrier. However, in the context of the new emission symbols, it is the modulation of the *main* carrier that determines the first symbol (type of modulation of the main carrier).

Amplitude modulation is often

Examples of CCIR Necessary Bandwidths

0.002	Hz = H002	6	kHz = 6K00	1.25	MHz = 1M25
0.1	Hz = H100	12.5	kHz = 12K5	2	MHz = 2M00
25.3	Hz = 25H3	180.4	kHz = 180K	10	MHz = 10M0
400	Hz = 400H	180.5	kHz = 181K	202	MHz = 202M
2.4	kHz = 2K40	180.7	kHz = 181K	5.65	GHz = 5G65

simplistically described as varying the amplitude of the carrier from a zero power level to a peak power level. This chapter includes some photographs of oscilloscope patterns that seem to prove this notion. In fact the oscilloscope pattern is a composite of the energy produced over a range of frequencies. The carrier itself stays at the same amplitude when modulated by an analog (such as voice) baseband signal. The modulation itself produces sidebands. They are bands of frequencies on both sides of

---

Emission Designators

Emissions are classified by the following basic characteristics:

(1) First symbol—type of modulation of the main carrier

(1.1) Emission of an unmodulated carrier — N

(1.2) Emission in which the main carrier is amplitude modulated (including cases where subcarriers are angle modulated)

   (1.2.1) Double sideband — A

   (1.2.2) Single sideband, full carrier — H

   (1.2.3) Single sideband, reduced or variable-level carrier — R

   (1.2.4) Single sideband, suppressed carrier — J

   (1.2.5) Independent sidebands — B

   (1.2.6) Vestigial sideband — C

(1.3) Emission in which the main carrier is angle modulated

   (1.3.1) Frequency modulation — F

   (1.3.2) Phase modulation — G

(1.4) Emission in which the main carrier is amplitude and angle modulated either simultaneously or in a pre-established sequence. — D

(1.5) Emission of pulses[1]

   (1.5.1) Sequence of unmodulated pulses — P

   (1.5.2) A sequence of pulses

      (1.5.2.1) modulated in amplitude — K

      (1.5.2.2) modulated in width/duration — L

      (1.5.2.3) modulated in position/phase — M

      (1.5.2.4) in which the carrier is angle modulated during the period of the pulse — Q

      (1.5.2.5) which is the combination of the foregoing or is produced by other means — V

(1.6) Cases not covered above, in which an emission consists of the main carrier modulated, either simultaneously or in a preestablished sequence, in a combination of two or more of the following modes: amplitude, angle, pulse — W

(1.7) Cases not otherwise covered — X

(2) Second symbol—nature of signal(s) modulating the main carrier

(2.1) No modulating signal — 0

(2.2) A single channel containing quantized or digital information without the use of a modulating subcarrier[2] — 1

(2.3) A single channel containing quantized or digital information with the use of a modulating subcarrier[2] — 2

(2.4) A single channel containing analog information — 3

(2.5) Two or more channels containing quantized or digital information — 7

(2.6) Two or more channels containing analog information — 8

(2.7) Composite system with one or more channels containing quantized or digital information, together with one or more channels containing analog information — 9

(2.8) Cases not otherwise covered — X

(3) Third symbol—type of information to be transmitted[3]

(3.1) No information transmitted — N

(3.2) Telegraphy—for aural reception — A

(3.3) Telegraphy—for automatic reception — B

(3.4) Facsimile — C

(3.5) Data transmission, telemetry, telecommand — D

(3.6) Telephony (including sound broadcasting) — E

(3.7) Television (video) — F

(3.8) Combination of the above — W

(3.9) Cases not otherwise covered — X

The following two optional characteristics may be added for a more complete description of an emission:

(4) Fourth symbol—detail of signal(s)

(4.1) Two-condition code with elements of differing numbers and/or durations — A

(4.2) Two-condition code with elements of the same number and duration without error correction — B

(4.3) Two-condition code with elements of the same number and duration with error correction — C

(4.4) Four-condition code in which each condition represents a signal element (of one or more bits) — D

(4.5) Multi-condition code in which each condition represents a signal element (of one or more bits) — E

(4.6) Multi-condition code in which each condition or combination of conditions represents a character — F

(4.7) Sound of broadcasting quality (monophonic) — G

(4.8) Sound of broadcasting quality (stereophonic or quadraphonic) — H

(4.9) Sound of commercial quality (excluding categories K and L below) — J

(4.10) Sound of commercial quality with the use of frequency inversion or band-splitting — K

(4.11) Sound of commercial quality with separate frequency-modulated signals to control the level of demodulated signal — L

(4.12) Monochrome — M

(4.13) Color — N

(4.14) Combination of the above — W

(4.15) Cases not otherwise covered — X

(5) Fifth symbol—nature of multiplexing

(5.1) None — N

(5.2) Code-division multiplex[4] — C

(5.3) Frequency-division multiplex — F

(5.4) Time-division multiplex — T

(5.5) Combination of frequency-division multiplex and time-division multiplex — W

(5.6) Other types of multiplexing — X

Notes

[1] Emissions where the main carrier is directly modulated by a signal that has been coded into quantized form (for example, pulse code modulation) should be designated under (1.2) or (1.3).

[2] This excludes time-division multiplex.

[3] In this context the word "information" does not include information of a constant, unvarying nature such as is provided by standard-frequency emissions, continuous-wave and pulse radars, and so forth.

[4] This includes bandwidth-expansion techniques.

Emission Types

Emissions may also be referred to by the following emission types:

CW
First Symbol: A, C, H, J or R
Second Symbol: 1
Third Symbol: A or B
Also J2A and J2B.

MCW
First Symbol: A, C, D, F, G or R
Second Symbol: 2
Third Symbol: A or B

Phone
First Symbol: A, C, D, F, G, H, J or R
Second Symbol: 1, 2 or 3
Third Symbol: E
Also first symbol B and second symbol 7, 8 or 9.

Image
First Symbol: A, C, D, F, G, H, J or R
Second Symbol: 1, 2 or 3
Third Symbol: C or F
Also first symbol B; second symbol 7, 8 or 9; and third symbol W.

RTTY/Data
First Symbol: A, C, D, F, G, H, J or R
Second Symbol: 1 (2, 7 or 9 above 51 MHz)
Third Symbol: B (RTTY) or D (Data) (W above 51 MHz)
J2B is permitted anywhere F1B is permitted; J2D is permitted anywhere F1D is permitted.

Pulse
First Symbol: P, K, L, M, Q, V or W
Second Symbol: 0, 1, 2, 3, 7, 8, 9 or X
Third Symbol: A, B, C, D, E, F, N, W or X

SS (Spread Spectrum)
First Symbol: A, C, D, F, G, H, J or R
Second Symbol: X
Third Symbol: X

Test (Emissions containing no information)
First Symbol: Any
Second Symbol: Any
Third Symbol: N

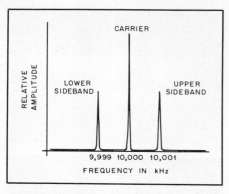

Fig. 1 — A 10-MHz carrier modulated by a 1-kHz sine wave.

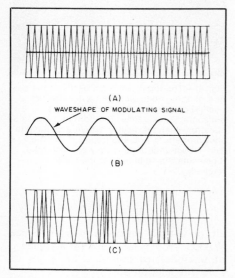

Fig. 2 — Graphical representation of frequency modulation. In the unmodulated carrier at A, each RF cycle occupies the same amount of time. When the modulating signal, B, is applied, the radio frequency is increased and decreased according to the amplitude and polarity of the modulating signal.

the carrier frequency. AM is basically a process of heterodyning or nonlinear mixing. As in any mixer, when a carrier and baseband modulation are combined, there are three products in the frequency range of interest: (1) the carrier, (2) the lower sideband (LSB), and (3) the upper sideband (USB). Thus, if a carrier of 10 MHz were modulated by a 1-kHz sine wave, the outputs would be as shown in Fig. 1.

The bandwidth of the modulated signal in this example would be 2 kHz, the difference between the lowest and highest frequencies. In AM, the difference between the carrier and farthest component of the sideband is determined by the highest frequency component contained in the baseband modulating signal.

Angle Modulation

Two particular forms of angle modulation are *frequency modulation* (FM) and *phase modulation* (PM).

The term frequency modulation is often used to cover various forms of angle modulation. Amateurs use FM when referring to angle-modulated VHF/UHF radios which may use either FM or PM. The pre-WARC '79 emission symbol, F, was used for both FM and PM. However, the post-WARC '79 symbols are F for FM and G for PM.

Frequency and phase modulation are not independent, since the frequency cannot be varied without also varying the phase, and vice versa.

The communications effectiveness of FM and PM depends almost entirely on the receiving methods. If the receiver will respond to frequency and phase changes but is insensitive to amplitude changes, it will discriminate against most forms of noise, particularly impulse noise such as that from ignition systems.

Frequency Modulation

Fig. 2 is a representation of frequency modulation. When a modulating signal is applied, the carrier frequency is increased during one half cycle of the modulating signal and decreased during the half cycle of the opposite polarity. This is indicated in the drawing by the fact that the RF cycles occupy less time (higher frequency) when the modulating signal is positive, and more time (lower frequency) when the modulating signal is negative.

The change in the carrier frequency (*frequency deviation*) is proportional to the instantaneous amplitude of the modulating signal. Thus, the deviation is small when the instantaneous amplitude of the modulating signal is small, and is greatest when the modulating signal reaches its peak, either positive or negative. The drawing shows the amplitude of the RF signal does not change during modulation. This is an oversimplification and is true only in the overall sense, as the amplitude of both the carrier and sidebands varies with frequency modulation. FM is capable of conveying dc levels, as it can maintain a specific frequency.

Phase Modulation

In phase modulation, the characteristic varied is the carrier phase from a reference value. In PM systems, the demodulator responds only to instantaneous changes in frequency. PM cannot convey changes in dc levels unless special phase-reference techniques are used. The amount of frequency change, or deviation, is directly proportional to how rapidly the phase is changing and the total amount of the phase change. The rapidity of the phase change is directly proportional to the frequency of the modulating signal and to the instantaneous amplitude of the modulating signal. This means that in a PM system, deviation increases with both the instantaneous amplitude and frequency of the modulating signal. Thus, PM modulators have a built-in *pre-emphasis*, where devia-

tion increases with modulating frequency. By way of contrast, deviation in FM systems is proportional only to the amplitude of the modulating signal. Apart from this characteristic it is difficult to distinguish between the two.

Angle-Modulation Sidebands

In AM there is a single set of sidebands above and below the carrier frequency. FM and PM produce many sets of sidebands that occur at integral multiples of the modulating frequency on both sides of the carrier. An angle-modulation signal therefore inherently occupies a wider channel than an AM signal.

In angle modulation, the number of sidebands depends on the relationship between the modulating frequency, frequency deviation and *modulation index*. For angle modulation with a sinusoidal modulating function

$$\chi = \frac{D}{m} = \phi \qquad \text{(Eq. 1)}$$

where

χ = modulation index
D = peak deviation (half the difference between the maximum and minimum values of the instantaneous frequency
m = modulation frequency in hertz
ϕ = phase deviation in radians (a radian = $180/\pi$ or approximately 57.3 degrees)

For example: The peak frequency deviation of an FM transmitter is 3000 Hz either side of the carrier frequency. The modulation index when modulated by a sine wave of 1000 Hz is

$$\text{modulation index} = \frac{3000}{1000} = 3$$

When modulated with a 3000-Hz sine wave at the same deviation the index would be 1; at 100 Hz the index would be 30, and so on.

Given a constant input level to the modulator, in PM the modulation index is constant regardless of the modulating frequency; in FM it varies with the modulating frequency, as shown in the above example. In an FM system the ratio of the *maximum* carrier-frequency deviation to the *highest* modulating frequency is called the *deviation ratio*. Thus

$$\text{deviation ratio} = \frac{D}{M} \qquad \text{(Eq. 2)}$$

where

D = peak deviation
M = maximum modulation frequency in hertz

For example: The deviation ratio for narrow-band FM is 5000 Hz (peak deviation) divided by 3000 Hz (maximum modulation frequency) and is 1.67.

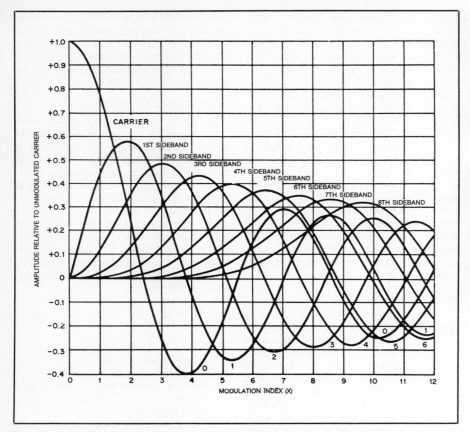

Fig. 3 — Amplitude variation of the carrier and sideband pairs with modulation index. This is a graphical representation of mathematical functions developed by F. W. Bessel. Note that the carrier completely disappears at modulation indexes of 2.405, 5.52 and 8.654.

Fig. 4 — The top photo is an oscilloscope pattern of an unmodulated RF carrier. The vertical (Y) axis shows amplitude, and the horizontal (X) axis time. The bottom photo is a spectrum-analyzer display, where amplitude is shown on the Y axis and frequency on the X axis. Notice that there is only one line that represents the amplitude at the carrier frequency.

Fig. 3 shows how the amplitudes of the carrier and the various sidebands vary with the modulation index. This is for single-tone modulation; the first-order sidebands (a pair, one above and one below the carrier frequency) are displaced from the carrier by an amount equal to the modulating frequency, the second is twice the modulating frequency away from the carrier, and so on. For example, if the modulating frequency is 2000 Hz and the carrier frequency is 29,500 kHz, the first sideband pair is at 29,498 and 29,502 kHz, the second pair is at 29,496 and 29,504 kHz, the third at 29,494 and 29,506 kHz, and so on. The amplitudes of these sidebands depend on the modulation index, not on the frequency deviation.

Note that as shown in Fig. 3, the carrier strength varies with the modulation index. (In amplitude modulation the carrier strength is constant; only the sideband amplitude varies.) At a modulation index of 2.405, the carrier disappears entirely. It then becomes "negative" at a higher index, meaning that its phase is reversed compared to the phase without modulation. In angle modulation, the energy that goes into the sidebands is taken from the carrier, the *total* power remaining the same regardless of the modulation index.

Since there is no change in total amplitude with modulation, an FM or PM signal can be amplified without distortion by an ordinary class-C amplifier. The modulation can take place in a very low-level stage, and the signal can then be amplified by either frequency multipliers or straight-through amplifiers.

If the modulated signal is passed through one or more frequency multipliers, the modulation index is multiplied by the same factor as the carrier frequency. For example, if modulation is applied at 3.5 MHz and the final output is on 28 MHz, the total frequency multiplication is eight times, so if the frequency deviation is 500 Hz at 3.5 MHz it will be 4000 Hz at 28 MHz.

Pulse Modulation

FCC rules restrict pulse modulation to the microwave region. Because of this it is not in common usage among amateurs. Pulse-modulated signals are usually sent as a series of short pulses separated by relatively long stretches of time with no signal being transmitted. (A typical pulse transmission might use 1-μs pulses with a 1000-Hz pulse rate. Thus, the peak power of a pulse transmission is usually much greater than its average power.

The pre-WARC '79 emission symbol for all pulse-type emissions was P. Since WARC '79, P is used only for a sequence of unmodulated pulses. Other types of pulse modulation are:

- Emission symbol K — pulse-amplitude modulation (PAM)
- Emission symbol L — pulse-width modulation (PWM) or pulse-duration modulation (PDM)
- Emission symbol M — pulse position/phase modulation (PPM)
- Emission symbol Q — angle modulation during the pulse
- Emission symbol V — combination of the above or by other means

AMATEUR RADIO MODULATION SYSTEMS

Specific modulation systems of general interest to radio amateurs are discussed below. Pre- and post-WARC '79 emission designations and graphic illustrations are included.

UNMODULATED CARRIER

Just as number systems include the digit 0, RF carriers have their unmodulated state. The emission symbol for an unmodulated carrier is N0N (formerly A0 or F0). N0N emission is permitted in all amateur bands above 51 MHz. In addition, it is permitted for beacon operation in bands above 28.2 MHz specified by FCC rules. N0N may also be used on any amateur band below 51 MHz for short

Fig. 5 — Voice-modulated AM DSB signal. On top is a dual-trace oscilloscope pattern of amplitude (Y axis) vs. time (X axis). The lower trace is a baseband voice signal. The upper trace is the carrier 100% modulated by the voice signal. The bottom photo is the spectrum-anaylzer display of amplitude (Y axis) vs. frequency (X axis).

periods of time when required for authorized remote control purposes or for experimental purposes (such as for transmitter tuning).

The bandwidth of an N0N emission is 0 Hz except for the transient sidebands that occur when the carrier is turned on or off. Fig. 4 shows an oscilloscope amplitude vs. time display and a spectrum analyzer amplitude vs. frequency display of an unmodulated carrier.

ANALOG TELEPHONY

Modulation systems for transmission of a single analog channel of telephony (including sound broadcasting) are identified by the post-WARC '79 symbols — 3E. The dash is replaced by a letter representing the type of modulation of the main carrier. Types of modulation for speech transmission that are commonly used in the Amateur Radio Service follow.

Double-Sideband Amplitude-Modulated Telephony

Double-sideband (DSB) amplitude-modulated (AM) telephony is generated by varying the amplitude of the carrier by a voice-frequency analog speech signal. Its post-WARC '79 designation is A3E (formerly A3). The full designation for commercial or amateur quality is 6K00A3EJN, meaning: 6 kHz bandwidth, DSB AM, telephony, sound of commercial quality, no multiplexing. In this case, the highest modulating frequency is 3 kHz,

resulting in 3-kHz sidebands above and below the carrier.

While DSB AM was the primary phone modulation system used in the early days of Amateur Radio, very few amateurs use it today. DSB AM has been virtually replaced by single-sideband amplitude modulation (SSB AM) in the HF bands. Angle (frequency or phase) modulation and SSB telephony are used on the VHF and UHF bands. Nevertheless, the most popular way of producing an SSB signal is to first generate a DSB AM signal and filter out the unwanted sideband.

Fig. 5 shows an oscilloscope amplitude vs. time display and a spectrum-analyzer amplitude vs. frequency display of a voice-modulated AM DSB signal. The signal in Fig. 5 is said to be 100% modulated on peaks, which is the maximum that the FCC permits. Modulation above 100% is unproductive because it adds distortion and generates unwanted sidebands, called *splatter*. Modulation with peaks much below 100% is undesirable because signal-to-noise ratio suffers.

At 100% modulation, voltage of each of the sidebands is half that of the carrier. Therefore, the power in each sideband is $(\frac{1}{2})^2$ times or ¼ that of the carrier. For a transmitter with a carrier output power of 100 watts, the power in each sideband is 25 watts, and the total sideband power is 50 watts. Fig. 6 illustrates the power in the carrier and sidebands of a 100%-modulated AM DSB signal. However, the same 100-watt AM DSB transmitter produces instantaneous peaks of 400 watts as illustrated in the vector diagram of Fig. 7. The bandwidth of a double-sideband AM telephony signal is calculated

$$B_n = 2M \qquad\qquad (Eq. 3)$$

where

B_n = necessary bandwidth in hertz
M = maximum modulation frequency in hertz

Receiving DSB AM Telephony

A double-sideband voice-modulated signal with carrier can be demodulated to audio by means of a half-wave or full-wave rectifier; simply one or more diodes. When the modulated signal passes through a nonlinear device, the carrier mixes with the two sidebands and produces an audio output.

On HF, multipath propagation causes AM DSB signals to fade in amplitude. Fading can be overcome to some extent by using an automatic gain control (AGC) loop circuit to keep the audio output at a constant level. Another multipath effect is selective fading, which has the effect of periodically distorting the demodulated audio. This type of distortion may be virtually eliminated by independent-sideband detection of the upper and lower sidebands and by representing the USB and LSB outputs to separate earphones. Simple elec-

trical combination after detection will re-introduce the distortion.

Single-Sideband Suppressed-Carrier AM Telephony

As both sidebands of a DSB AM signal convey the same information, a single sideband (SSB) may be transmitted and received. Since the carrier contains no intelligence, it too may be suppressed prior to transmission and reinserted in the receiver. SSB transmission and reception adds complexity and cost to radio equipment. However, SSB has a number of advantages:

• *spectrum conservation* — two SSB signals can occupy the space of one DSB signal.

• *more talk power for a transmitter final stage* — the same transmitter illustrated in Figs. 6 and 7 that ran 100 W carrier, 400 W peak and 50 W of talk power (USB + LSB) in DSB AM service can run 400 W of peak SSB talk power. Thus for a given transmitter power amplifier, SSB is said to have a 400/50 = 8/1 = 9-dB advantage over DSB AM, considering transmitter peak power alone.

• *elimination of carrier interference* — this eliminates the possibility of a carrier heterodyning with an adjacent signal.

• *reduction in multipath distortion* — SSB does not suffer the audio distortion

Fig. 6 — Example of a carrier 100% modulated by a single 1-kHz tone.

Fig. 7 — Vector diagram of 100% modulation of an AM carrier at the instant when peak conditions exist. The broken vectors show the relationships at an instant when the modulating signal is somewhat below its peak.

Fig. 8 — Single-sideband suppressed-carrier voice modulation. At top is a dual-trace oscilloscope pattern of amplitude (Y axis) vs. time (X axis). The bottom trace is a baseband voice signal. The upper trace is the SSBSC RF telephony signal. The lower photo is the spectrum-analyzer display of amplitude (Y axis) vs. frequency (X axis).

(mushiness) heard when receiving a DSB AM signal where the USB and LSB propagate through separate ionospheric paths.

In the early days of Amateur Radio SSB, a favorite pastime was to calculate the overall effective advantage of SSB over DSB communications. Besides transmitter final amplifier peak power, other considerations are amplifier average power handling capability, the effects of impulse noise on SSB and DSB reception, fading and distortion resulting from multipath propagation, and reception in the presence of different types of interference. However, at risk of resurrecting an old controversy, the overall advantage of SSB over DSB is on the order of 12 dB.

Fig. 8 shows amplitude vs. time and amplitude vs. frequency displays of an SSB suppressed-carrier (SC) signal. The emission symbol is J3E (formerly A3J) for SSBSC. The necessary bandwidth is calculated

$$B_n = M - L \qquad \text{(Eq. 4)}$$

where

B_n = necessary bandwidth in hertz
M = maximum modulation frequency in hertz
L = lowest modulation frequency in hertz

The full emission designation for an SSBSC telephony signal modulated from

300 to 3000 Hz is 2K70J3EJN. On the end, J means commercial quality, and N signifies no multiplexing.

Receiving SSBSC Telephony

SSBSC signals can be demodulated by an ordinary AM detector and by using a beat-frequency oscillator to reinsert the carrier within a few hertz of where it should be relative to the sidebands. Better performance can be realized by using a product detector, which is explained in Chapter 18.

Amplitude-Compandored Single-Sideband Telephony

Amplitude *compression* and limiting are common speech-processing techniques used in most SSB transmission systems to limit peak amplitudes and keep the average speech level high. In some SSB receiving systems, an *expansion* circuit is included to restore the compressed speech to its full dynamic range. A circuit that handles both transmitting compression and receiving expansion is known as a compandor. Unless there is some coordination between the compressor and expander, the expander will not know when and how much to expand. In amplitude-compandored single sideband (ACSSB) the control information is sent as amplitude modulation of a 3.1-kHz pilot tone.

There is no special post-WARC '79 emission symbol for ACSSB. It would fall into the SSBSC category of J3E (formerly A3J), however. The necessary bandwidth would be calculated by

$$B_n = M - L \qquad \text{(Eq. 5)}$$

where

B_n = necessary bandwidth in hertz.
M = maximum modulation frequency in hertz, which in this case is that of the pilot tune
L = lowest modulation frequency in hertz.

Single-Sideband Full-Carrier Telephony

This type of modulation is the same as SSBSC except that a full carrier has been added. It is also known as *compatible AM* (CAM) because it can be received on an ordinary AM receiver with no beat-frequency oscillator. CAM has a number of additional advantages:

• receiver tuning is less critical than for SSBSC.
• bandwidth is half that of DSB AM.
• it is easy to generate using an SSBSC transmitter by the simple insertion of the carrier.

Disadvantages are:

• transmission of the full carrier reduces the peak power available for the intelligence-bearing sideband.
• carriers produce unnecessary beat notes in the phone bands.
• reception with an ordinary DSB AM

Fig. 9 — Displays of a single-sideband, full-carrier telephony, or compatible-AM (CAM), signal. At top is a dual-trace oscilloscope pattern of amplitude (Y axis) vs. time (X axis). The bottom trace is a baseband voice signal. The upper trace is the CAM RF signal. The lower photo is the spectrum-anaylzer display of amplitude (Y axis) vs. frequency (X axis).

receiver will be less effective than a receiver designed for SSB reception.

The post-WARC '79 emission symbol for single-sideband full-carrier telephony is H3E (formerly A3H). The full CCIR emission designation 3K00H3EJN would mean a bandwidth of 3 kHz, full-carrier, single-sideband telephony, commercial quality and no multiplexing. Necessary bandwidth is calculated by

$$B_n = M \qquad \text{(Eq. 6)}$$

where

B_n = necessary bandwidth in hertz
M = maximum modulation frequency in hertz

Fig. 9 shows oscilloscope and spectrum-analyzer displays of a sample CAM signal.

Angle-Modulated Telephony

Below 29.0 MHz, FCC rules limit the bandwidth of frequency- or phase-modulated telephony to that of an AM transmission having the same audio characteristics. The full emission designation for such a signal would be 6K00F3EJN for frequency modulation and 6K00G3EJN for phase modulation. These designations break into: 6-kHz bandwidth, F for frequency modulation or G for phase modulation, single-channel analog, telephony, sound of commercial quality and no multiplexing.

Because of the limitation not to exceed the bandwidth of an AM transmission of the same characteristics, the bandwidth is restricted to 2M (twice the maximum modulation frequency) or $2 \times 3000 = 6000$ Hz. You cannot use 5-kHz or even 3-kHz deviation without greatly exceeding the 6-kHz bandwidth limit. In fact, the usual FM bandwidth formulas will not work in this case, and it is necessary to examine the power in the second pair of sidebands and limit it to about 1% of the total. If this were done assuming sinusoidal modulation at 3000 Hz, the highest modulation index would be 0.4, and deviation would be limited to 1.2 kHz. In practice, however, the energy distribution in a complex (voice) wave is such that the modulation index for any one frequency component is reduced as compared to the index with a sine wave having the same peak amplitude as the voice wave. Thus, for voice, a modulation index of 0.6 and a 1.8-kHz deviation will ensure that the second pair of sidebands will be 27 dB below the unmodulated carrier level.

To obtain the benefits of this mode, a good FM receiver is required. As shown in Fig. 3, at an index of 0.6 the amplitude of the first pair of sidebands is about 25 percent of the unmodulated-carrier amplitude; this compares with a sideband amplitude of an AM transmitter modulated 100 percent.

Above 29.0 MHz, the standard FM deviation is 5 kHz. The formula for necessary bandwidth is

$$B_n = 2M + 2DK \qquad \text{(Eq. 7)}$$

where

  B_n = necessary bandwidth in hertz
  M = maximum modulation frequency in hertz
  D = peak deviation in hertz
  $K = 1$

For a maximum modulation frequency of 3000 Hz and a peak deviation of 5000 Hz, the necessary bandwidth is 16,000 Hz. The emission designation would be 16K0F3EJN for 16-kHz bandwidth, frequency modulation, analog, telephony, commercial quality, and no multiplexing. In the case of phase modulation, the designation would be 16K0G3EJN.

In the early 1970s, 15-kHz deviation was used extensively by amateurs. Using Eq. 7, the bandwidth would be 36 kHz, and the emission designations would be 36K0F3EJN and 36K0G3EJN for frequency modulation and phase modulation, respectively. Currently, 15-kHz deviation is used mostly on frequencies above 450 MHz. One exception is that some fast-scan ATV groups apply 15-kHz FM audio modulation to the video carrier on repeater input frequencies.

TV Sound

The sound channel for U.S. TV broadcasting has a maximum modulation fre-

quency of 15 kHz and uses a peak deviation of 25 kHz. Using Eq. 7, necessary bandwidth is calculated to be 2M + 2DK = $(2 \times 15) + (2 \times 25 \times 1) = 80$ kHz. The emission designation would be 80K0F3EGN, meaning: 80-kHz necessary bandwidth, frequency modulation, analog, telephony, sound of broadcasting quality (monophonic) and no multiplexing. This is of interest to amateurs who transmit ATV for reception by ordinary TV receivers. Amateurs may not be interested in transmitting the full 50- to 15,000-Hz audio range and can reproduce high-quality speech with a 250- to 6000-Hz audio passband. In this case, the necessary bandwidth would be reduced to 62 kHz. If the maximum modulation frequency were reduced to 3000 Hz, the necessary bandwidth would be 56 kHz.

FM Broadcasting

The characteristics of FM sound broadcasting are of interest to amateurs for special applications. Chapter 32 illustrates the use of an FM broadcast receiver as a demodulator in a Gunnplexer™ microwave communication system.

FM sound broadcasting uses a peak deviation of 75 kHz and a maximum modulation frequency of 15 kHz. Again using Eq. 7, the necessary bandwidth is 2M + 2DK = $2 \times 15 + 2 \times 75 \times 1 = 180$ kHz. The emission designation is 180KF3EGN, which breaks down to: 180-kHz necessary bandwidth, frequency modulation, analog, telephony, sound of broadcasting quality (monophonic), and no multiplexing. For stereophonic or quadraphonic sound, the G would be replaced by H. N would become F to indicate frequency-division multiplexing.

AMATEUR IMAGE COMMUNICATIONS MODULATION

Image communications systems used in the Amateur Radio Service are outlined in Chapter 20. Below is a discussion of the most popular modulation systems for these modes.

Fast-Scan Television

Two types of amplitude modulation are presently in use by Amateur Radio fast-scan television (FSTV) operators. One is double-sideband, and the other is vestigial sideband. Although most FSTV is in color, some monochrome (black and white) FSTV is still in use.

The simplest way to transmit FSTV is monochrome DSB AM. In this case, the necessary bandwidth can be calculated from

$$B_n = 2M \qquad \text{(Eq. 8)}$$

where

  B_n = necessary bandwidth in hertz
  M = maximum modulation frequency in hertz

Typically, monochrome FSTV has a video bandwidth (M in Eq. 8) of 2.5 MHz. The complete CCIR emission designation would be 5M00A3FMN for: 5-MHz necessary bandwidth, double-sideband AM, single-channel analog information, television, monochrome, and no multiplexing. This emission designation does not account for any audio channel — the possibilities include sending the audio independently or multiplexing it with the video transmission.

Using the NTSC color system, the video bandwidth needs to be about 4 MHz. Again using Eq. 8, the DSB AM necessary bandwidth would be 8 MHz. The emission designation becomes 8M00A3FNM, which stands for: an 8-MHz necessary bandwidth, double sideband AM, single-channel analog information, television, color and no multiplexing. Again, no audio channel is included.

Double-sideband AM transmission of either monochrome or color TV occupies a considerable amount of spectrum. So, it is desirable to use vestigial-sideband (VSB) transmission wherever possible for FSTV to reduce bandwidth. This is particularly important for FSTV repeater outputs because repeaters are generally well sited for wide-area coverage and may run several hundred watts of power. For vestigial-sideband FSTV, the necessary bandwidth of the visual transmission can be calculated from

$$B_n = M + V \qquad \text{(Eq. 9)}$$

where

  B_n = necessary bandwidth in hertz
  M = maximum modulation frequency in hertz
  V = bandwidth of the vestigial sideband (typically 1.25 MHz)

For example, the full emission designation for a VSB color TV transmission might be 5M25C3FNN, meaning: 5.25-MHz necessary bandwidth, vestigial-sideband AM, single-channel analog information, television, color, and no multiplexing. For monochrome VSB TV, the emission designation might be 4M00C3FMN, meaning: 4-MHz necessary bandwidth, vestigial-sideband AM, single-channel analog, television, monochrome and no multiplexing. Neither of these designations includes an audio channel which would most likely be 4.5 MHz above the video carrier and use 80K0F3EGN emission as discussed earlier in this chapter.

Analog Slow-Scan Television or Facsimile

Slow-scan television (SSTV) or facsimile (FAX) is typically transmitted by frequency modulating an audio oscillator and feeding that into a single-sideband suppressed-carrier transmitter. The bandwidth has to take into account both the frequency range over which the oscillator frequency is swung (such as from 1200 to

2300 Hz) and the number of picture elements (pixels) transmitted per second. The necessary bandwidth can be calculated from

$$B_n = 2M + 2DK \qquad \text{(Eq. 10)}$$

where
B_n = necessary bandwidth in hertz
M = N/2
N = number of pixels per second
K = 1.1 (typically)
D = peak deviation (half the difference between the maximum and minimum values of the instantaneous frequency)

For example, with a tone that can be swung from 1200 to 2300 Hz (a difference of 1100 Hz), D = half the difference, or 550 Hz. If the horizontal sweep rate is 15 Hz and there are 100 pixels per line, N = (15 × 100) = 1500 pixels/s, and M = 1500/2 = 750. Pouring these numbers in Eq. 10, B_n = (2 × 750) + (2 × 550 × 1.1) = 1500 + 1210 = 2710 Hz. If this were an SSTV transmission, the emission designator could be 2K71J3FMN, for: 2.71-kHz necessary bandwidth, single-sideband suppressed-carrier, single-channel analog information, monochrome and no multiplexing. For facsimile, it would be 2K71J3CMN — the C designating facsimile. Note that it is the SSBSC modulation of the main carrier that determines the basic type of emission (J), not the fact that the subcarrier is frequency modulated. On the other hand, if you directly frequency-modulate the main carrier, the J in the above designators would change to F.

Quantized Slow-Scan Television or Facsimile

Many amateurs are now using computers to generate *quantized* (rather than continuously varying signals). The bandwidth of quantized SSTV or FAX may be calculated using Eq. 15 provided that the transitions between quantized steps are smooth. For abrupt transitions between steps where image contouring is to be preserved, larger values of K should be used. If the modulation system is as described under Analog Slow-Scan Television or Facsimile, above, the emission designators for quantized SSTV or FAX would be changed by substituting the digit 2 (meaning quantized modulation of a tone) for the digit 3 (analog) in the third symbol.

TELEGRAPHY

These modulation systems include telegraphy for aural reception (Morse code) and telegraphy for automatic reception (radioteletype).

Continuous-Wave Morse Telegraphy

Telegraphy by *on-off keying* (OOK) of a carrier is the oldest radio modulation system. It is also known as CW (for continuous wave). While CW is used by

Fig. 10 — Shaping and timing in CW keying systems.

amateurs and other communicators to mean OOK telegraphy by Morse code, parts of the electronics industry use CW to signify an unmodulated carrier. OOK telegraphy is also known as *amplitude-shift keying* (ASK).

The emission symbol for Morse OOK of the main carrier is A1A (formerly A1). The first letter is A because keying a carrier on and off produces double (upper and lower) sidebands corresponding to the frequency components of the keying pulse. The amplitude of the RF signal rises from zero to full strength some time after the key is closed, and returns to zero some time after the key is opened. The lengths of these transition intervals and their wave shapes determine the bandwidth occupied by the signal.

In Fig. 10, the envelope rises from zero to full amplitude in 5 ms. The waveform during the rise time resembles 90 degrees of sine wave having a period of 20 ms, or a frequency of 50 Hz. Amplitude-modulation theory tells us that the occupied bandwidth will be 100 Hz; that is, 50 Hz for the lower sideband (LSB) and 50 Hz for the upper sideband (USB). If the waveform deviates from sinusoidal, harmonics are present, and the bandwidth will be some integral multiple of 100 Hz. The fall time is just as important as the rise time; whichever is shorter or has the greatest harmonic content will determine the bandwidth of the emission.

League publications have long promoted 5-ms rise and fall times for CW keying envelopes. This figure was not chosen arbitrarily. Appendix 6 of the CCIR Radio Regulations and section 2.202 of the FCC rules define the bandwidth for an A1A emission as

$$B_n = B K \qquad \text{(Eq. 11)}$$

where
B_n = necessary bandwidth in hertz
B = telegraph speed in bauds
K = an overall numerical factor that varies according to the emission and that depends on the allowable signal distortion.

The CCIR and FCC recommend K = 3 for nonfading circuits and K = 5 for fading circuits when using telegraphy for aural reception. If K = 3 is chosen, that means the frequency of the keying envelope rise is the third harmonic of the keying frequency. K = 3 is the minimum needed for aural reception because a K = 1 (although useful for machine recognition) sounds like the keying is too soft. K = 5 is more appropriate for fading circuits because the faster rise time helps the ear sense the transitions. Further, K = 5 says that the third *and* fifth harmonic of the keying pulses are present in both sidebands. Thus, if any of these harmonics are lost through *selective fading* caused by *multipath* propagation, the rest of the signal stands a good chance of getting through and being interpreted correctly by the receiving operator. Selective fading isn't usually a problem on HF at speeds below 50 bauds because the upper and lower sidebands are fairly close in frequency and are usually *correlated* (they fade together). Every now and then you can hear the exception, which sounds like the signal is in a barrel.

In Morse telegraphy a dot occupies one unit of time, as does a space. For a string of dots having a duration of 20 ms, there will be 25 such dots in a second, and the keying speed will be 50 bauds. We are more accustomed to words per minute (WPM)

Fig. 11 — Curves for determining 23-dB bandwidths and maximum telegraph speeds for various keying rise and fall times.

Fig. 12 — Displays of a CW OOK signal. At top is a dual-trace oscilloscope pattern of amplitude (Y axis) vs. time (X axis). The bottom trace is the CW keying input before shaping at 25 dots/s. The upper trace is the keyed RF carrier after keying has been shaped for approximately 5-ms rise and fall times. The bottom photo is the spectrum-analyzer display of amplitude (Y axis) vs. frequency (X axis) for the same signal.

than bauds when dealing with Morse code, so let's apply the following formulas.

WPM = 2.4 × dot/s
WPM = 1.2 B

where

WPM = telegraph speed in words per minute
2.4 = a constant calculated by comparing dots per second with plain-language Morse code sending the word PARIS
1.2 = a constant calculated by comparing the signaling rate in bauds with plain-language Morse code sending the word PARIS
B = telegraph speed in bauds

Thus a keying speed of 25 dot/s or 50 bauds is equal to 60 WPM. Returning to Eq. 11, on a nonfading circuit the necessary bandwidth will be 50 × 3 = 150 Hz. This value differs from the 100 Hz derived earlier because the formula is based on a larger energy spectrum and recognizes that the keying waveform isn't likely to be purely sinusoidal. Also, we defined the rise and fall times to include the complete transition interval for ease of illustration. Measuring the rise and fall times according to the 10% to 90% convention shortens the times somewhat and tends to further reconcile the two bandwidth values. Given a 150-Hz bandwidth, how fast can we communicate over a fading path? Setting B_n = 150 and K = 5, and solving Eq. 11 for B produces a telegraph speed of

30 bauds, which is 36 WPM (PARIS). You may conclude that 5-ms rise and fall times are suitable for up to 36 WPM on fading circuits and 60 WPM on nonfading circuits. These numbers can be scaled up or down according to your needs as shown in Fig. 11.

Fig. 12 shows an oscilloscope amplitude vs. time display and a spectrum-analyzer amplitude vs. frequency display of an OOK signal.

To complete the picture, the full CCIR emission designation for the Morse code keying just discussed is 150HA1AAN. The figure 150 is the necessary bandwidth in hertz (H); A = double-sideband amplitude modulation; 1 = a single channel containing quantized or digital information without the use of a modulating subcarrier; the second A = telegraphy — for aural reception; the third A = two-condition code with elements of differing numbers and/or durations; and N = no multiplexing.

Receiving Morse Telegraphy

Proper reception of a Morse-code transmission requires that the receiver bandwidth be at least that of the necessary bandwidth plus any frequency error. Thus, if you have 150-Hz receiver bandwidth, it would be necessary for you to carefully tune your receiver to receive a 150-Hz-bandwidth transmission. Or, if you want to have a fixed-frequency receiver, probably one that's crystal controlled, you will need to increase the 150-Hz bandwidth

by the combined error of both the transmitter and receiver frequencies.

For aural reception, a Morse-code OOK radio signal is not completely demodulated to its original dc pulse, since only thumping would be heard. Instead, it consists of simply heterodyning the RF signal down to an AF signal somewhere in the vicinity of 700 Hz. If the IF bandwidth is much greater than 150 Hz, the overall bandwidth can be reduced by adding an audio filter in the receiver AF circuits. These concepts and practical circuits are developed in Chapter 28.

Single-Sideband Suppressed Carrier Tone-Modulated Morse

Rather than keying a main carrier on and off, many modern transmitters generate a CW signal by keying an audio tone of about 700 or 800 Hz and feeding it to an SSBSC transmitter. The transmitter output looks just the same as though the main carrier had been keyed except for the suppressed carrier 700 or 800 Hz away. In fact, the carrier is so well suppressed that it cannot be heard any appreciable distance away from the transmitter. "If it looks like a duck, walks like a duck and quacks like a duck..." Well, not in this case. The transmitted signal is not classified as A1A but as J2A (formerly A2J). Eq. 11 can still be used to calculate bandwidth. Using the 5-ms rise-time example discussed under continuous-wave Morse telegraphy, the bandwidth would remain 150 Hz. Thus, the

ACSB® — Amplitude-compandored single sideband; registered trademark of Sideband Technology Inc. (See ACSSB.)

ACSSB — Amplitude-compandored single sideband.

ADM — Adaptive delta modulation.

AFSK — Audio-frequency-shift keying.

AM — Amplitude modulation.

Analog — Information in continuously variable quantities. (Opposite digital. Also see quantized.)

ANBFM — Adaptive narrow-band frequency modulation.

Apparent carrier — The frequency, f_0, at which the signal maximum appears.

APK — Amplitude phase keying. (Same as QAM.)

APCM — Adaptive pulse-code modulation.

ASK — Amplitude-shift keying.

AWGN — Additive white Gaussian noise.

Baseband — The band of frequencies of a signal (a) prior to modulation of the main carrier or (b) after demodulation of the main carrier.

Baud (Bd) — A unit of signaling speed equal to the number of discrete conditions or events per second. (If the duration of a pulse is 20 ms, the signaling rate is 50 bauds or the reciprocal of 0.02.)

Bit/s — A measure of the number of bits of data transmitted per second. (The prefixes k, M, or G may be added to denote higher speeds; for example 1 kbit/s is 1000 bits per second.)

BPSK — Binary phase-shift keying.

Carrier — A continuous radio frequency capable of being modulated by a baseband signal or subcarrier.

CDM — Companded delta modulation.

CDMA — Code-division multiple access.

CFSK — Coherent frequency-shift keying.

C/N — Carrier-to-noise ratio. (Expressed in dB.)

Compandor — A contraction of compressor-expander.

CPFSK — Continous-phase frequency-shift keying.

CPM — Continous-phase modulation.

CVSD — Continuously variable slope delta modulation. (Used to convert analog speech into compressed digital form.)

CW — Continuous wave. (In Amateur Radio, CW usually means a continuous carrier wave keyed on and off by Morse code.)

DAV — Data above voice.

DBPSK — Differentially binary phase-shift keying.

DCPSK — Differentially coherent phase-shift keying.

Demodulation — The process of deriving the original modulation signal from a modulated carrier wave.

DEBPSK — Differentially encoded binary phase-shift keying, with carrier recovery.

DECPSK — Differential encoded coherent phase-shift keying.

DFSK — Double frequency-shift keying.

Dibit — A group of two bits. (The possible states are 00, 01, 10 and 11. In phase modulation each dibit translates to one of four specific phases or transitions.)

Digital — Information in discrete states. (Opposite analog.)

DIV — Data in voice.

DLL — Delay-locked loop.

DPCM — Differential pulse-code modulation.

DPMM — Digitally processed multimode modulation.

DPSK — Differential phase-shift keying.

DS — Direct sequence. (A technique used in spread spectrum.)

DSB — Double sideband.

DSBSC — Double-sideband suppressed carrier.

DUV — Data under voice.

Envelope delay — The propagation time of the envelope of a wave.

Equalizer — A circuit with fixed or variable parameters for correction of amplitude or phase distortion.

Eye diagram — (Also called eye pattern). An oscilloscope display of a digital signal stream, triggered at the transmission bit rate, to show the received waveform. (The displayed waveform resembles an eye.)

FAX — Facsimile.

FDM — Frequency-division multiplexing. (Typically used to transmit a number of sub-carriers [each having its own frequency] over one carrier.)

FDMA — Frequency-division multiple access.

FFSK — Fast frequency-shift keying. (Same as MSK.)

FH — Frequency hopping. (A modulation technique used in spread spectrum.)

FM — Frequency modulation.

FSK — Frequency-shift keying.

FSTV — Fast-scan television.

GMSK — Gaussian-filtered minimum-shift keying.

Group delay — The rate of change with frequency of the phase shift during propagation from one point to another.

ICW — Interrupted continuous wave.

ISB — Independent sideband.

Isochronous distortion — The peak-to-peak phase jitter, which may be expressed in percentage of the unit interval.

Intersymbol interface (ISI) — Pulse stretching of one pulse into the next pulse.

Jitter — The peak-to-peak time difference between the ideal time and the actual time for a pulse transition.

LPC — Linear predictive coding. (A technique for converting analog speech to digital form using a small number of bits.)

LSB — Lower sideband.

---

complete emission designation would be 150HJ2AAN.

Amplitude Tone-Modulated Morse Telegraphy

This type of modulation, often called *modulated* CW (MCW), was lumped under an ambiguous pre-WARC '79 emission symbol of A2. MCW or A2 meant that a Morse-keyed tone modulated a double-sideband AM transmitter. The ambiguity was whether only the sidebands were keyed or the sidebands and the carrier. Carrier-keyed MCW is permitted in the Amateur Radio Service only on frequencies between 50.1 and 54 MHz and above 144.1 MHz. MCW produced by keying the tone but not the carrier can be operated on the frequencies just mentioned and as specified in §97.65(b) of the FCC rules: "Whenever code practice, in accordance with §97.91 (d), is conducted in bands authorized for A3 emission tone modulation of the radio telephone transmitter may be utilized when interspersed with appropriate voice instructions."

The post-WARC '79 emission symbol for MCW is A2A. Again, no distinction is made in the emission symbol to tell whether the carrier is keyed. The formula for necessary bandwidth is

$$B_n = BK + 2M \qquad \text{(Eq. 12)}$$

where

B_n = necessary bandwidth in hertz

B = modulation rate in bauds

M = maximum modulation frequency in hertz

K = 5 for fading circuits, 3 for non-fading circuits

For a 25-WPM ($B = 20$) transmission with $M = 1000$ and $K = 5$, the bandwidth will be 2.1 kHz. The full emission designation in this case will be 2K10A2AAN. Broken down, the designation stands for: 2.1 kHz bandwidth, double-sideband AM, a single channel containing quantized or digital information, telegraphy for aural reception, two-condition code with elements of differing numbers and/or durations, and no multiplexing.

Frequency-Shift-Keyed Telegraphy

On-off keying is effective for aurally received Morse-code transmissions because the ear is able to recognize the difference between the presence of a signal and noise (the absence of signal). Demodulators for teletypewriters and computers do much better with two positive conditions, each representing a specific logic state (1 or 0).

Frequency-shift keying (FSK) provides the two positive states just mentioned. The transmitter shifts between two predetermined frequencies, called *mark* (1) and *space* (0). In Amateur Radio Baudot and AMTOR systems, the standard shift is now 170 Hz. Deviation (usually abbreviated D) is measured from an imaginary center frequency and the mark or space frequencies, and is half the shift. Thus a 170-Hz shift equals a deviation of 85 Hz.

Sometimes you will see the abbreviation CP used in front of FSK. CP, meaning *continuous phase,* says that the mark and space frequencies as well as the dc pulses that switch between them are clocked in a way that ensures a continuous sinusoidal function. This avoids generating unwanted sidebands that would have resulted from waveform discontinuities.

To date, virtually all amateur FSK has been NCFSK, the NC standing for *non-coherent.* You can tell this quickly by looking at the signaling rate (in bauds) and the shift: If one is not an integral multiple of the other, the FSK will be noncoherent. For example, a 170-Hz-shift FSK system keyed at 45.45 bauds is noncoherent because 170 divided by 45.45 equals 3.740374 — far from a round number. Unless special design precautions are taken, an NCFSK signal could contain many unwanted sideband components (key clicks),

MAP — Maximum *a posteriori* probability. (A mathematical estimative technique used in data demodulation. See ML.)

Mark — The presence of a signal. (See space.)

M-ary — M is a variable representing the number of states (in modulation).

MCW — Modulated continuous wave. (In Amateur Radio, MCW usually means a tone-modulated carrier keyed on and off by Morse code.)

MASK — Multiple amplitude-shift keying.

MFSK — Multiple frequency-shift keying.

ML — Maximum likelihood. (A mathematical estimative technique used in data demodulation. See MAP.)

MPSK — Multiple phase-shift keying.

Modem — Modulator-demodulator.

Modulation — The process of varying some characteristic of a carrier wave to convey intelligence.

Modulation index — In frequency modulation, the number of sideband pairs for a given modulating frequency.

MSK — Minimum-shift keying. (Same as FFSK.)

MSTV — Medium-scan television.

MUX — Multiplex; multiplexer.

NBFM — Narrow-band frequency modulation.

NBPSK — Narrow-band phase-shift keying.

NCFSK — Noncoherent frequency-shift keying.

Necessary bandwidth — The bandwidth just sufficient to ensure the transmission of information at the rate and with the quality required.

NLA-QAM — Nonlinear amplified QAM.

NLF-OQPSK — Nonlinearly filtered QPSK; also known as Feher's QPSK.

Occupied bandwidth — The bandwidth the upper and lower limits of which have mean powers equal to a specified pecentage (0.5% unless otherwise specified) of the total mean power.

OOK — On-off keying.

OQPSK — Offset (or staggered) quadrature phase-shift keying.

PAM — Pulse-amplitude modulation.

PCM — Pulse-code modulation.

PDM — Pulse-duration modulation. (Same as PWM.)

PFM — Pulse-frequency modulation.

PLL — Phase-locked loop.

PM — Phase modulation.

PSK — Phase-shift keying.

Pulse spreading — Elongation of a received pulse as a result of multipath propagation.

PWM — Pulse-width modulation. (Same as PDM.)

QAM — Quadrature amplitude modulation. (Same as APK.)

QASK — Quadrature amplitude-shift keying.

Q-M/PSK — Quadrature suppressed-carrier AM added to quadrature carrier and hard limited.

QPPM — Quantized pulse-position modulation.

QPRS — Quadrature-partial-response modulation system.

QPSK — Quadrature phase-shift keying (quadraphase).

Quadbit — A group of 4 bits. In phase modulation each quadbit translates to one of 16 specific phases or transitions.)

Quantize — To divide the range of variables into a finite number of specific values or steps.

Raised cosine (RC) — A method of shaping a keying waveform to reduce bandwidth by following the cosine function with the negative peak of the wave raised (or biased) to 0-V dc.

Reduced carrier (RC) — A method of transmission wherein the carrier is reduced by a predetermined number of decibels.

SCPC — Single channel per carrier.

Sideband — The group of frequencies above or below the main carrier frequency which

contain the product of modulation.

S/N — Signal-to-noise ratio. (Expressed in dB.)

Space — The absence of a signal. (See mark.)

Splatter — Generation of unnecessary sidebands by exceeding 100% modulation in an AM system or by flat-topping.

SQAM — Staggered (or offset) quadrature amplitude modulation.

SQPSK — Staggered (or offset) quaternary phase-shift keying.

SSB — Single sideband.

SSBSC — Single-sideband suppressed carrier.

SSMA — Spread-spectrum multiple access.

SSTV — Slow-scan television.

Suppressed carrier (SC) — A method of transmission wherein the carrier is greatly attenuated.

TADI — Time assignment digital interpolation. (A technique for sending bursts of data during pauses in speech.)

TDM — Time-division multiplexing.

TDMA — Time-division multiple access.

TFM — Tamed frequency modulation.

TH — Time hopping. (A technique used in spread spectrum.)

Unit interval — The duration of the shortest signal element. (Expressed in seconds, the unit interval is the reciprocal of the signaling speed in bauds.)

USB — Upper sideband.

VF — Voice frequencies.

VFCT — Voice-frequency carrier telegraphy. (A technique for combining multiple telegraph channels in the frequency spectrum normally occupied by one voice channel.)

VSB — Vestigial sideband.

VSDM — Variable-slope delta modulation.

WBFM — Wideband frequency modulation.

WGN — White Gaussian noise.

WPM — Words per minute. (A unit of speed in telegraph systems.)

8PSK — Eight-ary or octal phase-shift keying.

---

which would interfere with nearby channels.

The pre-WARC '79 emission symbol for FSK was F1. The new designation still begins with F1 but includes a third letter (and the fourth and fifth letters if you care to add them). For conventional 170-Hz FSK 45.45-baud Baudot RTTY, the short-form emission symbol is F1B, the B standing for telegraphy — for automatic reception. The complete emission designation would be 249HF1BBN. The optional fourth letter means a two-condition code with elements of the same number and duration without error correction; the fifth letter N is for no multiplexing. For Baudot RTTY, the necessary bandwidth is calculated

$$B_n = B + 2DK \qquad \text{(Eq. 13)}$$

where

B_n = necessary bandwidth
B = modulation rate in bauds
D = peak deviation (half the frequency shift) in hertz
K = 1.2 (typically)

The complete emission designation for AMTOR FSK RTTY is 304HF1BCN. The bandwidth 304H is calculated using Eq. 13, above; in this case, B is 100 bauds. The optional fourth and fifth letters are: C for

two-condition code with elements of the same number and duration with error correction and N for no multiplexing.

For both Baudot and AMTOR RTTY, the third letter B, meaning telegraphy for automatic reception, implies *direct-printing* telegraphy. In CCIR lingo, direct-printing describes the traditional teletypewriter-to-teletypewriter circuit where what you type on one end comes out on a typewriter-like printer on the other end. However, when you depart from direct-printing telegraphy and enter the world of computers to generate FSK, you are entering the "twilight zone" of CCIR terminology. Thus, if you are transmitting ASCII from teletypewriter to teletypewriter, you are transmitting F1B emission. If, on the other hand, you are transmitting *data* (in this case loosely meaning that a computer generates it and it is probably received by a computer-like device at the other end), then the emission symbol is F1D. We suggest using the third symbol B for all narrow-band direct-printing telegraphy whether sent by a teletypewriter or a computer.

Audio-Frequency-Shift-Keyed Telegraphy

Audio-frequency-shift keying (AFSK) is more popular than direct FSK of the main carrier for both direct-printing telegraphy and data transmission in the Amateur

Radio Service. AFSK into an SSBSC transmitter is common for both the HF bands and via satellite. For Baudot and AMTOR, the emission designations of AFSK-generated signals would be 249HJ2BBN and 304HJ2BCN, respectively, using the same parameters as in the FSK examples given earlier.

Above 50 MHz, radioteletype transmissions are often sent by frequency-shift keying an audio tone and feeding the AFSK tone into the microphone input of an FM transmitter. Necessary bandwidth calculations get a bit tricky because of the double modulation. First, let us determine the baseband bandwidth of the frequency-shifted tones. That is done by using Eq. 13, which will yield bandwidths of 249 Hz for 45-baud Baudot, as calculated above. If the AFSK tones used are 2125 and 2295 Hz, you can determine the highest modulation frequency by finding the center frequency and adding half the bandwidth to that. As 2125 and 2295 Hz differ by 170 Hz, the center frequency is 2210 Hz. Half the 249-Hz bandwidth is 125 Hz (124.5 Hz rounded up), so 2210 + 125 = 2335. Thus the highest modulation frequency is 2335 Hz. To complete the bandwidth calculation, we then use the general necessary bandwidth formula for the main FM carrier

Fig. 13 — Power spectral density of BPSK, QPSK, MSK, GMSK and TFM relative to the mean power of the total emission. (After CCIR Rep. 767-1 and Steber, March 1984)
B_bT = normalized bandwidth of premodulation
Gaussian band-pass filter (GMSK)
f_c = center frequency
f_b = bandwidth (Hz)
P = spectral density (W/Hz)

Fig. 14 — Wide spectral displays of 1200-baud data transmissions. At top is a display of amplitude (Y axis) vs. frequency (X axis) of a 1200-baud signal produced by a Bell 202 modulator, which has a frequency shift of 1000 Hz. At center is a similar display of the output of a minimum-shift-keying (MSK) modulator, which has a shift of 600 Hz. At bottom is a display of a binary-phase-shift-keying (BPSK) modulator. Note that the top and bottom displays have spans of 20 kHz, while the center display span is 50 kHz.

$$B_n = 2M + 2DK \qquad (Eq.\ 10)$$

where

B_n = necessary bandwidth in hertz
M = maximum modulation frequency in hertz
D = peak deviation in hertz
K = 1

Thus, if a frequency deviation of 5 kHz is used, $B_n = (2 \times 2335) + (2 \times 5000 \times 1) = 4670 + 10,000 = 14,670$ Hz.

DATA, TELEMETRY AND TELECOMMAND

Data, telemetry and telecommand are identified by D as the third symbol of the emission designator. Included in this category are computer-to-computer data transfers, packet radio, telemetry from satellites, and remote control of models and other objects. Excluded from this category is narrow-band direct-printing telegraphy (conventional radioteletype).

Efficient Data Communications

A measure of data communication efficiency is the number of hertz or frequency shift (in an FSK system) per baud (Hz/Bd) — this is nothing more than FM modulation index. Narrow-band direct-printing RTTY transmissions use low signaling rates and small frequency shifts in absolute terms (Hz). Typically an RTTY signal uses a frequency shift of 170 hertz and signals at a rate of 45 bauds. This amounts to 170 Hz/45 Bd, which reduces to a modulation index of 3.78 (Hz/Bd). If we were to use the same modulation index for a 1200-baud data transmission, the frequency shift would be $3.78 \times 1200 = 4536$ Hz. Further, applying Eq. 13, the necessary bandwidth would be

$$B_n = B + 2DK = 1200 + (4536 \times 1.2)$$
$$= 1200 + 5443 = 6643 \text{ Hz.}$$

Clearly, it would not be good spectrum efficiency to use more than 6 kHz of bandwidth when existing technology permits transmission of a 1200-baud data signal in a much smaller bandwidth. Through this analysis, we have established that conventional RTTY, while not occupying much spectrum in absolute terms, is spectrally inefficient with respect to its signaling rate. Also, it can be concluded that data transmission at higher speeds must use spectrally efficient modulation techniques in order to find room in crowded Amateur Radio bands.

The FCC recognized this matter of spectrum efficiency in the rules, which state: "the . . . frequency shift (difference between the frequency for the "mark" signal and that for the "space" signal), as appropriate, shall not exceed 1000 Hz. When these emissions are used on frequencies above 50 MHz, the frequency shift, in hertz, shall not exceed the sending speed, in baud(s), of the transmission, or 1000 Hz, whichever is greater." The frequency shift (in Hz) not exceeding the sending speed (in Bd) means a limit of 1 Hz/Bd (a modulation index of 1) for signaling rates of 1000 Bd or more.

For 1200-Bd packet radio, it is common to use surplus Bell 202 compatible modems. As Bell 202 tones (1200 and 2200 Hz) shift 1000 Hz, the result is 1000/1200 or a modulation index of 0.83 (Hz/Bd). On HF packet radio, there is activity using Bell 103 tones (originate tones of 1070 and 1270 Hz or answer tones of 2025 and 2225 Hz) at a signaling speed of 300 bauds. This amounts to a modulation index of $(200/300) = 0.67$ (Hz/Bd). A frequency shift of 600 Hz at a signaling speed of 1200 bauds would give a modulation index of

Fig. 15 — Close-in spectral displays of same types of modulation as in Fig. 14. Bell 202 FSK (1000-Hz shift) at top; MSK (600-Hz shift) at center; and BPSK (180° phase shift) at bottom.

(600/1200) = 0.5 and would be called *minimum-shift keying* (MSK) or, less frequently, *fast frequency-shift keying* (FFSK).

Eq. 13 is considered a good rule of thumb for modulation indexes greater than 1. For modulation indexes below 1, Eq. 13 is inaccurate and yields excessively large necessary bandwidth figures. In such cases, we recommend either a literature search for the specific type of modulation or actual measurement with a spectrum analyzer to determine occupied bandwidth. For your convenience, Fig. 13 summarizes the spectral densities of a number of digital modulation schemes.

Multilevel Modulation

It is now commonplace to use more than one modulation system to generate a radio signal. As an example, you can use a digital stream to frequency modulate an audio tone that frequency-modulates the transmitter carrier. This technique is used for transmission of RTTY at VHF. In some texts, this complex modulation technique is abbreviated FM-FM (or FM/FM). The first term is the modulation applied to the subcarrier, while the second is the modulation of the main carrier.

Here are some examples of double modulation systems used in the Amateur Radio Service:

AFSK-SSB — A digital stream (Baudot, AMTOR, packet radio) modulating an audio-frequency-shift-keyed tone that modulates a single-sideband transmitter. (Emission designation: J2B or J2D.)

FM-SSB — A signal frequency modulating a subcarrier that modulates a single-sideband transmitter. (This is commonly used for SSTV and FAX on high-frequency transmitters; emission designations would be J3F and J3C, respectively.)

FM-VSB — A signal frequency modulating a subcarrier that modulates a vestigial-sideband transmitter. (Example: The aural subcarrier injected into a UHF fast-scan TV transmitter.)

FURTHER READING ON MODULATION, MULTIPLEXING AND DEMODULATION

Sandro Belline, et al., "Noncoherent Detection of Tamed Frequency Modulation," *IEEE Trans. on Communications,* March 1984.

CCIR, *Radio Regulations,* International Radio Consultative Committee, International Telecommunication Union, Geneva, 1982.

CCIR, *Recommendations and Reports of the CCIR, 1982,* "Efficient Digital Satellite Communications," Volume VIII, Rep. 767-1, International Radio Consultative Committee, International Telecommunication Union, Geneva, 1982.

Kah-Seng Chung, "Generalized Tamed Frequency Modulation and its Application for Mobile Radio Communications," *IEEE Trans.* on Vehicular Technology, August 1984.

Dennis Connors, KD2S, "Bibliography on Minimum-Shift Keying," *QEX,* March 1983.

John P. Costas, K2EN, "Synchronous Communications," *IRE Proc.,* December 1956.

FCC, "Part 2 — Frequency Allocations and Radio Treaty Matters; General Rules and Regulations, and Part 97 — Amateur Radio Service," *Rules and Regulations.*

Kamilo Feher, *Digital Communications Microwave Applications,* Prentice-Hall, Inc., Englewood Cliffs, NJ, 1981.

Kamilo Feher, *Digital Communications Satellite/Earth Station Engineering,* Prentice-Hall, Inc., Englewood Cliffs, NJ, 1983.

Roger L. Freeman, W1HIA, *Telecommunication Transmission Handbook,* John Wiley & Sons, New York, 1975.

Roger L. Freeman, *Reference Manual for Telecommunications Engineering,* John Wiley & Sons, New York, 1985.

Robert M. Gagliardi, *Satellite Communications,* Lifetime Learning Publications, Belmont, California, 1984.

NTIA, *Manual of Regulations and Procedures for Federal Radio Frequency Management,* Washington, DC, revised 1984.

Frank F. E. Owen, *PCM and Digital Transmission Systems,* McGraw-Hill Book Company, New York, 1982.

E. W. Pappenfus, et al., *Single Sideband Principles and Circuits,* McGraw-Hill Publications Company, New York, 1964.

Mischa Schwarz, *Information Transmission, Modulation, and Noise,* McGraw-Hill Publishing Company, New York, 1980.

James J. Spilker, Jr., *Digital Communications by Satellite,* Prentice-Hall, Inc., Englewood Cliffs, NJ, 1977.

William D. Stanley, *Electronic Communications Systems,* Reston Publishing Company, Inc., Reston, Virginia, 1982.

J. Mark Steber, "Understanding PSK Demodulation Techniques," *Microwaves & RF,* March and April 1984.

Chapter 10

Radio Frequency Oscillators and Synthesizers

RF oscillators and synthesizers are fundamental building blocks used in radio equipment of all kinds. The first stage in almost all simple transmitters is an oscillator. This stage determines on what particular frequency the transmitter will operate. In a similar manner, the various oscillators used in a superheterodyne communications receiver determine the frequency the receiver is tuned to. The simplest transmitter is a crystal-controlled oscillator. A full-feature transceiver may use a microprocessor-controlled frequency synthesizer to determine transmit and receive frequencies.

An oscillator is actually a special type of amplifier. The transistor or other active device used in the oscillator amplifies the signal applied to its input just as any amplifier circuit does. The basic difference is that a portion of the output from the device is fed back to the input of the amplifier so that it aids the applied signal. This is called positive feedback or regeneration. An example of this is the howling that sometimes occurs in a public-address system. Negative feedback or degeneration tends to oppose the input signal.

Crystal Oscillators

A crystal-controlled oscillator uses a piece of quartz that has been ground to a particular thickness, length and width. For the most part, the thickness determines the frequency at which the crystal oscillates, irrespective of the stray capacitance in the immediate circuit of the crystal. Stray capacitance has some effect on the operating frequency, but overall the effect is minor. The maximum power available from such an oscillator is restricted by the heat (caused by circulating RF current) the crystal can withstand before fracturing. The circulating current is determined by the amount of feedback required to ensure excitation. Excessive heating of the crystal causes frequency drift. The extent of the drift is related to the manner in which the quartz crystal is cut. It is for these reasons that the amount of feedback used should be held to only that level which provides quick oscillator starting and reliable opera-

Fig 1—Four types of popular solid-state crystal oscillators.

tion under load. The power necessary to excite a successive stage properly can be built up inexpensively by low-level amplifiers.

Although a wide variety of crystal-controlled oscillator circuits can provide acceptable performance in amateur equipment, only a few of the popular ones will be highlighted here. In the circuits offered as illustrations, the feedback must be sufficient to assure quick starting of the oscillator. Some circuits function well without the addition of external feedback components (internal capacitance within the transistor or tube being adequate). Other circuits need external feedback capacitors. Poor-quality (sluggish) crystals generally require larger amounts of feedback to provide operation comparable to that of lively crystals. Some surplus crystals are sluggish, as can be the case with those

which have been reground or etched for a different operating frequency. Therefore, some experimentation with feedback voltage may be necessary when optimizing a given circuit. As a rule of thumb it is necessary to use one-fourth of the oscillator output power as feedback power to ensure oscillation.

The active element in an oscillator can be a tube, transistor or IC. Some common examples of solid-state oscillators are shown in Fig 1. A Pierce oscillator that employs a JFET is illustrated at A. A bipolar transistor is used at B to form a Colpitts oscillator. The example in Fig 1C shows how to extract the harmonic of a crystal by tuning the collector circuit to the desired harmonic. Unless a band-pass filter is used after the tuned circuit, various harmonics of the crystal frequency will appear

Fig 2—Two common tube types of crystal oscillators.

Fig 3—Two methods for suppressing VHF and UHF parasitic oscillations. R1 at A damps the parasitics and Z1 at B (ferrite beads) serves that purpose.

Fig 4—The crystal-oscillator operating frequency can be shifted slightly by means of trimmer capacitors as shown at A and B. A series hookup (A) is used with transistors to help compensate for the relatively high input capacitance of the transistor.

in the output. Therefore, if good spectral purity is desired it is necessary to use a double-tuned collector tank to obtain a band-pass characteristic, or to employ the tank circuit shown and follow it with a harmonic filter.

An overtone oscillator is depicted in Fig 1 at D. The crystal oscillates near an odd multiple of the fundamental cut—usually the third or fifth harmonic. In this example the drain tank is tuned approximately to the desired overtone. Oscillation will begin when the tank is tuned slightly above the overtone frequency. A high-Q tuned circuit is necessary.

Vacuum-tube crystal oscillators are presented in Fig 2. A modified Pierce oscillator is shown at A. In this case the screen grid of V1 functions as the plate of a triode tube. Feedback is between the screen and control grids. C_{fb} will range from 10 to 100 pF for oscillators operating from 1.8 to 20 MHz. At lower frequencies the feedback capacitor may require a higher value.

A Colpitts style of tube oscillator is illustrated in Fig 2B. The feedback occurs between the grid and cathode by means of a capacitive divider (C1 and C2). The plate tank can be tuned to the crystal frequency or its harmonics. In the interest of good

oscillator stability, the supply voltage to the circuits of Figs 1 and 2 should be regulated. This is especially significant in the case of harmonic or overtone oscillators where small amounts of drift are multiplied by the chosen harmonic factor.

The usual cause of erratic oscillation, or no oscillation at all, is excessive loading on the oscillator output by the succeeding stage of circuit, insufficient feedback or a sluggish crystal. Concerning the latter, a crystal not ground to a uniform thickness and feathered carefully around the edges may be difficult to make oscillate. Attempts by amateurs inexperienced in grinding their own crystals may lead to this condition.

Some crystal oscillators develop unwanted VHF self-oscillation (parasitics) even though the circuits may be functioning normally otherwise. The result will be a VHF waveform when the RF voltage is viewed by means of an oscilloscope. Parasitics can cause TVI and specific problems elsewhere in the circuit in which the oscillator is used. Two simple methods for preventing VHF parasitics are shown in Fig 3. The technique at A calls for the insertion of a low-value resistance (R1) in the collector lead as close to the transistor body as possible. Typical resistance values are 10 to 27 ohms. The damping action of the resistor inhibits VHF oscillation. An alternative to the use of resistance for swamping VHF oscillation is illustrated at B in Fig 3. One or two high-mu miniature

ferrite beads (μ_i = 950) are placed near the transistor body in the lead to gate 1. The beads can be used in the drain lead when a tuned circuit or RF choke is used in that part of the circuit. Ferrite beads can be used in the base or collector lead of the circuit of Fig 3A, rather than employing R1. Similarly, R1 can be used at gate 1 of the oscillator.

Adjusting Frequency

It is necessary in some crystal oscillator applications to ensure spot accuracy of the operating frequency. Various reactances are present in most oscillator circuits, causing the operating frequency to differ somewhat from that marked on the crystal case. Addition of a trimmer capacitor will permit "rubbering" the crystal to a specified frequency within its range. This procedure is sometimes referred to as "netting" a crystal.

Fig 4 shows two circuits in which a trimmer capacitor might be used to compensate for differences in the operating frequency of the oscillator. At A the series capacitor (C1) is connected between the low side of the crystal and ground. The series hookup is used to help offset the high input capacitance of the oscillator. The input capacitance consists of the series value of feedback capacitors C2 and C3 plus the input capacitance (C_{in}) of Q1. Conversely, the input capacitance of the circuit at B in Fig 4 is quite low because a triode tube is employed. In this kind of circuit the trimmer capacitor is connected in parallel. The choice between series and parallel trimming will depend on the active device used and the amount of input capacitance present. This rule applies to tube oscillators as well as those which use transistors.

Fig 5 shows four practical oscillator circuits of this type. C1 is included for adjusting the crystal to the frequency for which it has been ground. In circuits where considerable shunt capacitance is present (Fig 5A and C) the trimmer is usually connected in series with the crystal. When there is minimal parallel capacitance (approximately 6 pF in the circuits at B and D, Fig 5) the netting trimmer can be placed in parallel with the crystal. Whether a series or parallel trimmer is used will depend also on the type of crystal used (load capacitance and other factors).

Feedback capacitance (C_{fb}) for the circuit at B in Fig 5 must be found experimentally. Generally, a value of 100 pF will suffice for operation from 3.5 to 20 MHz. As the operating frequency is lowered it may require additional capacitance. The drain RF choke should be self-resonant below the operating frequency.

A third-overtone crystal is illustrated at Fig 5D. Satisfactory operation can be had by inserting the crystal as shown by the dashed lines. This method is especially useful when low-activity crystals are used in the overtone circuit. However, C1 will have little effect if the crystal is connected from gate to drain, as shown. C2-L1 is adjusted slightly above the desired overtone frequency to ensure fast starting of the oscillator. The circuits shown in Fig 5 can be used with dual-gate MOSFETs also, assuming that gate 2 is biased with a positive 3 to 4 volts.

Crystal Switching

Although several crystals for a single oscillator can be selected by mechanical means, a switch must be contained in the RF path. This can impose severe restrictions on the layout of a piece of equipment. Furthermore, mechanical switches normally require that they be operated from the front panel of the transmitter or receiver. That restriction complicates the remote operation of such a unit. Also, the switch leads can introduce unwanted reactances in the crystal circuit. A better technique is illustrated in Fig 6, where D1 through D3—high-speed silicon switching diodes—are used to select one of three or more crystals from some remote point. As operating voltage is applied to one of the diodes by means of S1, it is forward biased into "hard" conduction, thereby completing the circuit between the crystal trimmer and ground. Some schemes actually call for reverse-biasing the unused diodes when they are not activated. This ensures almost complete cutoff, which may not be easy to achieve in the circuit shown because

Fig 5—Practical examples of crystal-controlled oscillators that can be frequency trimmed.

Fig 6—Method for changing crystals by means of diode switching.

of the existing RF voltage on the diode anodes.

VXO Circuits

Variable-frequency crystal oscillators (VXOs) are useful in place of conventional crystal oscillators when it is necessary to "rubber" the crystal frequency a few kilohertz. AT-cut crystals in HC-6/U type holders seem to provide the greatest frequency change when used in a VXO. To obtain maximum frequency shift it is vital to reduce stray circuit capacitance to the smallest possible amount. This calls for low-capacitance switches, low minimum-capacitance variable capacitors, and the avoidance of crystal sockets. The crystals should be spaced well away from nearby metal surfaces and circuit components to further reduce capacitance effects. The higher the crystal fundamental frequency, the greater the available frequency swing. For example, a 3.5-MHz crystal might be moved a total of 3 kHz, whereas a 7-MHz crystal could be shifted 10 kHz. Although shifts as great as 50 kHz at 7 MHz may be possible, they should be avoided. Under those conditions, the high-stability traits of a crystal oscillator are lost.

Fig 7 contains a simple VXO circuit at A. By adjusting X_L the operator can shift the crystal frequency. The range will start at the frequency for which the crystal is cut and move lower. In both circuits, D1 is included to stabilize the FET bias and reduce the transistor junction capacitance during the peak of the positive RF-voltage swing. It acts as a clamp, thereby limiting the transistor g_m at peak-voltage periods. This lowers the junction capacitance and provides greater VXO swing. D1 also reduces harmonic output from the VXO by restricting the nonlinear change in transistor junction capacitance—a contributing factor to the generation of harmonic currents. Clamp diodes are used for the same purpose in conventional FET VFOs. The circuit of Fig 7A will provide a swing of approximately 5 kHz at 7 MHz.

An improved type of VXO is presented

Fig 7—Circuits for two types of VXOs.

Fig 8—Technique for heterodyne frequency generation in a receiver.

Fig 9—Examples of Hartley VFOs. A MOSFET version is shown at A; a vacuum-tube type at B.

at B in Fig 7. Depending on the exact characteristics of the crystal used at Y1, swings as great as 15 kHz are possible at 7 MHz. X_L is set initially for a reactance value that will provide the maximum possible frequency shift when C1 is tuned through its range. The frequency shift should be only that which corresponds to true VXO control, even though greater range can be had after the circuit ceases to be a highly stable one. X_L is not adjusted again. A buffer stage should be used after either of the VXO circuits to prevent frequency pulling during load changes.

VXOs of this general type are useful in portable transmitters and receivers when full band coverage is sacrificed in exchange for stability and simplicity. Output from VXOs can be multiplied several times to provide LO energy for VHF and UHF receivers and transmitters. When that is done it is possible to realize 100 kHz or more of frequency change at 144 MHz.

VFO Circuits

Variable-frequency oscillators are similar to VXOs. The essential difference is that greater frequency coverage is possible, and no crystals are used. The practical upper frequency limits for good CW or SSB stability is between 7 and 10 MHz. For operation at higher frequencies, it is better to employ a heterodyne-type VFO. This calls for a VFO operating at, say, 5 MHz. The VFO output is heterodyned in a mixer with energy from a crystal-controlled oscillator. This provides a resultant or difference frequency at the desired LO-chain output frequency. A block diagram is given at Fig 8 to illustrate the concept as it might appear in a receiver. The same scheme could be used in a transmitter. The heterodyne oscillator has a crystal for each amateur band accommodated by the receiver. The crystals and appropriate band-pass filters are switched by a panel-mounted control. The band-pass filter (Fig 8) is desirable to prevent 5- and 12.3-MHz energy from reaching the receiver mixer. A doubly balanced mixer is recommended if minimum unwanted energy is desired at the mixer output.

Some typical VFOs are shown in Figs. 9 and 10. A vacuum-tube Hartley is compared to a similar one that utilizes a dual-gate MOSFET in Fig 9. The capacitor shown in dashed lines (C1) can be used in that part of the circuit rather than at the

Fig 10—Colpitts VFOs. A bipolar transistor type is seen at A, while an FET version is given at B.

low end of the tank coil if greater bandspread is desired. C1 is the main-tuning capacitor and C2 is the padder for calibrating the oscillator. The coil tap is approximately 25 percent of the total number of turns for proper feedback.

A comparison is drawn in Fig 10 between a bipolar transistor and JFET version of a series-tuned Colpitts oscillator (sometimes called a "series-tuned Clapp"). These VFO circuits can be scaled to other operating frequencies by using the values shown to determine the reactances of the capacitors. This information will enable the designer to select approximate values in picofarads for other frequencies.

Fundamental Stability Considerations

There are some specific measures that must be taken when designing a VFO. The form on which the VFO coil is wound is of special significance with regard to stability. Ideally, the use of metallic core material should be avoided. Therefore, powdered iron, brass, copper and ferrite slugs, or toroid cores for that matter, are not recommended when high stability is required. The reason is that the properties of such core materials are affected by changes in temperature and can cause a dramatic shift in the value of inductance that might not occur if an air-core coil was used. Furthermore, some styles of slug-tuned inductors are subject to mechanical instability in the presence of vibration. This can cause severe frequency jumping and a need for frequent recalibration of the VFO readout.

Regardless of the format selected for the VFO coil, the finished product should be coated with two or three applications of polystyrene cement (Q dope) or similar low-loss dopant. This will keep the coil turns secured in a permanent position—an aid to mechanical stability.

The VFO coil should be mounted well away from nearby conducting objects (cabinet walls, shield cans, and so on) to prevent frequency shifts which are likely to occur if the chassis or cabinet are stressed during routine handling or mobile operation. Movement of the chassis, cabinet walls and other nearby conductive objects can (if the coil is close by) change the coil inductance. Furthermore, the proximity effects of the conductive objects present an undefined value of capacitance between the coil and these objects. Changes in spacing will alter that capacitance, causing frequency shifts of an abrupt nature.

It follows that all forms of mechanical stability are of paramount importance if the VFO is to be of "solid" design. Thus, the trimmer or padder capacitors used in the circuit should be capable ot remaining at their preset values despite temperature changes and vibration. For this reason it is not wise to use ceramic or mica trimmers. Air-dielectric variable capacitors of the PC-board-mount subminiature type are recommended.

The main tuning element (capacitor or permeability tuner) needs to have substantial rigidity; it should be mounted in a secure manner. Variable capacitors used as main-tuning elements should be of the double-bearing variety. They should rotate easily (minimum torque) to minimize mechanical stress of the VFO assembly when they are adjusted. Variable capacitors with plated brass plates are preferred over those with aluminum plates. Compared with brass, aluminum is more subject to physical changes in the presence of temperature variations. The VFO tuning-capacitor rotor must be grounded at both ends as a preventive measure against instability. Some designers have found that a 1/8- to 1/4-inch-thick piece of aluminum or steel plate serves as an excellent base for the

VFO assembly. It greatly reduces instability that can be caused by stress on the main chassis of the equipment. The VFO module can be installed on shock mounts to enhance stability during mobile operation.

Electrical Stability

Apart from the mechanical considerations just discussed, the relative quality of the components used in a VFO circuit is of great importance. Fig 11 contains three illustrations of basic solid-state tunable oscillators suggested for amateur applications. The numbered components have a direct bearing on the short- and long-term stability of the VFO. That is, the type of component used at each specified circuit point must be selected with stability foremost in mind. The fixed-value capacitors, except for the drain bypass, should be temperature-stable types. NP0 ceramic capacitors are recommended for frequencies up to approximately 10 MHz. A second choice is the silver-mica capacitor (dipped or plain versions). Silver micas tend to have some unusual drift characteristics when subjected to changes in ambient temperature. Some increase in value while others decrease. Still others are relatively stable.

It is often necessary to experiment with several units of a given capacitance value in an effort to select a group of capacitors that are suitably temperature stable. The same is not true of polystyrene capacitors. When they are used with the commonly available slug-tuned coils, the temperature characteristics of the polystyrene capacitors and those of the inductor tend to cancel each other. This results in excellent frequency stability. If toriodal cores are used, they should be made of SF-type powdered iron material (Amidon mix 6). This material has a low temperature coefficient and when used with NP0-type ceramic capacitors produces very low drift oscillators. Ordinary disc-ceramic capacitors are unsuitable for use in stable VFOs. Those with specified temperature characteristics (N750 and similar) are useful, however, in compensating for drift.

The circuit of Fig 11A is capable of very stable operation if polystyrene capacitors are used at C3 through C8. A test model for 1.8 to 2.0 MHz exhibited only 1 Hz of drift from a cold start to a period some two hours later. Ambient temperature was 25° C. Q1 can be any high-g_m JFET for use at VHF or UHF. Capacitors C1 through C4 are used in parallel as means of distributing the RF current among them.

A single fixed-value capacitor in that part of the circuit would tend to change value because of the RF heating within it. Therefore, a distinct advantage exists when several capacitors can be used in parallel at such points in a VFO circuit. The same concept is generally true of C5, C6 and C7. In the interest of stability, C5 should be the smallest value that will permit reliable oscillation. Feedback capacitors C6 and C7 are typically the same value and have an X_c of roughly 60 Ω. Therefore, a suitable value for a 1.9-MHz VFO would be 1500 pF.

C8 of Fig 11A should be the smallest capacitance value practical with respect to ample oscillator drive to the succeeding stage. The smaller the value of C8, the less the chance for oscillator pulling during load changes. D1 is a gate-clamping diode for controlling the bias of the FET. Basically, it limits the positive swing of the sine wave. This action restricts the change in Q1 junction capacitance to minimize harmonic generation and changes in the amount of C associated with L1.

The reactance of RFC can be on the order of 10 kΩ. The drain bypass, C9, should have a maximum X_c of 10 ohms to ensure effective bypassing at the operating frequency. Ideally, an X_c of 1 ohm would be used (0.1 μF at 1.5 MHz). D2 is used to provide 9.1 volts, regulated, at the drain of Q1. Lower operating voltages aid stability through reduced RF-current heating, but at the expense of reduced oscillator output.

A Hartley oscillator is shown in Fig 11B. This circuit offers good stability also, and is one of the better circuits to use when the tank is parallel tuned. The tap on L1 is usually between 10 and 25 percent of the total coil turns, tapped above the grounded end. This ensures adequate feedback for reliable oscillation. The higher the FET g_m, the lower the feedback needed. Only that amount of feedback necessary to provide oscillation should be used: Excessive feedback will cause instability and prohibitive RF heating of the components. Most of the rules for the circuit of Fig 11A apply to the oscillator in Fig 11B.

Parallel tuning of the kind used in Fig 11B and C are suitable for use below 6 MHz, although the circuit at B can be used successfully into the VHF region. However, the Colpitts oscillators of A and C in Fig 11 have large amounts of shunt capacitance caused by C6 and C7 of A, and C5 and C6 of C. The smaller the coupling capacitor between L1 and the gate, the less pronounced is this effect. The net result is a relatively small value of inductance at L1, especially with respect to Fig 11C, which lowers the tank impedance and may prevent oscillation (high C-to-L ratio). The series-tuned circuit of Fig 11A solves the shunt-C problem nicely by requiring considerably greater inductance at L1 than would be acceptable in the circuit of Fig 11C. The circuit at A resembles the popular "Clapp" circuit of the early 1950s.

A suitable transistor for Q1 of Fig 11C is an RCA 40673. The Texas Instruments 3N211 is also ideal, as it has an extremely high g_m—approximately 30,000 microsiemens (μS). Dual-gate MOSFETs are suitable for the circuits of Fig 11A and B if biased as shown at C. Also, they can be used as single-gate FETs by simply connecting gates 1 and 2 together. No

Fig 11—Three common types of VFOs for use in receivers and transmitters.

external bias is required if this is done. Gate 2 of Q1 (Fig 11C) should by bypassed with a low-reactance capacitor (C4), as is the rule for the drain bypassing of all three examples given in Fig 11.

Bipolar transistors are satisfactory for use in the three VFOs just discussed. The principal disadvantage of bipolars in these circuits is the low base impedance and higher device input capacitance. Most FETs exhibit an input C of approximately 5 pF, but many bipolar transistors have a substantially higher capacitance, which tends to complicate a VFO design for the higher operating frequencies. The UHF small-signal transistors, such as the 2N5179, are best suited to the circuits under discussion.

Load Isolation for VFOs

Load changes after the oscillator have a pronounced effect on the operating frequency. Therefore, it is imperative to provide some form of buffering (isolating stage or stages) between the oscillator and the circuit to which it will be interfaced. The net effect of load changes, however minor, is a change in reactance which causes phase shifts. The latter affects the operating frequency to a considerable degree. Therefore, the more isolating stages which follow the oscillator (up to a practical number, of course), the less likelihood of load shifts being reflected back to the oscillator.

Buffer stages can perform double duty by affording a measure of RF amplification, as needed. But, care must be taken to avoid introducing narrow-band networks in the buffer/amplifier chain if considerable frequency range is planned, for example, 5.0 to 5.5 MHz. If suitable broadband characteristics are not inherent in the design, the oscillator-chain output will not be constant across the desired tuning range. This could seriously affect the conversion gain and dynamic range of a receiver mixer, or lower the output of a transmitter in some parts of a given band.

Fig 12A illustrates a typical RC coupled VFO buffer with broadband response. C1 is selected for minimum coupling to the oscillator, consistent with adequate drive to Q1. Q1 and Q2 should have high f_T and medium beta to ensure a slight RF-voltage gain. Devices such as the 2N2222A and 2N5179 are suggested.

Q2 of Fig 12A operates as an emitter-follower. The RF-voltage output will be approximately 0.9 of that supplied to the base. In a typical VFO chain, using an oscillator such as the one in Fig 11A, this buffer strip will deliver approximately 1 volt P-P across the 470-Ω emitter resistor of Q2.

A better circuit is offered in Fig 12B. Q1 is a JFET that has a high input impedance (1 MΩ or greater) by virtue of the FET-device characteristic. This minimizes loading of the oscillator. RFC1 is chosen to resonate broadly with the stray circuit capacitance (roughly 10 pF) at the mid-range frequency of the LO chain. Although this does not introduce significant selectivity, it does provide a rising characteristic in the RF-voltage level at the source of Q1.

Q2 functions as a fed-back amplifier with shunt feedback and source degeneration. The feedback stabilizes the amplifier and makes it broadband. The drain tank is designed as a pi network with a loaded Q of 3. The transformation ratio is on the order of 20:1 (1000-ohm drain to 50-ohm load). R1 is placed across L1 to further broaden the network response. The 50-ohm output level is recommended in the interest of immunity to load changes: The higher the output impedance of a buffer chain the greater the chance for oscillator pulling with load changes. P-P output across C3 should be on the order of 3 volts when using the oscillator of Fig 11A.

Fig 13 illustrates a composite VFO that

Fig 12—VFO buffer and buffer/amplifier sections, which provide isolation between the oscillator and the VFO-chain load. The circuit at B is recommended for most applications.

Fig 13—Suggested circuit for a stable series-tuned Colpitts VFO. Buffering follows the oscillator to increase the output level and provide load isolation.

has a buffer stage followed by an amplifier. D1 can be included to provide the necessary frequency offset when switching the receiver from upper to lower sideband. This is necessary to eliminate the need to readjust the calibration dial when changing sidebands. C1 is adjusted for the desired offset amount. The pi-network output from the amplifier stage is designed to transform 500 ohms to 50 ohms. The low-impedance output is desirable in the interest of minimum frequency pulling from load changes. A 3300 ohm swamping resistor is used across the pi-network inductor to broadband the tuned circuit and to prevent any tendency toward instability when a high-impedance load is attached to the circuit. Long-term drift measurements with this type of circuit at the frequency specified indicated a maximum shift of 60 Hz over a three-hour period. Output was measured at approximately 1 volt RMS across 50 ohms.

Other VFO Criteria

Apart from the stability considerations just treated, purity of emissions from VFOs is vital to most designers. It is prudent to minimize the harmonic output of a VFO chain and to ensure that VHF parasitic energy is not being generated within the LO system.

The pi-network output circuit of Fig 12B helps reduce harmonics because it is a low-pass network. Additional filtering can be added at the VFO-chain output by inserting a half-wave filter with a loaded Q of 1 (X_L and X_C = 50 for a 50-Ω line).

VHF parasitics are not uncommon in the oscillator or its buffer stages, especially when high f_T transistors are employed. The best preventive measures are keeping the signal leads as short as possible and adding parasitic suppressors as required. The parasitic energy can be seen as a superimposed sine wave riding on the VFO output waveform when a high-frequency scope is used.

A low-value resistor (10 to 22 ohms) can be placed directly at the gate or base of the oscillator transistor to stop parasitic oscillations. Alternatively, one or two ferrite beads (950 μ_i) can be slipped over the gate or base lead to resolve the problem. If VHF oscillations occur in the buffer stages, the same preventive measures can be taken.

VFO noise should be minimized as much as possible. A high-Q oscillator tank will normally limit the noise bandwidth adequately. Resistances placed in the signal path will often cause circuit noise. Therefore, it is best to avoid the temptation to control the RF excitation to a given LO stage by inserting a series resistor. The better method is to use small-value coupling capacitors.

A Hartley VFO circuit is shown in Fig 14. Operating frequency range with the components shown is 5.0 to 5.5 MHz, but the circuit will function well from 2.5 to 10 MHz. The design guidelines offered in the previous section will be useful for altering the circuit for other frequency ranges. More information about this VFO circuit can be found in the High-Performance Communications Receiver project in Chapter 30, and another practical VFO circuit is shown in the Band-Imaging Receiver project in Chapter 30. Other VFO circuits and design information appear in the ARRL publication *Solid-State Design for the Radio Amateur*.

Fig 14—Schematic diagram of a general-purpose Hartley VFO. The circuit will function well from 2.5 to 10 MHz; the tuning range with the components shown is 5.0 to 5.5 MHz.

C1—100-pF NP0 ceramic.
C2—82-pF NP0 ceramic.
C3—126-pF NP0 ceramic.
C4—365-pF air variable capacitor (broadcast replacement type).
L1—35 turns no. 28 enamel wire on a T-50-6

toroid core. Tap 8 turns from ground. Approximately 4.9-µH total inductance.
Q6—General-purpose JFET, MPF-102, 2N4416 or similar.
Q7—Dual-gate MOSFET, 40673, 3N140 or

similar.
T2—Ferrite transformer, 18-turn primary, 5-turn secondary, no. 28 enamel wire on an FT-37-43 core.
Z1—Ferrite bead on gate 2 lead of Q7. FB43-101 or similar.

Radio Frequency Synthesizers

This introduction to RF synthesizers was prepared by Robert J. Zavrel, Jr, W7SX. Receiver and transmitter local oscillators must be able to change frequency if you want to change the radio operating frequency. Analog (LC) VFO circuits filled this requirement until the phase-locked loop (PLL) synthesizer became a technically feasible alternative. The PLL allows digital control of a synthesizer in linear frequency steps. Furthermore, the PLL frequency accuracy is derived from a crystal oscillator reference. These attributes are impossible to achieve with a traditional analog VFO. A second type of digital synthesizer has also found its way into amateur equipment, the direct digital synthesizer (DDS). DDS and "hybrids" configured from DDS and PLL techniques have opened fantastic new possibilities for synthesizer designers.

Digital technology provides many advantages for synthesizer control. Frequencies can be "scanned" or "tuned" manually through rotary optical encoders or electronically through up-down counters. The "number" of VFOs available in a radio circuit is only limited by the number of digital memory addresses in the radio synthesizer. The operator can scan, tune or "program" a frequency and then store the digital number in a memory location. These advantages can be realized in both PLL and DDS systems.

RF-synthesizer engineering is like many other engineering problems. The optimum design will be a compromise. Indeed, most discussions involving any engineering problem evolve into a discussion of compromises. DDS is not a replacement for PLL synthesizers any more than the screwdriver was a replacement for the hammer. It is simply a better technique for some, but not all, synthesizer designs.

A brief comparison of the respective technical trade-offs of the DDS and PLL synthesizer architectures will help clarify the advantages and disadvantages of both. Table 1 lists some of the primary design considerations for PLL synthesizers and direct digital synthesizers.

In PLL synthesizers, smaller step size is achieved at the price of longer settling time and/or increased phase noise. (There is a detailed discussion about phase noise later in this chapter.) Since other types of noise are also included in practical phase-noise measurements, we refer to "composite noise" in Product Review equipment tests. Lower phase noise usually results in longer settling times or larger step sizes. Of course PLLs that produce less phase noise can be built if larger size, and higher cost and power consumption are permitted.

DDS has generated great excitement because the trade-offs associated with PLL synthesizers disappear. Phase noise, for practical purposes, disappears. Settling time is typically established by the bandwidth of an anti-alias filter, usually measured in nanoseconds. Frequency resolution is determined by the phase-accumulator bit size, with typical resolution being in fractions of one hertz, even into the UHF range. Furthermore, these three key specifications are mutually independent.

The major limitations of DDS architectures are the clock speed, which determines the bandwidth, and the quality of the digital-to-analog converter (DAC), which usually determines the spurious responses. Lower clock speed permits higher DAC bit resolution. As with PLLs, cost, power consumption and size can permit less compromise between these two specifications.

PHASE-LOCKED LOOP (PLL) SYNTHESIZERS

One common frequency-synthesis technique is called the "indirect" method. This method uses phase-locked loop (PLL). The description "indirect" refers to the fact that the output frequency is generated by stabilizing a voltage-controlled oscillator (VCO).

A simple phase-locked loop synthesizer block diagram is shown in Fig 15. Five elements make up the simple loop; a VCO, a programmable divider, a phase detector, a loop filter and a reference frequency source.

The purpose of the PLL synthesizer is to take a signal from a VCO, divide the frequency by an integer, and compare that result to a precise and stable reference frequency in a phase detector. The phase detector produces an electrical output that indicates positive or negative phase difference. The phase detector output is fed back to the VCO through a filter. The loop works to adjust the output of the phase detector to zero automatically. That means the output of the programmable divider is precisely on the same frequency as the reference. This can be described mathematically as:

$$F = NFr$$

where F is the output frequency, N is the value of the programmable divider, which is always an integer, and Fr is the reference frequency.

Depending on the reference frequency, phase comparison can take place at great speed. Frequency corrections can be made at such a rate that small and rapid deviations in frequency such as phase noise can be corrected. A control voltage correction can only be made once every cycle of the reference frequency. Therefore, the correction at the output of the phase detector is not a continuous function but rather a sampled function. The sample frequency is equal to the reference frequency. This signal is filtered to remove some of the energy at the reference frequency. Not all of the reference frequency energy can be

Table 1
Synthesizer Design Trade-offs

Trade-offs of PLL synthesizers
1. Frequency resolution
2. Setting time
3. Phase noise (spectral purity)

Trade-offs of Direct Digital Synthesizers
1. Bandwidth
2. Discrete spurious response (spectral purity)

Trade-offs of both DDS and PLL synthesizers
1. Synthesizer performance
2. Power consumption
3. Cost
4. Size

Fig 15—A simple single-loop PLL synthesizer.

removed; what remains is applied to the VCO control voltage. Any variation of the control voltage frequency modulates the VCO. This modulation causes sidebands to be generated. These sidebands appear not only at frequencies removed from the carrier by the reference frequency, but also at harmonics of the reference frequency. The amount of reference energy that is applied to the VCO is a function of the loop filter and the phase detector.

The loop filter has an effect not only on the reference sidebands of the PLL synthesizer, but also on the time and nature of the lock up. Fig 16 shows the three basic paths for PLL frequency change. In the first path the loop changes from the original to the new frequency directly without overshoot and in minimum time. This is called critically damped and is the usual path chosen in synthesizer design, especially if the frequency must change between transmit and receive. Curve B in Fig 16 shows the frequency rapidly changing to the desired frequency, overshooting the mark and continuing to oscillate around the desired frequency before becoming stable. This characteristic is called underdamped.

It may appear that this transient characteristic has no value in the design of synthesizers. A certain amount of underdamping can make the loop filter design easier for realizing low sideband levels in the system; this approach may be used when the synthesizer is not required to change frequency rapidly. Curve C in Fig 16 shows the overdamped case. In this case the frequency changes from the old frequency to the new frequency without overshoot, but the time required is considerably longer than in the critically damped case.

Several varieties of phase detectors are suitable for use in PLL systems. One very simple type of phase detector is the exclusive-OR circuit shown in Fig 17. The signals presented to the exclusive-OR phase detector must have exactly 50 percent duty cycle—a condition not difficult to generate when using IC dividers.

Fig 18 shows the input and output waveforms found in the exclusive-OR phase detector. When the phase angle between the two inputs is 90 degrees (Fig 18B), the average value of the output is 50 percent. When the phase angle is less, the average value of the output changes depending on which input is leading. Furthermore, the output is a pulse train with a frequency equal to twice the input frequency. It is important when using the simple exclusive-OR phase detector that the loop filter have sufficient rejection of the phase detector output frequency.

The exclusive-OR phase detector has one serious drawback that limits its use in certain types of frequency synthesizers: If there is any harmonic relationship between the two inputs to the phase detector, the output will allow the loop to lock up on an

incorrect output frequency. This can be used to advantage for PLL systems where harmonics are desired. In a PLL where only one frequency is desired, however, this possibility must be eliminated. There would be no problem if the frequency range of the VCO were limited to a ratio of less than 2 to 1. This limitation would preclude the VCO from ever locking on a harmonic because the VCO cannot generate the fundamental and the harmonic of any frequency.

A phase detector specifically designed for phase-locked loops is shown in Fig 19. This phase detector is not susceptible to harmonically related inputs; for that reason it is more accurately called a phase/frequency detector. The phase/frequency detector also has a three-state output. If the phase or frequency difference is such that a

Fig 16—Three transient frequency-change characteristics: critically damped at A, underdamped at B, overdamped at C.

Fig 17—Exclusive-OR type phase detector.

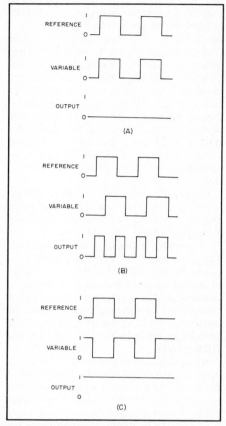

Fig 18—Waveforms associated with an exclusive-OR phase detector. Variable and reference are in phase at A. Variable leads reference by 90° at B. At C, variable and reference are 180° out of phase.

Fig 19—A phase/frequency detector specifically designed for phase-locked loop synthesizers.

positive output is required, the upper (P-channel) FET conducts supplying a current path from V_{DD} to the output. If the input phase relationship is such that a negative output is required, the lower (N-channel) FET conducts and provides a current path from the output to V_{SS}. If the phase angle is very close neither FET conducts and the output floats. Because the output has the capability of two "on" states as well as an "off" state, the amount of reference ripple in the output is much lower than with the exclusive-OR phase detector. The only significant disadvantage of this phase detector is the definition of where the phase angle between the two inputs is small enough for both output transistors to be off. In operation the loop will "bounce" between the two on states

and cause a low frequency noise that can be objectionable. The usual solution to this problem is to inject a small amount of current at the phase detector to force the phase detector out of this "dead zone."

Programmable Dividers

Programmable dividers are generally constructed from IC counters. The counter can be binary or decade depending on the source of programming information. Binary counters are suited to microprocessor programming where there is a binary output. For simple systems, where information is accepted from mechanical switches, binary-coded-decimal programming (BCD) is required. Therefore, both binary and BCD programmable dividers are used in synthesizer systems.

Fig 20 shows a programmable divider using ripple BCD counters as the dividers. A magnitude comparator accepts information from the programming switches and compares this input to the state of the counter. When the counter reaches the selected state, the "equals" output of the magnitude comparator provides a reset pulse to the counter. This type of programmable divider is frequency limited to only a few megahertz.

A higher frequency alternative is to use a synchronous counter with internal zero detect as shown in Fig 21. This programmable divider is preset to a number and then counts down to a value of one and then is preset to the same number. Normally, IC counters are provided with internal zero detection for the purpose of cascading counters. For use as a programmable divider, however, the detection of the count of one is required. This can be done simply by detecting the zero state for all of the cascaded counters except the least significant digit that detects the count of one.

The advantage of this type of programmable divider is a significant increase in operating speed. First, the propagation delay within the counter is much less than that of a ripple counter. Second, only one state of the counter must be decoded, a value of one, and the magnitude decoder required for that task is simpler and therefore, faster than a full-function magnitude comparator. A typical TTL programmable divider using synchronous down-counters can operate reliably at 15 MHz.

There are special programmable dividers using CMOS technology with special look-ahead decoding that can further increase the speed to a point where CMOS logic speed can approach that of TTL. These specialized circuits are typically used in synthesizer LSI chips.

Voltage-Controlled Oscillators

The VCO used for a PLL can be practically any one of the standard oscillator circuits with a varactor diode in the tuned circuit to allow voltage tuning. Fig 22 shows a Colpitts oscillator that has a varactor diode. The VCO must not only provide the output from the synthesizer, but also must provide drive for the programmable divider. Usually several buffer amplifier stages are used to isolate the VCO from the output of the synthesizer as well as the programmable divider. Changes in the VCO load can cause the generation of unwanted phase noise.

The noise level of a synthesizer will depend to a great extent on the design of the VCO. One method of reducing VCO phase noise is to use two varactor diodes back to back, as shown in Fig 22. This prevents the RF voltage at the VCO tuned circuit from being rectified in the varactor diode and changing the tuning voltage.

Fig 23A shows a spectrum-analyzer dis-

Fig 20—A programmable divider based on a ripple counter.

Fig 21—A programmable divider based on a synchronous down counter.

play of a typical VCO. The phase-noise reduction provided by a phase-locked loop is evident in the photo of Fig 23B.

PLL SYNTHESIZERS FOR HIGH-FREQUENCY COMMUNICATIONS SYSTEMS

The synthesizer required for high frequency communications systems presents several design problems. First, the operating frequency span is large, from 100 kHz to 30 MHz for general coverage. Also, the frequency resolution must be fine; and 100 Hz is considered the absolute maximum for SSB or CW operation and then only if a clarifier or receiver-incremental tuning (RIT) control is provided for SSB operation. For RTTY operation or SSB without the use of a clarifier control even better resolution is required, typically on the order of 25 Hz or less. Because 25-Hz steps are not easily displayed by the frequency display, some designs use 10-Hz resolution, which is sufficiently small to accommodate any type of operation. Narrow resolution and wide frequency coverage are two characteristics that are not complementary. That is, it would be easy to design a phase-locked loop with a narrow frequency range and narrow resolution. It is difficult to design a synthesizer that has a broad frequency range and narrow frequency resolution, while maintaining good noise performance and quick lock-up time.

Typical amateur HF operation involves continuous tuning for signals, as opposed to VHF FM where operation takes place on well-defined frequencies. Therefore, the time it takes the synthesizer to lock on the proper frequency is an important parameter and must be taken into account in the design of a high-frequency synthesizer. All of these requirements taken together dictate a system more complicated than a single-loop synthesizer.

The modern trend in receiver (and transceiver) design is up conversion, a scheme in which the first IF is higher than the highest received frequency. For coverage to 30 MHz, the minimum IF must be above 30 MHz. That places the local oscillator at 30.1 to 60 MHz for a 0.1- to 30-MHz input. In practice the first IF is 45 MHz, or higher, which dictates first local-oscillator coverage from 45 to 75 MHz—a span of less than an octave.

A ratio of two to one between the highest and the lowest frequency generated, or an octave, is about the maximum range that can be covered reliably by a single VCO. Greater frequency ratios are obtained by using several VCOs or band-switching the VCO with transistors or PIN diodes. It is especially important to minimize the VCO frequency range in the design of low-noise synthesizers. As previously mentioned, the exclusive-OR phase detector requires an input range of less than two to one. Essentially, a simple synthesizer cannot operate with a maximum to minimum frequency

ratio of more than two to one.

For a frequency resolution of 50 Hz a conventional, single-loop synthesizer requires a 50-Hz reference. The loop bandwidth must be considerably less than 50 Hz, in order to reduce the level of reference sidebands. Lock up time in this case would be too slow for manual tuning of amateur bands. Any frequency excursion of more than a few kilohertz would find the loop dragging behind the frequency display. To counteract this, multiple loop synthesizers are used. The output frequency of these

(A)

(B)

Fig 23—Spectrum analyzer photographs of a VCO. The VCO is disconnected from the phase-locked loop at A. The reduction of noise sidebands provided by the loop is shown at B.

Fig 22—A Colpitts oscillator with varactor tuning suitable for use as a VCO.

Fig 24—A two-loop synthesizer used in a high-frequency receiver or transceiver with a 45-MHz IF.

synthesizers is a function of two phase-locked loops.

Two-Loop Synthesizers

Fig 24 shows an example of a two-loop synthesizer for use with an up-converting receiver or transceiver with a 45-MHz first IF. In this example, a coarse-tune PLL provides an output at 50 to 80 MHz. This loop has a reference frequency of 100 kHz and a fast lock-up time. Because of the high reference frequency, this loop can provide a very clean output signal. The coarse-tune VCO output is mixed with the main VCO output. The output of the mixer is tuned to 5 MHz. For each frequency of the coarse-tune synthesizer, there are two possible frequencies of the main VCO that will provide a 5-MHz output; the sum and the difference.

To prevent the VCO from operating at the wrong frequency, a coarse-tune voltage is applied to the main VCO. This voltage sets the VCO to approximately the correct frequency. The mixer output is phase compared to the fine-tune PLL synthesizer output. The output of this phase detector is fed through a loop amplifier to the main VCO. Thus, the frequency difference between the coarse-tune loop and the main VCO is precisely equal to the output frequency of the fine-tune loop.

To avoid the lock-up time problems, the fine-tune loop does not operate in the 5-MHz range, but at 50 times that frequency, or 250 MHz. The required output frequency is 5.0000 MHz to 4.90005 MHz. This frequency variation is the reverse from the programming information; as the programming data is increased in value the frequency of the fine-tune VCO is decreased. This can be handled either by a microprocessor or with logic within the fine-tune synthesizer as shown in Fig 25.

Because the loop operates at 50 times the desired output frequency, the reference frequency is 50 times the desired frequency resolution—2500 Hz for 50-Hz resolution. It is not difficult to achieve a lock time of a few ms with a 2500-Hz reference. In addition, the noise and reference sidebands at 250 MHz are reduced 33 dB because of the frequency division.

Practically any division factor can be used for the fine-tune loop. For example, a standard ECL divide-by-40 chip could be used. The VCO would operate in the 200-MHz region; the reference would be 2000 Hz. Lock-up time would be slightly longer, but the programmable divider ratios would remain exactly the same as in the previous example.

General-coverage receivers and transceivers increase the need for frequency synthesis in HF equipment. A typical amateur-band-only transceiver of a few years ago used a crystal oscillator in conjunction with a conventional VFO. The VFO operated in the megahertz region and the crystal oscillator operated in the low-

Fig 25—Logic circuit for use with the fine-tune synthesizer within the system shown in Fig 24.

Fig 26—Frequency control for a partially synthesized transceiver for high-frequency operation.

VHF region. This scheme provides reasonable noise and stability performance. When more than a few frequency bands are covered, however, the cost of the required crystals becomes prohibitive. For a general-coverage receiver with the range divided into 500-kHz bands, approximately 59 crystals are required; that is totally unacceptable.

Partial Synthesis

One solution to the crystal problem is the partially synthesized transceiver (see Fig 26). Partially synthesized means that the operating frequency is set by both a synthesizer and a free-running VFO. This synthesizer consists of a single PLL. The 500-kHz reference frequency ensures that phase noise will be sufficiently low for SSB, RTTY and CW operation; the VFO ensures that the resolution is nearly infinite.

A VCO (actually three separate switchable oscillators) is the first local oscillator. It operates 48.05 MHz above the input frequency. The output of this VCO is mixed with a 45.05- to 45.55-MHz signal to produce a 3.0- to 33.0-MHz output. This output feeds the programmable divider. The 45.05- to 45.55-MHz signal is generated by mixing a 40-MHz oscillator with a 5.05- to 5.55-MHz VFO.

Output from the programmable divider feeds a phase detector, which also receives a 500-kHz reference frequency. The programmable divider works in a range from 6 to 65; that corresponds to frequency coverage from 0 to 29.5 MHz. The programmable divider sets the operating frequency of the transceiver in 500-kHz steps while the VFO adds from 0 to 500 kHz to the basic synthesizer frequency.

There are some significant disadvantages to this type of system. First, the frequency cannot be fully programmed externally. Because of the mechanically tuned VFO, only the 500-kHz bands can be programmed. Second, the frequency stability is not better than that of the VFO. Because the VFO is operating in the low MHz region, however, the stability will be acceptable for all but the most demanding operation. Finally, the frequency readout is a combination of digital inputs to the synthesizer and the dial of a VFO. This can be improved by using a frequency counter to display the frequency electronically.

VHF SYNTHESIZER APPLICATIONS

The requirements of a frequency synthesizer for VHF operation are generally less stringent than those for HF. Normally the synthesizer covers only one amateur band. That means a span that is a small percentage of the operating frequency. Resolution or channel separation is typically 5 or 10 kHz for FM operation and perhaps 100 Hz for SSB operation. A simple synthesizer would appear to suit the VHF transceiver. The problem is that conventional logic cannot operate at frequencies of 150 MHz. Even emitter-coupled logic (ECL) with propagation delays as short as a few nanoseconds cannot be used to construct programmable dividers to operate at 150 MHz.

One method of constructing a VHF PLL synthesizer is shown in Fig 27. In this example, the VCO output is divided by 10 in an ECL prescaler. ECL is fast enough to operate as a fixed divider at 150 MHz, but fails as a conventional programmable divider.

The major disadvantage of this synthesizer design method is that the loop reference frequency must be reduced by the same factor as the fixed-modulus divider. As an example, if a synthesizer for a 2-meter transceiver were designed with 5-kHz channel resolution using a simple phase-locked loop, a 5-kHz reference frequency could be used. If a fixed-modulus prescaler with a division of 10 were placed between the VCO and the programmable divider, the reference frequency would have to be reduced to 500 Hz.

It is important that the highest reference frequency possible be used in a PLL synthesizer for best noise performance and lowest reference sidebands. In this example, the output of the prescaler can be used to drive relatively low-speed logic in the programmable divider. However, even 15 MHz requires fast logic in a programmable divider. Fixed-modulus prescaler divisions of more than 10 are typically required with some low-power logic families. This means a less than 500-Hz reference frequency in the 2-meter synthesizer example. That would greatly compromise the synthesizer performance.

Dual-Modulus Programmable Dividers

One technique used in VHF synthesizers with conventional logic without reducing the reference to an unacceptable frequency is the dual-modulus programmable divider. The heart of the divider is the dual-modulus prescaler shown in Fig 28. This ECL chip can divide by two factors that differ by 1. The dual-modulus prescaler shown in Fig 28 can divide by either 10 or 11, depending on the state of the modulus control input. The 10/11 ratio has important applications in BCD-programmed synthesizers. They are available in a variety of frequency capabilities up to more than 500 MHz. Some standard ratios are: 5/6, 8/9, 15/16, 20/21, 32/33, 40/41 and 80/81. Other ratios can be created with one of these chips and some external logic.

The dual-modulus programmable divider consists of three parts: the main counter, the auxiliary counter and the dual-modulus prescaler (see Fig 29). Both the main and auxiliary counters are presettable; they are often down counters. At the beginning of the divider cycle both the main and auxiliary counters are preset to the respective programmed value. Both counters are clocked together from the output of the dual-modulus prescaler. If the auxiliary counter is preset to a value other than zero, the dual-modulus prescaler starts counting by the larger of its two divisors $(N + 1)$ at the beginning of the divider cycle. When the auxiliary counter reaches zero, the mode of the dual-modulus prescaler is changed to the smaller of the two divisors (N). The main counter continues to count

Fig 27—VHF synthesizer using a fixed-modulus prescaler.

Fig 28—Block diagram of a dual-modulus prescaler suitable for VHF synthesizers.

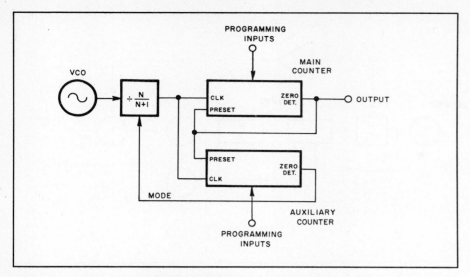

Fig 29—Block diagram of a dual-modulus divider.

Fig 30—Block diagram of a Motorola LSI synthesizer chip.

toward zero, while the auxiliary counter stops counting. When the main counter reaches zero both the main and auxiliary counters are preset, and the divider cycle starts anew.

The total number of VCO cycles required for a complete divider cycle can be calculated in the following manner. Assume the main counter is preset to the value, M, and the auxiliary counter is set to the value of A. Because the dual-modulus prescaler divides by N + 1 until the auxiliary counter

reaches zero, (N + 1)A VCO cycles are required to reach this point. The mode is then switched and the dual-modulus prescaler divides by N until the main counter reaches zero. The main counter requires (M − A) counts or N(M − A) VCO cycles to reach zero. The total cycles of the VCO required for the complete divider cycle is:

$$(N+1) A + N (M-A) = NM + A$$

From the equation, it can be seen that M has more effect on the division value of

the dual-modulus divider than A. In the case of a 10/11 prescaler, the effect of M is 10 times that of A. That ratio is an important advantage of the 10/11 prescaler. In BCD-programmed synthesizers such as those programmed directly from switches, some of the switches can program the main counter while others are used to program the auxiliary counter.

There are some restrictions on the possible values of M and A. Because the auxiliary counter must reach zero before or concurrent with the main counter, the value of M must be equal to or greater than A. There is also a limit on the minimum division factor. That limit is equal to N(N − 1). For example, the minimum division factor for a dual-modulus divider using a 10/11 prescaler is 90. As a proof, try to determine what numbers must be set into the main and auxiliary counters to create a division of 89. It is not possible to find two numbers that will work and satisfy the requirement that M be equal to or greater than A. This minimum does not usually cause any problems in VHF synthesizers in which the minimum division factor is usually quite high.

Integrated Circuits

One significant advancement in synthesizer design is the LSI chip made specifically for dual-modulus synthesizers. Chips such as the Motorola MC145156 and MC145152, when used with suitable prescalers, allow two-chip synthesizer designs to operate at more than 500 MHz. A block diagram of a Motorola chip is shown in Fig 30. This chip is unique; the frequency-programming information is entered into the chip serially to reduce the package size. This could be a disadvantage in some systems, but it can be handled easily by a microprocessor. The MC145152 is a parallel entry version of the MC145156; the '145152 is housed in a 24-pin package, while a 16-pin package serves for the '145156.

Another important advance in dual-modulus VHF synthesizer design came when low power ECL prescalers became available. Perhaps the most significant disadvantage of the divider was the cost and the power requirements of the dual-modulus prescaler. An early 150-MHz ECL dual-modulus prescaler required as much as 100 mA at 5 volts; the power requirement for a modern prescaler is as low as 7 mA. This makes the dual-modulus prescaler a possible contender for portable, battery-operated equipment.

Frequency Modulation

FM is accomplished in a PLL by modulating the oscillator control voltage. The loop normally will tend to remove any frequency variation. To prevent removing all of the applied modulation, the response of the loop is restricted to frequencies below the voice-frequency band or approximately 300 Hz. Unfortunately, this prevents the loop from removing mechanically induced FM of the VCO known as microphonics. When the loop frequency response is so limited, the VCO must have few microphonics. This requires rigid shields and components secured with adhesives or potting compounds.

When modulation is applied to the VCO control voltage the amount of frequency deviation depends on the VCO constant. In VHF synthesizers where the bandwidth is a small percentage of the operating frequency, the variation in VCO constant versus operating frequency is small. When the VCO frequency range is large compared to the operating frequency, such as the 4-MHz span of the 50-MHz band, VCO constant can be a significant problem.

Mixing in VHF Synthesizers

VHF synthesizers can also use some form of mixing. Mixing can achieve two goals simultaneously. It can reduce the VCO frequency to a value that can be handled by conventional logic. Mixing can also perform some of the synthesizer arithmetic such as providing the IF offset for receive.

Fig 31 shows a block diagram of a VHF synthesizer using a mixing technique. In this example, the VCO operates in two bands, 133.3 to 137.3 MHz which is the receiver local-oscillator range, and the transmitter range from 144 MHz to 147.995 MHz. The same VCO serves as the receiver local oscillator and the transmitter oscillator. The VCO is mixed with a 125.3-MHz oscillator for receive and a 136-MHz oscillator for simplex transmit. In Fig 31, the programmable divider division factor goes from 1600 at 144 MHz to 2399 at 147.995 MHz. No special code conversion is required for this synthesizer, and Fig 32 shows the logic diagram of the programmable divider. On simplex, the VCO frequency is changed by 10.7 MHz between transmit and receive, by switching crystals in the offset oscillator. For repeater operation, the crystal oscillator is changed to provide a transmit frequency 600 kHz up or down from the receive frequency. More crystals are required to operate with other splits. The disadvantage of this synthesizer is the number of required crystals. A 2-meter synthesizer with simplex, 600-kHz positive and negative repeater offsets and 1-MHz repeater split requires seven crystals including the reference-oscillator crystal. The output frequency is directly dependent on each crystal, unlike the dual-modulus synthesizer, in which frequency accuracy depends on only one crystal.

The VCO must shift approximately 10 MHz between transmit and receive. This requires the synthesizer to lock up quickly. The transmitter must be inhibited while the synthesizer is out of lock. To facilitate the frequency shift, a fixed capacitor can be switched in and out of the VCO tank circuit.

A variation of this synthesizer uses only

Fig 31—Block diagram of a VHF synthesizer using mixing techniques.

Fig 32—Logic diagram of the programmable divider for the synthesizer shown in Fig 33.

Fig 33—Block diagram of a microprocessor-controlled VHF synthesizer.

two crystal oscillators, including the 5-kHz reference. VCO shifts, transmit/receive switching and repeater offsets are controlled by a microprocessor. A block diagram of this synthesizer is shown in Fig 33. The VCO must still shift for transmit and receive; it shares this problem with the previous example. However, only two crystals are required—a significant advantage over the previous case.

One example of a synthesizer design that does not require a VCO shift between transmit and receive is shown in Fig 34. In this design, the VCO serves as the receiver local oscillator at all times. On transmit, the VCO is mixed with a crystal-controlled, frequency-modulated oscillator operating at the receiver IF. Repeater offsets are handled by the programmable divider. For repeater operation, the VCO has to shift between transmit and receive, but only 600 kHz or 1 MHz, depending on the offset. That is an improvement over the previous examples, where the VCO was required to shift an amount equal to the receiver IF plus any repeater offset.

Like any heterodyning transmitter there is a possibility of transmitting spurious signals. To minimize this chance, the receiver IF should be as high as practical. In the example shown, the receiver IF is 16.9 MHz. The local oscillator range is 127.1 to 131.095 MHz. LO output is mixed with a 16.9-MHz, frequency-modulated crystal oscillator to provide the transmitted frequency. Care must be taken to prevent local oscillator radiation. The 16.9-MHz signal is filtered easily. To effectively eliminate the local oscillator from the transmit signal requires a sharp tuned circuit. This circuit can be adjusted automatically with a varactor diode, tuned from the VCO control voltage. This technique usually reduces the spurious signal level to an acceptable limit.

Frequency synthesis at UHF uses similar techniques to those used at VHF, with some minor changes. The frequencies involved in this range limit the use of the dual-modulus synthesizer and make mixing schemes difficult. One acceptable method of UHF synthesis is to use a fixed-modulus prescaler. Because most modes of operation at UHF are broadband, the presence of the reference frequency in the PLL is not a significant problem. Simple frequency dividers such as divide by 2, 4 or 8 are available for operating frequencies as high as 2 GHz and are expected to become available for even higher frequencies.

DIRECT DIGITAL SYNTHESIZERS (DDS)

This information about direct digital synthesizers was prepared by Robert J. Zavrel, Jr, W7SX. Direct digital synthesis has recently become a viable technique for high-performance radio applications. The parameters of the synthesized waveform—frequency, phase, and amplitude—are defined or calculated digitally. DDS relies upon the fact that any frequency can be defined as a change in phase per unit time. We can write this mathematically as:

$$\omega = 2\pi f = \Delta\phi \, / \, \Delta t.$$

The Greek delta (Δ) means change. The higher the frequency, the faster the phase changes.

Fig 35 shows a block diagram of a simple DDS system. We will study the function and operation of each block to learn how the system works. Before going into the details of DDS, however, it may be helpful to relate some basic oscillator fundamentals to digital techniques.

It may help your understanding of oscillators to visualize a point on a rotating wheel. Each complete rotation of the wheel represents one cycle of the oscillator waveform. The rotation speed corresponds to the frequency, and if the wheel spins at a constant speed the oscillator produces a sine wave. Each point on the wheel corresponds to a particular phase point on the oscillator waveform, as Fig 36 shows.

A phase accumulator is a variable-modulus counter designed to add a single number to the value already in the accumulator every time the circuit receives a clock pulse. The accumulator defines the instantaneous phase point on the wheel. Eventu-

Fig 34—Block diagram of a synthesizer requiring only minimal VCO frequency shifting.

Fig. 35 — A basic DDS system. Frequency tuning can be provided by a microprocessor, memory, up-down counter, or simple switches. FM can be effected by adding or subtracting to that number. Likewise an adder or subtractor can provide PM when applied to the instantaneous phase number. AM is accomplished by placing a digital multiplier between the ROM and the DAC. Alternatively, analog AM can be realized through more conventional methods after the anti-alias filter.

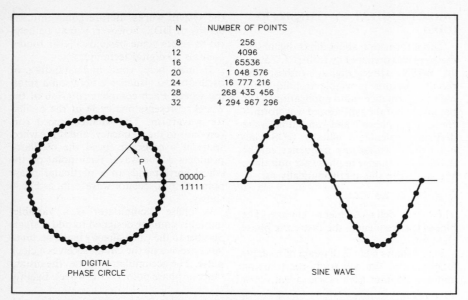

N	NUMBER OF POINTS
8	256
12	4096
16	65536
20	1 048 576
24	16 777 216
28	268 435 456
32	4 294 967 296

DIGITAL PHASE CIRCLE

SINE WAVE

Fig. 36 — Every point around a wheel can be related to a point on an oscillator output waveform. If these points are represented by binary digits, then the number of digits (N) relates to the number of points that can be represented (2^N).

ally, the counter will overflow, and this starts another trip around the digital phase circle.

The frequency-tuning word shown as an input to the phase accumulator in Fig 35 tells the accumulator what number to add to the stored value with each clock pulse. This sets the counter modulus, and represents the "jump size," which tells the accumulator how many points on the circle to skip when it goes to the next value. If M represents this jump size, which is the change in accumulated phase during the time between clock pulses, then we can write an equation to describe the frequency of the waveform being synthesized.

why the phase accumulator adds the same number to the stored value with each clock pulse. The output waveform is not a linear function, however. So the accumulator output does not represent the output signal. The lookup table contains the amplitude values that represent a sine wave output. Phase values from the accumulator tell the lookup table which amplitude value to select next. Taking fewer phase jumps increases the synthesizer frequency and taking more phase jumps decreases the output frequency for a fixed clock frequency.

The digital-to-analog converter (DAC) creates an instantaneous amplitude sample for the desired RF signal. The DAC receives its digital-word input from the lookup table. Following the DAC an anti-

alias filter removes the alias signals, thereby providing a sine-wave signal from the stair-step waveform at the DAC output. Therefore, the first analog signal appears at the synthesizer output.

There is one important limitation to the range of frequencies that we can generate with this simple DDS system. The sample rate, or clock frequency, must be at least twice the output frequency. (This is defined by the Nyquist theorem.) If we use only two phase points (180 degrees apart on our circle) we will define not only a sine wave at the desired frequency, but also higher-frequency signals called aliases. Selecting phase points more than 180° apart results in a signal that is *not* at the desired output frequency. There is more information about the Nyquist Sampling Theorem in the Digital Basics chapter of this *Handbook*.

If we want to build a 0- to 10-MHz DDS, we must use a system clock of at least 20 MHz. Practical limitations restrict the actual highest synthesized frequency to about ⅓ the clock frequency, but more on this later.

Fig 37 shows how a sine wave at any frequency can be synthesized from a fixed clock, within the restrictions of the Nyquist criteria. The DDS system is programmed for some value of ω. The phase accumulator then generates the appropriate $\Delta\phi / \Delta t$ sequence, which establishes how far through the cycle each amplitude sample occurs. The ROM lookup table converts the digital phase sample into a digital amplitude number and the DAC generates the analog amplitude progression from these digital amplitude values. Notice that when the phase changes little between samples a low-frequency waveform is generated but when there is a large phase change between samples a higher-frequency waveform is generated.

The Phase Accumulator

In its simplest form, the phase accumu-

$$\frac{\Delta\phi}{\Delta t} = \frac{\dfrac{M}{2^N}}{\dfrac{1}{f_{clk}}} = M \frac{f_{clk}}{2^N}$$

where

$\dfrac{\Delta\phi}{\Delta t}$ is the change in phase with respect to time (frequency) of the output signal.

f_{clk} is the clock frequency.

Three parameters determine the output frequency: the clock frequency, the phase accumulator bit size (N), and the tuning input (M). Each of these parameters can be carefully controlled.

The phase of a sine wave is a linear function of time for a fixed frequency. This is

BINARY DAC VALUE

11111111

10000000

0000000

FIXED CLOCK — SAMPLE RATE

Fig. 37 — Fixed clock-sample rate. Any combination of frequencies can be synthesized using DDS as long as the frequencies are lower than the Nyquist frequency. An 8-bit DAC provides 256 discrete amplitude values. The frequency resolution of a DDS system is determined by the size of the phase accumulator, not the DAC or ROM size.

lator is a binary variable-modulus counter. The input data (called the "tuning word" or "M") programs the counter to add a certain binary number value to the count with each clock cycle. A 24-bit counter can have up to 2^{24} (about 16.7 million) possible tuning states. The counter output is the desired output signal instantaneous phase value, defined by a 24-bit binary word. The rate of change of this word is given by:

$$\frac{\Delta\phi}{\Delta t} = \omega = 2\pi f$$

The frequency resolution or tuning step size of a DDS system is given by:

$$f(step) = \frac{f(clock)}{2^N}$$

where N is the number of bits in the phase-accumulator counter.

The tuning step size of a 24-bit phase accumulator clocked at 20 MHz is:

$$f(step) = \frac{20 \text{ MHz}}{2^{24}} = \frac{20 \times 10^6 \text{ Hz}}{16,777,216} \approx 1.2 \text{ Hz}$$

If we increase N to 48 bits the resolution becomes several nanohertz!

One advantage of running a digital counter from a stable quartz clock is that very linear phase progressions can be produced. Phase linearity is the same as the clock time progression linearity! Consequently, the phase noise in a DDS system is typically less than the phase noise of the reference oscillator. In effect, the DDS system is dividing the reference clock frequency by some number (K) greater than 2. The reduction in phase noise will be $20 \log_{10} K$. There is a phase noise limitation in all real DDS systems, however. For example, if we apply a theoretically noise-free clock to a real DDS system we will see some phase noise on the DDS signal. This phase noise "error" has been measured at about -120 dBc / Hz at 1 Hz offset, and settles in about -140 dBc / Hz a few hundred hertz away. Phase noise is not a practical problem in modern DDS designs. Phase errors arising from quantized approximations in the digital portion of a DDS system produce spurious responses at discrete frequencies. "Broadband" noise is generated in the DAC.

The Lookup Table

Phase is a linear time function for a given frequency, but the output-waveform amplitude is a sinusoid function. There is a constant relationship between phase and amplitude values, and digital sine-wave synthesizers make use of this fact. For example, 0 degrees corresponds with an amplitude of 0, 90 degrees corresponds with $+1$, 180 degrees gives an amplitude of 0 again, 270 degrees corresponds with -1, and so on.

The lookup table is a digital phase-to-amplitude converter usually configured from a read-only memory or ROM. The phase accumulator output is applied to the

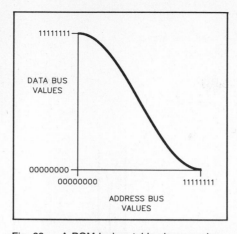

Fig. 38 — A ROM lookup table shows cosine data and address locations. The phase accumulator skips up and down the cosine values to provide the proper amplitude value to the DAC for each discrete value of time.

ROM address bus. The ROM data bus then provides the DAC with the corresponding amplitude value. Information could be included in the ROM for the full 360° of the sine wave, but ROM size can be decreased by including only 180 or 90 degrees of sine or cosine data. The phase accumulator then runs in both directions through the ROM and the output sign is set accordingly. Fig 38 shows the sinusoidal relationship between the address-bus and data-bus values.

Frequency Resolution and Spurious Response

The relationship between phase-accumulator bit size (defining frequency resolution) and DAC bit size (defining spectral purity) is often confused. It is not necessary to provide a 24-bit DAC to realize 24-bit frequency resolution. Indeed, a one-bit DAC could be used with any desired level of frequency resolution (48 bits, for example). A one-bit DAC can be simulated by the most significant bit (MSB) from the phase accumulator. The time-domain output of the MSB is a digital waveform whose individual components are multiple divisions of the clock frequency. (A rise or fall along any digital waveform in the system can only occur on the rise or fall of the clock signal.)

When viewed on a spectrum analyzer, the most significant spectral component of the MSB will be the desired output frequency, regardless of the tuned setting. Many other spectral components, often close-in to the desired signal, will also appear. These may be only 10 dB below the desired signal amplitude. The MSB of the phase accumulator provides a very poor-quality RF generator for the local oscillator of a radio. The only exception to the large spurious rule for one-bit DAC operation is when the phase accumulator is tuned to an even integer division of the clock. In these cases, the phase accumulator is simply dividing

the clock by an integer, just as a flip-flop divides by two. Then the MSB waveform is symmetrical, and the spurious signals disappear.

The effect of adding more bit resolution to the DAC is to reduce the spurious signal response amplitude of the system. This is accomplished by providing a closer approximation of the desired instantaneous amplitude value.

The Anti-Alias Filter

A pure sine wave has only one spectral component. Other waveforms will have additional frequency components, as viewed on a spectrum analyzer. The DAC produces a "stair-step" waveform, so we should expect multiple spectral lines. Indeed, besides the fundamental frequency, "alias" signals will appear on either side of the clock and multiples of the clock frequency. For example, if we generate a 1.5-MHz signal from a 20-MHz clock, the first pair of alias signals will appear at 18.5 and 21.5 MHz. See Figs 39 and 40.

As we increase the fundamental frequency, the frequency of the lowest alias signal decreases. For example, with a 20-MHz clock and 9.5-MHz output, the first alias signal will appear at 10.5 MHz. Filtering a signal 1 MHz away from the desired signal may not seem too difficult, but as we operate closer to the Nyquist limit (10 MHz in this example), the filtering task becomes more difficult. For this reason, the practical maximum operating frequency is about ⅓ clock in DDS systems.

A near-perfect sine wave can be recovered from the DAC output by using a low-pass anti-alias filter with a cut-off frequency near or slightly above ⅓ clock. The alias-signal amplitude conforms nicely to a SIN(X) / X curve. The required filter roll-off characteristics can be calculated from the operating and clock frequencies and the desired alias-signal suppression.

DDS Spurious Responses

The frequency resolution of a DDS system is determined by the system clock and the number of bits in the phase accumulator. The spectral purity derived from a DDS system is determined mainly by the

Fig. 39 — The time-domain output of a DAC in a DDS system using a 20-MHz clock.

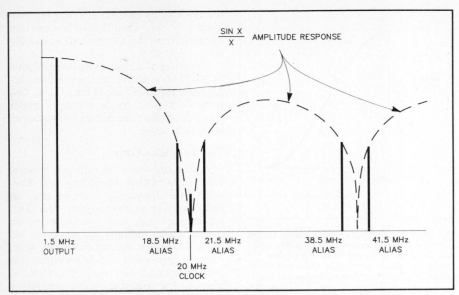

Fig. 40 — The frequency-domain output of the waveform shown in Fig 39. Notice that the amplitude of the spurious signals closely follows a SIN (X) / X response.

linearity and bit resolution of the DAC. The ROM should provide at least the same number of amplitude bits as the DAC resolution affords. There is some advantage in providing greater address-bit resolution than DAC resolution to minimize quantization errors, but there doesn't seem to be much advantage to extending the address two bits beyond the DAC resolution. For example, if an 8-bit DAC is to be used, the suggested ROM size for minimum spurious levels would be 10 address bits and 8 data bits. We could use 9 address bits if 180 degrees of mapping is provided, the tenth bit then being the up-down condition of the counter.

The major spectral impurity components of direct digital synthesizers consist of spurs at discrete frequencies rather than the "broad band" noise of PLL synthesizers[1]. The spurious signals are harmonically related to the fundamental output signal. These harmonics are "folded back" at the Nyquist frequency and at dc. For example, suppose we synthesize a 6-MHz signal from a 20-MHz clock. The Nyquist frequency is 20 MHz / 2, or 10 MHz. The second harmonic of the output should appear at 12 MHz, but is "folded back" to 8 MHz (2 MHz below the Nyquist frequency). The third harmonic (18 MHz) will appear at 2 MHz because that is 8 MHz below the Nyquist frequency. The fourth harmonic (24 MHz) will appear at 4 MHz because it can't go below zero, and so is "folded back" again from that point. The effect is that the discrete spurs are harmonics of the fundamental, which are mirrored between dc and the Nyquist frequency.

Another significant point is that as the synthesizer output changes, the spurs change by an amount equal to the harmonic multiple of the frequency change. For example, if we increase the output signal by 100 kHz, from 6 MHz to 6.1 MHz, the second-harmonic spur decreases by 200 kHz, from 8 MHz to 7.8 MHz. The third-harmonic spur decreases from 2 MHz to 1.7 MHz and the fourth-harmonic spur increases from 4 MHz to 4.4 MHz.

Now suppose we tune the output signal to exactly ¼ the clock frequency. The spurs disappear because all the odd-order harmonics fall on the fundamental frequency (5 MHz with a 20-MHz clock). The even-order harmonics either appear at 10 MHz, or as a dc offset error. (If you aren't sure of this try calculating the harmonic frequencies and where the spurs fall between dc and the Nyquist frequency.) If we tune slightly off 5 MHz, however, the odd-order spurs will "accumulate" around the main signal. All the odd-order harmonics "cross over" the main carrier signal at ¼ clock. (Alternate odd-order harmonics fall on opposite sides of the main signal.) See Fig 41. If we tune the DDS output to near ⅓ clock (the worst-case) even-order and many odd-order spurs appear close-in. See Fig 42.

We can derive an excellent view of the spurious response of a DDS system by looking at these two key operating frequencies. Most of the worst-case spurs will fall in two narrow-bandwidth windows. This evaluation technique is very roughly equivalent to the derivation of second and third-order intercept points. Mixer or amplifier performance can be very accurately predicted if intercept points and other parameters are known. Likewise, DDS performance can be predicted accurately at nearly any frequency if the ¼ and ⅓ "cross-over" spurs are known. Figures 41 and 42 show typical spectrum-analyzer displays at ¼ and ⅓ crossover frequencies. The amplitudes of these spurs remain relatively constant as they "bounce" back and forth between the Nyquist frequency and dc.

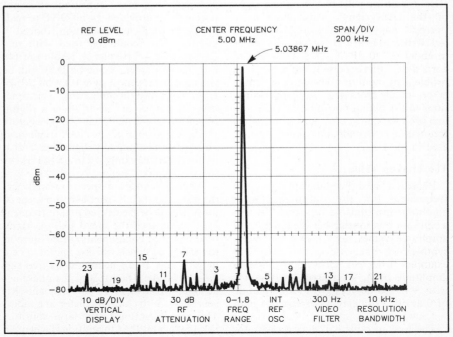

Fig. 41 — Crossover spur measurement at ¼ clock frequency with a 20-MHz clock. The spurs along the bottom of the display are numbered according to their harmonic order. The synthesizer output is 5.03867 MHz.

[1]T. Sheffer, John Fluke Mfg Co, "Introduction to Direct Digital Synthesis," *Proceedings of RF Expo East*, 1989.

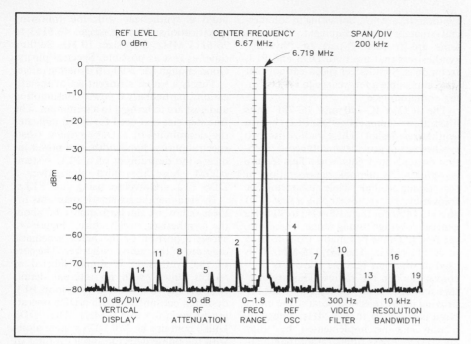

REF LEVEL   CENTER FREQUENCY   SPAN/DIV
0 dBm   6.67 MHz   200 kHz

Fig. 42 — Crossover spur measurement at ⅓ clock frequency with a 20-MHz clock. The spurs along the bottom of the display are numbered according to their harmonic order. The synthesizer output is 6.719 MHz.

Two factors cause spurious-signal generation in a DDS system. Since the DAC provides a quantized approximation of the sampled amplitude value, error is inherent to the technique. Even if a "perfect" DAC is used, spurs will appear in the system. Since there is no perfect DAC, additional errors will be realized because of the technical limitations of the DAC. Both quantized and DAC errors show themselves as the harmonically related spurs explained above.

It is possible to achieve excellent receiver performance using DDS. The frequency schemes must be selected carefully and the best available DAC should be used.[2]

DDS Settling Time

At first glance, the settling time to move a DDS system from one frequency to another is zero. There is a practical limitation, however. The anti-alias filter and additional filters must have a finite bandwidth. There are no loop time constants to contend with as in PLL systems, but there is a time response inherent in any DDS system.

The frequency tuning "word" must be loaded into the phase accumulator. Many controllers use serial or 8-bit bus architectures to load the 24, 32, or whatever number of bits needed to control the frequency. Unless parallel bus tuning is used, it will take several clock periods to load the tuning word. Once it has been loaded, the tuning

word must change the modulus of the counter. The number of clock periods required for this operation will depend on the controller. It may take from 2 or 3 up to 40 or 50 clock periods. A 20-MHz clock has a period of 50 ns. If we multiply this by 40 or 50, we begin to see performance levels approaching PLL designs. (Most DDS designs are superior to the time response of PLL synthesizers, however.) There may be further delays in latches between the accumulator and ROM, between the ROM and DAC, and in the DAC itself. The total time required to move the synthesizer from one frequency to another is the settling time, $T_{settling}$.

Quadrature Generation

Sometimes we have a need to generate two signals that will maintain a 90° phase relationship between each other, such as a sine and cosine waveform. Such signals are in *quadrature*. DDS systems provide a convenient way to generate signals in quadrature.

If two lookup tables and DACs are used with the same phase accumulator, quadrature signals can be generated. The ROMs must be loaded with sine and cosine data. The great advantage of quadrature synthesis using DDS is that the two signals stay exactly 90° out of phase with each other from dc to the Nyquist frequency.

The practical limitation in maintaining excellent quadrature lies in building tracking anti-alias filters. Maintaining 1 degree accuracy above ¼ clock while attenuating the first alias by 60 dB or so is an exceedingly difficult filter tracking problem.

Quadrature accuracy becomes progressively easier as lower frequencies are generated for a given alias attenuation. The filter tracking considerations are often overlooked when designing a quadrature generator.

For many applications where quadrature synthesis and DDS are desired, a single DDS unit working in conjunction with more conventional quadrature synthesizer techniques might be advised. A fast TTL dual divide-by-four flip-flop can provide excellent quadrature response and is inherently broadbanded, rendering it an excellent companion to a DDS synthesizer. Fast TTL is preferred over CMOS or ECL.[3,4]

Numeric Modulation in DDS Systems

We learned earlier that all three parameters of the output waveform (frequency, phase and amplitude) from a DDS are defined by binary digital words. We can effect all known forms of modulation (FM, PM, and AM) by "modulating" these digital words. In fact, virtually any known waveform can be generated using DDS techniques! The only limitation is bandwidth and creative software to combine FM, PM, and/or AM.

We can frequency modulate the DDS output by adding to or subtracting from the frequency tuning word. A digitized analog modulating waveform (such as audio, video, fax or other signal) is applied to the tuning port after adding it to a "center" or "start" frequency tuning word. Since the modulator adds and subtracts directly, the linearity is limited only by the bit resolution of the modulator. For example, 16 bit linearity comparable to compact disc (CD) quality should be easily achieved for very high quality broadcast exciters.[5]

FSK systems with 2, 4, 8, 16, 32, or more bits are easily configured by simply "keying" the appropriate bits on the tuning port. Furthermore, "soft" or minimum shift keying (MSK) can be achieved by sequencing discrete frequency values. Any frequency can be accurately defined and implemented by sequencing a control ROM.

Extremely linear sweep generators can be built by controlling the frequency port with a counter. In fact, if the sweep generator is a second-variable-modulus counter, 2^N sweep rates can be realized! Furthermore, start and stop frequencies are easily set by functions on the controlling counter.

[2]R. Zavrel, Jr, "A Direct Digital Synthesis VFO," *Ham Radio*, Sept 1988.

[3]R. Zavrel, Jr, "New Low-Power Single Sideband Circuits," Signetics Corp Application Note AN1981, 1988.

[4]M. Bomford, Telemus Electronic Systems, Inc, "Selection of Dividers for Microwave PLL Applications," *Proceedings of RF Expo East*, 1989.

[5]R. Zavrel, Jr, "A Completely Digital FM Broadcast Stereo System," *43rd Annual Broadcast Engineering Conference Proceedings*, NAB, 1989.

We can phase modulate the synthesized signal by placing an adder at the output of the phase accumulator. The same rules apply to PM as FM regarding linearity, linear and digital modulating waveforms. It should even be possible to frequency modulate and phase modulate a signal simultaneously, if anyone would want to do such a thing.

Amplitude modulation takes place after the lookup table. Place a digital multiplier between the ROM and the DAC. A four-quadrant multiplier will produce a double-sideband, suppressed-carrier signal, while single-quadrant multiplication yields full-carrier DSB. Carrier suppression exceeds 50 dB for 8-bit DSB four-quadrant multiplication. Of course AM can be combined with FM and/or PM with exceptional linearity to produce any digital or analog modulating waveform.

HYBRID DDS/PLL SYNTHESIZERS

Standing alone, the DDS technique is remarkably flexible. When used in combination with traditional RF techniques, including PLL techniques, there is a whole new world of possibilities. Direct digital synthesizers are now appearing in commercial Amateur Radio equipment. These systems are frequently part of "hybrid" synthesizers that use both DDS and PLL techniques. Synthesizer specifications that were impossible a few years ago are becoming commonplace.

The ICOM IC-780 and IC-781 units illustrate a complex DDS/PLL hybrid synthesizer design. These radios use two synthesizers to provide simultaneous reception on separate frequencies. This feature is useful in DX pile-ups, net operation, or for "tuning around" while monitoring one frequency. The radios employ a first IF of 46.5115 MHz for their 100-kHz to 30-MHz general-coverage tuning range. Therefore, the first LO must be tunable from 46.6115 to 76.5115 MHz. The 46.5115-MHz IF is used in what has become known as "up-conversion" in HF radios. This architecture simplifies front-end filtering while improving image rejection because the image band is about 93 to 123 MHz. Image rejection can be implemented by using 30-MHz low-pass filters rather than high-Q resonant tanks.

The challenge for the LO designer is to build a synthesizer with the following specifications: Tuning range: 46.6115 to 76.5115 MHz. Step size: 10 Hz. Settling time: as fast as possible. Spectral purity: Good enough for >90-dB dynamic range.

This is a rather stringent set of specifications, particularly if power consumption and cost are to be held to a minimum. The fine step size and need for speed indicates the desirability of a DDS system. Cost, spectral purity, bandwidth, and power indicate the desirability of a PLL system. ICOM chose the third alternative, a DDS/PLL architecture using dual PLLs.

By studying the schematic diagrams for these radios, we can learn quite a bit about the synthesizer architecture. Figure 43 shows a portion of the block/schematic diagram of the radio synthesizer. The core of the synthesizer is simply labeled as "DDS Unit," with no internal details shown. The radios use a twin-loop PLL design in conjunction with a DDS operating between 0.5 to 1.0 MHz. The "DDS Unit" contains an MF DDS system along with the phase detector and loop filter of the first PLL.

The actual DDS unit has three possible

Fig. 43 — A partial block diagram of the ICOM IC-780 and IC-781 synthesizer architecture using a DDS and dual PLLs. Most filters, buffers and related circuitry have been omitted for simplicity.

configurations: a clock of 10.48576 MHz and a 20-bit counter, a 5.24288-MHz clock and 19-bit counter, or a 2.62144-MHz clock with an 18-bit counter and the schematic shows a 10.48576-MHz source applied to the "DDS Unit."

The "DDS Unit" output is a dc control voltage for the first PLL VCO. This first VCO operates from 42.0115 to 42.5115 MHz. A 41.5115-MHz source is provided by a rather complex set of fixed PLLs and mixers all mastered from a 12.5-MHz reference oscillator. This 41.5115-MHz signal is then mixed with the VCO output to provide a 0.5- to 1.0-MHz product. This low-frequency signal is fed back to the "DDS Unit" where the phase is compared with the 0.5- to 1.0-MHz DDS output. Consequently, the VHF output of the first PLL is phase-locked to the MF DDS signal without suffering spectral degradation caused by frequency multiplication. A loop filter with a relatively wide bandwidth can be employed, allowing settling times under 10 μs. This is considerably slower than the DDS system, and phase noise will be added by the PLL in this design.

The second PLL uses a similar scheme. The 42.0115- to 42.5115-MHz output from the first loop is mixed with the 46.6115- to 76.5115-MHz output of the second PLL. This produces a 4.500- to 34.000-MHz product that is divided by an integer in the range from 9 to 68 to produce a 500-kHz signal. The phase of this 500-kHz signal is then compared with a 500-kHz signal provided by the 12.5-MHz reference and divide-by-25 circuit.

The second PLL provides the required LO signal for the receiver first mixer. The entire synthesizer circuit actually appears twice in the radio, thus providing the two LOs necessary for simultaneous dual-channel operation.

To summarize the IC-780/781 DDS/PLL architecture, two PLLs are used in conjunction with a DDS. The DDS provides exact 10-Hz steps between 0.5 and 1.0 MHz. This low-frequency signal with a 500-kHz range is translated to 42.0115 to 42.5115 MHz in the first PLL. The second PLL, in effect provides the general-coverage function by generating a signal with a 29.9-MHz range, from 46.6115 to 76.5115 MHz. Fine tuning is provided by the first loop, and 500-kHz steps are provided by the second loop for full-band coverage.

Special Considerations for Receiver Designs

There are two other important points when considering DDS/PLL hybrids. With careful analysis, you can prove that the closest a spur can come to the output frequency in a DDS system is equal to the frequency resolution of the least-significant bit used in the tuning bus. For example, assume we use a 2^{24} Hz clock (16.777216 MHz) and a 24-bit phase accumulator. The tuning resolution of this system is therefore exactly 1 Hz. If we only use the 12 most-significant bits of the phase accumulator, we establish a step size of 4096 Hz. Therefore, the closest a spur can come to the carrier is 4096 Hz. If a PLL is used in conjunction with this DDS system, *all* spurs can be effectively eliminated if the loop bandwidth filter is narrower than the 4096 Hz value! In other words, where $T_{settling} > 1 / f_{resolution}$ all spurs can be attenuated by the loop bandwidth filter.

The second point is that even when tight resolution is required (such as 10 Hz for an HF radio) spurs can be greatly reduced. Spurs that are typically −50 dBc can be devastating to a receiver dynamic range specification. A −50-dBc spur *inside* the receiver bandpass filter will simply contribute to intermodulation distortion of the baseband signal. For an SSB or FM receiver with a 1% THD audio specification a −50-dBc spur inside the baseband will not cause significant effects. For cases where $T_{settling} > 1 / f_{bandwidth\ of\ baseband}$ spurs can be eliminated from affecting the mixing specifications. For a typical SSB receiver, $T_{settling}$ must be greater than about 1 / 3.2 kHz or about 300 μs.

SYNTHESIZER BIBLIOGRAPHY

Brewer, John, Earl W. McCune Jr, Robert J. Zavrel Jr, Peter Stokes, Collection of Application Notes on direct digital synthesis AN1002, AN1004, AN1005, AN1007, AN4001, AN8001, AN8002, AN3006, AN3007, and AN3002, Digital RF Solutions, Inc, 1988-1989.

Bomford, Mark, Telemus Electronic Systems, Inc, "Selection of Dividers for Microwave PLL Applications," *Proceedings of RF Expo East,* 1989.

Hayward, W., "Variations in a Single-Loop Frequency Synthesizer," *QST*, September 1981.

Helfrick, A. D., *Amateur Radio Equipment Fundamentals*, Englewood Cliffs, NJ: Prentice Hall, 1982, pp 111-119.

Helfrick, A. D., *Practical Repair and Maintenance of Communications Equipment*, Englewood Cliffs, NJ: Prentice Hall, 1983, Chapter 5.

Helfrick, A. D., "A High-Performance Synthesized 2-Meter Transmitter," *QST*, September 1980.

Helfrick, A. D., "The Universal Synthesizer," *QST*, September 1981.

Helfrick, A. D., "A Modern Up-Converting General-Coverage Receiver," *QST*, December 1981.

Helfrick, A. D., "Versatile Communications Receiver," *Ham Radio*, July 1982.

Helfrick, A. D., "A Modern Synthesizer for Portable VHF Transceivers," *QST*, April 1982.

McCune, Earl W., "Frequency Modulation Design for Direct Digital Synthesizers," *Proceedings of RF Expo East*, 1989.

Rohde, Ulrich L., *Digital PLL Frequency Synthesizers*, Englewood Cliffs, NJ: Prentice Hall, 1983.

Sabin, Shoenike, et al, *Single-Sideband Systems and Circuits*, McGraw-Hill, 1988.

Williams, Fred, "A Digital Frequency Synthesizer," *QST*, April, 1984.

Zavrel, Robert J., Jr and Gwyn Edwards, *DDS Handbook*, Stanford Telecommunications, 1990.

Zavrel, Robert J., Jr, and Earl W. McCune Jr, "Low Spurious Techniques and Measurements for DDS Systems," *Proceedings of RF Expo East*, 1988.

Zavrel, Robert J., Jr, "New Low-Power Single Sideband Circuits," Signetics Corp. Application Note AN1981, 1988.

Zavrel, Robert J., Jr, "A Completely Digital FM Broadcast Stereo System," *43rd Annual Broadcast Engineering Conference Proceedings*, NAB, 1989.

Zavrel, Robert J., Jr, "Digital Modulation Using the NCMO," *RF Design,* March, 1988.

Zavrel, Robert J., Jr, "A Direct Digital Synthesis VFO," *Ham Radio*, September, 1988.

Oscillator Phase Noise

The following material on phase noise was written by John Grebenkemper, KI6WX, and first appeared as a two-part article in March and April 1988 *QST*.

Oscillators have formed the basis of most radio communications systems since spark-gap transmitters were retired. Originally, these oscillators used piezoelectric crystals or high-Q LC tuned circuits as resonant elements. More recently, *phase-locked loops* (PLLs) have been used in radios with synthesized local oscillators. There is no theoretical reason that prevents a phase-locked oscillator from having better phase-noise characteristics than a free-running oscillator using an LC tuned circuit.

An ideal oscillator would generate a sine wave at a given frequency with no deviation in amplitude or phase over time. If we looked at this signal with an ideal spectrum analyzer, we would see all of the energy concentrated at the fundamental frequency and none at any other frequency. If ideal oscillators existed, problems with phase noise wouldn't exist.

Oscillator signals vary in both amplitude and phase as a function of time. These variations are referred to as *amplitude noise* and *phase noise*. Amplitude noise is an undesired variation in the *amplitude* of an oscillator signal. If we use an oscilloscope to look at oscillator output, we can see that the amplitude peaks of the sine wave vary with time (Fig 44).

Phase noise is an undesired variation in the phase of the signal. In this case, an oscilloscope shows that the time between zero crossings of the signal varies over time when compared to the zero crossings of an ideal sine wave. An exaggerated example of phase noise is shown in Fig 45.

Several factors combine to make amplitude noise much less important than phase noise. The first is that most oscillators tend to produce less amplitude noise than phase noise. This occurs because the active devices in most oscillators are operated in a gain-saturated condition. Gain saturation occurs when increasing the input to a device or stage results in no further increase in output. If a device or stage is sufficiently gain saturated, small changes in the amplitude of the input signal (amplitude noise, in other words) produce no change in the output level.

Amplitude noise is secondary in importance to phase noise for another reason. Most modern ham rigs use mixers in their signal-generation schemes. Because mixers are usually operated with their local-oscillator input ports gain saturated, any amplitude noise on the input signal generally does not appear on the mixer output.

SPECIFYING PHASE NOISE LEVELS

There are many ways to display oscillator phase noise. The most common presentation is called single-sideband (SSB) phase noise. This is simply a display of the phase-noise characteristics on one side of the carrier. The SSB phase-noise presentation has probably achieved its widespread use because SSB phase noise is easy to measure and interpret for the average person who is familiar with RF measurement techniques. The display of SSB phase noise is exactly what you would see if the oscillator was observed using an ideal spectrum analyzer with a 1-Hz sampling bandwidth.

The vertical axis is the SSB phase noise measured in units of "dBc/Hz." The "dBc" means that we are measuring the power in the phase noise relative to the power in the carrier. The "Hz" implies that we are making this measurement in a 1-Hz bandwidth. (Phase noise is usually not actually *measured* in a 1-Hz bandwidth, for reasons of instrumentation limitations.)

The horizontal axis represents the difference between the measurement and oscillator frequencies, and is usually referred to as the *offset frequency*. Offset frequency is measured in Hz, and it is usually plotted on a logarithmic scale. An offset of 1 kHz means that we are measuring the phase noise 1 kHz from the carrier; an offset of 10 kHz is 10 kHz from the carrier, and so on. A 10-kHz offset from a 10-MHz carrier means that we are making measurements at 9.99 MHz or 10.01 MHz.

Two typical phase-noise measurements are shown in Fig 46. At an offset frequency of 0 Hz, the SSB phase noise is always 0 dBc/Hz, because we are measuring the carrier power, which is the reference for these measurements. At any other offset, the SSB phase noise is always a negative dB value.

Phase noise in a communications system can be divided into two different regions. The *in-band* or *close-in* phase noise is the component that is *within the modulation bandwidth* of the signal. The *out-of-band* or *far-out* phase noise is the component that is *beyond* the modulation bandwidth of the signal. The modulation bandwidth of an amateur SSB signal is 3 kHz. Therefore, we can define the close-in phase noise of an SSB signal as the noise at offsets of less than 3 kHz, and the far-out phase noise as the phase noise at offsets greater than that. The difference between close-in and far-out phase noise is similarly defined for modes with different modulation bandwidths.

The example used in Fig 46 shows the phase noise for two different synthesized oscillators. The phase-noise plot labeled "good" is the phase noise from an excellent synthesized local oscillator. These

Fig 44—Oscillator amplitude noise effects as viewed on an oscilloscope. The broken line shows the output of an ideal oscillator; the solid line shows the output waveform of an oscillator with a large amount of amplitude noise.

Fig 45—Oscillator phase-noise effects as viewed on an oscilloscope. The broken line shows the output of an ideal oscillator; the solid line shows the output waveform of an oscillator with a large amount of phase noise.

Fig 46—Phase-noise characteristics of two synthesized oscillators. The lower curve represents the output of a well-designed synthesized oscillator. The upper curve represents that of a poorly designed synthesized oscillator. Note the broad peak at 1 kHz, and the spikes visible near 60 and 120 Hz, and 11 and 22 kHz. (See text.)

phase-noise characteristics are considered the best presently obtainable for oscillators used in HF receivers. The phase noise from this oscillator rapidly decreases with increasing offset frequency, reaching −160 dBc/Hz at an offset frequency of 100 kHz. The slight flattening of the phase-noise plot near 1 kHz results from the natural frequency of the PLL (the natural frequency produces optimum loop response). (It is normal for a synthesized oscillator to show flattening or a few dB of peaking of the phase noise at the natural frequency of the PLL.) This oscillator would present only minor phase-noise problems in amateur applications.

The phase-noise plot labeled "poor" is typical of what one would expect from an inferior synthesized oscillator. The characteristics of such an oscillator include strong spurious signals, an underdamped PLL (lack of sufficient negative feedback), and a high phase-noise floor. Large spurious signals are shown at harmonics of 60 Hz and 11 kHz. These signals result from frequency modulation of the oscillator in the PLL, and are generally caused by inadequate shielding or poor loop design. The broad peak at 1 kHz results from an underdamped PLL. Any peaking greater than this is indicative of a poorly designed phase-locked oscillator.

The phase noise of the poorer oscillator in Fig 46 is only −130 dBc/Hz at a 100-kHz offset. This is generally caused by deficient design of the phase-locked oscillator. Any of the above forms of degradation in the phase noise of an oscillator compromise the performance of a transmitter (and/or receiver).

EFFECTS OF OSCILLATOR PHASE NOISE

In order to understand the effects of phase noise, we have to keep some basic principles in mind. The term *communications system* used here refers to the receiver, the transmitter to which the receiver is tuned, and other nearby transmitters. The term *system* is used to convey that phase-noise effects can result from *both the receiver and transmitters*, not just the affected receiver.

Principle 1: Whenever a carrier is passed through a mixer, the phase noise of the oscillator driving that mixer is *added* to the carrier. This means that the oscillator SSB phase-noise power at a given offset frequency is added to the phase noise already present on the carrier at the same offset frequency. For instance, suppose we pass an ideal carrier (one with no phase noise) through two mixers, each driven by an oscillator with an SSB phase noise of −130 dBc/Hz at a 10-kHz offset. After passing the carrier through the first mixer, the SSB phase noise on the carrier is −130 dBc/Hz. After passing the carrier through the second mixer, the phase noise on the carrier is −127 dBc/Hz. This is the *sum* of the phase-noise *power* of the carrier and local oscillators at the 10-kHz offset frequency. (Summing two equal powers is a doubling of either power, or a 3-dB increase. −127 dBc is twice as much power as −130 dBc.) This example illustrates that *the oscillator with the worst phase-noise characteristics limits the performance of the system*. This principle holds for both transmitters and receivers.

Principle 2: *Phase noise on a transmitted signal causes effects identical to phase noise generated in a receiver*. (Of course, transmitter-generated phase noise can affect many users of the radio spectrum, while receiver-generated phase noise only affects the person using that receiver!)

Principle 3: Passing an oscillator signal through a filter *reduces* the phase noise in accordance with the filter bandwidth and attenuation characteristics. For instance, passing a carrier through a filter (centered on the carrier frequency) with a bandwidth of 20 kHz reduces the phase noise for offset frequencies greater than 10 kHz. As a result of this, transmitters and receivers have an *apparent phase noise* that is usually less than the sum of their local oscillator phase-noise levels. The *apparent* phase noise is what limits the *system* performance.

This effect must be applied with a good understanding of exactly what the filtering does. For instance, in receivers, filtering *before* a mixer determines the apparent phase noise; in transmitters, filtering *after* a mixer determines apparent phase noise. The improvement in the apparent phase-noise floor achievable with filtering depends on the power level of the signal being filtered. A normal filter at room temperature generates thermal-noise power of about −170 dBm/Hz. A 10-dBm signal passed through this filter can achieve a noise floor no lower than −160 dBc/Hz.

CLOSE-IN VERSUS FAR-OUT PHASE NOISE

The close-in and far-out phase-noise components act on a communications system in different ways. Close-in phase noise limits the performance of the system even when there is plenty of signal present. With an AM or FM signal, the close-in phase noise limits the maximum signal-to-noise ratio (SNR) that can be achieved by the system. With a frequency-shift-keyed or a phase-shift-keyed signal, the close-in phase noise limits the maximum bit error rate that the system can achieve. Both of these effects can be quantified once the communications system is defined. With an SSB voice signal, the effects are much harder to predict, but excessive phase noise does degrade SSB signal intelligibility to some extent.

The effect of close-in phase noise on FM signals is relatively easy to calculate, and makes a good case study of the effects of phase noise, because of the wide use of FM by amateurs in the VHF and UHF bands. Oscillator phase-noise limits derived from the FM case should be adequate for most other modulation modes, with the possible exception of phase-shift keyed modulation.

Phase noise on an oscillator signal has exactly the same effect as frequency modulating the oscillator with noise. In fact, given the SSB phase noise of an oscillator, it is possible to calculate the equivalent frequency deviation. This deviation is called the *incidental frequency modulation* (IFM) of the oscillator.

The phase noise in an FM communications system causes a constant noise level to appear at the receiver output, regardless of the strength of the received signal. This noise imposes a maximum SNR that the communications system can achieve.

It takes an oscillator with a very high level of close-in phase noise to degrade amateur communications systems. Most amateur communications are accomplished with marginal signal to noise ratios, and the close-in phase noise would have to be *very* strong to cause problems in such situations. Therefore, for most amateur applications, close-in phase noise is relatively unimportant.

Far-out phase noise, however, can have a significant impact on amateur communications. Its main effect is to degrade the dynamic range of a communications system. This degradation can result from phase noise in either the receiver or the transmitter. If the transmitter has excessive phase noise, transmitted signals are partly composed of broadband FM noise. The phase-noise emissions of some current amateur equipment are capable of significantly increasing the noise level on an entire amateur band! The effect of this is generally experienced only by amateurs living within a few miles of the offending transmitter, because the power level of the phase noise is quite low. A kilowatt transmitter with a high level of phase noise produces only a few microwatts in a typical amateur receiving bandwidth. As low as this may seem, however, it can be quite a problem for nearby receivers when you consider that a typical HF receiver is capable of detecting signals of less than 10^{-15} watts!

Far-out phase noise in a receiver oscillator is less destructive, because it affects only the receiver in which it is generated. The net effect, however, is the same: Any signal that reaches a mixer in the receiver is modulated by the phase noise in the local oscillator driving that mixer. As such, the signal appears to have at least as much phase noise as the local oscillator. Thus, sufficiently strong signals *off* the receiving frequency can degrade receiver sensitivity by raising the noise floor *at* the receiving frequency. Receiver dynamic range is reduced as the noise floor rises.

As an example, suppose that a transmitter has a power output of 1 kW and an SSB phase noise of -100 dBc/Hz at a given offset frequency. At that offset frequency, the transmitter radiates noise at a level of -40 dBm/Hz. In a 2-kHz bandwidth, this is equivalent to a noise level of -7 dBm, or 200 μW. This is sufficient power to cause significant interference to local receivers. *The effect on a receiver is the same as if the transmitter had low phase noise and the receiver had an SSB phase noise of -100 dBc/Hz.* Fortunately, the oscillators in most amateur equipment don't have this much SSB phase noise at offset frequen-

cies greater than a few kilohertz.

The effect of phase noise on an amateur communications system can be calculated with reasonable accuracy if a few simple assumptions are made. From the calculated effects, we can calculate the oscillator performance necessary to meet our requirements. The assumptions are:

1) The transmitter is located 1 mile from the receiver.

2) The EIRP (effective isotropic radiated power) of the transmitter is 100 W ($+50$ dBm).

3) The loss from the transmit antenna to the receive antenna is the same as in free space. (This isn't strictly true for signals propagated above ground, but it gives an approximation of the expected signal attenuation. The actual attenuation is almost impossible to calculate because of the effects of the local terrain.)

4) The receive antenna gain is 0 dBi in all directions.

5) Our goal is a phase-noise level that does not significantly degrade the performance of the communications system. That is, the received noise resulting from oscillator phase noise should be equal to or less than the background noise normally picked up by an antenna on a given amateur band. (Background noise is composed of radio emissions from our galaxy, as well as man-made noise and atmospheric noise, and varies with frequency.)

Table 1 shows the results of these calculations. The table shows values for both 14 MHz (representative of the HF bands) and 144 MHz (representative of the VHF bands). As can be seen from these calculations, the phase noise must be less than -140 dBc/Hz if there is to be no noticeable interference. A higher EIRP or less transmitter-to-receiver antenna separation would require even better phase-noise performance to guarantee no significant interference. The graph of Fig 47 shows phase-noise interference generated at

14 MHz as a function of transmitter-to-receiver antenna separation, and the apparent SSB phase noise of the system. The interference level is plotted in S units, assuming S9 is equal to 50 μV and each S unit is 6 dB. As you can see from the graph, an SSB phase noise of -120 dBc/Hz at a distance of 500 feet produces nearly an S9 signal. This graph may be applied to local situations to estimate the interference potential that could result from oscillator phase noise.

PHASE NOISE LEVELS IN AMATEUR EQUIPMENT

Equipment cost limits the extent to which we can minimize phase noise in communications systems; with this in mind, we can set rough phase-noise performance standards for equipment in various price ranges.

Curves showing recommendations for such standards appear in Fig 48. These curves represent tools for comparison of phase-noise performance in amateur equipment.

Four curves are shown: "excellent," "good," "fair" and "poor." When the phase-noise characteristics of a radio are known, they can be compared to the curves in Fig 48. The worst curve that a radio's phase-noise characteristics pass through should be considered the performance of that radio. The "excellent" curve approximates the best performance that can be expected from modern HF and VHF synthesized oscillators. For amateur equipment, this curve is approached by free-running LC and crystal oscillators, and by the very best transceivers.

The "good" curve represents what is achieved by most well-designed amateur equipment. It doesn't cost a great deal more to design a radio that meets this curve (as opposed to the "poor" or "fair" curves). A radio with phase-noise performance that only meets the "fair" curve

Table 1
Typical Maximum Tolerable Phase-Noise Levels

	14 MHz	144 MHz
EIRP	+50 dBm	+50 dBm
Loss from transmitter to receiver (distance = 1 mile)	60 dB	80 dB
Signal power at receiving antenna (0-dBi gain receiving antenna)	−10 dBm	−30 dBm
Noise power at receiving antenna (background noise)	−150 dBm/Hz	−172 dBm/Hz
Equivalent SSB phase noise	−140 dBc/Hz	−142 dBc/Hz

This table shows maximum phase-noise levels tolerable in a communications system before dynamic range is significantly degraded. In both cases, EIRP is 100 W; separation between transmitting and receiving antennas is 1 mile; the receiving antenna is omnidirectional and has 0 dBi gain; and the receiver is sensitive enough to detect the noise.

At 14 MHz, path loss and received noise power allow the receiver to detect any phase noise stronger than −140 dBc/Hz. At 144 MHz, background noise is lower and path loss is higher, resulting in a tolerable equivalent phase-noise level of −142 dBc/Hz at this frequency. See text for additional information.

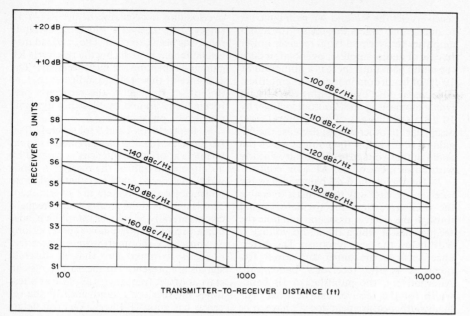

Fig 47—Phase-noise interference at 14 MHz as a function of the distance between transmitting and receiving antennas. The curves are based on a transmitter EIRP of 100 W and a receiving bandwidth of 2 kHz. The path loss from the transmit antenna to the receive antenna is assumed to follow the free-space attenuation curve. S9 is equivalent to 50 μV.

Fig 48—Phase-noise performance levels for amateur equipment. The curves from top to bottom represent poor, fair, good and excellent phase-noise performance. (See text.)

Fig 49—Block diagram of test setup for measuring the SSB phase noise of an SSB or CW receiver.

hasn't been designed with much regard for minimizing phase noise. The "poor" curve represents a design that is *so* poor that a transmitter with this performance shouldn't be used on the amateur bands because of the great amount of interference it can generate.

The close-in phase-noise characteristics shown in the curves of Fig 48 are relatively easy for most oscillators to achieve. The close-in regions of the curves were derived mainly from the effects of IFM on the limiting FM SNR. Table 2 lists the close-in phase-noise IFM integrated from 10 Hz to 10 kHz for each of these curves. (Even a radio generating the IFM level corresponding to phase noise matching the "poor" curve provides adequate voice communications capability.)

MEASURING PHASE NOISE

Equipment capable of measuring low levels of far-out phase noise is quite expensive. It is not unusual for commercial enterprises to invest $100,000 in good phase-noise measurement equipment. Inexpensive techniques are, however, available for measuring the apparent phase noise of communications receivers and transmitters. The equipment necessary to measure *receiver* phase noise can be built by enterprising amateurs for well under $100.

Measuring Receiver Phase Noise

A block diagram of a receiver phase-noise measurement setup is shown in Fig 49. The test setup consists of an oscillator, a step attenuator and an ac voltmeter. The output of the oscillator is fed through the attenuator to the receiver's RF input. The ac voltmeter is connected to the audio output of the receiver. The receiver is operated in SSB or CW mode with the AGC disabled.

The oscillator and step attenuator must be carefully constructed (well shielded, minimum necessary lead lengths and so on) for proper operation of this test setup. A simple oscillator circuit suitable for use in this application appears on page 126 of the ARRL publication *Solid State Design for the Radio Amateur*. The oscillator provides the reference signal for measuring phase noise. The phase noise of the oscillator

Table 2
Incidental Frequency Modulation

Curve	IFM
Excellent	0.4 Hz
Good	2.5 Hz
Fair	20 Hz
Poor	160 Hz

Incidental frequency modulation (IFM) resulting from the phase-noise levels shown in Fig 48. The IFM was calculated for the frequency range from 10 Hz to 10 kHz.

must be less than that of the receiver if we are to measure receiver phase noise accurately. The oscillator should have a power output of at least +10 dBm (10 mW) into 50 Ω. Less power than this may limit the accuracy of the measurement setup at low phase-noise levels. The oscillator should be constructed in a metal box and powered by an internal 9-V battery to minimize unwanted signal leakage.

The step attenuator must have a maximum attenuation of at least 140 dB. Preferably, it should be adjustable in 1-dB steps. It is difficult to design a single attenuator circuit that provides this much attenuation, so a step attenuator with a maximum of 60 or 70 dB of attenuation should be used in series with fixed attenuators to obtain the maximum value. A design for a suitable step attenuator is given in the Test Equipment and Measurements chapter. Each of the fixed attenuators can be constructed in a shielded enclosure using standard Pi or T resistor configurations to achieve the desired attenuation. Use BNC connectors on the oscillator and step attenuator; they have better shielding properties than UHF connectors. Commercial step attenuators and in-line coaxial attenuators are sometimes available on the surplus market. If you choose to build attenuators, use 5% (or better) precision resistors. The accuracy of the phase-noise measurements depend to a great extent on the accuracy of the attenuators.

The ac voltmeter is used to measure the audio output level from the receiver. The voltmeter should measure true RMS voltage, but commonly available peak-reading ac voltmeters are adequate for this application.

Phase-noise measurements are done on the band for which the oscillator is built. Measurements should be made in each amateur band, since phase-noise levels of many receivers vary from one amateur band to another. Briefly, the measurement procedure is as follows: A reference audio output level is established by tuning the receiver to the oscillator frequency and measuring the audio output voltage. The receiver is then tuned above (or below) the oscillator frequency in increments of the desired offset frequency. The attenuation is then decreased until the noise voltage at the audio output is the same as the reference level. The difference in the two attenuator settings is then corrected for the receiver bandwidth to give the SSB phase noise at that offset frequency. The process is then repeated for several different offset frequencies. The step-by-step measurement procedure follows.

Step-By-Step Measurement Procedure

1) Connect the test equipment as shown in Fig 49. Set the step attenuator to its maximum attenuation. Switch the oscillator out of the line. Set the receiver for SSB or CW reception with the AGC disabled. Preamplifiers or input attenuators in the receiver should be disabled, if possible. Use the narrowest IF bandwidth available in the

receiver. Set the RF and AF gain controls to maximum, unless this causes the audio amplifier to overload from receiver noise. In case of audio-amplifier overload, reduce the audio gain until there is a minimum of 10 dB of headroom in the audio amplifier. This can be done by decreasing the AF gain (while monitoring audio output voltage) by 10 dB after all signs of gain compression disappear. In other words, decrease the AF gain to 10 dB below the point at which the audio output voltage begins to vary linearly with adjustment of the AF gain control.

2) Determine the 6-dB bandwidth of the receiver. An easy way to do this is to enable the oscillator, tune the oscillator signal through the receiver passband and note the frequencies at which the audio voltage is 6 dB below the peak response. The difference between the upper and lower frequencies is the receiver's bandwidth. Alternatively, the published 6-dB bandwidth for the receiver can be used. The bandwidth measurement doesn't have to be very accurate—a 25% error in the bandwidth factor affects the phase-noise measurement by only 1 dB. Record the receiver bandwidth (Δf).

3) Switch the oscillator into the line. Center the oscillator signal in the receiver passband. Switch the oscillator out of the line and measure and record the audio output voltage. Switch the oscillator into the line again, and adjust the step attenuator until the audio voltage increases by 41% (3 dB) from the no-signal value. The signal is now at the receiver's MDS (minimum discernible signal) level. This setting is a compromise: A higher setting allows more precise measurement of the audio output voltage; a lower setting decreases the possibility of overloading the receiver front end. Record the frequency to which the receiver is tuned (fo), the setting of the step attenuator (A_0), and the audio output voltage (V_0).

4) Measure the phase noise by first tuning the receiver to the desired offset frequency, given by fo + f, where f is the offset frequency. Then, adjust the attenuator until the audio output voltage is as close as possible to (V_0). Record the total attenuation (A_1) and the audio voltage (V_1). The SSB phase noise at this offset frequency is found by

$$L(f) = A_1 - A_0 - 10 \log (\Delta f)$$

where

$$L(f) = \text{SSB phase noise in dBc/Hz}$$

5) Determine if the receiver is overloaded at this offset frequency as follows: Decrease the attenuation by 3 dB. Note the audio voltage at the new attenuator setting (V_2). The audio output voltage of the receiver should increase by approximately 22% (1.7 dB) from V_1. If it increases by less than 18% (1.4 dB), it is likely that some stage in the receiver is overloaded, and the SSB phase-noise measurement is inaccurate. If the overload is in the audio stages, it can be eliminated by decreasing the audio gain and repeating the measurements. If the

overloading is occurring in the RF or IF stages, the receiver's blocking dynamic range has been exceeded. The overload may be eliminated by reducing the receiver's RF gain and repeating the measurements. The existence of this problem indicates that, at this offset frequency, the receiver's performance is limited by blocking dynamic range, not phase noise.

6) Repeat steps 4 and 5 for several offset frequencies. Ideally, measurements should be made at offset frequencies separated by no more than half of the receiver's bandwidth, in order to make sure that no discrete phase-noise components are overlooked. This is tedious at the greater offset frequencies. Generally, a coarser sampling is adequate to plot the phase-noise curve, as long as you check the intermediate offset frequencies to make sure that no discrete signals are present. The measurements can start at offset frequencies as close as a few times the receiver's bandwidth, if the receiver has good IF filters. You can determine if the offset is too small by disconnecting the audio voltmeter from the receiver and listening to the audio. If you can hear the carrier signal at all, the offset is too small. All that should be present is noise if the measurement is to be accurate. Increase the offset until no trace of carrier remains in the audio to be sure of the measurement.

The technique outlined in the steps above is quite accurate. SSB phase-noise levels of less than −160 dBc/Hz can be measured on a receiver that has good sensitivity and a high gain-compression point (good dynamic range), as determined in step 5. It is difficult to construct an oscillator that has a noise floor much below this level, and, as mentioned earlier, the oscillator phase-noise level limits the accuracy of the measurement setup.

This measurement technique has advantages and disadvantages. One of its major advantages is that it measures the *apparent* phase noise of the receiver. Apparent phase noise includes the effects of filters; it is the phase noise that actually limits a receiver's dynamic range.

One disadvantage of this measurement technique is that it doesn't allow *direct* measurement of the phase noise of an oscillator. Therefore, it can't be used to directly measure the phase noise of a transmitter. This limitation can be overcome by using a receiver with known phase-noise characteristics to measure the phase noise of a transmitter. The transmitter is substituted for the oscillator in the test setup, and its output is attenuated to the power level of the oscillator. As long as the transmitter phase noise is greater than that of the receiver, measurements of the transmitter's phase noise will be accurate.

Another disadvantage is that, at some offset frequencies, the receiver's dynamic range may make phase-noise measurement impossible. Precision in this measurement technique requires that the oscillator output be variable from a very low level to a very high level, in small, precise steps.

Fig 50—Measured SSB phase noise of an ICOM IC-745 transceiver (serial number 01528).

Table 3

SSB Phase Noise of ICOM IC-745 Receiver Section

Oscillator output power = −3 dBm (0.5 mW)
Receiver bandwidth (Δf) = 1.8 kHz
Audio noise voltage = 0.070 V
Audio reference voltage (V_0) = 0.105 V
Reference attenuation (A_0) = 121 dB

Offset Frequency (kHz)	Attenuation (A_1) (dB)	Audio V_1 (volts)	Audio V_2 (volts)	Ratio V_2/V_1	SSB Phase Noise (dBc/Hz)
4	35	0.102	0.122	1.20	−119
5	32	0.104	0.120	1.15	−122*
6	30	0.104	0.118	1.13	−124*
8	27	0.100	0.116	1.16	−127*
10	25	0.106	0.122	1.15	−129*
15	21	0.100	0.116	1.16	−133*
20	17	0.102	0.120	1.18	−137
25	14	0.102	0.122	1.20	−140
30	13	0.102	0.122	1.20	−141
40	10	0.104	0.124	1.19	−144
50	8	0.102	0.122	1.20	−146
60	6	0.104	0.124	1.19	−148
80	4	0.102	0.126	1.24	−150
100	3	0.102	0.126	1.24	−151
150	3	0.102	0.124	1.22	−151
200	0	0.104			−154
250	0	0.100			−154
300	0	0.098			< −154
400	0	0.096			< −154
500	0	0.096			< −154
600	0	0.097			< −154
800	0	0.096			< −154
1000	0	0.096			< −154

Asterisks indicate measurements possibly affected by receiver overload (see text).

Table 3 and Fig 50 show phase-noise characteristics measured in the receiver section of an ICOM IC-745 transceiver using this method. Table 3 includes the attenuation and voltage values to show their relationships to phase-noise levels in the IC-745 over this range of offset frequencies. The data obtained from the ratio of V_2 to V_1 indicates that the receiver was probably overloaded at offset frequencies from 5 kHz to 15 kHz. This measurement was limited to an SSB phase-noise floor of −154 dBc/Hz because of the low power-output level of the oscillator. Fig 50 is based on the far-out phase noise data obtained from Table 3, as well as the close-in phase noise measured using laboratory test equipment and the same IC-745. The data obtained using the method described earlier and that obtained from the laboratory test equipment closely track each other. The phase-noise performance of this transceiver generally exceeds that indicated by the "good" curve in Fig 48.

TRANSMITTER PHASE-NOISE MEASUREMENT IN THE ARRL LAB

The system used to measure transmitter phase noise in the ARRL Lab essentially consists of a direct-conversion receiver with very good phase-noise characteristics. As shown in Fig 51, an attenuator is used after the transmitter, a Mini-Circuits ZAY-1 mixer, a Hewlett-Packard 8640B signal generator, a bandpass filter and an audio-frequency spectrum analyzer (HP 8556A/8552B) to make the measurements. The transmitter signal is mixed with the output of the signal generator, and signals produced in the mixing process that are not required for the measurement process are filtered out. The spectrum analyzer then displays the transmitted phase-noise spectrum. The 100 mW output of the HP 8640B is barely enough to drive the mixer—the setup would work better with 200 or even 400 mW of drive. To test the phase noise of an HP 8640B, we use a second '8640B as a reference source. It is quite important to be sure that the phase noise of the reference source is lower than that of the signal under test, because what is actually being

Fig 51—ARRL transmitter phase-noise measurement setup.

measured is the combined phase-noise output of the signal generator and the transmitter. It would be quite embarrassing to publish phase-noise plots of the reference generator instead of the transmitter under test! The HP 8640B has much cleaner spectral output than most transmitters.

Fig 52 shows a phase noise photograph for ICOM 745 serial number 03101. This

photograph was taken directly from the spectrum-analyzer display, using the test setup shown in Fig 51. The photo does not necessarily reflect the phase-noise characteristics of all ICOM 745 transceivers.

The carrier is not shown in the photograph because it is nulled by heterodyning and bandpass filtering. The log reference level (the top horizontal line on the scale

Fig 52—ICOM IC-745 (serial number 03101) phase-noise characteristics. Measurement frequency: 3.5 MHz, power output: 100 W.

in the photos) represents −60 dBc/Hz. It is common in industry to use a 0-dBc log reference, but such a reference level would not allow measurement of phase-noise levels below −80 dBc/Hz. The actual measurement bandwidth used on the spectrum analyzer is 100 Hz, but the reference is scaled for a 1-Hz bandwidth. This allows phase-noise levels to be read directly from the display in dBc/Hz. Because each vertical division represents 10 dB, the photos show the noise level between −60 dBc and −140 dBc. The horizontal scale is 2 kHz per division.

What do the Phase-Noise Pictures Mean?

Although they are useful for comparing different radios, phase-noise photographs can also be used to calculate the amount of interference you may receive from a nearby transmitter with known phase-noise characteristics. An approximation is given by

Interfering signal level = NL + 10 × log BW

where

Interfering signal level is in dBc
NL is the noise level on the receiving frequency
BW is receiver IF bandwidth in Hz

For instance, if the noise level is −90 dBc and you are using a 2.5-kHz SSB filter, the interfering signal will be −56 dBc. In other words, if the transmitted signal is 20 dB over S9, and each S unit is 6 dB, the interfering signal will be as strong as an S3 signal.

The measurements made in the ARRL Lab apply only to transmitted signals. It is reasonable to assume that the phase-noise characteristics of most transceivers are similar on transmit and receive, because the same oscillators are generally used in the local-oscillator (LO) chain.

In some cases, the receiver may have better phase-noise characteristics than the transmitter. Why the possible difference? The most obvious reason is that circuits often perform less than optimally in strong RF fields, as anyone who has experienced RFI problems can tell you. A less-obvious reason results from the way that many high dynamic-range receivers work. To get good dynamic range, a sharp crystal filter is often placed immediately after the first mixer in the receive line. This filter removes all but a small slice of spectrum for further signal processing. If the desired filtered signal is a product of mixing an incoming signal with a noisy oscillator, signals far away from the desired one can end up in this slice. Once this slice of spectrum is obtained, however, unwanted signals cannot be reintroduced, no matter how noisy the oscillators used in further signal processing. As a result, some oscillators in receivers don't affect phase noise.

The difference between this situation and that in transmitters is that crystal filters are seldom used for reduction of phase noise in transmitting because of the high cost involved. Equipment designers have enough trouble getting smooth, click-free break-in operation in transceivers without having to worry about switching crystal filters in and out of circuits at 40-WPM keying speeds!

CONCLUSION

Close-in phase noise generally has little effect on the performance of amateur communications systems. However, far-out phase noise *can* significantly reduce the dynamic range of a receiver. Far-out phase-noise performance has effects just as critical as blocking dynamic range and two-tone dynamic range performance of receivers. Ideally, these measurements should be made for a range of offset frequencies. Far-out phase noise in receivers can be measured with relatively inexpensive test equipment, as long as care is taken to perform the measurements properly.

Chapter 11

Radio Transmitting Principles

Even though some modern transmitters and transceivers contain only solid-state devices, it is still practical to use a hybrid circuit that contains a mixture of tubes and active semiconductor stages. Typically, the unit has transistors, diodes and ICs up to the driver stage of the transmitter. At that point one will find a tube driver used to supply RF power to a vacuum-tube amplifier. The amplifier might consist of a pair of 6146Bs.

The principal advantage of tube amplifiers is that they are somewhat less subject to damage from excessive drive levels and mismatched loads. However, a properly designed solid-state driver and PA section should be immune to output mismatch damage, provided an SWR-protection circuit has been included in the transmitter. A solid-state amplifier is slightly more difficult to design and have work correctly than is a tube amplifier of equivalent power. This is because purity of emissions is harder to achieve when transistor power stages are employed. Transistors generate considerably more harmonic energy than tubes do, and are prone to self-oscillation at LF, VLF and audio frequencies unless some careful design work is done. This is not generally true of tube amplifiers.

If one is to ignore these problems and concentrate mainly on cost and convenience, transistors may have the edge over tubes. A 13.6-volt design can be operated directly from an automotive or solar-electric supply, whereas a tube amplifier requires a high-voltage power supply for mobile, portable and fixed-station use. When an ac power source is required, the cost of a high-voltage, medium-current supply for tubes versus a low-voltage, high-current power source for transistors is similar, provided new components are used in both. At power-output levels in excess of approximately 150 watts, the transistor-amplifier power supply becomes rather expensive because of complex regulator-

circuit requirements. This is why most amateurs use vacuum tubes in high-power HF and VHF amplifiers. The number of power transistors required (plus combiners) to generate a l-kW signal may run considerably higher in cost than a tube or tubes for an amplifier of equivalent power. The price of large heat sinks versus a cooling fan may place the solid-state amplifier in a prohibitive price class also.

The decision to buy or build a transmitter is founded on some basic considerations: cost compared to features; professional appearance contrasted to that of homemade equipment; the knowledge and satisfaction gained from building equipment, as weighed against buying commercially made gear and simply becoming an operator. The judgment must fit the amateur's objectives and affluence. Home-built transmitters are usually easier to service than commercial ones because the builder knows the circuit layout and how each stage functions. Futhermore, the cost of maintenance is markedly lower for homemade equipment than for most factory-built gear. But the greatest significance to home-built circuits is the knowledge gained from constructing a project and the pride that goes with using it on the air!

Not all parts of a transmitter are covered in depth in this chapter. A discussion of frequency-generating circuits is found in Chapter 10. For information on RF power amplifiers, see Chapter 15.

Above 50 MHz

The frequencies above 50 MHz were once a world apart from the rest of Amateur Radio — in equipment required, in modes of operation and in results obtained. Today these worlds blend increasingly.

The almost universal use of SSB for voice work in the HF range has had a major impact on equipment design for the VHF and even UHF bands. Many amateurs have

a considerable investment in HF sideband gear. This equipment provides accurate frequency calibration and good mechanical and electrical stability. It is effective in CW as well as SSB communication. These qualities are attractive to VHF operators, so it is natural for them to look for ways to use HF gear on frequencies above 50 MHz.

Use of VHF accessory devices, both ready made and homebuilt, is increasing. This started years ago with the VHF receiving converter. Similar conversion equipment for transmitting has been widely used since SSB has been on the HF bands. Today the HF trend is to one-package stations, transceivers. The obvious move for many VHF operators is a companion box to perform both transmitting and receiving conversion functions. Known as transverters, these are offered by several manufacturers. They are also relatively simple to build, and are thus attractive projects for the home-builder of VHF gear.

CW, SSB and FM are the predominant modes on the VHF bands. Each method of communication has certain transmitter requirements. In general equipment used for FM is of the oscillator-multiplier type. The multiplier stages are needed to realize the desired deviation.

Because SSB cannot be passed satisfactorily through a frequency-multiplication stage, generation of VHF SSB signals requires the use of one or more mixer stages. VHF CW may be generated either by mixing or by frequency multiplying. Recently, manufacturers of amateur FM transceivers have been using a combination of both approaches. In the multimode VHF transceiver, which offers the operator a choice of CW, SSB, FM and often AM, we find both approaches to signal generation.

Transmitter Basics

The most basic type of transmitter is one that contains a single stage, is crystal con-

Fig. 1 — A transistor oscillator is shown at A. The example at B illustrates a type of crystal oscillator.

Fig. 2 — Circuit example of a simple, solid-state CW transmitter.

trolled, and is designed for CW operation. A circuit example is given in Fig. 1. This kind of transmitter is not especially suitable for use on the air because it is inefficient and is prone to generating a chirpy CW signal unless loaded lightly. But the same circuit is entirely acceptable when followed by an isolating stage (buffer-amplifier) as shown in Fig. 2. The second stage not only builds up the power level, but also gives the oscillator a relatively constant load to look into. The constant load helps to prevent oscillator pulling and attendant chirping of the CW note.

Fig. 3 illustrates the basic types of transmitters for CW and RTTY work. The drawing at A represents the general circuit given in Fig. 2. Illustration B is an expansion of that circuit and inclues a frequency multiplier. A heterodyne type of generator, which is currently popular for multiband transmitters and tranceivers, is shown as the exciter section of a transmitter in drawing C. A frequency synthesizer is shown as the RF generator at D.

For operation on AM, any of the lineups given in Fig. 3 is suitable, provided a modulator is added. It is used to modulate the operating voltage to the PA stage, or in some designs the operating voltage to the PA and the stage immediately before it.

The block diagram of Fig. 4 outlines the functional stages of an SSB transmitter. Zl can be a simple VFO, a heterodyne generator (Fig. 3C) or a frequency synthesizer. The essential difference between this type of transmitter and one that would be used for CW/RTTY is that the RF amplifiers must operate in Class A, AB or B (linear), rather than in Class C, which is suitable for CW work. However, linear amplifiers are entirely satisfactory for any transmission mode at a sacrifice in efficiency. Once the SSB signal is generated it cannot be passed through a frequency multiplier. All post-filter stages must operate straight through. Class C amplifiers are generally used in FM transmitters as well as in CW and RTTY transmitters.

Fig. 5 illustrates two approaches to VHF FM transmitters. Shown at A is a transmitter that uses phase modulation, also known as indirect FM. Multiplier stages bring the signal to the operating frequency and increase the deviation to the desired range. A frequency-synthesized direct FM transmitter is shown at B. Fewer multiplier stages are required for this method because greater deviation can be realized at the modulator. Audio is amplitude limited and the frequency response is shaped before modulation in both transmitters.

Crystal Switching

Although several crystals for a single oscillator can be selected by mechanical means, a switch must be contained in the RF path. This can impose severe restrictions on the equipment layout. Furthermore, mechanical switches normally require that they be operated from the front panel of the transmitter or receiver. That type of format complicates the remote operation of such a unit. Also, the switch leads can introduce unwanted reactances in the crystal circuit. A better technique is illustrated in Fig. 6, where D1 and D2 — high-speed silicon switching diodes — are used to select one of two or more crystals from some remote point. As operating voltage is applied to one of the diodes by means of S1, it is forward biased into "hard" conduction, thereby completing the circuit between the crystal trimmer and ground. Some schemes actually call for reverse-biasing the unused diode or diodes when they are not activated. This ensures almost complete cutoff, which may not be easy to obtain in the circuit shown because of the existing RF voltage on the anodes of D1 and D2.

VARIABLE-FREQUENCY OSCILLATORS

The theory and general application of variable-frequency oscillators is treated in Chapter 10. The circuit principles are the same regardless of the VFO application.

Some additional considerations pertain to the use of VFOs in transmitters as compared to a VFO in a receiver. Generally, heating of the interior of a transmitter cabinet is greater than in a receiver. This is because considerably more power is being dissipated in the transmitter. Therefore, greater care must be given to oscillator long-term stability. Temperature-compensating capacitors are often needed in the frequency-determining portion of the oscillator to level off the long-term stability factor. Some oscillators are designed for use with a temperature-control oven for the purpose of maintaining a relatively constant ambient temperature in the oscillator compartment — even while the equipment is otherwise turned off. Another design

Fig. 3 — Block diagrams of various transmitters that use specific frequency-generation methods.

Fig. 4 — Block diagram of a heterodyne type of SSB transmitter.

Fig. 5 — Block diagrams of indirect (A) and direct (B) FM VHF transmitters.

Fig. 6 — A method for selecting one of two (or several) crystals by means of diode switching. D1 and D2 are the switches.

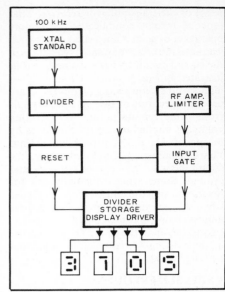

Fig. 7 — Frequency counter block diagram.

matter related to a transmitter-contained VFO is RF shielding of the oscillator and the attendant low-level buffer-isolation stages that follow it. Fairly high levels of stray RF can be present in a transmitter and some of that energy may migrate to the oscillator section by means of stray radiation or conduction along wiring leads or circuit-board elements. Thus, it is important to provide as much physical and electrical isolation as possible. The VFO should be housed in a rigid metal box. All dc leads entering the enclosure require RF-decoupling networks that are effective at all frequencies involved in the transmitter design. The VFO box needs to be fastened securely to the metal chassis on which it rests to ensure good electrical contact. Excessive stray RF entering the VFO circuitry can cause severe instability and erratic oscillator operation.

VFO Dials

One of the tasks facing an amateur builder is the difficulty of finding a suitable dial and drive assembly for a VFO. A dial should provide a sufficiently slow rate of tuning — 10 to 25 kHz per knob revolution is considered optimum — without backlash. Planetary drives are popular because of their low cost; however, they often develop objectional backlash after a short period of use. Several types of two-speed drives are available. They are well suited to home-made amateur equipment. The Eddystone 898 precision dial has long been a favorite with amateurs, although the need to elevate the VFO far above the chassis introduces some mechanical stability problems. If a permeability-tuned oscillator (PTO) is used, one of the many types of turn counters made for vacuum variable capacitors or rotary inductors may be employed.

Linear Readout

If a linear-dial frequency readout is

desired, the variable capacitor must be only a small portion of the total capacitance in the oscillator tank. Capacitors tend to be very nonlinear near the ends of rotation. A gear drive providing a 1.5:1 reduction should be employed so that only the center of the capacitor range is used. Then, as a final adjustment, the plates of the capacitor must be filed until linear readout is achieved. In a PTO, the pitch of the oscillator coil winding may be varied so that a linear frequency change results from the travel of the tuning slug. A different approach is to use a variable-capacitance diode (Varicap) as the VFO tuning element. A meter that reads the voltage applied to the Varicap is calibrated to indicate the VFO frequency.

Electronic Dials

An electronic dial consists of a simplified frequency counter that reads either the VFO or operating frequency of a transmitter or receiver. The advantage of an electronic dial is the excellent accuracy (to 1 hertz, if desired) and the fact that VFO tuning does not have to be linear. The readout section of the dial may use neon-glow tubes called Nixies® or a seven-segment display using incandescent lamps, filament wires in a vacuum tube, LCDs (liquid crystal display), LEDs (light-emitting diodes) or fluorescent displays. The use of MSI and LSI circuits, some containing as many as 200 transistors on a single chip, reduces the size required for an electronic dial to a few square inches of circuit-board space.

A typical counter circuit is given in Fig. 7. The accuracy of the counter is determined by a crystal standard, often referred to as a clock. The output from a 100-kHz calibration oscillator, the type often used in receivers and transceivers, may be employed if an accuracy of 100 Hz is sufficient. For readout down to 1 Hz, a 1- to 10-MHz AT-cut crystal should be chosen,

because this type of high-accuracy crystal exhibits the best temperature stability. The clock output energy is divided in decade-counter ICs to provide the pulse that opens the input gate of the counter for a preset time.

The number of RF cycles that pass through the gate while it is open are counted and stored. Storage is used so the readout does not blink. At the end of each counting cycle, the stored information activates the display LEDs, which present the numbers counted until another count cycle is complete. A complete electronic dial arranged to be combined with an existing transmitter or receiver was described in October 1970 *QST*. Also, Macleish et al. reported an adapter that allows a commercially made frequency counter to be mated with ham gear so the counter performs as an electronic dial (May 1971 *QST*).

Frequency Multiplication

If it is necessary to use frequency multipliers at some point after the VFO or other frequency generator in a transmitter, the circuits of Fig. 8 can be applied. Of course, vacuum-tube multipliers are entirely suitable if the design is not one that uses semiconductors. The fundamental principles for frequency multiplication are applicable to tubes and transistors alike. The requirement is to operate the devices in Class C. Although a transistor circuit may be operated with forward bias applied to a frequency multiplier, the stage must be driven hard enough to override the bias and operate Class C. Forward bias is sometimes used in a multiplier stage (solid state) to lower the excitation requirements. Negative voltage (reverse bias) is often used on the grid of a vacuum-tube multiplier, but forward bias is not.

The circuit of Fig. 8A is probably the least suitable for frequency multiplication. Typically, the efficiency of a doubler of this type is 50 percent, a tripler is 33 percent and a quadrupler is 25 percent. Additionally, harmonics other than the one to which the output tank is tuned will appear in the output unless effective band-pass filtering is applied. The collector tap on L1 of Fig. 8A is placed at a point that offers a reasonable compromise between power output and spectral purity. The lower the tap with respect to V_{cc}, the lighter the collector loading on L1 and the greater the filtering action of the tuned circuit. The trade-off is, however, a reduction in output power as the mismatch of the collector to the load increases.

A push-push doubler is shown at Fig. 8B. Because of the conduction angle of this type of circuit the efficiency is similar to that of a straight amplifier operating in Class C. Also, the driving frequency (f) will be well attenuated at the doubler output if electrical balance and component symmetry are ensured. A 12AU7A tube will work nicely in this type of circuit well into the VHF region. T1 in this example is a trifilar-wound, broad-band toroidal transformer. It drives the gates of Q1 and Q2 in push-pull (opposite phase). The drains are in parallel and are tuned to 2f. R1 is used to establish electrical balance between Q1 and Q2. R1 is set while the doubler is being fully driven. Diode doublers can be used in a similar circuit; see Chapter 4.

A push-pull tripler is illustrated in Fig. 8C. The matter of electrical balance and symmetry is important to proper operation. The circuit discriminates against even harmonics, aiding spectral purity. The efficiency is somewhat better than a tripler using the circuit of Fig. 8A. If vacuum tubes are used in the circuits of Fig. 8, the input ports should employ high-impedance tuned circuits for best performance.

The Oscillator-Multiplier VHF Transmitter

This type of transmitter, which may be used for FM or CW, generally starts with a crystal oscillator operating in the HF range, followed by one or more frequency-multiplier stages and at least one amplifier stage. While relatively simple to construct, such transmitters can cause much grief unless the builder takes precautions to prevent undesired multiples of the oscillator and the multiplier stages from being radiated. For frequencies below 450 MHz the transmitting mixer is not difficult to construct and is recommended for most applications. Spurious-signal radiation is much easier to prevent with the mixer, although it does not lend itself to compact FM equipment design. For operation on the amateur UHF bands, the oscillator-multiplier approach offers definite advantages. Fig. 9 shows how the harmonics of a 144-MHz signal may be multiplied to permit operation on amateur UHF and microwave bands. Stability at 144 MHz is easy to realize with current technology, making stable microwave signals simple to generate. Varactor diodes are used as

frequency-multiplying devices. They are installed in resonant cavities. Operation will probably be crystal controlled, as even the best transceiver/transverter combination used to generate the 144-MHz signal may create problems when the output is multiplied in frequency 40 times! A frequency synthesizer with a stable reference oscillator may be used to generate the 144-MHz signal, but its output should be well filtered to eliminate noise.

Fig. 8 — Single-ended multiplier (A), push-push doubler (B) and push-pull tripler (C).

Fig. 9 — Multiplier scheme for generating RF on weak-signal communication frequencies at UHF and above. All frequencies are in megahertz. An 1152-MHz LO can be used to drive microwave multiplier circuits or serve as an LO for a 1296-MHz transverter with a 144-MHz IF.

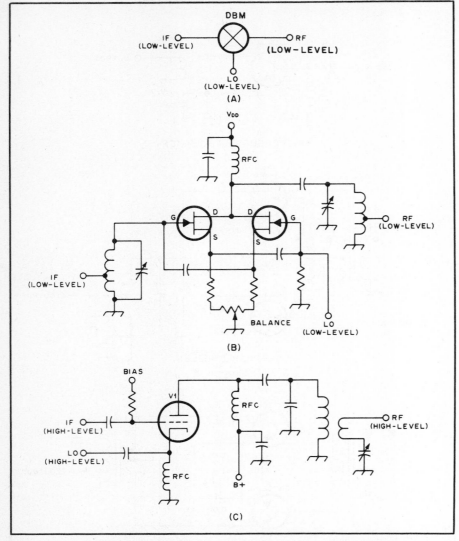

Fig. 10 — A trio of commonly used VHF transmitting mixers. At A, perhaps the simplest, a commercially available diode doubly balanced mixer. RF output is low, requiring the use of several stages of amplification to reach a useful level. At B, a singly balanced mixer using FETs. Adjustment of this circuit is critical to prevent the local-oscillator signal from leaking through. A mixer of this type can supply slightly more output than a diode mixer (3 dBm, as opposed to 1 dBm for the mixer shown at A). At C, a high-level mixer using a vacuum-tube triode is shown. In this case, V1 might be a type 2C39 or 7289 tube. With the correct circuit constants this mixer could provide an SSB output of 15 watts on 1296 MHz. Power input would be about 100 watts! In addition, 10 watts of LO and 5 watts of IF drive would be needed. Despite these requirements, such a circuit provides a relatively low-cost means of generating high-level microwave SSB. Spurious outputs at the LO and image frequencies will be quite strong. To attenuate them, a strip-line or cavity filter should be used at the mixer output.

Although spurious outputs of the various multiplier stages may not cause harmful interference, that is no excuse for not removing them. In most cases, the Q of successive cavities will suffice. A band-pass filter may be used to filter the final multiplier stage.

Transmitting Mixers

With the possible exception of the power levels involved, there is no reason to consider transmitting mixers differently than their receiving counterparts. One thing to keep in mind is that many deficiencies in the transmitter mixer will show up on the air. Receiver mixer troubles are *your* problem. Transmitter mixer troubles become everyone's problem!

A trio of popular types of transmitting mixers is shown is Fig. 10. The doubly balanced diode mixer at A may be built using discrete components or the phase relationship between ports may be established using etched-circuit strip lines. Miniature DBMs are available at low cost from several manufacturers. They offer an almost foolproof method of generating VHF SSB. Another popular mixer uses a pair of FETs in a singly balanced configuration. If care is taken in construction and adjustment, local-oscillator rejection will be adequate with this circuit. To be safe, a series-tuned trap, designed to attenuate the LO leakage even further,

should follow this stage. A typical FET balanced mixer is shown in Fig. 10B.

Finally, we see a typical vacuum-tube mixer (Fig. 10C). Because it can handle more power, the tube mixer has endured at VHF. Its higher output, when compared to most solid-state mixers, reduces the number of subsequent amplifier stages needed to reach a specific power level. This is the only advantage of using them as mixers, at least on the lower VHF bands.

High-Level Transmitting Mixers

When you are designing a transmitting converter for VHF, the trade-offs between the advantages of mixing at a low power level, such as in a diode-ring mixer, and using several stages of linear amplification must be weighed against the cost of amplifying devices. On 432 MHz and above, it may be desirable to mix the IF and local-oscillator signals at a fairly high level. This method makes it unnecessary to use costly linear devices to reach the same power level. High-level mixing results in a slightly distorted signal, so it should be used only when essential.

Fig. 11 gives the schematic diagram of a typical 432-MHz high-level mixer. V1 is the final amplifier tube of a retired commercial 450-MHz FM transmitter. The oscillator and multiplier stages now produce local-oscillator injection voltage, which is applied to the grid as before. The major change is in the cathode circuit. Instead of being directly at ground, a parallel LC circuit is inserted and tuned to the IF. In this case 10-meters was chosen. With the exception of 144 MHz, any amateur band could serve as the IF. A 144-MHz IF is unsuitable because the third harmonic would appear at the output, where it would combine with the desired signal. For that reason, some additional output filtering is needed with this circuit. The original crystal in the transmitter is replaced with one yielding an output at the desired local-oscillator frequency, then the intermediate stages are retuned.

One disadvantage of the high-level mixer is the relatively large amount of local-oscillator injection required. In many cases it is simpler to mix at a lower level and use linear amplifiers than to construct the local-oscillator chain. On the higher bands, it may be feasible to generate local-oscillator energy at a lower frequency and use a passive varactor mixer to reach the injection frequency. In this case the previous statements about diode-multiplier spurious outputs apply. If the local-oscillator injection is impure, the mixer output will be also. For further information on mixers see Chapters 4 and 12 of this publication and *Solid State Design for the Radio Amateur*, an ARRL publication.

Output Filtering

Output purity from oscillators, multipliers and amplifiers is of paramount importance to the performance of numerous circuits. In the interest of compliance with current FCC regulations, wherein all spurious emissions from a transmitter must be 40 dB or greater below the peak power of the desired signal at HF and 60 dB or greater between 30 and 225 MHz, filtering is important. The type of filter used — band-pass, notch, low-pass or high-pass — will depend on the application. Band-pass filters afford protection against spurious responses above and below the amateur band for which they have been designed. Low-pass filters attenuate energy above the desired output frequency, while high-pass filters reduce energy below the band of interest.

It is common practice to include a harmonic filter at the output of a VFO chain to ensure purity of the driving voltage to a mixer or amplifier stage. The filter bandwidth must be adequate for the tuning range of the VFO in order to prevent attenuation of the output energy within the desired band. For this reason, some designers prefer to use a low-pass type of filter instead of a band-pass one.

The Electrical Fundamentals chapter includes detailed information about designing suitable filters. Tables of component values allow you to select a particular design or scale the values for different frequencies and impedance ranges.

Driver Stages

The choice between tubes and transistors in low-level amplifier and driver stages will depend on the nature of the composite transmitter. Some designs contain a mixture (hybrid) of tubes and semiconductors, while other circuits have no vacuum tubes at all. If tubes are used in a hybrid circuit, they are generally restricted to the driver and PA sections of the transmitter.

There is no reason why tubes should be used in preference to power transistors for output powers up to say, 150 watts, despite the prevailing myth that tubes are more rugged, operate more stably and produce less spurious output. It is true that transistors are less tolerant than tubes to SWR levels in excess of 2:1, but a correctly designed transistor amplifier can be operated safely if SWR-protection circuitry is included. Furthermore, spectral purity can be just as good from a solid-state amplifier as it is from a vacuum-tube amplifier. A harmonic filter normally follows a solid-state power stage, whereas this measure may not be required when tubes are used. Amplifier IMD (third- and fifth-order products) in solid-state power stages which operate linearly is fully as acceptable as that observed in most tube types of linear amplifiers. Typically, if a design is correct, the IMD will be on the order of −33 dB from the reference power value.

The major area of concern when designing a solid-state driver or PA section is to prevent low-frequency self-oscillations. Such parasitics tend to modulate the carrier and appear as spurious responses within the

Fig. 11 — Partial schematic diagram of a 70-cm (432-MHz) mixer, built from a converted FM transmitter. The original oscillator-multiplier-driver stages of the unit now provide LO injection. A stripline filter should be used at the output of the mixer to prevent radiation of spurious products.

amplifier passband. The low-frequency parasitics occur as a result of the extremely high gain exhibited by HF and VHF transistors at the low-frequency end of the spectrum. The theoretical gain increase for a given transistor is 6 dB per octave as the operating frequency is lowered. The same is not true of vacuum tubes. Therefore, it is necessary to employ quality decoupling and bypassing in the circuit. It is similarly important to use low-Q, low-inductance RF chokes and matching networks to discourage low-frequency tuned-base, tuned-collector oscillations. The suppression concepts just discussed are illustrated in Fig 12 at B and C. In the circuit at B there are two 950-mu ferrite beads added over the pigtail of RFC1 to swamp the Q of the choke. Three bypass capacitors (0.001, 0.01 and 0.1 μF) are used with RFC2 of Fig 12B to provide effective RF decoupling from VHF to MF. A 22-μF capacitor is used near RFC2 to bypass the +V_cc line at low frequency and audio. This method is recommended for each high-gain solid-state stage in a transmitter.

Driver Circuits

The circuits of Fig 12A and 12B are typical of those that would be employed to excite a tube-type PA stage. The 6GK6 tube driver at A can be biased for Class C or Class AB operation, making it suitable for CW or SSB service. Of course, the AB mode would be suitable for CW and SSB,

and would require considerably less excitation power than would the same stage operating in Class C. Other tubes that perform well in this circuit are the 6CL6, 12BY7A and 5763. The output tank is designed for high impedance so it will interface properly with the high-impedance grid of the PA. It may be necessary to include a neutralization circuit with this type of amplifier, especially if care is not exercised in the layout. The high transconductance of the 6GK6 series encourages self-oscillation near the operating frequency. Z1 is a parasitic choke that should be included as a matter of course to prevent VHF parasitics.

A transistor amplifier suitable for driving a Class C tube PA is presented in Fig 12B. Q1 operates Class C, so it is not satisfactory for amplifying SSB energy. However, forward bias (approximately 0.7 volt) can be added between the emitter and ground to move the operating curve into the Class AB (linear) region, thereby making the stage suitable for SSB signal amplification. A 1.5-ohm resistor can be added between the emitter and ground to help prevent thermal runaway and to introduce degeneration (feedback) for enhancing stability. No bypass capacitor would be used from emitter to ground if this were done. T1 is a narrow-band toroidal RF transformer that has a turns ratio suitable for transforming the collector impedance to the grid impedance (determined by the value of the

Fig 12 — Circuit examples of transistor and tube driver stages for use in transmitters.

Shunt feedback is used between the base and collector to enhance stability and contribute to the broadband characteristic of the circuit. T1 is a conventional broadband transformer wound on a toroid core. The turns ratio is adjusted to match the approximate 200-ohm collector impedance to the base impedance of the transistor PA stage — typically less than 5 ohms. Heat sinks are required for the transistors of Fig 12B and C. The primary of T1 should have a reactance of roughly four times the collector impedance at the lowest proposed operating frequency. Therefore, for 1.8 MHz the primary winding would be 70 μH (X_L = 800 ohms). This can be achieved easily by using an FT50-43 Amidon core. The primary advantage to a broadband driver is that it need not be band-switched or peaked by means of a front-panel control. The transistor selected for broadband service should have very high f_T and beta ratings. Transistors designed for UHF service are excellent as HF amplifiers when broadbanding is contemplated. Neutralization is not necessary when using bipolar-transistor amplifiers.

A practical three-stage broadband amplifier strip is shown schematically in Fig 13. With an input level of 10 mW, it is possible to obtain 1.4 watts of output from 3.5 to 29 MHz. A keying transistor (Q4) is included for turning the amplifier off by means of a VOX, or for keying it during CW operation.

RMS and dc voltages are noted on the diagram of Fig 13 to aid in troubleshooting. Overall gain for the strip at 7 MHz is 31 dB, with slight gain variations elsewhere in the passband. T1 consists of 30 turns of no. 28 enameled wire (primary) on an FT50-43 toroid core. The secondary has four turns of no. 28 wire. T2 uses 16 turns of no. 28 enameled wire (primary) looped through an Amidon BLN-43-302 ferrite balun core. The secondary contains four turns of no. 28 wire. RFC1, RFC2 and RFC3 are 250-μH units. They are made by winding 20 turns of no. 28 enameled wire on FT37-43 toroid cores. D1 and D2 are 1-A, 50-PIV rectifier diodes. This driver was designed to excite a Motorola MRF449A PA stage to a power-output range from 15 to 30 watts. C1 at the emitter of Q1 can be selected to provide the overall gain needed in this strip. The value given at C1 proved suitable for the ARRL version of this amplifier. The final value will depend on the gain of the individual transistors acquired for this circuit.

Coupling Between Transmitter Stages

Correct impedance matching between a stage and its load provides maximum transfer of power. The load can be an antenna or a succeeding stage in a transmitter. Thus, the output impedance of a stage must be matched to the input of the following stage. Various forms of coupling networks are popular for use in tube or transistor circuits. The choice will depend on a

grid resistor of the PA) of the final amplifier. The secondary winding of T1 is tuned to resonance at the operating frequency. Approximately 1 watt of output can be taken from Q1 in the HF region when a 12-volt V_{cc} is used. This is ample power for driving a pair of 6146B tubes in Class AB1.

A broadband solid-state driver is shown in Fig 12C. The trade-off for broadband operation (1.8 to 30 MHz in this example) is a reduction in maximum available gain. Therefore, the output from Q1 of Fig 12C will be less than 1 watt. The stage operates Class A, making it linear. The emitter is unbypassed to provide emitter degeneration.

Fig 13 — Practical circuit for a three-stage broadband amplifier/driver. See text.

number of considerations — available driving power versus tolerable mismatch, the selectivity required and impedance matching can be approximated by

$$Z = \frac{V_{cc}^2}{2P_o}$$

where Z is in ohms and P_o is the power output from the stage. However, determining the input impedance of the base of the following stage is difficult to do without expensive laboratory equipment. Generally, when the PA delivers more than 2 watts of output power, the base impedance of that stage will be less than 10 ohms — frequently just 1 or 2 ohms. For this reason, some kinds of LC matching networks do not lend themselves to the application. Furthermore, with the precise input impedance of a transistor power amplifier not known, it becomes desirable to use what is sometimes referred to as a "sloppy" matching network. This is an LC network in which both the inductance and capacitance elements are variable to allow a wide range of adjustment for matching. On the other hand, some designers purposely introduce a mismatch between stages to control the power distribution and aid stability. When this technique is used, it is necessary to have more driving power than would be needed under a matched condition. An intentional mismatch results in a trade-off between gain and the desired end effect of introducing a mismatch.

In the interest of stability, it is common practice to use low-Q networks between stages in a solid-state transmitter. The penalty for using a low-Q resonant network is poor selectivity; there is little attenuation of harmonic or other spurious energy.

Fig 14 — Typical coupling methods for use between amplifier stages. See text.

Conversely, tube stages operate at relatively high plate and grid impedance levels and can be neutralized easily (not true of transistors). This permits the use of high-Q networks between stages, which in turn provide good selectivity. Most solid-state amplifiers use matching networks with loaded Qs of 5 or less. Tube stages more commonly contain networks with loaded Qs of 10 to 15. The higher the Q, up to a practical limit, the greater the attenuation of frequencies other than the desired ones. In all cases, the input and output capacitances of tubes and transmitters must be included in the network constants, or to use the engineering vernacular, "absorbed" into the network. The best source of information on the input and output capacitances of power transistors is the manufacturer's data sheet. The impedance values depend on the operating frequency and power level of the transistor — a very complex set of curves. Most data sheets list specific values of input and output capacitance, which do not vary with the operating frequency or power level.

The interstage coupling method shown in Fig 14A is a common one when vacuum tubes are employed. The driver plate has a tuned circuit that is resonant at the operating frequency. A low-value coupling capacitor (100 pF in this example) routes the drive from the plate of V1 to the grid of V2 across a high-impedance element, RFC2. RFC1 is used as part of the de-coupling network for the supply voltage to V1.

Band-pass coupling between tube stages is demonstrated at Fig 14B. C1 has a very small capacitance value and is chosen to provide a single-hump response when the two resonators (L1 and L2) are peaked to the operating frequency. The principal advantage to this circuit over that of Fig 14A is greater purity of the driving energy to V2 by virtue of increased selectivity. As an alternative to capacitive coupling (C1), link coupling can be used between the cold ends of L1 and L2. Similar band-pass networks are applicable to transistor stages. The collector and base of the driver and PA stages, respectively, would be tapped down on L1 and L2 to minimize loading. This helps preserve the loaded Q of the tuned circuits, aiding selectivity.

A common form of transformer coupling is shown in Fig 14C. T1 is usually a toroidal inductor for use up to approximately 30 MHz. At higher frequencies it is often difficult to obtain a correct impedance ratio. Depending on the total number of transformer turns used, the secondary might call for less than one turn, which is impractical. However, for most of the spectrum up to 30 MHz this technique is entirely satisfactory. The primary tap on T1 is chosen to transform the collector impedance of Q1 to the base impedance of Q2 by means of the turns ratio between the tapped section and the secondary winding of the transformer. If there is a tendency

toward self-oscillation, R1 may be added in shunt with the secondary to stabilize Q2. The value used will be in the 5- to 27-ohm range for most circuits. The rule of thumb is to use just enough resistance to tame the instability.

A method for coupling between stages by means of a capacitive divider is illustrated in Fig 14D. The net value of C1 and C2 in series must be added to the capacitance of C3 when determining the inductance required for resonance with L1. The basic equation for calculating the capacitance ratio of C1 and C2 is included in the diagram. RFC1 serves as a dc return for the base of Q2. The Q of the RF choke is degraded intentionally by the addition of two 950-mu ferrite beads. This aids stability, as discussed earlier in this chapter. An advantage to using this type of circuit is that VHF and UHF parasitics are discouraged and harmonic currents are attenuated when C2 is fairly high in capacitance. This is not true of the circuit in Fig 14C.

When the impedance levels to be matched are of the proper value to permit

Fig 15 — Circuit and mathematical solution for matching network no. 1. Actual circuit (A), parallel equivalent (B) and series equivalent (C).

Fig 16 — Circuit and equations for network no. 2. Actual circuit (A) and series equivalent (B).

Fig 17 — Network-solution equations and circuit for network no. 3. Actual circuit (A) and series equivalent (B).

employing specific-ratio broadband transformers, the circuit of Fig 14E is useful. In this example, two 4:1 transformers are used in cascade to provide a 16:1 transformation ratio. This satisfies the match between the

Fig 18 — Parallel and series equivalent circuits and the formulas used for conversion.

$$R_S = \frac{R_{OUT}}{1 + (R_{OUT}/X_P)^2}$$

$$X_S = R_S\left(\frac{R_{OUT}}{X_P}\right)$$

PARALLEL EQUIVALENT

SERIES EQUIVALENT

80-ohm collector of Q1 and the 5-ohm base of Q2. The shortcoming of this technique is the lack of selectivity between stages, but the advantage is in the broadband characteristic of the coupling system. The phasing dots on the diagram near T1 and T2 indicate the correct electrical relationship of the transformer windings.

Network Equations

The three networks shown in Figs 15, 16 and 17 will provide practical solutions to many of the impedance-matching problems encountered by amateurs. In each of the figures it is assumed that the output impedance being matched is lower than the input impedance of the following stage. If this is not the case, the network (the circuit elements between the points marked A and B) can be turned around to provide the correct transformation.

Normally, the output impedance of a transistor is given as a resistance in parallel with a capacitance, C_{out}. To use the design equations for these three networks, the output impedance must first be converted from the parallel form (R_{out} and C_{out}) to the equivalent series form (R_s and C_s). These equivalent circuits and the equations for conversion are given in Fig 18. Often the output capacitance is small enough that it may be neglected; the resulting error is compensated for by using variable components in the network.

The low-pass T network (Fig 17) has the advantage of matching a wide range of impedances with practical component values. Some designers feel that of the various networks used in solid-state work, the T network is best in terms of collector efficiency. The harmonic suppression afforded by the T network varies with the transformation ratio and the total Q of the network. For stages feeding an antenna, additional harmonic suppression will normally be needed. This is also true for networks 1 and 2. These three networks are covered in detail in *Motorola Application Note AN-267*. Another excellent paper on the subject was written by Becciolini, *Motorola Application Note AN-271*.

The equations for networks 1, 2 and 3 were taken from AN-267. That paper con-

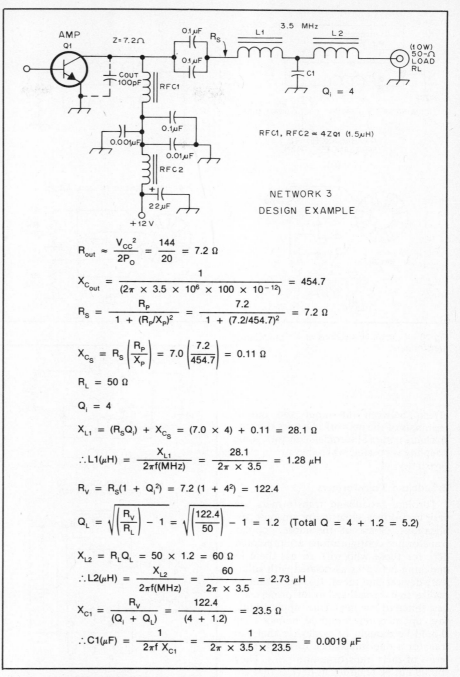

$$R_{out} \approx \frac{V_{CC}^2}{2P_O} = \frac{144}{20} = 7.2\ \Omega$$

$$X_{C_{out}} = \frac{1}{(2\pi \times 3.5 \times 10^6 \times 100 \times 10^{-12})} = 454.7$$

$$R_S = \frac{R_P}{1 + (R_P/X_P)^2} = \frac{7.2}{1 + (7.2/454.7)^2} = 7.2\ \Omega$$

$$X_{C_S} = R_S\left(\frac{R_P}{X_P}\right) = 7.0\left(\frac{7.2}{454.7}\right) = 0.11\ \Omega$$

$$R_L = 50\ \Omega$$

$$Q_i = 4$$

$$X_{L1} = (R_S Q_i) + X_{C_S} = (7.0 \times 4) + 0.11 = 28.1\ \Omega$$

$$\therefore L1(\mu H) = \frac{X_{L1}}{2\pi f(MHz)} = \frac{28.1}{2\pi \times 3.5} = 1.28\ \mu H$$

$$R_V = R_S(1 + Q_i^2) = 7.2\ (1 + 4^2) = 122.4$$

$$Q_L = \sqrt{\left(\frac{R_V}{R_L}\right) - 1} = \sqrt{\left(\frac{122.4}{50}\right) - 1} = 1.2\quad (\text{Total } Q = 4 + 1.2 = 5.2)$$

$$X_{L2} = R_L Q_L = 50 \times 1.2 = 60\ \Omega$$

$$\therefore L2(\mu H) = \frac{X_{L2}}{2\pi f(MHz)} = \frac{60}{2\pi \times 3.5} = 2.73\ \mu H$$

$$X_{C1} = \frac{R_V}{(Q_i + Q_L)} = \frac{122.4}{(4 + 1.2)} = 23.5\ \Omega$$

$$\therefore C1(\mu F) = \frac{1}{2\pi f\ X_{C1}} = \frac{1}{2\pi \times 3.5 \times 23.5} = 0.0019\ \mu F$$

Fig 19 — A practical example of network no. 3 and the solution to the network design.

tains computer solutions to these networks and others, with tabular information for various values of Q and source impedances. A fixed load value of 50 ohms is the base for the tabular data.

A design example for network 3 is given in Fig 19. The solutions for the other two networks follow the same general trend, so examples for networks 1 and 2 will not be given. In Fig 19 the component "C_{out}" is taken from the manufacturer's data sheet. If it is not available, it can be ignored at the expense of a slight mathematical error in the network determination. By making C1 variable the network can be made to approximate the correct transformation

ratio. At the lower frequencies C1 will be fairly large in value. This may require a fixed-value silver-mica capacitor in parallel with a mica compression trimmer to obtain the exact value of capacitance needed. The equations will seldom yield standard values of capacitance.

L1 and L2 of Fig 19 can be wound on powdered-iron toroid cores of suitable cross-sectional area for the power involved. This is explained in an earlier chapter of this book. L1 and L2 should be separated by mounting them apart and at right angles. Alternatively, a shield can be used between the inductors. This will prevent unwanted capacitive and inductive coupling

Fig 20 — Circuit illustrations of 4:1 broadband transformers.

effects between the input and output terminals of the network. Despite the self-shielding nature of toroidal inductors, some coupling is possible when they are in close proximity.

Broadband Transformers

Toroidal broadband transformers are very useful in a great many amateur applications. Some of the more popular transformer configurations are presented here for those who wish to use them in matching networks associated with solid-state devices and tubes. It is important to realize that broadband transformers are best suited to low-impedance applications, say, up to a few hundred ohms. They should be thought of as devices that can transform one impedance to another, in terms of their transformation ratio. They should not be regarded as devices that are built for some specified pair of impedances, such as 200 ohms to 50 ohms in the case of a 4:1 transformer. The term "balun" pertains only to a broadband transformer that converts a balanced condition to one that is unbalanced, or vice versa.

The broadband transformers illustrated in Figs 20, 21 and 22 are suitable for use in solid-state circuits, as matching devices between circuit modules and in antenna-matching networks. For low power levels the choice of core material is often ferrite. Powdered-iron is more often the designer's preference when working with high power levels. The primary reason to avoid ferrite at high power is the potential for damage to the core material during saturation and overheating. This can alter the permeability factor of the core material permanently.

Fig 21 — Circuit examples of 9:1 broadband transformers (A and C) and a variable-impedance transformer (E).

Fig 22 — Assorted broadband transformers.

Powdered-iron is more tolerant in this regard.

Fig 20 shows two types of 4:1 transformers, plus a method for connecting two of them in series to effect a 16:1 transformation. The circuit at E is often used between a 50-ohm source and the base of an RF power transistor.

Two styles of 9:1 transformer are shown in Fig 21 at A and C. They are also found at the input to transistor amplifiers and between the collector and the load. The variable-ratio transformer of Fig 21E is excellent for obtaining a host of impedance transformations. This transformer was developed by W2FMI for use in matching ground-mounted vertical antennas.

Phase-reversal, 1:1 balun and hybrid-combiner transformers are shown in Fig 22. The circuit at E of Fig 22 is useful when it is necessary to feed two signals to a single load. When the input signals are on different frequencies, the power is split evenly between R3 and R4. When the input voltages are on the same frequency (as with two transistor amplifiers feeding a single load), with the amplitudes and phase identical, all of the power is delivered to R4. The amplifiers are effectively isolated from each other.

Chapter 12

Radio Receiving Principles

How good should receiver performance be? A suitable answer might be, "As good as is possible, consistent with the state of the amateur art and the money available to the purchaser." That opens up a wide area for debate, but the statement is not meant to imply that a receiver has to be costly or complex to provide good performance: Some very basic, inexpensive homemade receivers offer outstanding performance.

For many years the evolution of commerical amateur receivers seemed to stagnate except for the window dressing and frills added to the front panels. Emphasis was placed on "sensitivity" (whatever was really meant by that term) in the advertising. Some amateurs concluded (as a result of the strong push for sensitive receivers) that the mark of a good unit was seen when atmospheric noise on the HF bands could push the S-meter needle up to an S2 or S3. Very little thought, if any, was given to the important parameters of a receiver — high dynamic range, fine readout resolution and frequency stability. Instead, receivers were placed on the market with 5- or 10-kHz dial increments and excessive amounts of front-end gain. The excessive gain caused the mixer (or mixers) to collapse in the presence of moderate and strong signals.

Double-conversion superheterodyne receivers were for a long time the choice of manufacturers and amateurs. The second IF was often 100 or 50 kHz, thereby enabling the designer to get fairly reasonable orders of selectivity by means of high-Q IF transformers. That concept predated the availability of crystal-lattice and mechanical filters. The low-frequency second IF dictated the use of a double-conversion circuit in order to minimize image responses.

Single-conversion receivers offer much cleaner performance in terms of spurious responses and dynamic range. Although their performance is acceptable in many instances, there is considerable room for improvement. At least there is only one mixer to cause intermodulation-distortion (IMD) and overloading problems in a single-conversion superheterodyne receiver. A strong doubly balanced mixer (DBM) and careful gain distribution in such a receiver can yield superb performance. Of course, the local oscillator should be stable and low in noise components to further enhance performance. Thus far, not many commerically built amateur receivers meet these criteria. In terms of dynamic range, some manufactured receivers exhibit an MDS (minimum discernible signal) of − 145 dBm (referenced to the noise floor); blocking of the desired signal does not occur (1 dB of compression) until the adjacent test signal is some 116-dB above the noise floor, and the two-tone IMD dynamic range is on the order of 85 dB. Greater detail concerning this measurement technique is given in Chapter 25. A receiver with the approximate figures just given is considered to be an acceptable one for use where fairly strong signals prevail. However, improvements over those numbers have been achieved by amateurs who designed and built their own receivers.

VHF and UHF

Adequate receiving capability is essential in VHF and UHF communications. This is true whether the station is a transceiver or a combination of separate transmitting and receiving units, regardless of the modulation system used. Transceivers and FM receivers are treated separately in this Handbook, but their performance involves basic principles that apply to all receivers for frequencies above 30 MHz. Important attributes are good signal-to-noise ratio (low noise figure), adequate gain, stability and freedom from overloading and other spurious responses.

A VHF station often has an HF-band communications receiver, with a crystal-controlled converter for the desired VHF band ahead of it. The HF receiver serves as a tunable IF system, complete with detector, noise limiter, BFO and audio amplifier.

Choice of a suitable communications receiver for use with converters should not be made lightly. A good receiver for this purpose has all the characteristics of a good HF receiver. The special requirements of FM phone are discussed in Chapter 18.

Good mechanical design and frequency stability are important. Image rejection should be high in the converter output range. This may rule out 28 MHz with single-conversion receivers having 455-kHz IF systems.

This suggests strongly that amateurs consider designing and building their own receivers. Certainly, this is within the capability of many experimenters. The satisfaction derived from such an effort can't be measured. The following sections of this chapter are written for those who wish to acquire a better understanding of how a practical receiver operates. Design data and related philosophy are included for those who are inspired toward developing a homemade receiver.

Sensitivity

One of the least understood terms among amateurs is sensitivity. In a casual definition the word refers to the ability of a receiver to respond to incoming signals. It is proper to conclude from this that the better the sensitivity, the more responsive the receiver will be to weak signals. The popular misconception is that the greater the receiver front-end gain, the higher the sensitivity. An amateur who subscribes to this concept can ruin the performance of a good receiver by installing a high-gain preamplifier ahead of it. Although this will cause the S meter to read much higher on all signals, it can actually degrade the receiver sensitivity if the preamplifier is of inferior design (noisy).

A true measure of receiver sensitivity is obtained when the input signal is referenced to the noise generated within the receiver. Since the significant noise generated inside a receiver of good design originates in the RF and mixer stages (sometimes in the post-mixer amplifier), a low-noise front end is vital to high sensitivity. The necessary receiver gain can be developed after the mixer — usually in the IF amplifier section. The internal noise is generated by the thermal agitation of electrons inside the tubes, transistors or ICs. It is evident from this discussion that a receiver of high sensitivity could be one with relatively low front-end gain. This thought should be kept in

Fig. 1 — Relationship between noise figure and noise temperature.

a temperature above absolute zero ($-273°$ C or 0 K). Electrons move in a random fashion colliding with relatively immobile ions that make up the bulk of the material. The final effect is that in most substances there is no net current in any particular direction on a long-term average, but rather a series of random pulses. These pulses produce what is called thermal agitation noise, thermal noise or Johnson noise.

As the currents caused by electron movement increase with temperature, so does the noise power. Also, as the pulses are random, they spread out over a broad frequency spectrum. As it turns out, if we examine the power contained in a given passband, the value of that power is independent of the center frequency of the passband. This is expressed as

$$p = kTB$$

where p is the thermal noise power, k is Boltzmann's constant (1.38×10^{-23} joule per K), T is absolute temperature in kelvins and B is the bandwidth in hertz. Notice that the power is directly proportional to temperature, and at 0 K the noise power is zero.

Active devices normally exhibit noise temperatures different from their ambient temperatures. The thermal noise produced by a semiconductor device will limit its ability to respond to input signals below the level of the internally generated noise. Noise temperature, noise factor and noise figure are all measures of this device noise. The results are expressed in terms of temperature, ratios and decibels, respectively.

Consider a 50-ohm termination connected to the input of a device with the termination cooled to absolute zero. There would be no noise produced by this source, and the noise output from the device would be that of the internally generated noise. If the termination were now heated to a temperature that would raise the output noise of the device by 3 dB (thermal agitation noise equal to the internally generated noise of the device) and the temperature of the termination measured, the effective input noise temperature (T_E) of the device would be this value. The noise temperature specification is independent of bandwidth and is directly proportional to noise power. For example, if we were to halve the noise temperature we would double the signal-to-noise ratio.

In order to convert a noise temperature measurement to noise figure, an intermediate calculation is required — noise factor (f). Noise factor is by definition the ratio of the total output noise power to the input noise power when the termination is at the standard temperature of 290 K ($17°$ C). The noise power caused only by the input noise of the termination is simply the noise power of the source multiplied by the gain of the device. Mathematically

$$N_{power\ input} = GkBT_o$$

where G is the gain of the device and T_o is 290 K. The total noise caused by the input noise of the termination and the internally generated noise is simply the sum of the two noise sources multiplied by the gain of the device, or

$$N_{power\ total} = GkB(T_o + T_E)$$

where T_E is the effective input noise temperature and T_o is 290 K. The noise factor (f) is calculated as

$$f = \frac{N_{power\ total}}{N_{power\ input}}$$

where T_E is the effective input noise temperature and T_o is 290 K. Noise figure can then be calculated as follows:

$$NF = 10\ \log_{10} f = 10\ \log_{10} \left(1 + \frac{T_E}{T_o}\right)$$

where noise figure is expressed in decibels. Should the noise figure of the device be known and it is desired to find the noise temperature, the equation can be rearranged as follows:

$$T_E = 290\ [antilog(NF/10) - 1]K$$

where noise figure is expressed in decibels. A graph illustrating the relationship between noise figure and noise temperature is given in Fig. 1.

Noise factor can also be represented in terms of signal-to-noise ratios as

$$f = \frac{S/N\ at\ input}{S/N\ at\ output}$$

and noise figure can be found from

$$NF = 10\ \log_{10} f$$
$$= 10\ \log_{10} \frac{S/N\ at\ input}{S/N\ at\ output}$$

A receiving system consists of an interconnection of individual stages, some noisier than others. Each stage's noise contribution to the reduction of signal-to-noise ratio can be expressed as a noise figure. How much the noise figure of a particular stage affects system noise figure depends on the gain of the stages between that stage and the antenna. That is, if a stage's gain is sufficiently large, its noise figure will tend to override or "mask" the noise contribution of the stage following it. Mathematically, the noise factor of a receiving system can be expressed as

$$F = f_1 + \frac{f_2 - 1}{G_1} + \frac{f_3 - 1}{G_1\ G_2} +$$
$$\dots + \frac{f_n - 1}{G_n \dots G_2\ G_1}$$

where
  f_n = noise factor of the nth stage
  G_n = gain of the nth stage.

mind as we enter the discussion of dynamic range and noise figure.

Noise Temperature, Noise Factor and Noise Figure

The lower the receiver noise figure (NF), the more sensitive it is. Receiver noise figures are established primarily in the RF amplifier and/or mixer stages. Low-noise active devices (tubes or transistors) should be used in the receiver front end to help obtain a low noise figure. The unwanted noise, in effect, masks the weaker signals and makes them difficult to copy. Noise generated in the receiver front end is amplified in the succeeding stages along with the signal energy. Therefore, in the interest of sensitivity, internal noise should be kept as low as possible.

Don't confuse external noise (man-made and atmospheric, which comes in on the antenna) with receiver noise during discussions of noise figure. Although the ratio of the external noise to the incoming signal level has a lot to do with reception, external noise does not relate to this general discussion. It is because external noise levels are quite high on 160, 80, 40 and 20 meters that emphasis is seldom placed on a low receiver noise figure for those bands. However, as the operating frequency is increased from 15 meters up through the microwave spectrum, the matter of receiver noise becomes a primary consideration. At these higher frequencies the receiver noise almost always exceeds that from external sources, especially at 2 meters and above.

Receiver noise is produced by the movement of electrons in any substance (such as resistors, transistors and FETs) that has

Brief analysis of this equation shows that the first stage of a receiving system is the most important with regard to noise figure. If the gain of this and succeeding stages is greater than unity, the denominator of each successive term becomes greater. The numerical value of terms beyond the second or third approaches zero and can be ignored.

It might seem that the more gain an RF amplifier has, the better the signal-to-noise ratio and therefore the better the reception. This is not necessarily true. The primary function of an RF amplifier is to establish the noise figure of the system. One good RF stage is usually adequate unless the mixer is a passive type with loss instead of gain. Two RF stages are the usual maximum requirement.

Once the system noise figure is established, any further gain necessary to bring a signal to audible levels may be obtained from intermediate-frequency stages or in the audio channel. Use the minimum gain necessary to set the overall receiver noise figure; this will help avoid overloading and spurious signals in subsequent stages.

Further examination of the equation points out the desirability of mounting the first stage of the receiver system at the antenna for VHF and UHF. The transmission line from the antenna to the receiver can be considered as a stage in the receiving system. The first stage of a receiving system makes the major contribution of noise figure to the system, so it is highly desirable that the first stage be a low-noise amplifier with gain. A transmission line is a "lossy" amplifier, and if placed at the first stage of a receiving system, automatically limits the system noise figure to that of the transmission line, at best. If the first RF amplifier is placed before the lossy transmission line stage, at the antenna, the amplifier gain will tend to mask the noise added by the transmission line.

Noise-Figure Measurements

Amateurs can use a thermal noise source for determining receiver noise figure. The resistance of the noise-generator output must match that of the receiver input, 50 ohms to 50 ohms, for example. Fig. 2 shows a setup for making these measurements. The first reading is taken with the noise generator turned off. The receiver audio gain is adjusted for a convenient noise reading in decibels, as observed on the audio power meter. The noise generator is turned on next, and its output is increased until a convenient power ratio, expressed by N2/N1, is observed. The ratio N2/N1 is referred to as the "Y-factor", and this noise figure measurement technique is commonly called the Y-factor method. From the Y-factor and output power of the noise generator, the noise figure can be calculated

$$NR = ENR - 10 \log_{10}(Y - 1)$$

where

NF = noise figure in decibels
ENR = excess noise ratio of the noise generator in decibels
Y = output noise ratio, N2/N1.

The excess noise ratio of the generator is

$$ENR = 10 \log_{10}\left(\frac{P2}{P1} - 1\right)$$

where

P2 = noise power of the generator
P1 = noise power from a resistor at 290 kelvins.

If a thermionic diode such as a 5722 tube is used as the noise source, and if the circuit is operated in the "temperature-limited mode" (portion of the tube curve where saturation occurs, dependent on cathode temperature and plate voltage), the (excess) decibels can be calculated by

$$(excess)\ dB = 10 \log_{10}(20\ Rd\ Id)$$

where

Rd = the noise source output resistance
Id = the diode current in amperes.

Most manufacturers of amateur communications receivers rate the noise characteristics with respect to signal input. A common expression is S + Noise/Noise, or the signal-to-noise ratio. Usually the sensitivity is given as the number of microvolts required for an S + Noise/Noise ratio of 10 dB. Sensitivity can also be expressed in terms of the minimum discernible signal (MDS) or noise floor of the receiver. (See Chapter 25.)

Typically, the noise figure for a good receiver operating below 30 MHz runs about 5 to 10 dB. Lower noise figures can be obtained, but they are of no real value because of the external noise arriving from the antenna. It is important to remember also that optimum noise figure in an RF amplifier does not always coincide with maximum stage gain, especially at VHF and higher. This is why actual noise measurements must be used to peak for best noise performance.

Selectivity

Many amateurs regard the expression "selectivity" as equating to the ability of a receiver to separate signals. This is a fundamental truth, particularly with respect to IF selectivity which has been established by means of high-Q filters (LC, crystal, monolithic or mechanical). But in a broader sense, selectivity can be employed to reject unwanted signal energy in any part of a receiver — the front end, IF section, audio circuit or local-oscillator chain. Selectivity is a relative term, since the degree of bandwidth can vary from a few hertz to more than a megahertz, depending on the design objectives. Therefore, it is not uncommon to hear terms like "broadband

Fig. 2 — Block diagram of a noise measurement setup.

Fig. 3 — A curve and equation for determining the unloaded Q of a tuned circuit.

filter" or "narrow-band filter."

The degree of selectivity is determined by the bandwidth of a filter network. The bandwidth is normally specified for the minus 3-dB points on the filter response curve; the frequencies where the filter output power is half the peak output elsewhere in the passband. The difference in frequency between a minus 3-dB point and the filter center frequency is known as Δf. The bandwidth of the filter then becomes 2 Δ f. Fig. 3 illustrates this principle and shows how the unloaded Q of a tuned circuit or resonator relates to the bandwidth characteristic.

If a tuned circuit is used as a filter, the higher its loaded Q, the greater the selectivity. To make the skirts of the response curve steeper, several high-Q resonators can be used in cascade. This aids the selectivity by providing greater rejection of signals close in frequency to the desired one. The desirable effect of cascaded filter sections can be seen in Fig. 4. The circuit is that of a tunable Cohn type of three-pole filter for use in the front end of a 160-meter receiver. The response curve is included to illustrate the selectivity obtained.

An ideal receiver with selectivity applied to various significant parts of the circuit might be structured something like this:

a) Selective front end for rejecting out-of-band signals to prevent overloading and spurious responses.

Fig. 4 — A tunable Cohn-type filter is shown at A. L5 and L6 are the bottom-coupling inductors (1.45 μH). L1 and L4 are 70 pH and L2, L3 are 140 μH. A response curve for the tunable filter is given at B.

b) Selective IF circuit (two IF filters: one for 2.4-kHz SSB bandwidth and one for 300-Hz CW and RTTY bandwidth).

c) RC active or passive audio filter for audio selectivity to reduce wideband noise and provide audio selectivity in the range from 300 to 2700 Hz (SSB), 2100 to 2300 Hz (or 1250 to 1450 Hz), for RTTY and a very narrow bandwidth, such as 750 to 850 Hz, for CW.

d) Selective circuits or filters in the local oscillator chain to reject all mixer injection energy other than the desired frequency.

This illustrates clearly that selectivity means more than the ability of a receiver to separate one amateur signal from another that is nearby in frequency. Specifically, it means that selectivity can be used to select one frequency or band of frequencies while rejecting others.

Selectivity at VHF

Ever-increasing occupancy of the radio spectrum brings with it a parade of receiver overload and spurious responses. Overloading problems can be minimized by the use of high-dynamic-range receiving techniques, but spurious responses such as

Fig. 5 — Round and square helical resonators, showing principal dimensions. Diameter, D (for side, S) is determined by the desired unloaded Q. Other dimensions are expressed in terms of D (or S) as described in the text.

the image frequency must be filtered out before mixing occurs. Conventional tuned circuits cannot provide the selectivity necessary to eliminate the plethora of signals found in most urban and many suburban neighborhoods. Other filtering techniques must be used.

Although some amateurs use quarter-wavelength coaxial cavities on 50, 144 and 220 MHz, the helical resonators shown in Fig. 5 are usually a better choice as they are smaller and easier to build. In the frequency range from 30 to 100 MHz, where it's difficult to build high-Q inductors, and because coaxial cavities are very large, the helical resonator is an excellent choice. At 50 MHz, for example, a capacitively tuned, quarter-wavelength coaxial cavity with an unloaded Q of 3000 would be about 4 inches in diameter and nearly 5 feet long. On the other hand, a helical resonator with the same unloaded Q is about 8.5 inches in diameter and 11.3 inches long. Even at 432 MHz, where coaxial cavities are common, the use of a helical resonator will result in substantial size reductions. The following design information on helical resonators originally appeared in a June 1976 QST article by W1HR.

The helical resonator has often been described simply as a coil surrounded by a shield, but it is actually a shielded, resonant section of helically wound transmission line with relatively high characteristic impedance and low axial propagation velocity. The electrical length is about 94 percent of an axial quarter wavelength, or 84.6 electrical degrees. One lead of the helical winding is connected directly to the shield, and the other end is open circuited as shown in Fig. 5. Although the shield may be any shape, only round and square shields will be considered in this section.

Design

The unloaded Q of a helical resonator is determined primarily by the size of the shield. For a round resonator with a copper coil on a low-loss form, mounted in a copper shield, the unloaded Q is given by

$$Q_u = 50 \, D \sqrt{f_o}$$

where D = inside diameter of the shield in inches and f_o = frequency in MHz.

If the shield can is square, assume D to be 1.2 times the width of one side. This formula, which includes the effects of losses and imperfections in practical materials, yields values of unloaded Q which are easily attained in practice. Silver plating of the shield and coil will increase the unloaded Q by about three percent over that predicted by the equation. At VHF and UHF, however, it is more practical to increase slightly the shield size (i.e., increase the selected Q_u by about three percent before making the calculation). The fringing capacitance at the open-circuited end of the helix is about 0.15D pF (i.e., approximately 0.3 pF for a shield 2 inches in diameter).

Once the required shield size has been determined, the total number of turns, N, winding pitch, P, and characteristic impedance, Z_o, for round and square helical resonators with air dielectric between the helix and shield, are given by

$$N = \frac{1908}{f_o D} \qquad P = \frac{f_o D^2}{2312} \qquad Z_o = \frac{99,000}{f_o D}$$

$$N = \frac{1590}{f_o S} \qquad P = \frac{f_o S^2}{1606} \qquad Z_o = \frac{82,500}{f_o S}$$

In these equations, dimensions D and S are in inches, and f_o is in megahertz. The design nomograph for round helical resonators in Fig. 6, which can be used with slide-rule accuracy, is based on these formulas.

Although there are many variables to consider when designing helical resonators, certain ratios of shield size and length, and coil diameter and length, will provide optimum results. For helix diameter, d = 0.55D, or d = 0.66S. To determine helix length, b = 0.825D, or b = 0.99S. For shield length, B = 1.325D and H = 1.60S.

Calculation of these dimensions is simplified by the design chart of Fig. 7. Note that these ratios result in a helix with a length 1.5 times its diameter, the condition for maximum Q. The shield is about 60 percent longer than the helix — although it can be made longer — to completely contain the electric field at the top of the helix and the magnetic field at the bottom.

It should be mentioned that the winding pitch, P, is used primarily to determine the required conductor size. During actual construction the length of the coil is adjusted to that given by the equations for helix length. Conductor size ranges from 0.4P to 0.6P for both round and square resonators and is plotted graphically in Fig. 8.

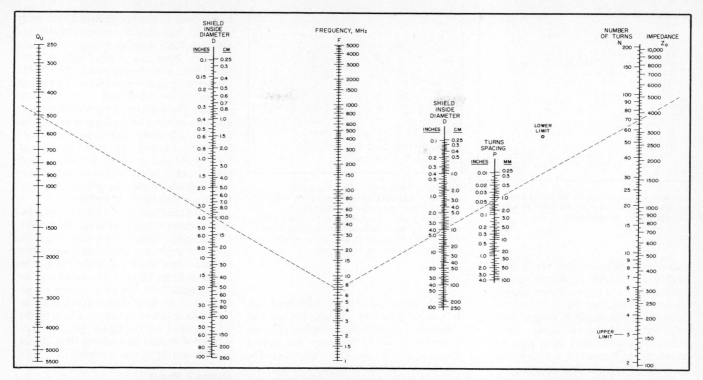

Fig. 6 — Design nomograph for round helical resonators. After selecting unloaded Q_u, required shield diameter is indicated by index line from Q_u scale to frequency scale (dashed index line here indicates a shield of about 3.8 inches for an unloaded Q of 500 at 7 MHz). Number of turns, N, winding pitch, P, and characteristic impedance, Z_o, are determined by index line from the frequency scale through previously determined shield diameter on right-hand side of the chart (index line indicates P = 0.047 inch, N = 70 turns, and Z_n = 3600 ohms).

Obviously, an area exists (in terms of frequency and unloaded Q) where the designer must make a choice between a conventional cavity (or lumped LC circuit) and a helical resonator. At the higher frequencies, where cavities might be considered, the choice is affected by shape factor: a coaxial resonator is long and relatively small in diameter, while the length of a helical resonator is not much greater than its diameter. A second consideration is that point where the winding pitch, P, is less than the radius of the helix (otherwise the structure tends to be nonhelical). This condition occurs when the helix has fewer than three turns ("upper limit" on the design nomograph of Fig. 6).

Construction

To obtain as high an unloaded Q as possible, the shield should should not have any seams parallel to the axis of the helix. This is usually not a problem with round resonators because large-diameter copper tubing is used for the shield, but square resonators require at least one seam and usually more. However, the effect on unloaded Q is minimal if the seam is silver soldered carefully from one end to the other.

Best results are obtained when little or no dielectric is used inside the shield. This is usually no problem at VHF and UHF because the conductors are large enough that a supporting coil form is not required. The lower end of the helix should be soldered to the inside of the shield at a

Fig. 7 — Helical resonator design chart. After the shield diameter has been determined, helix diameter, d, helix length, b, and shield length, B, can be determined with this graph. Index line indicates that a shield diameter of 3.8 inches requires helix mean diameter of 2.1 inches, helix length of 3.1 inches, and shield length of 5 inches.

point directly opposite from the bottom of the coil.

Although the external field is minimized by the use of top and bottom covers, the top and bottom of the shield may be left open with negligible effect on frequency or unloaded Q. If covers are provided, however, they should make good electrical contact with the shield. In those resonators where the helix is connected to the bottom

Fig. 8 — Helix conductor size vs. winding pitch, P. A winding pitch of 0.047 inch for example, dictates a conductor diameter between 0.019 and 0.028 inch (number 22 or 24 AWG).

cover, that must be soldered solidly to the shield to minimize losses.

Tuning

A helical resonator designed from the nomograph of Fig. 6, if carefully built, will resonate very close to the design frequency. Resonance can be adjusted over a small range by slightly compressing or expanding the helix. If the helix is made slightly longer than that called for in Fig. 7, the resonator can be tuned by pruning the open end of the coil. However, neither of these methods is recommended for wide frequency excursions because any major deviation in helix length will degrade the unloaded Q of the resonator.

Most helical resonators are tuned by

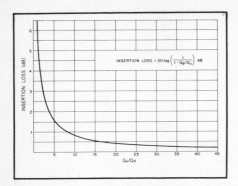

Fig. 9 — Insertion loss of all tuned resonant circuits is determined by the ratio of loaded to unloaded Q as shown here.

Fig. 10 — Response curve for a single-resonator 432-MHz filter showing the effects of capacitive and inductive input/output coupling. Response curve can be made symmetrical on each side of resonance by combining the two methods (inductive input and capacitive output, or vice versa).

means of a brass tuning screw or high quality air-variable capacitor across the open end of the helix. Piston capacitors also work well, but the Q of the tuning capacitor should ideally be several times the unloaded Q of the resonator. Varactor diodes have sometimes been used where remote tuning is required, but varactors can generate unwanted harmonics and other spurious signals if they are excited by strong, nearby signals.

When a helical resonator is to be tuned by a variable capacitor, the shield size is based on the chosen unloaded Q at the operating frequency. Then the number of turns, N, and the winding pitch, P, are based on resonance at $1.5f_o$. Tune the resonator to the desired operating frequency, f_o.

Insertion Loss

The insertion loss (dissipation loss), IL, in decibels, of all resonant circuits is given by

$$IL = 20 \log_{10} \left(\frac{1}{1 - Q_d/Q_u} \right) dB$$

where

Q_d = loaded Q
Q_u = unloaded Q.

This is plotted in Fig. 9. For the most practical cases ($Q_d > 5$), this can be closely approximated by $IL \approx 9.0 (Q_d/Q_u)$ dB. The selection of a loaded Q for a tuned circuit is dictated primarily by the required selectivity of the circuit. However, to keep dissipation loss to 0.5 dB or less (as is the case for low-noise VHF receivers), the unloaded Q must be at least 18 times the loaded Q. Although this may be difficult to achieve in practice, it points up the necessity of considering both selectivity and insertion loss before choosing the unloaded Q of any resonant tuned circuit.

Coupling

Signals may be coupled into and out of helical resonators with inductive loops at the bottom of the helix, direct taps on the coil or any combination of these. Although the correct tap point can be calculated easily, coupling by loops and probes must be determined experimentally. When only one resonator is used, the input and output coupling is often provided by probes. For maximum isolation the probes are positioned on opposite sides of the resonator.

When coupling loops are used, the plane of the loop should be perpendicular to the axis of the helix and separated a small distance from the bottom of the coil. For resonators with only a few turns, the plane of the loop can be tilted slightly so it is parallel with the slope of the adjacent conductor. Helical resonators with inductive coupling (loops) will exhibit more attenuation to signals above the resonant frequency (as compared to attenuation below resonance), whereas resonators with capacitive coupling (probes) exhibit more attenuation below the passband, as shown for a typical 432-MHz resonator in Fig. 10. This characteristic may be a consideration when choosing a coupling method. The passband can be made more symmetrical by using a combination of coupling methods (inductive input and capacitive output, for example).

If more than one helical resonator is required to obtain a desired band-pass characteristic, adjacent resonators may be coupled through apertures in the shield wall between the two resonators. Unfortunately, the size and location of the aperture must be found empirically, so this method of coupling is not very practical unless you're building a large number of identical units.

Since the loaded Q of a resonator is determined by the external loading, this must be considered when selecting a tap (or position of a loop or probe). The ratio of this external loading, R_b, to the characteristic impedance, Z_o, for a quarter-wavelength resonator is calculated from

$$K = \frac{R_b}{Z_o} = 0.785 \left(\frac{1}{Q_d} - \frac{1}{Q_u} \right)$$

Even when filters are designed and built properly, they may be rendered totally ineffective if not installed properly. Leakage around a filter can be quite high at VHF and UHF, where wavelengths are short. Proper attention to shielding and good grounding is mandatory for minimum leakage. Poor coaxial cable shield connection into and out of the filter is one of the greatest offenders with regard to filter leakage. Proper dc lead bypassing throughout the receiving system is good practice, especially at VHF and above. Ferrite beads placed over the dc leads may help to reduce leakage even further.

Proper termination of a filter is a necessity if minimum loss is desired. Most VHF RF amplifiers optimized for noise figure do not have a 50-ohm terminating input impedance. As a result, any filter attached to the input of an RF amplifier optimized for noise figure will not be properly terminated, and the filter's loss may rise substantially. As this loss is directly added to the RF amplifier's noise figure, prudent consideration should be made of filter choice and placement in the receiver.

Dynamic Range

Here is another term which seems to confuse some amateurs and even some receiver manufacturers. The confusion concerns true dynamic range (as treated briefly at the start of this chapter) and the AGC control range in a receiver. That is, if a receiver AGC circuit has the capability of controlling the overall receiver gain by some 100 dB from a no-signal to a large-signal condition, a misinformed individual might claim that the dynamic range of the receiver is 100 dB. A receiver with a true dynamic range of 100 dB would be a very fine piece of equipment, indeed!

Dynamic range relates specifically to the amplitude levels of multiple signals that can be accommodated during reception. This is expressed as a numeric ratio, generally in decibels. The present state of the receiver art provides optimum dynamic ranges of up to 100 dB. This is the maximum dynamic range attainable when the distortion products are at the sensitivity limit of the receiver. Simply stated, dynamic range is the decibel difference (or ratio) between the largest tolerable receiver input signal (without causing audible distortion products) and the minimum discernible signal (sensitivity).

Poor dynamic range can cause a host of receiving problems when strong signals appear within the front-end passband. Notable among the maladies is cross modulation of the desired signal. Another effect is desensitization of the receiver from a strong unwanted signal. Spurious signals may appear in the receiver tuning range when a strong signal is elsewhere in the band. This is caused by IMD products from the mixer. Clearly, strong signals cause undesired interference and distortion of the desired signal when a receiver's dynamic range is poor. Design features of importance to high-dynamic-range receivers will appear in this chapter.

TRF Receivers

Tuned-radio-frequency receivers have little value in Amateur Radio today, but in the early days they were suitable for the reception of spark and AM signals. They consisted mainly of a couple of stages of selective RF amplification, an AM detector and an audio amplifier. Variations were developed as regenerative and super-regenerative receivers.

The straight regenerative detector was simply a self-oscillating detector that provided increased sensitivity (similar in function to a product detector) and a beat note for CW reception. Amplitude-modulated signals could be copied, if they were loud, when the regeneration control was set for a nonoscillating condition. For weak-signal AM reception the regeneration control was advanced to increase the detector sensitivity, and the signal was tuned in at zero beat, thereby eliminating the heterodyne from the carrier. Present-day uses for the TRF receiver are restricted mainly to reception of AM broadcast signals, for hi-fi reception and for field-strength indicators of CW or AM signals.

Superregenerative receivers were quite popular among VHF and UHF amateurs in the '30s, '40s and early '50s. The principle of operation was an oscillating detector that had its oscillation interrupted (quenched) by a low-frequency voltage slightly above the audible range (20 to 50 kHz being typical). Some superregenerative detectors employed a so-called self-quenching trait, brought about by means of an RC network of the appropriate time constant. The more esoteric "supergenny" or "rushbox" detectors used an outboard quench oscillator. This circuit was more sensitive than the straight regenerative detector, but was best suited for reception of AM and wide-band FM signals. Because of the quenching action and frequency, the detector response was extremely broad, making it unsuitable for narrow-band signals versus audio recovery. High-Q input tuned circuits helped make them more selective, but a typical superregenerative receiver that used a tuned cavity at the detector input could accommodate only ten 1000-μV, 30-percent-modulated AM signals in a range from 144 to 148 MHz without signal overlap. These tests were performed in the ARRL laboratory with the 10 signals separated from one another by equal amounts.

A major problem associated with the use of regenerative and superregenerative receivers was oscillator (detector) radiation. The isolation between the detector and the antenna was extremely poor, even when an RF amplifier was employed ahead of the detector. In many instances the radiated energy could be heard for several miles, causing intense interference to other

Fig. 11 — Typical detectors that can be used in the front ends of direct-conversion receivers. A passive diode is shown in A. The active detector (B) provides considerable conversion gain. An example of a practical direct-conversion receiver is shown in C.

amateurs in the community.

Direct-Conversion Receivers

A more satisfactory simple receiver for CW or SSB is called the direct-conversion or synchrodyne type. Although there is a distinct possiblity of signal radiation, it is considerably lower in level than with regenerative receivers. This results from better isolation between the antenna and the source of oscillation. A modern direct-conversion receiver uses a separate oscillator and a balanced or doubly balanced detector. Both features help to reduce unwanted radiation.

The detection stage of this receiver is actually a product detector that operates at the desired signal frequency. The product-detector circuits described in Chapter 18 are suitable in this kind of receiver. A tuned RF amplifier is useful ahead of the detector at 14 MHz and higher, but it is seldom necessary from 160 through 40 meters. This is because the atmospheric and man-made noise from the resonant antenna usually exceeds that of the detector below 14 MHz. When no RF stage is used, it is desirable to include a tuned network ahead of the detector.

Fig. 11 shows typical front ends for direct-conversion receivers. One circuit (A) employs a passive detector. The other (B) contains an active detector. Circuit B is desirable in the interest of increased gain. More information about product detectors can be found in Chapter 18.

The circuit of Fig. 11A shows a singly balanced passive detector. Front-end selectivity is provided by a tuned circuit. T1 is a broadband, trifilar-wound toroid transformer. It is tapped on the input tuned circuit at the approximate 50-ohm point. An RF filter is used after D1 and D2 to prevent LO energy from being passed on to the audio amplifier.

Fig. 11B illustrates an active singly balanced IC detector. The input impedance across pins 1 and 5 is roughly 1000 ohms. However, the secondary winding of the input tuned circuit can be made lower than 1000 ohms to reduce the signal amount to the detector. This will ensure improved dynamic range through a deliberate mismatch. Such a practice is useful when an RF amplifier precedes the detector. For maximum sensitivity when no RF amplifier is included, it is more practical to use a 1000-ohm transformation from the 50-ohm antenna (larger link at the detector input). An audio transformer is used at the detector output. The primary winding should have low dc resistance to provide dc balance between the collectors of the differential-amplifier pair in the IC. Alternatively, a center-tapped primary can be used. If this is done, pin 8 should be connected to one end of the winding and the B+ fed to the center tap. The impedance between pins 6 and 8 is approximately 8000 ohms.

In order to obtain ample headphone volume during reception of weak signals,

Fig. 12 — A method for eliminating common-mode hum in a direct-conversion receiver, as described by W7ZOI.

it is necessary to use an audio amplifier that has between 80 and 100 dB of gain. The first AF amplifier should be low-noise type, such as a JFET. The audio-gain control should follow the first audio amplifier. Selectivity for SSB and CW reception can be had by including a passive or RC active audio filter after the gain control. Fig. 11C contains a circuit that shows a typical direct-conversion receiver in its entirety. As was stated earlier, the detector is operating as a product detector rather than a mixer, and the VFO is serving as a BFO. The difference frequency between the incoming 7-MHz signal and the 7-MHz BFO injection voltage is at audio frequency (zero IF). This is amplified by Q1, filtered through a passive LC audio network, then amplified by two 40-dB op-amp stages. It is possible to copy AM signals with this type of receiver by tuning the signal in at zero beat.

Direct-conversion receivers of the type illustrated in Fig. 11 provide double-signal reception; that is, a CW beat note will appear either side of the zero beat. This is useful during sideband reception, wherein the upper sideband is received on one side of zero beat and the lower sideband will appear on the opposite side of zero beat. QRM will be greater, of course, with this kind of receiver because there is no rejection of the unwanted sideband. Some designers have contrived elaborate circuits that, by means of phasing networks, provide single-signal reception. Unfortunately, the circuit becomes nearly as complex as that of superheterodyne. The benefits obtained are probably not worth the effort.

Direct-conversion receivers are not especially suitable above 14 MHz because it is difficult to secure adequate BFO stability at so high a frequency. A practical solution to the problem is the employment of a heterodyne BFO chain in which a 5-MHz VFO is heterodyned with crystal-controlled oscillators. Direct-conversion receivers are ideal for use in simple transceivers because the BFO can be used also as the frequency source for the transmitter, provided the appropriate frequency offset is included between transmit and receive to permit copy of SSB and CW signals without readjusting the BFO.

Characteristic Faults

A major difficulty connected with direct-conversion receivers is microphonics. The effect is noted when the operating receiver is bumped or moved. An annoying ringing sound is heard in the receiver output until the mechanical vibration ceases. The simple act of peaking the front end or adjusting the volume control can set off a microphonic response. This trait is caused by the extremely high gain needed in the audio amplifier. Slight electrical noises in the receiver front end, caused by small vibrations, are amplified many times by the audio channel. They are quite loud by the time they reach the speaker or phones. The best precautionary measure to reduce microphonics is to make all of the detector and BFO circuit leads and components as rigid as possible. Addition of an RF amplifier stage ahead of the detector will also help by virtue of increasing the front-end gain. This reduces the amount of audio gain needed to copy a signal, thereby diminishing the loudness of the microphonics.

The other common problem inherent in direct-conversion receivers is hum (Fig. 12). The fault is most pronounced when an ac power supply is used. The hum becomes progressively worse as the operating frequency is increased. For the most part, this is caused by ac ground loops in the system. The ac modulates the BFO voltage, and the hum-modulated energy is introduced directly into the detector, as well as being radiated and picked up by the antenna. The most practical steps toward a cure are to affix an effective earth ground to the receiver chassis and power supply, use a battery power supply and feed the antenna with coaxial cable. End-fed wire antennas increase the possiblity of hum if they are voltage fed (high impedance at the receiver end). Decoupling the ac power supply leads (dc leads to the receiver) is also an effective preventive measure for hum. The cure described by Wes Hayward, W7ZOI, is to add a toroidal decoupling choke, bifilar wound, in the plus and minus dc leads from the power supply. This will prevent high-impedance RF paths between the power supply and receiver. The effect is to prevent BFO energy from entering the power supply, being modulated by the rectifier diodes and reradiated by the ac line. This form of buzz is called ''common-mode hum.''

Superheterodyne Receivers

Nearly all of the present-day communications receivers are structured as superheterodyne types. Fig. 13 shows a simple block diagram of a single-conversion superheterodyne circuit. This basic design has been popular since the 1930s, and only a few general circuit enhancements have been introduced in recent years. Sophisticated versions of this type of receiver use alternatives to the circuits indicated in the block diagram. The local oscillator, for example, might utilize a phase-locked loop or synthesizer LO chain rather than a straight VFO. Digital readout is used in many models in place of the more traditional analog readout method. RF noise blankers (often very complex) are chosen by some designers in preference to simple shunt audio noise limiters. An assortment of techniques is being used to improve the overall selectivity of these receivers — elaborate IF filtering, RC active or LC passive audio filters. However, the basic circuit concept remains unchanged. The advancement of greatest significance in recent years is the changeover from vacuum tubes to semiconductors. This has increased the life span of the equipment, improved overall efficiency, aided stability (through reduced heating) and contributed to greater ruggedness and miniaturization.

Some manufacturers still produce double- or multiconversion superheterodyne receivers, but the circuits are similar to that of Fig. 13. Multiconversion receivers have a second mixer and LO chain for the purpose of making the second IF lower than the first. This helps to increase the overall selectivity in some designs, but it often degrades the receiver dynamic range through the addition of a second mixer. Multiconversion receivers are more prone to spurious responses than are single-conversion designs, owing to the additional oscillator and mixing frequencies involved. The "cleanest" performance is obtained from properly designed single-conversion receivers.

Circuit Function

In the example of Fig. 13 it is assumed that the receiver is adjusted to receive the 20-meter band. Front-end selectivity is provided by the resonant networks before and after the RF amplifier stage. This part of the receiver is often called the preselector, meaning that it affords a specific degree of front-end selectivity at the operating frequency. The RF amplifier increases the level of the signal from the antenna before it reaches the mixer. The amount of amplification is set by the designer, consistent with the overall circuit requirements (gain distribution). Generally, the gain will be from a few decibels to as much as 25 dB.

When the incoming signal reaches the mixer it is heterodyned with the local-oscillator frequency to establish an IF (intermediate frequency). The IF can be the sum or the difference of the two frequencies. In the example given, the IF is the difference frequency, or 9 MHz.

An IF filter (crystal lattice or ceramic monolithic) is used after the mixer. At low intermediate frequencies (455 kHz and similar), mechanical filters are often used. The IF filter sets the overall receiver selectivity. For SSB reception it is usually 2.4 kHz wide at the 3-dB points of the filter response curve. For CW reception it is be-

Fig. 13 — Block diagram of a single-conversion superheterodyne receiver for 20 meters. The arrows indicate the direction of signal and voltage components.

Fig. 14 — Layout of a typical amateur superheterodyne receiver.

tween 200 and 500 Hz in bandwidth, depending on the design objective and the operator preference. A good bandwidth for CW and RTTY reception is 300 Hz. Wider filters are available for AM and FM reception.

Output from the IF filter is increased by one or more amplifier stages. The overall gain of most IF strips varies from 50 to 100 dB. The amount of signal gain is determined by the design objective, the type of amplifier devices used and the number of gain stages.

The amplified IF energy is routed to a product detector, where it is mixed with the beat-frequency oscillator output. This produces an audio frequency voltage, which is amplified and fed to a speaker or headphones. The BFO is adjusted for reception of the upper or lower sideband, depending on which is appropriate at the time. In either case the BFO frequency is offset slightly from the center frequency of the IF filter. For SSB reception it is usually offset approximately 1.5 kHz, in which case it falls on the slope of the IF response curve. For CW reception the BFO is offset approximately 800 Hz from the IF filter center frequency to produce an 800-Hz peak audio tone in the speaker. Other values of CW offset are common, but 800 Hz is preferred by many CW operators.

The overall gain of the receiver can be adjusted manually (by means of a panel-mounted control) or automatically (by means of an AGC circuit). Energy can be sampled from the IF amplifier output or the audio amplifier. Depending on the method used, the resultant AGC is called *IF derived* or *audio derived*. There are many arguments pro and con about which

method is best. They shall not be considered here. In Fig. 13 the AGC voltage is sampled from the IF strip, amplified by the AGC amplifier and then rectified to provide a dc control voltage. A dc amplifier is used to drive the AGC terminals of the RF and IF amplifiers. It can also be used to operate an S meter for observing relative signal-strength levels. When the incoming signal is weak the gain-controlled stages operate fully. As the incoming signal becomes stronger the AGC circuit starts lowering the gain of the RF and IF stages, thereby leveling the audio output at the speaker. A well-designed AGC system will provide a uniform level of audio output (at a given AF-gain control setting) over an incoming signal-level variation of 100 dB. The net effect is to prevent overloading of some of the receiver stages and to protect the operator from the startling effect of tuning from a weak signal to an extremely loud one. Fig. 14 shows the front panel and controls for a typical amateur-band superheterodyne receiver.

Local Oscillators

A good communications receiver contains oscillators that operate in a stable and spectrally pure manner. Poor oscillator performance can spoil the best of receivers even though all other parts of the circuit are functioning in elegant fashion. Not only should the oscillator be stable with regard to short- and long-term drift, it should have minimum noise in the output (at least 80 dB below the peak value of the fundamental energy) and be reasonably free of spurious responses. Concerning the latter, it is not difficult to design an oscillator that has all harmonics attenuated by 60 or 70

dB. Another important characteristic of an oscillator is quick starting when operating voltage is applied.

Oscillator instability can result from a host of poor design practices. To improve the stability characteristics it is useful to observe the following:

1) Use well-filtered regulated operating voltages.

2) Use temperature-stable, fixed-value capacitors in the frequency-determining part of the circuit. Polystyrene and silver mica capacitors are recommended.

3) Ensure that all mechanical and electrical components are secured rigidly in their part of the circuit. This will lessen the chance for mechanical instability.

4) Build the oscillator on firm, flex-free material.

5) When practical, enclose the oscillator in its own shield compartment and use RF filtering in the dc supply leads. The more constant the ambient temperature surrounding the oscillator, the greater will be the frequency stability.

Precautions should be taken to ensure that the oscillator in a receiver looks into a constant load impedance. Even minute load changes will cause phase shifts which can affect the oscillator frequency. The effect is more pronounced with VFOs than it is with crystal-controlled oscillators. Because of these conditions it is good design practice to couple very lightly to the oscillator stage. The power level can be increased by adding one or more buffer/amplifiers before the oscillator signal is applied to the mixer or detector.

Changes in operating voltage will result in frequency shifts. It is for this reason that regulated voltage is recommended for oscillators. Zener diodes are adequate for the purpose.

Magnetic cores, such as those in slug-tuned coils, change their properties with variations in ambient temperature, thereby causing inductance changes that can severely affect the oscillator frequency. Furthermore, mechanical instability can result if the slugs are not affixed securely in the coil forms.

Oscillator noise can be held to an acceptable level by employing high-Q tuned circuits. The higher the tank Q, the narrower the bandwidth and, hence, the lower the noise output voltage. Excessive LO noise will have a serious effect on mixer performance.

High amounts of harmonic current in the LO-chain output can cause unwanted mixer injection. If the receiver front-end selectivity is not of high magnitude, spurious signals from outside the band of interest will be heard along with the desired ones. Harmonic energy can degrade the performance of some kinds of mixers, making it worthwhile to use suitable filtering at the LO-chain output.

Receiver Front Ends

The designer has a number of options

available when planning the input section of a receiver. The band-pass characteristics of the input tuned circuits are of considerable significance if strong out-of-band signals are to be rejected — an ideal design criterion. Many of the commerical receivers available to the amateur use tuned circuits that can be adjusted from the front panel of the equipment. The greater the network Q, the sharper the frequency response and, hence, the better the adjacent-frequency rejection. For a given network design the bandwidth doubles for each octave higher. That is, an 80-meter front-end network may have a 3-dB bandwidth of 100 kHz for a given Q and load factor. At 40 meters the same type of network would be 200-kHz wide at the 3-dB points of the response curve. This is the reason that most receivers have a tunable front-end section (preselector). If fixed-tuned filters were used, at least two such filters would be necessary to cover from 3.5 to 4 MHz or 1.8 to 2.0 MHz. This would complicate the design and increase the equipment cost.

Fig. 15 shows the two concepts just discussed. The circuit at A covers all of the 80-meter band, and if selective enough offers some in-band rejection. A pair of Butterworth band-pass filters might be used at FL1 and FL2 of Fig. 15B to cover all of the 80-meter band. A lot of additional components would be required, and the in-band rejection of unwanted signals would be less than in the case of circuit A. The principal advantage of the circuit at B is that front-panel peaking adjustments would not be necessary once the trimmers in the filters were set for the desired response. A similar tuned circuit for either example in Fig. 15 would be used between the RF amplifier and the mixer.

Regardless of the type of LC input network used, a built-in step attenuator is worth considering. It can be used for measuring changes in signal level, or to reduce overloading effects when strong signals appear in the receiver passband. Fig. 16 shows how this can be done. The example at A is suitable for simple receivers when calibration in decibels is not a requisite, and when maintaining an impedance match between the tuned circuit and the antenna is not vital. The circuit at B is preferred because the pads are of 50-ohm impedance. In the circuit shown three steps are available: 6, 12 and 18 dB, depending on how the switches are thrown. The resistance values specified are the closest standard ones to the actual values needed to provide precisely 6 or 12 dB of attenuation. For amateur work the accuracy is adequate. Front-end attenuators are useful when VHF converters are used ahead of the station receiver. If the converters have a significant amount of overall gain they can degrade the dynamic range of the main receiver when strong signals are present. The attenuators can be set to simulate a condition of unity gain through the converter, thereby aiding receiver dynamic

Fig. 15 — Method for selecting band-pass filters for 75 and 80 meters at the input to an RF amplifier.

Fig. 16 — Front-end attenuators. A simple type is given at A and a step-attenuator version is shown at B.

Fig. 17 — Narrowband RF amplifiers are shown from A to C. A fed-back broadband RF amplifier is shown at D.

range. It is worth remembering, however, that an attenuator used at the input of a receiver when no converter is attached will degrade receiver sensitivity and noise figure. A receiver used frequently for antenna and received-signal decibel measurements might have several 3-dB pads included, thereby providing greater resolution during measurements.

RF Amplifiers

It was implied earlier in the chapter that RF amplifiers are useful primarily to improve the receiver noise figure. When atmospheric and man-made noise levels exceed that of the mixer it should be possible to realize better dynamic range by not having an RF amplifier. The gain of the RF stage, when one is used, should be set for whatever level is needed to override the mixer noise. Sometimes that is only a few decibels. A good low-noise active device should be employed as the RF amplifier in such instances.

A well-designed receiver should not have AGC applied to the RF amplifier. The best noise figure and RF-stage dynamic range will result when AGC is not applied. This is because the AGC voltage changes the operating characteristics of the RF amplifier from Class A to a less-linear mode.

Fig. 17 shows some typical RF amplifiers for use in amateur receivers. Tube-type circuits have not been included because they do not offer any particular advantage over solid-state amplifiers.

The circuit at A in Fig. 17 is likely to be the least subject to self-oscillaton of the four examples given. The common-gate hookup helps to ensure stability if the gate lead is kept as short as is physically possible. The gain from a common-gate amplifier of this type is lower than that of a common-source amplifier. However, gains up to 15 dB are typical. The drain of the FET need not be tapped down on the drain coil, but if it is there will be less loading on the tuned circuit, thereby permitting somewhat greater tuned-circuit selectivity: The lower the drain tap, the less the stage gain.

All of the FET amplifiers in Fig. 17 are capable of providing low-noise operation and good dynamic range. The common-source circuits at illustrations B and C can provide up to 25 dB of gain. However, they are more prone to instability than is the circuit at A. Therefore, the gates are shown tapped down on the gate tank: Placing the input at a low impedance point on the tuned circuit will discourage self-oscillation. The same is true of the drain tap. JFETs will hold up under considerable

RF input voltage before being damaged. Laboratory test of the MPF102 showed that 80 volts P-P (gate to source) was required to destroy the device. However, in the interest of good operating practices the P-P voltage should be kept below 10. Tapping the gate down on the input tuned circuit will result in lower levels of P-P input voltage, in addition to aiding stability.

A broadband bipolar-transistor RF amplifier is shown in Fig. 17 at D. This type of amplifier will yield approximately 16 dB of gain up to 148 MHz, and it will be unconditionally stable because of the degenerative feedback in the emitter and the negative feedback in the base circuit. A broadband 4:1 transformer is used in the collector to step the impedance down to approximately 50 ohms at the amplifier output. A 50-ohm characteristic exists at the input to the 2N5179 also. A band-pass filter should be used at the input and output of the amplifier to provide selectivity. The 4:1 transformer helps to ensure a collector load of 200 ohms, which is preferred in an amplifier of this type. This style of amplifier is used in CATV applications where the transformation from collector to load is 300 to 75 ohms.

Stability

Excessive gain or undesired feedback

may cause amplifier instability. Oscillation may occur in unstable amplifiers under certain conditions. Damage to the active device from overdissipation is only the most obvious effect of oscillation. Deterioration of noise figure, spurious signals generated by the oscillation, and reradiation of the oscillation through the antenna, causing RFI to other services, can also occur from amplifier instability.

Neutralization or other forms of feedback may be required in RF amplifiers to reach stability. Amplifier neutralization is achieved by feeding energy from the amplifier output circuit back to the input in such an amount and phase as to cancel out the effects of device internal capacitance and other unwanted input-output coupling. Care in termination of both the input and output can produce stable results from an otherwise unstable amplifier. Attention to proper grounding and proper isolation of the input from the output by means of shielding can also yield stable operating conditions.

Overloading and Spurious Signals

Normally, the RF amplifier is not a significant contributor to overloading problems in VHF receiving systems. The RF amplifiers in the first or second stage of a receiving system operate in a linear service, and if properly designed require a substantial signal input to cause deviation from linearity. Overloading usually occurs in the naturally nonlinear mixer stages. Images and other responses to out-of-band signals can be reduced or eliminated by proper filtering at the amplifier input.

In general, unwanted spurious signals and overloading increase as the signal levels rise at the input to the offending stage. Consequently, minimum gain prior to the stage minimizes overloading. Since noise figure may suffer at reduced gain, a compromise between optimum noise figure and minimum overloading must often be made. Especially in areas of high amateur activity, sacrificing noise figure somewhat may result in increased weak-signal reception effectiveness if the lower noise-figure system is easily overloaded.

Typical Circuits for VHF and Above

Common circuits for the RF amplifiers used at VHF and UHF are illustrated in Figs. 18 through 21. The termination impedances of both the input and output of these examples are low (50 ohms), suiting them well to preamplifier service. Preamplifiers are useful for improving the noise figure of existing equipment.

The choice of active device has a profound effect on the weak-signal performance of an RF amplifier. Although tubes can be used on the VHF and UHF bands, their use is seldom seen, as solid-state devices provide far better performance at lower cost. Bipolar transistors can provide excellent noise figures up through 4 GHz if chosen and used properly. The

Fig. 18 — Typical grounded-source RF amplifiers. The dual-gate MOSFET, A, is useful below 500 MHz. The junction FET, B, and neutralized MOSFET, C, work well on all VHF bands. Except where given, component values depend on frequency.

JFET is usable through 450 MHz, although the most commonly available ones drop off in performance quickly beyond that frequency. Dual-gate MOSFETs also are usable through 450 MHz. The GaAsFET provides superior noise figures past 1300 MHz.

Most RF amplifiers for use below 225 MHz use FETs rather than bipolars. Unless bipolar transistors are run at relatively high standing currents they are prone to overloading from strong signals. Additionally, their lower terminating impedances can present somewhat awkward design considerations to the builder. The FET minimizes these problems while presenting an acceptable noise figure.

Above 225 MHz, inexpensive FETs cannot provide the low noise figure attainable from bipolars. The wavelength at these higher frequencies also allows the convenient use of tuned lines rather than conventional coils, easing the possible design difficulties of the lower terminating impedances of bipolars.

The input network of an RF amplifier should be as low in loss as possible to assure a low noise figure, since any loss before the first stage is effectively added to the noise figure. High-selectivity circuits often have significant losses and should be avoided at the front end. L networks usually provide the least loss while achieving proper impedance matching. High-quality components should also be employed in the input circuit to further reduce losses.

It should be pointed out that the terminating impedance of transistors for optimum noise figure is usually not the same as that for optimum power transfer (gain). This complicates the design and tuning procedures somewhat, but careful

Fig. 19 — Grounded-gate-FET preamplifier tends to have lower gain and broader frequency response than other amplifiers described.

Fig. 20 — Cascode amplifier circuit combines grounded-source and grounded-gate stages, for high gain and low noise figure. Though JFETs are shown, the cascode principle is useful with MOSFETs as well.

measurements and adjustment can compensate for these shortcomings. The dual-gate MOSFET has different internal geometry, so optimum noise match is virtually identical to optimum gain match. This means that adjusting a dual-gate MOSFET amplifier for maximum gain usually provides best noise figure.

Some examples of common-source amplifiers are shown in Fig. 18. Many properly designed dual-gate MOSFET amplifiers do not require neutralization to achieve stability and best noise figure. An

example of this approach is shown in Fig. 18A. Neutralization may be required; Fig. 18C shows capacitive neutralization applied to a dual-gate-MOSFET amplifier. Common-source JFET amplifiers usually require neutralization to attain satisfactory operation. Inductive neutralization as shown in Fig. 18B is commonly used.

Using the gate as the common stage element introduces negative feedback and eliminates the need for neutralization in a common-gate amplifier, as shown in Fig. 19. The feedback reduces the stage

gain and lowers the input impedance, increasing the bandwidth of the stage. An additional benefit of common-gate amplifiers is reduced susceptibility to overload as compared to common-source amplifiers.

The cascode circuit of Fig. 20 combines the common-source and the common-gate amplifiers, securing some of the advantages of each. Increased gain over a single stage is its greatest asset.

Fig. 21 shows typical bipolar amplifiers for the UHF range. Fig. 21A illustrates a common-emitter amplifier, analogous to the common-source FET amplifier. The common-base amplifier of Fig. 21B can similarly be compared to a common-gate FET amplifier.

Front-End Protection

The first amplifier of a receiver is susceptible to damage or complete burnout through application of excessive voltage to its input element by way of the antenna. This can be the result of lightning discharges (not necessarily in the immediate vicinity), RF leakage from the station transmitter through a faulty send-receive relay or switch, or RF power from a nearby transmitter and antenna system. Bipolar transistors often used in low-noise UHF amplifiers are particularly sensitive to this trouble. The degradation may be gradual, going unnoticed until the receiving sensitivity has become very poor.

No equipment is likely to survive a direct hit from lightning, but casual damage can be prevented by connecting diodes back-to-back across the input circuit. Either germanium or silicon VHF diodes can be used. Both have the thresholds of conduction well above any normal signal level, about 0.2 volt for germanium and 0.6 volt for silicon. The diodes used should have fast switching times. Diodes such as the 1N914 and hot-carrier types are suitable. A check on weak-signal reception should be made before and after connection of the diodes.

MIXERS

Conversion of the received energy to a lower frequency, so it can be amplified more efficiently than would be possible at the signal frequency, is a basic principle of the superheterodyne receiver. The stage in which this is done may be called a converter or frequency converter, but we will use the more common term, mixer, to avoid confusion with converter, as applied to a complete VHF receiving accessory. Mixers perform similar functions in both transmitting and receiving circuits.

The mixer is one of the most important parts of a high-performance receiver. It is at this point where the greatest consideration for dynamic range exists. For best receiver performance the mixer should receive only enough preamplification to overcome the mixer noise. When excessive amounts of signal energy are permitted to reach the mixer, there will be desensitization, cross-modulation and IMD products in the mixer. When these effects are severe enough the receiver can be rendered useless. Therefore, it is advantageous to utilize what is often called a "strong mixer." That is, one which can handle high signal levels without being affected adversely.

Generally speaking, diode-ring passive mixers fare the best in this regard. However, they are fairly noisy and require considerably more LO injection than is the case with active mixers. For the less sophisticated types of receivers, it is adequate to use single-ended active mixers, provided the gain distribution between the antenna and mixer is proper for the mixer device used. Field-effect transistors are preferred by most designers; bipolar-transistor mixers are seldom used.

The primary advantage of an active mixer is that it has conversion gain rather than loss. This means that the stages following the mixer need not have as much gain as when diode mixers are used. A typical doubly balanced diode mixer will have a conversion loss of some 8 dB, whereas an FET active mixer may exhibit a conversion gain as great as 15 dB. The cost of gain stages is relatively small. This consideration easily justifies the use of strong passive mixers in the interest of high dynamic range.

An LC, crystal-lattice, or mechanical type of band-pass filter is almost always used after the mixer or the post-mixer amplifier. This helps to establish the overall selectivity of the receiver. It also rejects unwanted mixer products that fall outside the passband of the filter.

In the interest of optimum mixer performance, the LO energy supplied to it should be reasonably clean with respect to unwanted frequencies. Many designers, for this reason, use a band-pass filter between the LO output and the mixer input. Excessive LO noise will seriously degrade receiver performance. LO noise should be 80 dB or more below the peak output level. Excessive noise will appear as noise sidebands in the receiver output.

A receiver for 50 MHz or higher usually has at least two mixer stages: one in the VHF or UHF converter, and usually two or more in the communications receiver that follows it. We are primarily concerned here with the first mixer.

The ideal mixer would convert any input signal to another chosen frequency with no distortion, and would have a noise figure of 0 dB. Unfortunately, a mixer such as that exists only in a dream world. The mixer that has a 0-dB noise figure (or equivalent loss) has yet to be conceived. This means that the proper use of RF amplification and perhaps post-mixer amplification is necessary for maximum receiver performance with regard to sensitivity. Poor sensitivity is the least difficult of the mixer failings to mend.

Because the mixer operates in a nonlinear mode, reduction of distortion becomes a major design problem. As the mixer input

Fig. 21 — Examples of VHF amplifiers using bipolar transistors.

Fig. 22 — Two styles of active mixers using FETs.

Fig. 23 — An active singly balanced FET mixer.

Fig. 24 — Singly and doubly balanced diode mixers.

level is increased, a point is reached where the output no longer increases linearly with input. A phenomenon known as compression occurs. When the compression point is reached, the sensitivity of the mixer is reduced for every signal in the passband. This is manifested as desensing. Different types of mixers characteristically reach their compression points at different input levels, so proper mixer choice can minimize this type of distortion. Any amplifier before the mixer will increase the input levels to the mixer, lowering the point where the input level to the receiving system will cause compression. Therefore, a builder should not use more gain than is necessary to establish system noise figure prior to the mixer.

If more than one signal is present in the passband going into the mixer, they may mix to produce spurious responses known as intermodulation distortion (IMD) products. As the input levels increase further, higher-order IMD products may appear, seemingly filling the passband. Proper mixer operating conditions will alleviate IMD problems and also reduce gain-compression problems.

A third type of distortion is cross modulation. This is most readily observed on AM signals. When the carrier is on, cross modulation is evidenced by modulation characteristics of another signal being superimposed on the received carrier. Techniques to improve IMD characteristics also improve cross-modulation performance.

A problem inherent in all mixing systems is image generation. Whenever two signals are mixed, components are produced at the sum and difference of the two signal frequencies and at multiples of these frequencies. For receiving applications amateurs typically want to detect only one of the mixing products, usually the first-order mixing product. Filtering must be applied to separate the desired signal from the rest. Post-mixer filtering is not adequate, as input images can be mixed to the same intermediate frequency as the desired signal. Input filtering discriminates against these images and prevents unwanted out-of-band signals from overloading the mixer.

Typical HF Mixer Circuits

Fig. 22 shows two single-ended active mixers that offer good performance. The example at A employs a JFET with LO injection supplied to the source across a 560-ohm resistor. This injection mode requires somewhat more LO power than would be used if injection was done at the gate. However, there is less occasion for LO pulling when source injection is used, and there is better isolation between the LO and antenna than would be the case with gate injection.

The circuit at B in Fig. 22 is similar in general performance to that at A. The major difference is that a dual-gate MOSFET is used to permit injection of the LO energy at gate 2. Since there is considerable signal isolation between gates 1 and 2, LO pulling is minimized, and antenna-to-LO isolation is good.

A singly balanced active mixer is illustrated in Fig. 23. Two 40673 dual-gate MOSFETs are connected in push-pull, but with the LO frequency injected in parallel at gate 2 of each device. A potentiometer is used in the sources of the transistors to permit circuit balance. This mixer offers performance superior to that of the mixers shown in Fig. 22.

One of the least complicated and inexpensive mixers is the two-diode version (singly balanced) seen in Fig. 24A. A trifilar-wound broadband toroidal transformer is used at the mixer input. The shortcoming of this mixer over the one at B is that signal isolation between all three mixer ports is not possible. A better version is that at B in Fig. 24. In this case all three mixer ports are well isolated from one another. This greatly reduces the probability of spurious responses in the receiver. Conversion loss with these mixers is approximately 8 dB. The impedance of the mixer ports is approximately 50 ohms.

Fig. 25 — Method for diplexing the mixer output to improve the IMD characteristics.

Improved IMD characteristics can be had from a diode-ring mixer, by placing a diplexer after the mixer as shown in Fig. 25. The diplexer consists of a high-pass network (L1) and a low-pass one (L2). L2 is tuned to the IF and serves as a matching network between 50 ohms and R_L, the FET gate resistor. L1 and the associated series capacitors are tuned to three times the IF and terminated in 50 ohms. This gives the mixer a proper resistive termination without degrading the 9-MHz IF. The high-pass network has a loaded Q of 1.

IC Mixers

Although numerous ICs are available for use as mixers, only three are shown here. Fig. 26 shows a CA3028A singly balanced active mixer. The diagram at B shows the inner workings of the IC. The LO is in-

Fig. 26 — CA3028A singly balanced mixer. The circuit for the IC is given at B.

Fig. 27 — MC1496G doubly balanced mixer and circuit of the IC.

Fig. 28 — Plessey SL6440C doubly balanced mixer. R1 is selected for a bias current of about 12 mA. T1 and T2 are broadband transformers wound on ferrite toroidal cores.

Fig. 29 — Examples of single-ended mixers. The diode mixer, A, is usable through the microwave region. FET mixers, B and C, offer conversion gain and low noise figure.

jected at pin 2 of the IC. Conversion gain is on the order of 15 dB.

Fig. 27A illustrates a doubly balanced IC active mixer that employs an MC1496G. A schematic diagram of the IC is shown at B. The performance of this mixer is excellent, but is it not as strong a mixer as that of Fig. 24. However, it has good conversion gain and a fairly low noise figure.

The Plessey SL6440C programmable high-level doubly balanced mixer is shown in Fig. 28 in a broadband circuit. This configuration produces a conversion gain of 8 dB and a third-order output intercept of approximately +22 dBm. The single-sideband noise figure was found to be 11 dB. If the mixer input and output ports are terminated in 50 ohms, rather than 200 ohms as shown in Fig. 28, the typical conversion gain will be − 1 dB.

Single-ended Mixers for VHF and UHF

The simplest type of mixer is the diode mixer. The signal and the heterodyning frequency are fed into the mixer, and the mixer output includes both the sum and the difference frequencies of the two. In the case of the circuit shown in Fig. 29A the difference frequency is retained, so the 1296-MHz input signal is converted down to 28 MHz. The sum frequency is filtered out by the 28-MHz tuned circuits.

A quality diode (such as the hot-carrier type) has a fairly low noise figure up through the microwave region. Since most active mixers fall off in performance above 500 MHz, the diode mixer is the one most commonly found in amateur microwave service. Unfortunately, all diode mixers have conversion loss. The loss must be added to the noise figure of the stage following the mixer to determine the system noise figure. A low-noise stage following the mixer is necessary for good weak-signal reception. The noise figure of most communications receivers is far higher than what is needed for a low-noise-figure system; if not, RF amplification is used.

Bipolar transistors are not good square-law type devices, and thus are not favored for single-ended applications. Their major use is in switching-type mixers of the balanced variety.

Field-effect transistors have good square-law response and are very popular VHF mixers. The dual-gate MOSFET is a common mixer found in VHF amateur equipment. The MOSFET can provide considerable conversion gain, while at the same time maintaining a reasonable noise figure. MOSFET overload characteristics are suitable for the vast majority of applications. Local-oscillator energy can be applied at one of the MOSFET gates, effectively isolating the local oscillator from the other signals. The gate impedance is high, so relatively little injection is needed for maximum conversion gain. A typical example is shown in Fig. 29B.

JFETs are close to the MOSFET in mixer performance but are more difficult to apply in practical hardware. As with the MOSFET, input impedance to a JFET mixer is high, and substantial conversion gain is available. JFET bias for mixer service is critical and must be adjusted for best results. The output impedance of a JFET is lower than a dual-gate MOSFET; typically around 10 kΩ. Although other possibilities exist, local-oscillator injection should be made at the JFET source for best results. The source is a low-impedance point, so considerably more local-oscillator power is required than if a dual-gate MOSFET were used as the mixer. Noise figures as low as 4 dB are possible with circuits like that shown in Fig. 29C.

The injection level of the local oscillator affects mixer performance. Raising the LO level increases conversion gain in an FET mixer. The local-oscillator signal should be as large as possible without pushing the FET into its pinchoff region. The gate junction of the FET should never conduct in mixer applications. Increased IMD products result from either of these conditions and should be avoided. The local-oscillator energy should be as pure as possible. Distorted injection energy not only increases IMD production but also increases stage noise figure.

Proper termination of the output of an FET mixer optimizes overload performance. If the impedance seen at the drain of an FET mixer is too high at any of the mixer product frequencies, large voltage excursions can occur on the FET drain. If the voltage excursion on the drain is large enough, output distortion will be evident. Often these high-voltage excursions occur at frequencies outside the desired passband, causing distortion from signals not even detectable by the receiver. A resistor within the output matching network may be used to limit the broadband impedance to a suitably low level.

Balanced Mixers

Use of more than one device in either a singly or doubly balanced mixer offers many advantages over a single-ended mixer. The balance prevents energy injected into a mixer port from appearing at another port. The implications of this are significant when minimum mixer distortion is sought. The port-to-port isolation inhibits any signals other than the mixing products from reaching subsequent stages where they might be mixed and cause undesirable products. The usually large local-oscillator signal is kept away from the RF amplifier stages where it might cause gain compression because of its magnitude. Any amplitude-modulated noise found on the local-oscillator signal is suppressed at the mixer output, where it might be later detected. In a singly balanced mixer only one port, usually the local-oscillator input, is isolated from the other two. A doubly balanced mixer isolates all three ports from each other.

The most common balanced mixer uses

Fig. 30 — Balanced mixers for VHF and UHF. The singly balanced mixer, A, provides isolation of the local oscillator from the output. The doubly balanced diode mixer, B, has all ports isolated from each other, and is broadband throughout VHF. A special dual JFET is used at C to give high dynamic range with low noise figure.

Fig. 31 — Typical crystal oscillator for VHF use, A. The diode frequency doubler, B, provides good rejection of the fundamental signal.

diodes. The disadvantages presented earlier with respect to single-ended diode mixers apply here also. A singly balanced diode mixer is shown in Fig. 30A. Hot-carrier diodes are normally used for D1 and D2, as they can handle high currents, have a low noise figure, and are available for use up through several gigahertz.

The doubly balanced mixer is more common today. Commercial modules, very reasonably priced, are often used instead of homemade circuits. Large-scale manufacturing can usually offer electrical balance not so easily attained with the homemade units. Isolation of 35 to 40 dB is typical at VHF, with only 6 to 7 dB of conversion loss. High local-oscillator injection is needed to reach optimum performance with these mixers. Proper broadband termination of all the mixer ports is necessary to prevent unwanted signals from being reflected into the mixer "rat race," only to emerge at another port. The IF port (shown in Fig. 30B) is the most critical with respect to termination and should be terminated at 50 + j0 ohms. Transmission line transformers provide the necessary phase shift, as half the bridge is fed 180 degrees out of phase with respect to the

other half. These can be wound on ferrite toroidal forms to effect a broadband response. Careful winding of the transformers improves balance in the circuit, which in turn improves port-to-port isolation.

Active devices can be used very effectively in balanced mixers. Both FETs and bipolars can be used successfully. Active balanced mixers offer all the benefits of balanced diode mixers, plus the added advantage of conversion gain rather than loss. Because of this conversion gain, less RF amplification is needed to establish a lower system noise figure than would be needed with a diode mixer. Low gain prior to the mixer keeps mixer-input levels low, maximizing mixer overload resistance. High-dissipation active devices can be used, yielding better mixer performance than is available from diode balanced mixers. Fig. 30C shows a dual FET which has been specially designed for mixer applications. R1 allows for electrical balance adjustment in the circuit. A sharp null in local oscillator output at the mixer output can be observed when R1 is set to the optimum point, showing that electrical balance has been achieved.

Injection Stages

Oscillator and multiplier stages supplying heterodyning energy to the mixer should be as stable and free of unwanted frequencies as possible. Proper application of crystal control gives the stability needed. Two major factors influence oscillator stability: temperature and operating voltage. As the temperature of a component changes, its internal geometry is altered somewhat as the constituent materials expand or contract. This typically results in internal capacitance changes that affect the resonant frequency of the tuned circuits controlling the oscillator frequency. Use of quality components that have good temperature characteristics helps in this regard. Minimum power should be extracted from the oscillator as excessive heat dissipation within either the crystal or the transistor will cause internal capacitance changes in those devices, moving the resonant frequency. Voltage to the transistor should be regulated for best stability. Simple Zener-diode regulation is sufficient, or a three-terminal regulator IC can be used.

Any unwanted injection frequencies will mix with signals present in the mixer, creating spurious outputs at the mixer output. A clean local oscillator will prevent these unwanted outputs. The oscillator chain output can be heavily filtered to cut down the harmonic content of the oscillator. Good planning and design will minimize the unwanted energy, making the filtering job less demanding. A high-frequency crystal in the oscillator minimizes the number of times that the fundamental oscillator frequency has to be multiplied to reach the converter injection frequency. Proper use of doublers rather than triplers can eliminate any odd oscillator frequency multiples, so a low-pass filter at the output has to filter only the fourth harmonic and beyond. A band-pass filter would be needed at the output of a tripler to eliminate the second harmonic and the higher ones. Finally, good shielding and power-line filtering should be used throughout to prevent any line noise from reaching the mixer or causing RFI problems elsewhere.

Fig. 31A shows a typical circuit useful for providing the 116-MHz injection energy necessary to convert a 144-MHz signal down to 28 MHz. R_z dampens the crystal action somewhat, assuring that the proper overtone is the actual oscillation frequency. The collector tank network is parallel tuned and can be wound on a toroidal core to reduce radiation. The output is link coupled from the tank, minimizing harmonic coupling. This oscillator would be followed by a buffer to bring the signal up to that level needed and to purify the oscillator signal further.

A similar oscillator could be used in a 220-MHz converter. Since crystals are not available at 192 MHz, the frequency required for conversion to 28-MHz converter output, the most logical approach is to use a 96-MHz oscillator and double its output. Fig. 31B shows a diode frequency doubler suitable for the application. The phase-shifting transformer can be made from a trifilar winding on a ferrite core. Hot-carrier diodes allow the use of a doubler like this up through at least 500 MHz. There is a loss of about 8 dB through the doubler, so amplification is needed to raise the injection signal to the appropriate level. Fundamental energy is down by as much as 40 dB from the second harmonic with a balanced diode doubler such as this. All of the odd harmonics are well down in amplitude also, without using tuned circuits. A low-pass filter can be used to eliminate the undesired harmonics from the output.

DOUBLY BALANCED MIXERS

Advances in technology have provided the amateur builder with many new choices of hardware to use in the building of receivers, converters or preamplifiers. The broadband doubly balanced mixer (DBM) package is a fine example of this progress. As amateurs gain an understanding of the capabilities of this device, they are incorporating this type of mixer in many pieces of equipment, especially receiving mixers. The combined mixer/amplifier described here was presented originally in March 1975 *QST* by K1AGB.

Mixer Comparisons

Is a DBM really better than other types? What does it offer, and what are its disadvantages? To answer these questions, another look at more conventional active (voltages applied) mixing techniques and some of their problems is in order. Briefly, common single-device active mixers with gain at VHF and UHF are beset with problems of noise, desensitization and insufficient local-oscillator (LO) isolation from the RF and IF "ports." As mixers, most devices have noise figures in excess of those published for them as RF amplifiers and will not provide sufficient

sensitivity for weak-signal work. To minimize noise, mixer-device current is generally maintained at a low level. This can reduce dynamic range and increase overload potential. Gain contributions of RF amplifiers (used to establish a low system noise figure) further complicate the overload problem. LO-noise leakage to the RF and IF ports adversely affects system performance. Mixer dynamic range can be limited by conversion of this noise to the IF, placing a lower limit on mixer system sensitivity. Generally 20 dB of mixer midband interport isolation is required, and most passive DBMs can offer greater than 40 dB.

A commercially manufactured doubly balanced diode mixer offers performance predictability, circuit simplicity and flexibility. Closely matched Schottky-barrier hot-carrier diodes, commonly used in most inexpensive mixers of this type, provide outstanding strong-signal mixer performance (up to about 0 dBm at the RF input port) and add little (0.5 dB or so) to the mixer noise figure. Essentially, diode conversion loss from RF to IF, listed in Table 1, represents most of the mixer contribution to system noise figure. Midband isolation between the LO port and the RF and IF ports of a DBM is typically > 35 dB — far greater than that achievable with conventional single-device active-mixing schemes. This isolation is particularly advantageous in dealing with low-level local-oscillator harmonic and noise content. Of course, selection of LO devices with low audio noise figures, and proper RF filtering in the LO output, will reduce problems from this source.

Often-listed disadvantages of a diode DBM are (a) conversion loss, (b) LO power requirements, and (c) IF-interface problems. The first two points are closely interrelated. Conversion loss necessitates some low-noise RF amplification to establish a useful weak-signal system noise figure. Additional LO power is fairly easy to generate, filter and measure. If we accept the fact that more LO power is

necessary for the DBM than is used in conventional single-device active mixing circuits, we leave only two real obstacles to be overcome in the DBM, those of conversion loss and IF output interfacing.

To minimize conversion loss in a DBM, the diodes are driven by the LO beyond their square-law region, producing an output spectrum which in general includes the terms[2]

1) Fundamental frequencies fLO and fRF
2) All of their harmonics
3) The desired IF output, fLO $\pm$ fRF
4) All higher order products of nfLO $\pm$ mfRF, where n and m are integers.

The DBM, by virtue of its symmetry and internal transformer balance, suppresses a large number of the harmonic modulation products. In the system described here, f LO is on the low side of fRF; therefore, numerically, the desired IF output is fRF − fLO. Nonetheless, the term fLO + fRF appears at the IF output port equal in amplitude to the desired IF signal, and this unused energy must be effectively terminated to obtain no more than the specified mixer-conversion loss. This is not the image frequency, fLO − fIF, which will be discussed later.

In any mixer design, all RF port signal components must be bypassed effectively for best conversion efficiency (minimum loss). Energy not "converted" by mixing action will reduce conversion gain in active systems, and increase conversion loss in passive systems such as the diode DBM. RF bypassing also prevents spurious resonances and other undesired phenomena from affecting mixer performance. In this sytem, RF bypassing at the IF output port will be provided by the input capacitance of the IF interface. The DBM is not a panacea for mixing ills, and its effectiveness can be reduced drastically if all ports are not properly terminated.

[2]See appendix at the end of this section on mixers.

Table 1
Doubly Balanced Mixers

Manufacturer	WJC	M/A-Com Anzac	MCL	MCL	MCL	MCL
Model	M6F	MD-108	SRA-1	SRA-1H	RAY-1	MA-1
Frequency Range (MHz)						
LO	2-500	5-500	5-500	5-500	5-500	1-2500
RF	2-500	5-500	51-500	5-500	5-500	1-2500
IF	DC-500	DC-500	DC-500	DC-500	DC-500	DC-1000
Conversion loss Mid-range	9 dB max.	7.5 dB max.	6.5 dB typ.	6.5 dB typ.	7.5 dB typ.	8.0 dB typ.
Isolation, LO-RF	34-40 dB min.	40 dB min.	45 dB typ.	45 dB typ.	40 dB typ.	40 dB typ.
Mid-range LO-IF	25-35 dB min.	35 dB-min.	40 dB typ.	40 dB typ.	40 dB typ.	40 dB typ.
Total input power	50 mW	400 mW	500 mW	500 mW	1W	50 mW
LO power requirement	+7 dBm (5 mW)	+7 dBm (5 mW)	+7 dBm (5 mW)	+17 dBm (50 mW)	+23 dBm (200 mW)	+10 dBm (10 mW)
Signal 2-dB compression level	Not spec.	Not spec.	+1 dBm	+10 dBm	+15 dBm	+7 dBm
Impedance, all ports	50 ohms	50 ohms	50 ohms	50 ohms	50 ohms	50 ohms

All specifications apply only at stated LO power level.

WJC—Watkins Johnson Co, Components Division
MCL—Mini-Circuits Lab

For manufacturers' addresses, see the ARRL Parts Suppliers List in the Component Data chapter of this *Handbook*.

Fig. 32 — The IF port of a doubly balanced mixer, matched at fLO − fRF and reactive at fLO + fRF. In this configuration conversion loss, RF compression and desensitization levels can vary ±3dB while harmonic modulation and third-order IMD products can vary ±20 dB.

DBM-Port Termination

Most DBM performance inconsistencies occur because system source and load impedances presented to the mixer are not matched at all frequencies encountered in normal operation. The terminations (attenuator pads) used in conjunction with test equipment by manufacturers to measure published performance characteristics are closely matched over a wide range of frequencies. Reactive mixer terminations can cause system problems, and multiple reactive terminations can usually compound these problems to the point where performance is very difficult to predict. Let's see how we can deal with reactive terminations.

The IF Port

The IF port is very sensitive to mismatch conditions. Reflections from the mixer/IF-amplifier interface (the pi network in Fig. 33) can cause the conversion loss to vary as much as 6 dB. Also greatly affected are third-order intermodulation-product ratio and the suppression of spurious signals, both of which may vary ± 10 dB or more. It is ironic that the IF port is the most sensitive to a reactive termination, as this is a receiving system point where sharp-skirted filters are often desired.

Briefly, here is what happens with a reactive IF port termination. Fig. 32 shows a DBM with "high side" LO injection and an IF termination matched at fLO − fRF but reactive to fLO + fRF. The latter term re-enters the mixer, again combines with the LO, and produces terms that exit at the RF port, namely 2fLO + fRF, a dc term, and fLO + fRF − fLO (the original RF-port input frequency). This condition affects conversion loss, as mentioned earlier, in addition to RF-port VSWR, depending on the phase of the reflected signal. The term 2fLO + fRF also affects the harmonic spectrum resulting in spurious responses.

One solution to the IF interface problem is the use of a broadband 50-ohm resistive termination, like a pad, to minimize reflec-

tions. In deference to increased post-conversion system noise figure, it seems impractical to place such a termination at the mixer IF output port. While a complementary filter or diplexer (high-pass/low-pass filters appropriately terminated) can be used to terminate both fRF + fLO and fRF − fLO[†], a simpler method can be used if fRF + fLO is less than 1 GHz and (fRF + fLO)/(fRF − fLO) ≥ 10. Place a short-circuit termination to fRF + fLO, like a simple lumped capacitance, directly at the mixer IF terminal. This approach is easiest for the amateur to implement and duplicate, so a form of it was tried — with success. In our circuit, C1 serves a dual purpose. Its reactance at fRF + fLO is small enough to provide a low-impedance "short-circuit" condition to this term for proper mixer operation. Additionally, it is part of the input reactance of the mixer IF amplifier interface. Fortunately, the network impedance-transformation ratio is large enough, and in the proper direction, to permit a fairly large amount of capacitance (low reactance) at the mixer IF-output port. The capacitor, in its dual role, must be of good quality at VHF/UHF (specifically fRF + fLO), with short leads, to be effective. The mixer condition (fRF + fLO)/(fRF − fLO) ≥ 10 is met at 432 and 220 MHz with a 404/192 MHz LO (28-MHz IF) and on 144 MHz with a 130-MHz LO (14-MHz IF). At 50 MHz, with a 36-MHz LO, we are slightly shy of the requirement, but no problems were encountered in an operating unit. The pi-type interface circuit assures a decreasing impedance as IF operation departs from midband, lessening IMD problems.

The LO Port

The primary effect of a reactive LO source is an increase in harmonic modulation and third-order IMD products. If the drive level is adequate, no effect is noted on conversion loss, RF compression and desensitization levels. A reactive LO source can be mitigated by simply padding the LO port with a 3- or 6-dB pad and increasing the LO drive a like amount. If excess LO power is not available, matching the LO source to the mixer will improve performance. This method is acceptable for single-frequency LO applications, when appropriate test equipment is available to evaluate matching results. For simplicity, a 3-dB pad was incorporated at the LO-input port as an interface in both versions of the mixer. Thus the LO port is presented with a reasonably broadband termination, and is relatively insensitive to applied frequency, as long as it is below about 500 MHz. This implies that frequencies other than amateur assignments may be covered — and such is indeed the case when ap-

†Presentation and calculation format of these terms is based on "low-side" LO injection; see the appendix for explanation.

Table 2
DBM IF Amplifier Parts List

	14 MHz IF output	28 MHz IF output
C1	470 pF JFD 471J or equiv.	300 pF JFD 301J or equiv.
C2	390 pF SM	not used
C3	180 pF SM	51 pF SM
C4	39 pF SM	18 pF SM
C5	56 pF SM	27 pF SM
C6	300 pF SM	150 pF SM
L1	9 turns no. 18 enam., close wound on a 3/8-inch diameter red-slug coil form.	9 turns no. 24 enam., close wound on a 1/4-inch diameter green-slug coil form.
L2	18 turns no. 26 enam., close wound on a 3/8-inch diameter red-slug coil form. Tap down 7 turns from top for 3N140 drain connection. See text.	12 turns no. 26 enam., close wound on a 1/4-inch diameter green-slug coil form. No tap used
L3	Same as L2 but no tap, spaced 1-1/8 inch center-to-center with L2.	Same as L2, spaced 1 inch center-to-center with L2.
R1, R3	300-ohm 1/4 W	430 ohm, 1/4 W
R2	16 ohm, 1/4 W	11 ohm, 1/4 W

Ferrite beads can be replaced by a 10-ohm, 1/4-W carbon resistor at one end of the choke, if desired.

SM = Silver Mica.

propriate LO frequencies and RF amplifiers are used. Remotely located LOs, when adjusted for a 50-ohm load, can be connected to the mixer without severe SWR and reflective-loss problems in the transmission line.

Broadband mixers exhibit different characteristics at different frequencies, owing to circuit resonances and changes in diode impedances resulting from LO power-level changes. Input impedances of the various ports are load dependent, even though they are isolated from each other physically, and by at least 35 dB electrically. At higher frequencies, this effect is more noticeable, since isolation tends to drop as frequency increases. For this reason, it is important to maintain the LO power at its appropriate level, once other ports are matched.

The RF Port

A reactive RF source is not too detrimental to system performance. This is good, since the output impedance of most amateur preamplifiers is seldom 50 ohms resistive. A 3-dB pad is used at the RF port in the 50- and 144- to 14-MHz mixers, and a 2-dB pad is used in the 220/432- to 28-MHz units, although they add directly to mixer noise figure. RF inputs between about 80 and 200 MHz are practical in the 14-MHz-IF-output model, while the 28-MHz-output unit is most useful from 175 to 500 MHz. Mixer contribution to system noise figure will be almost completely overcome by a low-noise RF amplifier with sufficient gain and adequate image rejection.

Image Response

Any broadband mixing scheme will have a potential image-response problem. In most amateur VHF/UHF receiver systems (as in these units), single-conversion techniques are employed. The LO is placed below the desired RF channel for noninverting down-conversion to IF. Conversion is related to both IF and LO frequencies. Because of the broadband nature of the DBM, input signals at the RF image frequency (numerically $fLO - fRF$ in our case) will legitimately appear inverted at the IF-output port, unless proper filtering is used to reduce them at the mixer RF-input port. For example, a 144-MHz converter with a 28-MHz IF output (116-MHz LO) will have RF image-response potential in the 84- to 88-MHz range. TV channel 6 wideband-FM audio will indeed appear at the IF-output port near 28 MHz unless appropriate RF- input filtering is used to eliminate it. While octave-bandwidth VHF/UHF "imageless mixer" techniques can improve system noise performance by about 3 dB (image noise reduction), and image signal rejection by 20 dB — and much greater with the use of a simple gating scheme — such a system is a bit esoteric for our application. Double- or multiple-conversion techniques can be used to advantage, but they further complicate an otherwise simple system. Image noise and signal rejection will depend on the effectiveness of the filtering provided in the RF-amplifier chain.

Mixer Selection

The mixer used in this system is a Relcom M6F, with specifications of the M6F and suitable substitutes given in Table 1. While mixers are available with connectors attached; they are more expensive. The MF6 and substitutes are designed for printed-circuit applications. Their short leads assure a proper interface between the mixer and the IF amplifier. The combining of mixer and IF amplifier in one converter package was done for that reason. Along these lines, the modular approach permits good signal isolation and enables the mixer-amplifier/IF system to be used at a variety of RF and LO-input frequencies, as mentioned earlier.

Most commonly available, inexpensive DBMs are not constructed to take advantage of LO powers much above + 10 dBm (10 mW). To do so requires additional circuitry, which could degrade other mixer characteristics, specifically conversion loss and interport isolation. The advantage of higher LO power is primarily one of improved strong-signal-handling performance. At least one manufacturer advertises a moderately priced "high-level" receiving DBM that can use up to + 23 dBm (200 mW) LO power, and still retain the excellent conversion loss and isolation characteristics shown in Table 1. The usefulness of mixers with LO power requirements above the commonly available + 7 dBm (5 mW) level in amateur receiving applications may be a bit moot, as succeeding stages in most amateur receivers will likely overload before the DBM does. Overdesign is not necessary.

In general, mixer selection is based on the lowest practical LO level requirement that will meet the application, as it is more economical and results in the least LO leakage within the system. As a first-order approximation, LO power should be 10 dB greater than the highest anticipated input-signal level at the RF port. Mixers with LO requirements of + 7 dBm are adequate for amateur receiving applications.

Application Design Guidelines

While the material just presented only scratches the surface in terms of DBM theory and utilization in amateur VHF/UHF receiving systems, some practical solutions to the mixer-port mismatch problem have been offered. To achieve best performance from most commerically manufactured broadband DBMs in amateur receiver service, the following guidelines are suggested:

1) Choose IF and LO frequencies that will provide maximum freedom from interference problems. Don't guess; go through the numbers!

2) Provide a proper IF-output termination (most critical).

3) Increase the LO-input power to RF-input power ratio to a value that will provide the required suppression of any in-band interfering products. The specified LO power (+ 7 dBm) will generally accomplish this.

4) Provide as good an LO match as possible.

5) Include adequate premixer RF-image filtering at the RF port.

When the mixer ports are terminated properly, performance usually in excess of published specifications will be achieved — and this is more than adequate for most amateur VHF/UHF receiver mixing applications.

THE COMBINED DBM/IF AMPLIFIER

A low-noise IF amplifier (2 dB or less) following the DBM helps ensure an acceptable system noise figure when the mixer is preceded by a low-noise RF amplifier.

Fig. 33 — A schematic diagram for the doubly balanced mixer and IF post amplifier. The IF can be either 14 or 28 MHz. Parts values are given in Table 2.

A pi-network matching system used between the mixer IF-output port and gate 1 of the 3N140 transforms the nominal 50-ohm mixer-output impedance to a 1500-ohm gate-input impedance (at 28 MHz) specifically for best noise performance. The network forms a narrow-band mixer/IF-output circuit, which serves two other importance functions: It helps achieve the necessary isolation between RF and IF signal components, and serves as a 3-pole filter, resulting in a monotonic decrease in match impedances as the operating IF departs from midband. This action aids in suppression of harmonic-distortion products.

The combined DBM/IF amplifier is shown schematically in Fig. 33 and pictorially in the photographs. In the 14-MHz model, the 3N140 drain is tapped down on its associated inductance to provide a lower impedance for better strong-signal-handling ability. The 3N140 produces about 19 dB gain across a 700-kHz passband, flat within 1 dB between 13.8 and 14.5 MHz. A 2-MHz passband is used for the 28-MHz model, and the device drain is connected directly to the high-impedance end of its associated inductance. Both amplifiers were tuned independently of their mixers, and checked for noise figure as well as gain. With each IF amplifier pretuned and connected to its mixer, signals were applied to the LO- and RF-input ports. The pi-network inductance in the IF interface was adjusted carefully to see if performance had been altered. No change was noted. IF gain is controlled by the externally accessible potentiometer. Passband tuning adjustments in the drain circuit are best made with a sweep generator, but single-signal tuning techniques will be adequate. While there should be no difficulty with the non-gate-protected 3N140, a 40673 may be substituted directly if desired.

DBM/IF Amplifier IMD Evaluation

Classical laboratory IMD measurements were made on the DBM/IF amplifier using two − 10 dBm signals, closely spaced in the 144-MHz range. The LO power used was + 7 dBm. Conversion loss was 5 dB and the calculated third-order output intercept point was + 15 dBm. In operation, as simulated by these test conditions, equivalent output signal levels at J3 would be strong enough to severely overload most amateur receivers.

A high-performance, small-signal, VHF/UHF receiving amplifier optimized for IMD reduction and useful noise figure is only as good as any succeeding receiving-system stage, in terms of overload. The DBM/IF-amplifier combination presented significantly reduces common first-mixer overload problems, leaving the station receiver as the potentially weak link in the system. When properly understood and employed, the broadband DBM followed by a selective low-noise IF amplifier can be a useful tool for the amateur VHF/UHF receiver experimenter.

APPENDIX

Mixer Terminology

*f*RF — RF input frequency
*f*LO — local-oscillator input frequency
*f*IF — IF output frequency

By convention, mixing signals and their products are referred to the LO frequency for calculations. In the mixer system, *f*RF is always above *f*LO, so we will refer our signals to *f*RF, with the exception of Fig. 32 which used the *f*LO reference.

Overload

A generic term covering most undesired operating phenomena associated with device nonlinearity.

Harmonic Modulation Products

Output responses caused by harmonics of *f*LO and *f*RF and their mixing products.

RF Compression Level

The absolute single-signal RF input-power level that causes conversion loss to increase by 1 dB.

RF Desensitization Level

The RF input power of an interfering signal that causes the small-signal conversion loss to increase by 1 dB, i.e., reducing a weak received signal by 1 dB.

Intermodulation Products

Distortion products caused by multiple RF signals and their harmonics mixing with each other and the LO, producing new output frequencies.

Mixer Intermodulation Intercept Point

Because mixers are nonlinear devices, all signals applied will generate others. When two signals (or tones), F1 and F2, are applied simultaneously to the RF-input port, additional signals are generated and appear in the output as *f*LO ± (*n*F1 + *m*F2). These signals are most troublesome when *n* + *m* is a low odd number, as the resulting product will lie close to the desired output. For *n* − 1 (or 2) and *m* − 2 (or 1), the result is three (3), and is called the two-tone/third-order intermodulation products. When F1 and F2 are separated by 1 MHz, the third-order products will lie 1 MHz above and below the desired output. Intermodulation is generally specified under anticipated operating conditions since performance varies over the broad mixer-frequency ranges. Intermodulation products may be specified at levels required (i.e., 50 dB below the desired outputs for two 0-dBm input signals) or by the intercept point.

The intercept point is a ficitious point determined by the fact that an increase of level of two input tones by 10 dB will cause the desired output to increase by 10 dB, but the third-order output will increase by 30 dB. If the mixer exhibited no compression, there would be a point at which the level of the desired output would be equal to that of the third-order product. This is called the third-order-intercept point.

Noise Figure

Noise figure (NF) is a relative measurement based on excess noise power available from a termination (input resistor) at a particular temperature (290 K). When measuring the NF of a doubly balanced mixer with an automatic system, such as the HP-342A, a correction may be necessary to make the meter reading consistent with the accepted definition of receiver noise figure.

In a broadband DBM, the actual noise bandwith consists of two IF passbands, one on each side of the local-oscillator frequency (*f*LO + *f*IF and *f*LO − *f*IF). This double-sideband (DSB) IF response includes the RF channel and its image. In general, only the RF channel is desired for further amplification. The image contributes nothing but receiver and background noise.

When making an automatic noise-figure measurement using a wideband noise source, the excess noise is applied through both sidebands in a broadband DBM. Thus the instrument meter indicates NF as based on both sidebands. This means that the noise in the RF and image sidebands is combined in the mixer IF-output port to give double contribution (3 dB greater than under SSB conditions). For equal RF-sideband responses, which is a reasonable assumption, and in the absence of preselectors, filters or other image rejection elements, the automatic NF meter readings are 3 dB lower than the actual NF for DBM measurements.

The noise figure for receivers (and most DBM) is generally specified with only one sideband for the useful signal. As mentioned in the text, most DBM diodes add no more than 0.5 dB (in the form of NF) to conversion loss, which is generally measured under single-signal RF-input (SSB) conditions. Assuming DBM conversion efficiency (or loss) to be within specifications, there is an excellent probability that the SSB NF is also satisfactory. Noise-figure calculations in the text were made using a graphical solution of the well known noise-figure formula:

$$f_T = f_1 + \frac{f_2 - 1}{g_1}$$

converted to decibels.

Improved Wideband IF Responses

The following information was developed in achieving broad-band performance in the mixer-to-amplifier circuitry. In cases where only a small portion of a band is of interest the original circuit values are adequate. For those who need to receive over a considerable portion of a band, say 1 to 2 MHz, a change of some component will provide improved performance over a broad range while maintaining an acceptable noise figure.

Ther term "nominal 50-ohm impedance" applied to diode DBM ports is a misnomer, as their reflective impedance is rarely 50 ohms + j_0, and a VSWR of 1 is almost never achieved. Mixer performance specified by the manufacturer is measured in a 50-ohm broadband system, and it is up to the designer to provide an equivalent termination to ensure that the unit will meet specifications. Appropriate matching techniques at the RF and LO ports will reduce conversion loss and LO-power requirements. Complex filter synthesis can improve the IF output match. However, if one does not have the necessary equipment to evaluate these efforts, they may be wasted. Simple, effective, easily reproduced reduced circuitry was desired as long as the trade-offs were acceptable. Measurements indicate this to be the case.

The most critical circuit in the combined unit is the interface between mixer and IF amplifier. It must be low-pass in nature to satisfy VHF signal component bypassing requirements at the mixer IF port. For best mixer IMD characteristics and low conversion loss, it must present to the IF port a nominal 50-ohm impedance at the desired frequency, and this impedance value must not be allowed to increase as IF operation departs from midband. The impedance at the IF-amplifier end of the interface network must be in the optimum region for minimum cross-modulation and low noise. A dual-gate device offers two important advantages over most bipolars. Very little, if any, power gain is sacrificed in achieving best noise figure, and both parameters (gain and NF) are relatively independent of source resistance in the optimum region. As a result, the designer has a great deal of flexibility in choosing a source impedance. In general, a 3:1 change in source resistance results in only a 1-dB change in NF. With minimum cross-modulation as a prime system consideration, this 3:1 change (reduction) in source resistance implies a 3:1 improvement in cross-modulation and total harmonic distortion.

Tests in the 3N201 dual-gate MOSFET have shown device noise performance to be excellent for source impedances in the 1000- to 2000-ohm region. For optimum noise and good cross-modulation performance, the nominal 50-ohm mixer-IF-output impedance is stepped up to about 1500 ohms for IF-amplifier gate 1, using the familiar low-pass pi network. This is a mismatched condition for gate 1, as the device input impedance for best gain in the HF region is on the order of 10 kΩ. Network loaded-Q values in the article are a bit higher than necessary, and a design for lower Q_L is preferred. Suggested modified component values are listed in Fig. 34. High-frequency attenuation is reduced somewhat, but satisfactory noise and bandwidth perfor-

Fig. 34 — Suggested changes in the mixer-to-3N140 pi-network interface circuit, producing lower Q_L and better performance.

Fig. 35 — Methods for applying AGC to a bipolar IF amplifier (A) and a dual-gate-MOSFET IF stage (B).

mance are more easily obtained. Coil-form size is the same, so no layout changes are required for the modification. Components in the interface must be of high Q and few in number to limit their noise contribution through losses. The 28-MHz values provide satisfactory interface network performance over a 2-MHz bandwidth. A higher Q_L in the 28-MHz interface can be useful if one narrows the output network and covers only a few hundred kilohertz bandwidth, as is commonly done in 432-MHz weak-signal work.

Device biasing and gain control methods

were chosen for simplicity and adequate performance. Some sort of gain adjustment is desirable for drain-circuit overload protection. It is also a handy way to "set" the receiver S meter. A good method for gain adjustment is reduction of the gate-2 bias voltage from its initial optimum-gain bias point (greater than +4 V dc), producing a remote-cutoff characteristic (a gradual reduction in drain current with decreasing gate bias). The initial gain-reduction rate is higher with a slight forward bias on gate 1, than for $V_{g_1s} = 0$. Input- and output-circuit detuning resulting from gain reduc-

Fig. 36 — An IC type of IF amplifier with AGC applied.

Fig. 37 — AGC is applied to an MC1590G IC.

tion (Miller effect) are inconsequential as the gate-1 and drain susceptances change very little over a wide range of $V_{g_2}s$ and I_D at both choices of IF. Best intermodulation figure for the 3N201 was obtained with a small forward bias on gate 1. The bias-circuit modification shown in Fig. 34 may be tried, if desired.

IF Amplifiers

The amount of amplification used in a receiver will depend on how much signal level is available at the input to the IF strip. Sufficient gain is needed to ensure ample audio output consistent with driving headphones or a speaker. Another consideration is the amount of AGC-initiated IF gain range. The more IF stages used (a maximum of two is typical), the greater the gain change caused by AGC action. The range is on the order of 80 dB when two CA3028A ICs are used in the IF strip. A pair of MC1590G ICs will provide up to 120 dB of gain variation with AGC applied.

Nearly all modern receiver circuits utilize ICs as IF amplifiers. Numerous types of ICs are available to provide linear RF and IF amplification at low cost. The CA3028A and MC1590G ICs are the most popular ones for amateur work because they are easy to obtain and are inexpensive. With careful layout techniques either device will operate in a stable manner. Bypassing should be done as near to the IC pins as possible. Input and output circuit elements must be separated to prevent mutual coupling which can cause unstable operation. If IC sockets are used they should be of the low-profile variety with short socket conductors.

Fig. 35 contains examples of bipolar transistor and FET IF amplifiers. Typical component values are given. A CA3028A IC, connected for differential-amplifier operation, is shown in Fig. 36 as an IF amplifier. Up to 40 dB of gain is possible with this circuit. The IC is useful up to 120 MHz and has a low noise figure.

A Motorola MC1590G IC will provide up to 50 dB of gain when used as an IF amplifier. An example of the circuit is given in Fig. 37. AGC operates in the reverse of that which is applied to a CA3028A. With the CA3028A, the gain will be maximum with maximum AGC voltage. An MC1590G delivers maximum gain at the low AGC voltage level.

With both amplifiers (Figs. 36 and 37) the input impedance is on the order of 1000 ohms. The output impedance is close to 4000 ohms. These values are for single-ended operation, as shown. The values are doubled when either device is operated in push-pull with respect to input and output tuned circuits.

Choice of Frequency

The selection of an intermediate frequency is a compromise between conflicting factors. The lower the IF the higher the selectivity and gain, but a low IF brings the image nearer the desired signal and hence decreases the image ratio. A low IF also increases pulling of the oscillator frequency. A high IF improves the image ratio and reduces pulling, but the gain is lowered and selectivity is harder to obtain by simple means.

An IF of the order of 455 kHz gives good selectivity and is satisfactory from the standpoint of image ratio and oscillator pulling at frequencies up to 7 MHz. The image ratio is poor at 14 MHz when the mixer is connected to the antenna, but adequate when there is a tuned RF amplifier between the antenna and mixer. At 28 MHz and at very high frequencies, the image ratio is very poor unless several RF stages are used. Above 14 MHz, pulling is likely to be bad without very loose coupling between mixer and oscillator. Tuned-circuit shielding also helps.

With an IF of about 1600 kHz, satisfactory image ratios can be secured on 14, 21 and 28 MHz with one RF stage of good design. For frequencies of 28 MHz and higher, a common solution is to use double conversion, choosing one high IF for image reduction (9 MHz is frequently used) and a lower one for gain and selectivity.

In choosing an IF it is wise to avoid frequencies on which there are strong signals, such as broadcast bands, since such signals may get into the IF amplifier by conduction or radiation pickup. Shifting the IF or better shielding are solutions to this interference problem.

Fidelity: Sideband Cutting

If the selectivity is too great to permit uniform amplification over the band of frequencies occupied by the modulated signal, some of the sidebands are "cut." While sideband cutting reduces fidelity, it is frequently done to favor communications effectiveness.

IF Selectivity

Assuming that all stages are properly designed, IF selectivity is the most significant selectivity in a receiver. This selectivity separates signals and reduces QRM. At intermediate frequencies above 500 kHz it is common practice to use crystal filters. These can be designed with just one crystal (Fig. 38A), or with two or more crystals. Fig. 38B illustrates a two-crystal, half-lattice filter. A cascaded half-lattice filter is shown at C of Fig. 38. Table 4 lists various crystal filters manufactured by Spectrum International.

The single-crystal example shown at A of Fig. 38 is best suited for simple receivers intended mainly for CW use. C1 is adjusted to provide the bandpass characteristic shown adjacent to the circuit. When the BFO frequency is placed on the part of the low-frequency slope (left) which gives the desired beat note respective to f_o (approximately 800 Hz), single-signal reception will result. To the right of f_o in Fig. 38A the response drops sharply to reduce output on the unwanted side of zero beat, thereby making single-signal reception possible. If no IF filter were used, or if the BFO frequency fell at f_o, nearly equal response would exist on either side of zero beat (double-signal response) as is the case with direct-conversion receivers. QRM on the unwanted-response side of the IF passband would interfere with reception. The single-crystal filter shown is capable of at least 30 dB of rejection on the high-frequency side of zero beat. The filter termination, R_T, has a marked effect on the response curve. It is necessary to experiment with the resistance value until the desired response is obtained. Values can range from 1500 to 10,000 ohms.

A half-lattice filter is shown at B in Fig. 38. The response curve is symmetrical, and there is a slight dip at center frequency. The dip is minimized by proper selection of R_T. Y1 and Y2 are separated in frequency by the amount needed to obtain CW or SSB selectivity. The bandwidth at the 3-dB points will be approximately 1.5 times the crystal-frequency spacing. For upper- or lower-sideband reception, Y1 and Y2 would be 1.5 kHz apart, yielding a 3-dB bandwidth of approximately 2.25 kHz. For CW work, a crystal spacing of 0.4 kHz would result in a bandwidth of roughly 600

Fig. 38 — A comparison among crystal IF filters. The selectivity is increased as crystals are added.

Table 3
Collins Radio Mechanical Filters

Part & Type Numbers	Min. 3 dB BW @ 25° (kHz)	Min. 4 dB CBW OTR (kHz)	Max. 60 dB BW @ 25°C (kHz)	Max. 60 dB BW OTR (dB)	Max. RV @ 25°C (dB)	Max. RV OTR (dB)	Max. IL @ 25°C (dB)	Max. IL COTR (dB)	Min. 60 dB SBR (kHz)	S & L −5% ohms	Res. Cap. +5% (pF)
526-9689-010 F455FD-04	0.375	0.375	3.5	4.0	3.0	4.0	10.0	12.0	455-F60L F6OH-465	2000 350	350
526-9690-010 F455FD-12	1.2	1.2	8.7	9.5	3.0	4.0	10.0	12.0	445-F6OL F6OH-465	2000 350	350
F526-9691-010 F455FD-19	1.9	1.9	5.4	5.9	3.0	4.0	10.0	12.0	445-F6OL F60H-465	2000	330 350
526-9692-010 F455FD-25	2.5	2.5	6.5	7.0	3.0	4.0	10.0	12.0	445-F60L F6OH-465	2000 510	510
526-9693-010 F455FD-29	2.9	2.9	7.0	8.0	3.0	4.0	10.0	12.0	445-F6OL F6OH-465	2000 510	510
526-9694-010 F455FD-38	3.8	3.8	9.0	10.0	3.0	4.0	10.0	12.0	445-F6OL F6OH-465	2000 1000	1000
526-9695-010 F455FD-58	5.8	5.8	14.0	15.0	3.0	4.0	10.0	12.0	445-F6OL F6OH-465	2000 1100	1100

OTR = Operating Temperature Range, RV = Ripple Voltage, IL = Insertion loss, SBR = Stop Band Range, S & L = Source and Load
Courtesy of Collins Radio Co.

Table 4
Crystal Filters

Application	SSB Tran.	SSB Rec.	CW or Digital Data	AM	AM	CW	FM
Filter Type	XF-9A	XF-9B	XF-9NB	XF-9C	XF-9D	XF-9M	XF-9E
No. of crystals	5	8	8	8	8	4	8
6-dB of bandwidth	2.5 kHz	2.4 kHz	0.5 kHz	3.75 kHz	5.0 kHz	0.5 kHz	12 kHz
Passband ripple	<1 dB	<2 dB	<0.5 dB	<2 dB	<2 dB	<1 dB	<2 dB
Insertion loss	<3 dB	<3.5 dB	<6.5 dB	<3.5 dB	<3.5 dB	<5 dB	<3 dB
Term. impedance	500 Ω	500 Ω	500 Ω	500 Ω	500 Ω	500 Ω	1200 Ω
Ripple capacitors	30 pF	30 pF	30 pF	30 pF	30 pF	30 pF	30 pF
Shape factor	6:50 dB 1.7	6:60 dB 1.8	6:60 dB 2.2	6:60 dB 1.8	6:60 dB 1.8	6:60 dB 4.4	6:60 dB 1.8
Stop-band atten.	>45 dB	>100 dB	>90 dB	>100 dB	>100 dB	>90 dB	>90 dB

Courtesy of Spectrum International

Fig. 39 — Block diagram of a mechanical filter (Collins Radio).

Fig. 40 — Crystal IF filters can be used at both ends of the IF strip. FL2 greatly reduces wideband IF noise.

Hz. The skirts of the curve are fairly wide with a single half-lattice filter, which uses crystals in the HF region.

The skirts can be steepened by placing two half-lattice filters in cascade, as shown in Fig. 38C. R1 and R_T must be selected to provide minimum ripple at the center of the passband. The same rule applies for frequency spacing between the crystals. C1 is adjusted for a symmetrical response.

The circuits of Fig. 38 can be built easily and inexpensively by amateurs. The transformers shown are tuned to center frequency. They are wound bifilar or trifilar on ferrite or powdered-iron cores of appropriate frequency characteristics.

A technique that has recently gained favor with amateurs is that of building crystal filters in the form of a ladder network, in which all crystals are cut to the same frequency. TV color-burst and CB crystals are commonly used to fabricate low-cost filters having high performance. The design procedure involves analysis of a quartz crystal in terms of its lumped-constant equivalent circuit. These lumped-constant values are then used to design a modern Chebyshev or Butterworth band-pass filter. Wes Hayward, W7ZOI, described the procedure in detail in "A Unified Approach to the Design of Crystal Ladder Filters" in May 1982 *QST* (pp. 21-27).

An illustration of how a mechanical filter operates is provided in Fig. 39. Perhaps the most significant feature of a mechanical filter is the high Q of the resonant metallic disks it contains. A Q figure of 10,000 is the nominal value obtained with this kind of resonator. If L and C constants were employed to acquire a bandwidth equivalent to that possible with a mechanical filter, the IF would have to be below 50 kHz. Table 3 lists various mechanical filters that are manufactured by Collins Radio Co.

Mechanical filters have excellent frequency-stability characteristics. This makes it possible to fabricate them for fractional bandwidths of a few hundred hertz. Bandwidths down to 0.1 percent can be obtained with these filters. This means that a filter having a center frequency of 455 kHz could have a bandwidth as small as 455 Hz. By inserting a wire through the centers of several resonator disks, thereby coupling them, the fractional bandwidth can be made as great as 10 percent of the center frequency. The upper limit is governed primarily by occurrence of unwanted spurious filter responses adjacent to the desired passband.

Mechanical filters can be built for center frequencies from 60 to 600 kHz. The main limiting factor is disk size. At the low end of the range, the disks become prohibitively large. At the high limit of the range, the disks become too small to be practical.

The principle of operation is shown in Fig. 39. As the incoming IF signal passes through the input transducer, the signal is converted to mechanical energy. This energy is passed through the disk resonators to filter out the undesired frequencies, then through the output transducer where the mechanical energy is converted back to the original electrical form.

The transducers serve a second function: They reflect the source and load impedances into the mechanical portion of the circuit, thereby providing a termination for the filter.

Mechanical filters require external resonating capacitors, which are used across the transducers. If the filters are not resonated, there will be an increase in insertion loss and degradation of the passband characteristics. Concerning the latter, there will be various unwanted dips in the nose response (ripple), which can lead to undesirable effects. The exact amount of

shunt capacitance will depend on the filter model used. The manufacturer's data sheet specifies the proper capacitor values.

Collins mechanical filters are available with center frequencies from 64 to 500 kHz and in a variety of bandwidths. Insertion loss ranges from 2 dB to 12 dB, depending on the style of filter used. Of greatest interest to amateurs are the 455-kHz mechanical filters with the prefix F455. They are available in bandwidths of 0.375, 1.2, 1.9, 2.5, 2.9, 3.8 and 5.8 kHz. Maximum insertion loss is 10 dB, and the characteristic impedance is 2000 ohms. Different values of resonating capacitance are required for the various models, ranging from 350 to 1100 pF. Although some mechanical filters are terminated internally, this series requires external source and load termination of 2000 ohms. The F455 filters are the least expensive of the Collins line.

Most modern receivers have selectable IF filters to provide suitable bandwidths for SSB and CW. Most commercial receivers use a 250- to 600-Hz bandwidth filter for CW and a 1.8- to 2.7-kHz bandwidth for SSB. CW or SSB filters are used to receive RTTY. The input and output ends of a filter should be well isolated from one another if the filter characteristics are to be realized. Leakage across a filter will negate the otherwise good performance of the unit. The problem becomes worse as the filter frequency is increased. Mechanical switches are not recommended above 455 kHz for filter selection because of leakage across the switch wafers and sections. Diode switching is preferred by most designers. The switching diodes for the filter that is out of the circuit are usually back-biased to ensure minimum leakthrough.

In the interest of reducing wideband noise from the IF amplifier strip, it is worthwhile to use a second filter that has exactly the same center frequency as the first. The second filter is placed at the end of the IF strip, ahead of the product detector. This is shown in Fig. 40. The technique was described by W7ZOI in March and April 1974 *QST*. The second filter, FL2, has somewhat wider skirts than the first, FL1. An RC active audio filter after the product detector has a similar effect, but the results are not quite as spectacular as when two IF filters are used. The overall signal-to-noise ratio is enhanced greatly by this method.

Automatic Gain Control

Automatic regulation of the gain of the receiver in inverse proportion to the signal strength is an operating convenience in reception, because it tends to keep the output level of the receiver constant regardless of input-signal strength. The average rectified dc voltage, developed by the received signal across a resistance in a detector circuit, is used to vary the bias on the RF and IF amplifier stages. Since this voltage is proportional to the average amplitude of the signal, the gain is reduced as the signal strength increases. The control will be more complete and the output more constant as the number of stages to which the AGC bias is applied is increased. Control of at least two stages is advisable.

Various schemes from simple to extravagant have been conceived to develop AGC voltage in receivers. Some perform poorly because the attack time of the circuits is wrong for CW work, resulting in "clicky" or "pumping" AGC. The first significant advance toward curing the problem was presented by Goodman, W1DX, "Better AVC for SSB and Code Reception," January 1957 *QST*. He coined the term "hang" AVC, and the technique has been adopted by many amateurs who have built their own receiving equipment. The objective is to make the AGC take hold as quickly as possible to avoid the ailments mentioned earlier.

For best receiver performance the IF filters should be contained within the AGC loop, which strongly suggests the use of RF-derived AGC. Most commercial receivers follow this rule. However, good results can be obtained with audio-derived AGC, despite the tendency toward a clicky response. If RC active audio filters are used to obtain receiver selectivity, they should be contained within the audio-AGC loop if possible.

Fig. 41 illustrates the general concept of an AGC circuit. RF energy is sampled from the output of the last IF by means of light coupling. This minimizes loading on the tuned circuit of the IF amplifier. The IF energy is amplified by the AGC amplifier, then convert to dc by means of an AGC rectifier. R1 and C1 are selected to provide a suitable decay time constant (about 1 second for SSB and CW). Q1 and Q2 function as dc amplifiers to develop the voltage needed for AGC control of the IF (and sometimes, RF) amplifier stages. The developed AGC voltage can be used to drive an S meter. A level control can be placed at the input of the AGC amplifier to establish the signal input level (receiver front end), which turns on the AGC system. Most designers prefer to have this happen when a received signal level is between 0.25 and 1 μV. The exact parameters are based somewhat on subjectivity.

An AF-derived AGC loop is shown in Fig. 42. It is suitable for use with CA3028A IF-amplifier ICs. Provision is made for manual IF-gain control. D1 functions as a gating diode to prevent the manual-control circuitry from affecting the normal AGC action. This circuit was first used in a receiver described by DeMaw in June and July 1976 *QST*.

An RF-derived AGC system is seen in Fig. 43. It operates on a principle similar to that shown in Fig. 42, except that an op amp is used in place of the discrete bipolar dc amplifiers. Current changes are sampled across the 10-kΩ FET source resistor by

Fig. 41 — A system for developing receiver AGC voltage.

Fig. 42 — A practical circuit for developing AGC voltage for a CA3028A IF amplifier.

means of the op amp difference amplifier. With the values of resistance given, the output dc swing of the op amp is the desired + 2 to + 9 volts for controlling CA3028A IF amplifiers. This system was also used in the DeMaw receiver.

It certainly is not essential to have AGC in a receiver. If the operator is willing to adjust the gain manually, good performance is certain to result. AGC is mainly an operator convenience: It prevents loud signals from blasting out of the speaker or headphones when the operator tunes the band at a given AF-gain setting.

Beat-Frequency Oscillators

The circuits given for crystal-controlled oscillators in Chapter 10 are suitable for use in BFO circuits. A beat oscillator generates energy that is supplied to a product detector for reception of CW and SSB signals. The BFO frequency is offset by the appropriate amount with respect to the center frequency of the IF filter. For example, a BFO used during CW reception is usually some 800 Hz above or below the IF center frequency. During SSB reception the offset is slightly more — approximately 1.5 kHz above or below the IF center frequency, depending upon the need for upper or lower sideband operation. Typically, the BFO is placed roughly 20 dB down on the slope of the IF passband curve for SSB reception or transmission.

Fig. 43 — An AGC system for CA3028A IF amplifiers. An op amp is used as difference amplifier to provide AGC voltage while operating an S meter.

A BFO need not be crystal controlled. It can use a VFO circuit, or it can be tuned by means of a Varactor diode. Elimination of the crystals represents a cost savings to the builder, but frequency stability may not be as good as when crystal control is employed.

When the BFO is operated at frequencies above 3 MHz it is helpful to use a buffer stage after the oscillator to minimize the effects of pulling. Furthermore, if a passive product detector is used in the receiver, a substantial amount of BFO output power will be required — approximately +7 dBm. The buffer/amplifier helps to boost the oscillator output to satisfy this requirement.

S Meters

Signal-strength meters are useful when there is a need to make comparative readings. Such might be the case when another operator asks for a comparison between two antennas being tested. Because S meters are relative-reading instruments, signal reporting based on the amount of needle deflection is generally without meaning. No two receivers render the same reading a given signal, unless by coincidence. This is because the gain distribution within an amateur receiver varies from band to band. Since most S meters are activated from the AGC line in a receiver, what might be S9 on one ham band could easily become S6 or 10 dB over S9 on another band. A receiver that rendered accurate readings on each band it covered would be extremely esoteric and complex.

An attempt was made by at least one receiver manufacturer in the early 1940s to establish some significant numbers for S meters. S9 was to be equivalent to 50 μV, and each S unit would have been equal to 6 dB. The scale readings above S9 were given in dB. The system never took hold in the manufacturing world, probably for the reasons given earlier.

In addition to the example shown in Fig. 43, some typical S-meter circuits are offered in Fig. 44. The example at C can be used with RF- or audio-derived AGC.

NOISE REDUCTION

The only known approach to reducing tube, transistor and circuit noise is through

Fig. 44 — Various methods for using an S meter. At A, V1 is a meter amplifier. As the AGC voltage increases, the plate current decreases to lower the voltage drop across R1. An up-scale meter reading results as the current through the meter increases. At B, the negative-going AGC voltage is inverted and amplified by an operational amplifier circuit. R1 establishes the dB-per-S-unit sensitivity; R2 is the meter-zeroing adjustment. R3 and D1 compress the readings over S9. This circuit is well suited to an IF amplifier having a gain control characteristic that is linear in dB/volt, such as one using dual-gate MOSFETs. At C, the negative AGC voltage forward biases the transistor to cause an increase in collector current, thereby deflecting the meter upward with signal increases.

Fig. 45 — A simple audio limiter/clipper. R1 sets the bias on the diodes for the desired limiting level.

Fig. 46 — Examples of RF and audio ANL circuits. Positive and negative clipping takes place in both circuits. The circuit at A is self-adjusting.

the choice of low-noise, front-end, active components and through more overall selectivity.

In addition to the active-device and circuit noise, much of the noise interference experienced in reception of high-frequency signals is caused by domestic or industrial electrical equipment and by automobile ignition systems. The interference is of two types in its effects. The first is "hiss," consisting of overlapping pulses similar in nature to the receiver noise. It is largely reduced by high selectivity in the receiver, especially for code reception. The second is the "pistol-shot" or "machine-gun" type, consisting of separated impulses of high amplitude. The hiss type of interference usually is caused by commutator sparking in dc and series-wound ac motors, while the shot type results from separated spark discharges (ac power leaks, switch and key clicks, ignition sparks and the like).

Impulse Noise

Impulse noise, because of the short duration of the pulses compared with the time between them, must have high amplitude to contain much average energy. Hence, noise of this type strong enough to cause much interference generally has an instantaneous amplitude much higher than that of the signal being received. The general principle of devices intended to reduce such noise is to allow the desired signal to pass through the receiver unaffected, but to make the receiver inoperative for amplitudes greater than that of the signal. The greater the amplitude of the pulse compared with its time of duration, the more successful the noise reduction.

Another approach is to "silence" (render inoperative) the receiver during the short duration time of any individual pulse. The listener will not hear the "hole" because of its short duration, and very effective noise reduction is obtained. Such devices are called "blankers" rather than "limiters."

In passing through selective receiver circuits, the time duration of the impulses is increased, because of the bandwidth of the circuits. Thus, the more selectivity ahead of the noise-reducing device, the more dif-

Fig. 47 — Diagram of a noise blanker. C1 and L1 are tuned to the receiver IF.

ficult it becomes to secure good pulse-type noise suppression.

Audio Limiting

A considerable degree of noise reduction in CW and RTTY reception can be accomplished by amplitude-limiting arrangements applied to the audio-output circuit of a receiver. Such limiters also maintain the signal output nearly constant during fading. These output-limiter systems are simple, and are readily adaptable to most receivers without any modification of the receiver itself. However, they cannot prevent noise peaks from overloading previous stages.

Noise-Limiter Circuits

Pulse-type noise can be eliminated to an extent which makes the reception of even the weakest of signals possible. The noise pulses can be clipped or limited in amplitude, at either an RF or AF point in the receiver circuit. Both methods are used by receiver manufacturers; both are effective.

A simple audio noise limiter is shown at Fig. 45. It can be plugged into the headphone jack of the receiver and a pair of headphones connected to the output of the limiter. D1 and D2 are wired to clip both the positive and negative peaks of the audio signal, thus removing the high spikes of pulse noise. The diodes are back-biased by 1.5-volt batteries permitting R1 to serve as a clipping-level control. This circuit also limits the amount of audio reaching the headphones. When tuning across the band, strong signals will not be ear shattering and will appear to be the same strength as the weaker ones. S1 is open when the circuit is not in use to prevent battery drain. D1 and D2 can be germanium or silicon diodes, but 1N34As or 1N914s are generally used. This circuit is usable with only high-impedance headphones.

The usual practice in communication receivers is to use low-level limiting, Fig. 46. The limiting can be carried out at RF or AF points in the receiver, as shown. Limiting at RF does not cause poor audio quality as is sometimes experienced with series or shunt AF limiters. Limiting at audio affects the normal AF signal peaks as well as the noise pulses, giving an unpleasant audio quality to strong signals.

In a series-limiting circuit, a normally conducting element (or elements) is connected in the circuit in series and operated in such a manner that it becomes nonconductive above a given signal level. In a shunt limiting circuit, a nonconducting element is connected in shunt across the circuit and operated so that it becomes conductive above a given signal level, thus short-circuiting the signal and preventing its being transmitted to the remainder of the amplifier. The usual conducting element will be a forward-biased diode, and the usual nonconducting element will be a back-biased diode. In many applications, the value of bias is set manually by the operator; usually the clipping level will be set at about 1 to 10 volts.

The AF shunt limiter at A and the RF shunt limiter at B operate in the same manner. A pair of self-biased diodes are connected across the AF line at A, and across an RF inductor at B. When a steady CW signal is present the diodes barely conduct, but when a noise pulse rides in on the incoming signal, it is heavily clipped because capacitors C1 and C2 tend to hold the diode bias constant for the duration of the noise pulse. For this reason the diodes conduct heavily in the presense of noise and maintain a fairly constant signal output level. Considerable clipping of CW signal peaks occurs with this type of limiter, but no apparent deterioration of the signal quality results. L1 at B is tuned to the IF of the receiver. An IF transformer with a conventional secondary winding could be used in place of L1, the clipper circuit being connected to the secondary winding; the plate of the 6BA6 would connect to the primary winding in the usual fashion.

IF Noise Silencer

The IF noise silencer circuit shown in Fig. 47 is designed to be used ahead of the high-selectivity section of the receiver. Noise pulses are amplified and rectified, and the resulting negative-going dc pulses are used to cut off an amplifier stage during the pulse. A manual "threshold" control is set by the operator to a level that only permits rectification of the noise pulses that rise above the peak amplitude of the desired signal. The clamp transistor, Q3, short circuits the positive-going pulse "overshoot." Running the 40673 controlled IF amplifier at zero gate 2 voltage allows the direct application of AGC voltage.

Chapter 13

Radio Transceivers

Transceivers have taken the place of separate transmitter/receiver combinations in nearly every Amateur Radio station. Some of the reasons for this are cost, compactness, portability and ease of operation.

The three previous chapters (10, 11 and 12) covered the fundamentals of frequency generation, transmitting and receiving principles. The transceiver brings these concepts together in an integrated package.

Circuit Considerations

Every transceiver, whether simple or complex, uses some of the same circuitry for transmitting and receiving. Shared stages frequently include oscillators, mixers, amplifiers, filters and tuned circuits. Usually, sharing is achieved by switching the input and output of a particular stage from the receiver to the transmitter. Shared circuitry may result in more economical and compact equipment.

The designer must determine whether any transmitting and receiving stages are sufficiently alike to permit their replacement by a single circuit. To do this, three conditions must be satisfied.

First, the stages must operate in the same frequency range. Depending on the circuit, that range may be wide or narrow.

Second, input and output power levels must be comparable. Often, the low level of IF signal processing that takes place in SSB transmitters allows one or more of the same IF amplifiers to be used by the receiver. However, there are other stages, such as the receiver RF amplifier and transmitter final power amplifier, that are never replaced by a single circuit. Because linearity, efficiency and heat dissipation are major concerns in SSB power amplifier design, the transistors chosen for these stages have internal geometries that optimize their power-handling capability. Receiver RF amplifiers, however, process much smaller signal levels, so power-handling capability is less important. Instead, great care is taken to ensure that the stage exhibits low distortion and good noise figure.

Finally, impedances must be matched. This is often done by designing each stage

A full-featured, 100-W, 160- through 10-m transceiver, the Ten-Tec Omni V Model 562 was designed for serious operators—contesters and DXers. Its signal-generation scheme minimizes local-oscillator phase noise. It transmits and receives CW, SSB, FSK and AFSK. FM is optional.

for an input and output impedance of 50 Ω. Even when sharing is possible, it may not always be desirable. The cost and complexity of the required switching circuitry and the additional effort that may be needed to align the transceiving stage must be taken into account. The designer can weigh these factors against the reduction in size, weight and component count that the transceiving approach makes possible.

Historical Developments

In the early days of radio, great constructional differences existed between transmitters and receivers. The spark-gap transmitter had little in common with the crystal or electrolytic receiver-detector.

The invention of the vacuum tube and development of continuous-wave (CW) transmission led to transmitters and receivers that used amplification. However, differences in power levels and frequency schemes prohibited circuit sharing. Fig. 1 shows the block diagram of a typical AM transmitter. Each block represents a different stage employing one or more tubes. A stable, low-frequency signal is generated by the crystal oscillator, and is isolated from later stages by a buffer amplifier. This signal is then raised to the desired frequency using a nonlinear multiplying stage. Finally, the multiplier output is filtered and then amplified by an RF amplifier. Audio from the microphone is amplified and then de-

livered to the RF power amplifier, where voice information is impressed on the carrier. Audio circuits use linear (Class A, AB, or B) amplifiers to avoid distortion. RF amplifiers and frequency multipliers use nonlinear (Class C) stages.

In contrast, a typical AM receiver appears in Fig. 2. There are several important differences. Instead of nonlinear multiplying, the receiver uses heterodyning methods for frequency conversion. Also, frequencies and power levels are generally different from those used in the AM transmitter. The only stages performing the same function are the audio stages. Depending on transmitter power, a microphone amplifier or even the modulator could be used for audio amplification in the receiver.

The development of circuitry for single-sideband suppressed-carrier communication led to many similarities between transmitters and receivers. The AM receiver of Fig. 3A requires only a BFO to demodulate SSB signals. The block diagram of an SSB transmitter, shown in Fig. 3B, more closely resembles that of a heterodyne receiver than an AM transmitter. In fact, the major difference between block diagrams of an SSB heterodyne transmitter and receiver is the direction of signal flow. Both use similar oscillator frequencies, mixing schemes and power levels to process SSB signals, leading to many opportunities for circuit sharing.

Fig. 1 — Block diagram of a conventional AM transmitter.

Block Diagram Basics

Analyzing a transceiver reveals how the concept of block sharing has been realized. By minimizing circuitry, size, cost and energy consumption can be reduced. Fig. 4 shows how compatible signal levels and frequency schemes were successfully used to eliminate duplicate circuitry in the Ten-Tec Argosy II transceiver. From left to right, the first shared circuits are the local-oscillator (LO) stages, comprising the VFO and crystal oscillators, a premixer and a band-pass filter (BPF).

Both receiver and transmitter are tuned by the same VFO/crystal-oscillator combination. One section of the band switch selects the correct crystal for each band. The LO band-pass filter attenuates undesired mixing products. The LO stages have been largely replaced on more-recent designs by *frequency synthesizers* using voltage-controlled oscillators (VCOs) and phase-locked loops (PLLs), which offer more flexibility in operating frequency.

In this transceiver the intermediate frequency is 9 MHz. The LO output equals the operating frequency minus the intermediate frequency. For receiving, the output of the band-pass filter is mixed with incoming signals in the RCVE MIXER. VFO frequency can be varied slightly to provide receiver incremental tuning (RIT). For transmitting, the same output is mixed with the transmitter IF signal in the XMIT MIXER. This stage produces a low-level signal at the operating frequency.

A digital frequency counter measures the LO output frequency. Only the kHz digits are displayed; the MHz element of the operating frequency is indicated by the band switch position marked on the front panel.

A crystal filter, an expensive item, is shared between transmit and receive. On transmit, it passes only one sideband of the double-sideband signal and provides additional carrier suppression. On receive, the steep-skirted passband response of the filter provides sharp selectivity. While the transmit and receive mixers might also have been combined into one shared stage, Ten-Tec

chose to use separate devices.

Transmit gain is controlled by an automatic level control (ALC) bias voltage developed in the final amplifier stage. This bias ensures maximum transmitter output without overdriving the amplifiers. On receive, an automatic gain control (AGC) voltage similarly controls the gain of the receive IF amplifier, to produce a relatively constant volume level.

Below the mixer stages in Fig. 4 is the receiver intermediate-frequency amplifier. Additional crystal filters to improve receive-only selectivity may be installed there. The receiver product detector mixes receive-IF signals with the output of the carrier oscillator, to provide an audio signal. The carrier oscillator also provides the RF signal for the transmit balanced modulator. The product detector and balanced modulator are mixers. The carrier oscillator signal mixed with the receive IF signal in the product detector produces an audio signal. The microphone audio mixed with the carrier oscillator signal in the balanced modulator produces a 9-MHz double-sideband signal.

Use of broadband tuned circuits in modern equipment greatly simplifies band switching. In the Argosy II, the band switch selects a crystal and its associated band-pass filter, an additional band-pass filter at the operating frequency and the transmitting low-pass filter. The operating frequency band-pass filter attenuates image-frequency signals on transmit and receive.

Design Considerations

Circuit sharing in a transceiver helps to streamline a design, but the switching circuitry is sometimes rather extensive. The receiver audio amplifier must be cut off and sensitive small-signal stages of the receiver must be protected during transmit. Linear transmit stages are biased such that "idling" current flows even when no signal is applied. The broadband noise generated by these stages would interfere with recep-

Fig. 2 — A superheterodyne AM receiver.

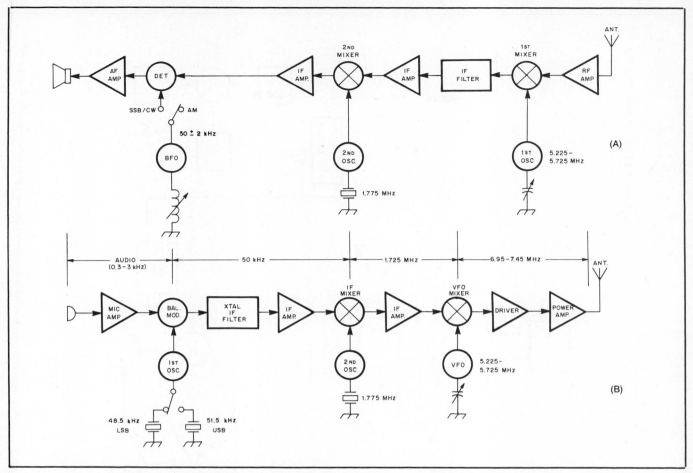

Fig. 3 — Block diagrams show similarities between a superheterodyne AM/SSB receiver (A) and a heterodyne SSB transmitter (B).

tion, so they must be biased to cut off idling current, or turned off completely during receive.

Most transceivers use a combination of relays and switching diodes to perform the required switching. PIN diodes, which can be biased to appear as either open or closed switches to RF energy, are especially useful. By placing them at the required circuit location, long and potentially troublesome RF interconnections may be avoided.

Most transceiver circuits require some form of sequencing to ensure that the receiver is properly muted before the transmitter is energized. This involves shutting off and turning on various transmitting and receiving stages in a pre-determined sequence. Yaesu used such time-delay sequencing circuitry in their FT-ONE transceiver. Fig. 5 shows a section of this circuitry. During CW operation, key closures are detected by the KEY line and applied to two inverter gates, U14e and U14f. The RC time constant on U14f delays the keying signal before it can pass through buffer U13d to actuate Q20, the transmit bias switch. The TX SIG line, whose logical state changes at the same time as the KEY line, has many functions. It supplies the third input to the transmit bias

switch (U14d) and provides a proper voltage to the RC network on the input of Q12. This RC time constant delays operation of the receiver zero-voltage reference switch (RX 0). The TX SIG line supplies inputs to several other sequentially delayed gates. These control the transmit zero-voltage reference switch (Q11), both transmit and receive 13.5-volt supply switches (Q19 and Q22) and the receiver bias switches (Q15, Q16). The antenna relay, powered by relay drivers Q25 and Q26, is also controlled by the TX SIG line.

TRANSCEIVER FEATURES

The basic transceiver is fine for casual sideband and CW work, but it has limitations in more rigorous operation, such as DX chasing and contesting. Fortunately, most transceivers today offer built-in features to help increase their flexibility.

RIT and XIT

Receiver incremental tuning (RIT) has become an almost universal transceiver feature that allows adjustment of the receive frequency without changing the transmit frequency. One important use of this feature is correcting for an operator who tunes to a beat note that differs from

the transceiver's built-in frequency offset on CW or who prefers to listen to slightly different-sounding voice characteristics on SSB. By using the RIT control instead of the VFO dial, the pitch of the received audio can be changed while leaving the transmit frequency undisturbed. Otherwise, if during a QSO one operator adjusts the VFO to fine tune the receiver, he will also adjust the transmit frequency. The other operator will likely compensate for this frequency shift by similarly adjusting the VFO. Before long, such frequency leapfrogging may move both stations far enough to cause interference with other ongoing communications.

Some RIT controls permit the receive frequency to be shifted as much as 10 kHz. These controls can be used as a second VFO, allowing split-frequency operation.

XIT (Transmitter Incremental Tuning) is closely related to RIT, permitting the transmitter frequency to be shifted a few kilohertz away from the receive frequency. Many transceivers use the same knob for controlling both the RIT and XIT functions to permit listening on the transmitter offset frequency.

Fig. 6A is a schematic diagram of an RIT similar to that used in the Kenwood

Fig. 4—Block diagram of the Ten-Tec Argosy II transceiver.

The Ten-Tec Argosy is an SSB/CW transceiver capable of 5- or 50-W output power. Adjusting the DRIVE control allows for lower power. This early-'80s vintage radio popular with QRP operators includes the 10-MHz band. Its successor, the Argosy II, sports a digital frequency readout.

The ICOM IC-735 offers SSB, CW, AM and FM modes, a 100-W transmitter, versatile memory system and general-coverage receiver in a compact package.

TS-520S and TS-820S transceivers. D1 is a varactor diode. Because it forms part of the VFO tuning circuitry, any change of dc bias on D1 will cause a shift in VFO frequency. Potentiometer R1 is used as the RIT frequency-shift control. It forms part of a voltage divider with R3 and R4 when the RIT is switched on, allowing a variable bias to be applied to D1 (Fig. 6B). When the RIT is off, or when the transceiver is in transmit, however, a fixed bias is applied to D1 (Fig. 6C). When R1 is at the center of its range, the transmit and receive frequencies should coincide. R2, an internal trimmer potentiometer, ensures this by providing limited adjustment of the fixed varactor dc bias, eliminating any frequency difference.

XIT circuits operate in the same manner, except that the potentiometer that applies dc bias to the varactor diode is switched into operation during transmit instead of receive. Generally, RIT and XIT circuits use relays or solid-state devices for switching.

IF Shift

This useful receiver feature, sometimes called passband tuning, effectively changes the center frequency of the receiver passband without changing the frequency to which the receiver is tuned. By leaving the pitch of the received signal or signals undisturbed, IF shift permits optimum placement of the available receiver selectivity around an SSB or CW signal.

Although IF shift can be viewed as changing the center frequency of the receiver IF filter, this filter operates on only one fixed frequency. Instead, the IF signal is shifted above and below this passband. Fig. 7 is a block diagram of a simple IF shift system. A tunable oscillator provides an 8.455-MHz signal to the mixers. The first mixer uses this signal to convert the incoming 455-kHz IF to the 8.000-MHz

filter frequency. The second mixer then converts this 8.000-MHz signal back down to 455 kHz. By varying the oscillator frequency, the position of the desired signal within the filter passband can be changed.

When properly tuned, a received signal will pass through the center of the IF filter. Interference to one side of this desired signal may be removed by several methods. Fig. 8A shows such an interfering signal and its relationship to the passband filter. If the transceiver is tuned upward 250 Hz (Fig. 8B), the interfering signal will no longer fall within the passband. This is an effective and practical interference cure on CW, requiring only that the operator listen to a CW note 250 Hz lower than normal. On SSB, however, this solution is impractical, because it leaves the voice signal unintelligible. By using the IF shift control, the interfering signal may still be eliminated (Fig. 8C), and signal intelligibility retained.

In practice, an IF shift circuit may not be as simple as the one shown in Fig. 7. The Kenwood TS-820 HF transceiver incorporates an IF shift circuit that is also part of the phase-locked-loop (PLL) frequency synthesizer. In the block diagram (see Fig. 9) operation on 14.250 MHz is shown.

In the synthesizer, the heterodyne oscillator supplies a fixed 19.5-MHz signal to the heterodyne mixer. This is mixed with a 23.08-MHz signal from the voltage controlled oscillator (VCO) to produce a difference frequency of 3.58 MHz. With the IF shift off, this 3.58-MHz difference frequency mixes with an 8.8315-MHz carrier oscillator signal in the carrier mixer to produce a 5.2515-MHz difference frequency.

The phase detector compares this signal with the 5.2515-MHz signal generated by the VFO. If any phase difference between these two signals is detected, an appropriate dc voltage will be produced by the phase detector and applied to the voltage-controlled oscillator. The VCO will respond by changing frequency slightly, in a direction that reduces this phase difference. The net effect is that the VCO remains locked to the 5.2515-MHz VFO signal.

The PLL has two outputs. One supplies the 23.08-MHz VCO signal to the RF mixer. This mixes with the desired RF input signal (14.250 MHz) to produce an 8.83-MHz IF signal. The other output is at 8.8315 MHz; it mixes with the filtered 8.83-MHz IF signal in a product detector, producing audio at 1.5 kHz.

As the VFO is moved up in frequency, an error voltage will be produced in the phase detector, causing the VCO frequency to shift down by the same amount. This relationship is a result of the mixing scheme, which uses difference frequencies instead of sum frequencies. The result is a lower frequency being tuned in by the transceiver.

Consider the transceiver once again tuned to 14.25 MHz. As the IF shift con-

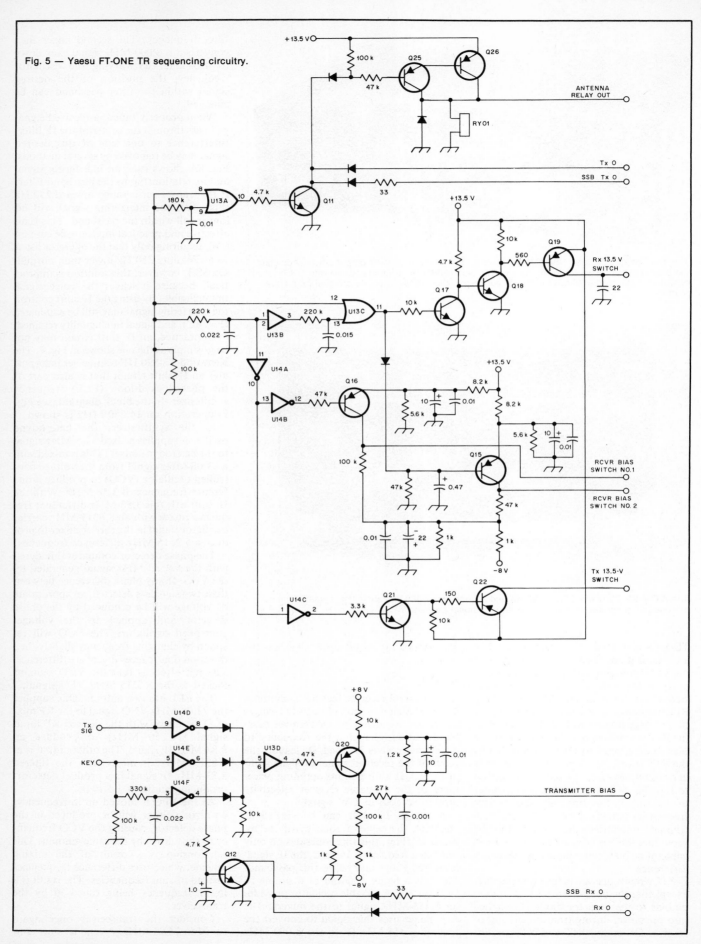

Fig. 5 — Yaesu FT-ONE TR sequencing circuitry.

Fig. 6 — RIT circuit similar to that used in the Kenwood TS-520S and TS-820S series transceivers (A). At B is the equivalent circuit formed when the RIT is switched on. At C is the circuit when RIT is off or during transmit.

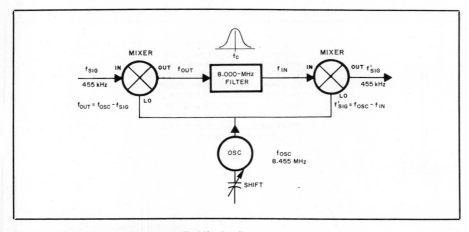

Fig. 7 — Block diagram of a simple IF-shift circuit.

Fig. 8 — At A, receiver tuning places desired signal in center of the 500-Hz-wide CW passband filter. Another signal 250 Hz away will also fall within the passband, causing interference. At B, interfering signal has been removed by tuning receiver up 250 Hz. Desired signal will now have a 250-Hz lower pitch, however. At C, IF shift permits the passband to be moved, eliminating the interfering signal without changing the pitch of the desired signal.

trol is adjusted to raise the carrier oscillator 500 Hz to 8.832 MHz, a higher difference frequency will be produced by the carrier mixer. The phase detector will in turn detect this frequency difference and force the VCO up 500 Hz, to 23.0805 MHz, to compensate. At this point, the higher VCO frequency injected into the RF mixer will cause a portion of the 20 meter amateur band 500-Hz higher to pass through the crystal filter, just as a 500-Hz adjustment of the VFO would. (Keep in mind, however, that the VFO frequency has not been changed.)

After filtering, the resultant IF signal is mixed in the product detector with the IF-shifted carrier oscillator signal. This 500 Hz higher carrier-oscillator signal effectively compensates for the 500 Hz higher VCO signal, producing demodulated, IF-shifted audio. If the carrier oscillator had not been shifted up 500 Hz, the net effect would be exactly as if the VFO had been used to shift the receiver frequency up 500 Hz to 14.2505 MHz.

IF shift is also useful for improving reception of radioteletype (RTTY) and other data signals. Ordinarily, a reasonably wide

SSB filter is used to recover the standard RTTY modem or terminal unit (TU) audio tones of 2295 and 2125 Hz. Unfortunately, BFO placement relative to the center frequencies of many such SSB filters allows recovery of audio frequencies from 300 to 3000 Hz (Fig. 10A). Only the higher frequencies are important here, so the lower 300 to 2000 Hz response represents unneeded bandwidth that only makes the receiver more susceptible to interference from adjacent signals.

To get around this, a 500-Hz CW filter might be used, but such filters are generally used with BFO placements allowing an 800-Hz beat note with signal at filter center. The two RTTY tones separated by only 170 Hz would still be heard, but their recovered audio frequencies would be centered about 800 Hz (885 and 715 Hz, respectively) — totally unacceptable to the RTTY demodulators (Fig. 10B). The solution, IF shift, allows the recovered-audio pitch at filter

Fig. 9 — TS-820 IF shift block diagram. Frequencies given in the boxes indicate ranges for the parts of the synthesizer. For further discussions see text.

Fig. 10 — Receiver tuning needed to demodulate a RTTY signal. At A, a 3-kHz sideband filter is used. Note that an interfering signal also falls within the passband. At B, RTTY tones are received using a 500-Hz CW filter. The receiver has been tuned upward in frequency to place the desired signal in this narrow passband, and the RTTY tones now fall at 715 and 885 Hz. At C, a 500 Hz CW filter and IF shift are used together to recover the required RTTY frequencies of 2125 and 2295 Hz. Interference is rejected by the narrow 500-Hz passband.

Fig. 11 — Variable-bandwidth tuning can be obtained by placing a second filter at the input or output of the IF shift circuit shown in Fig. 7.

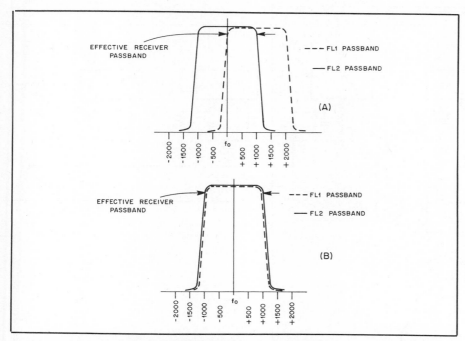

Fig. 12 — Variable-bandwidth tuning requires the use of two passbands. By moving the center frequency of one passband, the overall bandwidth is reduced.

Fig. 13 — A basic VOX system.

center to be varied at will — from 800 to 2210 Hz, for example. This allows reception of audio tones at 2295 and 2125 Hz, and provides a narrow passband response (Fig. 10C).

Frequently, an SSB or a special FSK mode is used by transceivers for RTTY transmission and reception. When poor band conditions make reception difficult with the SSB filter, a narrow CW filter and

IF shift can improve copy. However, in most transceiver designs, the CW filter can be used only in the CW mode. This situation requires the operator to switch back and forth between modes when transmitting and receiving RTTY.

Variable-Bandwidth Tuning

To avoid the expense of equipping a transceiver with several IF filters, variable-bandwidth tuning (VBT) has been developed. This circuit is similar to IF shift. However, instead of shifting the IF passband, VBT permits adjustment of the IF width to optimize reception under various operating conditions. VBT also provides reasonable receiver CW selectivity in transceivers equipped only with SSB filters.

One way of implementing VBT is by taking the simple IF-shift system of Fig. 7 and placing a second IF filter at its output. The resulting VBT system is shown in Fig. 11. By shifting the passband of the first filter with respect to the second, the effective system bandwidth may be reduced (Fig. 12A). When two equal-bandwidth filters are exactly aligned, the overall system bandwidth will be at a maximum (Fig. 12B).

Notch Filtering

Another way of reducing interference is to notch, or reject, the offending signal. A notch filter reduces receiver response over a narrow band of frequencies. The notch frequency is adjustable, so it can be tuned to the interfering signal frequency, eliminating unwanted CW or AM carrier tones, while preserving the desired signal's audio response.

Today, two types of notch filters are found in amateur transceivers. One type, the IF notch, operates at the receiver IF. The other type is the audio notch filter. IF notch filters are most often employed at relatively low frequencies, such as 455 or 50 kHz, where the high circuit Q required for a narrow bandwidth notch can be easily obtained. In a single-conversion receiver that uses an IF in the 8- to 10-MHz range, notch filtering is generally provided by means of audio filters.

Both filter types can be effective, although some audio notch filters do not provide the attenuation or notch depth afforded by typical IF notch filters. Typical values of attenuation range from 30 to 60 dB. If a filter has only a 30-dB notch, it will attenuate a 20-dB-over-S9 signal to a level equivalent to about S7. A 60-dB notch would reduce the same signal to approximately S2.

Audio Peak Filters

Another type of filter found in some receivers is the audio peak filter (APF). These filters are narrow-bandwidth bandpass filters. Usually, the bandwidth is a few hundred hertz (or less), and the center frequency is adjustable.

An APF can offer a significant improve-

Fig. 14 — Schematic diagram of a transceiver IF module constructed from integrated-circuit building blocks.

ment in overall selectivity, even in a receiver equipped with a narrow bandwidth IF filter. There may be some problems, however, if an APF is used instead of an IF crystal filter for CW reception. Because the APF is located in the receiver audio section, a strong signal outside the APF passband can still be amplified to a very high level in the receiver IF stages. In fact, the signal level can overload some receiver stages, producing distortion and reducing receiver sensitivity. An IF filter prevents this problem by removing the undesired signal before it reaches the IF amplifiers. Even a receiver that is not overloaded may suffer from an undesired signal activating the AGC circuit and reducing receiver sensi-

tivity to the point where a weak signal will not be heard. Sometimes this problem can be overcome by disabling the AGC circuitry.

VOX

A transceiver equipped with VOX (voice operated switch) may be changed from receive to transmit by merely speaking into the microphone. Fig. 13 is a block diagram of a basic VOX system. It consists of a differential amplifier, variable time-delay circuit and transmit-receive (TR) switch. Audio energy from the microphone, controlled by the VOX-gain potentiometer, is applied to one of the two input terminals of a differential amplifier. Audio input

level is adjusted so the operator's normal voice intensity will energize the TR switch. The time delay circuit keeps the TR switch energized during short pauses in speech. Without the time delay, the switch would alternate rapidly between transmit and receive. Proper adjustment of the VOX delay prevents this annoying condition.

A problem may develop when audio from the speaker reaches the microphone. If it is as loud as the operator's voice, it will turn on the transmitter. A solution might be to place the speaker and microphone at opposite ends of the shack, or to wear headphones. Fortunately, a more convenient solution, anti-VOX, makes this unnecessary. With anti-VOX, a portion of the

Owing to its large list of standard features, including a built-in power supply, ICOM's IC-781 160- through 10-m transceiver weighs in at more than 50 pounds. The display provides information on frequency, mode, VFO and filter, transmit/receive offset and memory. Those desiring further details can choose from data in 17 different menus, displayed at the bottom of the screen. Want to know if a band is open? A scope display shows signals ± 25, 50 or 100 kHz from the frequency you're using. Output power is in the 150-W range.

receiver audio is applied to the other input of the differential amplifier. Signal level is determined by the anti-VOX (or anti-trip) potentiometer. When the anti-VOX potentiometer is set properly, any speaker audio picked up by the microphone will be cancelled by this anti-VOX signal, preventing the receiver from keying the transmitter.

FUTURE TRENDS

The latest transceiver designs are strongly influenced by recent developments in RF and computer technology. Complete receiver subsystems are now available in single IC packages. Improved fabrication techniques promise to increase device reliability while decreasing cost. These changes are sure to have an effect on the Amateur Radio equipment of tomorrow.

Building Block Basics

It is already possible to assemble a transceiver from IC building blocks, adding only a few discrete components (individual resistors, capacitors, transistors, etc.). The schematic diagram in Fig. 14 bears strong resemblance to a block diagram, since the circuitry needed for each stage function (mixer, amplifier), is entirely contained within IC modules.

This single-conversion design is described in the RSGB *Radio Communications Handbook*. It can be used as the foundation for either a single- or multi-band HF transceiver. Audio at the transmitter microphone input will produce a 70-mV RMS, 9-MHz SSB output. Similarly, the receiver will accept a 9-MHz SSB input signal and convert it down to audio, providing 65 mW of power to a speaker or external power amplifier. Fig. 15 is a schematic diagram showing how the basic transceiver may be expanded into a fully operational HF communications system.

This circuit design illustrates an important shift away from conventional transceiver design philosophy. There is practically no sharing of circuitry. This approach may well be more economical than trying to use a single chip for both transmitting and receiving, for several reasons. First of all, it is much easier to merely switch supply voltage from the receiver circuitry to the transmitter circuitry than to develop extensive RF switching arrangements for each shared chip. Second, the cost of switching circuitry might easily add up to more than the cost of the chips they were designed to eliminate! Additionally, alignment is sure to be quicker and easier when transmitting and receiving circuitry can be isolated from one another.

Digital Aspects

Digital electronics plays an extensive role in Amateur Radio today. For the amateur transceiver, digital methods are used both externally, for generating and interpreting various modes of digital communications, and internally, for performing such circuit functions as stabilizing the operating frequency, storing and recalling control set-

The Yaesu FT-736R is a 144- and 430-MHz multimode radio that accepts optional modules for 50-54, 222-225 and 1240-1300 MHz. Its standard features include a built-in ac power supply (a cable allowing for dc operation is optional), full-duplex satellite operation, IF shift and notch filter, speech processor, memories and scanning, VOX, and provisions for an optional internal keyer.

Fig. 15 — A complete transceiver, using the IF module of Fig. 14.

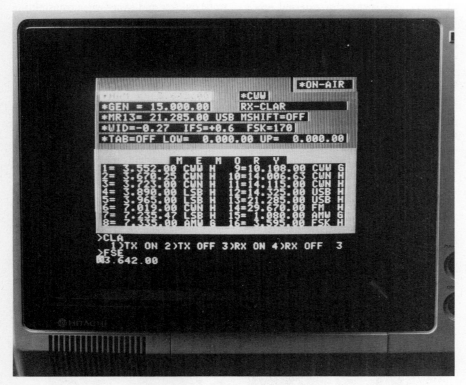

Fig. 16 — Computer graphic display from the Yaesu FT-980 transceiver controller program.

features of the digital frequency controller include push-button frequency tuning and tab setting. This tab function permits an operator to partition an amateur band to avoid accidental transmissions on unauthorized frequencies.

The '980 can be connected to a personal computer through an appropriate interface. This arrangement makes it possible to tune the radio and store and manipulate frequencies from the computer keyboard. Control of such important operating features as RIT, IF shift, mode control, IF width, FSK shift, and even TR switching may be performed by the computer.

Fig. 16 is the graphic display from an FT-980 controller program. This particular program, as supplied by Yaesu, is designed to be run on an Apple II computer. Complete transceiver diagnostics are given, and any listed parameter may be changed at will, making the transceiver front panel unnecessary. In fact, practically every front panel control is disabled when the computer program runs.

A more complex program might not only control the transceiver, but also format and send RTTY text. Or, the computer might serve as a processor for voice signals, permitting fingertip control of compression, frequency response, and so on. The possibilities are limited only by the skill and imagination of the software designer.

Two relatively new forms of digital communications, AMTOR and packet radio, make computer control necessary both for generating and interpreting data and for

tings from memory, and preventing out-of-band operation.

The Yaesu FT-980, for example, has a built-in microprocessor that allows up to

16 frequencies to be stored and instantly recalled from memory. Mode and VFO information for each channel is simultaneously programmed and stored. Other

Fig. 17 — A transceiver of the future?

transmit/receive mode switching. Close synchronization is required among the various hardware and software elements within each system, and among all active systems comprising a network. A transceiver used in an AMTOR system, for example, must exhibit quick recovery time (on the order of 10 ms) when switching from receive to transmit. Care must be taken to ensure that circuit time constants are short enough to permit this type of high-speed operation.

Tomorrow's Transceiver

As digital methods improve and digital logic increases in speed, it may only be a matter of time before amateur signals are exclusively digitally processed. The transceiver of tomorrow may employ a receiver consisting of an analog-to-digital (A/D) converter at the antenna or IF input and a digital-to-analog (D/A) converter/amplifier or a line driver at the audio/baseband output to accommodate voice or data signals, respectively (Fig. 17). In between, all information would be processed as digital data. When the

The Kenwood TS-950SD 160- through 10-meter transceiver features digital signal processing in its audio variable-bandwidth tuning circuit. A voice synthesizer that announces tuned frequency is optional. A computer interface is built in, as is an automatic antenna tuner and 100 memories. Output power is in the range of 150 W.

transceiver is transmitting, the process would simply be reversed, with audio from a microphone applied to an analog-to-digital converter, digitally processed up to the operating frequency, and transmitted using conventional RF techniques. With the ever-increasing speeds of microcomputers, the transceiver of today may tomorrow be reduced to little more than packaged software, with the necessary RF A/D and D/A conversion tasks handled by small plug-in interface modules.

Chapter 14

Repeaters

Repeaters—strategically placed stations that automatically retransmit received signals—are a mainstay of Amateur Radio. Many new amateurs excitedly anticipate their first hand-held transceiver (HT). They see an HT as a key to mainstream Amateur Radio, but those small, convenient transceivers would hold little import without repeaters to extend their range and capabilities. Repeaters are a key resource for local public-service activities and Amateur Radio in general.

The most familiar repeater system receives on one frequency and simultaneously retransmits on another frequency. We call these dual-frequency repeaters. In fact, there are two other repeating schemes in amateur use.

Linear translators simultaneously receive and retransmit passbands that are wide enough to accommodate several channels, which may carry more than one form of modulation. Amateurs use linear translators primarily as satellite transponders. Linear translators and transponders are covered at the end of this chapter.

Packet radio uses digipeaters, which receive digital information from one station, store it and then retransmit it (usually on the same frequency) to a different station. Dual-frequency repeaters use two frequencies at one time, while digipeaters use two times with one frequency. Digipeaters are discussed in the Digital Communications chapter of this book and in *Your Gateway to Packet Radio*, published by ARRL.

Here we deal with the technical side of repeaters: their basic construction and operating requirements. Because most amateur repeaters operate from 144-148 MHz, the discussion will center around an FM-voice repeater for use on that band. In general, the techniques apply to all dual-frequency repeaters.

If you are a present or prospective repeater user, you can find information about repeater use in the Operating Aids chapter of this *Handbook*, *The ARRL Repeater Directory*, *The ARRL Operating Manual* and *The FCC Rule Book*, all published by ARRL.

A BASIC REPEATER

A simple repeater needs only a receiver,

Fig 1—A is a pictorial of frequency usage in a dual-frequency repeater system. Both stations, A and B, transmit on frequency X and receive on frequency Y; the repeater receives on X and transmits on Y. Solid arrows show the path when station A transmits; dashed arrows indicate the path when station B transmits. Repeater reception and transmission occur simultaneously. B shows a block diagram of a dual-frequency repeater.

transmitter, power supply, antenna and control circuitry on an appropriate site. Fig 1 shows a simple dual-frequency repeater, which uses a duplexer to simultaneously transmit and receive on one antenna (more on this later).

The components shown allow a repeater to operate under automatic control, as defined by the FCC in Part 97 §§97.205(d), 97.109(d) and 97.3(a)(6). Stations under automatic control usually have no provision to change frequency or inhibit transmission if their transmit frequency is in use, so various other means have been established to minimize interference: Repeater operation is restricted to certain amateur subbands. Control circuitry is usually designed so that: (1) equipment failure disables the transmitter and (2) there is some means of remotely overriding automatic control.

PLANNING A REPEATER

Resources

A successful repeater requires a lot of planning and more information sources than this book. If you are considering installation of a repeater, you should acquire:

The ARRL Repeater Directory—The latest edition contains a timely catalog of registered repeaters in your area, repeater registration cards and a list of local frequency coordinators.

US Geological Survey (USGS) map (scale 1:250,000)—The map shows roads and elevations that you need in order to determine a suitable repeater location, its height above mean sea level (AMSL) and the repeater height above average terrain (HAAT).

The FCC Rule Book (published by ARRL)—This book contains FCC Part 97 Rules and Regulations, along with a detailed discussion about the meaning and application of those rules. One whole chapter is devoted to "Repeaters and Control."

The ARRL Antenna Book—Chapters about "Repeater Antenna Systems" and "Radio Wave Propagation" tell how to tailor the antenna system to your service area and how to determine the service area that your repeater will reliably cover (for normal terrain).

Manufacturers' Catalogs—Some makers of repeater equipment have design aids to help communications-system designers.

The First Steps

First, set some goals for your repeater.

What need will it serve? What area should it cover? Quickly review the listed repeaters in your area to determine possible frequencies you might use. Also contact your frequency coordinator to let him know of your plans. Although you do not yet have enough information to get a coordinated frequency, the coordinator knows of repeaters that are not listed in the repeater directory, and he may have valuable suggestions about coordination issues in your area.

Choosing a Site

Plot the area you wish to serve on the map. Use the printed elevations and contour lines to select a location capable of serving the area. The highest hill, building or mountain in the area usually provides maximum coverage, but you may need to restrict coverage to avoid interference in areas with many existing repeaters. *Antenna Book* information about ground-wave propagation and repeater antenna patterns may help you overcome coverage problems. For example, a site at a mountain peak might serve your valley well, but it might also interfere with existing repeaters in the neighboring valley (see Fig 2). A location somewhere on the near mountain side, or a directional antenna at the peak, would be better.

Next, travel to the area and look for suitable sites and structures. An ideal site would have an access road, a tower, and a building with electric and telephone service. Luckily, many good locations in the US have already been spotted by other radio services, so a tower and the necessary utilities may be in place. When you find a promising location, find the landlord and begin negotiations. While commercial users often pay rent for radio sites, you may be able to negotiate reduced rent based on the emergency-communication and community-service benefits of an amateur repeater (be sure to keep any promises you make). As an example, the US Forest Service (USFS) recently set fees for amateur use of their communications sites at $75 per year (in six of the nine USFS Regions—see November 1989 *QST*, p 56 and the August 23, 1989 *Federal Register* for details).

Frequency Coordination

Repeater frequency assignments are coordinated by regionally recognized groups of amateur volunteers known as frequency coordinators. Frequency coordinators keep extensive records of repeater input, output and control frequencies that aid them in recommending frequency assignments to minimize interference.

The FCC recognized the frequency-coordinating system when placing the responsibility for resolution of interference between repeaters. Responsibility for resolving interference between coordinated repeaters is mutual. When there is interference between a frequency-coordinated repeater and one that is not, the responsi-

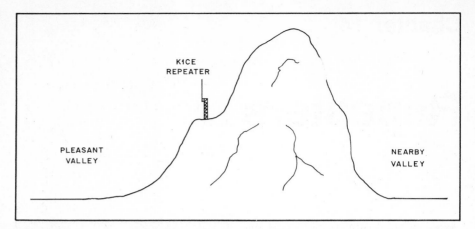

Fig 2—Location of K1CE repeater halfway up the mountain gives desired coverage of Pleasant Valley, while reducing co-channel interference from signals originating in Nearby Valley.

bility for resolving the interference falls upon the repeater that is not coordinated.

In order to determine a coordinated frequency, a frequency coordinator needs several pieces of information. Although practices may vary with each frequency coordinator, you can make a good start with a registration form from the latest *ARRL Repeater Directory*.

Several items on the repeater registration card bear discussion. Height AMSL, longitude and latitude can be read from the USGS map mentioned earlier. EIRP and HAAT can be computed as explained below. With this information in hand, you are ready to contact the frequency coordinator for a coordinated frequency pair.

Effective Radiated Power (ERP)

ERP is the effective radiated power of a station with respect to some standard radiator. *Measured* antenna performance is usually compared to a dipole. *Calculated* antenna performance is usually compared to a either dipole or an isotropic radiator. (An isotropic radiator is an imaginary antenna with a spherical radiation pattern.) Since a dipole has a theoretical gain of 2.14 dB over an isotropic radiator, you can translate from dipole to isotropic (EIRP) reference by adding 2.14 dB. (Subtract 2.14 dB from isotropic to get dipole-reference gain.)

To calculate ERP, total the gains and losses in the transmitter and antenna system. Here is an example calculated for a 200-W transmitter feeding a duplexer with 2.2 dB loss, a feed line with 1.8 dB loss and an antenna with 6-dB gain over an isotropic radiator (dBi):

$$EIRP = G_{TX} - L_{DUP} - L_{FL} + G_{ANT}$$
$$= 23 \text{ dBW} - 2.2 \text{ dB} - 1.8 \text{ dB}$$
$$+ 6 \text{ dBi} = 25 \text{ dBW} = 316.2 \text{ W}$$

where

G_{TX} = Transmitter power, in dB, with respect to 1 W (200 W = 23 dBW)

L_{DUP} = Duplexer loss in dB

L_{FL} = Feed line loss in dB

G_{ANT} = Antenna gain with respect to an isotropic radiator

If compared to a dipole, the antenna gain would be 6 − 2.14 = 3.86 dBd. The ERP would then be 22.86 dBW, or about 193.2 W. Remember that the field strength is *not* changing, only the reference for antenna gain. That is, a 316.2-W transmitter feeding an isotropic radiator, a 193.2-W transmitter feeding a dipole (both through loss-less feed lines) and the repeater system described above all produce exactly the same signal strength.

Height Above Average Terrain (HAAT)

HAAT is a measure of antenna height that reflects the characteristics of terrain surrounding the antenna site. On the USGS map mentioned earlier, lay out eight evenly spaced radials (0, 45, 90, 135, 180, 225, 270 and 315 degrees) that extend 10 miles from the antenna location. Read and record the terrain elevation at the map contour line closest to each radial at distances of 2, 4, 6, 8 and 10 miles from the antenna location. Total the elevations and divide by 40 (the number of measurements you've made) to compute the average height of the terrain surrounding the antenna, AT. HAAT is then the height (AMSL) of the antenna center of radiation less the computed average height of terrain (see Table 1 for an example).

Equipment

Repeater equipment often serves under severe conditions. All components may operate around the clock in times of emergency, and failure is unacceptable. Hence, all equipment should be designed for 100% duty cycle. If the repeater environment is not temperature controlled, the frequency-determining circuits should be stable over the temperature range expected. Provide security for the equipment at the site. If the area is open to unauthorized persons, install the equipment in a locking cabinet to prevent tampering. Most repeater owners choose to buy the transmitter and receiver as a complete assembly. If so, the buyer has no control over design choices and individual performance characteristics of these components. Nonetheless, the buyer should know important performance factors and consider them when purchasing a repeater.

The Receiver

The receiver should have a wide dynamic range so that it is less susceptible to front-end overload (more on this later). Sensitivity choices should consider the users you wish to serve. Receiver sensitivity is not an issue if you want to serve a minimal 1-W HT over a distance of 25 miles or less. Place your antenna so that the served area is within the VHF radio horizon, which can be determined from:

$$d = 1.415 \sqrt{h} \qquad \text{(Eq 1)}$$

where

d = distance in miles
h = antenna HAAT in feet

For example, a typical repeater receiver (0.3 μV sensitivity) should easily serve a 20-mile radius from an HAAT of 200 feet—even with a unity-gain antenna.

If you want to cover a much larger area, consider path gain v path loss for the path from the user's transmitter to the repeater receiver. There are path gains associated with user's transmitter power, the antennas, antenna heights and repeater receiver sensitivity. Losses are associated with feed lines, the duplexer and propagation medium. Read the discussion of reliable VHF coverage and station-gain calculations in the Radio Wave Propagation chapter of the *Antenna Book*. Use the technique described there to perform a station-gain calculation for a typical user station (1-5 W for HTs, 25-100 W for mobile stations) transmitting at the coverage fringe. If the path gain is insufficient, it can be improved by increasing receiver sensitivity, antenna gain, antenna height or

user transmitter power. A receiver preamplifier might help in marginal situations, but it may increase problems with desensitization, IMD and co-channel interference. Losses may be reduced by using better feed lines or a better duplexer.

The Transmitter

Spectral purity is a major factor when choosing a repeater transmitter. Because the transmitter operates simultaneously with the receiver, very near the receive frequency and is located close to the receiver, spurious emissions must be minimal. Nearly all repeater transmitters are crystal controlled to provide the cleanest, most stable signal possible.

How much RF power should the transmitter produce? When we consider path gains v losses for the path from repeater transmitter to user receiver, the factors associated with antennas, heights and feed lines are the same as those for the receive path. Further, the user receiver sensitivity will probably equal that of the repeater receiver unless the repeater uses a receiver preamplifier. Thus, the repeater transmit power should equal that of the user station for equal transmit and receive communication paths. Stronger-than-typical user stations, however, will be able to reach the repeater from beyond the typical fringe area. If you wish to serve such stations, set the transmitter power to equal that of the strongest expected distant user. Small-area repeaters usually transmit 10-25 W (PEP), while wide-coverage repeaters transmit 100 W (PEP) or more.

The Antenna System

It is tempting to oversimplify the choice of a repeater antenna. Since the majority of repeater users—mobile and hand-held radio operators—use vertically polarized antennas, you could install a simple ¼-λ vertical antenna and go home.

While many repeaters begin life with a simple antenna (usually for early tests at the owner's home), several factors should

affect the final installation. If you do want a true omnidirectional pattern, a single side-mounted vertical antenna can't supply it. Arrays of vertical dipoles may be arranged around the tower to provide an omnidirectional pattern, positioned to favor a desired area or to suppress interference if needed. Directional antennas may be used along with an omnidirectional antenna to cover specific narrow areas or overcome difficult terrain. High-gain omnidirectional arrays have limited vertical beamwidth. In some cases coverage can be improved by tilting the beam via appropriate phasing arrangements. *The ARRL Antenna Book* gives details of these techniques and a list of repeater antenna manufacturers.

Current on the outside of the feed line should be eliminated to preserve antenna radiation patterns and improve isolation. Therefore, it is better to use two sets of radials, separated by ¼-λ, at the base of ground-plane antennas. Similarly, top-mounted antennas should not be mounted flush with the tower top, but ¼-λ above it. Fig 3 illustrates the double-radial technique and also a schematic of a coaxial-sleeve balun ("bazooka") that prevents current on transmission lines.

A "bazooka" is a ¼-λ coaxial sleeve that is attached to the feed-line shield at the sleeve end farthest from the antenna. It forms a section of transmission line with the outer surface of the feed-line shield and suppresses current there.

Feed line should be chosen for minimum loss and maximum shield continuity consistent with your cost limits. Rigid (Hardline) or semi-rigid (Heliax) cables with air dielectric yield minimum loss. The chief disadvantage with such cables is the expense of the special connectors they require. George Chaney, W5JTL, described several ways to make connectors for popular Hardline and Heliax cables in his *QST* article, "Hardline Coaxial Connectors You Can Make" (April 1987, pp 32-35).

Rigid and semi-rigid cables may not be

Table 1

Computing Height Above Average Terrain (HAAT)

				Height Data				
Distance (Miles)	0°	45°	90°	135°	180°	225°	270°	315°
2	1500	1400	1400	1500	1500	1400	1450	1500
4	1450	1250	1300	1400	1350	1400	1350	1350
6	1300	1150	1200	1250	1250	1200	1200	1250
8	1100	1000	1000	1000	1050	1000	900	1000
10	1000	900	800	750	750	850	850	925
	6350 +	5700 +	5700 +	5900 +	5900 +	5850 +	5750 +	6025 = 47175

Tower base is 1450 ft AMSL.
Antenna center of radiation is 63 ft above tower base.

Computation
AT = 47175 ÷ 40 = 1179.375 ft AMSL
HAAT = 1450 + 63 − 1179 = 334 ft

flexible enough for use inside the repeater cabinet, but any flexible cable used there should have 100% shield coverage. In the past, some amateurs added a second shield to short cables by removing a length of braid from a second cable, sliding it over the first braid and securing the ends with solder or automotive hose clamps. While that practice may improve shield coverage, leakage is still possible. Commercial

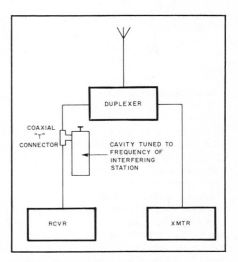

double-shielded cables (such as Belden 9913) do a much better job because the foil shield layer offers 100% coverage. In addition, some manufacturers now make "super-flexible" Heliax, with additional air around the foam dielectric that allows a tighter-than-normal bending radius.

INTEGRATING THE RF SYSTEM

Dual-frequency repeaters differ from other amateur stations in that they transmit and receive simultaneously. In addition, they are often located very near other active transmitters. These conditions can lead to two major problems and numerous others.

Overload (Desensitization)

The repeater transmitter or other transmitters at or near the repeater site may overload the receiver. Because overload reduces receiver sensitivity, the condition is sometimes called *desensitization* or simply "desense." Desensitization is indicated when a weak incoming signal breaks the repeater squelch, but disappears when the offending transmitter switches on. If the problem is within the repeater, the transmitter will cycle on and off as long as the weak signal remains. If another transmitter is affecting the receiver, the loss of signal will follow the transmissions of the offending transmitter. To prevent desensitization, we must provide adequate isolation between the receiver and all other transmitters at or near the repeater site. Helical resonators are compact resonant circuits that are used to block multiple interfering signals (see the Radio Receiving Principles chapter). Several offending signals may be adequately attenuated by open ¼-λ transmission-line stubs (one stub for each frequency) connected in parallel with the receiver feed line. A flexible-cable or Hardline stub is sufficient in many cases; use a tuned cavity for extreme situations (see Fig 4).

Intermodulation Distortion (IMD or "Intermod")

IMD is another hazard of locating transmitters and receivers that operate simultaneously in close proximity. The product is spurious signals that may fall at or near the repeater receive frequency. If off frequency, the resulting signal may desensitize the receiver; on-frequency IMD may capture the receiver and hold the squelch open. IMD occurs most often in the repeater receiver or the output circuit of a nearby transmitter, although it can happen in an impromptu diode resulting from poor electrical contact anywhere near the site. (A primer on intermod appears in David W. Potter, W2GZD's "Intermodulation Reviewed," May 1983 *QST*, pp 17-18.)

If the IMD occurs in the repeater receiver front end, solutions described for desensitization will work. IMD in the repeater transmitter can be cured with tuned-cavity notch filters or a terminated circulator (isolator).

A circulator is a three-port device which passes energy from each port to the next (from 1 to 2, 2 to 3 and 3 to 1) in only one direction. An isolator is formed when one of the ports is terminated with a resistor. If a transmitter is connected to port 1, an antenna to port 2 and a resistor (usually 50 Ω) to port 3, transmission occurs with little loss, but any energy flowing from antenna to transmitter dissipated in the resistor. Install an isolator only in the transmit path; an isolator in the receive path would prevent signals from reaching the receiver.

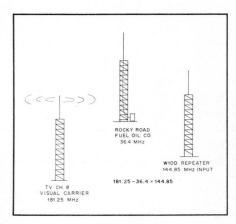

Fig 4—A single resonant cavity is used to "notch" out an interfering signal.

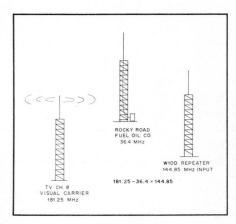

Fig 5—A pictorial representation of a typical repeater IMD problem. When energy from the channel-8 visual carrier mixes with the Rocky Road Fuel Oil Co signal in the Rocky Road transmitter output stage, it produces IMD products at the sum and difference frequencies (181.25 + 36.4 = 217.65 MHz and 181.25 − 36.4 = 144.85 MHz). One of these intermod products is the input frequency of the W1OD repeater and could key up that repeater. A cure must be applied at the Rocky Road transmitter to eliminate the problem (see text).

Fig 3—At A, a typical 2-meter FM antenna with two sets of radials spaced ¼-λ apart. At B, the coaxial-sleeve, or "bazooka," balun for isolating the feed line from the antenna.

When IMD occurs outside the repeater hardware, however, no modification to the repeater will help. In that case, diplomatic skills may be crucial.

Begin by determining the frequencies of other transmitters in the area. Remember that adjacent broadcast transmitters may mix with other signals to produce the problem (Fig 5 shows an example). When IMD is not created in the receiver, direction-finding techniques can be used to locate the source. Monitor suspect transmitters while listening to the repeater to confirm the source. Once likely culprits have been identified, work with the technicians who service that equipment to achieve a cure. Only modifications to the offending installations will solve the problem. Although it may be the legal responsibility of the owners to pay for the necessary service, it is often difficult or impossible to force action. In such cases it may be expedient for you to provide some of the needed resources.

Transmitter/Receiver Isolation

Each time the repeater transmitter switches on, the receiver is subject to severe overload. For a 2-m repeater with a 10-W transmitter offset 600 kHz from a receiver with squelch sensitivity of 0.3 μV, the required isolation is 72 dB. (Typical isolation requirements range from 55 to 90 dB.) It is the foremost challenge of repeater design and maintenance to provide and maintain such isolation.

There are two approaches to achieving adequate isolation in dual-frequency repeaters: one separates the transmit and receive antennas; the other uses an assembly of tuned cavities called a duplexer.

Antenna Separation

Most repeater owners consider antenna separation as an isolation method because new commercial duplexers cost $1500 or more. Conflicting needs and constraints, however, quickly complicate the installation and result in numerous disadvantages and extra costs. Generally, a cost advantage may be realized when there is a very tall support available.

For good performance, the repeater transmit and receive coverage should be nearly identical. That goal is difficult to achieve with any significant antenna separation. About ½ mile of horizontal separation is needed to achieve the 72 dB of isolation mentioned earlier. The added expense of a second repeater site and communication (for both control and baseband information) between them may exceed the cost of a duplexer.

Much less vertical antenna separation is required (25 feet yields 64 dB), but 72 dB may not be achievable because one feed line must pass through the field of the other antenna.

Equal transmit and receive coverage requires that antenna separation is an insignificant portion of the antenna heights. For example, if the receive antenna is mounted at 50 ft and the transmit antenna at 25 ft, the radio horizons would be 10 and 7 miles, respectively. The receive-coverage area would be 78 square miles—the transmit area only 38. If we limit the coverage difference to 10% of the served area with 25 ft of antenna separation, the receive and transmit antennas would be mounted at 250 and 225 ft, respectively.

A Duplexer

Most amateur repeaters (in the 144- to 925-MHz range) use a duplexer to provide the necessary isolation. When a duplexer is used, the repeater simultaneously transmits and receives on a single antenna. This saves the cost of separate sites, antennas and feed lines. Also, transmit and receive coverage is identical except for differences between the transmit- and receive-system gains.

A typical 2-m duplexer consists of six tuned cavities: three at the receiver input and three at the transmitter output. (Four cavities may be sufficient on other bands, where the repeater offset is a greater percentage of the operating frequency—see Table 2.) The two banks of three are connected to the antenna feed line in parallel. Let's look at the characteristics of a single cavity from the assembly.

Table 2

Typical Frequency Offsets for Amateur Repeaters

Band (MHz)	Offset		Offset ÷ Frequency
29	100	kHz	0.0034
50	1.0	MHz	0.0196
144	600	kHz	0.0042
220	1.6	MHz	0.0073
440	5.0	MHz	0.0112
902	13.0	MHz	0.0143
1270	12.0	MHz	0.0094

The cavity is ¼-λ long (plus ½ of its diameter). The center-conductor length is variable by means of a threaded rod, which is used to tune the cavity. Each cavity functions as a series-resonant (band-pass) circuit. A capacitor connected across a cavity provides an anti-resonant notch below the resonant frequency (f_0), while an inductor produces a notch above. Both shunt components also shift f_0. The shunt-component value determines the distance between the notch and f_0.

A commercial 144-MHz duplexer can provide 100 dB of isolation for 2.2 dB of insertion loss, at a price near $2000. Amateurs can build a duplexer with similar performance from information in *The ARRL Antenna Book*. The project requires some machine-shop work and care in assembly; parts quality and construction accuracy are critical to duplexer performance. Use only high-quality connectors and cable (cable length between cavities is important).

Several external factors affect duplexer performance. Ambient temperature variations change cavity dimensions. Humidity changes the cavity dielectric constant. Localized heating (from power dissipated through insertion loss) can distort the cavity. Mechanical shock or vibration can move the plunger within the cavity. Thus, it is best to provide a safe, temperature-stable environment for the duplexer; duplexers should be periodically aligned, at the repeater site if possible. Minor impedance mismatch significantly affects duplexer performance. Any slight change in antenna SWR may cause great changes in insertion loss and isolation.

Construction Practices

After the receiver and transmitter antenna ports have been isolated, there still may be problems as a result of stray RF in the equipment room or cabinet. These may appear as erratic control operation, echo and other frustrating problems that would convince you that gremlins are real.

Use thorough shielding techniques throughout the installation. The transmitter and receiver should be located in RF-tight boxes; all dc and audio leads should enter or exit the boxes via feed-through capacitors. Use shielded cable for all audio and control leads. Ground each piece of equipment to the cabinet, and provide an adequate RF ground for the system. Where RF lines must pass near audio or control lines they should cross at 90° to minimize coupling.

BASIC CONTROL FUNCTIONS

Transmitter Control (COR/CAS)

Transmitter control is the primary repeater control function. It is performed by monitoring a receiver line that indicates the presence of an incoming signal (squelch on an FM receiver) and keying the transmitter when that line is active. The circuit that performs this function is known as a carrier-operated relay (COR), carrier-activated switch (CAS) or one of several other names such as squelch relay or signal relay. Fig 6 shows an appropriate COR circuit and a timer.

The receiver squelch circuit should exhibit some hysteresis: It should take a stronger signal to open the squelch than it does to hold it open (see Fig 7). This ensures that stations too weak for viable communication cannot open the squelch.

A VOX circuit, similar to that used on SSB equipment can be connected to the CAS. VOX requires that there be audio (voice or tone), as well as carrier, present to activate the transmitter. This is appropriate for modes other than FM or when interference from unmodulated

Fig 6—A shows a COR/CAS circuit for repeater use. CR1 is a silicon diode. K2 may be any relay with a 12-V coil (a long-life reed relay is best). R2 sets the length of time that K2 remains closed after the input voltage disappears (hang time). B shows a timer circuit. Values shown for R1 and C1 should provide timing up to four minutes or so. C1 should be a low-leakage capacitor; Q1 is a silicon-controlled rectifier, ECG-5452 or equivalent. K1 may be any miniature relay with a 12-volt coil. The timer is reset when the supply voltage is momentarily interrupted. The switch must be in the RESET position for the remote reset to work.

Fig 7—The function of hysteresis in a squelch circuit. The upper line represents variations in the signal strength, while the lower line represents the squelch action. Notice that it takes a stronger signal to open the squelch than it does to keep it open.

repeater without identifying. Rapidly fading signals cycle the repeater on and off. A noise burst appears with each incoming-carrier drop during a contact. Users are continually "stepped on" by the identifier circuit (IDer). Finally, there is no means to suppress very long transmissions resulting from interference or long-winded users. Appropriate timing would make the repeater much more pleasurable to use. Let's look at some basic timing functions and circuits.

Basic Timing Functions

A "kerchunk filter" is a timer that delays transmitter-PTT activation by ½ second or so when the squelch first opens. This delay requires a significant user transmission to key the transmitter; hence, the user is encouraged to identify. The filter also suppresses short noise bursts on the receive frequency.

A "hang timer" keeps the PTT active a few seconds after the incoming carrier drops. If the operators use proper procedures to change between transmitting and receiving stations, there is no need to wait for the repeater transmitter carrier to drop. Noise bursts between exchanges will be nearly eliminated.

A "time-out" timer begins timing when the receiver squelch becomes active. When the set time-out period (usually three minutes) has elapsed, the timer disables the PTT line until the incoming carrier drops.

The "ID timer" should be enabled when both the PTT and receiver squelch lines are active (this prevents enablement by the IDer). After 10 minutes, it activates the IDer and resets itself.

Timing Methods

There are two basic methods to perform timing functions. RC networks are the most practical timing method for analog repeater-control systems. RC timing uses the charge across a capacitor to activate a transistor, relay or both. Where switching components already exist, delays can be added with simple RC networks (components C1 and R2 in Fig 6A perform the hang-timer function). RC components can also be used with a transistor, IC or relay to perform independent timed switching functions (see Fig 8). Although RC circuits are tiresome to adjust for long intervals, and the interval changes with temperature, they are the best choice where microprocessor control is not available.

Fig 8 shows a time-out timer constructed with a 555 IC. It is a good example of RC timing and the logic associated with repeater timers. The design assumes that the receiver squelch circuit presents a positive voltage (well above 0.7 V) when there is a carrier present and the transmitter is active when the PTT line is grounded. When a carrier is received, the CAS grounds PTT IN, which triggers U1 and activates K1, routing the transmitter PTT line to ground through the CAS; timing be-

carriers is a problem on FM repeaters.

Timers

Basic repeater control could be accomplished with no timers. A simple switching interface between the receiver squelch and transmitter PTT circuit would allow immediate retransmission of whatever the receiver "hears." A CW identifier could transmit every time the carrier drops.

Such a system would be legal, but very annoying to users—imagine: any noise on the receive frequency immediately appears on every monitoring user radio. This invites "kerchunking," a natural, but undesirable, user practice of momentarily keying the

Fig 8—An elementary time-out timer circuit using a 555 IC. Components shown allow timing from 5 seconds to about 4½ minutes. The coil of K1 should draw less than 200 mA. See text for details of operation.

Fig 9—A simple digital timer circuit. Ten output lines are provided by the last 4017 IC; this allows the user to select outputs at one-minute intervals from one to ten minutes. The three-minute output is useful for time-out timers, while the seven-, nine- or ten-minute outputs could be used to time an identifier circuit.

gins. If the received carrier drops during the timing cycle, the base of Q1 is grounded, switching on Q2, which discharges C1 and restarts the time-out interval. If the carrier does not drop before the time-out period has elapsed, pin 3 of U1 goes low, K1 releases and the transmitter PTT line is left open. Once timed out, K1 cannot be activated until PTT IN has opened. Thus, the receiver must be quiet for a period greater than the CAS hang time to reset the time-out condition.

Digital timers count clock pulses to measure a desired interval. They offer much greater precision than RC timing circuits, but that precision is not needed in repeater control circuits. Compared to RC timing, parts count, circuit complexity and dollar cost are all higher for stand-alone digital timers. Fig 9 shows a digital-timing circuit that provides separate output lines for intervals from 1 to 10 minutes and a 1-minute clock.

Repeater Identification (IDer)

FCC rules now permit many forms of identification. CW and voice identification are acceptable on all repeaters, but stations transmitting RTTY, data or image communications may identify in those modes (see *The FCC Rule Book* for details). Automatic identifiers for those modes are beyond the scope of this work, but a circuit for a CW IDer is shown in Fig 10.

An RS flip-flop (U1A and U1B) latches the input COR signal. The flip-flop gates a divide-by-ten counter (U2), which counts one-minute (1/60 Hz) input signals from a divider circuit like the one shown in Fig 9. When the selected time is reached by the counter, the output goes high, resetting the RS flip-flop and a binary counter (U4). When the binary counter is reset, its clock (U3A) is allowed to run. The binary counter clocks the address lines of a memory chip (U5), and the data programmed into the EPROM appears at pin 9. This data is used to gate the tone os-

Fig 10—A simple Morse code identifier circuit. See text for details.

cillator (U3B) to produce the Morse code ID. When U4 reaches binary 10000000, its Q8 output is high, and this stops the U3A clock until the counter is again reset by U2.

Only the least-significant bit of each data word in the EPROM is used in this application. The ID is programmed into the EPROM by burning a one for tone on and a zero for tone off. Three ones in a row makes a dash, and three zeros makes a character space. Six or seven zeros in a row can be used as a word space. Programming for "de AA2Z" is shown in Fig 11. The remaining seven bits in the data word are ignored.

The beauty of this approach is its flexibility. Other IDs or messages could be programmed into the EPROM, using the seven unused data bits. A simple logic circuit could then be used to select which bit of the data word is used to gate the tone oscillator. Other circuit modifications will probably be obvious to more advanced builders.

Ideally, an identifier circuit should in-

corporate means for the operator to vary the speed, pitch and amplitude of the Morse code being sent. FCC rules require that the code be sent at a speed no greater than 20 WPM and that it have sufficient deviation to be understandable when a voice is simultaneously being transmitted. Most operators prefer the ability to "fine tune" such things. Another desirable feature will inhibit the identifier from starting while a carrier is being received. Assuming the time-out timer of such a system is set for three minutes, the identifier timer should be set for no greater than seven minutes to ensure strict adherence to FCC identification rules.

Voice identification is also permitted. In the past, the most common form of voice ID used a tape player and prerecorded cassettes or cartridges. Obviously, circuitry must be employed to start the tape player, key the transmitter while the tape is running, and shut off the player and release the transmitter at the end of the tape message. A modern version of the voice ID

relies on digital speech synthesis techniques, which is beyond the scope of this chapter.

MICROPROCESSOR CONTROL

Microprocessors are ideally suited to the tasks of repeater control. Although a myriad of special circuits could be built to control the many functions common in modern repeaters, the interface logic for the circuits must be built in. A microprocessor controller allows software control, which is much more easily modified as the repeater grows. Each circuit board need only supply control lines for interface to the controller.

Figs 12 through 19 show flow charts of the functions required for repeater control. ("About the Flow Charts" contains some additional information to help understand them.) Fig 20 shows the audio lines and switching necessary to work with the flow charts. The charts should be helpful in programming a dedicated microprocessor controller such as "The ARRL Microcontroller" (J. Bloom, KE3Z, July 1986

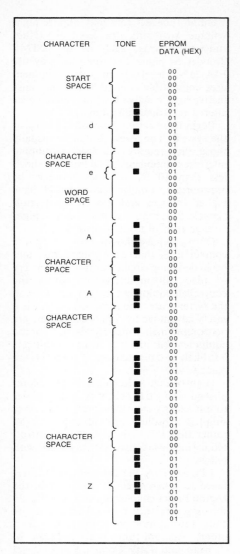

Fig 11—The message "DE AA2Z" programmed into an EPROM for use in the identifier circuit. A one indicates "tone on," a zero "no tone."

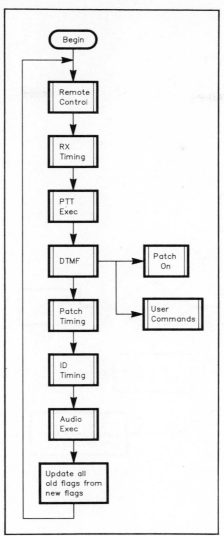

Fig 12—*Main Program*—Program flow for a computer repeater controller. "Patch On" is a routine to initiate an autopatch, which is called from the DTMF Command module. A multitude of user and control commands may be added through DTMF Command as indicated by the "User Commands" subroutine. See "About the Flow Charts" for an explanation of the action in the last procedure.

QST, pp 14-19) or the "8052AH-BASIC Micro Project Controller" (R. Hinrichs, WM6H, October 1988 *QEX*, pp 3-9 and 15).

Personal computers have become practical for use as repeater controllers. With some computers, the control program must be placed in a ROM cartridge so that it is not lost when power fails. IBM® PC clones, with a single disk drive, are available at very reasonable cost. Disk storage and the ability to execute a program automatically after a power failure are very attractive attributes for a controller. Along with a computer, you will need an interface card with enough input and output lines to cover the features you plan. Figs 12 through 20 show flow charts and audio-control circuitry applicable to personal computers. Many hams are capable of writing software for their favorite computer.

REMOTE CONTROL

Although the FCC does not require that a repeater have remote-control capability, it is a good idea to have some minimum capacity in this area. *Remote control* takes the repeater from automatic control and places it under the direct control of a control operator at some other location. Functions that aid, but are not essential to, repeater operation may be radio controlled on the repeater input frequency. The simplest means of remote control is a telephone line to the repeater site.

Remote Control by Telephone

The telephone-line interface project shown at the end of this chapter provides a TTL ring indicator. We can "watch" that line with a high-level controller or dedicated logic circuit. The simplest form of control merely toggles the repeater operation, from enabled to disabled and back, when a single ring is detected. For increased security, some special conditions could be added. For example, one single ring could enable control for a predetermined time period and a second single ring, within that period, toggles the repeater.

For more sophisticated control, the phone can be electronically "lifted" off hook and the audio passed to a DTMF decoder, such as shown in the Station Accessories chapter of this volume. (Note that the decoder ICs used are very sensitive to noise on the power-supply line. Such noise should be reduced to less than 10 mV P-P.) The decoded signals can be processed by discrete logic circuits or a high-level controller to provide sophisticated remote repeater control. The processing circuitry should provide the control operator with confirmation of the action taken. An inexpensive response circuit appears in "Mnemonic Encoder—Lets You Know What Your Repeater is Up To" June 1981 *QST*, pp 15-17. A block diagram of a sophisticated telephone control link appears in Fig 21.

When a computer with a modem is used as a controller, the software could include a terminal subroutine. This would allow remote control via telephone modem.

Remote Control by Radio

Remote control can also be achieved by radio. The control techniques outlined for telephone control may be used for radio control as well. A remote-control transmitter is an auxiliary station as defined by the FCC: It can only operate on amateur bands above 220.5 MHz and not on the 431-433 or 435-438 MHz bands. There must be a definite transition from automatic to remote control and back; under remote control, operation must cease within three minutes if the control link fails. The control transmitter must be protected against unauthorized use. The control receiver is subject to the same problems (desensitization, IMD and so on) as the repeater receiver, and the same cures apply. A block diagram of an RF control link appears in Fig 22.

INTEGRATING THE CONTROL SYSTEM

Once the component circuits for a repeater have been acquired, they must be integrated into a functional system. Typically, the RF components operate from a +12-V dc supply and require either +12-V or 0-V control signals, while the repeater controller produces TTL signals.

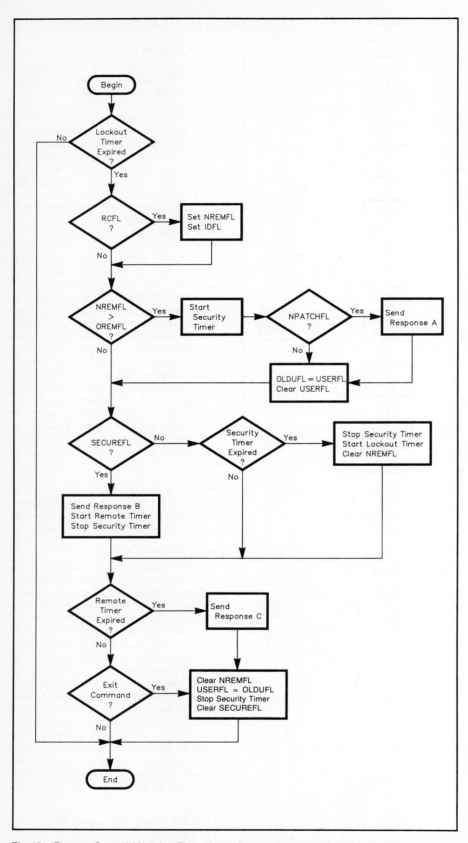

Fig 13—*Remote Control Module*—Flow chart of controller action for timing and remote-control functions. Typical timer values would be: SECURITY 30 seconds, LOCKOUT 5 minutes and REMOTE 5 minutes. Since all responses cause transmissions, IDFL is set when remote control begins so that the transmitter will identify after remote operation. The module is written for remote control by radio. For telephone control, RCFL would come from a telephone ring-detect circuit; a timer would then measure a time before answering, and the phone must then be electrically "lifted off the hook."

Vacuum-tube RF gear may require high-voltage switching for control. Other function boards, such as the DTMF decoder or phone-line interface may use EIA-232-D levels. Even if all equipment uses compatible control levels, the sense (active high v active low) may need to be altered for some functions.

Begin by selecting the control levels for the system. The levels chosen are usually those that require the least additional interface components. If all leads are short, less than 10 ft, TTL levels might be appropriate. Longer leads should have higher voltages and less stringent load-capacitance requirements. Avoid high-voltage control leads if possible.

Once you have chosen a system, list the control lines that need interfacing, and begin designing circuits for installation. Try to place all modifications within the controlled equipment so that all cables in the system carry the same levels. This is a safety advantage for you because there are no exposed high-voltage leads, and for the equipment because a mistake in cabling is less likely to cause damage if the levels are compatible.

High-voltage switching may be accomplished with FETs, but it is usually easier to use relays because the design process is simpler. Absolute ground (where 0 V, rather than 0.7 V, is needed for control) requirements are also best controlled with relays.

TTL and EIA-232-D levels can be interfaced to other levels as discussed in the Digital Basics chapter of this book. Fig 23 shows several other useful interface circuits. Information about interfacing with older, vacuum-tube gear appears in "Cheap and Easy Control-Signal Level Converters," by J. Galm, WB8WTS, in February 1990 *QST*, pp 24-27.

ADDITIONAL REPEATER FEATURES

Emergency Power

A typical emergency power supply consists of a storage battery capable of powering the repeater for at least several hours when commercial power is interrupted.

Many repeater operators mistakenly install a lead-acid battery intended for automobile use. Such batteries are designed to supply a large current for very short durations, and are not well suited to the task at hand—supplying several amperes, on and off, over a period of a few hours or days. A deep-discharge "marine" battery is far better suited for repeater service. Marine batteries are sold at stores that cater to boating enthusiasts. The price, size and capacity specifications are similar to automotive batteries, but their performance in emergency back-up service is far superior.

Simple continuous-charge circuits may damage the emergency battery. Constant charging, even at a "trickle," can boil away

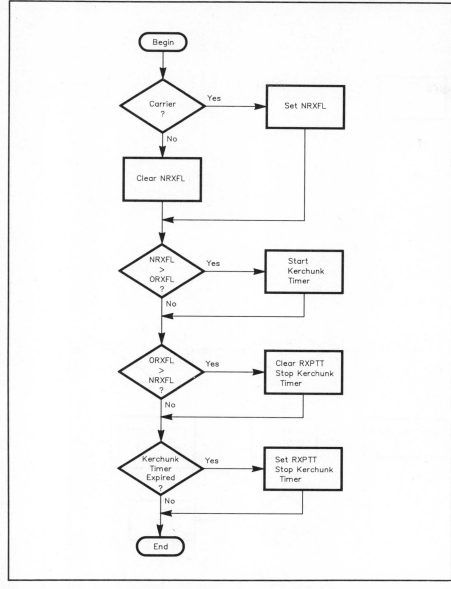

Fig 14—*RX Timing Module*—Repeater receiver timing flow. Typical timer value: KERCHUNK 0.3 second.

In order to implement an autopatch, you need telephone service to the repeater site, a phone-line interface (one appears at the end of this chapter), a remote-control link (third-party traffic is not permitted under automatic control, except by packet radio) and logic circuits to control the process.

Legally, remote-control must be either by radio or a second telephone line, *so that control is effective while the autopatch is active.* A typical patch-equipped repeater has control operators on duty when the patch is likely to be used. When a control operator comes on duty, he or she sends the controller a code that permits users to activate the patch; a similar code is sent to disable the patch when the control operator goes off duty.

The patch-control circuits must provide several functions:

- *Enable/disable patch*—accessible via remote control only.
- *Activate patch* (typically a DTMF "*")—disconnect receiver audio from transmitter, connect transmitter and receiver to telephone line, lift phone "off hook" and activate PTT for duration of call. At this point, the user hears the dial tone over the air and may dial the desired phone number.
- *Hang up* (typically a DTMF "#")—Place phone on hook, disconnect transmitter and receiver from telephone line, reconnect receiver audio to transmitter and return PTT control to the CAS.

Radio-link noise may create DTMF-dialing problems. Sophisticated controllers can reduce these problems by delaying the connection of receiver audio to the telephone line until after dialing is complete. The controller then decodes the incoming tones, and generates clean tones for dialing. Where only pulse dialing is available, the controller must decode the incoming DTMF tones and translate them into pulses for dialing.

Some autopatch controllers monitor the dialing tones and terminate the call if the first digit is a "1." This prevents long-distance calls in some areas.

Courtesy Tones

Many controllers trigger an audio tone when the time-out timer is reset. This lets users know that the incoming carrier has dropped, so that the conversation may continue before the CAS hang time has elapsed. Sometimes the tone is used to convey other information as well. For example, a tone similar to a telephone dial tone, or the Morse character "P" might indicate that the patch is active. Keep the range of tones small. Few users take the time to learn a complex set of tones, so no information is conveyed.

Monitor and Alert Functions

While the FCC forbids retransmission of broadcasts from other services (except for NASA shuttle transmissions—see *The FCC Rule Book* for details), creative repeater

electrolyte during hot summer months. A lead-acid battery may survive one or two such episodes, but its capacity will be diminished and it will require premature replacement. Some commercial repeater controllers provide diode switching and a trickle charge. If the trickle is too great, the battery may be destroyed.

Fig 24 shows a simple, inexpensive device that isolates the battery from the repeater until the commercial power mains fail. Once the power is interrupted, the battery is automatically switched in and remains on line until the power is restored. Since the battery is isolated from the repeater, a separate trickle charger will be required. The trickle charger can be connected to a programmable light timer to control the

amount of charge the battery receives each day. Some experimentation with a hydrometer will determine the minimum daily charging time. After an extended period on battery power, recharge the battery with a regular charger—the trickle charger is insufficient to restore the charge quickly.

Autopatch

Autopatch is a function that allows repeater connection to commercial telephone lines, thus permitting users to place telephone calls. This is the most common form of third-party traffic on voice repeaters. Autopatch greatly enhances the public-service utility of most repeaters because it allows radio access to police and other public-service agencies.

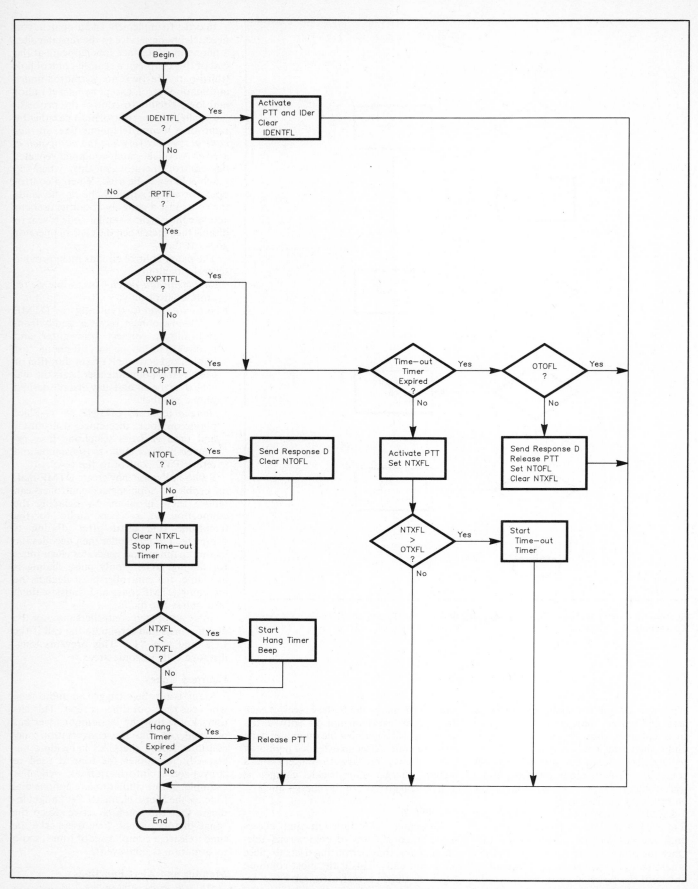

Fig 15—*PTT Exec Module*—PTT control and time-out timing flow. Typical timer values: TIME OUT 3 minutes, HANG 2 seconds. The time-out message is sent immediately on time out and again when the received carrier and autopatch are clear. A courtesy tone BEEP is sent when the time-out timer is reset. Time out limits autopatch calls as well as PTT activity, and it is not reset while the patch is active.

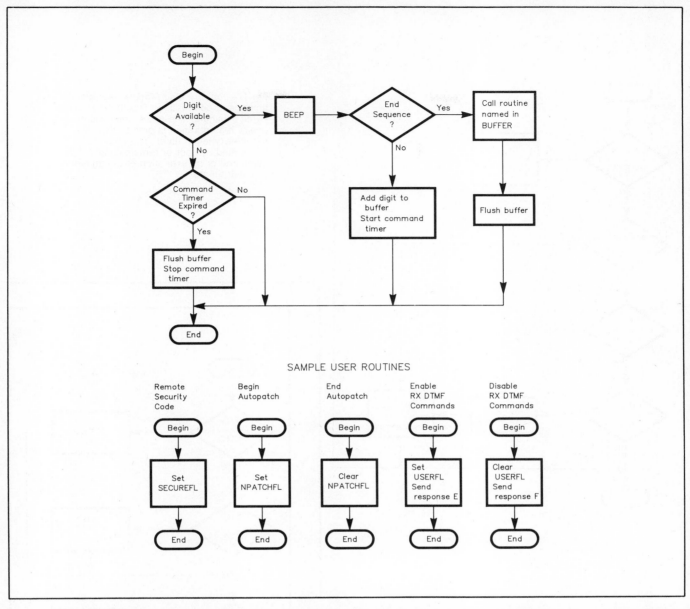

SAMPLE USER ROUTINES

Fig 16—*DTMF Command Module*—DTMF command interpreting flow. The command timer rejects sequences with an unreasonable delay (set it to 1 or 2 seconds) between digits and those not followed by a predetermined end-of-sequence code (usually "#") or other indicator.

operators have developed legal alternatives that allow repeater announcement of significant events. For example, Fig 25 shows an aircraft emergency-locator-transmitter (ELT) monitor and alert circuit.

When the circuit receives an ELT transmission (they transmit on 121.5 MHz and 243 MHz) that exceeds six minutes duration, it keys the repeater PTT and transmits an alert tone for approximately two minutes. This lets repeater users know that an aircraft is down and needs immediate help. The circuit originally appeared in the June 1980 issue of *QST* on pp 42 and 43; details of circuit operation appear there.

Similar circuits could monitor National Weather Service transmissions for warning tones and alert amateurs to extreme weather conditions.

Linked Repeaters

The term "link," in Amateur Radio, generally applies to a repeater or auxiliary station in a network. Control links allow remote control of a repeater or allow two repeaters to work together. "Linked" repeaters work together to extend coverage of frequency or distance.

Rules changes have given Novice operators access to repeaters on the 220- and

1270-MHz bands. This has led many repeater operators to link (parallel connect) their 220-MHz repeaters with those on other bands. There are several positive results:

- Novices are quickly drawn into mainstream Amateur Radio, which encourages them to upgrade. (In fact, most growth from this rule change has been in the Technician, not Novice, class.)
- A significant increase in manpower (Novices) for public-service activities.
- With combined repeaters, equipment band-coverage problems are eliminated: hams equipped for 2 meters and those

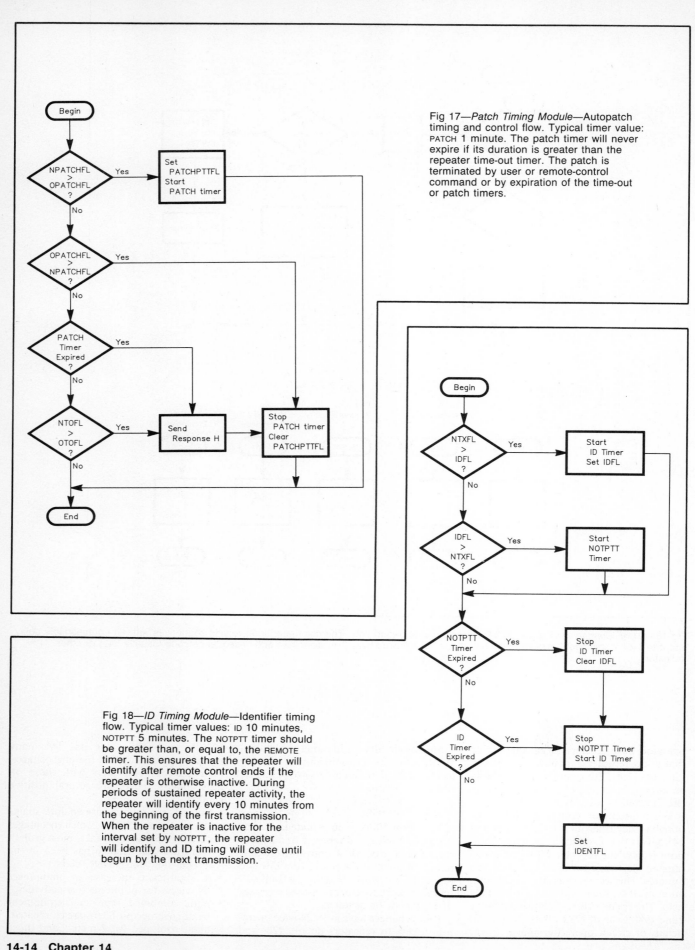

Fig 17—*Patch Timing Module*—Autopatch timing and control flow. Typical timer value: PATCH 1 minute. The patch timer will never expire if its duration is greater than the repeater time-out timer. The patch is terminated by user or remote-control command or by expiration of the time-out or patch timers.

Fig 18—*ID Timing Module*—Identifier timing flow. Typical timer values: ID 10 minutes, NOTPTT 5 minutes. The NOTPTT timer should be greater than, or equal to, the REMOTE timer. This ensures that the repeater will identify after remote control ends if the repeater is otherwise inactive. During periods of sustained repeater activity, the repeater will identify every 10 minutes from the beginning of the first transmission. When the repeater is inactive for the interval set by NOTPTT, the repeater will identify and ID timing will cease until begun by the next transmission.

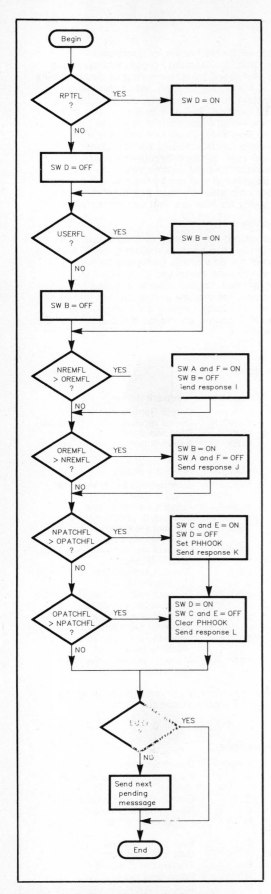

Fig 19—*Audio Exec Module*—Audio- and Response-circuit-control flow. See Fig 20 and Table B in "About the Flow Charts" for the actions of sw A through sw F.

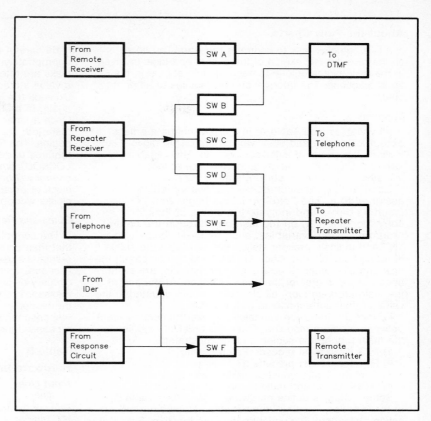

Fig 20—A block diagram of audio-control circuits. Note that Response messages *always* go to the transmitter.

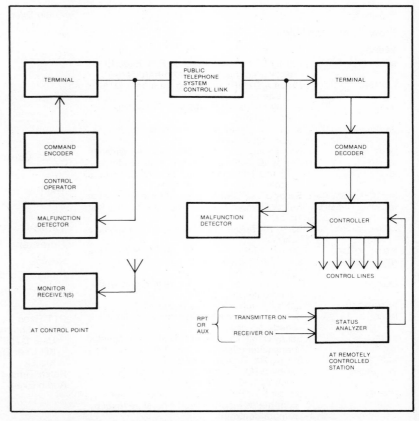

Fig 21—Block diagram of a public-telephone-system control link.

About the Flow Charts

It is a complex task to control a repeater. The flow charts give a basic sketch of the events and logic involved in the task. Notes unique to each module appear in the figure captions. The information here applies to all of the charts.

Variables

All variables (see Table A) in the flow charts are flags except for BUFFER and DIGIT, which hold DTMF digits. Flags indicate the status of significant events. The variables: xRXFL, xTOFL, xTXFL, xREMFL and xPATCHFL reflect transitions as well as current status.

Each of the transition cases has two variables assigned to it. The "old" variables begin with "O" (such as ORXFL) and indicate the status of their corresponding flag on the last loop through the control program. "New" variables, such as NRXFL, begin with "N" and indicate present status. We can tell if the status of a flag has changed since the last loop by comparing the new and old values. If new is greater than old, the event began; if old is greater than new, it ended. At the end of the main program loop, all old variables are updated to the value of their corresponding new variable.

Four of the transition variables are used to communicate between program modules. Thus, the order of modules in the main program is subject to four constraints:
1) PTT Exec must precede Patch Timing
2) PTT Exec must precede ID Timing
3) Remote Control must precede Audio Exec
4) DTMF Command must precede Audio Exec

Some variables define hardware actions (see Table B). In these cases, "setting" the variable actuates the named action, "clearing" the variable ends the function. For example, when PTT is set, the repeater should transmit. When PHHOOK is set, hardware should electrically "lift the phone off the hook."

Table A
Flow-Chart Variables

Variable	Meaning
BEEP	Set by DTMF Command or PTT Exec to request courtesy tone from hardware
BUFFER	Holds a DTMF digit string naming a DTMF routine for execution
BUSY	Set by hardware to indicate Response circuit is busy
CARRIER	Set by hardware when the repeater is receiving a carrier
DIGIT	Holds a digit from the DTMF-decoder hardware
IDENTFL	Set by ID Timing when it is time to identify
IDFL	Set by ID Timing routine when the ID timer is running
NPATCHFL, OPATCHFL	Set by DTMF Command to control the autopatch
NREMFL, OREMFL	Set by Remote Control when the control link is active
NRXFL, ORXFL	Set by RX Timing when the repeater is receiving a carrier
NTOFL, OTOFL	Set by PTT Exec when the repeater is timed out
NTXFL, OTXFL	Set by PTT Exec when the repeater is transmitting
OLDUFL	Holds value of USERFL for restoration when remote control ceases
PATCHPTTFL	Set by Patch Timing to request PTT
RCFL	Set by hardware when the remote-control link needs service
RPTFL	Set by DTMF Command to enable the repeater transmitter (clear RPTFL to kill the transmitter)
RXPTT	Set by RX Timing to request PTT
SECUREFL	Set by DTMF Command when the correct security code is received
USERFL	Set by DTMF Command to enable user commands (once cleared it must be reset by remote control)

Timers

Be careful that all timers handle long intervals appropriately. In machine-language programming, timing tasks are often performed by incrementing or decrementing a value stored in a memory location. When the value exceeds the location numeric capacity, counting begins again: In an 8-bit location, 255 + 1 is 0, 0 − 1 is 255. Once a timer expires, stop counting until it is to be restarted; set the beginning count just before counting begins. The Remote Control module LOCKOUT timer requires particular care. *When the program begins, the LOCKOUT timer must hold the expired value, or remote control will be disabled.* If you are working with a real-time clock or personal computer, be sure that any timers or clocks work properly for intervals that include midnight.

Command Responses

The controller should notify users or control operators that their commands have been executed. Table C lists the responses used in the flow charts (indicated by SEND RESPONSE and appropriate meanings). The response circuitry or programming should provide a queue for messages to be sent (so that messages are not lost when the response circuit is busy sending a message). The response circuit PTT control should be wired directly to the repeater transmitter.

Table B
Hardware Interface

Input Lines

Routine	Variable	Hardware Action
Remote Control	RCFL	Detect Remote carrier
RX Timing	CARRIER	Detect repeater receiver carrier
DTMF Command	DIGIT	Decoded DTMF digit
Audio Exec	BUSY	Detect Response circuit busy

Output Lines

Routine	Variable	Hardware Action
PTT Exec	PTT	Activate repeater transmitter
	IDENTIFY	Activate IDer
	BEEP	Activate courtesy tone
Audio Exec	PHHOOK	Connect to telephone line
	SW A	Connect Remote receiver audio to DTMF decoder
	SW B	Connect repeater receiver audio to DTMF decoder
	SW C	Connect repeater receiver audio to telephone
	SW D	Connect repeater receiver audio to repeater transmitter
	SW E	Connect telephone audio to repeater transmitter
	SW F	Connect Response audio to Remote transmitter
DTMF Command	BEEP	Activate courtesy tone (after each digit)

The IDer and Response-circuit PTT-control lines should be wired directly to the repeater transmitter PTT line.

Table C
Command Responses

Routine	Variable	Communication
Remote Control	A	Patch is active. Do you want to kill it?
	B	Control Operator connected
	C	Remote Control time out
PTT Exec	D	Repeater time out
DTMF Command		
User DTMF	E	User command on
Kill User DTMF	F	User command off
Kill TX	G	Transmitter disabled
Patch Timing	H	Patch time out
Audio Exec	I	User command off. Control link on
	J	Control link off
	K	Autopatch on
	L	Autopatch off

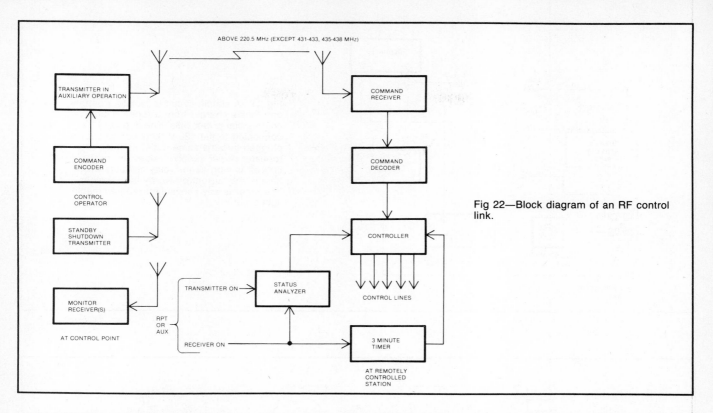

Fig 22—Block diagram of an RF control link.

Fig 23—Several examples of control interface circuits. A shows a circuit that can serve as a buffer amplifier (if +V = 5) for TTL or as a level converter depending on +V and the device used. With +V = 12, a high TTL input produces a 12-V output; low TTL in yields 0 V out. Circuit B uses a steering diode and voltage divider so that an EIA-232-D input can safely drive a transistor. When +V = 5 V, output is TTL; +V = 12 V yields 12 V for high, 0 V for low, inputs. Circuit C inverts the input. Output range depends on +V as in the other circuits. For supplies up to 15 V, use general-purpose switching transistors. All circuits can drive 12-V low-current relays.

Fig 24—A simple circuit to isolate a battery and trickle charger from a repeater until commercial power fails. The line cord connected to the 120-V relay coil should be plugged into the same outlet as the repeater power supply. Values are not critical as long as the relay contacts will handle the current drawn by the repeater. The timer is any convenient programmable light timer.

Fig 25—The W7VEW ELT monitor control circuit. Resistors may be ¼ watt.

on 220 MHz can operate as one net.

Logic and audio circuits to combine two or more repeaters must perform several functions:

1) logically OR the CAS signals.
2) combine the receive audio signals with a level control for each signal
3) distribute the combined audio to the transmitters with a level control for each transmitter.

For maximum utility, linked repeaters should be able to operate independently when the combination is disabled. Analog switch ICs, such as 4051s, are extremely useful in constructing the link audio interface.

Aside from the Novice/220-MHz issue, some repeater owners have linked repeaters into networks that expand repeater coverage. One network was discussed in "FM/RPT," Jan 1987 *QST*, p 61. The network was established by Sergio Marino, KG1C, and Frank Duffy, K1MOQ. It links 2-meter, 220- and 450-MHz repeaters in Massachusetts, New Hampshire, Rhode Island and Vermont with coverage extending into Canada, Connecticut and New York. Plans for a linking controller appear in "A Repeater-Linking Controller" by J. Bednar, WB3ESS, in December 1989 *QST*, pp 22-27.

Both combined and linked repeaters potentially allow transmission of voice signals from multiple sources simultaneously. Sophisticated controllers can poll the incoming lines and select the audio to be transmitted either by a preset priority (2 meters over 220 MHz, for example) or according to signal strength.

Linear Translators and Transponders

A linear translator is similar to a repeater in many ways. Each is a combination of a receiver and a transmitter that is used to extend the range of mobile, portable and fixed stations. A typical FM voice repeater receives on a single frequency or channel and retransmits what it receives on another channel. By contrast, a typical translator receiver passband is wide enough to include many channels. Received signals are amplified, shifted to a new frequency range and retransmitted by the translator. Fig 26 shows block diagrams for a simple voice repeater and a simple translator.

By comparing block diagrams, you can see that the major hardware difference between a repeater and a translator is signal detection. In a repeater, the signal is reduced to baseband (audio) before it is retransmitted. In a translator, signals in the passband are moved to an IF for amplification and retransmission.

A MULTI-MODE MACHINE

Operationally, the contrast is much greater. An FM voice repeater is a one signal, one mode input and one signal, one mode output device. A translator can receive several signals at once and convert (or translate) them to a new range. Further, a linear translator can be thought of as a multi-mode repeater. It is said of computers, "garbage in—garbage out." In a similar manner, whatever goes into a linear translator is what comes out. A linear translator can be used for AM, SSB, ACSB, FM, SSTV and CW—either single or mixed modes and in any combination.

TRANSLATOR APPLICATIONS

For a variety of reasons, linear translators have not been used very often in commercial applications. For that reason, there is not much surplus equipment and practical knowledge to be found. This is one area where the amateur community has taken the lead, especially in satellite communications.

Some work has been done with linear translators for terrestrial Amateur Radio communication, particularly on the West Coast of the USA. For most of us, however, the more familiar application is in the amateur communication satellites.

TRANSPONDERS

By convention, any linear translator that is installed in a satellite is called a transponder. Because of the universal availability of satellite communications to amateurs, the remainder of this chapter will refer to linear translators as transponders. For more information on communicating through satellites, see the Space Communications chapter.

A transponder aboard a satellite may have 130-dB gain and an output power of 1 watt. In that regard, it is much like a communications receiver. The main difference is that the receiver has an audio output and the transponder an RF output.

All stations using a transponder must share the limited power available. For that reason, high-duty-cycle modes such as RTTY and SSTV are limited to specific calling frequencies.

Repeaters are often referred to by their operating frequencies. For example, a .34/.94 machine receives on 146.34 MHz and transmits on 146.94 MHz. A different convention applies to transponders: The input band is given, followed by the corresponding output band. For example, a 2-m/10-m transponder would have an input passband centered near 146 MHz and an output passband centered near 29 MHz. Transponders are usually identified by mode—not mode of transmission such as SSB or CW. Mode has an entirely different meaning in this case. The various frequency band combinations used for uplink and downlink are referred to as modes. See Table 3.

A block diagram of a simple transponder is shown in Fig 27. For several reasons, transponders used aboard satellites are more complex than the one shown. Just as a receiver design provides band-pass filtering, image rejection, AGC and overall gain, a transponder design must meet similar

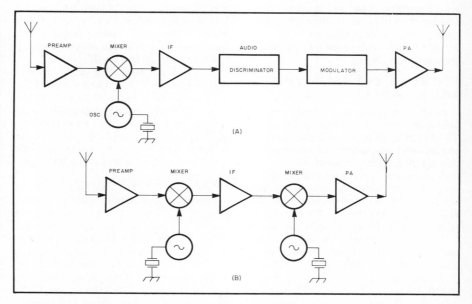

Fig 26—Block diagram of an FM voice repeater at A; of a linear translator at B.

Fig 27—Block diagram of a simple 2-m/10-m linear transponder.

Table 3
Transponder Mode Designations

Mode	Ground station transmit band (uplink)[1,2]	Ground station receive band (downlink)[1,2]
A	145 MHz	29 MHz
B	435 MHz	145 MHz
J	145 MHz	435 MHz
JA[3]	145 MHz	435 MHz
JD[4]	145 MHz	435 MHz
JL	1.2 GHz & 145 MHz	435 MHz
K	21 MHz	29 MHz
KA	21 MHz & 145 MHz	29 MHz
KT	21 MHz	29 MHz & 145 MHz
L	1.2 GHz	435 MHz
S	1.2 GHz	2.4 GHz
T	21 MHz	145 MHz

U[5] (see Mode B)

Notes

[1]Uplink is always specified first.
[2]Each spacecraft transponder uses a portion of the band. See the Space Communications chapter of this *Handbook* for specific frequency information.
[3]JA is short for J (A)nalog. Same as Mode J.
[4]JD is short for J (D)igital. Same input/ output frequency bands as Mode J.
[5]This is the same as Mode B. Since the West German amateurs who built the 435/145-MHz transponder often refer to it as the U-transponder, Mode B is sometimes referred to as Mode U.

considerations. For that reason, transponder designers use multiple-frequency conversions. A block diagram of the basic Mode-A transponder used on OSCAR 8 is shown in Fig 28.

INVERTING AND NONINVERTING TRANSPONDERS

In any conversion stage, the LO may be above or below the incoming frequency. The LO frequencies in a single- or multi-conversion transponder may be chosen so that entering signals are inverted. That type design changes upper-sideband signals into lower-sideband (and vice versa), transposes relative mark-space placement in RTTY, and so on. When this scheme is used, the result is called an inverting transponder.

The major benefit of an inverting transponder is that Doppler shifts on the uplink and downlink are in opposite directions and will, to a limited extent, cancel. With the 146/29-MHz Mode A link combination, Doppler is not serious; transponders using this frequency combination are typically noninverting. Transponders using higher frequency combinations are usually inverting.

POWER AND BANDWIDTH

The power output, bandwidth and operating frequencies of a transponder must be compatible. When a transponder is fully loaded with equal-strength signals, each signal should provide an adequate signal-to-noise ratio at the Earth's surface.

Low-altitude (800-1500 km) satellites perform well with from 1 to 4 watts of PEP at frequencies between 29 and 435 MHz, using a 100-kHz-wide transponder. More sophisticated, high-altitude (35,000 km) satellites provide acceptable performance with 35 watts PEP using a 500-kHz-wide transponder downlink at 146 or 435 MHz.

DYNAMIC RANGE

Dynamic-range requirements for a transponder may appear to be less severe than for an HF receiver. An HF receiver will handle signals differing in level by as much as 100 dB. A low-altitude satellite will encounter signals in its passband differing by perhaps 40 dB. That, however, is only part of the story. The HF receiver filters out all but the desired signal before introducing most of the gain. All transponder users must be accommodated simultaneously—quite a different situation. In one sense, all stations share a single channel. Transponder gain can, therefore, be limited by the strongest signal in the passband.

When a strong station is driving the satellite transponder to full power output, stations more than 22 dB lower than that level will not be heard on the downlink. That is true even if the weaker stations are perfectly readable when the strong signal is not present! User stations must cooperate by using only the minimum power necessary for communication through the satellites.

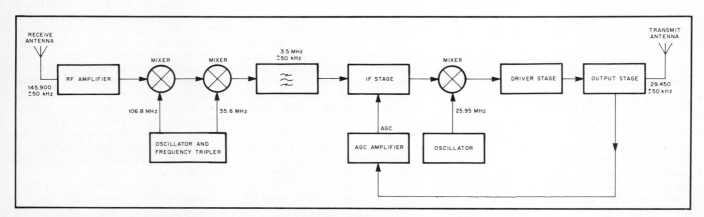

Fig 28—Block diagram of the Mode A transponder used on AMSAT-OSCAR 8.

A Solid-State Phone-Line Interface

This project, by Scott Mazar, WBØOOD, and Noel J. Petit, WBØBGI, originally appeared in the October 1981 issue of *QST*. Before constructing the interface, review information about connection to the public telephone system in the Audio and Video Equipment chapter.

The basic telephone company requirements for interface equipment appear in Table 4. The telephone company requires that phone lines be isolated from voltages in the user's system; this is to prevent unwanted noise and voltage on their equipment. Therefore, any equipment connected to the phone line must be dc isolated. This normally requires transformers and relays, but here we use optoisolators (with an isolation rating of 2.5 kV) instead.

CIRCUIT OPERATION

The circuit in Fig 29 has three basic sections: ring/connect, transmit and receive. A ring-detector circuit indicates whether the phone line is ringing. The ringing waveform passes through C1 (used to block the dc on the phone line) and is rectified by the diode bridge (D1 through D4). Direct current passes through DS1 to indicate ring voltage on the line, and U4 for external electrical sensing. (The bridge rectifier is necessary because DS1 and U4 can only withstand about 3 V of reverse voltage.)

When U4 turns on, it discharges C2, bringing the inputs of U1A and U1B low. These inverters electrically indicate the presence of a ring signal. The combination

Table 4

Telephone Interface Specifications

Frequency Range	Maximum Noise
DC	0.5 mA
Voice Range	
(300-3000 Hz)	−3 dBm*
2450-2750	Minimize if long-distance calls are to be made
3995 to 4005 Hz	18 dB below voice level
4.0 to 10.0 kHz	−16 dBm
10.0 to 25.0 kHz	−24 dBm
25.0 to 40.0 kHz	−36 dBm
above 40.0 kHz	−50 dBm

Loop Signals

On Hook—minimum 30 kΩ, line to line.
Off Hook—maximum 200 Ω, line to line.

*dBm is relative to 1 mW across 600 ohms.

Fig 29—Schematic diagram of the phone-line interface. Fixed-value resistors are ¼-W metal-film or carbon units. Variable resistors are ¼-W trimmers. C1, C4 and C5 are metalized polyester capacitors. C2 and C3 are electrolytic, 10-V or greater. DS1-DS4, inclusive, are red 10-mA LEDs. U4-U8, inclusive, are 4N28 optoisolators. U1 is a 7404 hex inverter.

of R2 and C2 on the inputs of the inverters provides a long time constant for the ring signal. DS3 indicates the ring signal. The output of U1A is the digital ring signal sent to external equipment.

The interface connection is accomplished by applying a high logic level to the "pick up the phone" input, energizing U5, U6 and DS4. An LED indicates the input signal. U5 and U6 are connected in series to prevent breakdown of the phototransistors when the ring voltage is present (a typical collector-emitter breakdown voltage is about 100 V for one transistor). The optoisolator transistors then conduct, causing Q1 to conduct. This turns on Q2, which then has about 20 mA flowing through it. This connects the phone interface to the telephone system.

Audio Receiver

The second basic section of the interface is the audio receiver. U7 conducts most of the line current through its diode, lighting it to a constant brilliancy. Audio from the telephone system modulates the dc loop current. The audio passes through U7 and is amplified to a useful level (0 dBm) by U3. R20 sets the received-audio level, which depends on the particular phone line in use.

Audio Transmitter

The final section is the audio transmitter. To inject audio back into the phone line, the loop current is modulated by the repeater audio. Since Q2 is in series with the 20-mA current loop, perturbing its base current (by shunting some of the current to ground through U8) will modulate the loop current. The collector current of Q2 is proportional to the transistor base current. The circuit driving U8 is a constant-current source to ensure linear transmission of the audio. Typically, the voltage variation at the phone line terminals is less than 0.5 V P-P for transmitted and received audio. This low level is insufficient to trigger the ring-detection circuit, which requires about 3 V to fire.

OTHER FEATURES

The circuit has two additional noteworthy features. The reverse-polarity LED informs you when the line is connected to the wrong polarity (the LED may also light during ringing). Also, the diode and capacitor regulator (D7 and C3) isolate hash on the −5-V dc supply to provide a noise-free signal to the input of U2 and U3. This is especially important if the negative supply is used for other computer components.

CONSTRUCTION NOTES

The prototype was constructed on a 4- × 5-inch perforated circuit board with a 22-pin edge connector. Component placement is not critical. The LEDs are along the front edge for easy viewing. Control signals are all TTL levels. Since most repeaters suppress long-distance calls, this circuit does not filter the 2450- to 2750-Hz disconnect tone (see Table 4). Also, most amateur receivers filter audio above 3000 Hz, so no filters are provided in the interface unit. If your particular installation does not meet these conditions, provide additional filtering to meet phone-company specifications.

ADJUSTMENT

Once constructed, the circuit should be tested on the actual phone line to be used because impedance and audio levels vary from line to line. The ring-detect, pick-up-the-phone and reverse-polarity-indicator sections require no adjustment, but they should be checked before the audio levels are adjusted.

Connect the interface audio-output terminal to the repeater transmitter audio input, apply a pick-up-the-phone signal and use the dial tone to set the output level (R21). Next, connect the repeater receiver (0 dBm) to the interface audio-input connection. Hang up the interface (remove the pick-up signal), and dial it from another phone. Apply the pick-up signal, and adjust the input level (R25) and input bias (R22) until clear, loud audio is heard on the phone line with about 20 mA of loop current; the two adjustments will interact. Once the interface input adjustments are finished, recheck the audio reproduction of the interface output. The output level may have changed if the magnitude of the loop current has changed.

CONCLUSION

As installed, a microprocessor control system checks the ring-detect output each quarter second. If a ring signal is sensed, the repeater branches to a subroutine that allows remote control of the computer. A signal from the repeater receiver initiates the autopatch function. The computer picks up the phone and passes the dial signals and voice audio to the phone interface during the autopatch.

There are other applications for this interface. The circuit can be used as a phone patch for HF radios.

Chapter 15

RF Power Amplifiers

RF power amplifiers present significant design challenges to the radio amateur. A power amplifier in an amateur station may be called upon to develop as much as 1500 watts of RF output power, the legal maximum in the United States. The voltages and currents needed to perform this feat are much higher than those found in other amateur equipment; the voltage and current levels are potentially lethal, in fact. Every component in an RF power amplifier must be carefully selected to endure these high electrical power levels without failing. Large quantities of heat are produced in the amplifier and have to be dissipated safely. Spurious signal generation must be minimized, not only for legal reasons, but also for sound neighbor relations. Every one of these challenges has to be overcome to produce a loud, clear signal from a safe and reliable amplifier.

TYPES OF POWER AMPLIFIERS

Power amplifiers are categorized by their power level, intended frequencies of operation, device type, class of operation and circuit configuration. Within each of these categories there usually is a wide range of circuit options. Choosing from almost all the possibilities to arrive at a suitable combination is the entire concept of design.

Solid State versus Vacuum Tubes

Today, most items of commercially manufactured amateur equipment use solid-state devices exclusively. A few manufacturers still offer HF transceivers with tubes in the final transmitter output stage, but their popularity is dwindling. Using transistors exclusively offers the manufacturers several advantages:

1) Compact design — Even with their heat sinks, transistors are smaller than tubes, allowing smaller packages.

2) Power-supply simplification — Tube amplifiers need a multitude of voltages to function. The filament requires a low voltage, high current supply; the plate circuit, several hundred volts. To meet these needs requires additional power supply components, beyond what the rest of the transceiver needs.

3) "No-tune-up" operation — By their nature transistors lend themselves to low impedance, broadband operation. Harmonic energy suppression can be performed by fixed-tuned, low-pass filters; these can be switched when changing bands. Tube amplifiers must be retuned on each band, and even for significant frequency movement within a band.

4) Long life — Nothing in a transistor wears out. Unless the device is defective, or damage is inflicted on it because its ratings are exceeded, transistors can last virtually forever. Vacuum tubes wear out as their filaments deteriorate from continued operation.

5) Manufacturing ease — Transistors are ideally suited for printed-circuit-board fabrication. The low voltages and low impedances encountered with transistor circuitry work very well on printed circuits (some circuits use the circuit board traces themselves as circuit elements); the high impedances found with vacuum tubes do not. The transistor's physical size and shape also works well with printed circuits; the device can be soldered right to the board, an impossible task with a vacuum tube. These advantages in fabrication mean reduced manufacturing costs.

Based on all this reasoning, it seems there would be no place for vacuum tubes in a transistorized world. Transistors do have significant limitations, however, especially in a practical sense. Individual transistors available today cannot develop more than approximately 150-W output. Pairs of transistors or even pairs of pairs are usually employed in practical designs, even at the 100-W level. Present-day transistors just cannot withstand the high currents needed for high power levels, so the current must be divided among several devices. Beyond the 300-W output level, somewhat exotic (at least for radio amateurs) techniques of power combination from multiple amplifiers must be used. Although this has been successfully done, it is an expensive proposition.[1] Even if one ignores the challenge of the RF portions of a high power transistor amplifier, there is the dc power supply to consider. A solid-state amplifier capable of delivering 1 kilowatt of RF output might require regulated 50 volts at more than 40 amperes. Developing that much current is a formidable and expensive task. These limitations considered, solid-state amplifiers are practical up to a couple of hundred watts output. Beyond that point, the vacuum tube still reigns.

CLASSES OF OPERATION

The class of operation of an amplifier stage is defined by its output current conditions. This, in turn, determines the amplifier's efficiency, linearity and operating impedances.

• Class A: The RF drive level and dc bias are set so there is device output current all the time. The conduction angle is $360°$ (see Fig. 1A). (The conduction angle of an amplifier is defined as the angular portion of a drive cycle over which there is output current. Conduction angle is measured in degrees; a full sine-wave cycle is $360°$.) The active device in a Class A amplifier acts as a variable resistor. Output voltage is generated by the varying current flowing through the load resistance. Maximum linearity is achieved in a Class A amplifier, but the efficiency of the stage is low. In theory, maximum efficiency is 50%, but in practice it usually runs about 25 to 30%.

• Class AB: Drive level and dc bias are adjusted so output current flows appreciably more than half the drive cycle, but less than the whole drive cycle. The

[1]Granberg, "One KW — Solid-State Style," *QST*, April 1976, p. 11; May 1976, p. 28.

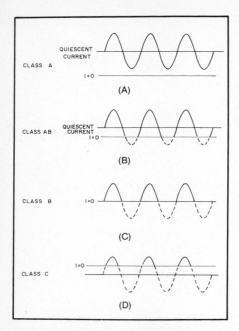

Fig. 1 — Amplifying device output current for various classes of operation. All assume a sinusoidal drive signal.

Fig. 2 — The fundamental circuit for a generator and a load includes the internal power source resistance (R_1), the load resistance (R_2), and associated reactances (X_1 and X_2). A network is used to "match" the impedances.

Fig. 3 — Efficiency is dependent on the ratio of the load resistance to the source resistance.

operating angle is much greater than 180° but less than 360° (see Fig. 1B). Efficiency is much better than Class A, averaging over 50%. Class AB linearity is not as good as that found in Class A, but is very acceptable for even the most rigorous SSB applications.

• Class B: Bias and RF drive are at a level where the device is just cut off (see Fig. 1C) and output current flows during one half of the drive cycle (conduction angle = 180°). Improved efficiency is attained, up to 65%, and acceptable linearity is still maintained.

• Class C: The dc bias is adjusted so that the device is cut off. Output current flows only during peaks in the drive cycle (see Fig. 1D). The output current consists of pulses at the drive frequency; the conduction angle is considerably less than 180°. Since the output device is cut off for more than half the operating cycle, efficiency is relatively high, up to 80%. Linearity is extremely poor, though.

There are other amplifier classes not usually found in amateur service. Most amplifiers that use Class D through H operate at audio frequencies. Their prime virtue is high efficiency. Manufacturers of audio equipment use these amplifier classes to reduce power supply requirements and the associated high costs in high-power stereo amplifiers. Sophisticated techniques would be required to implement these operating classes in radio-frequency amplifiers, particularly at high power levels. The additional complexity and cost is difficult to justify for amateur RF service.

The class of operation is independent of device type and circuit configuration. The active amplifying device and the circuit

itself must be uniquely applied for each operating class, but amplifier linearity and efficiency are limited by the class of operation. Clever amplifier design cannot improve on these fundamental limits. Poor design and implementation, though, can certainly prevent an amplifier from approaching its potential in efficiency and linearity.

IMPEDANCE MATCHING

All power sources, such as the tube or transistor in a power amplifier, have an internal impedance. The impedance usually consists of a resistance in combination with some reactance. Current flowing through this internal resistance in the process of generating power is converted to heat. The electrical power consumed by the internal resistance is unavailable to the load, and only goes to heating up the power source. It can be proven algebraically that the maximum power available from a power source is transferred to the load resistance when the load resistance is equal to the source resistance. If the source has reactance associated with it, then the load impedance must be equal to the complex conjugate of the source impedance.

Usually, neither the source impedance nor the load impedance can be changed. In order to achieve maximum power transfer, a matching network is used between the source and the load to transform the load impedance to the source impedance (and vice versa). This is illustrated in Fig. 2.

The total power generated by the source is

$$P_{IN} = P_{OUT} + P_D$$

where
  P_{IN} = the source power input
  P_{OUT} = the power delivered to the load
  P_D = the power dissipated in the source resistance.

The efficiency (the ratio of output power to total power generated) is

$$Eff. = \frac{P_{OUT}}{P_{IN}} \text{ or } \frac{P_{OUT}}{P_{OUT} + P_D}$$

Efficiency is usually expressed as a percentage.

When the source impedance is matched to the load impedance, each impedance consumes the same amount of power (simple Ohm's Law: $P = I^2R$, the current being the same through both series impedances). It then follows that half the power generated is transferred to the load, and half is dissipated by the source. Efficiency is 50% when the source resistance is equal to the load resistance.

One of the main objectives in power amplifier design is to transfer as much fundamental frequency power to the load as possible, without exceeding the amplifier's active device ratings. In other words, maximum efficiency is needed. As illustrated in Fig. 3, efficiency improves as the load resistance to source resistance ratio increases. The usual practice in RF power amplifier design is to select an optimum load resistance that will provide the highest power output, while staying within the amplifying device's power rating.

The optimum load resistance is determined by the amplifying device's current transfer characteristics, and in the case of vacuum tubes, by the amplifier's class of operation. For a transistor amplifier, the optimum load resistance is

$$R_L = \frac{V_{cc}^2}{2P_O}$$

Where R_L (the load resistance) is equal to the dc collector voltage (V_{cc}) squared, divided by two times P_O (the amplifier power output in watts). Vacuum tubes have more complex current transfer characteristics and each class of operation produces different RMS values of RF current through the load impedance. The optimum load resistance for vacuum tube amplifiers can be approximated by the ratio of the dc plate voltage to the dc plate current, divided by a constant, appropriate to each class of operation (and this in turn determines the maximum efficiency each class of operation can provide). The optimum tube load resistance is

$$R_L = \frac{V_P}{KI_P}$$

where

R_L = the appropriate load resistance
V_P = the dc plate potential in volts
I_P = the dc plate current in amperes
K = a constant that approximates the RMS current to dc current ratio appropriate for each class. For the different classes of operation

Class A, $K \approx 1.3$
Class AB, $K \approx 1.5$
Class B, $K \approx 1.57$
Class C, $K \approx 2$

The load resistance for an RF power amplifier usually is a transmission line connected to an antenna, or the input of another amplifier. It isn't practical, or usually even possible, to modify either of these load resistances to the optimum value needed for high-efficiency operation. A matching network is normally used to transform the true load resistance to the optimum load resistance for the amplifying device. The matching network is also used to cancel any reactance in the two impedances (source and load). Two types of matching networks are found in RF power amplifiers: tank circuits and transformers.

TANK CIRCUITS

Parallel resonant circuits and their equivalents have the ability to store energy. Capacitors store electrical energy in the electric field between their plates; inductors store energy in the magnetic field induced by the coil winding. These circuits are referred to as tank circuits, since they act as storage "tanks" for RF energy.

The energy stored in the individual tank circuit components varies with time. At some point the capacitor in a tank circuit is fully charged, and the current through the capacitor is zero. All the energy in the tank is stored in the capacitor's electric field. Since the inductor is connected directly across the capacitor, the capacitor then starts to discharge through the inductor (since the inductor has no energy stored in it, there is no magnetic field and the voltage potential across the inductor is zero).

The current flowing into the inductor creates a magnetic field; energy now is being stored in the inductor's magnetic field. Assuming there is no resistance in the tank circuit, the increase in energy stored in the inductor's magnetic field is balanced by the decrease in the energy stored in the capacitor's electric field. The total energy stored in the tank circuit stays constant; some is stored in the inductor, some in the capacitor. As the energy level rises in the inductor, the voltage potential across the

Fig. 4 — There are two currents in a tank circuit: the line current (I_{LINE}) and the circulating current ($I_{CIRCULATING}$). The circulating current is dependent on tank Q.

inductor will climb from its original zero voltage condition. According to Lenz's law, the voltage produced is in opposition to the increasing current flowing into the inductor. Eventually, the induced voltage is large enough to totally oppose the current created by the transfer of energy from the capacitor to the inductor. The capacitor's electric field is depleted at this point, and all the tank circuit's energy is stored in the magnetic field of the inductor.

The voltage potential across the inductor, which is in parallel with the capacitor, then starts to recharge the capacitor (the polarity is now reversed from the original condition). Eventually, the capacitor charges fully, and all the energy is then stored in the capacitor's electric field instead of in the inductor's magnetic field. Again, the capacitor discharges into the inductor, where a voltage in opposition to the current develops across the inductor. Once the potential is high enough, the capacitor again recharges. The flow of energy into the inductor from the capacitor and back again is an alternating current. It can be mathematically shown that this alternating current is sinusoidal, and has a frequency of

$$F = \frac{1}{2\pi \sqrt{LC}}$$

which of course is the resonant frequency of the tank circuit. In the absence of a load or any losses to dissipate tank energy, the tank circuit current would oscillate forever.

A typical tank circuit is shown in Fig. 4. The values for L and C are chosen so that the reactance at L (X_L) is equal to the reactance of C (X_C) at the frequency of the signal generated by the ac voltage source. Since X_L is equal to X_C, the line current, I_{LINE}, as measured by meter M1 is close to zero; only the leakage through C is measurable. However, the current, $I_{circulating}$, in the loop defined by L, R and C is definitely not zero. Examine what would happen if the circuit were suddenly broken at points A and B. The circuit is now comprised of L, C, R and M2, all in

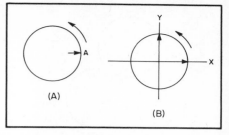

Fig. 5 — The rotation of a point on a flywheel defines a sine wave.

series. X_L is equal to X_C, so they are series resonant. The current in the circuit (if some voltage were applied between points A and B), the circulating current, is only limited by the resistance R. If R is equal to zero, the circulating current would be infinite!

The Flywheel Effect

A tank circuit can be likened to a flywheel — a mechanical device for storing energy. The energy in a flywheel is stored in the angular momentum of the wheel. Most flywheels are very heavy, and concentrate their mass as close to their outer rim as possible to maximize angular momentum. A perfect, unloaded flywheel is unaffected by friction or air resistance. It would spin forever once given an initial shot of energy to start it turning. No energy is expended heating up bearings or moving air; all the energy is stored in the flywheel's rotation.

But, as soon as a load of some sort is attached, the wheel starts to slow or even stop. Some of the energy stored in the spinning flywheel is now being transferred to the load. In order to keep the flywheel turning at a constant speed, the energy drained by the load has to be replenished. Energy has to be added to the flywheel from some external source. If sufficient energy is added to the flywheel, it maintains its constant rotation.

In the real world, of course, flywheels suffer from the same fate as tank circuits; there are system losses that dissipate some of the stored energy without performing any useful work. Air resistance and friction in the bearings slow the flywheel. In a tank circuit, resistive losses drain energy.

The comparison between a flywheel and a tank circuit is more accurate than first appearances might suggest. Fig. 5A shows the side view of a flywheel. This particular flywheel has no load attached, and happens to be in an environment where there is no friction or air resistance (perhaps in outer space). It is already spinning. Since there are no losses and no load draining energy from it, the wheel rotates at a constant speed and probably has been doing so for a long time.

At some particular time, point A is exactly at the three o'clock position. The time it takes for the wheel to make one complete revolution so that point A is again at ex-

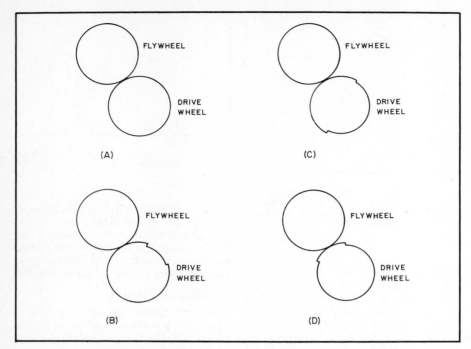

Fig. 6 — Equivalent amounts of energy can be coupled into a flywheel over varying operating angles.

actly three o'clock is called the period of rotation. The frequency of rotation is the reciprocal of this; instead of the number of time units it takes for the flywheel to rotate once, the motion is expressed as the number of rotation units the wheel makes in one time unit. In order to measure this properly, some reference points are required. A set of axes, passing through the shaft of the flywheel, is convenient. One is labeled X, one is Y. When point A is exactly at three o'clock, it lies exactly on the X axis. At that instant, point A has a Y coordinate of zero, because it is at the same point along the Y axis as the origin of the flywheel shaft. One quarter revolution later, point A now is exactly on the Y axis. The flywheel happens to have a radius of 1 unit, so the Y coordinate of A at one quarter revolution (90° of rotation) is 1.

One quarter turn later, point A is again on the X axis, but opposite from where it started. It has rotated one half turn or 180°. The Y coordinate is again zero. Another quarter turn of rotation later, point A has again rotated 90°, for a total of 270°. It's again on the Y axis, but directly opposite its position one half turn ago. The Y coordinate is now −1, to indicate that point A's position is below the flywheel shaft rather than above it. Another one-quarter rotation, for a total of 360° since first measured, and point A is back to its position along the X axis. The Y coordinate is again zero, since point A is again vertically level with the flywheel shaft. All further rotations of the wheel follow precisely the same pattern.

By careful measurement, the Y coordinate of point A could be plotted for the entire rotation of the flywheel, rather than just every quarter turn. The plot would be of a sine wave, just like the circulating current in a tank circuit. This is no mere coincidence; the circulating current in the tank circuit is exactly analogous to the rotation of the flywheel. The circulating current in the tank circuit is the result of the rotation of an electromagnetic field vector as energy is transferred back and forth between the tank circuit's inductor and capacitor.

Fig. 6 illustrates a variety of techniques that can be used to replace the energy transferred to a load from a flywheel. A drive wheel, powered by an electric motor of some type, is coupled to the flywheel. The coupling can be through gear teeth, friction drive or any number of other ways. In this case, the flywheel and drive wheel are coupled together by a 100% efficient friction drive. The drive wheel is shown in Fig. 6A. With no load attached to the flywheel, the energy in the (perfect) flywheel remains constant, demanding no additional energy from the drive wheel and the drive motor. The drive motor uses no electrical current.

As soon as a load is attached, energy flows from the flywheel into the load. In order to maintain the flywheel's energy and thus its rotation, this energy must be replaced. The only source of energy available to the flywheel is the drive wheel, so energy flows from the drive wheel into the flywheel. The drive wheel derives its energy from its drive motor, which in turn takes externally generated electricity and converts it to mechanical energy. A loss in available energy anywhere along this chain causes a similar loss for the remainder of the linkage. In scientific terms, energy must be conserved.

Conversely, if additional energy becomes available anywhere along the chain, perhaps caused by an increase in electrical power at the drive motor, the additional energy is transferred down the line to the load. This implies that controlling the energy supplied to the drive motor affects the energy levels throughout the linkage, and the energy ultimately supplied to the load. The energy available to the load can then be varied, or modulated, by varying the energy supplied to the drive motor.

Another drive system that requires less energy from the drive motor is shown in Fig. 6B. Part of the drive wheel has been cut away so that the drive wheel engages the flywheel for only a part of the drive wheel's rotation. When the drive wheel contacts the flywheel, it supplies energy to the flywheel. The drive motor draws electrical current since it has to provide the energy for the drive wheel. During the portion of the rotation when the cutout on the drive wheel faces the flywheel (that portion of the rotation when the drive wheel would still contact the flywheel if there were no cutout), the drive motor can coast. The motor draws no current. No energy is being transferred from the drive wheel to the flywheel, and the drive motor coasts until the cutout is passed. When the wheels again engage, the drive wheel transfers energy to the flywheel and the drive motor again draws current.

Since the drive motor draws current only during a portion of the flywheel rotation (because of the cutout), the average current consumption per flywheel rotation is reduced. System efficiency improves, but with one drawback — the drive wheel has no control over the flywheel while the cutout faces the flywheel. However, since the uncontrolled portion of the flywheel rotation is short compared to the overall flywheel rotational period, any corrections can be made during the much longer time frame when the two wheels are in contact.

Fig. 6C represents a drive wheel-flywheel system in which the drive wheel contacts and drives the flywheel for only half of the flywheel rotation. During the other half, the drive wheel coasts and drive motor current goes to zero. The low drive-motor duty cycle makes this scheme the most efficient so far. The bad part is that control of the flywheel is lost for half the rotation period.

A limiting case of this efficiency concept is shown in Fig. 6D. Here the drive wheel only "kicks" the flywheel for a short portion of the flywheel rotation period. The duty cycle is low, but there is almost no control of the flywheel except during the short contact period.

The flywheel drive systems just described are analogous to the different classes under which an amplifier can be run. Fig. 6A is just like Class A operation. During the entire flywheel rotation period, the drive wheel provides energy to the flywheel, just as the output device in a Class A amplifier transfers current into its tank circuit. The efficiency is not very good, but the control over the flywheel, or tank circuit circulating current, is as tight as it can be. For an amplifier, this translates to faithful reproduction of the drive signal with low distortion. Classes AB, B, and C are represented by Figs. 6B, 6C and 6D, respectively.

Progressively with each class, the drive wheel actually drives the flywheel for shorter segments of the flywheel rotation period. In Fig. 6C the contact is for one half the rotation; the conduction angle is 180°. So it is also in an amplifier. In a Class B amplifier, device output current flows for half the drive cycle or 180°. What is important in both the flywheel system and the RF power amplifier is that the drive system supplies enough energy to keep the flywheel turning or the tank current circulating. It is also important to note that as the conducting angle decreases, control of the flywheel or tank circuit is given up. The amount of energy transferred from the flywheel or tank circuit into the load is decreasingly controlled by the drive system. Reproduction of changes in the drive energy level at the load (also referred to as modulation), deteriorates as the conduction angle decreases. In an RF power amplifier this is called distortion.

Tank Circuit Q

In order to quantify the ability of a tank circuit or even a flywheel to store energy, a quality factor, Q, is defined. Q is the ratio of energy stored in a system to energy lost.

$$Q = 2\pi \frac{W_S}{W_L}$$

where
  W_S = is the energy stored by the flywheel or tank circuit
  W_L = the energy lost to heat and the load.

By algebraic substitution and appropriate integration, the Q for a tank circuit can be expressed as

$$Q = \frac{X}{R}$$

where
  X = the reactance of either the inductor or the capacitor
  R = the series resistance.

Since both circulating current and Q are proportional to $1/R$, circulating current is therefore proportional to Q. The tank circulating current is equal to the line current multiplied by Q. If the line current is 100 mA, and the tank Q is 10, then the circulating current through the tank is 1 ampere. (This also implies, according to Ohm's Law, that the voltage potentials across the components in a tank circuit are also proportional to Q.)

When there is no load connected to the tank, the only resistances contributing to

R are the losses in the tank circuit. The unloaded Q_U in that case is

$$Q = \frac{X}{R_{Loss}}$$

where
  X = the reactance of either the inductor or capacitor
  R_{Loss} = the loss resistance in the circuit.

To the tank circuit, a load acts exactly the same as circuit losses. Both consume energy. It just happens that energy consumed by the circuit losses becomes heat. The only difference is the use the energy is put to. When energy is coupled out of the tank circuit into a load resistor, the unloaded tank circuit Q (Q_L) is

$$Q_L = \frac{X}{R_{Loss} + R_{Load}}$$

where R_{Load} is the load resistance. Energy dissipated in R_{Loss} is wasted as heat; ideally, all the tank circuit energy should be dissipated in R_{Load}. This implies that R_{Loss} should be as small as possible; the unloaded Q will rise accordingly.

Tank Circuit Efficiency

The efficiency of a tank circuit is the ratio of power dissipated in the load resistance, R_{Load} (the useful power) to the total power dissipated in the tank circuit (by R_{Load} and R_{Loss}). Within the tank circuit, R_{Load} and R_{Loss} are in series, and the circulating current flows through both. The power dissipated by each is therefore proportional to their resistance. The loaded tank efficiency can therefore be defined as

$$\text{Tank efficiency} = \frac{R_{Load}}{R_{Load} + R_{Loss}} \times 100$$

where efficiency is measured as a percentage. By algebraic substitution, the loaded tank efficiency can also be expressed as

$$\text{Tank Efficiency} = (1 - \frac{Q_L}{Q_U}) \times 100$$

where
  Q_L = the tank circuit loaded Q
  Q_U = the unloaded Q of the tank circuit.
It follows then that tank efficiency can be maximized by keeping Q_L low, which keeps the circulating current low and the I^2R losses down. The unloaded Q should be maximized for best efficiency; this means keeping the circuit losses low.

The selectivity provided by a tank circuit helps suppress harmonic currents generated by the amplifier. The amount of harmonic suppression is dependent upon circuit Q, so a conflict exists for the amplifier designer. A low Q_L is desirable for best tank efficiency, but low Q_L yields poor harmonic suppression. High Q_L keeps amplifier harmonic levels low, but tank ef-

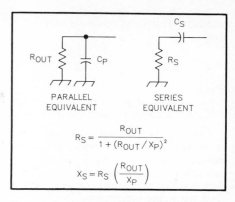

Fig. 7 — Parallel and series equivalent circuits and the formulas used for conversion.

ficiency suffers. At HF, Q_L can usually be chosen as a compromise value where tank efficiency remains high and harmonic suppression is also reasonable. At the higher frequencies the tank Q_L is not as controllable. However, unloaded Q can always be optimized, regardless of frequency, by keeping circuit losses low.

Large-diameter coil conductors help keep circuit losses low by reducing skin-effect losses. Silver-plated conductors also reduce skin-effect losses. Other ways to keep circuit losses low include using large-diameter interconnecting wires and capacitors with a large plate surface area.

Matching Circuits

Tank circuit type matching networks need not take the form of a capacitor directly connected in parallel with an inductor. A number of equivalent circuits can be used to match the impedances normally encountered in a power amplifier. Most are operationally more flexible than a parallel resonant tank. Each has it virtues and failings, but the final choice usually is based on the actual component values needed to implement a particular network. Different networks may require unreasonably high or low inductance or capacitance values. In that case, a change to another type of network or to a different value of Q_L may be required. Several different networks may have to be investigated before the final design is reached.

Normally, the impedances of active amplifying devices are given as a resistance in parallel with the reactance. The equivalence between parallel impedance and series impedance is the basis for all matching network design. The equivalent circuits and the equations for conversion are given in Fig. 7. In order to use most design equations for computing matching networks, the parallel impedance must first be converted to its equivalent series form.

The Q_L of a parallel impedance can be converted from the series form as well. Substitution of the usual formula for calculating Q into the equations from Fig 7 gives

$$Q_L = \frac{R_P}{X_P}$$

where

R_P = the parallel equivalent resistance
X_P = the parallel equivalent reactance.

Several impedance-matching networks are shown in the Radio Transmitting Principles chapter. A low-pass T network and two low-pass L networks are included. Both types of matching networks provide good harmonic suppression.

The pi network may also be used in amplifier matching. Harmonic suppression in a pi network is a function of the impedance transformation ratio and the Q_L of the circuit. Second harmonic attenuation is approximately 35 dB for a load impedance of 2000 Ω in a pi network with a Q_L of 10. The third harmonic is typically 10 dB lower and the fourth harmonic approximately 7 below that. Again, the techniques described earlier in the book can be used to calculate exact theoretical values for different impedances and Q_L values. A typical pi network as used in the output circuit of a tube amplifier is shown in Fig 8. The component values for a pi network with a Q_L of 12 are stated in Table 1. Other values of Q_L can be used by applying the formulas

$$\frac{Q_N}{12} = \frac{C_N}{C_{12}} \quad \text{and} \quad \frac{Q_N}{12} = \frac{L_{12}}{L_N}$$

where

Q_N = the new Q_L value for the network
C_{12} and L_{12} = the different component values taken from Table 1
C_N and L_N = the component values for a pi network with a Q_L of Q_N.

The pi-L network is a combination of a pi network followed by an L network. The pi network transforms the load resistance to an intermediate impedance level called the image impedance. Typically, the image impedance is chosen to be between 300 and 700 Ω. The L section then transforms from the image impedance down to 50 Ω. The output capacitor of the pi network is combined with the input capacitor for the L network, as shown in Fig 9. The pi-L configuration attenuates harmonics better than a pi network. Second harmonic levels for a pi-L network with a Q_L of 10 is approximately 52 dB down from the fundamental. The third harmonic is attenuated 65 dB and the fourth harmonic approximately 75 dB. Component values for a pi-L network with a Q_L of 12 are given in Table 2. Other component values can be calculated for different values of Q_L by using the formulas described previously for the pi network.

The values for L and C in Tables 1 and 2 are based on purely resistive impedances.

Fig 8 — A pi matching network used at the output of a tetrode power amplifier. RFC2 is used for protective purposes in the event C_{BLOCK} fails.

Table 1

Pi-Network Values for Various Plate Impedances with a Loaded Q of 12

	MHz	1500(12)	2000(12)	2500(12)	3000(12)	3500(12)	4000(12)	5000(13)	6000(14)	8000(16)
C1	1.8	708	531	424	354	303	264	229	206	177
	3.5	364	273	218	182	156	136	118	106	91
	7	182	136	109	91	78	68	59	53	46
	14	91	68	55	46	39	34	30	27	23
	21	61	46	36	30	26	23	20	18	15
	28	46	34	27	23	20	17	15	13	11
C2	1.8	3413	2829	2415	2092	1828	1600	1489	1431	1392
	3.5	1755	1455	1242	1076	940	823	766	736	716
	7	877	728	621	538	470	411	383	368	358
	14	439	364	310	269	235	206	192	184	179
	21	293	243	207	179	157	137	128	123	119
	28	279	182	155	135	117	103	96	92	90
L1	1.8	12.81	16.6	20.46	24.21	27.90	31.50	36.09	39.96	46.30
	3.5	6.59	8.57	10.52	12.45	14.35	16.23	18.56	20.55	23.81
	7	3.29	4.29	5.26	6.22	7.18	8.12	9.28	10.26	11.90
	14	1.64	2.14	2.63	3.11	3.59	4.06	4.64	5.14	5.95
	21	1.10	1.43	1.75	2.07	2.39	2.71	3.09	3.43	3.97
	28	0.82	1.07	1.32	1.56	1.79	2.03	2.32	2.57	2.98

These component values are for use with the circuit of Fig 8 and were provided by W6FFC and K1JX.

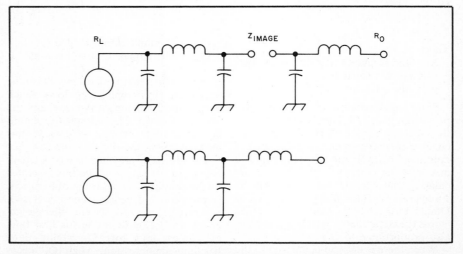

Fig 9 — The pi-L network uses a pi network to transform the input impedance (R_L) to the image impedance (Z_{IMAGE}). An L network transforms Z_{IMAGE} to R_o.

Table 2
Pi-L-network Values for Various Plate Impedance and Frequencies
These values are based on a loaded Q of 12.

Zin (Ohms)	Freq. (MHz)	C1 (pf)	L1 (µH)	C2 (pF)	L2 (µH)
1500	1.80	784.	14.047	2621.	8.917
1500	2.00	636.	14.047	1982.	8.917
1500	3.50	403.	7.117	1348.	4.518
1500	4.00	318.	7.117	991.	4.518
1500	7.30	174.	3.900	543.	2.476
1500	7.00	188.	3.900	596.	2.476
1500	14.00	93.	1.984	292.	1.259
1500	14.35	89.	1.984	276.	1.259
1500	21.00	62.	1.327	191.	0.843
1500	21.45	59.	1.327	185.	0.843
1500	28.00	48.	0.959	152.	0.609
1500	29.70	43.	0.959	134.	0.609
2000	1.80	591.	17.933	2355.	8.917
2000	2.00	478.	17.933	1788.	8.917
2000	3.50	304.	9.086	1211.	4.518
2000	4.00	239.	9.086	894.	4.518
2000	7.00	142.	4.978	534.	2.476
2000	7.30	131.	4.978	490.	2.476
2000	14.00	70.	2.533	264.	1.259
2000	14.35	67.	2.533	249.	1.259
2000	21.00	47.	1.694	173.	0.843
2000	21.45	45.	1.694	167.	0.843
2000	28.00	36.	1.224	135.	0.609
2000	29.70	32.	1.224	120.	0.609
2500	1.80	474.	21.730	2168.	8.917
2500	2.00	382.	21.730	1654.	8.917
2500	3.50	244.	11.010	1115.	4.518
2500	4.00	191.	11.010	827.	4.518
2500	7.00	114.	6.033	493.	2.476
2500	7.30	105.	6.033	453.	2.476
2500	14.00	56.	3.069	240.	1.259
2500	14.35	53.	3.069	230.	1.259
2500	21.00	38.	2.053	158.	0.843
2500	21.45	36.	2.053	154.	0.843
2500	28.00	29.	1.483	127.	0.609
2500	29.70	26.	1.483	111.	0.609
3000	1.80	397.	25.466	2026.	8.917
3000	2.00	318.	25.466	1554.	8.917
3000	3.50	204.	12.903	1042.	4.518
3000	4.00	159.	12.903	777.	4.518
3000	7.00	94.	7.070	468.	2.476
3000	7.30	87.	7.070	426.	2.476
3000	14.00	47.	3.597	222.	1.259
3000	14.35	44.	3.597	217.	1.259
3000	21.00	32.	2.406	146.	0.843
3000	21.45	30.	2.406	145.	0.843
3000	28.00	24.	1.738	115.	0.609
3000	29.70	21.	1.738	105.	0.609
3500	1.80	338.	29.155	1939.	8.917
3500	2.00	272.	29.155	1476.	8.917
3500	3.50	174.	14.772	997.	4.518
3500	4.00	136.	14.772	738.	4.518
3500	7.00	81.	8.094	444.	2.476
3500	7.30	75.	8.094	404.	2.476
3500	14.00	40.	4.118	215.	1.259
3500	14.35	38.	4.118	206.	1.259
3500	21.00	27.	2.755	136.	0.843
3500	21.45	25.	2.755	138.	0.843
3500	28.00	21.	1.989	106.	0.609
3500	29.70	18.	1.989	99.	0.609
4000	1.80	297.	32.805	1841.	8.917
4000	2.00	238.	32.805	1412.	8.917
4000	3.50	153.	16.621	947.	4.518
4000	4.00	119.	16.621	706.	4.518
4000	7.00	71.	9.107	418.	2.476
4000	7.30	65.	9.107	387.	2.476
4000	14.00	35.	4.633	204.	1.259
4000	14.35	33.	4.633	197.	1.259
4000	21.00	23.	3.099	137.	0.843
4000	21.45	22.	3.099	132.	0.843
4000	28.00	18.	2.238	107.	0.609
4000	29.70	16.	2.238	95.	0.609
5000	1.80	239.	40.011	1696.	8.917
5000	2.00	190.	40.011	1316.	8.917
5000	3.50	123.	20.272	872.	4.518
5000	4.00	95.	20.272	658.	4.518
5000	7.00	57.	11.108	387.	2.476
5000	7.30	52.	11.108	360.	2.476
5000	14.00	29.	5.651	186.	1.259
5000	14.35	27.	5.651	183.	1.259
5000	21.00	19.	3.780	125.	0.843
5000	21.45	18.	3.780	123.	0.843
5000	28.00	15.	2.730	95.	0.609
5000	29.70	13.	2.730	89.	0.609
6000	1.80	200.	47.118	1612.	8.917
6000	2.00	160.	47.118	1242.	8.917
6000	3.50	103.	23.873	829.	4.518
6000	4.00	80.	23.873	621.	4.518
6000	7.00	48.	13.081	368.	2.476
6000	7.30	44.	13.081	340.	2.476
6000	14.00	24.	6.655	172.	1.259
6000	14.35	22.	6.655	173.	1.259
6000	21.00	16.	4.452	117.	0.843
6000	21.45	15.	4.452	116.	0.843
6000	28.00	13.	3.215	87.	0.609
6000	29.70	11.	3.215	84.	0.609
8000	1.80	152.	61.119	1453.	8.917
8000	2.00	120.	61.119	1138.	8.917
8000	3.50	78.	30.967	747.	4.518
8000	4.00	60.	30.967	569.	4.518
8000	7.00	36.	16.968	337.	2.476
8000	7.30	33.	16.968	312.	2.476
8000	14.00	18.	8.632	165.	1.259
8000	14.35	17.	8.632	159.	1.259
8000	21.00	12.	5.775	104.	0.843
8000	21.45	11.	5.775	106.	0.843
8000	28.00	9.	4.171	86.	0.609
8000	29.70	8.	4.171	77.	0.609

Operating Q — 12. Output load — 52 ohms. Computer data provided by Bill Imamura, JA6GW and Clarke Greene, K1JX.

Any reactance modifies these values. Stray circuit reactances as well as tube or capacitor reactances all should be included as part of the matching network. Very often these reactances will render most of the matching circuits impractical. Either unacceptable loaded Q values or unrealistic component values are required. A compromise must be made once all the matching network alternatives have been investigated and found unacceptable.

Above 30 MHz, transistor and tube reactances completely dominate circuit impedances. At the lower impedances found in transistor circuits, the standard networks can be applied as long as suitable components are used. Capacitors rarely exhibit their marked values above 50 MHz because of internal reactances in addition to lead inductance, and must be compensated for. Tuned circuits frequently take the form of strip lines or other transmission lines in order to obtain "pure" inductances. The choice of components is often more significant than the type of network used.

The high impedances encountered in VHF tube amplifier plate circuits are not easily matched with the typical networks. The tube output capacitance is usually of such a high value that most matching networks are unsuitable. The usual practice is to resonate the tube output capacitance with a low-loss inductance connected in parallel. The result is a very high Q tank circuit. Component losses must be kept to an absolute minimum in order to achieve reasonable tank efficiency. Output impedance transformation is usually performed by a link inductively coupled to the tank circuit or by a parallel transformation of the output resistance through a series capacitor.

Transformers

Broadband transformers are often used in matching to the input impedance or optimum load impedance in a power amplifier. Multioctave power amplifier performance can be achieved by appropriate application of these transformers. The input and output transformers are two of the most critical components in a broadband amplifier. Amplifier efficiency, gain flatness, input SWR and even linearity are all affected by the transformer design and use. There are two transformer types, as described in the Electrical Fundamentals chapter; the conventional transformer and the transmission-line transformer.

The conventional transformer is wound much the same way as a power transformer. The primary and secondary windings are wound around a high-permeability core, usually made from a ferrite or powdered-iron material. Coupling between the secondary and primary is made as tight as possible to minimize leakage inductance. At low frequencies, the coupling between windings is predominantly magnetic. As the frequency rises, the permeability in the core decreases and the leakage inductance increases; transformer losses increase as well.

Typical examples of conventional transformers are shown in Fig 10. In Fig 10A, the primary windings consist of brass or copper tubes, inserted into ferrite sleeves. The tubes are shorted together at one end by a piece of copper-clad printed circuit board material. The secondary winding is threaded through the tubes. Since the low-impedance winding is only a single turn, the transformation ratio is limited to the squares of integers — 1, 4, 9, 16, etc. The lowest effective transformer frequency is determined by the inductance of the one-turn winding. It should have a reactance at least four times greater than the impedance it is connected to, for extended low-frequency response.

The coupling coefficient between the two windings is a function of the primary tube diameter and its length, and the diameters and insulation thickness of the wire used in the high-impedance winding. High impedance ratios, greater than 36:1, should use large-diameter secondary windings. Miniature coaxial cable (using only the braid as the conductor) works very well. Another use for coaxial cable braid is illustrated in Fig 10B. Instead of using tubing for the primary winding, the secondary winding is threaded through copper braid. Performance of the two units is almost identical.

The cores used must be large enough so the core material will not saturate at the power level applied to the transformer. Core saturation can cause permanent changes to the core permeability, as well as

(A)   (B)

Fig 10 — The two methods of constructing the transformers as outlined in the text. At (A), the one-turn loop is made from brass tubing; at (B), a piece of coaxial cable braid is used for the loop.

overheating. Transformer nonlinearity also develops at core saturation. Harmonics and other distortion products are produced, clearly an undesirable situation. Multiple cores can be used to increase the power capabilities of the transformer. The core size required can be calculated through the use of formulas presented in the Electrical Fundamentals chapter of this *Handbook* in the discussion of ferromagnetic transformers.

Transmission line transformers are similar to conventional transformers, but can be used over wider frequency ranges. In a conventional transformer, the high-frequency losses are caused by leakage inductance, rising with frequency. In a transmission line transformer, the windings are arranged so there is tight capacitive coupling between the two. A high coupling coefficient is maintained up to a high frequency.

The Radio Transmitting Principles chapter includes additional information about broadband transformers. Transformers with a variety of impedance-transformation ratios are illustrated there.

Output Filtering

Filtering of the amplifier output is sometimes necessary to meet spurious-signal requirements. Broadband amplifiers, by definition, provide little if any suppression of harmonic energy. Amplifiers using tank circuits in their output often require further attenuation of undesired harmonics. High level signals, particularly at multiple transmitter sites, can travel down the feed line and mix in a power amplifier, causing spurious outputs. For example, an HF transceiver signal radiated from a triband beam is picked up by a VHF FM antenna on the same mast. The signal saturates the low-power FM transceiver output stage, even with power off, and is reradiated by the VHF antenna. Proper use of filters can reduce spurious energy considerably.

The type of filter used will depend on the application and the level of spurious attenuation needed. Band-pass filters attenuate spurious signals above and below the band for which they are designed. Low-pass filters attenuate signals above the desired output frequency, while high-pass

filters reduce energy below the design frequency.

The Electrical Fundamentals chapter includes detailed information about designing suitable filters. Tables of component values allow you to select a particular design or scale the values for different frequencies and impedance ranges.

TRANSMITTING DEVICE RATINGS

Plate Dissipation

The ultimate determination of the power-handling capability of a tube is its plate dissipation. It is the measure of how many watts of heat the tube can safely dissipate without exceeding critical temperatures. Excessive temperature can weaken or even melt internal tube connections or the seals that retain vacuum in the tube. The result — tube failure. The same tube may have different ratings, depending on the conditions under which it is operated, but all the ratings are based primarily upon the heat that the tube can safely dissipate.

Efficiency for amplifiers runs between 25 and 75 percent, depending on the operating class. The efficiency indicates how much of the stage's power is useful RF; the rest is wasted power in the form of heat, dissipated through the plate. By knowing the plate-dissipation limit of the tube, and the efficiency expected from the chosen class of operation, the maximum power output and input levels can be determined. The maximum power output possible is

$$P_{OUT} = \frac{P_D N_P}{100 - N_P}$$

where
P_{OUT} = the power output in watts
P_D = the plate dissipation in watts
N_P = the efficiency (as a percentage).

The dc input power would simply be

$$P_{IN} = \frac{100 \, P_{OUT}}{N_P}$$

Almost all tube-type power amplifiers in amateur service today operate as linear amplifiers (Class AB or B) with an efficiency of approximately 60%. That means a useful power output of approximately 1.5 times the plate dissipation can be reliably expected from a linear amplifier (assuming everything else works right).

The amplifier duty cycle determines the dissipation rating. Some types of operation are less efficient than others, meaning that the tube must dissipate more heat. Some forms of modulation, such as CW or SSB are intermittent in nature, causing less average heating than modulation formats in which there is continuous transmission, such as RTTY. Power tube manufacturers use two different rating systems to allow for the variations in service. CCS — Continuous Commercial Service — is the more conservative rating and is used for specifying tubes that are in constant use. The second rating system is based on intermittent, low-duty-cycle operation, and is known as ICAS — Intermittent Commercial and Amateur Service. ICAS ratings are normally used by amateurs who wish to obtain maximum power output with reasonable tube life in CW and SSB service. The conservative CCS ratings should be used for FM, RTTY and SSTV applications. (Plate power transformers for amateur service are also rated in CCS and ICAS terms.)

Maximum Ratings

Tube manufacturers publish sets of maximum values for the tubes they produce. No single maximum value should ever be used, unless all other ratings are simultaneously held substantially below their maximum values. As an example, a tube may have a maximum plate-voltage rating of 2000, a maximum plate-current rating of 300 mA, and a maximum plate power-input rating of 400 W. Therefore, if the maximum plate voltage of 2000 is used, then the plate current should be limited to 200 mA (not 300 mA) to stay within the maximum power-input rating of 400 W.

The manufacturers also publish sets of typical operating values that should result in good efficiency and long tube life. These values for many tubes can also be found in the Component Data chapter.

TRANSISTOR POWER DISSIPATION

RF power amplifier transistors are limited in power-handling capability by the amount of heat the device can safely dissipate. Power dissipation for a transistor is expressed symbolically as P_D. The maximum rating is based on maintaining a case temperature of 25 °C. If greater temperatures are anticipated, the device has to be derated in milliwatts per °C, as specified by the manufacturer for that particular device. The efficiency considerations described earlier in reference to plate dissipation apply here, also. A rule of thumb for selecting a P_D rating suitable for a given RF power output level is to choose a transistor that has a maximum

dissipation of twice the desired output power.

Maximum Transistor Ratings

Transistor data sheets specify the maximum operating voltage for several conditions. Of particular interest is the V_{CEO} specification (collector to emitter voltage, with the base open). In RF amplifier service the collector to emitter voltage can rise to twice the dc supply potential. Thus, if a 12-V supply is used, the transistor should have a V_{CEO} of 24 or greater to preclude damage.

The maximum collector current is also specified by the manufacturer. This specification is actually limited by the current-carrying capabilities of the internal bonding wires. Of course, the collector current must stay below the level that generates heat higher than the allowable device power dissipation. Many transistors are also rated for the load mismatch they can safely withstand. A typical specification might be for a transistor to tolerate a 30:1 SWR at all phase angles.

Transistor manufacturers publish data sheets that describe all the appropriate device ratings. Typical operating results are also given in these data sheets. In addition, many manufacturers publish application notes illustrating the use of their devices in practical circuits. Construction details are usually given. Perhaps owing to the popularity of Amateur Radio among electrical engineers, most of the notes describe applications especially suited to the Amateur Service. Specifications for some of the more popular RF power transistors are found in the Component Data chapter.

PASSIVE COMPONENT RATINGS

Output Tank Capacitor Ratings

The tank capacitor in a high-power amplifier should be chosen to allow sufficient spacing between plates to preclude high-voltage breakdown. The peak RF voltage present across a tank circuit under load, but without modulation, may be taken conservatively as being equal to the dc plate or collector voltage. If the dc supply voltage also appears across the tank capacitor, this must be added to the peak RF voltage, making the total peak voltage twice the dc supply voltage. At the higher voltages, it is usually desirable to design the

tank circuit so that the dc supply voltages do not appear across the tank capacitor, thereby allowing the use of a smaller capacitor with less plate spacing. Capacitor manufacturers usually rate their products in terms of the peak voltage between plates. Typical plate spacings are given in Table 3.

Output tank capacitors should be mounted as close to the tube as temperature considerations will permit, to make possible the shortest capacitive path from plate to cathode. Especially at the higher frequencies, where minimum circuit capacitance becomes important, the capacitor should be mounted with its stator plates well spaced from the chassis or other shielding. In circuits in which the rotor must be insulated from ground, the capacitor should be mounted on ceramic insulators of a size commensurate with the plate voltage involved and — most important of all, from the viewpoint of safety to the operator — a well-insulated coupling should be used between the capacitor shaft and the dial. The section of the shaft attached to the dial should be well grounded. This can be done conveniently through the use of panel shaft-bearing units.

High-Frequency Tank Coils

Tank coils should be mounted at least their diameter away from shielding to prevent a marked loss in Q. Except perhaps at 28 MHz, it is not important that the coil be mounted quite close to the tank capacitor. Leads up to 6 or 8 inches are permissible. It is more important to keep the tank capacitor, as well as other components, out of the immediate field of the coil. For this reason, it is preferable to mount the coil so that its axis is parallel to the capacitor shaft, either alongside the capacitor or above it.

Many factors must be taken into consideration in determining the size of wire (see Table 4) that should be used in winding a tank coil. The considerations of form factor and wire size which will produce a coil of minimum loss are often of less importance in practice than the coil size that will fit into available space or that will handle the required power without excessive heating. This is particularly true in the case of input circuits for screen-grid tubes where the relatively small driving power required can be easily obtained even if the losses in the driver are quite high. It may

Table 3
Typical Tank-Capacitor Plate Spacings

Spacing Inches	Peak Voltage	Spacing Inches	Peak Voltage	Spacing Inches	Peak Voltage
0.015	1000	0.07	3000	0.175	7000
0.02	1200	0.08	3500	0.25	9000
0.03	1500	0.125	4500	0.35	11000
0.05	2000	0.15	6000	0.5	13000

Table 4

Wire Sizes for Transmitting Coils for Tube Transmitters

Power Input (Watts)	Band (MHz)	Wire Size
1000	28-21	6
	14.7	8
	3.5-1.8	10
500	28-21	8
	14-7	12
	3.5-1.8	14
150	28-21	12
	14-7	14
	3.5-1.8	18
75	28-21	14
	14-7	18
	3.5-1.8	22
25 or less*	28-21	18
	14-7	24
	3.5-1.8	28

*Wire size limited principally by consideration of Q.

be considered preferable to take the power loss if the physical size can be kept down by making the coils small.

The wire sizes in Table 4 are larger than those typically used in modern commercial and home-built equipment. That is because their values were derived for AM service, where there is a continuous carrier and modulation peaks have a PEP four times the carrier value. Thus, the no. 10 wire required for 1000-W input on 75-meter AM would be adequate for at least 4-kW PEP in SSB service.

Larger wire size than required for current handling capabilities is often used to maximize unloaded Q. Particularly at higher frequencies where skin depth considerations increase losses, the greater surface area of large diameter windings can be beneficial. Small-diameter copper tubing, up to 0.25-in outer diameter, can be used successfully for tank coils up through the lower VHF range. Silver plating the tubing further reduces losses. This is especially true as the tubing ages, and oxidizes. Silver oxide is a much better conductor than copper oxides, so silver-plated tank coils maintain their low-loss characteristics even after years of use.

At VHF and above, tank circuits take on forms less reminiscent of the familiar coil inductor. The inductances required to resonate tank circuits of reasonable Q at these higher frequencies is small enough that only strip lines or coaxial lines are practical. Since these are constructed from sheet metal or large-diameter tubing, current-handling capabilities normally are not a relevant factor.

RF Chokes

The characteristics of any RF choke will vary with frequency, from characteristics resembling those of a parallel-resonant circuit of high impedance, to those of a series-resonant circuit, where the impedance is lowest. In between these extremes, the choke will show varying amounts of inductive or capacitive reactance.

In series-feed circuits, these characteristics are of relatively small importance because the RF voltage across the choke is negligible. In a parallel-feed circuit, however, the choke is shunted across the tank circuit, and is subject to the full tank RF voltage. If the choke does not present a sufficiently high impedance, enough power will be absorbed by the choke to burn it out. To avoid this, the choke must have a sufficiently high reactance to be effective at the lowest frequency, and yet have no series resonances near the higher frequency bands. These potential resonances should be carefully investigated with a dip meter. A resonant choke failure in a high power amplifier can be very dramatic and damaging!

Blocking Capacitors

A series capacitor is usually used at the input of every amplifier output circuit. Its purpose is to block dc from appearing on any of the matching circuit components and the antenna. As mentioned in the section on tank capacitors, output circuit component ratings can be relaxed somewhat when only the ac component of the output voltage is present.

The voltage rating for a blocking capacitor should be equal to at least twice the dc voltage applied. The peak voltage in a tank circuit can approach this value. A large safety margin is desirable, since blocking capacitor failure can bring catastrophic results.

The blocking capacitor should be low impedance at the amplifier operating frequencies. Since all the amplifier RF output current flows through the capacitor, a low impedance is necessary to avoid dissipation of RF power in the capacitor, caused by the resistive loss of the capacitor. Not only is that power wasted, but also the power-dissipation capabilities of most capacitors is minimal. A reasonable capacitance value for a blocking capacitor is one that limits its dissipation to less than 0.1% of the amplifier output power. This implies a capacitive reactance less than one thousandth the circuit impedance.

The current flowing through the blocking capacitor is dependent on circuit loaded Q. High levels of current flow in typical power amplifier output circuits. The capacitor must be capable of withstanding these currents. Below a couple of hundred watts at the high frequencies, suitable voltage rating disc ceramic capacitors work well in high-impedance tube amplifier output circuits. Above that power level and at VHF, ceramic doorknob capacitors are needed for their low losses and high current handling capabilities. The so-called "TV doorknob" breaks down at high RF current levels and should be avoided.

The very high values of Q_L found in many VHF and UHF tube-type amplifier tank circuits often require custom fabrication of the blocking capacitor. This can usually be accommodated through the use of a Teflon "sandwich" capacitor. Here, the blocking capacitor is formed from two parallel plates separated by a thin layer of Teflon. This capacitor often is part of the tank circuit itself, forming a very low-loss blocking capacitor. Teflon is rated for a minimum breakdown voltage of 2000 volts per mil of thickness, so voltage breakdown should not be a factor in any practically realized circuit.

The capacitance formed from such a Teflon sandwich can be calculated from the information presented in the Electrical Fundamentals chapter (use a dielectric constant of 2.1 for Teflon). In order to prevent any potential irregularities caused by dielectric thickness variations (including air gaps), Dow-Corning DC-4 silicone grease should be evenly applied to both sides of the Teflon dielectric. This grease has similar properties to Teflon, and will fill in any surface irregularities that might cause problems.

The very low impedances found in transistorized amplifiers present special problems. In order to achieve the desired low blocking capacitor impedance, large-value capacitors are required. Special ceramic chips and mica capacitors are available that meet the requirements for high capacitance, large current carrying capability, and low associated inductance. These capacitors are more costly than standard disc-ceramic or silver-mica units, but their level of performance easily justifies their price. Most of these special-purpose capacitors can be identified by the fact that they are either leadless or come with wide straps instead of normal wire leads. Disc-ceramic and other wire-lead capacitors are generally not suitable for transistor power amplifier service.

SOURCES OF OPERATING VOLTAGES

Tube Filament or Heater Voltage

The heater voltage for the indirectly heated cathode-type tubes found in low-power classifications may vary 10 percent above or below rating without seriously reducing the life of the tube. The voltage of the higher-power, filament-type tubes should be held closely between the rated voltages as a minimum and five percent above rating as a maximum. Because of internal tube heating at UHF and higher, the manufacturers' rated filament voltage often is reduced at these higher frequencies. The derated filament voltages should be followed carefully to maximize tube life. Series dropping resistors may be required in the filament circuit to attain the correct voltage. The voltage should be measured at the filament pins of the tube socket while the amplifier is running. The filament choke and the interconnecting wiring all have voltage drops associated with them. The high current drawn by a power tube heater circuit causes substantial voltage drops to occur across even a small resistance. Also, make sure that the plate power drawn from the power line does not cause a drop in filament voltage below the proper value when plate power is applied.

Thoriated-type filaments lose emission when the tube is overloaded appreciably. If the overload has not been too prolonged, emission sometimes may be restored by operating the filament at rated voltage with all other voltages removed for a period of 10 minutes, or at 20% above rated voltage for a few minutes.

Vacuum Tube Plate Voltage

Dc plate voltage for the operation of RF amplifiers is most often obtained from a transformer-rectifier-filter system (see Chapters 6 and 27) designed to deliver the required plate voltage at the required current. It is not unusual for a power tube to arc over internally. This is usually caused by the intrusion of a charged subatomic particle into the tube. The flashover by itself is not normally dangerous to the tube, as long as the event is short lived. Damage, to both the high-voltage supply and the tube, usually occurs when the flashover totally discharges the power supply capacitor bank. The subsequent high-current discharge into the tube not only damages the tube, but also frequently destroys the rectifiers in the power supply.

A good preventative measure against this is the inclusion of a 50- to 100-Ω, high-wattage power resistor in series with the plate voltage circuit. The additional resistance in the line lengthens the time constant associated with the capacitor-load resistance circuit. Short-duration flashovers are dampened by the RC low-pass action of the plate circuit, once the resistor is added. Any future flashovers probably will go undetected. Even at high plate-current levels, the addition of the resistor does little to affect the dynamic regulation of the plate supply. The wattage rating of the resistor may be calculated from the expected maximum dc plate current drawn by the tube. A safety factor of at least two should be applied to ensure resistor reliability.

Grid Bias

The grid bias for a linear amplifier should be highly filtered and very well regulated. Any ripple or other voltage change in the bias circuit modulates the amplifier. This causes hum to appear on the signal as well as distortion. Since most linear amplifiers draw only small amounts of grid current, these bias supply requirements are not hard to meet.

Fixed bias is usually obtained from a variable-voltage regulated supply. Voltage adjustment allows setting bias level to give the desired resting plate current. Fig 11

Fig 11 — Various techniques for providing operating bias with tube amplifiers.

shows a simple Zener-diode-regulated bias supply. The dropping resistor is chosen to allow approximately 10 mA of Zener current. Bias is then regulated for all drive conditions up to a grid current level of about 5 mA. The potentiometer allows the bias level to be adjusted between V_{Zener} to approximately 15 volts higher. This range is usually adequate to allow for variations in the operating conditions between different tubes. Under stand-by conditions, when it is desirable to cut off the tube entirely, the Zener ground return is interrupted so the full bias supply voltage is applied to the grid.

In Fig 11B and C, bias is obtained from the voltage drop across a Zener diode in the cathode (or filament center-tap) lead. Operating bias is obtained by the voltage drop across D1 as a result of plate (and screen) current flow. The diode voltage drop effectively raises the cathode potential relative to the grid. The grid is therefore lower in potential than the cathode by the Zener voltage of the diode. Assigning an arbitrary potential of zero to the cathode gives a grid bias equal to the Zener drop. The Zener-diode wattage rating should be twice the product of the maximum cathode current times the developed bias. There-

fore, a tube requiring 15 volts of bias during a maximum cathode current flow of 100 mA would dissipate 1.5 W in the Zener diode. The diode rating, to allow a suitable safety factor, would be 3 W or greater. The circuit of Fig 11C illustrates how D1 would be used with a cathode driven (grounded grid) amplifier as opposed to the grid-driven example at B.

In all cases the Zener diode should be bypassed by a 0.01 μF capacitor of suitable voltage rating. Current through any type of diode generates shot noise. If not bypassed, this noise would modulate the amplified signal, causing distortion in the amplifier output.

Screen Voltage For Tubes

Power tetrode screen current varies widely with both excitation and loading. The current may be either positive or negative. In a linear amplifier the screen voltage should be well regulated for all values of screen current. The power output from a tetrode is very sensitive to screen voltage, and any dynamic change in the screen potential can cause distorted output. Voltage regulator tubes or Zener diodes are usually used for screen regulation.

Fig 12 — A Zener-regulated screen supply for use with a tetrode. Protection is provided by a fuse and a varistor.

Fig 12 shows a typical example of a regulated screen supply for a power tetrode amplifier. The voltage from a fixed dc supply is dropped to the Zener stack voltage by the current-limiting resistor. A screen bleeder resistor is connected in parallel with the Zener stack to allow for the negative screen current developed under certain tube operating conditions. The bleeder current is chosen to be somewhat greater than the expected maximum negative screen current. For external anode tubes in the 4CX250 family, a typical value would be 20 mA. For the 4CX1000 family, a screen bleeder current of 70 mA is required. The idling current for the Zeners is set to be approximately 10 mA higher than the expected maximum screen current, plus the screen bleeder-resistor current. The screen voltage is then regulated for all values of current between maximum negative screen current and maximum positive screen current.

A tetrode should never be operated without plate voltage and load; otherwise the screen would act like an anode and draw excessive current. Supplying the screen through a series dropping resistor from the plate supply affords a measure of protection, since the screen voltage only appears when there is plate voltage. Alternatively, a fuse can be placed between the regulator and the bleeder resistor. The fuse should not be installed between the bleeder resistor and the tube, because the tube should never be operated without a load on the screen. Without a load, the screen potential tends to rise to the anode voltage. Any screen bypass capacitors or other associated circuitry would likely be damaged by this high voltage.

In Fig 12, a varistor is connected from screen to ground. If, because of some circuit failure, the screen voltage should rise substantially above its nominal level, the varistor will conduct and clamp the screen voltage to ground. This usually causes a fuse to blow in the power supply, and power is interrupted before any damage occurs. The varistor voltage should be chosen to be approximately 50 percent higher than normal screen voltage.

Fig 13 — Biasing methods for use with transistor amplifiers.

Table 5

Specifications of Some Popular Tubes, Sockets and Chimneys

Tube	CFM	Back Pressure (inches)	Socket	Chimney
3-400Z/8163	13	0.13	SK-400, SK-410	SK-416
3-500Z	13	0.082	SK-400, SK-410	SK-406
3CX800A7	19	0.35	EIMAC P/N 154353	
3-1000Z/8164	25	0.38	SK-500, SK-510	SK-516
3CX1500/8877	35	0.41	SK-2200, SK-2210	SK-2216
4-250A/5D22	2	0.1	SK-400, SK-410	SK-406
4-400A/8438	14	0.25	SK-400, SK-410	SK-406
4-1000A/8166	20	0.6	SK-500,SK-510	SK-506
4CX250R/7850W	6.4	0.59	SK-600, SK-600A, SK-602A, SK-610, SK-610A, SK-611, SK-612, SK-620, SK-620A SK-621, SK-630	SK-606 SK-626
4CX300A/8167	7.2	0.58	SK-700, SK-710, SK-711A, SK-712A, SK-740, SK-760, SK-761, SK-770	SK-606
4CX350A/8321	7.8	1.2	Same as 4CX250R	
4CX1000A/8168	25	0.2	SK-800B, SK-810B, SK-890B	SK-806
4CX1500/8660				
8874	8.6	0.37		

These values are for sea-level elevation. For locations well above sea level (Denver, Colorado, for example), add an additional 20% to the figure listed.

Transistor Biasing

Solid-state power amplifiers generally operate in Class C or AB. When some bias is desired during Class C operation (Fig 13A), a resistance of the appropriate value can be placed in the emitter return as shown. Most transistors will operate in Class C without adding bias externally, but in some instances the amplifier efficiency can be improved by means of emitter bias. Reverse bias supplied to the base of the Class C transistor should be avoided because it will lead to internal breakdown of the device during peak drive periods. The damage is frequently a cumulative phenomenon, leading to gradual destruction of the transistor junction.

A simple method for Class AB biasing is shown in Fig 13B. D1 is a silicon diode that acts as a bias clamp at approximately 0.7 V. The forward bias establishes linear-amplification conditions. That value of bias is not always optimum for a specified transistor in terms of IMD. Variable bias of the type illustrated in Fig 13C permits the designer sufficient variance to locate the operating point for best linearity. The diode clamp or the reference for another type of regulator is usually thermally bonded to the power transistor. The bias level then tracks the thermal characteristics of the output transistor. Since a transistor's current transfer characteristics are a function of

temperature, thermal tracking of the bias is necessary to maintain device linearity and to prevent thermal runaway and the subsequent destruction of the transistor.

AMPLIFIER COOLING

Tube Cooling

Vacuum tubes must be operated within the temperature range specified by the manufacturer if long tube life is to be achieved. Tubes with glass envelopes rated at up to 25 W plate dissipation may be run without forced-air cooling, if a moderate amount of cooling by convection can be arranged. If a perforated metal enclosure is used, and a ring of ¼-inch-diameter holes are placed around the tube socket, normal air flow can be relied on to remove excess heat at room temperatures.

For tubes with greater plate dissipation, or those operated with plate currents in excess of the manufacturer's ratings, forced-air cooling with a fan or blower is needed. Most manufacturers rate tube cooling requirements for continuous-duty operation. Their literature will indicate the required volume of air flow, in cubic feet per minute (CFM), at some particular back pressure.

Back pressure is the pressure that is built up inside an imperfect air passage when pressurized by an air source such as a blower. A perfect air passage offers no resistance to air flow, so the volume of air entering the passage flows out at the same rate. Any practical air passage is finite in size, and restricts the volume of air that can flow through. The difference between the potential volume of air that is available for flow through the air passage and the volume that actually flows manifests itself as back pressure. Anything that represents resistance to the air flow develops back pressure.

Tubes and their associated components are obstacles to the free passage of air and so develop back pressure to an air stream. The exact amount of pressure will depend on the blower, tube socket, tube and chimney characteristics. Blowers vary in their ability to work against back pressure so the matter of blower selection should not be taken lightly.

Values of CFM and back pressure for some of the more popular tubes, sockets and chimneys are given in Table 5. The back pressure is specified in inches of water and can be measured easily in an operational air passage as indicated in Figs 14 and 15. The pressure differential between the air passage and the atmospheric pressure is measured with a device called a manometer. A manometer is nothing more than a piece of clear tubing, open at both ends and fashioned in the shape of a "U." The manometer is temporarily connected to the chassis and is removed after the measurements are completed. As shown in the diagrams, a small amount of water is placed in the tube. At Fig 15A the blower is "off" and the water will seek its own level, because the air pressure (ordinary atmospheric pressure) is the same at both ends of the manometer tube. At B, the blower is "on" (socket, tube and chimney in place) and the pressure difference, in terms of inches of water, is measured. For most applications a standard scale can be used for the measurement and the results will be sufficiently accurate.

Table 6 illustrates the performance specifications for Dayton blowers, which are available through W. W. Grainger outlets throughout the U.S. Blowers having wheel diameters similar to those in Table 6 will likely have similar flow and back-

Fig 14 — Air is forced into the chassis by the blower and exits through the tube socket. The manometer is used to measure system back pressure, which is an important factor in determining the proper size blower.

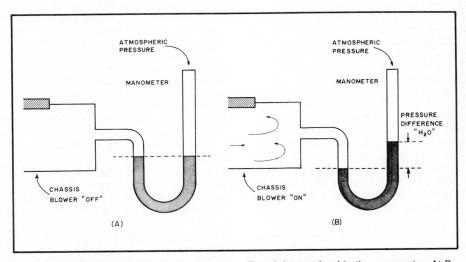

Fig 15 — At A the blower is "off" and the water will seek its own level in the manometer. At B the blower is "on" and the amount of back pressure in terms of inches of water can be measured as indicated.

Table 6
Blower Performance Specifications

Wheel Dia.	Wheel Width	RPM	Free Air	Back Pressure (inches) 0.1	0.2	0.3	0.4	0.5	Cutoff	Stock No.
2″	1″	3160	15	13	4	—	—	—	0.22	2C782
3″	1-15/32″	3340	54	48	43	36	25	17	0.67	4C012
3″	1-7/8″	3030	60	57	54	49	39	23	0.60	4C440
3″	1-7/8″	2880	76	70	63	56	45	8	0.55	4C004
3-13/16″	1-7/8″	2870	100	98	95	90	85	80	0.80	4C443
3-13/16″	2-1/2″	3160	148	141	135	129	121	114	1.04	4C005

Fig 16 — Anode compartment pressurization is more efficient than grid compartment pressurization. Air exits through the tube anode, through a chimney, and through the tube socket.

pressure characteristics. If in doubt about specifications, consult the manufacturer. The setup of Fig 15 is the authoritative determinant of cooling adequacy. As an example, assume that an amplifier is to be built using a 3-1000Z tube. A blower capable of supplying 25 CFM at a back pressure of 0.38 inch of water is required. It appears (from Table 6) that the second blower listed would be suitable, although it may be marginal since it can supply only 25 CFM into a back pressure of 0.4 inch of water. The next larger size would provide a margin of safety.

When a pair of tubes is used, the CFM rating is doubled, but the back pressure remains the same as that for one tube. A pair of 3-1000Z tubes, for example, would require 50 CFM at a back pressure of 0.38 inch of water. In this case the fifth blower listed in the table would be suitable since it can supply 85 CFM at a back pressure of 0.4 inch of water. Always choose a blower that can supply at least the required amount of air. Smaller blowers will almost certainly lead to shortened tube life.

One method for directing the flow of air around a tube envelope or through tube cooling fins involves the use of a pressurized chassis. This system is shown in Fig 14. A blower is attached to the chassis and forces air up through the tube socket and around the tube. A chimney (not shown in this drawing) is used to guide the air around the tube as it leaves the socket. A chimney will prevent the air from being dispersed as it hits the envelope or cooling fins, concentrating the flow for maximum cooling.

A less conventional approach is shown in Fig 16. Here the anode compartment is pressurized by the blower. A special chimney is installed between the anode heat exchanger and a ventilation hole in the compartment cover. The blower pressurizes the anode compartment, and the only paths for air flow are through the anode and its chimney, and through the air system socket. Measurements by Dick Jansson, WD4FAB, indicate a nearly even split of the air flow between the anode and the air system socket. The pressure losses in a test made on an amplifier using a 4CX250 indicates a back pressure of only 0.33 inch

of water with this scheme. This compares to a measured back pressure of 0.76 inch of water encountered by conventional base-to-anode cooling. Blower requirements are reduced considerably.

Table 5 also contains the part numbers for air-system sockets and chimneys to be used with the tubes that are listed. The builder should investigate which of the sockets listed for the 4CX250R, 4CX300A, 4CX1000A and 4CX1500A best fit the circuit needs. Some of the sockets have certain tube elements grounded internally through the socket. Others have elements bypassed to ground through capacitors that are integral parts of the sockets.

Depending on one's design philosophy and tube sources, some compromises in the cooling system may be appropriate. For example, if glass tubes are available inexpensively as broadcast pulls, a shorter lifespan may be acceptable. In such a case, an increase of convenience and a reduction in cost, noise and complexity can be had by using a pair of "muffin" fans. One fan may be used for the filament seals and one for the anode seal, dispensing with a blower and air-system socket and chimney. The air flow path for this scheme is not as uniform as with the use of a chimney. The tube envelope cylinder mounted in a cross flow has flow stagnation points and low heat transfer in certain regions of the cylinder. These points become hotter than the rest of the envelope. The use of multiple fans to disturb the cross air flow can significantly reduce this problem. Many amateurs have used this cooling method successfully in low-duty-cycle CW and SSB operation, but it is not recommended for AM, SSTV or RTTY service.

The true test of the effectiveness of a forced air cooling system is the amount of heat conducted away from the tube by the air stream. The power dissipated can be calculated from the air flow temperatures. The dissipated power is

$$P = 169Q_A [(T_2/T_1) - 1]$$

where
P = the dissipated power in watts
Q_A = the air flow in CFM
T_1 = the inlet air temperature (normally room temperature)
T_2 = the amplifier exhaust temperature.

The exhaust temperature can be measured with a cooking thermometer at the air outlet. The thermometer should not be placed inside the anode compartment because of the high voltage present.

Transistor Cooling

Transistors used in power amplifiers dissipate significant amounts of power, and the heat so generated must be effectively removed to maintain acceptable device temperatures. Some bipolar power transistors have the collector connected directly to the case of the device, as the collector

must dissipate most of the heat generated when the transistor is in operation. Others have the emitter connected to the case. However, even the larger case designs cannot conduct heat away fast enough to keep the operating temperature of the device within the safe area, the maximum temperature that a device can stand without damage. Safe area is usually specified in a device data sheet, often in graphical form. Germanium power transistors may be operated at up to 100°C while the silicon types may be run at up to 200°C. Leakage currents in germanium devices can be very high at elevated temperatures; thus, silicon transistors are preferred for power applications.

A thermal sink, properly chosen, will remove heat at a rate that keeps the transistor junction temperature in the safe area. For low-power applications a simple clip-on heat sink will suffice, while for 100-W input power a massive cast-aluminum finned radiator will be necessary. The appropriate size heat sink can be calculated based on the thermal resistance of the transistor case to ambient temperature. The first step is to calculate the total power dissipated by the transistor:

$$P_D = P_{DC} + P_{RFin} - P_{RFout}$$

where
P_D = the total power dissipated by the transistor in watts
P_{DC} = the dc power into the transistor in watts
P_{RFin} = the RF power into the transistor in watts
P_{RFout} = the RF output power from the transistor in watts.

The value of P_D is then used to obtain the Θ_{CA} value from

$$\Theta_{CA} = \frac{T_C - T_A}{P_D}$$

where
Θ_{CA} = the thermal resistance of the device case to ambient
T_C = the device case temperature
T_A = the ambient temperature (room temperature).

A suitable heat sink can then be chosen from the manufacturer's specifications for Θ_{CA}. The heat generated by the transistor must be radiated to the ambient by the heat sink so a low Θ_{CA} is needed. A well designed heat sink system minimizes thermal path lengths and has a large cross-sectional area. The thermal bonding of the transistor to the heat sink should have minimum thermal loss. In general, the heat sink mounting surface must be flat and the transistor firmly attached to the heat sink so intimate contact is made between the two. The use of thermal silicone based heat sink compounds offer considerable improvement in thermal transfer. The thermal resistance of this grease is considerably less than that of air, but is not nearly as good as that of aluminum. The quantity of grease should be kept to an absolute minimum. Enough should be used only to fill in any air gaps between the transistor and the heat sink surface.

The maximum temperature rise in the transistor junction may easily be calculated by using the equation

$$T_J = (\Theta_{JC} + \Theta_{CA}) P_D + T_A$$

where

T_J = the transistor junction temperature

Θ_{JC} = the manufacturer's published thermal resistance of the transistor from junction to case

Θ_{CA} = the thermal resistance of the device case to ambient

P_D = the power dissipated by the transistor

T_A = the ambient temperature.

The value of T_J must be kept below the manufacturer's recommended junction temperature to prevent transistor failure. Measured values of the ambient temperature and the device case temperature can be used in the preceding formulas to calculate junction temperature.

Design Guidelines and Examples

Most of the design problems facing an amplifier builder are not theoretical, but have to do with real-world component limitations. There is no such thing as a "pure" resistance or "pure" inductance or capacitance. The tubes and transistors used in RF amplifiers have stray reactances and resistances associated with every element of their construction. Every passive component has stray reactance and resistance to go along with its "advertised" function. Some of these factors can be ignored at some frequencies, but successful design and construction accounts for all of these "facts of life" and their effects.

A simplified equivalent schematic of an amplifying device is shown in Fig 17A. The input is represented by a resistance in parallel with a capacitance. The output consists of a current generator in parallel with a resistance and capacitance. This is an accurate description of both a transistor and a vacuum tube, regardless of circuit configuration (as demonstrated in Fig 17B and C). Both the input and output impedances have a resistive component in parallel with a reactive component.

The amplifier input and output matching networks must transform the complex impedances found in the amplifying device to the transmission line impedance (usually 50 ohms). Other impedances associated with the amplifier circuit, such as the impedance of a dc-supply choke, must also be included in the matching-network design. The matching networks and the associated components are influenced by each other's presence, and proper consideration must be made to account for their effects.

Perhaps the best way to explain the design considerations necessary to implement a particular amplifier function is through example. The following examples are representative of the various problems associated with power amplifier design. They are not intended to be detailed con-

Fig 17 — The electrical equivalents for power amplifiers. In A, the input is represented by a resistor in parallel with a capacitor and the output is a current source in parallel with another resistor and capacitor. These effects are applied to tubes and transistors in B and C.

struction plans; they only demonstrate the approach one would take in designing similar projects.

DESIGN EXAMPLE 1: A HIGH-POWER VACUUM TUBE HF AMPLIFIER

Most popular HF transceivers produce approximately 100-W output. According to the manufacturer's specifications, the EIMAC 8877 is a suitable candidate for use in a power amplifier capable of the maximum legal power output with this much

excitation. The 8877 can develop 1500-W output for approximately 60-W of drive when used in a grounded grid circuit. Grounded-grid operation is usually the easiest tube amplifier circuit to implement. The input impedance is relatively low, not too different from 50 Ω. The negative feedback inherent in the grounded-grid configuration reduces the likelihood of amplifier instability. Fewer supply voltages are needed in this configuration compared to others; only high-voltage dc for the plate and low-voltage ac for the filament are needed.

The first step in the amplifier design process is to verify that the tube is actually capable of producing the anticipated results, and still stay within manufacturer's ratings. The plate dissipation expected during normal operation of the amplifier is computed first. Since the amplifier will be used for SSB operation among others, a class of operation producing linear amplification must be used. Class AB operation is a very good compromise between linearity and good efficiency, with an expected efficiency of about 60%. Based on efficiency formulas presented earlier, an input power of 2500 W is needed to produce the desired 1500-W output. Operated under these conditions, the tube dissipates 1000 W — well within the manufacturer's specifications.

The specification for maximum grid current must be adhered to closely in high-mu triodes, for maximum tube life. The grid structure in these tubes is the most fragile element, since it is closely spaced to the cathode and carefully aligned to achieve high current gains. For a fixed level of drive, grid current tends to decrease with increasing plate potential. The maximum plate voltage allowable for the 8877 is specified to be 4000 V. A plate potential of 3500 V is chosen to minimize grid current, which is well within the published guidelines. In order to reach the 2500-W input power, 714 mA of plate current must be drawn at this plate voltage.

The next step in the design process is to calculate the optimum plate load resistance at this plate voltage and current for Class AB operation. From the earlier equations, R_L is calculated to be 3268 Ω. This result is approximate since the value for K in Class AB is only approximately 1.5. For ease in further calculations, the plate resistance can be rounded off to 3500 Ω.

The first decision that has to be made is to choose input and output matching networks. Almost any network can be used at the output to transform the 3500-Ω plate impedance down to 50 Ω, but experience shows that the pi and pi-L networks yield the most practical component values. Additionally, these two networks provide reasonable harmonic attenuation. The pi-L does give significantly greater harmonic attenuation than the pi, so it is usually a better choice. The penalty of using a pi-L network is the additional burden of the "L" inductor and band-switching this inductor in multiband amplifiers.

The input impedance of a grounded-grid 8877 is specified to be approximately 54 Ω. While this is close enough to 50 Ω to cause only minimal SWR at the input, the impedance varies with drive level. The fluctuating impedance can present problems for the exciter output matching network, increasing the intermodulation distortion level from the exciter. A tank circuit matching network at the amplifier input can stabilize the impedance through its "flywheel effect." The matching circuit must have a Q_L of at least two for this to occur. The pi network is a suitable choice for this application.

Fig 18 illustrates these input and output networks applied in the amplifier circuit. The schematic shows the major components in the amplifier RF section, but with band switching omitted. C1 and C2 and L1 form the input pi network. C3 is a blocking capacitor to keep the cathode dc potential isolated from the exciter.

The filament in an 8877 is in close proximity to the cathode — it has to be to adequately heat the cathode. A capacitance of several picofarads is formed between the two. Particularly at high frequencies where these few picofarads represent a relatively low reactance, RF drive intended for the cathode can be capacitively coupled into the filament, where it becomes heat. To keep the drive where it belongs in the cathode, the filament must be kept at a high RF impedance above ground. The high impedance minimizes RF current flow in the filament circuit; RF dissipated in the filament becomes virtually zero. The dc resistance should be kept to a minimum to lessen voltage drops in the high-current filament circuit.

The best type of choke for use in this application is a pair of heavy gauge bifilar windings over a ferrite rod. The ferrite core raises the inductive reactance throughout

Fig 18 — A simplified schematic of a grounded-grid amplifier using a pi network input and a pi-L network output.

Fig 19 — The effective reactances for the amplifier in Fig 18.

the HF region so that a minimum of wire is needed, keeping filament-circuit voltage drops low. The bifilar winding technique adds to the bandwidth of the choke and assures that both filament terminals are at the same RF potential.

Plate voltage is supplied to the tube through RFC2. C5 is the plate blocking capacitor. The output pi-L network is composed of tuning capacitor C6, loading capacitor C7, pi coil L2 and L coil L3. RFC3 is a high-inductance RF choke placed at the output for safety purposes. Its value, usually 1 to 2 millihenrys, is high enough so that it appears as an open circuit across the output connector for RF. However, should the plate blocking capacitor fail and allow high voltage onto the output matching network, RFC3 would short the dc to ground and blow the power-supply fuse. This prevents dangerous high voltage from appearing on the feed line or antenna.

The next calculations to be made involve the design of the input and output matching networks. The resistances to be matched have already been defined. The tube input resistance is specified by the manufacturer

to be 54 Ω. The calculated plate resistance is 3500 Ω. Both have to be transformed to 50 Ω, the impedance of the connecting cables. Unfortunately, neither of these impedances is purely resistive. As shown in Fig 17, the tube input and output impedances are composed of both resistance and internal capacitances. These capacitances must be taken into account when designing the matching networks. Additionally, any reactance introduced into the networks by dc supply line chokes and interconnecting leads must be accounted for.

Fig 19 shows the various reactances in the amplifier circuit. At the tube input, the impedance is 54 ohms in parallel with C_{IN}, 26 pF. In the output circuit C_{OUT} is the tube output capacitance, 10 pF. The reactance presented by the plate choke is shown as L_{CHOKE}. C_{STRAY} represents the combined stray capacitances of the interconnecting leads in the output circuit, the enclosure metal work in proximity to the tube, and the parasitic reactances in the tuning capacitor. The rest of the components C_{TUNE}, C_{LOAD} and the two Ls form the pi-L network.

Design of the input matching circuit is straightforward. The pi network circuit equations from the Electrical Fundamentals chapter are used to calculate component values. A Q_L of between two and three should be used. Higher Q values reduce the network's bandwidth, perhaps requiring the inclusion of a front-panel control for use across an entire amateur band. The purpose of this input network is to stabilize the impedance presented to the exciter, not to offer selectivity. The value of the capacitor at the tube input end of the pi network should be reduced by 26 pF; that value of capacitance is automatically added in parallel to the pi-network capacitor by the tube input impedance.

The output matching network is usually the most difficult section of an amplifier to design. The tables presented earlier in the chapter greatly simplify the effort. Both the pi and pi-L design tables were calculated around a loaded Q value of 12. Loaded Qs lower than 10 do not provide adequate harmonic suppression; values much higher than 18 increase matching network losses caused by high circulating currents. A Q_L value of 12 is a good compromise between harmonic suppression and circuit losses. Theoretical matching network component values can be taken right from the chart for the 3500-Ω plate impedance. These values can then be adjusted to allow for the previously described circuit reactances.

First, the low frequency component values should be examined. At 3.5 MHz the tuning capacitor value from Table 2 is 174 pF. Fig 19 shows three reactances directly in parallel with C_{TUNE}. The tube output capacitance, C_{OUT}, adds 10 pF directly in parallel to C_{TUNE}. Strays in the circuit, represented by C_{STRAY}, also are directly added in parallel to C_{TUNE}. An exact value for C_{STRAY} is difficult to define, so an educated guess must be thought of. In a well constructed, carefully thought out power amplifier, C_{STRAY} can be estimated to be approximately 10 pF. Between C_{OUT} and C_{STRAY}, 20 pF of pi-L network input capacitance is already accounted for. The inductance of the plate choke is also in parallel with C_{TUNE}. A popular plate choke used in many amplifiers has an inductance of 90 μH. At 3.5 MHz this is an inductive reactance of 1979 Ω. When combined in parallel with the 174 pF (261 Ω at 3.5 MHz) at the input of the pi-L network, an effective capacitance of 151 pF results. Since the pi-L network requires an effective capacitance of 174 pF at its input, the value of C_{TUNE} must be increased to compensate for the plate choke inductance. A total capacitance at the pi-L input of 197 pF, in parallel with the 90-μH plate choke, gives an effective capacitance of 174 pF. Of the 197 pF required, 10 pF comes from circuit strays, 10 pF comes from C_{OUT}, and 177 pF must come from the tuning capacitor, C_{TUNE}. A tuning capacitor with a maximum capacitance

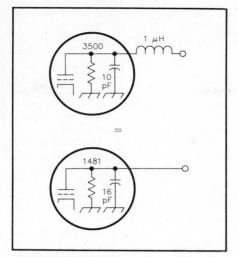

Fig 20 — The effect of a series inductance in vacuum tube output circuit. In this case, the 3500-Ω plate resistance is transformed down to 1481 ohms.

around 200 pF should be used to allow for loads with higher than a 1:1 SWR.

The component values for the high end of the amplifier frequency range should also be examined. At 29.7 MHz, Table 2 calls for an input capacitance of 18 pF. Since C_{OUT} and C_{STRAY} already account for 20 pF of pi-L input capacitance, a problem exists. Nothing can be done to reduce C_{OUT}; C_{STRAY} presumably is at a minimum also. Additionally, the tuning capacitor probably has a minimum capacitance around 15 pF. The minimum circuit capacitance found at the pi-L input is already 35 pF, nearly twice the required value.

There are potentially three solutions to this dilemma. The first is probably the simplest to implement. A higher loaded Q for the pi-L network will require more capacitance at the input. Raising Q_L to 24 changes the input capacitance requirement to 36 pF, which is within the range of the circuit as described. Many amplifier builders, both commercial and amateur, take this approach. The major drawback is substantially increased tank circuit losses caused by the increased Q.

Another potential solution is to reduce the minimum capacitance provided by C_{TUNE}. Vacuum variable capacitors have minimum capacitances as low as three to five pF, and can be used at C_{TUNE}. This reduces the minimum effective circuit capacitance to 25 pF. A pi-L network with a loaded Q of 17 needs only 26 pF at its input. While not optimum, a Q_L of 17 is perfectly acceptable from a tank circuit loss perspective. Unfortunately, vacuum variables are very expensive and cumbersome mechanically.

A third possibility is the use of an additional reactance in the output circuit. An inductance connected in series between the tube and the tuning capacitor will act as an L network in conjunction with C_{OUT} and

transform the plate load resistance to a lower value. This is shown in Fig 20. Lower input impedance-matching networks require higher input capacitances while maintaining a Q_L of 12. For example, a matching network designed for a plate impedance of 1500 Ω requires 43 pF of input capacitance at 29.7 MHz. In order to calculate the L network, the series equivalent impedance for the tube must be computed. The plate impedance is 3500 Ω in parallel with 10 pF (C_{OUT}). At 10 meters, this is 3500 Ω in parallel with − j535 ohms.

Using the equivalence formulas described earlier, this converts to an equivalent series impedance of 80 − j523 Ω. A 1-μH inductor, having an impedance of j187 ohms at 29.7 MHz, can be added as the series inductance for the L network. A series equivalent resistance of 80 − j523 plus j187 or 80 − j336 Ω results. This converts to an equivalent parallel impedance of 1491 Ω in parallel with − j355 Ω, which is equal to 1491 ohms (rounded to 1500 Ω) in parallel with 15 pF at 29.7 MHz. This new impedance is what the pi-L must now match. C_{OUT} is now effectively 15 pF, and when combined with the 10 pF of C_{STRAY} and the 15 pF minimum capacitance of C_{TUNE}, gives an effective input capacitance of 40 pF. C_{TUNE} must be adjusted to a value of 18 pF to give the required pi-L input capacitance of 43 pF for this new impedance level. The L inductor should be a high-Q coil wound from copper tubing to keep losses low. The L inductor has a decreasing yet significant effect on progressively lower frequencies. A similar calculation to the above should be made on each band to determine the transformed equivalent plate impedance, before referring to Table 2.

The 90-μH plate choke still remains in parallel with C_{TUNE}. At 29.7 MHz its impedance is in excess of 16,000 ohms and has very little effect on the RF characteristics of the circuit.

An analysis like this should be performed on every band the amplifier will operate on. Only then can the actual impedance levels be calculated and acted upon. Since the other components in the circuit, L2, L3 and C7, have no other reactances associated with them, their use is straightforward.

This amplifier is made operational on multiple bands by switching in additional inductances for L2 and L3 as the operating frequency is lowered. The usual practice is to use a shorting switch that will short out the unused portions of the total inductors for the band in use. The wiring to the switch and the switch itself add stray inductance and capacitance to the circuit. To minimize these effects at the higher frequencies, the unswitched 10-meter L2 should be placed closest to the high-impedance end of the network at C6. The effects of stray reactance diminish as the impedance level goes down. Reactances associated with the switch are effectively placed in parallel with C7 where the impedance level is between 300 and 700 ohms. The coil taps are best determined in an empirical fashion.

The impedance match in both the input and output networks can be checked without applying dc voltage, once the amplifier is built. In actual operation, the tube input and output resistances are the product of current flow through the tube. Without dc present, these resistances don't exist; the tube is an open circuit for dc. The input and output resistances can be easily simulated by ordinary quarter- or half-watt resistors (not wirewound, though; they are more inductive than resistive at RF). Resistors having the same value as the input and output resistances, connected in parallel with the tube input and output, present the same termination resistances to the matching networks as the tube does in operation. C_{IN} and C_{OUT} are physical properties of the tube, and are there whether dc is applied or not.

With the termination resistors in place, the impedance matches achieved by the matching networks can be measured by means of a noise bridge or return loss measurement set-up. For measuring the input match, the bridge is connected to the amplifier input. The matching network can then be adjusted for the desired match. To measure the output match, the bridge is connected to the amplifier output. Since the output matching network is bilateral (it works in both directions), the matching effectiveness of the network can be measured in either direction; obviously it's easier to measure from the 50-Ω end of the network. The taps on the inductors are then determined experimentally, adjusting the taps and the variable capacitors for best match. Once the best tap points are found, the connecting wires can be soldered in place and the termination resistors removed. The amplifier is now ready for full-voltage testing.

Design Example 2: A Medium Power 144-MHz Amplifier

For several decades the 4CX250 family of power tetrodes has been used successfully up through 500 MHz. The latest versions in the family are still state-of-the-art products. They are relatively inexpensive, produce high gain and lend themselves to relatively simple amplifier designs. In amateur service at VHF, the 4CX250 is a particularly attractive choice for an amplifier. Most VHF exciters used now by amateurs are solid-state and usually develop 10 W or less output. The drive requirement for the 4CX250 in grounded cathode, Class AB operation ranges between 2 and 8 watts for full power output, depending on frequency. At 144 MHz, manufacturer's specifications suggest an available output power of over 300 W. This is clearly a substantial level improvement over 10 W, so a 4CX250B will be used in this amplifier.

The first design step is the same as performed in the previous example — verify that the proposed tube will perform as desired while staying within the manufacturer's ratings. Again assuming a basic amplifier efficiency of 60% for Class AB operation, 300 W of output requires a plate input power of 500 W. Tube dissipation is rated at 250 W, so plate dissipation is apparently not a problem as the tube will only be dissipating 200 W in this amplifier. The recommended maximum plate potential is 2000 V; the tube will be running near its maximum ratings. Plate current for 500-W input is then 250 mA, which is within the manufacturer's ratings. The plate load resistance can now be calculated. Using the same formula as before, the value is determined to be 5333 Ω.

The next step is to investigate the output circuit. The manufacturer's specification for C_{OUT} is 4.7 pF. The inevitable circuit strays along with the tuning capacitor add to the circuit capacitance. A carefully built amplifier might only have 7 pF of stray capacitance, and a specially-made tuning capacitor can be fabricated to have a mid-range value of 3 pF. The total circuit capacitance adds up to about 15 pF. At 144 MHz this represents a capacitive reactance of only 74 Ω. The Q_L of a tank circuit with this reactance in parallel with a plate load resistance of 5333 Ω is over 72. A pi output matching network would be totally impractical. The L required would be extremely small and circuit losses would be prohibitive. The best solution is the simplest: Connect an inductor in parallel with the circuit capacitance to form a parallel-resonant tank circuit.

To keep tank circuit losses low with such a high Q_L, a very high Q inductor must be used. The lowest loss inductors are formed from transmission line sections. These can take the form of either coaxial lines or strip lines. Both have their advantages and disadvantages, but the strip line is so much easier to fabricate that it is almost exclusively used in VHF tank circuits today.

The reactance of a terminated transmission line section is a function of both its characteristic impedance and its length (see the Transmission Lines chapter). The reactance of a line terminated in a short circuit is

$$X_{in} = Z_o \tan \ell$$

where
  X = is the circuit reactance
  Z_o = the line impedance
  ℓ = the transmission line length in degrees.

For lines shorter than a quarter wavelength (90°) the circuit reactance is inductive.

In order to resonate with the tank circuit capacitive reactance the transmission line reactance must be the same value, but inductive. This requires an inductive reactance of 74 ohms. Examination of the formula for transmission-line circuit reactance suggests that a wide range of lengths can yield the same inductive reactance as long as the line Z_o is appropriately scaled. Based on circuit Q considerations, the best bandwidth in a tank circuit results when the ratio of Z_o to X_{in} is between one and two. This implies that transmission line lengths between 26.5° and 45° give the best bandwidth. Between these two limits, and with some adjustment of Z_o, practical transmission lines can be designed. A transmission line length of 35° is 8 inches long at 144 MHz, which is a workable dimension mechanically. Substi-

Fig 21 — The simplified schematic for a VHF power amplifier using a power tetrode. The output circuit is a parallel-tuned tank circuit with series reactance output matching.

tution of this value into the transmission line equation gives a Z_o of 105 Ω for the transmission line.

The width of the strip line and its placement relative to the ground planes determine the line impedance. Other stray capacitances such as mounting standoffs also affect the impedance. Accurate calculation of the line impedance for most physical configurations requires extensive application of Maxwell's equations and is beyond the scope of this book. The specialized case in which the strip line is parallel to and located halfway between two ground planes has been documented in *ITT Reference Data for Radio Engineers*. According to charts presented in that book, a 105-Ω strip line impedance is obtained by placing a line with a width of approximately 0.4 times the ground plane separation halfway between the ground planes. Assuming the use of a standard 3-inch-deep chassis for the plate compartment, this yields a strip line width of 1.2 in. A strip line 1.2 in. wide located 1.5 in. above the chassis floor and grounded at one end has an inductive reactance of 74 ohms at 144 MHz.

The resulting amplifier schematic diagram is shown in Fig 21. L2 is the strip-line inductance just described. C3 is the tuning capacitor, made from two parallel brass plates whose spacing is adjustable. One of the plates is connected directly to the strip line while the other is connected to ground through a wide, low-inductance strap. C2 is the plate blocking capacitor. This can be either a ceramic doorknob capacitor such as the Centralab 850 series or a homemade "Teflon sandwich." Both are equally effective at 144 MHz.

Impedance matching from the plate resistance down to 50 ohms can be either through an inductive link or through capacitive reactance matching. Mechanically, the capacitive approach is simpler to implement. Fig 22 shows the development of reactance matching through a series capacitor (C4 in Fig 21). By using the parallel equivalent of the capacitor in series with the 50-Ω load, the load resistance can be transformed to the 5333-Ω plate resistance. Substitution of the known values into the parallel-to-series equivalence formulas reveals that a 2.15 pF capacitor at C4 matches the 50-Ω load to the plate resistance. The resulting parallel equivalent for the load is 5333 Ω in parallel with

2.13 pF. The 2.13-pF capacitor is effectively in parallel with the tank circuit.

A new plate line length must now be calculated to allow for the additional capacitance. The equivalent circuit diagram containing all the various reactances is shown in Fig 23. The total circuit capacitance is now just over 17 pF, which is a reactance of 64 Ω. Keeping the strip-line width and thus its impedance constant at 105 Ω dictates a new resonant line length of 31°. This calculates to be 7.14 inches for 144 MHz.

The alternative coupling scheme is through the use of an inductive link. The link can be either tuned or untuned. The length of the link can be estimated based on the amplifier output impedance, in this case 50 Ω. For an untuned link, the inductive reactance of the link itself should be approximately equal to the output impedance, 50 Ω. For a tuned link, the length depends on the link Q_L. The link Q_L should generally be greater than two, but usually less than five. For a Q_L of three this implies a capacitive reactance of 150 Ω, which at 144 MHz is just over 7 pF. The self inductance of the link should of course

be such that its impedance at 144 MHz is 150 Ω (0.166 μH) at 144 MHz. Adjustment of the link placement determines the transformation ratio of the circuit line. Some fine adjustment of this parameter can be made through adjustment of the link series tuning capacitor. Placement of the link relative to the plate inductor is an empirical process.

The input circuit is shown in Figs 21 and 23. C_{IN} is specified to be 18.5 pF for the 4CX250. This is only 60 Ω at 2 meters, so the pi network again is unsuitable. Since a surplus of drive is available with a 10-W exciter, circuit losses at the amplifier input are not as important as at the output. An old-fashioned "split stator" tuned input can be used. L1 in Fig 21 is series tuned by C_{IN} and C1. The two capacitors are effectively in series (through the ground return). A 20-pF variable at C1 set to 18.5 pF gives an effective circuit capacitance of 9.25 pF. This will resonate at 144 MHz with an inductance of 0.13 μH at L1. L1 can be wound on a toroid core for mechanical convenience. The 50-Ω input impedance is then matched by link coupling to the toroid. The grid impedance

Fig 23 — The reactances and resistances for the amplifier in Fig 21

Fig 22 — Series reactance matching as applied to the amplifier in Fig 21.

Fig 24 — A simplified schematic of a broadband HF transistorized power amplifier. T1 and T2 are 4:1 broadband transformers to match the low input impedance of the transistor.

is primarily determined by the value for R1, the grid bias feed resistor.

Design Example 3: A Broadband HF Solid-State Amplifier

Linear power amplifier design using transistors at HF is a fundamentally simple process. An appropriate transistor meeting the desired design specifications is selected on the basis of dissipation and power output. The transistor manufacturers greatly simplify the design by specifying each RF power transistor according to its frequency range and power output. The amplifier designer need only match to the device input and output and provide appropriate dc bias currents to the transistor.

The Motorola MRF464 is an RF power transistor capable of 80-W PEP output with low distortion. Its usable frequency range is up through 30 MHz. At a collector potential of 28 V, a collector efficiency of 40% is possible.

Fig 24 shows the schematic diagram of a 2- to 30-MHz broadband linear amplifier using the MRF464. The input impedance of the transistor is specified by the manufacturer to be $1.4 - j0.30\ \Omega$ at 30 MHz and drops down to $9.0 - j5.40$ at 2 MHz. Transformers T1 and T2 match the 50-ohm amplifier input impedance to an approximate median value of the transistor input impedance. They are both 4:1 step-down ratio transmission-line transformers. A single 16:1 transformer could be used in place of T1 and T2, but 16:1 transformers are more difficult to fabricate for broadband service.

The manufacturer specifies the transistor output resistance to be approximately 6 ohms (in parallel with an equivalent output capacitance) across the frequency range. T3 is a ferrite-loaded conventional transformer with a step-up ratio of approximately 8:1. This matches the transistor output to 50 Ω.

The amplifier has a falling gain characteristic with rising frequency. To flatten out the gain across the frequency range, negative feedback could be applied. However, most power transistors have highly reactive input impedances and large phase errors would occur in the feedback loop. Instability could potentially occur.

A better solution is to use an input correction network. This network is used as a frequency-selective attenuator for amplifier drive. At 30 MHz, where transistor gain is least, the input power loss is designed to be minimal (less than 2 dB). The loss increases lower in frequency to compensate for the increased transistor gain. The MRF464 has approximately 12 dB more gain at 1.8 MHz than at 30 MHz; the compensation network is designed to have 12 dB loss at 1.8 MHz. A properly designed compensation network will result in an overall gain flatness of approximately 1 dB.

AMPLIFIER STABILIZATION

Stable Operating Conditions

Purity of emissions and the useful life of the active devices in a tube or transistor circuit depend heavily on stability during operation. Oscillations can occur at the operating frequency or far from it because of undesired positive feedback in the amplifier. Unchecked, these oscillations pollute the RF spectrum and can lead to tube or transistor overdissipation and subsequent failure. Each type of oscillation has its own cause and its own cure.

A linear amplifier operates with its input and output circuits tuned to the same frequency. Unless the coupling between these two circuits is kept to a minimum, some energy from the output will be coupled in phase back to the input and the amplifier will oscillate. Care should be used in arranging components and wiring of the two circuits so that there will be negligible opportunity for coupling external to the tube or transistor itself. Complete shielding between input and output circuits usually is required. All RF leads should be kept as short as possible, and particular attention should be paid to the RF return paths from input and output tank circuits to emitter or cathode.

In general, the best arrangement using a tube is one in which the input circuit and the output circuit are on opposite sides of the chassis. Individual compartments for the input and output circuitry add to the isolation. Transistor circuits are somewhat more forgiving, since all the impedances are relatively low. However, the high currents found on most amplifier circuit boards can easily couple into unintended circuits. Proper layout, the use of double-sided circuit board material (with one side used exclusively as a ground plane and low-inductance ground return), and heavy doses of bypassing on the dc supply lines can keep most solid-state amplifiers from oscillating.

VHF and UHF Parasitic Oscillations

Z1 of Fig 25 is a parasitic choke. This network will help dampen oscillations at VHF and UHF. It acts as a high series impedance at these frequencies to break up the unwanted VHF/UHF circuit path causing oscillation. Z1 consists of a non-inductive resistor, between 51 and 100 Ω, with a coil wound around the resistor body. This forms a broadband RF choke that presents a high impedance at VHF and higher, but looks like a low reactance in the HF region and lower. The resistance in parallel with the inductor lowers the Q of the choke, and dissipates undesired VHF energy.

A typical parasitic suppressor for a power level up to 150 W uses 6 to 8 turns of no. 20 wire wound around a 56-Ω, 1-W composition resistor. The coil ends are soldered to the resistor pigtails near the body of the resistor. Z1 is then placed in series with the output circuit, as close to the tube plate pin or cap as possible. For higher RF powers a high-wattage Globar resistor, or a 25-W noninductive (NIT) power resistor in parallel with the minimum inductance that will stop the oscillations should be used. Larger inductances will affect operation at the upper end of HF (particularly 10 meters). A few turns of no. 12 or 14 wire around the resistor body should suffice. Additional parasitic suppression can be attained, if needed, by connecting a low value resistor (10 to 51 Ω) in series with the tube input, near the tube socket. This is illustrated by R1 of Fig 25.

Parasitic oscillations can be dampened in low-power solid-state amplifiers by using a small amount of resistance in series with the base or collector lead as shown in Fig. 26A. The value of R1 or R2 typically should be between 10 and 22 Ω. The use of both resistors is seldom necessary, but an empirical determination must be made. R1 or R2 should be located as close to the transistor as practical.

At power levels in excess of approximately 0.5 W, the technique of parasitic suppression shown in Fig 26B is effective. The voltage drop across a resistor would be prohibitive at the higher power levels, so one or more ferrite beads placed over connecting leads can be substituted (Z1 and Z2). A bead permeability of 125 presents a high impedance at VHF and above with-

Fig 25 — Single-ended, neutralized RF amplifier. Z1 is a parasitic suppressor, see text.

Fig 26 — Suppression methods for VHF and UHF parasitics in solid-state amplifiers.

Fig 27 — Illustration of shunt feedback in a transistor amplifier. C1 and R3 comprise the feedback network.

out affecting HF performance. The beads need not be used at both circuit locations. Generally, the terminal carrying the least current is the best place for these suppression devices. This suggests that the resistor or ferrite beads should be connected in the base lead of the transistor.

C3 of Fig 27 can be added to some power amplifiers to dampen VHF/UHF parasitic oscillations. The capacitor should be low in reactance at VHF and UHF, but must present a high reactance at the operating frequency. The exact value selected will depend upon the collector impedance. A reasonable estimate is to use an X_c of 10 times the collector impedance at the operating frequency. Silver-mica or ceramic chip capacitors are suggested for this application. An additional advantage is seen in the bypassing action for VHF and UHF harmonic energy in the collector circuit. C3 should be placed as close to the collector terminal as possible, using short leads. The effects of C3 in a broadband amplifier are relatively insignificant at the operating frequency. However, when a narrow-band collector network is used, the added capacitance of C3 must be absorbed into the network design in the same manner as the C_{OUT} of the transistor.

Low-Frequency Instability

Bipolar transistors exhibit a rising gain characteristic as the operating frequency is lowered. To preclude low-frequency instabilities because of the high gain, shunt and degenerative feedback are often used. In the regions where low-frequency self-oscillations are most likely to occur, the feedback increases by nature of the feedback network, reducing the amplifier gain. In the circuit of Fig 27, C1 and R3 provide negative feedback, which increases progressively as the frequency is lowered. The network has a small effect at the desired operating frequency but has a pronounced effect at the lower frequencies. The values for C1 and R3 are usually chosen experimentally. C1 will usually be between 220 pF and 0.0015 μF for HF-band amplifiers while R3 may be a value from 51 to 5600 Ω.

R2 of Fig 27 develops emitter degeneration at low frequencies. The bypass capacitor, C2, is chosen for adequate RF bypassing at the intended operating frequency. The impedance of C2 rises progressively as the frequency is lowered, thereby increasing the degenerative feedback caused by R2. This lowers the amplifier gain. R2 in a power stage is seldom greater than 10 Ω, and may be as low as 1 Ω. It is important to consider that under some operating and layout conditions R2 can cause instability. This form of feedback should be used only in those circuits in which unconditional stability can be achieved.

R1 of Fig 27 is useful in swamping the input of an amplifier. This reduces the chance for low-frequency self-oscillations, but has an effect on amplifier performance in the desired operating range. Values from 3 to 27 Ω are typical. When connected in shunt with the normally low base impedance of a power amplifier, the resistors lower the effective device input impedance slightly. R1 should be located as close to the transistor base terminal as possible, and the connecting leads must be kept short to minimize stray reactances. The use of two resistors in parallel reduces the amount of inductive reactance introduced compared to a single resistor.

Although the same concepts can be applied to tube-type amplifiers, the possibility of self-oscillations at frequencies lower than VHF is significantly lower than in solid-state amplifiers. Tube amplifiers will usually operate stably as long as the input-to-output isolation is greater than the stage gain. Proper shielding and dc power lead bypassing essentially eliminate feedback paths, except for those through the tube itself.

Amplifier Neutralization

Depending on the inner electrode capacitances of tubes, a neutralization circuit may be necessary. Output energy

Fig 28 — The equivalent feedback path due to the internal capacitance of the tube grid plate structure in a power amplifier.

Fig 29 — Example of neutralization of a single-ended RF amplifier.

can be capacitively coupled back to the input as shown in Fig 28. Neutralization involves coupling a small amount of the output energy (which by the tube phase relationships is out of phase with the input energy) and feeding it back to the amplifier input. There the neutralization circuit energy cancels the unwanted in-phase (positive) feedback. A typical circuit is given in Fig 29. L2 provides a 180° phase reversal because it is center tapped. C1 is connected between the plate and the lower half of the grid tank. C1 is then adjusted so that the energy coupled from the tube output through the neutralization circuit is equal in amplitude and exactly 180° out of phase with the energy coupled from the output back through the tube. The two signals then cancel and the oscillation ceases.

The easiest way to adjust a neutralization circuit is to connect an RF source to the amplifier output tuned to the amplifier operating frequency. An RF detector of some kind is then connected to the amplifier input. The amplifier should remain turned off for this test. The amplifier tuning and loading controls, as well as any input network adjustments should then be peaked for maximum indication on the RF detector connected at the input. C1 is then adjusted for minimum response on the detector. This null indicates that the neutralization circuit is canceling energy coupled back to the amplifier input through the tube (or transistor) internal capacitances.

Screen-Grid Tube Neutralizing Circuits

The plate-to-grid capacitance in a screen-grid tube is reduced to a fraction of a picofarad by the interposed grounded screen. Nevertheless, the power sensitivity of these tubes is so great that only a very small amount of feedback is necessary to start oscillation. To assure a stable tetrode amplifier, it is usually necessary to load the grid circuit, or to use a neutralizing circuit.

A capacitive neutralizing system for screen-grid tubes is shown in Fig 30. C1 is the neutralizing capacitor. The value of C1

Fig 30 — A neutralization circuit may use either C1 or C2 to cancel the effect of the tube internal capacitance.

should be chosen so that at some adjustment of C1,

$$\frac{C1}{C3} =$$

$$\frac{\text{Tube grid-plate capacitance (or } C_{gp})}{\text{Tube input capacitance (or } C_{IN})}$$

The grid-to-cathode capacitance must include all strays directly across the tube capacitance, including the capacitance of the tuning capacitor stator to ground. This may amount to 5 to 20 pF.

Grid Loading

The use of a neutralizing circuit may often be avoided by loading the grid circuit if the driving stage has some power capacity to spare. Loading by tapping the grid down on the grid tank coil or by a resistor from grid to cathode is effective in stabilizing an amplifier. Either measure reduces the gain

and the sensitivity of the amplifier somewhat, lessening the possibility of oscillation. Substitution of a resistor for the grid circuit bias supply choke accomplishes the same goal.

BIBLIOGRAPHY

Belcher, "RF Matching Techniques, Design and Example," *QST,* October 1972, pp 24-30.

Feynman, *Lectures on Physics,* Vol. I, Addison-Wesley Publishing Co, 1977.

Goodman, "My Feed Line Tunes My Antenna," *QST,* April 1977, pp 40-42.

Granberg, "Build This Solid-State Titan," *QST,* June 1977, pp 27-31 (Part 1); *QST,* July 1977, pp 27-29 (Part 2).

Granberg, "One KW-Solid-State Style," *QST,* April 1976, pp 11-14 (Part 1); *QST,* May 1976, pp 28-30 (Part 2).

Hejhall, "Broadband Solid-State Power Amplifiers for SSB Service," *QST,* March 1972, pp 36-43.

Johnson and Artigo, "Fundamentals of Solid-State Power-Amplifier Design," *QST,* September 1972, pp 29-36 (Part 1); *QST,* November 1972, pp 16-20 (Part 2); *QST,* April 1973, pp 28-34 (Part 3).

Johnson, "Heat Losses in Power Transformers," *QST,* May 1973, pp 31-34.

Knadle, "A Strip-line Kilowatt Amplifier for 432 MHz," *QST,* April 1972, pp 49-55.

Meade, "A High-Performance 50-MHz Amplifier," *QST,* September 1975, pp 34-38.

Meade, "A 2-KW PEP Amplifier for 144 MHz," *QST,* December 1973, pp 34-38.

Olsen, "Designing Solid-State RF Power Circuits," *QST,* August 1977, pp 28-32 (Part 1); *QST,* September 1977, pp 15-18 (Part 2); *QST,* October 1977, pp 22-24 (Part 3).

Orr, *Radio Handbook,* 22nd Ed, Howard W. Sams & Co, Inc, 1981.

Potter and Fich, *Theory of Networks and Lines,* Prentice-Hall, Inc, 1963.

Reference Data for Radio Engineers, ITT, Howard & Sams Co, Inc.

RF Data Manual, Motorola, Inc, 1982.

Simpson, *Introductory Electronics for Scientists and Engineers,* Allyn and Bacon, Inc, 1975.

Solid State Power Circuits, *RCA Designer's* Handbook, 1972.

White, "Thermal Design of Transistor Circuits," *QST,* April 1972, pp 30-34.

Chapter 16

Transmission Lines

The place where RF power is generated is very frequently not the place where it will be used. A transmitter and its antenna are a good example. To radiate well, the antenna should be high above the ground and should be kept clear of trees, buildings and other objects that might absorb energy. The transmitter itself, however, is most conveniently installed indoors, where it is readily accessible.

A *transmission line* is the means by which RF energy is conveyed from one point to another. The types of transmission lines include simple two-conductor configurations, such as the familiar coaxial cable and TV parallel-wire line. Such lines are useful from power-line frequencies to well into the microwave region, and they form the most commonly used class. Waveguide is representative of a second type. Here the conductor configuration is complex, and ordinary concepts such as voltage and current tend to become obscure. As a consequence, various waveguide parameters are expressed in terms of the electric and magnetic fields associated with the line. The propagation of electromagnetic energy through waveguides is closely related to similar phenomena in space itself.

Transmission Lines and Circuits

A transmission line differs from an ordinary circuit in one very important aspect. *Propagation delays* exist from one end of the transmission line to the other. The speed at which electrical energy travels, while tremendously high when compared to mechanical motion, is not infinite. Propagation times are often of no significance in circuit design, as the layout dimensions are small in terms of signal wavelength. This is not true for transmission-line considerations, where finite propagation time becomes a factor of paramount importance. This is illustrated in Fig. 1. A transmission line connects a source at point S to a load at point L, separated by a distance ℓ.

Suppose that the distance ℓ is 300 meters (nearly 1000 feet). Also suppose for a moment that the source is a battery, rather than the RF generator shown at the left in Fig. 1. At the instant the battery is connected to the two wires of the transmission line, an electric current can be detected in

Fig. 1—Source and load connected by means of a transmission line. VF (velocity factor) and Z_0 (characteristic impedance) are properties of the line, as discussed in the text.

the wires near the battery terminals. This current does not flow instantaneously throughout the length of the wires, however.

The electric field that causes the current cannot travel faster than the speed of light, so a measurable interval of time elapses before the currents become evident even a relatively short distance away. The current could not be detected at the load, 300 meters away, until one microsecond (one millionth of a second) after the connection was made. By ordinary standards this is a very short length of time, but in terms of radio frequencies it represents the time for one complete cycle of a 1-MHz radio signal. It also represents the time for 10 complete cycles of a 10-MHz signal.

In a practical transmission line the energy travels somewhat slower than the speed of light (typically from 65 to 97 percent of light speed), depending on the type of transmission line. This line characteristic is called the *velocity factor* (VF) of the line.

The transmission-line current charges the capacitance between the two wires. The conductors of this "linear" capacitor also have inductance, however. The transmission line may be thought of as being composed of a whole series of small inductors and capacitors connected as shown in Fig. 2. Each inductor represents the inductance of a very short section of one wire, and each capacitor represents the capacitance between two such short sections.

CHARACTERISTIC IMPEDANCE

Consider an infinitely long chain of inductors and capacitors connected as shown in Fig. 2. All the small inductors have the same value, as do all the small capacitors. This line has an important property. To an electrical impulse applied at one end, the combination appears to have an impedance. This is called the *characteristic impedance* or *surge impedance*, often abbreviated Z_0. Its value is approximately equal to $\sqrt{L/C}$, where L and C are the inductance and capacitance per unit length.

In the equivalent transmission line of Fig. 2 there are no resistors, and thus no power is lost in the line. In this case, Z_0 becomes a pure resistance, R_0. (Lost power is represented by I^2R, or power dissipated in the line.) With no resistance, there is no power loss no matter what the line length may be. This may not seem consistent with calling the impedance a pure resistance, because the word *resistance* implies that some power will be dissipated if current flows. But with an infinitely long line, the effect (as far as the source of power is concerned) is exactly the same as if the line were replaced by a pure resistance. This is because the energy leaves

Fig. 2—Equivalent of a transmission line in lumped circuit constants.

the source and travels outward forever along the line.

The characteristic impedance of a line determines the amount of current that can flow when a given voltage is applied to an infinitely long line. The impedance limits the flow of current in the same way that a definite value of actual resistance limits current flow when a voltage is applied.

All practical transmission lines exhibit some power loss. These losses occur in the resistance that is inherent in the conductors that make up the line, and from leakage currents flowing in the dielectric material between the conductors. Because of these losses, the characteristic impedance (or Z_0) of practical lines contains a small reactive component. This component is usually capacitive, but it is small enough that its effects may be disregarded in Amateur Radio applications.

The inductance and capacitance per unit length of line depend on the size of the conductors and the spacing between them. The smaller the spacing between the two conductors and the greater their diameter, the higher the capacitance and the lower the inductance. A line with closely spaced large conductors will have low impedance, while one with widely spaced small conductors will have relatively high impedance.

Matched Lines

Actual transmission lines do not extend to infinity, but have a definite length. In use they are connected to, or *terminate* in, a load at the output end of the line, as illustrated in Fig. 1. If the load is a pure resistance of a value equal to the characteristic impedance of the line, the line is said to be *matched*. To current traveling along the line, such a load just looks like still more transmission line of the same characteristic impedance.

In other words, a short line terminated in a purely resistive load equal to the characteristic impedance of the line acts just as if the line was infinitely long. In a matched transmission line, energy travels outward along the line from the source until it reaches the load, where it is completely absorbed.

RF on Lines

Assume now that a very short burst of power is emitted from the source in Fig. 1. This is represented by the vertical line at the left of the series of lines in Fig. 3. As the pulse voltage appears across the load Z_a of Fig. 1, all the energy may be absorbed, or part of it may be reflected in much the same manner that energy in a water wave is reflected as the wave hits a steep breakwater or the end of a container. This reflected wave is represented by the second line in the series, and the arrow above the line indicates the direction of travel. As the second wave reaches the source, the process is repeated, with all

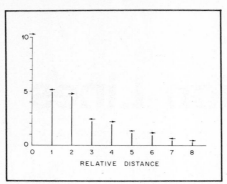

Fig. 3—Component magnitudes for forward and reverse traveling waves produced by a short pulse on a transmission line.

of the energy being either absorbed or partially reflected.

Even though the back-and-forth cycle is actually infinite, after a few reflections the intensity of the traveling wave becomes very small. If, instead of a short pulse, a continuous RF voltage is applied to the terminals of a transmission line, the voltage at any point along the line will consist of a sum of voltages—the composite of waves traveling toward the right and waves traveling toward the left. The sum of the waves traveling toward the right is called the *forward wave* or incident wave, while the one traveling toward the left is called the *reflected wave*. If Z_a contains resistance, there will be a net flow of energy from the source to the load.

Line Factors and Equations

In practical applications of transmission lines, one factor is very important: the manner in which the source and load are connected. Some "impedance lump" effects may arise from connectors and from the method of connecting the source and the load. These effects may cause the line to "see" a different impedance than would be indicated if the measurements were made directly at the load terminals. This is shown in Fig. 1 by the abrupt change in dimensions at each end of the line, ℓ. Even though the short line connecting the generator to the main transmission line (and the one connecting the load to the line) might have the same characteristic impedance, a mismatch will still occur if the physical sizes are different, unless the adapter connecting the lines is tapered to effect a smooth change between the different dimensions. This effect can usually be neglected at HF, but it becomes important as the frequency of operation is extended into the VHF region and above.

In the example shown in Fig. 3, the ratio of the voltage in the reflected wave to the voltage in the incident wave is defined as the voltage reflection coefficient. This coefficient is designated by the Greek letter rho (ρ). The relationship between the out-

put resistance (R_a), the output reactance (X_a), the line impedance (Z_0) and the magnitude of the reflection coefficient is

$$\rho = \sqrt{\frac{(R_a - R_0)^2 + X_a^2}{(R_0 + R_a)^2 + X_a^2}} \qquad \text{(Eq. 1)}$$

Note that if R_a is equal to R_0 and X_a is 0, the reflection coefficient is 0. This represents a matched condition where all the energy in the incident wave is transferred to the load. In effect, it is as if there is an infinite line of characteristic impedance Z_0 connected at A. On the other hand, if R_a is 0, regardless of the value of X_a, the reflection coefficient is 1.0. This means that *all* the power is reflected, in much the same manner as radiant energy is reflected from a mirror.

If there are no reflections from the load, the voltage distribution along the line is constant or "flat." A line operating under these conditions is often referred to as a *flat line*. If reflections exist, a voltage standing-wave pattern will result. The ratio of the maximum voltage on the line to the minimum value (provided the line is longer than a quarter wavelength) is defined as the *voltage standing wave ratio*, or VSWR. Reflections from the load also result in a standing-wave pattern of current flowing in the line. The ratio of maximum to minimum current, or ISWR, is identical to the VSWR in a given line. In amateur literature the abbreviation SWR is commonly used for standing-wave ratio, as the results are identical when taken from proper measurements of either current or voltage. The SWR is related to the reflection coefficient by

$$\text{SWR} = \frac{1 + \rho}{1 - \rho} \qquad \text{(Eq. 2)}$$

and

$$\rho = \frac{\text{SWR} - 1}{\text{SWR} + 1} \qquad \text{(Eq. 3)}$$

The definition of Eq. 3 is a more general one, valid for any line length. Often, the actual load impedance is unknown. An alternative way of expressing the reflection coefficient is

$$\rho = \sqrt{\frac{P_r}{P_f}} \qquad \text{(Eq. 4)}$$

where
P_r = the power in the reflected wave
P_f = the power in the forward wave

The parameters are relatively easy to measure with a directional RF wattmeter (power meter), either homemade or purchased. It should be obvious, however, that there can be no other power sources at the load if the definition above is to hold. For instance, assume the reflection coefficient (ρ) of the generator in the example shown in Fig. 3 is 0.9. This value could be obtained by substituting the generator resistance and reactance into Eq. 1, but not by measurement if the source is activated.

It is possible to determine the input resistance and reactance of a terminated line if the load resistance and reactance are known. The line length and characteristic impedance must also be known. The equations are

$$R_{in} = \frac{R_a (1 + \tan^2\ell)}{\left(1 - \frac{X_a}{Z_0}\tan\ell\right)^2 + \left(\frac{R_a}{Z_0}\tan\ell\right)^2}$$

(Eq. 5)

$$X_{in} = \frac{X_a (1 - \tan^2\ell) + \left(Z_0 - \frac{R_a^2 + X_a^2}{Z_0}\right)\tan\ell}{\left(1 - \frac{X_a}{Z_0}\tan\ell\right)^2 + \left(\frac{R_a}{Z_0}\tan\ell\right)^2}$$

(Eq. 6)

where
X_{in} = resistive component of the impedance at the input end of the line
X_{in} = reactive component of the impedance at the input end of the line
R_a = load resistance
X_a = load reactance
ℓ = electrical line length in degrees or radians

To determine the value of the tangent function, the line length, along with the frequency in MHz and the velocity factor (VF), can be substituted into the following expression:

$$\ell \text{ (degrees)} = 0.366f_{(MHz)} \times \ell_{(feet)}/VF$$

(Eq. 7)

Lost Power

Often it is mistakenly assumed that power reflected from a load represents power that is lost in some way. With proper matching at the input end of the line, this is true only if there is considerable loss in the line itself. In addition to the forward loss, some reflected power is dissipated on the way back to the source.

If the terminating resistance is zero, the input reactance consists of a pure reactance, which is given by

$$X_{in} = Z_0 \tan\ell$$

(Eq. 8)

If the line termination is infinite in value (an open circuit), the input reactance is given by

$$X_{in} = Z_0 \cot\ell$$

(Eq. 9)

A short length of line (less than a quarter wavelength) with a short circuit as a terminating load appears as an inductance, while an open-circuited line appears as a capacitance.

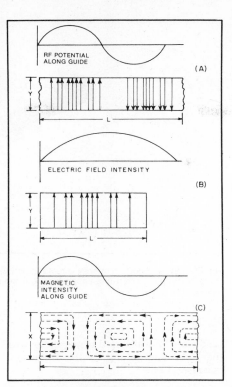

Fig. 4 — Field distribution in a rectangular waveguide. The TE$_{1,0}$ mode of propagation is depicted.

Waveguides

A waveguide is a conducting tube through which energy is transmitted in the form of electromagnetic waves. The tube is not considered as carrying a current in the same sense that the wires of a two-conductor line do, but rather a boundary which confines the waves to the enclosed space. Skin effect prevents any electro-magnetic effects from being evident outside the guide. The energy is injected at one end, either through capacitive or inductive coupling or by radiation, and is received at the other end. The waveguide merely confines the energy of the fields, which are propagated through it to the receiving end by means of reflections against its inner walls.

Analysis of waveguide operation is based on the assumption that the guide material is a perfect conductor of electricity. Typical distributions of electric and magnetic fields in a rectangular guide are shown in Fig. 4. It will be observed that the intensity of the electric field is greatest (as indicated by closer spacing of the lines of force) at the center along the X dimension, Fig. 4B, diminishes to zero at the end walls. Zero field intensity is a necessary condition at the end walls, since the existence of any electric field parallel to the walls at the surface would cause an infinite current to flow in a perfect conductor. This represents an impossible situation.

Modes of Propagation

Fig. 4 represents a relatively simple

Table 1
Wavelength Formulas for Waveguide

	Rectangular	Circular
Cut-off wavelength	2X	3.41R
Longest wavelength transmitted with little attenuation	1.6X	3.2R
Shortest wavelength before next mode becomes possible	1.1X	2.8R

distribution of the electric and magnetic fields. An infinite number of ways exist in which the fields can arrange themselves in a guide, as long as there is no upper limit to the frequency to be transmitted. Each field configuration is called a mode. All modes may be separated into two general groups. One group, designated TM (trans-verse magnetic), has the magnetic field entirely transverse to the direction of propagation, but has a component of electric field in that direction. The other type, designated TE (transverse electric) has the electric field entirely transverse, but has a component of magnetic field in the direction of propagation. TM waves are sometimes called E waves, and TE waves are sometimes called H waves. The TM and TE designations are preferred, however.

The particular mode of tranmission is identified by the group letters followed by subscript numerals; for example TE$_{1,0}$, TM$_{1,1}$, etc. The number of possible modes increases with frequency for a given size of guide. There is only one possible mode (called the dominant mode) for the lowest frequency that can be transmitted. The dominant mode is the one normally used in practical work.

Waveguide Dimensions

In the rectangular guide the critical dimension in Fig. 4C is X; this dimension must be more than one-half wavelength at the lowest frequency to be transmitted. In practice, the Y dimension usually is made about equal to ½ X to avoid the possibility of operation at other than the dominant mode. Other cross-sectional shapes than the rectangle can be used, the most important being the circular pipe. Many of the same considerations apply as in the rectangular shape.

Wavelength formulas for rectangular and circular guides are given in Table 1, where X is the width of a rectangular guide and R is the radius of a circular guide. All figures are in terms of the dominant mode.

Coupling to Waveguides

Energy may be introduced into or extracted from a waveguide or resonator by means of either the electric or magnetic field. The energy transfer takes place frequently through a coaxial line. Two methods for coupling are shown in Fig. 5. The probe at A is simply a short extension

Fig. 5 — Coupling to waveguide and resonators.

Fig. 6 — At its cutoff frequency a rectangular waveguide can be analyzed as a parallel two-conductor transmission line supported from top and bottom by an infinite number of quarter-wavelength stubs.

of the inner conductor of the coaxial line, oriented so it is parallel to the electric lines of force. The loop shown at B is arranged to enclose some of the magnetic lines of force. The point at which maximum coupling will be obtained depends on the particular mode of propagation in the guide or cavity; the coupling will be maximum when the coupling device is in the most intense field.

Coupling can be varied by rotating the probe or loop through 90 degrees. When the probe is perpendicular to the electric lines the coupling will be minimum; similarly, when the plane of the loop is parallel to the magnetic lines, the coupling will be minimum.

Evolution of a Waveguide

Suppose an open-wire line is used to carry VHF energy from a generator to a load. If the line has any appreciable length, it must be well insulated from the supports to avoid high losses. Since high-quality insulators are difficult to make for microwave frequencies, it is logical to support the transmission line with quarter-wavelength stubs, shorted at the far end. The open end of such a stub presents an infinite impedance to the transmission line, provided the shorted stub is nonreactive. However, the shorting link has finite length and, therefore, some inductance. This inductance can be nullified by making the RF current flow on the surface of a plate rather than through a thin wire. If the plate is large enough, it will prevent the magnetic lines of force from encircling the RF current.

An infinite number of these quarter-wave stubs may be connected in parallel without affecting the standing waves of voltage and current. The transmission line may be supported from the top as well as the bottom, and when infinitely many supports are added, they form the walls of a waveguide at its cutoff frequency. Fig. 6 illustrates how a rectangular waveguide evolves from a two-wire parallel transmission line. This simplified analysis also shows why the cutoff dimension is a half wavelength.

While the operation of waveguides is usually described in terms of fields, current flows on the inside walls, just as fields exist between the conductors of a two-wire transmission line. At the waveguide cutoff frequency, the current is concentrated in the center of the walls, and disperses toward the floor and ceiling as the frequency increases.

MATCHING THE ANTENNA TO THE LINE

The load for a transmission line may be any device capable of dissipating RF energy. When lines are used in applications involving transmitters, the most common load is an antenna. When a transmission line is connected between an antenna and a receiver, the receiver input circuit is the load (not the antenna), because the power taken from a passing wave is delivered to the receiver.

Whatever the application, the conditions existing at the load, and *only* the load, determine the standing-wave ratio on the line. If the load is purely resistive and equal to the characteristic impedance of the line, there will be no standing waves. If the load is not purely resistive, or is not equal to the line Z_0, there will be standing waves. No adjustments can be made at the input end of the line to change the VSWR. Neither is the VSWR affected by changing the line length.

Only in a few special cases is the load inherently of the proper value to match a practicable transmission line. In all other cases it is necessary either to operate with a mismatch and accept the VSWR that results, or else to take steps to bring about a proper match between the line and load by means of transformers or similar devices. Impedance-matching transformers may take a variety of physical forms, depending on the circumstances.

Note that it is essential, if the VSWR is to be made as low as possible, that the load at the point of connection to the transmission line be purely resistive. In general, this requires that the load be tuned to resonance. If the load itself is not resonant at the operating frequency, the tuning can

Fig. 7 — "Q" matching section, a quarter-wave impedance transformer.

sometimes be accomplished in the matching system.

The Antenna as a Load

Every antenna system, no matter what its physical form, will have a definite value of impedance at the point where the line is connected. The problem is to transform this antenna input impedance to the proper value to match the line. In this respect there is no "best" type of line for a particular antenna system, because it is possible to transform impedances in any desired ratio. Consequently, any type of line may be used with any type of antenna. There are frequently reasons other than impedance matching that dictate the use of one type of line in preference to another, such as ease of installation, inherent loss in the line, and so on, but these are not considered in this section.

Although the input impedance of an antenna system is seldom known accurately, it is often possible to make a close estimate of its value. Matching circuits can be built with ordinary coils and capacitors, but these are not used extensively because they must be supported at the antenna and must be weatherproofed. The systems described below use *linear transformers*.

The Quarter-Wave Transformer or "Q" Section

As mentioned previously, a quarter-wave

transmission line may be used as an impedance transformer. See Fig. 7. If the antenna impedance and the characteristic impedance of the line to be matched are known, the characteristic impedance of a matching section is

$$Z = \sqrt{Z_1 Z_0}$$

where

Z_1 = antenna impedance
Z_0 = characteristic impedance of the line to which it is to be matched.

Example: To match a 600-ohm line to an antenna presenting a 72-ohm load, the quarter-wave matching section would require a characteristic impedance of

$$\sqrt{72 \times 600} = \sqrt{43,200} = 208 \text{ ohms}$$

The spacing between conductors and the conductor size determine the characteristic impedance of the transmission line. As an example, for the 208-ohm transmission line required above, the line could be made from ½-inch-diameter tubing spaced 1.5 inches between conductors.

The length of the quarter-wave matching section may be calculated from

$$\text{Length (feet)} = \frac{246 \text{ VF}}{f}$$

$$\text{Length (meters)} = \frac{75 \text{ VF}}{f}$$

where

VF = velocity factor
f = frequency in MHz

Example: A quarter-wave transformer of RG-11 is to be used at 28.7 MHz. From Table 2, VF = 0.66.

$$\text{Length} = \frac{246 \times 0.66}{28.7} = 5.66 \text{ feet}$$

$$= 5 \text{ feet 8 inches}$$

The antenna must be resonant at the operating frequency. Setting the antenna length by formula is accurate enough with single-wire antennas, but in other systems, particularly close-spaced arrays, the antenna should be adjusted to resonance before the matching section is connected.

When the antenna input impedance is not accurately known, it is advisable to construct the matching section so the spacing between conductors can be changed. The spacing may then be adjusted to give the lowest SWR on the transmission line.

Series-Section Transformers

The *series-section transformer* has advantages over the quarter-wave transformer. The material in this section is based on a July 1978 *QST* article by Frank A. Regier, OD5CG/WA1ZQC. The transformer illustrated in Fig. 8 closely resembles the ¼-wave transformer. (Actually, the ¼-wave transformer is a special case of the series-section transformer.) The important differences are: first, that the matching section

Fig. 8 — Series section transformer Z_1 for matching transmission-line Z_0 to load, Z_L.

need not be located exactly at the load; second, that it may be less than a quarter wavelength long; and third, that there is great freedom in the choice of the characteristic impedance of the matching section.

In fact, the matching section can have any characteristic impedance that is not too close to that of the main line. Because of this freedom, it is almost always possible to find a length of commercially available line that will be suitable as a matching section. As an example, consider a 75-Ω line, a 300-Ω matching section, and a purely resistive load. It can be shown that such a section may be used to match any resistance between 5 Ω and 1200 Ω to the main line.

The design of a series-section transformer consists of determining (1) the length $\ell2$ of the series or matching section and (2) the distance $\ell1$ from the load to the point where the section should be inserted into the main line. Three quantities must be known: the characteristic impedances of the main line and of the matching section, both assumed purely resistive, and the complex load impedance, Z_L.

The two lengths, $\ell1$ and $\ell2$, are to be determined from the characteristic impedances of the main line and the matching section, Z_0 and Z_1, respectively, and from the load impedance ($Z_L = R_L + jX_L$). The first step is to determine the normalized impedances.

$$n = \frac{Z_1}{Z_0}$$

$$r = \frac{R_L}{Z_0}$$

$$x = \frac{X_L}{Z_0}$$

Next, $\ell2$ and $\ell1$ are determined from

$$\ell2 = \arctan B$$
$$\ell1 = \arctan A$$

where

$$B = \pm \sqrt{\frac{(r-1)^2 + x^2}{r\left(n - \frac{1}{n}\right)^2 - (r-1)^2 - x^2}}$$

$$A = \frac{\left(n - \frac{r}{n}\right)B + x}{r + xnB - 1}$$

Lengths $\ell2$ and $\ell1$ thus determined are electrical lengths in degrees. Actual lengths are obtained by dividing by 360° and multiplying by the wavelength measured along the line (main line or matching

Fig. 9 — Example of series-section matching. A 38-Ω antenna is matched to 50-Ω coax by means of a length of 75-Ω cable.

section, as the case may be), taking the velocity factor of the line into account.

The sign of B may be chosen either positive or negative, but the positive sign is preferred because it results in a shorter matching section. The sign of A may not be chosen, but may turn out to be either positive or negative. If a negative sign occurs and an electronic calculator is used to determine $\ell1$, a negative electric length will result. If this happens, add 180°. The resultant electrical length will be correct both physically and mathematically.

In calculating B, if the quantity under the radical is negative, an imaginary value for B results. This means that Z_1, the impedance of the matching section, is too close to Z_0 and should be changed.

Limits on the characteristic impedance of Z_1 may be calculated in terms of the standing-wave ratio produced by the load on the main line without matching. For matching to occur, Z should either be greater than $Z_0\sqrt{\text{VSWR}}$ or less than $Z_0\sqrt{\text{VSWR}}$.

An Example

Suppose we want to feed a 29-MHz ground-plane vertical antenna with RG-58-type foam-dielectric coax (Fig. 9). We'll assume the antenna impedance to be 38 ohms pure resistance, and use a length of RG-59 foam-dielectric coax as the series section.

Z_0 is 50 ohms, Z_1 is 75 ohms, and both cables have a velocity factor of 0.79. (From above, Z_1 must have an impedance greater than 57.4 Ω or less than 43.6 Ω.) The design steps are as follows.

From the earlier equations, n = 1.5, r = 0.76 and x = 0.

Further, B = 0.3500 (positive sign chosen), $\ell2$ = 19.29° and A = −1.4486. Calculating $\ell1$ yields −55.38°. Adding 180° to obtain a positive result gives $\ell1$ = 124.62°.

To find the physical lengths $\ell1'$ and $\ell2'$, we first find the free-space wavelength.

$$\lambda_o = \frac{984}{f_{\text{MHz}}} \text{ feet}$$

and the transmission-line wavelength

$$\lambda = \lambda_o \times \text{velocity factor}$$

In the present case we find λ = 26.81 ft. Finally, we have

$$\ell 1' = \frac{\ell 1 \times \lambda}{360} = 9.28 \text{ ft, and}$$

$$\ell 2' = \frac{\ell 2 \times \lambda}{360} = 1.44 \text{ ft.}$$

This completes the calculations. Construction consists of cutting the main coax at a point 9.28 ft from the antenna and adding a 1.44-ft length of the 75-Ω cable.

The Quarter-Wave Transformer

The antenna in the preceding example could have been matched by a ¼-λ transformer at the load. Such a transformer would have a characteristic impedance of 43.6 Ω. It is interesting to see what happens in the design of a series-section transformer if this value is chosen as the characteristic impedance of the series section.

Following the same steps as before, we find n = 0.872, r = 0.76 and x = 0. From these values we find B = ∞ and ℓ2 = 90°. Further, A = 0 and ℓ1 = 0°. These results represent a quarter-wave section at the load, and indicate that, as stated earlier, the quarter-wave transformer is indeed a special case of the series-section transformer.

Folded Dipoles

If a half-wave antenna element is split into two or more parallel conductors, it can be made to match various line impedances. The transmission line is attached at the center of only one conductor. Various forms of such "folded dipoles" are shown in Fig. 10. Currents in all conductors are in phase in a folded dipole and, since the conductor spacing is small, the folded dipole is equivalent in radiating properties to an ordinary single-conductor dipole. However, the current flowing into the input terminals of the antenna from the line is the current in one conductor only, and the entire power from the line is delivered at this value of current. This is equivalent to saying that the input impedance of the antenna has been raised by splitting it up into two or more conductors.

The ratio by which the input impedance of the antenna is stepped up depends not only on the number of conductors in the folded dipole but also on their relative diameters, since the distribution of current between conductors is a function of their diameters. (When one conductor is larger than the other, as in Fig. 10C, the larger one carries the greater current.) The ratio also depends on the spacing between the conductors, as shown by the graphs of Figs. 11 and 12. An important special case is the two-conductor dipole with conductors of equal diameter; as a simple antenna, not a part of a directive array, it has an input impedance close enough to 300 ohms to afford a good match to 300-ohm twin-lead.

Fig. 11 indicates the required ratio of conductor diameters in a 2-conductor

Fig. 10 — The folded dipole, a method for using the antenna element itself to provide an impedance transformation. Depending on the velocity factor of the line used for the flat top, the conductors should be shorted part-way in from the end. This is because the sections must be resonant both as quarter-wave transmission-line stubs and quarter-wavelength single-wire radiators. A flat top made from 300-ohm twin-lead would have shorting straps at about 85 percent of the distance from center to end. However, no straps are necessary when open-wire line is used in the flat top. This is because the velocity factor of the line (about 97 percent) is very close to the percentage of a physical half wavelength needed for electrical resonance in the "thick" antenna thus created.

Fig. 11 — Impedance transformation ratio, two-conductor folded dipole. The dimensions d1, d2 and s are shown on the inset drawing. Curves show the ratio of the impedance (resistive) seen by the transmission line to the radiation resistance of the resonant antenna system.

dipole to give a desired impedance ratio. Similar information for a three-conductor dipole is given in Fig. 12. This graph applies if all the three conductors are in the same plane. The two conductors not con-

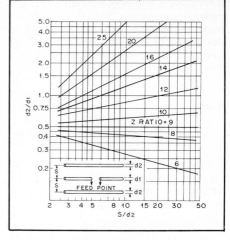

Fig. 12 — Impedance transformation ratio, three-conductor folded dipole. The dimensions d1, d2 and s are shown on the inset drawing. Curves show the ratio of the impedance (resistive) seen by the transmission line to the radiation resistance of the resonant antenna system.

Fig. 13 — The T match and gamma match.

nected to the transmission line must be equally spaced from the fed conductor, and must have equal diameters. The fed conductor may have a different diameter, however. The unequal-conductor method has been found particularly useful in matching to low-impedance antennas such as directive arrays using close-spaced parasitic elements.

The antenna element should be approximately self-resonant at the median operating frequency. The length is seldom critical, because a folded dipole tends to have the characteristics of a "thick" antenna and thus has a relatively broad frequency-response curve.

T and Gamma Matching Sections

The method of matching shown in Fig. 13A is based on the fact that the impedance between any two points equidistant from the center along a resonant antenna is resistive, and has a value that depends on the spacing between the two points. It is therefore possible to choose a pair of points between which the impedance will have the right value to match a transmission line. In practice, the line cannot be connected directly at these points because the distance between them is much greater than the conductor spacing of a practical transmission line. The T arrangement in Fig. 13 overcomes this difficulty by using a second conductor paralleling the antenna to form a matching section to which the line may be connected.

The T is particularly suited to use with a parallel-conductor line. The operation of this system is somewhat complex. Each T conductor (Y in the drawing) forms a short section of transmission line with the antenna conductor opposite it. Each of these transmission-line sections can be considered to be terminated in the impedance that exits at the point of connection to the antenna. Thus, the part of the antenna between the two points carries a transmission-line current in addition to the normal antenna current. The two transmission-line matching sections are in series, as seen by the main transmission line.

If the antenna by itself is resonant at the operating frequency, its impedance will be purely resistive. In this case the matching-section lines are terminated in a resistive load. As transmission-line sections, these matching sections are terminated in a short, and are shorter than a quarter wavelength. Thus their input impedance, i.e., the impedance seen by the main transmission line looking into the matching-section terminals, will be reactive as well as resistive. This prevents a perfect match to the main transmission line, since its load must be purely resistive for perfect matching. The reactive component of the input impedance must be tuned out before a proper match can be obtained.

One way to do this is to detune the antenna just enough, by changing its length, to cause reactance of the opposite kind to be reflected to the input terminals of the matching section, thus canceling the reactance introduced. Another method, which is considerably easier to adjust, is to insert a variable capacitor in series with each matching section where it connects to the transmission line, as shown in Chapter 19. The capacitors must be protected from the weather.

The method of adjustment commonly used is to cut the antenna for approximate resonance and then make the spacing X some value that is convenient constructionally. The distance Y is then adjusted, while maintaining symmetry with respect to the center, until the VSWR on the transmission line is as low as possible. If the VSWR is not below 2:1 after this adjustment, the antenna length should be changed slightly and the matching section taps adjusted again. This procedure may be continued until the VSWR is close to 1:1.

When the series-capacitor method of reactance compensation is used, the anten-

Fig. 14 — Radiator with coaxial feed (A) and methods of preventing unbalanced currents from flowing on the outside of the transmission line (B and C). The half-wave phasing section shown at D is used for coupling between an unbalanced circuit when a 4:1 impedance ratio is desired or can be accepted.

na should be the proper length for resonance at the operating frequency. Trial positions of the matching-section taps are then taken, each time adjusting the capacitor for minimum VSWR, until the standing waves on the transmission line are brought down to the lowest possible value. The unbalanced (gamma) arrangement in Fig. 13B is similar in principle to the T, but is adapted for use with single coax line. The method of adjustment is the same.

LOADS AND BALANCING DEVICES

The most important practical load for a transmission line is an antenna, which in most cases will be "balanced" — that is, constructed symmetrically with respect to the feed point. A balanced antenna should be fed with a balanced feeder system in order to preserve symmetry with respect to ground. This will avoid difficulties with unbalanced currents on the line and consequent undesirable radiation from the transmission line itself. Line radiation can be prevented by a number of devices that detune or decouple the line for "antenna" currents, and thus greatly reduce their amplitude.

Often the antenna is fed through coaxial line, which is inherently unbalanced. In such a case, some method should be used for connecting the line to the antenna without upsetting the symmetry of the antenna itself. This requires a circuit that will isolate the balanced load from the unbalanced line while providing efficient power transfer. Devices for doing this are

called baluns (a contraction for "balanced to unbalanced").

An antenna with open ends, of which the half-wave dipole is an example, is inherently a balanced radiator. When the antenna is opened at the center and fed with a parallel-conductor line, this balance is maintained throughout the system, as long as external causes of unbalance are avoided.

If the antenna is fed at the center through a coaxial line, as indicated in Fig. 14A, this balance is upset because one side of the radiator is connected to the shield while the other is connected to the inner conductor. On the side connected to the shield, current can flow down over the outside of the coaxial line. The fields thus set up cannot be canceled by the fields from the inner conductor because the inside fields cannot escape through the shielding of the outer conductor. Hence these "antenna" currents flowing on the outside of the line will be responsible for radiation.

Linear Baluns

Fig. 14B shows a balun arrangement known as a *bazooka,* which uses a sleeve over the transmission line. The sleeve, with the outside of the outer conductor, forms a shorted quarter-wave line section. As described earlier in this chapter, the impedance looking into the open end of such a section is very high, so the end of the outer conductor of the coaxial line is effectively isolated from the part of the line below the sleeve. The length is an electrical quarter wave, and may be physically shorter if the insulation between the sleeve and the line is other than air. The bazooka (and the balun form shown in Fig 14C) have no effect on antenna impedance at the frequency where the ¼-wave sleeve (and the line section in C) are resonant. However, the sleeve and line section both add inductive shunt reactance at frequencies lower, and capacitive shunt reactance at frequencies higher than the ¼-wave-resonant frequency.

Another method that gives an equivalent effect is shown at C. Since the voltages at the antenna terminals are equal and opposite (with reference to ground), equal and opposite currents flow on the surfaces of the line and second conductor. Beyond the shorting point, in the direction of the transmitter, these currents combine to cancel out. The balancing section "looks like" an open circuit to the antenna, since it is a quarter-wave parallel-conductor line shorted at the far end, and thus has no effect on the normal antenna operation. This is not essential to the line-balancing function of the device, however, and baluns of this type are sometimes made shorter than a quarter wavelength to provide the shunt inductive reactance required in certain matching systems.

Fig 14D shows a third balun, in which equal and opposite voltages, balanced to ground, are taken from the inner conductors of the main transmission line and half-wave phasing section. Since the voltages at the balanced end are in series while the voltages at the unbalanced end are in parallel, there is a 4:1 step-down in impedance from the balanced to the unbalanced side. This arrangement is useful for coupling between a 300-ohm balanced line and a 75-ohm coaxial line, for example.

Voltage Baluns

The narrowband linear baluns described in the preceding section are seldom employed at frequencies below VHF because of their physical size. Instead, broadband baluns generally are used. These can be divided into two distinct categories: voltage baluns and choke, or current, baluns. Examples of the two types of baluns are shown in Fig 15.

The voltage baluns of Fig 15A and B cause equal and opposite voltages to appear at the two output terminals, relative to the voltage at the "cold" side of the input. If the two antenna halves are perfectly balanced with respect to ground, the currents flowing from the output terminals will be equal and opposite and no "antenna" current will flow on the line. (This means that, if the line is coaxial, there will be no current on the outside; if the line is balanced, the currents in the two conductors will be equal and opposite. These are the conditions for a nonradiating line.) Under this condition, the 1:1 voltage balun of Fig 15A performs exactly the same function as the current balun of Fig 15C, as there is no current in winding b. If the

Fig 15—(A) 1:1 voltage balun; (B) 4:1 voltage balun; (C) 1:1 current balun; and (D) 4:1 current transformer. (D) is wound on two cores, which are separated.

antenna isn't perfectly symmetrical, however, unequal currents will appear at the balun output, causing antenna current to flow on the line, an undesirable condition. Another potential shortcoming of the 1:1 voltage balun is that winding b appears across the line. If this winding has insufficient impedance (a common problem, particularly near the lower-frequency end of its range), the system SWR will be degraded. The choke or current balun is recommended for use at the junction of the antenna and feed line. However, voltage baluns still are commonly used in this application and may serve a useful function if the user is aware of their shortcomings.

Choke (Current) Baluns

While voltage baluns cause equal and opposite voltages to appear at their outputs, choke or current baluns cause equal and opposite currents to flow. The result is that antenna currents are effectively reduced, or "choked off," even if the antenna is not perfectly balanced. If winding impedances become marginal at lower frequencies, the balun's ability to eliminate antenna currents is reduced, but (for the 1:1 balun) no winding impedance appears across the line. When feeding a balanced antenna with a coaxial line, the choke balun is most effective when placed at the antenna feed point. If induced current on the line is a problem, additional baluns can be placed at approximately ¼-λ intervals along the line. Current baluns are also useful for feeding asymmetrical antennas with balanced line and for eliminating line antenna currents that occur for any reason.

Although it may not be apparent from the diagrams, the voltage balun of Fig 15A is identical to the current balun of Fig 15C if its third, or tertiary, winding (winding b) is removed. This winding is the cause of the different fundamental operation of the two 1:1 balun types.

Construction

Either type of broadband balun can be constructed using a variety of techniques. Construction of choke (current) baluns is described here. The objective is to obtain a high impedance for currents that tend to flow on the line. Values of a few hundred to over a thousand ohms are readily achieved. These baluns work best when used with antennas having feed-point impedances less than 100 ohms or so (400 ohms for 4:1 baluns). This is because the winding impedance must be high relative to the antenna impedance for effective operation, and higher impedances are difficult to achieve. In some cases, a balun can be effective when inserted on the transmitter side of a Transmatch being used with a nonresonant antenna.

Air-Core Baluns

The simplest construction method for a 1:1 balun for coaxial line is simply to wind a portion of the line into a coil. (See Fig 16.) Currents on the outside of the line encounter the coil's impedance, while currents on the inside are unaffected. A flat coil (like a coil of rope) shows a broad resonance that easily covers three bands. Some geometries are reasonably effective over the entire HF range. If particular problems are encountered on a single band, a coil that is resonant at that band may be added. The coils shown in Table 2 were constructed to have a high impedance at the indicated frequencies, as measured with an impedance meter. Many other geometries can also be effective. This construction technique is not effective with twin lead because of coupling between adjacent turns. An air-core 4:1 choke balun is shown in Fig 17.

Ferrite-Core Baluns

Ferrite-core baluns can provide a high impedance over the entire HF range. They may be wound either with two conductors in bifilar fashion, or with a single coaxial cable. Rod or toroidal cores may be used. Current through a choke balun winding is the "antenna current" on the line; if the balun is effective, this current is small. Baluns used for high-power operation should be tested by checking for temperature rise before being put into full service. If the core overheats, turns must be added or a larger or lower-loss core must be used. It also would be wise to investigate the cause of such high line antenna currents. Type 72, 73 or 77 ferrite will give the greatest impedance over the HF range. Type 43 ferrite has lower loss, but somewhat less impedance. Core saturation is not a problem with these ferrites at HF; they will overheat due to loss at flux levels well below saturation. Eight to ten turns on a toroidal core or 10-15 turns on a rod are typical values for the HF range. Winding impedance increases approximately as the square of the number of turns.

The W2DU Balun

Another type of choke balun that is very effective was originated by M. Walter Maxwell, W2DU. A number of small ferrite cores may be placed directly over the coax where it is connected to the antenna. The bead balun in Fig 18 consists of 50 Amidon no. FB-73-2401 ferrite beads slipped over a 1-foot length of RG-58A coax. The beads fit nicely over the insulating jacket of the coax and occupy a total

Fig 16—An RF choke formed by coiling the feed line at the point of connection to the antenna. The inductance of the choke isolates the antenna from the remainder of the feed line.

Table 2
Effective Choke (Current) Baluns

Wind the indicated length of coaxial feed line into a coil (like a coil of rope) and secure with electrical tape. The balun is most effective when the coil is near the antenna. Lengths are not highly critical.

Single Band (Very Effective)

Freq, MHz	RG-213, RG-8	RG-58
3.5	22 ft, 8 turns	20 ft, 6-8 turns
7	22 ft, 10 turns	15 ft, 6 turns
10	12 ft, 10 turns	10 ft, 7 turns
14	10 ft, 4 turns	8 ft, 8 turns
21	8 ft, 6-8 turns	6 ft, 8 turns
28	6 ft, 6-8 turns	4 ft, 6-8 turns

Multiple Band

Freq, MHz	RG-8, 58, 59, 8X, 213
3.5-30	10 ft, 7 turns
3.5-10	18 ft, 9-10 turns
14-30	8 ft, 6-7 turns

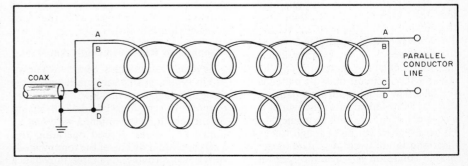

Fig 17—A 4:1 air-core current balun.

Fig 18—A bead balun consisting of 50 Amidon no. FB-73-2401 ferrite beads over a length of RG-58A coax. See text for details.

Fig 19 — Networks for matching a low-impedance transmitter output to a random-length end-fed wire antenna.

Fig 20 — Simple circuits for coupling a transmitter to a balanced line that presents a load different than the transmitter output impedance. A and B respectively are series- and parallel-tuned circuits using variable inductive coupling between coils. C and D are similar but use fixed inductive coupling and a variable series capacitor, C1. A series-tuned circuit works well with a low-impedance load; the parallel circuit is better with high-impedance loads (several hundred ohms or more).

length of 9½ inches. Twelve Amidon FB-77-1024 or equivalent beads will come close to doing the same job using RG-8 or RG-213 coax. Type 73 material is recommended for 1.8-30 MHz use, but type 77 material may be substituted; use type 43 material for 30-250 MHz. The cores present a high impedance to any RF current that would otherwise flow on the outside of the shield. The total impedance is in approximate proportion to the stacked length of the cores. Like the ferrite-core baluns described above, the impedance stays fairly constant over a wide range of frequencies. Again, 70-series ferrites are a good choice for the HF range, with type 43 being useful if heating is a problem. Type 43 or 61 is the best choice for the VHF range. Cores of various materials can be used in combination, permitting construction of baluns effective over a very wide frequency range, such as from 2 to 250 MHz.

Nonradiating Loads

Not all loads terminating transmission lines are radiators. Typical examples of nonradiating loads are the grid circuit of a power amplifier, the input circuit of a receiver and another transmission line. This last case includes the "antenna tuner." (Some prefer the term "antenna coupler" because such a device is used to couple a transmission line to a transmitter. ARRL publications use the word *Transmatch*, a coined word covering devices that match the transmitter output to whatever load it sees.)

Coupling to a Receiver

A good match between an antenna and its transmission line does not guarantee a low standing-wave ratio on the line when the antenna system is used for receiving. The VSWR is determined wholly by what the line "sees" at the receiver antenna-input terminals. For minimum VSWR the receiver input circuit must be matched to the line. The rated input impedance of a receiver is a nominal value that varies over a considerable range with frequency. Most HF receivers are sensitive enough that exact matching is not necessary. The most desirable condition is when the receiver is matched to the Z_0 of the line, which in

turn is matched to the antenna. This transfers maximum power from the antenna to the receiver with the least transmission line loss.

Coupling to Random-Length Antennas

Several Transmatch schemes are shown in Fig 19, permitting random-length wires to be matched to normal low-Z transmitter outputs. The circuit to be used will depend on the length of the antenna wire and its impedance at the desired operating frequency. Ordinarily one of the four methods shown will provide a suitable impedance match to an end-fed random wire, but the

configuration will have to be determined experimentally. A VSWR bridge should be used as a match indicator.

Coupling the Transmitter to the Line

The type of coupling system needed to transfer maximum power from the final RF amplifier to the transmission line depends almost entirely on the input impedance of the line. The input impedance is determined by the standing-wave ratio, the line length and the Z_0 of the line. The simplest case is that in which the line is terminated in its characteristic impedance. In this case the VSWR is 1:1 and the input impedance is equal to the Z_0 of the line, regardless of line length. For this condition the line is said to be "flat."

Coupling systems that will deliver power into a flat line can be readily designed. For practical purposes the line can be considered flat if the VSWR is no greater than about 1.5:1. That is, a coupling system designed to work into a pure resistance equal to the line Z_0 will have enough leeway to take care of the small variations in input impedance that will occur when the line length is changed, if the VSWR is higher than 1:1 but no greater than 1.5:1.

Current practice in transmitter design is to provide an output circuit that will work into such a line, usually a coaxial line of 50 to 75 ohms characteristic impedance. If the input impedance of the transmission line differs appreciably from the transmitter output design impedance, then a matching network must be inserted between the transmitter and the line input terminals.

Impedance-Matching Circuits for Transmission Lines

As shown earlier in this chapter, the input impedance of a line that is operating with a high standing-wave ratio can vary over quite wide limits. The simplest type of circuit that will match such a range of impedances to 50 or 75 ohms is a simple series- or parallel-tuned circuit, approximately resonant at the operating frequency. If the load presented by the line at the operating frequency is low (below a few hundred ohms), a series-tuned circuit should be used. When the load is higher than this, the parallel-tuned circuit is easier to use.

Typical simple circuits for coupling between the transmitter with 50- to 75-ohm coaxial-line output and a balanced transmission line are shown in Fig 20. The inductor L1 should have a reactance of about 60 ohms when adjustable inductive coupling is used (Figs 20A and 20B). When a variable series capacitor is used, L1 should have a reactance of about 120 ohms. The variable capacitor, C1, should have a reactance at maximum capacitance of about 100 ohms.

On the secondary side, L_s and C_s should be capable of being tuned to resonance at about 80 percent of the operating frequency. In the series-tuned circuits, for a given low-impedance load, looser coupling can be used between L1 and L_s as the L_s-to-C_s ratio is increased. In the parallel-tuned circuits, for a given high-impedance load, looser coupling can be used between L1 and L_p as the C_p-to-L_p ratio is increased. The constants are not critical; the rules of thumb are mentioned to assist in correcting a marginal condition where sufficient transmitter loading cannot be obtained.

Coupling to a coaxial line that has a high VSWR, and that consequently may present the transmitter with a load it cannot couple to, is done with an unbalanced version of the series-tuned circuit, as shown in Fig 21.

Fig 21 — Coupling from a transmitter designed for 50- to 75-ohm output to a coaxial line with a 3 or 4:1 VSWR is readily accomplished with these circuits. Essential difference between the circuits is adjustable inductive coupling at A, and fixed inductive coupling with variable series capacitor at B. In either case the circuit can be adjusted to give a 1:1 VSWR in the line to the transmitter. The coil ends marked X should be adjacent, for minimum capacitive coupling.

The rule given above for coupling ease and L_s-to-C_s ratio applies to these circuits as well.

The most satisfactory way to set up any of the circuits of Fig 20 or 21 initially is to connect a coaxial VSWR indicator in the line to the transmitter, as shown in Fig 21. The RF-wattmeter type of bridge, which can handle the full transmitter power and may be left in the line for continuous monitoring, is excellent for this purpose. A simple resistance bridge is perfectly adequate, however, requiring only that the transmitter output be reduced to a very low value so the bridge will not be overloaded. To adjust the circuit, make a trial setting of the coupling (coil spacing in Figs 20A and B and 21A, C1 setting in others) and adjust C_s or C_p for minimum VSWR as indicated by the bridge. If the VSWR is not 1:1, readjust the coupling and retune C_s or C_p, continuing this procedure until the VSWR is at or near 1:1. The settings may then be logged for future reference.

In the series-tuned circuits of Figs 20A and C, the two capacitors should be adjusted for similar settings. The "$2C_s$" indicates that a balanced series-tuned coupler requires twice the capacitance in each of two capacitors as does an unbalanced series-tuned circuit, all other things being equal.

It is possible to use circuits of this type without initially setting them up with a VSWR bridge. In such a case it is a matter of cut and try until adequate power transfer

between the amplifier and main transmission line is obtained. Initial tuning can be done by listening on a receiver tuned to the intended operating frequency, and adjusting for maximum band noise or received signal strengths. Tuning without an SWR bridge, however, frequently results in high VSWR in the link with consequent power loss, "hot spots" in the coaxial cable and tuning that is critical with frequency. The VSWR indicator method is simple and gives the optimum operating conditions quickly and with certainty.

THE CONJUGATE MATCH AND THE Z_0 MATCH

One purpose of matching impedances is to enable a power source or generator, having an optimum load impedance, to deliver its maximum available power to a load having a different impedance, usually through a transmission line having still another impedance. The same principles apply, and the same wave actions and reflections occur, whether the matching device is a stub on a line, a quarter-wave line transformer, or a network of lumped reactances such as a pi-network tank circuit or a Transmatch. (In ARRL literature, a Transmatch is considered to be a matching device used between the transmitter and the feed line.) To aid in understanding the principles of matching, we shall consider transmission lines and reactance components of the Transmatch as lossless elements, and then treat the effects of loss later.

The conjugate match is defined by the National Institute for Standards and Technology (NIST) as the condition for maximum power absorption by a load, in which the impedance seen looking toward the load at a point in the circuit is the complex conjugate of that seen looking toward the source. The Z_0 match is the condition in which the impedance seen looking into a transmission line is equal to the characteristic impedance of the line.

If a generator, a load, and an ideal lossless line connecting them all have the same Z_0, both a Z_0 match and a conjugate match exist. (A Z_0 match is also a special condition of the conjugate match.) Under these conditions the generator delivers its maximum available power into the line, which transfers it to the load where it is completely absorbed.

If the Z_0 load is now replaced by another, such as an antenna having an impedance $Z_L = R + jX \neq Z_0$, we have two mismatches at the load, a Z_0 mismatch and a conjugate mismatch. The Z_0 mismatch creates a reflection having a magnitude

$$\rho = \frac{Z_L - Z_0}{Z_L + Z_0}$$

causing a reflection loss ρ^2 that is referred back along the line to the generator. This in turn causes the generator to see the same magnitude of Z_0 mismatch at the line input. This referred Z_0 mismatch causes the generator to deliver less than its maximum available power by the amount equal to the reflection loss. There is no power lost in the line — only a reduction of power delivered. And all of the reduced power delivered is absorbed by the load.

If a matching device is now inserted between the line and the load, the device provides a conjugate match at the load by supplying a reflection gain which cancels the reflection loss, so the line sees a Z_0 match at the input of the matching device. Since the line is terminated in a Z_0 match, the generator now sees a Z_0 match at the line input, and will again deliver its maximum available power into the line, to be completely absorbed by the load.

However, if a Transmatch is inserted between the generator and the line instead of a matching device at the load, the Transmatch provides the conjugate match at the line input, and the generator sees a Z_0 match at the Transmatch input. At the load, the line now sees a conjugate match, but also sees a Z_0 mismatch. The Z_0 mismatch again causes a reflection loss that is referred back to the line input as before. With the Transmatch at the line input, the reflection gain, which again cancels the reflection loss, shields the generator from seeing the referred Z_0 mismatch again appearing at the line input.

The reflection gain of the Transmatch also creates the conjugate match at the load, and thus enables the load to absorb the maximum available power delivered by the generator. Since the generator sees a Z_0 match at the Transmatch input, it continues delivering its maximum available power into the line through the Transmatch, and the power is still completely absorbed by the load because of the conjugate match.

The amount of forward power flowing on a lossless line is determined by the expression

$$\frac{1}{1 - \rho^2}$$

where ρ = voltage coefficient of reflection.

On a real line with attenuation, forward power at the conjugate matching point is

$$\frac{1}{1 - \rho^2 e^{-4\alpha}}$$

where

α = line attenuation in nepers
  = dB/8.686

e = 2.71828..., the base of natural logarithms

The power arriving at the mismatched load with attenuation in the line is

$$\frac{e^{-2\alpha}}{1 - \rho^2 e^{-4\alpha}}$$

and the power absorbed in the load is

$$\frac{(1 - \rho^2) e^{-2\alpha}}{1 - \rho^2 e^{-4\alpha}}$$

The power reflected is

$$\frac{\rho^2 e^{-2\alpha}}{1 - \rho^2 e^{-4\alpha}}$$

The Conjugate Matching Theorem

To understand how a conjugate match is created at the load with the Transmatch at the line input, examine the Conjugate Matching Theorem and the wave actions which produce the conjugate match. It is the conjugate match that enables the load to absorb the maximum available power from the generator despite the Z_0 load mismatch.

"If a group of four-terminal networks containing only reactances (or lossless lines) are arranged in tandem to connect a generator to its load, then if at any junction there is a conjugate match of impedances, there will be a conjugate match of impedances at every other junction in the system."

To paraphrase from the NIST definition, "conjugate match" means that if in one direction from a junction the impedance has the dimensions R + jX, then in the opposite direction the impedance will have the dimensions R − jX. And according to the theorem, when a conjugate match is accomplished at any of the junctions in the system, any reactance appearing at any junction is canceled by an equal and opposite reactance, which also includes any reactance appearing in the load. This reactance cancellation results in a net system reactance of zero, establishing resonance in the entire system. In this resonant condition the generator delivers its maximum available power to the load, which is why an antenna operated away from its natural resonant frequency is tuned to resonance by a Transmatch connected at the input to the transmission line.

Conjugate matching is obtained through a controlled wave interference between two sets of reflected waves. One set of waves is reflected by the load mismatch, and the other by a complementary mismatch introduced by the reactances in the Transmatch. The mismatch introduced by the reactances of the Transmatch creates reflected waves of voltage and current at the matching point (the Transmatch input). These waves are equal in magnitude but opposite in phase relative to those arriving from the load mismatch. The two sets of reflected voltage and current waves created by the two mismatches combine at the matching point to produce resultant waves of voltage and current that are respectively at 0° and 180° in phase relative to the source wave.

The phase relationship of 180° between the resultant voltage and current waves creates a virtual open circuit to waves traveling toward the source, which totally re-reflects both sets of reflected waves back into the line. This re-reflection prevents the reflected waves from traveling beyond the matching point, which is the reason an SWR indicator connected at the input of

the Transmatch shows zero reflected power at the conclusion of the tune-up procedure. On re-reflection the voltage and current components of the reflected waves emerge in phase with the corresponding components of the source wave, so by superposition, all of the power contained in the reflected waves is added to the power in the source wave. Consequently, the forward power in the line is greater than the source power whenever the line is terminated in a Z_0 mismatch. This is why the forward-power wattmeter connected at the output of the Transmatch indicates a value higher than the source power, by the amount equal to the reflected power.

This enlargement of the forward power is called "reflection gain." Reflection gain cancels the reflection loss, creating the conjugate match that enables the Z_0-mismatched load to absorb the maximum available power delivered by the generator. When the source power enlarged by the reflected power reaches the Z_0-mismatched load, Z_L, the power previously reflected and added to the source power is again subtracted by the Z_0 mismatch reflection, leaving the source power to be completely absorbed by the load. This is why all power entering the line is absorbed in the load, regardless of the mismatch or SWR.

In lines having attenuation, all power entering the line is absorbed in the load, except for that lost because of attenuation. When the matching is performed at the line input, the attenuation increases as the Z_0 load mismatch increases because, in addition to the attenuation of the forward power, the reflected power is also attenuated in the same proportion. However, when the matched-line attenuation is low, as it is in typical amateur installations, the additional loss because of Z_0 mismatch is small. The additional losses are so low that even with moderate to high SWR values, the difference in power radiated compared to that with a 1:1 SWR is too small to be discerned by the receiving station. Information for calculating the additional power lost versus SWR is available from the graph in Fig 24, Chapter 16 of this *Handbook*, and from Fig. 9 in December 1974 *QST*, p. 12.

THE CONJUGATE MATCH AND THE PI-NETWORK TANK

In transceivers having tubes in the RF output stage, the pi network serves as a matching network as well as a harmonic-controlling tank circuit. When properly adjusted, the pi network matches the optimum load resistance of the tubes to the impedance seen at the input of the coaxial line connected to the output of the network.

In the ever-present quest for the perfect 1:1 SWR, many amateurs are unaware that the pi network is usually capable of matching the optimum tube load resistance to a wider range of output load impedances than defined by a 2:1 SWR; some will match to as high as 3:1, and sometimes

Table 3
Characteristics of Commonly Used Transmission Lines

Type of line	Z_0 Ohms	VF %	pF per foot	OD	Dielectric Material	Max Operating Volts (RMS)
Coaxial Line						
RG-6	75.0	75	18.6	0.266	Foam PE	—
RG-8X	52.0	75	26.0	0.242	Foam PE	—
RG-8	52.0	66	29.5	0.405	PE	4000
RG-8 foam	50.0	80	25.4	0.405	Foam PE	1500
RG-8A	52.0	66	29.5	0.405	PE	5000
RG-9	51.0	66	30.0	0.420	PE	4000
RG-9A	51.0	66	30.0	0.420	PE	4000
RG-9B	50.0	66	30.8	0.420	PE	5000
RG-11	75.0	66	20.6	0.405	PE	4000
RG-11 foam	75.0	80	16.9	0.405	Foam PE	1600
RG-11A	75.0	66	20.6	0.405	PE	5000
RG-12	75.0	66	20.6	0.475	PE	4000
RG-12A	75.0	66	20.6	0.475	PE	5000
RG-17	52.0	66	29.5	0.870	PE	11000
RG-17A	52.0	66	29.5	0.870	PE	11000
RG-55	53.5	66	28.5	0.216	PE	1900
RG-55A	50.0	66	30.8	0.216	PE	1900
RG-55B	53.5	66	28.5	0.216	PE	1900
RG-58	53.5	66	28.5	0.195	PE	1900
RG-58 foam	53.5	79	28.5	0.195	Foam PE	600
RG-58A	53.5	66	28.5	0.195	PE	1900
RG-58B	53.5	66	28.5	0.195	PE	1900
RG-58C	50.0	66	30.8	0.195	PE	1900
RG-59	73.0	66	21.0	0.242	PE	2300
RG-59 foam	75.0	79	16.9	0.242	Foam PE	800
RG-59A	73.0	66	21.0	0.242	PE	2300
RG-62	93.0	86	13.5	0.242	Air space PE	750
RG-62 foam	95.0	79	13.4	0.242	Foam PE	700
RG-62A	93.0	86	13.5	0.242	Air space PE	750
RG-62B	93.0	86	13.5	0.242	Air space PE	750
RG-133A	95.0	66	16.2	0.405	PE	4000
RG-141	50.0	70	29.4	0.190	PTFE	1900
RG-141A	50.0	70	29.4	0.190	PTFE	1900
RG-142	50.0	70	29.4	0.206	PTFE	1900
RG-142A	50.0	70	29.4	0.206	PTFE	1900
RG-142B	50.0	70	29.4	0.195	PTFE	1900
RG-174	50.0	66	30.8	0.100	PE	1500
RG-213	50.0	66	30.8	0.405	PE	5000
RG-214*	50.0	66	30.8	0.425	PE	5000
RG-215	50.0	66	30.8	0.475	PE	5000
RG-216	75.0	66	20.6	0.425	PE	5000
RG-223*	50.0	66	30.8	0.212	PE	1900
9913 (Belden)*	50.0	84	24.0	0.405	Air space PE	—
9914 (Belden)*	50.0	78	26.0	0.405	Foam PE	—
Aluminum Jacket, Foam Dielectric						
1/2 inch	50.0	81	25.0	0.500		2500
3/4 inch	50.0	81	25.0	0.750		4000
7/8 inch	50.0	81	25.0	0.875		4500
1/2 inch	75.0	81	16.7	0.500		2500
3/4 inch	75.0	81	16.7	0.750		3500
7/8 inch	75.0	81	16.7	0.875		4000
Parallel Line						
Open wire	—	97	—	—		—
75-ohm transmitting twin lead	75.0	67	19.0	—		—
300-ohm twin lead	300.0	82	5.8	—		—
300-ohm tubular	300.0	80	4.6	—		—
Open Wire, TV Type						
1/2 inch	300.0	95	—	—		—
1 inch	450.0	95	—	—		—

Dielectric Designation	Name	Temperature Limits
PE	Polyethylene	−65° to +80°C
Foam PE	Foamed polyethylene	−65° to +80°C
PTFE	Polytetrafluoroethylene (Teflon)	−250° to +250°C

*Double shield

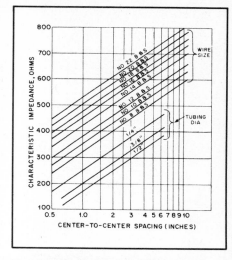

Fig 22 — Chart showing the characteristic impedance of spaced-conductor parallel transmission lines with air dielectric. Tubing sizes are given for outside diameters.

even 4:1. During tune-up, if a resonance dip in plate current can be obtained at the proper loaded value of current within the range of the tuning and loading capacitors in the pi network, the network has correctly matched the tubes to whatever impedance is seen at the output. This is true no matter how high the SWR. When correctly tuned to the plate-current dip, the tubes see the desired load, the network has supplied a match, and any reflected power as shown by an SWR indicator has been re-reflected in the same manner as described above for the Transmatch. In other words, the pi network can serve as the Transmatch for whatever SWR it can load properly.

TRANSMISSION LINE CHARACTERISTICS

Each type of line has a characteristic velocity factor, related to its insulating-material properties. The velocity factor must be taken into account when cutting a transmission line to a specific part of a wavelength — such as with a quarter-wavelength transformer. For example, if RG-8A were used to make a quarter-wavelength line at 3.5 MHz, the line dimension should be 0.66 × 246/f (MHz), because RG-8A has a velocity factor of 0.66. Thus, the line would be 46.4 feet long instead of the free-space length of 70.3 feet. Table 3 shows various velocity factors for the transmission lines commonly used by amateurs. Open-wire line has a velocity factor of essentially unity because it lacks a substantial amount of solid insulating material. Conversely, molded 300-ohm TV line has a velocity factor of 0.80 to 0.82.

Amateurs can construct their own parallel transmission lines by following the chart contained in Fig 22. With wire conductors it is easy to fabricate open-wire feed lines. Spacers made of high-quality insulating

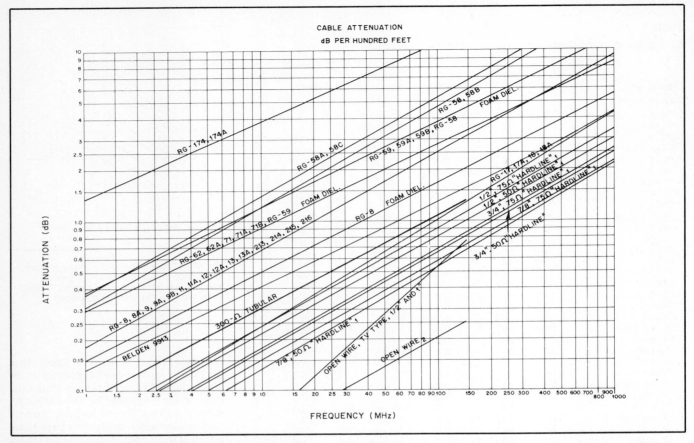

CABLE ATTENUATION
dB PER HUNDRED FEET

FREQUENCY (MHz)

Fig 23 — This graph displays the attenuation in decibels per 100-foot lengths of many popular transmission lines. The vertical axis represents attenuation and the horizontal axis frequency. Note that these loss figures are only accurate for properly matched transmission lines.

material are used at appropriate distances apart to maintain the spacing between the wires.

Characteristic Impedance

Too great a distance between insulating spacers may yield variations in line impedance because of nonconstant conductor spacing, and may permit the conductors to short out. These considerations are more important in outdoor installations in windy weather. The characteristic impedance of an air-insulated parallel-conductor line, neglecting the effect of the insulating spacers, is given by

$$Z_0 = 276 \log \frac{2S}{d}$$

where

Z_0 = characteristic impedance
S = center-to-center distance between conductors
d = diameter of conductor (in same units as S)

The characteristic impedance of an air-insulated coaxial line is given by the formula

$$Z_0 = 138 \log \frac{b}{a}$$

where

Z_0 = characteristic impedance
b = inside diameter of outer conductors
a = outside diameter of inner conductor (in same units as b)

It does not matter what units are used for a and b as long as they are the same units. The characteristic impedance of any transmission line can be expressed as a function of the distributed capacitance and inductance:

$$Z_0 = \sqrt{L/C}$$

where

Z_0 = characteristic impedance
L = inductance (henrys) per unit length
C = capacitance (farads) per unit length

Line Losses

The power loss in a transmission line is not directly proportional to the line length, but varies logarithmically with the length. That is, if 10% of the input power is lost in a section of line having a certain length, then 10% of the remaining power will be lost in the next section of the same length. For this reason it is customary to express line losses in terms of decibels per unit

length, because the decibel is a logarithmic unit. Calculations are simple because the total loss in a line is merely the loss per unit length multiplied by the total number of units. Line loss is usually expressed in decibels per hundred feet. It is necessary to specify the frequency for which the loss applies, because the loss varies with frequency.

Fig 23 shows the loss (or attenuation) per hundred feet versus frequency for several common types of lines, both coaxial and balanced types.

Effect of VSWR

The power lost in a line is lowest when the line is terminated in a resistance equal to its characteristic impedance, and increases with an increase in the standing-wave ratio. This is because the average values of both current and voltage become larger as the VSWR becomes greater. The increase in effective current raises the I^2R (ohmic) losses in the conductors, and the increase in effective voltage increases the E^2/R losses in the dielectric.

The increased loss caused by a VSWR greater than 1 may or may not be serious. If the VSWR at the load is not greater than 2, the *additional* loss caused by the standing

Fig 24—Increase in line loss because of standing waves (VSWR measured at the load). To determine the total loss in decibels in a line having a VSWR greater than 1, first determine the loss for the particular type of line, length and frequency, on the assumption that the line is perfectly matched (Fig 23). Locate this point on the horizontal axis and move up to the curve corresponding to the actual VSWR. The corresponding value on the vertical axis gives the additional loss in decibels caused by the standing waves.

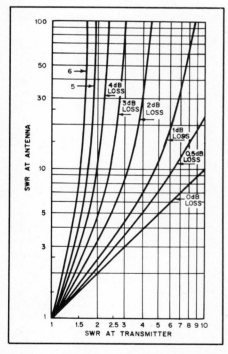

Fig 25—VSWR at input end of transmission line vs. VSWR at load end for various values of matched-line loss.

waves, as compared with the loss when the line is perfectly matched, does not amount to more than about ½ dB even on very long lines. Since ½ dB is an undetectable change in signal strength a VSWR of 2 or less is every bit as good as a perfect match, as far as losses are concerned.

The effect of VSWR on line loss is shown in Fig 24. The horizontal axis is the attenuation, in decibels, of the line when perfectly matched. The vertical axis gives the *additional* attenuation. For example, if the loss in a certain line is 1 dB when perfectly matched, a VSWR of 3 on that same line will cause an additional loss of approximately 0.5 dB. The total loss on the poorly matched line is therefore 1 + 0.5 = 1.5 dB. If the VSWR were 10 instead of 3, the additional loss would be 2.5 dB, and the total loss 1 + 2.5 = 3.5 dB.

It is important to note that the curves in Fig 24 that represent VSWR are the values that exist *at the load*. In most cases of amateur operation, this will be at the antenna end of a length of transmission line. The VSWR as measured at the input or transmitter end of the line will be less, depending on the line attenuation. It is not always convenient to measure VSWR directly at the antenna. By using the graph shown in Fig 25, however, you can obtain the VSWR at the load by measuring it at the input to the transmission line and using the known (or estimated) loss of the transmission line. For example, if the VSWR at the transmitter end of a line is measured as 3 to 1 and the line is known to have a total attenuation (under matched conditions) of 1 dB, the VSWR at the load end of the line will be 4.4 to 1. From Fig 24, the additional loss is nearly 1 dB because of the presence of the VSWR. The total line loss in this case is 2 dB.

Fig 26 shows the actual power delivered to the antenna (assuming 100 W is the input to the transmission line) as a function of the measured VSWR at the *input* end of the transmission line. The loss figures represent the line loss when perfectly matched; the power actually delivered to the antenna takes into account the additional losses caused by the *true* VSWR at the load (which is higher than that measured at the input of the transmission line). For example, when using a transmission line having a matched loss of 2 dB and a *measured* VSWR at the input end of the transmission line of 3:1, only 31.3 W of the 100-W output is actually delivered to the antenna.

Fig 26—The power actually delivered to the antenna (assuming 100-W output) as a function of VSWR measured at the input end of the transmission line. The loss figures represent line loss for perfectly matched transmission lines.

Bibliography

Everitt, W. L., *Communication Engineering*, 2nd edition, New York: McGraw-Hill, 1937.

Friis, H. T., and S. A. Schelkunoff, *Antennas: Theory and Practice*, New York: John Wiley and Sons, 1952.

Maxwell, M. W., *Reflections: Transmission Lines and Antennas*, Newington, CT: ARRL, 1990.

Regier, F. A., "Series-Section Transmission Line Impedance Matching," *QST*, Jul 1978, pp 14-16.

Roehm, Albert A., W2OBJ, "Some Additional Aspects of the Balun Problem," *The ARRL Antenna Compendium, Vol 2*, p 172.

Smith, P. H., *Electronic Applications of the Smith Chart in Waveguide, Circuit and Component Analysis*, New York: McGraw-Hill.

The ARRL Antenna Book, 15th edition, ed. G. L. Hall, Newington: American Radio Relay League, 1988.

Chapter 17

Antenna Fundamentals

An antenna system is comprised of all the components used between the transmitter or receiver and the actual radiator. Therefore, such items as the antenna proper, transmission line, matching transformers, baluns and Transmatch qualify as parts of an antenna system.

In a well designed system, only the antenna does the radiating. It is noteworthy that any type of feed line can be utilized with a given antenna, provided the following conditions are met. A suitable matching device must be used to ensure a low standing-wave ratio (SWR) between the feed line and the antenna, and another between the feed line and the transmitter (or receiver).

Some antennas possess an input impedance at the feed point close to that of certain transmission lines. For example, a half-wavelength, center-fed dipole, placed at a correct height above ground, will have a feed-point impedance of approximately 75 ohms. In such a case it is practical to use a 75-ohm coaxial or balanced line to feed the antenna. But few amateur half-wavelength dipoles actually exhibit a 75-ohm impedance. This is because at the lower end of the high-frequency spectrum the typical height above ground is rarely more than ¼ wavelength. The 75-ohm characteristic is most likely to be realized in a practical installation when the horizontal dipole is approximately one-half, three-quarters or one wavelength above ground. At lower heights the approximate feed-point resistance may be obtained from Fig. 1, but values may vary at different locations because of differences in ground conductivity.

Fig. 1 shows the difference between the effects of perfect ground and real earth at low antenna heights. The effect on the resistance of a horizontal half-wave antenna is negligible only as long as the height of the antenna is greater than 0.2 wavelength. Below this height, while decreasing rapidly to zero over perfectly conducting ground, the resistance decreases less rapidly with height over actual ground. At lower heights the resistance stops decreasing at around 0.15 wavelength, and thereafter increases as height decreases further. The reason for the increasing resistance is that more and more of the induction field of the antenna is absorbed by

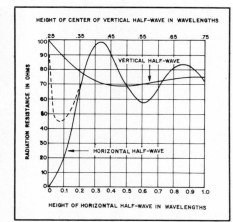

Fig. 1 — Curves showing the radiation resistance of vertical and horizontal half-wavelength dipoles at various heights above ground. The broken-line portion of the curve for a horizontal dipole shows the resistance over real earth, the solid line for perfectly conducting ground.

the lossy ground as the height drops below ¼ wavelength.

For a half-wave vertical antenna, the center of which is ¼ wavelength or more above the surface, differences between the effects of perfect ground and real earth on the impedance is negligible. The resistance of a vertical dipole at various heights above real and perfectly conducting ground is shown in Fig. 1.

The Antenna Choice

The amount of available space should be high on the list of factors to consider when selecting an antenna. Those who live in urban areas often must accept a compromise type of antenna for the HF bands because the city lot won't accommodate full-size wire dipoles, end-fed systems or high supporting structures. Other constrictions are imposed by the amount of money available for an antenna system (including supporting hardware), the number of amateur bands to be worked and local zoning ordinances.

Finally, the operation objective comes into play; to dedicate one's self to DXing, or to settle for a general type of operation that will yield short- and long-haul QSOs during periods of good propagation.

Because of these influences, it is impos-

sible to suggest one type of antenna system over another. A rule of thumb might be to erect the biggest and best collection of antennas that space and finances will allow. If a modest system is the order of the day, then use whatever is practical and accept less than optimum performance. Practically any radiator will enable the operator to make good contacts under some conditions of propagation, assuming the radiator is able to accept power and radiate it at some useful angle respective to earth.

In general, the height of the antenna above ground is the most critical factor at the higher end of the HF spectrum — 14 through 30 MHz. This is because the antenna should be clear of conductive objects such as power lines, phone wires, gutters and the like, plus high enough to have a low radiation angle. This is not nearly as important at 2 to 10 MHz, but lower frequency antennas still should be well away from conductive objects and as high above ground as possible in the interest of good performance. The exception is a ground-mounted vertical antenna. Ground-plane verticals, however, should be installed as high above ground as possible so their performance will not be degraded by conductive objects.

Antenna Polarization

Most HF-band antennas are either vertically or horizontally polarized, although circular polarization is possible, just as it is at VHF and UHF. The polarization is determined by the position of the radiating element or wire with respect to earth. Thus, a radiator that is parallel to the earth radiates horizontally, while an antenna at a right angle to the earth (vertical) radiates a vertical wave. If a wire antenna is slanted above earth, it radiates waves that are between vertical and horizontal in nature.

During line-of-sight communications, maximum signals will exist when the antennas at both ends of the circuit have the same polarity; cross polarization results in many decibels of signal reduction. During propagation via the ionosphere (sky wave), however, it is not essential to have the same polarization as the station at the opposite end of the circuit. This is because the radiated wave is bent and it tumbles considerably during its travel through the atmospheric layer from which it is refracted. At the far end of the communications path the wave may be horizontal, vertical or somewhere in between at a given instant. On multihop transmissions, in which the signal is refracted more than once from the atmosphere, and similarly reflected from the earth's surface during its travel, considerable polarization shift will occur. Therefore, the main consideration for a good DX antenna is a low angle of radiation rather than the polarization. It should be said, however, that most DX antennas for HF work are horizontally polarized. The major exception is the ground-plane vertical and phased vertical arrays.

Impedance

The impedance at a given point in the antenna is determined by the ratio of the voltage to the current at that point. For example, if there were 100 RF volts and 1.4 amperes of current at a specified point in an antenna and if they were in phase, the impedance would be approximately 71 ohms.

The impedance is significant with regard to matching the feeder to the feed point: Maximum power transfer takes place under a perfectly matched condition. As the mismatch increases, so does the reflected power. If the feed line is not too lossy or long, good performance can be had at HF when the standing-wave ratio (SWR) is 3:1 or less. When the feeder loss is very low — as with open-wire transmission line — much higher SWR is not detrimental to performance if the transmitter is able to work into the mismatched condition satisfactorily. In this regard, a Transmatch (matching network between the transmitter and the feed line) is often employed to compensate for the mismatch condition, enabling the operator to load the transmitter to its full rated power.

Antenna impedance can be either resistive or complex (containing resistance and reactance). This will depend on whether or not the antenna is resonant at the operating frequency. Many operators mistakenly believe that a mismatch, however small, is a serious matter, and that their signals won't be heard well even if the SWR is as low as 1.3:1. This unfortunate fallacy has cost much wasted time and money among some amateur groups as individuals attempted to obtain a perfect match. A perfect match, however ideal the concept may be, is not necessary. The significance of a perfect match becomes more pronounced only at VHF and higher, where feed-line losses are a major problem.

Antenna Bandwidth

The bandwidth of an antenna refers generally to the range of frequencies over which the antenna can be used to obtain good performance. The bandwidth is usually referenced to some SWR value, such as, "The 2:1 SWR bandwidth is 3.5 to 3.8 MHz." Some more specific bandwidth terms are used also, such as the gain bandwidth and the front-to-back ratio

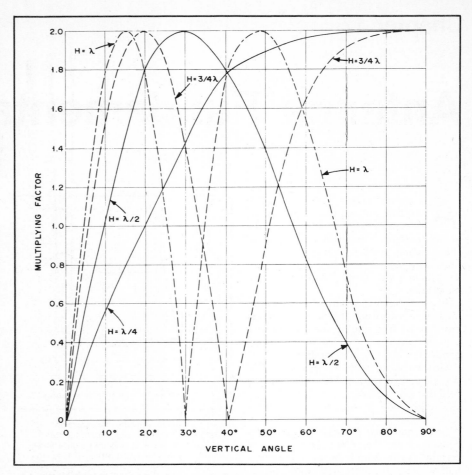

Fig. 2 — Effect of ground on the radiation of horizontal antennas at vertical angles for four antenna heights. These data are based on perfectly conducting ground.

bandwidth. The gain bandwidth is significant because the higher the antenna gain, the narrower the gain bandwidth will be for a given gain-bandwidth product.

For the most part, the lower the operating frequency of a given antenna design, the narrower the bandwidth. This follows the rule that the bandwidth of a resonant circuit doubles as the frequency of operation is increased by one octave (or doubled), assuming the Q is the same for each case. Therefore, it is often difficult to obtain sufficient bandwidth to cover all of the 160- to 80-meter bands with a dipole antenna cut for each of those bands. The situation can be aided by applying broadbanding techniques, such as fanning the far ends of a dipole to simulate a conical type of dipole.

Radiation Angle

The vertical angle of maximum radiation is of primary importance, especially at the higher frequencies. It is advantageous, therefore, to erect the antenna at a height that will take advantage of ground reflection so as to reinforce the space radiation at the most desirable angle. Since low angles usually are most effective, this generally means that the antenna should be high. The height should be at least one-half

wavelength at 14 MHz, and preferably three-quarters or one wavelength. At 28 MHz the height should be at least one wavelength, and preferably higher.

The physical height required for a given height in wavelengths decreases as the frequency is increased, so that acceptable heights are not impractical; a half wavelength at 14 MHz is only 35 feet, while the same height represents a full wavelength at 28 MHz. At 10 MHz and lower, the higher radiation angles are effective, so a useful antenna height is not difficult to attain. But greater height is important at 10 MHz and below when it is desired to work DX consistently. Heights between 35 and 70 feet are suitable for the upper bands, the higher figures being preferable. It is well to remember that most simple horizontally polarized antennas do not exhibit the directivity they are capable of unless they are one-half wavelength or more above ground. Therefore, with dipole-type antennas it is not important to choose a favored broadside direction unless the antenna is at least one-half wavelength above ground.

Imperfect Ground

Fig. 2 is based on ground having perfect conductivity, whereas the earth is not a perfect conductor. The principal effect of actual ground is to make the curves inaccurate at the lowest angles; appreciable high-frequency radiation at angles smaller than a few degrees is practically impossible to obtain over horizontal ground. Above 15 degrees, however, the curves are accurate enough for all practical purposes, and may be taken as indicative of the result to be expected at angles between 5 and 15 degrees.

The effective ground plane — that is, the plane from which ground reflections can be considered to take place — seldom is the actual surface of the ground. Instead, it is several inches to a few feet below it, depending on the characteristics of the soil.

Current and Voltage Distribution

When power is fed to an antenna, the current and voltage vary along its length. The current is maximum (loop) at the center and nearly zero (node) at the ends. The opposite is true of the RF voltage. The current does not actually reach zero at the current nodes, because of the end effect. Similarly, the voltage is not zero at its node because of the resistance of the antenna, which consists of both the RF resistance of the wire (ohmic resistance) and the radiation resistance. The radiation resistance is the equivalent resistance that would dissipate the power the antenna radiates, with a current flowing in it equal to the antenna current at a current loop (maximum). The ohmic resistance of a half-wavelength antenna is ordinarily small enough, compared with the radiation resistance, to be neglected for all practical purposes.

Conductor Size

The impedance of the antenna also depends on the diameter of the conductor in relation to the wavelength, as indicated in Fig. 3. If the diameter of the conductor is increased, the capacitance per unit length increases and the inductance per unit length decreases. Since the radiation resistance is affected relatively little, the decreased L/C ratio causes the Q of the antenna to decrease so that the resonance curve becomes less sharp. Hence, the antenna is capable of working over a wide frequency range. This effect is greater as the diameter is increased, and is a property of some importance at the very high frequencies where the wavelength is small.

THE HALF-WAVELENGTH ANTENNA

A fundamental form of antenna is a single wire whose length is approximately equal to half the transmitting wavelength. It is the unit from which many more complex forms of antennas are constructed and is known as a dipole antenna.

The length of a half-wave in free space is

$$Length\ (ft) = \frac{492}{f\ (MHz)} \qquad (Eq.\ 1)$$

The actual length of a resonant half-

wavelength antenna will not be exactly equal to the half wavelength in space, but depends on the thickness of the conductor in relation to the wavelength. The relationship is shown in Fig. 3, where K is a factor that must be multiplied by the half wavelength in free space to obtain the resonant antenna length. An additional shortening effect occurs with wire antennas supported by insulators at the ends because of the capacitance added to the system by the insulators (end effect). The following formula is sufficiently accurate for wire antennas for frequencies up to 30 MHz.

Length of half-wave antenna (ft) =

$$\frac{492 \times 0.95}{f\ (MHz)} = \frac{468}{f\ (MHz)} \qquad (Eq.\ 2)$$

Example: A half-wave antenna for 7150 kHz (7.15 MHz) is 468/7.15 = 65.45 ft, or 65 ft 5 in.

Above 30 MHz the following formulas should be used, particularly for antennas constructed from rod or tubing. K is taken from Fig. 3.

Length of half-wave antenna (ft) =

$$\frac{492 \times K}{f(MHz)} \qquad (Eq.\ 3)$$

$$Length\ (in) = \frac{5904 \times K}{f\ (MHz)} \qquad (Eq.\ 4)$$

Example: Find the length of a half-wavelength antenna at 28.7 MHz, if the antenna is made of ½-inch-diameter tubing. At 28.7 MHz, a half wavelength in space is

$$\frac{492}{28.7} = 17.14\ ft$$

from Eq. 1. The ratio of half wavelength to conductor diameter (changing wavelength to inches) is

$$\frac{(17.14 \times 12)}{0.5\ in.} = 411$$

From Fig. 3, K = 0.97 for this ratio. The length of the antenna, from Eq. 3 is

$$\frac{492 \times 0.97}{28.7} = 16.63\ ft$$

or 16 feet 7½ inches. The answer is obtained directly in inches by substitution in Eq. 4

$$\frac{5904 \times 0.97}{28.7} = 199.5\ inches$$

The length of a half wavelength antenna is affected also by the proximity of the dipole ends to nearby conductive and semi-conductive objects. In practice, it is often necessary after cutting the antenna to the computed length to do some experimental "pruning" of the wire, lengthening or shortening it in increments to obtain a low

Fig. 3 — Effect of antenna diameter on length for half-wavelength resonance, shown as a multiplying factor, K, to be applied to the free-space, half-wavelength equation (Eq. 1 of text). The effect of conductor diameter on the center feed-point impedance is shown here also.

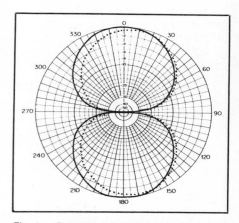

Fig. 4 — Response of a dipole antenna in free space, looking at the plane of the conductor, solid line. If the currents in the halves of the dipole are not in phase, some distortion of the pattern will occur, broken line. (Pattern calculation courtesy of "Annie.")

SWR. This can be done by applying RF power through an SWR indicator and observing the reflected-power reading. When the lowest SWR is obtained for the desired part of an amateur band, the antenna is resonant at that frequency. The value of the SWR indicates the quality of the match between the antenna and the feed line. With feed-line impedances of 50 or 75 ohms, the SWR at resonance should fall between 1.1:1 and 1.7:1 for antennas of average height that are clear of nearby conductive objects. If the lowest SWR obtainable is too high for use with solid-state rigs, a Transmatch or line-input matching network may be used, as described in Chapter 16.

Radiation Characteristics

The classic radiation pattern of a dipole antenna is most intense perpendicular to the wire. A figure-8 pattern (Fig. 4) can be

'Annie, a commercially available program for plotting antenna patterns on the Apple II series of computers, is available from Sonnet Software, Dept. QH, 4397 Luna Course, Liverpool, NY 13088.

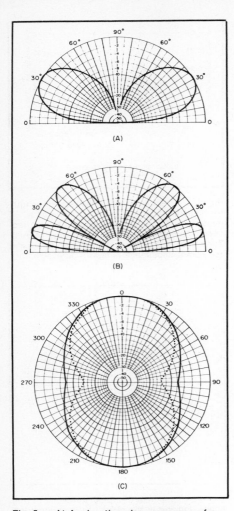

Fig. 5 — At A, elevation-plane response of a dipole antenna placed ½ wavelength above a perfectly conducting ground, and B, the pattern for the same antenna when it is raised to one wavelength height. C shows the azimuth patterns of the dipole for the two heights at the most favored elevation angle, the solid-line plot for the ½-λ height at an elevation angle of 30 degrees, and the broken-line plot for the 1-λ height at an elevation angle of 15 degrees. (Pattern calculation courtesy of "Annie.")

Fig. 6 — Method for affixing the feed line to the center of a dipole antenna. A plastic block is used as a center insulator. The coaxial cable is held in place by means of a metal clamp.

Fig. 7 — Construction details for a folded-dipole antenna. TV ribbon line is used as the dipole and feed line. Two pieces of plastic form an insulator/sandwich at the center to hold the conductor junction secure. When ribbon line is used for the flat top, the two conductors should be shorted at about 82% of the distance from the feed point to the ends.

assumed off the broad side of the antenna (bidirectional pattern) if the dipole is ½ wavelength or greater above earth and is not degraded by nearby conductive objects. This assumption is based also on a symmetrical feed system. In practice, a coaxial feed line may distort this pattern slightly, as shown in Fig. 4. Minimum horizontal radiation occurs off the ends of the dipole. This discussion applies to a half-wavelength antenna that is parallel to the earth. If the dipole is erected vertically, however, uniform radiation in all compass directions will result in a doughnut pattern if it could be viewed from above the antenna.

Many beginners assume that a dipole antenna will exhibit a broadside pattern at any height above ground. In fact, as the antenna is brought closer to ground, the radiation pattern deteriorates until the antenna is, for the most part, an omnidirec-

tional radiator of high-angle waves. Many are tempted to use any convenient height, such as 20 or 30 feet above ground, for an 80-meter dipole, only to learn that the system is effective in all directions over a relatively short distance (out to 500 or 1000 miles under good conditions).

It can be seen from this that height above ground is important for a host of reasons. Fig. 5 illustrates clearly the advantage gained from antenna height. The radiation angle of Fig. 5A is 30 degrees, whereas at a height of one wavelength (Fig. 5B) the lobes split and the lower ones provide a good DX-communications angle of 15 degrees. The directivity of the antenna at the two heights is shown in Fig. 5C. The solid line shows the azimuth pattern at a radiation angle of 30 degrees for a ½-λ dipole height, and corresponds to the plot in Fig. 5A. The broken line shows the pattern for a radiation angle of 15 degrees and a 1-λ height, corresponding to the plot of Fig. 5B. Fig. 5C illustrates that there is significant radiation off the ends of a low horizontal dipole, even at the most favored elevation angle. For the ½-λ height (solid line), the radiation off the ends is only 7.6 dB lower than that in the broadside direction.

The higher angle lobes of the pattern of Fig. 5B (50 degrees) are useful for short-haul communications and compare favorably in practice with the lobe angle

shown in Fig. 5A. At heights appreciably lower than ½ wavelength, the lobe angle becomes higher. Eventually the two lobes converge to create the discrete "ball of radiation" which has a very high-angle nature (poor for long-distance communications).

Feed Methods

Most amateur single-wire dipole antennas (half wavelength) have a feed-point impedance between 50 and 75 ohms, depending on the installation. Therefore, standard coaxial cable is suitable for most installations. The smaller types of cable (RG-58 and RG-59) are satisfactory for power levels up to a few hundred watts if the SWR of the system is low. For high-power stations (RG-8 or RG-11) larger cables should be used.

These cables can be connected at the center of the antenna, as shown in Fig. 6. A plastic insulating block is used as central reinforcement for the cable and the dipole wires. The coax shield braid is connected to one leg of the dipole and the center conductor is soldered to the remaining leg. The exposed end of the cable should be sealed against dirt and moisture to prevent degradation of the transmission line.

Symmetrical feed can be obtained by inserting a 1:1 balun transformer at the dipole feed point. If one is not used, it is unlikely that the slight pattern skew resulting from nonsymmetrical feed will be noticed. The effects of unbalanced feed are most significant in beam antennas at VHF and higher. The narrower the beam pattern, the more annoying the condition will be.

The characteristic impedance of a dipole antenna can be increased by using a two-wire or folded dipole of the type shown in Fig. 7. This antenna offers a good match to 300-ohm TV ribbon. Alternatively, two pieces of wire can be used to form the equivalent of the TV-line dipole. If this is done it will be necessary to locate insulating spacers every few feet along the length of the dipole to keep the wires spaced apart uniformly and to prevent short circuiting. Open-wire TV ladder line is excellent for use in a 300-ohm folded dipole antenna, both for the radiator and the feed line. Feeder losses with this type of construction will be very low as opposed to molded TV twin-lead.

A dipole antenna can be used as an all-band radiator by using tuned open wire feed line. This principle is shown in Fig. 8A. In this example the dipole is cut to a half wavelength for the lowest desired amateur band. It is operated on its harmonics when used for the other chosen amateur bands. A typical antenna of this type might be utilized from 80 through 10 meters. This style of radiator is known by some amateurs as the center-fed Zepp. An end-fed version (end-fed Zepp) is shown in Fig. 8 at B. This version is not quite as

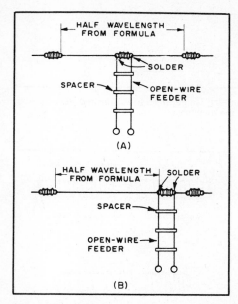

Fig. 8 — Center fed Zepp antenna (A) and an end-fed Zepp at B.

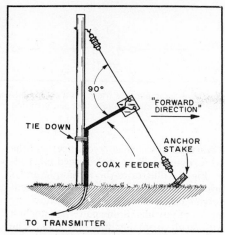

Fig. 9 — Example of a sloping half-wavelength dipole. On the lower HF bands over poor to average earth, maximum radiation is off the sides and in the "forward direction" indicated here, if a nonconductive support is used. A metal support will alter this pattern by acting as a parasitic element, depending on its electrical height.

Fig. 10 — At A, details for a drooping dipole which can be used for multiband HF operation. A Transmatch is shown at B, suitable for matching the antenna to the transmitter over a wide frequency range.

desirable as the center-fed version because the feed system is not symmetrical. This can cause feeder radiation and a distortion of the antenna radiation pattern.

Both types of Zepp antenna require a matching network (Transmatch) at the transmitter end of the line to convert the feeder impedance to 50 ohms, and to change the balanced condition to an unbalanced one. Although the feed line may be anything from 200 ohms up to 600 ohms (not critical), losses will be insignificant when open-wire line is used. This is true despite the variations in antenna feed-point impedance from band to band. The feed-point impedance for the dipole will be high at even harmonics and will be low at the lowest operating frequency and at odd harmonics thereof. For example, if the dipole is cut for 40 meters, the feed-point impedance will be low on 40 and 15 meters, but it will be high at 20 and 10 meters.

With a dipole antenna the feed line should be routed away from the antenna at a right angle for as great a distance as possible. This will help prevent current imbalance in the line caused by RF pickup from the dipole. A right-angle departure of 1/4 wavelength or greater is suggested.

Under some circumstances it may be necessary to experiment with the length of the open-wire feeders when using an all-band Zepp. This is because at some operating frequencies the line may present an "awkward" impedance to the Transmatch, making it impossible to obtain a suitable load condition for the transmitter. This will depend on the capability of the Transmatch being used.

Dipole Variations

The physical application of dipoles can be varied to obtain radiation properties that differ from those of the more conventional horizontal dipole. Furthermore, the nature and amount of property at the site will often dictate departures from the conventional means of erecting a dipole.

A sloping dipole can be useful for DX work on the lower HF bands because of its low angle of radiation. A sloping dipole is shown in Fig. 9. Excellent results can be had when the ground end of the antenna is only a few feet above the earth. When the antenna is supported with a nonconducting mast over poor to average earth, the radiation pattern tends to be cardioid shaped, but without a sharp null at the back. Maximum response is off the sides and in the "forward direction" as indicated in Fig. 9. The front-to-back ratio of the sloping dipole depends on the frequency and the conductivity of the earth, as well as the amount of slope and the vertical elevation angle of concern. Surprisingly, the sloping dipole becomes an omnidirectional radiator over a perfectly conducting earth.

If a metal mast or tower is used, it will alter the shape of the radiation pattern by acting as a parasitic element. Best results as a reflector seem to be obtained when the support is grounded and is approximately a quarter wave in physical height, supporting rotary beam or other antennas at the top. Some amateurs install four slopers for a given amateur band, spaced equidistantly around the tower. A feed-line switching system is used to obtain directivity in the chosen direction.

Drooping Dipole (Inverted V)

Another popular type of dipole antenna is the so-called inverted V, or drooping dipole. Because it has no characteristics of a true V antenna, the name inverted V is misleading. A drooping dipole is shown in Fig. 10. Newcomers to Amateur Radio are frequently led to regard this antenna as a panacea, but there is nothing magical or superior about a drooping dipole. In fact, its performance is inferior to that of a horizontal dipole at the same height as the apex. The main attribute is that it requires only one supporting structure. As with a horizontal dipole, it can be used for single or multiband operation.

Contrary to popular belief, the radiation off the ends of the drooping dipole is essentially no greater than that of a horizontal dipole at the same height as the apex. This myth probably arises because the drooping dipole is not an efficient radiator in the broadside direction, so it merely seems by comparison to its broadside performance that it is a good radiator off the ends. As is true of a horizontal dipole, the higher the drooping dipole is mounted above the ground, the better it will perform respective to low-angle, long-distance communications.

Best results are obtained when the enclosed angle of the drooping dipole is 90° or more. At angles less than 90°, considerable cancellation takes place, and reduced antenna performance results. At angles greater than 120° the antenna begins to function as a horizontal dipole.

When the ends of the drooping dipole are relatively close to the earth, pruning of the dipole legs may be necessary to compensate for the capacitive effect to ground.

Fig. 11 — When limited space is available for a dipole antenna the ends can be bent downward as at A, or back on the radiator as shown at B. The drooping dipole at C can be erected with the ends bent parallel with the ground when the available supporting structure is not high enough to permit an enclosed angle of approximately 90°.

Thus, if the dipole is cut to length by means of the standard half-wavelength equation, it may be too long as a drooping dipole. Incremental trimming of each end of the dipole can be done while using an SWR indicator. This will show when the lowest SWR is obtained. A 50-ohm feed line offers a good match for drooping dipoles when single-band operation is desired. For multiband use, the antenna can be fed with open-wire line and matched to the transmitter with a Transmatch.

The most ideal supporting structure for a drooping dipole is a wooden or other nonconductive one. This type of support will have the least effect on the antenna pattern and performance.

Drooping dipoles are effective when used for a single band, the one for which it has been cut. Good results can also be had for two-band operation. An 80-meter dipole can be fed with open-wire line and used also on 40 meters as two half waves in phase. On 40 meters its performance at low radiation angles off the ends will be slightly superior to that of a 40-meter *half-wave* horizontal dipole at the same height as the apex.

Bent Dipoles and Trap Dipoles

When there is insufficient real estate to permit the erection of a full-size horizontal or drooping dipole, certain compromises are possible in the interest of getting an antenna installed. The voltage ends (far ends) of a dipole can be bent downward

toward earth to effect resonance, and the performance will not be reduced markedly. Fig. 11 illustrates the technique under discussion. At A the dipole ends are bent downward and secured to anchors by means of guy line. Some pattern distortion will result from bending the ends. The dipole ends can also be bent back over the wire halves of the antenna, as shown at B in Fig. 11. This causes some signal cancellation (more severe than with the system of Fig. 11A), so it is not a preferred technique.

Fig. 11C demonstrates a bending technique for drooping dipoles when the available supporting mast or tree is too short to permit normal installation. The ends of the dipole are guyed off by means of insulators and wires, as shown. Alternatively, but not preferred, is the fold-back method at B in Fig. 11.

All of the shortening systems highlighted in Fig. 11 will have an effect on the overall length of the dipole. Therefore, some cutting and testing will be necessary to ensure a low SWR in the favored part of the amateur band for which the antenna is built. If open-wire feeders and a Transmatch are used, the dipole length will not be critical, provided it is close to the length required for a fully extended half-wavelength dipole. Pruning will be required if single-band operation with coaxial feed line is planned.

Trap dipoles offer one solution to multiband operation with a shortened radiator. The concept is shown in Fig. 12. In this example the dipole is structured for two-band use. Assuming that the antenna is made for operation on 80 and 40 meters, the overall radiator (including the traps) must be resonant at the center of the chosen section of the 80-meter band. The traps add loading to the dipole, so the length from the feed point to the far end of each leg will be somewhat shorter than normal. During 40-meter operation the traps present a high impedance to the signal and divorce the wires beyond the traps. Therefore, the wire length from the feed point to each trap is approximately what it would be if the dipole were cut for just 40 meters, with no traps in the line.

This principle can be extended for additional bands, using a new set of traps for each band. Since there is considerable interaction between the various segments of a multiband trap dipole, considerable experimentation with the wire lengths between the traps and beyond will be necessary.

Fig. 12 — Example of a trap dipole antenna. L1 and C1 can be tuned to the desired frequency by means of a dip meter before they are installed in the antenna.

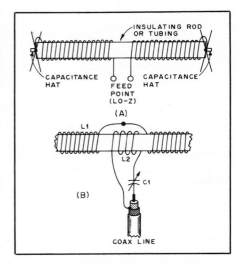

Fig. 13 — A helically wound dipole is illustrated at A. As shown, the radiation resistance will be very low and will require a broadband matching transformer. The coupling method shown at B is more satisfactory for providing a matched condition.

The trap capacitors (C1) should be high-voltage and high-current units. Transmitting mica capacitors offer good performance. Transmitting ceramic capacitors are usable, but change value with extreme changes of temperature. Therefore, they are more suitable for use in regions where the climate is fairly constant throughout the year. The coils (L1) should be reasonably heavy wire gauge to minimize I^2R losses. The X_L and X_C values in traps are not critical. Generally the reactance can be on the order of 100 to 300 ohms. The traps should be checked for resonance before they are installed in the antenna system. This can be done with a dip meter and a calibrated receiver. Weatherproofing should be added to the traps as a measure against detuning and damage from ice, snow and dirt.

Helically Wound Dipoles

The overall length of a half-wavelength dipole can be reduced considerably by using helically wound elements. Fig. 13A shows the general form taken with this type of antenna. A length of insulating rod or tubing (fiberglass or phenolic) is used to contain the wire turns of the dipole. The material should be of high dielectric quality. Varnished bamboo has been used successfully by some in lieu of the more expensive materials. A hardwood pole from a lumber yard can be used after being coated one or more times with exterior spar varnish.

To minimize losses, the wire used should be of the largest diameter practical. The turns can be close-wound or spaced apart, with little difference in performance. The ends of the helical dipole should contain capacitance hats (disks or wire spokes preferred) of the largest size practical. The hats will lower the Q of the antenna and broaden its response. If no disks are used, extremely high RF voltage can appear at the ends of the antenna. At medium power levels and higher the insulating material can burn when no hats are used. The voltage effect is similar to that of a Tesla coil.

The feed-point impedance of helical dipoles or verticals is quite low. Therefore, it may be necessary to use some form of matching network to interface the antenna with 50-ohm coaxial cable. A broadband, variable-impedance transformer is convenient for determining the turns ratio of the final transformer used. The feed method shown at B of Fig. 13 can be used to obtain a matched condition. L2 is wound over L1, or between the two halves of L1, as illustrated. C1 is adjusted for an SWR of 1 at the center of the desired operating range. The bandwidth of this type of antenna is quite narrow. A 40-meter version with an 18-foot overall length exhibited a 2:1 SWR bandwidth of 50 kHz. The capacitance hats on that model were merely 18-inch lengths (whiskers) of no. 8 Copperweld wire. Greater bandwidth would result with larger capacitance hats.

To obtain half-wavelength performance it is necessary to wind approximately one wavelength of wire on the tubing. Final pruning can be done while observing an SWR indicator placed in the transmission line. Proximity to nearby conductive objects and the earth will have a significant effect on the resonance of the antenna. Ideally, final adjustments should be made with the antenna situated where it will be during use. Marine spar varnish should be painted on the elements after all tuning is finished. This will protect the antenna from the weather and will lock the turns in place so that detuning will not occur later.

A reasonably linear current and voltage distribution will result when using a helically wound dipole or vertical. The same is not true of center-, mid- or end-loaded (lumped inductance) dipoles. The efficiency of the helically wound antenna will be somewhat less than a full-size dipole. The performance will suffer as the helices are made shorter. Despite the gain-length trade-off, this antenna is capable of good performance when there is no room for a full-size dipole.

LONG-WIRE ANTENNAS

An antenna will be resonant so long as an integral number of standing waves of current and voltage can exist along its length; in other words, so long as its length

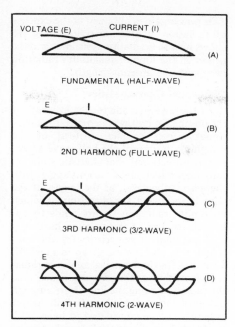

Fig. 14 — Standing-wave current and voltage distribution along an antenna when it is operated at various harmonics of its fundamental resonant frequency.

is some integral multiple of a half wavelength. When the antenna is more than one wavelength long it usually is called a long-wire antenna, or a harmonic antenna.

Current and Voltage Distribution

Fig. 14 shows the current and voltage distribution along a wire operating at its fundamental frequency (where its length is equal to a half wavelength) and at its second, third and fourth harmonics. For example, if the fundamental frequency of the antenna is 7 MHz, the current and voltage distribution will be as shown at A. The same antenna excited at 14 MHz would have current and voltage distribution as shown at B. At 21 MHz, the third harmonic of 7 MHz, the current and voltage distribution would be as in C; and at 28 MHz, the fourth harmonic, as in D. The number of the harmonic is the number of half waves contained in the antenna at the particular operating frequency.

The polarity of current or voltage in each standing wave is opposite to that in the adjacent standing waves. This is shown in the figure by drawing the current and voltage curves successively above and below the antenna (taken as a zero reference line), to indicate that the polarity reverses when the current or voltage goes through zero. Currents flowing in the same direction are in phase; in opposite directions, out of phase.

It is evident that one antenna may be used for harmonically related frequencies, such as the various amateur bands. The long-wire or harmonic antenna is the basis of multiband operation with one antenna.

Physical Length

The length of a long-wire antenna is not

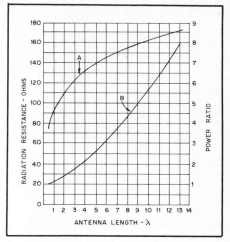

Fig. 15 — Curve A shows the variation in radiation resistance with antenna length when the antenna is fed at a current maximum. Curve B shows power in the lobes of maximum radiation for long-wire antennas as a ratio to the maximum radiation for a half-wave antenna.

an exact multiple of that of a half-wave antenna because the end effects operate only on the end sections of the antenna; in other parts of the wire these effects are absent, and the wire length is approximately that of an equivalent portion of the wave in space. The formula for the length of a long-wire antenna, therefore is

$$\text{Length (feet)} = \frac{492 \, (N - 0.05)}{f \, (\text{MHz})}$$

where N is the number of half waves on the antenna.

Example: An antenna 4 half waves long at 14.2 MHz would be

$$\frac{492 \, (4 - 0.05)}{14.2} = \frac{492 \, (3.95)}{14.2}$$

= 136.9 feet, or 136 feet 10 inches.

It is apparent that an antenna cut as a halfwave for a given frequency will be slightly off resonance at exactly twice that frequency (the second harmonic), because of the decreased influence of the end effects when the antenna is more than one-half wavelength long. The effect is not important, except for a possible unbalance in the feeder system and consequent radiation from the feed line. If the antenna is fed in the exact center, no unbalance will occur at any frequency, but end-fed systems will show an unbalance on all but one frequency in each harmonic range.

Impedance and Power Gain

The radiation resistance as measured at a current loop becomes higher as the antenna length is increased. Also, a long-wire antenna radiates more power in its most favorable direction than does a half-wave antenna in its most favorable direction.

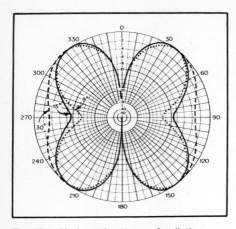

Fig. 16 — Horizontal patterns of radiation from a full-wave antenna. The solid line shows the pattern for a vertical angle of 15°; broken lines show deviation from the 15° pattern at 9° and 30°. All three patterns are drawn to the same relative scale; actual amplitudes will depend on the height of the antenna.

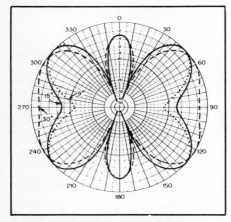

Fig. 17 — Horizontal patterns of radiation from an antenna three half-waves long. The solid line shows the pattern for a vertical angle of 15°; broken lines show deviation from the 15° pattern at 9° and 30°. Minor lobes coincide for all three angles.

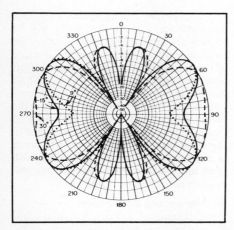

Fig. 18 — Horizontal patterns of radiation from an antenna 2 wavelengths long. The solid line shows the pattern for a vertical angle of 15°; broken lines show deviation from the 15° pattern at 9° and 30°. The minor lobes nearly coincide for all three angles.

This power gain is obtained at the expense of radiation in other directions. Fig. 15 shows how the radiation resistance and the power in the lobe of maximum radiation vary with the antenna length.

Directional Characteristics

As the wire is made longer in terms of the number of half wavelengths, the directional effects change. Instead of the doughnut pattern of the half-wave antenna, the directional characteristic splits up into lobes which make various angles with the wire. In general, as the length of the wire is increased the direction in which maximum radiation occurs tends to approach the line of the antenna itself.

Directional characteristics for antennas 1 λ, 1½ λ, and 2 λ are given in Figs. 16, 17 and 18 for three vertical angles of radiation. Note that, as the wire length increases, the radiation along the line of the antenna becomes more pronounced. Still longer antennas can be considered to have practically end-on directional characteristics, even at the lower radiation angles.

When a long-wire antenna is fed at one end or at the current loop closest to that end, the radiation is most pronounced from the long section. This unidirectional pattern can be accentuated by terminating the far end in a load resistance to ground. The load resistor will dissipate energy that would ordinarily be radiated toward the feed point. Depending on the pattern symmetry of the unterminated antenna, this resistor must handle up to half the power delivered to the feed point. The exact resistance must be determined empirically, but the voltage-to-current ratio at a current node is a good starting value. A quarter-wavelength wire beyond the resistor can serve as a pseudo ground for the system. Low-angle radiation from a long wire can be enhanced by sloping the wire down toward the favored direction.

Methods of Feeding

In a long-wire antenna, the currents in adjacent half-wave sections must be out of phase, as shown in Fig. 14. The feeder system must not upset this phase relationship. This is satisfied by feeding the antenna at either end or at any current loop. A two-wire feeder cannot be inserted at a current node, however, because this invariably brings the currents in two adjacent half-wave sections in phase. A long-wire antenna is usually made a half wavelength at the lowest frequency and fed at the end.

Long-Wire Directive Arrays

Two long wires can be combined in the form of a horizontal V, in the form of a horizontal rhombus, or in parallel, to provide a long-wire directive array. In the V and rhombic antennas the main lobes reinforce along a line bisecting the acute angle between the wires; in the parallel antenna the reinforcement is along the line of the lobe. This reinforcement provides both gain and directivity along the line, since the lobes in other directions tend to cancel. When the proper configuration for a given length and height above ground is used, the power gain depends on the length (in wavelengths) of the wires.

Rhombic and V antennas are normally bidirectional along the bisector line mentioned above. They can be made unidirectional by terminating the ends of the wires away from the feed point in the proper value of resistance. When properly terminated, V and rhombic antennas of sufficient length work well over a three-to-one or four-to-one frequency range and hence are useful for multiband operation.

Antenna gains of the order of 10 to 15 dB can be obtained with properly constructed long-wire arrays. The pattern is rather sharp with gains of this order, however, and rhombic and V beams are not used by amateurs as commonly as they once were, having been displaced by the rotatable multielement Yagi beam. Futher information on these antennas can be found the *The ARRL Antenna Book*.

BEAMS WITH DRIVEN ELEMENTS

By combining individual half-wave antennas into an array with suitable spacing between the antennas (called elements) and feeding power to them simultaneously, it is possible to make the radiation from the elements add up along a single direction and form a beam. In other directions the radiation tends to cancel, so a power gain is obtained in one direction at the expense of radiation in other directions.

There are several methods of arranging the elements. If they are strung end to end, so that all lie on the same straight line, the elements are said to be collinear. If they are parallel and all lying in the same plane, the elements are said to be broadside when the phase of the current is the same in all, and end-fire when the currents are not in phase.

Collinear Arrays

Simple forms of collinear arrays, with current distribution, are shown in Fig. 19. The two-element array at A is popularly known as a Franklin array, two half-waves in phase or a double Zepp antenna. It will be recognized as simply a center-fed dipole operated at its second harmonic.

By extending the antenna, as at B, the additional gain of an extended double Zepp antenna can be obtained. Carrying the length beyond that shown will result in an X-shaped pattern that no longer has the maximum radiation at right angles to the wire.

Collinear arrays may be mounted either horizontally or vertically. Horizontal mounting gives increased azimuthal directivity, while the vertical directivity remains the same as for a single element at the same height. Vertical mounting gives the same horizontal pattern as a single element, but improves the low-angle radiation.

Fig. 19 — Collinear antennas in phase. The system at A is known as two half waves in phase and has a gain of 1.8 dB over a half-wave antenna. By lengthening the antenna slightly, as in B, the gain can be increased to 3 dB. Maximum radiation is at right angles to the antenna. The antenna at A is sometimes called a double Zepp antenna, and that of B is known as an extended double Zepp.

Fig. 20 — Simple broadside array using horizontal elements. By making the spacing S equal to 3/8 wavelength, the antenna at A can be used at the corresponding frequency and up to twice that frequency. Thus when designed for 14 MHz it can also be used on 18, 21, 25 and 28 MHz. The antenna at B can be used on only the design band. This array is bidirectional, with maximum radiation broadside or perpendicular to the antenna plane (perpendicularly through this page). Gain varies with the spacing S, running from 2½ to almost 5 dB. (See Fig. 22.)

Fig. 21 — Top view of a horizontal end-fire array. The system is fed with an open-wire line at X and Y; the line can be of any length. Feed points X and Y are equidistant from the two insulators, and the feed line should drop down vertically from the antenna. The gain of the system will vary with the spacing, as shown in Fig. 22, and is a maximum at 1/8 wavelength. By using a length of 33 feet and a spacing of 8 feet, the antenna will work on 20, 17, 15, 12 and 10 meters.

Fig. 22 — Gain vs. spacing for two parallel half-wave elements combined as either broadside or end-fire arrays.

Broadside Arrays

Parallel antenna elements with currents in phase may be combined as shown in Fig. 20 to form a broadside array, so named because the direction of maximum radiation is broadside to the plane containing the antennas. The gain and directivity depend on the spacing of the elements.

Broadside arrays may be suspended either with the elements all vertical or with them horizontal and one above the other (stacked). In the case of vertical elements, the horizontal pattern becomes quite sharp, while the vertical pattern is the same as that of one element alone. If the array is suspended horizontally, the horizontal pattern is equivalent to that of one element while the vertical pattern is sharpened, giving low-angle radiation.

Broadside arrays may be fed either by tuned open-wire lines or through quarter-wave matching sections and flat lines. In Fig. 20B, note the crossing over of the phasing section, which is necessary to bring the elements into proper phase relationship.

End-Fire Arrays

Fig. 21 shows a pair of parallel half-wave elements with currents out of phase. This is known as an end-fire array because it radiates best along the plane of the antennas, as shown. The end-fire principle was first demonstrated by John Kraus, W8JK, and 2-element arrays of this type are often called "8JK" antennas.

The end-fire array may be used either vertically or horizontally (elements at the same height), and is well adapted to amateur work because it gives maximum gain with relatively close element spacing. Fig. 22 shows how the gain varies with spacing. End-fire elements may be combined with additional collinear and broadside elements to give a further increase in gain and directivity.

Either tuned or untuned lines may be used with this type of array. Untuned lines preferably are matched to the antenna through a quarter-wave matching section or phasing stub.

Fig. 23 — Unidirectional two-element end-fire array and method of obtaining 90° phasing.

Fig. 24 — A four-element combination broadside collinear array, popularly known as the lazy-H antenna. A closed quarter-wave stub may be used at the feed point to match into an untuned transmission line, or tuned feeders may be attached at the point indicated. The gain over a half-wave antenna is 5 to 6 dB.

Fig. 25 — Radiation resistance (solid curve) and reactance (dotted curve) of vertical antennas as a function of physical height.

Unidirectional End-Fire Arrays

Two parallel elements spaced ¼ wavelength apart and fed equal currents 90° out of phase will have a directional pattern in the plane of the array at right angles to the elements. The maximum radiation is in the direction from the element in which the current lags. In the opposite direction the fields from the two elements cancel.

One way in which the 90° phase difference can be obtained is shown in Fig. 23. Each element must be matched to its transmission line, the two lines being of the same type except that one is an electrical quarter wavelength longer than the other. The length L can be any convenient value. Open quarter-wave matching sections could be used instead. The two transmission lines are connected in parallel at the transmitter coupling circuit.

When the currents in the elements are neither in phase nor 180° out of phase the radiation resistances of the elements are not equal. This complicates the problem of feeding equal currents to the elements. If the currents are not equal, one or more minor lobes will appear in the pattern and decrease the front-to-back ratio. The adjustment process is likely to be tedious and requires field-strength measurements in order to get the best performance.

More than two elements can be used in unidirectional end-fire arrays. The requirement for unidirectivity is that there must be a progressive phase shift in the element currents. The shift must equal the spacing between the elements in electrical degrees, and the current amplitudes also must be properly related. This requires binominal current distribution — i.e., the ratios of the currents in the elements must be proportional to the coefficients of the binominal series. In the case of three elements, this requires that the current in the center element be twice that in the two outside elements, for 90° (quarter-wave spacing and element current phasing. This antenna has an overall length of ½ wavelength.

Combined Arrays

Broadside, collinear and end-fire arrays may be combined to give both horizontal and vertical directivity, as well as additional gain. The lower angle of radiation resulting from stacking elements in the vertical plane is desirable at the higher frequencies. In general, doubling the number of elements in an array by stacking will raise the gain from 2 to 4 dB, depending on the spacing.

Although arrays can be fed at one end as in Fig. 20B, it is not especially desirable in the case of large arrays. Better distribution of energy between elements, and hence better overall performance, will result when the feeders are attached as nearly as possible to the center of the array.

A 4-element array, known as the lazy-H antenna, is a popular configuration. This arrangement is shown with the feed point indicated, in Fig. 24. (Compare with Fig. 20B.) For best results, the bottom section should be at least a half wavelength above ground.

It will usually suffice to make the length of each element equal to that given by the dipole formula. The phasing line between the parallel elements should be of open-wire construction and its length can be calculated from:

Length of half-wave line (feet)

$$= \frac{480}{f\ (MHz)}$$

Example: A half-wavelength phasing line for 28.8 MHz would be

$$\frac{480}{28.8} = 16.67 \text{ feet} = 16 \text{ feet } 8 \text{ inches}$$

The spacing between elements can be made equal to the length of the phasing line. No special adjustments of line or element length or spacing are needed, provided the formulas are followed closely.

THE VERTICAL ANTENNA

One of the more popular amateur antennas is the vertical type. With this style of antenna it is possible to obtain low-angle radiation for ground-wave and DX work.

Additionally, vertical antennas occupy a relatively small amount of space, making them ideal for city-lot property and apartment buildings. The principal limitation in performance is the omnidirectional pattern. This means that QRM can't be nulled out from the directions that are not of interest at a given period. The exception is, of course, when arrays of vertical elements are used. Despite the limitation of a single vertical element with a ground screen or radial system, cost versus performance is an incentive that inspires many antenna builders.

For use on the lower frequency amateur bands — notably 160 and 80 meters — it is not always practical to erect a full-size vertical. In such instances it is satisfactory to accept a shorter radiating element and employ some form of loading to obtain an electrical length of one's choice. Most constructors design a system that contains a ¼-wavelength driven element. However, good results and lower radiation angles are sometimes realized when using a 3/8- or ½-wavelength vertical. At the lower amateur frequencies the larger verticals become prohibitive, especially in urban areas where zoning ordinances may exist, and where limited acreage may rule out the installation of guy-wire systems.

Fig. 25 provides curves for the physical height of verticals in wavelength versus radiation resistance and reactance. The plots are based on perfectly conducting ground, a condition seldom realized in practical installations. It can be seen that the shorter the radiator, the lower the radiation resistance — with 6 ohms being typical for a 0.1-wavelength antenna. The lower the radiation resistance, the more the antenna efficiency depends on ground conductivity. Also, the bandwidth decreases markedly as the length is reduced toward the left of the scale in Fig. 25. Difficulty is also experienced in developing a suitable matching network when the radiation resistance is very low.

Illustrations of various vertical-antenna radiation patterns are given in Fig. 26. The example at A is for a quarter-wavelength radiator over a theoretically ideal ground. The dashed lines show the current distribution, including the image portion below ground. The image can be equated to one half of a dipole antenna, with the vertical radiator representing the remaining dipole half.

The illustration at B characterizes the pattern of a half-wavelength vertical. It can be seen that the radiation angle is somewhat lower than that of the quarter-wavelength version at A. The lower angles enhance the DX capability of the antenna. Two half wavelengths in phase are shown in Fig. 26 at C and D. From a practical point of view, few amateurs could erect such an antenna unless it was built for use on the higher HF bands, such as 20, 15 or 10 meters. The very low radiation angle is excellent for DXing, however.

Full-Size Vertical Antennas

When it is practical to erect a full-size vertical antenna, the forms shown in Fig. 27 are worthy of consideration. The example at A is the well-known vertical ground plane. The ground system consists of four or more above-ground radial wires against which the driven element is worked. The length of the radials and the driven element is derived from the standard equation

$$L \text{ (feet)} = \frac{234}{f \text{ (MHz)}}$$

It has been established generally that with four equidistant radial wires drooped at approximately 45° (Fig. 27A) the feed-point impedance is roughly 50 ohms. When the radials are at right angles to the radiator (Fig. 27B) the impedance approaches 36 ohms. The major advantage in this type of vertical antenna over a ground-mounted type is that the system can be elevated well above nearby conductive objects (power lines, trees, buildings, etc.). When drooping radials are utilized they can be used as guy wires for the mast that supports the antenna. The coaxial cable shield braid is connected to the radials, and the center conductor is common to the driven element.

The Marconi antenna shown in Fig. 27C is the classic form taken by a ground-mounted vertical. It can be grounded at the base and shunt fed, or it can be isolated from ground, as shown, and series fed. This antenna depends on an effective ground system for efficient performance. The subject of ground screens is treated later in this chapter. If a perfect ground were located below the antenna, the feed impedance would be near 36 ohms. In a practical case, owing to imperfect ground, the impedance is more apt to be in the vicinity of 50 to 75 ohms.

A gamma feed system for a grounded ¼-wavelength vertical is presented in Fig. 27D. Some rules of thumb for arriving at workable gamma-arm and capacitor di-

Fig. 26 — Elevation plane responses for a quarter-wavelength vertical antenna (A), a ½-wavelength type (B) and two half waves in phase (C and D). It can be seen that the examples at B and D provide more radiated power at low radiation angles than the version at A.

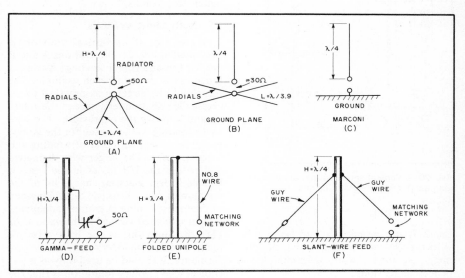

Fig. 27 — Various types of vertical antennas.

mensions are to make the rod length 0.04 to 0.05 wavelength, its diameter ⅓ to ½ that of the driven element and the center-to-center spacing between the gamma arm and the driven element roughly 0.007 wavelength. The capacitance of C1 at a 50-ohm matched condition will be some 7 pF per meter. The absolute value at C1 will depend on whether the vertical is resonant and on the precise value of the radiation resistance. Generally, best results can be had when the radiator is approximately three percent shorter than the resonant length.

Amateur antenna towers lend themselves well to use as shunt-fed verticals, even though an HF band beam antenna may be mounted on the tower. The overall system should be close to resonance at the desired operating frequency if gamma feed is to be used. The HF-band beam will contribute somewhat to top loading of the tower. The natural resonance of such a system can be checked by dropping a no. 12 or 14 wire down from the top of the tower (making it common to the tower top) to form a folded unipole (Fig. 27E). A four- or five-turn link can be inserted between the lower end of the drop wire and the ground system, then a dip meter inserted in the link to observe the resonant frequency. If the tower is equipped with guy wires, they should be broken up with strain insulators to prevent unwanted loading of the vertical. In such cases where the tower and beam antennas are not able to provide ¼-wavelength resonance, portions of the top guy wires can be used as top-loading capaci-

Fig. 28 — Vertical antennas that are less than one quarter wavelength in height.

Fig. 29 — At A are the details for the tubing section of the loading assembly. Illustration B shows the top hat and its spokes. The longer the spokes, the better.

tance. It will be necessary to experiment with the guy-wire lengths (using the dip-meter technique) while determining the proper dimensions.

A folded-unipole type of vertical is depicted at E of Fig. 27. This system has the advantage of increased feed-point impedance. Furthermore, a Transmatch can be connected between the bottom of the drop wire and the ground system to permit operation on more than one band. For example, if the tower is resonant on 80 meters, it can be used as shown on 160 and 40 meters with reasonable results, even though it is not electrically long enough on 160. The drop wire need not be a specific distance from the tower, but spacings between 12 and 30 inches are suggested.

The method of feed shown at Fig. 27F is commonly referred to as "slant-wire feed." The guy wires and the tower combine to provide quarter-wave resonance. A matching network is placed between the lower end of one guy wire and ground and adjusted for an SWR of 1. It does not matter at which level on the tower the guy wires are connected, assuming that

the Transmatch is capable of effecting a match to 50 ohms.

Physically Short Verticals

A group of short vertical radiators is presented in Fig. 28. Illustrations A and B are for top and center loading. A capacitance hat is shown in each example. The hat should be as large as practical to increase the radiation resistance of the antenna and improve the bandwidth. The wire in the loading coil is chosen for the largest gauge consistent with ease of winding and coil-form size. The larger wire diameters will reduce the I^2R losses in the system. The coil-form material should be of the medium or high dielectric type. Phenolic or fiberglass tubing is entirely adequate.

A base-loaded vertical is shown at C of Fig. 28. Since this is the least effective method of loading in terms of antenna performance, it should be used only as a last choice. The primary limitation is that the current portion of the vertical exists in the coil rather than the driven element. With center loading the portion of the antenna below the coil carries current, and with the top loading version the entire vertical element carries current. Since the current part of the antenna is responsible for most of the radiating, base loading is the least effective of the three methods. The radiation resistance of the coil-loaded antennas shown in Fig. 28 is usually less than 16 ohms.

A method for using guy wires to top load a short vertical is illustrated in Fig. 28 at D. This system works well with gamma feed. The loading wires are trimmed to provide an electrical quarter wavelength for the overall system. This method of loading will result in a higher radiation resistance and greater bandwidth than the systems shown at A through C of Fig. 28. If any HF band or VHF array is atop the tower, it will simply contribute to the top loading.

A tri-wire unipole is shown at E of Fig.

28. Two no. 8 drop wires are connected to the top of the tower and brought to ground level. The wires can be spaced any convenient distance from the tower — normally 12 to 30 inches from one side. C1 is adjusted for an SWR of 1. This type of vertical has a fairly narrow bandwidth, but because C1 can be motor driven and controlled from the operating position, QSY-ing is accomplished easily. This technique will not be suitable for matching to 50-ohm line unless the tower is less than an electrical quarter wavelength high.

A different method for top loading is shown at F of Fig. 28. W9UCW described this system in "The Minooka Special," December 1974 *QST*. An extension is used at the top of the tower to effect an electrical quarter-wavelength vertical. L1 is a loading coil with sufficient inductance to provide antenna resonance. This type of antenna lends itself nicely to operation on 160 meters.

A method for effecting the top-loading shown in Fig. 28F is illustrated in the drawing of Fig. 29. Pipe section D is mated with the mast above the HF-band beam antenna. A loading coil is wound on solid Plexiglas rod or phenolic rod (item C), then clamped inside the collet (B). An aluminum slug (part A) is clamped inside item B. The top part of A is bored and threaded for a 3/8 inch × 24 thread stud. This will permit a standard 8-foot stainless-steel mobile whip to be threaded into item A above the loading coil. The capacitance hat (Fig. 29B) can be made from a 1/4-inch-thick brass or aluminum plate. It may be round or square. Lengths of 1/8-inch brazing rod can be threaded for a 6-32 format to permit the rods to be screwed into the edge of the aluminum plate. The plate contains a row of holes along its perimeter, each having been tapped for a 6-32 thread. The capacitance hat is affixed to item A by means of the 8-foot whip antenna. The whip will increase the effective height of the vertical antenna.

Cables and Control Wires on Towers

Most vertical antennas of the type shown in Fig. 28 consist of towers and HF or VHF beam antennas. The rotator control wires and the coaxial feeders to the top of the tower will not affect antenna performance adversely. In fact, they become a part of the composite antenna. To prevent unwanted rf currents from following the wires into the shack, simply dress them close to the tower legs and bring them to ground level. This decouples the wires at RF. The wires should then be routed along the earth surface (or buried underground) to the operating position. It is not necessary to use bypass capacitors or RF chokes in the rotator control leads if this is done, even when maximum legal power is employed.

Variations in Verticals

A number of configurations qualify for use as vertical antennas even though the radiators are fashioned from lengths of wire. Fig. 30A shows a flat-top T vertical. Dimension H should be as tall as possible for best results. The horizontal section, L, is adjusted to a length which provides resonance. Maximum radiation is polarized vertically despite the horizontal top-loading wire. A variation of the T antenna is depicted at B of Fig. 30. This antenna is commonly referred to as an inverted L. Vertical member H should be as long as possible. L is added to provide an electrical quarter wavelength overall. Some amateurs believe that a 3/8-wavelength version of this antenna is more effective, since the current portion of the wire is elevated higher above ground than is the case with a quarter-wavelength wire.

Half-Sloper Antenna

A basic-half sloper antenna is shown at C of Fig. 30. The wire portion represents one half of a dipole. The feed point is between the tower leg and the upper end of the slope wire, with the coax shield braid being connected to the tower. The feed-point impedance is generally between 30 and 60 ohms, depending on the length of the wire, the tower height and the enclosed angle between the slope wire and the tower. The tower constitutes a portion of this antenna, and will have a voltage maximum somewhere between the feed point and ground. The half sloper has been found useful for close-in work as well as for DXing. A VSWR as low as 1.5:1 can be obtained (using 50-ohm coax feed line) with the system of Fig. 30C by experimenting with the slope-wire length and the enclosed angle. This assumes there are no guy wires that are common to the tower. If guys are used they should be insulated from the tower and broken into nonresonant lengths for the band of operation.

Many amateurs are likely to have towers that support HF-band Yagis or quad

beams. The conductors situated above the sloper feed point have a marked effect on the tuning of the sloper system. The beam antenna becomes a portion of the overall tower/sloper system. Although the presence of the beam seems to have no appreciable effect on the radiation pattern of the sloper, it does greatly affect the VSWR. If a low VSWR can't be obtained for a given amateur antenna installation, the system illustrated in Fig. 30D can be applied.

The sloper is erected in the usual manner, but a second wire (L2) is added. It is connected to the tower at the antenna feed point, but insulated at the low end. L2 plus the tower constitutes the missing half of the dipole. This half is effectively a fanned element (similar to a conical element) and tends to increase the bandwidth of the sloper system over that which can be obtained with the version at C. The "compensating wire" (L2) is spaced approximately 90° from L1, and is roughly 30° away from the side of the tower. The VSWR can be brought to a low value (usually 1:1) by varying the L2/tower and L1/L2 enclosed angles. The degree of these angles will depend on the tower height, the beam atop the tower and the ground condition below the system.

Tests indicate the sloper to be effective on its harmonics for DX and local work. If harmonic operation is planned, the 50-ohm coaxial feeder should be replaced with open-wire line, which is coupled to the transmitter by means of a Transmatch. With open-wire feed, the L2 compensating wire of Fig. 30D will not be necessary.

Best performance will be had when the base of the tower is well grounded. Buried radials are highly recommended as part of the ground system. Operation on 160 meters can be had by feeding the low end of L2. The bandwidth of the system in Fig. 30 will be approximately 50 kHz on 160 meters, 100 kHz on 80 meters, 200 kHz on 40 meters, and so on, between 2:1 VSWR points.

Ground Systems

The importance of an effective ground system for vertical antennas cannot be emphasized too strongly. However, is it not always possible to install a radial network that approaches the ideal. A poor ground is better than no ground at all, and therefore the amateur should experiment with whatever is physically possible rather than ruling out vertical antennas. It is often possible to obtain excellent DX results with practically no ground system at all.

Although the matter of less-than-optimum ground systems could be debated almost endlessly, some practical rules of thumb are in order for those wishing to erect vertical antennas. Generally a large number of shorter radials offers a better ground system than a few longer ones. For example, 8 radials of 1/8 λ are preferred over 4 radials of ¼ λ. If the physical height

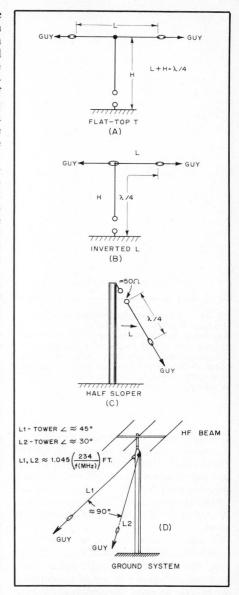

Fig. 30 — Some variations in vertical antennas that offer excellent performance.

of the vertical is an eighth wavelength, the radial wires should be of the same length and dispersed uniformly from the base of the tower.

The conductor size of the radials is not especially significant. Wire gauges from no. 4 to no. 20 have been used successfully by amateurs. Copper wire is preferred, but where soil is low in acid or alkali, aluminum wire can be used. The wires can be bare or insulated, and they can be laid on the earth's surface or buried a few inches below ground. The insulated wires will have greater longevity by virtue of reduced corrosion and dissolution from soil chemicals.

If time and expense are not prime considerations, the amateur should bury as much ground wire as possible. Some operators have literally miles of wire buried radially beneath their vertical antennas.

Fig. 31 — A two-band trap vertical antenna. The trap should be resonated as a parallel resonant circuit at the center of the operating range for the higher frequency band; typical component reactances range from 100 to 300 ohms. At the lower frequency the trap will act as a loading inductor, adding electrical length to the total antenna.

When property dimensions do not allow a classic installation of equally spaced radial wires, they can be placed in the ground wherever space will permit. They may run away from the antenna in only one or two compass directions. Results will still exceed those of when no ground system is used.

A single ground rod, or group of them bonded together, is seldom as effective as a collection of random-length radial wires. In some instances a group of short radial wires can be used in combination with ground rods driven into the soil near the base of the antenna. Bear in mind, though, that RF currents at MF and HF seldom penetrate the earth more than several inches. The power company ground can be tied in, and if a metal fence skirts the property it can also be used as part of the ground system. A good rule is to use anything that will serve as a ground when developing a radial ground system.

All radial wires must be connected together at the base of the vertical antenna. The electrical bond needs to be of low resistance. Best results will be obtained when the wires are soldered together at the junction point. When a grounded vertical is used, the ground wires should be affixed securely to the base of the driven element. A lawn edging tool is excellent for cutting slits in the soil when laying radial wires.

Trap Verticals

Although a full-size, single-band antenna is more effective than a lumped-constant one, there is justification for using trap types of multiband antennas. The concept is especially useful to operators who have limited antenna space on their property. Multiband compromise antennas are also appealing to persons who engage in portable operation and are unwilling to transport large amounts of antenna hardware to the field.

The 2-band trap vertical antenna of Fig. 31 operates in much the same manner as a trap dipole or trap-style Yagi. The notable difference is that the vertical is one half of a dipole. The radial system (in-ground or above ground) functions as a ground plane for the antenna, and represents the missing half of the dipole. Therefore, the more effective the ground system, the better the antenna performance.

Trap verticals are adjusted as quarter-wavelength radiators. The portion of the antenna below the trap is adjusted as a quarter-wavelength radiator at the higher proposed operating frequency. That is, a 20/15-meter trap vertical would be a resonant quarter wavelength at 15 meters from the feed point to the bottom of the trap. The trap and that portion of the antenna above the trap (plus the 15-meter section below the trap) constitute the complete antenna during 20-meter operation. But because the trap is in the circuit, the overall physical length of the vertical antenna will be slightly less than that of a single-band, full-size 20-meter vertical.

Traps

The trap functions as the name implies: It traps the 15-meter energy and confines it to the part of the antenna below the trap. During 20-meter operation it allows the RF energy to reach all of the antenna. Therefore, the trap in this example should be tuned as a parallel resonant circuit to 21 MHz. At this frequency it divorces the top section of the vertical from the lower section because it presents a high-impedance (barrier) at 21 MHz. Generally, the trap inductor and capacitor have a reactance of 100 to 300 ohms. Within that range it is not critical.

The trap is built and adjusted separately from the antenna. It should be resonated at the center of the portion of the band to be operated. Thus, if one's favorite part of the 15-meter band is between 21,000 and 21,100 kHz, the trap would be tuned to 21,050 kHz.

Resonance is checked by using a dip meter and detecting the dipper signal in a calibrated receiver. Once the trap is adjusted it can be installed in the antenna, and no further adjustment will be required. It is easy, however, to be misled after the system is assembled: Attempts to check the trap with a dip meter will suggest that the trap has moved much lower in frequency (approximately 5 MHz lower in a 20/15-meter vertical). This is because the trap has become absorbed into the overall antenna, and the resultant resonance is that of the total antenna. Ignore this phenomenon.

Multiband operation for three or four bands is quite practical by using the appropriate number of traps and tubing sections. The construction and adjustment procedure is the same, regardless of the number of bands covered. The highest frequency trap is always closest to the feed end of the antenna, and the next to lowest frequency trap is always the farthest from the feed point. As the operating frequency is progressively lowered, more traps and more tubing sections become a functional part of the antenna.

The trap should be weatherproofed to prevent moisture from detuning it. Several coatings of high dielectric compound, such as Polystyrene Q Dope, are effective. Alternatively, a protective sleeve of heat-shrink tubing can be applied to the coil after completion. The coil form for the trap should be of high dielectric quality and be rugged enough to sustain stress during periods of wind.

The trap capacitor must be capable of withstanding the RF voltage developed across it. The amount of voltage present will depend on the operating power of the transmitter. Fixed-value ceramic transmitting capacitors are suitable for most power levels if they are rated at 5000 to 10,000 volts. A length of RG-58/U or RG-59/U coax cable can be used successfully up to 200 watts. (Check to see how many picofarads per foot your cable is rated at before cutting it for the trap.) RG-8/U or RG-11/U cable is recommended for the trap capacitor at powers in excess of 200 watts. The advantage of using coax cable is that it can be trimmed easily to adjust the trap capacitance.

Large-diameter copper magnet wire is suggested for the trap coil. The heavier the wire gauge the lower the trap losses and the higher the Q. The larger wire sizes will reduce coil heating.

YAGI AND QUAD DIRECTIVE ANTENNAS

Most of the antennas described earlier in this chapter have unity gain or just slightly more. For the purpose of obtaining gain and directivity it is convenient to use the Yagi-Uda or cubical quad types of HF-band beam antennas. The former is commonly called a Yagi and the latter is referred to as a quad in the amateur vernacular.

Most operators prefer to erect these antennas for horizontal polarization, but they can be used as vertically polarized arrays as well merely by rotating the elements by 90°. In effect, the beam antenna is turned on its side for vertical polarity. The number of elements employed will depend on the gain desired and the capability of the supporting structure to contain the array safely. Many amateurs obtain satisfactory results with only two elements in a beam antenna, while others have several

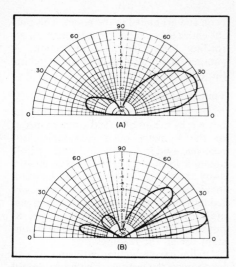

Fig. 32 — Elevation-plane response of a three-element Yagi placed ½ wavelength above a perfect ground (A) and the same antenna spaced one wavelength above ground (B). Pattern calculations courtesy of "Annie." [2]

elements operating for a single amateur band.

Regardless of the number of elements used, the height-above-ground considerations discussed earlier for dipole antennas remain valid with respect to the angle of radiation. This is demonstrated in Fig. 32 at A and B where a comparison of radiation characteristics is given for a three-element Yagi at one-half and one wavelength above a perfectly conducting ground. It can be seen that the higher antennas (Fig. 32B) has a lobe that is more favorable for DX work (roughly 15°) than the larger lobe of Fig. 32A (approximately 30°). The pattern at B shows that some useful high-angle radiation exists also, and the higher lobe is suitable for short-skip contacts when propagation conditions dictate the need.

A free-space azimuth pattern for the same antenna is provided in Fig. 33. The back-lobe pattern reveals that most of the power is concentrated in the forward lobe. The power difference dictates the front-to-back ratio in decibels. It is infrequent that two 3-element Yagis with different element spacings will yield the same lobe patterns. The pattern of Fig. 33 is shown only for illustrative purposes.

Parasitic Excitation

In most of these arrangements the additional elements receive power by induction or radiation from the driven element and reradiate it in the proper phase relationship to give the desired effect. These elements are called parasitic elements, as contrasted to the driven elements, which receive power directly from the transmitter through the transmission line.

The parasitic element is called a director when it reinforces radiation on a line

²See footnote 1 earlier in this chapter.

pointing to it from the driven element, and a reflector when the reverse is the case. Whether the parasitic element is a director or reflector depends on the parasitic-element tuning, which usually is adjusted by changing its length.

Gain vs. Spacing

The gain of an antenna with parasitic elements varies with the spacing and tuning of the elements. Thus, for any given spacing, there is a tuning condition that will give maximum gain at this spacing. The maximum front-to-back ratio seldom, if ever, occurs at the same condition that gives maximum forward gain. The impedance of the driven element also varies with the tuning and spacing, and thus the antenna system must be tuned to its final condition before the match between the line and the antenna can be completed. The tuning and matching may interact to some extent, however, and it is usually necessary to run through the adjustments several times to ensure that the best possible tuning has been obtained.

Two-Element Beams

A two-element beam is useful where space or other considerations prevent the use of the larger structure required for a three-element beam. The general practice is to tune the parasitic element as a reflector and space it about 0.15 wavelength from the driven element, although some successful antennas have been built with 0.1-wavelength spacing and director tuning. Gain vs. element spacing for a two-element antenna is given in Fig. 34 for the special case where the parasitic element is resonant. It is indicative of the performance to be expected under maximum-gain tuning conditions.

Three-Element Beams

A theoretical investigation of the three-element case (director, driven element and reflector) has indicated a maximum gain of slightly more than 7 dB. A number of experimental investigations has shown that the optimum spacing between the driven element and reflector is in the region of 0.15 to 0.25 wavelength, with 0.2 wavelength representing probably the best overall choice. With 0.2-wavelength reflec-

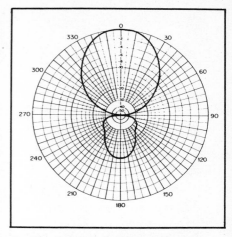

Fig. 33 — Azimuth-plane pattern of a three-element Yagi in free space. Pattern calculation courtesy of "Annie."

Fig. 34 — Gain vs. element spacing for an antenna and one parasitic element. The reference point, 0 dB, is the field strength from a half-wave antenna alone. The greatest gain is in the direction A at spacings of less than 0.14 wavelength, and in direction B at greater spacings. The front-to-back ratio is the difference in decibels between curves A and B. Variation in radiation resistance of the driven element is also shown. These curves are for a self-resonant parasitic element. At most spacings the gain as a reflector can be increased by slight lengthening of the parasitic element; the gain as a director can be increased by shortening. This also improves the front-to-back ratio.

tor spacing, Fig. 35 shows that the gain variation with director spacing is not especially critical. Also, the overall length of the array (boom length in the case of a

Fig. 35 — General relationship of gain of three-element Yagi versus director spacing, the reflector being fixed at 0.2 wavelength.

Fig. 36 — Element lengths for a three-element beam. These lengths will hold closely for the tubing elements supported at or near the center.

rotatable antenna) can be anywhere between 0.35 and 0.45 wavelength with no appreciable difference in gain.

Wide spacing of both elements is desirable not only because it results in high gain but also because adjustment of tuning or element length is less critical and the input resistance of the driven element is higher than with close spacing. A higher input resistance improves the efficiency of the antenna and makes a greater bandwidth possible. However, a total antenna length, director to reflector, of more than 0.3

wavelength at frequencies of the order of 14 MHz introduces considerable difficulty from a construction standpoint. Lengths of 0.25 to 0.3 wavelength are therefore used frequently for this band, even though they are less than optimum.

In general, the antenna gain drops off less rapidly when the reflector length is increased beyond the optimum value than it does for a corresponding decrease below the optimum value. The opposite is true of a director. It is therefore advisable to err, if necessary, on the long side for a reflector and on the short side for a director. This also tends to make the antenna performance less dependent on the exact frequency at which it is operated: An increase above the design frequency has the same effect as increasing the length of both parasitic elements, while a decrease in frequency has the same effect as shortening both elements. By making the director slightly short and the reflector slightly long, there will be a greater spread between the upper and lower frequencies at which the gain starts to show a rapid decrease.

When the overall length has been decided on, the element lengths can be found by referring to Fig. 36. The lengths determined by these charts will vary slightly in actual practice with the element diameter and the method of supporting the elements. The tuning of a beam should always be checked after installation. However, the lengths obtained by the use of the charts will be close to correct in practically all cases, and they can be used without checking if the beam is difficult to access.

Table 1 can be used to determine the lengths needed for 4-element Yagis. Both CW and phone lengths are included for the three bands, 20, 15 and 10 meters. The 0.2-wavelength spacing will provide greater bandwidth than the 0.15 spacing. Antenna gain is essentially the same with either spacing. The element lengths given will be the same whether the beam has two, three or four elements. It is recommended that plumbers delight type construction be used, where all the elements are mounted directly on and grounded to the boom. This puts the entire array at dc ground potential, affording better lightning protection. A gamma section can be used for matching the feed line to the array.

Tuning Adjustments

The preferable method for checking the beam is by means of a field-strength meter, or the S meter of a communications receiver, used in conjunction with a dipole antenna located at least 10 wavelengths away and as high or higher than the beam that is being checked. A few watts of power fed into the antenna will give a useful signal at the observation point, and the power input to the transmitter should be held constant for all the readings.

Preliminary matching adjustments can be done on the ground. The beam should be set up so the reflector element rests on the earth, with the remaining elements in a vertical configuration. In other words, the beam should be aimed straight up. The matching system is then adjusted for a 1:1 SWR between the feed line and driven element. When the antenna is raised to its operating height, only slight touch-up of the matching network should be required.

A great deal has been printed about the need for tuning elements of a Yagi-type beam. However, experience has shown that for Yagi arrays made from metal tubing, the lengths given in Fig. 36 and Table 1 are close enough to the desired length that no further tuning should be required.

Simple Systems — The Rotary Beam

Two- and three-element systems are popular for rotary-beam antennas, where the entire antenna system is rotated, to permit its gain and directivity to be utilized for any compass direction. The antennas may be mounted either horizontally (with the plane containing the elements parallel to the earth) or vertically.

A four-element beam will give still more gain than a three-element one, provided the support is sufficient for about 0.2 wavelength spacing between elements. The

---

Table 1

Element Lengths for 20, 15 and 10 Meters, Phone and CW

Freq. (kHz)	Driven Element		Reflector		First Director		Second Director	
	A	B	A	B	A	B	A	B
14,050	33' 5-3/8''	33' 8''	35' 2-1/2''	35' 5-1/4'	31' 9-3/8''	31' 11-5/8''	31' 1-1/4''	31' 3-5/8''
14,250	32' 11-3/4''	33' 2-1/4''	34' 8-1/2''	34' 11-1/4''	31' 4''	31' 6-3/8''	30' 8''	30' 10-1/2''
21,050	22' 4''	22' 5-5/8''	23' 6''	23' 7-3/4''	21' 2-3/4''	21' 4''	20' 9-1/8''	20' 10-7/8''
21,300	22' 3/4''	22' 2-3/8''	23' 2-5/8''	23' 4-1/2''	20' 11-1/2''	21' 1''	20' 6-1/4''	20' 7-3/4''
28,050	16' 9''	16' 10-1/4''	17' 7-5/8''	17' 8-7/8''	15' 11''	16'	15' 7''	15' 9-1/2''
28,600	16' 5-1/4''	16' 6-3/8''	17' 3-1/2''	17' 4-3/4''	15' 7-1/4''	15' 8-1/2''	15' 3-3/8''	15' 4-1/2''

A: | 0.2 | 0.2 | 0.2 |

B: | 0.15 | 0.15 | 0.15 |

These lengths are for 0.2- or 0.15-wavelength element spacing.

To convert ft to meters multiply ft × 0.3048.
Convert in to mm by multiplying in × 25.4.

tuning for maximum gain involves many variables, and complete gain and tuning data are elusive.

The elements in close-spaced arrays (less than ¼-wavelength element spacing) preferably should be made of tubing of ½ to 1 inch diameter. A conductor of large diameter not only has less ohmic resistance but also has lower Q; both these factors are important in close-spaced arrays because the impedance of the driven element usually is quite low compared to that of a simple dipole antenna. With three- and four-element close-spaced arrays the radiation resistance of the driven element may be so low that ohmic losses in the conductor can consume an appreciable fraction of the power.

Feeding the Rotary Beam

Any of the usual methods of feed (described later under Impedance Matching) can be applied to the driven element of a rotary beam. The popular choices for feeding a beam are the gamma match with series capacitor, the T match with series capacitors, and a half-wavelength phasing section, as shown in Fig. 37. These methods are preferred over any others because they permit adjustment of the matching and the use of coaxial-line feed. The variable capacitors can be housed in small plastic cups for weatherproofing; receiving types with close spacing can be used at powers up to a few hundred watts. Maximum capacitance required is usually 140 pF at 14 MHz and proportionally less at the higher frequencies.

If physically possible, it is better to adjust the matching device after the antenna has been installed at its ultimate height, since a match made with the antenna near the ground may not hold for the same antenna in the air.

Sharpness of Resonance

Peak performance of a multielement parasitic array depends on proper phasing or tuning of the elements, which can be exact for one frequency only. Close-spaced arrays usually are quite sharp-tuning because of the low radiation resistance. The frequency range over which optimum results can be obtained is only of the order of one or two percent of the resonant frequency, or up to about 500 kHz at 28 MHz. However, the antenna can be made to work satisfactorily over a wider frequency range by adjusting the director or directors to give maximum gain at the highest frequency to be covered, and by adjusting the reflector to give optimum gain at the lowest frequency. This sacrifices some gain at all frequencies but maintains more uniform gain over a wider frequency range.

The use of large-diameter conductors will broaden the response curve of an array, because a larger diameter lowers the Q. This causes the reactances of the elements to change rather slowly with frequency, with the result that the tuning stays near

Fig. 37 — Illustrations of gamma and T matching systems. At A, the gamma rod is adjusted along with C until the lowest SWR is obtained. A T match is shown at B. It is the same as two gamma-match rods. The rods and C1 and C2 are adjusted alternately for a 1:1 SWR. A coaxial 4:1 balun transformer is shown at C. A toroidal balun can be used in place of the coax model shown. The toroidal version has a broader frequency range than the coaxial one. The T match is adjusted for 200 ohms and the balun steps this balanced value down to 50 ohms, unbalanced. Or the T match can be set for 300 ohms, and the balun used to step this down to 75 ohms unbalanced. Dimensions for the gamma and T match rods are not given by formula. Their lengths and spacing will depend on the tubing size used, and the spacing of the parasitic elements of the beam. Capacitors C, C1 and C2 can be 140 pF for 14-MHz beams. Somewhat less capacitance will be needed at 21 and 28 MHz.

Fig. 38 — Information on building a quad or a delta-loop antenna. The antennas are electrically similar, but the delta-loop uses plumber's delight construction.

optimum over a considerably wider frequency range than with wire conductors.

Delta Loops and Quad Beams

One of the more effective DX arrays is called the cubical quad, or simply, quad antenna. It consists of two or more square loops of wire, each supported by a bamboo or fiberglass cross-arm assembly. The loops are a quarter wavelength per side (full wavelength overall). One loop is driven and the other serves as a parasitic element — usually a reflector. A variation of the quad is called the delta loop. The electrical properties of both antennas are the same, generally speaking, though some operators report better DX results with the delta loop. Both antennas are shown in Fig. 38. They differ mainly in their physical properties,

one being of plumber's delight construction, while the other uses insulating support members. One or more directors can be added to either antenna if additional gain and directivity is desired, though most operators use the two-element arrangement.

It is possible to interlace quads or "deltas" for two or more bands, but if this is done the formulas given in Fig. 38 may have to be changed slightly to compensate for the proximity effect of the second antenna. For quads the length of the full-wave loop can be computed from

$$\text{Full-wave loop (ft)} = \frac{1005}{f \text{ (MHz)}}$$

If multiple arrays are used, each antenna should be tuned separately for maximum forward gain, as noted on a field-strength meter. The reflector stub on the quad should be adjusted for this condition. The delta loop gamma match should be adjusted for a 1:1 SWR. No reflector tuning is needed. The delta loop antenna has a broader frequency response than the quad, and holds at an SWR of 1.5:1 or better across the band for which it is constructed.

The resonance of the quad antenna can be found by checking the frequency at which the lowest SWR occurs. The element length (driven element) can be adjusted for resonance in the most-used portion of the band by lengthening or shortening it.

A two-element quad or delta loop anten-na compares favorably with a three-element Yagi array in terms of gain (see *QST,* May 1963 and January 1969, for additional information). The quad and delta-loop antennas perform very well at 50 and 144 MHz. A discussion of radiation patterns and gain, quads vs. Yagis, was presented by Lindsay in May 1968 *QST.*

VHF and UHF Antennas

Improving an antenna system is one of the most productive moves open to the VHF enthusiast. It can increase transmitting range, improve reception, reduce interference problems and bring other practical benefits. The work itself is by no means the least attractive part of the job. Even with high-gain antennas, experimentation is greatly simplified at VHF and UHF because an array is a workable size, and much can be learned about the nature and adjustment of antennas. No large investment in test equipment is necessary.

Whether we buy or build our antennas, we soon find that there is no one "best" design for all purposes. Selecting the antenna best suited to our needs involves much more than scanning gain figures and prices in a manufacturer's catalog. The first step should be to establish priorities.

Gain

Shaping the pattern of an antenna to concentrate radiated energy, or received-signal pickup, in some directions at the expense of others is the only possible way to develop gain. This is best explained by starting with the hypothetical isotropic antenna, which would radiate equally in all directions. A point source of light illuminating the inside of a globe uniformly, from its center, is a visual analogy. No practical antenna can do this, so all antennas have gain over isotropic (dBi). A half-wave dipole in free space has a gain of 2.1 dBi. If we can plot the radiation pattern of an antenna in all planes, we can compute its gain, so quoting it with respect to isotropic is a logical base for agreement and understanding. It is rarely possible to erect a half-wave antenna that has anything approaching a free-space pattern; this fact is responsible for much of the confusion about true antenna gain.

Radiation patterns can be controlled in various ways. One is to use two or more driven elements, fed in phase. Such collinear arrays provide gain without markedly sharpening the frequency response, compared to that of a single element. More gain per element, but with a sacrifice in frequency coverage, is obtained by placing parasitic elements, longer and shorter than the driven one, in the plane of the first element, but not driven from the feed line. The reflector and directors of a Yagi array are highly frequency sensitive and such an antenna is at its best over frequency changes of less than one percent of the operating frequency.

Frequency Response

Ability to work over an entire VHF band may be important in some type of work. The response of an antenna element can be broadened somewhat by increasing the conductor diameter, and by tapering it to something approximating a cigar shape, but this is done mainly with simple antennas. More practically, wide frequency coverage may be a reason to select a collinear array, rather than a Yagi. On the other hand, the growing tendency to channelize operations in small segments of our bands tends to place broad frequency coverage low on the priority list of most VHF stations.

Radiation Pattern

Antenna radiation can be made omnidirectional, bidirectional, practically unidirectional, or anything between these conditions. A VHF net operator may find an omnidirectional system almost a necessity, but it may be a poor choice otherwise. Noise pickup and other interference problems tend to be greater with such antennas, and those having some gain are especially bad in these respects. Maximum gain and low radiation angle are usually prime interests of the weak-signal DX aspirant. A clean pattern, with lowest possible pickup and radiation off the sides and back, may be important in high-activity areas, or where the noise level is high.

Height Gain

In general, the higher an antenna is installed, the better in VHF antenna installations. If raising the antenna clears its view over nearby obstructions, it may make dramatic improvements in coverage. Within reason, greater height is almost always worth its cost, but height gain must be balanced against increased transmission-line loss. Line losses are considerable at VHF, and they increase with frequency. The best available line may be none too good, if the run is long in terms of wavelength. Give line-loss information, shown in table form in Chapter 16, close scrutiny in any antenna planning.

Physical Size

A given antenna design for 432 MHz will have the same gain as one for 144 MHz, but being only one-third the size it will intercept only one-third as much energy in receiving. Thus, to be equal in communication effectiveness, the 432-MHz array should be at least equal in size to the 144-MHz one, which will require roughly three times as many elements. With all the extra difficulties involved in going higher in frequency, it is well to be on the big side in building an antenna for the higher bands.

DESIGN FACTORS

Having sorted out objectives in a general way, we face decisions on specifics, such as polarization, type of transmission line, matching methods and mechanical design.

Polarization

Whether to position the antenna elements vertically or horizontally has been a moot point since early VHF pioneering. Tests show little evidence on which to set up a uniform polarization policy. On long paths there is no consistent advantage, either way. Shorter paths tend to yield higher signal levels with horizontal in some kinds of terrain. Man-made noise, especially ignition interference, tends to be lower with horizontal. Verticals are markedly simpler to use in omnidirectional systems and in mobile work.

Early VHF communication was largely vertical, but horizontal gained favor when directional arrays became widely used. The major trend to FM and repeaters, particularly in the 144-MHz band, has tipped the balance in favor of verticals in mobile work and for repeaters. Horizontal predominates in other communication on 50 MHz and higher frequencies. It is well to check in advance in any new area in which you expect to operate, however, as some localities still use vertical almost exclusively. A circuit loss of 20 dB or more can be expected with cross-polarization.

Transmission Lines

There are two main categories of

transmission lines, balanced and unbalanced. Balanced lines include open-wire lines separated by insulating spreaders, and twin-lead, in which the wires are embedded in solid or foamed insulation. Line losses result from ohmic resistance, radiation from the line and deficiencies in the insulation. Large conductors, closely spaced in terms of wavelength, and using a minimum of insulation, make the best balanced lines. Impedances are mainly 300 to 500 ohms. Balanced lines are best in straight runs. If bends are unavoidable, the angles should be as obtuse as possible. Care should be taken to prevent one wire from coming closer to metal objects than the other. Wire spacing should be less than 1/20 wavelength.

Properly built open-wire line can operate with very low loss in VHF and even UHF installations. A total line loss under 2 dB per hundred feet at 432 MHz is readily obtained. A line made of no. 12 wire, spaced ¾ inch or less with Teflon spreaders, and running essentially straight from antenna to station, can be better than anything but the most expensive coax, at a fraction of the cost. This assumes the use of baluns to match into and out of the line, with a short length of quality coax for the moving section from the top of the tower to the antenna. A similar 144-MHz setup could have a line loss under 1 dB.

Small coax such as RG-58/U or -59/U should never be used in VHF work if the run is more than a few feet. Half-inch lines (RG-8/U or -11/U) work fairly well at 50 MHz, and are acceptable for 144-MHz runs of 50 feet or less. If these lines have foam rather than solid insulation they are about 30 percent better. Aluminum-jacket lines with large inner conductors and foam insulation are well worth their cost. They are readily waterproofed, and can last almost indefinitely. Beware of any "bargains" in coax. Lost transmitter power can be made up to some extent by increasing power, but once lost, a weak signal can never be recovered in the receiver.

Effects of weather should not be ignored. A well-constructed open-wire line works well in nearly any weather, and it stands up well. Twin-lead is almost useless in heavy rain, wet snow or icing. The best grades of coax are impervious to weather. They can be run underground, fastened to metal towers without insulation, or bent into any convenient position, with no adverse effects on performance.

Impedance Matching

Theory and practice in impedance matching are given in detail in earlier chapters, and theory, at least, is the same for frequencies above 50 MHz. Practice may be similar, but physical size can be a major modifying factor in choice of methods.

Universal Stub

As its name implies, the double-

Fig. 39 — Matching methods commonly used in VHF antennas. The universal stub, A, combines tuning and matching. The adjustable short on the stub and the points of connection of the transmission line are adjusted for minimum reflected power in the line. In the delta match, B and C, the line is fanned out to tap on the dipole at the point of best impedance match. Impedances need not be known in A, B and C. The gamma match, D, is for direct connection of coax. C1 tunes out inductance in the arm. Folded dipole of uniform conductor size, E, steps up antenna impedance by a factor of four. Using a larger conductor in the unbroken portion of the folded dipole, E, gives higher orders of impedance transformation.

adjustment stub of Fig. 39A is useful for many matching purposes. The stub length is varied to resonate the system, and the transmission line and stub impedances are equal. In practice this involves moving both the sliding short and the point of line connection for zero reflected power, as indicated on an SWR indicator connected in the line.

The universal stub allows for tuning out any small reactance present in the driven part of the system. It permits matching the antenna to the line without knowledge of the actual impedances involved. The position of the short yielding the best match gives some indication of how much reactance is present. With little or no reactive component to be tuned out, the stub will be approximately a half wavelength from load to short.

The stub should be stiff bare wire or rod, spaced no more than 1/20 wavelength. Preferably it should be mounted rigidly, on insulators. Once the position of the short is determined, the center of the short can be grounded, if desired, and the portion of

the stub no longer needed can be removed.

It is not necessary that the stub be connected directly to the driven element. It can be made part of an open-wire line, as a device to match into or out of the line with coax. It can be connected to the lower end of a delta match, or placed at the feed point of a phased array. Examples of these uses are given later.

Delta Match

Probably the first impedance match was made when the ends of an open line were fanned out and tapped onto a half-wave antenna at the point of most efficient power transfer, as in Fig. 39B. Both the side length and the points of connection either side of the center of the element must be adjusted for minimum reflected power in the line, but as with the universal stub, the impedances need not be known. The delta makes no provision for tuning out reactance, so the universal stub is often used as a termination for it, to this end.

Once thought to be inferior for VHF applications because of its tendency to radiate if adjusted improperly, the delta has come back to favor now that we have good methods for measuring the effects of matching. It is very handy for phasing multiple-bay arrays with open lines, and its dimensions in this use are not particularly critical. It should be checked out carefully in applications like that of Fig. 39C which have no tuning device.

Gamma Match

The gamma match is shown in Fig. 39D. There being no RF voltage at the center of a half-wave dipole, the outer conductor of the coax is connected to the element at this point, which may also be the junction with a metallic or wooden boom. The inner conductor, carrying the RF current, is tapped out on the element at the matching point. Inductance of the arm is canceled by means of C1, resulting in electrical balance. Both the point of contact with the element and the setting of the capacitor are adjusted for zero reflected power, with a bridge connected in the coaxial line.

The capacitor can be made variable temporarily, then replaced with a suitable fixed unit when the required capacitance value is found, or C1 can be mounted in a waterproof box. Maximum capacitance should be about 100 pF for 50 MHz and 35 to 50 pF for 144. The capacitor and arm can be combined with the arm connecting to the driven element by means of a sliding clamp, and the inner end of the arm sliding inside a sleeve connected to the inner conductor of the coax. One can be constructed from concentric pieces of tubing, insulated by plastic sleeving. RF voltage across the capacitor is low, once the match is adjusted properly, so with a good dielectric, insulation presents no great problem, if the initial adjustment is made with low power. A clean, permanent, high-conductivity bond between arm and element is important, as the RF current is high at this point.

Folded Dipole

The impedance of a half-wave antenna broken at its center is 72 ohms. If a single conductor of uniform size is folded to make a half-wave dipole, as shown in Fig. 39E, the impedance is stepped up four times. Such a folded dipole can thus be fed directly with 300-ohm line with no appreciable mismatch. Coaxial line of 70 to 75 ohms impedance may also be used if a 4:1 balun is added. (See balun information in Chapter 16.) Higher impedance step-up can be obtained if the unbroken portion is made larger in cross-section than the fed portion, as in Fig. 39F. For design information see Chapter 16.

Baluns and Transmatches

Conversion from balanced loads to unbalanced lines, or vice versa, can be performed with electrical circuits, or their equivalents made of coaxial line. A balun made from flexible coax is shown in Fig. 40A. The looped portion is an electrical

Fig. 40 — Conversion from unbalanced coax to a balanced load can be done with a half-wave coaxial balun, A. Electrical length of the looped section should be checked with a dip meter, with ends shorted, B. The half-wave balun gives a 4:1 impedance step up.

Fig. 41 — The balun conversion function, with no impedance change, is accomplished with quarter-wave lines, open at the top and connected to the coax outer conductor at the bottom. The coaxial sleeve, A, is preferred.

half-wavelength. The physical length depends on the propagation factor of the line used, so it is well to check its resonant frequency, as shown at B. The two ends are shorted, and the loop at one end is coupled to a dip-meter coil. This type of balun gives an impedance step-up of 4:1 in impedance, 50 to 200 ohms, or 75 to 300 ohms typically.

Coaxial baluns giving a 1:1 impedance transfer are shown in Fig. 41. The coaxial sleeve, open at the top and connected to the outer conductor of the line at the lower end (A) is the preferred type. A conductor of approximately the same size as the line is used with the outer conductor to form a quarter-wave stub, in B. Another piece of coax, using only the outer conductor, will serve this purpose. Both baluns are intended to present an infinite impedance to any RF current that might otherwise tend to flow on the outer conductor of the coax.

The functions of the balun and the impedance transformer can be handled by various tuned circuits. Such a device, commonly called an antenna coupler or Transmatch, can provide a wide range of impedance transformations. Additional

selectivity inherent to the Transmatch can reduce RFI problems.

Stacking Yagis

Where suitable provision can be made for supporting them, two Yagis mounted one above the other and fed in phase may be preferable to one long Yagi having the same theoretical or measured gain. The pair will require a much smaller turning space for the same gain, and their lower radiation angle can provide interesting results. On long ionospheric paths a stacked pair occasionally may show an apparent gain much greater than the 2 to 3 dB that can be measured locally as the gain from stacking.

Optimum spacing for Yagis of five elements or more is one wavelength, but this may be too much for many builders of 50-MHz antennas to handle. Worthwhile results can be obtained with as little as one-half wavelength (10 feet), but 5/8 wavelength (12 feet) is markedly better. The difference between 12 and 20 feet may not be worth the added structural problems involved in the wider spacing, at 50 MHz at least. The closer spacings give lowered

Fig. 42 — A method for feeding a stacked Yagi array.

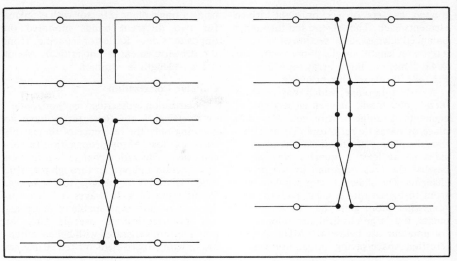

Fig. 43 — Element arrangements for 8, 12 and 16-element collinear arrays. Parasitic reflectors, omitted here for clarity, are five percent longer and 0.2 wavelength in back of the driven elements. Feed points are indicated by black dots. Open circles are recommended support points. The elements can run through wood or metal booms, without insulation, if supported at their centers in this way. Insulators at the element ends (points of high RF voltage) tend to detune and unbalance the system.

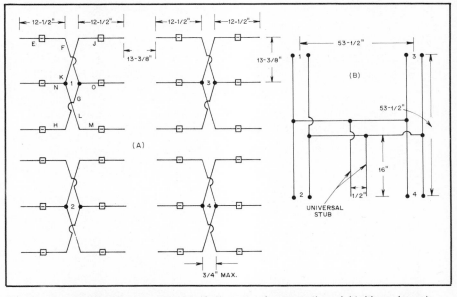

Fig. 44 — Large collinear arrays should be fed as sets of no more than eight driven elements each, interconnected by phasing lines. This 48-element array for 432 MHz (A) is treated as if it were four 12-element collinears. Reflector elements are omitted for clarity. Phasing harness is shown at B.

measured gain, but the antenna patterns are cleaner (less power in the high-angle lobes) than will be obtained with one-wavelength spacing. The extra gain with wider spacings is usually the objective on 144 MHz and higher bands, where the structural problems are not severe.

One method for feeding two 50-ohm antennas, as might be used in a stacked Yagi array, is shown in Fig. 42. The transmission lines from each antenna to the common feed point must be equal in length and an odd multiple of a quarter wavelength. This line acts as an impedance transformer and raises the feed impedance of each antenna to 100 ohms. When the two antennas are connected in parallel at the coaxial T fitting, the resulting impedance is close to 50 ohms.

COLLINEAR ANTENNAS

Information given thus far is mainly on parasitic arrays, but the collinear antenna has much to recommend it. Inherently broad in frequency response, it is a logical choice where coverage of an entire band is wanted. This tolerance also makes a collinear array easy to build and adjust for any VHF application. The use of many driven elements is popular in very large phased arrays, such as may be required for moonbounce (EME) communication.

Large Collinear Arrays

Bidirectional curtain of arrays of four, six and eight half-waves in phase are shown in Fig. 43. Usually reflector elements are added, normally at about 0.2 wavelength in back of each driven element, for more gain and a unidirectional pattern. Such

parasitic elements are omitted from the sketch in the interest of clarity.

When parasitic elements are added, the feed impedance is low enough for direct connection to open line or twin-lead, connected at the points indicated by black dots. With coaxial line and a balun, it is suggested that the universal stub match, Fig. 39A, be used at the feedpoint. All elements should be mounted at their electrical centers, as indicated by open circles in Fig. 43. The framework can be metal or insulating material, with equally good results. The metal supporting structure is entirely in back of the plane of the reflector

elements. Sheet-metal clamps can be cut from scraps of aluminum to make this kind of assembly, which is very light in weight and rugged as well. Collinear elements should always be mounted at their centers, where RF voltage is zero — never at their ends, where the voltage is high and insulation losses and detuning can be very harmful.

Collinear arrays of 32, 48, 64 and even 128 elements can be made to give outstanding performance. Any collinear should be fed at the center of the system, for balanced current distribution. This is very important in large arrays, which are treated as sets of six or eight driven elements each. The sets are fed through a balanced harness, each section of which is a resonant length, usually of open-wire line. A 48-element collinear array for 432 MHz, Fig. 44, illustrates this principle.

A reflecting plane, which may be sheet metal, wire mesh, or even closely spaced elements of tubing or wire, can be used in place of parasitic reflectors. To be effective, the plane reflector must extend on all sides to at least a quarter wavelength beyond the area occupied by the driven elements. The plane reflector provides high front-to-back ratio, a clean pattern, and somewhat more gain than parasitic elements, but large physical size rules it out for amateur use below 420 MHz. An interesting space-saving possibility lies in using a single plane reflector with elements for two different bands mounted on opposite sides. Reflector spacing from the driven element is not critical. About 0.2 wavelength is common.

Circular Polarization

Polarization is described as "horizontal" or "vertical," but these terms have no meaning once the reference of the earth's surface is lost. Many propagation factors can cause polarization change — reflection or refraction and passage through magnetic fields (Faraday rotation), for example. Polarization of VHF waves is often random, so an antenna capable of accepting any polarization is useful. Circular polarization, generated with helical antennas or with crossed elements fed 90 degrees out of phase, will respond to any linear polarization.

The circularly polarized wave, in effect, threads its way through space, and it can be left- or right-hand polarized. These polarization senses are mutually exclusive, but either will respond to any plane polarization. A wave generated with right-hand polarization, when reflected from the moon, comes back with left-hand, a fact to be borne in mind in setting up EME circuits. Stations communicating on direct paths should have the same polarization sense.

Both senses can be generated with crossed dipoles, with the aid of a switchable phasing harness. With helical arrays, both senses are provided with two antennas, wound in opposite directions.

Chapter 18

Voice Communications

The history of radiotelephony is indeed interesting. Way back in 1878, Bell and Tainter devised a system to voice-modulate a light beam! Called the photophone, it relied on a silvered plane mirror mounted so that it could be vibrated by sound waves. Detection was by a light-sensitive selenium cell in the receiver. By using a focusing lens and a parabolic mirror, this method spanned 250 yards.

Radio voice communications owe credit to Fessenden. In 1902, he developed a system to modulate continuous waves with the human voice. Before this time, most voice transmissions were attempts at modulating spark transmitters, with generally poor results.

Frequency modulation (FM) was first technically addressed by John R. Carson in *Proceedings of the IRE*, in February 1922. By mathematical analysis, he "proved" FM inferior to AM on two counts: bandwidth requirements and distortion.

The Carson analysis held until May 1936, when another paper on FM appeared in the same journal. In this work, Major Edwin H. Armstrong set the stage for viable FM communications. Some of his ideas are still in use today!

Eleven years later, single-sideband suppressed-carrier (SSB) came on the amateur scene. On September 21, 1947, Oswald G. Villard, W6QYT, operating W6YX, worked Winfield G. Wagener, W6VQD on the 75-meter band. The SSB era had begun.

Recently, a new single-sideband technique, Amplitude Compandored Single Sideband (ACSSB) has been introduced. Intended for the Land Mobile Service, ACSSB has some of the advantages of FM and SSB. Its use remains limited, however, but may one day be used in amateur satellite work.

Single Sideband

On the high-frequency amateur bands, single sideband is the most widely used radiotelephony mode. Since SSB is a sophisticated (or simplified, depending on one's point of view) form of amplitude modulation, it is worthwhile to take a brief look at some AM fundamentals. Modulation is a mixing process. When RF and AF signals are combined in a standard AM transmitter (such as one used for commercial broadcasting) four output signals are generated: the original carrier or RF signal, the original AF signal, and two sidebands, whose frequencies are the sum and difference of the original RF and AF signals, and whose amplitudes are proportional to that of the original AF signal. The sum component is called the upper sideband. It is erect, in that increasing the frequency of the modulating audio signal causes a corresponding increase in the frequency of the RF output signal. The difference component is called the lower sideband, and is inverted, meaning an increase in the modulating frequency results in a decrease in the output frequency. The amplitude and frequency of the carrier are unchanged by the modulation process, and the original AF signal is rejected by the RF output network. The RF envelope (sum of sidebands and carrier), as viewed on an oscilloscope, has the shape of the modulating waveform.

Fig. 1B shows the envelope of an RF

(A)

(B)

Fig. 1 — Electronic displays of AM signals in the frequency and time domains. (A) Unmodulated carrier or single-tone SSB signal. (B) Full-carrier AM signal with single-tone sinusoidal modulation.

Fig. 2 — Typical balanced modulator circuits. The representative parts values should serve as a basis for designing one's own equipment.

signal that is modulated 20 percent by an AF sine wave. The envelope varies in amplitude because it is the vector sum of the carrier and the sidebands. A spectrum analyzer or selective receiver will show the carrier to be constant. The spectral photograph also shows that the bandwidth of an AM signal is twice the highest frequency component of the modulating wave.

An amplitude-modulated signal cannot be frequency multiplied without special processing because the phase/frequency relationship of the components of the modulating waveform would be severely distorted. For this reason, once an AM signal has been generated, it can be moved in frequency only by heterodyning.

All of the intelligence is contained in the sidebands, but two-thirds of the RF power is in the carrier. The carrier serves only to demodulate the signal in the receiver. If this carrier is suppressed in the transmitter and reinserted in the proper phase in the receiver, several significant communications advantages accrue. If the reinserted carrier is strong compared to the incoming double-sideband signal, exalted carrier reception is achieved in which distortion caused by frequency-selective fading is reduced greatly. A refinement of this technique, called synchronous detection, uses a phase-locked loop to enhance the rejection of interference. Also, the lack of a transmitted carrier eliminates the heterodyne interference common to adjacent AM signals. Perhaps the most important advantage of eliminating the carrier is that the overall efficiency of the transmitter is increased. The power consumed by the carrier can be put to better use in the sidebands. The power in the carrier is continuous, and an AM transmitter requires a heavy-duty power supply. An SSB transmitter having the same power output as an AM transmitter can use a much lighter power supply because the duty cycle of voice operation is low.

Balanced Modulators

The carrier can be suppressed or nearly eliminated by using a balanced modulator or an extremely sharp filter. In SSB transmitters it is common practice to use both devices. The basic principle of any balanced modulator is to introduce the carrier in such a way that only the sidebands will appear in the output. The type of balanced-modulator circuit chosen by the builder will depend on the constructional considerations, cost, and the active devices to be employed.

In any balanced-modulator circuit there will be no output with no audio signal. When audio is applied, the balance is upset, and one branch will conduct more than the other. Since any modulation process is the same as "mixing," sum and difference frequencies (sidebands) will be generated. The modulator is not balanced for the

Table 1

Forward-to-Reverse Resistance Ratio for Different Classes of Solid-State Diodes

Diode Type	Ratio M = 1,000,000	
Point-contact germanium (1N98)	500	
Small-junction germanium (1N270)	0.1	M
Low-conductance silicon (1N457)	48	M
High-conductance silicon (1N645)	480	M
Hot-carrier (HPA-2800)	2000	M

sidebands, and they will appear in the output.

A rectifier-type balanced modulator is shown in Fig. 2, at A and B. If they have equal forward resistances, the diode rectifiers are connected so that no RF can pass from the carrier source to the output circuit by either of the two possible paths. The net effect is that no RF energy appears in the output. When audio is applied, it unbalances the circuit by biasing the diode (or diodes) in one path, depending on the instantaneous polarity of the audio, and hence some RF will appear in the output. The RF energy in the output will appear as a double-sideband suppressed-carrier signal.

For minimum distortion in any diode modulator, the RF voltage should be at least six to eight times the peak audio voltage. The usual operation involves a fraction of a volt of audio and several volts of RF. Desirable diode characteristics for balanced modulator and mixer service include: low noise, low forward resistance, high reverse resistance, good temperature stability and fast switching time (for high-frequency operation).

Table 1 lists the different classes of diodes, giving the ratio of forward-to-reverse resistance of each. This ratio is an important criterion in the selection of

diodes. Also, the individual diodes used should have closely matched forward and reverse resistances; an ohmmeter can be used to select matched pairs or quads.

One of the simplest diode balanced modulators in use is that of Fig. 2A. Its use is usually limited to low-cost portable equipment in which a high degree of carrier suppression is not vital. A ring balanced modulator, shown in Fig. 2B, offers good carrier suppression at low cost. Diodes D1 through D4 should be well matched and can be 1N270s or similar. C1 and R1 are adjusted for best RF balance as evidenced by maximum carrier null. It may be necessary to adjust each control several times alternately to secure optimum carrier suppression.

Varactor diodes are part of the unusual circuit shown in Fig. 2C. This arrangement allows single-ended input of nearly equal levels of audio and carrier. Excellent carrier suppression, 50 dB or more, and a simple method of unbalancing the modulator for CW operation are features of this design. D1 and D2 should be rated at 20 pF for a bias of −4 V. R1 can be adjusted to cancel any mismatch in the diode characteristics, so it isn't necessary that the varactors be well matched. T1 is wound on a small-diameter toroid core. The tap on the primary winding of this transformer is at the center of the winding.

A bipolar-transistor balanced modulator is shown in Fig. 2D. This circuit is similar to one used by Galaxy Electronics and uses closely matched transistors at Q1 and Q2. A phase splitter (inverter), Q3, is used to feed audio to the balanced modulator in push-pull. The carrier is supplied to the circuit in parallel and the output is taken in push-pull. D1 is a Zener diode and is used to stabilize the dc voltage. Controls R1 and R2 are adjusted for best carrier suppression.

The circuit at E offers superior carrier suppression and uses a 7360 beam-deflec-

Fig. 3 — Additional balanced-modulator circuits in which integrated circuits are used.

Table 2

Guidelines for Amateur SSB Signal Quality

Parameter	Suggested Standard
Carrier suppression	At least 40-dB below PEP
Opposite-sideband suppression	At least 40-dB below PEP
Hum and noise	At least 40-dB below PEP
Third-order intermodulation distortion	At least 30-dB below PEP
Higher-order intermodulation distortion	At least 35-dB below PEP
Long-term frequency stability	At most 100-Hz drift per hour
Short-term frequency stability	At most 10-Hz P-P deviation in a 2-kHz bandwidth

Fig. 4 — Balanced-modulator design using hot-carrier diodes.

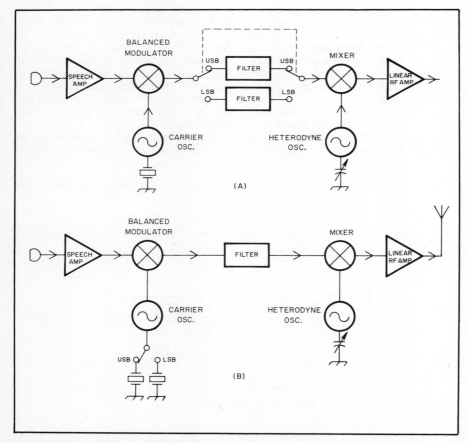

Fig. 5 — The filter method of SSB generation. Two sideband selection schemes are commonly used.

tion tube as a balanced modulator. This tube is capable of providing as much as 60 dB of carrier suppression. When it is used with mechanical or crystal-lattice filters, the total carrier suppression can be as great as 80 dB. Most well-designed balanced modulators can provide between 30 and 50 dB of carrier suppression. The primary of transformer T1 should be bifilar wound for best results.

Vacuum-tube balanced modulators can be operated at high power levels and the double-sideband output can be used directly into the antenna. Past issues of *QST* have given construction details on such transmitters.

IC Balanced Modulators

Integrated circuits (ICs) are presently available for use in balanced-modulator and mixer circuits. A diode array such as the RCA CA3039 is ideally suited for use in circuits such as that of Fig. 3A. Since all diodes are formed on a common silicon chip, their characteristics are extremely well matched. This fact makes the IC ideal in a circuit where good balance is required. The hot-carrier diode also has closely matched characteristics and excellent temperature stability. Using broadband toroidal-wound transformers, it is possible to construct a circuit similar to that of Fig. 4 that will have 40 dB of carrier suppression without the need for balance controls. T1 and T2 consist of trifilar windings, 12 turns of no. 32 enam. wire wound on a ½-inch toroid core. Another device with good inherent balance is the special IC made for modulator/mixer service, such as the Motorola MC1496G or Signetics S5596. A sample circuit using the MC1496 is shown in Fig. 3B. R1 is adjusted for best carrier balance. The amount of energy delivered from the carrier generator affects the level of carrier suppression; 100 mV of injection is about optimum, producing up to 55 dB of carrier suppression.

SINGLE-SIDEBAND EMISSION

A further improvement in communications effectiveness can be obtained by transmitting only one of the sidebands. When the proper receiver bandwidth is used, a single-sideband signal will show an effective gain of up to 9 dB over an AM signal of the same peak power. Because the redundant information is eliminated, the required bandwidth of an SSB signal is half that of a comparable AM or DSB emission. Unlike DSB, the phase of the local carrier generated in the receiver is unimportant.

Generating the SSB Signal: The Filter Method

If the DSB signal from the balanced modulator is applied to a band-pass filter, one of the sidebands can be greatly attenuated. Because a filter cannot have infinitely steep skirts, to obtain adequate suppression of the unwanted sideband the response of the filter must begin to roll off within about 300 Hz of the phantom carrier. This effect limits the ability to transmit bass frequencies, but these frequencies have little communications value. The filter rolloff can be used to obtain an additional 20 dB of carrier suppression. The bandwidth of an SSB filter is selected for the specific application. For voice communications, typical values are 1.8 to 3.0 kHz.

Fig. 5 illustrates two variations of the filter method of SSB generation. The heterodyne oscillator is represented as a simple VFO, but may be a premixing system or synthesizer. The scheme at B is perhaps less expensive than that of A, but the heterodyne-oscillator frequency must be shifted when changing sidebands if the dial calibration is to be maintained. The ultimate sense (erect or inverted) of the final output signal is influenced as much by the relationship of the heterodyne-oscillator frequency to the fixed SSB frequency as by the filter or carrier frequency selection. The heterodyne-oscillator frequency must be chosen to allow the best image rejection. This consideration requires that the heterodyne-oscillator frequency be above the fixed SSB frequency on some bands and below it on others. To reduce circuit complexity, early amateur filter types of SSB transmitters did not include a sideband selection switch. The result was that the output was LSB on 160, 75 and 40 meters, and USB on the higher bands. This convention persists despite the flexibility of most modern amateur SSB equipment.

Filter Types

For carrier frequencies in the 50- to 100-kHz region, a satisfactory filter can be made up of lumped-constant LC sections. High quality components and careful adjustment are required for good results with this type of filter. An alternate possibility is a "synthesized" filter comprised of high-performance operational amplifiers used as gyrators or "active inductors." A further drawback of SSB generation in this frequency range is that multiple conversion is necessary to reach the desired output frequency with adequate suppression of spurious mixing products.

Mechanical filters are an excellent choice for SSB generation in the 400- to 500-kHz region. These filters are described in some detail in the receiving chapter. For wide-dynamic-range receiving applications, the more modern types using piezoelectric transducers are preferred for lowest intermodulation distortion. In transmitters, where the signal levels can be closely predicted, the types using magnetostrictive transducers are entirely suitable.

Quartz crystal filters are commonly used in systems in which the SSB signal is generated in the high-frequency range. Some successful amateur designs have also employed crystals at 455 kHz. Generally, four or more crystal elements are required to obtain adequate selectivity for SSB

transmission. Crystal-filter design is a sophisticated subject, and the more esoteric aspects are beyond the scope of this *Handbook*. The discussion of piezoelectric crystal theory in Chapter 4 is sufficient background material for the general understanding of the concepts outlined in this section.

A fundamental crystal-filter section is the half-lattice, shown in Fig. 6. The passband of this type of filter is slightly wider than the frequency spacing between the crystals. The antiresonant (parallel resonant) frequency or pole of the low-frequency crystal must be equal to the series-resonant frequency or zero of the high-frequency crystal. Such a filter is useful for casual receiving purposes, but the ultimate stopband attenuation is poor, and numerous spurious responses will exist just outside the passband. Cascading two of these sections back to back, as in Fig. 7, will greatly suppress these parasitic resonances and steepen the skirts without materially affecting the passband. An important factor in the design of this type of filter is the coefficient

of coupling between the two halves of the transformer. The coupling must approach unity for proper operation. A twisted bifilar winding on a high-permeability ferrite core most nearly approximates this ideal. Some crystal filters have tuned input and output transformers. The flatness of the passband is heavily dependent on the terminating resistances. Lattice filters exhibit fairly symmetrical response curves and can be used for LSB or USB selection by means of placing the carrier frequency on the upper or lower skirt.

An asymmetrical filter is shown in Fig. 8. Using this approach, good unwanted sideband suppression can be obtained with only two crystals. The crystals are ground for the same frequency. The potential bandwidth here is only half that obtained with a half-lattice design. The maximum bandwidth of almost any crystal filter can be increased by using plated crystals intended for overtone operation.

The home construction of crystal filters can be very time consuming, if not expensive. The reason for this is that one must

Fig. 6 — The half-lattice crystal filter. Crystals A and B should be chosen so that the parallel-resonant frequency of one is the same as the series-resonant frequency of the other. Very tight coupling between the two halves of the secondary of T1 is required for optimum results. The theoretical attenuation-vs.-frequency curve of a half-lattice filter shows a flat passband between the lower series-resonant frequency and higher parallel-resonant frequency of the pair of crystals.

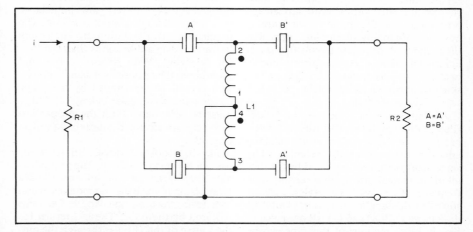

Fig. 7 — Half-lattice filters cascaded in a back-to-back arrangement. The theoretical curve of such a filter has increased skirt selectivity and fewer spurious responses, as compared with a simple half lattice, but the same passband as the simple circuit.

Fig. 8 — An asymmetrical filter and theoretical attenuation curve.

Fig. 9 — Some ladder filters based on CB crystals, with the response that can be expected from the 6-pole unit.

experiment with a large number of crystals to produce a filter with satisfactory performance. Crystal grinding and etching can be a fascinating and highly educational activity, but most home builders would prefer to spend their time on other aspects of equipment design. High-quality filters are available from several manufacturers. Most amateurs who build their own SSB equipment adopt a "systems engineering" approach and design their circuits around filters of known performance. Some filter suppliers are listed in the Component Data chapter. It is still worthwhile to have an appreciation for the basic design ideas, however, for many of the less expensive filters can be improved markedly by the addition of a couple of crystals external to the package. The technique is to steepen the skirts by grouping sharp notches on either side of the passband.

An important exception is the ladder filter. Although this type of filter is treated in textbooks, it has received attention in the amateur literature only recently. The significant feature of ladder filters is that all of the crystals are ground for the same frequency. Low-cost CB crystals are ideally suited to this application. Representative designs by F6BQP and G3JIR are given in Fig. 9. Filter sections of this type can be cascaded for improved shape factor with very little effect on the 3-dB bandwidth.

Ladder filters having six or more elements are suitable for SSB transmitting and receiving service. In general, the bandwidth is inversely proportional to the values of the shunt capacitors and directly proportional to the terminal impedances. Table 3 lists the frequencies of the CB channels. Overtone crystals for CB service have fundamental resonance at approximately one third of the listed frequency.

Filter Applications

The important considerations in circuits using band-pass filters are impedance matching and input/output isolation. The requirements for isolation are less severe in transmitting applications than they are for receiving. With proper layout and grounding, the opposite sideband suppression should be determined by the shape factor rather than signal leakage. The filter must be terminated with the proper impedances to ensure a smooth bandpass response.

Fig. 10A shows a typical SSB generator using a KVG crystal filter. The grounded-gate JFET presents a broadband 50-ohm termination to the balanced modulator and transforms the impedance to the 500 ohms required by the filter. The DC return for the source of the JFET is through the output transformer of the modulator. The tank circuit is broadly resonant at 9 MHz

and rejects any spurious signals generated in the modulator that might be propagated through the filter. Crystal filters should be isolated from any dc voltages present in the circuit.

A circuit using a Collins mechanical filter is illustrated in Fig. 10B. The IF transformer prevents spurious responses and

Table 3
CB Frequencies

Channel	Frequency (MHz)	Channel	Frequency (MHz)
1	26.965	21	27.215
2	26.975	22	27.225
3	26.985	23	27.255
4	27.005	24	27.235
5	27.015	25	27.245
6	27.025	26	27.265
7	27.035	27	27.275
8	27.055	28	27.285
9	27.065	29	27.295
10	27.075	30	27.305
11	27.085	31	27.315
12	27.105	32	27.325
13	27.115	33	27.335
14	27.125	34	27.345
15	27.135	35	27.355
16	27.155	36	27.365
17	27.165	37	27.375
18	27.175	38	27.385
19	27.185	39	27.395
20	27.205	40	27.405

Fig. 10 — Connecting a packaged filter into an SSB generator. (A) 9-MHz crystal filter, (B) 455-kHz mechanical filter.

Fig. 11 — The phasing system of SSB generation.

Table 4

Unwanted Sideband Suppression as a Function of Phase Error

Phase Error (deg.)	Suppression (dB)
0.125	59.25
0.25	53.24
0.5	47.16
1.0	41.11
2.0	35.01
3.0	31.42
4.0	28.85
5.0	26.85
10.0	20.50
15.0	16.69
20.0	13.93
30.0	9.98
45.0	6.0

removes dc bias. The output terminating network does double duty as the bias network for the transistor amplifier stage. The filter output transformer is the dc return for the base circuit. This technique is legitimate so long as the current is limited to 2 mA.

SSB Generation: The Phasing Method

Fig. 11 shows another method for obtaining a single-sideband signal. The audio and carrier signals are each split into components separated 90° in phase and applied to balanced modulators. When the DSB outputs of the modulators are combined, one sideband is reinforced and the other is cancelled. The figure shows sideband selection by means of transposing the audio leads, but the same result can be had by means of switching the carrier leads.

The phasing method was used in many pre-1960 amateur SSB exciters, but became less popular after the introduction of relatively inexpensive high-performance band-pass filters. The phase shift and amplitude balance of the two channels must be very accurate if the unwanted sideband is to be adequately attenuated. Table 4 shows the required phase accuracy of one channel (AF or RF) for various levels of opposite sideband suppression. The numbers given assume perfect amplitude balance and phase accuracy in the other channel. It can be seen from the table that a phase accuracy of ±1° must be maintained if the signal quality is to satisfy the criteria tabulated at the beginning of this chapter. It is difficult to achieve this level of overall accuracy over the entire speech band. Note, however, that speech has a complex spectrum with a large gap in the octave from 700 to 1400 Hz. The phase-accuracy tolerance can be loosened to ±2° if the peak deviations can be made to occur within the spectral gap.

The major advantage of the phasing system is that the SSB signal can be generated at the operating frequency without the need for heterodyning. Phasing can be used to good advantage even in fixed-frequency systems. A loose-tolerance (±4°) phasing exciter followed by a simple two-pole crystal filter can generate a high-quality signal at very low cost.

Audio Phasing Networks

It would be difficult to design a two-port network having a quadrature (90°) phase relationship between input and output with constant-amplitude response over a decade of bandwidth. A practical approach, pioneered by Robert Dome, W2WAM, is to use two networks having a differential phase shift of 90°. This differential can be closely maintained in a simple circuit if precision components are used. The 350/2Q4 audio phase shift network manufactured by Barker and Williamson is such a circuit. The 2Q4 is a 1950 vintage component but it is still useful. A modern design using this device is given in Fig. 12. The insertion loss of the 2Q4 is 30 dB, and the phase-shift accuracy is ±1.5° over the 300-3000 Hz speech band.

The tolerances of the components can be relaxed considerably if several phase-shift sections are cascaded. A sixth-order network designed by HA5WH is shown in Fig. 13. Using common ±10% tolerance components, this phase shifter provides approximately 60 dB of opposite-sideband attenuation over the range of 300 to 3000 Hz.

Numerous circuits have been developed to synthesize the required 90° phase shift electronically. Active-filter techniques are used in most of these systems, but precision components are needed for good results. An interesting phasing system described in *Electronics* for April 13, 1978, makes use of a tapped analog delay line. These "bucket brigade" devices are becoming available at reasonable prices on the surplus market.

RF Phasing Networks

If the SSB signal is to be generated at a fixed frequency, the RF phasing problem is trivial; any method that produces the proper phase shift can be used. If the signal is produced at the operating frequency, problems similar to those in the audio networks must be overcome.

A differential RF phase shifter is shown in Fig. 14. The amplitudes of the quadrature signals won't be equal over an entire phone band, but this is of little consequence as long as the signals are strong enough to saturate the modulators.

Where percentage bandwidths are small, such as in the 144.1- to 145-MHz range, the RF phase shift can be obtained convenient-

Fig. 12 — A circuit using the B&W 2Q4 audio phase shift network.

Fig. 13 — A high-performance audio phase shifter made from ordinary loose-tolerance components.

R : 12k ±10%
C1 : 0.044 μF (2 x 0.022 μF)
C2 : 0.033 μF
C3 : 0.02 μF
C4 : 0.01 μF
C5 : 5600 pF
C6 : 4700 pF

U1, U2 : HIGH PERFORMANCE OPERATIONAL AMPLIFIER

Fig. 14 — A simple RF phase shifter. One of the capacitors can be variable for precise alignment.

Fig. 15 — Block diagram of a phase-locked-loop phase-shifting system capable of maintaining quadrature over a wide bandwidth. The doubly balanced mixer is used as a phase detector.

ly by means of transmission-line methods. If one balanced-modulator feed line is made an electrical quarter wavelength longer than the other, the two signals will be 90° out of phase. It is important that the cables be properly terminated.

One method for obtaining a 90° phase shift over a wide bandwidth is to generate the quadrature signals at a fixed frequency and heterodyne them individually to any desired operating frequency. Quadrature hybrids having multioctave bandwidths are manufactured commercially, but they cost hundreds of dollars. Another practical approach is to use two VFOs in a master-slave phase-locked-loop system. Many phase detectors lock the two signals in phase quadrature. A doubly balanced mixer has this property. One usually thinks of a phase-locked loop as having a VCO locked to a reference signal, but a phase dif-

ferential can be controlled independently of the oscillator. The circuit in Fig. 15 illustrates this principle. Two digital phase shifters are sketched in Fig. 16. If ECL ICs are used, this system can work over the entire HF spectrum.

DETECTORS

Diode Detectors

The simplest detector for AM is the

diode. A germanium or silicon crystal is an imperfect form of diode (a small current can usually pass in the reverse direction), but the principle of detection in a semiconductor diode is similar to that in a vacuum-tube diode.

Circuits for both half-wave and full-wave diodes are given in Fig. 17. The simplified half-wave circuit at Fig. 17A includes the RF tuned circuit, L2C1, a coupling coil, L1, from which the RF

Fig. 16 — Digital RF phase shift networks. The circuit at A uses JK flip flops, and the circuit at B uses D flip flops. In each case the desired carrier frequency must be quadrupled before it is processed by the phase-shift network.

Fig. 17 — Simplified and practical diode detector circuits. A, the elementary half-wave diode detector; B, a practical circuit with RF filtering and audio output coupling; C, full-wave diode detector, with output coupling indicated. The circuit, L2C1, is tuned to the signal frequency; typical values for C2 and R1 in A and C are 250 pF and 250 kΩ, respectively; in B, C2 and C3 are 100 pF each; R1, 50 Ω, and R2 250 Ω. C4 is 0.1 pF.

Fig. 18 — Illustrations of the detection process.

energy is fed to L2C1, and the diode, D1, with its load resistance, R1, and bypass capacitor, C2.

The progress of the signal through the detector or rectifier is shown in Fig. 18. A typical modulated signal as it exists in the tuned circuit is shown at A. When this signal is applied to the rectifier, current will flow only during the part of the RF cycle when the anode is positive with respect to cathode, so that the output of the rectifier consists of half-cycles of RF. These current pulses flow in the load circuit comprised of R1 and C2. C2 charges to the peak value of the rectified voltage on each pulse and retains enough charge between pulses so that the voltage across R1 is smoothed out, as shown in C. C2 thus acts as a filter for the radio-frequency component of the output of the rectifier, leaving a dc component that varies in the same way as the modulation on the original signal. When this varying dc voltage is applied to a following amplifier through a coupling capacitor (C4 in Fig. 17), only the variations in voltage are transferred, so the final output signal is ac, as shown in D.

In the circuit at 17B, R1 and C2 have been divided for the purpose of providing a more effective filter for RF. It is important to prevent the appearance of any RF voltage in the output of the detector, because it may cause overloading of a succeeding amplifier stage. The audio-

frequency variations can be transferred to another circuit through a coupling capacitor, C4. R2 is usually a "potentiometer" so the audio volume can be adjusted to a desired level.

Coupling from the potentiometer (volume control) through a capacitor also avoids any flow of dc through the moving contact of the control. The flow of dc through a high-resistance volume control often tends to make the control noisy (scratchy) after a short while.

The full-wave diode circuit at Fig. 17C differs in operation from the half-wave circuit only in that both halves of the RF cycle are utilized. The full-wave circuit has the advantage that RF filtering is easier than in the half-wave circuit. As a result, less attenuation of the higher audio frequencies will be obtained for any given degree of RF filtering.

The reactance of C2 must be small compared to the resistance of R1 at the radio frequency being rectified, but at audio frequencies must be relatively large compared to R1. If the capacitance of C2 is too large, response at the higher audio frequencies will be lowered.

Compared with most other detectors, the gain of the diode is low, normally running around 0.8 in audio work. Since the diode consumes power, the Q of the tuned circuit is reduced, bringing about a reduction in selectivity. The loading effect of the

Fig. 19 — Plate-detection circuits. In each example the input circuit is tuned to the signal frequency. Typical R1 values for the tube circuit at A are 1000 to 5600 ohms. For the FET circuit at B, R1 is on the order of 100 to 3900 ohms.

Fig. 20 — An infinite-impedance detector.

diode is close to one half the load resistance. The detector linearity is good, and the signal-handling capability is high.

Plate Detectors

The plate detector is arranged so that rectification of the RF signal takes place in the plate circuit of the tube or the drain of the FET. Sufficient negative bias is applied to the grid to bring the plate current nearly to the cutoff point, so that application of a signal to the grid circuit causes an increase in average plate current. The average plate current follows the changes in the signal in a fashion similar to the rectified current in a diode detector.

In general, transformer coupling from the plate circuit of a plate detector is not satisfactory, because the plate impedance of any tube is very high when the bias is near the plate-current cutoff point. The same is true of a JFET or MOSFET. Impedance coupling may be used in place of the resistance coupling shown in Fig. 19. Usually 100 henrys or more of inductance is required.

The plate detector is more sensitive than the diode detector because there is some amplifying action in the tube or transistor. It will handle large signals, but is not as tolerant as the diode. Linearity, with the self-biased circuits shown, is good. Up to

the overload point the detector takes no power from the tuned circuit, and so does not affect its Q and selectivity.

Infinite-Impedance Detector

The circuit of Fig. 20 combines the high signal-handling capabilities of the diode detector with the low distortion and, like the plate detector, does not load the tuned circuit it connects to. The circuit resembles that of the plate detector, except that the load resistance, 27 kΩ, is connected between source and ground and thus is common on both gate and drain circuits, giving negative feedback for the audio frequencies. The source resistor is bypassed for RF but not for audio, while the drain circuit is bypassed to ground for both audio and radio frequencies. An RF filter can be connected between the source and the output coupling capacitor to eliminate any RF that might otherwise appear in the output.

The drain current is very low with no signal but increases with signal as in the case of the plate detector. The voltage drop across the source resistor consequently increases with signal. Because of this and the large initial drop across this resistor, the signal usually cannot drive the gate positive with respect to the source.

Product Detectors

A product detector is similar in function to a balanced or product modulator. It is also similar to a mixer. In fact, the latter is sometimes called a "first detector" in a receiver circuit. Product detectors are used principally for SSB, CW and RTTY FSK signal detection. Essentially, it is a detector whose output is equal to the product of the beat-frequency oscillator (BFO) and the RF signals applied to it. Output from the product detector is at audio frequency. Some RF filtering is necessary at the detector output to prevent unwanted IF or BFO voltage from reaching the audio amplifier which follows the detector. LC or RC RF decoupling networks are satisfactory, and they need not be elaborate. Fig. 22 illustrates this type of filtering.

Diode Product Detectors

The product detectors shown in Fig. 21 are called "passive." The term means that the devices used do not require an operating voltage. Active devices (transistors, ICs and tubes) do require an operating voltage. Passive mixers and detectors exhibit a conversion loss, whereas active detectors can provide conversion gain. Passive detectors usually require a substantially greater level of BFO injection voltage than is the case with active detectors. Therefore, the primary drawbacks to the use of diodes in these circuits are the loss in gain and the high injection level required. A typical conversion loss for a two-diode detector (Fig. 21A) is 5 dB. The four-diode detectors have a loss of approximately 8 dB. The BFO injection level for each of the diode detectors shown in Fig. 21 is +13 dBm, or 20 mW.

Fig. 21 — Examples of diode product detectors. Singly balanced types are shown at A and B. A doubly balanced version is illustrated at C.

detector is shown at B. Two diodes have been added to improve the circuit balance while presenting a more symmetrical load to the BFO. The result is better isolation between the BFO and IF input ports.

Two broadband transformers are used to provide the doubly balanced detector of Fig. 21C. The advantage with this configuration is that all three ports are effectively isolated from one another.

Simple Active Product Detectors

Fig. 22 contains two examples of single-ended active detectors that employ FETs. They are quite acceptable for use in simple receivers that do not require high performance characteristics. The circuit at A uses a JFET which has BFO injection voltage supplied across the source resistor. Because the source is not bypassed, instability can occur if the circuit is used as a mixer which has an IF that is close to the signal frequency. This problem is not apt to become manifest when the output is at audio frequency. Slightly more injection power is needed for circuit A than is necessary for the detector at B. An RMS voltage of roughly 0.8 is typical (6.5 mW).

The detector of Fig. 22B operates in a similar fashion to that of A, but the BFO is injected on control gate no. 2. Approximately 1 volt RMS is needed (0.1 mW). FETs with proper injection levels and moderate signal-input amounts have excellent IMD characteristics. Generally, they are preferred to single-ended, bipolar-transistor detectors. The circuits at A and B contain RF chokes and bypass capacitors in the drain leads to minimize the transfer of BFO energy to the succeeding audio stage. The bypass capacitors are also useful for rolling off the unwanted high-frequency audio components.

Active Balanced Product Detectors

Examples of active IC product detectors are given in Fig. 23. A singly balanced version is shown at A. It uses an RCA differential-pair IC. Except for its conversion gain, it performs similarly to the singly balanced diode detector of Fig. 21B. Doubly balanced active detectors are seen at B and C of Fig. 23. These ICs contain two sets of differential amplifiers each. The "diffamps" are cross-connected in the examples shown to obtain double balanced circuits. The virtues of these detectors are similar to the equivalent four-diode types, but they exhibit several decibels of conversion gain. The MC1496G is made by Motorola, and the CA3102E is an RCA device.

Other SSB Modes

An SSB transmitter is simply a frequency translator. Any frequency- or amplitude-varying signal (within the bandwidth capabilities of the transmitter) applied to the input will be translated intact (although frequency inversion takes place in LSB) to the chosen radio frequency. If amplitude-

Since the terminal impedance of the detector is roughly 50 ohms, an RMS BFO voltage of 1, or P-P voltage of 2.8, is required.

The advantages to the use of diodes in a product detector are circuit simplicity, low cost, broadband characteristics, low noise figure and good port-to-port signal isolation. This type of detector is excellent at the input of a direct-conversion receiver (to be treated later in the chapter).

The transformers shown in the circuits of Fig. 21 are broadband, toroidally wound types. The black dots near the windings of T1 and T2 indicate the phasing required. The core material is ferrite, and the windings are trifilar. Core permeability can be

950 for most applications, although some designers use cores with less initial permeability. An Amidon FT-50-43 is entirely suitable as a transformer core for the circuits shown. Fifteen trifilar turns are ample for each transformer.

High-speed silicon switching diodes are satisfactory for use in the circuits of Fig. 21. They should be as closely matched as possible for forward and back resistance. Closely matched diodes can be had by using a diode-array IC, such as the RCA CA3019 or 3039. Hot-carrier diodes are excellent for the circuits shown. Matched 1N914s are the choice of many amateur designers.

A singly balanced detector is shown at A in Fig. 21. An improved singly balanced

Fig. 22 — Active product detectors. A JFET example is provided at A and a dual-gate MOSFET type is at B.

limited tones corresponding to the video information of a slow-scan television picture are fed into the microphone input, F3F emission will result. Two alternating tones from an AFSK RTTY keyer will cause the transmitter to produce an F1B signal. A keyed audio tone will be translated into an A1A signal. This technique is a perfectly legitimate way to operate CW with an SSB transceiver, and is simpler than the more traditional method of upsetting the balanced modulator for carrier leakage. One can vary the transmitting frequency independently of the receiving frequency by means of changing the audio tone. The strength of the tone determines the transmitter power output. Good engineering practice requires that the tone be frequency-stable and that the total harmonic distortion be less than 1%. Also, the carrier and opposite sideband must be suppressed at least 40 dB. Of course the rise and decay times of the audio envelope must be controlled to avoid key clicks.

Independent-Sideband Emission

If two SSB exciters, one USB and the other LSB, share a common carrier oscillator, two channels of information can be transmitted from one antenna. Methods for ISB generation in filter and phasing transmitters are shown in Fig. 24. May 1977 QST carried an article on converting the popular Drake TR-4C to ISB.

Many commercially manufactured SSB transceivers have provisions for controlling the transmit or receive frequency with an external VFO or receiver. With slight modification it should be possible to slave two transceivers to a single VFO for ISB operation. The oscillators in the transceivers must be aligned precisely.

The most obvious amateur application for independent sideband is the transmission of slow-scan television with simultaneous audio commentary. On the VHF bands, other combinations are possible, such as voice and code or SSTV and RTTY.

Power Ratings of SSB Transmitters

Fig. 25A is more or less typical of a few voice-frequency cycles of the modulation envelope of a single-sideband signal. Two amplitude values associated with it are of particular interest. One is the maximum peak amplitude, the greatest amplitude reached by the envelope at any time. The other is the average amplitude, which is the average of all the amplitude values contained in the envelope over some significant period of time, such as the time of one syllable of speech.

The power contained in the signal at the maximum peak amplitude is the basic transmitter rating. It is called the peak-

envelope power, abbreviated PEP. The peak-envelope power of a given transmitter is intimately related to the distortion considered tolerable. The lower the signal-to-distortion ratio the lower the attainable peak-envelope power as a general rule. For splatter reduction, an S/D ratio of 25 dB is considered a border-line minimum, and better figures are desirable.

The signal power, S, in the classical definition of S/D ratio is the power in one tone of a two-tone test signal. This is 6 dB below the peak-envelope power in the same signal. Manufacturers of amateur SSB equipment usually base their published S/D ratios on PEP, thereby getting an S/D ratio that looks 6 dB better than one based on the classical definition. QST product reviews also use the PEP reference. In comparing distortion-product ratings of different transmitters or amplifiers, first make sure the ratios have the same base.

Peak vs. Average Power

Envelope peaks occur only sporadically during voice transmission, and have no direct relationship to meter readings. The meters respond to the amplitude (current or voltage) of the signal averaged over several cycles of the modulation envelope. (This is true in practically all cases, even though the transmitter RF output meter may be calibrated in watts. Unfortunately, such a calibration means little in voice transmission since the meter can be calibrated in watts only by using a sine wave — which a voice-modulated signal definitely is not.)

The ratio of peak-to-average amplitude varies widely with voices of different characteristics. In the case shown in Fig. 25 the average amplitude, found graphically, is such that the peak-to-average ratio of amplitudes is almost 3:1. The ratio of peak power to average power is something else again. There is no simple relationship between the meter reading and actual average power, for the reason mentioned earlier. See Chapter 2 for a complete discussion of computing PEP.

Testing a Sideband Transmitter

There are three commonly used methods for testing an SSB transmitter. These include the wattmeter, oscilloscope and spectrum-analyzer techniques. In each case, a two-tone test signal is fed into the mic input to simulate a speech signal. From the measurements, information concerning such quantities as PEP and inter-modulation-distortion-product (IMD) levels can be obtained. Depending on the technique used, other aspects of transmitter operation (such as hum problems and carrier balance) can also be checked.

As might be expected, each technique has both advantages and disadvantages and the suitability of a particular method will depend on the desired application. The wattmeter method is perhaps the simplest one but it also provides the least amount of in-

Fig. 23 — Examples of IC product detectors. At A is a singly balanced version, while those at B and C are doubly balanced.

method (using a two-tone test input signal), the power output is multiplied by two.

A spectrum analyzer is capable of giving the most information (of the three methods considered here), but it is also the most costly method and the one with the greatest chance of misinterpretation. Basically, a spectrum analyzer is a receiver with a readout that provides a plot of signal amplitude vs. frequency. The readout could be in the form of a paper chart but usually it is presented as a trace on a CRT. For a spectrum analyzer to provide accurate information about a signal, that signal must be well within the linear dynamic range of the analyzer. For an explanation of the function and application of this instrument see Chapter 25.

Two-Tone Tests and Scope Patterns

A very practical method for amateur applications is to use a two-tone test signal (usually audio) and sample the transmitter output. The sample is then applied directly to the vertical-deflection plates in an oscilloscope. An alternative method is to use an RF probe and detector to sample the waveform and apply the resulting audio signal to the vertical-deflection amplifier input.

If the amplifier has good linearity, the resulting envelope will approach a perfect sine wave pattern (see Fig. 26A). As a comparison, a spectrum-analyzer display for the same transmitter and under the same conditions is shown in Fig. 26B. In this case, spurious products approximately 30 dB below the amplitude of each of the tones can be seen.

As the distortion increases, so does the level of the spurious products, and the resulting waveform departs from a true sine-wave function. This can be seen in Fig. 26C. One of the disadvantages of the scope and two-tone test method is that a relatively high level of IMD-product voltage is required before the waveform seems distorted to the eye. For instance, the waveform in Fig. 26C doesn't seem too much different from the one in Fig. 26A but the IMD level is only 17 dB below the level of the desired signal (see analyzer display in Fig. 26D). A 17- to 20-dB level corresponds to approximately 10% distortion in the voltage waveform. Consequently, a "good" waveform means the IMD products are at least 30 dB below the desired tones. Any noticeable departure from the waveform in Fig. 26A should be suspect, and the transmitter operation should be checked.

The relation between the level at which distortion begins for the two-tone test signal and an actual voice signal is a rather simple one. The maximum deflection on the scope is noted (for an acceptable two-tone test waveform) and the transmitter is then operated such that voice peaks are kept below this level. If the voice peaks go above this level, a type of distortion called "flattopping" will occur. Results are shown for a two-tone test signal in

formation. RF wattmeters suitable for single-tone or CW operation may not be accurate with a two-tone test signal. A suitable wattmeter for the latter case must have a reading that is proportional to the actual power consumed by the load. The reading must be independent of signal waveform. A thermocouple ammeter connected in series with the load would be a typical example of such a system. The output power would be equal to I^2R, where I is the current in the ammeter and R is the load resistance (usually 50 ohms). In order to find the PEP output with the latter

Fig. 24 — Independent-sideband generators. (A) Filter system. (B) Phasing system. The block marked "RF combiner" can be a hybrid combiner or a summing amplifier.

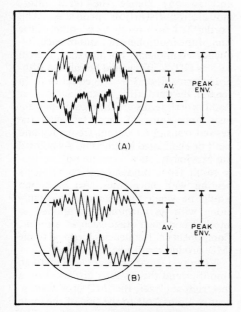

Fig. 25 — (A) Typical SSB voice-modulated signal might have an envelope of the general nature shown, where the RF amplitude (current or voltage) is plotted as a function of time, which increases to the right horizontally. (B) Envelope pattern after speech processing to increase the average level of power output.

Fig. 26E. IMD-product levels rise very rapidly when flattopping occurs. For instance, third-order product levels will increase 30 dB for every 10-dB increase in desired output as the flattopping region is approached, and fifth-order terms will increase by 50 dB.

Interpreting Distortion Measurements

Unfortunately, considerable confusion has grown concerning the interpretation and importance of distortion in SSB gear. Distortion is a very serious problem when high spurious-product levels exist at frequencies removed from the passband of the desired channel. In this case, such distortion may cause needless interference to other channels ("splatter"), and should be avoided. This can be seen quite clearly in Fig. 26F, where the flattopping region is approached and the fifth and higher order terms increase dramatically. The situation is less serious if such products fall within the bandwidth of operation.

On the other hand, attempting to suppress in-band products more than necessary is not only difficult to achieve but may not result in any noticeable increase in signal quality. In addition, measures required to suppress in-band IMD often cause problems at the expense of other qualities such as efficiency. This can lead to serious difficulties such as shortened tube life or transistor heat-dissipation problems.

The two primary causes of distortion can be seen in Fig. 27. While the waveform is for a single-tone input signal, similar effects occur for the two-tone case. As the drive signal is increased, a point is reached at which the output current (or voltage) cannot follow the input, and the amplifier saturates. As mentioned earlier, this condition is often referred to as flattopping. It can be prevented by ensuring that excessive drive doesn't occur; the usual means of accomplishing this is by ALC action. The ALC provides a signal that is used to lower the gain of earlier stages in the transmitter.

The second type of distortion is called "crossover" distortion and occurs at low signal levels. (See Fig. 27.) Increasing the idling plate or collector current is one way of reducing the effect of crossover distortion in regards to producing undesirable components near the operating frequency. Instead, the components occur at frequencies considerably removed from the

(A)

(B)

(C)

(D)

(E)

(F)

Fig. 26 — Scope patterns for a two-tone test signal and corresponding spectrum-analyzer displays. The pattern in A is for a properly adjusted transmitter and consequently the IMD products are relatively low as can be seen on the analyzer display. At C, the PA bias was set to zero idling current and considerable distortion can be observed. Note how the pattern has changed on the scope and the increase in IMD level. At E, the drive level was increased until the flattopping region was approached. This is the most serious distortion of all since the width of the IMD spectrum increases considerably, causing splatter (F).

Fig. 28 — Speech pattern of the word "X" in a properly adjusted SSB transmitter.

Fig. 29 — Severe clipping (same transmitter as Fig. 22 but with high drive and ALC disabled).

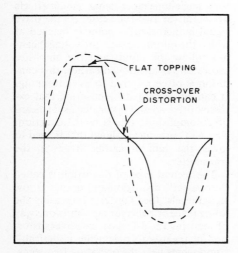

Fig. 27 — Waveform of an amplifier with a single-tone input showing flattopping and crossover distortion.

operating frequency and can be eliminated by filtering.

As implied in the earlier discussion, the effect of distortion is to generate frequency components that add or subtract in order to make up the complex waveform. A more familiar example would be the harmonic generation caused by the nonlinearities often encountered in amplifiers. However, a common misconception that should be avoided is that IMD is caused by fundamental-signal components beating with harmonics. Generally speaking, no such simple relation exists. For instance, single-ended stages have relatively poor second-harmonic suppression but with proper biasing to increase the idling current, such stages can have very good IMD-suppression qualities.

However, a definite mathematical relation does exist between the desired components in an SSB signal and the "distortion signals." Whenever nonlinearities exist, products between the individual components which make up the desired signal will occur. The mathematical result of such multiplication is to generate other signals of the form $(2f1 - f2)$, $(3f1)$, $(5f2 - f1)$ and so on. Hence the term intermodulation-distortion products. The "order" of such products is equal to the sum of the multipliers in front of each frequency component. For instance, a term such as $(3f1 - 2f2)$ would be called a fifth-order term, since $3 + 2$ is equal to 5. In general, the third, fifth, seventh and similar "odd-order" terms are the most important ones since some of these fall near the desired transmitter output frequency and can't be eliminated by filtering. As pointed out previously, such terms do not normally result from fundamental components beating with harmonics. An exception would be when the fundamental signal along with its harmonics is applied to another nonlinear stage such as a mixer. Components at frequencies identical to the IMD products will result.

When two equal tones are applied to an amplifier and the result is displayed on a spectrum analyzer, the IMD products appear as "pips" off to the side of the main signal components (Fig. 26). The amplitudes associated with each tone and the IMD products are merely the decibel difference between the particular product and one tone. However, each desired tone is 3 dB down from the average power output and 6 dB down from the PEP output.

Since PEP represents the most important quantity as far as IMD is concerned, relating IMD-product levels to PEP is one logical way of specifying the "quality" of a transmitter or amplifier in regard to low distortion. For instance, IMD levels are referenced to PEP in "Product Review" specifications of commercially made gear in *QST*. PEP output can be found by multiplying the PEP input by the efficiency of the amplifier. The input PEP for a two-tone test signal is given by

$$PEP = \frac{E_p I_p}{n} \left[1.57 - 0.57 \frac{I_o}{I_p} \right]$$

where

E_p = plate voltage

I_p = average plate current
I_o = idling (zero signal) plate current
n = duty cycle of test tones ($=1.0$ for steady two-tone test, 0.5 for 50% duty cycle, etc)

The inclusion of a factor for test-tone duty cycle allows calculation of amplifier PEP input with the application of *pulsed* test tones. (Pulsed tones result in lower average power input, and this allows longer test periods if the amplifier under test cannot tolerate continuous operation at maximum PEP input. See Goodman, "Pulsed Signals Through S.S.B. Transmitters," *QST*, Sept 1965, pp 18-19.) If continuous test tones are used, $n = 1.0$.

Generally speaking, most actual voice patterns will look alike (in the presence of distortion) except in the case where severe flattopping occurs. This condition is not too common since most rigs have an ALC system, which prevents overdriving the amplifiers. However, the voice pattern in a properly adjusted transmitter usually has a "Christmas tree" shape when observed on a scope; an example is shown in Fig. 28.

More Information

Further discussion on measurements, including FCC power measurement procedures, can be found in Chapter 25. For a discussion of voice processing see Chapter 7. Equipment and accessory construction projects are presented in Chapters 27 through 34.

Amplitude Compandored Single Sideband

There has not been much said about Amplitude Compandored Single Sideband (ACSSB) in Amateur Radio literature. However, amateur experimenters should be aware of ACSSB developments now underway in the land-mobile communications industry.

SSB is the standard mode for HF voice communications. Amateurs have used SSB at VHF and UHF with good success but usually between fixed locations and experienced operators. When SSB was tried in the Land Mobile Service, several problems were noticed. One was that the users (who are not trained operators) couldn't master the control known as CLARIFIER to land-mobile people and receiver incremental tuning or RIT to amateurs. In addition, the users were annoyed by the fading and noise experienced with SSB over the FM they were familiar with. So, to get the spectrum savings of SSB over FM, the land-mobile engineers had to come up with a form of SSB that gave the land-mobile users everything that they were accustomed to with FM, including signaling.

Pilot Tone

A conventional SSB transmission has a suppressed carrier. In order to demodulate the signal at the receiver, the missing carrier is replaced. At higher frequencies it is unrealistic to expect the original carrier at the transmitter and that reinserted at the receiver to be exactly the same. As mentioned above, adding a knob to compensate for the error is unacceptable for landmobile service. So manufacturers have added a pilot tone to the audio, sufficiently separated in frequency and filtered so that the two do not interfere with each other. The pilot tone is usually 3.1 kHz. As shown

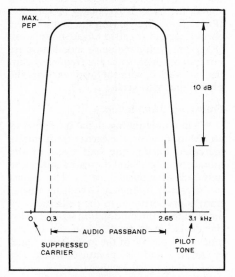

Fig. 30 — Bandwidth of an ACSSB signal is 3.1 kHz.

in Fig. 30, the pilot power level is about 10 dB below the voice peak power. Thus, the transmitter has an output power of approximately 1/10th of maximum when there is no voice modulation.

At the receiver, the pilot tone is compared with an internal reference oscillator in a phase-locked-loop circuit. The difference voltage thus produced is used to shift the receiver local oscillator until the frequency error is eliminated. The time constant of the phase-locked loop is short enough to be ignored by the user and to be compatible with tone decoders used for signaling purposes.

The pilot tone serves other functions than locking the receiver on frequency. It is used to control squelch and AGC circuits as well. The pilot tone can also be modu-

lated for signaling or telemetry transmission — a useful feature in logic-controlled systems.

Amplitude Compandoring

Compression of voice signals is common in Amateur Radio SSB. What is not common in amateur SSB is to employ an expandor at the receiving end. The term "compandor" is a fusion of the terms "compressor" and "expandor." When signal levels are high, ACSSB and NBFM produce similar results. As distance between stations increases beyond primary service areas, however, both modes suffer, but in different ways: In the near fringe area, NBFM degrades quickly, which is manifested by annoying noise and fading, followed by a complete loss of audio. ACSSB audio tends to degrade gradually over much greater distances, and fading results in transitory distortion.

ACSSB Potential

Although ACSSB has some potential in earth-to-space and space-to-earth communications, its land-based potential is limited by several factors. A CCIR (International Radio Consultative Committee) study comparing ACSSB with NBFM found that ACSSB was not any more spectrum efficient than NBFM in congested environments. In addition, co-channel interference was found to be significantly higher with ACSSB. Finally, unlike NBFM, ACSSB equipment is not interoperable with existing FM equipment.

Further Reading on ACSSB

J. S. Belrose, VE2CV, "On SSB Radio Communications," *QEX*, July 1982, pp. 3-4.

F. B. Childs, "ACSB—Filling the Gaps Between FM Channels," *Mobile Radio, Technology,* January/February 1983, pp. 60-66.

"Comparison of Selected Narrowband Modulation Systems," CCIR Study Group 1, Document No. 1/6, Oct 30, 1987.

B. Snyder, W9GT, "What ACSB Means to you," *Business Radio Action,* June 1982, pp. 13-17.

Haller and Van Deursen, "Amplitude Compandored Sideband Compared to Conventional Frequency Modulation for VHF Mobile Radio: Laboratory and Field Testing Results," *OST Technical Memorandum FCC/OST TM83-7,* Federal Communications Commission, Washington, DC, October 1983.

Frequency Modulation

Methods of radiotelephone communication by frequency modulation were developed in the 1930s by Major Edwin Armstrong in an attempt to reduce the problems of static and noise associated with receiving AM broadcast transmissions. The primary advantage of FM, the ability to produce a high signal-to-noise ratio when receiving a signal of only moderate strength, has made FM the mode chosen for mobile communications services and quality broadcasting. The disadvantages (the wide bandwidth required and the sometimes poor results obtained when an FM signal is propagated via the ionosphere because of phase distortion), have limited the use of frequency modulation to the 10-meter band and the VHF/UHF section of the spectrum.

FM has some impressive advantages for VHF operation, especially when compared to AM. With FM, the modulation process takes place in a low-level stage and remains the same, regardless of transmitter power. The signal may be frequency multiplied after modulation, and the PA stage can be operated Class C for best efficiency, as the "final" need not be linear.

In recent years there has been increasing use of FM by amateurs operating around 29.6 MHz. The VHF spectrum now in popular use includes 52 to 54 MHz, 146 to 148 MHz, 222 to 225 MHz, and 440 to 450 MHz.

Frequency and Phase Modulation

It is possible to convey intelligence by modulating any property of a carrier, including its frequency and phase. When the frequency of the carrier is varied in accordance with the variations in a modulating signal, the result is frequency modulation (FM). Similarly, varying the phase of the carrier current is called phase modulation (PM). Frequency and phase modulation are not independent, since the frequency cannot be varied without also varying the phase, and vice versa.

Frequency Modulation

When a modulating signal is applied to an FM modulator, the carrier frequency is increased during one half cycle of the modulating signal and decreased during the half cycle of opposite polarity. The change in the carrier frequency (frequency deviation) is proportional to the instantaneous amplitude of the modulating signal. Thus, the deviation is small when the instantaneous amplitude of the modulating signal is small, and is greatest when the modulating signal reaches its peak, either positive or negative.

Phase Modulation

If the phase of the current in a circuit shifts, there is an instantaneous frequency change during the time that the phase is shifting. The amount of frequency change, or deviation, is directly proportional to how rapidly the phase is shifting and the total amount of the phase shift. The rapidity of the phase shift is directly proportional to the frequency of the modulating signal. Further, in a properly operating PM system the amount of phase shift is proportional to the instantaneous amplitude of the modulating signal. This means that the amount of frequency change, or deviation, caused by a phase modulator, is directly proportional to both the instantaneous voltage and the frequency of the modulating signal. This is the outstanding difference between FM and PM, since in FM the frequency deviation is proportional only to the amplitude of the modulating signal. See Chapter 9 for further discussion of this and related topics.

FREQUENCY MODULATION METHODS

Direct FM

A simple, satisfactory device for producing FM in an amateur transmitter is the reactance modulator. This is a vacuum tube or transistor connected to the RF tank circuit of an oscillator in such a way as to act as a variable inductance or capacitance.

Fig. 32A is a representative circuit. Gate 1 of the modulator MOSFET is connected across the oscillator tank circuit, C1/L1, through resistor R1 and blocking capacitor C2. C3 represents the input capacitance of the modulator transistor. The resistance of R1 is large compared to the reactance of C3, so the RF current through R1/C3 will be practically in phase with the RF voltage appearing at the terminals of the tank circuit. However, the voltage across C3 will lag the current by 90 degrees. The RF current in the drain circuit of the modulator will be in phase with the grid voltage, and consequently is 90 degrees behind the current through C3, or 90 degrees behind the RF tank voltage. This lagging current is drawn through the oscillator tank, giving the same effect as though an inductance were connected across the tank. The frequency increases in proportion to the amplitude of the lagging plate current of the modulator. The audio voltage, introduced through a radio-frequency choke, varies the transconductance of the transistor and thereby varies the RF drain current.

The modulated oscillator usually is operated on a relatively low frequency, so a high order of carrier stability can be secured. Frequency multipliers are used to raise the frequency to the final frequency desired.

A reactance modulator can be connected to a crystal oscillator as well as to the self-controlled type as shown in Fig. 32B. However, the resulting signal can be more phase-modulated than it is frequency-

Fig. 31 — Portability and reliability make 2-meter FM hand-held operation a natural for supplying communications during emergencies, particularly when normal lines of communication are disrupted and access to the affected area is limited. (*KB4GJH photo*)

Fig. 32 — Reactance modulators using (A) a high-transconductance MOSFET and (B) a varactor diode.

Fig. 33 — (A) The phase-shifter type of phase modulator. (B) preemphasis and (C) deemphasis circuits.

modulated, because the frequency deviation that can be secured by varying the frequency of a crystal oscillator is quite small.

The sensitivity of the modulator (frequency change per unit change in modulating voltage) depends on the transconductance of the modulator transistor. It increases when R1 is made smaller in comparison with C3. It also increases with an increase in LC ratio in the oscillator tank circuit. However, for highest carrier stability it is desirable to use the largest tank capacitance that will permit the desired deviation to be secured while keeping within the limits of linear operation.

A change in any of the voltages on the modulator transistor will cause a change in RF drain current, and consequently a frequency change. Therefore it is advisable to use a regulated power supply for both modulator and oscillator.

Indirect FM

The same type of reactance-tube circuit that is used to vary the tuning of the oscillator tank in FM can be used to vary the tuning of an amplifier tank and thus vary the phase of the tank current for PM.

Hence the modulator circuit of Fig. 32A or 33A can be used for PM if the reactance transistor or tube works on an amplifier tank instead of directly on a self-controlled oscillator. If audio shaping is used in the speech amplifier, as described above, an FM-compatible signal will be generated by the phase modulator.

The phase shift that occurs when a circuit is detuned from resonance depends on the amount of detuning and the Q of the circuit. The higher the Q, the smaller the amount of detuning needed to secure a given number of degrees of phase shift. If the Q is at least 10, the relationship between phase shift and detuning (in kilohertz either side of the resonant frequency) will be substantially linear over a phase-shift range of about 25 degrees.

From the standpoint of modulator sensitivity, the tuned circuit Q on which the modulator operates should be as high as possible. On the other hand, the effective Q of the circuit will not be very high if the amplifier is delivering power to a load since the load resistance reduces the Q. There must therefore be a compromise between modulator sensitivity and RF power out-

put from the modulated amplifier. An optimum Q figure appears to be about 20; this allows reasonable loading of the modulated amplifier, and the necessary tuning variation can be secured from a reactance modulator without difficulty. It is advisable to modulate at a low power level.

Reactance modulation of an amplifier stage usually results in simultaneous amplitude modulation because the modulated stage is detuned from resonance as the phase is shifted. This must be eliminated by feeding the modulated signal through an amplitude limiter or one or more saturating stages — that is, amplifiers that are operated Class C and driven hard enough so that variations in the amplitude of the input excitation produce no appreciable variations in the output amplitude.

For the same type of reactance modulator, the speech-amplifier gain required is the same for PM as for FM. However, since the actual frequency deviation increases with the modulating audio frequency in PM, it is necessary to cut off the frequencies above about 3000 Hz before modulation takes place. If this is not done,

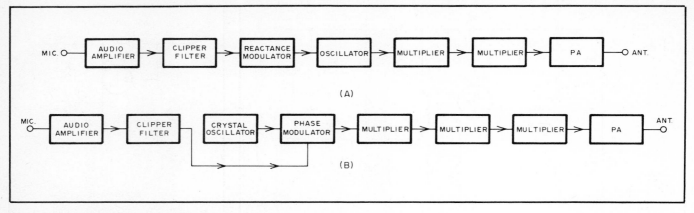

Fig. 34 — Block diagrams of typical FM exciters.

unnecessary sidebands will be generated at frequencies considerably removed from the carrier.

Speech Processing for FM

The speech amplifier that feeds the modulator is of ordinary design, except that no power is taken from it and the AF voltage required by the modulator input usually is small — only a volt or two for transistors. Because of these modest requirements, only a few speech stages are needed; a two-stage amplifier consisting of two bipolar transistors, both resistance-coupled, will more than suffice for crystal ceramic or Hi-Z dynamic microphones.

Several forms of speech processing produce worthwhile improvements in FM system performance. It is desirable to limit the peak amplitude of the audio signal applied to an FM or PM modulator, so that the deviation of the FM transmitter will not exceed a preset value. This peak limiting is usually accomplished with a simple audio clipper placed between the speech amplifier and modulator.

The clipping process produces high-order harmonics which, if allowed to pass through to the modulator stage, would create unwanted sidebands. Therefore, an audio low-pass filter with a cut-off frequency between 2.5 and 3 kHz is needed at the output of the clipper. Excess clipping can cause severe distortion of the voice signal. An audio processor consisting of a compressor and a clipper has been found to produce audio with a better sound (less distortion) than a clipper alone.

To reduce the amount of noise in some FM communication systems, an audio shaping network called preemphasis is added at the transmitter to proportionally attenuate the lower audio frequencies, giving an even spread to the energy in the audio band. This results in an FM signal of nearly constant energy distribution. Preemphasis applied to an FM transmitter will give the emission the deviation characteristics of PM. The reverse process, called deemphasis, is accomplished at the receiver to restore the audio to its original

relative proportions. See Fig. 33.

FM Exciters

FM exciters and transmitters take two general forms. One, shown at Fig. 34A, consists of a reactance modulator which shifts the frequency of an oscillator to generate an FM signal directly. Successive multiplier stages provide output on the desired frequency, which is amplified by a PA stage. This system has a disadvantage in that, if the oscillator is free running, it is difficult to achieve sufficient stability for VHF use. If a crystal-controlled oscillator is employed, because the amount that the crystal frequency is changed is kept small, it is difficult to achieve equal amounts of frequency swing.

The indirect method of generating FM shown in Fig. 34B is currently popular. Shaped audio is applied to a phase modulator to generate FM. Since the amount of deviation produced is very small, a large number of multiplier stages is needed to achieve wide-band deviation at the operating frequency. In general, the system shown at A will require a less complex circuit than that at B, but the indirect method (B) often produces superior results.

Testing an FM Transmitter

Accurate checking of the operation of an FM or PM transmitter requires different methods than the corresponding checks on an AM or SSB set. This is because the common forms of measuring devices either indicate amplitude variations only (a milliammeter, for example), or because their indications are most easily interpreted in terms of amplitude.

The quantities to be checked in an FM transmitter are the linearity and frequency deviation and the output frequency, if the unit uses crystal control. The methods of checking differ in detail.

Frequency Checking

Channelized FM operation requires that a transmitter be held within a few hundred hertz of the desired channel even in the wide-band system. Having the transmitter

on the proper frequency is particularly important when operating through a repeater. The rigors of mobile and portable operation make a frequency check of a channelized transceiver a good idea at three-month intervals.

Frequency meters generally fall into two categories, the heterodyne type and the digital counter. Today the digital counter is used almost universally; units counting to over 500 MHz are available at relatively low cost in kit form. Even less expensive low-frequency counters can be employed by using a prescaler, a device that divides an input frequency by a preset ratio, usually 10 or 100. Many prescalers may be used at 148 MHz or higher, using a counter with a 2-MHz (or more) upper frequency limit. If the counting system does not have a sufficient upper frequency limit to measure the output of an FM transmitter directly, one of the frequency-multiplier stages can be sampled to provide a signal in the range of the measurement device. Alternatively, a crystal-controlled converter feeding an HF receiver that has accurate frequency readout can be employed, if a secondary standard is available to calibrate the receiving system.

Deviation and Deviation Linearity

A simple deviation meter can be assembled following the diagram of Fig. 35A. This circuit was designed by K6VKZ. The output of a wide-band receiver discriminator (before any deemphasis) is fed to two amplifier transistors. The output of the amplifier section is transformer coupled to a pair of rectifier diodes to develop a dc voltage for the meter, M1. There will be an indication on the meter with no signal input because of detected noise, so the accuracy of the instrument will be poor on weak signals.

To calibrate the unit, signals of known deviation will be required. If the meter is to be set to read 0-15 kHz, then a 7.5-kHz deviation test signal should be employed. R1 is then adjusted until M1 reads half scale, 50 μA. To check the peak deviation of an incoming signal, close both S1 and

Fig. 35 — (A) Schematic diagram of the deviation meter. Resistors are ½-watt composition, and capacitors are ceramic, except those with polarity marked, which are electrolytic. D1-D3, incl., are high-speed silicon switching diodes. R1 is a linear-taper composition control, and S1, S2 are SPST toggle switches. T1 is a miniature audio transformer with 10-kΩ primary and 20-kΩ center-tapped secondary (Triad A31X). (B) Chart of audio frequencies that will produce a carrier null when the deviation of an FM transmitter is set for the values given.

PEAK DEVIATION METER
(A)

Audio Frequency	Deviation Produced		
	1st Null	2nd Null	3rd Null
905.8 Hz	±2.18 kHz	± 5.00 kHz	± 7.84 kHz
1000.0 Hz	±2.40 kHz	± 5.52 kHz	± 8.65 kHz
1500.0 Hz	±3.61 kHz	± 8.28 kHz	±12.98 kHz
1811.0 Hz	±4.35 kHz	±10.00 kHz	±15.67 kHz
2000.0 Hz	±4.81 kHz	±11.04 kHz	±17.31 kHz
2079.2 Hz	±5.00 kHz	±11.48 kHz	±17.99 kHz
2805.0 Hz	±6.75 kHz (B)	±15.48 kHz	±24.27 kHz

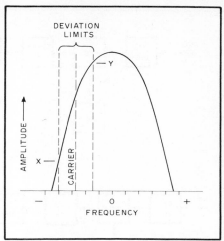

Fig. 36 — FM detector characteristics. Slope detection, using the sloping side of the receiver's selectivity curve to convert FM to AM for subsequent detection.

S2. Then, read the meter. Opening first one switch and then the other will indicate the amount of positive and negative deviation of the signal, a check of deviation linearity.

Measurement of Deviation Using Bessel Functions

Using a mathematical relationship known as the Bessel Function it is possible to predict the points at which, with certain audio-input frequencies and predetermined deviation settings, the carrier output of an FM transmitter will disappear completely. Thus, by monitoring the carrier frequency with a receiver, it will be possible to identify aurally the deviation at which the carrier is nulled. A heterodyne signal at either the input or receiver IF is required so the carrier will produce a beat note that can be identified easily. Other tones will be produced in the modulation process, so some concentration is required when making the test. With an audio tone selected from the chart (Fig. 35B), advance the deviation control slowly until the first null is heard. If a higher-order null is desired, continue advancing the control further until the second, and then the third, null is heard. Using a carrier null beyond the third is generally not practical.

For example, if a 905.8-Hz tone is used, the transmitter will be set for 5-kHz deviation when the second null is reached. The second null achieved with a 2805-Hz audio

input will set the transmitter deviation at 15.48 kHz. The Bessel-function approach can be used to calibrate a deviation meter, such as the unit shown in Fig. 35A.

Reception of FM Signals

Receivers for FM signals differ from others principally in two features — there is no need for linearity preceding detection (it is, in fact, advantageous if amplitude variations in signal and background noise can be minimized). Also, the detector must be capable of converting frequency variations of the incoming signal into amplitude variations.

Frequency-modulated signals can be received after a fashion on any ordinary receiver. The receiver is tuned to put the carrier frequency partway down on one side of the selectivity curve. When the frequency of the signal varies with modulation it swings as indicated in Fig. 36, resulting in an AM output varying between X and Y. This is then rectified as an AM signal.

With receivers having steep-sided selectivity curves, the method is not very satisfactory because the distortion is quite severe unless the frequency deviation is small, since the frequency deviation and output amplitude is linear over only a small part of the selectivity curve.

The FM Receiver

Block diagrams of an AM/SSB and an

FM receiver are shown in Fig. 37. Fundamentally, to achieve a sensitivity of less than 1 μV, an FM receiver requires a gain of several million — too much total gain to be accomplished with stability on a single frequency. Thus, the use of the super-heterodyne circuit has become standard practice. Three major differences will be apparent from a comparison of the two block diagrams. The FM receiver employs a wider-bandwidth filter and a different detector, and has a limiter stage added between the IF amplifier and the detector. Otherwise the functions, and often the circuits, of the RF, oscillator, mixer and audio stages will be the same in either receiver.

In operation, the noticeable difference between the two receivers is the effect of noise and interference on an incoming signal. From the time of the first spark transmitters, QRN has been a major problem for amateurs. The limiter and discriminator stages in an FM set can eliminate a good deal of impulse noise, except noise that manages to acquire a frequency-modulation characteristic. Accurate alignment of the receiver IF system and phase tuning of the detector are required to achieve good noise suppression. FM receivers perform in an unusual manner when QRM is present, exhibiting a characteristic known as the capture effect. The loudest signal received, even if it is only two or three times stronger than other stations on the same frequency, will be the only transmission demodulated. By comparison, an S9 AM or CW signal can suffer noticeable interference from an S2 carrier.

Bandwidth

Most FM sets that use tubes achieve IF selectivity by using a number of over-coupled transformers. The wide bandwidth and phase-response characteristic needed in the IF system dictate careful design and

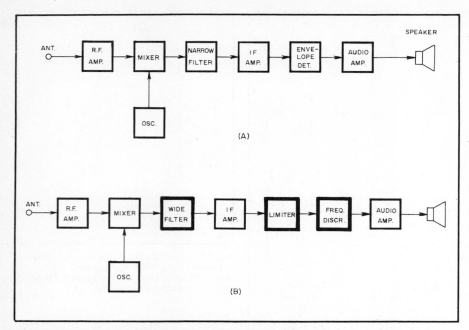

Fig. 37 — Block diagrams of (A) an AM, (B) an FM receiver. Dark borders outline the sections that are different in the FM set.

Fig. 38 — (A) Input wave form to a limiter stage shows AM and noise. (B) The same signal, after passing through two limiter stages, is devoid of AM components.

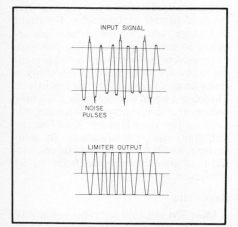

Fig. 39 — Representation of limiter action. Amplitude variations on the signal are removed by the diode action of the grid- and plate-current saturation.

alignment of all interstage transformers.

For the average ham, the use of a high-selectivity filter in a homemade receiver offers some simplification of the alignment task. Following the techniques used in SSB receivers, a crystal or ceramic filter should be placed in the circuit as close as possible to the antenna connector — at the output of the first mixer, in most cases. Table 5 lists a number of suitable filters available to amateurs. Experimenters who wish to build their own can use surplus HF crystals or ceramic resonators.

One item of concern to every amateur FM user is the choice of IF bandwidth for the receiver. Deviation of 5 kHz is now standard on the amateur bands above 29 MHz. A wide-band receiver can receive narrow-band signals, suffering only some loss of audio level in the detection process. Naturally, it also will be subject to adjacent-channel interference, especially in congested areas.

Limiters

When FM was first introduced, the main selling point for the new mode was that noise-free reception was possible. The circuit in the FM receiver that has the task of chopping off noise and amplitude modulation from an incoming signal is the limiter. Most types of FM detectors respond to both frequency and amplitude variations of the signal. Thus, the limiter stages preceding the detector are included so only the desired frequency modulation will be demodulated. This action can be seen in Fig. 38.

Limiter stages can be designed using tubes, transistors or ICs. For an amplifier to act as a limiter, the applied voltages are chosen so the stage will overload easily, even with a small amount of signal input. As shown in Fig. 39, the input signal limits when it is of sufficient amplitude so that diode action of the input voltage and output current saturation clip both sides of the input signal, producing a constant-amplitude output voltage.

Obviously, a signal of considerable strength is required at the input of the limiter to assure full clipping, typically 1 volt for transistors and several hundred microvolts for ICs. Limiting action should start with an RF input of 0.2 μV or less, so a large amount of gain is required between the antenna terminal and the limiter stages. For example, many commercial solid-state receivers use nine transistor stages for sufficient gain before the first limiter. The new ICs offer some simplification of the IF system, as they pack a lot of gain into a single package.

When sufficient signal arrives at the receiver to start limiting action, the set quiets — that is, the background noise disappears. The sensitivity of an FM receiver is rated in terms of the amount of input signal required to produce a given amount of quieting, usually 20 dB. Use of solid-state devices allows receivers to achieve 20 dB quieting with 0.15 to 0.5 μV of input signal.

A single transistor amplifier stage will not provide good limiting over a wide range of input signals. Two stages, with different input time constants, are a minimum requirement. The first stage is set to handle impulse noise satisfactorily while the second is designed to limit the range of signals passed on by the first. At frequencies below 1 MHz it is useful to employ untuned RC-coupled limiters that provide sufficient gain without oscillation.

Fig. 40A shows a two-stage limiter using transistors in two stages biased for limiter service. The base bias on either transistor may be varied to provide limiting at a desired level. The input-signal voltage required to start limiting action is called the limiting knee. This refers to the point at which collector current ceases to rise with

Table 5
FM-bandwidth Filters Available to Amateurs

Manufacturer	Model	Center Frequency	Nominal Bandwidth	Ultimate Rejection	Impedance Ω In	Out	Insertion Loss	Crystal Discriminator
KVG (1)	XF-9E	9.0 MHz	12 kHz	90 dB	1200	1200	3 dB	XD9-02
KVG (1)	XF-107A	10.7 MHz	12 kHz	90 dB	820	820	3.5 dB	XD107-01
KVG (1)	XF-107B	10.7 MHz	15 kHz	90 dB	910	910	3.5 dB	XD107-01
KVG (1)	XF-107C	10.7 MHz	30 kHz	90 dB	2000	2000	4.5 dB	XD107-01
CDI (2)	-	21.5 MHz	15 kHz	90 dB	550	550	3 dB	—
CDI (2)	-	21.5 MHz	30 kHz	90 dB	1100	1100	2 dB	—
Clevite (3)	TCF4-12D3CA	455 kHz	12 kHz	60 dB	40 k	2200	6 dB	—
Clevite (3)	TCF4-18G45A	455 kHz	18 kHz	50 dB	40 k	2200	6 dB	—
Clevite (3)	TCF6-30D55A	455 kHz	30 kHz	60 dB	20 k	1000	5 dB	—

Manufacturers' addresses are as follows: (1) Spectrum International, P.O. Box 1084, Concord, MA 01742, tel. 617-263-2145; (2) Crystal Devices, Inc. (CDI), 6050 N. 52nd Ave., Glendale, AZ 85301, tel. 602-934-5234; (3) Semiconductor Specialists, Inc., P.O. Box 66125, O'Hare International Airport, Elmhurst, IL 60126, tel. 312-279-1000.

Fig. 40 — Typical limiter circuits using (A) transistors, (B) a differential IC, (C) a high-gain linear IC.

increased input signal. Modern ICs have limiting knees of 100 mV for the circuit shown in Fig. 40C, using the RCA CA3028A or Motorola MC1550G, or 200 mV for the MC1590G of Fig. 40D. Because the high-gain ICs such as the CA3076 and MC1590G contain as many as six or eight active stages that will saturate with sufficient input, one of these devices pro-

vides superior limiter performance compared to a pair of transistors.

Detectors

The first type of FM detector to gain popularity was the frequency discriminator. The characteristic of such a detector is shown in Fig. 41. When the FM signal has no modulation, and the carrier is at point

0, the detector has no output. When audio input to the FM transmitter swings the signal higher in frequency, the rectified output increases in the positive direction. When the frequency swings lower, the output amplitude increases in the negative direction. Over a range where the discriminator is linear (shown as the straight portion of the line), the conversion

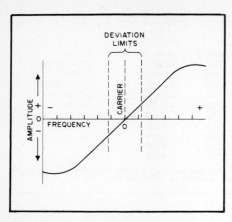

Fig. 41 — The characteristic of an FM discriminator.

Fig. 42 — Typical frequency-discriminator circuit used for FM detection. T1 is a Miller 12-C45.

Fig. 43 — A ratio detector of the type often used in entertainment radio and TV sets. T1 is a ratio-detector transformer such as the Miller 1606.

Fig. 44 — Crystal discriminator, C1 and L1 are resonant at the intermediate frequency. C2 is equal in value to C3. C4 corrects any circuit imbalance so equal amounts of signal are fed to the detector diodes.

of FM to AM will also be linear.

A practical discriminator circuit is shown in Fig. 42. The voltage induced in the T1 secondary is 90 degrees out of phase with the current in the primary. The primary signal is introduced through a center tap on the secondary, coupled through a capacitor. The secondary voltages combine on each side of the center tap so that the voltage on one side leads the primary signal while the other side lags by the same amount. When rectified, these two voltages are equal and of opposite polarity, resulting in zero-voltage output. A shift in input frequency causes a shift in the phase of the voltage components that results in an increase of output amplitude on one side of the secondary, and a corresponding decrease on the other side. The differences in the two changing voltages, after rectification, constitute the audio output.

In the search for a simplified FM detector, RCA developed a circuit that became standard in entertainment radios; it eliminated the need for a preceding limiter stage. Known as the ratio detector, this circuit is based on the idea of dividing a dc voltage into a ratio that is equal to the ratio of the amplitudes from either side of a discriminator-transformer secondary. With a detector that responds only to ratios, the input signal may vary in strength over a wide range without causing a change in the level of output voltage — FM can be detected, but not AM. In the actual ratio detector, Fig. 43, the required dc voltage is developed across two load resistors, shunted by an electrolytic capacitor. Other differences include the two diodes, which are wired in series aiding rather than series opposing, as in the standard discriminator circuit. The recovered audio is taken from a tertiary winding that is tightly coupled to the primary of the transformer. Diode-load resistor values are selected to be lower (5000 ohms or less) than for the discriminator.

The sensitivity of the ratio detector is one-half that of the discriminator. In general, however, the transformer design values for Q, primary-secondary coupling

Fig. 45 — (A) Block diagram of a PLL demodulator. (B) Complete PLL circuit.

and load will vary greatly, so the actual performance differences between these two types of FM detectors are usually not significant. Either circuit can provide excellent results. In operation, the ratio detector will not provide sufficient limiting for communications service, so this detector also is usually preceded by at least a single limiting stage.

Other Detector Designs

The difficulties often encountered in building and aligning LC discriminators have inspired research that has resulted in a number of adjustment-free FM detector designs. The crystal discriminator utilizes a quartz resonator, shunted by an inductor, in place of the tuned-circuit secondary used in a discriminator transformer. A typical circuit is shown in Fig. 44. Some commercially made crystal discriminators have the input-circuit inductor, L1, built in (C1 must be added), while in other types both L1 and C2 must be supplied by the builder. Fig. 44 shows typical component values; unmarked parts are chosen to give the desired bandwidth. Sources for crystal discriminators are listed in Table 5.

The PLL

Since the phase-locked loop (PLL) was reduced to a single IC package, it has made significant impact on receiver design. Signetics first introduced a PLL in a single flat-pack IC. Motorola and Fairchild are making the PLL in separate building-block ICs. These allow a builder to assemble an FM receiving system with a minimum of bother.

A basic phase-locked loop consists of a phase detector, a filter, a dc amplifier and a voltage-controlled oscillator (VCO). The VCO runs at a frequency close to that of an incoming signal. The phase detector produces an error voltage if any frequency difference exists between the VCO and the IF signal. This error voltage is applied to the VCO. Any changes in the frequency of the incoming signal are sensed at the detector and the error voltage readjusts the VCO frequency so it remains locked to the intermediate frequency. The bandwidth of the system is determined by a filter on the error-voltage line. See Fig. 45.

Because the error voltage is a copy of the audio variations originally used to shift the frequency of the transmitter, the PLL functions directly as an FM detector. The sensitivity achieved with the Signetics NE565 PLL is good — about 1 mV for a typical circuit. No transformers or tuned circuits are required. The PLL bandwidth is usually 2 to 10 percent of the IF for FM detection. Components R1/C1 set the VCO close to the desired frequency. C2 is the loop-filter capacitor, which determines the capture range — that range of frequencies over which the loop will acquire lock with an unlocked input signal. The NE565 has an upper frequency limit of 500 kHz.

Chapter 19

Digital Communications

There is a growing trend away from analog transmission methods and toward digital communications. This is not limited to systems, such as computers, that use digital codes in their native language. Digital types of transmission are increasingly used for signals that are analog in origin and must be delivered to the ultimate user in analog form.

This chapter covers not only Baudot, AMTOR, ASCII and other radioteletype (RTTY) or computer-to-computer communications, but the granddaddy of them all—Morse code. It may be convenient to label these different digital codes and tuck them away in separate categories. To do so, however, limits one's thinking to what already has been done.

Digital communication will change rapidly. Distinctions between the present categories will become increasingly blurred, and there will be a scramble for new terminology to keep up with technological change. Looking to the future, the FCC has given the Amateur Service wide latitude for the use of digital communications techniques.

Fig. 1 — A family portrait of telegraph keyers used over this century. At front left is a hand key or straight key. Next is a semiautomatic key, usually called a *bug*, which produced a series of dots automatically but not dashes (which had to be formed individually by the operator). At front right is an electronic paddle keyer that produced both dots and dashes automatically when initiated by the operator. At rear left, a keyboard-operated electronic keyer. At right is a personal computer that has been programmed to generate and receive Morse code.

Rules and Regulations

Emission types such as data, RTTY, CW and MCW are defined in §97.3 of the FCC Rules. These emission types are defined in terms of the possible emission type designators, such as: "§97.3(c)(2) *Data*. Telemetry, telecommand and computer communications emissions having designators with A, C, D, F, G, H, J or R as the first symbol; 1 as the second symbol; D as the third symbol; and emission J2D. Only a digital code of a type specifically authorized in this Part may be transmitted."

Technical details of the transmitted signals are specified in §97.307. Permitted signaling rates and frequency shifts vary with operating frequency. For example, for frequencies below 28 MHz, §97.307(f)(3) says, "Only a RTTY or data emission using a specified digital code listed in §97.309(a) of this Part may be transmitted. The symbol rate must not exceed 300 bauds, or for frequency-shift keying, the frequency

shift between mark and space must not exceed 1 kHz." The digital codes specified in §97.309(a) are Baudot, AMTOR and ASCII, defined as:

(1) the 5-unit, start-stop, International Telegraph Alphabet No. 2 code, defined in International Telegraph and Telephone Consultative Committee (CCITT) Recommendation F.1, Division C;

(2) The 7-unit code specified in International Radio Consultative Committee (CCIR) Recommendation CCIR 476-2 (1978), 476-3 (1982, 476-4 (1986) or 625 (1986);

(3) The 7-unit code, defined in American National Standards Institute X3.4-1977 or International Alphabet No. 5, defined in CCITT recommendation T.50 or in International Organization for Standardization, ISO 646 (1983), and extensions as provided for in CCITT Recommendation T.61 (Malaga-Torremolinos, 1984).

Current rules permit transmission rates up to 19.6 kilobauds between 50 and 220 MHz and 56 kilobauds above 220 MHz. Rather than set maximum speeds for other digital codes, the FCC specifies a maximum bandwidth of 20 kHz between 50 and 220 MHz, and 100 kHz between 220 and 1240 MHz.

A Bit of History

The term "radioteletype" originally meant communications between typewriter-like *machines* using a telegraph code known as Baudot (or Murray). Before 1975, few amateurs thought about any terminal other than a teletypewriter for RTTY communications.

Affordable personal computers first became available around 1975. A number of radio amateurs acquired computers (which used an eight-bit code) and immediately thought of interfacing them to

Baudot teleprinters (which used five information bits). One application was to use a teleprinter to produce a paper printout (hard copy) for their computer. Another was to use the computer to send and receive Baudot RTTY and CW on the amateur bands.

In 1980 the FCC legalized Amateur Radio transmission of the American National Standard Code for Information Interchange (ASCII), which is the code used by these computers. Then in 1982, in response to an ARRL petition (RM-3788), the FCC amended its rules to permit any digital code to be used above 50 MHz. In response to another ARRL petition (RM-4122), the FCC amended its rules in 1983 to permit amateurs to use *AM*ateur *T*eleprinting *O*ver *R*adio (AMTOR) in the high-frequency bands.

Another FCC order, which was effective on June 15, 1983, made several other changes that affected digital communications. The maximum audio- or radio-frequency shift was redefined as not to exceed 1000 Hz (between the mark and space frequencies) below 50 MHz, also that the frequency shift in hertz shall not exceed the sending speed in bauds or 1000 Hz, whichever is greater. The same order eliminated the need for CW or voice identification of digital transmissions and authorized stations to identify in Baudot, AMTOR or ASCII, whichever code is used for all or part of the communication below 50 MHz or when any digital code is used above 50 MHz.

These regulatory changes have done much to clear the way for significant changes in Amateur Radio digital communications. No doubt, there will be more Rules changes designed to facilitate new forms of digital communications.

Morse Code

Radiotelegraphy by Morse code is the original modulation method used in Amateur Radio. The code is named after its inventor, Samuel F. B. Morse, 1791-1872, an American artist and promoter of the telegraph. Unlike codes designed for teletypewriters, the Morse code consists of elements of unequal length. The short pulse is called a dot (often sounded *dit*), and the long pulse is a dash (sounded *dah*). There are unique combinations of dots and dashes for the letters of the alphabet, numerals, punctuation marks and procedure signals (prosigns). A comprehensive list of the code combinations and their meanings appears in Table 1. The list shows code combinations for languages that use the Latin alphabet and includes accented letters,

---

Table 1
Morse Code Character Set[1]

A	didah	• —	I	didit	••	S	dididit	•••			
B	dahdididit	— •••	J	didahdahdah	• — — —	T	dah	—			
C	dahdidahdit	— • — •	K	dahdidah	— • —	U	dididah	•• —			
D	dahdidit	— ••	L	didahdidit	• — ••	V	didididah	••• —			
E	dit	•	M	dahdah	— —	W	didahdah	• — —			
F	dididahdit	•• — •	N	dahdit	— •	X	dahdididah	— •• —			
G	dahdahdit	— — •	O	dahdahdah	— — —	Y	dahdidahdah	— • — —			
H	didididit	••••	P	didahdahdit	• — — •	Z	dahdahdidit	— — ••			
			Q	dahdahdidah	— — • —						
			R	didahdit	• — •						

1	didahdahdahdah	• — — — —	4	didididah	•••• —	8	dahdahdahdidit	— — — ••
2	dididahdahdah	•• — — —	5	didididit	•••••	9	dahdahdahdahdit	— — — — •
3	didididahdah	••• — —	6	dahdidididit	— ••••	0	dahdahdahdahdah	— — — — —
			7	dahdahdididit	— — •••			

Period [.]:	didahdidahdidah	• — • — • —	A̅A̅A̅	*Fraction bar [/]:*	dahdididahdit	— •• — •	D̅N̅
Comma [,]:	dahdahdididahdah	— — •• — —	M̅I̅M̅	*Quotation marks ["]:*	didahdididahdit	• — •• — •	A̅F̅
Question mark				*Dollar sign [$]:*	didididahdididah	••• — •• —	S̅X̅
or request for				*Apostrophe [']:*	didahdahdahdahdit	• — — — — •	W̅G̅
repetition [?]:	dididahdahdidit	•• — — ••	I̅M̅I̅	*Paragraph [¶]:*	didahdahdididit	• — — •••	A̅L̅
Error:	dididididididit	•••••••	H̅H̅	*Underline [__]:*	didididahdahdit	•• — — •	I̅Q̅
Hyphen or dash [—]:	dahdidididdidah	— •••• —	D̅U̅	*Starting signal:*	dahdidahdidah	— • — • —	K̅A̅
Double dash [=]:	dahdidididah	— ••• —	B̅T̅	*Wait:*	didahdididit	• — •••	A̅S̅
Colon [:]:	dahdahdahdididit	— — — •••	O̅S̅	*End of message or cross [+]:*	didahdidahdit	• — • — •	A̅R̅
Semicolon [;]:	dahdidahdidahdit	— • — • — •	K̅R̅	*Invitation to transmit [K]:*	dahdidah	— • —	K
Left parenthesis [(]:	dahdidahdahdit	— • — — •	K̅N̅	*End of work:*	didididahdidah	••• — • —	S̅K̅
Right parenthesis [)]:	dahdidahdahdidah	— • — — • —	K̅K̅	*Understood:*	dididahdidit	•• — •	S̅N̅

Notes
1. Not all Morse characters shown are used in FCC code tests. License applicants are responsible for knowing, and may be tested on, the 26 letters, the numerals 0 to 9, the period, the comma, the question mark, A̅R̅, S̅K̅, B̅T̅ and fraction bar [D̅N̅].
2. The following letters are used in certain European languages which use the Latin alphabet:

Ä, Ą	didahdidah	• — • —	Ö, Ø, Ó	dahdahdahdit	— — — •		
Á, Å, À, Â	didahdahdidah	• — — • —	Ñ	dahdahdidahdah	— — • — —		
Ç, Ć	dahdidahdidit	— • — ••	Ü	dididahdah	•• — —		
É, È, Ę	dididahdidit	•• — ••	Ż	dahdahdidit	— — ••		
È	didahdididah	• — ••• —	Ź	dahdahdidahdit	— — • — •		
Ê	dahdidididahdit	— •••• •	CH, Ş	dahdahdahdah	— — — —		

3. Special Esperanto characters:

Ĉ	dahdidahdidit	— • — ••
Ŝ	didididahdit	••• — •
Ĝ	didahdahdidit	• — — ••
Ĥ	dahdidahdahdit	— • — — •
Ŭ	dididahdah	•• — —

4. Signals used in other radio services:

Interrogatory	dididahdidah	•• — • —		I̅N̅T̅
Emergency silence	dididididahdah	•••• — —		H̅M̅
Executive follows	dididahdidah	•• — • —		I̅X̅
Break-in signal	dahdahdahdahdah	— — — — —		T̅T̅T̅T̅T̅
Emergency signal	didididahdahdahdididit	••• — — — •••		S̅O̅S̅
Relay of distress	dahdidididahdididahdidit	— ••• — •• — ••		D̅D̅D̅

which are needed in some languages.

The listing of all of the code combinations does not imply that amateurs should learn and use all of them. In fact, to satisfy FCC testing requirements and for general use on the ham bands, you need to learn only the 26 letters, 10 numerals, the period, the comma, the question mark, fraction bar (D̄N̄), ĀR, S̄K and B̄T. If you do not already know these Morse characters, it is advisable to learn the code in an orderly manner, preferably with the help of an instructor. After you have learned the basic characters and have some on-the-air experience, you may wish to expand your vocabulary of Morse code characters as you hear them or have need to send them.

Table 1 will also prove useful to those wishing to develop computer programs to send and receive Morse code. Some such programs have been flawed by omissions of valid characters and bogus combinations resulting from an incomplete listing of existing assignments.

Table 2 lists Morse code combinations for languages that are not based on the Latin alphabet. While most Amateur Radio

Table 2
Morse Codes for Other Languages

Code	Japanese	Thai	Korean	Arabic	Hebrew	Russian	Greek
•	ヘ he	ๅ sara-a	ㅏ a		ו vav	Е,Э E	E epsilon
—	ム mu	ต tor-tow	ㅓ ŏ	ت ta	תת tav	Т T	T tau
••	゛ nigori	ะ sara-e	ㅑ ya	ي ya	י yod	И I	I iota
•—	イ i	⅃ sara-r	ㅗ o	ا alif	א aleph	А A	A alpha
—•	タ ta	น nor-nu	ㅛ yo	ن noon	נן nun	Н N	N nu
——	ヨ yo	ม mor-ma	ㅁ m	م meem	מם mem	М M	M mu
•••	ラ ra	ส sor-sue	ㅕ yŏ	س seen	שׁ shin	С S	Σ sigma
••—	ウ u	ไ mai-ek		ط ta	ט tet	У U	OΥ omicron ypsilon
•—•	ナ na	ร roe-rue	ㅠ yu	ر ra	ר reish	Р R	P rho
•——	ヤ ya	ว vor-van	ㅂ p(b)	و waw	צץ tzadi	В V	Ω omega
—••	ホ ho	ด door-dek		د dal	ד dalet	Д D	Δ delta
—•—	ワ wa	ค kor-kwai	ㅇ -ng	ك kaf	ךכ chaf	К K	K kappa
——•	リ ri	ก go-kai		غ ghain	ג gimmel	Г G	Γ gamma
———	レ re	โ sara-o		خ kha	ה heh	О O	O omicron
••••	ヌ nu	ห hor-heep	ㅜ u	ح ha	ח chet	Х H	H eta
•••—	ク ku	ั mai-tho	ㄹ r-(-l)	ض dad		Ж J	HΥ eta ypsilon
••—•	チ ti	ฟ for-fun	ㄴ n	ف fa	ףפ feh	Ф F	Φ phi
••——	ノ no	ึ sara-eu				Ю yu	AΥ alpha ypsilon
•—••	カ ka	ล law-ling	ㄱ k(g)	ل lam	ל lamed	Л L	Λ lambda
•—•—	ロ ro	ๅ sara-air		ع ain		Я ya	AI alpha iota
•——•	ツ tu	ป por-pla			פ peh	П P	Π pi
•———	ヲ wo	ญ yor-ying	ㅈ ch(j)	ج jeem	ע ayen	Й Y	ΥI ypsilon iota
—•••	ハ ha	บ bor-baimai	ㅎ h	ب ba	בב bet	Б B	B beta
—••—	マ ma	ช chor-chang	ㄷ t(d)	ص sad		ь,ъ mute	Ξ xi
—•—•	ニ ni	ข kho-khai	ㅋ k'	ث tha	ם samech	Ц TS	Θ theta
—•——	ケ ke	ย yor-yak	ㅊ ch'	ظ za		Ы I	Υ ypsilon
——••	フ hu	ซ zor-zo	ㅔ e	ذ dhal	ז zain	З Z	Z zeta
——•—	ネ ne	ผ pho-phueng	ㅌ t'	ق qaf		Щ SHCH	Ψ psi
———•	ソ so	ุ sara-u	ㅐ ae	ز zay	ק kof	Ч CH	EΥ epsilon ypsilon
————	コ ko	ฉ choe-ching		ش sheen		Ш SH	X khi
••—••	ト to	ี sara-ie		ه he			
••—•—	ミ mi	่ sara-au					
••——•	° han-nigori	้ sara-aue					
•—•••	オ o	็ sara-ar					
•—••—	井 (w)i	ไ sara-i					
•—•—•	ン n	๋ mai-jatawa					
•—•——	テ te	ฤ row-rue					
•——••	ヱ (w)e	ฬ por-pan					
•——•—	- hyphen	่ mai-han agas					
•———•	セ se	้ maitho han agas					
—••••	メ me	อ or-ang					
—••—•	モ mo	จ jor-jan					
—••——	ユ yu	ฑ tor-tahan					
—•—••	キ ki	ฏ tor-tung					
—•—•—	サ sa						
—•——•	ル ru	ง ngor-ngoo					
—•———	エ e						
——••—	ヒ hi						
——•—•	シ si						
——•——	ア a	ฮ hor-nok hook					
———•—	ス su						
•—•••—				ﻻ lam-alif			

Fig. 2 — Timing of Morse code elements and spaces. The word PARIS is used as the typical word in English plain-language text. CODEX is typical of random-letter groups.

CW communications use the International Morse Code (Table 1), you can occasionally hear hams native in the same language chat with one another in the codes listed in Table 2.

Timing of Morse Code

The basic unit of time in Morse code is the length of the dot. The duration of the dash is three times that of the dot. The term *element* is used to include both dots and dashes. The space between two elements forming the same character is the same as for the dot. The space between characters is equal to three dots. The space between words or groups is equal to seven dots. These relationships are illustrated in Fig. 2.

Note that the length of characters varies. The letter E is the shortest because it is used most frequently in English plain-language text. T and I are next in line, and the codes get longer for letters that are less frequently used.

Analysis of English plain-language text indicates that the average word (including the space between words) is 50 units long. The word PARIS is of this length and is used to accurately set transmission speed. For example, if you wish to transmit at 10 WPM, adjust the keying speed until the word PARIS is sent 10 times in one minute. If you were to set the speed for PARIS but then send random-letter groups for code practice, you would find that the number of groups sent per minute is smaller. The reason is that the average length of random-letter groups is 60 units — the length of the group CODEX. The code speed for plain-language English can be found from

$$\text{speed (WPM)} = \frac{\text{dots/min}}{25}$$

$$= 2.4 \times \text{dots/s}$$

For example, a properly adjusted keyer gives a string of dots that are counted at 10 dots per second: speed = $2.4 \times 10 =$ 24 WPM. For these keyers the code speed may be determined directly from the clock frequency

$$\text{speed (WPM)} = 1.2 \times \text{clock freq. (Hz)}$$

For a quick and simple means of determining the code speed, send a continuous string of dashes and count the number of dashes that occur in a five-second period. This number, to a close approximation, is the code speed in words per minute. A method for checking the speed of a Morse keyboard is to send a continuous string of zeros, with proper interletter spacing. Most keyboards will automatically insert the correct space if the key is released and re-activated before the end of the character. If zeros are sent for one minute, the speed is approximately

$$\text{speed (WPM)} = (\text{zeros/min}) \times 0.44.$$

Cutting Numbers

You will notice that the numerals 0 through 9 in Morse code are longer than letters. That's fine as long as numbers are only an incidental part of the transmission.

Radio services that send lots of numeric text, such as weather information, usually cut the length of the codes for numbers. Table 3 lists both long numbers and cut number substitutions. Cut numbers should be used sparingly whenever in doubt that the receiving operator will understand them. Also, only the long numbers are legal for identification purposes. Cut numbers are not in widespread use by amateurs except for sending RST reports. Even there, usually only the numeral 9 is sent in cut form. Another exception is that the cut form of zero is frequently used in rag-chewing. The long form of zero should be sent in call signs and in message headings.

MORSE KEYING AND SWITCHING

Two basic problems involved with Morse code radiotelegraphy are keying the transmitter on and off and switching between transmit and receive states. If the transmitter is switched on and off too slowly, the resultant RF signal will be difficult to read because the keying sounds too soft. If the transitions are too fast, extraneous sidebands, called *key clicks*, are generated. It is the responsibility of the transmitter operator to ensure that unnecessary key clicks are not transmitted.

Ideally, a transceiver should quickly change from receive to transmit states when the key is pressed. Similarly, it should revert to the receiving state as soon as the key is opened. This is called *break-in keying* and allows the sending operator to hear between keying elements in the event that the receiving station is trying to interrupt. This is an important feature for the serious CW operator and is attainable by careful transceiver design.

Power-Supply Regulation for CW Keying

It is impractical to control the shape of the RF keying envelope unless the transmitter power supply is properly filtered and regulated. Improper regulation could cause the effect shown in Fig. 3D. This type of wave is even richer in harmonics than a square wave. The severity of the problem is a function of power supply load regulation. Note that in a class-C amplifier the change in power output related to plate or collector voltage regulation is proportional to the *square* of the voltage change. The power supply for a solid-state transmitter

Table 3
Morse Cut Numbers

Numeral	Long Number		Cut Number		Equivalent Character
1	didahdahdahdah	•－－－－	didah	•－	A
2	dididahdahdah	••－－－	dididah	••－	U
3	didididahdah	•••－－	didididah	•••－	V
4	didididahdah	••••－	didididdah	••••－	4
5	dididididit	•••••	didididit	••••• or •	5 or E
6	dahdidididit	－••••	dahdidididit	－••••	6
7	dahdahdididit	－－•••	dahdidididit	－•••	B
8	dahdahdahdidit	－－－••	dahdidit	－••	D
9	dahdahdahdahdit	－－－－•	dahdit	－•	N
0	dahdahdahdahdah	－－－－－	dah	－	T

Note: These cut numbers are not legal for use in call signs. They should be used only where there is agreement between operators and when no confusion will result.

may be regulated easily and inexpensively by electronic means, but such a scheme applied to a high-power tube type of transmitter is costly and dissipates considerable power. Fortunately, the plate voltage waveform can be corrected with a passive circuit (see Dome, May 1977 *QST*). Note also that the power source must be nearly pure dc to ensure that the transmitter output signal is not broadened by hum modulation.

RF Envelope Shaping

On-off keying is a form of amplitude modulation and, as such, generates sidebands whose spacing from the carrier is a function of envelope rise and fall times, which are the highest-frequency components of the keying waveform. An untreated keying waveform approaches *square-wave* modulation, consisting of the keying frequency plus *all of its odd harmonics*. These harmonics create key clicks extending many kilohertz either side of the carrier. Adjusting the rise and fall times of the keying waveform to about 5 ms controls key clicks yet allows a wide range of practical keying speeds, as explained in Chapter 9.

Once the power supply voltage has been brought under control, it is a simple matter to shape the keying envelope with an RC network. The figures in this section illustrate the application of time-constant circuits to various keying methods.

When a circuit carrying current is opened or closed mechanically, a spark is generated. This spark causes the circuit to radiate energy throughout the electromagnetic spectrum. When a transmitter is keyed manually or through a relay, the spark at the contacts can cause local BCI, *but this spark has no effect on the RF output signal*. A simple filter (0.01-μF capacitor in series with 10 ohms) across the key or relay contacts will usually reduce the

(A) (B) (C) (D)

Fig. 3 — These photos show CW signals as observed on an oscilloscope. At A is a dot generated at 46 bauds with no intentional shaping, while at B the shaping circuits have been adjusted for approximately 5-ms rise and decay times. Vertical lines are from a 1-kHz signal applied to the Z or intensity axis for timing. Shown at C is a shaped signal with the intensity modulation of the pattern removed. For each of these photos, sampled RF from the transmitter was fed directly to the deflection plates of the oscilloscope.

A received signal having essentially no shaping is shown at D. The spike at the leading edge is typical of poor power-supply regulation, as is also the immediately following dip and rise in amplitude. The clicks were quite pronounced. This pattern is typical of many observed signals, although not by any means a worst case. The signal was taken from the receiver's IF amplifier (before detection) using a hand-operated sweep circuit to reduce the sweep time to the order of one second. (Photos from October and November 1966 *QST*.)

local clicks to a tolerable level. Solid-state switching methods significantly reduce the current and voltage that must be switched mechanically, thereby reducing local clicks and enhancing operator safety. Modern transistorized transmitters incorporate this type of keying. With proper device selection, solid-state keying may be implemented in older tube designs as well.

Amplifier tubes may be keyed in the cathode (filament transformer center-tap for directly heated types), grid-bias supply or screen. Transistors should be keyed in one leg of the collector supply. The low impedance of RF power transistor circuits usually requires the emitter to be grounded

Fig. 4 — Cathode keying. Envelope shaping is accomplished by means of the RC network. Q1 must be able to withstand the plate voltage of the keyed stage. Some suitable types are: DTS-423, 2N6457 (400V), SDT 13305 (500V), DTS-801 (800V), MJ12010 (950V), 2SC1308K, ECG 238 (1500V). These are high-energy devices and are capable of switching any value of plate current the tube is likely to draw. For plate voltages below about 350, the 2N3439 is adequate (and much less expensive).

Fig. 5 — Blocked-grid keying. The rise time of the keying pulse is determined by C1 and its associated network. The decay time is governed by the R1C2 product. R_g is the existing grid leak. Typical values for R1 and C2 are 220 kΩ and 0.022 μF. Some transistors suitable for Q1 are: 2N5415 (200 V), MM4003 (250 V), MJE350 (300 V), 2N5416, RCS882 (350 V), 2N6213 (375 V), 2N6214 (425 V).

Fig. 6 — If a suitable high-voltage PNP transistor cannot be obtained, an NPN unit can be used with an optical isolator. The rise time of the keying envelope is controlled by the "integrating" capacitor connected to the base of the phototransistor.

Fig. 7 — Circuit to interface digital logic with positive or negative key lines. Q1 and Q2 must be able to withstand the expected negative and positive keying voltages and currents.

Fig. 8 — Keying circuit for solid-state class-C amplifiers in the 100-watt class, such as those sold for VHF FM service. Q1 must be able to pass the amplifier collector current without dropping too much voltage. Types 2N6246, SK3173 and RS2043 are good for currents up to 15 amperes.

Fig. 9 — Keying a dual-gate MOSFET oscillator. The 741 op amp is used as a comparator. With the input resistors shown, the circuit can be triggered by any +5-volt logic device.

Fig. 10 — Keying a doubly balanced modulator in a CW-SSB transmitter.

Fig. 11 — Debouncing circuit for hand keys and relay contacts. The minimum dot length is determined by the R1C1 product.

as directly as possible; therefore, no solid-state analog of cathode keying exists. Similarly, blocked-grid keying has no transistor equivalent, because a reverse bias suf-ficient to cut the stage off in the presence of heavy excitation would cause breakdown of the base-emitter junction.

Mechanical contacts frequently bounce several times before stabilizing in the closed state. The beginnings of keying pulses formed by bouncing contacts are poorly defined. This defect can degrade the readability of a code signal under adverse conditions. Relays and semiautomatic keys are especially prone to this malady. The circuit of Fig. 11 will help clean up the pulses generated by mechanical contacts.

A satisfactory CW RF envelope can be amplified by means of a *linear* amplifier without affecting the keying characteristics. If, however, the signal is amplified by one or more nonlinear stages (e.g., a class-C multiplier or amplifier), the signal envelope will be modified, possibly introducing significant key clicks. It is possible to compensate for this effect by using longer-than-normal rise and decay times in the exciter and letting the amplifier modify the signal to an acceptable one. Any clicks generated by a linear amplifier are likely to be the result of low-frequency parasitic oscillations.

Oscillator Keying

A change in frequency at the beginning of a keying pulse is called a *chirp*. If the oscillator isn't keyed, chirp is the result of changing dc operating potentials or changing RF load conditions on the oscillator. The voltage to the oscillator can be regulated easily, as most transmitters use fairly low-power oscillators. If the oscillator frequency is pulled by the loading effect of subsequent keyed stages, better load isolation is indicated.

If break-in operation is desired (see below), it may be necessary to key the transmitter's oscillator. Oscillators may be keyed by the same methods used for amplifiers, but greater care is required to obtain good results. In general, the goals of clickless and chirpless oscillator keying are mutually exclusive. This is because a key-click filter will cause the operating voltage to be applied *slowly*, thereby creating a chirp. Crystal oscillators may be keyed satisfactorily if active crystals are used. A keyed oscillator may exhibit a continuous frequency change during a keying pulse. This defect is called a *yoop*. It is caused by RF heating in the tank circuit or crystal. Yoop is usually an indication of a faulty component or excessive oscillator power.

Break-in operation with a VFO-controlled transmitter usually dictates some form of *differential* keying. In this system, the oscillator is turned on as quickly as possible and the amplifier is keyed after the oscillator has stabilized. When the key is released, the oscillator operates until the amplifier output has decayed to zero. Shaping of the keying envelope is accomplished in the amplifier keying circuit. In the past, break-in operation was implemented with VR tubes and relays. The complexity of such systems frightened many hams away from this convenient mode. With modern circuitry, break-in can be simple, quiet and safe. One method of break-in keying is shown in Fig. 12.

A few notes concerning oscillator keying are in order. Do not attempt to key an oscillator unless it is stable while running

Fig. 12 — Differential (sequential) keying system for fast break-in with oscillator-multiplier transmitters.

free, at the same time the other stages are keyed. If the oscillator frequency is multiplied, chirps and yoops will be multiplied also. The transmitter signal should be checked at the highest operating frequency. It may be found that the signal quality is satisfactory on 160 meters but leaves something to be desired on 10. Modern transmitters and transceivers provide multi-band operation by the heterodyne method and should be stable on all bands.

Backwave

If the transmitter oscillators run continuously, they may be audible as a *backwave* between keying pulses. A strong backwave may indicate the need for neutralizing one or more transmitter stages. In general, if the backwave conforms to the −40 dB spurious signal rule, it won't be objectionable.

Practical Keying Circuits

The circuits of Figs 4 through 12 illustrate methods by which various solid-state and thermionic devices may be keyed. In these circuits, the armature of the hand key is at ground potential and the voltage across the key is imperceptible. The current through the key is generally less than 1 milliampere. A neon bulb with a proper series resistor across the key will alert the operator to junction breakdown of the high-voltage transistors. As long as safety is given due consideration, the key-at-ground convention need not be followed, but this standardization is useful for equipment interconnections. Digital control is shown in all of the examples. This feature simplifies the simultaneous keying of transmitter stages, TR switches, sidetone oscillators and muting systems. The ICs used to perform the control functions are plentiful and inexpensive. These systems use a

logic high to indicate a keydown condition.

Break-In

Break-in (QSK) is a system of radiotelegraph transmission in which the station receiver is sensitive to other signals between the transmitted keying pulses. This capability is very important to traffic handlers, but can be used to great advantage in ragchewing as well. Break-in gives CW communication the dimension of more natural conversation.

Most commercially manufactured transceivers feature a "semi break-in" mode in which the first key closure actuates the VOX relay. The VOX controls are usually adjusted to hold the relay closed between letters. With proper VOX adjustment, it is possible for the other operator to break your transmission between words, but this system is a poor substitute for true break-in.

Separate Antennas

The simplest way to implement break-in is to use a separate antenna for receiving. If the transmitter output power is low (below 50 watts or so) and the isolation between transmitting and receiving antennas is good, this method can be satisfactory. Best isolation is obtained by mounting the antennas as far apart as possible and at right angles. Smooth break-in involves protecting the receiver from damage by the transmitter power and assuring that the receiver will "recover" fast enough to be sensitive between keying pulses. If the receiver recovers fast enough but the transmitter clicks are bothersome (they may be caused by receiver overload and so exist only in the receiver), their effect on the operator can be minimized through the use

Fig. 13 — A TR switch can be connected to the input side of the transmitter pi network. For powers up to about 100 W, C1 can be a 5-10 pF, 1000-V mica unit. For high-power operation a smaller "gimmick" capacitor made from a short length of coaxial cable should be used.

Fig. 14 — An external TR switch. The primary of T1 is 50 turns of no. 30 enameled wire on an FT37-43 toroid core. The secondary is 15 turns of no. 30 wound over the primary.

of an output limiter. The separate antenna method is most useful on the 160-, 80- and 40-meter bands, where the directional effects of the antennas aren't pronounced.

Switching a Common Antenna

When powers above about 50 watts are used, where two antennas are not available, or when it is desired to use the same antenna for transmitting and receiving (a "must" when directional antennas are used), special treatment is required for quiet break-in operation on the transmitter frequency.

Vacuum relays or reed switches may be used to switch the antenna between the transmitter and receiver in step with the keying. This method is satisfactory for power levels up to the legal limit, but the relays are expensive and the system timing is critical.

Perhaps the most modern and elegant approach is the use of PIN diodes to switch the antenna. These devices are available in power ratings up to about 100 watts, but are quite expensive at present. There are no keying-speed constraints when PIN diodes are used, and if the proper devices are selected, the spectral purity of the output signal won't be affected. The important electrical parameter in this regard is *carrier lifetime*.

An easy and economical way to implement break-in with a single antenna is to use an electronic *TR switch*. With such a device the antenna is connected to the transmitter at all times. In the most common type of electronic TR switch, a tube is used to couple the antenna to the receiver. When the transmitter is keyed, the RF output causes the tube to draw grid current through a high-resistance grid leak. The high negative bias thus developed cuts off the plate current, limiting the signal delivered to the receiver.

Unfortunately, when the grid circuit is driven into rectification, harmonics are generated. A low-pass filter between the TR

switch and the antenna can help to eliminate TVI caused by the harmonics, but the lower-order harmonics may cause interference to other communications. Another common shortcoming of TR switches is that the transmitter output circuit may "suck out" the received signal. In a transmitter having a high-impedance tuned-output tank circuit, both of these problems can be circumvented by connecting the TR switch to the *input* side of the tank circuit. With this configuration, the grid rectification harmonics are suppressed and the received signal peaked by means of the tuned circuit. Fig. 13 shows a MOSFET TR switch that works on this principle.

A TR switch for use external to any transmitter is shown in Fig. 14. The tube is grid-block keyed, and the fixed-value bias prevents any grid current flow at power levels up to 800 watts. This power figure assumes a 50-ohm system with a unity SWR. The circuit can withstand peak RF voltages up to 300. The power capability must be derated if the impedance at the point of connection is higher than 50 ohms.

Although the signal path has a diode, it is effectively "linearized" by the high-value series resistor, and should not significantly degrade the spectral purity of the transmitter output.

External TR switches should be well shielded and the power leads carefully filtered. In general, the coaxial cable to the transmitter should be as short as possible, but some experimenting may be necessary to eliminate "suck out" of the received signal. It is commonly stated that electronic TR switches are usable only with transmitters having class-C output stages because the "diode noise" generated by the resting current of a linear amplifier will mask weak signals. Actually, the class-of-service designation is not related to key-up conditions, so there is no reason a linear amplifier can't be biased off during key-up periods.

Reduction of Receiver Gain During Transmission

For absolutely smooth break-in operation with no clicks or thumps, means must be provided for momentarily reducing the

Fig. 15 — A diode attenuator for receiver gain reduction during keying. The logic threshold is determined by

$$\frac{R2}{R1 + R2}(+ V_{cc}).$$

For ± 15-volt CMOS logic, R1 = R2 = 1M. For ±5-volt TTL operation, R1 = 130 kΩ, R2 = 15 kΩ.

Fig. 17 — A 555 universal timer used as a sidetone generator. Pin 4 is taken to ground to interrupt the tone. The frequency of oscillation is about 500 Hz with the constants shown.

Fig. 16 — Gain-reduction circuit for receivers using a fixed-bias dual-gate MOSFET in the first stage. As much as 40 dB of attenuation is possible with this method. The logic threshold is calculated as in Fig. 15.

gain through the receiver. A muting function completely disables the receiver audio during key-down periods. Assuming the transmitter signal at the receiver is held below the damage level, muting the audio output can be an effective means of achieving smooth break-in *provided no AGC is used*. AGC systems suitable for CW operation are characterized by long "hang" times. Unless the transmitter signal in the receiver is at a level similar to that of the other station, the AGC system will seriously desense the receiver, rendering the break-in system useless. A diode attenuator suitable for use with TR switches or separate antennas is shown in Fig. 15. If the receiver uses a dual-gate MOSFET with no AGC in the first stage, the method of Fig. 16 may be used.

Monitoring

If the receiver output is muted, an audio sidetone oscillator must be used to monitor one's sending. A 555 timer connected as an astable multivibrator is commonly used for this purpose. This device delivers rectangular output pulses, and the resulting signal often sounds quite raucous. A variation of the standard 555 circuit appears in Fig. 17. The diodes maintain the symmetry of the waveform independently of the pitch and the RF filter removes many of the objectional harmonics. A keying monitor can be powered by the RF output of the transmitter. Such a circuit is shown in Fig. 18. Keying monitors often have built-in loudspeakers, but it is less expensive and

more convenient to inject the monitor signal into the audio output stage of the receiver. With this system one always hears the sidetone from the same source (speaker or headphones) as the other station's signal.

If the audio output isn't muted, the receiver can be used to monitor one's keying, provided both stations are on the

same frequency. Some DX operators transmit and listen on separate frequencies. When using your receiver as a monitor, you should be careful about drawing any conclusions concerning the quality of your signal. The signal reaching the receiver must be free of any line voltage effects induced by the transmitter. To be certain of your signal quality you should listen to your station from a distance. Trading stations with a nearby amateur is a good way to make signal checks.

Fig. 18 — An RF-powered keying monitor suitable for power outputs from about 20 to 100 W. This circuit should be installed inside the transmitter or a shielded enclosure to minimize RFI.

Narrow-Band Direct-Printing Telegraphy (RTTY)

RTTY stands for radioteleprinter communication; the R stands for *radio* and TTY is a common abbreviation for *teleprinter* or *teletypewriter*. RTTY consists of

three main modes of operation: Baudot, AMTOR and ASCII. The Baudot signal format is directly compatible with mechanical teleprinters, even though most radio

amateurs no longer use them. AMTOR is an extension of Baudot operation that makes use of error detection and correction along with other "computerized" enhancements. ASCII RTTY employs the digital code computers use to communicate, although it is not used much on the ham bands. The advantages and disadvantages of ASCII RTTY are discussed later in this chapter.

The term "narrow-band direct-printing telegraphy" (NBDP) is used by the International Telecommunication Union (ITU) to mean communications between two teleprinters. In general, NBDP and RTTY refer to radio signals that are intended to be printed directly on paper by a mechanical teleprinter. That is what the term *direct printing* refers to. Even though most operators now use a video terminal to view the data, the on-the-air signals are identical to the signals from a mechanical teleprinter. By FCC and ITU definitions, NBDP/RTTY includes AMTOR and Baudot. It also includes ASCII when using an asynchronous transmission system with start and stop pulses. (ASCII is most commonly used as part of packet-radio systems, discussed later in this chapter.)

BAUDOT RADIO TELEPRINTING

The commercial- or military-surplus Baudot-encoded teleprinter (TTY) was the mainstay of amateur RTTY operators from 1946 through the late '70s. There are still numerous TTY machines in use, but many RTTY operators are now using computer-based terminals. In some cases the terminal was designed to include RTTY and CW as part of a multimode system. In others, amateurs adapted personal computers to send and receive the Baudot code.

The Baudot Telegraph Code

Current FCC rules in §97.309(a)(1) identify the Baudot code as the International Telegraph Alphabet Number 2 (ITA2). This code is recognized by the International Telegraph and Telephone Consultative Committee (CCITT), and allows for national variations, principally to accommodate foreign-language alphabets. The ITA2 coded character set is shown in Table 4. A variation of this code, recog-

nized in §97.309(a)(2) as the code specified in the International Radio Consultative Committee (CCIR) Recommendations 476 and 625, is also shown in Table 4. This code is used for AMTOR communications, covered later in this chapter.

Each action command for the teleprinter is contained within a transmitted data frame. The action might be to print the symbol "A," ring the bell or advance the paper a line. Fig 19 shows a pictorial of such a frame arranged in left-to-right order, as it would be observed on an oscilloscope. With the Baudot code, each "frame" consists of seven timing elements. For most Baudot teleprinters, which send at a signaling rate of about 45 bauds, each of the first six timing elements is 22 milliseconds in duration. The last timing element may be from 1 to 1.5 times longer than the others.

During the first timing element there is no current regardless of what code combination is being transmitted. This first element is called the *start pulse* because it indicates the start of a frame. The receiving TTY detects the beginning of the start pulse (no current) and starts a mechanical timer that determines when to sample all following elements within that frame.

After the start pulse element, the transmitting TTY sends five data elements; the on/off current state during these elements demotes the transmitted character. (The no-current condition is called SPACE and the condition with current is called MARK.) Because there are five variable data elements, it is possible to transmit one of 32 combinations. Following the five variable data elements is the *stop pulse* element, during which there is always current.

ITA2 is a five-level code, and there are only two conditions for each level (A or Z, space or mark, binary 0 or 1). Therefore, a total of $2 \times 2 \times 2 \times 2 \times 2 = 2^5 = 32$ different code combinations are possible. Because it is necessary to provide 26 Latin letters, 10 numerals and punctuations, the 32 code combinations are not sufficient. This problem is solved by using the codes twice; once in the *letters* (LTRS) case and again in the *figures* (FIGS) case. Two special characters, LTRS and FIGS are used to indicate whether subsequent characters will be in letters or figures case. (You can think of the LTRS and FIGS keys as similar to the SHIFT LOCK key on a typewriter or keyboard.) The receiving terminal stores the last received LTRS or FIGS characters so it remains in the last-received case until changed.

Refer to Table 4 for the following example. Suppose combination 2 is received by a teleprinter. The machine will print "B" if the last case character received was LTRS, or it will print "?" if the last case character was FIGS. The transmitting TTY must ensure that the letters and figures combinations are transmitted in the right places so the receiving TTY prints the correct symbols.

Table 4

ITA2 (Baudot) and CCIR Rec. 476 (AMTOR) Codes

Combination No.	ITA2[1] Code Bit No. 43210	Hex	CCIR 476[2] Code Bit No. 6543210	Hex	Character Set Letters Case	Figures Case ITA2	Figures Case U.S. TTYs[3]
1	00011	03	1000111	47	A	—	—
2	11001	19	1110010	72	B	?	?
3	01110	0E	0011101	1D	C	:	:
4	01001	09	1010011	53	D	5[5]	$
5	00001	01	1010110	56	E	3	3
6	01101	0D	0011011	1B	F	4[4]	!
7	11010	1A	0110101	35	G	4[4]	&
8	10100	14	1101001	69	H	4[4]	# or motor stop
9	00110	06	1001101	4D	I	8	8
10	01011	0B	0010111	17	J	BELL	'
11	01111	0F	0011110	1E	K	(	(
12	10010	12	1100101	65	L	)	)
13	11100	1C	0111001	39	M	.	.
14	01100	0C	1011001	59	N	,	,
15	11000	18	1110001	71	O	9	9
16	10110	16	0101101	2D	P	0	0
17	10111	17	0101110	2E	Q	1	1
18	01010	0A	1010101	55	R	4	4
19	00101	05	1001011	4B	S	'	BELL
20	10000	10	1110100	74	T	5	5
21	00111	07	1001110	4E	U	7	7
22	11110	1E	0111100	3C	V	=	;
23	10011	13	0100111	27	W	2	2
24	11101	1D	0111010	3A	X	/	/
25	10101	15	0101011	2B	Y	6	6
26	10001	11	1100011	63	Z	+	"
27	01000	08	1111000	78	← CR (Carriage return)		
28	00010	02	1101100	6C	≡ LF (Line feed)		
29	11111	1F	1011010	5A	↓ LTRS (Letter shift)		
30	11011	1B	0110110	36	↑ FIGS (Figure shift)		
31	00100	04	1011100	5C	SP (Space)		
32	00000	00	1101010	6A	BLK (Blank)		

Notes

[1] 1 represents the mark condition (shown as Z in ITU recommendations) which is the higher emitted radio frequency for FSK, the lower audio frequency for AFSK. 0 represents the space condition (shown as A in ITU documents). Bits are numbered 0 (least significant bit) through 4 (most-significant bit). The order of bit transmission is LSB first, MSB last. Symbols A and Z are defined in CCIR Rec. R.140.

[2] 1 represents the mark condition (shown as B in CCIR recommendations), which is the higher emitted radio frequency for FSK, the lower audio frequency for AFSK). 0 represents the space condition (shown as Y in CCIR recommendations). Bits are numbered 0 (LSB) through 6 (MSB). The order of bit transmission is LSB first, MSB last.

[3] Many U.S. teletypewriters have these figures case characters.

[4] At present unassigned. Reception of these signals, however, should not initiate a request for repetition.

[5] The pictorial representations of ⊠ or ⌖ indicate WRU (Who are you?), which is used for an answer-back function in telex networks.

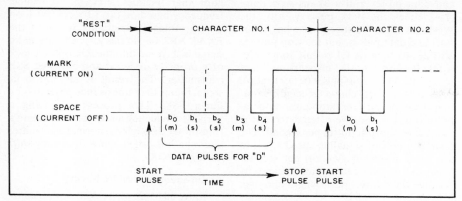

Fig. 19 — Time sequence of typical Baudot character, the letter D.

Fig 20 — A simple TTY loop circuit is shown. The current supply uses a 175 V dc source and a 3000-Ω resistor to reduce the time constant associated with the selector-magnet inductance.

Table 5
Baudot Signaling Rates and Speeds

Signaling Rate (bauds)	Data Pulse (ms)	Stop Pulse (ms)	Speed (WPM)	Common Name
45.45	22.0	22.0	65.00	Western Union
	22.0	31.0	61.33	"60 speed"
	22.0	33.0	60.61	45 bauds
50.00	20.0	30.0	66.67	European; 50 bauds
56.92	17.57	25.00	76.68	"75 speed"
	17.57	26.36	75.89	57 bauds
74.20	13.47	19.18	100.00	"100 speed"
	13.47	20.21	98.98	74 bauds
100.0	10.00	15.00	133.33	100 bauds

Control functions such as LTRS, FIGS, carriage return (CR), line feed (LF), space (SP) and blank are assigned to both the letters and figures cases so that they can be used in either case. The remaining 26 code combinations have different character meanings, depending on whether they are preceded by a LTRS or FIGS character.

ITA2 figures case positions not used for numerals and the slant sign or fraction bar may be used for the remote control of receiving printers or other purposes. The *Character Set* columns of Table 4 show some of the variations between ITA2 and many teleprinters found in the US.

There are a couple of things to note here. This type of data communications, using a start pulse and a stop pulse to control timing, is called "start/stop asynchronous framing." It is called *asynchronous* because the receiving TTY isn't *synchronized* to the sending TTY between frames. Instead, the receiving TTY measures time relative to the start pulse of each frame and uses that information to determine when later elements within that frame have arrived. Although these examples give specific values for the number of bits per frame and the duration of each element within the frame, there is nothing to say that other parameters would not work as well. ASCII teleprinters such as the Teletype Model 33, for example, use 9 (sometimes 10) bits per frame and an element duration of 9.09 ms.

Baudot Teletypewriters

Mechanical teletypewriter equipment consists of these basic components:

A *printer* prints on a continuous supply of paper (in a roll or fan folded) about the width of letter-size paper.

A *keyboard* is used by an operator to originate messages. Most mechanical keyboards have encoders to send out the character code in start-stop (asynchronous) sequence. A teleprinter with keyboard and printer may be known as *KSR*, which stands for *Keyboard Send-Receive* terminal.

A *perforator* is a unit that punches paper tape and may be controlled by direct mechanical connection to a keyboard. The term *reperforator (reperf)* signifies that the perforator punches tape from electrically received signals and usually prints the corresponding characters on the tape. A *Receive-Only Typing Reperforator (ROTR)* receives serial data and perforates and prints on the tape.

A *Transmitter-Distributor (TD)* set is a tape reader that senses the perforations in the tape and produces encoded start-stop pulses. A teletypewriter with a tape capability may be called *Automatic Send-Receive* or *ASR*.

Teletypewriter Loop Circuits

In a mechanical TTY, the keyboard and

printer each have their own independent current circuits or *loops*. The TTY does not generate the current; instead, it interrupts the current (keyboard) and detects current (printer). This means an external current generator is hooked in series with both the keyboard and printer loops. Fig 20 shows a simplified diagram of such a "local loop" setup.

The TTY keyboard loop is simply a mechanical switch contact. When a key is pressed, the switch interrupts the current to generate properly timed current pulses to represent that character. In the printer, the current is detected by a relay called the selector magnet. When there is current through the magnet a force is exerted on an armature that decodes the data elements. The currents are small, usually 60 mA, although some newer TTYs use 20-mA loop currents.

You might expect a fairly low voltage for the loop supply, but most machines use a supply in the range of 100 to 300 V dc. The higher voltage is used with a series resistor, primarily to reduce the circuit time constant associated with the selector-magnet inductance (which is on the order of several henrys).

Computer-Based Baudot Terminals

Electronic Baudot terminal equipment, as shown in the photo, is similar to counterpart mechanical teletypewriter units. These electronic units come in two basic formats:

Many RTTY operators now use all electronic systems.

as a complete dedicated RTTY terminal with keyboard and display capability or as an external modem (modulator/demodulator) used with a personal computer system. If the external modem is part of a multimode data controller that includes a packet-radio TNC, then the software to encode and decode the RTTY signal is built into the modem. If a simple modem is used then the computer system encodes and decodes the RTTY signals.

A *microprocessor* is the foundation of the system, either as part of a dedicated system or multimode data controller or as the heart of a *microcomputer*. The microprocessor encodes and decodes ASCII characters, converts them to and from the comparable Baudot codes, and provides the start-stop code sequence for transmission and reception. There is also *random-access memory (RAM)* for volatile (temporary) storage of data and *read-only memory (ROM)* for nonvolatile (permanent) storage. *Erasable programmable read-only memory (EPROM)* is nonvolatile but can be erased and reprogrammed.

The other units described below can be considered *peripherals* from the standpoint of the microcomputer.

A *keyboard* usually produces an ASCII-encoded parallel output.

A *video-display terminal* or *VDT* is the normal display device. Many VDTs use cathode-ray tubes (CRTs), but flat-screen character displays are coming into use.

A *character printer* is used when a paper (hard) copy is desired.

A *disk drive* may be added to the system to store text or software on flexible (floppy) diskettes. Alternatively, an audio cassette tape recorder may be used. (The audio cassette recorder may also be used to record the received audio signals, and these can be fed through the modem later for decoding.)

Baudot Speeds and Signaling Rates

The operating speed of mechanical teleprinter machines is determined by motor speed and gearing ratios or electronic timing circuits. Common speeds are 60, 67, 75 or 100 WPM. See Table 5 for the relationship of speeds and signaling rates and pulse times.

The speed is given in the *approximate* number of five-letter-plus-space combinations transmitted in a *continuous sequence* in start-stop format over a one-minute interval. Convenient choices of gearing ratios and motor-shaft speeds have resulted in noninteger WPM rates. Common usage, however, has rounded the exact speeds to easily remembered numbers. Thus, "60 speed" Baudot actually is sent at 61.33 WPM, and "75 speed" is really 76.67 WPM.

There is a problem with using words per minute or characters per second to specify TTY speed because of the varying length of stop pulses in use. For example, "60 speed" Baudot TTY has 22-ms-long start

and data pulses and a 31-ms stop pulse (1.42 times the data pulse width); the Western Union "65 speed" also has 22-ms start and data pulses, but the stop pulse is also 22 ms long (a 1:1 ratio); some electronic terminals use 22-ms start and data pulses and 33-ms stop pulses (a 1.5:1 ratio).

In light of these character-length variations from the different stop-pulse-to-data-pulse ratios in use, we often refer to the number of shortest pulses per second. The *baud* is a unit of signaling speed equal to one pulse (event or symbol) per second. You can find the signaling rate in bauds by dividing the shortest pulse length into one; for example, $1 / 0.022 = 45.45$, commonly abbreviated to 45.5 or even 45 bauds.

RTTY MODEMS

The term *modem* is a contraction of *modulator-demodulator*. Some amateurs use the term *terminal unit* or *TU* to mean modem or sometimes just a demodulator.

The modulator portion of a modem takes the digital data from a TTY or computer system and converts it to analog information for the transmitter. The demodulator portion takes the analog information from the receiver and converts it to digital data for the computer or TTY. There are two common methods of modulating the transmitter, *frequency-shift keying (FSK)* and *audio-frequency-shift keying (AFSK)*.

Frequency-Shift Keying

With frequency-shift keying (FSK), an RF carrier of constant output power is always present during a transmission. The carrier frequency is always at one of two values. One value (typically the higher radio frequency) indicates the mark, or current-on condition. The other value (typically the lower radio frequency) indicates the space or no-current condition. The difference between these frequencies is called the *frequency shift*.

Early FSK systems used 850-Hz shift because it was more tolerant of transmitter and receiver frequency drift. Today most radio amateurs use 170-Hz shift for their FSK systems, to help conserve spectrum.

Below 50 MHz, FSK is normally used for Baudot RTTY. FCC Rules specify that below 28 MHz the symbol-transmission rate must not exceed 300 bauds or the frequency shift must not exceed 1 kHz. On the 10-meter band the maximum symbol rate is 1200 bauds or a maximum frequency shift of 1 kHz.

Direct frequency-shift keying of HF transmitters is possible using a diode and a variable capacitor or a voltage-variable-capacitance diode (varactor diode) in the transmitter VFO circuit. Some commercial HF transceivers have frequency-shift keyers of this type built in. The FCC emission designator for this *direct FSK* system is F1B.

There is another method of developing an FSK signal. It uses an audio-tone oscil-

lator that includes a circuit to change frequency based on the TTY current-loop keying. Integrated circuits (such as the EXAR XR2206) do this job well. The audio signal is then fed into the microphone jack of a properly designed and adjusted SSB transmitter. The result is an on-the-air signal that is the same as that generated by direct FSK. This process of having a variable-frequency audio tone modulate a transmitter through the normal transmitter audio path is called *audio-frequency-shift keying (AFSK)*.

Audio-Frequency-Shift Keying

Above 50 MHz where A2B or F2B emissions are used, audio-frequency-shift keying (AFSK) of an FM transmitter is the common modulation method. Again, the RF carrier stays on the air throughout the transmission and a modulating audio tone is shifted in frequency. US amateurs traditionally have used an audio frequency of 2125 Hz for mark and a somewhat higher frequency for space. At one time, when 850-Hz shift was used by amateurs on HF, this same shift was used for VHF AFSK, making the space tone 2975 Hz. After the shift on HF was reduced to 170 Hz, the common VHF AFSK space frequency was changed to 2295 Hz.

AFSK of SSB Transmitters

Many HF RTTY stations simply feed AFSK tones to the microphone input of an SSB transmitter or transceiver. The FCC emission designator for this type of transmission is J2B. When properly designed and adjusted, however, this modulation method cannot be distinguished from an F1B (FSK) emission on the air.

The user should make certain that audio distortion, carrier and unwanted sidebands are not present to the degree of causing interference. The user should also make certain that *the equipment is capable of withstanding the 100-percent duty cycle needed for the duration of an RTTY transmission*. For safe operation, it is often necessary to reduce the transmitter power output to 25 to 50 percent of the power level that is safe for CW operation.

Such a system is simple to use and ensures that the transceivers operate on the same transmit and receive frequencies. The disadvantage of AFSK is that imperfections in the sideband filters may permit splatter to be transmitted if the audio tone generator is distorted or overdrives the transmitter.

The same modems are frequently used for both VHF AFSK and HF FSK via an SSB transmitter. This proved difficult when the 850-Hz-shift tones of 2125-Hz mark and 2975-Hz space were used because of the narrow filtering used in most SSB equipment. So some amateurs, particularly those in IARU Region 1 (Europe and Africa), began using the "low tones" of 1275-Hz mark and 2125-Hz space to operate more in the center of the SSB filter passbands. When the shift was reduced to 170 Hz, 1275 Hz was retained for mark, and 1445 Hz was used for space. Both high and low tones can be used interchangeably on the HF bands because only the amount of shift is important. The slight frequency difference is unnoticed on the air because each station tunes their transmitters and receivers for best results. On VHF AFSK, however, the high and low tone pairs are not compatible.

To tune an exact RTTY frequency, remember that most SSB radio equipment will display the frequency of its (suppressed) carrier, not the frequency of the mark signal. For example, if you want to operate on 14,083 kHz and you are using a 2125-Hz AFSK mark frequency, your SSB radio (suppressed-carrier) frequency should be 14,083 + 2.125 = 14,085.125 kHz.

On HF, the *higher* frequency is the mark condition, but AFSK modems use the *lower* frequency for mark. Because of this, the *lower sideband* mode is used for RTTY on SSB equipment. The lower sideband inverts the relationship of the input tones, so the mark frequency becomes the higher transmitted frequency.

Modern SSB transceivers frequently label the sideband-selection knob as NORMAL and REVERSE. To operate RTTY on the bands above 10 MHz you will have to select the REVERSE sideband position on such a radio. If you are not using the correct sideband your signal will be "upside down" (the space tone will be the higher-frequency tone) and other operators will have to invert the signals to copy them. Some, but not all, data controllers are able to do this, so it is best to be certain you are transmitting signals that are "right-side up."

AFSK Modulators

The audio tone produced by an AFSK modulator must be nearly sinusoidal. A nonsinusoidal waveform contains harmonics of the fundamental frequency. If, for example, a nonsinusoidal (low) tone of 1275 Hz is used, the audio outputs will be 1275, 2550 and 3825 Hz. A properly designed SSB transmitter might be expected to filter out 3825 Hz, but may not be able to reduce 2550 Hz to an acceptable level, depending on the filter characteristics.

Particularly when using the low tones, the harmonic distortion of the tones should be kept to a few percent. As mentioned earlier, the audio tones are frequently generated by an IC. The EXAR XR-2206 is a monolithic function generator capable of producing the required sine-wave signals, and is often used in AFSK modulators.

FSK Demodulators

FSK reception is normally done in two steps. The first step is to convert the RF FSK signal to an audio FSK (AFSK) signal. The easiest way to do this is with an SSB receiver. If the mark and space signals are 14070.085 kHz and 14069.915 kHz, respectively, and the SSB receiver is set to LSB with a carrier frequency of 14072.210 kHz, then the mark frequency will be converted to 2125 Hz and the space frequency to 2295 Hz. These audio signals are then passed to the demodulator. Since we now have an AFSK signal, the demodulator is the same as would be used with an AFSK RTTY system on VHF.

AFSK Demodulators

An AFSK demodulator takes the shifting tones from the audio output of a receiver and produces TTY keying pulses. These pulses can be used to drive the selector magnets of a mechanical TTY or the data can be displayed on a microprocessor-based system.

Many AFSK demodulators are of the FM type. A phased-locked loop (PLL) can be used to demodulate the signal, but most FM demodulators make use of filters with either active or passive devices and a discriminator.

The typical filter demodulator consists of five major function blocks, as shown in Fig 21. The first section is a band-pass filter that passes both the mark and space tones and rejects signals above and below these frequencies. The output of this filter then drives a limiter, which increases the difference between a strong desired signal and any weaker undesired signals and also reduces any amplitude variations of the desired signal. The limiter output drives a tuned discriminator that decides if the audio signal is closer to the mark or the space frequency. The diode following the

mark filter produces positive pulses and the one following the space filter produces negative pulses. The larger signal from the discriminator overrides the other, and drives a low-pass filter with a cutoff frequency just above the keying rate. The signal then goes to a slicer, or comparator, which drives the TTY loop to control the selector magnets or feeds the signal on to a computer system for display.

Other demodulator designs use AM (limiter-less) detectors in place of a discriminator or PLL. These types of demodulators, when properly designed, permit continuous copy even when the mark or space frequency fades out completely. At 170-Hz shift, however, the mark and space frequencies tend to fade more at the same time than they do independently. In other words, when one fades chances are that the other will fade about the same time. For this reason, FM and AM types of demodulators are comparable at 170-Hz shift. At wider shifts (say 425 Hz and above), the independently fading mark and space signals can achieve an *in-band frequency-diversity* effect if the demodulator is capable of processing it. To conserve spectrum, it is generally desirable to stay with 170-Hz shift for 45-baud Baudot and forego the possible in-band frequency-diversity gain. The in-band frequency-diversity gain should be kept in mind for higher signaling rates that would justify greater shift.

DIVERSITY RECEPTION

Diversity reception of RTTY signals refers to the ability to use a variety of techniques to demodulate the signal. Normally you must receive both mark and space tones to demodulate the signal reliably. The frequency diversity mentioned in the last section is one example of a way to demodulate the signal if one of the tones fades.

Another type of diversity can be achieved by using two antennas, two receivers and a dual demodulator. Some amateurs are using such a setup with excellent results. One of the antennas would be the normal station antenna for that band. The second antenna could be either another antenna of the same polarization located at least 3/8-wavelength away, or an antenna of the opposite polarization located at the first an-

Fig 21 — An AFSK filter demodulator circuit. The 2125-Hz band-pass filter selects the mark signal and the 2295-Hz filter selects the space signal. The diodes product positive pulses from mark signals and negative pulses from space signals.

tenna or anywhere nearby. One difficulty is how to get both receivers on the same frequency without having to tune both carefully. Some RTTY diversity enthusiasts have located slaved receivers on the surplus market. Other methods could include a computer controlling two receivers so that both would track.

Two demodulators are needed for this type of diversity. Also, some type of diversity combiner or selector is needed. Many commercial or military RTTY demodulators are equipped for diversity reception.

The payoff for using diversity is a worthwhile improvement in copy. Depending on fading conditions, adding diversity may be equivalent to raising transmitter power sevenfold (8 dB).

Further Reading on Baudot RTTY

DATACOM, British Amateur Radio Teledata Group (BARTG), c/o Ian Brothwell, G4EAN/G4ATG, 56 Arnot Hill Rd, Arnold, Nottingham NG5 6LQ, England, published quarterly.

Henry, G. W. "Bill," "RTTY Demodulators," *CQ,* Nov 1983, pp 20-24; reprints available from HAL Communications, PO Box 365, Urbana, IL 61801.

Hobbs, Yeomanson and Gee, *Teleprinter Handbook,* Radio Society of Great Britain, Alma House, Cranborne Rd, Potters Bar, Herts EN6 3JW, England, 1983.

Ingram, *RTTY Today,* Universal Electronics, Inc, 4555 Groves Rd, Suite 3, Columbus, OH 43232, 1984.

Kretzman, *The New RTTY Handbook,* Cowan Publishing Corp, 14 Vanderventer Ave, Port Washington, NY, 1962.

Nagle, "Diversity Reception: an Answer to High Frequency Signal Fading," *Ham Radio,* November 1979, pp 48-55.

RTTY Journal, 9085 La Casita Ave, Fountain Valley, CA 92708.

Schwartz, "An RTTY Primer," *CQ,* issues of August 1977, November 1977, February 1978, May 1978 and August 1978.

Tucker, *RTTY from A to Z,* Cowan Publishing Corp, 14 Vanderventer Ave, Port Washington, NY, 1970.

AMTOR—AN ERROR REDUCTION SYSTEM FOR RTTY

AMTOR (AMateur Teleprinting Over Radio) is a specialized form of RTTY that reduces the number of errors as compared to conventional RTTY systems. RTTY circuits are plagued with problems of fading and noise unless something is done to mitigate these effects. Conventional diversity techniques (frequency, polarization and/or space diversity) are often used at the receiving station to provide two or more simultaneous versions of the transmission. The receiver then chooses the best of these two signals to forward to the teleprinter for printing. The decision-making process is usually accomplished by analog circuitry or a microcomputer.

An AMTOR operating position.

An error-detecting and correcting direct-printing telegraphy system is described in a recommendation from the International Radio Consultative Committee (CCIR). There have been several revisions of the AMTOR system over the years. Current FCC Rules permit US amateurs to use the code found in Recommendations 476-2 (1978), 476-3 (1982), 476-4 (1986) and 625 (1986); all other parameters may be changed. CCIR Recommendation 625-1 (1990) has recently been released by the CCIR. To ensure compatibility between AMTOR implementations, these systems generally conform to the CCIR Recommendations.

AMTOR is Time Diversity

Another method of getting more than one opportunity to see a given transmission is time diversity. The same signal sent at different times will experience different fading and noise conditions. AMTOR makes use of time diversity to provide communications that have fewer errors than conventional Baudot RTTY.

AMTOR provides two major modes of communications, ARQ and FEC; both make use of time diversity. ARQ stands for "*A*utomatic *R*epeat re*Q*uest." In the ARQ mode, the "sending" station transmits a block of three characters and the "receiving" station replies with a one-character ACK (ACKnowledgment—okay to send the block) or a NAK (Negative Acknowlegment—I missed the last block, send it again). Because of the ACK/NAK handshaking, only two stations can be in an ARQ QSO. Other stations can monitor the QSO, but they don't get the benefit of error reduction. When speaking of ARQ communications, the terms "sending" and

"receiving" can be confusing because the radios of both stations are constantly switching from receive to transmit and back again. When you hear ARQ on the air it sounds like birds chirping because of the "send-a-block" "receive-a-block" on/off transmissions.

FEC stands for "*Forward Error Correction.*" In FEC, each character is transmitted twice, but with the second transmission displaced in time from the first by 350 ms. Note that both ARQ and FEC make use of time diversity. In the case of ARQ, if the receiving station didn't copy a block of three characters correctly, it asks the sending station to repeat the block. That repeat takes place later in time than the first try; that's the time diversity for ARQ. For FEC, the second copy of a character, 350 ms after the first transmission, provides the time diversity.

AMTOR Modes

ARQ and FEC are the major modes of AMTOR. However, there are two other minor modes of AMTOR: SELFEC and LISTEN. SELFEC is very similar to plain old FEC, except that SELFEC sends a SELCAL at the beginning of its transmission and then inverts the data. This allows a transmitting station to send to a single station (or selected group of stations) without wasting everyone's paper. The LISTEN mode is a monitor-only mode that's used to monitor ARQ communications.

The CCIR documentation has specific names for ARQ, FEC and SELFEC. The proper titles that are used in the CCIR documentation haven't really caught on in the amateur or commercial radio services. CCIR calls ARQ "Mode A," while FEC

Table 6

CCIR Rec 625 Service Information Signals[1]

Mode A (ARQ)	Bit No. 6543210	Mode B (FEC)
Control signal 1 (CS1)	1100101	
Control signal 2 (CS2)	1101010	
Control signal 3 (CS3)	1011101	
Control signal 4 (CS4)	0110101	
Control signal 5 (CS5)	1101001	
Idle signal β	0110011	Idle signal β
Idle signal α	0001111	Phasing signal 1, idle signal α
Signal repetition (RQ)	1100110	Phasing signal 2

[1] 1 represents the mark condition (shown as B in CCIR recommendations), which is the higher emitted radio frequency for FSK, the lower audio frequency for AFSK.
0 represents the space condition (shown as Y in CCIR recommendations). Bits are numbered 0 (LSB) through 6 (MSB). The order of bit transmission is LSB first, MSB last.

is called "Mode B Collective" and SELFEC is called "Mode B Selective." The CCIR documentation doesn't specify any sort of LISTEN mode—that's strictly an Amateur Radio invention.

AMTOR Origins

AMTOR was popularized for Amateur Radio by Peter Martinez, G3PLX, who designed and built the first low-cost AMTOR code converter.[1] The AMTOR protocol is the same as the commercial SITOR protocol[2] that is used for MF/HF marine TELEX applications. The only difference in features between AMTOR and SITOR is that AMTOR includes the LISTEN mode to monitor ARQ QSOs.[3]

CCIR 625 Adds New Features

The inclusion of the CCIR 625 protocol provides a new wrinkle to the AMTOR system. In a nutshell, CCIR 625 is the same as CCIR 476, but it provides better definition of how the protocol should operate as well as the ability to use longer SELCALs. An additional feature of CCIR 625 is that the calling station is identified automatically to the called station at the time of connection or reconnection. CCIR 625 is a superset of the original CCIR 476 protocol. Devices that conform to CCIR 625 are able to communicate with CCIR 476 devices.

Error-Detection Mechanism

The seven-bit AMTOR code is created by taking the 5-bit ITA2 (Baudot) code and adding two bits to each character. The two additional bits are assigned values such that the total number of ones in a seven-bit word is equal to four. For some characters, the values of more than just the two new bits need to be adjusted to get a "4 ones, 3 zeros" ratio. There is a one-for-one correspondence between the ITA2 (5-bit) and AMTOR (7-bit) codes for all 32 combinations of the 5-unit code, as can be seen in Table 4. Ordinarily, a 7-unit code has 2^7 or 128 possible combinations, but for AMTOR, only those combinations that

have four bits high and three bits low are used. Because each AMTOR character has four bits high and three bits low, it is referred to as a "constant ratio code." If a received character does not have this constant ratio, the receiving station knows there is an error. This may sound like a flimsy error-detection system, but in practice it works well on MF and HF channels.

Of the possible 128 combinations formed by a 7-bit code, only 35 combinations have the "4 ones, 3 zeros" constant ratio code. So, 32 of the combinations equate to the 32 ITA2 combinations, with three remaining for service information signals as shown in Table 6.

These three unique combinations are Idle Signal Beta (β), Idle Signal Alpha (α) and Repeat Request (RQ). In addition to these three unique service information signals, three others (CS1, CS2 and CS3) are not unique, but are borrowed from the 32 combinations that equate to ITA2 (CCIR 625 adds CS4 and CS5 to the AMTOR protocol). They are not confused with the message characters because they are sent only in the reverse direction.

ARQ (Mode A)

This is a synchronous system, transmitting blocks of three characters from the Information Sending Station (ISS) to the Information Receiving Station (IRS). Both stations transmit radio signals for each data block transferred. The terms ISS and IRS describe which station is sending information (ISS) and which is sending ACK/NAK responses (IRS). The station that initiates the QSO is known as the Master Station (MS) and the station that receives the call is known as the Slave station (SS). The MS first sends the selective call characters (SELCAL) of the called station in blocks of three characters, listening between blocks. CCIR 476 uses calls of two blocks (4 characters plus padding) while CCIR 625 uses calls of three blocks (7 characters plus padding). These SELCALs are arbitrary

groups of characters that are used only to initiate ARQ calls. Four-letter SELCALs are used for CCIR 476 AMTOR and are normally derived from the first character and the last three letters of the station call sign. As an example, for a call sign of W1AW the four character AMTOR SELCAL would be WWAW. When the Slave Station (SS) recognizes its SELCAL, it answers that it is ready. The MS now becomes the Information Sending Station and will send traffic as soon as the Information Receiving Station says it is ready.

After contact is established, the ISS sends its message in groups of three characters and pauses between groups for a reply from the IRS. Each character is sent at a rate of 100 bauds, or 210 ms for a three-character information block and 70 ms for a one-character ACK/NAK block. The block repetition cycle is 450 ms, so there are 240 ms during each cycle that the ISS is not sending. This 240-ms period is taken up by propagation time from the ISS to the IRS, 70 ms for the IRS to send its service information signal, and the return trip back to the ISS. Turn-around or switching time associated with the modem and the radio transmitter and receiver (known as equipment delay) must occur within this 240-ms period. A receive-transmit turnaround time of less than 20 ms is desirable.[4] When an ISS is done sending information, it can enable the other station to become the ISS by sending the three-character sequence FIGS Z B (the characters + and ?). A station may end the contact by sending an "end of communication signal" consisting of three Idle Signal Alphas (α α α).

On the air, AMTOR Mode A signals have a characteristic chirp-chirp sound to them. Because of the 210/240-ms on/off timing, Mode A can be used with some transmitters at full power levels.

FEC (Mode B, Collective Broadcast)

When transmitting to more than one station (for example calling CQ, sending bulletins or participating in a net), there is no (one) station to act as IRS to send ACK/NAKs in the reverse direction. Even if there were one, that station's ability to receive without error may not be representative of other stations that also want to copy the signal.

FEC uses a simple Forward Error Correction (FEC) technique of sending each character twice. If the repetition were sent immediately, a single noise burst or quick fade could mutilate both. Burst errors can be virtually eliminated by delaying the repetition for a period thought to exceed the duration of most noise bursts. In AMTOR, the first transmission of a character (called DX) is followed by four other characters, after which the retransmission (called RX) of the first character occurs. At 70 ms per character, this leaves 280 ms between the end of the first transmission and the beginning of the second. From the start of the first to the start of the second, the duration is 350 ms.

In FEC, the receiving station tests each received character for the constant 4/3 ratio code. Characters with the 4/3 ratio are printed while those characters where both the first and second transmission are mutilated are replaced with an error symbol (typically an underscore or space character).

The sending station's transmitter must be capable of 100%-duty-cycle operation for FEC transmissions, just like conventional Baudot RTTY. Thus, it may be necessary to reduce transmitter power to a level of 50% of full rating, or even less.

AMTOR Operation

Thanks to multi-mode controllers, more than 50,000 Ámateur Radio stations are now "AMTOR capable"; many of these are quite active on AMTOR. Common practice is to use the 170-Hz frequency shift and 100-baud signaling rate that the CCIR 476/625 protocol calls for. Although most AMTOR operators make use of commercial multi-mode controllers, a few prefer to roll-their-own.[1,5,6]

Typically, AMTOR operations are at the bottom end of the RTTY segment on each HF band. On 20 meters, AMTOR BBS operation is typically below 14075 kHz, while person-to-person AMTOR operation is above 14075 kHz.

Here's a brief sketch of AMTOR operation. Further details can be found in *The ARRL Operating Manual* and in a guide to AMTOR operation written by Paul Newland.[7]

As with most other modes, when you want to make a contact, look for a quiet frequency and inquire (using FEC) if the frequency is in use. If nothing is heard, then give a CQ call. Don't send RYRYRY, as is often done with Baudot systems. Instead, once you are in the transmit FEC mode, just let your system send idle (phasing) signals for 15 to 45 seconds. The rhythm created by the idle signals attracts just as much attention as a Baudot RYRYRY. Better yet, the idle signals allow all stations to synchronize easily with your transmission. After sending some idle characters, then send a few lines of CQ followed by a line with your call and the SELCAL you have selected for your station. The other station can call you back using either FEC or ARQ and you are on your way!

AMTOR Mailboxes

An attractive feature of AMTOR is that it lends itself to mailbox operation. AMTOR mailboxes allow you and your ham friends to exchange messages over radio without requiring that you both be active at the same instant on the same frequency, and it works over paths of many thousand kilometers. You can check into an AMTOR mailbox and be told if you have any messages waiting for you, plus you can leave messages for others—all error-free using HF radio. NTS operators have found this to be helpful to some of their traffic-handling efforts. FCC Rules do not permit unattended automatic control of an HF AMTOR station at this time.

APLink

The most popular AMTOR Mailbox is the APLink system, designed by Vic Poor, W5SMM. APLink stands for AMTOR-Packet-Link. The APLink system operates on an IBM PC® (or clone) using two serial ports. One port is connected to an AMTOR controller and HF radio while the other port is connected to a packet controller and VHF radio. Local users can connect on VHF using packet and, more importantly, messages from the VHF packet network can be forwarded to the APLink system. Distant users can connect on HF using AMTOR and retrieve their messages. Thus, messages can come and go from distant stations via HF AMTOR or from nearby or network stations using the VHF packet network.

TEX/AMTEX/NAVTEX

TEX is a generic term used to refer to bulletin-dissemination systems that make use of AMTOR FEC and special headers. These special headers permit receiving equipment to identify and ignore messages that have already been received without error. Specific TEX systems are the AMTEX system that W1AW uses to transmit bulletins to radio amateurs and the NAVTEX system that the US Coast Guard uses on 518 kHz to transmit bulletins to ships in coastal areas.[8]

For TEX systems, each bulletin or message begins with a special header and ends with the group "NNNN." The special header looks like "ZCZC XYnn." The "ZCZC" group marks the beginning of the message while the "XYnn" group identifies special characteristics of the message.

For AMTEX, the letter used in position "X" of the special header denotes the source of the message (ARRL, AMSAT, etc) while the letter used in position "Y" denotes the type of message (propagation bulletin, satellite bulletin, etc). The characters "nn" denote a two-digit serial number. TEX receiving equipment makes use of this header information to remember bulletins that it has already received correctly. Any repeats of that bulletin will be ignored because the receiving equipment will recognize that a message with that header has already been received correctly. Additionally, bulletins on topics not of interest can be ignored so that they are never printed.

AMTOR/SITOR SWL Operation

Decades ago, the HF commercial bands had plenty of interesting RTTY traffic. Press reports, weather reports and so on were commonplace. Today, much traffic has shifted to satellites and that which remains on HF is often encrypted. Yet there are still some frequencies that provide interesting copy. Most are in the commercial marine bands.

Press can often be seen in the evening hours in the ARQ mode. Look from 8415 to 8435 kHz and 12580 to 12630 kHz for such traffic. Another good place to look is 518 kHz, just below the AM broadcast band. The US Coast Guard transmits information to ships in coastal areas four times each day from each of six transmitters in the lower 48 states on 518 kHz. Marine shore stations transmit traffic lists and weather forecasts using FEC on 4343.0, 6416.0, 8051.5, 8087.0, 8514.0, 12886.5, 17021.6 and 22487.0 kHz.

Don't forget that W1AW, the flagship station of the ARRL, transmits Amateur Radio bulletins at least three times a day, every day of the week, on the amateur HF bands. Check a recent issue of *QST* to find the latest W1AW operating schedule.

AMTOR References

[1] P. Martinez, "Amtor, An Improved RTTY System Using a Microprocessor," *Radio Communication*, RSGB, Aug 1979.

[2] CCIR, Recommendations 625-1 (1990) and 476-4 (1986), "Direct-Printing Telegraph Equipment in the Maritime Mobile Service," reprint available from ARRL.

[3] P. Newland, "An Introduction to AMTOR," *QST*, Jul 1983.

[4] P. Newland, "How to Measure Transceiver TR Switching Times," *QEX*, Mar 1987.

[5] P. Newland, "Z-AMTOR: An Advanced AMTOR Code Converter," *QST*, Feb 1984.

[6] P. Newland, "Algorithms and Methods for SITOR/AMTOR Systems," *QEX*, Jul 1988.

[7] P. Newland, "A User's Guide to AMTOR Operation," *QST*, Oct 1985.

[8] P. Newland, "AMTEX, NAVTEX-Like Dissemination Procedures for Amateur Radio," *Proceedings of the ARRL Amateur Radio 8th Computer Networking Conference*, pp 182-188.

American National Standard Code for Information Interchange (ASCII)

The American National Standard Code for Information Interchange (ASCII) is a coded character set used for information-processing systems, communications systems and related equipment. Current FCC regulations provide that amateur use of ASCII shall conform to ASCII as defined in American National Standards Institute (ANSI) Standard X3.4-1968. ANSI has issued a revision X3.4-1977, which differs only in terminology and elimination of two choices for certain graphics. Its international counterparts are International Organization for Standardization Standard ISO 646-1973 and International Alphabet No. 5 (IA5) as specified in CCITT Recommendation V.3.

ASCII uses seven bits to represent letters, figures, symbols and control characters. Unlike ITA2 (Baudot), ASCII has both upper- and lower-case letters. The ASCII coded character set is shown in Table 7.

The bits in the table are arranged according to standard binary representation (b_6 through b_0). In the international counterpart codes, £ usually replaces #, and $ may be replaced by the international currency sign ¤.

Some early video display terminals and teleprinters, such as the Teletype Corp. Model 33, implemented only the upper-case letters. They usually display the upper-case letters when the lower-case letters are

ASCII Char.	Keyboard Character	Dec	Hex	Binary 6543210	Name	Graphic Symbol

Logical Communication Control Group

SOH Control A 1 01 0000001 Start of Heading
Used at the beginning of a message heading.

STX Control B 2 02 0000010 Start of Text
Used at the beginning of a message heading.

ETX Control C 3 03 0000011 End of Text
Terminates text.

EOT Control D 4 04 0000100 End of Transmission
Indicates conclusion of a transmission, which may have contained one or more texts and any associated headings. It may be used to turn off the receiving device.

ENQ Control E 5 05 0000101 Enquiry
Requests a response from a remote station. The response may be the remote station's identification (Who are you?).

DLE Control P 16 10 0010000 Data Link Escape
Changes the meaning of a limited number of continuously following characters. It is used exclusively to provide supplementary controls in data-communication networks. DLE is normally terminated by a shift in (SI) character.

NAK Control U 21 15 0010101 Negative Acknowledgment
Transmitted by a receiver as a negative response to a sender.

SYN Control V 22 16 0010110 Synchronous Idle
Used by a synchronous transmission system in the absence of any other character to provide a signal from which synchronization may be achieved or retained.

ETB Control W 23 17 0010111 End of Transmission Block
Used to indicate the end of a block of data for communication purposes.

Physical Communication Group

NUL Control @ 0 00 0000000 Null
Media or time fill. It may be inserted into, or removed from, a stream of data without affecting the information content of that stream.

CAN Control X 24 18 0011000 Cancel
Indicates that the data with which it is sent is in error or is to be disregarded. It usually means cancel the line (data back to the last CR).

EM Control Y 25 19 0011001 End of Medium
Identifies the physical end of the medium, or the end of the used or wanted portion of information recorded.

SUB Control Z 26 1A 0011010 Substitute
A substitute for another character in the same position to keep data fields correct.

Device Control Group

BEL Control G 7 07 0000111 Bell
Used to call for operator attention. It may trigger an alarm or other attention devices.

BS Control H 8 08 0001000 Backspace
A format effector that controls the movement of the printing position to one space backward on the same printing line. It is used for things such as: underlining, restriking for boldness and forming composite characters by overstriking. It is a very unpredictable character, that is implemented differently on printers and video-display terminals.

HT Control I 9 09 0001001 Horizontal Tab
A format effector that controls the movement of the printing position to the next in a series of predetermined positions along the same printing line.

LF Control J 10 0A 0001010 Line Feed
A format effector that controls the movement of the printing position to the next printing line.

VT Control K 11 0B 0001011 Vertical Tab
A format effector that controls the movement of the printing position to the next in a series of predetermined printing lines.

FF Control L 12 0C 0001100 Form Feed
A format effector that controls the movement of the printing position to the first predetermined printing line on the next form or page.

CR Control M 13 0D 0001101 Carriage Return
A format effector that controls the movement of the printing position to the first printing position on the same printing line. In some cases, the CR will incorporate an automatic line feed (LF) as either a default or an option. This feature, called New Line (NL), is used to make computer keyboards more like those of typewriters.

DC1 Control Q 17 11 0010001 Device Control 1

DC2 Control R 18 12 0010010 Device Control 2

DC3 Control S 19 13 0010011 Device Control 3

DC4 Control T 20 14 0010100 Device Control 4

These are the control of ancillary devices associated with data processing or telecommunications systems, especially for switching devices on or off. While DC1 and DC3 are often used to start and stop the flow of data, these control signals are "wild cards" that are used for nearly any switching purposes.

Information Separators

FS Control \ 28 1C 0011100 File Separator

GS Control] 29 1D 0011101 Group Separator

RS Control ∧ 30 1E 0011110 Record Separator

US Control — 31 1F 0011111 Unit Separator

FS, GS, RS and US is a hierarchical group of information separators used for formatting and string processing. FS is the most inclusive, and US the least inclusive. A *file* is a grouping of all related records. A *group* is a collection of *records* within a file. A record is a collection of related fields of data. A *unit* is a number of fields 1 to 80 characters long.

Code Extension Group

SO Control N 14 0E 0001110 Shift Out
Indicates that the code combinations that follow are to be interpreted as outside of the standard character set until a shift in (SI) character is reached.

SI Control O 15 0F 0001111 Shift In
Indicates that the code combinations that follow are to be interpreted according to the standard code table.

ESC ESC 27 1B 0011011 Escape
Intended to provide code extension (supplementary characters). The ESC character itself is a prefix affecting the interpretation of a limited number of continuously following characters. It may be terminated by a shift in (SI) character.

Table 7
The ASCII Coded Character Set

Bit 3	Bit 2	Bit 1	Bit 0	Hex 2nd	0	1	2	3	4	5	6	7
				Bit 6 →	0	0	0	0	1	1	1	1
				Bit 5 →	0	0	1	1	0	0	1	1
				Bit 4 →	0	1	0	1	0	1	0	1
				Hex 1st →	0	1	2	3	4	5	6	7
0	0	0	0	0	NUL	DLE	SP	0	@	P	`	p
0	0	0	1	1	SOH	DC1	!	1	A	Q	a	q
0	0	1	0	2	STX	DC2	"	2	B	R	b	r
0	0	1	1	3	ETX	DC3	#	3	C	S	c	s
0	1	0	0	4	EOT	DC4	$	4	D	T	d	t
0	1	0	1	5	ENQ	NAK	%	5	E	U	e	u
0	1	1	0	6	ACK	SYN	&	6	F	V	f	v
0	1	1	1	7	BEL	ETB	'	7	G	W	g	w
1	0	0	0	8	BS	CAN	(	8	H	X	h	x
1	0	0	1	9	HT	EM	)	9	I	Y	i	y
1	0	1	0	A	LF	SUB	*	:	J	Z	j	z
1	0	1	1	B	VT	ESC	+	;	K	[	k	{
1	1	0	0	C	FF	FS	,	<	L	\	l	|
1	1	0	1	D	CR	GS	-	=	M	]	m	}
1	1	1	0	E	SO	RS	.	>	N	^	n	~
1	1	1	1	F	SI	US	/	?	O	_	o	DEL

ACK	= acknowledge	FF	= form feed
BEL	= bell	FS	= file separator
BS	= backspace	GS	= group separator
CAN	= cancel	HT	= horizontal tab
CR	= carriage return	LF	= line feed
DC1	= device control 1	NAK	= negative acknowledge
DC2	= device control 2	NUL	= null
DC3	= device control 3	RS	= record separator
DC4	= device control 4	SI	= shift in
DEL	= (delete)	SO	= shift out
DLE	= data link escape	SOH	= start of heading
ENQ	= enquiry	SP	= space
EM	= end of medium	STX	= start of text
EOT	= end of transmission	SUB	= substitute
ESC	= escape	SYN	= synchronous idle
ETB	= end of block	US	= unit separator
ETX	= end of text	VT	= vertical tab

Notes

1. "1" = mark, "0" = space.
2. Bit 6 is the most-significant bit (MSB). bit 0 the lest-significant bit (LSB).

Fig. 22 — Time sequence of typical ASCII character, the letter S sent serially.

received. On newer terminal equipment, a CAPS-LOCK feature on the keyboard may be used to shift all letters to upper case.

Control Characters

ASCII has 32 *control characters* plus the special characters for space and delete. They are not consistently used as specified in the ANSI X3.4 standard. However, it will be helpful to know the standard uses. There are five groups in the control set: Logical Communication Control, Physical Communication, Device Control, Information Separators and Code Extension. Below is an explanation of each control character. The first line of each entry follows the format shown in the table on the previous page.

Parity

While not strictly a part of ASCII (ANSI X3.4), an eighth bit (P) may be added for *parity* checking. FCC rules permit optional use of the parity bit. The applicable U.S. standard (ANSI X3.16-1976) and international standard (CCITT Rec. V.4) recommend an *even* parity sense for asynchronous data communication and *odd* parity sense for synchronous data communication. However, there is very little standardization within the computer industry, and you will find five variations:

(1) no parity, (2) always mark, (3) always space, (4) odd parity or (5) even parity. See Chapter 8 for details of parity checking.

Code Extensions

By sacrificing parity, the eighth bit can be used to extend the ASCII 128-character code to one having 256 possibilities. Work is now underway to produce an international standard on extended coded character sets for text communication that will provide supplementary sets of graphic characters. Use of these extended character sets by U.S. amateurs is permitted above 50 MHz but not below 50 MHz where only specified codes (Baudot, AMTOR and ASCII) are authorized by FCC rules.

ASCII Serial Transmission

Serial transmission of ASCII is covered in ANSI Standards X3.15 and X3.16, and CCITT Recommendations V.4 and X.4. They specify that the bit sequence for serial transmission of an ASCII character shall be least-significant bit first to most-significant bit or b_0 through b_6 (plus the parity bit P if used).

Serial transmission may be either *synchronous* or *asynchronous*. In synchronous transmissions, only the information bits (and optional parity bit) are sent, as shown in Fig. 22A.

Asynchronous (start-stop) serial transmission adds a *start pulse* at the beginning and a *stop pulse* at the end of each character. The start pulse is the same length as for the information pulses. The stop pulse may be one or two bit periods long. Although there is some variation, the convention is that the stop pulse is one bit period long except for 110-baud transmissions where mechanical teletypewriters may be involved.

ASCII Data Rates

Personal computers usually provide a choice of ASCII serial input/output data rates ranging from 110 to 19,200 bits per second, as shown in Table 8.

Data communications signaling rates depend largely on the medium and the state of the art when the equipment was selected. Numerous national and international standards that recommend different data rates, are listed in Table 9. The most-used rates tend to progress in 2:1 steps from 300 to 9600 bits per second and in 8000 bits-per-second increments from 16,000 bits per second. For Amateur Radio serial ASCII transmissions the data rates of 75, 110, 150,

Table 8
ASCII Asynchronous Signaling Rates

Bits per Second	Data Pulse (ms)	Stop Pulse (ms)	CPS	WPM
110	9.091	18.182	10.0	100
150	6.667	6.667	15.0	150
300	3.333	3.333	30.0	300
600	1.667	1.667	60.0	600
1200	0.8333	0.8333	120	1200
2400	0.4167	0.4167	240	2400
4800	0.2083	0.2083	480	4800
9600	0.1041	0.1041	960	9600
19200	0.0520	0.0520	1920	19200

CPS = characters per second

$$= \frac{1}{START + 7\ (DATA) + PARITY + STOP}$$

WPM = words per minute = $\frac{CPS}{6} \times 60$

= number of 5-letter-plus-space groups per minute

Table 9
Data Transmission Signaling-Rate Standards

Standard	Signaling Rates (bit/s)	Tolerance
CCITT		
V.5	600, 1200, 2400, 4800	± 0.01%
V.6	Preferred: 600, 1200, 2400, 3600, 4800, 7200, 9600	± 0.01%
	Supplementary: 1800, 3000, 4200, 5400, 6000, 6600, 7800, 8400, 9000, 10200, 10800	
V.21	200	≤ 200 bit/s
	300 (where possible)	≤ 300 bit/s
V.23	600	≤ 600 bit/s
	1200	≤ 1200 bit/s
	75 (backward channel)	≤ 75 bit/s
V.35	Preferred: 48000	± 1 bit/s
	When necessary: 40800	± 1 bit/s
V.36	Recommended for international use: 48,000	
	Certain applications: 56000, 64000, 72000	
X.3	Packet assembly/disassembly speeds: 50, 75, 100, 110, 134.5, 150, 200, 300, 600, 1200, 1200/75, 1800, 2400, 4800, 9600, 19200, 48000, 56000, 64000	
ANSI		
X3.1	Serial: 75, 150, 300, 600, 1200, 2400, 4800, 7200, 9600	
	Parallel: 75, 150, 300, 600, 900, 1200	
X3.36	Above 9600 bit/s, signaling rates shall be in integral multiples of 8000 bit/s.	
	Selected standard rates: 16000, 56000, 1344000 and 1544000	
	Recognized for international use: 48000	
EIA		
RS-269-B	(Same as ANSI X3.1)	
FED STD		
-1001	(Same as ANSI X3.36) For foreign communications: 64000	
-1041	2400, 4800, 9600	

300, 600, 1200, 2400, 4800, 9600, 16,000, 19,200 and 56,000 bits per second are suggested.

Bauds vs. Bits Per Second

The term *baud* is a unit of signaling speed equal to one discrete condition or event per second. In single-channel transmission, such as the FCC prescribes for Baudot transmissions, the signaling rate in bauds equals the data rate in bits per second. However, the FCC does not limit ASCII to single-channel transmission. There are digital modulation systems that have more than two (mark and space) states. In *dibit* modulation two ASCII bits are sampled at a time. The four possible states for a dibit are 00, 01, 10 and 11. In four-phase modulation, each state is assigned an individual phase of 0, 90, 180 and 270 degrees, respectively. Using dibit phase modulation, the signaling speed in bauds is half the information-transfer rate in bits per second. As the FCC specifies the digital sending speed in bauds, amateurs may transmit ASCII at higher information rates by using digital modulation systems that encode more bits per signaling element. This technology is open for exploration by Amateur Radio experimenters.

Amateur ASCII RTTY Operations

On April 17, 1980 the FCC first permitted ASCII in the Amateur Radio Service. U.S. amateurs have been slow to abandon Baudot in favor of asynchronous serial ASCII.

Some of the reluctance to use it arises from the reasoning that asynchronous ASCII has two (or three with a parity bit added) more bits than asynchronous Baudot and is usually sent at higher speeds. Thus, it was felt that the greater data rates and increased bandwidth needed for ASCII would make its reliability lower than that of Baudot. This is true as far as it goes but

does not exhaust the theoretical possibilities, which will be discussed below.

On the practical side, some amateurs tried ASCII on the air and experienced poor results. In some cases, this can be traced to the use of modems that were optimized for 45-baud operation. At 110 or 300 bauds, the 45-baud mark and space filters are too narrow. On the HF bands, speeds above 50 or 75 bauds are subject to intersymbol interference (ISI) (slurring one pulse into the next) from multipath propagation. Multiple paths can be avoided by operating at the maximum usable frequency (MUF) where there is only one ray path. The amount of multipath delay varies according to operating frequency with respect to the MUF and path distance. Paths in the 600- to 5000-mile range are generally less bothered by multipath than shorter or longer ones, with paths of 250 miles or less being difficult from a multipath standpoint. As a result, successful operation at the higher ASCII speeds depends on using the highest frequency band possible as well as having suitable modems at both ends of the circuit.

Returning to the theoretical comparison of Baudot and ASCII, recall that the FCC requires asynchronous (start-stop)

transmission of Baudot. This means that the five information pulses must be sent with a start pulse and a stop pulse, usually of 1.42 times the length of the information pulse. Thus, an asynchronous Baudot transmitted character requires 7.42 units. In contrast, 7 bits of ASCII plus a parity bit, a start and a two-unit stop pulse has 11 units. However, it is possible to send only the 7 ASCII information bits synchronously (without start and stop pulses), making the number of units that must be transmitted (7 vs. 7.42) slightly smaller for ASCII than for Baudot. Or, it is possible to synchronously transmit 8 bits (7 ASCII bits plus a parity bit) and take advantage of the error-detection capability of parity. Also, there is nothing to prevent ASCII from being sent at a lower speed such as 50 or 75 bauds, to make it as immune to multipath as 45- or 50-baud Baudot RTTY is. So it is easy to see that ASCII can be as reliable as Baudot RTTY if care is used in system design.

While 45- or 50-baud RTTY circuits can provide reliable communications, this range of signaling speeds does not make full use of the HF medium. Speeds ranging from 75 to 1200 bauds can be achieved on HF with error-detection and error-correction techniques similar to those used in AMTOR. Reliable transmission at these higher speeds can be accomplished by means of packet radio, which is described later in this chapter.

Bibliography on ASCII

ANSI X3.4-1977, "Code for information interchange," American National Standards Institute, 1430 Broadway, New York, NY 10018.

ANSI X3.15-1976, "Bit sequencing of the American national standard code for information interchange in serial-by-bit data transmission."

ANSI X3.16-1976, "Character structure and character parity sense for serial-by-bit data communication information interchange."

ANSI X3.25-1976, "Character structure and character parity sense for parallel-by-bit communication in American national standard code for information interchange.

Bemer, "Inside ASCII," *Interface Age*, May, June and July 1978.

CCITT V.3, "International Alphabet No. 5," International Telegraph and Telephone Consultative Committee, CCITT volumes with recommendations prefixed with the letters V and X are available from United Nations Bookstore, Room 32B, UN General Assembly Building, New York, NY 10017 or from International Telecommunication Union, General Secretariat, Sales Service, Place des Nations, CH 1211, Geneva 20, Switzerland.

CCITT V.4, "General structure of signals of International Alphabet No. 5 code for data transmission over the public telephone network."

ISO 646-1973 (E), "7-bit coded character set for information processing interchange," International Organization for Standardization, available from ANSI, 1430 Broadway, New York, NY 10018.

Mackenzie, *Coded Character Sets, History and Development,* Addison-Wesley Publishing Co., 1980.

Code Conversion

Conversion between International Morse, Baudot and ASCII is tricky business. In fact, it is virtually impossible to come up with a perfect conversion between any two of these codes, let alone all three. Anyone who has given this serious consideration will confirm this.

The root of the problem is that each code has a somewhat different character set. All three have all the numerals (0-9), a word space, certain punctuation marks and the Latin alphabet upper case in common. If you have original text with upper- and lower-case letters in ASCII, the case information will be lost when converting to Baudot or Morse, both of which assume that all letters are in upper case. Once lost, the case information cannot be regained except, perhaps, by a computer program designed to guess the case.

Another problem with code conversion is that the conversion tables cannot be bilateral. Using the case example, above, both upper- and lower-case ASCII will translate to upper-case Baudot and Morse, but Baudot and Morse letters cannot translate to both ASCII cases. There are some subtleties to this game. Thus, if you want to design a versatile code-conversion scheme, it is useful to build unilateral conversion tables, one for translating code a to b, another for converting code b to a.

The differences between the international and national implementations of Baudot add some further complications. On most U.S. teletypewriters, the figures-case characters for D, F, G and H are used for $, !, & and # (or motor stop), respectively. In ITA2, these characters are unassigned, meaning they are set aside for national use. So, you can't use these characters for international communications unless you have an agreement with the other station as to what each means. Perhaps even worse is that the figures-case characters for J, S, V and Z, while specified to be audible signal (bell), ', = and +, respectively, for ITA2, show up as ', bell, ; and " on many U.S.

TTYs. You can use these characters internationally as long as you bear in mind that hams in other countries will probably interpret them within their ITA2 meanings.

There are some more complications when considering conversion to and from ASCII or its international versions, IA5 and ISO 646. The ASCII characters #, $, @, [, \ ,], ^ , ` , {, |, } and ~ may be assigned to different graphic characters in other countries. Some languages need these wild cards for accented letters.

Morse code presents a few dilemmas too. One is that few hams know the complete Morse character set shown in Table 1. To limit the character set to just those known by most amateurs might be advisable for QSOs that will be aurally read by the average operator. However, it could be unnecessarily restrictive when sending to the expert operator or to a computer that knows the whole code. A code-conversion program that produces Morse might include a menu-selectable feature to vary the conversion table according to the receiving audience.

Code Conversion Standards

International standards, ISO/DIS 6936 and CCITT Rec. S.18, exist for conversion from ITA2 to ASCII and the reverse. They include direct conversion for all common characters and change both upper- and lower-case ASCII into upper-case ITA2 in a straightforward manner. When translating from ITA2 to ASCII, ITA2 characters for which there are no corresponding ASCII characters are translated to SUB. Going the other way around, SOH, STX, ETX, EOT, ACK, DLE, NAK, SYN, ETB and DEL are removed; the other nontranslatable characters are replaced by the question mark (?). Bear in mind that ISO/DIS 6936 is based on ITA2, not the version of Baudot that is found on many U.S. teletypewriters.

Limiting code conversion simply to direct equivalents may not be the best approach for Amateur Radio. In this respect, it is important to note that some characters (in Morse, Baudot and ASCII) change their meanings according to the context, or protocol, in which they are used. For example, the Morse code combination •–•– is an accented letter A for certain European languages but is also used as a separator in Amateur Radio message headings. The meanings of ASCII control characters change as different implementors of computer systems or data-communications networks reassign them to meet specific needs. What is ETX (end of text) to one system is Control C (crash the program) to another.

To go beyond the direct equivalents requires that the context(s) be carefully defined and standardized. In other words, if you know how a certain character (or sequence of characters) is used in one code using one protocol, there must be a corresponding character or set of characters in the other code and protocol.

Now that you're completely confused, let's look at how to say that a message is coming. ASCII has its SOH (start of heading) — just one control character can do the job. In Baudot it's a problem, but not insurmountable. CCITT Rec. S.4 comes to the rescue by using ZCZC as the start of the heading. And in Morse — ah Morse! — we have two possibilities: HR (meaning here is, or hear the following message) and $\overline{KA}$, a starting signal. There are similar correspondences between ASCII EOT, Baudot (CCITT Rec. S.4) NNNN, and Morse $\overline{AR}$.

These examples illustrate the practicality of developing contextual code-conversion tables for Amateur Radio. This is not to suggest that everyone rush out there and implement one on the assumption that any right-thinking person would go along with your conversion table. Beware of the mines, quicksand, traps and low doorways! How many programmers made up their own ASCII character for the Morse code com-

Table 10
Conversion from Morse to ASCII and Baudot

Int'l Morse Code	Char.	ASCII Code 6543210	Char.	Baudot Code '43210	Char.²
•	E	1000101	E	↓00001	E
—	T	1010100	T	↓10000	T
••	I	1001001	I	↓00110	I
•—	A	1000001	A	↓00011	A
—•	N	1001110	N	↓01100	N
——	M	1001101	M	↓11100	M
•••	S	1010011	S	↓00101	S
••—	U	1010101	U	↓00111	U
•—•	R	1010010	R	↓01010	R
•——	W	1010111	W	↓10011	W
—••	D	1000100	D	↓01001	D
—•—	K	1001011	K	↓01111	K
——•	G	1000111	G	↓11010	G
——•'•	O	1001111	O	↓11000	O
••••	H	1001000	H	↓10100	H
•••—	V	1010110	V	↓11110	V
••—•	F	1000110	F	↓01101	F
••——	Ü				
•—••	L	1001100	L	↓10010	L
•—•—	Ä				
•——•	P	1010000	P	↓10110	P
•———	J	1001010	J	↓01011	J
—•••	B	1000010	B	↓11001	B
—••—	X	1011000	X	↓11111	X
—•—•	C	1000011	C	↓01110	C
—•——	Y	1011001	Y	↓10101	Y
——••	Z	1011010	Z	↓10001	Z
——•—	Q	1010001	Q	↓10111	Q
———•	Ö				
————	CH				
•••••	5	0110101	5	↑10000	5
••••—	4	0110100	4	↑01010	4
•••——	SN				
•••—•	3	0110011	3	↑00001	3
••—••	ÉÊE̦				
••—•—	INT				
••——•					
••———	2	0110010	2	↑10011	2
•—•••	AS				
•—••—	AU				
•—•—•	AR +	0101011	+	↑10001	+ (ITA)
•—•——					
•——••	ÁÀÂÅ				
•——•—					
•———•					
•————	1	0110001	1	↑10111	1
—••••	6	0110110	6	↑10101	6
—•••—	BT =	0111101	=	↑11110	= (ITA)
—••—•	DN /	0101111	/	↑11101	/
—••——					
—•—••	Ç				
—•—•—	KA				
—•——•	KN (	0101000	(	↑01111	(
—•———					
——•••	7	0110111	7	↑00111	7
——••—	Ź				
——•—•	Ñ				
——•——	8	0111000	8	↑00110	8
———••	9	0111001	9	↑11000	9
———•—	0	0110000	0	↑10110	0
••••——	HM				
•••—•—	SK				
••—••—	IX				
••——••	IMI ?	0111111	?	↑11001	?
••——•—	IQ __	10111'1	—		
•—••—•	AF "	0100010	"	↑10001	" (U.S.A.)
•—•—•—	AL ¶				
•—•—•—	AAA .	0101110	.	↑11100	.
•————	WG '	0100111	'	↑00101 / ↑01011	' (ITA) / ' (U.S.)
—••••—	DU -	0101101	—	↑00011	-
—•—•—•	KR ;	0111011	;	↑11110	; (U.S.)
—•—•—	KK)	0101001	)	↑10010	)
——••——	MIM ,	0101100	,	↑01100	,
———•••	OS :	0111010	:	↑01110	:
•••—••—	SX $	0100100	$	↑01001	$ (U.S.)
••••••••	Error				

Notes
1. In Baudot code, it is necessary to check to see if the terminal is in the correct case (↓ = letters, ↑ = figures). If not, a LTRS or FIGS must be inserted before the code shown.
2. Figures-case characters are the same for both ITA 2 and U.S. teletypewriters except where indicated. If only (U.S.) is shown, this is an unassigned character in ITA 2.

Table 11
Conversion from Baudot to ASCII and Morse

Baudot Code ¹ 43210	Char.²	ASCII Code 6543210	Char.	Int'l Morse Code	Char.
↓↑00000	Blank	0000000	NUL		
↓00001	E	1000101	E	•	E
↑00001	3	0110011	3	•••——	3
↓↑00010	LF	0001010	LF		
↓00011	A	1000001	A	•—	A
↑00011	—	0101101	—	—••••—	—
↓↑00100	SP	0100000	SP		space
↓00101	S	1010011	S	•••	S
↑00101	' (ITA)	0100111	'	•———•	'
↑00101	Bell (U.S.)	0000111	BEL		
↓00110	I	1001001	I	••	I
↑00110	8	0111000	8	———••	8
↓00111	U	1010101	U	••—	U
↑00111	7	0110111	7	——•••	7
↓↑01000	CR	0001101	CR		
↓01001	D	1000100	D	—••	D
↑01001	WRU (ITA)	0000101	ENQ		
↑01001	$ (U.S.)	0100100	$	•••—••—	$
↓01010	R	1010010	R	•—•	R
↑01010	4	0110100	4	••••—	4
↓01011	J	1001010	J	•———	J
↑01011	Bell (ITA)	0000111	BEL		
↑01011	' (U.S.)	0100111	'	•———•	'
↓01100	N	1001110	N	—•	N
↑01100	,	0101100	,	——••——	,
↓01101	F	1000110	F	••—•	F
↑01101	! (U.S.)	0100001	!		
↓01110	C	1000011	C	—•—•	C
↑01110	:	0111010	:	———•••	:
↓01111	K	1001011	K	—•—	K
↑01111	(	0101000	(	—•——•	KN (
↓10000	T	1010100	T	—	T
↑10000	5	0110101	5	•••••	5
↓10001	Z	1011010	Z	——••	Z
↑10001	+ (ITA)	0101011	+	•—•—•	AR +
↑10001	" (U.S.)	0100010	"	•—••—•	AF "
↓10010	L	1001100	L	•—••	L
↑10010	)	0101001	)	—•——•—	KK)
↓10011	W	1010111	W	•——	W
↑10011	2	0110010	2	••———	2
↓10100	H	1001000	H	••••	H
↑10100	# (U.S.)	0100011	#		
↓10101	Y	1011001	Y	—•——	Y
↑10101	6	0110110	6	—••••	6
↓10110	P	1010000	P	•——•	P
↑10110	0	0110000	0	———•—	0
↓10111	Q	1010001	Q	——•—	Q
↑10111	1	0110001	1	•————	1
↓11000	O	1001111	O	———	O
↑11000	9	0111001	9	———••	9
↓11001	B	1000010	B	—•••	B
↑11001	?	0111111	?	••——••	IMI ?
↓11010	G	1001101	G	——•	G
↑11010	& (U.S.)	0100110	&		
↓↑11011	FIGS				
↓11100	M	1001101	M	——	M
↑11100	.	0101110	.	•—•—•—	AAA .
↓11101	X	1011000	X	—••—	X
↑11101	/	0101111	/	—••—•	DN /
↓11110	V	1010110	V	•••—	V
↑11110	= (ITA)	0111101	=	—•••—	BT =
↑11110	; (U.S.)	0111011	;	—•—•—•	KR ;
↓↑11111	LTRS				

Notes
1. In Baudot code, it is necessary to check to see what the current case is before conversion (↓ = letters, ↑ = figures, ↓↑ = either).
2. Figures-case characters are the same for both ITA 2 and U.S. teletypewriters except where indicated. If only (U.S.) is shown, this is an unassigned character in ITA 2.

Table 12

Conversion from ASCII to Morse and Baudot

ASCII Code 6543210	Char.	Int'l Morse Code	Int'l Morse Char.	Baudot ¹ 43210	Baudot Char.²
0000000	NUL			↓↑ 00000	Blank
0000001	SOH				
0000010	STX				
0000011	ETX				
0000100	EOT				
0000101	ENQ			↑ 01001	WRU (ITA)
0000110	ACK				
0000111	BEL			↑ 01011	Bell (ITA)
				↑ 00101	Bell (U.S.)
0001000	BS				
0001001	HT				
0001010	LF			↓↑ 00010	LF
0001011	VT				
0001100	FF				
0001101	CR			↓↑ 01000	CR
0001110	SO				
0001111	SI				
0010000	DLE				
0010001	DC1				
0010010	DC2				
0010011	DC3				
0010100	DC4				
0010101	NAK				
0010110	SYN				
0010111	ETB				
0011000	CAN				
0011001	EM				
0011010	SUB				
0011011	ESC				
0011100	FS				
0011101	GS				
0011110	RS				
0011111	US				
0100000	SP	Space		00100	SP
0100001	!				
0100010	"	•—••—•	$\overline{AF}$ "	↑ 10001	" (U.S.)
0100011	#			↑ 10100	# (U.S.)
0100100	$	•••—••—	$\overline{SX}$ $	↑ 01001	$ (U.S.)
0100101	%				
0100110	&				
0100111	'	•————•	$\overline{WG}$ '	↑ 00101	' (ITA)
				↑ 01011	' (U.S.)
0101000	(	—•——•	$\overline{KN}$ (	↑ 01111	(
0101001	)	—•——•—	$\overline{KK}$)	↑ 10010	)
0101010	*				
0101011	+	•—•—•	$\overline{AR}$ +	↑ 10001	+ (ITA)
0101100	,	——••——	$\overline{MIM}$,	↑ 01100	,
0101101	-	—••••—	$\overline{DU}$ —	↑ 00011	—
0101110	.	•—•—•—	$\overline{AAA}$.	↑ 11100	.
0101111	/	—••—•	$\overline{DN}$ /	↑ 11101	/
0110000	0	—————	0	↑ 10110	0
0110001	1	•————	1	↑ 10111	1
0110010	2	••———	2	↑ 10011	2
0110011	3	•••——	3	↑ 00001	3
0110100	4	••••—	4	↑ 01010	4
0110101	5	•••••	5	↑ 10000	5
0110110	6	—••••	6	↑ 10101	6
0110111	7	——•••	7	↑ 00111	7
0111000	8	———••	8	↑ 00110	8
0111001	9	————•	9	↑ 11000	9
0111010	:	———•••	$\overline{OS}$:	↑ 01110	:
0111011	;	—•—•—•	$\overline{KR}$;	↑ 11110	; (U.S.)
0111100	<				
0111101	=	—•••—	$\overline{BT}$ =	↑ 11110	= (ITA)
0111110	>				
0111111	?	••——••	$\overline{IMI}$?	↑ 11001	?
1000000	@				

ASCII Code 6543210	Char.	Int'l Morse Code	Int'l Morse Char.	Baudot ¹ 43210	Baudot Char.²
1000001	A	•—	A	↓ 00011	A
1000010	B	—•••	B	↓ 11001	B
1000011	C	—•—•	C	↓ 01110	C
1000100	D	—••	D	↓ 01001	D
1000101	E	•	E	↓ 00001	E
1000110	F	••—•	F	↓ 01101	F
1000111	G	——•	G	↓ 11010	G
1001000	H	••••	H	↓ 10100	H
1001001	I	••	I	↓ 00110	I
1001010	J	•———	J	↓ 01011	J
1001011	K	—•—	K	↓ 01111	K
1001100	L	•—••	L	↓ 10010	L
1001101	M	——	M	↓ 11100	M
1001110	N	—•	N	↓ 01100	N
1001111	O	———	O	↓ 11000	O
1010000	P	•——•	P	↓ 10110	P
1010001	Q	——•—	Q	↓ 10111	Q
1010010	R	•—•	R	↓ 01010	R
1010011	S	•••	S	↓ 00101	S
1010100	T	—	T	↓ 10000	T
1010101	U	••—	U	↓ 00111	U
1010110	V	•••—	V	↓ 11110	V
1010111	W	•——	W	↓ 10011	W
1011000	X	—••—	X	↓ 11101	X
1011001	Y	—•——	Y	↓ 10101	Y
1011010	Z	——••	Z	↓ 10001	Z
1011011	[				
1011100	\				
1011101	]				
1011110	^				
1011111	_	•——•—•	$\overline{IQ}$ _		
1100000	`				
1100001	a	•—	A	↓ 00011	A
1100010	b	—•••	B	↓ 11001	B
1100011	c	—•—•	C	↓ 01110	C
1100100	d	—••	D	↓ 01001	D
1100101	e	•	E	↓ 00001	E
1100110	f	••—•	F	↓ 01101	F
1100111	g	——•	G	↓ 11010	G
1101000	h	••••	H	↓ 10100	H
1101001	i	••	I	↓ 00110	I
1101010	j	•———	J	↓ 01011	J
1101011	k	—•—	K	↓ 01111	K
1101100	l	•—••	L	↓ 10010	L
1101101	m	——	M	↓ 11100	M
1101110	n	—•	N	↓ 01100	N
1101111	o	———	O	↓ 11000	O
1110000	p	•——•	P	↓ 10110	P
1110001	q	——•—	Q	↓ 10111	Q
1110010	r	•—•	R	↓ 01010	R
1110011	s	•••	S	↓ 00101	S
1110100	t	—	T	↓ 10000	T
1110101	u	••—	U	↓ 00111	U
1110110	v	•••—	V	↓ 11110	V
1110111	w	•——	W	↓ 10011	W
1111000	x	—••—	X	↓ 11101	X
1111001	y	—•——	Y	↓ 10101	Y
1111010	z	——••	Z	↓ 10001	Z
1111011	{				
1111100	|				
1111101	}				
1111110	~				
1111111	DEL				

Notes

¹ In Baudot code, it is necessary to check to see what the current case is before conversion (↓ = letters, ↑ = figures, ↓↑ = either case).

² Figures-case characters are the same for both ITA 2 and U.S. teletypewriters except where indicated.

bination —•——• ($\overline{KN}$) when left parenthesis [(] was part of International Morse? Many other radio services, even other IARU Member Societies, have been using —•——• for left parenthesis all along.

The ARRL Digital Communications Committee will be working on standardized code-conversion tables for use by amateurs. This will dovetail with other work on standardizing message formats.

CODE-CONVERSION TABLES

Tables 10 through 13 are based on direct character-for-character translations between Morse, Baudot and ASCII. They are conservative and do not conflict with international standards. Conversions between ITA2 and ASCII comply with ISO/DIS 6936. The tables have numerous blanks where there are no exact equivalents in the other codes. The order of characters for each table is determined by the digital value of the code from which conversion is to be made.

Table 13
Code Conversion, ITA1 through 4 (Notes 1 and 2)

Combination No.	ITA1 Bit No. 43210	Figure Case ITA1	Letter Case All Codes	Figure Case ITA2-4	ITA2 Bit No. 43210	ITA3 Bit No. 6543210	ITA4 Bit No. 543210
1	+ + + + −	1	A	—	00011	0101100	000110
2	+ − − + +	8	B	?	11001	1001100	110010
3	+ − − + −	9	C	:	01110	0011001	011100
4	+ − − − −	0	D	Note 4	01001	0011100	010010
5	+ + + − +	2	E	3	00001	0001110	000010
6	+ − − − +	Note 3	F	Note 4	01101	1100100	011010
7	+ − + − +	7	G	Note 4	11010	1000011	110100
8	+ − + − −	+	H	Note 4	10100	0100101	101000
9	+ + − − +	Note 3	I	8	00110	0000111	001100
10	+ − + + −	6	J	BELL	01011	1100010	010110
11	− − + + −	(	K	(	01111	1101000	011110
12	− − + − −	=	L	)	10010	0100011	100100
13	− − + − +	)	M	.	11100	1000101	111000
14	− − − − +	Note 3	N	,	01100	0010101	011000
15	+ + − − −	5	O	9	11000	0110001	110000
16	− − − − −	%	P	0	10110	0101001	101100
17	− − − − +	/	Q	1	10111	1011000	101110
18	− − − + +	−	R	4	01010	0010011	010100
19	− + − + +	.	S	'	00101	0101010	001010
20	− + − + −	Note 3	T	5	10000	1010001	100000
21	+ + + − −	4	U	7	00111	0100110	001110
22	− + − − −	'	V	=	11110	1001001	111100
23	− + − − +	?	W	2	10011	1010010	100110
24	− + − + −	,	X	/	11101	0110100	111010
25	+ + − + +	3	Y	6	10101	1010100	101010
26	− + + − −	:	Z	+	10001	1000110	100010
27	+ + + − −	Carriage return		Carriage return	01000	1100001	010000
28	− + + + −	Line feed		Line feed	00010	0001101	000100
29	− + + + +	Letter blank (space)		Letter shift	11111	0111000	111110
30	+ − + + +	Figure blank (space)		Figure shift	11011	0110010	110110
31	− − + + +	Error		Space	00100	0001011	001000
32	+ + + + +	Instrument at rest		Blank	00000	1110000	000001
— —				Phasing signal	—	—	110011
— —				Signal repetition	—	0010110	—
— —				Signal alpha	Note 5	1001010	000000
— —				Signal beta	Note 6	0011010	111111

Note 1: For complete specifications of these codes see the following International Telecommunication Union documents: ITA1 and 2 — Telegraph Regulations (Geneva Revision, 1958), ITA3 — CCITT Rec. S.13, ITA4 — CCITT Rec. R.44.

Note 2: In ITA1, + indicates positive current, − negative current. In ITA2 through ITA4, 1 represents mark condition (shown as Z in ITU recommendations, which is the higher emitted radio frequency for FSK, the lower for AFSK). 0 represents the space condition (shown as A in ITU recommendations). For meanings of A and Z see CCITT Rec. 140. The normal order of bit transmission is lowest significant bit (LSB) first.

Note 3: At the disposal of each administration for its internal service.

Note 4: At present unassigned. Reception of these signals, however, should not initiate a request for repetition. See CCITT Rec. S.4.

Note 5: Permanent 0 polarity.

Note 6: Permanent 1 polarity.

Conversion from Morse to ASCII and Baudot

Table 10 starts with the Morse E and progresses through the code to the longest characters. This progression has been used in code-conversion programs written in BASIC. All Morse Latin letters translate directly to Baudot letters and upper-case ASCII letters. All direct equivalents of punctuation marks are included. International Morse has specific code combinations for accented letters. However, they cannot be translated out of context to either Baudot or ASCII because individual national implementations of these codes place them differently.

The programmer is left to determine how to display nonconvertible Morse characters. For example, an incoming S̄K̄ cannot be displayed or printed as such because an overlining capability is not usually provided in computer peripherals. Perhaps it could be shown as SK if there is an underlining capability or <END OF WORK> if not. Alternatively, it could be ignored at the expense of losing that meaning.

When converting from Morse (or ASCII) to Baudot, the program has to check to see what case the Baudot is in. If, for example, you just received WB and the next character is 4, you have to check to see that the device is in letters case before giving it the B. In this case it is so no LTRS function need be issued. Then, having checked or remembered that the device is in letters case for the B, a FIGS function must be sent before sending the Baudot device the 4.

Conversion from Baudot to ASCII and Morse

Table 11 is arranged by binary progression starting with 00000 (blank). Note that blank translates to an ASCII NUL, but the letters-shift (LTRS) character does not convert to an ASCII DEL. When a mistake is made during preparation of paper tape, the operator may backspace the tape and use LTRS or DEL to punch all hole positions to erase erroneous characters. If this is done when preparing Baudot tapes, the LTRS function will be read as a change from figure case (if it was there) to letter

case. If letter case was not wanted, a figures-shift character must be inserted after the LTRS functions. DEL causes no case change, so LTRS and DEL are not equivalent.

The bell and apostrophe (') translate nicely from ITA2 to ASCII. But note that these codes in ITA2 are just exactly reversed in the code used in most U.S. Baudot TTYs. Because of this difference, it is usually desirable to send both characters in Baudot. This causes both ITA2 and U.S. machines to ring the bell and print an apostrophe. In that other stations may send one code, the other or both together, this makes an interesting puzzle for the code conversion programmer.

The WRU (Who are you?) character in ITA2 converts to ENQ (enquiry) in ASCII. They are both used to request the identity of the other terminal. However, ENQ may also be used to request the status of the other terminal.

Figures H (10100) is messy. It is unassigned in ITA2 and available for national use. On U.S. TTYs, it is probably a pound sign (#), and thus will translate # to an ASCII #. On older machines, it may be used as a motor stop.

When using figures case, you should be aware of a feature called *unshift on space* that may be implemented on some Baudot terminals. If you send a group of numbers and a space, the machine will print letters-case characters after the space if it has the unshift-on-space feature. To avoid this problem, it is a good idea always to send a FIGS just before each group of figures that are preceded by a space.

Some terminals have a "nonoverline" feature. An automatic LF is sent every time a CR is received. Others have a "wrap-around" feature that automatically moves to the first printing position of the new line when the old line is full. If your terminal has these features, don't assume everyone has them.

Conversion from ASCII to Morse and Baudot

This conversion is probably the most-needed one because many amateurs are using, or would like to use, an ASCII keyboard to generate Morse and Baudot codes. Table 12 shows that most code combinations needed in Morse and Baudot can be translated from the ASCII character set. However, there are some Morse characters (accented letters, $\overline{SN}$, $\overline{INT}$, $\overline{AS}$, $\overline{AU}$, $\overline{HM}$, $\overline{SK}$, $\overline{IX}$, or $\overline{HH}$) that don't appear on an ASCII keyboard. Some of the control characters or graphic characters could be used until an Amateur Radio standard code conversion table is developed.

Code Conversion ITA1 through 4

Table 13 gives character-for-character code equivalents for these CCITT codes. ITA1 was used on cables. ITA2 is in standard use in the Amateur Service and in telex services worldwide. ITA3 is found in Table A-1 of Annex A to CCITT Recommendation S.13, "Use on Radio Circuits of 7-Unit Synchronous Systems Giving Error Correction by Automatic Repetition." ITA4 is specified in Annex A to CCIR Rec. R.44 entitled "6-Unit Synchronous Time-Division 2-3-Channel Multiplex Telegraph System for Use over FMVFT Channels Spaced at 120 Hz for Connection to Standardized Teleprinter Networks." The abbreviation FMVFT means frequency modulated voice-frequency telegraph. ITA1, 3 and 4 are not currently used in the Amateur Radio Service but would be legal in the U.S. above 50 MHz. They are included herein primarily for information.

Packet Radio

Data communications is telecommunications between computers. *Packet switching* is a form of data communications that transfers data by subdividing it into "packets," and *packet radio* is packet switching using the medium of radio.

Packet radio has its roots in the Hawaiian Islands, where the University of Hawaii began using the mode in 1970 to transfer data to its remote sites dispersed throughout the islands. Amateur packet radio began in Canada after the Canadian Department of Communications permitted amateurs to use the mode in 1978. (The Federal Communications Commission permitted amateur packet radio south of the 49th parallel in 1980.)

In the first half of the 1980s, packet radio was the habitat of experimenters and those few communicators who did not mind communicating with a limited number of potential fellow packet communicators. In the second half of the decade, packet radio took off as the experimenters built a network that increased the potential number of packet stations that could intercommunicate and thus attracted tens of thousands of communicators who wanted to take advantage of this potential. Today, packet radio is one of the most popular modes of Amateur Radio communications, because it is a very effective means of communication.

• It provides error-free communications. The receiving station receives information exactly as the transmitting station sends it, so you do not waste time deciphering communication errors caused by electrical interference or changes in propagation.

• It uses time efficiently, since packet bulletin-board systems permit packet operators to store information for later retrieval by other amateurs.

• It uses the radio spectrum efficiently, since one radio channel may be used for multiple communications simultaneously or one radio channel may be used to interconnect a number of packet stations to form a "cluster" that provides for the distribution of information to all of the clustered stations.

• Each local channel may be connected to other local channels to form a network that affords interstate and international data communications. This network can be used by interlinked packet bulletin-board systems to transfer information, messages and third-party traffic via HF, VHF, UHF and satellite links.

• It uses other stations efficiently, since any packet-radio station can use one or more other packet-radio stations to relay data to its intended destination.

• It uses current station transmitting and receiving equipment efficiently, since the same equipment that is used for voice communications may be used for packet communications. The outlay for the additional equipment necessary to make your voice station a packet-radio station may be as little as $100. It also allows you to use that same equipment as an alternative to costly landline data communications links for transferring data between computers.

With these attributes, it is no wonder that packet radio is so popular.

OPEN SYSTEMS INTERCONNECTION REFERENCE MODEL

Introduced in 1978, the Open Systems Interconnection (OSI) Reference Model (RM) is a long-term project of the International Organization for Standardization (ISO) to promote compatible communications among a wide variety of systems. It specifies a communications structure of seven distinct levels or layers. Although the terms *level* and *layer* are used synonymously in the OSI-RM context, more often than not level refers to the function and layer refers to the name. This usage appears in the following list of the seven levels of the OSI-RM:

• Level 7—Application Layer (highest level)
• Level 6—Presentation Layer
• Level 5—Session Layer
• Level 4—Transport Layer
• Level 3—Network Layer
• Level 2—Link Layer
• Level 1—Physical Layer (lowest level)

One advantage of OSI-RM is that its levels are modular. As a result, different people can work on individual levels with some assurance that the various levels will work together in a system. Modularity also permits more than one protocol per level. Each level must communicate with the level(s) above and below it and must follow agreed rules for these interlevel interfaces. In order for distant systems to communicate, *peer* levels (for example, the link layer on one system and the link layer on the other) must exchange data in an agreed protocol. The interlevel and peer-to-peer relationships between two systems in direct communication are shown in the "apartment-house" diagram in Fig 23.

Although the protocols for each level are in various stages of development, the OSI-RM has won international acceptance in the telecommunications industry and in some amateur packet-radio circles. ISO 7498 and CCITT Recommendation X.200 are the primary documents for the OSI-RM.

Level 1—The Physical Layer

The function of the physical layer, the lowest level in the OSI-RM, is to send and receive *bits* (binary ones and zeros—marks and spaces). This level is concerned with the following:

• Physical connections—duplex or half-duplex transmission
• Physical service data units (PSDUs)—one bit in serial transmission, "n" bits in parallel transmission
• Circuit identification
• Bit sequencing
• Notification of fault conditions
• Deriving quality-of-service parameters

In addition, the following functions are associated with the physical layer:

• Modulation and demodulation (modems)
• Signaling speed
• Transmission of data and handshaking signals
• Characterization of communications media (radio circuit)

The physical layer is the only level that maintains an actual electrical connection with its peers. The other levels communi-

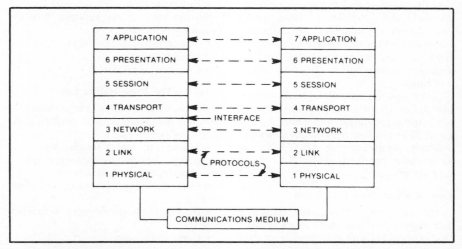

Fig 23 — Open Systems Interconnection reference model protocol levels. The solid lines between layers, as shown between 3 and 4, are interfaces. The dashed lines indicate logical communications between peer layers.

cate with their peers through *logical* or *virtual* connections.

Level 2—The Link Layer

The link layer or Data-Link Control Layer arranges the bits into *frames*. Its most common protocol is ISO High-Level Data Link Control Procedures (ISO 3309). The link layer performs the following functions:

• Establishes and releases one or more link connections
• Exchanges data-link service data units (DLSDUs)—frames
• Identifies end-points
• Keeps DLSDUs/frames in proper sequence
• Notifies the network layer when errors are detected
• Controls data flow
• Selects optional quality-of-service parameters

Level 3—The Network Layer

The network layer arranges data into packets (in other words, frames with network information added). In CCITT X.25 protocol, the network layer is called the *packet layer*. The functions provided by the network layer are:

• Network addressing and identifiers
• Network connections and release
• Transmission of network service data units (NSDUs)—packets
• Quality-of-service parameters
• Notifies the transport layer of errors
• Flow control
• Expedited service through network
• May provide sequenced delivery

Basically, there are two types of network-layer protocols: *connection* and *connectionless*. Connection protocols set up a *virtual circuit* (VC) between the two end points. Connectionless protocols use a *datagram* (DG), which contains complete addressing information in each packet so that it can use any available route through a network. The advantage of connection protocols is that since each packet does not contain complete addressing information, its overhead is lower. The advantage of the connectionless protocol is that packets may freely choose the best available routes for their transfer, rather than being stuck on a virtual circuit whose quality may vary at any time.

Some view the network layer as two sublayers: Level 3 (or Level 3A)—the network (or *intranet*) sublayer and Level 3.5 (or Level 3B)—the internetworking (*internet*) sublayer. As an example, CCITT X.25 is an intranet protocol, while X.75 is an internet protocol.

Level 4—The Transport Layer

The transport layer organizes data into a *transport protocol data unit* (TPDU), that is, a packet with transport-layer data added. This layer ensures that all data sent is received completely and in proper sequence at the destination. The following functions are performed by the transport layer:

• Transmission of TPDUs—messages.
• Multiplexing and demultiplexing—to share a network connection between two or more transport connections
• Error detection—detect lost, garbled, duplicated, misdelivered or missequenced TPDUs
• Error recovery—recovery from detected errors.

Other functions are:

• Connection establishment
• Data transfer
• Release—disconnection of transport connection

The CCITT transport protocol in Recommendation X.224 specifies transport service in five classes, which are designed according to the error behavior of network connections. They are:

• Class 0—Simple class
• Class 1—Basic error-recovery class
• Class 2—Multiplexing class
• Class 3—Error-recovery and multiplexing class
• Class 4—Error-detection and recovery class

The amount of work to be done at the transport layer is dependent on the protocol (virtual circuit or datagram) used at the network layer. Because individual datagrams may arrive via different routes through a network, the transport layer in a connectionless network needs to buffer messages and put them in their original sequence. Connection networks permit the use of a leaner transport layer.

Level 5—The Session Layer

The session layer organizes data into *session protocol data units* (SPDUs). This layer is concerned with:

• Dialog management
• Data-flow synchronization and resynchronization
• Mapping addresses with names (so users may retain a name if they move)
• Graceful or abrupt disconnection
• Buffering data until delivery time

Session services are grouped into the following phases:

• Connection establishment
• Data transfer
• Connection release

Level 6—The Presentation Layer

The presentation layer is responsible for terminal management and performs the following functions:

• Transfer of syntax for character sets, text strings, data display formats, graphics, file organization and data types
• Data encoding, decoding and compacting
• Interpret character sets (example: ASCII)
• Code conversion

Level 7—The Application Layer

The application layer is a window between the OSI communications environment and the application process. It is the only level that does not interface with a higher one. The application layer provides the following functions:

• Log-in—identification of communications partners
• Password checks and authority to communicate
• Determine adequacy of resources
• Determine acceptable quality of service
• Synchronization of applications programs
• Selecting the dialog procedures
• Agreement on error-recovery responsibility
• Procedures for control of data integrity
• Identifying data syntax constraints

Application-layer protocols fall into five groups:

• Group 1—System-management protocols
• Group 2—Application-management protocols
• Group 3—System protocols
• Group 4—Industry-specific protocols
• Group 5—Enterprise-specific protocols

PHYSICAL-LAYER CONSIDERATIONS —DATA INTERFACE STANDARDS

Layer 1 of the OSI model defines the electrical and mechanical standards such as connector configuration and which pins are used for different signals. The physical layer is responsible for getting individual *bits* transferred from one piece of equipment through the communications medium to the other equipment.

Digital communications equipment commonly has one or more serial binary data ports for connection to the next piece of equipment. Serial ports send and receive data one bit at a time. The Electronic Industries Association (EIA) and CCITT define serial ports as *interchange circuits* at the interface between the *data terminal equipment* (DTE) and the *data circuit-terminating equipment* (DCE) for the transfer of binary data, control and timing signals, and analog signals where appropriate. A DTE may be a video display terminal (VDT) or a computer that serves as or emulates a data terminal. Typically, a DCE is a modulator-demodulator (modem) that terminates the analog communications circuit.

With some equipment configurations it is difficult to tell which is the DTE and which is the DCE. It is necessary to know one from the other in order to know how to interpret the standard. A fairly safe rule is that the DTE is the farthest from the communications channel. So in a setup with a terminal, a computer, a packet-assembler/disassembler (PAD) and a modem:

• at the terminal-computer interface, the terminal is the DTE, and the computer is the DCE.

• at the computer-PAD interface, the

computer is the DTE, and the PAD is the DCE.

• at the PAD-modem interface, the PAD is the DTE, and the modem is the DCE.

Internationally, data-interchange interfaces are defined in CCITT Recommendations V.24 and V.28 for data rates up to 20,000 bit/s. V.35, which is primarily a 48-kbit/s modem specification, is also being used as a standard for data rates above 20,000 bit/s.

In the United States, the most common standard is EIA-232-D for speeds up to 20,000 bit/s. EIA also has issued other standards, known as EIA-422, EIA-423 and EIA-449. When considering surplus military equipment, bear in mind that interfaces may be designed to military interface standards such as MIL-STD-188C (similar to EIA-232-D), MIL-STD-188-114 (similar to EIA-422), MIL-STD-188-144 (similar to EIA-423) and MIL-STD-1397 (42 and 250 kbit/s).

Some parallel ports are also found in amateur digital equipment. In parallel ports, the eight bits in a byte move in and out of the equipment simultaneously on eight separate wires. Two parallel-interface standards of interest to amateurs are the Centronics parallel interface, a de facto standard interface for parallel printer ports, and the Institute of Electronics and Electrical Engineers (IEEE) Standard 488, also known as the IEEE 488 bus, IEC 625, Hewlett-Packard Interface Bus (HPIB) and General Purpose Interface Bus (GPIB).

Balanced vs Unbalanced Interfaces

As in RF circuits, balanced and unbalanced circuits are used in digital interfaces. In fact, data signals sent at speeds of megabytes per second *are* RF and need to be treated as such. The rise and fall transitions of much slower data rates may be in the RF range. Like any transmission line, if the line is not terminated at both ends in its characteristic impedance, the conductors will radiate. Also, the line will be susceptible to electromagnetic interference from nearby conductors.

An unbalanced circuit has one signal conductor and perhaps one or more timing- and control-signal conductors; the return path for each is through a common signal ground. Unbalanced circuits are commonly used for circuits operating at speeds below 20,000 bit/s and for wire lines not exceeding 50 feet or 15 meters, as in EIA-232-D. In this standard, longer cables may be used if the load capacitance does not exceed 2500 pF; twisted-pair EIA-232-D cables have been run successfully as long as 500 feet, although the standard guarantees only 50 feet.

Balanced interface circuits use two conductors balanced to ground. When one wire is positive, the other is negative. Balanced circuits support higher data rates over longer distances with less tendency for interference and should be considered

Fig 24 — Several DB25 connectors, as used with the EIA-232-D data interface standard.

for data rates over 20,000 bit/s.

Bipolar vs Neutral Interfaces

Most data interface circuits between equipment use bipolar signaling; that is, the circuit switches between a positive voltage (say 5 V dc) for a binary 0 and a negative voltage (say −5 V dc) for a binary 1. A problem with bipolar signaling is that the power supply must supply positive and negative voltages, thus adding to its complexity and cost. Another problem is that ICs called line drivers and line receivers are needed to convert the neutral signals to and from the polar signals.

Some designers avoid these problems by transferring neutral signals between equipment, typically at "TTL levels" of approximately 0 and +5 V dc. Neutral TTL-level signaling suffers from poor noise immunity and signal distortion. Such interfacing is viable only for short lines and where the equipment at the other end of the line is also using TTL levels instead of a standard interface circuit.

EIA-232-D, V.24 and V.28

EIA-232-D and its predecessor RS-232-C is the interface standard of the age. Its DB25 connector, shown in Fig 24, is everywhere you go these days. Avid packeteers are known to have EIA-232-D receptacles in various rooms of the house, even the bathroom.

EIA-232-D's international counterparts are CCITT Recommendations V.24 and V.28. V.24 describes the functions of each circuit and V.28 specifies the electrical parameters: voltages, impedances, load capacitance and signal characteristics. Specifications for the 25-pin connector are found in ISO 2210, which also assigns pin numbers to V.24 circuits. The male pin connector (DB25P) is normally installed on the DTE and the female connector (DB25S)

on the DCE. Pin assignments for EIA-232-D and V.24 are shown in Table 15.

Signal Levels

The voltage ranges for EIA-232-D and V.24 are shown in Fig 25. Most signals higher than +5 V and lower than −5 V will function with the circuit successfully. Common practice is to supply +12-V and −12-V power to MC1488 quad line drivers, which are used in conjunction with MC1489 quad line receivers.

Nine pins (1 through 8 and 20) are used in most interfacing applications. The remaining pins are sometimes used, depending on the circumstances. You will find EIA-232-D cables with anywhere from 5 to all 25 lines. Similarly, modems and other digital equipment advertised as "EIA-232-D compatible" can be expected to use signal voltage levels specified in EIA-232-D and V.28 and at least not violate the standard. They may not implement the entire standard, however, and may leave out control lines that may or may not be needed for your applications. Where space is at a premium, a connector smaller than the DB25 may be used.

DB25 connectors come in varieties designed for mounting on panels or printed-circuit boards and for terminating cable assemblies. Use shielded hoods and cables to reduce the possibility of electromagnetic interference.

Gender Changes

Although the standard is that the male DB25P goes on the DTE and the female DB25S on the DCE, it is not uncommon to see equipment with only the female DB25S connectors and cable assemblies with male DB25Ps. Therefore, a gender changer is handy when connecting non-standard equipment. One can be made easily by connecting two DB25Ss or

Table 15
Data Interface Connections

Pin	Ckt	EIA-232-D Description	V.24 No.	Name	Common Abbr.*
1	—	Shield			
2	BA	Transmitted Data	103	Transmitted Data	TxD
3	BB	Received Data	104	Received Data	RxD
4	CA	Request to Send	105	Request to Send	RTS
5	CB	Clear to Send	106	Clear to Send	CTS
6	CC	DCE Ready	107	Data Set Ready	DSR
7	AB	Signal Ground	102	Signal Ground	SG
8	CF	Received Line Signal Detector	109	Data Carrier Detect	CD
9	—	(Reserved for Testing)			
10	—	(Reserved for Testing)			
11	—	Unassigned			
12	SCF/CI	Sec. Rec'd Line Sig. Detector/ Data Sig. Rate Select (DCE Source)	122	Backward Channel Received Line Signal Detector	SCD
13	SCB	Sec. Clear to Send	121	Backward Channel Ready	SCTS
14	SBA	Sec. Transmitted Data	118	Transmitted Backward Channel Data	STxD
15	DB	Transmission Signal Element Timing (DCE Source)	114	Transmitter Signal Element Timing (DCE Source)	TxC
16	SBB	Sec. Received Data	119	Received Backward Channel Data	SRxD
17	DD	Receiver Signal Element Timing (DCE Source)	115	Receiver Signal Element	RxC
18	LL	Local Loopback			
19	SCA	Sec. Request to Send	120	Transmitted Backward Line Signal	SRTS
20	CD	DTE Ready	108/2	Data Terminal Ready	DTR
21	RL/CG	Remote Loopback/Signal Quality Detector	110	Data Signal Quality Detector	SQ
22	CE	Ring Indicator	125	Calling Indicator	RI
23	CH/CI	Data Signal Rate Select (DTE/ DCE Source)	111 112	Data Rate Selector Data Rate Selector	
24	DA	Transmit Signal Element Timing (DTE Source)	113	Transmitter Signal Element Timing, (DTE Source)	ETxC
25	TM	Test Mode			

*Most abbreviations in this column are generally recognized by association with their full names. Exceptions are: ETxC = External Transmitter Clock, RxC = Receiver Clock and TxC = Transmitter Clock.

Table 16
EIA-449 37-Pin Connector Assignments

Pin	Direction	Mnemonic	Circuit name
1	—	SHIELD	
2	from DCE	SI	Signaling rate indicator
3	—	SPARE	
4	to DCE	SD	Send data
5	from DCE	ST	Send timing
6	from DCE	RD	Receive data
7	to DCE	RS	Request to send
8	from DCE	RT	Receive timing
9	from DCE	CS	Clear to send
10	to DCE	LL	Local loopback
11	from DCE	DM	Data mode
12	to DCE	TR	Terminal ready
13	from DCE	RR	Receiver ready
14	to DCE	RL	Remote loopback
15	from DCE	IC	Incoming call
16	to DCE	SF/SR	Select frequency Signaling rate selector
17	to DCE	TT	Terminal timing
18	from DCE	TM	Test mode
19	—	SG	Signal ground
20	from DCE	RC	Receive common
21	—	SPARE	
22	to DCE	SD	Send data
23	from DCE	ST	Send timing
24	from DCE	RD	Receive data
25	to DCE	RS	Request to send
26	from DCE	RT	Receive timing
27	from DCE	CS	Clear to send
28	to DCE	IS	Terminal in service
29	from DCE	DM	Data mode
30	to DCE	TR	Terminal ready
31	from DCE	RR	Receiver ready
32	to DCE	SS	Select standby
33	from DCE	SQ	Signal quality
34	to DCE	NS	New signal
35	to DCE	TT	Terminal timing
36	from DCE	SB	Standby indicator
37	to DCE	SC	Send common

Fig 25 — EIA-232-D and V.28 voltage limits.

DB25Ps back to back with ribbon cable or individual wires connecting correspondingly numbered pins.

Null Modems

Another useful gadget is a *null modem*, which is a pair of DB25 connectors of the appropriate gender(s) mounted back-to-back and wired pin-for-pin except that pins 2 (transmit data) and 3 (received data) are crossed and pins 4 (request to send) and 5 (clear to send) are crossed. This solves the problem of connecting two pieces of equipment both wired as DCEs or DTEs.

EIA-422-A, V.11 and X.27

EIA-422-A specifies differential, balanced circuits for rates up to 100 kilobauds at distances up to 4000 feet or 10 megabauds at distances up to 40 feet using D-Subminiature DB37 (37-pin) connectors wired according to ISO 4902. EIA-422-A is compatible with CCITT Recommendations V.11 and X.27, but is not interoperable with EIA-232-D, MIL-STD-188C or CCITT V.28 and V.35, and is not compatible with EIA-423-A without reconfiguration.

EIA-423-A, V.10 and X.26

EIA-423-A is an unbalanced, bipolar circuit capable of distances up to 4000 feet at 3 kilobauds or 40 feet at 300 kilobauds. It is compatible with CCITT Recommendations V.10 and X.26 and can interoperate with EIA-232-D circuits. EIA-423-A and V.10/X.26 use D-Subminiature DB37 (37-pin) connectors wired according to ISO 4902.

EIA-449

EIA-449 is capable of signaling rates up to 2 Mbit/s at a cable length of 667 feet. The standard specifies two connectors, a D-Subminiature DB37 and DB9 (37- and 9-pin). See Tables 16 and 17.

V.35

CCITT Recommendation V.35 is a standard for 48-kbit/s modems, but its interface specifications and the 34-pin Winchester rack-and-panel connector (specified in ISO 2593) have become standard in the United States for interchange circuits operating at 48, 56 and 64 kbit/s. The ISO 2593 connector is shown in Fig 26. Table 18 shows the pin labels and functions for this connector.

IEEE 488 Parallel Interface

This is a parallel bus for limited distances (67 feet). It is of interest as a control bus for test equipment and some communications equipment. The Commodore PET personal computer used the IEEE 488 bus to control its peripherals. Most industrial-use test instruments have the IEEE 488 bus for computer-controlled testing. See Table 19 for more information about this connector. This bus uses a unique 24-pin connector shown in Fig 27.

OPERATIONAL MODES

A number of terms describe the opera-

Table 17
EIA-449 9-Pin Connector Assignments

Pin	Direction	Mnemonic	Circuit name
1	—	SHIELD	
2	from DCE	SRR	Secondary receiver ready
3	to DCE	SSD	Secondary send data
4	from DCE	SRD	Secondary receive data
5	—	SG	Signal ground
6	—	RC	Receive common
7	to DCE	SRS	Secondary request to send
8	from DCE	SCS	Secondary clear to send
9	to DCE	SC	Send common

Fig 26 — ISO 2593 rack-and-panel connector. This connector is usually identified with V.35 and is found on modems operating at speeds in excess of 20,000 bit/s.

Table 19
IEEE 488 Bus Pin Allocations

Pin	Mnemonic	Signal
1	D101	Data line 1
2	D102	Data line 2
3	D103	Data line 3
4	D104	Data line 4
5	EOI(24)	End or identify
6	DAV	Data valid
7	NRFD	Not ready for data
8	NDAC	Not data accepted
9	IFC	Interface clear
10	SRQ	Service request
11	ATN	Attention
12	SHIELD	Shield
13	D105	Data line 5
14	D106	Data line 6
15	D107	Data line 7
16	D108	Data line 8
17	REN(24)	Remote enable
18	GND(6)	Ground for pin 6
19	GND(7)	Ground for pin 7
20	GND(8)	Ground for pin 8
21	GND(9)	Ground for pin 9
22	GND(10)	Ground for pin 10
23	GND(11)	Ground for pin 11
24	GND(logic)	Ground for pins 5 and 27

tion of circuits or connections, grouped under the category variously called *operational*, *communication* or *transmission* modes. There are some minor differences between data-communications and telephone-company usage within the United States, and between US and international usage. Since packet radio is used internationally, it is important to remember that different interpretations of the same terms may cause problems in understanding terminology between packeteers in different countries. Also, some confusion can occur between the operational mode of the communications and how many radio frequencies are being used. For example, a half-duplex data exchange may use one frequency (often called simplex) or two frequencies (called duplex).

Although this subject is treated here under physical-layer considerations, there are parallel uses of the terms defined below at higher ISO protocol levels. Fig 28 will help in understanding these terms.

Simplex (SX)

According to the IEEE, simplex opera-tion is a "method of operation in which communication between two stations takes place in one direction at a time." The ITU Radio Regulations define it as an "operating method in which transmission is made possible alternately in each direction of a *telecommunication* channel..." A footnote says that simplex operation may use either one or two frequencies. CCIR Rec R.140 says "simplex (circuit) permitting the transmission of signals in either direction, but not simultaneously."

Radio amateurs often use the term simplex to indicate that only one frequency is used for a VHF-FM circuit. This is the current amateur digital transmission mode, where two or more stations involved in a contact operate on exactly the same frequency and take turns transmitting and receiving. Simplex operation minimizes equipment requirements by permitting the sharing of equipment for both transmitting and receiving. A transceiver (as opposed to a separate receiver and transmitter) and a common antenna may be used.

In other uses of the term, simplex transmission is in only one direction with no reverse direction. CCIR R.140 calls this a *unidirectional connection*. One-way operation is seldom used in data communications, since there is no return channel or way of reversing the channel to detect and correct errors. Nevertheless, there are some Amateur Radio one-way transmission applications, usually point to multipoint, such as bulletin and beacon operations.

Half Duplex (HDX)

A half-duplex circuit can transmit in either direction, but only one direction at a time according to the IEEE and other references. Although this sounds like

Table 18
ISO 2593 Pin Allocations for V.35 Interfaces

Pin	Circuit	Direction	Function	Pin	Circuit	Direction	Function
A	101	Common	Protective ground or earth	AA	114	to DTE	Transmitter signal element timing B-wire
B	102	Common	Signal ground or common return	P	103	from DTE	Transmitted data A-wire
C	105	from DTE	Request to send	S	103	from DTE	Transmitted data B-wire
D	106	to DTE	Ready for sending	U	113	from DTE	Transmitter signal element timing A-wire
E	107	to DTE	Data set ready				
F	109	from DTE	Data channel received line signal detector	Z	—	—	F_3
H	108/1	from DTE	Connect data set to line	W	113	from DTE	Transmitter signal element timing B-wire
	108/2	from DTE	Data terminal ready				
	125	to DTE	Calling indicator	BB	—	—	F_3
K	—	—	F_1	CC	—	—	F_4
L	—	—	F_2	DD	—	—	F_5
M	—	—	F_1	EE	—	—	F_4
N	—	—	F_2	FF	—	—	F_5
R	104	to DTE	Received data A-wire	HH	—	—	N_1
T	104	to DTE	Received data B-wire	JJ	—	—	N_2
V	115	to DTE	Receiver signal element timing A-wire	KK	—	—	N_1
X	115	to DTE	Receiver signal element timing B-wire	LL	—	—	N_2
Y	114	to DTE	Transmitter signal element timing A-wire	MM	—	—	F
				NN	—	—	F

N = Pins permanently reserved for national use.
Pins HH, JJ and KK are used in the U.K. for transmitter-clock control.

F = Pins reserved by ISO, not for national use.
Subscripts indicate pins to form pairs.

Table 20
American and International Interface Standards

American	Circuits	Electrical	Connector
EIA-232-D	CCITT V.24	CCITT V.28	ISO 2110
EIA-449/422-A	CCITT V.24	CCITT V.10	ISO 4902
EIA-449/422-A	CCITT V.24	CCITT V.11	ISO 4902
(no equivalent)	CCITT V.24	CCITT V.35	ISO 2593

Fig 27 — 24-pin connector used for IEEE 488 cables.

simplex, the clue to understanding the difference between simplex and half-duplex operation is in the CCITT R.140 definition of half duplex: "a circuit (or connection) capable of duplex operation, but which, on account of the nature of its termination, can be operated alternately only." In other words, the channel is capable of simultaneous operation in both directions, but the terminal equipment can only send or receive, not both, simultaneously.

Full Duplex (FDX)

In a full-duplex circuit, information can flow both ways simultaneously. The IEEE and CCIR definitions agree on this, although CCIR calls it simply *duplex* operation. A CCIR Radio Regulations footnote states that "duplex operation require(s) two frequencies in radio communication." CCIR Rec R.140 has another term: "duplex, two way simplex (connection)—a circuit permitting the exchange of signals in both directions."

Full-duplex operation is not in general use in packet radio, but will be required for high-speed packet trunks where simplex or half-duplex circuits cannot provide sufficient peak capacity. Full duplex is more complex than simplex because the transmitter and receiver must operate simultaneously at the same site. This requires separation or duplexing of the receiving and transmitting antennas, as is normal practice in FM-voice repeater applications.

Semi-Duplex

This is a term found in the ITU Radio Regulations to describe a "method which is *simplex* operation at one end and *duplex* operation at the other."

Diplex

CCIR Rec R.140 defines this as "permitting simultaneously and in the same direction, the transmission or reception of two signals over a circuit or channel."

MODEMS

Modem is a contraction of *modulator-demodulator*. In telephone terminology, it is also called a *data set*. A modem is used to convert digital baseband signals to and from analog form for transmission over analog media.

Analog communications systems that transmit speech have an analog baseband

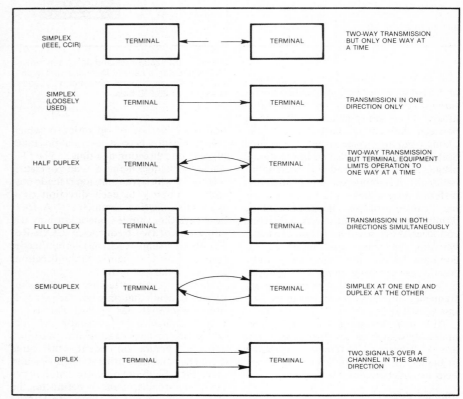

Fig 28 — Operational modes. US and international usage of these terms varies. See discussion in text.

bandwidth of approximately 3 kHz. A relationship exists between this bandwidth and the data rates that it can accommodate. A 3-kHz analog channel can accommodate 1200-bit/s operation easily and speeds as high as 9600 bit/s with more difficulty using complex modulation techniques. Typically, these higher speeds require circuits with higher signal-to-noise ratios, so when the circuit is not optimum, the higher-speed modems *fallback* to slower speeds.

Modem Parameters

There are a variety of parameters encompassing the modem world; these are discussed in the following paragraphs.

Modulation

Binary frequency-shift keying (FSK) is the most common form of modulation for Amateur Radio data transmissions. This technique translates a binary 1 to a mark tone (at 1200 Hz, for example) and a binary 0 to a space tone (at 2200 Hz, for example). Minimum-shift keying (MSK) is a form of FSK in which the frequency shift in hertz is one half the signaling rate in bauds. Thus, a 1200-baud signal shifted by 600 Hz is MSK.

Phase-shift keying (PSK) is another form of modulation used for data transmission. Its use in Amateur Radio has been limited to satellite operation and some low-speed terrestrial operation, but interest is growing in using PSK for high-speed packet radio. While binary phase-shift keying (BPSK) is robust, it is not particularly spectrum efficient. *M-ary* PSK schemes, such as 4-ary PSK (4PSK) or 8-ary PSK (8PSK), permit transmission of more bits per second at a lower baud rate and are used in high-speed telephone modems.

Amplitude-shift keying (ASK) is not used

in amateur packet radio, but in combination with PSK, may achieve high speeds within relatively narrow bandwidths.

Demodulation

The function of a demodulator in a data modem is to convert the analog signal back to its digital baseband. Modem designers admit that the modulator is the easy part of modem design; demodulators are more difficult.

FSK demodulators are among the simpler ones. There are two main design approaches: FM and AM. The FM demodulator hard-limits the signal to a constant amplitude to eliminate amplitude variations, then looks for zero crossings to produce a square-wave output. Many FSK demodulators use phase-locked loops. FM demodulators suffer from dropouts when either the mark or space frequency fade below a certain threshold level. AM demodulators have separate filters for the mark and space frequencies. The demodulator compares the amplitudes of the filter outputs to see which frequency is present. A properly designed AM-type demodulator can produce good digital output during periods when only one signal (mark or space) can be received.

PSK demodulators need some way to determine phase shifts. There is no ready source of absolute phase reference at the demodulator, so some phase reference must be derived by the demodulator. In normal PSK, it is necessary to compare the phase of the received signal with a fixed phase-reference source. Some systems transmit phase-reference information in short bursts. Differential phase-shift keying (DPSK) demodulation does not need a fixed phase-reference signal, but decides whether a phase shift has occurred by comparing one symbol with the last symbol received.

Synchrony

Most lower-speed modems are asynchronous and operate at a variable rate (for example, 0-300 bit/s). This designation indicates that the modem is capable of maintaining a 0 or 1 logic state indefinitely. When each character is started and when transitions may occur therein are functions of the data keying the modulator. When receiving data, the demodulator recognizes changes of state that occur at any time, perhaps within certain limits to reject noise.

Higher-speed modems are usually synchronous. The modulator clocks out data at a fixed rate. The demodulator duplicates or regenerates the clock from the received data. Bit-synchronous demodulators have the advantage of knowing when a bit is supposed to occur and can use various decision strategies to determine which of two binary states (or 4 dibit states, 8 tribit states, and so on) was received. Synchronous demodulators usually have a 3-dB

S/N advantage over asynchronous demodulators.

Frequency Modes: Originate and Answer

Full-duplex telephone modems divide the audio-frequency spectrum into high- and low-frequency bands. Transmission in one direction is possible by modulating a tone (or tones) in the higher-frequency band, while transmission in the opposite direction is possible using lower-frequency tone(s). To eliminate confusion on the telephone, the calling (originating) station transmits on the low tone(s), for example, and the called (answering) station transmits on the high tone(s). The two stations stick with the tone(s) they chose when the circuit was established throughout the communications session.

In the early days of time-shared computers, many terminals were equipped with *originate-only* modems because they only called the computer center and never answered calls. Similarly, computer centers that only answered calls minimized cost by installing *answer-only* modems. These one-way modems saved money, but when they became available on the surplus market, they were a source of frustration for personal-computer users who wanted to both originate and answer calls. Amateur Radio operators modified these modems to change the tones to the same frequency band (high or low) for packet-radio simplex operation.

Carrier Detection

Most demodulators have an output for Received Line Signal Detector, also known more commonly as Carrier-Detect (CD). In telephone modems, a 0 CD condition indicates that no signal is being received or that the received signal is unsuitable for demodulation. In a half-duplex circuit, whenever there is a 1 CD output, the modem is inhibited from transmitting. This informs the modem that there is a live modem of its own species on the other end of the circuit.

In Amateur Radio, CD serves a different purpose. We want the modem to know when there is anyone else using the channel in order to prevent packet collisions. When an amateur packet modem detects a signal, CD inhibits the modem from transmitting until no signal is present.

Transmission Impairments

Frequency Response

Many radios have amplitude-vs-frequency responses that are not uniform. Fig 29 illustrates an audio-frequency response that might be seen through a radio system. This may be the result of roll-off of high frequencies in an audio amplifier or using too narrow an IF filter. Low-frequency losses could be caused by using a capacitor having too small a value of

capacitance for interstage coupling in an amplifier. An IF filter with excessive ripple in the passband could wreak havoc with the frequency response; similar problems could be the fault of poor IF alignment. Virtually all voice radios can be used for packet operation—many without modification of any kind. Others may require some minor surgery to make them suitable for data communications.

Phase-Shift and Envelope-Delay Distortion

Propagation through an audio communications channel should vary uniformly with frequency. If the propagation time is not uniform, the components of a complex waveform (for example, the fundamental frequency and several harmonics) will arrive out of their proper phase relationships and result in a distorted waveform. Fig 30 illustrates linear and nonlinear phase-shift characteristics, as well as the corresponding envelope delays.

Amplitude Nonlinearity

This is not usually a serious problem

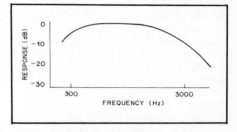

Fig 29 — Amplitude-vs.-frequency response of a radio system designed for voice communications. Note the attenuation of both highs and lows.

Fig 30 — At A is the phase-shift-vs.-frequency response of a radio system. B shows the corresponding envelope delay distortion.

when using voice radios for data communications systems with binary amplitude states. Any nonlinear distortion in the voice-frequency channel adds harmonics to the fundamental modulating signal, however. Amateur Radio transmitter microphone-input circuits typically have substantial amounts of compression, with the time constants optimized for speech. Unwanted products may be generated, especially if a data signal is at a level high enough to be well into the compression or clipping region.

Nonlinear distortion becomes serious in certain high-speed modems which use quantized AM, possibly in combination with PSK. In such modems, nonlinear response in the channel makes the amplitude differences between adjacent levels uneven and could result in falsing, particularly in the presence of noise.

Equalization

Various forms of distortion, such as nonuniform frequency response and envelope-delay distortion, can be corrected by equalization. An equalizer is a circuit that compensates for undesired amplitude-frequency and/or phase-frequency characteristics. Equalizers can overcome the poor response in a radio receiver or an entire system if the distortion at the transmitter and that introduced by the medium are known. An equalizer works by setting the gains of an audio-frequency filter. *Automatic equalization* and *adaptive equalization* are techniques that automatically compensate for circuit distortion. Automatic equalizers adjust to circuit conditions upon reception of a special bit sequence, called *training*, sent before the transmission of data. Adaptive equalizers make continuous adjustments during reception.

Frequency-Translation Error

When an FM-voice radio is used with an AF modem, the received tones are at the exact frequencies produced by the modulator at the transmitting station. However, if the modulator and demodulator are not tuned to precisely the same frequencies, some distortion in the received data should be expected, particularly under conditions of poor S/N ratio.

When data is transmitted with AF modems through SSB-voice radios, even a small mistuning of the receiver relative to the transmitter frequency can cause distortion. Doppler shift, if not corrected, can also corrupt received data. Under these circumstances, accurate frequency control and a demodulator tuning indicator are recommended.

Noise

Periodic or random noise affects the performance of a digital demodulator. Some types of noise, particularly transients,

may simply be an annoyance to voice communications; however, it takes only one bit error to corrupt a packet. Impulse noise on the order of 1-ms duration and decaying over 4 ms will likely have little effect on a 45-baud RTTY signal with a 22-ms data pulse, but at 1200 bauds, that same pulse could wipe out 1 to 4 bits.

As in any other radio application, it is necessary to minimize the noise level presented to the data demodulator. Proper siting, use of directive antennas with minimal noise pick-up, and low-noise receiving preamps are desirable for packet-radio stations. Careful selection of demodulator input-filter shape and bandwidth can contribute to reducing the impact of the noise received by the modem. While most demodulators perform flawlessly in the absence of noise, some fail sooner than others as the signal-to-noise ratio is decreased. What separates the best radio modems from the rest of the pack is their ability to perform in the presence of interference.

Jitter

Jitter comes in many flavors and may be introduced almost anywhere in a system. *Phase jitter* consists of abrupt variations in phase or unwanted angle modulation. It can be described as the received data signal zero crossings occurring at the wrong time. Phase jitter can be introduced in the modulation process by power-supply hum modulating the master oscillator or by the data modulator clocking on the wrong pulse in a train. Jitter of 15 degrees or more can cause misinterpretation of data by a demodulator, depending on how sampling is performed. If the demodulator is designed to look for edges of pulses, any jitter is likely to introduce errors. If the demodulator samples in the middle of the pulse period or integrates energy over the entire pulse period, jitter may not be a serious problem. In addition to phase jitter, which may occur throughout a transmission, phase hits are a transient unwanted angle modulation that may last 4 ms or longer, according to the telephone definition.

Amplitude jitter is not usually a problem for angle-modulated data communications, but it could be for systems using quantized AM. In telephone terminology, *gain hits* are transient phenomena lasting 4 ms or more where changes in amplitude exceed 12 dB. Gain hits in the negative direction are called *dropouts*.

Modem Standards

AT&T and CCITT have written the lion's share of modem standards. Table 23 summarizes these standards. Many modems were developed by AT&T for different applications and are known by their Bell designations (for example, Bell 103). CCITT modems closely parallel Bell

types, but are not necessarily interoperable with them. For example, both the Bell 103 and the CCITT V.21 operate at 300 bit/s and are alike in many respects, but the two use different sets of tone frequencies and cannot intercommunicate. There is the same similarity and incompatibility between Bell 202 and CCITT V.23.

Bell 103/113 Family

Bell 103/113, usually shortened to Bell 103, are part of the Bell 100-series data sets and are also called the Bell 103/113 family. Model number 103 designates an originate/answer modem, whereas the letter suffix denotes the configuration. Model number 113 can be either originate or answer, as differentiated by the letter suffix. Specific models are:

103A: Older originate/answer, single-channel modem for installation in Model 33 or 35 Teletype® equipment.

103E (Computer Site): Originate/answer, up to 40 in a cabinet.

103F: For leased lines only.

103G: Originate/answer, single-channel modem that includes an integrated telephone set.

103H: Originate/answer, single-channel modem for direct installation in Model 37 Teletype sets.

103J, 103JR: Originate/answer, single-channel modem. The 103J was the model used prior to the FCC Registration Program. The "R" suffix indicates registration under Part 68 of the FCC rules.

113A: Originate-only, single-channel "bare-bones" modem for terminal installations. Early 113A-L1 and -L1A versions did not require ac power supplies as they were powered from the telephone line. Later models with L1/2 and L1A/2 suffixes require ac power supplies.

113AR: Registered version of the 113A.

113C: Full-featured originate-only, single-channel modem used prior to registration.

113CR: Registered version of 113C.

113B: Answer only, in 20-channel increments. Older modem used in multiline computer installations.

113D: Unregistered version of 113DR.

113DR: Answer-only registered modem available in individual and multiline configurations.

The Bell 103/113 family operates at speeds up to 300 bit/s. Although used since its introduction for 110-bit/s ASCII teleprinters, it is used now almost exclusively for low-speed computer communications.

The spectrum is divided into two bands, each with a carrier using FSK between two frequencies. The two lower-band frequencies are called F1M (frequency 1 mark) and F1S (space). The higher-band frequencies are called F2M and F2S. The originating station transmits on F1 and receives on F2, while the answering station transmits on F2 and receives on F1. See Table 21 and Fig 31.

Bell 103/113 modems normally use the EIA RS-232-C or EIA-232-D interface, depending on their age. The Clear-to-Send circuit (from modem to DTE) is on when the modem establishes a connection. The Transmitted Data circuit can be used only when Clear to Send is on. Received Data (modem to DTE) is the circuit that delivers the data received from the other modem. When Carrier Detect (modem to DTE) is on, it indicates that the data carrier is being received from the modem at the other end of the circuit. When Carrier Detect is off, this circuit is held in a marking condition. An on condition on the Data Set Ready circuit (modem to DTE) indicates that the modem is connected to the telephone line and in the data mode. An on condition on the Ring Indicator (modem to DTE) circuit indicates that a ringing signal has been received. Data Terminal Ready (DTE to modem), when on, permits the modem to answer incoming calls automatically. An off condition tells the modem to disconnect from the line when the call is completed.

CCITT V.21

This is the modem used for low-speed (110, 200 and 300-bit/s) asynchronous data transmission outside of North America. The frequency scheme for the V.21 is shown in Table 22 and Fig 32. V.21 is similar to, but incompatible with, Bell 103/113. A Bell 103 modem can, however, communicate with a V.21 modem when using HF packet radio, because the mark and space frequencies of each are 200 Hz apart, although the specific frequencies are different.

Bell 202

In the beginning of amateur packet radio, the Vancouver Amateur Digital Communications Group (VADCG) selected the Bell-202 modem for their 2-meter packet-radio network because some of these units were available on the surplus market. Today they are widely used throughout the world for VHF packet radio using AFSK with an FM transceiver and on 10 meters using FSK (AFSK to an SSB transceiver).

Bell 202 is a half-duplex modem designed for asynchronous, binary, serial data transmission at speeds up to 1200 bit/s. The maximum bit rate is also a function of the transmission circuit; Bell-202 modems can handle up to 1800 bit/s on conditioned lines. It uses FSK modulation with mark and space frequencies of 1200 and 2200 Hz, respectively. See Fig 33. Some models have a 5-bit/s on/off-keyed (OOK) reverse channel on 387 Hz used for a break signal to indicate when to turn the circuit around and for certain forms of error control. To defeat long-distance telephone line echo suppressors, the modem sends a 2025-Hz echo-suppressor disabling tone for 300 ms, ±50 ms. Since echo suppressors turn on

Table 21
Bell 103/113 Modem Frequency Scheme

Mode	Originate	Answer
Transmit	F1M 1270 Hz mark	F2M 2225 Hz mark
	F1S 1070 Hz space	F2S 2025 Hz space
Receive	F2M 2225 Hz mark	F1M 1270 Hz mark
	F2S 2025 Hz space	F1S 1070 Hz space

Fig 31 — Bell 103/133 modem frequencies. The call-originating station transmits on the lower-frequency band and receives on the higher-frequency band. The called (answering) station does the opposite.

Table 22
CCITT V.21 Modem Frequency Scheme

Mode	Channel 1 (Calling station)	Channel 2 (Called station)
Transmit	F$_A$ 1180 Hz 0 bit	F$_A$ 1850 Hz 0 bit
	F$_Z$ 980 Hz 1 bit	F$_Z$ 1650 Hz 1 bit
Receive	F$_A$ 1850 Hz 0 bit	F$_A$ 1180 Hz 0 bit
	F$_Z$ 1650 Hz 1 bit	F$_Z$ 980 Hz 1 bit

Fig 32 — CCITT V.21 modem frequencies. The call-originating station transmits on the lower-frequency band and receives on the higher-frequency band similar to Bell 103/113 modems.

Fig 33 — Bell 202 modem frequencies. The 387-Hz reverse channel on some Bell 202 modems is not used for amateur packet radio.

after 100 ms of no signal, the modem keeps its forward- or reverse-channel transmitter on at all times. Bell-202 modems use EIA RS-232-A, -B, -C or EIA-232-D interfaces, according to when they were designed.

Specific Bell model numbers are:

202A and 202B: Superseded by 202C and 202D.

202C: Older modem with handset, single channel, self-contained. Switched lines—0-1200 bit/s. Leased lines—0-1800 bit/s.

202C5, 9 or 11: Without reverse channel.

202C6, 10 or 12: With reverse channel.

202D: Same as 202C without handset; requires 804A auxiliary set.

202E: Older transmit-only data set with telephone set. Optional reverse channel.

202R: 0-1800 bit/s modem similar to 202D, no auto answer.

202S: 0-1200 bit/s auto answer before FCC registration.

202SR: Registered version of 202S.

202T: 0-1800 bit/s, for leased lines, 1 to 8 in housing.

There are some newer Bell 202-compatible modems with 75-baud or 150-baud reverse channels. This feature has been added for leased-line and videotex service. The Am7911 is a single-chip modem with a 150-baud reverse channel in both Bell-202 and V.23 modes.

CCITT V.23

CCITT V.23 is similar to Bell 202. Although V.23 1200-baud mark and space frequencies are 100 Hz different than those of the 202, the two modems are interoperable under certain conditions. In addition, V.23 has a fallback speed of 600 bauds and uses a different space frequency for that speed. Another difference is that the V.23 backward channel uses FSK and is capable of data rates up to 75 bauds. V.23 frequencies are shown in Fig 34. V.23 also has an echo-suppressor disabling tone of 2100 Hz. V.23 modems use the V.24 interface. Pin 23, data signaling rate selector (circuit no. 111), tells the modem to change speed.

Bell 212A

In late 1976, Bell introduced a full-duplex 1200-bit/s modem, the Bell 212A. Bell 212AR denotes the FCC-registered version now in use. To achieve this within the audio passband of a telephone channel, the bandwidth of each 1200-bit/s signal was reduced by using *dibit*-encoded, differential phase-shift keying (DPSK). In dibit encoding of a PSK signal, two bits are used to determine the phase of the transmitted signal:

Dibit	Phase
00	90°
01	0°
10	180°
11	270°

The originating station transmits on 1200 Hz and the answering station transmits on

Fig 34 — CCITT V.23 modem frequencies.
Those for Mode 1 (600 bauds) are at A.
Mode 2 (1200-baud) frequencies are at B.

Fig 35 — Bell 212A model frequencies for
1200-bit/s full-duplex operation. See Fig. 31
for frequencies when in the Bell 103 mode.

2400 Hz, as shown in Fig 35. In addition, the 212A has a low-speed FSK modem for communication with Bell-103 modems. The operating speed is selected by the modem originating the call. An answering 212A can tell the type of the originating modem and automatically adjust to the right speed and protocol.

Bell 212A uses a bit-sequence encoder, called a *scrambler*, to prevent transmitting a pathological bit sequence (such as a long string of 0s). The scrambler operates according to a fixed algorithm designed to produce a pseudorandom bit pattern, thus providing control over the shape of the spectrum produced by keying. Without scrambling, the demodulator would lose synchronization with the dibit clock.

Although Bell-212A modems are popular for telephone-line use, little or no experimentation with the 212A for packet radio is known as this is written.

CCITT V.22

CCITT V.22 is similar to Bell 212A, and the two can interoperate synchronously at 1200 bit/s. V.22 uses the same frequencies as the 212A, 1200 Hz (channel 1) for the

Table 23
Summary of Bell and CCITT Modem Characteristics

Standard	Forward	Fallback	Reverse	Sync/async	Modulation	Transmitting frequencies
Bell 103/113	0-300			Async	FSK	Originate: 1070 Hz space 1270 Hz mark Answer: 2025 Hz space 2225 Hz mark
CCITT V.21	0-300			Async	FSK	Originate: 980 Hz mark 1080 Hz space Answer: 1650 Hz mark 1850 Hz space
Bell 202	1200			Async	FSK	Forward: 1200 Hz mark 2200 Hz space
			5		OOK	Reverse: 387 Hz
CCITT V.23	1200			Async	FSK	Forward: 1300 Hz mark 2100 Hz space
		600			FSK	Fallback: 1300 Hz mark 1700 Hz space
			75		FSK	Reverse: 390 Hz mark 450 Hz space
Bell 212A	1200			Sync	4DPSK	Originate: 1200 Hz Answer: 2400 Hz
		300			FSK	Same as Bell 103
CCITT V.22	1200			Both	4DPSK	Modes I and II: Originate: 1200 Hz Answer: 2400 Hz
		600			2DPSK	Modes II and IV: Originate: 1200 Answer: 2400
		300			FSK	Same as V.21
Bell 201CR	4800			Sync	4DPSK	Carrier: 1800 Hz
CCITT V.22bis	2400			Both	QAM	Originate: 1200 Hz Answer: 2400 Hz
		1200		Both	4DPSK	Same as V.22
CCITT V.26	2400			Sync	4DPSK	Carrier: 1800 Hz
			75	Async	FSK	Same as V.23
CCITT V.26bis	2400			Sync	4DPSK	Carrier: 1800 Hz
		1200		Sync	2DPSK	
			75	Async	FSK	Same as V.23
CCITT V.26ter	2400			Sync	4DPSK	Carrier: 1800 Hz
		1200		Sync	2DPSK	
			75	Async	FSK	Same as V.23
Bell 208BR	4800			Sync	8DPSK	Carrier: 1800 Hz
CCITT V.27	4800			Sync	8DPSK	Carrier: 1800 Hz
			75	Async	FSK	Same as V.23
CCITT V.27bis	4800			Sync	8DPSK	Carrier: 1800 Hz
		2400		Sync	4DPSK	
			75	Async	FSK	Same as V.23
CCITT V.27ter	4800			Sync	8DPSK	Carrier: 1800 Hz
		2400		Sync	4DPSK	
			75	Async	FSK	Same as V.23
Bell 203	3600 4800 5400 6400 7200 9600 10800			Sync		
Bell 209A	9600			Sync	QAM	
CCITT V.29	9600			Sync	QAM	Carrier: 1700 Hz
		7200		Sync	QAM	
		4800		Sync	QAM	
CCITT V.32	9600			Sync	QAM	Carrier: 1800
		4800		Sync	QAM	
		2400		Sync	QAM	(Further study)
CCITT V.35	48000			Sync	SSBSC	Carrier: 100 kHz
		40800				
CCITT V.36	48000 56000 64000 72000			Sync	SSBSC	Carrier: 100 kHz
CCITT V.37	72000- 160000					

calling station (originate) and 2400 Hz (channel 2) for the called station (answer). Whenever channel 2 is in use, V.22 modems transmit an 1800-Hz guard tone at all times to suppress in-band telephone signaling.

V.22 has the following alternative modes:

Mode	Operation
I	1200-bit/s sync
II	1200-bit/s async
III	600-bit/s sync
IV	600-bit/s async
V	1200 and 0-300 bit/s async

Like the 212A, V.22 uses dibit DPSK. Below are phase changes for the various modes:

Mode	00	01	10	11 (dibits)
I, II	90°	0°	270°	180°
V	270°	180°	90°	0°

Mode	0	1 (bits)
III, V	90°	270°

V.22 modems come in various configurations. Alternative A is synchronous, B is A plus asynchronous, and C is B with Mode V added. Some V.22 modems do not have the 600-bit/s fallback speed.

Although the V.22 is widely used in Europe, there is no known packet-radio use at this time.

Amateur Packet-Radio Modems

Bell-202 modems dominate 1200-baud VHF packet-radio operation. These units were a good choice initially for VHF-FM packet radio because of their surplus availability. The Bell 202 has some problems, however. It is North American standard, not international, although it is to some extent interoperable with CCITT V.23 modems. Also, there is a general consensus that the Bell 202 is too slow and should be replaced. On HF, the Bell-202 frequency shift of 1000 Hz, while legal in the US, is excessive for operation at 300 bauds—the speed limit below 28 MHz. Even at 1200 bauds, 1000-Hz shift is not necessary, and a narrower shift of 800 Hz (CCITT V.23) or 600 Hz (minimum-shift keying—MSK) would be in the interest of spectral efficiency. Therefore, Bell-103 modems are used for 300-baud HF packet-radio communications because of their reasonably narrow 200-Hz frequency shift.

1200-Baud Modems

The Vancouver Amateur Digital Communications Group (VADCG) terminal-node controller (TNC) was designed without a modem because surplus Bell-202 modems were available. In late 1982, VADCG produced a Bell-202-like modem in both kit and PC-board-only form using an Exar XR-2206 function generator as the modulator and an XR-2211 phase-locked loop as the demodulator.

When Tucson Amateur Packet Radio (TAPR) designed their TNC 1, they added the modem to the TNC board to simplify getting on the air. The same Exar chips were used, but with a National MF10 switched-capacitor filter (SCF) for equalization to compensate for the audio responses of different VHF radios. A modem-disconnect arrangement was included to permit use of an external modem. This same modem design was carried over to the TAPR TNC 2. The TAPR modem can be reconfigured for 300-baud, 200-Hz FSK.

Leaving these modems in the dust are a number of faster modems that have been developed during the first decade of amateur packet radio. Some of these designs have been placed in operation to speed up internetworking and some are also being used at the user-level for satellite and terrestrial work.

2400-Baud Modems

The DRSI 2400-baud modem is a 2400-bit/s DPSK (differential phase-shift keying) modem designed for use with the DRSI PC*Packet Adapter™ Type 1. The 2400-bit/s signal rate is derived from a dibit (a group of two bits) data stream operating at 1200 bauds.

The Kantronics 2400 modem is a 2400-bit/s DPSK modem designed for installation in the Kantronics KPC-4 and KAM controllers. The 2400-bit/s signal rate is derived in the same manner as in DRSI's 2400-baud modem. The Kantronics 2400-TNC modem is a 1200-baud BPSK/2400-baud QPSK modem designed for installation in TNC 1s, TNC 2s and their clones. The Kantronics QPSK modem is a 1200-baud BPSK/2400-baud QPSK modem designed for installation in the Kantronics KPC-4 and KAM controllers. The Kantronics TNC-2400 modem is a 2400-bit/s DPSK modem designed for installation in TNC 1s, TNC 2s and their clones. The 2400-bit/s signal rate is derived in the same manner as in DRSI's 2400-baud modem.

4800-Baud Modem

The HAPN 4800-Bit/S modem is a 4800-baud modem designed by the Hamilton (Ontario) Area Packet Network.

9600-Baud Modem

The G3RUH 9600-Baud modem, designed by James Miller, G3RUH, is a 9600-baud modem intended for use with amateur voice-band NBFM (narrowband FM) radios. The Hamtronics 9600-Baud Digital RF Link is a 9600-baud 220- or 450-MHz transceiver with selectable 50- or 15-watt output. The K9NG 9600-Baud modem is a 9600-bit/s FSK modem designed by Steve Goode, K9NG.

Higher-Speed Modems

The AEA RFM-220 radio modem is a 19,200-baud FSK 220-MHz transceiver with a 25-watt output. The GLB Netlink 220 Data Transceiver is a 19,200-baud FSK 220-MHz digital transceiver with an output of 2 watts.

The Heatherington 56 KB RF modem is a 56,000-baud MSK transceiver intended for use with 50, 144, 220, 430, 902 or 1296-MHz linear transverters. It was designed by Dale Heatherington, WA4DSY, and is distributed by Georgia Radio Amateur Packet Enthusiast Society (GRAPES).

Modem Testing

Bit Error Rate

Bit-error-rate (BER) testing (BERT) is done by sending a known pseudorandom bit sequence, comparing the received bit sequence with the known one and analyzing the results. BER is the basic (but not the only) measure of performance of a digital communications system. BER is the probability of not properly receiving a bit and is expressed in terms of the number of errors $\times$ 10^{-n} or as a percentage.

Fig 36 shows a test setup, described by Steve Goode, K9NG, in the August 1983 issue of *QEX*. It tested the BER performance of the TAPR TNC 1 modem. Fig 37 presents the results of the TNC 1 modem test and Fig 38 shows the BERT results of the K9NG 9600-bit/s modem.

Block Error Rate

Block error rate (BLER, also sometimes seen as BKER) is more meaningful in packet radio than BER. "Block" refers to a transmission block, that is, the length of one transmission—in this case the length of a packet. Thus, BLER testing (BLERT) indicates how many transmission blocks can be sent without error. You can expect a typical VHF-FM radio channel with a

Fig 36 — K9NG's bit-error-rate-test setup for the TAPR TNC 1 modem.

Fig 37 — BER results of test setup in Fig. 36. BER for 1200 bit/s and 300 bit/s are shown at A and B, respectively. In both tests, an RF input signal of −121 dBm represents 20 dBq (decibels of quieting).

Fig 38 — BER results of testing the K9NG 9600-bit/s modem.

transmitted data to the horizontal trigger input of the oscilloscope. The oscilloscope is then set up to begin a trace when triggered and the horizontal sweep period is set to an integral multiple of the bit period. If you have only a single-trace oscilloscope, then connect the received data to the oscilloscope's vertical input as shown in Fig 40.

In the case of the K9NG eye patterns, a dual-trace oscilloscope was used. The upper trace in each photograph displays the digital baseband signal prior to modulation. Note that the top trace in the photo at A has smooth transitions between the upper and lower rails, but there is some flattopping on the rails. As the bit rate increases, the data looks less like a square wave and becomes sinusoidal in the top

full-quieting signal to allow a BER of 1×10^{-5} or higher. That means that, on average, an error would occur every 100,000 bits. If you send a 2000-bit packet repeatedly, on average one out of every 50 packets (100,000/2000 = 50) would be rejected because of a bit error introduced by the channel. Such a circuit would have a BLER of 2×10^{-2} (1/50 = 2×10^{-2}).

While typically random, bit errors tend to occur in bursts. Three bit errors may be clustered and destroy only one block, not three. Thus, BER and BLER are not necessarily proportional.

Modem Testing Techniques

Some telephone modems have a *self-test* feature, which may activate automatically upon power-up or manually when the operator pushes a test button. Upon test initiation, the test circuitry generates a test message that is routed through the modem back to the test circuitry, which compares the received message to the original test message and informs the operator of the results.

Loopback testing connects the modulator's output to the demodulator's input, either inside the modem or through a full-duplex communications channel. The operator sends a test message through the loopback route and compares the received message with the transmitted message for errors.

In packet radio, *remote testing* of the entire packet-radio system can be accomplished by "connecting to yourself" through another station (for example, a network node or digipeater). Simply make the connection, then send a test sequence on the keyboard and observe the results on

the screen. If errors occur in transmission, it is extremely unlikely that the sequence will be repeated by the other station.

Another packet-radio testing method for equipment and the propagational path has provided some interesting results. Two stations agree that one station is to send a series of brief packets. In order to tell which packets get through and which do not, the data sent in the packet is simply the time in hours, minutes and seconds. The receiving station saves the times received on disk and can use the times for statistical analysis of the system over the path.

EIA-232-D Break-Out Box

Aside from the bit-error-rate tester, the most powerful diagnostic tool for modem testing is the break-out box. In addition to modem testing, a break-out box is useful for checking any EIA-232-D interfacing problem. Sooner or later you will run into an interfacing problem that you can't fix by switching lines 2 and 3 and performing connector gender-change operations. Sometimes the control lines, particularly pins 8 and 20, need to be reversed, or signals may not be appearing on various EIA-232-D lines at the right times. A break-out box can also help you monitor what the modem is doing or not doing.

Eye Patterns

An essential diagnostic technique for modem design and testing is the *eye pattern* or *eye diagram* display on an oscilloscope. The eye-pattern display compares transmitted and received data signals. Some eye patterns photographed by K9NG appear in Fig 39.

To produce an eye pattern, connect the

(A)

(B)

(C)

Fig 39 — K9NG photographs of eye patterns using his 9600-bit/s modem. Upper trace on each of the above represents the digital baseband signal before modulation. The lower trace on each photo is the received data after demodulation. Data rates were 9.6, 12 and 16 kbit/s at A, B and C, respectively.

Fig 40 — Oscilloscope connections for eye patterns. A single-trace 'scope is shown. If available, a dual-trace 'scope can be used to display eye patterns prior to modulation and subsequent to demodulation.

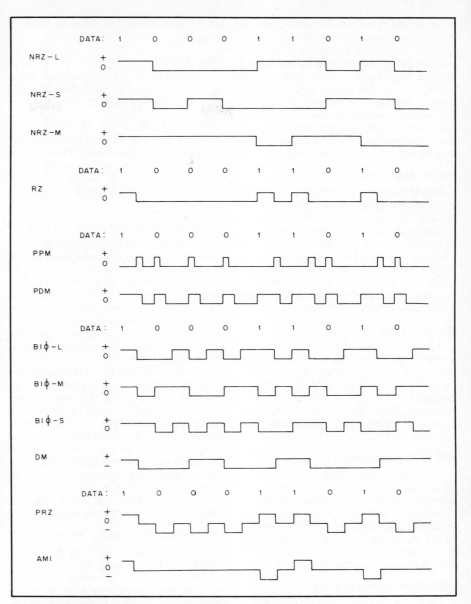

Fig 41 — Pulses produced by various binary baseband codes.

trace at C. The lower traces were produced by feeding the received data out of the demodulator into the second vertical channel input of the oscilloscope. In the lower trace at A, the eye pattern looks good with only minor amplitude and phase jitter. Amplitude jitter is seen by thickening or separation of the trace(s) in the vertical direction, while phase jitter appears as thickening or separation of the line(s) horizontally. Note how both amplitude and phase jitter increases as the data rate through the modem increases.

BINARY BASEBAND CODING

In the early days of digital signaling, 1s and 0s were translated directly to marks and spaces. However, experience with wire lines, missile telemetry and digital magnetic recording spawned the development of different binary baseband encoding techniques, also called line coding, transmission coding, channel coding, baseband data format and pulse-code modulation (PCM). A number of popular baseband codes are described below and illustrated in Fig 41.

NRZ-L (Nonreturn-to-zero—level)

NRZ-L, or simply NRZ, represents a 1 by one level and a 0 by the other level. Although Baudot and AMTOR RTTY normally use this type of coding, it is not suitable for transmission or recording systems incapable of handling dc levels. Without transitions, there is a tendency for the baseline to shift and cause signal-detection errors.

NRZ-S (Nonreturn-to-zero—space)

The term familiar to packet-radio operators is NRZI (nonreturn-to-zero—inverted). A 0 produces a change in level, while a 1 causes no change. It makes no difference whether a keying sequence begins on one tone or the other (usually called mark and space); only the transitions between the tones are important. In NRZ-S, long sequences of 1 bits cause no transitions, giving this code a strong dc component. In packet radio, however, *bit stuffing* or *zero insertion* after 5 continuous 1 bits limits the dc component to some extent. This is the predominant binary baseband

code used for packet radio at this time. It is supported by numerous protocol-controller chips, including the Intel 8273, Zilog 8530 and Western Digital 1933.

NRZ-M (Nonreturn-to-zero—mark)

This is also sometimes called NRZI, chiefly in digital recording, but it is the opposite of NRZ-S. A 1 produces a change in level, while a 0 causes no change. NRZ-M has a strong dc component whenever there are long sequences of 0 bits.

RZ (Return-to-zero)

A 1 produces a half-bit-period pulse and a 0 produces no pulse. RZ has a strong dc component, because no pulses are produced for 0 bits. The half-bit-period pulses require twice the bandwidth of codes

that transmit only full-bit-period pulses.

PPM (Pulse-position modulation)

A 1 produces a pulse in the middle of the symbol period, while a 0 produces a pulse at the beginning of the symbol period. PPM eliminates the dc component, but requires greater bandwidth than codes that transmit only full-bit-period pulses.

PDM (Pulse-duration modulation)

A 1 causes a long pulse, a 0 a shorter pulse. PDM has no dc component, but requires greater bandwidth than codes that transmit only full-bit-period pulses.

Biφ-L (Biphase-Level)

Biφ-L is often called "Manchester." More precisely, it is Manchester II," as it is the second code developed at Manchester, England. It is also referred to as "split phase." A 1 produces a half-bit-period 1 pulse followed by a half-bit-period 0 pulse during the symbol period. A 0 produces a half-bit-period pulse sequence of 01. Biφ-L eliminates the dc component, but requires twice the bandwidth of codes that transmit only full-bit period pulses. Biφ-L has been used for AMSAT data links and by packet-radio experimenters.

Biφ-M (Biphase-Mark)

Biφ-M is also called Manchester I, PE-M (phase encoding-mark), diphase and DF (double-frequency) and FM (frequency modulation) recording. There is a transition at the start of every bit period. A 1 causes a second transition halfway through the bit period, but a 0 does not cause a second transition. Biφ-M has no dc component, but requires twice the bandwidth of codes that transmit only full-bit-period pulses.

Biφ-S (Biphase-Space)

There is a transition at the beginning of every bit period in Biφ-S, which is also known as phase encoding. A 0 causes a second transition halfway through the bit period, but a 1 does not cause a second transition. Biφ-S has no dc component, but requires twice the bandwidth of codes that transmit only full-bit-period pulses.

DM (Delay Modulation)

DM is often called *Miller Code* or MFM (modified frequency modulation). A 1 causes a transition halfway through the bit period and a 0 causes no transition unless another 0 immediately follows, in which case a transition occurs at the end of the first bit period. DM is dc free and does not send pulses of less than one bit period.

PRZ (Polar return-to-zero)

PRZ is a pseudoternary or multilevel-binary (MLB) code in which a 1 produces a half-bit-period pulse of one polarity and a 0 produces a half-bit period pulse of the opposite polarity. PRZ has no dc component.

AMI (Alternate-mark-inversion)

AMI, also known as BP (bipolar), is in the pseudoternary or multi-level-binary (MLB) class of codes. A 1 causes a positive pulse for the first half of the bit period and a 0 for the second half. A 0 produces a 0-level output. AMI has no dc component, but lacks clocking information during long sequences of zeros.

HDBn (High-density bipolar codes)

To overcome timing problems associated with AMI, HDBn limits the maximum number of 0s to n. If $n + 1$ consecutive 0s occur in the data, the $n + 1$th 0 is replaced by a pulse of the same polarity as the pulse produced by the most-recent 1 bit.

HDB3 (where $n = 3$) is the most popular form.

Other Codes

There are other binary baseband codes, each having a particular combination of spectral and timing-recovery characteristics.

CIRCUIT TURNAROUND TIME

Circuit turnaround time is the interval between the last bit transmitted by a station and the first bit the station receiver can properly process. It is comprised of two parts: transceiver switching delays and propagation delay.

Transceiver Switching Delay

Transceiver switching delay is the time it takes a transceiver to change from receive to transmit or vice versa and stabilize at full performance in the new condition. For design purposes, it is necessary to analyze the transceiver switching delay in terms of its four components: (1) transmitter on time, (2) transmitter off time, (3) receiver on time and (4) receiver off time. Worst case measurements have been in the vicinity of 400 ms. Most HF and VHF radios can be modified to reduce the switching time to the 10- to 20-ms range. The requirements for HF/VHF packet radio are essentially the same as for AMTOR. For higher-speed packet radio (above 1200 bauds), a better design goal would be on the order of 1 ms. This 1-ms goal has been achieved in radio designs appearing recently. Once these designs are put in operation throughout the packet-radio network, transceiver switching delay problems will be minimized.

HF Skywave Propagation Delay

The worst-case propagation delay for a skywave path to the other side of the earth (12,000 miles) is about 70 ms. You can calculate the approximate delay in ms by dividing the distance in statute miles by 186 (in km by 300). Additional delay needs to be added to account for the distance traveled by the wave from earth to the ionosphere and back to earth again. That distance is more significant than the distance along the ground for near vertical-incidence skywave paths and can amount to as much as 260 mi (1.4-ms delay).

VHF/UHF Terrestrial Propagation Delay

You can calculate the VHF/UHF delay in ms by dividing the distance in miles by 186. For example, a 32-mile path has a propagation delay of 0.17 ms, which is usually insignificant compared to the equipment switching delay.

Meteor-Scatter Propagation Delay

Meteor-scatter paths are limited to around 1200 miles as a result of the curvature of the earth. Meteor trails range from about 50 to 80 miles above the earth. Propagation delays run from approxi-

mately 0.3 to 6.7 ms, depending on path length.

CHANNEL ACCESS

ALOHA, named after early packet-radio experiments at the University of Hawaii, is a channel-access method wherein a station transmits without checking to see if the channel is free. When a *collision* occurs, the TNC waits a random length of time and retries until it gets the frame through and receives an acknowledgment from the other station. Because of collisions, the maximum channel loading is approximately 18%, which is acceptable if traffic on a frequency is light.

More sophisticated access arbitration schemes involve listening before transmitting. For example, packet-radio TNCs look for the carrier-detect signal from the modem before transmitting. This is not absolute insurance against collisions, because two stations could transmit at exactly the same moment. Also, propagation delay makes it impossible to tell if a distant station is transmitting until some milliseconds after transmission began.

THE LINK LAYER

The link layer defines the protocol for error-free transmission and reception between two points that are at two ends of a communications medium. In packet radio, that means two stations that are connected directly (not through a network). Whereas the job of the physical layer is to get bits from one place to another through modems, radio transceivers and the propagation medium as reliably as possible, the function of the link layer is to move frames from one place to another through the physical layer and the communications medium. If the physical layer gets some bits wrong, the link layer detects these errors and keeps trying until the correct frame gets to the other station.

AX.25 LEVEL 2 PROTOCOL

On October 26, 1984, the ARRL Board of Directors approved the AX.25 Amateur Packet-Radio Link-Layer Protocol (Version 2.0). The AX.25 level 2 protocol follows, in principle, CCITT Recommendation X.25 with the following exceptions: the address field was extended to accommodate Amateur Radio call signs and an Unnumbered Information (UI) frame feature was added. It also follows the principles of CCITT Rec Q.921 (LAPD) in the use of multiple links, distinguished by the address field, on a single shared channel. With the exception of an extended address, it could be considered a subset of the ANSI Advanced Data Communications Control Protocol (ADCCP), balanced mode. It also follows the frame structure of High-Level Data Link Control Procedures (HDLC) per ISO 3309.

The AX.25 link-layer protocol formally

specifies the format of a packet-radio frame and the actions a packet-radio station must take when it transmits or receives a frame.

At the link layer, data is sent in transmission blocks called frames. In addition to data, each frame contains addressing, error-checking and control information. The addressing information lists the station sending the frame, the station receiving the frame and, optionally, the station(s) relaying the frame. This addressing technique allows many stations to share the same frequency. A station can monitor and display all the activity on a channel, no matter who the frames are addressed to, or a station may accept only frames intended for it and ignore the rest. The error-checking information in the frame allows the receiving station to determine whether the frame contains any errors. If the frame is error-free, the receiving station accepts it and sends an acknowledgment to the transmitting station. If the frame contains errors, the receiving station ignores it and waits for the sending station to retransmit it.

AX.25 Link-Layer Format

Link-layer packet-radio transmissions are sent in frames. Each frame is divided into *fields*. Fig 42 shows the frame format. Frame transmission is normally preceded by 16 bit reversals for synchronization. The frame consists of the beginning flag, address field, control field, network protocol identifier (PID), information field, frame-check sequence (FCS) and an ending flag.

Flag Field

Each frame starts and ends with a *flag* that has a unique bit pattern: 01111110. To assure that this pattern only appears at the beginning and end of frames, the sending station inserts a 0 bit and the receiving station removes it whenever five 1 bits show up anywhere else in a frame. This is called zero insertion or bit stuffing, as illustrated in Fig 43.

Address Field

The *address field* consists of from 2 to 10 specially encoded Amateur Radio call signs. The first address is the intended receiving station and the second is the source or originating station. If the two stations are in direct contact, that's all there is to the address field. If not, the call signs of 1 to 8 relaying stations or *digipeaters* may follow.

Each call sign takes up six character spaces. Call signs are made up of uppercase alphanumeric ASCII characters; shorter call signs are padded with ASCII spaces. A seventh character, called a *Secondary Station Identifier* (SSID), permits up to 16 different packet-radio stations to operate under one call sign. For example, W1AW-5 is a digipeater, while W1AW-4 is a bulletin-board station.

The SSID *octet* (8 bits) in the repeater address, when used, differs from the others

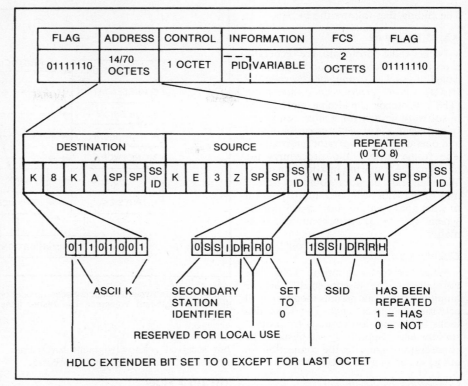

Fig 42 — AX.25 frame format. The repeater address field is optional and may contain as many as eight repeater call signs.

Fig 43 — The HDLC controller chip uses zero-insertion or bit-stuffing to eliminate the possibility of flags appearing within a frame. The transmitter examines the content between flags and inserts a 0 bit after all sequences of contiguous 1 bits to ensure that a flag sequence is not simulated. The receiver discards any 0 bit that directly follows 5 contiguous 1 bits that occur between the flag sequences.

because its last bit, "H," indicates whether a frame has been repeated. This is necessary to prevent the reception of identical frames, one direct and one from the repeater. In Fig 42, the two bits marked "R" are reserved and may be used in an agreed-upon manner in individual networks. When not implemented, they are set to 1.

Control Field

The *control field* contains a bit pattern that indicates the kind of frame it is (*information* or *supervisory*) and a frame number (0 to 7) for acknowledgments. It signals a connection request, ready/not-ready conditions, frame numbering and the specific mode of operation.

Protocol Identifier Field

The *Protocol Identifier Field* (PID) is actually part of the information field, as shown in Fig 42. It only appears in information (I) and unnumbered information

(UI) frames and identifies the kind of network-layer protocol, if any, that is in use.

Information Field

The *information field* (I field) contains the data to be transmitted. It can have any integral number of octets, from 1 to 256, of information. Octets at the beginning of the I field may be used for addressing and control for those levels by the network- and higher-protocol levels.

Frame-Check Sequence Field

The *frame-check sequence* (FCS) is a 16-bit number calculated by both the sender and receiver of a frame following an algorithm published in ISO 3309 (HDLC). Upon receipt of a frame, the receiver calculates the FCS on the basis of the received data and then compares its answer with the FCS calculated by the sender. If the two match, that frame is acknowledged.

The ending flag follows the FCS.

AX.25 Procedure

Packet-radio protocols are generally executed in a microprocessor-based device called a *packet assembler/disassembler* (PAD) or a *terminal-node controller* (TNC). Protocols can also be implemented in software written for a microcomputer. In any event, the procedures are automatic and operate without operator intervention. The frame format and procedures for handling the frame are link-layer matters. What appears on your computer screen may or may not be a close approximation of what goes on at the link layer, since the screen display is a presentation-layer matter.

Disconnected State

When power is applied, TNCs are normally in the disconnected state or monitor mode. This permits monitoring all activities on the channel. The TNC also looks for connection requests from other stations and responds by establishing the connection or ignoring the connection request, depending on circumstances.

Connection Establishment

When one station wishes to connect with another, it sends a command frame to the other station and starts a time-out timer. If the other station is on the air and able to connect, it sends an acknowledgment frame. If the called station does not respond before the timer runs out, the calling station resends the request a number of times.

Information Transfer

After the link connection is established, the TNCs enter the information transfer state, which permits the two stations to exchange information and supervisory frames.

Disconnection

While in the information-transfer state, either station may request to disconnect. Disconnection occurs after the other station responds or if it does not respond after several disconnect attempts.

Connectionless Operation

This procedure permits roundtables and bulletin transmissions via packet radio. The normal method of connection is not practical when multiple stations are involved, so the stations broadcast unnumbered information (UI) frames. Without frame numbering, the TNCs do not request retransmissions of bad frames as they do when connected.

Frame Acknowledgments

Each frame's control field includes the number (0 to 7) of the last frame correctly received from the other station. If the sending station had sent frame number 5,

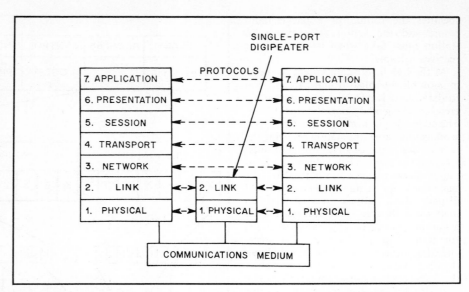

Fig 44 — Open Systems interconnection model of two packet-radio stations communicating through a single-port digipeater. The dashed lines represent logical communications between peer layers.

but received acknowledgment for frame number 4, it resends frame number 5.

DIGIPEATERS

A digipeater is a packet-radio station capable of recognizing and selectively repeating frames. An equivalent term used in industry is *bridge*. Virtually any TNC can be used as a single-port digipeater, because the digipeater function is included in the AX.25 Level 2 protocol firmware. An "apartment-house" diagram of how two packet-radio stations connect through a single-port or multiport digipeater is shown in Fig 44. Although the use of digipeaters is waning today as network nodes take their place, the digipeater function is handy when you need a relay and no node is available, or for on-the-air testing.

THE NETWORK LAYER

The network layer gets packets to their destination through a network. A number of networking standards currently exist. There is some disagreement among packet-radio experimenters on what form the network layer should take—virtual connections or datagrams, both of which are discussed below.

Fig 45A illustrates the classical Open Systems Interconnection model of how two computers communicate through a network. Note the peer-to-peer (for example, transport-to-transport) protocol relationships between the two end points and how the physical, link and network-layer protocols involve the relay station, called a *router*. The idea is that both end points have computers with software for each of the protocol layers. The full 7-story apartment-house protocol structure may indeed become the pattern for *hosts*—those stations that will provide substantial computer services to the network.

At the moment, however, most packet-radio stations are equipped with TNCs that have only a modest capability. They implement the physical layer (modem) and the link layer (frame assembly and disassembly), and have a rather basic presentation layer. The presentation-layer code takes care of the commands and responses between the terminal and the TNC. The network, transport and application layers are skipped—often called *null layers*. Some future TNCs may eventually implement all protocol levels. But for the moment, none do.

There is general agreement that however elaborate the network may become, network designers should take care not to disenfranchise the user with a present-day TNC. Furthermore, such users should be able to enjoy the full capabilities of the worldwide packet-radio network. Just how this will be accomplished is a matter of speculation. Yet it stands to reason that if all the fancy protocols are not in the user's TNC or personal computer, then they are likely to be in some superstation nearby.

Fig 45B may be closer to reality for amateur packet radio—certainly for the near future. The dashed lines forming the network- and transport-layer boxes in the router indicate some uncertainty of whether only the network layer or both the network and transport layers will be implemented. That depends largely on the outcome of the controversy between virtual connection and datagram approaches described below. If virtual connection is the approach chosen, only the network layer need be implemented. If datagram, then both need to be included.

The data-communications industry uses the term *local-area network* (LAN). That term, while perhaps okay when describing a 2-meter packet network, is inappropriate

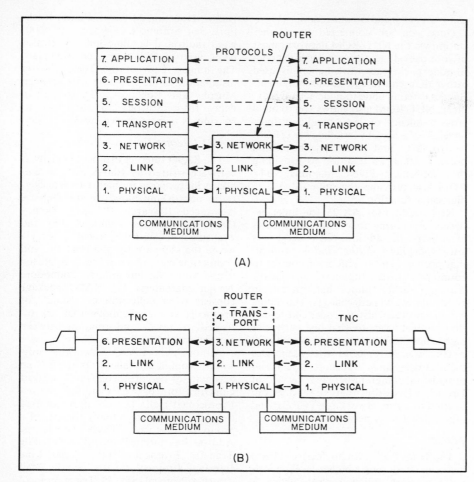

Fig 45 — Possible packet-radio networking modules. A shows the classical OSI model of two stations communicating through one or more network routers. This model will likely apply only to hosts that provide a service to the network. B represents a more modest idea of how users with present TNCs may communicate through a network. Dotted lines around the transport-layer box indicate that a transport-layer protocol may be required at the router if a datagram networking protocol is adopted. Dashed lines show logical communications between peer levels of protocol.

for packet-radio nets that might span half the globe, as they can on HF or via satellite. So, the term intranet was coined to mean a (level 3) network with one net controller (router) and a bunch of user stations. The term internet, on the other hand, is widely used to denote communication between (intra)nets. If the network goes the virtual-connection route, there will be both intranets and internets. If it goes datagram, there may or may not be intranets. Regardless of the outcome, it is hoped that we will end up with one worldwide standard. To do otherwise would mean that high-level *gateways* would have to be established between networks using different protocols. Unfortunately, when this is done, the unique advantages and enhancements in one network cannot be translated to networks not having the protocols to support them. In other words, communication between dissimilar networks becomes a matter of the least common denominator —something to avoid like grid current.

NETWORK PROTOCOL

Protocol(s) for the network layer have been developed using two different approaches: virtual circuit and datagram protocols.

Virtual-Circuit Protocol

Terry Fox, WB4JFI, presented one of the first proposals for higher-level packet radio at the Third ARRL Amateur Radio Computer Networking Conference in April 1984. His proposal for a virtual circuit network was based on the CCITT X.25 protocol.

A virtual circuit gives the appearance of providing a direct connection between you and another packet-radio station. Before communications commence, a "call setup" packet is sent through the network to set up a fixed path to the other station. Once the path is established, data packets may be sent through the circuit. These data packets are not burdened by a header

containing the full address of the desired path (like AX.25 packets that include digipeater routing information), because the network attempts to maintain the path for the duration of the communications. When communications are completed, the virtual circuit is cleared by removing the information about the path from the memory of each device along the communication path.

The virtual-circuit approach has the advantage of less overhead in the packet header and making the network (not the end user) responsible for acknowledgment of packets. In a virtual circuit, only the first packet establishing a virtual connection has the complete information needed by the network to route packets in the network header. Subsequent packets have an abbreviated network header. The RATS Open System Environment is amateur packet radio's implementation of the virtual circuit protocol.

RATS Open System Environment

The RATS Open System Environment (ROSE) was developed over a number of years by The Radio Amateur Telecommunications Society (RATS) of New Jersey. It is a firmware replacement for the TNC-2 class of TNCs that causes the TNC to act as a packet switch.

ROSE's function is to let the network do the work when trying to establish a packet-radio communications circuit. The network performs the task of determining the path between stations, not the user. ROSE uses *node-to-node packet acknowledgment* rather than *end-to-end packet acknowledgment*. When a user sends a packet from one point to another via the AX.25 digipeater network, his packet is simply handed off from one digipeater to another. If the intended destination station receives the packet without error, it sends an acknowledgment back along the same hand-to-hand path. Anywhere along the path, the packet or acknowledgment may collide with another packet and be lost. If the packet is lost, the originating station does not receive an acknowledgment from the destination station, so it resends the packet along the entire path again.

When a user sends a packet through a network using node-to-node acknowledgment, things are done differently. Each time the packet is transferred to a new node, that node sends an acknowledgment back to the previous node. If a packet or acknowledgment is lost, only the unacknowledged node has to resend the packet (to the next node). The originating station does not have to send the packet through the entire path.

Tom Moulton, W2VY, wrote the ROSE code, which permits you to contact another station in the network as long as you know the other station's call sign and the ROSE node number used by the other station; you do not have to specify the network path between you and the other station.

To specify a network node, ROSE uses the CCITT X.121 country code numbering system; in North America, the system is based on the telephone numbering system (area codes and local dialing prefixes in the United States and Canada). The ROSE node number consists of the three-digit area code followed by the three-digit local dialing prefix of the node, for a total of six digits. For example, "203666" would represent the area code for Connecticut (203) and the local dialing prefix for Newington (666).

Datagram Protocol Proposal

Phil Karn, KA9Q, proposed using a datagram type of network protocol based on the IP (Internet Protocol) developed by the Defense Advanced Research Projects Agency (DARPA). In a datagram protocol, each packet contains complete network addressing/routing information. There is more overhead per packet, but the advantage is that packets will reach the destination via any route still open, even in an unreliable network. The datagram protocol has been implemented in a number of amateur packet-radio networking protocols, including NET/ROM, TexNet and KA9Q Internet Protocol Package.

NET/ROM

Ron Raikes, WA8DED, and Mike Busch, W6IXU, developed new firmware for the TNC 2 (and TNC-2 clones) that supports Levels 3 and 4, the Network and Transport layers of the packet-radio network. NET/ROM replaces the TNC-2 EPROM (that contains the TAPR TNC-2 firmware) and converts the TNC into a *network node controller (NNC)* for use at wide- and medium-coverage digipeater sites. Since it is so easy to convert an off-the-shelf TNC into an NNC via the NET/ROM route, NET/ROM has become the most popular network implementation in the packet-radio world and has been installed at most dedicated digipeater stations, thus propelling the standard AX.25 digipeater into packet-radio history.

The NET/ROM network user no longer has to be concerned with the digipeater path required to get from one point to another. All the user needs to know is the local node of the station he wishes to contact. NET/ROM knows what path is required, and if one path is not working or breaks down for some reason, NET/ROM will switch to an alternative path, if one exists. The user can be assured that NET/ROM is on top of things, because each NET/ROM node automatically updates its node list periodically, and whenever a new node comes on the air, the other NET/ROM nodes become aware of the new node's existence. In addition to automatic route updating, routing information may also be updated manually by means of a terminal keyboard or remotely

using a packet-radio connection.

Once you are connected to another station via the NET/ROM network, most of your packets get through because node-to-node packet acknowledgment is used rather than end-to-end acknowledgment. Besides offering node-to-node acknowledgment, NET/ROM also allows you to build cross-frequency or cross-band multiport nodes. This is done by installing NET/ROM in two TNCs and connecting their serial ports together. In addition to providing these sophisticated NNC functions, NET/ROM also provides the standard AX.25 digipeater function.

NET/ROM uses AX.25 for links between neighboring nodes and links with its local users. In addition, NET/ROM uses a transport layer *sliding window protocol* that provides end-to-end error control to counteract lost, duplicate or out-of-sequence packet frames that result from node failures and path changes. The sliding window protocol also provides end-to-end flow control to assure that one particular path is not disproportionately loaded with traffic. Since NET/ROM strictly separates the Network and Transport layers and provides a datagram-network service at Level 3, it is possible that NET/ROM can be used as a subnetwork for TCP/IP and other higher-level network systems.

TexNet

The Texas Packet Radio Society (TPRS) has been developing a higher-level packet-radio network called TexNet, which is composed of dual-port *network-control processors (NCP)* that provide AX.25-compatible 1200-baud user access on 2 meters and node-to-node linking at 9600 baud on 70 cm. TexNet firmware can support 256 nodes within one network and each node can provide several user services, including access to TexNet, a bulletin board, digipeaters, weather information and a conference bridge that provides connected-mode roundtable service.

Each NCP contains a Z80 microprocessor with 24 kbytes of ROM to contain the firmware, 40 kbytes of RAM, a timer circuit and input/output ports. Each NCP is battery powered for emergency communications and has provisions for the addition of a hard-disk controller for more versatility. The firmware provides a Level 3 Network layer that uses datagrams with node-to-node acknowledgments.

Access to any TexNet service is accomplished by connecting to a local node using the node's call sign and a specific SSID. An SSID of -0 accesses a digipeater, an SSID of -2 accesses the first conference bridge, SSID -3 accesses the second conference bridge and SSID -4 accesses the network. Use of the various services can occur simultaneously on the same node, with a maximum of 20 users.

TexNet presently interconnects the Texas communities of Austin, Corpus Christi,

Dallas, Houston, Midland, Plano, Rockport, San Antonio and Waco with 9600-baud radio and landline links. It is also being used in Oklahoma and Michigan. The longest path of the Texas TexNet installation is the 240-mile trip between Murphy and Rockport. The round-trip delay from Murphy to Rockport to Murphy is a mere six seconds!

KA9Q Internet Protocol Package

The KA9Q Internet Protocol Package is software written by Phil Karn that embodies his proposal for higher-level packet-radio networking based on the Defense Advanced Research Projects Agency (DARPA) Internet Protocol (IP) and Transmission Control Protocol (TCP). He wrote the software for the IBM PC and compatible computers; it has been ported to the Apple Macintosh and Commodore Amiga computers. The KA9Q package consists of a collection or "suite" of protocols and applications that are intended to transfer information between computers.

Although the KA9Q networking software is commonly called "TCP/IP," an acronym for two protocols, the Transport Control Protocol (TCP) and the Internet Protocol (IP), the TCP/IP protocol used in KA9Q's software actually consists of a group of protocols. These include the Address Resolution Protocol (ARP), File Transfer Protocol (FTP), Serial Line Interface Protocol (SLIP), Simple Mail Transfer Protocol (SMTP), Telnet protocol and the User Datagram Protocol (UDP), as well as TCP and IP.

IP (Internet Protocol) is a Level 3 or Network layer protocol that keeps track of the network node addresses, while routing outgoing packets and recognizing packets that are intended for the local node. IP is assisted by ARP (Address Resolution Protocol), which provides the datagram address format that is required by IP, while still being aware of any manually generated routing tables that were created for the datagram routing function. (Users may specify the datagram route, just as a user specifies a digipeater route using the AX.25 Connect command.)

IP uses a 32-bit binary number to address a packet. Each network node, that is, each computer at each packet-radio station in the TCP/IP network, has a unique *IP address* that has been assigned by the local IP address coordinator. ARPANET assigned the address block starting with the digits 44 to amateur packet radio (as well as naming the amateur TCP/IP packet-radio network *AMPRNET*). As a result, the first two digits of all amateur packet-radio IP addresses are 44 (for example, the IP address of KA9Q is 44.64.0.1).

When a connect request is initiated, IP uses the IP address for the destination network node rather than a call sign. The destination node uses its call sign in response and, thereafter, the destination call sign is used for outgoing frames at AX.25 level 2 in order to conform with FCC regulations with regard to call signs.

TCP (Transport Control Protocol) is a Level 4 or Transport layer protocol that provides data integrity between the data's points of origination and destination, whenever such integrity is required. It assembles data for transmission into packets and disassembles received packets into data, while checking for errors and managing packet transmissions on the network. When TCP is not required, *UDP* (*User Datagram Protocol*) is available at Level 4 to perform other functions. For example, UDP is used by messages to determine for which applications, within a destination computer, the messages are intended.

SLIP (*Serial Line Interface Protocol*) is a Level 2 or Link layer protocol that provides a simple serial data transfer between the Network layer protocols and the EIA-232 interface of the Physical layer. *KISS*, for "Keep It Simple, Stupid," is a Link layer non-protocol for serial input and output that was written by Mike Chepponis, K3MC. KISS is a firmware replacement for TAPR TNCs (and TAPR TNC clones) that supports SLIP rather than the Link-layer connections of AX.25. As a result, no AX.25 connection is established with the other end of the circuit. Instead, KISS accepts serial data from the computer and sends it as AX.25 unconnected information (UI) packet frames (the packet-radio equivalent of the datagram). Received datagrams are transferred directly to the computer for disassembly by TCP. In effect, the KA9Q package performs much of the work that, up to now, has been performed by our TNCs.

In addition to these communications functions, the KA9Q package includes applications for use during communication sessions. Since the KA9Q package has the capability to perform multiple tasks simultaneously, several of these applications can be used at the same time.

FTP (*File Transfer Protocol*) allows the user to transfer files to or from the computer at another node. Since the data is transparent to TCP, any kind of data may be transferred. FTP provides password protection and three levels of file security: (1) read-only, (2) read-only, write new files, and (3) read-only, write new files, overwrite old files.

SMTP (*Simple Mail Transfer Protocol*) provides an automatic message-forwarding function. After the user enters a message for another station and saves it on disk, SMTP automatically attempts to establish communications with that other station and sends the message once communication is established. The drawback with using SMTP is that it requires specific message formatting. To alleviate this drawback, *Bdale's Mailer* (*BM*) is included in the

KA9Q package as a front-end to SMTP to perform the specific formatting task required by that protocol. BM was written by Bdale Garbee, N3EUA.

Finally, *Telnet* is a terminal-emulation protocol that provides a user-to-user "chat" function for communications with the live operator of another node (rather than with the station computer).

THE TRANSPORT LAYER

The transport layer makes sure that the data passed to and from higher layers is all there and in the right order. In datagram protocols, it is possible that a packet sent after another packet could beat the earlier packet to the destination. The transport layer buffers incoming packets and re-assembles them in the correct sequence. The transport header adds overhead to the packet to perform the transport layer functions.

THE SESSION LAYER

The session layer is responsible for connection establishment and termination. It can set up\multiple connections to the same or several different places. This protocol is not yet under active study.

THE PRESENTATION LAYER

The presentation layer comes close to a three-ring circus. It talks to the session layer to send and receive messages from distant computers. It deals with data files, code conversion and text strings, and is the traffic cop for computer peripherals. This layer also serves all the programs that might be running at the application layer.

THE APPLICATION LAYER

This layer runs one or more application programs—the real work of a computer in the user's view. Whereas some computers run one program that offers a service to the packet-radio network, others are user-oriented and use the network to communicate needed information to and from other computers in the network.

Some of these applications include packet-radio bulletin boards, weather servers, message forwarding, satellite gateways, call-sign directory servers and DX/contest spotting clusters. Future applications are limited only by our imaginations.

PACKET-RADIO BIBLIOGRAPHY

Abrams, C., "From TUs to Communications Processors," *QST*, Apr 1988.

ARRL, *First ARRL Amateur Radio Computer Networking Conference*, Volumes 1 and 2, ARRL, 1981.

ARRL, *Second ARRL Amateur Radio Computer Networking Conference*, ARRL, 1983.

ARRL, *Third ARRL Amateur Radio Computer Networking Conference*, ARRL, 1984.

ARRL, *Fourth ARRL Amateur Radio Computer Networking Conference*, ARRL, 1985.

ARRL, *Fifth ARRL Amateur Radio Computer Networking Conference*, ARRL, 1986.

ARRL, *Sixth ARRL Amateur Radio Computer Networking Conference*, ARRL, 1987.

ARRL, *Seventh ARRL Amateur Radio Computer Networking Conference*, ARRL, 1988.

ARRL, *Eighth ARRL Amateur Radio Computer Networking Conference*, ARRL, 1989.

ARRL, *Ninth ARRL Amateur Radio Computer Networking Conference*, ARRL, 1990.

Aschenbrenner, T. and T. McDermott, "The TEXNET Packet-Switching Network, Parts 1-3," *Ham Radio*, Mar, Apr and Jun 1987.

Borden, D. and P. Rinaldo, "The Making of an Amateur Packet-Radio Network," *QST*, Oct 1981.

Carpenter, R., "Routine Packet-Radio Meteor Burst Contacts on Six Meters," *QEX*, Oct 1984.

Connors, D. and T. Clark, "PACSAT - A New AMSAT Satellite Project," *QEX*, Nov 1982.

Cupp, F., "A 220-MHz 9600-Baud Data Radio System for Packet," *Ham Radio*, Feb 1989.

Deasington, R., *X.25 Explained: Protocols For Packet Switching Networks*, Second Edition, Ellis Horwood Ltd, 1986.

Electronic Industries Association, *EIA Standard, Interface Between Data Terminal Equipment And Data Circuit-Terminating Equipment Employing Serial Binary Data Interchange, EIA-232-D*, Electronic Industries Association, 1987.

Electronic Industries Association, *EIA Standard, Interface Between Data Terminal Equipment And Data Communication Equipment Employing Serial Binary Data Interchange, RS-232-C*, Electronic Industries Association, 1969.

Fox, T., *AX.25 Amateur Packet-Radio Link-Layer Protocol, Version 2, October 1984*, ARRL, 1984.

Friend, G., J. Fike, H. Baker and J. Bellamy, *Understanding Data Communications*, Texas Instruments Inc, 1984.

Grubbs, J., *Digital Communications with Amateur Radio*, Master Publishing, Inc, 1988.

Grubbs, J., *Get ***Connected To Packet Radio*, QSKY Publishing, 1986.

Horzepa, S., "Gateway" column, monthly, *QEX*.

Horzepa, S., "Packet Perspective" column, *QST*.

Horzepa, S., "Packet Radio" chapter of *The ARRL Operating Manual,* Fourth Edition, ARRL, 1991.

Horzepa, S., "The Shopper's Guide To Packet Radio TNCs," *QST*, Mar 1987.

Horzepa, S., *Your Gateway to Packet Radio*, 2nd Edition, ARRL, 1989.

Ingram, D., *Mastering Packet Radio*, Howard W. Sams & Co, 1988.

International Standards Organization, *Reference Model of Open Systems Architecture*, ISO, 1979.

Johnson, L., "Join the Packet-Radio Revolution," *73*, Nov 1983-Jan 1984.

Johnson, L., "The TAPR PSK Modem," *QEX*, Sep 1987.

Kesteloot, A. and D. Borden, "Xerox 820-1 Compendium," *QEX*, Jun 1986-Jan 1987.

Latta, G., "HF Packet: Comments and Tips," *QEX*, Dec 1986.

Loughmiller, D. and B. McGwier, "Microsat: The Next Generation of OSCAR Satellites, Parts 1 and 2," *QST*, May and Jun 1989.

Magnuski, H., "National Standards for Amateur Packet Radio Networks," *Conference Proceedings of the Eighth West Coast Computer Faire*, 1983.

Mayo, J., "Amateur Packet Radio Networking and Protocols, Parts 1-3," *Ham Radio*, Feb, Mar and Apr 1988.

Mayo, J., *The Packet Radio Handbook*, 2nd Edition, Tab Books, Inc, 1989.

McLarnon, B., "New Directions in HF Data Transmission Systems, Parts 1 and 2," *QEX*, Dec 1987 and Jan 1988.

Meijer, A. and P. Peeters, *Computer Network Architecture*, Computer Science Press, 1982.

Meinzer, K., "Packet Radio and Radio Communication Requirements," *QEX*, Mar 1983.

Miller, J., "A Packet Radio PSK Modem for JAS-1/FO-12," *Ham Radio*, Feb 1987.

Moore, J., "Packet Meteor Scatter Communications," *QEX*, Dec 1983.

Morrison, M., D. Morrison and L. Johnson, "Amateur Packet Radio: Parts 1 and 2," *Ham Radio*, Jul and Aug 1983.

Pechura, M., "Exploring Packet Radio with KISS," *Ham Radio*, Oct 1988.

Pratt, C., and V. Yarbrough, "Pictures by Packet," *QST*, May 1988.

Price, H., "Packet Radio—A Closer Look," *QST*, Aug 1985.

Price, H., "What's All This Racket About Packet," *QST*, Jul 1985.

Richardson, R., *Synchronous Packet Radio Using The Software Approach, Volume I*, Richcraft Engineering Ltd, 1983.

Richardson, R., *Synchronous Packet Radio Using The Software Approach, Volume II*, Richcraft Engineering Ltd, 1984.

Rinaldo, P., *Operating an Amateur Radio Station*, ARRL, 1989.

Rinaldo, P., Ed., *QEX: ARRL Experimenters' Exchange*, monthly, ARRL.

Rinaldo, P., "The Great 1989 HF Packet Design Quest," *QST*, May 1989.

Rogers, G., *Packet User's Notebook*, CQ Communications, Inc, 1988.

Rouleau, R. and I. Hodgson, *Packet Radio*, Tab Books, Inc, 1981.

Sanford, J., "Decoding Data Signals," *Ham Radio*, Dec 1988.

Stallings, W., *Tutorial: Computer Communications: Architectures, Protocols, and Standards*, IEEE Computer Society, 1985.

Tanenbaum, A., *Computer Networks*, Prentice-Hall, Inc, 1981.

Wade, B., "Packet Radio Conference Bridge," *Ham Radio*, Apr 1987.

Winter, P., "Packet Radio in Emergency Communications," *QST*, Sep 1986.

Yamashita, F., "A PSK Demodulator for the JAS-1 Satellite," *QEX*, Aug 1986.

Glossary of Digital Communications Terminology

ACK — Acknowledgment, the control signal sent to indicate the correct receipt of a transmission block.

Address — A character or group of characters that identifies a source or destination.

AFSK — Audio frequency-shift keying.

ALOHA — A channel-access technique wherein each packet-radio station transmits without first checking to see if the channel is free; named after early packet-radio experiments at the University of Hawaii.

AMICON — AMSAT International Computer Network — Packet-radio operation on SSC L1 of AMSAT-OSCAR 10 to provide networking of ground stations acting as gateways to terrestrial packet-radio networks.

AMRAD — Amateur Radio Research and Development Corporation, a nonprofit organization involved in packet-radio development (P.O. Drawer 6148, McLean, VA 22106).

AMTOR — Amateur Teleprinting Over Radio, an amateur radioteletype transmission technique employing error correction as specified in CCIR 476-2 or 476-3. CCIR Rec. 476-3 is reprinted in the proceedings of the Third ARRL Amateur Radio Computer Networking Conference, available from ARRL Hq.

ANSI — American National Standards Institute (1430 Broadway, New York, NY 10018.)

Answer — The station intended to receive a call. In modem usage, the *called* station or modem tones associated therewith.

ARQ — Automatic Repeat Request, an error-control technique in which a sending station, after transmitting a data block, awaits a reply (ACK or NAK) to determine whether to repeat the last block or proceed to the next.

ASCII — American National Standard Code for Information Interchange, a code consisting of seven information bits.

ASR — An Automatic Send-Receive teletypewriter.

Autostart — A device that automatically senses presence of a signal and turns on a printer motor.

AX.25[SM pend.] — Amateur packet-radio link-layer protocol approved by ARRL Board of Directors in October 1984. Copies of protocol specification are available from ARRL Hq for $8 U.S., $9 Canada and elsewhere.

Backwave — An unwanted signal emitted between the pulses of an on/off-keyed signal.

Balanced — A relationship in which two stations communicate with one another as equals; that is, neither is a primary (master) or secondary (slave).

Baud — A unit of signaling speed equal to the number of discrete conditions or events per second. (If the duration of a pulse is 20 ms, the signaling rate is 50 bauds or the reciprocal of 0.02.) (abbreviated Bd)

Baudot code — A coded character set in which five bits represent one character. Used in the U.S. to refer to ITA2.

Bell 103 — A 300-baud full-duplex modem using 200-Hz-shift FSK of tones centered at 1170 and 2125 Hz.

Bell 202 — A 1200-baud modem standard with 1200-Hz mark, 2200-Hz space, used for VHF FM packet radio.

BERT — Bit-error-rate test.

BER — Bit error rate.

Bit — Binary digit, a single symbol, in binary terms either a one or zero.

Bit stuffing — Insertion and deletion of 0s in a frame to preclude accidental occurrences of flags other than at the beginning and end of frames.

BLER — Block error rate.

BLERT — Block-error-rate test.

Break-in — The ability to hear between elements or words of a keyed signal.

Byte — A group of bits, usually eight.

Carrier Detect — Formally, Received Line Signal Detector, a physical-level interface signal that indicates that the receiver section of the modem is receiving tones from the distant modem.

CCIR — International Radio Consultative Committee, an International telecommunication Union agency.

CCIR Rec. 476-3 — The CCIR Recommendation used as the basis of AMTOR and incorporated by reference into the FCC rules.

CCITT — International Telegraph and Telephone Consultative Committee, an ITU agency. CCIR and CCITT recommendations are available from the U.N. Bookstore, United Nations Building, New York, NY 10017.

Chirp — Incidental frequency modulation of a carrier as a result of oscillator instability during keying.

Clear to Send — A physical-level interface circuit generated by the DCE that when ON indicates the signals presented on the Transmitted Data circuit can be transmitted.

Collision — A condition that occurs when two or more transmissions occur at the same time and cause interference to the intended receivers.

Connection — A logical communication channel established between peer levels of two packet-radio stations.

Contention — A condition on a communications channel that occurs when two or more stations try to transmit at the same time.

Control field — An 8-bit pattern in an HDLC frame containing commands or responses, and sequence numbers.

CRC — Cyclic Redundancy Check, a mathematical operation in which the results are sent with a transmission block to enable the receiving station to check the integrity of the data.

CSMA — Carrier Sense Multiple Access, a channel access arbitration scheme in which packet-radio stations listen on a channel for the presence of a carrier before transmitting a frame.

Cut numbers — In Morse code, shortening of codes sent for numerals.

DARPA — Defense Advanced Research Projects Agency; formerly ARPA, sponsors of ARPANET.

Datagram — A mode of packet networking in which each packet contains complete addressing and control information. (compare Virtual Circuit)

Data Set — Modem.

Destination — In packet radio, the station that is the intended receiver of the frame sent over a radio link either directly or via a repeater.

DCE — Data Circuit-Terminating Equipment, the equipment (for example, a modem) that provides communication between the DTE and the line radio equipment.

Digipeater — A link-level gateway station capable of repeating frames. The term "bridge" is used in industry.

Domain — In packet radio, the combination of a frequency and a geographical service area.

DTE — Data Terminal Equipment, for example a VDU or teleprinter.

DXE — In AX.25, Data Switching Equipment, a peer (neither master nor slave) station in balanced mode at the link layer.

EASTNET — A series of digipeaters along the U.S. East Coast.

EIA — Electronic Industries Association. (2001 Eye St., N.W., Washington, DC 20006.)

EIA-232-D — A standard physical-level interface between DTE (terminal) and DCE (modem), using 25-pin connectors.

Envelope-delay distortion — In a complex waveform, unequal propagation delay for different frequency components.

Equalization — Correction for amplitude-frequency and/or phase-frequency distortion.

Eye pattern — An oscilloscope display in the shape of one or more eyes for observing the shape of a serial digital stream and any impairments.

FADCA — Florida Amateur Digital Communications Association, c/o Gwyn Reedy, W1BEL, 812 Childers Loop, Brandon, FL 33511.

FCS — Frame Check Sequence. (See CRC.)

FEC — Forward Error Correction, an error-control technique in which the transmitted data is sufficiently redundant to permit the receiving station to correct some errors.

Field — In packet radio, at the link layer, a subdivision of a frame, consisting of one or more octets.

Flag — In packet switching, a link-level octet (01111110) used to initiate and terminate a frame.

Frame — In packet radio, a transmission block consisting of opening flag, address, control, information, frame-check-sequence and ending flag fields.

FSK — Frequency-Shift Keying.

Gateway — In packet radio, an interchange point.

HDLC — High-level Data Link Control Procedures as specified in ISO 3309.

Host — As used in packet radio, a computer with applications programs accessible by remote stations.

IA5 — International Alphabet Number 5, a 7-bit coded character set, CCITT version of ASCII.

Information field — Any sequence of bits containing the intelligence to be conveyed.

ISI — Intersymbol interference; slurring of one symbol into the next as a result of multipath propagation.

ISO — International Organization for Standardization.

ITA2 — International Telegraph Alphabet Number 2, a CCITT 5-bit coded character set commonly called the Baudot or Murray code.

JAS-1 — JAMSAT/JARL amateur satellite having packet-radio capability.

Jitter — Unwanted variations in amplitude or phase in a digital signal.

Key clicks — Unwanted transients beyond the necessary bandwidth of a keyed radio signal.

KSR — Keyboard Send-Receive teletypewriter.

LAP — Link Access Procedure, CCITT X.25 unbalanced-mode communications.

LAPB — Link Access Procedure, Balanced, CCITT X.25 balanced-mode communications.

Layer — In communications protocols, one of the strata or levels in a reference model.

Level 1 — Physical layer of the OSI reference model.

Level 2 — Link layer of the OSI reference model.

Level 3 — Network layer of the OSI reference model.

Level 4 — Transport layer of the OSI reference model.

Level 5 — Session layer of the OSI reference model.

Level 6 — Presentation layer of the OSI reference model.

Level 7 — Application layer of the OSI reference model.

Loopback — A test performed by connecting the output of a modulator to the input of a demodulator.

LSB — Least-significant bit.

Mode A — In AMTOR, an Automatic Repeat Request transmission method.

Mode B — In AMTOR, a Forward Error Correction transmission method.

Modem — Modulator-Demodulator, a device that connects between a data terminal and communication line (or radio). Also called Data Set.

MSB — Most-significant bit.

MSK — Frequency-shift keying where the shift in Hertz is equal to half the signaling rate in bits per second.

NAK — Negative Acknowledge. (opposite of ACK)

NAPLPS — ANSI X3.110-1983 Videotex/Teletext Presentation Level Protocol Syntax.

NBDP — Narrow-band direct-printing telegraphy.

NEPRA — New England Packet Radio Association, P.O. Box 15, Bedford, MA 01730.

Node — A point within a network, usually where two or more links come together, performing switching, routine and concentrating functions.

NRZI — Nonreturn to zero. A binary baseband code in which output transitions result from data 0s but not from 1s. Formal designation is NRZ-S (nonreturn-to-zero — space).

Null modem — A device to interconnect two devices both wired as DCEs or DTEs; in EIA RS-232-C interfacing, back-to-back DB25 connectors with pin-for-pin connections except that Received Data (pin 3) on one connector is wired to Transmitted Data (pin 3) on the other.

Octet — A group of eight bits.

OOK — On-off keying.

Originate — The station initiating a call. In modem usage, the *calling* station or modem tones associated therewith.

OSI-RM — Open Systems Interconnection Reference Model specified in ISO 7498 and CCITT Rec. X.200.

Packet Radio — A digital communications technique involving radio transmission of short bursts (frames) of data containing addressing, control and error-checking information in each transmission.

PACSAT — Proposed AMSAT packet-radio satellite with store-and-forward capability.

PAD — Packet Assembler/Disassembler, a device that assembles and disassembles packets (frames). It is connected between a data terminal (or computer) and a modem in a packet-radio station. (see also TNC)

Parity Check — Addition of noninformation bits to data, making the number of ones in a group of bits always either even or odd.

PID — Protocol identifier. Used in AX.25 to specify the network-layer protocol used.

PPRS — Pacific Packet Radio Society, P.O. Box 51562, Palo Alto, CA 94303.

Primary — The master station in a master-slave relationship; the master maintains control and is able to perform actions that the slave cannot. (Compare secondary.)

Protocol — A formal set of rules and procedures for the exchange of information within a network.

PSK — Phase-Shift Keying.

RAM — Random Access Memory.

Received Data — Physical-level signals generated by the DCE are sent to the DTE on this circuit. (abbreviated RxD)

Request to Send — Physical-level signal used to control the direction of data transmission of the local DCE. (abbreviated RTS)

RO — Receive-Only teletypewriter.

ROM — Read-Only Memory.

ROTR — Receive-Only Typing Reperforator Set.

Router — A network packet switch. In packet radio, a network-level relay station capable of routing packets.

RS-232-C — An EIA standard physical-level interface between DTE (terminal) and DCE (modem), using 25-pin connectors.

RTTY — Radioteletype.

Secondary — The slave in a master-slave relationship. Compare primary.

SOFTNET — An experimental packet-radio network at the University of Linköping, Sweden.

Source — In packet radio, the station transmitting the frame over a direct radio link or via a repeater.

SSID — Secondary Station Identifier. In AX.25 link-layer protocol, a multipurpose octet to identify several packet-radio stations operating under the same call sign.

SOUTHNET — A series of digipeaters along the U.S. Southeast Coast.

TAPR — Tucson Amateur Packet Radio Corporation, a nonprofit organization involved in packet-radio development (P.O. Box 22888, Tucson, AZ 85734).

TD — Tape Transmitter-Distributor Set, a paper tape reader.

Teleport — A radio station that acts as a relay between terrestrial radio stations and a communications satellite.

Teleprinter — Trademark of ITT/Creed. A printing teletypewriter.

Teletype — Trademark of the Teletype Corporation, usually used to refer to teletypewriters.

Teletypewriter — Generic term for printing telegraph equipment. (For specific types see ASR, KSR, RO, ROTR and TD.) (abbreviated TTY)

TNC — Terminal Node Controller, a device that assembles and disassembles packets (frames). (used interchangeably with PAD)

TR switch — Transmit-receive switch to allow automatic selection between receive and transmitter for one antenna.

Transmitted Data — Physical-level data signals transferred on a circuit from the DTE to the DCE. (abbreviated TxD)

TTY — Teletypewriter.

TU — Terminal Unit, a radioteletype modem or demodulator.

Turnaround time — The time required to reverse the direction of a half-duplex circuit, required by propagation, modem reversal and transmit-receive switching time of a transceiver.

UI — Unnumbered Information frame.

VADCG — Vancouver Amateur Digital Communications Group. (c/o Doug Lockhart, VE7APU, 9531 Odlin Rd., Richmond, BC V6X 1E1, Canada.)

VDT — Video-display terminal.

VDU — Video Display Unit, a device used to display data, usually provided with a keyboard for data entry.

Videotex — A presentation-layer protocol for two-way transmission of graphics.

Virtual Circuit — A mode of packet networking in which a logical connection that emulates a point-to-point circuit is established. (compare datagram)

V.24 — A CCITT standard defining physical-level interface circuits between a DTE (terminal) and DCE (modem), equivalent to EIA RS-232-C.

V.28 — A CCITT standard defining electrical characteristics for V.24 interface.

WESTNET — A series of digipeaters along the U.S. West Coast.

Window — In packet radio at the link layer, the range of frame numbers within the control field used to set the maximum number of frames that the sender may transmit before it receives an acknowledgment from the receiver.

X.25 — CCITT packet-switching protocol.

Chapter 20

Image Communications

Judging by the upsurge of amateur interest in systems that can send and receive pictures, many hams must be taking to heart the old Chinese proverb, "one picture is worth a thousand words." This, along with the availability of inexpensive video components, may explain why so many hams are motivated to use and experiment actively with systems capable of exchanging pictures.

There are three basic image communications systems in popular use by the amateur community. Each approach has unique features, capabilities and applications:

• *Fast-scan television (FSTV)*: Moving pictures are displayed on a standard TV set; includes sound. Its performance is similar to commercial broadcast TV pictures. It is used predominately in the UHF bands (70 and 23 cm) to provide local area coverage.

• *Slow-scan television (SSTV)*: Low-resolution still pictures are displayed on a standard TV set. Used in the HF bands, it provides worldwide coverage.

• *Facsimile (FAX)*: High-resolution still picture produced on paper or photographic film. It is used for weather-satellite reception and in the HF bands to provide worldwide coverage.

The recent amateur interest in image communications essentially reflects the current video orientation of our society. This is evidenced by the huge sales of home consumer items such as color TV sets, video cassette recorders, TV cameras, video games and computer graphics displays. Many of these consumer devices can be used in your shack as a foundation for building a complete amateur image communications system.

Fast-Scan Amateur Television

Fast-scan TV (FSTV), also referred to simply as amateur television (ATV), uses a transmission format fully compatible with video equipment designed for the home consumer market. The video is amplitude modulated; the audio is frequency modulated. Each video frame consists of 525 horizontal lines with 30 frames transmitted each second. (See Chapter 7 for more details on the scanning process.) Translated into simple terms, this means that an FSTV picture displays full motion, has a simultaneous sound channel, can be in color and has excellent detail just like commercial TV pictures.

Amateur television offers a major advantage over broadcast TV, though, and that is rooted in our ability to communicate interactively or two ways. Amateur television people have been communicating in round table nets for many years — long before industry discovered the benefits of interactive video or, as it's called, "teleconferencing."

Because the signals occupy several megahertz of bandwidth, the FCC does not permit FSTV on bands below 420 MHz. Most ATV is performed in the 420- to 440-MHz and 1240- to 1294-MHz segments of the 70- and 23-cm bands. Some ATV activity can be found in the 902-928 MHz band. These frequencies generally limit FSTV range to line of sight with extended

Fig. 1 — Fast-scan ATV station assembled using circuits described in this chapter plus a home-video camera and standard TV set.

coverage possible when ducting conditions exist or repeaters are used.

A Technician class or higher license is required to transmit FSTV below 1240 MHz. Novices may operate ATV in the 1270-1295 MHz portion of the 23-cm band. All you need is a home-video type camera, microphone, ATV transmitter and antenna. Depending on your application, a personal computer terminal or video tape recorder can be used instead of a camera. You don't even have to provide external synchronization. Sync pulses are part of the composite video signal from the camera, video cassette recorder or computer. No

modification to these devices is necessary.

To receive, all you need is an antenna, RF converter (also called a downconverter, it shifts the received signal to a standard VHF TV channel) and an unmodified home TV set. No scan converters are required. The basic elements of a fast-scan ATV station are shown in Fig. 1.

In keeping with the ham tradition for both public service and inventiveness in communications, ATVers have been using their live action video systems in many exciting applications. For example, the Southern California ATVers annually help coordinate and monitor the Tournament of Roses Parade and local marathons. During the Christmas season, amateurs have taken their systems into hospitals to permit children to see and talk with Santa Claus over live TV. Warren Weldon, W5DFU, uses his ATV cameras on a tall tower to search the Oklahoma skies for "killer tornadoes" while transmitting the pictures directly to the Weather Service to provide a valuable early-warning capability. Amateurs have transmitted ATV from Civil Air Patrol airplanes and even hot-air balloons. ATV has also been used in radio-controlled model airplanes and robots to provide the necessary feedback to aid the operator. Most recently, the FCC has permitted ATVers to retransmit the spectacular Space Shuttle video provided on

Fig. 2 — Aft end of STS-9 Shuttle cargo bay as seen via fast-scan ATV.

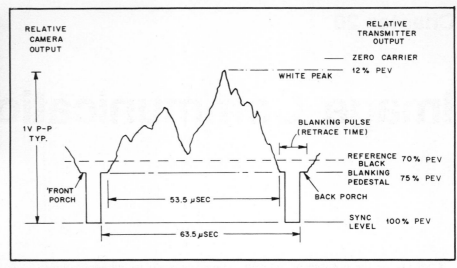

Fig. 3 — TV Waveform. Camera and corresponding transmitter RF output power levels during one horizontal line scan for black-and-white TV. (A color camera would generate a "burst" of 8 cycles at 3.58 MHz on the back porch of the blanking pedestal.) Note that "black" corresponds to a higher transmitter output power than "white."

NASA's public information channel on Satcom 1R (Fig. 2).

On a day-to-day basis, there are many down-to-earth uses for ATV. You can show off your shack, your family, home movies, video tapes and travel slides. You do run the risk of putting fellow ATV watchers to sleep! Some amateurs exchange video tape copies of their contacts with hams in other countries.

Your home computer system and ATV station make an ideal marriage. By simply taking the video output of your home computer into the video input of your ATV transmitter, the computer may be used to show still and animated graphics, teach computer programming and debugging, repeat W1AW RTTY bulletins and display bulletin-board messages. Serial data can also be placed on the TV sound subcarrier for exchanging computer programs.

Since ATVers share the bands with other types of emissions and amateur interests, frequencies have evolved through formal frequency-coordination organizations that minimize mutual interference to all band users in any given area. Before you start transmitting, check with local ATVers and the *ARRL Repeater Directory*. The *Repeater Directory* also lists your area frequency-coordination committee.

TV Waveforms

Thanks to the availability of off-the-shelf cameras, and receiving converters that preclude the need to perform surgery on your home TV set, it is not necessary to understand the inner workings of a camera or TV set. It is only necessary for you to know what the waveform at the output of a camera, computer or video tape recorder will look like to help you adjust your ATV station properly.

Fig. 3 shows what a single horizontal line of video looks like at the camera and transmitter output. Two basic elements can be seen in the waveform: the synchronization pulses and the video.

• Synchronization pulses — These are used in the TV receiver to synchronize the CRT electron beam scan with that of the camera (see Chapter 7). Although only "horizontal" pulses are shown in the figure, there are also "vertical" pulses,

which occur 60 times a second to ensure that the top of the received picture lines up properly with the top of image as seen by the camera. It is only important for you to know that the proper amplitude of these synchronization pulses must be maintained in the transmission process. The transmitter and linear amplifier must be adjusted properly to ensure that the sync is not overly compressed or clipped.

• Video — Between the synchronization pulses lies the video information that controls the intensity of the beam as it scans across the receiver picture tube. The signal level determines whether an individual picture element (pixel) shall be white, black or a given shade of gray. This concept is shown in Figs. 4 and 5.

Color TV is more complicated than black-and-white TV. The transmitting and receiving equipment is the same for black and white transmission, except that a color camera and TV receiver are required. The corresponding frequency spectrum of the color TV signal is shown in Fig. 6.

A brief discussion of color TV can be found in Chapter 7. An excellent source of more complete information on the basics of both monochrome and color television techniques may be found in the book *Television Handbook for the Amateur* by Biagio Presti. See the bibliography at the end of this section.

FSTV System Elements

As previously emphasized, standard, unmodified, off-the-shelf video components are used to generate and display the ATV pictures. A block diagram of a typical FSTV station is shown in Fig. 7. The most important part of the system is the antenna and coax. Since vegetation greatly attenuates UHF signals, mounting the antenna above tree tops is highly desirable. DX

Fig. 4 — The video signal resulting from viewing a gray-scale pattern ranging from black to white level.

Fig. 5 — A single line of the TV picture at A has its voltage waveform shown at B.

Fig. 6 — Frequency spectrum of a color TV signal shown in diagram at (A) and on a spectrum analyzer at (B). Each vertical division represents 10 dB; horizontal divisions are 1 MHz. Spectrum power density will vary with picture content, but typically 90% of sideband power is within the first megahertz.

Fig. 7 — Fast-scan ATV station.

will vary with terrain, trees and temperature inversion characteristics (ducting). Because the bandwidth of an FSTV system is considerably wider than a narrow-band voice circuit operating on the same frequency at the same power level, it is necessary to compensate for the accompanying decrease in received signal-to-noise by using relatively high-gain antennas, low-loss transmission lines and low-noise preamplifiers. One should not compare ATV performance with UHF broadcast TV reception. Commercial and public stations transmit a million, or more, watts of effective radiated power. Amateurs use considerably lower power levels, of course.

Antennas

The antenna must have both high gain and broad bandwidth. For the home-brew enthusiast, the 15-element quagi is popular (see Chapter 33). The MBM48/70 J Beam and several KLM models are good, high-gain, commercially constructed beams that are specially designed for broadband work. For portable applications, a small Yagi antenna, or omnidirectional antennas such as the AEA Isopole are used.

Polarization used by ATVers varies throughout the country. In general, most DX operations use horizontal, while most repeaters use vertical polarization. Check with local ATVers to determine the polarization used in your area before setting up an antenna.

Transmission Line

At 420 MHz, cable loss can be quite high, especially for long cable runs. Types such as RG-58 are very lossy at UHF (15-dB loss/100 feet at 420 MHz) and are not used for ATV work except for short equipment interconnects in the shack. Up to 50 feet, RG-8, -213 or -214 (5 dB/100 ft) are acceptable, but for longer runs, ½-inch Hardline such as Phelps-Dodge PD-FX 12-50H (2.1 dB/100 ft) or low-loss coax such as Belden 8214, Belden 9913, Belden 9914, or Saxton 8285 (3.8 dB/100 ft) is recommended. The exception to this is when the receive preamp can be mast-mounted at the antenna. The type of connector used (UHF or N) is not as important as proper installation and weatherproofing.

Receiver

The purpose of the receive converter is to shift the UHF signal to a frequency that is tunable on a standard TV set. The output is fed into the VHF antenna terminals on the set. No modification to the TV is required.

A preamplifier may be included as part of the converter or as a separate mast-mounted unit. The use of GaAsFET front ends for preamps, by virtue of their wide dynamic input range and related immunity from self-generated intermodulation components, has reduced the requirements for filtering ahead of the preamp. A popular commercial preamp for ATV use is Advanced Receiver Research model P432VDG.

Video Transmitter

A video transmitter is very similar in design to a UHF FM voice transmitter except that the constant dc voltage on the final RF amplifier stage is replaced with the amplitude-varying output of a video modulator to produce amplitude modulation. The principle is identical to plate (or collector) modulation prevalent in the pre-SSB era.

The transmitter is modulated with the video and synchronization signals provided by a camera. The modulator gain must be adjusted to provide the proper modulation level. Too little gain will produce a picture lacking contrast; too much gain may cause the picture to "white out" or clip off sync. Proper set-up of modulation level is just as important as transmitter power level. A strong received signal exhibiting poor contrast may look worse than a weak signal with excellent contrast. The modulator must have the bandwidth to pass the 3.58-MHz color-burst signal provided by the camera and for a 4.5-MHz sound subcarrier. Most solid-state UHF transmitters have output matching circuits that pass the wide-bandwidth ATV signals.

Power Amplification

To increase the power output from the video transmitter, a linear amplifier is used. Tube amplifiers generally provide better linearity than solid-state units, while solid-state amplifiers tend to have broader bandwidths.

Proper sync-to-video ratio and picture linearity are the main concerns when using a high-power transistor amplifier. A sync stretcher in the video modulator is used to compensate for gain compression (nonlinearity at high power levels) typically found in solid-state amplifiers. By exaggerating the sync level at the amplifier input, the proper sync-to-video relationship will result at the amplifier output as shown in Fig. 8. Transistor amplifiers, by virtue of their low loaded Qs, have sufficient bandwidth for ATV. This is generally not the case with

Fig. 8 — Oscilloscope used to observe the video waveform. The lower trace is the video signal as it comes out of the sync stretcher. The upper trace is the signal from the Mirage D1010-N amplifier.

tube amplifiers. At UHF, many tetrode high-power amps using 4CX250-type tubes have too high a loaded Q at the grid and plate to pass the color and sound subcarriers without significant attenuation. This can be overcome by control-grid modulation of the final stage and increased loading of the plate circuit. Grounded-grid triodes like the 7289 are less bandwidth restrictive in the linear mode because of the lower impedances associated with cathode drive. However, direct cathode modulation is usually preferred and much simpler. Sync stretching is normally not necessary with tube amplifiers, as their linearity is excellent.

For more discussion on the special considerations for linear amplifiers used in a television role, see "The Care and Feeding of Linear Amplifiers for ATV," *QST*, August 1982, p. 24.

Audio Transmission Techniques

Sound can be transmitted on FSTV using two main approaches. One method is to FM audio modulate the AM video carrier frequency. This permits a rather simple transmitter design, but the penalty is paid at the receiving end since a standard TV will not be able to pick up the audio. A separate FM receiver, tuned to the video frequency, must be used to recover the audio.

A more popular approach is to provide FM audio at a frequency 4.5 MHz above the video carrier using a separate transmitter or using a subcarrier generator that feeds the input of the video modulator. The advantage of this approach is that no separate receiver is required since a conventional TV set includes the circuitry to demodulate the 4.5-MHz subcarrier.

In addition to either technique, a separate 2-meter circuit has proven highly beneficial for talk back and coordination. By using 2 meters to establish a full-duplex audio link, the receiving station can provide valuable picture-quality reports to the TV transmitting station. Also, a casual 2-meter listener is intrigued when hearing the comments about a picture that cannot be seen on 2 meters, and is surprised to even

find out that there is ATV activity in the area. Many 2-meter enthusiasts have been drawn into ATV in this manner.

ATV Repeaters

There are two types of ATV repeaters on the air. Most are in-band machines with input and output in the 70-cm band. The other type of repeater is cross band. The input is in the 70-cm band and the output is in the 23-cm band. Exact frequencies are listed in the *ARRL Repeater Directory*. Cross band has an advantage of full-duplex monitoring of the received repeater video since receive system desense, a normal problem with in-band repeaters, is virtually eliminated. This allows an operator to make picture adjustments without relying on descriptions from other station operators.

Vertical polarization is predominant for repeater antennas because it is much easier to build or purchase commercial high-gain omnidirectional vertical antennas than horizontal types. Also it is easier for communication with mobile units which almost exclusively use vertical whip antennas.

To conserve transmitted signal bandwidth and prevent receiver desense, ATV repeaters use vestigial sideband, which is also used in commercial broadcasting. A filter at the output of the transmitter is used to suppress the lower sideband beyond 1.25 MHz while allowing up to 4.75 MHz on the upper sideband. This creates an ATV signal with 6-MHz bandwidth. Filtering can be accomplished using an interdigital filter of the type described by Fisher, "Interdigital Bandpass Filters for Amateur VHF/UHF Applications," *QST*, March 1968. (A commercially built interdigital filter is available from Spectrum International, model PSF-ATV.) Filtering can also be performed using a group of cavities tuned to provide a flat low-loss response over several megahertz but having very sharp skirts to perform the necessary out-of-band attenuation. (Such a multicavity filter is commercially available from TX-RX Systems Inc., model 19-66-79154-2.)

Amateur TV repeater design is described in more detail in Brown, "The WR4AAG ATV Repeater," *QST*, October 1975, p. 98; also Pasternak/Morris, *The Practical Handbook of Amateur Radio FM and Repeaters*, Tab Books, 1980; and *Everything You Always Wanted To Know About Amateur Television*, QCD Publications.

Constructing a Basic ATV System

An ATV station can be assembled using four basic circuit boards. (These boards may be purchased built and tested from PC Electronics, 2522 S. Paxson La., Arcadia, CA 91006.) This approach will enable the transmission and reception of full-color television with sound.

Shown in Figs. 9 through 12, all boards run from a common 13.8-V dc, 3 A regulated power source. The complete system can be mounted in a 12 × 8 × 3 inch

chassis. At the builder's option, the receive converter and TR relay can be mounted at the antenna in an outside weatherproof electrical box and controlled from the transmitter location.

Shielded connections between modules are made with the small RG-174 50-ohm coax. At UHF, the center conductor of the coax should not be more than ¼ inch past the shield for all board connections to minimize SWR and radiation. Power and signal connections are made with no. 24 vinyl-covered wire except to the 10-watt power module, which is no. 18.

RECEIVING PREAMP AND CONVERTER

The converter, shown in Fig. 10, tunes the 420- to 450-MHz band and shifts the received signal to TV Channel 3 (video carrier at 61.25 MHz) or Channel 2 or 4 if Channel 3 is used in your area. Trimmer capacitor, C3, which sets the varactor-diode-controlled oscillator range, sets the received frequency. The lead length from the board to the 10-kΩ frequency-tuning pot is not critical. This allows remote tuning if desired. The board, however, must be in a shielded enclosure to minimize stray pickup of unwanted adjacent TV channels.

A Mini-Circuits Lab SBL-1 doubly balanced mixer module is followed by an 80-MHz low-pass filter to reduce intermodulation from other strong signals. Ahead of the mixer is a low-noise MRF901 or NE64535 preamp stage. The MRF901 has a typical noise figure of 1.7 dB with 15-dB gain, while the NE64535 exhibits a 0.9-dB NF and 18-dB gain.

Coaxial cable with an impedance of 75 ohms is recommended to connect the unit to the TV-set VHF antenna input. Twin lead can act as an antenna bringing in strong adjacent-channel interference.

To align the converter, preset the three trimmer capacitors and the 10-kΩ VCO pot to their center positions. Set the 5-kΩ preamp transistor bias pot for 0.5-volt drop across the 100-Ω collector resistor if the MRF901 is used, or 0.8 volt with the NE64535. Have a nearby ATV station transmit a picture to you or use a signal generator. Use an insulated tuning tool to carefully adjust C3 for best reception of the signal. Watch your TV set as you adjust C3. You may find reception possible in two positions — one on the high side of the local oscillator injection frequency, the other on the low side. You want the low side. To do this, select the position with the most capacity on C3 (plates meshed). Next, fine tune with the 10-kΩ pot for best picture and finally peak C1 and C2.

TRANSMITTING CIRCUITS

Three circuit boards are used to transmit video and sound at approximately 12-watts PEP output. The exciter/modulator generates 80 milliwatts of AM, which drives a sealed broad-band power module.

Fig. 9 — ATV system-interconnection and power-supply schematic diagram using circuit board designs described in the text. See also Figs. 10, 11 and 12. The boards are also available fully built from P. C. Electronics. Output from the converter connects to a standard TV set. Video input is from a standard 1-volt peak-to-peak, 75-ohm source such as camera, video tape recorder or computer.

Fig. 10 — The circuit of the ATV receiving converter (TVC-1b) consists of a low-noise, high-gain RF amplifier, a doubly balanced mixer and a varicap-tuned VCO. Remote tuning of the converter permits it to be mounted at the antenna if desired. Variable capacitors are Arco 400, 1-10 pF, or equiv. L1 consists of a horseshoe-shaped loop of no. 18 wire, 4.5-inches long and 0.75 inch wide. Loop ends are soldered to a ground plane; a right-angle bend 0.5 inch from the grounded ends causes the rest of the loop to be parallel to the ground plane. Taps are made 0.75 inch from the ends. L2 consists of 1½ turns of no. 18 wire, 0.375-inch diameter, tapped at 0.5 inch from the lower end. L3 is a hairpin loop, 0.5 inch across the bottom and 0.625 inch high. It is made with no. 18 bus wire.

Fig. 11 — Diagram of the ATV exciter (TXA5). Variable capacitors are Arco 400, 1- to 10-pF, or equiv. All coils are wound from no. 24 bus wire, using a 10-24 screw for a winding form. Coupled coil pairs are placed 1/16 inch apart. Each stage is tuned with a voltmeter monitoring and peaking the next stage's emitter voltage. If peaked correctly, the voltages should be at or above those noted at each emitter. The 1-kΩ blanking pedestal bias pot is backed down to give 75% of the maximum unmodulated RF power output for proper video to sync ratio setup.

Another module generates the 4.5-MHz sound subcarrier.

The exciter/modulator, shown in Fig. 11, contains a fifth overtone crystal oscillator in the 100-MHz range. Following the oscillator are two doublers, the last of which is collector modulated along with the final. The bypass capacitors are chosen to remove 400-MHz energy but not attenuate the video below 8 MHz. This gives high-resolution and color even for 64-character-per-line computer video. The pedestal bias pot controls the blanking clamp level and

sets the proper video-to-sync ratio. A sync stretcher in the modulator circuit is used to compensate for nonlinearities in the final amplifier module. The stretcher circuit pulls the applied voltage on the modulated stages up to almost full V_{cc} during sync times. This is necessary since the input-vs.-output characteristic curves of UHF transistor amplifiers generally show gain compression in their upper power range. Typically, the last 3-dB increase in power output takes 6 dB of input power increase. Without sync stretching to compensate,

power output would have to be set to less than half the rated capability to maintain sync level and picture stability at the receiver.

The power amplifier consists of an MHW 710-2 or Amprex BGY41B power module with a heat sink and printed-circuit board for the line filtering parts (Fig. 9). Filtering of V_{cc} at the RF amplifier module under video modulation is critical. The supply impedance must be very low at video frequencies up to 5 MHz where the resistance and inductance of the supply

Fig. 12 — This ATV sound-subcarrier generator (FM-A5) permits both voice and video to be transmitted. U1 is either a National LF353N or Texas Instruments TL082CP. The MV2115 is a Motorola varicap of 100 pF at 4 volts.

leads are significant. The power modules are designed for 15 watts using FM, and are sufficiently linear for ATV.

The subcarrier sound generator, shown in Fig. 12, has a high-gain dynamic microphone amplifier consisting of a dual-section, FET-input op amp and soft limiter. A second input is used for mixing high-level audio from a VCR or color camera microphone. A 4.5-MHz oscillator is varactor modulated by the output of the audio amplifier. The deviation is fixed at 25 kHz by soft limiting back-to-back diodes. The 1-kΩ pot on the emitter follower adjusts the sound subcarrier injection level. The sound subcarrier is usually set about 15 dB below the video carrier level. This corresponds to around midpoint on the pot or 0.5 volt P-P on a scope. Too much injection will give a beat pattern in a color picture, and not enough will give a low audio level. The oscillator frequency should be set by adjusting the 18-μH inductor slug to within 3 kHz of 4.5 MHz using a counter connected to the 1-kΩ pot output.

Transmitter Tuning

Tune-up requires a voltmeter, UHF RF power meter and a low-SWR antenna or dummy load. Adjust each trimmer on the exciter/modulator board for peak emitter voltage on the following stage. There should be no video or subcarrier connected during the RF tune up. Set the pedestal clamp bias pot for maximum voltage on the emitter of the 2N2219A modulator transistor. When some power is indicated by the wattmeter, carefully peak C6 and C7 followed by C4 and C5 for maximum power. With 13.8-V dc, the PEP output should be at least 10 watts. To establish the proper video-to-sync ratio (Fig. 8), reduce the measured power output by 75% by adjusting the pedestal bias pot. For example, if the maximum power output is 12 watts, the blanking pedestal power setting should be adjusted for a 9-watt output. The sync stretcher will pull the power back up to 12 watts during sync time when video is applied. An average-reading wattmeter has little significance when measuring video-modulated RF since the reading will fluctuate greatly depending upon video gain setting, camera setup and image content. As previously described, the wattmeter reading is valid for adjusting the blanking pedestal and determining the PEP level with no video applied.

Connect any source of composite video (typically 1 volt peak-to-peak) to the input and adjust the 100-Ω video-gain pot for best picture at another ATVer's location, preferably at least 1 mile away. Picture monitoring on a TV set in your own shack can give a false indication due to overload and reflections. Use of a two-meter talk-back channel and a distant viewer will facilitate a rapid and accurate adjustment. It is best to use a scene or display with lots of white for proper modulation depth adjustment. Increase the gain until the white areas begin to smear; then back off until the smearing stops. Overmodulation will cut off the carrier during white areas of the picture causing undesirable buzzing in the received audio.

Proper video-to-sync ratio and picture linearity are major concerns when adding a high-power transistor linear amplifier, such as the Mirage D1010N. Setup is basically similar to that previously described using the 10-watt PEP module. However, the blanking pedestal pot should be adjusted for an output not exceeding 75 watts even though 100 watts is possible. With 75 watts measured at the amplifier output, the drive power to the final amplifier will be about 4 watts. The sync stretcher will still put the sync tip at over 10 watts drive to compensate for the high-power amplifier gain compression. The end result is to provide a 100-watt sync tip and the proper video-to-sync ratio at the amplifier output as shown in Fig 8.

FSTV Bibliography

Presti, *Television Handbook for the Amateur*, Aptron Labs, 1978; Available from QCD Publications, PO Box H, Lowden, IA 52255-0408.

Everything You Always Wanted To Know About Amateur Television, 3rd Edition, 1982, QCD Publications.

SPEC-COM, QCD Publications.

Brown and Wood, *Amateur Television Handbook Volume 1*, 1981, British Amateur Television Club

Brown, *Amateur Television Handbook Volume 2*, 1982, British Amateur Television Club

Frequency-Modulated Amateur Television (FMTV)

In the previous section, we described the use of amplitude modulation for fast-scan television. Another method just beginning to make inroads into the amateur community is frequency-modulated (fast-scan) television (FMTV). There are performance advantages possible with FMTV.

In the U.S., FMTV is used above 420 MHz, with the majority of activity found in the 1240-1260 MHz segment of the 24-cm band. Despite the additional path losses encountered at these higher frequencies, excellent performance can be achieved because of (1) the overall processing gain advantages afforded by FM; (2) the ability to use relatively compact high-gain antennas; and (3) the availability of interference-free channels.

Frequency-modulated television offers several exciting opportunities for amateurs to experiment with new modulation enhancement techniques, and also motivates fresh exploration into the relatively untouched microwave regions. In this section, the primary focus will be on 24-cm operation; however, the FMTV principles can be readily transferred to the higher-frequency bands.

History

The concept of transmitting fast-scan television pictures via FM is not exactly new. In fact, the possibilities of using FM for television were suggested as early as 1929.[1] The first quantitative analysis was reported in 1940 and was immediately followed by hardware development focused on using FM to relay commercial broadcast television between cities.[2,3,4] During World War II, the military sponsored research into FMTV and in the late 40s

FCC investigated FMTV for possible application in commercial UHF broadcasting.[5] During the 1950s and 60s research continued into various techniques such as pre-emphasis and de-emphasis, improved limiter and discriminator designs, and extensive investigations into bandwidth requirements. In the late 60s and early 70s interest in FMTV heightened as it became the primary mode for transmitting television through communications satellites and also in terrestrial communication applications for sending pictures from commercial news-gathering remote units back to their TV stations.[6]

In the amateur world, European hams have been at the forefront of FMTV experimentation and equipment development. Virtually all commercially-built amateur FMTV equipment is produced in Europe, with patches of FMTV just beginning to sprout in the United States.

24-cm FMTV Transmitters

The two basic techniques for generating a 24-cm FMTV signal are shown in Fig. 13. One method is to use a varactor to triple the amplified signal from a voltage-controlled 416-433 MHz oscillator that has been video modulated. The other approach is to simply amplify the output from a video-modulated 24-cm VCO. In either case, a standard composite video signal provided from a TV camera, video tape machine or computer is processed through a pre-emphasis filter which accentuates the high video frequencies to improve the overall system signal-to-noise ratio. The video signal is then combined with an audio subcarrier signal, typically at 5.8 or

6.0 MHz. With AM FSTV, the audio subcarrier is at 4.5 MHz. Experimentation has shown that a higher subcarrier frequency is required for good FMTV per-

(A)

(B)

Fig. 14 — FMTV transmitter components using a varactor tripler technique. At A, a Wood & Douglas 416-MHz voltage-controlled oscillator (UFM01) is used to drive a 10-W UHF amplifier (70LIN10). At B, a varactor tripler is used to produce approximately 3 W at 24 cm. This technique requires an external audio subcarrier generator and video pre-emphasis circuit. The boards are available fully assembled but require mounting and heat sinking.

Fig. 13 — Two methods of generating a 24-cm FMTV signal.

Fig. 15 — This 1-W FMTV transmitter kit from Solent Scientific employs a 24-cm VCO and amplifier. The design includes an on-board audio subcarrier generator and video pre-emphasis filter. The output may be amplified to 8 W using an optional power amplifier kit.

Fig. 16 — This experimental 24-cm transmitter from Wood and Douglas uses a phase-locked loop and reference crystal oscillator for precise frequency stability. The unit which produces a 20-mW output, has a built-in audio subcarrier generator but does not use video pre-emphasis.

formance. The audio subcarrier design shown in Fig. 13 can be easily set on 5.8 or 6.0 MHz for this purpose. The amplitude-varying signal, consisting of the FM audio riding the video envelope, controls the frequency of a voltage-controlled oscillator to generate the video FM signal. The signal is amplified (and tripled, if it was originally generated in the lower portion of the 400-MHz band) and then transmitted. Figs. 14, 15 and 16 show FMTV hardware using both transmission techniques.

24-cm FMTV Receivers

While a 24-cm FM transmitter is really not much more complicated than an AM transmitter, this is not the case with the receiver. The additional complexity in the receiver design is readily apparent in the block diagram in Fig. 17. For AM FSTV, it was only necessary to employ a converter which could produce a signal in the frequency range that could be tuned by a standard TV set. The TV possessed all of the necessary circuitry to demodulate the video and audio. With FM, much of this circuitry must be provided external to the TV set.

A converter, like the one shown in Fig. 18, is used to translate the signal to an intermediate frequency. Depending on the receiver design, the IF may be anywhere from 45 to 70 MHz. Typically, a phase-locked loop or doubly-balanced mixer is used as a discriminator to demodulate the signal to baseband video where the audio subcarrier is removed and further demodulated to baseband audio. This function is usually contained on an IF/video demodulator board, as shown in Fig. 19. The video portion is de-emphasized (high noise component attenuated) and made available for display on a video

Fig. 18 — This Wood and Douglas 24-cm to VHF converter (1250DC50) is fully built and packaged.

Fig. 19 — This Wood and Douglas video IF board (VIDIF) is used to demodulate the signal at the IF to baseband video. An external subcarrier demodulator and de-emphasis unit is required, and the board requires mounting in a suitable enclosure, as shown.

monitor. A Channel 3 or 4 RF modulator may be used to upconvert the baseband audio and video signals into a format viewable on a standard TV set.

Fig. 17 — Block diagram of an FMTV receiving system.

Fig. 20 — Two approaches to 24-cm FMTV receiver design. The design at A uses components designed for amateur use. At B, a modified 70-MHz satellite TV IF strip is used. See text.

Fig. 21 — This complete 24-cm FMTV receiver contains a preamplifier, converter, video IF strip, audio subcarrier demodulator, video de-emphasis filter and 12-V power supply.

Two possible receiver configurations based on commercially-available equipment are shown in Fig. 20. A complete 24-cm FMTV receiver corresponding to the Fig. 20A design is shown in Fig. 21. The schematic for the sound-subcarrier demodulator is shown in Fig. 22 while the circuit for the de-emphasis network will be described later in the text.

It is of interest to note that the operation of the FMTV receiver is almost identical to that used for home satellite TV reception except for the lower microwave carrier frequency and lower FM deviation levels typically used by amateurs operating in the 24-cm band. The 70-MHz satellite TV IF strips that are just beginning to become available on the surplus market can be

adapted for amateur use. If the strip is to be used on 24 cm to receive a nominal 4-MHz peak deviation signal, there are two basic modifications that are required. First, the surface acoustic wave (SAW) bandpass filter in the IF, typically exhibiting a 28 MHz bandpass, must be changed to one 12 to 16 MHz wide to better match the lower bandwidth occupied by amateur signals. This will improve sensitivity and reduce interference. Secondly, the overall gain of the discriminator and/or video amplifier circuits must be increased to compensate for the substantially lower amateur deviation levels to maintain the 1 V peak to peak video output needed for driving a standard TV monitor. If the strip is to be used to receive a signal exhibiting an 8-12 MHz deviation, which may be more common with 10-GHz operation, no modification will be required.

There are some satellite units called "block receivers" that directly cover the 950-1450 MHz range. At first glance, it would seem that this receiver would be ideal for amateurs since it could directly tune across the 24-cm amateur band; however, experimentation has shown that this receiver class has very poor sensitivity. (In normal satellite applications, the receiver depends on a high-gain, low-noise front end to convert the 3.7-4.2 GHz satellite band to 950-1450 MHz.) Unless a very high-gain and low noise figure pre-amplifier, along with a 12 to 16 MHz wide 24-cm bandpass filter, can be used at its front end, this type of receiver is not recommended.

24-cm Antennas and Transmission Line

Generally, the main requirement for an antenna system is that it must possess sufficient bandwidth to support FMTV. Most commercial and homebrew designs are adequate as long as they are cut for

Fig. 22 — Schematic diagram of an audio subcarrier demodulator circuit that converts 5.8-6.8 MHz audio subcarrier to baseband audio.

resonance at the transmit carrier frequency. A very popular antenna for ATV use world-wide is the French-built F9FT or TONNA antenna shown in Fig. 23. It is available built for three different frequencies: 1296, 1269 and 1248 MHz. Another possibility is the loop Yagi described in Chapter 32.

Transmission line losses at 24 cm can be quite formidable. If it is not possible to mount the receiver preamplifier, transmitter power amp or varactor tripler directly at the antenna mast, very low-loss transmission line must be used. For long runs, 7/8-inch Hardline (2.1 dB attenuation per 100 feet for foam dielectric and 1.5 dB/100 feet for air dielectric) should be used. For shorter lengths, ½-inch Hardline (3.5 dB attenuation per 100 feet for foam dielectric and 2.9 dB for air) or Belden 9913 (4.6 dB/100 feet) can be used. For very short hookups between equipment in the shack, ¼-inch foam dielectric, flexible Hardline (7 dB/100 feet) is ideal, but RG-8/-214 (12 dB/100 ft) or RG-58 (22 dB/100 feet) can be used as a more practical, cost-effective alternative.

Test Equipment

Good low-cost test equipment for 24 cm is generally scarce. One exception is the availability of 24-cm test generators that produce a video-modulated signal in the 10-80 mW range. Fig. 24 shows some commercially available units. These devices are not only invaluable in checking out FMTV receivers, but are also small enough to be built into a camera or installed in model airplanes to provide a compact mobile transmit capability over short ranges. For measuring frequencies in the 24-cm band, the Ramsey PS-10B prescaler has proven to be a highly cost-effective adjunct to a low-frequency counter.

Comparison of 24-cm FM-ATV with 70-cm FSTV

Given some of the apparent complexities of FM and some of the drawbacks of transmission on frequencies above 1 GHz, why use FMTV rather than stick with the venerable AM FSTV using readily available 70-cm gear? To fully examine the pros and cons of these systems, it is useful to first examine the relative merits of FM versus AM video and then compare 24-versus 70-cm propagation. Finally, we will look at the combined picture.

FM versus AM TV

A comparison between these two modulation modes has been the subject of university research and numerous studies in industry and the military. The specific advantages of FM television include:
• Better linearity and greater average transmitted power. Amplifiers can be operated in class-C mode and operated at full power using FM. Thus it is possible to obtain two to three times greater average output from a solid state amplifier oper-

Fig. 23 — The F9FT TONNA antenna is popular worldwide for FMTV work. Versions are available for 1248, 1269 and 1296 MHz.

(A)

(B)

Fig. 24 — 24-cm video test generators are helpful for checking out receivers. The 10-mW transmitter shown at A is fully built and packaged by Solent Scientific. The 80-mW transmitter board from PC Electronics, shown at B, requires an additional video inverter board to obtain the proper transmitted signal polarity.

ating in FM rather than AM. Another advantage is that sync compression, which is a common malady with improperly adjusted AM systems, is not a major problem when communicating with FMTV. These systems are therefore very easy to initially set up and operate.
• Signal-to-noise ratio improvement at demodulator output. With amplitude-modulated systems, the resulting video output signal-to-noise ratio will generally be the same as the receiver input carrier-to-noise ratio. In the case of FM, the video output signal-to-noise ratio will be significantly greater than the input carrier-to-noise ratio. The actual level depends on the input carrier-to-noise ratio being above a

"threshold level," typically 7-12 dB, and also on the value of the deviation index (the ratio of the peak deviation to the highest modulating frequency). Several studies have specifically examined the gain advantages that FM can provide over AM television.[7-10] Additional studies have examined tradeoffs of various parameters such as bandwidth and deviation to further optimize system performance.[11-16]
• Increased signal-to-noise performance through pre-emphasis and de-emphasis. As is shown in Fig. 6B, the high-frequency components of a video signal are considerably lower in amplitude than the low-frequency components. These higher frequencies, therefore, contribute very little to the overall transmitted bandwidth. Studies and analyses have demonstrated that it is useful to emphasize these higher-frequency components prior to transmission and then de-emphasize them at the receiver to restore the signal to its original composition.[17-20] While performing this de-emphasis, the higher-frequency components of the noise are attenuated, which effectively increases signal-to-noise ratio. (A good discussion of the overall concept of pre-emphasis and de-emphasis can be found in Reference 21.)
• Improved co-channel interference immunity. Studies have clearly demonstrated that FM television is more resistant than AM to a wide variety of interference sources.[22-24]
• Immunity from fading. Because the FM receiver uses hard limiting, any amplitude variations in the received signal caused by flutter normally associated with ATV mobile operations are reduced. This greater immunity from fast fading provides more solidly locked pictures.

Of course, with every set of advantages, you can always expect some disadvantages. The specific disadvantages of FMTV are:
• Equipment complexity. As previously described, the receiving equipment is more complex and expensive than that required to receive AM.
• Greater signal bandwidth. The transmitted signal bandwidth is greater than for vestigial AM FSTV. The microwave frequencies that can accommodate this bandwidth exhibit greater propagation losses.
• Poor weak-signal performance. FMTV performance for very weak signals will be worse than AM because of the FM receiver threshold effect.
• Degradation from multi-path interference. FMTV can be more susceptible to degradation from severe multi-path effects. While an amplitude-modulated TV shows ghosting in the face of multipath, FMTV degradation manifests itself as picture distortion such as a portion of the image appearing like a photographic negative.

70 cm versus 24 cm

• Although path losses are greater on 24 cm than 70 cm, these losses can be somewhat compensated by the fact that higher-gain 24-cm antennas can be constructed for the

same boom length as a 70-cm design.
- Vegetation and buildings tend to attenuate 24 cm more than 70 cm, making 24-cm antenna placement more critical.
- As 70 cm becomes more populated with narrowband voice repeaters that can put fundamentals and intermodulation products in the video receiver passband (degrading picture quality), system performance may become limited by interference more than by receiver noise figure. On the other hand, the amateur microwave frequencies are relatively free of mutual amateur interference sources. The major problem besetting the 23/24-cm amateur allocation is FAA Air Route Surveillance Radars which operate at 4 megawatts ERP and occupy an 8 MHz bandwidth in a variety of locations and center frequencies throughout the country.
- Test equipment for 24 cm is generally expensive. As amateur interest in the microwave regions begins to grow, however, new low-cost equipment should become available.

On balance, then, what does this all mean? In short, the higher path losses of 24 cm can be compensated for through higher-gain antennas, by the inherent system processing gains afforded through the use of FM and by the availability of more interference-free channels. In practical use, given paths that are at or near line-of-sight, and comparing transmitters operating at equal peak power levels, 24-cm FM-ATV will usually equal or outperform 70-cm FSTV. In cases involving large amounts of vegetation, rough terrain or man-made obstacles, or in situations normally involving very weak signal work, the 70-cm FSTV will be better.

FMTV Operating Parameters

Amateur standards for FMTV using

Table 1

Typical FMTV Amateur Operating Parameters

1. *Signal Polarity:* A black-to-white transition in the video causes an instantaneous increase in transmitted carrier frequency.
2. *Transmit Pre-emphasis:* In accordance with CCIR Recommendation 405-1 for 525 line systems
3. *Receiver De-emphasis:* In accordance with CCIR Recommendation 405-1 for 525 line systems
4. *Deviation:* 4 MHz Peak (8 MHz Peak-to-Peak)
5. *Sound subcarrier frequency:* 5.8 MHz or 6 MHz
6. *Sound subcarrier level:* 10 dB below video

A listing of countries using the 525-line format is provided in Table 2.

Table 2

Countries Using 525-Line Television Systems

United States	Mexico
Canada	Netherlands Antilles
Japan	Panama
Korea	Peru

525-line systems are beginning to evolve. Table 1 shows typical operating parameters.

The purpose of developing standards is to foster interoperability between stations, to promote operation with equipment exhibiting uniformly good performance, and to aid equipment manufacturers and builders in developing equipment that can best suit the needs of the amateur community. The local nature of microwave operation permits each local amateur group to establish its own operating parameters and standards to best suit local needs. The operating parameters shown in Table 1 represent a typical system. The values were derived based on both amateur experimentation in the U.S. and research into previous industrial and military investigations.

Tradeoffs in performance, bandwidth and cost must be considered when selecting operating parameters. A major goal is to operate with the minimum bandwidth practical for good performance. Minimum bandwidth is desirable not only from the standpoint of spectrum conservation, but also from concern to avoid sideband overlap with the 8-MHz-wide FCC Air Route Surveillance Radars, the 1240-MHz band edge, 1296-MHz DX/EME stations and 1269-MHz satellite uplinks. Careful selection of operating parameters also permits the effective use (with appropriate modifications) of low-cost off-the-shelf FMTV equipment available in Europe and satellite-TV 70-MHz IF receiver strips available in the U.S.

The specific rationale for the parameters in Table 1 is as follows:
- Signal Polarity: A "Black-to-White/Low-to-High Frequency" polarity was selected because this is the predominant mode for commercial FMTV satellite systems and amateur FMTV systems used in Europe. No modification to the video polarity of these units is needed.
- Transmit pre-emphasis and de-emphasis was selected in accordance with the International Telecommunication Union (ITU) International Radio Consultative Committee (CCIR) Recommendation 405-1. Pre-emphasis and de-emphasis is very inexpensive to implement, yet is a highly effective means of substantially improving the performance of FMTV systems. The circuit shown in Fig. 25, which uses readily-available parts, is a practical and low-cost implementation of the CCIR 405-1 pre-emphasis network suitable for 525-line Amateur Radio FMTV systems. Table 2 shows the countries using a 525-line standard. The performance characteristics of the circuit are shown in Fig. 26. The actual network losses are provided for design guidance; however, it is the relative losses, i.e., curve shape, that primarily affect system performance. The

Fig. 25 — Schematic diagram of a practical 525-line video pre-emphasis network for transmitter input, based on CCIR Recommendation 405-1. The capacitors should be plastic-film or mica for good stability. L1 is 56t no. 30 enam. wire on a T-50-2 core, or a Coilcraft SLOT-10-1-09.

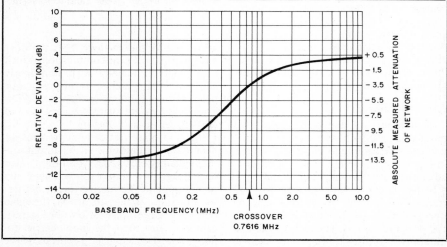

Fig. 26 — Characteristic response curve for a video pre-emphasis network.

Fig. 27 — Schematic diagram of a 525-line video de-emphasis network for receiver output. The capacitors should be plastic-film or mica for good stability. L1 is 52t no. 30 on a T-44-3 core, or a Coilcraft SLOT-10-1-12.

matching de-emphasis network for use at the receiver is shown in Fig. 27.

• A 4-MHz peak deviation is fairly standard world-wide for terrestrial (non-satellite) FMTV communications.[25] This deviation provides good picture quality at a lower bandwidth and deviation than is used by satellite TV systems. If a smaller deviation was used, the receiver processing gain advantages would rapidly diminish. A greater deviation, although improving system performance, would occupy excessive bandwidth; particularly for the 1240-1300 MHz (23/24-cm) amateur band. For some of the higher microwave regions

where sufficient bandwidth exists, particularly at 3.3 GHz and above, experimentation with greater deviations would be not only practical but highly desirable. Using higher deviation levels would permit the use of unmodified 70-MHz IF strips in the receiver design.

• A sound subcarrier frequency of 5.8 MHz (used by satellites) or 6.0 MHz (used by European FMTV hams) is high enough to avoid interference with the chroma signal yet low enough to minimize total transmit bandwidth.

• The −10 dB sound subcarrier level will allow good audio reception for P3.5 and better pictures. This level is referenced to the video level at the output of the pre-emphasis filter with a 1-V peak-to-peak 762-kHz sine wave applied to the transmitter video input. Increasing the subcarrier level too much can degrade picture quality while setting it too low may prevent the sound from being received under less than P5 conditions.

Practical FMTV Measurement Techniques

To assist in setting up the FMTV transmit parameters shown in Table 1 using test equipment affordable by amateurs, the following procedures are provided.

Transmit Video Deviation

To properly set the deviation of a transmitter using pre-emphasis, attention must be paid to using the proper input test frequency as well as voltage level. The following procedure may be used to establish a 4-MHz peak deviation with a 1 V

Table 3

Derivation of the Test Voltage Level for the 4 MHz Peak Deviation Adjustment:

For FM signals:

$$\text{modulation index} = \frac{\text{peak deviation}}{\text{modulating frequency}}$$

A Bessel function chart shows the relation between carrier and sideband amplitudes of the modulated signal as a function of the modulation index. At a specified value of the modulation index, the carrier and various sidebands go to zero.[26, 27]

By theory:

$$\text{modulation index} = 2.40 \text{ for first carrier null}$$

At the pre-emphasis crossover frequency of 762 kHz, the peak deviation of the first carrier null will be:

$$2.40 \times 0.762 \text{ MHz} = 1.8288 \text{ MHz}$$

Since the desired transmitter performance is 4 MHz peak deviation with a 1 V peak to peak input and assuming that the transmitter VCO performance is linear such that input voltage is directly proportional to transmit deviation, the results can be scaled:

$$\frac{1 \text{ V}_{P-P}}{4 \text{ MHz}} = \frac{X \text{ V}_{P-P}}{1.8288 \text{ MHz}}$$

cross multiplying:

$$1.8288 = 4X$$

and dividing:

$$\frac{1.8288}{4} = X$$

$$0.457 \text{ V} = X$$

peak to peak input for transmitters employing CCIR Rec 405-1 525-line pre-emphasis. It is based on the Bessel function null measurement technique and is founded on the theory that the transmitted signal carrier for an FM signal will be nulled when the ratio of the peak deviation to the modulating frequency is equal to 2.40.[26,27]

Step 1 — Set the signal generator to the pre-emphasis crossover frequency of 762 kHz and the level to 0.46 V peak to peak (See Table 3) using the set-up shown in Fig. 28.

Step 2 — Set the spectrum analyzer (or a receiver with a signal strength meter) to monitor the transmitted signal. Use a resolution bandwidth of 200 kHz or less. Starting with the transmit deviation control at the lowest possible level, slowly increase the deviation. The carrier amplitude will increase and rise above the upper and lower sidebands as shown in Fig. 29A.

Step 3 — Eventually the carrier will begin to drop with increasing deviation. Set the deviation control at the point the carrier is lowest (null). See Fig. 29B. The deviation is now properly set for 4-MHz peak. You may note that if you continue increasing the deviation, there will be other settings

Fig. 28 — Block diagram of the test configuration for setting video deviation.

Table 4
FMTV Equipment Sources

Solent Scientific c/o Worthing and District Repeater Group, ''Toftwood,'' Mill Lane, High Salvington, Worthing, Sussex BN13 3DF, England, tel. 011 44 903 67228 (transmitters).

Wood and Douglas, Unit 13 Youngs Industrial Estate, Aldermaston, Reading, England RG7 4PQ, tel. 011 44 735 671444 (24-cm video transmitters and receivers). US Representative: Tactical Communications, P.O. Box 1743, Melbourne, FL 32902, tel. 305-676-6907.

The PX Shack, 52 Stonewyck Drive, Belle Mead, NJ 08502, tel. 201-6013 (F9FT Tonna antennas).

PC Electronics, Tom O'Hara, W6ORG, 2522 Paxson La., Arcadia, CA 91006, tel. 818-447-4565 (24-cm test generator).

Science Workshop, Box 393, Bethpage, NY 11714 (''Poor Man's'' spectrum analyzer).

Additional reading on FM TV is contained in CQ-TV Magazine of the British Amateur Television Club. Write D. Lawton, Grenehurst, Pinewood Road, High Wycombe HP12 4DD, England, tel. 011 44 494 28899

Fig. 30 — A block diagram of the test configuration for measuring audio-subcarrier level relative to the video level.

Fig. 29 — Spectrum pictures of transmitter output observed on the Science Workshop ''Poor Man's Analyzer'' while adjusting transmitter deviation. As the deviation is first increased, the carrier and sideband levels will increase in amplitude, as shown at A; just before the desired deviation is reached, however, the carrier level will begin to drop. At the proper deviation level, the carrier will be nulled, as shown at B.

that will also achieve a null. The setting that is desired is the one with the lowest deviation; i.e., the first null.

Step 4 — To set up additional transmitters with the properly adjusted unit, send a test signal with the calibrated transmitter and then note the resulting peak-to-peak amplitude output on a receiver. For

another transmitter, deviation can be rapidly set by adjusting its deviation control to produce the same receiver output levels.

When transmitting a normal camera-produced picture, if the transmitter deviation exceeds the dynamic range of the receiver demodulator, you will note the presence of undesirable ''sparklies'' on the screen. These are shimmering black spots which appear in the white areas of the scene. If the receiving station cannot eliminate the sparklies through careful tuning, it may be necessary for the transmitting station to slightly reduce deviation.

Transmit Audio Level

The test set-up for measuring the audio subcarrier level with reference to the video level is shown in Fig. 30.

Step 1 — With the audio subcarrier turned off, apply a 1-V peak-to-peak 762-kHz signal at the video input to the transmitter's pre-emphasis filter. Measure the resulting peak-to-peak voltage level at the test point where the video and audio are summed, typically at the output of the pre-emphasis filter. This establishes the video reference level.

Step 2 — Turn off the signal generator and activate the audio subcarrier generator. Measure the peak-to-peak voltage level.

Step 3 — Divide the audio subcarrier level by the video reference level. This will yield the relative audio subcarrier level. An audio level 10 dB down from video will correspond to a voltage ratio of 0.32.

FMTV Bibliography

[1]J.H.O. Harries, ''Can Frequency and Phase-Change Modulation Reduce Interference?,'' *Television*, Vol. 2, no. 18, Aug. 1929, pp. 310-314.

[2]C.W. Carnahan, ''F-M Applied to a Television System,'' *Electronics*, Feb. 1940, pp. 29-32.

[3]F.H. Kroger et al, ''A 500-Megacycle Radio-Relay Distribution System for Television,'' *RCA Review*, Vol. 5, Jul. 1940, pp. 31-50.

[4]C.W. Hansell, ''Development of Radio Relay Systems,'' *RCA Review*, 1947, pp. 367-384.

[5]W.C. Boese, ''Survey Report on the use of Frequency Modulation for Television Transmission,'' *Technical Research and Technical Information Reports*, Part 2, Federal Communications Commission, May 25, 1950.

[6]L.S. Golding and J.E.D. Ball, ''Satellite Television Covers the World,'' *IEEE Spectrum*, Vol. 10, No. 8, Aug. 1973, pp. 24-31.

[7]H. Drysdale, ''A Comparison of the Performance of Television Transmission Systems Using Amplitude Modulation and Frequency Modulation,'' Royal Aircraft Establishment, *Technical Memorandum No. WE1201(E)*, Feb. 1966.

[8]K.G. Johannsen and E.A. Enriquez, ''Investigation of Surface Educational Television Distribution,'' *IEEE Transactions of Broadcasting*, Vol. BC-22, No. 2, Jun. 1976, pp. 45-52.

[9]D.O. Cummings, ''Some Considerations for Amplifier Spacing for AM and FM Supertrunks,'' *IEEE Transactions on Cable Television*, Vol. CATV-1, No. 1, Oct. 1976, pp. 63-73.

[10]P.R.J. Court, ''A Frequency Modulation System for Cable Transmission of Video or Other Wideband Signals,'' *IEEE Transactions on Cable Television*, Vol. CATV-3, No. 1, Jan. 1978, pp. 24-35.

[11]G.W. Beakley, ''Television to Small Earth Stations,'' *IEEE Transactions on Broadcasting*, Vol. BC-22, No. 3, Sep. 1976, pp. 96-100.

[12]L. Clayton, ''FM Television Signal-to-Noise,'' *IEEE Transactions on Cable Television*, Vol. CATV-1, No. 1, Oct. 1976, pp. 25-30.

[13]K.G. Johannsen et al, ''Television Sound Subcarrier Transmission in Space Communication,'' *IEEE Transactions*

on Broadcasting, Vol. BC-20, No. 3, Sep. 1974, pp. 42-48.

[14]D.W. Halayko and R.W. Huck, "Small Television Receive-Only 12 GHz Ground Terminals," *IEEE Transactions on Cable Television,* Vol. CATV-3, No. 3, Jul. 1978, pp. 112-119.

[15]"Broadcasting-Satellite Service (Sound and Television)," CCIR Documents of the XVth Plenary Assembly, Geneva, 1982, Volumes X and XI, Part 2, Recommendation 215-1.

[16]"Transmission de la Television en Modulation de Frequence," France Cables sous Marine et de Radio, Paris, 1984.

[17]C. Loo, "S/N Improvement of an FM Signal At or Near Threshold Due to De-Emphasis and Noise Weighting," *IEEE Transactions on Broadcasting,* Vol. BC-23, No. 3, Sep. 1977, pp. 65-70.

[18]"Pre-Emphasis Characteristics for Frequency Modulation Radio-Relay Systems for Television," CCIR Documents of the XVth Plenary Assembly, Geneva, 1982, Vol. 4, Recommendation 405-1.

[19]C. Loo, "Optimum Pre-Emphasis Network for Satellite Transmission of an FM TV Signal Near or at Threshold," *IEEE Transactions on Broadcasting,* Vol. BC-28, No. 2, Jun. 1982, pp. 37-43.

[20]W. F. Thorn, "FM Transmission of Television from Rockets and Balloons," Northeastern University, Electronics Research Laboratory, Boston, Scientific Report No. 3, 11 Jul. 1979.

[21]Mischa Schwartz, "Information Transmission, Modulation, and Noise," Polytechnic Institute of Brooklyn, 1959, pp. 305-311.

[22]P.R. Groumpos and B.D. Dimitriadis, "On the Subjective Evaluation of Protection-Ratios' Measurements for Co-Channel FM-TV Interference Under Variable (S/N) Ratios," *IEEE Transactions on Broadcasting,* Vol. BC-29, No. 3, Sep. 1983, pp. 101-105.

[23]"Broadcasting-Satellite Service (Sound and Television), Measured Interference Protection Ratios for Planning Television Broadcasting Systems," CCIR Documents of the XVth Plenary Assembly, Geneva, 1982, Volumes X and XI, Part 2, Recommendation 634-2.

[24]S. P. Barnes and E. F. Miller, "Carrier-Interference Ratios for Frequency Sharing Between Frequency-Modulated and Amplitude-Modulated-Vestigial Sideband Television Systems," Lewis Research Center, Cleveland, *NASA Technical Paper 1264,* Aug. 1978.

[25]"Frequency Deviation and the Sense of Modulation for Analogue Radio-Relay Systems for Television," CCIR Documents of the XVth Plenary Assembly, Geneva, 1982, Vol. 4, Recommendation 276-2.

[26]Murray G. Crosby, "A Method of Measuring Frequency Deviation," *RCA Review,* 1940, pp. 473-477.

[27]"Spectrum Analysis Amplitude and Frequency Modulation," Hewlett Packard Spectrum Analyzer Application Note No. 150-1, Nov. 1971.

Slow-Scan Television

Slow-scan television (SSTV) started in 1958 as the effort of a small band of Amateur Radio operators led by Copthorne Macdonald, VE1BFL. The intention of the project was to send television pictures on the HF amateur bands. By virtue of HF radio design and propagation characteristics, the SSTV system design is tailored to allow operation in a 3-kHz bandwidth — considerably less than the 6-MHz width of a commercial TV channel.

To meet the objective, bandwidth was decreased by reducing the information rate. Instead of 30 pictures a second, SSTV takes 8 seconds to send one picture. Instead of 525 lines, an SSTV picture is composed of 120 lines. The video is sent as a frequency-modulated subcarrier, which varies between 1500 Hz for black elements and 2300 Hz for white elements. Vertical and horizontal synchronizing signals are sent as bursts of 1200-Hz tones. Table 5 summarizes the SSTV standards for black-and-white TV operation.

In the early years of SSTV, the picture was displayed on surplus P7 radar tubes that could hold a slowly decaying picture for about 8 seconds when viewed in a darkened room. Special shuttered vidicons or flying spot scanners were used as the video sources. By 1974, several amateurs had built digital scan converters that permitted viewing a nondecaying picture in full daylight. The digital scan converter was designed so that the SSTV image could be stored in solid-state memory, and displayed on an unmodified black-and-white TV set. Fig. 31 shows an example of SSTV picture

Table 5
SSTV Standards

Frame Time	8 seconds
Lines per frame	120
Duration of line	67 ms
Duration of V sync	30 ms
Duration of H sync	5 ms
H or V sync frequency	1200 Hz
Black frequency	1500 Hz
White frequency	2300 Hz

quality using this technique. The converter also can be used to change the video output from a fast-scan camera into an SSTV-compatible signal. Thus, the scan converter is an interface between the slow-scan TV and fast-scan TV formats. A few years later, several commercial companies began producing these rather complex converters for amateur SSTV use.

Station Operation

As shown in Fig. 32, a typical SSTV station uses a standard transceiver, scan converter, TV camera and TV set. The TV receiver can be used for monitoring both the received signal and image to be transmitted.

Reception of SSTV is quite simple. The SSB voice of the transmitting amateur is tuned in so it sounds "natural." When the SSTV transmission begins, the signal should be in tune. The picture can be improved by using a transceiver that has passband tuning. Under ideal conditions the audio highs can be boosted to give some-

Fig. 31 — SSTV picture as seen on a standard TV set using digital scan converter.

what higher resolution. When poorer conditions exist, the passband can be tuned to minimize interference.

A General class or higher license is required to operate SSTV. It can be used on every band. The most popular frequency band is 20 meters, especially on 14.230 MHz, where an SSTV net meets each Saturday afternoon. Operators on the lower HF bands often experience poor quality because of multipath distortion, while the VHF and UHF bands limit the operational range.

Scan-Converter Design

The scan converter plays an integral part in both receiving and transmitting SSTV. The heart of the SSTV scan converter is the memory system. Most present systems use dynamic RAM ICs that contain enough bits

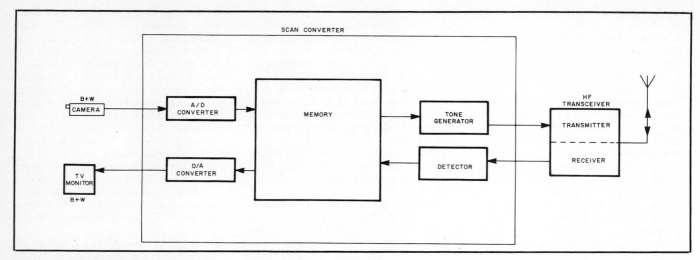

Fig. 32 — Basic SSTV station.

Fig. 33 — Color SSTV station.

to adequately resolve the picture elements and their gray scales. Sixty-five thousand bits (65 kbits) is the minimum considered acceptable for a single black-and-white picture.

Receiving

The converter has input detection circuitry to translate the SSTV audio-frequency variations from the receiver audio output into digital pulses. These contain horizontal and vertical synchronization as well as binary values representing the gray scales being sent. The pulses are stored in memory. The information is then sent to a digital-to-analog converter, which converts the stored data into an analog video signal fully compatible with a standard TV monitor to produce a nondecaying image.

Transmitting

Output from a black-and-white TV camera is converted into horizontal and vertical pulses along with digitized gray-scale values. The image is "snapped" in 1/60 of a second from the TV camera. The information is stored in memory. The digital output from memory goes to circuitry that produces the audio-frequency-modulated signal conforming to the SSTV standards. This SSTV output is then fed to the microphone input of the transceiver. Since the SSTV FM audio signal to the transmitter is continuous, the transceiver/linear amplifier RF power should be reduced to safe dissipation levels under this high-duty cycle operation.

Color SSTV

SSTVers have been experimenting with color since before the advent of the scan converters. In the initial experiments, red, green and blue filters were placed in front of the black and white TV camera and the face of the P7 monitor. The output of the filtered P7 monitor was captured on a color Polaroid® camera. The transmitting station sent a set of three 8-second SSTV frames that were received and recorded on film as a color picture, presuming the critical photographic camera alignment was not disturbed.

The scan converter offers a vast improvement over that interesting, but error-prone, technique for color SSTV. If two more memories are added to the black and white scan converter (195 kbits total), as shown in Fig. 33, each memory can be dedicated to a color. A black and white camera with a Red no. 25 filter, a Green no. 58 filter and a Blue no. 47B filter successively placed in front of the lens then sends one or more SSTV frames of each color. (A color TV camera is often used — that avoids the filter changing, but generally at a higher cost!) The receiving SSTV station switches the output of the SSTV detector to load the appropriate "color" memory. This is referred to as multiframe color SSTV. The outputs of the three color memories are translated from their digital gray-scale values into analog voltage levels capable of directly driving the gun drivers of a color TV monitor. Other designs translate the digital gray-scale values into composite-

Fig. 34 — Color SSTV station capable of storing multiple images.

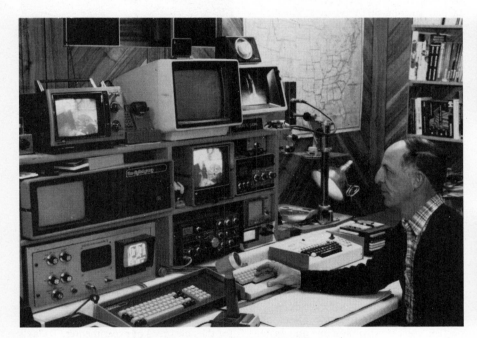

Fig. 35 — Microprocessor-based color SSTV station of WØLMD.

(A)

(B)

Fig. 36 — Noise caused by adjacent-channel interference is shown at A. Picture improvement when noise is removed by digital noise clipping is shown at B.

video levels and sends them to a conventional color TV set. The composite TV method simplifies the cabling and avoids TV set modification, at the cost of reduced bandwidth and resolution.

Recent Developments

Since the advent of the microprocessor, and because of the interest in more applications of the SSTV scan converters, systems are continuing to evolve in complexity and capability.

Multiple Image Storage

Since memories are continually getting larger and cheaper, present scan converters are being designed to hold four or more color pictures simultaneously (Fig. 34). This means a good received picture stored in a single memory does not have to be destroyed to make way for a new picture. If memories with 256 kbit capacity are used, the whole scan-converter memory can be built from three ICs. (A similar design 10 years ago would have required 768 of the 1-kbit memories used at that time.)

Increasing Resolution

The large array of memory opens up several design possibilities. The memory can be used for double vertical and double horizontal resolution if a single high-resolution picture for reception of schematics or weather satellite images is required.

Improved Color SSTV

In color SSTV applications, a microprocessor can be used to assign automatically the incoming SSTV color frame to the correct memory. The microprocessor also opens the way for even better transmission schemes such as sending all of the color information required for each line before the next line is sent. This results in a single-frame color SSTV system. Several techniques have been proposed for transmitting the color information. One system is described in "8 and 12 Second Single-Frame Color SSTV," *A5 Magazine*, November 1982, p. 32; another is described in "Robot Model 450-C Composite Single Frame Color Specification," *A5 Magazine*, February 1984, p. 28. A major objective is to maintain compatibility with existing black and white SSTV systems.

Fax Compatibility

Fax and weather satellite images can be seen on an SSTV scan converter if a format translator is attached to the input of the scan converter. Facsimile and weather satellite pictures, typically use over 1000 picture elements per line and over 1000 lines per picture. Since even high-resolution SSTV converters only have 256 × 256 resolution, the full quality of facsimile cannot be achieved. Nevertheless, the quality will be adequate for most experimenters.

Image Processing

The microprocessor may also be utilized for digital image processing to remove transmission noise from received pictures, and to boost the contrast of weak pictures. Since SSTV is much slower in data rate than conventional fast-scan ATV, the microprocessor has a chance to operate on the received images without resorting to very expensive high-speed digital signal-processing hardware. A highly sophisticated microprocessor-controlled color SSTV station is shown in Fig. 35.

A picture is often distorted significantly when it arrives at the receive station after HF transmission. A picture may have "buckshot noise" from adjacent-signal interference, as shown in Fig. 36A. A digital signal-processing algorithm known as a threshold noise clipper may be utilized to reduce the visibility of the noise interference. This algorithm compares the gray-scale value of each picture element (pixel) with the eight picture elements surrounding it. If the gray-scale value is significantly different from the average of the eight neighbors, then the average gray-scale value of the eight neighbors is taken instead of the original value of the center pixel. The restored picture is shown in Fig. 36B.

Another example of digital image processing is with SSTV pictures received with weak contrast as shown in Fig. 37A. This

means that the picture did not go either completely black or completely white. Often the problem is also compounded by marginal-signal conditions that inject considerable noise into the already weak picture. The restored picture in Fig. 37B shows what can be expected after a digital contrast-enhancing algorithm is used. The algorithm first derives a histogram of all the shades of gray that it finds in the received picture. Then it calculates the gray shade that represents the 10% point of the blackest picture elements, and the gray shade that represents the 10% point of all the white picture elements. Next a look-up table of expanded gray-scale values is made so that the weak shades are expanded linearly to full black and white. The microprocessor now modifies each picture element according to the expanded gray-scale values. While the effect is impressive on black-and-white pictures, it is very spectacular on color SSTV pictures. The microprocessor can also be used to electronically title an SSTV picture, as shown in the figures.

Future SSTV

The design of the scan converters is continuing to evolve. Now that image-processing techniques are becoming available in commercial SSTV scan converters, the next step will be scan-converter systems that are multitasking. This means that the scan converter can be simultaneously processing one picture, receiving a new picture and retrieving a picture from hard-disk memory for later transmission. A split-screen image could monitor all activities or concentrate on any one of them.

Another area of development will be simultaneous voice and video. This will involve sending the SSTV image during intervals of silence in the operator's voice transmission.

Standard digital silence-detecting algorithms can produce the effect of a perfect voice-control system, and instantaneously select voice or video modes along with a mode-change header. Several amateurs in Australia and New Zealand have been experimenting with low-resolution, narrow-bandwidth motion

(A)

(B)

Fig. 37 — Weak-contrast picture (A) and the same picture after digital contrast enhancement (B).

systems. These systems are designed to operate in voice grade bandwidth, making them applicable for long-distance HF transmission. Techniques such as these may permit the visual transmission of sign language images by Amateur Radio operators with speech or hearing difficulties.

SSTV today represents a wide open field for the new breed of experimenter. Today's SSTV systems involve microprocessors and software development. For those wanting to experiment with uncharted fields, the digital imaging possibilities within SSTV offer a tremendous challenge.

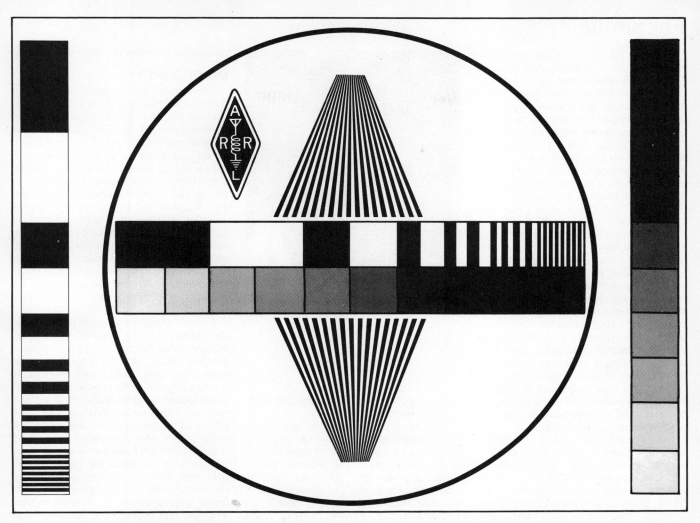

Fig. 38 — A test chart such as this can be used to check out a TV camera or an entire ATV transmitter system. It provides patterns for horizontal and vertical resolution and gray-scale testing. An 11 × 14-inch high-quality version printed on heavy paper is available from ARRL Hq. for $3 postpaid. You can personalize the ARRL test chart by adding your call letters, location and a photograph in the white space provided.

Facsimile

The text for this facsimile section was prepared by Jeff Wallach, N5ITU.

The earliest operational system for image transmission, facsimile (fax) networks date back to the late '20s and early '30s. Like any other imaging system, fax compromises in some areas to gain advantages in others. Conventional fast-scan TV is capable of handling moving images of moderate resolution, but the rapid image repetition rate requires several megahertz of signal bandwidth, which confines it to the UHF range. SSTV sacrifices resolution and motion to transmit relatively low resolution images in an 8-second frame within the bandwidth constraints of conventional SSB transceivers. The more advanced SSTV formats used on personal computer systems available in the marketplace today have resolution capabilities approaching fast scan but, given bandwidth restrictions, this is achieved by lengthening the transmission time for still frames to 17 or 188 seconds.

By comparison, fax represents a high-resolution service with pictures ranging from 800 to several thousand lines per frame. This high resolution is achieved within the constraints of audio bandwidths by using relatively long transmission times ranging from 3.3 to 15 minutes.

Fax is used widely in a number of services. Weather chart distribution is perhaps the most common, using both HF and landline links to weather service and forecast centers throughout the world. News photographs, sometimes called "wirephotos," are also distributed throughout the world in a similar manner. A wide variety of weather satellites transmit visible and infra-red imagery to ground stations using facsimile-type transmissions. Inexpensive systems are now common in business offices, schools, and law enforcement agencies to facilitate the transfer of documents, photographs, signatures, and fingerprints, etc. Facsimile machines are now even commonly used in the home for tasks like shopping by fax and ordering food from the local pizzeria!

Amateur fax work has been limited, primarily because of historical regulatory factors. During the post-WW II years, the 11-meter band was the only amateur HF assignment authorized for fax operation. The subsequent loss of 11 meters left the amateur fraternity with no regular fax operating privileges on HF. With the recent authorization of fax on all amateur bands and the proliferation of personal computers with fax interfaces, amateur interest has been rising rapidly.

IMAGE TRANSMISSION

A typical fax mechanical transmitter consists of a drum driven by a synchronous motor operating from a crystal or tuning-fork frequency standard. The material to be transmitted is wrapped around the

Fig 39—A typical fax picture.

drum, which rotates at a constant speed. A small spot of light is focused on the printed material (photo, text, map, etc.), and the light reflected from the subject is picked up by a photocell, photomultiplier or phototransistor. The rotation of the drum provides the equivalent of the "horizontal scanning" of the material. A carriage, supporting the light source and pickup assembly, is moved along the drum at a constant rate, providing the "vertical scanning." The carriage is usually operated by a threaded rod driven by another synchronous motor. As the carriage travels from one end of the drum to the other, the entire picture area is scanned. The voltage variations from the light pickup are amplified and used to modulate an audio subcarrier, using either amplitude or frequency modulation. For positive AM, the modulation is proportional to brightness, which typically ranges from 4% for black through 90 to 100% for white. Negative modulation reverses this relationship with minimum modulation level corresponding to white, and maximum to black.

Amplitude-modulated-subcarrier systems are typically used with VHF and microwave FM links (weather satellites using positive amplitude modulation) or weather chart and photo transmission via landline (typically negative frequency modulation). FM-subcarrier operation uses the voltage variations from the light pickup to shift the subcarrier frequency. Black material results in a 1500-Hz frequency, rising in linear fashion to 2300 Hz for white. The FM format is used with all fax systems that operate on HF, reducing problems caused by the fading that is inevitable on any long-distance short-wave transmission circuit.

IMAGE DISPLAY

The options for image display are far more varied than those for transmission. The device that displays the picture is known generically as the "recorder" and is found in a wide variety of configurations. Drum-type recorders hold a single sheet of the recording medium on a drum that is quite similar to that used in the transmitter. By contrast, continuous-feed fax recorders are designed to display pictures using material fed from a roll. Such recorders do not require that material be reloaded for each picture but are typically more complex than drum-type recorders. The newer fax systems use computer monitors or video terminals to display the document or photographic image at a very high resolution.

Facsimile recorders also differ widely in the nature of the recording medium. Photographic systems use film or photographic paper that is exposed by a modulated light source and lens. Such systems require a darkroom and photographic-processing chemicals and are not well suited for high-volume use. The most advanced photographic systems use a dry silver paper and modulated laser light source. These are usually continuous read-out machines in which the paper is heat processed prior to emerging from the recorder. Such systems provide superb image quality and are convenient to use. They are very expensive to purchase new, however, and are not yet available on the surplus market.

Weather chart recorders are typically of the continuous-feed type and employ a damp, chemically treated paper that is "exposed" using an electrolytic process that creates a dark line when current is passed through the paper. These systems are ideal for maps and charts and can provide a reasonable gray scale for continuous-tone images.

Another medium is electrosensitive paper in which printing is accomplished by applying a high voltage to a printing wire or stylus. The paper is dry and has a black base layer with a white coating. The applied voltage will cause varying amounts of the surface material to be burned away, thus creating a trace that can be varied from white (no coating removed) to black (all the coating burned away). With the proper choice of paper and printing electronics a fine gray scale can be obtained with images approaching photographic quality.

Yet another recording medium involves the use of a combination of carbon and white paper with the printing electronics driving a mechanical system that exerts varying pressure on the carbon to produce a trace on the white paper beneath. The image quality is marginal, not to mention all of the wasted carbon paper that is discarded. Long-term availability of the specialized paper may also be a problem.

Modern office fax machines utilize a photocopier method that offers up to 64 levels of gray scale for high-quality printed images.

STANDARDS

The essential standards for a fax unit are defined by three parameters: drum speed (helix speed in the case of continuous readout recorders), carriage or paper feed rate, and modulation characteristics. To be suitable for use in a given class of service, a piece of equipment must match the characteristics of the service.

Drum Speed

Drum speed is expressed in terms of revolutions per minute (r/min), which is equivalent to the scanning line frequency (line/min). Several "standard" speeds may be found in surplus commercial equipment with some units having multiple speed options:

• 60 line/min—standard speed for old wirephoto and chart recorders. Few modern services use this line rate and it is unsuitable for amateur use because of the extended periods required for image transmission with standard frame rates.

• 100 line/min—This speed was used for a considerable period with various wirephoto services and some machines still on the surplus market. Not used by current services so conversion to 120 or 240 line/min would be required.

• 120 line/min—Standard speed for HF and landline weather charts, some wirephoto services and weather satellite use. This line rate is marginal for amateur use since transmission times will range from 7 to 15 minutes depending on the other system specifications.

• 180 line/min—Used by some office fax systems such as the Xerox Model 400. It is acceptable for point-to-point links on VHF but for general HF use, weather charts and satellite reception, conversion to 120 or 240 line/min will be required.

• 240 line/min—Standard for weather satellite use and used by more modern wirephoto and chart transmissions. This is a good rate for amateur HF use since detailed pictures (800 lines) can be transmitted in as little as 3.3 minutes.

Other speeds can be found in specialized gear, and all will require conversion to either 120 or 240 line/min to be useful for amateur work.

Scanning Density

Scanning density is usually expressed by the number of lines per inch (line/in), or picture elements (pixels) per inch on a computer or video display. There are two different ways in which the scanning density can be used.

The first case is where the frame-time parameters of a signal format are known and you wish to obtain the appropriate scanning density for proper image display. An example might be the WEFAX weather satellite format in which the image has a 1:1 aspect ratio (square), a line rate of 240 line/min, and a frame time of 200 seconds, producing an 800-line image (4 lines/s × 200 seconds). Obviously the recorder should have a 240-r/min drum speed, but in choosing a recorder the proper scanning density must be determined. To compute the required scanning density, you need to know the width of the image format on the recorder. If you have some sample printouts, you can simply measure the width. In the case of a drum-type system, the width can be approximated by the relationship:

$$L = 3.14 \, D$$

where
  L = length of the scanning line (width)
  D = drum diameter

Since domestic recorders are calibrated in terms of lines/inch, your measurements should be in inches or converted to inches from the metric equivalents. In the case of a continuous readout system, the image width is usually slightly less than the width of the paper.

Another parameter is the aspect ratio of the image format (ratio of image width to image height). For the WEFAX example, the aspect ratio (A) is 1:1 or simply 1. The required scanning density can be computed from:

$$F = (t \times R) / (L / A)$$

where
  F = scanning density in line/in
  t = frame time in minutes
  R = scanning line frequency in line/min
  L = length of scanning line in inches
  A = aspect ratio

In the case of our WEFAX example, the scanning density for an 11-inch recorder is:

$$F = (3.33 \times 240) / (11 / 1) = 800 / 11 = 72.7$$

The scanning line frequency is not a particularly critical factor. If the value is within 10% of nominal, the distortion in the aspect ratio will not be noticeable. In the case of 240-line/min recorders, a scanning density of 75 line/in is commonly available and will produce an essentially perfect picture. Many of the recorders that found their way onto the surplus market recently use 96 line/in. This rate will compress the image vertically—it will not be as tall as it is wide—but the picture is acceptable.

A second use for the scanning density is the computation of the transmission time using a specific format or the computation of the line/in requirement when using a recorder with a different image width. As an example, we might consider computing the transmission time for a 19-inch weather chart recorder operating with a scanning frequency of 120 r/min and a 96-line/in scanning density, which is standard for weather chart service. Since width (19 in) and scanning density (96 line/in) are given and if we specify the aspect ratio of the image (A), we can compute the transmission/reception time (t) in minutes by rearranging the previous equation as:

$$t = ((L / A) \times F) / R$$

where
  t = transmission or reception time in minutes
  L = length of scanning line (width) in inches
  A = aspect ratio
  F = scanning density in line/min
  R = scanning line frequency in r/min

If the image is square (A = 1), then the time can be computed from:

$$t = ((19 / 1) \times 96) / 120 = (19 \times 96) / 120$$
$$t = 1824 / 120 = 15.2 \text{ minutes}$$

If A is greater than 1 (width > height), the transmission time will be reduced. Likewise if A is less than 1 (width < height), the transmission time will be increased.

If we know the drum speed and scanning density specifications for a specific format for one recorder, we can readily compute the required scanning density (line/in) setting for other recorders. In the previous case, we noted that 96 line/in is the standard setting for 120-r/min weather charts using a 19-inch recorder. The scanning density for other recorder widths can be calculated as follows:

$$F' = (F \times L) / L'$$

where
  F' = unknown scanning density in line/in
  F = reference scanning density in line/in
  L = reference line width
  L' = line width of new format

If we had access to an 11-inch recorder and wished to copy 120-r/min weather charts (F = 96 and L = 19), the required scanning density can be computed as follows:

$$F' = (96 \times 19) / 11 = 1824 / 11 = 165.8$$

If you were to check the specification of the 11-inch recorder, you would find a 166-line/in scanning density switch setting. That should work fine!

MODULATION FORMAT

The various modulation formats have already been briefly discussed. Chart recorders designed for landline use will usually have negative amplitude modulation. Weather satellite systems require positive amplitude modulation, while HF systems use FM subcarrier modulation. Some units will have several switch-selectable modulation formats. Ideally, a recorder or computer system should have complete selection for AM, FM, and positive and negative formats.

SURPLUS EQUIPMENT

Surplus commercial equipment is an excellent way to acquire fax hardware since the systems are well constructed (often to MIL specs), and the cost is low. The ideal unit will have multiple drum speeds, scanning densities and demodulation formats. In practice, some conversion will probably be needed. Before you consider conversion, factors such as documentation, circuit type and media should be considered. The modification process will require information about motor drive frequencies, control signals, circuit configurations, etc. A good technical manual containing schematics is a must! Unless you are going to use the system only for the mechanics (with a complete replacement of the electronics), you should not consider a unit for which a manual is unobtainable.

The nature of the electronic circuits is another important factor. Tube-type units are typical surplus items because they have been phased out of service in favor of solid-state equipment. Although the price may look appealing, consider carefully the present cost and availability of replacement tubes. You should not necessarily reject a tube system, but you can expect to do some circuit replacement as tubes become either too expensive or unavailable.

Finally, check out the recording medium. Electrolytic and electrostatic papers of various sorts will be around for quite some time, but some specialized media such as carbon-paper systems may be in short supply in the near future.

Modulation Format

Most surplus units will have amplitude-modulation capability, usually with both positive and negative formats. In some systems, shifting polarity is as simple as reversing diodes and changing the bias on a video stage. Addition of an FM capability to an AM-only unit can be achieved by using a standard SSTV demodulator with a suitable interface buffer to meet your circuit requirements.

Equipment Sources

Conversion requirements for surplus equipment can range from nothing to complete replacement of electronics and even mechanical changes. You should carefully study the requirements of the mode that you are interested in and evaluate the cost and conversion requirements of surplus equipment. The equipment can be found at the larger hamfests, through dealers or directly from the manufacturers. Three sources of equipment are:

Alden Electronic and Impulse Recording
    Equipment, Inc
        Washington St
        Westboro, MA 01581
Muirhead Inc
    1101 Bristol Rd
    Mountainside, NJ 07092
Atlantic Surplus
    3730 Nautilus Ave
    Brooklyn, NY 11224

MODERN OFFICE FAX MACHINES

There has been a tremendous revolutionary growth in the technology, and a concurrent reduction in price. This has led to a dramatic increase in the number of office/home fax machines in use today. This growth is akin to that witnessed in the home video tape recorder market 10 years ago. Very large scale integration, robotics, and mass production have brought down the price of a sophisticated, high resolution fax machine to less than that of a good color television set.

Modern fax machines offer a variety of options for high-speed delivery of documents and photographs. Many machines can receive and send documents unattended, have large digital memories for document storage, and allow store and forward processing of multiple documents via telephone, without human intervention. Fax machines can also double as a photocopier and/or telephone answering machine. The more sophisticated fax devices can screen an incoming telephone call, determine whether it is a voice call, another fax machine, or a computer modem, and make the appropriate connection.

Fax Machine Grouping

Fax machine technology is often correlated with a specific "group," such as Group 1, 2, 3, or 4. The fax group number refers to the generation or sequence in the technological evolution of hardware that the fax machine belongs to. The group number matches the age of the hardware technology. Group 1 is the oldest, and Group 4 the most modern technology.

There are several elements that define the technology, including the graphics resolution, the speed at which the document or image is transmitted, how the data is scanned and stored prior to transmission, and so on. One of the primary elements is how the image is scanned and the data compression method used. Data compression will be discussed later in this chapter. Recommendations formulated by the International Telegraph and Telephone Consultative Committee (CCITT) on how images are scanned, encoded, transmitted, and decoded for printing have resulted in the group standards. These international standards ensure communications compatibility for fax machines world-wide.

About 90% of the fax machines in use today are Group 3 machines. Group 3 fax machines scan and store the images as digital data. Group 1 and 2 machines used strictly analog scanning techniques. Group 3 devices print a much finer-resolution image than Group 1 or 2 machines, and can scan and transmit documents at much higher speeds (from 2400 bit/s to 9600 bit/s). Group 3 fax uses analog data transmission over standard telephone voice circuits, with maximum speeds of 9600 bit/s.

Group 4 fax machines are extremely sophisticated and expensive devices. Group 4 fax machines scan and transmit the image in a digital mode, at very high transmission speeds. Specialized digital telephone networks (Integrated Service Digital Network—ISDN) are required for digital data transmission at speeds in excess of 56,000 bit/s. For this reason Group 4 machines cannot communicate with Group 3 machines. Compatibility of the communication standards is a key element to consider when purchasing a machine.

Compatibility

Most of the older Group 2 fax machines remain in service because of their initial high costs, and the costs of replacement. Many Group 3 machines have some limited compatibility with the Group 2 fax format. Scanning densities and communications standards may limit the compatibility but basic functions are possible.

SUBSYSTEMS

A modern digital fax machine scans a document (text, photograph, graphics) and translates the image into a binary signal via the *scanner*. The binary signal is converted to an analog voltage, sent to the integrated telephone modem, and transmitted as a series of tones over analog phone lines. The fax machine at the other end of the phone line demodulates these tones, converts them to binary data, and reproduces the original image on a built-in printer. Therefore, the basic components of the modern-day fax machine are the scanner, modem, and printing device.

Scanners

Scanners convert the actual image on a sheet of paper into a series of binary digits (bits), which are sent to the modem for telephone transmission. They typically use a photoelectric element (photodiode) to detect the relative brightness of the white, black, and gray areas within the document or photo. Each small area is digitized by the scanner as one bit. Less expensive fax scanners only have a two-state digitizer (white or black), but the more sophisticated scanners have half-tone or gray-scale capabilities, distinguishing up to 64 different shades of gray.

Volumes of data are produced in scanning, storing, and transmitting a document image. Some type of data compression is needed to make it economically feasible to send a document using fax.

The CCITT compression standards are based on the statistical nature of scanned binary document imagery. The scanned document normally consists of large amounts of white space, with groupings of black in the text and line drawings (and gray in photographs). Because of the distribution of the white and black areas, it is statistically possible to use a technique called *run length encoding* to achieve image compression, saving space and transmission time. This technique involves replacement of scanned pixel values with code words representing the run lengths of black and white pixels along an individual scanned line. These coded representations are designed to require fewer bits than the original bit strings they represent. Group 3 compression uses a combination of run length encoding and a two-dimensional encoding system based on bit reversals between adjacent lines. Group 3 fax machines can discriminate 98, 196 or 391 pixels in a vertical inch, and 98 or 208 pixels in a horizontal inch. The Group 4 compression standard involves only the two-dimensional coding based on a bit reversal technique.

Modems

The fax MOdulator/DEModulator (modem) converts the digitized image (as binary data bits) into analog audio tones, with a bandwidth of approximately 3000 Hz. Group 3 fax modems will transmit these tones from 2400 bit/s to 9600 bit/s. Some machines can automatically revert to a slower speed if there is excessive noise on the telephone line, causing multiple line errors. The modem connects to the telephone line through a standard RJ-11 phone jack. Some fax machines also have error correction mode (ECM), an optional feature whereby the receiving machine communicates information about the data it has received back to the sending machine. The sending machine will send the same page of information again if it determines that errors have occurred in the transmission.

Printers

There are four basic printer types used in fax machines: thermal printers, electrostatic printers, dot-matrix printers, and laser printers. Laser printers yield the highest quality output, with up to 300 dots per inch resolution. This can add about $2000 to the cost of the fax machine, however. Thermal printers are heat sensitive, and tend to deteriorate over time. Electrostatic printers are similar to photocopiers, in which a black toner fluid is bonded to the paper whenever an electrical charge is generated by the print head. Dot matrix printers are the same ones used by personal computers. Fine wires on the print head strike a ribbon and leave a series of fine dots on the paper, generating individual characters or dots in a photograph.

HOME CONSTRUCTION

Effective fax systems can be built from scratch with performance equal to commercial equipment. Such projects are an interesting combination of electronics and mechanics. *The Weather Satellite Handbook* describes a complete direct-readout recorder for use with satellite imagery.[1] This system is completely solid state and

uses dry electrostatic paper. The documentation includes circuit changes for photographic printing if desired. C. B. Lee described a continuous-readout electrolytic recorder for weather charts.[2] Either system could be adapted for other services with the addition of different demodulators and drive motors. Anyone seriously considering building the fax mechanical subsystem should obtain the Hurst catalog (Hurst Manufacturing Company, 1551 E Broadway, Princeton, IN 47670). Hurst is one of the largest manufacturers of synchronous motors and carries a large line of stock and built-to-order units.

SERVICES

Services of potential interest to amateurs include weather satellites, weather chart HF transmissions and two-way amateur operation. Table 6 summarizes the standardized recorder requirements for each service.

Table 6
Standards For Various Classes of FAX Service

Service	Drum (Scan) Speed (r/min or line/min)	Size (in)	Scan Density (line/in)
WEFAX Satellite	240	11	75
APT Satellite	240	11	166
Weather Charts	120	19	96

Satellites

Amateurs have been very active in this area since the inception of the satellite program in the '60s and have made many valuable contributions. Reception and display of both geostationary and polar-orbiting satellite signals is entirely practical, but does involve antennas, receivers, tracking and a knowledge of the various satellite systems in addition to fax techniques. *The Weather Satellite Handbook* provides a complete guide to setting up a station, including construction projects.[1] *A Teacher's Guide for Building Weather Satellite Ground Stations* also provides a system overview with valuable information on the conversion of surplus fax gear.[3] *Facsimile for the Radio Amateur* and *The Satellite Experimenter's Handbook* provide some additional sources of information as well as a very broad overview of amateur satellite activities.[4, 5] There is a detailed overview of weather satellite ground stations later in this chapter.

Weather Charts

Weather charts are transmitted on literally dozens of HF channels throughout the day. Reception requires a stable general-coverage SSB receiver or a ham receiver with suitable frequency converter. Standard USB HF frequencies include 3357, 4975, 8080, 10,865, 12,125, and 20,015 kHz.

Two-way Amateur FAX

One of the greatest difficulties for two-

way operation has been locating fax transmitters. While surplus fax recorders are available, fax transmitters are much rarer. Office fax machines may require some conversion, but they usually include a transmitter and receiver in the same package.

The multimode digital controllers that connect to a personal computer (AEA, Kantronics, MFJ) provide a new way into amateur fax. These outboard digital units connect to the serial communications port on a personal computer, and offer reception and transmission of Packet, RTTY, AMTOR, CW, SSTV, and fax modes. Some units have gray level modems built in. With the appropriate computer software, you can transmit and receive high resolution (640 pixels × 480 lines × 16 shades of gray) SSTV and fax pictures. Once the picture is received on the computer, additional paint programs may color the image, digitally enhance the quality of the fax image, and retransmit to other appropriately equipped stations. The fax images can be displayed directly on the screen or sent to the printer for hard copy output. Many amateurs store these fax images on a hard disk, and electronically transmit them over telephone lines to computer bulletin board systems around the country.

A number of amateurs participate in an HF fax net every Sunday on 14.245 MHz at 2000 UTC. Many local clubs transmit fax pictures on VHF and UHF repeaters using the digital multimode units or other computer fax systems.

COMPUTERS

Digital scan converters have revolutionized SSTV and are about to do the same with fax. The use of home computers offers an exciting challenge for use as "intelligent" scan converters. An example of such a system is one developed by WB8DQT and K6AEP for use with the Radio Shack TRS-80C Color Computer.[6] The system has four elements: a fax interface circuit, a high-resolution display board, the computer with 64-kbyte RAM and a software package. The input signals are processed by the interface board and the computer, which samples the image, loads it into memory and passes the picture information to a display board for presentation on a standard TV monitor. The picture is displayed in a 256 × 256 format with 16 gray-scale levels.

A new system developed by AEA, the Amiga Video Terminal (AVT), uses a Commodore Amiga® computer to offer over 55 SSTV modes, nine fax modes with resolutions up to 1024 pixels by 1200 lines in 16 gray levels. This is an extremely sophisticated system that offers every known SSTV commercial and experimental mode, as well as fax at 60, 120, and 240 lines/min, WEFAX and other digital image processing capabilities. The AVT system has full autostart capability for both receive and transmit. It uses a 300 Hz white-black sweep for start, and 32 "phasing" pulses are transmitted. The system can pick up these signals from other AVT or commercial fax stations and synchronize immediately. The fax images can be panned, flipped, rotated, and imported to other paint programs for digital enhancement.

With the rapidly declining cost of personal computers, and the flexibility of using a computer in the ham shack, the days of modifying an older mechanical fax machine for amateur use are soon to be history. Additional computer-based fax systems are listed in the reference section at the end of this chapter.

WEATHER SATELLITES

The amateur community has been receiving and displaying weather satellite imagery since the earliest days of the US meteorological satellite program. Over the past few years there has been an explosive growth in the number of private ground stations being constructed, as well as a marked improvement in the technologies of RF subsystems, and an enhanced resolution of the imagery display instrumentation.

Amateurs world-wide are routinely displaying real-time imagery from American and Soviet polar-orbiting and geosynchronous weather satellites, storing the images digitally on their personal computers, and utilizing sophisticated digital image enhancement routines identical to those being employed by the NASA Voyager spacecraft! The high resolution weather satellite imagery now received in the ham shack rivals the quality of commercial systems costing tens of thousands of dollars. Much of the equipment needed to track the satellite, receive the radio signals, and display the imagery is similar or identical to that currently used in OSCAR satellite stations. Therefore, many hams are well situated to receive weather satellite facsimile, and develop the capability of a "personal eye in space"!

Modern weather-imaging platforms fall into two general categories: polar-orbiting and geostationary satellites. Fig 40 illustrates these two types of satellite orbits. The imaging techniques used by these satellite types are different, and are discussed separately in the following text.

Polar-Orbiting Satellites

Polar-orbiting spacecraft include the TIROS-N series operated by the United States and the METEOR 2 and 3 series spacecraft operated by the Soviet Union. In addition, the People's Republic of China has launched a polar-orbiting weather satellite, Feng Yun I, utilizing similar data transmission formats as the TIROS-N and METEOR series.

The operational concept of environmental polar-orbiting satellites is to maintain several spacecraft in a near-polar orbit at all times. The altitude and inclination of the orbit are selected to produce a sun-synchronous orbit, which means the satellite will pass over the same spot on the Earth at approximately the same time each day. One spacecraft will pass over a receiving ground station as the satellite travels from north to south (descending node) during the morning. A second spacecraft will pass from south to north (ascending node) over the same ground

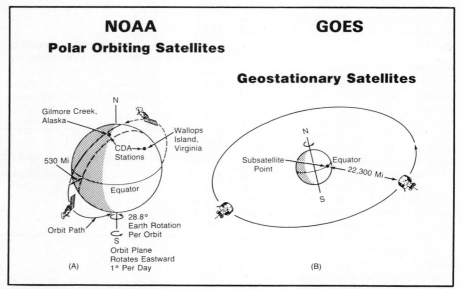

Fig 40—Schematic representation of polar-orbiting and geostationary weather satellite orbital tracks.

Fig 41—Meteorological satellites view the Earth through rotating mirrors to produce APT and HRPT images.

Advanced TIROS — N (ATN)

LEGEND	
AVHRR/2	ADVANCED VERY HIGH RESOLUTION RADIOMETER
BDA	BEACON/COMMAND ANTENNA
ESA	EARTH SENSOR ASSEMBLY
HIRS/2I	HIGH-RESOLUTION INFRARED SOUNDER
IMP	INSTRUMENT MOUNTING PLATFORM
IMU	INERTIAL MEASUREMENT UNIT
MSU	MICROWAVE SOUNDING UNIT
REA	REACTION ENGINE ASSEMBLY
SAD	SOLAR-ARRAY DRIVE
SBA	S-BAND ANTENNA
SBUV/2	SOLAR BACKSCATTER ULTRAVIOLET SPECTRAL RADIOMETER
SLA	SEARCH-AND-RESCUE TRANSMITTING ANTENNA (L-BAND)
SOA	S-BAND OMNI ANTENNA
SRA	SEARCH-AND-RESCUE RECEIVING ANTENNA
SSD	SUN SENSOR DETECTOR
SSU	STRATOSPHERIC SOUNDING UNIT
UDA	ULTRA-HIGH-FREQUENCY DATA COLLECTION SYSTEM ANTENNA
VRA	VERY-HIGH-FREQUENCY REAL-TIME ANTENNA
SEM	SPACE ENVIRONMENT MONITOR (DUMMY)

Fig 42—Diagram of an Advanced TIROS-N weather satellite platform. The sensors called out on the drawing are for various satellite purposes. *(drawing courtesy of NOAA)*

station during the afternoon.

Each of the satellites will pass over the same areas approximately 12 hours later traveling in the opposite direction. Because the Earth rotates beneath the orbiter during each orbital period, the satellite sensors observe a different portion of the surface of the Earth during each orbit. Fig 40A shows a sun-synchronous polar orbit.

The polar-orbiting weather satellites carry an array of instruments that sample a variety of environmental and meteorological events. They can transmit this data in real time on VHF, UHF, and SHF to direct-readout stations within view.

The primary imaging instrument on the TIROS-N spacecraft is the Advanced Very High Resolution Radiometer (AVHRR). This radiation-detection instrument is designed to scan a narrow strip of the Earth, using a mirror rotating at 360 r/min. Each mirror rotation scans one line of the image, and the spacecraft transmits the image one line at a time. Fig 41 illustrates this process. As the mirror rotates, the spacecraft moves through space; each rotation of the mirror covers a new portion of the Earth. In this way the satellite produces a long, continuous image (in five spectral ranges of light) with clearly defined side borders, but no definite top or bottom.

The reception of the radio signal is limited to the "line of sight" of the re-

Table 7

Currently Active Meteorological Spacecraft With APT Service

(Table Update by Grant Zehr, WA9TFB)

Spacecraft	Operating Country	Orbit Type	Inclination (Degrees)	Orbital Period	Frequencies (MHz)	Image Format	Line Rate lines/min
TIROS-N series	USA-NOAA	polar	98	102 min		SR*	120 (Visible & IR)
NOAA 10 (#16969)					137.500		
NOAA 11 (#19531)					137.620		
Meteor 2 series	USSR	polar	82	104 min		SR**	120 (Visible)
							20 (IR)
Meteor 2-16 (#18312)					137.400***		
Meteor 2-17 (#18820)					137.400***		
Meteor 2-18 (#19851)					137.300***		
Meteor 3 series	USSR	polar	82	110 min			120 (Visible & IR)
Meteor 3-2 (#19336)					137.850***		
Meteor 3-3 (#20305)					137.850***		
GOES Series	USA-NOAA	Geostat	0	24 hrs	1691	WEFAX	240
GOES-Imaging		98° W				(no WEFAX)	
GOES-7 (#17561)							
GOES-E****		65° W				(east WEFAX relay)	
GOES-5 (#12472)							
GOES-W****		135° W				(west WEFAX relay	
GOES-6 (#14050)							
METEOSAT	ESA	Geostat	0	24 hrs	1691	WEFAX	240
METEOSAT 4 (#19876)			0				

*Scanning radiometer format
**120 line per minute visible mode imagery available on a regular basis. 20 line per minute infrared imagery sometimes available at night
***Alternate frequencies for Meteor series spacecraft are 137.300 MHz, 137.400 MHz and 137.850 MHz.
****GOES-E and GOES-W refer to the spacecraft locations. GOES-(number) refer to particular spacecraft.

ceiving ground station, and can only be acquired when the satellite is above the horizon for that particular location. Current US and Soviet polar orbiters have an altitude ranging from 870 km (US) to 1200 km (USSR), providing a maximum time of signal reception of around 16 minutes. During acquisition of signal (AOS) the receiving station can display an image that is about 5800 km (3600 miles) long.

Fig 42 is a diagram of a typical TIROS-N satellite showing the primary instruments and RF transmitters. Note the location of the AVHRR instrument at the left of the diagram. The other sensors called out in the drawing are for other products.

Polar-Orbiting Satellite Facsimile Products

The AVHRR instrument detectors are sensitive to radiant energy of the visible, near infra-red, and infra-red (IR) spectrum. This combined analog information is digitized to 10-bit samples and transmitted to receiving stations as two types of imagery "products": a lower resolution (4 km) Automatic Picture Transmission (APT) image, and a High Resolution Picture Transmission (HRPT) with 1.1 km resolution.

APT

Early in the meteorological satellite program it became apparent that for users in remote areas to have access to satellite imagery on a timely basis, the satellite would have to transmit directly to the remote receiving station. The APT format was developed to meet this need. The first APT system was pioneered on TIROS VIII, launched on Dec 21, 1963. By 1965, radio amateurs were designing stations for home reception and distributing the plans to hams around the world.

The APT imagery was designed with a simple format that could be received and displayed on relatively inexpensive and easily obtained ground-station equipment. Active polar-orbiting satellites launched by the US, Soviet Union, and China continue to transmit images of the Earth via the APT analog format. Because of this international cooperation, the same equipment (with minor adjustments) can be used for reception of imagery from all of these spacecraft.

The APT mode, like facsimile, allows the transmission of a relatively high resolution image (4 km) in a moderate bandwidth by using a longer time for image transmission. With APT transmissions, the detected VHF FM signal (137 MHz) contains a subcarrier, the video image, and a 2400-Hz tone that is amplitude modulated. The amplitude peaks on the subcarrier represent the lighter portions of the image, and the low amplitude portions correspond to the darkest areas of the image. Intermediate portions of the subcarrier correspond to shades of the gray scale needed to produce the complete image. Thus, APT imagery is transmitted as an analog signal, at 120 lines per minute (lines/min) or 240 lines/min (see Table 7).

The US polar-orbiting spacecraft use 2400 Hz as the subcarrier frequency. With these satellites, the signal is always modulated at least 5%. If a noise-free signal is available, the user can employ a phase-locked loop circuit to track the subcarrier and use that information for detection and synchronization of the 120-lines/min or 240-lines/min image transmission. Soviet spacecraft use a 2500-Hz subcarrier frequency. On some Soviet platforms, the subcarrier modulation falls below 5% during the scan line. For this reason, it is not always possible to lock on to the subcarrier of these spacecraft with a PLL.

The TIROS-N analog signal is derived from the original digital data of the AVHRR instrument and multiplexed so that two of the five spectral channels are displayed in the APT image. The two spectral channels appear side by side, including a gray scale, minute markers and synchronization telemetry data.

Ground control stations select the visual channel and an infra-red channel during daylight passes. During the nighttime passes, two IR channels are usually found in the APT image. Infra-red imagery represents cold objects (clouds, ice) as light colors and warmer objects (oceans, land, vegetation) as darker shades of gray or black. Fig 43 shows an example of the visual APT channel from the NOAA 9 spacecraft. Fig 44 is a combined visual and IR APT image of Northern Europe taken by NOAA 9. Note the white minute markers against the black background and the gray scale for display calibration.

Soviet APT imagery consists of a single

Fig 43—Visual APT imagery of central US and Mexico imaged by NOAA 9.

Fig 45—APT image from Soviet METEOR-Priroda satellite showing the Southeastern US. There is a telemetry band along the right side.

Fig 44—Visual and IR imagery of Northern Europe taken by NOAA 9.

Fig 46—HRPT image of Northeastern US taken by NOAA 10.

visual image, with gray scale and a telemetry band, scanned at 240 lines/min. During nighttime passes, some Soviet polar orbiters switch to either a 20 lines/min IR format, or a newer 120 lines/min IR mode. Soviet COSMOS and OKEAN platforms also transmit radar imagery at 240 lines/min that may be received in an APT-like format. These spacecraft usually only transmit when in view of a Soviet ground station or ocean tracking vessel. European amateurs can frequently receive these APT radar images from the spacecraft as they transmit the data to receiving stations directly within the Soviet Union. Fig 45 is from a Soviet METEOR spacecraft and shows the southeastern US, with the telemetry data on the right side of the image.

HRPT

In contrast to the lower resolution of the 4 km APT VHF signal, the high-speed digital format of the HRPT offers an outstanding 1.1 km high-resolution image product. The HRPT digital image contains all five spectral channels and telemetry data from the AVHRR instrument (two visual, three IR). Data is transmitted in the SHF band (1698 and 1707 MHz) at 665 kilobits/s, requiring a scan rate of 360 lines/min. Until recently almost all HRPT ground stations were manufactured commercially, costing several hundred thousand dollars.

Development efforts by Dr John DuBois and Ed Murashie have resulted in a low cost, easy to construct amateur HRPT station based on the IBM® personal computer bus.[7] It is now entirely feasible to receive the exceptional HRPT imagery on an IBM PC using much of the same equipment required for the APT imagery. HRPT station requirements will be discussed in greater detail in the next section, but the essential requirements are an S band antenna, preamplifier, down-converter to 137 MHz, HRPT demodulation board, bit and frame synchronizer board (to separate clock and data lines), 137-MHz receiver, and an IBM PC. Fig 46 shows an HRPT image of the northeast coast of the US taken by the NOAA 10 satellite.

Geostationary Satellites

The second type of orbit commonly used for weather satellites is the geostationary orbit. A geostationary satellite is launched into a circular orbit in which the orbital track is directly above the equatorial plane of the Earth, at an altitude of 22,250 miles. At this altitude, the satellite has an orbital period of 24 hours, and appears to maintain the same relative position over the surface of the Earth. Thus, as seen from a receiving station on the ground, the geostationary satellite maintains a fixed position in the sky. This type of orbit is advantageous for remote sensing of meteorological phenomena, since the same area of the Earth can be imaged continuously. Fig 40B illustrates a geostationary orbit.

There are several geostationary weather satellites in orbit. These include the US Geostationary Operational Environmental Satellite (GOES) series, the European Meteosat, Japanese GMS, and Soviet Union GOMS spacecraft.

The primary meteorological instrument on the GOES satellite is the Visible and Infrared Spin Scan Radiometer (VISSR) Atmospheric Sounder (all shortened to VAS). Similar in function to the AVHRR instrument on the polar orbiters, the VAS produces several image products (low and high resolution) available for ground reception.

Geostationary Satellite Facsimile Products

WEFAX

The facsimile format that most amateurs receive is the weather facsimile (WEFAX) product. WEFAX refers to both a com-munications subsystem and a service provided by the GOES satellite. These transmissions are in the 1691 MHz (US) and 1694 MHz (European) bands. Remotely sensed measurements originally acquired by the VISSR instrument on the GOES spacecraft are first transmitted at high data rates to the National Oceanic and Atmospheric Administration (NOAA) command and data acquisition (CDA) ground stations. Visible and IR data of the full Earth disc are reformatted, calibrated, digitally enhanced, and geographically gridded by the CDA computers. These images are then immediately transmitted back to the GOES satellite.

The processed WEFAX images include visible and IR images (7-km resolution) of quadrants of the Earth, operational messages for ground stations, technical bulletins, weather maps from the National Meteorological Center, and processed mosaics of the polar-orbiter APT imagery. The original data source of these final WEFAX images may or may not be the same spacecraft from which they are received.

WEFAX imagery is transmitted at 1691 MHz as an FM signal with a 2400-Hz AM subcarrier. The beginning of the image is marked by a 300-Hz start tone lasting three seconds. A phasing signal lasting five seconds permits automatic synchronization by the display equipment. An image of 800 lines is transmitted for 200 seconds (at 240 lines/min), then followed by a 450-Hz stop tone lasting for five seconds. Note how this format differs from the continuous APT transmission of the polar orbiters.

WEFAX imagery is also rebroadcast on the HF bands, primarily to provide weather information to ships at sea and weather forecasters. These signals differ from those transmitted directly by the satellite in that they are frequency modulated, and require an FM (not AM) demodulator to capture the video data on the display device. Fig 47 shows a typical WEFAX image from the Meteosat 2 geostationary satellite.

VAS

High resolution cloud and temperature imagery in both visible and IR spectra are accomplished through the Visual Atmospheric Sounder (VAS) instrument. VAS provides both day and night two-dimensional cloud and Earth mapping capability with a satellite subpoint resolution of approximately 0.9 km in the visible range, and 6.9 km for the IR image.

The visible and IR VAS images are created simultaneously when light from the Earth falls on a vertical scanning mirror. The radiation then passes through an optical telescope system and various filters focus it on the respective visible and IR sensors. The image is formed by scanning from west to east by the rotation of the spinning spacecraft. The spin rate is 100 r/min or 600 milliseconds per scan line. After each revolution the vertical mirror is stepped to bring the next "strip" of Earth into view (north to south) of the sensors. Scanning the entire image takes 18.2 minutes, with two IR and eight visible samples being taken for each scan line. Synchronizing signals are also sent in the VAS data stream so that images will be

Fig 47—WEFAX image of Southern Europe and Northern Africa taken by the METEOSAT 2 spacecraft. (*photo courtesy of Gottfried Goldner*)

displayed correctly by ground station equipment.

The high speed VAS digital data is transmitted at 1687.1 MHz. The data is modulated on the carrier as bi-phase modulation (BPSK) at 2.11 megabits/s. Because of the wide-band signal, high data rate, and complexity of decoding the imagery, very few people have built systems capable of displaying the VAS imagery directly. WEFAX, which is derived from the complex VAS digital data, is the product that most amateurs receive from GOES.

Commercial ground stations, costing several hundred thousand dollars, are used by many television stations to display VAS imagery on the evening news. The color represented on the VAS image (usually an IR shot), and the 3-D representation of cloud heights is provided by image processing equipment at the television station, not by the satellite itself. (Weather satellite images are transmitted as shades of gray, not colors.)

RF Receiving Equipment

The weather satellite imagery is downlinked in two major frequency bands. The low resolution APT imagery is transmitted in the VHF (137-MHz) frequency range. The high resolution HRPT is transmitted on 1698 and 1707 MHz, GOES WEFAX on 1698 MHz, GOES VAS imagery on 1687.1 MHz, and Meteosat on 1694 MHz. Downconverters for these SHF frequencies are typically used to bring the signal down to a 137-MHz receiver, already being used for the APT direct-readout imagery. Commonly used frequencies are listed in Table 7.

There are a number of commercially manufactured receivers designed specifically to receive weather satellite signals. Both crystal controlled and fully synthesized scanning receivers (136-138 MHz) are available at moderate prices. Several critical factors, including sensitivity of the receiver, selectivity, and receiver IF bandwidth determine the ultimate quality of the image received. Receivers with a front-end sensitivity of 0.2 to 0.5 microvolts for 20 dB of quieting will produce noise-free signals when used with a good preamplifier and omnidirectional antenna.

The receiver IF bandwidth is a very important factor in obtaining good video from weather satellites. To reproduce quality APT imagery, the IF bandwidth must be wide enough to pass the entire signal waveform (the white and black upper and lower peaks). Otherwise, distortion and loss of picture resolution will occur. Too much bandwidth will result in excessive noise in the signal, producing a "snowy" picture.

The bandwidth requirement is influenced by two factors: the satellite transmitter deviation and the Doppler effect. The NOAA platforms have a signal deviation of about 17 kHz, and the Soviet METEOR spacecraft deviation is approximately 15 kHz.

Adding a Doppler shift of ± 4.5 kHz at the time of closest approach, a full IF bandwidth of 30 to 50 kHz is optimal. Most scanners have IF bandwidths of 15 kHz (narrowband FM) and 150 kHz (wideband FM). Since the receiver IF bandwidth is typically established by filters in the IF section, modifications can be easily made to readily available scanners to develop the required 30- to 50-kHz bandwidth. Some people have reported excellent results with unmodified scanners. "Building a Weather Satellite Ground Station: A Primer" includes a complete listing of ground station equipment sources.[8]

Antennas

The antenna design for the APT (137 MHz) signals is not critical, and many commercial two-meter antennas work very well at 137 MHz. The satellite RF signal is right-hand circularly polarized, and severe fading may occur with standard omnidirectional antennas that have nulls in the radiation pattern. A pair of crossed dipoles worked against a ground plane works fine in many cases. Such an antenna is described in the *Weather Satellite Handbook*. A mast-mounted preamplifier can improve reception with such an antenna.

Some amateurs have had good success with ½-λ vertical antennas such as the J-pole antenna for low-Earth-orbit satellites. The Space Communications chapter of this *ARRL Handbook* describes a two-band J-pole antenna for use with the Microsat satellites, and discusses some of the advantages of such an antenna. It should be rather easy to build a single-band version of this antenna scaled to 137 MHz. *The ARRL Antenna Book* provides further design information about J antennas.

Some amateurs use high-gain, satellite-tracking antenna systems (including OSCAR and moonbounce arrays) to receive the polar-orbiting weather-satellite signals. Crossed Yagi directional antennas are quite popular for APT ground stations. A quadrifilar helical antenna is another choice that demonstrates sufficient gain and a good radiation pattern. (You may find that a lot less antenna provides fine reception, however, so it is probably worth experimenting with some of the simpler antennas before building a high-gain array. If you already have a directional array set up for OSCAR work, you might as well use it for APT signal reception, however.)

Although the satellite must be tracked when using a directional antenna, there are interfaces available for personal computers that control the azimuth and elevation angles of the antenna, through the rotator, using a graphics satellite tracking program on the personal computer.[8] *The ARRL Antenna Book* and *The Satellite Experimenter's Handbook*, also published by ARRL, offer many excellent antenna construction projects for use in satellite signal reception.

For the geostationary satellites you will

need a larger antenna, but you have the advantage that you don't need to track the satellite during reception. You will have to reposition the antenna for each satellite, however. A 4-foot or larger diameter parabolic dish, crossed Yagis or loop Yagis with right-hand circular polarization are the most common. Many amateurs use satellite TV dishes and attach their own home-made 1691-MHz feed horn and preamplifier.

Preamplifiers

It is highly recommended that a good preamplifier be used in the RF subsystem. There are a variety of commercial designs available including those using bipolar and GaAsFET devices. For optimum results, the preamp should be mounted at the antenna, and use a good quality coax (such as Belden 9913) with N-connectors for low signal loss. Many two-meter preamps designed for OSCAR satellite use function extremely well at 137 MHz.

Downconverters for SHF Signals

Receiving imagery from GOES WE-FAX, VAS, NOAA HRPT, and Meteosat S-band signals requires some additional RF hardware as compared to APT signals. In general, all of this imagery is transmitted in the 1691- to 1707-MHz range. To receive these S-band signals, a downconverter tuned for the specific frequency is installed at the antenna, and the IF output (at 137.500 MHz) of the converter is fed into the 137-MHz receiver. Thus, the same radio may be used for APT and the high resolution weather satellite signals.

Image Display Systems

Several types of systems are currently available for displaying weather satellite images. These systems vary widely in resolution capabilities, recording and printing functions, digital image enhancement of the satellite imagery, and overall cost of construction. There are four practical methods to display the direct-readout imagery: photographic drum recorders, electrostatic recorders, cathode ray tube (CRT) displays and digital (computer) display systems.

Photographic Drum Recorders

The drum type recorders were described many years ago in *QST* by Wendell Anderson.[9] High quality APT imagery may be displayed by rotating-drum facsimile machines. Light-sensitive photographic paper is wrapped around a long cylinder (drum). The drum spins at exactly the same rate as the satellite-image line rate. If the satellite transmits data at 120 lines/min, for example, the drum must be rotated at exactly 120 revolutions/min. The sensitized paper is exposed one line at a time by an intensity-modulated light source, which is slowly drawn along the length of the drum. In this way the entire length of the paper is exposed. By modulating the light source with the APT or WEFAX tones from the satellites, the video signal is transformed into variations of brightness. After exposure, the photographic paper is developed using standard photographic finishing techniques.

Electrostatic Recorders

Similar printing techniques for reproducing weather satellite imagery can be used on electrostatic facsimile recorders. Electrostatic paper is used on a rotating drum, and an electrical current is passed through the paper. A chemical reaction induces a coloration of the paper, with the amount of coloration directly related with the amount of current flow. Many commercial electrostatic recorders, such as the older Xerox 400, Western Union Desk-Fax, and the K-550 can be modified for weather satellite imagery display.

CRT Monitors

Cathode ray tubes (CRT) may be modified for APT imagery display. The demodulated APT signal is applied as a varying voltage across the tube at the proper rate of speed and line deflection. The image is drawn on the CRT slowly, one line at a time. Because of the time required to draw an entire image on the face of the CRT, a time-lapse photograph of the screen must be taken while the signal is being fed into the display device. A photograph with the varied level of brightness (gray scale) represents the actual satellite image.

Digital Display Systems

With the advent of high-resolution graphics displays, low-cost digital memory chips and disk drives, and digital image-enhancement software for personal computers, digital storage and display of satellite imagery has become the preferred method for the satellite enthusiast. A digital image display system has many advantages over an analog display system (such as the electrostatic recorder), and provides some outstanding functionality and flexibility to store and digitally manipulate the original image. Functions including mass storage of imagery with no loss of data, high resolution graphical displays, digital image processing and color enhancement of the video, zooming, and image animation are all possible.

There are a great variety of personal computers available at costs ranging from several hundred to several thousand dollars. Almost any computer can be adapted for weather satellite image display, storage, and processing. The techniques discussed here focus primarily on processing APT and WEFAX imagery. The underlying methods of capturing the image, storing it digitally on disk, and computer enhancement of the video may be generically applied to the higher resolution HRPT and VAS products as well.

Fig 48 demonstrates the general concept of using a personal computer for APT and WEFAX imagery. Audio output from the

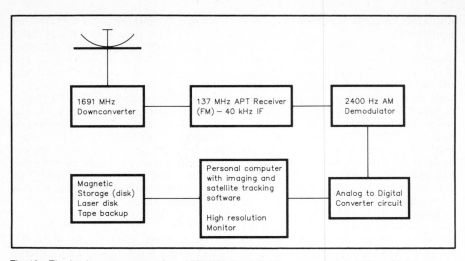

Fig 48—The basic components of an APT/WEFAX digital imagery ground station with image enhancement and storage capabilities are shown.

receiver is fed into an AM demodulator circuit (either an external circuit board or as a card within the PC). The imagery is represented at this point by the changing amplitude of the 2400-Hz modulated tone (video subcarrier). The 2400-Hz subcarrier must be removed (demodulated), leaving only the amplitude variations of the carrier (the actual video). The demodulated video, which consists of a varying analog voltage, must be converted into a digital signal the computer can understand.

An analog-to-digital (A/D) converter circuit will change the varying voltage into relative digital values that can be stored in the computer memory. Typically, the A/D circuit output is 8 binary digits (bits), giving values between 0 and 255 ($2^8 = 256$ values). Each one of these digital values represents one of 256 levels of gray in the satellite image. These 256 digital values must then be converted into a discrete picture element (pixel), which when displayed collectively on the computer monitor, form a coherent satellite image. This step, and those outlined below, require a computer program written for the specific personal computer in use.

The 256 values are assigned a specific level of intensity or brightness that correlates with the original video-signal amplitude. Typically, pure black is assigned a value of 0, with pure white a value of 255. All values in between represent 254 levels of gray. The computer software can also assign specific colors to these 256 values, creating a false coloration of the image. (Each one of the 256 levels also represents a specific temperature level, allowing for software determination of the temperature within clouds, sea and lake temperatures, ocean currents, etc.[10])

The screen display is divided into individual pixels, arranged horizontally across a scan line and into lines vertically down the screen. The number of pixels on

a single line is a function of the resolution of the computer graphics display card and the monitor. The scan lines must be precisely aligned to form a final coherent image on the display. The computer software must be able to detect the beginning of each scan line, position the line in the proper location on the screen, and provide the proper aspect ratio to the entire satellite image. The aspect ratio is in part determined by the scan rate of the software. For the NOAA APT imagery, 120 lines are scanned across the screen every minute.

The actual image resolution displayed on the screen depends on two major factors: the sampling frequency of the original satellite image, and the hardware resolution of the computer graphics card and monitor. Most software APT-capture routines sample at least 2400 samples per line. Higher sampling rates (4800 or 9600 samples per line) provide better resolution during zoom operations, but require a much larger data file to be stored in memory or on disk. The display resolution is very crucial for high resolution imagery. The number of pixels displayed on each line, the number of lines on the screen, and the number of levels of gray scale (or colors) that can be simultaneously displayed will determine the satellite imagery resolution that can be viewed.

Display systems for the IBM PC include the Enhanced Graphics adapter (EGA), which provides a resolution of 640 pixels horizontally by 350 lines and 16 colors (but no gray shades), and the higher resolution Video Graphics Adapter (VGA) with a resolution of 640 pixels horizontally by 480 lines and 25 shades of gray or colors, and the Super VGA with 1024 pixels horizontally by 768 lines and 256 gray shades or colors. A minimum of 16 gray-scale levels is required to resolve the small lakes, rivers, and mountains in the APT direct-readout imagery.

APT and WEFAX software and hardware interfaces are commercially available for the IBM® PC, Apple® // series and Macintosh®, Commodore Amiga®, and other computer systems.[8] Setting up a digital APT/WEFAX computer system can be as simple as installing the interface card (AM demodulator, filters, and A/D converter) in an available slot inside the PC bus, loading the software, plugging in the receiver, and waiting for acquisition of the signal! There have been many articles written in the popular magazines on the construction of APT and WEFAX computer stations.[6, 7, 11, 12, 13]

The basic WEFAX computer system can be upgraded to display HRPT digital imagery. Additional hardware components including a demodulation board, bit synchronizer board (to separate the clock and data signals), and software that scans at 360 lines/min are required. Fig 49 diagrams a basic HRPT station based on the IBM PC. Since the HRPT digital imagery is downlinked at 665 kbits/s, a 16-minute pass will create a raw data file of 80 megabytes. Thus, a large hard disk will be required on the PC.[7]

The digital multimode controllers discussed in the previous section will not copy WEFAX or APT imagery directly from the satellite. These units are manufactured to receive the HF rebroadcasts of the WEFAX data, and employ an FM demodulator for this purpose. An AM demodulator is required to decode the imagery directly from the weather satellites.

Digital Image Enhancement

The satellite imagery is stored in the computer as a digital data file, so it is possible to use image processing software routines to manipulate the data, and enhance the quality of the image. Image processing generally pertains to the alterations and analysis of pictorial information. The digital image is represented by discrete points of defined brightness. Each point has a numeric location within the image file, as well as a numeric brightness (or color). By manipulating these values of brightness within the image, you can carry out complex numeric transformations that can result in a brighter, clearer picture. You can also have the computer add false coloring, edge detection, 3-dimensional effects, animation, and a host of other quantitative and qualitative manipulations. Thus, digital image-display systems can process and manipulate the imagery using methods not available on non-digital display systems, such as the hard copy recorders and fax machines.

Digital image enhancement routines were developed on large mainframe computers during the early days of NASA's planetary

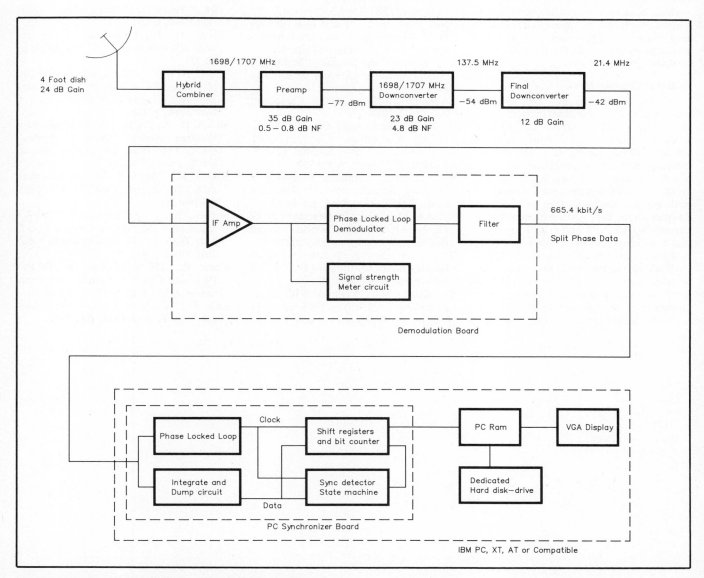

Fig 49—HRPT station block diagram based on the IBM® PC bus.

probe programs. Today there are inexpensive image processing programs for personal computers (some have actually been integrated into the APT software routines) that rival the power and flexibility of those used for the Voyager Neptune encounter!

Satellite Tracking

Another function of the personal computer in a satellite ground station is that of satellite tracking. Predicting the satellite AOS and LOS times used to be a labor intensive effort. Sophisticated graphical satellite tracking programs that display a map of the Earth and the current satellite position are available for the personal computer. These programs can also calculate the correct azimuth and elevation angle for any location. This data is then sent to an interface card that will automatically track the satellite and turn the antennas as the satellite passes overhead.

Satellite Keplerian elements, provided by NASA, may be obtained from computer bulletin board systems (BBS) nationwide. These elements can be automatically loaded into the tracking program, and updated positions of the satellite will be instantly available to the hobbyist.

National Organizations

Interested amateurs may wish to learn about national organizations that are active in weather-satellite-imagery capture and analysis. The Dallas Remote Imaging Group (DRIG) serves as a nationwide clearinghouse of information on new weather satellite launches, image display systems, digital image processing techniques, and satellite tracking. (See note 8.) A 24-hour phone BBS is available containing current NOAA APT and HRPT imagery, and the group also publishes a quarterly newsletter on remote imaging satellites. AMSAT also carries timely information on weather satellites, and markets several satellite tracking programs for personal computers. Through the use of BBS file-transfer techniques, weather satellite imagery received by US ground stations may be "traded" with European stations by transmitting the files over the phone lines. This way imagery not accessible at a particular geographic location may be viewed and compared to the local direct-readout imagery.

REFERENCES

[1]R. Taggart, *Weather Satellite Handbook*, 4th Edition, Available from ARRL and local Amateur Radio dealers.

[2]C. B. Lee, "Build A FAX From Scratch," *73*, July 1976, pp 44-50.

[3]R. J. Summers, T. Gottwald, *Teacher's Guide for Building Weather Satellite Ground Stations*, NASA EP-184 Office of Public Affairs, NASA Goddard Space Flight Center, Greenbelt, MD 20770.

[4]R. Dean, "Facsimile for the Radio Amateur," *73*, Sept 1976, pp 66-77.

[5]M. R. Davidoff, *The Satellite Experimenter's Handbook*, ARRL, 1986. (Second Edition in press.)

[6]C. Abrams, and R. Taggart, "A Color Computer SSTV/FAX System," *73*, Nov 1984, pp 10-21 and Dec 1984, pp 18-32. The computer program offered in this article is no longer available.

[7]J. DuBois, and E. Murashie, "Building an HRPT Station," *Journal of Environmental Satellite Amateur Users Group*, April 1990. PO Box 117088, Carrollton, TX 75011-7088.

[8]Dallas Remote Imaging Group, PO Box 117088, Carrollton, TX 75011-7088, *Building a Weather Satellite Ground Station: A Primer*, April 1990.

[9]W. Anderson, "Amateur Reception of Weather Satellite Picture Transmissions," *QST*, Nov 1965, pp 11-17.

[10]NOAA Technical Memorandum NESS 95, NOAA/NESDIS, World Weather Building, Washington, DC 20233.

[11]H. P. Shuch, "A Weather-Facsimile Display Board for the IBM PC," *QEX*, Sept 1988 pp 3-7 and 15.

[12]G. Zehr, "The VIP: A VIC Image Processor," *QST*, Aug 1985, pp 25-31.

[13]J. Dahl, "A Weather-Facsimile Package for the IBM-PC," Part 1, *QST*, April 1990, pp 15-24, Part 2, *QST*, May 1990, pp 17-21.

Selected Fax Bibliography for Additional Reading

Abrams, C., "In Search of the Perfect Picture," *QST*, Dec 1985, pp 14-17 and Jan 1986, pp 18-24; Feedback, *QST*, Dec 1986, p 47 and *QST*, Feb 1987, p 43.

Emiliani, G. and M. Righini, "An S-band Receiving System for Weather Satellites," *QST*, Aug 1980, pp 28-33; Feedback, *QST*, Nov 1980, p 53.

Emiliani, G. and M. Righini, "Printing Pictures from 'Your' Weather Geostationary Satellite," *QST*, Apr 1981, pp 20-25.

Isleib, G., "WeatherFAX Gray-Scale Generator," *QST*, Nov 1986, pp 22-25 and 29; Feedback, *QST*, Jan 1987, p 37.

Schwittek, E., and W. Schwittek, "WEFAX Pictures on Your IBM PC," *QST*, June 1985, pp 14-18.

Schwittek, E., "HF WEFAX on the IBM PC," Technical Correspondence, *QST*, Dec 1986, p 46.

Shuch, H. P., "Variable Tuning for WEFAX Receivers," *73*, Dec 1979, pp 70-75.

Shuch, H. P., "A Weather-Facsimile Display Board for the IBM PC," *QEX*, Sept 1988, pp 3-7 and 15; Feedback, *QEX*, Nov 1988, p 14.

Shuch, H. P., "A Low-Noise Preamp for Weather Satellite VISSR Reception," *QEX*, Feb 1989, pp 3-9; Feedback, *QEX*, June 1989, p 11.

Sueker, K., "Apple FAX: Weather Maps on a Video Screen," *BYTE*, June 1984, pp 146-151.

Sueker, K., "Real-Time HF WEFAX Maps on a Dot-Matrix Printer," *QST*, Mar 1986, pp 15-20; Feedback, *QST*, July 1986, p 43.

Vester, B., "HF WEFAX for the IBM PC, PCjr and C64," Technical Correspondence, *QST*, May 1987, pp 40-43.

Zehr, G., "The VIP: A VIC Image Processor," *QST*, Aug 1985, pp 25-31.

Chapter 21

Special Modulation Techniques

A mateur Radio is not limited to sending telegraphy, voice or images by conventional modulation systems. There are numerous uses for telecommand (remote control) and telemetry (distant reading of a sensor), both of which may use a variety of signaling techniques. In some applications, telecommand or telemetry signals are sent over a radio link dedicated to that purpose. In others, signaling is sent along with telegraph, voice or image communications in a secondary or incidental way, usually to facilitate communications. This chapter will cover some of the signaling techniques of interest to amateurs. Also, this chapter contains information about uses of experimental transmission techniques by radio amateurs.

RADIO COMMAND AND CONTROL

Amateur Radio may be used for remotely controlling an object or another radio station. Although command and control transmissions may not be used indiscriminately on the amateur bands, FCC rules include a number of special provisions for different applications. Before designing or attempting to operate new telecommand systems, it is a good idea to check *The FCC Rule Book*, available from the ARRL.

According to §97.3(l) of the FCC rules, *radio control operation* is one-way radio communication for remotely controlling objects or apparatus other than Amateur Radio stations. Reading further in §97.3(m), *control* means techniques used for accomplishing the immediate operation of an Amateur Radio station. Control includes one or more of the following: *local control*, *remote control* and *automatic control*. Remote control is defined by §97.3(m) (2) as manual control, with the other control operator monitoring the operation on duty at a control point located elsewhere than at the station transmitter, such that the associated operating adjustment(s) are accessible through a *control link*. §97.3(n) defines a control link as apparatus for effecting remote control be-

Fig. 1 — A typical radio-controlled model airplane with its accompanying control transmitter. The operator works the joysticks, and his or her actions are translated into commands that operate servos to control the airplane.

tween a control point and a remotely controlled station.

Whether controlling objects, apparatus or other Amateur Radio stations, bear in mind that N0N (formerly A0 or F0) emission (an unmodulated carrier) is not permitted below 51 MHz. This would apply to control transmissions that send control signals only occasionally but with the carrier left on continuously.

RADIO CONTROL OF A REMOTE MODEL AIRCRAFT OR VEHICLE

Radio control (R/C) of remote model aircraft or vehicles by hobbyists was started in the 1930s. ARRL's Ross Hull with R. B. Bourne, Clinton DeSoto, Byron Goodman, Harner Selvidge and H. M. Plummer did some early work, as did Walt and William Good. The Good brothers used a radio system to steer the free-flight type of model airplanes back to the launch point. The system was big, and not totally reliable, but it showed definite potential. A large tube-type transmitter on the ground sent a steering pulse on command to a tube-type receiver in the model airplane.

All of the early experimenting was carried on by Amateur Radio operators because amateur frequencies were the only frequencies available. Later, in the early 1950s, Citizen Band spots at 27.255 and 465 MHz were opened by the FCC for shared use by R/C hobbyists. This caused rapid growth of the R/C hobby due to the simpler license.

When the Citizens Band was formed from the old 11-meter amateur band, certain frequencies were set aside for or shared by the R/C enthusiasts. However, since many of the early receivers were wideband superregenerative types, many fliers found their airplanes crashing because of adjacent CB interference. Many became amateurs as a result, and operate to this day at the top of the 6-meter band, a territory unused by most amateurs because of its proximity to TV Channel 2.

Recent pressure by 6-meter FM repeater operators to use this upper area has resulted in the suggested R/C frequencies being moved to the bottom end of 6 meters. Some amateur R/C operators use 10 meters by obtaining new crystals and retuning the

Fig. 2 — Sample signal from an R/C transmitter.

Fig. 3 — The signal seen by each servo.

Fig. 4 — Example of a PCM-encoded signal.

older 27-MHz CB R/C equipment. The bulk of R/C operation occurs on the new license-free radio-control bands at 72-73 and 75-76 MHz.

The license-free frequencies do get overcrowded at many flying fields, so most amateurs who are R/C hobbyists purchase 6-meter R/C transmitters and receivers.

Uses

The majority of R/C systems are used for controlling the flight of model airplanes, as shown in Fig. 1. Other applications include R/C cars and R/C motorboats and sailboats. The airplanes vary in size from about a pound in weight with a 1-foot wingspan to gigantic multi-engine models weighing over 50 pounds with 15-foot wingspans. Many modelers fly large-wingspan gliders. R/C cars may have electric motors or be gas-engine driven.

The operator controls the model from a transmitter that has control sticks. Miniature receivers are built into the model to receive signals from the transmitter. The action of the control sticks is sent through the transmitter and receiver to servos located in the model. These translate the stick movement into some mechanical movement which produces the desired control. The operator can control movements such as ailerons, elevator, rudder or throttle in an airplane. The operator may control the steering, throttle, rudder or a sail winch in a model car or boat. Often, more sophisticated scale models have other systems controlled remotely, such as retracting wheels, "bomb dropping," flaps, battleship guns that turn and fire, anchors that raise and lower, and many other interesting actions.

Because R/C systems are widely available at low cost, amateurs can use them for many unique applications around the station that may require some kind of mechanical adjustment. The amateur TV station can have its TV cameras panned, zoomed or focused using R/C. Potentiometers or tuning knobs can be turned by R/C. Miniature antennas could be turned by some of the special high-thrust servos intended for very large model airplanes. Several amateurs active on SSTV use R/C servos to swing in color filters over their black-and-white TV cameras.

Design

Most current R/C designs consist of a low-power transmitter that sends out a repeating series of width-modulated pulses to the R/C receiver. Each width-modulated pulse represents a single channel, for example the rudder channel. An R/C system is rated by the number of channels it supports, based on how many of these width-modulated pulses are involved. See Fig. 2. For example, systems are called 4-channel systems, 7-channel systems, and so on. An R/C system also may be sending out more than "4 channels," but only have four servos or four control sticks included with the system, so it is still known as a "4 channel." The series of pulses repeat about 50 times a second, so that any control stick movement can quickly result in an appropriate servo movement.

Each channel's servo monitors a positive pulse that varies in duration between 1 and 2 milliseconds, centered at 1.5 ms. See Fig. 3. The servo's electronics are designed so a 1.5-ms pulse will cause the motor to move the control arm to a centered position. If the pulse width changes to 1 ms, the servo control arm will turn 45 degrees in one direction. If the pulse width had changed to 2 ms, the servo control arm would have turned 45 degrees in the other direction. The servo quickly reacts to any change in the transmitter control stick, and maintains position if no new stick movement has occurred. Depending on manufacturer and type, the precise pulse duration and amount may vary slightly.

Some servos are very small and light, with little torque. Others are larger with considerable torque. Most of the newer servos have three leads — a ground or common lead, a +4.8-volt lead, and the pulse lead. Prices vary from $10 to $50 per servo.

Some recent systems utilize pulse-coded modulation (PCM) instead of the traditional pulse-width modulation scheme. See Fig. 4. PCM sends the absolute position of each channel, encoded as bits (similar to ASCII), plus a check bit. The receiver is then able to reject any faulty or corrupted signal, and use the last good position setting. If no good positions arrive over a predetermined short period of time, the system can reset the servos to an assumed safe postion, such as low throttle and neutral control surfaces, until the system once again obtains acceptable PCM codes.

Most of the existing R/C transmitters use discrete components to encode the pulses. Fig. 1 shows a prototype transmitter that uses a CMOS microprocessor for the encoding task. The block diagram of such a transmitter is shown in Fig. 5. This transmitter has the ability to have totally new control features and options added by simply replacing the program in EPROM. This transmitter can retain the flight trim

Fig. 5 — Simplified block diagram of a microprocessor-encoded R/C transmitter.

Fig. 6 — UoSAT-OSCAR command station, G3YJO, at the University of Surrey, Guildford, Surrey, England. At A is the 2-m, 70-cm and 23-cm az-el antenna array. Inside the station, at B, are the digital command and display consoles alongside the transmitting and receiving equipment.

settings of four different airplanes, or it could provide an unlimited number of channels for unique applications such as scale boats or robotics.

Because of the potentially lethal nature of R/C airplanes flying often in excess of 100 mi/h, 6-meter repeater operators on 50 MHz or 53 MHz should coordinate their frequencies with the local R/C clubs. The most commonly used Amateur Radio R/C frequencies are: 53.1, 53.2, 53.3, 53.4, 53.5, 53.6, 53.7, 53.8 and 53.9 MHz. Most current Amateur Radio R/C activities occur on 53.1 to 53.5. Frequencies expected to be used in the future are:

Frequency	Channel No.
50.80	00
50.82	01
50.84	02
50.86	03
50.88	04
50.90	05
50.92	06
50.94	07
50.96	08
50.98	09

RADIO REMOTE CONTROL OF AN AMATEUR RADIO STATION

Radio communication for remotely controlling another Amateur Radio station is considered *auxiliary operation* by the FCC. All Amateur Radio bands above 220.5 MHz (excluding 431 to 433 and 435 to 438 MHz) are available for auxiliary operation. FCC rules specify that the remotely controlled station must have provisions to limit transmission to a period of no more than 3 minutes in the event of malfunction in the control link.

Remote Control of a Repeater

When remotely controlling a station in *repeater operation*, the control link must use frequencies above 220.5 MHz and may not use the input (receiving) frequencies of the repeater, according to FCC rules. For

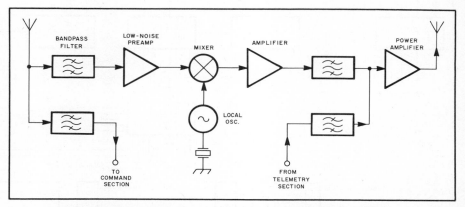

Fig. 7 — Functional block diagram of a typical satellite transponder showing telecommand and telemetry channels.

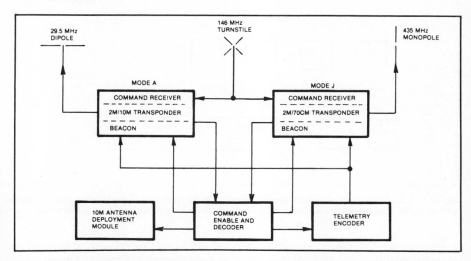

Fig. 8 — AMSAT-OSCAR 8 satellite functional block diagram. OSCAR 8 telemetry was sent using 20-WPM Morse code. A complete set of data required about 20 seconds to send.

a discussion of repeater-control methods see Chapter 14.

Telecommand of a Satellite

The FCC defines *telecommand operation* as earth-to-space Amateur Radio communication to initiate, modify or terminate functions of a station in space operation (that is, an Amateur Radio communications satellite).

The following frequencies are available for telecommand operation: 7.0-7.1, 14.0-14.25, 21.0-21.45, 24.89-24.99, 28.0-29.7, 144-146, 435-438 and 24,000-24,050 MHz.

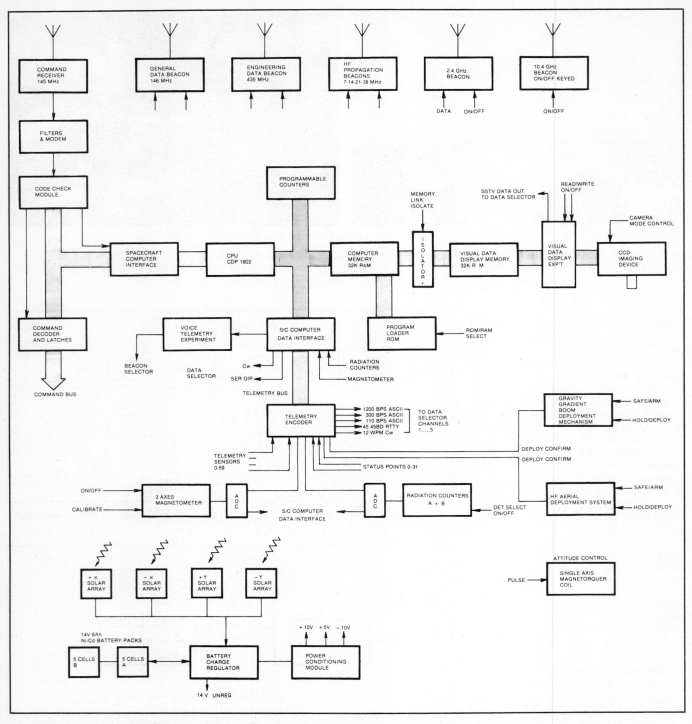

Fig. 9 — UoSAT-OSCAR 9 functional block diagram. The OSCAR 9 telemetry system has provisions for monitoring 60 analog sensor channels and 45 digital status points. Telemetry data can be sent on Morse code, RTTY (Baudot code) or ASCII.

Stations in telecommand operation are exempt from station identification requirements and may transmit special codes intended to obscure the meaning of command messages to the satellite, according to §97.421 of the FCC rules.

Telecommand links are used to switch OSCAR satellites from one operating mode to another and to turn off a malfunctioning transmitter that might cause interference. In addition, the ability to telecommand subsystems prolongs the useful life of the satellite by turning off parts of the satellite to conserve energy. Command frequencies, codes and transmission formats are confidential and provided only to AMSAT-approved command stations.

There are volunteer command stations in more than 8 countries. Fig. 6 shows the UoSAT-OSCAR command station at the University of Surrey, England.

TELEMETRY

Telemetry is the process of measuring a quantity, transmitting the result to a distant station, and there indicating or recording the measured quantity. It is strongly associated with rocketry and satellites but has many other applications. In many instances where radio is used to telecommand or control a distant radio station, a telemetry link is needed to monitor conditions at the remote station. When a command is sent, telemetry provides the feedback necessary to see whether the command was carried out and to monitor conditions afterwards to ensure the desired results.

AMATEUR-SATELLITE TELEMETRY

In §97.403(d) of the FCC rules, telemetry is defined as space-to-earth transmissions, by a station in space operation, of results of measurements made in the station, including those relating to the function of the station. The FCC considers telemetry transmissions by amateur satellites to be permissible one-way communications and says that such transmissions may consist of specially coded messages intended to facilitate communications.

Telemetered information typically includes satellite temperature, solar-cell current, battery temperature and voltage, and other parameters that describe the electrical and mechanical conditions of the satellite. Telemetry data may also include the results of scientific observations in the case of amateur satellites with a research mission.

Telemetry is transmitted by means of a beacon, usually just outside the satellite's communications passband. Beacon transmitters typically have output power levels of 50 mW to 1 W depending on the altitude of the spacecraft. Telemetry encoding methods vary, but OSCAR satellites have used Morse code, Baudot radioteletype, "advanced encoding techniques" (ASCII for computer processing) and digitized speech.

SIGNALING

Signaling systems for command, control and telemetry must be designed with high reliability in mind. Many early signaling systems used analog transmission techniques to represent continuously variable quantities by the amplitude, frequency or duration of a tone. Most new systems use some type of digital transmission technique and often include a degree of redundancy for detection and correction of errors.

Multiplexing

Most signaling systems are capable of sending more than one piece of information in the same transmission. For example, the telemetry from a satellite might routinely include a complete system check with readings from numerous sensors. Combining two or more streams of information on one radio carrier is called *multiplexing*.

Frequency-division multiplexing (FDM) is a method of sending each of the information streams over separate subcarriers, each at a different frequency. The subcarriers could be modulated in various ways, according to the nature of the information. Fig. 10 illustrates the baseband of an FDM signal.

Time-division multiplexing (TDM) uses only one channel but assigns the different data streams to different time slots. For example, telemetry from sensor 1 could be followed in turn by that of sensors 2, 3, and

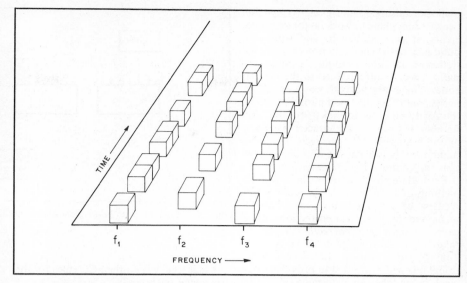

Fig. 10 — Frequency-division multiplexing (FDM). Each block represents a logical 1 being transmitted. The spaces in between are 0s. Four streams of data are being sent, each on a separate frequency.

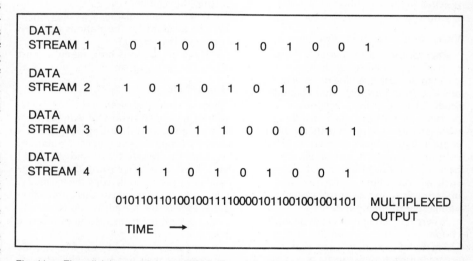

Fig. 11 — Time-division multiplexing (TDM). Four data streams are interleaved to produce one multiplexed data stream at four times the individual data rate.

so forth, as shown in Fig. 11.

Coding

Essentially every signaling system, whether for control or telemetry, requires some type of encoding at the sending station and decoding at the receiving station. A voltage or current reading cannot be transmitted in its original form but could be used to frequency-modulate an audio tone suitable for transmission. The signal can be demodulated by a frequency-to-voltage converter. Alternatively, the original signal could have been fed to an analog-to-digital converter to produce a digital code that, in turn, could frequency-shift key an audio tone. This signal could be received by an FSK demodulator and decoded by a digital-to-analog converter.

In general, FCC rules permit codes where they facilitate communication rather than obscure meaning. A careful reading of *The*

FCC Rule Book is advised before using specific coding and modulation systems.

Error Control

When designing a signaling system, particularly one for command and control, serious attention should be given to the possibility of errors and the consequences of those errors causing undesirable results. There is no such thing as an error-free communications channel, although some approach the level of perfection. Amateur Radio channels are subject to noise, interference and fading, so some errors may be encountered from time to time. It is best to ensure that the communications channel has a basic reliability well into the 90% range before considering it for control purposes.

It is worthwhile to consider at least some type of *error detection* scheme to prevent the decoder from accepting erroneous commands or falsing on no signal. To give the decoder something to work on for detecting errors, it is necessary to add some redundancy to the encoding process prior to transmission. For example, a single-bit parity check is often added to the ASCII code. There are several ways of using parity, but using the ''odd parity'' system, the parity bit is set to make sure that the number of 1 bits in the character is always an odd number. If, on reception, the number of 1s is even, the decoder knows that the command contains an error.

Error-detection systems are simply methods of confirming the (probable) correctness of a signal. More sophisticated techniques provide error correction, often called *forward error correction (FEC)*. It takes more than 1 bit of redundancy for a 7-bit code to implement FEC. Several additional bits will be needed to provide sufficient redundancy to determine what the correct signal should have been. The exact ratio of parity bits to original coding bits varies according to the specific type of FEC system and the percentage of errors that the system can correct on its own.

Encryption and Authentication

Encryption is a technique of encoding each symbol against a changing key in order to obscure meaning or prevent someone else from knowing what command to send. The FCC has recognized its importance as a safeguard against tampering with satellites and permits its use for telecommand of amateur spacecraft. The FCC rules do not presently permit encryption to be used for other Amateur Radio purposes, such as controlling a repeater. Yet, it is undesirable to use a control system that is vulnerable to manipulation.

Where tampering is a threat, an *authentication* technique should be considered. Using this approach, you can send the same command each time but have a changing element appended to the end for authentication purposes. For example, if the command for turning on the autopatch is OA, then the first transmission of that command might be OA7, the next one OAR, the third OAM, and so forth, the third character being selected from a sequence known only to the encoder and decoder.

SPECIFIC SIGNALING TECHNIQUES

Before settling on a specific signaling technique, it is useful to consider some of the trade-offs. Here is a suggested checklist:

• What is the original form of the data to be transmitted?
• Does it need to be converted to a transmissible format?
• Will the modulation fit within a standard voice channel, on-off or frequency-shift-key a transmitter, or does it need a special modulator?
• What type of demodulator is required?
• Does the data need to be converted after demodulation?

Fig. 12 — Block diagram of a typical AMSAT-OSCAR Morse code telemetry encoder.

• Is it legal within the FCC rules for the frequency purposes?
• Is frequency coordination needed?
• Will the encoding/modulating equipment be accessible to the stations transmitting the signals?
• Will the demodulating/decoding equipment be available to the stations expected to receive the signals?
• Have precautions been taken against errors, tampering or simple loss of control?

Morse Code

Morse code has been used for transmitting telemetry from OSCAR satellites because no special decoding equipment is needed to copy the telemetry information. See Fig. 12. Speeds of 10 and 20 WPM have been used to ensure that a large number of people could copy the telemetry. The chief disadvantage of this application is that speeds that are easily copied aurally do not permit the transmission of massive data.

If sent using on-off keying, Morse-code transmission may not be reliable enough for command and control purposes. Use of frequency-shift keying would overcome that problem. Computers can be used for both the generation and decoding of Morse characters.

Baudot Code

ITA2 (commonly called Baudot) is normally a direct-printing telegraph system. However, §97.69 of the FCC rules provides that ITA2 figures-case characters except the numerals and slant bar may be used for remote control of receiving printers and other objects. The purpose of doing so must be to facilitate communication, not to obscure meaning. The codes available for control purposes are the figures-case positions corresponding to the following letters: A, S, D, F, G, H, J, K, L, Z, C, V, B, N and M.

For telemetry purposes, the complete ITA2 character set may be used. Numerous amateurs throughout the world are equipped to receive and print these transmissions.

The complete ITA2 character set is given in Chapter 19.

AMTOR

What was said about ITA2 applies to AMTOR, as AMTOR uses the ITA2 character set. However, AMTOR has two optional error-control modes (ARQ and FEC), which may be valuable for control or telemetry transmissions.

ASCII

ASCII has a larger character set than ITA2. Further, it is usually sent at speeds much higher than ITA2 or AMTOR. Also, it is the native code for most microcomputers, making code conversion unnecessary. These advantages make ASCII suitable for many telemetry applications.

The same FCC rule provision for controlling printers or other objects mentioned above for Baudot applies even more so in this case. The reason is that ASCII has a much larger number of control characters already built into the code. See Chapter 19 for the complete ASCII character set.

Digitized Speech

UoSAT-OSCAR 9 first used digitized speech for telemetry. It has the advantage that anyone who knows the English language can instantly decode the meaning. It is particularly useful for educational demonstrations involving students in the lower grades. Its low data rate for easy listening makes it unsuitable for most telemetry applications.

Amateur Television

It may seem strange to consider amateur television (both slow scan and fast scan) as a signaling system, but don't overlook it as a possibility. Image communications systems are excellent for some types of telemetry. TV could be used to look at meter faces, confirm that an antenna system is still there and pointing in the right direction, or could look at the weather situation at a remote location. The camera can be remotely controlled so it can view

Fig. 13 — DTMF key pad layout. Whenever a key is pressed, the pad produces two AF tones, one from the low group and one from the high group. Twelve-button key pads are standard. Optional 16-button key pads are available on some hand-held radios.

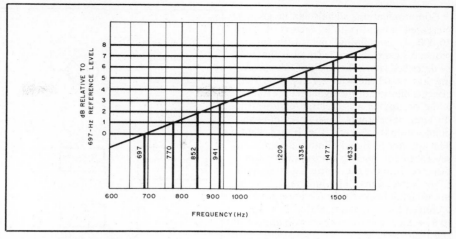

Fig. 14 — The effect of pre-emphasis on DTMF tones.

different scenes, zoom in on items of interest, and so forth. Fast-scan ATV might also be the "eyes" for remote control of models.

Dual-Tone Multifrequency Signaling

In the late 1940s, Bell Laboratories developed the Touch-Tone® signaling system to replace telephone pulse dialing. The dual-tone multifrequency (DTMF) signaling system, as it is known generically, became widely used in Amateur Radio with the introduction of autopatches to 2-meter FM repeaters. Repeater operators also found many control applications for DTMF. These aspects of DTMF signaling are covered in Chapter 14.

The fact that many amateurs own VHF/UHF transceivers with built-in DTMF encoders makes DTMF an attractive candidate for a variety of control purposes. However, this is simply a one-way advantage (that is, from a hand-held transceiver to a base unit) because the hand-held radios do not presently include DTMF decoders. Such decoders would be used for selective-calling purposes in order to mute the hand-held receiver until a prearranged tone sequence is received.

The standard 12-button DTMF key pad is a 2-out-of-7 tone encoder, meaning that the encoder selects one tone from the low group of 697, 770, 852 or 941 Hz and a second from the high group of 1209, 1336 or 1477 Hz. An optional 16-button DTMF key pad is also available; it is a 2-out-of-8 tone encoder. The 16-button variety uses the additional high-group frequency of 1633 Hz. The key pad layout with tones related to character assignments is shown in Fig. 13.

A number of amateurs have puzzled over how to encode the 26 Latin letters on a DTMF pad. There is an encoding scheme that was originally devised to enable the deaf to use a DTMF pad on a telephone to report a fire to the local fire department. In this system, two buttons are pressed for each letter. First, push the button with the letter printed on it — that would be the "2"

button for A, B and C. The result would be ambiguous, so press *, 0 or # to indicate whether it is A, B or C, respectively. The only problem left is what to do with Q or Z, which do not appear anywhere on the key pad. The solution is to send ** for Q and ## for Z. They're easy to remember because they fall directly below the keys (PRS) and (WXY) where they were omitted. As an example, 225 Main St. would be encoded

$$\frac{2}{2}\ \frac{2}{2}\ \frac{5}{5}\ \frac{M}{6*}\ \frac{A}{2*}\ \frac{I}{4\#}\ \frac{N}{60}\ \frac{S}{7\#}\ \frac{T}{8*}$$

DTMF signals may be encoded with either a manual key pad or an automatic dialer. With manual keying, the duration of the tone depends on how long the key is pressed, and the length of the wait between tones is a function of how long the operator takes to press the next key. A minimum dwell time of 30 to 40 ms is necessary to ensure that most DTMF decoders will properly recognize the tones. Typical decoders need at least 10 ms delay between tones and may reset themselves if the next tones are not received within 2.5 seconds. Thus, a decoder designed for 35 ms dwell time and 15 ms of spacing could decode up to 20 digits per second. Automatic dialers are programmed to transmit one or more telephone numbers in rapid sequence. Repertory dialers are automatic dialers that store a large quantity of telephone numbers, any one of which can be recalled by a few key strokes.

Twist or tone differential refers to the relative amplitude difference between the low-group and high-group tones, expressed in decibels. DTMF tone encoders are usually designed to produce a twist of 3 dB, where the high group is at the higher amplitude. Some DTMF key pads have an internal adjustment that can vary the low or high group as much as ±5 dB. DTMF decoders can tolerate a certain amount of twist, sometimes as much as 12 dB, without malfunctioning, in order to allow latitude for misadjustment of the encoder and fre-

quency distortion in the communications channel.

When DTMF tones are fed into the audio input stage of an FM transmitter, the levels of all tones should be about equal at that point. The DTMF tones should emerge from the audio-processing stage of the transmitter without clipping. Any clipping at this point will generate intermodulation products that could cause interference and may hinder proper decoding at the receiving station. In a normal FM transmitter, the modulation is pre-emphasized by 6 dB per octave. This means that a frequency of 1394 Hz would be 6 dB higher after pre-emphasis than a 697-Hz tone, assuming that both tones were of the same amplitude before pre-emphasis. Fig. 14 shows the relative amplitudes of the DTMF tones after pre-emphasis. It can be seen that the combination of the highest tone from the low group (941 Hz) and the highest from the high group (1477 Hz on a 12-button key pad and 1633 on a 16-button key pad) will produce the greatest frequency deviation. So when you set the peak deviation for DTMF signaling on an FM transmitter, it is necessary to do so at the highest tones from the low and high groups. On a 12-digit key pad use the pound sign (#) to adjust the deviation to about 3 kHz (for a transmitter designed for 5-kHz deviation on voice peaks).

At the receiving end, 6-dB-per-octave de-emphasis does the job of restoring the DTMF tones to an equal level.

SPREAD-SPECTRUM COMMUNICATIONS

The common rule of thumb for judging the efficiency of a modulation scheme is to examine how tightly it concentrates the energy of the signal for a given rate of information. While the compactness of the signal appeals to the conventional wisdom, spread-spectrum modulation techniques take the exact opposite approach — that of spreading the signal out over a very wide bandwidth.

Communications signals can be greatly increased in bandwidth by factors of 10 to 10,000 by combining them with binary sequences using several techniques that will be described later. The result of this spreading has two beneficial effects. The first effect is dilution of the signal energy so that while occupying a very large bandwidth, the amount of power density present at any point within the spread signal is very slight. The amount of signal dilution depends on several factors such as transmitting power, distance from the transmitter and the width of the spread signal. The dilution may result in the signal being below the noise floor of a conventional receiver, and thus invisible to it, while it can be received with a spread-spectrum receiver!

The second beneficial effect of the signal spreading process is that the receiver can reject strong undesired signals—even those much stronger than the desired spread-spectrum signal power density. This is because the desired receiver has a copy of the spreading sequence and uses it to "despread" the signal. Nonspread signals are then suppressed in the processing. The effectiveness of spread spectrum's interference-rejection property has made it a popular military antijamming technique.

Conventional signals such as narrow-band FM, SSB and CW are rejected, as are other spread-spectrum signals not bearing the desired pseudonoise (PN) coding sequence. The result is a type of private channel, one in which only the spread-spectrum signal using the same pseudonoise sequence will be accepted by the spread-spectrum receiver. A two-party conversation can take place, or if the code sequence is known to a number of people, net-type operations are possible.

The use of different binary sequences allows several spread-spectrum systems to operate independently of each other within the same band. This is a form of sharing called code-division multiple access. If the system parameters are chosen judiciously and if the right conditions exist, conventional users in the same band space will experience very little interference from spread-spectrum users. This allows more signals to be packed into a band; however, each additional signal, conventional or spread spectrum, will add some interference to all users.

Benefits for Spectrum Managers

Effective spectrum management attempts to use a band as fully as possible while keeping interference to a minimum. A limit exists as to how many signals can be put in a band. When the allocation is used up, additional stations that use conventional modes may cause interference that degrades or blocks communications by other users. Additional spread-spectrum signals, however, may not cause severe interference; they just raise the background noise level. The limit to the number of spread-spectrum signals that can occupy a

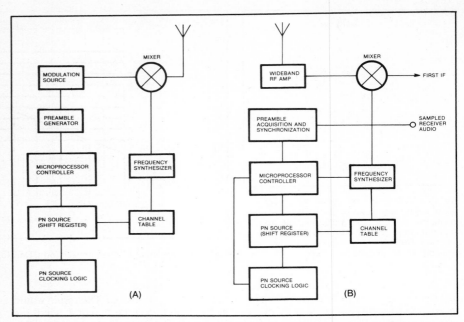

Fig. 15 — The block diagram of a frequency-hopping (FH) transmitter is shown at A. The channel table contains frequencies that the FH transmitter will visit as it hops through the band. These channels are selected to avoid interference to fixed band users (such as repeaters). The preamble employs the falling edge of an audio tone to trigger hopping. Conventional modulation, such as SSB, is employed. The block diagram at B is for an FH receiver. Preamble acquisition and synchronization trigger the beginning of the hopping mode and keep the receiver channel changes in step with the transmitter.

Fig. 16 — A graphic representation of the distribution of power as the signal bandwidth increases. The unspread signal (A) contains most of its energy around a center frequency. As the bandwidth increases (B), the power about the center frequency falls. At C and D, more energy is being distributed in the spread signal's wider bandwidth. At E, the energy is diluted as the spreading achieves a very wide bandwidth. Bandwidth is roughly twice the bit speed of the PN code generator.

band is sometimes called a "soft" limit because the effects of over allocation are not as severe as the rapid degradation caused by over allocation of conventional users.

Overlay is a spectrum-management concept that takes advantage of the spread-spectrum signal rarification and interference-rejection effects to share a band with conventional modulation users. In bands that are channelized and are fully allocated by assigned users such as repeaters, there are few ways to accommodate new users. Yet, viewing such a band on a spectrum analyzer reveals that much of the spectrum is only lightly used because of the intermittent use of many repeaters and the presence of numerous guard bands between fixed channels.

In the overlay concept, the spread-spectrum signal is continuously spread over a shared band. It can exist in both the unused guard bands and on intermittently used repeater channels. It is, in effect a form of frequency diversity that takes advantage of whatever unused spectrum space is available within its spreading width.

Spread spectrum possesses a number of additional advantages. Spread spectrum provides a degree of protection against fading (a large variation in received signal strength caused by reflections, as in TV "ghosts"). Frequency-selective fading typically affects a relatively narrow band of frequencies. The spread carrier offers a form of frequency diversity that can offset the faded frequencies by those within the spread-spectrum signals that do not experience the same fading. The effects of reflective or multipath interference, which result from several parts of the same signal arriving at the spread-spectrum receiver at slightly different times, can be largely reduced. Signals that arrive late at the spread-spectrum receiver will not match the spreading code currently being used to decode the signal. Hence they are rejected as interference.

Finally, spread spectrum can be used to construct very precise ranging and radar systems. The spread carrier, modulated with the PN sequence, permits the receiver to measure very precisely the time the signal was sent; thus, spread spectrum can be used to time the distance to a transmitter for ranging, or to an object as in the case of a radar reflection. Both applications have been commonly used in the aerospace field for many years.

Types of Spread Spectrum

There are numerous ways to cause a carrier to spread; however, all spread-spectrum systems can be viewed as two modulation processes. First, the information to be transmitted is applied. A conventional form of modulation, either analog or digital, is commonly used for this step. Second, the carrier is modulated by the spreading code, causing it to spread out over a large bandwidth. Four spreading techniques are commonly used in military and space communications, but amateurs are currently authorized to use only the frequency hopping and direct sequence techniques.

Frequency Hopping

Frequency hopping (FH) is a form of spreading in which the center frequency of a conventional carrier is altered many times a second in accordance with a pseudo-random list of channels. See Fig. 15. The amount of time the signal is present on any single channel is called the dwell time. To avoid interference both to a conventional user and from conventional users, the dwell time must be very short, commonly less than 10 milliseconds.

Direct Sequence

Direct sequence (DS) is a second form of spreading in which a very fast binary bit stream is used to shift the phase of an RF carrier. This binary sequence is designed to appear to be random (that is, a mix of approximately equal numbers of zeroes and ones), but is generated by a digital circuit. This binary sequence can be duplicated and synchronized at the transmitter and receiver. Such sequences are called pseudo-noise or PN. See Fig. 16. Each PN code bit is called a *chip*. The phase shifting is commonly done in a balanced mixer that typically shifts the RF carrier between 0 and 180 degrees; this is called binary phase-shift keying (BPSK). Other types of phase-shift keying are also used. For example, quad-rature phase-shift keying (QPSK) shifts between four different phases.

DS spread spectrum is typically used to transmit digital information. See Figs. 17 and 18. A common practice in DS systems is to mix the digital information stream with the PN code. The result of this mixing causes the PN code to be either inverted for a number of PN chips for an information bit of one or left unchanged for an information bit of zero. This modulation process is called bit-inversion modulation for obvious reasons. The resulting PN code is mixed with the RF carrier to produce the DS signal.

Chirp

The third spreading method employs a carrier that is swept over a range of frequencies. This method is called *chirp* spread spectrum and finds its primary application in ranging and radar systems.

Time Hopping

The last spreading method is called *time hopping*. In a time-hopped signal, the carrier is on-off keyed by the PN sequence, resulting in a very low duty cycle. The speed of keying determines the amount of signal spreading.

A hybrid system is formed by combining two or more forms of spread spectrum into a single system. Typically, a hybrid system combines the best points of two or more spread-spectrum systems. The performance

Fig. 17 — In bit-inversion modulation, a digital information stream is combined with a PN bit stream, which is clocked at four times the information rate. The combination is the exclusive-OR sum of the two. Notice that an information bit of one inverts the PN bits in the combination, while an information bit of zero causes the PN bits to be transmitted without inversion. The combination bit stream has the speed characteristics of the original PN sequence, so it has a wider bandwidth than the information stream.

Fig. 18 — The block diagram of a direct sequence transmitter is shown at A. The digital modulation source is mixed with a combination of the PN sequence mixed with the carrier oscillator. The PN sequence is clocked at a much faster rate than the digital modulation; a very fast composite signal emerges as a result of the mixing. The preamble is selected at the start of transmission. Part B shows a direct sequence receiver. The wideband signal is translated down to a baseband (common) frequency. The processes form a correlator, mixing a baseband oscillator with the PN source and then mixing the result against the incoming baseband RF. The synchronization process keeps the PN sequence in step by varying the clock for optimal lock. After mixing, the information is contained as a digital output signal and all interference is spread to noise. The low-pass filter removes some of this noise. Notice that the transmitter and receiver employ very similar designs, one to perform spreading, the other to despread.

tests devised to identify random sequences. Codes that have random-like properties are called pseudorandom or pseudonoise sequences.

Correlation

Correlation is a fundamental process in a spread-spectrum system and forms a common method of receiving signals. Correlation measures how alike two signals are; that is, how similar in appearance they are to each other. The degree of likeness is often expressed as a number between zero and one. A perfect match is typically indicated by a one, while no match may be indicated by a zero. Partial matches yield values between one and zero, depending upon likeness.

In a spread-spectrum receiver, correlation is often used to identify a signal that has been coded with a desired PN sequence. Correlation is usually done with a circuit known as a correlator. A correlator is typically composed of a mixer followed by a low-pass filter that performs averaging. The mixer is where the two signals to be compared are multiplied together. A match yields a high value of output; but if the two mixed signals differ, the output will be lower depending on how different the signals are. The averaging circuit reports the average output of the mixer. This value is therefore the average likeness of the two signals.

In a DS system, the correlator is used to identify and detect signals with the desired spreading code. Signals spread with other PN codes, or signals not spread at all, will differ statistically from the desired signal and give a lower output from the correlator. The desired signal will have a strong match with locally generated PN code and yield a larger output from the correlator.

Notice that the averaging circuit of the correlator gives the average mixer value over time. If noise or interference is present, some of the received signal will be corrupted. After mixing, the interfering signals are spread and resemble noise, while the desired signal is despread and narrowband. The averaging circuit of the correlator then performs a low-pass filter function, thereby reducing the noise while passing the desired narrowband information. This is the heart of the DS interference-rejection process.

Correlation action in an FH system is implemented differently, but the concept is the same. In a frequency-hopping system, the transmitter carrier frequency is being moved about many times a second according to the spreading sequence. The receiver uses the same spreading sequence to follow the transmitter, moving from channel to channel in exact step with the signal. If the receiver is out of step with the signal, it cannot recover the information being transmitted.

FH signals that are under the control of a different PN sequence will be received only randomly, by the chance that both the

of a hybrid system is usually better than can be obtained with a single spread-spectrum technique for the same cost. The most common hybrids combine both frequency-hopping and direct-sequence techniques.

Spreading Sequences

One of the most important aspects of spread spectrum is the PN sequence used to spread the RF carrier. The spreading sequence determines how well the various properties of spread spectrum will perform.

The spreading sequence takes a form geared to the type of spread spectrum being used. For frequency hopping, the spreading code is a stream of numbers that represent the channels to which the frequency hopper will travel. In a DS system, the spreading code is a very fast bit stream generated by a digital circuit. In both cases, the PN code is generated to resemble random activity and passes many of the desired and undesired PN codes have a channel in common at that moment. Narrowband signals will be visited occasionally by the hopping signal and should not be a cause of interference.

Despreading and Detection

In DS systems, collapsing the spread-spectrum signal by removing the effects of the spreading sequence is called despreading. If the DS signal is viewed as a signal with two types of modulation impressed on it (one for spreading and the other containing information) then despreading is a demodulation step aimed at the spreading sequence. What remains after the removal of the spreading sequence is the digital information stream.

The despreading process is in fact performed by a correlator containing a mixer and an averaging circuit. In the correlator, like signals produce a high value while unlike signals produce lower values. Thus signals that are the same produce high outputs because the signals reinforce each other. Signals that are unlike cannot reinforce each other and therefore form lower-valued products.

Bit-inversion modulation is detected by this correlator action since an information bit of "1" caused the PN code to be inverted, while a "0" leaves the PN code unchanged. In the correlator, a "0" information bit generates an uninverted PN code stream that closely correlates with the local PN code. Comparatively, a "1" results in a complete decorrelation since the PN code is inverted for this information bit. Through this action the correlator recovers the transmitted information.

Undesired signals in the DS receiver passband are not correlated with the local PN code. Within the correlator, the undesired signals randomly fall in and out of match on a bit-by-bit basis. Here the mixer output resembles noise that is filtered by the correlator low-pass filter. In comparison, the mixer will produce a stream of ones for an uninverted PN sequence or a stream of zeros for the inverted PN sequence.

Thus, the mixing process despreads the desired spread-spectrum signal and causes the undesired signals to spread to noise. It is mainly through the mixing process that interference is rejected within a spread-spectrum receiver.

Spreading Sequence Generators

Generation of the PN sequence is commonly done with linear-feedback shift registers (LFSR). See Fig. 19. The shift register consists of a number of one-bit memory registers that shift their contents to the right with each clock pulse. New values are introduced at the left-most stage while output is commonly taken from the right-most stage.

The shift register can be used to generate a wide variety of sequences. Generation of a linear sequence is typically done by tapping the values of certain cells and com-

Fig. 19 — Various PN sequences. At A, a three-stage shift register with (1,3) stages tapped. There are seven unique code words, each as wide as the shift register. At B, a three-stage shift register with (2,3) stages tapped produces a somewhat different arrangement of code words. At C, two nonmaximal-length cycles result from the tap choices of (1,2) for the three-stage register. A and B are maximal-length cycles. At D is a three-stage linear feedback shift register. The stages to be combined with exclusive-OR to produce feedback are selected by S1-S3.

bining the values using an exclusive-OR (one-bit addition without carry) gate. The combined output is then fed back to the input of the left-most cell.

The LFSR sequence is a repeating sequence whose maximun length is related to the number of stages (N) in the shift register by the equation: length = $2^N - 1$. This equation determines the maximum length; not all tap choices produce the longest sequence, however. There are two cases to consider: the maximal-length sequence or m-sequence and the nonmaximal-length or composite sequences.

The length of an m-sequence is given by the equation $2^N - 1$ and is the longest possible for a given register length. Since the output repeats after producing $2^N - 1$ bits, the entire sequence can be viewed as a cycle (see Fig. 19).

Initializing the register with any sequence of consecutive bits from the cycle will generate the entire cycle from that point. A cycle is commonly started by an initial value of all zeros followed by a one such as 0000001 for a seven-stage register. Other starting values still generate the same sequence but are said to be phase shifted from the zeros followed by a one initial starting point. A run of bits selected from the sequence that is the same length as the generating shift register is called a code

word of the sequence. All code words from an m-sequence are unique with no repeats, and no code word contains all zeros.

Comparatively, the length of the non-maximal sequence is always shorter than $2^N - 1$, and its outputs form a number of distinct short cycles. Code words are not unique for this type of sequence. The nonmaximal sequences are called a composite sequence because a composite sequence can be expressed as a combination of shorter maximal-length sequences. The nonmaximal-sequence length is in fact the product of the length of the smaller m-sequences of which it is composed.

Determining whether a given tap sequence will produce a maximal or composite sequence is quite complicated. Most efforts have been carried out by computer search methods, and a number of excellent tables are available for the designer.

A maximal-length sequence seven-stage shift register can easily be built with two ICs, as shown in Fig. 20. A more complete description of this shift register appeared in October 1986 *QEX*.

Orthogonality

An important consideration in choosing a sequence for a spread-spectrum system is the amount of statistical similarity a sequence has with conventional signals and with sequences employed by other spread-spectrum systems. The greater the degree of similarity, the less able the spread-spectrum receiver will be able to reject interference.

The ideal sequence will show a very low correlation when compared with undesired sequences. Moreover, the PN sequence should also have a low correlation with shifted versions of itself. A measure of a sequence's self-correlation is measured by its autocorrelation function (ACF). The ACF measures how much interference will be received from other spread-spectrum units using the same PN sequence but with different starting points within the PN code cycle.

Two code families that have found common usage are the m-sequences and Gold codes. Gold codes are a family of spreading codes generated by exclusive-OR combining the output of two "preferred" m-sequence generators. Many other PN codes can be used with spread spectrum — Dixon lists a number of such codes.

Synchronization

Synchronization is the most difficult issue for spread-spectrum systems. For a spread-spectrum receiver to demodulate the desired signal, it must be able to synchronize the locally generated PN code reference with the one used by the transmitter. This operation commonly takes place at very high speeds. It is usually viewed as two processes: rough synchronization which searches and acquires the receiver's PN code within one bit or channel of the transmitter's, and fine synchronization which maintains bit or channel dwell timing.

In rough synchronization, the receiver attempts to line up the local PN code as close as possible to the transmitters. There are two methods. The first is called epoch synchronization, in which the transmitter periodically sends a special synchronization sequence. Commonly, this synchronization sequence is a unique short bit sequence chosen because it is easily detected by a simple correlator known as a digital matched filter. This filter consists of a shift register that clocks the received sequence by one bit at a time and compares it against the unique sequence. The output of the matched filter is highest when the unique word is found in the input bit stream.

A second method of synchronization is known as phase synchronization. Here, the receiver attempts to determine which of the $2^N - 1$ phases the m-sequence could be in. To determine the phase, and thereby the synchronization, at least N bits would have to be received without error. Noisy signals may require more than N bits depending on the signal-to-noise ratio.

PN codes with short cycle times will exhibit several repetitions in a short amount of time. A digital matched filter can be constructed to signal the presence of a unique code word from this short spread-

ing code sequence. This is essentially a form of epoch synchronization.

Longer sequences require more-complex synchronization methods. One method uses a sequence based on the time of day. The receiver sets up a digital matched filter with a value several seconds ahead of the current time and waits for this unique code word to appear. The procedure may be useful for net operations in which stations can enter or leave a net at will.

There are a number of specially developed sequences available for rapid synchronization; however, they fall beyond the scope of this brief discussion.

Preamble

A preamble signal is commonly sent by the spread-spectrum transmitter immediately before the transmitter enters the spread mode. The preamble signal alerts the receiver to set up its synchronizing procedure to acquire the spread signal. The format of the preamble is different from system to system.

In slow frequency hopping, which has hop rates of less than 100 times a second, a tone appearing on a prearranged frequency or home channel can be used. The falling edge of the tone signals the beginning of hopping. At faster speeds, the precise instant the tone falls may be difficult to measure accurately; other preamble methods are typically employed. One such method calls for the frequency hopping receiver to examine a specific set of channels continually. A frequency-hopping transmitter would hop on these channels a prearranged number of times to allow the receiver to synchronize.

In direct-sequence transmissions the preamble performs three functions. First, the RF carrier must be acquired by the receiver. This may be done by transmitting a run of all zero bits, which reveals the carrier's center frequency to the receiver. Second, local clock synchronization is established by transmitting a sequence of alternating ones and zeros. The receiver will detect these transitions and derive bit timing from them. Last, the spreading code itself must be synchronized. This can be

done by an epoch synchronization procedure.

Once rough synchronization is established, the spread-spectrum receiver must track and maintain bit timing or channel dwell timing. There are several techniques to accomplish fine synchronization; however, the underlying mechanism is a feedback loop that attempts to minimize the timing error between the transmitter and receiver PN code at the fraction of a bit time.

The feedback loop itself commonly consists of a differencing circuit that calculates the actual bit difference and a feedback path that adjusts the receiver spreading code clock. In one technique called dithering, the spreading-code clock speed is continually rocked back and forth around the synchronization point, causing the receiver to periodically move in and out of synchronization a small amount. The point at which best synchronization is achieved is used to synchronize the receiver clock. Dithering can track a spreading code whose timing may be changing, perhaps because the transmitter is mobile, or in the case of HF spread spectrum, with changes in the height of the reflecting layers of the ionosphere.

Spectrum of Spread Spectrum

The spectrum of each type of spread-spectrum signal depends on several factors, such as the speed at which the spreading code is clocked, the type of spreading code used, whether frequency hopping or direct sequence is being used, the modulation bandwidth and the method of modulation.

Fig. 21 is the spectrum of a BPSK DS sequence. The signal is symmetric around the center frequency and contains several peaks that are called lobes. The main lobe is maximum at the center frequency but falls rapidly. The point at which the main lobe falls to its low point is called the first zero; subsequent lobes are called spectral sidelobes. The main lobe of a DS signal contains the majority of power, about 90 percent, while the remaining 10 percent is distributed over the side lobes. In many systems, the side lobes are clipped since

Fig. 20 — A maximal-length sequence seven-stage shift register. A complete description of this circuit appeared in October 1986 *QEX*.

Fig. 21 — Power vs. frequency for a direct-sequence-modulated spread-spectrum signal. The envelope assumes the shape of a sin x^2 divide by x curve. With proper modulating techniques, the carrier is suppressed.

Fig. 22 — Power vs. frequency for frequency-hopping spread-spectrum signals. Emissions jump around in pseudorandom fashion to discrete frequencies.

they tend to extend out over a large span of spectrum but carry little of the DS signal's power.

The chip rate determines the overall spread of the DS signal. The overall size of the DS carrier expands as the chip rate increases, while lower chip rates collapse the signal into a nonspread conventional PSK signal. In addition, the chip rate determines the size of the DS main lobe and the location of the zeros. The main lobe is 2/chip-rate wide, centered about the DS carrier's center frequency. Zeros occur at multiples of 1/chip-rate, symmetrically on either side of the center frequency.

The spectrum of an FH signal is shown in Fig. 22. The spectrum structure is not as complex as in the DS signal, but depends on the spreading bandwidth and type of modulation used. The spectrum of FH signals consists of a carrier that moves pseudorandomly among many channels. As the speed of hopping increases, channels are visited more frequently with less time spent on a channel. At very fast hopping speeds, significant sidebands can be observed on the FH signal. These sidebands are generated from the pulse-like behavior that the FH signal exhibits at high speeds.

The amount of power the frequency-hopping transmitter delivers per channel is related to how often the channel is visited and the dwell time. The amount of power per channel is greater with fewer channels; conversely, a large number of channels decreases the frequency of visits, hence a lower power per channel. In sum, the larger the number of channels, the lower the signal power per channel.

Last, the method of modulation has a marked effect on the spectrum of an FH signal. For example NBFM produces a constant-amplitude signal and generates a relatively flat spectrum. SSB, however, emits energy only when there is information to transmit, and hence less energy is emitted overall.

Near vs. Far-Field Strength

Spread-spectrum signals exhibit some unusual but logical signal effects. Close to the transmitter, a spread-spectrum signal may be observed readily on a conventional receiver; however, at a distance (50-100 miles) the signal may be noticed only with careful measurement. This results in a property called *low probability of intercept* (LPI). Some authors dispute the notion of LPI, saying that spread-spectrum signal energy is in fact intercepted by the receiving station's antennas and receivers; however, there is a low probability that the listener will recognize the presence of spread spectrum. The term *low probability of recognition* (LPR) has been suggested in place of LPI.

This radical difference in signal strength between close-in and distant observers is quite logical. The power of a narrow-band signal is typically concentrated about a center frequency; hence, a conventional narrow-band receiver will be in a position to collect much of the original power subject to path loss. In the DS spread-spectrum case, the same power is distributed over a band of frequencies, giving less power per hertz. A narrow-band receiver can collect only as much of this distributed power as the width of its IF passband; consequently, it registers a much weaker signal. A spread-spectrum receiver's passband is quite wide, allowing it to receive the entire bandwidth containing the spread-spectrum signal. This power is concentrated by the despreading process, making the output signal-to-noise ratio at least equal to the narrow-band signal's.

In the case of FH spread spectrum, a full-power narrow-band carrier is hopped among many channels. The concentrated power of the carrier can be observed at a distance equal to that of a nonhopping narrow-band signal; however, a conventional receiver will only catch a glimpse of the FH signal as it briefly visits the currently received channel.

FH Frequency Generation

Generation of FH frequencies is commonly done with a synthesizer that operates in one of several ways. The most popular amateur synthesizer technique uses a phase-locked loop (PLL) in which a voltage-controlled oscillator (VCO) generates the frequency of interest. The VCO is typically locked to a multiple of a reference crystal that also determines the channel spacing. The loop is established by sampling the VCO output frequency and dividing it down so its divided frequency matches the reference-oscillator frequency.

The error voltage generated by the phase comparator holds the VCO on the desired multiple of the reference oscillator.

This approach is limited because of the time required for the loop to settle. Various modifications are possible such as replacing the loop's low-pass filter with an active low-pass filter; however, the settling-time problem is difficult to overcome. One successful method has been to use two or more synthesizers, alternately allowing one to settle while using the other to control the current channel. The increase in hopping speed can be found by calculating one minus the number of synthesizers multiplied by the ratio of dwell to settling time.

Another enhancement to the basic PLL synthesizer comes by inserting a D/A converter into the PLL. The D/A takes a digital word from a computer which represents a voltage feed to the VCO. The voltage has been selected so the VCO will produce a desired frequency. The PLL and reference oscillator are used to lock the VCO output to a precise channel; however, the large settling time, attributed mainly to the loop tracking large jumps in frequency, is absent.

A different approach to FH generation can be found in the direct-synthesis approach. Here, a large number of samples are taken of a sine wave that is stored in a ROM. A signal is generated by feeding these samples into a wide-band D/A converter, producing an RF sine wave. The frequency of the RF sine wave is determined by the rate at which the samples are fed to the D/A. A synthesizer of this type is capable of hopping many thousands of times per second and commonly has a resolution of 1-hertz steps.

Self Policing and Enforcement

Spread spectrum belongs to the general class of wideband signals that are new to many Amateur Radio operators. Traditionally, amateur experience has been with narrow-band signals that can be easily received with conventional receiving equipment. Wideband signals require larger IF bandwidths and some new ways of thinking.

Spread spectrum employs a carrier with a very wide bandwidth. In addition, the carrier is coded with a PN sequence. These two factors make conventional amateur receivers unsuitable for spread-spectrum reception. There are, however, many techniques available that recognize, locate and recover the transmitted information for amateur spread-spectrum users.

Amateur operators are interested in experiments that enhance communications; hence, system parameters are chosen to facilitate communications. Amateur systems are designed so they can be received without too much difficulty. Conversely, military users are interested in signal hiding — to prevent reception by unauthorized users — so military system parameters are set with this objective in mind.

When a spread-spectrum signal is above the noise level, it can be received with a wideband receiver, and direction-finding techniques can be used to locate the signal source. Interference to other amateur operations or TVI complaints are resolved easily because a signal strong enough to cause interference is far enough above the noise that it can be located with conventional DF techniques. In particular, a directional antenna can be connected to the receiver that is being interfered with. Rotation of the antenna can be used to help locate the source. Moreover, the periodic identification required of all amateur signals can aid the interference-determination process.

Currently, the FCC has authorized two types of spread-spectrum communications for amateurs. The user must identify with narrow-band transmissions on one frequency in the band being used. Alternatively, the station ID may be transmitted while in spread-spectrum operation if the transmission is changed so that CW, SSB or narrow-band FM receivers can be used to identify the station. One proposed identification procedure is for the stations involved to send call signs by on-off keying of the spread-spectrum carrier. This will provide a method to readily identify an amateur spread-spectrum user.

Sometimes it is necessary to monitor the contents of an amateur spread-spectrum transmission to determine if the amateur station is being used properly. This is possible when the signal is above the noise; a wideband receiver and appropriate detector to demodulate the signal are necessary. Other signals in the passband can cause interference, so a sharp beam antenna is required to reduce the effects of the undesired signal.

In DS spread-spectrum transmissions, both the spreading PN code and the transmitted information are digital in nature and are often mixed before being used to modulate the RF carrier. The signal must be despread before the digital information can be recovered; however, the PN code must be known in advance. In the spread-spectrum rules, the FCC defines three m-sequence PN codes for amateur use. These codes are generated by three shift-register configurations: a seven-stage register tapped at stages (7,1); a 13-stage register tapped at stages (13,4,3,1); and a 19-stage register tapped at stages (19,5,2,1). These three sequences are the only ones that amateurs are allowed to use. It is not difficult to test all three sequences against a received amateur DS signal to determine which is in use. Once the sequence is identified and synchronized, the transmitted digital information can be recovered.

Amateur SS Experimentation

Spread-spectrum development for jamproof military communications began in the late 1940s. John P. Costas, W2CRR, was the first person to recognize non-

military applications for SS. Costas presented a paper entitled "Poisson, Shannon, and the Radio Amateur," in the *Proceedings of the IRE* for December 1959. (Poisson and Shannon developed mathematical models for communications systems — all analytical studies in communication theory and information theory are based on their results.)

In this paper, Costas explained that congested band operation presents an interesting problem in analysis that can be solved by statistical methods. He showed that in spite of the bandwidth economy of SSB, there are definite advantages to using very broadband techniques. Costas concluded that broadband techniques would result in more efficient use of the spectrum and an increase in the number of available channels. At the time, Costas' statements were revolutionary, for they challenged the conventional theory that congestion in the radio spectrum can be relieved only by the use of smaller transmission bandwidths.

In 1980, Dr. Michael Marcus of the FCC Office of Science and Technology (OST) suggested that radio amateurs experiment with spread-spectrum modulation techniques. The rationale was that (a) the civil radio services could take advantage of the spread-spectrum pioneering of the military, (b) design of spread-spectrum systems by the private sector was slow because of the high cost of development vs. return on investment, (c) more experimentation was needed in areas such as designing for low-cost and on-the-air testing in congested frequency bands, and (d) radio amateurs could perform useful experiments without the need for either governmental or industrial research and development money.

The Amateur Radio Research and Development Corporation (AMRAD) requested, and the FCC granted, a Special Temporary Authority (STA) to permit spread-spectrum tests in the amateur bands by a small number of amateurs, for one year beginning in March 1981. Under the STA, the first Amateur Radio SS tests were conducted by W4RI in McLean, Virginia and K2SZE in Rochester, New York. Later, WA3ZXW in Annapolis, Maryland ran additional on-the-air tests with K2SZE. The equipment used was capable of hopping over a frequency range up to 100 kHz at rates of 1, 2, 5 and 10 hops per second. RF power output levels of 100 and 500 watts were used into dipole antennas.

These particular radios functioned best at 5 hops per second. This was subjectively judged on the basis of least-bothersome interference from the various signals at the different hopping frequencies. It was observed that frequency hopping was more successful in the presence of heavy CW interference than it was in the presence of heavy SSB interference. In comparison, conventional SSB usually provided better communications than frequency-hopped SSB whenever a single clear channel could be found for the conventional SSB.

However, the conventional SSB could be disrupted by strong interference on that channel. While hampered by cyclic interference when busy frequencies were revisited, the frequency-hopped link could be maintained despite band congestion.

Although the tests were announced beforehand in Amateur Radio publications and on the air from W1AW, no correspondence was received indicating that the frequency-hopping tests either interfered with, or were heard by, other Amateur Radio stations. The only exception was that several amateurs in the Northern Virginia area could recognize the presence of the frequency-hopped transmissions on conventional SSB receivers after learning what the signal sounded like. All were within five miles of W4RI and were able to hear both ends.

AMRAD member Chuck Phillips, N4EZV, built a VHF frequency-hopping radio in 1980. The design consisted of a modified VHF-Engineering scanner board capable of switching between four different crystal oscillators. By tripling the clocking speed, the transmitter was made to hop at 12 hops per second. The oscillators were arranged to operate continuously, and were switched in and out by using high-isolation solid-state switches. Sometime in 1981, the Motorola synthesizer chip showed up in a GLB add-on synthesizer board. N4EZV modified a couple of those boards and managed to reach 15 hops per second. Later that year, N4EZV tried a new synthesizer, working at lower frequencies, by modifying some Heathkit HW2031s. The synthesizer signal was then heterodyned to the desired output frequency. Both the transmitter and receiver were equipped with identical frequency "look-up tables" stored in EEPROMs. When the push-to-talk microphone switch was depressed, a short audio tone burst was transmitted and then decoded at the receiver. At the end of the burst, both transmitter and receiver started hopping to the frequencies pre-loaded in the look-up tables. The hopping rate was derived by dividing down from the reference crystal used to pilot the whole setup. When the microphone push-to-talk button was released at the end of a transmission, another tone was sent, which stopped the hoppers. If the receiver detected only noise, (caused by interference), it would automatically revert to its "home frequency" where it would wait for another transmission. This system seems to operate well up to about 100 hops per second over a 4-megahertz frequency range.

Experiments run by AMRAD in 1985 used a Commodore computer to control the frequency of an ICOM IC-2AT. Very little interference to conventional 2-meter users was created by the spread spectrum transmissions. The signals were inaudible to amateurs involved in regular QSOs, but the transmissions did cause some interference by keying some repeaters that did not have a carrier-sense activation delay.

This interference affected only a few repeaters out of many in the Northern Virginia area, and the problem was cured by removing the appropriate repeater input frequencies from the table of frequencies used in the frequency-hopping scheme.

In 1987, AMRAD member Elton Sanders, WB5MMB used the direct-synthesis oscillator described by Fred Williams in the February 1985 issue of *QST* to build a frequency hopper. The frequency of the direct-synthesis oscillator was determined by a program written by David Borden, K8MMO, to run on an IBM® PC-XT clone, and the oscillator output was limited to frequencies within the 6.15 to 6.25 MHz band. This output was then multiplied by 72, and fed to a 70-centimeter output amplifier. (Hopping rates ranging between 250 and 1000 hops per second were obtained by this method.)

Initial discussions with the FCC concerning the second STA revealed that the FCC Field Operations Bureau was interested in conducting monitoring and direction-finding exercises against amateur spread-spectrum transmissions. In February 1985, FCC personnel conducted a "fox hunt" to find an amateur spread-spectrum transmitter operating at an undisclosed site. Using the standard FCC spectrum analysis van and enforcement car, FCC personnel located the transmitter within 25 minutes, proving that they can DF amateur spread-spectrum transmissions if necessary.

On May 9, 1985, the FCC amended the rules to permit SS operation on the amateur bands above 420 MHz at power output levels no greater than 100-W PEP for domestic communications. These rules became effective in June 1986. The amateur community is working toward establishing a set of standards for amateur SS operation. The current rules authorize three PN sequences, and both FH and DS are allowed. Hybrid spread-spectrum techniques are not permitted. Bandwidths may be as large as the amateur band of operation. Also, SS users are specifically prohibited from causing interference to other users of the band.

Under these new rules, amateurs engaging in SS operation must maintain a log with the following information.

1) A technical description of the transmitted signal.

2) Signal parameters including the frequency or frequencies of operation, the chip rate, the code, the code rate, the spreading function, the transmission protocol(s) including the method of achieving synchronization, and the modulation type.

3) A general description of the type of information being conveyed; for example, voice, text, memory dump, facsimile, television and so on.

4) The method and, if applicable, the frequencies used for station identification.

5) The beginning date and ending date of use of each type of transmitted signal.

Throughout 1986 and 1987, AMRAD continued to devise and run experiments designed to bring this spread-spectrum technology within the reach of the average radio amateur, by utilizing only parts and technologies readily available to everyone. In June 1986, AMRAD member Andre Kesteloot, N4ICK, demonstrated a way to derive clock signals (suitable for frequency-hopping) by using broadcast TV signals. The complete experiment is described in October 1986 *QEX*, pp 4-7. With the equipment described, the trailing edge of an audio tone burst was used to derive original

synchronization, and the two sets hopped at 15 hops per second for more than one hour without losing sync.

In September 1986, N4ICK demonstrated an experimental board allowing for the transmission of data with direct-sequence spread spectrum. Synchronization was obtained by using a sliding correlator, fully described in the December 1986 issue of *QEX*. In 1987, N4ICK developed a method for deriving precise clock signals from AM radio broadcast transmitters (see October 1987 *QEX*) which was used in an interesting experiment conducted in January 1988. This experiment (see May 1988 *QEX*) can be summarized as follows (see Fig. 23): N4ICK used two hand-held transceivers operating on 445 MHz. At both sites, PN generators were driven by clock pulses derived from the same AM radio transmitter. These two PN sequences were thus driven by synchronous clocks (it was still necessary to correlate them). At the receiver end, additional pulses were fed into the clock pulse stream, making that clock operate slightly faster than the transmitting clock. The receiver output was connected to a DTMF decoder. In the absence of a valid tone, the receiver clock would continue to operate faster than the transmitter clock. If a DTMF tone was sent at the transmitter for a certain duration of time, there would necessarily be a moment when the transmitting and the receiving PN sequences would be in phase. At that moment, the output of the receiver's doubly balanced mixer would be correlated, and a signal would reach the DTMF decoder. A valid output from the DTMF decoder would be used to slow the receiver clock-pulse generator down to its normal speed. Although the overall synchronization process was relatively slow

Fig. 23 — Block diagram of one of N4ICK's spread-spectrum experiments.

(it could take up to 45 seconds to reach sync) once synchronization was reached both stations would remain in lock for hours.

These AMRAD experiments all relied on a clock derived from an external reference. A major problem, one common to all spread-spectrum systems, remained. How can the transmitter clock signal be recovered directly from the received signal? Because the received signal appears to be noise (Fig 24B) this can be a formidable challenge. In the May 1989 issue of *QST*, Andre Kesteloot described his design of a complete UHF direct-sequence transmitter and receiver, offering a remarkably simple solution to the problem of synchronization. (Because of its simplicity, the solution does not offer all the anti-jamming properties of more sophisticated systems, but this should not be of concern to Amateur Radio operators.)

The block diagram is shown in Fig 25. At the transmitter site, the output of a 446 MHz generator is fed to one of the input ports of a doubly balanced mixer (DBM). The other input port of the mixer is connected to a PN sequence generator, which is clocked at a submultiple of the transmitter carrier frequency. Since the carrier and the clock are harmonically related, recovering either one will be sufficient to derive the other.

At the receiver end of the link, a sliding correlator is used as follows: The output of a free-running "synchronized oscillator" is divided to create a clock signal at a frequency close to that of the transmitter clock. This locally generated clock is used to drive a PN generator identical to that used at the transmitter site. The resulting PN sequence is mixed with the incoming RF in a doubly balanced mixer. The free-running frequency of the synchronized oscillator can be adjusted to run the receiver PN sequence slightly faster or slower than the transmitter oscillator (which is fixed). Although they are not synchronized, the transmitter and receiver PN sequences are identical. They do differ in speed, however, so the receiver sequence "slides by" the transmitter sequence, somewhat like two wheels rotating at different speeds on the same shaft. One of the wheels can thus be thought of as "catching up" with the other. There will necessarily be one instant when the two PN sequences are momentarily in phase. At that moment, correlation, or "despreading" occurs, and the output of the receiver DBM duplicates the original carrier, as shown in Fig 24C. This carrier is fed to the input of the synchronized oscillator, which locks on the incoming signal. Since the recovered carrier is now synchronized to the transmitter oscillator, the receiver PN generator (which is a submultiple of the carrier) remains in phase with that at the transmitter, and the loop is closed. The original clock has been regenerated and the system stays locked. With a seven-stage shift register as described in the article, search-and-lock at the receiver is almost instantaneous (on the order of a few milliseconds).

Fig 24—(A) The envelope of the unfiltered biphase-modulated spread-spectrum signal as viewed on a spectrum analyzer. In the practical system described, band-pass filtering is used to confine the spread-spectrum signal to the amateur band. (B) At the receiver end of the link, the filtered spread-spectrum signal is apparent only as a 10-dB hump in the noise floor. (C) The despread signal at the output of the receiver DBM. The original carrier—and any modulation components that accompany it—has been recovered. The peak carrier is about 45 dB above the noise floor—more than 30 dB above the hump shown at B. (These spectrograms were made at a sweep rate of 0.1 s/div and an analyzer bandwidth of 30 kHz; the horizontal scale is 1 MHz/div.)

Fig 25—A block diagram of the practical spread-spectrum link. The success of this arrangement lies in the use of a synchronized oscillator (right) to recover the transmitter clock signal at the receiving site.

Selected SS Bibliography

Reading material on spread spectrum may be difficult to obtain for the average amateur. Below are references that can be mail ordered. Spread-spectrum papers have also been published in *IEEE Transactions on Communications, on Aerospace and Electronic Systems* and *on Vehicular Technology.*

Dixon, *Spread Spectrum Systems*, second edition, 1984, Wiley Interscience, 605 Third Ave., New York, NY 10016.

Dixon, *Spread Spectrum Techniques*, IEEE Service Center, 445 Hoes La., Piscataway, NJ 08854.

Golomb, *Shift Register Sequences*, 1982, Aegean Park Press, Laguna Hills, CA.

Hershey, *Proposed Direct Sequence Spread Spectrum Voice Techniques for Amateur Radio Service*, 1982, U.S. Department of Commerce, NTIA Report 82-111.

Holmes, *Coherent Spread Spectrum Systems*, 1982, Wiley Interscience, New York.

The *AMRAD Newsletter* carries a monthly column on spread spectrum and reviews ongoing AMRAD experiments. In addition, the following articles on SS have appeared in Amateur Radio publications:

Feinstein, "Spread Spectrum — A report from AMRAD," *73*, November 1981.

Feinstein, "Amateur Spread Spectrum Experiments," *CQ*, July 1982.

Kesteloot, ed., *The ARRL Spread Spectrum Sourcebook* (Newington, CT: ARRL, 1990). Includes Hershey, *QST* and *QEX* material listed separately here.

Kesteloot, "Practical Spread Spectrum: A Simple Clock Synchronization Scheme," *QEX*, October 1986.

Kesteloot, "Experimenting with Direct Sequence Spread Spectrum," *QEX*, December 1986.

Kesteloot, "Extracting Stable Clock Signals from AM Broadcast Carriers for Amateur Spread Spectrum Applications," *QEX* October 1987.

Kesteloot, "Practical Spread Spectrum: Achieving Synchronization with the Slip-Pulse Generator," *QEX,* May 1988.

Kesteloot, "A Practical Direct-Sequence Spread-Spectrum UHF Link," *QST*, May 1989.

Kesteloot, "Practical Spread Spectrum: Clock Recovery With the Synchronous Oscillator," *QEX,* June 1989.

Rhode, "Digital HF Radio: A Sampling of Techniques," *Ham Radio*, April 1985.

Rinaldo, "Spread Spectrum and the Radio Amateur," *QST*, November 1980.

Sabin, "Spread Spectrum Applications in Amateur Radio," *QST*, July 1983.

Williams, "A Digital Frequency Synthesizer," *QST*, April 1984.

Williams, "A Microprocessor Controller for the Digital Frequency Synthesizer," *QST*, February 1985.

Chapter 22

Radio Frequencies and Propagation

Although great advances in understanding the many modes of radio wave propagation have been made in recent years, the number of variables affecting long distance communication are very complex and not entirely predictable. Amateur attempts to schedule operating times and frequencies for optimum results may not always succeed, but familiarity with the nature of radio propagation can improve your chances for success and add greatly to your enjoyment of the pursuit of distant communications. Indeed, personal computer technology now allows the average radio amateur to more accurately assess how day-to-day propagation changes will influence his operation and provides guidelines for frequency and operating time selections.

The sun, ultimate source of life and energy on Earth, influences all radio communication beyond ground-wave or line-of-sight ranges. Conditions vary with such obvious sun-related cycles as time of day and season of the year. Since these conditions differ for appreciable changes in latitude and longitude, and everything is constantly changing as the Earth rotates, almost every communications circuit has unique features with respect to the band of frequencies that are useful and the quality of signals in portions of that band.

Historically, propagation forecasting has been somewhat of a mystery, consisting of a combination of experience, "old wives' tales" and reference manuals. Today the radio amateur has new tools to perform rational frequency management, so frequency selection need not be a hit or miss proposition. In this chapter we will look at sky wave propagation and what influences it. We will also look at some ways that radio amateurs can reduce the mystery and even use the idiosyncrasies of propagation to their advantage.

As we study the various modes and conditions that affect the propagation of radio waves, we need to be sure that we understand the terms being used. Reflection and refraction are two words that often seem to be used interchangeably, even though they describe quite different phenomena.

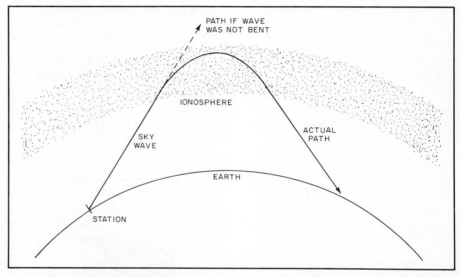

Fig. 1 — Because radio waves are bent in the ionosphere, they return to Earth far from their origin. Without refraction in the ionosphere, radio waves would pass into space.

Reflection occurs at any boundary between materials with different dielectric constants. Familiar examples with light are reflections from water surfaces, window glass and mirrors. Both water and glass are transparent for light, but their dielectric constants are very different from that of air. Some of the light energy that hits either material will bounce off, or be reflected. Radio waves, having much longer wavelengths than light, are practically unaffected by a thin layer of glass, but their behavior upon encountering water may vary, depending on the purity of the water. Distilled water is a good insulator; salt water is a relatively good conductor.

Depending on their wavelength (or frequency), radio waves may be reflected by buildings, trees, vehicles, the ground, water, ionized layers in the outer atmosphere, or at boundaries between air masses having different temperatures and moisture content. Some of the radio energy will be absorbed in the medium that the wave hits, and some of it may pass into (or through) the material. *Medium* is the term used to

refer to a material that a wave is traveling through.

Refraction is the bending of a wave as it passes from one medium into another. (If the wave is moving in a direction that is at a right angle to the boundary between the two materials, the wave will not be bent.) This bending occurs because the wave travels at a different speed in the new material. If you place a straight object into water at an angle, the object will appear to be bent at the water's surface. (You can try this with a pencil and a glass of water.) This is an example of refraction of light waves.

Radio waves bend when they pass from one material into another in the same way that light waves do. The degree of bending depends on the difference in speeds at which the waves move through the two materials. The amount of bending also increases at higher frequencies. As radio waves travel through different areas of the atmosphere, there may be gradual changes in the speed of the waves as the temperature, air density and levels of ionization change. This will result in a gradual bending of the radio waves. Most amateur communication on the HF bands depends on this bending of radio waves, so it is a very important concept. Fig. 1 illustrates the refraction of a radio wave as it is returned to Earth.

THE IONOSPHERE

On frequencies below 30 MHz, long distance communication is the result of refraction (bending) of the wave in the ionosphere. The ionosphere is a region 30 to 260 miles above the Earth's surface where free ions and electrons exist in sufficient quantity to affect the direction of wave travel. Depending on the frequency used and the time of day, the ionosphere can support communications from very short ranges of less than 60 miles (called Near Vertical Incidence Signals — NVIS) to distances of greater than 6000 miles.

Ionization of the upper atmosphere is attributed to ultraviolet radiation from the sun. The result is not a single ionized region, but several layers of varying densities at various heights surrounding the Earth. Each layer has a central region of maximum electron density, which tapers off both above and below that altitude.

Ionospheric Layers

The ionospheric layers that most influence HF communications are the D, E, E_s, F_1 and F_2 layers. Of these, the D layer acts as a large RF sponge that absorbs signals passing through it. Depending on frequency and time of day, the remaining four are useful to the communicator.

The D layer, which is between 45 and 55 miles above the Earth, is most pronounced during daylight hours with its ionization being directly proportional to how high the sun is in the sky. Because absorption is inversely proportional to frequency, wave energy in the two lowest amateur bands (1.8 and 3.5 MHz) is almost completely absorbed by this layer during daylight hours. The rise and fall of the D layer dictates the lowest usable frequency (LUF) over a given path. While the effects of the D region are reasonably well known, the exact chemistry and physics of how this layer behaves are not well known or defined.

The lowest region of the ionosphere useful for returning radio signals to the Earth is the E layer. Its average height of maximum ionization is from 65 to 75 miles. The atmosphere here is still dense enough so that ions and electrons set free by solar radiation do not have to travel far before they meet and recombine to form neutral particles. For this reason the layer can maintain its ability to bend radio waves only in the presence of sunlight. Ionization is thus greatest around local noon, and it practically disappears after sundown.

A nomadic cousin of the E region is called sporadic-E. The sporadic-E region consists of relatively dense patches of ionization that literally drift around about 70 miles above the Earth. The effects of sporadic-E become confused with those of other types of ionization on the lower amateur frequencies, but they stand out above 21 MHz and into the VHF region. This is especially true during a solar minimum, when the bands above 21 MHz are rarely open. Sporadic-E propagation is covered in more detail in the VHF/UHF section of this chapter.

The region of ionization mainly responsible for long distance communication is the F-layer. Its altitudes of ionization range from about 90 to 250 miles. It ionizes very rapidly at sunrise, reaching peak electron density early in the afternoon at the middle of the propagation path. The ionization decays very slowly after sunset, reaching the minimum value just before sunrise. This period, called the pre-sunrise depression, is the time when the lowest MUF over the path is observed. During the day, the F region is split into two layers, the F_1 and the F_2.

The F_1 layer is not an important propagation medium. Its refracting heights are between 90 and 120 miles, and it forms and decays in direct correlation to the passage of the sun. After sunset, the F_1 layer decays and it is replaced by a broadened F_2 layer.

The F_2 region is the primary medium supporting amateur HF communications. The thickness of this layer ranges from a relatively thin layer (50 miles) during the day to a broad layer (95 miles) centered at about 200 miles above the Earth at night. The daytime layer is very dense and has very complex combination/recombination characteristics. Because of Earth/ionospheric geometry, the maximum range of a single hop off the F_2 region is about 2500 miles. Fig. 2 summarizes day to night variations of the layers and shows approximate heights for them.

Traditionally, the ionospheric layers are characterized as nice, well behaved, stratified layers. Recent technologies allow very high resolution measurements of the medium to be made, and indicate that the ionospheric layers are in continual horizontal and vertical motion. You should recognize that these variations are a routine situation that must be dealt with. Periods of very high solar activity, with their disruptions, may present the opportunity for unusual propagation periods. Use the winter solar minimum periods to exploit 160 meters and use the uncertainties of HF propagation to your advantage.

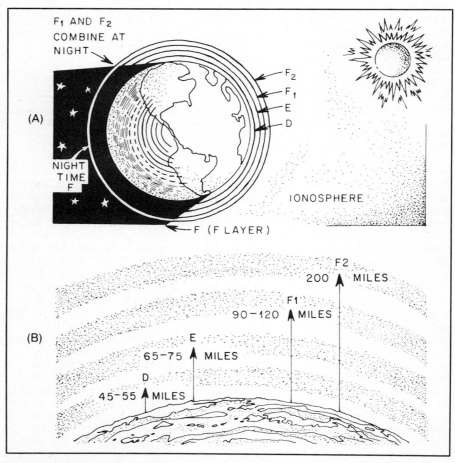

Fig. 2 — The ionosphere consists of several layers of ionized particles at different heights above the Earth. At night, the D and E layers disappear and the F_1 and F_2 layers combine to form a single F layer.

Virtual Height

An ionospheric layer is a region of considerable depth, but for practical purposes it is convenient to think of each layer as having a definite height. The height from which a simple reflection from the layer would give the same effects (observed from the ground) as the effects of the gradual bending that actually takes place is called the virtual height of that layer. Fig. 3 illustrates the virtual height of a layer in the ionosphere.

The virtual height of an ionospheric layer for various frequencies is determined with a variable-frequency sounding device (called an ionosonde) that directs energy vertically and measures the time required for the round-trip path. As frequency is increased, a point is reached where no energy will be returned from the ionosphere. The frequency where radio waves will penetrate a layer of the ionosphere instead of returning to Earth is called the critical frequency for that layer.

TYPES OF PROPAGATION

Depending on the propagation method, radio waves can be classified as ionospheric waves (sky waves), tropospheric waves or ground waves (surface waves). The sky wave is that main portion of the total radiation leaving the antenna at angles above the horizon. Without the refracting (bending) qualities of the ionosphere, these signals would be lost in space. The tropospheric wave is that portion of the radiation kept close to the Earth's surface as a result of bending in the lower atmosphere. This normally occurs only at the higher HF or lower VHF frequencies. The ground wave is that portion of the radiation directly affected by the surface of the Earth. It has two components — an Earth-guided surface wave and the space wave. Ground wave propagation is vertically polarized and its absorption increases with frequency. At equal power levels, a surface-wave signal over water will travel tens to hundreds of miles farther than the same signal over land.

Nearly all amateur communication on frequencies below 30 MHz is by means of sky waves. After leaving the transmitting antenna, this type of wave travels from the Earth's surface at an angle that would send it out into space if its path were not bent enough to bring it back to Earth. As the radio wave travels outward from the Earth, it encounters ionized particles in the ionosphere. The ionosphere refracts (or bends) radio waves, and at some frequencies the radio waves are refracted enough so they return to Earth at a point far from the originating station.

Because most amateur operation uses the sky wave mode of propagation, let's try to visualize just what is happening over a typical HF circuit. The *propagating bandwidth* is that band of frequencies which are propagating or usable between two points. This band of frequencies is constantly changing throughout the day, as shown in Fig. 4. This day/night plot (called a diurnal plot) shows how the band of propagating frequencies changes as a function of day and night. The upper boundary is called the maximum usable frequency (MUF).

The MUF is a function of how highly ionized the F region is. During a solar maximum, the MUF can rise above 30 MHz during daylight hours. Fig. 4 was developed from data taken during a solar minimum between Cycles 20 and 21.

The low-frequency boundary on Fig. 4 is called the lowest usable frequency (LUF). The LUF is a function of absorption, signal-to-noise ratio, power and transmission mode. Note that the change in LUF directly correlates to the movement of the sun over the path, and peaks at noon at the midpoint of the path. The vertical axis in Fig. 4 shows relative signal amplitude. The irregularity is due to the various multihop modes that can exist between the MUF and LUF.

It is important to remember that the definitions of LUF and MUF are for a specific communications path. For example, the frequencies useful for communications from your location to western Europe may be quite different from the frequencies useful for communications to Australia.

Multihop Propagation

When an ionospherically propagated wave returns to Earth, it can be reflected upward from the ground, travel again to the ionosphere, and be refracted to Earth. This process can be repeated several times under ideal conditions, leading to very long distance communications. Ordinarily, ionospheric absorption and ground-reflection losses exact tolls in signal level and quality, so multiple-hop propagation usually yields lower signal levels and more distorted modulation than single hop

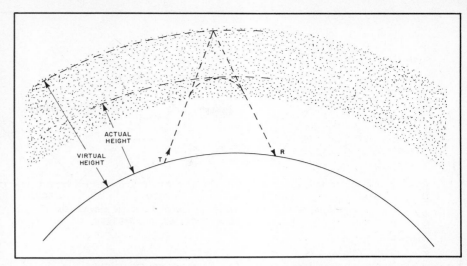

Fig. 3 — The virtual height of a layer in the ionosphere is the height at which a simple reflection would return the wave to the same point as the gradual bending that actually takes place.

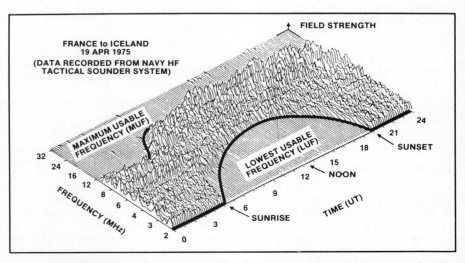

Fig. 4 — Day-Night characteristics of typical HF sky wave propagation. (Courtesy Naval Ocean Systems Center.)

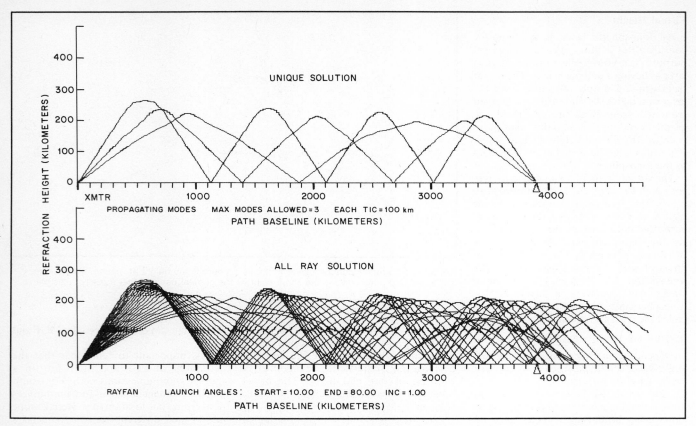

UNIQUE SOLUTION

PROPAGATING MODES   MAX MODES ALLOWED = 3   EACH TIC = 100 km
PATH BASELINE (KILOMETERS)

ALL RAY SOLUTION

RAYFAN   LAUNCH ANGLES: START = 10.00   END = 80.00   INC = 1.00
PATH BASELINE (KILOMETERS)

Fig. 5 — Ray trace of 14.0-MHz Signals over the Hawaii to California path at 1800 UTC on February 21, 1973. (Courtesy Naval Ocean Systems Center.)

signals. There are exceptions, however, and under ideal conditions even communications using long path signals are possible. These signals are discussed in the next section.

The same signal can be propagated over a given path via several different numbers of hops. The example in Fig. 5 shows that 2-hop, 3-hop, and 4-hop F_2 modes existed at the same time for a 14-MHz path. The receiver sees these three signals all arriving at very slightly different times, causing signal distortion. On CW, there is no real problem. On SSB, the signal is distorted slightly due to time spreading. On RTTY the distortion may be sufficient to degrade the signal to the point that it is useless. Table 1 shows the difference in these three signals, their angles of arrival, path loss and signal to noise ratio. This data was prepared using a sophisticated computer analysis known as Advanced PROPHET, a FORTRAN program run on mainframe computers.

Ionospheric Sounder Data

Propagation conditions between the MUF and the LUF are explored by using an ionospheric sounder. The oblique incidence sounder ionogram shown in Fig. 6 was produced by sweeping the entire HF spectrum at the transmitter and measuring all the propagating energy at the receiver. This shows that six modes of propagation

Table 1

Multimode Parameters — Advanced PROPHET Ray Trace Synopsis

DATE: 2/17/73	TIME: 18:00 UT	ATMOSPHERIC NOISE: YES	BWIDTH: 3,000 KHz
FREQ: 14.0	SSN: 126.4	PK: 1.0	MAN-MADE NOISE: QM	SNR REQD: 12.0 db
XMTR: HONO	LAT: 21.4	LON: 158.2°	ANT: 101 @ *OMNI*	PWR: 100.00 W
RCVR: SFRAN	LAT: 38.1°	LON: 122.3°	ANT: 161 @ 261.9°	RANGE: 3893.6 KM
IONOSPHERE:	FOE = 2.6 MHz	FOF1 = 3.6 MHz	FOF2 = 8.2
	HMF2 = 326 KM	YMF2 = 108.9 KM	

NHOP	2	3	4	0	0	0
MODE	3300000	3330000	3333000	0000000	0000000	0000000
ANGLE	13.75	19.55	29.10	0.00	0.00	0.00
DELAY (MSEC)	13.930	14.302	15.498	0.000	0.000	0.000
LOSS (DB)	163.08	161.98	152.04	0.00	0.00	0.00
1HZ SNR (DB)	28.44	29.53	39.48	0.00	0.00	0.00
ADJ SNR (DB)	−6.33	−5.24	4.71	0.00	0.00	0.00
HT1 (KM)	312.74	298.03	356.96	0.00	0.00	0.00
HT2 (KM)	345.78	270.95	304.13	0.00	0.00	0.00
HT3 (KM)	0.00	254.85	282.81	0.00	0.00	0.00
(VIRTUAL HEIGHTS)						

exist for this particular path, each covering a different part of the HF spectrum with some overlapping. For example, if 14.3 MHz was used on this path between California and Hawaii, the signal would arrive at three discreet times, one signal from the two-hop mode, one from the three-hop mode and one from the four-hop mode. At the receiver, the three modes arriving at slightly different times would cause distortion of the signal. It is im-

portant to note that the characteristics seen in Fig. 6 are unique to this HF sky wave circuit. Each and every different point to point circuit will have its own mode structure as a function of time of day. This means that every HF propagation problem has a totally unique solution.

Depending on how intensely the F region is ionized, an HF signal will be refracted in the ionosphere and reflected from the ground several times before it gets to the

Fig. 6 — HF oblique sounder ionogram. This photo shows a typical chirpsounder measurement on a 2500-mile path during midmorning in March.

desired receiver. Fig. 5 illustrates how several propagation modes can be expected, depending on the vertical radiation pattern of the transmitting antenna. The height of the refracting medium, the distance to the desired receiver and the signal radiation angle from the transmitter create the geometry of a path. If a receiver is too close to the transmitter, it will be in the skip zone where the ionosphere is not ionized enough to return very steep angles of signal radiation. There may be places along the transmission path where the signal cannot be heard because of the *geometry* of the situation, even though the transmission frequency is between the MUF and LUF.

The higher the radiation angle, the deeper into the ionosphere the signal penetrates before it is bent back to Earth. In order to establish a successful communications link, a user must choose a frequency between the MUF and the LUF, the antenna radiation pattern must meet the path geometry requirements and the signal must exceed the required signal-to-noise ratio.

SOLAR PHENOMENA

Man's interest in the sun is older than recorded history. Records of sunspot observations translatable into modern terms go back nearly 300 years. The first complete sunspot cycle to be recorded began in 1755, and is referred to as Cycle 1. Sunspot cycles have been numbered consecutively since then, so we are at the beginning of Cycle 22 now.

Current observations are statistically *smoothed*, or averaged, to maintain a

continuous record in the form of the International Sunspot Number (ISN). (The smoothed number means that it is an average of the values for six months before and six months after the month in question — International Sunspot Numbers are always six months behind the present date. For example, the latest ISN on January 1, 1987 is for July 1, 1986.) This number is the basis for traditional HF propagation predictions. In this section we will describe solar radiation, how it influences propagation, and how radio amateurs can use the knowledge of its day to day variations to select operating times and frequencies.

Solar Cycles

The periodic rise and fall of sunspot

numbers had been studied for many years before their correlation with radio-propagation variations was well known. Sunspot cycles average 10.7 years in length (we usually refer to an 11-year cycle), but have been as short as 7.3 years and as long as 17.1 years. The highs and lows also vary greatly. Cycle 19 peaked in 1958 with a sunspot number of over 200. Cycle 20, of more average intensity, reached 120 in 1969, while Cycle 21 rose to 164.5 in December 1979. By contrast, one of the lowest cycles, Cycle 14, peaked at only 60 in 1907. Several cycle lows, called solar minimums, have not reached zero levels on the International scale for any appreciable period, while little or no activity occurs for several months during the minimum of some cycles. (The minimum period of 1985 is a good example of a time with almost no activity.)

What does this mean to the radio amateur? At solar maxima (high sunspot number), the radiation from all the active regions around the sunspots makes the ionosphere capable of returning higher-frequency radio signals to the Earth instead of allowing them to pass through. This means that frequencies up to 40 MHz or higher are usable for long-distance communication. During periods of minimum solar activity, the amount of radiation is reduced, and frequencies above 20 MHz become unreliable for long-distance communication on a day-to-day basis. For this reason, the radio amateur needs to be aware of the current solar cycle status.

Navy scientists have recently revised their predictions for the next five solar cycles, which extends through the year 2040. Fig. 7 shows a graph of sunspot numbers for Solar Cycles 17 through 21 and predictions for Cycles 22 through 26. Fig. 7 predicts that the next solar maximum will occur around 1991-1992 with a peak level similar to Cycle 20 (1969).

Note that the cycles do not have a sine-wave shape. The rise time is shorter than the decay time, but neither is clearly defined. There are no absolutes at either solar maximum or solar minimum; periods

Fig. 7 — Solar sunspot number prediction for the next five sunspot cycles, from the Naval Ocean Systems Center.

of extremely intense activity have been observed from a single sunspot region during solar minimum. This can cause short term openings on the higher frequencies. Large numbers of very low radiation sunspots have also been observed during a solar maximum. This allows unexpected propagation conditions to exist at either solar minimum or maximum.

A useful indication of overall solar activity is the solar-flux index, a number associated with the measured radio noise coming from the sun at 2800 MHz. One such measurement is made at 1700 UTC daily in Ottawa, Canada. The latest solar-flux index is transmitted at 18 minutes past every hour by WWV. Because it is a current measurement for solar activity, it tends to be more useful in predicting propagation conditions than the more traditional sunspot number. This solar flux, more commonly called *10.7-cm solar flux* or *2800-MHz solar flux* can be directly related to sunspot number using the chart shown in Fig. 8.

Solar Radiation

There are two types of radiation from the sun that influence propagation; electromagnetic and particle emissions. The electromagnetic emissions include X-rays, ultraviolet (UV) and extreme ultraviolet (EUV). Each has an impact on a different part of the ionosphere. Particle emissions come in two forms: high-energy particles (high-energy protons and alpha particles) and low-energy particles (low-energy protons and electrons). The different types of radiation travel from the Earth to the sun at different speeds and have varying effects on sky-wave propagation. The time it takes for each type of radiation to travel from the sun to the Earth is shown in Fig. 9. The effects that result from each radiation type are also summarized in this figure.

EUV ionizes the ionospheric F region and is always present at some level. During solar maxima, the increased number of active regions on the sun provide for increased EUV, which in turn increases the F-region ionization and allows the use of higher frequencies for long-distance communication. UV and X-ray emissions ionize the D region, which absorbs HF energy. During solar flares, UV and X-ray emissions increase, causing increased signal loss on those HF circuits facing the sun. It takes about 8 minutes for electromagnetic emissions from the sun to travel to the Earth, because this energy travels at the speed of light.

High-energy particle radiation travels more slowly than light, and reaches the Earth from 15 minutes to several hours after a large solar flare. The high-energy particle emissions cause much higher absorption in the Earth's polar regions. They also create a radiation hazard to satellite systems and personnel orbiting the Earth in spacecraft. The lower-energy

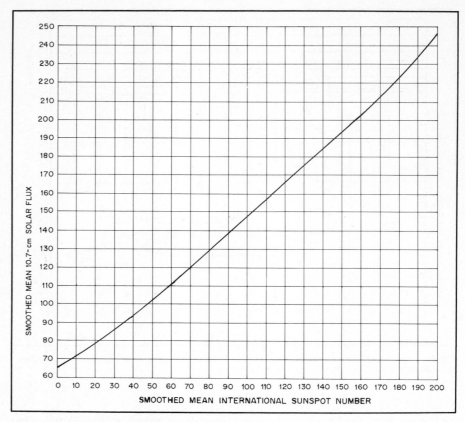

Fig. 8 — Relationship between the smoothed mean sunspot number and the 2800-MHz (10.7-cm) solar flux. In the low months of a solar cycle, flux values run between about 66 and 86. Intermediate years may see values of 85 to 150. The peak years of Cycle 21 brought readings between 140 and 380, in 1979 and 1980.

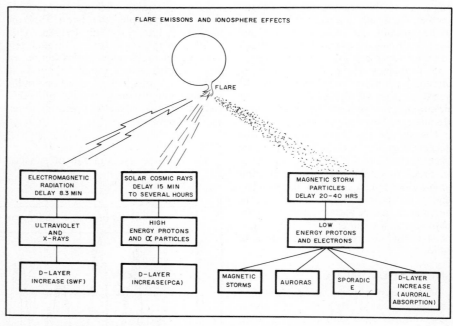

Fig. 9 — A summary of solar flare emissions and ionospheric effects.

particles travel even more slowly, and cause magnetic disturbances, auroras, sporadic E and increased polar-region absorption. These emissions arrive 20 to 40 hours after the solar flare has occurred.

It is difficult to compare solar activity to ionospheric variations because the chief ionizing agent for the F-region of the ionosphere is EUV, and this makes the traditional solar sunspot number (SSN) a poor short-term measure of solar effects on the ionosphere. EUV must be measured from satellite platforms, so relatively little is known about its variability. There is evidence, however, that EUV varies in much the same way as the 10.7-cm solar flux, which can be measured at ground level. For that reason, the solar-flux index is replacing the SSN as a short-term measure of solar activity.

Variations in the level of solar radiation can be gradual, as with the passage of sunspot groups and other long-lived activity centers across the solar surface, or the variations may be sudden and abrupt as with solar flares. Because the rotational period of the sun is approximately 28 days, a region of high activity that is on the disk (that region of the sun facing the Earth) will be in a position of affecting propagation for about 14 days and then hidden for about 14 days. A very active region can produce short-term radio blackouts for the full 14 days of its transit across the disk, but will produce particle events such as magnetic storms and radio aurora for only about seven days. Generally, until an active region crosses the central meridian of the sun, a strong flare cannot produce particle disturbances on the Earth because of the Earth/sun trajectory.

Absorption

When moving particles collide with each other, the one with the higher amount of energy will generally lose some of its energy to the other particle. As a radio wave travels through the ionosphere, it bumps into ionized particles and gives up some of its energy to those particles as it sets them in motion. The ionosphere absorbs energy from the radio wave. Such absorption is greater at lower frequencies, because it is proportional to the inverse square of frequency. It is this absorption that defines the LUF of a circuit. (If too much energy is absorbed, the signal will be too weak to be heard at the receiving station.)

Absorption is caused by X-rays and UV radiation, and it increases markedly during solar flares and auroral disturbances. A signal loses strength every time it passes through the D region. For this reason, a three-hop signal will have more path loss, (or less signal at the destination), than a one-hop signal. In order to minimize absorption, amateurs should use frequencies as near the MUF as possible.

EFFECTS OF THE EARTH'S MAGNETIC FIELD

The ionosphere has been discussed thus far in terms of simple bending, or refraction. An understanding of long-distance propagation must also take the Earth's magnetic field into account. Because of the Earth's magnetic field, the ionosphere is a double refracting medium that breaks up plane-polarized waves into what are known as the ordinary and extraordinary waves. This helps to explain the dispersal of plane polarization encountered in most ionospheric communication.

The Earth's magnetic field is disturbed by particle emissions from the sun. These emissions cause the magnetic field to vary, which causes loss of signals in the polar regions, increased aurora, and depleted F_2 ionization (called an ionospheric storm) at mid latitudes. Ionospheric storms tend to migrate southward from the polar region 36 to 72 hours after the actual solar event. This depletion of the ionosphere tends to affect most ham bands, resulting in generally poor operating conditions for the duration of the storm. An indicator of this happening is when the K index, also announced at 18 minutes after the hour on WWV, rises above 3. Remember that K_p is on a scale of 0 to 9, with 9 being the most disturbed condition.

RADIATION ANGLE AND SKIP DISTANCE

The lower the angle above the horizon at which a wave leaves the antenna, the less refraction in the ionosphere is required to bring it back to Earth, or to maintain useful signal level. This is the basis for the emphasis on low radiation angles in the pursuit of DX on the HF and VHF bands.

Some of the effects of radiation angle are illustrated in Fig. 10. The high-angle waves from the transmitter, T, are bent only slightly in the ionosphere, and so pass through it. The wave at a somewhat lower angle is just capable of being returned by the ionosphere.

This radiation angle from the antenna is called the critical angle. Radiation at angles more than the critical angle above the horizon will not be returned to Earth, while radiation at angles less than the critical angle will be returned farther from the transmitter. In daylight, if the frequency is low enough, the wave might be returned by the E layer, reaching R1. If the wave is returned from the F_2 layer, it will reach R2. The higher angle wave is returned closer to the transmitting point, T, than is the lowest-angle wave, which returns to R3.

The area between R1 and the outer reaches of the ground wave, near the transmitter, is called the skip zone. If R2 is at the shortest distance where energy returned from the F_2 layer is usable, the distance between R2 and T is the skip distance. The actual distances to both R1 and R2 depend on the ionization density, the radiation angle at T, and on the frequency in use. Table 2 has been included to provide a general indication of typical F-layer skip distances for the MF and HF amateur bands. Because these values can vary as much as 50% or more, they should be used only for comparison.

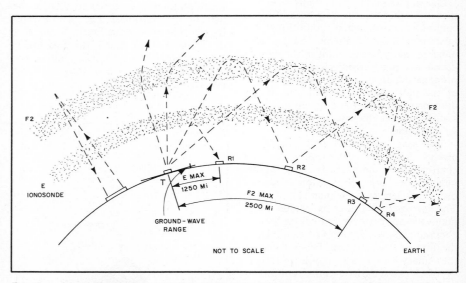

Fig. 10 — A vertical incidence sounder, shown at the left, measures virtual height and critical frequency of the F_2 layer. The transmitter, T, is shown radiating signals at four different angles. At the two highest radiation angles, the waves pass through the ionosphere after slight refraction. The lower-angle wave is returned to Earth by the E layer, if the frequency is low enough, at a maximum distance of 1250 miles. The signals are returned from the F_2 layer at a maximum distance of about 2500 miles, depending on the radiation angle. The signal may make a double hop, going from R2 to R4, which is beyond the maximum single-hop range. The lowest-angle wave reaches the maximum practical single-hop distance at R3.

LONG-PATH PROPAGATION

Propagation between any two points on the Earth's surface is usually by the shortest direct route, which is a great-circle path between the two points. A great circle is an imaginary line drawn around the Earth, formed by a plane passing through the center of the Earth. The diameter of a great circle is equal to the diameter of the Earth. You can find a great-circle path between two points by stretching a string tightly between those two points on a globe. If a rubber band is used to mark the entire great circle, you can see that there are really two great-circle paths. See Fig. 11.

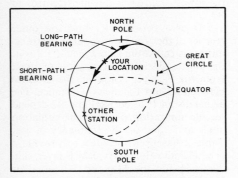

Fig. 11 — A sketch of the Earth, showing a great-circle path between two stations. Short-path and long-path bearings are shown from the northern-hemisphere station.

One of those paths will usually be longer than the other, and it may be useful for communications when conditions are favorable. Of course you must have a beam antenna that you can point in the desired direction to make effective use of long-path propagation. The station at the other end of the path must also point his or her antenna in the long-path direction to your station to make the best use of this propagation mode.

The long- and short-path directions always differ by 180°. Since the circumference of the Earth is about 24,000 miles, short-path propagation is always over a path length of less than 12,000 miles. The long-path distance is 24,000 miles minus the short-path distance for a specific communications circuit. For example, if the distance from Gordon, Pennsylvania to the Canary Islands is 3510 miles at a bearing of 85°, then the long-path circuit would be a distance of 20,490 miles at a bearing of 265°. (Chapter 16 of *The ARRL Antenna Book* contains information about distance and bearing calculations.)

Normally, radio signals propagate most effectively along the great-circle path that provides the least absorption. Since the D layer of the ionosphere is most responsible for signal absorption, the amount of sunlight that the signal must travel through

helps determine how strong the signals will be. So at times, your signal will be stronger at the receiving station when it travels over the nighttime side of the Earth.

For paths less than about 6000 miles, the short-path signal will almost always be stronger, because of the increased losses caused by multiple-hop ground-reflection losses and ionospheric absorption over the long path. When the short path is more than 6000 miles, however, long-path propagation will usually be observed either along the "gray line" between darkness and light, or over the nighttime side of the Earth.

While signals will generally travel best along the great-circle path, there is often some deviation from the exact predicted beam heading. Ionospheric conditions can cause radio signals to reflect or refract in unexpected ways. So it is always a good idea to rock your rotator control back and forth around the expected beam heading, and listen for the peak signal strength. If the strongest signals come from a direction that is significantly different from the great-circle headings, then we say the signals are following a crooked path. Anytime signals are not following a great-circle path, you have crooked-path propagation.

GRAY-LINE PROPAGATION

The *gray line* (sometimes called the *twilight zone*) is a band around the Earth that separates the daylight from darkness. Astronomers call this the terminator. It is a somewhat fuzzy region because the Earth's atmosphere tends to diffuse the light into the darkness. Fig. 12 illustrates the gray line around the Earth. Notice that on one side of the Earth, the gray line is coming into daylight (sunrise), and on the other side it is coming into darkness (sunset).

Propagation along the gray line is very efficient. One major reason for this is that the D layer, which absorbs HF signals, disappears rapidly on the sunset side of the gray line, and it has not yet built up on the sunrise side.

The gray line runs generally north and south, but varies as much as 23° either side of the north-south line. This variation is caused by the tilt of the Earth's axis relative to its orbital plane around the sun. The gray line will be exactly north and south at the equinoxes (March 21 and September 21). On the first day of summer in the northern hemisphere (June 21) it is tilted a maximum of 23° one way and on the first day of winter (December 21) it is tilted a maximum of 23° the other way. Fig. 13 illustrates the changing gray-line tilt. The tilt angle will be between these extremes during the rest of the year.

One way to describe the gray-line tilt is as an angle measured upward from the equator, looking east. It is important to note that if you measure an angle greater than 90° at sunrise, then you will measure an angle less than 90° at sunset on the same day. For example, at sunrise on April 16 the gray line makes an angle of approximately 99° with the equator, and at sunset it makes an angle of 81°. This means you can work into a different area of the world using gray-line propagation at sunset than you could at sunrise on the same day.

FADING

Changes in signal level, called fading, arise from a variety of phenomena, some natural and some man-made. Two or more parts of the wave may follow different paths, causing phase differences between wave components at the receiving end. Total field strength may be greater or less than the strength of one component. This

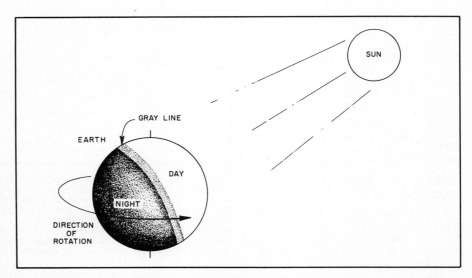

Fig. 12 — The gray line is a transition region between daylight and darkness. One side of the Earth is coming into sunrise, and the other side is just past sunset.

Fig. 13 — The angle with which the gray line crosses the equator depends on the time of year, and on whether it is at sunset or sunrise. A shows that the gray line is perpendicular to the equator twice a year, at the vernal equinox and the autumnal equinox. B indicates that the north pole is tilted toward the sun at an angle of 23° at the summer solstice, and C shows that it is tilted away from the sun at an angle of 23° at the winter solstice. These changes in the sun's position relative to the poles cause the gray line to shift position.

type of fading is called multipath interference. Fluctuating signal levels also result from the changing nature of the wave path, as in the case of moving air-mass boundaries in tropospheric propagation on the higher frequencies. Man-made sources of fading include reflections from aircraft and ionospheric discontinuities produced by exhaust from large rocket engines. Routinely, most fading comes from natural sources, like multipath interference.

Under some circumstances the wave path may vary with very small changes in frequency, so that modulation sidebands arrive at the receiver out of phase, causing mild or severe distortion. Called selective fading, this problem increases with signal bandwidth. Double-sideband AM signals suffer much more from selective fading than do single-sideband, suppressed-carrier signals.

THE SCATTER MODES

Much long-distance propagation can be described in terms of discrete reflection, though the analogy is never precise since true reflection would be possible only with perfect mirrors in a vacuum. All electromagnetic wave propagation is subject to scattering influences that alter idealized patterns to a great degree. The Earth's atmospheric and ionospheric layers, and objects in the wave path all act to scatter the signal. Strong returns are thought of as reflections and weaker ones as scattering, but both influence wave propagation. Scatter modes are useful in many kinds of communications.

Forward Scatter

We describe the skip zone as if there were no signal heard between the end of useful ground-wave range and the points R1 or R2 of Fig. 10. But actually, the transmitted signal can be detected over much of the skip zone, if sufficiently sensitive devices and methods are used. A small portion of the transmitted energy is scattered back to Earth in several ways, depending on the frequency.

Tropospheric scatter extends the local communications range to an increasing degree with frequencies above 20 MHz, becoming most useful in the VHF range. *Ionospheric scatter,* mostly used from the height of the E region, is most marked at frequencies up to about 60 or 70 MHz. *VHF tropospheric scatter* is usable within the limits of amateur power levels and antenna techniques, out to nearly 500 miles. *Ionospheric forward scatter* is discernible in the skip zone at distances up to 1200 miles or so.

A major component of ionospheric scatter is that contributed by short-lived columns of ionized particles formed around meteors entering the Earth's atmosphere. This can be anything from very short burst of little communications value to sustained periods of usable signal level, lasting up to a minute or more. Most common in the early morning hours, meteor scatter can be an interesting adjunct to amateur communication at 21 MHz and higher, especially in periods of low solar activity. It is at its best during major meteor showers.

Backscatter

A complex form of scatter is readily observed when working near the maximum usable frequency for the F layer over a particular path at a given time. The transmitted wave is refracted back to Earth at some distant point, which may be an ocean area or a land mass. A small portion of the transmitted signal may be reflected back into the ionosphere toward the transmitter when it reaches the Earth. The reflected wave helps fill in the skip zone, as shown in Fig. 14.

Backscatter signals are generally very weak, but there is no evidence of fading. Voice signals have a hollow, barrel-like sound. With optimum equipment, such signals are usable at distances from just beyond the reliable local range out to several hundred miles. Under ideal conditions, backscatter communications are possible over 3000 miles or more, though the term *sidescatter* is more descriptive of what happens on such long paths.

The scatter modes contribute to the usefulness of the higher parts of the DX spectrum, especially during periods of low solar activity when the normal ionospheric modes are often less available.

MF AND HF PROPAGATION

The amateur MF and HF bands (160 meters being the sole MF entry) are distinct in their propagation characteristics, but share one common bond: All of them utilize the F_2 layer for the primary mode of long-distance propagation. Here are capsule descriptions of propagation on those bands:

• The 1.8-MHz (160-meter) band suffers from extreme daytime D-layer absorption. Therefore, the top band is primarily useful at night. Only daytime signals entering the ionosphere at very high angles will be returned to Earth, which limits communications to 75 miles or so. At night, the D layer dissipates, and lower-angle signals are propagated. Under these conditions, communications over several thousands miles are possible.

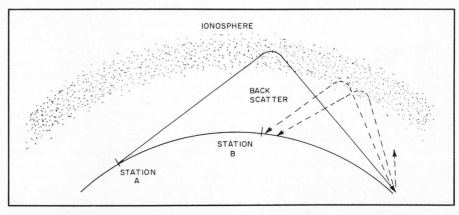

Fig. 14 — When radio waves pass into the ionosphere, some energy may be scattered back into the skip zone.

Another factor affecting propagation on this band is noise, both atmospheric and man-made. Since warm weather and noise producing thunderstorms often go hand-in-hand, winter is generally the best time to work DX on 160 meters.

• The 3.5-MHz (80-meter) band is similar to the 1.8-MHz band in many respects. Daytime absorption is significant, but not quite as extreme as on 1.8 MHz. Remember, absorption is proportional to the inverse square of frequency so as frequency is increased, D-layer effects are reduced. Typically, daytime communications range is approximately 250 miles. During nighttime, signals are often propagated halfway around the world. As on 1.8 MHz, atmospheric noise tends to be high, making winter the most attractive season for the 80 meter DXer.

• The 7-MHz (40-meter) band is the lowest frequency band that shows appreciable skip distance (see Table 2). During the day, a typical amateur station can cover a radius of approximately 500 miles. At night, reliable world-wide communications are possible on 40 meters. Atmospheric noise is somewhat more diminished, compared to 80 meters, but still presents a problem during the summer months. However, 40-meter DX signals are often of sufficient amplitude to override even high-level summer static. It is for that reason that 40 meters is the lowest-frequency amateur band considered reliable for year-round DX communication.

Table 2

Approximate Minimum Skip Distances for the Amateur MF and HF Bands

Band	Noon*	Midnight*
160 m	0	0
80 m	0	0
40 m	0	300 mi
30 m	200 mi	600 mi
20 m	500 mi	1000 mi
17 m	750 mi	(Daytime only)
15 m	800 mi	(Daytime only)
12 m	1000 mi	(Daytime only)
10 m	1200 mi	(Daytime only)

*Local time at the midpoint of the path.

• The 10-MHz (30-meter) band is unique in that it shares characteristics of both daytime and nighttime bands. Communications of up to 1000 miles are typical during the daytime, with this distance extending halfway around the world at night. In this respect, the band is generally useful on a 24-hour basis. During a solar minimum, the MUF on some DX paths may drop below 10 MHz during the night. Under these conditions, 30 meters adopts the characteristics of the higher frequency, daytime bands described below. Because the 30-meter band is a transitional band that is usable during both the day and night

for long-distance communications, it also shows the least variation in conditions during the swing between solar maximum and solar minimum.

• The 14-MHz (20-meter) band is traditionally regarded as the amateurs' primary long-haul DX band. Regardless of our position in the 11-year cycle, 20 meters can be depended on for world-wide propagation during the daylight hours. During solar maximum periods, 20 meters will often stay open to distant locations throughout the night. Skip distance is appreciable on the band (see Table 2), and is always present to some degree. Atmospheric noise is not too much of a consideration on the band, even in the summer. Because of its popularity, 20 meters tends to be very congested during the daylight hours.

• The 18-MHz (17-meter) band is similar to the 15-meter band in many respects, but the effects of fluctuating solar activity are not quite as pronounced. During the years of high solar activity, 17 meters is reliable for daytime and early-evening long-range communications, often lasting well after sunset. During moderate years, this band resembles 15 meters, opening during sunlight hours and closing shortly after sunset. During solar minimum periods, 17 meters will open to middle and equatorial latitudes, but only for short periods during midday on north-south paths.

• The 21-MHz (15-meter) band has characteristics similar to the 20-meter band, but shows greater fluctuation with changing solar activity. During peak years, 15 meters is reliable for daytime long-distance communications, and will often stay open well into the night. Twenty-four hour, continuous DX operation is possible on occasion, although less often than on 20 meters, and only during the peak of a solar maximum. In periods of moderate solar activity, 15 meters is basically a daytime-only band, closing shortly after sunset. During solar minimum periods, 15 meters may not open at all except for infrequent north-south transequatorial circuits. Sporadic-E is observed occasionally in early summer and mid-winter, although this is not common and the effects are not as pronounced as on the higher frequencies.

• The 24-MHz (12-meter) band offers propagation that combines the best of the 10- and 15-meter bands. While 12 meters is primarily a daytime band during low and moderate sunspot years, periods of solar activity find the band open well after sunset, often over long paths. During years of moderate solar activity, 12 meters opens to the low and middle latitudes during the daytime hours, but seldom remains open after sunset. Unlike 10 meters, periods of low solar activity seldom cause this band to go completely dead except at higher latitudes. Occasional daytime openings, especially in the lower latitudes, have been noted over north-south paths. The main sporadic-E season on 24 MHz lasts from late spring through summer and short

openings may be observed in mid-winter.

• The 28-MHz (10-meter) band is well known for extreme variations in characteristics. During a solar maximum, long-distance propagation is so efficient that very low powers can produce very loud signals half-way around the globe. DX is abundant with very modest equipment. Many a new DXer has been born on 10 meters. During a solar maximum, 10 meters is a daytime band remaining open a few hours past sunset. During periods of moderate solar activity, 10 usually opens only to low and transequatorial latitudes around midday. During a solar minimum, 10 meters is completely dead all day. There are anomalous openings (scatter, meteor burst, sporadic-E) during solar minimum that go unnoticed because most of the amateur population has migrated to lower frequencies. This lack of occupancy tends to enhance the dead appearance of the band. Amateurs who specialize in 10-meter operation make contacts throughout the solar cycle.

Sporadic-E propagation is fairly common on 10 meters, occurring between late April and early August. This phenomenon occurs regardless of F-layer conditions, and provides single-hop communications out to 1300 miles and multiple-hop communications to 2600 miles.

PROPAGATION PREDICTION

To the casual amateur, part of the thrill in ham radio is the challenge of finding an open frequency to operate on. The more serious amateur, interested in DX or traffic handling, wants to know, in advance, the band that will have the best stability and hearability in the geographical area of interest. Today's amateur has several options in planning his or her operations. These include the propagation charts in *The ARRL Operating Manual,* home computer predictions and the use of HF reference beacons. When these three techniques are used together, they can take a lot of mystery out of propagation conditions.

In December 1982, *QST* published the first MUF prediction program, called MINIMUF, for the ham microcomputer. Response throughout the amateur community was positive and the program quickly proliferated through many of the common home computers. In the early 1980's, a new generation of synthesized, digital HF receivers and transceivers provided full coverage for the entire HF spectrum causing renewed interest in shortwave broadcast listening. With these resources, today's enlightened amateur can schedule his or her operating activities using the long term predictions in *The ARRL Operating Manual,* fine tune them with short term predictions from a home computer and calibrate these signal predictions made in advance with on-the-air observations of known shortwave broadcasters. *The ARRL Operating Manual* contains an extensive set of propagation prediction charts, with complete information on how to use them to make a realistic estimate of propagation conditions

MUF Prediction on the Home Computer Using MINIMUF

Traditionally, the prediction of the maximum usable frequency (MUF) is done by a large, complex computer model, nominally consisting of 150,000 to 200,000 bytes of computer code. In 1977, a simple model was developed to emulate the dynamics of the MUF and its sensitivity to solar activity and seasonal changes. Simple is an understatement; the original model consisted of 80 BASIC program steps! Since that time many military, industrial, commercial and amateur HF users have successfully implemented and used MINIMUF.

The initial verification was done by comparing the prediction with oblique-incidence sounder data, which is the only way to observe the actual MUF boundary. The original sounder data base encompassed 196 path months (4074 test points) of observed maximum usable frequencies measured over 23 different HF sounder paths. MINIMUF was found to have an rms error of ± 3.8 MHz. Current users find it useful from 2 MHz to 50 MHz for MUF predictions out to 6000 miles. However, accuracy degrades for ranges of less than 250 miles.

As one can imagine, anything as simple as MINIMUF invites tinkering. Numerous experimenters have made attempts to improve the model with such features as adding an E and F_1 layer (MINIMUF is a single-layer model), changing constants to reflect local conditions and giving it more diurnal variation. All of these revisions, when compared against oblique-sounder data, degraded the accuracy and made the program more complicated. These exercises only serve to prove the old adage, "If it works, don't fix it." The version of MINIMUF described in this *Handbook* was first published in 1978 (see bibliography) and is still the principal version in use.

Application Tips

As solar activity varies, user interest in updating the MINIMUF prediction to reflect current conditions also increases. The updating method found to be most effective was to vary the sunspot number input parameter as a function of the 10.7-cm solar flux. Because of the lag in F-layer response to a rapid increase in solar activity, it is best to use either a 5-day, 15-day or 90-day running average of the 10.7-cm flux. The type of application will determine which is best. The 5-day mean is a short term, more dynamic input while the 90-day mean is more applicable for long term planning. As was indicated in a previous section, the current 10.7-cm solar flux information is transmitted at 18 minutes after every hour on WWV. The

conversion curve to translate the 10.7-cm flux to sunspot number is shown in Fig. 8.

Two other points are borne out by field testing. First, MINIMUF is an F-region approximation. Any intervention by E-region modes of propagation, either as multiple E or EF modes is not predictable by MINIMUF. Such operational situations are proving to represent only a small percentage of the total, however. Second, MINIMUF has the greatest accuracy within the one- and three-hop ranges between 300 miles and 7500 miles. Predictions for transmission paths longer than this should be used with some caution.

Many different conversions of the original MINIMUF article in December 1982 *QST* were received by the Program Exchange Department at ARRL Headquarters. In addition, input was received from numerous amateurs on its modification (see bibliography). A printed listing of an enhanced version of MINIMUF, which includes an LUF-plotting routine, written in BASIC, is available for $2.00 and an SASE. Write to ARRL Headquarters, Technical Department, 225 Main St., Newington, CT 06111. A table of benchmark data is also included to assure correct program loading.

Further Notes on Use

After you have a version of MINIMUF running on your computer, there are countless ways to test it yourself. One method is to observe the passage of the MUF through a frequency where a reference transmitter operates. WWV, WWVH and many shortwave broadcast signals will do nicely. Normally, ± 30 minutes from the predicted time of MUF passage (either the signal appears or goes away) is a good window.

Do not be mislead by comparing your prediction to published propagation charts. All HF prediction programs do well on some paths and poorly on others (and not necessarily the same paths). Comparing one HF prediction program against another is not valid unless all of the assumptions within the models are approached in the same manner. Such comparisons should be used with great caution because they are comparisons of apples and strawberries.

For those that are interested in calculating the Frequency of Optimum Transmission (FOT) and the LUF, two simplified approaches may suffice. The FOT may be approximated by 0.85 × MUF. This is the frequency which is supposed to have the highest circuit reliability and the least multipath interference. The LUF may be approximated by 0.25 × MUF with an upper limit of 12 MHz. After sunset, the LUF drops to below 2 MHz and remains there until sunrise.

HF Reference Beacons

Another method to assist day to day operations is establishing the habit of monitoring an HF signal that regularly

appears on the same frequency, at the same time, and maintains fairly constant transmission characteristics. The three most available sources of signals to monitor are (1) HF shortwave broadcasters; (2) time standard stations; and (3) amateur beacons. This method of environmental assessment is made even more attractive by a new generation of fully synthesized, programmable, general-coverage receivers, both in receive-only and transceive configurations. In general, these receivers are state-of-the-art, sensitive and very frequency agile. Stations to be monitored may be programmed in any order, with almost any revisit time and dwell time. This allows you to browse around the HF spectrum. You will find a whole new world of interesting signals; commercial, military, business, affairs of state, and broadcast; signals most amateurs don't normally listen to.

The most prolific HF signals that are useful for routinely monitoring conditions are those of the high power broadcasters. Most countries in the world maintain a foreign radio service to transmit news, music, and shows of interest from that country to large portions of the world. These signals, mostly double-sideband, amplitude modulation (AM), have 100 kW or more power and use large directive antennas. It takes effective radiated powers such as this to maintain broadcast quality at HF. The main advantage of using these signals is that they transmit on several frequencies simultaneously, allowing a listener to estimate the propagating bandwidth (LUF to MUF) over a given reference path.

While there are literally hundreds of these stations, some of the stronger signals to listen for in the USA are Voice of America (USA), BBC (UK), Radio Moscow (USSR), Deutsche-Welle (FDR), Radio Canada International (Canada), Radio South Africa (South Africa), Radio Nacional Buenos Aires (Argentina) and Radio Australia (Australia). The most useful frequencies to listen on are 5.9 to 6.2 MHz, 7.1 to 7.3 MHz, 9.5 to 9.775 MHz, 11.7 to 11.975 MHz, 15.1 to 15.4 MHz, 17.7 to 17.9 MHz, 21.4 to 21.75 MHz, and 25.6 to 26.1 MHz.

To use these broadcasts, one must establish routine listening habits and monitor the same transmissions at the same time each day. Develop a sense of trend. Are conditions improving or degrading? Monitoring several different signals can yield a picture of global conditions. Are BBC's signals making it over the Polar regions? Can you hear both the 6.0- MHz and 9.5-MHz signals from Radio Australia, and are they of equal strength?

In general, there are HF broadcasters in almost any part of the world an amateur may be interested in. If they are properly monitored they can provide an excellent assessment of global propagation. You should be aware, however, that the programs from some of these stations are transmitted from locations outside of the country. So if you hear a program from Radio Moscow, the Voice of America or the BBC, for example, you may not be listening to radio signals coming from Moscow, the USA or Great Britain. Shortwave listener's guides can help you learn where the broadcast is coming from, and program schedules from the stations themselves will often list the transmitter locations.

Time Standard Stations

Probably the most-used HF reference signals are the US Time Standard signals from WWV and WWVH. The Department of Commerce, National Oceanic and Atmospheric Administration, Environmental Research Laboratories in Boulder, Colorado maintain time standard stations at Ft. Collins, Colorado (WWV) and Kauai, Hawaii (WWVH). These stations transmit standard "tic" pulses each second, with minute announcements and special bulletins periodically (such as 10.7 cm flux at 18 minutes after the hour on WWV and 45 minutes after the hour on WWVH, updated daily at 2118 and 2145 UTC, respectively). WWV and WWVH transmit on 1.5, 5, 10, 15 and 20 MHz with very precise time and frequency stability. For amateurs in the USA, these signals are very useful to calibrate MINIMUF predictions, and to assess day to day communications reliability over one-hop ranges.

Amateur Beacon Stations

Historically, DX clubs and experimenters have established special interest beacons to alert DX operators of new long-range openings. There is a series of beacons on 10 meters between 28.1 and 28.5 MHz. These beacons have been established to alert 10-meter fans to long-haul openings or a sporadic-E opening. DX organizations are now establishing beacons at lower frequencies to optimize their DX-search operations.

Because these beacons emerge and leave the ham bands on a sporadic basis, no attempt will be made to list them here. A current list of beacons appears periodically in the "How's DX?" column of QST.

SELECTED HF-PROPAGATION REFERENCES

Anderson, John E., "MINIMUF for the Ham and the IBM Personal Computer," QEX, Nov. 1983, pp. 7-14.

Bramwell, Denton, "Technical Correspondence — More MINIMUF Mods," QST, May 1983, p. 43.

Horzepa, Stan, "On Line — Translating BASIC," QST, Aug. 1983, p. 64.

Paul, Dr. Adolf K., "NOSC Scientist Predicts Sunspot Activity," Technical Briefs, Naval Ocean System Center, 17 Feb. 1986.

Rose, Robert B., J. N. Martin and P. H. Levine, "MINIMUF-3: A Simplified HF MUF-Prediction Algorithm," Naval Ocean Systems Center Technical Report TR-186, Feb. 1, 1978.

Rose, Robert B., "MINIMUF: A Simplified MUF-Prediction Program for Microcomputers," QST, Dec. 1982, pp. 36-38.

Rose, Robert B., "Technical Correspondence — MINIMUF Revisited," QST, Mar. 1984, p. 46.

Rose, Robert B., "New Initiatives in HF-Signal Coverage Assessment," Ionospheric Effects Symposium, Naval Research Laboratory, Washington, DC, June 1984.

Shallon, Sheldon C., "Technical Correspondence — MINIMUF on Polar Paths," QST, Oct. 1983, p. 48.

Shallon, Sheldon C., MINIPROP, a commercially prepared program written for Amateur Radio users; 11058 Queensland St., Los Angeles, CA 90034-3029.

THE WORLD ABOVE 50 MHz

50-54 MHz (6-meter band)

The lowest amateur VHF band shares many of the characteristics of both lower and higher frequencies. Nearly every form of propagation is found in the 6-meter band, which contributes greatly to its popularity. In the absence of any favorable propagation conditions, well-equipped 50-MHz stations work regularly over a radius of at least 300 miles, depending on terrain, power, receiver capabilities, and antenna. Weak-signal tropo scatter allows the very best stations to make 500-mile contacts nearly any time. Weather effects may extend the normal range by a few hundred miles, especially during the summer months, but true ducting is rare.

Sporadic-E is probably the most common and certainly the most popular form of propagation on the 6-meter band. Single-hop E-skip openings may last many hours for contacts in the 400- to 1300-mile range, primarily during the spring and early summer. Multiple-hop sporadic-E provides transcontinental contacts several times a year, and contacts between the U.S. and South America, Europe, and Japan via multiple-hop E-skip have been made on rare occasions. During the peak of the 11-year sunspot cycle, world-wide 50-MHz DX is possible due to F_2 reflections during daylight hours. F_2 backscatter provides an additional propagation mode for contacts up to 2000 miles when the maximum usable frequency (MUF) is just below 50 MHz.

Other types of ionospheric propagation make 6 meters an exciting band. Aurora effects in the temperate latitudes allow contacts up to 1300 miles and sometimes farther. In the early morning hours, meteor scatter is a popular 50-MHz endeavor that provides brief contacts in the 500- to 1300-mile range. Transequatorial spread F (TE) creates 50-MHz paths as long as 5000 miles across the equator during peak sunspot years. Propagation by field-aligned irregularities (FAI) may provide additional hours of contacts at distances of up to 1300 miles.

144-148 MHz (2-meter band)

Ionospheric effects are significantly reduced at 144 MHz, but they are far from absent. F-layer propagation is unknown except for TE, which is responsible for the current 144-MHz terrestrial DX record of nearly 5000 miles. Sporadic-E occurs as high as 144 MHz about a tenth as often as at 50 MHz, but the maximum single-hop distance is the same, about 1300 miles. Sporadic-E contacts greater than 2000 miles have been made across the U.S. and Canada, as well as in Europe, but they are rare.

Auroral propagation is quite similar to that found on 50 MHz, except that signals tend to be weaker and more distorted. Meteor-scatter contacts up to 1300 miles are limited primarily to the periods of the great annual meteor showers. Contacts have been made via FAI on 144 MHz, but its potential has not been fully explored.

Tropospheric effects improve with increasing frequency, and 144 MHz is the lowest VHF band at which weather plays an important propagation role. Weather-induced enhancements may extend the normal 300- to 400-mile range of well equipped stations to 500 miles and more, especially in the summer and early fall. Tropospheric ducting makes it possible for contacts of more than 1200 miles over the continent and at least 2500 miles over water.

220-225 MHz (135-cm band)

The 135-cm band shares many characteristics with the 2-meter band. The normal working range of better 220-MHz stations is nearly as good as comparably equipped 144-MHz stations. The 135-cm band is slightly more sensitive to tropospheric effects, but ionospheric modes are more difficult to use.

Aurora and meteor-scatter signals are somewhat weaker than on 144 MHz. Sporadic-E contacts on 220 MHz are extremely rare, but may become more common as use of this band increases. TE is well within the possibilities of 220 MHz, and FAI may be possible as well. Increased activity on the 135-cm band will surely reveal the extent of 220-MHz propagation modes.

420-450-MHz (70-cm band)

The lowest amateur UHF band marks the highest frequency on which ionospheric propagation is commonly observed. Aurora signals are much weaker, and the range is usually less, than on 144 or 220 MHz. Meteor scatter is much more difficult than on the lower bands because signals are significantly weaker and of much shorter duration. Although sporadic-E and FAI are unknown as high as 432 MHz and probably impossible, TE may be useful. TE reception has been observed on this band, but no two-way 432-MHz contacts have been reported.

Well equipped 432-MHz stations can expect to work over a radius of at least 300 miles in the absence of any propagation enhancement. Tropospheric bending is more pronounced at 432 MHz and provides the most frequent and useful means of extended range contacts. Tropospheric ducting supports contacts of 1000 miles and farther over land and more than 2500 miles over water. The current 432-MHz terrestrial DX record of 2550 miles was accomplished via ducting over water. Reflections from airplanes, mountains and other stationary objects may also be useful adjuncts to 70-cm propagation.

902-928 MHz (33-cm band) and Higher

Ionospheric modes of propagation are nearly unknown in the UHF bands above 902 MHz. Aurora scatter may be within the range of amateur power levels at 902 and 1296 MHz, but signal levels will be well below those at 432 MHz. Doppler shift and distortion will be considerable, and the signal bandwidth may be quite wide. No other ionospheric propagation modes are likely.

Almost all extended distance work in the UHF and microwave bands is accomplished with the aid of tropospheric enhancements. The frequencies above 902 MHz are very sensitive to changes in the weather. Tropospheric ducting is more common than in the VHF bands. Contacts up to 2500 miles have been made on 1296 MHz and more than 1000 miles on 10 GHz by ducting. Limited amateur experiences have shown that well equipped stations can work reliably up to 200 miles and farther on 1296 MHz, but in general, normal working ranges are reduced with increasing frequency. Above 10 GHz, attenuation caused by atmospheric water vapor and oxygen become the most significant limiting factors in long-distance communications.

VHF/UHF/MICROWAVE PROPAGATION MODES

There is a wide variety of means by which radio frequencies above 50 MHz may be propagated beyond the horizon. They can be divided into three broad categories: propagation modes involving the ionosphere, such as F_2-layer reflections and meteor scatter; those limited to the troposphere (the weather-producing lower 10 miles of the atmosphere), such as ducting; and reflections from large solid objects, such as mountains and airplanes. Each of these is discussed in turn. Table 3 summarizes the characteristics of these propagation effects.

F2-Layer Reflections

Most long-distance radio communications in the HF range (3-30 MHz) result from one or more reflections in the F_2-layer of the ionosphere, 150 to 250 miles in altitude. The MUF of F_2 reflections reaches only as high as 70 MHz during the peak years of the sunspot cycle, making 6 meters the only useful VHF band for this type of communications. The skip distance at 50 MHz is usually between 1800 and 2500 miles, but multiple-hop paths make world-wide DX possible. The MUF often exceeds 50 MHz during a 3-year period around the peak of the 11-year solar maximum. During the period from 1989 to 1991, thousands of intercontinental 6-meter contacts were made from all parts of the globe, coinciding with the peak of cycle 22. The solar maximum for cycle 23 is expected about the year 2000, when once again 50-MHz worldwide contacts may be possible via the F_2 layer.

The MUF follows seasonal and daily cycles as well as the sunspot cycle. Even during the peak sunspot years, the MUF may reach 50 MHz in the northern hemisphere only from October through May. Six-meter F_2 contacts are generally completed only over paths entirely in daylight, because the MUF declines sharply after sunset. Stations running a few watts and simple antennas can work F_2 DX when conditions are favorable.

It is possible to forecast F_2-layer MUF using 2800-MHz solar flux values broadcast by WWV at 18 minutes after each hour. The MUF may approach 50 MHz at midday when the solar flux exceeds 175 (equivalent to a sunspot number of 125). The MUF can be followed more directly from the high frequencies through 50 MHz using a suitable general-coverage receiver.

Just before the MUF reaches 50 MHz F_2 backscatter is often evident on the

---

Table 3

VHF, UHF and Microwave Propagation

Propagation Mode	Useful Frequency	Expected Distances	Most Favorable Times
Ionospheric Modes			
F_2 Backscatter	50 MHz	100-2000 miles	Daylight during peak sunspot years
F_2 Reflection	50 MHz	1800-12,500 miles	Daylight during peak sunspot years
Transequatorial Spread-F	50-432 MHz	2000-5000 miles	1700-2200 local time during peak sunspot years
Sporadic-E	50-220 MHz	400-2500 miles and farther	Anytime, but common late mornings and early evenings May-July and December-January
Field-aligned irregularities	50-144 MHz, possibly 220 MHz	400-1300 miles	During and just after intense sporadic-E sessions
Aurora	50-432 MHz, possibly to 1296 MHz	100-1300 miles	Anytime, but more likely late afternoons during March-April and September-October
Meteor scatter	50-432 MHz	500-1300 miles	Early mornings, especially during one of the great annual meteor showers
Tropospheric Modes			
Line of sight	50 MHz-300 GHz	1-200 miles	Anytime, but cold weather better for bands above 10 GHz
Tropo scatter	50 MHz-300 GHz	50-500 miles	Anytime
Rain scatter	1296 MHz-10 GHz	5-100 miles	During periods of heavy rain
Ducting	50 MHz-300 GHz	100-2500 miles and farther	During favorable weather conditions
Reflection and diffraction by solid objects			
Stationary object reflections	144 MHz-300 GHz	5-150 miles	Anytime. Objects must be above the radio horizon for both stations
Airplane reflection	144 MHz-300 GHz	5-400 miles	During passage of an airplane between two stations
Earth-moon-earth reflection	50 MHz-2304 MHz, and higher	100-12,500 miles	When the moon is at perigee and within sight of the two stations
Knife-edge diffraction	432 MHz-300 GHz	5-200 miles	Anytime. Hills or mountains must lie between the two stations

6-meter band. Signals transmitted in the direction of an F_2 region with an MUF just below 50 MHz will be scattered back toward the transmitter over a wide area. Backscatter may provide another useful way of making contacts up to 2000 miles and farther. Backscattered signals are generally weak and have a characteristic hollow or ringing sound to them. High power and directive antennas are usually required to make backscatter contacts.

Transequatorial Spread-F

Discovered in 1947, *transequatorial spread-F (TE)* propagation makes it possible for contacts between 3000 and 5000 miles across the equator on frequencies as high as 432 MHz. Stations attempting TE contacts must be nearly equidistant from the geomagnetic equator. Many contacts have been made on 50 and 144 MHz between Europe and South Africa, Japan and Australia, and the Caribbean region and South America. Fewer contacts have been made on the 220-MHz band. TE signals have been heard on 432 MHz, but so far, no two-way contacts have resulted.

Unfortunately, for most continental U.S. stations, the geomagnetic equator dips south of the geographic equator in the western hemisphere, making only the most southerly portions of Florida and Texas within TE range. TE contacts from the southeast part of the country may be possible with Argentina, Chile, and even South Africa.

Limited experience with TE indicates that it peaks between 1700 and 2200 local time during years with high sunspot numbers. Signals have a rough aurora-like note. High power and large antennas are not required to work TE, as stations with 100 watts and single long Yagis have been successful.

The physics of TE propagation is not well understood, but a popular hypothesis suggests that during peak sunspot years, the F_2 layer near the equator bulges and intensifies slightly. The MUF late in the day may increase to 1.5 times its normal level 15° either side of the magnetic equator. VHF and UHF signals are refracted twice over the magnetic equatorial region at angles that normally would be insufficient to reflect the signals back toward Earth. The geometry is such, however, that two shallow reflections in the F_2 layer can create north-south terrestrial paths up to 5000 miles.

Sporadic-E

"Short skip," long familiar on the 10-meter band during the summer months, also affects the VHF bands as high as 220 MHz. *Sporadic-E*, as it is more properly called, propagates 50- and 144-MHz signals between 400 and 1300 miles. Multiple-hop sporadic-E has supported contacts up to 5000 miles on 50 MHz and more than 2000

miles on 144 MHz. The first confirmed 220-MHz sporadic-E contact was made in June 1987, but such contacts are likely to be very rare in the future.

Although sporadic-E is most common during the months of May, June and July, with a less-intense season at the end of December and early January, it can appear anytime. It is apparently unaffected by the sunspot cycle, and its association with the weather is highly uncertain. It is most likely to occur from 0900 to 1200 and again early in the evening between 1700 and 2000 local time.

Efforts to predict sporadic-E openings have not been highly successful, probably because its causes are not well understood. Studies have demonstrated that small and unusually dense patches of ionization in the E-layer, between 50 and 60 miles in altitude, are responsible for sporadic-E reflections. These sporadic-E clouds, as they are called, may form suddenly, move quickly from their birthplace, and dissipate within a few hours.

Sporadic-E clouds also exhibit an MUF that can be followed from 28 MHz through the 50-MHz band and higher. When the skip distance on 28 MHz is as short as 300 or 400 miles, it is a good sign that the MUF has reached 50 MHz. Contacts at the maximum sporadic-E distance, about 1300 miles, should then be possible at 50 MHz. E-skip contacts as short as 400 miles on 50 MHz, in turn, may be a sign that 144-MHz contacts in the 1200-mile range can be completed. Backscatter from sporadic-E clouds may also be evident on frequencies just below the MUF of the cloud.

The alert VHF operator will monitor

6-meter openings for signs that the MUF may be approaching 144 MHz. Hearing a 50-MHz station work progressively shorter paths suggests that the MUF is rising rapidly and gives clues to possible 144-MHz paths. See Fig. 15. The MUF can also be followed through TV channels 2 through 6 (56-88 MHz), the FM broadcast band (88-108 MHz), and into the aircraft band above that. Sporadic-E openings occur about a tenth as often on 144 MHz as on 50 MHz and for much shorter periods. It is common for the 6-meter band to be open for hours via sporadic-E, but 2-meter openings typically last only a matter of minutes. A few spectacular 2-meter sporadic-E sessions have lasted for longer than an hour. Sporadic-E may also affect the frequencies above the 2-meter band; this can be followed on TV channels 6 through 13 (174-216 MHz). The MUF for sporadic-E has been observed to exceed 200 MHz on a few occasions, but 220-MHz contacts are still very rare events.

Field-Aligned Irregularities

Amateurs have experimented with a little-known scattering mode known as *field-aligned irregularities (F AI)* on 50 and 144 MHz since 1978. Propagation via FAI accompanies sporadic-E openings and may persist for several hours after E-skip as disappeared. There are indications that 2000 to 2400 local time may be the most productive for FAI. Stations attempting FAI contacts direct their antennas toward a common scattering region that corresponds to a known sporadic-E reflection point. They need not be along a single great-circle path. Stations in southern

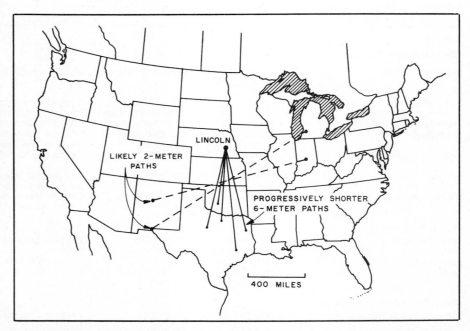

Fig. 15 — Sporadic-E contacts of 400 miles on 50 MHz indicate that 1200-mile paths may be open on 144 MHz. Hearing a 50-MHz station in Lincoln, Nebraska, work progressively shorter paths into Texas and Oklahoma (solid lines) suggests that 144-MHz contacts (dashed lines) may be possible. The midpoint of all paths is the same area of high-MUF, sporadic-E activity, in this case just north of the Kansas-Oklahoma border.

Florida, for example, have completed 144-MHz FAI contacts with Dallas, Texas, when all participating stations were beamed toward a common scattering region over northern Alabama.

FAI-propagated signals are weak and fluttery, reminiscent of aurora signals. Doppler shifts of as much as 3 kHz have been observed in some tests. Stations running as little as 100 watts and a single Yagi should be able to complete FAI contacts during the most favorable times, but higher power and larger antennas may yield better results. Contacts have been made on 50 and 144 MHz, and 220-MHz FAI seems probable as well. Expected maximum distances should be similar to other forms of E-layer propagation — up to 1300 miles.

Aurora

Radio signals with frequencies as high as 3000 MHz have been scattered by the aurora borealis or northern lights (aurora australis in the Southern Hemisphere), but amateur *aurora* contacts have been reported only through 432 MHz. By pointing directional antennas toward the center of aurora activity (generally north in the Northern Hemisphere) contacts up to 1300 miles distant are possible. Stations north of 42° latitude experience many aurora openings each year, while those in the Gulf Coast states may hear aurora signals no more than once a year, if that often.

The appearance of aurora is closely linked to solar activity. During massive solar storms, high energy streams of electrons and protons spew out from the sun. These high-energy particles are trapped by the Earth's magnetic field in the polar regions. They ionize the gases of the E-layer and higher, giving rise to spectacular visual displays as well as affecting radio communications. Aurora generally absorbs radio signals below 20 MHz, while those above 20 MHz are scattered and reflected.

Auroras occur most often around the spring and fall equinoxes (March-April and September-October), but aurora may appear in any month. Radio aurora activity generally peaks between 1600 and 2000 local time and may reappear later in the evening. Aurora may be anticipated by following the A- and K-index reports on WWV at 18 minutes after each hour. A K-index of 4 or greater and an A-index of at least 30 are indications that a geomagnetic solar storm is in progress and an aurora likely. The probability, intensity, and southerly extent of aurora increase as the two index numbers rise. Weak and watery signals on the AM broadcast band through the 40-meter band late in the afternoon may be an indication that an aurora is already in progress. The 20-meter band may close down altogether. Satellite operators have also noticed that 144-MHz downlink signals are often weak and distorted when satellites pass near the polar regions during magnetic storms.

You do not have to able to see an aurora to make aurora contacts. Useful aurora may be as distant as 650 miles and well below the visual horizon. Auroras scatter radio signals back toward the transmitter over a very wide area, making possible contacts with stations up to 1300 miles away. Antennas should be pointed generally north and then used to probe east and west to peak signals. Offsets from north are usually greatest when the aurora is closest. There may be some advantage to antennas that can be elevated, especially when auroras are nearby. High power and large antennas are not necessary to work aurora. Stations with as little as 10 watts output have made aurora contacts on frequencies as high as 432 MHz.

Aurora-scattered signals are easy to identify. On 50-MHz SSB, signals sound very distorted and somewhat wider than normal; on 144 MHz and above, the distortion may be so severe that only CW is useful. Aurora CW signals have a distinctive note variously described as a buzz, hiss, or mushy sound. Doppler shifts of 1 kHz may be evident on 144 MHz and several kHz on 432 MHz. Signal strength dramatically decreases with higher frequencies, while Doppler shift and distortion increase. Especially strong aurora may evolve into a mode known as auroral-E on 50 MHz. Distortion disappears and path lengths may increase well beyond the usual 1300-mile limit for aurora.

Meteor Scatter

Contacts between 500 and 1300 miles distance can be made on 50 through 432 MHz via reflections from the ionized trails left by meteors as they travel through the ionosphere. The kinetic energy of meteors no larger than peas, and more commonly the size of grains of sand, are sufficient to ionize a column of air up to 12 miles long in the E-layer. The particle itself evaporates and never reaches the ground, but the ionized column may persist for a few seconds to a minute or more before it dissipates. This is enough time to make very brief contacts by reflections from the ionized trails. Hundreds of thousands of meteors enter the Earth's atmosphere every day, but relatively few have the required size, speed, and orientation to the Earth to make them useful for *meteor-scatter* propagation.

Radio signals in the 30- to 100-MHz range are reflected best by meteor trails, making the 50-MHz band prime for meteor-scatter work. The early morning hours around dawn are the most productive, because the Earth's rotation sweeps up incoming meteors and contributes to their apparent velocity. Meteor contacts ranging from a second or two to more than a minute can be made nearly any morning on 50 MHz. Meteor-scatter contacts on 144 MHz and higher are more difficult because reflected signal strength and duration drop sharply with increasing frequency. A meteor trail that provides 30 seconds of communication on 50 MHz will last only 3 seconds on 144 MHz and less than 1 second on 432 MHz.

Meteor scatter may be somewhat better during July and August because the average number of meteors entering the Earth's atmosphere peaks during those months. The very best times are during one of the great annual meteor showers, when the number of useful meteors may increase 50-fold over the normal rate of one or two per hour. See Table 4. A meteor shower occurs when the Earth passes through a relatively dense stream of particles, thought to be the remnants of a comet, that are also in orbit around the sun. The greatest showers are relatively consistent from year to year, both in their recurrence and meteor density.

Table 4

Prominent Annual Meteor Showers

Name	Peak dates	Rate, meteors/hour
Quadrantids	January 3	50
Arietids	June 7-8	60
Perseids	August 12-13	50
Geminids	December 12-13	60

Because meteors provide only fleeting moments of communication even during one of the great meteor showers, especially on 144 MHz and above, special operating techniques are often used to increase the chances of completing a contact. Prearranged schedules between two stations establish times, frequencies, and precise operating standards. Usually, each station transmits on alternate 15-second periods until enough information is pieced together a bit at a time to confirm contact. Nonscheduled random meteor contacts are quite common on 50 MHz and 144 MHz during meteor showers, but short transmissions and alert operating habits are required.

It is helpful to run several hundred watts to a large antenna, but meteor-scatter can be used by modest stations under optimal conditions. During the best showers, a few watts and a small Yagi are sufficient on 50 MHz. On 144 MHz, at least 100 watts output and a long Yagi are needed for consistent results. Proportionately higher power is required for 220 and 432 MHz even under the best conditions.

Line of Sight

At one time it was thought that communications in the VHF range and higher would be restricted to "line of sight" paths. Although this has not proven to be the case even in the microwave region, the concept of line of sight is still useful in understanding propagation. In the absence of any kind of enhancement, radio waves traveling through the weather-producing lower few thousand feet of the atmosphere, called the troposphere, do not travel in straight lines. Radio waves are normally refracted, or bent, slightly earthward. The reason is not hard to understand. The normal drop in temperature, pressure, and water vapor content of air with increasing altitude affects the refractive properties of the atmosphere. Just as light is refracted as it crosses the boundary between two dissimilar media, such as water and air, radio waves are refracted as they pass through an atmosphere whose refractive properties change with altitude. Under average conditions, radio waves are refracted toward Earth enough to make the horizon appear 1.34 times farther away than the visual horizon.

A simple formula can be used to estimate the distance to the radio horizon under average conditions:

$$d = \sqrt{2h}$$

where

    d = distance to the radio horizon in miles

    h = height above average terrain in feet

The distance to the radio horizon for an antenna 100 feet above average terrain is thus 14.1 miles; a station on top of a 5000-foot mountain would have a radio horizon of 100 miles. The line-of-sight distance for any pair of stations is their combined distance to a common horizon. Stations on top of two 5000-foot mountains no more than 200 miles distant would be within each other's radio horizon.

Tropospheric Scatter

Contacts beyond the horizon are made every day on the VHF bands and higher without the aid of obvious propagation enhancement. "Ground wave," a term that is more appropriate to propagation on the frequencies below 3 MHz, plays no important role above 50 MHz. Beyond-the-horizon communication in the VHF range and higher is possible because a tiny portion of the transmitted signal is scattered by small changes in the index of refraction of air, and by dust, clouds, and other naturally occurring particles in the troposphere. Most amateurs are unaware that they use *tropo scatter,* even though it plays an essential role in most ordinary VHF and UHF communication. The normal ranges for well equipped stations provided in the propagation summaries of each band, for example, are really the maximum distances commonly worked via tropo scatter.

The theoretical maximum distance that can be worked via tropo scatter is limited ultimately by the line-of-sight distance two stations have of the same scattering region

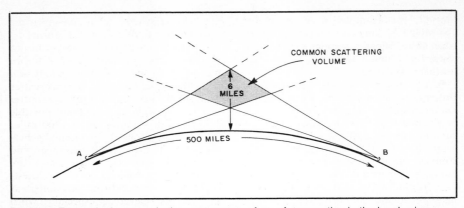

Fig. 16 — Tropospheric scatter is the most common form of propagation in the bands above 50 MHz. A small portion of transmitted signals is scattered by the atmosphere, but only that portion scattered within sight of two stations — the common scattering volume — provides the vital tropo-scatter link. The maximum theoretical range of 500 miles for tropo scatter is limited by the highest part of the atmosphere useful for scattering, about 6 miles in altitude. At 6 miles, the radio horizon is 250 miles distant.

of the troposphere. See Fig. 16. The highest altitude for which scattering is efficient at amateur power levels is about 6 miles. An application of the distance-to-horizon formula shows that 500 miles is the maximum distance for stations relying only on tropo scatter at any frequency.

In practice, tropo scatter paths are shorter than 500 miles because most stations are less than optimal, and scattering path losses increase with frequency. Almost all extended-distance tropo scatter work involves weak signals and considerable fading. Scatter may be worked any time or season. Weather affects scattering efficiency, but its effects are nearly impossible to predict over any given path.

Rain scatter is a special case of tropo scatter that is practical in the 1296 MHz to 10 GHz range. Stations simply point their antennas toward a common area of rain. A certain portion of radio energy is scattered by the raindrops, making over-the-horizon or obstructed-path contacts possible, even with low power. The theoretical range for rain scatter is as great as 400 miles, but the experiences of amateurs in the microwave bands suggests that expected ranges are less than 100 miles. Snow and hail make less efficient scattering media unless the ice particles are partially melted. Smoke and dust particles are too small for extraordinary scattering, even in the microwave bands.

Tropospheric Enhancement and Ducting

Weather dramatically affects tropospheric refraction, and specific weather conditions can be linked to enhanced propagation. Enhancement refers to tropospheric refraction that is greater than normal but insufficient to bend radio waves back to the surface of the Earth. Increased signal strength and extended path distances to the limits of tropo scatter, or about 500 miles, result from enhanced tropospheric conditions. Ducting takes place when refraction is so great that radio

signals are bent all the way back to the surface of the Earth. When ducting conditions in the troposphere exist over a wide geographic area, signals may remain very strong over distances of 1000 miles or more. Higher frequencies are more sensitive to tropospheric refraction, and effects may be observed in the microwave bands before they affect the lower frequencies.

Enhancement and ducting occur when the normal lapse in air temperature with altitude is reversed, that is when temperature increases with altitude. This condition is known as a temperature inversion. Temperature inversions are often accompanied by unusual drying of air with altitude, which contributes to increased refractivity. A large number of weather conditions are known to create temperature inversions. Some of the more common and most useful inversion-producing weather conditions are discussed in turn.

Radiation inversions are probably the most common and widespread of the various weather conditions useful to propagation. Radiation inversions form only over land after sunset as a result of progressive cooling of the air near the Earth's surface. As the Earth cools by radiating heat into space, the air just above the ground is cooled in turn. At higher altitudes, the air remains relatively warmer, thus creating the inversion. The cooling process may continue through the evening and predawn hours, creating inversions that extend as high as 1500 feet. Radiation inversions are most common during clear, calm, summer evenings. They are more distinct in dry climates, in valleys, and over open ground. Their formation is inhibited by wind, wet ground, and cloud cover. Although such inversions are common and widespread, they are rarely strong enough to cause true ducting. The enhanced conditions so often observed on summer evenings are usually a result of radiation inversions.

Large, sluggish, *high-pressure systems*

(or anticyclones) create the most dramatic and widespread tropospheric ducts. Inversions in high-pressure systems are created by the sinking and compressing of air within the high. Useful inversions appear between 1000 and 5000 feet. Ducts intensify during the evening and early morning hours. The longest and strongest radio paths usually lie to the south and southwest of the high-pressure centers. See Fig. 17.

Over continental areas, sluggish high-pressure systems that are likely to contain strong temperature inversions are most common in late summer over the eastern half of the U.S. They move very slowly out of Canada, generally southeastward, and may linger for days, providing many hours of extended propagation. The southeastern part of the country, including the Gulf and the lower Midwest, experiences the most high-pressure openings; the upper Midwest and East Coast somewhat less frequently; the mountain states and the West Coast rarely.

Semipermanent high-pressure systems — nearly constant climatic features in certain parts of the world — have created the longest and most exciting ducting paths. The Eastern Pacific High, which migrates northward off the coast of California during the summer, has been responsible for the longest ducting paths reported to date, more than 2500 miles on 144 MHz through 1296 MHz between California and Hawaii. The Bermuda High is a nearly permanent feature in the Caribbean area. During the summer, it too moves north and often covers the southeastern U.S. It has produced contacts in excess of 1800 miles from Florida and the Carolinas to the West Indies, but its potential has not been exploited. Other semipermanent highs lie in the Indian Ocean, the western Pacific, and off the coast of west Africa.

The *wave cyclone* is a more dynamic weather system seen primarily during the spring months over the middle part of the American continent. The wave begins as a disturbance in a long continental front, which creates two distinct parts. On the western leg, a cold front forms and moves rapidly eastward; to the east, a warm front moves slowly northward. When the wave is in its open position, as shown in Fig. 18, north-south radio paths 1000 miles and longer may be possible in the warm sector — that area to the east of the cold front and south of the warm front. East-west paths nearly as long may also open up in the southerly parts of the warm sector. Evening and early morning are generally the best times. Wave cyclones are rarely productive for more than 24 to 36 hours, because the eastward moving cold front eventually closes off the warm sector. Temperature inversions associated with wave cyclones are created by a fast stream of warm, dry air above 3000 feet that covers relatively cooler and moister Gulf air flowing northward near the Earth's surface in the warm sector.

Fig. 17 — Sprawling, slow-moving, high-pressure systems, a common feature in the eastern half of the country during the late summer, provide the majority of extended tropospheric ducts. Shown here are the surface weather features on September 8, 1984, when many contacts of 1000 miles or more were made on all bands from 144 MHz through 1296 MHz. Solid lines represent typical paths reported during the early evening hours. Note that long paths appeared to the southwest of the high-pressure center. For more details about this tropospheric event, see January 1985 *QST*, pp. 74-77; and March 1986 *QEX*, pp. 5-12.

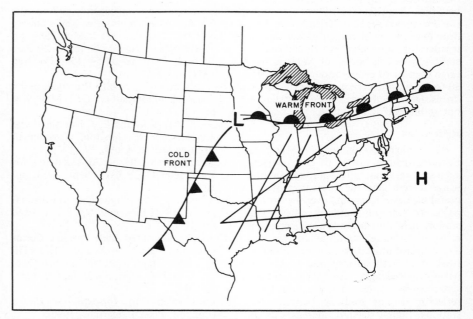

Fig. 18 — The wave cyclone also creates tropospheric ducts that support contacts in excess of 1000 miles in the bands above 144 MHz. Shown here is a wave that formed on June 2, 1980. Solid lines show typical contacts made on 144 MHz and 432 MHz. Similar contacts were made on the following day, before the wave collapsed. Another wave formed along the same continental front on June 6-7 and that provided an additional period of VHF and UHF DX.

Warm fronts and *cold fronts* sometimes bring enhanced conditions, but rarely true ducting. A warm front marks the surface boundary between a mass of warm air flowing over an area of relatively cooler and more stationary air. Inversion conditions may be stable enough for several hundred miles ahead of the warm front to bring enhancement and sometimes ducting. A cold front marks the surface boundary between a mass of cool air that is trying to wedge itself under more stationary warm air. The warmer air is pushed aloft in a narrow band behind the cold front, creating a strong but highly unstable temperature inversion. The best chance for enhancement occurs during the two or three hours after the front passes. Long paths, if they are possible, will open parallel to the passing front.

Certain kinds of wind may also create useful inversions. The *Chinook wind* of the American high plains (and similar winds in other parts of the world) floods the eastern slopes of the Rockies and the Great Plains with warm and very dry air, primarily in the springtime. Inversion effects may be felt from Canada to Texas and east to the Mississippi River. *Land breezes,* the cool air that blows in from the ocean in coastal areas after sunset during the warmer months, is accompanied by a return flow of warm air at 1000 feet or so in altitude. Land breeze inversions often bring enhanced conditions and occasionally allow contacts in excess of 500 miles along the East Coast and other coastal areas. In southern Europe, a hot, dry wind known as the *sirocco* that blows northward from the Sahara Desert across the Mediterranean has probably been responsible for record-breaking microwave contacts in excess of 1000 miles.

Over warm water areas, such as the Caribbean and other tropical waters, *evaporation inversions* may create ducts that are useful only in the microwave region between 3.3 and 24 GHz. These are among the few inversions that depend on a sharp drop in water-vapor content rather than on temperature inversion. Air just above the surface of warm bodies of water is saturated because of evaporation. Within 10 to 30 feet in altitude, the water-vapor content drops significantly, creating a very shallow but stable and strong duct.

Reflections

At frequencies above 144 MHz, reflections from a variety of large objects, such as buildings, airplanes, mountains, water towers, and the like can provide a useful means of extending over-the-horizon paths to several hundred miles. Two stations need only beam toward a common reflector, whether stationary or moving. The reflector must be within the radio line-of-sight of both stations and be large in terms of wavelength. Contrary to common sense notions, the best position for a reflector is not midway between two stations. Signal strength increases as the reflector approaches one end of the path; the reflector may even be positioned on the far side of one station with good result.

The maximum range is limited by the line-of-sight distance of both stations to the reflector and to a lesser extent by reflector size. A water tower on top of a hill 500 feet above average terrain could extend reliable microwave coverage of a station in a nearby valley to more than 30 miles. The extreme limit for airplane reflections is about 550 miles, assuming the largest jets fly no higher than 40,000 feet. Actual airplane reflection contacts are likely to be considerably shorter.

In addition to making fair reflectors, hills and mountains can also serve as effective knife-edge diffractors at VHF and higher. A small portion of signals traveling over the crest of a mountain range or a line of hills at least 100 wavelengths long will be diffracted downward on the far side. (Diffraction is a bending of the wave as it passes across the edge of a well defined object.) Only a small portion of the signal energy will be diffracted into the "shadow" area, but it may make it possible to complete paths up to 100 miles or more that might otherwise be obstructed by the terrain.

The moon has also been used as reflector on 50 MHz through at least 2304 MHz. Very high power and large antennas, along with the very best receivers, are required to overcome the extreme losses involved in Earth-Moon-Earth (EME) paths. Contacts from one side of the Earth to the other, 12,500 miles, are possible. The techniques of EME communication are specialized enough to be discussed in detail elsewhere in the *Handbook.*

SELECTED VHF/UHF PROPAGATION BIBLIOGRAPHY

Bacon, Jim, "An Introduction to Sporadic E," *Radio Communication,* Radio Society of Great Britain, Part I: May 1989, pp 37-41; Part II: June 1989, pp 37-39; Part III: July 1989, pp 51-54; Part IV: Aug 1989, pp 48-52.

Bain, Walter F., "VHF Propagation by Meteor-Trail Ionization," *QST,* May 1974, pp. 41-47, 176.

Bean, Bradford R. and E. J. Dutton, *Radio Meteorology* (Washington: Government Printing Office, 1968).

Collier, James S., "Upper-Air Conditions for Two-Meter DX," *QST,* Sept. 1955, pp. 16-18.

Cracknell, R. G., "Transequatorial Propagation of V.H.F. Signals,"*QST,* Dec. 1959, pp. 11-17.

Cracknell, Ray, Fred Anderson, and Costas Fimerelis, "The Euro-Asia to Africa VHF Transequatorial Circuit During Solar Cycle 21,"*QST,* Nov. 1981, pp. 31-36; Dec. 1981, pp. 23-27.

Davies, Kenneth, *Ionospheric Radio* (London: Peter Peregrinus, 1990).

Gannaway, J. N., "Tropospheric Scatter Propagation," *QST,* Nov. 1983, pp. 43-48.

Greene, Clarke, "Meteor-Scatter Communications," *QST,* Jan. 1986, pp. 14-17.

Jessop, G. R., ed., *VHF/UHF Manual,* 4th edition (Hertfordshire, England: Radio Society of Great Britain, 1983).

Kneisel, Thomas F., "Ionospheric Scatter by Field-Aligned Irregularities at 144 MHz," *QST,* Jan. 1982, pp. 30-32.

Newton, Charlie, *Radio Auroras* (Potters Bar, England: RSGB, 1990).

Owen, Michael R., "VHF Meteor Scatter — An Astronomical Perspective," *QST,* June 1986, pp. 14-20.

Owen, Michael R., "The Great Spordic-E Opening of June 14, 1987," *QST,* May 1988, pp. 21-29.

Pocock, Emil, "The Weather that Brings VHF DX," *QST,* May 1983, pp. 11-16.

Pocock, Emil, "Sporadic-E Propagation at VHF: A Review of Progress and Prospects." *QST,* April 1988, pp. 33-39.

Pocock, Emil, "Auroral-E Propagation at 144 MHz," *QST,* Dec. 1989, pp. 28-32.

Pocock, Emil, "Practical Radio Aurora," *QST,* Mar 1990, pp 20-25.

Reisert, Joseph H. and Gene Pfeffer, "A Newly Discovered Mode of VHF Propagation,"*QST,* Oct. 1978, pp. 11-14.

Reisert, Joseph, "Improving Meteor Scatter Communications," *Ham Radio* June 1984, pp. 82-92.

Wilson, Melvin S., "Midlatitude Intense Sporadic-E Propagation," *QST,* Dec. 1970, pp. 52-55 and Mar. 1971, pp. 54-57.

NEWSLETTERS WITH VHF/UHF PROPAGATION NEWS

Feed Point, North Texas Microwave Society, Wes Atchison, WA5TKU, Rte 4, Box 565, Sanger, TX 76266 (bimonthly, $12/year).

50 MHz DX Bulletin, Harry A. Schools, KA3B, 1606 Newkirk St, Philadelphia, PA 19145 (monthly, $25/year).

432 and Above EME News, Allen Katz, K2UYH, Electrical Engineering Dept, Trenton State College, Trenton, NJ 08650 (enclose an SASE with inquiries).

Northeast VHF News, Northeast VHF Assn, Lewis D. Collins, W1GXT, 10 Marshall Terr, Wayland, MA 01778 (bi-annually, $4/year).

Pack Rats' Cheese Bits, Mt Airy VHF Radio Club, Rick Connor, WC2K, 412 Carranza Rd, Tabernacle, NJ 08088 (monthly, $7/year).

Rochester VHF Group Journal, Rochester VHF Group, PO Box 92122, Rochester, NY 14692 (monthly, $10/year).

Sidewinders on Two Bulletin, Howard Hallman, WD5DJT, 3230 Springfield, Lancaster, TX 75134 (monthly, $10/year).

Six News, UK Six Metre Group, Ted Collins, G4UPS, 27 Parklands, Hemyock, Devon EX15 3RY, England (monthly).

2 Meter EME Bulletin, Robert E. Turner, 14826 Daisy Ln, Tampa, FL 33613 ($18/year).

220 Notes, Walt Altus, AA9AW, W6539 Birch St, Onalaska, WI 54650 (bimonthly, $6.50/year).

VHF/UHF Newsletter, RSGB, Alma House, Cranbourne Rd, Potters Bar, Hertfordshire EN6 3JW, England.

West Coast VHFer, Bob Cerasuolo, WA6IJZ, PO Box 74, Sun Valley, AZ 86029 (monthly, $10/year).

Chapter 23

Space Communications

Radio communication distances are essentially limited by the curvature of the Earth, unless various propagation enhancements are utilized. Propagation effects that are dependent upon the atmosphere or ionosphere can be conditionally (and sometimes unpredictably) used to transmit radio signals around the Earth's curvature, thus thwarting the straight-line radio range concept, even at VHF and UHF frequencies. Communicating beyond line-of-sight distances, however, may require the use of high power and gain antennas. These types of communications are defined as "terrestrial communications."

Because objects in space are visible from a number of locations on the Earth at the same time, communications between stations within this "circle of visibility" is possible in a predictable manner. This can be achieved by using the space object as a passive reflector for radio energy, or if the space object contains a transponding radio transmitter/receiver, it can act as an radio relay. The predictable signal path to the space object and back avoids the uncertain attenuation inherent in terrestrial propagation.

Amateur Radio space communications have two major facets: artificial satellites and the natural satellite, the Moon. Together, they make VHF and higher frequencies usable for amateur intercontinental communications and push today's technology to the limit.

SATELLITE COMMUNICATIONS

The excitement of global VHF/UHF long distance communication (DX) is within the reach of nearly every amateur, and can be experienced with small antennas, low power and relatively simple equipment. The amateur satellite program has been developing for more than a quarter of a century. It began in 1961 and has been enhanced with every launch. The rich history of the amateur satellite program is well covered in *The Satellite Experimenter's Handbook*, published by the ARRL. Presented here is detailed information on setting up a ground station for this fascinating facet of Amateur Radio. With the satellite tracking and operating techniques presented in *The ARRL Operating Manual*, amateurs now have the most up-to-date information available on satellite communications.

Spacecraft

Amateurs currently enjoy intercontinental communications through a class of high-altitude OSCAR (Orbiting Satellite Carrying Amateur Radio) satellites, called Phase III. These satellites are characterized by their highly elliptical orbits that provide operating windows of up to 10 hours, with wide-ranging geographical coverage. Two Phase III satellites are available as of this writing: the fully operational OSCAR 13, in a high-inclination (Molniya) orbit, and its ailing, partially operational cousin, OSCAR 10 (AO-10). These two satellites have demonstrated to the world a noteworthy capability for global communications since AO-10 was first made available in August 1983.

Amateur satellites employ a full-duplex transmitter/receiver combination called a transponder. This transponder allows operators to hear their own signals in real time, as well as those of other operators—great for multistation intercontinental round tables. A satellite operator will transmit on one band (uplink) and receive on another band (downlink). AO-13 provides transponder service in Mode B (145 MHz uplink, 435 MHz downlink), as does AO-10 (when available). AO-13 also supports a pair of transponders for both Mode J (144 MHz uplink, 435 MHz downlink) and Mode L (1269 MHz uplink, 435 MHz downlink), which commonly operate simultaneously and are referred to as Mode JL. See Tables 1 and 2. Both transponders offer noise-free 70-cm downlinks.

Amateurs in several countries are now participating in the process of designing and constructing spacecraft. In 1986, the first Japanese amateur satellite, JAS-1, now Fuji-OSCAR 12 (FO-12), was orbited. In 1990, the same group launched into orbit JAS-2, now Fuji-OSCAR 20 (FO-20). Fuji-OSCAR 12 is now defunct, but FO-20 is doing very well in its low Earth orbit (LEO) at an altitude of 1500 km. Satellites in this type of orbit are termed Phase II spacecraft. FO-20 carries a Mode-J transponder that serves two functions: linear SSB service, and an advanced packet store-and-forward global message service with a 1.5-megabyte RAM storage bank.

Soviet amateurs have updated their aging fleet of Radio Sputnik (RS) satellites with RS-10/11. This transponder satellite, like its predecessor, resides in a Phase-II circular orbit. The Soviet spacecraft designs have concentrated more on HF communications links to accommodate the kinds of equipment readily available in that country.

A cluster of six packet and educational Phase-II, low-Earth-orbit satellites were launched in January 1990. These supersmall satellites represent the first in a series of new OSCAR satellites. Dubbed *Microsat* because of their small size, these spacecraft are cubes approximately 230 mm (9 inches) on a side, with a mass in the neighborhood of 10 kg (22 pounds). Microsats employ the most advanced electronic technology of any OSCAR satellite. This effort was sponsored and conducted by a consortium of organizations: AMSAT-NA (AMSAT North America), BRAMSAT (AMSAT Brazil), AMSAT-LU (AMSAT Argentina), Weber State College, ARRL and TAPR. See Fig 1.

In a long-term development effort, AMSAT-NA is working on a large spacecraft for placement in geostationary Earth orbit (GEO). This Phase-IV satellite will provide 24-hour service to its coverage area. With amateur satellites in GEO, operators will not have to track the satellite actively, but simply point their antennas at a fixed point in space. AMSAT-DL (AMSAT Germany) amateurs have also started a project, termed Phase IIID, that will provide coverage much like OSCARs 10 and 13. Plans are for this spacecraft to have six times the transponder power of AO-13 and gain antennas pointing at the earth for a majority of the orbit, providing superior communications from a highly elliptical orbit.

Operating Frequencies

Early OSCARs used Mode-A (145 MHz

Table 1
OSCAR Operating Modes

Mode	Uplink Band	Downlink Band
A	2 m (145 MHz)	10 m (29 MHz)
B	70 cm (435 MHz)	2 m (145 MHz)
J	2 m (145 MHz)	70 cm (435 MHz)
L	24 cm (1269 MHz)	70 cm (436 MHz)
S	70 cm/24 cm	13 cm (2401 MHz)
LJ	2 m/23 cm	70 cm
K	15 m	10 m

Table 2
Spacecraft Frequencies

OSCAR 10

	Uplink (MHz)	Downlink (MHz)	Beacon (MHz)
Mode B	435.025-435.175	145.975-145.825	General 145.810 Engrg 145.990

OSCAR 11

VHF Beacon	145.825 MHz NBFM FSK telemetry	
UHF Beacon	435.025 MHz NBFM FSK, PSK telemetry	
S-Band Beacon	2401.5 MHz AFSK, PSK	

OSCAR 13

	Uplink (MHz)	Downlink (MHz)	Beacon (MHz)
Mode B	435.423-435.573	145.975-145.825	General 145.8125 Engrg 145.975
Mode J	144.423-144.473	435.990-435.940	General 435.651 (Note 1) Engrg 436.020
Mode L	1269.351-1269.731	436.005-435.677	General 435.651 Engrg 436.020
Digital Mode L	1269.675	435.675 (Note 2)	
Mode S	435.602-436.636	2400.715-2400.749	2400.664 (Note 3)

FO-20

	Uplink (MHz)	Downlink (MHz)	Beacon (MHz)
Linear Mode J	145.900-146.000	435.900-435.800	435.795 (Note 5)
Packet Mode J	145.850, 145.870, 145.890, 145.910	435.910 (Note 4)	435.910 (Note 6)

Notes
*See Table 7 for OSCARs 14-19.
1) Mode L is always commanded when Mode J is active. There may be times that Mode L is active without Mode J.
2) RUDAK is a digital-only transponder that uses PSK encoding. Mode S is a soft-limited FM transponder that can also accommodate up to four SSB signals. The AO-13 Mode S transponder is non-inverting, unlike other AO-13 transponders.
3) Mode S is a soft-limited FM transponder that can also accommodate up to four SSB signals. The AO-13 transponder is non-inverting, unlike other AO-13 transponders.
4) NRZI/PSK, 1200 bit/s
5) JA beacon: Frequency nominal, CW, PSK or NØN
6) JD telemetry: Frequency nominal, PSK

STORE—AND—FORWARD
RELAYING OF
DIGITAL SIGNALS

Fig 1—The Microsat PACSATs provide multiple satellites in sun-synchronous orbits for global digital store-and-forward capability.

uplink, 29 MHz downlink) transponders that were affected by F2-layer ionization phenomena during periods of high solar activity. Table 1 shows the relationships of the various transmitting and receiving frequencies (Modes) for ground stations communicating through satellite transponders. When the ionosphere is active, communications from 10-meter satellite downlinks (and lower) can be seriously impaired.

Newer classes of amateur satellites have

been designed to use higher-frequency amateur bands for a number of reasons. In addition to avoiding ionospheric effects, spectrum capacity and attainable antenna directivity are among some of the other reasons for moving to the UHF region for future satellites. OSCAR 13 features a combination of Mode B, Mode J, Mode L and Mode S transponders.

Future high-altitude satellites, such as in the Phase IIID and Phase IV program, will carry a combination of Modes J, L and S,

with a heavy emphasis on Mode-S operation (see Table 2). From GEO altitude, more than 45% of the Earth's surface can be viewed at one time, so the potential number of users is tremendous. A span of several hundred kilohertz to more than one megahertz is needed to afford sufficient spectrum for these users, and this much free spectrum space can only be found in the UHF region.

Another reason for using UHF with OSCARs is that high-gain, directional antennas are needed to make communications possible over such long paths. Since satellites are powered by batteries and solar cells, there are limitations on the amount of power the satellite transmitter can consume. The most efficient way get to the needed ERP is through the use of high-gain, narrow-beamwidth antennas. Such antennas would be too large and heavy at HF and VHF for the strict size and mass constraints imposed by the launch vehicle.

While there has been a great deal of interest and effort aimed at high-altitude satellites, recent technological advances have made the resurgence of the LEO satellite of particular interest for specialized missions. The global store-and-forward PACSAT is just such a spacecraft. These satellites are quite small and inexpensive, but have enormous capabilities. The specific mission does not inherently require concurrent satellite access, even for stations that might have such geographical situations that would permit such access. Of notable interest to ground stations is that the transmitter output of 4 W is concentrated on a single SSB frequency, not a band segment. Thus, the power output does not have to be shared by multiple stations at the same time. The impact of this situation is that the satellite should be easily heard by ground stations with the simplest of equipment, as will be discussed later.

Communications Methods

Amateurs who use satellites for communications must be alert to the needs of using that resource efficiently. Only narrow-bandwidth modulation methods, such as CW and SSB, should be used for general QSOs. NBFM is not an efficient use of the limited satellite transponder spectrum. Also, the 100% duty cycle of FM voice is a very inefficient use of transponder RF power. Conventional RTTY is allowed on AO-13 in Mode B. Packet radio is the preferred data-transmission mode, though, because the information-rate/duty-cycle ratio is much higher.

Most satellites have recommended use patterns for their transponders. Attention is placed on voluntarily devoting portions of the bandwidth of the transponder to various uses. Typical band segments include CW only, mixed CW and SSB and SSB only. Fig 2 shows a generalized band plan for Modes B and J for AO-10 and AO-13. Satellite users should consult *The*

ARRL Operating Manual for operating information for amateur satellites.

Another interesting use of the global communications capabilities of high-altitude satellites is the service provided by "gateway" stations. A gateway station provides an interface between differing services. In the case of AO-10 and AO-13, some amateur communities of VHF FM operators have been served by gateways that translate FM repeater signals into satellite SSB signals, and vice-versa. Global and transcontinental contacts have been made through AO-10 and AO-13 by operators using VHF hand-held transceivers.

Fig 3 shows the block diagram of a manually operated gateway that has been active from Illinois. Another interesting form of gateway is the land-based linear translator that provides a portion of the

Fig 3—The K9NO satellite gateway allows FM repeater users to work stations through OSCAR 13. All the user needs is an FM transceiver for 2 m and 70 cm, and the ability to reach the repeater. This scheme allows many users to share one satellite ground station.

Fig 2—The OSCAR satellite band plan allows for CW-only, mixed CW/SSB, and SSB-only operation. Courteous operators observe this voluntary band plan at all times.

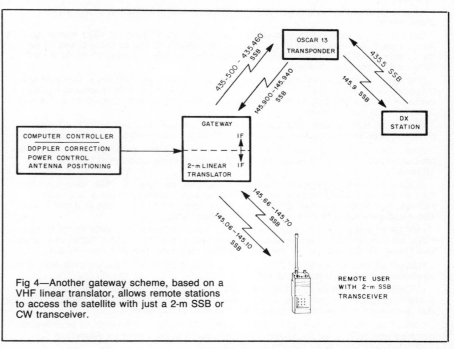

Fig 4—Another gateway scheme, based on a VHF linear translator, allows remote stations to access the satellite with just a 2-m SSB or CW transceiver.

AO-13 passband for operators with limited resources for satellite operation. One particular translator gateway provides a 40-kHz-wide band segment for SSB service as shown in Fig 4. Both of these gateways operate in half-duplex for the remote user. Other schemes permit a remote user to operate full duplex, but at the expense of more equipment.

COMMUNICATIONS REQUIREMENTS

Most long-distance communications depend on natural propagation phenomena. Some days, a kilowatt and high Yagi are needed to establish communications; at other times, 5 W and a long wire will do

the trick. Stations designed to take advantage of ionospheric propagation are largely a matter of personal preference. Bigger stations usually mean bigger signals.

Operation through a satellite is somewhat different. Fixed conditions such as transponder receiver sensitivity and power output, and variable conditions such as spacecraft attitude and path losses, are the dominating factors in establishing mini-

mum ground-station requirements. Once the minimum requirements are met, you can have reliable communications any time the satellite is in view, regardless of changing propagation phenomena. The communications requirements for AO-10 and AO-13 have been well defined since these spacecraft have become operational. Unlike other areas of amateur interest, an inadequate station won't merely limit your ability to communicate—it will probably prohibit successful communications entirely.

Satisfactory satellite communications might be possible with an existing station, but planning the ground station around certain parameters will enhance its effectiveness. Ground stations for Phase III satellites, such as AO-10 and AO-13, need to consider such subtleties as low-loss feed line, a low-noise GaAsFET preamplifier and high-gain VHF/UHF antennas that can be pointed accurately.

The parameters that should be considered for a Phase III OSCAR ground station are:

1) 146-MHz antenna gain of at least 13 dBic, circularly polarized. Right-hand circular polarization (RHCP) that is switchable to left-hand circular polarization (LHCP) is a must for effective operation, with a preference for RHCP if the antenna is not switchable. More antenna gain is always desirable for better performance. Antenna gain of much more than 18 dBi, however, is not cost effective—satellite transponder noise floors limit further benefits.

2) 435-MHz antenna gain of at least 13 dBic, circularly polarized. For this band, it is highly desirable to be able to switch between RHCP and LHCP. Gains of 14 to 18 dBic are preferred for AO-10 Mode B, and AO-13 Modes B, J and L.

3) 1269-MHz antenna gain of 20+ dBic is very useful for AO-10 Mode L, using low power (15-40 W). Current AO-13 users are having success with linear antenna polarization, even though the spacecraft antenna uses RHCP, but the link is decidedly improved by using circular polarization.

4) Circularly polarized antennas must be mounted on nonmetallic booms so antenna performance is not degraded by having a metal boom in the antenna field. Similarly, coaxial feed lines must be routed axially rearward past the antenna reflector to avoid pattern distortion.

5) Feed-line loss of less than 2 dB is needed; less than 1 dB is better. This can be effectively achieved (for receiving purposes) without expensive Hardline through the use of antenna-mounted preamplifiers and other equipment.

6) 435-MHz EIRP (effective isotropic radiated power) of no more than 1000 W, in Mode B. Most operations can be conducted with 100- to 300-W EIRP, and at times it's possible to use only 10-W EIRP.

7) 144-MHz EIRP of no more than 1000 W for AO-13 Mode J. Again, most operations can be conducted with 100- to 300-W EIRP.

8) 1269-MHz EIRP of at least 3000 to 5000 W for AO-13 Mode L, preferably RHCP. Some operators do use higher EIRP (10,000 to 25,000 W) and they have substantial return signals. Although these power levels will not saturate the Mode-L transponder, they are acceptable, but not necessary.

9) 435-MHz EIRP of about 1 kW for AO-13 Mode S—about the same as Mode B.

10) 146-MHz receive system noise figure no greater than 2 dB. Noise figures less than 1 dB are not warranted because of the limitations imposed by terrestrial noise sources.

11) 2400-MHz AO-13 Mode-S receive system antenna gain of 26 dB (a nominal 4-foot-diameter parabolic reflector) and a receive noise figure less than 1 dB.

12) 435-MHz receive system noise figure

of less than 1 dB. Terrestrial noise levels are not a limiting factor on this band.

13) Frequency readout resolution of 1 kHz on transmit and receive. Accurate frequency readout allows you to find your signal on the downlink without causing needless QRM.

14) An accurate means of determining antenna direction at all times during an orbit. This means knowing where the antennas are pointed, and where to point them. It is achievable through graphical plotting or a computer printout of pointing angles.

Like many other aspects of Amateur Radio, trade-offs can be made to minimize expenditure of time and money. Up to a point, antenna gain is easier to obtain than transmitter power. It is easier to put up a bigger Yagi to increase your EIRP than to build or buy an amplifier. For example, a commercially available 40-element 435-MHz crossed Yagi provides enough EIRP for AO-13 Mode-B communications with only 50 W at the antenna. Often, 5 to 25 W is all that is necessary.

Better antennas also improve receive performance. All things considered, it is much more cost effective—and desirable from a performance standpoint—to optimize the receiving set-up before investing in greater transmit EIRP.

The parameters that should be considered for LEO OSCAR PACSAT ground stations are:

1) 146-MHz FM transmitting, and 437-MHz SSB receiving antennas that do not need human attention during a satellite pass. Because the orbit access time of a LEO satellite is relatively short, the operator will need to pay attention to the packet communications, rather than to pointing antennas or tuning radios. Antennas can be either computer controlled, or better still, omnidirectional designs that concentrate most of the RF energy toward the horizon, where the path length is the greatest. A 5/8-wave antenna over a ground plane or a J-pole antenna should fill the bill for this application.

2) 437-MHz receive system noise figure of less than 1 dB.

Circular Polarization

In the HF bands, polarization differences between antennas are not really noticeable because of the nonlinearities of ionospheric reflections. On the VHF and UHF bands, however, there is little ionospheric reflection. Cross-polarized stations (one using a vertical antenna, the other a horizontal antenna) often find considerable difficulty, with upwards of 20-dB of loss. Such linearly polarized antennas are "horizontal" or "vertical" in terms the antenna's position relative to the surface of the Earth—a reference that loses its meaning in space.

The use of circularly polarized (CP) antennas for space communications is well established. If spacecraft antennas used linear polarization, ground stations would

Table 3
Polarization and Gain of AO-10 and AO-13 Antennas

Frequency (MHz)	High Gain Antennas		Omni Antennas	
	Polarization	Gain (dBi)	Polarization	Gain (dBi)
146	RHCP	9.0	Linear	0.0
436	RHCP	9.5	Linear	2.1
1269	RHCP	12.0	RHCP	0.0

(Adapted from *The AMSAT-Phase III Satellite Operations Manual*, prepared by AMSAT and Project OSCAR)

Fig 5—This diagram shows the far-field radiation pattern (undeformed) for the 2-meter high-gain antenna on AO-10 and AO-13. (Adapted from *The AMSAT-Phase III Satellite Operations Manual*, prepared by AMSAT and Project OSCAR.)

not be able to maintain polarization alignment with the spacecraft because of changing orientation. Ground stations using CP antennas are not sensitive to the polarization motions of the spacecraft antenna, and therefore will maintain a better communications link.

All AO-10 and AO-13 gain antennas (for 2 m, 70 cm, 24 cm and 13 cm) are configured for RHCP operation along their maximum gain direction. See Table 3 and Fig 5. Since this direction is also the main antenna lobe along the spacecraft +Z axis, the best communications with AO-10 and AO-13 will also be along that direction. Since AO-10 and AO-13 radiations are RHCP, ground stations should also use RHCP for optimum communications.

There are times, however, when LHCP provides a better satellite link. AO-13 is designed so that the main antenna lobe is oriented toward the center of the Earth when the satellite is at apogee. AO-10 is not under active orientation control at the time of this writing because of a failure of the flight computer memory. Thus, the AO-10 main-lobe orientation is a matter of chance. AO-13 is only oriented toward the Earth's center for a few hours either side of apogee,

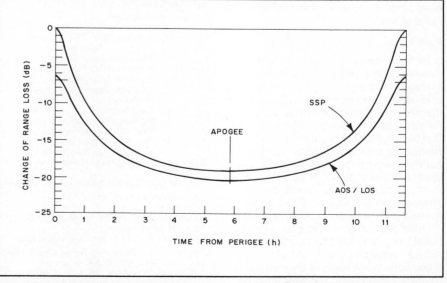

Fig 6—Range loss of signal strength during the 11.7-hour elliptical orbit of OSCAR 10. OSCAR 13 performance is very similar. (Adapted from *The AMSAT-Phase III Satellite Operations Manual*, prepared by AMSAT and Project OSCAR.)

however. As the satellite moves away from apogee, the orientation changes and the RHCP main lobe is not centered on Earth. At other times, ground command stations have to orient the spacecraft at odd angles to maintain proper sunlight on the solar cells that are used for prime power. Again, at such times the satellite antenna's main lobe is not pointed directly at Earth.

During the periods when the main lobe is directed away from Earth, communications are still possible through the use of AO-13's antenna side lobes. CP antenna patterns, however, exhibit side lobes that can be polarized in the opposite sense to the main lobe. At times when only LHCP side lobes are available, ground stations must be able to switch to LHCP to maintain optimum communications.

Independently switchable RHCP/LHCP antenna circularity is necessary, especially for 70 cm. It is not required for 24-cm operation on AO-13 because Mode-L operations are only conducted on the main lobe. Switchable RHCP/LHCP on 2 m is very convenient for significant Mode-B operations.

Spin Modulation

A characteristic of the AO-10 and AO-13 designs is that the 2-m and 70-cm high-gain array patterns have three side lobes located along the spin axis that are only about 3 dB weaker than the primary axial lobe. The effective radiation pattern intended for this antenna is shown in Fig 5. Lobes in the off-axis antenna patterns produce amplitude modulation of signal strength as the spacecraft spins about its axis. Off-axis operations of AO-10 and AO-13 are an established fact of life, creating spin modulation frequencies of about 0.5 Hz from a 10 r/min spin rate.

Stations using CP antennas are much less affected by spin modulation than those using linearly polarized antennas. Good signals are maintainable off-axis from the main lobe, if the ground station is using switchable CP.

Path Loss

In free space, a station located at a distance from an RF source will receive an average power flow from that source that is inversely proportional to the square of the distance. Doubling the range will reduce the signal by 6 dB. Because Phase III satellites have substantially elliptical orbits, the changes in path length (slant range) and path loss is correspondingly sizable. Fig 6 illustrates the changes in path length of AO-13 signals for all conditions from apogee to perigee, and for direct overhead passes (SSP location) at AOS or LOS.

Other physical processes introduce additional losses in signals traveling to and from AO-13 through the troposphere and ionosphere. While many of these effects are frequency dependent, the additional path losses for AO-13 signals are small compared to the slant-range path losses. Table 4 summarizes the path losses for each band used on AO-13.

Link Budget

Link-budget computations can be deceiving to the unwary observer. The problems arise from the application of wide-bandwidth spacecraft transponders to handle a wide variety of complex, time-averaged, narrow-bandwidth QSOs. The

---

Table 4

Summary of One-Way Transmission Losses for Communications Paths Between Earth and Phase III Spacecraft at Apogee in an 11.7 Hour Elliptical Orbit, as Viewed Near AOS-LOS Range

Loss Mechanism	Attenuation (dB) 2 m	70 cm	24 cm
Path Loss	168.07	177.57	186.86
Tropo/Ionospheric Refraction	0.002	0.0003	0.0002
Tropo Absorption	0.1	0.7	1.65
Ionospheric Absorption (by category)			
D-Layer	0.12	0.013	0.002
F-Layer	0.12	0.013	0.002
Aurora	0.13	0.014	0.002
Polar Cap Absorption (a rare D-layer event)	0.47	0.053	0.006
Field-Aligned Irregularities	†	†	†

†Little data available, characterized by rapid amplitude and phase fluctuations.

(Adapted from *The AMSAT-Phase III Satellite Operations Manual* prepared by AMSAT and Project OSCAR)

Table 5

Link Budget Computations for Mode-B and Mode-L Transponders on OSCAR 10 and OSCAR 13 at Apogee and AOS-LOS Range

Ground Station Uplink

Symbol	Parameter	Mode B (70 cm uplink)	Mode L (24 cm uplink)
N_f	Sat Receiver Noise Floor	–136.7 dBm	–137.4 dBm
SNR	Avg Signal-to-Noise Ratio	15.0 dB	15.0 dB
P_s	Signal at Satellite	–121.7 dBm	–122.4 dBm
G_r	Satellite Antenna Gain	9.0 dBi	12.0 dBi
P_a	Signal at Sat Antenna	–130.7 dBm	–134.4 dBm
P_L	Path Loss	177.57 dB	186.86 dB
$L_{i,t}$	Iono/Tropo Loss	0.73 dB	1.65 dB
$L_{p,p}$	Pointing/Polarization Loss	1.5 dB	1.5 dB
$P_t + G_t$	Reqd Gnd Stn avg ERP	19.10 dBW	25.61 dBW
	or:	81.3 W	363.9 W
	Gnd Stn PEP ERP	25.10 dBW	31.61 dBW
	or:	323.6 W	1448.8 W
G_t	Gnd Station Antenna Gain	16.0 dBi	19.0 dBi
P_t	Gnd Stn PEP Power Output	9.1 dBW	13.6 dBW
	or:	8.1 W	18.2 W

Satellite Downlink

Symbol	Parameter	Mode B (2 m downlink)	Mode L (70 cm downlink)
P_t	Satellite Max. PEP Output	16.99 dBW	16.99 dBW
	Average Output	10.99 dBW	10.99 dBW
L_m	Multi-user Load Share	–15.0 dB	–20.0 dB
G_s	Satellite AGC Compression	0.0 dB	0.0 dB
G_t	Satellite Antenna Gain	9.0 dBi	9.5 dBi
P_u	Average User ERP Output	34.99 dBm	30.49 dBm
P_L	Path Loss	168.07 dB	177.57 dB
$L_{i,t}$	Iono/Tropo Loss	0.33 dB	0.73 dB
$L_{p,p}$	Pointing/Polarization Loss	1.5 dB	1.5 dB
G_r	Receiving Antenna Gain	12.0 dBi	16.0 dBi
P_s	Received Signal Level	–122.91 dBm	–133.31 dBm
P_n	Noise in Rcv Bandwidth	–137.76 dBm	–146.67 dBm
SNR	Avg Signal-to-Noise Ratio	14.8 dB	13.4 dB

Link computations are based on the following parameters:

11.7 hour elliptical orbit
Eccentricity = 0.6
Slant range = 41,395 km at AOS/LOS
2.4 kHz SSB Signal
6 dB peak (PEP) to average signal ratio

Ground Station Receiving Noise Characteristics:
at 2 m: T = 505 K, NF = 4.4 dB
at 70 cm: T = 65 K, NF = 0.9 dB

(Adapted from *The AMSAT-Phase III Satellite Operations Manual*, prepared by AMSAT and Project OSCAR)

analysis presented in Table 5 employs a somewhat lower signal-to-noise ratio than the source information. Actual on-the-air experience has shown these lower values to be workable. The computation is also performed on the basis of averaged RF power levels. The conversion to PEP is done at the end, assuming a 6-dB relationship between PEP and average power.

In the link computations, no allowances have been made for ground station transmission line attenuation. Information on attenuation of a variety of popular feed lines is shown in Chapter 16. If you measure RF power near the antenna and have a tower-mounted, low-noise preamp, the link computations can be used as presented. The computation is based on two possible worst-case conditions: maximum slant range values at AOS/LOS, and the spacecraft at apogee. An important assumption is that the spacecraft antenna pattern is on-axis to the communications path—a highly unusual condition. Of course, an infinite number of cases could be presented in such a tabular assessment.

Another highly variable parameter that must be taken into account is pointing and polarization loss. With the wide variety of AO-10 and AO-13 offset pointing situations that are seen in typical operation, pointing and polarization losses can easily reach values of 10 dB or more. Nevertheless, the presentation in Table 5 is in the ballpark for Mode-B operations for typical power levels and signal conditions.

Consistent AO-13 Mode-L performance, with the spacecraft near apogee, can be attained with uplink power in the range of 3 to 5 kW EIRP, preferably circularly polarized. Also required is a good receiving setup, with 70-cm downlink antenna gain about 18 dBic and a low-noise GaAsFET preamp at (or very near) the antenna.

Table 5 also provides a good implicit guide for link operations for AO-13 Mode J.

EQUIPPING A STATION

Perhaps the biggest difference between terrestrial and satellite communications is that the latter is full-duplex. This means that you transmit and receive simultaneously. You can hear your own downlink signal while transmitting, as well as that of the station being worked. Full duplex provides the opportunity for a fully interactive conversation, as if the other station is in the same room.

Successful satellite operation demands that you locate and hear your own signal from the spacecraft. Choose equipment with this goal in mind. Equipping a station for full-duplex operation is not too difficult because the transmitter is on a different band than the receiver. Ground-station configurations for high-altitude satellites vary according to the communications "mode" being used. Figs 7, 8 and 9 show several different configurations suitable for both AO-10 Mode B, and AO-13 Modes B, J and L.

Operating through one of the LEO PACSATs will require the same basic Mode-J equipment shown in Fig 9. The packet equipment required is covered in Chapter 19. The standard protocol, adopted for FO-12 and planned for PACSAT, is an uplink using AFSK-FM—the same protocol used for terrestrial packet. Downlinks, however, will use Manchestered PSK, greatly enhancing the downlink signal-to-noise ratio over that of AFSK-FM. Manchestered PSK decoding requires the use of an SSB receiver and a special modem connected to the TNC. One benefit of the PSK modem is that it can operate in AFC mode to automatically correct for satellite downlink Doppler shift. Uplink Doppler shift does not need correction for 1200-baud packet service, because satellite

Fig 7—Several different Mode-B satellite-station configurations are shown here. At A, separate VHF/UHF multimode transceivers are used for transmitting and receiving. The configuration shown at B uses transmitting and receiving converters or transverters with HF equipment. At C, a multimode, multiband transceiver can perform both transmitting and receiving functions, full duplex, in one package. The Ten-Tec 2510 shown at D contains a 435-MHz transmitter and a 2-meter-to-10-meter receiving converter.

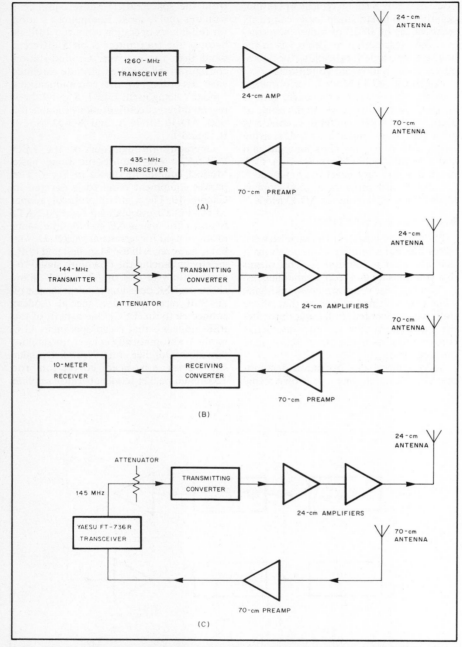

Fig 8—Several different Mode-L satellite-station configurations. At A, separate VHF/UHF multimode transceivers are used for transmitting and receiving. The configuration shown at B uses transmitting and receiving converters or transverters with HF equipment. At C, a multimode, multiband transceiver can be used for full duplex receiving and transmitting (with the addition of a 2-meter-to-24-cm transmitting converter).

receiver bandwidth is adequate to cover those frequency excursions. These modems are available from several sources. Fig 10 shows the equipment configuration needed for PACSAT operations.

Receivers

Receiving requirements for AO-10 and AO-13 are demanding, but satisfying results can be achieved with the right equipment. Do not expect to find 60-dB-over-S9 signals on the downlink. OSCAR operation is a weak-signal environment. Contacts can be made with signals that are

only 4 dB stronger than the noise. Conversational quality can be assured with signals that are at least 6 to 9 dB stronger than the noise.

The old adage "you can't work 'em if you can't hear 'em" especially applies to satellite work. The first step that should be taken toward gearing up for AO-10 and AO-13 is to assemble the best receiving setup possible. There is no point in worrying about transmitting capability until satellite signals can be heard comfortably.

There are a number of options for start-

ing a satellite station from scratch. You may wish to try building almost any part of the station—from a simple controller, to a complete station. Alternatively, the busy operator may wish to purchase everything. All of the necessary components are readily available from commercial suppliers.

Amateurs active on 2 meters with a multimode transceiver already have the basic building block for receiving Mode B and transmitting on Modes J and L (with an additional transmitting converter). If you currently have no VHF equipment, consider that a multimode, multiband transceiver will also allow you to explore the exciting world of terrestrial 2-meter and 70-centimeter SSB operations. The basic requirements are that the rig include SSB and CW modes, and that it covers the entire 2-m and (most of the) 70-cm band. A multimode transceiver also makes an excellent replacement for an FM-only 2-meter rig.

The major equipment manufacturers listed in Table 6 all make suitable transceivers, either single-band or multiband units. The current crop of base-station rigs includes the Kenwood single-band transceivers TS-711A (2 m) and TS-811 (70 cm), and multiband transceiver TS-790A. ICOM has the single-band transceivers IC-271A and IC-275A (2 m), and IC-471H and IC-475H. Yaesu offers its multiband FT-726R and FT-736R transceivers. There are also several compact multimode radios intended for mobile use that are quite usable. These include the Yaesu single-band FT-290R and FT-790R, Kenwood single-band TR-751A and TR-851A, and the ICOM single-band IC-290H. In addition, there are often good buys on the used market, if you're interested in an older radio. Gear such as the Kenwood TS-700 series, Yaesu FT-225RD and ICOM IC-251 are still popular. Many of these transceivers have been reviewed in *QST*.

Users of the AO-13 Mode L may want to consider using a transceiver for 24-cm transmissions. Such a unit will also allow operations on the popular 23-cm section (1296 MHz) of the band. Kenwood and Yaesu offer 23-cm modules for their multiband transceivers for this service. ICOM also offers the single-band IC-1271A. Alternatively, there are some 24-cm transmitting converters and transverters that employ a 2-meter IF.

An excellent solution for receiving Modes B, J and L satellite signals can be found in the form of receiving converters used with your quality HF transceiver or receiver. The 2-m and 70-cm receiving converter consists of a mixer and a local oscillator and may contain a preamplifier. The local-oscillator frequency is usually chosen so that signals will be converted for reception by any receiver that covers the 10-meter band. In addition, a number of manufacturers offer transverters that include a receiving converter and transmit-

(A)

(B)

(C)

PACSAT GROUND STATION CONFIGURATION

Fig 9—Several different Mode-J satellite-station configurations are shown here. At A, separate VHF/UHF multimode transceivers are used for transmitting and receiving. The configuration shown at B uses transmitting and receiving converters or transverters with HF equipment. At C, a multimode, multiband transceiver can perform both transmitting and receiving functions, full duplex, in one package.

ting converter in the same package.

Even though satellite receiving performance may be improved through the use of converters and HF receivers, the amateur assembling a satellite station must keep in mind the need for a separate VHF/UHF transmitting capability.

Receiving converters are available commercially from several suppliers listed in Table 6. For those who enjoy building equipment, there are several suitable construction projects in Chapter 31.

There are several advantages to using a receiving converter. Modern HF transceivers and receivers have excellent frequency stability, frequency readout in 1 kHz or smaller steps, good SSB and CW crystal filters, an effective noise blanker and high dynamic range. Chances are good that a multimode VHF transceiver will offer some, but not all, of these features.

Cost is another factor. If you already own an HF rig, but are not interested in terrestrial VHF/UHF SSB operation (you don't need 2-meter transmit capability for Mode B), the cost of building or buying a superior receiving converter will be significantly less than that of even an older multimode transceiver. One commercial example of a Mode-B only unit is the Ten-Tec 2510B, providing an excellent 2-m receiving converter and a complete 70-cm SSB/CW transmitter, all with coupled VFOs for simultaneous tracking on both bands. While the '2510 is an economical way to get into satellite operation, it must be remembered that it is limited to Mode-B service.

Experience has often shown that daytime noise will often raise the practical 2-meter receiver noise floor by 10 to 20 dB, making Mode-B daytime communications difficult, at best. In general, noise is not a problem at 70 cm (for Mode-J and Mode-L reception), but in some areas interference from airport radar can be troublesome. In addition, local FM repeaters may be heard in the satellite passband of the ground-based receiver because the VHF transceiver may offer poor rejection of strong nearby signals. Use of a high-dynamic-range receiving converter with a good HF transceiver

Fig 10—The PACSAT RF equipment configuration is similar to other Mode-J stations. Added equipment is needed for the terminal, TNC and PSK Modem.

Table 6

Suppliers of Equipment of Interest to Satellite Operators

Multimode VHF and UHF Transceivers and Specialty Equipment
ICOM America, Inc, 2380-116th Ave NE, Bellevue, WA 98004.
Ten-Tec Inc, Sevierville, TN 37862.
Kenwood USA Corp, PO Box 22745, 2201 East Dominguez St, Long Beach, CA 90801-5745.
Yaesu Electronics Corp, 17210 Edwards Rd, Cerritos, CA 90701.

Converters, Transverters and Preamplifiers
Advanced Receiver Research, Box 1242, Burlington, CT 06013.
Angle Linear, PO Box 35, Lomita, CA 90717 (preamps only).
Hamtronics, Inc, 65-E Moul Rd, Hilton, NY 14468.
Henry Radio, 2050 S Bundy Dr, Los Angeles, CA 90025.
The PX Shack, 52 Stonewyck Dr, Belle Mead, NJ 08502.
Radio Kit, Box 411, Greenville, NH 03048.
Spectrum International, PO Box 1084, Concord, MA 01742.
Transverters Unlimited, Box 6286, Station A, Toronto, ON M5W 1P3, Canada.

Power Amplifiers
Alinco Electronics, PO Box 20009, Reno, NV 89515.
Communications Concepts, Inc, 2648 North Aragon Ave, Dayton, OH 45420.
Down East Microwave, Box 1655A, RFD 1, Burnham, ME 04922.
Encomm, 1506 Capitol Ave, Plano, TX 75074.
Falcon Communications, PO Box 8979, Newport Beach, CA 92658.
Mirage Communications, PO Box 1000, Morgan Hill, CA 95037.
TE Systems, PO Box 25845, Los Angeles, CA 90025.

Antennas
Cushcraft Corp, 48 Perimeter Rd, Manchester, NH 03108.
Down East Microwave, Box 1655A, RFD 1, Burnham, ME 04922.
KLM Electronics, Inc, PO Box 816, Morgan Hill, CA 95037.
Telex Communications, Inc, 9600 Aldrich Ave S, Minneapolis, MN 55420

Note: This is a partial list. The ARRL does not endorse specific products.

ICOM IC-275A/H is typical of the 2-meter multimode transceivers on the market today. It can be used for AO-10 and AO-13 Mode-B downlinks and Mode-J uplinks. The IC-475A/H, virtually identical in appearance, offers a matching 70-cm signal for the uplink.

has been shown to solve both of these problems. The lesson here is that many VHF transceiver noise blankers are inadequate for VHF/UHF satellite operation, and that some VHF transceivers do not work well in areas with many strong, nearby signals. Better results may be had with a receiving converter than with a VHF multimode transceiver.

Preamplifiers

No discussion of satellite receiving systems would be complete without mentioning preamplifiers. Good, low-noise preamplifiers are essential for receiving weak downlink signals.

Multimode rigs and most transverters will hear much better with the addition of a GaAsFET preamplifier ahead of the receiver, albeit at the expense of a considerable reduction in the receiver's third-order intercept point. While a preamplifier can be added at the receiver, it may not do much good. Considerably better results can be obtained if the preamp is mounted near the antenna. Losses in the feed line will seriously degrade the noise figure of even the best preamplifier (mounted at the receiver), while an antenna-mounted preamplifier can overcome nearly all of these noise figure problems.

Table 6 lists several sources of commercially built preamplifiers. These are available in several configurations. Some models are designed to be mounted in a receive-only line, for use with a receiving converter or transverter. Others, designed with multimode transceivers in mind, have built-in relays and circuitry that automatically switch the preamplifier out of the antenna line during transmit operation. Still others are housed, with relays, in weatherproof enclosures that mount right at the antenna. For the equipment builder, several suitable designs appear in Chapter 31, and in *The Satellite Experimenter's Handbook*.

Transmitters

AO-10 and AO-13 Mode-B uplinks require a controllable 5 to 50 W of 435-MHz RF power at the antenna. Feed-line losses in a typical 435-MHz installation

For amateurs with HF receivers or transceivers who have no desire for transceive operation on 2 meters, a receiving converter such as this Advanced Receiver Research R144VDA may be the answer. Shown with matching low-noise GaAsFET preamplifier, this unit converts 2-meter AO-10 and AO-13 Mode-B downlink signals for reception on any receiver that can tune to 29 MHz.

A low-noise GaAsFET preamplifier on 2 m and 70 cm, such as this Angle Linear model, is essential if you want to maximize your downlink reception. The preamplifier should be mounted at the antenna for best results.

can easily reach 3 dB, so you'll need anywhere between 10- and 100-W output from your transmitter. AO-13 Mode L, has an uplink requirement of 15 to 100 W, depending upon antenna gain.

Since the possible number of combinations of transmitter power and antenna gain needed to give a satisfactory signal through AO-10 and AO-13 is infinite, satellite users generally talk about their uplink capability in terms of *effective radiated power* (ERP). ERP takes into account antenna gain, feed-line loss and RF output power. For example, a 10-W signal fed into a 3-dB-gain antenna will have an ERP of 20 W (3 dB greater than, or twice as strong as, 10 W). This assumes no loss in the feed line and all 10 W from the transmitter reaches the antenna. If the signal is 10 W into a 10-dB-gain antenna, the ERP is 100 W. The same 100-W ERP can be achieved with a 50-W transmitter and a 3-dB-gain antenna.

Stations with an uplink ERP as low as 10 W can be copied through AO-10 and AO-13, Modes B and J, but ERP levels of 100 to 400 W are the norm. No matter what your ERP, your signal on the downlink should never be stronger than the AO-10 and AO-13 general beacon at 145.81 MHz (Mode B) and 435.65 MHz (Mode J). As a reminder, satellite service ground stations do not have to be as strong as the beacon to provide excellent communications, good operators will adjust their signals to the level needed for the QSO. You must have a way of adjusting your uplink signal power so that your downlink is no stronger than

the beacon. These points are discussed in detail in *The ARRL Operating Manual.*

If a Mode-B satellite ground station has a 10-W transmitter, a short run of low-loss feed line and good antenna gain, an additional amplifier will probably not be needed. If losses and gains do not add up to enough station ERP, a 30- to 40-W amplifier may be needed. Some operators have 100-W amplifiers, but with the antennas available today, use of that much power is guaranteed to create an uplink signal that far exceeds the beacon level. This is considered by good operators to be an antisocial action. Considerate operators with 100-W amplifiers quickly reduce drive power to reduce their ERP to acceptable levels.

Most satellite operators use UHF multimode transceivers to generate Mode-B uplink signals. The manufacturers listed in Table 6 make 70-cm multimode transceivers that are similar to the 2-meter units as described earlier. Although most of these transceivers provide 10-W output, some can deliver 25 W or more.

Earlier satellites in the AMSAT lineup created and fostered the need for good multimode 2-m transceivers—they formed the nucleus of the satellite station. Current and future satellite programs will feature the 70-cm transceiver as the focal point of the satellite station, emphasizing the trend to even higher frequencies. Note that the 70-cm transceiver is involved in all of the AO-13 operating modes.

For Mode-L transmitting, there are several transmitting converters, transvert-

ers, amplifiers and even a multimode transceiver available from the suppliers listed in Table 6. Chapter 32 details several construction projects that will get you on Mode L. AO-13 Mode-L operation can use the power levels offered by a tube-type amplifier, but useful results can be obtained using power levels that can be generated by transistors.

Specialty Equipment

Separate transceivers or transmitting and receiving converters are no longer the only way to go. Modern equipment offered by Kenwood, Yaesu and Ten-Tec, tailored for the satellite user, does it all one package.

The Kenwood TR-790A and Yaesu FT-726R and FT-736R units start out as 2-meter multimode transceivers. They are, however, expandable to other bands with the addition of optional modules. The Mode-B satellite operator would most likely be interested in the TR-790A or FT-726R/FT-736R with the stock 144-MHz and 430-MHz modules. These RF modules will also serve well for Mode J (directly), and Mode L using an outboard 23-cm transmitting converter. Both manufacturers also offer 23-cm transceive modules for Mode L. To tie it all together, the Kenwood and Yaesu transceivers also offer satellite modules (stock or optional) that allow the amateur to transmit on one band for the uplink while receiving on another band for the downlink. This is full duplex operation; the effect is the same as having two separate radios in one box.

Antennas

The best antennas for use in the amateur satellite service are circularly polarized (CP). Helical antennas like the ones shown in Fig 11 were used for AO-7 and AO-8 (Phase II) satellites. An 8-turn helical for 70 cm and a huge 6-turn helical for 2 meters provided excellent results. For AO-10 and AO-13, however, more gain is needed at 2 m and 70 cm than a reasonably sized helical antenna can supply. In addition, successful AO-10 and AO-13 operations require the ability to switch conveniently from RHCP to LHCP.

The present trend in satellite arrays uses a different method to achieve circular polarization for Modes B and J. These antennas, shown in Fig 12, are essentially two complete Yagis mounted perpendicular to each other on the same boom. One set of elements is mounted ¼ wavelength ahead of the other. The antennas are fed in phase and are switchable from RHCP to LHCP. These particular antennas, manufactured by KLM, have proved to be excellent performers. Cushcraft and Telex/ HyGain also manufacture crossed-Yagi satellite antennas for OSCAR service. Emphasis must be placed on achieving CP operation on single-boom antennas, rather than with multiple separate Yagis mounted orthogonally to each other. The latter can lead to somewhat uncertain circularity.

Satellite antennas should be mounted as close to the station as possible. Height above ground makes no difference for satellite work, except that the antennas must be mounted high enough that trees and other obstructions do not block the view of the satellite at low elevations. A low mount allows use of shorter feed lines (lower losses) and often reduces noise pickup by the antennas. Many operators are able to set up their antennas on a 10- to 15-foot mast right next to the shack, and have only 20 feet of feed line. Plan to use good-quality, low-loss coaxial cable from the start, such as Belden 9913. Hardline coaxial cable, available from a number of manufacturers, is even better.

Mode-L transmitting antennas have taken numerous forms, mostly based on the technology needed for EME communications. Loop Yagis, such as those presented in Chapter 32, are popular, but you must stack at least two in an array to achieve the 20 + dBi gain necessary for AO-13 Mode L. Also popular are large parabolic reflector antennas, as seen in EME and TVRO services. For AO-13 Mode L, some of these higher-gain antennas provide good results. Although higher gain means lower transmitter power, the narrow beamwidths require the operator to reposition the antenna more often.

Although a practical CP Yagi for 24 cm has not yet been demonstrated, such an approach may be feasible. Because AO-13 Mode L is only operated near satellite apogee, RHCP is the only CP sense needed, thus making the use of helical antennas attractive. A home-built Mode-L helical antenna array is shown in Fig 12, and is presented later in this chapter. Active Mode-L operators have also found that a small parabolic dish (6 feet in diameter, or larger) with a circularly polarized feed can make a fine Mode-L antenna. A number of reasonably priced TVRO dishes are available, and they require only the addition of a suitable feed for Mode-L service. For TVRO dishes of 12 feet in diameter, a dual-band (70 cm and 24 cm) feed for Mode L is being done, as the gain at 70 cm is sufficient for excellent reception, and the gain is very substantial for QRP 24-cm transmissions.

While circular polarization will be helpful on the PACSAT uplink and downlink, there are some interesting trade-offs. For Phase II OSCARs of the past, the turnstile-over-reflector (T/R) was an interesting and useful CP antenna. The T/R antenna, however, has poor gain at elevation angles below about 25°, and a lot of LEO satellite operations happen at low elevations. Studies have shown that LEO slant ranges and system gains demand high gain at low elevation angles. The importance of this

The Kenwood TS-790A is a multiband, multimode transceiver for 2-meter (45 W) and 70-cm (40 W) that can be used for AO-10 Mode B and AO-13 Modes B and J full-duplex transmitting and receiving operations. A 23-cm module is available for AO-13 Mode-L uplink. For owners of the TS-790A, this unit would be the only radio needed in the shack for satellite communications.

Fig 11—Helical antennas such as these are excellent for low-orbiting Phase II satellites.

Another means of generating a 435-MHz uplink signal is with an HF transceiver and a 10-meter-to-70-cm transverter such as this SSB Electronics TV28-432.

Usually, a little more than 10 W uplink power is required for a good downlink signal. Solid-state "brick" amplifiers such as this Mirage D1010 provide the extra power needed. Care must be taken, however, to use only the minimum power necessary to maintain reliable communications.

low-elevation antenna gain outweighs the desirability of circular polarization. For omnidirectional station antennas, a good low-angle antenna such as the 5/8-wave length vertical or a J-pole antenna is recommended. These concentrate radiation on the horizon, but still perform well at close-in slant ranges and high-elevation passes. Separate antennas for 2-m transmit and 70-cm receive are recommended. These can be easily placed on the roof of the QTH, rather than involving expensive tower supports.

STATION ACCESSORIES

Satellite communications, like any other specialized facet of Amateur Radio, requires some specialized station accessories. Having the best equipment does not necessarily guarantee success. There are a number of "hints-and-kinks" type ideas that can make OSCAR operation far more satisfying. These items convert a basic receiver, transmitter and a pair of antennas into a very workable operating position. Some of the items discussed here will provide capabilities beyond that of satellite operation. They also apply to VHF and UHF terrestrial work. Design your station to suit your own needs.

Antenna Rotators

Unlike stations located on the surface of the Earth, AO-10 and AO-13 will be found somewhere in the sky above. Operators commonly aim antennas toward another station by changing the pointing angle, or azimuth (sometimes called az). Aiming antennas toward AO-10 and AO-13 requires the control of antenna elevation (el). Satellite antennas must be able to rotate from side to side and up and down simultaneously. See Fig 12.

Although the use of electrically controlled antenna rotators will be discussed here, it might noted that Phase III satellite motions are slow enough that hand-operated "armstrong" antenna control is feasible. At times, the antennas may not need repositioning for periods of up to four hours.

Azimuth Rotators

Azimuth rotators are commonly used for positioning terrestrial HF and VHF antennas. Antennas for OSCAR 8 and other low-orbit satellites were on the smaller and lighter side, so light-duty TV-antenna rotators such as those sold by Alliance, Channel Master, Radio Shack and others could be used for the azimuth rotator.

Today's high-gain satellite arrays are a bit large for these light-duty rotators. Look for something more robust, such as a rotator recommended for turning a small HF beam or VHF array. Various models manufactured by Alliance, Daiwa, Kenpro, Telex and others are advertised in *QST*.

Elevation Rotators

Elevation rotator selection is somewhat more limited, but there are some interesting things that can be done. Commercially manufactured models are available. The Kenpro KR500, designed specifically for elevating small- to medium-size VHF or UHF arrays, is quite popular among satellite operators, as is the Kenpro KR5400, both of which are combined az-el rotators. Home-brewed elevation mounts are more the rule, using TVRO antenna jack-screw motion controls or other similar devices.

A lower-cost, commercially manufactured alternative is the Alliance U110 TV-antenna rotator, designed for lightweight antenna arrays. Rotators of this type have been used by satellite operators for years. Despite its relatively light-duty construction, the U110 will handle antenna loads of up to 40 pounds. The key to success is to achieve a static balance of the antenna

Fig 12—A very popular commercially manufactured antenna array for AO-10 and AO-13, Modes B and J, is a pair of KLM crossed Yagis. Shown also are Mode-L helical antennas. The large box on the mast contains a 2-meter and 70-cm preamplifier, coaxial relays, a 24-cm transverter and power amplifier, and power-supply regulators.

Yaesu's FT-736R is a multiband, multimode transceiver for 2-meter (25 W) and 70-cm (25 W) that can be used for AO-10 Mode B and AO-13 Modes B and J full-duplex transmitting and receiving operations. A 23-cm module is available for AO-13 Mode-L uplink. For owners of the FT-736R, this unit would be the only radio needed in the shack for satellite communications.

The Ten-Tec 2510 Mode-B satellite station is designed specifically for Mode-B operation. The box contains a 435-MHz SSB and CW transmitter, as well as a 145-to-28-MHz receiving converter with a low-noise front end.

mass so that the rotator does not have to elevate a "dead" load. A highly attractive feature of the elevation rotators noted above is that the boom to be rotated passes completely through the rotator. This allows the mounting of one antenna on each side of center, and the adjustment of their respective positions for a side-to-side balanced load.

Fig 14 shows one particular method of mounting the U110. The rotator is clamped to the mast (the one that the azimuth rotator turns) with a plate that permits it to mount 90° from its normal orientation. With the rotator mounted in this position, it is not protected from rain or snow as well as it is in the normal position. A cover (an appropriately sized plastic dishpan or bucket is ideal) is added to afford protection from the elements. A problem with

polyethylene plastics, commonly used in kitchenware, is that solar radiation quickly deteriorates their polymeric structure and causes the plastic to break apart. As shown, the plastic cover has been protected from the sun with an aluminum-foil baking pan.

Another, more robust elevation axis is shown in Fig 15. This mount is based upon some rugged journal-block self-aligning ball bearings that were found at a local surplus shop. The bearings found have a bore of 1-15/16 inch, just right to fit the OD of a piece of 1-1/2-inch (nominal) galvanized steel pipe. Another surplus item was found in the form of a linear-screw mechanism, used for TVRO dish positioning. It moves through a distance of 8 inches in a period of 60 seconds and is attached to the azimuth mast and an arm on the elevation axis.

Antenna Cross Boom Construction

One requirement not commonly discussed is that of using a nonmetallic elevation axis boom for antennas that have their boom-to-mast mounting hardware in the center of the boom. A metal cross boom will seriously distort the beam pattern of a circularly polarized antenna, so it is important to make those portions of the cross boom nearest to the antennas from nonmetallic materials.

From a structural standpoint, the best nonmetallic material for this job is glass-epoxy composite tubing. Lengths of this material may be found at an industrial supply house that specializes in plastics. Also, KLM sells lengths of 1½-inch-OD fiberglass masting for this purpose, and Telex/HyGain includes fiberglass masting with their OSCAR antennas. If you have

Fig 14—Close-up of an Alliance U110. Note how the unit is protected from the elements by plastic and aluminum covers. Note the PVC pipe that slides over the steel stub protruding from the rotator.

Fig 15—For heavy-duty elevation axis service, a stronger mount can be made from 1-1/2-inch pipe and 1-15/16-inch self-aligning bearing assemblies. The axis is moved through 0° to 90° degrees with a TVRO linear dish drive coupled to an arm on the pipe axis. Fiberglass extensions fit into the ends of the pipe to provide the needed antenna mounts. This photograph shows the axis in an inverted position, as it is mounted on a tilt-over tower.

a rotator that will accept a 1½-inch elevation boom, then your best bet is to use a single piece of this tubing. The 1½-inch-OD fiberglass tubing also sides into the ID of the 1½-inch pipe used for the heavy-duty elevation axis.

A less expensive alternative is to make the cross boom from a combination of metallic and nonmetallic tubing. For strength and stiffness, use a short length of steel or aluminum tubing through the middle of the rotator. Let the metal tubing extend for about 6 inches on each side of the rotator. Then, install nonmetallic masting, such as common PVC pipe, over the steel stubs.

The elevation boom pictured in Figs 12 to 14 was constructed with this method. The center piece that fits through the U110 is a 2-foot section of 1.33-inch-OD steel tubing that was originally part of the top support rail of a chain-link fence. Attached to the steel stub on each side of the rotator is 4-foot length of 1¼-inch, schedule-40 PVC pipe. PVC pipe is specified by the nominal ID, here 1¼ inches. There are several varieties of 1¼-inch PVC pipe—schedule 40 indicates a thick-wall, heavy-duty version. This pipe slipped nicely over the center stub. The fit is perfect—no machining was needed.

Unlike glass-epoxy tubing, PVC pipe is not very stiff; it needs help. The secret to making PVC pipe capable of supporting satellite Yagis is to insert a wooden dowel into the PVC pipe, along its entire length. The finished dimension of 1-3/8-inch wooden clothes-rod dowel (the kind you might hang inside a closet) is just perfect for a slide fit into the pipe. This material is available from most lumber yards. Add a few ¼-inch bolts to each side to secure the pieces, and you've got a sturdy, inexpensive, nonmetallic elevation boom.

Position Indicators

You may notice additional hardware around the elevation rotator shown in the photos. With the use of high-directivity antennas, the accuracy of the U110 control box is questionable. Adding a single-turn, 1-kΩ precision potentiometer provides the ability to closely control and position the elevation boom. See Fig 16. The potentiometer (a large surplus instrumentation model) is attached to the elevation axis with a U-bolt and angle bracket. A metal arm with lead weights at the end is attached to the potentiometer shaft. The weighted arm and gravity hold the shaft motionless while the potentiometer body turns with the elevation boom.

A simple circuit, shown in Fig 17, is all that is needed to control the U110 and to use signals from the precision potentiometer (R3) for an accurate position indicator. R1 is used to zero the scale, while R2 calibrates the range of the indicator.

The value of R2 will depend on the value of the voltmeter you use. For example, a 0- to 100-mV meter might be used, adjusted so that 10 mV equals 10° elevation, 30 mV equals 30° elevation, and so on.

Tower-Mounted Preamplifiers

To get the most out of your satellite station, you'll need to mount a low-noise preamplifier on the tower or mast, near the antenna, so that feed-line losses do not degrade low-noise performance. Feed-line losses ahead of the preamplifier add directly to receiver noise figure. A preamp with a 0.5-dB noise figure will not do you much good if there is 3 dB of feed-line loss between it and the antenna.

There are a variety of good preamplifiers available. Chapters 31 and 32 detail several suitable construction projects, and Table 6 lists many commercial suppliers.

Mast mounting of sensitive electronic equipment has been a fact of life for the serious VHF/UHFer for years, although it may seem to be a strange or difficult technology for many HF operators. A mast-mounted preamp is not difficult to construct, and there are a growing number of commercially available models as well. See the list of equipment suppliers in Table 6.

Take another look at Fig 12. The large white box located below the elevation rotator can't be missed. Fig 18 shows the interior of this box: It contains a lot of

Fig 16—Details of the position potentiometer mounting and weighted arm.

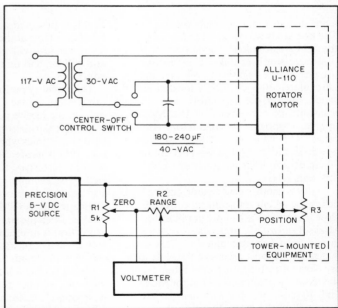

Fig 17—Block diagram of the elevation rotator direction control and position readout.

Fig 18—Interior of the tower-mounted equipment rack with the cover removed. The 70-cm equipment is on the left, while power-supply regulators, a 24-cm transmit converter and a 2-meter preamp are mounted on the right.

Fig 19—Close-up of the 2-meter preamplifier, relays and 24-cm transmit converter.

items in addition to a simple preamplifier. The box holds two racks of equipment. On the right are dc voltage regulators with their pass-transistor heat sinks. These regulators provide on-site-regulated 12-V dc from an unregulated 30-V dc supply located in the shack. Below the regulators is a 24-cm transmitting converter for the Mode-L uplink. Opposite the regulators on the other rack panel is a 70-cm solid-state power amplifier for the Mode-B uplink, a 70-cm preamplifier for the Mode-L downlink and relays.

Fig 19 is another view that details the area below the 24-cm transmitting converter. A close look shows a 2-m preamplifier for the Mode-B downlink, and relays to switch it in and out of the antenna line. This setup is designed to beat excessive feed-line losses. Normal installations may require only the receiving preamplifier (2 m for Mode B, and 70 cm for Modes J and L) to be mounted on the mast. More on the transmitting equipment later.

Station Control Circuitry

Fig 20 is a schematic diagram of the control circuitry for the 2-meter tower-mounted rack. Parts of this diagram will be helpful, even if only the preamp is mounted at the antenna. Note that this circuit is designed around surplus coaxial relays available at the time of construction. Your version will probably be different, and will depend on the relays available to you.

This circuitry performs several functions. For starters, it places the preamp in the line only during receive periods, and takes it out of the line during transmit periods, as well as at those times when the station is not in use. This is needed if the satellite array is used for terrestrial transceive operation as well. The switching arrangement shown also protects the preamp from stray electromagnetic pulses (EMP), such as lightning strokes, when the station is not in use. EMP protection is desirable even if the antenna and preamp are used only for receiving OSCAR-10 signals.

Fig 20 is only a little more complicated than the average mast-mounted preamp setup because it also allows 2-m RF to drive a 24-cm, Mode-L transmitting converter. An extra relay (K3) is used to switch between 2-m and 24-cm operation. K1, a SPDT transfer relay, switches the antenna between the input of the preamp and a through-line to K2. K2, another SPDT relay, switches the feed line from the shack, between the preamp output and K1. The relays are connected so that they must be energized to place the preamp in line, thus insuring that the preamp is disconnected when not in use.

Tower-Mounted Equipment Shelters

Many amateurs seem apprehensive about placing their valuable radio equipment outdoors. Such fears are unfounded if adequate care is taken to protect the equipment from the elements. The equipment shown in the photos has been outdoors for years without any adverse effects.

The present mast-mounted enclosure shown earlier is a welded aluminum box purchased from a surplus dealer. It was used because it was available and the price was right. You don't really need a big box like this if you just want to protect a preamp and relays.

Fig 21 shows the basic scheme for weatherproofing tower-mounted equipment. The fundamental concept is to provide a cover to shelter equipment from rain. A deep-drawn aluminum pan can make an excellent shelter. A trip to the housewares section of the local department store will reveal a variety of plastic and aluminum trays and pans that can make suitable rain covers. As mentioned before, polyethylene plastic does not stand up too well in sunlight. Clear polystyrene refrigerator

Fig 20—Control circuitry for the mast-mounted 2-meter preamplifier and 24-cm Mode-L transmitter. K1-K3 are surplus coaxial relays.

Fig 21—Protection for tower-mounted equipment need not be elaborate. Be sure to dress the cables as shown so that water drips off the cable jacket before it reaches the enclosure.

containers work better than those made of polyethylene, and aluminum is best of all. Choose a cover that is large enough for your equipment; remember to leave room for connecting cables.

The bottom of the rain cover is open to the elements. This is done on purpose and will not cause any problems. Do not try to hermetically seal the enclosure. By leaving the bottom open, adequate ventilation will prevent accumulation of water condensation. Just make sure that water cannot run into the enclosure by way of cables coming from above. Form the cables as shown in Fig 21 to provide drip loops. Adding a piece of window screen over the opening should be considered to avoid infestations of insects and small animals.

Transmitting Accessories

Fig 22 shows the 70-cm rack from the mast-mounted equipment box. The 70-cm power amplifier (built on the heat sink at the left of the photo) is mounted in the box near the antenna to avoid feed-line losses. Tower mounting of a transmitter is probably unnecessary for 70 cm, but becomes much more important for higher frequencies. Feed-line losses at 70 cm are generally twice as great than those at 2 m. Losses at 24 cm are about twice as great as those at 70 cm, or four times as great as those at 2 meters. For an 80-foot-long feed line, losses at 24 cm can easily reach 6 dB. Under such conditions, a 100-W amplifier in the shack will only yield 25 W at the antenna. A good alternative is to place the transmitting converter and a 20-W solid-state amplifier in the tower-mounted box. The results are nearly the same, and you avoid the time and money needed to generate high power that will just be lost in the feed line anyway.

A coaxial RF sampler is connected to the output of the 70-cm amplifier, also shown in Fig 22. It is good amateur practice to monitor the power at the antenna to be sure that everything is working properly. To the right of the power amplifier is a 70-cm preamp and coaxial relay used for Mode-J and Mode-L reception, and for terrestrial communications.

One important aspect of using GaAsFET preamps with transmitting equipment is getting everything to switch at the proper time. If transmitters, amplifiers and antenna relays are keyed simultaneously, it's likely that RF will be applied to the feed line before the relays are fully connected to the antenna load. Such hot switching can

Fig 22—The 70-cm equipment panel holds a power amplifier, preamp and TR relays.

easily arc the contacts on expensive coaxial relays. In addition, if the TR relay is not fully closed, RF may be applied to the preamplifier. Such bursts of RF energy are guaranteed to destroy the GaAsFET in the preamplifier. Many pieces of transmitting equipment (especially multimode transceivers) emit a short burst of RF power when switched on or off, so there is the risk of transmitting into your preamp even if you are careful to pause before keying.

Ideally, keying of a transmitter should follow a timing sequence that will ensure the safety of the equipment. When you switch into transmit from receive, the coaxial relays change state to remove the preamplifier from the line. Next, the power amplifier is keyed on. The last thing that happens is that the transmitter RF is enabled. When switching back to receive, the sequence is reversed. First, the transmitter RF is switched off, the power amplifier is disabled, and then the TR relays change state to place the preamp back in service.

Solid-state sequencers to control station TR switching are shown in Chapters 31 and 32. In addition, a unit designed specifically for use with the Yaesu FT-726R and FT-736R units is presented elsewhere in this chapter.

Receiving Accessories

Additional useful equipment applies to those stations using a receiving converter and an HF receiver for downlink reception. An in-line switchable attenuator can be installed between the converter output and the antenna input of the 10-meter receiver. Such an attenuator can be used to lower the AGC level and improve the perceived signal-to-noise ratio. In addition, by adjusting the attenuator so that the S meter on the HF rig rests at zero at no signal, more accurate signal reports can be given. The attenuator circuit is shown in Chapter 25. A modified version is useful; it has only three steps: 5, 10 and 20 dB. These three settings allow attenuation in 5-dB steps from 0 to 35 dB.

Antenna Accessories

Long-boom Yagis, such as the KLM antennas shown in Figs 12 and 13, can suffer from boom sag that might cause pattern distortion and pointing errors. In addition, a boom support is desirable in areas where high winds or ice are a problem. To avoid possible interference with the antenna pattern, the boom brace must be made from nonconductive material such as Phillystran™ HPTG2100 guy cable.

Details are shown in Fig 23. The vertical boom-brace support member is also nonconductive, made from a fiberglass fishing rod blank. A short piece of threaded stainless-steel rod inserted in the top of the tube is used to adjust tension on the boom brace. A 2-inch piece of 5/16-inch copper tubing brazed across the threaded rod in a "T" fashion holds the cable in place. Jam

Fig 23—A boom brace may be desirable for long Yagis. This arrangement is made from nonconductive material to prevent undesirable effects on the antenna pattern.

nuts secure the threaded rod once the boom is straight.

Experience with the exposed polarization-changing relays used on some commercial antennas has shown that they are prone to failure caused by an elusive mechanism known as "diurnal pumping." The relay is covered with a plastic case, and the seam between the case and PC board is sealed with a silicone sealant. It is not hermetically sealed, however. As a result, the day/night temperature swings pump air and moisture in and out of the relay case. Under the right conditions, moisture from the air will con-

Fig 24—KLM 2M-22C antenna CP switching relay with relocated balun and protective cover.

dense inside the relay case when the air cools. Water builds up inside the case, promoting extensive corrosion and unwanted electrical conduction, seriously degrading relay performance in a short time.

A good rain shelter keeps water from falling directly on the equipment, yet allows the enclosure to "breathe," eliminating water buildup. Equipment in such an enclosure will stay dry and healthy, with the exception of minor corrosion of unprotected steel.

If you have antennas with sealed plastic relays, such as the KLM CX series, you can avoid problems by making the modifications shown in Fig 24. Relocate the 4:1 balun as shown, and place a clear polystyrene plastic refrigerator container over the relay. Notch the container edges for the driven element and the boom so that the container will sit down over the relay, sheltering it from the elements. Bond the container in place with a few dabs of RTV adhesive sealant.

Position the antenna in an "X" orientation, so that neither set of elements is parallel to the ground. The switcher board should now be canted at an angle, and one side of the relay case should be lower than the other. Carefully drill (by hand) a pair of 3/32-inch holes through the lower side to vent the relay case. The added cover keeps rain water off the relay, and the holes will prevent any buildup condensation inside the relay case. Relays so treated have remained clean and operational over periods of years without any problems.

Station Control

Depending on the complexity of your satellite station, you might want to combine most of the switching and control circuitry into a single box that provides ready access to all controls. Fig 25 shows a box cut to a low profile (beneath the multi-antenna rotator control unit) that contains all of the switches needed to control the station accessories. It houses the TR sequencer circuit board as well.

This box controls the following functions: change antenna polarization from RHCP to LHCP on 2 m and 70 cm, switch the 2-m and 70-cm preamplifiers in and out of the circuit, and switch the power amplifier in or out of the line. The box also contains a high-performance 2-m receive converter, for use with an HF transceiver, when Mode-B conditions become difficult. As shown, home-built control unit boxes can be dressed-up with the addition of a plotted or printed label on white paper. The label is bonded to the panel with thin, double-sided adhesive tape. A covering of clear tape protects the label from smudges and dirt.

Fig 25—The satellite station at WD4FAB, with the Antenna Controller mounted above a low-profile station controller. On the right is a Yaesu FT-726R transceiver, with a power meter, clock and 23-cm transverter mounted on top.

Automatic Antenna Controller

This project was designed by Dick Jansson, WD4FAB.

Integrated-circuit technology and the availability of personal computers have combined to inject some interesting aspects of electronic technology into the up-to-date satellite station. At the same time, the antenna gains used in the satellite station place substantial demands upon the ability to control the positioning of the antennas accurately. Aside from the station control equipment shown in Fig 25, a digital display antenna controller is shown for three rotators (azimuth and elevation for satellite antennas and azimuth for an HF antenna).

This section will detail the electronic aspects of that controller and its coupling to a personal computer to provide automatic antenna tracking of satellites and digital displays of antenna position. This antenna controller assembly can be used effectively with or without the computer connection and can be used even if satellite tracking is not an interest.

The closed loop positioning of devices such as satellite antennas can involve many complex technologies, depending upon how closely the positioning is needed and achieved. If the antennas had extremely narrow beamwidths, the positioning requirements would be very high, and even the flexibility of the antennas and mounts could drive such a controller into instability. Fortunately, the antenna beamwidths used for VHF, UHF and microwave antennas in the Amateur Satellite Service run from ±25° down to ±5°, at the lowest end.

These generous beamwidths allow for very substantial reductions in the control requirements on the total system; in fact, a servo system engineer would consider the control system to be "sloppy." The pointing requirements are, however, sufficiently demanding that most commercial antenna controllers do not provide sufficient control and/or position information to satisfy the needs. The antenna controller shown in Fig 25 overcomes these limitations by providing an accurate antenna position digital display. It allows three operating modes: manual position control, commanded position control and computer position control.

CIRCUIT DETAILS

The schematics for this antenna controller project, Figs 26-29, may look complex, but they are truly elementary in function. The controller is merely an updated implementation of the antenna position readout of Fig 17. The overall assembly, schematically illustrated in Fig 26, shows two (of the three) controllers, the needed power supplies, brake controls and the digital panel meters (DPM). The only

ROTATOR CONNECTIONS

HY—GAIN (CDE) ROTATOR CONNECTIONS

Fig 26—The overall assembly, showing two of the three controllers, the power supplies, brake controls and digital panel meters. Radio Shack part numbers are in parentheses.

44-position card edge connector (A/R) (276-1551).
44-position plug-in perf board (A/R) (276-154).
DB25S connector (276-1548).
Control activity LED (A/R) (276-041).
12.6-Vac 300-mA transformer (273-1385).
25.2-Vac CT 2.0-A transformer (273-1512).
25.2-Vac CT 450-mA transformer (if required) (273-1366).
1-kΩ 1-turn linear potentiometer.
1-kΩ 10-turn linear potentiometer.
Turns counting potentiometer dials.

SPDT momentary center off switch (manual control).
SPST switch (enable control).
SPST switch (power).
Fuse holder (270-364).
Fuse, 2 A (270-1275).
0.01-mF 2-kV disc ceramic capacitors (272-160).
Rotator phasing capacitor (A/R).
Power line cord.
Digital panel meter (A/R, see text).
Ferrite bead filters, FB43-101.
Connectors and cabinet (A/R).

Fig 27—The Power-Supply Card. For capacitors not listed below, use 0.1-mF miniature bypass units with 0.25-in. lead centers. Radio Shack part numbers are in parentheses.

C1, C3, C5, C6, C10—0.1 mF/50 Vdc (272-109).
C2, C4—1000 mF/35 Vdc (272-1019).
C8—100 pF/50 Vdc disc (272-123).
C9—1 μF/25 Vdc (272-1434).
C11—100 mF/35 Vdc (272-1016).
D1—1N4696 9-V Zener.

Q1—TIP31 transistor (276-2017).
R1—2.15 kΩ, 1%.
R2—4.99 kΩ, 1%. Adjust value for any changes in +5 Vdc output.
R3—6.2 Ω, ¼ W.
R4—1.5 kΩ, ¼ W.
R5—470 Ω, ½ W (271-019).

U1, U5—CSB rectifier (276-1161).
U2—7812 regulator (276-1771).
U4—LM723 regulator (276-1740).

Misc

IC socket—14-pin DIP (276-1999).
Heat sinks (3)—TO-220 (276-1363).

digital functions of this controller are in the DPM displays, a fact that will surely disappoint the digital purist. The analog approach up to the DPM units is an easy route to take, however. It can provide good results with available low cost components, including the antenna position-determining components. Commercially available DPM units are used as basic 0-200 mVdc meters. Supply them with analog voltages suitable for the proper digital display of rotator angular position: 0-90 mV for elevation and 0-36 mV for azimuth. Three-place digital display is achieved on each axis.

Accommodating a wide variety of commercially available rotators presents some real challenges for the designer, as one of the most popular of the rotators, the Hy-Gain (formerly CDE), employs some unconventional internal circuitry. The Hy-Gain unit not only grounds the ac common line, used for the brake and motor circuits, but also ties the position potentiometer slider to the chassis ground. These connections prevent the isolation of the ac circuitry from the grounded dc circuits and place a sensitive position-determining circuit on the same lead as the high-current ac components. The circuitry shown over-

comes these problems, but required some innovations to solve.

The ac and dc common leads being joined in the Hy-Gain rotator require that the supply transformers for the ac and dc circuits be two separate devices. Were the commons not joined in the rotator, the constructor could use a single 25 Vac transformer to power the entire unit, as the ac switches are optoisolated from the dc circuitry. This optoisolation even allows the use of 117 Vac drives to rotators, provided grounds are carefully observed. The ac and dc common lines being joined in the Hy-Gain rotator also require that the position potentiometer leads be run separately from the rotator terminal block to avoid the excessive errors caused by the voltage losses of high current leads.

The grounding of the slider of the position potentiometer in the Hy-Gain rotators prevent that component from being used as a conventional voltage divider for position measurement, as is done for other rotators. The Hy-Gain position potentiometer is, instead, used as a variable resistor and is provided with a simple constant current source, so there is a linear relationship between the voltage across the resistor

Fig 28—Channel Control Card. R1, R3, R6, R7, R9 and R11 must be precision 1% metal-film units. R12, R17-23, R25-29 are ¼-W, carbon-composition units. All capacitors are miniature 0.1-mF, 50 Vdc, 0.25-in. lead-center units. Part numbers in parentheses are Radio Shack.

C1, C2, C4-12, C15-23—0.1 mF/50 Vdc (272-109).
D1, D2—1N914 diode (276-1122).
Q1, Q2—2N2222 transistor (276-2009).
Q3, Q4—SC141B Triac (276-1020).
R1, R3, R11—10.0 kΩ 1%.
R2, R4—1-kΩ 15-turn Trimpot (271-342).
R5, R10—10-kΩ, 15-turn Trimpot (271-343).
R6—12.1 kΩ 1%.
R7—100 Ω 1% (for 36-mV azimuth readout), or 1 kΩ 1% (for 90-mV elevation readout).
R8—10 kΩ ¼ W (271-1335).
R9—8.25 kΩ 1%.
R12, R17—1 MΩ ¼ W (271-1356).
R14, R15—See text.
R18, R19-21, R27—3.3 kΩ ¼ W (271-1328).
R22, R23—470 Ω ¼ W (271-1317).
R24—470 Ω ½ W carbon composition (271-019).
R25, R26—180 Ω ¼ W.
R28, R29—470 kΩ ¼ W (271-1354).
U1—LM324 quad op amp (276-1711).
U2—LM339 quad comparator (276-1712).
U3, U4—MOC3010 optocoupler (276-134).

Misc

IC sockets (3)—14-pin DIP (276-1999).
Heat sinks (2)—TO-220 heat sink (276-1363).

Fig 29—Brake Control Card, needed for rotators (such as Hy-Gain) that have separate brakes to prevent wind-driven rotations. Radio Shack part numbers are in parentheses.

C1, C4-6, C8—0.1 mF/50 Vdc (272-109).
C3—100 mF/35 Vdc (272-1016).
C7, C9—1 mF/25 Vdc (272-1434).
Q1—2N2907 PNP (276-2023).
Q2—2N2222 NPN (276-2009).
Q3—SC141B Triac (276-1020).
R1—470 kΩ ¼ W (271-1354).

R2—3.9 kΩ ¼ W.
R3—10 kΩ ¼ W (271-1335).
R4—470 Ω ½ W (271-019).
R5—180 Ω ¼ W.
R6—100 Ω ¼ W (271-1311).
R7—1 kΩ 15-turn Trimpot (271-342).

R8—220 Ω ¼ W (271-1313).
U1—MOC3010 optocoupler (276-134).
U2—LM317T regulator (276-1740).

Misc

IC sockets—7-pin (modified 8-pin) (276-1995).
Heat sinks (2)—TO-220 heat sink (276-1363).

and the rotational position of the rotator (this neat solution is to the credit of ARRL Laboratory Supervisor Jon Bloom). The connections to a conventional rotator and to a Hy-Gain rotator are both shown in Fig 26.

One additional caveat in using the Hy-Gain rotator is that the "grounding" of the potentiometer slider is done directly to the rotating case of the assembly, and measuring circuit continuity depends upon electrical conduction through the main ball bearing. This continuity is only happenstance and can be intermittent. The situation can be improved considerably by providing several turns of shielding braid as a conductive strap between the rotating case and the base.

The Power Supply Card, shown in Fig 27, provides outputs of ±12 Vdc, to supply the comparators and op amps, and a tightly regulated +5 Vdc for the measuring circuits. The +5 Vdc supply is also current limited at approx 100 mA so if there is an external short in the antenna rotator system, the supply will not destroy itself. An additional isolated 9 Vdc supply is included to power the DPM units, as they generally cannot be powered from the same reference supply they are measuring.

The Channel Control Card, Fig 28, is the schematic that looks complicated, but is

really just an assembly of several very simple circuits. U1A and U1D are voltage followers and merely isolate the position-measuring circuits from the following circuits. U1B and U1C are not much more than voltage followers, but in some cases they have low gain values configured to give the needed outputs to the control circuits and the Kansas City Tracker (KCT) unit in the PC. The KCT is the key unit for the automatic control. U2A and U2B are comparators configured for very high gain switching sensing for signals ±16 mV from the reference. The outputs of U2 drive following transistor switches which, in turn, drive the optoisolator LEDs. AC switching is done with great efficiency with triac devices.

R14 and R15 are gain-setting resistors for maximizing output drive to the KCT controller. Set resistors as follows:

Azimuth drive with full 5 Vdc from position potentiometer—R14 = 0 (jumper wire), R15 = 10k.

Elevation drive with less than 5 Vdc available—R14 = 10k 1%, set R15 for gain needed to reach <5 Vdc. Gain = 4, R15 = 3.4k; gain = 3, R15 = 5.11k; gain = 2, R15 = 10k.

The user needs to be aware of the basis of the control, as these precepts affect the gain settings of the Control Card. These conditions are:

Fig 30—The Antenna Controller control PC-board assembly. The double-sided PC-board concept with the top surface as all ground plane has shown itself to be quite RFI-resistant.

1) Elevation axis position potentiometer with a 5 Vdc supply but operates only over ¼th of its motion range, 0°-90°, yielding a position indication output of only approx 0-1.25 Vdc.

2) The KCT analog input needs to cover most of the full 0-5 Vdc range for full 256-bit digital resolution of the rotator position. This requires that the elevation

Fig 31—Power-supply PC-board assembly, providing the specialized power conditioning needed for the control board.

Fig 32—Brake-control PC-board assembly needed for such rotators as the Hy-Gain (CDE) line.

Fig 33—Antenna Controller assembly with the case removed, showing the board assembly for the three control channels.

axis analog position signal be increased by about a factor of 4.

3) The azimuth position command potentiometer, a 10-turn unit, is operated over only 3.6 turns and has an output of only 0.36×5 Vdc, or approx 1.8 Vdc, necessitating a controlled gain to have the effective output near the 5 Vdc of the position potentiometer. The 3.6-turn range of the azimuth command potentiometer gives a command dial reading directly in degrees.

All of these various conditions can be accommodated with the adjustable resistors R2, R4, R5 and R10, and the three fixed resistors R7, R14 and R15. Other situations are easily met with the flexibilities built into the card; all that is needed is some simple arithmetic to determine the voltage divider ratios and op amp gains.

For rotators that have separate brakes to prevent unwanted, wind-driven rotations, such as the Hy-Gain units, the Brake Control Card is needed (Fig 29). This card senses any drive activity from the Control Card and releases the brake as needed. The brake is re-engaged after a three-second time delay following the cessation of drive activity. The brake drive is also opto-isolated and triac driven. Also contained on this card is the adjustable current source for the position potentiometer operated as a variable resistor in the Hy-Gain rotators. The current output is set to give slightly less than 5 Vdc output signal to the measuring circuit when the antenna is at its maximum rotational position, 360°.

CONSTRUCTION

The vast majority of the electronic components for this controller are available from Radio Shack. While printed-circuit assemblies are shown, these very same cards can be constructed on 4.5- × 4-inch 44-position plug-in perfboards, also from Radio Shack (276-154). Component-placement templates for the boards are available from the Technical Secretary, ARRL HQ (request Publication No. 144, the *Handbook* Antenna Controller template package). A kit containing the PC boards and most parts is available from Ocean State Electronics, PO Box 1458, Westerly, RI 02891, tel 800-866-6626. (The ARRL in no way warrants this offer.)

Photographs of the completed assemblies are shown in Figs 30-33. These card assemblies are not so large as to require a card cage to contain them; they can simply be plugged into the proper connectors (Radio Shack 276-1551) mounted into a common aluminum chassis behind the front panel of the cabinet.

The digital panel meters shown in Fig 25 were obtained some years ago, and their manufacturer appears to be no longer in business. Similar DPM units (CMI Modutec) are listed, at low cost, in the Newark Electronics catalog, however. These units are shown to be available with ranges of ±5 V and ±200 mV. If other than the ±200 mV range is used, the voltage divider and gain ranges will need to be adjusted. The use of the ±5 V range looks as if it would produce interesting results, using the 3.6 V range for azimuth and 0.9 V for elevation. The decimal point on all of these

DPM units are hard wire selectable to the location desired.

Switches used for the controls are a pair of Switchcraft lever switches, as their "feel" is good for the service. The MANUAL switch is a Momentary-Off-Momentary control, while the ENABLE switch is latched "On" in the enable position. The lever switches can easily be adjusted to operate in either the latched or momentary modes. The lever switches are not the smallest that could be used, but their operator tactile performance outweighed miniaturization factors.

Transformers for the conversion of line power to operating voltages are available from Radio Shack. The DPM supply can be the smallest possible 12.6 Vac transformer, and the controller dc supply can also be a small 25 Vac transformer. Power for the rotator motors should come from a fairly husky transformer, which could also be the same one from the original rotator control box. Also rescue the ac phasing capacitor from the rotator control box, if it is contained in that assembly.

Position Command Potentiometers are standard 10-turn units for azimuth control and a one-turn unit for the elevation control. These controls both use available turns counting dials from Clarostat, Bourns or Spectrol, all listed in the Newark Electronics catalog. The LED units shown are standard low-cost panel-mount display diodes that not only indicate activity but also take active part in the electrical performance of the control unit.

Using the Microsats

The following material was written by Dick Jansson, WD4FAB.

Within a three-week period in early 1990, the Amateur Radio world was presented with the spectacular delivery to orbit of seven new communications satellites in two launches. One launch provided two UoSATs (UO-14 and UO-15) and four AMSAT Microsats (PACSAT, AO-16; LUSAT, LO-19; DOVE, DO-17; and WEBERSAT, WO-18). A second launch provided us with a new Japanese amateur satellite, Fuji-OSCAR 20. Aside from the achievement of orbital insertion of so many satellites, these launches signal the beginning of some very-high-technology communications, basically in the digital store-and-forward packet world. While the following discussion will describe the ground-station needs for communicating with the Microsats, this information is equally applicable for all of the newly launched satellites, and even the NASA "ham-in-space" Space Shuttle missions.

Communicating with low-Earth-orbiting (LEO) satellites, such as the Microsats, has been found to be easier than previously imagined. Examinations of ground antenna requirements for LEO satellites have caused some new thinking and some purging of old ideas. Let us examine this information and see just what a good antenna should look like, and how to build one.

Engineers who completed the assembly and tests on the Microsats found that using a PSK modem with a TNC can be just a little tricky if the incoming signal is too strong. They found that the modem could lock up on one of the sidebands of the signal, with the result that the decoded signal is not understood by the TNC. If the received signal is not too strong, this tracking of the wrong sideband should not be too much of a problem. The signals from Microsats are strong and the use of high-gain antennas is unnecessary. Low-gain omnidirectional antennas are in order. The use of omnidirectional antennas removes the need for expensive equipment to track a satellite with the station antennas.

Use of excessive transmitter power and antenna gain on the Microsat uplink is a socially unacceptable practice, just as it is in other Amateur Radio communications. Too much uplink power "captures" the spacecraft receiver, making it unusable by others.

One low-gain antenna that was commonly promoted for LEO service in the early days of the OSCAR program was the circularly polarized (CP) Turnstile-over-Reflector antenna. A number were built for the 1983 STS-9 mission of the Space Shuttle *Columbia*, with Owen Garriott, W5LFL, on board. The turnstile was supposed to be a good antenna to use for that mission, but the operators in their automobiles with 5/8-wavelength antennas clearly outper-

Table 7
Microsat Frequencies and Modes

Satellite	Uplink(s) (MHz)	Downlink(s) (MHz)	Data Format
UoSAT-OSCAR-14	145.975	435.07	1200 bit/s AFSK (FM) (9600 bit/s FSK, switchable)
UoSAT-OSCAR-15	None	435.12	1200 bit/s AFSK (FM) (9600 bit/s FSK, switchable)
AMSAT-OSCAR-16	145.90 145.92 145.94 145.96	437.025 437.05 2401.10	1200 bit/s PSK AX.25 (4800 bit/s, switchable)
DOVE-OSCAR-17	None	145.825 2401.200	Digitized voice with 1200 bit/s AFSK AX.25 (FM) telemetry
WEBERSAT-OSCAR-18	None	437.075 437.100	1200 bit/s PSK AX.25
LUSAT-OSCAR-19	145.84 145.86 145.88 145.90	437.125 437.150	1200 bit/s PSK AX.25 (4800 bit/s, switchable)

Fig 34—Microsat visibility v elevation angle. Note the minuscule percentage of time the spacecraft is visible at high elevation angles.

formed the turnstile antenna with their reception of *Columbia* on the horizon.

This antenna problem was pointed out in "A Method for Evaluating Antennas For a Low Earth Orbit Mission," by Courtney Duncan, N5BF, in the *AMSAT-NA Technical Journal*, V1, N2, Winter 1987-88. His conclusions about the location of a LEO satellite with respect to a ground station are shown in Fig 34. This partial polar plot shows that a LEO satellite will be below 10° elevation about 52% of the time, below 20° 76% of the time, and below 30° about 90% of the time. Visibility time above 60° elevation is very small. One look in an *ARRL Antenna Book* at the vertical radiation polar plot for a turnstile antenna will show that it does not receive signals very well below 30°, negating its usefulness for LEO satellites.

There is another problem with the use of a CP antenna, like the turnstile, on a LEO satellite. The spacecraft transmitted signals may be circularly polarized but that is only from one position of the spacecraft. Attitude control of the Microsats provide for a magnetically induced tumble of 2 revolutions per orbit, and a sun-driven spin of 0.2 to 1.0 revolution per minute. This results in a very complex spacecraft motion. Operations with AMSAT-OSCAR

8 found that the sense of circularity on the received signal at any ground station changed as the spacecraft traveled along its orbit, and there was no consistency in the CP sense. The building of a fixed-sense (RHCP or LHCP) receiving antenna is viewed as counterproductive to good communications.

Let us now consider antennas that do perform well at low angles of radiation. The elementary ½-wavelength vertical is the fundamental antenna. It has no ground plane or collinear arrangements. Fig 35 shows the relative gain performance for a vertical ½-wavelength antenna as a function of elevation angle above the horizon, and it is not bad for the first 60°. Also shown in Fig 35 is the reduction of signal path loss from the satellite, which gets closer to the ground station as it becomes higher in the sky. A reduction of path loss (a "double" negative notation) is a gain in overall performance, and this gain is happening faster than the loss of the ½-wavelength antenna. Plotting the sum of these losses (or gains) gives us the third curve on Fig 35, or the total system performance. Note that this system performance does not return to 0 dB until an elevation angle of 70° is reached. This means that much more than 95% of the visibility

Fig 35—Plot showing the relative gain performance of a ½-wavelength vertical antenna, the change in satellite path loss and the resultant total system performance.

time for a LEO satellite is covered by useful omnidirectional antenna performance.

An additional note of caution is that vertical omnidirectional antennas can be overdone. The use of multi-element vertical collinear antennas provides too much gain on the horizon because the main lobe of those antennas is below an elevation angle of 30°. The user of such an antenna would have to do the cross plot for the system performance shown in Fig 35 to know how the collinear will perform.

A 70-cm AND 2-m J-POLE SATELLITE ANTENNA

This discussion about antenna performance leads one to ask if there is some antenna configuration that will do the job, is low in cost and, most important of all, is simple. A possible solution was spotted in an old copy of the ARRL book *FM and Repeaters for the Radio Amateur*, 3rd printing, 1976. Page 95 describes "A Combination 6- and 2-Meter J Pole" antenna, with credit given to W5WEU. This dual-band J-pole antenna scheme looked like it was just the item that was needed, and a 2-m and 70-cm version was quickly built.

The J-pole antenna is fundamentally an end-fed ½-wavelength antenna that uses a ¼-wavelength-long transformer section to supply the very high feed voltage. It is an ideal end-mounted, single-mast antenna. (Another candidate would be the coaxial antenna, but building a dual-band, single-unit assembly might present a bit of a problem.)

The dual J-pole antenna appears to be a good answer for the single assembly of two ½-wavelength antennas. The upper 70-cm antenna does not know the lower 2-m antenna exists; it is just a support for the 70-cm unit. Similarly, the 2-m antenna just has a bit of a fat top that does not affect tuning at all.

A lot was found out about J-pole antennas in trimming this job. Nearby conductors within 2 wavelengths can detune the J pole, and the mast and J elements want to be very close to theoretical free-space measurements for best performance. The result of this design and test effort is shown in Figs 36 through 41. Materials chosen for this antenna are obtainable from common sources. Just about every hardware store has 1.0-inch OD aluminum tube, or

shower-curtain rod, and the design was built around a 72-inch long piece. The J elements are of ½-inch tube from the same aluminum rack.

The remaining pieces needed are shown in Figs 36 and 37, and should be readily available. Note that the clamps used for holding the pieces together are taken from common aluminum clamps that have rubber bushings to be used for wire bundles. The rubber parts are removed and the aluminum clamp is reshaped, using a pair of water pump pliers, over a solid piece of aluminum bar the same sizes as the tubing. Clamp the bar stock in a vise and the task can be done in a few minutes. The holes in the clamp may need to be redrilled to make sure it will tightly grab the tubing. Use of all stainless-steel screws, nuts, flat washers and lock washers is highly recommended. Most hardware stores have this hardware readily available.

Carefully tuning the antenna by adjusting the dimensions noted with an asterisk (*) can result in a performance with near zero reflected power at the design center frequencies. Fig 38 shows the completed assembly. Figs 39, 40 and 41 show some of the details of the 70-cm and 2-m feed points and brackets. It is very important to use the RG-142/U coaxial cable for these feed points, as the center conductor of the coaxial feed line is exposed to the weather. The RG-142/U is an all-Teflon construction that will withstand the weathering without adverse effects. Any less weather-resistant coaxial cable can be expected to deteriorate in short order.

Further protection of the coaxial cable from the effects of weather elements can be obtained by using a suitable mastic, such as Coax Seal® around the center conductor where it exits the outer jacket. The purist may also want to close the top ends of the tubing. Small wooden plugs carved to fit and bonded into the tube ends with RTV sealant would do the job very well.

Operating experience with signals from the cluster of Microsats shows that when the antenna is in the clear (not blocked by trees, buildings or other objects), it provides resounding reception of the satellites once they are clear of ground clutter. This

Fig 36—Construction details for the dual-band J-pole antenna.

NO. 6—32 BLIND THREAD INSERT, 2 PLACES

1.00" CABLE CLAMP, MS21919DG—16, 2 EA
(REMOVE RUBBER BUSHING, RESHAPE CLAMP)
NO. 10—32 x 0.62" SS SCREWS, 2 EA
NO. 10 SS FLAT WASHER, 4 EA
NO. 10 SS LOCK WASHER, 2 EA
NO. 10—32 SS NUT, 2 EA

0.50" CABLE CLAMP, MS21919DG—8, 2 EA
(REMOVE RUBBER BUSHING, RESHAPE CLAMP)
NO. 10—32 x 0.62" SS SCREWS, 2 EA
NO. 10 SS FLAT WASHER, 4 EA
NO. 10 SS LOCK WASHER, 2 EA
NO. 10—32 SS NUT, 2 EA

0.38" DIA THRU, DIMPLE TUBE FOR RELIEF
ON COAXIAL CABLE EXIT

0.196" DIA THRU, 4 PLACES

1.50"   2.00"

0.25"

2.625"   0.25"

3.13"

(A)

NO. 6—32 BLIND THREAD INSERT, 2 PLACES

0.50" CABLE CLAMP, MS21919DG—8, 3 EA
(REMOVE RUBBER BUSHING, RESHAPE CLAMP)
NO. 10—32 x 0.62" SS SCREWS, 3 EA
NO. 10 SS FLAT WASHER, 6 EA
NO. 10 SS LOCK WASHER, 3 EA
NO. 10—32 SS NUT, 3 EA

1—3/8" U BOLT, 2 EA
5/16"—18 SS NUT, 4 EA
5/16" SS FLAT WASHER, 4 EA
5/16" SS LOCK WASHER, 4 EA

1.00" CABLE CLAMP, MS21919DG—16, 4 EA
(REMOVE RUBBER BUSHING, RESHAPE CLAMP)
NO. 10—32 x 0.62" SS SCREWS, 4 EA
NO. 10 SS FLAT WASHER, 8 EA
NO. 10 SS LOCK WASHER, 4 EA
NO. 10—32 SS NUT, 4 EA

0.344" DIA THRU, 4 PLACES
0.196" DIA THRU, 7 PLACES

0.50"

1.56"   1.660"   2.12"

0.295"   5.00"

1.62"   0.50"   2.13"

0.25"

0.25"   1.75"

0.50"

3.31"   (B)

1.00"

0.25"

Fig 37—A: Construction details for the plate of the 70-cm part of the antenna. B: 2-m antenna plate details. 0.125-in.-thick aluminum should be used for both plates.

Fig 38—The completed antenna. The J-pole design is a simple and effective means of getting started in Microsat communications. The joint at the center provides a convenient means to shorten the length for transporting the antenna. A short length of smaller-diameter tubing fits inside the antenna. Hose clamps tighten the antenna tubing to the inner tubing.

reception is within 30 seconds of rising above the local horizon. While PSK packet can be obtained with rather noisy signals, reception is enhanced with the use of a modest 1-dB-NF GaAsFET preamplifier.

JUST WHAT IS A PACSAT?

The following material has been provided by Mike Crisler, N4IFD, and is extracted from the AMSAT-NA *PACSAT Beginner's Guide*.

A PACSAT is an amateur satellite capable of operating similarly to land-based packet radio. The real advantage is that this digipeater/radio bulletin board service (RBBS) is in orbit, with its "footprint" (antenna pattern) covering the entire

Fig 39—Lower antenna (2-meter) feed point and mounting-bracket assembly. Note the use of #12 TW house wire as a cable wrap to hold the RG-142/U coax cable in place on the base. Also note the use of the small cable clamp soldered to the coax braid at its attachment point. Both the center conductor and braid attachment are held to the elements with no. 6-32 stainless-steel screws into aluminum blind nuts purchased at the hardware store. All intermetallic contacts are coated with an aluminum joint compound to prevent corrosion and poor electrical properties. Thomas & Betts Catalog No. 21059 is a very good compound to use. (Dept G, 920 Rte 202, Raritan, NJ 08869).

Fig 40—Rear view of the 2-meter base bracket, showing the U bolts provided for mast mounting. This bracket has an "L" bend to prevent the antenna from sliding down the mast.

Fig 41—Top antenna (70-cm) feed point, a simple plate and clamps. An easy exit should be provided for the RG-142/U coaxial cable at this point, as the coax is pretty stiff. Drill a 3/8-inch hold and carefully deburr all edges. Then insert a ¼-inch pin punch (or similar metal object) into the hole to dimple the tubing underneath and pry it up a little on top.

surface area of the earth several times daily. The altitude of a PACSAT (equivalent to the height of a digipeater antenna) is over 500 miles, allowing an operator in Florida to digipeat directly with another in California or Canada! Since a PACSAT moves so fast, this type of QSO can last several minutes at best. Considering the way most of us type, not much information is likely to be exchanged. This was not the intended use of the PACSATs.

PACSATs are intended to relay messages and files that are *uploaded* from land-based stations. Their polar orbits allow stations located at low latitudes to have at least four to five access periods a day to each of the PACSATs. At higher latitudes the number of access periods per day increases.

EQUIPMENT

The equipment required for operating the AO-16 (sometimes called PACSAT) and LO-19 (sometimes called LUSAT) spacecraft is pretty simple. Fig 10 illustrates a typical setup. Nearly every station has low-band SSB receive capability that can be tuned to the 437-MHz satellite downlink receive frequency through the use of a low-cost receive converter. Similarly, many stations have a 2-m FM transmitter and a packet TNC. Adding a PSK modem to the TNC completes the hardware requirements. With software available from AMSAT, a PACSAT ground station can be on the air in a short time.

The equipment characteristics necessary

for a good satellite operating station apply equally to any PACSAT station. Placing a band-pass filter on the receive antenna feed line is highly recommended, especially if a single antenna, such as the dual-band J-pole antenna shown elsewhere in this chapter, is used. The 4 × 3 × 5 filter (also shown elsewhere in this chapter) has proven to be very effective. It has a high rejection of the 2-m transmitter signal, and prevents overload of the 70-cm GaAsFET pre-amplifier.

A terminal node controller (TNC) translates and exchanges digital information between the computer, the transmitter and the receiver. A TNC will allow the station computer and radio to converse with the computer aboard the satellite. Most TNCs will easily interface with the 2-m transmitter and 70-cm receiver required for PACSAT communications. Several changes from the standard packet setup will be needed since PACSAT operation is crossband full duplex. For example, an outboard PSK modem is needed to complement the TNC for PACSAT service.

Terrestrial packet operations are discussed in the Digital Communications chapter of this book. A discussion of the KISS mode is in order here, as the satellite station TNC must be in this mode to talk to the PACSATs. Normal packet operations use a protocol (a group of specific operating instructions) called AX.25. This protocol presents a set of instructions to the TNC for handling data in an error-free manner. It was felt at the time of the PACSAT launch that the AX.25 protocol would limit operating options after launch. KISS is a version of TNC operating software that bypasses many of the control functions of the TNC. It relinquishes control to the computer itself, giving much more flexibility to the user. When the operator uses the software available from AMSAT, KISS operations are automated; the software will activate KISS automatically and shut it off when exiting the program.

Make sure the TNC unit used for PACSAT operation will operate in the KISS mode. Many of the older TNC 2s and TNC 1s do not have KISS software incorporated in the EPROM within the TNC. Many can be modified to run KISS, however.

A second thing needed by the TNC is the ability to interface with a modem other than the one built into the TNC. The onboard modem in most TNCs uses AFSK (audio-frequency shift keying). However, the PACSATs use a phase-shift keying (PSK) technique. PSK-coded digital signals can be decoded at much lower signal-to-noise levels than AFSK or FSK can. PSK-coded signals can be detected and decoded even when the signal is buried in the noise. That level of performance is simply not available with AFSK. Therefore, the internal modem of the TNC must be disconnected and an outboard PSK modem connected in its place. This is not as hard as it sounds. Some TNCs such as the TAPR kit feature a plug-in interface header that permits easy switch selection of either the internal AFSK or the external PSK modem for operation.

As for the PSK unit itself, there are several options. A complete unit is available from PacComm in Tampa, Florida. It is basically an improved, commercially built version of the TAPR PSK modem kit. The unit comes with an instruction booklet that gives step-by-step details to interface the modem with many different radios and TNCs. Also available is the G3RUH modem from Radiokit in New Hampshire and the TAPR PSK unit. Both the September 1987 issue of *QEX* and the March 1990 issue of *The AMSAT Journal* have reviews on the construction of the TAPR PSK modem.

The connection between the computer and the TNC needs to be the full EIA-232 connection since the operating software, called PG (short for PACSAT ground-station software) requires all of the EIA-232 handshaking signals with the TNC. The VHF radio will require full transmit and receive cabling if you intend to use your unit for standard 2-m packet as well as PACSAT. The downlink receiver will require receive cabling along with AFC (automatic frequency control) capability. If the receiver has the ability to change frequency remotely (typically through the microphone connection or via the UP and DOWN buttons on the microphone), the AFC feature can be used to correct for Doppler shift of the downlink signal. Doppler shift for the microsats is about 15-20 kHz in a 10- to 15-minute period. For example, AO-16 shows up around 437.035 MHz and disappears around 437.017 MHz.

During a pass, tuning is somewhat critical. Casual tuning in on the downlink signal may only result in a carrier lock on a satellite transmitter sideband rather than the true signal. These sidebands will not decode properly. If no data starts coming through, try retuning. By utilizing the AFC feature on the PSK unit, the modem will lock on the signal as soon as it is acquired and will tune the receiver automatically throughout the rest of the pass.

SOFTWARE

The AMSAT PACSAT diskette contains all the software needed to work the PAC-SATs. The disk is set up to load into directories that will be needed on the IBM-compatible computer. These are: \ AO16, \ LO19 and \ PACDOC. \ AO16 is the operating directory for AO-16 and \ LO19 is the operating directory for LO-19. The \ PACDOC directory contains the program documentation files. These are extremely important and should be read thoroughly before attempting to use the birds.

One of the files located in each of the two satellite directories is called "pg.cfg" and

looks like this for AO-16:

```
ao16access 30660
bdcstcall Pacsat-11
bbscall Pacsat-12
mycall N4IFD-0
port 1
speed 9600
graball 1
log_kiss 1
log 1
maxdupes 10
restart_delay 54
break_delay 36
maxsel 30
```

A couple of things need to be done to this file before running the rest of the programs: Your own station call sign must appear after "mycall"; the TNC must be communicating with the PC at 9600 bauds (if not, change the value accordingly); and, finally, make sure that "port 1" is appropriate for the PC's serial port. Make these same changes in the similar file in the \ LO19 directory, and the TNC is ready to copy the first pass.

The present release of the PACSAT Ground Station Software consists of four programs that implement the PACSAT protocol suite described in papers by Harold Price, NK6K, and Jeff Ward, G0/K8KA, in the *ARRL Computer Networking Conference Proceedings*. These protocols and programs introduce a new type of "BBS" operation to amateur packet radio. In standard BBS operation, the operator connects to the BBS station and is treated like a remote terminal user. In the PACSAT system, however, the ground-station computer connects to the satellite computer and the two exchange messages efficiently using automated procedures.

This automated approach requires standardization of procedures and data formats. The protocol specifications—collectively called the PACSAT Protocol Suite—specify a standard file header format, a broadcast protocol and a connected-mode file-transfer protocol.

This software package includes the following programs:

PB.EXE—Receives broadcasts from PAC-SAT. After a broadcast file is received, it must be processed with PHS.EXE.

PHS.EXE—Displays PACSAT File headers, and removes headers from files that have been downloaded from PACSAT. PHS.EXE is the complementary program to PFHADD.EXE.

PFHADD.EXE—Prepares files for uploading. Only files that have been processed by PFHADD.EXE may be uploaded to PACSAT.

PG.EXE—Implements the connected-mode file transfer protocol called FTL0. PG.EXE can be used to get lists of files which are on PACSAT, to download files from PACSAT, and to upload files to PACSAT. Before uploading a file to PACSAT, the operator must prepare it with PFHADD.EXE. After downloading a file from PACSAT, it must be

processed with PHS.EXE.

Users of the PACSATs should do their best to keep up with changing versions of these programs. New versions will have bug fixes and some will contain enhancements. For as long as it remains practical to do so, the newest versions of these programs will be available on the satellite. Of course, when diskettes are ordered from AMSAT, users can be assured of getting the latest version.

There are several executable files in these directories that need explanation before being run. Be aware that some of these programs (PG and PB) will not run unless the PC is connected to the PSK/TNC!

PB Program

Try running PB first. Get into the \ AO16 directory, and type in the PB command. You will eventually wind up with a nice screen that looks like the one shown in the photo. If it doesn't, there is probably a communication problem with the TNC or PSK. Recheck all of the cabling, try the TNC in the Terminal mode and reread the instruction books. If this doesn't work, you might want to consider the AMSAT booklet, the *PACSAT Beginner's Guide*; it has an appendix of Elmers who will gladly help you troubleshoot any problems you may encounter.

PB is the program used to "recognize" the satellite downlink and copy the bulletin information being transmitted. It requires less time to get up and running because it operates in the receive mode only. After the screen information is displayed, press the letter H to tell the program to display all the file headers as they are broadcast. The G and K commands have already been invoked by the software setup commands. The G or Grab command is the one of interest, as it allows capture of all the files being broadcast by the satellite. All you have to do is tune the downlink receiver as the satellite comes over the horizon. When the station receiver locks onto the correct downlink signal, data starts to scroll down the lower half of the PB screen. (The "H" command must be toggled on for this to happen.)

Tuning can sometimes be a bit tricky. It works best when the downlink receiver is on USB and the audio level is set a little lower than normal. Start tuning well above the frequency where the satellite signal is expected (about 437.035 MHz for AO-16), and slowly tune down toward the *published* downlink frequency—437.025 MHz for AO-16. Keep going back and forth like this until the downlink is heard. This process is much less time consuming if current Keplerian elements are used in the tracking program and an accurate time source is available in the shack.

About the time the tracking program indicates that the satellite should rise above the horizon, its PSK signal should soon be audible. Keep tuning above where this sound is first heard and slowly tune down

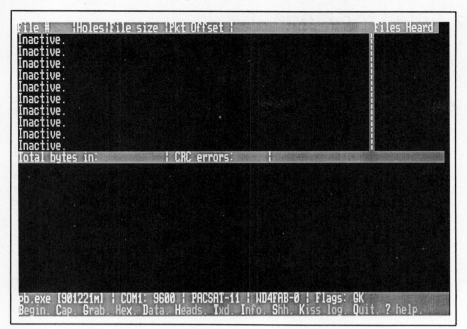

File #	Holes	File size	Pkt Offset		Files Heard

```
Inactive.
Inactive.
Inactive.
Inactive.
Inactive.
Inactive.
Inactive.
Inactive.
Inactive.
Inactive.
```

Total bytes in: | CRC errors:

```
pb.exe [901221m] | COM1: 9600 | PACSAT-11 | WD4FAB-0 | Flags: GK
Begin. Cap. Grab. Hex. Data. Heads. Txd. Info. Shh. Kiss log. Quit. ? help.
```

After getting into the \ AO16 directory and entering PB, you should see a screen that looks like this.

while watching the display LEDs on the front of the PSK modem. They will indicate "lock" as the PSK modem locks onto the PSK downlink. At this point there may not be any received text scrolling across your screen. If this is the case, the TNC is probably locked onto one of the sidebands of the downlink signal.

Keep tuning slowly downward until the next lock occurs. This should be the proper signal. The computer screen will indicate that the data files being transmitted by the satellite are being captured, and they should scroll down the lower half of the screen. If this did not work the first time, don't give up. Just keep tuning slowly from above the signal until lock is achieved and data begins to appear.

When locked onto the center of the downlink signal, the PSK modem will take over the tuning chores and there will be no need for manual tuning of the VFO. Just sit back and watch the files come down. As the files are downloaded, the upper right hand part of the computer screen will begin to fill up with the hex file names. In the upper center portion of the screen the number of holes in the file will be tracked (for future downloading) and the lower portion of the screen will basically perform

like your packet screen does when you have the MONitor command set to ON.

When the pass is over, you will be able to read what has been received from the PACSAT. As the PB program is asked to "Quit" it will write something called "hole files" to the disk. These tell it what partial files were captured during this pass so it will only look for "fills" on those files next time around. The files that are successfully downloaded will be stored as a hexadecimal number followed by the extension ".dl" indicating they are complete downloaded files. These files can then be read by using another one of the executable programs on the diskette—the PACSAT Header Show routine or PHS.EXE. Some of the ".dl" files have been included on the AMSAT diskette for practice. Frequently these files are "Zipped" (compressed) and need to have PKUNZIP used to open them up.

PG Program

Now comes the real challenge—using PG to select files from the directory aboard the PACSAT and ask for downloads of those files. After you are comfortable with the PB program and have the transmitter adjusted and ready to operate, you can try the PG program. This program creates a screen very much like PB, but allows the transmission of uplink files to the satellite as well as the reception of directories and downloading of specific files.

The documentation associated with the PB/PG suite of programs is in the directory called \ PACDOC on the diskette. It gives the specifics of just how to prepare a file for upload. For further information, please contact AMSAT for their *Beginner's Guide*.

The 4 × 3 × 5 MHz Filter for Mode J

If your 435-MHz receive system is sensitive enough to experience desense from your 2-meter uplink, this filter should solve the problem. Most Mode J OSCAR users have experienced some difficulty getting satisfactory results on this mode. Being able to receive well is the secret. Adding this filter should narrow the passband enough to allow rejection of unwanted noise and birdies. Insert it before any preamp or converter in the antenna feed line. If the third harmonic level is high, it may be necessary to use a similar filter built for 2 meters after your uplink 2-meter rig.

Most plumbing-supply outlets can supply you with the material for the ¾- and 3-inch copper pipe. The only other item of cost is the type of coax receptacle you want to use. Make it adaptable to your system, without sacrificing loss. The filter should cost less than $10.

Be careful when you solder double-sided PC board. Direct the heat of your torch at the pipe and enough heat will transfer to the board to allow the solder to flow. It is not necessary to use PC board, as copper or brass that is thick enough to support the unit will do. If copper or brass is not available, a soup can you can solder to works

well. The more stable the structure, the better.

The filter has a narrow passband, but with a good high-gain, low-noise system you should be able to peak up the noise with no signal. A low-power 145.050-MHz signal into a dummy load should give you a test signal to peak the filter.

The insertion loss measured in the ARRL Lab was around 0.4 to 0.5 dB. If you want to improve this figure, use silver braze and silver plating. This filter was fashioned after a design by Joe Reisert, W1JR, and was built by Jay Rusgrove, W1VD.

Parts List

Piece No.

DRILL OR PUNCH TO FIT COAX CONNECTOR 3-3/4" FROM BOTTOM

3-3/4"

1	Pipe, copper 3″ diam, 5″ long	Cut ends square. Drill or punch for connectors 3¾″ from bottom.
2	Pipe, copper 3/4″ diam, 4″ long	AgSn (plumbing alloy) solder to center of 10.
3	Disk, copper ¾″ diam 1/16″-1/8″ thick	Drill through center. Solder solid hook-up wire between disk and connector to space disk 3/16″ from piece 2.
4	Disk, copper ¾″ diam 1/16″-1/8″ thick	Drill through center. Solder solid hook-up wire between disk and connector to space disk 3/16″ from piece 2.
5	Connector, coax	BNC, SMA or N type. Solder to prevent turning. For large connector, use chassis punch.
6	Same as 5	
7	Nut, brass ¼″-20 hex	
8	Nut, brass ¼″-20 hex	
9	PC board, double-sided. Top 4″ × 4″.	Drill hole in center to clear ¼-20 bolt. Solder 7 and 8 each side of hole. (Use bolt 11 to hold nuts in place when soldering.)
10	PC board, double-sided. Bottom 4″ × 4″.	Solder 2 in center.
11	Bolt, brass ¼-20 × 3″	Insert through 12, then through 7 and 8
12	Locking nut, brass, ¼-20 hex	To hold piece 11 after resonance adjustment.

A Digital TR Sequencer for Satellite Work

The need for properly controlling the timing, or sequence, of events in switching a station from transmit to receive is covered in detail in Chapters 31 and 32. The main advantage of sequencing, rather than just switching everything simultaneously, is to protect equipment from damage. For example, sequencing will prevent you from transmitting into a preamplifier or hot switching relays. The TR sequencer described here can be used for other aspects of VHF and UHF operation, but it was built with full-duplex (on two bands) satellite operation in mind, by Dick Jansson, WD4FAB.

Circuit Details

Fig 42 is a schematic diagram of the sequencer. The component count is quite low. Most of the discrete components have been added to protect the circuit from RFI problems. U1 and U2 provide control signal conditioning and digital switching logic, while U3 provides both the key-down and key-release timing. Darlington-connected transistors were used for each relay driver (Q1-Q12) so that practically any garden-variety transistors can be used. The tabs of the TO-220 transistors are mounted to a heat sink for conservative operation. Although most of the switching needs in a modern amateur station require transistors that can handle a few milliamperes of current, some surplus coaxial relays require 500 mA or more. These

Fig 42—Schematic diagram of the digital TR sequencer. All resistors are ¼ W unless noted. Capacitors are disc ceramic unless noted. Capacitors marked with polarity are electrolytic. The output switching transistors (Q1-Q12) can be just about anything that will handle the current requirements.

"generic" control transistors will handle all jobs.

This sequencer provides a 50-ms delay for the transmitter and power amplifier outputs, giving the preamp relays time to settle. Another 50-ms delay is provided for returning the preamps to the line after the transmitter and power amplifier have been turned off. These time delays are conservative, but not at all noticeable in operation. If 50 ms is too long, the 3.3-μF timing capacitors could be reduced to 2.2 μF to provide a 30-ms delay.

Construction and Installation

Construction is straightforward. All components are mounted on a PC board as shown in Fig 43. Etched circuit boards and partial parts kits are available from A & A Engineering (see the ARRL parts suppliers list in the Component Data chapter). The output transistors are mounted so that they hang over the edge of the board and can be mounted to the

Fig 44—The digital TR sequencer is built on a PC board. The output switching transistors can be mounted to the chassis for improved thermal dissipation.

Fig 43—Parts placement diagram for the digital TR sequencer. A full-size etching pattern is given at the back of this book.

chassis to dissipate heat. See the detail in Fig 43. Fig 44 is a photo of the finished unit.

Although this unit was designed with the FT-726R and FT-736R in mind, it can be used with any equipment. If you wish to use it with the FT-726R/FT-736R, Fig 45 shows the preferred way to connect everything. This modification allows you to intercept the TR switching for each FT-726R RF module, but it requires no drilling or irreversible modifications. Each RF module in the Yaesu rig has a TR relay and driver transistor that are on separate PC boards within the module. A small three-wire cable and connector join them. Simply break the lead and run wires out through the louvers on the bottom of the transceiver. It is convenient to place a small connector at the end of this pig-tail lead, allowing the separation of the transceiver and sequencer. Small 3- or 4-pin connectors can be found at model airplane hobby stores, in the radio-controlled (R/C) model section, as they are used to connect R/C servos to receivers.

Fig 45—The Yaesu FT-726R/FT-736-R can be modified so that the TR sequencer can be used to switch it into transit.

A Mode-L Helical Antenna Array for OSCAR-13

OSCAR 13 Mode-L operations require a modest gain antenna for the uplink on 1269 MHz. the antenna gain and ERP required is not nearly as high as it was for OSCAR 10. Solid conversational signal levels need only be 50 to 6 dB out of the noise, and need not be as strong as the Mode-L beacon, which is nearly 20 dB out of the noise. Experiments show that 10 W and a single 45-element loop Yagi return a signal-to-noise ratio of only 2 to 3 dB. The RHCP approach was taken to gain 3 + dB over the previous results, achieving satisfactory results using only 15 W of RF. The antenna presented here can be easily built by the home constructor. This 4-element helical array was designed and built by Dick Jansson, WD4FAB.

Helical Antenna Design

The helical antenna was invented and exploited by Dr John Kraus, W8JK, in the 1940s. Dr Kraus has amply described many facets of this interesting antenna in his texts, which were employed extensively in this effort. Fig 12 shows this array mounted between the 2-m and 70-cm satellite antennas. Fig 46 is a closer view of the helical array.

Helical antennas have their own terminology, as explained in Fig 47. A helical antenna is very broadband, and can be used over a range of frequencies much greater than that encompassing the 1240-to-1300

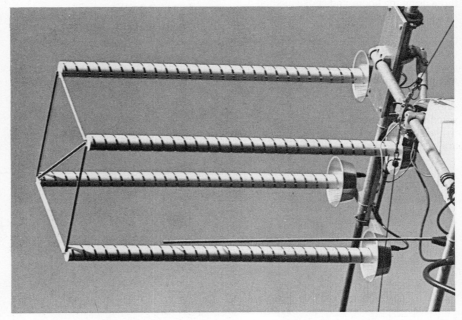

Fig 46—The quad array of 6-λ helical antennas, poised and ready for service on AO-13 Mode L.

MHz ham band. Since there is interest in communicating on 1296 MHz, as well as the Mode-L uplink at 1269 MHz, it was decided to target the antenna's center frequency at

1280 MHz. For long helical antennas, gain values nominally peak with the circumference, C, of the "cylinder" measuring approximately 1.09 wavelengths. The free-

Fig 47—Helical antenna nomenclature as defined by John Kraus, W8JK.

space wavelength at 1280 MHz is:

$\lambda = 23.42$ cm

The design value of C is then:

$C = 1.09* \lambda = 25.53$ cm $= 10.05$ inches.

The design diameter for the helical cylinder is:

$D = C/\pi = 8.13$ cm $= 3.20$ inches.

Helical antennas for lower frequencies can be difficult to construct, especially those using the boom-and-spoke method to support the element. For 24-cm operation, the boom-and-spoke design becomes nearly impractical. A design shown in Kraus' textbook employs a dielectric cylinder with a ribbon element wound on the outside—an approach that is simple to implement.

In a conversation with Dr Kraus, it was suggested that if the helical element is wound on a dielectric substrate, the dielectric will contribute a loading of the element and reduce the velocity of the RF energy,

much like conventional coaxial cable. It was guessed that a 10 to 15% velocity-factor reduction would be in order. Therefore, the antenna is designed to resonate 10 to 15% higher in frequency, making the helical diameter a bit smaller than a free-space design. Reducing the diameter makes the new target:

$D = (1.0 - 0.1) * D_{fs} = 0.9 * 3.20 = 2.88$ inches.

Helical element gain was calculated:

$G = 84 = 19.2$ dBic.

Array spacing, based on the computed gain, is:

4-element spacing $= 2.59\lambda = 23.86$ inches.

A rounded spacing of 24 inches was used.

Materials

The outside diameter of a 2½-inch (nominal) PVC pipe is 2.875 inches, quite close to the estimated target of D = 2.88

inches. Concern has been expressed about the use of PVC in an RF environment. A simple check of a piece of PVC pipe in the microwave oven showed only a small amount of heating.

PVC irrigation pipe is available in standard lengths of 20 feet. Four "boom tubes" of the required length can be obtained from one 20-foot-long pipe. Boom sag is insignificant, despite the limber nature of PVC. The four elements are each 6.4 λ.

Construction

Supporting the helical antenna requires that the entire length be supported from the root, or reflector end, of the boom tube. A search through the plumber's storage shelves for a suitable PVC fitting uncovered plenty of caps for PVC pipe, but no plugs. A PVC threaded plug for 2½-inch pipe was located, however, and with a little filing and trimming, fit into the bore of the boom tube, leaving the outside diameter clear for the ribbon element. Figs 48, 49 and 50 show the boom tube as trimmed for service, and the plug with its embedded screws for attaching the assembly to the support structure.

An important consideration when building any antenna array is that all antennas be as similar as possible. In the construction of the helical array, this means that the windings of the ribbon element on each antenna must be accurately duplicated. Fig 51 shows that each boom tube is scribed with a reference line along the right quadrant. In keeping with the helicals being wound for RHCP, and the antenna feed point being located above the top of the boom tube, the right quadrant point is really the starting point of the element at the root of the boom tube. The precision of this duplicity cannot be over emphasized. After scribing the longitudinal line, cross mark scribes were made at each crossing point of the ribbon element. Fig 51

Fig 48—Fabrication details for the helical antenna PVC boom.

Fig 49—Parts for the helical antenna reflector-end PVC construction are shown before being glued together.

Fig 50—The helical antenna reflector end assembly.

shows the dimensions of the helix.

Nickel-plated copper ribbon, 0.004 inch thick and 3/8 inch wide, is used to wind the helical elements. The boom tube is supported by a simple fixture that allows it to slowly rotate while the ribbon is wound on the tube, it is taped down at nearly every turn. Each turn is checked for uniformity, and after the entire 28.5 turns are applied and the ribbon cut, it is rechecked. The element is then bonded to the boom tube with a cyanoacrylate adhesive such as ZAP/CA, available at most hobby shops. After the adhesive is fully set and the masking tape tabs removed, the element solder area is masked with tape and the entire boom tube assembly is protected with a coating of clear Krylon acrylic spray coating.

Supporting the array is an H-frame, constructed of 2-inch aluminum channel (see Fig 52). This channel is about the lightest that can be used, considering the cantilever design of the antenna elements. The clamping of a cross member to the 1½-inch pipe elevation axis, as shown in Figs 53A and 53B, considerably reduces torsional stiffness problems.

Notice also in Figs 52 and 53, that the array is clamped to the elevation axis with U bolts made from 5/16-inch stainless-steel

threaded rod stock. Most of the plated-steel U bolts quickly rust beyond usefulness, with the exception of some well-galvanized marine hardware, which is not generally available in the amateur market.

The stiffness of the H frame is not overly abundant. Adding a set of non-metallic (dielectric) outboard struts increases stability, Fig 54 shows the dimensions of these struts, which are made from fiberglass-epoxy composite angle stock. PVC or other suitable non-metallic material will suffice, as long as the material is light and stiff. Fig 55 shows the attachment points for these struts on the outer ends of the boom tubes. The strut attachments are made of fiberglass-epoxy board (see Fig 48). This end plate has captive nuts riveted to the inside to allow easy strut attachment.

Reflector designs for helical antennas vary from flat circular planes to deep conical surfaces. A common practice for helical arrays is to use a single plane surface for all of the elements. The wind resistance of such plane reflectors, even of mesh, is notable, so individual reflectors are used instead. The required plane diameter is 3/4 λ, while other configurations are shown as "cup" reflectors with a depth of 3/8 λ. A ready-made reflector was found in the "pudding pan" shown in Fig 56. Details

HELIX PROPERTIES:
D = 2.880"
C = 9.048"
S = 2.062"
α = 12.84°
L = 9.280"
n = 28.5 turns
A = 59.16"
d = 0.375" x 0.004" Ribbon

Fig 51—All of the normally complicated element supports for helical antennas are unnecessary with the use of a copper-ribbon element.

Fig 52—Details of the H-frame support for the array, made from 2 × 1-inch aluminum channel stock.

(A)   (B)

Fig 53—Two views of the homemade stainless steel U-bolt, made from threaded rod stock.

Fig 54—Details of the outboard antenna struts.

APPLICATION	L	QUAN.
SPACER STRUT	23.00"	4
DIAGONAL STRUT	32.94"	1

NOTES:
1) MATERIAL: FIBERGLASS—EPOXY COMPOSITE, PVC, OR ANY OTHER WEATHER RESISTANT NON—CONDUCTING MATERIAL.

2) CROSS—SECTION DIMENSIONS ARE REFERENCED ONLY TO INDICATE THAT THE STRUT CONFIGURATION NEEDS TO BE STIFF, YET LIGHTWEIGHT.

Fig 55—The outboard end of the helix booms are closed to prevent animals from setting up housekeeping in the antenna. Also shown are the rivets holding the threaded inserts onto the 1/16-inch fiberglass-epoxy board. These provide attachment points for the dielectric braces on the boom ends.

(A)

(B)

Fig 57—Two views of the antenna reflector and matching section.

for mounting the boom tube and reflector to the H frame are also shown in Fig 56.

Matching the helical array to a 50-Ω feed line necessitates some choices. The nominal feed impedance of a helical antenna of 140 Ω can be realized with a tapered-impedance, open-line matching transition to a 50-Ω feed point. Using open feed lines in some environments is asking for trouble, so it was decided to match each individual antenna to a 50-Ω feed, and then use a four-port power divider to equally divide the power from a single feed line.

The peripheral, or tangential, antenna feed has been sucessfully used by amateurs. This feed scheme requires that the antenna element turn nearest the reflector be kept on its helical path until it intercepts the reflector, at which point the coaxial cable connector is mounted. Furthermore, the closest ¼-turn of the element is also used (with transmission line capacitive tuning) to match the feed to 50 Ω. Some aspects of this method would be difficult to employ with the dielectric boom-tube structure. Instead, a ¼-λ transition exits the boom tube toward the connector, across a controlled dielectric path—a sheet of 0.10-inch-thick Teflon.

Aside from the matching details shown in Fig 56, Figs 57A and 57B show the short section of copper ribbon soldered to the connector and to the element ribbon. This matching section is easy to build and adjust. No more than five minutes was consumed in measuring and adjusting the match. The ribbon is held as tightly to the Teflon as is possible, essentially creating a stripline conductor from the element to the connector.

With each antenna presenting a 50-Ω load, the task remained to connect all four feeds to a single 50-Ω feed line. There are a couple of ways to construct a four-port feed. Commercial power splitters are available, as noted in *QST* advertisements. George Chaney's (W5JTL) works of the past clearly show another way to construct the needed hardware to provide an "Extended/Expanded Power Divider."

This device, shown in Fig 58, consists of a pair of 50-Ω ¼-λ Q sections, which transform two 50-Ω antenna feeds to a 100-Ω impedance point. The Q sections are then joined to two equal (but not specific) length 100-Ω coaxial lines which, when combined at the center at the main feed line, look like

Fig 56—Details of the antenna reflector and feed matching. This reflector is made from a 3-quart "pudding pan" found in the housewares department of a hardware store.

Fig 58—Details of the four-port power divider.

50 Ω again. For convenience, this air-dielectric coaxial line was fabricated of square brass tubing, making for easy soldering of the connectors.

Fig 59 shows the coaxial line assembly mounted on the rear of the antenna H frame, by means of threaded rods that are silver brazed to the tube. Also shown in Fig 59 is the short 7-foot-long feed line from the power divider to the transmitter, contained inside the white box near the top of the tower. The antenna ports of the power divider are coupled to each antenna through four 2-λ lengths of Belden 9913 coax.

Some of the internal details of the power divider are further illustrated in Figs 60A and 60B. The lengths of the Q sections are based on free-space wavelengths, not allowing for any velocity constant. While this computation may not be the best, there was no better information available. The proof was in the testing. Four 50-Ω, 5-W, dc-to-10-GHz terminations were attached to the antenna ports of the jumper lines, and 15 W of RF was fed to the main feed port. No reflected power was observed at the main feed port, meaning that the match was probably better than 1.15:1, using available instrumentation.

(A)

(B)

Fig 59—The four-port power divider is mounted behind the H-frame with 2-λ jumpers made from Belden 9913 coaxial cable. The jumpers connect the divider to each antenna.

Fig 60—Two views of the construction details of the power divider.

Selected References

Satellite Equipment Selection

D. DeMaw, "Trio-Kenwood TS-700S 2-Meter Transceiver," *QST*, Feb 1978, pp 31-32.

C. Hutchinson, "TEN-TEC 2510 Mode B Satellite Station," *QST*, Oct 1985, pp 41-43.

D. Ingram, "The Ten-Tec 2510 OSCAR Satellite Station/Converter," *CQ Magazine*, Feb 1985, pp 44-46.

J. Kleinman, "ICOM IC-290H All-Mode 2-Meter Transceiver," *QST*, May 1983, pp 36-37.

J. Lindholm, "ICOM IC-471A 70-cm Transceiver," *QST*, Aug 1985, pp 38-39.

R. Schetgen, Ed., *The ARRL Radio Buyer's Sourcebook* (Newington: ARRL, 1991). A compilation of product reviews from *QST*.

M. Wilson, "ICOM IC-271A 2-Meter Multimode Transceiver," *QST*, May 1985, pp 40-41.

M. Wilson, "Yaesu Electronics Corp. FT-726R VHF/UHF Transceiver," *QST*, May 1984, pp 40-42.

M. Wilson, "Yaesu FT-480R 2-Meter Multimode Transceiver," *QST*, Oct 1981, pp 46-47.

H. Winard and R. Soderman, "A Survey of OSCAR Station Equipment," *Orbit*, No. 16, Nov-Dec 1983, pp 13-16 and No. 18, Mar-Apr 1984, pp 12-16.

Antennas

M. Davidoff, "Off-Axis Circular Polarization of Two Orthogonal Linearly Polarized Antennas," *Orbit*, No. 15, Sep-Oct 1983, pp 14-15.

J. L. DuBois, "A Simple Dish for Mode-L," *Orbit*, No. 13, Mar-Apr 1983, pp 4-6.

B. Glassmeyer, "Circular Polarization and OSCAR Communications," *QST*, May 1980, pp 11-15.

G. L. Hall, ed., *The ARRL Antenna Book* (Newington: ARRL, 1991). Available from your local radio store or from ARRL.

R. Jansson, "Helical Antenna Construction for 146 MHz," *Orbit*, May-June 1981, pp 12-15.

R. Jansson, "KLM 2M-22C and KLM 435-40CX Yagi Antennas," *QST*, Oct 1985, pp 43-44.

R. Jansson, "70-Cm Satellite Antenna Techniques," *Orbit*, No. 1, Mar 1980, pp 24-26.

C. Richards, "The Chopstick Helical," *Orbit*, No. 5, Jan-Feb 1981, pp 8-9.

V. Riportella, "Amateur Satellite Communications," *QST*, May 1986, pp 70-71.

G. Schrick, "Antenna Polarization," *The ARRL Antenna Compendium*, Vol 1 (Newington: ARRL 1985), pp 152-156.

A. Zoller, "Tilt Rather Than Twist," *Orbit*, No. 15, Sep-Oct 1983, pp 7-8.

Microsats

Loughmiller, D. and B. McGwier, "Microsat: The Next Generation of OSCAR Satellites." Part 1: *QST*, May 1989, pp 37-40. Part 2: *QST*, Jun 1989, pp 53-54, 70.

Loughmiller, D., "Successful OSCAR Launch Ushers in the '90s," *QST*, Apr 1990, pp 52-53.

Loughmiller, D., "DOVE: The Digital Orbiting Voice Encoder," *QST*, May 1990, pp 40-41.

Loughmiller, D., "WEBERSAT-OSCAR 18: Amateur Radio's Newest Eye in the Sky," *QST*, Jun 1990, pp 50-51.

Fuji-OSCARs

JARL, "Introduction of JAS-1b," *QEX*, Sep 1989, pp 12-15. Background and specifications for FO-12 and, before its launch, FO-20.

General Texts

M. Davidoff, *The Satellite Experimenter's Handbook* (Newington: ARRL, 1990.)

The ARRL Operating Manual (Newington: ARRL.)

The AMSAT-Phase III Satellite Operations Manual, prepared by Radio Amateur Satellite Corp and Project OSCAR, Inc, 1985. Available from AMSAT, 850 Sligo Ave, Silver Spring, MD 20910.

Glossary of Satellite Terminology

AMSAT — A registered trademark of the Radio Amateur Satellite Corporation, a nonprofit scientific/educational organization located in Washington, DC. It builds and operates Amateur Radio satellites and has sponsored the OSCAR program since the launch of OSCAR 5. (AMSAT, PO Box 27, Washington, DC 20044.)

Anomalistic period — The elapsed time between two successive perigees of a satellite.

AO-# — The designator used for AMSAT OSCAR spacecraft in flight, by sequence number.

AOS — Acquisition of signal — The time at which radio signals are first heard from a satellite, usually just after it rises above the horizon.

Apogee — The point in a satellite's orbit where it is farthest from Earth.

Area coordinators — An AMSAT corps of volunteers who organize and coordinate amateur satellite user activity in their particular state, municipality, region, or country. This is the AMSAT grassroots organization set up to assist all current and prospective OSCAR users.

Argument of perigee — The polar angle that locates the perigee point of a satellite in the orbital plane; drawn between the ascending node, geocenter, and perigee; and measured from the ascending node in the direction of satellite motion.

Ascending node — The point on the ground track of the satellite orbit where the subsatellite point (SSP) crosses the equator from the Southern Hemisphere into the Northern Hemisphere.

Az-el mount — An antenna mount that allows antenna positioning in both the azimuth and elevation planes.

Azimuth — Direction (side-to-side in the horizontal plane) from a given point on Earth, usually expressed in degrees. North = 0° or 360°; East = 90°; South = 180°; West = 270°.

Circular polarization (CP) — A special case of radio energy emission where the electric and magnetic field vectors rotate about the central axis of radiation. As viewed along the radiation path, the rotation directions are considered to be right-hand (RHCP) if the rotation is clockwise, and left-hand (LHCP) if the rotation is counterclockwise.

Descending node — The point on the ground track of the satellite orbit where the subsatellite point (SSP) crosses the equator from the Northern Hemisphere into the Southern Hemisphere.

Desense — A problem characteristic of many radio receivers in which a strong RF signal overloads the receiver, reducing sensitivity.

Doppler effect — An apparent shift in frequency caused by satellite movement toward or away from your location.

Downlink — The frequency on which radio signals originate from a satellite for reception by stations on Earth.

Eccentricity — The orbital parameter used to describe the geometric shape of an elliptical orbit; eccentricity values vary from e = 0 to e = 1, where e = 0 describes a circle and e = 1 describes a straight line.

EIRP — Effective isotropic radiated power. Same as ERP except the antenna reference is an isotropic radiator.

Elliptical orbit — Those orbits in which the satellite path describes an ellipse with the Earth at one focus.

Elevation — Angle above the local horizontal plane, usually specified in degrees. (0° = plane of the Earth's surface at your location; 90° = straight up, perpendicular to the plane of the Earth).

Epoch — The reference time at which a particular set of parameters describing satellite motion (Keplerian elements) are defined.

EQX — The reference equator crossing of the ascending node of a satellite orbit, usually specified in UTC time and degrees of longitude of the crossing.

ERP — Effective radiated power — System power output after transmission-line losses and antenna gain (referenced to a dipole) are considered.

ESA — European Space Agency — A consortium of European governmental groups pooling resources for space exploration and development.

FO-# — The designator used for Japanese

amateur satellites, by sequence number. Fuji-OSCAR 12 and Fuji-OSCAR 20 are the first two such spacecraft.

Geocenter — The center of the Earth.

Geostationary orbit — A satellite orbit at such an altitude (approximately 22,300 miles) over the equator that the satellite appears to be fixed above a given point.

Ground station — A radio station, on or near the surface of the earth, designed to transmit or receive to/from a spacecraft.

Groundtrack — The imaginary line traced on the surface of the Earth by the subsatellite point (SSP).

Inclination — The angle between the orbital plane of a satellite and the equatorial plane of the Earth.

Increment — The change in longitude of ascending node between two successive passes of a specified satellite, measured in degrees West per orbit.

Iskra — Soviet low-orbit satellites launched manually by cosmonauts aboard Salyut missions. Iskra means "spark" in Russian.

JAMSAT — Japan AMSAT organization.

Keplerian Elements — The classical set of six orbital element numbers used to define and compute satellite orbital motions. The set is comprised of inclination, Right Ascension of Ascending Node (RAAN), eccentricity, argument of perigee, mean anomaly and mean motion, all specified at a particular epoch or reference year, day and time. Additionally, a decay rate or drag factor is usually included to refine the computation.

LHCP — Left hand circular polarization.

LOS — Loss of signal — The time when a satellite passes out of range and signals from it can no longer be heard. This usually occurs just after the satellite goes below the horizon.

Mean anomaly (MA) — An angle that increases uniformly with time, starting at perigee, used to indicate where a satellite is located along its orbit. MA is usually specified at the reference epoch time where the Keplerian elements are defined. For AO-10 the orbital time is divided into 256 parts, rather than degrees of a circle, and MA (sometimes called phase) is specified from 0 to 255. Perigee is therefore at MA = 0 with apogee at MA = 128.

Mean motion — The Keplerian element to indicate the complete number of orbits a satellite makes in a day.

Microsat — Collective name given to a series of small amateur satellites having store-and-forward capability (OSCARs 14-19, for example).

NASA — National Aeronautics and Space Administration, the U.S. space agency.

Nodal period — The amount of time between two successive ascending nodes of a satellite orbit.

Orbital elements — See Keplerian Elements.

Orbital plane — An imaginary plane, extending throughout space, that contains the satellite orbit.

OSCAR — Orbiting Satellite Carrying Amateur Radio.

OSCARLOCATOR — A graphical satellite tracking device used to locate a satellite in its orbit and aid in pointing antennas.

Pass — An orbit of a satellite.

Passband — The range of frequencies handled by a satellite translator or transponder.

Perigee — The point in a satellite's orbit where it is closest to Earth.

Period — The time required for a satellite to make one complete revolution about the Earth. See Anomalistic period and Nodal period.

Phase I — The term given to the earliest, short-lived OSCAR satellites that were not equipped with solar cells. When their batteries were depleted, they ceased operating.

Phase II — Low altitude OSCAR satellites. Equipped with solar panels that powered the spacecraft systems and recharged their batteries, these satellites have been shown to be capable of lasting up to five years (OSCARs 6, 7 and 8, for example).

Phase III — Extended-range, high-orbit OSCAR satellites with very long-lived solar power systems (OSCARs 10 and 13, for example).

Phase IV — Proposed OSCAR satellites in geostationary orbits.

Precession — An effect that is characteristic of AO-10 and Phase III orbits. The satellite apogee SSP will gradually change over time.

Project OSCAR — The California-based group, among the first to recognize the potential of space for Amateur Radio; responsible for OSCARs I through IV.

QRP days — Special orbits set aside for very low power uplink operating through the satellites.

RAAN — Right Ascension of Ascending Node. The Keplerian element specifying the angular distance, measured eastward along the celestial equator, between the vernal equinox and the hour circle of the ascending node of a spacecraft. This can be simplified to mean roughly the longitude of the ascending node.

Radio Sputnik — Soviet Amateur Radio satellites (see RS #).

Reference orbit — The orbit of Phase II satellites beginning with the first ascending node during that UTC day.

RHCP — Right hand circular polarization.

RS # — The designator used for most Soviet Amateur Radio satellites (RS-1 through RS-13, for example).

Satellipse — A graphical tracking device, similar to OSCARLOCATOR, designed to be used with satellites in elliptical orbits.

Satellite pass — Segment of orbit during which the satellite "passes" nearby and in range of a particular ground station.

Sidereal day — The amount of time required for the Earth to rotate exactly 360 degrees about it's axis with respect to the "fixed" stars. The sidereal day contains 1436.07 minutes (see Solar day).

Solar day — The solar day, by definition, contains exactly 24 hours (1440 minutes). During the solar day, the Earth rotates slightly more than 360 degrees about its axis with respect to "fixed" stars (see Sidereal day).

Spin modulation — Periodic amplitude fade-and-peak resulting from the rotation of a satellite's antennas about its spin axis, rotating the antenna peaks-and-nulls.

SSC — Special service channels. Frequencies in the downlink passband of AO-10 that are set aside for authorized, scheduled use in such areas as education, data exchange, scientific experimentation, bulletins and official traffic.

SSP — Subsatellite point — Point on the surface of the Earth directly between the satellite and the geocenter.

Telemetry — Radio signals, originating at a satellite, that convey information on the performance or status of onboard subsystems. Also refers to the information itself.

Transponder — A device onboard a satellite that receives radio signals in one segment of the spectrum, amplifies them, translates (shifts) their frequency to another segment of the spectrum and retransmits them. Also called linear translator.

UoSAT-OSCAR (UO #) — Amateur Radio satellites built under the coordination of radio amateurs and educators at the University of Surrey, England.

Uplink — The frequency at which signals are transmitted from ground stations to a satellite.

Window — Overlap region between acquisition circles of two ground stations referenced to a specific satellite. Communication between two stations is possible when the subsatellite point is within the window.

Earth-Moon-Earth

EME communications, also known as "moonbounce," has become a popular form of space communication. The concept is simple: The moon is used as a passive reflector for VHF and UHF signals. With a total path length of nearly 500,000 miles, EME is the ultimate DX. EME is a natural and passive propagation phenomenon, and EME QSOs count toward the WAS, DXCC and VUCC awards. EME opens up the VHF and UHF bands to a new universe of worldwide DX.

The first demonstration of EME capability was done by the US Army Signal Corps just after WW II. In the 1950s, using 400 MW of effective rdiated power, the US Navy established a moon relay link between Washington, DC and Hawaii which could handle four multiplexed Teletype (RTTY) channels. The first successful amateur reception of EME signals occurred in 1953 by W4AO and W3GKP.

It took until 1960 for 2-way amateur communications to take place. Using surplus parabolic dish antennas and high-power klystron amplifiers, the Eimac Radio Club, W6HB, and the Rhododendron Swamp VHF Society, W1BU, accomplished this milestone in July 1960 on 1296 MHz. In the 1960s, the first wave of amateur EME enthusiasts established amateur-to-amateur contacts on 144 MHz and 432 MHz. In April 1964, W6DNG and OH1NL made the first 144-MHz EME QSO. 432-MHz EME experimentation was delayed by the 50-W power limit (removed January 2, 1963). Only one month after the first 144-MHz QSO was made, the 100-foot-diameter dish at Arecibo, Puerto Rico, was used to demonstrate the viability of 432-MHz EME, when a contact was made between KB4BPZ and W1BU. The first amateur-to-amateur 432-MHz EME QSO occurred in July 1964, between W1BU and KH6UK.

The widespread availability of reliable low-noise semiconductor devices along with significant improvements in Yagi arrays ushered in the second wave of amateur activity in the 1970s. Contacts between stations entirely built by amateurs became the norm instead of the exception. In 1970, the first 220- and 2304-MHz EME QSOs were made, followed by the first 50-MHz EME QSO in 1972. 1970s activity was still concentrated on 144 and 432 MHz, although 1296-MHz activity grew.

As the 1980s approached, another quantum leap in receive performance occurred with the use of GaAsFET preamplifiers. This, and improvements in Yagi performance (led by DL6WU's log-taper design work), and the new US amateur power-output limit of 1500 W have put EME in the grasp of most serious VHF and UHF operators. The 1980s saw 144- and 432-MHz WAS and WAC become a reality for a great number of operators. The 1980s also witnessed the first EME QSOs on 3456 MHz and 5760 MHz (1987), followed by EME QSOs on 902 MHz and 10 GHz (1988).

EME activity is still primarily a CW mode. As stations have improved, SSB is now more popular. Regardless of the transmission mode, successful EME operating requires:

1) As close to the legal power output as possible.

2) A fairly large array (compared to OSCAR antennas).

3) Accurate azimuth and elevation rotation.

4) Minimal transmission-line losses.

5) A low system noise figure, preferably with the preamplifier mounted at the array.

Choosing an EME Band

Making EME QSOs is a natural progression for many weak-signal terrestrial operators. Looking at EME path loss v frequency (Fig 61), it may seem as if the lowest frequency is best, because of reduced path loss. This is not entirely true. The path-loss graph does not account for the effects of cosmic and man-made noise, nor does it relate the effects of ionospheric scattering and absorption. Both short- and long-term fading effects also must be overcome.

50-MHz EME is quite a challenge as the required arrays are very large. In addition, sky noise limits receiver sensitivity at this frequency. Because of power and licensing restrictions, it is not likely that many foreign countries will be able to get on 50-MHz EME.

144 MHz is probably the easiest EME band to start on. It supports the largest number of EME operators. Commerical equipment is widely available; a 144-MHz EME station can almost be completely assembled from off-the-shelf equipment.

222 MHz is a good frequency for EME, but there are only a handful of active stations, and 222 MHz is available only in ITU Region 2.

432 MHz is the most active EME band after 144 MHz. Libration fading is more of a problem than at 144 MHz, but sky noise is more than an order of magnitude less than on 144 MHz. The improved receive signal-to-noise ratio may more than make up for the more rapid fading. However, 432-MHz activity is most concentrated into the one or two weekends a month when conditions are expected to be best.

902 MHz and above should be considered if you primarily enjoy experimenting and building equipment. If you plan to operate at these frequencies, an unobstructed moon window is a must. The antenna used is almost certain to be a dish. 902 MHz has the same problem that 222 MHz has—it's not an international band. Equipment and activity is expected to be limited for many years.

1296 MHz currently has a good amount of activity from all over the world. Recent equipment improvements indicate 1296 MHz should experience a significant growth in activity over the next few years. 2300 MHz has received renewed interest. It suffers from nonaligned international

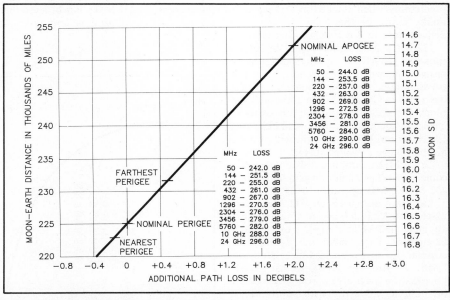

Fig 61—Variations in EME path loss can be determined from this graph. SD refers to semi-diameter of the moon, which is indicated for each day of the year in t he *The Nautical Almanac*.

band assignments and restrictions in different parts of the world.

Antenna Requirements

The tremendous path loss incurred over the EME circuit requires a high-power transmitter, a low-noise receiver and a high-performance antenna array. Although single-Yagi QSOs are possible, most new EME operators will rapidly become frustrated unless they are able to work many different stations on a regular basis. Because of libration fading and the nature of weak signals, a 1- or 2-dB increase in array gain will often be perceived as being much greater. An important antenna parameter in EME communications is the antenna noise temperature. This refers to the amount of noise received by the array. The noise comes from cosmic noise (noise generated by stars other than the sun), earth noise (thermal noise radiated by the earth), and noise generate by man-made sources such as power line leaks and other broadband RF sources.

Yagi antennas are almost universally used on 144 MHz. Although dish antennas as small as 24 feet in diameter have been successfully used, they offer poor gain-to-size trade-offs at 144 MHz. The minimum array gain for reliable operation is about 18 dBd (20.1 dBi). The minimum array gain should also allow a station to hear its own echoes on a regular basis. This is possible by using four 2.2-λ Yagis. The 12-element 2.5-λ Yagi described in Chapter 33 is an excellent choice. When considering a Yagi design, you should avoid old-technology Yagis, that is, designs that use either constant-width spacings, constant-length directors or a combination of both. These old-design Yagis will have significantly poorer side lobes, a narrower gain bandwidth and a sharper SWR bandwidth than modern log-taper designs. Modern wideband designs will behave much more predictably when stacked in arrays, and, unlike many of the older designs, will deliver close to 3 dB of stacking gain.

222-MHz requirements are similar to those of 144 MHz. Although dish antennas are somewhat more practical, Yagis still predominate. The 16-element 3.8-λ Yagi described in Chapter 33 is a good building block for 222-MHz EME. Four of these Yagis are adequate for a minimal 222-MHz EME station, but six or eight will provide a much more substantial signal.

At 432 MHz, parabolic-dish antennas become viable. The minimum gain for reliable 432-MHz EME operation is 24 dBi.

Yagis are also used on 432 MHz. the 22-element Yagi detailed in Chapter 33 is an ideal 432-MHz design. Four of the 22-element Yagis meet the 24-dBi-gain criteria, and have been used successfully on EME. If you are going to use fixed-polarization Yagi array, you should plan on building an array with substantially more than 24-dBi gain if you desire reliable contacts with small stations. This extra gain

is needed to overcome polarization misalignment.

At 902 MHz and above, the only antenna worthy of consideration is a parabolic dish. While it has been proven that Yagi antennas are capable of making EME QSOs at 1296 MHz, Yagi antennas, whether they use rod or loop elements, are simply not practical.

EME QSOs have been made at 1296 MHz with dishes as small as 6 feet in diameter. For reliable EME operation with similarly equipped stations, a 12-foot-diameter dish (31 dBi gain at 1296 MHz) is a practical minimum. TVRO dishes, which are designed to operate at 3 GHz, make excellent antennas, provided they have an accurate surface area. The one drawback of TVRO dishes is that they usually have an undesirable F/d ratio. More information on dish construction and feeds can be found in the *ARRL Antenna Book*.

Polarization Effects

All of the close attention paid to operating at the best time, such as nighttime perigee, with high moon declination and low sky temperatures is of little use if signals are not aligned in polarization between the two stations attempting to make contact. There are two basic polarization effects. The first is called spatial polarization. Simply stated, two stations (using az-el mounts and fixed linear polarization) that are located far apart, will usually not have their arrays aligned in polarization as seen by the moon. Spatial polarization can easily be predicted, given the location of both stations and the position of the moon.

The second effect is Faraday rotation. This is an actual rotation of the radio waves in space, and is caused by the charge level of the earth's ionosphere. At 1296 MHz and above, Faraday rotation is virtually nonexistent. At 432 MHz, it is believed that up to a 360° rotation is common. At 144 MHz, it is believed that the wavefront can actually rotate seven or more complete 360° revolutions. When Faraday rotation is combined with spatial polarization, there are four possible results:

1) Both stations hear each other and can QSO.

2) Station A hears station B, station B does not hear station A.

3) Station B hears station A, station A does not hear station B.

4) Neither station A not station B hear each other.

At 144 MHz, there are so many revolutions of the signal, and the amount of Faraday rotation changes so fast that, generally, hour-long schedules are arranged. At 432 MHz, Faraday rotation can take hours to change. Because of this, half-hour schedules are used. During the day time, you can count on 90 to 180° of rotation. If both stations are operating during hours of darkness, there will be little Faraday rotation, and the amount of spatial polarization determines if a schedule should be attempted.

At 1296 MHz and above, circular polarization is standard. The predominant array is a parabolic reflector, which makes circular polarization easy to obtain. Although the use of circular polarization would make one expect signals to be constant, except for the effect of the moon's distance, long-term fading of 6 to 9 dB is frequently observed.

With improved long-Yagi designs, for years the solution to overcoming polarization misalignment has been to make the array larger. Making your station's system gain 5 or 6 dB greater than required for minimal EME QSOs will allow you to work more stations, simply by moving you farther down the polarization loss curve. After about 60° of misalignment, however, making your station large enough to overcome the added losses quickly becomes a lifetime project! See Fig 62.

At 432 MHz and lower, Yagis are widely used, making the linear polarization

ATTENUATION V POLARIZATION MISALIGNMENT

ANGLE	—	LOSS
0°	—	0 dB
10°	—	0.13 dB
20°	—	0.54 dB
30°	—	1.25 dB
40°	—	2.32 dB
50°	—	3.84 dB
60°	—	6.02 dB
70°	—	9.32 dB
80°	—	15.2 dB
90°	—	∞

Fig 62—The graph shows how quickly loss because of polarization misalignment increases after 45°. The curve repeats through 360°, showing no loss at 0° and maximum loss at 90° and 270°.

standard. Although circular polarization may seem like a simple solution to polarization problems, when signals are reflected off the moon, the polarization sense of circularly polarized radio wave is reversed, requiring two arrays of opposite polarization sense be used. Initially, crossed Yagis with switchable polarization may also look attractive. Unfortunately, 432-MHz Yagis are physically small enough that the extra feed lines and switching devices become complicated, and usually adversely affect array performance. Keep in mind that even at 144 MHz, Yagis cannot tolerate metal mounting masts and frames in line with the Yagi elements.

When starting out on EME, keep in mind that it is best to use a simple system. You will still be able to work many of the larger fixed-polarization stations and those who have polarization adjustment (only one station needs to have polarization control). Once you gain understanding and confidence in your simple array, a more complex array such as one with polarization rotation can be attempted.

Receiver Requirements

A low-noise receiving setup is essential for successful EME work. Many EME signals are barely, but not always, out of the noise. To determine actual receiver performance, any phasing line and feed line losses, along with the noise generated in the receiver, must be added to the array noise reception. When all losses are considered, a system noise figure of 0.5 dB (35 K) will deliver about all the performance that can be used at 144 MHz, even when low-loss phasing lines and a quiet array are used.

The sky noise at 432 MHz and above is low enough (cold sky is < 15 K at 432 MHz, and 5 K at 1296 MHz) so the lowest possible noise figure is desired. Current high-performance arrays will have array temperatures near 30 K when unwanted noise pickup is added in. Phasing line losses must also be included, along with any relay losses. Even at 432 MHz, it is impossible to make receiver noise insignificant without the use of a liquid-cooled preamplifier. Current technology gives a minimum obtainable GaAsFET preamplifier noise figure, at room temperature, of about 0.35 dB (24 K). See Fig 63.

GaAsFET preamps have also been standard on 1296 MHz and above for several years. Noise figures range from about 0.4 dB at 1296 MHz (30 K) to about 2 dB (170 K at 10 GHz). HEMT devices are now available to amateurs, but are of little use below 902 MHz because of 1/f noise. At higher frequencies, HEMT devices have already shown impressively low noise figures. Current HEMT devices are capable of noise figures close to 1.2 dB at 10 GHz (93 K) without liquid cooling.

At 1296 MHz, a new noise-limiting factor appears. The physical temperature of the moon is 210 K. This means that just like the earth, it is a black-body radiator.

Fig 63—Two systems for switching a preamplifier in and out of the receive line. At A, a single length of cable is used for both the transmit and receive line. At B is a slightly more sophisticated system that uses two separate transmission lines. At C, a high-isolation relay is used for TR switching. The energized position is normally used on receive.

The additional noise source is the reflection of sun noise off the moon. Just as a full moon reflects sunlight light to earth, the rest of the electromagnetic spectrum is also reflected. On 144 and 432 MHz, the beamwidth of a typical array is wide enough (15° is typical for 144 MHz, 7° for 432 MHz) that the moon, which subtends a 0.5° area, is small enough to be insignificant in the array's pattern. At 1296 MHz, beamwidths approach 2°, and moon-noise figures of up to 5 dB are typical at full moon. Stations operating at 2300 MHz and above have such narrow array patterns that many operators actually use moon noise to assure that their arrays are pointed on the moon!

A new weak-signal operator is encouraged to experiment with receivers and filters. A radio with passband tuning or IF-shift capability is desired. These features are used to center the passband and the pitch of the CW signal to the frequency at which the operator's ears perform best. Some operators also use audio filtering. Audio filtering is efective in eliminating high-frequency noise generated in the radio's audio or IF stages. This noise can be very fatiguing during extended weak signal operation. The switched-capacitor audio filter has become popular with many operators.

Transmitter Requirements

Although the maximum legal power (1500 W out) is desirable, the actual power required can be considerably less, depending on the frequency of operation and size of the array. Given the minimum array-gain requirements previously discussed, the power levels recommended for reasonable success are shown in Table 8.

The amplifier and power supply should be constructed with adequate cooling and safety margins to allow extended slow-speed CW operation without failure. The transmitter must also be free from drift and chirp. The CW note must be pure and properly shaped. Signals that drift and chirp are harder to copy. They are especially annoying to operators who use narrow CW filters. A stable, clean signal will improve your EME success rate.

Calculating EME Capabilities

Once all station parameters are known, the expected strength of the moon echoes

---

Table 8

Transmitter Power Required for EME Success

Power at the array

50 MHz	1500 W
144 MHz	1000 W
222 MHz	750 W
432 MHz	500 W
902 MHz	200 W
1296 MHz	200 W
2300 MHz and above	100 W

can be calculated given the path loss for the band in use (see Fig 61). The formula for the received signal-to-noise ratio is:

$$S/N = P_p - L_t + G_t - P_l + G_r - P_n \quad \text{(Eq 1)}$$

where

P_o = transmitter output power (dBW)
L_t = transmitter feed-line loss (dB)
G_t = transmitting antenna gain (dBi)
P_l = total path loss (dB)
G_r = receiving antenna gain (dBi)
P_n = receiver noise power (dBW)

Receiver noise power, P_n, is determined by the following:

$$P_n = 10 \log_{10} K \times B \times T_s \quad \text{(Eq 2)}$$

where

K = 1.38×10^{-23} (Boltzmann's constant)
B = bandwidth (Hz)
T_s = receiving system noise temperature (K)

Receiving system noise temperature, T_s, can be found from:

$$T_s = T_a + (L_r - 1) T_l + L_r T_r \quad \text{(Eq 3)}$$

where

T_a = antenna temperature (K)
L_r = receiving feed-line loss (ratio)
T_l = physical temperature of feed line (normally 290 K)
T_r = receiver noise temperature (K)

An example calculation for a typical 432-MHz EME link is:

P_o = +30 dBW (1000 W)
L_t = 1.0 dB
G_t = 26.4 dBi (8 × 6.1-λ 22-el Yagis)
P_l = 262 dB
G_r = 23.5 dBi (15 ′ parabolic)
T_a = 60 K
L_r = 1.02 (0.1-dB preamp at antenna)
T_l = 290 K
T_r = 35.4 K (NT = 0.5 dB)
T_s = 101.9 K
P_n = −188.5 dB
S/N = +5.4 dB

It is obvious that EME is no place for a compromise station. Even relatively sophisticated equipment provides less-than-optimum results.

Fig 64 gives parabolic dish gain for a perfect dish. The best Yagi antennas will not exceed the gain curve shown in Chapter 33. If you are using modern, log-taper Yagis, properly spaced, figure about 2.8 to 2.9 dB of stacking gain. For old-technology Yagis, 2.5 dB may be closer to reality. Any phasing line and power divider losses must also be subtracted from the array gain.

Locating the Moon

The moon orbits the earth once in approximately 28 days, a lunar month. Because the plane of the moon's orbit is tilted from the earth's equatorial plane by approximately 23.5°, the moon swings in a sine-wave pattern both north and south of the equator. The angle of departure of the moon's position at a given time from the equatorial plane is termed *declination* (abbreviated decl). Declination angles of the moon, which are continually changing (a few degrees a day), indicate the latitude on the earth's surface where the moon will be at zenith. For this presentation, positive declination angles are used when the moon is north of the equator, and negative angles when south.

The longitude on the earth's surface where the moon will be at zenith is related to the moon's *Greenwich Hour Angle*, abbreviated G.H.A. or GHA. "Hour angle" is defined as the angle in degrees to the west of the meridian. If the GHA of the moon were zero degrees, it would be directly over the Greenwich meridian. If the moon's GHA were 15 degrees, the moon would be directly over the meridian designated as 15° W longitude on a globe. As one can readily understand, the GHA of the moon is continually changing, too, because of both the orbital velocity of the moon and the earth's rotation inside the moon's orbit. The moon's GHA changes at the rate of approximately 347° per day.

GHA and declination are terms that may be applied to any celestial body. *The Nautical Almanac* and other publications list the GHA and decl of the sun and moon (as well as for other celestial bodies that may be used for navigation) for every hour of the year. This information may be used to point an antenna when the moon is not visible. Almanac tables for the sun may be useful for calibrating remote-readout systems.

Using the Almanac

The Nautical Almanac and other almanacs show the GHA and declination of the sun or moon at hourly intervals for every day of the period covered by the book. Instructions are included in such books for interpolating the positions of the sun or moon for any time on a given date. The orbital velocity of the moon is not constant, and therefore precise interpolations are not linear.

Fortunately, linear interpolations from one hour to the next, or even from one day to the next, will result in data that is entirely adequate for Amateur Radio purposes. If linear interpolations are made from 0000 UTC on one day to 0000 UTC on the next, worse-case conditions exist when apogee or perigee occurs near mid-day on the next date in question. Under such conditions, the total angular error in the position of the moon may be as much as a sixth of a degree. Because it takes a full year for the earth to orbit the sun, the similar error for determining the position of the sun will be no more than a few hundredths of a degree.

If a polar mount (a system having one axis parallel to the earth's axis) is used, information from the *Almanac* may be used directly to point the antenna array. The local hour angle (LHA) is simply the GHA plus or minus the observer's longitude (plus if east long., minus if west). The LHA is the angle west of the observer's meridian at which the celestial body is located. LHA and declination information may be translated to an EME window by taking local obstructions and any other constraints into account.

Azimuth and Elevation

An antenna system that is positioned in azimuth (compass direction) and elevation (angle above the horizon) is called an *az-el* system. For such a system, some additional work will be necessary to convert the almanac data into useful information. The GHA and decl information may be converted into azimuth and elevation angles with the mathematical equations that follow. An electronic calculator or computer that treats trigonometric functions may be used. CAUTION: Most

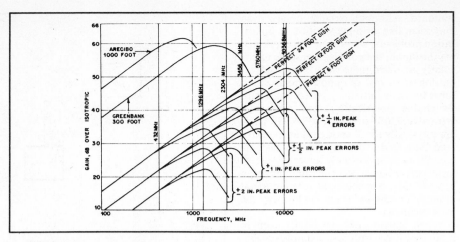

Fig 64—Parabolic-antenna gain v size, frequency and surface errors. All curves assumed 60/ aperture efficiency and 10-dB power taper. References: J. Ruze, British IEEE.

almanacs list data in degrees, minutes, and either decimal minutes or seconds. Computer or calculator programs generally require this information in degrees and decimal fractions, so a conversion may be necessary before the almanac data is entered.

Determining az-el data from equations follows a procedure similar to calculating great-circle bearings and distances for two points on the earth's surface. There is one additional factor, however. Visualize two observers on opposite sides of the earth who are pointing their antennas at the moon. Imaginary lines representing the boresights of the two antennas will converge at the moon at an angle of approximately 2°. Now assume both observers aim their antennas at some distant star. The boresight lines now may be considered to be parallel, each observer having raised his antenna in elevation by approximately 1°. The reason for the necessary change in elevation is that the earth's diameter in comparison to its distance from the moon is significant. The same is not true for distant stars, or for the sun.

Equations for az-el calculations are:

$$\sin E = \sin L \sin D + \cos L \cos D \cos LHA \qquad \text{(Eq 4)}$$

$$\tan F = \frac{\sin E - K}{\cos E} \qquad \text{(Eq 5)}$$

$$\cos C = \frac{\sin D - \sin E \sin L}{\cos E \cos L} \qquad \text{(Eq 6)}$$

where

E = elevation angle for the sun
L = your latitude (negative if south)
D = declination of the celestial body
LHA = local hour angle = GHA plus or minus your longitude (plus if east long., minus if west long.)
F = elevation angle for the moon
K = 0.01657, a constant (see text that follows)
C = true azimuth from north if sin LHA is negative; if sin LHA is positive, then the azimuth = 360 minus C

Assume our location is 50° N lat, 100° W long. Further assume that the GHA of the moon is 140° and its declination is 10°. To determine the az-el information we first find the LHA, which is 140 minus 100 or 40°. Then we solve Eq 4:

$$\sin E = \sin 50 \sin 10 + \cos 50 \cos 10 \cos 40$$

$$\sin E = 0.61795 \text{ and } E = 38.2°$$

Solving Eq 5 for F, we proceed. (The value for sin E has already been determined in Eq 4.)

$$\tan F = \frac{0.61795 - 0.06175}{\cos 38.2}$$

$$= 0.76489$$

From this, F, the moon's elevation angle, is 37.4°.

We continue by solving Eq 6 for C. (The value of sin E has already been determined.)

$$\cos C = \frac{\sin 10 - 0.61795 \sin 50}{\cos 38.2 \cos 50}$$

$$= -0.59308$$

C therefore equals 126.4°. To determine if C is the actual azimuth, we find the polarity for sin LHA, which is sin 40° and has a positive value. The actual azimuth then is 360 − C = 233.6°.

If az-el data is being determined for the sun, use of Eq 5 must be omitted; Eq 5 takes into account the nearness of the moon. The solar elevation angle may be determined from Eq 4 alone. In the above example, this angle is 38.2°.

The mathematical procedure is the same for any location on the earth's surface. Remember to use negative values for southerly latitudes. If solving Eq 4 or 5 yields a negative value for E or F, this indicates the celestial body below the horizon.

These equations may also be used to determine az-el data for man-made satellites, but a different value for the constant, K, must be used. K is defined as the ratio of the earth's radius to the distance from the earth's center to the satellite.

The value for K as given above, 0.01657, is based on an average earth-moon distance of 239,000 miles. The actual earth-moon distance varies from approximately 225,000 to 253,000 mi. When this change in distance is taken into account, it yields a change in elevation angle of approximately 0.1° when the moon is near the horizon. For greater precision in determining the correct elevation angle for the moon, the moon's distance from the earth may be taken as:

$$D = -15,074.5 \times SD + 474,332$$

where

D = moon's distance in miles
SD = moon's semi-diameter, from the almanac.

Calculator and Computer Programs

As has been mentioned, a calculator or computer may be used in solving the equations for azimuth and elevation. Tables in this section list suitable programs. The program of Table 9 is for Hewlett-Packard HP-25 and similar calculators using reverse Polish notation (RPN). With this program, the GHA and declination of a celestial body are entered for a particular time of day, and the calculator computes the azimuth and elevation for that time. Calculations must then be repeated for a different time of day, by using different GHA and declination values, as appropriate. For EME work, it is convenient to calculate az-el data at 30-minute intervals or so, and to keep the results of all calculations handy during the EME window. Necessary antenna-position corrections can then be made periodically.

Table 10 is a BASIC language program

Table 9

Calculator Program for Determining Azimuth and Elevation of Celestial Bodies

Line	Key Entry
01	RCL 1
02	−
03	STO 4
04	f cos
05	x ≥ y
06	STO 5
07	f cos
08	X
09	RCL 0
10	f cos
11	STO 6
12	X
13	RCL 0
14	f sin
15	STO 7
16	RCL 5
17	f sin
18	STO 5
19	X
20	+
21	STO X 7
22	Enter ↑
23	g sin⁻¹
24	f cos
25	STO X 6

Use these program steps for the moon (lines 21-25)

Use these program steps for the sun and distant bodies

26	g 1/x	26	f Last x
27	x ≥ y	27	GTO 32

28	RCL 3
29	−
30	X
31	g tan⁻¹
32	RCL 5
33	RCL 7
34	−
35	RCL 6
36	÷
37	g cos⁻¹
38	RCL 4
39	f sin
40	g x ≥ 0
41	GTO 44
42	R↓
43	GTO 00 (or R/S)
44	R↓
45	CHS
46	RCL 2
47	+
48	GTO 00 (or R/S)

Instructions

1) Load the program, selecting lines 26 and 27 for either the moon or for more distant bodies. Switch to RUN.

2) Initialize: f PRGM; f FIX 1; g DEG

3) Store constants: 360 STO 2; 0.01657 STO 3

4) Store data
Your latitude (degrees and decimal; negative if east) STO 0
Your longitude (degrees and decimal; negative if east) STO 1

5) Input data:
Decl. of celestial body (degrees and decimal) Enter ↑
GHA of celestial body (degrees and decimal) R/S
The result displayed after a few seconds is the azimuth or bearing in degrees clockwise from north.
Depressing x ≥ y displays the elevation angle above the horizon. (The body is below the horizon if a negative angle is displayed.)

6) For another az-el calculation from the same location, go to step 5.

7) For az-el calculations from a different location on the earth's surface, go to step 4 using new latitude and longitude.

Table 10

Computer Program for Determining Azimuth and Elevation of Celestial Bodies

```
10 REM * * * MOONTRAK.BAS * * *
20 CLS:PRINT"PROGRAM TO CALCULATE AZ-EL DATA FOR THE SUN OR MOON"
30 PRINT:PRINT"Program by J. Hall, K1TD, ARRL Hq., Rev 1.1, June 1983":PRINT
40 PRINT"This program may be reproduced without prior permission"
50 PRINT"provided The ARRL Handbook is credited.":PRINT
60 B$="###.#":I=57.2958:K=.01657
70 PRINT"Enter negative values for southerly latitudes."
80 PRINT"Enter negative values for easterly longitudes."
90 PRINT:INPUT"Your latitude (degrees and decimal)";A
100 INPUT"Your longitude (degrees and decimal)";L1
110 D=SIN(A/I):F=COS(A/I)
120 INPUT"UTC date (no comma, please)";A$
130 INPUT"Data for which, sun or moon";C$:PRINT
140 PRINT A$" GHA of ";C$;" at 0000 UTC":INPUT"   (degrees and decimal)";L2
150 PRINT A$" declination at 0000 UTC":INPUT"   (degrees and decimal)";B1
160 PRINT A$" GHA at 2400 UTC":INPUT"   (degrees and decimal)";L3
170 PRINT A$" declination at 2400 UTC":INPUT"   (degrees and decimal)";B2
180 GI=(L3+360-L2)/24
190 BI=(B2-B1)/24
200 J%=0:GOSUB 330
210 FOR A%=0 TO 48:G=SIN(B1/I):L=L2-L1
220 E=D*G+F*COS(B1/I)*COS(L/I):C=(G-D*E)/F:J=E
230 IF E>=1 THEN E=1.5708:GOTO 250
240 IF E<=-1 THEN E=-1.5708 ELSE E=ATN(E/SQR(ABS(1-E*E)))
250 C=C/COS(E):IF C>=1 THEN C=0:GOTO 270
260 IF C<=-1 THEN C=180 ELSE C=I*(-ATN(C/SQR(ABS(1-C*C)))+1.5708)
270 IF LEFT$(C$,1)="M" OR LEFT$(C$,1)="m" THEN GOSUB 430
280 E=I*E:IF J%=8 AND E>=0 THEN GOSUB 410
290 IF E>=0 THEN GOSUB 360
300 B1=B1+BI/2:L2=L2+GI/2:IF L2>360 THEN L2=L2-360
310 NEXT:PRINT:PRINT"Data for ";A$;" is completed for the ";C$
320 INPUT"To continue, press enter";J%:CLS:PRINT"Next ";:GOTO 120
330 CLS:PRINT"Data for the ";C$" from ";A;"deg. lat., ";L1;"deg. long."
340 PRINT"for ";A$:PRINT
350 PRINT"Time, UTC","Azimuth","Elevation":PRINT:RETURN
360 IF INT(A%/2)=A%/2 THEN D$=STR$(50*A%) ELSE D$=STR$(50*A%-20)
370 D$=RIGHT$(D$,LEN(D$)-1)
380 IF LEN(D$)<4 THEN D$="0"+D$:GOTO 380
390 PRINT D$,:IF SIN(L/I)<=0 THEN PRINT USING B$;C; ELSE PRINT USING B$;360-C;
400 PRINT TAB(32);:PRINT USING B$;E:J%=J%+1:RETURN
410 PRINT:INPUT"For more data press enter";J%
420 J%=0:GOSUB 330:RETURN
430 J=(J-K)/COS(E):E=ATN(J):RETURN
440 REM NOTE:  % = integer
```

for the IBM PC. This program provides azimuth and elevation information for half-hour intervals during a UTC day when the celestial body is above the horizon. The program makes a linear interpolation of GHA and declination values (discussed earlier) during the period of the UTC day.

With the program of Table 10 in operation, the computer first asks for various data to be entered via the keyboard, including GHA and declination for 2400 UTC for the date of the calculations. This data, of course, will be the same as for 0000 UTC for the following day from the almanac. After all data is entered, the computer performs calculations for each half hour. Only those results for which the body is above the horizon are displayed, so there may be a period of 15 seconds or more during which nothing appears to be happening. This is normal. The program may be modified to print the results of calculations on paper if a line printer is available, or to adapt it for use on other computers with variations in BASIC language.

Either of these programs may be used for determining the azimuth and elevation for more distant bodies, by using program steps 26 and 27 for the sun in Table 9, or by entering SUN at the keyboard for statement 130 in Table 10. Further, Table 9 may be used for determining the positiions of man-made satellites for a given time, if the appropriate value for the constant K is stored in register 3. For this application, the coordinates of the sub-satellite point are used in place of GHA and declination.

Libration Fading of EME Signals

One of the most troublesome aspects of receiving a moonbounce signal, besides the enormous path loss and Faraday rotation fading, is *libration fading*. This section will deal with libration (pronounced lie-*bray*-shun) fading, its cause and effects, and possible measures to minimize it.

Libration fading of an EME signal is characterized in general as fluttery, rapid, irregular fading not unlike that observed in tropospheric scatter propagation. Fading can be very deep, 20 dB or more, and the maximum fading will depend on the operating frequency. At 1296 MHz the maximum fading rate is about 10 Hz, and scales directly with frequency.

On a weak CW EME signal, libration fading gives the impression of a randomly keyed signal. In fact on very slow CW telegraphy the effect is as though the keying is being done at a much faster speed. On very weak signals only the peaks of libration fading are heard in the form of occasional short bursts or "pings."

Fig 65 shows samples of a typical EME echo signal at 1296 MHz. These recordings, made at W2NFA, show the wild fading characteristics with sufficient S/N ratio to record the deep fades. Circular polarization was used to eliminate Faraday fading; thus these recordings are of libration fading only. The recording bandwidth was limited to about 40 Hz to minimize the higher sideband-frequency components of libration fading that exist but are much smaller in amplitude. For those who would like a better statistical description, libration fading is Raleigh distributed. In the recordings shown in Fig 65, the average signal-return level computed from path loss and mean reflection coefficient of the moon is at about the +15 dB S/N level.

It is clear that enhancement of echoes far in excess of this average level is observed. This point should be kept clearly in mind when attempting to obtain echoes or receive EME signals with marginal equipment. The probability of hearing an occasional peak is quite good since random enhancement as much as 10 dB is possible. Under these conditions, however, the amount of useful information that can be copied will be near zero. Enthusiastic newcomers to EME communications will be stymied by this effect since they know they can hear the signal strong enough on peaks to copy but can't make any sense out of what they try to copy.

What causes libration fading? Very simply, multipath scattering of the radio

Fig 65—Chart recording of moon echoes received at W2FNA on July 26, 1973, at 1630 UTC. Antenna gain 44 dBi, transmitting power 400 watts and system temperature 400 K.

waves from the very large (2000-mile diameter) and rough moon surface combined with the relative motion between earth and moon called librations.

To understand these effects, assume first that the earth and moon are stationary (no libration) and that a plane wave front arrives at the moon from your earthbound station as shown in Fig 66A.

The reflected wave shown in Fig 66B consists of many scattered contributions from the rough moon surface. It is perhaps easier to visualize the process as if the scattering were from many small individual flat mirrors on the moon that reflect small portions (amplitudes) of the incident wave energy in different directions (paths) and with different path lengths (phase). Those paths directed toward the moon arrive at your antenna as a collection of small wave fronts (field vectors) of various amplitudes and phases. The vector summation of all these coherent (same frequency) returned waves (and there is a near-infinite array of them) takes place at the feed point of your antenna (the collecting point in your antenna system). The level of the final summation as measured by a receiver can, of course, have any value from zero to some maximum. Remember that we assumed the earth and moon were stationary, which means that the final summation of these multipath signal returns from the moon will be one fixed value. The condition of zero relative motion between earth and moon is a rare event that will be discussed later in this section.

Consider now that the earth and moon are moving relative to each other (as they are in nature), so the incident radio wave "sees" a slightly different surface of the moon from moment to moment. Since the lunar surface is very irregular, the reflected wave will be equally irregular, changing in

Fig 66—How the rough surface of the moon reflects a plane wave as one having many field vectors.

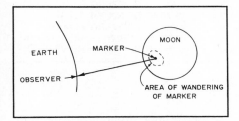

Fig 67—The moon appears to "wander" in its orbit about the earth. Thus a fixed marker on the moon's surface will appear to move about in a circular area.

amplitude and phase from moment to moment. The resultant continuous summation of the varying multipath signals at your antenna feed point produces the effect called libration fading of the moon-reflected signal.

The term libration is used to describe small perturbations in the movement of celestial bodies. Each libration consists mainly of its diurnal rotation; moon libration consists mainly of its 28-day rotation, which appears as a very slight rocking motion with respect to an observer on earth.

This rocking motion can be visualized as follows: Place a marker on the surface of the moon at the center of the moon disc, which is the point closest to the observer, as shown in Fig 67. Over time, we will observe that this marker wanders around within a small area. This means the surface of the moon as seen from the earth is not quite fixed but changes slightly as different areas of the periphery are exposed because of this rocking motion. Moon libration is very slow (on the order of 10^{-7} radians per second) and can be determined with some difficulty from published moon ephemeris tables.

Although the libration motions are very small and slow, the larger surface area of the moon has nearly an infinite number of scattering points (small area). This means that even slight geometric movements can alter the total summation of the returned multipath echo by a significant amount. Since the librations of the earth and moon are calculable, it is only logical to ask if there ever occurs a time when the total libration is zero or near zero. The answer is yes, and it has been observed and verified experimentally on radar echoes that minimum fading rate (not depth of fade) is coincident with minimum total libration. Calculation of minimum total libration is at best tedious and can only be done successfully by means of a computer. It is a problem in extrapolation of rates of change in coordinate motion and in small differences of large numbers.

EME OPERATING TECHNIQUES

Many EME signals are near the threshold of readability, a condition caused by a combination of path loss, Faraday rotation and libration fading. This weakness and unpredictability of the signals has led to the development of techniques for the exchange of EME information that differ from those used for normal terrestrial work. The fading of EME signals chops dashes into pieces and renders strings of dots incomplete. This led to the use of the "T M O R" reporting system. Different, but similar, systems are used on the low bands (50 and 144 MHz) and the high bands (432 MHz and above). Tables 11 and 12 summarize the differences between the two systems.

As equipment and techniques have improved, the use of normal RST signal reports has become more common. It is now quite common for two stations working for the first time to go straight to RST reports if signals are strong enough. These normal reports let stations compare signals from one night to the next. EME QSOs are often made during the ARRL VHF contests. These contacts require the exchange of 4-digit grid locators. On 432 MHz and above, the sending of "GGGG" has come to mean "Please send me your grid square," or conversely, "I am now going to send my grid square."

The length of transmit and receive periods is also different between the bands. On 50 and 144 MHz, 2-minute sequences are used. That is, stations transmit for two full minutes, and then receive for two full minutes. One-hour schedules are used, with the eastern-most station (referenced to the international date line) transmitting first. Table 13 gives the 2-minute sequence procedure. On 222 MHz, both the 144-MHz and 432-MHz systems are used.

On 432 MHz and above, 2½-minute sequences are standard. The longer period is used to let stations with variable polarization have adequate time to peak the signal. The last 30 seconds is reserved for signal reports only. Table 14 provides more information on the 432-MHz EME QSO sequence. The western-most station usually transmits first. However, if one of the stations has variable polarization, it may elect to transmit second, to take the opportunity to use the first sequence to peak the signal. If both stations have variable polarization, the station that transmits first should leave its polarization fixed on transmit, to avoid "polarization chasing."

CW sending speed is usually in the 10- to 13-WPM range. It is often best to use greater-than-normal spacing between individual dits and dahs, as well as between complete letters. This helps to overcome libration fading effects. The libration fading rate will be different from one band to another. This makes the optimum CW speed for one band different from another. Keep in mind that characters sent too slowly will be chopped up by typical EME fading. Morse code sent too fast will simply be jumbled. Pay attention to the sending practices of the more successful stations, and try to emulate them.

Doppler shift must also be understood. As the moon rises or sets it is moving

Table 11
Signal Reports Used on 144-MHz EME

T — Signal just detectable
M — Portions of call copied
O — Complete call set has been received
R — Both "O" report and call sets have been received
$\overline{SK}$ — End of contact

Table 12
Signal Reports Used on 432-MHz EME

T — Portions of call copied
M — Complete calls copied
O — Good signal—solid copy (possibly enough for SSB work)
R — Calls and reports copied
$\overline{SK}$ — End of contact

Table 13
144-MHz Procedure—2-Minute Sequence

Period	1½ minutes	30 seconds
1	Calls (W6XXX DE W1XXX)	
2	W1XXX DE W6XXX	T T T T
3	W6XXX DE W1XXX	O O O O
4	RO RO RO RO	DE W1XXX K
5	R R R R R	DE W6XXX K
6	QRZ? EME	DE W1XXX K

Table 14
432-MHz Procedure—2½-Minute Sequence

Period	2 minutes	30 seconds
1	VE7BBG DE K2UYH	
2	K2UYH DE VE7BBG	
3	VE7BBG DE K2UYH	T T T
4	K2UYH DE VE7BBG	M M M
5	RM RM RM RM	DE K2UYH K
6	R R R R R	DE VE7BBG $\overline{SK}$

towards or away from objects on earth. This leads to a frequency shift in the moon echoes. The amount of Doppler shift is directly proportional to frequency. At 144 MHz, about 500 Hz is the maximum shift. On 432 MHz, the maximum shift is 1.5 kHz. The shift is upward on moonrise and downward on moon set. When the moon is due south, your own echoes will have no Doppler shift, but stations located far away will still be affected. For scheduling, the accepted practice is to transmit zero beat on the schedule frequency, and tune to compensate for the Doppler shift. Be careful—most transmitters and transceivers have a built in CW offset. Some radios read this offset when transmitting, and others don't. Find out how your transmitter operates and compensate as required.

Random operation has become popular

in recent years. In the ARRL EME contest, many of the big guns will not even accept schedules during the contest periods, because they can slow down the pace of their contest contacts.

EME Operating Times

Obviously, the first requirement for EME operation is to have the moon visible by both EME stations. This requirement not only consists of times when the moon is above the horizon, but when it is actually clear of obstructions such as trees and buildings. It helps to know your exact EME operating window, specified in the form of beginning and ending GHAs (Greenwich Hour Angle) for different moon declinations. This information allows two different stations to quickly determine if they can simultaneously see the moon.

Once your moon window is determined, the next step is to decide on the best times during that window to schedule or operate. Operating at perigee is preferable because of the reduced path loss. Fig 61 shows that not all perigees are equal. There is about a 0.6-dB difference between the closest and farthest perigee points. The next concern is operating when the moon is in a quiet spot of the sky. Usually, northern declinations are preferred, as the sky is quietest at high declinations. If the moon is too close to the sun, your array will pick up sun noise and reduce the sensitivity off your receiver. Finally, choosing days with minimal libration fading is also desirable.

Perigee and apogee days can be determined from the *Nautical Almanac* by inspecting the tables headed "S.D." (semidiameter of the moon in minutes of arc). These semi-diameter numbers can be compared to Fig 61 to obtain the approximate moon distance. Many computer programs for locating the moon now give the moon's distance. The expected best weekends to operate on 432 MHz and the higher bands are normally printed well in advance in various EME newsletters.

When the moon passes through the galactic plane, sky temperature is at its maximum. Even on the higher bands this is one of the least desirable times to operate. The areas of the sky to avoid are the constellations of Orion and Gemini (during northern declinations), and Sagittarius and Scorpius (during southern declinations). The position of the moon relative to these constellations can be checked with information supplied in the *Nautical Alamanac* or *Sky and Telescope* magazine.

Frequencies and Scheduling

According to the ARRL-sponsored band plan, the lower edge of most bands is reserved for EME operation. On 144 MHz, EME frequencies are primarily between 144.000 and 144.080 MHz for CW, and 144.100 and 144.120 MHz for SSB. Random CW activity is usually between 144.000 and 144.020 MHz. In the US,

144.000 to 144.100 MHz is a CW subband, so SSB QSOs often take place by QSYing up 100 kHz after a CW contact has been established. Because of the large number of active 144-MHz stations, coordinating schedules in the small EME window is not simple. The more active stations usually have assigned frequencies for their schedules.

On 432 MHz, the international EME CW calling frequency is 432.010 MHz. Random SSB calling is done on 432.015 MHz. Random activity primarily takes place between 432.000 and 432.020 MHz. The greater Doppler shift on 432 MHz requires greater separation between schedule frequencies than on 144 MHz. Normally 432.000 MHz, 432.020 MHz and each 5-kHz increment up to 432.070 MHz are used for schedules.

Activity on 1296 MHz is centered between 1296.000 and 1296.040 MHz. The random calling frequency is 1296.010 MHz. Operation on the other bands requires more specific coordination. Activity on 33 cm is split between 902 and 903 MHz. Activity on 2300 MHz has to accommodate split-band procedures because of the different band assignments around the world.

EME Net Information

An EME net meets on 14.345 MHz on weekends for the purpose of arranging schedules and exchanging EME information. The net meets at 1600 UTC. OSCAR satellites are becoming more popular for EME information exchange. When Mode B is available, a downlink frequency of 145.950 MHz is where the EME group gathers. On Mode L and Mode JL, the downlink frequency is 435.975 MHz.

Other Modes

Most EME contacts are still made on CW, although SSB has gained in popularity and it is now common to hear SSB QSOs on any activity weekend. The ability to work SSB can easily be calculated from Eq 1. The proper receiver bandwidth (2.3 kHz) is substituted. SSB usually requires a +3-dB signal-to-noise ratio, whereas slow-speed CW contacts can be made with a 0-dB signal-to-noise ratio. Slow-scan television and packet communication has been attempted between some of the larger stations. Success has been limited because of the greater signal-to-noise ratios required for these modes, and severe signal distortion from libration fading.

Chapter 24

Construction Techniques

While a better job can be done with a variety of tools, by taking little care it is possible to turn out a fine piece of equipment with only a few common hand tools. A list of tools that are indispensable in the construction of electronic equipment is found on this page. With these tools it should be possible to prepare panels and metal chassis for assembly and wiring. It is an excellent idea for the amateur who builds gear to add tools from time to time as finances permit.

RECOMMENDED TOOLS AND MATERIALS

Long-nose pliers, 6- and 4-inch
Diagonal cutters, 6- and 4-inch
Combination pliers, 6-inch
Screwdriver 6- to 7-inch, 1/4-inch blade
Screwdriver, 4- to 5-inch, 1/8-inch blade
Phillips screwdriver, 6- to 7-inch
Phillips screwdriver, 3- to 4-inch
Long-shank screwdriver with holding clip on blade
Scratch awl or scriber for marking metal
Combination square, 12-inch, for layout work
Hand drill, 1/4-inch chuck or larger
Soldering pencil, 30-watt, 1/8-inch tip
Soldering iron, 200-watt, 5/8-inch tip
Hacksaw and 12-inch blades
Hand nibbling tool, for chassis-hole cutting
Hammer, ball-peen, 1-lb head
Heavy-duty jackknife
File set, flat, round, half-round, and triangular. Large and miniature types recommended
High-speed drill bits, no. 60 through 3/8-inch diameter
Set of Spintite socket wrenches for hex nuts
Adjustable wrenches, 6- and 10-inch
Machine-screw taps, 4-40 through 10-32 thread
Socket punches, 1/2 in, 5/8 in, 3/4 in, 1-1/8 in, 1-1/4 in, and 1-1/2 in
Tapered reamer, T-handle, 1/2-inch maximum width
Bench vise, 4-inch jaws or larger
Medium-weight machine oil
Tin shears, 10-inch
Motor-driven emery wheel for grinding

Table 1
Numbered Drill Sizes

No.	Diameter (Mils)	Will Clear Screw	Drilled for Tapping from Steel or Brass
1	228.0	12-24	—
2	221.0	—	—
3	213.0	—	14-24
4	209.0	12-20	—
5	205.0	—	—
6	204.0	—	—
7	201.0	—	—
8	199.0	—	—
9	196.0	—	—
10	193.5	—	—
11	191.0	10-24 10-32	—
12	189.0	—	—
13	185.0	—	—
14	182.0	—	—
15	180.0	—	—
16	177.0	—	12-24
17	173.0	—	—
18	169.5	—	—
19	166.0	8-32	12-20
20	161.0	—	—
21	159.0	—	10-32
22	157.0	—	—
23	154.0	—	—
24	152.0	—	—
25	149.5	—	10-24
26	147.0	—	—
27	144.0	—	—
28	140.0	6-32	—
29	136.0	—	8-32
30	128.5	—	—
31	120.0	—	—
32	116.0	—	—
33	113.0	4-40	—
34	111.0	—	—
35	110.0	—	—
36	106.5	—	6-32
37	104.0	—	—
38	101.5	—	—
39	099.5	3-48	—
40	098.0	—	—
41	096.0	—	—
42	093.5	—	—
43	089.0	—	4-40
44	086.0	2-56	—
45	082.0	—	—
46	081.0	—	—
47	078.5	—	3-48
48	076.0	—	—
49	073.0	—	—
50	070.0	—	2-56
51	067.0	—	—
52	063.5	—	—
53	059.5	—	—
54	055.0	—	—

Solder, *rosin core only*
Contact cleaner, liquid or spray can
Duco cement or equivalent
Electrical tape, vinyl plastic

Radio-supply houses, mail-order retail stores and most hardware stores carry the various tools required for building or servicing Amateur Radio equipment. While power tools (electric drill or drill press, grinding wheel, etc.) are very useful and will save a lot of time, they are not essential.

Twist Drills

Twist drills are made of either high-speed steel or carbon steel. The latter type is more common and will usually be supplied unless a specific request is made for high-speed drills. The carbon drill will suffice for most equipment construction work and costs less than the high-speed type.

While twist drills are available in a number of sizes, those listed in bold type in Table 1 will be most commonly used in construction of amateur equipment. It is usually desirable to purchase several of each of the commonly used sizes rather than a standard set, most of which will be used infrequently, if at all.

Although Table 1 lists drills down to no. 54, the series extends to no. 80. No. 68 and no. 70 are useful for drilling printed-circuit boards for component leads.

Care of Tools

The proper care of tools is not only a matter of pride to a good worker. Energy is saved and annoyance avoided by possessing a full kit of well-kept, sharp-edged tools.

Drills should be sharpened at frequent intervals so grinding is kept at a minimum each time. This makes it easier to maintain the rather critical surface angles required for best cutting with least wear. Occasional oilstoning of the cutting edges of a drill or reamer will extend the time between grindings.

The soldering iron can be kept in good condition by keeping the tip well tinned with solder and not allowing it to run at

Fig. 1 — A compact assembly of commonly available items, this soldering station sanitizes the electronics assembly process. Miniature toggle switches are used because of the minimal force required to manipulate them. The force required to operate standard-size switches could destabilize the unit.

Fig. 2 — View of the chassis underside with the bottom plate removed. No. 24 hookup wire is adequate for all connections. Use sleeving wherever the possibility of a short circuit exists. The diode may be installed in either direction.

full voltage for long periods when it is not being used. After each period of use, the tip should be removed and cleaned of any scale that may have accumulated. An oxidized tip may be cleaned by dipping it in sal ammoniac (ammonium chloride) while hot and then wiping it clean with a rag. If a copper tip becomes pitted, it should be filed until smooth and bright and then tinned immediately with solder. Most modern soldering iron tips are iron-clad and cannot be filed.

Useful Materials

Small stocks of various miscellaneous materials will be required in constructing radio apparatus. Most of these are available from hardware or radio-supply stores. A representative list follows:

Sheet aluminum, solid and perforated, 16 or 18 gauge, for brackets and shielding.

Aluminum angle stock, 1/2 × 1/2-inch

1/4-inch-diameter round brass or aluminum rod for shaft extensions.

Machine screws: Round-head and flat head, with nuts to fit. Most useful sizes: 4-40, 6-32 and 8-32, in lengths from 1/4-inch to 1-1/2 inches. (Nickel-plated steel will be found satisfactory except in strong RF fields, where brass should be used.)

Bakelite, Lucite, polystyrene and copper-clad PC-board scraps.

Soldering lugs, panel bearings, rubber grommets, terminal-lug wiring strips,

varnished-cambric insulating tubing, heat-shrinkable tubing.

Shielded and unshielded wire.

Tinned bare wire, nos. 22, 14 and 12.

Machine screws, nuts, washers, soldering lugs, etc., are most reasonably purchased in quantities of a gross. Many radio-supply stores sell small quantities and assortments that come in handy.

A DELUXE SOLDERING STATION

The simple device shown on this page can enhance the versatility and longevity of a soldering iron as well as make electronic

assembly more convenient. Fig. 1 depicts the obvious convenience features — a protective heat sink and case, and a tip-cleaning sponge rigidly attached to a sturdy base for efficient one-handed operation. Inside the chassis are some electrical refinements that justify the sophisticated name soldering station.

Soldering iron tips and heating elements last longer if operated at a lower-than-maximum temperature when idling. In the unit described here, temperature reduction is accomplished by halving the duty cycle of the applied ac voltage. D1 in Fig. 3 con-

Fig. 3 — Schematic diagram of the soldering station. D1 is a silicon power rectifier, 1-A, 400-PIV. S1 is a miniature SPST toggle switch rated 3 at 125 V. This current is satisfactory for use with irons having power ratings up to 100 W.

ducts only when the hot ac line is positive with respect to neutral. If the diode were reversed, the soldering iron would be heated only on the negative half cycles, but the result would be the same. This is one of the rare applications of rectifier diodes where the polarity is not important. With current flowing only in one direction, only one electrode of the neon bulb will glow. Closing S1 short-circuits the diode and applies full power to the soldering iron, igniting both bulb electrodes brightly.

CMOS ICs are prone to damage by static charges, so they should be soldered with an iron having a grounded tip. This requirement is fulfilled by most irons having 3-wire power cords.

The base for the unit is a 2 × 6 × 4-inch (HWD) aluminum chassis (Bud AC-431 or equivalent). An Ungar model 8000 soldering iron fits neatly on the chassis top. The holder has two mounting holes in each foot. A sponge tray nests between the feet and the case. In this model, a sardine tin is used for the sponge tray. A suitable watertight enclosure can also be fabricated from strips of copper-clad circuit-board material. The tray and iron holder are secured to the chassis by 6-32 × 1/2-inch pan-head machine screws and nuts, with flat washers under the screw heads (sponge tray) and lock washers under the nuts (chassis underside). One of these nuts fastens a 6-lug tie point strip to the chassis bottom. Use the soldering iron holder base as a template for drilling the chassis and sponge tray. The floor of the sponge tray must be sealed around the screw heads to prevent moisture from leaking into the electrical components below the chassis. RTV compound was used for this purpose in the unit pictured.

Purchase a separate 3-wire cord for the power input. Merely splicing the soldering station into existing soldering iron cord will shorten the operating radius of the iron and make it awkward to use. Heyco bushings were used to anchor both cords in the unit described. If these aren't available, grommets and cable clamps will work as well. Knotting the cords inside the chassis is a simple expedient that normally provides adequate strain relief.

The underchassis assembly is shown in Fig. 2. The neon bulb is forced through a 3/16-inch-ID grommet. The leads are sleeved to prevent short circuits. If you mount the bulb in a fixture or socket, use a clear lens to ensure that the electrodes are distinctly visible. Fit a cover to the bottom of the chassis to prevent accidental contact with the live ac wiring. Stick-on rubber feet will ensure a skid-free unit that won't mar your work surface.

SOLDERING-IRON TEMPERATURE CONTROL

Greater flexibility can be realized by installing a temperature rather than an idle control for your soldering iron. An incandescent-light dimmer can be used to

Fig. 4 — An incandescent-light dimmer controls soldering iron tip temperature. Only one of the duplex outlets is connected through the dimmer.

control the working temperature of the tip. Shown in Fig. 4 is a temperature control that can be built into an electrical box. A dimmer and a duplex outlet are mounted in the box; the wiring diagram is shown in Fig. 5. Be sure to break the link that connects the two hot terminals of the duplex outlet. The hot terminal is narrower than the neutral one. Neutral terminals may remain interconnected.

The dimmer shown in Fig. 4 was purchased at Radio Shack. It looks like a switch but it is really a variable control. Finer adjustment could be realized with a knob-controlled unit, but this one works fine.

When soldering static-sensitive devices, two or three jumpers can be used to ground you, the work and the iron. If the iron does not have a ground wire in the power cord, clip a jumper from the metal part of the iron near the handle to the metal box that houses the temperature control. Another jumper connects from the box to the work. Finally, a jumper goes from the box to your metal watch band. 3M makes an elastic wrist band for static grounding. This wrist band is equipped with a snap-on ground lead. Also, a 1-MΩ resistor is built into the snap of the strap to protect the user should a live circuit be contacted while using the strap. A similar resistor should be built into any homemade ground strap to protect the operator. It's not good practice to work on live circuits, however. This resistor will pro-

Fig. 5 — Schematic diagram of the soldering-iron temperature control.

tect you, but you should make sure that all power is removed from a circuit before working on it. Remember: even 24 V can be lethal! This technique works well for soldering CMOS ICs and GaAsFETs.

Chassis Working

With a few essential tools and proper procedure, building radio gear on a metal chassis is a relatively simple matter. Aluminum is preferred to steel, not only because it is a superior shielding material, but because it is much easier to work and provides good chassis contacts.

The placement of components on the chassis is shown clearly in the photographs in this *Handbook*. Aside from certain essential dimensions, which usually are given in the text, exact duplication is not necessary.

Fig. 6 — Method of measuring the heights of capacitor shafts. If the square is adjustable, the end of the scale should be set flush with the face of the head.

Much trouble and energy can be saved by spending sufficient time in planning the job. When all details are worked out beforehand, the actual construction is greatly simplified.

Cover the top of the chassis with a piece of wrapping paper, or, preferably, cross-section paper. Fold the edges down over the sides of the chassis and fasten with adhesive tape. Then assemble the parts to be mounted on top of the chassis and move them about until a satisfactory arrangement has been found, keeping in mind any parts to be mounted underneath, so interference in mounting can be avoided. Place capacitors and other parts with shafts extending through the panel first, and arrange them so the controls will form the desired pattern of the panel. Be sure to line up the shafts squarely with the chassis front. Locate any partition shields and panel brackets next, and then sockets and any other parts. Mark the mounting-hole centers of each accurately on the paper. Watch out for capacitors whose shafts are off center and do not line up with the mounting holes. Do not forget to mark the centers of socket holes and holes for wiring leads. The small holes for socket-mounted screws are best located and center-punched, using the socket itself as a template, after

Fig. 7 — To cut rectangular holes in a chassis corner, holes may be filed out as shown in the shaded portion of B, making it possible to start the hacksaw blade along the cutting line. A shows how a single-ended handle may be constructed for a hacksaw blade.

the main center hole has been cut.

Use the square to indicate the centers of shafts. These should be extended to the chassis front and marked on the panel at the chassis line, the panel being fastened on temporarily. The hole centers may then be punched in the chassis with the center punch. After drilling, the parts that require mounting underneath may be located and the mounting holes drilled, making sure by trial that no interferences exist with parts mounted on top. Mounting holes along the front edge of the chassis should be transferred to the panel by once again fastening the panel to the chassis and marking it from the rear.

Next, mount on the chassis the capacitors and any other parts with shafts extending to the panel, and measure accurately the height of the center of each shaft above the chassis, as illustrated in Fig. 6. The horizontal displacement of shafts having already been marked on the chassis line on the panel, the vertical displacement can be measured from this line. The shaft centers may now be marked on the back of the panel, and the holes drilled. Holes for any other panel equipment coming above the chassis line may then be marked and drilled, and the remainder of the apparatus mounted. Holes for terminals and other parts of the rear edge of the chassis should also be marked at this time.

Drilling and Cutting Holes

When drilling holes in metal with a hand drill it is important that the centers first be located with a center punch, so the drill point will not "walk" away from the center when starting the hole. When the drill starts to break through, special care must be used. Often it is an advantage to shift a two-speed drill to low gear at this point. Holes more than ¼-inch in diameter should be started with a smaller drill and reamed out with the larger drill.

The chuck on the usual type of hand drill is limited to ¼-inch drills. The ¼-inch hole may be filed out to larger diameters with a round file. Another method possible with limited tools is to drill a series of small holes with the hand drill along the inside of the circumference of the large hole, placing the holes as close together as possible. The center may then be knocked out with a cold chisel and the edges smoothed with a file.

Taper reamers which fit into the carpenter's brace will make the job easier. A large rat-tail file clamped in the brace makes a good reamer for holes up to the diameter of the file.

For socket holes and other large holes in an aluminum chassis, socket-hole punches should be used. They require first drilling a guide hole to pass the bolt that is turned to squeeze the punch through the chassis. The threads of the bolt should be oiled occasionally.

Large holes in steel panels or chassis are best cut with an adjustable circle cutter ("flycutter"). Occasional application of machine oil in the cutting groove will help. The cutter first should be tried out on a block of wood or scrap material to make sure it is set for the right diameter.

The burrs or rough edges that usually result after drilling or cutting holes may be removed with a file, or sometimes more conveniently with a sharp knife or chisel. It is a good idea to keep an old wood chisel sharpened and available for this purpose.

Rectangular Holes

Square or rectangular holes may be cut out by making a row of small holes as previously described, but is more easily done by drilling a ½-inch hole inside each corner, as illustrated in Fig. 7, and using these holes for starting and turning the hacksaw. The socket-hole punch and the square punches that are now available also may be of considerable assistance in cutting out large openings.

Semiconductor Heat Sinks

Homemade heat sinks can be fashioned from brass, copper or aluminum stock with ordinary workshop tools. The dimensions of the heat sink will depend on the type of device used and the amount of heat that must be conducted away from the body of the semiconductor.

Fig. 8 shows the order of progression for forming a large heat sink from aluminum or brass channels of near-equal height and depth. The width is lessened in parts B and C so each channel will fit into the preceding one as shown in the completed model at D. The three pieces are bolted together with 8-32 screws and nuts. Dimensions given are for illustrative purposes only.

Heat sinks for smaller transistors can be

Fig. 8 — Details for forming channel-type heat sinks.

fabricated as shown in Fig. 9. Select a drill bit that is one size smaller than the diameter of the transistor case and form the heat sink from 1/16-inch-thick brass, copper or aluminum stock as shown in steps A, B and C. Form the stock around the drill bit by compressing it in a vise (A). The completed heat sink is press-fitted over the body of the semiconductor as illustrated at D. The larger the heat sink area, the greater the amount of heat conducted away from the transistor body. In some applications, such as power transistor stages, the heat sinks shown in Fig. 9 may be 2 or 3 inches in height.

Another technique for making heat sinks for TO-5 type transistors and larger models is shown in Fig. 10. This style of heat sink will dissipate considerably more heat than will the type shown in Fig. 9. The main body of the sink is fashioned from a piece of 1/8-inch-thick aluminum angle bracket — available from most hardware stores. A hole is bored in the angle stock to allow the transistor case to fit *snugly* into it. The transistor is held in place by a small metal plate whose center hole is slightly smaller in diameter than the case of the transistor. Details are given in Fig. 10.

A thin coating of silicone grease, available from most electronic supply houses, can be applied between the case of the transistor and the part of the heat sink with which it comes in contact. The silicone grease will aid the transfer of heat from the transistor to the sink. Electrically conductive and nonconductive grease is available. Do not use conductive grease for applications where the device is insulated from the heat sink. This practice can be applied to all models shown here. In the example given in Fig. 8, the grease should be applied between the three channels before they are bolted together, as well as between the transistor and the channel it contacts.

Construction Notes

If a control shaft must be extended or insulated, a flexible shaft coupling with adequate insulation should be used. Satisfactory support for the shaft extension, as well as electrical contact for safety, can be provided by means of a metal panel bushing made for the purpose. These can be obtained singly for use with existing shafts, or they can be bought with a captive extension shaft included. In either case the panel bushing gives a solid feel to the control. The use of fiber washers between ceramic insulation and metal brackets, screws or nuts will prevent the ceramic parts from breaking.

Cutting and Bending Sheet Metal

If a metal sheet is too large to be cut conveniently with a hacksaw, it may be marked with scratches as deep as possible along the line of the cut on both sides of the sheet, and then clamped in a vise and worked back and forth until the sheet breaks at the line. Do not carry the bending too far until

Fig. 9 — Steps used in constructing heat sinks for small transistors.

Fig. 10 — Layout and assembly details of another homemade heat sink. The completed assembly can be insulated from the main chassis of the transmitter by using insulating washers.

the break begins to weaken; otherwise the edge of the sheet may become bent. A pair of iron bars or pieces of heavy angle stock, as long or longer than the width of the sheet, to hold it in the vise, will make the job easier. C clamps may be used to keep the bars from spreading at the ends. Bends may be made similarly. The rough edges may be smoothed with a file or by placing a large piece of emery cloth or sandpaper on a flat surface and running the edge of the metal back and forth over the sheet.

Much of the tedium of sheet metal work can be relieved by using copper-clad printed-circuit board material wherever possible. Copper-clad stock is manufac-

tured with phenolic, FR-4 fiberglass and Teflon base materials in thicknesses up to 1/8 inch. While it is manufactured in large sheets for industrial use, some hobby electronics stores and surplus outlets market usable scraps at reasonable prices. PC-board stock is easily cut with a small hacksaw. Because the nonmetallic base material isn't malleable, it can't be bent in the usual way. However, corners are easily formed by holding two pieces at right angles and soldering the seam. Excellent RF-tight enclosures can be fabricated in this manner. Many projects in this Handbook were constructed using this technique. If mechanical rigidity is required of a large

Table 2

Standard Metal Gauges

Gauge No.	American or BS†	U.S. Standard††	Birmingham or Stubs†††
1	0.2893	0.28125	0.300
2	0.2576	0.265625	0.284
3	0.2294	0.25	0.259
4	0.2043	0.234375	0.238
5	0.1819	0.21875	0.220
6	0.1620	0.203125	0.203
7	0.1443	0.1875	0.180
8	0.1285	0.171875	0.165
9	0.1144	0.15625	0.148
10	0.1019	0.140625	0.134
11	0.09074	0.125	0.120
12	0.08081	0.109375	0.109
13	0.07196	0.09375	0.095
14	0.06408	0.078125	0.083
15	0.05707	0.0703125	0.072
16	0.05082	0.0625	0.065
17	0.04526	0.05625	0.058
18	0.04030	0.05	0.049
19	0.03589	0.04375	0.042
20	0.03196	0.0375	0.035
21	0.02846	0.034375	0.032
22	0.02535	0.03125	0.028
23	0.02257	0.028125	0.025
24	0.02010	0.025	0.022
25	0.01790	0.021875	0.020
26	0.01594	0.01875	0.018
27	0.01420	0.0171875	0.016
28	0.01264	0.015625	0.014
29	0.01126	0.0140625	0.013
30	0.01003	0.0125	0.012
31	0.008928	0.0109375	0.010
32	0.007950	0.01015625	0.009
33	0.007080	0.009375	0.008
34	0.006350	0.00859375	0.007
35	0.005615	0.0078125	0.005
36	0.005000	0.00703125	0.004
37	0.004453	0.006640626	—
38	0.003965	0.00625	—
39	0.003531	—	—
40	0.003145	—	—

†Used for aluminum, copper, brass and nonferrous alloy sheets, wire and rods.
††Used for iron, steel, nickel and ferrous alloy sheets, wire and rods.
†††Used for seamless tubes; also by some manufacturers for copper and brass.

---

copper-clad surface, stiffening ribs may be soldered at right angles to the sheet.

Finishing Aluminum

Aluminum chassis, panels and parts may be given a sheen finish by treating them in a caustic bath. An enameled or plastic container, such as a dishpan or infant's bathtub, should be used for the solution. Dissolve ordinary household lye in cold water in a proportion of one-quarter to one-half can of lye per gallon of water. The stronger solution will do the job more rapidly. Stir the solution with a stick of wood until the lye crystals are completely dissolved. Be very careful to avoid skin contact with the solution. It is also harmful to clothing. Sufficient solution should be prepared to cover the piece completely. When the aluminum is immersed, a very pronounced bubbling takes place and ventilation should be provided to disperse the escaping gas. A half hour to two hours in the bath should be sufficient, depending on the strength of the solution and the desired surface.

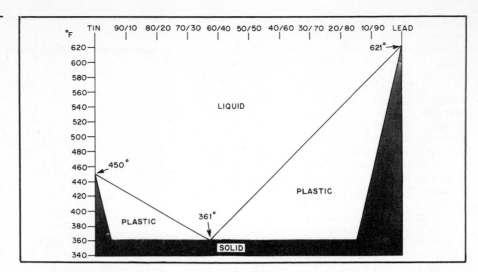

Fig. 11 — State diagram for tin-lead solder alloys. Courtesy of Litton Industries, Inc., Kester Solder Co.

Raw aluminum can be prepared for painting by abrading the surface with medium-grade sandpaper, making certain the strokes are applied in the same direction (not circular or random). This process will create tiny grooves on the otherwise smooth surface. As a result, paint or lacquer will adhere well. Before painting, wash the abraded aluminum with alcohol or soap and hot water, then dry thoroughly. Avoid touching the prepared surface before painting it. One or two coats of zinc chromate primer applied before the finish paint will ensure good adherence.

Soldering

The secret of good soldering is to use the right amount of heat. Solders have different melting points, depending on the ratio of tin to lead. Tin melts at 450 °F and lead at 621 °F (see Fig. 11). Solder with 63% tin and 37% lead melts at 361 °F, the lowest melting point for a tin and lead mixture. Called 63-37, this ratio also provides the most rapid solid to liquid transition and best stress resistance.

As shown in Fig. 11, solder that is not 63-37 goes through a *plastic* state. If the solder is deformed while it is in the plastic state, that deformation will remain when the solder freezes into the solid state. Any stress or motion applied to "plastic solder" will result in poor solder joint.

A 60-40 solder has the best *wetting* qualities. Wetting is the ability to spread rapidly and alloy uniformly. Soldering is not like glueing. The solder does more than bind pieces of metal together and provide an electrically conductive path between them. In the soldering process, the materials being joined and the solder combine to form an alloy. This effect is illustrated in Fig. 12. Because of its low melting point, small plastic area and excellent wetting characteristics, 60-40 solder is the most commonly used alloy in electronics.

Fig. 12 — An alloy layer exists in a good solder joint.

Various solder alloys are used for special purposes. Other tin-lead alloys are 50-50 and 40-60. A low-melting-point solder, 50-32-18 (tin-lead-cadmium) has a melting temperature of under 300 °F. This alloy is used for heat sensitive components.

Some connections carrying very high current can't be made with ordinary tin-lead solder because the heat generated by the joint resistance would melt the solder. Automotive starter brushes and UHF transmitter tank circuits are two cases in which this situation can occur. High-melting-point silver solder prevents this condition. A typical alloy contains 5-93.5-1.5 (tin-lead-silver) and the melting point is about 600 °F.

To prevent the silver plating on some components from leaching into the solder, some silver is added to the solder. A typical alloy contains 62-36-2 (tin-lead-silver) and melts at 354 °F. Another silver solder is 96.3-3.7 (tin-silver); it contains no lead and melts at 430 °F.

Always use rosin-core solder; never acid-core. The rosin is a flux. Flux removes oxide by suspending it in solution and floating it to the top. Flux is not a cleaning agent! The work must be cleaned before soldering. Flux is not a part of a soldered connection — it merely aids the soldering process. After soldering, any remaining flux should be removed. Alcohol is a good solvent for the job. A toothbrush is an excellent tool for applying the alcohol and scrubbing the excess flux away.

The two key factors in quality soldering are time and temperature. Generally, rapid heating is desired. If heat is applied too long, the flux may become used up and surface oxidation can become a problem. Further, thin coating may dissolve from leads and components, or components may be harmed. The soldering-iron tip should be hot enough to readily melt the solder without burning, charring or discoloring components, PC boards or wires. Usually, a tip temperature about 100°F above the solder melting point is about right for mounting components on PC boards.

When soldering, apply the solder to the joint — not to the iron. A small amount of solder on the tip will improve heat transfer. The iron and the solder should be applied simultaneously to the joint. Keep the iron clean by brushing the tip with a cloth towel or a moist sponge. Allow the joints to cool in air at room temperature. Make sure there is no movement or stress on joints during cooling and solidification of the solder.

When you solder transistors, crystal diodes or small resistors, the lead should be gripped with a pair of pliers up close to the unit so that the heat will be conducted away. Overheating of a transistor or diode while soldering can cause permanent damage. Also, mechanical stress will have a similar effect. Therefore, a small unit should be mounted so there is no appreciable mechanical strain on the leads.

Trouble is sometimes experienced soldering to the pins of coil forms or male cable plugs. It helps if the pins are first cleaned on the inside with a suitable twist drill and then tinned by flowing rosin-core solder into them. Immediately clear the surplus solder from each hot pin by a whipping motion or by blowing through the pin from the inside of the form or plug. Before inserting the wire in the pin, file the nickel plate from the pin tip. After soldering, remove excess solder with a file.

When soldering to the pins of polystyrene coil forms, hold the pin to be soldered with a pair of heavy pliers to form a heat sink and ensure that the pin does not heat enough in the coil form to loosen and become misaligned.

Just as important as soldering is desoldering to remove components. Commercially made wicking material (braid) will soak up excess solder from a joint. Another useful tool is an air-suction solder remover. Or, you can heat the joint and "flick" the wet solder off. Keep a large cardboard box handy to flick the solder into, or you'll get solder splashes everywhere.

Wiring

The wire used in connecting amateur equipment should be selected by considering both the maximum current it will be

called on to handle and the voltage its insulation must stand without breakdown. Also, from the consideration of TVI, the power wiring of all transmitters should be done with wire that has a braided shielding cover. Receiver and audio circuits may also require the use of shielded wire at some points for stability or the elimination of hum.

No. 20 stranded wired is commonly used for most receiver wiring (except for the high-frequency circuits) where the current does not exceed 2 or 3 amperes. For higher-current heater circuits, no. 18 is available. Wire with cellulose acetate insulation is good for voltages up to about 500. For higher voltages, Teflon-insulated or other special HV wire should be used. Teflon insulation has the additional advantage of not melting when a soldering iron is applied. This makes it particularly helpful in tight places or large harnesses. Although Teflon-insulated wire is more expensive, it is often available from industrial surplus houses. Inexpensive wire strippers make the removal of insulation from hookup wire an easy job.

When power leads have several branches in the chassis, it is convenient to use fiber-insulated multiple tie points as anchorages of junction points. Strips of this type are also useful as insulated supports for resistors, RF chokes and capacitors. Exposed points of high-voltage wiring should be held to a minimum; those that cannot be avoided should be made as inaccessible as possible to accidental contact or short-circuit.

Where shielded wire is called for and capacitance to ground is not a factor, Belden type 8885 shielded grid wire may be used. If capacitance must be minimized, it may be necessary to use a piece of car radio low-capacitance lead-in wire or coaxial cable.

For wiring high-frequency circuits, rigid wire is often used. Bare soft-drawn tinned wire, size 22 to 12 (depending on mechanical requirements) is suitable. Kinks can be avoided by stretching a piece 10 or 15 feet long and then cutting it into short lengths that can be handled conveniently. RF wiring should be run directly from point to point with a minimum of sharp bends and the wire kept well spaced from the chassis or other grounded metal surfaces. Where the wiring must pass through the chassis or a partition, a clearance hole should be cut and lined with a rubber grommet. If insulation is necessary, varnished cambric tubing (spaghetti) can be slipped over the wire.

In transmitters in which the peak voltage does not exceed 2500, the shielded grid wire mentioned above should be satisfactory for power circuits. For higher voltages, Belden type 8656, Birnbach type 1820, or shielded ignition cable can be used. In the case of filament circuits carrying heavy current, it may be necessary to use no. 10 or 12 bare or enameled wire, slipped through

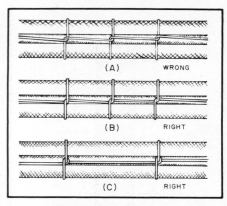

Fig. 13 — Methods of lacing cables. The method shown at C is more secure, but takes more time than the method of B. The latter is usually adequate for most amateur requirements.

Fig. 14 — Plastic products are used to form and secure wires into a cable.

Fig. 15 — Adhesive-backed blocks and plastic wraps used to make wiring cables. Some wraps are reusable.

spaghetti, and then covered with copper braid pulled tightly over the spaghetti. If the shielding is simply slid back over the insulation and solder flowed into the end of the braid, the braid usually will stay in place without the necessity for cutting it back or binding it in place. The braid should be cleaned first so solder will take with a minimum of heat. RF wiring in transmitters usually follows the methods described above for receivers with due respect to the voltages involved.

Where power or control leads run together for more than a few inches, they will present a better appearance when bound together in a single cable. The correct technique is illustrated in Fig. 13; both

Fig. 16 — Pictorial diagram of a heavy-duty plate choke for the HF bands. No. 26 enameled wire is used for the winding. Low-loss material should be used for the form.

plastic and waxed-linen lacing cords are available. A variety of plastic devices are available to bundle wires into cables and to clamp or secure them in place. Figs. 14 and 15 show some of the products and techniques that you might use. Check with your local electronic parts supplier for items that are in stock.

To give a commercial look to the wiring of any unit, run any cabled leads along the edge of the chassis. If this isn't possible, the cabled leads should then run parallel to an edge of the chassis. Further, the generous use of the tie points mounted parallel to an edge of the chassis, for the support of one or both ends of a resistor or fixed capacitor, will add to the appearance of the finished unit. In a similar manner, arrange the small components so that they are parallel to the panel or sides of the chassis.

Winding Coils

Close-wound coils are readily wound on the specified form by anchoring one end of the length of wire (in a vise or to a doorknob) and the other end to the coil form. Straighten any kinks in the wire and then pull to keep the wire under slight tension. Wind the coil to the required number of turns while walking toward the anchor,

always maintaining a slight tension on the wire.

To space-wind the coil, wind the coil simultaneously with a suitable spacing medium (heavy thread, string or wire) in the manner described above. When the winding is complete, secure the end of the coil to the coil-form terminal and then carefully unwind the spacing material. If the coil is wound under suitable tension, the spacing material can be easily removed without disturbing the winding. Finish the space-wound coil by judicious applications of Duco cement to hold the turns in place.

The cold end of a coil is the end at or close to chassis or ground potential. Coupling links should be wound on the cold end of a coil to minimize capacitive coupling.

RF chokes must often present a high impedance over a broad frequency range. This requirement calls for the avoidance of series resonances within the range. Such resonances can be avoided in single-layer solenoids by separating the winding into progressively shorter sections. A practical choke suitable for HF amateur service at plate impedances up to 51-kΩ and currents up to 600 mA is shown in Fig. 16.

Another way to build a broadband choke is to wind a small number of turns on a high-permeability ferrite rod (such as the type used for antennas in some portable radios). The magnetic core supplies a large inductance with a small winding. Keeping the number of turns small reduces the distributed capacitance and raises the self-resonant frequency of the choke. Ferrite chokes are best suited to low-impedance applications. A bifilar (this term is explained in the following paragraphs) filament choke for grounded-grid kilowatt HF amplifiers appears in Fig. 17.

Toroidal inductors and transformers are specified for many projects in this *Handbook*. The advantages of this type of winding include compactness and a self-shielding property. Figs. 18 and 19 illustrate the proper way to wind and count the turns on a toroidal core.

A *bifilar* winding is one that has two identical lengths of wire, which when placed on the core result in the same number of turns for each wire. The two wires can be put on the core side by side at the same time, just as if a single winding were being applied. An easier and more popular method is to twist the two wires (8 to 15 times per inch will suffice), then

Fig. 18 — The suggested winding method for a single-layer toroid as shown at A. A 30° gap is recommended (see text). Wrong methods are shown at B and C. At D is a method for placing a tap on the coil.

Fig. 19 — The view at A shows how the turns on a toroid should be counted. The large black dots in the diagram at B are used to indicate the polarity (phasing) of the windings.

Fig. 20 — Schematic and pictorial presentation of a bifilar-wound toroidal transformer.

wind the pair on the core. The wires can be twisted handily by placing one end of the length of two wires in a bench vise. The remaining wire-pair ends are tightened into the chuck of a small hand drill, and the twisting is done.

A *trifilar* winding has three wires, and a *quadrifilar* winding has four. The procedure for preparation and winding is otherwise the same as for a bifilar winding. Fig. 20 shows a bifilar type of toroid in schematic and pictorial form. The wires have been twisted together prior to placing them on the core. It is helpful, though by no means essential, to use wires of different color when multifilar-winding a core. The more wires used, the more perplexing it is

Fig. 17 — Bifilar filament choke wound on a ferrite rod. Heat-shrink tubing will help anchor the winding. If enameled wire is used, the form should be insulated before winding.

to identify the end of the windings correctly once the core has been wound. There are various colors of enamel insulation available, but it is not easy for amateurs to find this wire locally or in small-quantity lots. This problem can be solved by taking lengths of wire (enameled magnet wire), cleaning them to remove dirt and grease, then spray-painting them. Ordinary aerosol-can spray enamel works fine. Spray lacquer is not as satisfactory because it is brittle when dry and tends to flake off the wire.

The winding sense of a multifilar toroidal transformer is important in most circuits. Fig. 19B illustrates this principle. The black dots (called phasing dots) at the top of the T1 windings indicate polarity. That is, points a and c are both start or finish ends of their respective windings. In this example, points a and d are of opposite phase (180° phase difference) to provide push-pull voltage feed to Q1 and Q2.

CIRCUIT-BOARD FABRICATION

Modern-day builders prefer the neatness and miniaturization made possible by the use of etched printed-circuit boards. There are additional benefits to be realized from the use of circuit boards: Low lead inductances, excellent physical stability of the components and interconnecting leads, and good repeatability of the basic layout of a given project. The repeatability factor makes the use of circuit boards ideal for group projects.

Planning and Layout

The constructor should first plan the physical layout of the circuit by sketching a pictorial diagram on paper, drawing it to scale. Once this has been done, the interconnecting leads can be inked in to represent the copper strips that will remain on the etched board. The Vector Company sells layout paper for this purpose. It is marked with the same patterns used on their perforated boards.

After the basic etched-circuit design has been completed, the designer should go over the proposed layout several times to insure against errors. When that has been done, the pattern can be painted on the copper surface of the board to be etched. Etch-resistant solutions are available from commercial suppliers and can be selected from their catalogs. Some builders prefer to use India ink for this purpose. Perhaps the most readily available material for use in etch-resist applications is ordinary exterior enamel paint. The portions of the board to be retained are covered with a layer of paint applied with an artist's brush, duplicating the pattern that was drawn on the layout paper. The job is made a bit easier by tracing over the original layout with a ballpoint pen and carbon paper while the pattern is taped to the copper side of the unetched circuit board. The carbon paper is placed between the pattern and the

Fig. 21 — A homemade stand for processing etched-circuit boards. The heat lamp maintains the etchant-bath temperature between 90 and 115°F (32 and 46°C) and is mounted on an adjustable arm. The tray for the bath is raised and lowered at one end by the action of a motor-driven eccentric disc, providing the necessary agitation of the chemical solution. A darkroom thermometer monitors the temperature of the bath.

Fig. 22 — Schematic diagram of an audio amplifier.

circuit board. After the paint has been applied, it should be allowed to dry for at least 24 hours prior to the etching process. The Vector Company produces a rub-on transfer material that can also be used as etch-resist when laying out circuit-board patterns. Thin strips of ordinary masking tape, cut to size and firmly applied, serve nicely as etch-resist material too.

To make a single PC board, it is convenient to cover the copper surface with masking tape, transfer the circuit pattern by means of carbon paper, then cut out and remove the sections of masking tape where the copper is to be etched away. An X-acto® hobby knife is excellent for the purpose. Masking tape, securely applied, serves as a fine etch-resist material.

Many magazine articles feature printed-circuit layouts. The more-complex patterns (those containing ICs and high component densities) are difficult to duplicate accurately by hand. A photographic pro-

cess is the most efficient way to transfer a layout from a magazine page to a circuit board. A Thermofax transparency-producing machine (most schools have these) will copy the circuit on a clear plastic sheet for use as a negative. Pressing this negative against a photosensitive copper-clad board with a piece of glass and exposing the assembly to sunlight for about 90 seconds will deactivate the etchant resist on the exposed part of the board. The portion of the copper that is shielded from the light by the negative will resist etching. Photosensitive PC-board material is manufactured by Kepro Company.

The Etching Process

Almost any strong acid bath will serve as an etchant, but the two chemical preparations recommended here are the safest to use. A bath can be prepared by mixing one part ammonium persulphate crystals with two parts clear water. A normal quantity of working solution for most Amateur Radio applications is composed of one cup of crystals and two cups of water. To this mixture add ¼ teaspoon of mercuric chloride crystals; this serves as an activator for the bath. Ready-made etchant kits that use these chemicals are available from Vector. Complete kits that contain circuit boards, etchant powders, etch-resist transfers, layout paper, and plastic etchant bags are also available from Vector at moderate prices.

Another chemical bath that works satisfactorily for copper etching is made up from one part ferric chloride crystals and two parts water. No activator is required with this bath. Ready-made solutions (one-pint and one-gallon sizes) are available through some mail-order houses at low cost. They are manufactured by Kepro Company and carry stock numbers E-1PT and E-1G, respectively.

Etchant solutions become exhausted after a certain amount of copper has been processed. Therefore, it is wise to keep a quantity of the bath on hand if frequent use is anticipated. With either chemical bath, the working solution should be maintained at a temperature between 90 and 115°F. A heat lamp can be directed toward the bath during the etching period, its distance set to maintain the required temperature. A darkroom thermometer is handy for monitoring the temperature of the bath.

While the circuit is immersed in the solution, it should be agitated continuously to permit uniform reaction to the chemicals. This action will also speed up the etching process somewhat. Normally, the circuit board should be placed in the bath with the copper side facing down, toward the bottom of the tray. The tray should be nonmetallic, preferably a Pyrex dish or a photographic darkroom tray.

Fig. 21 shows a homemade etching stand made up from a heat lamp, some lumber, and an 8-r/min motor. An eccentric disc has been mounted on the motor shaft and butts against the bottom of the etchant tray. As the motor turns, the eccentric disc raises and lowers one end of the tray, thus providing continuous agitation of the solution. The heat lamp is mounted on an adjustable, slotted wooden arm. Its height above the solution tray is adjusted to provide the desired bath temperature. Because the etching process takes between 15 minutes and one hour — dependent on the strength and the temperature of the bath — such an accessory is convenient.

After the etching process is completed, the board is removed from the tray and washed thoroughly with fresh, clear water. The etch-resist material can then be rubbed off by applying a few brisk strokes with medium-grade steel wool. WARNING: *Always use rubber gloves when working with etchant powders and solutions. Should the acid bath come in contact with the body, immediately wash the affected area with clear water. Protect the eyes when using acid baths.*

No-Etch PC Boards

Some would-be builders express revulsion at the prospect of PC-board fabrication. The distaste for chemical processes should not deter a person, however, for several alternatives exist.

A construction technique that is practically indistinguishable from true printed circuitry is excavating a copper-clad board with hand-held grinding tool, such as the Moto-tool manufactured by the Dremel Company. The simpler circuits can be cut out of the board with an X-acto knife. Unwanted copper can be removed by heating it with a soldering iron and lifting it off with a knife while it is still hot.

Alternative Construction Methods

Many methods can be used to construct a circuit. Say, for example, you wish to build the audio amplifier shown in Fig. 22. What construction method would you use? Many possibilities exist — some of them will be covered in this section.

You can build the audio amplifier on an etched PC board. That technique was described earlier. The results might look like the board shown in Fig. 23. For a complicated project, a lot of work can go into getting one perfect PC board. However, after that first one is perfected, dozens more can be made with relative ease.

Solderless Prototyping Board

An etched PC board is not always the best way to construct a circuit. That is especially true when you are developing a circuit. It can be frustrating to have to make another PC board for every circuit variation you want to try. A better method for experimental circuit construction is to use a solderless prototyping board. Several models are available from many sources. One of these is illustrated in Fig. 24.

(A)

(B)

Fig. 23 — Audio amplifier built on a PC board. Top view at A; bottom view at B.

Fig. 24 — The audio amplifier of Fig. 22 has been built on this solderless prototyping board.

Metal strips inside the board grip inserted component leads and hookup wire. The strips are arranged in short columns along the center of the board and in long rows at the top and bottom. Circuit components and hookup wire are used to interconnect the strips and make the circuit. This is a fast and easy way to test an idea and work on modifications. Component and interconnection changes can be readily made.

There are some minor disadvantages to these solderless boards. Because of the capacitance between the finger-stock strips, the boards are not good for building RF circuits. Also, to prevent deforming the

finger stock when using components with heavy leads, you must add short lead extensions of small diameter wire.

Perforated Construction Board

Perhaps the least complicated approach to circuit-board fabrication is the use of unclad perforated board. Perforated board is available with many different hole patterns. Your choice will depend on your needs.

A great deal of time can be spent laying out and etching a single PC board. Circuit construction on perforated board is much easier. Start by placing the components on the board and moving them about until a satisfactory layout is obtained. Component leads are then pushed through the holes, connected with bus or hookup wire and soldered. The audio amplifier of Fig. 22 is shown constructed with this technique in Fig. 25.

Perforated boards and accessories are manufactured by several companies. Accessories include mounting hardware and a variety of connection terminals for solder and solderless construction. These products are widely available.

Utility PC Boards

Utility PC boards offer a hybrid alternative to the custom-designed etched PC board. They offer the flexibility of perforated board construction and the mechanical and electrical advantages of etched circuit connection pads. Utility PC boards can be used to build anything from simple passive filter circuits to computers.

(A)

(B)

Fig. 25 — Audio amplifier built on perforated board. Top view at A; bottom view at B.

Fig. 26—Etching pattern for the universal breadboard. Black represents copper; the pattern is shown actual size. You can etch your own from this pattern or purchase a board from Circuit Board Specialists. See the Parts Suppliers list in Chapter 35.

Fig. 27—Utility PC boards like these are available from Oak Hills Research. See the Parts Suppliers list in Chapter 35.

(A)

(B)

Fig. 28 — Audio amplifier built on a multipurpose PC breadboard. Top view at A; bottom view at B.

Circuits can be built on boards on which the copper cladding has been divided into connection pads. Power supply voltages can be distributed on bus strips. The etching pattern for a board of this type can be found in Fig. 26. Boards like those shown in Fig. 27 are commercially available.

The example audio amplifier is shown in Fig. 28. This time the amplifier was built on a Radio Shack board that is designed for building circuits with ICs. Component leads are inserted into the board and soldered to the etched pads. Wire jumpers connect the pads together to complete the circuit.

Utility boards with one or more etched plugs for use in computer-bus, interface and general purpose applications are widely available. Connectors, mounting hardware and other accessories are also available. Check with your parts supplier for details.

Plug-in boards facilitate maintenance and repair.

Wire Wrap

Wire-wrap construction can be used to construct a circuit quickly and without solder. Low- and medium-speed digital circuits are often assembled on a wire-wrap board. The technique is not limited to digital circuits, however. Fig. 29 shows the example audio amplifier built using wire wrap. Circuit changes can be easily made, and yet the method is suitable for permanent assemblies.

Wire wrap basically consists of twisting or wrapping a wire around a post to make each connection. The wrapping tool resembles a thick pencil. Powered wire-wrap guns are used when many connections must be made. The wire is almost always no. 30 and has a thin insulation on it. Two wire-wrap methods are used: the standard

and the modified wrap (Fig. 30). The modified wrap is more secure and should be used for no. 30 wire. The wrap-post terminals are usually square; they should be long enough for at least two connections. For proper wire-wrap technique, see Figs. 30 and 31.

When wire wrapping, small components can be mounted on an IC header plug. The plug is then inserted into a wire-wrap IC socket, as shown in Fig. 29. The large capacitor in that figure has its leads soldered to Y-shaped wrap posts. Wire wrap works only on posts with sharp corners!

Ugly or Dead-Bug Construction

The term "ugly construction" was coined by Wes Hayward, W7ZOI. "Dead-bug construction" gets its name from the appearance of an IC with its leads sticking up in the air. This technique uses copper-clad circuit-board material as a foundation and ground plane on which to build a circuit using point-to-point wiring.

This method is flexible. The builder may use the parts on hand, something that is often difficult to do with the projects that use etched boards. The circuit may be changed easily; that aids experimentation. Speed is the greatest virtue of ugly construction. A moderately complex project (like a QRP transmitter) can be built in half the time, or less, than that required for the

(A)

Fig. 31 — Improper wire-wrap connections. Insufficient insulation for modified wrap is shown at A; a spiral wrap at B; an open wrap at C and an over wrap at D.

stand-off insulators. One resistor lead is soldered to the copper ground plane, the other lead is used as a circuit connection point. You can use ¼- or ½-watt resistors in values from 220 kΩ to several megohms. The high-ohmage resistors act more like *insulators* than true resistors. Therefore, the higher the resistance the better for this application. As a rule of thumb, the resistor being used as a stand-off insulator should have a value that is at least 10 times the circuit impedance or value or resistance used at that circuit point. For example, if a resistor is used as a tie point at the 50-Ω part of a circuit, the resistor should be 500 Ω or greater.

Fig. 33A illustrates pictorially how one might apply the stand-off technique to wire the circuit shown at C of Fig. 33. Illustration B demonstrates how the resistor pigtails are bent before the component is

(B)

Fig. 29 — Audio amplifier built using wire-wrap techniques.

Fig. 32 — Audio amplifier built using ugly or dead bug construction.

Fig. 34 — Cordwood modules make compact subassemblies. This broad-band amplifier consists of two transistors, two capacitors and six resistors.

Fig. 30 — Wire-wrap connections. Standard wrap is shown at A; modified wrap at B. The modified wrap should be used with no. 30 wire.

same project using boards that have to be etched and drilled.

Components are mounted just above the copper-clad board. (See Fig. 32.) Copper on the board becomes the circuit ground. Ground connections are made directly, thereby minimizing component lead lengths. Short lead lengths and a low-impedance ground conductor help prevent circuit instability. For that reason, ugly construction is particularly good for RF circuits — and for sensitive circuits, better than etched circuit boards.

High-ohmage resistors can be used as

Fig. 33 — Pictorial view of a circuit board that uses ugly construction is shown at A. A closeup view of one of the standoff resistors is shown at B. Note how the pigtails are bent. The schematic diagram at C shows the assembled circuit displayed at A.

soldered to the PC-board material. Components E1 through E5 are resistors that are used as stand-off insulators. They do not appear in the schematic diagram. The base circuitry at Q1 of Fig. 33A is stretched out excessively. This was done to reduce clutter in the drawing. In a practical circuit all of the signal leads should be kept as short as possible. E4 would, therefore, be placed much closer to Q1 than the drawing indicates.

R1 and R2 of Fig. 33 actually serve two purposes: They are not only the normal circuit resistances, but function as stand-off posts as well. This practice should be followed wherever a capacitor or resistor can be employed in the dual role.

Space Savers.

Compact assemblies can be made using cordwood modules. A cordwood module resembles a sandwich. On the outside are the end pieces. In the center are the circuit

Fig. 35 — Surface-mounted components take up little space on this thick-film module. *(Courtesy Tactical RF Inc., Norfolk, Massachusetts.)*

components. The end pieces have holes for the component leads to pass through. Etched traces or point-to-point wiring can be used for circuit connections. Component leads can be used to make connections to the module. This construction method is particularly useful for making small

subassemblies. A broad-band amplifier with two transistors, two capacitors and six resistors built with this technique is shown in Fig. 34.

Another space-saving technique is the use of surface-mounted or chip components. Most UHF and microwave enthusiasts know about chip resistors and capacitors. Other devices, such as transistors and diode arrays, are also available in this space-saving format.

Surface-mounted components take up very little space on a PC board. Even less space is required when circuit traces and components are placed on a piece of ceramic substrate material to make a thick-film module. It is possible for the advanced amateur builder to construct thick-film modules at home. The techniques used today are beyond the scope of this book. Fig. 35 shows what can be done using thick-film technology for making miniature circuits.

Chapter 25

Test Equipment and Measurements

Measurement and testing go hand in hand, but it is useful to make a distinction between measuring and testing. Measurement is commonly considered to give a meaningful quantitative result, while for testing a simple indication of satisfactory or unsatisfactory may suffice. In any event, the accurate calibration associated with real measuring equipment is seldom necessary for simple test apparatus.

Certain items of measuring equipment that are useful to amateurs are readily available in kit form, at prices that represent a genuine saving over the cost of identical parts. Included are volt-ohm-milli-ammeter combinations, vacuum-tube and transistor voltmeters, oscilloscopes and the like. The coordination of electrical and mechanical design, components and appearance make it far preferable to purchase such equipment than to attempt to build one's own.

However, some test gear can easily be built at home. This chapter considers the principles of the more useful types of measuring equipment and concludes with the descriptions of several pieces that not only can be built satisfactorily at home but also will facilitate operation of the amateur station.

The Direct-Current Instrument

In measuring instruments and test equipment suitable for amateur purposes, the ultimate readout is generally based on a measurement of direct current. A meter for measuring dc uses electromagnetic means to deflect a pointer over a calibrated scale in proportion to the current flowing through the instrument.

In the D'Arsonval type, a coil of wire to which the pointer is attached is pivoted between the poles of a permanent magnet. When current flows through the coil, it sets up a magnetic field that interacts with the field of the magnet to cause the coil to turn. The design of the instrument normally makes the pointer deflect in direct proportion to the current.

A less expensive type of instrument is the moving-vane type, in which a pivoted soft-iron vane is pulled into a coil of wire by the magnetic field set up when current flows through the coil. The farther the vane extends into the coil, the greater the magnetic pull on it for a given change in current. This type of instrument thus does not have linear deflection. The intervals of equal current change are crowded together at the low-current end and spread out at the high-current end of the scale.

Current Ranges

The sensitivity of an instrument is usually expressed in terms of the current required for full-scale deflection of the pointer.

Fig 1—Use of a shunt to extend the calibration range of a current-reading instrument.

Although a very wide variety of ranges is available, the meters of interest in amateur work have basic movements that will give maximum deflection with currents measured in microamperes or milliamperes. They are called microammeters and milli-ammeters, respectively.

Thanks to the relationships between current, voltage and resistance expressed by Ohm's Law, it becomes possible to use a single low-range instrument—e.g., 1 milliampere or less full-scale pointer deflection—for a variety of direct-current measurements. Through its ability to measure current, the instrument can also be used indirectly to measure voltage. Likewise, a measurement of both current and voltage will obviously yield a value of resistance. These measurement functions are often combined in a single instrument—the volt-ohm-milliammeter or VOM, a multirange meter that is one of the most useful pieces of measuring and test equipment an amateur can possess.

Accuracy

The accuracy of a dc meter of the D'Arsonval type is specified by the manufacturer. A common specification is 2 percent of full scale, meaning that a 0-100 microammeter, for example, will be correct to within 2 microamperes at any part of the scale. There are very few cases in amateur work where accuracy greater than this is needed. However, when the instrument is part of a more complex measuring circuit, the design and components can all cause error, reducing the overall accuracy of the complete device.

Extending the Current Range

Because of the way current divides between two resistances in parallel, it is possible to increase the range (more specifically, to decrease the sensitivity) of a dc micro-ammeter or milliammeter. The meter itself has an inherent resistance—its internal resistance—which determines the full-scale current passing through it when its rated voltage is applied. (This rated voltage is on

Fig 2—A safe method for determining the internal resistance of a meter.

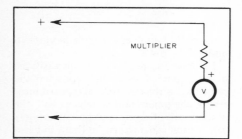

Fig 3—A voltmeter is a current-indicating instrument in series with a high resistance, the "multiplier."

Fig 4—Effect of voltmeter resistance on accuracy of readings. It is assumed that the dc resistance of the screen circuit is constant at 100 kilohms. The actual current and voltage without the voltmeter connected are 1 mA and 100 volts. The voltmeter readings will differ because the different types of meters draw different amounts of current through the 150-kΩ resistor.

the order of a few millivolts.) By connecting an external resistance in parallel with the internal resistance, as in Fig 1, the current will divide between the two, with the meter responding only to that part of the current that flows through the internal resistance of its movement. Thus, it reads only part of the total current; the effect is to make more total current necessary for a full-scale meter reading. The added resistance is called a shunt.

It is necessary to know the meter's internal resistance before the required value for a shunt can be calculated. It may vary from a fraction of an ohm to a few thousand ohms, with the higher resistance values associated with higher sensitivity. When this resistance is known, it can be used in the formula below to determine the re-

quired shunt for a given multiplication:

$$R = \frac{R_m}{n - 1}$$

where
  R = the shunt
  R_m = internal resistance
  n = the factor by which the original meter scale is to be multiplied.

Often the internal resistance of a particular meter will be unknown. This is usually the case when the meter is purchased at a flea market or is obtained from a commercial piece of equipment. Unfortunately, the internal resistance of the meter can not be measured directly with a VOM or VTVM without risk of damage to the meter movement.

Most modern digital multimeters *can* be used to measure the internal resistance of a meter directly.

Fig 2 shows another method that can be used safely to determine the internal resistance of a meter. A calibrated meter capable of measuring the same current as the unknown meter is required. The system works as follows: S1 is placed in the open position and R2 is set for maximum resistance. A supply of constant voltage is connected to the terminals + and − (a battery will work fine) and R2 is adjusted so that the unknown meter reads exactly full scale. Note the current shown on M2. Close S1 and alternately adjust R1 and R2 so that the unknown meter (M1) reads exactly half scale and the known meter (M2) reads the same value as in the step above. At this point the current in the circuit flows through M1 and half through R1. To determine the internal resistance of the meter, simply open S1 and read the resistance of R1 with a VTVM, VOM or digital voltohmmeter.

The values of R1 and R2 will depend on the meter sensitivity and the supply voltage. The maximum resistance value for R1 should be approximately twice the expected internal resistance of the meter. For highly sensitive meters (10 μA and less) 1 kilohm should be adequate. For less sensitive meters 100 ohms should suffice. Use no more supply voltage than necessary.

The value for minimum resistance at R2 can be calculated using Ohm's Law. For example, if the meter is a 0-1 mA type and the supply is a 1.5-volt battery, the minimum resistance required at R2 will be

$$R2 = \frac{1.5}{0.001}$$

R2(min) = 1500 ohms

In practice a 2- or 2.5-kΩ potentiometer would be used.

Making Shunts

Homemade shunts can be constructed from any of various special kinds of resistance wire, or from ordinary copper wire if no resistance wire is available. The copper wire table in this handbook gives

the resistance per 1000 feet for various sizes of copper wire. After computing the resistance required, determine the smallest wire size that will carry the full-scale current (250 circular mils per ampere is a satisfactory figure for this purpose). Measure off enough wire to provide the required resistance. A high-resistance 1- or 2-watt carbon-composition resistor makes an excellent form on which to wind the wire. It is recommended that you use the largest size copper wire that is practical to keep the effects of the temperature coefficient of copper to a minimum.

The Voltmeter

If a large resistance is connected in series with a current-reading meter, as in Fig 3, the current multiplied by the resistance will be the voltage drop across the resistance. This is known as a multiplier. An instrument used in this way is calibrated in terms of the voltage drop across the multiplier resistor and is called a voltmeter.

Sensitivity

Voltmeter sensitivity is usually expressed in ohms per volt, meaning that the meter full-scale reading multiplied by the sensitivity will give the total resistance of the voltmeter. For example, the resistance of a 1-kΩ-per-volt voltmeter is 1000 times the full-scale calibration voltage, and by Ohm's Law the current required for full-scale deflection is 1 milliampere. A sensitivity of 20 kΩ per volt, a commonly used value, means that the instrument is a 50-microampere meter.

The higher the resistance of the voltmeter, the more accurate the measurements, especially in high-resistance circuits. Current flowing through the voltmeter will cause a change in the voltage between the points where the meter is connected, compared with the voltage with the meter absent. This is illustrated in Fig 4.

Multipliers

The required multiplier resistance is found by dividing the desired full-scale voltage by the current, in amperes, required for full-scale deflection of the meter alone. Strictly, the internal resistance of the meter should be subtracted from the calculated value but this is seldom necessary (except perhaps for very low ranges), since the meter resistance will be negligible compared with the multiplier resistance. An exception is when the instrument is already a voltmeter and is provided with an internal multiplier, in which case the multiplier resistance required to extend the range is

$$R = R_m (n - 1)$$

where
  R_m = total resistance of the instrument
  n = factor by which the scale is to be multiplied

For example, if a 1-kΩ-per-volt voltmeter

having a calibrated range of 0-10 volts is to be extended to 1000 volts, R_m is $1000 \times 10 = 10$ kΩ, n is $1000/10 = 100$, and $R = 10,000 (100 - 1) = 990$ kΩ.

When extending the range of a voltmeter or converting a low-range meter into a voltmeter, the rated accuracy of the instrument is retained only when the muliplier resistance is precise. Precision wire-wound resistors are used in the mulipliers of high-quality instruments. These are relatively expensive, but the home constructor can do quite well with 1-percent-tolerance composition resistors. They should be derated when used for this purpose—that is, the actual power dissipated in the resistor should be not more than ¼ to ½ the rated dissipation—and care should be used to avoid overheating the body of the resistor when soldering to the leads. These precautions will help prevent permanent change in the resistance of the unit.

Ordinary composition resistors are generally furnished in 10- or 5-percent-tolerance ratings. If possible errors of this order can be accepted, resistors of this type may be used as multipliers. They should be operated below the rated power dissipation figure, in the interest of long-term stability.

DC MEASUREMENT CIRCUITS

The Voltmeter

A current-measuring instrument should have very low resistance compared with the resistance of the circuit being measured; otherwise, inserting the instrument will cause the current to differ from its value with the instrument out of the circuit. The resistance of many circuits in radio equipment is high and the circuit operation is affected little, if at all, by adding as much as a few hundred ohms in series. In such cases the voltmeter method of measuring current, shown in Fig 5, is frequently convenient. A voltmeter (or low-range milliammeter provided with a multiplier and operating as a voltmeter) having a full-scale voltage range of a few volts is used to measure the voltage drop across a suitable value of resistance acting as a shunt.

The value of shunt resistance must be calculated from the known or estimated maximum current expected in the circuit (allowing a safe margin) and the voltage required for full-scale deflection of the meter with its multiplier.

Power

Power in direct-current circuits is determined by measuring the current and voltage. When these are known, the power is equal to the voltage in volts multiplied by the current in amperes. If the current is measured with a milliammeter, the reading of the instrument must be divided by 1000 to convert it to amperes.

The setup for measuring power is shown in Fig 6, where R is any dc load, not necessarily an actual resistor.

Resistance

Obviously, if both voltage and current are measured in a circuit such as that in Fig 6, the value of resistance R (in case it is unknown) can be calculated from Ohm's Law. For accurate results, the internal resistance of the ammeter or milliammeter, mA, should be very low compared with the resistance, R, being measured. This is because the voltage read by the voltmeter, V, is the voltage across mA and R in series. The instruments and the dc voltage should be chosen so that readings are in the upper half of the scale, if possible, since the percentage error is less in this region.

The Ohmmeter

Although Fig 6 suffices for occasional resistance measurements, it is inconvenient when frequent measurements over a wide range of resistance are to be made. The device generally used for this purpose is the ohmmeter. This consists fundamentally of a voltmeter (or milliammeter, depending on the circuit used) and a small battery, the meter being calibrated so the value of an unknown resistance can be read directly from the scale. Typical ohmmeter circuits are shown in Fig 7. In the simplest type, Fig 7A, the meter and battery are connected in series with the unknown resistance. If a given deflection is obtained with terminals A-B shorted, inserting the resistance to be measured will cause the meter reading to decrease. When the resistance of the voltmeter is known, the following formula can be applied.

$$R = \frac{eR_m}{E} - R_m$$

where

R = resistance to be found
e = voltage applied (A-B shorted)
E = voltmeter reading with R connected, and
R_m = resistance of the voltmeter.

The circuit of Fig 7A is not suited to measuring low values of resistance (below a hundred ohms or so) with a high-resistance voltmeter. For such measurements the circuit of Fig 7B can be used. The unknown resistance is

$$R = \frac{I_2 R_m}{I_1 - I_2}$$

where

R = the unknown resistance
R_m = the internal resistance of the milliammeter
I_1 = current with R disconnected from terminals A-B
I_2 = current with R connected

The formula is based on the assumption that the current in the complete circuit will be essentially constant whether or not the

Fig 5—Voltmeter method of measuring current. This method permits using relatively large values of resistance in the shunt, standard values of fixed resistors frequently being usable. If the multiplier resistance is 20 (or more) times the shunt resistance, the error in assuming that all the current flows through the shunt will not be of consequence in most practical applications.

Fig 6—Measurement of power requires both current and voltage measurements; once these values are known, the power is equal to the product P = EI. The same circuit can be used for measurement of an unknown resistance.

Fig 7—Ohmmeter circuits. Values are discussed in the text. →

Fig 8—The Wheatstone bridge circuit. It is frequently drawn as at B for emphasizing its special function.

Fig 9—The IC voltmeter mounted in a small plastic case. This basic instrument measures only dc voltages, but with an RF probe as described later in this chapter, it can be used for RF measurements as well. It may also be used for resistance measurements, by using techniques described in the previous section. DS1, mounted between the binding posts, is a power-on indicator.

unknown terminals are short-circuited. This requires that R1 be very large compared with R_m, e.g., 3000 ohms for a 1-mA meter having an internal resistance of perhaps 50 ohms. A 3-volt battery would be necessary in this case in order to obtain a full-scale deflection with the *unknown* terminals open. R1 can be an adjustable resistor, to permit setting the open-terminal current to exact full scale.

A third circuit for measuring resistance is shown in Fig 7C. In this case a high-resistance voltmeter is used to measure the voltage drop across a reference resistor, R2, when the unknown resistor is connected so that current flows through it, R2 and the battery in series. By suitable choice of R2 (low values for low-resistance, high values for high-resistance unknowns), this circuit will give equally good results on all resistance values in the range from one ohm to several megohms. That is provided that the voltmeter resistance, R_m, is always very high (50 times or more) compared with the resistance of R2. A 20-kΩ-per-volt instrument (50-μA movement) is generally used. Assuming that the current through

the voltmeter is negligible compared with the current through R2, the formula for the unknown is

$$R = \frac{eR2}{E} - R2$$

where

R and R2 are shown in Fig 7C
e = the voltmeter reading with A-B open circuited
E = voltmeter reading with R connected.

The zero adjuster, R1, is used to set the voltmeter reading exactly to full scale when the meter is calibrated in ohms. A 10-kΩ variable resistor is suitable with a 20-kΩ-per-volt meter. The battery voltage is usually 3 volts for ranges up to 100 kΩ or so and 6 volts for higher ranges.

Bridge Circuits

An important class of measurement circuits is the bridge. A desired result is obtained by balancing the voltages at two different points in the circuit against each other so there is zero potential difference between them. A voltmeter bridged between the two points will read zero (null) when this balance exists, but will indicate some definite value of voltage when the bridge is not balanced.

Bridge circuits are useful both on direct current and on ac of all frequencies. The majority of amateur applications are at radio frequencies, as shown later in this chapter. However, the principles of bridge operation are most easily introduced in

Fig 10—A high impedance voltmeter need not be complex. This circuit uses a single IC. BT1 and BT2 can be 2 AAA (or AA) cells in a holder or 9-V transistor radio batteries (see text).

D1—LED, 5-V, 20 mA; Radio Shack 276-041 or equiv.
J1, J2—Banana jacks, 500-V insulation (see text), RS 274-662 or equiv.
M1—50-μA dc meter
R1—1.0-MΩ, 1/2-W, 5% resistor.
R2—4.7-MΩ and 300-kΩ, 1/4-W, 5% resistors in series.
R3—3.9-MΩ and 100-kΩ, 1/4-W, 5% resistors in series.
R4—470-kΩ and 30-kΩ, 1/4-W, 5% resistors in series.

R5—390-kΩ and 10-kΩ, 1/4-W, 5% resistors in series.
R6—47-kΩ and 3-kΩ, 1/4-W, 5% resistors in series.
R7—39-kΩ and 1-kΩ, 1/4-W, 5% resistors in series.
R8—10-kΩ, 1/4-W, 5% resistor.
R9—10-kΩ, 1/4-W PC-mount potentiometer, RS 271-218 or equiv.
R10—10-kΩ, panel-mount potentiometer, RS 271-1722.

R11—Current-limiting resistor; 680 Ω for 3-V batteries at BT1 and BT2, or 1.6 kΩ for 9-V batteries.
S1—1-pole, 7-position rotary switch (see text), RS 275-1385 or equiv.
S2—2-pole, 2-position toggle switch, RS 275-614 or equiv.
U1—LF353N dual JFET op amp, RS 276-1715 or equiv.

terms of dc, where the bridge takes its simplest form.

The Wheatstone Bridge

The simple resistance bridge, known as the Wheatstone bridge, is shown in Fig 8. All other bridge circuits—some of which are rather elaborate, especially those designed for ac—derive from this. The four resistors, R1, R2, R3 and R4 shown in A, are known as the bridge arms. For the voltmeter reading to be zero, the voltages across R3 and R4 in series must add algebraically to zero; that is, E1 must equal E2. R1 with R3 and R2 with R4 form voltage dividers across the dc source, so if

$$\frac{R1}{R3} = \frac{R2}{R4} \quad \text{then}$$

$$E1 = E2$$

The circuit is customarily drawn as shown at Fig 8B when used for resistance measurement. The equation above can be rewritten

$$R_x = R_s \frac{R2}{R1}$$

to find R_x, the unknown resistance. R1 and R2 are frequently made equal; then the calibrated adjustable resistance (the standard), R_s, will have the same value as R_x when R_s is set to show a null on the voltmeter.

Note that the resistance *ratios*, rather than the actual resistance values, determine the voltage balance. However, the values do have important practical effects on the sensitivity and power consumption. The bridge sensitivity is the readiness with which the meter responds to small amounts of unbalance about the null point; the sharper the null the more accurate the setting of R_s at balance.

The Wheatstone bridge is rarely used by amateurs for resistance measurement, the ohmmeter being the favorite instrument for that purpose. However, it is worthwhile to understand its operation because it is the basis of more complex bridges.

Electronic Voltmeters

It has been pointed out that for many purposes the resistance of a voltmeter must be extremely high in order to avoid "loading" errors caused by the current that necessarily flows through the meter. The use of high-resistance meters tends to cause difficulty in measuring relatively low voltages (under perhaps 1000 volts) because progressively smaller multiplier resistance is needed as the voltage range is lowered.

The voltmeter resistance can be made independent of the voltage range by using vacuum tubes or field-effect transistors as electronic dc amplifiers between the circuit being measured and the indicator, which may be a conventional meter movement or a digital display. As the input resistance of the electronic devices is extremely high—hundreds of megohms—they have essen-tially no loading effect on the circuit to which they are connected. They do, however, require a closed dc path in their input circuits (although this path can have very high resistance). They are also limited in the amplitude of voltage that their input circuits can handle. Because of this, the device actually measures a small voltage across a portion of a high-resistance voltage divider connected to the circuit being measured. Various voltage ranges are obtained by appropriate taps on the voltage divider.

In the design of electronic voltmeters it has become standard practice to use a voltage divider having a resistance of 10 megohms, tapped as required, in series with a 1-megohm resistor incorporated in the meter. The total voltmeter resistance, including probe, is therefore 11 megohms. The 1-megohm resistor serves to isolate the voltmeter circuit from the active circuit.

Hybrid Digital Meters

Over the years since digital meters (DMMs) came in to the price range of experimenters, the one argument against DMMs has been the lack of a facility for peaking and nulling circuits. The conversion and display times of most digital meters are slow enough that slight peaks and dips are almost impossible to observe without going to ridiculous extremes. Because of this, most experimenters still have a good old VOM or VTVM on the bench. In the past few years, manufacturers have taken various steps to make the digital meter more attractive to the user who needs peaking and nulling facilities. Three approaches have come into use:

1) Putting a small analog meter on the front panel of the DMM to give trends indication. This meter tends to be coarsely calibrated. This method allows the user to see the peaks and nulls and still have the accuracy of the digital display available in one package. Examples of this type of meter are the Heath IM-2264 and the Simpson 460-3.

2) Addition of a bar graph on the display. This bar graph usually takes the form of 20 to 40 dots in a row which are lit in proportion to the percentage of the range that is inputted. For example, if the meter had a 2-V range and a 20-dot bar graph, a dot would light for every 0.1-V increase. So if this meter has an input of 0.6 V on its leads, the six left-hand dots would light. This may seem a bit coarse, but it is useful in practice. Examples of this type of meter are the Fluke 70 series (sold by Heath as the SM77) and the Simpson 467.

3) The third method is using peak and null LEDs. In this case, there are two LEDs: one is for peaking and one is for nulling. As a signal is peaked, the peaking LED will glow brighter. When the peak occurs, both LEDs will glow equally. As the peak is passed, the null LED will brighten. This is probably the most difficult to interpret of the three methods. An example of this type of meter is the Sencore DVM56A.

The individual will have to decide which method best suits his or her personal taste and budget, when selecting this type of meter. But, with the steady improvement in measurement technology, the day may not be far off when mechanical meter movements may completely disappear from electrical and electronic applications.

AN IC VOLTMETER

One of the fundamental troubleshooting techniques is to check the voltage present at various points in the circuit. The measured voltage is compared with the voltage we expect to find at that point. Knowing what to expect is important. If we don't have some idea of what the voltage should be, measuring it won't tell us very much. Often the voltages we measure in a circuit will not agree exactly with our expected values. Small variations are normal and do not mean the circuit is not operating as it should. Component tolerance and meter errors are the primary causes for these variations.

Shown in Figs 9 through 12 is an easy-to-build, high-impedance dc voltmeter, first described by George Collins, KC1V, in January 1982 *QST*. All of the parts for the voltmeter are readily available. Calibration is simple and the cost is low. Construction of this meter can be considered as an easy weekend project. The input-impedance is 11 MΩ, and accuracy is better than 15%. With the RF probe shown later in this chapter, this meter can be used to make reasonably accurate RF voltage measurements at frequencies up to 30 MHz.

Circuit Details

The input impedance of the meter is determined by the total resistance of the range-selector voltage divider (R1 through R8). The values of the individual resistors have been selected to provide the desired full-scale voltage ranges and a total resistance of 11 MΩ. Some of the resistance values needed for the divider are not found in the standard series of 5%-tolerance resistor values. To avoid having to buy expensive (and hard to find) 1% resistors, two 5% units are used in series for each of the nonstandard values.

To keep the meter movement from loading the 11-MΩ divider, an operational amplifier (op amp) with JFET inputs is used to drive the meter. The LF353N IC (U1) contains two of these op amps in the same package. U1B drives the meter movement, while U1A serves as an adjustable voltage reference point. Both of the op amps are connected as voltage followers. This means that the input and output voltages are the same (a gain of 1). What makes the voltage follower useful is that the output can supply several milliamperes of current while the input draws a very small current (the input impedance is high).

Fig 11—Inside view of the IC voltmeter. This version was built from an available parts kit. Other components and construction styles can be used as well.

Fig 12—Parts-placement guide for the FET voltmeter. Parts are placed on the nonfoil side of the board; the shaded area represents an X-ray view of the copper pattern. A full-size etching pattern can be found at the back of this book.

By varying the voltage at pin 3 of U1 with R10, the zero setting of the meter can be adjusted to compensate for changes in battery voltage and room temperature. The fact that both op amps are in the same package helps reduce drift caused by temperature changes. R10 is mounted on the front panel so the operator can adjust it easily. R9 is the calibration control; it adjusts the meter sensitivity. R9 does not require frequent adjustment, so it is mounted inside the case.

Two batteries are used to power the meter circuit. Any battery potential between 3 and 9 V can be used without changes in the circuit. In the unit shown, four AAA penlight cells are used. These give the needed 3 V and have long life. Two 9-V transistor radio batteries will also be suitable.

Construction

Almost any type of case can be used to house the voltmeter. The exact size needed will depend on the dimensions of the batteries, meter movement and switches used. A plastic case, only 2-7/8 × 4 × 1-5/8 inches, houses the meter shown in the photographs. If a larger meter movement is used, an enclosure measuring 2-5/8 × 5-1/6 × 1-5/8 inches will be more satis-

factory. If you use a case with a metal panel, it is best if the negative jack (J2) is not connected to the panel. This permits voltage measurements below ground potential without having a voltage on the meter case.

The voltage-divider resistors are mounted on the range selector switch S1, as shown in Fig 11. If the switch has any spare lugs, they can be used as tie points for the series-connected resistors. If no lugs are available, simply solder the leads together; the remaining leads will support the resistors. The other components can be mounted on a small printed-circuit board,* although any method of wiring can be used. A quick and simple way of wiring the IC is to use a general-purpose IC-prototyping board, such as the Radio Shack 276-159.

The builder should be aware that very minute leakage currents between pins of the op-amp IC can cause improper operation

*A printed-circuit board and parts for the voltmeter, including a small circuit board for an RF probe, are available from Circuit Board Specialists, P.O. Box 951, Pueblo, CO 81002-0951.

of the instrument. If a circuit board is used, be sure to clean the rosin flux from around these pins after soldering is completed. Use a suitable solvent, such as denatured alcohol. Further, the circuit board should not be allowed to rest on any type of supporting material; even nonconducting foam may yield unexpected results.

With the resistor values shown in Fig 10, the highest full-scale range is 500 V. If this range is included, be sure the input connectors (J1 and J2) and the range switch (S1) are rated for 500 V or more. J1 and J2 should also be able to handle 500 volts safely. Only thin, fiber washers are used to insulate some type of jacks from the panel. These are fine for up to 100 V, but are not recommended for higher voltages. If the 500-V range is not needed, R7 and R8 can be connected in series or replaced by a 50-kΩ resistor (the same as R6).

Calibration

Only the sensitivity control, R9, needs to be adjusted before the meter can be used. A good method of calibration is to use two fresh carbon-zinc batteries in series to form a source of known potential. Each cell, when new, should produce 1.54 V. To adjust R9, turn the meter on, and set it to the 5-V range. With the meter leads shorted together, adjust the zero control (R10) so that the meter shows zero. Connect the two cells to the meter, and adjust R9 so the meter reads 3.1 V. This completes the voltmeter, and it is ready to use.

AC Instruments and Circuits

Although purely electromagnetic instruments that operate directly from alternating current are available, they are seen infrequently in present-day amateur equipment. For one thing, their use is not feasible above power-line frequencies.

Common instruments for audio and radio frequencies generally use a dc meter movement in conjunction with a rectifier. Voltage measurements suffice for nearly all test purposes. Current, as such, is seldom measured in the AF range. When RF current is measured the instrument used is a thermocouple milliammeter or ammeter.

The Thermocouple Meter

In a thermocouple meter the alternating current flows through a low-resistance heating element. The power lost in the resistance generates heat that warms a thermocouple, a junction of certain dissimilar metals that has the property of developing a small dc voltage when heated. This voltage is applied to a dc milliammeter calibrated in suitable ac units. The heater-thermocouple-dc meter combination is usually housed in a regular meter case.

Thermocouple meters can be obtained in ranges from about 100 mA to many amperes. Their useful upper frequency limit is in the neighborhood of 100 MHz. Their principal value in amateur work is in measuring current into a known load resistance for calculating the RF power delivered to the load.

Rectifier Instruments

The response of a rectifier-type meter is proportional (depending on the design) to either the peak amplitude or average amplitude of the rectified ac wave, and never directly responsive to the RMS value. The meter therefore cannot be calibrated in RMS without preknowledge of the relationship that happens to exist between the real reading and the RMS value. This relationship, in general, is not known, except in the case of single-frequency ac (a sine wave). Many practical measurements involve nonsinusoidal wave forms, so it is necessary to know what kind of instrument you have, and what it is actually reading, in order to make measurements intelligently.

Peak and Average with Sine-Wave Rectification

Fig 13 shows the relative peak and average values in the output of half- and full-wave rectifiers (see Chapter 6 for further details). As the positive and negative half cycles of the sine wave have the same shape, A, half-wave rectification of either the positive half, B or the negative half, C, gives exactly the same result. With full-wave rectification, D, the peak is still the same, but the average is doubled, since

Fig 13—Sine-wave alternating current or voltage, A, with half-wave rectification of the positive half cycle, B, and negative half cycle, C. At D—full-wave rectification. Average values are shown with relation to a peak value of 1.

there are twice as many half cycles per unit of time.

Unsymmetrical Wave Forms

A nonsinusoidal waveform is shown in Fig 14A. When the positive half cycles of this wave are rectified, the peak and average values are shown at B. If the polarity is reversed and the negative half cycles are rectified, the peak value is different but the average value is unchanged. The fact that the average of the positive side is equal to the average of the negative side is true of all ac waveforms, but different waveforms have different averages. Full-wave rectification of such a lopsided wave doubles the average value, but the peak reading is always the same as it is with the half cycle that produces the highest peak in half-wave rectification.

Effective-Value Calibration

The actual scale calibration of commercially made rectifier-type voltmeters is very often (almost always, in fact) in terms of RMS values. For sine waves this is satisfactory, and useful since RMS is the standard measure at power-line frequency. It is also useful for many RF applications where the waveform is often close to sinusoidal. But in other cases, particularly in the AF range, the error may be considerable when the waveform is not pure.

Turn-Over

From Fig 14 it is apparent that the calibration of an average-reading meter will

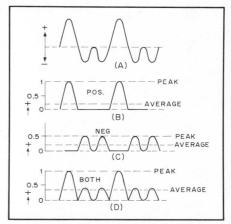

Fig 14—Same as Fig 13 for an unsymmetrical waveform. The peak values are different with positive and negative half-cycle rectification.

be the same whether the positive or negative sides are rectified. A half-wave peak-reading instrument, however, will indicate different values when its connections to the circuit are reversed (turn-over effect). Very often readings are taken both ways, in which case the sum of the two is the peak-to-peak (P-P) value, a useful figure in much audio and video work.

Average- and Peak-Reading Circuits

The basic difference between average- and peak-reading rectifier circuits is that the output is not filtered for averaged readings, while a filter capacitor is charged up to the peak value of the output voltage for measuring peaks. Fig 15A shows typical average-reading circuits, one half-wave and the other full-wave. In the absence of dc filtering the meter responds to wave forms such as are shown at B, C and D in Figs. 14 and 15, and since the inertia of the pointer system makes it unable to follow the rapid variations in current, it averages them out mechanically.

In Fig 15A, D1 actuates the meter; D2 provides a low-resistance dc return in the meter circuit on the negative half cycles. R1 is the voltmeter multiplier resistance. R2 forms a voltage divider with R1 (through D1), which prevents more than a few ac volts from appearing across the rectifier-meter combination. A corresponding resistor can be used across the full-wave bridge circuit.

In these two circuits no provision is made for isolating the meter from any dc voltage that may be on the circuit under measurement. The error caused by this can be avoided by connecting a large capacitor (not electrolytic!) in series with the hot lead. The reactance must be low compared with the meter impedance (see next section) in order for the full ac voltage to be applied

Fig 15—At A, half-wave and full-wave rectification for an instrument intended to operate on average values. At B, half-wave circuits for a peak-reading meter.

Fig 16—Typical semiconductor diode characteristic. Actual current and voltage values vary with the type of diode, but the forward-current curve would be in its steep part with only a volt or so applied. Note the change in the current scale for reverse current. Breakdown voltage, again depending on diode type, may range from 15 or 20 volts to several hundred.

to the meter circuit. As much as 1 µF may be required at line frequencies with some meters. The capacitor is not usually included in a VOM.

Series and shunt peak-reading circuits are shown in Fig 15B. C1 isolates the rectifier from dc voltage on the circuit under measurement. In the series circuit (which is seldom used) the time constant of the C2-R1-R2 combination must be very large compared with the period of the lowest ac frequency to be measured; similarly with C1-R1-R2 in the shunt circuit. The reason is that the capacitor is charged to the peak value of voltage when the ac wave reaches its maximum, and then must hold the charge (so it can register on a dc meter) until the next maximum of the same polarity. If the time constant is 20 times the ac period, the charge will have decreased by about five percent by the time the next charge occurs. The average drop will be smaller, so the error is appreciably less. The error will decrease rapidly with increasing frequency, assuming no change in the circuit values, but will increase at lower frequencies.

In Fig 15B, R1 and R2 form a voltage divider that reduces the peak dc voltage to 71 percent of its actual value. This converts the peak reading to RMS on sine-wave ac. Since the peak-reading circuits are incapable of delivering appreciable current without considerable error, R2 is usually the 11-megohm input resistance of an electronic voltmeter. R1 is therefore approximately 4.7 megohms, making the total resistance approach 16 megohms. A capacitance of 0.05 µF is sufficient for low audio frequencies under these conditions. Much smaller values of capacitance suffice for radio frequencies, obviously.

Voltmeter Impedance

The impedance of the voltmeter at the frequency being measured may have an effect on the accuracy similar to the error

caused by the resistance of a dc voltmeter, as discussed earlier. The ac meter acts like a resistance in parallel with a capacitance, and since the capacitive reactance decreases with increasing frequency, the impedance also decreases with frequency. The resistance is subject to some variation with voltage level, particularly at very low voltages (on the order of 10 volts or less) depending on the sensitivity of the meter movement and the kind of rectifier used.

The ac load resistance represented by a diode rectifier is approximately equal to one-half its dc load resistance. In Fig 15A the dc load is essentially the meter resistance, which is generally quite low compared with the multiplier resistance R1, so the total resistance will be about the same as the multiplier resistance. The capacitance depends on the components and construction, test lead length and disposition, and other such factors. In general, it has little or no effect at lower line and low audio frequencies, but the ordinary VOM loses accuracy at the high audio frequencies and is of little use at RF. For radio frequencies it is necessary to use a rectifier having very low inherent capacitance.

Similar limitations apply to the peak-reading circuits. In the parallel circuit the resistive component of the impedance is smaller than in the series circuit because the dc load resistance, R1/R2, is directly across the circuit being measured, and is therefore in parallel with the diode ac load resistance. In both peak-reading circuits the effective capacitance may range from 1 or 2 to a few hundred picofarads. Values of the order of 100 pF are to be expected in electronic voltmeters of customary design and construction.

Linearity

Fig 16, a typical current/voltage characteristic of a small semiconductor rectifier, indicates that the forward dynamic

resistance of the diode is not constant, but rapidly decreases as the forward voltage is increased from zero. The transition from high to low resistance occurs at considerably less than 1 volt, but is in the range of voltage required by the associated dc meter. With an average-reading circuit the current tends to be proportional to the square of the applied voltage. This crowds the calibration points at the low end of the meter scale. For most measurement purposes, however, it is far more desirable for the output to be linear; that is, for the reading to be directly proportional to the applied voltage.

To obtain linearity it is necessary to use a relatively large load resistance for the diode—large enough so this resistance, rather than the diode's own resistance, will govern the current flow. A linear or equally spaced scale is thus gained at the expense of sensitivity. The amount of resistance needed depends on the type of diode; 5000 to 50,000 ohms usually suffices for a germanium rectifier, depending on the dc meter sensitivity, but several times as much may be needed for silicon. The higher the resistance, the greater the meter sensitivity required; i.e., the basic meter must be a microammeter rather than a low-range milliammeter.

Reverse Current

When voltage is applied in the reverse direction there is a small leakage current in semiconductor diodes. This is equivalent to a resistance connected across the rectifier, allowing current to flow during the half cycle that should be completely nonconducting and causing an error in the dc meter reading. This back resistance is so high as to be practically unimportant with silicon diodes, but may be less than 100 kΩ with germanium.

The practical effect of semiconductor back resistance is to limit the amount of resistance than can be used in the dc load. This in turn affects the linearity of the

Fig 17—RF probe for use with an electronic voltmeter. The case of the probe is constructed from a seven-pin ceramic tube socket and a 2¼-inch tube shield. A half-inch grommet at the top of the tube shield prevents the output lead from chafing. A flexible copper-braid grounding lead and alligator clip provide a low-inductance return path from the test circuit.

meter scale. The back resistance of vacuum-tube diodes is infinite, for practical purposes.

RF Voltage

Special precautions must be taken to minimize the capacitive component of the voltmeter impedance at radio frequencies. If possible, the rectifier circuit should be installed permanently at the point where the RF voltage is to be measured, using the shortest possible RF connections. The dc meter can be remotely located, however.

For general RF measurements an RF probe is used in conjunction with an 11-MΩ electronic voltmeter, substituted for the dc probe mentioned earlier. The circuit of Fig 18, essentially the peak-reading shunt circuit of Fig 15B, is generally used. The series resistor, installed in the probe close to the rectifier, prevents RF from being fed through the probe cable to the electronic voltmeter. RF is further reduced from reaching the voltmeter by the cable capacitance. This resistor, in conjunction with the 10-MΩ divider resistance of the electronic voltmeter, also reduces the peak rectified voltage to a dc value equivalent to the RMS of the RF signal, to make the RF readings consistent with the regular dc calibration.

Of the diodes readily available to amateurs, the germanium point-contact or Schottky type is preferred for RF applications. It has low capacitance (on the

Fig 18—The RF probe circuit.

order of 1 pF) and in the high-back-resistance types the reverse current is not serious. The principal limitation is that its safe reverse voltage is only about 50-75 volts, which limits the RMS applied voltage to 15 or 20 volts. Diodes can be connected in series to raise the overall rating.

Fig 19—Inside the probe. The 1N34A diode, calibration resistor and input capacitor are mounted tight to the terminal strip with the shortest possible leads. Spaghetti tubing is placed on the diode leads to prevent accidental short circuits. The tube-shield spring and flexible copper grounding lead are soldered to the cable braid (the cable is RG-58 coax). The tip can be either a phone tip or a short pointed piece of stiff wire.

AN RF PROBE FOR ELECTRONIC VOLTMETERS

The isolation capacitor, C1, crystal diode and filter/divider resistor are mounted on a bakelite five-lug terminal strip, as shown in Fig 20. One end lug should be rotated 90 degrees so it extends off the end of the strip. All other lugs should be cut off flush with the edge of the strip. Where the inner conductor connects to the terminal lug, unravel the shield three-quarters of an inch, slip a piece of spaghetti tubing over it and then solder the braid to the ground lug on the terminal strip. Remove the spring from the tube shield, slide it over the cable, and crimp it to the remaining quarter inch of shield braid. Solder both the spring and a 12-inch length of flexible copper braid to the shield.

Fig 20—Component mounting details.

Next, cut off the pins on a seven-pin miniature shield-base tube socket. Use a socket with a cylindrical center post. Crimp the terminal lug previously bent out at the end of the strip and insert it into the center post of the tube socket from the top. Insert the end of a phone tip or a pointed piece of heavy wire into the bottom of the tube

socket center post, and solder the lug and tip to the center post. Insert a half-inch grommet at the top of the tube shield, sliding it over the cable and flexible braid down into the tube socket. The spring should make good contact with the tube shield to assure that the tube shield (probe case) is grounded. Solder an alligator clip to the other end of the flexible braid and mount a phone plug on the free end of the shielded wire.

Mount components close to the terminal strip, to keep lead lengths as short as possible and minimize stray capacitance. Use spaghetti tubing over all wires to prevent accidental shorts.

The phone plug on the probe cable plugs into the dc input jack of the electronic voltmeter and RMS voltages are read on the voltmeter negative dc scale.

The accuracy of the probe is within ±10 percent from 50 kHz to 250 MHz. The approximate input impedance is 6000 ohms shunted by 1.75 pF (at 200 MHz).

RF Power

Power at radio frequencies can be measured by means of an accurately calibrated RF voltmeter connected across the load in which the power is being dissipated. If the load is a known pure resistance, the power, by Ohm's Law, is equal to E^2/R, where E is the RMS value of the voltage.

If the load is not a pure resistance, the above method indicates only apparent power. The load can be a terminated transmission line, tuned with the aid of bridge circuits such as are described in the next section to act as a known resistance. An alternative load is a dummy antenna, a known pure resistance capable of dissipating the RF power safely.

AC Bridges

In its simplest form, the ac bridge is exactly the same as the Wheatstone bridge discussed earlier. However, complex impedances can be substituted for resistances, as suggested by Fig 21A. The same bridge equation holds if Z is substituted for R in each arm. For the equation to be true, however, the phase angles as well as the numerical values of the impedances must balance; otherwise, a true null voltage is impossible to obtain. This means that a bridge with all "pure" arms (pure resistance or reactance) cannot measure complex impedances; a combination of R and X must be present in at least one arm aside from the unknown.

The actual circuits of ac bridges take many forms, depending on the type of measurement intended and on the frequency range to be covered. As the frequency is raised, stray effects (unwanted capacitances and inductances) become more pronounced. At radio frequencies, special attention must be paid to minimizing them.

Most amateur-built bridges are used for

Fig 21—(A) Generalized form of bridge circuit for either ac or dc. (B) One form of ac bridge frequently used for RF measurements. (C) SWR bridge for use in transmission lines. This circuit is often calibrated in watts rather than volts.

RF measurements, especially SWR measurements on transmission lines. The circuits at Fig 21B and C are favorites for this purpose.

Fig 21B is useful for measuring both transmission lines and lumped constant components. Combinations of resistance and capacitance are often used in one or more arms; this may be required for eliminating the effects of stray capacitance.

The bridge shown in Fig 21C is used only on transmission lines, and only on those lines having the characteristic impedance for which the bridge is designed.

SWR Measurement—the Reflectometer

In measuring the standing-wave ratio, advantage is taken of the fact that the voltage on a transmission line consists of two components traveling in opposite directions. The power going from the transmitter to the load is represented by one voltage (designated incident or forward) and the power reflected from the load by the other. Because the relative amplitudes and phase relationships are definitely established by the line's characteristic

impedance, its length and the load impedance in which it is terminated, a bridge circuit can separate the incident and reflected voltages for measurement. This is sufficient for determining the SWR. Bridges designed for this purpose are frequently called reflectometers.

Refer to Fig 21A. If R1 and R2 are made equal, the bridge will be balanced when $R_x = R_s$. This is true whether R_x is an actual resistor or the input resistance of a perfectly matched transmission line, provided R_s is chosen to equal the characteristic impedance of the line. Even if the line is not properly matched, the bridge will still be balanced for power traveling outward on the line, since outward-going power sees only the Z_0 of the line until it reaches the load. However, power reflected back from the load does not see a bridge circuit, and the reflected voltage registers on the voltmeter. From the known relationship between the incident and reflected voltages the SWR is easily calculated:

$$SWR = \frac{V_o + V_r}{V_o - V_r}$$

where

V_o = incident voltage
V_r = reflected voltage

The Reflected Power Meter

Fig 21C makes use of mutual inductance between the primary and secondary of T1 to establish a balancing circuit. C1 and C2 form a voltage divider in which the voltage across C2 is in the same phase as the voltage at that point on the transmission line. The relative phase of the voltage across R1 is determined by the phase of the current in the line. If a pure resistance equal to the design impedance of the bridge is connected to the RF OUT terminals, the voltages across R1 and C2 will be out of phase and the voltmeter reading will be minimum. If the amplitudes of the two voltages are also equal (they are made so by bridge adjustment) the voltmeter will read zero. Any other value of resistance or impedance connected to the RF OUT terminals will result in a finite voltmeter reading. When used in a transmission line this reading is proportional to the reflected voltage. To measure the incident voltage, the secondary terminals of T1 should be reversed. To function as described, the secondary-winding reactance of T1 must be very large compared to the resistance of R1.

Instruments of this type are usually designed for convenient switching between forward and reflected power, and are often calibrated to read watts in the specified characteristic impedance. As the power

calibration is made at an SWR of 1:1, the actual power transmitted to the load must be calculated from the difference between the forward and reflected readings when the SWR is other than 1:1. A reading of 400 watts forward and 300 watts reflected means that 400 W − 300 W = 100 W has been delivered to the load. The SWR can be calculated from the formula

$$SWR = \frac{1 + \sqrt{\dfrac{\text{reflected power}}{\text{forward power}}}}{1 - \sqrt{\dfrac{\text{reflected power}}{\text{forward power}}}}$$

$$SWR = \frac{1 + \sqrt{\dfrac{300}{400}}}{1 - \sqrt{\dfrac{300}{400}}} = 13.9$$

Both of these calculations assume that the loss in the transmission line is very small; information on correcting for line loss is given in Chapter 16.

Sensitivity and Frequency

In all of the circuits in Fig 21 the sensitivity is independent of the applied frequency, within practical limits. Stray capacitances and couplings generally limit the performance of all three at the high-frequency end of the useful range. Fig 21A will work right down to dc, but the low-frequency performance of Fig 21B is degraded when the capacitive reactances become so large that voltmeter impedance becomes low in comparison. (In all these bridge circuits, it is assumed that the voltmeter impedance is high compared with the impedance of the bridge arms.) In Fig 21C the performance is limited at low frequencies by the fact that the transformer reactance decreases with frequency, so that eventually the reactance is not very high in comparison with the resistance of R1.

The Monimatch

A type of bridge that is simple to make, but in which the sensitivity rises directly with frequency, is the Monimatch and its various offspring. The circuit cannot be described in terms of lumped constants, as it makes use of the distributed mutual inductance and capacitance between the center conductor of a transmission line and a wire placed parallel to it. The wire is terminated in a resistance approximating the characteristic impedance of the transmission line at one end and feeds a diode rectifier at the other.

Frequency Measurement

The regulations governing amateur operation require that the transmitted signal be maintained inside the limits of certain bands of frequencies.[1] The exact frequency need not be known, as long as it is not outside the limits. On this last point there are no tolerances: It is up to the individual amateur to see that he stays safely inside.

This is not difficult to do, but requires some simple apparatus and the exercise of some care. The apparatus commonly used is the frequency-marker generator, and the method involves use of the station receiver, as shown in Fig 22.

Fig 22—Setup for using a frequency standard. It is necessary that the transmitter signal be weak in the receiver—of the same order of strength as the marker signal from the standard. This requirement can usually be met by turning on just the transmitter oscillator, leaving all power off any succeeding stages. In some cases it may also be necessary to disconnect the antenna from the receiver.

The Frequency Marker

The marker generator in its simplest form is a high-stability oscillator generating a series of signals which, when detected in the receiver, mark the exact edges of the amateur assignments. It does this by oscillating at a low frequency that has harmonics falling on the desired frequencies.

Most US amateur band limits are exact multiples of 25 kHz, whether at the extremes of a band or at points marking the subdivisions between types of emission, license privileges, and so on. A 25-kHz fundamental frequency therefore will produce the desired marker signals if its harmonics at the higher frequencies are strong enough. But since harmonics appear at 25-kHz intervals throughout the spectrum, along with the desired markers, the problem of identifying a particular marker arises. This is easily solved if the receiver has a reasonably good calibration. If not, most marker circuits provide for a choice of fundamental outputs of 100 and 50 kHz as well as 25 kHz, so the question can be narrowed down to initial identification of 100-kHz intervals. From these, the desired

[1]These limits depend on the type of emission and class of license held, as well as on international agreements. See the latest edition of *The FCC Rule Book* for current status.

25-kHz (or 50-kHz) points can easily be spotted. Coarser frequency intervals are rarely required; there are usually signals available from stations of known frequency, and the 100-kHz points can be counted off from them.

Transmitter Checking

In checking one's own transmitter frequency, the signal from the transmitter is first tuned in on the receiver and the dial setting at which it is heard is noted. Then the nearest marker frequencies above and below the transmitter signal are tuned in and identified. The transmitter frequency is obviously between these two known frequencies.

If the marker frequencies are accurate, this is all that needs to be known—except that the transmitter frequency must not be so close to a band (subband) edge that sideband frequencies, especially in phone transmission, will extend over the edge.

If the transmitter signal is inside a marker at the edge of an assignment, to the extent that there is an audible beat note with the receiver BFO turned off, normal CW sidebands are safely inside the edge. (This statement does not take into account abnormal sidebands such as those caused by clicks and chirps.) For phone the safety allowance is usually taken to be about 3 kHz, the nominal width of one sideband. A frequency difference of this order can be estimated by noting the receiver dial settings for the two 25-kHz markers that bracket the signal and dividing 25 by the number of dial divisions between them. This will give the number of kilohertz per dial division.

Transceivers

The method described above is applicable when the receiver and transmitter are separate pieces of equipment. When a transceiver is used and the transmitting frequency is automatically the same as that to which the receiver is tuned, setting the tuning dial to a spot between two known marker frequencies is all that is required. The RIT control must be turned off.

The proper dial settings for the markers are those at which, with the BFO on, the signal is tuned to zero beat—the spot where the beat disappears as the tuning makes the beat tone progressively lower. Exact zero beat can be determined by a very slow rise and fall of background noise, caused by a beat of a cycle or less per second. In receivers with high selectivity it may not be possible to detect an exact zero beat, because low audio frequencies from beat notes may be prevented from reaching the speaker or headphones.

Frequency-Marker Circuits

The basic frequency-determining element in most amateur frequency markers is a

100-kHz or 1-MHz crystal. Although the marker generator should produce harmonics at 25-kHz and 50-kHz intervals, crystals (or other high-stability devices) for frequencies lower than 100 kHz are expensive and difficult to obtain. However, there is really no need for them, since it is easy to divide the basic frequency down to whatever one desires; 50 and 25 kHz require only two successive divisions, each by two. In the division process, the harmonic output of the generator is greatly enhanced, making the generator useful at frequencies well into the VHF range.

Simple Crystal Oscillators

Fig 23 illustrates two of the simpler circuits. C1 in both circuits is used for exact adjustment of the oscillating frequency to 100 kHz, which is done by using the receiver for comparing one of the oscillator's harmonics with a standard frequency transmitted by WWV, WWVH or a similar station.

Fig 23A shows a field-effect transistor analog of a vacuum-tube circuit. However, it requires a 10-mH coil to operate well, and since the harmonic output is not strong at the higher frequencies the circuit is given principally as an example of a simple transistor arrangement. A much better oscillator is shown at B. This is a cross-connected pair of transistors forming a multivibrator of the free-running or asynchronous type, locked at 100 kHz by using the crystal as one of the coupling elements. While it can use two separate bipolar transistors as shown, it is much simpler to use an integrated-circuit dual gate, which contains all necessary parts except the crystal and capacitors. Further, it is considerably less expensive and more compact than the separate components.

Frequency Dividers

Electronic division is accomplished by a bistable flip-flop or cross-coupled circuit that produces one output change for every two impulses applied to its input circuit, thus dividing the applied frequency by two. All division therefore must be in terms of some power of two. In practice this is no handicap since with modern integrated-circuit flip-flops, circuit arrangements can be worked out for division by any desired number.

As flip-flops and gates in integrated circuits come in compatible series—meaning that they work at the same supply voltage and can be directly connected together—a combination of a dual-gate version of Fig 23B and a dual flip-flop makes an attractive simple combination for the marker generator. A circuit using a similar arrangement appears in Chapter 34.

There are several different basic types of flip-flops, the variations having to do with methods of driving (dc or pulse operation)

Fig 23—Two simple 100-kHz oscillator circuits. B is the most suitable of available transistor circuits (for marker generators) and is recommended where solid-state construction is to be used. In both circuits C1 is for fine frequency adjustment. The output coupling capacitor, C3 is generally small—20 to 50 pF—a compromise to avoid loading the oscillator by the receiver antenna input while maintaining adequate coupling for good harmonic strength.

and control of the counting function. Information on the operating principles and ratings of a specific type usually can be obtained from the manufacturer. The counting-control functions are not needed in using the flip-flop in a simple marker generator, although they come into play when dividing by some number other than a power of two.

Other Methods of Frequency Checking

The simplest possible frequency-measuring device is an absorption frequency-meter—a parallel LC circuit, tunable over a desired frequency range, with its tuning dial calibrated in frequency. It can be used only for checking circuits in which at least a small amount of RF power is present, because the energy required to give a detectable indication is not available in the LC circuit itself; it has to be extracted from the circuit being measured. Hence the name absorption frequency meter. What is actually measured is the frequency of the RF energy, not the frequency to which the circuit under test may be tuned.

The measurement accuracy of such an instrument is low, compared with the accuracy of a marker generator, because the Q of a practicable LC circuit is not high enough to make precise dial readings possible. Also, any two circuits coupled together react on each other's tuning. (This can be minimized by using the loosest

coupling that will give an adequate indication.)

The absorption frequency meter has one useful advantage over the marker generator —it will respond only to the frequency to which it is tuned, or to a band of frequencies very close to it. Thus there is no harmonic ambiguity, as there sometimes is with a marker generator.

Absorption Circuit

A typical absorption frequency-meter circuit is shown in Fig 24. In addition to the adjustable tuned circuit, L1-C1, it includes a pickup coil, L2, wound over L1, a high-frequency semiconductor diode, D1, and a microammeter or low-range (usually not more than 0-1 mA) milliammeter. A phone jack is included so the device can be used for listening to the signal.

Fig 24—Absorption frequency-meter circuit. The closed-circuit phone jack may be omitted if listening is not wanted, in which case the positive terminal of M1 goes to common ground.

The sensitivity of the frequency meter depends on the sensitivity of the dc meter movement and the size of L2 in relation to L1. There is an optimum size for this coil that must be found by experimentation. An alternative is to make the rectifier connection to an adjustable tap on L1, in which case there is an optimum tap point. In general, the rectifier coupling should be a little below (that is, less tight than) the point that gives maximum response, since this will make the indication sharper.

Calibration

The absorption frequency meter must be calibrated by taking a series of readings from circuits carrying RF power at known frequencies. The frequency of the RF energy may be determined by means such as a marker generator and receiver. The setting of the dial that gives the highest meter indication is the calibration point for that frequency. This point should be determined by tuning through it with loose coupling to the circuit being measured.

Frequency Standards

The difference between a marker generator and a frequency standard is that special pains are taken to make the frequency-standard oscillator frequency as stable as possible. Variations in temperature, humidity, line voltage and other factors can cause a small change in frequency.

While there are no definite criteria that distinguish the two in this respect, a circuit designated as a standard for amateur purposes should be capable of maintaining frequency within at least a few parts per million in ambient conditions, without adjustment. Commercially made receivers that employ synthesizers use frequency standards with a tolerance of 1 part in 100,000,000. A simple marker generator using a 100-kHz crystal can be expected to have frequency variations 10 times (or more) greater under similar conditions. It can of course be adjusted to exact frequency at any time the WWV (or equivalent) signal is available.

The design considerations of high-precision frequency standards are outside the scope of this chapter, but information is available from time to time in periodicals.

Frequency Counters

One of the most accurate means of measuring frequency is the frequency counter. This instrument is capable of numerically displaying the frequency of the signal supplied to its input. For example, if an oscillator operating at 8.244 MHz is connected to the counter input, 8.244 would be displayed. At present, there are counters that are usable well up into the gigahertz range. Most counters that are used at high frequencies make use of a prescaler ahead of a basic low-frequency counter. Essentially, the prescaler divides the high-frequency signal by 10, 100, 1000 or some other amount so the low-frequency counter can display the operating frequency.

The accuracy of the counter depends on an internal crystal reference. The more accurate the crystal reference, the more accurate the readings will be. Crystals for frequency counters are manufactured to close tolerances. Most counters have a trimmer capacitor so the crystal can be set exactly on frequency. Crystal frequencies of 1 MHz, 5 MHz or 10 MHz have become more or less standard. Harmonics of the crystal can be compared to WWV or WWVH signals at 5, 10, 15 MHz, etc., and adjusted for zero beat.

Many frequency counters offer options to increase the accuracy of the counter's timebase; this directly increases the counter's accuracy. These options usually employ temperature-compensated crystal oscillators (TCXOs) or crystals mounted in constant temperature ovens that keep the crystal from being affected by changes in ambient (room) temperature. Counters with these options are capable of obtaining accuracies of 0.1 ppm (part per million) or better. For example, a counter with a timebase with an accuracy of 5.0 ppm and a second counter with a TCXO with an accuracy of 0.1 ppm are available to check a 436-MHz CW transmitter for satellite use. The counter with the 5-ppm timebase could have a frequency error of as much as 2.18 kHz, while the possible error of the counter with the 0.1-ppm timebase is only 0.0436 kHz.

A 500-MHz FREQUENCY COUNTER

The advent of LSI (large-scale-integration) integrated-circuit technology has reduced the construction costs of many electronic products. The frequency counter shown in Figs 25 through 34 was designed and built in the ARRL lab by Ed Hare, KA1CV and Tom Miller, NK1P. It uses an Intersil ICM7226A 10-MHz frequency counter to obtain a lot of performance for relatively little cost. With some careful shopping it can be built for about $150.00, including the cabinet. It is usable from audio through UHF, and its sensitivity of 30 mV makes it a useful station accessory and troubleshooting tool.

Two input connectors are provided. The 10-MHz input has a high impedance, with a usable range of 20 Hz to over 10 MHz. The sensitivity is reduced to about 100 mV at the low-frequency end. The 500-MHz input has a 50-ohm impedance, and it is used for frequencies from 400 kHz to over 500 MHz. A SENSitivity control allows this input to accommodate signals of up to 2 V RMS.

The project incorporates a prescaler that works with the range switch to automatically select a divide-by-10 or divide-by-100 function. This prescaler can also be built as a separate project to extend the range of an existing frequency counter. The ½-inch digital readout is easy to read in almost any lighting conditions; a GATE

Fig 25—Exterior view of the 500-MHz frequency counter. Clear red plastic has been put in front of the LED display to make it easier to read in bright light.

LED is included for those who like to watch "das-blinkenlights."

Technical Details

This project was designed in modules. Fig 26 shows the schematic of the prescaler. The 10 MHz input uses Q1 and its associated circuitry as a high-input-impedance preamplifier, with input protection provided by D1 and D2. U1 is a high-speed comparator used to obtain fast-rising square waves from the output of Q1. The output of this stage is coupled into Q2 to obtain the TTL voltage levels required by U5.

U2 is a MAR-6 MMIC preamplifier stage for the 500-MHz input. Other MMICs were tried successfully at U2, requiring only a change in the value of R10. (For more information on MMIC devices, see February and March 1987 *QST*). An 11C90 is used at U3 as a high-speed divide-by-10 stage. R12, R13 and R14 are optional components; they allow a fine adjustment of the V$_{REF}$ voltage output from U3, increasing the counter sensitivity. If the resistors are left out of the circuit the sensitivity will decrease to about 100 mV.

The output of U3 feeds U4 and U5, another divide-by-10 stage. A 74S160 binary counter is used in this stage. A 74LS160 can be substituted here, but this limits the counter response to about 350 MHz.

U5 selects either the 10-MHz direct input or the 500-MHz input divided by 10 or 100. This selection is accomplished through the appropriate A, B or C inputs of the 74LS151. If the prescaler is built as a separate module these signals must be provided. Table 1 shows a truth table for this stage. The output of this stage is a TTL voltage level.

The prescaler module requires +4.75 to +5.25 V at 450 mA and +12 to +18 V at 120 mA. The +12 to +18 V is regulated to +10 V by D5. Extensive power-supply bypassing has been used throughout.

The power-supply schematic is shown in Fig 27. A full-wave bridge rectifier is used to generate +12 to +18 V. This is

regulated to +5 V by U1. The builder has quite a bit of latitude when selecting components for the power-supply circuit. Any 12.6-V transformer with at least a 450-mA current rating may be used at T1. U2 can be rated at 50 V or higher, 1 A or better. The values for C1 and C3 are approximate and could easily vary by 50%. The capacitor voltage ratings shown are the minimum that should be used, however.

The 10-MHz counter section has been designed to make use of the counter feature available in the Intersil ICM7226A frequency counter IC. The schematic for this module is shown on Fig 28. The internal 10-MHz oscillator can be adjusted to zero-beat with WWV. It is important to use a high-quality capacitor at C103; a mica or polystyrene capacitor is best. If a ceramic capacitor is used, the oscillator frequency is apt to be fairly sensitive to temperature changes, and this degrades counter accuracy. C102 can be any small trimmer capacitor that has a capacitance of at least 50 pF (a 6 to 70 pF unit was used in the ARRL counter). The RESET switch allows the user to restart the counter, a useful feature on longer gate times. The HOLD feature stops the counting and maintains the last reading on the LED display. The display uses GI MAN6710 dual displays, and the display PC board is designed to accommodate this (or an equivalent) display. Experienced builders could substitute a different LED display, but the ICM7226A is specified to sink a maximum of 25 mA, so the substitution must be made accordingly. The gate LED (DS101) lights when the counter is sampling the input signal.

The ICM7226A replaces the ICM7216C that was used in an earlier version of this counter. The ICM7226A has BCD outputs available. Pads have been placed on the printed-circuit board for these outputs to facilitate custom modifications using these signals.

The counter features six ranges. Gate times are 10 s, 1 s, 100 ms and 10 ms, with 100 ms used on the two prescaled ranges. Ultimate resolution is 0.1 Hz. The left decimal point indicates that the input signal

Fig 26—Schematic diagram of the prescaler module. All resistors are ¼ W, 5% tolerance, unless noted. Polarized capacitors are electrolytic.

R11—5-kΩ linear panel-mount potentiometer.
R12—500-Ω single-turn trimmer potentiometer.
Q1—MPF102 JFET.
Q2—2N3904 NPN transistor.
U1—LM360 high-speed comparator. (Available from Jameco or BCD Electro, see Chapter 35).

U2—MAR-6 or MSA-685 MMIC (see text) Available from Microwave Components of Michigan, see Chapter 35).
U3—11C90 Prescaler (Available from Circuit Board Specialists, see Chapter 35).

U4—74S160 Schottky decade counter (see text).
U5—74LS151 8-input multiplexer.
D1-D4—Small-signal diode: 1N4148, 1N914 etc.
D5—10-V, 1-W Zener diode.

is over-range. The external decimal point mode of the ICM7226A is used, automatically switching the decimal point to accommodate Hz, kHz and the two prescaled MHz ranges.

The ICM7226A accomplishes range and decimal point changes by connecting the RANGE and DP IN inputs to the various digit-multiplex outputs and internally evaluating the multiplex relationship. The TTL circuitry of U102, U103 and U104 is designed to automatically generate the

Table 1
Prescaler Control Logic

Inputs			Result
A	B	C	
H	L	L	divide by 10
L	H	L	divide by 100
X	X	H	direct (no prescale)

H = > 2.7 V
L = < 0.8 V
X = don't care

signals required to switch the prescaler into its various modes. U102 is configured as a flip-flop, changing state as the range switch is set to the 100-MHz or 500-MHz range by detecting a simultaneous occurrence of DP IN and digit 6 for divide-by-10 or digit 5 for divide-by-100. U103 and U104 set the 10-MHz output high on all other ranges. U102 and U103 must be CMOS, 74C00 or 74HC00. The use of a low-power Schottky device here will result in excessive loading of the multiplexing lines. C104 and

Fig 27—Schematic diagram of the power supply. Polarized capacitors are electrolytic.
S1—SPST switch.
T1—Power transformer, 120-V primary, 12.6-V, 450-mA secondary.
U1—7805 voltage regulator IC.
U2—50-V, 1-A bridge rectifier.

C105 are used to smooth out multiplexing glitches that would otherwise result in false switching of the flip-flop outputs. U104 can be CMOS or low-power Schottky. The ARRL version uses a 74C74 here.

Construction Details

The counter and prescaler should be constructed using the PC artwork that is found in the back of this book. Circuit layout is important to the proper operation of the 10 MHz squaring circuit and the 11C90 divide-by-10 IC. Fig 29 shows the component-side parts-placement diagram for the counter/prescaler board. Use insulated wire jumpers at the places marked W on the component-placement diagram.

Some additional components must be mounted on the bottom side of the board, and it is easier to do this after all of the component-side parts have been installed. U2 is a surface-mount MMIC; the cut pin is the input. The bypass capacitors are installed on pads on the PC board. Refer to Fig 30 for the solder-side parts-placement diagram. Fig 31 shows how the bypass capacitors have been mounted using heat-shrink tubing to keep the component leads from shorting to any of the PC board traces.

A 16-pin DIP socket is used for J101, and a 16-pin DIP connector and ribbon cable form the mating connector. Fig 33 shows this ribbon cable going to the display board. Insulation displacement connector (IDC) headers are easy to install on a length of ribbon cable.

Sockets are recommended for all of the DIP ICs because it is a good idea to verify proper voltages at the power pins of the ICs before they are installed. Sockets also make IC replacement easier.

If the PC board is used for the power supply, the parts should be installed on the board as shown in the power-supply component-placement diagram, Fig 32. Pay close attention to the orientation of U1 (mount it with the tab flush against the PC board—part number facing up) and to the polarity markings on the electrolytic capacitors and the bridge rectifier. U1 requires a small heat sink similar to that shown in the upper left corner of Fig 33.

The component-placement diagram for the display board is shown in Fig 34. A 16-pin DIP socket may be installed at J102 if desired, or the wires from J101 may be directly soldered through the appropriate holes. Pin 1 on J101 should be connected to pin 1 on J102. Install wire jumpers at the places marked W on the parts-placement diagram.

The display board mounts directly to the front panel. If ½-inch spacers are used to mount the display board, the LEDs will be flush with the front panel. For those builders who wish to exactly duplicate the ARRL version of the counter, a dimensional diagram and actual-size layout of the front panel lettering are available from the ARRL Technical Department secretary for an SASE and $1.00.

The ARRL version of the counter was built in a Bud AC-406 chassis (2 × 9 × 7 inches HWD) with a BPA-1593 bottom plate. The HOLD and RESET switches and the GATE LED are mounted between the display board and the front panel, so these must be mounted before the display board is installed. It is probably easier to install the wires on the PC board and solder them to the front-panel components after they are mounted. C6, C7, D3 and D4 are mounted off-board, and should be installed directly at J2 using short leads. Short pieces of RG-174 coaxial cable are used to connect J1 and J2 to the appropriate points on the PC board. The sensitivity control should be wired so that clockwise rotation decreases the resistance. The remainder of the layout is not critical, so the builder can easily determine the layout best suited to the components used. The interior photograph, Fig 33 shows the arrangement used in the ARRL version.

Alignment and Troubleshooting

There is little alignment that needs to be performed on this circuit. Lab tests indicate that the counter has completely stabilized after a warm-up time of 60 minutes, showing 170 Hz drift at 10 MHz during the warm-up period. To align the counter, allow an hour for warm-up and tune in WWV (10 MHz or 20 MHz) on a general-coverage receiver. Next, tune in the signal from the counter's internal oscillator on the receiver. It may be necessary to use an external antenna placed near the counter circuitry to pick up enough signal from the ICM7226A oscillator. Adjust C102 so that the oscillator is zero-beat with the WWV carrier.

A second calibrated frequency counter could also be used to set the 10-MHz oscillator if desired. Couple a signal from the ICM7226A 10-MHz oscillator by placing the second counter's probe near the oscillator components. Adjust C102 for a 10-MHz reading on the second counter.

If a variable-output VHF/UHF generator is available, the prescale sensitivity control (R12), may be adjusted for maximum sensitivity. Set the front-panel SENSitivity control fully clockwise and start with about 100 mV at 500 MHz into the 500 MHz input. Gradually decrease the output from the signal generator while adjusting R12 to maintain an accurate reading. With somewhere around 30 mV input, the prescale sensitivity control will not give further improvement. R12 may be left at this setting; it should not require any further adjustment. It is best to use an external attenuator to reduce strong signals to about 100 mV or so, but the front-panel SENSitivity control can be used for input signals up to 2 V RMS. The 10-MHz input can withstand input voltages of about 20 V RMS. The front-panel SENSitivity control has no effect on the 10 MHz input.

If the circuit fails to function refer to Chapter 26 for general troubleshooting information. The signals are divided by 10 at U3 and U4; keep this in mind if signal tracing is being performed.

U106 U105 LSD

EXCEPT AS INDICATED, DECIMAL
VALUES OF CAPACITANCE ARE
IN MICROFARADS (μF); OTHERS
ARE IN PICOFARADS (pF);
RESISTANCES ARE IN OHMS;
k = 1000, M = 1000 000.

Fig 28—Schematic diagram of the 10-MHz counter module. All resistors are ¼ W, 5% tolerance. Polarized capacitors are electrolytic.

C102—6-70 pF ceramic trimmer (see text).
C103—39-pF, 50-V silver mica or polystyrene.
Q101—2N3906 PNP transistor.
S101—Double-pole, six-position, non-shorting rotary switch.
S102, S103—SPST momentary contact panel-mount push-button switch.
U101—Intersil ICM7226A common-anode frequency counter. (Available from Digi-Key; see Chapter 35).
U102, U103—74C00 CMOS quad-NAND gate (see text).
U104—74C74 CMOS dual D flip-flop (see text).
U105-U108—Dual 7-segment LED display; General Instrument MAN6710, Panasonic LN524RA or ECG3074 (Available from Digi-Key or Mouser, see Chapter 35).
Y101—10-MHz crystal, 30 pF load.

Fig 29—Parts-placement diagram for the prescaler and counter board, as seen from the component side of the board. Additional parts are mounted on the solder side of the board. A full-size etching pattern is included at the back of this book.

Fig 30—Parts-placement diagram for the prescaler and counter board, as seen from the foil side of the board. Ensure that U2 is mounted as shown; the cut lead is the input pin.

Fig 31—View of the solder side of the prescaler and counter board. Heat-shrink tubing has been used to ensure that the capacitor leads will not short circuit to the PC board traces.

Fig 32—Parts-placement diagram for the power supply board, as seen from the component side of the board. A full-size etching pattern is included at the back of this book.

Fig 33—Interior view of the completed 500-MHz frequency counter. Ribbon cable and IDC headers have been used to connect the display board to the prescaler and counter board.

Fig 34—Parts-placement diagram for the display board, as seen from the component side of the board. There is a full-size etching pattern at the back of this book.

Other Instruments and Measurements

Many measurements require a source of ac power of adjustable frequency (and sometimes adjustable amplitude) in addition to what is already available from the transmitter and receiver. RF and AF test oscillators, for example, provide signals for purposes such as receiver alignment, testing of phone transmitters, and so on. Another valuable adjunct to the station is the oscilloscope, essential for checking waveforms.

RF Oscillators for Circuit Alignment

Receiver testing and alignment, covered in an earlier chapter, uses equipment common to ordinary radio service work. Inexpensive RF signal generators are available, both complete and in kit form. However, any source of signal that is weak enough to avoid overloading the receiver usually will serve for alignment work. The frequency marker generator is a satisfactory signal source. In addition, its frequencies, although not continuously adjustable, are known far more precisely, since the usual signal-generator calibration is not highly accurate. For rough work a gate-dip or grid-dip meter is sufficient.

AUDIO-FREQUENCY OSCILLATORS

Tests requiring an audio-frequency signal generally call for one that is a reasonably good sine wave. The best oscillator circuits for this use are RC-coupled, operating as close to a class-A amplifier as possible. Variable frequencies covering the entire audio range are needed for determining frequency response of audio amplifiers.

For most phone-transmitter testing, and for simple trouble shooting in AF amplifiers, an oscillator generating one or two frequencies with good waveform is adequate. A two-tone (dual) oscillator is particularly useful for testing sideband transmitters and adjusting them for on-the-air use.

The circuit of a simple RC oscillator that is useful for general test purposes is given in Fig 35. This Twin-T arrangement gives a waveform that is satisfactory for most purposes, and by choice of circuit constants the oscillator can be operated at any frequency in the audio range. R1, R2 and C1 form a low-pass type network, while C2, C3 and R3 form a high-pass network. As the phase shifts are opposite, there is only one frequency at which the total phase shift from collector to base is 180 degrees; oscillation will occur at this frequency. Optimum operation results when C1 is approximately twice the capacitance of C2 or C3, and R3 has a resistance about 0.1 that of R1 or R2 (C2 = C3 and R1 = R2). Output is taken across C1, where the harmonic distortion is least. A relatively high impedance load should be used—100 kΩ or more.

A small-signal AF transistor is suitable for Q1. Either NPN or PNP types can be

Fig 35—Twin-T audio oscillator circuit. Representative values for R1-R2 and C1 range from 18 kΩ and 0.05 μF for 750 Hz to 15 kΩ and 0.02 μF for 1800 Hz. For the same frequency range, R3 and C2-C3 vary from 1800 ohms and 0.02 μF to 1500 ohms and 0.01 μF. R4 should be approximately 3300 ohms. C4, the output coupling capacitor, can be 0.05 μF for high-impedance loads.

used, with due regard for supply polarity. R4, the collector load resistor, must be large enough for normal amplification, and may be varied somewhat to adjust the operating conditions for best waveform.

A WIDE-RANGE AUDIO OSCILLATOR

A wide-range audio oscillator that will provide a moderate output level can be built from a single 741 operational amplifier (Fig 36). Power is supplied by two 9-volt batteries, from which the circuit draws 4 mA. The frequency range is selectable from 8 Hz to 150 kHz. Distortion is approximately one percent. The output level under a light load (10 kΩ) is 4 to 5 volts. This can be increased by using higher battery voltages, up to a maximum of plus and minus 18 volts, with a corresponding adjustment of R_f.

Pin connections shown are for the TO-5 case. If another package configuration is used, the pin connections may be different. R_f is trimmed for an output level about five percent below clipping. This should be done for the temperature

Fig 36—A simple audio oscillator that provides a selectable frequency range.

at which the oscillator will normally operate, as the lamp is sensitive to ambient temperature. This unit was originally described by Schultz in November 1974 *QST*; it was later modified by Neben as reported in June 1983 *QST*.

A TWO-TONE AUDIO GENERATOR

The audio frequency generator shown in Figs. 37 and 38 makes a very convenient signal source for testing the linearity of a single-sideband transmitter. To be suitable for transmitter evaluation, a generator of this type must produce two nonharmonically related tones of equal amplitude. The level of harmonic and intermodulation distortion must be sufficiently low so as not to confuse the measurement. The frequencies used in this generator are 700 and 1900 Hz, both well inside the normal audio passband of an SSB transmitter. Spectral analysis and practical application with many different transmitters has shown this generator to meet all of the requirements mentioned above. While designed specifically for transmitter testing, it is also useful any time a fixed-frequency, low-level audio tone is needed. Details on distortion measurement and the two-tone test can be found in Chapter 18.

Circuit Details

Each of the two tones is generated by a separate Wein bridge oscillator, U1B and U2B. The oscillators are followed by RC active low-pass filters, U1A and U2A. Because the filters require nonstandard capacitor values, provisions have been made on the circuit board for placing two capacitors in parallel in those cases where standard values cannot be used. The oscillator and filter capacitors should be polystyrene or Mylar film types if available. Two tones are combined at op amp U3A. This amplifier has a variable resistor, R4, in its feedback loop which serves as the ouput LEVEL control. While R4 varies both tones together, R3, the BALANCE control, allows the level of tone A to be changed without affecting the level of tone B. This is necessary because some transmitters do not have equal audio response at both frequencies. Following the summing amplifier is a step attenuator; S3 controls the output level in 10-dB steps. The use of two output level controls, R4 and S3, allows the output to cover a wide range and still be easy to set to a specific level. The remaining op amp, U3B, is connected as a voltage follower and serves to buffer the output while providing a high-impedance load for the step attenuator. Either a high or a low output impedance can be selected by S4.

Fig 37—Exterior view of the two-tone audio generator.

The values shown are suitable for most transmitters using either high- or low-impedance microphones.

Construction and Adjustment

Component layout and wiring are not critical, and any type of construction can be used with good results. For those who wish to use a printed-circuit board, a parts-placement guide is shown in Fig 39. Because the generator will normally be used near a transmitter, it should be enclosed in some type of metal case for shielding. Battery power was chosen to reduce the possibility of RF entering the unit through the ac line. With careful shielding and filtering, the builder should be able to use an ac power supply in place of the batteries.

The only adjustment required before use is the setting of the oscillator feedback trimmers, R1 and R2. These should be set so that the output of each oscillator, measured at pin 7 of U1 and U2, is about 0.5 volt RMS. A VTVM or oscilloscope can be used for this measurement. If neither of these is available, the feedback should be adjusted to the minimum level that allows the oscillators to start reliably and stabilize quickly. When the oscillators are first turned on, they take a few seconds before they will have a stable output amplitude. This is caused by the lamps, DS1 and DS2, used in the oscillator feedback circuit. This is normal and should cause no difficulty. The connection to the transmitter should be through a shielded cable.

Resistors at Radio Frequencies

Measuring equipment often requires essentially pure resistance in some part of its circuit—that is, resistance exhibiting only negligible reactive effects on the frequencies at which measurement is intended. Of the resistors available to amateurs, this requirement is met only by small composition (carbon) resistors. The inductance of wire-wound resistors makes them useless for amateur frequencies.

The reactances to be considered arise from the inherent inductance of the resistor itself and its leads, and from small stray capacitances from one part of the resistor to another and to surrounding conductors. Although both the inductance and capacitance are small, their reactances become increasingly important as the frequency is raised. Small composition resistors, properly mounted, show negligible capacitive reactance up to 100 MHz or so in resistance values up to a few hundred ohms; similarly, the inductive reactance is negligible in values higher than a few hundred ohms. The optimum resistance region in this respect is 50 to 200 ohms.

Proper mounting includes reducing lead length as much as possible, and keeping the resistor separated from other resistors and conductors. Care must also be taken in some applications to ensure that the resistor, with its associated components, does not form a closed loop into which a voltage could be induced magnetically.

So installed, the resistance is essentially pure. In composition resistors the skin effect is very small, and the RF resistance up to VHF is nearly the same as the dc resistance.

Dummy Antennas

A dummy antenna is simply a resistor that can be substituted for an antenna or transmission line for test purposes. The dummy must exhibit the same resistance as the antenna or line it is to replace. It permits leisurely transmitter testing without radiating a signal. (Amateur regulations strictly limit the amount of on-the-air testing that may be done.) A dummy antenna is useful in testing receivers, in that electrically it resembles an antenna, but does not pick up external noise and signals, a desirable feature in some tests.

For transmitter tests the dummy antenna must be capable of dissipating safely the entire power output of the transmitter. For most testing it is desirable that the dummy simulate a perfectly matched transmission line; it should be a pure resistance of approximately 50 or 75 ohms. This is a severe limitation in home construction, because nonreactive resistors rated at more than a few watts' safe dissipation are very difficult to obtain. Tubular carborundum nonreactive resistors can often be found in military surplus transmitters and antenna tuners. These resistors usually are rated at

Fig 38—Schematic diagram of the two-tone audio generator. All resistors are ¼-W composition type.

BT1, BT2—Four AA cells.
C1A, B—Total capacitance of 0.0054 µF, ±5%.
C2A, B—Total capacitance of 0.034 µF, ±5%.
C3A, B—Total capacitance of 0.002 µF, ±5%.

C4A, B—Total capacitance of 0.012 µF, ±5%.
DS1, DS2—12-V, 25-mA lamp.
R1, R2—500-Ω, 10-turn trim potentiometer.
R3—500-Ω, panel-mount potentiometer.
R4—1-kΩ, panel-mount potentiometer.

S1, S2—SPST toggle switch.
S3—Single-pole, 6-position rotary switch.
S4—SPDT toggle switch.
S5—DPDT toggle switch.
U1, U2, U3—Dual JFET op amp, type LF353N or TL082.

Fig 39—Parts-placement diagram for the two-tone audio generator, shown from the component side of the board. A full-size etching pattern can be found at the back of this book.

50 to 100 W. Check surplus catalogs. (There are, however, dummy antenna kits available that can handle up to a kilowatt.)

For receiver and minipower transmitter testing an excellent dummy antenna can be made by installing a 51- or 75-ohm composition resistor in a PL-259 fitting, as shown in Fig 40. Sizes from one-half to two watts are satisfactory. The disc at the end helps reduce lead inductance and completes the shielding. Dummy antennas made in this way have good characteristics through the VHF bands as well as at all lower frequencies.

Increasing Power Ratings

More power can be handled by using a number of 2-watt resistors in parallel, or series-parallel, but at the expense of introducing some reactance. Nevertheless, if some departure from the ideal impedance characteristics can be tolerated, this is a practical method for getting increased dissipation in a dummy antenna. The principal problem is stray inductance, which can be minimized by mounting the resistors on flat copper strips or sheets, as indicated in Fig 41.

The power rating on resistors is a continuous rating in free air. In practice, the maximum power dissipated can be increased in proportion to the reduction in duty cycle. Thus with keying, which has a duty cycle of about one half, the rating can be doubled. With sideband the duty cycle is usually not over about one-third. The best way of judging is to feel the resistors occasionally (with power off); if too hot to touch, they may be dissipating more power than they are rated for.

Fig 40—Dummy antenna made by mounting a composition resistor in a PL-259 coaxial plug. Only the inner portion of the plug is shown; the cap screws on after assembly is completed.

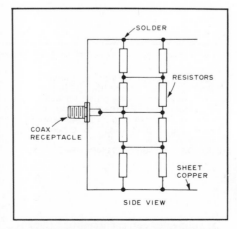

Fig 41—Use of resistors in series-parallel to increase the power rating of a small dummy antenna. Mounted in this way on pieces of flat copper, inductance is reduced to a minimum. Eight 100-ohm, 2-watt composition resistors in two groups, each four resistors in parallel, can be connected in series to form a 50-ohm dummy. The open construction shown permits free air circulation.

The dummy load shown in Fig 42 was constructed to test the feasibility of using a large number of 2-watt resistors to form a high-power load. This example uses 66 carbon resistors of 3.3 kΩ. The load will handle power levels up to 100 watts for reasonable lengths of time, and the SWR is less than 1.3 to 1 at frequencies up to 30 MHz. Because variations in construction may affect the stray reactances, it is recommended that the builder follow the general layout shown in the photograph. Complete details can be found in January 1981 *QST*.

A SIMPLE INDUCTANCE METER

The inductance meter shown in Figs 43 through 47 measures the relative Q of a coil as well as its inductance. The Q/L meter is based on a design by Doug DeMaw, W1FB; this version was built by Zachary Lau, KH6CP, in the ARRL Lab. Simple LC Hartley oscillators replace the crystal oscillators used in the original design, eliminating the need for low-pass filters and reducing circuit complexity and cost. The accuracy of the meter is approximately ±10 percent using the dial layout shown. Greater accuracy can be obtained by calibrating the meter against known high-accuracy standards.

Circuit Details

The schematic of the Q/L meter is shown in Fig 43. A low-level RF signal is generated using an oscillator and an amplifier (Q1 through Q5). This signal is then applied to a tuned circuit consisting of the inductor under test and a calibrated capacitor. The voltage across the tuned circuit is measured using Q6 and displayed on M1, a 200-μA meter. When the capacitor is adjusted for resonance at the frequency of the RF signal, the voltage across the tuned circuit is maximized, resulting in a peak indication on the meter.

The crystal oscillators used in the original versions were replaced with Hartley LC oscillators as a cost-cutting measure. While the Hartley oscillators do not have the great stability of crystal oscillators, they are adequate for this application. The output of the LC oscillators is relatively clean, and no additional filtering is needed. The potentiometers from source to ground

Fig 42—100-watt dummy antenna made up of 66, 2-watt carbon resistors.

Fig 43—Schematic diagram of the inductance meter. Fixed-value capacitors are disk ceramic unless otherwise noted. Fixed-value resistors are ¼ or ½ W units.

C1, C2, C4, C5, C7, C8, C10 and C11—NPØ disc, silver mica or polystyrene.
C17—365 pF air variable, Radiokit BC-01 with Jackson Brothers 4511/DAF vernier or equiv.
D1-D4—High-speed silicon diode; 1N914 or 1N4148.
L1—17t no. 26 enam wire on an Amidon T-30-6 core. Tap 5 turns from ground.

L2—28t no. 28 enam wire on an Amidon T-30-2 core. Tap 7 turns from ground.
L3—47t no. 28 enam wire on an Amidon T-50-2 core. Tap 12 turns from ground.
L4—58t no. 28 enam wire on an Amidon T-50-1 core. Tap 14 turns from ground.
M1—200-µA meter.
Q1-Q4, Q6—2N5486 or 2N5484 JFET.

Q5—2N3866 or 2N5109 NPN transistor.
R16—Three 1-Ω ¼ or ½ W resistors in parallel.
S1—2-pole, 4-position rotary switch.
S2—SPDT center-off toggle switch.
T1—23t no. 26 enam wire on an Amidon FT-50-43 core. 1 turn no. 22 hookup wire secondary.

allow control of the power to the buffer amplifier.

The buffer amplifier is a broadband class-A amplifier with shunt and emitter feedback. T1 is used to match the 0.33-ohm load to the amplifier, as the load tends to swamp out the frequency dependence of the circuit.

A voltage-to-current amplifier (Q6) is used to determine the amount of RF present at J1. For best sensitivity, a small amount of current should always flow through the meter. Two meter shunts are used to select different Q ranges, and the 78L05 voltage regulator supplies Q6 with a constant voltage.

Construction

Construction of the Q/L meter is fairly straightforward. The parts-placement diagram is shown in Fig 45. The toroids must be wound carefully; the total number of turns on the coils is determined by counting the number of times the wire passes through the hole in the toroid.

Fig 44—This inductance meter features a direct readout over an inductance range from 0.12 μH to 1.8 mH.

Fig 45—Parts-placement diagram for the inductance meter.

Fig 46—Interior view of the inductance meter. An L-shaped bracket supports the variable capacitor.

test inductor closer together and use the given dial layout if a series compensation inductor is used. The accuracy of the dial shown here may differ because of minor differences in construction and components.

The capacitor is mounted three inches from the terminals on an L-shaped mounting bracket below a vernier drive. The 6-to-1 vernier drive is used to prevent the tuning rate from being too fast for high Q inductors. A piece of plastic scored with a sharp knife is used as a dial pointer. The cabinet used is a Ten-Tec SE-7.

Testing

An RF probe or oscilloscope should be used to verify that the oscillators are working. The peak-to-peak voltage at the input of the buffer amplifier should not exceed 0.40 V to allow the buffer amplifier to operate linearly. The potentiometers in the oscillator circuit, (R3, R5, R7 and R9), are used to adjust the oscillator output levels. They can be adjusted while measuring the oscillator output, or simply adjusted for an adequate meter deflection while measuring an inductor. If multiple peak indications are noted, the potentiometer is set too high and should be adjusted for less meter deflection. The oscillator output voltage depends somewhat on the FETs used; it may be as low as 0.20 V. R19, the high-Q shunt, should be set for a much lower meter reading than the low-Q shunt, R20.

Operation

After connecting the unknown inductor to the test jacks, the sensitivity control is adjusted for a small quiescent meter current between 5 and 25 microamperes. If this

The most critical construction detail is the mounting of the capacitor and the terminals for the test inductor. See Fig 46. The ungrounded capacitor lead is connected to J1 with a piece of no. 14 wire.

The distance from the capacitor to J1 in the version shown here is 2¼ inches, and the dial layout shown in Fig 47 may be used if this terminal spacing is duplicated. It may be possible to position the capacitor and is not done, it may be impossible to find a peak, as the detector may be essentially turned off! The low-Q setting is most useful in finding the value of an unknown inductor. The capacitor is then adjusted for a peak meter reading. If no peak can be found, a different range should be tried.

Limitations

The meter will not be very accurate for inductances below 0.3 μH; at inductances this low, the measurements are greatly affected by lead length and parts layout. It may be possible to calibrate the unit in terms of Q; the meter is most useful as a measure of *relative* Q, however. The unit shown here was not calibrated for Q, as the meter reading is affected by the setting of the quiescent point. In addition, Q should always be measured at the frequency of interest, as it varies markedly with frequency. The inductance measurements are not absolute; it is not unusual for the inductance of a ferrite-core inductor to vary with frequency. Despite these limitations, this Q/L meter is quite useful in obtaining approximate inductance values.

OSCILLOSCOPES

Most engineers and technicians will tell you that the most useful single piece of test and design equipment is the modern triggered-sweep oscilloscope (commonly called just a "scope"). This is because not only can the oscilloscope measure voltage, but it can display voltage relative to time, showing the waveform pictures we are all familiar with from electronics textbooks. Over the past 10 years, the advances in semiconductor technology have brought the price of a good high-frequency scope within the affordable price range for most hams.

Fig 48 shows a simplified diagram of a triggered-sweep oscilloscope. The heart of the scope is the cathode ray tube (CRT) display. The CRT allows the visual display of an electronic signal by taking two electric signals and using them to deflect a beam of electrons. This beam is then deflected to a particular place on the phosphorescent screen of the CRT where it causes a small spot to glow. The particular location of the spot is determined by the value of the voltage applied to the vertical and horizontal inputs.

All the other circuits in the scope are used to take the real world signal and convert it to a form usable by the CRT. Let's take a look at how a signal travels through the oscilloscope circuitry. We will assume the trigger select switch is in the INTERNAL position (see Fig 48).

The first thing the input signal comes to is the input coupling switch. The switch allows the coupling of low-level ac signals that are superimposed on a large dc signal (this is often the case in audio amplifiers). In the AC position the dc component is blocked from reaching the vertical amplifier chain and saturating it (this would

cause distortion that would make the displayed ac signals meaningless). It is important to note that at frequencies below 30 Hz it is not advisable to use ac coupling because the value of the blocking capacitor represents a considerable series impedance to very low-frequency signals. After the coupling switch, the signal next comes to a calibrated attenuator which is used to reduce the signal to a level that can be tolerated by the scope's vertical amplifier. The vertical amplifier amplifies the signal to a level that can drive the CRT and also adds a bias component to properly position the waveform on the screen.

A small sample of the signal from the vertical amplifier is sent to the trigger circuitry. The trigger circuit feeds a start pulse to the sweep generator when the input signal reaches a certain level. The sweep generator gives a precisely timed signal that looks like a triangle (see Fig 49). This triangular signal causes the scope trace to sweep from left to right, with the zero voltage point representing the left side of the screen and the maximum voltage representing the right side of the screen.

Fig 47—Full-size dial template.

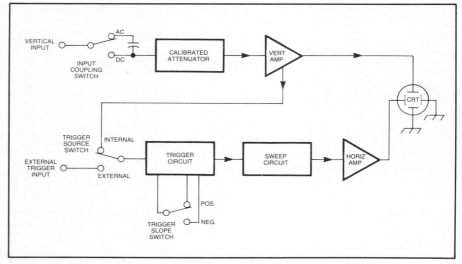

Fig 48—A block diagram of a simple triggered-sweep oscilloscope.

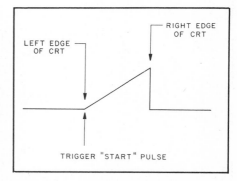

Fig 49—The sweep circuit produces a ramp pulse that is used to sweep the CRT electron beam from side to side.

The sweep circuit feeds the horizontal amplifier, which in turn drives the CRT. It is also possible to trigger the sweep system from an external source (such as the system clock in a digital system). This is done by using an external input jack with the trigger select switch in the EXTERNAL position.

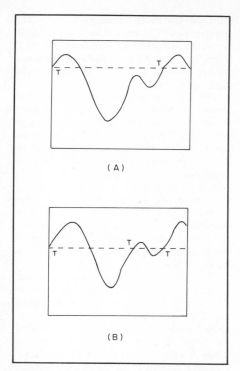

Fig 50—Selection of the trigger point is very important. Selecting the trigger point in A produces a stable display, but the trigger shown at B will produce a display that "jitters" from side to side.

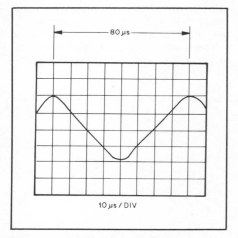

Fig 51—Oscilloscopes can be used to measure frequency. Here the displayed wave has a period of 80 microseconds (8 divisions × 10 microseconds per division) and a frequency of 12.5 kHz (1/80 μs).

Fig 52—Block diagram of a modern dual-trace oscilloscope.

An explanation of the operation of the trigger system may be useful at this point. Basically, the trigger system looks at the reference signal (internal or external) to determine if it is positive- or negative-going and to see if the signal has passed a particular level. Fig 50A shows a typical signal, the dotted line on the figure representing the trigger level. If we assume that the trigger slope switch is set to the POSITIVE position it is obvious that the only points where a trigger will occur are the points marked "T." It is important to note that once a trigger circuit is "fired" it cannot fire again until the sweep has completed one complete traversal of the screen from left to right. It is also important that the trigger level be chosen properly so the display "locks" in place.

Fig 50B shows a situation where the level has not been properly selected. Because there are two points during a single cycle of the waveform that meet the triggering requirements, the trigger circuit will have a tendency to jump from one trigger point to another. This will cause the waveform to appear to jitter from left to right. Simple adjustment of the trigger level control will solve this problem.

Up to now we have not discussed what the travel across the horizontal axis represents. This axis is calibrated in units of time. This is especially helpful because knowing the time of one cycle can give us the frequency of the waveform. In Fig 51, for example, if we know that the sweep speed selector is set at 10 μs/division and we count the number of divisions (vertical bars) between peaks of the waveform (or any similar well-defined points that occur once per cycle) we can determine the period of one cycle. In this case it is 80 μs. This means that the frequency of the waveform is 12,500 Hz (1/80 μs). The accuracy of the measured frequency depends on the accuracy of the scope's sweep oscillator (usually approximately 5%) and the linearity of the ramp generator. Obviously, this accuracy cannot compete with even the least expensive frequency counter, but the scope can still be used to determine that a circuit is functioning properly.

Unfortunately, if we wanted to compare two signals (like the input and the output of an amplifier) we would have to alternately connect the scope input to each of the two points to be measured. This inconvenience can be solved by using a *dual-trace* oscilloscope. This scope has two vertical input channels which can be displayed either individually or simultaneously.

Fig 52 shows a simplified block diagram of a dual-trace triggered-sweep oscilloscope. The only differences between this scope and our previous example are the additional vertical amplifier and the "channel switching circuit." This block selects whether we display channel A, channel B or both (simultaneously). The dual display is not a true dual display (there is only one electron gun in the CRT) but the dual traces are synthesized in the scope. True dual-trace dual-beam scopes are rare and very expensive.

There are two methods of synthesizing a dual-trace display from a single-beam scope. These two methods are referred to as "chopped mode" and "alternate mode." In the chopped mode a small portion of the channel A waveform is written to the CRT, then a corresponding portion of the channel B waveform is written to the CRT. This procedure is continued until both waveforms are completely written on the CRT. The chopped mode is especially useful where an actual measure of the time difference between the two waveforms is required. The chopped mode is usually most useful on slow sweep speeds (times greater than a few microseconds per division).

In the alternate mode, the complete

channel A waveform is written to the CRT followed immediately by the complete channel B waveform. This occurs so quickly that it appears that the waveforms are displayed simultaneously. This mode of operation is used to measure the absolute phase difference between two signals by triggering both sweeps from the same vertical input signal. Unfortunately, this mode of operation is not useful at very slow sweep speeds, but is good at most other sweep speeds.

Most dual-trace oscilloscopes also have a feature called "X-Y" operation. This feature allows one channel to drive the horizontal amplifier of the scope (called the X channel) while the other channel (called Y in this mode of operation) drives the vertical amplifier. Some oscilloscopes also have an external Y input. X-Y operation allows the scope to display Lissajous patterns for frequency and phase comparison, and to use specialized test adapters such as curve tracers, spectrum analyzer front ends, etc. Because of frequency limitations of most scope horizontal amplifiers the X channel is usually limited to a 5- or 10-MHz bandwidth.

The oscilloscope has limits, like every other device. For most purposes the voltage range of the scope can be expanded by the use of appropriate probes (which we will cover later). The most important limiting factor for most oscilloscopes is the *frequency response* (also called the *bandwidth*) of the oscilloscope. At the specified maximum response frequency, the response will be down 3 dB (0.707 voltage). For example, if we put a 100-MHz 1-V sine wave into a 100-MHz bandwidth scope we will read approximately 0.707 V on the scope display. The same scope at frequencies below 30 MHz (down to dc) should be accurate to about 5%.

Directly related to bandwidth is a parameter called *rise time*. This term refers to the fact that if a very sharp and square waveform is put into a scope input the display will appear to take a finite amount of time to rise to a specified fraction of the input voltage level. The rise time is usually defined as the time required for the display to show a transition from the 10% to 90% points of the input waveform, as shown in Fig 53. The mathematical definition of rise time is given by:

$$t_r = \frac{0.35}{BW}$$

where

t_r = rise time (μs)
BW = bandwidth (MHz)

It is also important to note that all but the most modern (and expensive) scopes are not designed for precise measurement of either time or frequency. At best they will not have better than 5% accuracy in these applications. This does not diminish the usefulness of even a moderately priced oscilloscope, however.

Fig 53—Oscilloscope bandwidth has a limiting effect on the rise time of the signals displayed on the scope.

Oscilloscope Probes

Connecting the signal to be measured to the input of the oscilloscope requires some form of electrical connection, preferably a shielded connection. Your first thought would probably lead you to a piece of small-diameter coax cable. Unfortunately, as we go higher in frequency the capacitance of the cable would produce a capacitive reactance considerably lower than the one-megohm input impedance of the oscilloscope. In addition, the scope has a certain built-in capacitance at its input terminals (usually between 5 and 35 pF). These two capacitances cause problems if we are probing a circuit with a relatively high impedance.

The simplest method of connecting the signal to the scope is to use a specially designed probe. The most common scope probe is a "×10" probe (called a "times ten probe"). This probe forms a 10 to 1 voltage divider using the built-in resistance of the probe and the input resistance of the scope. When you use a times ten probe you must multiply the value of the calibrated attenuator by 10. For example, if your scope is on the 1-V/div range and you were using an ×10 probe the actual readings on the scope face would be 10 V/div.

Unfortunately, if we just put a resistor in series with the scope input it seriously degrades the scope's rise-time performance and therefore its bandwidth. This is because the scope's input looks like a parallel RC circuit and the series resistor feeding it causes a significant reduction in available charging current from the source. We can correct this by using a compensating capacitor in parallel with the series resistor. This in fact forms two dividers: one resistive voltage divider and one capacitive voltage divider. With these two dividers connected in parallel with the RC relationships shown in Fig 54, the probe and scope should have a flat response curve through the whole bandwidth of the scope.

To account for manufacturing tolerances in the scope and the probe the com-

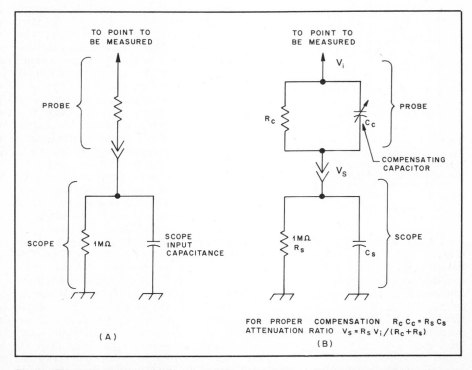

Fig 54—The probe at A is uncompensated; the compensating capacitor in the probe shown at B can be used to "tweak" the probe to compensate for circuit capacitances (see text for details).

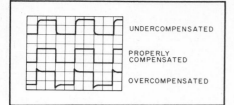

Fig 55—Oscilloscope displays showing a squarewave input and undercompensated, overcompensated and properly compensated probes. Refer to the text for a discussion of the figure.

Fig 56—Block diagram of a dual-trace digital oscilloscope.

pensating capacitor is made variable and is used to "tweak" the probe and scope for proper response when they are connected together. Most scopes provide a "calibrator" output that produces a known-frequency square wave for the purpose of adjusting the compensating capacitor in a probe. Fig 55 shows possible responses when the probe is connected to the oscilloscope's calibrator jack. We can see that the leading edge shown in the top and bottom traces of Fig 55 is incorrect. If you get these pictures from the calibrator jack, adjust the compensating capacitor until you get a perfectly square display as is shown in the middle trace of the figure.

If the probe cable is too short, do not attempt to extend the length of the cable by adding a piece of common coaxial cable. There are two reasons for this. First, the compensating capacitor is chosen to compensate for the provided length of cable. It usually will not have enough range to compensate for extra lengths. Additionally, the cable used to make a scope probe is of specialized construction and electrical characteristics. Its requirements are significantly different than normal coax cable.

Another important point in scope probe use is to use the shortest ground lead possible. Long ground leads are inductors at high frequencies. In these circuits they cause ringing and other undesirable effects.

Digital Oscilloscopes

Up to now we have discussed versions of the classic oscilloscope that has existed for over 30 years. As we have noted, the cost of the oscilloscope has dropped with the widespread use of semiconductor technology. This is not the only change that semiconductors have brought to the oscilloscope market, however. In the past five years the *digital oscilloscope* has appeared in laboratories around the world. This type of oscilloscope has quickly gone from a laboratory oddity to an affordable tool in reach of the active experimenter. The design of a digital oscilloscope relies heavily on microcomputer technology, and the prominence and affordability of digital scopes has roughly paralleled the microcomputer market. We will not spend significant space on this type of scope only because almost any details we give will be quickly overtaken by technological advances. A basic primer may be of interest, however.

A block diagram of the basic digital oscilloscope is given in Fig 56. The only thing we have previously not seen are the blocks labeled *sample and hold* (S/H), *analog to digital converter* (ADC) and *microcontroller*. These blocks take the analog signal and convert it to a sequence of digital bits which can be used to represent the waveform. Processing the signals in this way means that the information can then be passed to a computer where it can be stored (on floppy disks) or analyzed using advanced mathematical techniques (such as Fast Fourier Transforms). In fact, most digital oscilloscopes that are in the price range of the experimenter do not even have a CRT; they use the computer terminal to display their result. Measurement parameters are adjusted via the computer keyboard, rather than with front-panel knobs and switches. Fig 57 shows a picture of a digital oscilloscope of this type. In the parlance of the engineer they are sometimes referred to as *waveform digitizers*, or *scope front ends*.

Referring to the block diagram, we can discuss the operation of the digital oscilloscope. Like most digital devices, the digital scope has a microprocessor "brain." The microprocessor commands the sample and hold circuit to sample the amplitude of the input signal at regular intervals. The sample and hold circuit then holds this value while the analog to digital converter converts the sampled value to its digital

Fig 57—A digital "oscilloscope front end" for a personal computer. Other digital oscilloscopes take the form of a circuit board that plugs into an expansion slot in the computer *(photo courtesy of Heath Co)*.

(A)

(B)

Fig 58—Two displays of the same waveform. The display at A was produced with an analog storage scope. The display at B was produced with a digital oscilloscope. Notice that the digital display is not continuous, leaving the actual shape of the rising and falling edges open to interpretation.

equivalent. This digital equivalent and information representing the time at which the sample was taken can either be sent to internal RAM for later use or can be sent out to the host microcomputer. The whole process is repeated a number of times until the waveform is duplicated.

Unfortunately, if the sample rate is not high enough, very fast signal perturbations between sampling points do not appear on the display. For example Fig 58A and 58B show the same signal as measured on an analog and digital scope. As you can see, there are large spikes in the analog scope that do not seem to show up on the digital scope. Some of the more expensive digital scopes use special methods to overcome this problem, but these methods are unlikely to come to lower priced units for a few years.

Some digital oscilloscopes are now appearing on the market in a portable form; these scopes employ a liquid-crystal display (LCD) very similar to that used on many lap-top computers. This type of digital scope requires no outboard computer and is usually battery operated. It is important to note that these scopes display the waveform as a series of unconnected dots. In certain very complex waveforms this

may cause some difficulty in interpretation. Also, as a consequence of other circuitry restrictions these hand-held scopes usually have very limited bandwidth (in the 100 to 500 kHz range) which means they are only useful in audio and slow digital work. Undoubtedly as technology advances, the performance of these scopes will improve considerably.

As with all new technology items, specifications are sometimes misleading because of lack of standard definitions for terms. If you are considering buying a digital scope we recommend you either attempt to see the unit you are interested in in operation or consult with a local ham in the electronics business who can offer some experienced advice.

Storage Oscilloscopes

Storage scopes are now showing up on the surplus markets at prices available to many amateurs. Storage scopes are analog instruments with special long-persistence phosphor CRTs that allow them to capture single-shot events. For example, if you wanted to determine the switching time of an antenna sequencer you would trigger the scope from the control signal input to the sequencer and monitor the contacts with the vertical input to determine when the relay had switched. With a regular oscilloscope the trace would be gone from the CRT before you could determine the switching time, but with the storage scope's long-persistence CRT for a reasonable time (15 to 120 seconds) you can observe the switching action before the trace fades from the screen.

A newer version of the storage scope is the *digital storage oscilloscope* (DSO). The DSO uses a high-speed semiconductor memory which is continually read back to the display so that the waveform can be viewed for as long as necessary. The DSO is a relatively straightforward extension of the digital oscilloscopes we have previously discussed.

Lissajous Figures

When sinusoidal ac voltages are applied to both sets of deflecting plates in the oscilloscope, the resultant pattern depends on the relative amplitudes, frequencies and phases of the two voltages. If the ratio between the two frequencies is constant and can be expressed in integers, a stationary pattern will be produced.

The stationary patterns obtained in this way are called Lissajous figures. Examples of some of the simpler Lissajous figures are given in Fig 59. The frequency ratio is found by counting the number of loops along two adjacent edges. Thus in C there are three loops along a horizontal edge and only one along the vertical, so the ratio of the vertical frequency to the horizontal frequency is 3:1. Similarly, in E there are four loops along the horizontal edge and three along the vertical edge, giving a ratio of 4:3.

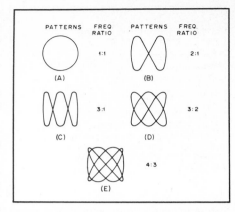

Fig 59—Lissajous figures and corresponding frequency ratios for a 90-degree phase relationship between the voltages applied to the two sets of deflecting plates.

Assuming that the known frequency is applied to the horizontal plates, the unknown frequency is

$$f2 = \frac{n2}{n1}\ f1$$

where

f1 = known frequency applied to horizontal plates

f2 = unknown frequency applied to vertical plates

n1 = number of loops along a vertical edge

n2 = number of loops along a horizontal edge.

An important application of Lissajous figures is in the calibration of audio-frequency signal generators. For very low frequencies the 60-Hz power-line frequency is held accurately enough to be used as a standard in most localities. The medium audio-frequency range can be covered by comparison with the 440- and 600-Hz modulation on WWV transmissions. It is possible to calibrate over a 10:1 range, both upward and downward from these frequencies and thus cover the audio range useful for voice communication.

An oscilloscope having both horizontal and vertical amplifiers is desirable, since it is convenient to have a means for adjusting the voltages applied to the deflection plates to secure a suitable pattern size.

Oscilloscope Bibliography

vanErk, R., *Oscilloscopes, Functional Operation and Measuring Examples*, McGraw-Hill Book Co, New York 1978.

Bunze, V., "Probing in Prospective-Application Note 152," Hewlett-Packard Co, Colorado Springs, CO 1972 (Pub No. 5952-1892)

The XYZs of Using a Scope, Tektronix, Inc, Portland, OR 1981 (Pub No. 41AX-4758)

"Basic Techniques of Waveform Measurement (Parts 1 and 2)," Hewlett-Packard Co, Colorado Springs, CO 1980 (Pub No. 5953-3873)

Millman, J. and Taub, H., *Pulse Digital and Switching Waveforms*, McGraw-Hill Book Co, New York 1965, pp 50-54.

Martin, V., "A Detailed Look at Probes," *Ham Radio*, September 1985, pp 75-86.

Operation and Service Manual for Model IC-4802 Computer Oscilloscope, Heath Co, Benton Harbor, MI 1986 (Pub No. 595-3458-1)

HF ADAPTER FOR NARROW-BANDWIDTH OSCILLOSCOPES

Fig 60 shows the circuit of a simple piece of test equipment that will allow you to display signals that are beyond the normal bandwidth of an inexpensive oscilloscope. This circuit was built to monitor modulation of a 10-meter signal on a scope that has a 5-MHz upper-frequency limit. This design features a Mini-Circuits Laboratory SRA-1 mixer. Any stable oscillator or VFO with an output of 10 dBm can be used for the local oscillator (LO), which mixes with the HF signal to produce an IF in the range of the oscilloscope.

The mixer can handle RF signal levels up to −3 dBm without clipping, so this was set as an upper limit for the RF input. A toroidal-transformer coupler is constructed by winding a 31-turn secondary of no. 28-AWG wire on a 3E2A core, which has a 0.038-inch diameter. The Amidon FT-37-75 is an equivalent core. The primary is a piece of coaxial cable through the core center. The coupler gives 30-dB attenuation and has a flat response from 0.5 to 100 MHz. An additional 20-dB attenuation was added for a total of 50 dB before the mixer. One-watt resistors will do fine for the attenuator. The completed adapter should be built into a shielded box.

This circuit, with the 25-MHz LO frequency, is useful on frequencies in the 20- to 30-MHz range with transmitters of up to 50-W power output. By changing the frequency of the LO, any frequency in the range of the coupler can be displayed on a 5-MHz-bandwidth oscilloscope. More attenuation will be required for higher-power transmitters. This circuit was described by Kenneth Stringham Jr., AE1X in the Hints and Kinks column in February 1982 *QST*.

A GATED NOISE SOURCE

The circuit of Fig 61 may be used to construct a simple low-cost device to optimize a converter for best noise figure. The simplicity of this system makes effective alignment possible without a lot of test equipment.

Numerous articles have described units where noise-figure tests may be made. With the exception of certain thermal-limited diodes (5722, for example), an absolute value of noise figure is not obtainable with these units; this device is no exception.

Anyone using a classic noise-figure meter soon learns that the tune-up of a system is a cut-and-try procedure where an adjustment is made and its influence is observed by calibrating the system. Then the excess-noise source is applied and the effect evaluated. This is basically an after-the-fact method of testing after an adjustment is made, and is consequently time consuming.

Fig 60—Schematic diagram of an adapter to display RF signals on a narrow-bandwidth oscilloscope, including a 10-dBm 25-MHz LO, −30-dB coupler, 20-dB attenuator and diode-ring mixer.
T1—See text.

The gated noise source doesn't require a special detector, or any detector at all other than your ear. By turning the noise source on and off at an audio rate, the ratio of noise contributed by the system to noise of the system plus excess noise appears as an audio note. The louder the note, the greater the differential in levels. Hence, the greater the influence of the excess noise, the better the noise figure.

If greater precision is desired than that obtained by subjectively listening to the signal, an oscilloscope may be used. Connect the scope vertical input to any point in the audio system of the receiver, such as the speaker terminals. Adjust the scope for a display of several multiples of the train of square pulses. Proceed by adjusting the device(s) being tested for greatest vertical deflection.

Fig 61—Schematic diagram of the gated noise source.
BT1, BT2—9-volt battery, Eveready 216 or equiv.
C5—0.001-μF feedthrough capacitor, Sprague BH-340.

S1—Double-pole, single-throw miniature toggle.

The result of an adjustment is instantly visible as an increase or decrease in the recovered audio. This method of noise evaluation is by no means new. Most modern automatic noise-figure meters turn the excess-noise source on and off and then, through rather sophisticated methods, evaluate the results. This technique is sometimes called Y-parameter testing.

While the method and circuit described here are not exceptional, they represent a fresh approach to noise evaluation. This approach does not require long-term integrating detectors and tedious "twice-power" measurements that, without absolute calibration, can result in no more than simply optimizing the system.

In some cases the available noise generated by this unit may be too great. The output may be reduced by inserting attenuators between the generator output and the device under test or by adding a 2000-ohm potentiometer at the point marked in Fig 61. The use of an attenuator is preferred because it reduces the apparent output VSWR of the generator by increasing the return loss. If a control is used it must be returned to its minimum insertion-loss position when starting a test or no signal may be heard.

This circuit uses readily available junk-box parts and may be easily duplicated. The lead placement in and around the diode itself should follow good VHF practices with short leads and direct placement.

Theory of Operation

Q1 and Q2 are used in a cross-coupled multivibrator circuit, operating at approximately 700 Hz. The value of C1 is greater than C2 to cause the duty cycle to favor the conduction of Q2 slightly. When Q2 conducts, the pulse is coupled to Q3 via C3, turning on Q3 and causing current flow through R7, D1 and R8.

The diode generates broadband noise that is passed through R9 to the output. R7, C4 and C5 form a low-pass filter to prevent high-order harmonics from the switching pulses from appearing in the output.

The influence of stray RF signals entering the device under test through the generator may be minimized by shielding the components shown. A simple box may be built by using PC-board scraps. For best match, this source should be connected directly to the input of the device under test; therefore, the unit is equipped with a male connector. This matching becomes a greater consideration as the frequency of interest increases.

Operation on Other Than AM

Some contemporary receivers and transceivers cannot be operated in the AM mode, and consequently the noise source seems unusable. The detection of noise is the process by which the noise source operates; therefore, it will not work through an FM detector, nor will it work

Fig 62—A simple detector that can be used when aligning SSB and FM receivers (see text for details).

through a product detector since one of the terms of the detection (the noise) is not coherent.

The SCOPE jack on most receivers is loosely coupled to the IF amplifier, preceding the detector. A wide-band scope connected to this point will show the train of pulses and eliminate the need for aural detection. The alignment of the later IF stages of a system should have the least impact on the noise performance, and maximum signal response will always occur at the same setting. Therefore, the simple detector of Fig 62 will generally work for aural AM detection. Connect point A to the last IF amplifier plate or collector. Connect point B to the audio amplifier, at or near the volume control, and ground point C. With this arrangement the normal detector output is turned down with the volume control, and the temporary detector provides AM detection.

The gated noise source has been used for literally hundreds of applications and has proved to be a powerful yet simple addition to the test bench. While no guarantee of duplication may be made, these units develop approximately 18 dB of excess noise in the region of 50-300 MHz. This unit was originally described by Hartsen in January 1977 *QST*.

A NOISE BRIDGE FOR 1.8 THROUGH 30 MHz

The noise bridge, sometimes referred to as an antenna noise bridge, or RX noise bridge, is an instrument that measures the impedances of antennas or other electrical circuits. The unit shown here provides adequate accuracy for most measurements in the 1.8- through 30-MHz range. Battery operation and small physical size make this unit ideal for remote-location use. Tone modulation is applied to the wide-band noise generator as an aid for obtaining a null indication. This noise bridge includes general improvements to noise bridges and techniques for calibration described by John Grebenkemper, KI6WX, in August 1989 *QST*, pp 27-32 and 52. Additional information about using the noise bridge for transmission-line measurements appears in that article and in the Transmission Line and Antenna Measurements chapter of *The ARRL Antenna Book* (16th ed). A detector, such as the station receiver, is required for operation.

The noise bridge consists of two parts—

Fig 63—Interior and exterior views of the noise bridge. The unit is finished in red enamel. Press-on lettering is used for the calibration marks. Note that the potentiometer must be isolated from ground.

the noise generator and the bridge circuitry. See Fig 64. A 6.8-volt Zener diode serves as the noise source. U1 generates an approximate 50% duty cycle, 1000-Hz, square-wave signal that is applied to the cathode of the Zener diode. The 1000-Hz modulation appears on the noise signal and enhances null detection. The broadband-noise signal is amplified by Q1, Q2 and associated components to produce an approximate S9 signal in the receiver. Slightly more noise is available at the low end of the frequency range, as no frequency compensation is applied to the amplifier. Roughly 20 mA of current is drawn from the 9-volt battery, thus ensuring long battery life—providing the power is switched off after use!

The bridge portion of the circuit consists of T1, C1, C2 and R1. T1 is a ferrite binocular core wound as shown in the Fig 64 detail. This design eliminates phase shift, and the ferrite core has sufficient permeability to eliminate low-frequency resistance shift. One winding of T1 couples noise energy into the bridge circuit. The remaining two windings are each one in an arm of the bridge. C1 and R1 complete the known arm; the UNKNOWN circuit with C3 and C4 comprise the remainder of the bridge. The terminal labeled RCVR is for connection to the detector.

The reactance range of a noise bridge depends on several factors, including operating frequency, value of the series capacitor (C3 or C3 plus C4 in Fig 64) and the range of the variable capacitor (C1 in

Fig 64—Schematic diagram of the noise bridge. Resistors are ¼-watt composition types. Capacitors are miniature ceramic units unless indicated otherwise. Component designations indicated in the schematic but not called out in the parts list are for text and parts-placement reference only.

BT1—9-volt battery, NEDA 1604A or equiv.
C1—15- to 150-pF variable.
C2—20-pF mica.
C3—47-pF mica.
C4—82-pF mica.
J1, J2—Coaxial connector.

R1—Linear, 250 ohm, AB type. Use a good grade of resistor.
S1, S2—Toggle, SPST.
T1—Transformer: 3 windings on an Amidon BLN-43-2402 ferrite binocular core. Each winding is three turns of no. 30 enameled

wire. One turn is equal to the wire passing once through both holes in the core. The primary winding starts on one side of the transformer, and the secondary and tertiary winding start on the other side.
U1—Timer, NE555 or equiv.

Fig 64). The RANGE switch selects reactance measurements weighted toward either capacitance or inductance by placing C4 in parallel with C3. The zero-reactance point occurs when C1 is either nearly fully meshed or fully unmeshed. The RANGE switch nearly doubles the resolution of the reactance readings.

CONSTRUCTION

The noise bridge is contained in a homemade aluminum enclosure that measures 5 × 2-3/8 × 3-3/4 inches. Many of the circuit components are mounted on a circuit board that is fastened to the rear wall of the cabinet. The circuit-board layout is such that the lead lengths to the board from the bridge and coaxial connectors are at a minimum. A parts-placement guide for the circuit board is shown in Fig 65.

Care must be taken when mounting the potentiometer, R1. For accurate readings the potentiometer must be well insulated

Fig 65—Parts-placement guide for the noise bridge as viewed from the component or top side of the board. Mounting holes are located in two corners of the board, as shown. A full-size etching pattern can be found at the back of this book.

from ground. In the unit shown, this was accomplished by mounting the control on a piece of Plexiglas, which in turn was fastened to the chassis with a piece of aluminum angle stock. Additionally, a ¼-inch control-shaft coupling and a length of phenolic rod were used to further isolate the control from ground where the shaft passes through the front panel. Use a high-quality potentiometer to ensure good measurement results.

There is no such problem when mounting the variable capacitor because the rotor is grounded. Use a high-quality capacitor; do not try to save money on that component. Two female RF fittings on the rear panel are connected to a detector (receiver) and to the UNKNOWN circuit. Do not use plastic-insulated phono connectors (they might influence bridge accuracy at higher frequencies). Use miniature coaxial cable (RG-174) between the RCVR connector and circuit board. Attach one end of C3 to the circuit board and the other directly to the UNKNOWN circuit connector.

Bridge Compensation

Stray capacitance and inductance in the bridge circuit can affect impedance readings. If a very accurate bridge is required, use the following steps to counter the effects of stray reactance. Because the physical location of the board, connectors and controls in the cabinet determine where compensation is needed, there is no provision for the compensation components on the printed circuit board.

Good calibration loads are necessary to check the accuracy of the noise bridge. Four are needed here: a 0-Ω (short-circuit) load, a 50-Ω load, a 180-Ω load and a variable-resistance load. The short-circuit and fixed-resistance loads are used to check the accuracy of the noise bridge; the variable-resistance load is used when measuring coaxial-cable loss.

Construction details of the loads are shown in Fig 66. Each load is constructed inside a connector. When building the loads, keep leads as short as possible to minimize parasitic effects. The resistors must be noninductive (*not* wirewound). Quarter-watt, carbon-composition resistors should work fine. The potentiometer in the variable-resistance load is a miniature PC-mount unit with a maximum resistance of 100 Ω or less. The potentiometer wiper and one of the end leads are connected to the center pin of the connector; the other lead is connected to ground.

Stray Capacitance

Stray capacitance on the variable-resistor side of the bridge tends to be higher than that on the unknown side. This is so because the parasitic capacitance in the variable resistor, R1, is comparatively high.

The effect of parasitic capacitance is most easily detected using the 180-Ω load. Measure and record the actual resistance of the load, $R/L\frac{1}{2}$. Connect the load to

Fig 66—Construction details of the resistive loads used to check and calibrate a noise bridge. Each of the loads is constructed inside a coaxial connector that matches those on the bridge. (Views shown are cross-sections of PL-259 bodies; the sleeves are not shown.) Leads should be kept as short as possible to minimize parasitic inductance. (A) is a short circuit; (B) depicts a 50-Ω load; (C) is a 180-Ω load; (D) shows a variable-resistance load used to determine the loss in a coaxial cable.

the UNKNOWN connector, place S2 in the X_L position, tune the receiver to 1.8 MHz, and null the bridge. (See "Finding the Null" below for tips.) Use an ohmmeter across R1 to measure its dc resistance. The magnitude of the stray capacitance can be calculated by

$$C_p = C2 \left(\sqrt{\frac{R1}{R_L}} - 1 \right)$$

where
R_L = load resistance (as measured)
R1 = resistance of the variable resistor
C3 = series capacitance

We can compensate for C_p by placing a variable capacitor, C_c, in the side of the bridge with lesser stray capacitance. If R1 is greater than R_L, stray capacitance is greater on the variable resistor side of the bridge: Place C_c between point U (on the circuit board) and ground. If R1 is less than R_L, stray capacitance is greater on the unknown side: Place C_c between point B and ground.

If the required compensating capacitance is only a few picofarads, you can use a gimmick capacitor (made by twisting two short pieces of insulated, solid wire together) for C_c. A gimmick capacitor is adjusted by trimming its length.

Compensate the bridge by setting the dc

resistance of R1 equal to R_L. With the bridge at 1.8 MHz, alternately adjust C_c and C1 to obtain a null.

Stray Inductance

Parasitic inductance, if present, should be only a few tens of nanohenrys. This represents a few ohms of inductive reactance at 30 MHz. The effect is best observed by reading the reactance of the 0-Ω test load at 1.8 MHz and 30 MHz; the indicated reactance should be the same at both frequencies.

If the reactance reading decreases as frequency is increased, parasitic inductance is greater in the known arm, and compensating inductance is needed between point U and C3. If the reactance increases with frequency, the unknown-arm inductance is greater, and compensating inductance should be placed between point B and R1.

Compensate for stray inductance by placing a single-turn coil, made from a 1- to 2-inch length of solid wire, in the appropriate arm of the bridge. Adjust the size of this coil until the reactance reading remains constant from 1.8 to 30 MHz.

Calibration

Good calibration accuracy is necessary for accurate noise-bridge measurements. Calibration of the resistance scale is straightforward. To do this, tune the receiver to a frequency near 10 MHz. Attach the 0-Ω load to the UNKNOWN connector and null the bridge. This is the zero-resistance point; mark it on the front-panel resistance scale. The rest of the resistance range is calibrated by adjusting R1, measuring R1 with an accurate ohmmeter, calculating the increase from the zero point and marking the increase on the front panel.

Most bridges have the reactance scale marked in capacitance because capacitance does not vary with frequency. Unfortunately, that requires calibration curves or nontrivial calculations to arrive at the load reactance. An alternative method is to mark the reactance scale in *ohms* at a reference frequency of 10 MHz. This method calibrates the bridge near the center of its range and displays reactance directly, but it requires a simple calculation to scale the reactance reading for frequencies other than 10 MHz. The scaling equation is:

$$X_{u(f)} = X_{u(10)} \frac{10}{f}$$

where
f = frequency in MHz
$X_{u(10)}$ = reactance of the unknown load at 10 MHz.
$X_{u(f)}$ = reactance of the unknown load at f.

A shorted piece of coaxial cable serves as a reactance source. (The reactance of a shorted, low-loss coaxial cable is dependent only on the cable length, the measurement frequency and the cable characteristic impedance.) Radio Shack RG-8M is used here because it is readily available, has relatively low loss and has an almost purely resistive characteristic impedance.

Prepare the calibration cable as follows:

1) Cut a length of coaxial cable that is slightly longer than $\lambda/4$ at 10 MHz (about 20 feet for RG-8M). Attach a suitable connector to one end of the cable; leave the other end open-circuited.

2) Connect the 0-Ω load to the noise bridge UNKNOWN connector and set the receiver frequency to 10 MHz. Adjust the noise bridge for a null. Do not adjust the reactance control after the null is found.

3) Connect the calibration cable to the bridge UNKNOWN terminal. Null the bridge by adjusting *only* the variable resistor and the receiver frequency. The receiver frequency should be less than 10 MHz; if it is above 10 MHz, the cable is too short, and you need to prepare a longer one.

4) Gradually cut short lengths from the end of the coaxial cable until you obtain a null at 10 MHz by adjusting only the resistance control. Then connect the cable center and shield conductors at the open end with a short length of braid. Verify that the bridge nulls with zero reactance at 20 MHz.

5) The reactance of the coaxial cable (normalized to 10 MHz) can be calculated from:

$$X_{i(10)} = R_0 \, \frac{f}{10} \, \tan\left(2\,\pi\,\frac{f}{40}\right)$$

where

$X_{i(10)}$ = cable reactance at 10 MHz
R_0 = characteristic resistance of the coaxial cable (52.5 Ω for Radio Shack RG-8M)
f = frequency in MHz

The results have less than 5% error for reactances less than 500 Ω, as long as the test-cable loss is less than 0.2 dB. This error becomes significantly less at lower reactances (2% error at 300 Ω for a 0.2-dB-loss cable). The loss in 18 feet of RG-8M is 0.13 dB at 10 MHz. Reactance data for Radio Shack RG-8M is given in Table 2.

With the prepared cable and calibration values on hand, proceed to calibrate the reactance scale. Tune the receiver to the appropriate frequency for the desired reactance (given in Table 2, or found using the equation). Adjust the resistance and reactance controls to null the bridge. Mark the reactance reading on the front panel. Repeat this process until all desired reactance values have been marked. The resistance values needed to null the bridge during this calibration procedure may be significant (more than 100 Ω) at the higher reactances.

This calibration method is much more accurate than using fixed capacitors across the UNKNOWN connector. Also, you can

Table 2

Noise Bridge Calibration Data: Coaxial-Cable Method

This data is for Radio Shack RG-8M cable ($R_0 = 52.5\ \Omega$) cut to exactly $\lambda/4$ at 10 MHz; the reactances and capacitances shown correspond to this frequency.

| \multicolumn{4}{c}{Reactance} | \multicolumn{2}{c}{Capacitance} |
X_i	f(MHz)	X_i	f(MHz)	C(pF)	f(MHz)
10	3.318	−10	19.376	10	9.798
20	4.484	−20	18.722	20	9.612
30	5.262	−30	18.048	30	9.440
40	5.838	−40	17.368	40	9.280
50	6.286	−50	16.701	50	9.130
60	6.647	−60	16.062	60	8.990
70	6.943	−70	15.471	70	8.859
80	7.191	−80	14.936	80	8.735
90	7.404	−90	14.462	90	8.618
100	7.586	−100	14.044	100	8.508
110	7.747	−110	13.682	110	8.403
120	7.884	−120	13.369	120	8.304
130	8.009	−130	13.097	130	8.209
140	8.119	−140	12.861	140	8.119
150	8.217	−150	12.654		
160	8.306	−160	12.473		
170	8.387	−170	12.313		
180	8.460	−180	12.172		
190	8.527	−190	12.045		
200	8.588	−200	11.932	C(pF)	f(MHz)
210	8.645	−210	11.831	−10	10.219
220	8.697	−220	11.739	−20	10.459
230	8.746	−230	11.655	−30	10.721
240	8.791	−240	11.579	−40	11.010
250	8.832	−250	11.510	−50	11.328
260	8.872	−260	11.446	−60	11.679
270	8.908	−270	11.387	−70	12.064
280	8.942	−280	11.333	−80	12.484
290	8.975	−290	11.283	−90	12.935
300	9.005	−300	11.236	−100	13.407
350	9.133	−350	11.045	−110	13.887
400	9.232	−400	10.905	−120	14.357
450	9.311	−450	10.798	−130	14.801
500	9.375	−500	10.713	−140	15.211

calibrate a noise bridge in less than an hour using this method.

Finding the Null

In use, a receiver is attached to the RCVR connector and some load of unknown value is connected to the UNKNOWN terminal. The receiver allows us to hear the noise present across the bridge arms at the frequency of the receiver passband. The strength of the noise signal depends on the strength of the noise-bridge battery, the receiver bandwidth/sensitivity and the impedance difference between the known and unknown bridge arms. The noise is stronger and the null more obvious with wide receiver passbands. Set the receiver to the widest bandwidth AM mode available.

The noise-bridge output is heard as a 1000-Hz tone. When the impedances of the known and unknown bridge arms are equal, the voltage across the receiver is minimized; this is a null. In use, the null may be difficult to find because it appears only when both bridge controls approach the values needed to balance the bridge.

To find the null, set C1 to mid-scale, sweep R1 slowly through its range and listen for a reduction in noise (it's also helpful to watch the S meter). If no reduction

is heard, set R1 to mid-range and sweep C1. If there is still no reduction, begin at one end of the C1 range and sweep R1. Increment C1 about 10% and sweep R1 with each increment until some noise reduction appears. Once noise reduction begins, adjust C1 and R1 alternately for minimum signal.

SIGNAL GENERATORS FOR RECEIVER TESTING

The oscillator shown in Figs 67 and 68 was designed for testing high-performance receivers. Parts cost for the oscillator has been kept to a minimum by careful design. While the stability is slightly less than that of a well-designed crystal oscillator, the stability of the unit should be adequate for measurements of most amateur receivers. In addition, the ability to shift frequency is important when dealing with receivers that have spurious responses. More importantly, LC oscillators with high-Q components often have superior phase noise performance compared to crystal oscillators, because of power limitations in the crystal oscillators (crystals are easily damaged by excessive power).

The circuit is a Hartley oscillator

followed by a class-A buffer amplifier. To keep the frequency of the oscillator somewhat independent of the supply voltage, a 5-V regulator is used. The amplifier is cleaned up by a seven-element Chebyshev low-pass filter which is terminated by a 6-dB attenuator. The attenuator ensures that the filter works properly, even with a receiver that has an input impedance other than 50 ohms. A receiver designed to work with a 50-ohm system may not have a 50-ohm input impedance. The +4 dBm of output is adequate for most receiver measurements. It may even be too much for some receivers; the potential exists for damage to narrow crystal filters following amplifiers. It is assumed that the user will use a step attenuator to lower the output level to an appropriate value.

Construction

This unit was built in a box made of double-sided circuit board. The box used in the prototype has inside dimensions of $1 \times 2.2 \times 5$ inches (HWD). The copper foil of the circuit board makes an excellent shield, while the fiberglass helps temperature stability. Capacitor C2 should be soldered directly across L1 to insure high Q. As with any RF circuit, the component leads should be kept short. While silver mica capacitors have slightly better Q, NPØ capacitors may offer better stability. Mounting the three inductors orthoganally (axis of the inductors 90 degrees from each other) reduced the 2nd order harmonic by 2 dB compared to an initial prototype.

Alignment and Testing

The output of the regulator should be +5 V. The output of the oscillator should

Fig 67—This LC oscillator for receiver measurements offers good performance at relatively low cost.

Fig 68—Schematic diagram of the 3.7-MHz oscillator. All resistors are ¼ W, 5% units.

C1—1.4 to 9.2 pF air trimmer (value and type not critical)
C2—270 pF silver-mica or NPØ capacitor. Value may be changed slightly to compensate for variations in L1.
C3—56 pF silver mica or NPØ capacitor. Value may be changed to adjust output power.
C4—1000 pF solder-in feedthrough capacitor.

Available from Microwave Components of Michigan (see Chapter 35).
C5-C8—Silver-mica, NPØ disc or polystyrene capacitor.
D1—1N914, 1N4148.
L1—31t no. 18 enam wire on Amidon T-94-6 core. Tap 8 turns from ground end (7.5 μH).
L2, L4—21t no. 22 enam wire on an Amidon T-50-2 core (2.5 μH, 2.43 μH ideal).

L3—23t no. 22 enam wire on an Amidon T-50-2 core. (2.9 μH, 3.01 μH ideal).
T1—7t no. 22 enam wire bifilar wound on an Amidon FT-37-43 core.
Q1—2N5486 JFET. MPF102 may give reduced output.
Q2—2N5109.
U1—78L05 low-current 5-V regulator.

be +4 dBm (2.5 milliwatts) into a 50-ohm load. Increasing the value of C3 will increase the power output to a maximum of about 10 milliwatts. The frequency should be around 3.7 MHz. Adding additional capacitance across inductor L1 (in parallel with C2) will lower the frequency if desired, while the trimmer capacitor (C1) specified will allow adjustment to a specific frequency. The drift of one of the prototypes was 5 Hz over 25 minutes after a few minutes of warm up. If the warm-up drift is large, changing C2 may improve the situation somewhat. For most receivers, a drift of 100 Hz during the measurement period has a negligible effect on measurements.

HYBRID COMBINERS FOR SIGNAL GENERATORS

Many receiver performance measurements require two signal generators to be attached simultaneously to a receiver. A combiner that isolates the two signal generators is necessary to keep one generator from being frequency or phase modulated by the other. Commercially made hybrid combiners are available from Mini-Circuits, PO Box 350166, Brooklyn NY 11235-0003. Hybrid combiners are not difficult to construct, however, as the following project shows.

The combiners described here provide 40 to 50 dB of isolation between ports while attenuating the desired signal paths (each input to output) by 6 dB. A second feature of these combiners is that of maintaining the 50-ohm impedance of the system—very important if accurate measurements are to be made.

The combiners are constructed in small boxes made from double-sided circuit-board material. Each piece is soldered to the adjacent one along the entire length of the seam. This makes an essentially RF-tight enclosure. BNC coaxial fittings are used on the units shown. However, any type of coaxial connector can be used. Leads must be kept as short as possible and precision resistors (or matched units from the junk box) should be used. The circuit diagram for the combiners is shown in Fig 70.

Fig 69—Exterior view of the two hybrid combiners. The one on the left is designed to cover the 1 to 50 MHz range; the one on the right 50 to 500 MHz.

Fig 70—Schematic diagram of the hybrid combiners. For the 1- to 50-MHz model, T1 is 10 turns of no. 30 enameled wire bifilar wound on an FT-23-72 ferrite core. For the 50 to 500 MHz model, T1 consists of 10 turns of no. 30 enameled wire bifilar wound on an FT-23-63 ferrite core. Keep all leads as short as possible when constructing these units.

LOW-POWER STEP ATTENUATORS

A step attenuator is a useful and important tool for receiver testing. Step attenuators may often be found at flea markets for reasonable prices; in addition, the construction of an attenuator is well within the capabilities of most builders. Described here is a simple low-power step attenuator suitable for receiver front-end protection, and as a calibrated attenuator for receiver performance evaluation. This attenuator uses double-pole, double-throw slide switches to select different amounts of attenuation. Coaxial fittings are used at each end of the attenuator.

Description

Fig 71 is the schematic diagram of the attenuator. Eight pi-network resistive sections are employed; the attenuation is variable in 1-dB steps. A total attenuation value of 81 dB is available with all the sections switched in. The maximum attenuation of any single section is limited to 20 dB because leak-through would probably degrade the effect of higher attenuation sections and result in inaccuracy.

This is a low-power attenuator; it is not designed for use at power levels exceeding ¼ watt. If for some reason the attenuator will be connected to a transceiver, a means of bypassing the unit during transmit periods must be devised.

Parts

All the switches are DPDT standard size slide types. Stackpole S-5022CD03-0 units are used here. Other switch types may work as well, but have not been tested. The use of subminiature switches should be avoided.

Carbon-composition or film, ¼-watt, 5%-tolerance resistors are used. Ideally, the resistors should be selected using a reliable ohmmeter; this will ensure accuracy.

Double-sided PC board is used for the enclosure. Dimensions for the model described here are given in Fig 72. The attenuator has identification lettering etched into the top surface (or front panel) of the unit. This adds a nice touch, and is a permanent means of labeling. Of course, rub-on transfers or Dymo tape labels could be used as well.

Female BNC single-hole, chassis-mount connectors are used at each end of the

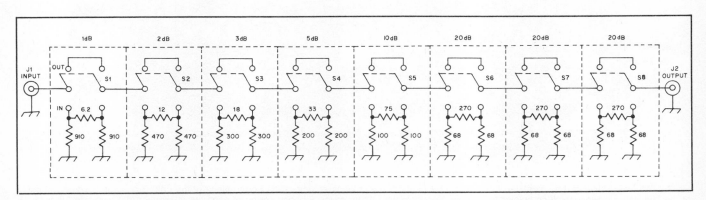

Fig 71—Schematic diagram of the attenuator. Resistors are ¼-W, 5%-tolerance, carbon-composition or film types. Resistances are given in ohms.

Fig 72—Mechanical dimensions of the attenuator enclosure.

Fig 73—Close-up of the switch detail.

enclosure. These connectors are small and easy to mount, have excellent RF qualities, and provide a means of easily connecting and disconnecting the attenuator by a simple twist of the wrist.

Construction

After all the box parts are cut to size and the necessary holes are made, scribe light lines to locate the inner partitions. Carefully tack-solder all partitions in position. Dress any PC-board parts that do not fit squarely. Once everything is in proper position, run a solder bead all the way around the joints. Caution: Do not use an excessive amount of solder, as the switches must later be fit flat inside the sections. The top, sides, ends and partitions can be completed. Dress the outside of the box to suit your taste. For instance, you might wish to bevel the box edges. Buff the copper with steel wool, add lettering, and finish off the work

with a coat of clear lacquer or polyurethane varnish.

Using a little lacquer thinner or acetone (and a lot of caution), soak the switches to remove the grease that was added during the manufacture. When dry, spray the inside of the switches lightly with a TV-tuner cleaner/lubricant. Using a sharp drill bit (about 3/16 inch will do), countersink the mounting holes on the actuator side of the switch mounting plate. This ensures that the switches will fit flush against the top plate. At one end of each switch, bend the two lugs over and solder them together. Cut off the upper halves of the remaining switch lugs. (A look at Fig 73 will help clarify these steps.)

Solder the horizontal members of the pi sections between the appropriate switch lugs. Try to keep the lead lengths as short as possible, and do not overheat the resistors. Now solder the switches in place

to the top section of the enclosure by flowing solder through the mounting holes and onto the circuit-board material. Be certain that you place the switches in their proper positions; correlate the resistor values with the degree of attenuation. Otherwise, you may wind up with the 1-dB step at the wrong end of the box.

Once the switches are installed, thread a piece of no. 18 bare-copper wire through the center lugs of all the switches, passing it through the holes in the partitions. Solder the wire at each switch terminal. Cut the wire between the poles of each individual switch, leaving the wire connecting one switch pole to that of the neighboring one on the other side of the partition, as shown in Fig 74.

At each of the two end switch terminals, leave a wire length of approximately 1/8 inch. Install the BNC connectors, and solder the wire pieces to the connector center conductors.

Now install the resistors that comprise the grounded legs of each pi section. Use short lead lengths. Remember that physical

Fig 74—An inside view of the completed attenuator. Use of short, direct leads enhances the performance of the unit. Brass nuts soldered at each of the four corners allow machine screws to be used to secure the bottom cover. File one corner of each nut to permit a flat, two-sided fit within the enclosure.

symmetry is conducive to good performance. Do not use excessive amounts of heat when soldering.

Solder a no. 4-40 brass nut at each inside corner of the enclosure. Recess the nuts approximately 1/16 inch from the bottom edge of the box to allow sufficient room for the bottom panel to fit flush. Secure the bottom panel with four no. 4-40, 1/4-inch machine screws and you're done!

This circuit was described by Shriner and Pagel in September 1982 *QST*. Resistance values for pi- and T-network resistive attenuators are given in Tables 3 and 4. Values are for use in 50-ohm unbalanced systems. These values can be scaled for use in other systems by dividing the resistance values by 50 and then multiplying by the system resistance. The resistances shown in Fig 71 are the nearest standard values to those resistances appearing in Tables 3 and 4, taking 5% tolerances into account. Although some of the values are a few ohms off, they are quite acceptable for amateur work.

MEASURING RECEIVER PERFORMANCE

Comparing the performance of one receiver to another is difficult at best. The features of one receiver may outweigh a second, even though its performance under some conditions is not as good as it should be. Although the final decision on which receiver to own will more than likely be based on personal preference, there are ways to compare receiver performance characteristics. The most important parameters are noise floor, intermodulation distortion, blocking (gain compression) and cross modulation.

Table 3
Pi-Network Resistive Attenuator (50 Ω)

dB Atten.	R1 (Ohms)	R2 (Ohms)
1	870.0	5.8
2	436.0	11.6
3	292.0	17.6
4	221.0	23.8
5	178.6	30.4
6	150.5	37.3
7	130.7	44.8
8	116.0	52.8
9	105.0	61.6
10	96.2	71.2
11	89.2	81.6
12	83.5	93.2
13	78.8	106.0
14	74.9	120.3
15	71.6	136.1
16	68.8	153.8
17	66.4	173.4
18	64.4	195.4
19	62.6	220.0
20	61.0	247.5
21	59.7	278.2
22	58.6	312.7
23	57.6	351.9
24	56.7	394.6
25	56.0	443.1
30	53.2	789.7
35	51.8	1405.4
40	51.0	2500.0
45	50.5	4446.0
50	50.3	7905.6
55	50.2	14,058.0
60	50.1	25,000.0

Table 4
T-Network Resistive Attenuator (50 Ω)

dB Atten.	R1 (Ohms)	R2 (Ohms)
1	2.9	433.3
2	5.7	215.2
3	8.5	141.9
4	11.3	104.8
5	14.0	82.2
6	16.6	66.9
7	19.0	55.8
8	21.5	47.3
9	23.8	40.6
10	26.0	35.0
11	28.0	30.6
12	30.0	26.8
13	31.7	23.5
14	33.3	20.8
15	35.0	18.4
16	36.3	16.2
17	37.6	14.4
18	38.8	12.8
19	40.0	11.4
20	41.0	10.0
21	41.8	9.0
22	42.6	8.0
23	43.4	7.1
24	44.0	6.3
25	44.7	5.6
30	47.0	3.2
35	48.2	1.8
40	49.0	1.0
45	49.4	0.56
50	49.7	0.32
55	49.8	0.18
60	49.9	0.10

Fig 75—General test setup used for evaluating receiver performance. Two signal generators (calibrated), a hybrid combiner, a step attenuator and an audio voltmeter are required for the measurements.

The general test setup is shown in Fig 75. Two calibrated signal generators are required, along with a hybrid combiner, a step attenuator and an ac voltmeter. A hybrid combiner is essentially a unit with three ports. This device is used to combine the signals from a pair of generators. It has the characteristic that signals applied at ports 1 or 2 appear at port 3, and are attenuated by 6 dB. However, a signal from port 1 is attenuated 30 or 40 dB when sampled at port 2. Similarly, signals applied at port 2 are isolated from port 1 some 30 to 40 dB. The isolating properties of the box prevent one signal generator from being frequency or phase modulated by the other. A second feature of a hybrid combiner is that a 50-ohm impedance level is maintained throughout the system. A commercial example of a directional bridge of this kind is an HP-8721A.

The signal generators used in the test setup must be calibrated accurately in dBm or microvolts. The generators should have extremely low leakage. That is, when the output of the generator is disconnected, no signal should be detected at the operating frequency with a sensitive receiver. Ideally, at least one of the signal generators should be capable of amplitude modulation. A suitable lab-quality piece would be the HP-8640B.

While most signal generators are calibrated in terms of microvolts, the real concern is not with the voltage from the generator but with the power available. The fundamental unit of power is the watt. However, the unit which is used for most low-level RF work is the milliwatt, and power is often specified in decibels with respect to 1 milliwatt (dBm). Hence, 0 dBm would be 1 milliwatt. The dBm level, in a 50-ohm load, can be calculated with the aid of the following equation

$$dBm = 10 \log_{10} [20 (V_{RMS})^2]$$

where dBm is the power with respect to 1 milliwatt and V is the RMS voltage available at the output of the signal generator.

The convenience of a logarithmic power unit like the dBm becomes apparent when signals are amplified or attenuated. For example, a −107-dBm signal that is applied to an amplifier with a gain of 20 dB will result in an output of −107 dBm + 20 dB, or −87 dBm. Similarly, a −107-dBm signal applied to an attenuator with a loss of 10 dB will result in an output of −107 dBm − 10 dB, or −117 dBm.

Noise-Floor Measurement

A generator that is tuned to the same frequency as the receiver is used for noise-floor measurements. Output from the generator is increased until the ac voltmeter at the audio-output jack of the receiver shows a 3-dB increase. This measurement indicates the minimum discernible signal (MDS) that can be detected with the receiver. This level is defined as that which

Fig 76—General test setup for measuring receiver noise floor. Signal levels for a hypothetical measurement are indicated. See text for a detailed discussion.

Fig 77—Test setup for measuring receiver blocking performance. Hypothetical measurements are included on the drawing.

will produce the same audio-output power as the internally generated receiver noise. Hence, the term "noise floor." As a hypothetical example, say the output of the signal generator is −127 dBm, the loss through the combiner is fixed at 6 dB and the step attenuator is set to 4 dB. The equivalent noise floor can then be calculated as follows:

Noise floor = −127 dBm − 6 dB − 4 dB
            = −137 dBm

where the noise floor is the power available at the receiver antenna terminal, −6 dB is the loss through the coupler and −4 dB is the loss through the attenuator. Refer to Fig 76.

Blocking

Blocking concerns gain compression. Both signal generators are used. One is set for a weak signal of roughly −110 dBm and the receiver is tuned to this frequency. The other generator is set to a frequency of 20 kHz away and is increased in amplitude until the receiver output drops by 1 dB, as measured with the ac voltmeter. A blocking measurement is indicative of the signal level that can be tolerated at the receiver antenna terminal before desensitization will occur.

As an example, say that the output of the generator is −27 dBm, the loss through the combiner is fixed at 6 dB and there is 0 dB attenuation through the attenuator (effec-

tively switched out of the line). See Fig 77. The signal level at the receiver terminal that will cause gain compression is calculated as follows:

Blocking level = −27 dBm − 6 dB
               = −33 dBm

This can be expressed as dynamic range when this level is referenced to the receiver noise floor that was calculated earlier. This term can be called "receiver blocking dynamic range." Calculate it as follows:

Blocking dynamic range
= noise floor − blocking level
= −137 dBm − (− 33 dBm)
= −104 dB

This value is usually taken in terms of absolute value and would be referred to as 104 dB.

Two-Tone IMD Test

One of the most significant parameters that can be specified for a receiver is a measure of the range of signals that can be tolerated while producing essentially no undesired spurious responses. The evaluation is made with a two-tone intermodulation-distortion (IMD) test. It is generally a conservative evaluation for other effects, such as blocking, which will occur only for signals well outside the IMD dynamic range of the receiver.

Two signals of equal level spaced 20 kHz

apart are injected into the input of the receiver. Call these frequencies f1 and f2. The so-called third-order intermodulation-distortion products will appear at frequencies of (2f1-f2) and (2f2-f1). Assume that the two input frequencies are 14.040 and 14.060 MHz. The third-order products will be at 14.020 and 14.080 MHz.

The step attenuator will be useful in this experiment. Adjust the two generators for an output of − 10 dBm each at frequencies spaced 20 kHz. Tune the receiver to either of the third-order IMD products. Adjust the step attenuator until the IMD product produces an output 3 dB above the noise level as read on the ac voltmeter.

For an example, say the output of the generator is − 10 dBm, the loss through the combiner is 6 dB and the amount of attenuation used is 40 dB. See Fig 78. The signal level at the receiver antenna terminal that just begins to cause IMD problems is calculated as:

$$\text{IMD level} = -10 \text{ dBm} - 6 \text{ dB} - 40 \text{ dB}$$
$$= -56 \text{ dBm}$$

This can be expressed as a dynamic range when this level is referenced to the noise floor. This term is referred to as "IMD dynamic range" and can be calculated

IMD dynamic range
$$= \text{noise floor} - \text{IM level}$$
$$= -137 \text{ dBm} - (-56 \text{ dBm})$$
$$= -81 \text{ dB}$$

Therefore, the IMD dynamic range of this receiver would be 81 dB.

Evaluating the Data

Thus far, a fair amount of data has been gathered with no mention of what the numbers really mean. It is somewhat easier to understand exactly what is happening by arranging the data in a form something like that in Fig 79. The base line is just a power line with a very small level of power at the left and a higher level (0 dBm) at the right.

The noise floor of the hypothetical receiver is drawn in at − 137 dBm, the IMD level (the level at which signals will begin to create spurious responses) at − 56 dBm and the blocking level (the level at which signals will begin to desense the receiver) at − 33 dBm. As can be seen, the IMD dynamic range is some 23 dB smaller than the blocking dynamic range. This means IMD products will be heard across the band long before the receiver will begin to desense − some 23 dB sooner.

The figures for the hypothetical receiver represent those which would be expected from a typical communications receiver on the market today. It is interesting to note that it is possible for the home constructor to build a receiver that will outperform commercially available units (even the high-priced ones).

THE SPECTRUM ANALYZER

The spectrum analyzer is like an

Fig 78—Receiver IMD performance test setup. Signal levels for a hypothetical measurement are given. A detailed discussion of this measurement is given in the text.

Fig 79—This graph displays the performance of a hypothetical (though typical) receiver under test. The noise floor is − 137 dBm, blocking level is − 33 dBm and the IMD level is − 56 dBm. This corresponds to a receiver blocking dynamic range of 104 dB and an IMD dynamic range of 81 dB.

oscilloscope in that both present an electrical signal through graphical representation. The oscilloscope is used to observe electrical signals in the time domain (amplitude as a function of time). However, not all signals can be represented properly in only the time domain. Amplifiers, mixers, oscillators, detectors, modulators and filters are best characterized in terms of their frequency response. This information is obtained by viewing electrical signals in the frequency domain (amplitude as a function of frequency). One instrument that can display the frequency domain is the spectrum analyzer.

Time and Frequency Domain

To better understand the concepts of time and frequency domain, see Fig 80. The three-dimensional coordinates show time (as the line sloping toward the bottom right), frequency (as the line rising toward the top right) and amplitude (as the vertical axis). The two discrete frequencies shown are harmonically related, so we'll refer to them as f_1 and $2f_1$.

In the representation of time domain at Fig 80B, all frequency components of a signal are summed together. In fact, if the two discrete frequencies shown were applied to the input of an oscilloscope, we would see the solid line (which corresponds to $f_1 + 2f_1$) on the display.

In the frequency domain, complex signals (signals composed of more than one frequency) are separated into their individual frequency components. Additionally, a measurement is made as to the power level at each discrete frequency. The display depicted at Fig 80 C is typical of that obtained with a spectrum analyzer.

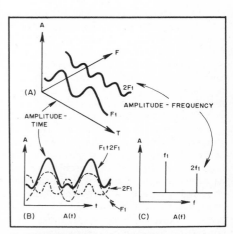

Fig 80—Different ways in which a complex signal may be characterized. At A is a three-dimensional display of amplitude, time and frequency. At B, this information is shown only in the time domain as would be seen on an oscilloscope. At C the same information is shown in the frequency domain as it would be viewed on a spectrum analyzer.

Fig 81—A block diagram of a superheterodyne spectrum analyzer.

The frequency domain can contain information not found in the time domain and therefore the spectrum analyzer offers advantages over the oscilloscope for certain measurements. As might be expected, there are some measurements that require data gathering to be done in the time domain. In these cases, the oscilloscope is an invaluable instrument.

Spectrum Analyzer Basics

There are several different types of spectrum analyzers, but by far the most common is nothing more than an electronically-tuned superheterodyne receiver. The receiver is tuned using a ramp voltage; this ramp voltage performs two functions: First, the ramp voltage sweeps the frequency of the analyzer local oscillator. Second, the ramp is used to deflect the horizontal axis of a CRT display, as shown in Fig 81. The vertical axis of the CRT display is provided deflection from the signal strength of the received signal. In this way, the CRT display has frequency on the horizontal axis and signal strength on the vertical axis.

Most spectrum analyzers use the up-converting technique so that a fixed-tuned input filter is capable of removing the image. Only the first local oscillator need be tuned to tune the receiver. In the up-conversion design, a wideband input is converted to an IF higher than the highest input frequency. As with most up-converting communications receivers, it is not easy to achieve the desired ultimate selectivity at the first IF, because of the rather high frequency. For this reason, dual or higher orders of conversion are used to generate an IF low enough that the desired selectivity can be achieved practically. In the example of Fig 81 dual conversion is used; the first IF is at 400 MHz with a second IF at 10.7 MHz.

In the example spectrum analyzer, the first local oscillator is swept from 400 MHz to 700 MHz; this converts the input (from nearly 0 MHz to 300 MHz) to the first IF of 400 MHz. The usual rule of thumb for varactor-tuned oscillators is that the maximum practical tuning ratio (the ratio of the highest frequency to the lowest frequency) is an octave or a two-to-one ratio. As it can be seen from the example spectrum analyzer, the tuning ratio of the first local oscillator is 1.75 to one, which meets this specification.

The image frequency spans 800 MHz to 1100 MHz and is easily eliminated using a low-pass filter with a cut-off frequency around 300 MHz. The 400-MHz first IF is converted to 10.7 MHz where the ultimate selectivity of the analyzer is obtained. The image of the second conversion, (421.4 MHz), is eliminated by the first IF filter. The attenuation of the image should be rather great, on the order of 60 to 80 dB. This requires a first IF filter with a high Q; this is achieved by using helical resonators, SAW resonators or cavity-type filters. Another method of eliminating the image problem is to use triple conversion; converting first to an intermediate IF such as 50 MHz and then to 10.7 MHz. As with any receiver, an additional frequency conversion requires added circuitry and produces further potential spurious responses.

Most of the signal amplification takes place at the lowest IF; in the case of the example analyzer this is 10.7 MHz. This is where the communications receiver and the spectrum analyzer differ. A communications receiver demodulates the incoming signal so that the modulation can be heard or further demodulated for RTTY or packet or other mode of operation. In the spectrum analyzer, only the signal strength is needed.

In order for the spectrum analyzer to be most useful, it should be convenient to display signals of widely different levels. As an example, signals differing by 60 dB, which is a thousand to one difference in voltage or a million to one in power, would be difficult to display. This would mean that if power were displayed, one signal would be one million times larger than the other (in the case of voltage one signal would be a thousand times larger). In either case it would be difficult to display both signals on a CRT. The solution to this problem is to use a logarithmic display and to display the relative signal levels in decibels. Using this technique, a one-thousand-to-one ratio of voltage reduces to a sixty-decibel difference.

The conversion of the signal to a logarithm is usually performed in the IF amplifier or detector, resulting in an output voltage proportional to the logarithm of the input RF level. This output voltage is then used to drive the CRT display.

Spectrum Analyzer Performance Specifications

The performance parameters of a spectrum analyzer are specified in terms similar to those used for radio receivers, in spite of the fact that there are many differences between a receiver and a spectrum analyzer.

The *sensitivity* of a receiver is often specified as the minimum detectable signal, which means the smallest signal that can be heard. In the case of the spectrum analyzer, it is not the smallest signal that can be heard, but the smallest signal that can be seen. The *dynamic range* of the spectrum analyzer determines the largest and smallest signals that can be viewed on the analyzer. As with a receiver, there are several factors that can affect dynamic range, such as intermodulation distortion, 2nd and 3rd order distortion and blocking. *IMD dynamic range* is the maximum difference in signal level between the minimum detectable signal and the level of two signals of equal strength that generate an intermodulation product equal to the minimum detectable signal.

This is a good point to explain another of the significant differences between a communications receiver and a spectrum analyzer. Although the communications receiver is an excellent example to introduce the spectrum analyzer, there are several differences such as the previously explained lack of a demodulator. Unlike the communications receiver, the spectrum analyzer is not a sensitive radio receiver. To preserve a wide dynamic range, the spectrum analyzer often uses passive mixers for the first and second mixers. Therefore, referring to Fig 81, the noise figure of the analyzer is no better than the losses of the input low pass filter plus the first mixer, the first IF filter, the second mixer and the loss of the second IF filter. This often results in a combined noise figure of more than 20 dB. With that kind of noise figure the spectrum analyzer is obviously not a communications receiver for extracting very weak signals from the noise but a measuring instrument for the analysis of frequency spectrum.

The *selectivity* of the analyzer is called the *resolution bandwidth*. This term refers to the minimum frequency separation of two signals of equal level that can be resolved so that there is a 3-dB dip between the two. The IF filters used in a spectrum analyzer differ from a communications receiver in that the filters in a spectrum analyzer have very gentle skirts and rounded passbands, rather than the flat passband and very steep skirts used on an IF filter in a high-quality communications receiver. This rounded passband is necessary because the signals pass into the filter passband as the spectrum analyzer scans the desired frequency range. If the signals suddenly pop into the passband (as they would if the filter had steep skirts), the filter tends to ring; a filter with gentle skirts is less likely to ring. This ringing, called *scan loss*, distorts the display and requires that the analyzer not be swept in frequency at an excessive rate. All this means that the scan rate must be checked periodically to be certain that the signal amplitude is not affected by excessive rate.

Spectrum Analyzer Applications

When and where is a spectrum analyzer used? Spectrum analyzers are used in situations where the signals to be analyzed are very complex and an oscilloscope display would be an undecipherable jumble. The spectrum analyzer is also used when the frequency of the signals to be analyzed is very high. Although high-performance oscilloscopes are capable of operation into the UHF region, moderately-priced spectrum analyzers can be used well into the GHz region.

The spectrum analyzer can also be used to view very low-level signals. For an oscilloscope to display a VHF waveform, the bandwidth of the oscilloscope must extend from zero to the frequency of the waveform. If harmonic distortion and other higher-frequency distortions are to be seen the bandwidth of the oscilloscope must exceed the fundamental frequency of the waveform. This broad bandwidth can also admit a lot of noise power. The spectrum analyzer, on the other hand, analyzes the waveform using a narrow bandwidth; thus

it is capable of reducing the noise power admitted.

Probably the most common application of the spectrum analyzer is the measurement of the harmonic content and other spurious signals in the output of a radio transmitter. Fig 82 shows two ways to connect the transmitter and spectrum analyzer. The method shown at A should not be used for wide-band measurements since most line-sampling devices do not exhibit a constant-amplitude output over a broad frequency range. Using a line sampler is fine for narrow-band measurements, however. The method shown at B is used in the ARRL Lab.

The attenuator must be capable of dissipating the transmitter power, and it must have sufficient attenuation to protect the spectrum analyzer input. Many spectrum analyzer mixers can be damaged by only a few milliwatts, so most analyzers

Fig 82—Two commonly used setups for observing the output of a transmitter or amplifier on a spectrum analyzer. The system at A uses a line sampler to pick off a small amount of the transmitter or amplifier power. At B, the majority of the transmitter power is dissipated in the power attenuator.

Fig 83—ARRL laboratory test setup for transmitters or amplifiers with several different power levels.

have an adjustable input attenuator that will provide a reasonable amount of attenuation to protect the sensitive input mixer from damage. The power limitation of the attenuator itself is usually on the order of a watt or so, however. This means that 20 dB of additional attenuation is required for a 100 watt transmitter, 30 dB for a 1000 watt transmitter, and so on, to limit the input to the spectrum analyzer to one watt. There are specialized attenuators that are made for transmitter testing; these attenuators provide the necessary power dissipation and attenuation in the 20 to 30 dB range.

The test setup used in the ARRL laboratory for measuring an HF transmitter or amplifier is shown in Fig 83. As can be seen, different power levels dictate different amounts of attenuation between the transmitter or amplifier and the spectrum analyzer.

When using a spectrum analyzer it is very important that the maximum amount of attenuation be applied before a measurement is made. In addition, it is a good practice to view the entire spectrum of a signal before the attenuator is adjusted. The signal being viewed could appear to be at a safe level, but another spectral component, which is not visible, could be above the damage limit. It is also very important to limit the input power to the analyzer when pulse power is being measured. The *average* power may be small enough so that the input attenuator is not damaged, but the *peak* pulse power, which may not be readily visible on the analyzer display, can destroy a mixer, literally in microseconds.

Fig 84 shows the broadband spectrum of a transmitter, showing the harmonics in the output. The horizontal (frequency) scale is 5 MHz per division; the main output of the transmitter at 7 MHz can be seen about 1.5 major divisions from the left of the trace. A very large apparent signal is seen at the extreme left of the trace. This occurs at what would be zero frequency and it is caused by the first local oscillator frequency being exactly the first IF. All up-converting superheterodyne spectrum analyzers have this IF feedthrough; in addition, this signal is occasionally accompanied by smaller spurious signals generated within the analyzer. To determine what part of the displayed signal is a spurious response caused by IF feedthrough and what is an actual input signal, simply remove the input signal and observe the trace.

It is not necessary or desirable that the transmitter be modulated for this broadband test. Investigating the sidebands from a modulated transmitter requires a narrow band spectrum analysis and produces displays similar to that shown in Fig 85. The test setup used to produce this display is shown in Fig 86. In this example a two-tone test signal is used to modulate the transmitter. Fig 85 shows the two test tones plus some of the intermodulation produced by the single-sideband transmitter.

(A)   (B)

Fig 84—Spectrum analyzer display of two different transmitters on the 40-meter band. Each horizontal division represents 5 MHz and each vertical division is 10 dB. The photograph at A shows a clean transmitted signal; the transmitter at B shows more spurious signal content. Both transmitters are legal, however, according to current FCC spectral purity requirements.

Fig 85—Spectrum analyzer photograph showing the result of an SSB transmitter two-tone test. Each horizontal division represents 1 kHz and each vertical division is 10 dB. The third-order products are 30 dB below the PEP (top line), the fifth-order products are down 37 dB and seventh-order products are down 44 dB. This represents acceptable (but not ideal) performance.

When using a spectrum analyzer it is necessary to ensure that the analyzer does not generate additional spurious signals that are then attributed to the system under test. Some of the spurious signals that can be generated by a spectrum analyzer are harmonics and intermodulation distortion. If it is desired to measure the harmonic levels of a transmitter at a level below the spurious level of the analyzer itself, a notch filter can be inserted between the attenuator and the spectrum analyzer as shown in Fig 87. This reduces the level of the fundamental signal and prevents that signal from generating harmonics within the analyzer, while still allowing the harmonics from the transmitter to pass through to the analyzer without attenuation. Caution should be used when using this technique; detuning the notch filter or inadvertently changing the transmitter frequency will allow potentially high levels of power to enter the analyzer. In addition, care must be exercised with the choice of filters; some filters (such as cavity filters) will respond not only to the fundamental but will notch out odd harmonics as well.

It is good practice to check for the generation of spurious signals within the spectrum analyzer. When a spurious signal is generated by a spectrum analyzer, adding attenuation at the analyzer input will cause the internally generated spurious signals to decrease by an amount greater than the added attenuation. If attenuation added ahead of the analyzer causes all of the visible signals to decrease by the same amount, this indicates a spurious-free display.

The input impedance for most RF spectrum analyzers is 50 ohms; not all circuits

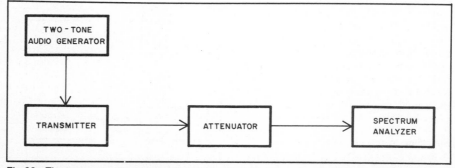

Fig 86—The test setup used in the ARRL laboratory for measuring the IMD performance of transmitters and amplifiers.

Fig 87—A notch filter can be used to reduce the level of a transmitter's fundamental signal so that the fundamental does not generate harmonics within the analyzer.

Fig 89—An inductive pickup loop, called a "sniffer" probe. This probe does not load the circuit under test. See text for details.

Fig 88—A voltage probe designed for use with a spectrum analyzer.

have convenient 50-ohm connections that can be accessed for testing purposes, however. Using a probe such as the one shown in Fig 88 allows the analyzer to be used as a troubleshooting tool. The probe can be used to track down signals within a transmitter or receiver, much like an oscilloscope is used. The probe shown offers a 100-to-one voltage reduction and provides a loading to the circuit of 5000 ohms.

A different type of probe is shown in Fig 89. This inductive pickup coil (sometimes called a "sniffer") is very handy for troubleshooting. The coil is used to couple signals from the radiated magnetic field of a circuit into the analyzer. A short length of miniature coax is wound into a pick-up loop and soldered to a larger piece of coax. The use of the coax shields the loop from coupling energy from the electric field component. The dimensions of the loop are not critical, but the smaller the dimensions of the loop, the more accurate the loop will be in locating the source of radiation of RF energy. The shield of the coax provides a complete electrostatic shield without introducing a shorted turn.

The sniffer allows the spectrum analyzer to sense RF energy without contacting the circuit being analyzed. If the loop is brought near an oscillator coil, the oscillator can be tuned without directly contacting (and thus disturbing) the circuit. The oscillator can then be checked for reliable starting and the generation of spurious sidebands. With the coil brought near the tuned circuits of amplifiers or frequency multipliers, those stages can be tuned using a similar technique.

Even though the sniffer does not contact the circuit being evaluated, it does extract some energy from the circuit. for this reason, the loop should be placed as far from the tuned circuit as is practical. If the loop is placed too far from the circuit, the signal will be too weak or the pick-up loop will pick up energy from other parts of the circuit and not give an accurate indication of the circuit under test.

One very handy application of the sniffer is to locate sources of RF leakage. By probing the shields and cabinets of RF generating equipment (such as transmitters) egress and ingress points of RF energy can be identified by indications on the analyzer display.

One very powerful characteristic of the spectrum analyzer is the instrument's capability to measure very low-level signals. This characteristic is very advantageous when very high levels of attenuation are measured. Fig 90 shows the set-up for tuning the notch and bandpass of a VHF duplexer. The spectrum analyzer, being capable of viewing signals well into the low microvolt region, is capable of measuring the insertion loss of the notch cavity more than 100 dB below the signal generator output. Making a measurement of this sort requires care in the interconnection of the equipment and a well-designed spectrum analyzer and signal generator. RF energy

leaking from the signal generator from the cabinet, the line cord or even the coax itself, can leak into the spectrum analyzer through similar paths and corrupt the measurement. This leakage can make the measurement look either better or worse than the actual attenuation depending on the phase relationship of the leaked signal.

Extensions of Spectral Analysis

What if a signal generator is connected to a spectrum analyzer so that the signal generator output frequency is exactly the same as the receiving frequency of the spectrum analyzer? It would certainly appear to be a real convenience not to have to continually reset the signal generator to the desired frequency. It is, however more than a convenience. A signal generator connected in this way is called a *tracking generator* because the output frequency tracks the spectrum analyzer input frequency. The tracking generator makes it possible to make sweep-frequency measurements of the attenuation characteristics of circuits, even when the attenuation involved is large as the bandpass of narrow filters such as the cavity described in the previous example.

Fig 91 shows the connection of a tracking generator to a circuit under test. In order for the tracking generator to create an output frequency exactly equal to the input frequency of the spectrum analyzer, the internal local oscillator frequencies of the spectrum analyzer must be known; this is the reason for the interconnections between the tracking generator and the spectrum analyzer. The test set-up of Fig 91 will measure the gain or loss of the circuit under test. Only the magnitude of the gain or loss is available; in some cases, the phase angle between the input and output would also be an important and necessary parameter.

The spectrum analyzer is not sensitive to the phase angle of the tracking generator output. In the process of generating the tracking generator output, there were no guarantees that the phase of the tracking generator would be either known or constant. This is especially true of VHF spectrum analyzers/tracking generators where a few inches of coaxial cable represents a

(A)

TUNING THE BANDPASS

(B)

TUNING THE NOTCH

Fig 90—A spectrum analyzer and signal generator can be used to tune the bandpass and notch filters of a duplexer. Leakage around the duplexer must be kept to a minimum.

Fig 91—Filter response over a range of frequencies can be plotted by tracking a signal generator with the local oscillator of the spectrum analyzer.

Fig 92—A network analyzer can measure both the phase and magnitude of the filter input and output signals. See text for details.

number of degrees of phase shift.

One effective way of measuring the phase angle between the input and output of a device under test is to sample the phase of the signal applied to the device under test and apply the sample to a phase detector. The phase of the output of the device under test is also sampled and applied to the phase detector. Fig 92 shows a block diagram of this technique. An instrument that can measure both the magnitude and phase of a signal is called a *vector network analyzer*, or simply a network analyzer.

The magnitude and phase can be displayed either separately or together. When the magnitude and phase are displayed together the two can be presented as two separate traces similar to the two traces on a dual-trace oscilloscope. A much more useful method of display is to present the magnitude and phase as a polar plot where the locus of the points of a vector having the length of the magnitude and the angle of the phase are displayed. Very sophisticated network analyzers can display all of the S parameters of a circuit in either a polar format or a Smith Chart format.

Chapter 26

Troubleshooting and Repair

Traditionally, the radio amateur has maintained a working knowledge of station equipment. This knowledge, and the resourcefulness to make repairs with whatever supplies are available, keeps amateur installations operating when all other communications fail. The radio amateur's ability to troubleshoot and repair equipment is not only a tradition; it is fundamental to the existence of the service.

Every amateur must make a decision when faced with equipment failure. Not everyone is an electronics wizard; your set may end up at the repair shop. The theory you learned for the FCC examinations and the information in this handbook can help you make an intelligent choice. If the problem is something simple (and most are), why not avoid the effort of shipping the radio to the manufacturer? Although the saving of time and money is gratifying, the experience and confidence gained may prove far more valuable. Especially when a problem appears during an emergency.

Troubleshooting and repair of electronic gear need not be a mystical subject. It is more like detective work. A knowledge of complex math is not required. However, one must have, or develop, the ability to read a schematic diagram and to visualize signal flow through the circuit. A working knowledge of resistors, capacitors, inductors and semiconductor devices, and how they affect the dc resistance of a network, is also necessary. The fundamental concepts are covered elsewhere in this book.

We are all a bit nervous when we enter new territory. Do not be intimidated by the intricate circuits of a modern radio. Even the most complex transceiver is made up of relatively simple circuits. As you gain experience, you will develop a first-hand understanding of circuit functions. This insight, and the confidence gained from experience, distinguish the skillful troubleshooter.

SAFETY FIRST

Always! Death is permanent. Before we

Table 1
Safety Rules

1) Keep one hand in your pocket when working on "live" circuits or checking to see that capacitors are discharged.
2) Include a conveniently located ground-fault-interrupter/circuit breaker in the work-bench wiring.
3) Use grounded plugs and receptacles on all equipment that is not double insulated.
4) Use double-insulated equipment when working:
  a) outdoors.
  b) on a concrete or dirt floor.
  c) near standing water.
5) Use an isolation transformer when working on ac/dc devices.
6) Switch off the power, ground the positive lead from the supply and discharge capacitors when making circuit changes.
7) Do not subject electrolytic capacitors to:
  a) excessive voltage.
  b) ac.
  c) reverse voltage.
8) Test leads should be well insulated.
9) Do not work alone!
10) Wear safety glasses for protection against sparks and metal fragments.
11) Always use a safety belt when working above ground level.
12) Wear shoes with nonslip soles that will support your feet when climbing.
13) Wear a hard hat when someone is working above you.
14) Be careful with tools that may cause short circuits.
15) Replace fuses only with those having proper ratings.

begin considering the equipment and techniques of troubleshooting, we must discuss the preservation of the worker and his tools.

Electricity can be lethal. Only 50 mA flowing through the body is painful; 100 to 500 mA is usually fatal. Under certain conditions, as little as 24 V can kill. Keep one hand in your pocket while working on "live" circuits to prevent the possibility of resting your free hand on a ground. This reduces the risk of electricity passing

through your chest (the most fatal current path). A list of safety rules can be found in Table 1.

TEST EQUIPMENT

Test equipment is required for efficient troubleshooting. We cannot see electrons flow. Electrons do affect various devices in our equipment, however, with results that we can see.

Many fear that repairing their own ham gear means purchasing a bench full of expensive test instruments. This is not so! In fact, you probably already own the most important instruments. Some others may be purchased inexpensively, rented, borrowed or built at home. A shortage of test gear may limit the kind of repairs you attempt, but do not let it stop you from making repairs that *are* within your capabilities.

Most hams elect to buy test gear. Before buying, consider whether your use of the item merits the expense. Instruments that do not give sufficient return for an individual, may for a club. Expensive test instruments look more reasonable when the cost is split among the members of a club (and a pool of test gear may also serve to pull a sleepy club out of the doldrums).

I mentioned that you already own some of the most important instruments. We each have some of these natural test instruments.

• Eyes — Use them to search for evidence of heat or arcing. Often these conditions are indicated by discoloration or charring of components and circuit boards.

• Ears — Gross distortion can be detected by ear. The "snaps" and "pops" of arcing or the sizzling of a burning component may help you track down circuit faults.

• Nose — Arcing in a circuit produces ozone (what you sometimes smell in the air during a thunderstorm). Smoke from hot components can usually be smelled before it is seen. Some components emit a "hot" smell when overheated. This

Table 2
Sources of Equipment Manuals

HI Manuals, Inc.†
P.O. Box Q-802
Council Bluffs, IA 51502

Howard Sams Publications
4300 W. 62nd St.
Indianapolis, IN 46205

Collins Telecommunications Products
  Division,
Rockwell International
Cedar Rapids, IA 52406

R. L. Drake Co.
P.O. Box 112
911 Springboro Pike
Miamisburg, OH 45342
513-866-2421

Hallicrafters Manuals
Ardco Electronics††
P.O. Box 95, Dept. Q
Berwyn, IL 60402

Hammarlund Manuals
Irving J. Abend
P.O. Box 426
Bergenfield, NJ 07621
201-384-7589

Hammarlund Manuals
Pax Manufacturing Co.
Attn: Peter Kjeldsen
100 East Montauk Hwy.
Lindenhurst, NY 11757

ICOM America, Inc.
2380-116th Ave. NE
Bellevue, WA 98004
206-454-8155

Swan Division of Cubic Communications
305 Airport Rd.
Oceanside, CA 92054
619-757-7525

Ten-Tec, Inc.
Hwy. 411 East
Sevierville, TN 37862
615-453-7172

Kenwood USA Corp.
2201 East Dominguez St.
Long Beach, CA 90810
213-639-4200

U.S. Government Surplus
General Services Administration
National Archives and Record Services
Washington, DC 20408

U.S. Government Surplus
Slep Electronics Co.††
P.O. Box 100
Otto, NC 28763

Yaesu Electronics Corp.
17210 Edwards Rd.
Cerritos, CA 90701
213-404-2700

†HI Manuals will not answer requests for information unless a $5 research fee is included. Order their catalogue ($1) to see if they have the manual you need.
††Write for manual prices (specify model).

---

smell remains long after power is removed. Nerves in the nose are extremely sensitive; heat that generates no smell can be felt when brought within 1 or 2 inches of the nose.

- Fingers — Use your fingers to measure low heat levels in components. Solid-state devices are temperature sensitive; if you can hold your finger on them while they are operating (be careful!), they are cool enough. If an operating device is too hot to hold, check for excessive current flow; additional heat sinks may be required.

- Brain — More troubleshooting problems have been solved with a VOM and a brain than with the most expensive spectrum analyzer. Use your brain to assemble information and analyze data collected by other instruments. (The magnifying glass did not make Sherlock Holmes famous; it was his mind!)

Information

There is a sea of information available (a bibliography is included at the end of this chapter). Sometimes it is difficult to find information on a specific item, but remember that Amateur Radio offers a great resource to each of us. Check into a few roundtable QSOs and ask for help. There are over 400,000 hams in the U.S.; chances are someone else has had the same trouble you are experiencing. Look in

Amateur Radio publications; ownership clubs for particular radios may advertise.

Before beginning work, obtain a manual for the radio. An owner's manual or schematic is mandatory; a service manual is better. Some sources of manuals are listed in Table 2.

ARRL members have other resources. ARRL Hq. may be able to provide copies of manuals that are in the ARRL files, and equipment-modification references for back issues of *QST*.[1] Place a "HamAds" listing in *QST* when searching for a rare manual.

The ARRL Technical Coordinator (TC) program may also be able to help. TCs and Assistant Technical Coordinators (ATCs) are volunteers who are willing to help hams with technical questions. For the name of a local ATC, contact your Section Manager (listed on page 8 of any issue of *QST)*.

ELECTRONIC TEST EQUIPMENT

Simple test gear is frequently included in the equipment under repair. Nearly all receivers include a speaker. An S meter is usually connected ahead of the audio chain. If the S meter shows signals, the RF chain is probably functioning. The antenna jack of a receiver can serve as a crude signal in-

[1]Write to ARRL Headquarters for information on costs and availability of specific manuals, copies and back issues.

jector. (Noise should be heard from the speaker when a test lead is rubbed against the center conductor of the antenna jack.) Some receivers include a calibrator. The calibrator signal, which is rich in harmonics, is injected in the RF chain close to the antenna jack and may be used for signal tracing and alignment. Every transmitter has an oscillator that may be used as a signal generator.

Spare components enable you to test by substitution. A lot of troubleshooting may be done without what is normally called test equipment.

Here is a summary of test instruments and their applications. Some items serve several purposes and may substitute for others on the list. The list does not cover all equipment available, only the most common and useful instruments.

- Multimeters — This group includes vacuum-tube voltmeters (VTVMs), volt-ohm-milliammeters (VOMs), field-effect-transistor VOMs (FETVOMs), digital multimeters (DMMs). Meter operation and use is explained in Chapter 25.

Look for a meter with an input impedance of 20 kΩ/V or better. Reasonably priced models are available with 30 kΩ/V ($35) and 50 kΩ/V ($40).

The high-Z input characteristic of FETVOMs, VTVMs and other electronic voltmeters makes them the preferred instruments for voltage measurements. DMMs are usually high-Z meters, but they may be sensitive to RF. Most technicians keep an analog-display VOM handy for use near RF equipment.

Multimeters are used to read bias voltage, circuit resistance, presence and level of signal (with an appropriate probe). They can test resistors, capacitors (within certain limitations), diodes and transistors.

- Test Leads — Keep an assortment of leads that terminate in medium and small alligator clips. It is best to make your own leads because ready-made leads use small wire that is not soldered to the clips.

Open wire leads (Fig. 1A) can pick up RFI that disturbs measurements. RFI is reduced somewhat if the leads are twisted together (Fig. 1B). A coaxial cable lead (Fig. 1C) *increases* RFI problems *if* the shield is *not* grounded. The cable shield must be grounded to reduce RFI.

Low capacitance, or ×10, probes (Fig. 1D) are used to reduce the effect of instrument-input and shield capacitance on the circuit under test. A network in the probe serves as a 10:1 divider and compensates for frequency distortion in the cable and test instrument. The trimmer capacitor on ×10 and ×100 oscilloscope probes should be adjusted for the best-looking square wave from the internal calibrator. See Fig. 1H.

Demodulator probes (see Fig. 1E and Chapter 25) convert ac voltages to dc for measurement. They are also used to allow scope triggering from a modulation envelope.

Fig. 1 — An array of test probes for use with various test instruments.

A capacitively coupled probe (Fig. 1F) can be made from a connector and a length of coax cable. Remove about ¾ inch of the cable jacket at one end. Trim the shield to ½ inch from the end and tin it. Use some RTV (room-temperature-vulcanizing) adhesive to seal the end against moisture. Install the connector at the other end of the cable.

Capacitive coupling increases with proximity and potential at the test point. Be very careful with this probe around high voltage. (The dielectric strength of air is about 80 V per 0.001 inch.)

A probe for inductive coupling (Fig. 1G) can be made in similar fashion. Connect a two- or three-turn loop across the center conductor and shield before sealing the end. The inductive pick up is useful for coupling to high-current points.

• SWR Meter — Every shack should have one! It can be the first indicator of antenna trouble. The SWR meter can also be used between an exciter and power amplifier to spot an impedance mismatch.

Simple meters indicate relative SWR and are fine for Transmatch adjustment and

Fig. 2 — Optimum inductive and capacitive dip-meter coupling.

Fig. 3 — An oscilloscope display showing the relationship of the time-base setting and graticule lines.

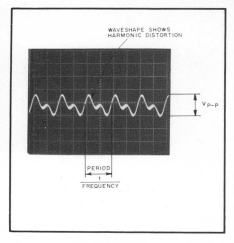

Fig. 4 — Information available from a typical oscilloscope display of a waveform.

line monitoring. However, if you want to make accurate measurements of antenna impedance or calculate SWR at the antenna feed point, a calibrated wattmeter with a directional coupler is required (one is shown in Chapter 25).

• Dummy Load — This is a necessity! Do not put a signal on the air while repairing equipment. Courtesy demands that we spare other amateurs from the QRM of tests until we are reasonably sure of the repair. More important, before a transmitter is fixed, we have no idea what spurious emissions it may generate. A dummy load also works to the technician's benefit by providing a known, matched load for use during adjustments.

When buying a dummy load, avoid used, oil-cooled dummy loads unless you can be sure that the oil does not contain PCBs. This biologically hazardous compound was common in transformer oil until a few years ago.

• Dip Meter — This device is often called a transistor dip meter or a grid-dip oscillator (from vacuum-tube days). Principles of dip-meter operation are covered in Chapter 25.

Most dip meters can also serve as an absorption frequency meter (in this mode, measurements are read at the current peak, rather than the dip). Further, some meters have a connection for headphones. The operator can usually hear signals that do not register on the meter. Because the dip meter is an oscillator, it can be used as a signal generator in certain cases where high accuracy or stability are not required.

A dip meter may be coupled to a circuit either inductively or capacitively. Inductive coupling results from the magnetic field generated by current flow. Therefore, inductive coupling should be used when a

conductor with relatively high current flow is convenient. Maximum inductive coupling results when the axis of the pick-up coil is placed perpendicular to a nearby current path (see Fig. 2A).

Capacitive coupling is required when current paths are magnetically confined or shielded. (Toroidal inductors and coaxial cables are common examples of magnetic self shielding.) Capacitive coupling depends on the electric field produced by voltage. Use capacitive coupling when a point of relatively high voltage is convenient. Capacitive coupling is maximum when the end of the pick-up coil is near a point of high voltage (see Fig. 2B). In either case, the circuit under test is affected by the presence of the dip meter. Always use the minimum coupling that yields a noticeable indication.

Use the following procedure to make reliable measurements. First, bring the dip meter gradually closer to the circuit while slowly varying the dip-meter frequency. When a current dip occurs, hold the meter steady and tune for minimum current. Once the dip is found, move the meter away from the circuit and confirm that the dip comes from the circuit under test (the current reading should increase with distance from the circuit until the dip is gone). Finally, move the meter back toward the circuit until the dip is just noticed. Retune the meter for minimum current and read the dip-meter frequency with a calibrated receiver or frequency meter.

The current dip of a good measurement is smooth and symmetrical. A non-symmetrical dip indicates that the dip-meter oscillator frequency is being significantly influenced by the test circuit. Such conditions do not yield usable readings.

When purchasing a dip meter, look for one that is mechanically and electrically stable. The coils should be in good condition. A headphone connection is helpful. Battery-operated models are easier to use for antenna measurements.

• Oscilloscope — A picture is worth a

thousand words, and the moving trace of a 'scope can give us more information about a signal than any other piece of test gear. A discussion of oscilloscope basics appears in Chapter 25.

The simplest way to display a waveform is to connect the vertical amplifier of the 'scope to a point in the circuit through a simple test lead. (When viewing RF, use a low-capacitance probe that has been "matched" to (compensated for) the 'scope amplifier.) See Fig. 1F. First, check to make sure that the circuit under test is isolated from the ac line by a transformer. Set the vertical-amplifier sensitivity so the circuit voltage will cover about half of the CRT screen. Connect the 'scope leads. Set the sweep-rate (sometimes called the TIME-BASE control so that one or more cycles are shown (see Fig. 3). Adjust the SYNC and SYNC-LEVEL controls for a stable display. Line sync only "locks" signals that are some multiple of 60 Hz.

An examination of the waveform gives peak-to-peak voltage (if calibrated), approximate period (frequency is the reciprocal of the period) and a rough idea of signal purity (see Fig. 4). If the 'scope has dual trace (can display two signals at once) capability, a second waveform may be displayed and compared to the first. When the two signals are taken from the input and output of a stage, stage linearity and phase shift can be checked (see Fig. 5).

Other display techniques are covered in previous chapters and later in this chapter. For more information, see the bibliography at the end of this chapter.

A primary performance characteristic of a 'scope is amplifier bandwidth. This specification tells us the frequency at which amplifier response has dropped 3 dB. The instrument will display higher frequencies, but cannot be used for accurate measurement of them. Expect an accuracy of no better than 3% when a 'scope is used well below its rated bandwidth. Most 'scope applications in Amateur Radio, however, do not require accurate measurements. Thus,

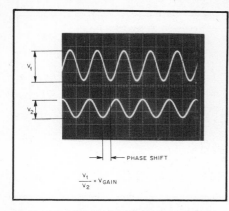

Fig. 5 — A dual-trace scope display of amplifier input and output waveforms.

$$\frac{V_1}{V_2} = V_{GAIN}$$

PHASE SHIFT

1-kHz SQUARE WAVE OSCILLATOR

NOISE AMPLIFIER

Fig. 6 — Schematic and parts-placement diagram of the AF/RF signal injector. All resistors are ¼ W, 5% carbon types, and all capacitors are disc ceramic. A full-size etching pattern can be found at the back of this book.

BT1 — 9-V transistor radio battery.
D1, D2 — Silicon switching diode, 1N914 or equiv.
D3 — 6.2-V, 400 mW Zener diode.
J1, J2 — Banana jack.

Q1-Q4 — General purpose silicon NPN transistors, 2N2222 or equiv.
R1 — 1-kΩ panel-mount control.
S1 — SPST toggle switch.

'scopes are useful to hams well beyond the specifications. Do not believe that transmitter emissions are clean based only on a 'scope display. A bandwidth of 250 to 500 MHz is required to display all significant harmonics from an HF transmitter.

When buying a 'scope, get the greatest bandwidth you can afford. Old and wide is better than new and narrow, with respect to bandwidth. Old Hewlett Packard or Tektronix scopes of great bandwidth are occasionally sold at hamfests. Keep to well-known manufacturers when buying a used scope, or any test equipment for that matter.

• Signal Generators — Although signal generators are used for sophisticated circuit tests, their role in troubleshooting is limited to use in signal injection and alignment techniques. An AF/RF signal-injector schematic is shown in Fig. 6. For those instances where more accuracy is needed, the crystal-controlled signal source of Fig. 7 can be used. The AF/RF circuit provides usable harmonics up to 30 MHz, while the crystal-controlled oscillator will function with crystals from 1 to 15 MHz. These two projects are not meant to compete with standard signal generators, but they are adequate for signal injection.[2] A better generator is required for receiver alignment or for receiver quality testing.

When shopping for a signal generator, look for one with a pure sine-wave signal. A good signal generator is double or triple shielded against leakage. Fixed-frequency audio should be available for modulation of the RF and for injection into audio stages. The frequency control of a good generator does not slip or exhibit backlash. Signal level should be controlled by a switch, labeled in dBm, not a potentiometer. The output jack should be a coaxial connector (usually a BNC), not the kind used for microphone connections. Some older, high-quality units are common. Look for World War II surplus units of the

CRYSTAL OSC

Fig. 7 — Schematic and parts-placement diagram of the crystal-controlled signal source. All resistors are ¼ W, 5% carbon types, and all capacitors are disc ceramic. A full-size etching pattern can be found at the back of this book.

BT1 — 9-V transistor radio battery.
J1 — Crystal socket to match the crystal type used.
J2 — RCA phono jack or equiv.
Q1, Q2 — General purpose silicon NPN

transistor, 2N2222 or equiv.
R1 — 500-Ω panel-mount control.
S1 — SPST toggle switch.
Y1 — 1- to 15-MHz crystal.

[2]More information about the signal injector and signal source appears in, Some Basics of Equipment Servicing," Feb. 1982 *QST* (Feedback, May 1982).

Fig. 8 — A typical radio converted for signal-tracer use. R1, R2 and R3 must be chosen to provide appropriate loads for the preceding stages.
S1 — SPST switch.   S2, S3, S4 — 2P3T slide switches.

URM series, Hewlett Packard/Boonton model 202, Measurements Inc. model 80 and 65, military units TS-497 and BC-221 and Hewlett Packard model 606. (The Technical Department at ARRL Headquarters has a bibliography of articles about the BC-221 that includes a solid-state conversion and calibration technique.) Home-built signal generators may be quite good, but make sure to check construction techniques, level control and shielding quality. Some 1000-Hz square-wave generators produce harmonics that are useful up to 10 MHz.

• Signal Tracers — Signals can be traced with a voltmeter and an RF probe, a dip meter or an oscilloscope, but there are some devices made especially for signal tracing. Most convert the traced signal to audio (often using a voltmeter RF probe) and apply the amplified audio to a speaker. The tracer must function as a receiver and detector for each frequency range in the test circuit. A high-impedance tracer input is necessary to prevent circuit loading.

An old radio can be converted into a signal injector/tracer for use with common IFs (Fig. 8). Modify the radio so a test probe can be connected to each functional block. If the stages preceding the test probe are disabled, the set is a signal tracer; if the preceding stages are operating, the set is a signal injector. (Use a step attenuator to adjust injected-signal level.) Avoid ac/dc radios for this use.

A general-coverage receiver can be used to trace signals in radios with uncommon IFs. Most receivers, however, have a low-impedance input that severely loads the test circuit. To minimize loading, use a capacitive probe. When the probe is held near the circuit, signals will be picked up and carried to the receiver. It may also pick up stray RF; make sure you are listening to the correct signal by switching the circuit under test on and off while listening.

Dedicated signal tracers are limited test instruments. All things considered, a dip meter, with an absorptive mode and a headphone connection, is a much better value.

• Tube Tester — Two types of tube testers are common. The first is the emission tester. As the name implies, this tester checks the tube by measuring the amount of electron emission from the cathode (cathode current, I_c). Each grid is shorted to the plate through a switch and the current is observed while the tube operates as a diode. By opening the switches from each grid to the plate (one at a time) we can check for opens and shorts. If the plate current does not drop slightly as a switch is opened, the element connected to that switch is either open or shorted to another element. We cannot tell an open from a short with this test. The emission tester does not indicate the ability of a tube to amplify.

The other common tube tester checks transconductance. Some transconductance testers read plate current with a fixed bias network. Others use an ac signal to drive the tube while measuring plate current. Both of these tests are meant to indicate the transconductance (amplification) of a tube.

Leakage is another tube fault that testers often check. Contamination inside the tube envelope may result in current leakage between elements. The paths can have high resistance (250 kΩ), and may result from gas or deposits of electron-emitting material that have been transferred from the cathode. Leakage can be checked with an ohmmeter using the ×1M range, depending on the actual spacing of tube elements. Tube testers use a moderate voltage to check for leakage. Beware: This voltage may *cause* shorts in tubes with very close element spacings (6AK5, GL-2C51 and GL-5670).

Use the same caution in the purchase of a tube tester that you would with any other used equipment. Know the testing method, make sure the manual is included and see that it checks the tubes you want to check.

• Transistor Tester — Transistor testers are similar to transconductance tube testers. Collector current is measured while the device is biased into conduction or while an ac signal is applied at the control terminal.

Most transistor failures appear as either an open or shorted junction. Opens and shorts can be found easily with an ohm-meter; a special tester is not required. Transistor gain characteristics vary widely, however, even between units with the same device number.

Testers are useful to determine the characteristics of a particular transistor. A tester that uses no ac signal can read the transistor dc alpha and beta, while testers that apply an ac signal show the ac alpha or beta. The tester can help you decide if a particular transistor has sufficient gain for use as a replacement. It may also help when matched transistors are required.

Transistor testers are inexpensive, so purchase of a used instrument is unnecessary. The functions of a dc tester can be performed with a power supply and a meter (details are shown later in this chapter under "Components").

• Frequency Meter — Various instruments for frequency measurement, their construction and operation are covered in Chapter 25.

Almost any digital frequency counter is good enough for troubleshooting and repair work. No special temperature compensation is necessary unless you require accuracy greater than 1 part per million. Used equipment should be in good working order with no signs of damage or abuse.

• Power supplies — A well-equipped test bench should include a means of varying the ac-line voltage, a variable-voltage regulated dc supply and an isolation transformer. If you want to work on vacuum-tube gear, the maximum voltage available from the dc supply should be high enough to serve as a bias supply for common tubes.

Ac-line voltage varies slightly with load. An autotransformer with a movable tap lets you boost or reduce the line voltage slightly. This is helpful when testing equipment supply-voltage tolerance.

A variable-voltage dc supply may be used to power various small items under repair and as a variable bias supply for testing active devices. Construction details for a laboratory power supply appear in Chapter 27.

As mentioned earlier, ac/dc radios must be isolated from the ac line during testing and repair. Keep an isolation transformer handy if you want to work on table-model broadcast radios or television sets. Some transceivers of the 1960s also used the ac/dc power supply.

• Accessories — There are a few small items that may be used in troubleshooting. You may want to keep them handy.

A cold source is useful when searching for intermittent connections. Most parts suppliers carry some kind of cooling agent in a spray can. Poor connections frequently become open circuits when cooled.

A heat source helps locate components that fail only when hot. A small incandescent lamp can be mounted in a large piece of sleeve insulation to produce localized

Fig. 9 — A source of local heat made from insulating sleeve and a small dial lamp.

heat for test purposes (see Fig. 9).

A stethoscope (with the pickup removed — Fig. 10) or a long piece of sleeve insulation can be used to listen for arcing or sizzling in a circuit.

Fig. 10 — A stethoscope, with the pickup removed, used to listen for arcing in crowded circuits.

Troubleshooting Procedures

Connector faults are more common than component troubles. Consider poor connections as prime suspects in our troubleshooting detective work. Begin every job with an inspection of the connections. Is the antenna connected? How about the speaker, fuses and TR switch? Are transistors and ICs firmly seated in their sockets? Are all interconnection cables sound and securely connected? After checking the obvious, begin an in-depth investigation.

To begin that investigation, define the problem accurately. Ask yourself these questions:

1) What functions of the equipment do not work as they should; what does not work at all?

2) What kind of performance can you realistically expect?

3) Is there anything in the operational history of the equipment that could have caused the trouble?

4) Has the trouble occurred in the past? (Keep a record of troubles, maintenance and repair in the owner's manual or log book.)

Write the answers to the questions. The information will help with your work, and help service personnel if their advice or professional service is required.

SEARCHING AT THE BLOCK LEVEL

The block diagram is a road map. It shows the signal paths for each circuit function. These paths may run together, they may cross occasionally, or not at all. Those blocks that are not in the paths of faulty functions can be eliminated as suspects. Sometimes the symptoms point to a single block, and no further search is necessary.

In cases where more than one block is suspect, several approaches may be used. Each requires that a block, or stage, be tested. Signal injection, signal tracing or a combination of both techniques may be used for this purpose.

THE INSTINCTIVE APPROACH

First, consider an instinctive approach. The check for connector problems mentioned at the beginning of this section is an example of this procedure. Experience has shown connector faults to be so common that they should be checked even before a systematic approach begins.

When instinct springs from a base of experience, search by instinct may be the fastest procedure. If instinct is correct,

Table 3

Symptoms and Their Causes for All Electronic Equipment

Symptom	Cause
Power Supply Problems	
No output voltage	Open circuit (usually a fuse or transformer winding).
Hum or ripple	Faulty regulator, capacitor or rectifier, low-frequency oscillation.
Amplifiers	
Low gain	Transistor, coupling capacitors, emitter-bypass capacitor, AGC component, alignment.
Noise Transistors, Coupling capacitors, resistors	
Oscillations	Dirt on variable capacitor or chassis, shorted op-amp input.
Untuned (oscillations do not change with frequency)	Audio stages.
Tuned	RF, IF and mixer stages.
Squeal	Open AGC-bypass capacitor.
Static-like crashes	Arcing trimmer capacitors, poor connections.
Static in FM receiver	Faulty limiter stage, open capacitor in ratio detector, weak RF stage, weak incoming signal.
Intermittent noise	All components and connections, band-switch contacts, potentiometers (especially in dc circuits), trimmer capacitors, poor antenna connections.
Distortion (constant)	Oscillation, overload, faulty AGC, leaky transistor, open lead in tab-mount transistor, dirty potentiometer, leaky coupling capacitor, open bypass capacitors, imbalance in tuned FM detector, IF oscillations, RF feedback (cables).
Distortion (strong signals only)	Open AGC line, open AGC diode.
Frequency change	Physical or electrical variations, dirty or faulty variable capacitor, broken switch, loose compartment parts, poor voltage regulation, oscillator tuning (trouble when switching bands).
No Signals	
All bands	Dead VFO or heterodyne oscillator.
One band only	Defective crystal, oscillator out of tune, band switch.
No function control	Faulty switch, poor connection, defective switching diode or circuit.
Improper Dial Tracking	
Constant error across dial	Dial drive.
Error grows worse along dial	Circuit adjustment.

Table 4
Transmitter Problems

Symptom	Cause
Key clicks	Keying filter, distortion in stages after keying.
Modulation problems	
Loss of modulation	Broken cable (microphone, PTT, power), open circuit in audio chain, defective modulator.
Distortion on transmit	Defective microphone, RF feedback from: lead dress, modulator imbalance, bypass capacitor, improper bias, excessive drive.
Arcing	Dampness, dirt, improper lead dress.
Low output	Incorrect control settings, improper carrier shift (CW signal outside of passband), audio oscillator failure, transistor or tube failure, SWR protection circuit.
Antenna Problems	
Poor SWR	Damaged antenna element, matching network, feed line, balun failure (see below), resonant conductor near antenna, poor connection at antenna.
Balun failure	Excessive SWR, weather or cold-flow damage in coil choke, broken wire.
RFI	Arcing or poor connections anywhere in antenna system or nearby conductors.

Table 5
Transceiver Problems

Symptom	Cause
Inoperative S meter	Faulty relay
PA noise in receiver	
Excessive current on receive	
Arcing in the PA tank	
Reduced signal strength on transmit and receive	IF failure
Poor VOX operation	VOX amplifiers and diodes
Poor VOX timing	Adjustment, component failure in VOX timing circuits or amplifiers
VOX consistently tripped by receiver audio	AntiVOX circuits or adjustment

repair time and effort may be reduced substantially. As experience and confidence grow, the merits of the instinctive approach grow with them. However, the inexperienced technician who chooses this approach is at the mercy of chance.

As an example, suppose an AM receiver suddenly begins producing weak and distorted audio. An inexperienced person frequently suspects poor alignment as a common problem. Even though the manufacturer's instructions and the proper equipment are not available, our friend begins twiddling the transformer cores. Before long, the set is hopelessly misaligned. Now our misguided ham must send the radio to a shop for an alignment that was not needed before repairs were attempted.

Alignment does not shift suddenly. A normal signal-tracing procedure would have shown that the signal was good up to the detector, but badly distorted after that stage. The defective detector diode that caused the problem would have been easily found and quickly replaced.

Tables 3 through 6 list common symptoms, and their probable causes. Background information about the items in the tables and symptoms that cannot be itemized appear in the text. These servicing hints have been collected from many sources and may save some time if similar troubles are encountered. The tables list only problems that occur often in troubleshooting and repair. If a problem matches one listed, proceed to testing at the component level. If a particular symptom is not found in the tables, continue at the block level with a systematic approach.

The Power Supply

Many equipment failures are caused by trouble in the power supply. Fortunately, most power-supply problems are easy to find and repair (see Fig. 11). First, use a voltmeter to measure output. Loss of output voltage is usually caused by an open circuit. (A short circuit draws excessive current that opens the fuse, thus becoming an open circuit.) If the fuse has opened, turn off the power, replace the fuse and measure the load-circuit dc resistance. The measured resistance should be consistent with the power-supply ratings:

$$R \geq \frac{E}{I}$$

where
R = load-circuit resistance
E = supply voltage
I = maximum supply current

If R is too low, check the load circuit with an ohmmeter to locate the trouble. (Nominal circuit resistances are included in most equipment manuals.) If the load-circuit resistance is normal, look for a shorted filter capacitor or defective regulator IC. Electrolytic capacitors fail with long (two years) disuse; the electrolytic layer may be re-formed as explained later in this chapter.

IC regulators are often victims of oscillations in their high-gain amplifiers. Such oscillations are normally prevented by capacitors that connect the IC input and output pins to the adjustment or ground pin. Check or replace these capacitors whenever a regulator has failed.

Ac ripple, or hum, is caused by feedback, poor regulation or defective filter components. Look for a defective

Fig. 11 — A schematic of a typical power supply showing the components mentioned in the text.

Table 6
Receiver Problems

Symptom	Cause
Low sensitivity	Semiconductor contamination weak tube, alignment
Signals and calibrator heard weakly (low S-meter readings) (strong S-meter readings)	RF chain
	AF chain, detector
No signals or calibrator heard, only hissing	RF oscillators

Distortion	
On strong signals only	AGC fault
AGC fault	Active device cut off or saturated
Difficult tuning	AGC fault
Inability to receive	Detector fault
AM weak and distorted	Poor detector, power or ground connection
CW/SSB unintelligible	BFO off frequency or dead
FM distorted	Open detector diode

(A)

(B)

Fig. 12 — Equipment set up for amplifier gain testing. Connect the equipment as shown in A and adjust the 'scope display so that the waveform peaks are at graticule lines. Move the 'scope probe to the amplifier output and increase attenuation until the envelope size matches that of the input signal. Stage gain, independent of 'scope calibration, is shown on the step attenuator.

regulator, a shorted choke or open capacitor in the filter. In new construction projects make sure RF is not getting into the power supply.

Once the faulty component is found, inspect the surrounding circuit and consider what may have caused the problem. Referred symptoms (where a faulty component is the result of another failure, rather than the cause) are often encountered. For example, a shorted filter capacitor will increase current flow and burn out a rectifier diode. The defective diode is easy to find but the capacitor may show no visible damage. When a component has been subjected to excess current or voltage, as a result of another failure, check it.

Amplifiers

Amplifiers are the most common circuits in electronics. The output of an ideal amplifier would match the input signal in every respect except magnitude: No distortion or noise would be added. Real amplifiers *always* add noise and distortion.

Gain

Gain is the measure of amplification and it is usually expressed in decibels (dB) over a specified frequency range, known as the bandwidth or passband of the amplifier. When an amplifier is used to provide a stable load for the preceding stage, or as an impedance transformer, there may be little or no power gain. Amplifier failure usually results in a loss of gain or excessive distortion at the amplifier output. In either case, check external connections first. Is there power to the stage? Has the fuse opened? Check the speaker and leads in audio output stages, the microphone and push-to-talk (PTT)

line in transmitter audio sections.

Excess voltage, excess current or thermal runaway lead to sudden failure of semiconductors. The failure may appear as either a short, or open, circuit of one or more PN junctions.

Thermal runaway is characteristic of bipolar transistors. If degenerative feedback (the emitter resistor reduces base-emitter voltage as conduction increases) is insufficient, thermal runaway will allow excessive current flow and device failure. Check transistors by substitution, if possible.

Faulty coupling components can reduce amplifier output. Look for component failures that would increase series, or decrease shunt, impedance in the coupling network. Coupling faults can be located by signal tracing or parts substitution. Other passive-component defects reduce amplifier output by shifting bias or causing active-device failure. These failures are evident when the dc operating voltages are measured.

A fault in the AGC loop may force a transistor into cutoff or saturation. Open the AGC line to the device and substitute a variable voltage for the AGC signal. If amplifier action varies with voltage, suspect the AGC components; otherwise, suspect the amplifier.

Gain bandwidth measurements can be

made with a stable signal source, step attenuator and oscilloscope. See Fig. 12.

Noise

A slight hiss is normal in all electronic circuits. This noise is produced whenever current flows through a conductor that is warmer than absolute zero. Noise is compounded and amplified by succeeding stages. Repair is necessary only when noise threatens to obscure normally clear signals.

Semiconductors can produce hiss in two ways. First, faulty devices frequently produce excessive hiss under normal conditions. Second, any semiconductor junction produces white noise (hiss) when reverse biased. Both conditions worsen with increased temperature, so localized heat may help you find the source. Hiss can also be traced with an oscilloscope. Hissing from a resistor may increase when the component is tapped with a pencil or other insulator.

Typical sources of impulse noise are resistors, capacitors, semiconductors, vacuum tubes and connections. Poor connections and arcing are the most common causes of impulse noise.

Use signal-tracing techniques and substitution to locate noise sources. Physical shock and temperature increase noise from faulty components. A stethoscope lets you hear arcing in crowded

Fig. 13 — An in-circuit test for noise in active devices/coupling components. R1 should duplicate the collector-ground impedance of the active device.

(A)

(B)

(C)

Fig. 14 — Examples of distorted wave forms. The result of clipping is shown in A and non-linear amplification at B. A pure sine wave is shown in C for comparison. An example of harmonic distortion is shown in Fig. 4, earlier in this chapter.

circuits. Check connections at cables, sockets and switches. Look for dirty variable-capacitor wipers and potentiometers. Procedures for cleaning parts are given later in this chapter.

Rotary switches may be tested by bridging the contacts with a clip lead. Loose contacts may sometimes be repaired by gluing them to the switch deck. Operate variable components through their range while observing the noise level at the circuit output.

Potentiometers are particularly noise prone when used in dc circuits. Clean them with spray cleaner and rotate the shaft several times.

Mica trimmer capacitors often sound like lightning when arcing occurs. Test them by installing a series 0.01-μF capacitor. If the noise disappears, replace the trimmer.

Noise in transformers and loads can be spotted by substituting a suitable current-limiting resistor for the active device (Fig. 13). If the noise stops, the active component is at fault.

Oscillations

An amplifier oscillates whenever there is sufficient positive feedback. Oscillation may occur at any frequency from a slow audio buzz (often called "motorboating") up to the frequency where active-device gain is zero. Unwanted oscillations are usually the result of changes in the active device (increased junction or interelectrode capacitance), failure of an oscillation-suppressing component (open decoupling or bypass capacitors, neutralizing components) or new feedback paths (improper lead dress, dirt on the chassis or components). A shift in bias or drive levels may aggravate oscillation problems.

Oscillations that occur in audio stages do not change as the radio is tuned because the operating frequency, and therefore the component impedances, do not change. However, RF and IF oscillations vary in amplitude as operating frequency is changed.

Oscillation stops when the output circuit of the offending stage is changed enough to upset the feedback amplitude or phase. An additional bypass capacitor may pro-

duce such a change. The defective stage can be found more reliably with a signal tracer or oscilloscope.

Distortion

Distortion is the product of nonlinear operation. The resultant waveform contains not only the input signal, but new signals, at other frequencies as well. All of the frequencies combine to produce the distorted waveform. Distortion in a transmitter gives rise to splatter, harmonics and RFI.

Fig. 14 shows some typical cases of distortion. Clipping (also called flat-topping — Fig. 14A) is the consequence of excessive drive. The corners on the waveform show that harmonics are present. (A square wave contains the fundamental and all odd harmonics.) These odd harmonics would be evident as splatter above and below the operating frequency, possibly outside the amateur band. Key clicks are similar to clipping.

Harmonic distortion produces radiation at frequencies far removed from the fundamental. Harmonic distortion is a

major cause of RFI; it is the product of improper neutralization or ineffective harmonic suppression.

Incorrect bias brings about unequal amplification of the positive and negative wave sections. Consequences similar to those of clipping or harmonic distortion may be present.

In most cases, the amateur's ability to detect and measure distortion is limited by available test equipment. (Instruments used for distortion measurement are the distortion meter, noise meter, spectrum analyzer and phase meter.) However, some rough measurements of distortion can be made with a function generator and an oscilloscope.

Distortion Measurement

First, set the generator for a square wave and view it on the 'scope. Use a low-capacitance probe. The wave should show square corners and a flat top. Next, inject a square wave at the amplifier input and again view the input wave on the 'scope. Any new distortion is a result of the test circuit loading the generator output. (If the wave shape is severely distorted, the test is not valid.) Now, move the test probe to the test circuit output and read the waveform. Refer to Fig. 15 to estimate circuit distortion and its cause.

The above applies only to audio amplifiers without frequency tailoring. In RF gear, the transmitter may have a very narrow audio passband, so inserting a square wave into the mic input may result in an output that is difficult to interpret. The frequency of the square wave will have a significant effect.

All components listed as sources of impulse noise may also produce distortion. Check variable capacitors and resistors, switches, connectors and sockets for dirt or corrosion. Distortion that only affects strong signals usually indicates an AGC defect.

Leaky transistors produce distorted signals. A vacuum tube with an interelectrode short also causes distortion. These semiconductor and vaccum-tube conditions may mimic AGC trouble.

IF oscillations may produce distortion. They cause constant, full AGC action. (This is evident on a 'scope display or in bias measurements.) The S meter shows strong signals even with the antenna disconnected. AGC and conduction levels in RF sections are nearly constant as the operating frequency is varied.

Improper bias often results from an overheated or open resistor. Heat causes resistor values to permanently increase. Leaky, or shorted capacitors and RF feedback can also produce distortion by disturbing bias levels. Distortion is also caused by circuit imbalance in Class AB or B amplifiers.

Oscillators

While the loss of oscillator output

Fig. 15 — Square wave distortion and probable causes.

usually has drastic effects on equipment operation, the effects do not point directly to oscillator failure. Whenever there is weakening or complete loss of signal, check oscillator operation and frequency. There are several methods:

- Use a receiver with a coaxial probe to listen for the oscillator signal.
- A dip meter can be used to check oscillators. In the absorptive mode, tune the dip meter to within ± 15 kHz of the oscillator, couple it to the circuit, and listen for a beat note in the dip-meter headphones.

A dip meter in the active mode can be set to the oscillator frequency and coupled to the oscillator output. If the oscillator is dead, the dip-meter signal will restore circuit operation. Tune the dip meter slowly, or you may pass stations so quickly that they sound like "birdies."

- Oscillator waveform shows on a 'scope. However, operating frequency cannot be determined accurately. Use a low-capacitance (10X) probe for oscillator observations.
- Tube oscillators usually have no grid bias at startup, but negative bias when oscillating. Use a high-impedance voltmeter to measure grid bias. The bias also changes with frequency.
- Emitter current varies with frequency in transistor oscillators. Use a sensitive, high-impedance voltmeter across the emitter resistor to observe the current level.
- Control voltage changes with oscillation (for both tubes and transistors) in a crystal oscillator. Measure the control (either grid, or base) voltage while shunting the crystal with a 0.001-μF capacitor; if the stage is oscillating, the level will vary when the capacitor is added. Do not short the crystal!

Stability

Judge stability by the standards in practice when the circuit was made. Drift of several kilohertz per hour was quite normal years ago. Your needs may demand more stability, and modifications may be in order, but drift that is consistent with the equipment design is not a defect. This applies to new equipment as well as old. It is normal for some digital displays to flash back and forth between two values for the least-significant digit.

Drift is caused by variations in the oscillator. Poor voltage regulation and heat are the most common culprits. Check regulation with a voltmeter (use one that is not affected by RF). Regulators are usually part of the oscillator circuit. Check them by substitution. Check bypass capacitors by bridging them with good capacitors.

Solid-state replacements for tubes may improve oscillator stability by reducing heat and, therefore, temperature change in the circuit.[3] Long warm-up times can be avoided by keeping the oscillator compartment warm constantly. A small lamp, such as that used in a night light, mounted in the oscillator compartment keeps components near normal operating temperature. Wire the lamp so that it is on when the receiver is off, and off when the receiver is on.

Chirp is a form of rapid drift that is usually caused by excessive oscillator loading or poor power-supply regulation. When troubleshooting chirp, look for defects in buffer stages that affect the oscillator load. (For example, a shorted coupling capacitor increases loading drastically.) Also check lead dress, tubes and switches for new feedback paths (feedback defeats buffer action).

Frequency instability may also result from defects in feedback components. Too much feedback may produce spurious

signals, while too little makes oscillator startup unreliable.

Sudden frequency changes are frequently the result of physical variations. Loose components or connections are probable causes. Check for arcing or dirt on printed-circuit boards, trimmers and variable capacitors, loose switch contacts, bad solder joints or loose connectors.

Many older rigs used rivets to hold terminal strips, tube mounting rings and transistor sockets against ground. Rivets made a fine connection to chassis ground when the rigs were new. But, as time goes on, corrosion and mechanical weakening cause intermittent or high-impedance ground connections. To locate this type of problem, use a short piece of flexible, insulated wire (such as the braid from a piece of RG-174) with a piece of insulated tubing over it. Attach an alligator clip to each end. Connect one alligator clip to the suspect terminal and the other clip to the nearest chassis ground point. If the problem disappears, drill out the offending rivet and replace it with a machine screw, lockwasher and nut of the appropriate size.

A similar problem occurs when the screws around the edge of a PC board are used to connect the board to the chassis ground. If you run into this problem, remove the mounting screws and lightly sand the edge of the circuit board with fine sandpaper. Also clean the portions of the chassis that make contact with the board and its mounting screws. Remount the board to the chassis with machine screws, lockwashers and nuts.

Dial Tracking

Dial tracking errors may be associated with oscillator operation. Misadjustments in the frequency-determining components make dial accuracy worse at the ends of the dial. Tracking errors that are constant everywhere in the passband arise from slippage in the dial drive. This is usually cured

[3]Background design tips are in the reference for Sartori at the end of this chapter.

Fig. 16 — A schematic of a simple oscillator showing the locations of trimmer and padder capacitors.

Fig. 17 — Diode switching selects oscillator crystals at A. A transistor switch is used to key a power amplifier at B.

by a simple mechanical or calibration adjustment.

Tracking at the high-frequency end of the dial is controlled by trimmer capacitors. A trimmer is a variable capacitor connected in parallel with the main tuning capacitor (see Fig. 16). The trimmer represents a higher percentage of the total capacitance at the high end of the tuning range. It has little effect on tuning characteristics at the low-frequency end of the dial.

Low-end tracking is adjusted by a padder capacitor. A padder is a variable capacitor that is connected in series with the main tuning capacitor. Padder capacitance has a greater effect at the low-frequency end of the dial. The padder capacitor is often eliminated to save money. In that case, the low-frequency tracking is adjusted by the main tuning coil.

Controls

Semiconductors have made it practical to place a transistor or diode at each point where switching is required and run only dc leads to that point. This eliminates many problems caused by long leads.

Mechanical switches are relatively rugged. They can withstand substantial voltage and current surges. The environment does not drastically affect them, and there is usually visible damage when they fail.

Semiconductor switching offers inexpensive, high-speed operation. When subjected to excess voltage or current, most transistors and diodes silently expire. Occasionally, one sends up a smoke signal to mark its passing.

Temperature alters semiconductor characteristics. A normally adequate control signal may not be effective when transistor beta is lowered by a cold environment. Heat may cause a control voltage regulator to produce an improper control signal.

The control signal is actually a bias for the semiconductor switch. Forward-biased diodes and transistors act as closed switches while reverse biased components simulate open switches. If the control (bias) signal is not strong enough to completely saturate the semiconductor, conduction may not continue through a full ac cycle. Severe distortion results.

When dc control leads provide unwanted feedback paths, switching transistors may become modulators or mixers. Additionally, any reverse-biased semiconductor junction is a potential source of white noise.

Semiconductor switching usually reduces the cost and complexity of switching components. Switching speed is increased, contact corrosion and breakage are eliminated. In exchange, troubleshooting is complicated by additional support components such as voltage regulators and decoupling capacitors (see Fig. 17). The technician must consider many more components and symptoms when working with diode- and transistor-switched circuits.

Another kind of control circuit is becoming common in amateur equipment. Nearly every new transceiver is controlled by a miniature computer. Microprocessor control is beyond the scope of this chapter. For successful repair of microprocessor-controlled circuits, the technician should have the knowledge and test equipment necessary for computer repair. Familiarity with machine-language programming may also be desirable.

Transmitters

Many transmitter faults have already been covered. However, there are few techniques used to ensure stable operation of RF amplifiers in transmitters that are not covered elsewhere.

A parasitic choke frequently consists of

a 51- to 100-Ω non-inductive resistor with a coil wound around the body and connected to the leads. It is used to prevent VHF and UHF oscillations in a vacuum-tube amplifier. The coil has a low impedance at the operating frequency, but effectively blocks VHF and UHF oscillations. The choke is placed in the plate lead, close to the plate connection. Parasitic chokes often fail from excessive current flow. In these cases, the resistor is charred. Occasionally, physical shock or corrosion will produce an open circuit in the coil; test for continuity with an ohmmeter. Low-frequency oscillations are usually not a problem with vacuum-tube amplifiers.

Transistor amplifiers are protected against parasitic oscillations by low-value resistors or ferrite beads in the base or collector leads. Resistors are used only at low power levels (about 0.5 W), and both methods work best when applied to the base lead. Negative feedback is used to prevent oscillations at lower frequencies. An open component in the feedback loop may cause low-frequency oscillation, especially in broadband amplifiers.

Keying

The simplest form of modulation is on/off keying. Although it may seem that there cannot be much trouble with such an elementary form of modulation, two very important transmitter faults are the result of keying problems.

Key clicks are produced by fast rise and decay times of the keying waveform. Most transmitters include an RF filter across the key connections to shape the waveform and prevent clicks. In order to prevent clicks, all amplifiers following the last keyed stage must maintain linear operation. When clicks are experienced, check the keying filter components first, then the succeeding stages. An improperly biased power amplifier, or a Class C amplifier that is not keyed, may produce key clicks even though the keying waveform is correct. Clicks caused by a linear amplifier are a sign of low-frequency parasitic oscillations.

The other modulation problem associated with on/off keying is called backwave. Backwave is a condition in which the signal is heard (usually at a reduced level) even when the key is up. This occurs when the oscillator signal feeds through a keyed amplifier; neutralization of the keyed amplifier may be necessary.

Arcing

Although the sound and smell of arcs may conjure up nostalgic memories of the days when radios were made of wood, and operators of steel, it is a sign of trouble in modern gear. Arc sites are usually easy to find because an arc that generates visible light or noticeable sound also pits and discolors conductors.

Arcing is often caused by dampness, dirt or lead dress. If the dampness is temporary, dry the area and resume operation. Dirt

Fig. 18 — Test points used when tracing an antenna system circuit.

may be cleaned from the chassis with a residue-free cleaner. Arrange leads so high-voltage conductors are isolated. Keep them away from sharp corners and screw points.

Operating practice occasionally causes some arcing in control components. Arcing occurs in capacitors when the working voltage is exceeded. Air-dielectric variable capacitors can sustain occasional arcs without damage, but arcing indicates operation beyond circuit limits. Transmatches working beyond their ability may suffer from arcing.

Low Output Power

Some transmitters automatically reduce power in the TUNE mode. Check the owner's manual to see if the condition is normal. Check the control settings. Transmitters that use broad-bandwidth amplifiers require so little effort from the operator that control settings are seldom noticed. The CARRIER (or DRIVE) control may have been bumped. Remember to adjust tuned amplifiers after a significant change in operating frequency (usually 50 to 100 kHz).

Low power output in a transmitter may also spring from a misadjusted carrier oscillator or defective SWR protection circuit. If the carrier oscillator is set to a frequency well outside the transmitter passband, there may be no measurable output. Output power will increase steadily as the frequency is moved into the passband.

Complete loss of signal occurs when the carrier oscillator stops, although loss of the tone oscillator signal (in transmitters that use an audio tone to generate CW) may have the same effect. The tone oscillator may also be used to produce a CW sidetone. Loss of sidetone together with a loss of RF output indicates a defective tone oscillator.

Transistors may fail if the SWR protection circuit malfunctions. An open circuit in the "reflected" side of the sensing circuit leaves the transistors unprotected, a short "shuts them down."

Antennas

Begin antenna troubleshooting with a visual inspection of the antenna and surrounding area. Look for resonant conduc-

tors within a few wavelengths of the antenna. (Conductors that are perpendicular to the antenna are not significant.) If there are no obvious problems, test the antenna system.

To test the antenna system, transfer the antenna end of the feed line from the antenna to a dummy load (see Fig. 18). If the SWR appears normal, the problem must lie with the antenna itself. Make a closer inspection; look for corroded connections or an element that has slipped or broken. Check the components in any matching network at the feedpoint. Water in traps, and insects in variable capacitors or coils are common culprits.

If the SWR is still poor, move the dummy load to the next feed-line coupling that is closer to the transmitter and check the SWR again. Repeat this procedure until the SWR returns to normal. The faulty system component is the last one disconnected. Don't forget that SWR meters may have defects also. When in doubt, confirm readings with a second meter.

Balun Failures

Symptoms of balun failure include burned insulation and arcing between turns. Replace the damaged balun and avoid high-SWR operation.

A coaxial choke (usually 10 turns, 6-inch diameter for RG-58/U, larger cables require larger diameters) serves the same purpose as a balun. Falling branches, weather and so on may damage coaxial-choke baluns. Another threat to the coaxial choke is a phenomenon known as cold flow. The action is very similar to a piece of wire slicing through cheese. The center conductor slowly moves, cutting through the core dielectric as a result of the stress in the bent cable. This problem is most common in foam-dielectric cables, and is aggravated by warm weather.

RFI

RFI can be produced in any part of the antenna system. The cause is usually poor connections. Almost any metal-to-metal joint can form a diode junction. When RF is induced across the junction, rectification and strong harmonics result. Luckily, only conductors that are of a significant elec-

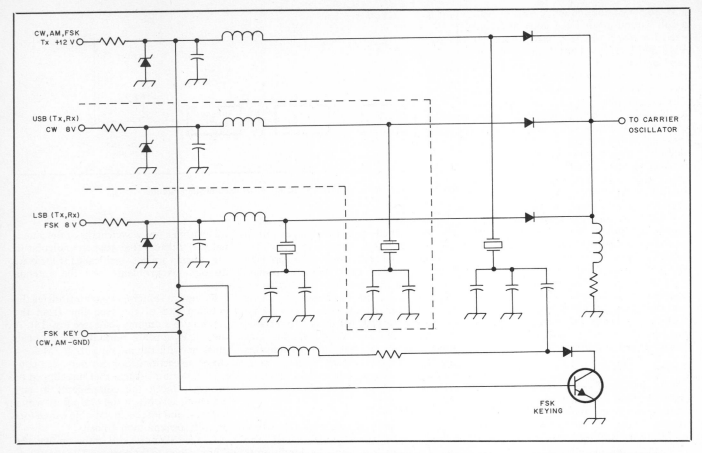

Fig. 19 — Partial schematic of a transceiver oscillator. The symptoms described in the text are caused by one or more components inside the dashed lines or a faulty USB/CW control signal.

trical length develop enough power to radiate the harmonics produced. The most likely troublemakers are tower sections, TV line amplifiers, antenna and feed-line connections, video recorders, guy wires and metal gutters. Less obvious sources can be located with direction-finding techniques. As you get closer to the RFI source, it is possible to hear the noise on higher harmonics. Switch to a higher band to prevent overload as you draw near the source. Once the source is located, correct the problem by electrically bonding the parts together. More information about RFI problems and cures appears in Chapter 40.

Transceivers

Elaborate switching schemes are used in transceivers for signal control. Many transceiver malfunctions can be attributed to relay or switching problems. Suspect the switching controls when:

- The S meter is inoperative.
- There is arcing in the tank circuit.
- Plate current is high during reception.
- There is PA noise in the receiver.
- Received signals are erratic or weak.

Since transceiver circuits are shared, stage defects frequently affect both the transmit and receive modes, although the symptoms may change with mode.

Oscillator problems usually affect both transmit and receive modes, but different oscillators, or frequencies, may be used for different emissions. Check the block diagram.

For example, one particular transceiver uses a single carrier oscillator with three different crystals (see Fig. 19). One crystal sets the carrier frequency for CW, AM and FSK transmit. Another sets USB transmit and USB/CW receive, and a third sets LSB transmit and LSB/FSK receive. This radio showed a strange symptom. After several hours of CW operation, the receiver produced only a light hiss on USB and CW. Reception was good in other modes, and the power meter showed full output during CW transmission. An examination of the block diagram and schematic showed that only one of the crystals (and seven support components) was capable of causing the problem.

Another potential trouble area is VOX control. If there is difficulty in switching to transmit, check the VOX-SENSITIVITY and ANTI-VOX control settings. Next, see if the PTT and manual (MOX) transmitter controls work. If the PTT and MOX controls function, examine the VOX-control diodes and amplifiers. Test the switches, control lines and control voltage if the transmitter does not respond to other TR controls. VOX SENSITIVITY and ANTI-VOX settings

should also be checked when the transmitter switches on in response to received audio. Suspect the anti-VOX circuitry next. Unacceptable VOX timing results from a poor VOX-delay adjustment, or a bad resistor or capacitor in the timing circuit or VOX amplifiers.

Alignment

The mixing scheme of the modern SSB transceiver is complicated. The signal passes through many mixers, oscillators and filters. Satisfactory SSB communication requires accurate adjustment of each stage. Do not attempt any alignment without a copy of the manufacturer's instructions and the necessary test equipment.

Receivers

The important characteristics of a receiver are selectivity, sensitivity, stability and fidelity. Receiver malfunctions ordinarily affect one or more of these areas.

Selectivity

Tuned transformers may develop a shorted turn, capacitors can fail and alignment is required occasionally. Such defects are accompanied by a loss of sensitivity. Filters may fall victim to physical damage from external forces. Cavities and resonators are subject to similar hazards. Except in cases of catastrophic failure (where either the filter passes all signals, or none), it is difficult to spot a loss of selectivity. Bandwidth and insertion-loss measurements are necessary to judge filter performance.

Sensitivity

A gradual loss of sensitivity results from gradual failure of an active device or faulty alignment. Sudden, partial sensitivity reductions are the effect of low RF-amplifier output, or a shift in the frequency of an oscillator or a filter passband. Complete and sudden loss of sensitivity is caused by an open circuit anywhere in the signal path or by a "dead" oscillator.

Stability

The stability of a receiver depends on its oscillators. See the section on oscillators earlier in this chapter.

Distortion

Causes of distortion are covered earlier in this chapter. Distortion may be the effect of poor connections or faulty components in the signal path. AGC circuits produce many receiver defects that appear as distortion or insensitivity.

AGC

Distortion that affects only strong signals is the normal symptom of AGC failure. All stages operate at maximum gain when the AGC influence is removed. An S meter can help diagnose AGC failure because it is operated by the AGC loop.

An open AGC bypass capacitor forces feedback through the loop and usually a squeal (oscillation). Changes in the loop time constant affect tuning. If stations consistently blast, or are too weak, the time constant is too fast. An excessively slow time constant makes tuning difficult, and stations fade after tuning. When loop problems are extreme, AGC-controlled stages may be forced into cut off or saturation.

Some AGC circuit designs provide a shunt Zener diode to clamp loop voltage and prevent cut off or saturation. The protection diode is called an AGC gate.

Detector Problems

Detector trouble usually appears as distortion of the received signal. AM, SSB and CW signals may be weak and unintelligible, FM signals distorted. Suspect an open circuit in the detector near the detector diodes. If tests of the detector parts indicate no trouble, look for a poor connection in the power-supply or ground leads. A BFO that is "dead" or off frequency prevents SSB and CW reception.

Alignment

Unfortunately, IF transformers are as enticing to the neophyte technician as a carburetor is to a shade-tree mechanic. In truth, radio alignment (and for that matter, carburetor repair) is seldom required. Circuit alignment may be justified under the following conditions:

• The set is very old and has not been adjusted in many years.

• The circuit has been subject to abusive treatment or environment.

• There is obvious misalignment from a previous repair.

• Tuned-circuit components or crystals have been replaced.

• There is a malfunction, but *all* other circuit conditions are normal. (Faulty transformers can be located because they will not tune.)

Even if one of the above conditions is met, do not attempt alignment unless you have the proper equipment.

Receiver alignment should progress from the detector to the antenna terminals. When working on an FM receiver, align the detector first, then the IF and limiter stages, and finally the RF and local oscillator stages. For an AM receiver, align the IF stages first, then the RF and oscillator stages.

Both AM and FM receivers can be aligned in much the same manner:

1) Set the receiver RF GAIN to maximum, BFO control to zero (or center) and tune to the high end of the receiver passband.

2) Disable the AGC.

3) Set the signal source to the center of the IF passband, with no modulation and minimum signal level.

4) Connect the signal source to the input of the IF section.

5) Connect a voltmeter to the IF output as shown in Fig. 20.

6) Adjust the signal-source level for a slight indication on the voltmeter.

7) Peak each transformer in order, from the meter to the signal source.

The adjustments interact; repeat steps 6 and 7 until adjustment brings no noticeable improvement.

8) Remove the signal source from the IF-section input, reduce the level to minimum, set the frequency to that shown on the receiver dial and connect the source to the antenna terminals.

9) Adjust the signal level to give a slight reading on the voltmeter.

10) Adjust the trimmer capacitor of the RF amplifier for a peak reading of the test signal. (Verify that you are reading the correct signal by switching the source on and off.)

11) Reset the signal source and the

Fig. 20 — Typical receiver alignment test points. To align the entire radio, connect a dc voltmeter at TP4. Inject an IF signal at TP2, and adjust the IF transformers. Move the signal generator to TP1 and inject RF for alignment of the RF and oscillator stages. To align a single stage, place the generator at the input and an RF voltmeter at the output: TP1/TP2 for RF, TP2/TP3 for IF.

receiver tuning for the low end of the passband.

12) Adjust the local-oscillator padder for peak reading.

13) Repeat steps 8 through 11 until the settings do not change.

Digital Equipment

Few ham shacks across the country show no signs of the digital revolution. The inscrutable number crunchers have brought automated precision to everything from desk clocks to computer-controlled EME antenna arrays. Although every aspect of their operation may be resolved to a simple 1 or 0, the symptoms of their failure are far more complicated. As with other equipment:

• Observe the operating characteristics.
• Study the block diagram and the schematic.
• Test.
• Replace defective parts.

Problems in digital circuits have two elementary causes. First, the circuit may give false counts because of electrical noise at the input. Second, the gates may lock in one state.

False counts from noise are especially likely in a ham shack. (A 15- to 20-μsec voltage spike can trigger a TTL flip-flop.) Amateur Radio equipment often switches heavy loads; the attendant transients can follow the ac line or radiate directly to nearby digital equipment. Ringing in filters or leads or oscillation in the digital circuit can also produce false counts.

The effects of extra counts are determined by the design of the digital equipment: A station clock may run fast, but a microprocessor-controlled transceiver may "decide" that it is only a receiver. It might even be difficult to determine that there is a problem without a logic analyzer or multitrace 'scope and a thorough understanding of circuit operation.

Begin by removing the faulty equipment from RF fields. If the symptoms cease with the removal from RF, it will be necessary to shield the equipment against such fields. When it is possible to move the device, distance may be a permanent answer. In other cases, bypass or filter the power, input and output lines of the digital circuit.

Microprocessors use clock speeds of 1 to 10 MHz; it may be impossible to filter RF from the lines when the RF is near the clock frequency. In these cases, the best approach is to shield the digital circuit and all lines running to it.

RFI to nearby equipment may also be a sign that the station is radiating spurious signals. Inspect the station ground and all connections when such problems appear. Also check for radiation from chassis or ac lines with an absorptive wavemeter or a field-strength meter with a capacitive probe.

Strong RF fields may also cause lock up. Deal with this problem in the same

Fig. 21 — Simple digital circuits can be tested with a few components. In this case, an AND gate is tested. Open and close S1 and S2 while comparing the VOLTS reading with a truth table for the device.

manner as with RF-induced noise. Lockup may also be the result of a short, or open, circuit.

Check for the correct voltages at the pins of each chip. (Make the measurements at the pins of the IC, not the socket pins.) Next, smell and feel each IC for heat. Excessive heat is often evidence of a shorted IC.

Repair any power faults, replace overheated components and check for restored operation. If there is still a malfunction, test the circuit board and sockets for open or shorted connections.

Record the placement and orientation of any active devices installed in sockets, then remove them from the circuit board to prevent damage during testing. (Follow the handling precautions for MOS devices.) Consider the maximum voltage specifications of any devices that cannot be removed before testing. Some devices can be damaged by 0.6 V on certain pins. After these precautions, proceed to test the board with an ohmmeter.

Last, lockup can be the effect of a failed logic gate or IC. In clocked circuits, listen for the clock signal with a coax probe and a suitable receiver. If the signal is found at the clock chip, trace it to each of the other ICs, to be sure that the clock system is intact.

If a suitable scope (15-MHz bandwidth, with storage capability and a x10 probe) is available, check pulse timing and duration against circuit specifications. Pay special attention at analog-to-digital converters.

Logic gates, flip-flops and counters may be tested (see Fig. 21) by triggering them, manually, with a power supply (4 to 5 V is a safe level). Diodes may be checked with an ohmmeter. Testing of more complicated ICs requires the use of a logic analyzer, multitrace scope or a dedicated IC tester.

Check repaired circuits for restored operation. Test frequency counters against another counter or a calibrated signal generator.

SYSTEMATIC APPROACHES

The instinctive approach works well for those with years of troubleshooting experience. Those of us who are new to this game need some guidance. A systematic approach is a disciplined procedure that allows us to tackle problems in unfamiliar equipment with a reasonable hope of success.

There are two common systematic approaches to troubleshooting at the block level. The first is signal tracing; the second is signal injection. The two techniques are very similar. Differences in test equipment and the circuit under test determine which method is best in a given situation.

Signal Tracing

This approach is best for testing transmitters, solid-state and high-impedance circuits. Signal tracing is the best way to check transmitter blocks because the necessary signals are present by design. Most signal generators cannot supply the wide range of signal levels required to test a transmitter.

Signal tracing requires that a steady signal be present in the circuit passband. (An off-the-air signal may be used when testing a receiver. When the receiver is completely disabled, the signal tracer may be connected at the output of the first RF stage as an indicator of incoming signals.) A signal generator or other *stable* signal source may be used. Use a signal of −80 dBm (22 μV) for most amateur receivers. Higher signal levels (7 dBm, 0.5 V) may damage sensitive components.

Signal Tracing Equipment

A voltmeter, with an RF probe, is the most common instrument used for signal tracing. Low-level signals cannot be measured accurately with this instrument. Signals that do not exceed the junction drop of the diode, in the probe, will not register at all, but the presence, or absence, of larger signals can be observed.

A dedicated signal tracer can also be used. It is a simple instrument that may not have adjustable sensitivity. Signal information is usually presented as audio. An experienced technician may be able to judge the level and distortion of the signal by ear; only gross changes will be noticeable.

Absorptive wavemeters may be used for signal tracing if they are sufficiently sensitive and have a suitable probe. Use a wavemeter with headphones to trace weak signals. The frequency selectivity of a wavemeter is an advantage in signal tracing. Tracing a crowded circuit, however, may be impossible unless the instrument has provision for a capacitive probe.

An oscilloscope is the most versatile signal tracer. It offers high input impedance, variable sensitivity, and a constant display of the traced waveform. A demodulator probe permits observation of the modulation envelope in RF circuits. Dual-trace scopes can display the waveforms present at the input and output of a circuit simultaneously. Gross distor-

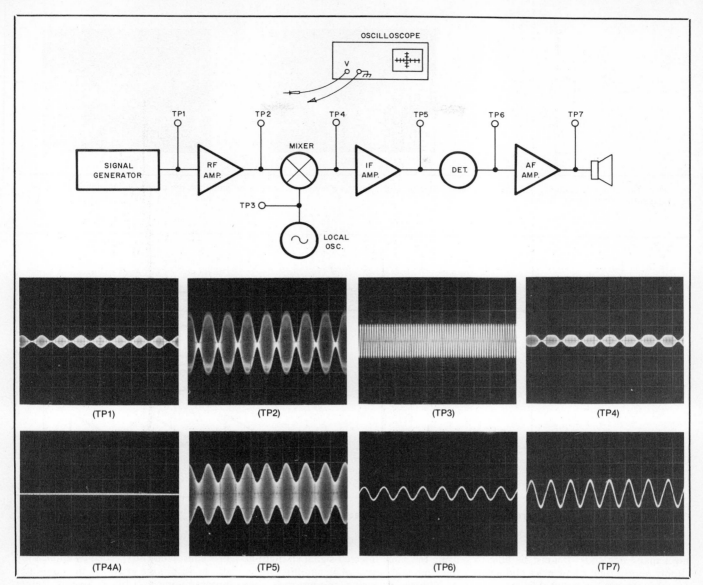

Fig. 22 — Signal tracing in a simple receiver. Photos TP1 through TP6 show typical patterns for a 'scope connected to the corresponding test points. TP1 through TP4 show 0.5 V per vertical division; TP5 through TP7 show 2.0 V per division. TP4A is TP4 with signal source removed. All patterns were made with a 10X probe and a 2-mS-per division sweep rate.

tion and phase relationship are visible on a dual-trace display.

Signal-Tracing Procedure

First, make sure that the circuit under test and test instruments are isolated from the ac line by transformers. Set the signal source to an appropriate level and frequency. Switch on power to the test circuit and connect the signal-source output to the test-circuit input. Place the tracer probe at the circuit input and check for presence of the test signal; observe the characteristics of the signal if you are using a 'scope (see Fig. 22). Compare the detected signal to the source signal during tracing. Move the tracer probe to the output of the next stage and observe the signal. Signal level should increase in amplifier stages and may decrease slightly in other stages. The signal will not be present at the output of a "dead" stage.

Low-impedance test points may not provide sufficient signal to drive a high-impedance signal tracer; tracer sensitivity is important. Also, the circuit/probe impedance relationship may make the output level appear low in stages where there is a radical impedance change from input to output (see Fig. 23). It is important to note that the circuit in Fig. 23 is a current amplifier, and that within reason the voltages at TP1 and TP2 are equal and in phase. Remember that there are two signals (the test signal and the local oscillator signal) present in a mixer stage. Switch the signal source on and off repeatedly to make sure that the tracer reading varies (it need not disappear) with source switching.

Signal Injection

Like signal tracing, signal injection is particularly suited to some situations. Signal injection is a good choice for receiver troubleshooting because a detector is already provided as part of the design. Also, the required signal-injection levels vary less widely in a receiver than in a transmitter. Signal injection is also better for vacuum-tube circuits. Low-impedance circuits may not produce enough signal to drive available signal tracers; signal injection may then be the best technique.

Signal-Injection Equipment

If you are testing equipment that does not include a suitable detector as part of the circuit, some form of signal detector is required. Any of the instruments used for signal tracing are adequate. Remember to consider the signal level at the test point when choosing an instrument.

The signal source used for injection must

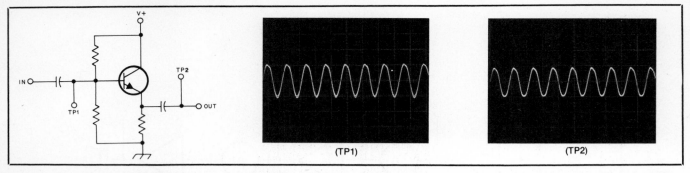

Fig. 23 — The effect of circuit impedance on a 'scope display. Although the circuit functions as an amplifier, the change in impedance from TP1 to TP2 results in the traces shown.

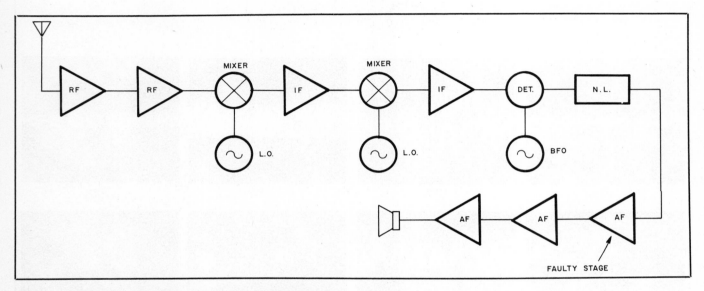

Fig. 24 — The 18-tube receiver diagnosed by the "divide and conquer" technique.

meet many demands. It must be able to supply appropriate frequencies and levels for each stage to be tested. For example, a typical superhet receiver requires AF, IF and RF signals that vary from 6 volts at AF, to 0.2 µV at RF. Each conversion stage used in a receiver requires another IF from the signal source.

Signal-Injection Procedure

If an external detector is required, set it to the proper level and connect it to the test circuit. Set the signal source for AF and inject a signal directly into the signal detector to test operation of the injector and detector.

Move the signal source to the input of the preceding stage and observe the signal. Continue moving the signal source to the inputs of successive stages. (Use a 50-Ω resistor, in series with the signal-source lead to inject a signal at the input of an inverting amplifier.) The detected signal disappears when the source is at the input of a defective stage. Prevent stage overload by reducing the level of the injected signal as testing progresses through the circuit. Remember to use suitable frequencies for each tested stage.

Make a rough check of stage gain by using the same injected-signal strength at the input and output of an amplifier stage. As with signal tracing, this test may yield misleading results if there is a radical difference in impedance from stage input to output. Understand circuit operation before testing!

Mixer stages present a special problem because they have two inputs, rather than one. A lack of signal at the test detector may result from either a faulty mixer or a faulty local oscillator (LO). Check oscillator operation with a 'scope, absorption wavemeter or by listening on another receiver. If none of these instruments are handy, inject the frequency of the LO at the LO output. If a dead oscillator is the only problem, this should restore operation.

If the oscillator is operating, but off frequency, a multitude of spurious responses will appear. A simple signal injector that produces many frequencies simultaneously is not suitable for this test. Use a well-shielded signal generator set to an appropriate level at the LO frequency.

Divide and Conquer

Both signal tracing and signal-injection procedures may be speeded by application of a technique known in computer programming as a binary search. Rather than check each stage sequentially, check a point halfway through the nonfunctioning section. As an example:

A surplus 18-tube receiver is not working. All of the filaments light, but there is absolutely no response from the speaker.

First, substitute a suitable speaker — still no sound. Next, check the high-voltage supply — no problem there. No clues indicate any particular stage. Signal tracing or injection must provide the answer.

Get out the signal generator and switch it on. Once the signal is stable, set the generator for a low-level RF signal, switch the RF OFF and connect the output to the receiver. Switch the RF ON again and place a high-Z signal-tracer probe at the lug of the antenna connection. Instantly, the tracer emits a strong audio note. Good; the test equipment is functioning.

Now, move the probe to the input of the receiver detector. As the tracer probe touches the circuit the familiar note sounds. Next, set the tracer for audio and place the probe halfway through the audio chain. It is silent! Move the probe halfway back to the detector, and the note appears once again. Yet, no signal is present at the output of the stage. The third audio stage is faulty.

Saving Time

Under certain conditions, the block search may be speeded by testing at the middle of successively smaller circuit sections. Each test limits the fault to one half of the remaining circuit (see Fig. 24). The receiver has 18 stages and the fault is in stage 12. This approach requires only four tests to locate the faulty stage, a substantial saving of time.

The divide-and-conquer tactic cannot be used in equipment in which the signal path splits during processing. Test readings taken inside feedback loops are misleading unless you understand the circuit and the waveform to be expected at each point in the test circuit. It is best to consider all stages within a feedback loop as a single block during the block search.

TESTING WITHIN A STAGE

The search is now nearing an end. A few dc measurements will usually pinpoint one or more specific components that need adjustment or replacement. First, check the active device. If the device can be tested easily in the circuit, do so; otherwise, go on to check dc voltages.

Look in the service manual to determine if the circuit is controlled by AGC. The service manual should either give test procedures for the stage with the AGC active, or have instructions for disabling the AGC.

Check the parts in the circuit against the schematic diagram to be sure that they are reasonably close to the design values (someone may have changed them during repairs). Next, make some calculations to see what the voltage should be. It is important to consider the effect of the meter in these calculations. Remember, however, that the calculated voltages are nominal; measured voltages may vary from the calculations. When making measurements, remember the following points:

• Make measurements at device leads, not at circuit-board traces or socket lugs.
• Use small test probes to prevent accidental shorts.
• Never connect or disconnect power to solid-state circuits with the switch on.

Symptoms and Faults in a Typical Amplifier Circuit

Fig. 25 is a schematic of a common-emitter transistor amplifier. The emitter, base and collector leads are labeled e, b and c, respectively. Important dc voltages are measured at these points and designated V_e, V_b and V_e. Similarly, the important currents are I_e, I_b and I_c. V+ indicates the supply voltage. Emitter-base internal resistance, R_b, is approximated by the formula:

$$R_b = \frac{26 \beta}{I_e} \qquad \text{(Eq. 2)}$$

Fig. 25 — A typical common-emitter amplifier (audio).

where I_e is expressed in milliamperes. The "junction drop," V_j, is the potential measured across a semiconductor junction that is conducting. V_j is typically 0.6 V for silicon and 0.2 V for germanium transistors.

R1 and R2 form a voltage divider that supplies dc bias (V_b) for the transistor. Normally, V_e, will be equal to V_b less the e-b junction drop. R4 provides degenerative dc bias, while C3 provides a low-impedance path for the signal. From this information, normal operating voltages can be calculated:

$$V_b = \frac{(V+)R2}{(R1 + R2)} = 1.09 \text{ V} \qquad \text{(Eq. 3)}$$

$$V_e = V_b - V_j = 0.49 \text{ V} \qquad \text{(Eq. 4)}$$

$$I_e = \frac{V_e}{R4} = 0.001 \text{ A} \qquad \text{(Eq. 5)}$$

$$I_c = \frac{I_e \beta}{(\beta + 1)} = 0.001 \text{ A} \qquad \text{(Eq. 6)}$$

$$V_c = (V+) - (I_c \times R3) = 7.14 \text{ V} \qquad \text{(Eq. 7)}$$

Refer to Fig. 25 while reading the symptoms associated with failure of various components in the circuit.

• R1 open:
$V_b = 0$, $V_e = 0$, $V_c = 12$

V_b drops to ground potential because current through the voltage divider stops. When $V_b < V_e + V_j$, the transistor stops conducting. V_c rises to V+.

• R1 short:
$V_b = 12$, $V_e = 11.4$, $V_c < V_b$

Since the resistance of R1 is zero, $V_b = V+$. This biases the transistor into saturation (full on), usually resulting in destruction of the transistor, R3 or R4.

• R2 open:
$V_b = 1.7$, $V_e = 1.1$, $V_c < V_b$

The voltage divider becomes R1 in series with R4 and R_b. The combination of R1, R4 and R_b sets V_b at saturation, so that V_c is approximately equal to V_e.

• R2 short:
$V_b = 0$, $V_e = 0$, $V_c = 12$

A short in R2 has the same effect as an open R1.

• R3 open:
$V_b = 0.62$, $V_e = 0.02$, $V_c < V_b$

No output. Since R3 is open there is no I_c. This reduces I_e and V_e. The difference between V_e and V_b forward biases the e-b junction and the series combination of R4 + R_b appears in parallel with R2 divider. The circuit stabilizes with V_e close to zero and V_b equal to V_e plus V_j. V_c is approximately equal to V_e.

• R3 short:
$V_b = 1.09$, $V_e = 0.49$, $V_c = 12$

No output. If R3 = 0, then the output voltage $V_c = (V+) - (IC \times 0) = V+$.

• R4 open:
$V_b = 1.09$, $V_e = 0$, $V_c = 12$

No I_e can flow, therefore $I_b = I_c = 0$. V_c rises to V+. V_b changes imperceptibly. Attempts to measure V_e will indicate V_e slightly less than V_b because the meter provides a high-Z path for a small I_e.

• C1 or C2 open:
$V_b = 1.09$, $V_e = 0.49$, $V_c = 7.14$

Bias is normal; but the signal is gone. Loss of signal with normal bias can only be caused by a coupling capacitor. A 'scope or signal tracer can be used to show presence of signal and locate the faulty capacitor.

• C3 open:
$V_b = 1.09$, $V_e = 0.49$, $V_c = 7.14$

When C3 opens, impedance to the signal is increased and gain is reduced. The voltage gain becomes R3/R4.

• C3 short:
$V_b = 0.7$, $V_e = 0$, $V_c < V_b$

This shorts R4, so V_e becomes 0 V. I_b increases until V_b is equal to V_j. The transistor is saturated, so V_c is approximately equal to V_e.

• c-b junction open:
$V_b = 0.62$, $V_e = 0.02$, $V_c = 12$

No I_c flows, so V_c rises to V+. Other symptoms simulate an open R3.

• c-b short:
$V_b = 1.64$, $V_e = 1.04$, $V_c = 1.64$
$V_c = V_b$ because of the short.
$I_e = V+ /(R3 + R4)$; $V_e = R4 \times I_e$.
$V_b = V_e + V_j$.

• e-b open:
$V_b = 1.09$, $V_e = 0$, $V_c = 12$

No I_b and, therefore, no I_e can flow. $V_c = V+$; $V_e = 0$. V_b is normal.

• e-b short:
$V_b = 0.05$, $V_e = 0.05$, $V_c = 12$

$V_b = V_e$; V_e is at a low value because R4 is in parallel with R2, thus lowering V_b. Since the e-b junction is shorted, R_b is 0; all emitter current flows through the base.

There is no I_c; $V_c = V+$.
- e-c short:
$V_b = 1.09$, $V_e = 1.09$, $V_c = 1.09$, $V_c = V_e$. Since the emitter-collector path has no resistance, all I_e flows to the collector and there is no I_b. V_b is normal, but $V_e = V_c$ as determined by the R3/R4 voltage divider.

Voltage Levels

There are two voltage levels in most cir-cuits. Most component failures (opens and shorts) will force one of the dc measurements very close to one of these levels. Typical failures that show up as incorrect dc voltages include: open coupling transformers; shorted capacitors; open, shorted or overheated resistors and open or shorted semiconductors.

For example, consider the circuit of Fig. 25. If R2 failed open, the voltage-divider action at the base would stop. V_b would rise to 12 V (R1 becomes a pull-up resistor) and bias the e-b junction on. With the e-b junction conducting, a new divider network is formed of R1 in series with the internal base resistance of the transistor and R4. V_b will stabilize based on this new divider — if the transistor is not destroyed while saturated. Now proceed to test the suspected parts and make the repair.

Components

Each electronic component has a function. This section acquaints you with the functions, failure modes and test procedures of resistors, capacitors, inductors and other components. Test the components implicated by symptoms and stage-level testing. In most cases, a particular faulty component will be located by these tests. If a faulty component is not indicated, check the circuit adjustments. As a last resort, use a shotgun approach. Replace all parts in the problem area with components that are known to be good.

Wires and Connectors

Short circuits are caused by physical damage to insulation or by conductive contamination. Damaged insulation is usually apparent during a close visual inspection of the conductor or connector. Look carefully where conductors come close to corners or sharp objects. Consider areas where wires and connectors are subject to stress.

Conductive contaminants range from water to metal filings. Most can be removed by a thorough cleaning. Any of the residue-free cleaners can be used, but remember that the cleaner may also be conductive. Do not apply power to the circuit until the area is completely dry. Keep the cleaners away from the variable-capacitor plates, transformers and parts that may be harmed by the chemical. The most common conductive contaminant is solder.

Increased resistance and open connections are most often the outgrowth of repeated flexing. Nearly everyone has broken a wire by bending it back and forth, and broken wires are usually easy to detect. Connector failure is more insidious. Most connectors maintain contact as a result of spring tension that forces two conductors together. As the parts age, they become brittle and lose tension.

Any connection may deteriorate because of nonconductive corrosion at the contacts. Solder helps prevent this problem but even soldered joints suffer from corrosion when exposed to weather.

Since poor connections increase joint resistance, the dissipated power (I^2R) in the joint increases. Signs of excess heat often surround poor connections in circuits that carry moderate current.

Check for short and open circuits with an ohmmeter or continuity tester. Repair worn insulation by replacing the wire or securing an insulating sleeve (spaghetti) or heat-shrink tubing over the worn area. Clean those connections that short as a result of contamination. Replace broken wires. Occasionally, corroded connectors may be repaired by cleaning, but replacement of the conductor/connector is usually required. Solder all connections that may be subject to harsh environments and protect them with acrylic enamel, RTV compound, or a similar coating.

When replacing conductors, use the same material and size, if possible. Substitute only wire of greater cross-sectional area (smaller gauge number) or material of greater conductivity. Insulated wire should be rated at the same, or higher, temperature and voltage as the wire it replaces. Replacement connectors should be chosen with consideration given to voltage and current ratings. Use connectors with symmetrical pin arrangements only where correct insertion is not critical.

Resistors

Resistors are used to limit or divide current and to divide voltage. They fail by increasing resistance (often becoming an open circuit) or developing leakage. Excessive heat causes most resistors to permanently change value. Such heat may come from external sources or from power dissipated within the resistor. Sufficient heat burns the resistor until it becomes an open circuit. Resistors also fracture (become an open circuit) as a result of physical shock.

Leakage is only a problem with resistors of very high value (100 kΩ or more). Leakage current actually flows through dirt paths on the outside of the resistor body, mounts or circuit board, not through the resistor itself.

Resistors that have permanently changed value may be replaced, or repaired by connecting an appropriate resistor in parallel with the faulty part. Leakage is cured by cleaning the resistor body and surrounding area.

Potentiometers suffer from noise (especially in dc circuits) in addition to the problems of fixed-value resistors. Dirt often causes intermittent contact between the wiper and resistive element. To cure the problem, spray cleaner into the potentiometer (through holes in the case) and rotate the shaft a few times. The resistive element in wire-wound potentiometers eventually wears and breaks from the sliding action of the wiper.

Replacement resistors should be of the same value, tolerance, type and power rating as the original. The value should stay within tolerance: Suppose a 10-kΩ resistor with a 20% tolerance, fails. Resistors of closer tolerance need not have the same nominal value as the original, as long as their value, plus or minus their tolerance, falls within the tolerance range (10,000 × 0.8 = 8000 Ω to 10,000 × 1.2 = 12,000 Ω) of the original. A 9100-Ω, 5%-tolerance resistor should have a value between 9100 × 0.95 = 8645 Ω and 9100 × 1.05 = 9555 Ω. Thus, the 5% resistor is a suitable replacement.

Replacement resistors may be of a different type than the original, if the characteristics of the replacement are consistent with circuit requirements. Some resistor families and their characteristics are:
- Carbon composition — Carbon-composition resistor values are moderately stable from 0° to 60° C (their resistance increases above *and below* this temperature range). They are not inductive, but they are relatively noisy, and have wide tolerances.
- Wire wound — These resistors are very stable in value, and are made to close tolerances. They are, however, small coils of wire and exhibit inductance when used in ac circuits.
- Metal film — Metal film resistors are exceptionally stable in value. They are made to close tolerances, are noninductive and create little noise. High-power (above 3 W) versions are not available.
- Carbon film — Carbon film resistors

are not as stable, nor are their tolerances as close, as those of metal-film resistors. They are noninductive. Carbon-film resistors are especially useful because they have a *negative* temperature characteristic. That is, their resistance decreases with temperature. They are often used in temperature-compensation circuits.

Substitute resistors may have a greater power rating than the original, except in high-power emitter circuits where the resistor also acts as a fuse.

Potentiometers should be replaced with the same type (carbon or wire wound) and taper (linear, log, reverse log, and so on) as the original. Keep the same, or better tolerance, but be mindful of the power rating. Potentiometer power ratings are specified for the entire resistive element. A 10-W potentiometer can dissipate 10 W only when set for maximum resistance. The allowable dissipation for a segment of the resistor is proportional to the resistance of that segment, depending on taper. If the wiper of a 10-W unit were set to 30% of the total resistance, it could only dissipate 3 W in that portion of the element.

In all cases, mount high-temperature resistors away from heat-sensitive components. Also, keep carbon resistors away from heat sources. This will extend their life and assure minimum resistance variations.

Fuses

Always use exact replacement fuses. It is important for maximum safety that the current, voltage and timing (fast-, normal- or slow-blow) be identical to the original. Also, the replacement fuse should be the same physical size. Never attempt to force a fuse that is almost the right physical size to fit into the fuse-holder. The substitution of a bar, wire or penny for a fuse invites a "smoke party."

Capacitors

Capacitors are used to store energy (in the electrostatic field between the plates) or block the flow of dc. They fail as a result of excess current, voltage or temperature. Dielectric failure or a permanent shift of capacitance are symptoms of current overload. Voltage overload may produce internal corona or puncture the dielectric. Excess heat may come from nearby heat-generating components, excessive current, an operating frequency well beyond the capacitor design frequency or a lossy dielectric. Leakage occurs directly, through the dielectric, or through leakage paths (dirt) across the component body or chassis surface.

Testing

The easiest way to test capacitors (out of circuit) is with an ohmmeter. In this test, the resistance of the meter forms a timing circuit with the capacitor to be checked. Capacitors from 0.01 μF to 1.0 μF can be tested with common ohmmeters. Set the meter to its highest range and connect the test leads across the discharged capacitor. When the leads are connected, current

Fig. 26 — Fixture for testing capacitors and reforming the dielectric or electrolytic capacitors. Use 12 V for testing and the capacitor working voltage for reformation.

begins to flow. The capacitor passes current easily when discharged, but less easily as the charge builds. We see this on the meter as a low resistance that builds, over time, to infinity. The speed of the resistance build up corresponds to capacitance, small capacitance values seem to achieve infinite resistance instantly. A 0.01-μF capacitor checked with a 11-MΩ FETVOM would increase from zero to a two-thirds scale reading in 0.11 second, while a 1-μF unit would require 11 seconds to reach the same reading. If the tested capacitor does not reach infinity within five times the period taken to reach the two-thirds point, it has excess leakage. If the meter reads infinite resistance immediately, the capacitor is open. (Aluminum electrolytic capacitors cannot be measured by this method because they often give erroneous high-leakage readings.)

Fig. 26 shows a circuit that may be used to test capacitors. Make sure that the power supply is off, set S1 to CHARGE and S2 to TEST, then connect the capacitor to the circuit. Switch on the power supply and allow the capacitor to charge until the voltmeter reading stabilizes. Next, switch S1 to TEST and watch the meter for a few seconds. If the capacitor is good, the meter will show no potential. (In fact, there will be some voltage drop, but the meter will not be able to measure it.) Any appreciable voltage indicates excess leakage. After testing, set S1 to CHARGE, switch off the power supply, and press the DISCHARGE button until the meter shows 0 V, then remove the capacitor from the test circuit.

Capacitance can be measured with a capacitance meter, an RX bridge or a dip meter. An RX bridge (see "A Noise Bridge for 160 through 10 Meters," Chapter 25) can be used to measure capacitance by placing a 50-Ω resistor in series with the capacitor. The procedure is similar to that explained for calibrating the bridge.

To determine capacitance with a dip meter, a parallel-resonant circuit should be constructed using the capacitor of unknown value and an inductor of known value. Measure the resonant frequency of the circuit, and calculate the value of the

Fig. 27 — Partial view of an air-dielectric variable capacitor. Apply cleaning fluid where the wiper contacts the rotor plates.

unknown component, using the formula:

$$\text{unknown} = \frac{\left(\dfrac{1000}{2\pi\, f_o}\right)^2}{\text{known}} \qquad \text{(Eq. 9)}$$

where

f_o = resonant frequency in MHz
known = the value (L in μH, C in pF) of the known component

This formula works for unknowns of either C or L.

It is best to keep a collection of known components that have been measured on accurate L or C meters. Alternatively, a "standard" value might be taken as the average value of several (10 or more) components with the same marked value (disregard parts with values that differ greatly from the rest), or that of a section of coaxial cable. (Capacitance per unit length is usually specified.) Prewound, air-dielectric coils, such as Miniductor®, Polycoil®, and Air-dux® are high-Q inductors with reliable values. The accuracy of tests made with any of these alternatives depends on the accuracy of the "standard" value component. Further information on this technique appears in Bartlett's article, "Calculating Component Values," in the Nov. 1978 *QST*.

Cleaning

The only variety of common capacitor that can be repaired is the air-dielectric variable capacitor. Electrical connection to the moving plates is made through a spring-wiper arrangement (see Fig. 27). Dirt normally builds on the contact area, and cleaning is occasionally required.

Before cleaning the wiper/contact, use gentle air pressure and a soft brush to remove all dust and dirt from the capacitor plates. Then use a screwdriver blade to lift the wiper gently from the rotor plate and apply some cleaning fluid. Rotate the shaft quickly several times to work in the fluid and establish contact. Use the cleaning fluid sparingly, and keep it off the plates except at the contact point.

Replacement Capacitors

Replacement capacitors should match the original in value, tolerance, dielectric, working voltage and temperature coefficient. If exact replacements are not available, substitutes may vary from the original part in the following respects.

Bypass capacitors may vary from one to three times the capacitance of the original. Coupling capacitors may vary from one-half to twice the value of the original. Capacitance values in tuned circuits (especially filters) must be held constant, and any replacement will probably require circuit alignment.

If the same type of capacitor is not available, use one with better dielectric characteristics; however, do not use mica capacitors to block high dc voltages. Also, do not substitute polarized capacitors for nonpolarized parts. Capacitors with a higher working voltage may be used, unless the replacement is an electrolytic. When choosing substitute capacitors, consider the characteristics of each type:

• Air dielectric — Air-dielectric capacitors are large when compared to other types of the same value. They are very stable over a wide temperature range. Losses are low, and a high Q can be obtained. Humidity and atmospheric pressure can cause arcing. Consider plate shape when choosing replacement air variable capacitors; correct plate shape assures proper dial tracking.

• Ceramic — There are two types of ceramic capacitors. Those with a low dielectric constant are relatively large, but very stable and nearly as good as mica capacitors at HF.

High dielectric constant ceramic capacitors are physically small for their capacitance, but their value is not as stable. Their dielectric properties vary with temperature, applied voltage and operating frequency. Use them only in coupling and bypass roles. Tolerances are usually +100% and −20%.

Ceramic capacitors are produced with values from 100 pF to 0.1 μF. They are not polarized.

• Electrolytic — Electrolytic capacitors are popular because they provide high capacitance values in small packages at a reasonable cost. Leakage is high, as is inductance, and they are polarized. Internal inductance restricts foil electrolytics to low-frequency applications. They are available

with values from 1 to 500,000 μF.

A dielectric is "formed" by the voltage applied to the capacitor. As a consequence, electrolytics should not be used where the dc potential is well below the capacitor working voltage. It is best to slowly walk the voltage up, increasing about 10% every 10-15 minutes.

The dielectric must be re-formed when the capacitor has been stored, or operated at low voltage for long periods (two years or more). Re-formation is accomplished by applying full working voltage to the capacitor, with current limited, until the dielectric strength is restored.

The circuit shown in Fig. 26 can be used for this purpose. Set S2 to REFORM, S1 to REFORM and R2 to maximum resistance. Place the capacitor in the circuit, turn on the power supply and set it to the capacitor working voltage. Adjust CURRENT for a 10-mA reading and leave the power on until the voltmeter shows the full supply voltage across the capacitor. It may take several days to complete the re-formation; if full supply voltage is not achieved, the capacitor must be replaced.

Tantalum electrolytic capacitors perform better than aluminum units but their cost is higher. They are smaller, lighter and more stable, with less leakage and inductance than their aluminum counterparts. Re-formation problems are less frequent, but working voltages are not as high as with aluminum units.

• Paper dielectric — Paper capacitors are inexpensive; capacitances from 500 pF to 50 μF are available. High working voltages are possible, but paper-dielectric capacitors have high leakage rates and tolerances are no better than 10 to 20%.

Paper-dielectric capacitors are not polarized; however, the body of the capacitor is usually marked with a color band at one end. The band indicates the terminal that is connected to the outermost plate of the capacitor. This terminal is represented by a curved line in the schematic symbol for a capacitor; it should be connected to ground, or the side of the circuit with least potential, as a safety precaution.

• Plastic film — Capacitors with plastic-film (polystyrene, polyethelyne or Mylar) dielectrics have the same characteristics as paper capacitors in most respects. They are more expensive than paper capacitors, but have much lower leakage rates (even at high temperatures). Capacitance is more stable than that of paper capacitors; low temperature coefficients are possible. Plastic-film capacitors are not polarized.

• Mica — The capacitance of mica capacitors is very stable with respect to time, temperature and electrical stress. Leakage and losses are very low. Values range from 1 pF to 0.1 μF, with tolerances from ±1% to ±20%. High working voltages are possible, but they must be derated severely as operating frequency increases. Mica capacitors are not polarized.

Fig. 28 — Dip-meter coupling to inductors.

Silver mica capacitors are made by depositing a thin layer of silver on the mica dielectric. This makes the value even more stable, but it presents the possibility of silver migration through the dielectric. The migration problem worsens with increased dc voltage, temperature and humidity. Avoid using silver-mica capacitors under such conditions.

Inductors and Transformers

Inductors store energy (in a magnetic field) or restrict the flow of ac. They can fail in several ways. The most common failure is a broken conductor. A short circuit across one or more turns of a coil will impair operation. Inductors that are used to block ac signals may "leak." (The ac signal may couple magnetically or capacitively through a faulty shield can, poor lead dress or distributed capacitance in the inductor.) Inductance may change as a result of shorted turns or physical damage to the coil or core material. Excessive tank-circuit current generates enough heat to melt plastics used as coil forms.

Inductors may be checked for open-circuit failure with an ohmmeter. Dc resistance will rarely exceed a few ohms. Shorted turns and other changes in inductance show only during alignment or inductance measurement. The procedure for measurement of inductance with a dip meter is the same as that given for capacitance measurement, except that a capacitor of known value is used in the resonant circuit. Fig. 28 shows the proper dip-meter orientation with respect to various coil configurations.

Replacement inductors must have the same inductance as the original, but that is only the first requirement. They must also carry the same current, withstand the same voltage and present nearly the same Q as the original part. Given the original as a pattern, the amateur can duplicate these qualities for many inductors. Note that inductors with cores are frequency-sensitive, so the replacement must have the same core material.

If the coil is of simple construction, with the form and core undamaged, carefully observe (and record) the number of turns and their placement on the form. Also note how the coil leads are arranged and connected to the circuit. Then determine the wire size and insulation used. (There is little hope of matching coil characteristics unless the wire is duplicated exactly in the new part.) Next, remove the old winding (be careful not to damage the form) and apply a new winding in its place. Be sure to dress all coil leads and connections in exactly the same manner as the original. Apply Q dope to hold the finished winding in place. Follow the same procedure in cases where the form or core is damaged, except that a suitable replacement form or core (same dimensions and permeability) must be found.

Ready-made inductors may be used as replacements if the characteristics of the original and the replacement are known and compatible. Unfortunately, many inductors are poorly marked. Thus, some comparisons and measurements are necessary.

Wire diameter, insulation and turn spacing are critical to the current and voltage ratings of an inductor. Next, eliminate those parts that bear no physical resemblance to the original part. This may seem an odd procedure, but the Q of an inductor depends on its physical dimensions and the permeability of the core material. Inductors of the same value, but of vastly different size or shape, will likely have a great difference in Q.

The Q of the new inductor can be checked by installing it in the circuit, aligning the stage and performing the manufacturer's passband tests. Although this practice is all right in a pinch, it does not yield an accurate Q measurement.

A better measurement of effective, unloaded Q can be made with a dip meter and an RF voltmeter (or a dc voltmeter with an RF probe). Make a parallel-resonant circuit using the replacement inductor and a capacitance equal to that of the tuned circuit under repair. Connect the voltmeter across this parallel combination and measure the resonant frequency. Adjust the dip-meter/circuit coupling for a convenient reading on the voltmeter, then maintain this dip-meter/circuit relationship for the remainder of the test. Vary the dip-meter frequency until the voltmeter reading drops to 0.707 times that at resonance. Note the frequency of the dip meter and repeat the process, this time varying the frequency on the opposite side of resonance. The difference between the two dip meter readings is the test-circuit bandwidth. This can be used to calculate the circuit Q:

$$Q = \frac{f_o}{Bw} \qquad \text{(Eq. 10)}$$

where
f_o = operating frequency
Bw = measured bandwidth in the same units as the operating frequency.

Fig. 29 — Test circuits to determine the winding '"sense" of transformers. Observe the sense dots.

Once the replacement inductor is found, install it in the circuit. Duplicate the placement, orientation and wiring of the original. Ground-lead length and arrangement should not be changed.

Isolation and magnetic shielding can be improved by replacing solenoid inductors with toroids; however, it is likely that many circuit adjustments will be needed to compensate for reduced coupling and mutual inductance. Alignment is required whenever a tuned-circuit component is replaced.

A transformer consists of two inductors that are magnetically coupled. Transformers are used to change voltage and current levels (this changes impedance also). Failure usually occurs as an open circuit or short circuit of one or more windings.

Amateur testing of power transformers is limited to ohmmeter tests for open circuits and voltmeter checks of secondary voltage. Make sure that the power-line voltage is correct, then check the secondary voltage against that specified. There should be less than 10% difference between open-circuit and full-load secondary voltage.

Replacement transformers must match the original in voltage, volt-ampere (VA), duty cycle and operating frequency ratings. (All transformer windings should be insulated for the full power-supply voltage.) Transformer windings are color coded; see Chapter 35 for more information. If it is necessary to determine the phase relationship of transformer leads, the tests illustrated in Fig. 29 can be used.

Relays

Although relays are being replaced by semiconductor switching in low-power circuits, they are still used extensively for control of high-power RF in transceivers and amplifiers. Relay action may become sluggish. Ac relays can buzz (with adjustment becoming impossible). A binding armature or weak springs can cause intermittent switching. Excessive duty cycle ruins contacts and shortens relay life.

Relays can be tested with a voltmeter or by jumping across contacts with a test lead (power on, in circuit) or with an ohmmeter (out of circuit). Look for erratic readings across the contacts, open or short circuits at contacts or an open circuit at the coil.

Most failures of simple relays can be repaired by a thorough cleaning. Clean contacts and mechanical parts with a residue-free cleaner. Keep it away from the coil and plastic parts that may be damaged. Dry the contacts with lint-free paper, such as a business card; then burnish them with a smooth steel blade. Do not use a file to clean contacts.

Replacement relays should match or exceed the original specifications for voltage, current, switching time and impedance (impedance is significant in RF circuits only). Many relays used in transceivers are specially made for the manufacturer. Substitutes may not be available from any other source.

Before replacing a multicontact relay, make a drawing of the relay, its position, the leads and their routings through the surrounding parts. This drawing allows you to complete the installation properly, even if you are distracted during the delicate operation. RF leads must be dressed exactly

Fig. 30 — A diode conduction, leakage and Zener-point test fixture. The ammeter should read mA for conduction and Zener-point, µA for leakage tests.

as they were on the original part, or alignment may be required.

SEMICONDUCTORS

Diodes

The primary function of a diode is to pass current in one direction only. Zener diodes are made with a predictable reverse-breakdown voltage and used as voltage regulators. Varactor diodes are specially made for use as voltage-controlled variable capacitors. (Any semiconductor diode may be used as a voltage-variable capacitance, but the value will not be as predictable as of a varactor.) A Diac is a special-purpose diode that passes only pulses of current in each direction.

Rectifier diodes fail by becoming an open circuit, a short circuit, by developing excess reverse leakage or by losing the ability to switch on and off quickly. Zener diodes may also fail by shifting their avalanche (reverse-breakdown) point. Varactor diodes fail in the same fashion as capacitors.

There are three basic tests for most diodes. First, is it a diode? That is, does it conduct in one direction and block current flow in the other? An ohmmeter is suitable for this test in most cases.

Before tests begin, make sure the meter uses a voltage of more than 0.7 V and less than 1.5 V to measure resistance. Next, use a good diode to determine the meter polarity: Set the meter to read ohms ×100 and connect the test probes across the diode. When the negative terminal of the ohmmeter battery is connected to the cathode, the meter will show 200 to 300 Ω (forward resistance) for a good silicon diode, 200 to 400 Ω for a good germanium diode. Reverse the lead polarity and set the meter to ohms ×1M (times one million, or the highest scale available on the meter) to measure diode reverse resistance. Good diodes should show 100- to 1000-MΩ and 100-k to 1-MΩ for silicon and germanium, respectively. When done, mark the meter lead polarity for future reference.

To check a suspected diode, disconnect one end of the diode from the circuit, then measure the forward and reverse resistance. Diode-quality is shown by the ratio of reverse to forward resistance. A ratio of 100:1 is typical for small-signal diodes. The ratio may go as low as 10:1 for power diodes.

This procedure measures the junction resistances at low voltage. If the Zener point of a rectifier diode has shifted to a low value, it may not show in this test. The defect might show in the leakage-current measurement, but substitution is the only dependable test.

The second diode test measures the forward voltage drop across the diode junction. This measurement is made while the diode is conducting. Use a test circuit like that shown in Fig. 30, connect the diode, adjust the supply voltage until the current through the diode matches the manufacturer's specification and compare the junction drop to that specified. Silicon junctions usually show about 0.6 V, while germanium is typically 0.2 V. Junction voltage drop increases with current flow. The results of this test can be used to choose diodes that are matched with respect to forward resistance at a given current level.

The final simple diode test measures diode leakage current. Place the diode in the circuit used above, but with reverse polarity. Set the specified reverse voltage and read the leakage current on the ammeter. (The currents and voltages measured in the junction voltage-drop and leakage tests vary by several orders of magnitude.)

The major criterion of Zener diodes is the Zener voltage. The Zener-voltage test also uses the circuit of Fig. 30. Place the diode in the circuit (so that it is reverse biased), increase the voltage until there is a large increase in current flow, then read the Zener voltage from the voltmeter.

Replacement rectifier diodes should have the same current and peak inverse voltage (PIV) as the original. Series combinations of diodes are often used in high-voltage rectifiers. Good engineering practice demands that the voltage be distributed equally across each diode. This is accomplished by placing a resistor and capacitor across each diode. When a diode fails, check the associated components also.

Switching diodes may be replaced with diodes that have equal or greater current ratings and a PIV greater than twice the peak-to-peak voltage of the signal they switch. Switching time requirements are not critical except in logic and some keying circuits. RF switching diodes used near resonant circuits must have exact replacements, as the diode resistance and capacitance will affect the tuned circuit. Logic circuits require exact replacements to assure compatible switching and load characteristics.

Voltage, current and capacitance characteristics must be considered when replacing varactor diodes. Once again, exact replacements are best.

Zener diodes should be replaced with parts having the same Zener voltage and equal or better current, power, impedance and tolerance specifications. Check the associated current-limiting resistor when replacing a Zener diode.

Bipolar Transistors

The fundamental purposes of transistors are to switch and to amplify. Transistor failures occur as an open junction, a shorted junction, excess leakage or a change in amplification performance.

Transistor tests are not performed at the planned operating frequency. Tests are made at dc or a low frequency (usually 1000 Hz). This practice is based on the assumption that the semiconductor meets all of its specifications equally well. That is, if it functions at low frequencies, it functions equally well at high frequencies. When special RF circuits (such as oscillators) are planned, build a circuit to test prospective devices at the operating frequency. The circuit under repair is the best test of a potential replacement part.

The simplest and probably the most telling of bipolar-transistor tests is performed with a test lead, a 10-kΩ resistor and a voltmeter, while the transistor is in a circuit with the power on. Connect the voltmeter across the emitter/collector leads and read the voltage. Then use the test lead to connect the base and emitter leads (Fig. 31A). Under these conditions, conduction of a good transistor will be cut off and the meter should show nearly the entire supply voltage across the emitter/collector leads. Next, remove the clip lead and connect the 10-kΩ resistor from the base to the collector. This should bias the transistor into conduction and the emitter/collector voltage should drop. (Fig. 31B) (This test indicates transistor response to changes in bias voltage.)

Transistors can be tested (out of circuit) with an ohmmeter in the same manner as diodes. Look up the device characteristics before testing and consider the consequences of the ohmmeter-transistor circuit. Limit junction current to 1 to 5 mA for small-signal transistors. Transistor destruction or inaccurate measurements may result from careless testing.

Use the ohms ×100 and ohms ×1000 ranges for small-signal transistors. For high-power transistors use the ohms ×1 or ohms ×10 ranges. The reverse-to-forward resistance ratio for good transistors may vary from 30:1 to 100:1. Germanium transistors sometimes show low reverse resistance when tested with an ohmmeter.

Bipolar transistor leakage may be specified from the collector to the base, emitter to base or emitter to collector (with the junction reverse biased in all cases). The specification may be identified as I_{cbo}, I_{bo}, collector cutoff current or collector leakage for the base-collector junction, I_{ebo}, and so on for other junctions.[4]

---

[4]The term, "I_{cbo}" means, "Current from collector to base with emitter open." The subscript notation indicates the status of the three device terminals. The terminals concerned in the measurement are listed first, with the remaining terminal specified as "s," shorted, or "o" open.

Fig. 31 — An in-circuit semiconductor test with a clip lead, resistor and voltmeter. The meter should read V+ at (A), and anything from a slight variation to 0 V at (B).

Fig. 32 — A test circuit for measuring collector-base leakage with the emitter shorted, open or shorted through a (variable) resistance, depending on the setting of S1. See the transistor manufacturer's instructions for test conditions and the value of R1 (if used). Reverse battery polarity for PNP transistors.

Manufacturers may require that tests be made with the emitter lead unconnected, shorted to the base or connected to the base through a resistor. Temperature is critical to this test. Allowable leakage current increases with junction temperature.

A suitable test fixture for base-collector leakage measurements is shown in Fig. 32. Make the required connections and set the voltage as stated in the transistor specifications and compare the measured leakage current with that specified. Small-signal germanium transistors exhibit I_{cbo} and I_{ebo} leakage currents of about 15 μA. Leakage increases to 90 μA or more in high-power

Fig. 33 — A test circuit for measuring transistor beta. Values for R1 and R2 will vary widely with the transistor tested. Reverse the battery polarities for PNP transistors.

components (germanium power transistors can develop excess leakage while sitting on the shelf.) Leakage currents for silicon NPN transistors are seldom more than 1 μA. Leakage current tends to double for every 10° C increase above 25° C.

Breakdown-voltage tests actually measure leakage at a specified voltage, rather true breakdown voltage. Breakdown voltage is known as BV_{cbo}, BV_{ces} (emitter shorted to base) or BV_{ceo}. Use the same test fixture shown for leakage tests, adjust the power supply until the specified leakage current flows, and compare the junction voltage against that specified.

A circuit to measure dc current gain is shown in Fig. 33. Current gain is also known as:

- (alpha) $= \dfrac{\Delta I_c}{\Delta I_e}$

in a common-base amplifier

- (beta) $= \dfrac{\Delta I_c}{\Delta I_b}$

in a common-emitter amplifier; "collector-to-base current gain," "forward current-transfer ratio,"

- h_{FE} = (ac current gain).
- h_{fe} = (dc current gain).

Conditions for gain testing are dictated by the manufacturer's data sheet. When testing, do not exceed the voltage, current (especially in the base circuit) or dissipated-power rating of the transistor. Make sure that the load resistor is capable of dissipating the power generated in the test. When I_c is high, measure the emitter-collector leakage current (with emitter shorted to base) first, and subtract the leakage from I_c before calculating gain. Do not neglect the effect of the meter resistance on the circuit.

RF devices should be tested at RF. Most component manufacturers include a test-circuit schematic on the data sheet. The test circuit is usually an RF amplifier that operates near the high end of the device frequency range.

Semiconductor failure is nearly always the result of environmental conditions. Open junctions, excess leakage (except with germanium transistors) and changes in amplification performance result from overload or excessive current. Shorted junctions are caused by voltage spikes.

Fig. 34 — Ohmmeter tests of a JFET. The junction is reverse biased at A and forward biased at B.

Check surrounding parts for the cause of the transistor's demise, and correct the problem before installing a replacement.

JFETs

Junction FETs can be tested, out of circuit, with an ohmmeter in much the same way as bipolar transistors (see Fig. 34). Connect the negative ohmmeter lead to the gate of an N-channel JFET and check the resistance to both source and drain. The JFET is reverse biased by the ohmmeter battery, and resistance across each junction should be several megohms or more (using the ohms X1M scale). Then reverse the lead polarity to measure the forward resistance of each junction, which should be 500 to 1000 Ω. P-channel JFETs can be checked in the same manner with the test-lead polarity reversed for both tests.

MOSFETs

MOS (metal-oxide semiconductor) layers are extremely fragile. Normal body static is enough to puncture this delicate insulator. Even gate-protected (a diode is placed across the MOS layer to clamp voltage) MOSFETs may be destroyed by 6 V. Make sure the power is off, capacitors discharged and the leads of a MOSFET are shorted together before installing or removing it from a circuit. Use a voltmeter to be sure the chassis is near ground potential, then touch the chassis before and during MOSFET installation and removal. This assures that there is no difference of potential between your body and the MOSFET leads. Follow this equalization procedure whenever a MOSFET may contact another object. Ground the soldering-iron tip with a clip lead when soldering MOS devices. The source should be the first lead connected and the last disconnected to a circuit.

The insulating layers in MOSFETs prevent testing with an ohmmeter. They can be checked for operation with the transistor tester shown in Chapter 25. The test, however, is only a general check for operation, substitution is the only practical means for amateur testing of MOSFETs.

FET Considerations

Replacement FETs should be of the same kind as the original part. That is, JFET or MOSFET, P-channel or N-channel, enhancement or depletion characteristics should be chosen to match the original.

Next consider the breakdown voltage required by the circuit. Always allow for twice to four times the signal voltage in amplifiers. Provision should be made for transients of 10 times the line voltage in power supplies. Breakdown voltages are usually specified as $V_{(BR)GSS}$ or $V_{(BR)GDO}$.

Gate-voltage specifications indicate the bias or signals required for operation. The specification usually gives the gate voltage required to cut off or initiate channel current (depending on the mode of operation). Gate voltages are usually listed as V_{GS} (OFF), V_p (pinch off), V_{TH} (threshold) or I_D (ON) or I_{TH}.

Gate leakage is a measure of FET input impedance. MOSFET gate leakage is extremely small; JFET leakage is greater. Leakage does not increase appreciably with temperature in either device. The characteristic may be called I_{GSS} (leakage from gate to source with drain shorted to source), I_{GSO} or I_{GDO}. (The first term is the preferred measurement, as the GSS configuration results in greater leakage.)

Dual-gate MOSFET characteristics are complicated by interaction of the two gates. Cutoff voltage, breakdown voltage and gate leakage are the important traits of each gate. V_{GIS} (OFF) is the cutoff voltage designation for gate 1, while $V_{(BR)GISS}$ and I_{GISS} are the gate-1 breakdown voltage and leakage current designators, respectively.

Semiconductor Substitution

In all cases try to obtain exact replacement semiconductors. Specifications vary slightly from one manufacturer to the next. Also, device specifications are minimums; some units far exceed them. Obtain replacements for PA devices (and others that are not common) from the equipment manufacturer. Some parts are specially selected for a particular characteristic by the maker.

Crossover equivalents are useful, but not infallible. Before using an equivalent, check the specifications against those for the original part. When choosing a replacement, consider:

- Is it silicon or germanium?
- Is it a PNP or an NPN?
- Operating frequency and input/output capacitance.
- Dissipated power (often less than $V_{max} \times I_{max}$).
- Will it fit the original mount?
- Unusual circuit demands (low noise and so on).
- The gain-bandwidth product.

Remember that crossover equivalents are listed without testing, and manufacturer's numbers are not necessarily unique. Derate power specifications, as recommended by the manufacturer, for high-temperature operation.

INTEGRATED CIRCUITS

The basics of integrated circuits are covered in Chapter 4. Amateurs seldom have the sophisticated equipment required to test ICs. Even a multitrace 'scope can view only their simplest functions. We must be content to check every other possible cause, and only then assume that the problem lies with an IC.

There are two major classes of ICs: Linear and digital. Linear ICs are best replaced with identical units. Do not overlook equipment manufacturers as a source of replacements; they are the only source with a reason to stockpile obsolete or custom-made items. If substitution of an IC is unavoidable, look in one of the many books written about ICs, their use and traits. Understanding and assessing the necessary characteristics can be as difficult as redesigning the entire circuit. In fact, extensive modifications of the coupling circuits and wiring may be required to conform to the new device connections. The concept of the electronic building block, which implies some degree of interchangeability, is fundamental to IC production, but the intricacies of comparison make substitution difficult.

Substitution of digital and array ICs is somewhat easier than that of linear ICs because there are fewer significant characteristics to consider. Digital signals, because of their on/off nature, demand only speed and slight power, not fidelity, from a device.

First, review the explanation of the various logic families and their electrical characteristics in Chapter 8. Interface circuits and their limitations are covered there also. Consider interface and logic requirements, switching time and fan-out when choosing substitute parts. Check supply voltages, at the lead to the IC pin, once again before installing any new IC. It is a good idea to check the potential on each trace to the bad component. The old IC may have "died" as a result of a lethal voltage. Measure twice — repair once! Of course, in-circuit performance is the final test of any substitution.

TUBES

The most common tube failures in amateur service are cathode depletion and gas contamination. Whenever a tube is operated, the coating on the cathode loses some of its ability to produce electrons. It is time to replace the tube when electron production (cathode current, I_c) falls to 50 to 60% of that exhibited by a new tube. This kind of tube failure is accelerated by exceeding the recommended duty cycle, as is often the case when sweep tubes are pressed into amateur service. High-gain power-amplifier tubes often fail from cathode depletion when filament voltage is not adequately regulated.

A gas-contaminated tube can be spotted because there is often a glow *between* the elements during operation. The gas reduces tube resistance and leads to runaway plate current evidenced by a red glow from the anode, interelectrode arcing or a blown power-supply fuse. Runaway plate current is most likely to occur during long transmissions at higher operating frequencies.

Less common tube failures include an open filament, broken envelope and interelectrode shorts. Use an ohmmeter to check for an open filament (remove the tube from the circuit first). A broken envelope is visually obvious, although a cracked envelope may appear as a gassy tube. Interelectrode shorts are evident during voltage checks on the operating stage. Any two elements that show the same voltage are shorted. (Remember that some interelectrode shorts, such as the cathode-suppressor grid, are normal.) Confirm that the tube is shorted, and not the circuit, by removing the tube.

Substitution is the best test of a tube. First, check the tube for opens and shorts on a tester. If the tube has an open element, check the surrounding circuits for shorts, then try a new tube. When you suspect that tubes are weak, check them by substitution. Place a new tube in the circuit and leave it in place only if there is a noticeable improvement. In power-supply circuits, measure the B+ with the old tube in place. If a new tube increases the B+ by 10% or more, leave the replacement in the circuit. Remember that no tube tester can adequately test a tube for use as an oscillator.

The "life test" is meant to determine if a tube will fail in the near future. Connect the tube to an emission tester and reduce the filament voltage by 20% from normal. If the plate current drops below that of a good tube, the service life of the tube is nearly over. Also, the cathodic emission of a strong tube falls slowly when filament voltage is removed; emission in a weak tube stops immediately.

Tube testers are covered earlier in this chapter. Look there for more information about testers and tips on their use.

Generally, a tube may be replaced with another that has the same basic model number, but look at data sheets for the respective tubes to verify their compatibility. Consider the base configuration and pinout, interelectrode capacitances (a small variation is okay except for tubes in oscillator service), dissipated power ratings of the plate and screen grid and current limitations (both peak and average).

For example, the 6146A may be replaced with a 6146B (heavy duty), but the B-suffix tube should not be replaced with an A-suffix version. (See the tetrode and pentode transmitting tube specifications in Chapter 35: A 6146B can dissipate 35 W safely, while a 6146A is rated at only 25 W.) In some cases, the difference denotes differences in filament voltages, or even base styles, so check *all* specifications before making a replacement.

As usual, the best course is an exact replacement from the equipment manufacturer; especially for tubes used in RF-power and oscillator circuits. (These are sometimes hand-picked or close-tolerance versions of standard models. Even tubes of the same model number, prefix and suffix vary slightly, in some respects, from one supplier to the next.)

CHECKOUT

Inspect each circuit visually when repairs are complete. Look for cold solder joints and signs of damage incurred during the repair. Use a bright light close behind printed circuit boards to check for breaks in the copper foil. Double check the position, leads and polarity of diodes, transistors and electrolytic capacitors that were removed or replaced. Make sure that all ICs have pin 1 in the proper spot. Test fuse continuity with an ohmmeter and verify that its current rating matches the circuit specification.

Observe the lead dress. Place wires clear of screw points and sharp edges. Separate the leads that carry dc, RF, input and output as much as possible. Plug-in circuit boards should be firmly seated with screws tightened and star washers installed if so specified. Shields and ground straps should be installed just as they were on the original.

For Transmitters Only

Since the signal produced by an HF transmitter can be heard the world over,

a thorough check is demanded after any service. Follow the procedure below to make sure the transmitter operates properly. Do not exceed the transmitter duty cycle while testing. Limit transmissions to 10 to 20 seconds unless otherwise specified by the owner's manual.

1) Set all controls as specified in the operation manual, or at mid scale.

2) Connect a dummy load and a power meter to the transmitter output.

3) Set the drive or carrier control for low output.

4) Switch the power on.

5) Transmit and quickly set the final-amplifier bias to specifications.

6) Slowly tune the output network through resonance. The current dip should be smooth and repeatable. It should occur simultaneously with the maximum power output. If these characteristics are not present, the amplifier is unstable. Adjust the neutralization circuit (see details in Chapter 15) if one is present or check for oscillation. An amplifier requires neutralization whenever active devices, components or lead dress (that affect the output/input capacitance) are changed.

7) Check to see that the output power is consistent with the amplifier class used in the PA (efficiency should be about 25% for Class A, 50 to 60% for Class AB or B, and 70 to 75% for Class C.)

8) Repeat steps 4 through 6 for each band of operation from lowest to highest frequency.

9) Check the carrier balance (in SSB transmitters only) and adjust for minimum power output with maximum RF drive and no microphone gain.

10) Adjust the VOX controls.

11) Measure the passband and distortion levels if equipment (wide-bandwidth 'scope or spectrum analyzer) is available.

All Other Repaired Circuits

After completing all of the preliminary checks, remove any test equipment, set the circuit controls per the manufacturer's specifications (or to midrange if specifications are not available), and switch the power on. Watch and smell for smoke, and listen for odd sounds such as arcing or hum. Operate and observe the circuit for a few minutes, consistent with allowable duty cycle. Vary all operating controls through their full range (consistent with operating instructions); see that they have the desired effects. Measure the gain and distortion of repaired amplifiers.

If the circuit appears to be operating normally, vary the power-supply voltage ±10% while checking for intermittent connections. Check for intermittents by subjecting the circuit to heat, cold and slight flexure. Also, tap or jiggle the chassis lightly with an alignment tool or other insulator. If the equipment is meant for mobile or portable service, operate it through an appropriate temperature range. Many mobile radios do not work on cold

Fig. 35 — Ship equipment packed securely in a box within a box.

mornings, or on hot afternoons, because a temperature-dependent intermittent was not found during repairs.

FACTORY REPAIRS

This chapter does not tell how to perform all repairs. Those repairs that deal with very complex and temperamental circuits, or that require sophisticated test equipment, should be passed on to a professional.

You should have opened a dialog with the manufacturer early in the repair work: If you did not, do so now. Notify the repair center before shipping any equipment. Get authorization for shipping and an identification name or number for the package.

Begin the packing procedure by blocking and tying down all heavy components. Large vacuum tubes should be wrapped in packing material or shipped separately. Make sure that all circuit boards and parts are firmly attached. Enclose a statement of the trouble, a short history of operation and any test results that may help the service technician.

Use a box within a box for shipping. (See Fig. 35) Place the equipment and some packing material inside a box. Seal the box with tape, address it, and mark it "Fragile — Electronic Equipment." Place that box inside another that is at least six inches larger in each dimension. Fill the gap with packing material, seal, address and mark the outer box. Choose a good freight carrier and insure the package.

Used Equipment

There is a certain thrill we all feel as we enter the flea market at our favorite hamfest. Vikings, "Gooney birds," Warriors and the venerable S-Line appeal to almost everyone. Equally tempting is the allure of a bargain; few hams can resist one.

Keep an eye on the classified section of radio magazines. Know the going price for radios that interest you and never pay that price without a demonstration. Try to buy equipment that was of high quality when it was new. It will serve you well when it is old.

Any gear that has been in storage may need repair. When you are looking for a bargain, gear that needs repair is usually the best buy unless:

- It is heavily damaged.
- Expensive test gear is needed for repair.
- No manual or parts are available.

Recently Built Equipment

First, do not buy unless you know the manufacturer. Know the equipment and whether parts and manuals are available. See that the manual is included in the sale — manuals are difficult to locate and expensive.

When a good prospect is found, open the cabinet. Look for missing parts, evidence of fire or damage. Purchase modified equipment if you trust the seller, or if the modifications can be easily removed. Modifications are as good as the skill of the person who installed them. Check the meter functions; the readings can tell you much.

Older Gear

Gear made before 1970 is usually suitable only for CW operation. Once again, do not overpay, watch for modifications and get the manual. Check for missing parts, and do not waste time on equipment that was inferior when new.

Beware of power supplies that do not use an isolation transformer. Such gear is difficult to modify. Connection of accessories, such as a keyer, keyboard or Q multiplier, is dangerous.

Restoration

First, open the cabinet and replace any parts that show signs of physical damage. Electrolytic capacitors often fail with age. Visual failure signs include bulges and leakage of a thick fluid or a white, gray or brownish paste or powder. Even if none of these signs are present, an electrolytic capacitor may be destroyed when power is first applied after long disuse. This may be prevented by re-forming the dielectric layer before applying power (see earlier section of this chapter).

Paper capacitors (wax or plastic coated) fail by leakage. They exude fluid or develop cracks in their coating. Replace faulty paper capacitors with dipped-Mylar units of the same, or higher, working voltage.

Mica and ceramic capacitors survive storage better than their tubular counterparts, but they require more exact replacements. Replacements must match not only the capacitance and working voltage of the original, but also the tolerance and temperature coefficient in all but bypass applications.

Remove dust and dirt with a small brush and a vacuum cleaner while inspecting the circuitry. Use extreme care around variable capacitors, inductors and rotary switches. Clean potentiometers and rotary switches with residue-free spray cleaner. Service air-dielectric variable capacitors as described earlier in this chapter. An eraser will clean stubborn dirt from rotary switch contacts,

but be very gentle and do not disturb lead dress around the switch. If leads to RF circuits are disturbed during cleaning, alignment may be affected.

After all visible problems have been corrected, disconnect one of the transformer secondary leads and measure the dc resistance from the power-supply output to ground. If the resistance is not consistent with the power ratings of the supply, locate the reason before applying power. If all is well, reconnect the transformer secondary and use a variable-voltage transformer to apply power gradually to the circuit. Listen and watch for arcs in the circuit as power is applied. Equipment that has been in storage should be "burned in" before proceeding. Operate the circuit (within duty-cycle limits) several hours each day for a week. Stay near the gear during this period to make sure that the "burn in" does not become a "burn down."

Once the basic clean up is completed, note any troubles as instructed earlier in this chapter and begin the normal repair routine. Once the equipment is repaired, clean the cabinet, instrument panel and knobs with household or automotive cleaner and a small brush. Smooth surfaces may be brightened by an application of automotive wax.

A SPECIAL CASE — NEW CONSTRUCTION

In most repair work, the technician is aided by the knowledge that the circuit once worked. It is only necessary to find the faulty part(s) and replace it. This is not so with newly constructed equipment. Repair of equipment with no working history is a special, and difficult, case.

Try to tackle the project one stage at a time. Consider each stage as two halves: Input and output. Look for any active device that is either saturated or cut off. Problems with the bias circuit are usually evident even with no input signal.

Use this procedure to set the bias of a high-gain amplifier. Set up the amplifier with a suitable dummy load and an oscilloscope on the output. Feed the input with a sine wave through an appropriate matching network. Increase the drive until the output waveform is clipped to a nearly square wave (See Fig. 36). Adjust the bias so that the positive and negative sections of the wave have equal duty cycles. Decrease the drive level slowly while making fine bias adjustment to maintain the duty cycle.

If equal clipping is not possible, suspect the component values or design. Nonlinear operation can be cured by adjusting values in the bias network, unless the active device is unsuitable for the circuit. When the circuit will only operate near saturation or cut off, try reducing positive feedback.

Once the bias is adjusted, check carefully for oscillations or noise. Oscillations are most likely to start with maximum gain and the amplifier input shorted. Any noise that

(A)

(B)

(C)

Fig. 36 — Waveforms seen while adjusting amplifier bias. The amplifier is overdriven at A, adjusted for proper duty cycle at B and operating normally at C.

is induced by 60-Hz sources can be seen with a 'scope synchronized to the ac line. Test with the supply voltage varied by ±10% (high-gain circuits are sensitive to supply-voltage changes).

RF oscillations should be cured with changes of lead dress or circuit components. Separate input leads from output leads; use coaxial cable to carry RF between stages; neutralize inter-element or junction capacitance. Ferrite beads on the control element of the active device often stop unwanted oscillations.

Low-frequency oscillations ("motorboating") indicate poor stage isolation or inadequate power-supply filtering. Try a better lead-dress arrangement and/or increase decoupling capacitance. Use larger capacitors at the power-supply lead, increase the number of capacitors or use separate decoupling capacitors at each stage.

Coupling capacitors that are too low in value cause poor low-frequency response. Poor response to high frequencies is frequently caused by transistor input capacitance. The input capacitance of a transistor decreases with frequency; this lowers stage gain. Reducing the stage gain at lower frequencies will help, as will using a better transistor.

References

Bartlett, J., "Calculating Component Values," *QST*, Nov. 1978.

Carr, J., *How to Troubleshoot and Repair Amateur Radio Equipment*, Blue Ridge Summit, PA: Tab Books Inc., 1980.

DeMaw, D., "Understanding Coils and Measuring their Inductance," *QST*, Oct. 1983.

Gibson, H., *Test Equipment for the Radio Amateur*, London, England: Radio Society of Great Britain, 1974.

Gilmore, C., *Understanding and Using Modern Electronic Servicing Test Equipment*, TAB Books, Inc., 1976.

Glass, F., *Owner Repair of Amateur Radio Equipment*, Los Gatos, CA: RQ Service Center, 1978.

Goodman, R., *Practical Troubleshooting with the Modern Oscilloscope*, TAB Books, Inc., 1979.

Haas, A., *Oscilloscope Techniques*, New York, NY: Gernsback Library, Inc., 1958.

Hallmark, C., *Understanding and Using the Oscilloscope*, TAB Books, Inc., 1973.

Helfrick, A., *Amateur Radio Equipment Fundamentals*, Englewood Cliffs, NJ: Prentice-Hall, Inc., 1982.

Henney, K., and Walsh, C., *Electronic Components Handbook*, New York, NY: McGraw-Hill Book Company, 1957.

Klein, L., and Gilmore, K., *It's Easy to Use Electronic Test Equipment*, New York, NY: John R. Rider, Publisher, Inc. (A division of Hayden Publishing Company), 1962.

Lenk, J., *Handbook of Electronic Test Procedures*, Prentice-Hall, Inc., 1982.

Loveday, G., and Seidman, A., *Troubleshooting Solid-State Circuits*, New York, NY: John Wiley and Sons, 1981.

Margolis, A., *Modern Radio Repair Techniques*, Tab Books Inc., 1971.

Neben, H., "An Ohmmeter with a Linear Scale," *QST*, Nov. 1982.

Neben, H., "A Simple Capacitance Meter You Can Build," *QST*, Jan. 1983.

Noble, F., "A Simple L-C Meter," *QST*, Feb. 1983.

Priedigkeit, J., "Measuring Inductance and Capacitance with a Reflection-Coefficient Bridge," *QST*, May 1982.

Sartori, H., "Solid Tubes — A New Life for Old Designs," *QST*, Apr. 1977; "Questions on Solid Tubes Answered," Technical Correspondence, *QST*, Sept. 1977.

Wedlock, B., and Roberge, J., *Electronic Components and Measurements*, Prentice-Hall, Inc., 1969.

"Some Basics of Equipment Servicing," series, *QST*, Dec. 1981, Jan.-Mar. 1982, feedback May 1982.

Chapter 27

Power Supply Projects

Construction of a power supply can be one of the most rewarding projects undertaken by a radio amateur. Whether it's a charger for the NiCds in a VHF hand-held transceiver, a low-voltage, high-current monster for a new 100-watt solid-state transceiver, or a high-voltage supply for a new linear amplifier, a power supply is basic to all of the radio equipment we enjoy and operate. Power-supply projects are especially inviting to amateurs new to rolling their own. Unlike transmitters and receivers, layout and wiring of power supplies is not particularly important to proper operation. Parts for many power-supply projects are readily available in many areas, either through local retail outlets or at flea markets and hamfests. The power-supply project requiring a special, hard-to-find part is the exception, rather than the rule. In addition, final testing and adjustment of most power-supply projects requires only a voltmeter, and perhaps an oscilloscope — tools commonly available to most amateurs.

Additional information on power-supply design and theory may be found in Chapter 6. General construction techniques that may be helpful in building the projects in this chapter are outlined in Chapter 24. Chapters 2, 3, 4 and 5 contain basic information on the components that make up power supplies.

Safety must always be carefully considered during design and construction of any power supply. Power supplies contain potentially lethal voltages, and care must be taken to guard against accidental exposure. For example, electrical tape, insulated tubing (spaghetti) or heat-shrink tubing is recommended for covering exposed wires, component leads, component solder terminals and tie-down points. Whenever possible, connectors used to mate the power supply to the outside world should be of an insulated type designed to prevent accidental contact.

Connectors and wire should be checked for voltage and current ratings. Always use wire with an insulation rating higher than the working voltages in the power supply. Special high-voltage wire is available for use in B+ supplies. Chapter 35 contains a table showing the current-carrying capability of various wire sizes. Scrimping on wire and connectors to save money could result in a flashover, meltdown or fire.

All fuses and switches should be placed in the hot leg(s) only. The neutral leg should not be interrupted. Use of a three-wire (grounded) power connection will greatly reduce the chance of accidental shock. The proper wiring color code for 117-V circuits is: black — hot; white — neutral; and green — ground.

Power Supply Primary Circuit Connector Standard

The International Commission on Rules for the Approval of Electrical Equipment (CEE) standard for power supply primary circuit connectors for use with detachable cable assemblies is the CEE-22 (see Fig. 1). The CEE-22 has been recognized by the ARRL and standards agencies of many countries. Rated for up to 250 V, 6 A at 65°C, the CEE-22 is the most commonly used three-wire (grounded), chassis-mount

Fig. 1 — CEE-22 connectors are available with built-in line filters and fuse holders.

primary circuit connector for electronic equipment in North America and Europe. It is often used in Japan and Australia as well.

When building a power supply requiring 6 A or less from the primary supply, a builder would do well to consider using a CEE-22 connector and an appropriate cable assembly, rather than a permanently installed line cord. Use of a detachable line cord makes replacement easy in case of damage. CEE-22 compatible cable assemblies are available with a wide variety of power plugs including most types used overseas.

Some manufacturers even supply the CEE-22 connector with a built-in line filter. These connector/filter combinations are especially useful in supplies that are operated in RF fields. They are also useful in digital equipment to minimize conducted interference to the power lines.

CEE-22 connectors are available in many styles for chassis or PC-board mounting. Some have screw terminals; others have solder terminals. Some styles even contain built-in fuse holders.

A 5-A Switching-Regulator Supply

This section describes a practical 13.8-volt, 5-ampere switching power supply suitable for use with transceivers in the 25-watt-output class. Circuit simplicity and easy parts acquisition were the major design goals. The supply was built and tested in the ARRL laboratory by Greg Bonaguide, WA1VUG. A 10-watt-output 220-MHz FM transceiver was used as a load with no apparent degradation of the RF output spectral purity. The line and load regulation are acceptable, and the unit

is slightly more efficient than an equivalent linear supply. With the heat sink specified, the unit can withstand 3-minute FM transmissions interspersed with 1-minute listening periods. Because of the simple circuit configuration, conventional preregulation components are used. Therefore, this

Fig. 2 — Front panel of the switching power supply. The cabinet is by Apollo and has a built-in power switch.

Fig. 3 — Interior view of the switching power supply. The main switch transistor heat sink and fuse are mounted on the rear panel.

Fig. 5 — Parts-placement guide for the PC board of the switching-regulator supply control board. The component side is shown with an X-ray view of the foil. A full-size etching pattern can be found at the back of this book.

power supply offers no particular economic advantage over one using linear regulation. This project was intended to demonstrate the switching principle as applied to voltage regulation, and it serves that purpose well. However, it is not in any way represented to be a state-of-the-art design.

A more nearly technically correct name for this project might be "A 5-A Power Supply Using a Switching Regulator." However, it's not necessary to belabor the distinction between supplies and regulators in casual work.

Fig. 2 shows the cosmetic aspects of the front panel, while Fig. 3 reveals one satisfactory arrangement of internal com-ponents. The schematic diagram is given in Fig. 4. Stud-mount rectifiers are used in a full-wave bridge. A PC board for the diodes is visible in Fig. 3, but the etching pattern is not printed here because of its simplicity. The component-placement guide for the electronics board is given in Fig. 5. A full-size etching pattern can be found at the back of this book.

Fig. 4 — A switching power supply suitable for use with medium-power amateur transceivers. At full load the switching rate is approximately 50 kHz. Resistance values are in ohms, and capacitance values are in microfarads.

D1 — 6 A, 600 PIV, anode common to case, ECG 5863 or equiv.

L1 — 33 turns no. 14 enam. on Amidon FT 240-43 toroidal core.

Q1 Heat sink — 4 × 3 inches with ½-inch fins extruded from flat surfaces.
Q2 Heat sink — TO-5 clip-on unit.

A 28-V, High-Current Power Supply

Many modern high-power transistors used in RF power amplifiers require 28-V dc collector supplies, rather than the traditional 12-V supply. By going to 28 V (or even 50 V), designers significantly reduce the amount of current required for an amplifier in the 100-W or higher output class. The power supply shown in Figs. 14 through 18 is conservatively rated for 28 V at 10 A (enough for a 150-W output amplifier) — continuous duty! It was designed with simplicity and readily-available components in mind. Mark Wilson, AA2Z, built this project in the ARRL lab.

Circuit Details

The schematic diagram of the 28-V supply is shown in Fig. 15. T1 was designed by Avatar Magnetics specifically for this project. The primary requires 117-V ac, but a dual-primary (117/234 V) version is available. The secondary is rated for 32 V at 15 A, continuous duty. The primary is bypassed by two 0.01-μF capacitors and protected from line transients by an MOV.

U1 is a 25-A bridge module available

Fig. 14 — The front panel of the 28-V power supply sports only a power switch, pilot lamp and binding posts for the voltage output. There is room for a voltmeter, should another builder desire one.

from Radio Shack or a number of other suppliers. It requires a heat sink in this application. Filter capacitor C1 is a computer-grade 22,000-μF electrolytic. Bleeder resistor R1 is included for safety because

of the high value of C1; bleeder current is about 12 mA.

There is a trade-off between the secondary voltage of the transformer and the value of the filter capacitor. To maintain regulation, the minimum supply voltage to the regulator circuitry must remain above approximately 31 V. Ripple voltage must be taken into account. If the voltage on the bus drops below 31 V in ripple valleys, regulation may be lost.

In this supply, the transformer secondary voltage was chosen to allow use of a commonly-available filter value. The builder found that 50-V electrolytic capacitors of up to about 25,000 μF were common and the prices reasonable; few dealers stocked capacitors above that value, and the prices increased dramatically. If you have a larger filter capacitor, you can use a transformer with a lower secondary voltage; similarly, if you have a transformer in the 28- to 35-V range, you can calculate the size of the filter capacitor required. Chapter 6 contains the formulas needed to calculate ripple for different filter

NOTE: POINTS A-D REFER TO INTERCONNECTIONS WITH THE CROWBAR CIRCUIT IN FIG. 16. IF THE CROWBAR IS NOT USED, JUMPER POINTS A AND B.

EXCEPT AS INDICATED, DECIMAL VALUES OF CAPACITANCE ARE IN MICROFARADS (μF); OTHERS ARE IN PICOFARADS (pF OR $\mu\mu$F); RESISTANCES ARE IN OHMS; k = 1000, M = 1000 000.
T = TANTALUM

Fig. 15 — Schematic diagram of the 28-V, high-current power supply. Resistors are ¼-W, 5% types unless otherwise noted. Capacitors are disc ceramic unless noted; capacitors marked with polarity are electrolytic. Parts numbers given in parenthesis that are preceded by the letters RS are Radio Shack catalog numbers.

C1 — Electrolytic capacitor, 22,000 μF, 50 V (Mallory CGS223UO50X4C or equiv., avail. from Mouser Electronics).
DS1 — Pilot lamp, 117-V ac (RS 272-705).
Q1-Q5 — NPN power transistor, 2N3055 or equiv. (RS 276-2041).
R2-R5 — Power resistor, 0.1 Ω, 5 W (or greater), 5% tolerance.
R7 — Power resistor, 0.05 Ω, 10 W (or greater), made from two 0.1-Ω, 5-W resistors in parallel.
T1 — Power transformer. Primary, 117-V ac; secondary, 32 V, 15 A. (Avatar Magnetics AV-430 or equiv. Dual primary version is part no. AV-431. Available from Avatar Magnetics.
U1 — Bridge rectifier, 50 PIV, 25 A (RS 276-1185).
U2 — Three-terminal adjustable voltage regulator, 100 mA (LM-317L or equiv.). See text.
U3 — 723-type adjustable voltage regulator IC, 14-pin DIP package (LM-723, MC1723, etc., RS 276-1740).
Z1 — 130-V MOV (RS 276-570).

and transformer values.

The regulator circuitry takes advantage of commonly-available parts. The heart of the circuit is U3, a 723 voltage regulator IC. The values of R8, R9 and R10 were chosen to allow the output voltage to be varied from 20 to 30 V. The 723 has a maximum input voltage rating of 40 V, somewhat lower than the filtered bus voltage. U2 is an adjustable 3-terminal regulator; it is set to provide approximately 35 V to power U3. U3 drives the base of Q1, which in turn drives pass transistors Q2-Q5. This arrangement was selected to take advantage of common components. At first glance, the number of pass transistors seems high for a 10-A supply. Input voltage is high enough that the pass transistors must dissipate about 120 W (worst case), so thermal considerations dictate the use of four transistors. See Chapter 6 for a complete discussion of thermal design. If you use a transformer with a significantly different secondary potential, refer to the Chapter 6 thermal tutorial to verify the size heat sink required for safe operation.

R9 is used to adjust supply output voltage. Since this supply was designed primarily for 28-V applications, R9 is a "set and forget" control mounted internally. A 25-turn potentiometer is used here to allow precise voltage adjustment. Another builder may wish to mount this control, and perhaps a voltmeter, on the front panel to easily vary the output voltage.

The 723 features current foldback if the load draws excessive current. Foldback current, set by R7, is approximately 14 A, so F2 should blow if a problem occurs. The output terminals, however, may be shorted indefinitely without damage to any power-supply components.

If the regulator circuitry should fail, or if a pass transistor should short, the unregulated supply voltage will appear at the output terminals. Most 28-V RF transistors would fail with 40-plus volts on the collector, so a prospective builder might wish to incorporate the overvoltage protection circuit shown in Fig. 16 in the power supply. This circuit is optional. If you choose to use the "crowbar," make the interconnections as shown. Note that R11 and F3 of Fig. 16 are added between points A and B of Fig. 15. If the crowbar is not used, place a wire jumper between points A and B of Fig. 15.

This crowbar circuit is taken from Motorola application notes for the MC3423 overvoltage sensor IC. The chip contains a 2.5-V reference and two comparators. When the voltage at pin 2 (sense terminal) reaches 2.5 V, the output goes high (from 0.0 V to the positive bus voltage) to drive the gate of Q6, a high-current SCR. Q6 turns on, shorting the supply output terminals. This circuit is inexpensive and easy to implement, yet it allows the builder to precisely set the trip voltage. It provides excellent gate drive to the SCR, and is somewhat quicker and more reliable than

Fig. 16 — Schematic diagram of the over-voltage protection circuit. Resistors are ¼-W, 5% carbon types unless noted.

Q6 — 20-A, 100-V stud-mount SCR (RCA SK6502 or equiv.).
R12 — 5-kΩ, 10-turn potentiometer in series
with a 24-kΩ, ¼-W resistor.
U4 — Overvoltage sensor IC, Motorola MC3423 (RS 276-1717).

Fig. 17 — Interior of the 28-V, high-current power supply. The cooling fan is necessary only if the pass transistors and heat sink are mounted inside the cabinet. See text.

crowbar circuits that use Zener diodes. R11 and F3 protect the pass transistors from damage in case of high-current transients.

The trip voltage is determined from the equation

$$V_{TRIP} \approx 2.5 \left(1 + \frac{R11}{R12}\right)$$

The application notes recommend that R13 be less than 10 kΩ for minimum drift and suggest a value of 2.7 kΩ. In this version, R12 is preset with a 24-kΩ resistor, and a 5-kΩ, 10-turn potentiometer dials in the precise trip point.

Construction

Fig. 17 shows the interior of the 28-V supply. It is built in a Hammond 1401K enclosure. All parts mount inside the box. The regulator components are mounted on a small PC board that is attached to the rear of the front panel. See Fig. 18. Most of the parts were purchased at local electronics stores or from suppliers listed in Chapter 35. Many parts, such as the heat sink, pass transistors, 0.1-Ω power resistors and filter capacitor can be obtained from scrap computer power supplies found at flea markets.

Q2-Q5 are mounted on a Wakefield model 441K heat sink. The transistors are mounted to the heat sink with isulating washers and thermal heat-sink compound to aid heat transfer. Radio Shack TO-3 sockets make electrical connections easier. The heat sink surface under the transistors must be absolutely smooth. Carefully deburr all holes after drilling and lightly sand the edges with fine emery cloth.

A five-inch fan circulates air past the heat sink inside the cabinet. Forced-air cooling is necessary only because the heat sink is mounted inside the cabinet. If the heat sink was mounted on the rear panel with the fins vertical, natural convection would provide adequate cooling and no fan would be required.

U1 is mounted to the inside of the rear panel with heat-sink compound. Its heat sink is bolted to the outside of the rear panel to take advantage of convection cooling.

U2 may prove difficult to find. The 317L is a 100-mA version of the popular 317-series 1.5-A adjustable regulator. The 317L is packaged in a TO-92 case, while the normal 317 is usually packaged in a larger TO-220 case. Many of the suppliers listed in Chapter 35 sell them, and RCA SK7644 or Sylvania ECG1900 direct replacements are available from many local electronics shops. If you can't find a 317L, you can use a regular 317 (available from Radio Shack, among others).

R7 is made from two 0.1-Ω, 5-W resistors connected in parallel. These resistors get warm under sustained operation, so they

Fig. 18 — Parts-placement diagram for the 28-V power supply. A full-size etching pattern appears at the back of this book.

are mounted approximately 1/16 inch above the circuit board to allow air to circulate and to prevent the PC board from becoming discolored. Similarly, R6 gets warm to the touch, so it is mounted away from the board to allow air to circulate. Q1 becomes slightly warm during sustained operation, so it is mounted to a small TO-3 PC board heat sink.

Not obvious from the photograph is the use of a single-point ground to avoid ground-loop problems. The PC-board ground connection and the minus lead of the supply are tied directly to the minus terminal of C1, rather than to a chassis ground.

The crowbar circuit is mounted on a small heat sink near the output terminals. Q6 is a stud-mount SCR and is insulated from the heat sink. An RCA replacement SCR was used here because it was readily available, but any 20-A or greater SCR that can handle at least 50 V will work. The other components are mounted on a small circuit board that is attached to the heat sink with angle brackets. U4 is available from Radio Shack.

Although the output current is not extremely high, no. 14 or no. 12 wire should be used for all high-current runs, including the wiring between C1 and the collectors of Q2-Q5; between R2-R5 and R7; between F2 and the positive output terminal; and between C1 and the negative output terminal. Similar wire should be used between the output terminals and the load.

Testing

First, connect T1, U1 and C1 and verify that the no-load voltage is approximately 44-V dc. Then, connect unregulated voltage to the PC board and pass transistors. Leave the gate lead of Q6 disconnected from pin 8 of U4 at this time. You should be able to adjust the output voltage between approximately 20 and 30 V. Set the output to 28 V.

Next, set the crowbar to fire at 29 V or whatever trip voltage you desire. Set the potentiometer of R12 for maximum resistance. Connect a voltmeter to U4, pin 8. The voltmeter should indicate 0.0 V. Increase supply voltage to 29 V and adjust R12 until pin 8 goes high, to approximately 28 V. Back off the supply voltage; pin 8 should go low again. Connect the gate lead of Q6 and again increase supply voltage to 29 V. The crowbar should fire, shorting the supply output. Slight adjustment of R12 may be necessary. Remove power and turn R9 to reduce supply voltage below the trip point. Apply power and reset the output voltage to 28 V.

Next, short the output terminals to verify that the current foldback is working. Voltage should return to 28 when the shorting wire is disconnected. This completes testing and setup.

The supply shown in the photographs dropped approximately 0.1 V between no load and a 12-A resistive load. During testing in the ARRL lab, this supply was run for four hours continuously with a 12-A resistive load on several occasions without any difficulty.

A 1.2- to 15-Volt, 5-Ampere Supply

The power supply shown in Figs. 19 to 23 is intended for general-purpose, test-bench applications. The output is adjustable from 1.2 to 17 volts at currents up to 6 amperes. Metering is provided for voltage levels up to 15 volts and current levels up to 5 amperes. Most of the components used in this supply are of the junk-box variety with the possible exception of U2, the three-terminal voltage regulator. The circuit will tolerate fairly wide component substitutions and still offer good performance. The majority of the circuit components are mounted on a 2¾ × 4½-inch circuit board. All controls, including the

mains fuse are located on the front panel for easy access.

The Circuit

As shown in Fig. 20, two power

transformers are used in parallel to feed U1, the full-wave bridge rectifier assembly. The transformers specified are rated at 2 amperes each. The prospective builder might question the wisdom of using only

Fig. 19 — A simple 1.2- to 15-volt, 5-ampere power supply. All controls are mounted on the front panel for easy access. The milliammeter reading is multiplied by 100 to obtain the true output current.

Fig. 21 — Inside view of the power supply. Component placement is not at all critical; however, the layout shown here provides a neat appearance.

Fig. 20 — Schematic diagram of the 5-ampere power supply. Component designations on the schematic diagram but not shown in the parts list are for text or placement guide reference only.

C1 — 3300-µF, 35-volt, axial leads.
J1, J2 — Binding posts.
M1 — 0-50 mA, Calectro DI-914 or equiv.
M2 — 0-15 V, Calectro DI-920 or equiv.
Q1 — Silicon PNP power, Radio Shack 276-2043 or equiv.

R1 — Meter shunt, 13 inches no. 22 enameled wire wound on a high-value, 1-watt resistor. (Resistor used only as a form for the wire.)
R6 — 2500 ohms, 2 watts, panel mount.
S1 — SPST, toggle.

S2 — DPDT, toggle. Both sections connected in parallel.
T1, T2 — 117-V primary, 18-V CT secondary. Radio Shack 273-1515.
U1 — Bridge-rectifier assembly, 50 V, 25 A.
U2 — Regulator, LM-317K.

Fig. 22 — For voltage and current requirements that fall to the left of the diagonal line, the power supply may be operated in the LO mode. Pass-transistor dissipation will be reduced when the supply is operated in this manner.

Fig. 23 — Circuit-board layout pattern as viewed from the component side of the board. A full-size etching pattern can be found at the back of this book.

in selecting the HI or LO mode of operation.

The regulator consists of a pass transistor "wrapped around" an adjustable voltage regulator. Circuit operation can be understood by noting the values of R3 and R2. The majority of the three-terminal regulator current will flow through R3 and D1. The offset voltage in D1 is approximately equal to the emitter-base potential of Q1. Because of this, the voltage drop across R3 will be the same as that across R2. Since the ohmic value of R2 is 0.33 of R3, three times as much current will flow in Q1 as in U2. The net result is that the current capability of the overall circuit is increased by a factor of four. In addition, the current-limiting characteristics of the three-terminal regulator are transferred directly to the composite circuit.

M1 and its associated shunt resistor are placed at the input to the regulator circuit so that the voltage drop across the resistor will not adversely alter the supply voltage regulation. The relatively small current drawn by the regulator circuitry does not seriously affect the meter accuracy. M2 measures supply output voltage.

Construction

The power supply is housed in a homemade enclosure that was fabricated from sheet aluminum. Fig. 21 shows the parts layout. Dimensions of the enclosure are 5½ × 6 × 8 inches, although any cabinet that will house the components may be used. Circuit board layout information is given in Fig. 23. The completed circuit board is mounted vertically to the chassis using space lugs and no. 6 hardware. A small heat sink for the LM317K regulator was made from a scrap piece of aluminum. The pass transistor is mounted to a larger heat sink which is bolted to the rear panel of the power supply. Here, a Motorola MS-10 was used. Bear in mind that the transistor must be insulated from the sink. Use a small amount of heat-sink compound between the transistor and the sink for a good thermal bond.

Since the power supply can deliver up to 6 amperes, fairly heavy wire should be used for those runs carrying the bulk of the current. No. 18 wire was used in this unit and it appeared to be adequate.

The completed power supply may be "crowbarred" without worry of regulator or pass transistor destruction. Perhaps the only precaution that should be mentioned is that of the exposed collector of the pass transistor. Although no damage will occur if the case is shorted to ground, it will cause the loss of output voltage. This could occur if the power supply is mounted on a test bench with a number of leads dangling behind the unit. A simple fix for this would be to mount a plastic TO-3 transistor cover over the case.

4 amperes worth of transformer in a 5-ampere supply. This is a valid question. With a 5-ampere load connected to the output of the supply, the transformers deliver more than their rated secondary voltage and do not become unreasonably warm to the touch even after continuous-duty operation. If transformers of different manufacture are used, it might be wise to select units having a higher current rating — just to be sure.

S2 is included in the design so that either half or all of the secondary voltage may be applied to U1. This feature was included so that the dissipation of the pass transistor may be reduced when using the supply with low-voltage, high-current loads. The graph displayed in Fig. 22 can be used as a guide

The Perfect 10: A Battery Eliminator for FM Portables

In an effort to reduce the size of FM portable equipment, some manufacturers have opted to reduce the number of batteries in the battery pack. Now, a typical portable rig operates from a pack containing eight cells (nominal 9.6-V potential). Operating these rigs from an external supply, typically 12-V from an automobile electrical system or commonly used home power supply, can be risky. Pete O'Dell, KB1N, presents the following solution for those amateurs wishing to power their portables from a source other than internal batteries. The "Perfect 10," shown in Figs. 46 through 50, was originally presented in March 1984 *QST*.

The Regulator Circuit

Fig. 47 shows a circuit for use with the 12-V electrical system of an automobile (or any other 12-V dc source capable of supplying about 500 mA). Both the input and the output are fused for added safety. The mounting tab of U1 (internally connected to pin 2) is bolted to the metal cabinet that houses the circuit. Heat-sink compound is applied between the tab and the cabinet to aid heat transfer. The metal of the cabinet should be more than adequate as a heat sink because the input voltage is only 2 to 4 volts above the output voltage.

Two alternatives are available for U1. The 10-V fixed regulator is not very common, but is available from Texas Instruments distributors. You could also use an LM317 adjustable regulator (available from Radio Shack and other sources). Adjust the 2-kΩ potentiometer for a supply output of 10 V.

D1 provides protection for the regulator chip in the event that the output terminal potential of U1 rises above that at the input terminal. Without D1, the regulator can be destroyed. That condition can occur easily. The capacitor on the input of U1 charges (assuming S1 is open). DS1 lights, then slowly extinguishes as the capacitor discharges. U1 may survive the small reverse current, but why take chances?

The two capacitors should be mounted as close to the regulator IC as possible.

Fig. 47 — Schematic diagram of the regulator circuit. The resistor is a carbon-composition type. Capacitance is in microfarads. The input capacitor is electrolytic. Parts numbers in parentheses are from Radio Shack.

D1 — Silicon power diode, 1N4001 or equiv.
DS1 — Green LED (276-022).
F1,F2 — Fast-acting fuse, 1 A (270-1273).
S1 — SPST toggle (275-602).

U1 — 10-V, 1-A, three-terminal regulator, Texas Instruments 7810 or equiv. or 1-A adjustable three-terminal regulator (LM317 or equiv.).

Fig. 48 — Schematic diagram of the base-station version of the battery eliminator. Components used in the regulator circuit are identical with those in Fig. 47. Consult the Fig. 47 parts list for component values.

T1 — Filament transformer; primary: 117-V ac, 60 Hz; secondary: 12.6-V ac, 1.2 A (173-1505).

U2 — Bridge rectifier, 4 A, 100 PIV (276-1171).

Fig. 49 — Internal view of the regulated supplies. Construction is straightforward; layout is not critical.

Some manufacturers recommend lead lengths no greater than ¼ inch. U1, D1 and the capacitors mount in a small aluminum box. A mounting tab on the box permits it to be secured under the dash, out of sight. F1 and F2 are housed in in-line fuse holders. S1 and DS1 are mounted on a small home-made bracket that is attached to the dash.

A Base-Station Supply

Fig. 48 shows a version of the circuit that operates directly from 117-V ac. The regulator circuit is identical to that of Fig. 47. DS2 is located on the output and provides a quick visual check of the output status. The fuse holders are the panel-mounted variety instead of the in-line type. All the components are mounted inside a small aluminum box (Fig. 49). Again, the cabinet serves as the heat sink for the regulator chip.

Initially, a 1000-μF capacitor was tried for the input of the regulator. No problems were encountered when using the supply with a 2.5-W portable. However, at the 5-W level, some hum was noticeable on the signal. A 5000-μF unit cured the problem.

Making Connections

Fig. 50 shows one method of connecting the battery eliminator to a portable rig. J1 is a miniature plastic-enclosed, closed-circuit phone jack (Radio Shack 274-296 or similar). P1 is a matching plug. As a phone

Fig. 46 — Two versions of the Perfect 10. The mobile unit bracket with ON/OFF switch attaches to a convenient spot on the dashboard, while the box housing the regulator mounts out of sight.

Fig. 50 — Block diagram of the connections between the battery pack, radio circuit board and battery eliminator for the Tempo S5 and similar portable units.

plug is inserted into a jack, the tip will cause a short, initially, between the elements of the jack. This results in a momentary short from the positive terminal of the battery to ground, which will not damage the battery pack (as long as the short is momentary). The event may cause a fuse in series with the battery to blow. If your radio incorporates a fuse in series with the battery pack, you should consider a different plug-and-jack system.

Finding a place to mount the jack in a small radio can be a chore. Carefully measure the openings and distances before drilling the mounting hole. Use liberal amounts of heat-shrink tubing to cover bare wires or terminals.

This method should work for most portables on the market — those that do not have slide-on battery packs. For rigs with the slide-on packs, the easiest approach is to obtain an empty pack and construct the circuit inside it.

Two ferrite beads are added to the power leads near the circuit board in Fig. 50. These minimize the possibility of RF getting back into the portable-rig circuit through the battery eliminator. If the eliminator is constructed in a slide-on pack, the beads should be placed on the output wires that are soldered to the terminal inside the pack.

Before applying power, double check all wiring. With the radio ON/OFF switch in the OFF position, apply power to the eliminator circuit and check the voltage at the power input of the radio. If everything is all right, proceed with final assembly. There is nothing to adjust. Just use and enjoy.

The AA6PZ Power Charger

The battery charger shown in Figs. 52 through 58 combines the best features of constant-current and constant-voltage NiCd chargers. This charger was originally described by Paul Zander, AA6PZ, in December 1982 *QST*.

The Power Charger

As shown in Fig. 53, when the battery voltage is low, the current available from the charger is high enough to keep the transmitter on the air. As the battery voltage increases, the charging current decreases in order to avoid overcharging the battery. Finally, as the battery approaches full charge the current tapers off more slowly with increasing voltage. This action provides a topping-off charge with some latitude for variations in battery voltage.

Fig. 54 shows what happens when a discharged battery is connected to the Power Charger. The initial current is high, charging the battery to 25 to 30% of its capacity in the first hour. The current drops off as the battery is charged. After approximately 6 hours the battery is fully charged. Then, as continued charging pushes the battery voltage higher, the current decreases to a few milliamperes. If you forget to disconnect the Power Charger after the battery is charged, the final charge rate is actually less stressful to the battery than if you were using a constant-current trickle charger.

What happens if you operate with the Power Charger connected? When the transmitter draws current from the battery the battery voltage drops, and more current is available from the Power Charger.

Fig. 52 — Interior view of the Power Charger. The three LEDs are mounted on long leads so they protrude through the top cover.

Fig. 53 — Output characteristics of the Power Charger circuit.

When the battery is less than three quarters charged the charger supplies most, if not all, of the transmitter current.

Rapid-charging capability, by itself, is of limited utility if the charger must be plugged into a wall outlet. The Power Charger can be operated with a wide variety of sources that supply from 12 to 30 volts. For mobile operation the car battery can supply the power from the cigarette lighter. For extended portable or emergency operation, lead-acid storage batteries may be useful. For fixed-station use, a simple ac-operated supply can be used.

Circuit Description

A simplified schematic diagram of the Power Charger is shown in Fig. 55. A full schematic is shown in Fig. 56. A PNP series-pass transistor, Q1, is used to control the charging current, and a 1-Ω resistor (R1) is used to monitor that current. When Q1 has enough base drive it will have 0.2 V or less between collector and emitter. This, combined with the voltage drop across R1, allows the circuit to have a minimal difference between the input and output voltages. Although it might be possible to use an IC voltage regulator in place of Q1 and some of the other parts, most IC regulators have a minimum of 2 or 3 V between the input and output. This makes them unsuited for mobile and portable operation where there is not much voltage to spare.

Q2 and Q3 control the base drive to Q1. Q3 receives input from Q4 if the charging current is too high — and from Q5 if the output voltage is too high. In response to either of these inputs, Q3 reduces the Q2 base current. This, in turn, reduces the base drive to Q1 so that the proper output voltage and current are maintained.

Q4 and the associated components monitor the output current. The base-

Fig. 54 — Typical charging performance of the Power Charger. Shown at A is the percentage of full charge obtained as a function of charging time. The charging current, as a function of time, is shown at B.

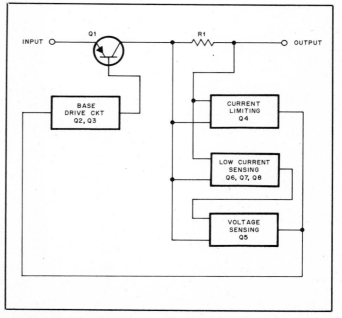

Fig. 55 — Block diagram of the Power Charger.

emitter junction of Q4 is connected across R1. When the current is more than 700 mA, Q4 is turned on. This sends a signal through the other transistors to reduce the base drive to Q1 so the current cannot go higher. In practice, this much current will only be drawn by the transceiver if you are transmitting while the battery is discharged. If the 700-mA current limit is not high enough for your transmitter it can be increased by connecting R5 between the emitter and base of Q4. The formula

$$R5 = \frac{70}{R1 \times I_{MAX} - 0.7}$$

can be used to determine the correct value. For example, a 680-Ω resistor would increase the current limit to 800 mA. Any variation in the tolerance of R1 and other resistors will affect the current limit markedly, so measure to value of your particular resistor and compute the value of R5 accordingly.

During most of the charging cycle Q5 and the 4.7-V Zener diode act as a voltage-sensing circuit. The combination of Q1, Q2, Q3 and Q5 regulate the collector voltage of Q1 at 11.2 V. There is, however, a resistor (R1) between that point and the battery. When the output current is 500 mA there is 0.5 V across R1, so the output is only 10.7 volts. At 200 mA, the drop across R1 is 0.2 volt, and the output is 11.0 volts. Viewed from the battery terminals, as the voltage increases the charging current decreases.

As we have just seen, R1 determines the slope of the voltage-current relation shown in Fig. 53. A value of 1 Ω works well with NiCd batteries having a capacity of 450 mAh. For batteries having a smaller capacity, the value of R1 should be increased. For example, when one is charging 250-mAh batteries, R1 should be 1.8 Ω.

Using a 330-Ω resistor for R5 would give a maximum current of 500 mA.

The remainder of the circuit is used to provide the topping-off part of the charging cycle. Q6 and Q7 form an amplifier that senses the voltage drop caused by charging current flowing through R1. When the current approaches 100 mA, Q7 starts to turn off and Q6 begins to turn on. The collector output of Q6 is connected to the base circuit of Q5. This causes the charger voltage to rise slightly. The output voltage is allowed to increase more as the current drops further. Eventually, a point of equilibrium is reached at which the current is only a few milliamperes. This current is unable to push the battery voltage higher. With this method, the battery can be fully charged safely and quickly.

As the output voltage increases at the end of the charging cycle, the base drive to Q8 is reduced. This causes the CHARGING LED to dim and eventually go out when charging is complete.

If the input voltage is too low the LOW-VOLTAGE LED turns on to signal that you will be unable to fully charge the battery. This is most likely to occur when using an external storage battery to supply the Power Charger. A similar situation can occur when using the Power Charger with rigs that do not have an internal diode in series with the battery. If the power-charger input is accidentally disconnected, Q1 might conduct some current in the reverse direction. The LOW VOLTAGE LED will light as a warning. If, under these circumstances, the input terminals should be accidentally short-circuited, Q2 and Q1 turn off as a safety measure to avoid damaging the radio. The residual current drain on the NiCd battery will be only a few milliamperes.

The last items in the schematic diagram

are the input and output fuses. As we have just seen, the power-charger circuit has current limiting, so perhaps the fuses are not necessary. However, consider that a fully charged NiCd battery can deliver many amperes to a short circuit, and that an automobile battery is designed to deliver peak currents of 200 A or more. In this environment a couple of 20-cent fuses seem like a good idea to prevent unwanted fireworks!

Construction

In designing the Power Charger circuit, consideration was given to using parts that are readily available. The only critical part is Q1, which should be an 2N4918. The fuse clips are Littlefuse no. 102071 or a similar part by another manufacturer. Alternatively, fuses with wire leads can be soldered directly to the board.

All of the components can be mounted on a 1.9- × 3.9-inch etched circuit board. An etching pattern for this board appears at the back of this book. This size fits comfortably inside a 2 × 4 × 1-inch aluminum box. A parts-placement diagram is shown in Fig. 58. Q1 is mounted with an insulating washer between it and the box. The mounting provides heat sinking for Q1 and mechanical support for one end of the circuit board. The other end of the board is supported by a no. 4-40 machine screw and three nuts. The first nut holds the screw securely to the box. The remaining nuts go above and below the board to hold it level in the box. The head of the same screw can be used to mount a rubber foot on the outside of the box.

Probably the only construction difficulty you will encounter is determining the proper charging connector for your transceiver. There seem to be as many different connectors as there are transceivers. Then there

Fig. 56 — Schematic diagram of the Power Charger. Except as indicated all resistors are ¼-W, 5% carbon types. Capacitors are disc ceramic units rated at 50 V or greater. Polarized capacitors are 25-V electrolytic types.

Fig. 57 — A simple ac adapter, such as the one shown here, can be used to power the charger for fixed-station use.

Fig. 58 — Parts-placement guide for the Power Charger. This view is from the component side of the board. Gray areas represent an X-ray view of the unetched foil. The etching pattern appears at the back of this book.

are several transceivers that are intended for use with a drop-in charger. A mating connector can be made from pieces of plastic and screws for the contacts. The challenge with the drop-in connector is to maintain contact when you transmit. Otherwise, the Power Charger cannot supply power directly to the transmitter, but can only recharge the battery when you set the transceiver back in the charger.

Another concern arises when you try to use one Power Charger with two transceivers. If the transceivers have a different number of cells in their battery packs, then the charging voltage must be different for each transceiver. It might be possible to build the Power Charger for the transceiver with the greater number of cells, and use an adapter containing two series silicon diodes for the other transceiver. The pair of diodes has a drop of approximately 1.4 V, which is similar to that of one charged NiCd cell. A compromise adjustment of the output voltage would then allow use of the Power Charger with either transceiver.

Adjustment

There are two variable resistors to adjust for proper operation of the Power Charger. Make sure the input voltage is high enough that the LOW INPUT VOLTAGE LED remains off while these adjustments are being performed. The initial adjustment procedure is based on voltage measurements. The

final adjustment procedure measures the specific charging current.

For the initial adjustment, turn R2 fully counterclockwise and R3 fully clockwise. Connect the Power Charger input to a convenient dc supply and the output to a dc voltmeter. Both the ON LED and the CHARGING LED should be lit. Adjust R2 for 11.2 volts (1.4 volts per cell). If your transceiver has an internal diode, increase the voltage by 0.7 volt to compensate for the voltage drop in the diode. If you are unsure about the accuracy of your voltmeter it is advisable to adjust R2 for a voltage reading that is a little on the low side. Next, slowly turn R3 counterclockwise. The CHARGING LED should become dim and go out. Adjust R3 to the point where the CHARGING LED is so dim you can barely see it. Then turn R3 a quarter turn counterclockwise. The output should increase by about 1 volt as R3 is adjusted.

The final adjustment takes care of small errors in setting the voltage, and adjusts the Power Charger to compensate for a diode or other components that may be between the transceiver charging connector and the battery.

Next, connect a milliammeter in place of the circuit board jumper between the CHARGING LED and R1. This is the best place to measure the charging current accurately. If, instead, the meter were connected directly to the output of the Power Charger, it is likely that the voltage drop

caused by the internal resistance of the meter would adversely affect the adjustment. A meter connected in place of the jumper will measure the current drawn by Q5, Q6, Q7 and the associated parts. This current, which is about 10 mA, can be measured when the Power Charger output is disconnected. When the battery is connected the true charging current can be found by subtracting the transistor current from the meter reading.

It may be tempting to measure the Power Charger input current instead, but an ammeter connected at the input would read the current drawn by the ON LED, the CHARGING LED and the base of Q1. This current could be from 20 to 100 mA, thus making an accurate determination of the charging current impossible.

Now, with the ammeter connected and the Power Charger turned on, it is time for the big moment. Connect the transceiver containing the charged NiCd battery to the Power Charger. The initial current surge may be 100 mA or more, but the current should fall quickly to less than 45 mA, which is the trickle-charge rate. Adjust R2 for a charging current between 20 and 30 mA. Adjust R3 until the CHARGING LED is so dim you can barely see it. Some interaction between these adjustments is normal, so you will probably have to repeat them several times until the current and the brightness of the CHARGING LED are correct.

Since continued charging will cause the current to decrease slowly with time, the adjustments should be completed within a minute or two of connecting the battery. If this can't be done disconnect the transceiver for a few minutes to allow the battery to recover, then try again. If you plan to use your Power Charger with more than one battery, a compromise adjustment of R2 may be necessary to compensate for construction differences in the batteries.

If you encounter difficulty with this adjustment you may have a bad component or a wiring error. Power resistors in values from 10 to 200 Ω may be used as loads to verify that your Power Charger has an output similar to that shown in Fig. 53.

Sam Bases, K2IUV, offered these additional thoughts on calibration of the Power Charger in Technical Correspondence in September 1983 QST.

Calibration of the output voltage is extremely critical, and most inexpensive VOMs are definitely not accurate enough to do the job. Furthermore, typical milliammeters have a relatively high series resistance and will affect the charge current when removed from the circuit. Here's why: To charge the battery to 100% of capacity, the individual cell voltage must reach a minimum of 1.42 V at a charge rate of 0.1C, or 11.36 V for an 8-cell battery without an internal diode. A set point of 11.20 V, or 1.40 V per cell (as suggested), will result in only 15-37% of full charge. I experienced an apparent loss of battery capacity, which was actually due to insufficient charge current at 11.20 V. Similarly, voltmeter errors as little as 0.16 V or milliammeter-induced voltage drops of the same amount will result in failure to charge the battery properly.

The charge rate must taper to the normal charge rate of 0.05C to 0.1C at 1.42 to 1.44 V per cell, or 22.5 to 45 mA for a 450-mAh battery. This charge rate may be left on indefinitely. A charge rate of 0.02C is a trickle charge, and it is used only to maintain a battery that previously has been fully charged. The power charger should not taper below 0.05C, or the battery will never reach 100% capacity; 0.1C is a better minimum value.

You may wish to calibrate the charger with a digital voltmeter as follows:

1) Using the slow-rate "wall charger," give your battery a 16-hour charge.

2) Connect the battery to the power charger for at least one-half hour. Monitor the current with a meter having a resistance of less than 0.2 Ω. You may use a current-sampling resistor of 0.1 Ω in series with the charger, and measure the voltage drop across it with a *good* DVM. For example, a reading of 0.0045 V indicates a charging current of 45 mA. (This measurement is usually beyond the means of anything but laboratory-grade instruments.)

3) If a laboratory-grade DVM is not available, connect the charger directly to the battery, without any series resistor or ammeter, using the leads intended to be permanent. Measure the battery voltage with a DVM or laboratory-grade analog meter. Adjust R2 for a battery voltage of 1.42-1.44 V per cell, adding 0.7 V if your battery pack has an internal diode. Adjust R3 so the yellow LED barely glows, then readjust R2 (because of interaction). Alternatively, measure the voltage across R1 and adjust R2 and R3 to give a reading corresponding to 0.05C-0.1C. V = R1 × 0.1C, so for a 450-mAh, 8-cell battery, V = 1.0 × 0.045 A = 0.045 V.

As a final thought, I strongly suggest the use of a multifingered or other effective heat sink and thermally conductive grease together on Q1. Without them, excessive temperatures and thermal cycling will eventually damage the transistor, possibly damaging your battery from overcharge.

Operation

Operation of the Power Charger is simple. Connect it to a convenient power source between 12 and 30 V dc. If the polarity is correct, the ON LED will light. If the voltage is high enough, the LOW INPUT VOLTAGE LED will be off. Connect the transceiver and the CHARGING LED will come on. When charging is complete the CHARGING LED will go out. Disconnect the Power Charger first from the transceiver and then from the power source. Fig. 57 shows a suggested supply if you don't have a suitable ac power supply. It has some ac ripple, but that is no problem since the charger acts as an electronic voltage regulator.

If a supply of 20 V or more is used to power the charger, an external 10- or 20-Ω power resistor should be used to reduce the power dissipation in Q1. The value of R4 should also be increased to keep the current through the ON LED below 20 mA.

The Power Charger can be used to charge the battery or to maintain the charge in the battery while the transceiver is being used. It is recommended that the latter mode of operation not be used on an exclusive basis, however. If the NiCd batteries are not allowed to cycle occasionally between a fully discharged and fully charged condition, they will suffer a temporary reduction in capacity. Although it is not necessary, a good procedure is to let the battery run down before connecting the Power Charger. This will maintain maximum battery capacity.

The last consideration is temperature. NiCd batteries are not designed for wide temperature extremes. With the exception of some special cells, most NiCds vent if they are allowed to exceed 45 °C (113 °F). Especially avoid leaving them in a closed car on a sunny day. Also, at low temperatures the chemical activity in the battery slows down. NiCds can be used below freezing, but the capacity is reduced. For these reasons, charging of any type should be minimized when the battery is very warm or very cold.

A Controlled Battery Charger for Emergency Power Supplies

It's essential to use proper charging methods to maintain emergency battery power supplies in a ready-to-be-used condition. It's possible to keep a lead-acid battery continuously connected to a charger — provided the charger incorporates features to prevent the battery from overcharge! This project, presented by Dick Jansson, WD4FAB, describes the design and construction of a battery charger that may be left connected to a lead-acid battery at all times, whether in storage or at an emergency site. The battery is kept fully charged and ready for use if commercial power fails. Figs. 59 through 63 accompany this project. A number of these chargers have been built by the Orange County, FL, ARES group.

The Circuit

Today's commonly available voltage-regulator ICs make the construction of a

Fig. 59 — The controlled battery charger can be built in several configurations. Size depends on the intended application.

Table 1
Limiting Resistors for Controlled Battery Charger

Current Limit (mA)	R2 Value (Ohms)
1000	0.62
280	2.2
100	6.2
26	24.0

Voltage Limit (V)	R3 Value (Ohms)
10.5	3.40 k
11.9	4.75 k
13.8	6.80 k

Fig. 60 — Schematic diagram of the controlled battery charger. Radio Shack part numbers are given in parentheses.

C1 — Electrolytic capacitor, 470 μF, 35 V (272-1018).
C2 — Ceramic disc capacitor, 100 pF (272-123).
C3 — Ceramic disc capacitor, 0.001 μF (272-126).
D1 — Silicon diode, 50 PIV, 3 A (1N5400 or equiv. 276-1141).
F1 — Fuse, 125 V, 2 A (270-1275) in a chassis-mount holder (270-307).
Q1 — Power transistor, NPN, 40 W, TO-220 case (TIP31 or equiv. 276-2017).

R1 — Resistor, 1.8 kΩ, ¼ W (271-1324).
R2 — Resistor, ½ or 1 W. See text and Table 1.
R3 — Resistor, ¼ W, 1%. See text and Table 1.
R4 — Resistor, 7.15 kΩ, ¼ W, 1%. See text.
T1 — Filament transformer. Primary, 117 V; secondary 12.6 V at 300 mA or 1.2 A. See text. (273-1505 or 273-1385).
U1 — Bridge rectifier, 50 PIV, 3 A (276-1151).
U2 — Regulator IC, type 723 (276-1740).

Fig. 61 — Parts-placement guide for the controlled battery charger. A full-size etching pattern appears at the back of this book.

sophisticated charger relatively easy. Fig. 60 is a schematic diagram of the charger. The unit is constructed from parts available from Radio Shack, except for the precision resistors needed to set the values for voltage limiting (R3 and R4). Several values for voltage- and current-limiting resistors are given in Table 1. The builder may customize the charger for a specific need based on the information given. For example, a builder may wish to build one charger for lead-acid batteries and another to provide controlled charging for a NiCd battery pack.

The charger has two possible inputs. For operation from 117-V ac, T1 provides 12.6-V ac to U1, a full-wave bridge rectifier, and filter C1. Filtered output is approximately 18-V dc. The charger may also

be powered from a 12- to 16-V dc source connected to the DC INPUT terminals. This feature is especially handy for charging a NiCd battery pack from a car battery. U2, a 723-type (LM723, μA723, MC1723CP and so on) voltage-regulator IC, regulates the dc and controls voltage and current limits. If the battery voltage falls below the voltage limit set by the ratio of R3 and R4, the charger provides a constant-current output whose value is set by R2. When the battery charges to the voltage limit, the current "folds over" to hold that voltage limit. U2 can safely provide currents up to 100 mA. For applications requiring more current, up to 1 A, pass transistor Q1 is needed. If you do not use Q1, connect pins 2 and 10 of U2. Higher-current applications can be adapted by using a properly sized

transformer and an appropriate pass transistor with an adequate heat sink.

Construction

Although this simple circuit does not require a PC board, one was designed to simplify construction of a number of these chargers for the local ARES group. Fig. 61 is a parts-placement guide; a full-size etching pattern appears at the back of this book. Two versions of the finished unit are shown in Fig. 62. Both are built into small aluminum boxes purchased at Radio Shack. One unit was built with a 1.2-A transformer and is used for charging lead-acid batteries. Q1 is used here, and the tab is thermally connected to the box with insulating hardware. Q1 gets only comfortably warm, so no other heat sink is necessary.

The other charger uses two of the regulator boards to charge two different sizes of NiCd battery packs for hand-held transceivers. A 300-mA transformer is used for this application, and only one rectifier/filter (located on the lower PC board) is needed for both regulated outputs. Q1 is not used here, so a wire jumper is used to connect the PC board pads normally connected to the Q1 base and emitter. Insert the jumper between U2, pin 2 and U2, pin 10.

Adjustment

The most critical value to be adjusted is the output limiting voltage. With no battery load connected, turn on the charger and measure the open-circuit voltage with an accurate voltmeter. If possible, use a digital voltmeter with 0.1% accuracy. If the voltage is not exactly what you need, you will have to experiment with the value of R3. Major voltage adjustments should be made by changing the value of this resistor. Minor output voltage trimming may be accomplished by shunting R3 with a high-ohmage carbon resistor to lower the voltage, or by shunting R4 to raise the voltage.

For a six-cell lead-acid battery, set the voltage to approximately 13.75 V. This value was chosen to hold electrolyte vaporization to an acceptable level. Voltage limits for NiCd battery packs are nominally set to 1.43 V per cell. Some commercially

Fig. 63 — The controlled battery charger, attached to a deep-discharge lead-acid battery in a waterproof enclosure, is ready to be transported to an emergency site.

Fig. 62 — Two versions of the controlled battery charger. The unit at the left is designed to charge a lead-acid storage battery. The one at the right is designed to charge two different low-current NiCd packs. See text for a complete explanation.

made packs have built-in protective series diodes, so 0.7 V must be added to the total battery voltage to compensate for the drop across the diode.

About Batteries

The best type of battery for long-term emergency use is the deep-cycle lead-acid battery. Designed to power electrical fishing boat motors and accessories in recreational vehicles, these batteries are designed to be discharged over a long period at a steady rate. Normal automotive batteries are designed to discharge partially at a very high rate (to start the car), and then be recharged promptly while the alternator is also carrying the load.

Fig. 63 shows a Sears no. 9601 deep-discharge battery in its companion waterproof case. The charger is housed in the box attached to the case. In an emergency, the entire 25-pound assembly can be picked up by the handle and taken to the field complete with charger. This setup gives reliable service at a moment's notice.

Emergency Gelled-Electrolyte Battery Pack

Since loss of commercial power is often encountered in an emergency, it's a good idea to have a fully charged prime power source on hand. The battery pack and charger described here is designed to operate a 10-W (output) transceiver for 8 hours, 80% of which is standby, 10% receiving and 10% transmitting. This project, shown in Figs. 64 through 68, was designed and built by Warren Dion, N1BBH.

Calculations indicate that a 2 ampere-hour (Ah) battery should be adequate. A battery with twice that capacity was selected, however for the following reasons:

1) Published ampere-hour ratings are based on a steady 20-hour drain. Occasional high-current bursts required for transmitting lower capacity.

2) A battery left on FLOAT (see below) will not be charged to full capacity.

3) Some 12-V gear won't work well at the battery manufacturer's 10.5 end-voltage.

4) Aging reduces battery capacity.

Accordingly, the following project uses

Fig. 64 — Both the battery pack and companion charger are built in identical, compact enclosures.

a 4-Ah battery. While larger batteries may be substituted, smaller ones are not recommended.

Lead-acid batteries with a gelled electrolyte were selected for this project. These batteries may be left on a trickle charge for extended periods without damage, and they may be deep-discharged if necessary. The gelled electrolyte helps the user avoid leaking liquids and escaping gas normally associated with liquid-electrolyte lead-acid batteries. In addition, these cells may be operated in any position without the worry of leakage through vent holes.

The Battery Pack

The battery pack, shown in Fig. 65, is little more than two batteries in a case. A few notes apply, however. The batteries are held together with two cable ties connected end to end to provide enough length. Blocks of wood (or any smooth material) locate the batteries and keep them away from protruding screws, cables, fuse holder, etc. The blocks are braced against the sides of the case and glued to keep them from shifting. Do not expect the glue alone to keep the blocks in place. These batteries fit the selected case closely, so that its cover clamps them securely.

Lead-acid batteries easily produce currents of insulation-melting proportions. The 5-A fuse will limit damage caused by a dead short. The connector, an Anderson Power Products 1300 series, is one chosen

Fig. 65 — Interior of the battery pack. Care is taken to secure the batteries to keep them from moving.

for its performance and versatility. Being hermaphroditic and polarized, the same connector is used on both the battery and charger cables.

The Charger

The charger is a "bulletproof" design offering the following features:

1) Voltage limiting to prevent overcharging.
2) Current limiting to protect batteries that are heavily discharged.
3) A worst-case current limit of 1.5 A.
4) A thermal limit to protect the regulator.
5) FULL and FLOAT charging options.
6) Isolation from the power line.

A battery in any state of charge may be connected and left on charge without risk of damage to the charger or battery. With the FULL-FLOAT switch on float, the battery may be left on charge indefinitely, trading off a little capacity for this convenience. The LED turns on to indicate that the battery is fully charged.

The Circuit

The charger schematic diagram is shown in Fig. 66. Most components are available from Radio Shack. Since the final charging voltage must be held to within 0.1 volt, and precision components are impractical, 5% tolerances are prescribed throughout. The two trimmer potentiometers, R4 and R8, provide sufficient range to set the charging voltage and indicator light precisely.

Regulator U1 is the key component, maintaining the final charging voltage, and

in cooperation with Q1, limiting the charging current. The output voltage is approximately $1.25 \times (R7 + R8)/R6$. R9 is in series with the charging current. When this current reaches about 0.6 A, the voltage across R9 is sufficient to forward bias the base-emitter junction of Q1, which conducts, shunting the R7 + R8 combination. This pulls down the output voltage to a value that will just maintain a 0.6-A charging current.

The *absolute maximum* charging current is ¼ the rated ampere-hours, in this case 1.0 A. The recommended charging current is 0.15 to 0.20 times the Ah rating, 0.6 to 0.8 A in this case. If a faster charging rate is desired, or a larger battery is used, the charging rate can best be adjusted by shunting R9. Refer to the following table:

R9A	Current Limit
None	0.6 A
6.2-6.8	0.7
3.0-3.3	0.8
2.0-2.2	0.9
1.0	1.2

Full vs. Float

When a "12-V" battery is fully charged, its terminal voltage reaches 14.4, while accepting a low maintenance current from the charger. Long periods in this state will damage the battery. Therefore, if the battery is to be left on charge for extended periods, the voltage must be reduced by about 0.1 V per cell. In a "12-V" battery this figures out to 13.8 V, which is, conveniently, 0.6 V lower than full charge. A

Fig. 66 — Schematic diagram of the battery pack and charger. All resistors are ¼ W, 5% tolerance, unless noted. Parts numbers given in parentheses are Radio Shack catalog numbers.

BT1, BT2 — Gelled-electrolyte, lead-acid battery, 6 V, 4 Ah (Yuasa NP4-6 or equiv. Available from Glynn Electronics, Box 800, Middleboro, MA 02346).
C1 — Electrolytic capacitor, 470 μF, 35 V (272-1030).
D1 — Silicon rectifier, 50 PIV, 3 A (276-1141).
D2 — Zener diode, 5.1 V, 1 W, 5% tolerance (276-565).
D3 — Red LED (276-062).

F1 — Fuse, 0.5 A, 250 V (270-1271).
F2 — Fuse, 5 A, 250 V (270-1278).
Q1 — Transistor, NPN, 2N2222 (276-1617).
R4 — Trimmer potentiometer, 100 kΩ. PC-board mount (271-220).
R8 — Trimmer potentiometer, 500 Ω, PC-board mount (271-226).
R9 — Resistor, 1 ohm, 2 to 5 W.
R9A — Optional resistor, see text.
S1 — Slide switch, SPST (275-401).

T1 — Transformer; primary 117 V, secondary 18 V, 1.2 A (modified Radio Shack 273-1480, see text; or Radio Shack 273-1515, with 18-V secondary).
U1 — Adjustable three-terminal regulator, LM317T (276-1778).
U2 — Quad op amp, LM3900 (276-1713).
U3 — Full-wave bridge rectifier, 100 PIV, 4 A (276-1171).

Fig. 67 — Interior view of the battery charger. Although perforated board is used in this version, a PC-board layout is shown in Fig. 68.

silicon-junction rectifier in series with the output supplies the needed drop, and requires only one adjustment for both the voltage limit and indicator light settings.

Charger Indicator

Full charge is signaled by the state of two variables, namely, terminal voltage and end-of-charge current. The current is affected by battery condition and temperature; therefore, terminal voltage is the chosen indicator. The LM3900 op amp (U2) used in this portion of the circuit is a current-sensitive device. The voltage from any forward-biased pin to common is an almost constant 0.6 V. For this application Zener D2 provides a reference voltage. The current through R2 $[(5.1 - 0.6)/100,000$

$= 45~\mu A]$ is fed to pin 3. When this exceeds the current into pin 2, U2 output is pulled down and D3 is not lit. When the charger output voltage reaches 14.4, trimmer R4 is adjusted so that the current into pin 2 is slightly greater than $45~\mu A$. At this point U2 toggles, and the light turns on. R11 provides positive feedback to sharpen the switching point.

Construction Notes

Construction of the charger, shown in Fig. 67, is conventional, and parts location not critical. Perforated board construction obviates the need for a printed circuit, but the layout is directly transferable to a one-sided etched board. For builders wishing to use a PC board, a full-size etching pattern may be found at the back of this book. Parts placement is shown in Fig. 68. It is best to socket the LM3900. The LM317T requires a heat sink. In this design it is screwed to the cabinet using a mica washer insulator. Radio Shack 3 × 5 × 5-7/8-in cabinets (No. 270-253) are used for both battery pack and charger.

Reworking T1

Transformers with 18-V secondaries are not as easy to find as the popular 12.6 and 25.2 styles. The 12.6-V types will not supply enough voltage to bias the regulator properly, and will cause the regulator to overheat. A secondary value of 16-18 V RMS is ideal. This can be obtained by pruning the secondary of the recommended 25.2-V transformer, if a suitable 18-V transformer is not available.

Place the transformer on its back and pry up the four tabs that lock the "U" frame mounting strap. Pull the legs of the frame apart and lift out the core with its windings.

The core is built up of laminations shaped as letters E and I. Run a thin-bladed

knife between one of the outside I laminations and the stack. Remove the lamination and save it. Next run the knife between the abutting E lamination and the stack, especially where it passes through the coil window. Next, place the stack on the edge of the bench with the legs of the E facing upward and the loosened lamination just clear of the edge. Place a screwdriver blade against the center leg of the E, and tap gently on the handle until the lamination slides free. Carefully pull the lamination out of the stack.

In the same manner, remove the rest of the laminations and save them. Bent laminations can be straightened by placing them on a smooth, flat surface and *tapping* gently with a hammer.

Next, unwind the plastic insulating tapes and save them. Find the outside turn of the secondary and remove it from its solder lug. Unwind *55 turns*. Cut off the excess wire, clean the end and resolder it to its lug. Replace the tapes.

Reassemble the core alternating E laminations end-for-end, and interleaving the I laminations. It will be necessary to squeeze the stack a little to get the last lamination into the coil window. Place the stack on a flat surface and tap the edges of the stack with a hammer, turning so that all four sides are tapped. This will make the stack square and even.

Wrap the mounting strap back around the core and clamp the legs tightly against the sides. Bend in the four lugs, and hammer them down well. Connect the primary to 117 V, 60 Hz and measure the secondary voltage. It should be between 16 and 20 V RMS.

Initial Tests and Adjustments

Before connecting the battery, do the following:
1) Check the circuit for correctness.
2) Connect a 1000-ohm resistor across the output.
3) Turn trimmer R8 until the output voltage is exactly 14.4.
4) Turn trimmer R4 until the light turns off and then back R4 off until the light just comes back on.
5) Repeat 3 and 4, above.
Most moving-pointer (D'Arsonval) meters are not accurate enough for these adjustments. Use a digital meter in good condition with at least 2½ (preferably 3½) digits.

To Charge a Battery

Plug the battery pack into the charger and the charger into the power line. The charging light should be on. Select FULL or FLOAT, as required. If fully discharged, a recharge should take 6 to 8 hours. If partially discharged, it will take about the same number of hours that the battery has been in service since its last charge. When the light turns on, disconnect the battery. If the battery is to be left on charge, be sure it is switched to FLOAT.

Fig. 68 — Parts-placement guide for the emergency battery pack. A full-size etching pattern is given at the back of this book.

A 2000-Volt Power Supply

The power supply shown in Figs. 69 through 72 is capable of supplying 2000 volts at 1 ampere in conservative operation. Many ceramic tubes, such as the 8874, 3CX800A7 and 4CX250 family, require 2-kV plate supplies. This project is intended to illustrate various design techniques used in high-voltage (HV) supplies. Although all of the parts used here are readily available from commercial suppliers, sufficient information is presented for a builder to adapt the project to suit individual needs and to incorporate components on hand. This power supply was designed and built in the ARRL lab by Mark Wilson, AA2Z.

Circuit Details

The heart of this supply, shown schematically in Fig. 70, is an Avatar Magnetics AV-415 transformer. Although the AV-415 has a dual primary, use of 234 V is essential to good regulation. The secondary has taps for 1375, 1515 and 1650 V to allow the builder to optimize the output voltage for the filter capacitor used. A full-value secondary was chosen, rather than a lower voltage secondary and voltage-doubler circuit, to aid voltage regulation. The transformer is rated for 1.2 A, continuous duty.

Fig. 69 — The completed 2000-V, 1-A power supply.

This supply is intended to be placed away from the operating position in an inconspicuous spot, perhaps under the operating table, so it may be activated remotely by J1. If J1 is jumpered, the supply may be activated by S1. When S1 and J1 are both closed, the coil of K1 is energized, closing the contacts and applying primary power. R1 and R2 in the primary feed to T1 provide inrush current protection. At turn-on, the filter capacitors are discharged and look like a dead short. The

Fig. 70 — Schematic diagram of the 2-kV, 1-A supply.

C2-C7 — Electrolytic capacitor, 240 μF, 450 V (Mallory CG241T450V4C or equiv.).
F1 — High-voltage fuse, 5 kV, 2 A (Buss HVJ2).
J1 — Two-conductor socket (Cinch S-402-AB or equiv.).
J2,J3 — Chassis-mount female MHV

connector (Amphenol 27000).
K1 — Relay, DPDT, 240-V ac coil, 240-V, 25-A contacts (Potter and Brumfield PRD11AYO-240V or equiv.).
K2 — Relay, DPDT, 24-V dc coil, 240-V, 25-A contacts (Potter and Brumfield PRD11DYO-24V or equiv.).

S1 — Switch, SPST, 240-V.
T1 — Power transformer; primary 117/234 V, secondary 1650-V,1.2-A Continuous Commercial Service (CCS) (Avatar Magnetics AV-415 or equiv. Available from Avatar Magnetics

Fig. 71 — The primary components of the 2-kV supply are mounted on the rear panel.

ALL CAPACITORS
0.01 μF, 1 kV

ALL RESISTORS
390 kΩ, 1 W

ALL DIODES
1 kV, 3-A

Fig. 72 — Parts placement for the rectifier board. The full-size etching pattern appears at the back of this book.

charging current surge is high enough that the rectifier diodes may rupture, so R1 and R2 are necessary to limit the inrush current to a safe value. After a 0.6-second time delay (determined by C1 and R3), K2 closes and shorts out R1 and R2. Full primary power is now available. K1 and K2 both have high-current contacts.

A full-wave bridge rectifier follows the transformer. The bridge is made from a number of individual diodes with a 1000-PIV rating. Each diode is shunted with a 0.01-μF capacitor to suppress transient voltage spikes and a 390-kΩ equalizing resistor. Although three of the 1000-PIV diodes would allow an ample safety margin for a 2-kV supply, the limiting factor is the 500-V breakdown rating of 1-W metal film resistors. Using five diode/capacitor/resistor sets in each leg of the bridge presents 400 V to each resistor.

Filtering is accomplished with a string of six 240-μF, 450-V capacitors connected in series. The nominal rating of this string is 40 μF at 2.7 kV. This value of capacitance was chosen to keep the ripple under 3% and was calculated using the formula

$$C = \frac{1}{2\sqrt{3}\ f_r\ R_L\ (\text{Ripple Factor})}$$

where

C = capacitance in farads
f_r = ripple frequency in hertz
R_L = load resistance in ohms

In this application, F_r = 120 (full-wave rectification), R_L = 2000 (2000 V divided by 1 A) and the ripple factor = 0.03 (3%). Plugging these values into the equation yields 40.1 μF for the target value. The 240-μF capacitors (6 in series = 40 μF total) were the closest readily available value. The total 2.7-kV rating includes a safety margin.

A 40-kΩ, 11-W resistor shunts each filter capacitor. The actual value of electrolytic capacitors may vary as much as ±20% of the rated value, so these resistors are necessary to equalize the voltage across each capacitor in the string. The shunt resistance should be about 100 ohms per volt of supply output. In this case, 2000 V × 100 Ω/V = 200,000 ohms total. Six resistors are used, so each should be 200,000 divided by 6, or 33.3 kΩ each. The closest readily available value, 40 kΩ, was selected. The power rating of each resistor is determined from Ohm's Law (E^2 divided by R). In this case, E = 333 (2000 V divided by 6 resistors), and R = 40 kΩ, resulting in a power requirement of 2.8 W. The 11-W resistors chosen give an adequate safety margin. The equalizing resistors also form the bleeder.

Two protective devices follow the filter. F1 is a special 5-kV, 2-A fuse made by Buss. This fuse is 5 inches long and has a ceramic body. It will open if sustained excess current is drawn. R4 is a current-limiting resistor used to protect the power supply and amplifier in case of a high-voltage arc. R5 keeps the negative lead a few ohms above ground for current-metering purposes in the amplifier.

Construction

The final weight of this supply is about 60 pounds, so construction on an ordinary lightweight aluminum chassis is less than optimum. To avoid chassis-flexing problems, a framework was constructed from aluminum angle stock. Top and side panels then bolt to the framework. The bottom panel is made from 1/8-in-thick aluminum, adding to the rigidity of the structure. The power supply measures 9 × 8½ × 20 inches (HWD). The framework is easily fabricated with hand tools, and the angle stock is available from most hardware stores. The side and top panels may be cut and filed by hand, but many sheet metal suppliers will shear panels to the correct size for little or no additional cost.

All of the primary circuitry, including K1, K2, J1, S1, R1-R3 and C1 are all mounted on the rear panel (Fig. 71). Liberal use of solder lugs adds to a neat appearance. All primary wiring was done with no. 12 wire.

The bridge rectifier diodes and associated components are mounted on a glass-epoxy circuit board. The diodes and resistors are mounted slightly above the board to allow airflow to all sides for cooling. The PC board is mounted vertically on ceramic standoff insulators. Parts placement for the rectifier board is shown in Fig. 72, and a full-size etching pattern may be found at the back of this book.

Filter capacitors and equalizing resistors are mounted on a sandwich made from acrylic sheet. In addition to securing the capacitors, the acrylic provides additional insulation between the capacitors and chassis. Copper straps interconnect the capacitors, and the 40-kΩ resistors are mounted far enough above the capacitors to allow adequate airflow for cooling.

F1 and R4 are mounted on ceramic standoffs bolted to the front panel. Amphenol MHV high-voltage receptacles, similar to BNC connectors but designed for use up to 5 kV at 5 A, are used for the output. No. 18 test lead wire with insulation rated to 5 kV is used for all secondary wiring.

Care in mounting and wiring the components in a high-voltage supply is essential for safety. Any components and connections carrying high voltage should be kept well away from the chassis to avoid accidental arcs. High-voltage supplies should be fully enclosed to prevent accidental contact. Safety and common sense are the watchwords — *HV is lethal*!

A 3500-Volt Power Supply

The high-voltage power supply shown in Figs. 73 through 75 will loaf along during legal-power-limit operation. Capable of powering amplifiers employing such tubes as the 3-1000Z, 3CX1200A7, 4CX1000, and 8877, this supply is rated for 3500 V at 1 A output. Mark Wilson, AA2Z, built this project in the ARRL lab.

Circuit Details

Fig. 73 is the schematic diagram of this supply. The transformer used here is manufactured by the Peter W. Dahl Co. It features a 220/240-V primary and a 2650-V secondary rated at 1.5 A Intermittent Commercial and Amateur Service (ICAS). The core material is hipersil, which represents a significant weight saving over conventional material. One of the design goals was good regulation under heavy loads, so a 117-V primary wasn't even considered. Similarly, use of a full-value secondary and bridge rectifier, rather than a voltage-doubler scheme, aids in good regulation. Of course, a center-tapped secondary (2650-0-2650 V) would work just as well.

This supply was built to power several amplifiers requiring different voltages, so a variable autotransformer is used on the primary. Supply output can be varied between 0 and approximately 4 kV.

High-voltage block-type rectifiers are used here, rather than strings of individual 1-kV devices. These rectifiers are rated at 14 kV at 1 A and have a 250-A surge-

Fig. 73 — Front view of the completed 3500-V power supply.

current rating. If a builder were to purchase new the individual diodes, resistors and capacitors necessary to make a bridge rectifier suitable for this power supply, the cost could easily exceed that of the block rectifiers. Additionally, these HV rectifiers are compact and much easier to replace should they fail.

The filter capacitor used here is a 25-μF, 4-kV oil-filled unit made by Condensor

Products Corp. This capacitor does not contain any of the carcinogenic chemical PCB, but many oil-filled capacitors available at flea markets do, so be wary if another capacitor is substituted. Oil-filled capacitors have some advantages over HV filter capacitors made from strings of individual electrolytics. Oil-filled capacitors are sealed and will not dry out after years of service. They may be used all the way

Fig. 74 — Schematic diagram of the 3500-V power supply.

C2 — Filter capacitor, 25 μF, 4 kV (Condenser Products KMOC 4M25ES-1 or equiv. Available from Condenser Products Corp., P.O. Box 997, Brooksville, FL 33512).

D1-D4 — Rectifier diode, 14 kV, 1A (K2AW HV14-1 or equiv. Available from K2AW's Silicon Alley, 175 Friends La., Westbury,

NY 11590).

F3 — High-voltage fuse, 5 kV, 2 A (Buss HVJ2 or equiv.).

J1,J2 — High-voltage connector (Millen 37001 or equiv.).

R7 — Multiplier resistor made from five 2-MΩ, 2-W resistors in series.

T1 — Variable autotransformer, 0-280 V, 10 A

(Superior Electric 236B Powerstat® or equiv.).

T2 — Power transformer; primary, 220/240 V, secondary 2650 V, 1.5-A ICAS (Dahl ARRL-001 or equiv. Available from Peter W. Dahl Co. See Chapter 35 parts-suppliers list.

Fig. 75 — Interior view of the 3500-V power supply.

they are mounted on a circuit board behind the meter.

Construction

This supply is built on a homemade chassis and cabinet measuring 9 × 17 × 14 inches (HWD). The bottom plate, which supports most of the components, is made from 0.125-inch-thick aluminum sheet. Aluminum angle brackets bolted to the bottom plate provide additional strength, as well as allow for attachment of the panels. The front and rear panels are made from 0.062-inch-thick aluminum sheet. The top and side panels are made from two pieces of aluminum sheet, each bent 90 degrees. The two top/side halves meet in the center where they are screwed to a bracket running between the front and rear panels. The entire chassis and cabinet could be made with hand tools, but a trip to the local aluminum supplier with a list of needed panel dimensions will probably yield the nicely sheared, square panels necessary for a professional-looking project.

As shown in Fig. 75, all components mount on the front and bottom panels. Even the line cord passes through the front panel, leaving the rear panel empty so the supply may be placed on the floor against a wall in the shack. The line cord and primary wiring are no. 12 wire. The transformer is securely bolted to the bottom plate by ¼-in bolts. The block rectifiers are mounted to the bottom panel with silicone heat-sink compound to aid in cooling.

F3 and R1-R6 all mount on a circuit board that is mounted on ceramic stand-offs above C2. Be sure that this board is mounted well-away from the chassis or other components.

All secondary wiring is done with no. 18 test lead wire with insulation rated at 5000 V. The output connectors, mounted on the front panel, are of the Millen 37001 type and are rated for 7000 V.

As with any project incorporating high voltage, lead dressing is important. High-voltage can bridge small air gaps, so care must be taken to keep component terminals and wires away from the chassis. Only wire with suitable insulation should be used, because HV will arc through insulation designed for lower voltages.

up to their maximum voltage ratings, and they often take up less space than a stack of electrolytics. Oil-filled capacitors are somewhat more expensive initially — in this case about 30% more than a comparable string of electrolytics; however, they do last a long time and are definitely worth considering.

R1-R4 act as a bleeder. Four 100-kΩ, 25-W units are used to minimize the voltage across any individual resistor. If one large resistor was used, arcing could occur between the turns of wire that make up the resistor.

Like the 2000-V supply, this circuit employs a high-voltage fuse and a series resistor in the HV output lead to protect against overcurrent and arcs. A homemade fuse can be made from a piece of no. 30 tinned wire suspended on ceramic stand-offs. The minus lead is kept a few ohms above ground for metering purposes in the companion amplifier.

A 0-5-kV meter is included. The basic movement is 0-500 μA, so a 10-MΩ shunt resistor is necessary. Be careful to mount the resistors away from the chassis. Here,

Chapter 28

Audio and Video Equipment

The story of radio begins with amateurs transmitting and receiving dots and dashes. Soon hams were communicating by voice. Amateurs were transmitting pictures 20 years before commercial TV came into being. Hams still communicate by Morse code, voice and TV. The techniques they use have changed and other modes have been added. All that communication activity has created a demand for a wide variety of electronic equipment. This chapter describes a number of projects for audio and video.

A Simple, High-Performance CW Filter

This inductor-capacitor CW filter uses one stack of the familiar 88-mH inductors and two 44-mH inductors in a five-resonator circuit that gives high performance at low cost. The center frequency is fixed at 750 Hz because most transceivers use this sidetone frequency, but sidetones between 700 and 800 Hz can be received with less than 1 dB attenuation relative to the center frequency. Ed Wetherhold, W3NQN, designed and built the filter presented here. The author can provide parts for this project at nominal cost. Write E. E. Wetherhold, W3NQN, 1426 Catlyn Place, Annapolis, MD 21401 for more information. If you need a design for a different center frequency, the author can provide that as well. Be sure to include a self-addressed, stamped 9½- × 4-inch envelope with your request.

One feature of this filter is a 3-dB bandwidth of 236 Hz. This bandwidth is narrow enough to give good selectivity, and yet broad enough for easy tuning with no ringing. Five high-Q resonator circuits provide good skirt selectivity that is equal to or better than most commercial active filters costing more than $80. In comparison, this CW filter can be built for less than $15. Simple construction, low cost and good performance make this filter an ideal first project for anyone interested in putting together a useful station accessory.

Design

Fig 1 shows the filter schematic diagram and component values. These values were selected for a center frequency of 750 Hz and for a filter impedance level of 230 ohms. The filter sees a 230-ohm source impedance consisting of the 200-ohm source (transformed from 8 ohms), a 22-ohm transformer winding resistance and an 8-ohm inductor resistance. In a similar way, the filter sees a load impedance of 230 ohms. This design was selected so that only one turn needs to be removed from both windings of a standard 44-mH inductor to give the required L2 and L4 values.

Construction

Fig 2 is a pictorial diagram showing the filter wiring. Note the 44-mH lead connection, as well as the connections between the capacitor leads, the 88-mH stack terminals and the 44-mH inductor leads. Fig 3 shows the finished filter installed in an aluminum box. Before beginning construction, obtain one 88-mH five-inductor stack with a mounting clip and two 44-mH inductors, and then follow steps 1 to 5.

1) Remove one turn from each of the two windings of one 44-mH inductor to get 43.5 mH (total turns removed is two). Carefully scrape off the film insulation and connect the start lead (with sleeve) of one

Fig 1—Schematic diagram of 750-Hz CW filter. Use 1% tolerance capacitors for best results.

C1, C5—0.512 µF capacitor.
C2, C4—1.036 µF capacitor.
C3—170.7 nF capacitor.
J1—Phone jack, or jack to match your headphones.
L1, L5—88-mH toroid (part of toroid stack, see text).

L2, L4—43.5 mH toroid (modified 44-mH toroid, see text).
L3—264-mH toroid (part of toroid stack, see text).
P1—Phone plug, or plug to match your receiver.

R1—Zero to 220-ohm, ½-W, 10% resistor (see text).
S1—DPDT switch.
T1, T2—8-ohm to 200-ohm impedance-matching transformer, 0.4-W.

Fig 2—Pictorial diagram showing L2 and L4 lead connection and wiring of inductor stack (L1, L3, L5).

Fig 3—The assembled filter is shown installed in a CR-800 aluminum box. The thru/bypass switch (S1) and input/output transformers (T1, T2) are at the left end of the box.

winding to the finish lead (no sleeve) of the adjacent winding to make the center tap as shown in Fig 2. Do the same for the second 44-mH inductor.

2) Fasten both of the 43.5-mH inductors to opposite ends of the 88-mH stack using clear silicone-rubber sealant, available from most hardware stores.

3) Position the 43.5-mH inductors so their leads can be easily connected to the rest of the circuit. Solder the capacitor leads to the stack terminals as shown in Fig 2.

4) Obtain a suitable box and make holes for the inductor mounting clip, the DPDT switch, and the phone jack and phone cord. First, install matching transformers T1 and T2 and the inductor stack with capacitors. Fasten the transformers (with leads pointing up) to the bottom of the box with silicone rubber sealant. Secure the stack to the bottom of the box with a 1-3/8-inch component mounting clip and two no. 6-32 × 5/16-inch screws. Instead of the 8 × 3 × 2¾-inch aluminum box shown in Fig 3 (Mouser Stock No. 537-CR-800), a small cardboard box may be used to minimize cost.

5) Complete the wiring of the transformers, the DPDT switch with resistor R1, and the phone jack and phone plug. Then check the correctness of your wiring by measuring and comparing the filter node-to-node resistances with the values listed in Table 1.

Installation

T1 and T2 match the filter to the receiver low-impedance audio output and to an 8-ohm headset or speaker. If your headset is high impedance, T2 may be omitted. In this case, connect a 10%, ½ W resistor from node 9 (C5 output lead) to ground. Choose the resistor value so the parallel combination of the headset and resistor gives the correct filter termination im-

Table 1
Node-to-Node Resistances for the CW Audio Filter

Nodes		Components	Resistance (ohms)
From	To		
1	GND	T1 hi-Z winding	12
2	GND	L1 and ½ L2	10
3	GND	L2	4
4	GND	½ L2	2
5	GND	L3 and ½ L4	26
6	GND	½ L4	2
7	GND	L4	4
8	GND	L5 and ½ L4	10
9	GND	T2 hi-Z winding	12
2	4	L1	8
5	6	L3	24
6	8	L5	8
2	3	L1 and ½ L2	10
8	7	L5 and ½ L4	10

Notes

1) See Figs 1 and 2 for the filter node locations.

2) Check your wiring using the resistance values in Table 1. If there is a significant difference between your measured values and the table values, you have a wiring error that must be corrected.

3) For accurate measurements, use a digital VOM or an analog VOM (such as a Triplett Model 630) that has a scale center of about 5 ohms on the ×1 ohmmeter range.

pedance (within 10 percent of 230 ohms).

Performance

The measured 30-dB and 3-dB bandwidths are about 511 and 235 Hz, respectively, and the 30-dB/3-dB shape factor is 2.17. This factor can be used to compare the performance of this filter with others. The measured insertion loss at 750 Hz is less than 3 dB and is typical of passive filters of this type. This small loss is compensated by slightly increasing the receiver audio gain. R1 helps to maintain a constant audio level when the filter is switched out of the circuit. The correct value of R1 for your audio system should be determined by experiment. Start with a short circuit for R1 and then gradually increase the resistance until the audio level

appears to be the same with the filter in or out of the circuit.

More than 700 hams have constructed this five-resonator filter (using either the 2-stack or the newer 1-stack arrangement) and many have commented on its excellent performance and lack of hiss and ringing.

References

Wetherhold, "Modern Design of a CW Filter using 88- and 44-mH Surplus Inductors," *QST*, Dec. 1980 and Feedback, *QST*, Jan. 1981, p. 43.

Wetherhold, "High Performance CW Filter," *Ham Radio*, Apr 1981.

Radio Handbook, 23rd edition, W. Orr, ed., Howard W. Sams & Co, 1987 (1-Stack CW Filter), p. 13-4.

A Passive Audio Filter for SSB

While audio filters are most often used during CW reception, the SSB operator can also benefit from their use. Shown in Figs 4 and 5 is a passive band-pass filter designed by Ed Wetherhold, W3NQN, for phone operation. This filter was described in Dec. 1979 *QST*. W3NQN can provide parts for the filter at nominal cost. Write for more information and prices. (Please include an SASE.) His address appears on page 28-1.

All of the inductors are the surplus 88-mH toroidal type with their windings wired either in series or parallel to get the required 88 or 22 mH of inductance. The series connection is shown in Fig 2. The 0.319-μF capacitors were selected from several 0.33-μF capacitors that were about 3 percent on the low side. The 0.638-μF value was obtained with a single 0.68-μF capacitor that was about 6 percent on the low side. The 1.276-μF values were obtained by paralleling selected 1-μF and 0.33-μF capacitors.

Fig 5 shows the measured and calculated attenuation responses of the filter. The difference between the measured and calculated responses at the low frequency side of the passband is probably caused by the much lower Q of the inductors at these frequencies.

The necessary termination resistance of this filter is 206 ohms. While this is not a standard value, it should not be too difficult for most amateurs to accommodate. If low-impedance headphones are used, a matching transformer can be used to provide the correct termination. A suitable transformer is available from Mouser Electronics (see Chapter 35 parts-suppliers list). The part number is 42TU200, and it is a 200-ohm CT to 8-ohm CT unit.

Fig 4—Schematic diagram of the SSB band-pass filter (A). Shown in B is a pictorial wiring diagram of the terminal board on the inductor stack.

Fig 5—Response curves of the SSB band-pass filter.

RC Active Audio Filters

The active audio filter is more popular than the passive type shown in Figs 1 and 4. The primary advantages of active filters are (1) unity gain or greater (passive filters have some insertion loss), and (2) that they are more compact than LC filters. Another advantage of RC active filters is that they can be made with variable Q and variable center or cutoff frequencies. These two features can be controlled at the front panel of the receiver by means of potentiometers.

Most RC active filters are designed for a gain of 1 to 5. A recommended gain is 2 for most amateur applications. The more filter sections placed in cascade, the better the skirt selectivity. The maximum number of usable RC filter sections is typically four. The minimum acceptable number is two for CW work, but a single-section RC active filter is often suitable for SSB reception in simple receivers. As the Q and number of filter sections increases there is a strong tendency toward "ringing." This appears in the speaker or earphones as a howling sound, which can be most unpleasant to hear. The

same is true of passive audio filters that have extremely high loaded-Q values.

Op amp ICs are used as the active devices in most RC active filters. The 741, LM301 and 747 ICs are suggested for that applica-tion. However, discrete devices can be used with equal success if the builder so desires. Fig 6 shows one section of an active filter that uses transistors. Q1 serves as a source-follower at the input and Q2 is one section

Fig 6—Circuit example of one pole section of an RC active audio filter that uses discrete active devices, Q1 and Q2.

LOW-PASS FILTER

$$C_1 \leq \frac{[a^2 + 4b(K - 1)]C_2}{4b}$$

$$R_1 = \frac{2}{[aC_2 + \sqrt{[a^2 + 4b(K - 1)]C_2{}^2 - 4bC_1C_2}]\omega_c}$$

$$R_2 = \frac{1}{bC_1C_2R_1\omega_c{}^2}$$

$$R_3 = \frac{K(R_1 + R_2)}{K - 1} \quad (K > 1)$$

$$R_4 = K(R_1 + R_2)$$

where

K = gain
f_c = −3 dB cutoff point
$\omega_c = 2\pi f_c$
$a = 0.765367$ (see text)
$b = 1$
C_2 = a standard value near $10 / f_c$ μF

Note: For unity gain, short R4 and omit R3.

Example:

$K = 2$
$f = 4000$ Hz
$\omega_c = 25,132.74$
$C_2 \approx 0.0025$ μF
$C_1 \leq 0.003$ μF
$R_1 = 19,254 \ \Omega$ (use 20 kΩ)
$R_2 = 11,278 \ \Omega$ (use 11 kΩ)
$R_3 = 61,066 \ \Omega$ (use 62 kΩ)
$R_4 = 61,066 \ \Omega$ (use 62 kΩ)

HIGH-PASS FILTER

$$R_1 = \frac{4b}{[a + \sqrt{a^2 + 8b(K - 1)}]\omega_c C}$$

$$R_2 = \frac{b}{\omega_c{}^2 C^2 R_1}$$

$$R_3 = \frac{KR_1}{K - 1} \quad (K > 1)$$

$$R_4 = KR_1$$

where

K = gain
f_c = −3 dB cutoff point
$\omega_c = 2\pi f_c$
$a = 0.765367$ (see text)
$b = 1$
C = a standard value near $10 / f_c$ μF

Note: For unity gain, short R4 and omit R3.

Example:

$K = 4$
$f = 250$ Hz
$\omega_c = 1570.8$
$C \approx 0.04$ μF (use 0.039 μF)
$R_1 = 11,407 \ \Omega$ (use 11 kΩ)
$R_2 = 23,358 \ \Omega$ (use 24 kΩ)
$R_3 = 15,210 \ \Omega$ (use 15 kΩ)
$R_4 = 45,630 \ \Omega$ (use 47 kΩ)

BAND-PASS FILTER

Pick K, Q, $\omega_o = 2\pi f_c$
where f_c = center freq.
Choose C

Then $R1 = \dfrac{Q}{K_o\omega_o C}$

$$R2 = \frac{Q}{(2Q^2 - K_o)\omega_o C}$$

$$R3 = \frac{2Q}{\omega_o C}$$

Example:

$K = 2$, $f_o = 800$ Hz, $Q = 5$ and
$C = 0.022$ μF
$R1 = 22.6$ kΩ (use 22 kΩ)
$R2 = 942 \ \Omega$ (use 1000 Ω)
$R3 = 90.4$ kΩ (use 91 kΩ or 100 kΩ)

Fig 7—Equations for designing a low-pass RC active audio filter are given at A. B, C and D show design information for high-pass, band-pass and band-reject filters, respectively. All of these filters will exhibit a Butterworth-type response.

Fig 8—Practical circuit for a two-pole CW RC active filter, showing how it can be switched into and out of the audio channel of a receiver.

BAND-REJECT FILTER

$$f_o = \frac{1}{2\pi \, R1 \, C2}$$

where
R2 = R3 = $\frac{R1}{2}$
C1 = 2C2
C2 = C3

Example:
f_o = 500 Hz
R1 = 150 kΩ
Then
R2 = R3 = 75 kΩ
C2 = 2122 pF (choose 2000 pF
    or 2200 pF)
C2 = 4244 pF (choose 4300 pF)

of the filter. Additional cascaded filter sections would consist of the circuit that is common to Q2. The values of R1 and R2 would be changed to modify the center frequency (f_c) of the filter. The lower the resistance value the higher the f_c. A dual potentiometer could be used in place of R1 and R2 to provide variable frequency response.

Design data for second-order Butterworth VCVS low-pass and high-pass filters is shown in Figs 7A and 7B respectively. The desired filter gain is designated K, and the frequency at the −3 dB points is designated f. To design one of these filters, start by selecting the gain (K) and cutoff frequency (f_c). Then start plugging the variables into the formulas in the order given. Second-order calculations are shown, and these give approximately 40 dB per decade of attenuation outside the passband. If greater attenuation is desired, cascade another second-order section, this time substituting 1.847759 for a in the second section. This second section attenuates unwanted frequencies an additional 40 dB per decade.

Design data for a band-pass active filter using a single op amp is shown in Fig 7C. Only one pole is shown for clarity. The term K represents the desired gain of the filter. Gains of 1 (unity) and 2 are most common. The desired filter Q can be calculated by dividing the center frequency by the bandwidth (delta f) at the −3 dB points.

Fig 7D shows a simple band-reject filter using a single op amp. Many applications for a band-reject filter will call for an adjustable reject frequency. This filter won't fill those needs, but does illustrate the filter concept. Select the desired notch center frequency and a standard resistor or capacitor value. Then use the equations to calculate values for the other components. If the calculated values aren't close to standard values you can select another starting value and try again, or you can combine components to reach the design values.

High-Q, stable capacitors are imperative to proper filter performance. Polystyrene capacitors are recommended for use at C of Figs 6 and 7. The frequency-determining resistors and capacitors should be as close to the design values as possible. Variations greater than 5 percent in resistance and capacitance in a multipole filter will widen the 3-dB bandwidth and cause dips in the nose of the response curve. In other words, f_c should be exactly the same for *all* filter sections in an ideal example.

A practical example of a two-pole RC active filter that uses a dual op-amp IC is given in Fig 8. It is switched in and out of the audio amplifier by means of S1. As shown, the filter represents the minimum acceptable design for most CW work. A three- or four-section filter of this type would be more desirable for CW work under adverse band conditions (QRM or weak signals).

An Audio Amplifier with AGC for Simple Receivers

Many excellent articles describing simple receivers have appeared in the amateur literature. In many respects these receivers perform well. However, most of the designs lack an automatic gain control (AGC) circuit. This amplifier module was first described in April 1983 *QST* by Rick Littlefield, K1BQT.

There are several ICs on the market that satisfy amateur receiver audio requirements. The LM-386 is well suited for amateur use. This chip features low distortion, plenty of gain (up to 200), low current drain and high stability. With a 9-V supply it delivers 200 mW of audio power, more than sufficient to drive a speaker.

Automatic Gain Control

IF-derived AGC is probably the best. However, deriving a control signal from the IF stage may not be practical in simple designs in which the IF signal levels are low and BFO leakage is common. Audio-derived AGC is usually a safer choice. But deriving AGC from a receiver that employs a single high-gain audio chip can also present a problem. The only voltage-sampling point before the volume control is at the output of the product detector, where the voltage level is very low. Thus, a functional AGC circuit would require the addition of high-gain circuitry to develop a usable control voltage.

The simplest alternative is to derive the control voltage at the audio-amplifier output, where the signal level is high. The AGC circuit then keeps the amplifier from being driven past a predetermined output level. Limiting is set somewhere below the maximum undistorted output level of the audio amplifier at a comfortable "maximum" volume level for the radio. A drawback to this approach is that AGC action does not occur at very low gain settings. This should not be a problem in quiet listening environments — the human ear can adapt easily to changes of 20 dB or more in normal conversation. In noisy environments the radio would be operated at a higher volume level, and heavy AGC action would keep the output more constant. This is a compromise compared to a 90-dB AGC system operating independently of the audio gain control; but it works and does not add much to the complexity of the receiver circuit.

Circuit Information

The circuit shown in Fig 9 has been used successfully in several small receivers. The LM386 audio section is compact and stable. Miniature 220-μF, 16-V capacitors (available from Radio Shack) contribute to the small size of the layout. The circuit is designed to drive an 8-ohm speaker. Operation with headphones is possible by adding a simple attenuator similar to those used in transistor radios. A 10-ohm resistor

Fig 9—Circuit diagram of a simple audio amplifier and AGC module for use with homemade receivers.

Fig 10—Parts-placement guide for the audio module. This view is from the component side of the board. Gray areas represent an X-ray view of the unetched foil. A full-size etching pattern can be found in the back of this book.

replaces the speaker, and a 470-ohm series resistor drops the output to a comfortable listening level.

The AGC design was borrowed from a more conventional audio-derived configuration and adapted for this application. This circuit has some interesting features that make it universal. First, it samples a wide range of audio levels while remaining virtually transparent to the circuit because of the high input impedance. Second, it can be used with either a bipolar or an IC-based IF section that requires a positive bias-voltage swing, or with MOSFET stages, which employ a negative bias-voltage swing.

Since Q1 will respond to either positive or negative voltage, the polarity of D1 determines the direction of the bias-voltage swing. R2 sets the resting-bias level. Adjust this level to the point where AGC action begins to lower the receiver background noise on a quiet frequency. R1 is used to adjust the drive. It should be set for smooth response. Overdrive will cause a pronounced overshoot or a cracking sound when strong signals come on. Lack of drive will cause insufficient limiting, and the audio amplifier will be driven into distortion. A substitution box can be used to determine a value for R1 that will work best with your radio. Or, start with a 50-kΩ potentiometer and measure the required resistance.

An Expandable Headphone Mixer

From time to time, active amateurs find themselves wanting to listen to two or more rigs simultaneously with one set of headphones. For example, a DXer might want to comb the bands looking for new ones while keeping an ear on the local 2-meter DX repeater. Or, a contester might want to work 20 meters in the morning while keeping another receiver tuned to 15 meters waiting for that band to open. There are a number of possible uses for a headphone mixer in the ham shack.

The mixer shown in Figs 11 through 13 will allow simultaneous monitoring of up to three rigs. Level controls for each channel allow the audio in one channel to be prominent, while the others are kept in the background. Although this project was built for operation with three different rigs, the builder may vary the number of input sections to suit particular station requirements. This mixer was built in the ARRL lab by Mark Wilson, AA2Z.

Circuit Details

The heart of the mixer is an LM386 low-power audio amplifier IC. This 8-pin device is capable of up to 400 mW output at 8 ohms — more than enough for headphone listening. The LM386 will operate from 4- to 12-V dc, so almost any station power supply, or even a battery, will power it.

As shown in Fig 12, the input circuitry for each channel consists of an 8.2-ohm resistor (R1-R3) to provide proper termination for the audio stage of each transceiver, a 5000-ohm level control (R4-R6) and a 5600-ohm resistor (R7-R9) for isolation between channels. C1 sets the gain of the LM386 to 46 dB. With pins 1 and 8 open, the gain would be 26 dB. Feedback resistor R10 was chosen experimentally for minimum amplifier total harmonic distortion

Fig 11—The 3-channel headphone mixer is built on a small PC board. Note that the lead length was kept to a minimum to aid stability.

(THD). C2 and R11 form a "snubber" to prevent high-frequency oscillation, adding to amplifier stability. None of the parts values are particularly critical, except R1-R3, which should be as close to 8 ohms as possible.

Construction

Most of the components are arranged on a small PC board. Parts placement is shown in Fig 13, and a full-size etching pattern is shown in the back of this book. Perfboard will work fine also, but some attention to detail is necessary because of the high gain of the LM386. Liberal use of ground connections, short lead lengths and a bypass capacitor on the power-supply line

all add to amplifier stability.

The mixer was built in a small diecast box. Tantalum capacitors and ¼-W resistors were used to keep size to a minimum. The '386 IC is available from Radio Shack (cat. no. 276-1731). A 0.01-μF capacitor and a ferrite bead on the power lead help keep RF out of the circuit. In addition, shielded cable is highly recommended for all connections to the mixer. The output jack is wired to accept stereo headphones.

Output power is about 250 mW at 5% THD into an 8-ohm load. The output waveform faithfully reproduces the input waveform, and no signs of oscillation or instability are apparent.

Fig 12—Schematic diagram of the LM386 headphone mixer. All resistors are ¼ W. Capacitors are disc ceramic unless noted.

Fig 13—Parts-placement diagram for the LM386 headphone mixer. A full-size etching pattern appears in the back of this book.

An ATV Monitoring Instrument

To maintain high-quality video images, amateur television enthusiasts must monitor their transmissions. RF sampling is often used to siphon a portion of the transmitter's RF output from the transmission line for monitoring purposes. This relatively easy-to-build video sampler, shown in Figs 14 through 21, is based on this technique, but goes several steps further. By employing a directional coupler, it not only provides low-level output to a TV monitor, but also permits percentage modulation and relative SWR measurements. Biagio Presti, of Aptron Laboratories, Inc., designed and built this instrument. John Gereke of Southwest Sound also contributed to this project.

Circuit Description

Fig 14 is a schematic diagram of the unit. The stripline directional coupler provides detection of both forward and reverse power. When S1 is in the VIDEO position, modulation is detected and routed to chopper IC U1. The IC switches inside U1 are connected as shown in Fig 15.

If S3 is also placed in the VID position, then IC switch 1-2 is always closed, and IC switches 3-4 and 9-8 are always open. Detected video is then routed to the input of the video amplifier consisting of Q2, Q3 and Q4. The output from Q4 is capable of driving a TV monitor input and must be terminated in 75 ohms. For percentage modulation measurements, this output is

connected to an oscilloscope.

If S3 is placed in the CHOP position, then IC switches 3-4 and 9-8 are turned off and on at a 60-Hz rate by Q1. In this configuration, the connections of switch 9-8 form a 60-Hz inverter that drives IC switch 1-2. This produces a ground reference on the face of an oscilloscope connected to the video output terminal and set to view the signal at the horizontal TV rate.

Placing S1 in the SWR position allows making SWR measurements.

PC Board Assembly

Fig 16 shows the PC-board parts placement. The board is made from 1/16-inch, double-sided glass-epoxy stock, so the

Fig 14—Schematic diagram of the ATV monitoring instrument. Resistors are ¼ W, 5% types unless otherwise noted. Capacitors are disc ceramic unless noted. Capacitors marked with polarity are electrolytic.

C1, C2 — 220-μF, 35-V miniature PC-mount electrolytic capacitor.
C3, C4, C7, C8 — 0.22-μF epoxy-coated monolithic ceramic capacitor.
C5 — 100-pF feedthrough capacitor.
C6 — 0.001-μF feedthrough capacitor.
C9, C10 — 220-μF, 16-V miniature electrolytic capacitor, axial leads.

D1, D2 — 1N34 diode.
D3, D4 — 1N4003 diode.
D5 — LED in a panel-mount holder.
J1, J2 — Chassis-mount female Type-N connector.
J3 — Chassis-mount female BNC connector.
M1 — Microammeter, 200 μA full scale.
Q1 — VN10KM FET.
Q2, Q3 — General-purpose NPN silicon

transistor, 2N4124 or equiv.
Q4 — Small-signal PNP amplifier transistor, 2N4126 or equiv.
T1 — Power transformer. Primary, 117-V ac. Secondary, 12.6-V ac, 100 mA.
U1 — Quad bilateral switch IC, CD4066.
U2 — 12-V, 1.5-A three-terminal regulator (LM7812 or equiv.).

component side acts as a groundplane. If you can make double-sided boards, use the etching pattern provided for the component side to clear away unwanted copper from around component holes. If you cannot make double-sided boards, leave the component side unetched. After drilling all lead holes, clear away the component-side copper from holes for component leads that are not grounded. A 1/8-inch drill bit turned by hand works well for clearing holes.

The PC board mounts vertically to the rear plate of the case used. The Type-N connector center pins connect directly to the PC board, so the board must be mounted very close to the panel. This means some components must be mounted on the circuit side of the PC board. All of the resistors, small bypass capacitors, rectifier diodes and U1 mount on the component side. The remainder of parts and wiring mount on the circuit side. Any component leads that are grounded should be soldered to the groundplane of the board as well as the circuit trace.

When mounting the parts on the circuit side, be sure to orient U2 and the transistors properly. Leave the body of the electrolytics elevated above the board to allow soldering of the leads to the pads as shown in Fig 17A. Remember to clip leads on the opposite side to avoid shorts.

The case used should be at least three inches deep to allow room for the switches and meter to mount to the front panel. The power transformer can be mounted to the case bottom plate. Use sensible wiring

Fig 15—Schematic diagram of the switches inside the CD4066.

practice in wiring the ac leads to the switch and fuse.

A short piece of 75-ohm coaxial cable should be used to connect the video from the board to J3. A grounding lug should be used on the video connector to bring the coax shield to ground without relying on the case metal for ground.

When mounting the stripline diodes (D1 and D2) and the 33-ohm resistor, be careful not to allow solder blobs to accumulate. The leads for the diode and resistor to the stripline should be very short to the body of the component, and the leads should not

extend beyond the stripline area as shown in Fig 17B.

The 1N34 diodes should be a matched pair for best results. You can match such diodes adequately by using an ohmmeter and measuring the forward drop of a number of diodes until two are found that read the same or nearly so.

Metal Parts

The area of construction requiring some care is the mechanical placement of the Type-N connectors to the rear panel and the metal shield parts. The reason is that

Fig 16—Parts-placement diagram of the ATV monitoring instrument. Components that mount on the circuit side of the board are drawn with solid lines. Components represented by dashed lines mount on the component side of the board. See text. A full-size etching pattern appears at the back of this book.

Fig 17—Component-mounting details. At A, components that mount to the circuit side of the board must be spaced away from the board so you can solder the leads to the circuit traces. Any leads that go to ground are also soldered to the foil groundplane on the component side of the board. At B, details of the components that mount to the stripline may be seen.

Fig 18—The pieces of the PC board shield are made from tin plate (or thin sheet brass or copper). The piece at A solders to the PC board circuit side to form three sides of the stripline compartment shield. The connector shield piece, shown at B, forms the fourth side of the shield. It is held in place by the connector-mounting hardware. See Fig 19C. The shield cover piece shown at C completes the stripline enclosure.

once the connectors are mounted, along with the shield piece associated with the connector mounting, the nuts holding these pieces are no longer reachable when the PC board is slipped into position. The PC mounting holes for the center conductor of the connectors must then slip perfectly into place or the PC board will not fit, and the shield associated with the connector will not butt properly to the PC board shield piece. See Figs 18 and 19.

How to Use the Instrument

It is a simple matter to use the instrument to monitor video. First, connect the video output to a monitor terminated in 75 ohms. Place the VID/CHOP switch in the VID position. Adjust video gain for suitable contrast. If you have a multiburst signal available, then the quality of transmitter performance can be checked as well.

To Check for Percentage Modulation

A properly designed TV transmitter has a clamping circuit that establishes the sync tip to a constant value. Because the RF amplitude of the signal approaches zero for "white-going" signals, any overmodulating white peaks will bring the carrier to zero, causing "sync buzz." To avoid this condition, peak white modulation is set to 87.5%.

First, connect the transmitter output to the IN Type-N connector and the antenna line to the OUT Type-N connector. Next, connect the video output to an oscilloscope with sufficient bandwidth to view video (10 MHz) and terminate the output in

Fig 19—Assembly of the shield. At A, the stripline shield is soldered to the component side of the PC board. At first, the shield is tack soldered in place. Next, the connector shield piece is attached to the rear case wall. At final assembly, all seams will be soldered to make an RF-tight enclosure. As shown at B, the PC board is spaced ¼ inch away from the rear wall of the case. The center conductor of the connector inserts in the stripline hole just enough to make a good solder connection to the circuit trace. Dimensions for mounting the connectors are given at C.

75 ohms. You can make an adequate termination by using a ¼-watt, 5%, 75-ohm resistor with one lead soldered to the center pin of a BNC male connector and the opposite end of the resistor soldered to the shell. By using a BNC T connector, you can then make the connection to the scope. TV monitors general-

ly provide 75-ohm terminations, but if not, then the same scheme can be used for the monitor as well. Then, set the scope horizontal sweep rate to allow two or three TV lines to be viewed.

The ideal signal to use for modulating the transmitter is a test-generator stairstep signal since the "white" step is clearly de-

fined. If, however, you do not have a test signal, a black card with a white square in the center can be used in conjunction with your camera. The idea is to have a clear white video reference with which to set the percentage modulation.

Set the VID/CHOP switch to CHOP. Set the VID/SWR switch to VID. With every-

Fig 20—When you have set up the monitoring instrument with a test generator to check percentage modulation, the scope display should look like this.

Fig 21—Use this graph to determine SWR from the meter readings. See text.

flection from the chopper reference bar to the tip of sync, then each cm of deflection represents 25%. Setting the tip of sync to video white at 3.5 cm is equivalent to 87.5% modulation.

Adjust the *transmitter* video level and sync stretch for proper sync to video ratio and percentage modulation.

To Monitor SWR

Set the VID/SWR switch to SWR and the FWD/REV switch to FWD. Adjust the SET control for full-scale reading on the meter (200 μA).

Now switch the FWD/REV switch to REV and read the meter. The ratio of the reverse to forward reading is used by referring to the SWR chart in Fig 21 or calculate using

$$\frac{F + R}{F - R}$$

where
  F = forward reading
  R = reverse reading

For example, if the reverse reading is 40 μA, then the ratio is 40/200 or 0.2. Referring to Fig 21, read 0.2 on the RATIO scale to the curve and then to the SWR scale and read 1.5 SWR.

The instrument will handle more than 50 watts and can be left in place without degradation to the quality of transmission or power output.

thing turned on, the scope display should appear as in Fig 20.

Adjust the scope vertical gain and the instrument video gain to a calibrated vertical deflection. For example, if the scope display is set to a 4-cm vertical de-

Telephone Equipment

This section was written by J. P. Neil, KN6B, a Professional Engineer with many years of telephone-system-design and laboratory-testing experience.

There are a number of amateur-related devices besides telephones (such as modems, repeater controls, phone-patches, computers, and so on) that require telephone-company-line intercommunication. Because of this, a basic knowledge of telephone practices is desirable. The following text outlines some of the main, important characteristics and switched-network interface design parameters.

THE TELEPHONE COMPANY INTERFACE

The interface involves two key portions: the central office (CO) and the terminal device (often abbreviated CPE for "customer premises equipment"). Since these must work together efficiently, certain basic requirements must be observed. Part 68 of the FCC technical rules to prevent "Harms To The Network" must be observed. More about these rules later.

Central Office Basics

The CO consists primarily of switching equipment, which is nearly all computerized electronics. A few rural areas and independent telephone companies may still use the older electromechanical switching equipment, but overall, the operations are essentially the same. The CO is called "inside plant." The "outside plant" consists mainly of multi-pair cables going to the "subscribers."

For our purposes, we are only interested in "loop" systems. We are interested in two operating modes. Under the normal idle condition ("on-hook") there is no current from the CO. In the "off-hook" operating mode, there is loop current flowing through the system. That current is supplied by the CO batteries. This battery voltage is normally about 48 V dc, but can be as high as 56.5 V dc or as low as around 42.5 V dc, in the on-hook condition. Typical loop current is from about 25 to 40 mA, but may be from 20 to 120 mA, depending upon proximity to the CO "exchange."

Fig 22 shows a narrow window of off-hook terminal voltage versus loop current and resistance. The optimum terminal loop resistance is about 200 ohms, but must be within the window to avoid marginal operation of the CO line relays.

The equipment leads are called "tip" and "ring," or just T and R. For the idle or on-hook state, the tip (positive) lead (green) is grounded. The CO ringing generator and the −48 V dc supply connect to the ring lead (red). When the CO ringing voltage is on the line, the tip is still grounded and the ring lead is hot. The ringing voltage *at the CO* is typically about 130 V RMS, but more likely 60 to 80 V RMS at the terminal end

Fig 22—This graph shows the allowable range of off-hook resistances for terminal interface equipment.

Fig 23—A basic data access arrangement (DAA) telephone interface circuit.

C1—Non-polarized capacitor, 0.2 μF to 0.47 μF, 400 V dc or greater.
K1—Clare MHC (SPST) or equivalent normally open relay.
R1, R2—Standard value nearest to calculated value, ¼ or ½ W (see text).
R3—5.6 kΩ to 10 kΩ, ¼ to ½ W.
T1—600-ohm to 600-ohm telephone line

matching transformer (Microtran PM32F or equivalent).
U1—TIL181 opto-isolator, or similar opto-isolator with 1.5 kV dc or higher isolation.
Z1—Gas surge protector, 250 to 350 V dc breakdown, such as Siemens, Joslyn, Shinko or TII devices.

because of cable and equipment resistance. Incidentally, the CO ac (signal) impedance is 900 ohms, not 600 ohms as normally provided at the CPE end. This mismatch is intentional, so don't worry about it.

Terminal Interface Equipment

There are several important parameters to be considered. Primarily these are: input lightning and power line surge (and leakage) protection; dc loop resistance; ac (600 ohm) signal impedance; pulse and/or dual-tone, multifrequency (DTMF) signaling; longitudinal balance; and sometimes return loss. Fig 23 shows a typical interface for some device other than a telephone. (The phone company calls a telephone a "subset" or "station.") There is a bit more information about this circuit later.

There are usually more surges from T and R (or both) to ground, than across the T/R pairs. Protection should be not only across the T/R pairs, but from T and R to (earth) ground if possible. If the device is in a nonmetallic case, a protector only across T and R is better than nothing, but not a substitute for full metallic and longitudinal (ground) protection.

Adequate longitudinal balance, needed to minimize crosstalk on the cables, is essentially the difference in the ac signal voltage measured from T and R to ground. This must be at least 40 dB (the voltages not more than 1% apart). The FCC requires 60 dB from 200 Hz to 1 kHz.

Return loss (measured in dB) is essentially the suppression of a reflected (mismatched) signal coming back towards the source.

Return loss is related to SWR. Higher return-loss values correspond to lower values of SWR.

Interface Design Notes

Fig 23 illustrates a typical telephone company interface for almost any device except telephone company subsets. Note that this circuit utilizes a standard 1:1 (600 to 600 ohm) repeat coil (line transformer). Some manufacturers, for economy reasons, use very small transformers not intended to carry the loop current. Instead, they capacitively couple to one side of the T or R line, and substitute a solid-state "holding circuit" to pass the off-hook dc loop current. If one elects to do this, the holding circuit should have a dc resistance of around 200 ohms, but an ac impedance of 6000 ohms (or higher) impedance.

The suggested surge protector (Z1) is a telephone-type, 3-terminal gas-filled unit. (Examples are the Joslyn Trigard® 2022-44 protectors, Siemens SVP® T61-C350, Shinko 2P-13 and Clare PMT 3(310) devices.) These are small, approximately ¼ inch × ¼ inch, and easily mounted on a PC board. Varistors or TransZorbs® can be substituted. Note that varistors are usually marked in volts RMS, whereas the gas types show the actual dc breakdown voltage. The breakdown voltage should be not less than 250 V dc, nor greater than 350 V dc (or peak ac).

Next in line is the ring detector. This must be capacitively coupled for dc loop-voltage isolation. Opto-isolators are normally used to provide this isolation. They are inexpensive and should have a minimum of 1.5 kV insulation capability. Sometimes a reverse diode is used in shunt with the photo diode, but it isn't mandatory.

The relay, normally in the open or on-hook mode is also available for dial-pulsing, network-switching purposes. Control of this relay is from any suitable source (manual or automatic) as desired. If opening and closing of the relay contacts causes problem voltage spikes, they can be bypassed by an R-C (series) "snubber" circuit in parallel with the contacts.

Note the two resistors in series with the transformer (T1) line side winding. Since such transformers typically have dc resistances of from 50 to about 90 ohms, additional resistance will have to be added to make up the difference with the optimum 200-Ω value. While a single resistor will work, using two of half the calculated value makes for better line balance. These resistors also provide extra protection below the breakdown voltage of the protector. You can calculate the required value for these resistors by subtracting the transformer coil resistance from 200, and then dividing by 2. For the circuit of Fig 23 assume a coil resistance of 50 Ω. Then:

$$R = 200 \ \Omega - 50 \ \Omega = 150 \ \Omega$$
$$R1 = R2 = R \ / \ 2 = 150 \ \Omega \ / \ 2 = 75 \ \Omega$$

This value is not critical, so 82 Ω, 10% units will also work.

The "load" or network on the hybrid (logic) side of T1 should be adjusted to reflect a 600-ohm (or matching) impedance into the telephone company line. The effect of the series resistors on the telephone company side is negligible, but if one is concerned, they can be bypassed with capacitors.

Further data on telephone company interface circuits are available from various sources knowledgeable about telephone company practices. Be warned that some semiconductor manufacturers and others have published interface circuits that are questionable. Some are missing necessary components, and some include unnecessary components. One Radio Shack book gives data on British telephone circuits rather than data based on US Standards, for example.

Since the tip/ring wires constitute a "2-wire" pair with signals in both directions, the line-balancing network (NET) on the logic side must provide a 2- to 4-wire "hybrid combiner" to permit both send and receive operations. Hybrids can be either transformer-coupled or solid-state (op-amp) types.

Telephones

Telephones must also convert 2-wire telephone company pairs into 4-wire capability inside the subset. In the more conventional types like the 500 or 2500 series (pulse or tone) units, the hybrid for this purpose is made up of a 3-winding transformer, with a little leakage to permit hearing a "side-tone" to indicate the set is alive. (Side-tone is the small amount of signal from the telephone transmitter that you can hear in the telephone receiver.) These POTS (plain old telephone system) phones use a transmitter (microphone) containing carbon granules. When vibrated by sounds, there is a direct current through them, and the transformer converts this variable dc into ac. The receiver is electro-dynamic, similar to a small speaker.

Many of the sets now sold, including those made for AT&T, Bell companies and independents, use electronic, semiconductor construction and they are more vulnerable to surge damage than the older types. The microphones are usually of the electret (transistorized) variety. These are okay, except when used on the same line with the transformer (POTS) types. In this case the carbon transmitters "rob" so much of the off-hook dc voltage that there isn't enough

Fig 24—A shows a basic Wheatstone Bridge configuration for a telephone bridge circuit. B shows the practical construction of a hybrid coupler circuit in which the four bridge inductors are combined into two center-tapped inductors.

left to operate the electret mike. The result is often completely distorted, unintelligible speech from the electret unit. If electret types are only used on the same line with other electret mikes, there is normally no problem. Just don't "mix and match."

Fig 24A illustrates the basic bridge circuit of a POTS phone. The electronic units use various types of electronic hybrids, now available in IC form.

Although the basic modified Wheatstone Bridge circuit shows five windings, in practice this is reduced to only three windings. See Fig 24B. POTS types also contain varistors, capacitors and resistors for equalization and level control, not shown in the basic bridge of Fig 24A or B.

Evaluation of the Fig 24A and B bridge circuits indicates that the dc loop current from the CO flows only through two hybrid windings and the transmitter (mike). The current is blocked in the NET circuit by the 2.16 μF capacitor. The ac signal flows through all the windings, however. They are wound opposed to each other in each branch, on a common core. This prevents feedback between the send and receive branches (but only when the NET is exactly matched to the telephone line impedance). A side-tone mismatch is incorporated.

FCC PART 68 RULES

In 1976, the FCC instituted Part 68 rules and regulations concerning "Customer-Provided Equipment." In essence, this defines rules and test requirements to prevent "Harms to the Network" for *all* devices connected to the switched, and later, also private-line networks. Legally, the FCC is not concerned about whether a terminal device works well. These rules also legally apply whether or not the devices are manufactured in quantity for public sale, or privately made in single quantities for personal use.

If you make a device which causes a problem to the telephone company, the FCC can take legal action against you for violation of Part 68. The technical parameters include: surge protection; ac power-line leakage; hazardous voltages; signal and harmonic levels; longitudinal balance; on-hook impedance and "billing protection." Billing protection is a two-second delay after the answering phone goes off hook, before the telephone company equipment begins to bill the call. No signal greater than -55 dBm may be transmitted during these two seconds. Modems and other interface devices must have a built-in 2-second delay. You are advised to obtain a copy of FCC Part 68 from the Government Printing Office, and read Sub-Part D before connecting any home-made device to the telephone line.

Among other tests, telephone company line transformers and interface relays must pass a 1 kV RMS leakage test for 60 seconds, respectively from windings to windings and to the core, and from coil to contacts (not between contacts). The device must pass a 1 kV RMS test between T and R shorted and grounded to external metallic materials. Also under the same conditions, it must survive a longitudinal simulated lightning surge with 1.5 kV dc source (both polarities) with a 10 μs maximum rise time and 160 μs minimum decay time to half crest; and a "metallic" surge of 800 V dc (both polarities), across T and R, both on and off hook, at 10 μs maximum rise time and 560 μs minimum decay time to half crest. These surge sources must have a minimum output of 100 A capability. This indicates the need for adequate "front-end" protection against line surges.

Phone Patches

At one time phone patches were illegal under AT&T pressure on the FCC. For some years now, however, they have been tacitly ignored by telephone companies, if properly designed. Possibly one good reason for dropping this opposition was that in many cases the phone patches generated extra toll calls that would not otherwise have been made. As long as the patches cause no network problems they are usually tolerated. All devices must meet FCC Part 68 rules, and commercially made units for public sale must be FCC registered.

Phone patches can be simple, manually operated types, or more sophisticated units with telephone line VOX control. The latter require built-in line null-balancing circuits. In either case, provision can be made to include an integral speaker (if desired), with muting of the receiver speaker.

Fig 25 illustrates a relatively simple

Fig 25—This diagram shows a basic phone-patch circuit. Manual or VOX transmitter operation is possible with this circuit. The text describes how to adjust the network for proper operation. Be sure to also read the information about Part 68 of the FCC Rules in the text.

D1-D4—1N4002 diodes or bridge rectifier, such as Radio Shack 276-1152.
L1, L2—2.5 mH RFC.
S1—3PDT switch.

S2—DPDT switch.
S3—SP3T switch.
T1, T2—Telephone interface transformers, 600/300/300 ohm windings (see text).

Z1—Gas surge protector, 3-wire, 250 to 350 V dc breakdown, such as Siemens, Joslyn, Shinko or TII devices (see text).

phone-patch circuit that meets telephone company and FCC Part 68 requirements. It includes a 2-transformer (2-wire to 4-wire) "hybrid" conversion circuit comprised of two 600/300/300-ohm telephone line transformers (such as Microtran T9317 coupling transformers). A meter provides line-level monitoring (with a bridge rectifier). There is a NET null-balancing circuit, an RF line filter and send/receive level controls. This design includes both manual and VOX transmitter operation.

Overall operation of the phone patch should be reasonably evident for both manual and VOX telephone transmissions. The receiver AF output is based on 600 ohms. It can be modified to suit other impedance values. The patch output to the transmitter microphone-input jack is based on a high-impedance match. This too can be altered to suit other input values.

The monitor meter can be either a high-impedance built-in VU or dB type meter, or an external bench meter (DVM) or other high-impedance instrument with a dB scale. To calibrate an uncalibrated scale, set an AF signal generator at 1 kHz and terminate it with a 600-Ω resistor. Connect the meter (with a variable series resistance) across the 600-Ω resistor. Connect a high-impedance ac voltmeter in parallel with the meter being calibrated. Adjust the generator level until you read 0.775 V RMS on the ac voltmeter. This represents 0 dBm. Adjust the meter series resistance so the meter indication is less than full scale, and mark 0 dBm at that point. To calibrate several other points on the scale, see Table 2 for a listing of RMS voltages and dBm values.

When meter calibration is complete, determine a fixed series meter-calibration resistance. Then wire the Monitor/Null circuit as shown. Next, you will have to adjust the audio input levels from the

Table 2

Power Ratio (in dBm) for Various Voltages Across a 600-Ohm Load

$dB = 20 \log (E1 / E2)$,
0 dBm across 600 Ω = 0.775 V RMS

dBm	V RMS	V P-P
+2	0.976	2.760
+1	0.870	2.460
0	0.775	2.192
−1	0.691	1.954
−2	0.616	1.741
−3	0.549	1.552
−4	0.489	1.383
−5	0.436	1.233
−6	0.388	1.099
−7	0.346	0.979
−8	0.309	0.873
−9	0.275	0.778
−10	0.245	0.693
−11	0.218	0.618
−12	0.195	0.551
−13	0.174	0.491
−14	0.155	0.437
−15	0.138	0.390
−16	0.123	0.347
−17	0.109	0.310
−18	0.0976	0.276
−19	0.0870	0.246
−20	0.0775	0.219

receiver to the phone patch. To do this, set the phone-patch AF gain control to maximum and set switch S3 to MON. Temporarily connect the 1-kHz signal source to the AF input of the patch and adjust it to show −9 dBm at the T/R line output termination.

The maximum allowable level on the CO tip/ring terminals (often called the CO "trunk" pair) under FCC Part 68 rules is −9 dBm. Incidentally, note that with any devices using DTMF *network signaling*, under Part 68 rules, the level may not exceed 0 dBm. A good practical DTMF level is about −2 to −4 dBm.

The next step is to adjust the network balance. This is especially important for VOX operation, where crosstalk from the received audio line would appear on the transmitter microphone lead and could trip the transmitter VOX circuit. Set S3 at NULL and connect the patch AF output to the transmitter mike input. Put a 600-Ω resistor across the T/R connector (with the phone line disconnected). Now adjust the network R/C controls for *minimum* meter reading. Incidentally, before commencing any actual VOX telephone patch operations, it is essential to have a telephone set (off-hook) connected to the telephone company line for both line loading and aural monitoring purposes.

Do not switch the patch on to an unterminated telephone company line in the idle (on-hook) condition. Ringing signals and line noises could trip the transmitter VOX circuit. Additional manual-only switches can be added if desired.

Actually, it would be better to build a breadboard patch first to experiment for optimum values. Regarding the NET balance circuit, use a capacitance decade box (or equivalent unit) with an actual off-hook telephone company (off-hook telephone-set-loaded) line termination. While the average R/C NET 600 ohms in series with a 2.16 µF capacitor is a typical standard, it is desirable to determine the best R/C (series) combination values by "cut and try" for any given telephone company line. These values should then be selected for the final patch NET unit in order to obtain the best possible hybrid NULL. Telephone company line impedance can change from time to time depending on weather (leakage), telephone company "bridge taps," and other factors, so adjustable selection is occasionally needed. It is desirable to completely shield the final patch to minimize RFI.

Chapter 29

Digital Equipment

Digital techniques are finding more and more application in Amateur Radio with each passing year. In addition to enhancing projects for the "standard" modes, such as CW and Baudot RTTY, digital technology is leading amateurs into new areas such as AMTOR and packet radio. As time passes, amateurs are thinking of new ways to interface their radio equipment with computers for even more enjoyment, creating the need for modems specifically designed for radio applications. Chapters 8 and 19 contain related information that may be helpful in understanding the projects in this chapter.

A Simple CMOS Iambic Keyer

The keyer shown in Figs 1 through 3 features iambic operation, dot and dash memories and internal sidetone generation. The keyer was designed and built by Paul Newland, AD7I, and originally appeared in June 1988 *QST*.

Circuit Details

Fig 2 shows the schematic of the CMOS keyer. The clock circuit was designed by Roy Lewallen, W7EL, and was used in his keyer project that first appeared in an issue of *SPRAT*—a QRP journal—several years ago. This clock has the advantage of good asynchronous starting without elongating the first clock period. Exclusive-OR gates U1B and U1C are used for the dot and dash memories. A Schmitt-trigger gate (U2D) configured as an AF oscillator serves as a handy, low-cost, minimum parts-count sidetone generator.

The keyer circuit is composed of five major sub-circuits. They are:
• Dot timer
• Dash timer
• Dot memory
• Dash memory
• Asynchronous clock

First, let's focus on the dot and dash timers. The heart of each timer is a CMOS 4017 decade counter. This chip's count advances on the rising edge of the clock input when both the reset and inhibit inputs are low. If the inhibit line is high, clock signals are ignored. When the reset line is high, the counter immediately goes to the zero state. The outputs of this counter are decoded; when the counter output is in the zero state, the zero output is high and all other outputs are low. When the counter is in the two state, the two output is high and all other outputs are low, and so on.

The dot and dash timers operate in a similar way. For clarity, we'll cover just the dash timer. When no dashes are desired,

Fig 1—This simple CMOS keyer uses four common ICs, seven diodes, four transistors, 21 resistors, 13 capacitors and two potentiometers.

the timer is in the four state and is held there because the inhibit input is tied to the four output. If both the dot and dash timers are inhibited, both inputs of U2A are high and the clock is disabled. When in the idle state, the outputs of both the dot memory (U1B) and dash memory (U1C) are high. Note that when the dot memory is idle, D5 is reverse biased, and when the dash timer is idle, D6 is reverse biased.

The only thing keeping the dash timer from being reset is that D4 is forward biased, holding the dash timer's reset input low (inactive). When the dash paddle is closed, the output of the dash memory formed by U1C, R6 and R7 goes low (C4 bypasses stray RF). This signal is inverted by U1D, and D4 is then reverse biased. Because all diodes at the reset input of the dash timer are reverse biased, the reset signal goes high, forcing the counter to go from four to zero.

When the dash timer is in the zero state, the keying transistor, Q1, is biased on by the current flowing through R9. Because of the low base-emitter voltage drop of Q1, most of R9's current goes into the base-emitter junction of Q1. When the state-four output of the dash timer goes low (when the timer leaves the four state), the clock signal from U2B goes from high to low and quickly back to high. (The speed of this process is determined by how fast C7 discharges through D7.) The time constant provided by R8 and C6 ensures that the dash timer remains reset long enough to ignore the first rising edge of the clock. (If this time constant is too short, the first dash

Fig 2—Schematic of the simple CMOS keyer. The portion of the circuit enclosed by the shaded line is optional. If you choose not to include the sidetone circuit, be sure to ground the unused inputs of U2 (pins 8, 9, 12 and 13).

C7—0.22 μF tantalum or ceramic. Q1, Q3—2N3904, 2N2222 or equiv. U1—CD4070.
J1—¼-in. three-conductor jack. Q2, Q4—2N3906, 2N2907 or equiv. U2—CD4093.
LS1—8-Ω or 100-Ω speaker. R14—1 MΩ potentiometer. U3, U4—CD4017.

would only be two Morse elements in length instead of the requisite three.) On the second rising edge of the clock, the dash timer moves from state zero to state one. Now the bias current for Q1 is provided by R10 instead of R9. Similarly, R11 provides bias current for state two. State three provides the space for the inter-element timing period.

The next rising edge of the clock moves the dash timer into the idle state (state four) and disables the clock. A reset pulse from the dash timer's state-four output also tries to reset the dash memory (U1C) via C5. If the paddle is open, this pulse clears the memory to a high state. If the paddle is still closed, the pulse momentarily clears the dash memory, but because of the remaining key closure, the memory is set again as soon as the charge on C5 is dissipated through R6.

If the dot paddle is closed while a dash is being sent, the dot memory is set before the dash timer reaches state four. During the period when C5 is trying to reset the dash memory, the dot timer is reset (D4, D5 and D6 all reverse biased). This makes the keyer send a dot followed by a space immediately after the dash/space combination is finished. Voila—iambic operation! During the time when the dot timer is active, the dash timer is held idle by forward-biased D5, until the dot-timer cycle finishes.

Construction

The prototype keyer was built on a piece of perf board. A PC board has since been developed; Fig 3 shows the parts-placement diagram. The PC board and a kit of parts are available from A&A Engineering[1]. Nothing about the layout is particularly critical, so the layout shown in Fig 3 can be modified to suit your needs. Just about any construction method is fine; dead bug, wire wrap, point-to-point and etched PC-board wiring are all fine. One caution you need to observe is the sensitivity of CMOS ICs to static electricity. Always use a grounding wrist strap or its equivalent to protect the ICs during handling. Also, if you elect not to use the PC-board layout shown in Fig 3, be sure to place the bypass capacitors as close as possible to their respective IC pins. The signal levels in the keyer are very small, and poor RF by-passing can make the keyer do some mighty strange things.

A word of caution about C7, the clock capacitor: the keyer uses CMOS ICs to provide keying at minimal current drain.

[1]PC boards and kits of parts are available from A & A Engineering, 2521 W La Palma Ave, Unit K, Anaheim, CA 92801, tel 714-952-2114.

Fig 3—Parts-placement diagram for the keyer. Parts are mounted on the non-foil side of the board; the shaded area represents an X-ray view of the copper pattern. A full-size etching pattern appears at the back of the book.

Because of this, no on/off switch is included. Be sure to use a low-leakage capacitor for C7 (either ceramic or tantalum). Don't use a garden-variety electrolytic here if the keyer will be battery powered; these are often very leaky. The keyer will work fine if you use a leaky cap for C7, but battery life will be markedly reduced.

Optional Circuitry

The optional circuitry enclosed by the shaded line in Fig 2, including the keying amplifier and the sidetone circuit, is not essential. CMOS gates were used because of their flexibility, as well as the low current drain already mentioned. These devices can be powered from anything between 3 and 15 V (74HC-series parts could also be used, but over a norrower supply-voltage range). The problem is that these devices can only supply a few hundred microamps of current from their outputs for a guaranteed logic level. If these gates are used to drive a transistor with a gain of 50 or so, only a small amount of keying current will be available to drive a transmitter. Often this is too little current for anything but QRP rigs. Q2 and Q3 (with associated resistors) form the keying amplifier, and increase available current to levels suitable for keying almost any transmitter. The value of drive current can be controlled by changing the values of R17 and R18. In general, decreasing the value of R17 will increase the available keying current.

The second optional item is the sidetone generator formed by a Schmitt-trigger gate

(U2D) with an RC circuit for feedback. The sidetone frequency can be changed by varying R22. As the resistance of R22 is increased the frequency of the sidetone decreases. Low-level audio output is available to drive an audio amplifier (such as the one in a transceiver), and the high-level output is suitable for driving a small speaker. Try to avoid using the high-level output to drive a speaker if you are running the keyer from a 9-V battery. The sidetone circuit itself doesn't draw much current, but a speaker sure does! Whenever possible, let the rig provide the sidetone, or you'll be feeding the keyer an awful lot of batteries.

Operation

The keyer operates just like any other electronic keyer. The circuit has one anomaly that you should be aware of, however. When power is first applied (when you connect a battery, or turn on your rig if the keyer is built into it), a reset pulse is not always sent to the dot or dash counter chips. The lack of a reset signal can cause more than one of the counters to be in active states at the same time, and the keyer will stick in the key-down mode. All it takes to "un-stick" the keyer is to squeeze the paddle after power is applied. This anomaly generally isn't a problem because battery life is long, and the power is only cycled when changing cells. If you build the keyer into a rig, however, this key-down bug can be more objectionable. In this case, try a different set of 4017 counters at U3 and U4.

CW on a Chip

Fig 4 shows a single-chip electronic keyer that can easily be built in a weekend, thanks to the Curtis keyer-on-a-chip. This IC has made it possible to construct a quality, flexible keying system with a minimum of additional discrete components. This project first appeared in an article by Paul Pagel, N1FB, and Bob Shriner, WA0UZO, in December 1983 *QST*.

Fig 4—View of the single-IC iambic keyer. The unit shown here was built around the Curtis 8044M integrated circuit, and features an analog speed readout.

The Curtis Chip

There are four versions of the Curtis 8044 CMOS IC. Two of these (8044/8044B) are contained in a 16-pin package and the others (8044M/8044BM) in an 18-pin package.[1] The additional pins are connected to internal circuitry that provides a keyer sending speed monitoring function by means of a meter and a few other external components. The whole family of ICs features contact debouncing, RF immunity and self-completing character generation. A weight control, sidetone output and dot memory are also included. The memory function helps to prevent dot loss if the operator "leads" the keyer. With a quiescent current drain of about 50 μA, an on/off switch is not really required.

The "plain vanilla" (no suffix) and B-suffix ICs offer two slightly different iambic (squeeze) keying methods in addition to single-lever (non-squeeze) keying.[2,3] With the no-suffix IC, a dot or dash being sent when the paddles are released is completed and nothing else is sent. The B-suffix IC completes the dot or dash being sent upon paddle release, and then sends an opposite element; that is, a dot after a dash or a dash after a dot. Many squeeze-key operators prefer the latter method of iambic operation. If only single-lever paddle operation is desired, either IC should suffice.

Board Design

To make the keyer as universal in application as possible, the board is patterned so that any of the ICs mentioned earlier can be used with or without some of their inherent capabilities.[4,5] The board is single sided, and is small enough to fit inside almost any transmitter or transceiver.

Any or all of the variable controls may be mounted on the board or brought out for external adjustment. Two on-board output keying options are provided: reed relay output (with or without arc suppression components across the contacts) or a transistor-keyed output that can be con-

[1]Curtis Electro Devices, Inc. generously supplied the ICs used in this project.
[2]L. Fay, "The Iambic Gambit," July 1981 *QST*.
[3]Curtis Electro Devices Lil' Bugger, Product Review, March 1981, *QST*.

[4]An etched circuit board and a complete kit of parts is available from Circuit Board Specialists, P.O. Box 969, Pueblo, CO 81002.
[5]The keyer ICs are available from Curtis Electro Devices, Inc., Box 4090, Mountain View, CA 94040. Be sure to specify IC type when ordering.

Fig 5—Schematic diagram of the keyer. All resistors shown are ¼-W, 5% types.

figured to fit station keying requirements.

Assembly

Construction details are given in Figs 5 and 6. A parts-placement guide appears in Fig 7.[6] All components except the IC should be soldered to the PC board. The integrated circuit should be installed last. A socket is recommented to avoid overheating the chip. Use an 18-pin socket, so either the 16- or 18-pin version may be used. If the 16-pin chip is used, the two extra positions on the socket are left empty; just be sure to install the IC correctly.

The keyer should be built to suit the user's requirements. Any components associated with unwanted features may be eliminated. These may include: sidetone output, level and pitch control, and the speed-meter function. If transistor-output keying is desired, the relay arc-suppression network may be deleted. A 5.6-kΩ resistor between pins 15 and 16 of U1 will eliminate the WEIGHT control, if a variable unit is not needed. If the weighting appears to be too heavy, reduce the value of C6 or eliminate it altogether. The MANUAL KEY input can be used as a TUNE function; an SPST switch that brings the line to ground will create a key-down condition.

If an IC with the speed-meter function is chosen, any meter with a full-scale deflection range of 50 to 500 μA (with a linear scale) can be used. In the unit shown, a modified VU meter was used. A new meter scale was made with two-words-per minute increments between 0 and 100. With the 100-kΩ resistor shown in series with the SPEED potentiometer in Fig 2, the maximum speed of the keyer is about 50 WPM. Alter the value of the fixed resistor to modify the speed range. The top-end speed for this unit is about 80 WPM.

A switch is included to turn the keyer and/or the transistor audio amplifier (Q2) on and off. To increase battery life, the audio amplifier can be left off. The side-tone oscillator will probably not be required, since most modern transmitters and transceivers have built-in sidetone monitoring circuits. The keyer monitor does serve as a good indicator of battery condition: as the battery becomes depleted, the note will become quite chirpy.

Relay-Contact Arc Suppression

Some transmitter keying lines may require the inclusion of an arc-suppression network across the keying relay contacts. Most modern transmitters and transceivers should not need this network (C10, R19), as they are usually operated at low voltage levels. But keying some transmitters and transceivers using tubes in the final amplifier may require the relay contact

[6]Templates for the sloping-panel keyer cabinet are availabe from ARRL HQ for a business-size envelope and $2 to cover template and postage costs.

Fig 6—Some possible output circuit arrangements. The jumper (W) shown at (A) and (C) is inserted in place of D3. D3 is included to ensure rapid energization of K1; it may not be needed. Q3 and the components to the right of the dashed line in (C) are not mounted on the keyer circuit board.

Fig 7—Parts-placement guide for the Curtis-IC keyer. Parts are placed on the nonfoil side of the board; the shaded area represents an X-ray view of the copper pattern. A full-size etching pattern appears at the back of this book.

Table 1
Series Resistor Values

Voltage	Value (ohms)
70	100
100	200
150	450
200	800

protection. The prototype keyer has been successfully used with a Kenwood TS-820S transceiver without the arc-suppression network; no problems resulted. The key line voltage in that rig is −65-V dc. The information presented in Table 1 should assist prospective users to determine the required network values.

Calibrating the Speed Control

Sending speed can be determined by counting the number of dashes (dahs) sent in a five-second period. This number is the code speed in words per minute. A more refined measurement method uses an oscilloscope or a frequency counter connected to pin 12 of U1.
The formula is

$$speed = \frac{f}{1.2}$$

where speed is in WPM and f is the dot frequency measured at pin 12 of U1. Thus, for speeds of 10, 25 and 50 WPM, the frequency counter should display dot frequencies of 8.33, 20.8 and 41.6 Hz, respectively.

Keyer Case Construction

Two enclosure styles have been tried. The first—the rectangular configuration—is easy to assemble. The control labels may be difficult to read at some angles, however. The sloping-panel version is more attractive, but a bit more difficult to put together. Either case style is available from Circuit Board Specialists; case style desired should be mentioned when ordering.

Double-sided PC board material is used for the enclosure. Once the box parts have been cut to size, they should be burnished with fine steel wool. The edges must be beveled for a good fit. Use caution to avoid removing too much material from the parts.

The speaker should be laid on a flat surface and the grill pressed into position. Quick-drying epoxy cement secures the grill.

After the box parts are prepared, they should be tack soldered together and checked for alignment and correct fit. If all is well, lay a bead of solder around each seam. A 25- to 45-W soldering iron should be sufficient.

A light coat of clear polyurethane varnish over most of the box will help maintain a pleasant sheen. The prototype cabinet was accented with light-blue epoxy spray paint.

Install the panel mounted controls, jacks, meter and speaker. The keyer board should be mounted with the meter-calibration potentiometer on the bottom.

Appendix

Most modern Amateur Radio transmitters, particularly solid-state designs, do not require additional relay-contact protection. When using this keyer with such a low-voltage transmitter, R18 can be removed or jumpered.

Some grid-block-keyed transmitters will require additional relay-contact protection in the form of an added series-connected resistor if the key-line voltage exceeds 70 and a large-value bypass capacitor is tied between the key line and ground. The appropriate resistor value can be determined from Table 1. Resistor power rating can be calculated by multiplying the resistor value by the square of the key-down circuit current in amperes. This resistor can often be placed within the body of the key-line plug. A silicon diode should be connected across the contacts of K1 (in place of C10, R19) to absorb the "kick" when keying inductive loads (such as another relay).

The CMOS Super Keyer II

The original CMOS Super Keyer built by Jeff Russell, KC0Q, and Bud Southard, N0II, appeared in October 1981 *QST*[1] and several editions of *The ARRL Handbook*. Now, their CMOS Super Keyer II—a worthy successor—is here. (This project originally appeared in the November 1990 issue of *QST*.) As you'll see, modern technology allows much more to be done with a minimal amount of hardware, a smaller PC board and simplified construction.[2] The pre-programmed microprocessor,

Fig 8—The CMOS Super Keyer II is packed with features—and has fewer parts than the original design.

[1] J. Russell and C. Southard, "The CMOS Super Keyer," *QST*, Oct 1981, pp 11-17.
[2] A detailed operating manual and parts kit for the PC-board-mounted parts (programmed CPU IC, IC socket, ceramic resonator, transistors, resistors, capacitors and etched PC board) are available from Idiom Press, Box 583, Deerfield, IL 60015. Price: $45 (subject to change without notice). Add $3 shipping and handling in the US, $5 for surface-mail foreign orders. Credit cards are not accepted. (The ARRL in no way warrants this offer.) As a service to the visually impaired, an operating manual is available on disk free of charge. To obtain the manual-on-disk, send a PC- or MS-DOS-formatted, 3½ or 5¼-inch floppy disk and self-addressed, stamped mailer to Idiom Press. When corresponding with the authors or Idiom Press, include a business-size, self-addressed, envelope with one unit of First Class postage. [At press time, a chip upgrade for the Super Keyer II was announced. For details, contact Idiom Press.—*Ed.*]

available from the source listed in footnote 2, serves as the keyer.

A glance at Fig 8 is all it takes to realize that the keyer doesn't need a keypad or a myriad of switches and knobs to control it. But don't conclude from this that it's just a bare-bones memory keyer! In fact, this keyer will satisfy the needs of casual ragchewers as well as avid DXers and contest operators. Because there are so few controls necessary to operate this keyer, handicapped amateurs will find it

easy to handle. As an aid to the handicapped, a manual-on-disk is available—see footnote 2.

FEATURES

Peek inside the Super Keyer II (see Fig 9) and you'll see that the small (1.4 × 2.4-inch) PC board contains only one IC, a couple of transistors and a few other components. It's the program in the IC that really makes this keyer remarkable. It provides:

Fig 9—An inside view of the Super Keyer II. Around the speaker, three AA, single-cell holders are glued to the box bottom. A pair of ¾-inch spacers support the PC board at the rear of the cabinet. The analog speed control (R13) is center-mounted on the front panel. On the back panel are the paddle and key-line jacks. As shown in Fig 8, the four push-button switches are mounted on the top half of the cabinet, two on each side of R13.

- An iambic keyer with dot and dash memories.
- Four 48-character messages.
- Character and Real-Time messages.
- Timed pauses within messages.
- Messages that can call other messages and contain operational commands.
- Message-loop capability for continuous play.
- Message break-in to allow for paddle-inserted text.
- Input queue to store multiple message activation.
- Contest serial numbering (000-9999).
- Digital and linear analog speed control (6-60 WPM).
- Adjustable weighting (dot/dash ratio) of 25-75%.
- A built-in 700-Hz sidetone monitor.
- A transmitter key-down (tune) function.
- Hand-key mode.
- Compensation for transmitter-induced keying distortion.
- Selectable automatic character spacing.
- Keyer-status inquiry functions.
- Ultra-low power consumption for battery operation.

How does the Super Keyer II provide all this flexibility without a keypad or a bunch of switches and knobs? Simple: Commands are sent to the keyer in Morse code—using the paddles!

A detailed explanation of the operational features of the keyer will be given later. First, let's have a look at the schematic diagram (Fig 10) and find out how easy it is to build your own Super Keyer II.

CIRCUIT DESCRIPTION

The keyer schematic is shown in Fig 10. The main component is the Motorola MC68HC705C8P CMOS microcomputer (U1). This IC contains an 8-bit central-processing unit, timer, bidirectional I/O lines, 304 bytes of RAM and nearly 8 kbytes of PROM. A 2-MHz clock is employed, with the frequency set by a ceramic resonator (Z1).

Dot, dash and message-input lines are pulled up by R2-R7 and momentarily grounded by paddle or button closures. Analog speed is controlled by a software analog-to-digital converter (ADC) in conjunction with R8, C8 and R13. C8 is charged quickly through R8 with PA2 configured as an output. PA2 is then made an input, and the discharge time through R13 is measured.

A software-generated 700-Hz sidetone is selectively output on PA5. Q2 is a voltage follower that provides speaker drive through R9. Transmitter keying is done by Q1, which will handle low-voltage, positive-key-line rigs only. Take care not to exceed any of the maximum ratings of the 2N2222 transistor used at Q1 (V_{CEO} = 30, I_C = 800 mA, P_D = 1.2 W). If your transceiver has a negative key line or one that exceeds Q1's limits (likely if you own an older transceiver with a vacuum-tube final amplifier), use an interface circuit between the keyer and the transceiver; suitable circuits were described in *QST*.[3]

[3]See J. Galm, "Cheap and Easy Control-Signal Level Converters," *QST*, Feb 1990, pp 24-27, for a means of interfacing this keyer with negative-key-line transmitters—*Ed*.

The CMOS Super Keyer II is designed for low power consumption. When idle, the microcomputer "sleeps"—not even the clock runs—yielding a current drain of under *10 μA!* Thus, there's no need for an on/off switch. While the keyer is active, its current consumption rises to about 5 mA (with the sidetone monitor turned off), but after two seconds of inactivity, the keyer automatically goes back to sleep. The monitor is the major power consumer, requiring peak currents of about 40 mA. So, to extend battery life, the monitor should normally be turned off, and the rig's sidetone used to monitor sending.

The keyer works with any supply voltage in the range of 3 to 5.5. Three series-connected, AA alkaline cells provide a nominal 4.5 V and will yield many months of service under normal operating conditions. You could also use four series-connected, rechargeable NiCd cells to supply 4.8 V, an approach similar to that taken with the original Super Keyer.

BUILD YOUR OWN

The PC board and associated components are available as a partial kit (see footnote 2). A parts-placement guide is shown in Fig 11. A full-scale etching pattern appears at the back of this book. Chassis-mounted parts, as used in the unit shown here, are all available from Radio Shack. Similar components are also stocked by mail-order electronics parts suppliers.[4]

A 1.5 × 5.08 × 5.25-inch plastic enclosure obtained at a local hamfest houses the keyer shown in the accompanying photos. With miniature switches and connectors and tighter packaging, a considerably smaller box would suffice. If you so desire, you can use remotely located message buttons instead of (or in parallel with) the chassis-mounted switches.

Though housed in a plastic box, the keyer has not shown any allergic reactions to RF even when it was used adjacent to a kilowatt amplifier driving coax-fed antennas. But if your shack (or Field Day site) is hot with RF, consider the use of a metal enclosure and shielded cables.

The keyer can be built without the manual speed control, R13. If you opt to do this, also use a 100-kΩ resistor for R8 and install a jumper wire in place of C8. Then, only digital speed control is available, so you might find this procedure useful: Program messages 1 and 2 with /SU2 and /SD2, respectively, so simple button pushes provide convenient up/down speed control in 2-WPM steps. (The /SU and /SD commands are described later.)

OPERATIONAL DESCRIPTION

When power is first applied to the keyer, it responds by sending OK in Morse code. The initialization state of the keyer is:

[4]Mouser Electronics, 2401 Hwy 287 N, Mansfield, TX 76063, tel 800-346-6873.

Fig 10—Schematic diagram of the keyer. All capacitors are 25-V units. Resistors are ¼-W carbon-composition or metal-film units. RS part numbers in parentheses are Radio Shack.

BT1—Three 1.5-V AA alkaline cells (RS 23-552) wired in series; NiCd cells can also be used—see text.
J1—¼-inch, three-circuit key jack (RS 274-312).
J2—Phono jack (RS 274-346).
LS1—2-inch diam, 8-Ω speaker (RS 40-245).
Q1,Q2—2N2222 or similar NPN (RS 276-2009).
R13—100-kΩ pot, linear taper (RS 271-092).

S1-S4—SPST push-button switch (RS 275-1566).
U1—Motorola MC68HC705C8P (must be pre-programmed; see footnote 2).
Z1—2-MHz resonator with built-in capacitor (Digi-Key part no. PX200; available from Digi-Key Corp, 701 Brooks Ave S, Thief River Falls, MN 56701, tel 800-344-4539).
Enclosure—Pac-Tec CM5-125 used for prototype shown here. (Pac-Tec boxes are

available from Electronic Precepts of Florida, 7401 114th Ave N, Suite 502A, Largo, FL 34643, tel 800-367-4649. The CM5-125 case comes in four colors: black, gray, tan and PC bone (an off-white). Price: $13.09 plus shipping and handling in quantities of 1 to 39. (The ARRL in no way warrants this offer.)
Two ¾-inch standoffs
Three single-cell battery holders (RS 270-401)
Knob (RS 274-416)

Fig 11—Parts-placement guide for the CMOS Super Keyer II. Parts are placed on the nonfoil side of the board; the shaded area represents an X-ray view of the copper pattern. An etching pattern appears at the back of this book.

- Speed: 20 WPM (at the current knob position).
- Weighting: 50%.
- Monitor: on.
- Auto-space: off.
- Messages: empty.
- Load mode: Character.
- Input queue: on.
- Serial number: 001.
- Number option: 0.
- Function speed: 20 WPM.

Speed Control

Speed range, determined by the software, is 6 to 60 WPM. The analog control (R13) varies the speed over a 3-to-1 range. Software compensation allows the speed to vary *linearly* with knob rotation—this rare feature makes speed adjustment easy. As you might expect, operating speed can also be set digitally. When speed is set digitally, it is assigned to the current knob position. This allows you to tailor the absolute speed range of the analog control to suit your operating needs. For example, at KCØQ, the fully counterclockwise position of the knob is programmed to be 13 WPM. Speed then increases linearly with clockwise rotation to a maximum of about 39 WPM.

To make function control easy, another—independent—speed can be programmed for use when entering commands. For example, even if you're operating at 35 WPM, function-controlling commands can be entered at 20 WPM or any other speed you choose. Alternatively, the command-entry speed can be made to default to the current operating speed. (See the explanation of the Reset mode under *Button Functions*.)

Keyer Commands

All paddle-entered keyer commands are sent in Morse code; they are summarized in alphabetical order in Tables 1-3. If you enter an invalid command, or an incorrect parameter for a command, the keyer emits a burst of rapid dots [which sound like an electronic raspberry!—Ed.] Multiple commands cannot be entered at one time. That is, each command must be entered separately and preceded by the simultaneous press of buttons 1 and 2. The presence of one or more *d*s represents the need for a digit(s) as part of the command.

Function Commands

Most function commands (see Table 1) are employed only once to customize the keyer to your preferences. The keyer's functions are controlled using the push-button switches and the paddles. From left to right (see Fig 8) the buttons are designated as 1, 2, 3 and 4. To alert the keyer that a command is to be entered, momentarily and simultaneously press buttons 1 and 2. The keyer automatically disables transmitter keying, enables the sidetone, switches to the current command-entry speed, and acknowledges your request by sending F. Then, key in the desired command characters. For example, entering S25 sets the operating speed to 25 WPM. When the command is completed (the keyer knows when this occurs; no other action is necessary), the transmitter key line is again enabled and the speed and sidetone return to their previous state.

The K*dd* command is included to compensate for keying distortion that may be introduced by your transmitter or amplifier. As is shown clearly in some *QST* product reviews, semi-break-in and full-break-in (QSK) operation can significantly shorten the keying on-time. This is caused by internal sequencing delays when changing between receive and transmit. The result is a light or choppy CW envelope. Although increasing the duty cycle with the weight command (W*dd*) helps, it is correct for only one speed. However, keying compensation (K*dd*) corrects the problem for all speeds by increasing the on-time of the keyer output, and commensurately decreas-

ing the off-time, by a period of up to 25 milliseconds.

The Z*d* command selects various treatments for zeros when playing the contest serial number. Leading zeros may be inhibited or replaced by an *O* or *T*. Independently, an *O* or *T* can also replace any other zeros, and an *N* can be substituted for the number *9*.

Inquiry Commands

See Table 2. In addition to the commands that change settings and modes, there is a full set of keyer inquiry commands you can use. Inquiry commands allow you to determine the current state of the keyer. State information is sent to you in Morse code with the monitor automati-

---

Table 1

Paddle-Entered Commands and Associated Functions

Command	Function
A	Auto-space—toggles the automatic character spacing feature on or off. The keyer confirms the new state by sending ON or OFF. When on, Auto-space aids the operator in forming properly spaced characters within a word. Character crowding is prevented by forcing at least three space elements whenever more than one space has been detected. This effect is very noticeable at low speeds and can be felt by high-speed operators as well. Without Auto-space, character spaces are determined by the operator.
D	Decrement—decrements the serial number by one, effectively canceling the automatic increment applied when last played from a message. The decrement function accommodates resending the last serial number, as might be needed when a repeat of a contest exchange is requested.
F*dd*	Function speed—sets the speed used to control keyer functions to *dd* WPM, where *dd* represents two digits in the range of 6 to 30 (leading zeros must be used for speeds less than 10 WPM). This speed is employed for entering commands and loading messages. It is independent of the operating speed and is unaffected by the analog speed control. Alternatively, the function speed can be made to follow the operating speed by setting *dd* = 00.
H	Hand key—causes the keyer to enter the hand-key mode. Keying output follows closures of the dot or dash paddle levers when either (or both) are used as a straight key. Normal iambic keyer operation is regained by pressing any of the four push-button switches.
K *dd*	Keying compensation—increases keying on-time and decreases keying off-time by *dd* milliseconds, where *dd* represents two digits in the range 00 to 25. Although similar to increasing weighting, the time adjustment is independent of speed.
L	Load mode—toggles the load mode between Character and Real-Time. The keyer confirms the new mode by sending C or R as appropriate.
M	Monitor—alternately enables and disables the 700-Hz sidetone monitor. To conserve battery power, use the rig's sidetone and operate the keyer with its monitor off.
N*dddd*	Number—initializes the contest serial number to *dddd*, where *dddd* represents four digits in the range of 0000 to 9999. Note that *four digits must be entered* even though only *three digits are sent for numbers less than 1000;* use leading zeros when appropriate. Also, it is possible—but not practical—to set the count to 000.
Q	Queue—toggles the input queue between on and off. The keyer confirms the new mode by sending ON or OFF as appropriate. When off, message-button closures are acted upon immediately, canceling any message in progress. When on, up to eight button presses are sequentially recalled and acted upon in sequence as each message completes.
RV	ReVerse—reverses the sense of the dot and dash paddles as may be desired by left-handed operators.
S*dd*	Speed—sets the current operating speed to *dd* WPM, where *dd* represents two digits in the range 6 to 60. Thus, keyer speed can be controlled in a precise, digital manner. In addition, the speed function establishes the current position of the manual speed control (R13) to correspond to the entered speed. The pot control knob can then be used to vary the speed faster or slower over a total range of 3 to 1. Control via the knob is linear and increases speed in a clockwise direction.
SU*d*	Speed Up—increases the operating speed by *d* WPM, where *d* is a single digit in the range of 0 to 9.
SD*d*	Slow Down—decreases the operating speed by *d* WPM, where *d* is a single digit in the range of 0 to 9.
W*dd*	Weight—sets the code weighting to *dd* percent, where *dd* represents two digits in the range of 25 to 75. Weight is the duty cycle of a continuous string of dots, which is 50% for perfectly sent code. A higher weighting percentage produces a "heavier" sound, and a lower weighting percentage causes characters to sound "lighter." Weighting is adjusted to the operator's preference as well as to compensate for transmitter distortion. Once set, weighting remains constant and independent of speed.
X	Xmit (tune)—causes a continuous key-down condition of the output key line for purposes of transmitter and amplifier adjustment. The keyer's monitor is *not* active in this mode. Opening the key line is accomplished by simply tapping the dot or dash paddle.
Z*d*	Zeros and Nines—controls the way that zeros and nines are sent in the serial number (see text).

cally enabled (even if it was disabled) and keying output disabled. Inquiries are initiated by momentarily and simultaneously pressing buttons 1 and 2. After receiving the F reply from the keyer, enter the desired inquiry with a leading question mark. For example, ?S asks what the current operating speed is; the keyer responds by sending two digits. Other inquiries evoke responses of ON, OFF or other meaningful characters as appropriate. The complete set of inquiries is: ?A, ?F, ?K, ?L, ?N, ?Q, ?S, ?W, ?Z, ?1, ?2, ?3 and ?4. The last four are message inquiries that play the contents of message buffers 1 through 4, respectively. None of the inquiry responses key the transmitter.

Embedded Commands

A summary of these commands and their functions is presented in Table 3. Character-mode messages (described later) can contain embedded commands. To distinguish the commands from normal text, the command strings are prefixed by a slash bar (/) and entered as a separate word. When encountered during a message playback, the desired function is executed.

Break (/B) suspends the message for paddle entry and then automatically resumes the message when an exaggerated word space is detected. It makes constructing contest message loops a breeze!

Gap (/Gd) allows spacing to be modified when emphasis is desirable. Expanded gaps can be used, for example, in call signs like W0EJ and W0IZ, to make the E or I easier to copy. It can also be used to shorten or lengthen the space between words.

Relative speed changes (/SUd, /SDd) can be very useful. For example, the message /SU5 QRZ TEST DE W0IZ /SD5 is played at increased speed, but leaves the normal operating speed unchanged.

Messages

Four message buffers are provided. Each can hold 48 bytes (384 bits), which is generous enough, for example, to store *the quick brown fox jumped over the lazy dogs back*. The message buffers are volatile: If power is removed from the keyer, the messages will be erased.

A message-editing feature is included. If you make a mistake while entering a message, send a stream of seven or more dots. This tells the keyer to locate the last word and erase it. The keyer then plays back the previous word (if any) so you know where you left off. You can erase as many words as necessary. When you've reached the desired position, simply continue with the entry.

Loading a message is easy. Just press and hold one of the four buttons. After two seconds, the sidetone is enabled and the keyer emits a tone to signify that transmitter keying is inhibited. The keyer then sends an R or C to tell you if it's in Real-Time or Character mode, then message loading may begin. Enter the message text

Table 2
Inquiry Commands

Command	Function
?A	Inquire Auto-space—the keyer responds by sending ON or OFF as appropriate.
?F	Inquire Function Speed—the keyer sends the current function speed setting in WPM as two digits.
?K	Inquire Keying Compensation—the keyer sends the current compensation in milliseconds as two digits.
?L	Inquire Load mode—the keyer responds by sending C if in Character mode, or R if in Real-Time mode.
?N	Inquire Number—the keyer plays the current contest serial number (but does not increment it).
?Q	Inquire Queue—the keyer responds with ON or OFF as appropriate.
?S	Inquire Speed—the keyer sends the current operating speed in WPM as two digits.
?W	Inquire Weighting—the current weighting percentage is reported by the keyer using two digits.
?Z	Inquire Zeros and Nines: the keyer responds with the option number (0-9) currently in effect.
?1	Inquire Message 1—message 1 is played.
?2	Inquire Message 2—message 2 is played.
?3	Inquire Message 3—message 3 is played.
?4	Inquire Message 4—message 4 is played.

Table 3
Embedded Commands and Associated Functions

Command	Function
/B	Break—message play is suspended to allow insertion of paddle text. The operator may then insert one or more words using the paddle. Once paddle input has begun, the Break function is canceled when inactivity exceeding a word space is detected. The interrupted message is then resumed. A Break may also be aborted by pressing one of the four pushbuttons, which causes the corresponding message to play immediately.
/D	Decrement—decrements the contest serial number by one.
/Gd	Gap—the normal 7-element interword space is modified to 3 + d, where d is a digit in the range of 0 to 9. It is used to exaggerate intercharacter or interword spacing. For example, a call like W0EJ can be entered with slight stretching of the character space around the E for emphasis, making it easier to copy. Note that /G0 yields a normal character space; /G4 yields a normal word space.
/N	Number—the current value of the contest serial number is played. Its value is then automatically incremented by one.
/Pdd	Pause—a speed-independent pause of d.d seconds is inserted, where dd represents two digits in the range of 00 to 99. For example, /P35 results in a delay of 3.5 seconds. Pauses greater than 9.9 seconds are obtained by using consecutive commands that total the desired value.
/Sdd	Speed—the operating speed is set to dd WPM, where dd represents two digits in the range of 6 to 60.
/SUd	Speed Up—increases the operating speed by d WPM, where d is a single digit in the range of 0 to 9.
/SDd	Slow Down—decreases the operating speed by d WPM, where d is a single digit in the range of 0 to 9.
/1	Message 1—message 1 is played followed by the resumption of the current message. If the current message is 1, a continuous loop is created. All four messages work this way.
/2	Message 2—message 2 is played followed by the resumption of the current message.
/3	Message 3—message 3 is played followed by the resumption of the current message.
/4	Message 4—message 4 is played followed by the resumption of the current message.

via the paddles. When you're done, terminate the message by simply tapping the same button again. If the message-buffer capacity is exceeded in either mode, the message is terminated automatically.

A message is played by tapping one of the four push-button switches. If the input-queue feature is enabled, the keyer will remember as many as eight button closures and play the messages in turn. Or, with the queue disabled, a button closure cancels any ongoing message and immediately starts the new one. Messages are aborted whenever a paddle is closed, allowing instant interruption for manual sending.

Real-Time Mode

The Real-Time mode works like it does in the original CMOS Super Keyer: What goes in is what comes out. You determine the spacing, so it will be as perfectly timed, compressed or exaggerated as you make it.

In this mode, pauses are stored as spaces. It's important to know this because those spaces consume memory. After you've asked the keyer to accept a message, you don't have to rush the first entry because the keyer won't start storing pause-spaces until the first paddle closure is made. Once message entry begins, however, the keyer loads continuously: any pauses introduced are stored as spaces in the message. The elapsed time between the end of the last character entered to message termination is stored as a space at the end of the message. Real-Time mode does *not* permit the use of embedded function commands.

Character Mode

In the Character mode, complete character encodings are stored (rather than just bits to represent dots, dashes and spaces). The software sanitizes your sending and produces perfectly timed Morse code when the message is played. Also, there is no

need to worry about word spacing. Just stop sending after every word—the keyer will prompt you by sending an I (this doesn't appear as output) and wait for you to send the next word. Unlike Real-Time mode, there is no limit to the elapsed time between words, so there's no need to rush your entry.

Messages entered using the Character mode can contain embedded function commands for greater operating flexibility. These commands include those for speed changes, playing and incrementing the serial number, decrementing the serial number for repeats, and more (see Table 3).

A message can call any other message, allowing the messages to be linked, if desired. If a message calls itself, directly or via another called message, a continuous loop results.

Loops are useful for beacons, calling CQ, moonbounce and meteor-scatter operation, and in contesting. Loops are even more useful with the embedded Pause and Break functions. Speed-independent pauses in multiples of 0.1 second can be inserted anywhere, and the message resumes automatically after the time expires. A message Break allows you to insert one or more words manually. The message then resumes after a pause that exceeds a normal word space.

Button Functions

As mentioned earlier, single-button closures activate messages, and the 1-2 combination readies the keyer to accept paddle-entry functions. For added convenience, certain keyer function commands are duplicated by other double-button closures. The 2-3 combination is acknowledged by the keyer sending D, and decrements the serial number. Pressing 2-4 enables the Xmit (tune) function and is ac-

knowledged by an X from the keyer. Similarly, pressing 1-3 sets the hand-key mode (preferred by some operators when tuning up their rigs), and is acknowledged by the keyer sending an H. The 3-4 button pair is for inquiry, and waits for paddle entry after acknowledging with ?. Finally, pressing buttons 1 and 4 simultaneously is acknowledged by the keyer as RV and causes a reversal in paddle sense (swapping the dot and dash sides of the paddle).

One four-button combination is recognized: 1-2-3-4. It's a Reset mode. It comes in handy, for instance, if you've mistakenly set the command-entry speed so high that you find you can't make further entries! If such a mistake occurs, don't panic or pull the batteries. Just press all four buttons simultaneously. The operating speed is reset to 20 WPM at the current knob position and the function-entry speed defaults to follow the knob setting. You can then decrease the speed to a comfortable value.

SUMMARY AND ACKNOWLEDGMENTS

Within a few months after this keyer appeared in *QST*, over 900 kits had been sold. A small number of builders reported problems. These problems were traced to transistors that were installed backwards or the builder's use of normally closed instead of normally open switches. Double-check your work!

The CMOS Super Keyer II is designed to be versatile yet simple and affordable. It has the advantage of battery operation and can serve your needs from a basic iambic keyer to a powerful contest machine.

Designs such as this are never done in a vacuum. We gratefully acknowledge the assistance, suggestions and encouragement offered by Bob, W9KNI; Joe, NØBB; Dale, WØIZ; Barry, WAØRJT and Jim, WØSR.

An LSI Modem for Amateur Radio

Whether you are trying to get on the air with a complex packet-radio terminal node controller or simply hooking up your home computer to copy RTTY, you will need an interface to change the analog output of your radio to digital input for your computer, and to change the digital output from your computer to analog input for your radio. This interface MODulates input to the radio and DEModulates output from the radio, so it is called a *modem*. This project, shown in Figs 12 through 15, presents a modem designed around an Advanced Micro Devices Am7910 IC.[1] Use of this large scale integrated (LSI) circuit device greatly simplifies construction of an inexpensive and simple, yet versatile and noise-immune, modem. Jeff Ward, K8KA, designed and built this project in the ARRL lab.

The Am7910

The Am7910 is a complete modem in a 28-pin DIP package. The chip requires no external filters or control circuits. Fig 12 shows that all of the control and data lines for a full-duplex FSK modem are available right on the chip. Five "mode-control" pins allow the selection of various FSK tone pairs and filter parameters. External circuitry is needed only to buffer the input and output signals and to provide operating voltage to the Am7910.

The modulator and demodulator in the chip employ both analog and digital signal-processing circuits. The incoming signal first passes through an analog prefilter, then is converted by an analog-to-digital (A/D) converter, then passes through digital band-pass filters, and finally is

[1]Devices, application notes and information are available from Advanced Micro Devices, 901 Thompson Pl, PO Box 3453, Sunnyvale, CA 94088.

Fig 12—The Am7910 is a complete, full-duplex modem in a 28-pin DIP package.

Table 1
Am7910 Modes Used in Amateur Radio

S5	S4	S3	S2	S1	
MC4	MC3	MC2	MC1	MC0	Mode
1	0	0	0	0	Bell 103 originate loop-back.
1	0	0	0	1	Bell 103 answer loop-back.
1	0	0	1	0	Bell 202 main loop-back.
1	0	0	1	1	Bell 202 with equalizer loop-back.

†1 indicates an open switch; 0 a closed switch.

digitally demodulated. The modulator is a digital sine synthesizer, followed by digital band-pass filters, a digital-to-analog converter (DAC) and an analog post filter. As a result of this mixture of analog and digital circuitry, the Am7910 has a clean, stable modulator and a selective demodulator.

Modes and Mode Control

The mode-control pins (pins 17-21) on the Am7910 deserve some explanation. These pins should be thought of as five binary bits. Changing the voltages on the pins changes the binary word which they represent. Different "control words" cause the modem to enter different modes.

Four of the available modes are used in radio communication. Table 1 shows the switch settings and binary codes for these modes. Bell 202 is a 1200-baud FSK protocol found on most packet-radio networks. The only difference between the two Bell 202 implementations is in demodulator filter response.

Bell 103 is a 200-Hz shift FSK protocol. It is used for packet radio on the HF bands, and is also very close to the 170-Hz shift used by standard amateur RTTY stations. Bell 103 is a full-duplex protocol—the modem receives on one pair of tones while simultaneously transmitting on another pair. Unfortunately, for Amateur Radio use, we need to have the modem receive and transmit on the same tone pair. On most modems, this means changing a switch setting every time the station is switched from transmit to receive or vice versa. However, the "loopback" modes on the Am7910 solve this problem. These modes are usually used for testing the modem. For that purpose, the modem transmitter and receiver are put on the same tone pair. Since this is what is desired in the half-duplex radio environment, the loop-back modes are used for normal Amateur Radio operation.

Circuit Description

Using discrete components to build a modem as versatile as the Am7910 would be a costly and delicate task. In contrast, only 10 components and a power supply are needed to put the Am7910 in operation. The circuit presented here (Fig 13) is

not the bare-bones implementation of the Am7910. To make the modem easy to use, this circuit adds two ICs and a few other components to the minimum configuration.

While the Am7910 uses 0 V for a logic low and +5 V for a logic high, computer equipment which adheres to the RS-232-C interface standard normally uses +12 V for logic high and −12 V for logic low. U2 and U3, a 1489 RS-232-C line receiver and a 1488 RS-232-C line driver, make the modem RS-232-C compatible.

A single DIP package contains S1 through S5, the mode-control switches. These switches make it easy to use any of the modes available on the AM7910. The mode-control pins are TTL compatible and draw little current. When one of the switches (S1-S5) is open, the corresponding mode-control pin is set to +5 V (logic high) via one of resistors R1-R5. When one of the switches is closed, the corresponding pin is grounded (logic low). In the grounded position, the high value chosen for R1-R5 reduces current drain from the +5 V supply. Of course, the mode of operation could be hard-wired into the circuit, but why sacrifice versatility?

The rest of the chip is wired as specified in Advanced Micro Devices' application notes for the Am7910, ignoring all but one of the "back-channel" connections. The one back-channel control line which must be connected is Back Request To Send (BRTS), pin 11. This pin must be set to

Table 2
Pin-outs for P1 and P2

P1		P2	
Pin	Signal	Pin	Signal
1	GND	1	Transmit carrier (TC)
2	TD	2	GND
3	RD	3	GND
4	RTS	4	Receive carrier (RC)
5	CD		
6	CTS		
7	NC		
8	DTR		

P1 has pin 1 toward the power supply, while P2 has pin 4 toward the power supply.

Fig 13—Schematic diagram for the Am7910-based modem and power supply. All resistors are ¼ W.

C1,C2,C25—220 μF, 35-V electrolytic, radial leads.
C3-C10—1 μF tantalum.
C11-C14—0.01μF disc ceramic.
C15-C18—10 μF, 50-V electrolytic, axial leads.
C19—22 pF silver mica.
C20—15 pF silver mica.
C21—0.033 μF disc ceramic.
C22,C24—0.68 μF disc ceramic.
C23—2000 pF disc ceramic.
P1—8-pin locking header (GC-41-088 or equiv.).
P2—4-pin locking header (GC-41-084 or equiv.).

P3—CEE-22 male, chassis mount.
R10—100 Ω, 2 W.
S1-S5—SPST, contained on a single DIP switch.
S6—SPST.
T1—Power transformer; 117-V primary, 30-V CT secondary (Cat. no. 102.152; available from Toroid Corp. of Maryland, 4720-Q Boston Way, Lanham, MD 20706).
U1—Advanced Micro Devices Am7910 (see text).
U2—1488 RS-232-C line driver. For TTL interfacing, use jumpers shown at A in detail. See text.
U3—1489 RS-232-C line receiver. For TTL

interfacing, use jumpers shown at B in detail. See text.
U4—Bridge rectifier (Radio Shack 276-1146 or equiv.).
U5—LM7805 +5-V, 1-A voltage regulator.
U6—LM78L12 +12-V, 100-mA voltage regulator.
U7—LM79L12 −12-V, 100-mA voltage regulator.
U8—LM79L05 −5-V, 100-mA voltage regulator.
Y1—2.4576-MHz crystal (M-Tron MP-2 or equiv. Available from M-Tron Industries Inc., P.O. Box 630, Yankton, SD 57078.).

Fig 14—Using the toroidal power transformer, the modem and the power supply fit neatly on a small PC board.

+5 V, unasserting BRTS; otherwise the back channel would take control of the modem. A copy of the applications notes for the Am7910 will help you to better understand the circuit.

Power Supply

Since the Am7910 runs on ±5 V and the RS-232-C interface demands ±12 V, the circuit includes a four-voltage regulated power supply. Regulators rated at 100 mA are used on all but the +5 V supply. The +5-V supply must provide more than 100 mA, so a 1-A regulator and a small heat-sink are employed. To keep the supply small, a toroidal power transformer was used. If you do not intend to mount your modem in a small box, any transformer with a 25-V, center-tapped secondary could be used. The combination of C25 and R10 causes a 5-ms rise time on the +5-V supply,

as required by the Am7910. The rest of the power supply design is standard, with special attention paid to the selection and placement of bypass capacitors. For a complete discussion of regulated power supplies, see Chapter 6.

Construction Technique

Although the circuit can be built on a perforated board using point-to-point wiring, it is recommended that you use the circuit-board layout provided (Fig 14). Use of the circuit board not only speeds construction and trouble-shooting, but results in a stable, reproducible circuit. Sockets are used for all ICs, and for the DIP switch (S1-S5). Locking, polarized connectors are used for all digital and analog signals to and from the modem. See Table 2. Parts placement for the PC board is shown in Fig 15, and a full-size etching pattern appears at the back of this book.

The circuit board is mounted on the bottom plate of an 8 × 10 × 2-in chassis. Appropriate digital, audio and power connectors, and an ON/OFF switch are mounted on the chassis itself, and the chassis is then attached to the bottom plate, over the circuit board. Of particular interest is the use of a CEE-22 power connector with integral fuse holder, which saves some precious rear-panel space.

Circuit Check-Out

Once you have mounted all of the components on your PC board, make some tests before putting any of the ICs in their sockets. Check for properly regulated voltages at the ungrounded ends of C15,

C16, C17 and C18. Check to see that there is +5 V on pin 2 of U1 and pin 14 of U2. Check that −5 V is on pin 4 of U1. Pin 1 of U3 should be at −12 V, and pin 14 of U3 should be at +12 V. Once you have made these measurements, turn off the supply and insert U2 and U3 in their sockets. Turn on the supply, and measure the voltage at every pin on the socket for U1. None of these pins should have a voltage greater than +5 V or less than −5 V. If any of these pins are outside of the ±5 V range, check to see that U2 and U3 are in the correct sockets, and that all PC-board jumpers are installed correctly. Only when you have ensured that no voltages too high or too low are being applied to the socket for U1 should you install U1 and attempt to use the modem. It may be hard to resist the temptation to simply plug everything in at once and "go for it"—but remember, the Am7910 is the single most expensive component on the board. Its protection is worth a few minutes' delay.

Modem Operation

Once you have completed the preliminary check-out of your modem, connect it to a computer or (preferably) an EIA-232-D break-out box. Set the mode-control switches to Bell 202 main loopback (switches 1, 3 and 4 in the ON position; switches 2 and 5 OFF). Now set RTS and DTR to +12 V. The modem should respond by setting CTS to +12 V. CD should remain at −12 V. If you now connect pins 1 and 4 on the audio connector (connecting the transmit output to the receive input) CD should go to +12 V, and whatever voltage is on TD should also appear at RD. If all goes as predicted, hook the modem to your rig, and you're on the air!

Troubleshooting

Although the Am7910 is a complex chip, and not all possible problems can be covered here, a few common problems should be mentioned.

If the modem operates well on the test bench, but erratically when connected to a radio, you have RFI problems. If the modem is not in a box, put it in one. Ground the box, and put ferrite beads on all lines into and out of the modem. Shield all of the I/O cables. Unless you have unusual amounts of RF in your shack, these precautions should eliminate the RFI.

If CTS does not go to +12 V when you set RTS and DTR, momentarily ground the case of the crystal (Y1). If this solves the problem, your crystal is not starting to oscillate when you turn on the modem. Although there is no sure fix for this problem, try varying the values of C19 and C20. Experiment with asymmetrical values between 10 and 20 pF. A high value (1-MΩ) resistor across the leads of Y1 may also result in consistent oscillator start-up. If oscillator start-up does not seem to be the

Fig 15—Parts-placement guide for the Am7910-based modem and power supply, shown from the component side of the board. A full-size etching pattern appears at the back of this book.

problem, check to see that you have indeed sent the correct voltages to U1: pin 12 and pin 16 should see 0.0 V (resulting from the +12-V signals on RTS and DTR being inverted and buffered by U2). Pin 11 and pin 1 (BRTS and RING) should be at +5 V, disabling the back channel and enabling the modem. If all of these conditions are met, and your modem still does not work, get the application notes from the manufacturer and start troubleshooting.

Non-RS-232-C Operation

Some home computers do not have true RS-232-C (or EIA-232-D) interface signals. These machines commonly use +5 V and 0 V for I/O. Since the Am7910 uses these same signal levels, such computers can be interfaced to the modem without U2 and U3, the RS-232-C transmitter and receiver. U2 and U3 should be replaced with jumpers as shown in Fig. 13. Remember that control signals will now be considered ON when

they are at 0 V and OFF when they are at +5 V. Check to see that this is how your computer's control signals are defined. If they send +5 V when they are ON you will have to invert them before sending them to the Am7910.

Experiments

If you're interested in experimentation, there are some interesting things that can be tried with the Am7910. Both of these experiments should allow the modem to be used on 170-Hz RTTY. The simplest way to use the Am7910 on 170-Hz RTTY is to use one of the 200-Hz shift Bell 103 loopback modes. The 30-Hz difference between the amateur tones and the Bell 103 tones does not degrade performance very much. Try it and see!

Another way to put the Am7910 on 170-Hz shift would be to change the frequency of Y1. Since Y1 is the frequency

reference for the entire modem, lowering the frequency of Y1 by 15% should change the 200-Hz shift to 170-Hz. This modification has not been tried yet, but that is what home-brewing is all about! If you are going to use your Am7910 modem on HF, be sure you understand what RF tones will result if you use an SSB transmitter with the AF tones from the modem. You will want to be sure that you are listening and transmitting on the same frequencies.

Conclusion

The Am7910 modem, using the circuit presented here, has been in use for some time on a packet-radio repeater at ARRL Headquarters. If you are interested in many facets of digital communication, this modem, with its many modes, could be the solution to your interface problems. For a state-of-the-art project that's easy to build and useful in the shack, the Am7910 "World Chip" fills the bill.

The W2IHY Audio Memory Keyer

A digital voice recorder (called a DVR, or audio keyer) is the audio equivalent of a CW memory keyer. A CW memory keyer stores Morse code messages for retransmitting. A DVR stores digitized audio messages for retransmission. Digital voice recorders are gaining popularity with SSB/FM contesters. With a DVR, memory segments can be loaded with short, frequently used messages (such as CQs and contest exchanges). These messages can then be easily retransmitted. Other uses for the audio keyer include record and playback of received audio during a QSO and voice identification for a repeater. In a few years audio keyers will be as common a station accessory as CW memory keyers are today.

The audio keyer shown in Figs 16 through 18 was designed and built by Julius Jones, W2IHY.

W2IHY thanks Herb and Barbara Sweet, (K2GBH and WA2KCL) for their assistance with the project writeup. The audio keyer has the following features:

1) Four message memories each capable of storing up to 10 seconds of digitized audio
2) A message write/read (record/send) indicator
3) A microphone gain indicator
4) A built-in audio monitor
5) The ability to repeatedly read (send) a selected memory
6) Adjustable delays between repeats
7) Electronic control of transmitter push to talk (PTT)
8) Adjustable PTT sensitivity and delay controls
9) Voice-activated reset (VAR)
10) Adjustable VAR sensitivity control
11) Battery back-up capability

The audio keyer is designed using commonly available components, including 74HC series high-speed CMOS, 256k × 1-bit dynamic random-access memory (DRAM) chips, LM1458N operational amplifiers, linear voltage regulators and an Analog Devices eight-bit analog-to-digital / digital-to-analog converter (ADC7569JN) containing an on-chip track and hold circuit.

The audio keyer can be constructed, using all new parts, for about $185. A single-message version can be built for about $130 by replacing the 256k DRAM ICs with 64k ICs (150 ns or 120 ns). The single-message keyer may be later upgraded to full capacity simply by installing 256k ICs. All the parts are available from Jameco Electronics[1] and Mouser Electronics[2],

except the A-to-D converter which is available from Analog Devices[3].

The keyer has been used in high RF environments without any problems. It has also been used in a multiband SSB contest. On-the-air tests indicate that other stations find it difficult to distinguish between live signals and keyer-generated signals.

Circuit Description

The schematic of the DVR is shown in Fig 17, and a block diagram of the keyer is shown in Fig 18. Audio from the microphone is amplified through two cascaded operational amplifiers. The audio microphone level control (R49) sets the gain of the second stage of amplification.

The output of the microphone amplifier is sent to a six-pole unity-gain low-pass filter and to an analog audio switch. (The audio switch will be discussed later.) The low-pass filter removes high frequencies present in the amplified microphone signal. The 3-dB cut-off frequency of the filter is 1.8 kHz.

The output of the microphone low-pass filter is sent to the analog-to-digital converter (ADC), microphone-level indication circuitry and VAR circuitry. The ADC samples the low-pass filter output and converts it into an 8-bit data word.

Signals sampled by the ADC exceeding ± 1.25 volts will be clipped to ± 1.25 volts. The microphone level LED (DS1) provides visual indication when the input level to the ADC is near + 1.25 V. The microphone-level indicator is turned on when the ADC is sent a signal from the microphone low-pass filter exceeding 0.9 V. The microphone

low-pass filter output is also sent to the voice-activated reset (VAR) circuitry. When activated, VAR allows the audio keyer to be reset when you speak into the microphone. This is analogous to resetting a CW memory keyer by tapping the paddle. VAR sensitivity potentiometer R47 establishes the microphone low-pass filter level that will reset the keyer.

The output of the ADC is sent to eight 256k × 1 DRAM chips. The control circuits allow the digitized microphone input to be stored in the memory.

To send (play back) data stored in memory, an eight-bit word is read from memory and sent to the DAC, where the data is restored to analog form.

The output of the DAC is sent to a six-pole low-pass filter. (The DAC low-pass filter is identical to the microphone low-pass filter.) This filter removes high-frequency components from the DAC-generated analog signal.

The output of the DAC low-pass filter is sent to the analog audio switch and to the push-to-talk controls. During playback, audio in analog form is gated from the DAC low-pass filter through the analog switch (transistor Q2). When the keyer is not sending or writing, the analog switch selects audio from the microphone amplifier (transistor Q1). During a write operation neither the microphone amplifier nor the DAC low-pass filter are gated through the analog audio switch.

Audio gated through the analog switch is sent to output level control R44 and to the speaker monitor amplifier. T1 provides isolation between the keyer audio output and the microphone input of the transceiver. R44 is adjusted to drive the attached transceiver to the appropriate audio level. The output of the analog switch is also sent to the speaker monitor. Control R48 adjusts the monitor volume.

The PTT controls detect audio sent from the DAC low-pass filter. When audio is

Fig 16—The W2IHY Audio Memory Keyer can store four messages, each containing up to 10 seconds of audio.

[1]Jameco Electronics, 1355 Shoreway Road, Belmont, CA 94002, tel 415-592-8121.
[2]Mouser Electronics, 2401 Hwy 287 North, Mansfield, TX 76063, tel 1-800-346-6873.

[3]Analog Devices Inc, Rt 1 Industrial Park, Norwood, MA 02062-9106, tel 617-329-4700. (AD7569JN may be phone ordered).
[4]PC boards and information available from: Julius D. Jones (W2IHY), 15 Vanessa Lane, Staatsburg, NY 12580, tel 914-889-4933.

detected, transistor Q3 grounds the transceiver's PTT. Adjustment of the PTT sensitivity control (R45) determines the DAC low-pass filter level that will ground the transceiver's PTT. The delay (PTT) control (R46) determines the length of time Q3 is grounded after the absence of detected audio from the DAC low-pass filter.

The control circuits provide the following functions:

1) crystal control timebase
2) refresh control for the dynamic RAMS
3) interfaces to various front-panel controls including memory select pushbuttons (S1-S4), reset pushbutton (S5), repeat switch (S7), repeat delay (R59) and send/write switch (S6).

When a memory button is pressed, the position of the send/write switch (S6) determines whether the selected memory is loaded with microphone audio or played to the transceiver. During a write operation, the VAR and repeat functions are disabled and the audio being recorded is not gated through the audio switch.

Sending recorded data with repeat on causes the selected memory to be continuously read. Sending (with or without repeat on) may be stopped by pushing the reset button, pushing (enabling) the microphone PTT or using the voice activated reset (VAR). The repeat delay function allows the user to select the amount of time between delays. The repeat delay time-out begins when the microphone PTT is disabled (transceiver PTT unkeyed). Enabling the microphone PTT prior to completion of the repeat time-out resets the timer.

The following example is meant to clarify the operation of repeat delay. Each memory may contain up to 10 seconds of audio. Suppose that memory number one contains six seconds of audio followed by four seconds of no audio. Memory number two contains four seconds of audio followed by two seconds of no audio, followed by three seconds of audio and one second of no audio. Repeat is on and repeat delay is set to six seconds. If memory number one is read, the message will be repeated every 12 seconds. If memory number two is read, the message will be repeated every 15 seconds. The minimum delay in a repeat time-out is a few milliseconds. The maximum delay in a repeat time-out is about 20 seconds.

The Memory In Use LED (DS2) is turned on during a send/write operation. At the completion of reading from or writing to memory, the LED is turned off. During a repeat operation that takes more than 10 seconds, the Memory In Use LED stays on for only the first 10 seconds of the operation (only when the memory is being read). Referring to the previous example, if memory number one is read with repeat on, the Memory In Use LED will remain on for 10 seconds and will be turned off for two seconds. If memory number two

was read, the Memory In Use LED would remain on for 10 seconds and would be turned off for five seconds.

Construction

Point-to-point or wire-wrap methods can be used to construct the keyer. A glass-epoxy double-sided board with plated-through holes, solder mask, and a silk-screened parts-placement pattern is available from W2IHY[4]. With this board it is recommended that sockets be used for all of the ICs. Also, all components should be soldered to the board with a low-wattage soldering iron (25 to 40 watts). The board measures 5.5 by 9.375 inches.

Wiring most switches and potentiometers to the PC board is accomplished through 16-pin IC sockets J4 and J5. Two single-ended 24-inch 16-pin DIP jumpers are connected between the various panel LEDs, potentiometers and switches and the sockets on the PC board. The schematic diagram and Table 1 provide details of the connections.

The memory select and reset pushbuttons S1 through S5 can be connected to the board through either IC socket. If one socket is used to connect front-panel switches to the board, the other socket may be connected to an external source (through a connector) to provide remote control of the keyer. It is important to use shielded cables as shown on the schematic. Decoupling capacitors must be used at the power connectors (0.1 μF) and at the microphone input connections (0.1 μF) to the keyer. Spurious signals will be heard if the capacitors are omitted. Power (ac or dc) entering the keyer must first be grounded on the PC board to prevent ground loops. In the prototype, this was accomplished by using a three-conductor miniature stereo plug and jack for the power connectors.

Power Supply

The audio keyer may be powered by either a 9 to 12 V ac supply or a 10 to 20 V dc supply. Battery backup may also be used for short periods. If only 12 V dc or battery backup operation is desired, diode D14 may be removed. If only ac operation (without battery backup) is desired, components D11, D12, D15, U36, R41, R42, C8, C13 and C14 are not necessary. The battery backup voltage should never exceed the voltage on capacitor C47.

Crystal Frequency Selection

The crystal frequency should be selected to optimize audio bandwidth and message size while considering the minimum refresh rate. All memory cells must be refreshed within 4 milliseconds. The minimum crystal frequency that will do this is 2.048 MHz. The following equation defines (for a given crystal frequency) the message length in seconds.

Message Time (in seconds) =

$$\frac{\text{Memory Size} \times 1024}{2 \times \text{Crystal Frequency (in hertz)}}$$

Using a 3.2768 MHz crystal, it will take 10.24 seconds to load one 65,536 × 8-bit-word memory segment. It is recommended that a crystal between the frequencies of 3.0 MHz and 3.6 MHz be used. Using a crystal with a frequency below 3 MHz will require modifying the response of the low-pass filters.

Wiring Options

Microphone Impedance—The microphone amplifier shown in the schematic is designed to work with a low-impedance microphone. A high-impedance microphone may be used if the following

---

Table 1

J4 and J5 Pin-outs

J4		J5	
Pin	Signal	Pin	Signal
1	VAR sensitivity R47	1	Repeat delay potentiometer R59
2	VAR reset to switch S10	2	Memory pushbutton S2
3	PTT sensitivity potentiometer R45	3	Memory pushbutton S4
4	PTT delay potentiometer R46	4	Memory In Use LED DS2
5	PTT from microphone	5	Send/write switch S6
6	Memory pushbutton S1	6	Ground
7	Memory pushbutton S3	7	Repeat switch S7
8	Keyer pushbutton S5	8	Keyer Reset pushbutton S5
9	Audio out to speaker	9	Repeat switch S7
10	Memory pushbutton S4	10	Power on LED DS3
11	Memory pushbutton S2	11	Microphone Level LED DS1
12	PTT out to transceiver (to S11)	12	SEND/WRITE switch S6
13	Ground	13	Not used
14	PTT sensitivity potentiometer R45	14	Memory pushbutton S3
15	VAR reset (from switch S16)	15	Memory pushbutton S1
16	+5 V VAR sensitivity potentiometer R47	16	+5 V to repeat delay potentiometer R59

Fig 17 (sheet 1 of 3)

Fig 17 (sheet 2 of 3)

Fig 17 (sheet 3 of 3)

Fig 17—Schematic diagram of the W2IHY audio keyer. All resistors are ¼ W, 5% units unless noted. Capacitors are disc ceramic units unless noted. Capacitors marked with polarity are radial electrolytic. PC boards for this project are available from W2IHY[4].

C1-C8, C53—4.7 µF, 16 V radial electrolytic.
C9-C12, C66, C67—0.01 µF, 50 V Mylar 10%.
C13, C14, C29-C45, C56-C65—0.1 µF, 25 V Mylar 10%.
C46—100 pF, 50 V disc ceramic.
C23,C24,C26-C28,C51,C52,C54,C55—100 µF, 16 V radial electrolytic.
C15-C18—0.033 µF, 50 V Mylar 10%.
C19-C22—0.001 µF, 50 V Mylar 10%.
C47, 48—3300 µF, 25 V radial electrolytic.
C49,C50—1000 µF, 25 V radial electrolytic.
D1-D10, D16-D18—Silicon diode (1N914 or 1N4148).
D11-D15—1N4001.
J1,J2—Female microphone connector (choose to match your equipment).
J3—RCA phono plug.
J4,J5—16-pin IC socket.
R1-R29, R56-R58—10 kΩ.
R31- R34—1 kΩ.
R43—820 Ω.
R38, R50-R55—100 Ω.
R41—330 Ω.
R39,R40—470 Ω.
R37—2.2 kΩ.
R30—300 kΩ.
R35—47 kΩ.
R36—4.7 kΩ.
R42—680 Ω.
R49—25 kΩ potentiometer.
R44-R48—10 kΩ potentiometer, ½ W.
R59—1 MΩ potentiometer.
S1-S5—Single-pole momentary pushbutton switch.
S6,S8—DPDT toggle switch.
S7—SPDT toggle switch.
S9—4PDT toggle switch.
S10, S11—SPST toggle switch.
T1—Audio transformer, 600 Ω 1:1 (Mouser 42TM016).
T2—117 V ac primary, 9 V ac 500 mA secondary.
Q1-Q3—2N2222A.
U1-U4, U6—LM1458N.
U5—LM386N.
U7—AD7569JN A/D and D/A converter IC; Analog Devices Inc[3].
U8-U15—41256 256k × 1-bit dynamic RAM.
U16, U18, U20, U34—74HC4040.
U17, U19, U21—74HC244.
U22, U25, U29—74HC00.
U23, U30—74HC04.
U24, U28, U31—74HC10.
U26—74LS123.
U27, U35—74HC73.
U32, U33—74HC20.
U36—LM555.
Y1—3.2768 MHz crystal.

Fig 18—Block diagram of the audio keyer. See text for a discussion of this diagram.

component values are used: R31 = 47k, R35 = 47Ok, R32 = 47k.

Microphone Level—Control of the microphone amplifier gain is provided by potentiometer R49. Increasing the value of R49 increases the microphone amplifier gain.

PTT Sensitivity—Potentiometer R45 controls the sensitivity of the PTT circuitry. Increasing the value of R45 increases the PTT sensitivity.

PTT Delay—Potentiometer R46 controls the hold time of the push to talk circuit. Increasing the resistance of R46 increases the PTT hold time.

Audio Output Level—Potentiometer R44 controls the audio keyer output level. Increasing the resistance of R44 increases the keyer analog output level.

Monitor Volume—Potentiometer R48 controls the monitor audio output volume. Increasing the resistance of R48 will increase the monitor volume.

Voice Activated Reset Sensitivity—VAR sensitivity controls the microphone audio level that resets the audio keyer. As R47 is increased, lower microphone audio levels are required to reset the keyer.

Repeat Delay—Potentiometer R59 controls the delay between reading and re-reading the memory. Increasing R59 increases the delay between repeats.

Operating the Audio Keyer

When power is first applied to the keyer, it may be sending or writing. Press the reset button or microphone PTT to cancel these operations. This will return the keyer to a known state.

Message Writing

While you talk into the microphone, adjust the microphone level control (R49) until the microphone level indicator (DS1) begins to light. Next set the send/write switch (S6) to the write position. Push one of 4 memory push buttons to load (write) a memory. *Do not press your PTT button at this point*; this will reset the keyer. The Memory In Use indicator (DS2) will stay on until the selected memory is full. It takes about 10 seconds to load a particular memory. During write operations, the repeat, monitor output and VAR functions are automatically disabled.

Message Sending

Set the send/write switch (S6) to the send position. Turn off the repeat and VAR switches. Press one of the four memory pushbuttons to begin the send operation. The Memory In Use indicator (DS2) will stay on until the memory read operation is completed. Again, do not press the PTT switch at this point; this will reset the keyer.

PTT Sensitivity and PTT Delay

Follow the message sending procedure. Adjust the PTT delay to mid scale. Adjust the PTT sensitivity (R45) until the transceiver's push to talk is enabled. Adjust the PTT delay potentiometer (R46) for the desired hold time, and readjust the PTT sensitivity control if necessary.

Repeat and Repeat Delay

PTT sensitivity and PTT delay *must* be adjusted for desired operation. Turn on the repeat switch (S7). Follow the message sending procedure. Adjust R59 to obtain the desired spacing between messages.

VAR and VAR Sensitivity

Turn on the Voice Activated Reset (VAR) switch (S10). Follow the message sending procedure. Talk into the microphone. Adjust the VAR sensitivity control (R47) until the keyer is reset.

Transceiver PTT Operation

Transceiver PTT operations may be activated by turning on switch S11 and either sending a message from the keyer or by pushing the microphone PTT. When the microphone PTT is depressed, the keyer is reset. Audio from the microphone is amplified and sent to the transceiver and the transceiver PTT is grounded (activated). Switch S11 should be turned off if VOX operation is desired.

Keyer Bypass

A four-pole double-throw switch (S9) is used to switch either the audio keyer or the microphone to the audio output jack. If S9 has switched the microphone directly to the transceiver, the keyer need not be powered on for the microphone and its PTT to be used with the transceiver.

Audio Output

The audio output control (R44) should be adjusted to drive the transceiver to the same audio level that is obtained from a directly connected microphone.

BOB—An EIA-232-D Break-Out Box

The EIA-232-D interface standard greatly simplifies the interconnection of digital devices. When something goes wrong at a 232-D interface, however, the 25 signal lines and two equipment configurations—data terminal equipment (DTE) and data-circuit terminating equipment (DCE)—can easily confuse the troubleshooter. The EIA-232-D break-out box (BOB) is a piece of test equipment used to simplify troubleshooting. Jeff Ward, K8KA, designed and built the breakout box described here in the ARRL lab.

Break-out boxes can be simple or very complex. In its simplest form, a break-out box displays the polarity of the voltage on an EIA-232-D line. Deluxe break-out boxes monitor and change the voltages on several EIA-232-D lines and alter the wiring at the interface between two EIA-232-D devices. The deluxe break-out box is powerful, but expensive. Fortunately, many of the problems that amateurs will encounter can be diagnosed with a relatively simple break-out box.

BOB

This project (Figs 19-23) describes the construction and use of BOB, an average break-out box. BOB is inexpensive, yet useful in many situations. It has the following features: a male and a female DB-25 connector at each end; a patch bay that allows any of the 7 most important lines at one

Fig 19—The final version of the EIA-232-D break-out box uses PC-board construction. The prototype, built on a perforated board using wire-wrap techniques, performed just as well.

end to be patched to any of the lines at the other end; the ability to set any line to +12 V or −12 V; and bi-color LEDs to indicate the polarity of the voltage on each line.

The circuit (Fig 20) is simple. Each of the signal lines (2,3,4,5,6,8 and 20) is brought from the DB-25 connectors to the DIP socket in the center of the BOB. The DIP socket acts as a patch bay. Any line from one pair of connectors can be patched to any line on the other pair. Each line is attached to a DPDT center-off toggle switch. One position of the switch sets the line to +12 V; the other position sets the line to −12 V. The OFF position lets the line "float" at the voltage applied to it by devices attached to BOB. Bi-color, polarity-indicating LEDs with current limiting resistors display the polarity of each line.

If BOB is to be used to set voltage levels on EIA-232-D lines, an external ±12-V power supply is needed. In this case, the ground from BOB should be connected to the power supply ground. Otherwise, BOB should be grounded to the unit(s) under test.

Construction

The prototype for BOB was built on a perforated-board chassis using wire-wrap techniques. The LEDs were mounted on the top of the board, while the switches were mounted through the board using standard mounting hardware. Although

Fig 20—Schematic diagram for the EIA-232-D breakout box. The same circuit is used for pins 2, 3, 4, 5, 6, 8 and 20.

D1-D14—Bi-color LEDs (Jameco #XC5491 or equiv.).

J1, J2—DB-25-F (AMP 206584-2 or equiv.).

J3—14-pin DIP socket (3M 214-3339 or equiv.).

P1, P2—DB-25-M (AMP 206604-1 or equiv.).

R1-R14—1.2 kΩ, ¼ W.

Fig 22—The zero-insertion-force DIP socket in the center of the break-out box can hold DIP headers with various jumper configurations.

Fig 21—Parts-placement guide for the EIA-232-D break-out box, shown from the component side of the board. A full-size etching pattern appears at the back of this book.

not as refined as later PC-board models, the prototype performed well in the ARRL lab.

To avoid the complicated, time-consuming wire-wrap process, a printed circuit board was designed for BOB. All components, including the switches, LEDs and DB-25 connectors, are mounted directly on top of the board. Because the board is single sided, some jumpers are necessary. Parts placement is shown in Fig 21. Be careful to insert all of the LEDs in the same direction, with their longer leads toward the center of the board. A full-size etching

pattern for this board can be found at the back of this book.

Partial Construction

If you do not want to invest in a complete set of parts for BOB, you can construct part of the circuit. If you populate one-half of the board, you will be able to use your BOB for everything but in-line monitoring. Installing only the LEDs results in a fine EIA-232-D monitoring device. Of course, you can leave one of the DB-25 connectors off of each end and simply have a less versatile BOB. If you

initially construct a partial BOB, you can add the remaining components at any time.

The Patch Bay

The prototype had a female DB-25 connector in the center of the board for use as a patch bay. The PC-board version uses a 14-pin zero-insertion-force (ZIF) DIP socket (Fig 22). The DIP socket, although smaller and more delicate than the DB-25, is the better choice. A 7-circuit DIP switch can be inserted into the socket and used to switch through or interrupt any of the 7 EIA-232-D lines. DIP component headers can also be used to wire various patch bay configurations. Although any 14-pin DIP socket will work, one with zero- or low-insertion force makes changing patches or switches much easier.

Potential Problems

Before you use BOB, you should understand two circuit shortcomings. First, BOB draws current from the unit under test. Second, unless you are careful, you can use BOB to create short circuits.

BOB draws current from the circuit under test to light the polarity-indicating LEDs. Using current from the circuit being monitored eliminates the need for active buffers, transistor switches, and a power supply. However, it means that BOB loads the EIA-232-D device hooked to it. In extreme cases, this loading may interfere with circuit testing. If you suspect this is the case, use an oscilloscope or VOM to check circuit voltages. If positive voltages are much below 12 V or negative voltages are much above – 12 V, the circuit is overloaded.

It is possible to switch a line to + 12 V on one side of the patch bay, patch it across to the other side, and then switch it to – 12 V. This will short-circuit your power supply. You will also cause a short circuit if you attempt to reverse the polarity of an

Fig 23—A shows how to use the break-out box to activate a DCE device. To activate a DTE device, use the switch settings shown at B. The jumpers and switch settings shown at C configure the break-out box for connecting two DTE devices.

scriptions of a few common problems and how BOB is used to solve them can help you learn how to use it.

Activating DCE

It is often necessary to test a modem or other piece of data-circuit terminating equipment (DCE) without having it attached to a computer. To activate a DCE, lines 20 and 4 must be set to +12 V. To do this, use BOB with no jumpers in the patch bay and a power supply attached. Put all of BOB's switches in the OFF position. Connect the DCE to one of BOB's DB-25 connectors, and set the switches for pins 4 and 20 to the +12 position (Fig 23A). Be sure to use the switches on the same side of the patch bay as the DB-25 that you are using. Now, assuming that the DCE is a modem, you should see a carrier at its analog output. By setting the switch for line 2 (transmitted data) to +12 V you should be able to change the tone coming from the modem.

LEDs should indicate that the modem is setting pins 5 and 6 to +12 V. These lines are used to activate equipment attached to the modem. If they are inactive, or remain at −12 V, then a device attached to the modem might never send any data.

If the modem does not respond correctly, then you have learned that it is not operating as a standard DCE device. Further troubleshooting is in order. If the modem does respond as predicted, you know that any problems you have are caused by some other piece of equipment.

Activating DTE

BOB can also be used to activate a data terminal equipment (DTE) device, such as a terminal, to see if it is operating correctly. When BOB is configured as shown in Fig 23B, data sent by the DTE should appear as flickering of the LED on line 2.

If the data does appear, there are still some things you should use BOB to determine: Does the DTE set line 20 to +12 V? Many DCE devices must have this line set to +12 V. Does the DTE under test set line 4 to +12 V before sending data? How does the DTE react to changes on lines 5, 6 and 8? You can answer these questions quickly by changing switches and observing LEDs. The answers will come in handy when you wish to interface the DTE to other equipment.

Connecting Like Devices

It is sometimes necessary to connect two EIA-232-D devices with the same configuration (DCE or DTE). If two terminals (DTE devices) are simply wired together, they would both attempt to transmit on line 2 and to receive on line 3. The transmitted signals would collide and no received signals would be heard. Also, both units

EIA-232-D line which is being driven by the equipment under test. Be sure that you do not attempt to set one line to two levels, and be sure that the equipment under test is not setting a line that you are trying to set with BOB. If you are careful, you will not be bothered by the economies in BOB's design.

Using The Break-out Box

You should become familiar with the material in Chapter 19 concerning the EIA-232-D interface. While only the numbers for the various lines will be referred to here, the full names of the lines can often give insight into their functions. It is also valuable to know which type of device, DCE or DTE, generates each signal.

When you are familiar with the EIA-232-D interface, and familiar enough with BOB to understand its limitations, you will be able to begin using it. It is impossible to anticipate every configuration of BOB that will be useful. However, de-would be setting line 4 to +12 V, but lines 5, 6 and 8 would be set by neither. This would not work.

With the aid of BOB, and a DIP header wired as shown in Fig 23C, two DTE devices can be connected with no problems. In this configuration BOB is called a "null modem," since it replaces the modems that would usually connect two terminals. Two DCE devices can be connected in a similar manner.

Conclusion

These are only a few of the things you can do with BOB. BOB is a powerful device for monitoring and changing signals at an EIA-232-D interface. If you are careful to avoid short circuits, BOB can teach you about EIA-232-D interfaces and help solve confusing problems.

Chapter 30

HF Radio Equipment

In this chapter you will find descriptions of radio equipment that you can build for the amateur bands below 30 MHz. The projects fall into three broad categories: receivers, transmitters and power amplifiers.

There is much personal pride and satisfaction in building and using a piece of radio equipment. The knowledge you gain of the workings on both sides of the front panel is another source of pleasure.

The theory necessary to understand the operation of the equipment described in this chapter is found elsewhere in this book. Some of the chapters you may wish to review are: Chapter 10, Radio Frequency Oscillators and Synthesizers; Chapter 11, Radio Transmitting Principles; Chapter 12, Radio Receiving Principles and Chapter 15, Radio Frequency Power Amplifiers.

A Band-Imaging CW Receiver for 10 and 18 MHz

Band imaging has long been used in Amateur Radio as a means of making a stable local oscillator (LO) do double duty. Instead of building equipment using only one LO-to-RF relationship for frequency conversion—with, for instance, only the *difference* between the LO and higher-frequency incoming signals giving output at the IF—*two* of several LO-to-RF relationships can be exploited for two-band coverage. A band-imaging receiver appeared in every edition of this *Handbook* from 1953 through 1966, from "A Two-Band Four-Tube Superheterodyne" in 1953 to "The HB-65 Five-Band Receiver" in 1966. Each of these receivers converted the 80- and 40-meter amateur bands to a 1.7-MHz IF by means of a 5.2-5.7-MHz LO. On 80 meters, the conversion relationship in such a receiver is LO − RF = IF; on 40, the relationship is RF − LO = IF. Both bands "tune in the same direction" with this system: The received frequencies of 3.5 and 6.9 MHz correspond to the lower limit of the LO tuning range.

Band imaging can also be used to cover the 80- and 20-meter amateur bands: A 5.0-5.5-MHz LO is used to convert each band to a 9-MHz IF. In such a system, the LO-to-RF relationship on 80 meters is RF + LO = IF; on 20, RF − LO = IF. The drawback to this band-imaging system is that the lower band "tunes backwards": The lower limit of the LO tuning range corresponds to 4.0 MHz on 80 meters and 14.0 MHz on 20. Nonetheless, the 80/20 band-imaging system has also been popular with radio amateurs because of the inherent sideband inversion between the image bands: The BFO-to-IF relationship that affords LSB reception on 80 meters demodulates USB on 20.

Fig. 1 — The band-imaging receiver covers the CW segments of the 10- and 18-MHz amateur bands with good stability, sensitivity and single-signal selectivity. Larger controls are (l-r) TUNING, IF GAIN and AF GAIN. The two smaller controls, separated by the PHONES jack, are BAND and SIDETONE LEVEL. The TUNING scale is drawn on contact paper applied to an aluminum disc.

With this overview of band-imaging techniques in place, we present a band-imaging CW receiver for 10 and 18 MHz (see Fig. 1). Using a 14-MHz LO, it converts the entire 10-MHz amateur band, and the CW portion of the 18-MHz amateur band, to a 4-MHz IF. Both bands tune in the same direction. At 4 MHz, a four-crystal ladder filter provides single-signal selectivity. The design emphasizes good basic receiver performance with an eye toward compactness; hence, features such as a digital frequency display, AGC and active audio filtering have been omitted. Alignment and checkout of the band-imaging receiver requires only (1) a 51-ohm resistor; (2) a receiver capable of CW reception at 14.0-14.2 MHz and 4 MHz ±1 kHz with an S-meter and frequency display resolution of 1 kHz or greater; and (3) a crystal-controlled marker generator capable of providing 10-kHz markers. The performance measurements given later in this article were obtained from a receiver aligned *by ear* with such test equipment. You need not have access to a radio lab to enjoy similar results. David Newkirk, AK7M, designed and built this project in the ARRL lab.

Circuit Description: RF Amplifiers

A separate 40673 RF amplifier is used for each band. (See Fig. 2). The circuit is electrically identical to that used for the RF amplifiers in "A High-Performance Communications Receiver," presented later in this chapter. Several other circuits in the band-imaging receiver are based on the K5IRK/W7ZOI high-performance design. To simplify alignment of the band-imaging

Fig. 2 — Schematic of the RF amplifiers for the band-imaging receiver. A separate amplifier is used for each band. The low- and band-pass filters may be aligned with the aid of a crystal-controlled marker generator; see text. Capacitors are disc ceramic unless otherwise noted. Capacitors marked with polarity are electrolytic. All resistors are ¼-W, 10% units unless otherwise noted.

C1, C2, C4, C7 — Silver mica, polystyrene or ceramic capacitor; see Table 1 for values.
C3, C5, C6 — Ceramic or mica compression trimmer. Mouser Electronics ceramic trimmer 24AA067 (12-100 pF) used for 100 pF; Mouser 24AA064 (5-45 pF) used for 45 pF.
J1 — Coaxial RF connector.

L1-L4 — Wound on Amidon T-50-6 powdered-iron toroid core or equiv. All inductors use no. 22 enameled wire with one exception: For L2 at 10 MHz, use no. 24 enameled wire. See Table 1 for number of turns.
Q1 — 40673 dual-gate MOSFET.
S1 — 3PDT toggle (Radio Shack 275-661 or equiv).

T1 — Transformer wound with no. 28 enameled wire on Amidon FT-37-43 ferrite toroid core or equiv. Primary (168 μH), 20 turns; secondary (6.7 μH), 4 turns.
Z1 — Ferrite bead on Gate 2 lead of Q1, Amidon FB-43-101 or equiv.

Table 1

Component Values for the Band-Imaging Receiver RF Amplifiers

MHz	C1	L1	C2	L2	C3	C4, C7	L3, L4	C5, C6
10	300	13	680	29	100	33	17	100
18	180	10	390	22	45	22	10	100

Values listed for capacitors are capacitance in pF. Values listed for inductors are number of turns of wire required.

receiver, the variable coupling capacitor (C15 in Ch. 30, Fig. 12) between the two sections of the output filter is replaced by three 12-pF capacitors in series. Gain of this circuit is 12 to 15 dB, depending on alignment and the characteristics of Q1. Band changing is accomplished by switching RF input, RF output and dc connections between the 10- and 18-MHz amplifier boards via S1, a 3PDT toggle. Input and output (I/O) impedances of each RF amplifier board are 50 ohms.

Mixer, IF Filter and IF Amplifiers

See Fig. 3. The band-imaging receiver uses a Mini-Circuits SBL-1 doubly balanced diode-ring mixer (U1) followed by a strong bipolar-transistor IF amplifier (Q2).[1] This is the circuit used in the K5IRK/W7ZOI receiver, with several modifications. In the band-imaging receiver, the bifilar 4:1 collector transformer in the original design has been replaced with a toroidal monofilar choke,

RFC1. The supply end of the 1-kΩ Q2 base bias resistor is now connected directly to the 12-V dc line at the cold end of RFC1. This removes the RF feedback present in the original circuit. Surprisingly, this feed-backless configuration results in better sensitivity *and* two-tone 3rd-order IMD dynamic range than the unmodified circuit affords *at a 4-MHz IF*. The original circuit, intended for use at an IF of 9 MHz, did not provide a comparable performance even when the inductance of its 4:1 collector transformer was scaled for 4 MHz.

The post-mixer amplifier feeds a four-crystal ladder filter via a 6-dB pad. The I/O impedances of the crystal filter are 200 ohms. Because this is a good match for the collector impedance of Q2, the step-down transformer in the original post-mixer amplifier circuit is not required. The 50-ohm 6-dB attenuator of the original circuit has been scaled to 200 ohms. This pad should *not* be replaced with one of lower attenuation: It assures a nonreactive wideband termination for Q2 *and* the crystal filter. Less attenuation here results in reduced IMD dynamic range, as confirmed by lab tests.

The crystal filter was designed using Hayward's technique (see "Simple Cohn Crystal Filters," *QST*, July 1987, pp 24-29). Measured selectivity of the prototype filter was 405 Hz at −6 dB and 1850 Hz at −60 dB, resulting in a −60 dB/−6 dB shape factor of 4.57. Insertion loss was 2 dB, and passband ripple was less than 0.4 dB. As is characteristic of simple ladder crystal filters, the upper passband slope is steeper. Because of this, the BFO must be set on the *upper* side of the filter for best single-signal reception. With the BFO set to provide a 550-Hz beat note for signals at IF center, rejection of the audio image in the prototype receiver was 73 dB. Ultimate attenuation was 90 dB.

No filter adjustment is necessary, but it *is* important that you use the specified crystals if you intend to duplicate the post-mixer-amplifier/pad/filter arrangement shown in Fig. 3. Substitutions at Y1-Y4 will require filter capacitors of other than 300 pF, resulting in I/O impedances of other than 200 ohms. Hayward states that the series-resonant frequencies of the four filter crystals must fall within a spread of no more than 10% of the desired *3-dB* filter bandwidth. We chose to evaluate the performance of the filter in the more popular terms of −60 and −6 dB bandwidths; it follows that 10% spread is too generous where a given *−6 dB* filter bandwidth is the target. Experiments with various new and surplus 4-MHz microprocessor-clock crystals in the ARRL lab showed that the new International Crystal Mfg. (ICM) crystals provided the best

---

[1]Mini-Circuits, see ARRL Parts Suppliers List at the end of the Component Data chapter.

performance overall. Shape factors (−60 dB/−6 dB) for the clock-crystal filters were rarely less than 5, and sometimes more than 6. I/O impedances were between 300 and 400 ohms. Several times, four crystals within a suitably narrow frequency spread could be found only by grading *10 or more* clock crystals. Custom-ground crystals offer the added advantage of resonating —within tolerance, of course—on the frequency you specify. Their unit price is higher, but they come closest to guaranteeing that your filter will perform as predicted.

Post-filter IF amplification is provided by U2, an MC1350P video amplifier IC. The 200-ohm resistor between pins 4 and 6 of U2, in conjunction with the 0.1 µF bypass capacitor at pin 6, terminates the crystal filter output. Manual gain control is achieved by applying a variable positive voltage to pin 5 of U2 through a 27-kΩ

resistor and IF GAIN control R1. Receiver muting is accomplished by means of Q3: Grounding the MUTE terminal (center conductor at J2) applies maximum gain-reduction voltage to U2. The supply voltage (nominally 12) appears across J2 with the receiver unmuted; current through the grounded MUTE line is 5 mA. IF output (Z ≈ 50 ohms) is available at the secondary of T2.

Local Oscillator

The schematic of the band-imaging receiver LO is shown in Fig. 4. An MPF102 JFET, Q4, operates as a Colpitts oscillator. The oscillator signal is amplified by Q5, a 40673 dual-gate MOSFET. Bandspread is achieved by tapping the tuning capacitor, C9, down on LO tank inductor L5. Tuning range of the circuit is approximately 14.060 to 14.153 MHz. Air-dielectric trimmer C10 shifts this range for dial calibration.

Fig. 3 — Schematic of the mixer, crystal filter and IF amplifier stages of the band-imaging receiver. Capacitors are disc ceramic unless otherwise noted. Capacitors marked with polarity are electrolytic. All resistors are ¼-W, 10% units unless otherwise noted.

C8 — 350-pF compression trimmer (Arco 428 or equiv).
J2 — Phono jack.
Q2 — 2N3866 or 2N5109. Use a small heat sink on this transistor.
Q3 — 2N3906.
R1 — 10-kΩ linear potentiometer.
RFC1 — 95 µH; 15 turns no. 24 enameled

wire on Amidon FT-37-43 ferrite toroid core.
T2 — Transformer wound on Amidon T-68-1 powered-iron toroid core, or equiv. Primary (12.9 µH): 36 turns no. 26 enameled wire, center-tapped; secondary (0.9 µH): 3 turns no. 26 enameled wire over center of primary.

U1 — Mini-Circuits SBL-1 doubly balanced diode-ring mixer.
U2 — MC1350P video amplifier IC.
Y1-Y4 — 4.000000-MHz custom-etched crystal, 26°C calibration temperature, grade CS-1 (0.001% tolerance), F-700 holder, series resonant. International Crystal Mfg Co type 433340. See text.

Fig. 4 — Schematic of the band-imaging receiver LO and buffer circuit. Capacitors are disc ceramic unless otherwise noted. Capacitors marked with polarity are electrolytic. All resistors are ¼-W, 10% units unless otherwise noted. At A, an LM317L adjustable regulator is used at U3. The inset at B shows connections for an 78L07 regulator at U3. For best stability, use only NP0 (C0G) capacitors in the circuitry associated with the gate and source leads of Q4. Space L5 by at least its diameter from other components and the LO shield box. See text and Fig. 8.

C9 — 50-pF air variable (Jackson Bros 4667-50 or equiv).
C10 — 17-pF air trimmer (Johnson 189-506-5 or equiv).
L5 — 1.4 µH: 11 turns no. 22 tinned wire, 24 turns per inch (Barker & Williamson 3038 Miniductor). Tap at 2 or 3 turns from ground end. See text and Figs. 8 and 9B.

Q4 — MPF102 JFET.
Q5 — 40673 dual-gate MOSFET.
RFC2 — 39 µH: Miller 70F395AI, or 24 turns no. 26 enameled wire on Amidon FT-50-61 ferrite toroid core.
T3 — Transformer wound on Amidon FT-37-43 ferrite toroid core or equiv.

Primary (50 µH): 11 turns no. 26 enameled wire. Secondary (3.8 µH): 3 turns no. 26 enameled wire.
U3 — Voltage regulator, LM317LH, LM317LZ or (with circuit changes shown at inset B) 78L07.
Z2 — Ferrite bead on Gate 2 lead of Q2, Amidon FB-43-101 or equiv.

Despite the relatively high LO operating frequency, stability is good. Measured drift of the point-to-point-wired prototype oscillator was −530 Hz in the 45-minute period after turn-on, 460 Hz of which occurred in the first ten minutes. Over the next three hours, this oscillator drifted approximately −20 Hz. Stability was even better with the circuit rebuilt on an etched circuit board: Drift for the ten minutes after turn-on was only −256 Hz. *The key to this stability is the use of NP0 (C0G) ceramic units for all fixed capacitors associated with the gate and source of Q4.* Although silver-mica or polystyrene capacitors may be hand-picked for low drift, only NP0 capacitors offer minimum drift "off the shelf." Oscillator stability is further improved by the use of a three-terminal regulator to stabilize Q4's drain supply, and by enclosing LO and buffer in a shield box to slow the effect of changes in ambient air temperature.

BFO, Detector and Audio Stages

The K5IRK/W7ZOI crystal-controlled BFO is used in this receiver with one modification: The secondary of T4 in Fig. 5 carries only RF and no dc. Y5 is an inexpensive 4-MHz microprocessor clock crystal. Every such crystal we tried worked well in this circuit; a custom-ground crystal is unnecessary here.

The detector and AF stages of the band-imaging receiver are shown in Fig. 6. The product detector (U4) is a Mini-Circuits SBL-1 doubly balanced diode-ring mixer. RFC3 and the 0.001-µF capacitor provide RF filtering ahead of the AF preamp, U5, an NE5534 low-noise audio op amp. The

parts list for Fig. 6 specifies a "wind-it-yourself" toroidal choke for RFC3; pi-wound chokes tried here were prone to pickup of 60-Hz harmonics.

U6, an LM380N-8, serves as the AF power amplifier. Its output is connected to a front-panel stereo headphone jack, J4,

and a rear-panel phono connector, J5. J4 is wired to accept stereo headphones; monaural phones may be used if inserted no farther than the first detent. The 1-kΩ resistor from the output lead to ground serves to charge U6's 470-µF output coupling capacitor at power-up if a head-

Fig. 5 — Schematic of the band-imaging receiver BFO. Capacitors are disc ceramic unless otherwise noted. Capacitors marked with polarity are electrolytic. All resistors are ¼-W, 10% units unless otherwise noted.

C11, C12 — 100-pF ceramic or mica compression trimmer. Mouser Electronics 24AA067 (12-100 pF) suitable.
Q6 — 2N3904.
T4 — Transformer wound on Amidon T-68-2

powdered-iron toroid core or equiv. Primary (19.8 µH): 59 turns no. 28 enameled wire, tapped at 12 turns. Secondary (0.98 µH): 9 turns no. 28 enameled wire over tap end of primary.

Fig. 6 — Schematic of the product detector and audio amplifiers for the band-imaging receiver. Capacitors are disc ceramic unless otherwise noted. Capacitors marked with polarity are electrolytic. All resistors are ¼-W, 10% units unless otherwise noted.

J3, J5 — Phono jack.
J4 — Stereo headphone jack.
R2, R3 — 10-kΩ audio-taper potentiometer.

RFC3 — 1-mH RF choke: 34 turns no. 30 enameled wire on Amidon FT-37-72 ferrite toroid core or equiv.
U4 — Mini-Circuits SBL-1 doubly balanced

diode-ring mixer.
U5 — NE5534 low-noise audio op amp.
U6 — LM380N-8 audio power amp.

phone or speaker load has not already been installed at J4 or J5. Without this resistor, the capacitor would charge on connection of the audio transducer, resulting in a loud thump.

As mentioned earlier, no active audio filtering is included in the band-imaging receiver. The higher audio components in detected IF amplifier hiss are reduced by the 0.05-µF capacitor connected between the hot end of the AF GAIN control, R3, and ground.

Sidetone can be injected into the audio chain at J3. Sidetone level is adjusted from the front panel by R2. Setting R2 to minimum shunts the AF GAIN control with a 33-kΩ resistor; this reduces overall audio gain by less than 1 dB. A 400-mV signal at J3 provides more than enough sidetone audio at normal AF GAIN settings.

This receiver requires, but does not include, a regulated dc power supply capable of providing a maximum of 220 mA at 12 V. See Chapter 27, Power Supply Projects, for suitable circuits.

Construction

The receiver was prototyped using point-to-point and "dead bug" modular construction (see Fig. 7). Later, circuit boards were designed and debugged.[2] You may use either method for building your receiver, with good results. The following construction hints are based on the circuit-board version of the receiver, but much of the information here will be of use to builders using either style of construction.

Parts for this receiver are available from

[2]Circuit-board templates are available from the ARRL Technical Department secretary for $3.00 and a no. 10 s.a.s.e.

Fig. 7 — The band-imaging receiver prototype. The LO is in the left foreground; just behind it, the 10- and 18-MHz RF amplifiers. At center, the mixer/filter/IF amplifier module, with the detector/AF amplifier module at far right. The smallest module, upper right, is the BFO. Performance was good even though etched circuit boards were not used.

a number of sources. Virtually everything can be obtained from Mouser, Radio Shack, DigiKey and Circuit Specialists. See the parts suppliers list at the end of Chapter 35 for addresses and telephone numbers of these suppliers.

See Fig. 8. The receiver is housed in a Hammond 1590F diecast aluminum box (approximately 7¼ × 7¼ × 2½ inches). Threaded standoffs are used to mount all circuit boards except the detector/audio board; spade lugs are used to mount this module vertically. Miniature 50-ohm coaxial cable (RG-174) is used for all RF connections between modules except the LO-mixer line. Here, miniature Teflon®-dielectric cable is used because of

Teflon's high melting point (see Fig. 9A). RG-174 is also used to connect J3, SIDETONE INPUT, to the detector/audio board. Connections from this board to the AF GAIN and SIDETONE LEVEL controls are made with stranded hookup wire in three colors. This makes for more compact wiring than miniature coax allows and causes no problems with hum or crosstalk. The IF GAIN control and audio output connections are also made in this way. Dc wiring is stranded hookup wire; binding posts are used to bring dc into the receiver.

We recommend that you build, test and install the band-imaging receiver modules in this order: (1) LO; (2) detector/audio and BFO; (3) mixer/filter/IF amplifier; (4)

Fig. 8 — The band-imaging receiver just fits into a Hammond 1590F diecast aluminum box. In this top view, the LO (in its shield box, shown here with cover removed) dominates the layout. The RF amplifier boards are at top, one above the other. The BFO is to the left of the LO, with the detector/audio amplifier board (edge-on) to the right. At far right, the mixer/filter/IF amplifier board. The two capacitors and resistor beneath the mixer/AF board have since been incorporated into the board design. For a similar view of the band-imaging receiver in full color, see the cover of July 1987 *QST*.

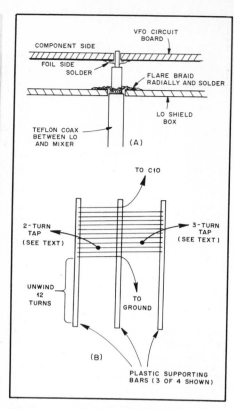

Fig. 9 — The detail drawing at A shows installation of the LO output lead. Miniature Teflon coax is recommended here because its dielectric will not melt during soldering. The shield must be flared and soldered to the *inner* wall of the LO shield box. At B, details of the LO inductor, L5, are shown. Taps are made by pushing in adjacent turns of the coil stock. The untrimmed plastic bars preserve the Q of L5 by holding the Miniductor away from the shield box bottom. Before counting the 11 turns necessary for the coil, unwind enough turns from the uncut Miniductor stock to allow L5 to stand above the shield-box bottom by its diameter. The plastic bars are fragile; they may be impregnated with Duco or similar cement for greater strength. The completed L5 is cemented to the shield-box bottom after the LO tuning range has been set.

RF amplifiers. The LO comes first because its installation entails the majority of the metalwork necessary to build the receiver. The sequence allows you to use completed modules as part of your test equipment for the modules later in the sequence.

The LO shield box is made of double-sided copper-clad circuit board. The 10:1 epicyclic reduction drive is a Jackson Bros 5857. Because the sides of the Hammond diecast aluminum box are not perpendicular to the bottom, special construction techniques are needed to ensure that the TUNING capacitor shaft is perpendicular to the front panel of the box. The following construction sequence resulted in a smooth-tuning, no-backlash LO installation in the ARRL lab version of the band-imaging receiver:

1) Mount the 10:1 reduction drive on the front panel.

2) Build the LO shield box (four sides and bottom), soldering only the side and rear pieces into place on the bottom. The front and rear pieces of the shield box must butt the shield box sides as shown in Fig. 8. *Tape* the front side into place. Drill four mounting holes in the shield box bottom plate.

3) Chisel the molded-in printing from the center of the diecast-box bottom to smooth the box floor. Sanding may also be necessary to achieve this.

4) Locate the C9 (TUNING capacitor) mounting hole in the LO shield box front by pushing the box up against the reduction-drive coupler. Size this hole slightly larger than the capacitor mounting bushing. This allows later adjustment of C9's position. Temporarily mount the capacitor in the front side of the shield box and keep this assembly taped to the rest of the box.

5) Place the LO box in the diecast box so that C9 is inserted into the reduction-drive coupler. By feel, be sure that the

capacitor is about 1/16-inch short of full insertion into the coupler sleeve. This allows leeway for later adjustment. Mark the diecast box to pass the LO mounting screws through the holes in the shield-box bottom plate. Drill these holes now.

6a) Remove the taped-on front of the shield box. Build and install the LO/buffer circuit board, including the LO output cable and 12-V dc line, in the partially completed shield box. The output cable consists of a 6-inch piece of miniature Teflon coaxial cable (see Fig. 9A) Fig. 9B shows how to prepare LO inductor L5 from a length of B & W Miniductor.

6b) Temporarily install C9, C10, L5 and the 27-pF NP0 LO-tuned-circuit capacitor to the LO/buffer board by short leads. Terminate the LO output cable with a 51-ohm resistor. Verify operation of the LO/buffer board by applying dc power and tuning in the LO signal on the 14-MHz test receiver. Adjust C9 and C10 as necessary to bring the signal into your receiver's tuning range. You may need to add or remove fixed capacitors in the LO tuned circuit. Don't spend time now on setting the LO tuning range; that comes later.

6c) Once LO performance has been verified, disconnect C9, C10, L5 and the fixed tuned-circuit capacitor from the LO/buffer board. Install the board into the LO shield box.

7) Install C10 flat to the shield box floor by soldering down its rotor tab. Be sure to allow clearance for C9. Bend the C10 stator tab up to clear the box bottom. Connect C10 to the LO/buffer circuit board with tinned no. 18 solid wire. Solder L5 into the circuit; it will be cemented to the box floor later, but do not do this yet.

8) Bolt the LO into the diecast box. Loosely mount C9 in the front side of the LO box. Slide the front LO box side into place, and at the same time, slide the C9 shaft into the reduction-drive coupler to about 1/16 inch short of full insertion. *Do not* tape the LO box front into place as before.

9) Adjust the reduction drive to bring its coupler worm screws to approximately 10 and 2 o'clock. Set C9 to maximum capacitance without disturbing the reduction drive. Now, with C9 loose in its mounting hole, tighten the worm screws in the reduction-drive coupler.

10) Tighten C9 to the front of the LO shield box.

11) Using the reduction drive, turn C9 back and forth through its range several times to settle the LO box front into position. Depending on how tightly the front is held in place by the LO box sides, you may need to push the sides apart slightly to free the front piece. By eye, the front of the LO box should appear parallel to the front of the diecast box. If all looks well,

12) Solder the front side of the LO box into position.

Final tuning-range and anti-backlash adjustments will be made during alignment and testing of the receiver.

The circuit board placement shown in Fig. 8 works well. Although the position of the LO shield box left little choice as to the placement of the rest of the circuit boards, maximum spacing between the BFO and mixer/filter/IF amplifier boards was decided on *beforehand* to keep the BFO signal out of the IF amplifier circuitry.

Alignment

Test equipment necessary for aligning the band-imaging receiver is a 51-ohm resistor, a receiver capable of CW reception at 14.0-14.2 MHz and 4 MHz ±1 kHz with an S-meter and frequency display resolution of 1 kHz or greater, and a crystal-controlled marker generator capable of

providing 10-kHz markers. Equip the coaxial input of the test receiver with a short test cable terminated with alligator clips.

Detector/audio amplifier and BFO. The audio amplifiers require no adjustment. Align the BFO as follows: Without connecting the BFO to the detector, connect a 51-ohm resistor across the secondary of T4. Set C11 (FREQ ADJ) and C12 (OUTPUT TUNE) to midrange. Apply 12 V dc to the BFO. Set the test receiver for CW reception at 4000 kHz and attach the shield clip of its test cable to the BFO ground foil. Leave the center-conductor clip unconnected. Next, tune in the BFO on the test receiver. Adjust C12 for maximum received signal as indicated by the test receiver S-meter. Adjust C11 to put the BFO at approximately 4000.5 kHz. This completes alignment of the BFO for now. Remove the 51-ohm resistor from the T4 secondary and connect the BFO to the detector with RG-174 cable.

Mixer, filter and IF amplifier. The IF amplifier requires only one adjustment: With 12 V applied to the mixer/filter/IF amplifier board and later stages, adjust C8, IF TUNE, for maximum noise in the speaker or headphones.

Local oscillator tuning range. Connect the LO output cable to the mixer, and apply 12 V to the LO. Tune C9 to the low end of its range, and set the test receiver to 14.060 MHz. Connect the test cable shield clip to the LO box, but leave the center-conductor clip unconnected. Adjust C10 until you hear the LO in the test receiver. Be sure that the unconnected test-cable lead is far enough from the LO tuned circuit to have no effect on the LO frequency. Set the test receiver to 14.155 MHz. Tune the LO upward in frequency until you hear it in the test receiver. With luck, the TUNING capacitor will be nearly at minimum capacitance. Depending on the exact values of the capacitors in the Q4 gate circuitry, however, your LO may not have enough tuning range, requiring that you search downward for it with the test receiver even with the TUNING capacitor at minimum capacitance. If this is so, move the tap on L5 from 2 to 3 turns above ground and readjust the 14.060-MHz band edge with C10. This will increase the tuning range. (You may need to add capacitance in parallel with the 27-pF LO tuned-circuit capacitor to allow C9 to hit the band edge.) C10's tuning range is much larger than that of the TUNING capacitor, so adjust it carefully. With experimentation, you should be able to achieve a TUNING range of between 90 and 150 kHz. Remember that you'll need to make your final band-edge adjustment *after* installation of the LO box cover; be sure to provide a hole in the cover for this purpose, but leave the cover off for now. After you have set the LO tuning range, cement the base of each L5 pillar to

the shield-box bottom with Duco® (or similar) cement.

RF amplifiers. Install the 10-MHz RF amplifier in the receiver, and solder a 51-ohm resistor from the center conductor of J1 to ground. Connect the crystal calibrator, set for 10-kHz markers, to J1. Set the BAND switch to 10 MHz. Tune in a marker near the center of the tuning range and adjust C3 for maximum signal. Tune in the lowest marker in the range; adjust C5 for maximum signal. Tune in the highest marker in the range; adjust C6 for maximum signal. Because the C5 and C6 adjustments interlock somewhat, repeat them several times for good measure. Now, install the 18-MHz RF amplifier board and repeat this procedure at 18 MHz with C3 (at band center), C5 (at the lowest marker) and C6 (at the highest marker). This completes alignment of the RF amplifier boards.

Anti-backlash adjustment. With luck, the TUNING control will turn freely and require the same input torque across the tuning range. Backlash should be imperceptible throughout the range. If backlash is present, try loosening the reduction-drive coupler screws and tightening them again. Backlash in the ARRL lab version of this receiver was done away with by loosening and retightening the tuning capacitor in its mounting hole, *and* by slipping the TUNING capacitor several degrees to one side in the drive coupling sleeve before retightening the coupler worm screws.

Dial calibration. Calibrate the tuning dial *after* the tuning range has been set *and* any backlash has been ironed out. In the model shown in Fig. 1, calibration of the 10- and 18-MHz TUNING scales differs by the width of a dial marking. The left edge of each mark is used during 18-MHz tuning (18 MHz L); the right edge is used during 10-MHz reception (10 MHz R). Calibration of the full TUNING capacitor rotation (360°; 180° for each band) would make this unnecessary, but one band would tune "backward" relative to the other.

Performance

Measured performance of the band-imaging receiver at 10 MHz: Minimum discernible signal (MDS), −140.5 dBm; two-tone 3rd-order IMD dynamic range (20-kHz spacing), 89.5 dB; blocking dynamic range, 134 dB; image rejection, 74 dB. At 18 MHz: MDS, −140.0 dBm; two-tone 3rd-order IMD dynamic range, (20-kHz spacing), 90.0 dB; blocking dynamic range, 131 dB; image rejection, 82 dB. With a signal tuned in on the 10-MHz band, dropping the receiver three inches to the operating table produced *no discernible shift* in the pitch of the received signal. Maximum audio output was 0.66 W into an 8.2-Ω test load. Current drain at 12 V dc was 95.1 mA with no input signal, 220 mA at maximum audio output.

A High-Performance Communications Receiver

The receiver described here is the work of W7ZOI and K5IRK, and was presented in November 1981 *QST*. A progressive system was used in the *QST* version, starting with a simple (but very useable) direct conversion receiver and concluding with a multiband superheterodyne. This approach is highly recommended for those who may lack construction experience.

(A)

(B)

Fig. 10 — A 5-band, SSB version of the high-performance communications receiver constructed by K5IRK. In the top view, the VFO is located in the center with the input filter, mixer and IF boards to the left. The board at the far right contains the product detector and audio stages. The two boards to the right of the VFO are active audio filters (A). The bottom view shows the converter and oscillator boards. The BFO is contained in the shielded box at the left and the mixer board is at the lower center (B).

Fig. 11 — Block diagram of the W7ZOI/K5IRK communications receiver.

Shown in Figs. 10 through 19 is the receiver in its final form. The overall layout is shown in the block diagram, Fig. 11. On 80 meters the receiver functions as a single-conversion superheterodyne, with reception of the higher bands provided by higher-performance crystal-controlled converters. All of the converters use the same mixer module, switching only the converter filter and crystal oscillator modules. As shown, the 40-meter converter does not use an RF amplifier — it is unnecessary and it degrades dynamic range. The lower noise figure obtained with the RF stage is required on the bands above 7 MHz, however.

Many criteria were used in the design of this receiving system, but first and foremost were simplicity and ease of duplication. To this end, readily available components were used throughout. Alternative components are suggested where appropriate, and the circuits are insensitive to transistor type, allowing freedom in substitution. This does not in any way imply that the performance has been compromised; indeed, this receiver can equal the strong-signal performance of many of the high-priced receivers on the market today.

Circuit Description: The Converter, Filter and RF Amplifier

Preselection for the individual converter sections is provided by the circuit shown in Fig. 12. The optional RF amplifier is shown in A, and the version without the amplifier is shown in B. The same circuit board layout can be used for both versions.

Each filter module uses two types of filters. The first is a 5-pole low-pass, necessary to prevent spurious reponses from VHF TV and FM broadcast signals. The second filter provides the majority of the front-end selectivity. It is a double-tuned circuit comprised of L7, L8 and their related capacitors. A variable capacitor is used at C15 because the small, non-standard values required here are difficult to obtain; a 1- to 5-pF variable is readily available and can be preset to the value given in Table 1 or adjusted during alignment.

The RF amplifier uses a dual gate MOSFET and modified-input low-pass filter. The first section is a simple low-pass filter, while the second section is a pi net-work that transforms from 50 to 2000 ohms with a Q of 10. This provides an optimum driving impedance for the amplifier. The output uses a broadband transformer to provide a 50-ohm output impedance, ensuring proper termination for the following double-tuned circuit.

The filters may be aligned with a signal generator or crystal calibrator. If a calibrator is used, the input of the receiver should be terminated with a 50-ohm resistor. Initially, C15 is set near minimum capacitance, and the receiver is tuned to the center of the band. C14 and C17 are then adjusted for maximum response. C15 is then partially meshed, and C14 and C17 are again peaked for maximum response. The filter bandwidth is estimated by observing the reponse as the receiver is tuned toward band edges. This procedure is repeated until the desired bandwidth is realized. The input pi network used with the RF amplifier is adjusted by setting C22 for maximum response at the center of the band.

Mixer Module

The two mixer modules used in the composite receiver are identical, each being comprised of a doubly balanced diode-ring mixer, U2 of Fig. 13, followed by a 9-MHz IF amplifier. The IF amplifier, Q9, is one of the more critical stages in the receiver. It must have a reasonable noise figure, low IMD, and a 50-ohm input and output impedance. A bipolar transistor with negative feedback is used to establish the gain and impedances. The 6-dB pad at the output preserves the input and output match of the stage. The moderately high bias current used ensures low distortion.

The transistor type used for Q9 *is critical*. It should have an F_t of at least 500 MHz. The 2N5109, 2N3866 and 2SC1252 are all suitable.

Amplifier gain, including the loss of the pad, is about 16 dB. The mixer has a loss of about 6 dB, leaving a net module gain of 10 dB. The amplifier output intercept is about + 30 dBm. Careful measurements have shown that a diplexer is not required between the mixer and the amplifier.

Crystal Oscillator Module

Shown in Fig. 14 is the circuit used for all of the crystal oscillators in the receiver. One or two of the modules are used for the BFO, and one module is used with each converter. The circuit is a Hartley oscillator with the crystal in series with the feedback tap from the coil. A trimmer capacitor in series with the crystal adjusts the operating frequency of the oscillator. If a single BFO is used, the 12-volt operating bias is applied through the output link as shown in Fig. 14B. When more than one module is used, as with the converters, operating voltage is applied through the bandswitch, Fig. 14C. Only the oscillator in use has power applied to it.

This circuit will deliver an output power

Fig. 12 — Circuit diagram of the converter filter and optional RF amplifier used in the W7ZOI/K5IRK receiver. The circuit using the RF amplifier is shown in A, while the configuration without the amplifier is shown in B.

C12, C13, C16, C18-21 — Silver mica or
  ceramic, see Table 1 for values.
C14, C17, C22 — Mica compression trimmer
  or similar variable, see Table 1 for values.
C15 — Air variable, 1 to 5 pF.

L7-10 — No. 22 enamel wire wound on
  Amidon T50-6 core, see Table 1 for number
  of turns.
Q10 — Dual gate MOSFET, 40673, 3N211,

3SK40 or similar.
T5 — Ferrite transformer, 20 turns primary,
  4 turns secondary, on Amidon FT37-43 core.
Z6 — Ferrite bead on lead of Q10. Amidon
  type FB43-101.

of about +10 dBm, which is more than enough to drive the diode mixers. Adjustment of the oscillators should be done with the mixer attached. C11 is tuned for maximum output and proper starting of the oscillator. The series capacitor is then adjusted for the correct operating frequency. This capacitor may be eliminated in those modules used with the converters. In these cases, the crystal is connected directly to ground.

80-Meter Preselector Filter

The 80-meter preselector filter is shown in Fig. 15. It consists of two cascaded filters: The first is a 7-pole, high-pass (3-MHz cutoff), composed of the components between the two 650-pF capacitors. This filter suppresses spurious responses from AM broadcast signals. The second part of the filter, while basically a low-pass type, was designed for a very pronounced peak, resulting in a sharp, bandpass-like response. C6 is a 365-pF broadcast capacitor mounted on the front panel.

VFO Module

The variable frequency oscillator, Fig. 16, uses a JFET in a Hartley circuit, followed by a dual-gate MOSFET buffer. For best temperature stability, type SF material (Amidon -6 code) is used for the inductor

core, as this material has a lower temperature coefficient than the usual slug-tuned inductor. All of the capacitors in the tuned circuit should be NP0 ceramics, as they have the lowest temperature coefficient of any readily available type. Silver mica and polystyrene types should not be used in this circuit.

The resonator (tuned circuit) should be

lightly loaded; to this end, the coupling capacitor to the gate of the JFET is kept as small as possible. If the specified 2.7-pF NP0 ceramic cannot be obtained, a small air variable of similar value can be substituted. Following these precautions will ensure excellent stability. Typical warm-up drift is under 200 Hz over a period of 10 minutes. After warm-up, drift

Table 1
Component Data for W7ZOI/K5IRK Receiver Converter Filters

Parts for filter without amplifier:

F, MHz	C19 C21	C20	L9 L10	C12 C18	C13 C16	C14 C17	C15	L7 L8
7.1	430	860	17	42	50	180	4.6	25
10.6	300	600	13	32	50	180	4.1	17
14.2	220	430	12	20	—	180	2.3	17
18.2	180	360	10	22	50	180	3.9	10
21.2	150	300	10	18	—	180	3.0	10
24.2	130	270	9	14	—	180	2.1	10
28.5	110	220	8	12	—	180	1.6	10

Parts for filter with RF amplifier:

F, MHz	C19	C20	C21	C22	L9	L10
10.6	300	680	33	50	13	29
14.2	220	500	22	50	12	25
18.2	180	390	—	50	10	22
21.2	150	330	—	50	10	20
24.2	130	300	—	50	9	19
28.5	110	250	—	50	8	17

Note: Other filter parts are identical to that without the amplifier. Values listed for capacitors are capacitance in pF. Values listed for inductors are the number of turns of wire required.

Fig. 13 — Diagram of the mixer module. Two of these modules are used in the completed receiver. One is for 80-meter input, with its output at 9 MHz. The second is used with the converters; its output is at 80 meters.

Q9 — TO-39 CATV type bipolar transistor, F_T = 1 GHz or greater. 2N5109, 2SC1252 2SC1365 or 2N3866 suitable. A small heat sink is used on this transistor.

T4 — Broadband ferrite transformer, 10 bifilar turns no. 28 enamel on Amidon FT37-43 core.

U2 — Mini Circuits Lab doubly balanced mixer, type SBL-1. Type SRA-1 is also suitable, as are similar units from other manufacturers.

is no more than 10 or 20 Hz in a 5-minute period.

The buffer stage, Q7, is conventional with the exception of the broadband output transformer, T2. The buffer provides good isolation for the oscillator and an output power of between +5 and +8 dBm.

Intermediate Frequency Amplifier

The heart of this receiver is its IF section. This design uses an IF of 9 MHz, with selectivity provided by a crystal filter of the builder's choice. The circuitry shown in Fig. 17 is designed for a filter requiring 500-ohm input and output terminations.

The input is a pi network which transforms the 50-ohm source impedance of the mixer module to the 500 ohms required by the filter. The filter output is terminated in a 560-ohm resistor.

The majority of the IF gain is provided by two dual-gate MOSFETs, Q11 and Q12. The bias on these stages is shifted upward by a pair of silicon diodes. This extends the gain control range as the gate 2 bias is altered. The last IF stage is a differential pair of PNP transistors, Q13 and Q14. Outputs are available from each of the collectors. The one from Q14 is routed through coaxial cable to the product detector.

The other IF output drives the detector,

Fig. 14 — Crystal oscillator module used for BFO and converter oscillators.

C10 — Silver mica or ceramic. See Table 2 for values.

C11 — Mica compression or similar trimmer. See Table 2 for values.

Q8 — General-purpose NPN, 2N3904, 2N2222A or similar.

RFC2, RFC3 — 20 turns no. 28 enamel on Amidon FT-37-43 core.

S1 — Part of bandswitch or sideband selection switch. See text.

T3 — No. 22 wire on Amidon core, see Table 2 for number of turns and type of core.

Y1 — Series-resonant crystal. See Table 2 for frequency. For 9-MHz BFO applications, a KVG type XF-903 can be used for either USB or LSB.

D1. When large signals are present, the detected voltage from D1 appears at the base of Q16, discharging the timing capacitor, C24. The voltage change at C24 is coupled to the line through a diode, and reduces the gain of Q11 and Q12. R10, the "AGC set," is adjusted for a dc potential of 0.4- to 0.5-volt at the base of Q16. This adjustment is made with the AGC on, with no signals present. When measured with a high-impedance voltmeter, the AGC line should show about 6 volts at maximum gain.

Two transistor switches are contained in the amplifier. Q17 is used to defeat the

Table 2
Component Data for W7ZOI/K5IRK Receiver Crystal Oscillator Module

Band (m)	Y1 (MHz)	C10 (pF)	C11 (pF)	Core	primary	T3 tap (turns)	secondary
40	3.3	100	90	T-68-2	65	13	10
30	6.5	100	60	T-50-6	35	7	6
BFO	9.0	56	60	T-50-6	35	7	6
20	10.5	56	60	T-50-6	30	7	6
17	14.5	33	60	T-50-6	23	5	4
15	17.5	33	60	T-50-6	23	5	4
12	21.0	—	60	T-50-6	20	4	4
10	24.5	—	60	T-50-6	20	4	4
10	25.0	—	60	T-50-6	20	4	4
10	25.5	—	60	T-50-6	20	4	4
10	26.0	—	60	T-50-6	20	4	4

Fig. 15 — 80-meter preselector filter. The input section is a high-pass filter and output section forms a peaked low-pass filter. The variable capacitor is mounted on the front panel.

C5 — 560-pF, silver mica.
C6 — 365-pF or larger broadcast replacement type air variable.
L2, L4 — 21 turns, no. 22 enamel wire on Amidon type T50-2 core.
L3 — 20 turns, no. 22 enamel wire on Amidon T50-2 core.
L5, L6 — 30 turns, no. 22 enamel wire on Amidon T68-2 core.

EXCEPT AS INDICATED, DECIMAL VALUES OF CAPACITANCE ARE IN MICROFARADS (µF); OTHERS ARE IN PICOFARADS (pF); RESISTANCES ARE IN OHMS. ALL CAPACITORS ARE DISC CERAMIC AND RESISTORS ARE 1/4-WATT, 5% COMPOSITION OR METAL FILM TYPES, UNLESS OTHERWISE SPECIFIED.

Fig. 16 — Schematic diagram of the VFO used in the W7ZOI/K5IRK receiver. This circuit will function well from 2.5 to 10 MHz. The tuning range using the components listed is 5.0 to 5.5 MHz.

C1 — 100-pF NP0 ceramic.
C2 — 82-pF NP0 ceramic.
C3 — 126-pF NP0 ceramic.
C4 — Air variable, 365-pF broadcast replacement type.
L1 — 35 turns no. 28 enamel wire on Amidon T50-6 core. Tap 8 turns from ground. Approximately 4.9-µH total inductance.
Q6 — General-purpose JFET, MPF-102, 2N4416 TIS-88, 2SK19GR or similar.
Q7 — Dual gate MOSFET, 40673, 3N140, 3N211, 3SK40 or similar.
T2 — Ferrite transformer, 18-turn primary, 5-turn secondary, no. 28 enamel wire on Amidon FT37-43 core.
Z1 — Ferrite bead on lead of Q7. Amidon FB43-101 or similar.

Fig. 17 — Schematic diagram of the 9-MHz IF amplifier.

C23 — 90-pF compression trimmer or similar variable.
C25 — 470-pF silver mica or ceramic.
C26 — 130-pF silver mica or ceramic.
L10 — 23 turns, no. 22 enamel wire on Amidon T50-6 core.
L11, L12 — 15 turns, no. 22 enamel wire on Amidon FT37-43 core.
Q11, Q12 — Dual-gate MOSFET, 40673,

3N140, 3N211, 3SK40 or similar.
Q13, Q14 — PNP silicon transistor, 2N2907A, 2N3906, 2N4403 or similar.
Q15-17 — NPN silicon transistor, 2N2222A, 2N3904, 2N4401 or similar.
R10 — 1-kΩ PC-board mount variable resistor linear taper.
T6 — Ferrite transformer, 15-turn primary, 3-turn secondary, no. 28 enamel wire on

Amidon FT37-43 core.
Z3 — 9-MHz crystal filter, 500 ohm impedance level: For SSB, KVG type XF-9B, Yaesu XF-92A or International Radio and Computers, eq. For CW, KVG type XF-9M or XF-9NB, Yaesu XF-90C or International Radio and Computers, eq.
Z4, Z5 — Ferrite bead on lead of MOSFET, Amidon FB43-101 or similar.

AGC. It is activated by a positive voltage applied to the "AGC off" line. The other switch, Q15, is attached directly to the AGC line. A positive voltage applied to its input shorts the AGC line to ground, muting the receiver. The extra diodes allow muting to occur quickly while not discharging C24. The IF returns rapidly to full gain after muting periods.

The AGC response is more than adequate and overshoot is minimal. Recovery time is relatively independent of signal level. The recovery time may be shortened by decreasing the value of C24 or the associated 1-megohm resistor.

Detector Audio Module

The IF section of the receiver is followed by the detector and audio amplifiers, shown in Fig. 18. The detector used here is a doubly balanced diode-ring mixer, a Mini-Circuits Labs SBL-1. Mixers from other manufacturers or homemade equivalents will work as well. The excellent balance provided by this type of mixer helps eliminate problems with the AGC system caused by BFO leakage.

The detector output is applied to a diplexer network formed by RFC1 and related components. This network ensures that the detector is properly terminated at all frequencies from audio to VHF.

The first audio amplifier is somewhat unusual in that it uses the common-base configuration. When biased for an emitter current of about 0.5 mA, it provides the

50-ohm input impedance necessary to properly terminate the detector. The second audio stage, Q2, is a direct-coupled PNP amplifier. The receiver may be muted by shorting the collector of Q2 to ground. This is done by applying a positive voltage to the muting input, saturating Q5. The output of Q2 drives the audio gain control, which is mounted on the front panel. If the optional RC active filter is used, it is connected between the output of Q2 and the gain control.

Q3 functions as a common-emitter amplifier, while Q4 is an emitter follower. Q4, biased for an emitter current of about 30 mA, provides sufficient audio output to drive low-impedance (4 to 16 ohms) headphones. If high-impedance headphones are

Fig. 18 — Schematic diagram of the product detector and audio amplifer. If high-impedance headphones are to be used, the output circuit shown in B is recommended.

Q1, Q3 — Low-noise NPN, 2N3565 or similar.
Q2 — General-purpose PNP, 2N3906 or similar.

Q4 — TO-5 or TO-39 NPN, 2N3053 or similar with small heat sink.
R3 — 10-kΩ audio taper.

RFC1 — 20 turns no. 28 enamel wire on Amidon FT37-43 ferrite toroidal core.

Fig. 19 — Schematic diagram of the optional RC active audio filter. A 4-pole low-pass filter is shown here. Additional sections may be added for improved performance.

C6, C8 — 0.01-μF, 10% or better tolerance, ceramic or polystyrene.

C7, C9 — 0.0022-μF, 10% or better tolerance, ceramic or polystyrene.
R4-9 — 33-kΩ for CW or 15-kΩ for SSB filter.

U1 — 1458 or similar, dual op-amp.
U2 — 741, or similar, op-amp.

to be used, a step-up transformer should be used to increase the system voltage gain. This is shown in Fig. 18B. An auxiliary input to the audio amplifier is provided for injection of a sidetone signal for CW monitoring.

The optional RC active filter shown in Fig. 19 can be used to improve selectivity during CW reception, especially when the

IF filter is of bandwidth suitable for SSB operation. As shown in Fig. 19, the filter has a single pole of high-pass filtering and four poles of low-pass response. The cutoff frequency is about 1-kHz for CW or 2-kHz for SSB. The filter bandwidth is determined through proper choice of resistor values. Values for both bandwidths are given in Fig. 19. The filter may be expanded to

many more sections for improved skirt selectivity.

Construction

Mechanical details, such as the type of cabinet and dial drive, are left to the discretion of the builder. Band switching is not critical, as all of the switched points occur at low impedance levels. A multi-wafer

Table 3

Measured and Calculated Receiver Performance Characteristics

Circuit	RF Amp.	Bandwidth, Hz	NF, dB	IP_{in}, dBm	MDS, dBm	DR, dB
Single Conv.*	no	500	16	+ 18	− 131	99
Single Conv.	no	2500	16	+ 18	− 124	94
Single Conv.	yes	500	5	+ 2	− 142	96
Single Conv.	yes	2500	5	+ 2	− 135	92
Dual Conv.	no	500	18	+ 12	− 129	94
Dual Conv.*	no	2500	18	+ 12	− 122	89
Dual Conv.	yes	500	6	− 2	− 141	92
Dual Conv.*	yes	2500	6	− 2	− 141	88

RF amplifier assumed to have a 3 dB noise figure, a 15 dB gain and a + 22 dBm output intercept. Circuits marked with (*) are measured cases. All measurements done at 14 MHz.

rotary switch will work well. Small coaxial cable, such as RG-174/U, should be used for all signal lines.

The version shown here was built by K5IRK. The bulk of the 80-meter part of the receiver is mounted above the chassis. The VFO is contained in an aluminum box, providing both shielding and mechanical strength. The BFOs are below the chassis in a box constructed of scrap circuit-board material. The converters are mounted below the chassis.

Homemade, etched circuit boards were used in the K5IRK model, while "ugly-but-quick" breadboards were utilized by W7ZOI in the construction of his receiver.[1,2] "Ugly boards" are easily built, with scraps of unetched circuit-board material serving as ground foil. The circuitry is supported by those components that are normally grounded. Additional support is provided by suitable tie points. Large-value resistors serve well for this purpose, especially in RF circuits where the impedance level is low. All of the circuitry for the receiver was initially breadboarded using this method. While not as "professional" in appearance, the performance was identical to that of later circuit board versions. In few cases where a performance difference could be detected, the ugly breadboards were superior, usually a result of improved grounding.

Performance

It should be emphasized that, although relatively simple, this receiver is not a toy. It features excellent stability, selectivity consistent with the filter used by the builder, adequate sensitivity, and a dynamic range that rivals or exceeds that of many commercially available equivalents. The only major compromise is the utilization of dual conversion on the higher bands. The penalty is small, because the gain distribution has been carefully planned.

System measurements were made on the receiver at various stages of development.

This data is summarized in Table 3. Both measured data and calculated results are presented to give the prospective builder some feel for the performance to be expected. The table shows the system noise figure, input intercept, minimum detectable signal and the two-tone dynamic range. Both CW and SSB bandwidths are considered in both single- and dual-conversion designs, with and without an RF amplifier. Measurements and calculations generally agree within 1 dB.

Table 3 reveals no surprises. The nature of the trade-off between single and dual conversion is well illustrated, as is the effect of adding an RF amplifier. The system showing the largest dynamic range is the single-converson design without an RF amplifier. It should be noted that this data pertains only to the modules described. Changes in gain, noise figure or intercept of any stage will change the results. The table should not be used for general comparisons.

The dual-conversion systems are about 5 dB "weaker" than the single conversion ones; this is typical. It should be understood that this observation applies only to dual-conversion systems with a wide bandwidth first IF. Modern systems using a crystal filter at the first IF will display performance much the same as a single-conversion receiver, even if they utilize several conversions. No gain compression was measureable in the single-conversion model with no RF amplifier, even with an input signal of − 10 dBm. VFO phase noise was measured to be − 152 dBc/Hz at a spacing of 10 kHz.

Operationally, the receiver is pleasing to use, offering a clean, crisp sound that is not always found in commercial equivalents. Of greatest significance is that the receiver should be easily duplicated at a cost well under that of commercial units.

[1]Circuit board templates are available from ARRL for $1 and a large s.a.s.e.

[2]Circuit boards, negatives and many parts for this receiver are available from Circuit Board Specialists. See the Parts Suppliers list in Chapter 35.

A BC-Band Energy-Rejection Filter

Inadequate front-end selectivity, or poorly performing RF amplifier and mixer stages, can result in unwanted cross-talk and overloading from adjacent commercial or amateur stations. An appropriate filter between the antenna and receiver can attenuate the out-of-band signals but pass those of interest with little or no attenuation.

For reception of frequencies both below and above the broadcast band, a 550- to 1600-kHz band-stop filter is required. However, because a majority of ham receivers are used only for reception above 1600 kHz, a high-pass filter provides the needed attenuation with less cost and complexity than a band-stop filter. That solution is presented here.

Since the signal strength of local broadcast stations can be quite high, the stop-band attenuation of the high-pass filter should also be high. The filter shown here provides about 60 dB of stop-band attenuation with less than 1 dB of attenuation above 1800 kHz. The filter input and output ports match 50 ohms with a maximum SWR of 1.353:1 (reflection coefficient = 0.15). A 10-element filter yields adequate stop-band attenuation and a reasonable rate of attenuation rise. Finally, to simplify construction, only those designs permitting the use of standard-value capacitors were considered.

Building the Filter

The filter parts layout, schematic diagram, response curve and component values are shown in Fig 20. The standard capacitor values listed are within 2.8 percent of the design values. There should be little difficulty in obtaining the desired filter response. If the attenuation peaks (f2, f4 and f6) do not fall at 0.677, 1.293 and 1.111 MHz, tune the series-resonant circuits by slightly squeezing or separating of the toroidal-inductor windings.

Construction of the filter is relatively simple, as shown in Fig 21. Use Panasonic NP0 ceramic disk capacitors (ECC series,

class 1) for values between 10 and 270 pF. For values between 330 pF and 0.033 μF, use Panasonic P-series polypropylene (type ECQ-P) capacitors. These capacitors are available through Digi-key (see the ARRL Parts Suppliers List) and other suppliers. The powdered-iron T-50-2 toroidal cores are available through either Amidon or Palomar Engineers.

The filter may be adapted for a 3.4-MHz cutoff frequency by doubling the L and C values. (This effectively doubles the frequency-label values in Fig 20.) For the 80-meter version, L2 through L6 should be 20 to 25 turns each, wound on T-50-6 (yellow) cores. The actual turns required may vary one or two from the calculated values. Parallel-connect capacitors as needed to achieve the non-standard capacitor values needed for this filter.

Filter Performance

The stop-band attenuation is 58.3 dB. The measured cutoff frequency (0.0988 dB attenuation) is 1.7 MHz. The measured passband loss is less than 0.8 dB from 1.8 to 10 MHz. Between 10 and 100 MHz, the insertion loss of the filter gradually increases to 2 dB. Input impedance was measured between 1.7 and 4.2 MHz. Over the range tested, the input impedance of the filter remained within the 37 to 67.7 ohm input-impedance window (equivalent to a maximum SWR of 1.353:1). This material originally appeared in a February 1978 *QST* article by Ed Wetherhold, W3NQN.

Fig 20—Filter-response curve, insertion loss, layout and schematic diagram.

Fig 21—The filter is built on perfboard in a 2 × 2 × 5-inch aluminum box. The filter can be made smaller if desired, and other coaxial connectors can be used in place of the BNC fittings shown.

A "Cubic Incher" for 80, 40 and 30 Meters

Good things do, indeed, come in small packages. Dennis Monticelli, AE6C, squeezed a lot of circuitry into a cubic inch of space when he built his popular 40-meter QRP transmitter.[1] Later, Greg Bonaguide, WA1VUG, of the ARRL staff repackaged the transmitter and added 80-meter operation for earlier editions of *The ARRL Handbook*. Here is a small transmitter based on those projects that provides 30-meter coverage, better output filtering and a shaped keying waveform. This description is condensed from an article by Doug DeMaw, W1FB, in Sep 1990 *QST*.

Circuit Description

Refer to Fig 23. C2 controls oscillator feedback. Too much feedback in this part of the circuit encourages a "chirpy" CW note and contributes to spurious emissions. Also, too much current through Y1 can destroy the crystal. C2 should be the minimum capacitance that ensures reliable oscillator starting, consistent with maximum output power.

C4 reduces unwanted VHF currents in the collector circuit. Transmitter output power increased approximately 0.1 W when C4 was added. C4 also improves the RF output quality. Its reactance (X_C) is 478 ohms at the operating frequency.

The original Cubic Incher circuit in *QST* has no harmonic filtering. The circuit shown in earlier *Handbook* editions uses a single pi-section low-pass output filter in order to comply with FCC regulations for spectral purity. In this version, a half-wave low-pass filter reduces spurious energy to about 50 dB below carrier power (see Fig 24). The filter values were derived from the normalized filter tables elsewhere in this volume. C5, C6 and C7 are not the exact computed values for the half-wave filter. Rather, they are the nearest standard capacitance values.

Fig 22—A top view of the Cubic Incher for 30 meters. Q1 and its heat sink are at the upper left. C3 is at bottom center, and the output filter is at lower right.

Fig 23—Schematic diagram of the Cubic Incher for 80, 40 or 30 meters. See Table 1 for component values not listed here. Fixed-value capacitors are silver mica or disc ceramic. Resistors are ¼-W carbon composition.

C3—80-600 pF mica compression trimmer for 80 meters. 10-100 pF trimmer for 30 and 40 meters.
D1—1N914 switching diode or equiv.
FB1—Miniature 850 μ_i ferrite bead (Amidon).
Q1—NPN RF power transistor, NEC 2SC1957. See text.
Q2—PNP switching transistor, TIP-30 or -30C. See text.
T1—Tuned RF transformer. See Table 1.
Y1—Fundamental crystal in HC-6/U holder, 30 pF load capacitance.

Except as indicated, decimal values of capacitance are in microfarads (μF); others are in picofarads (pF); resistances are in ohms; k= 1,000.

[1]"Build a 40-M Cubic Incher," *QST*, July 1982, pp 34-36.

Fig 24—Spectral photograph of the 30-meter Cubic Incher. Each horizontal division represents 10 MHz. Each vertical division represents 10 dB. As tested in the ARRL Lab, the second harmonic is −51 dB below the carrier at 1.5 W output. This transmitter meets FCC spectral requirements.

Table 1

Component Values and Coil Winding Information for 80, 40 and 30 Meter Operation

Band (meters)	C1 (pF)	C2 (pF)	C4 (pF)	C5, C7 (pF)	C6 (pF)	L1	L2	L3	L4, L5
80	1000	100	100	820	1600	4 turns no. 26 over L2	38 turns no. 26 on a T-50-2 toroid (7 μH)	4 turns no. 26 over L2	24 turns no. 26 on T-37-2 toroid (2.3 μH)
40	470	56	47	470	1000	Same as above	Same as above	Same as above	17 turns no. 26 on T-37-2 toroid (1.1 μH)
30	300	18	33	220	470	3 turns no. 26 over L2	27 turns no. 26 on T-50-6 toroid (3 μH)	4 turns no. 26 over L2	18 turns no. 26 on T-37-6 toroid (0.97 μH)

The keying transistor (dc switch Q2) permits CW-waveform shaping. (Any PNP switching transistor that can accommodate the current of Q1 is satisfactory.) The waveform shape is determined by C8, C9, R1 and R2. The values shown provide acceptable keying rise and fall times. CW shaping is also affected by the adjustment of C3. Fortunately, the best waveform shaping coincided with maximum power output for the prototype 30-meter circuit. This may not always be so; tune C3 for a click-free note while monitoring the signal with a receiver that has the AGC disabled and the RF gain turned down to simulate a weak signal.

The original Cubic Incher uses a Motorola MRF-472 transistor for Q1. An NEC 2SC1957 was used in the prototype 30-meter transmitter. It works fine, although greater output power can be obtained from an MRF-472 or similar transistor (Sylvania lists ECG 295 as equivalent to MRF-472). Use any RF power transistor with an f_T of 100 MHz or greater and a power rating equivalent to, or greater than, that of an MRF472.

Constructing the Transmitter

This project was assembled using point-to-point wiring on a universal breadboard. An etching pattern appears at the back of this book, and similar boards are available from many sources.

A 1-1/4 × 3/4 × 1/16-inch-thick piece of "L"-shaped aluminum serves as a heat sink for Q1. Standard aluminum angle stock is acceptable.

The circuit shown is not crowded on the breadboard. A skilled builder can fit the parts into half of the area taken by the prototype. Keep the RF leads on the board as short as possible (less than 1 in.). There should be room on the breadboard for two or even three Cubic Incher circuits, for a two- or three-band QRP rig. Alternatively, a direct-conversion receiver and a Cubic Incher could be constructed on a single breadboard to provide a trans-receiver.

Alignment

Alignment requires a dummy load (two 2-W, 100-Ω resistors in parallel work fine), a 0-1 A meter, and a monitoring receiver. Connect the ammeter in the +12 V line (be sure the meter polarity is correct). Next, attach the dummy load, insert a crystal, switch on the transmitter power supply, ground the key line and tune the monitoring receiver around the crystal frequency. If nothing is heard, and significant current is drawn (200 mA for 2SC1957, 250 to 450 mA for MRF-472), adjust C3 until the crystal begins to oscillate. Next, attach a straight key, send a string of dits and dahs, and adjust C3 for the best sounding CW note. It should be stable and chirp free. Finally, attach an antenna and readjust C3 slightly.

Performance

The output power and collector current of Q1 of Fig 23 vary with the operating voltage. The prototype yielded 1.75 W of filtered output with a 14-V dc supply and 1.25 W with a 12-V supply. The circuit performs well with supply voltages as low as 8.

There was no damage to the 2SC1957[2] while keying the transmitter into an open or shorted termination. This is because it has a high maximum V_{CE} rating of +75 V.

Oscillator frequency varies with load changes. This is characteristic of single-stage transmitters. There is normally no problem unless the antenna is moved toward and away from conductive objects by the wind.

[2]2SC1957 and other NEC RF power transistors are available from Oak Hills Research (see the ARRL Parts Suppliers List at the end of the Component Data chapter).

The QRP Three-Bander CW Transceiver for 18, 21 and 24 MHz

This low-power CW transceiver is easy to use, sensitive enough to receive weak QRP stations, and includes audio limiting to protect your ears from loud local stations. Moving from band to band with this rig is easy: Just change crystals and re-peak its receiver input. Key down, the QRP Three-Bander produces its own sidetone—and RF, too: 1.25 to 4 watts, depending on the band, the dc supply voltage and the particular transistors used in the transmitter. And you can build the QRP Three-Bander your way: with a printed circuit board, or ground-plane construction.[1] This material is taken from an article by Zack Lau, KH6CP, in Oct 1989 *QST*.

Circuit Description

Fig 26 shows the transceiver circuit. U1, an NE602N doubly balanced mixer IC, operates as a direct-conversion (D-C) product detector, converting the incoming signal directly to audio by mixing it with energy from Q2, a bipolar-junction-transistor (BJT) variable crystal oscillator (VXO). Although the NE602 achieves its conversion gain and low noise figure at the expense of dynamic range, it rejects AM-broadcast-band signals well when a capacitor is present across its differential output (pins 4 and 5).

To help prevent hum pickup, the NE602's audio output is amplified by a differential amplifier (U2A, half of an NE5532 low-noise, audio-op-amp IC), which feeds a moderate-gain filter stage (U2B). The final audio-amplifier stage (U3A, half of another NE5532) drives low-impedance stereo headphones at a comfortable level. Q1, a 2N5486 junction-field-effect-transistor (JFET) used as a switch, breaks the connection between U2B and U3A in transmit to keep keying clicks and thumps out of the headphones.

The QRP Three-Bander uses audio amplitude limiting instead of automatic gain control (AGC): Diodes in the filter and final-audio-amplifier stages (D1-D2, and D3-D4, respectively), and R18 (between the final audio amplifier and J2), provide ear and headphone protection by clipping the transceiver's audio output on strong signals.

Transmitter RF is generated by Q3, an MPS918 (or 2N5179) BJT operating as a

(A)

(B)

Fig 25—Front and top views of the QRP Three Bander.

[1]This technique, also known by the unfortunate pejorative terms *ugly* or *dead-bug construction*, entails supporting circuit components—connected directly to each other by short leads—above a thin copper sheet (ground plane). Despite their appearance, circuits built in this way generally work better than their PC-board-built counterparts because air is a better dielectric than fiberglass or phenolic. Builders well-versed in ground-plane construction can generally build the ground-plane version of a given circuit faster than its circuit-board equivalent.

VXO. Q3's output signal drives a buffer amplifier consisting of two BJTs: Q5, a 2N2222, and Q6, a 2N5109 (or selected 2N2222A). The buffer circuit is based on a design by Lewallen;[2] this version is re-

[2]R. Lewallen, "An Optimized QRP Transceiver," Feedback, *QST*, Nov 1980, p 53.

biased for higher power output to make it more suitable for transmitters. The transmitter power amplifier, Q8, is an MRF237 BJT running class C. A seven-element low-pass filter (L1 through L3, and C37 through C40) reduces the harmonic content of the transmitted signal. Because this filter's cutoff frequency is high enough to

Fig 26—Schematic of the QRP Three-Bander. All resistors are ¼ W, carbon film. The inset, B, shows how to replace C1 with a switch (S2) and three trimmer capacitors (C44-C46); if you use this variation, peak C44 at 24 MHz *before* adjusting C45 and C46 for maximum received-signal strength at 21 and 18 MHz.

C1—50 pF, air dielectric, variable (Millen 21050 7- to 45-pF ceramic trimmers, used in ground-plane version, and switch and trimmers [S2 and C44-C46, Fig 1B] have been used successfully). See text.
C2, C24—0.0056 μF, ceramic.
C3, C8, C10, C19-C21, C23, C27, C29, C32-C35, C43—0.022 μF, ceramic.
C4, C11, C18—1-μF, 35-V tantalum electrolytic.
C5, C6, C15—0.22 μF, metal film.
C7, C9—0.0022 μF, metal film (Bessel AF filtering). Use 0.0027 μF for tighter, Chebyshev filtering.
C12, C13—0.010 μF, metal film (Bessel AF filtering). Use 0.012 μF for tighter, Chebyshev filter.
C14—0.056 μF, metal film.
C16—0.0015 μF, polypropylene.
C17, C31—4.7-μF, 35-V, tantalum electrolytic.
C22, C28—14 pF, air dielectric, variable. (Millen 21015 capacitors and Johnson 189-series trimmers have been used successfully. Several months of on-air-use caused severe wear in the RX FREQ Johnson 189-series capacitor, however; use a tuning, not trimmer, capacitor at RX FREQ for longest capacitor life.) See text.
C25—0.015 μF, metal film.
C26, C30—0.082 μF, metal film.
C36, C42—15 pF, silver mica.
C37—100 pF, silver mica.
C38, C39—240 pF, silver mica.
C40—120 pF, silver mica.
C41—220 pF, silver mica.
C44-C46—30-pF plastic trimmer (optional). Used in conjunction with S2, these capacitors replace C1. See text.
D1-D9—1N914 or 1N4148 silicon switching diode.
J1—Phono jack.
J2—1/8-inch stereo phone jack.
J3—BNC jack. See text.
L1, L3—Toroidal inductor, 12 turns of no. 26 enam wire on a T-25-6 powered-iron core (0.46 μH).
L2—Toroidal inductor, 13 turns of no. 26 enam wire on a T-25-6 powdered-iron core (0.52 μH).
L4, L6—Toroidal inductor, 26 turns of no. 24 enam wire on a T-44-2 powdered-iron core (3.8 μH).
L5—Toroidal inductor, 9 turns of no. 24 enam wire on a T-25-6 powdered-iron core (0.26 μH).
Q1—2N5486 JFET. A 2N4416, 2N5485, 2N5484 or MPF102 should also work.
Q2—2N3904 BJT.
Q3—BJT, MPS918 or 2N5179 recommended. A 2N3904 will work, but may exhibit faster keying rise and fall times at 24 MHz than those shown in Fig 3, and the transceiver's RF power output may be suboptimal.
Q4, Q7—2N3906 BJT.
Q5—2N2222 BJT. A 2N3904 will also work.
Q6—2N5109 RF-power BJT. A selected metal-cased (TO-18) 2N2222A will work; some 2N2222As may not have enough gain for optimum power output at 24 MHz. See text.
Q8—Motorola MRF237 RF-power BJT.
R1, R6, R17, R18, R21, R27, R41—100 Ω.
R2, R3, R12—2.2-kΩ (Bessel AF filtering). Use 3.3-kΩ for tighter, Chebyshev filtering.
R4, R5—75 kΩ.
R7, R22, R29, R38—4.7 kΩ.

R8—75 kΩ (Bessel AF filtering). Use 56-kΩ for tighter, Chebyshev filtering.
R9, R20, R23, R30, R32—1 kΩ.
R10, R14, R31—10 kΩ.
R11—1 MΩ.
R13—100-kΩ, audio-taper potentiometer.
R15, R16, R35, R36—47 kΩ.
R19—10-kΩ, audio-taper potentiometer.
R24, R37, R42—47 Ω.
R25, R33, R34—100 kΩ.
R26—22 kΩ.
R28—270 Ω.
R39—470 Ω.
R40—15 kΩ.
RFC1—Toroidal RF choke. Use 6 turns of no. 26 enam wire on an FT-37-43 ferrite toroid (10 μH).
S1—Normally open, momentary push-button.
S2—SPDT, center-off toggle (optional). Use only if C1 is replaced with C44, C45 and C46. See text.
T1—Narrow-band transformer, 10.5:1 turns ratio; 21 turns of no. 26 enam wire on a T-30-6 powdered-iron toroid (primary, 1.75 μH). Secondary has 2 turns of no. 24 or 26 enam wire over primary winding.
T2—Broadband transformer, 10:1 turns ratio; 20 turns of no. 26 enam wire on an FT-37-43 ferrite toroid (primary). Tap is 13 turns from the collector. Secondary has 2 turns of no. 24 or 26 enam wire over primary winding.
T3—Broadband transformer, 5:1 turns ratio; 20 turns of no. 26 enam wire on an FT-37-43 ferrite toroid (primary); tap at 13 turns from the collector end. Secondary has 4 turns of no. 24 or 26 enam wire over primary winding.
T4—Broadband transformer, 3:1 turns ratio; 9 turns of no. 26 enam wire on an FT-37-43 ferrite toroid (primary). Secondary has 4 turns of no 24 or 26 enam wire over primary winding.
U1—NE602 mixer IC.
U2, U3—NE5532 dual low-noise op-amp IC.
U4—78L05 5-V regulator IC.
Y1, Y2—Fundamental crystal, HC-25/U holder, parallel resonance, 20- or 32-pF load capacitance. See text for discussion of frequency choice.

The title photo version of the QRP Three-Bander uses the switch-and-capacitors scheme shown at Fig 26B instead of C1, and Johnson air-dielectric trimmers for RX FREQ (C22) and TX FREQ (C28). Acrylic blocks machined to take set screws and the trimmers' 3/16-inch-diameter shafts serve as tuning knobs. The board is 4 × 5-3/8 inches in size.

pass the transceiver's 24-MHz output with little loss and yet is low enough to reduce harmonics of the rig's 18-MHz signal to a legal level, it requires no adjustment for band changes. Fig 27 shows the output spectrum of the Three-Bander's transmitter.

Full-break-in, relay-less TR switching is one of the QRP Three-Bander's finer points. The TR switch is a wide-bandwidth version of the switch used by Lewallen in his Optimized QRP Transceiver.[3] If you model this switch or measure its characteristics, you'll notice lots of passband ripple: The filter (C36, C41, C42, L4, L5 and L6) has steep skirts and three peaks corresponding to the bands covered by the

[3]R. Lewallen, "An Optimized QRP Transceiver," QST, Aug 1980, pp 14-19.

Fig 27—Worst-case spectral display of the QRP Three-Bander. Each horizontal division represents 10 MHz; each vertical division represents 10 dB. The spike at far left (the spectrum analyzer's first-local-oscillator signal) serves as a convenient "0 MHz" reference. When this spectrogram was taken, the QRP Three-Bander was producing 4 W (14.08-V dc supply) at 18.07 MHz. All harmonics and spurious emissions are at least 36 dB below peak fundamental output. The QRP Three-Bander complies with current FCC specifications for spectral purity.

transceiver. Although the calculated safe maximum-power-handling capability of this switch is just 1.4 W at 24.9 MHz, it seems to handle the transceiver output just fine. (A PIN-diode switch with appropriate biasing could handle more power, but PIN diodes are more difficult to find than ordinary switching diodes.)

The Three-Bander's transmitter section uses *differential keying*—a method of time-sequencing the keying of multiple transmitter stages to achieve a desired effect. As implemented in this circuit, differential keying helps eliminate chirp by turning on the transmit oscillator (Q3) before the buffer amplifier (Q5-Q6) comes on. This sequence is reversed at key up: The buffer amplifier turns off before the oscillator stops. Turning the oscillator on before the buffer gives the oscillator time to stabilize before the transmitter puts out RF; keeping the oscillator on after the buffer turns off assures that frequency changes by the turning-off oscillator won't be present in the transmitted signal.

To avoid key clicks—which would make the Three-Bander's signal wider than necessary for effective CW communication—the waveform of the transmitted signal is shaped in the buffer amplifier. Even though the transmitter power amplifier is nonlinear and tends to shorten the rise and fall times of its driving signal, the Three-Bander's transceiver's RF-output waveform is well-shaped, as shown in Fig 28. The open-circuit voltage at the KEY jack is positive, and about 0.5 V less than the transceiver's dc supply voltage; 1.3 mA flows in the keying circuit line when the KEY jack is shorted.

Getting the Parts

The tough part of building has nothing to do with soldering or making holes in

Fig 28—The QRP Three-Bander's CW-keying waveform at 18.07 MHz. The upper trace is the RF envelope; the lower trace depicts the actual key closure. Each horizontal division represents 5 ms.

metal: It's finding the parts! Fortunately, all the parts used in this project are sold by a number of suppliers.

Parts availability is one thing; parts cost is another. Aside from the crystals, variable capacitors C1 (RX PEAK), C22 (RX FREQ) and C28 (TX FREQ) are probably the most expensive components in this project. You can save money by purchasing these capacitors from a surplus outlet or flea market, although they are still available new. In this application, the voltage rating and physical size of C1, C22 and C28 are relatively unimportant; these capacitors need only cover the necessary capacitance range. C1 must cover the range from 15 to 45 pF. VXO capacitors C22 and C28 should have a maximum capacitance of 10 to 50 pF (10 to 15 pF is optimum) and have a minimum capacitance of just a few picofarads—the lower the minimum capacitance, the better.[4] If you can't find air-dielectric variables at an affordable price, you can replace a given variable capacitor with a switch and several trimmer capacitors, as shown in Fig 26B for C1, RX PEAK; the transceiver shown in the title photo uses this arrangement. You may prefer the Fig 26B solution to C1 because flipping a switch is easier than peaking a tuning control; on the other hand, a front-panel peaking control can help you minimize interference from strong shortwave broadcasters, as discussed later in "Using the Radio on the Air." This switch-and-trimmers idea can also be applied to the transceiver VXOs; you can readjust the trimmers if your preset frequencies are occupied.

[4]Most of the frequency variation provided by C22 and C28 occurs at the low-capacitance end of their capacitance spans. Thus, achieving the smallest possible minimum capacitance at C22 and C28 is especially important to builders who duplicate this project with ground-plane construction because of the generally lower stray capacitances this construction method affords. Less stray capacitance in the VXO circuit maximizes the VXO tuning capacitor's contribution to capacitance *change* in the circuit.

The crystal frequencies you choose depend somewhat on the particular VXO tuning capacitors you use. A VXO with a maximum tuning capacitance of many tens or even hundreds of picofarads (so much capacitance that the crystal is essentially shorted to ground with the tuning capacitance at maximum) may oscillate as much as 10 kHz below the frequency marked on the crystal. If, however, you use capacitors with maximum capacitances in the range specified, your VXOs should oscillate within a few kilohertz of the crystal frequency.

If you want to get your transceiver working on all three of its bands with minimal experimentation, use a 2N5109 at Q6 to ensure adequate drive to the final amplifier at 24 MHz. A *metal-cased* (TO-18) 2N2222A may work if you're willing to try several transistors at Q6 before settling on one. (Metal-cased 2N2222As worked in two out of the three QRP Three-Banders built at HQ.) If you're interested in using your Three-Bander only at 18 and 21 MHz, *any* TO-18 2N2222A will probably work at Q6.

One benefit of home-brewing is that you can use connectors of your choice. BNC connectors are used as antenna jacks here. UHF and N connectors are also suitable. This transceiver uses phono jacks for power and keying connections. (Beware of using phono jacks with batteries—phono plugs can short-circuit all too easily. Molex connectors and fuses are safer.) The presence of identical keying and power-supply connectors isn't a problem with this rig: Nothing blows up if the key and power-supply cables are interchanged.

Construction Details

Fig 29 is a parts-placement diagram. Decide early on whether you'll build the transceiver over a ground plane or on a PC board. If you decide to build a PC-board version, glass-epoxy (G-10 or FR-4), copper-clad circuit board is better than cheap phenolic board because of glass-

Fig 29—A parts-placement diagram for the QRP Three Bander transceiver. The component side of the board is shown, with an X-ray view of the circuit foil. A full-size etching pattern appears at the back of this book.

epoxy's generally higher quality—and because glass-epoxy's greater heat tolerance allows the desoldering and replacement of components with minimal damage to the board. (This is especially important if you're new to building; you may need to fix wiring goofs.) The copper pads for the wires between the board and off-board components are extra large, just in case you have to do a lot of resoldering. (Small pads tend to lift off the board if subjected to too much soldering heat.) This is a trade-off in the case of the VXO-capacitor wires, though: The narrower the pads for C22 and C28 wires, the wider the VXO tuning range per crystal.

Whether you build your transceiver on a PC board or with ground-plane construction, the transceiver circuitry should be completely shielded when in use. It's important that there be grounded metal between the VXO capacitors and your fingers. Otherwise, you may experience the magic-wand effect that long-time hams call *hand capacitance*. (The VXO-capacitor stators [immovable plates] are at a high impedance above ground, and nearby objects—including you—can be "seen" by those circuit points unless a grounded shield is interposed. You shouldn't be able to tune your receiver just by bringing your hand close to the tuning knob!) Complete shielding of the transceiver circuitry also helps minimize hum and microphonics in the NE602 detector, especially when the transceiver is used with a poor RF ground.

Wind your inductors and transformers before you start wiring the circuit. Amateur radio-equipment builders commonly count coil turns wrong; this usually results in coils wound with one turn too many. (Hint: With toroids, just passing the wire through the core counts as one turn.)[5,6]

Because this is an RF project, keep component leads short, as shown in the photographs. Long leads can induce excessive noise and hum into the circuit. (If you're *really* unlucky, overlong leads may cause the circuit to oscillate when it should be amplifying.) Transformers T1 through T3 aren't critical with regard to mounting—they can either lie flat or stand upright. Use screws, lock washers and ¼-inch-long

metal spacers to mount the transceiver boards in their boxes.

Q8, the transmitter power amplifier, must be heat-sinked. Because the MRF237's case is connected to the transistor emitter (instead of the collector, as is usually the case with metal-cased BJTs), you can heat-sink Q8 merely by soldering its case to the circuit-board ground foil (or to the ground plane, if you're undertaking ground-plane construction.) One small solder joint does the job; you needn't solder the entire case perimeter.

Use three-hole-mount phono jacks (two holes for mounting screws and one for the jack barrel) because they don't loosen with use as easily as single-hole mount types do. Drill the extra holes necessary to seat the anti-rotation tabs on the GAIN and SIDETONE LEVEL controls because seating the tabs—instead of breaking them off—results in controls that almost never work loose from the panel.[7]

Testing

None of the Three-Bander's circuits need be trimmed or aligned beyond the adjustments possible with its panel controls, so you need only verify that it works. Power the transceiver with a small supply during testing—a 12- to 15-V regulated power supply capable of producing no more than 0.5 to 1 A is fine. (A supply capable of sourcing 7 or 10 A invites the possibility of serious smoke and component destruction if you make a wiring mistake. Don't use batteries, either: Short-circuited, they can source enough current to melt wires!)

The first test is to determine whether or not the Three-Bander can hear its own transmit oscillator. Set the GAIN control to the middle of its rotation. Plug in crystals at Y1 and Y2, both on the same frequency, and set the RX PEAK, RX FREQ and TX FREQ capacitors so that their plates are half meshed. Press the SPOT button and adjust RX FREQ to find the transmitter signal. If you're lucky, you now have an expensive code-practice oscillator! If you can't hear anything at all, even after trying the entire range of the GAIN control, there's a fault in the receiver audio chain.

If you can meter your power supply's output current, you can confirm that the transmitter works by attaching a 50-Ω dummy load to (a 2-W carbon or metal-oxide resistor) and briefly shorting the KEY jack. If the transmitter is working, the transceiver's current drain should increase to 200 or 300 mA with keying. You can also use an oscilloscope, RF wattmeter or RF voltmeter to measure the transmitter output.

Using the Radio on the Air

The ultimate test of a home-brew rig is

making contacts. Although D-C receivers are notorious for fooling their operators into transmitting on the wrong frequency, the QRP Three-Bander's independent transmitter and receiver oscillators can help you avoid this problem. Perhaps the easiest way is to let other stations tune you in properly by calling CQ on a clear frequency! The second way to be sure you've spotted your transmitter on the other station's frequency is to adjust TX FREQ so that your spotting signal (1) has the same pitch as the incoming signal and (2) "tunes the same way" as the incoming signal. In other words, if, once you've spotted your transmitter, adjusting RX FREQ causes your spotting signal to rise in pitch as the incoming station falls in pitch, or vice versa, you've set your transmitter to the wrong frequency and must readjust it to "the other side of zero beat" to put your signal in the other station's receiver.[8] Another approach is to adjust RX FREQ for zero beat with the incoming signal, press SPOT, and adjust TX FREQ to zero beat your transmitter to your receiver *and* the incoming signal. Once you've done this, adjust RX FREQ to receive the incoming signal at the pitch you want. This latter approach works well on a busy band: After you've spotted your transmitter, readjust RX FREQ to receive the less-interfered-with "side" of the received signal. (Incidentally, you can zero-beat your transmitter to fairly strong incoming stations by pulling out the receive crystal [Y1] and adjusting the spotting signal to zero beat. In this case, the spotting signal acts as the receiver local oscillator. The spotting and incoming signals will have exactly the same pitch when you plug the receive crystal back in.)

Adjust RX PEAK for maximum received-signal strength. If no man-made signals are audible, adjust RX PEAK for maximum background noise. You can also use this control as an attenuator by mistuning it—a useful feature when strong signals overload the rig's mixer. Usually, detuning RX PEAK just enough to reduce the culprit signal below the overload point preserves sufficient desired-signal sensitivity for you to keep operating.

Adjust the GAIN control for a comfortable listening level; this control does not affect the sidetone level. For finding stations, adjust GAIN so you can just hear the background noise.

The SIDETONE LEVEL control adjusts what its name implies. Although a sidetone is unnecessary with a straight key, it's quite handy—if not essential—with electronic keyers.

---

[5]Chapter 2 of this volume shows several aspects of toroid construction, including how to count toroid turns accurately, and how to wind a toroidal transformer (like T1, T2 and T3 in this project).

[6]The inductances listed for L1 through L6 are *measured* values. If you attempt to verify these inductances by using well-known toroid-inductance formulas to work backward from the core and turns values given, you'll come up with different inductance values. This is so because simple formulas for calculating the inductance of toroids tend to overestimate the inductance. (Such formulas are easy to spot: They fail to take wire thickness into account, returning the same inductance whether you use wire so thick you can barely wind it, or hairlike wire that's nearly invisible!)

[7]These are important considerations in portable QRP operation because you've usually left the necessary retightening tools at home!

[8]Because the days when radio amateurs routinely tuned for replies over a significant portion of a band are long gone, accurately spotting your transmitter is important. Spotted on "the wrong side of zero beat," but at the same pitch as the incoming signal, your transmitter is twice that pitch away from the incoming signal—for example, *1.4 kHz away* from an incoming signal tuned to produce a 700-Hz pitch.

The SPOT button turns on the QRP Three-Bander's transmit oscillator, allowing you to adjust your transmit frequency without actually transmitting a signal on the air. (Sweeping a signal across a band is considered poor amateur practice—even for antenna testing.)

Performance

The performance of the QRP Three-Bander varies with band, dc supply voltage and the particular active devices used. Two versions of the Three-Bander exhibit a receive sensitivity (minimum discernible signal, or MDS) between −124 and −128 dBm, and 3rd-order-IMD dynamic ranges between 71 and 74 dB. A third Three-Bander exhibits an MDS between −112 and −120 dBm, and a 3rd-order-IMD dynamic range between 67 and 69 dB. Operated at 13.8 V and using an MPS918 at Q3, two QRP Three-Banders produce 2.6 and 4.0 W at 18 MHz, 2.6 and 3.4 W at 21 MHz, and 1.7 and 2.5 W at 24 MHz. A third Three-Bander (with a hand-picked 2N3904 at Q3) produces 3.8 W at 18 MHz, 3.1 W at 21 MHz and 2.4 W at 24 MHz when operating at 13.8 V. Operating the Three-Bander at 13.8 V provides 3 to 70% more transmitter output power than that available with a 13.0-V supply.

Although the Three-Bander's receiver isn't unduly sensitive or crunch-proof, it's adequate for routine amateur communication. There was no difficulty in making 3rd-order-IMD dynamic-range measurements on the Three-Bander's receiver at the ARRL lab's standard 20-kHz spacing.

The frequency swing afforded by the Three-Bander's VXOs varies with the band, stray capacitances and the particular crystals and VXO tuning capacitors used. The crystals I used allowed swings of 8.9 to 16.2 kHz at 18 MHz, 8.4 to 17.6 kHz at 21 MHz, and 14.1 to 23.4 kHz at 24 MHz.

On the Air

The QRP Three-Bander's receiver is more than satisfactory, considering its simplicity. There's audio to spare. The receiver is a bit microphonic, but not annoyingly so. There may be a bit of hum at some settings of the RX PEAK control when using an ac-operated power supply in conjunction with a poor RF ground.

Full break-in is fun with the QRP Three-Bander. Zack Lau has solved several problems at once by incorporating audio limiting into this transceiver: "De-thumping" the rig's TR switching, protecting the operator's ears and headphones from overdrive, and ridding the rig's side-tone of monotony. (In transmit, you hear the sidetone [assuming that you've set its SIDETONE LEVEL control to allow this, of course], a tone corresponding to the frequency difference between the receive and transmit VXOs, and the products of intermodulation between these signals as they mix in the Three Bander's audio-limiting circuitry. Result: The rig's "sidetone" rarely sounds the same two QSOs in a row!)

The QRP Three-Bander's differential keying is a class act. It sounds absolutely A1 at 18, 21 and 24 MHz. (No "Sure the keying's too hard—but heck, it's QRP" excuses are necessary for this low-power rig.) If you must key an oscillator for CW, this is how to do it.

Other Bands?

Many builders may like this transceiver to cover different bands—14 or 28 MHz, for instance. Here are some untested modification hints for the adventurous.

First of all, most of the QRP Three-Bander's RF circuits are broadbanded enough to cover the HF spectrum without modification. The exceptions are the NE602's tuned input circuit (C1-T1), the transmitter-output low-pass filter (C37-C40, L1-L3), and the TR switch filter (C36, C41, C42, and L4-L6). The variable crystal oscillators should work fine from 3.5 to 28 MHz with fundamental-mode crystals; keep in mind, however, that a VXO's tuning range generally decreases as the crystal frequency is lowered.

You may need to add a few more turns to T4's primary winding on the low bands, but T4 is pretty broadband, too.

The TR switch is a bit tricky to design—you can't get the peaks in a high-ripple band-pass filter to fall exactly where you want them merely by poking at a calculator—but you can always use Lewallen's single-band version (see footnote 4). If you use a band switch for the TR circuit, receiver front end and transmitter output filter, getting the QRP Three-Bander to cover five or six bands shouldn't be too difficult.

A Portable QRP CW Transceiver for 20 and 30 Meters

This transceiver was designed for 20-meter backpack operation in the mountains of Colorado. It offers:

- A single-signal receiver.
- Transceive operation and VFO tuning.
- AGC for listening comfort.
- 5 watts output.
- Semi-QSK TR switching.
- CW sidetone.
- A signal-strength meter.
- Adaptation to 30-meter operation.
- Easy construction.
- Kit availability.[1]

This transceiver was designed by Gary Breed, K9AY, and described by him in Dec 1990 and Jan 1991 *QST*.

The text describes operation of the 20-meter version; the 30-meter version operates similarly. Table 1 lists the component values that change with the band of operation.

The Receiver Circuit

At the heart of the receiver is a multi-function VHF FM receiver IC, the Motorola MC3362. This chip provides all the functions of a complete dual-conversion superhet VHF FM receiver, requiring no other active devices except an audio power amplifier (see the block diagram in Fig 31). The MC3362 has two oscillator/mixer sections with buffer amplifiers at the outputs, a six-stage limiting amplifier, quadrature detector, RSSI (received-signal-strength indicator) output, and a comparator for use in data reception. CW and SSB performance is good, and the external RF circuitry requirements are minimal.

The receiver schematic is shown in Fig 32. Starting at the antenna input, a double-tuned preselector provides input selectivity. The coupling method uses tapped capacitors instead of the more common link or tapped-coil approach. This method allows the use of shielded, slug-tuned inductors for easy construction and repeatable performance. Light coupling is used between the two parallel tuned resonators. With only a narrow band to cover, a sharply peaked response is desirable.

The capacitors in the parallel tuned circuits are selected so that the total capacitance (in series) resonates with the coils, while the ratio of capacitance matches the 50-Ω antenna impedance and the 200-Ω input of the MC3362 (U1). The same formula used for tapped coils yields the appropriate capacitor-value ratio:

$$C1/C2 \text{ or } C3/C4 = \sqrt{(Z_{in} \div Z_{out})} \quad \text{(Eq 1)}$$

At 20 meters, the circuit's loaded Q (about 32) and the reactance of the resonat-

Fig 30—A front view of the Portable QRP CW Transceiver (20-meter version).

ing elements (125 Ω) result in an impedance across the coils of around 4 kΩ, requiring a 0.11 ratio for C1/C2 and 0.22 for C3/C4. I selected standard-value capacitors close to this ratio, and I modeled the circuit using a network-analysis program.[2] The result is a filter with a −6-dB passband of 13.4 to 14.3 MHz and a low input SWR.

The mixers in U1 are the doubly balanced Gilbert-cell type used in virtually all IC mixers (like the MC1496, SL6440C and NE602). The first mixer is internally connected to a unique differential oscillator that has on-chip varactor tuning diodes. The oscillator requires only a parallel tuned circuit to operate. That's all—just one capacitor and one coil. Tuning is accomplished by adjusting the voltage at the junction of the varactors. VFO construction is typically quite critical, but almost anyone can build this simple VFO.

The VFO is tuned using a voltage taken from a +6-V bus that's stabilized by a 78L06 regulator (U5). Frequency increases with tuning voltage, but according to a nonlinear function. Two resistors are used to set the tuning range: R1 limits the upper range and R2 avoids operation at zero volts, keeping the tuning control in the most linear range. The varactors have a linear range of only about 5 pF, so the tuned-circuit LC ratio determines how wide the tuning range will be. The varactors don't exhibit great temperature stability, so a smaller tuning range (high C) gives the best stability.

Two pots do the tuning. One serves as

Table 1

Component Values for 20- and 30-Meter Operation

Component	Band	
	20m	30m
Receiver		
R1	33 kΩ	150 kΩ
R2	470 kΩ	22 kΩ
C6	470 pF	56 pF
L1, L2	1.4 μH	2.4 μH
Transmitter		
C1, C3	270 pF	680 pF
C2	430 pF	820 pF
L3, L4	1.4 μH	2.4 μH
L1, L2	12 t no. 24 on T-37-2 toroid core	14 t no. 24 on T-37-2 toroid core

the main tuning control, covering about 50 kHz from end to end. This tuning rate is too fast, so a second pot was added as a fine-tuning control. It allows ±2-kHz adjustment. Smaller tuning ranges could be covered with a single tuning pot. It's possible to use a vernier drive and a single-turn pot in this application, but most inexpensive verniers have a lot of backlash, and better ones would dramatically increase the cost.

The mixer is followed by a buffer amplifier whose output goes to a four-crystal filter. The filter is of a Cohn design described by Wes Hayward, W7ZOI.[3] This filter uses four 8.0-MHz microprocessor crystals from the same manufacturing

[1]PC boards and parts kits for the transceiver are available from A&A Engineering, 2521 W LaPalma, Unit K, Anaheim, CA 92801, tel 714-952-2114.

[2]RF Notes No. 4, ETRON RF Enterprises, PO Box 4042, Diamond Bar, CA 91765.

[3]W. Hayward, "Designing and Building Simple Crystal Filters," *QST*, Jul 1987, pp 24-29.

lot, selected for oscillation frequencies within 25 Hz of each other. The capacitors yield a −3-dB passband about 400-Hz-wide. The impedances of the buffer stage output and next mixer input are 180 and 330 Ω, respectively, which are in the ballpark range for the Cohn filters. Some operators may prefer a wider bandwidth, such as 600 to 800 Hz, and might try 220-pF capacitors in the filter. Details on selecting appropriate capacitors are given in Hayward's article.

The second mixer stage in U1 is used as the product detector, and its associated oscillator serves as the BFO. This oscillator is a conventional Colpitts type. Because the active devices involved are biased internally, the crystal and feedback capacitors at pins 3 and 4 of U1 are the only external components required. The 8-MHz BFO crystal is from the same batch as the filter crystals, "rubbered" with a trimmer capacitor to 800 Hz above the center of the filter passband to get the desired CW beat note.

The product-detector output goes to the audio stages. None of U1's other functions are used.

The audio stages provide three functions: bandpass filtering, AGC and power amplification. Two sections of an LM324 quad op amp (U2A and U2B) are used as an active filter with two low-pass poles (1200-Hz cutoff), and two high-pass poles (600-Hz cutoff). This high-pass/low-pass combination has excellent ultimate rejection, and it avoids the ringing that occurs in most narrow bandpass filters. Scaling the capacitor values in these filter sections allows use at other bandwidths, such as 2.7 kHz (300 to 3000 Hz) for SSB.

An MC3340P audio-gain-control IC (U3) is used with U2C and U2D as an AGC circuit. One op-amp section amplifies U3's output and isolates the AGC rectifier from the audio path. Another op amp serves as a dc amplifier that drives U3's gain-control pin and the S meter.

The low output impedance of the buffer (U2C) allows a fast attack time by rapidly charging the 470-kΩ/4.7-µF resistor/capacitor time-delay circuit. The high input impedance of the following dc amplifier (U2D) follows the natural decay time of the RC network, giving a fast-attack, slow-release AGC. The attack time is slow enough to be audible on the first code element of a strong signal, but a fairly long decay time eliminates much subsequent popping until the signal ceases long enough for the RC network to discharge. The AGC control range is 50 dB or more.

The 2.7-kΩ resistor at pin 2 of U3 sets the no-signal gain, and is chosen so there is a bit of linear range before the onset of AGC action. (This keeps the receiver quiet when it's tuned between stations.) Receiver muting is provided by applying +12 V to U3's gain-control pin through an isolating resistor, pulling gain to minimum. The resting potential at the op-amp output is around 0.8 V; a 1N4148 diode in series with

Fig 31—Pinout and block diagram of the MC3362 receiver IC. Input and output resistances are indicated for the ports of the MC3362's two mixers.

this output eliminates the offset. A surplus 200-µA meter serves as an S meter.

A conventional audio power amplifier, using an LM386 (U4), is included. The keyed sidetone from the transmitter is fed to U4 *after* the AGC and AF-gain control, so its level is unaffected by their actions. The speaker or headphones should match the low (4 to 16) Ω audio-output impedance.

Construction and Tune-Up

A 3- × 5-inch PC board holds the receiver circuit (see Fig 33). The low parts count in the RF stages allows plenty of ground-plane area on the single-sided board. Construction is ordinary through-the-hole PC-board assembly. Use sockets for the ICs. The shielded coils require no special treatment, and because most of the circuit operates at audio, construction is not critical. Keep leads short; components

should be mounted as close to the board as possible.

To adjust the receiver, a stable signal source in the band is required, along with a frequency counter or receiver to indicate the VFO frequency. With patience, it is possible to use only the in-band signal source—if you know its frequency. A transmitter (such as your main rig), running a few watts into a dummy load with a nearby pickup wire for coupling to the receiver's antenna input, represents the minimum required test equipment.

Tune-up is simple; there are only four adjustments. First, adjust the VFO-coil (L3) slug for the lowest desired frequency with both tuning pots set to minimum resistance (lowest tuning voltage). The receiver uses an 8000-kHz IF and the VFO tunes from about 6015 to 6065 kHz, which corresponds to 14015- to 14065-kHz cover-

Fig 32—Circuit diagram of the receiver. Values shown are for 20-meter operation. Capacitors are disc ceramic unless noted otherewise. The following lines connect to the transmitter: to TR Relay, VFO OUT, Sidetone In, Mute. The values for R1, R2, C6, L1 and L2 are given in Table 1.

C1, C4—100 pF.
C2—820 pF.
C3—2.5 pF.
C5—560 pF.
C_F—300 pF.

age. Using the values shown, the tuning range is about 50 kHz, with ±2-kHz fine tuning. A frequency counter connected at the VFO output terminals is the best calibration setup to use. If a counter is unavailable, a strong signal at the desired frequency can be tuned in using the VFO slug, but this approach takes patience and the right touch with a tuning tool.

Once the range is set, adjust the input coils (L1 and L2) for a peak at the band center. Before their final adjustment, adjust the BFO trimmer so the signal peaks with a 750- to 800-Hz note. Input tuning can then be completed. The coils are best tuned for a peak S-meter reading using a reasonably strong signal. (This is easier than tuning by ear with weak signals.) Mark the MAIN TUNING dial in the desired increments.

At this point, the job is almost done. All that you may need to do is change R4 to obtain the deflection range you prefer on the S meter. The 22-kΩ value shown was used for a 200-μA meter. Other meters may need

a different resistor value for the desired deflection range. In some cases, a second 1N4148 diode in series with the meter may be needed to get a proper zero.

The dial can be calibrated using either a counter or the calibrated external signal. The even-megahertz IF also makes it possible to use a counter as a frequency display. Just drop the megahertz digits (ie, 6042-kHz VFO = 14042-kHz receiver frequency). The counter described by Doug Bainbridge, NØHPK, in February 1989 *QST*,[4] would work well here. If you use such a counter, be sure to shield it to keep the harmonics of its clock and display-multiplexing signals out of the receiver.

Performance

This receiver is plenty sensitive, with a minimum discernible signal of about

[4]D. Bainbridge, ''A Low-Cost Frequency Counter,'' *QST*, Feb 1989, pp 21-26. Also see Feedback, *QST*, Apr 1989, p 43.

−123 dBm. Its measured third-order IMD dynamic range is 70 dB; not exceptional, but it's good for such a simple receiver. The AGC operation is reasonably smooth for an audio-derived system, and despite its limitations, it is a vast improvement in operating comfort over no AGC at all.

Selectivity is good, with the crystal and audio filters resulting in a 400-Hz-wide passband at −3 dB and 1325 Hz at −30 dB. However, opposite sideband rejection is only a little under 40 dB. With an 8-MHz IF, the isolation of the chip and filter circuitry is insufficient to allow better performance. The pins on the IC for filter input and output are only 0.2 inches apart, and some coupling across the filter occurs. Versions constructed for other bands, using lower-frequency IFs (with proportionally less coupling), demonstrated much better skirt selectivity. Fortunately, the AGC action pushes down the weaker unwanted signals and minimizes the problem.

This receiver's only real weakness is temperature stability. In a stable environ-

Additional Possibilities

This receiver can be adapted to almost any frequency range, as long as a few limitations are observed. The MC3362 first mixer and oscillator will go to 200 MHz or higher, but the first IF is designed for operation below 12 MHz, with internal roll-off capacitors limiting its upper frequency. Also, the small capacitance range of the varactors limits tuning range at lower VFO frequencies. The VFO works at 9 MHz with excellent short-term stability. Operation up through 15 meters should be possible.

Because this design does not use the limiting IF and quadrature detector in the MC3362 (and their associated limiting of the signal waveform), this receiver works very well for SSB. Excellent results were obtained in experiments with commercial crystal and ceramic IF filters on several HF bands. All that is needed for SSB is a widening of the audio-filter passband and impedance matching for the SSB filter. AGC parameters are fine as they are for voice operation. This receiver makes an excellent net monitor, or it can be used as a bedside monitor for your favorite DX frequency. If the band isn't open, you needn't waste time wandering to the shack!

The voltage-tuned VFO lends itself to synthesizer control. Some of the synthesizer chips on the market could probably be made to work with relatively simple circuitry. Another way to make use of voltage tuning is to add RIT. A small relay driven by the transmit/receive control could switch a pot in and out of the circuit, connected like the one used for fine tuning.

ment, such as a ham shack, there is no trouble with VFO stability; it holds within a few tens of hertz for hours on end. When operated in the variable outdoor weather, however, noticeable frequency changes can occur, although short-term stability is still good as long as the temperature is fairly constant. The problem is due to the temperature variation of the varactors, with some contribution from the other VFO components. Dial calibration can be off by a few kilohertz in extremely cold or hot situations. Attempts to correct this problem with temperature-compensation capacitors severely worsened short-term stability, so the problem remains.

This transceiver has a built-in band-edge warning. Because the rig uses an even-megahertz IF with a BFO operating just above the passband, a strong spurious signal is located about 1.5 kHz above the lower band edge. This is an annoyance when operating at the band edge, but it's also a convenient reference point. Of course, if you don't select coverage down to the lower band edge, you'll have to live with some calibration error (General and Advanced operators need to be careful). Accepting this shortcoming is a small price to pay for simplicity.

Fig 33—Parts-placement diagram for the receiver circuit board. The component side of the board is shown, with an X-ray view of the circuit foil. A full-size etching pattern appears at the back of this book.

Fig 35—Circuit diagram of the transmitter. Values of components marked ** vary with the band of operation; see Table 1. See text for information about winding the inductors.

Fig 34—A top view of the 20-meter transceiver. The receiver board is mounted closest to the front panel (left). The transmitter board is nearest to the RF connector (right).

The Transmitter Circuit

Refer to Fig 35. Because the receiver is a superhet, on transmit, the VFO needs to be converted to the operating frequency, but offset by 800 Hz from the receiver frequency. To do this simply, an NE602 oscillator/mixer IC (U1) is used with an external crystal tuned to the center of the receiver's filter passband. (The crystal is from the same batch as those in the receiver filter and BFO; its frequency is adjusted by a series inductor and a trimmer in the feedback circuit.) U1 operates on Zener-regulated 6 V derived from a 12-V line that's switched by TR relay K1. This switching arrangement keeps the transmitter from delivering power until *after* the TR relay has been switched to the transmit position.

The mixer output contains the VFO and crystal frequencies and their sum and difference. A double-tuned filter after the mixer passes only the 14-MHz output. The NE602 is a low-level device, so the VFO input to U1, pin 1, is reduced with a series resistor. (If this was not done, the NE602 would generate substantial spurious signals.)

A typical problem in circuit design is impedance matching. This circuit has to match the very high impedance of the tuned circuits in the filter to the low impedance of the RF-amplification stages. Usually, this is done with tapped coils, link coupling, or another matching network. An FET source follower can also accomplish the task. This circuit uses yet another method: an IC video buffer.

Recently, op amps, buffers and other "low-frequency" ICs with bandwidths into the hundreds of megahertz have become available. One of these ICs, National Semiconductor's LM6321 (U2) has an input impedance of 5 MΩ and a very low output impedance. The LM6321's voltage gain is one, but it has plenty of current gain, and thus power gain. U2 requires almost no external parts: a pair of 1-MΩ resistors to bias the input, plus bypass and coupling capacitors, are all that's needed. A series resistor at the input minimizes this chip's tendency to oscillate with inductive inputs.

Except as indicated, decimal values of capacitance are in microfarads (μF); others are in picofarads (pF); resistances are in ohms; k= 1,000, M= 1,000,000.
∗ Heat Sink.
∗∗ See Caption
IC pins not shown are unused.

Fig 36—The QRP transceiver's keyed waveform. The upper trace is the RF envelope; the lower trace is the key closure. Each horizontal division is 5 ms. The transceiver was being operated at 6 W output.

The convenient low-impedance output of the buffer drives a class-A 2N3866 driver amplifier (Q1) with negative feedback. Class-A operation allows higher gain than class C, and the use of feedback ensures stable input and output impedances. Thus, the harmonics generated in this stage are not severe, and a simple broadband transformer (T1) can be used to couple it to the final stage. The driver and the preceding buffer stage are keyed, as explained later.

The final amplifier (Q2) uses the popular MRF475, a rugged NPN power transistor capable of 12 W output. This final transistor can handle momentary shorts and opens at its output in this application. All of is occasionally hook some outrageous load to a rig's antenna terminal!

At 5 W output, the collector-load impedance is close to 12 Ω, as determined by the general equation:

$$R_L = (V_{CE} - V_{SAT})^2 \div (2\ P_O)\quad (Eq\ 2)$$

Assuming a 12-V supply, $(V_{CE} - V_{SAT})$ is about 11 V. Thus, the impedance is 12.1 Ω, which can be easily and closely matched to 50 Ω by a 4:1 transformer. A five-pole low-pass filter at the output reduces the harmonic content to an acceptable level.

Control Circuits

Transmit/receive switching, keying circuitry and the sidetone oscillator are all on the transmitter board. TR switching is done by keying a 2N3906 transistor (Q4), which drives an RC network through a blocking diode. The rapidly charged RC network turns on Q5, pulling in the TR relay. The discharge time of the RC network is controlled by a trimmer pot, DELAY, that you can set for the desired hold-in time. The relay is a small DIP-outline DPDT unit. One set of contacts switches the antenna and the other feeds power to U1 and the receiver-muting circuit.

Keying begins with two sections of a 4001 CMOS quad NOR gate (U3). Its 12-V out-put drives a TIP110 Darlington power transistor (Q3) that switches dc to U2 and the 2N3866 driver stage. A series-R, shunt-C network to ground from the keying transistor's base shapes the keyed waveform. A photo of the rig's keyed output is shown in Fig 36.

The sidetone is generated in U3A and U3B, which form a keyed square-wave oscillator. The components shown yield an 800-Hz note with a 12-V supply, which assists in zero-beating incoming signals. Some variation in pitch occurs with different 4001s and changing supply voltage. The oscillator's high output level is attenuated by a 470-kΩ resistor in series with the 5-kΩ SIDETONE LEVEL control.

Coils and Transformers

The transmitter uses five inductors. Wind the driver-output transformer (T1) on a 43-material, ¼- × ¼-inch, two-hole balun core. The primary consists of three turns of no. 28 wire (the wire passes three times through each of the core's two holes). The secondary is a single turn "hairpin loop" of no. 24 wire. The power-amplifier RF choke (RFC1) is made of three turns of no. 24 wire on a large 73-material ferrite bead. The output transformer (T2) has eight bifilar turns of no. 28 wire on an FT-37-43 ferrite toroid. The two coils in the low-pass filter are identical: See Table 1 for winding information.

Construction

Transmitter assembly is straightforward, using common through-hole PC-board construction. See Fig 37. As with all RF circuitry, keep component leads short and make good solder joints. A single-sided PC board with plenty of ground-plane area, combined with a compact but uncrowded layout, assures good stability.

The order of assembly is a bit more important with the transmitter than the receiver, as some larger components are used in the transmitter. Install U3's socket and the 0.01-μF bypass capacitors first. The driver- and final-stage output transformers, low-pass filter coils and ferrite-bead RF

Fig 37—Parts-placement diagram for the transmitter circuit board. The component side of the board is shown, with an X-ray view of the circuit foil. A full-size etching pattern appears at the back of this book.

Fig 38—Spectrum analyzer display of the QRP transmitter's output. Horizontal divisions are each 10 MHz; vertical divisions are each 10 dB. Output power is approximately 6 W. All harmonics and spurious emissions are at least 42 dB below peak fundamental output. The transceiver complies with current FCC specifications for spectral purity for equipment in this power-output class and frequency range.

choke should go in next. The crystal, resistors, other capacitors and diodes can then be placed on the board. Then install the relay and shielded coils. You can solder in the connector pins for the power, antenna and control lines at any time.

Finally, install the transistors and ICs. For best performance, the NE602 and LM6321 should be soldered directly to the board—don't use sockets. The 2N3866 (Q1) uses a finned radial heat sink and should be mounted about 3/16 inch above the board to clear the surrounding components. The heat-sink fins should straddle the emitter-bypass capacitor. Solder Q2's heat sink into place, then mount the MRF475 to it with a mica insulator and heat-sink compound. After you've mounted and checked the device for shorts, solder in and trim the transistor leads.

Mount the board in the case on metal standoffs at each of its four corners. Like all transmitters, the board needs to be well-grounded to ensure stability. Most of the wires interconnecting the transmitter and receiver sections can be routed under the PC boards for neatest layout.

Alignment

An oscilloscope is the preferred test equipment for transmitter adjustments, but you can get satisfactory results with just a power indicator, such as a wattmeter or an RF-voltage probe. Begin checkout with the separate +12-V power to the final amplifier *disconnected*.

Keying the rig should mute the receiver and enable the sidetone. Adjust the sidetone-level control for the desired level. If the pitch is too high or low, increase or decrease the value of the 51-kΩ resistor between pins 2 and 3 of U3.

Temporarily disconnect the muting line. Keying should now produce two tones: the sidetone and the beat note between the receiver BFO and the transmitter-mixer crystal. Adjust the trimmer on the transmitter crystal to match the tone pitches as closely as possible. Reconnect the mute line.

If you have access to an oscilloscope, hook the probe to pin 7 of U2. With the transmitter keyed, adjust the two coils (L3 and L4) following the mixer for maximum level and the cleanest waveform. If this is not a smooth adjustment, make sure that all the components are installed with the shortest possible leads and that all solder joints are good. Repeat with the scope across the final-amplifier base resistor. (If you don't have an oscilloscope, move to the next step.)

Connect the power lead to the final amplifier. If possible, monitor the current in the supply lead to the rig. If you aren't using an oscilloscope, key the rig and adjust L3 and L4 for maximum power output. The peak may be quite broad, so adjust them carefully for the exact peak. The rig should draw between 0.8 and 1.25 A from a 12.0-V supply, generating 3 to 8 W output. Output can be trimmed for best efficiency by squeezing and spreading the turns on low-pass filter coils L1 and L2 (this changes the impedance match). Output level can be adjusted by changing Q1's emitter resistor.

Transmitter Performance

The transmitter typically keys smoothly, with no significant shortening of the first dot. The sidetone is adjustable from quiet to earsplitting, and the TR turnaround can be set between near QSK and a sizable fraction of a second.

Even when critical reports were requested, the on-the-air reports have been good. The only difficulty has been erratic performance when the rig is operating into a high-SWR antenna. The stray RF that floats around under such conditions seems to create problems. No such problems occur when the rig feeds antenna systems with SWRs of 1.5:1 or better. Some antennas with 2:1 SWRs have worked well with the rig, but others have not.

The transmitter's spectral purity meets FCC requirements, as shown in Fig 38.

The "Ugly Weekender"—A 7-MHz QRP Transmitter

Here is a simple, VFO-controlled 40-meter transmitter with 1.5 W of RF output. Beyond its value as an easily built transmitter that covers more than the few-kilohertz offered by typical VXO-controlled designs, it serves as an excellent introduction to "ugly" or "dead bug" construction techniques. This description, by Roger Hayward, KA7EXM, and Wes Hayward, W7ZOI, first appeared in the August 1981 *QST*.

Simple transmitters often use crystal control, but this is somewhat impractical because of the high cost of crystals: you can build a VFO for the price of a few crystals. The greatest obstacle to some builders, however, is printed-circuit layout. The use of printed circuit boards has become so popular that many amateurs are afraid to attempt a project that is not accompanied by an etching pattern or a source of etched boards. This is unfortunate!

Numerous methods may be used in the construction of electronic equipment. The assumption that a design might function better if built on an etched and drilled circuit board is false.

Fig 39—The "Ugly Weekender" transmitter. The lower box houses the VFO and buffer stages, while the upper box holds the driver and PA stages.

Fig 40—Schematic diagram of the VFO and control circuits for the QRP transmitter. Fixed-value capacitors are disc ceramic unless specified otherwise. Resistors are ½-W 10% carbon units.

C1, C2—Miniature air variable, 80 pF max.
D1, D2, D3—Silicon switching diode, 1N914, 1N4152 or equiv.
D4—Zener diode, 1N937 or equiv.
J1—Phone jack.
J2—Phono jack or coaxial connector of builder's choice.

L1—25 turns no. 22 enameled wire on Amidon T-50-6 powdered-iron toroid core. Tap 6 turns from ground end.
L2—20 turns no. 26 enameled wire on Amidon ferrite core, FT-37-43.
Q1—JFET, 2N4416, TIS88 or equiv. (see text).
Q2, Q3—General-purpose NPN transistor, such as 2N2222 or 2N3904.
Q4, Q5—General-purpose PNP transistor, such as 2N2907 or 2N3906.

R1-R5—High-value resistors used as standoffs (see text).
T1—Broadband transformer. Collector winding is 20 turns no. 28 enameled wire on an Amidon FT-37-43 core. J2 winding is 5 turns no. 28 enameled wire over the primary winding.

Fig 41—Schematic diagram of the driver and power-amplifier portion of the QRP transmitter. Fixed-value capacitors are disc ceramic unless noted otherwise. Polarized capacitors are electrolytic or tantalum. Fixed-value resistors are ½-W 10% composition units.

D5—Zener diode, 1N973B or equiv.
D6, D7—Silicon switching diode, 1N914, 1N4152 or equiv.
J3, J4—Phono jack or coaxial connector of builder's choice.
L3—RF choke, 35 turns no. 22 enameled wire on an Amidon T-68-2 core.

L4, L5—16 turns no. 22 enameled wire on an Amidon T-50-6 core.
L6—45 turns no. 26 enameled wire on an Amidon T-50-2 core.
Q6—NPN transistor, 2N2222, 2N3904, or equiv.
Q7—RF power transistor, 2N3553, 2N3866 or equiv. Use a heat sink.

R6-R7—High-value resistors used as standoffs (see text).
R8—100-Ω ½-W composition potentiometer (see text).
T2, T3—Transmission-line transformer, 10 bifilar-wound turns no. 28 enameled wire on an Amidon FT-37-43 ferrite core.

The "Ugly" Method

The purpose of this article is to present a simple, good-performance QRP transmitter design, and to illustrate some "ugly" construction methods that may be used for whatever project the builder might want to assemble. These methods are especially attractive for small projects.

"Ugly" construction has several advantages over printed circuits. It is very flexible. The builder may use parts on hand, a practice that is often difficult with projects built on etched boards. The circuit may be easily changed for experimentation. Stray capacitance with circuit-board material as the dielectric is eliminated. Speedy construction is the greatest virtue of "ugly" methods.

This transmitter was designed and built in two winter afternoons. Contacts were made before the end of that period. Estimated construction time was less than half that required for projects using etched boards.

Overall Design

The transmitter shown in Figs 40 and 41 operates in the 7-MHz CW sub-band. VFO control is used for operating flexibility and economy. The VFO signal is well buffered before it is routed to a second enclosure that contains the keyed driver and a power amplifier (PA) stage. Shaped keying provides a click-free signal. Efficiency was considered important for battery conservation because the authors often take their rigs backpacking. Finally, electronic TR switching allows for near-QSK operation, and it's less expensive than a relay. Slight modifications allow use as a direct-conversion transceiver. This transmitter is based largely on a transceiver designed and built (with "ugly" methods) by Roy Lewallen, W7EL. The reader should review Roy's article (which immediately follows this work) for design details. Departures from the W7EL circuit are noted in this description. This transmitter is not as compact as Roy's—but then few are!

Circuit Details and Construction

The transmitter is built by means of point-to-point wiring (Fig 42). The foundation is a pair of small aluminum boxes, 1½ × 3 × 5½ inches. The boxes are bolted together, and each contains a scrap of unetched copper-clad circuit-board material bolted directly to the box. The boards serve as low-impedance ground for all of the circuitry.

Numerous components are attached to ground. Each serves the desired circuit function and provides mechanical support for other components that are attached to its ungrounded ends. Where additional support is required, high-value resistors serve as effective standoffs. The exact value of the resistors is not critical so long as it is high enough to prevent significant loss through the resistor. (Let's say, ten times the circuit impedance at the resistor.) The resistor standoffs here are 1.1-MΩ, ½-W resistors. Any value from 220-kΩ upward (½ or ¼ watt) will function well. The resistors are shown in the schematic diagrams as R1-R7. They have no bearing on circuit operation, except to provide mechanical support.

Tuning is provided by a pair of 80-pF air-variable capacitors from the authors' junk box. C2 is the main tuning control, and C1 is a coarse band-set adjustment. C2 spans about 80 kHz with the components shown (see Fig 43). Substitutions are possible. For example, the main tuning capacitor, C2, may be a standard 365-pF broadcast-band replacement type. C3 should then be in-

Fig 42—Close-up view of the assembly technique discussed in this article. Components are soldered to the circuit-board material and used as standoffs.

Fig 43—Interior view of the transmitter VFO and buffer stages. The variable capacitors are at left.

creased to 220 pF to retain the present 8-kHz tuning range.

The FET used at Q1 is not especially critical, but oscillator output may be low when the popular MPF102 is used: Use a 2N4416. A TIS-88 (essentially a plastic version of the 2N4416) is used here.

For optimum stability, use NP0 ceramic discs for all fixed-value capacitors in the VFO. Avoid silver-mica capacitors. Polystyrene capacitors are probably suitable, but they may degrade VFO stability.

Most VFO drift occurs when the power is initially applied. Drift in operation is minimized by allowing the VFO to run continuously. The VFO frequency is shifted downward by adding a 2.7-pF capacitor to the oscillator tuned circuit (via Q4 and D2) during key-down periods. The timing components associated with Q4 inhibit the oscillator shift between characters, but shift frequency about 25 kHz upward during longer key-up periods.

The VFO output is buffered with a two-transistor feedback amplifier, Q2 and Q3. This circuit provides 10 to 15 mW of output, which is more than enough to drive the following stage. The reverse isolation is excellent. This circuit is a refinement of Lewallen's circuit.

Transistor selection is not critical: 2N2222As or 2N3904s will work well at Q2, Q3, and Q6. Be careful about transistors purchased at local electronics stores, however, often devices sold as a "2N2222A" do not meet actual 2N2222A specifications. The keying transistor, Q5, is located on the VFO board. A capacitor between the collector and base provides an integrator action that ensures clean keying.

Construction of the VFO is not critical. Builders are often advised to keep all leads as short as possible. This is generally an exaggeration, especially for HF equipment. Some leads must be short, while others may be relatively long with no harm. Specifi-

cally, bypass-capacitor leads should be short.

Consider the buffer amplifier, a circuit with two bypass capacitors. One decouples the positive supply from the circuit. That capacitor should have a short lead to circuit ground. The other end should be connected directly to T1 and Q2. Similarly, the emitter bypass on Q3 needs to have reasonably short leads. Leads of other components may be longer, with no ill effects.

The output stages are shown in Fig 41. This part of the circuit is built in the second box. The isolation afforded by a separate enclosure increases VFO stability and reduces load variations that shift the oscillator frequency.

Three holes for leads (between boxes) are drilled through the two boxes and the circuit boards. One is located near Q5 for the keyed + 12 V line to the driver. The second is near the PA for an unkeyed + 12 V line. The third is near T1, and it carries RF to the DRIVE control (R8). Insulated wire is used for these three connections. In addition, the two circuit boards (ground) are connected by a bare wire through the hole near T1 and R8. The bare wire is soldered to both boards.

The value of the DRIVE control (R8) is not critical. Values from 100 to 1000 ohms are suitable. The driver stage is a departure from the W7EL design: The original circuit was tuned. Since there is no need for selectivity at this point, a broadband design is used. The original circuit had a tendency toward instability (self-oscillation). This is eliminated by using an amplifier with negative shunt feedback from collector to base, via the 2.2-kΩ resistor.

Two bifilar-wound transformers are used at T2 and T3. The winding details are shown in the insert of Fig 41. The two wires forming each bifilar winding may be twisted together, but this is not important at 7 MHz. Use ferrite cores (not powdered

iron) for all three transformers.

The final amplifier is virtually identical to that described by W7EL. The emitter lead on Q7 should be short, although it is moderately long in the prototype to accommodate the method used to mount the transistor. The 385-pF capacitor at the collector of Q7 should be attached close to the transistor.

L4 and L5 form a double pi-network for output filtering. The network is designed to present an impedance of 50 ohms to the collector of Q7. The TR circuit is formed by L6 and the 51-pF capacitor. The two components are series resonant at 7 MHz, so there is minimum attenuation during receive periods. High RF voltages appear at the collector of Q7 when transmitting. This causes the TR switching diodes, D6 and D7, to conduct alternately. The 51-pF capacitor then becomes part of the transmitter output network. There is less than 1 mW of power available at the receiver coax connector during key-down periods: This level will not damage most receivers. The receiver should have an excellent AGC system or separate muting facilities if QSK operation is desired.

It is a good idea to build and test construction projects in stages whenever possible. Problems are much more easily identified and cured that way. Build and test this transmitter in a sequential manner, as follows:

Build the VFO first. Apply power, and check the actions of C1 and C2 by listening to the signal in a receiver.

Construct and test the buffer (Q2 and Q3). Measure the buffer output power into a 50-ohm load using an RF probe and a voltmeter.

Build the keying circuit, including the frequency-offset components. Test it by observing: (1) the control signal with a dc voltmeter, and (2) the frequency shift with a receiver.

Fig 44—Photo of the driver and PA assembly. The DRIVE control, R8, is visible at the lower left.

Fig 45—Worst-case spectral display of the transmitter output with a 14-V supply. The second harmonic is −34 dBc. This transmitter complies with FCC requirements for spectral purity.

Next, build the driver stage (see Fig 44), and measure the output into a 50-ohm load (about 70 mW with R8 at maximum). This measurement was performed on the prototype with an RF probe and attenuators.

Construct the PA next. Measure the output power as with the driver circuit. The total power-supply current was also measured. The DRIVE control was set for 1.5 W of RF output with a corresponding supply current of 200 to 250 mA. This indicates reasonable (50%) efficiency.

After testing, the transmitter is ready for use. The one shown here yielded numerous contacts with stations up and down the West Coast of the US and Canada (from Oregon) in just a few days of casual oper-

ation. Reports indicated that the note was stable, clean and crisp—certainly far from ugly! (See Fig 45.)

What Next?

Output power may be increased to over 2 watts by advancing the DRIVE control. The current rises to over 500 mA, however, which indicates poor efficiency. The output network should be redesigned if higher output is desired. A different transistor could then be used at Q7. Some of the devices intended for the output stage of CB transmitters should yield 5 to 10 watts. The available power from the driver can be increased to 150 mW by changing R9 to 15 ohms.

You may wish to convert this unit to a direct-conversion transceiver. An auxiliary VFO output is shown in Fig 40. The power from this point is suitable to drive a diode-ring product detector, as used in the Optimized QRP Transceiver. The 25-kHz VFO offset, may be easily reduced to the 800 Hz needed for a direct-conversion transceiver by shunting D2 with a 150-pF capacitor.

Conclusion

Whatever you are building, it is worth questioning the need for an etched circuit board. More often than not, the "ugly" methods presented here will do as well, with considerable time and money savings and absolutely no performance compromise. Construction is also simpler than with printed-circuit methods—if you avoid extreme miniaturization.

An Optimized QRP Transceiver for 7 MHz

Here is a rig that provides real challenge for the QRP home builder. Nonetheless, this is a classic circuit and a favorite in the QRP community. Even though this project (designed and built by Roy Lewallen, W7EL) was first published in August 1980 *QST*, it is still the best available portable QRP rig in many respects. This presentation has been condensed somewhat from the original and it includes Roy's circuit updates through July 1990.

It is quite a feat to build this circuit into the package shown. The less adventuresome reader can elect to build this rig into a larger package. If you are a beginning home builder or unfamiliar with "ugly" construction techniques, look at The Ugly Weekender that precedes this project. That article explains the basics of the "ugly" or "dead bug" construction style and describes a slightly more tame transmitter that could be substituted for the transmit section of this project.

Many QRP rigs have been described in Amateur Radio publications over the years. The distinguishing characteristic of this transceiver is that it was designed and then optimized for high performance. It's relatively easy to build something that works, but it usually requires a great deal more effort to produce something that works really well. That effort has gone into this rig, and the result is a 40-meter CW transceiver with the following characteristics:

- clean keying and smooth, quiet transceive operation
- stable VFO coverage from 7.0 to 7.15 MHz
- receiver incremental tuning (RIT)
- 1.5 W RF output
- receive current drain less than 20 mA
- high-performance direct-conversion receiver
- small size (1½ × 2½ × 3½ in.)

Some Underlying Philosophy

"High-performance direct-conversion receiver" may seem to be self-contradictory. After all, direct-conversion (DC) receivers are so simple they can't possibly compete with a good superhet, right? Wrong! DC receivers have only one significant disadvantage when compared to superhets: the presence of an audio image which doubles the amount of noise and interference heard.

The only other inherent disadvantage is the inability to generate RF- or IF-derived AGC. The same careful attention to detail and potential problems is required in designing the DC receiver as is required for a top-quality superhet, if comparable performance is to be realized. This last point is frequently overlooked, and that may be one reason why the DC receiver is often seen as a mediocre performer.

All other problems can be overcome with careful design, and even the two inherent disadvantages can be overcome to some extent. For CW, narrow AF filters may be

Fig 46—This diminutive QRP transceiver is a joy to operate. It features a high-dynamic-range receiver, smooth break-in operation, RIT and a host of other high-performance features.

used, reducing the image bandwidth along with the desired signal bandwidth. RIT helps also: When an image signal produces the same beat note as the desired signal, adjusting the RIT moves one up in pitch and the other down, thus separating them.

As for AGC, this rig does perfectly well without it. This receiver is on a par with all but the best superhet for any type of operation, except perhaps during contests in conjunction with a high-power transmitter. Yet it has but a fraction of the superhet's complexity. Note also that to use a superhet in a transceiver, an additional oscillator and mixer are necessary to convert the VFO to the transmit frequency. In a transceiver using a DC receiver the required shift is only a few hundred hertz, which can be easily accomplished by pulling the VFO.

Since this rig was designed for portable use, current drain was a major consideration. Experience indicates that many solid contacts are possible using simple antennas and operating at night with 1.5 W on 40 meters. This power level is also more than adequate for short-range daytime operation. Power drain is low-enough that the rig will run for about a week of evening operation from one charge on ten NiCd "A" cells (660 mAh).

The VFO

The oscillator (Fig 47) is a good example of the principle that a circuit need not be complex to work well, if properly designed. This simple Hartley circuit exhibits less than 200-Hz warm-up drift, with about half of that within one minute after turn-on. This drift performance is completely repeatable, as shown by the building of many such oscillators. The circuit used here is the result of considerable experimentation directed toward identifying sources of drift in such VFOs. The following guidelines result:

- Build VFOs with point-to-point wiring

over a ground plane of copper foil. Use circuit board, but copper side uppermost.
- Use NP0 ceramic capacitors.
- A gate diode (D2 here) is essential.
- The inductor is best wound on a type-6 powdered-iron toroidal core. It helps to anneal the coil after winding by boiling it in water a short while and letting it cool in free air.

If rapid temperature changes are expected, you may want to temperature compensate the VFO. Do this by replacing part of the fixed capacitance with negative temperature-coefficient (TC) capacitors, such as polystyrene or negative-TC ceramic units.

The VFO buffer, although designed for low current drain, is the major power consumer in the receiver, requiring 10 mA. The key to efficiency in this sort of buffer is to choose the transformer turns ratio to sustain as large a voltage swing at the output stage collector (or drain) as possible. Buffer voltage gain is approximately one half, providing about 2.5 volts P-P output.

The RIT circuit uses a Zener diode as a voltage-variable capacitor. While Zener diodes are inexpensive and readily available, their nominal capacitances may vary a great deal with different manufacturers. The circuit may be empirically adapted to an individual diode by changing the value of the capacitor (here 15 pF) in series with the diode. Select the capacitor value to yield a tuning range of about 1300 Hz with a diode reverse-bias variation of about 9 to 4 volts. When the RIT control is adjusted to the center of its range, the frequency shift should equal the center frequency of the receive audio filter (about 650 Hz). During transmit, or when the ZERO button is depressed, the shift is removed, causing the transmit frequency to be the same as that of a received signal peaked at the audio-filter center and tuned to the correct side of zero beat.

C1—1 µF, 3-V non-polarized ceramic.
D1—Zener, 15-V, 400-mW, 1N965 or equiv.
D2, D3, D5-D13—Silicon general-purpose/switching diode; 1N914, 1N4152 or equiv.
D4—Zener, 33-V, 400-mW, 1N973 or equiv.
D14—Zener, 10-V, 400-mW, 1N961 or equiv.
L1—Approximately 3 µH; 26 turns on a T-44-6 core. Tap at seven turns from ground end.
L2—Approximately 10 µH, 43 turns on a T-50-2 core.
L3, L4—1 µH; 19 turns on a T-37-6 core.
L5—9.4 µH; 58 turns on a T-37-6 core.
Q1, Q11—Silicon N-channel JFET, 300 mW, 2N4416.
Q2, Q3, Q10—General purpose, silicon NPN, 310-mW, 2N3904.
Q4—General purpose, silicon NPN, 1.8 W, 2N2222.
Q5—RF power, silicon NPN, 7 W, 2N3553 or 2N5859.
Q6, Q7—General purpose, silicon PNP, 310 mW, 2N3906.
Q8—General purpose, NPN, 310 mW, 2N4124 or 2N3565.
Q9—General purpose, silicon NPN, 310 mW, 2N3565. For a better noise figure, use a 2N4124 or 2N3904.
RFC1—100-µH subminiature choke, wound on a ¼-watt-resistor-sized ferrite form. Dc resistance is approximately 8 Ω.
T1—Primary 10 turns, secondary 2 turns. Wound on a BLN-43-2402 core or primary 15 turns, secondary 3 turns on an FT-37-72 core.
T2—Primary 39 turns (approximately 6.7 µH), secondary 5 turns. Wound on a T-44-6 core.
T3, T4—Five trifilar turns on a BLN-43-2402 core. (If size is not a concern, it is easier to wind five trifilar turns on a T-37-72 core.)
U1—op amp, LM301.
U2, U3—Dual op amp, LM358N (one section unused).

The Transmitter

The transmitter is a fairly efficient (75%) class C design. The Zener diode (D4) was added to protect the output transistor after it was twice destroyed by inadvertently transmitting with the antenna disconnected. Some caution is necessary when using a Zener diode at the output-stage collector, as many Zener diodes have a large shunt capacitance. When adding the diode, the collector capacitance must be reduced by an amount approximately equal to the capacitance of the diode when it is reverse biased by the collector supply voltage. In this transmitter, the total capacitance at the collector should equal approximately 450 pF, including the fixed capacitor, the 51-pF receiver pick-off capacitor, the Zener diode and the transistor (about 10 pF). If the capacitance of the diode can't be measured, make the 385-pF fixed capacitor variable and adjust it for best transmitter efficiency.

The value of L2 is not critical, as long as it's not much smaller than the 10 µH shown. Conventional solenoid RF chokes work fine, but toroids help reduce mutual coupling in a tightly packed rig.

In some versions of the transceiver, the VFO is pulled off frequency during receive-transmit TR switching. This occurs because some transmit RF is coupled into the VFO tank circuit.

The frequency can be measured with a frequency counter or a stable receiver. Connect a counter to the secondary of T1 or listen to the VFO on the receiver (connect a short wire to T1 if needed). Without transmitting, push the ZERO (spot) button. At one end of the RIT range, the VFO frequency should not change. Leave the RIT setting there and transmit. Any frequency shift results from unwanted RF coupling into the VFO.

RF may couple via radiation or conduction. Build the VFO inside a shielded box (inside the rig) to minimize radiation problems. A full ground plane in the VFO compartment helps, and locate the VFO tank-component (L1 and the 510-pF capacitor are the most important) ground connections at the same point to minimize conduction problems. This assures that the components are not part of an RF ground loop.

If the output power is less than 2 W, low VFO output (less than 4 V P-P) is the probable cause. VFO output is low when the pinch-off voltage of the FET (Q1) is less than 3.5 V. Most, but not all, 2N4416s are adequate. (Do not substitute MPF-102s, many of which have inadequate pinch-off voltages.)

The Receiver

More time has been spent improving the receiver than any other part of the rig. The end result is no more complex than the first version, but the improvement has been great, again showing that complexity and performance don't equate.

The receiver signal is taken through the 51-pF capacitor from the transmitter output filter. When transmitting, the diodes protect the receiver and cause the 51-pF capacitor to become part of the transmitter output network. When receiving, the capacitor and L5 make up a fairly low-Q series-resonant network to reduce signal attenuation by maintaining an approximately 50-ohm source impedance to the mixer. The additional filtering it provides is helpful also. A conventional and doubly balanced mixer is used.

A diplexer follows the mixer. It provides a wide-band 50-Ω termination for both RF and AF, while preventing RF energy from reaching the AF amplifier and preventing AF energy from being wasted in the RF termination. The RF termination is a 0.1-µF capacitor and a 51-Ω resistor; RFC1 and the 0.47-µF capacitor form a low-pass filter which prevents any residual RF from reaching Q10, thus greatly enhancing immunity to AM interference. Q10 presents an input impedance of approximately 50 Ω for maximum power transfer.

Receiver Audio

Because the receiver audio gain exceeds 100 dB, great care must be taken to prevent feedback or amplification of power-supply hum. This receiver uses an active decoupling circuit (consisting of Q9 and associated parts) to avoid these problems in the input stage, where the sensitivity is greatest.

An active audio filter follows the AF preamp. The filter has a peaked low-pass response with a Q of five—low enough to keep ringing unnoticeable. It is simple, noncritical and adequate for general operating. The peak frequency is about 650 Hz, which corresponds to the transmit-receive frequency offset with the RIT control centered. An LM301 op amp was used because of its low noise and relatively low current drain. A TL071 or TL072 should give comparable performance, and one section of an LM358 may be used with a 2-dB increase in noise figure.

The last two stages are conventional AF amplifier stages. Their frequency response rolls off below 150 Hz and above 1500 Hz.

Builders may want to add a low-impedance audio output. This may be done by reducing the gain of U2B (change the 270-pF capacitor to 560 pF and the 390-kΩ resistor to 20 kΩ) and routing the U2B output to an LM386 amplifier circuit.

A low-impedance audio output increases a D-C receiver's tendency to oscillate (squeal) because output-return signals feedback to early audio stages through circuit ground. The tendency can be reduced through careful grounding techniques (see the double-starred components in Fig 47), or isolate the low-impedance return path from circuit ground (insulate the output jack mounting from circuit ground and connect the output return directly to the ground terminal of the output amplifier).

Unwanted audio may also feedback through the VFO and mixer stages. Such feedback can be reduced by operating the VFO at half of the output frequency and feeding the mixer through a doubler stage. Schematics and discussions of a suitable low-impedance output stage and a VFO-doubler arrangement are available as "Optimized Options" (publication no. 143—send an SASE) from ARRL HQ.

U3 is a sidetone oscillator. The injection level is set by the 100-kΩ resistor at pin 6 of U2B. The level may be varied to suit individual taste by changing the resistor value.

Keying and TR Switching

Three events must occur when this kind of transceiver is keyed, and they must occur in the proper sequence if operation is to be clean. They are, in order: (1) receiver mutes, (2) VFO shifts frequency, and (3) transmitter keys. These events must occur in reverse sequence when switching back from transmit to receive. The sidetone oscillator must also be keyed, but its timing isn't as critical.

Fig 48—High component density is necessary to squeeze all the circuitry of the transceiver into such a small package. Point-to-point wiring is used. The transmitter circuitry is at the upper left in the photo. The output transistor, which is bolted to the case, is hidden below the top layer of components.

Fig 49—The output spectrum of the optimized QRP transceiver. Vertical divisions are each 10 dB; horizontal divisions are each 5 MHz. The second harmonic is about −37 dBc. The transmitter meets FCC spectral purity requirements for a 5-W transmitter.

Attention to this sequence and proper transmitter waveform shaping makes the difference between a poor-sounding rig and a really clean one. Many people have been surprised to learn my power level—because "it doesn't sound like a QRP rig." Only a few parts are required to accomplish this. In addition, it's easier to copy a clean weak signal than a poor one, so good keying and freedom from chirp, clicks and roughness are particularly important for QRP transmitters.

The receiver is muted by Q11 which acts as a series gate. Q9, U1 and U2A are all driven to saturation for a while when the transmitter is keyed—and again when the key is released. Q11 is turned off immediately when the transmitter is keyed, then turned back on after the disturbance is over, about 60 ms after the key is released. The diodes around U2A prevent the output of U2A from swinging to ground during the disturbance, a condition which turns Q11 on when it should be off. I find the 60-ms delay to be ideal, as it removes distractions between dits and dahs at medium speeds, while it is short enough to provide essentially instantaneous break-in. The disturbance (hence, required delay) could possibly be reduced further by limiting the swing of either or both Q9 and U1 or by biasing the U1 and U2A outputs closer to the positive supply voltage.

Oscillator frequency shift is obtained by changing the bias on the Zener diode (used as a voltage-variable capacitor) in the VFO circuit. Q7 provides the timing; it switches on quickly when the key is closed, but switches off some 5 ms after the transmitter output drops to zero following the release of the key. Shaped keying is provided by Q6 and the associated components. Simultaneous base and collector keying of the driver stage is required to give the desired rise and fall times (a few ms) at the transmitter output. The sidetone oscillator is keyed from the same line.

Construction

Fig 48 shows the interior of the transceiver. It would be very difficult to duplicate the unit exactly, because many hard-to-find miniature components are used. Get a good idea of the placement of controls, connectors and large components before you begin. Since it's difficult to troubleshoot or modify such a rig once built, construct and operate a large breadboard version first.

Build the circuitry on small pieces of perfboard and mount the boards vertically for dense packing. It helps a great deal to mount components on both sides of each board and ignore the convention of placing parts in neat rows. A surprising amount of space was saved by using 1/8-W resistors rather than 1/4-W units. Tantalum electrolytic capacitors also save a great deal of space over their aluminum counterparts. Small parts are nearly always more expensive and less available than their larger counterparts, so each builder must decide if the trade-off is a good one.

Adjustment and Operation

Only three controls require adjustments: (1) Set the VFO trimmer so that the lowest VFO frequency is at the lower band edge. (2) Adjust the drive-level pot for 1.5 W of output power (no major problem will arise if driven at higher or lower levels, but efficiency may drop slightly). (3) Peak the transmitter driver tank circuit at the center of the frequency range. None of these should require attention once set. Fig 49 shows the spectral output of the transceiver.

Operation is simple by design. The only point worth noting is that (as with any direct-conversion receiver) signals must be tuned on the correct side of zero beat so that the transmitter will be on the same frequency. Guest operators usually pick this up in a few minutes, so the SPOT button is seldom used. When the rig is new, however, it's nice to know just where the transmitter will be when the key is pressed.

A Legal-Limit Amplifier for 160 through 10 Meters

The amplifier described here is an update of the 1500-W output legal-limit amplifier described in the 1985 and 1986 *ARRL Handbooks*. It uses the EIMAC 8877 (3CX1500A7) high-mu triode in grounded-grid service. The 8877 will easily deliver 1500-W RF output with the drive levels afforded by most 100-W-class transceivers. Operating at 1500-W output, tube dissipation is well within the manufacturer's specification.

Shown in Figs. 50 through 61, this amplifier covers 160 through 10 meters, not including the WARC bands. Operation on the 24-MHz WARC band is possible with the band switch in the 28-MHz position, but the input SWR will be a little higher than on the other bands. Many of the components used were purchased at flea markets and from mail-order dealers. The names and addresses of the parts suppliers are detailed at the end of the Component Data chapter. Amplifier parts are expensive. The builder is encouraged to substitute components from surplus dealers or flea markets where possible if cost is a problem. Be sure, however, to use only components with adequate ratings. The dc and RF power levels found in this project are capable of destroying parts with insufficient ratings.

Dick Stevens, W1QWJ, designed and built this project. The power supply and RF deck are built on separate chassis because of the size and weight of the power supply. Standard 19-inch rack panels are used for the front panels, so both pieces may be rack mounted if desired.

Power Supply

The high-voltage power supply delivers 1 A continuously at user-selectable voltages of 2.5, 3 or 3.5 kV. During normal operation, only the 3-kV position is used, but a lower level is available for tuneup, and a higher level is available if line sag is a problem. Circuits are provided for protection, automatic start and PTT line control. Fig. 51 is the power-supply schematic diagram, and the unit is pictured in Figs. 52 and 53.

Circuit Details

The secondary side of the power supply is conventional. T1 is a Hipersil transformer with a 234-V primary and secondary taps at 1770, 2125 and 2475 V. S3 is a high-voltage switch with large contacts and ceramic insulation used to select among the taps. The 234-V primary and full-value secondary contribute to good voltage regulation. D2 through D5 are 14-kV, 1-A rectifiers connected in a full-wave bridge. C2 is a surplus 53-µF, 3.5-kV oil-filled capacitor. If the builder cannot locate one of these units, a suitable replacement

Fig. 50 — The 8877 HF amplifier uses a standard rack-type front panel. The tuning and loading capacitors are controlled by venier drives with turns counters. Once the settings for each band are determined, they can be recorded for quick band changes.

should be at least 25 µF at a similar voltage rating. R4, the 200-kΩ bleeder resistor, is made up of eight 25-kΩ, 25-W units connected in series.

A high-voltage meter (M1) is included in the supply. The value of R_M, the multiplier resistor, will depend on the value of the basic meter movement. See Chapter 25 for information on meter multipliers and shunts. The B− lead floats above chassis ground. R3 is included to keep the B− near ground potential. The floating B− allows plate current to be metered in the negative lead for safety. C4 and C5 are bypass capacitors.

Power enters the supply from the 234-V line through a 20-A, 2-pole circuit breaker. DS1 will light when the circuit breaker is closed. With S1 in AUTOMATIC and S2 in START, a 24-V signal at J4 from the amplifier control circuitry will energize K1. K1A closes, energizing K2. DS2 lights. K2A and K2B apply reduced primary voltage to T1 through R2. After a second or so, C1 charges and energizes K3. K3A closes, shorting across R2, to apply full primary voltage to T1. This circuit protects D2-D5 from damage by effectively limiting inrush current through the rectifiers while C2 charges. R1 adjusts the charging time for C1. DS3 lights, signaling that the power supply is ready for service. An additional protective feature is that K1B is in the exciter PTT line to prevent keying the amplifier without high voltage present. Note that the supply can be activated manually (not by the amplifier control circuit) by placing S1 in the OFF position

and using S2 to turn the supply on and off. PTT line protection is lost in the manual mode, however.

J1 is a grounded, polarized 117-V ac receptacle used to provide power to the RF deck. Correct 117-V ac wiring must be used here. The ground (green) wire is connected to the chassis ground. The neutral (white) wire is connected to the 234-V line neutral. The hot side (black) is connected to one side of the 234-V line. Likewise, standard wiring must be used in the RF deck.

J1 and J2 are Millen connectors rated at 7 kV. Test prod wire (5-kV insulation) is used for the B+ and B− runs to the RF deck. A braid ground strap bonds the power supply and RF deck chassis together for added protection.

Construction

The power supply is built behind a standard 12½-inch-high, 19-inch-wide rack panel. It is designed to fit inside a Bud Prestige series cabinet. T1 needs a good base to support the weight, so the bottom plate is made from a piece of ¼-inch-thick aluminum plate that is approximately 14 inches square. The size and shape of the power supply enclosure will depend on the actual components used. Be sure that it is sturdy, and allow sufficient room for air to circulate.

T1 and C2 are bolted to the bottom plate. The rectifiers, control relays and other parts mount on a shelf above C2. The eight 25-W resistors that make up the bleeder are mounted to two vertical strips of phenolic stock.

Fig. 51 — Schematic diagram of the high-voltage power supply. Capacitors are disc ceramic unless noted. Possible parts sources are listed in parentheses. See the Component Data chapter for the addresses of the parts suppliers.

C2 — Oil-filled capacitor, 53 μF, 3.5 kV (Electronic Emporium cat. no. 4W308T or equiv.).
D2-D5 — Rectifier, 14 kV, 1 A (K2AW's Silicon Alley HV-14 or equiv.).
DS1-DS5 — Neon pilot lamp, 120 V, with built-in dropping resistor (Radio Shack).
J1, J2 — High-voltage connector (Millen 37001 or equiv.).
J3 — Chassis-mount three-wire 117-V ac socket.
J4 — Two-conductor Jones socket.
J5 — Chassis-mount phono jack.

K1 — 4PDT relay, 24-V dc coil, 2-A contact. (Potter & Brumfield KH4703-1 or equiv.).
K2, K3 — DPST relay, 120-V ac coil, 20-A contacts. (Potter & Brumfield PRD7AYO or equiv.).
M1 — 0 to 50 μA meter with suitable multiplier resistor (R_M). See text.
R_M — Meter multiplier resistor. Exact value will depend on meter movement used. See text and the Test Equipment chapter for information on meter multipliers.

R1 — Adjustable resistor, slider type, 1-kΩ, 25 W.
R4 — 200-kΩ, 200-W bleeder made from eight 25-kΩ, 25-W resistors in series (see text).
S1 — SPDT switch, 117-V, 3-A contacts.
S2 — SPST switch, 117-V, 3-A contacts.
S3 — High-voltage switch (see text).
T1 — Power transformer; 234-V primary, secondary taps at 1770, 2125 and 2475 V, 1.5 A, continuous duty (Peter W. Dahl Co. no. PT-2475 or equiv.).
Z1, Z2 — 130-V metal-oxide varistor (Radio Shack).

Fig. 52 — Front panel view of the 8877 amplifier high-voltage supply. It is built on a 12½-inch high rack panel and mounted in a Bud Prestige cabinet. Output voltages of 2.5, 3 and 3.5 kV are switch-selectable from the front panel.

RF Deck

The RF deck houses the 8877 and associated RF circuitry as well as the amplifier-control circuit board. This amplifier uses a tuned input circuit and a pi-L output circuit. The filament transformer (T1) and antenna relay (K6) are built in. Cooling is provided by blower B1. Fig. 54 is a schematic diagram of the control circuitry, and Fig. 55 shows the RF circuitry.

Control Circuits and Metering

The control circuits are somewhat involved and are designed to protect the expensive 8877 tube from excessive fila-

Fig. 53 — Interior of the high-voltage power supply cabinet.

ment inrush current, excessive grid current, and application of drive in the absence of plate voltage. A three-minute delay circuit prevents keying the amplifier until the tube gets up to operating temperature, and another time-delay circuit keeps the blower running for a short while after power is removed.

When S1 of Fig. 54 (POWER) is closed, several things happen. First, 117-V ac is applied through R2 to the primary of filament transformer T1. R2 limits inrush current and is in the line until C2 charges, energizing K2. K2A shorts across R2, applying full primary voltage to T1. K2B lights the FILS LED. Note that T1 has several primary taps to allow adjustment of the filament voltage (measured at the socket) to 5.0 V, ±0.25 V, as specified by the tube manufacturer. At the same time filament power is applied, blower B1 starts and time-delay relay K1 starts to heat. K1A does nothing at this time. When power is turned off, however, K1A will stay closed for several minutes to run the blower and cool the tube after filament voltage is removed. K1 does not control the blower

directly, but rather does so through K8, a relay with contacts heavy enough to handle the current needed by the blower motor.

S1 also starts K3, a three-minute time-delay relay. When K3 energizes, the OPERATE LED lights. Finally, S1 applies primary voltage to T2 of the 24-V dc control-relay supply. When S2, RESET, is closed, 24 V is applied to various points in the control circuit. A 24-V signal is sent through relay contacts K4B and K3A to energize K1 in the high-voltage power supply. K3A also allows 24 V to reach K5, the PTT relay, so that the amplifier may be keyed from the PTT line. Note that since K3A is in the line to the HV-supply control relay and the PTT relay, the HV supply cannot be turned on and the PTT line cannot be keyed until after the three-minute warmup period.

The transceiver PTT control connects to the HV power supply, and K1B in the power supply activates K5 in the RF deck to prevent keying the amplifier in the absence of B+. K5A applies operating bias to the 8877, and K5B operates the antenna TR re-

lays (K6, K7). K6 has a slight time delay, provided by C5. This feature assures that K7 will close before K6 to prevent hot switching.

Protection from excessive grid current is provided by Q1 and associated components. When the grid current exceeds a certain amount (set to approximately 70 mA by R5), Q1 fires and operates K4. K4C lights the TRIP LED. K4B opens, shutting off the HV supply and opening the PTT circuitry to protect the tube. To reset the amplifier, switch S2 off and then on again and everything will restart automatically. S2 can also be used to place the amplifier in standby if operation with the transceiver only is desired.

M1 and M2 of Fig. 55 monitor grid current and plate current. Plate current is monitored in the B− lead, rather than in the B+ lead, for safety. A pair of back-to-back diodes and 0.01-μF capacitors protect the meters from transients and RF voltages.

Input Circuitry

The RF input appears at J1 of Fig. 55. If the amplifier is turned off or bypassed by S2 of the control circuit, the input signal is routed directly to the output connector, J2. When the amplifier is in operation, the input signal goes to the tuned input circuitry and then to the 8877 cathode. Although the 8877 input impedance is close to 50 ohms and RF drive could be connected directly to the 8877 cathode, the tuned input is used for improved linearity and lower drive requirements.

There is a separate pi network (C1, L1, C2) for each band. S1 selects the appropriate network for the band in use. The input networks were designed with a Q of approximately 2 to be broadly resonant on each band. For clarity, only one pi network is shown in Fig. 55. Table 1 presents the complete input network data.

The coil (L1) for each band is wound on a 3/8-inch slug-tuned form. The slugs were purchased from a surplus dealer, but any 3/8-inch slug-tuned form with a red core should work. Table 1 gives both calculated capacitor values and the real-world values used in this amplifier.

Output Circuitry

B+ enters the RF deck through J3 and is routed through RFC2 and RFC3. The B+ line is bypassed by C8 and C9. C7 is a dc blocking capacitor that keeps dc voltages out of the tank circuit and off the feed

Fig. 54 — Schematic diagram of the 8877 amplifier control circuitry. Resistors are ¼-W types unless noted. Capacitors are disc-ceramic types unless noted. Capacitors marked with polarity are electrolytic. See the Component Data chapter for the addresses of the parts suppliers.

B1—Blower, 54 CFM (Dayton 4C012A or equiv.).
DS1-DS3—LED.
D4—Stud-mount Zener diode, 8 V, 50 W (1N3303 or equiv.).
K1—Time-delay relay with a 2-3 minute delay on release, 115-V ac coil (Amperite 115NO69 or equiv.).
K2—DPDT relay, 12-V dc coil with 120-V, 10-A contacts (Radio Shack).

K3—Time-delay relay with a 3-minute delay on operate, 115-V ac coil (Amperite 115NO180 or equiv.).
K4, K5—4PDT relay, 24-V dc coil with 2-A contacts (Potter & Brumfield KH4703-1 or equiv.).
K6, K7—Dow Key Model 60 coaxial antenna relays with 24-V dc coils.
K8—DPDT relay, 120-V ac coil with 125-V ac, 10-A contacts (Radio Shack).

T1—Filament transformer. Primary: 120-V with taps for ±4% and ±8%; secondary: 5 V, 10.5 A (Avatar Magnetics AV-454 or equiv.).
P1—Two-conductor Jones plug to match J4 in the HV power supply (Fig. 59).
T2—Power transformer. Primary: 117-V; secondary: 18 V, 2 A.
U1—Bridge rectifier module, 50 PIV, 1 A (Radio Shack).
Z1—130-V metal-oxide varistor (Radio Shack).

Fig. 55 — Schematic diagram of the 8877 amplifier RF deck. Resistors are ¼-W types unless noted. Capacitors are disc-ceramic types unless noted. Capacitors marked with polarity are electrolytic. See the Component Data chapter for addresses of parts suppliers.

C1, C2—See Table 1.
C7—1200-pF, 30-kV RF-type doorknob capacitor (Electronic Emporium).
C10—1000-pF, 5-kV vacuum variable capacitor (Jennings UCSL 1000-5 or equiv.).
C11—Two 800-pF, 5-kV doorknob capacitors in parallel.
C12—1000-pF, 1.5kV air variable (Cardwell 154-30 or equiv.).
C13—400-pF, 5-kV doorknob capacitor.
J1, J2—Female UHF connector (in this case, part of K6 and K7).

J3, J4—High-voltage connector (Millen 37001 or equiv.).
K6, K7—See Control-circuit schematic.
L1—See Table 1.
L2, L3—See Fig. 56.
RFC1—50 μH; 39T no. 24 enam. wire close wound on a ¼-inch powdered rion core.
RFC-2—No. 24 enam. close wound on a 1-inch Teflon form. The form is 5 inches long; the winding is 4 inches long. Measured inductance is 195 μH.
RFC3—8.2 μH (Ohmite Z50 or equiv.).
RFC4—2.5 mH (Millen 4537 or equiv.).

S1—Single wafer, 2-pole, 6-position ceramic rotary switch with indexing to match S2.
S2—Six position, two section, high-power ceramic RF switch with non-shorting contacts and 60-degree indexing (Model 86, avail. from Radio Switch Corp., Rt. 79, Marlboro, NJ 07746). Section S2C is a homemade addition. See Fig. 61.
Z1—Parasitic suppressor. Made from 2T of ½-inch wide copper strap, ½-inch ID. Shunt the strap with two 100-Ω, 2-W carbon-composition resistors in parallel.

Table 1
Input Coil Data

Band	L1 (μH) (Calculated)	L1 Winding Information†	C14, C15 (pF) (Calculated)	C14, C15 (pF) (Values Used)
160	4.2	27T no. 24	1640	1120 + 560 = 1680
80	2.07	16T no. 22	820	820
40	1.18	9T no. 20	430	210 + 210 = 420
20	0.59	7T no. 20	220	210
15	0.39	5T no. 20	150	150
10	0.30	4T no. 20	100	100

†All coils wound on 3/8-in-diameter form; slug-tuned with red core. Available from Electronic Emporium, part number PLS5-B-2.

line and antenna. Should C22 short, placing dangerous voltage on the output connector, RFC4 will short the B + line to ground and blow the power-supply circuit breaker.

This amplifier uses a pi-L tank circuit for better suppression of harmonic energy. To get a better Q and improved efficiency on 10 and 160 meters, a 1000-pF vacuum-variable capacitor was chosen for C10 (TUNE).

C12 (LOAD), a 1000-pF air variable, does not have enough capacitance for operation on 160 and 80 meters. A spare contact on S2A switches C11 into the circuit for 160-meter operation, while S2C switches C13 into the circuit for 80-meter operation.

L2 is made from a section of ¼-inch copper tubing for 10 meters and a section of B&W Pi Dux stock for the other bands. The L coil, L3, is also made from a small section of Pi Dux stock. S2 switches the taps for use on the various bands. Fig. 56 is a detailed diagram of the tank coil connections.

Construction

The completed RF deck is shown in Figs. 57 and 58. The main support for the components is a standard 4- × 17- × 10-inch (HWD) chassis (Bud AC-427). Like the power supply, the chassis is mounted

L2A = 6T OF 0.25-INCH DIAMETER COPPER TUBING, 1.75 INCHES ID, CLOSE WOUND (10 METERS).

L2B = 21T OF B&W 2406A PiDUX COIL STOCK TAP AT 3T FOR 15m, 5T FOR 20m, 7T FOR 40m, 13T FOR 80m AND 21T FOR 160m. TAPS MEASURED FROM THE JUNCTION WITH L2A.

L3 = 15.5T OF B&W 1411A PiDUX COIL STOCK TAP AT 1T FOR 10m, 1.5T FOR 15m, 2T FOR 20m, 4T FOR 40m, 8T FOR 80m AND 15.5T FOR 160m

Fig. 56 — Details of the pi-L coils, L2 and L3 of Fig. 55.

Fig. 57 — Underside of the 8877 amplifier chassis.

to a 19-inch-wide, 12½-inch-high rack panel. For RF shielding, sidewalls 4¾ inches high are mounted to the chassis with aluminum angle stock. A top cover bolts to aluminum angle stock that is connected to the sidewalls. Similar aluminum-sheet-and-angle-stock construction is used to enclose the tube socket underneath the chassis.

A separate enclosure that is bolted to the amplifier top cover houses the input circuitry. This enclosure is positioned so that its band switch is directly above the main band switch in the output network. A simple chain drive from the main band switch makes both input and output switches turn in unison from a single front-panel control. The sprockets (part no. RCS-12) and chain (RCX-25) are available from Small Parts, Inc. See the parts suppliers list in the Component Data chapter. Align the chain drive with both switches in the 10-meter position. Leave some slack in the chain to allow the detents in both switches to function effectively.

The underside of the chassis is shown in Fig. 57. A single circuit board in the lower half of the photo contains the bias and control circuitry. The antenna relays are mounted to the rear chassis wall, to the right of the control circuitry. The filament and control circuit transformers are mounted at the top left of the photo, near the front panel, and the tube socket is to the right of the transformers. A Dayton blower pressurizes the enclosed cathode compartment, and air exits through the tube anode cooler. A Teflon chimney directs the exhaust air.

Although an EIMAC SK-2200 series socket could be used, the socket used for this amplifier was homemade. It is built around a Johnson type 247 and an aluminum plate. Complete details of this plate, along with a full-size template, are shown in Fig. 59. This socket assembly can be made with hand tools — there is no fancy or complex metal work required.

The relative positions of the output-network components is shown in Fig. 58. The tuning capacitor is mounted close to the tube, and the loading capacitor is on the other side of the chassis. Both of these capacitors use Groth turns-counter dials with vernier drives for smooth tuning. These drives were purchased from Robert H. Bauman Sales, P.O. Box 122, Itasca, IL 60143.

The band switch is in the center of the chassis. S2C, to switch in additional loading capacitance for 80 meters, is a homemade addition to the band switch. It consists of two Barker and Williamson high-power switch contacts (available from B&W — see the Component Data chapter) and a wafer made from a piece of double-sided PC-board material. See Fig. 61. S2C is attached to the main band-switch shaft.

The pi coil, L2, may be seen to the left of the 8877. The two coil pieces are supported by a rectangular piece of glass-epoxy circuit board material with all copper removed. The coil assembly is mounted

Fig. 58 — Interior of the 8877 amplifier RF deck. The input compartment, which was attached to the top cover, has been removed. The chain-drive sprocket on the main band-switch shaft is visible between the chassis and the front panel.

above the chassis with ceramic standoffs. The L coil is mounted with a similar arrangement to the left of the band switch and perpendicular to the pi coil. The two coils must be mounted at right angles to prevent undesired coupling. All plate circuit connections are made with copper straps.

In this amplifier, it was necessary to provide a ½-inch wide ground strap between the tuning and loading capacitors to prevent ground-loop currents. Connect the frame of the loading capacitor to the lead-screw mechanism of the vacuum variable. Do not ground this strap to the chassis.

Tuneup and Operation

Check the high-voltage power supply for proper operation before connecting it to the RF deck. Check all circuit paths in the B+ supply and RF deck for possible short circuits. Verify the operation of all control circuitry with the high-voltage off and with the tube removed from the socket. If everything works, apply power to the filament transformer, blower and control circuitry, and measure the filament voltage at the tube socket. If all is well, remove power from the RF deck and install the covers. Connect the high-voltage supply. Connect an exciter capable of delivering about 100 W to the input through a wattmeter and connect the amplifier output to a suitable dummy load through a second wattmeter.

Place the power-supply switches in AUTOMATIC and START. Close the RESET switch on the RF deck and turn the POWER switch on. The blower will start and filament power will be applied. The FILS lamp will light. After three minutes, K3 will close and the high-voltage supply will turn on. Press the transceiver PTT switch. M2 should indicate about 150 mA resting plate current.

Apply about 10 to 20 W of drive and adjust the TUNE and LOAD controls until the grid-current meter reads about 70 mA. Adjust R5 until the grid-trip circuit functions. Reset the circuit and verify that the grid-trip circuit functions at about 70 to 80 mA.

Apply about 10-W drive and adjust the slugs of the coils in the input pi networks for lowest SWR at the center of each band. Adjust the TUNE and LOAD controls for maximum output. Tuning of a pi-L circuit is similar to that for a conventional pi circuit, except that the setting of the LOAD capacitor is much more critical. Gradually increase drive until the power output reaches 1500 W. Recheck the input SWR on each band with the amplifier running at full output.

Table 2 shows the operating parameters for this amplifier as measured in the ARRL lab. Fig. 60 shows the exceptionally clean spectral output from the pi-L network.

Fig. 59— Details of the homemade socket for the 8877 tube. All hardware is no. 6-32. A full-size template for the aluminum plate is shown at A. Connection to the grid is made through four spring fingers made from spring brass or copper. Details of these clips are shown at B. Assembly of the socket is shown at C. Assemble as follows. Insert four 1-inch no. 6-32 machine screws through the plate. Slip a 3/8-inch by 3/8-inch-OD aluminum bushing over each screw. Place a spring finger on each screw, followed by a nylon washer. Slide the Johnson 247 socket onto the screws, and secure each screw with a nylon washer, metal lock washer and nut. Align the spring fingers for good contact with the grid ring and tighten. Connections to the bottom of the socket are shown at D.

Table 2
8877 Amplifier Operating Characteristics

Band	Power Output (W)	Plate Voltage (V)	Plate Current (mA)	Grid Current (mA)	Drive Power (W)	Input SWR
160	1500	2700	1000	30	65	1.1:1
80	1500	2800	900	35	65	1.2:1
40	1500	2800	900	40	65	1.1:1
20	1500	2800	1000	40	65	1.2:1
15	1500	2800	1000	45	65	1.2:1
12	1500	2800	1000	50	65	1.5:1
10	1500	2800	980	50	65	1.4:1

Fig. 60 — Worst-case spectral photograph of the 8877 amplifier. Power output is 1500 W on 3.5 MHz. Each vertical division is 10 dB, and each horizontal division is 1 MHz. All harmonics and spurious emissions are at least 54 dB down. This amplifier complies with current FCC spectral-purity requirements.

¼-IN HOLE

NO. 11 DRILL

COPPER

(A)

Drill and tap for set screws

¼-IN HOLE

NO. 11 HOLE

MATERIAL: ¼″ ALUM. PLATE CUT TO SHAPE OF SWITCH WAFER

(B)

4-1/4″ SQ. X 1/4″-THICK PLEXIGLAS SHEET

1/4″ HOLE

WAFER

B&W SWITCH CONTACTS

STRAP TO C13

ADJUST WAFER ON SHAFT SO IT CONNECTS ONLY IN THE 80 M POSITION

STRAP TO GROUND

(C)

Fig. 61 — Details of the homemade switch used for S2C. At A is a full-size template of the wafer. Material is double-sided circuit board. Remove all copper but that indicated by the shaded area; the pattern should be the same on each side of the board. The aluminum piece that mates the switch wafer to the band-switch shaft is shown at B. At C, the entire switch is assembled on a Plexiglas sheet.

A 1500-W Linear Amplifier Using 3-500Z Tubes

Here is a modern linear amplifier with features not always available on commercial amplifiers. The amplifier uses a pair of 3-500Z high-mu power triodes, and operates on the 80, 40, 20, 17, 15, 12 and 10-meter bands. It produces 1500-W PEP with about 100 W of drive. Information is included to take you through the steps necessary to ensure that the amplifier functions properly when completed. Dick Stevens, W1QWJ, designed and built this amplifier.

Fig 62 shows the completed amplifier on top of the power supply cabinet. The amplifier cabinet is homemade, using sheet aluminum and aluminum angle stock. The power supply cabinet is much larger than necessary, but it is one the author had available, and it provides a solid base for the amplifier. The combination fits nicely beside the operating table or desk.

There are many practical reasons for building your own amplifier. You can build an amplifier that will perform better than many lower-priced commercial amplifiers. Using off-the-shelf new parts, the cost of this 1.5-kW amplifier should be around $1000. Searching flea markets for parts will reduce the cost even further. One word of caution: *do not buy used tubes*. The ARRL Parts Suppliers List at the end of the Component Data chapter lists addresses of possible component suppliers for this amplifier.

FEATURES

When you buy a pair of 3-500Z tubes for approximately $250, you need to provide protective circuits to ensure long tube life. Filament in-rush current is a common concern. When the filaments are cold their resistance is very low, and the initial filament current can be high. This shortens tube life. Remember, you will switch the filaments on and off many times over the life of your amplifier. A relay, resistor and a few other small parts provide a protective circuit.

No matter how careful you are when tuning the amplifier, it is very easy to exceed the maximum grid-current rating. A transistor, relay and a few small parts provide a "grid trip" circuit to protect the grid from excessive current. You may be surprised how many times the grid-trip circuit operates during initial tuning and testing.

Sequential keying protects the amplifier against "hot" relay switching. With this circuit, the antenna transfer relays are switched and the amplifier is in a ready condition before *any* RF is applied to the tubes. This circuit also protects the driving transceiver, which in many cases can sink a limited amount of external TR current. This sequential keying circuit requires less than 5 mA, and works with any modern transceiver.

Automatic level control (ALC) is also

Fig 62—The (2)3-500Z amplifier and HV supply.

provided. This circuit helps prevent excessive drive to the amplifier. Do not, however, run the transceiver and amplifier "flat out" and expect the ALC to perform miracles. Remember that the amplifier can be overdriven before the ALC circuit does its job. The short delay before drive is reduced can introduce distortion. If you build a clean amplifier and run it conservatively, it will help ensure a clean signal.

Parasitic suppression is a beast that haunts all modern vacuum-tube amplifiers, whether commercial or home built. Parasitic oscillation destroys more vacuum tubes than any other cause. Richard Measures, AG6K, has explained the cure of this beast in great detail. See his article, "Improved Anode Parasitic Suppression for Modern Amplifier Tubes," *QST*, Oct 1988, pp 36-38, 66, 89. The Sep and Oct 1990 issues of *QST* contain a follow-up series by Measures, "Parasites Revisited." This amplifier incorporates his very successful method of parasitic suppression in the plate circuit. The suppressors are described in more detail later in this write-up.

POWER-SUPPLY DESCRIPTION

The high-voltage (HV) power supply is a full-wave-bridge design that delivers 2.5, 3.0, or 3.5 kV dc at 1 amp. The voltage regulation is excellent, credited in part to

a Peter Dahl Hypersil transformer and a large 53-μF, 3.5-kV, oil-filled filter capacitor. (If the builder cannot locate such a capacitor, a suitable replacement should be at least 25 μF at a similar voltage rating.)

Transformer T201 has a 240 V ac primary with a 220 V input tap, and output taps at 1770, 2125 and 2500 V. The transformer is rated at 1.5 A for intermittent commercial and amateur service (ICAS).

Fig 63A is the schematic diagram of the HV supply. (The HV circuit is hand wired, the photo shows general parts-placement information.) A protective circuit limits the in-rush current when the supply is initially switched on. S203 is a high-voltage switch (with large contacts and ceramic insulation) used to select the output voltage. Under normal conditions, the 3-kV (dc) position is selected. The 2.5-kV position can be used while tuning, and the 3.5-kV position may be selected if your line voltage is a bit low.

Along with the HV supply, the power-supply cabinet also houses the filament transformer and in-rush current-protection relay. (Fig 63 also shows these circuits.) There is not sufficient room on the amplifier chassis to mount the transformer.

The 15 V dc control-circuit power supply is also located in the power-supply cabi-

Fig 63—The high-voltage power supply is shown at A. B shows the filament transformer and in-rush current protection circuit. Addresses for parts suppliers are given at the end of the Component Data chapter.

C202—Oil-filled capacitor, 53 μF, 3.5 kV. If a similar unit cannot be found, the replacement should have at least 25 μF and an equal or higher voltage rating.

D201-D204—Rectifier, 8 kV, 1 A (K2AW's Silicon Alley HV-8 or equiv) or higher-voltage rating.

J1-J12—Pin numbers of 12-pin female Jones connector used for connections between the amplifier and power supply.

J13—Phono jack or other suitable connector for VOX/MOX line from transceiver.

J14—High-voltage connector (female).

K201, K202—DPST relay, 240 V ac, 25 A contacts, 120 V ac coil (Potter and Brumfield PR7AYO or equiv).

K203—DPST relay, 125 V ac, 10 A contacts, 12 V dc coil (Radio Shack 275-218 or equiv).

K204—SPST relay, 125 V ac, 10 A contacts, 12 V dc coil.

M201—High-voltage supply meter, 0-1 mA movement.

S201—DPST 20 A, 220 V switch (local electrical-supply stores).

S202—SPST rocker switch, 6 A, 120 V (Radio Shack 275-690 or equiv).

S203—High-voltage selector switch, see text.

T201—Hypersil power transformer, 220, 240 V ac primary; 1770, 2125, 2500 V ac, 1.5 A secondary, ICAS (Peter W. Dahl Co no. ARRL-002 or equiv).

T202—Filament transformer, 120 V ac primary; 5 V ac, 30 A center-tapped secondary (Hammond type 167 X5 or equiv).

Fig 64—Schematic diagram of the 3-500Z amplifier control circuitry. Resistors are ¼ W unless noted. Capacitors are disk ceramic unless noted, and those marked with a + are electrolytic. Addresses for parts suppliers are given at the end of the Component Data chapter.

B101, B102—Blower, 4-in. 120 V ac fan (Radio Shack 273-241 or equiv).

D101-D103, D106-D109, D111—Small-signal switching diodes, 1N914 or equiv.

D104, D105—1 A, 100 PIV, such as 1N4002.

D110—Zener diode, 10 V, 50 W, 1N2808, 1N3309 or equiv.

K102—DPDT relay, 125 V ac, 10 A contacts; 160 Ω, 12 V dc coil (Radio Shack 275-218 or equiv).

K103, K104—SPST relay, 125 V ac, 10 A contacts; 320 Ω, 12 V dc coil (Radio Shack 275-248 or equiv).

M101—Plate-current meter, 0-1 A movement.

M102—Grid-current meter, 0-500 mA movement.

P1-P6, P10, P11—Pin numbers of male 12-pin Jones connector used for connections between the amplifier and power supply.

Q101-Q105—2N2222 or equiv.

S103-S105—SPST rocker switch, 6 A, 120 V (Radio Shack 275-690 or equiv).

U101—Bridge rectifier, 4 A, 100 PIV (Radio Shack 276-1171 or equiv).

U102—15-V positive voltage regulator, UA7815C (Radio Shack 276-1772 or equiv).

Fig 65—Interior view of the power-supply cabinet. The high-voltage supply is at the bottom. The filter capacitor and bleeder resistor are visible at the left and the high-voltage transformer is at the right. The filament transformer and 15-V dc supply for the control circuit are mounted on the shelf in the top-right corner. The high-voltage SELECTOR switch is clearly visible in the center of the photo.

Fig 66—Photo of the amplifier chassis bottom. The chain-drive arrangement visible at the bottom of the photo connects the input-filter band switch (S3 on Fig 68) with the output network BAND switch (S2 on Fig 68). One knob on the front panel operates both switches. The control-circuit board is visible in the lower-right corner of the chassis and the ALC board is along the left edge. The input-filter circuits (and band switch S3) are near the top of the photo. The B & W low-pass filter is at the top of the photo. The bifilar filament choke is across the center of the chassis.

Fig 67—Photo of the top side of the amplifier deck. The neat, uncluttered appearance of the RF section is evident. Notice the plate choke at right and the harmonic suppressors at the tube plates. The modified RADIOKIT capacitor is at the left, and the inductors are in the center. Careful inspection of the coil shows the different turns spacing of the two coils, as well as the solder joint between the two sections. The 10-meter coil mounts perpendicular to the other coils. The chain-driven band-switch arrangement is at the bottom of the photo, but the output BAND switch is hidden by the inductors.

net, although this circuit is shown as part of the control circuit in Fig 64. (The control circuit is built on perfboard; no etching pattern or parts-placement diagram is needed.) Fig 65 shows the layout inside the power-supply cabinet. The high-voltage supply is at the bottom; the filament transformer and 15 V dc supply are on the shelf. Notice the 53-μF filter capacitor and the 100-kΩ bleeder resistor at the left side.

The B+ (plate-voltage) lead to the amplifier is made from high-voltage insulated wire (30-kV insulation, no. 22 wire) and a high-voltage connector. A braid ground strap bonds the power supply to the amplifier chassis.

Circuit Operation

When switch S201 is closed, 240 V ac is available to the power supply. Neon bulb DS201 lights, showing that power is available to the power supply, and 120 V ac is available to the amplifier via pin 1 of the 12-pin Jones connector.

When the filament switch (S104 in the control-circuit diagram, Fig 64) is closed, 120 V ac is applied (through pin 2 of the Jones plug and R209) to the filament transformer, T202. The resistor limits the filament in-rush current. The control circuit also applies 15 V dc to R210 and relay K204. When capacitor C204 has charged sufficiently to operate the relay, contacts K204A close, applying the full 120 V to T202.

To energize the HV supply, switches S103 and S202 must be closed. This applies 15 V dc from the control circuit to relay K203. Relay K203 operates and closes contacts K203A, sending 120 V ac to K201. When K201 operates, it closes contacts K201A and B, sending 240 V through resistors R201 and R202 to the primary of T201. Indicator DS202 lights.

Resistors R201 and R202 limit the charging current through diodes D201-D204, protecting them from the high charging-current demands of the filter capacitor, C202. The ac voltage applied to diode D205 is rectified and passed to the RC filter consisting of R203 and C201. In about one second the voltage across C201 reaches 15 to 20 V dc, and relay K202 activates. Contacts K202A and K202B then close, applying the full 240 V ac to T201. Diodes across the relay coils suppress voltage spikes.

The negative return (B−) is isolated slightly above ground by R204. This is required for amplifier metering purposes. R207 acts somewhat like a high-voltage fuse and protects the 3-500Z amplifier tubes in case of an arc over. Meter M201 measures plate voltage; it is a 0-1 mA movement with a 5-MΩ multiplier resistor, R206. R206 consists of five series-connected 1-MΩ, 2-W, 2% resistors. If a different meter movement is used, a new value for the multiplier resistor must be calculated. R205 is a 100-kΩ, 200-W bleeder resistor. To protect the amplifier from drive without plate voltage on the tubes, the VOX/MOX signal from the transceiver is routed through power-supply control relay contacts, K203B. Unless the HV supply is operating, a VOX/MOX signal from the transceiver won't reach the input and output relays, so the amplifier is bypassed.

RF DECK

The RF deck includes two 3-500Z triodes, the control circuit board, ALC board, input filters and the output pi network. It is built into an aluminum cabinet. A pair of small muffin fans blow air directly onto the tubes, and there is a vent hole directly over the tubes. A piece of aluminum screen covers the hole; no. 6 hardware holds the screen in place. The screen edges are covered with glass-fiber electrical tape to prevent fraying. Figs 66 and 67 show the internal construction of the amplifier.

To avoid a cluttered diagram, only part of the input circuit is shown in Fig 68. Each band has its own input filter, and component values for these filters are given in Fig 69. One capacitor in each filter is adjustable, so the filters can be tuned for lowest SWR (1.5:1 or better). The inductors are wound on toroids. The core and winding information is also given in Fig 69.

The filter board is mounted facing the rear panel. An access hole cut in the panel allows easy adjustment. A piece of aluminum serves as a cover plate; it is held in place by two machine screws and PEM nuts (which press fit into holes in the panel).

Each tube has a parasitic-suppression network connected directly to the plate lead. Each network includes a choke, which consists of 3 turns of no. 18 nichrome or stainless-steel wire with a 7 mm inside diameter. Two 100-Ω, 2-W metal-film resistors are parallel connected to each other and the coil. *It is important that the resistors do not go through the center of the coil.* This network is clearly visible in Fig 67.

Fig 68—Schematic diagram of the 3-500Z amplifier RF deck. Resistors are ¼ W unless noted. Capacitors are disc ceramic unless noted, and those marked with a + are electrolytic. See Fig 69 for details of the input filters. Addresses for parts suppliers are given at the end of the Component Data chapter.

C18—12.5 to 43 pF, 4500 V, section of modified RADIOKIT no. 245 capacitor (or equiv). See the sidebar for modification instructions.

C19—30.5 to 200 pF, 4500 V, section of modified RADIOKIT capacitor.

C20—40 to 1500 pF, 1700 V, air-variable capacitor, such as RADIOKIT no. 1600 (or equiv).

J15, J16—RF connectors to suit builder. The author used a BNC input connector and a coaxial relay with an N connector at the output.

J17—Phono jack or suitable connector for ALC line to transceiver.

K5—SPDT relay, 12 V dc coil (Radio Shack 275-248 is suitable).

K6—SPDT coaxial relay, 12 V dc, 160 mA coil (To.Tsu. Electric Co Ltd CX-600 N, or equiv.).

P7, P8, P9, P12—Pin numbers of male 12-pin Jones connector used for connections between the amplifier and power supply.

P14—High-voltage connector (male) and cable (see text).

RFC1—Plate choke, wound on ¾-in. diameter Teflon rod. See text for winding details.

RFC2—30 A filament choke, such as B & W FC-25A.

RFC3—2 ½-mH choke.

S2—Output rotary switch, nonshorting 2-section, 7-position high-voltage ceramic-wafer switch with 30° indexing. (The author used 2 wafers of a Radio Switch Corporation Model 86-4-8-30 4-wafer, 8-position switch.)

S3—Input rotary switch, nonshorting 2-section, 7-position ceramic wafer switch with 30° indexing. The author used an 11-position Centralab 2513 switch.

The amplifier output is routed through a low-pass filter (B & W Model FL-10/1500) to reduce any harmonic energy. This filter is mounted on the back panel.

ALC Circuit

The ALC circuit samples RF drive through a voltage divider circuit, C1 and C2. The sampled voltage is rectified by diode D2, and filtered by C8. R1 sets the threshold voltage, or operating point, of the ALC. When the rectified sample voltage exceeds the threshold set by R1, a dc voltage is sent to the transceiver to reduce its output. The threshold voltage is adjustable to cover nearly any operating condition of any transceiver.

There is a full-size etching pattern for the ALC board in the circuit-board patterns at the back of this *Handbook*. Fig 70 is the ALC board parts-placement diagram.

Control Circuit

The control circuit is shown in Fig 64. When the transceiver VOX/MOX line is grounded (transmit), pin 4 of the Jones connector (P4) is grounded. This ground is connected through K102B to diodes D106, D107, D108 and D109.

This causes Q104 and Q102 to stop conducting. Q105 then conducts, and relay K104 activates, sending 15 V dc to the antenna changeover relays (K5 and K6 on the RF deck; see Fig 68). A short time later Q103 conducts, operating relay K103, which puts the amplifier in the operating condition. (The delay is set by the time it takes C111 to charge after Q102 stops conducting. This time delay allows the antenna relays to close before the amplifier is keyed.)

Fig 69—Details of the eight input filters. Each filter connects to the appropriate position on the band switch. The chart gives capacitor values and inductor winding information. Output capacitors (C_O) are all silver-mica units. Input capacitors (C_I) are mica compression trimmers. The 80-meter input capacitor has a 390 pF silver-mica capacitor in parallel with the trimmer. ARCO part numbers for the trimmer capacitors are: 240-700 pF, 4215; 95-350 pF, 428; 55-250 pF, 426.

Filter Band (meters)	C_I (pF)	C_O (pF)	L_n core	L_n turns (no. 20 wire)
80	390+240−700	820	T−50−2	21
40	240−700	390	T−50−2	15
20	95−350	220	T−50−2	11
17	55−250	150	T−50−6	16
15	55−250	120	T−50−6	9
12	55−250	110	T−50−6	8
10	55−250	110	T−50−6	7

Fig 70—Parts-placement diagram for the ALC circuit board. The component side of the board is shown, with an X-ray view of the circuit foil. A full-size etching pattern is included at the back of this *Handbook*.

Grid-current protection is provided by Q101. Grid current is sensed from the voltage drop across R101. The trip level is set by R107. When the grid current reaches 215 mA, Q101 conducts, causing relay K102 to activate. This opens contacts K102B in the VOX/MOX line and switches the amplifier off. Contacts K102A close to light DS102 (indicating a grid-trip condition) and provide a latched ground for the relay coil through S105. K102 remains active until the RESET switch, S105, is opened or the power supply is switched off.

The control circuits are made on a printed circuit board. A full-size etching pattern is given at the back of this *Handbook*. Fig 71 is the control board parts-placement diagram. The author's amplifier exhibited an RFI problem in the control circuit during 80-meter operation. The control-circuit relays cycled on and off when the amplifier output exceeded about 500 W with the plate voltage set to 3 or 3.5 kV. A few circuit modifications were made to cure this problem. Each lead to the control circuit board was filtered with an FB-73-801 bead

and a 0.01-μF disc capacitor to ground (see Fig 71). Several other bypass capacitors were added at various points in the circuit. In addition, 47-kΩ resistors were added between the base and emitter leads of Q102 and Q104. A 15-kΩ resistor was added between the base and emitter of Q101. The capacitors and resestors were added to the underside of the circuit board, and are shown with dashed lines on Fig 64 and the parts-placement diagram.

Construction Hints

The most difficult part of building this amplifier is the homemade enclosure, but if the aluminum stock is cut carefully it will go together without too much problem. Be prepared to do quite a bit of cutting and filing, however!

A 10 × 14 × 3-in. chassis is the basic foundation for the amplifier, with the 14-in. side at the front and back. A cabinet made from 16-gauge aluminum completes the amplifier enclosure. The enclosure is 11½ in. high. To build a similar cabinet you need the following sheet-aluminum pieces:

1   14¼- × 11½-in. (front panel)
2   12 × 11½ in. (sides)
1   14- × 11½-in. (inner front panel)
2   14 × 12 in. (top and bottom)
1   14- × 8½- in. (back)
1   cover to fit the input-filter access opening

The inner front panel and both sides cover three sides of the chassis. The back extends from the top of the chassis to the cabinet top. The pieces are connected by means of ½-in. aluminum angle, drilled and tapped for no. 6-32 machine screws.

An opening in the back of the amplifier chassis allows access to the input-filter assembly for adjustment. An aluminum plate covers this opening. The RF INPUT and BYPASS BNC connectors, antenna relay (RF OUTPUT) and ALC output phono connectors and the Jones connector for filament and control-circuit power are all located on the rear chassis panel, as are the GRID TRIP and ALC LEVEL controls.

The 3-500Z tubes are 4 in. from the right side of the cabinet and are centered 4 in. apart. Locate the BAND switch and coil assembly 8 in. from the right side of the cabinet. The tuning capacitors are 2½ in. from the left side of the cabinet. The LOAD capacitor is centered (6¾ in. down from the top), and the TUNE capacitor is centered (3 in. down from the top). Dimensions are given as a guide; alter them as needed for different components.

The input band switch operates by means of a chain-drive linkage to the output BAND switch. The drive linkage is located between the two front panels, as shown in Figs 66 and 67.

The TUNE capacitor is a modified RADIOKIT part (no. 245 or equiv). The sidebar describes the required modifications.

The tank coil is made in three sections

Fig 71—Parts-placement diagram for the control-circuit board. The component side of the board is shown, with an X-ray view of the circuit foil. Some components were added to the board to solve an RFI problem; these were soldered to the foil side of the board. They are shown with dashed lines. A full-size etching pattern is included at the back of this *Handbook*.

FB = FB-73-801

Table 1

Plate Tank Circuit Inductor Information

Band	Inductance (mH)	Tap Point
10 meters	1.4	Junction of L1 and L2
12 meters	1.6	½ turn on L2 (B & W 2404T)
15 meters	1.9	1½ turns on L2
17 meters	2.2	2½ turns on L2
20 meters	2.8	3½ turns on L2
40 meters	5.6	4½ turns on L3 (B & W 2406T)
80 meters	11	Complete L1, L2, L3

(see Fig 67). The 10-meter section consists of five turns of ¼-in. copper tubing (1½-in. ID, 2½ in. long). The second section is a piece of B & W 2404T coil stock (5½ turns), and the third section is a piece of B & W 2406T stock (8½ turns). Table 1 lists the coil inductance and posi-

CONVERSION OF RADIOKIT NO. 245 CAPACITOR TO A TWO-SECTION CAPACITOR

Step 1. Make two tie-rod-support plates as shown in the figure. The back tie-rod plate has a half circle notch at the bottom to clear the ground-lug rivet.

Step 2. Locate the hole between the two rivets that hold the stator supports. This hole is predrilled with a no. 35 bit. Tap this hole with a no. 6-32 tap.

Step 3. Mount the front and back tie-rod plates to the capacitor with no. 6-32 × ½-in. machine screws.

Step 4. Measure the distance between the inside faces of the tie-rod plates. (This distance should be very close to 8¾ in.) Cut a piece of ¼-in. aluminum rod to just fit between the tie-rod plates. With a no. 35 bit, drill a hole in the end of the ¼-in. rod to a depth of ½ in. Tap this hole for a no. 6-32 screw. Mount the completed tie rod between the tie-rod mounting plates.

Step 5. The new tie rod will hold the capacitor together for the next operation. Remove all nuts on the stator tie rods and remove the tie rods. All stator plates and spacers will come loose. Be careful not to lose any of these parts.

Step 6. Using the brass stator tie rods as stock, cut two new tie rods 6-7/8 in. long and two new tie rods 2¾ in. long. With a no. 10-32 die, cut new threads on the plain ends to a length of ½ in.

Step 7. Slide a shaft collar over the ¼-in. rotor shaft all the way to the front end plate. Lock the setscrew to hold

Fig A—Make two end plates as shown to hold the modified capacitor together after the stator-support rods have been cut to form the two sections.

the shaft to the front end plate. This will prevent the small ball bearings from falling out of position. Remove all three ¼-in. tie rods for complete disassembly of the capacitor. Be very careful not to lose the single ball bearing that centers the rotor shaft to the rear bearing. Loosen and remove the nut that holds the rotor plates to the shaft. Count from the rear of the rotor shaft and remove the sixth rotor plate. Where the sixth plate was you

should now have two spacers. Replace the nut and tighten it. Reassemble the capacitor and the rotor, securing the frame with the three ¼-in. tie rods. Be sure to replace the single ball bearing at the rear of the rotor.

Step 8. Reassemble the front stator. Count off 21 stator plates and 40 spacers. Using the 6-7/8-in. brass tie rod, assemble the stator. Install the finished stator on the front support insulators. Install no. 10 nylon washers between the locking nuts and the insulators to prevent the insulators from breaking. Slide the 2¾-in. tie rods into the rear insulators. Add one no. 10 nylon washer and two no. 10-32 nuts. Next, add one plate and then a spacer. Continue adding plates and spacers until you have four plates and three spacers. Lock the assembly together with no. 10-32 nuts. Add a no. 10 nylon washer and a no. 10-32 nut to the outside of the tie rods.

Step 9. Adjust the no. 10-32 nuts so you have proper spacing between the stator and rotor plates, and tighten all locking nuts to hold the assembly in proper alignment.

The measured capacitance of the larger section should be 200 pF maximum and 30 pF minimum. The measured capacitance of the smaller section should be 43 pF maximum and 12 pF minimum.

The finished capacitor should have 5 rotor and 4 stator plates on the rear section and 21 rotor and 21 stator plates on the front section.

tions of the band-switch taps for each band. Cut the pieces of coil stock and solder them together. Wind the 10-meter coil.

Cut a piece of 1/4-in. Plexiglas 2-7/8 in. wide by 8 in. long. File the Plexiglas edges so it will fit inside the coil stock as shown in the photo. Slide the Plexiglas through the center of the B & W coil-stock pieces. Mount the 10-meter coil on the end nearest the 2404T coil stock. The assembled coil is supported by 3/8- × 4-3/8-in. fiber-reinforced plastic rods drilled and tapped for no. 6-32 machine screws. The BAND switch is mounted directly under the coil assembly.

The plate RF choke is wound on a 4-in.-long piece of ¾-in. Teflon rod. The design is taken from a *QST* article by Doug DeMaw, W1FB, "Save Money—Build Your Own RF Choke!" April 1979, pp 30-31. The choke is centered between the 3-500Z tubes and mounted 2½ in. down from the top of the right cabinet side. One end of the Teflon coil form is drilled and tapped so the coil can be fastened to the cabinet with a nylon machine screw.

Wind the choke using no. 24 enameled wire. There are four close-wound sections with a ¼-in. × ½-turn gap between sections. Starting from the B+ end, close wind 30 turns (this should occupy about 11/16 in.) The next section is 46 turns (about 1-1/16 in.). Wind 21 turns (a little less than ½ in.) for the third section. The last section is 17 turns (about 3/8 in.). Complete the plate choke with a protective coating of Q-dope or similar varnish.

TUNING AND OPERATION

Use an ohmmeter to check all circuit paths in the power supply and RF deck for possible short circuits. Check the HV supply for proper operation before connecting it to the RF deck. Before installing the tubes in their sockets, verify the operation of all control circuits. Connect the Jones power-supply cable and a heavy braid ground strap between the amplifier and power-supply cabinets. (Don't connect the high-voltage lead between the RF deck and the power-supply cabinet. With the jack of the HV connector mounted on the supply cabinet, you needn't worry about a live high-voltage lead accidentally touching the chassis or operator. You must, however, activate the HV supply to make the control circuit operational.)

Turn on the power-supply main power switch and the amplifier POWER switch. The blowers should run and you should measure about 5 V at the tube sockets. Switch on PLATE VOLTAGE at the power supply and then the PLATE voltage switch on the amplifier. After a few seconds the relays should engage. Next, ground the amplifier VOX/MOX line and check to see that the control-circuit relays activate as expected. When everything is working properly, turn off all power and carefully install the tubes. Install the top and bot-

Table 2
Amplifier Operating Conditions Measured in ARRL Lab

V_P = 2500

Frequency (MHz)	Grid Current (mA)	Drive (W)	Output (W)
3.8	230	115	940
7.1	140	100	930
14.2	140	100	940
18.1	150	100	960
21.2	140	100	960
24.9	150	100	800
28.5	120	100	720

V_P = 3000

Frequency (MHz)	Grid Current (mA)	Drive (W)	Output (W)
3.8	160	110	1250
7.1	160	100	1250
14.2	140	100	1120
18.1	140	100	1070
21.2	150	100	1110
24.9	150	100	930
28.5	160	100	800

V_P = 3500

Frequency (MHz)	Grid Current (mA)	Drive (W)	Output (W)
3.8	180	110	1480
7.1	180	100	1470
14.2	150	100	1320
18.1	160	100	1280
21.2	160	100	1080
24.9	160	100	1290
28.5	140	100	940

Note: Amplifier was loaded to a maximum I_{plate} of 800 mA in all cases. For an unloaded plate voltage (V_P) of 2500, the loaded V_P was 2250, at 3000 V it was 2700 V and at 3500 V it was 3100 V.

Fig 72—Worst-case spectral photograph of the 3-500Z amplifier. Power output is 950 W on 7.1 MHz with the plate voltage set at 2500 V. Each vertical division is 10 dB and each horizontal division is 5 MHz. All harmonics and spurious emissions are at least 46 dB below the peak fundamental output. This amplifier complies with current FCC spectral-purity requirements.

Fig 73—Worst-case spectral display of the amplifier output during two-tone intermodulation distortion (IMD) testing. The third-order products are approximately 40 dB below PEP output. Vertical divisions are 10 dB; horizontal divisions are 2 kHz. The amplifier was operated at 900 W PEP output on 14.1 MHz with the plate voltage set at 2500 V.

tom covers on the amplifier chassis.

Connect the HV lead to the amplifier. Attach a transceiver (capable of delivering about 100 W) through a wattmeter to the RF INPUT. Route the amplifier RF OUTPUT through a second wattmeter to a suitable dummy load. Install a VOX/MOX lead from the transceiver to the amplifier jack, or simply ground the amplifier VOX/MOX line to make the amplifier transmit during the test.

Flip on the power-supply main power switch and then the amplifier POWER switch to activate the filament supply. You should see the tubes begin to glow. Set the high-voltage SELECTOR switch to 2500, and then close the PLATE VOLTAGE switch on the power supply followed by the PLATE switch on the amplifier. *(CAUTION: Never operate the high-voltage SELECTOR switch with the plate voltage on! Severe*

arcing will occur across the switch contacts, and you may destroy the switch.) With the exciter set to transmit SSB, press the mike PTT switch and note the amplifier plate-current reading. It should be about 120 mA.

With the amplifier set to operate on 80 meters, apply about 10 W of CW drive and adjust the input-filter capacitor for that band to achieve the lowest possible SWR. (You should have no trouble adjusting the filter for an SWR of 2:1 or better.) Now adjust the TUNE and LOAD controls for maximum output. (The easiest way to tune this amplifier is to observe a wattmeter connected to the output and tune for maximum power.) Recheck the input SWR with the amplifier running at full output.

Adjust the input filter for each band in turn. Turn off the PLATE VOLTAGE and select 3000 V (and then 3500 V), running through the amplifier-tuning process again each time. Keep detailed notes of the plate and grid currents for each band at each plate-voltage setting. You should normally operate with 3000 V (use the 3500-V switch position to get 3000 V if the line voltage is low at your location).

Table 2 summarizes the operating conditions measured in the ARRL Lab. Fig 72 shows the spectral output of the amplifier with the signals run through the B & W FL-10/1500 low-pass filter. Fig 73 shows the worst-case results of the Lab's intermodulation-distortion (IMD) testing.

Chapter 31

VHF Radio Equipment

The bands at 50, 144 and 220 MHz each contain more spectrum space than the total of *all* bands below 50 MHz! Little wonder that the VHF bands are popular favorites with many hams.

This chapter contains projects for the VHFer. In it you will find preamplifiers and converters for receiving. You will also find transmitting converters and transverters (used for transmitting and receiving). Most hams will be interested in the RF power amplifiers. Perhaps you will find what you are looking for.

For a discussion of RF amplifier theory see Chapter 15. Transmitter and receiver theory is covered in Chapters 11 and 12.

Dual-Gate MOSFET Preamplifiers for 28, 50, 144 and 220 MHz

The performance of many older receivers can be improved with a simple preamplifier in the front end. The simple design shown in Figs. 1 through 5 uses a dual-gate MOSFET to provide about 20-dB gain with associated noise figures of 1 to 1.5 dB on 28, 50, 144 and 220 MHz. They can be used for weak-signal or satellite work, and they can help put some life into an older 144- or 220-MHz FM transceiver. This is a simple, stable design. When built with a 3SK48, 3SK51 or 3N204, it will hold its own with all but the best GaAsFET designs. Kent Britain, WA5VJB, designed and built these preamplifiers.

Circuit Details

The basic circuit for the 28- and 50-MHz designs is shown in Fig. 1. Fig. 2 shows the 144- and 220-MHz versions. Q1 is a VHF dual-gate MOSFET. Many devices will work in this circuit. The author has successfully used the following devices (listed in order of preference): 3SK48, 3SK51, 3N204, 3SK40, 3N211. L1 and C1 tune the input. C6 and L2 tune the output of the 144- and 220-MHz versions. The 28- and 50-MHz preamplifiers use an untuned resistive output. R1 and R2 provide gate-2 bias.

Construction

The preamps shown here were built

Fig. 1 — Schematic diagram of the 28- and 50-MHz dual-gate MOSFET preamplifiers. Resistors are ¼-W carbon types.

C1 — Ceramic or piston trimmer capacitor, 20- to 25-pF max.
C2, C3 — 500- to 1000-pF feedthrough capacitor, solder-in type preferred.
C4 — 500- to 1000-pF feedthrough capacitor.
C5 — 100- to 200-pF silver-mica or ceramic capacitor.

J1, J2 — Female chassis-mount RF connectors, BNC preferred.
L1 — 28 MHz: 23t no. 24 enam. on ¼-inch slug-tuned coil form. 50 MHz: Same, but 10t.
Q1 — Dual-gate MOSFET such as 3SK51 or 3N204. See text.

Fig. 2 — Schematic diagram of the 144- and 220-MHz dual-gate MOSFET preamplifiers. Resistors are ¼-W carbon types.

C1, C6 — Ceramic or piston trimmer capacitor, 10- to 15-pF max.
C2, C3 — 500- to 1000-pF feedthrough capacitor, solder-in type preferred.
C4 — 500- to 1000-pF feedthrough capacitor.
C5 — 50- to 200-pF silver-mica or ceramic capacitor.
J1, J2 — Female chassis-mount RF connectors, BNC preferred.
L1 — 144 MHz: 8t no. 18 wire, 3/16-inch ID, 1/2-inch long. 220 MHz: 5t no. 18 wire, 3/16-inch ID, 1/2-inch long.
L2 — 144 MHz: 8t no. 18 wire, 3/16-inch ID, 1/2-inch long. Tap at 1t. 220 MHz: 5t no. 18 wire, 3/16-inch ID, 1/2-inch long. Tap at 1/2t.
Q1 — Dual-gate MOSFET such as 3SK51 or 3N204. See text.

EXCEPT AS INDICATED, DECIMAL VALUES OF CAPACITANCE ARE IN MICROFARADS (µF); OTHERS ARE IN PICOFARADS (pF OR µµF); RESISTANCES ARE IN OHMS; k = 1000, M = 1000 000.

Fig. 3 — RF component side of the board of a 2-meter version of the dual-gate MOSFET preamplifier.

Fig. 4 — Another view of the 2-meter MOSFET preamp showing the dc components mounted on the other side of the board.

"dead bug" style on a piece of unetched double-sided circuit-board material. The foil acts as a ground plane, and all ground connections are made directly to it. The finished preamp fits inside a small Minibox. See Figs. 3 and 4. Fig. 5 shows the general layout. Dc components, including C4, D1, R1 and R2 mount on one side of the board. Voltage is fed to the transistor through C2 and C3. Parts placement is not at all critical. Solder the case of Q1 to the ground plane.

Parts for this project are available from many of the suppliers listed in Chapter 35. One source for 3SK51 transistors is Fuji-Svea, P.O. Box 3375, Torrance, CA 90510.

Adjustment is easy. Simply tune in a weak signal and adjust C1 and L1 (28- and 50-MHz models) or C1 and C6 (144- and 220-MHz models) for best signal-to-noise ratio.

Fig. 5 — Suggested board layout for the MOSFET preamplifier. There are slight differences between the 28- and 50-MHz versions and the 144- and 220-MHz units. See text. Parts outlined with dashed lines are mounted on the back of the board. Component numbers refer to Figs. 1 and 2.

Dual-Gate GaAsFET Preamplifiers for 28, 50, 144 and 220 MHz

Dual-gate GaAsFET devices offer builders the opportunity to experiment with the latest technology — low-noise GaAsFETs — for a modest investment. The preamplifiers described here use GaAsFETs that cost less than $5 each, yet the preamplifiers offer noise figures well under 1 dB with gains ranging from 20 to 24 dB. Kent Britain, WA5VJB, designed and built the preamplifiers shown in Figs. 6 through 10.

Circuit Details

The basic circuit for the 28- and 50-MHz designs is shown in Fig. 6. Fig. 7 shows the 144- and 220-MHz versions. Q1 is a dual-gate GaAsFET. Many devices will work in this circuit, including the NEC NE41137 and NE25137, Motorola MRF966/967 and Mitsubishi MGF1100. Parts values are given for all of these devices so the builder can use whatever transistor is easiest to find. L1, C1 and C2 tune the input. C5 and L2 tune the output of the 144- and 220-MHz versions. The 28- and 50-MHz preamplifiers use an untuned resistive output. R1 and R2 provide gate-2 bias.

Variable capacitors can be miniature ceramic trimmer capacitors or piston trimmers. The exact value is not critical; any trimmer with a maximum value around that specified will do. C7, the output coupling capacitor, can be any small silver-mica around the specified value. For stability, it is important to use good-quality

capacitors for the gate 2 and source bypasses. Ceramic chip or leadless disc-ceramic types are necessary to provide a low-impedance ground.

Occasional instability in 144-MHz versions of this preamplifier can be eliminated by adding R5 or FB1 (Figures 7 and 10).

Construction

The dual-gate GaAsFET preamplifiers are built "dead bug" style on a piece of double-sided PC board material. See Figs. 8 and 9. The circuit board acts as a low-impedance ground plane, and all ground connections are made directly to it. J1, J2 and C9 also secure the circuit board to the lid of the enclosure. The enclosure can be any aluminum diecast box (Bud CU-124; Hammond 1490B) or Mini-box (Bud CU-3002A) approximately 4 by 2 inches, or you can make one by soldering pieces of circuit board material together.

Q1 is supported above the ground plane by its gate 2 and source leads, which are soldered directly to C3 and C4. The other ends of these capacitors are soldered to the ground plane. R4 should be soldered in place with essentially no lead length. Placement for the rest of the parts is not critical, but keep the leads short. A layout that has proven successful is shown in Fig. 10.

GaAsFETs are static-sensitive, so handle them accordingly. See Chapter 24 for information on working with static-sensitive devices. It's best to assemble the rest of the circuit and install Q1 last. Use a grounded iron if possible, and solder the leads quickly.

Parts for this project are available from Microwave Components of Michigan and Applied Invention, both listed in Chapter 35. NEC transistors are available from California Eastern Laboratories, 3260 Jay St., Santa Clara, CA 95050.

Table 1

L1 and L2 Values for 144- and 220-MHz Dual-Gate GaAsFET Preamplifiers

Device	L1 144 MHz	L1 220 MHz	L2 144 MHz	L2 220 MHz
NE41137/NE25137	7t	5t	7t, tap at 2t	5t, tap at 1½t
3SK97 and MGF1100	5t	3½t	7t, tap at 2t	5t, tap at 1½t
MRF966/967	12t	8t	8t, tap at 2t	5t, tap at 1½t

Note: All coils are no. 20 to 24 wire, 3/16-inch ID, spaced one wire dia.

Fig. 6 — Schematic diagram of the 28- and 50-MHz dual-gate GaAsFET preamplifiers. Resistors are ¼-W carbon types unless noted.

C1 — Ceramic or piston trimmer capacitor, 10-pF max.
C2 — Ceramic or piston trimmer capacitor, 20- to 25-pF max.
C3, C4 — 200- to 1000-pF chip capacitor.
C6, C10 — 500- to 1000-pF feedthrough capacitor, solder-in type preferred.

C7 — 200- to 500-pF silver-mica or disc-ceramic capacitor.
C8 — 5- to 25-µF electrolytic capacitor.
C9 — 500- to 1000-pF feedthrough capacitor.
D1 — 5.1-V, 1-W Zener diode (1N4733 or equiv.).
D2 — 1N914, 1N4148 or any diode with ratings

of 25 PIV and 50 mA or greater.
J1, J2 — Female-chassis mount RF connectors, BNC preferred.
L1 — 28 MHz: 13t no. 24 enam. on ¼-inch slug-tuned coil form. 50 MHz: Same, but 9t.
Q1 — Dual-gate GaAsFET, NEC NE41137, Mitsubishi MGF1100 or 3SK97.

Fig. 7 — Schematic diagram of the 144- and 220-MHz dual-gate GaAsFET preamplifiers. The same circuit is used for all versions, but some parts values are different. See Table 1. Resistors are ¼-W carbon-composition types unless otherwise noted.

C1, C2 — 10-pF (max.) ceramic or piston trimmer capacitor.
C3, C4 — 200- to 1000-pF ceramic chip capacitor or leadless disc-ceramic capacitor.
C5 — For 144 MHz: 20 pF trimmer capacitor. For 220 MHz: 10-pF trimmer capacitor.
C6, C9 — 400- to 1000-pF feedthrough capacitor.
C7 — 50- to 100-pF silver-mica capacitor.
C8 — 1- to 25-μF, 25-V electrolytic capacitor.

D1 — 5.1-V, 1-W Zener diode (1N4733 or equiv.)
D2 — 1N914, 1N4148 or any diode with ratings of 25 PIV and 50 mA or greater.
FB1 — FB-43-101 ferrite bead (for 144 MHz only; see text).
J1, J2 — Female chassis-mount BNC or Type-N connector.
L1 — See Table 1.
L2 — See Table 1.
Q1 — NEC NE41137, NE25137, Motorola

MRF966/967, Mitsubishi MGF 1100 or 3SK97 dual-gate GaAsFET.
R1 — For NE41137, NE25137, MGF1100, 3SK97: 10 kΩ; for MRF966/967: 4.7 kΩ.
R2 — 10 kΩ for all devices.
R3 — 150- to 250-ohm, 1- or 2-W resistor.
R4 — For NE41137, NE25137, MGF1100, 3SK97: 47 Ω; for MRF966/967: 100 Ω.
R5 — For 144-MHz only. See text.

Fig. 8 — This version of the 50-MHz dual-gate GaAsFET preamplifier is built in a small diecast box. Construction of the 28-MHz preamp is identical. A suggested parts placement is shown in Fig. 10.

Fig. 9 — This 144-MHz dual-gate GaAsFET preamp uses an NE41137 and is built on the lid of an aluminum diecast box. The 220-MHz version is similar. See Fig. 10 for a suggested parts placement.

Fig. 10 — Suggested board layout for the dual-gate GaAsFET preamplifier. There are slight differences between the 28- and 50-MHz versions and the 144- and 220-MHz units. See text. Component numbers refer to Figs. 6 and 7.

GaAsFET Preamplifiers for 144 and 220 MHz

GaAsFET devices enable amateurs to build preamplifiers with very low noise figures for terrestrial, satellite and EME work. In addition, GaAsFETs offer superior strong-signal IMD performance — a characteristic that is important on our crowded bands. Described here and shown in Figs. 11 through 13 are preamplifiers for 144 and 220 MHz that use readily available Mitsubishi MGF1402 or MGF1202 devices. Other single-gate GaAsFETs such as the Dexcel 1500 and 2500 series, or the NEC 700 series, also work well. Gain is typically 20 to 24 dB with noise figures of about 0.5 dB. Kent Britain, WA5VJB, designed and built these preamplifiers.

Circuit Details

Fig. 11 is a schematic diagram of the preamplifier. The circuit is the same for both bands, although some component values are different. L1, C1 and C2 tune the input. C5 and L2 tune the output. Variable capacitors can be miniature ceramic trimmer capacitors or piston trimmers; piston types are recommended. The exact value is not critical; any trimmer with a maximum value around that specified will do. C6, the output coupling capacitor, can be any small silver-mica around the specified value. For stability, it is important to use good-quality capacitors for the source bypasses. Note that there are two

Fig. 11 — Schematic diagram of the 144- and 220-MHz MGF1402 GaAsFET preamplifiers.

C1, C2 — 10-pF (max.) ceramic or piston trimmer capacitor (piston trimmer preferred).
C3, C4 — 200- to 1000-pF ceramic chip capacitor or leadless disc-ceramic capacitor.
C5 — For 144 MHz: 20 pF trimmer capacitor. For 220 MHz: 10-pF trimmer capacitor (piston trimmer preferred).
C6 — 100- to 200-pF silver-mica capacitor.
C7, C9 — 400- to 1000-pF feedthrough capacitor.

C8 — 1- to 25-μF, 25-V electrolytic capacitor.
D1 — 3.9-V, 1-W Zener diode (1N4730 or equiv.).
D2 — 1N914, 1N4148 or any diode with ratings of 25 PIV and 50 mA or greater.
J1, J2 — Female chassis-mount BNC or Type-N connector.
L1 — For 144 MHz: 9t no. 20 wire, 3/16-inch ID, spaced 1 wire dia. For 220 MHz: same as

144 MHz, but 6t.
L2 — For 144 MHz: 6t no. 20 wire, 3/16-inch ID, spaced 1 wire dia. Tap at 1½t. For 220 MHz: 4t no. 20 wire, 3/16-inch ID, spaced 1 wire dia. Tap at 1t.
Q1 — Mitsubishi MGF1402 GaAsFET. Others usable (see text).
R1 — 100-Ω, 1/4- or 1/8-W resistor.
R2 — 150- to 250-ohm, 1- or 2-W resistor.

(A)

(B)

Fig. 12 — This 220-MHz GaAsFET preamplifier is built in a Hammond 1590A diecast box. All ground connections are made to the circuit-board ground plane. A suggested parts placement is shown in Fig. 13.

source leads and that each has a bypass capacitor. Ceramic chip or leadless disc-ceramic types are necessary to provide a low-impedance ground.

Construction

The GaAsFET preamplifiers are built "dead bug" style on a piece of double-sided PC board material. See Fig. 12. The circuit board acts as a low-impedance ground plane, and all ground connections are made directly to it. J1, J2 and C9 also secure the circuit board to the lid of the enclosure. The enclosure can be any aluminum diecast box (Bud CU-124; Hammond 1590B) or Minibox (Bud CU-3002A) approximately 4 by 2 inches, or you can make one by soldering pieces of circuit board material together.

Q1 is mounted to the shield by its source leads, which are soldered directly to C3 and C4. The other ends of these capacitors are soldered to the ground plane. R4 should be soldered in place with essentially no lead length. A layout that has proven successful is shown in Fig. 13. To help prevent L1 and L2 from coupling, wind one coil in the left-hand direction and the other in the right-hand direction.

GaAsFETs are static-sensitive, so handle

Fig. 13 — Suggested board layout for the MGF1402 144- and 220-MHz GaAsFET preamplifier. Component numbers refer to Fig. 11.

them accordingly. See Chapter 24 for information on working with static-sensitive devices. It's best to assemble the rest of the circuit and install Q1 last. Use a grounded iron if possible, and solder the leads quickly.

Parts for this project are available from Microwave Components of Michigan and Applied Invention, both listed in Chapter 35. MGF1402 transistors are available from Advanced Receiver Research, Box 1242, Burlington, CT 06013.

Remote Preamplifier-Switching System

The preamplifier-switching system described here and shown in Figs. 14 through 16 is intended primarily for EME applications. Serious VHF and UHF operators may wish to consider similar systems for terrestrial work, as a tower-mounted preamplifier usually means a noticeable reduction in system noise figure.

The Circuit

The relay-switching system is separated into two parts. One section is mounted at the tower, and the other, the control circuitry and power supply, is mounted at the station. A length of four-conductor, TV-type rotator cable can be used to inter-

connect the two units. The package mounted at the tower consists of two RF coaxial relays and a preamplifier. As shown in Fig. 15, K1 is used to switch the antenna between the transmit line and a line that connects K1 with K2. K2 switches the preamplifier to either the antenna or a 50-ohm termination. With the system shown, it is impossible to transmit accidentally into the preamplifier.

K1 must be able to handle the full transmitter power. Relays rated for high power at VHF and UHF include the Dow-Key DK-60 series and the Transco Y and D series. These relays are expensive when purchased new, but they often show up at

Fig. 14 — A preamplifier relay switching system suitable for EME work. The relay box is mounted at the antenna and the control box is located in the station. A length of four-conductor wire connects the two units.

Fig. 15 — Schematic diagram of the preamplifier switching system. The diagram is divided into two parts; the top portion for the circuitry at the antenna and the bottom for use in the station.

DS1 — Neon indicator light with built-in dropping resistor.
K1, K2 — RF-coaxial relays suitable for the frequency range to be used.
K3 — SPDT relay with contacts to carry

voltage/current needed for coils of K1, K2.
R1 — Termination, 50 ohms, noninductive. Resistor built into a PL-259 connector.
S1, S2 — Toggle SPST.

T1 — Isolation transformer, 117-V ac primary, 117-V ac secondary, 15 VA, Stancor P-6411 or equiv.
TB1-TB3, incl. — Terminal block, screw connection, four terminals.

flea markets. K2 is used only to switch the receive line, so it may be a low-power relay. Typical surplus relays have BNC connectors. The project shown here uses two Dow-Key relays.

Relay isolation is an important consideration. High power levels can leak through the unused relay contacts and damage the receive preamplifier, so the use of two relays helps keep the level of RF that appears at the preamp to a minimum.

Generally, no more than 10 mW or RF should be allowed to reach the preamp input. Use of a 0.1- to 0.25-wavelength section of cable between K1 and K2, instead of the double-male connector shown here, would substantially increase isolation.

The control circuit is set up so that the relays must be energized to receive. This offers two advantages. When the station is not in use, the preamp is terminated in a 50-ohm load rather than the antenna. This

protects the preamp from static charges from nearby lightning strikes. Also, if the tower-mounted preamp or one of the relays should fail, the transmit line would be connected directly to the antenna. Another TR relay can be installed at the station end of the transmit line and operation could continue (although without the benefit of a tower-mounted preamp).

S2 allows the operator to switch the relays without putting the station into transmit. The preamp input can be switched between the 50-ohm load and the antenna. This allows for sun-noise measurements.

A method of sequencing the relays and the other components is recommended so that the relays are not "hot switched" with RF power applied. A TR sequencer is described elsewhere in this chapter.

The portion of the system mounted at the station is essentially a power supply and control circuitry. A line-isolation transformer is used to power the 117-V relay coils. A pilot light, fuse and ON/OFF switch are provided in this design. Many surplus relays have 26-V dc coils, so a suitable dc power supply will be necessary in some cases.

Construction

The items to be mounted at the tower are enclosed in an ordinary chassis and bottom plate assembly. Fig. 16 indicates the general layout. Short lead lengths are used throughout. Bulkhead UHF feed-through connectors are used to ensure an RF- and watertight enclosure. The item shown at the bottom center of the enclosure is a commercial preamplifier. Power for the preamplifier (12-V dc) is fed through the fourth wire of the four-wire cable that connects the two modules (tower and station). When all components are mounted properly, the chassis is sealed with silicone rubber (RTV). A terminal block provides for connection to the four-conductor cable. Two 0.01-μF capacitors are mounted across

Fig. 16 — Interior view of the package mounted at the antenna. The object at the bottom center of the chassis is a commercial preamplifier.

the relay coils at terminal block TB3.

The station circuitry is mounted in a small aluminum cabinet. A neon indicator, on/off power and termination switch are mounted to the front panel. The fuse and interconnection terminal blocks TB1 and TB2 are mounted on the rear apron. Component layout is not at all critical.

TR Time-Delay Generator

If you've ever blown up your new GaAsFET preamp or hard-to-find coaxial relay, or are just plain worried about it, this transmit/receive (TR) time-delay generator is for you. This little circuit makes it simple to put some reliability into your present station or to get that new VHF or UHF transverter on the air fast, safe and simple. Its primary application is for VHF/UHF transverter, amplifier and antenna switching, but it can be used in any amplifier-antenna scheme. An enable signal to the TR generator will produce sequential output commands to a receive relay, a TR relay, an amplifier and a transverter — automatically. All you do is sit back and work DX! This project, shown in Figs. 17 through 23, was designed and built by Chip Angle, N6CA.

Why Sequence?

In stations using transverters, extra power amplifiers and external antenna-mounted TR relays, several problems may arise. The block diagram of a typical station is shown in Fig. 17. When the HF exciter is switched into transmit by the PTT or VOX line, it immediately puts out a ground (or in some cases a positive voltage) command for relay control and an RF signal.

If voltage is applied to the transverter, amplifier and antenna relays simultaneously, RF can be applied as the relay contacts bounce. In most cases, RF will be applied before a relay can make full closure. This can easily arc contacts on dc and RF relays and cause permanent damage. In addition, if the TR relay is not fully closed before RF from the power amplifier is applied, excessive RF may leak into the receive side of the relay. The likely result — preamplifier failure!

The TR time-delay generator supplies commands, one after another, going into transmit and going back to receive from transmit, to turn on all station relays in the right order, eliminating the problems just described.

Circuit Details

Here's how it works. See the schematic diagram in Fig. 19. Assume we're in receive and are going to transmit. A ground command to Q2 (or a positive voltage command to Q1) turns Q2 off. This allows C1 to charge through R1 plus 1.5 kΩ. This rising voltage is applied to all positive (+) inputs of U1, a quad comparator. The ladder network on all negative (−) inputs of U1 sets the threshold point of each comparator at a successively higher level. As C1 charges up, each comparator, starting with U1A, will sequentially change output states.

The comparator outputs are fed into U2, a quad exclusive-OR gate. This was in-

Fig. 17 — A typical VHF or UHF station arrangement with transverter, preamp and power amp. As shown, most TR relays change at the same time.

Fig. 18 — Block diagram of a VHF/UHF station with a remote-mounted preamp and antenna relays. The TR time-delay generator makes sure that everything turns on in the right order.

EXCEPT AS INDICATED, DECIMAL
VALUES OF CAPACITANCE ARE
IN MICROFARADS (μF) ; OTHERS
ARE IN PICOFARADS (pF OR μμF) ;
RESISTANCES ARE IN OHMS ;
k = 1000, M = 1 000 000

* ADDING JUMPER INVERTS
  OUTPUT STATE

cluded in the design to allow "state programming" of the various relays throughout the system. Because of the wide variety of available relays, primarily coaxial, you may be stuck with a relay that's exactly what you need — except its contacts are open when it's energized! To use this relay, you merely invert the output state of the delay generator by inserting a jumper between the appropriate OR-gate input and ground. Now, the relay will be "on" during receive and "off" during transmit. This might seem kind of strange; however, high-quality coaxial relays are hard to come by and if "backwards" relays are all you have, you'd better use them.

The outputs of U2 drive transistors Q3-Q6, which are "on" in the receive mode. Drive from the OR gates turns these

transistors "off." This causes the collectors of Q3-Q6 to go high, allowing the base-to-emitter junctions of Q7-Q10 to be forward-biased through the LEDs to turn on the relays in sequential order. The LEDs serve as built-in indicators to check performance and sequencing of the generator. This is convenient if any state changes are made.

When the output transistors (Q7-Q10) are turned on, they pull the return side of the relay coils to ground. These output transistors were selected because of their high beta, very low saturation voltage (V_{CE}) and low cost. They can switch (and have been tested at) 35 V at 600 mA for many days of continuous operation. If substitutions are planned, test one of the new transistors with the relays you plan to

use to be sure that the transistor will be able to power the relay for long periods.

To go from transmit to receive, the sequencing order is reversed. This gives additional protection to the various system components. C1 discharges through R1 and Q2 to ground.

Fig. 20 shows the relative states and duration of the four output commands when enabled. With the values specified for R1 and C1, there will be intervals of 30 to 50 milliseconds between the four output commands. Exact timing will vary because of component tolerances. Most likely everything will be okay with the values shown, but it's a good idea to check the timing with an oscilloscope just to be sure. Minor changes to the value of R1 may be necessary.

Fig. 19 — Schematic diagram of the TR time-delay generator. Resistors are ¼ W. Capacitors are disc ceramic. Capacitors marked with polarity are electrolytic.

D1-D4 — Red LED (MV55, HP 5082-4482 or equiv.).

D5-D8 — 33-V, 500-mW Zener diode (1N973A or equiv.).

C1 — 1.5-µF, 16-V or greater, axial-lead electrolytic capacitor. See text.

Q1-Q6 — General purpose NPN transistor (2N3904 or equiv.).

Q7-Q10 — Low-power NPN amplifier transistor, MPS6531 or equiv. Must be able to switch up to 35 V at 600 mA continuously. See text.

R1 — 47-kΩ, ¼-W resistor. This resistor sets the TR delay time constant and may have to be varied slightly to achieve the desired delay. See text.

U1 — Quad comparator, LM339 or equiv.

U2 — Quad, 2-input exclusive OR gate (74C86N, CD4030A or equiv.).

Most relays, especially coaxial, will require about 10 ms to change states and stop bouncing. The 30-ms delay will give adequate time for all closures to occur.

Construction and Hookup

One of the more popular antenna changeover schemes uses two coaxial relays — one for actual TR switching and one for receiver/preamplifier protection. See

Fig. 20 — The relative states and durations of the four output commands when enabled. This diagram shows the sequence of events when going from receive to transmit and back to receive. The TR delay generator allows about 30 to 50 ms for each relay to close before activating the next one in line.

Fig. 21 — The TR time-delay generator can also be used to sequence the relays in an HF power amplifier.

Fig. 22 — Parts placement diagram of the TR time-delay generator. A full-size etching pattern is given at the back of this book.

Fig. 23 — The completed time-delay generator fits in a small aluminum box.

Fig. 18. A project using this scheme is presented elsewhere in this chapter.

Many RF relays have very poor isolation, especially at VHF and UHF frequencies. Some of the more popular surplus relays have only 40 dB isolation at 144 MHz or higher. If you are running high power, say 1000 W (+60 dBm) at the relay, the receive side of the relay will see +20 dBm (100 mW) when the station is transmitting. This power level is enough to inflict fatal damage on your favorite preamplifier.

Adding a second relay, called the RX isolation relay here, terminates the preamp in a 50-ohm load during transmission and increases the isolation significantly. Also, in the event of TR relay failure, this extra relay will protect the receive preamplifier.

As shown in Fig. 18, both relays can be controlled with three wires. This scheme provides maximum protection for the receiver. If high-quality relays are used and

verified to be in working order, relay losses can be kept well below 0.1 dB, even at 1296 MHz. The three-conductor cable to the remote relays should be shielded to eliminate transients or other interference.

By reversing the RX-TX state of the TR relays (that is, connecting the transmitter hardline and 50-ohm preamp termination to the normally open relay ports instead of the normally closed side), receiver protection can be provided. When the station is not in use and the system is turned off, the receiver preamplifier will be terminated in 50 Ω instead of being connected to the antenna. The relays must be energized to receive. This might seem a little backward; however, if you are having static-charge-induced preamplifier failures, this may solve your problem.

Most coaxial relays aren't designed to be energized continuously. Therefore, adequate heat sinking of coaxial relays must be considered. A pair of Transco Y relays can be energized for several hours when mounted to an aluminum plate 12 inches square and ¼ inch thick. Thermal paste will give better heat transfer to the plate. For long-winded operators, it is a good idea to heat sink the relays even when they are energized only in transmit.

Fig. 21 shows typical HF power amplifier interconnections. In this application, amplifier in/out and sequencing are all provided. The amplifier will always have an antenna connected to its output before drive is applied.

Many TR change-over schemes are possible depending on system requirements. Most are easily satisfied with this TR delay generator.

The TR delay generator is built on a 2½ × 3¼ inch PC board. See Fig. 22. The board can be mounted in a small aluminum case, as shown in Fig. 23. Connections to the rest of the system are made through feedthrough capacitors. Do not use feedthrough capacitors larger than 2000 pF because peak current through the output switching transistors may be excessive.

Three-Watt Transmitting Converter for 6 Meters

The linear transmitting converter shown in Figs. 36 through 39 is a simple, low-cost way to extend the coverage of any 28-MHz transmitter to the 6-meter band. Output power is 3 watts PEP and the 28-MHz drive requirement is 1 mW. This drive level is compatible with the transverter outputs found on many current HF transceivers. By selecting the appropriate resistor values, the input attenuator can easily be adjusted for drive levels as high as 100 mW.

Particular care was taken during the design stage to ensure that spurious emissions are at a minimum. The IMD performance is such that this unit can be used to drive a high-power linear amplifier without generating excessive adjacent-channel interference.

Circuit Description

LO injection is supplied to the mixer by a crystal oscillator operating at 22 MHz. The output of the oscillator is filtered to reduce harmonics to approximately -40 dBc and is then applied to a power splitter, T2. One port of the splitter feeds the mixer, and the other output is connected to J1. This output can be used to supply LO to a receiving converter for transceiver operation. A 3-dB attenuator between the splitter and the mixer provides a wideband termination for the mixer LO port. The power delivered to the mixer is $+7$ dBm.

A commercial diode-ring module is used for the mixer. The excellent balance of this type of mixer reduces the band-pass filter requirements following the mixer. The IMD performance is also very good; the third-order products are 40 dB below each tone of the two-tone output signal when the input signal is at the recommended level of -10 dBm (each tone). The attenuator at the IF port prevents overdriving the mixer. The 20-dB pad shown in Fig. 37 allows a driving signal of 30 to 40 mW (PEP) to be used. This attenuator should be adjusted if other drive levels are desired.

The mixer is followed by a broadband amplifier, 6-dB pad and a 3-pole band-pass filter. The amplifier has a gain of nearly 20 dB at 50 MHz and provides a good termination for the mixer. Signal level at the filter output is about -10 dBm. Two more stages of class-A amplification follow the band-pass filter, bringing the signal level up to the $+16$ dBm necessary to drive the power-amplifier stage.

The power amplifier uses a Motorola MRF476 transistor operating class AB. The MRF476, a low-cost device in a plastic TO-220 package, will deliver a minimum of 3 watts PEP with good linearity at 50 MHz. A CW output of up to 4 watts can be obtained from this converter, but the key-down time should be limited to 60 seconds. This is because of the relatively small heat sink used in this unit. The power-amplifier input and output networks

Fig. 36 — Six-meter transmitting converter and 3-W PEP amplifier.

are both designed to match the transistor to 50 ohms. Their design was based on data supplied in the *Motorola RF Data Manual* (2nd edition). The amplifier output is filtered by a 7-pole low-pass filter designed for a cutoff frequency of 56 MHz and a ripple factor of 0.17 dB.

Construction

The converter is constructed in two sections: the low-level section consisting of the LO, mixer, band-pass filter and class-A amplifiers and the power-amplifier/low-pass filter section. No printed circuit board is needed for the low-level section; rather, the components are mounted directly on a piece of etched copper-clad board. The component leads going to ground support the components above the board. Among the many advantages to this style of construction is the ease with which the circuits can be modified. Also, if a printed-circuit board is used, the components used to lay out the board, such as variable capacitors,

are likely to be the only types that can be used. This makes it difficult for the builder to use junk box components.

Note that the LO and its filter are completely enclosed by a shield made of double-sided circuit-board material. This was found to be necessary to ensure that 22-MHz LO energy does not find its way into the amplifier stages. It was expected that a 1-inch-high shield around the LO would provide sufficient isolation — this is not the case; a complete enclosure is required. It is recommended that a shield enclosure be constructed around the remaining portion of the low-level section. This will prevent feedback from the power-amplifier board to the class-A stages. It was not necessary to do this in the prototype shown in the photographs, but is good practice when the two boards are mounted in the same enclosure (such as an aluminum chassis).

The power-amplifier board is constructed on a printed board (Fig. 38). It is

Fig. 37 — Schematic diagram of the 6-meter transmitting converter.

C2, C3, C5-C7, incl. — 2- to 25-pF air or foil-
  dielectric trimmer.
C8, C9, C11 — 15-115 pF mica trimmer (Arco
  406 or equiv.)
C10 — 1.5- to 20-pF mica trimmer (Arco 402 or

equiv.)
FB — Ferrite bead, Amidon FB101-43.
L1, L2 — 7 turns, no. 28 enamel on T25-6 core.
L3-L5, incl. — 12 turns, no. 28 enamel on
  T37-6 core.

L6 — 6½ turns, no. 26 enamel on T37-12 core.
L7 — 9½ turns, no. 22 enamel on T50-12 core.
L8, L10 — 8 turns, no. 22 enamel on T50-12
  core.
L9 — 8 turns, no. 22 enamel on T50-12 core.

not necessary that the board be etched. The
layout shown can be used as a guide and
the copper clad cut away with a sharp
X-acto® knife. After cutting through the
copper with the knife, applying heat from
a soldering iron allows the foil to be lifted
off easily. The heat sink for the MRF476
is made from a 3½ × 1-inch strip of
1/16-inch aluminum folded into a U shape.
Use a small amount of heat-sink compound
between the transistor body and the heat

sink. The MRF476, unlike many RF transistors, has the collector connected to the
mounting tab; thus the heat sink is hot for
both RF and dc. The center pin of the transistor is also connected to the collector, but
it is not used. Connection to the collector
is made through the mounting tab. The
unused pin should be cut off at the point
where it becomes wider (about 1/8 inch
from the transistor body). The other pins
are bent down to make connection to the

circuit board at this same point. Connection between the two boards can be made
with a short length of RG-174 coaxial
cable.

Tune-Up and Operation

The low-level stages are aligned before
connecting the power-amplifier stage. A
50-ohm resistor is connected through the
0.01-μF blocking capacitor to the output of
the last class-A amplifier and 12 volts is ap-

BAND-PASS FILTER

* HEAT SINK

Compress winding to cover half of core.
R1 — 220-ohm, 1-W resistor in series with a
   500-ohm, ½-W trimmer.
RFC1 — 10-µH solenoid type RF choke (Miller
   74F105AP or equiv.).
RFC2 — 1.2-µH solenoid type RF choke (Miller

74F126AP or equiv.).
T1 — 27 turns primary, 5 turns secondary,
   no. 28 enamel on T37-6 core.
T2 — 5 bifilar turns, no. 26 enamel on FT37-61
   core.

T3 — 7 bifilar turns, no. 28 enamel on FT23-43
   core.
T4, T5 — 5 bifilar turns, no. 26 enamel on
   FT37-61 core.
U1 — Mini-Circuits SRA-1 doubly balanced
   mixer.

plied to the oscillator and class-A amplifiers. The oscillator is adjusted by setting C2 at mid-range. Next, C3 is tuned for maximum output as measured with a VTVM and RF probe connected to pin 8 of the mixer. C2 can then be adjusted to bring the frequency to exactly 22 MHz. If a frequency counter with a high-impedance input is used, it should be connected to pin 8 of the mixer. If the counter has a 50-ohm input it can be connected to J1.

The adjustment of C2 and C3 will interact so the procedure should be repeated. J1 should always be connected to a load close to 50 ohms. If a receive converter is not being used, a 50-ohm resistor, mounted in a BNC connector, should be connected to J1.

The band-pass filter is aligned by applying a 28.7-MHz CW signal to the input of the converter and adjusting C5, C6 and C7 for maximum output at the output of the

last amplifier. Check the frequency response of the filter by varying the frequency of the input signal from 28 to 29 MHz. The output power should not vary more than 1 dB within the passband of the filter. The 50-ohm resistor at the output of the last class-A amplifier should now be removed and the power amplifier connected through a short length of coaxial cable.

To align the input and output networks

Fig. 38 — Parts-placement guide for the 6-meter transmitting converter. All components mount on the foil side of the board. A full-size etching pattern can be found at the back of this book.

(A) (B) (C)

Fig. 39 — Spectral analysis of 6-meter transmitting converter. Display at A shows the fundamental and second harmonic. The harmonic is 73 dB below the 3-watt carrier. The fundamental has been notched 30 dB to prevent overload of the spectrum analyzer. Each horizontal division is 20 MHz. A close-in display is shown in B: Each horizontal division is 2 MHz and the center frequency is 50 MHz. The 2 × 28-MHz spurious product (which falls in channel 2) is attenuated more than 75 dB relative to the carrier power. The two-tone IMD spectrum is shown in C; the third-order products are 34 dB below PEP. Each horizontal division is 2 kHz. In all three displays each vertical division is 10 dB.

of the final, connect the amplifier output to a wattmeter and 50-ohm load. Attach the amplifier to a 12-volt, 1-A power supply (maximum current drain is approximately 750 mA for the complete converter) and place a milliammeter in the collector supply line at the point marked × in Fig. 37. With no drive applied, turn on the dc power and adjust R1 for a collector current of 35 to 40 mA. Apply just enough 29-MHz drive to the input of the converter to get an indication on the wattmeter and peak C8 through C11 for maximum output. Now increase the drive slowly, keeping the networks peaked, until the output power is 4 watts. Do not maintain the output at 4 watts any longer than is necessary. It is important that the output network be adjusted while the output is at the 3.5- to 4-watt level. If it is adjusted at a lower level the IMD performance will be degraded. When the output is adjusted as described above, the third-order IMD products should be at least 32 dB below the 3-watt-PEP level (Fig. 39C).

Linear Transverters for 144 and 220 MHz

The CW and SSB portions of the 144- and 220-MHz bands have swelled with activity during the past few years. Although there is plenty of commercially made CW and SSB gear for 144 MHz, there is little available for 220. Paul Drexler, WB3JYO, designed and built the linear transverters described here and shown in Figs. 40 through 62. These projects enable the use of a standard 28-MHz transceiver as a tunable IF for 144- or 220-MHz operation. Construction is less complicated than building a complete transceiver, and all of the good features of the HF rig (such as a clean SSB source, stable VFO and good crystal filters) are incorporated. Chapters 11 and 12 contain additional information on transverter theory. Although these transverters may be tuned for any segment of operation, they were designed mainly to cover the lower portion of each band (144 to 145 MHz and 220 to 221 MHz). A 12-V power supply and an antenna are the only other equipment necessary to complete the VHF station.

The complete transverter design includes a minimum of hard-to-find components and should be easily reproducible. Although the text and illustrations center around the 220-MHz transverter, component values are given for the 144-MHz unit as well. Except for the local oscillator (LO), all circuits are common to both designs.

The receive converter has a 0.6-dB noise figure and an overall conversion gain of 28 dB. These figures were verified on an HP8970A noise-figure meter with an HP346A noise source. Transmit-converter power output is a conservative 1 W under linear operation. The companion amplifier produces 8 to 10 W of linear output power. Much care was taken to make the transmit chain as clean as possible, and the receive converter incorporates techniques to maximize sensitivity and dynamic range.

CIRCUIT DESCRIPTION

Fig. 41 shows the transverter block diagram. The main difference between the 144- and 220-MHz versions is the LO. Although transceive operation is depicted, the experimenter may choose to limit construction to either transmit only or receive only. LO energy is injected into a high-level (+17 dBm) doubly balanced mixer during receive. Received signals are amplified by a GaAsFET preamplifier and then filtered before entering the mixer. The 28-MHz

Fig. 40 — The 144- or 220-MHz transverter is built using a modular circuit approach. Each circuit is boxed and mounted on a chassis with interconnections of short lengths of 50-ohm coaxial cable.

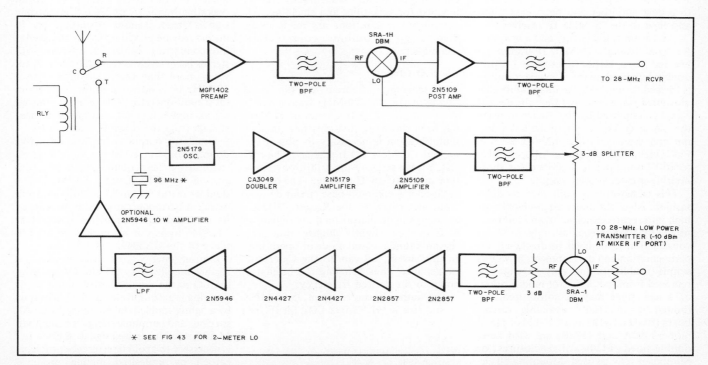

Fig. 41 — Block diagram of the 144- and 220-MHz transverters. All blocks but the local oscillator are common to both bands.

Fig. 42 — Schematic diagram of the 192-MHz local oscillator. All resistors are ¼-W carbon-composition types unless otherwise noted. Capacitors are silver-mica or miniature monolithic ceramic types unless otherwise noted. Capacitors marked with polarity are electrolytic.

C1 — 25-pF (max.) miniature ceramic trimmer.
C2, C3, C4 — 9-pF (max.) miniature ceramic trimmer.
C5, C7 — 10-pF (max.) ceramic piston trimmer or miniature ceramic trimmer.
C6 — 0.5-pF ceramic chip or gimmick capacitor. See text.

J1, J2 — Chassis-mount female BNC connector.
L1 — 10t no. 24 enam., 0.100-inch ID, close wound.
L2 — 15t no. 28 enam. on T25-6 toroid core.
L3, L4 — 5t no. 24 enam., 0.125-inch ID, close wound.

L5 — 4t no. 24 enam., 0.125-inch ID, close wound.
L6, L7 — 5t no. 18 tinned, 0.250-inch ID, spaced one wire dia. Tap at 1t from ground.
Q2 — RCA CA3049 transistor array. CA3054 or Motorola MC3346 are acceptable substitutes.
RFC1-RFC4 — 2.2-µH molded miniature RF

signal at the output port of the mixer is sent to a post amplifier and band-pass filter, and then to the 28-MHz IF receiver.

On transmit, LO energy and a low-level RF signal from the 28-MHz IF transceiver are fed to a standard-level (+7 dBm) doubly balanced mixer. The mixer output is filtered to eliminate the image and other unwanted responses, and then the desired signal is amplified by five stages to reach the 1-W level. The output of the 1-W transmit converter is further filtered to meet FCC rules and regulations. An optional 8- to 10-W amplifier is described for those desiring greater power output.

This transverter is built in a modular fashion. All of the major circuit blocks are built into separate enclosures and interconnected by 50-ohm coaxial cable. Modular construction lends itself to on-the-air experimentation and development, as well as simple troubleshooting. Any stage may be removed from the circuit for modification, or a new stage may be substituted. Although commercially available diecast boxes (BUD CU-123 and CU-124 or Hammond 1590A and 1590B) are used here, double-sided PC-board enclosures or Miniboxes may be used. Mounting all circuits in individual boxes is highly recommended for versatility and shielding. All component connections are made using direct, point-to-point construction techniques.

Local Oscillator

A schematic diagram of the local oscillator for the 220-MHz transverter is shown in Fig. 42. A frequency of 96 MHz has been chosen so that only one stage of multiplication is necessary to obtain the needed 192-MHz LO frequency. The crystal, Y1, is a series-resonant, fifth-overtone type in an HC-18/U package. The oscillator used is a common-base circuit derived from an article by Joe Reisert, W1JR.[1] Most crystal oscillators tend to oscillate at a frequency slightly higher than the crystal's fundamental mode of operation. In this circuit, L2 cancels the C_o crystal capacitance, thus bringing the oscillator down to the desired frequency.

The author chose to use a 95.95-MHz crystal (for a 191.9-MHz LO); an IF fre-

quency of 28.1 MHz corresponds to an operating frequency of 220.0 MHz. Strong signals from stations operating on 10 meters may be picked up by the transverter interconnecting cables, interfering with signals being received from 220 MHz. Also, when more than one transverter with a 28-MHz IF is operated in the same room (at a multioperator VHF contest station, for example), it is not uncommon to hear signals from the other IF transceivers.

Oscillator output is fed into an active doubler constructed with a CA3049 transistor array. This circuit is based on a suggestion by Bill Strunk, K3ZMA. The doubler features as much as 7-dB gain and excellent harmonic suppression because of its balanced input circuit. A CA3054 or MC3346 transistor array may be used in place of the CA3049.

Output energy from the doubler is further amplified by Q3 and Q4 to bring the LO to the required mixer input level. Filtering is accomplished at the LO output by a lightly coupled double-tuned filter. All spurious and harmonic energy is better than 55 dB below the desired signal. A clean LO is necessary to avoid interference problems caused by undesired mixing products

[1]Reisert, Joe, "VHF/UHF Receivers," Ham Radio, March 1984, pp. 42-46.

choke.

T1 — 7t no. 30 enam., trifilar wound on T25-12 core or Mini-Circuits T4-1 transformer. See text.

U1 — Three-terminal voltage regulator, 8 V, 100 mA (LM78L08 or equiv.).

Y1 — Fifth-overtone, 96-MHz series-resonant crystal, HC-18/U holder.

during receive and transmit.

After the filter, a resistive power divider is used to drive the transmit and receive mixers. Resistive pads attenuate the LO signal to the proper level while providing a 50-Ω impedance for the mixer input.

Although a similar lineup could be employed for 144 MHz, a three-stage 116-MHz oscillator is shown schematically in Fig. 43. The 144-MHz transverter uses a 116-MHz series-resonant crystal (Y1) to avoid frequency multipliers. Oscillator output is amplified by Q2 and Q3 until it reaches the level necessary to drive both the transmit and receive mixers. LO output is filtered by a double-tuned band-pass filter. After the filter, a resistive power divider is used to drive the transmit and receive mixers; again, pads attenuate the signal to the proper level.

With the filters properly adjusted, all spurious outputs from the LO are about 58 dB below the fundamental. Fig. 44 shows the spectral output from the LO receive port.

Receive Converter

The 144- and 220-MHz receive converters are identical, except for the tuned

circuits in the front end. In each case, the converter consists of a GaAsFET preamplifier, a mixer/diplexer circuit and an optional 28-MHz post amplifier. The mixer/diplexer and post amplifier circuits are the same, regardless of band. Each of the three receive converter blocks is built into a separate module. This was done to facilitate experimentation and development of each stage. Of course, it is possible to build all three circuits in one box. This subject will be addressed in the construction portion of this article.

Mixer

The heart of the receive converter is a Mini-Circuits SRA-1H high-level, doubly balanced mixer (DBM). See Fig. 45. This mixer requires an LO injection level of + 17 dBm, compared with the + 7 dBm injection level required for standard mixers. The high-level mixer offers superior strong-signal handling characteristics while maintaining the port-to-port isolation, image suppression and simplicity inherent in a DBM. The SRA-1H is modestly priced and available in small quantities directly from the manufacturer.

Reactive terminations can ruin the excellent IMD characteristics of a DBM.[2,3] The IF port, in particular, is most sensitive to a nonresistive 50-ohm termination. Anything short of a 20-dB resistive pad at the IF port will result in increased IMD products and a lower third-order-intercept point. Feeding the output of a DBM directly into a narrowband amplifier will decrease the mixer's third-order intercept point as compared to a purely resistive termination. The diplexer circuit shown in Fig. 45 represents one solution to the problem of proper mixer termination. The diplexer's low-pass response presents a 20-dB return loss at 28 MHz and terminates higher frequencies into 50 ohms.

RF Preamplifier

A low-noise, high-dynamic-range GaAsFET preamplifier is used in front of the mixer to overcome mixer conversion loss. The GaAsFET device offers exceptional performance, compared with most bipolars and MOSFETs, and designs abound.[4,5] The circuit in Fig. 46 has proven reliable during many hours of on-the-air operation. This simple design offers a noise figure of 0.4 dB, as measured on an HP8970A noise-figure meter with the HP346A noise source. This noise figure is much lower than the feed line loss preceding the preamplifier; performance is exceptional for all applications short of in-

[2] Will, Peter, "Reactive Loads — The Big Mixer Menace," *Microwaves*, April 1971, pp. 38-42.
[3] Cheadle, Dan, "Selecting Mixers for Best Intermod Performance," *Microwaves*, Nov. and Dec. 1973.
[4] Kraus, Geoff, "VHF and UHF Low Noise Preamplifiers," *QEX*, Dec. 1981, p. 3.
[5] Reisert, Joe, "Low Noise GaAsFET Technology," *Ham Radio*, Dec. 1984, pp. 99-112.

tensive EME receiving. A 30-mA bias current achieves optimum signal-handling capability. The third-order-intercept point is + 25 dBm. Gain is 24 dB.

The double-tuned filter between the preamp and mixer provides a reasonable degree of filtering. A trap (L2) is used to attenuate the 164-MHz (188 MHz for the 2-meter version) image. Fig. 47A shows the swept frequency response of the 220-MHz version. A comb line or helical filter might be used if greater selectivity is required.

28-MHz Post Amplifier

For most amateur applications, a 28-MHz post amplifier is not necessary. It serves to amplify the 28-MHz IF signal to increase S-meter readings. The author lives among several of the "big gun" VHF stations in southeastern Pennsylvania, so high dynamic range is essential to avoid overload problems. The receive converter operates nicely without any post amplification, thereby preserving the IF receiver's dynamic range.

The 28-MHz post amplifier shown in Fig. 48 has been included here for those operators fortunate enough to live away from strong in-band signals. The 2N5109 is readily available and provides good performance at low cost. In this circuit, the device is biased to provide 13-dB gain with a third-order-intercept point of + 26 dBm. The design features a tuned input circuit and a broadband output transformer. A double-tuned band-pass filter at the output assures a clean signal for the IF receiver. Fig. 47B shows the swept frequency response of the post amplifier.

If you live in an area with loud local signals, yet want to use a post amplifier, a pad may be used between the post amplifier and the IF receiver to reduce the converter gain to a level that the IF receiver can handle. The value of attenuation will depend on the IF receiver's ability to handle large signals. When you first connect the receive converter to the IF receiver, you will probably notice that the S-meter on the receiver moves up to S3 or higher (a lot depends on the nature of your specific receiver), even with no signals present. To determine the right pad value for your application, place a variable step attenuator in the line between post amp and IF receiver and increase the attenuation until the IF receiver S-meter is just above zero. If you want to leave the step attenuator in the line, fine. If not, you can build a pad with the correct value from the attenuator tables given in Chapter 25 of this *Handbook*.

Transmit Converter

A schematic diagram for the 1-W transmit converter is shown in Fig. 49. The 192-MHz LO (116-MHz LO for the 144-MHz version) and 28-MHz signals are mixed in a Mini-Circuits SRA-1 standard-level DBM. A pad is necessary to limit the 28-MHz input to a maximum level of − 10 dBm, ensuring good linearity and

Fig. 43 — Schematic diagram of the 116-MHz local oscillator for the 2-meter transverter. All resistors are ¼-W, carbon-composition types unless otherwise noted. Capacitors are silver-mica or miniature monolithic ceramic types unless otherwise noted. Capacitors marked with polarity are electrolytic.

C1 — 25-pF (max.) miniature ceramic trimmer.
C2, C3 — 15-pF (max.) miniature ceramic trimmer.
C4, C5 — 10-pF (max.) ceramic piston trimmer or miniature ceramic trimmer.
C6 — 0.5-pF ceramic chip or gimmick capacitor. See text.

J1, J2 — Chassis-mount female BNC connector.
L1 — 8t no. 24 enam., 0.100-inch ID, close wound.
L2 — 13t no. 28 enam. on T25-6 toroid core.
L3, L4 — 7t no. 24 enam., 0.125-inch ID, close wound.
L5, L6 — 8t no. 18 tinned, 0.250-inch ID,

spaced one wire dia. Tap at 1t from ground.
RFC1-RFC3 — 2.7-μH molded miniature RF choke.
U1 — Three-terminal voltage regulator, 8 V, 100 mA (LM78L08 or equiv.).
Y1 — Fifth-overtone, 116-MHz series-resonant crystal, HC-18/U holder.

spectral purity. No parts values are shown for the IF pad; the exact resistor values will depend on the amount of 28-MHz drive available from the transverter output of your IF transceiver. For example, if your IF rig delivers 20 mW (+13 dBm) at the transverter output, you would need to build a 23-dB pad. See Chapter 25 for tables listing resistor values for different levels of attenuation.

Mixer output is fed through a resistive pad for proper termination, and then filtered by a double-tuned band-pass filter to reduce the image and other undesired mixing products. Two 2N2857 amplifier stages follow the filter, followed by two 2N4427 stages. The final amplifier stage is a 2N5946. All stages are biased for linear operation. The 2N5946 may be substituted with a lower-power 2N5945 or 2N5944 device; if you substitute, you may have to alter the input and output matching, as well as the bias circuit. A 7-element Chebyshev low-pass filter (Fig. 50) follows the 2N5946. Swept filter response is shown in Fig. 51B. The output is exceptionally clean; a spec-

tral plot is shown in Fig. 51A.

Although some designers may question the use of five stages to achieve 1-watt output, there are several good reasons for doing so. This transmit converter is rated

Fig. 44 — Spectral output of the 192-MHz LO receive port. All harmonic and spurious outputs are at least 58 dB below peak fundamental output.

for conservative operation at a healthy, filtered 1-W output. It is not "almost" a watt, like some four-stage designs. All stages are run below their maximum possible output level, ensuring clean, linear

Fig. 45 — Schematic diagram of the receive mixer and diplexer filter. Capacitors are silver-mica. Resistors are ¼-W carbon-composition types.

J1-J3 — Chassis-mount female BNC connector.
L1 — 0.35 µH; 6t no. 24 enam. on T50-6 toroid core.
L2 — 0.205 µH; 5t no. 24 enam. on T50-6 toroid core.
L3 — 0.18 µH; 5t no. 24 enam. on T37-6 toroid core.
U1 — Mini-Circuits SRA-1H high-level, doubly balanced mixer. Available directly from the manufacturer. See text.

Fig. 47 — Swept response of the 220-MHz preamplifier (A) and the 28-MHz post amplifier (B). The image filter at the output of the 220-MHz preamplifier produces a deep null at 164 MHz.

Fig. 46 — Schematic diagram of the 144- or 220-MHz GaAsFET preamplifier. All resistors are ¼-W carbon composition types unless otherwise noted. Capacitors are silver-mica or miniature monolithic ceramic types unless otherwise noted. Capacitors marked with polarity are electrolytic.

C1, C2, C5, C7 — 10-pF (max.) ceramic piston trimmer or miniature ceramic trimmer.
C3, C4 — 500-pF ceramic chip capacitor.
C6 — 0.3 to 3 pF ceramic piston trimmer.
J1, J2 — Chassis-mount female BNC connector.
L1 — 220 MHz: 3t no. 18 enam., 0.250-inch ID, close wound. 144 MHz: 5t.
L2 — 220 MHz: 13t no. 24 enam. on T44-10 toroid core; 144 MHz: 27t no. 26 enam. on T37-10 toroid core.

L3, L4 — 220 MHz: 5t no. 18 tinned wire, 0.250-inch ID, spaced one wire dia. Tap at 1t from ground. 144 MHz: same as 220 MHz, except coil is 7t.
Q1 — Single-gate GaAsFET, MGF1402.
RFC1 — 68-µH molded miniature RF choke.
T1 — 4t no. 28 enam. bifilar wound on T25-12 toroid core.
U1 — Three-terminal voltage regulator, 5 V, 100 mA (LM78L05 or equiv.).

Fig. 48 — Schematic diagram of the 28-MHz post amplifier. All resistors are ¼-W carbon-composition types unless otherwise noted. Capacitors are silver-mica or miniature monolithic ceramic types unless otherwise noted. Capacitors marked with polarity are electrolytic.

C1, C2, C3 — 15-pF (max.) miniature ceramic trimmer.
J1, J2 — Chassis-mount female BNC connector.
L1 — 12t no. 26 enam. on T37-6 toroid core.

L2, L3 — 15t no. 26 enam. on T37-6 toroid core. Tap at 4t from ground.
RFC1 — 10-µH miniature molded RF choke.
T1 — 20t no. 30 enam. bifilar wound on T37-10 toroid core.

Fig. 49 — Schematic diagram of the 144- and 220-MHz transmit converter. All resistors are ¼-W carbon-composition types unless otherwise noted. Capacitors are silver-mica or miniature monolithic ceramic types unless otherwise noted. Capacitors marked with polarity are electrolytic.

C1, C3, C5, C6, C7 — Miniature ceramic trimmer, 220 MHz: 8 pF (max.); 144 MHz: 25 pF (max.).

C2 — Silver-mica capacitor, 220 MHz: 2 pF; 144 MHz: 3 pF.

C4 — Silver-mica capacitor, 220 MHz: 3 pF; 144 MHz: 5 pF.

C8 — Miniature ceramic trimmer, 220 MHz:

15 pF (max.); 144 MHz: 25 pF (max.).

C9, C10 — 25-pF (max.) miniature ceramic trimmer (same for both bands).

C11, C12 — Ceramic piston trimmer or miniature ceramic trimmer, 220 MHz: 10 pF (max.); 144 MHz: 25 pF (max.).

J1-J3 — Chassis-mount female BNC connector.

L1, L2 — 220 MHz: 4t no. 20 tinned, 0.250-inch ID, spaced one wire dia. Tap at 1t from ground. 144 MHz: Same as 220 MHz except coil is 6t.

L3, L4, L5 — 220 MHz: 3t no. 20 tinned, 0.250-inch ID, spaced one wire dia. 144 MHz: Same as 220 MHz except coil is 5t.

L6 — 220 MHz: 1t no. 20 tinned, 0.250-inch ID.

Fig. 50 — Schematic diagram of 7-element Chebyshev low-pass filter. Capacitors are silver-mica types.

C1, C3 — 220 MHz: 15 pF; 144 MHz: 27 pF.
C2 — 220 MHz: 18 pF; 144 MHz: 30 pF.
L1, L4 — 220 MHz: 3t no. 22 enam., 3/16-inch ID, close wound; 144 MHz also 3t.
L2, L3 — 220 MHz: 4t no. 22 enam., 3/16-inch ID, close wound; 144 MHz: 5t.

operation. The gain from the extra stage also allows the use of the filters after the mixer and at the output. The author lives in an area where the VHF bands are congested, so clean, linear operation is a must for sound relations with other amateurs sharing the band.

Power Amplifier

An optional 8- to 10-W linear power amplifier is shown schematically in Fig. 52. This amplifier uses another 2N5946 transistor. The design is relatively simple. Input matching is accomplished by C1, C2 and L1. L2, C3 and C4 match the output. The only differences between the 220-MHz and 144-MHz versions are the values of L1 and L2.

The bias circuit, suggested by Dave Mascaro, WA3JUF, uses an LM317 adjustable regulator to provide a stiff bias supply. The LM317 circuit is capable of providing 30- to 40-mA of stable bias current.

Switching

Fig. 53 is a schematic diagram of the transverter switching circuitry. K1 is used to switch power to the transverter modules in transmit and receive. When the trans-

Fig. 51 — The plot at A shows the spectral output of the 1-W, 220-MHz transmit converter after filtering. All harmonics and spurious emissions are at least 60 dB below the fundamental output. This transmit converter meets current FCC spectral-purity specifications. The plot at B is the swept frequency response of the low-pass filter shown in Fig. 50.

144 MHz: 2t no. 20 tinned, 0.250-inch ID, spaced one wire dia.
L7 — 220 MHz: 1t no. 20 tinned, 0.250-inch ID. 144 MHz: 3t no. 20 tinned, 0.250-inch ID, spaced one wire dia.
L8 — 220 MHz: 6t no. 20 enam., 0.250-inch ID, close wound. 144 MHz: Same as 220 MHz except coil is 8t.
L9, L10 — 15 t no. 22 enam. on T44-10 toroid

core (same for both bands).
R1 — Start with 68-ohm, 2-W resistor; vary for proper bias. See text.
RFC1-RFC4 — 220 MHz: 1.8-μH miniature molded RF choke; 144 MHz: 2.2-μH miniature molded RFC.
U1 — Mini-Circuits SRA-1 standard level, doubly balanced mixer. Available directly from the manufacturer. See text.

verter is powered on, 12.5-V dc is applied directly to the LO and through K1 to the VHF preamplifier and 28-MHz post amplifier. When J2 is closed, K1 removes power from the preamplifier and post amplifier and applies 12.5-V dc to the transmit converter and power amplifier. The LO, used for transmit and receive, is always on.

When J2 is closed, K2 is also energized. K2, an RF relay, switches the antenna between the VHF preamplifier input and the power amplifier output. Relays of this type are generally available at flea markets at modest prices. Since most HF transceivers have separate transverter input and output connections, no relay switching for the IF rig is included. The transmit converter IF input is connected directly to the transverter output on the HF transceiver, while the post amplifier output is connected directly to the transverter input on the HF transceiver.

Relays with 26-V dc coils were used here

since most surplus coaxial relays require this voltage. While relays with any coil voltage could be used, it is a good idea to run relays and electronics from separate power supplies to avoid possible problems caused by voltage transients that occur when the relay coils are switched. The diode and capacitor connected across the relay coil power line help to alleviate transients.

CONSTRUCTION TECHNIQUES

Although this project is not intended for a first-time effort, anyone having a reasonable amount of VHF construction experience should encounter no difficulty. As with all VHF circuits, a certain amount of construction care is required.

Proper grounding techniques, RF bypassing and shielding will ensure stable operation. Feedthrough grounding is used to provide a low-inductance ground return to both sides of the PC board. Basically, this means drilling a hole through the PC

board at key points where components must have a good RF ground and installing a rivet or piece of no. 20 tinned wire soldered to both sides of the board. See Fig. 54. Check the schematic diagrams for each circuit and install ground feed-throughs accordingly.

High-quality, low-inductance capacitors ensure a good RF bypass. Ceramic chip capacitors work best. These can be expensive, however, so they are used only where absolutely necessary. Epoxy encapsulated, miniature, monolithic ceramic capacitors work quite well as bypass capacitors.

Tight shielding between the input and output of each stage of the transmit converter eliminates the likelihood of feedback. Shielding was only found necessary on the transmit converter.

The variable capacitors used in each stage are miniature ceramic or piston trimmers. The value of these capacitors is not critical as long as you use capacitors with maximum values close to those specified in the schematic diagram. For example, there are many capacitors available with a range from 2 to 8 pF or 2 to 12 pF. Any of these will work fine in circuits that call for 9- or 10-pF-maximum variables. Ceramic piston trimmers are most convenient for building the double-tuned band-pass filters. Johan-

Fig. 52 — Schematic diagram of the 8- to 10-W power amplifier. Capacitors are monolithic ceramic types unless otherwise noted. Capacitors marked with polarity are electrolytic.

C1, C4 — 10-100 pF mica trimmer (Arco 406 or equiv.).
C2, C3 — 5-75 pF mica trimmer (Arco 405 or equiv.).
C5 — 51 pF metal-clad book-mica capacitor. See text.
C6, C7 — 1000 pF metal-clad book-mica capacitor. See text.
J1, J2 — Chassis-mount female BNC connector.
L1 — 220 MHz: ½t no. 20 tinned, 0.250-inch ID ("hairpin loop"); 144 MHz: 1t no. 20 tinned,

0.250-inch ID.
L2 — 220 MHz: 1t no. 20 tinned, 0.250-inch ID; 144 MHz: 2t no. 20 tinned, 0.250-inch ID, spaced one wire dia.
L3 — VK-200 wideband RF choke.
L4 — 8t no. 20 enam., 0.250-inch ID, close wound.
Q1 — 2N5946 or Thompson-CSF SD1160 RF power transistor.
U1 — Three-terminal adjustable voltage regulator, 1 A (LM317 or equiv.).

Fig. 53 — Schematic diagram of the transverter switching arrangement.

J1, J2 — Chassis-mount female Cinch-Jones power plug.
J3 — Chassis-mount phono jack.
K1 — DPDT power relay, 3-A contacts, 26-V dc

coil.
K2 — SPDT coaxial antenna changeover relay, BNC connectors, 26-V dc coil.
S1 — SPDT switch, 5-A contacts.

son, Trimtronics or Voltronics all manufacture 8- to 10-pF maximum piston trimmers suitable for these filters.

"Dead bug" layout is best suited for VHF/UHF construction. As shown in the accompanying photographs, components are supported by their leads above the

ground plane. In most cases, component leads are soldered directly to the leads of other components, keeping the length of each interconnection to a minimum. A low-inductance RF ground is achieved since the component leads are soldered directly to the ground plane. This construction

Fig. 54 — Detail of the feedthrough grounding used to achieve a good RF ground. See text for details.

method eliminates the need for designing an etched PC board, a task not easily accomplished at VHF and above.

Each circuit, or "module," is built on a piece of double-sided circuit board stock and mounted in a separate metal enclosure. In the transverter shown in the photographs, each module is built into a small Hammond 1590 series diecast box. In each case, the box cover has been discarded. The circuit board holding the components has been shaped to fit the box tightly in place of the cover. Each module has BNC connectors for RF input and output. Voltage is supplied through a feedthrough capacitor. The result is an RF-tight enclosure for each part of the circuit. Since the 1-W transmit converter board is large, and a suitable diecast box is expensive, the transmit converter is mounted under the chassis that supports the rest of the modules.

Finding Parts

These days, it is becoming increasingly difficult to find parts. This transverter makes use of parts available from a number of sources. The parts suppliers table in Chapter 35 lists many possible sources, and still others advertise in *QST* and other amateur magazines. Some parts sources are listed below. You can find addresses and other information in Chapter 35 for companies that are listed by name only here. This list is by no means complete; these are sources that the author knows of that will sell to individuals in small quantities.

- Advanced Receiver Research, Box 1242, Burlington, CT 06013 (MGF1402 GaAsFETs)
- Amidon Associates (toroid cores, ferrite beads, VK-200 chokes)
- Applied Invention (piston trimmers, chip caps)
- MHz Electronics, 3802 N. 27th Ave., Phoenix, AZ 85017 (transistors, book-mica capacitors)
- Microwave Components of Michigan (trimmers, piston trimmers, GaAsFETs, chip caps, feedthrough caps, diecast boxes)
- Mini-Circuits, P.O. Box 166, Brooklyn, NY 11235 (mixers, T1 in 192-MHz LO)
- Mouser Electronics (resistors, capacitors, ceramic trimmers, molded RF chokes, diecast boxes)
- Radiokit (toroid cores, ferrite beads, Arco variables, diecast boxes)

• R.F. Gain, Ltd. (transistors)

Local Oscillator

Build the local oscillator first; you'll need LO energy to test most of the other stages. Before soldering anything, gather all of the necessary components and lay them out on the board in order to plan adequate room before constructing. Follow the schematic diagram and refer to Fig. 55 for an idea of how to lay out the board. Although the 192-MHz LO for the 220-MHz transverter is shown, layout is similar for the 116-MHz version.

Once the general layout scheme has been achieved, the components may be soldered together, beginning with Q1. Keep component leads short, but leave enough room so that you can change components if necessary. Make sure that the leads of Y1 are as short as possible and that the crystal will not touch the box that the LO will be installed in. A dab of silicone sealant will hold the crystal in place.

Q1, Q2 and Q3 are mounted "belly up" with their leads sticking into the air. Note that Q1 and Q3 have a lead that is connected to the case. Solder this lead to ground. The collector of Q4 is tied to the case, so it is mounted with the leads facing the ground plane. Make sure that the case of Q4 does not touch the ground plane or other components.

Dc power for the LO enters the case through a feedthrough capacitor. Miniature molded RF chokes and bypass capacitors decouple the power line at each stage. In Fig. 55, these RFCs and capacitors are arranged in a horizontal line that traverses the top of the board. Q1 is powered through an 8-V, three-terminal regulator IC. Mount the associated bypass capacitors as close to the IC body as possible.

Q2 has several unused sections. Cut off all unused leads before soldering it into the circuit. T1 is a trifilar-wound transformer on a T25-12 toroid core. See Fig. 56 for details. Although the transformer used here was wound by hand, a Mini-Circuits model T4-1 may also be used.

The output filter uses two ceramic piston trimmer capacitors mounted through the circuit board. These piston trimmers make it convenient to mount L6 and L7; common ceramic trimmers like those used in the rest of the circuit will also work here. A shield made from a piece of double-sided circuit-board material separates L6 and L7, eliminating overcoupling and ensuring a "clean" filter response. Although a 0.5-pF ceramic chip capacitor was used to couple the two filter sections, a ¼-inch-long gimmick capacitor made from two pieces of no. 28 enameled wire twisted tightly together will work here.

One of the advantages of dead bug construction — one that you should take advantage of — is that each stage can be tested individually. After you build the basic oscillator (Q1 and associated components), you can test for 96 (or 116) MHz

Fig. 55 — The 192-MHz local oscillator is laid out in the order it is drawn on the schematic diagram. Q1 is at the far left; Q4 is near the center of the board. The band-pass filter is at the right, next to J1 and J2. The resistors used for the power divider and pad are soldered into the circuit with virtually no lead length.

Fig. 56 — Winding details for T1 in the 192-MHz LO. Label one end of three 5-inch pieces of enameled wire as shown. Holding all three wires flat, in parallel, begin threading the toroid starting with the unlabeled end of the three wires. Carefully wind the toroid by feeding the entire group of wires in parallel. Once seven turns have been wound, use an ohmmeter to trace the unlabeled ends. Label the end of wire A by A', and so on. After the windings have been properly labeled, connect T1 as shown.

Fig. 57 — Closeup of the VHF RF preamplifier. The input components at the left of the board are mounted with as little lead length as possible, to minimize losses.

output by capacitively coupling into a receiver or spectrum analyzer from the 50-ohm pad at the output of the stage. When you are sure Q1 is working, build the next stage and test it. Proceed alternately building and testing each stage until you reach the final output stage.

When all of the LO stages are complete, check the operating frequency with a counter or spectrum analyzer. Tune each stage for maximum output. Tuning is somewhat interactive, so recheck each stage after you have done the initial tuneup. Each variable capacitor should have a definite peak. If you have a method of checking low power levels, check the output at the receive and transmit ports. Power output should be as indicated on the drawings.

All other stages are constructed in a like manner. Lay the board out in advance; start at the input and work toward the output. Test each stage after you build it, and fix any problems before continuing to the next stage.

Preamplifier

The GaAsFET transistor requires special handling care because it is especially sensitive to static electricity. Solder the transistor into the circuit last; use a grounded-tip, low-temperature soldering iron. If a static-free work station is unavailable, ground yourself before removing the MGF1402 from its protective package to prevent static buildup from destroying the device.

Although an MGF1402 is specified, you can use other devices if you change the biasing resistors accordingly. Consult the references listed at the end of this project writeup before attempting a substitution. The MGF1402 is a fairly common transistor and is available from several of the suppliers listed in Chapter 35.

The general layout is shown in Fig. 57. Although BNC connectors were used here, Type-N or SMA connectors may be employed. A number of ground feedthroughs are used at points indicated on the schematic diagram. These feedthroughs are necessary for stable operation and optimum performance; they must be used. See Fig. 54.

Ceramic chip capacitors are mandatory for the source bypass on the MGF1402. Do not attempt to substitute low-grade capacitors here! Chip capacitors provide a low-impedance source ground; this is of particular importance for stable operation with high-gain devices such as the microwave GaAsFET used here. The MGF1402 is mounted directly to the source bypass capacitors by its source leads. First, solder one end of each chip capacitor to the ground plane. Then solder one source lead to each chip capacitor. See the preamplifier projects that appear earlier in this chapter for complete details of this mounting scheme.

The output filter is similar to the one described in the local-oscillator section. In

Fig. 58 — Closeup of the 28-MHz post amplifier. Q1 uses a push-on finned heat sink. The transistor case is tied to the collector, so the heat sink must be positioned away from the case and nearby components.

Fig. 59 — Closeup of the receive mixer and diplexer filter. RG-174 cable is used between the mixer and input connectors.

this case, however, the coupling capacitor is a 0.3- to 3-pF trimmer. A toroidal coil is added for the 164-MHz image trap.

28-MHz Post Amplifier

The 2N5109 post amplifier shown in Fig. 58 requires little special care. Note, however, the use of a push-on, finned heat sink. Keep the heat sink away from the circuit board and other components since the 2N5109 case is tied to the transistor collector.

Receive Mixer

The receive mixer and diplexer filter may be housed in one enclosure, as shown in Fig. 59. The SRA-1H is best mounted on top of the circuit board with the pins protruding through to the component side. Carefully mark and drill eight holes using

a no. 59 drill bit. All holes on top of the board are deburred with a 1/8-inch drill bit; turn the bit by hand to remove the copper from around the hole. This allows for ample clearance where leads are close to touching the board. Deburr the holes for pins 1, 3, 4 and 8 on the component side of the board. The other pins are grounded and should be soldered directly to the ground plane.

Transmit Converter

Construction of the transmit converter requires a little extra planning for component layout because of the number of stages involved. Position the SRA-1 and the five transistors to allow sufficient room for the remaining components. It is better to allow extra room than to be cramped for space. Refer to Fig. 60 for ideas on board layout.

Fig. 60 — The transmit converter incorporates extensive bypassing and shielding. J1 and J2 are at the bottom left. Q1, Q2 and Q3 are arranged along the lower edge of the board, below the horizontal shield. Q4 and Q5 are above that shield; Q4 is to the right. The two emitter leads of Q5 are soldered directly to the ground plane near the center of the board. The low-pass filter is between Q5 and the output connector.

Drill any mounting holes as you go along. Start by mounting the SRA-1 using the same technique described above. Then mount J1 and J2. Build the mixer bandpass filter first, and then work stage-by-stage toward the output.

Q1, Q2 and Q3 should be shielded by placing a small piece of sheet metal or double-sided circuit-board material over each transistor. Cut a U-shaped notch in the shield to clear the transistor case. Each shield may be soldered directly to the ground plane. Q1 and Q2 are mounted "belly up," while Q3 and Q4 are mounted "right side up." Cut the Q3 and Q4 emitter lead to ¼ inch before soldering the transistor in place. Note that Q1 and Q2 have four leads; one is tied directly to the transistor case and must be soldered to the ground plane. The case of Q3, however, is connected to the collector, so be sure to leave adequate clearance between the case and the shield. Q4 must have a push-on, finned heat sink. The heat sink should not touch any other components. Again, keep all leads as short as possible.

Q5 is a stud-mounted power transistor. Drill a hole just large enough to pass the threaded stud and transistor base through the circuit board. The emitter leads should lay almost flat on the component side of the board. Cut the collector and base leads to half of the original length, while leaving the emitter leads full length. The heat sink for Q5 is made from a U-shaped piece of brass sheet (the same material used for the circuit-board shields). Mount D1 on top of the heat sink for good thermal contact;

Fig. 61 — Space is a bit tight, but the 10-W amplifier will fit inside a small diecast box. Q1 is mounted at the center of the board. Input circuitry is to the left, output to the right. U1 and associated bias circuitry are behind the shield adjacent to J1.

solder the ground end of D1 directly to the heat sink.

The value of R1 must be determined experimentally. Start with a 68-ohm, 2-W resistor. Measure the quiescent current of Q5 by inserting a milliammeter in the circuit at the cold end of L8. The quiescent current should be between 20 and 40 mA; adjust the value of R1 until proper bias is achieved.

The transmit converter is tuned by applying 12.5-V dc, LO energy and a 28-MHz signal attenuated to provide −10 dBm at the mixer input. Peak the double-tuned filter for maximum 220-MHz (or 144-MHz) output. If a spectrum analyzer is available, tune for a balance between maximum 220-MHz (or 144-MHz) energy and minimum spurious output. Next, peak C1 through C3. Alternately peak C5 and C6 for maximum output. C7, C8, C9 and C10 are adjusted in the same manner. Although a wattmeter may be used for tuning purposes, a spectrum analyzer tells the full story. Tune each stage for a compromise between output power and spectral purity.

Harmonics are 60-dB down after filtering. After you're through adjusting the transmit converter, power output should be 1 watt.

Power Amplifier

The 10-W amplifier shown in Fig. 61 is mounted in its own diecast box. Ground feedthroughs are used beneath the 2N5946 emitter leads and at all variable capacitor grounds. The LM317 regulator IC must be attached to a heat sink. Bias should be adjusted for a quiescent current of 40 to 60 mA.

C5, C6 and C7 are Unelco metal-clad book-mica capacitors. These capacitors provide an excellent low-impedance RF ground and are designed to work at high-current points. For stable operation, it is important that you use book-mica capacitors at these points.

The heat sink is fashioned from two U-shaped pieces of aluminum sheet. Be careful when mounting the heat sink; lateral pressure on the 2N5946 stud may break the transistor.

Summary

The transverter modules are arranged on a chassis as shown in Figs. 40 and 62. Short runs of 50-ohm coaxial cable interconnect the units. Most of the dc power wiring is done underneath the chassis.

The 144/220-MHz transverter represents a low-cost, modern approach to getting on the VHF bands. Circuit construction is straightforward, and the design makes use

Fig. 62 — The transmit converter is mounted in a cutout portion of the chassis, component side down. Dc for the transmit and receive chains is brought in to K1 and from there to a barrier strip. Wires are routed from the barrier strip to each module.

of commercially available parts. The modular construction approach offers flexibility for easy troubleshooting and experimentation.

The author wishes to thank Ron Whitsel, WA3AXV, and other members of the Mount Airy VHF Radio Club "Packrats"

whose encouragement made this project possible.

References
Hardy, *High Frequency Circuit Design*. Reston, VA: Reston Publishing Co., Inc., 1979.
Hayward, *Introduction to Radio Frequency Design*. Englewood Cliffs, NJ: Prentice Hall, Inc., 1982.

144- or 220-MHz Band-Pass Filter

Spectral purity is necessary during transmitting. Tight filtering in a receiving system ensures the rejection of out-of-band signals. Those unwanted signals may otherwise lead to receiver overload and increased intermodulation-distortion (IMD) products that manifest themselves as annoying in-band "birdies."

The double-tuned band-pass filter is not new. Filter designs involving this circuit abound in amateur designs because they are simple, are easy to construct, offer a relatively narrow passband and are quite forgiving of resonator variations. This filter was designed by Paul Drexler, WB3JYO.

The filter shown in Fig. 77 includes a resonant trap coupled between the resonators to provide increased rejection of undesired frequencies. Many popular VHF conversion schemes use a 28-MHz intermediate frequency (IF).

Proper filtering of the image frequency is often overlooked in amateur designs. The low-side injection frequency used in 144-MHz mixing schemes is 116 MHz and the image frequency, 88 MHz, falls in the

Fig. 78 — Frequency-response of the 144-MHz band-pass filter. Image-reject notch is for a 28-MHz IF.

Fig. 79 — Frequency-response of the 220-MHz band-pass filter. Image-reject notch is for a 28-MHz IF.

Channel 6 television band. Inadequate rejection of a broadcast carrier at this frequency results in a strong, wideband signal present in the low end of the two-meter band. A similar problem exists on the transmit side that can cause TVI. The band-pass filters described have been effectively used to suppress undesired mixing products. See Figs. 78 and 79.

Circuit construction is easily accomplished using a double-sided copper-clad circuit board. Observing good construction techniques, component lead lengths must be kept to a minimum to eliminate resistive losses and unwanted stray coupling. The piston trimmers are mounted through the board with the coils soldered to the opposite end, parallel to the board. Placing a shield between L1 and L3 decreases mutual coupling and improves the frequency response. Peak C1 and C3 for optimum response. Component values are given in Table 2.

Fig. 77 — Schematic diagram of the double-tuned band-pass filter. Component values are given in Table 2.

Table 2
Component Values

	144 MHz	220 MHz
C2	1 pF	1 pF
C1, C3	1-7 pF piston	1-7 pF piston
L2	27t no. 26 enam. on T37-10	15t no. 24 enam. on T44-10
L1, L3	7t no. 18, ¼-in ID, tap 1½t	4t no. 18, ¼-in ID, tap 1½t

L1, C1, L3 and C3 form the tank circuits that resonate at the desired frequency. C2 and L2 reject the undesired energy while allowing the desired signal to pass. The tap points on L1 and L3 are for 50-ohm matching and may be adjusted for optimal energy transfer. Several filters have been constructed using a miniature variable capacitor in place of C2 so that the notch frequency could be varied.

RF Chokes for the VHF Bands

Many of the construction projects in this chapter call for fabricating one or more RF chokes. Specific instructions are given in each case, but additional guidance is often sought by those embarking on projects of their own design. The information presented here is a brief tutorial in theory and practice for those interested in constructing VHF equipment.

Distributed capacitance limits the range over which an RF choke will work. A coil wound with some spacing between the adjacent turns exhibits less distributed capacitance than one in which turns are close. This makes the space-wound choke superior to the close-wound one. A minimum of cement on the windings is also desirable. The space-wound 50-MHz choke in Table 3 and shown in the upper right of Fig. 80 is as good as you can make for that band, and better than most chokes you could buy. It is good at 144 MHz as well, and even serviceable at 220 MHz. A close-wound choke of fine wire, heavily doped with lacquer, might be usable on only one VHF band, and very likely it would not be too good even there.

To construct RF chokes you will need some wire: no. 22 enamel (Nycald or Formvar preferred); no. 28 enamel, silk or cotton covered; and no. 30 or 32, of any similar insulation. Silk- or cotton-covered wires take cement nicely, but enamel is okay otherwise, and it is usually most readily available.

High-value ½- or 1-watt carbon resistors make good winding forms for use at 144 MHz and higher. A 2-watt resistor is big enough for a 50-MHz choke, but Teflon or Nylon rod stock is better. Do not use polystyrene or Lucite, if any heat is to be involved. These materials will melt in the heat of an average transmitter enclosure.

Table 3

RF Chokes for 50-, 144- and 220-MHz Service

Frequency	Inductance	Description
50 MHz	7.8 to 9.5 μH	B&W miniductor no. 3004, 1-3/8 to 1-9/16 inch long.*
50 MHz	8.3 μH	No. 28 double silk covered (dsc), space-wound on ½-inch Teflon rod. Winding 1¾ inch long. See text.
50 MHz	7.2 μH	No. 28 dsc, close-wound on ¼-inch Teflon rod. Winding 1-7/16 inch long.
144 MHz	2.15 μH	No. 22 Nyclad, close-wound 1-3/16 inch on ¼-inch Teflon rod.
144 MHz	1.42 μH	31 turns no. 28 dsc, space-wound on ¼-inch dia self-supporting.
(The 144-MHz chokes work well on 220 MHz.)		
220 MHz	0.6 μH	13 turns no. 22 Nyclad on ¼-inch Teflon rod.
220 MHz	0.75 μH	17 turns no. 28 dsc space-wound on ¼-inch Teflon rod. Winding 5/8 inch long.
220 MHz	0.52 μH	22 turns no. 22 Nyclad close-wound on no. 24 drill, self-supporting.

*Excellent for use except where high temperatures are involved.

Fig. 81 — How a choke is positioned with respect to other circuits may be important. The choke at the top is coupled to the plate line of the transmitter tuned circuit. Outside the loop, as shown at the bottom, makes the choke far less subject to RF breakdown.

Fig. 82 — Transmitter applications for RF chokes vary markedly in regard to the quality of choke needed. In the grid circuit, RFC5 has no difficult job to do, and any choke suitable for low-power use is suitable. The shunt-feed choke, RFC6, must meet severe requirements, especially in high-powered amplifiers. It is effectively connected across the transmitter tank circuit, and is subjected to high temperature, current and voltage. The output choke, RFC7, is mainly a safety device, and it operates under much less stringent circumstances.

Fig. 80 — Typical handmade VHF chokes. At the rear are close-wound and space-wound chokes for 50 MHz wound on ¼-inch and ½-inch Teflon rod, drilled and tapped for end-mounting. Three 144-MHz chokes are shown in the center; the two at the left being excellent for high-current applications. In front are similar types to these, but for the 220-MHz band.

Teflon rod can be found in plastics supply houses, in ¼- and ½-inch diameter. It drills and taps nicely, it won't melt, and its insulating quality is excellent. Bakelite rod or even wood dowelling is good enough for the less-critical choke applications. The smallest-diameter prepared coil stock is usable for 50-MHz chokes, but it won't stand much heat.

Space-winding RF chokes is easy. First drill through the rod at spacings indicated under winding length in the table. Now measure off slightly more than a half wavelength of wire for the design frequency band. Double it back on itself and feed the end through one of the holes in the rod. Now wind the coil as if it were to be bifilar. If you clamp the other end of the double wire in a vise, or tie it down firmly otherwise, this can be done easily. Keep the wires under tension, and be sure they are not twisted at any point. Wind tightly and then feed the end through the other rod hole.

Now remove one of the wires by unwinding carefully, keeping it under tension throughout. The remaining wire will be space-wound as neatly as if done by machine. Apply a thin coating of polystyrene cement, using a bit more around the lead holes, and your choke is done.

Self-supporting chokes of excellent quality can be made by winding no. 22 or 24 wire tightly on various drill sizes, and then slipping the drill or other winding form out. If wound under tension the coil will hold its shape when slipped off the form. Turns can be spaced by running a thin knife blade between them.

You can tell a good choke from an inferior one easily enough. Connect it across your driver-stage tuned circuit, and see what it does to your final-stage grid current. Also note how much you have to retune the driver circuit to restore resonance. A perfect choke would have no harmful effects, and it would not heat up. You won't find one that good, but a well-designed choke will come close. If the choke is not a good one, don't run the test too long at any appreciable power level, or you won't have to look for indications — you'll smell them!

6-Meter Amplifier Using the 3CX800A7

The amplifier described here uses the new EIMAC 3CX800A7 in a grounded-grid circuit. With 2200 V on the plate and 25-W drive, it will provide about 700-W output — enough for weak-signal work such as meteor scatter. The 3CX800A7 is well suited for this application. It combines low drive requirements normally associated with tetrodes, yet it offers the stability of grounded-grid triodes. Figs. 83 through 88 depict the amplifier. Dick Stevens, W1QWJ, designed and built this project.

Circuit Details

Fig. 84 is a schematic diagram of the amplifier. The RF deck includes everything except the high-voltage power supply. Several suitable supplies are described elsewhere in this chapter and in Chapter 27. This amplifier requires 2000- to 2200-V at about half an ampere. The plate tank circuit is a pi-L network consisting of C11, C12, L3 and L4. This configuration gives somewhat better harmonic suppression than a standard pi network. The cathode input circuit is a T network consisting of L1, L2 and C8. A filament choke is recommended above 50 MHz to keep the filament above ground for RF. RFC2 is bifilar wound on a ferrite rod. According to sources at EIMAC, use of a center-tapped transformer at T1 is not necessary. If you have a transformer of the correct voltage, but without a center tap, go ahead and use it.

C13 and C14 bypass the B+ line. RFC3 is a hand-wound choke on a Teflon form, while RFC4 is an Ohmite Z-144. RFC5, an

Fig. 83 — The 3CX800A7 6-meter amplifier is mounted on a rack panel. Meters are mounted behind the panel with bezels.

Ohmite Z-50, is included for safety to prevent high voltage from appearing at the antenna connector if dc blocking capacitor C15 fails.

R1, in the B+ line, will protect the tube and power supply in case of a high-voltage arc. In this case, R1 was mounted in the power supply. It doesn't matter if you mount it in the power supply or the RF deck, but the use of this resistor is highly recommended.

Cathode bias is provided by a 5.1-V Zener diode, D5. R3 prevents the cathode voltage from soaring if D5 fails. F2 will blow if excessive cathode current is drawn. R4 nearly cuts the tube off on receive.

All metering is done in the negative return lead for safety. C9, C10, D3 and D4 protect the meters. The antenna relay is located externally but is powered from the amplifier.

A grid overcurrent trip circuit is included to protect the 3CX800A7 from damage. The cost of the tube makes protection circuitry a must! Grid current is sensed across R5. If the grid current exceeds a preset value, Q1 conducts and actuates K1. Contact K1A, in the K2 coil supply line, opens and removes power from K2, placing the amplifier in STANDBY. To restore normal circuit operation, turn S2 to the off position; this will reset K1. S2 is "on" for normal operation. This switch provides an additional function: It controls the VOX

Fig. 84 — Schematic diagram of the 6-meter amplifier using the 3CX800A7. Resistors are ¼-W carbon types unless noted. Capacitors are disc ceramic types unless noted. SM means silver-mica. Capacitors marked with polarity are electrolytic.

B1 — Dayton 4C012A 54-CFM blower.
C8 — 100-pF air variable (Millen 22100 or equiv.).
C11 — Modified air variable, 4 to 11 pF. See text.
C12 — 8- to 140-pF air variable, receive spacing (Cardwell 149-6 or equiv.).
C13, C14 — 1000-pF, 5-kV disc-ceramic capacitor.
C15 — 1500-pF, 5-kV RF-type doorknob capacitor.
C16 — 3300-pF, 500-V silver-mica capacitor.
D1-D4 — 600-PIV, 1-A silicon diode.
D5 — 5.1-V, 10-W Zener diode (1N3996 or equiv.).
DS1, DS2 — 12-V dc pilot light.
J1 — Chassis-mount female BNC connector.
J2 — Chassis-mount female Type-N connector.

J3, J6 — Chassis-mount phono jack.
J4, J5 — Millen 37001 high-voltage connector.
K1 — DPDT miniature relay, PC-board mount, 12-V dc coil (RS 275-213).
K2 — DPDT relay, 12-V dc coil, 10-A contacts.
L1, L2 — 10t no. 18 wire, 5/8-inch ID, 1 inch long.
L3 — 5t 1/8-inch copper tubing, 1-1/8 inches ID, 2½ inches long.
L4 — 5t no. 12 wire, 1/2-inch ID, 1-1/8 inches long.
M1 — 0-100 mA dc meter (Simpson Model 1327, avail. from Larson Instrument Co., Greenbush Rd., Orangeburg, NY 10962).
M2 — 0-1 A dc meter (Simpson Model 1327, avail. from Larson Instrument Co.).
Q1 — 2N2222 or equiv.
RFC1 — 10-μH RF choke. 40t no. 22 enam. on

a ¼-inch ferrite form or a Radio Shack no. 273-101.
RFC2 — 14t no. 16 enam. on a ½-inch-OD ferrite rod. See text.
RFC3 — 40t no. 22 enam. closewound on a 2-inch-long by ¾-inch OD Teflon rod. See text.
RFC4 — Ohmite Z-144 RF choke.
RFC5 — Ohmite Z-50 RF choke.
T1 — Filament transformer. 117-V ac primary; 13.5-V, 1.5-A center-tapped secondary (Avatar AV-440 or equiv. Available from Avatar Magnetics, 1147 N. Emerson St., Indianapolis, IN 46219).
T2 — Power transformer. 117-V ac primary; 12.6-V, 1.2-A secondary.
U1 — 50-PIV, 4-A bridge rectifier.
U2 — 12-V, 1.5-A three-terminal regulator (LM7812 or equiv.).

circuit and antenna bypass relay circuit, so the amplifier can be switched in and out of the line between antenna and transceiver.

Construction

The amplifier is built on a 10 × 12 × 3-inch chassis (LMB 10123C). For the best possible RF shielding, the plate circuitry is built inside its own 5 × 10 × 3-inch chassis (LMB 5103C) that is mounted on top of the main chassis. The chassis is attached to a standard 19 × 7 inch aluminum rack panel (Hammond PBPA 19 007). The meters are mounted to the front panel with bezels.

Most of the parts used in this project were purchased from Radio Shack, Semiconductor Surplus, 2822 N. 32nd St., Phoenix, AZ 85008 and RadioKit, P.O. Box 411, Greenville, NH 03048.

Considerable care must be given to the tank circuit construction to keep stray capacitance to a minimum. To this end, the plate tuning capacitor (C11) is rebuilt from a receiving type. All available commercial capacitors had too high a minimum capacitance.

The first step in construction is to fabricate the plate tuning capacitor. The capacitor is made from a stock Cardwell ER25AS split-stator capacitor having a maximum capacitance of 25 pF per section, with four stator and five rotor plates. The capacitor is 1-5/8 inches long between the end bearing plates and is made up of individual stator and rotor plates held together with spacers, washers and nuts.

Carefully disassemble the capacitor. Be careful not to lose any of the small parts. Two new no. 4-40 by 2-1/8-inch-long tie rod bolts are needed. Reassemble the capacitor as a single section with four stator and three rotor plates with three spacers between plates. The completed capacitor will have a spacing adequate for 3.5-kV breakdown. The minimum capacitance is 4 pF and the maximum is 11 pF. Any capacitor of this type construction in the same general capacitance range should work. Alternatively, a small vacuum variable will work.

The tuning and loading capacitors, as well as L3 and C15, are mounted on an aluminum subassembly, as shown in Fig. 85. C12, the plate loading capacitor, is a standard value and required no modification. L3 is made of 1/8-inch copper tubing and is suspended between C11 and C12. The bottom of L3 should be about ½ inch above the bottom of the subassembly. Additional details of the plate compartment may be seen in Fig. 86.

The subassembly is made from a piece of aluminum sheet that measures 4¾ × 5¾ inches. Fold up 2 inches on the longer side at a right angle to form an L bracket, as shown in Fig. 85. The capacitor shafts are mounted 1 inch in from each end, in the center of the 2-inch lip.

RFC3, the plate choke, is wound on a 2-inch length of ¾-inch-OD Teflon rod. Drill each end to a depth of ½ inch and

Fig. 85 — The output network mounts on a separate subassembly. C15 connects to the rest of the circuit with wide copper straps.

Fig. 86 — Top view of the 3CX800A7 6-meter amplifier with the plate-compartment cover removed. The blower pressurizes the plate compartment and air exhausts through a chimney made from Teflon sheet (not shown). A Dow-Key 260B is used here as a TR relay. T1 and K2 are mounted on top of the chassis.

tap for no. 10-32 hardware. Screw a 1-inch length of no. 10-32 threaded rod (or a bolt with the head cut off) into each end. Starting at ½ inch from one end of the rod, wind 40 turns of no. 22 enameled wire. Leave extra wire at each end for making connections. The winding should be about 1 inch long and is centered on the form.

Secure both ends of the winding with epoxy cement. Slip a no. 10 solder lug over one of the pieces of threaded rod and solder one end of the winding to it. This will be the end that attaches to C15.

The plate compartment is pressurized, and a chimney made from Teflon sheet that fits around the tube anode forces the air

Fig. 87 — The underside of the chassis is divided in half by a partition to shield the input circuit.

Fig. 88 — Spectral output of the 3CX800A7 6-meter amplifier. Power output is 700 W on 50 MHz. Each vertical division is 10 dB and each horizontal division is 10 MHz. All harmonics and spurious emissions are greater than 64 dB down. This amplifier complies with current FCC spectral purity requirements.

Table 4

Typical Operating Conditions for the 3CX800A7 6-Meter Amplifier

Plate supply voltage	2200 V
Zero-signal plate current	65 mA
Single-tone plate current	500 mA
Single-tone grid current	40 mA
Drive power	25 W
Output power	700 W
Efficiency	62%

up through the tube to an exhaust hole cut in the top of the plate compartment. The hole is shielded with aluminum screen. Details of this type of chimney and cooling system may be found in the 2-meter 8930 amplifier project presented later in this chapter.

Fig. 87 shows the underside of the amplifier chassis. A partition down the center of the chassis shields the input circuitry. The tube socket, input network and filament choke mount on one side of the partition. The dc components and control circuitry mount on the other. Operating voltages reach the tube through feedthrough capacitors in the partition.

To insure stability, the grid grounding straps should go from pin 4 to pin 7, and from pin 4 to pin 11. Ground pin 4 to the chassis at a solder lug at one of the tube-socket mounting screws. These pin numbers are for the EIMAC SK-1900 socket. Alternatively, EIMAC can supply a collet (part no. 720359) to ground the grid. The cathode straps should go between pins 1-8, 2-9 and 3-10. Solder these straps

together where they cross at the center of the socket and make the cathode RF connection to this point.

Filament choke RFC2 is wound on a ferrite core. Cut two 36-inch lengths of no. 16 enameled wire and bifilar wind them on a ½-inch wooden dowel. Dress the ends to make the winding 2 inches long. Cut a 3-inch length of ferrite rod and file the ends so there are no sharp edges. Carefully slide the bifilar winding off the dowel and onto the ferrite rod. After the winding is centered on the rod, give it a coat of epoxy cement to hold it in place. See Chapter 24 for more details on this type of RF choke.

The grid protection circuitry is built on a small piece of Radio Shack part no. 276-159 prototyping board. One half the board is used. Most of the other components mount to the chassis or to terminal strips.

Initial Tune-Up and Adjustment

Connect an SWR meter between a 6-meter transmitter capable of supplying 20 W and the amplifier input. Connect a wattmeter and a good 50-ohm dummy load capable of handling at least 700 W to the output connector. Close S1 and allow the 3CX800A7 to warm up for at least 3 minutes before applying plate voltage. Caution: never apply filament voltage without the blower running. Never apply drive without plate voltage and a load connected to the tube, or the tube grid-dissipation rating may be exceeded.

Apply low plate voltage, about 1 kV, and apply a watt or two of drive. Adjust C8 for

minimum input SWR. It might be necessary to spread or squeeze turns on L2 to get a 1.1:1 SWR.

Adjust C11 and C12 for maximum output. There is not much leeway with L3. It has to be the correct value to resonate with the output capacitance of the 3CX800A7 and the low capacitance of C11. Chances are that you may have to shut the amplifier off, disconnect the high voltage and spread the turns on L3 slightly to get the output circuit to resonate properly. The circuit should resonate with C11 set at ½ mesh.

When you get the output circuit to resonate at low power, bolt down all the covers and apply full plate voltage. Zero-signal plate current should be 65 to 70 ma. Apply a couple of watts drive and tune the amplifier for maximum output. Slowly increase the drive, keeping the output tuned for maximum. With 10-W drive from a typical multi-mode transceiver, output should be 400 to 500 W. With 25-W drive, output should be approximately 700 W. Table 4 lists typical operating conditions. Check the input SWR at full power and readjust as necessary.

Most likely the grid overcurrent trip circuit will operate at some point during the initial tune-up, placing the amplifier in STANDBY. Decrease the sensitivity by adjusting R2, mounted on the grid-trip circuit board. A hole is cut in the chassis bottom plate for access to this control. With the values shown, the circuit should trip at 20 mA with R2 set to a minimum. Adjust R2 slightly until the circuit holds at 40 to 50 mA of grid current. The tube's maximum grid-current rating is 60 mA.

A spectral photograph of the amplifier output is shown in Fig. 88. It meets current FCC spectral-purity requirements.

A 2-kW PEP Amplifier for 50 to 54 MHz

A number of manufacturers sell low-power-output (10-watt) transceivers and transverters for 6-meter operation. This particular power-output level is not in line with that required to drive the popular grounded-grid amplifiers. Even the high-mu triodes, such as those of the 8874 family, require at least 25 watts of drive for 1 kilowatt of input. Over 50 watts of drive may be required for 2-kilowatt service.

This leaves two options for owners of 10-watt-output rigs. One solution is to use a solid-state "brick" amplifier to drive the grounded-grid amplifier. This results in complex relay-switching systems not to mention the cost of the amplifier and a high-current supply to power it. The other approach is to use a tetrode such as the 4CX1000A in a grounded-cathode amplifier (see Figs. 89 through 97). In this circuit, 10 watts of drive will provide 2 kilowatts of input power, thereby eliminating an intermediate amplifier stage.

Circuit Description

The schematic diagram of the amplifier is shown in Fig. 90. As the 4CX1000A is a high-mu tube, care must be taken in the design and construction of the amplifier to prevent instability. In the circuit shown, this was accomplished without the need for neutralization — one of the drawbacks commonly associated with the use of these tubes.

The input network is series tuned. A link couples power from the exciter to the tube. Series tuning was chosen primarily because of the large input capacitance of the tube (roughly 100 pF). The tube socket and strays add an additional 20 pF. This tuning method places the tube input capacitance in series with the tuning capacitor, effectively reducing the tuning capacitance. A number of other networks were tried, including one somewhat exotic current-feed method, but none proved as simple and effective as the one shown. Bias voltage is shunt fed to the grid through R1. This resistor also heavily swamps the grid circuit and helps to provide amplifier stability without the need for neutralization. Should it be desired to increase the gain of the amplifier for use with lower power rigs, the value of R1 can be increased and the network components changed as appropriate. The cathode is grounded through short, heavy leads at the base of the SK-800B tube socket. A screen bypass capacitor is an integral part of this socket. The capacitor is 1500 pF, is rated for 400 volts and is of the mylar-film variety. Capacitors are connected between ground and each of the three filament-connection points.

The plate circuit used in this amplifier is of the common pi-network variety, with two exceptions. First, the internal tube plate capacitance, which is on the order of

10 pF, comprises what would be considered the "tuning" capacitor of the network. Since the tube capacitance is fixed, the inductor is used as an adjustable element. A compressible/expandable coil is used here. This arrangement allows the amplifier to cover the entire 6-meter band, whereas other designs using shorted-turn and slug-tuned techniques will cover little more than 1 MHz of tuning range. Additionally, the compressing and expanding of the coil does not have an adverse effect on the inductor Q, as typically occurs with the other systems. The tube capacitance dictates the circuit Q, which is roughly 14.

A single, multisecondary transformer provides power for the filament, bias and screen supplies. Although the filament winding is rated for 6.3 V at 8.8 A, the transformer delivers 6.0 V at 9.0 A — precisely that required by the 4CX1000A. The transformer was run for a period of 10 hours under these conditions and no appreciable heating of the wires or core was noted. Transformers of other manufacture or different voltage/current ratings should be carefully checked.

The high-voltage secondary of the transformer provides energy for the bias and screen supplies. Zener diodes limit the dissipation of the bias potentiometer. R6 cuts the amplifier off during receive periods. J5 is shorted for transmit.

The transformer secondary also feeds the screen supply. Here, a full-wave rectifier provides the dc energy. Q1, D3, R1 and R2 form a regulator that limits the current that can be drawn through the transistor to 40 mA. This extra circuitry is desirable in the event of high-voltage supply failure. No more than 40 mA of current can be drawn through the regulator, ensuring that the screen is protected. Without such a safety device, a failure of the high-voltage supply would mean that the screen dissipation might be pushed well above the specified 12-watt maximum rating. D4-D9, inclusive, make up the screen-voltage regulator.

M1, located in the −HV lead, continuously monitors cathode current. Meter shunts are provided in the bias and screen supplies. M2 can be switched between grid and screen by means of S2. This meter reads 0 to 10 mA for grid and 0 to 100 mA for screen current.

The amplifier requires a high-voltage supply. The design and construction of such supplies is covered in Chapter 27.

Construction

Many of the construction details can be seen in Fig. 91. The general layout is not especially critical, although good isolation between the grid and plate circuitry is a must. To this end, the Eimac SK-800B socket is used. The built-in screen-bypass capacitor is an important factor in amplifier stability. Other sockets without this

Fig. 89 — Front-panel view of the 2-kW, 6-meter amplifier.

capacitor should be avoided.

The amplifier is built on a 10 × 12 × 3-inch aluminum chassis that is attached to an 8¾ inch-high, 19-inch-wide rack panel. Sheet-aluminum panels are made so that the overall height of the amplifier enclosure is 7½ inches.

The grid compartment is constructed from a second aluminum chassis that measures 7 × 7 × 2 inches. It is easiest to cut the hole for the tube socket with the smaller chassis bolted in place. In this manner exact alignment can be guaranteed. A heavy-duty hand nibbler tool was used to make the large hole. All leads entering the grid compartment pass through 1000-pF feedthrough capacitors to ensure an RF-tight enclosure. The amplifier input connection is through a UG-625B (female) chassis-mount BNC connector, directly into the grid compartment. The general placement of the input-network components can be seen in the photograph. A perforated aluminum cover is placed over the smaller grid-compartment chassis. This piece must allow adequate air flow for proper tube cooling. It is a good idea to check air flow with and without this piece in place in order to determine whether the material is suitable.

The remainder of the bottom chassis houses the screen and bias power-supply components and the control circuitry. Many of the parts are contained on a single-sided circuit board. The parts-layout diagram is shown in Fig. 96. Zener diodes are mounted on an aluminum plate and the circuit board. While the aluminum provides some heat-sinking, cooling for the diodes is supplied primarily by the system blower, as the diode stack is mounted in the air flow path. Cooling for the tube is by means of a blower that is mounted external to the chassis. A plastic flange (Newtone 366, used with central vacuum cleaning systems) is suitable for use with 2-inch automobile heater/defroster hose. A length of this hose connects the pressurized chassis to the blower, which can be mounted at some convenient location. For ultra-quiet operation the blower can be mounted in a closet or in an adjoining room. Copper or brass screening is used to cover the flange opening, thus maintaining an RF-tight chassis. Information on how to select a

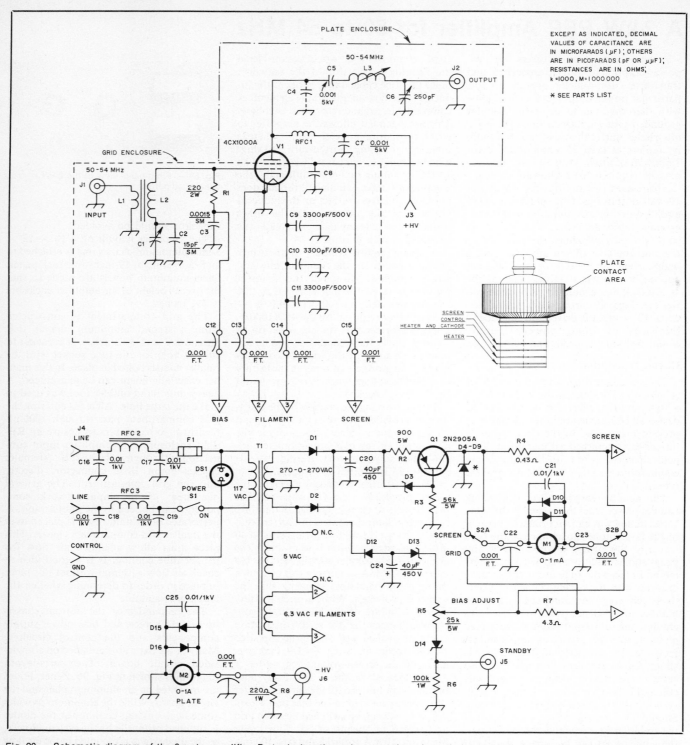

Fig. 90 — Schematic diagram of the 6-meter amplifier. Parts designations shown on the schematic but not called out in the parts list are for text reference only.

C1 — Miniature variable, panel mount, 32 pF maximum.
C2 — Silver mica, 15 pF, mounted directly across C1.
C4 — Tube internal plate capacitance.
C5, C7 — Transmitting capacitor, 0.001 μF, 5000 volt. Centralab 858S-1000 or equiv.
C6 — Transmitting variable, 250 pF maximum.
C8 — Screen bypass built into SK-800B socket.
C20, C24 — Electrolytic, 40 μF, 450 volt.
D1, D2, D10-D12, incl., D15, D16 — Silicon, 2.5 ampere, 1000 volt.
D3 — Zener diode, 45 volt, 1 watt.
D4-D9, incl. — Zener diode, stud mount, 56 volt, 10 watt. Connect in series.

D13 — Zener diode, 200 volt, 5 watt.
D14 — Zener diode, 30 volt, 1 watt.
DS1 — Neon indicator built into S1.
F1 — Fuse, 1 ampere.
J1 — Coaxial connector, BNC chassis mount, UG-625B or equiv.
J2 — Coaxial connector, type N chassis mount, UG-58 or equiv.
J3 — High-voltage connector, Millen 37001 or equiv.
J4 — 4 conductor.
J5, J6 — Phono connector.
L1 — 2 turns no. 24 enam. wire wound over L2.
L2 — 10 turns no. 24 enam. wire on a T-50-12 core.

L3 — See text and drawing.
M1 — 0.1 mA, Simpson 15070 or equiv.
M2 — 0.1 A, Simpson 15101 or equiv.
Q1 — 2N2905A or equiv.
R4 — Meter shunt, 19½ in of no. 34 enam. wire wound on a high-value, ½-watt resistor.
R5 — Potentiometer, 25k-ohm, 5 watt.
R7 — Meter shunt, 4.3 ohm, ¼ watt.
RFC1 — 36 turns no. 24 enam. wire on a 1-in-diameter Teflon rod.
RFC2, RFC3 — 6 turns no. 22 enam. wire on an FT-50-43 core.
S1 — SPST, rocker type with built-in neon indicator.
S2 — Rotary, 2 pole, 2 position.
T1 — Stancor P8356 or equiv. See text.

Fig. 91 — Underside of the amplifier. The grid-compartment chassis is normally enclosed by a perforated aluminum cover which was removed for this photograph.

Fig. 93 — Dimensional drawing of the inductor assembly. Delrin can be obtained from most plastic supply houses. Check the Yellow Pages of your local telephone directory for dealers.

Fig. 92 — Plate compartment of the amplifier. Details of the inductor are given in the text and in additional photographs and drawings.

Fig. 94 — Photograph of the assembled adjustable inductor. Make certain to use only plated brass hardware for pieces that come into contact with the coil.

Fig. 95 — Photo (A) and schematic diagram (B) of the low-pass filter that is used after the amplifier. The filter is built to fit inside a 2¼ × 2¼ × 5-in box. Good quality capacitors such as silver-mica types should be used.

C1-C4 — 110 pF silver mica, 1000 V.
L1, L3 — 4 turns no. 14 wire, 5/16-inch ID.
L2 — 5 turns no. 14 wire, 7/16-inch ID.

suitable blower is given in Chapter 15 of this *Handbook*. Connection to the meters is through 1000-pF feedthrough capacitors.

The plate compartment is somewhat less busy than the underside of the amplifier. See Fig. 92. The only component that needs explanation is the inductor. Details of the construction are shown in Fig. 93, and a photograph is shown in Fig. 94. Two pieces of 3/8-inch Delrin plate are used as the stationary end pieces. A ¼-inch control bushing is used at the center of each piece. A third piece of Delrin stock is used for the movable plate. This piece is tapped to accommodate the ¼-28 thread of the shaft that is used to move the plate. This shaft

is double nutted on each side of the rear support to prevent the shaft from moving in relation to either the front or rear supports. As the front-panel knob is turned, only the movable plate changes position to compress or expand the coil. The exact dimension of the coil is fairly critical, so it should be made as close to specification as possible. Once the coil has been wound it can be silver plated to prevent oxidation.

As a point of interest, the amplifier front panel was painted orange. Black press-on lettering was used to label the front panel controls. A light coat of clear lacquer was applied to protect the lettering.

Operation

It is a good idea initially to check out the various tube-element voltages without the tube in the socket. The screen voltage may

turn out to be different than the nominal 336 because of poor Zener-diode voltage tolerances. As long as the voltage is under 375 no problems should be encountered. Operation of the protective circuitry can be verified by loading the output of the screen supply with appropriate high-wattage resistors. Ensure that the bias control will allow adjustment between the values shown on the schematic. Set the voltage to roughly − 150 so that the tube will be cut off when

Fig. 96 — Parts-placement guide for the printed-circuit board as shown from the component side. A full-size etching pattern can be found at the back of this book.

Table 5

Operating Parameters

	1 kW	2 kW
Plate voltage	2100 V dc	3000 V dc
Plate current (single tone)	480 mA	667 mA
Plate current (idling)	50 mA	50 mA
Power input	1000 W	2000 W
Power output	620 W	1250 W
Efficiency	62 %	62.5 %
Drive power	4 W	9 W

Fig. 97 — Spectral photograph of the amplifier and filter adjusted for 1-kilowatt input. Each horizontal division represents 50 MHz and each vertical division is 10 dB. This amplifier complies with current FCC requirements for spectral purity.

the amplifier is first turned on. Eimac recommends that the 4CX1000A heater voltage be applied for a period of not less than three minutes before plate voltage and current are applied.

Connect a transmitter capable of supplying 10 watts of power to J1 through an SWR indicator. Also, connect a dummy load and power meter to J2. After the amplifier has warmed up for several minutes, short J5 and adjust the bias control for an idling current of 50 mA. Apply a small amount of drive power and adjust L3 and C6 for maximum power output. Next, adjust C1 for minimum reflected power as indicated by the input SWR indicator. Apply additional drive power and

continue adjusting L3 and C6 for maximum power output. Use the operating parameters given in Table 5 as a guide. For the amplifier described here an adjustable high-voltage supply was used. The voltage and current levels for 1-kW and 2-kW input level were chosen to equalize the plate impedance, thus requiring only a minimal change in the settings of L3 and C6 for changing power level. If the fixed-voltage supply is used to power this amplifier, similar efficiencies should be attained.

As with many amplifier designs for VHF operation, additional low-pass filtering is required to meet the FCC spectral-purity requirements (all spurious and harmonic emissions — 60 dB or greater below peak

power). A suitable filter circuit is shown in Fig. 95. The unit was constructed in a small aluminum box and is mounted directly at the output connector by means of a double-male adapter. With this filter the amplifier easily exceeds the FCC requirements. A spectral photograph is shown in Fig. 97.

A Medium-Power 144-MHz Amplifier

The typical 2-meter rig these days puts out 10 watts or so. While 10 W is adequate for local communications, it is not enough for reliable long-haul work. Although occasional band openings and enhanced conditions allow long-distance contacts with low power, something more is desirable for weak-signal work. The amplifier pictured in Figs. 98 through 110 will supply more than 300-W output for 10-W of drive. It is clean, easy to build and reliable. If the builder shops wisely, the entire amplifier can be built for less than the cost of a commercially manufactured 150-W "brick" amplifier and associated 20-A, 13.8-V regulated supply. This project was designed by Clarke Greene, K1JX, and built by Mark Wilson, AA2Z, in the ARRL lab.

Circuit Details

An 8930 tetrode (350-W plate dissipation) is used in this design. The 8930 is identical electrically to the 4CX250R, but it features a larger anode cooler for higher dissipation with lower air flow and pressure drop requirements. If the builder must purchase a new tube, the 8930 is a good choice because it is more rugged than the 4CX250. However, a commonly available 4CX250B will work fine in this circuit. Only minor mechanical changes are necessary to accommodate the 4CX250's smaller anode cooler. The amplifier and power supply are shown schematically in Figs. 99 and 100.

The input circuit consists of L2, which is series tuned by C2 and the tube input capacitance. C3 is used in parallel with C2 to preset the tuning range for a smooth vernier action. A single 15- or 20-pF variable may be used at C2, but the tuning will be more critical. Power is coupled to L2 through link L1.

Bias voltage is fed to the tube through R1. This resistor, which consists of three 820-ohm, 2-W carbon composition resistors in parallel, swamps the grid heavily. Heavy swamping is important for amplifier stability. It also raises the drive requirement to about 8 W for full output. The amplifier can be driven to full output with about 2 W if the grid swamping resistor is changed to 2000 ohms or so and the input matching is adjusted accordingly. Excessive drive, however, will make the tube run in the nonlinear region, causing splatter up and down the band. It is impossible to adequately control the drive power by adjusting the exciter mic gain control. An input circuit designed for the drive level available from the exciter makes it difficult to overdrive the amplifier, ensuring a clean signal and peaceful coexistence with nearby amateurs sharing the band.

The output circuitry consists of a quarter-wavelength strip line, L3, which is tuned by C9. A tuned link, L4 and C10, couples power to the output jack. High voltage is fed to the tube at the low-impedance (ground) end of the line through RFC1. C8 is the plate-blocking capacitor.

The filament, bias and screen voltages are all supplied by T1. EIMAC specifies filament voltage at 6.0 ±0.3 V, so R11 is included to drop the transformer voltage to the proper level.

T1 has a secondary winding of 270-0-270 V which is used for the screen and bias supplies. Screen voltage regulation is accomplished by five 60-V Zener diodes, D7 through D11. The voltage from the supply is dropped to the Zener stack voltage by current-limiting resistor R5. R7, a screen bleeder resistor, is connected in parallel with the Zener stack to allow for negative screen current developed under certain tube operating conditions.

A tetrode should not be operated without plate voltage and a load. Otherwise, the screen would act like the anode and draw excessive current. Should this happen accidentally, F2 will blow and protect the screen. F2 is placed between the Zener stack and the bleeder, rather than between the bleeder and the tube. If the tube were operated without a load on the screen, the screen potential would rise to the anode voltage, destroying the screen bypass capacitor. Should the screen voltage rise above 390 V, Z1, a metal-oxide varistor, will conduct and clamp the screen voltage to ground. The power-supply fuse should blow before any damage occurs.

Bias voltage is taken from the same secondary winding as the screen voltage. When the amplifier is in standby, − 200 V is applied to the grid to cut the tube off. In transmit, D12 is switched in, supplying operating bias. R9 is used to adjust operating bias from − 40 to − 60 V to allow for differences among tubes. D15 is included to minimize Zener voltage drift as D14 changes temperature.

The 5-V winding on T1 supplies coil voltage for K1. Contacts K1B switch the bias from standby to operate. K1C provides "dry" contacts for antenna relay switching.

S1 applies voltage to the blower motor, while S2 energizes T1. These two switches are connected so that the blower must be switched on before filament voltage is applied. The blower may be left on after the amplifier has been turned off.

The high-voltage supply is designed to deliver 2000 V under load. The heart of the supply is a heavy-duty Hammond transformer that will run cool even under continuous use. The 234-V primary and full-wave bridge rectifier in the secondary aid voltage regulation.

The B+ supply is turned on from the amplifier front panel, so the supply may be located away from the operating position. K1 is a heavy-duty power relay with contacts large enough to handle the supply current. R1 and R2 provide inrush current protection for the rectifiers. These resistors are shorted out by the contacts of K2, applying full primary voltage after a short delay. This delay is about 0.6 second, and is determined by R3 and C1.

D1 through D4 are high-voltage rectifiers provided by K2AW. They eliminate the need for a PC board full of individual 1000-PIV units with associated capacitors and equalizing resistors. C2 is a surplus oil-filled capacitor. Individual electrolytic capacitors would work fine, if enough units are connected in series to give about 40 μF at a voltage rating of at least 2500 V.

R4 through R6 make up the bleeder resistor. Several individual resistors are used, rather than one large unit, to keep the voltage across each resistor within ratings. F2 is a high-voltage fuse that will protect the power supply and amplifier in case of a short circuit. The negative lead of the power supply floats above chassis ground so that plate current may be monitored in the negative lead in the RF deck. R8 keeps the B − lead close to chassis potential. R9, in series with the B + lead, protects the tube and power supply from high-voltage flashovers.

Plate current is monitored by a 0- to 500-mA meter in the negative lead. A 0- to 5-mA meter monitors grid current and screen current. Shunt R6 increases the movement to a 50-mA range for the screen. The high-voltage supply has a separate 0- to 4-kV meter.

S3, used to turn on the high-voltage

Fig. 98 — The 8930 amplifier and accompanying high-voltage power supply are built behind standard 19-in rack panels.

Fig. 99 — Schematic diagram of the 8930 2-m amplifier RF deck. Screen, filament and bias supplies, as well as metering and switching, are built into the RF chassis. The companion high-voltage supply schematic is given in Fig. 100.

B1 — 54 CFM blower (Dayton 4C012A or equiv.).
C1, C4, C5 — Feedthrough capacitor, 2000 pF, 1 kV (Erie 1202-005 or equiv.).
C2 — Miniature air variable, 1.8 to 8.7 pF (Cardwell 160-104 or equiv.).
C6 — Feedthrough capacitor, 1500 pF, 2.5 kV (Erie 1280-060 or equiv.).
C8 — Plate dc blocking capacitor; part of plate line assembly. See text and Fig. 104.
C9 — Flapper capacitor. See text and Fig. 104.
C10 — Air variable, 2.8 to 7.5 pF (Millen 22006 or equiv.).
D1-D6, D12, D13, D15 — Silicon diode, 1 kV, 1 A (1N4007).
D7-D11 — Zener diode, 60 V, 10 W (RCA SK192).
D14 — Zener diode, 39 V, 5 W (1N5366).
DS1 — Meter illumination lamps (see text).
J1 — BNC chassis mount.

J2 — Type N chassis mount.
J3, J4 — High-voltage connector (Millen 37001 or equiv.).
J5 — CEE-22 chassis mount power connector.
J6 — Chassis-mount phono jack.
J7 — Two-conductor socket (Cinch S-402AB or equiv.).
J8 — Terminal strip, two conductor.
K1 — DPDT relay, 6-V dc coil.
L1 — 1 turn no. 16 enam. wound over center of L2.
L2 — 4 turns no. 16 tinned wire, 3/8-in ID, 5/8-in long.
L3 — Plate line. See text and Fig. 104.
L4 — Output coupling link. See text and Fig. 104.
M1 — Plate current meter, 0-500 mA (Simpson model 1327 with custom face; Cat. no. 10552, avail. from Larson Instrument Co., Greenbush Road, Orangeburg, NY 10962).

M2 — Grid and screen current meter, 0-5 mA movement (Simpson model 1327 with custom face; Larson Instruments Co., cat. no. 10551).
R1 — Three 820-Ω, 2 W carbon composition resistors in parallel. See text.
RFC1 — 1.72 μH, 600 mA RF choke (J. W. Miller RFC-144 or equiv.).
S1, S2, S4 — SPST rocker switch.
S3 — DPDT rocker switch.
S5 — Rotary switch, 2 circuit, 2 position, non-shorting (Mallory 3222J or equiv.).
T1 — Power transformer, 117-V ac primary; secondary: 270-0- 270-V at 120 mA, 6.3-V CT at 3.5 A, 5 V at 3 A (Stancor PC-8405 or equiv.).
U1 — Bridge rectifier, 50 V, 1A.
Z1 — Metal-oxide varistor, 370-V dc continuous, 390-470 V peak (Zenamic Z275LA40A or equiv.).

Fig. 100 — Schematic diagram of the high-voltage power supply for the 8930 2-m amplifier.

D1-D4 — High-voltage rectifier, 14 kV, 1 A (K2AW HV14-1 or equiv.).

F2 — High-voltage fuse, 5 kV, 2 A (Buss HVJ-2 or equiv.).

J1 — Two-conductor socket (Cinch S-402AB or equiv.).

J2, J3 — High-voltage connector (Millen 37001 or equiv.).

K1 — Power relay, DPST, 234-V ac coil, 277-V ac, 25-A contacts (Potter & Brumfield PRD7AYO-240V or equiv.).

K2 — Power relay, DPDT, 24-V dc coil, 277-V ac, 25-A contacts (Potter & Brumfield PRD11DYO-24V or equiv.).

T1 — Power transformer; primary 117/234-V; secondary 1600 V, 1.2 A (Hammond Mfg. 126270 or equiv.).

supply from the RF deck, is wired so it is impossible to key the amplifier until the B+ is applied. When S2 is thrown, the filaments, bias and screen supplies all come on together. If operating bias was placed on the tube (by keying the amplifier) and no B+ was present, the screen would draw excessive current, as described before. As long as the tube is cut off, having screen voltage present without plate voltage is not a problem.

Construction

The 8930 amplifier is built using three separate chassis (see Figs. 101 and 102). The main chassis measures 10 × 17 × 3-in and is bolted to a standard 19-in-wide, 8¾-in-high rack panel. The plate compartment is a 13 × 5 × 3-in chassis, while the input compartment is a 4 × 5 × 2-in chassis. Use of separate enclosures ensures good shielding.

Amplifier cooling is accomplished using a split airflow, rather than the conventional base-to-anode flow. The blower pressurizes the plate compartment. A special chimney, fabricated from Teflon sheet and phenolic tubing (see Fig. 105), seals the area between the tube cooler and the plate compartment top cover. Air enters the plate compartment and exits through the anode cooler. Some of the air exits through the tube socket to cool the tube seals and input compartment. Measurements by ARRL TA Dick Jansson, WD4FAB, indicate that this cooling system reduces blower back-pressure requirements by about 50 percent with this tube. The blower chosen is capable of supplying 25 cubic feet per minute at 0.4-in of static column pressure — more than enough to cool the amplifier, even at full dissipation.

An EIMAC SK-620A socket is used in this project. The SK-620A and SK-630A sockets feature built-in low-inductance screen bypass capacitors and screen

Fig. 101 — Top view of the 8930 2-m amplifier. The tube and plate circuitry are mounted in a separate chassis that bolts to the main chassis. The plate compartment top cover has been removed for clarity, although it must be installed during amplifier operation.

shielding rings. These features are essential to amplifier stability. If possible, an SK-630A should be used because it features grounded cathode pins. The SK-620A was used here because one was on hand. The four cathode pins are bent in toward the socket center ring and soldered to it, assuring a solid, low-inductance cathode ground.

The input compartment is centered on the tube socket. Filament, bias and screen voltages enter the input box through feedthrough capacitors. All leads are kept as short as possible. The swamping resistor is connected between the feedthrough capacitor and the grid terminal. Likewise, the 100-ohm screen isolation resistor connects the screen pin and the feedthrough capacitor. L2 is supported by C2 and the

socket grid pin. L1 is mounted on a small ceramic standoff insulator near L2. J1 is a panel-mount BNC connector attached to the rear panel and connected to L1 by a short length of 50-ohm coaxial cable.

The plate compartment is mounted along the rear of the main chassis. Fig. 103 shows the relationships of the pieces inside the compartment. Details of L3, L4, C8 and C9 are given in Fig. 104.

L3 is a ¼-wavelength strip line made from brass and aluminum sheet. Complete details are shown in Fig. 104. One end bolts to the chassis, while the other end is silver-soldered to a copper strap that clamps around the anode cooler. C8, the plate blocking capacitor, is a "sandwich" capacitor formed by the two pieces of the plate line. The dielectric is a piece of 0.01-in

Fig. 102 — Underside of the 8930 2-m amplifier. The input circuitry is enclosed in a separate chassis. The screen and bias supplies are built on small printed-circuit boards. D7-D11, the screen regulator Zener diodes, are mounted on a piece of ¼-in-thick aluminum plate for adequate heat-sinking.

Fig. 103 — Component mounting information for the plate compartment.

C9 is made from two brass plates. Fig. 104 gives complete mechanical details of the capacitor assembly. One plate is silver soldered to the anode clamp. The movable plate is attached to a ¼-in Delrin rod supported by bushings in the chassis walls. A wide, low-inductance strap made from 0.003-in thick brass shim stock connects the movable capacitor plate to the chassis. A length of ¼-in-square brass bar is drilled and tapped to hold the shim stock securely against the chassis. A Jackson 6:1 ball drive (available from RadioKit — see Chapter 35 parts suppliers list) is used on the capacitor support shaft to ensure smooth tuning. A 6-32 machine screw tapped into the Delrin shaft ensures a solid mechanical stop. The two capacitor plates must *not* be allowed to touch — one plate is at ground potential, while the other is at 2 kV.

The copper, brass, Teflon, Delrin and aluminum stock necessary for this project are available from Small Parts, Inc. (see Chapter 35 parts suppliers list). Brass or plated brass hardware should be used throughout the plate compartment. Steel is unacceptable for use in strong RF fields. After assembly, the anode clamp, C9 plates and brass half of the plate line were treated with rub-on silver plating.

L4 is made from a piece of no. 14 tinned wire suspended over the cold end of the plate line. Details are shown in Fig. 104. It is supported on the ends by J2 and C10. Greatest coupling occurs when the section of the link that runs parallel to the strip line is placed over the center of the line. In this amplifier, best coupling occurred with the link spaced about ¼-in above the line, but the builder should experiment with different spacings to find the optimum distance for best efficiency.

High-voltage enters the plate compartment through feedthrough C6. RFC1 is soldered between C6 and the cold end of the line. Carefully clean away all flux from the plate line after soldering. Any flux left near the end of the line may offer a path for a high-voltage arc across the sandwich capacitor.

Brass screen, soldered to a brass plate, covers the blower inlet to ensure good shielding. Similarly, a piece of screen soldered to a plate shields the hot air exhaust. A liberal number of machine screws are used to secure the plate compartment top cover to the chassis to keep the RF in. The machine screws thread into aluminum captive fasteners pressed into the chassis. These fasteners are available from Penn Engineering and Mfg. Co., Danboro, PA 18916.

All parts for the screen and bias supplies except D7 through D11 and their 0.01-μF bypass capacitors are mounted on printed-circuit boards. Parts layouts for these boards are given in Fig. 106, and full-size etching patterns are given at the back of this book. The resistors tend to run warm, so they are spaced about ¼-in off the board to allow airflow on all sides. D7

thick Teflon sheet. Three 6-32 brass screws hold the sandwich together. The top half of the line has B+ on it, and the bottom half is grounded, so Teflon shoulder washers are used to insulate the screws from the top half of the line. The shoulder washers used here were cut on a lathe from ¾-in-diameter Teflon rod. A light coating of Dow Corning DC-4 silicone grease is spread on each side of the Teflon sheet to fill in any irregularities.

In this amplifier, the bottom half of the plate line is formed from a single piece of aluminum sheet bent in a sheet metal brake. With patience and a good bench vise and hammer, it should be possible to get a clean bend. If the builder does not have sheet metal bending capability, the bottom half of the line may be made from two separate pieces bolted together. The plate line may be made from copper or brass if this method is used. The top half of the sandwich must be made from copper or brass because it is soldered to the tube clamp.

Fig. 104 — Construction and assembly of L3, L4, C8 and C9.

Fig. 105 — Chimney construction details.

Fig. 106 — Parts placement for the screen (A) and bias (B) power supply boards as seen from the component side. Full-size etching patterns are given at the back of this book.

Fig. 107 — Interior view of the high-voltage power supply for the 8930 2-meter amplifier.

Table 6

Operating Parameters, 8930 144-MHz Amplifier

Plate voltage	2000-V dc
Plate current (single tone)	290 mA
Plate current (idling)	90 mA
Screen current	15 mA
Power input	580 W
Power output	340 W
Efficiency	59%
Drive power	6 W

8½-in-high rack panel (see Fig. 107). The major power supply components are bolted to a 1/8-in-thick plate. The front, rear and side panels are attached to the bottom plate by pieces of aluminum angle stock. All connections are made via the rear panel. Only the high-voltage meter (to show that the secondary is on) and a pilot lamp (to show that primary energy is applied) are mounted on the front panel. The high-voltage projects in Chapter 27 show full details on this type of construction.

Tune Up and Operation

When the wiring is complete, check and recheck all connections. The voltages present in this amplifier are potentially dangerous. Disconnect the filament, bias and screen supplies at the feedthrough capacitors on the input compartment. Turn on T1, if possible through a variable autotransformer, and check the voltages. The filament should be about 6-V ac. The screen supply should be around 300 V, plus

through D11 are mounted with insulating hardware on a ¼-in-thick aluminum plate that is bolted to the chassis for heat sinking.

M1 and M2 are Simpson Model 1327 3½-in meters. They are mounted behind the front panel using Simpson mounting bezels and illumination kits. Larson Instruments designed custom meter scales drawn for this project. M2 has two scales;

the GRID CURRENT scale reads 0 to 5 mA, while the SCREEN CURRENT scale reads −10 0 10 20 30 40 mA. The screen supply bleeder resistor draws 10 mA, so the zero for the SCREEN scale is offset 10 mA. Ordering information for these meters is included in the parts list in Fig. 99.

The high-voltage supply is built on a separate chassis, also mounted behind an

(A)

(B)

Fig. 108 — Spectral photograph of the 8930 2-meter amplifier is given at A. Power output is 340 W. Horizontal divisions are each 100 MHz; vertical divisions are each 10 dB. A shorted ¼-wavelength stub (Fig. 109) is necessary to make the amplifier meet current FCC spectral-purity requirements. The spectral photograph at B, taken with the stub installed, shows that all spurious and harmonic emissions are at least 60 dB down. In both photos, the fundamental has been reduced in amplitude by 30 dB by means of notch filters to prevent analyzer overload.

or minus a few volts. This may change some as the Zeners heat up to their operating temperature. The bias voltage should be about − 200 V. Close the TR relay, K1. Bias voltage should change to somewhere around − 50 V. If everything checks out, unkey K1 and turn the power off.

Connect the filament voltage to the feed-through capacitor on the input box. Turn on the blower and check for airflow. Turn on T1 (remember, no voltages other than filament are applied to the tube). Use an accurate voltmeter to check the voltage at the socket filament pins. Adjust R11 until the filament voltage is exactly 6.0 volts. Turn off the filament voltage and blower, and connect the screen and bias supplies to the appropriate feedthrough capacitors. Put the cover on the input compartment.

Connect the high-voltage supply to the RF deck. Connect a dummy load to J2 through an accurate VHF wattmeter, such as a Bird Model 43. Connect a 2-meter rig capable of supplying about 10 W to J1 through another VHF wattmeter. If only one wattmeter is available, connect it to the input first for initial adjustments and con-

nect the output directly to a dummy load.

Start the blower and check for airflow. Turn on T1, again preferably through a variable autotransformer in case of trouble. The exhaust air should be slightly warm from the filament. The screen current meter should read 0 (10 mA upscale from the current drawn by R7). The plate and grid current meters should not move.

After a minute or so, gradually apply plate voltage. Bring the voltage up to 1000 V or so. Listen and watch for any signs of high-voltage arcing. If everything seems okay, key the amplifier at J6. Adjust the idling plate current to approximately 90 mA using R9. Screen and grid current should stay at zero.

Apply a few watts of drive and adjust C2 for minimum reflected power on the SWR meter connected to the input. If the SWR is not better than 1.2 or 1.3, shut off the amplifier. Disconnect the high voltage, open up the input compartment and adjust the position of the link. It may take several tries, but it is important that the input match be as good as possible for best IMD characteristics. If moving the link does not bring the input SWR close to 1.2, try adjusting the spacing of L2 slightly.

When the input is matched, turn on the amplifier and bring the plate voltage up to 2000 V. If no arcing is noticed, apply a small amount of drive and tune C9 and C10 for maximum output. Increase drive slowly, and readjust C9 and C10 for maximum output. Watch the screen and plate current, and do not exceed the manufacturer's ratings. Table 6 lists the normal operating parameters for this amplifier. Six watts of drive should produce about 340-W output. If the efficiency is very much different from that shown in the table, try adjusting the position of the link with respect to the plate line.

This amplifier is extremely stable. With operating voltages applied (and no drive), the controls were tuned through their ranges with no hint of instability. This amplifier is not neutralized, so maximum output may not occur with the plate dip. The grid, tuning and loading controls work smoothly. Their adjustment is not critical — in fact, tuning is smoother than on some commercially manufactured HF amplifiers.

Spectral photographs are shown in Figs. 108 and 110. In Fig. 108A the second and fourth harmonics are about 50 dB below the amplitude of the fundamental. The sixth is 58 dB down. By increasing the value of C10 and reducing the size of L4, it is possible to raise the link Q to the point where the amplifier meets FCC spectral-purity requirements (all spurious and harmonic emissions at least 60 dB down); however, the high-Q link makes retuning necessary for small excursions in the 2-meter band.

Addition of a simple shorted stub cut to an electrical quarter wavelength at 144 MHz (Fig. 109) results in the spectral

Fig. 109 — Details of the ¼-wavelength stub.

Fig. 110 — Two-tone spectral photograph of the 8930 2-meter amplifier. Power output is 340 W PEP.

photograph shown in Fig. 108B. At the transmitter end, the stub looks like an open circuit for RF at 144 MHz, but it looks like an RF short circuit at the even harmonics. The only visible harmonic energy is at the fourth, and this is just out of the analyzer noise floor at − 62 dB.

The shorted stub serves a second purpose as well. In the unlikely event that the link detaches from its mounting and falls on the top of the plate line, placing high voltage on the output connector, the stub will short the dc to ground and blow the power supply fuse.

A two-tone test of this amplifier is shown in Fig. 110. The test setup consisted of two RF tones, one at 144.200 MHz and the other at 144.201 MHz fed into a combiner and then into the amplifier input. Except for the third-order products, which are down 28 dB from PEP, all IMD products generated within the amplifier are lower in amplitude than those found in most 10-W, solid-state, 2-m transceivers.

A 144-MHz Amplifier Using the 3CX800A7

The amplifier described here and pictured in Figs. 111 through 118 is based on the 3CX800A7 triode. This tube has a plate dissipation of 800 W with modest cooling requirements. Requiring only 19-W drive for 700-W output, this amplifier is compatible with some of today's low-power, solid-state multi-mode transceivers.

This amplifier was originally presented in April 1984 *QST* by David D. Meacham, W6EMD. It is based on a design for the 8874 tube presented in January 1972 *QST* by Raymond F. Rinaudo, W6ZO. Most of the changes to the original design are to accommodate the larger size of the 3CX800A7 and its attendant higher capacitances and currents. Fig. 112 is the schematic diagram of the complete 3CX800A7 amplifier. A plate-current meter is not included in this design, but

Fig. 111 — Front-panel view of the 3CX800A7 2-meter amplifier.

there is room on the front panel if the builder wishes to add one.

Construction

The amplifier chassis is mounted in a standard 19-inch-wide, 5¼-inch-high aluminum rack panel (Bud No. SFA-1833). A 5 × 13 × 3-inch aluminum chassis (Bud No. AC-422) is spaced 1¾ inches behind the panel by two aluminum end brackets.

Fig. 112 — Schematic diagram of the 3XC800A7 amplifier.

B1 — Blower (Dayton 4C012 or equiv.); see text.
C1, C2 — 1.7-14.1 pF air variable (E. F. Johnson 189-505-4 or equiv.).
C4, C5, C6 — Ceramic feedthrough, 1000 pF, 500 V (Erie 357-001).
C7 — EMI feedthrough filter, 1500 pF, 2.5 kV (Erie 1280-060).
C8, C9 — 50 pF, 7.5 kV, NP0 (HEC HT-50 852).
C10, C11 — See text.
D1, D2 — 1N4001.
D3 — Zener diode, 5.1 V, 10 W (1N3996A).
DS1 — NE51 in holder with built-in dropping resistor.
F1 — Slow-blow fuse, 2 A (Buss MDL-2 or equiv.).
F2 — 1.5 A fuse (Buss AGC 1½ or equiv.).
J1 — BNC bulkhead feedthrough connector (UG-492 A/U).
J2 — Type N female connector (part of C10 assembly — see text).
J3, J4 — High-voltage connector (Millen 37001 or equiv.).
L1 — 8 turns no. 16 tinned wire, 3/8-in ID, 11/16 in long.
L2 — 6 turns no. 16 tinned wire, 3/8-in ID, 11/16 in long.
L3 — Plate line, 1-5/16 in wide, 8-3/16 in long. See text and Fig. 115.
R1, R4 — 200 ohms, 12 W.
R2 — 10 kΩ, 12 W.
R3 — 35 ohms, 12 W.
R5 — 50 ohms, 50 W.
RFC1 — 1.0 μH choke, 300 mA (Miller 4602).
RFC2, RFC3 — 11 turns no. 20 HF wire on 3/8-in Noryl rod.
RFC4 — 10 turns no. 16 tinned wire, ½-in ID, 1-3/16 in long.
T1 — Filament transformer, 14.0-V, 2-A secondary (Triad F-251X or equiv.).

Fig. 113 — Mechanical details of the chassis and end brackets. The end brackets are made from 0.032-in aluminum, 5052 alloy or softer.

cabinet chosen is a lightweight aluminum unit made by Ten-Tec (No. 19-0525).

Input Circuit

In the cathode-driven configuration, the input impedance of the 3CX800A7 appears as a nominal capacitance of 26.5 pF in parallel with a resistive component that varies with operating conditions but is typically about 49 ohms. The computer-designed input circuit of this amplifier operates at a loaded Q of about 2.1. It can be set anywhere in the 2-meter band for an SWR of less than 1.3:1. C1 and C2 are predominantly matching and tuning controls, respectively; there is some interaction between them, however. When the input is tuned at 144.5 MHz, the input SWR will be less than 1.4:1 from 144 to 145 MHz.

The tube socket is an EIMAC SK-1900 or a Johnson part No. 124-311-100. Its center is mounted 2 inches from the end of the input box, adjacent to the mounting bracket. The tube pins and input circuit are cooled by a small amount of air admitted to the input box from the pressurized output box. Three holes, made with a no. 50 drill, provide adequate flow. These holes are spaced in a close triangle and are located diagonally across from the variable capacitors. Air exhausts through the tuning holes. Fig. 114 shows details of the input circuitry.

The heater circuit includes two chokes, feedthrough capacitors, the filament transformer, a voltage-dropping resistor and a switch. The chokes are wound with a turn-to-turn spacing of about one-half the wire diameter. They are self-resonant (parallel resonant) just above the 2-meter band. Nominal heater voltage for the 3CX800A7 is 13.5 V. The closest available commercial transformer has a 14.0-V secondary, so R3 is used in the primary. Switching is set up so the blower must be on before the heater can be activated. Conversely, this arrangement allows the blower to be left on after switching off the heater — a highly recommended practice.

Cathode bias is provided by a 5.1-V Zener diode, D3. R1 prevents the cathode voltage from soaring if the Zener fails. F2 will blow if excessive cathode current is drawn. R2 nearly cuts off plate current on receive. Because the grid is at dc ground, the negative supply lead must be kept above ground for grid-current metering by M1. R4 keeps the negative side of the plate supply from rising if M1, D1 and D2 all open up. D1, D2 and C3 protect the meter from transients and RF voltages.

Output Circuit

The output tank circuit is a silver-plated quarter-wave strip line (Fig. 115) fore-shortened by the tube, loading and tuning capacitances at, and near, its open end. It operates at a loaded Q of approximately 20. The silver-plated anode collet (Fig. 115) is made of 0.062-inch-thick brass sheet with Tech-Etch 134B finger stock soldered on

A 3½ × 1-inch aluminum chassis (Bud No. AC-1402) houses the input circuitry and is mounted on the larger chassis between it and the front panel. The right-

hand end bracket has a large lip on the rear for mounting the heater transformer and connectors. Fig. 113 shows mechanical details of the chassis and end brackets. The

Fig. 114 — Close-up of the input circuitry and tube-socket wiring. Keep all leads as short as possible. Although L2 is shown here with 5 turns, the final version uses 6 turns, as described in the parts list.

the inside. It is supported by two Teflon® standoffs 1½ inch in diameter and 1 inch long. At the far end of the line, a silver-plated shorting block contacts the chassis and the strip line. This block (Fig. 115) is made from 7/16-inch-thick brass 1-5/16 inches wide and 1 inch high. EIMAC CF-800 finger stock is screwed and then soldered on both top and bottom. The chassis and strip line are both slotted to allow 5/16 inch of shorting-block travel to set the tuning range of the capacitive-tuning paddle. A 1-inch-long Teflon standoff supports the center of the line. Construction details may be seen in Fig. 117.

The tuning (C11) and loading (C10) paddles are 1-3/16-inch-diameter discs made from silver-plated, 1/16-inch-thick brass. They are spaced 1-3/8 inches center-to-center. The output loading paddle is nearest the tube, and its center is 1-13/16 inches from the tube cooler surface. Spacing between the paddle and line during operation is about 0.135 inch. The output tuning boss, EIMAC part no. 720362, is tapped

Fig. 115 — Mechanical details of the plate line, anode collet and shorting block. The plate line is made from 0.032-in-thick silver-plated brass, although copper or aluminum (5052 alloy or softer) of the same thickness may be used. The lip on the plate line is screwed to the one end of the blocking capacitors. The anode collet, which is made from 0.062-in-thick silver-plated brass, is screwed to the other ends of the blocking capacitors. Tech-Etch no. 134B finger stock soldered around the inside of the anode collet grips the 3CX800A7. Finger stock on the silver-plated brass shorting block ensures good contact between the chassis and plate line.

for a ¼-28 threaded rod. The output loading control and output connector are two separate EIMAC assemblies combined into one unit. They are available from EIMAC as Support Assembly No. 720361 and Sliding Probe Assembly No. 720407. For this amplifier, the outer conductor was lengthened to reach the front panel. The grid collet is also available from EIMAC as part No 720359.

In addition to RFC4 and feedthrough capacitor C7, an energy-absorbing resistor (R5) is wired in series with the dc plate supply. This resistor will protect the tube and power supply in the event of a high-voltage arc. It provides necessary protection while dissipating only 12.5 W at 500-mA dc plate current.

Cooling

The blower specified provides a measured 25 CFM airflow through the output box and tube cooler at 0.42 inch of water-column static pressure. This amount of cooling is sufficient for 800 W of plate dissipation at sea level with inlet air temperatures up to 35° C. It is adequate for the same dissipation at 5000 feet of altitude with inlet-air temperatures up to 25° C.

Not evident from the photographs is the care taken to separate outgoing hot air from incoming cool air. This is accomplished by the addition of a simple dividing wall inside the cabinet running from the rear chassis cover of the output box to the rear of the cabinet. The material used is rigid fiberglass insulation — the kind you

Fig. 116 — Mechanical details of the exhaust air RFI filter. The honeycomb material is soldered inside a 2¾-in OD, 0.065- in wall brass tube. The flange, which bolts to the chassis, is made from 0.125-in-thick brass sheet.

Fig. 117 — Various views of the completed 3CX800A7 amplifier.

Fig. 118 — Rear view of the amplifier with the plate-compartment cover in place. Note the honeycomb RFI filter at the hot-air exhaust.

cut with a saw. It provides a measure of blower-noise suppression in addition to assuring cool inlet air.

Hot air leaving the anode cooler is directed to a homemade "honeycomb" RFI filter through a chimney made from rolled-up Teflon sheet. The filter is made of brass tubing and sheet with the honeycomb material soldered in place. See Figs. 116 and 118 for construction details. This filter acts as a waveguide-beyond-cutoff having high attenuation at 144 MHz.

The equation for calculating attenuation by this type of filter is

$$A_a = 32 \frac{D}{d}$$

where

A_a = aperture attenuation (dB)
D = length of pipe
d = inside diameter of pipe.

In this case, the "pipe" is each cell of the honeycomb. The basic material for the honeycomb is cadmium-plated brass heat-radiator core.[1] Each hexagonal-shaped cell has a width between flat sides (diameter) of 0.100 inch. The material is ½ inch thick.

[1] One source for the honeycomb radiator core material is G-O-Metric, c/o Marty Manion, 909 Norwich Ave., Delran, NJ 08075.

Plugging these values into the equation yields an A_a of 160 dB — more than enough! From a practical stand-point, it is usually sufficient to make cell length at least three times the nominal cell diameter.

Tune-up

Initial work may be done with a dip meter, particularly on the output circuit. With the tube in place, but with no voltages applied, the shorting block on the end of the plate line should be set to give a paddle-tuning range that straddles the desired operating frequency. Bear in mind that when the tube is "hot," the resonant frequency will be somewhat lower than it is without electron flow.

The input-tuning capacitor can be dip-meter resonated with the matching capacitor set at one-half mesh for a start. Further work here must be done "hot" with an SWR measuring device on the input.

Set the initial spacing between the output paddle and the plate line to 1/8 inch. Connect the output to a 50-ohm dummy load capable of handling at least 700 W at 144 MHz through an accurate VHF wattmeter, such as a Bird model 43. Connect a driver capable of delivering about 20 W to the input through an SWR-measuring device.

The heater of the 3CX800A7 should be run for at least three minutes before applying plate voltage. After the warm-up, short the TR terminals and apply about 1000 V to the plate. This should result in a small amount of idling plate current. Next, apply enough drive to produce a rise in plate current, and adjust the plate tuning for a peak in output power. Now tune and match the input circuit for minimum input SWR. Next, adjust the output loading paddle for maximum power output while keeping the plate current dipped with the plate tuning paddle. Apply full plate voltage and

higher drive power, and then repeak the output tuning and loading controls. Touch up the input tuning and matching, and the amplifier is ready for service.

A few words of caution are in order. Remember that the heater voltage must never be applied without the blower running, and that the heater must warm up at least three minutes before applying plate voltage. Never exceed 60-mA dc grid current, even during tune-up. Also, because of the relatively low grid dissipation of the 3CX800A7, RF drive must *never* be applied unless plate voltage is applied to the tube and a suitable load is connected to the output. Following these simple rules will substantially increase tube life and amplifier reliability.

Typical Operating Conditions

With Zener-diode bias, the 3CX800A7 is best operated in Class AB_2 for linear service. The data in Table 7 represent measured performance in linear service at 144 MHz. Complete data sheets are available from EIMAC. This amplifier is easily capable of conservative operation at 700-W output. Two of these tubes will run at the 1500-W output legal limit.

Table 7

Operating Conditions for the 3CX800A7 Amplifier

Plate supply voltage	2200 V
Zero-signal plate current †	65 mA
Single-tone plate current	500 mA
Grid bias (Zener bias)	−5.1 V
Single-tone grid current †	40 mA
Driving power	18.5 W
Output power	707 W
Gain	15.8 dB
Efficiency ††	64%

†Values may vary considerably from tube to tube.
††Actual tube efficiency is about one percent higher because of power loss in the 50-ohm series resistor in the plate lead (R5).

A 2-kW PEP Amplifier for 144 MHz

Large external-anode triodes in a cathode-driven configuration offer outstanding reliability, stability and ease in obtaining high power at 144 MHz.

The techniques employed in the design and construction of the cathode-driven 3CX1500A7/8877 amplifier described here (Figs. 119 to 122) have removed many of the mechanical impositions of other designs. Those interested in obtaining complete construction details should refer to the two-part article by Edward L. Meade Jr., K1AGB, appearing in December 1973 and January 1974 *QST*.

Output Circuit

The plate tank operates with a loaded Q on the order of 40 at 2-kW PEP input and 80 at 1 kW. Typical loaded Q values of 10 to 15 are used in HF amplifiers. In comparison, we are dealing with a relatively high loaded Q, so losses in the strip-line tank-circuit components must be kept very low. To this end, small-diameter Teflon rods are used as mechanical drives for the tuning capacitor and for physical support as well as mechanical drive for the output-coupling capacitor. The tuning vane or flapper capacitor is solidly grounded through a wide flexible strap of negligible inductance, directly to the chassis in close proximity to the grid-return point. A flexible-strap arrangement, similar to that of the tuning capacitor, is used to connect the output-coupling capacitor to the center pin of a type-N coaxial connector mounted in the chassis base.

Ceramic (or Teflon) pillars, used to support the air strip line, are located under the middle set of plate-line dc isolation bushings. This places these pillars well out of the intense RF field associated with the tube, or high-impedance end of the line. In operation, plate tuning and loading is quite smooth and stable, so a high-loaded Q is apparently not bothersome in this respect.

In this amplifier, output coupling is accomplished by the capacitive probe method. Major advantages of capacitive-

Fig. 120 — The placement of input-circuit components and supporting bracket may be seen in this bottom view. When the bottom cover is in place, the screened air inlet allows the blower to pull air in, pressurizing the entire under-chassis area. The Minibox on the rear apron is a housing for the input reflectometer circuit.

Fig. 121 — The tube and plate line is in place with the top and side of the compartment removed for clarity. The plate-tuning vane is at bottom center. A bracket is attached to the side panel to support the rear of the Teflon rod supporting the tuning vane. The coil at the opposite end of the plate line is RFC1, connected between the high-voltage-bypass plate and the top section of the plate-line sandwich. Items outside the tube enclosure include the filament transformer, blower motor, relays and a power supply to operate a VOX-controlled relay system.

Fig. 119 — Front-panel layout of the 2-meter kilowatt amplifier.

Table 8
Performance Data

	1 kW	1.6 kW
Power input, watts	1000	1600
Plate voltage	2600	2450
Plate current (single tone)	385 mA	660 mA
Plate current (idling)	50 mA	50 mA
Grid bias	− 10 V	− 10 V
Grid current (single tone)	35 mA	54 mA
Drive power, watts	18	41
Efficiency (apparent)	59.5%	61.8%
Power gain (apparent)	15.2 dB	13.9 dB
Power output, watts	595	1000

probe coupling are loading linearity and elimination of moving-contact surfaces.

Capacitive-probe coupling is a form of reactive transformation matching whereby the feed-line (load) impedance is transformed to the tube resonant-load impedance (Z_o) of 1800 ohms (at the 2-kW level) by means of a series reactance (a capacitor in this case).

Support Electronics

An RF-output monitor is a virtual necessity in VHF amplifiers. In this amplifier, one of these built-in circuits is achieved quite handily. The circuit consists of a 10:1 resistive voltage divider, diode rectifier, filter and adjustable indicating instrument. Two 7500-ohm, 2-watt carbon resistors are located in the plate compartment connected between the type-N RF-output connector and a BNC connector, inside a Minibox, with the 1500-ohm, 1-watt composition resistor and the rectifier diode joined at this point. Relative output voltage is fed, via feedthrough capacitors, to the level-setting potentiometer and multimeter switch.

Testing and Operation

The amplifier is unconditionally stable, with no parasitics. To verify this, a zero-bias check for stability was made. This involved shorting out the Zener diode in the cathode return lead, reducing bias to essentially zero volts. Plate voltage was applied, allowing the tube to dissipate about 885 watts. The input and output circuits were then tuned through their ranges with no loads attached. There was no sign of out-

put on the relative output meter and no change in the plate and grid currents. As with most cathode-driven amplifiers, there is a slight interaction between grid and plate currents during normal tune-up under RF-applied conditions. This should not be misconstrued as amplifier instability.

Tolerances of the Zener diode used in the cathode return line will result in values of bias voltage and idling plate currents other than those listed in Table 8. The 1N3311,

a 20-percent-tolerance unit, is rated at 12 volts nominal but actually operates at 10 volts in this amplifier (within the 20-percent tolerance).

To commence routine operation, the variable capacitor in the input circuit should be set at the point where lowest input SWR was obtained during the cold-tube initial tune-up. The ability of the plate tank to resonate at 144-145 MHz with the top cover in place should be verified with

Fig. 122 — Schematic diagram of the 144-MHz amplifier. Included is information for the input reflectometer used as an aid to tuning the cathode circuit for low SWR. C7, C8 and C9 are fabricated as described in the text and Fig. 121.

B1 — Blower, Fasco 59752-IN or Dayton 2C610. Wheel diameter is 3-3/16 inches.
C2 — 5- to 30-pF air variable, Hammarlund HF-30-X or equiv.
C3, C4, C5, C6 — 0.1-μF, 600-V, 20-A feed-through capacitor. Sprague 80P3 or equiv.
J1, J2, J6 — Type BNC.
J3 — Type N.
J4 — Coaxial panel jack, UG-22B/U, Amphenol 82-62 or equiv.
J5 — HV connector, James Millen 37001 or equiv.
L1 — Double-sided PC board, 1-1/4 × 4-7/16 inches.
L2 — 4-1/4 inches of no. 18 wire. L1 and L2 are part of the input reflectometer circuit.
L3 — 6 turns no. 18 enam., 5/8-in long on 3/8-in-dia form (white slug).
L4 — 3 turns no. 14 enam., 5/8 in long × 9/16-in ID. Lead length to L3 is 5/8 in. Lead length to cathode bus is 3/4 in.
L5 — Air dielectric stripline. See text.
P1 — Type BNC.
P2 — Type N.
R1 — Meter range multiplier. Ten 500-kΩ, 2-W composition resistors in series.
RFC1 — 7 turns no. 16 tinned, 1/2-in. ID × 1-in long.
RFC2 — 18 turns no. 18 enam., close wound on 1-MΩ, 2-watt composition resistor.
RFC3, RFC4 — Each 2 ferrite beads on component leads.
RFC5, RFC6 — 10 turns no. 12 enam., bifilar wound, 5/8-in dia.
S1 — Single-pole, three-position rotary switch, non-shorting contacts.
T1 — 5-V, 10-A secondary, center tap not used, Stancor P-6135 or equiv.

a grid-dip meter. Use a one-turn link attached to the RF output connector. Top and bottom covers are then secured. As with all cathode driven amplifiers, *excitation should never be applied when the tube heater is activated and plate voltage is removed.* Next, turn on the tube heater and blower simultaneously, allowing 90 seconds for warm-up. A plate potential between 2400 and 3000 volts then may be applied and its presence verified on the multimeter. The power supply should be able to deliver

800 mA or so. With the VOX relay actuated, resting current should be indicated on the cathode meter.

A small amount of drive is applied and the plate-tank circuit tuned for an indication of maximum relative power output. The cathode circuit can now be resonated, tuning for minimum reflected power on the reflectometer, and not for maximum drive power transfer. Tuning and loading of the plate-tank circuit follows the standard sequence for any cathode driven amplifier.

Resonance is accompanied by a moderate dip in plate/cathode current, a rise in grid current and a considerable increase in relative power output. Plate-current dip is not absolutely coincident with maximum power output, but it is very close. Tuning and output-loading adjustments should be for maximum efficiency and output as indicated on the output-meter. Final adjustment for lowest SWR at amplifier input should be done when the desired plate input-power level has been reached.

A 220-MHz High-Power Amplifier

This amplifier employs the 3CX1500A7/8877 in a cathode-driven circuit. The grid is grounded directly to the chassis, adding to the stability. The amplifier (Figs. 123 to 127) is unconditionally stable — more so than some amplifiers built for the HF region.

Circuit Details

Fig. 124 is a schematic diagram of the amplifier. The input circuit consists of a T network. Medium values of Q were chosen to provide high efficiency. Both the cathode and the heater are operated at the same RF potential; the heater is held above

Fig. 124 — Schematic diagram of the 220-MHz amplifier. Unless otherwise specified, all capacitors are disc ceramic and resistors are 1/2-watt carbon composition.

C1 — Air variable, 15 pF.
C2, C3 — Button mica, 500-pF, 500-V rating.
C4-C9, inclusive — Teflon capacitor (use 10-mil Teflon sheet).
C10 — Doorknob capacitor, 500 pF, 5-kV rating.
D1-D4 — 1000 PIV, 3A.

J1, J2 — Coaxial receptacle, type N.
J3 — High-voltage connector (Millen).
L1 — 3 turns no. 14, 1/4-inch ID, 3/4-inch long.
L2 — 1/4-inch-wide, 2-3/8-inch-long copper flashing strap.
L3 — Plate inductor (see Fig. 125).
RFC1 — 8 turns no. 18 enam. 1/2-inch dia,

3/4-inch long.
RFC2, RFC3 — 10 turns no. 18 enam. bifilar wound on 3/4-inch Teflon rod close wound.
RFC4 — 5 turns no. 16 enam. wound on 1-MΩ, 2-watt composition resistor.
T1 — Filament transformer, 5.0 V at 10.5 A.

Fig. 123 — Front-panel layout of the 220-MHz kilowatt.

Fig. 125 — Bottom view of the amplifier. RFC2 and RFC3 can be seen above tube socket (bifilar winding). Copper strap is L2 shown connected to C1. Small coil is L1 and larger coil is RFC1. The grid of the tube should be grounded to the chassis with finger stock similar to that used in the plate line. Component mounted on the heat sink at left is the Zener diode used for biasing purposes.

RF ground by the impedance of the filament choke. The plate tank is a pair of quarter-wavelength striplines placed symmetrically about the tube. This arrangement permits a more uniform flow of current through the anode, preventing "hot spots" on the anode conducting surface. Additionally, tube output capacitance is effectively halved, as one-half the tube capacitance (13 pF) is used to load each stripline. Striplines act as low-pass circuit elements even with the high unloaded-Q conditions found at 220 MHz. Linear inductors also offer control of odd-mode harmonics. No spurious responses could be found in this amplifier up through the 900-MHz region.

A strip-line impedance can be varied by changing its width and relation to its ground planes. Physical dimensions of the tube limit the position of the stripline above one ground plane. In order to use a commercially available chassis, the stripline was placed 1¼ inch above one side of an inverted 4-inch-high chassis. This means that approximately 75 percent of the RF current flows through the chassis, but only 25 percent flows through the top shield cover. The small percentage flowing through the top reduces the effect of any mechanical anomalies associated with a removable cover.

For quarter-wavelength lines, the ratio of line impedance to reactance should be between 1.5 and 2.0 for the best bandwidth. Taking stray capacitance into account, expected tuning capacitance and tube output capacitance gives a value of 55 ohms for X_C. Values of line impedance versus line length for resonance at 222 MHz were computed on a programmable calculator for impedances between 30 and 100 ohms. These were plotted on a graph. Final dimensions were determined using this system, choosing dimensions that fell into the middle of the graph, thus allowing for any unpredicted effects.

Construction details are given in Figs. 125, 126 and 127. The plate blocking capacitor consists of a sandwich of brass plate and the stripline, with Teflon sheet as the dielectric. This forms a very-low-loss, high-voltage capacitor. The plate bypass capacitor is built along the same principles. A piece of circuit board was sandwiched with Teflon sheet to the side wall of the chassis. This technique is used effectively throughout as an inexpensive bypass or feedthrough capacitor at VHF.

Amplifier output is coupled through a capacitive probe. Transformation of the load impedance to the tube resonant-load impedance is achieved by means of a series reactance (the loading capacitor). The tuning capacitor is solidly grounded by means of a flexible strap of negligible inductance.

A rather elaborate metering system is employed. Although all of the meters provide useful data, only the plate and grid meters are necessary for proper amplifier use.

The anode exhaust-temperature metering circuit takes advantage of a thermal property of semiconductors. As the temperature changes, the forward resistance of a diode changes in a nearly linear manner. The diode sensor is made a part of a bridge circuit, allowing calibrated operation. Calibration may be determined by packing the diode in ice for the low point (0° C) and immersing it in boiling water for the high point (100° C). The amount of heat dissipated by the tube is inversely proportional to the efficiency for a given power input. Low heat dissipation yields longer tube life.

High-power amplifiers require considerable attention to cooling. The plate compartment is pressurized by air from an external blower. Holes in the chassis allow a portion of this air to pass through the grid and cathode structure. Most of the air

Fig. 126 — Construction details of the 220-MHz plate line and associated components.

flows through the anode, a handmade Teflon chimney, then out the top cover. Aluminum screening is tightly bonded around these two openings. No radiated RF could be detected around the chassis except within one inch of the anode exhaust hole.

To commence operation, the input should be adjusted for minimum SWR with no voltages applied. The covers should be in place whenever voltage is present. Drive should *never* be applied without plate voltage and a load connected if the filament is energized. Cooling air must always be supplied whenever the filament is turned on.

After a 60-second warmup, small amounts of drive may be applied. The plate circuit is then tuned for maximum output indication. The drive level is then increased. Tuning and loading follow the normal procedure for any cathode-driven amplifier: Adjustments are made for maximum output and efficiency. When the desired plate output power has been reached, the input circuit should be adjusted for minimum input SWR.

Fig. 127 — Interior view of the 220-MHz plate compartment. Contact of the tube with "hot side" of C6 is accomplished with suitable finger stock (available from the tube manufacturer). This conductor, in conjunction with a similar one separated by the Teflon insulator, forms the L3/C6 combination. The entire assembly is sandwiched together by means of four insulated bushings (approximately ¾-inch diameter). Placement of bushings is not critical. RFC4 can be seen at the right connected to C9. C8 is at the right of the photo and has a nominal spacing of 1 inch to a similar plate soldered to L3. Tuning capacitor C7 can be seen at the left connected to C6. Drive mechanism can be of builder's choice.

Chapter 32

UHF and Microwave Equipment

U HF and up represents a challenge to the experimenter and builder. The techniques used at HF and VHF do not always work here. Tuned circuits for this range rarely contain coils and capacitors as they do at HF and VHF. Sections of transmission line are used instead. Sometimes those line sections are in the form of cavity resonators. At other times, a section of line is a trace that has been etched on a PC board.

In this chapter you will find new techniques, and old, illustrated in the various construction projects. Those projects range from simple to sophisticated.

Dual-Gate GaAsFET Preamplifiers for 432 MHz

Dual-gate GaAsFET devices in plastic packages offer amateurs the opportunity to build inexpensive preamplifiers with good noise performance. Described here and shown in Figs. 1 through 3 are two preamplifiers that use GaAsFET devices costing only a few dollars each. These preamplifiers were designed and built by Kent Britain, WA5VJB.

Circuit Details

The basic circuit is shown in Fig. 2. Information is given so that the NEC NE41137, Motorola MRF966/967, Mitsubishi MGF1100 or 3SK97 devices may be used. C1, C2 and C5 can be miniature ceramic trimmer capacitors or piston trimmers. The exact value is not critical; any trimmer with a maximum value of 8 to 10 pF will do. C7, the output coupling capacitor, can be any small silver-mica unit between 50 and 100 pF. For stability, it is important to use good-quality capacitors for the gate 2 and source bypasses. Ceramic chip or leadless disc-ceramic types are necessary to provide a low-impedance ground.

Construction

The dual-gate GaAsFET preamplifiers are built "dead bug" style on a piece of double-sided PC board material. See Fig. 1. The circuit board acts as a low-impedance ground plane, and all ground connections are made directly to it. J1, J2 and C9 also secure the circuit board to the lid of the

Fig. 1 — The dual-gate GaAsFET 432-MHz preamplifier is built "dead bug" style on a piece of copper-clad circuit board material.

Fig. 2 — Schematic diagram of the 432-MHz dual-gate GaAsFET preamplifiers. The same circuit is used for either version, but some parts values are different. Resistors are ¼-W carbon composition types unless otherwise noted.

C1, C2, C5 — 10-pF (max.) trimmer capacitor. Piston trimmer preferred, but miniature ceramic trimmer will work fine.
C3, C4 — 200- to 1000-pF ceramic chip capacitor or leadless disc-ceramic capacitor.
C6, C9 — 400- to 1000-pF feedthrough capacitor.
C7 — 50- to 100-pF silver-mica capacitor.
C8 — 1- to 25-μF, 25-V electrolytic capacitor.
D1 — 5.1-V, 1-W Zener diode (1N4733 or equiv.).
D2 — 1N914, 1N4148 or any diode with ratings of 25 PIV and 50 mA or greater.
J1, J2 — Female chassis-mount BNC or Type-N connector.
L1 — For NE41137: 2½t no. 20 copper wire, 3/16-inch ID, spaced one wire dia. For

MRF966/967: 4t no. 20 copper wire, 3/16-inch ID, spaced one wire dia. For 3SK97 or MGF1100: 2t no. 20 copper wire, 3/16-inch ID, spaced 1 wire dia.
L2 — For NE41137, MGF1100 or 3SK97: 2t no. 20 copper wire, 3/16-inch ID, spaced one wire dia. Tap at 1t. For MRF966/967: 2t no. 20 copper wire, 3/16-inch ID, spaced one wire dia. Tap at ½t.
Q1 — NEC NE41137, Motorola MRF966/967, Mitsubishi MGF1100 or 3SK97. See text.
R1 — For NE41137, MGF1100 or 3SK97: 10 kΩ; for MRF966/967: 4.7 kΩ.
R2 — 10 kΩ for all versions.
R3 — 150- to 250-ohm, 1- or 2-W resistor.
R4 — For NE41137, MGF1100 or 3SK97: 47 Ω; for MRF966/967: 100 Ω.

enclosure. The enclosure can be any aluminum diecast box (Bud CU-124; Hammond 1490B) or Minibox (Bud CU-3002A) approximately 4 by 2 inches, or you can make one by soldering pieces of circuit-board material together.

Q1 is supported above the ground plane by its gate 2 and source leads, which are soldered directly to C3 and C4. The other ends of these capacitors are soldered to the ground plane. R4 should be soldered in place with essentially no lead length. Placement for the rest of the parts is not critical, but keep the leads short. A layout that has proven successful is shown in Fig. 3.

GaAsFETs are static-sensitive, so handle them accordingly. See Chapter 24 for information on working with static-sensitive devices. It's best to assemble the rest of the circuit and install Q1 last. Use a grounded iron if possible, and solder the leads quickly.

Parts for this project are available from Microwave Components of Michigan and Applied Invention, both listed in Chapter 35. NEC transistors are available from California Eastern Laboratories, 3260 Jay St., Santa Clara, CA 95050.

Peak the tuning capacitors on a weak signal and adjust for best signal-to-noise ratio. For best results, you should have access to a noise-figure meter. This preamplifier typically measures 0.7- to 0.9-dB noise figure and 22- to 24-dB gain with any of the listed devices.

Fig. 3 — Suggested layout for the dual-gate GaAsFET 432-MHz amplifier. The circuit board is approximately 1¾ × 3¾ inches. J1 and J2 are approximately 1¾ inches apart.

GaAsFET Preamplifier for 70 cm

The preamplifier described here and shown in Figs. 4 through 6 offers good noise performance and gain, and is suitable for terrestrial, EME and satellite applications at 432 and 435 MHz. Gain is approximately 15 dB and the noise figure is 0.55 dB, measured on an HP8970A noise-figure meter with the HP346A noise source. This preamplifier is easy to build and offers stable operation with little adjustment. It was designed by Chip Angle, N6CA. The version shown here was built and tested in the ARRL lab by Mark Wilson, AA2Z.

Circuit Details

The schematic diagram of the 70-cm GaAsFET preamplifier is shown in Fig. 5. The circuit was originally designed for an NEC NE21889 GaAsFET, but a Mitsubishi MGF1402 or MGF1202 device will work fine. The version shown here uses an MGF1402, but most single-gate GaAsFETs will work.

This preamplifier uses source feedback to bring the input impedance close to 50 ohms. Input and output return loss is typically better than 15 dB. This means that a band-pass filter can be used ahead of the preamplifier without introducing mismatch loss or instability.

The design uses plenty of decoupling capacitors and RF chokes. Good-quality bypass capacitors are a must for stable operation, so use chip capacitors where specified. D1 and D2 are included for reverse and overvoltage protection. Regulator U1 allows virtually any voltage greater than 9-V dc to be used.

Construction

The preamplifier is built on a G-10 glass-epoxy printed-circuit board using surface-mounting techniques. Layout is shown in Fig. 6. All components mount to the circuit traces. The other side of the board is unetched copper except around the connector center pins, and acts as a ground plane. All grounded pads on the etched side are connected to the ground plane with eyelets or pieces of tinned wire that pass through holes in the board and are soldered to both sides.

The board is mounted to the lid of a diecast box (Hammond 1590B or Bud CU-124) and is designed to accommodate Type-N connectors. Aluminum spacers for the connectors must be fabricated, as shown in Fig. 6. These spacers mount between the box lid and the ground plane of the PC board.

Q1 has two source leads. Only one is used on this board, and the extra lead may be clipped off. The ferrite bead on the drain lead mounts in a small hole cut in the board. The drain lead passes through this bead and is soldered to a pad.

GaAsFETs are static-sensitive, so handle them accordingly. See Chapter 24 for in-

Fig. 4 — The 70-cm GaAsFET preamplifier is built on a PC board that is mounted to the lid of a diecast box. This version uses a Zener diode instead of the 3-terminal regulator shown in Figs. 5 and 6. Connector mounting hardware also holds the board in place. Component layout is shown in Fig. 6.

Fig. 5 — Schematic diagram of the 70-cm GaAsFET preamplifier. Resistors are carbon-composition types. Resistor values are given in ohms; capacitor values are given in pF.

C1 — 5.6-pF silver-mica capacitor or same as C2.
C2 — 0.6- to 6-pF ceramic piston trimmer capacitor (Johanson 5700 series or equiv.).
C3, C4, C5 — 200-pF ceramic chip capacitor.
C6, C7 — 0.1-μF disc ceramic capacitor, 50 V or greater.
C8 — 15-pF silver-mica capacitor.
C9 — 500- to 1000-pF feedthrough capacitor.
D1 — 16- to 30-V, 500-mW Zener diode (1N966B or equiv.).
D2 — 1N914, 1N4148 or any diode with ratings of at least 25 PIV at 50 mA or greater.
J1, J2 — Female chassis-mount Type-N connectors, PTFE dielectric (UG-58 or equiv.).
L1, L2 — 3t no. 24 tinned wire, 0.110-inch ID, spaced 1 wire dia.
L3 — 5t no. 24 tinned wire, 3/16-inch ID,

spaced 1 wire dia. or closer. Slightly larger diameter (0.010 inch) may be required with some FETs.
L4 — 1t no. 24 tinned wire, 1/8-inch ID.
L5 — 4t no. 24 tinned wire, 1/8-inch ID, spaced 1 wire dia.
L6 — 1t no. 24 tinned wire, 1/8-inch ID.
Q1 — Mitsubishi MGF1402 (see text).
R1 — 200- or 500-Ω cermet potentiometer set to midrange initially.
R2 — 62-Ω, 1/4-W resistor.
R3 — 51-Ω, 1/8-W carbon composition resistor, 5% tolerance.
RFC1 — 5t no. 26 enam. wire on a ferrite bead.
U1 — 5-V, 100-mA 3-terminal regulator (LM78L05 or equiv. TO-92 package).

Fig. 6 — Parts placement diagram for the 70-cm preamplifier. A full-size etching pattern may be found at the back of this book.

formation on working with static-sensitive devices. It's best to assemble the rest of the circuit and install Q1 last. Use a grounded iron if possible, and solder the leads quickly.

Parts for this project are available from Microwave Components of Michigan and Applied Invention, both listed in Chapter 35. MGF1402 transistors are available from Advanced Receiver Research, Box 1242, Burlington, CT 06013. NEC transistors are available from California Eastern Labora-

tories, 3260 Jay St., Santa Clara, CA 95050.

Adjustment

The preamplifier shown in Fig. 4 was assembled in the ARRL lab and tested before any adjustments were made. For starters, C2 was set at midrange. As assembled, the preamp measured 13 dB gain with a 0.57-dB noise figure — perfectly acceptable performance for a device

such as this. After adjusting C2 and bending L3 and L5, the gain increased to 15.25 dB with a 0.54-dB noise figure. This is acceptable for all but perhaps the most demanding EME applications. No amount of spreading or compressing the coils could make the gain fall below 12 dB or the noise figure rise above 0.65 dB. At no time did the preamp display signs of instability. In short, this is a reproducible project. You can assemble it without test equipment and be reasonably sure of the performance.

1296-MHz Transverter

Presented here is a basic 1296-MHz transverter system which, with some additions, could serve in a 1296-MHz moonbounce system. The basic unit coupled with a good antenna is capable of reasonable terrestrial performance as well. Construction requires a minimum of special skills and test equipment.

The established design specifications are listed below:

1) The unit forms the basis of a 1296-MHz weak-signal/moonbounce system.

2) The unit must be easy to build and duplicate.

3) It must be as inexpensive as possible.

4) It must use a minimum of special microwave components.

5) It must have a 28-MHz tunable IF.

6) The receiver portion should exhibit a noise figure of 3 dB or less and sufficient gain to override noise in the tunable IF. Reasonable dynamic range is also a requirement.

7) The transmitter output should be 250 mW with all spurs and harmonics down at least 40 dB.

8) The LO should produce at least +15-dBm output with all spurs and harmonics down 30 dB or more. It must be easy to align without special instruments.

9) At low microwave frequencies lumped constants are not very effective, so microstrip techniques are used wherever possible. The microstrip portions of the circuit can be constructed easily with nothing more than a sheet of copper, some single-sided 0.062-inch G-10 (glass epoxy) board, a sharp pair of scissors, and a few tubes of Superglue! This eliminates the mess of etching PC boards.

The 1296 transverter presented here, designed and constructed by Dave Eckhardt, W6LEV, fulfills all of these requirements. The total price tag from start to

Fig. 14 — The completed 1296-MHz transverter consists of three circuit boards. The boards may be stacked as shown and mounted in a convenient enclosure.

finish should be less than half the cost of comparable commercial units.

Theory of Operation

Fig. 13 presents the block diagram of the transverter. It is broken into three major functional units. From top to bottom these are the receive chain, local oscillator (LO) and transmit chain. A photograph of the finished unit is shown in Fig. 14.

A good LO is the key to a clean transverter design. The LO used here is based on a design originally presented in *Ham Radio*.[1] This reference is all but required reading before tuning up the LO without special instruments. An International Crystal OE-5 modular oscillator forms the heart of the LO chain. It oscillates at 105.658333 MHz, which places 1296.000 MHz at 28.100 MHz on the tunable IF. This frequency was chosen because the band-pass filters in some receivers exhibit loss below 28 MHz. It also allows for some error in the exact LO frequency.

The output link of the OE-5 module (no longer available; see Fig 21) resonates at 105 MHz, and feeds the first doubler. This stage tunes to 211 MHz with

[1]Shuch, H. P., "Compact and Clean L-Band Local Oscillator," December 1979 *Ham Radio*, p. 40.

Fig. 13 — Block diagram of the 1296-MHz transverter.

a single parallel-tuned resonant circuit with the inductor tapped down to feed the second doubler. The second doubler feeds a band-pass filter consisting of two inductively coupled, capacitively shortened quarter-wave stripline resonators tuned for 422.6 MHz. Output from the 422.6 MHz filter is fed to a parametric tripler which has both its input and output tuned to 1268 MHz. This technique yields about 4 dB more gain and a cleaner output than a conventional tripler. The 1268-MHz energy then passes through a 3-stage filter constructed of 0.025-inch-thick brass sheet and UT-141 semi-rigid coax. This filter was designed by Chip Angle, N6CA. The output of the filter feeds an MRF911 amplifier where the level is brought up to approximately +15 dBm. From there, the 1268-MHz signal is applied to an in-phase (Wilkinson) power divider. Each of the two output ports of the divider supply roughly +7 dBm of 1268-MHz energy to the mixers in the receive and transmit chains.

All spurs and harmonics of the LO are down 40 dB from the 1268-MHz output when tuned with the aid of a spectrum analyzer. The builder can achieve −30 dB on spurs and harmonics by following the procedure (outlined in the referenced *Ham Radio* article) for alignment without special instruments. The LO is easy to tune and achieves a clean output. It is, however, the most critical of any of the circuits in the transverter. Meticulous adherence to the outlined tune-up procedure is a must!

The receiver nominally exhibits a 3-dB noise figure with 32 dB of conversion gain. The antenna feeds the first MRF901 amplifier, which is optimized for best noise figure. Builders may want to precede the first stage with a low-loss band-pass filter, T/R switching and a GaAsFET preamplifier. Output from the noise-optimized first stage is fed through a band-pass filter identical to the 1268-MHz filter in the LO. The signal then goes to the second MRF901 amplifier, which is optimized for gain. Another band-pass filter couples the second stage to the mixer. The singly balanced rat-race mixer also accepts +7 dBm of 1268-MHz energy from one of the ports of the power divider located at the output of the LO. This type of mixer functions well with as little as +1 to +2 dBm of LO energy, but linearity and dynamic range are enhanced with +7 to +10 dBm of LO injection.

A terminating network follows the IF port of the mixer and also serves as a low-Q band-pass filter for the required difference frequency of 28 MHz. This network presents the IF port of the mixer with a constant 50-ohm load over a wide frequency range. Postconversion amplification is by means of two J310 JFETs in a common-gate configuration, with the first stage optimized for noise performance. If the builder has a sensitive 28-MHz receiver, both stages of postconversion gain may not

be required. The final block in the receiver chain is a tight band-pass filter centered on 28.5 MHz, which precedes the tunable IF.

The gain-optimized MRF901 amplifier and the two stages of postamplification gain are unconditionally stable. The noise-optimized MRF901 stage may be open- or short-circuited at its input with no damage to the device.

The transmit mixer accepts inputs from the second port of the LO power divider and 0 to +3 dBm of 28-MHz energy from the tunable IF. A terminating network/BPF identical to that in the receive chain is used at the IF port of the mixer. This mixer is identical to the receive mixer, except that the sum frequency is used. The filter that follows the RF port is, therefore, tuned to 1296 MHz, and is identical to the filters in the LO and receiver chain. The filter response is typically 15 dB down at 1268 MHz (the LO frequency) when tuned to 1296 MHz. If more attenuation is needed, two filters can be cascaded, or a high-Q open quarter-wave line cut for 1268 MHz can be installed in shunt on the filter port away from the mixer. Three stages of amplification, each supplying roughly 10 dB of unconditionally stable gain, are fed by the filter. Final output from the transmitter is between 200 and 300 mW.

SPECIAL COMPONENTS AND TECHNIQUES

Several special techniques are used in building this transverter, but don't be alarmed! They are easy to master, and may be adapted to other UHF and microwave projects. Also, application of several special components greatly simplifies the process of building any piece of microwave gear.

Components

All microwave circuits require some special components, and this project is no exception. However, since most amateurs have a limited bank account (that's one reason we build), the number of special components has been kept to a minimum.

Variable capacitors that work well at microwave frequencies are quite expensive, so another method of tuning was devised. Tuning involves use of transmission-line sections and chip capacitors. The builder should have about 30 to 50 good microwave chip capacitors on hand. Not all of these will be used, but allow 30% more than needed to account for breakage or metallization separation during soldering. Don't skimp! In many cases these capacitors establish the low- and high-frequency stability of the circuits. They should *not* be the "series resonant" type, but should present a very low capacitive reactance from dc to at least 5 GHz. American Technical Ceramics makes a good line of microwave chips. Although a value of 0.01 μF is shown in the schematics, values ranging from 0.01 μF to 1000 pF should work well. Several of the ads in *QST* routinely carry good microwave chip capacitors ranging from $.50 to $1.50 each.

Special care must be exercised in soldering the chip capacitors. Fig. 15 illustrates a good technique. All surfaces should be clean and lightly tinned before you attempt to solder the chip. Position the chip in place and hold it with a toothpick. Do not use a screwdriver or tweezers, since the metal can easily damage the ceramic base of the capacitor. Lay the chisel side of the tip of a 15- to 20-watt soldering pen on the surface to which the capacitor is to be soldered, with the tip of the chisel just touch-

Fig. 15 — A typical chip capacitor is shown at A. The proper technique for holding and soldering the chip is shown at B. At C the final appearance of the capacitor in the circuit. Check for good solder flow, no metallization separation and no cracks or fractures in the ceramic.

ing the chip capacitor.

Touch and flow a minimum amount of solder between the chip and the soldering pen tip and pull the tip away at a low angle to the surface. Repeat the procedure on the other side of the chip. If you don't dump too much heat into the chip while soldering the second end, you may not have to hold it in place. Fig. 15C illustrates how the connection should look when done. Inspect the solder and the chip capacitor with a magnifier for good solder flow and lack of fractures and cracks. Don't overheat the chip or the metallization may separate from the ceramic and you'll have to discard the capacitor. Several attempts may be necessary, but the technique can be mastered after a few tries.

In addition to chip capacitors, several high-quality microwave variable capacitors are needed. These devices are also available from some of the advertisers in *QST*. Johanson or Triko units may be used. The Johansons are more expensive, but mechanically superior. If you can tune the circuit to "perfection" with only 5 to 8 tries use the Trikos. However, they will not withstand repeated tweaking. (Who can resist?) Don't make too many substitutions of critical components unless you have some good microwave test gear.

Several feet of UT-141 semi-rigid Teflon dielectric coax is also required for resonators in the filters and interconnection between boards. Roughly 2 feet is required for the filters. In 2-foot lengths, UT-141 costs between $1.35 to $3 per foot. A few advertisers in *QST* offer it for sale. It is also available from most microwave parts/cabling and connector supply houses. The formula for the crystal frequency is:

Frequency = (1296.000 − IF)/12

All frequencies are in megahertz. This should be considered if the builder desires 1296.000 MHz to fall at some frequency other than 28.100 MHz. Although I have not built this unit for the OSCAR transponder, a change in LO frequency could bring 1269 MHz in range of a 28-MHz tunable IF. All circuits should have a wide enough tuning range to accommodate the slightly lower LO and operating frequencies.

Circuit Boards, Microstrip and Tuning

As mentioned in a previous section, much of the RF circuitry uses microstrip transmission-line sections. This was done because lumped-constant matching networks are not very effective at microwave frequencies. Their size is a significant portion of a wavelength, so they no longer "look like" their lumped dc equivalents. Lumped elements are available to the microwave industry, but they are generally quite expensive. The use of transmission-line sections offers a versatile, simple and inexpensive way of impedance matching and routing RF around a board. Microstrip

transmission line is especially well suited because it may be etched from a double-sided copper-clad board or cut out with a sharp knife or a pair of scissors from sheet copper and mounted above the ground plane with an adhesive.

Fig. 16 shows microstrip parameters; characteristic impedance is given by Schneider.[2] This project assumes a dielectric constant of 4.5 for G-10 board and 1.0 for air. The width of the strip, spacing above the ground plane, and dielectric material are all variables that determine the impedance of the line and its electrical length. If a circuit is designed with this in mind, it can be tuned by tweaking the spacing or width of a line. In addition, a shunt line may be shortened or lengthened by sliding a chip capacitor up and down the line! This is the technique used to tune the transverter. It may sound odd to the uninitiated, but it works well and doesn't involve expensive gold-plated components! Most of the circuits that need tuning are designed with a shunt line and a series line with the 50-ohm port located at the end of the series line. The matching circuit variables are chosen so that the normal scatter of S-parameters from device variation is compensated for by sliding the chip capacitor up and down the shunt line until the stage is optimized. Remember to use a toothpick to hold the capacitor in place.

In the design stages of this project, this method was modeled on a Hewlett-Packard HP-41CV calculator with the aid of the Smith Chart. The method looked promising. When the original air-microstrip version was constructed, no stage took more than 5 minutes of sliding chip capacitors up and down the shunt line and "fine tuning" the spacing of the microstrip elements to optimize. When the G-10 version was constructed, the "sliding capacitor" technique proved quite adequate. This method may be applied to just about any large- or small-signal RF circuitry that uses transmission-line sections for matching.

Several characteristic line impedances are required. Table 1 presents these impedances with the required line widths and spacings. Absolute precision is not needed in cutting the line widths, but reasonable care is required. "Eyeballing" them with a ruler graduated in 0.01-inch increments is adequate. In the case of G-10 board, the spacing is always that of the board, 0.062 inches. This project may be built with air-microstrip lines, or the lines may be mounted directly on the dielectric side of the single-sided G-10 board. In the latter case, the line length for a given electrical length of air line must be shortened by the square root of the dielectric constant. For a given electrical line length, the G-10 line is 0.471 times $(1/\sqrt{4.5})$ the physical length of the

corresponding air line. Therefore, for a given electrical length of line, the G-10 version occupies less than half the board space of an air-microstrip version.

In either case, the lines are simply cut to the appropriate width and length from a sheet of 1- or 2-ounce copper. If the G-10

Table 1
Microstrip Parameters

Z_0	Air ($\epsilon_r = 1$) w	h	G-10 ($\epsilon_r = 4.5$) w	h = 0.062
10	1.0000	0.0313		
16	1.2813	0.0625	0.5000	
18	1.1250	0.0625	0.4375	
50	0.3125	0.0625	0.1000	
70	0.3750	0.1250	0.0600	
86			0.0370	
90	0.1250	0.0625	0.030	
115	0.1563	0.125	0.016	
125	0.1250	0.1250	0.013	

Fig. 16 — Microstripline physical parameters. See Table 1.

Fig. 17 — Mounting technique for microwave transistors. Collector and base leads are straight; emitter leads are bent and soldered to the ground plane. See text.

Fig. 18 — Photograph showing mounting technique for microwave transistors.

[2]Hewlett Packard, *HP-41CV Circuit Analysis Pac.*

Fig. 20 — Details of the band-pass filter shown in Fig. 19.

version is built, the line is simply glued in place with Superglue. The air line version requires small spacers of 0.032, 0.062 or 0.125 inches. These are made from small (1/8 × 1/8 inch) squares of clean (no copper) 0.032, 0.062 or 0.125-inch-thick glass-epoxy board. The spacers and air line are then glued in place. A minimum number of spacers should be used. What could be easier! The ground plane on the "business side" of the G-10 board is cut from the same copper sheet to fit around and frame the microstrip elements. It is also glued in place with Superglue. It is necessary to curl the top ground over the edge of the board and solder it to the bottom ground plane. Small holes to pass no. 18 wire are drilled through both ground planes at intervals of ¼ to ½ inch. This is especially important on ground-plane edges that frame microstrip elements. Short pieces of no. 18 wire (or metal grommets) are then

Fig. 19 — 1268- or 1296-MHz band-pass filter. See text.

Fig. 21 — Schematic diagram of the local oscillator.

FL1 — 1268-MHz BPF. See Fig. 28 and text.
L1 — 90 nH, 4 turns no. 18 enameled wire, 7/32 in ID turns spaced one wire diameter. Collector tap 2½ turns, output tap 2 turns from cold end.
L2 — 23 nH, 2 turns no. 18 enameled wire, 3/16 in ID, closewound.

L3 — 0.33 μH, 12 turns no. 24 enameled wire, 3/16 in ID, closewound.
Q1, Q2, Q3 — MRF901.
Q4 — MRF911.
RFC1, RFC2 — 8 turns no. 24 enameled wire, 1/8 in ID, closewound.

Y1 — International Crystal Manufacturing Company, Inc. Local Oscillator module. Model no. OE-5. Note: International Crystal no longer manufactures these modules. A suitable oscillator circuit is shown in Chapter 31, Fig. 43.

passed through each hole, crimped with pliers, and soldered to both sides of the board.

Active Devices

The transverter circuitry uses only four active device types. These are the MRF901, MRF911, BFR96 and J-310. The first three are bipolar transistors and are used in the microwave circuitry. The J-310 is a JFET and is used only in the post-conversion amplifier of the receiver chain. The bipolars require a few comments.

The proper way to mount microwave devices is a bit different than for HF devices. All leads must be as short as possible and ground returns must be as direct as possible with minimum series impedance. Figs. 17 and 18 illustrate the proper way to mount the microwave devices. A hole is first drilled in the board where the transistor is to be mounted. The hole should be slightly larger than the plastic "pill." Bend the emitter lead(s) of the active device toward the bottom of the device at the pill edge and at right angles to the pill. Insert the active device into the hole. Orient the base and collector leads properly, and bend the portion of the emitter lead(s) that protrude through the bottom of the board flat with the bottom ground plane. Solder the emitter leads to the bottom ground plane.

The dc parameters of a bipolar RF device generally do not depend on the RF parameters, but the RF parameters are dependent on the dc bias parameters. Each device is characterized by the manufacturer under specific bias conditions. Although the RF parameters at this bias level (specific V_{cc} and I_c) are closely controlled by the manufacturer, the dc parameters (h_{fe} or β) of the RF devices generally are not as closely controlled. Since dc gain may vary greatly from device to device, the bias circuit must be flexible enough to set the same dc quiescent bias point in all cases. In some cases noise and gain optimization of a device require slightly different bias conditions to accommodate different high-frequency parameters. This is another way of saying "best noise performance generally does not coincide with maximum gain."

Table 2 summarizes the dc bias conditions for each bipolar transistor used in this project. These should be adhered to closely. The bias resistors shown in the schematics are those used at W6LEV. Since dc gain is not a controlled parameter, however, some minor adjustments to the bias resistors may have to be made. The dc characteristics of the devices may be determined with dc instruments and no RF drive. It is a good idea, however, to terminate each stage as it is built and during set-up with a 50-ohm resistor at input and output. Remember to block dc with a capacitor. The important parameters are collector current and collector voltage (see Table 2). The dc current gain of each device may even be measured before installing it into the circuit and the bias network "tweaked" for this gain. Remember that bipolar transistors are current-controlled, not voltage-controlled, devices. The only stage that may present a biasing problem is the BFR96. Establish the bias parameters for temperature stability.

Allow the device to warm for a few seconds after application of power to reach the stable bias point given in Table 2. This technique is preferable to letting it thermally drift through that point and run away.

CONSTRUCTION

3-Element 12xx-MHz Filter

Figs. 19 and 20 illustrate the mechanical details of the 1268/1296-MHz filter that is used in four places in the transverter circuitry. The filter consists of three coupled, capacitively loaded quarter-wave resonators. The center conductor of the coax forms a tunable cylindrical capacitor at the Hi-Z end of each resonator. The only tools required are a large pair of tin snips capable of cutting 0.025-inch-thick brass sheet, a ruler, vise and 0.035- and 0.144-in drill bits. A small hammer will aid in bending the brass, and a sharp X-acto knife can be used to cut the semi-rigid UT-141 coax. All dimensions are in inches and are shown in Fig. 24. The dimensions should be followed closely — to a few hundredths of an inch is desirable.

The brass sheet should be marked and cut to size. The holes are drilled next. Do *not* bend the brass before drilling. When the brass work is finished, cut the appropriate lengths of UT-141 semi-rigid coax. It is critical to cut the correct length. Straighten a length of the coax and carefully mark off the required 1.250 inches. With the X-acto or other sharp knife, score the coax around its perimeter at the mark by rolling it on a flat surface while applying moderate pressure to the cutting edge. Once the cut has been defined around the periphery, the pressure is increased while rolling the coax until the copper tubing is cut. Be careful not to cut too deeply into the Teflon, since the center conductor should not be cut at this point. Carefully cut through the Teflon.

To remove the coax from the bulk of the straightened portion and the center conductor, grab the length of coax to be removed lightly with a pair of pliers and pull carefully while slowly twisting it. Don't break the center conductor, since it is used to tune the resonators. Once the length of tubing and Teflon is removed, cut off the center conductor and lay both pieces aside. Repeat this procedure until the required number of resonators has been cut; three are required for each filter. Set the brass filter box on edge on a flat surface with the large holes downward and insert the lengths of semi-rigid coax into the large holes. Lightly coat the center conductors with silicone grease and insert them through the top (small) holes of the structure and into the Teflon of each resonator. The silicone grease aids in sliding the conductor in and

---

Table 2
Transistor DC Bias Parameters

Device	Noise Match		Power Match	
	V_{cc} (Volts)	I_c (mA)	V_{cc} (Volts)	I_c (mA)
MRF901	6	6	10	15
MRF911			10	20
BFR 96			10	50

Z1, Z2 — 50-Ω microstripline, 1.5 × 0.10 in (length × width). Tapped at 0.3 in from cold end. Z1 to Z2 spacing is 0.25 in.
Z3 — 90-Ω microstripline, 1.0 × 0.03 in.
Z4 — 16-Ω microstripline, 0.397 × 0.50 in.

Z5 — 90-Ω microstripline, 1.044 × 0.03 in. Tune for maximum gain with sliding chip capacitor.
Z6 — 115-Ω microstripline, 0.78 × 0.016 in.
Z7, Z8 — 70-Ω microstripline, 1.228 × 0.06 in.

out of the Teflon when tuning each filter. Do not insert it more than a half inch. This will hold the resonator in place while the resonators are soldered to the brass structure. Confirm that the copper of each resonator element is flush with the outer bottom surface of the brass "box." Use a 150-watt soldering gun, and solder each resonator in place from the inside of the box, making sure that the elements are parallel with the box side (the large surface) and each other. Do *not* solder the center conductors at this time.

To install the filter, set it in place on the ground plane. Make sure the filter ground plane forms a complete sheet of copper under the filter assembly. When installed, the ground plane will form the fourth side of the box. Carefully solder the box to the ground plane continuously along each edge. Do not add so much heat that the resonators slump in position within the filter. Do not solder the center conductors.

Input and output connections to the filters are formed by soldering a short piece of large-gauge wire or a copper strip from the 50-ohm microstripline to the resonator at a point 0.250 inch from the cold end.

Filter tuning is straightforward. It is assumed that the builder has some method of sensing the amplitude of the required signal at either 1268 or 1296 MHz. This may be a selective absorption wavemeter (resonant cavity or quarter-wave line and RF probe) or a receiver (converter and tunable IF). Start with each center conductor pushed about 0.5 inch into each resonator. As the filter is tuned it is imperative that the center conductors keep good ground contact with the brass structure where they pass through it! If a good connection is not maintained, the filter will either not tune or will change tuning once the center conductors are soldered.

The builder may want to introduce a slight large radius bend in each center conductor to keep friction between the brass and each tuning element. Be sure that the center conductors are coated with silicone grease before inserting them into the resonators. Starting with the input resonator, move the tuning element (center conductor) *slowly* in and out to peak the filter. Repeat for the center and output resonator. The center resonator is relatively critical, so don't use an overdamped meter movement to indicate output. Repeat the process several times, since the adjustments are interactive. *Carefully* solder each tuning element in place and cut off the excess.

LO and Power Splitter

Fig. 21 shows the schematic of the LO and power splitter, while Fig. 22 presents the layout used in the prototype. If the layout is modified, try to stick relatively close to a left-to-right progression. This is important for a clean output. You can construct the LO a stage at a time, tune it and then proceed to the next stage until the unit is completed, or complete the unit and then

Fig. 22 — Local oscillator board layout. Microstripline sections marked "50" are 50 ohms, any length. C indicates location of a chip capacitor; X indicates a jumper from top to bottom ground planes. Wrap board edges with copper and solder top and bottom.

Fig. 23 — Rat-race mixer and IF-port terminator.
C1, C2 — 15- to 20-pF chip capacitor.
C3 — 22.7-pF silver mica capacitor.
C4 — 568-pF silver mica capacitor.
D1, D2 — Schottky diodes — see text.
L1 — 1.42 μH.

L2 — 56.8 nH.
L3, L4 — 1.0 in length of no. 30 wire, 1/8-in above ground plane. Must be equal lengths.
L5 — 0.6 μH, 10 turns no. 24 enameled wire on a T-37-6 core.

tune it up. The latter is preferred since many of the adjustments interact. It is recommended that all the microstrip elements be laid out first. Then cut and glue the ground plane in place. Before mounting any components, solder the top and bottom ground planes together as described earlier with copper tape and no. 18 wire (or metal grommets). The lengths of microstripline given in Fig. 21 are for G-10 board, 0.062 inch thick.

A copper box (with a hole punched in it for the single adjustment) should be fabricated to enclose the oscillator. This box should be soldered to the ground plane.

The LO is the only place where high quality Johanson trimmer capacitors are used. Triko units can be used, but they are not as rugged.

When the unit is finished the tune-up procedure of footnote 1 should be followed. This LO will *not* perform properly when simply tuned for maximum output on a broadband power meter! Careful alignment is a must! Resist the temptation to go back and tweak. Connection to the receiver and transmitter boards should be made with short lengths of semi-rigid Teflon cable, since RG-58 foam coax is leaky at 1268 MHz.

The power divider is a standard Wilkinson in-phase divider. No alignment is necessary. The mismatch resistor between the ports should be either a 1/8-watt carbon composition unit with extremely short leads or a chip resistor.

Mixer

The same rat-race singly balanced mixer and IF port terminator are used in both the receiver and transmitter. See Figs. 23 and 24. The LO (1268 MHz) is injected ¼ and ¾ wavelength from each diode (the diodes are 180 degrees out of phase with each other). The non-microstrip side of the diodes are placed at 1296-MHz ground, but at a high impedance for the 28-MHz IF. The IF is fed through a network which

theoretically maintains $50 \pm j0$ ohms everywhere, but is transparent within its passband. It keeps the IF port at a constant impedance, which is important for proper mixer operation. The design equations for this network are given in Fig. 25. The RF is fed midway (¼ wavelength) from each diode.

The hot-carrier Schottky diodes should be matched. This may be accomplished in a rough but satisfactory manner by choosing two diodes which exhibit the same forward dc voltage drop when biased with 5 to 10 mA of forward current.

Nominal values are given for the tuned components of the IF-port terminator. Since dip mica and chip capacitor values may vary by 5%, each tuned circuit should be adjusted to resonance with a dip meter or other means before installation. The inductor in each case may be adjusted by expanding or compressing turns. Be sure to tune each circuit with the same lead lengths that will be used when finally installed. The circuit for 28 MHz was modeled on an HP-41CV using the GNAP option of the Circuits Pac. Table 3 presents the results. Actual results on the high-frequency end will depend on component quality.

Postconversion Amplifier and BPF

Fig. 26 shows the two stages of postconversion amplification and output BPF. The first amplifier stage may be noisematched to 50 ohms, if desired. As previously stated, the builder may opt to incorporate only one stage if sufficient gain and a low noise figure are present in the 28-MHz tunable IF.

The output BPF tuned components are critical. They should be tuned individually to resonance with a dip meter and frequency counter or some other method. Be sure to tune them with the same lead lengths that will be used when finally installed in the circuit. The shunt elements are especially critical. This filter may be used on other converter projects as well. For reference,

Fig. 27 gives the modeled response of the filter (HP-41CV with the LNAP option of the Circuits Pac). Actual response is very close to ideal.

Transmitter

The transmitter board is prepared in the same manner as the LO board. See Figs. 28 and 29. It is desirable to construct the transmitter stage by stage, since problems are easier to isolate this way. The mixer, IF port terminator and first amplifier (MRF901) are constructed first. Always ter-

Fig. 24 — Photograph of the singly balanced rat-race mixer, see Fig. 23.

R_0 = CHARACTERISTIC IMPEDANCE (USUALLY 50 OHMS)
$X_{L1} = X_{C1} = R_0Q$
$X_{L2} = X_{C2} = R_0/Q$

Fig. 25 — IF-port terminator diagram and design equations. A good choice for Q is approximately 5.

Fig. 26 — Postconversion amplifier and band-pass filter. Total gain is 23 dB, NF is 1 dB.
FB — Ferrite bead.
L1 — 0.613 µH, 14 turns of no. 22 enameled wire, ¼ in ID, closewound.
L2, L3 — 1.35 µH, 20 turns of no. 24 enameled wire on a T-37-6 core. L2 tapped 3.5 turns from cold end; L3 tapped 1.5 turns from cold end.
L4, L6 — 56 nH, 4 turns of no. 18 enameled wire, 5/32-in ID, closewound.
L5 — 3.1 µH, 27 turns of no. 24 enameled wire on a T-50-6 core.

minate the output of the last constructed stage with a "leadless" 51-ohm ¼-watt carbon composition resistor. First apply dc power and set the bias resistors for the collector current previously noted. Be sure it is stable with temperature. Then apply RF and adjust the sliding capacitor shunt line for maximum gain. An absorption wavemeter (cavity or quarter-wave line plus RF probe) or spectrum analyzer may be used. *Always* solder a chip capacitor at the far end of the tuned shunt line before applying power. Leave this chip in place and use another chip to fine-tune the line. Be sure to include the multiple bypass capacitors, since a 0.01-µF chip capacitor does not supply sufficient decoupling for LF and HF.

Receiver

If the builder has a signal source and a means of quantitative measurement, he may opt to construct the receiver stage by stage. See Figs. 30 and 31. If not, it's best to construct the entire circuit and then do the tune-up. The tuned-shunt lines are peaked in the same manner as the transmitter board. The 1296-MHz filters are tuned as previously described. You may want to vary the LO injection level. Generally, somewhere between + 3 and + 10 dBm injection yields quietest mixer operation. If the receiver is preceded by a GaAsFET preamplifier, the difference will be slight but noticeable over the MRF901 alone.

Conclusion

This transverter is relatively easy and inexpensive to construct. It is also relatively easy to get operating, provided good RF and microwave construction practices are

Fig. 27 — Calculated response of the 28-MHz output filter.

Table 3

IF-Port Terminator Performance

Freq. (MHz)	Z_{in}	Phase Angle (Degrees)
5	49.87	0.09
10	49.39	0.29
15	48.11	1.04
20	44.44	5.08
25	44.76	43.19
26	60.90	61.13
27	115.69	76.65
28	831.0	88.26
29	173.3	− 81.63
30	78.6	− 70.18
31	52.25	− 56.38
35	39.62	− 15.78
40	44.00	− 4.38
45	46.35	− 1.89
50	47.53	− 1.03
100	49.63	− 0.10
200	49.92	− 0.03

Fig. 28 — Transmitter board layout. Microstripline section marked "50" is 50 ohms, any length. C indicates location of a chip capacitor; X indicates a jumper from top to bottom ground planes. Wrap board edges with copper and solder top and bottom.

Fig. 29 — Schematic diagram of the transmitter section. Z2, Z8 and Z9 are tuned for maximum gain with "sliding" chip capacitors.
FL1 — 1296-MHz filter. See Fig. 28 and text.
FB — Ferrite bead.
RFC — 8 turns of no. 24 enameled wire, 1/8-in ID, closewound.
Z1 — 16-Ω microstripline, 0.62 × 0.50 in
(length × width).
Z2 — 90-Ω microstripline, 1.113 × 0.03 in.
Z3 — 125-Ω microstripline, 0.779 × 0.013 in.
Z4 — 16-Ω microstripline, 0.397 × 0.50 in.
Z5 — 90-Ω microstripline, 1.044 × 0.03 in.
Z6 — 115-Ω microstripline, 0.78 × 0.016 in.
Z7 — 16-Ω microstripline, 0.384 × 0.50 in.
Z8 — 90-Ω microstripline, 0.974 × 0.03 in.
Z9 — 86-Ω microstripline, 0.992 × 0.037 in.

Fig. 30 — Schematic diagram of the receiver section. Z2 and Z5 are tuned for maximum gain with "sliding" chip capacitors.

FL1, FL2 — 1296-MHz band-pass filter — see Fig. 28 and text.

RFC — 8 turns of no. 24 enameled wire, 1/8-in ID, closewound.

Z1 — 18-Ω microstripline, 0.868 × 0.438 in (length × width).
Z2 — 90-Ω microstripline, 0.904 × 0.03 in.
Z3 — 125-Ω microstripline, 0.708 × 0.013 in.

Z4 — 16-Ω microstripline, 0.620 × 0.50 in.
Z5 — 90-Ω microstripline, 1.113 × 0.03 in.
Z6 — 125-Ω microstripline, 0.779 × 0.013 in.

Fig. 31 — Receiver board layout. Microstripline sections marked "50" are 50 ohms, any length. C indicates location of a chip capacitor; × indicates a jumper from top to bottom ground planes. Wrap board edges with copper and solder top and bottom.

Fig. 32 — Photograph of the transmitter board.

Fig. 33 — Photograph of the receiver board.

followed. Various views of the completed unit are shown in Figs. 32 and 35.

Useful test equipment to go along with this project include a low-pass filter and a signal source. The filter shown in Fig. 34 is taken from the RSGB *Radio Communication Handbook*. This unit has a measured insertion loss of 0.35 dB. Response is down 3 dB at 12 MHz either side of 1296 MHz and 23 dB at 1152 MHz.

The filter could be built into the transverter — a lower loss cavity filter would be better if you use a GaAsFET preamplifier.

Fig. 34 — Interdigital band-pass filter for 1296 MHz. From *Radio Communication Handbook* by RSGB. Walls and plates in the W6LEV version were made of 0.062-in double-sided, copper-clad PC board.

A Single Board No-Tuning 23-cm Transverter

This transverter uses bandpass filtering with printed hairpin filters. It will work with any MMICs capable of operating at 1.3 GHz at the appropriate input and output levels. New MMIC types may be easily substituted simply by changing the MMIC and its bias resistor. It was designed by Rick Campbell, KK7B.[1]

System Block Diagram

Fig 35 is the transverter block diagram and Fig 36 is the schematic diagram. Fig 37 shows the layout of the 5- × 7-inch G-10 board with all functional blocks labeled. In the transmit path, FL1 removes the image, LO (local oscillator) and higher order spurious outputs. FL3 selects the desired LO harmonic. The LO signal is filtered again in FL4 before the LO is split and applied to the transmit and receive mixers.

The received signal passes through FL5, which attenuates out-of-band signals. After amplification, image noise added to the received signal is attenuated by FL6.

One noteworthy feature of this transverter is that the choice of LO drive frequency is left to the builder. The filters are narrow enough to permit use of outputs at 1152, 576, 384, 288 and 230.4 MHz. Fig 37 shows component values for 576-MHz

drive from the LO board described in footnote 1. Other LO frequencies may require minor component changes.

Circuit Performance

Careful measurements show a mixer conversion loss of 5.5 dB. The output for 1-dB compression is 0 dBm. LO suppression is about 25 dB. The mixers compare favorably with more-expensive packaged units.

Transmit output is about 13 dBm, which is suitable for some applications without further amplification. A major advantage of the MMIC output stage is that it offers an unconditionally stable, near-50-ohm source to the following stage or antenna.

Receive noise figure is less than 4 dB. The unconditionally stable 50-ohm load presented by the input MMIC is useful for direct connection to an antenna, and ideal as the stage following an external GaAsFET preamp.

The filters allow coverage of the entire 1240- to 1300-MHz band with a 144-MHz IF and appropriate LO drive. The bandpass filters used, although not mechanically critical, remove significant spurious responses. The passband response of one RF and one LO filter section is shown in Fig 38.

Construction

All components are surface mounted on the etched side of the board. The most tedious step is drilling the holes next to the MMIC mounting pads and soldering the

"C" wires to provide a low-impedance ground. Plated-through holes would eliminate this step. After preparing the board with its "C" wires, mount the chip capacitors, inductors and connectors. Finally, install the MMICs and bias resistors.

The bottom of the hairpin U is a low-impedance point for signals in the filter passband. A bypass capacitor at that point has little effect on the filter passband but provides a ground path for VHF signals. Although 22-pF capacitors are specified, values from 12 to 30 pF gave good results in the prototypes.

The multiplier works best with drive levels of 0 to 10 dBm, without a bias resistor. For higher drive levels, the bias circuit described in footnote 2 will provide more output. With 10 dBm drive at 230.4 MHz, output from FL3 is about −20 dBm, so about 33 dB of additional gain is needed. With 10 dBm drive at 576-MHz, output from FL3 is −3 dBm, so only 16 dB of gain is required.

Pads are included on the board for up to three MMICs. Choose the appropriate number of MMICs based on available LO drive level and frequency. FL3 and FL4 must be isolated. If only one MMIC is used

[1]R. Campbell, "A Single Board No-Tuning 23 cm Transverter," Proceedings of the 23rd Conference of the Central States VHF Society (Newington: ARRL, 1989), pp 44-52.

[2]R. Campbell, "A Clean Microwave Local Oscillator," Proceedings of the 21st Conference of the Central States VHF Society (Newington: ARRL, 1987), pp 51-57.

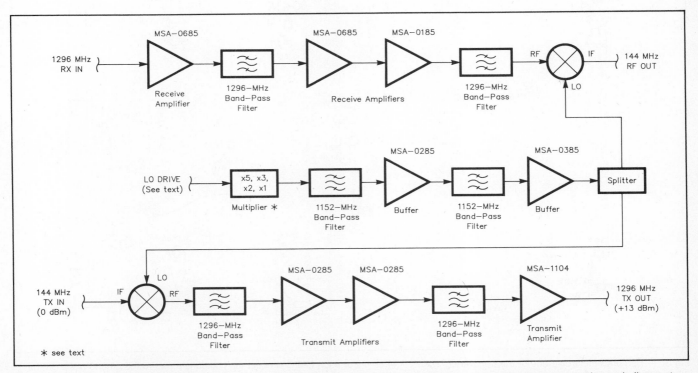

Fig. 35 — Block diagram of the single-board transverter. Extensive use of printed-circuit band-pass filters simplifies construction and alignment.

Fig. 36 — Schematic of the 1296-MHz transverter. All resistors and capacitors are chip types except as noted. Diodes D1 through D4 are HP 5082-2835. FL1 through FL6, the mixer tuned circuits and the Wilkinson power divider are etched on the circuit board.

Fig 37 — Part-placement diagram for the transverter. The "C" wires under each MMIC connect the component pad to the ground plane on the other side of the board.

Fig. 38 — Passband response of one LO filter (A) and one RF filter (B) in the transverter. With appropriate choice of LO frequency, the transverter is suitable for use across the entire 23-cm band.

it should be between them. If sufficient LO drive is already available at 1152 MHz, use a 6-dB attenuator pad between FL3 and FL4.

Alignment

The tuning components in the LO multiplier are quite broad: network Q is about 1. The 576-MHz network will also work for lower frequency inputs, but the component values can be optimized for each drive frequency. L1 and L2 may be increased to 3 turns for 384 MHz, 4 turns for 288 MHz and 5 turns for 230.4 MHz if necessary. If LO drive is sufficient to saturate U4, however, mixer performance will be relatively unaffected by small changes in LO level, and tuning is unnecessary. A high-level MMIC is recommended for the LO-output stage.

Parts and Circuit Boards

Components are available from Microwave Components of Michigan, whose address appears in the Component Data chapter. Etched and plated FR-4 circuit boards, complete kits and assembled transverters are available from Down East Microwave, Box 2310, RR-1, Troy, ME 04987.

The author acknowledges the assistance of Jim Davey, WA8NLC, John Miller of Michigan Technological University, Bob Dryden, W4OJK and John Molnar, WA3ETD.

A 1296-MHz Linear Power Amplifier

The linear power amplifier shown in Fig 39 uses a Mitsubishi power-amplifier module and a handful of other components to deliver up to 3-watts output from 1240 to 1300 MHz. It was designed and built by Bill Olson, W3HQT.

The M67715 module has 50-ohm input and output impedances. No impedance-matching networks are used, and no alignment is required. An input signal of 10 mW (10 dBm) will result in about 3-watts output. The M67715 is fairly rugged: Mitsubishi specifies it will tolerate an output VSWR of 20:1.

Fig 40 is the schematic diagram of the amplifier. The module requires two positive supply voltages and a regulated bias supply. The higher supply voltage (V_{cc2}) can be up to 16 V dc, but the lower voltage (V_{cc1}) cannot exceed 9 V dc. A 7809 three-terminal regulator connected to the V_{cc2} supply provides the 9-volt V_{cc1} and bias voltages. Chip capacitors are used to bypass the V_{cc} and bias terminals directly at the module. Fig 41 shows an inside view of the amplifier.

U1 and U2 are fastened directly to a piece of 2-inch aluminum channel, which is in turn attached to a heat sink. Mitsubishi specifies a total efficiency of about 25 percent for this module; for 3-watts output the module dissipates about 9 watts. The heat sink shown in Fig 39 may be conservative, but was of a convenient size. A U-shaped aluminum shield should be used to cover the aluminum channel when the amplifier is in use.

Parts, kits and complete amplifiers are available from Down East Microwave, Box 2310, RR-1, Troy, ME 04987.

Fig. 39 — A simple but rugged 1296-MHz linear power amplifier.

Fig. 40 — Schematic diagram of the 1296-MHz linear power amplifier.
C1, C6—10 μF, 16-Vdc chip electrolytic.
C2, C4—1000 pF, ceramic chip, NP0.
C3, C5—0.1 μF ceramic chip, NP0.
RFC1—5 turns no. 28 bare or enam wire on FB-43-5111.

Fig. 41 — Inside view of the amplifier. U1 is at the top and U2 at the bottom. Mount the circuit board to the heat sink before installing the type-N connectors.

1296-MHz Solid-State Power Amplifiers

With the ever-increasing number of commercial 1296 MHz transverters available on the market today, there exists an even greater demand for a simple and economical way to generate higher power. Most of the transverters presently available produce 0.5 to 1 watt of output. If this power level is used to drive a typical 2C39/7289 stripline or cavity amplifiers, the low power output is often disappointing. If the tube-type amplifier is run with at least 1 kV on the plate, typical gain is around 10 dB. This means that the 0.5 to 1 W is now at best 5 to 10 W output. One alternative is to cascade two of these amplifiers. We now could expect 50 to 100 W of output power.

This section describes two solid-state amplifiers that can replace the 2C39/7289 as the driver and provide 10-20 W — enough to drive a two-tube amplifier to full output. These amplifiers, shown in Figs. 68 through 72 were designed and built by Al Ward, WB5LUA.

The NEC NEL1306 and the NEL1320 were recently introduced as an economical solid state approach to generating moderate power (10-20 W) at 1269 and 1296 MHz. These amplifiers can be used for terrestrial or satellite work. When OSCAR 10 was designed, it was thought that 10 W into a modest gain antenna (20 dBi) would produce usable signals from the satellite.

Unfortunately, there were some problems and the sensitivity of AO-10 was not as originally expected for the Mode L uplink. These amplifiers can, however, be used as a driver for a higher-powered tube amplifier for Mode L service.

The NEL1306 is rated for 6-W output at 1296 MHz at the 1-dB compression point; the NEL1320 is rated at 20 W. One of the advantages of these devices is that they were designed for a V_{cc} of 12- to 13.6-V dc, making them ideal for portable and mobile operation. The NEL1306 is in the $26 price range, while the NEL1320 costs about $42. These are single-quantity prices, making the devices attractive to experimenters.

The performance of these amplifiers as built and tested by the author is shown in Table 7. The NEL1306 is a good buy. With 1.5 W input, 8 W output can be achieved. When tuned up at lower power levels, power gain can be as high as 10 dB. With 0.2 W drive from the transverter described earlier in this chapter, an output power level of 2.0 W is obtainable.

Power gains as high as 17 dB are possible with a two-stage amplifier (an NEL1306 driving an NEL1320). With a mere 200 mW of drive, 10-W output can be obtained. When driven with 1 W, the 1-dB compression point of 18 W will be achieved.

Circuit Details

The basic design, shown schematically in Fig. 68, is an adaption of a circuit described in the NEL1300 series data sheet. The design incorporates 30-ohm quarter-wavelength microstriplines on both the input and output. Shunt capacitors C3, C4, C7 and C8 form a pi network designed to match the low input impedance of the device to 50 ohms. C5, C6, C9 and C10 and the 30-ohm transmission line form an output pi network that matches the device to 50 ohms. C10 is not always necessary, depending on variations among devices and PC-board material. Glass-epoxy circuit-board material 0.031 inch thick was chosen for the dielectric material. A 30-ohm line

---

Table 7

Typical Operating Conditions for the 1296-MHz Solid-State Power Amplifiers

Device	NEL130681-12	NEL132081-12
P_{out} (1-dB C.P.)	7 W	18 W
Gain (1-dB C.P.)	6 dB typ.	5 dB typ.
Collector efficiency	40-50%	40-50%
Idling current	50 mA	150 mA
I_c @ 1-dB C.P.	1.1 A	3.0 A
V_{cc}	13.5 V	13.5 V
Power input	14.9 W	40.5 W

Fig. 68 — Schematic diagram of the NEL1306 and NEL1320 1296-MHz solid-state power amplifiers. The schematic is identical for both versions. Component values are the same except as noted.

C1, C2, C11, C17 — 10-pF chip capacitor.
C3, C4, C5, C6 — 3.6- to 5.0-pF chip capacitor.
C7, C8 — 1.8- to 6.0-pF miniature trimmer capacitor (Mouser 24AA070 or equiv.).
C9, C10 — Same as C7 and C8 for the NEL1306 amplifier. For the NEL1320 version, 0.8- to 10-pF piston trimmers are used (Johanson 5221 or 8053 or equiv.).
C12, C14 — 100-pF chip capacitor.

C13, C15 — 0.1-µF disc ceramic capacitor.
C16 — 10-µF electrolytic capacitor.
D1 — 1N4007 diode.
L1, L2 — 30-ohm microstripline, ¼ wavelength long (see text).
Q1 — NEC NEL130681-12 (6 W) or NEL132081-12 (18 W) transistor.
R1 — 82- to 100-Ω resistor, 2-W minimum. Vary for specified idling current.

R2 — 10-Ω, ¼-W carbon-composition resistor with "zero" lead length. See text.
R3 — 15-Ω, 1-W carbon-composition resistor.
RFC1 — 3t no. 24 wire, 0.125 inch ID, spaced 1 wire dia.
RFC2 — 1t no. 24 wire, 0.125 inch ID, spaced 1 wire dia.
RFC3 — 1-µH RF choke; 18t no. 24 enam. close-spaced on a T50-10 toroid core.

in this dielectric equates to a line width of 0.121 inches, which is equivalent to the width of both the collector and base leads of the NEL1300 series devices. This minimizes the discontinuity among L1, L2 and Q1.

Bias is provided by R1, R2 and D1. R1 can be optimized, if desired, to adjust the collector idling current.

RFC1 and RFC2 were selected by choosing the lowest possible reactance that will not affect power gain or output power. The RF chokes and the 10-pF bypass capacitors afford adequate decoupling at the frequency of operation. The values of RFC1 and RFC2 were purposely made different to avoid oscillations caused by bias choke coupling.

Keeping the high-frequency RF chokes in the collector as small as possible allows the parallel R3/RFC3 combination, in conjunction with bypass capacitors C14, C15, C16, to reduce the tendency of the transistor to generate low-frequency spurious signals. The 1-μH RF choke must be capable of handling 1 A for the NEL1306 and 3 A for the NEL1320. Special RF chokes were built to withstand the current.

Construction

The circuit is etched on 0.031-inch thick, double-sided, glass-epoxy circuit board. The layout is given in Fig. 69. Two separate boards are actually used — one for the input side and one for the output — and they are mirror images of each other. The copper is retained on the bottom side and serves as the ground plane. In addition, the grounded areas on the top side must be held at RF ground. This insures low-inductance grounding for the transistor emitter leads, matching capacitors and bias circuitry.

Several effective methods of grounding of the top ground plane to the bottom ground plane are summarized here.

1) Plated-through holes at the critical grounding areas mentioned above.

2) Use of pins or screws that penetrate through the circuit board and into the aluminum base plate at the critical areas.

3) Use of "wrap-around" foils on all edges of the ground plane.

Plated-through holes are often used in the commercial and military electronic marketplace but are not so easily reproduced in the average builder's circuit-board shop. The best technique is to use the "wrap-around" foils on all edges and use no. 4-40 screws to tie the circuit board to the base plate at the critical areas shown in Fig. 69. Solder the brass or copper foil to both ground planes.

It will be necessary to mill out a 0.240-inch-wide slot in the aluminum base plate to allow the transistor flange to be mounted 0.090 inch below the main surface, or to build up the input and output printed circuit boards with a 0.090-inch-thick aluminum plate. This is required since the transistor leads protrude from the device 0.165 inch above the bottom of the

flange, and the PC boards are only 0.031 inch high. These dimensions allow a wrap-around foil and solder buildup of 0.040 inch maximum.

One-inch screws are used to hold the transistor to the aluminum base plate. The base plate was drilled and tapped to accept the screws. The extra screw length that protrudes from the bottom of the base plate allows the use of an external heat sink, which is highly suggested if continous operation is desired.

The clearance holes in the NEL1300 devices are for no. 4-40 hardware. The holes were drilled out to accept no. 6-32 screws to make the assembly more rugged, although this may not be necessary. Be careful if you decide to drill out the holes to accept no. 6-32 hardware: the base plate is soft copper, and you could damage the device. Use a small vise to hold the transistor flange during the drilling operation.

The transistor leads should be soldered in place only after the circuit boards and transistor have been firmly bolted down to the base plate. This is necessary to minimize any buildup of stress in the transistor leads. Chip capacitors C3, C4, C5 and C6 should be soldered directly onto the leads of Q1 to ensure the shortest possible lead length.

In the original design of these amplifiers, Johanson piston trimmer capacitors (part

no. 5221 or 8053) were used for C7, C8, C9 and C10. These capacitors are fairly large, and in some instances the coupling between the bodies of C8 and C9 was enough to cause an in-band oscillation. Smaller variable capacitors should be used if at all possible. Mouser Electronics (see Chapter 35) part number 24A070, a 1.8- to 6.0-pF miniature trimmer capacitor, has been used successfully in the input and output networks of the NEL1306 with no performance degradation. The Johanson piston trimmers were used in the output network of the NEL1320 amplifier because of the high RF currents involved.

The original printed circuit board was designed to allow end-launch SMA-type connectors to be installed. Fig. 70 illustrates this technique. Four-hole, flange-mount SMA connectors can be mounted to the edge of the 0.250-inch-thick base plate using two of the four mounting holes. Drill and tap the base plate for no. 2-56 hardware. Extreme care must be exercised — it's easy to accidentally cross-thread or over-torque the no. 2-56 hardware.

An alternative approach is to mount the amplifier in an aluminum diecast box (Bud CU-124 or Hammond 1590B) and run miniature 50-ohm coaxial cable such as RG-174 from the amplifier board to the connector. The amplifiers shown in Figs.

Fig. 69 — Parts-placement diagram for the solid-state 1296-MHz power amplifiers. The same PC boards are used for each version. A full-size etching pattern may be found at the back of this book.

Fig. 70 — Construction details for the solid-state 1296-MHz power amplifiers. See text for additional information.

Fig. 71 — This NEL1306 amplifier was built inside a diecast box. Miniature coaxial cable runs to the connectors.

Fig. 72 — The NEL1320 amplifier is virtually identical to the NEL1306 version, except for the capacitors on the output stripline. C10 was not necessary on this version.

71 and 72 use the standard SMA connectors mounted to the walls of the metal box. BNC or Type-N connectors should work equally as well. When preparing each end of the coaxial cable, try to keep the pigtail leads as short as possible (1/8 inch or less); otherwise the mismatch will be difficult to tune out.

A performance comparison was made on one amplifier with end-launch connectors and another using the approach just described. No difference in gain or 1-dB compression point could be measured. Etched PC boards and parts kits are available from A & A Engineering.[3]

Tune-up and Operation

Initial setup of each amplifier is begun by terminating the input and output in good 50-ohm loads. Start with all capacitors at their minimum value. Apply 12- to 13.5-V dc to the V_{cc} and bias terminals. The collector idling current should be as shown in Table 7. R1 can be varied as required to obtain the correct idling current. For initial tuneup, it is suggested that a fuse be used in the collector lead to protect the device.

Measuring RF output power at this frequency can be difficult. The author used a calibrated 20-dB directional coupler along with enough attenuator pads to allow power to be read with a Hewlett Packard HP430C power meter and an HP477B thermistor mount. The HP431 power meter with its associated HP478A thermistor mount is a newer version of the HP430C.

[3]A & A Engineering. See the ARRL Parts Suppliers List at the end of the Component Data Chapter.

and does not suffer from temperature drift problems. Bird offers several low-power slugs for the popular model 43 in this frequency range. The 400-1000 MHz slugs can be used with decreased accuracy.

For the NEL1306 amplifier, start out with 50 to 100 mW of drive. Adjust the output network for maximum power output and then peak the input network for output power. Increase drive and repeak both matching networks for rated performance as shown in Table 7. Similarly, start out with approximately 1 W of drive for the NEL1320 and follow the same procedure. After a minute or two of operation at maximum power output, remove RF drive power and check to see that the collector idling current has not increased more than 25% over the initial setting. Keep D1 close to Q1. Thermal compound will enhance heat transfer to D1 to insure minimal drift in idling current with temperature changes.

Considerable effort was put forth to make sure that the amplifiers are stable. The devices have fairly high gain at the frequency of operation, so layout and good construction practices are very important. Here are some construction hints that can help ensure amplifier performance and stability.

1) Use the smallest (physical) size variable capacitors that will still handle the RF current.

2) Use wrap-around ground foils as noted. Grounding screws are required at the critical RF ground areas near the shunt variable capacitors, shunt bypass capacitors and Q1 emitters.

3) Connect braids from the coaxial cable jumpers to same ground as the shunt variable capacitors.

4) Use as little lead length as possible on R2 — less than 0.125 inch.

5) In some instances where the large piston trimmers are used, a shield approximately 0.75 inch high mounted on top of Q1 and grounded via the mounting screws can improve isolation between C8 and C9.

If transistor switching is being considered as a method of applying dc power to the power amplifier stages during transmit, the following technique is recommended. Keep 13.5-V dc applied to the V_{cc} terminal during receive and transmit. Use a series transistor switch to apply 12- to 13.5-V dc to the bias terminal during transmit. A power transistor capable of carrying only a few hundred milliamperes of bias current, as opposed to several amperes of collector current, will be required. More important, the voltage drop across the transistor switch in the V_{cc} line will be eliminated. This will ensure maximum power output of the NEL1300 devices by keeping V_{cc} at 13.5-V dc.

Several amplifiers of this design are currently in use. The NEL1300 series amplifiers offer a simple and efficient means of generating medium power on 1296 MHz. The 13.5-V dc requirement makes them ideal for mobile and portable operation.

Parts for this project are available from Applied Invention, Microwave Components of Michigan and Mouser Electronics (see the Component Data chapter). NEC transistors are available from California Eastern Laboratories, 3260 Jay St., Santa Clara, CA 95050.

The author wishes to thank everyone who offered technical advice, especially WA5TKU for helping with the construction and evaluation of the prototype amplifiers.

Simple Low-Noise Microwave Preamplifiers for 2.3 through 10 GHz

One of the hurdles to overcome in building a microwave station is construction of a good low-noise preamplifier. Techniques using lumped constants (capacitors and inductors) that work well at lower frequencies are often difficult to realize above 2304 MHz. Once a design is worked out and the preamplifier built, the unit must then be tuned for minimum noise figure (NF) before any sort of reasonable performance can be expected. Preamplifier tune-up itself presents a hurdle because many hams don't have access to NF test equipment that is accurate in the microwave region.

If these low-noise amplifiers (LNAs) are duplicated exactly from the information presented, no RF adjustments are required. Just bias their active devices properly, and the units are ready to go—with NFs under 1 dB at frequencies up to 5.7 GHz and around 1.5 dB at 10.368 GHz!

The 10-GHz amplifier is designed around the Avantek ATF-13135 GaAsFET, and the lower-frequency units are designed around the Avantek ATF-10135. Both devices have a nominal gate length of 0.3 micron. The ATF-10135 has a total gate periphery of 500 microns. The ATF-13135 has a gate periphery of 250 microns, making it more appropriate for higher-frequency operation. Best of all, these transistors are *not* high-priced exotics: The ATF-10135 sells for about $12.00, and the ATF-13135 is about $30.00 in small quantities.

Fig. 75 — Schematic of the 2.3-GHz preamplifier. Z1 through Z8 are microstriplines etched on the PC board. Shaded rectangles marked "50 Ω" are 50-Ω transmission lines etched on the PC board. All resistors and capacitors are chip types. C1, C2 and C5 can be 0.05- or 0.1-in. square. C4 and C7 enhance "low-frequency" bypassing. J1 and J2 are SMA female connectors; see text.

Fig. 76 — Schematic of the 3.4-GHz preamplifier. Z1 through Z11 are microstriplines etched on the PC board. Shaded rectangles marked "50 Ω" are 50-Ω transmission lines etched on the PC board. All resistors and capacitors are chip types. C1-C6 are 0.05-in. square. C8, C10, C12 and C14 enhance "low-frequency" bypassing. J1 and J2 are SMA female connectors; see text.

Fig. 77 — Schematic of the 5.7-GHz preamplifier. Z1 through Z12 are microstriplines etched on the PC board. Shaded rectangles marked "50 Ω" are 50-Ω transmission lines etched on the PC board. All resistors and capacitors are chip types. C1-C6 are 0.05-in. square. C8, C10, C12 and C14 enhance "low-frequency" bypassing. J1 and J2 are SMA female connectors; see text.

Fig. 78 — Schematic of the single-stage 10-GHz preamplifier. Z1 through Z7 are microstriplines etched on the PC board. Shaded rectangles marked "50 Ω" are 50-Ω transmission lines etched on the PC board. All resistors and capacitors are chip types. C1 and C2 are 0.05-in. square (ATC Type A capacitors are preferred). J1 and J2 are SMA female connectors; see text.

CIRCUIT DESCRIPTION

Schematics for the preamplifiers are shown in Figs 75 through 79. Fig 75 shows a single-stage 2.3-GHz design. Figs 76 and 77 show two-stage preamplifiers for 3.4 and 5.7 GHz. Figs 78 and 79 show single- and two-stage 10-GHz LNAs.

The same basic circuit configuration is used for each preamplifier. All impedance matching is accomplished with micro-striplines. None of the amplifiers contain adjustable RF components. Fixed-value capacitors are used for input, output and interstage coupling. Fixed-value capacitors and resistors are also used in the gate- and drain-bias decoupling circuitry.

I did the initial design for these pre-amplifiers with the aid of a Smith Chart and optimized them through computer simulation. LNA design is made considerably easier by computer-aided-design soft-ware. I was fortunate to have access to Touchstone®, an RF design program made by EESOF.

One of the most important parameters that the computer can analyze is stability. Proper choice of components in the bias decoupling networks and the use of source inductance in the form of source-lead length helps to maintain stability. The results are improved input and output SWR while maintaining low noise figure and moderate gain. In the case of the 3.4, 5.7 and 10-GHz amplifiers, the effect of the "through-the-board" mounting of the source leads is taken into account in the design so that no plated-through holes are necessary to achieve good performance.

BIAS NETWORKS

To minimize circuit losses, ground the GaAsFET source leads directly to the ground plane. To operate these devices with their source leads at dc ground, you must bias each device's gate negatively relative to its source. This can be done in a number of ways, so I left bias circuitry off the PC boards.

Three basic bias circuits are shown in Fig 80. Two are passive. The third—and most desirable—is an active bias network that uses a PNP transistor to set the GaAsFET drain voltage and current.

The simplest bias network, shown in Fig 80A, uses a 3.3-V Zener diode to set the drain voltage. A 1.5-V AA cell is used for the bias supply. Bias, applied through R1, sets the gate voltage, which in turn determines the drain current. Generally, the

Fig. 79 — Schematic of the two-stage 10-GHz preamplifier. Z1 through Z14 are microstriplines etched on the PC board. Shaded rectangles marked "50 Ω" are 50-Ω transmission lines etched on the PC board. All resistors and capacitors are chip types. C1-C3 are 0.05-in. square (ATC Type A capacitors are preferred). J1 and J2 are SMA female connectors; see text.

AA cell is connected so that there is always a negative voltage applied to the gate. The preamplifier is then turned on by connecting V_D to a positive voltage source. Because there is a 51-ohm resistor in series with the drain, there is some interaction between drain voltage and drain current: Greater drain current produces a lower drain voltage. The gate voltage required to properly bias the device varies from unit to unit because of slight variations in pinch-off voltage. (Pinch-off voltage is the gate voltage required to turn the FET off.) A disadvantage of this simple bias circuit is that it lacks compensation for bias changes over temperature variations. Although not optimum, this technique has been used at WB5LUA and WA5VJB with good results. A high-grade, long-life alkaline AA-size cell should last several months before its voltage drops low enough to cause the FET to draw excessive drain current.

An adaptation of the simple passive bias configuration is shown in Fig 80B. Drain voltage is again provided by a 3.3-V Zener diode, but this circuit replaces the AA cell with a positive-to-negative voltage inverter. Several manufacturers make suitable inverter ICs. A less-expensive approach is to use a common 555 timer in the simple inverter circuit shown. With simple battery bias, the negative supply is continuously applied to the FET gate. With the inverter of Fig 80B, gate and drain supplies are simultaneously applied to the FET. This approach has been used by manufacturers of satellite TV receiving equipment for years. Although there can be problems if the drain voltage is applied before the negative gate voltage, the 51-ohm resistor in series with the drain safely limits the maximum drain current—even if the application of gate voltage to the FET is delayed.

Fig. 80 — Bias circuits for the preamplifiers. See text for discussion. The passive circuit at A uses a 1.5-V cell for the gate supply and a Zener diode to stabilize the drain supply. The circuit at B, another passive arrangement, uses a 555 timer IC to generate negative gate bias, and a Zener diode to stabilize the drain supply. C shows an active bias circuit. The values of R1, R2 and R3 can be varied for different FET operating conditions; see text and Table 15. The value of R4 should be chosen so that 10-15 mA of Zener current flows when the FET (or FETs, for a two-stage design) is powered at rated bias.

Fig. 81 — Part-placement guides and etching patterns for the preamplifiers. PC board material is double-sided, 0.031-in-thick Rogers Duroid 5880 or Taconic TLY-5 (dielectric constant, 2.2). Black areas represent unetched copper foil. The back side of the board is left unetched to act as a ground plane. The part-placement guides are *not* shown at their actual size. All components mount on the etched side of the board.

An improvement on both passive circuits is the active bias circuit shown in Fig 80C. The negative gate supply uses the inverter of Fig 80B, but the drain supply employs an inexpensive PNP transistor in a circuit that effectively sets both the drain voltage and drain current regardless of device variations. It also offers a more constant bias over temperature than the passive designs. Drain voltage is set by R2 and R3, a voltage divider at the base of Q1. The voltage is then raised by the emitter/base junction voltage of Q1. Drain current is set by R1. The gate voltage required to sustain the drain voltage and current is set automatically by the voltage divider set up by the emitter/collector junction of Q1 and the negative voltage source. About -1 V is supplied to the FET gate.

Table 15 gives resistor values for various bias conditions. I suggest building a separate active bias network for each FET stage to properly set each device's bias point. I have, however, used a single active bias supply to power a two-stage amplifier with good success. If the devices are fairly

Table 15

Active Bias Circuit Values for Various Drain Currents

V_{DD} (V)	V_{DS} (V)	I_D (mA)	$R1$ (Ω)	$R2$ (kΩ)	$R3$ (kΩ)
3.5	2.5	20	75	2.2	2.8
3.25	2.5	15	117	2.2	2.3
4.0	3.0	20	50	2.2	4.3

Fig. 82 — This prototype two-stage 3.4-GHz preamplifier was built by the author. The enclosure is made from sheet brass soldered to the PC board (see text). The trimmer potentiometers are for adjustment of the gate supply for each stage.

Fig. 83 — A completed two-stage 10-GHz preamplifier.

Fig. 84 — The FET source leads are bent, inserted through slots cut in the PC board, and soldered to the ground plane. See text.

well dc matched (drain current v gate voltage), this technique will be okay. It will not, however, keep the device drain currents equal if they are not dc matched.

The active bias arrangement can also be used with a battery instead of the voltage inverter. Since the active bias network automatically adjusts gate voltage for a required bias condition, the circuit will adjust the gate voltage as it drops with battery age. The gate requires about -1 V, so the battery can age significantly before the FET bias condition is altered significantly. If this technique is used, it is best to start out with a 5- to 6-volt battery source. The active bias network will compensate for a battery voltage deteriorating to 1-1.5 V. Active bias networks are discussed in greater detail in Avantek application note AN-A002.[1]

CONSTRUCTION

Construction of all amplifiers is similar. Part-placement guides are shown in Fig 81. Etching patterns are given at the back of this book. All amplifiers are etched on 0.031-inch-thick Duroid 5880 or Taconic TLY-5 PC-board material with a dielectric constant of 2.2. The etched PC board can be installed in a housing such as a die-cast aluminum box. Another method, one that I prefer, is to solder thin (0.02-inch-thick) brass side walls to the PC board to form a shielded enclosure. The brass walls also connect the top and bottom ground planes, which is essential for low-loss "low-frequency" bypassing. Power connections for V_G and V_D can be made via 0.001-μF feedthrough capacitors soldered to the brass walls. See Figs 82 and 83.

SMA-type end-launch connectors are used for J1 and J2 to provide a low-loss transition from coaxial cable to the microstripline. Two- or four-hole gold-plated connectors are easily soldered to the PC board or brass side walls, depending on your assembly technique. End-launch connectors are preferred to the right-angle type because of the impedance discontinuity associated with the right-angle transition. Additional amplifier tuning may be required if right-angle connectors are used.

The type and size of the chip capacitors used in these amplifiers becomes increasingly important as frequency increases. For the blocking capacitors, I strongly recommend using good-quality RF-type ceramic chip capacitors, such as those made by ATC. The values specified are common and should not be hard to find. The physical size of the capacitors is especially critical at 10 GHz, where the 0.05-inch-square type *must* be used. Anything larger produces a sizable mismatch on the microstripline.

The value of the "low-frequency" bypass capacitors is less critical. Anything in the 820- to 1500-pF range will work fine. The value of the "high-frequency" bypass capacitors is somewhat more critical, though. Stay within 10% of the values indicated. Again, use good-quality capacitors for "high-frequency" bypassing.

To obtain a low noise figure, the preamp's FET source leads must be properly grounded. In the case of the 3456-MHz and higher-frequency preamplifiers, bend the FET source leads down right at the case and insert them through slots in the PC board. See Fig 84. The slots can be made with a sharp hobby knife or something similar. Be sure to clean up the area where the leads will pass through the slots by removing any extra dielectric material or copper. The source leads should be passed through the board, again bent at right angles and laid neatly along the bottom foil. Solder them to the bottom ground plane and try to force the solder to cover the length of the slot if possible.

Device installation is different with the 2304-MHz preamplifier because additional source-lead inductance is required. This inductance is added by making each FET source lead 0.07 inch long, rather than grounding them with the minimum possible lead length. Ground pads have been established on the artwork, and these pads must be properly connected to the bottom ground plane. Cut slots near the edge of the two pads closest to Q1. Insert a 0.1-inch-wide copper strap through the slots and solder top and bottom. Each source lead is then 0.07 inch long when Q1 is centered on the PC board.

Components for these preamplifiers, including chip capacitors, leadless capacitors, chip resistors and SMA connectors are available from Microwave Components of Michigan.[2] Avantek GaAsFETs are available from distributors around the country (see note 1). Etched PC boards are available from Down East Microwave.[3]

---

[1]Avantek AN-A002, as well as other Avantek application notes, are available from your local Avantek distributor. If you do not know the location of your local distributor, contact Avantek, 3175 Bowers Ave, Santa Clara, CA 95054-3292, tel 408-727-0700.

[2]See address in Component Data chapter.
[3]Down East Microwave, Box 2310, RR 1, Troy, ME 04987, tel 207-948-3741. ARRL in no way warrants this offer.

Table 16

Actual Preamplifier Performance Versus Computer Simulation and Projected Worst-Case Performance

Device	Freq (GHz)	Bias per device	Gain (dB)			Noise Figure (dB)		
			Typ	Worst Case	Simul	Typ	Worst Case	Simul
ATF-10135*	2.3	2 V @ 20 mA	13.5	12.0	13.9	0.5-0.6	0.8	0.60
ATF-10135**	2.3	2 V @ 20 mA	13.0	12.0	13.0	0.65	0.9	0.70
ATF-10135	3.4	2 V @ 20 mA	23.0	22.0	24.1	0.8-0.9	1.0	0.58
ATF-10135	5.7	2.5 V @ 15 mA	18.0	17.0	20.6	0.9-1.0	1.2	0.85
ATF-13135*	10.4	3 V @ 20 mA	8.5	7.5	10.6	1.25-1.5	1.7	1.25
ATF-13135	10.4	3 V @ 20 mA	18.0	15.0	21.9	1.5-1.7	2.0	1.35

*Single-stage amplifier
**Self-biased, single-stage amplifier

RESULTS

If the preamplifiers are built according to the information given in this article, RF adjustments should not be required. A slight adjustment can be made to the bias point if desired, but performance should be very close to that shown in Table 16 with the bias conditions shown. Based on test results obtained from preamplifiers built by a number of hams using available components, the average builder should be able to meet the worst-case gain and NF specifications shown in Table 16. If slightly different dielectric material or construction techniques have been used, the amplifier can be tuned by moving small capacitive tabs along the microstripline while monitoring NF and gain. A properly modified toothpick makes a handy low-loss tool for moving tabs around on the circuitry. Cut the end of a toothpick on a diagonal. Wet the end of the toothpick and use it to move small metal tabs around on the etch.

APPLICATIONS

The 2304-MHz preamplifier provides acceptable receive performance in the 2401-MHz OSCAR band with no modification. The NF at 2401 MHz should be only 0.1 or 0.2 dB greater than that obtainable at 2304 MHz, and LNA gain at both frequencies should agree to within a dB. Using a pair of these preamplifiers at the feed of my 2401-MHz satellite system, I see about 5 dB of sun noise and 10 to 15 dB of signal-to-noise ratio from the Mode S transponder aboard AMSAT-OSCAR 13. My antenna is a 4-foot-diameter UHF TV dish with ¼-inch mesh.

A similar two-stage 2304-MHz preamplifier is in use at the feed of my 24-foot home-brew stressed parabolic reflector. The measured NF of this preamp is 0.65 dB. With this system, I have worked W3IWI/8, SK6WM, OE9XXI, and W4HHK on 2304-MHz moonbounce (earth-moon-earth, EME).

VARIATIONS

In the original design, source leads were grounded directly to obtain the lowest possible noise figure. This necessitates the use of a dual-polarity supply as discussed earlier. The typical approach at VHF is to self-bias the FET by using a resistor connected in series between the source and ground. A capacitor is used to bypass the resistor at RF. As the frequency of operation increases, it becomes increasingly difficult to obtain high-quality, low-impedance bypassing. Although the self-biasing technique is simpler to build and uses a single power supply, some RF performance is sacrificed.

I evaluated self-biased versions with the help of the computer, and several prototypes were built and tested. The artwork was modified to include 0.075-inch-square pads to mount the FET source leads. Chip capacitors were then bridged between these pads and a ground pad. The ground pad

Fig. 85 — Schematic diagram of the self-biased version of the 2.3-GHz preamplifier. Z1 through Z8 are microstriplines etched on the PC board. Shaded rectangles marked "50 Ω" are 50-Ω transmission lines etched on the PC board. All capacitors are chip types.

C1, C2, C5—0.05- or 0.1-in. square capacitor.
C3, C4—470- or 1000-pF leadless, round, disc-ceramic capacitor (see text).
J1, J2—SMA female connectors (see text).

R1, R3—51-Ω chip resistor preferred; ¼-W carbon-film resistor with short leads should be okay.
R2—47-Ω ¼-W carbon-film resistor.

Fig. 86 — Parts-placement guide for the self-biased 2.3-GHz preamplifier. The etching pattern is the same as for the version that uses an external bias supply, except two pads are removed and Z3 must be lengthened. See text.

was then connected to the back ground plane by using 0.1-inch-wide ribbons through the board. This technique was tried on all preamplifiers except the 10-GHz models. With this configuration, the preamp NF at 2304 and 3456 MHz was 0.2 to 0.25 dB greater than that of the grounded source design. The gain of the 2304-MHz model decreased approximately 2 dB, while gain of the 3456-MHz model was reduced by slightly more than 3 dB. At 5760 MHz, performance deteriorated even further: NF increased by 0.8 dB, and gain decreased by 6 dB.

A computer simulation predicted similar results. In addition, the computer simulation indicated an oscillation in the 7- to 8-GHz range for all models. Apparently,

the inductance associated with the addition of the chip capacitors, associated mounting pads, and ribbon ground returns is great enough to cause instability at higher frequencies.

In looking for a way to avoid this oscillation, I tried using leadless round disc capacitors to bypass the source leads. I soldered the FET leads directly to the capacitors and soldered the capacitors to the bottom side of the PC board. This technique was tried on the 2304-MHz preamplifier; see Fig 85.

The bypassed-source 2304-MHz preamplifier uses the same artwork shown in Fig 81 for the grounded-source version. You'll need to make one change to the artwork, though. The input stub (Z3 of

Fig. 87 — The prototype self-biased 2.3-GHz preamplifier. The large rectangular pads near C3 and C4 are not needed and were dropped from the final artwork.

Fig 85) must be made slightly longer (increase its length from 0.22 to 0.38 inch) to help tune out the effect of the source bypass capacitors. Z3 can be extended by soldering a piece of copper foil to the end of the etched line. To mount C3 and C4, the source bypass capacitors, drill holes the diameter of the capacitors through the PC board as shown. See Fig 86. Be sure to place the holes so that the FET source leads are 0.070 inch long when Q1 is centered between Z1 and Z2. Solder a brass or copper sheet across the holes on the ground-plane side, and solder one side of C3 and C4 to the sheet. Then solder the Q1 source leads to the tops of C3 and C4. Fig 87 is a photograph of the finished unit.

According to the computer simulation, this technique yields unconditional stability in the 7- to 8-GHz range. The overall stability of a preamp built in this way is comparable to the grounded-source design. The *measured* performance of this configuration is good too. Compared to the grounded-source model, the gain of the bypassed-source LNA is within 1 dB, and the NF is within 0.1 dB, of that obtained with the grounded-source configuration—and no stability problems are evident. This technique is suggested for the 2304-MHz model only.

Although the preamplifier circuits are designed for minimum noise figure, the ATF-10135 and the ATF-13135 devices are capable of producing moderate power at microwave frequencies. When biased at 4 V and 70 mA, the ATF-10135 is capable of producing +20 dBm (100 mW)—operating at its 1-dB gain-compression point—at 4 GHz. Slightly less power can be expected at 5.7 GHz. At 12 GHz, the ATF-13135 is capable of producing +17.5 dBm at its 1-dB gain-compression point when biased at 4 V and 40 mA.

Summary

These amplifiers were designed by Al Ward, WB5LUA. They were originally described in *QST,* May 1989. Any one of them can be constructed easily in an evening. They offer low noise figure, acceptable gain, good input and output SWR, and good stability. Several dozen of these preamplifiers are already in use nationwide with good results. Copies of the 10.368-GHz preamplifiers, for instance, were used by WA5VJB and WA7CJO to make the first-ever 10-GHz EME QSO!

A Quarter Kilowatt 23-cm Amplifier

The amplifier project described here and shown in Figs. 99 through 123 offers the following features.

1) Covers 1240 to 1300 MHz.

2) Linear operation.

3) Grounded grid 7289/2C39 cavity amplifier, single tube.

4) Power gain ranges from 12 dB to 20 dB depending on output power, input power, loading, anode voltage and grid voltage.

5) 50-ohm input and output — no stub tuner required.

6) Power output greater than 200 W with about 12-W drive.

This project was designed and built by Chip Angle, N6CA. It was originally presented in March and April 1985 *QST*. All of the information given in the original article is reproduced here, including details of the design and construction of the RF deck and power supply, a practical water cooling system, testing and operation. The amplifier described here is a tried and proven design. It works well, is reliable and can be duplicated.

General Design Approach

A cavity amplifier is similar to a conventional amplifier designed for lower frequencies. The tube anode excites a resonant circuit, and power is in turn coupled into a load, usually 50 ohms. Instead of using coils and capacitors, as at lower frequencies, the cavity provides the resonant circuit necessary to tune the amplifier output.

The anode cavity of this amplifier is a squat cylinder. Cylinder height is set by mechanical tube requirements. The inside diameter of the cylinder sets the highest resonant frequency. Any capacitance added from the top to the bottom of the cavity will lower its resonant frequency, as will increasing the cavity diameter.

This amplifier uses 1/8-inch-thick copper plates for the cavity top and bottom and a thick-wall aluminum ring, cut from tubing, for the walls. This heavy construction virtually eliminates all resonant frequency variations caused by thermal and mechanical changes.

Fig. 100 is the schematic diagram of the cavity amplifier. The circuit is simple. Filament voltage enters the RF deck through C4, C5, RFC1 and RFC2. High voltage is fed to the anode through RFC3. C8, the anode bypass capacitor, is homemade from Teflon® dielectric sandwiched between a copper plate and the chassis.

The input pi network easily tunes the entire band at any power level. It is made from two Johanson piston trimmer capacitors and a "coil" made from copper wire. An input cavity is not necessary at 23 cm.

Output coupling is through a rotatable loop that serves as a variable loading control. This allows amplifier-tuning flexibility; it may be tuned for maximum gain

Fig. 99 — The completed 23-cm amplifier.

or for maximum power. Light loading can produce stable power gains of up to 20 dB.

Amplifier tuning is accomplished with a homemade cylindrical coaxial capacitor with Teflon dielectric (C6). There are no moving metal parts to cause erratic performance. The Teflon rod/tube screws in and out of the coaxial capacitor, increasing or decreasing the capacitance by changing the amount of Teflon dielectric inside the cylinder. With the rod all the way in, the dielectric is all Teflon; with the rod all the way out, the dielectric is all air.

Teflon has a relative dielectric constant (relative to air = 1) of 2.05, which means that the value of the capacitor with the Teflon rod all the way in is twice the value of the capacitor with the rod all the way out. Full capacitance will pull the resonant frequency of the amplifier down to 1240 MHz. Use of only one anode tuning adjustment means the amplifier will have more gain because shunt capacitance has been minimized.

Thermal Considerations

The cavity walls are formed by a thick-wall aluminum ring, which is sandwiched between two thick copper plates. RF and thermal properties of these two metals are reasonably close, whereas brass is rather poor in both respects. The 7289/2C39 tube used in this amplifier is being run at 2 to 2½ times its normal dissipation rating; therefore it's important to have a cavity that remains thermally stable.

Most previously described amplifiers

have used sheet brass in their construction. This has usually meant constant retuning of resonance to maintain output power at or near maximum.

The copper and aluminum construction in this amplifier has solved all thermal stability problems. The amplifier can easily be run key down for over an hour at 200-W output without retuning. This, of course, is obtained only with a good tube and water cooling.

Water cooling keeps the internal structure of the tube thermally stable. When air cooling is used for output levels of 100 to 150 W, output power fluctuations are a direct result of internal tube changes. These changes vary from tube to tube and must be tested for. In some cases, perfectly good RF tubes have had poor thermal stability. Such tubes can make good drivers at lower power levels.

Construction

Hand tools are great if you are skilled and patient. Most people want to hurry up and finish their new project. If that's you, then have a machine shop make all of the parts, leaving only the final assembly up to you. It should cost you about $200. The parts are not difficult to fabricate, but the process is time consuming. If you have the time and patience to do it yourself, this amplifier can be very inexpensive.

Gathering the Materials

All of the materials used in this amplifier are fairly common and should be available

Fig. 100 — Schematic diagram of the 23-cm amplifier.

C1 — 3-pF dipped mica capacitor.
C2, C3 — 1- to 10-pF piston trimmer capacitor (Johanson no. 3957, 5201 or equiv.).
C6 — Anode-tuning capacitor. See text and Fig. 110.
C7 — Anode-bypass capacitor, 90 pF. Homemade from copper plate and Teflon sheet.
C8 — Disc ceramic, 0.0047-µF, 3-kV capacitor.
J1 — 5-mm SMA connector, chassis mount, female.
J2 — Modified Type-N connector. See text and Fig. 106.
J3 — Female chassis-mount BNC connector.
L1 — Loop of no. 18 bus wire soldered between C2 and C3. See Fig. 114.
L2 — Output-coupling loop. Part of output-connector assembly. See text and Fig. 106.
RFC1, RFC2 — 5t no. 20 tinned, 3/16-inch ID.
RFC3 — 3t no. 20 tinned wound on a 20-ohm, 1-W carbon-composition resistor.

Fig. 101 — Complete dimensions for the aluminum template.

from suppliers in most metropolitan areas. Some suppliers have ''short sale'' racks where they sell odd pieces cut off standard lengths or sheets at reduced prices. The parts for this project are small enough that they may be fashioned from cutoff stock. Surplus-metal houses have some great buys, so start there if one is nearby.

The key to successfully completing this project is careful layout work before cutting or drilling any parts. Invest in a can of marking dye, a sharp scribe, an accurate rule, vernier calipers and several center punches. These tools are available at any machinists' supply shop. The marking dye will make cutting and filing lines much easier to see. Measure all dimensions as carefully as you can and then recheck them before cutting. Mark with a sharp scribe because the sharper the scribe, the finer the marked line, and the finer the marked line, the closer your cut will be to where it should be. Remember — the accuracy of your

drilled holes is only as good as your center-punching ability, so use a fine punch for the first mark and then a bigger one to enlarge the mark enough for drilling.

Access to a drill press is a must. It's extremely difficult to drill holes accurately with a hand drill. Although not absolutely necessary, you should have access to a lathe or milling machine to do the best possible job.

Other tools that will aid you with this project are a nibbling tool, a set of files and some sharp drill bits. If you don't already have one, purchase a file card to clean aluminum and copper shavings out of your files as you work. Clean, sharp files are faster and more accurate to work with. You'll also need an assortment of sand-paper for the final finishing work.

The Template Approach

It's best to fabricate a single template for marking and drilling the anode plate, anode bypass capacitor, cavity ring, grid plate and front panel. The template shown in Fig. 101 has all of the holes for these parts. If you use the template, you'll only have to make the careful measurements once — after that, it's simple to mark and drill the rest of the parts.

The template approach offers several other advantages. A template makes it much easier to maintain accuracy between the anode plate, cavity ring, grid plate and front panel; these parts will fit perfectly because they were all drilled from the same

master. The template approach also makes it possible to set up a small production line if you decide to build more than one of these amplifiers and combine them for higher power, or if a friend wants to build an amplifier along with you.

See Fig. 101 for complete template dimensions. Start with a piece of 1/16-inch-thick aluminum stock that is larger than you need and degrease it with soap and water. Dry it off and spray it with marking dye. Scribe a 4-inch square on the stock and cut the template to size. A shear will make this job much easier, but it can be cut with hand tools and filed to size.

Carefully measure and scribe all holes. Note that holes A and B are on the circumference of circles. Use a compass to scribe the circles, and then locate the holes. After you have marked and checked all holes, centerpunch and drill them. The holes should be drilled with a 1/16-inch or smaller bit. Recheck all measurements. If you goof, start again. The time you spend making the template as perfect as you can will save you much time and aggravation when you make and assemble the other parts.

When you finish the template, mark the front side for future reference. All plates that will be made from the template are marked and drilled from the front side (as viewed from the front panel).

Making the Copper Plates

Once you have completed the template,

ANODE PLATE
(VIEWED FROM FRONT PANEL)

1/8" COPPER

HOLE: A — 0.144-IN DIA. (NO. 27 DRILL). COUNTERSINK BACK SIDE TO
1/4-IN DIA. WITH A 100°C SINK.
B — 0.106-IN DIA. (NO. 36 DRILL), TAPPED NO. 6-32.
C — 5/32-IN DIA. (0.156). FOR ANODE TUNING POST, THIS SIDE.
F — 0.089-IN DIA. (NO. 43 DRILL). TAPPED NO. 4-40 FOR ANODE
BOX MOUNTING.
H — 1.500-IN DIA.

Fig. 102 — Drilling details for the anode plate. See Fig. 101 for additional information on hole location.

GRID PLATE
(VIEWED FROM FRONT PANEL)

1/8" COPPER

HOLE: A — 0.144-IN DIA. (NO. 27 DRILL).
C — 7/16-IN DIA. (0.438). ANODE TUNING COLLAR INSERTS FROM
THIS SIDE.
D — 1/8-IN DIA. (0.125). FOR CATHODE-GRID MOUNTING.
G — 0.144-IN DIA. (NO. 27 DRILL). FOR FRONT PANEL MOUNTING.
H — 7/8-IN DIA. FOR GRID FINGER STOCK. FINGERS PROTRUDE OUT
BACK SIDE.
NOTE: BRASS INPUT ENCLOSURE MOUNTS ON THIS SIDE.

Fig. 103 — Drilling details for the grid plate. See Fig. 101 for additional information on hole location.

ANODE-BYPASS-CAPACITOR PLATE
(VIEWED FROM FRONT PANEL)

1/8" COPPER

HOLES: B — 1/4-IN DIA.
E — 0.070-IN DIA. (NO. 50 DRILL). TAPPED FOR NO. 2-56 FOR
HIGH-VOLTAGE LUG.
H — 1-1/4-IN DIA. FOR ANODE FINGER STOCK; FINGERS PROTRUDE
OUT BACK SIDE.

Fig. 104 — Drilling details for the anode-bypass-capacitor plate. See Fig. 101 for additional information on hole location.

it will be easy to make the copper plates. The anode plate, grid plate and anode-bypass-capacitor plate are all made from 1/8-inch- thick copper. See Figs. 102, 103 and 104 for the dimensions of these pieces.

Measure and cut the three plates to the proper dimensions. Carefully break (deburr) all sharp edges to avoid small cuts to your fingers and hands.

Clean the plates with alcohol and spray them with marking dye. Clamp the aluminum template to each plate and carefully scribe the correct holes. Remember that all plates do not have the same holes. The anode plate uses holes A, B, C, F and H; the grid plate uses holes A,

C, D, G and H. The anode-bypass-capacitor plate uses holes B, E and H.

Use a small center punch to punch all holes accurately and lightly. If they then look accurate, enlarge them enough for drilling.

Copper isn't the easiest metal to work with. It's very stringy, and drilling it can be frustrating. You'll need the proper drill bits for best results. Special drills can be purchased, but that's not really necessary. You can use a grinder to carefully remove the sharp points on the outer edge of the cutting surface of each side of a standard drill bit. This will eliminate any tendency for the copper to grab. Practice on an old

bit and be sure to grind it symmetrically. Modified drill bits can still be used on aluminum and other metals.

Always start with a smaller drill and work up to the final hole size. It's safer and more accurate. The larger holes can be cut with a flycutter, or you can drill a series of smaller holes around the inside of a larger hole and file to finish. Either way is fine. Use lots of cutting fluid to lubricate the drill bit, and wear safety glasses and an old shirt. Remember, some cutting fluids are not to be used on aluminum.

Start with a no. 50 (0.070-inch) or smaller bit and drill pilot holes at each of your punched marks. The details for finishing each hole are listed in the drawings. Some holes are countersunk or tapped. Pay attention to the details and take your time.

When you are through drilling, you must deburr each hole. Copper is soft, so it tends to rise up around the hole during drilling and deburring. Use a flat file for the initial cut, and then remove any remaining material with a countersink. File the copper plates flat again because a flush fit on both sides of the aluminum ring is very important.

When all copper work is done, you should be able to stack the plates and see all pertinent holes align correctly. Enough tolerance is included in the dimensions to accommodate minor errors. After the holes are drilled, it can be difficult to tell which side of each plate is which, so mark the front side of each plate with a permanent marker.

Machining the Ring

The aluminum ring that forms the cavity

NO. 5/8-24 TAPPED
OR NOTE X

0.402"
0.402"

TEMPLATE
ALIGNMENT
NOTCH

TEMPLATE
FLUSH WITH RING

THICKEST
SECTION

0.390" TYP

SCRIBE
LINE

FAB. FROM
3½"-OD ALU. TUBING
WITH 3/8" WALL
≅2¾" ID.

SCRIBE
LINE

NOTE
(11 PLACES)

0.360" TYP

0.805"
± 0.005

CAVITY RING
(VIEWED FROM FRONT PANEL)

NOTE: HOLE A — 0.089-IN DIA. NO. 43 DRILL. DRILLED THRU AND TAPPED
GREATER THAN 3/8-IN DEEP WITH NO. 4-40 TAP FROM EACH SIDE.
NOTE X: NO. 5/8-24 TAPPED OR 5/8-IN-DIA. TUBING WITH SET SCREW FROM
GRID PLATE SIDE. (SEE TEXT).

Fig. 105 — Details of the cavity ring. See Fig. 101 for additional information on hole location.

wall is cut (sliced) from a length of 3½-inch OD tubing with a 3/8-inch wall thickness. See Fig. 105. The tubing ID is approximately 2¾ inches. The dimensions of the ring are the most critical in this amplifier. Tolerance of the ring thickness is ±0.005 inch to maintain full band coverage.

The ring can be hacksawed or bandsawed out of the tubing, but take extreme care to be accurate. Cutting tubing straight isn't easy. Clamp the tubing to prevent rotating on the bandsaw. The final finish cut is best done on a lathe or milling machine, but careful filing will work.

Once the ring is the correct thickness, deburr the sharp edges and spray it with marking dye. Notice that the outside and inside diameters are not concentric. This is normal for large tubing and is not a problem. Lay the ring flat and find the thickest wall section. Scribe a line across the wall at this point, across the center of the ring, and across the wall on the other side. The scribed lines on each side of the ring will be used to align the template. The output connector will be placed at the thick wall section.

Carefully align notch I on the template with the line scribed on the thickest wall section on the ring. Clamp the template onto the ring. Mark each of the 11 holes labeled A on the template. After you mark the holes and remove the template, check alignment with the copper plates just in case. If everything lines up, center punch all eleven holes on one side of the ring only, and drill each hole completely through the

ring. Use lots of cutting fluid. File the ring flat before and after deburring, taking care not to change the wall thickness. Tap each hole to accept no. 4-40 machine screws. Each hole will have to be tapped to a depth of at least 3/8-inch from both sides because long taps don't exist. The inside of the ring doesn't need to be polished.

The hole for mounting the output connector can now be drilled. There are two ways to mount this connector, and either scheme works fine. Read ahead to the section on making the output connector for more information. The first method of mounting the output connector involves tapping the ring with a no. 5/8-24 tap and using a lathe to cut matching threads on the output connector coupling sleeve. Large taps are expensive, but both a tap and die for Type-N connectors come in handy if you do a lot of building.

If you don't have access to a lathe or a large tap, the second method is easier. Make the output connector coupling sleeve from 5/8-inch-OD brass or copper tubing and drill the ring to just clear it. Then drill and tap the grid-plate side of the ring above the output connector to accept a setscrew. Use the setscrew to secure the output connector.

Output Connector

A standard Type-N chassis-mount female connector (silver plated) is used for the output probe/connector. See Fig. 106. First, remove the flange with a hacksaw and file flush with the connector body.

Next, make the output coupling sleeve that is right for your application (threaded or unthreaded, depending on how you fabricated the ring). The sleeve will be the same length in either case. The output coupling loop is fashioned from a piece of 0.032-inch-thick copper sheet that is 5/32 inch wide. Bend it to the dimensions shown in Fig. 106. We will solder the output connector together later.

Grid Compartment

The grid compartment measures 2 inches square by 1½ inches high. See Fig. 107. It is made from brass and can be sawed out of square tubing or bent from sheet stock. The cover can be made from any sheet metal.

Two small PC boards (Fig. 108) hold the finger stock that makes contact with the filament pin and cathode ring on the 2C39 tube. These boards are cut from 1/16-inch-thick, double-sided G-10 glass-epoxy stock. The copper pattern is identical for both sides of each piece. Mark and drill or file the holes first and then cut the boards to size. Small boards are difficult to hold while drilling them. Mark each side of each board and score the copper foil with a sharp knife.

The unwanted copper can be removed easily by heating the foil with a soldering iron and lifting it off. Use a flat file to deburr the boards. Do not use a countersink because the copper foil must be as close to the holes as possible to facilitate soldering the finger stock in place.

The input connector is a 5-mm SMA type. This is an excellent RF connector, especially for low-power UHF applications. Although an SMA is recommended, any small, screw-on connector will do. If you really feel you have to use a BNC then do so, but it's a lousy connector at frequencies above 200 MHz. Remember to move

REMOVE FLANGE

STANDARD N FEMALE CONNECTOR

5/8"
OD

7/16" ID

FAB. FROM 5/8" DIA.
BRASS ROD
(OR BRASS TUBING
SEE TEXT)

5/8"

OUTPUT COUPLING SLEEVE

END OF COUPLING
SLEEVE

OUTPUT
COUPLING SLEEVE

0.675"

0.525"

SOLDER

SOLDER IN PLACE

5/32"

FAB. FROM 0.032" COPPER SHEET

OUTPUT PROBE ASSEMBLY

Fig. 106 — Output-probe/connector assembly details.

Fig. 107 — Input compartment details.

the connector hole to accommodate its larger size.

The input connector must be as close as possible to the first input capacitor. Lead length of the input dc blocking capacitor must be as short as possible. The 3-pF capacitor is series resonant at 1200 MHz only with short (1/16-inch or less) leads.

Miscellaneous Bits and Pieces

There are still several small, but very important parts to fabricate. The front panel is shown in Fig. 109. It is made from a piece of 1/8-inch-thick aluminum sheet. Some builders may wish to mount the amplifier on a rack panel. Wash and dry your front-panel material and spray it with marking dye. Clamp it to the template and mark the holes. Check the hole alignment with the

Fig. 108 — Cathode and filament PC-board details.

Fig. 109 — Front-panel details.

Fig. 110 — Anode-tuning capacitor details.

Fig. 111 — Miscellaneous parts necessary to complete the amplifier.

Fig. 112 — Anode enclosure details.

Fig. 113 — Dimensions of the soldering fixture. See Fig. 101 for more information on hole location.

copper grid and anode plates. If all lines up correctly, center punch and drill the holes. The only front-panel control is for the anode tuning capacitor, which is adjusted by a ¼-inch shaft protruding through a 3/8-inch panel bushing in hole C.

The anode tuning collar, shown in Fig. 110A, is made from a piece of ½-inch-OD brass rod. This rod has a 3/8-inch hole drilled through its center, and it is turned down to 7/16-inch OD for half its length. The inside of the ½-inch-OD end is tapped to a depth of ¼ inch to accept 3/8-24 threads. This collar will be inserted into hole C on the grid plate.

Fig. 110B also shows the anode tuning post. It is simply a length of 5/32-inch-OD brass rod that inserts into hole C on the copper anode plate. This rod will form one plate of the anode tuning capacitor; the cavity wall is the other plate.

The anode tuner (Fig. 110C) is machined from a piece of 3/8-inch-OD Teflon rod. One end of the rod is drilled out with a no. 21 drill. The outer wall of this end is threaded with a no. 3/8-24 tap. This is the end that will thread into the anode tuning collar and slip over the anode tuning post. The other end is turned down to fit inside a ¼-inch shaft coupler.

Fig. 111 shows the remaining parts. The tuning shaft (A) is made from a piece of ¼-inch brass rod. A coupler (B) to connect the tuning shaft to the anode tuner may be purchased or made. This also applies to the front-panel spacers (C). The Teflon dielectric for the anode bypass capacitor (D) is made from 0.010-inch-thick Teflon sheet.

Use the template to locate holes B and H. Teflon washers and inserts (E) are used to insulate the mounting hardware for the anode bypass capacitor from the chassis. The inserts are made from ¼-inch-OD Teflon rod. The washers are made from Teflon sheet. Sharpen a piece of 3/8-inch OD tubing and chuck it up in a drill press. This tool will cut neat, round washers from the sheet.

The box that encloses the anode compartment (Fig. 112) is fabricated from a Bud AU-1083 utility cabinet. Clean the chassis and spray it with marking dye. Secure the template to the side of the enclosure that contacts the anode plate and scribe the holes labeled F. Make sure that these holes line up with the holes on the copper anode plate. If they do, center punch and drill them to size. If air cooling is used, the blower will mount to this box.

Soldering the Subassemblies

Once all copper and brass parts are drilled and deburred, they should be cleaned with alcohol and Scotch-Brite®, a nonmetallic pot cleaner, and washed in alcohol again. Set the pieces aside and avoid touching them. Fingerprints will inhibit soldering.

The best way to solder the heavy brass and copper parts is to first build the soldering fixture shown in Fig. 113. This soldering fixture, made from ½-inch-thick aluminum plate, will evenly heat the entire assembly to be soldered. Even heating will allow you to do a much better soldering job than you could otherwise.

The aluminum soldering fixture should be preheated on a stove or hot plate until bits of solder placed on its surface just melt. At this point, reduce the heat slightly. Avoid excessive heat. If the copper parts placed on the fixture suddenly turn dark, the heat is too high.

Solder the grid plate assembly first. You will need the copper grid plate, grid finger stock, anode tuning collar and brass input compartment.[1] Look at the drawings again to be sure that you know which parts go where. Insert the grid finger stock into hole H on the grid plate. As viewed from the front-panel side, the curved fingers will protrude out the back side, away from you. Apply liquid or paste flux and set the grid plate in the soldering fixture. The finger

[1]The finger stock for this project is available from Instrument Specialties, P.O. Box A, Delaware Water Gap, PA 18327. Contact them for the name of the closest distributor. The part numbers for this amplifier are: anode bypass capacitor plate, no. 97-70A; grid plate, no. 97-74A; cathode board, no. 97-420A; filament board, no. 97-280A.

stock will fit in hole H in the fixture, allowing the grid plate to rest flush with the surface of the fixture. Next, apply flux to the anode tuning collar and insert it in hole C of the grid plate. Part of the tuning collar will slip into hole C in the soldering fixture. Make sure the collar seats flush with the grid plate. The flux should start to bubble at this point. Carefully apply solder directly to the joints of the installed parts. The solder should melt almost immediately and flow bright and smooth. Next, place the square brass input compartment in place and apply flux. In a few seconds, it can be soldered by running solder around the joints, inside and outside. If you have trouble getting it to flow on both sides, merely tap the brass box aside (1/16 inch) and return it to its original position.

Now comes the hard part — getting the soldered assembly away from the heat without disturbing the alignment. A pair of forceps is recommended, but long pliers will do. Carefully lift the assembly off the soldering fixture and set on a cooling rack. Do this without moving any part. The cooling rack can be any two pieces of metal that will allow clearance for the protruding parts. You can expedite cooling by using an ordinary hair dryer in the "cool" position to gently blow air across the assembly.

While the grid assembly is cooling, assemble the output connector. See Fig. 106. Place the modified Type-N female connector, threaded end down, on the soldering fixture. Apply flux to the top and install the output coupling sleeve. Allow both parts to heat before applying solder. Carefully remove the soldered output connector from the fixture. When it has cooled, solder one end of the loop to the center pin of the N connector and the other to the output coupling sleeve.

Now place the anode plate on the soldering fixture and allow to heat. Apply flux to hole C. Insert the anode tuning post (5/32-inch-OD brass tube) and allow to heat; apply solder. Remove the parts and cool as before.

This completes the work with the soldering fixture. Be sure to let it cool off before handling! Save the fixture for future construction; you never know when you might want it again.

The anode plate and the anode-bypass-capacitor plate must be filed and then sanded flat on their butt surfaces to assure that there are no solder bumps or sharp points to puncture the Teflon dielectric. This must be done after soldering. The Teflon sheet is adequate insulation for many times the anode potential of this amplifier, but only if the surfaces it separates are smooth!

Next, clean the cathode and filament PC boards. Install the finger stock in hole H of the cathode board. Apply flux to both sides of the board. Heat with a hot iron and apply solder around the circumference of hole H, soldering the finger stock on both

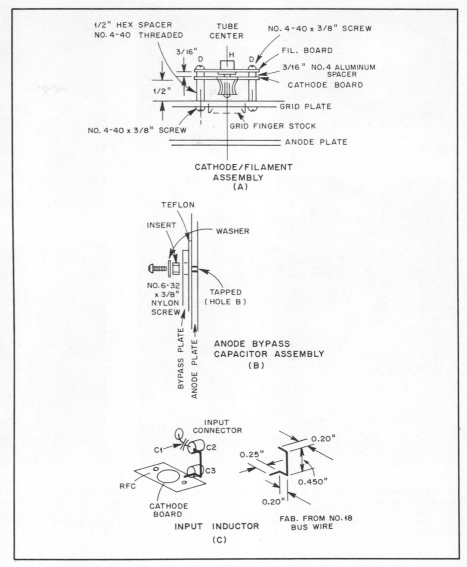

Fig. 114 — Assembly details for the filament and cathode boards (A), the anode-bypass capacitor (B) and the input pi network (C).

sides of the board. Use the same technique to install the filament pin.

After all parts have cooled, use a spray can of flux remover to clean them. Slight scrubbing with "Scotch-Brite" pot cleaner will finish them nicely. Congratulations: You have finished the pieces and are now ready to bolt the amplifier together.

Silver Plating

Over the years, many people have pushed silver plating as the only way to go. You may wish to silver plate the amplifier components before soldering them together, but it is not necessary. The RF skin conductivity of aluminum and copper is pretty good at 23 cm; these materials are much better than brass. In actual testing with four amplifiers, there was no difference in performance among tin-plated, silver-plated and unplated versions. A nickel-plated

amplifier exhibited 3-dB less gain than the others.

Assembly

After fabrication of all parts, assembly is simple. Figs. 114 through 116 show assembly details. Loosely fasten the grid and anode plates to the ring. Mount the input connector and capacitors on the input compartment. Loosely install the cathode and filament boards and their respective spacers. See Fig. 114A.

Now insert a 7289/2C39 tube. This will center up all finger stock. Place the Teflon anode tuner in its collar on the grid plate and screw it most of the way in. Now tighten all of the screws. The 7289/2C39 tube should slide in and out snugly, and the anode tuner should screw in and out smoothly.

The Teflon sheet and anode bypass

Fig. 115 — The completed cavity ring and anode plate with anode tuning post soldered in place are shown at A. The photo at B shows the grid plate with finger stock, input compartment and anode tuning collar soldered in place. The completed anode tuner is at the right. C shows the cavity ring attached to the anode plate. The anode-bypass capacitor is ready for installation. At D, the interior of the cavity as seen from the grid plate side is visible. The output probe/connector assembly is installed. The anode bypass capacitor and anode enclosure have been installed on the anode plate.

Fig. 116 — At A, the interior of the completed input compartment is visible. The photo at B shows the interior of the anode compartment with the anode bypass, RFC3, C8 and J3 installed.

Fig. 117 — Schematic diagram of the cavity amplifier filament and bias supplies. All resistors are ¼-W carbon types unless otherwise noted.

J1 — Female chassis-mount phono connector.
T1 — Filament transformer. Primary, 117-V; secondary, 6.3 V at 1 A.
T2 — Power transformer. Primary, 117-V;

secondary, 24 to 28 V at 50 mA or greater.
U1 — Bridge rectifier, 50 PIV, 1 A.
U2 — Adjustable 3-terminal regulator (LM317T or equiv.).

Z1, Z2 — 20-V unipolar metal-oxide varistor (General Semiconductor SA20 or equiv.) or two 20-V, 1-W Zener diodes.

capacitor plate can be installed now (Fig. 114B). Assemble the remaining input components, the filament feed-through capacitors and RFCs (Fig. 114C). Screw the output probe into the cavity ring (or push in the probe and tighten the set screw, depending on which method you chose). Install the high-voltage connector and other parts in the anode box. Mount the amplifier on the front panel and install the anode tuner shaft. This completes the assembly.

Power Supplies

The filament and bias supplies for the cavity amplifier are shown schematically in Fig. 117. The manufacturer's specification for the 7289/2C39 filament is 6.0-V ac at 1 A. The use of a standard 6.3-V ac, 1-A transformer only slightly increases the tube emission without much loss of tube life. The filament should be allowed to warm up before operating the amplifier, so the filament, bias and high-voltage supplies incorporate separate primary switches.

Biasing

Many biasing schemes have been published for grounded-grid amplifiers. Fig. 117 shows a bias network that satisfies all of the following operating requirements:

1) External bias supply referenced to ground.

2) Low-power components.

3) Variable bias to accommodate tube-to-tube variations.

4) TR switchable with relay contact or transistor to ground.

5) Bias-supply protection in case of a defective or shorted tube.

U2 provides a variable bias-voltage

source, adjustable by R1. The output of U2 drives the base of Q1, which is used to increase the current-handling capability of the bias supply. Q1 must be mounted on a heat sink. J1 is connected to the station TR switching system so that R1 is grounded on transmit and disconnected on receive. The approximate range of the bias supply is 6 to 20 V. Z1 and Z2 provide protection for R1 in case of a shorted tube. The amplifier can be run without Z1 and Z2 if you keep the anode voltage below 1100 V.

High-Voltage Power Supply

A safe, reliable high-voltage power supply is described here. Of course, you can use any readily available HV supply; keep in mind, however, that the 7289/2C39 anode potential should never exceed 1400-V dc at full load and that the amplifier will withstand 1900-V dc at low cathode current and cut-off-bias conditions. For maximum power output, assuming adequate drive power is available, anode voltage under full load should be about 1200- to 1400-V dc.

Fig. 118 is a schematic diagram of the high-voltage supply. A power transformer (T2) that delivers 900- to 1050-V ac is ideal. The type of rectifier circuit used will depend on the type of transformer chosen. Each leg of the rectifier is made from two 1000-PIV, 3-A silicon diodes connected in series. Each diode is shunted with a 0.01-μF capacitor to suppress transient voltage spikes, and a 470-kΩ equalizing resistor.

Filtering is accomplished with a string of four 360-μF, 450-V electrolytic capacitors connected in series. R3-R6 equalize the voltage across each capacitor in the string

and serve as bleeder resistors. Of course, a single oil-filled capacitor may be used here if available. Whatever type of filter you use, the total capacitance should be about 80 μF at a voltage rating of at least 1500-V dc. This value allows adequate "droop" of the anode voltage under high-current loads to protect the amplifier in case of RF overdrive or a defective tube.

Protective Circuitry

Some type of start-up protection should be incorporated in the primary. Fully discharged filter capacitors look like a dead short at supply turn-on. Initial surge current (until the capacitors charge) may be high enough to destroy the rectifiers. R1 and R2 provide some surge-current limiting, but either of the two primary configurations shown in Fig. 118 should be used. T1, a variable autotransformer (Variac and Powerstat are two common trade names), is ideal. In addition to allowing you to bring the primary up slowly, (and charging the capacitors gradually), it also allows full control of amplifier output power by varying anode voltage.

The second method, a "step-start" system, uses a resistor in the T2 primary to limit the turn-on surge current. When the capacitors have charged, K1 is energized, shorting out R11 and applying full voltage to the T2 primary.

F1 and R7 protect against high-voltage arc-overs or short circuits. If sustained overcurrent is drawn, F1 will open and remove B+ from the RF deck. Use a high-voltage fuse here; standard fuses may arc when blown and not interrupt the B+. R7

Fig. 118 — Schematic diagram of the amplifier high-voltage supply.

C1-C4 — Electrolytic capacitor, 360 μF, 450 V.
D1-D4 — Silicon rectifier, 1000 PIV, 3 A.
F1 — High-voltage fuse, 2 kV, 1 A.

J1 — Chassis mount female BNC or MHV connector.
R3-R6 — Wirewound resistor, 40 kΩ, 11 W.

T1 — Variable autotransformer, 500 VA.
T2 — High-voltage transformer. Primary, 117 V; secondary, 900 to 1050 V at 500 mA.

provides current limiting to protect the amplifier and power supply in case of a high-voltage arc.

Safety

An HV meter should always be used to monitor the status of the power supply. The values for R8-R10 shown in Fig. 118 will give a 1500-V dc full-scale reading on a 0-1 mA meter. RG-58 or -59 coaxial cable should be used for the high-voltage interconnection between the power supply and the RF deck. Ground the shield at both ends for safety and a good dc return.

Safety must be observed when working with all power supplies. These voltages are lethal! Always disconnect ac power and then discharge the filter capacitors before working on the power supply. Never guess or make assumptions about the status of a power supply. Assume it is hot.

Metering

Cathode-current monitoring is all that's really necessary for observing amplifier dc performance. Cathode current (I_K) is the sum of the plate (I_P) and grid (I_G) currents. Normally, when this amplifier is driven to 300- or 400-mA I_K, the grid current will be around 40 to 50 mA. The inclusion of a grid-current meter is not really necessary and only makes biasing and TR switching complicated.

Cooling

Desired output power and the level of drive power available will dictate what type of cooling to use. For intermittent duty (SSB, CW) at output levels less than 50 W, air cooling is satisfactory. Any small blower may be easily mounted to the aluminum box surrounding the tube anode. For high-duty-cycle modes and/or output levels

greater than 50 W, water cooling is highly recommended. Greater than twice the normal air-cooled output power can be obtained from a water-cooled tube, and water cooling is quiet.

Tube Modification and Water Jacket

The first step is to remove the air radiator from the tube. The air radiator screws on, so it may simply be unscrewed without damage to the tube.

First, place a hose clamp around the tube anode. Secure the radiator fins in a vise and grip the hose clamp with a pair of large pliers. Gently unscrew the tube from the radiator. If the hose clamp slips slightly, tighten it.

Some 7289/2C39 tubes use an air radiator that is attached with set screws. To remove the radiator, simply remove the set screws and pull the radiator off.

The air radiator will be replaced with a water jacket that allows water to be circulated past the tube anode and through a heat exchanger, where it is cooled and circulated past the tube anode again. Two different types of water jackets are described here.

The water jacket shown in Fig. 119 will work with any type of 7289/2C39. It is fabricated from a 1-inch-OD copper tubing cap and two short pieces of 9/32-inch OD brass tubing. The copper tubing cap should be available from a local hardware store or plumbing supply house. Brass tubing is available from many hobby stores and metal supply houses.

Mark and drill the copper cap so that the brass tubing is a snug fit. Thoroughly clean the parts until they shine. Push the tubing into the holes in the end cap and degrease the assembly with alcohol. Use plenty of flux and solder the seam around each sec-

tion of tubing. Allow the jacket assembly to cool.

Meanwhile, thoroughly clean the 7289/2C39 anode to a bright finish. Check the water jacket for fit. In some cases, you'll have to use a 0.005- to 0.010-inch-thick copper shim to fill the gap between the copper cap and the tube anode. This shim helps eliminate pin holes in the solder.

Using plenty of flux, solder the water jacket to the tube anode. Solder it quickly with a hot, high-wattage iron. Allow the tube to cool in the air after soldering to avoid thermal shock and possible breakage. After the tube has cooled, use plenty of alcohol to remove all traces of flux from the tube and water jacket.

The second type of water jacket is shown in Fig. 120. This jacket will work only with 7289/2C39 tubes that have a screw-on air radiator. It is designed to thread onto the tube anode just like the air radiator did. This jacket is machined from a piece of 1¼-inch aluminum rod. The water inlet

Fig. 119 — Details of the solder-on water jacket.

ALU. TUBING 9/32" OD, 1/4" ID 1" LENGTH

EPOXY IN PLACE

FAB. FROM 1-1/4" ALU. ROD

BOTTOM VIEW

RUBBER GASKET 1-3/16" OD, 3/4" ID 0.070" THICKNESS

ASSEMBLY

PINCH-OFF TUBE CLEARANCE

DETAIL AA

9/32"

9/32"

1/4" 19/32"
5/8" 7/8"

NO. 3/8-16 THREAD

1/2" 3/4"

5/16"

5/16"

THREAD DEPTH

0.594"

0.625"

7289 ANODE WATER JACKET

9/32" DIA.

3/16" DIA.

1/2" DIA.

Fig. 120 — Details of the screw-on water jacket.

and outlet tubes are made from 9/32-inch-OD, ¼-inch-ID aluminum tubing that is epoxied in place. A rubber gasket seals the jacket against leaks.

If you have access to a lathe, you should have no trouble duplicating the jacket. You could have one made up at a local machine shop. Complete screw-on water jackets are also available from Angle Linear.[2]

After you unscrew the air radiator from the 7289/2C39, check for and remove any burrs from the tube anode. The anode surface must be flat if the rubber gasket is to be effective. Screw the water jacket onto the tube. Tighten by hand only. Do not use any tools, or you could damage the tube or jacket! Do not use the water inlet and outlet tubes for leverage — they have thin walls and break easily.

Water System

Fig. 121 depicts the complete water-cooling system. Recommended pumps and accessories that have proven reliable and effective are listed in the caption.

Any small pump, such as a fountain pump, that can deliver 160 to 200 gallons

[2]25309 Andreo Ave., Lomita, CA 90717.

per hour can be used here. Most inexpensive pumps are not self-priming, which means that they won't pump water if they have air in the rotor. Although water can be forced through the pump for the initial prime, my system uses gravity priming. The water reservoir is a 2-foot length of 3-inch-OD plastic pipe that is available from hardware or plumbing stores. It is usually sold for use in residential sewer systems. The outlet is at the bottom and the inlet about halfway up the column. The inlet is located here to eliminate aeration that ionizes the water and reduces its effectiveness. The outlet feeds the pump directly. The pump and the reservoir outlet port should be mounted in the same plane. The pump should be oriented so that air bubbles will rise into the impeller output port and can be blown out once the pump starts running.

Flow Indicator and Heat Exchanger

Water cooling is best described as "super quiet." There is no noisy fan to hear to reassure you that the tube is receiving adequate cooling. If water flow is reduced or cut off during amplifier operation, tube damage is virtually assured.

Flow interlocks and switches to shut down the amplifier if water flow is reduced are hard to find and expensive. Flow in-

dicators, however, are inexpensive and reliable. A flow indicator has a spoked rotor that turns as water passes through the unit. If the wheel is turning, there is water flow; if not, you have a problem. Changes in flow rate can be observed by watching for speed changes in the rotor. A small lamp illuminates the flow indicator, making it easy to see rotation. The flow indicator should be mounted where it can be seen from the operating position and monitored during operation.

Heat exchangers, or radiators, remove the heat from water as it passes through. For this application, a small automobile transmission-oil cooler works great. Most auto-parts stores and speed shops have a good selection. Some come with mounting brackets. Look for a cooler with the input and output ports on the top so air bubbles will rise to the top and move on without becoming trapped. Trapped air degrades cooler performance.

If you use the amplifier for high-duty-cycle modes such as ATV or FM, or for long, slow-speed CW transmissions (EME, for example), you should use a small axial whisper fan to increase the effectiveness of the heat exchanger. A fan isn't necessary during normal operation, or even for sustained operation at moderate power levels, but is highly recommended if you plan prolonged operation at maximum power. Locate the fan so the warm exhaust air won't heat up other equipment.

Hoses and Fittings

Most hardware stores carry a complete line of brass fittings and adapters that can be used for this project. Brass, however, will eventually corrode and pollute the water supply. Plastic fittings are cheaper and don't corrode, but they are harder to find. Recreational vehicle suppliers are my main source for these parts. They are used extensively in drinking water systems for mobile homes and travel trailers. Procure the fittings when you have the rest of the parts in hand, as there are many variables to consider.

You can use any relatively soft, thin-wall vinyl tubing for all water lines. The main runs are made from 3/8-inch-ID hose, while ¼-inch-ID stock is used to connect to the 7289/2C39 water jacket. The ¼-inch-ID tubing fits snugly over the 9/32-inch-OD inlet and outlet tubes on the water jacket, so no clamps are required. All other hose connections should be secured with stainless-steel clamps to prevent leaks. Any leaks mean air in the system and deterioration of cooling performance.

Safety

The anode of the tube, and hence the water jacket and water, are in direct contact with the high-voltage supply, so some safety precautions must be observed. Approximately 12 to 18 inches of tubing should run between the 7289/2C39 jacket and any other component in the cooling

Fig. 121 — Details of the water-cooling system. Recommended pumps are: (1) Little Giant Pump Co. Model 1-42A or larger, available from most hardware stores; or (2) Calvert Engineering, Cal Pump Model 875S (160 gal/h), available from Calvert, 7051 Hayvenhurst Ave., Van Nuys, CA 91406, tel. 818-781-6029. The flow indicator (Model 15C; requires two ½-inch NPT connectors) is available from Proteus Industries, 240 Polaris Ave., Mountain View, CA 94043, tel. 415-964-4163.

system. This will allow enough resistance in the water to provide adequate current limiting, should the water contact any components that are grounded.

It is best to ground the water supply at the pump. This can be accomplished by replacing a short section of the tubing that runs to the flow indicator with a piece of brass or copper tubing. Solder a wire to this metal tubing and connect the other end of the wire to your station ground. Use at least 24 inches of vinyl tubing between the anode

cooling jacket and the ground point.

On the warm-water side of the 7289/2C39, run 12 inches of vinyl tubing to a small metal fitting or short section of metal tubing, and then another 12 inches of vinyl tubing to a grounded point (this can be at the heat exchanger). You can measure the water leakage current to ground by placing a microammeter between the metal fitting that connects the two vinyl hoses and ground. Leakage current should be less than 10 μA with clean

water and an anode potential of 1 kV. As the water ages, the leakage current will rise; when this happens, replace the water.

Grocery stores carry distilled water for use in steam irons. It may be deionized and not truly distilled, but it works fine for about four to six months in this application. Filters can be purchased from scientific supply houses, but it's not really worth it because deionized water is so cheap.

Do not use tap water under any circumstances! When you turn on the water system for the first time, run a gallon of water through it for half an hour to wash out fabrication impurities. Replace with clean water before using the system to cool the amplifier.

Water was chosen because it's inexpensive, nontoxic, nonflammable, and easy to clean up if you have a leak. Better liquid coolants are available, but they are toxic. Don't use them!

Cooling Performance

Fig. 122 is a graph of several transmit/receive cycles on a water-cooled, 500-W output, 23-cm power amplifier. For this test, two of the amplifiers described here were coupled with a hybrid combiner. This particular cooling system used one gallon of water. Experiments indicate that, during extended operation, the water temperature rises only 30 to 35 °F above ambient room temperature. Typically, the tube anode and water average 10 to 15 °F above ambient during casual operating.

Flow rates in this system are typically ⅓ gallon per minute per tube, which is more than adequate. At this rate, more than 300 W of dissipation from a single inefficient 7289/2C39 were required to boil the water in the water jacket. The water should not be allowed to boil because this will heat the rubber gasket.

Tubes

It is not really necessary to buy a new 7289/2C39. Used tubes can be found surplus for a few dollars and, in many cases, will perform as well as a new tube. Most used tubes have been sitting around for several years, so it's a good idea to run them through the dishwasher to clean them up and then run the filaments for about 24 hours. This will restore operation in many cases.

If you buy a new tube, you should be aware that the 7289/2C39 is being run far in excess of its ratings in this amplifier. The manufacturer's warranty will not cover tubes run in this application.

Contrary to popular opinion, glass tubes will work. Physically, they are not as rugged as the ceramic version, but the glass-to-metal seal seems to provide better shelf life than the ceramic seal. The glass tubes make great driver tubes and will work fine for power levels up to 100-W output. Pulse tubes (7815, 7211) are not recommended because of their poor thermal stability at high power levels. Also, they generally are

Fig. 122 — Performance graph of the water-cooling system.

30 to 40 MHz lower in resonant frequency in this amplifier compared to the 7289/2C39. Some 7289 tubes can be as much as 30 MHz lower in frequency. Minor length adjustment of the anode-tuning post may be required to accommodate amplifier and tube differences.

Tube Insertion

Extreme care must be exercised when inserting the 7289/2C39 tube. Never force the tube in place as damage (bending) of the cathode finger stock may result. Observe the layout of the finger stock to get an idea of how the tube inserts. Carefully position the tube so it is straight as you gently push. It should slide in snugly without any solid resistance.

Testing

After you have completed all of the parts for the amplifier, it's time to test everything before hooking it all together. Test the water-cooling system by turning it on and watching for steady water flow as indicated on the flow meter. The tube and water jacket can be removed from the cavity amplifier for this test.

Check all of the power-supply voltages first without connecting them to the RF deck. Then, without the tube in place, hook the bias and filament supplies to the cavity and check the voltages again at the tube finger-stock connections. Connect the high-voltage supply to the RF deck and bring the voltage up slowly with a variable autotransformer. Monitor the high-voltage on the anode bypass capacitor plate, and look and listen for any possible arcing between the anode-bypass-capacitor plate and ground. Use extreme care when measuring and testing the high-voltage supply. If everything looks okay with the power supplies, shut them off and disconnect them.

You can make a safe, low-power test of the cavity resonance without applying any voltage. With the tube in place, insert a 2-inch-long coupling loop on the end of a piece of coaxial cable between the spring fingers of the anode down into the cavity. Connect the amplifier output probe/connector to a device capable of detecting low-level RF at 23 cm (for example, a spectrum analyzer or microwattmeter). Feed a signal from an L-band signal generator into cable attached to the wire coupling loop that you inserted into the cavity. Set the signal generator for various frequencies in the 23-cm band and tune the amplifier anode tuner. There will be a sharp peak in output at cavity resonance.

This testing method can be used to determine cavity tuning range, anode-bypass-capacitor effectiveness and resonance of various tube types for use in this amplifier. Any cavity amplifier can be tested completely without ever applying high voltage. The better your test equipment, the easier the amplifier is to test. If all dimensions

were followed strictly, the amplifier will tune as designed.

Amplifier Hookup

Installation and operation of this amplifier is relatively straightforward, but as with any amplifier, several precautions must be followed. If these are adhered to, it will provide years of reliable service.

The amplifier is designed to be operated in a 50-ohm system and should never be turned on without a good 50-ohm load connected to the output connector. Never operate it into an antenna that has not been tuned to 50 ohms!

Drive power to the amplifier should never exceed 15 W. Never apply drive power in excess of 1 W unless all operating voltages are present and the tube is biased on. Otherwise, the tube grid-dissipation rating will be exceeded and you will probably ruin it.

As in all TR-switched systems, some type of interlock or sequencing of transmit and receive functions should be incorporated. In most systems, the sequence for going into transmit is something like this: First, switch the antenna changeover relay from the receiver to the power amplifier. Next, bias the power amplifier on. Last, key the exciter and apply drive to the amplifier. To go to receive, unkey the exciter, remove operating bias from the amplifier and switch the antenna relay back to the receiver. A TR sequencer is described in Chapter 31.

If the antenna relays are switched while the power amplifier is operating and putting out power, damage to the relay contacts and/or the amplifier is likely. If there is a momentary removal of the antenna while the power amplifier is biased on, it may oscillate. This can damage the TR relay, the tube, or even the receive preamplifier.

Fig. 123 — Performance of the cavity amplifier under different drive and plate-current conditions.

Tune Up and Operation

This is it — the big moment when you will see your project come to life! Connect an accurate UHF power meter and a 50-ohm antenna or load to the amplifier output connector. A Bird Model 43 wattmeter with a 100- or 250-W, 400- to 1000-MHz slug will give reasonable accuracy, depending on the purity of the drive signal. Apply filament power and tube cooling, and allow 3 to 5 minutes for the filaments to warm up. Turn on bias supply (the amplifier will draw maximum current if the anode voltage is applied without bias). Apply 300 to 400 V to the anode. There should be no current flowing in the tube as indicated on the cathode-current meter. Ground J1 on the bias supply to apply transmit bias and observe cathode current. As R1, the bias control, is turned clockwise, quiescent idling current should increase. Set for about 25 mA.

Apply 1 W of RF drive power. Turn the anode tuner while observing the RF output power meter and tune for maximum output. The output should go through a pronounced peak at cavity resonance. Adjust C2 and C3 on the input tuning network for maximum amplifier output. If possible, use a directional wattmeter between the driver and the amplifier input to check that best input SWR and maximum amplifier output occur at roughly the same setting.

Depending on the amount of drive power available, you may want to tune the amplifier for maximum power output or maximum gain. Fig. 123 shows what you can expect from different drive levels.

Once the amplifier is tuned for best input SWR and maximum output with 1 W of drive, anode voltage and drive power can be increased. Increase both in steps; be sure to keep the anode tuner peaked for maximum output power. When you get to the 100-W output level, very carefully readjust the input circuit for maximum output. The input capacitor closest to the cathode is critical and should need to be rotated less than 90 degrees maximum. Maximum output power will be roughly coincident with best input SWR.

Increase the drive power and keep the anode tuner peaked for maximum output. Increase the drive until you reach the desired output level, but do not exceed 400-mA I_K! At 1300-V dc and 350-mA I_K, output power with a good tube should be about 230 to 250 watts. At lower anode voltages, I_K will be higher for the same output power. Higher anode voltages result in higher gain, lower drive levels, lower grid current and lower plate current for a given output power.

The anode tuner's tuning rate is approximately 5 MHz per turn. Clockwise rotation of the tuner lowers the resonant frequency of the cavity. This control will require readjustment as you make large frequency excursions within the 23-cm band (for example, if you go from 1296 weak-signal work to the 1269-MHz satellite segment). You should also check the input SWR if you move more than 15 MHz. Generally, amplifier tuning does not change much after initial setup. You should be able to turn it on and use it without retuning as it heats up. Slight adjustments may be necessary, however, depending on cooling,

inherent thermal differences from tube to tube and duty cycle of the operating mode. Always keep the anode tuner peaked for maximum output, and check it from time to time, especially while you are first learning how the amplifier operates.

The output loading control is the output connector and probe assembly. Loading is changed by minor rotational adjustment of

the Type-N connector. First loosen the jam-nut (or set screw) slightly. While observing output power and keeping the anode tuner peaked, rotate the loading control ± 30 degrees maximum for greatest output power. This should be done only once and should not need repeating unless another tube is installed. Even then it may not be required.

10-GHz Gunnplexer Communications

The M/A-COM Gunnplexer transceiver shown in Fig. 129 will fit conveniently in your hand and is operated from a single 12-V power supply, either ac line operated or batteries! This makes the Gunnplexer ideal for fixed or portable operation.

The Gunnplexer is most often used in wide-band FM systems and is ideal for audio, full-color video and data transfer. With suitable peripheral equipment, systems for full-duplex audio, color video and up to several megabit data transfer are possible. Such high data rates should allow direct computer-to-computer memory transfer that would not be practical (or legal) on other lower-frequency amateur bands.

The Gunnplexer

The heart of the Gunnplexer is a Gunn diode oscillator, named after its inventor, John Gunn of IBM. A more detailed discussion of the Gunn diode is presented in Chapter 4. Refer to the cutaway drawing of the Gunnplexer, Fig. 130, for this discussion.

The Gunn diode is mounted with a varactor diode in a resonant cavity. When a regulated voltage is applied to the Gunn diode it oscillates; the frequency of oscillation is determined by the capacitance of the varactor diode and two mechanical tuning screws. The mechanical tuning screws can be likened to coarse tuning controls and are factory set for the appropri-

ate tuning range. The voltage applied to the varactor diode (1 to 20 V dc) tunes the frequency electronically a minimum of 60 MHz. Power is coupled out of the cavity through a small iris that has been designed as somewhat of a compromise between maximum power output and isolation from changes in diode impedance and load.

The Gunn oscillator is also used to provide the local-oscillator signal for the detector diode. A ferrite circulator couples an appropriate amount of energy into the low-noise Schottky mixer diode and isolates the transmitter and receiver. Because the Gunn oscillator functions as both the transmitter and the receiver local oscillator, the IF at each end must be at the same frequency.

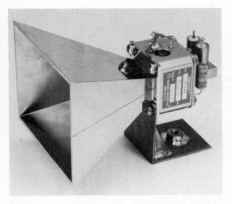

Fig. 129 — View of the Microwave Associates Gunnplexer. A protective resistor and diode are connected from the detector out-put to ground. A 50-μF electrolytic capacitor is connected from the Gunn diode terminal to ground. The Gunnplexer is designed to mate a UG-39/U waveguide flange when the horn antenna is removed.

Fig. 130 — Drawing of the Gunnplexer assembly. The Gunn oscillator assembly consists of a resonant cavity in which is mounted the Gunn diode and varactor diode. The cylinders contain the quarter-wave choke sections, which connect to the diodes. The Gunn oscillator assembly bolts to the mixer assembly, which contains the detector diode and ferrite circulator. A horn antenna bolts to the front of the mixer assembly. (Reproduced with permission from *Ham Radio Magazine*, January 1979.)

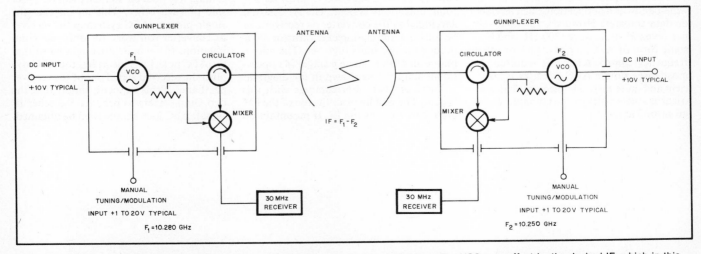

Fig. 131 — This drawing depicts a Gunnplexer communications system running full duplex. The VCOs are offset by the desired IF, which in this case is 30 MHz.

Table 12

Gunnplexer Specifications @ T_A = 25° C

Electrical Characteristics

RF Center Frequency	10.250 GHz[1]
Tuning	
Mechanical	± 50 MHz
Electronic	60 MHz min.
Linearity	1 to 40%
Frequency Stability	– 350 kHz/°C max.
RF Power vs. Temperature and Tuning Voltage	6 dB max.
Frequency Pushing	15 MHz/V max.
Input Requirements	
Dc Gunn Voltage Range[2]	+ 8.0 to + 10.0-V dc[2]
Maximum Operating Current	500 mA
Tuning Voltage	+ 1 to + 20 volts
Noise Figure[3]	< 12 dB

RF Output Power[1]

Model	P out (mW)
MA87141-1	10 min. 15 typ.
MA87141-2	20 min. 25 typ.
MA87141-3	35 min. 40 typ.

Notes

[1] Tuning voltage set at 4.0 volts.
[2] Operating voltage specified on each unit.
[3] 1.5 dB IF NF at 30 MHz.

Fig. 132 — Here is a complete bare-minimum communications system using the Gunnplexer transceiver. An inexpensive automobile FM converter or receiver is used for the receiver IF. A 7810 voltage regulator is used for the Gunn-diode supply, and a simple 741 op amp serves as the microphone stage. The frequency of operation is set by the potentiometer that biases the varactor diode. A 10-turn potentiometer provides a comfortable tuning rate.

Furthermore, the frequencies of the Gunnplexers must be separated by the IF. This is illustrated in Fig. 131. Intermediate frequencies of 30 MHz are more or less standard for audio work in the U.S. Both 45 and 70 MHz are used for video and high-speed data work.

As can be seen from Fig. 131, the Gunnplexer communications system is full duplex. In other words, both parties can talk and listen at the same time, without throwing switches. This is something that may take a while to get used to as most amateurs are programmed for VOX or PTT operation. In short, it is the ultimate break-in system!

One detail of the Gunnplexer that does require some specific attention is frequency control. The Gunnplexer has a frequency-stability specification of – 350 kHz frequency change per degree Celsius increase. This does not pose much of a problem with wide-bandwidth applications such as video or data transfer. However, for relatively narrowband audio work (200 kHz and less) some form of AFC, a phase-lock or other frequency-control scheme is required. In most cases simple AFC circuitry is sufficient and quite easy to implement. The electrical characteristics of the Gunnplexer are given in Table 12.

Bare Minimum Audio Communications System

The simplest of communications systems using the Gunnplexer transceivers can be formed with two 88- to 108-MHz FM receivers, two Gunnplexers, two microphones and associated amplifiers, and two sources of 12 V dc. A diagram of such a system is shown in Fig. 132. Some of the low-cost FM converters and receivers for automotive use make good IF strips for this communications system. The AFC signal developed in the converter or receiver can be routed to the Gunnplexer varactor diode to lock the two units together. The microphone amplifier can be a single 741 operational amplifier as shown in the diagram.

There are two shortcomings with this system. The first involves the use of the FM broadcast band as the IF. If mountaintop DXing is planned, it is likely that strong FM broadcast stations will be received no matter how short the lead between the detector and the FM converter or receiver is made. It will be necessary to select that part of the band where there are no strong signals present.

The second item involves AFC. Since it is possible to tune the Gunnplexers over a 60-MHz range with the varactor diode tuning, it is possible to tune them on either side of each other. This means that the single-polarity AFC system in the receiver or converter will work for only one combination. If the units are operated so that the AFC polarity is incorrect, the AFC will push the received signal out of the receiver passband. If this happens, simply tune the two Gunnplexers to produce the other IF signal. AFC lock should then be obtained.

A High-Performance Audio Communications System

The high-performance Gunnplexer audio system described here was developed by Advanced Receiver Research, and is sold as an amateur/commercial product.[1] The information is included here for those who wish to construct their own system.

This Gunnplexer support system has been specifically designed for use with the Microwave Associates Gunnplexers. The board contains a complete 30-MHz FM receiver, diode-switched IF filters, dual-polarity AFC system, Gunn-diode regulator and modulators for phone and CW. The system is suitable for fixed, portable or mobile operation. Power-supply requirements are a nominal 13 volts at 250 mA (this includes the current drawn by the Gunnplexer assembly). The circuit is specified for operation over the temperature range -25 to $+65\,°C$.

Theory of Operation

The circuit diagram is shown in Fig. 134, and an interconnection wiring guide in Fig. 135. Signal energy arriving at the IF input (pins 24 and 25) is routed to Q1, a low-noise RF amplifier. A band-pass filter, with a 3-dB bandwidth of 2 MHz, is located between the RF amplifier and mixer, Q2. LO injection for the mixer is provided by a crystal-controlled 40.7-MHz oscillator stage. Output from the mixer, at 10.7 MHz, is applied to either of two diode-switched ceramic filters. Supply voltage applied to pin 23 selects FL1 (supplied) and supply voltage applied to pin 22 selects FL2 (optional). Output from the filter is fed to IF amplifier stage Q3. Amplified 10.7-MHz energy is routed to the FM subsystem chip, U1, a CA3189E. Detected audio passes

[1]Advanced Receiver Research, Box 1242, Burlington, CT 06013, tel. 203-584-0776.

through an AF gain control (pins 16, 17 and 18) to U2, the audio amplifier. This stage has sufficient power to drive head-phones and/or a speaker.

Squelch control is available by U5A. U5B inverts the amplified AFC signal so that either polarity AFC may be selected by S3. Overall AFC gain is controlled by R_c. U5C sums the AFC information along with the manual tuning voltage. This composite signal is applied to the varactor terminal of the Gunnplexer. U5D functions as a meter driver. Its input can be switched for center-tuning (discriminator zero) and manual-tuning voltage. Input to the driver is selected by S1.

U3 is a microphone amplifier boosting the output from a microphone to a level suitable for modulating the Gunnplexer. U4 generates an approximate 500-Hz tone for MCW operation. Voice and MCW information is applied to the varactor of the Gunnplexer along with the AFC/tuning voltage. U6 is a three-terminal positive voltage regulator that provides an accurate 10-volt supply for the Gunn diode. A 1N4001 diode is included to protect against inadvertent application of reverse-polarity voltage.

It is advisable to mount the board in a well-shielded enclosure since the receiver is quite sensitive. The Gunnplexer unit can be mounted atop a tower and connected to the board through three lengths of coaxial cable. Although the Gunn diode and varactor line carry only dc and low-level audio signals, shielded cable is a must as even small-voltage pickups can produce relatively large modulating voltages, which are undesirable. In cases of severe pickup, small RF chokes may be required directly at the Gunn diode and varactor connections of the Gunnplexer. Lengths of cable of up to several hundred feet between the Gunnplexer and the board have been used with no problems. For long IF connection runs

it is desirable to install a 30-MHz preamplifier at the Gunnplexer to prevent the long cable run from adversely affecting the system noise figure.

The Gunnplexer system is capable of complete duplex communications, so good separation between the microphone and speaker is mandatory. The use of head-phones for this type of communications is generally advisable.

Alignment

1) Connect a signal generator capable of delivering a 30-MHz signal to the IF input connection.

2) Adjust the output level of the generator to a point where the signal-strength meter just begins to move up scale.

3) Adjust C_a, C_b and C_c for maximum indication on the meter.

4) Temporarily disconnect the signal generator from the input.

5) Place S1 in the discriminator position.

6) While switching S3 between the $+$ and $-$ AFC positions, adjust R_b so that the same meter reading is obtained in both switch positions. This reading should be mid scale on the discriminator meter.

7) Reconnect the signal generator to the input and center the signal in the receiver passband.

8) While switching S1 between the AFC ON and OFF positions, adjust C_d so that the same meter reading is obtained for both positions. This reading should be mid scale on the discriminator meter.

9) Adjust R_c for the desired AFC gain/locking range by shifting the signal-generator frequency away from the pass-band center.

10) R_c is adjusted while in communication with another station. Advance the level of this control to the point where distortion occurs. Back off the setting of the control to the point where distortion is no longer present.

Fig. 134 — Schematic diagram of the high-performance audio communications system. All capacitors specified in picofarads are silver mica, DM5 variety. All resistors are ¼-watt film types.

FL1 — Murata SFJ10. 7 mA, 10.7 MHz.
L1 — 25 turns no. 30 enam. wire on a T25-10 core.
L2, L3 — 13 turns no. 28 enam. wire on a T25-6 core.

L4, L5 — 25 turns no. 30 enam. wire on a T25-20 core.
L6 — 16 turns no. 28 enam. wire on a T25-10 core.
RFC1 — 10 turns no. 28 enam. wire on an FT23-43 core.

RFC2, RFC3 — 10 turns no. 28 enam. wire on an FT23-72 core.
RFC4 — 11 turns no. 28 enam. on an FT23-43 core.
Y1 — 40.7 MHz, third overtone.

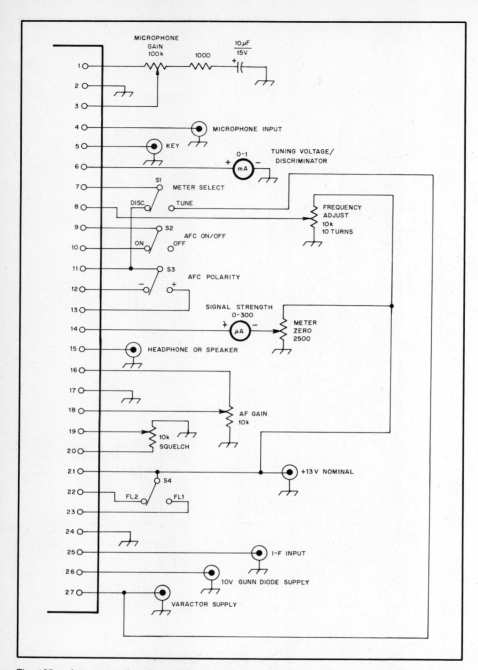

Fig. 135 — Interconnection diagram for the high-performance audio Gunnplexer communications system.

A 2-Mbit/s Microwave Data Link

One of the most exciting aspects of the microwave bands is the feasibility of using wideband signals there. One application of such signals is for very-high-speed digital data transmission. This section describes a microwave system that allows transmission of data at up to 2 million bits per second (Mbit/s). The system was designed by Glenn Elmore, N6GN, and Kevin Rowett, N6RCE. It was first described in "Inexpensive Multi-Megabaud Microwave Data Link," in *Ham Radio*, December 1989, pp 9-29. In addition to the data link, an analog voice channel is provided, which requires only an external microphone and speaker to allow simultaneous full-duplex audio communication. The link operates in the 10-GHz amateur band and uses an inexpensive commercial parabolic antenna along with a Doppler radar transceiver module to provide medium range communications at low cost.

Why go to the trouble of building a digital radio that is approximately 1000 times as fast as the 1200-baud systems currently in use? The answer is that doing so makes possible a whole spectrum of new applications for packet radio, including a nationwide—or even worldwide—digital amateur network. Once sufficient speed is available, almost any information can be transmitted digitally, including digital audio, facsimile, graphics and even digital television. Fortunately, microwaves and high speed communication fit together very well.

As the data rate increases, wider and wider bandwidths are required. Only when we go to the UHF and microwave amateur bands are signals permitted to have sufficient bandwidth for these very-high-speed digital signals. As frequency is increased, antennas of reasonable physical size are better able to focus the transmitted beam to just where it should go without wasting signal in different directions. In fact the amateur microwave bands, through 24 GHz, offer the best performance and cost available for such communication.

The link described here was built as an initial step in providing a moderate speed digital amateur network in Northern California to be used with a fledgling TCP/IP radio network. This was necessary to support some of the exciting applications intended for this network and to help advance use by amateurs of our valuable microwave spectrum, something we may lose if we do not learn to use it effectively. The original article described the use of this equipment with a surplus IBM PC plug-in card. By the time you read this, off-the-shelf amateur products should be available that negate the need of using such surplus boards.

SYSTEM DESIGN

Previous successes using 10-GHz Gunn-diode oscillators as local oscillators and transceivers for narrowband weak signal work suggested the possibility of using these inexpensive units for higher speed digital data transmission. In addition to low cost, these units, which are commonly used for motion detection (door openers and burglar alarms), speed measurement (police radar guns) and microwave receivers (radar detectors), have all of the microwave circuitry self contained. Fig 136 shows the system operation.

The 2-foot dish shown in Fig 137 has a gain of about 33 dB, or 2000 times, at 10.5 GHz. When driven by the microwave transceiver the effective radiated power is about the same as that of a 10-W 2-meter radio driving a quarter-wave whip.

The two ends of a link operate "split." One transceiver oscillator typically operates on 10,450 MHz while the other end is 105 MHz lower on 10,345 MHz. The difference between the two transmitter frequencies corresponds to the receiver first intermediate frequency. The receiver first IF signal on each end is generated by mixing the remotely transmitted signal (frequency modulated by the data to be transmitted) with the local transmitter signal. Thus each end uses its own transmitter as a receiver local oscillator, and each unit transmits continuously. Each receiver therefore sees the same IF. This is the same full-duplex arrangement described earlier in this chapter. Each transmitter produces 5 to 10 mW and is frequency modulated by varying its bias supply and using the frequency/voltage dependency of the transceiver to tune it.

The receiver first IF was selected at

Fig 136—System block diagram of the 2-Mbit/s, 10-GHz data link.

Fig 137—A 2-foot dish provides adequate gain at 10 GHz for a 30 to 40 mile path using this simple system. The dish used here was obtained from The Antenna Center, 505 Oak Street, Calumet, MI 49913, tel 906-337-5062.

Fig 138—The microwave assembly, including preamp.

introduced to the tuning depending upon whether the received data is a zero or a one.

The audio channel was added as an after-thought to provide for human communication, particularly while debugging the link and operating it with digital data the first time. An electret microphone is used to produce the transmit audio signal, which is amplified and limited prior to modulating the transmitter by way of high pass and low pass filters. Levels were selected to provide only small deviation compared to that of the digital channel. In this way the audio channel can operate without significantly interfering with or degrading the digital data. On receive, a volume control and speaker amplifier sufficient for driving headphones or a small speaker are provided.

An analog meter displays signal strength as carrier-to-noise ratio (C/N) or discriminator output to aid when manual frequency control is used. (The MC13055 FSK receiver chip has a built in logarithmic amplifier which can give a pretty accurate measure of C/N.) A switch allows either manual or automatic frequency control to be selected.

The microwave transceiver, modulator and receive preamplifier are mounted together in a box, shown in Fig 138, located at the prime focus of the parabolic antenna. A pyramidal horn was designed to simply and efficiently illuminate the dish antenna, obtaining nearly the maximum gain possible. The rest of the receiver is located in a separate enclosure along with circuits for the audio channel. This arrangement allows the antenna and microwave hardware to be located a considerable distance from the receiver for tower or mast mounting.

Emitter Coupled Logic (ECL) was used for incoming and outgoing data. These are differential lines that can be used even when there is considerable line length, such as when the microwave equipment is high on a tower or the receiver is to be located distant from the host computer. A standard 15-pin connector is used to connect to the radio hardware. Those familiar with Local Area Networks may recognize this connector and pinout as identical to that of a Media Access Unit, the device used to connect a computer to a coaxial cable connecting a building- or area-wide network. Only 12 V dc at approximately 350 mA, data input and data output need be supplied for operation of the entire radio link hardware.

CONSTRUCTION OF THE RADIO LINK

Antenna and Feedhorn

The antenna is mounted to a mast using a rear mounting bracket. This plate is cut from sheet aluminum and folded to produce four "feet" which attach to the dish, as shown in Fig 139. U clamps attach this plate to the mast. Minor elevation steering of the antenna is made possible by adding

105 MHz, with provision for tuning plus or minus 10 MHz to accommodate differential frequency drift of the free-running microwave transceivers with time or temperature. (Using an IF in this range also allows simple troubleshooting and testing with commonly available commercial FM broadcast receivers.) If both ends drift the same direction and amount, no correction is necessary since the resulting IF doesn't change. To correct for different drifts, automatic frequency control (AFC) is implemented by tuning the second LO, nominally at 150 MHz. The second LO output is mixed with the first IF signal to produce the second IF at 45 MHz, where detection takes place in a Motorola MC13055 FSK receiver chip. This chip is specified to operate at data rates up to 2 Mbit/s but has actually been used as high as 10 Mbit/s.

Along with the AFC circuit that tracks the frequency of a received signal, a search oscillator is also provided to allow the receiver to "find" the incoming signal when the link is first powered up or if signals are lost temporarily. The searching is controlled by the receiver's Data Carrier Detect (DCD) circuitry. Once the signal is found, the search oscillator is shut off and the AFC tunes the receiver correctly. Since the data is digital, an appropriate offset is

Fig 139—The antenna mounting bracket. The corners are bent to conform to the angle of the rear dish surface.

two extra sets of nuts to the clamps to allow adjusting the spacing between the mast and plate. Since the antenna has less than a four degree half-power beamwidth, this adjustment may be necessary, particularly when the two ends of the link are at different elevations and not too far apart.

The horn feed and microwave assembly attach to a plate and are held at the dish focal point by four ¼-inch diameter struts made from soft aluminum rod. This material was obtained at a local home supply store. Each rod is first cut to length and then drilled and tapped at each end for an 8-32 bolt. Finally, a tubing bender is used to shape it properly. Fig 140 shows the feed support struts.

The pyramidal horn feed is made by first cutting the sides and flange from copper or brass shim stock as shown in Fig 141. Since the material is thin, the whole assembly may first be tacked together with a medium-size soldering iron and then, when everything is in place, completely soldered.

The mounting plate, shown in Fig 142, has a short section of waveguide at its center. The waveguide section should be made by milling or drilling and filing a 0.40- by 0.90-inch rectangle in the plate. Great precision of construction for either the feed or the mounting plate is not necessary to obtain good performance. The feedhorn and transceiver mount on opposite sides of the mounting plate, and a small Bud box encloses the transmitter electronics.

Microwave Unit Assembly

Because the microwave transceiver is self contained, the RF electronics is not particularly critical or difficult to assemble. About the only sensitive circuitry is the receive preamplifier, and because this uses MMICs, short lead length and good grounding are the only requirements.

If printed circuit board material is used, the entire board can be made with a file and a small hobby knife. (Use board with copper on both sides.) 50-ohm microstrip transmission line is used to connect the MMICs. This line can be made by filing 0.005- to 0.010-inch slots 0.1-inch apart. The line is then cut into short sections and the components are soldered directly to it. Holes are drilled in the board to allow the MMIC leads to sit flush with the surface of the transmission lines. Holes are also drilled for all component ground leads, and the leads are soldered on the top and bottom of the board.

Layout of the regulator and modulator circuits is not critical, and the ECL IC may be "dead bug" mounted on top of the board. The board should be mounted to the aluminum box with short spacers. Use a twisted pair made from hookup wire to connect the board to the transceiver mixer diode. An approximate board layout is shown in Fig 143. Fig 144 shows the

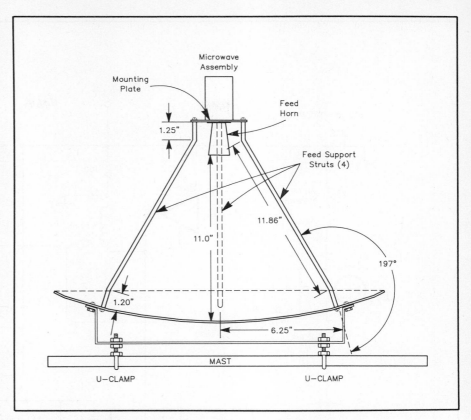

Fig 140—The dish assembly, showing the dimensions of the feed supports.

Fig 141—The feed horn is cut from a sheet of 0.03-inch thick copper or brass shim stock and soldered together.

Except as indicated, decimal
values of capacitance are
in microfarads (μF); others
are in picofarads (pF);
resistances are in ohms;
k= 1,000, M= 1,000,000

Connectors:

J1 BNC to microwave assembly

P1, P2, P3 0.1" spacing BERG
or similar

U4	MC10116		
Pin	Function	Pin	Function
1	$V_{cc}1$	9	$\overline{B_{in}}$
2	$\overline{A_{out}}$	10	B_{in}
3	A_{out}	11	V_{bb}
4	$\overline{A_{in}}$	12	$\overline{C_{in}}$
5	A_{in}	13	C_{in}
6	$\overline{B_{out}}$	14	$\overline{C_{out}}$
7	B_{out}	15	C_{out}
8	V_{ee}	16	$V_{cc}2$

U2	MC13055
PIN	FUNCTION
1	Comparator gnd
2	Comparator V_{cc}
3	IF ground
4	IF V_{cc}
5	Limiter input
6	Limiter bias
7	Limiter bias
8	Quad bias
9	Quad input
10	Detector out
11	Detector out
12	Meter drive
13	Carrier detect
14	− Comparator
15	+ Comparator
16	Data out

Fig 145—Schematic diagram of the receiver.

D1-4—1N914 diode.
D5—1N5139 varactor diode.
L1—330 nH shielded, slug-tuned coil (Digi-Key TK1406).
L2—410 nH shielded, slug-tuned coil (Digi-Key TK1407).

Q1—2N4416 N-channel JFET.
Q2—2N5116 P-channel JFET.
T1—80 nH slug-tuned coil (Digi-Key TK2101). The secondary is formed by wrapping one turn of hookup wire around the outside of the coil.

U1, U5—LM324 op amp (National).
U2—MC13055 FSK receiver IC (Motorola).
U3—LM386 audio amplifier (National).
U4—MC10116 line receiver (Motorola).
U6—LM317 voltage regulator (National).
U7—MAR-6 MMIC (Mini-Circuits Labs).

Fig 142—The feed mounting plate.

Fig 143—A suggested layout for the pre-amplifier board.

Pin	Function	Pin	Function
	U4	MC10116	
1	V_{cc} 1	9	$\overline{B_{in}}$
2	$\overline{A_{out}}$	10	B_{in}
3	A_{out}	11	V_{bb}
4	$\overline{A_{in}}$	12	$\overline{C_{in}}$
5	A_{in}	13	C_{in}
6	$\overline{B_{out}}$	14	$\overline{C_{out}}$
7	B_{out}	15	C_{out}
8	V_{ee}	16	V_{cc} 2

Except as indicated, decimal values of capacitance are in microfarads (μF); others are in picofarads (pF); resistances are in ohms; k= 1,000, M= 1,000,000

Fig 144—Schematic diagram of the microwave assembly and preamplifier.

A1—NEC ND751AAM 10-GHz Gunn transceiver (California Eastern Labs, 3260 Jay Street, Santa Clara, CA 95054, tel 408-980-3500). M/A-COM, Solfan and other units may be used.
D1—10 V, 1 W Zener diode.
U1, U2—MAR-6 MMIC (Mini-Circuits Labs).

U3—LM317 voltage regulator (National).
U4—MC10116 line receiver (Motorola).
U5—78M05 voltage regulator.

Fig 146—Interconnection diagram of the 10-GHz data link transceiver.

schematic diagram of the microwave assembly and preamplifier.

Receiver Assembly

Construction of the receiver assembly is also noncritical. Fig 145 shows the receiver schematic diagram. Use as much ground plane as possible on the component side of the board, and keep traces to the 45-MHz filter and discriminator as short as is reasonable. Otherwise, no special precautions need be taken. All ICs may be socketed for convenience. Fig 146 shows the connections between the transmitter and preamplifier board and the receiver assembly.

Tune-up and Testing

Unless a 10-GHz microwave signal generator is available, these units should be built as a pair, although two dishes are not necessary for short range use or testing. The bias voltage for the Gunn diode should be set to approximately 6.3 V with R102 before connecting the transceiver. Verify that the deviation control, R101, can be set to give a 0.25- to 0.5-V change in the diode bias when the ECL line receiver is toggled between states. Then hook up the transceiver. As shipped, most transceivers will be close to 10,525 MHz. With two transceiver/horn assemblies pointed at each other and separated a few feet, connect a frequency counter or general coverage receiver to the preamplifier output. Leaving one unit's tuning unchanged, tune the second unit while monitoring the IF signal with a counter or listening for it in a general coverage receiver. Turning the mechanical

tuning screw farther into the cavity will reduce frequency. As the unit is tuned 70 MHz or more lower than the other unit, a counter should be able to read the difference frequency. Using this technique, you should be able to "walk" the two units lower in frequency into the ham band by alternately adjusting the two units, ending with them spaced 105 MHz apart. If you get "lost" and don't know the absolute frequency, a local supermarket door opener can probably provide an appoximate 10,525-MHz reference. If a microwave frequency indicator is available adjustment is trivial.

Once the two ends are operating 105 MHz apart, the receivers may be aligned. Select MFC and set the tuning control, R5, to the middle of its range. Use a counter or 2-meter receiver to monitor the VCO frequency. Set the VCO to 148-150 MHz by adjusting T1. You should be able to tune several megahertz either side of this center with the manual tuning control. (AFC can tune it even further once the other circuits are operating.) Tune the VCO to 45 MHz above the previously measured frequency of the microwave IF (nominally 105 MHz) and adjust the 45-MHz bandpass coil, L1, for maximum C/N reading on the meter.

Tune the discriminator coil, L2, to center the detector output voltage on pin 10 or 11 of the MC13055. As you adjust the coil, note the minimum and maximum voltages at the extremes of the adjustment range, then set the ajdustment so that the voltage is midway between the minimum and maximum voltages.

During the next set of adjustments, it

may be necessary to attenuate the signals between the units to keep the C/N reading on scale. To do this, separate the units or use conductive foam material of the type used to protect ICs from electrostatic damage. The latter technique consists of placing a rectangular sheet of foam inside the feed horn such that it blocks the opening. If necessary, multiple layers of foam can be used in this manner.

With the squelch control set to its maximum resistance of (5 kΩ), a 0.35-V change at pin 12 of the MC13055 corresponds to a 10-dB change in received signal strength. While keeping the receiver tuned to center with the tuning control, adjust the position of the units and the absorbers to produce about 10 dB of C/N. Then adjust the squelch control so that the DCD light just extinguishes. Remeasure the squelch control resistance and calibrate your C/N reading by calculating sensitivity:

$$V_{p12} = 0.070 \times R_{squelch}$$

$R_{squelch}$ = squelch resistance in kilohms
V_{p12} = voltage at MC13055 pin 12 in volts per 10 dB change

Adjust the position of the units and the absorbers to give about as much C/N as you want to measure on your meter, then adjust R2 for zero with no signal and R3 for the appropriate meter reading with the signal present. (On a 4-V meter, for instance, you may want to adjust it so that each volt is equivalent to 10 dB C/N.)

Adjust the discriminator output sensitivity control, R4, for a full-scale reading on the tuning meter as the tuning control is used to tune across the incoming signal. Finally, select AFC and verify that the search oscillator runs when there is no incoming 105 MHz IF signal. Operation of the search oscillator can be observed as a sawtooth signal at P2-2.

The audio channel should work without further adjustment. Some background noise may be audible even when signal strength is high due to the phase noise of the microwave oscillators themselves, but the level should not be objectionable.

An oscilloscope should be used to verify data throughput and correct transmitter deviation setting. Monitor the discriminator output, P1-5, with the scope and set the oscilliscope sensitivity to give full screen display as the tuning control is used to tune through a signal in MFC mode. Now the transmitter may be modulated with data and the deviation adjusted with R101 to set the discriminator output to slightly less than full screen. It may be necessary to adjust the bias setting, R102, to keep the transceiver bias centered on 6.3 V.

At this point both the transmitter and receiver should be functioning properly and may be used for audio or digital communications. When units are separated by a great distance or signals are otherwise weak it may be beneficial to monitor the audio channel as an aid to link adjustment since audio communication will be possible even when noise is causing excessive errors on a data channel.

Performance, Results and Remaining Problems

Aligning the microwave dishes requires some skill. If you've not done this before, allow plenty of time for it, have solid mounts, and don't expect it to be like 2 meters. Use the audio channel to listen for receiver quieting and get a feel for how narrow the beamwidth is. Don't try to hand hold the antennas at both ends since both ends must be pointed correctly before either end hears anything. It may be useful to use manual frequency control at first too. If one end of the link can temporarily be located at a high location it is possible to power the other end from the 12 V dc in an automobile and drive around just to see what microwave communications feels like. Experience gained in these activities will help to make you a good judge of final locations for the digital link. Because these are low budget systems, line-of-sight is probably a requirement for anything other than fairly short links. One exception to this is if a good planar reflector is located close to one end of the link and can be used as an efficient mirror. This technique may be used to keep the hardware at ground level by using a mast- or tower-mounted "billboard" reflector. This has environmental advantages for the hardware too.

Measurements indicate that the unit passes data with a low error rate with signal strengths below 15 dB C/N. It is important that direct paths be used, however, since severe distortion can occur when multiple paths exist between the ends of the link. Such multipath conditions can cause link failure even with very large C/N. These units should provide low-error-rate data transmission on a line-of-sight path of more than 40 miles with well stirred air. In many locales, marine air layers and other causes of fading and ducting may require shortening the path to guarantee reliable throughput.

As with any ham project, there is certainly room for improvement of this hardware. Since the original RF design was for a 2 Mbit/s link, improvement should be possible through optimizing the receiver detector bandwidth. For all weather use, the equipment needs to be waterproofed if it's located on a mast. As an alternative, a coaxial-waveguide adapter could be mounted to the feedhorn and the microwave circuitry remotely located in a more protected environment. Low-loss semi-rigid coax cable should be used for connecting to the antenna if this is done.

Almost any surplus radar detector, motion detector or burglar alarm Gunn transceivers should work well. The M/A-COM Gunnplexers™, although more expensive, work very well too. With their built-in electronic tuning, they can even be modulated at higher rates for full 10 Mbit/s data links or ATV uses. It should be possible to frequency modulate them by driving the electronic tuning input from the ECL output, properly scaled and offset with a resistor network.

The first prototype of this link was actually built using 24-GHz radar transceivers and metal lamp reflectors for antennas. This arrangement works very well, and because of the modular system design, these microwave assemblies may be substituted for the 10 GHz ones described here with no other adjustments. The higher gain available for a given dish antenna size at 24 GHz can actually provide better performance over some paths.

For longer or more difficult paths a larger antenna may be used. If something other than a 0.5 focal length to diameter ratio reflector is used a new feed should be designed to produce maximum performance. Other diameters are available from the indicated supplier.

Chapter 33

Antenna Projects

Since the dawn of Amateur Radio, hams have been fascinated by antennas. Almost every ham has built at least one antenna, be it a dipole for one of the HF bands or a directional antenna for a VHF frequency. Through the years amateurs have tried countless possible configurations — everything from rain-gutter long wires, to balloon-supported wires, to full-size 80-meter beams. A quick scan of any of the ham bands will yield several discussions that attest to the popularity of antenna experimentation among amateurs.

This chapter presents projects for amateurs wishing to construct their own antennas. Related information can be found in Chapters 16 and 17. Chapter 37 tells how to get antennas into the air and keep them there safely.

Construction of Wire Antennas

There are many different types of wire antennas. The virtues of each, and the formulas for computing the right length for the desired operating frequency, are well documented in Chapter 17. The purpose of this section is to offer information on the actual physical construction of wire antennas. Because the dipole, in one of its configurations (Fig 1), is probably the most common amateur wire antenna, it is used in the following examples. The techniques described here, however, enhance the reliability and safety of all wire antennas.

Wire

Choosing the right type of wire for the project at hand is the key to a successful antenna—the kind that gets out like gangbusters and stays up in the face of a winter ice storm or a gusty spring wind storm. What gauge of wire to use is the first question to settle, and the answer depends on strength, ease of handling, cost, availability and visibility. Generally, antennas that are expected to support their own weight, plus the weight of the feed line, should be made from no. 12 wire. Horizontal dipoles, Zepps, some long wires and the like fall into this category. Antennas supported in the center, such as inverted-V dipoles and delta loops, may be made from lighter material, such as no. 14 wire—the minimum size called for in the National Electrical Code.

The type of wire to be used is the next important decision. Table 1 details several

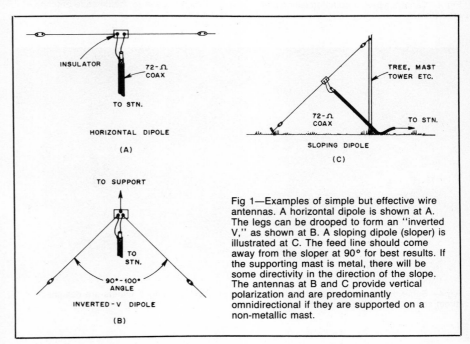

Fig 1—Examples of simple but effective wire antennas. A horizontal dipole is shown at A. The legs can be drooped to form an "inverted V," as shown at B. A sloping dipole (sloper) is illustrated at C. The feed line should come away from the sloper at 90° for best results. If the supporting mast is metal, there will be some directivity in the direction of the slope. The antennas at B and C provide vertical polarization and are predominantly omnidirectional if they are supported on a non-metallic mast.

popular wire styles and sizes. The strongest wire suitable for antenna service is copper-clad steel, also known as Copperweld®. The copper coating is necessary for RF service because steel is a relatively poor conductor. Practically all of the RF current is confined to the copper because of skin effect. Copper-clad steel is outstanding for permanent installations, but it can be difficult to work with. Kinking, which severely weakens the wire, is a constant threat when handling any solid conductor.

Solid-copper wire, either hard drawn or soft drawn, is another popular material. Easier to handle than copper-clad steel, solid copper is available in a wide range of sizes. It is generally more expensive, however, because it is all copper. Soft-

Table 1

Stressed Antenna Wire

American Wire Gauge	Recommended Tension[1] (pounds)		Weight (pounds per 1000 feet)	
	Copper-clad steel[2]	Hard-drawn copper	Copper-clad steel[2]	Hard-drawn Copper
4	495	214	115.8	126
6	310	130	72.9	79.5
8	195	84	45.5	50
10	120	52	28.8	31.4
12	75	32	18.1	19.8
14	50	20	11.4	12.4
16	31	13	7.1	7.8
18	19	8	4.5	4.9
20	12	5	2.8	3.1

[1]Approximately one-tenth the breaking load. Might be increased 50 percent if end supports are firm and there is no danger of ice loading.

[2]"Copperweld," 40 percent copper.

Fig 2—Various types of commercially made insulators.

Fig 3—Some ideas for homemade antenna insulators.

Fig 4—Some dipole center insulators have built-in SO-239 connectors. Others are designed for direct connection to the feed line.

drawn tends to stretch under tension, so periodic pruning of the antenna may be necessary in some cases.

Enamel-coated "magnet-wire" is a good choice for experimental antennas because it is easy to manage, and the coating protects the wire from the weather. Although it stretches under tension, the wire may be prestretched before final installation and adjustment. A local electric motor rebuilder might be a good source for magnet wire.

Hook-up wire, speaker wire or even ac lamp cord are suitable for temporary installations. Almost any copper wire may be used, as long as it is strong enough for the demands of the installation. Steel wire is a poor conductor and should be avoided. Aluminum may be suitable in some cases, although it is not usually very strong and is difficult to adequately connect a feed line to.

It matters not (in the HF region at least)

whether the wire chosen is insulated or bare. However, the wire should be either enameled or insulated to prevent corrosion. If exposed, the bare copper surface will corrode, causing a resistive loss in current, which flows only on the surface due to skin effect. If insulated wire is used, a 3 to 5% shortening beyond the standard 468/f length will be required to obtain resonance at the desired frequency, because of the increased distributed capacitance resulting from the dielectric constant of the plastic insulating material. The actual length for resonance must be determined experimentally by pruning and measuring because the dielectric constant of the insulating material varies from wire to wire. Portions that might come into contact with humans or animals should be insulated to reduce the chance of shock or burns. Several suppliers of wire suitable for the projects in this chapter are listed in Chapter 35.

Insulators

Wire antennas must be insulated at the ends. Generally, commercially available insulators are made from ceramic, glass or plastic. Some of the more common types are pictured in Fig 2. Insulators like these are available from many Amateur Radio dealers. Radio Shack and local hardware stores are other possible sources.

In a pinch, acceptable homemade insulators may be fashioned from a variety of material including (but not limited to) acrylic sheet or rod, PVC tubing, wood, fiberglass rod or even stiff plastic from a discarded container. Fig 3 shows some homemade insulators. Ceramic or glass insulators will usually outlast the wire, so they are highly recommended for a safe, reliable, permanent installation. Other materials may tear under stress or break down in the presence of sunlight. Many types of plastic do not weather well.

Many types of wire antennas require an insulator at the feed point. Although there are many ways to connect the feed line, there are a few things to keep in mind. If you feed your antenna with coaxial cable, you have two choices. You can install an SO-239 connector on the center insulator and use a PL-259 on the end of your coax, or you can separate the center conductor from the braid and connect the feed line directly to the antenna wire. Although the latter method is initially less costly, the former method offers several advantages.

Coaxial cable braid soaks up water like a sponge. If you do not adequately seal the antenna end of the feed line, water will find its way into the braid. Water in the feed line will lead to contamination, rendering the coax useless long before its normal lifetime is up. It is not uncommon for water to drip from the end of the coax inside the shack after a year or so of service if the antenna connection is not properly waterproofed. Use of a PL-259/SO-239 combination (or connector of your choice) makes the task of waterproofing connec-

Fig 5—Details of the dipole antenna. The end insulator connection is shown at A, while B illustrates the center insulator. Part C illustrates the completed antenna.

tions much easier. Another advantage to using the PL-259/SO-239 combination is that feed line replacement is much easier, should that become necessary.

Whether you use coaxial cable, open-wire "ladder line" or plastic-encased transmitting-type twin lead to feed your antenna, an often-overlooked consideration is the mechanical strength of the connection. Wire antennas and feed lines tend to move a lot in the breeze, and unless the feed line is attached securely, the connection will weaken with time. The resulting failure can range from a frustrating intermittent electrical connection to a complete separation of feed line and antenna. Fig 4 illustrates several different ways of attaching the feed line to the antenna.

Putting It Together

Fig 5 shows some of the finer points of antenna construction. Although a dipole is used for the examples, the techniques illustrated here apply to any type of wire antenna.

How well you put the pieces together is second only to the ultimate strength of the materials used in determining how well your antenna will work over the long term. Even the smallest details, such as how you connect the wire to the insulators (Fig 5A), contribute significantly to antenna longevity. By using plenty of wire at the insulator and wrapping it tightly, you will decrease the possibility of the wire pulling loose in the wind. There is no need to solder the wire once is it wrapped. There is no electrical connection here, only mechanical. The high heat needed for soldering can anneal the wire, significantly weakening it at the solder point.

Similarly, the feed line connection at the center insulator should be made to the antenna wires after they have been secured to the insulator (Fig 5B). This way, you will be assured of a good electrical connection between the antenna and feed line without compromising the mechanical strength. Do a good job of soldering the antenna and feed line connections. Use a heavy iron or a torch, and be sure to clean the materials thoroughly before starting the job. Proper planning should allow you to solder indoors at a workbench, where the best possible joints may be made. Poorly soldered or unsoldered connections will become a headache as the wire oxidizes and the electrical integrity degrades with time. Besides degrading your antenna performance, poorly made joints can be a cause of TVI because of rectification.

If made from the right materials, the dipole illustrated in Fig 5C should give the builder years of maintenance-free service —unless of course a tree falls on it! As you build your antenna, keep in mind that if you get it right the first time, you won't have to do it again for a long time.

Construction of Beams and Vertical Monopoles

Most beams and verticals are made from sections of aluminum tubing that have been extruded or drawn. Compromise beams have been fashioned from less-expensive materials such as electrical conduit (steel) or bamboo poles wrapped with conductive tape or aluminum foil. The steel conduit is heavy, is a poor conductor and is subject to rust. Similarly, bamboo with conducting material attached to it will deteriorate rapidly in the weather. Aluminum tubing is by far the best material for building antennas in the HF and VHF regions. Copper or brass may be used in some VHF and UHF applications, and this idea is discussed later in this chapter.

Aluminum tubing comes in a variety of sizes, detailed in Table 2. Such tubing is available in many metropolitan areas. Dealers may be found in the Yellow Pages under "Aluminum." Tubing usually comes in 12-foot lengths, although 20-foot lengths

are available in some sizes. Your aluminum dealer will probably also sell aluminum plate in various thicknesses needed for boom-to-mast and boom-to-element connections.

Aluminum is rated according to its hardness. The most common material used in antenna construction is grade 6061-T6. This material is relatively strong and has good workability. In addition, it will bend without taking a "set," an advantage in antenna applications where the pieces are constantly flexing in the wind. The softer grades (5051, 3003, etc) will bend much more easily, while harder grades (7075, etc) are more brittle.

Beam Elements

Beam elements are generally made from telescoping sections of aluminum tubing. The prime consideration when choosing tubing sizes is mechanical strength. Ob-

viously, a 66-foot-long 40-meter element would be made from much larger material than an 18-foot-long 10-meter element. Fig 6 shows generic element designs for 10, 15 and 20-meter elements. The exact length of each element will depend on the electrical design.

Wall thickness is of primary concern when selecting tubing. It is of utmost importance that the tubing fits snugly where the element sections join. Sloppy joints will make a mechanically unstable antenna. The magic wall thickness is 0.058 inch. For example (from Table 2), 1-inch outside diameter (OD) tubing with a 0.058-inch wall has an inside diameter (ID) of 0.884 inch. The next smaller size of tubing, 7/8 inch, has an OD of 0.875 inch. The 0.009-inch difference provides just the right amount of clearance for a snug fit.

Fig 7 shows several methods of fastening antenna element sections together. The slot

Table 2
Standard Sizes of Aluminum Tubing

6061-T6 (61S-T6) round aluminum tube in 12-foot lengths

OD (in)	Wall Thickness in	stubs ga	ID (in)	Approx Weight (lb) per ft	per length	OD (in)	Wall Thickness in	stubs ga	ID (in)	Approx Weight (lb) per ft	per length
3/16	.035	no. 20	.117	.019	.228	1	.083	no. 14	.834	.281	3.372
	.049	no. 18	.089	.025	.330	1-1/8	.035	no. 20	1.055	.139	1.668
1/4	.035	no. 20	.180	.027	.324		.058	no. 17	1.009	.228	2.736
	.049	no. 18	.152	.036	.432	1-1/4	.035	no. 20	1.180	.155	1.860
	.058	no. 17	.134	.041	492		.049	no. 18	1.152	.210	2.520
5/16	.035	no. 20	.242	.036	.432		.058	no. 17	1.134	.256	3.072
	.049	no. 18	.214	.047	.564		.065	no. 16	1.120	.284	3.408
	.058	no. 17	.196	.055	.660		.083	no. 14	1.084	.357	4.284
3/8	.035	no. 20	.305	.043	.516	1-3/8	.035	no. 20	1.305	.173	2.076
	.049	no. 18	.277	.060	.720		.058	no. 17	1.259	.282	3.384
	.058	no. 17	.259	.068	.816	1-1/2	.035	no. 20	1.430	.180	2.160
	.065	no. 16	.245	.074	.888		.049	no. 18	1.402	.260	3.120
7/16	.035	no. 20	.367	.051	.612		.058	no. 17	1.384	.309	3.708
	.049	no. 18	.339	.070	.840		.065	no. 16	1.370	.344	4.128
	.065	no. 16	.307	.089	1.068		.083	no. 14	1.334	.434	5.208
1/2	.028	no. 22	.444	.049	.588		*.125	1/8"	1.250	.630	7.416
	.035	no. 20	.430	.059	.708		*.250	1/4"	1.000	1.150	14.823
	.049	no. 18	.402	.082	.948	1-5/8	.035	no. 20	1.555	.206	2.472
	.058	no. 17	.384	.095	1.040		.058	no. 17	1.509	.336	4.032
	.065	no. 16	.370	.107	1.284	1-3/4	.058	no. 17	1.634	.363	4.356
5/8	.028	no. 22	.569	.061	.732		.083	no. 14	1.584	.510	6.120
	.035	no. 20	.555	.075	.900	1-7/8	.508	no. 17	1.759	.389	4.668
	.049	no. 18	.527	.106	1.272	2	.049	no. 18	1.902	.350	4.200
	.058	no. 17	.509	.121	1.452		.065	no. 16	1.870	.450	5.400
	.065	no. 16	.495	.137	1.644		.083	no. 14	1.834	.590	7.080
3/4	.035	no. 20	.680	.091	1.092		*.125	1/8"	1.750	.870	9.960
	.049	no. 18	.652	.125	1.500		*.250	1/4"	1.500	1.620	19.920
	.058	no. 17	.634	.148	1.776	2-1/4	.049	no. 18	2.152	.398	4.776
	.065	no. 16	.620	.160	1.920		.065	no. 16	2.120	.520	6.240
	.083	no. 14	.584	.204	2.448		.083	no. 14	2.084	.660	7.920
7/8	.035	no. 20	.805	.108	1.308	2-1/2	.065	no. 16	2.370	.587	7.044
	.049	no. 18	.777	.151	1.810		.083	no. 14	2.334	.740	8.880
	.058	no. 17	.759	.175	2.100		*.125	1/8"	2.250	1.100	12.720
	.065	no. 16	.745	.199	2.399		*.250	1/4"	2.000	2.080	25.440
1	.035	no. 20	.930	.123	1.467	3	.065	no. 16	2.870	.710	8.520
	.049	no. 18	.902	.170	2.040		*.125	1/8"	2.700	1.330	15.600
	.058	no. 17	.884	.202	2.424		*.250	1/4"	2.500	2.540	31.200
	.065	no. 16	.870	.220	2.640						

*These sizes are extruded; all other sizes are drawn tubes. Shown here are standard sizes of aluminum tubing that are stocked by most aluminum suppliers or distributors in the United States and Canada.

Fig 6—Element designs for Yagi antennas. (Use 0.058-inch-wall aluminum tubing except for end pieces where thinner-wall tubing may be used.)

Fig 7—Some methods of connecting telescoping tubing sections to build beam elements. See text for a discussion of each method.

Fig 8—A long boom needs both vertical and horizontal support. The crossbar mounted above the boom can support a double truss, which will help keep the antenna in position.

Fig 9—The boom-to-element plate at A uses muffler-clamp-type U-bolts and saddles to secure the round tubing to the flat plate. The boom-to-mast plate at B is similar to the boom-to-element plate. The main difference is the size of materials used.

and hose clamp method shown in Fig 7A is probably the best for joints where adjustments are needed. Generally, one adjustable joint per element half is sufficient to tune the antenna. Stainless steel hose clamps (beware—some "stainless steel" models do not have a stainless screw and will rust) are recommended for longest antenna life.

Figs 7B, 7C and 7D show possible fastening methods for joints that are not adjustable. At B, machine screws and nuts hold the elements in place. At C, sheet metal screws are used. At D, rivets secure the tubing. If the antenna is to be assembled permanently, rivets are the best choice. Once in place, they are permanent. They will never work free, regardless of vibration or wind. If aluminum rivets with aluminum mandrels are employed, they will never rust. Also, being aluminum, there is no danger of corrosion from interaction between dissimilar metals. If the antenna is to be disassembled and moved periodically, either B or C will work. If machine screws are used, however, take all possible

precautions to keep the nuts from vibrating free. Use of lock washers, lock nuts and flexible adhesive such as silicone bathtub sealant will keep the hardware in place.

Use of a conductive grease at the element joints is essential for long life. Left untreated, the aluminum surfaces will oxidize in the weather, resulting in a poor connection. Some trade names for this conductive grease are Penetrox, Noalox and Dow Corning Molykote 41. Many electrical supply houses carry these products.

Boom Material

The boom size for a rotatable Yagi or quad should be selected to provide stability to the entire system. The best diameter for the boom depends on several factors, but mostly the element weight, number of elements and overall length. Tubing diameters of 1¼ inches can easily support 3-element 10-meter arrays and perhaps a 2-element 15-meter system. For larger 10-meter antennas or for harsh weather conditions, and for antennas up to 3 elements on 20 meters or 4 elements on

15 meters, a 2-inch-diameter boom will be adequate. Two-inch-diameter booms should not be made any longer than 24 feet unless additional support is given to reduce both vertical and horizontal bending forces. Suitable reinforcement for a long 2-inch boom can consist of a truss or a truss and lateral support, as shown in Fig 8.

A boom length of 24 feet is about the point where a 3-inch diameter begins to be very worthwhile. This dimension provides a considerable amount of improvement in overall mechanical stability as well as increased clamping surface area for element hardware. The latter is extremely important if heavy icing is commonplace and rotation of elements around the boom is to be avoided. Pinning an element to the boom with a large bolt helps in this regard. On the smaller diameter booms, however, the elements sometimes work loose and tend to elongate the pinning holes in both the element and the boom. After some time the elements shift their positions slightly (sometimes from day to day!) and give a ragged appearance to the system, even though this may not harm the electrical performance.

A 3-inch-diameter boom with a wall thickness of 0.065 inch is very satisfactory for antennas up in size to about a 5-element, 20-meter array that is spaced on a 40-foot-long boom. A truss is recommended for any boom longer than 24 feet. One possible source for large boom material is irrigation tubing sold at farm supply houses.

Putting It Together

Once you assemble your boom and elements, the next step is to fasten the elements to the boom securely and then fasten the boom to the mast or supporting structure. Fig 9A shows the most practical method of attaching the elements to the boom. Of course, if the home constructor has access to a machine shop, there are any number of different ways to accomplish this. The size of the mounting plate will depend on the size of the boom and element materials used. Be sure to leave plenty of material on either side of the U-bolt holes. The U-bolts selected should be a snug fit for the tubing. If possible, purchase the muffler-clamp type U-bolts that come with

saddles.

The boom-to-mast plate shown in Fig 9B is similar to the boom-to-element plate. The size of the plate and number of U-bolts used will depend on the size of the antenna. Generally, antennas for the bands up through 20 meters require only two U-bolts each for the mast and boom. Longer antennas for 15 and 20 (35-foot booms and up) and most 40-meter beams should have four U-bolts each for the boom and mast because of the torque that the long booms and elements exert as the antennas move in the wind. When tightening the U-bolts, be careful not to crush the tubing. Once the wall begins to collapse, the connection begins to weaken. Many aluminum suppliers sell ¼-inch plate just right for this application. Often they will shear pieces to

the correct size on request. As with tubing, the relatively hard 6061-T6 grade is a good choice for mounting plates.

The antenna should be put together with good-quality hardware. Stainless steel is best for long life. Rust will attack plated steel hardware after a short while, making nuts difficult, if not impossible, to remove. If stainless muffler clamps are not available, the next best thing is to have them plated. If you can't get them plated, then at least paint them with a good zinc-chromate primer and a finish coat or two. Good-quality hardware is more expensive initially, but if you do it right the first time, you won't have to take the antenna down after a few years and replace the hardware. Also, when repairing or modifying an installation, nothing is more frustrating than fighting rusty hardware at the top of a tower.

The Loop Skywire

Here's a multiband HF antenna that's easy to build, costs nearly nothing and works great—yet relatively few amateurs use it. The antenna is the full-size horizontal loop—or, as this one's called—The Loop Skywire. The Skywire eliminates the need for multiple antennas to cover the HF bands, is made only of wire and coaxial cable (or open-wire line), and often needs no Transmatch. It's efficient and omni-directional over real earth, can be used on all harmonics of the fundamental frequency, and fits on almost every amateur's lot. The Skywire has been called "the best easy-to-build, multiband antenna around," and to those who now use the Loop Skywire, it's "the best kept secret in the amateur circle."

It is curious that many references to this antenna are brief pronouncements that it operates best as a high-angle radiator and is good for only short-distance contacts. This is not the case! Those who use the Loop Skywire know that its performance far exceeds the short haul. DX is easy to work. This antenna was originally featured in November 1985 *QST*, and was presented by Dave Fischer, WØMHS.

The Design

The Loop Skywire is shown in Fig 10. It is simply a full-wavelength loop antenna erected horizontal to the earth. Maximum enclosed area within the wire loop is the fundamental rule. The antenna has one wavelength of wire in its perimeter at the design or fundamental frequency. If you choose to calculate L_{total} in feet, the following equation should be used:

$$L_{total} = 1005/f$$

where f equals the frequency in MHz. (This is the standard formula for determining the length of full-wavelength loops.)

Given any length of wire, the maximum possible area the antenna can enclose is with the wire in the shape of a circle. Since it takes an infinite number of supports to hang a circular loop, the square loop (four supports) is the most practical. Further reducing the area enclosed by the wire loop (fewer supports) brings the antenna closer

to the properties of the folded dipole, and both harmonic-impedance and feed-line voltage problems can result. Loop geometries other than a square are thus possible, but remember the two fundamental requirements for the Loop Skywire—its horizontal position and maximum enclosed area.

Construction

The antenna's construction is simple. Although the loop can be made for any

Fig 10—A complete view of the Loop Skywire. The square loop is erected horizontal to the earth.

band or frequency of operation, the following two Loop Skywires are star performers. The 10-MHz band can also be operated on both.

3.5-MHz Loop Skywire: (3.5-28 MHz), total loop perimeter: 272 feet. Square side length: 68 feet.

7-MHz Loop Skywire: (7-28 MHz loop), total loop perimeter: 142 feet. Square side length: 35.5 feet.

The actual total length can vary by a few feet, as the length is not at all critical. Do not worry about tuning and pruning the loop to resonance. No signal difference will be detected on the other end.

Insulated, stranded copper wire—12 to 18 gauge—is usually used for the loop. Fig 11 shows the placement of the insulators at the loop corners. Either lock or tie the insulator in place with a loop wire tie, as shown in Fig 11A, or leave the insulator free to "float" or slide along the wire, Fig 11B. Most loop users float at least two insulators. This allows pulling the slack out of the loop once it is in the air, and eliminates the need to have all the supports exactly placed for proper tension in each leg. Floating two opposite corners is recommended. The feed point can be positioned anywhere along the loop. Most users feed the Skywire at a corner, however. Fig 12 shows a method of doing this. It is advantageous to keep the feed-point mechanicals away from the corner support. Feeding a foot or so from one corner allows the feed line to exit more freely. This method keeps the feed line free from the loop support.

Generally, a minimum of four supports is required. If trees are used for supports, then at least two of the ropes or guys used to support the insulators should be counterweighted and allowed to move freely. The feed-line corner is almost always tied down, however. Several loops have been constructed with bungie cords tied to three of the four insulators. This eliminates the need for counterweighting.

Recommended height for the antenna is 40 feet or more. The higher the better. However, successful local and DX operation has been reported in several cases with the loop as low as 25 feet.

If you are preoccupied with SWR, the reading will depend on your operating frequency and the type of feed line used. Coaxial cable is sufficient. Open-wire line works well, too. Most users feed the loop with RG-58. RG-8 is generally too cumbersome to use. The SWR from either of these loops is rarely over 3:1. If you are concerned about the SWR, use a Transmatch to eliminate all worries about power transfer and maximum signal strength. When constructing the loop, connect (solder) the coaxial feed line ends directly to the loop wire ends. Don't do anything else. Baluns or choke coils at the feed point are *unnecessary*. Don't let anyone talk you

into using them. The highest line SWR usually occurs at the second harmonic of the design frequency. The Loop Skywire is somewhat more broadband than corresponding dipoles, and is also more efficient. Do not expect SWR curves that are "dummy load" flat!

Using the Loop Skywire as a Vertical

Another interesting feature of this loop is its ability to be used as an all-band vertical antenna with top-hat loading. This is accomplished by keeping the feed-line run from the shack as vertical as possible and clear of metallic objects. Both feed-line conductors are then tied together (via a shorted SO-239 jack, for example), and the antenna is fed against a good ground system. This method allows excellent performance of the 40-meter loop on 80 meters, and the 80-meter loop on 160 meters. The feed arrangement for operating the loop as a vertical is shown in Fig 13.

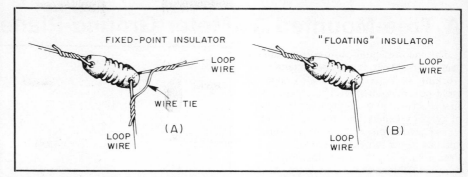

Fig 11—Two methods of installing the insulators at the corners of the loop.

Fig 12—Most users feed the Loop Skywire at the corner. Dimensions shown are approximate.

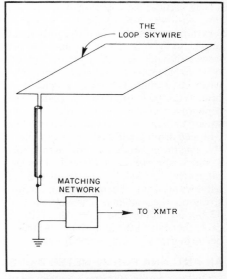

Fig 13—The feed arrangement for operating the loop as a vertical antenna.

A Tree-Mounted 30-Meter Ground-Plane Antenna

This inconspicuous, low-cost antenna is easy to build. It is a good antenna for working 30-meter DX and also makes a great portable antenna. The antenna was first described in the September 1984 issue of *QST* by Chuck Hutchinson, K8CH.

The evolution of this tree-mounted antenna began more than a decade ago. Al Francisco, K7NHV, was a doctoral candidate at Michigan State University. Al was living on campus and wanted to get on the air from his apartment. University rules did not permit outside antennas.

Al solved his problem by using an inconspicuous vertical antenna. He ran a piece of RG-58 cable from a bedroom window to the ground. From there, he slit a shallow trench to a nearby tree and buried the cable. At the base of the tree a pair of radials were soldered to the coax-line braid, then buried. Another piece of wire formed the main radiator of his 20-meter vertical. Despite having only two radials, the vertical worked well enough to solve Al's problem. The tree provided support and hid the vertical radiator without nullifying its performance.

Several years later K8CH moved to a new location. Dipoles for the 40- and 80-meter bands were hung in the trees. It was possible to work DX on 40 meters, but the low dipole worked too well on short skip; a vertical antenna with its low radiation angle would be a better alternative. Experience had proved that a vertical with 16 or more radials would be a good performer on the 40-meter band.

K8CH used a tree to support the vertical radiator the way K7NHV had. This time sections of TV mast, not wire, served as the vertical radiator. A full-grown walnut tree provided support for the antenna.

The vertical mast sections were placed into position close to the tree trunk. A length of treated 4- × 4-inch lumber was buried to serve as the base insulator. A large nail held the vertical mast in place. A short length of clothesline rope was wrapped around the mast at each tree branch that was to provide support. The rope was secured to the mast by tying four square knots, and the loose ends were then wrapped around and tied to the branches. By tying the extra square knots in the rope, a shock absorber was formed. This arrangement allowed the tree to move in the wind without transferring the motion into stress on the antenna. The vertical had 32 buried radials and a length of RG-8 cable that ran to the ham shack. Antenna performance was very good for DX.

AN ANTENNA FOR 30-METER DXING

On the day the 30-meter amateur band was opened by the FCC, K8CH (at yet another location) used a Transmatch and 40-meter dipole to make a few contacts. Later, he tried an 80-meter dipole. Both

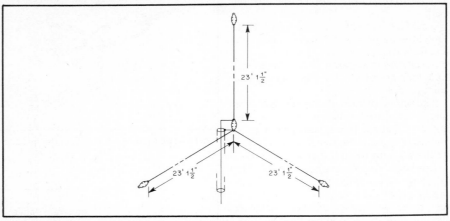

Fig 14—Dimensions and construction of a 30-meter ground-plane antenna.

were okay, but each worked too well on short skip. Stations within a couple of hundred miles were very loud—not the best situation for DXing!

A vertical antenna would tend to discriminate in favor of DX stations. One possibility was another version of the K7NHV special. There was a serious problem with that idea, however. Limited space and rocky soil meant that a good radial system would be almost impossible to install. So the decision was made to try a ground-plane antenna. The vertical radiator and two radials of the antenna would be made of wire.

The proper length of the elements is determined by the formula:

$$\text{Length}_{(feet)} = \frac{234}{f_{MHz}}$$

The vertical portion and each radial of the ground plane should be 23 feet 1½ inches for resonance at 10.12 MHz. Once you have the wire and insulators, it should not take long to assemble the antenna as shown in Fig 14. Be sure to solder the connection of coax cable to antenna wires.

The perfect tree for supporting the antennas was found at the back of the lot. Brush around the base of the tree made it hard to work around, but were great for camouflage. Only one obstacle stood in the way of speedy installation. How to get a line through the tree crotch 40 feet above the ground?

Getting a Line into a Tree

Many methods are used to get an antenna support line into the "right" crotch of a tree. You could use a bow and arrow or a slingshot. Attach an arrow to the end of a fishing line on a rod and reel. (Aluminum arrows with removable points work great.) Release the reel so line pulls off freely, and shoot. You can also use a slingshot, in which case you tie a lead fishing weight to the end of the line. (A half ounce to an ounce or so is about right.) A reel on a fishing rod works okay, but some

people attach a reel to the handle of their slingshot. This eliminates the need for a helper to hold the fishing rod.

There are a few tricks you should avoid learning "the hard way." First, make sure there is nothing breakable within range. Unless you are extremely fortunate, at least one attempt will go astray. Second, secure the free end of the line so it does not end up out of reach in the air. This is particularly frustrating when you have just managed to "hit the target."

When you miss your target, don't try to pull the weight back over a branch. It takes only a few seconds to let the weight fall to the ground, remove the weight and pull the line back through the tree. That way you get another try with the same weight.

Final Steps

It may take a few tries to get the line through that tree crotch at 40 feet. After that, tie the top insulator to the end of the line and haul it up to just below the crotch. A doubled-up section of the down-haul line can be wrapped around the tree at head level, and tied to support the antenna. Excess line can be secured in a coil a few feet above ground. Tie shorter lengths of line to the radial ends and secure the lines to convenient trees at a height above head level.

The procedure described above should only be used for temporary installations. This eventually results in abrasion to the rope and to the tree. Over time, girdling may occur leading to the loss of one or more of the branches. For permanent installations, use an eyescrew or a bolt through the branch to support this, or any other, wire antenna.

The tree-mounted ground-plane antenna works at least as well for DX as does a dipole at 60 feet. For stations less than a couple of hundred miles away there is pretty good rejection. (Use a horizontal antenna to work those closer stations.) You'll like the low cost, but perhaps best of all, the antenna is almost invisible.

A Multiband Inverted-V Antenna

The antenna shown in Fig 15 is popular among amateurs who prefer a single dipole for several bands of operation. Similar to the G5RV antenna, this antenna uses only open-wire line or 300-ohm ribbon-type feed line. The version shown in Fig 15 is erected as an inverted-V dipole. This is desirable because only one tall support pole, tower or tree is needed. Also, the antenna is relatively omnidirectional with vertical polarization. You may, however, choose to use this antenna as a horizontal radiator. The rules are the same for either type of installation. The length of the flat-top is not critical, but should be as long as possible (at least 100 feet or more for best results on the 80-meter band). For best operation, make sure the antenna is as symmetrical as possible.

The feed line for this antenna should be centered between the legs of the inverted V. It should come straight down to ground level, or nearly so. This ensures electrical symmetry. This is especially important when a metal mast or tower is used to support the antenna. The effects of the tower are canceled with a symmetrical installation. Three-hundred-ohm ribbon cable is usable to power levels of about 500 watts. Beyond that, open-wire line is a better choice. Best performance with this antenna will be had when the feed point is 60 or more feet above ground, but satisfactory

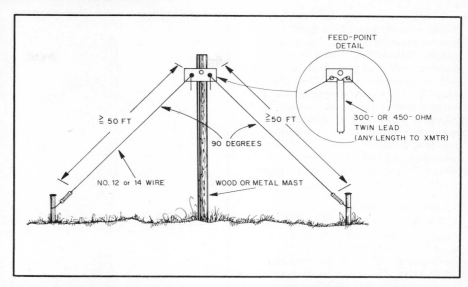

Fig 15—Details for constructing a multiband non-resonant inverted-V dipole with open-wire feeders. The feed line can be any convenient length. For best efficiency, the enclosed angle of the dipole should be between 90 and 110°.

results will be obtained if the apex is at least 30 feet high. An ideal installation would place the feed point of the antenna between 100 and 120 feet above ground, but this is generally beyond the realm of economic practicality for most amateurs.

Because most modern rigs are designed to operate into an unbalanced 50-ohm load, a Transmatch will have to be used to couple the transmitter to the antenna.

Universal Mounting Plate for Vertical Antennas

Fig 16 illustrates a mounting plate that will satisfy a host of conditions one might encounter when operating from an unfamiliar place. The hole size and spacing will depend on the U-bolts or muffler clamps used with the antenna. The lower set of holes (except the bottom-most two) permit using a supporting mast that is either vertical or horizontal. The holes in the top half of the plate permit the antenna to be mounted vertically or at 45° angle. Hole B is for a female-to-female bulkhead connector. The feed line attaches to one side of the fitting, and a banana plug fits into the center hole of the opposite end of the connector. This permits easy disconnection when disassembling the antenna. The radials are bolted to the two holes marked C, at the left and right center of the plate. The two holes (C) at the bottom

of the plate are for bolting an iron or aluminum angle stock to the plate. A second angle-stock piece is cut to the same size as the first and is used with the mounting hardware when it is convenient to clamp the mounting plate to a porch railing, window sill and so on. A pair of large C clamps can be used for this mounting technique.

The plate is made from ¼-inch aluminum. Brass or copper material could be used equally well if available.

Fig 16—Layout details for a universal mounting plate. The hole sizes and spacing will depend on the type of U-bolts used (see text).

Simple 5/8-Wave Verticals for 12 and 17 Meters

Thanks to the harmonic relationships between the HF ham bands, many antennas can be made to do "double duty." The simple verticals described here cover two bands at once, and provide an inexpensive way to get on the 12- and 17-meter bands. Here's how to turn a 30-meter quarter-wave vertical into a 5/8-wave vertical for the 12-meter band, and a 40-meter quarter-wave vertical into a 5/8-wave vertical for the new 17-meter band. These verticals were designed and constructed by John J. Reh, K7KGP. The write-up first appeared in April 1989 *QST*.

Construction Details

For the 30- and 12-meter vertical, an old aluminum multiband vertical was cut to a length of 25 feet, 3 inches. This corresponds to a design frequency of 24.95 MHz. The length-to-diameter ratio is approximately 460. The input impedance of a vertical that is substantially longer than a quarter wavelength (in this case 5/8 λ) is particularly sensitive to the λ/D ratio of the radiating element. If this antenna is duplicated with materials having a significantly different λ/D ratio, the results may be different.

After installing a good ground system (described later), the input impedance was measured and found to have a resistance of about 50 Ω, and a capacitance of about 155 Ω (at 24.95 MHz). At 10.125 MHz, the input impedance was just under 50 Ω, and purely resistive. To tune out the reactance at 24.95 MHz, a series inductor is installed (see Fig 17) and tapped to resonance at the design frequency. The easiest way to find resonance is by measuring the antenna SWR. Use a good-quality coil for the series inductor. The recommended coil has a diameter of 2½ inches, and has 6 turns per inch (B & W stock no. 3029). 3¼ turns were required to establish resonance on 12 meters. The SWR on 12 meters is 1.1:1, and

Fig 17—The 5/8-λ 17-meter / ¼-λ 40-meter vertical. A switch or relay can be used to remove the loading coil from the circuit for 40-meter operation. Move the coil tap for best SWR on the higher-frequency band. The radial system should be as extensive as possible. See *The ARRL Antenna Book*, Chapter 3, for more information on ground systems for vertical antennas.

on 30 meters, 1:1. To change bands from 12 to 30 meters, move the coil tap to the end of the coil closest to the vertical element. Alternatively, a single-pole switch or remotely operated relay can be installed at the base of the vertical for band switching.

The Ground System

The importance of a good ground system for vertical antennas cannot be overemphasized. Maximum RF current density—and therefore maximum ground

losses—for quarter-wave verticals occurs in the immediate area of the base of the antenna. Maximum ground loss for a 5/8-wave vertical occurs about 1/2 λ away from the base of the antenna. It's important to have the lowest possible losses in the immediate area for both types of verticals.

In addition to a ground radial system, 6- × 6-foot aluminum ground screen is used at the base of the antenna. The screen makes a good tie point for the radials and conducts ground currents efficiently. Seventeen wire radials, each about 33 feet long, are spaced evenly around the antenna. More radials would probably work better. Each radial is bolted to the screen using corrosion-resistant no. 10-24 hardware. (Do not attempt to connect copper directly to aluminum. The electrical connection between the two metals will quickly deteriorate.) The radials can be made of bare or insulated wire. Make sure the ground screen is bolted to the ground side of the antenna with heavy-gauge wire. Current flow is fairly heavy at this point.

Adapting the Antenna to the 17- and 40-Meter Bands

Table 3 gives specifications for the 5/8-wave vertical on 12 and 17 meters. If your existing 40-meter vertical is a few inches longer than 32 feet, 3 inches, try using it anyway—a few inches isn't too critical to performance on 17 meters.

Table 3

12- and 17-Meter Specifications for the 5/8-λ Vertical Antenna

Band	Height	Required Matching Inductance (μH)
12 meters	23' 5"	0.99
17 meters	32' 3"	1.36

An Extended Double Zepp for 12 Meters

This antenna was first described in December 1987 and December 1988 *QST*. The author is John J. Reh, K7KGP.

Zepp—short for Zeppelin—is a term applied to just about any resonant antenna end-fed by two-wire transmission line. The extended version of this antenna, although an old-fashioned design, provides 3-dB gain over a dipole—quite suitable for modern amateur needs. The extended double Zepp (EDZ) consists of two collinear 0.64-λ elements fed in phase. Fig 18 shows current distribution in an EDZ antenna, and Fig 19 shows its horizontal directivity pattern in free space.

Fig 20 shows the configuration of the 12-meter version, cut for 24.950 MHz. Each element is 25 feet, 3 inches long, and consists of no. 14 stranded copper wire. The antenna elements are center-fed by a short matching section made of a 5-foot, 5-inch length of 450-Ω open-wire line. Connection to a 52-Ω coaxial feed line is made by means of a 1:1 balun transformer.

Matching Section

The open-wire-line matching section is 52 electrical degrees long (0.145 λ). The matching section transforms the EDZ's input impedance to about 55 ohms, as measured with a noise bridge. The matching-section dimension given in Fig 20 assumes a velocity factor of 0.95 for the 450-Ω line.

Trimming the matching section to size is the only adjustment necessary with the EDZ. Make the transformer a little long to begin with, and shorten it an inch or two at a time to bring the system into resonance. (You can check resonance with a noise bridge or by monitoring the SWR.) Do *not* change the length of the elements—the EDZ's gain and directivity depend on its elements being 0.64 λ long.

Phasing Two EDZ's for More Gain and Directivity

Properly placed, two EDZ antennas can give improved gain and directivity over a single EDZ. Fig 21 compares the calculated horizontal directivity patterns of a single EDZ and an array consisting of two EDZs spaced at 1/8 λ and fed 180° out of phase. Fig 22 compares the vertical radiation patterns of the single and phased EDZs.

Fig 23 shows the dimensions of a practical two-EDZ configuration. With proper adjustment, it exhibits an SWR of 1.3:1 across the 24-MHz band. In the array at K7KGP, lightweight broom handles serve as spreaders between the element ends; the center spreader is a wooden slat. I used nylon rope to haul the array up between two trees. This antenna system works well; the contacts I have made with it have been entirely satisfactory.

The matching method shown in Fig 23

is somewhat clumsy because the combined length of the phasing lines is greater than the spacing between the EDZs. The feed method shown in Fig 24 should be easier to build because the combined length of the phasing lines equals the spacing between the EDZs.

Scaling for Other Bands

Assume you want to build an EDZ for 7.2 MHz. The 24.95-MHz antenna has element lengths of 25 feet, 3 inches and the matching-transformer line length is 5 feet, 5 inches. Use the following formula to scale the antenna dimensions to the desired band:

$$L2 = \frac{(f1 \times L1)}{f2}$$

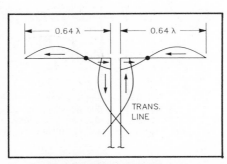

Fig 18—The extended double Zepp antenna consists of two 0.64-λ elements fed in phase.

where

L2 = length at the desired frequency
f1 = resonant frequency of the original antenna
L1 = length of interest at the resonant frequency of the original antenna
f2 = resonant frequency of the new antenna

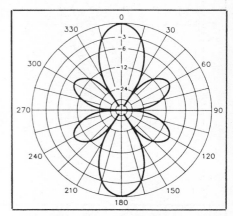

Fig 19—Horizontal directivity pattern for an extended double Zepp antenna in free space. Relative to a half-wave dipole, it exhibits a gain of approximately 3 dB. The antenna elements lie along the 90°-270° line.

Fig 20—The extended double Zepp at K7KGP, cut for 24.950 MHz. The 450-Ω matching section transforms the calculated input impedance (142 − *j*555 Ω) to 55 Ω (measured) for connection to 52-Ω coaxial cable by means of a 1:1 balun. The electrical length of the matching section is 52°; the linear dimension shown in the drawing assumes 450-Ω line with a velocity factor of 0.95.

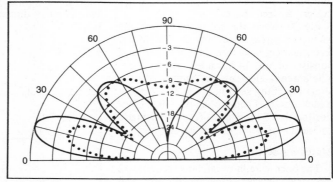

Fig 21—Comparison of calculated horizontal directivity patterns of one EDZ (dotted line) and two EDZs spaced a 1/8 λ and fed 180° out of phase (solid line). The antenna axes lie along the 0°-180° line, and the antennas are mounted 35 feet above average earth. The phased EDZs exhibit nearly 5 dB gain over a single EDZ. This is 7 to 8 dB gain over a half-wave dipole. Beamwidth of the two-EDZ array is 30°. The antenna axis is the same for the single EDZ and both EDZs in the phased array. The two-EDZ configuration characterized here is an *end-fire* array because maximum radiation occurs along its axis.

Fig 22—Comparison of the calculated vertical directivity patterns of the one EDZ (dotted line) and two EDZs spaced at 1/8 λ and fed 180° out of phase (solid line). The antenna axis lies along the 0° line.

Fig 23—One method of phasing two EDZs for greater gain and directivity. The array is bidirectional, with maximum radiation occurring along the array axis. The impedance across points X and Y is 50 Ω, balanced; with a 1:1 balun at XY, the array can be fed by means of 52-Ω coaxial cable. The stub, 1.5° long, cancels a capacitive reactance of approximately 13.5 Ω at the feed point. This array works well, but its matching system is clumsy because the combined length of the phasing lines is greater than the spacing of the two EDZs. Fig 24 shows a proposed feed method that takes up less space.

ANTENNA ELEMENTS ARE NO. 14 STRANDED COPPER WIRE.
PHASING LINE, MATCHING SECTION AND STUB ARE 450-Ω OPEN-WIRE LINE.

Fig 24—Alternative method of phasing two EDZs. In this arrangement, the length of each phasing line is half the EDZ spacing. Calculated impedance across points a and b is $15 - j112$ Ω. The matching section—11° in length—transforms this to a calculated impedance of approximately $55 - j32$ Ω (balanced) across points x and y. The stub, 4° long, cancels the capacitive reactance (32 Ω). A 1:1 balun transformer allows the array to be fed by means of 52-Ω coaxial cable. See text.

Lengths for L1 and L2 must be expressed in similar units (feet, meters, and so on); this also applies to units of measurement used for f1 and f2 (kHz, MHz, and so on).

Substituting the values for element length

$$L2 = \frac{24.95 \times 25.25}{7.2} = 87 \text{ feet, 6 inches}$$

and matching-transformer length

$$L2 = \frac{24.95 \times 5.417}{7.2} = 18 \text{ feet, 9 inches}$$

This scaling technique also works for element spacings. Velocity-factor considerations can be ignored because they were included in the initial design.

Simple Antennas for HF Portable Operation

The typical portable HF antenna is a random-length wire flung over a tree and end-fed through a Transmatch. QRP Transmatches can be quite compact, but each additional piece of equipment necessary makes portable operation less attractive. The station can be simplified by using resonant impedance-matched antennas for the bands of interest. Perhaps the simplest antenna of this type is the half-wave dipole, center-fed with 50- or 75-ohm coax. Unfortunately, RG-58, RG-59 or RG-8 cable is heavy and bulky for backpacking, and the miniature cables such as RG-174 are too lossy. A practical solution to the coax problem is to use folded dipoles made from lightweight TV twin lead. The characteristic impedance of this type of dipole is near 300 ohms, but it can be transformed to a 50-ohm source or load by means of a simple matching stub.

Fig 25 illustrates the construction method and important dimensions for the twin-lead dipole. A silver-mica capacitor is shown for the reactive element, but an open-end stub of twin lead can serve as well, provided it is dressed at right angles to the transmission line for some distance. The stub method has the advantage of easy adjustment of the system resonant frequency.

To preserve the balance of the feeder, a 1:1 balun must be used at the end of the feed line. In most applications the balance is not important, and the twin lead can be connected directly to a coaxial output jack, one lead to the center contact, and one lead to the shell. To preserve its low loss, the twin lead must be kept dry and free from bunching or coiling. Because of its higher impedance, a folded dipole exhibits a wider bandwidth than a single-conductor type.

Frequency	Length A	Length B	Length C	C_s	Stub Length
3.75 MHz	124' 9½"	104' 11½"	13' 0"	289 pF	37' 4"
7.15	65' 5½"	55' ½"	6' 10"	151 pF	19' 7"
10.125	46' 2½"	38' 10½"	4' 10"	107 pF	13' 10"
14.175	33' 0"	27' 9¼"	3' 5½"	76 pF	9' 10½"
18.118	25' 10"	21' 8¾"	2' 8½"	60 pF	7' 9"
21.225	22' ½"	18' 6½"	2' 3½"	51 pF	6' 7"
24.94	18' 9"	15' 9½"	1' 11½"	43 pF	5' 7½"
28.5	16' 5"	13' 9¾"	1' 8½"	38 pF	4' 11"

Fig 25—A twin-lead folded dipole makes an excellent portable antenna that is easily matched to 50-ohm stations.

The antennas described here are not as broad as a standard folded dipole because the impedance transformation mechanism is frequency selective. However, the bandwidth should be adequate. An antenna cut for 14.175 MHz, for example, will present an SWR of less than 2:1 over the entire 20-meter band.

Designing X-Beams

The X-beam is a high-performance broadband antenna that is ideal for radio operators with limited space. X-beams are inexpensive and easy to build. The X-beams described here were designed and built by Brice Anderson, W9PNE. This material first appeared in the *ARRL Antenna Compendium, Volume 1.*

The X-beam is a compact version of the 2-element Yagi; its performance equals or exceeds that of its conventional counterpart. X-beams are broadband, exhibit 5 to 6 dBd gain, and 15 to 18 dB front-to-back ratios. The formulas presented here will enable you to calculate X-beam dimensions for any frequency.

The X-beam's name is derived from its shape, shown in Fig 26. It consists of four arms, often built from aluminum tubing, and four wire loading tails. Because there is no boom, the antenna is usually mounted in a horizontal plane (like a cubical quad lying on its side), although a vertical-plane position can be used. X-beams are considerably smaller and lighter than comparable 2-element Yagis.

Construction

A square piece of heavy plywood, treated for weather protection, makes a suitable hub for 15- and 20-meter X-beams. The arms are secured to the hub with pipe brackets, and a nylon cord is strung tightly around the beam from tip to tip. This procedure strengthens the assembly and supports the tails.

An alternative method of construction is to use two pieces of aluminum angle stock bolted together as the X hub. The arms may then be clamped to the hub with hose clamps, using plastic tubing to insulate the driven arms. Tables 4 and 5 show X-beam dimensions for several amateur bands.

X-beam Types

Formulas are given for full-size and minimum-size X-beams. The full-size beam provides a close match to 50-ohm coax, and the greatest possible bandwidth. It is recommended for 10, 15 and 20 meters. The minimum-size beam offers similar performance, but the SWR is approximately 1.4:1. Because of the shorter arms, the ends of the tails nearly touch. It is generally used for 30 and 40 meters.

Many measurements on a large number of experimental X-beams were used to develop the formulas. The arms are made of tubing with a length-to-diameter ratio of about 200:1. Stranded no. 19 vinyl-covered wire is used for the tails. The use of larger tubing or larger wire will require slightly shorter tails than predicted by the formulas, and vice versa. The arms may be made of wire supported by nonconductive materials such as wood or bamboo. In this case, the tails will have to be made considerably longer.

Fig 26—Top and side views of the X-beam. The arms are made of aluminum tubing. Nylon cord is strung tightly around the perimeter of the antenna to strengthen the assembly and support the wire tails.

Formulas

For Full-size X-beams: Arm length (ft) = 195/f (MHz). Each arm is approximately 0.2 λ. Total driven element length (ft) = 603/f (MHz). Each X-beam driven element is approximately 27% longer than a conventional Yagi driven element. Driven element tail length (ft) = 106.5/f (MHz) (each tail). Total director element length (ft) = 575/f (MHz) (4.65% shorter than the driven element). Director tail length (ft) = 92.5/f (MHz) (each tail).

Do not use arms much longer than those calculated by the full-size formula. As the arms get longer and the tails get shorter, the pattern changes gradually to four broad lobes.

For Minimum-size X-beams: Arm-length (ft) = 177/f (MHz). Each arm is about 0.18 λ. Total driven element length (ft) = 603/f (MHz) (same as for full size X-beams). Driven element tail length (ft) = 125/f (MHz) (each tail). Total director element length (ft) = 575/f (MHz) (4.65% shorter than the driven element). Director tail length (ft) = 110.5/f (MHz) (each tail).

Tuning and Adjustment

The tails should be made a few inches longer than the calculated lengths (for tuning purposes). For tuning, the beam should be mounted on a pole at least 10 feet high. To determine resonance, an SWR bridge is placed in the coaxial feed line.

Using 5 W of power or less, quickly take several SWR measurements, starting at the low end of the band. Do not cause QRM! The lowest SWR occurs at the resonant

Table 4
Dimensions for Full-Size X-beams

Freq (MHz)	Arm Length	Driven Element Tail	Director Tail	Tail Difference
7.050	27' 8"	15' 1½"	13' 1½"	2'
10.125	19' 3"	10' 6"	9' 1½"	1' 4½"
14.100	13' 10"	7' 6½"	6' 6½"	1'
21.100	9' 3"	5' ½"	4' 4½"	8"
28.200	6' 11"	3' 9½"	3' 3½"	6"

Table 5
Dimensions for Minimum-Size X-beams

Freq (MHz)	Arm Length	Driven Element Tail	Director Tail	Tail Difference
7.050	25' 1½"	17' 9"	15' 9"	2'
10.125	17' 6"	12' 4"	10' 11"	1' 5"
14.100	12' 6½"	8' 10"	7' 10"	1'
21.100	8' 4½"	5' 11"	5' 3"	8"
28.200	6' 3½"	4' 5"	3' 11"	6"

frequency. If the resonant frequency is too low, cut one inch from each of the four tails (½ inch on 10 meters). Again determine resonance. Repeat this process until the antenna resonates at the desired frequency. The difference in tail length must be as shown in Tables 4 and 5. The resonant frequency will increase somewhat when the antenna is mounted on the tower.

The X-beam radiation pattern is slightly asymmetrical because of currents on the coax shield. While this only slightly affects antenna performance, purists may wish to connect a 1:1 balun to the driven element. For a balun, the coax can be coiled into a 6-inch-ID coil, taped together and attached to the mast under the beam. The coil should be 12 turns for 15 and 20 meters and 6 turns for 10 meters.

The performance of the simple X-beam is amazingly similar to larger, more conventional antennas. Put one up and challenge the "big guns."

HF Mobile Antennas

The antenna is perhaps the most important item in the successful operation of a mobile installation. Mobile antennas, whether designed for single or multiband use, should be securely mounted to the automobile, as far from the engine compartment as possible (for reducing noise pickup), and should be carefully matched to the coaxial feed line connecting them to the transmitter and receiver. All antenna connections should be tight and weatherproof. Mobile loading coils should be protected from dirt, rain and snow if they are to maintain their Q and resonant frequency. The greater the Q of the loading coil, the better the efficiency, but the narrower the bandwidth of the antenna system.

Though bumper-mounted mobile antennas are favored by some, it is better to place the antenna mount on the rear deck of the vehicle, near the rear window. This locates the antenna high and in the clear, assuring less detuning of the system when the antenna moves to and from the car body. *Never use a base-loaded antenna on a bumper mount.*

The choice of base or center loading a mobile antenna has been a matter of controversy for many years. In theory, the center-loaded whip presents a slightly higher base impedance than does the base-loaded antenna. However, with proper impedance-matching techniques employed there is no discernible difference in performance between the two methods. A base-loading coil requires fewer turns of wire than one for center loading, and this

Table 6
Approximate Values for 8-foot Mobile Whip

Base Loading

f(kHz)	Loading L(µH)	RC(Q50) Ohms	RC(Q300) Ohms	RR Ohms	Feed R* Ohms	Matching L(µH)
1800	345	77	13	0.1	23	3
3800	77	37	6.1	0.35	16	1.2
7200	20	18	3	1.35	15	0.6
14,200	4.5	7.7	1.3	5.7	12	0.28
21,250	1.25	3.4	0.5	14.8	16	0.28
29,000	—	—	—	—	36	0.23

Center Loading

f(kHz)	Loading L(µH)	RC(Q50) Ohms	RC(Q300) Ohms	RR Ohms	Feed R* Ohms	Matching L(µH)
1800	700	158	23	0.2	34	3.7
3800	150	72	12	0.8	22	1.4
7200	40	36	6	3.0	19	0.7
14,200	8.6	15	2.5	11.0	19	0.35
21,250	2.5	6.6	1.1	27.0	29	0.29

RC = Loading-coil resistance; RR = radiation resistance.
*Assuming loading coil Q = 300, and including estimated ground-loss resistance.
Suggested coil dimensions for the required loading inductance are shown in a following table.

is an electrical advantage because of reduced coil losses. A base-loaded antenna is more stable during wind loading and sway. If a homemade antenna system is contemplated, either system will provide good results, but the base-loaded antenna may be preferred for its mechanical advantages (see Table 6).

Loading Coils

There are many commercially built antenna systems available for mobile operation, and some manufacturers sell the coils as separate units. Air-wound coils of large wire diameter are excellent for use as load-

ing inductors. Large Miniductor coils can be installed on a solid phenolic rod and used as loading coils. Miniductors, because of their turns spacing, are easy to adjust when resonating the mobile antenna and provide excellent Q. Phenolic-impregnated paper or fabric tubing of large diameter is suitable for making homemade loading coils. It should be coated with liquid fiberglass, inside and out, to make it weatherproof. Brass insert plugs can be installed in each end, their centers drilled and tapped for a standard 3/8 × 24 thread to accommodate the mobile antenna sections. After the coil winding is pruned to resonance

(Table 7) it should be coated with a high-quality, low-loss compound to hold the turns securely in place and to protect the coil from the weather. Liquid polystyrene is excellent for this. Hobby stores commonly stock this material for use as a protective film for wall plaques and other artwork. Details for making a home-built loading coil are given in Fig 27.

Impedance Matching

Fig 28 illustrates the shunt-fed method of obtaining a match between the antenna and the coaxial feed line. For operation on 75 meters with a center-loaded whip, L2 will have approximately 18 turns of no. 14 wire, spaced one wire thickness between turns, and wound on a 1-inch-diameter form. Initially, the tap will be approximately five turns above the ground end of L2. Coil L2 can be inside the car body, at the base of the antenna, or it can be located at the base of the whip, outside the car body. The latter method is preferred.

Since L2 helps determine the resonance of the overall antenna, L1 should be tuned to resonance in the desired part of the band with L2 in the circuit. The adjustable top section of the whip can be telescoped until a maximum reading is noted on the field-strength meter. The tap is then adjusted on L2 for the lowest reflected-power reading on the SWR bridge. Repeat these two adjustments until no further increase in field strength can be obtained; this point should coincide with the lowest SWR. The number of turns needed for L2 will have to be determined experimentally for 40- and 20-meter operation. There will be proportionately fewer turns required.

Matching with an L Network

Any resonant mobile antenna that has a feed-point impedance less than the characteristic impedance of the transmission line can be matched to the line by means of a simple L network, as shown in Fig 29. The

Fig 27—Details for making a home-built mobile loading coil. A breakdown view of the assembly is given at A. Brass end plugs are snug-fit into the ends of the phenolic tubing, and each is held in place by four no. 6-32 brass screws. Center holes in the plugs are drilled and tapped for 3/8-24 thread. The tubing can be any diameter from 1 to 4 inches. The larger diameters are recommended. Illustration B shows the completed coil. Resonance can be obtained by installing the coil, applying transmitter power, then pruning the turns until the lowest SWR is obtained. Pruning the coil for maximum field-strength-meter indication will also serve as a resonance indication.

Fig 28—A mobile antenna using shunt-feed matching. Overall antenna resonance is determined by the combination of L1 and L2. Antenna resonance is set by pruning the turns of L1, or adjusting the top section of the whip, while observing the field-strength meter or SWR indicator. Then, adjust the tap on L2 for lowest SWR.

Table 7

Suggested Loading-Coil Dimensions

Required L (μH)	No. Turns	Wire Size	Dia In	Length In
700	190	22	3	10
345	135	18	3	10
150	100	16	2½	10
77	75	14	2½	10
77	29	12	5	4¼
40	28	16	2½	2
40	34	12	2½	4¼
20	17	16	2½	1¼
20	22	12	2½	2¾
8.6	16	14	2	2
8.6	15	12	2½	3
4.5	10	14	2	1¼
4.5	12	12	2½	4
2.5	8	12	2	2
2.5	8	6	2-3/8	4½
1.25	6	12	1¾	2
1.25	6	6	2-3/8	4½

network is composed of C_M and L_M. The required values of C_M and L_M may be determined from

$$C_M = \frac{\sqrt{R_A(Z_0 - R_A)}}{2\pi f \text{ (kHz) } R_A Z_0} \times 10^9 \text{ pF}$$

and

$$L_M = \frac{\sqrt{R_A(Z_0 - R_A)}}{2\pi f \text{ (kHz)}} \times 10^3 \text{ } \mu\text{H}$$

where
R_A = the antenna feed-point resistance
Z_0 = the characteristic impedance of the transmission line.

As an example, if the feed-point resistance is 20 ohms and the line is 50-ohm coaxial cable, then at 4000 kHz,

$$C_M = \frac{\sqrt{20 (50 - 20)}}{(6.28) (4000) (20) (50)} \times 10^9$$

$$= \frac{\sqrt{600}}{(6.28) (4) (2) (5)} \times 10^4$$

$$= \frac{24.5}{251.2} \times 10^4 = 975 \text{ pF}$$

$$L_M = \frac{\sqrt{20 (50 - 20)}}{(6.28) (4000)} \times 10^3$$

$$= \frac{\sqrt{600}}{25.12} = \frac{24.5}{25.12} = 0.97 \text{ } \mu\text{H}$$

The chart of Fig 30 shows the capacitive reactance of C_M and the inductive reactance of L_M necessary to match various antenna impedances to 50-ohm coaxial cable. The chart assumes the antenna element has been resonated.

In practice, L_M need not be a separate inductor. Its effect can be duplicated by adding an equivalent amount of inductance to the loading coil, regardless of whether the loading coil is at the base or at the center of the antenna.

Adjustment

In adjusting this system, at least part of C_M should be variable, the balance being made up of combinations of fixed mica

Fig 29—A whip antenna may also be matched to coax line by means of an L network. The inductive reactance of the L network can be combined in the loading coil, as indicated at the right.

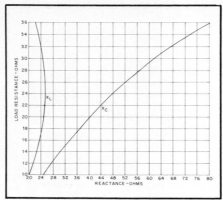

Fig 30—Curves showing inductive and capacitive reactances required to match a 50-ohm coax line to a variety of antenna resistances.

Fig 31—A capacitive hat can be used to improve the performance of base- or center-loaded whips. A solid metal disc can be used in place of the skeletal disc shown here.

capacitors in parallel as needed. A small, one-turn loop should be connected between C_M and the chassis of the car, and the loading coil should then be adjusted for resonance at the desired frequency as indicated by a dip meter coupled to the loop at the base. Then the transmission line should be connected, and a check made with an SWR indicator connected at the transmitter end of the line.

With the line disconnected from the antenna again, C_M should be readjusted and the antenna returned to resonance by readjustment of the loading coil. The line should be connected again, and another check made with the SWR bridge. If the SWR is less than it was on the first trial, C_M should be readjusted in the same direction until the point of minimum SWR is found. Then the coupling between the line and the transmitter can be adjusted for proper loading.

It will be noticed from Fig 30 that the inductive reactance varies only slightly over the range of antenna resistances likely to be encountered in mobile work. Therefore, most of the necessary adjustment is in the capacitor. The one-turn loop at the base should be removed at the conclusion of the adjustment and slight compensation made

at the loading coil to maintain resonance.

For manufactured loading coils that have no means for either adjusting or tapping into the inductance, here is a simple L-network matching method that requires no series inductor, and needs only a measurement of SWR to determine the value of the shunt matching capacitor C_M. By extending the whip slightly beyond its natural resonant length, the series inductance required for the L network appears in the feed-point impedance. At the correct length, the resulting parallel reactance component, X_L, causes the parallel resistance component, R_A, to equal the feed line characteristic impedance, Z_0 ohms. The match is accomplished by cancelling the parallel inductive reactance component, X_L, with shunt capacitor C_M, of equal but opposite reactance.

To perform the matching operation, first resonate the antenna at the desired frequency by adjusting the whip length for minimum SWR without the capacitor. The approximate value of X_L with the whip lengthened to make R_A equal to Z_0, may now be found from

$$X_L = Z_0 \times \sqrt{SWR}/(SWR - 1)$$

where SWR is that obtained at resonance. The reactance, X_C, of the shunt matching capacitor C_M is the negative of X_L. The capacitance of C_M may be determined for the desired frequency, f, in MHz from

$$C_M = 1 \times 10^6/2\pi f X_C \text{ pF}.$$

Form a capacitor, C_M, from a combination of fixed-mica capacitors in parallel, as needed, and connect the combination across the antenna input terminals as shown in Fig 30. Finally, increase the whip length in small increments until the minimum SWR is reached — it should be very low.

If a lower SWR is desired, a trimmer capacitor may be added to C_M, and by alternate adjustment of trimmer and whip length, a perfect 1:1 match can be obtained. Once C_M has been established for a given band, the antenna can then be matched at

other frequencies in the band by simply adjusting the whip length for minimum SWR. If an inductive rather than a capacitive shunt element is preferred, replace the capacitor with an inductor having the same absolute value of reactance, and shorten the whip instead of lengthening it from the natural resonant length.

Top-Loading Capacitance

Because the coil resistance varies with the inductance of the loading coil, the resistance can be reduced, beneficially, by reducing the number of turns on the coil. This can be done by adding capacitance to that portion of the mobile antenna that is *above* the loading coil (Fig 31). To achieve resonance, the inductance of the coil is reduced proportionally. Capacitive hats can consist of a single stiff wire, two wires or more, or a disc made up from several wires like the spokes of a wheel. A solid metal disc can also be used. The larger the capacitive hat, in terms of surface area, the greater the capacitance. The greater the capacitance, the smaller the amount of inductance needed in the loading coil for a given resonant frequency.

There are two schools of thought concerning the attributes of center-loading and base-loading. It has not been established that one system is superior to the other, especially in the lower part of the HF spectrum. For this reason both base and center-loading schemes are popular. Capacitive-hat loading is applicable to either system. Since more inductance is required for center-loaded whips to make them resonant at a given frequency, capacitive hats should be particularly useful in improving their efficiency.

The capacitance that is increased by the hat is the total antenna-to-ground and vehicle capacitance, which provides the path for the antenna currents to return to the generator or transmitter. To obtain optimum effectiveness, the hat should be placed at the top of the whip, which may require special mechanical considerations to keep the whip upright with wind loading. If the hat is large enough to be effective, only a negligible increase in capacitance will result from extending the whip above the hat. It is important to know that with center-loaded whips, the hat actually becomes more detrimental than helpful if placed directly above the loading coil. This incorrect placement causes an undesirable increase in hat-to-coil capacitance, which adds to the distributed capacitance of the coil, lowering the Q and increasing the coil resistance — just the opposite of the hat's intended purpose. Although often seen in this position, it is usually because of the mistaken notion that increased radiation results from the lower resonant SWR obtained by this incorrect placement. Such a placement does reduce feed-line load mismatch and SWR at resonance, but for the wrong reason. The total antenna-circuit load resistance is increased, bringing it closer to the 50-ohm impedance of the feed line. However, since this increase in load resistance is from the increased coil resistance, and not from an increase in radiation resistance, reducing the SWR in this manner increases the loss instead of the radiation. It is also for this reason that loading coils of the highest Q should be favored above the coils of lower Q used by some manufacturers to enable them to advertise a lower SWR. The rule to follow then, is that, since the coil with the highest Q has the lowest loss resistance, the coil that yields the highest SWR at resonance (without any matching circuitry) will produce the greatest radiation.

Building High-Performance VHF and UHF Yagis

This construction information is presented as an introduction to the three high-performance VHF/UHF Yagis that follow. All were designed and built by Steve Powlishen, K1FO.

For years the design of long Yagi antennas seemed to be a mystical black art. The problem of simultaneously optimizing 20 or more element spacings and element lengths presented an almost unsolvable set of simultaneous equations. With the unprecedented increase in computer power and widespread availability of antenna analysis software, we are now able to quickly examine many Yagi designs and determine which approaches work and which designs to avoid.

At 144 MHz and above, most operators desire Yagi antennas two or more wavelengths in length. This length (2 λ) is where most classical designs start to fall apart in terms of gain per boom length, bandwidth and pattern quality. Extensive computer and antenna range analysis has proven that the best possible design is a Yagi that has both varying element spacings and varying element lengths.

This logarithmic-design approach (pioneered by Gunter Hoch, DL6WU, and others) starts with closely spaced directors. The director spacings gradually increase until a constant spacing of about 0.4 λ is reached. Conversely, the director lengths start out longest with the first director and decrease in length in a decreasing rate of change until they are virtually constant in length. This method of construction results in a wide gain bandwidth. A bandwidth of 7% of the center frequency at the −1 dB forward-gain points is typical for these Yagis even when they are longer than 10 λ. The log-taper design also reduces the rate of change in driven-element impedance v frequency. This allows the use of simple dipole driven elements while still obtaining acceptable driven-element SWR over a wide frequency range. Another benefit is that the resonant frequency of the Yagi changes very little as the boom length is increased.

The driven-element impedance also changes moderately with boom length. The tapered approach creates a Yagi with a very clean radiation pattern. Typically, first side lobe levels of − 17 dB in the E plane, − 15 dB in the H plane, and all other lobes at − 20 dB or more are possible on designs from 2 λ to more than 14 λ.

The actual rate of change in element lengths is determined by the diameter of the elements (in wavelengths). The spacings can be optimized for an individual boom length or chosen as a best compromise for most boom lengths.

The gain of long Yagis has been the subject of much debate. Recent measurements and computer analysis by both amateurs and professionals indicates that given an optimum design, doubling a Yagi's boom length will result in a maximum theoretical gain increase of about 2.6 dB. In practice, the real gain increase may be even less because of escalating resistive losses and the greater possibility of construction error. Fig 32 shows the maximum possible gain per boom length expressed in decibels, referenced to an isotropic radiator. The actual number of directors does not play an important part in determining the gain v boom length as long as a reasonable number of directors are used. The use of more directors per boom length will normally give a wider gain bandwidth, however, a point exists where too many directors will adversely affect all performance aspects.

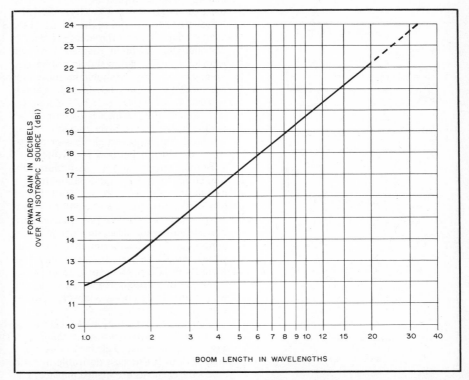

Fig 32—This chart shows maximum gain per boom length for optimally designed long Yagi antennas.

While short antennas (<1.5 λ) may show increased gain with the use of quad or loop elements, long Yagis (>2 λ) will not exhibit measurably greater forward gain or pattern integrity with loop-type elements. Similarly, loops used as driven elements and reflectors will not significantly change the properties of a long log-taper Yagi. Multiple-dipole driven-element assemblies will also not result in any significant gain increase per given boom length when compared to single-dipole feeds. Multiple-dipole feeds (such as log-periodic feeds), however, can be used to increase the SWR bandwidth of a Yagi.

Once a long-Yagi director string is properly tuned, the reflector becomes non critical. Reflector spacings between 0.15 λ and 0.2 λ are preferred. The spacing can be chosen for best pattern and driven-element impedance. Multiple-reflector arrangements will not significantly increase the forward gain of a Yagi which has its directors properly optimized for forward gain. Many multiple-reflector schemes such as tri-reflectors and corner reflectors have the disadvantage of lowering the driven-element impedance compared to a single optimum-length reflector. The plane or grid reflector, shown in Fig 33, may reduce the intensity of unwanted rear lobes. This can be used to reduce noise pickup on EME or satellite arrays. This type of reflector will usually increase the driven-element impedance compared to a single reflector. This sometimes makes driven-element matching easier. Keep in mind that even for EME, a plane reflector will add considerable wind

Fig 34—Yagi element correction v boom diameter. Curve A is for elements mounted through a round or square conductive boom, with the elements in mechanical contact with the boom. Curve B is for insulated elements mounted through a conductive boom, and for elements mounted on top of a conductive boom (elements make electrical contact with the boom). The patterns were corrected to computer simulations to determine Yagi tuning. The amount of element correction is not affected by element diameter.

Fig 33—Front and side views of a plane-reflector antenna.

load and weight for only a few tenths of a decibel of receive signal-to-noise improvement.

Yagi Construction

Normally, aluminum tubing or rod is used for Yagi elements. Hard-drawn enamel-covered copper wire can also be used on Yagis above 420 MHz. Resistive losses are proportional to the square of the element diameter and the square root of its conductivity. Element diameters of less than 3/16 inch or 4 mm should not be used on any band. The size should be chosen for reasonable strength. Half-inch diameter is suitable for 50 MHz, 3/16 to 3/8 inch for 144 MHz and 3/16 inch is recommended for the higher bands. Steel, including stainless steel and unprotected brass or copper wire, should not be used for elements.

Boom material may be aluminum tubing, either square or round. High-strength aluminum alloys such as 6061-T6 or 6063-T651 offer the best strength-to-weight advantages. Fiberglass poles have been used (where available as surplus). Wood is a popular low-cost boom material. The wood should be well seasoned and free from knots. Clear pine, spruce and Douglas fir are often used. The wood should be well treated to avoid water absorption and warping.

Elements may be mounted insulated or uninsulated, above or through the boom. Mounting uninsulated elements through a metal boom is the least desirable method unless the elements are welded in place. The Yagi elements will oscillate, even in moderate winds. Over several years this

element oscillation will work open the boom holes. This will allow the elements to move in the boom. This will create noise (in your receiver) when the wind blows, as the element contact changes. Eventually the element-to-boom junction will corrode (aluminum oxide is a good insulator). This loss of electrical contact between the boom and element will reduce the boom's effect and lower the resonant frequency of the Yagi.

Noninsulated elements mounted above the boom will perform fine as long as a good mechanical connection is made. Insulating blocks mounted above the boom will also work, but they require additional fabrication. One of the most popular construction methods is to mount the elements through the boom using insulating shoulder washers. This method is lightweight and durable. Its main disadvantage is difficult disassembly, making this method of limited use for portable arrays.

If a conductive boom is used, element lengths must be corrected for the mounting method used. The amount of correction is dependent upon the boom diameter in wavelengths. See Fig 34. Elements mounted through the boom and not insulated require the greatest correction. Mounting on top of or through the boom on insulated shoulder washers requires about half of the through-the-boom correction. Insulated elements mounted at least one element diameter above the boom require no correction over the free-space length.

The three following antennas have been optimized for typical boom lengths on each band.

A High-Performance 432-MHz Yagi

This 22-element, 6.1-λ, 432-MHz Yagi was originally designed for use in a 12-Yagi EME array built by K1FO. A lengthy evaluation and development process preceded its construction. Many designs were considered and then analyzed on the computer. Next, test models were constructed and evaluated on a home-made antenna range. The resulting design is based on W1EJ's computer-optimized spacings.

The attention paid to the design process has been worth the effort. The 22-element Yagi not only has exceptional forward gain (17.9 dBi), but has an unusually "clean" radiation pattern. The measured E-plane pattern is shown in Fig 35. Note that a 1-dB-per-division axis is used to show pattern detail. A complete description of the design process and construction methods appears in December 1987 and January 1988 QST.

Like other log-taper Yagi designs, this one can easily be adapted to other boom lengths. Versions of this Yagi have been built by several amateurs. Boom lengths ranged between 5.3 λ (20 elements) and 12.2 λ (37 elements).

The size of the original Yagi (169 inches long, 6.1 λ) was chosen so the antenna could be built from small-diameter boom material (7/8 inch and 1 inch round 6061-T6 aluminum) and still survive high winds and ice loading. The 22-element Yagi weighs about 3.5 pounds and has a wind load of approximately 0.8 square foot. This allows a high-gain EME array to be built with manageable wind load and weight. This same low wind load and weight lets the tropo operator add a high-performance 432-MHz array to an existing tower without sacrificing antennas on other bands.

Table 8 lists the gain and stacking specifications for the various length Yagis. The basic Yagi dimensions are shown in Table 9. These are free-space element lengths for 3/16-inch-diameter elements. Boom corrections for the element mounting method must be added in. The element-length correction column gives the length that must be added to keep the Yagi's center frequency optimized for use at 432 MHz. This correction is required to use the same spacing pattern over a wide range of boom lengths. Although any length Yagi will work well, this design is at its best when made with 18 elements or more (4.6 λ). Element material of less than 3/16-inch diameter is not recommended because resistive losses will reduce the gain by about 0.1 dB, and wet-weather performance will be worse.

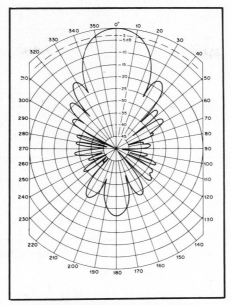

Fig 35—Measured E-plane pattern for the 22-element Yagi. Note: This antenna pattern is drawn on a linear dB grid, rather than on the standard ARRL log-periodic grid.

Quarter-inch-diameter elements could be used if all elements are shortened by 3 mm. The element lengths are intended for use with a slight chamfer (0.5 mm) cut into the element ends. The gain peak of the array is centered at 437 MHz. This allows acceptable wet-weather performance, while reducing the gain at 432 MHz by only 0.05 dB.

The gain bandwidth of the 22-element Yagi is 31 MHz (at the −1 dB points). The SWR of the Yagi is less than 1.4:1 between 420 and 440 MHz. Fig 36 is a network analyzer plot of the driven-element SWR v frequency. These numbers indicate just how wide the frequency response of a log-taper Yagi can be, even with a simple dipole driven element. In fact, at one antenna gain contest, some ATV operators conducted gain v frequency measurements from 420 to 440 MHz. The 22-element Yagi beat all entrants including those with so-called broadband feeds.

To peak the Yagi for use on 435 MHz (for satellite use), you may want to shorten all the elements by 2 mm. To peak it for use on 438 MHz (for ATV applications),

Table 8
Specifications for 432-MHz Yagi Family

No. of El	Boom length (λ)	Gain (dBi)*	FB ratio (dB)	DE impd (ohms)	Beamwidth E / H (°)	Stacking E / H (inches)
15	3.4	15.67	21	23	30 / 32	53 / 49
16	3.8	16.05	19	23	29 / 31	55 / 51
17	4.2	16.45	20	27	28 / 30	56 / 53
18	4.6	16.8	25	32	27 / 29	58 / 55
19	4.9	17.1	25	30	26 / 28	61 / 57
20	5.3	17.4	21	24	25.5 / 27	62 / 59
21	5.7	17.65	20	22	25 / 26.5	63 / 60
22	6.1	17.9	22	25	24 / 26	65 / 62
23	6.5	18.15	27	30	23.5 / 25	67 / 64
24	6.9	18.35	29	29	23 / 24	69 / 66
25	7.3	18.55	23	25	22.5 / 23.5	71 / 68
26	7.7	18.8	22	22	22 / 23	73 / 70
27	8.1	19.0	22	21	21.5 / 22.5	75 / 72
28	8.5	19.20	25	25	21 / 22	77 / 75
29	8.9	19.4	25	25	20.5 / 21.5	79 / 77
30	9.3	19.55	26	27	20 / 21	80 / 78
31	9.7	19.7	24	25	19.6 / 20.5	81 / 79
32	10.2	19.8	23	22	19.3 / 20	82 / 80
33	10.6	19.9	23	23	19 / 19.5	83 / 81
34	11.0	20.05	25	22	18.8 / 19.2	84 / 82
35	11.4	20.2	27	25	18.5 / 19.0	85 / 83
36	11.8	20.3	27	26	18.3 / 18.8	86 / 84
37	12.2	20.4	26	26	18.1 / 18.6	87 / 85
38	12.7	20.5	25	25	18.9 / 18.4	88 / 86
39	13.1	20.6	25	23	18.7 / 18.2	89 / 87
40	13.5	20.8	26	21	17.5 / 18	90 / 88

*Gain is approximate real gain based upon gain measurements made on six different-length Yagis.

Table 9

Free-Space Dimensions for 432-MHz Yagi Family

Element lengths are for 3/16-inch-diameter material.

El No.	Element Position (mm from rear of boom)	Element Length (mm)	Element Correction*
REF	0	340	
DE	104	334	
D1	146	315	
D2	224	306	
D3	332	299	
D4	466	295	
D5	622	291	
D6	798	289	
D7	990	287	
D8	1196	285	
D9	1414	283	
D10	1642	281	−2
D11	1879	279	−2
D12	2122	278	−2
D13	2373	277	−2
D14	2629	276	−2
D15	2890	275	−1
D16	3154	274	−1
D17	3422	273	−1
D18	3693	272	0
D19	3967	271	0
D20	4242	270	0
D21	4520	269	0
D22	4798	269	0
D23	5079	268	0
D24	5360	268	+1
D25	5642	267	+1
D26	5925	267	+1
D27	6209	266	+1
D28	6494	266	+1
D29	6779	265	+2
D30	7064	265	+2
D31	7350	264	+2
D32	7636	264	+2
D33	7922	263	+2
D34	8209	263	+2
D35	8496	262	+2
D36	8783	262	+2
D37	9070	261	+3
D38	9359	261	+3

*Element correction is the amount to shorten or lengthen all elements when building a Yagi of that length.

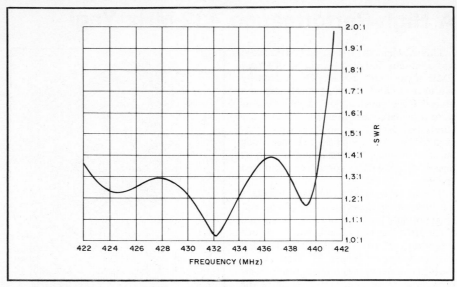

Fig 36—SWR performance of the 22-element Yagi in dry weather.

Fig 37—Element-mounting detail. Elements are mounted through the boom using plastic insulators. Push-nut retaining rings hold the element in place.

(A)

(B)

Fig 38—Several views of the driven element and T match.

shorten all elements by 4 mm. If you want to use the Yagi on FM between 440 MHz and 450 MHz, shorten all the elements by 10 mm. This will provide 17.6 dBi gain at 440 MHz, and 18.0 dBi gain at 450 MHz. The driven element may have to be adjusted if the element lengths are shortened.

Although this Yagi design is relatively broadband, it is suggested that close attention be paid to copying the design exactly as built. Metric dimensions are used because they are convenient for a Yagi sized for 432 MHz. Element holes should be drilled within ±2 mm. Element lengths should be kept within ±0.5 mm. Elements can be accurately constructed if they are first rough cut with a hack saw and then held in a vise and filed to the exact length.

The larger the array, the more attention you should pay to making all Yagis identical. Elements are mounted on shoulder insulators and run through the boom (see Fig 37). The element retainers are push nuts, preferably made from stainless steel. These are made by several companies, including Industrial Retaining Ring Co in Irvington, New Jersey, and AuVeco in Ft Mitchell, Kentucky. Local industrial hardware distributors can usually order them for you. The element insulators are not critical. Teflon® or black polyethylene are probably the best materials. The Yagi in the photographs is made with black Delryn insulators, available from Rutland Arrays in New Cumberland, Pennsylvania.

The driven element uses a UG-58A/U connector mounted on a small bracket. The UG-58A/U should be the type with the

Table 10

Dimensions for the 22-Element 432-MHz Yagi

Element Number	Element Position (mm from rear of boom)	Element Length (mm)	Boom Diam (in)
REF	30	346	
DE	134	340	
D1	176	321	
D2	254	311	7/8
D3	362	305	
D4	496	301	
D5	652	297	
D6	828	295	
D7	1020	293	
D8	1226	291	
D9	1444	289	
D10	1672	288	
D11	1909	286	1
D12	2152	285	
D13	2403	284	
D14	2659	283	
D15	2920	281	
D16	3184	280	
D17	3452	279	
D18	3723	278	7/8
D19	3997	277	
D20	4272	276	

Fig 39—Details of the driven element and T match for the 22-element Yagi. Lengths are given in millimeters to allow precise duplication of the antenna. See text.

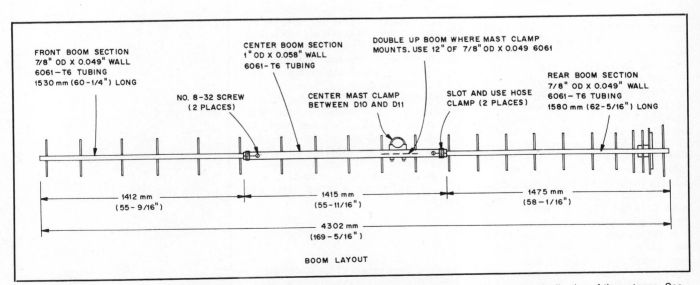

Fig 40—Boom-construction information for the 22-element Yagi. Lengths are given in millimeters to allow precise duplication of the antenna. See text.

Table 11

Dimensions for the 33-Element 432-MHz Yagi

Element Number	Element Position (mm from rear of boom)	Element Length (mm)	Boom Diam (in)
REF	30	348	
DE	134	342	
D1	176	323	
D2	254	313	
D3	362	307	
D4	496	303	1
D5	652	299	
D6	828	297	
D7	1020	295	
D8	1226	293	
D9	1444	291	
D10	1672	290	
D11	1909	288	
D12	2152	287	
D13	2403	286	1-1/8
D14	2659	285	
D15	2920	284	
D16	3184	284	
D17	3452	283	
D18	3723	282	1-1/4
D19	3997	281	
D20	4272	280	
D21	4550	278	
D22	4828	278	
D23	5109	277	1-1/8
D24	5390	277	
D25	5672	276	
D26	5956	275	
D27	6239	274	
D28	6524	274	
D29	6809	273	1
D30	7094	273	
D31	7380	272	

Fig 41—Boom-construction information for the 33-element Yagi. Lengths are given in millimeters to allow precise duplication of the antenna.

Fig 42—Details of the driven element and T match for the 33-element Yagi. Lengths are given in millimeters to allow precise duplication of the antenna.

press-in center pin. UG-58s with center pins held in by "C" clips will usually leak water. Some connectors use steel retaining clips, which will rust and leave a conductive stripe across the insulator. The T-match wires are supported by the UT-141 balun. RG-303/U or RG-142/U Teflon®-insulated cable could be used if UT-141 cannot be obtained. Figs 38A and 38B show details of the driven-element construction. Driven-element dimensions are given in Fig 39.

Dimensions for the 22-element Yagi are listed in Table 10. Fig 40 details the Yagi's boom layout. Element material can be either 3/16-inch 6061-T6 aluminum rod or hard aluminum welding rod.

A 24-foot-long, 10.6-λ, 33-element Yagi was also built. The construction methods used were the same as the 22-element Yagi. Telescoping round boom sections of 1, 1-1/8, and 1-1/4 inches in diameter were used. A boom support is required to keep

boom sag acceptable. At 432 MHz, if boom sag is much more than two or three inches, H-plane pattern distortion will occur. Greater amounts of boom sag will reduce the gain of a Yagi. Table 11 lists the proper dimensions for the antenna when built with the previously given boom diameters. The boom layout is shown in Fig 41, and the driven element is described in Fig 42. The 33-element Yagi exhibits the same clean pattern traits as the 22-element Yagi (see Fig 43). Measured gain of the 33-element Yagi is 19.9 dBi at 432 MHz. A measured gain sweep of the 33-element Yagi gave a −1 dB gain bandwidth of 14 MHz with the −1 dB points at 424.5 MHz and 438.5 MHz.

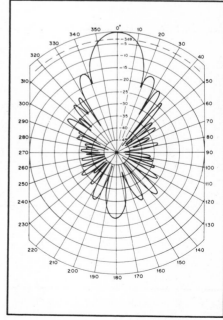

Fig 43—E-plane pattern for the 33-element Yagi. This pattern is drawn on a linear dB grid scale, rather than the standard ARRL log-periodic grid.

A High-Performance 144-MHz Yagi

This 144-MHz Yagi design utilizes the latest log-tapered element spacings and lengths. It offers near-theoretical gain per boom length, an extremely clean pattern and wide bandwidth.

The design is based upon the spacings used in a 4.5-λ 432-MHz computer-developed design by W1EJ. It is quite similar to the 432-MHz Yagi described elsewhere in this chapter. Refer to that project for additional construction diagrams and photographs.

Mathematical models do not always directly translate into real working examples. Although the computer design provided a good starting point, the author, Steve Powlishen, K1FO, built several test models before the final working Yagi was obtained. This hands-on tuning included changing the element-taper rate in order to obtain the flexibility that allows the Yagi to be built with different boom lengths.

The design is suitable for use from 1.8 λ (10 elements) to 5.1 λ (19 elements). When elements are added to a Yagi, the center frequency, feed impedance and front-to-back ratio will range up and down. A modern tapered design will minimize this effect and allow the builder to select any desired boom length. This Yagi's design capabilities per boom length are listed in Table 12.

The gain of any Yagi built around this design will be within 0.1 to 0.2 dB of the maximum theoretical gain at the design frequency of 144.2 MHz. The design is intentionally peaked high in frequency (calculated gain peak is about 144.7 MHz). It has been found that by doing this, the SWR bandwidth and pattern at 144.0 to 144.3 MHz will be better, the Yagi will

be less affected by weather and its performance in arrays will be more predictable. This design starts to drop off in performance if built with fewer than 10 elements. At less than 2 λ, more traditional designs perform well.

Table 13 gives free-space element lengths for ¼-inch-diameter elements. The use of metric notation allows for much easier dimensional changes during the design stage. Once you become familiar with the metric system, you'll probably find that construction is easier without the burden of cumbersome English fractional units. For 3/16-inch-diameter elements, lengthen all parasitic elements by 3 mm. If 3/8-inch-

diameter elements are used, shorten all of the directors and the reflector by 6 mm. The driven element will have to be adjusted for the individual Yagi if the 12-element design is not adhered to.

For the 12-element Yagi, ¼-inch-diameter elements were selected because smaller-diameter elements become rather flimsy at 2 meters. Other-diameter elements can be used as described previously. The 2.5-λ boom was chosen because it has an excellent size and wind load v gain and pattern trade-off. The size is also convenient; three 6-foot-long pieces of aluminum tubing can be used without any waste. The relatively large-diameter boom sizes (1-1/4

Table 12
Specifications for the 144-MHz Yagi Family

No. of El	Boom Length (λ)	Gain (dBd)	DE impd (ohms)	FB Ratio (dB)	Beamwidth E / H (°)	Stacking E / H (feet)
10	1.8	11.4	27	17	39 / 42	10.2 / 9.5
11	2.2	12.0	38	19	36 / 40	11.0 / 10.0
12	2.5	12.5	28	23	34 / 37	11.7 / 10.8
13	2.9	13.0	23	20	32 / 35	12.5 / 11.4
14	3.2	13.4	27	18	31 / 33	12.8 / 12.0
15	3.6	13.8	35	20	30 / 32	13.2 / 12.4
16	4.0	14.2	32	24	29 / 30	13.7 / 13.2
17	4.4	14.5	25	23	28 / 29	14.1 / 13.6
18	4.8	14.8	25	21	27 / 28.5	14.6 / 13.9
19	5.2	15.0	30	22	26 / 27.5	15.2 / 14.4

Table 13
Free-Space Dimensions for the 144-MHz Yagi Family

Element diameter is ¼ inch.

El No.	Element Position (mm from rear of boom)	Element Length (mm)
REF	0	1038
DE	312	955
D1	447	956
D2	699	932
D3	1050	916
D4	1482	906
D5	1986	897
D6	2553	891
D7	3168	887
D8	3831	883
D9	4527	879
D10	5259	875
D11	6015	870
D12	6786	865
D13	7566	861
D14	8352	857
D15	9144	853
D16	9942	849
D17	10744	845

Fig 44—Boom layout for the 12-element 144-MHz Yagi. Lengths are given in millimeters to allow precise duplication.

DRIVEN ELEMENT DETAIL 12 ELEMENT 144 MHz YAGI

INCHES = mm x 0.0394

Fig 45—Driven-element detail for the 12-element 144-MHz Yagi. Lengths are given in millimeters to allow precise duplication.

MATERIAL: RG-142/U OR RG-303/U
TEFLON-INSULATED COAXIAL CABLE

and 1-3/8 inches) were chosen, as they provide an extremely rugged Yagi that does not require a boom support. The 12-element 17-foot-long design has a calculated wind survival of close to 120 mi/h! The absence of a boom support also makes vertical polarization possible.

Longer versions could be made by telescoping smaller-size boom sections into the last section. Some sort of boom support will be required on versions longer than 22 feet. The elements are mounted on shoulder insulators and mounted through the boom. However, elements may be mounted, insulated or uninsulated, above or through the boom, as long as appropriate element-length corrections are made. Proper tuning can be verified by checking the depth of the nulls between the main lobe and first side lobes. The nulls should be 5 to 10 dB below the first side-lobe level at the primary operating frequency. The boom layout for the 12-element model is shown in Fig 44. The actual corrected element dimensions for the 12-element 2.5-λ Yagi are shown in Table 14.

The design may also be cut for use at 147 MHz. There is no need to change element spacings. The element lengths should be shortened by 17 mm for best operation between 146 and 148 MHz. Again, the driven element will have to be adjusted as required.

The driven-element size (½-inch diameter) was chosen to allow easy impedance matching. Any reasonably sized driven element could be used, as long as appropriate length and T-match adjustments are made. Different driven-element dimensions are required if you change the boom length. The calculated natural driven-element impedance is given as a guideline. A balanced T-match was chosen because it's easy to adjust for best SWR and provides a balanced radiation pattern. A 4:1 half-wave coaxial balun is used, although impedance-transforming quarter-wave

Table 14
Dimensions for the 12-Element 2.5-λ Yagi

Element Number	Element Position (mm from rear of boom)	Element Length (mm)	Boom Diam (in)
REF	0	1044	
DE	312	955	
D1	447	962	1-1/4
D2	699	938	
D3	1050	922	
D4	1482	912	
D5	1986	904	
D6	2553	898	1-3/8
D7	3168	894	
D8	3831	889	
D9	4527	885	1-1/4
D10	5259	882	

sleeve baluns could also be used. The calculated natural impedance will be useful in determining what impedance transformation will be required at the 200-ohm balanced feed point. *The ARRL Antenna Book* contains information on calculating folded-dipole and T-match driven-element parameters. A balanced feed is important for best operation. Gamma matches will severely distort the pattern balance. Other useful driven-element arrangements are the Delta match and the folded dipole, if you're willing to sacrifice some flexibility. Fig 45 details the driven-element dimensions.

A noninsulated driven element was chosen for mounting convenience. An insulated driven element may also be used. A grounded driven element may be less affected by static build-up. On the other hand, an insulated driven element allows the operator to easily check his feed lines for water or other contamination by the use of an ohmmeter from the shack.

Fig 46 shows computer-predicted E- and H-plane radiation patterns for the 12-element Yagi. The patterns are plotted on a 1-dB-per-division linear scale instead of the

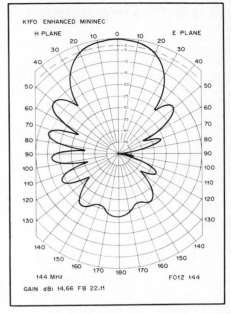

Fig 46—H- and E-plane pattern for the 12-element 144-MHz Yagi.

usual ARRL polar-plot graph. This expanded scale plot is used to show greater pattern detail. The pattern for the 12-element Yagi is so clean that a plot done in the standard ARRL format would be almost featureless, except for the main lobe and first sidelobes.

The excellent performance of the 12-element Yagi is demonstrated by the reception of Moon echoes from several of the larger 144-MHz EME stations with only one 12-element Yagi. Four of the 12-element Yagis will make an excellent starter EME array, capable of working many EME QSOs while being relatively small in size. The advanced antenna builder can use the information in Table 11 to design a "dream" array of virtually any size.

A High-Performance 222-MHz Yagi

Modern tapered Yagi designs are easily applied to 222 MHz. This design uses a spacing progression that is in between the 12-element 144-MHz design, and the 22-element 432-MHz design presented elsewhere in this chapter. The result is a design with maximum gain per boom length, a clean, symmetrical radiation pattern, and wide bandwidth. Although it was designed for weak-signal work (tropospheric scatter and EME), the design is suited to all modes of 222-MHz operation, such as packet radio, FM repeater operation and control links.

The spacings were chosen as the best compromise for a 3.9-λ 16-element Yagi. The 3.9-λ design was chosen, like the 12-element 144-MHz design, because it fits perfectly on a boom made from three 6-foot-long aluminum tubing sections. The design is quite extensible, and models from 12 elements (2.4 λ) to 22 elements (6.2 λ) can be built from the dimensions given in Table 15. Note that free-space lengths are given. They must be corrected for the element mounting method. Specifications for various boom lengths are shown in Table 16.

Construction

Large-diameter (1-1/4- and 1-3/8-inch-diameter) boom construction is used, eliminating the need for boom supports. The Yagi can also be used vertically polarized. Three-sixteenths-inch-diameter aluminum elements are used. The exact alloy is not critical; 6061-T6 was used, but hard aluminum welding rod is also suitable. Quarter-inch-diameter elements could also be used if all elements are shortened by 3 mm. Three-eighths-inch-diameter elements would require 10 mm shorter lengths. Elements smaller than 3/16-inch-diameter are not recommended. The elements are insulated and run through the boom. Plastic shoulder washers and stainless steel retainers are used to hold the elements in

place. The various pieces needed to build the Yagi may be obtained from Rutland Arrays, 1703 Warren St, New Cumberland, PA 17010. Fig 47 details the boom layout for the 16-element Yagi. Table 17 gives the dimensions for the 16-element Yagi as built. The driven element is fed with a T match and a 4:1 balun. See Fig 48 for construction details. See the 432-MHz Yagi project elsewhere in this chapter for additional photographs and construction diagrams.

The Yagi has a relatively broad gain and SWR curve, as is typical of a tapered design, making it usable over a wide frequency range. The example dimensions are intended for use at 222.0 to 222.5 MHz. The 16-element Yagi is quite usable to more than 223 MHz. The best compromise for covering the entire band is to shorten all parasitic elements by 4 mm. The driven element will have to be adjusted in length for best match. The position of the T-wire shorting straps may also have to be moved.

The aluminum boom provides superior strength, is lightweight, and has a low wind-load cross section. Aluminum is doubly attractive, as it will long outlast

Table 15
Free-Space Dimensions for the 222-MHz Yagi Family

Element diameter is 3/16-inch.

El No.	Element Position (mm from rear of boom)	Element Length (mm)
REF	0	676
DE	204	647
D1	292	623
D2	450	608
D3	668	594
D4	938	497
D5	1251	581
D6	1602	576
D7	1985	573
D8	2395	569
D9	2829	565
D10	3283	562
D11	3755	558
D12	4243	556
D13	4745	554
D14	5259	553
D15	5783	552
D16	6315	551
D17	6853	550
D18	7395	549
D19	7939	548
D20	8483	547

Table 16
Specifications for the 222-MHz Yagi Family

No. of El	Boom Length (λ)	Gain (dBd)	FB Ratio (dB)	DE Impd (ohms)	Beamwidth E / H (°)	Stacking E / H (feet)
12	2.4	12.3	22	23	37 / 39	7.1 / 6.7
13	2.8	12.8	19	28	33 / 36	7.8 / 7.2
14	3.1	13.2	20	34	32 / 34	8.1 / 7.6
15	3.5	13.6	24	30	30 / 33	8.6 / 7.8
16	3.9	14.0	23	23	29 / 31	8.9 / 8.3
17	4.3	14.35	20	24	28 / 30.5	9.3 / 8.5
18	4.6	14.7	20	29	27 / 29	9.6 / 8.9
19	5.0	15.0	22	33	26 / 28	9.9 / 9.3
20	5.4	15.3	24	29	25 / 27	10.3 / 9.6
21	5.8	15.55	23	24	24.5 / 26.5	10.5 / 9.8
22	6.2	15.8	21	23	24 / 26	10.7 / 10.2

Fig 47—Boom layout for the 16-element 222-MHz Yagi. Lengths are given in millimeters to allow precise duplication.

Table 17

Dimensions for 16-Element 3.9-λ 222-MHz Yagi

Element Number	Element Position (mm from rear of boom)	Element Length (mm)	Boom Diam (in)
REF		683	
DE	204	664	
D1	292	630	
D2	450	615	1-1/4"
D3	668	601	
D4	938	594	
D5	1251	588	
D6	1602	583	
D7	1985	580	
D8	2395	576	1-3/8"
D9	2829	572	
D10	3283	569	
D11	3755	565	
D12	4243	563	
D13	4745	561	1-1/4"
D14	5259	560	

Fig 48—Driven-element detail for the 16-element 222-MHz Yagi. Lengths are given in millimeters to allow precise duplication.

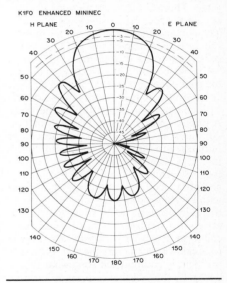

Fig 49—H- and E-plane patterns for the 16-element 222-MHz Yagi.

doubly attractive, as it will long outlast wood and fiberglass. Using state-of-the-art designs, it is unlikely that significant performance increases will be achieved in the next few years. Therefore, it's in your best interest to build an antenna that will last many years. If suitable wood or fiberglass poles are readily available, they may be used without any performance de-gradation, at least when the wood is new and dry. Use the free-space element lengths given in Table 16 for insulated-boom construction.

The pattern of the 16-element Yagi is shown in Fig 49. Like the 144-MHz Yagi, a 1-dB-per-division plot is used to detail the pattern accurately.

This 16-element design makes a good building block for EME or tropo DX arrays. Old-style narrow-band Yagis often perform unpredictably when used in arrays. The theoretical 3.0-dB stacking gain is rarely observed. The 16-element Yagi (and other versions of the design) reliably provides stacking gains of nearly 3 dB. (The spacing dimensions listed in Table 16 show just over 2.9 dB stacking gain.) This has been found to be the best compromise between gain, pattern integrity and array size. Any phasing line losses will subtract from the possible stacking gain. Mechanical misalignment will also degrade the performance of an array.

2-Meter, 5/8-Wavelength Vertical

Perhaps the most popular vertical antenna for FM mobile and fixed-station use is the 5/8-wavelength vertical. Compared to a 1/4-wavelength vertical, it has some gain over a dipole. Additionally, the so-called "picket fencing" type of flutter that results when the vehicle is in motion is greatly reduced when a 5/8-wavelength radiator is employed.

This style of antenna is suitable for mobile or fixed-station use because it is small, omnidirectional and can be used with radials or solid-plane ground (such as is afforded by the car body). If radials are used, they need be only ¼ wavelength or slightly longer. A 5 percent increase in length over ¼ wavelength is suggested for the radial wires or rods.

Construction

The antenna shown here is made from low-cost materials. Figs 50A and B show the base coil and aluminum mounting plate. The coil form is a piece of low-loss solid rod, such as Plexiglas or phenolic. The dimensions for this and other parts of the antenna are given in Fig 51. A length of brazing rod is used as the whip section.

The whip should be 47 inches long. Brazing rods come in standard 36-inch lengths, however, so it is necessary to solder an 11-inch extension to the top of the whip. A piece of no. 10 copper wire will suffice. Alternatively, a stainless-steel rod can be purchased to make a 47-inch whip. Shops that sell CB antennas should have such rods for replacement purposes on base-loaded antennas. The limitation one can expect with brazing rod is the relative fragility of the material, especially when the threads are cut for screwing the rod into the base-coil form. Excessive stress can cause the rod to break where it enters the coil form. The problem is complicated somewhat in this design by the fact that a spring is not used at the antenna mounting point. Innovators can find all manner of solutions to these problems by changing the physical design and using different materials when constructing the overall antenna. The main purpose of this description is to provide dimensions and tune-up data.

The aluminum mounting bracket must be shaped to fit the car with which it will be used. The bracket can be used to effect a "no-holes" mount. The inner lip of the vehicle trunk (or hood for front mounting) can be the point where the bracket attaches by means of no. 6 or no. 8 sheet-metal screws. The remainder of the bracket is bent so that when the trunk lid or car hood is raised and lowered, there is no contact between the bracket and the moving part. Details of the mounting unit are shown in Fig 51B. A 14-gauge metal thickness (or greater) is recommended for best rigidity.

There are 10½ turns of no. 10 or no. 12 copper wire wound on the ¾-inch-diameter

(A)

(B)

Fig 50—(A) A photograph of the 5/8-wavelength vertical base section. The matching coil is affixed to an aluminum bracket that screws onto the inner lip of the car trunk. (B) The completed assembly. The coil has been wrapped with electrical tape to prevent dirt and moisture from degrading performance.

Fig 51—Structural details for the 2-meter antenna are provided at A. The mounting bracket is shown at B and the equivalent circuit is given at C.

coil form. The tap on L1 is placed approximately four turns below the whip end. A secure solder joint is imperative.

Tune-Up

After the antenna has been affixed to the vehicle, insert an SWR indicator in the 50-Ω transmission line. Turn on the 2-meter transmitter and experiment with the coil-tap placement. If the whip section is 47 inches long, an SWR of 1:1 can be obtained

when the tap is at the right location. As an alternative to this method of adjustment, place the tap at four turns from the top of L1, make the whip 50 inches long and trim the whip length until an SWR of 1:1 is secured. Keep the antenna free of conductive objects or human bodies during tune-up, as conductive objects will detune the antenna and spoil the match. This antenna was described more completely in June 1979 *QST*, page 15.

A 5/8-Wavelength 222-MHz Mobile Antenna

This antenna, shown in Figs 52 and 53, was developed to fill the gap between a homemade ¼-wavelength mobile antenna and a commercially made 5/8-wavelength model. There have been other antennas made using modified CB models. This still presents the problem of cost in acquiring the original antenna. The major cost in this setup is the whip portion, which can be any tempered rod that will spring easily.

Construction

The base insulator portion is constructed of 1/2-inch Plexiglas rod. A few minutes work on a lathe was sufficient to shape and drill the rod. The bottom 1/2-inch of the rod is turned down to a diameter of 3/8 inch. This portion will now fit into a PL-259 UHF connector. A hole, 1/8-inch diameter, is drilled through the center of the rod. This hole will contain the wires that make the connections between the center conductor of the connector and the coil tap. The connection between the whip and the top of the coil is also run through this opening. A stud is force-fitted into the top of the Plexiglas rod. This allows the whip to be detached from the insulator portion.

The coil should be wound initially on a

Fig 52—Photograph of the 222-MHz, 5/8-wavelength mobile antenna. The bottom end of the coil is soldered to the coaxial connector.

form slightly smaller than the base insulator. When the coil is transferred to the Plexiglas rod it will keep its shape and will not readily move. After the tap point has been determined, a longitudinal hole is drilled into the center of the rod. A no. 22 wire can then be inserted through the center of the insulator into the connector. This method is also used to attach the whip to the top of the coil. After the whip has been fully assembled, a coating of epoxy cement

Fig 53—Diagram of the 222-MHz mobile antenna.

is applied. It seals the entire assembly and provides some additional strength. During a full winter's use there were no signs of cracking or mechanical failure. The adjustment procedure is the same as for the 2-meter antenna just described.

Quarter-Wave Vertical Antennas for 144, 222 and 440 MHz

Quarter-wave vertical antennas are useful for local communications when size, cost and ease of construction are important. For theoretical information about quarter-wave vertical antennas see the Antenna Fundamentals chapter of this book or *The ARRL Antenna Book*.

Construction Materials

The antennas shown in Figs 54 through 57 are each based on a coaxial connector. Use UHF or N connectors for the fixed-station antennas. BNC connectors are good for mobile antennas. BNC and N connectors are better than UHF connectors for VHF/UHF outdoor use because: (1) they provide a constant impedance over the frequencies of interest, and (2) they are weatherproof when the appropriate connector or cap is attached. The ground-plane antennas require a panel jack (it has mounting holes to hold the radials).

If the antenna is sheltered from weather, copper wire is sufficiently rigid for the element and radials. Antennas exposed to the weather should be made from 1/16- to 1/8-inch brass or stainless-steel rod.

Radials may be made from 3/16-inch aluminum rod or tubing and mounted on an aluminum sheet as shown in Fig 55. Do not use aluminum for the antenna element because it cannot be easily soldered to the coaxial-connector center pin.

Where the figures call for no. 4-40 hardware, stainless steel or brass is best. Use cadmium-plated hardware if stainless steel or brass is not available.

Fixed-Station Antennas

The ground-plane antenna in Fig 54 uses female chassis-mount connectors to support the element and four radials. If you have chosen large-diameter wire or tubing for the radials refer to Fig 55. Cut a metal sheet as shown (size is not critical, and the mounting tab is optional). Drill the sheet to accept the coaxial connector on hand (usually 11/16 inch) and the 4-40 hardware for the radials and connector. Bend the plate or radials as shown with the aid of a bench vise. Mount the coaxial connector and radials to the plate.

Small diameter (1/16-inch) radials may be attached directly to the mounting lugs of the coaxial connector with 4-40 hardware (Fig 57). To install 3/32- or 1/8-inch radials, bend a hook at one end of each radial for insertion through the connector lug. (You may need to enlarge the lug holes slightly for 1/8-inch rod.) Solder the radials (and hardware, if used) to the connector using a large soldering iron or propane torch.

Solder the element to the center pin of the connector. If the element does not fit inside the solder cup, use a short section of brass tubing as a coupler (a slotted

Fig 54—A simple ground-plane antenna for the 144, 222 and 440-MHz bands. The feed line and connector are inside the mast, and a hose clamp squeezes the slotted mast end to tightly grip the plug body. See Table 18 for element and radial measurements.

1/8-inch-ID tube will fit over an SO-239 or N-receptacle center pin).

One mounting method for fixed-station antennas appears in Fig 54. The method shown is probably the easiest and strongest. Alternatively, a tab (Fig 55D) or "L" bracket could be fastened to the side of a mast with a hose clamp. Once the antenna is mounted and tested, thoroughly seal the open side of the coaxial connector with RTV sealant, and weatherproof the connections with rust-preventative paint.

Mobile Applications

In order to achieve an omnidirectional radiation pattern, mobile vertical antennas should be located in the center of the vehicle roof. Practically, vertical antennas work

Table 18

¼-Wavelength Vertical Antenna Element and Radial Sizes

	Band		
	144 MHz	222 MHz	440 MHz
Lengths			
ℓ†	19¼″	12½″	6-5/16″
Diameters			
Brass rod	1/8″	3/32″	1/16″
Stainless-steel rod	3/32″	1/16″	1/16″

$$†\ell = \frac{234}{f}$$

where
ℓ = length, in ft
f = frequency, in MHz

Fig 55—Methods of mounting 3/16-inch aluminum-rod radials to a VHF/UHF ground-plane antenna. At A and B the radials are made approximately 1½ inches longer than ℓ, then bent (45°) and attached to a flat aluminum sheet. At C and D, the radials are somewhat shorter than ℓ, and the corners of the aluminum sheet are bent to provide the 45° angle. In both cases, ℓ is measured from the radial tip to the element. The size of the aluminum sheet is not critical. The mounting tab shown at D is optional; it could be added to the sheet in A and B, if desired.

well anywhere on a metal auto body (although the radiation pattern is not omnidirectional). In the interest of RF safety, antennas that are not mounted on the roof should be placed as far from the vehicle occupants as is practical.

The mobile antenna shown here is based on a mating pair of BNC connectors. (You could use similar techniques with N connectors.) If you plan to remove the antenna element, obtain a matching connector cap to protect the open jack from weather. The jack may be mounted directly through the vehicle body if you wish. If you do so, select a body panel with sufficient strength

to support the antenna, and be sure that there is adequate access to both sides of the panel for connector and cable installation.

Most home-made VHF and UHF mobile antennas are mounted on an 1/16-inch-thick aluminum L bracket, which is fastened to the side of the hood or trunk opening (see Fig 56A and B). If the opening lip slopes at the antenna location, the lower edge of the L bracket should match that slope. Hold the sheet against the inside of the opening lip, orient the sheet so that its top edge is parallel with the ground, and mark where the opening lip crosses the edges. Connect the marks with a straight

line, and cut the sheet on that line.

Drill the sheet as required for the coaxial connector, and bend as indicated. Mount the coaxial connector, and install the cable. Hold the bracket against the side of the opening, drill and secure it with two no. 6 or no. 8 sheet-metal screws and lock washers.

The antenna shown here was made for the 2-meter band. The element is about 19¼ inches of 1/8-inch brass rod (from a welding-supply store). Refer to Fig 56 and follow this procedure to install the element in the male BNC connector:
1) Prepare a special insulator from a 1-inch

(A)

BNC
PANEL
JACK

1-1/2"

VEHICLE HOOD
(SHOWN CLOSED)

1-1/2" MINIMUM

COAXIAL
CABLE

2 — NO, 6 OR NO. 8
SHEET—METAL
SCREWS

OPENING
LIP

(B)

OPENING LIP

(C)

SPECIAL INSULATOR (SEE TEXT)

3/32"   1/4"   1/2"

✱ SEE TABLE 18

INSTALL HEAT—SHRINK TUBING
IN THIS AREA

NO. 8 BRASS NUT
SOLDERED TO END
OF ELEMENT

(D)

1/8" BRASS ROD ELEMENT

ℓ ✱

Fig 56—Details of the mobile vertical mount and BNC center-pin connection. A shows a cross section of a typical vehicle hood opening with the hood closed. B shows the lower edge of the L bracket trimmed to match the slope of the hood (this ensures that the antenna is plumb). C shows the BNC center pin, the special insulator made from RG-58 and the end of the element shaped for connection. At D, the special insulator has been lashed to the element with fine bare wire and the center-pin positioned. The center-pin and lashing should be soldered, and the area indicated should be covered with heat-shrink tubing to prevent contact with the plug body when it is installed. The brass nut serves as eye protection.

Fig 57—A 440-MHz ground-plane antenna constructed using only an SO-239 connector, 4-40 hardware and 1/16-inch brass rod.

piece of RG-58 cable by removing all of the jacket and shield. Also remove the center-conductor insulation as shown.
2) File or grind an angle on the end of the brass rod.
3) Place the special insulator against the end of the brass rod and lash them together with fine bare wire.
4) Solder the wire, lashing and BNC center pin in place. (Use a light touch; too much heat causes the insulation to swell and makes it difficult to assemble the connector.)
5) Apply heat-shrink tubing to cover the special insulator and lashing. Place the tubing so that at least 1/8 inch of the special insulator remains exposed at the center-pin.
6) Place the element in the connector body and fill the back of the connector with epoxy to support the element. Install the BNC nut before the epoxy sets. (The BNC washer, clamp and gasket are discarded.)
7) Solder a no. 8 brass nut (or other rounded brass object) to the end of the element to serve as eye protection.

This general procedure can be adapted to all of the element materials recommended, and to N connectors as well.

Loop Yagis for 23 CM

Described here and shown in Figs 58 through 62 are loop Yagis for the 23-cm band. Several versions are described, so the builder can choose the boom length and frequency coverage desired for the task at hand. Mike Walters, G3JVL, brought the original loop Yagi design to the amateur community in the 1970s. Since then, many versions have been developed with different loop and boom dimensions. Chip Angle, N6CA, developed the antennas shown here.

Three sets of dimensions are given. Good performance can be expected if you follow the dimensions carefully. Recheck all dimensions before you cut or drill anything! The 1296-MHz version is intended for weak-signal operation at 1296 MHz, while the 1270-MHz version is optimized for FM and Mode L satellite work. The 1283-MHz antenna provides acceptable performance from 1280 to 1300 MHz.

These antennas have been built on 6- and 12-foot booms. Results of gain tests at VHF conferences and by individuals around the country peg the gain of the 6-footer at about 18 dBi, while the 12-foot version provides about 20.5 dBi. Swept measurements indicate that gain is about 2 dB down from maximum gain at ±30 MHz from the design frequency. SWR, however, deteriorates within a few megahertz on the low side of the design center frequency.

The Boom

The dimensions given here apply only to a ¾-inch-OD boom. If you change the boom size, the dimensions must be scaled accordingly. Many hardware stores carry aluminum tubing in 6- and 8-foot lengths, and that tubing is suitable for a short Yagi. If you plan a 12-foot antenna, you should find a piece of more rugged material, such as 6061-T6 grade aluminum. Do not use anodized tubing. The 12-foot antenna must be supported to minimize boom sag. The 6-foot version can be rear mounted. For rear mounting, allow 4.5 inches of boom behind the last reflector to eliminate SWR effects from the support.

The antenna is mounted to the mast with a gussett plate. The plate mounts at the boom center. See Fig 58. Drill the plate-mounting holes perpendicular to the element-mounting holes, assuming the antenna polarization is to be horizontal.

Elements will be mounted to the boom with no. 4-40 machine screws, so a series of no. 33 (0.113-inch) holes must be drilled along the center of the boom to accommodate this hardware. Fig 59 shows the

element spacings for different parts of the band. Tolerances should be followed as closely as possible.

Parasitic Elements

The reflectors and directors are cut from 0.0325-inch thick aluminum sheet and are ¼ inch wide. Fig 60 indicates the lengths for the various elements. These lengths apply only to elements cut from the specified material. For best results, the element strips should be cut with a shear. If you leave the edges sharp, birds won't sit on the elements!

Drill the mounting holes as shown in Fig 60. Measure carefully! After the holes are drilled, you must form each strap into a circle. This is easily done by wrapping the element around a round form (a small juice can works great).

Mount the loops to the boom with no. 4-40 × 1-inch machine screws, lock washers and nuts. See Fig 61. It's best to use stainless-steel or plated-brass hardware for everything. Although the initial cost is higher than for ordinary plated-steel hardware, stainless or brass hardware won't rust and need replacement after a few years. Unless the antenna is painted, it will definitely deteriorate.

Fig 58—Boom-to-mast plate details are given at A. B shows how the Yagi is mounted to the mast. A boom support for long antennas is shown in C. The arrangement shown in D and E may be used to rear mount antennas up to 6 or 7 feet long.

Driven Element

The driven element is cut from 0.0325-inch copper sheet and is ¼ inch wide. Drill three holes in the strap, as detailed in Fig 60. Trim the ends as shown and form the strap into a loop similar to the other elements. This antenna is like a quad; if the loop is fed at the top or bottom, it will be horizontally polarized.

Driven-element mounting details are shown in Fig 62. A mounting fixture is made from a ¼-20 × 1¼ inch brass bolt. File the bolt head to a thickness of 0.125 inch. Bore a 0.144-inch (no. 27 drill) hole lengthwise through the center of the bolt. A piece of 0.141-inch semi-rigid Hardline (UT-141 or equiv.) will mount through this hole and connect to the driven loop. The point at which the UT-141 passes through the copper loop and brass mounting fixture should be left unsoldered at this time to allow for matching adjustments when the antenna is completed, although the range of adjustment is not that great.

The UT-141 can be any convenient length. Attach the connector of your choice (preferably Type N). Use a short piece of low-loss RG-8 size cable (or better yet, ½-inch Hardline) for the run down the boom and mast to the main feed line. For best results, your main feed line should be the lowest-loss 50-ohm cable obtainable. Good 7/8-inch Hardline measures at 1.5 dB per 100 feet and virtually eliminates the need for remote mounting of the transmit amplifier.

Tuning the Driven Element

If you built the antenna carefully to the dimensions given, the SWR should be fine. Just to be sure, check the SWR if you have access to test equipment. You must be sure that your signal source is clean, however; wattmeters are often fooled by dirty signals and can give erroneous readings. If you have a problem, recheck all dimensions. If they look okay, a minor improvement may be realized by changing the shape of the driven element. Slight bending of reflector 2 may also help optimize SWR. When you have obtained the desired match, solder the point where the UT-141 jacket passes through the loop and brass bolt.

Quite a few people believe that practices common on lower frequencies can be used on 1296 MHz. That's the biggest reason that they don't work all the DX that there is to be worked!

First, when you have a design that's proven, copy it exactly—don't change it! This is especially true for antennas. Use the best feed line you can get. Why build an antenna if you are going to use lossy cable?

Here are some realistic measurements of common coaxial cables at 1296 MHz (loss per 100 feet): RG-8, 213, 214—11 dB;

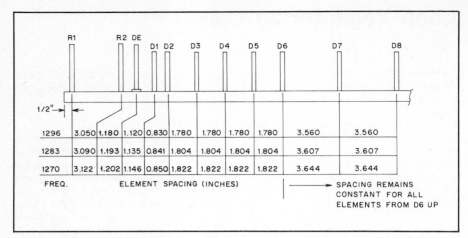

FREQ.	ELEMENT SPACING (INCHES)									
1296	3.050	1.180	1.120	0.830	1.780	1.780	1.780	1.780	3.560	3.560
1283	3.090	1.193	1.135	0.841	1.804	1.804	1.804	1.804	3.607	3.607
1270	3.122	1.202	1.146	0.850	1.822	1.822	1.822	1.822	3.644	3.644

SPACING REMAINS CONSTANT FOR ALL ELEMENTS FROM D6 UP

Fig 59—Boom drilling dimensions. Pick the version you want and follow these dimensions carefully. Spacing is the same for all directors after D6. Use as many as needed to fill up your boom.

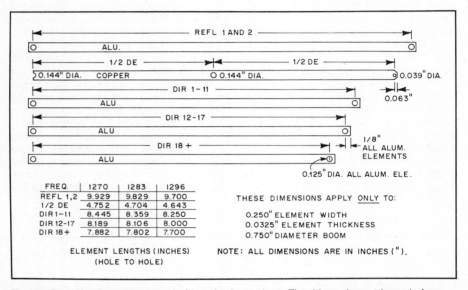

FREQ.	1270	1283	1296
REFL 1,2	9.929	9.829	9.700
1/2 DE	4.752	4.704	4.643
DIR 1–11	8.445	8.359	8.250
DIR 12–17	8.189	8.106	8.000
DIR 18+	7.882	7.802	7.700

ELEMENT LENGTHS (INCHES) (HOLE TO HOLE)

THESE DIMENSIONS APPLY ONLY TO:

0.250" ELEMENT WIDTH
0.0325" ELEMENT THICKNESS
0.750" DIAMETER BOOM

NOTE: ALL DIMENSIONS ARE IN INCHES (").

Fig 60—Parasitic elements are made from aluminum sheet. The driven element is made from copper sheet. The dimensions given are for ¼ inch wide by 0.0325-inch thick elements only. Lengths specified are hole-to-hole distances; the holes are located 0.125 inch in from each element end.

Fig 61—Element-to-boom mounting details.

½ inch foam/copper Hardline—4 dB; 7/8 inch foam/copper Hardline—1.5 dB.

Mount the antenna(s) to keep feed line loss to an absolute minimum. Antenna

DIELECTRIC 0.050"

SOLDER

Fig 62—Driven element details. See Fig 60 and the text for more information.

BOLT HEAD 1/8"

SOLDER

BOOM

1/4 - 20 BRASS BOLT

LOCKWASHER AND BRASS NUT

UT - 141 SEMI - RIGID COAX 52 Ω

TO CONNECTOR

height is less important than keeping the line losses low! Do not allow the mast to pass through the elements, like on antennas for lower frequencies! Cut all U-bolts to the minimum length needed—a quarter wavelength at 1296 MHz is a little over 2 inches! Avoid any unnecessary metal around the antenna.

Chapter 34

Station Accessories

An Amateur Radio station is much more than the major pieces of equipment found in the ham shack. The minor (only in size and complexity) pieces of equipment often determine the efficiency of the station and the pleasure of the operator.

In this chapter you will find descriptions of a number of accessory items. These represent the kind of projects amateurs like to build. For the most part, they are projects that do not require a lot of time and money to build. Projects of this type help to personalize your station.

A Homemade DTMF Encoder

To be compatible with all repeaters and telephone systems, a DTMF signal must be accurate and stable in frequency, and have a nearly sinusoidal waveform. Simpler encoders than the one described here can be built, but they will not provide its high performance.

This encoder features internal voltage regulation, allowing power to be taken from the rig it is used with; there is no need to depend on separate batteries for power. When a tone pair is selected by pressing the keyboard switch, the transmitter is keyed automatically. When the key switch is released, a delay timer keeps the transmitter on long enough for the next tone pair to be selected. It's no longer necessary to hang onto the push-to-talk switch while fumbling with the DTMF pad, and there are no squelch tails between digits. It has a low-impedance audio output which is electronically disconnected from the transmitter audio system when no keyboard switches are pressed. The encoder may be connected to the mic input of transceivers having either high- or low-impedance mic inputs, with negligible loading of the transmitter audio circuitry. The audio frequencies are crystal controlled, meaning there is minimal drift. This circuit was originally described by Roy Hejhall, K7QWR, in the February 1979 issue of QST.

Theory of Operation

Fig. 1 is a schematic diagram of the encoder. Tone generation is performed by U1, a CMOS IC. High-frequency tones from pin 15 are mixed with their low-frequency counterparts from pin 2 and passed through the level control, R1, before reaching emitter follower Q1. Q1 performs an impedance transformation, providing the low-impedance output mentioned previously. Q2, Q4 and Q5 are used as

Fig 1—Schematic diagram of the DTMF encoder. Any standard encoded keyboard may be used with this circuit, but those specified plug directly into a row of Molex pins soldered to the circuit board. Contact information for parts suppliers appears at the end of this chapter.

D1—5.1 V, 400 mW, Zener diode, 1N4733, HEP Z0406 or equiv.
D2—20 V, 1 W, Zener diode, 1N4747 or equiv.
Q1, Q2, Q4—Silicon NPN transistor, 2N4123 or equiv.
Q3—Silicon PNP transistor, 2N4125 or equiv.
Q5—Silicon NPN transistor, 2N4401 or equiv.
R1—10-kΩ, linear-taper, PCB trimmer potentiometer.

U1—MC14410 (Motorola) two of eight tone-encoder IC (supplier: Arrow Electronics).
Y1—1-MHz crystal in HC-18/U holder. Frequency tolerance 0.1%; series resistance 540 Ω; load capacitance 7 pF (supplier: Data Signal).
Z1—DTMF encoding keyboard. Digitran KL0054 (12 key), KL0049 (16 key) or equiv. (Suppliers: contact Bob Privell at Digitran for suppliers.)

switches. Q2 forces the audio-output impedance high when no keyboard switches are depressed, preventing the encoder from loading the transmitter mic input. Q4 and Q5 are operated as a Darlington pair, keying the transmitter push-to-talk (PTT) line when a keyboard switch is pressed. A single-package Darlington pair was originally used in this application, but its saturated collector voltage was high enough to prevent transmitter keying in some transceivers. Substituting discrete transistors solved the problem. Q2 and Q4 are driven by Q3, which is turned on by pulses from pin 7 of U1 when a keyboard switch is depressed.

U1 requires a 5-volt supply for proper operation. This is provided by the 470-ohm resistor and 1N4733 Zener diode, D1. With the exception of Q4, the remainder of the encoder circuit was also designed to operate from a 5-volt supply.

The length of time the transmitter remains keyed after a keyboard switch is released is determined by the 47-μF capacitor connected to the collector of Q3. On the prototype unit, a value of 47 μF provided a delay of just over one second. If you prefer a longer drop-out time, increase the value of this capacitor. Lowering its value will decrease drop-out time.

Construction and Testing

The prototype was built on a piece of perforated board, but a PC board is preferable. A parts-placement guide for a commercially available circuit board is shown in Fig. 2. U1 should be installed in a socket. The 0.001-μF disc capacitors connected to the base of Q4 and collector of Q5 should be installed as near the transistors as possible. Their function is to bypass RF from the transmitter, which can cause Q4 and Q5 to latch up in the keyed position.

A few simple checks will tell whether the circuit is functioning properly. The following tests may be performed before connecting the encoder to the radio, using only a 12-volt power supply, a high-impedance dc voltmeter and a scope, if one is available.

Fig 2—Parts-placement diagram for the DTMF encoder. A full-size etching pattern appears at the back of this book. Etched circuit boards are available from Lea Engineering (see "Contact Information" at the end of this chapter).

First ensure that D1 is regulating the encoder supply voltage at +5.1 V dc ±10 percent. U1 may be damaged if more than 6 volts is applied to pin 16.

The two operating states for the encoder are (1) no keyboard buttons depressed and (2) one or more buttons depressed. Connect the 12-V dc supply and measure the voltage at the test points shown on the schematic diagram. Voltages measured should be in accordance with those shown.

If any voltages are incorrect, look for wiring errors. If the collector voltage of Q2 is not at least 4 volts with no buttons pressed, the problem may be a leaky transistor at Q1 or Q2. If a scope is available it may be used to inspect the audio output. Pressing any one button should produce a two-tone signal, while depressing any two buttons simultaneously should produce a single tone.

Installation

The electrical portion of the installation simply involves running four wires from the encoder to the transceiver: +12 V, ground, push-to-talk (PTT) and audio output. Shielded audio cable is recommended for the audio output, which is connected to the transceiver mic input. The PTT lead is connected to the hot side of the mic PTT switch. The encoder PTT circuit is designed for rigs with an antenna relay coil connected to the +12 V bus and the PTT switch. The switch grounds the cold side of the relay coil during transmit. Ensure that your rig has this type of PTT circuit and that the relay coil draws less than 300 mA. Most of the popular VHF and UHF FM rigs have this type of PTT circuit. The mechanical details of the installation are left to the discretion of the builder.

Since the encoder will not load the audio system it should not be necessary to change the setting of any transmitter mic-level controls. Adjust only R1 in the encoder for proper tone deviation. The prototype unit has provided excellent performance on both a Tempo VHF/One 2-meter rig and a Kenwood TR-8300 UHF rig.

A Simple DTMF Decoder

A Touch Tone (dual-tone, multi-frequency, or DTMF) decoder can be a valuable link to a remotely controlled device, such as the phone patch in a repeater. Tone decoders of the past were rather large and unstable because they were constructed from discrete tone comparators such as the NE567. The '567 scheme also required rather expensive capacitors to keep the frequency even remotely accurate over a wide temperature range. Recently, Silicon Systems, Inc. introduced a new line of tone decoder ICs. They are hybrid devices, containing an audio filter, time base, tone decoders and TTL-compatible output drivers all on the same chip. Cost wise, it is less expensive to use the SSI IC as

Fig 3—The simple DTMF decoder uses a minimum of parts and fits on a compact PC board.

Fig 4—Schematic diagram of the tone decoder. All resistors are ¼-W units; all capacitors are disc ceramic. Note that on U1, uncircled pin numbers are for use with the SSI202 and SSI203, and circled pin numbers are for use with the SSI204. Contact information for parts suppliers appears at the end of this chapter.

C1-C4—0.1 μF
D1-D4—LED, color of your choice.
J1—Female, chassis-mount phono jack.
Q1-Q5—2N2222 or equiv.
R1—10 MΩ
R2—1 kΩ
R3-R7—10 kΩ
R8-R11—330 Ω
U1—SSI decoder IC (see text; suppliers: Silicon Systems Inc, Syntronics).
U2—4514 1-of-16 demultiplexer.
Y1—3.579545-MHz color-burst crystal.

opposed to other methods, and the finished unit is also considerably smaller. The project shown in Figs. 3 through 8, designed and built by Tom Miller, KA1JQW, in the ARRL Lab, uses the SSI202, SSI203 or SSI204 as a one-of-sixteen tone decoder.

Circuit Details

The decoder described here is designed so you can tailor the circuit to suit your needs. As mentioned before, three different SSI chips can be used. All produce the same results and are available from different sources at various prices. Fig. 4 shows the decoder schematic. Audio containing the DTMF tones is fed into the circuit at the AUD IN jack. The input amplitude should be between 20 and 600 mV RMS. The signal is ac-coupled and fed directly into the decoder IC. Notice that there are two sets of pin numbers for U1. The circled numbers are for use with the SSI204, and the uncircled numbers are for use with the SSI202 and '203.

Inside the decoder chip, the audio signal is filtered to rid it of noise and 60-Hz hum, and then split into two bands, one for high tones, and the other for low tones. From there, the two bands are further filtered and fed into the tone-detection circuits. The tone detection circuits compare the frequency of the incoming signal to that of an internal clock signal. This clock signal is generated by dividing down a crystal-controlled 3.579545 MHz oscillator (from a common color-burst crystal). Once detected, the outputs send the corresponding binary word and a strobe (called DV) for use by an external circuit.

The circuit described here uses a 4514 (1-of-16 decoder) to decode the binary output into 16 separate logic-level outputs. These outputs can be momentary (by installing a jumper between points A and B) or latched (by installing a jumper between points A and C). Some sort of driver circuitry must be used to prevent damage to the 4514. Examples of driver circuits are shown in Fig. 5.

The four data outputs from U1 are also available for use, and LEDs indicate activity. The strobe from the tone decoder is not specifically designated as an output on the circuit board. It can, however, be taken off the board from pin 1 of the 4514 or the collector of Q1 if the compliment is necessary. This will allow you to strobe the binary word onto a computer bus or other control device.

The circuit requires a single 5-V supply. It can readily run from 12-V dc or 117-V ac using the suggested power supply circuits shown in Fig. 6. Maximum current consumption at 5 V is 60 mA with all four LEDs lit, and 20 mA with no LEDs lit.

Fig 5—Suggested driver circuits for use with logic-level outputs. A typical relay or solenoid driver is shown at A, and B shows a typical high current/voltage driver with an optoisolated output stage. Resistors are ¼-W units.

D1—1N914 or 1N4148.
D2—1N4001 or equiv.
K1—Relay (application specific).
Q1, Q2—2N2222 or equiv.
Q3—2N3055 or equiv.

R1—10 kΩ.
R2—15 kΩ.
R3, R4—470 Ω.
U1—Optoisolator, Sylvania ECG3045 or equiv.

Fig 6—Suggested power supplies and regulator for use with the decoder. Decoder ICs are particularly sensitive to noise on the power-supply lines. If you have sporadic trouble with the decoder, add capacitors at the decoder-board "+5 V" connection until noise is suppressed to less than 10 mV P-P.

Table 1

Binary Output Table as Indicated by the LEDs

Tone Pair	Lit LEDs† D	C	B	A	Binary Word D	C	B	A
D	O	O	O	O	0	0	0	0
1	O	O	O	●	0	0	0	1
2	O	O	●	O	0	0	1	0
3	O	O	●	●	0	0	1	1
4	O	●	O	O	0	1	0	0
5	O	●	O	●	0	1	0	1
6	O	●	●	O	0	1	1	0
7	O	●	●	●	0	1	1	1
8	●	O	O	O	1	0	0	0
9	●	O	O	●	1	0	0	1
0	●	O	●	O	1	0	1	0
*	●	O	●	●	1	0	1	1
#	●	●	O	O	1	1	0	0
A	●	●	O	●	1	1	0	1
B	●	●	●	O	1	1	1	0
C	●	●	●	●	1	1	1	1

†O = not lit; ● = lit.

W = Jumper

Fig. 7—Parts placement guide for the DTMF decoder. This view is from the component side of the board. A full-size etching pattern appears at the back of this book.

Construction

The PC-board etching pattern is located at the back of this book. Fig. 7 shows the component layout from the component side of the board. Use sockets for the ICs, as this makes testing and repair easier. The board was designed for use with any of the SSI chips, so care should be taken when stuffing the circuit board—it is very easy to place the U1 in the wrong set of holes. If you are using the 14-pin variety decoder (SSI204), it should be located in the set of holes nearest to the crystal with pin 1 in the square pad. Conversely, if you are using one of the 18-pin decoders (SSI202 and '203) for U1, use the set of holes farthest from the crystal. Once again, be sure that pin 1 is located correctly. Fig. 8 shows two of the finished units, one using the SSI202, and the other using the SSI204. Notice the slight difference in location of the ICs; the two sets of holes are offset just enough to allow you to use one set and not the other.

If the decoder is to be used in a high-RF environment, such as that of a repeater controller, some precautions should be taken to ensure that there is no interference to the decoder. In this case, the unit should be housed in a closed aluminum chassis. Use a shielded wire and connector for the audio line, and install plenty of bypass capacitors in the power supply.

Testing/Set Up

Once the unit has been built, remove the ICs and apply 5-V dc to the power supply connections on the PC board. Then check the power-supply pins on the IC sockets with a voltmeter to be sure that the power supply is working properly and is correctly polarized. Then turn off the power and install the ICs. Although these steps might seem trivial, they can save a lot of grief from burned-out ICs.

Be sure that the right jumper (not both) is installed between point A and point B or

Fig. 8—Two finished units ready to go. Note the offset of the two decoder ICs.

C. Apply power once again. Next, you'll need a source of DTMF tones to test the unit. An easy source of the required tones is a pair of hand-held VHF transceivers. One must have a tone pad; this will be connected to a dummy load and used for transmitting the required tones. Connect the speaker output of the other hand-held transceiver to the decoder and set the audio output to low volume. Upon sending an audio tone pair to the decoder, the LEDs should indicate the corresponding binary word for as long as the tone is present. Table 1 shows the correlation between tone pairs and which LEDs are lit. Note that the output of the decoder IC is standard binary. The LED indication is not latched when a jumper is installed between points A and C; just the 1-of-16 outputs are latched. The completed unit is now ready for installation in the device to be controlled.

A Simple and Accurate QRP Directional Wattmeter

The directional wattmeter in Fig 9 gives accurate readings at power levels from 5 mW to 10 W. It is a bit tricky to achieve good low-power accuracy, but a simple compensation circuit handles the job. Roy Lewallen, W7EL, discusses low-voltage behavior of diodes at more length in his original description of this meter (February 1990 *QST*).

Fig 9—The QRP directional wattmeter provides accurate readings at power levels from 5 mW to 10 W.

CIRCUIT DESCRIPTION

A basic directional wattmeter has three major circuits: the directional coupler, detector and meter. Each circuit can be optimized for a particular application. Here's a description of each circuit.

Directional Coupler

Amateurs commonly use two types of directional couplers. The venerable Monimatch circuit (see McCoy's article in the bibliography at the end of this chapter) is simple and useful for SWR measurement, but it is not accurate as a wide-band wattmeter because it is frequency sensitive. The Bruene circuit (see bibliography) doesn't have this limitation, so is more suitable for our use. It's generally implemented with capacitive dividers to sense voltage, but transformers result in a simpler circuit that is adjustment free.

Several frequency-dependent effects can be reduced by maintaining a near-50-Ω line impedance through the wattmeter. A microstripline structure is effective for this application, and it is extremely simple to build.

Detector

Plain diode detectors, like the one shown in Fig 10, are simple to build and easy to use—*provided you don't require accurate results at low signal levels*. That is unfortunate, because this wattmeter is intended to provide good low-power accuracy. Five milliwatts provide only 145 mV (peak) at

Fig 10—Simple diode detector.

the detector, so detector accuracy must be maintained down to that level. Some diodes, such as back diodes and zero-bias Schottky types, are specially designed for detecting very small signals. These, however, aren't as readily available as common silicon, germanium, and medium-barrier silicon Schottky diodes, so only the latter three types were tested. Naturally, each has its deficiencies.

A simple germanium-diode detector is accurate for ac signals *only when the peak input signal level is above about 1 V*. A simple correction circuit is the secret to this wattmeter's accuracy. Common 1N34A germanium diodes purchased from Radio Shack are satisfactory for this detector; match them as shown in Fig 11. Additional information about diode compensation appears in articles by Grebenkemper listed in the bibliography at the end of this chapter.

Fig 11—Diode matching test setup. Diode forward voltage drops should match within a few millivolts.

The Meter Circuit

An op amp is a logical choice to provide a high load impedance for the detector and a low-impedance output. Most op amps, however, have enough input-bias current to produce a significant voltage across a high-value detector-load resistor, ruining the measurement. Fortunately, op amps with input-bias currents of only a few picoamperes—more than adequate for this application—are readily available. The CA3160 (and its externally compensated equivalent, the CA3130) has the desirable combination of extremely low input current, input- and output-voltage range down to the negative supply rail and moderately low current consumption. If you have another op amp that shares this set of features, you may substitute it for the CA3160 used at U1.

A second op amp (U2A in Fig 12), S3 and surrounding components select one of three power ranges for display. The important requirements for U2 are moderate current consumption and the ability to handle input and output signals near the negative supply rail (ground). An LM358 contains two such op amps; one section (U2B) is unused in this application. You could substitute ¼ of an LM324, another CA3160, or any other op amp with the required characteristics.

The diode-compensation circuit (D3 and R5 in Fig 12) creates an offset that approximately compensates for the drop across the detector diode. If dc was applied to detector D2/R4/C2, and if compensation resistor R5 and detector load resistor R4 were equal, perfect compensation would result (assuming that D2 and D3 were identical). However, the circuit actually compensates the detector *ac* drop with a *dc* drop, so more current must flow through compensation diode D3 than through D2. This is accomplished by making R5 smaller than R3 and R4. Although the compensation isn't perfect, it's extremely good, and a remarkable improvement for only two added components. Without the compensation circuit, the wattmeter error was 30-50% for small signals (5-50 mW); with the compensation circuit, measured error is less than 7% over the same range. In addition, the compensation circuit tracks well with temperature, an important consideration for portable use.

In Grebenkemper's Tandem Match circuit (see bibliography), an additional resistor and capacitor are used in the feedback network to ensure stability of the op amp. There are no signs of instability in the prototype, but if you experience instability problems, add the components marked with asterisks in Fig 12.

CONSTRUCTION

Directional Coupler

This wattmeter works best if there's a constant 50-Ω impedance from the input to the output, but it's not highly critical. There are always impedance bumps at the transitions between the coax connectors and the microstripline, and a larger bump at the coupler transformer, but these bumps can be made insignificant at HF with a little effort. Only the microstripline and directional coupler are sensitive to layout, and you have considerable latitude with these components if you know the rules.

The microstripline (see Fig 13) consists of a single trace on one side of the board and a ground plane on the other. There are at least three ways to fabricate this board: You can stick adhesive copper tape to the non-foil side of a single-sided board, you can etch a double-sided board or you can

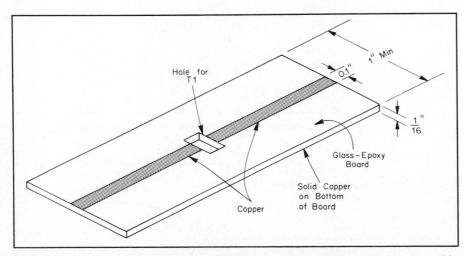

Fig 12—Schematic diagram of the QRP directional wattmeter. All fixed resistors are ¼-W, 5%-tolerance units. D1-D3 are common 1N34 germanium diodes; they should be matched (as shown in Fig 11) for best performance. T1-T3 are FT-37-72 ferrite cores with single-turn primaries (one pass through the core—see Fig 14). Each transformer has a single secondary winding consisting of 10 evenly spaced turns of no. 28 enameled wire. Do not substitute a different core for the FT-37-72. R6 can be any value between 10 kΩ and 100 kΩ. The resistor and capacitor (associated with U1) marked with asterisks may be necessary to eliminate instability (see text).

In schematic (Fig 12):
- Microstripline
- T1, T2, T3
- Directional Coupler
- R1 51, R2 51
- D1, D2
- Detectors, R3 100 k, R4 100 k
- C1 0.01, C2 0.01
- S2 FWD/REV
- Meter Circuits
- Except as indicated, decimal values of capacitance are in microfarads (μF); others are in picofarads (pF); resistances are in ohms; k=1,000, M=1,000,000.
- ● = phasing
- IC pins not shown are unused.
- U1 CA3160
- 0.01
- 10 μF / 16 V
- POWER S1
- 9 V
- 1 k *
- SENSITIVITY cw
- R6
- 0.001 *
- D3
- R5 12 k
- U2B
- U2A LM358
- CAL
- 5.6 k
- R7 2 k
- M1 0-1 mA
- CAL R8 10 k cw
- 18 k 1W
- 10W
- S3
- 5.1 k 0.1W
- R9 1 k cw
- CAL
- 51 k
- 0.01
- FULL SCALE SELECT

cut along the edges of the line with a knife and peel away the unwanted copper.

No matter which method you choose, start with a piece of 1/16-inch-thick, glass-epoxy PC board. Make the board long enough that you can solder it between watt-meter input and output connectors. The board should be at least 1 inch wide (wider is okay). The width of the microstrip (about 0.1 inch) determines the line impedance. Impedance doesn't change much as line width changes, and the impedance isn't too critical for this application. So if you don't have a decimal ruler, just make the trace a bit thinner than 1/8 inch—it'll be close enough. After making the board, cut a hole in the center just large enough to accommodate T1. The finished microstripline should look like that shown in Fig 14.

Mount the coupler components using *short* leads. (A suggested layout is shown in Fig 14.) Then assemble the rest of the wattmeter and mount the completed coupler between the input and output connectors. The connections from the connectors to the microstripline must be very short, particularly the ground connections. If possible, put a solder lug or lugs on the connector-mounting screws and solder the

Top of Board — T3, T2, T1, R2, R1, D2, R4, D1, R3, Ground Plane

Bottom of Board — Microstripline, T1

Fig 14—Close-up views of the completed directional coupler. T1's primary is a straight piece of insulated wire spanning the cut in the microstripline. T1's secondary winding is routed through the hole cut for T1. The top view shows the components comprising the directional coupler and detector. To achieve minimum lead lengths, R1-R4 are mounted vertically on the ground plane. C1 and C2 are not shown, although they should be mounted directly across R3 and R4, respectively.

Fig 13—Details of the microstripline on the directional-coupler circuit board (not drawn to scale).

In Fig 13:
- Hole for T1
- 0.1"
- 1" Min
- 1/16"
- Glass-Epoxy Board
- Solid Copper on Bottom of Board
- Copper

Fig 15—Use solder lugs to make a good connection to the ground side of the microstripline.

Table 2
Meter-Recalibration Data for the QRP Wattmeter

Power	Meter	SWR	Meter
0.0	0.0	1.0	0.0
0.05	0.224	1.6	0.200
0.1	0.316	2.0	0.333
0.2	0.447	3.0	0.500
0.3	0.548	4.0	0.600
0.4	0.633	5.0	0.667
0.5	0.707	7.0	0.750
0.6	0.775	10.0	0.818
0.7	0.837	∞	1.000
0.8	0.894		
0.9	0.949		
1.0	1.000		

The *Meter* column expresses fractions of full-scale reading on the original meter scale. For example, the new SWR = 3 mark should be placed at the same place as the half-scale (0.5) mark on the original meter face.

lugs directly to the bottom of the coupler board as shown in Fig 15.

Meter Circuit

Fig 16 shows a parts-placement diagram for the entire QRP wattmeter circuit. If you don't want to etch circuit boards, construct the microstripline board as described above and build the meter circuits using any construction style you like.

Meter Face

You need to make new scales for the meter or, at the very least, add markings to the existing scale. Table 2 gives data to mark POWER and SWR scales. If you decide to make new scales rather than add marks to the existing scale, record the correct places to make the new marks before you obliterate the old scale.

Refer to Fig 17. Attach the meter face to a large piece of paper. Trace around the face so you can exactly reposition it later. Find the meter pivot point by extending the scale end marks until they cross, and verify the pivot point by extending a couple of other points on the scale. Then draw lines from the pivot point through the meter face to an area beyond the face, labeling them appropriately, as shown. Then remove, repaint and replace the meter face. The new scale and marks can be hand drawn; press-on letters and numbers can be used, or the

Fig 16—Parts placement for the QRP wattmeter. A full-size etching pattern appears at the back of this book.

Fig 17—One means of recording meter-scale marking points before erasing the original scale (see text).

face may be made with a photographic process. When finished, the meter face should resemble Fig 18.

Tips

A small center-off toggle switch, wired for REVERSE-OFF-FORWARD operation, is a convenient way to combine S1 and S2.

Fig 18—Example of the finished meter face.

However, small toggle switches are amazing in their ability to turn themselves on at the slightest provocation—like being bumped around in a suitcase or backpack. So if you're going to use this wattmeter for portable operation, use some other kind of switch (a slide switch, for example) for, or in series with, S1.

Quite a few articles implement the Bruene directional-coupler circuit with a powdered-iron core (such as a T-68-2). The low winding impedance of such a transformer will ruin the accuracy of this circuit, so don't use powdered-iron cores for the transformers in this wattmeter.

Adjustments

All you'll need for adjustment is a high-impedance dc voltmeter. Connect the voltmeter between the wiper of the SENSITIVITY control (R6) and ground. Connect a temporary jumper between pins 7 and 3 of U1. Turn R6 fully ccw. Set the FULL SCALE SELECT switch (S3) to the 10-W position. Turn on the POWER switch (S1). Slowly turn R6 clockwise. As you do, the wattmeter and voltmeter readings should increase. If they do not, turn the wattmeter off and check the wiring.

Adjust R6 for a voltmeter reading of 6.49 V, then adjust R7 so the wattmeter reads full scale. Adjust R6 for a voltmeter reading of 2.05 V, then switch S3 to the 1-W position. Adjust R8 until the wattmeter indicates full scale. Adjust R6 for a voltmeter reading of 0.649 V, then switch S3 to the 0.1-W position. Adjust R9 for a full scale reading on the wattmeter. Turn the wattmeter off and *remove the temporary jumper between pins 3 and 7 of U1.* This completes the calibration. For maximum reliability, measure R7, R8 and R9 and replace them with fixed resistors of the measured values; readjustment should never be necessary.

If you need to measure SWR at levels very close to 1:1, you may want to tweak the wattmeter to show 0 W reflected power when connected to a reference dummy load. You may do so by adjusting R1 and R2. The theoretically correct value for these resistors is 49.5 Ω each. It's not necessary to readjust the wattmeter if you change the values of R1 and R2 slightly.

USE

To measure power, select the appropriate scale and turn S6 fully clockwise. The power flowing forward in the line is the forward reading minus the reverse reading. To measure SWR, switch S3 to the next more sensitive range and switch S2 to FORWARD. Adjust R6 for a full-scale meter reading. Flip S2 to REVERSE and read the SWR scale. To adjust a Transmatch, put the wattmeter between the transmitter and Transmatch and adjust the Transmatch for minimum reflected power.

The directional wattmeter can do anything an SWR meter can do, and many things besides. Because you can measure power anywhere in a system, you can use the wattmeter to find cable and Transmatch losses, measure transmitter power, and lots of other things. You'll be surprised how often you reach for it!

The Tandem Match—An Accurate Directional Wattmeter

Most SWR meters are not very accurate at low power levels because the detector diodes do not respond to low voltage in a linear fashion. This design uses a compensating circuit to cancel diode nonlinearity. It also provides peak detection for SSB operation and direct SWR readout that does not vary with power level. The following information is condensed from an article by John Grebenkemper, KI6WX, in January 1987 *QST*.

DESIGN PRINCIPLES

Directional wattmeters for Amateur Radio use consist of three basic elements: a directional coupler, a detector and a signal-processing and display circuit. A directional coupler samples forward- and reflected-power components on a transmission line. An ideal directional coupler would provide signals proportional to the forward and reflected voltages (independent of frequency), which could then be used to measure forward and reflected power over a wide frequency range. The best contemporary designs work over two decades of frequency.

The detector circuit provides a dc output voltage proportional to the ac input voltage. Most directional wattmeters use a single germanium diode as the detector ele-

Fig 19—The Tandem Match uses a pair of meters to display net forward power and true SWR simultaneously.

ment. A germanium, rather than silicon, diode is used to minimize diode nonlinearity at low power levels. Diode nonlinearity still causes SWR measurement errors unless it is compensated ahead of the display circuit. Most directional wattmeters do not work well at low power levels because of diode nonlinearity.

The signal-processing and display circuits compute and display the SWR. There are a number of ways to perform this function. Meters that display only the forward and reflected power require the operator to compute the SWR. Many instruments require that the operator adjust the meter to a reference level while measuring forward power, then switch to measure reflect-ed power on a special scale that indicates SWR. Meters that directly compute the SWR using analog signal-processing circuits have been described by Fayman, Perras, Leenerts and Bailey (see the bibliography at the end of this chapter).

Let's take a brief look at several popular circuits that accomplish the above functions and compare them to the circuits used in the Tandem Match. The design specifications of the Tandem Match are shown in Table 3, and a block diagram is shown in Fig 20.

Table 3
Performance Specifications for the Tandem Match

Power range:	1.5 to 1500 W
Frequency range:	1.8 to 54 MHz
Power accuracy:	Better than ± 10% (± 0.4 dB)
SWR accuracy:	Better than ± 5%
Minimum SWR:	Less than 1.05:1
Power display:	Linear, suitable for use with either analog or digital meters
SWR display:	Linear, suitable for use with either analog or digital meters
Calibration:	Requires only an accurate voltmeter

Fig 20—Block diagram of the Tandem Match.

CIRCUIT DESCRIPTION

A directional coupler consists of an input port, an output port and a coupled port. Ideally, a portion of the power flowing from the input to the output appears at the coupled port, but *none* of the power flowing from the output to the input appears at the coupled port. There are several terms that define the performance of a directional coupler:

1) *Insertion loss* is the amount of power that is lost as the signal flows from the input port to the output port. Insertion loss should be minimized so the coupler doesn't dissipate a significant amount of the transmitted power.

2) *Coupling factor* is the amount of power (or voltage) that appears at the coupled port relative to the amount of power (or voltage) transferred from the input port to the output port. The "flatness" (with frequency) of the coupling factor determines how accurately the directional wattmeter can determine forward and reflected power over a range of frequencies.

3) *Isolation* is the amount of power (or voltage) that appears at the coupled port relative to the amount of power (or voltage) transferred from the output port to the input port.

4) *Directivity* is the isolation less the coupling factor. Directivity dictates the minimum measurable SWR. A directional coupler with 20 dB of directivity measures a 1:1 SWR as 1.22:1, but one with 30 dB measures a 1:1 SWR as 1.07:1.

The directional coupler most common-ly used in Amateur Radio was first described in 1959 by Bruene in *QST* (see bibliography). The coupling factor was fairly flat (±1 dB), and the directivity was about 20 dB for a Bruene coupler measured from 3 to 30 MHz. Both factors limit the accuracy of the Bruene coupler for measuring low values of power and SWR. It is a simple directional coupler, however, and it works well over a wide frequency range if great precision is not required.

The coupler used in the Tandem Match (see Fig 21) consists of a pair of toroidal transformers connected in tandem. The configuration was patented by Carl G. Sontheimer and Raymond E. Fredrick (US Patent no. 3,426,298, issued February 4, 1969). It has been described by Perras, Spaulding (see bibliography) and others. With coupling factors of 20 dB or greater, this coupler is suitable to sample both forward and reflected power.

The configuration used in the Tandem Match works well over the frequency range of 1.8 to 54 MHz, with a nominal coupling factor of 30 dB. Over this range, insertion loss is less than 0.1 dB. The coupling factor is flat to within ±0.1 dB from 1.8 to 30 MHz, and increases to only ±0.3 dB at 50 MHz. Directivity exceeds 35 dB from 1.8 to 30 MHz and exceeds 26 dB at 50 MHz.

The low-frequency limit of this directional coupler is determined by the inductance of the transformer secondary windings. The inductive reactance should be greater than 150 Ω (three times the line characteristic impedance) to reduce insertion loss. The high-frequency limit of this directional coupler is determined by the length of the transformer windings. When the winding length approaches a significant fraction of a wavelength, coupler performance deteriorates.

The coupler described here may overheat at 1500 W on 160 meters (because of the high circulating current in the secondary of T2). The problem could be corrected by using a larger core or one with greater permeability. A larger core would require longer windings; that option would decrease the high-frequency limit.

DETECTOR CIRCUITS

Most amateur directional wattmeters use a germanium-diode detector to minimize the forward voltage drop. Detector voltage drop is still significant, however, and an uncompensated diode detector does not respond to small signals in a linear fashion. Many directional wattmeters compensate for diode nonlinearity by adjusting the meter scale.

The effect of underestimating detected power worsens at low power levels. Under these conditions, the ratio of the forward power to the reflected power is overestimated because the reflected power is always less than the forward power. This results in an instrument that underestimates SWR, particularly as power is reduced. A directional wattmeter can be checked for this effect by measuring SWR at several power levels. The SWR should be independent of power level.

Fig 21—Simplified diagram of the Tandem Match directional coupler. At A, a schematic of the two transformers. At B, an equivalent circuit.

Fig 22—Simplified diagram of the detector circuit used in the Tandem Match. The output voltage, V_0, is approximately equal to the input voltage. D1 and D2 must be a matched pair (see text). The op amp should have a low offset voltage (less than 1 mV), a low leakage current (less than 1 nA), and be stable over time and temperature. The resistor and capacitor in the feedback path assure that the op amp will be stable.

The Tandem Match uses a feedback circuit to compensate for diode nonlinearity. A simplified diagram of the compensated detector is shown in Fig 22. When used with the 30-dB directional coupler, the output voltage of this circuit tracks the square root of power over a range from 10 mW to 1.5 kW. The compensated diode detector tracks the peak input voltage down to 30 mV, while an uncompensated germanium-diode detector shows significant errors at peak inputs of 1 V and less. More information about compensated detectors appears in Grebenkemper's *QEX* article ''Calibrating Diode Detectors'' (see bibliography).

The compensation circuit uses the voltage across a feedback diode, D2, to compensate for the voltage drop across the detector diode, D1. (The diodes must be a matched pair.) The average current through D1 is determined by the detector-diode load resistor, R1. The peak current through this diode is several times larger than the average current; therefore, the current through

D2 must be several times larger than the average current through D1 to compensate adequately for the peak voltage drop across D1. This is accomplished by making the feedback-diode load resistor, R2, several times smaller than R1. The voltage at the output of the compensated detector approximates the peak RF voltage at the input. For Schottky-barrier diodes and a 1-MΩ detector-diode load resistor, a 5:1 ratio of R1 to R2 is nearly optimal.

SIGNAL-PROCESSING AND DISPLAY CIRCUITS

The signal-processing circuitry calculates and displays transmission-line power and SWR. When measuring forward power, most directional wattmeters display the actual forward power present in the transmission line, which is the sum of forward and reflected power if a conjugate match exists at the input end of the lines. Transmission-line forward power is very close to the net forward power (the actual power delivered to the line) so long as the SWR is low. As the SWR increases, however, forward power becomes an increasingly poor measure of the power delivered to the load. At an SWR of 3:1, a forward power reading of 100 W implies that only 75 W is delivered to the load (the reflected power is 25 W), assuming that transmission-line loss is zero. The Tandem Match differs from most wattmeters in that *it displays the net forward power, rather than the sum of forward and reflected power*. This is the quantity which must be optimized to result in maximum radiated power (and which concerns the FCC).

The Tandem Match directly computes and displays the transmission-line SWR on a linear scale. As the displayed SWR is not affected by changes in transmitter power, a matching network can be simply adjusted

to minimize SWR. Transmatch adjustment requires only a few watts.

The heart of the Tandem Match signal-processing circuit is the analog logarithm and antilogarithm circuitry shown in Fig 23. The circuit is based on the fact that collector current in a silicon transistor is proportional to the exponential (antilog) of its base-emitter voltage over a range of collector currents from a few nanoamperes to a few milliamperes when the collector-base voltage is zero (see Gibbons and Horn in the bibliography). Variations of this circuit are used in the squaring circuits to convert voltage to power and in the divider circuit used to compute the SWR. With good op amps, this circuit will work well for input voltages from less than 100 mV to greater than 10 V. (For the Tandem Match, ''good'' op amps are quad-packaged, low-power-consumption, unity-gain-stable parts with input bias less than 1 nA and offset voltage less than 5 mV. Op amps that

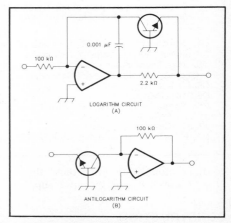

Fig 23—Simplified diagrams of the log circuit at A and the antilog circuit at B.

Fig 24—Schematic diagram of the Tandem Match directional wattmeter. Parts identified as RS are from Radio Shack. Contact information for parts suppliers appears at the end of this chapter.

D1, D2—Matched pair 1N5711, or equivalent
   (supplier: Surplus Sales of Nebraska).
D3, D4—Matched pair 1N5711, or equivalent
   (supplier: Surplus Sales of Nebraska).
D6, D7—1N34A.
D8-D14—1N914.
FB—Ferrite bead, Amidon FB-73-101 or equiv.
J1, J2—SO-239 connector.
J3, J4—Open-circuit jack.
M1, M2—50-μA panel meter, RS 270-1751.

Q1, Q3, Q4—2N2222 or equiv.
Q2—2N2907 or equiv.
R1, R2, R5—100-kΩ, 10-turn, cermet Trimpot.
R3, R4—10-kΩ, 10-turn, cermet Trimpot.
U1-U3—TLC27L4 or TLC27M4 op amp (Texas
   Instruments; supplier: Newark).

U4—TLC27L2 or TLC27M2 (Texas
   Instruments; supplier: Newark).
U5-U7—CA3146.
U8—LM334.
U9, U10—LM336.

CONSTRUCTION

The schematic diagram for the Tandem Match is shown in Fig 24. The circuit is designed to operate from batteries and draw very little power. Much of the circuitry is of high impedance, so take care to isolate it from RF fields. House the circuit in a metal case. Most problems in the prototype were caused by stray RF in the op-amp circuitry.

consume more power than those shown may require changes to the power supply.)

DIRECTIONAL COUPLER

The directional coupler is constructed in its own small, (2¾ × 2¾ × 2¼-inch) aluminum box (see Fig 25). Two pairs of SO-239 connectors are mounted on opposite sides of the box. A piece of PC board is run diagonally across the box to improve coupler directivity. The pieces of RG-8X coaxial cable pass through holes in the PC

board. (Note: Some brands of "mini 8" cable have extremely low breakdown voltage ratings and are unsuitable to carry even 100 W when the SWR exceeds 1:1. See "High-Power Operation" for details of a coupler made with RG-8 cable.)

Begin by constructing T1 and T2, which are identical except for their end connections. (Refer to Fig 25.) The primary for each transformer is the center conductor of a length of RG-8X coaxial cable. Cut two cable lengths sufficient for mounting as

Fig 25—Construction details for the directional coupler.

Fig 26—The parallel load resistors mounted on an SO-239 connector. Four 200-Ω resistors are mounted in parallel to provide a 50-Ω detector load.

shown in the figure. Strip the cable jacket, braid and dielectric as shown. The cable braid is used as a Faraday shield between the transformer windings, so it is only grounded at one end. *Important—connect the braid only at one end or the directional-coupler circuit will not work properly!* Wind two transformer secondaries, each 31 turns of no. 24 enameled wire on an Amidon T-50-3 or equivalent iron-powder core. Slip each core over one of the prepared cable pieces (including both the shield and the outer insulation). Mount and connect the transformers as shown in Fig 25, with the wires running through separate holes in the copper-clad PC board.

The directional coupler can be mounted separately from the rest of the circuitry if desired. If so, use two coaxial cables to carry the forward- and reflected-power signals from the directional coupler to the detector inputs. Be aware, however, that

any losses in the cables will affect power readings.

This directional coupler has not been used at power levels in excess of 100 W. For more information about using the Tandem Match at high power levels, see "High-Power Operation."

DETECTOR AND SIGNAL-PROCESSING CIRCUITS

The detector and signal-processing circuits were constructed on a perforated, copper-clad circuit board. These circuits use two separate grounds—*it is extremely important to isolate the grounds as shown in the circuit diagram.* Failure to do so may result in faulty circuit operation. Separate grounds prevent RF currents on the cable shield from affecting the op-amp circuitry.

The directional coupler requires good 50-Ω loads. They are constructed on the back of female UHF chassis connectors

where the cables from the directional coupler enter the wattmeter housing. Each load consists of four 200-Ω resistors connected from the center conductor of the UHF connector to the four holes on the mounting flange, as shown in Fig 26. The detector diode is then mounted from the center conductor of the connector to the 100-pF and 1000-pF bypass capacitors, which are located next to the connector. The response of this load and detector combination measures flat to beyond 500 MHz.

Schottky-barrier diodes (type 1N5711) were used in this design because they were readily available. Any RF-detector diode with a low forward voltage drop (less than 300 mV) and reverse breakdown voltage greater than 30 V could be used. (Germanium diodes could be used in this circuit, but performance will suffer. If germanium diodes are used, reduce the values of the detector-diode and feedback-diode load resistors by a factor of 10.)

The detector diodes must be matched. This can be done with dc, using the circuit shown in Fig 27. Use a high-impedance voltmeter (10 MΩ or greater). For this project, diodes are matched when their forward voltage drops are equal (within a few millivolts). In the prototype, diodes from the same production batch were sufficiently matched.

The rest of the circuit layout is not critical, but keep the lead lengths of the 0.001- and 0.01-μF bypass capacitors short. The capacitors provide additional bypass paths for the op-amp circuitry.

D6 and D7 form a voltage doubler to detect the presence of a carrier. When the forward power exceeds 1.5 W, Q3 switches on and stays on until about 10 seconds after the carrier drops. (A connection from TP7 to TP9 forces the unit on, even with no carrier present.) The regulated references of +2.5 V and −2.5 V generated by the LM334 and LM336 are critical. Zener-diode substitutes would significantly degrade performance.

The four op amps in U1 compensate for the nonlinearity of the detector diodes. D1-D2 and D3-D4 are the matched diode pairs discussed above. A RANGE switch selects the meter range. (A six-position switch was used here because it was handy.) The resistor values for the RANGE switch are shown in Table 4. Full-scale input power gives an output at U1C or U1D of 7.07 V. The forward- and reflected-power

Fig 27—Diode-matching test setup. Diode forward voltage drops should match within a few millivolts.

Table 4
Range-Switch Resistor Values

Full-Scale Power Level (W)	Range Resistor (1% Precision) (kΩ)
1	2.32
2	3.24
3	4.02
5	5.23
10	7.68
15	9.53
20	11.0
25	12.7
30	15.0
50	18.7
100	28.7
150	37.4
200	46.4
250	54.9
300	63.4
500	100.0
1000	237.0
1500	649.0
2000	open

detectors are zeroed with R1 and R2.

The forward- and reflected-detector voltages are squared by U2, U5 and U6 so that the output voltages are proportional to forward and reflected power. The gain constants are adjusted using R3 and R4 so that an input of 7.07 V to the squaring circuit gives an output of 5 V. The difference between these two voltages is used by U4B to yield an output that is proportional to the power delivered to the transmission line. This voltage is peak detected (by an RC circuit connected to the OPERATE position of the MODE switch) to indicate and hold the maximum power measurement during CW or SSB transmissions.

SWR is computed from the forward and reflected voltages by U3, U4 and U7. When no carrier is present, Q4 forces the SWR reading to be zero (that is, when the forward power is less than 2% of the full-scale setting of the RANGE switch). The SWR computation circuit gain is adjusted by R5. The output is peak detected in the OPERATE mode to steady the SWR reading during CW or SSB transmissions.

Transistor arrays (U5, U6 and U7) are used for the log and antilog circuits to guarantee that the transistors will be well matched. Discrete transistors may be used, but accuracy may suffer.

A three-position toggle switch selects the three operating modes. In the OPERATE mode, the power and SWR outputs are peak detected and held for a few seconds to allow meter reading during actual transmissions. In the TUNE mode, the meters display instantaneous output power and SWR.

A digital voltmeter is used to obtain more precise readings than are possible with analog meters. The output power range is 0 to 5 V (0 V = 0 W and 5 V = full scale). SWR output varies from 1 V (SWR = 1:1) to 5 V (SWR = 5:1). Voltages above 5 V are unreliable because of

voltage limiting in some of the op amp circuits.

CALIBRATION

The directional wattmeter can be calibrated with an accurate voltmeter. All calibration is done with dc voltages. The directional-coupler and detector circuits are inherently accurate if correctly built. To calibrate the wattmeter, use the following procedure:

1) Set the MODE switch to TUNE and the RANGE switch to 100 W or less.

2) Jumper TP7 to TP8. This turns the unit on.

3) Jumper TP1 to TP2. Adjust R1 for 0 V at TP3.

4) Jumper TP4 to TP5. Adjust R2 for 0 V at TP6.

5) Adjust R1 for 7.07 V at TP3.

6) Adjust R3 for 5.00 V at TP9, or a full-scale reading on M1.

7) Adjust R2 for 7.07 V at TP6.

8) Adjust R4 for 0 V at TP9, or a zero reading on M1.

9) Adjust R2 for 4.71 V at TP6.

10) Adjust R5 for 5.00 V at TP10, or a full-scale reading on M2.

11) Set the RANGE switch to its most sensitive scale.

12) Remove jumpers from TP1 to TP2 and TP4 to TP5.

13) Adjust R1 for 0 V at TP3.

14) Adjust R2 for 0 V at TP6.

15) Remove jumper from TP7 to TP8.

This completes the calibration procedure. This procedure has been found to equal calibration with expensive laboratory equipment. The directional wattmeter should now be ready for use.

ACCURACY

Performance of the Tandem Match has been compared to other well-known directional couplers and laboratory test equipment, and it equals any amateur directional wattmeter tested. Power measurement accuracy of the Tandem Match compares well to a Hewlett-Packard HP-436A power meter. The HP meter has a specified measurement error of less than ±0.05 dB. The Tandem Match tracked the 436A within ±0.5 dB from 10 mW to 100 W, and within ±0.1 dB from 1 W to 100 W. The unit was not tested above 100 W because a transmitter with a higher power rating was not available.

SWR performance was equally good when compared to the SWR calculated from measurements made with the 436A and a calibrated directional coupler. The Tandem Match tracked the calculated SWR within ±5% for SWR values from 1:1 to 5:1. SWR measurements were made at 8 W and 100 W.

OPERATION

Connect the Tandem Match in the 50-Ω line between the transmitter and the anten-

na matching network (or antenna if no matching network is used). Set the RANGE switch to a range greater than the transmitter output rating and the MODE switch to TUNE. When the transmitter is keyed, the Tandem Match automatically switches on and indicates both power delivered to the antenna and SWR on the transmission line. When no carrier is present, the OUTPUT POWER and SWR meters indicate zero.

The OPERATE mode includes RC circuitry to momentarily hold the peak-power and SWR readings during CW or SSB transmissions. The peak detectors are not ideal, so there could be about 10% variation from the actual power peaks and the SWR reading. The SWR × 10 mode increases the maximum readable SWR to 50:1. This range should be sufficient to cover any SWR value that occurs in amateur use. (A 50-ft open stub of RG-8 yields a measured SWR of only 43:1, or less, at 2.4 MHz because of cable loss. Higher frequencies and longer cables exhibit a smaller maximum SWR.)

It is easy to use the Tandem Match to adjust an antenna matching network. Adjust the transmitter for minimum output power (at least 1.5 W). With the carrier on and the MODE switch set to TUNE or SWR × 10, adjust the matching network for minimum SWR. Once minimum SWR is obtained, set the transmitter to the proper operating mode and output power. Place the Tandem Match in the OPERATE mode.

DESIGN VARIATIONS

There are several ways in which this design could be enhanced. The most important is to add UHF capability. This would require a new directional-coupler design for the band of interest. (The existing detector circuit should work to at least 500 MHz.)

Those who desire a low-power directional wattmeter can build a directional coupler with a 20-dB coupling factor by decreasing the transformer turns ratio to 10:1. That version should be capable of measuring output power from 1 mW to about 150 W (and it should switch on at about 150 mW). This change should also increase the maximum operating frequency to about 150 MHz (by virtue of the shorter transformer windings). If you desire 1.8-MHz operation, it may be necessary to change the toroidal core material for sufficient reactance (low insertion loss).

The Tandem Match circuit can accommodate coaxial cable with a characteristic impedance other than 50 Ω. The detector terminating resistors, transformer secondaries and range resistors must change to match the new design impedance.

The detector circuitry can be used (without the directional coupler) to measure low-level RF power in 50-Ω circuits. RF is fed directly to the forward detector (J1, Fig 24), and power is read from the OUTPUT POWER meter. The detector is

Fig 28—Schematic diagram of the high-power directional coupler. D1 and D2 are germanium diodes (1N34 or equiv). R1 and R2 are 47- or 51-Ω, ½-W resistors. C1 and C2 have 500-V ratings. The secondary windings of T1 and T2 each consist of 40 turns of no. 26 to 30 enameled wire on T-68-2 powdered-iron toroid cores. If the coupler is built into an existing antenna tuner, the primary of T1 can be part of the tuner coaxial output line. The remotely located meters (M1 and M2) are connected to the coupler box at J1 and J2 via P1 and P2.

quite linear from 10 μW to 1.5 W.

HIGH-POWER OPERATION

This material was condensed from a letter by Frank Van Zant, KL7IBA, which appears in July 1989 *QST* (pp 42-43). In April 1988, Zack Lau, KH6CP, described a directional-coupler circuit (based on the same principle as Grebenkemper's circuit) for a QRP transceiver (see the bibliography at the end of this chapter). The main advantage of Lau's circuit is very low parts count.

Grebenkemper uses complex log-antilog amplifiers to provide good measurement accuracy. This application gets away from complex circuitry, but retains reasonable measurement accuracy over the 1-1500 W range. It also forfeits the SWR-computation feature.

Lau's coupler uses ferrite toroids. It works great at low power levels, but the ferrite toroids heat excessively with high power, causing erratic meter readings and the potential for burned parts.

THE REVISED DESIGN

Powdered-iron toroids are used for the transformers in this version of Lau's basic circuit. The number of turns on the secon-

daries was increased to compensate for the lower permeability of powdered iron.

Two meters display reflected and forward power (see Fig 28). The germanium detector diodes (D1 and D2—1N34) pro-

vide fairly accurate meter readings, particularly if the meter is calibrated (using R3, R4 and R5) to place the normal transmitter output at mid scale. If the winding sense of the transformers is reversed, the meters

Fig 29—Directional-coupler construction details. Grommets or standoff insulators can be used to route the secondary windings of T1 and T2 through the PC-board shield. A 3½ × 3½ × 4-inch box serves as the enclosure.

are transposed (the forward-power meter becomes the reflected-power meter, and vice versa).

CONSTRUCTION

Fig 29 shows the physical layout of the coupler. The pickup unit is mounted in a $3\frac{1}{2} \times 3\frac{1}{2} \times 4$-inch box. The meters, PC-mount potentiometers and HIGH/LOW power switch are mounted in a separate box or a compartment in an antenna tuner.

The primary windings of T1 and T2 are constructed much as Grebenkemper described, but use RG-8 with its jacket removed so that the core and secondary winding may fit over the cable. The braid is wrapped with fiberglass tape to insulate it from the secondary winding. An excellent alternative to fiberglass tape—with even higher RF voltage-breakdown characteristics—is ordinary plumber's Teflon pipe tape, available at most hardware stores.

The transformer secondaries are wound on T-68-2 powdered-iron toroid cores. They are 40 turns of no. 26 to 30 enameled wire spread evenly around each core. By using no. 26 to 30 wire on the cores, the cores slip over the tape-wrapped RG-8 lines. With no. 26 wire on the toroids, a single layer of tape (slightly more with Teflon tape) over the braid provides an extremely snug fit for the core. Use care when fitting the cores onto the RG-8 assemblies. After the toroids are mounted on the RG-8 sections, coat the assembly with General Cement Corp Polystyrene Q Dope, or use a spot or two of RTV sealant to hold the windings in place and fix the transformers on the RG-8 primary windings.

Mount a PC-board shield in the center of the box, between T1 and T2, to minimize coupling between the transformers. Suspend T1 between the SO-239 connectors and T2 between two standoff insulators. The detector circuits (C1, C2, D1, D2, R1 and R2) are mounted inside the coupler box as shown.

CALIBRATION, TUNE UP AND OPERATION

The coupler has excellent directivity. Calibrate the meters for various power levels with an RF ammeter and a 50-Ω dummy load. Calculate I^2R for each power level, and mark the meter faces accordingly. Use R3, R4 and R5 to adjust the meter readings within the ranges. Diode nonlinearities are thus taken into account, and Grebenkemper's signal-processing circuits are not needed for relatively accurate power readings.

Start the tune-up process using about 10 W, adjust the antenna tuner for minimum reflected power, and increase power while adjusting the tuner to minimize reflected power.

This circuit has been built into several antenna tuners with good success. The bridge worked well at 1.5-kW output on 1.8 MHz. It also worked fine from 3.5 to 30 MHz with 1.2- and 1.5-kW output. The antenna is easily tuned for a 1:1 SWR using the null indication provided.

Amplifier settings for a matched antenna, as indicated with the wattmeter, closely agreed with those for a 50-Ω dummy load. Checks with a Palomar noise bridge and a Heath Antenna Scope also verified these findings. This circuit should handle more than 1.5 kW, *as long as the SWR on the feed line through the wattmeter is kept at or near 1:1.* (On one occasion high power was applied while the antenna tuner was not coupled to a load. Naturally the SWR was extremely high, and the output transformer secondary winding opened like a fuse. This resulted from the excessively high voltage across the secondary. The damage was easily and quickly repaired.)

A Transmatch for Balanced or Unbalanced Lines

Most modern transmitters are designed to operate into loads of approximately 50 ohms. Solid-state transmitters produce progressively lower output power as the SWR on the transmission line increases, owing to the built-in SWR protection circuits. Therefore, it is useful to employ a matching network between the transmitter and the antenna feeder when antennas with complex impedances are used.

One example of this need can be seen in the case of an 80-meter, coax-fed dipole antenna which has been cut for resonance at, say, 3.6 MHz. If this antenna were used in the 75-meter phone band, the SWR would be fairly high. A Transmatch could be used to give the transmitter a 50-ohm load, even though a significant mismatch was present at the antenna feed point.

It is important to remember that the Transmatch will not correct the actual SWR condition; it only conceals it as far as the transmitter is concerned. A Transmatch is useful also when using a single-wire antenna for multiband use. By means of a balun at the Transmatch output it is

Fig 30—Exterior view of the SPC Transmatch. Radio Shack vernier drives are used for the tuning capacitors. A James Millen turns-counter drive is coupled to the rotary inductor.

possible to operate the transmitter into a balanced transmission line, such as a 300- or 600-ohm feed system of the type that would be used with a multiband tuned dipole, V beam or rhombic antenna.

A secondary benefit can be realized from Transmatches of certain varieties: The matching network can, if it has a band-pass response, attenuate harmonics from the transmitter. The amount of attenuation is dependent upon the loaded Q (Q_L) of the network after the impedance has been matched. The higher the Q_L, the greater the attenuation. Some Transmatches, such as the Ultimate Transmatch of Fig. 31, can exhibit a high-pass response (undesirable), depending on the transformation ratio they are adjusted to accommodate. In a worst-case condition the attenuation of harmonic currents may be as low as 3 to 6 dB. Under different (better) conditions of impedance transformation, the attenuation can be as great as 20 to 25 dB.

The SPC Transmatch described here was developed to correct for the sometimes poor harmonic attenuation of the network in the Ultimate Transmatch. The SPC (series-parallel capacitance) circuit maintains a bandpass response under load conditions of less than 25 ohms to more than 1000 ohms (from a 50-ohm transmitter).

Fig 31—Circuit for the Ultimate Transmatch. The network can degenerate to a high-pass network under some conditions (see text). A T-network configuration provides identical matching range and does not require a split-stator capacitor at C1.

(A)

(B)

Fig 32—Schematic diagram of the SPC circuit. Capacitance is in pF. Contact information for parts suppliers appears at the end of this chapter.

C1—200-pF transmitting variable with plate spacing of 0.074 inch or greater (supplier: Oak Hills Research).
C2—Dual-section variable, 200 pF per section. Same plate spacing as C1 (supplier: Oak Hills Research).
J1, J2, J4—SO-239 coaxial connectors. J4 should have high-dielectric-strength insulation (such as Teflon) if high-Z single-wire antennas are used at J3.
J4—Ceramic feedthrough bushing.

L1—Rotary inductor, 25 μH minimum inductance (supplier: Oak Hills Research).
L2—Three turns no. 8 copper wire, 1 inch ID × 1½ inches long.
S1—Two-pole, four-position ceramic rotary wafer switch with heavy contacts. Two positions are unused.
Z1—Balun transformer: 12 turns no. 12 Formvar wire, trifilar, close-wound on 1-inch-OD phenolic or PVC-tubing form.

This is because a substantial amount of capacitance is always in parallel with the rotary inductor (C2B and L1 of Fig. 32). In comparison with the Ultimate circuit of Fig. 31, it can be seen that at high load impedances, the Ultimate Transmatch will have minimal effective output capacitance in shunt with the inductor, giving rise to a high-pass response.

Another advantage of the SPC Transmatch is its greater frequency range with the same component values used in the Ultimate Transmatch. The circuit of Fig. 32 operates from 1.8 to 30 MHz with the values shown. Only three-fourths of the available inductance of L1 is needed on 160 meters.

The notable difference in outward performance over the circuit in Fig. 31 is somewhat sharper tuning. This is because of the increased network Q. This is especially prominent at 40, 80 and 160 meters. For this reason there are vernier-drive dials on C1 and C2. They are also useful in logging the dial settings for changing bands or antennas.

Construction

Figs. 30 and 33 show the structural details of the Transmatch. The cabinet is homemade from 16-gauge aluminum sheeting. L brackets are affixed to the right and left sides of the lower part of the cabinet to permit attachment of the U-shaped cover.

The conductors which join the components should be of heavy-gauge material to minimize stray inductance and heating. Wide strips of flashing copper are suitable for the conductor straps. The center conductor and insulation from RG-59 polyfoam coaxial cable is used in this model for the wiring between the switch and the related components. The insulation is sufficient to prevent breakdown and arcing at 2 kW PEP input to the transmitter.

All leads should be kept as short as possible to help prevent degradation of the cir-

cuit Q. The stators of C1 and C2 should face toward the cabinet cover to minimize the stray capacitance between the capacitor plates and the bottom of the cabinet (important at the upper end of the Transmatch frequency range). Insulated ceramic shaft couplings are used between the vernier drives and C1 and C2, since the rotors of both capacitors are floating in this circuit. C1 and C2 are supported above the bottom plate on steatite cone insulators. S1

Fig 33—Interior view of the W1FB SPC Transmatch. L2 is mounted on the rear wall by means of two ceramic standoff insulators. C1 is on the right, and C2 is at the left. The coaxial connectors, ground post and J3 are on the lower part of the rear panel.

is attached to the rear apron of the cabinet by means of two metal standoff posts.

Operation

The SPC Transmatch is designed to handle the output from transmitters which operate up to 2 kW PEP input. L2 has been added to improve the circuit Q at 10 and 15 meters. However, it may be omitted from the circuit if the rotary inductor (L1) has a tapered pitch at the minimum-inductance end. It may be necessary to omit L2 if the stray wiring inductance of the builder's version is high. Otherwise, it may be impossible to obtain a matched condition at 28 MHz with certain loads.

An SWR indicator is used between the transmitter and the Transmatch to show when a matched condition is achieved. The builder may want to integrate an SWR meter in the Transmatch circuit between J2 and the arm of S1A (Fig. 32A). If this is done there should be room for an edgewise panel meter above the vernier drive for C2.

Initial transmitter tuning should be done with a dummy load connected to J1, and with S1 in the D position. This will prevent interference which could otherwise occur if tuning is done on the air. After the transmitter is properly tuned into the dummy load, unkey the transmitter and switch S1 to T (Transmatch). Never hot switch a Transmatch, as this can damage both transmitter and Transmatch. Set C1 and C2 at midrange. With a few watts of RF, adjust L1 for a decrease in reflected power. Then adjust C1 and C2 alternately for the lowest possible SWR. If the SWR cannot be reduced to 1:1, adjust L1 slightly and repeat the procedure. Finally, increase the transmitter power to maximum and touch up the Transmatch controls if necessary. When tuning, keep your transmissions brief and identify your station.

The air-wound balun of Fig. 32B can be used outboard from the Transmatch if a low-impedance balanced feeder is contemplated. Ferrite or powdered-iron core material is not used in the interest of avoiding TVI and harmonics that can result from core saturation.

The B position of S1 permits switched-through operation when the Transmatch is not needed. The G position is used for grounding the antenna system, as necessary; a quality earth ground should be attached at all times to the Transmatch chassis.

Final Comments

Surplus coils and capacitors are okay in this circuit. L1 should have at least 25 μH of inductance, and the tuning capacitors need to have 150 pF or more of capacitance per section. Insertion loss through this Transmatch was measured at less than 0.5 dB at 600 watts of RF power on 7 MHz.

A Link-Coupled Matching Network

Link coupling offers many advantages over the types of systems where a direct connection between the transmitter and antenna is required. This is particularly true on 80 meters, where commercial broadcast stations often induce sufficient voltage to cause either rectification or front-end overload. Transceivers and receivers that show this tendency can usually be cured by using only magnetic coupling between the transceiver and antenna system. There is no direct connection and better isolation results along with the inherent band-pass characteristics of magnetically coupled tuned circuits.

Although link coupling can be used with either single-ended or balanced antenna systems, its most common application is with balanced feed. The model shown here is designed for 80- through 10-meter operation.

The Circuit

The circuit shown in Fig. 35 and the accompanying photographs are those of a band-switched link coupler. L2 is the link and C1 is used to adjust the coupling. S1B

Fig 34—Exterior view of the band-switched link coupler. Alligator clips are used to select the proper tap positions of the coil.

Fig 35—Schematic diagram of the link coupler. The connections marked as "to balanced feed line" are steatite feedthrough insulators. The arrows on the other ends of these connections are alligator clips. Contact information for parts suppliers appears at the end of this chapter.

C1—350 pF maximum, 0.0435 inch plate spacing or greater.
C2—100 pF maximum, 0.0435 inch plate spacing or greater.
J1—Coaxial connector.
L1, L2, L3—B & W 3027 Miniductor stock, 2-inch diameter, 8 turns per inch, no. 14 wire. The coil assembly consists of 48 turns. L1 and L3 are each 17 turns tapped at 8 and 11 turns from outside ends. L2 is 14 turns tapped at 8 and 12 turns from the C1 end (see text for additional details).
S1—3-pole, 5-position ceramic rotary switch.

Fig 36—Interior view of the coupler showing the basic positions of the major components. Component placement is not critical, but the unit should be laid out for minimum lead lengths.

selects the proper amount of link inductance for each band. L1 and L3 are located on each side of the link and are the coils to which the antenna is connected. Alligator clips are used to connect the antenna to the coil because antennas of different impedances must be connected at different points (taps) along the coil. With many antennas it will be necessary to change taps for different bands of operation. C2 tunes L1 and L3 to resonance at the operating frequency.

Switch sections S1A and S1C select the amount of inductance necessary for each of the HF bands. The inductance of each of the coils has been optimized for antennas in the impedance range of roughly 20-600 ohms. Antennas that exhibit impedances well outside this range may require that some of the fixed connections to L1 and L3 be changed. Should this be necessary remember that the L1 and L3 sections must be kept symmetrical — the same number of turns on each coil.

Construction

The unit is housed in a homemade aluminum enclosure that measures 9 × 8 × 3½ inches. Any cabinet with similar dimensions that will accommodate the components may be used. L1, L2 and L3 are a one-piece assembly of B&W 3026 Miniductor stock. The individual coils are separated from each other by cutting two of the turns at the appropriate spots along the length of the coil. Then, the inner ends of the outer sections are joined by a short wire that is run through the center of L2. Position the wire so that it will not come into contact with L2. Each of the fixed tap points on L1, L2 and L3 is located and lengths of hookup wire are attached. The coil is mounted in the enclosure and the connections between the coil and the bandswitch are made. Every other turn of L1 and L3 is pressed in toward the center of the coil to facilitate connection of the alligator clips.

As can be seen from the schematic, C2 must be isolated from ground. This can be accomplished by mounting the capacitor on steatite cones or other suitable insulating material. Make sure the hole through the front panel for the shaft of C2 is large enough so the shaft does not come into contact with the chassis.

Tuneup

The transmitter should be connected to the input of the Transmatch through some sort of instrument that will indicate SWR. S1 is set to the band of operation and the balanced line is connected to the insulators on the rear panel of the coupler. The alligator clips are attached to the mid points of coils L1 and L3 and power is applied. Adjust C1 and C2 for minimum reflected power. If a good match is not obtained, move the antenna tap points either closer to the ends or center of the coils. Again apply power, and tune C1 and C2 until the best possible match is obtained. Continue moving the antenna taps until a 1-to-1 match is obtained.

The circuit described here is intended for power levels up to roughly 200 watts. Balance was checked by means of two RF ammeters, one in each leg of the feed line. Results showed the balance to be well within 1 dB.

A Balanced QRP Transmatch

The balanced QRP Transmatch shown in Figs 37 through 39 was designed and built by Zachary Lau, KH6CP, in the ARRL Lab. It is designed for use with balanced feed lines, although random-wire antennas can be fed if one of the antenna terminals is grounded. Unlike most Transmatches designed for use with balanced feed lines, this design features a balun at the input, rather than at the output. As a result, the balun sees impedances close to the design impedances once the Transmatch has been properly adjusted. This results in lower loss and freedom from core saturation at low power levels.

Since it is balanced currents that prevent feed-line radiation, this circuit was designed to balance currents rather than voltages. Some antenna systems use circuits that provide balanced voltages, making it necessary to make the system symmetrical in an effort to balance the currents. By going straight to balanced currents, instead of balanced voltages, it is possible to use a much simpler matching network. In addition, the actual current balance in typical amateur open-wire feed lines should be improved.

Construction

The inductor L1 and the capacitor C1 should be of the highest quality obtainable for best performance. Low-impedance loads will require a good inductor for efficient matching, while high-impedance loads will require a good capacitor.

L1 was wound with tinned copper wire to make it easier to adjust taps. It is necessary to wind the wire with spaces between turns to prevent shorts which may make the inductor lossy; no. 16 wire is heavy enough to stay in position on the toroid. The inductor used had a full-inductance Q of 420 at 7.9 MHz; the Q was 410 after the taps and switch were added. The use of clip lead taps is not recommended as they increase losses, although they may be useful in initially setting up tap positions.

Capacitor C1 should have a value of at least 250 pF, and larger capacitors will work even better, increasing the range of the Transmatch at low frequencies. Suitable capacitors are usually available at hamfests. The value of C2 and C3 should equal C1, and C4 should be twice the value of C1. If the calculated values of C2, C3 and C4 are not available, smaller values may be used.

Capacitor C1 must be insulated from the chassis, so it was mounted using ½-inch Plexiglas with tapped screw holes. An insulated shaft coupler was used to prevent high voltage from appearing on the knob set screw. The cabinet is a Ten-Tec MW-8 with a model 91-206 matching tilt-up bail. Although it is large for a QRP Transmatch, the cabinet matches the author's QRP rig

and allows the controls to be spaced apart for easy use. The logging scale is typewritten paper attached to the cabinet with a Plexiglas sheet.

T1 is a trifilar-wound transformer.

Fig 37—This QRP Transmatch for balanced feed lines features a balun at the input of the matching network.

Fig 38—Schematic diagram of the QRP Balanced Transmatch. Contact information for parts suppliers appears at the end of this chapter.

C1—330 pF variable capacitor, 500 V rating.
C2, C3—330 pF silver-mica capacitor, 500 V rating.
C4—600 pF silver-mica capacitor, 500 V rating.
J1—Female chassis-mount BNC connector.
J2—Two ceramic feedthrough insulators.
L1—36 turns no. 16 tinned wire on an Amidon T-200-6 core.

S1—Ceramic rotary switch, single wafer, 1 pole, 12 position.
S2—Ceramic rotary switch, single wafer, 2 pole, 6 position.
T1—12 trifilar turns on an Amidon FT-114-61 core. Primary, no. 16 enameled wire; secondary, no. 18 enameled wire.

Winding details are shown in Fig 38. It is possible to wind this coil with only two windings, eliminating the solder joint. The coil should be duplicated exactly with regard to the number of turns and core material unless the transformer can be tested at the operating frequency. Testing can be done by hooking up two baluns in series and measuring the insertion loss. The matching network will compensate for a poor balun, but efficiency will probably suffer. A toroidal choke balun would be recommended for a higher power version.

Switches S1 and S2 should be ceramic. Phenolic switches are not recommended, although they should work at low power levels on the order of a few watts. The switch positions should never be changed while more than a few watts of RF is applied.

Adjustment

Adjustment of the Transmatch is much easier if the approximate impedance of the load is known. In his article in *The ARRL Antenna Compendium, Volume 1*, "Mr. Smith's 'Other' Chart and Broadband Rigs" Roger Ghormley, WØKK, details how parts values for L networks can be calculated. Alternately, received signals can be peaked up by first adjusting the inductor and then the capacitor. As with any Transmatch, low power should be used in the initial adjustment. The actual power handling capability will depend on the load. The capacitor breakdown voltage is the limiting factor on high-impedance loads; a 2000-ohm load will cause the 500 V capacitors to reach their maximum rating at 62.5 W, while the maximum rating will be reached with 625 watts into a 200-ohm load. The current-handling capability of the wire is the limit on low-impedance loads;

Fig 39—Interior layout of the QRP Transmatch. The variable capacitor is mounted on a Plexiglas block.

a 40-ohm load will cause a 90-W signal to generate 1.5 A through the wire, while 450 watts will generate 1.5 A if the load is 200 ohms. These values are for resistive loads; a reactive load would require higher current and voltage ratings. The unit shown here has worked well in low-power operation (up to 4.5 watts).

A 50- to 75-Ohm Broadband Transformer

Shown in Figs. 40 through 42 is a simple 50- to 75-ohm or 75- to 50-ohm transformer that is suitable for operation in the 2- to 30-MHz frequency range. A pair of these transformers is ideal for using 75-ohm CATV Hardline in a 50-ohm system. In this application one transformer is used at each end of the cable run. At the antenna one transformer raises the 50-ohm impedance of the antenna to 75 ohms, thereby presenting a match to the 75-ohm cable. At the station end a transformer is used to step the 75-ohm line impedance down to 50 ohms.

The schematic diagram of the transformer is shown in Fig. 40, and the winding details are given in Fig. 41. C1 and C2 are compensating capacitors; the values shown were determined through swept return-loss measurements using a spectrum analyzer and tracking generator. The transformer consists of a trifilar winding of no. 14 enameled copper wire wound over an FT-240-61 (Q1 material) or equivalent core. As shown in Fig. 41, one winding has only half the number of turns of the other two. Care must be taken when connecting the loose ends so the proper phasing of the turns is maintained. Improper phasing will become apparent when power is applied to the transformer.

If the core has sharp edges it is a good idea either to sand the edges until they are relatively smooth or wrap the core with tape. The core shown in the photograph was wrapped with ordinary vinyl electrical tape, although glass-cloth insulating tape would be better. The idea is to prevent chafing of the wire insulation.

Construction

The easiest way to construct the transformer is wind the three lengths of wire on the core at the same time. Different color wires will aid in identifying the ends of the windings. After all three windings are securely in place, the appropriate wire may be unwound three turns as shown in the diagram. This wire is the 75-ohm connection point. Connections at the 50-ohm end are a bit tricky, but if the information in Fig. 41 is followed carefully no problems should be encountered. Use the shortest connections possible, as long leads will degrade the high-frequency performance.

The transformer is housed in a homemade aluminum enclosure measuring $3\frac{1}{2} \times 3\frac{3}{4} \times 1\frac{1}{4}$ inches. Any commercial cabinet of similar dimensions will work fine. In the unit shown in the photograph, several "blobs" of silicone seal (RTV) were used to hold the core in position. Alternatively, a piece of phenolic insulating material may be used between the core and the aluminum enclosure. Silicone seal is used to protect the inside of the unit from moisture. All joints and screw heads should receive a generous coating of RTV.

Checkout

Checkout of the completed transformer or transformers is quite simple. If a 75-ohm dummy load is available connect it to the 75-ohm terminal of the transformer. Connect a transmitter and SWR indicator (50 ohm) to the 50-ohm terminal of the transformer. Apply power (on each of the HF bands) and measure the SWR looking into the transformer. Readings should be well under 1.3 to 1 on each of the bands. If a 75-ohm load is not available and two transformers have been constructed they may be checked out simultaneously as follows. Connect the 75-ohm terminals of both transformers together, either directly through a coaxial adaptor or through a length of 75-ohm cable. Attach a 50-ohm load to one of the 50-ohm terminals and connect a transmitter and SWR indicator (50 ohm) to the remaining 50-ohm terminal. Apply power as outlined above and record the measurements. Readings should be under 1.3 to 1.

The transformers were checked in the ARRL laboratory under various mismatched conditions at the 1500-watt power level. No spurious signals (indicative of core saturation) could be found while

Fig 41—Pictorial drawing of the 50- to 75-ohm transformer showing details of the windings.

Fig 42—Packaging of the 50- to 75-ohm transformers.

viewing the LF, HF and VHF frequency range with a spectrum analyzer. A key-down, 1500-watt signal produced no increase in the temperature of the windings.

Using the Transformers

For indoor applications, the transformers can be assembled open style, without benefit of a protective enclosure. For outdoor installations, such as at the antenna feed point, the unit should be encapsulated in epoxy resin or mounted in a suitable weatherproof enclosure. A Minibox, sealed against moisture, works nicely for the latter.

Fig 40—Schematic diagram of the 50- to 75-ohm transformer described in the text. C1 and C2 are compensating capacitors.

C1—100 pF, silver mica.
C2—10 pF, silver mica.
J1, J2—Coaxial connectors, builder's choice.
T1—Transformer, 6 trifilar turns no. 14 enameled copper wire on an FT-240-61 (Q1 material, μ_i = 125) core. One winding has one-half the number of turns of the other two.

Super Dummy

Super Dummy is an RF load for use with full-power RF amplifiers. See Figs. 43 through 47. Designed by ARRL TA Dick Jansson, WD4FAB, this dummy load will "loaf" along at 1500 watts for 10 minutes without complaint. Super Dummy is not just a copy of the similar appearing Heathkit HN-31A Cantenna. A lot of development went into proving this design. These efforts concentrated on RF matching, heat transfer design and coolant selection.

It is not easy to design a dummy load for high-power operation. Heat must be safely dissipated and a good match maintained. Forced air cooling of 300 two-watt carbon resistors and running a Heath Cantenna with automobile antifreeze coolant were tried. Neither of these ideas proved satisfactory. Efforts were then turned to other directions. An improved dummy load evolved from this work. Super Dummy is suitable for HF and low VHF regions at 1500 watts.

The Bird Model 612 dummy load/wattmeter uses the type of construction shown in Fig. 44. This design ensures proper characteristic impedance (Z_0) along the structure. Starting with the coaxial connector, a tapered line is used to provide a constant impedance (50 ohms) to the resistor. The coaxial shield then decreases in size to

Fig 44—An RF load should have proper characteristic impedance along the entire structure for operation over a wide frequency range (see text).

Fig 43—Super Dummy is an RF load designed to handle 1.5 kW.

match the diminishing impedance to ground along the resistor. Coaxial line impedance can be determined from the formula:

$$Z_0 = \frac{138}{\sqrt{\epsilon}} \log \frac{D}{d}$$

where

Z_0 = coaxial line characteristic impedance
D = ID of coaxial shell
d = OD of coaxial conductor
ϵ = dielectric constant of coolant (air = 1.0)

This equation shows that as the impedance along the resistor diminishes following a straight-line curve, the shape of the coaxial shield or shell around the resistor follows a smooth logarithmic curve. That curve can be seen in Fig. 44.

A logarithmically tapered coaxial shell is difficult to form. At HF, we don't have to worry about the shape of the coaxial shell. Unless you are a purist, it is far easier to just use the straight tubing shown in Figs. 45 and 46. A straight shell proves quite usable into the VHF region. For a 50-ohm resistor, the coaxial shell is sized for a Z_0 of about 25 ohms.

RF Performance

The SWR of Super Dummy was measured in the ARRL lab. Fig. 47 shows the results, an excellent match through the HF region (SWR less than 1.05). SWR is only 1.08 at 50 MHz, rising to a tolerable 1.4 at 144 MHz.

Construction

Construction of Super Dummy is straightforward. Two one-gallon paint cans were obtained from a painting supply house. A 5.5-inch-diameter disc is removed from the closed end of the top can and four 0.120-inch holes are drilled equally spaced through the remaining bottom rim with matching holes in the top rim of the bottom can. The two cans can now be locked together with four no. 4 screws and nuts,

forming a "two high" can assembly. Carefully solder the rims of the cans to fully seal the assembly against oil leakage. Be sure to secure the cans with the screws as solder is dependable only for sealing and not for mechanical strength.

Mount the shield tube to the cover with four aluminum angle brackets. Space the tube 1.5 to 2 inches from the cover, allowing room for the coolant to flow out of the top. Clamp the copper straps to each end of the resistor. Under the top strap be sure to include the U-shaped strap that is used to connect the resistor and the SO-239 coaxial connector. Install the resistor in the tube, making sure that the U strap slides over the SO-239 connector center pin. Center and clamp the lower end firmly with four no. 6 brass screws and lock nuts. Solder the U strap to the connector pin after clamping the lower end.

Coolant

Selection of a coolant for the resistor involved a lengthy investigation. The use of PCB transformer oils is illegal and involves a serious health hazard. The investigation did identify several modern-day transformer and heat transfer oils that could be used, but none of these are available for purchase in any quantity less than a 55-gallon drum.[1] Transformer oil has lower viscosity. That means lower resistor temperatures, but at the penalty of using an oil with a 140 to 150°C flash point (vaporization temperature). Transformer oils are also treated to remove water, but maintaining this dry condition is difficult and expensive. Calculations of the fluid heat transfer show that turbulent nature convection flow exists for rated power levels. The use of higher viscosity oil produces higher resistor temperatures, but the gain in flash point temperature is greater than the rise in resistor temperature. Oils designed for heat transfer have flash points in the 230 to 250°C region.

[1]Shell Oil Co., "Thermia"; Chevron Oil Co., "Heat Transfer Oil No. 1"; Gulf Oil Co., Security No. 53; Texas Oil Co., "Thermia".

A — SO-239 COAXIAL CONNECTOR.
B — BRACKET MOUNTING HARDWARE: USE NO. 6 FOR THE TOP AND NO. 4 FOR THE TUBE.
C — TUBE MOUNTING BRACKET, ½ × 3 IN, BEND ½ INCH FROM END. FOUR REQUIRED.
D — COPPER STRAP, 0.88 × 0.010 × 5 IN.
E — COPPER STRAP, 0.88 × 0.010 × 3.5 IN, BEND ¼ INCH FROM EACH END. SECURE WITH THREE SETS OF NO. 4 HARDWARE. TWO REQUIRED.
F — ALUMINUM TUBE, 2.00 (OD) × 0.049 (WALL) × 12.0 IN (LONG).
G — RESISTOR, CARBORUNDUM PART NO. 889SP500K.
H — SEE TEXT.
I — NO. 6-32 × ¾-IN BRASS SCREW WITH 2 NUTS. FOUR REQUIRED.

Fig 45—X ray view of the interior of Super Dummy. To ensure proper cooling, coolant level should be higher than the top of the tube. Carborundum 889SP500K supplier: Carborundum. (Contact information for parts suppliers appears at the end of this chapter.)

Fig 46—View of the insides of Super Dummy. Construction details are given in Fig 45.

Fig 47—Super Dummy SWR curve. Measurements were made in the ARRL lab using swept return-loss techniques.

Heat transfer oils are composed predominantly of mineral oil. Highly refined or medicinal mineral oil has a usably high flash point but an undesirably high cost. Heat transfer oils contain small amounts of rust and oxidation inhibitors, making them preferable to mineral oils. Heat transfer oils are not available in small quantities, but in at least one case the very same product is relabeled and sold in 5 gallon cans for service as a "turbine oil." That product is sold by TEXACO distributors as Regal Oil R&O No. 46.

Use of automotive motor and transmission oils is undesirable. They are composed of a wide mixture of oils with differing flash points. Motor oil additives will damage the metal platings on an RF resistor. There is no danger in the short term use of automotive oils, but the long-term effects are a problem. Further, there are no economic advantages with automotive oils, as they cost as much as turbine oil.

Thermal Tests

Thermal performance tests were done with Super Dummy in mineral oil at a power level of 1.5 kW. The large resistor used in Super Dummy has a reasonable power density (3.5 watts/cm^2). That results in moderate operating temperatures and negligible resistance shift. Some tests were conducted without the coaxial shield tube. Considerable thermal stagnation of the oil was measured in these tests with temperatures in the range of 160 °C at the top and only 40 °C at the bottom of the container. The coaxial shield tube around the resistor performs another valuable function here. The tube enhances oil flow from the bottom of the can to the top, forcing better oil mixing in the can and effective use of the total thermal mass of the 2 gallons of coolant.

UHF Gallon Dummy

UHF Gallon Dummy is an RF load for use with VHF and UHF RF amplifiers up to 1.3 GHz and power outputs to 1 kW. See Figs. 48 through 56. Designed by ARRL TA Dick Jansson, WD4FAB, this dummy load is an extension of the work done with "Super Dummy," the HF legal-limit load presented earlier in this chapter. It will handle 1000 watts for five minutes without complaint. A lot of development went into proving this design, with efforts concentrated on RF matching, heat transfer design and coolant selection.

The Bird Model 612 dummy load/wattmeter uses the type of construction shown in Fig. 44. This design ensures proper characteristic impedance (Z_0) along the structure. Starting with the coaxial connector, a tapered line is used to provide a constant impedance (50 ohms) to the resistor, while expanding the transmission line size up to meet that of the resistor. The coaxial shield then decreases in size along the resistor to match the diminishing impedance-to-ground of the resistor. Coaxial line impedance can be determined from the formula

$$Z_0 = \frac{138}{\sqrt{\epsilon}} \log \frac{D}{d}$$

where
Z_0 = coaxial line characteristics impedance
D = ID of coaxial shell
d = OD of coaxial conductor
ϵ = dielectric constant of coolant (air = 1.0).

This equation shows that as the impedance along the resistor diminishes following a straight-line curve; the shape of the coaxial shield or shell around the resistor follows a smooth logarithmic curve. That curve can be seen in Fig. 44.

A logarithmically tapered coaxial shell is difficult to form, so most designers just use straight tubing at HF. This approach works just fine. For the VHF and UHF region, however, proper RF impedance matching is very important because the dimensions of the load become significantly sizable compared to the wavelengths of interest. UHF Gallon Dummy provides a close approach to the ideal shapes.

RF Performance

The SWR of the UHF Gallon Dummy was measured in the ARRL lab. Fig. 49 shows the results: An excellent match through 220 MHz (SWR less than 1.05). SWR is a tolerable 1.25 for the 70-cm band and less than 1.25 for the 23-cm band. To obtain these results, you *must* have UHF Gallon Dummy immersed in its coolant oil. The dielectric constant of the oil is approximately 2.3. UHF Gallon Dummy tested dry showed an SWR of approximately 2.0 across most of the spectrum. The change

is caused by the difference between the dielectric constant of the oil and that of air.

Deviations in performance from the target design are caused by some of the practicalities of constructing such a load. The builder can carefully watch, and avoid, such elements as the dimensional steps in the center conductor as it attaches to the connector, and at the junction with the

Fig 48—UHF Gallon Dummy is built into two one-gallon paint cans bolted and soldered together.

resistor. The lack of a logarithmically shaped resistor shell will, of course, provide an element of performance error. In short, paying attention to small details is important in obtaining the best performance from this load.

Construction

Although you can build the UHF dummy load shown here from parts purchased separately from suppliers, a good way to begin is to purchase a Heathkit HN-31A "Cantenna" dummy load and modify it. This way, you won't have to track down the power resistor, and you'll get one of the paint cans complete with a lid with a vent hole.

The housing for the UHF Gallon Dummy is made from two one-gallon paint cans obtained from a painting supply house. Remove a 5.5-inch-diameter disc from the closed (bottom) end of the top can. Drill four 0.120-inch holes, equally spaced, around the remaining bottom rim; drill matching holes in the top rim of the bottom can. The two cans can now be locked together with four no. 4 screws and nuts, forming a "two high" can assembly. Carefully solder the rims of the cans to fully seal the assembly against oil leakage. You must secure the cans with the screws, as solder is only dependable for sealing and not for mechanical strength. Prime and paint the exterior of this can assembly to resist the rigors of rust corrosion.

The interior parts of the UHF Gallon Dummy were built using hobby store brass shim stock, a 1-kW (rating with coolant) 50-ohm resistor (available from Carborundum or from a Heathkit HN-31A) and

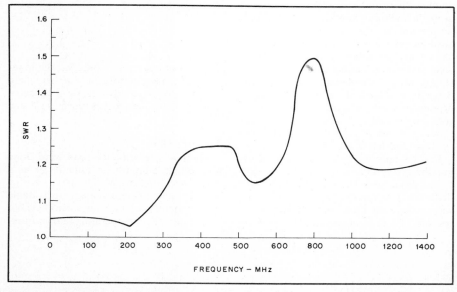

Fig 49—UHF Gallon Dummy SWR curve made in the ARRL lab using swept return-loss techniques. Measurements were made in the two-gallon can with turbine oil coolant.

some wooden dowels. Apart from an electric drill and a soldering iron, this double conical shape was formed entirely with hand tools. Fig. 50 is an X-ray view of the interior of the UHF Gallon Dummy showing the arrangement of the parts.

Make all of the parts before you begin assembly of any part of the load. Figs. 51 and 52 detail the flat layout of the sheet brass that will be used to make the transition and resistor cones. Fig. 53 shows the center-conductor cone, four braces and two clamp bands. These drawings are full-size templates. They may be photocopied and used directly to do the sheet-metal layout. Carefully lay out and cut these parts to size. Drill the no. 60 holes and cut the joining tabs.

Start assembly by forming the brass stock for the transition cone into a conical shape. The edges of the brass stock are lap-joined and soldered along the longitudinal seam. You will get better results if you drill some small holes in the tab where the two edges overlap and install 1/16-inch eyelets to act as rivets to hold the assembly together as you solder. Assemble the resistor cone the same way. Assembly of the conical copper center conductor is similar, except that it is just soldered along its seam (no rivets). Figs. 54 and 55 show how the pieces should look when finished and how they will attach to the paint can lid.

Drill a hole for the UG-680 hermetic Type-N connector in the center of the paint can lid. Attach the connector nut and securely tighten it in place. Solder the connector to the top of the lid, as shown in Fig. 56, to seal the connection against possible coolant leakage.

Solder the small end of the brass transition cone to a shortened nut from a PL-259 connector. This nut will screw onto the back-side threads of the UG-680 connector. Be sure to drill a small vent relief hole through the PL-259 nut to allow coolant oil into the upper section of the cone; see Fig. 54. Check this assembly on the UG-680 to be sure that it is perpendicular to the lid, but do not attach yet.

Clamp the large end of the conical center conductor to the resistor and check that it is straight and true. Check the small end of the center-conductor tube for fit on the UG-680 center conductor. Slide this cone-and-resistor subassembly into the brass transition shell; leave it loose. Carefully line up the tabs on the large end of the transition cone with the tabs on the large end of the resistor cone. When you are sure of the alignment, solder the tabs together to form one large double-conical shell. The cone-and-resistor subassembly will still be a loose part inside the shell assembly.

Slide the small end of the center-conductor cone through the small end of the transition cone and solder it to the center conductor of the UG-680 connector. Screw the double-cone shell assembly to the outside of the UG-680 connector. When the connector end is in place, the free end of

Fig 50—Cutaway view of UHF Gallon Dummy. Carborundum 889SP500K supplier: Carborundum. (Contact information for parts suppliers appears at the end of this chapter.)

the resistor should fit into the small end of the resistor cone, where it will be secured with a brass clamp band.

Add the four braces by soldering them between the lid and the transition cone to make a more rigid structure. Check your work at this point and make any corrections.

Coolant

Selection of a coolant for the resistor involved a lengthy investigation. The use of PCB transformer oils is illegal and involves a serious health hazard. The investigation did identify several modern-day transformer and heat transfer oils that could be used, but none of these are available for purchase in any quantity less than a 55-gallon drum.[1] Transformer oil has lower

[1]Shell Oil Co., "Thermia"; Chevron Oil Co., "Heat Transfer Oil #1"; Gulf Oil Co., "Security #53"; Texas Oil Co., "Thermia".

viscosity. That means lower resistor temperatures, but at the penalty of using an oil with a 140 to 150°C flash point (vaporization temperature). Calculations of the fluid heat transfer show that a turbulent natural convection flow exists for rated power levels. The use of higher viscosity oil produces higher resistor temperatures, but the gain in flash point temperature is greater than the rise in resistor temperature. Oils designed for heat transfer have flash points in the 230 to 250°C region. Transformer oils are treated to remove water, but maintaining this dry condition is difficult and expensive.

Heat transfer oils are composed mainly of mineral oil. Highly refined or medicinal mineral oil has a usably high flash point but an undesirably high cost. Heat transfer oils contain small desirable amounts of rust and oxidation inhibitors, making them preferable to mineral oils. Heat transfer oils are not available in small quantities, but in at

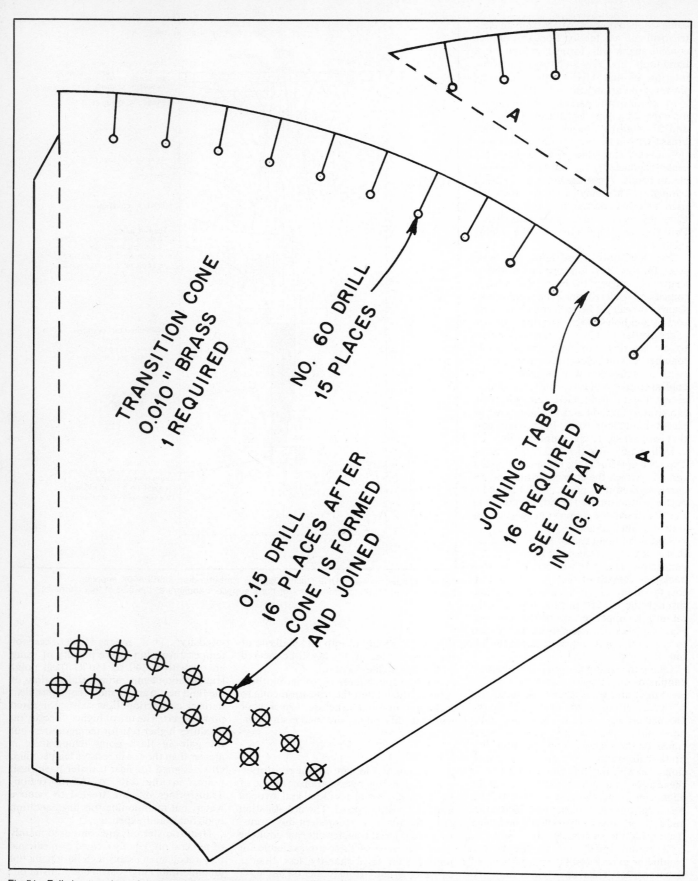

TRANSITION CONE
0.010" BRASS
1 REQUIRED

NO. 60 DRILL
15 PLACES

0.15 DRILL
16 PLACES AFTER
CONE IS FORMED
AND JOINED

JOINING TABS
16 REQUIRED
SEE DETAIL
IN FIG. 54

A

A

Fig 51—Full-size template of the transition cone. Make a copy of this page, cut out the two pieces and tape them together along edge A. You can use this template directly to lay out the transition cone on sheet brass.

0.54" APPROX.

CUTOUT NOTCH

TAB DETAIL

BEND LINE

NO. 60 DRILL 22 PLACES

NO. 60 DRILL 22 PLACES

8 TABS

JOINING TABS 16 REQUIRED SEE DETAIL

RESISTOR CONE

0.15" DRILL 16 PLACES AFTER CONE IS FORMED AND JOINED

Fig 52—Full-size template of the resistor cone. The tab detail applies to this cone and the transition cone of Fig 51.

CENTER CONDUCTOR
0.005 – 0.010" COPPER
1 REQUIRED

CLAMP BAND 0.01" BRASS
2 REQUIRED

0.109" DRILL
4 PLACES

NO. 60 DRILL
7 PLACES

BRACE 0.01" BRASS
4 REQUIRED

Fig 53—Full-size templates for the center conductor cone, braces and clamp bands.

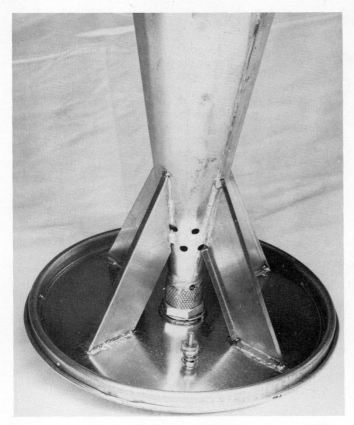

Fig 54—Four braces secure the transition cone to the lid of the paint can. Drill a hole in the PL-259 nut that solders to the transition cone and screws to the Type-N connector.

Fig 55—The resistor clamps to the end of the resistor cone (top of photo). At the bottom of the photo, the tabs on the resistor and transition cones are soldered together.

Fig 56—The UG-680/U Type-N connector is soldered to the lid of the paint can to seal the hole against leakage. To the right of the connector is a vent made from a no. 6-32 machine screw, a spring and a nut.

least one case the very same product is relabeled and sold in 5 gallon cans for service as a "turbine oil." That product is sold by the Texas Oil Company (TEXACO) distributors as Regal Oil R&O No. 46.

Use of automotive motor and transmission oils is undesirable. They are composed of a wide mixture of oils with differing flash points. Motor oil additives will damage the metal platings on an RF resistor. There is no danger in the short term use of automotive oils, but the long term effects are a problem. There are no economic advantages with automotive oils either; they cost just as much as turbine oil.

Thermal Tests

Thermal performance tests were done with the UHF Gallon Dummy with a 1-kW resistor (rating with coolant) in mineral oil at a power level of 1.5 kW. The tests were conducted with considerable apprehension, but no spectacular events occurred except for very vigorous convection flow of oil over the resistor. Don't use this size resistor at higher power levels than its 1 kW (cooled) rating. The resistor gets *very hot* at 1.5 kW, and substantial permanent resistance shifts have been measured.

Some tests were conducted without a coaxial shield tube. Considerable thermal stagnation of the oil was measured in these tests with temperatures in the range of 160 °C at the top and only 40 °C at the bottom of the container. The coaxial shield assembly at the top and only 40 °C at the bottom of the container. The coaxial shield assembly around the resistor performs another valuable function here. The shield enhances oil flow from the bottom of the can to the top, forcing better oil mixing in the can and effective use of the total thermal mass of the two gallons.

A Marker Generator for 100, 50 and 25 kHz

A marker generator that provides reference signals at 100-, 50-, and 25-kHz intervals is a useful addition to any ham shack. The generator can be used as a low-level signal source when testing receivers, or it can be installed inside a receiver and used to mark the edges of the amateur bands and subbands. When built into a receiver, the marker generator is usually called a crystal calibrator.

The standard design for a marker generator involves using a crystal oscillator operating at 100 kHz and then dividing this signal with flip-flops to get the 50- and 25-kHz signals. The 100-kHz crystals are rather expensive, however, and are difficult to locate.

Another way to produce marker signals is to use a crystal oscillator operating at a multiple of 1 MHz. Crystals for 1, 2 and 4 MHz are readily available at reasonable prices on the computer surplus market.

Fig 57—Front view of the 100, 50 and 25-kHz marker generator. A two-pole rotary switch was used in this unit; one section of the switch applies power to the generator, and the other selects the desired signal.

Low-cost TTL ICs can then be used to divide the signal down to 100, 50 and 25 kHz. This is the approach taken in the marker generator shown in Figs. 57 through 60. The marker generator is simple to build, and it provides a good introduction to the principles of digital circuits. The output of the generator is rich in harmonics and provides marker signals up into the 2-meter band. This project was designed and built by Bruce Hale, KB1MW, in the ARRL Lab.

Circuit Description

The schematic of the marker generator is shown in Fig. 58 Two of the NAND gates in a 7400 quad-NAND package, U1, are used as an oscillator. The crystal, Y1, sets the operating frequency at 1, 2 or 4 MHz, and C1 is used to trim the frequency during the calibration procedure. U1C acts as a buffer between the oscillator and the rest

Fig 58—Schematic diagram of the marker generator. All resistors are ¼-W, 5% types. All capacitors are disk ceramic unless noted. Capacitors marked with polarity are tantalum electrolytic.

C1—5-60 pF miniature trimmer capacitor.
C2—20 pF disk ceramic (see text).
U1—7400 or 74LS00 quad NAND gate.

U2, U4—7474 or 74LS74 dual D flip flop.
U3—7490 or 74LS90 decade counter.
U5—78L05, 7805 or LM340-T5 5 V voltage

regulator (see text).
Y1—1, 2 or 4-MHz crystal in HC-25, HC-33 or HC-6 holder.

Fig 59—The marker generator may be built using a 1 MHz, 2 MHz or 4 MHz crystal. With a 1 MHz crystal, U2 is not needed. The 4 MHz version was built using a 7805 regulator. All of the units built in the ARRL lab could be trimmed to within 50 Hz of 100 kHz, including a prototype built on perforated board.

Table 5

Marker Generator Jumper Placement

Crystal Frequency	Jumper Placement
1 MHz	A—F
	U2 not used
2 MHz	A—B, C—F
	Add a 1-Ω resistor from D to U2 pin 14
4 MHz	A—B, C—D, E—F

of the circuit; U1D is not used, so its inputs are grounded. Unused TTL gate inputs should always be connected either to ground or to V_{cc} through a pull-up resistor.

U2 is a 7474 dual D flip-flop. The two flip-flops in this package are used to divide the output of the oscillator down to 1 MHz. This circuit is designed so that crystals operating at 1, 2 or 4 MHz can be used, depending on what is available. If a 1-MHz crystal is used, U2 is not needed and can be left completely out of the circuit. If a 2-MHz crystal is used, one flip-flop of the two available is used, and the input of the second flip-flop is pulled high with a 1-kΩ resistor. Using a 4-MHz crystal requires both flip-flops for a 1-MHz output to U3. Notice the PRESET and CLEAR inputs (pins 1, 4, 10 and 13); these inputs can be pulled low to set and clear the flip-flops. During normal operation these inputs must be held high—a 1-kΩ pull-up resistor is connected from the PRESET and CLEAR inputs to V_{cc}.

U3 is a 7490 divide-by-ten counter (sometimes called a decade counter). A 1 MHz input to this IC produces a 100 kHz output signal at pin 12. We could stop here if we were building a 100-kHz signal generator.

Another 7474 dual flip-flop is used at U4 to divide the 100-kHz output of U3 down to 50 and 25 kHz. Again, the PRESET and CLEAR inputs must be pulled high. The outputs of U3, U4A and U4B are connected to switch S1A to select the desired output. C2 decouples the output jack from the circuit to prevent excessive loading.

U5 is a 78L05 low-current, 5-V regulator IC in a TO-92 package. The regulator input and the output are bypassed with 1-μF tantalum and 0.01-μF disc ceramic capacitors. A 9-V transistor battery provides the power source, and S1B is used as an on-off switch.

Construction

Construction of this project is straightforward. A PC board was used in the final versions shown in Fig. 59, but a prototype built on a Radio Shack perforated board worked well. Wire-wrap construction could also be used.

A PC component-placement diagram is shown in Fig. 60. The PC pattern shown can be used to build the marker generator using any of the three crystal frequencies by varying the placement of three jumper wires. Locations for the jumpers are clearly labeled on the PC pattern and they should be set as shown in Table 5, depending on the crystal frequency. Provision is made on the PC board for either crystals in small HC-25 holders or the larger HC-33 or HC-6 holders.

If low-power Schottky ICs are available, they should be used at U1, U2, U3 and U4, These ICs draw considerably less current than their standard TTL counterparts, and using them will reduce the drain on the battery. These devices are labeled with "LS" as part of their numerical designator; a low-power quad NAND gate is designated a 74LS00.

The value of the coupling capacitor, C2, is not critical. Any value between 10 and 100 pF will work, with the larger values providing a bit less signal at the output jack.

A standard 7805 regulator IC in a TO-220 package can be used at U5 if a 78L05 cannot be located. This is "overkill" in a way, since the 7805 is rated to pass at least an amp of current, and the marker generator draws only about 70 mA, even with standard TTL ICs. The 78L05 regulator should be available from the same companies that sell the TTL ICs used in this project.

Fig 60—Parts-placement diagram for the marker generator PC board. Consult Table 5 for information on placing the jumpers at points A, B, C, D, E and F. Extra pads in the oscillator section of the board allow for the use of a crystal in a small HC-25 holder or a larger HC-33 or HC-6 holder. Pads are also provided for different sizes of trimmer capacitor. A full-size etching pattern appears at the back of this book.

The input voltage to the regulator can be as high as 12-V dc; this may be desired if the marker generator is built inside a receiver using a 12-V power supply or some other source of 12-V dc is convenient. The low-power regulator may require a small press-on heat sink if 12-V dc is used, however.

A Radio Shack 2-pole 6-position rotary switch was used in this version of the marker generator, but any available rotary switch with at least four positions can be used. If a 2-pole switch is not available, a separate power switch can be used, but be careful to switch the generator off when it is not in use. An LED can be used as a power indicator.

Computer surplus crystals were used in all the units shown here, and all the generators could be trimmed to within 50 Hz of 100 kHz. These crystals are available from many of the electronics dealers listed in the Component Data chapter.

The value of C1 (the oscillator frequency trimmer) is not critical. Trimmers are available at Radio Shack in a 5 to 60 pF range—this is fine. Too small a value may not trim the oscillator frequency properly, and too large a value may prevent the oscillator from operating.

Adjustment and Calibration

To check the power supply section of the marker generator, measure the input and output voltages at U5. Input to the IC should be at least 8 V, and the output should be between 4.8 and 5.2 V.

Use an oscilloscope to observe the output waveform as S1 is rotated to select the 100, 50 and 25-kHz marker signals. The output should approximate a 3 to 5 V peak-to-peak square wave. The larger the value of the coupling capacitor C2, the less "square" the output will be as the higher-frequency harmonics are attenuated.

The easiest way to calibrate the marker generator is with a frequency counter. With the counter connected to the output of the calibrator, adjust C1 until the counter measures the frequency to the desired precision. Greater capacitance at C1 will lower the oscillator frequency; if the oscillator will not trim with C1 at maximum capacitance, a low-value capacitor can be added in parallel with C1 to further reduce the oscillator frequency.

If a frequency counter is not available, the generator can be calibrated using WWV. Tune in WWV and disconnect the receiver antenna. Switch the receiver to the CW position (or turn on the BFO) without changing the setting of the tuning dial. Connect a short piece of wire to the output of the generator and place it near the receiver. Adjust C1 until the marker generator can be clearly heard in the receiver.

Contact Information

The following companies or resources are mentioned in this chapter. Since amateurs often have access to obsolete parts through surplus dealers and hamfests, resources are not deleted from this list when the normal supplier ceases operation or discontinues a part. This list is changed when the chapter is revised, or when we receive reader feedback. A revision date follows each entry. More timely information about some companies may appear in The ARRL Parts Suppliers List (see the Component Data chapter of this volume).

All Electronics Corp, 15004 Oxnard St, Van Nuys, CA 91411, 800-826-5432 (Apr 91).

Amidon Associates, PO Box 956, Torrance, CA 90508, 213-763-5770 (Apr 91).

Arrow Electronics (Attn: Laura), 1860 Smithtown Ave, Ronkonkoma, NY 11779, 800-932-7769, fax 516-585-0878 (Apr 91).

B & W (Barker & Williamson), 10 Canal St, Bristol, PA 19007, 215-788-5581 (Apr 91).

BCD Electro, PO Box 450207, Garland, TX 75045-0207, 214-343-1770, fax 214-343-1854 (Apr 91).

Carborundum Co, Electrical Products Division, PO Box 339, Niagara Falls, NY 14302, 716-278-2521 (Apr 91).

Data Signal Inc, 2403 Commerce Ln, Albany, GA 31707 (Apr 91).

Digi-Key Corporation, 701 Brooks Ave S, PO Box 677, Thief River Falls, MN 56701, 800-344-4539 (Apr 91).

Digitran, 855 S Arroyo Pkwy, Pasadena, CA 91105, 213-449-3110 (contact: Bob Privell) (Apr 91).

Fair Radio Sales, PO Box 1105, Lima, OH 45802, 419-227-6573 (Apr 91).

Heathkit, Heath Co, Benton Harbor, MI 49022 (Apr 91).

International Crystal, PO Box 26330, Oklahoma City, OK 73126, 405-236-3741 (Apr 91).

James Millen Electronics, PO Box 4215BV, Andover, MA 01810-4215, 508-975-2711, fax 508-474-8949 (Apr 91).

JAN Crystals, 2341 Crystal Dr, PO Box 06017, Fort Myers, FL 33906-6017, 800-526-9825 (Apr 91).

Lea Engineering, 1230 Layola Dr, Tempe, AZ 85282 (Apr 91).

MEPCO/Centralab Corp Headquarters, A North American Philips Corp, 2001 W Blue Heron Blvd, Riviera Beach, FL 33404, 407-881-3200 (Apr 91).

Newark Electronics, 4801 N Ravenswood St, Chicago, IL 60640, 312-784-5100 (Apr 91).

Oak Hills Research, 20879 Madison, Big Rapids, MI 49307, 616-796-0920 (Apr 91).

Palomar Engineers, PO Box 455, Escondido, CA 92033 (Apr 91).

Radio Shack—see local yellow pages for the nearest store (Apr 91).

Silicon Systems Inc, 14351 Myford Rd, Tustin, CA 92680, 714-731-7110. Single units of the DTMF decoder ICs (SSI175T202-SSI175T204) are available as engineering samples from the Marketing Department. Pin-compatible ICs are made by Crystal Semiconductor Corp (CS202-CS204) and Harris Semiconductor (CD22202-CD22204) (Apr 91).

Surplus Sales of Nebraska, 1315 Jones St, Omaha, NE 68102 (Apr 91).

Sylvania—see local yellow pages under electronic parts. Sylvania may be listed as GTE or ECG parts (Apr 91).

Syntronics, 2143 Guaranty Dr, Nashville, TN 37214 (Apr 91).

Texaco—see local yellow pages for distributors (Apr 91).

BIBLIOGRAPHY

A. Bailey, "The Antenna Lab, Parts 1 and 2," *Radio Communication*, Aug and Sep 1983.

W. Bruene, "An Inside Picture of Directional Wattmeters," *QST*, Apr 1959.

D. Fayman, "A Simple Computing SWR Meter," *QST*, Jul 1973, pp 23-33.

J. Gibbons and H. Horn, "A Circuit With Logarithmic Response Over Nine Decades," *IEEE Transactions on Circuit Theory*, Vol CT-11, No. 3, Sep 1964, pp 378-384.

J. Grebenkemper, "The Tandem Match— An Accurate Directional Wattmeter," *QST*, Jan 1987, pp 18-26. Also see "Tandam Match Corrections," *QST* Technical Correspondence, Jan 1988, p 49.

J. Grebenkemper, "Calibrating Diode Detectors," *QEX*, Aug 1990, pp 3-8.

Z. Lau and C. Hutchinson, "Improving the HW-9 Transceiver," *QST*, Apr 1988, pp 26-29.

V. Leenerts, "Automatic VSWR and Power Meter," *Ham Radio*, May 1980.

L. McCoy, "The Monimatch," *QST*, Oct 1956.

H. Perras, "Broadband Power-Tracking VSWR Bridge," *Ham Radio*, Aug 1979.

W. Spaulding, "A Broadband Two-Port S-Parameter Test Set," *Hewlett-Packard Journal*, Nov 1984.

F. Van Zant, "High-Power Operation with the Tandem Match Directional Coupler," *QST*, Jul 1989, pp 42-43.

Chapter 35

Component Data

INDEX OF TABLES IN CHAPTER 35

Table Number	Title	Page Number
1	Resistor-Capacitor Color Code	35-1
2	Standard Values for Capacitors and Resistors	35-2
3	EIA Temperature Characteristic Code for Disc-Ceramic Capacitors	35-3
4	EIA Designations for Capacitor Temperature Coefficient	35-3
5	EIA Capacitance Tolerance Codes	35-3
6	Approximate Series-Resonant Frequencies of Disc-Ceramic Bypass Capacitors	35-4
7	Powdered-Iron Toroid Cores—Magnetic Properties	35-4
8	Powdered-Iron Toroid Cores—Dimensions	35-4
9	Color Code for Hookup Wire	35-5
10	Ferrite Toroid Cores—Properties	35-5
11	Copper-Wire Table	35-6
12	EIA Vacuum-Tube Base Diagrams	35-7
13	Triode Transmitting Tubes	35-8
14	Tetrode and Pentode Transmitting Tubes	35-9&10
15	TV Deflection Tubes	35-11
16	Semiconductor Diode Specifications	35-11
17	Voltage-Variable Capacitance Diodes	35-12
18	Zener Diodes	35-12—14
19	Metal-Oxide Varistors Transient Suppressors	35-15
20	Japanese Semiconductor Nomenclature	35-15
21	General-Purpose Transistors	35-15
22	Low-Noise Transistors	35-16
23	RF Power Transistors, High Frequency, Low Voltage Amplifier Transistors, Power FETs	35-16&17
24	VHF and UHF Class-A Linear Transistors	35-18
25	Suggested Small-Signal FETs	35-18
26	Power FETs	35-19
27	General Purpose Silicon Power Transistors	35-20&21
28	Package Information	35-22
29	Integrated Circuit Operational Amplifiers	35-23
30	IC Op Amp Base Diagrams	35-24&25
31	Three-Terminal Voltage Regulators	35-26&27
32	Coaxial Cable End Connectors	35-28&29
33	Cross-Family Adapters	35-29
34	Miniature Lamp Guide	35-30&31
35	Crystal Holders	35-32
36	Properties of Common Thermoplastics	35-33—35
37	TTL Families	35-35
38	Fractions of an inch with Metric Equivalents	35-36
39	Aluminum Numbers for Amateur Use	35-36
40	Voltage-to-Power Conversion Table	35-37
41	Equivalent Values of Relfection Coefficient, Attenuation, SWR and Return Loss	35-38
42	ARRL Parts Suppliers List	35-38&39

Few of us have the time or space to collect all the literature available on the many different commercially manufactured components. Even if we did, the task of keeping track of new and obsolete devices would surely be formidable. Fortunately, amateurs tend to use a limited number of component types. This chapter provides a source of information on the kinds of components most often encountered by the amateur experimenter.

Component Values

Values of composition resistors and small capacitors (mica and ceramic) are specified throughout this *Handbook* in terms of "preferred values." In the preferred-number system, all values represent (approximately) a constant-percentage increase over the next lower value. The base of the system is the number 10. Only two significant figures are used.

"Tolerance" means that a variation of plus or minus the percentage given is considered satisfactory. For example, the actual resistance of a "4700-ohm" 20-percent resistor can lie anywhere between 3700 and 5600 ohms, approximately. The permissible variation in the same resistance value with 5-percent tolerance would be in the range from 4500 to 4900 ohms, approximately.

In the component specifications in this *Handbook*, it is to be understood that when no tolerance is specified the *largest* tolerance available in that value will be satisfactory.

Table 1
Resistor-Capacitor Color Code

Color	Significant Figure	Decimal Multiplier	Tolerance (%)	Voltage Rating*
Black	0	1	–	–
Brown	1	10	1*	100
Red	2	100	2*	200
Orange	3	1,000	3*	300
Yellow	4	10,000	4*	400
Green	5	100,000	5*	500
Blue	6	1,000,000	6*	600
Violet	7	10,000,000	7*	700
Gray	8	100,000,000	8*	800
White	9	1,000,000,000	9*	900
Gold	–	0.1	5	1000
Silver	–	0.01	10	2000
No color	–	–	20	500

*Applies to capacitors only.

Values that do not easily fit into the preferred-number system (such as 500, 25,000) can be substituted. It is obvious, for example, that a 5000-ohm resistor falls well within the tolerance range of the 4700-ohm 20-percent resistor used in the example above. It would not, however, be usable if the tolerance were specified as 5 percent.

Component Markings

The values of small components such as capacitors and resistors are usually marked with standard color codes or cryptic abbreviations. If you have an ohmmeter and capacitor meter, you can quickly determine the value of an unknown component. If not, the information in the following section can help you identify the majority of components you're likely to encounter.

Table 1 shows the standard resistor-capacitor color code. From the information in Table 1, you can determine the value and tolerance of most resistors. You can also use this information to determine the value, tolerance and voltage rating of some capacitors, such as mica and molded paper types.

Table 2 shows standard values for resistors and capacitors. Note that these are the significant figures in the value and that these standard values may be multiplied by powers of 10. For example, 2.2 μF, 22 μF, 220 μF and 2200 μF are all standard capacitance values. Standard resistor values

Table 2

Standard Values for Capacitors and Resistors

*1.0	*1.5	*2.2	*3.3	*4.7	*6.8
1.1	1.6	2.4	3.6	5.1	7.5
*1.2	*1.8	*2.7	*3.9	*5.6	*8.2
1.3	2.0	3.0	4.3	6.2	9.1

Note: All values available in ±5%
     *Available in ±10%

include 1.5 Ω, 15 Ω, 150 Ω, 1.5 kΩ, 15 kΩ, 150 kΩ 1.5 MΩ and 15 MΩ.

Capacitor Markings

The value, tolerance, temperature characteristics and voltage rating of many small capacitors such as disc-ceramic, mica and tantalum types can be determined from a color code or from a combination of letters and numbers. Fig. 1 shows several popular marking systems.

In addition to the value, disc-ceramic capacitors may be marked with a letter/number combination signifying temperature characteristics. See Table 3. For example, a capacitor marked Z5U is suitable for use between +10 and +85°C, with a maximum capacitance change of −56% or +22%.

Capacitors with highly predictable temperature coefficients of capacitance are sometimes used in oscillators that must be frequency stable with temperature. If an application called for a temperature coefficient of −750 parts per million per degree Celsius (N750), a capacitor marked U2J would be suitable. These codes are listed in Table 4.

Some capacitors, such as dipped silver mica units, have a letter designating the capacitance tolerance. These letters are deciphered in Table 5.

Fixed-Value Resistors

Composition resistors (and small wire-wound units molded in cases identical to the composition type) are color-coded as shown in Fig. 2. Color bands are used on resistors having axial leads; on radial-lead resistors the colors are placed as shown in the drawing. When bands are used for color coding the body color has no significance.

Examples: A resistor of the type shown in the lower drawing of Fig. 2 has the fol-

Fig. 1 — Capacitors can be identified by color codes and markings. Shown here are identifying markings found on many common capacitor types.

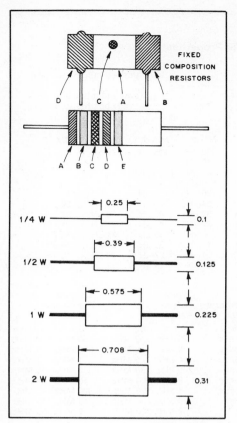

FIXED COMPOSITION RESISTORS

1/4 W — |← 0.25 →| / 0.1

1/2 W — |← 0.39 →| / 0.125

1 W — |← 0.575 →| / 0.225

2 W — |← 0.708 →| / 0.31

Fig. 2 — Color coding and body size for fixed resistors. The color code is given in Table 1. The colored areas have the following significance.

A — First significant figure of resistance in ohms.
B — Second significant figure.
C — Decimal multiplier.
D — Resistance tolerance in percent. If no color is shown the tolerance is ±20%.
E — Relative percent change in value per 1000 hours of operation; Brown, 1%; Red, 0.1%; Orange, 0.01%; Yellow, 0.001%.

Table 3
EIA Temperature Characteristic Code for Disc Ceramic Capacitors

Minimum Temperature		Maximum Temperature		Max. Cap. Change Over Temp. Range	
X	−55°C	2	+45°C	A	±1.0%
Y	−30°C	4	+65°C	B	±1.5%
Z	+10°C	5	+85°C	C	±2.2%
		6	+105°C	D	±3.3%
		7	+125°C	E	±4.7%
				F	±7.5%
				P	±10%
				R	±15%
				S	±22%
				T	−33%, +22%
				U	−56%, +22%
				V	−82%, +22%

Table 4
EIA Designations for Capacitor Temperature Coefficient

Industry	EIA
NP0	C0G
N033	S1G
N075	U1G
N150	P2G
N220	R2G
N330	S2H
N470	T2H
N750	U2J
N1500	P3K
N2200	R3L

Table 5
EIA Capacitance Tolerance Codes

C	±¼ pF
D	±½ pF
F	±1 pF or ±1%
G	±2 pF or ±2%
J	±5%
K	±10%
L	±15%
M	±20%
N	±30%
P	−0%, +100% or GMV
W	−20%, +40%
Y	−20%, +50%
Z	−20%, +80%

lowing color bands: A, red; B, red; C, orange; D, no color. The significant figures are 2,2 (22) and the decimal multiplier is 1000. The value of resistance is therefore 22,000 ohms and the tolerance is ±20 percent.

A resistor of the type shown in the upper drawing of Fig. 2 has the following colors: Body (A), blue; end (B), gray; dot, red; end (D), gold. The significant figures are 6, 8 (68) and the decimal multiplier is 100, so the resistance is 6800 ohms. The tolerance is ±5 percent.

The preferred values over one decade are given in Table 2. All resistance values (from less than 1 ohm to about 22 megohms) are available in ±2% metal film and ±5% carbon-composition units.

Carbon composition and metal film resistors have standard power ratings of 1/10, 1/8, 1/4, 1/2, 1 and 2 watts. The 1/10- and 1/8-watt sizes are expensive and difficult to purchase in small quantity.

They are used only where miniaturization is essential. The 1/4-, 1/2-, 1- and 2-watt composition resistors are drawn to scale in Fig. 2. Metal film resistors are usually slightly smaller than carbon units of the same power rating. Film resistors can often be distinguished by a glossy vitreous enamel coating and an hourglass profile as opposed to a right circular cylinder. They are the most commonly available type today, but the resistive film is often deposited in the form of a solenoid. Thus, they can be highly inductive and therefore less desirable than carbon-composition resistors in RF circuits.

Power Transformers

1) Primary Leads: black
   If tapped:
      Common: black
      Tap: black and yellow striped
      Finish: black and red striped
2) High-Voltage Plate Winding; red
   Center-Tap: red and yellow striped
3) Rectifier Filament Winding: yellow
   Center-Tap: yellow and blue striped
4) Filament Winding no. 1: green
   Center-Tap: green and yellow striped
5) Filament Winding no. 2: brown
   Center-Tap: brown and yellow striped
6) Filament Winding no. 3: slate
   Center-Tap: slate and yellow striped

IF Transformers

Plate lead — *blue*
B-plus lead — *red*
Grid (or diode) lead — *green*
Grid (or diode) return — *black*
   Note: If the secondary of the IF transformer is center-tapped, the second diode plate lead is green-and-black striped, and black is used for the center-tap lead.

Audio Transformers

Plate (finish) lead of primary — *blue*
B-plus lead (this applies whether the primary is plain or center-tapped) — *red*
Plate (start) lead on center-tapped primaries. (Blue may be used for this lead if polarity is not important) — *brown*
Grid (finish) lead to secondary — *green*
Grid return (this applies whether the secondary is plain or center-tapped) — *black*
Grid (start) lead on center-tapped secondaries (Green may be used for this lead if polarity is not important) — *yellow*

   Note: These markings apply also to line-to-grid and tube-to-line transformers.

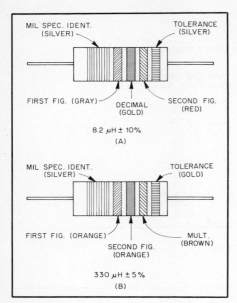

Fig. 3 — Color coding for tubular encapsulated RF chokes. At A, an example of the coding for an 8.2-μH choke is given. At B, the color bands for a 330-μH inductor are illustrated. The color code is given in Table 1.

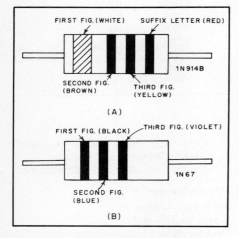

Fig. 4 — Color coding for semiconductor diodes. At A, the cathode is identified by the double-width first band. At B, the bands are grouped toward the cathode. Two-figure designations are signified by a black first band. The color code is given in Table 1. The suffix-letter code is: A — brown, B — red, C — orange, D — yellow, E — green, F — blue. The 1N prefix is understood.

Table 6

Approximate Series-Resonant Frequencies of Disc Ceramic Bypass Capacitors

Capacitance	Freq.[1]	Freq.[2]
0.01 μF	13 MHz	15 MHz
0.0047	18	22
0.002	31	38
0.001	46	55
0.0005	65	80
0.0001	135	165

[1]Total lead length of 1 inch
[2]Total lead length of 1/2 inch

Table 7

Powdered-Iron Toroid Cores — Magnetic Properties

Inductance and Turns Formula

The number of turns (N) necessary to obtain a specific inductance (L) can be calculated by

$$N = 100 \sqrt{\frac{L}{L_{100}}}$$

L = desired inductance (μH)

L_{100} = core inductance (μH per 100 turns)

Inductance Per 100 Turns ±5%

No.	MIX-41	MIX-3	MIX-15	MIX-1	MIX-2	MIX-6	MIX-10	MIX-12
T-200	755 μH	360 μH			120 μH	105 μH		
T-184	1640 μH	720 μH			240 μH			
T-157	970 μH	420 μH			140 μH	115 μH		
T-130	785 μH	330 μH	250 μH	200 μH	110 μH	96 μH		
T-106	900 μH	405 μH	330 μH	280 μH	135 μH	116 μH		
T-94	590 μH	248 μH		160 μH	84 μH	70 μH	58 μH	32 μH
T-80	450 μH	180 μH	170 μH	115 μH	55 μH	45 μH	34 μH	22 μH
T-68	420 μH	195 μH	180 μH	115 μH	57 μH	47 μH	32 μH	21 μH
T-50	320 μH	175 μH	135 μH	100 μH	50 μH	40 μH	31 μH	18 μH
T-37	240 μH	110 μH	90 μH	80 μH	42 μH	30 μH	25 μH	15 μH
T-25	200 μH	100 μH	85 μH	70 μH	34 μH	27 μH	19 μH	13 μH
T-12	90 μH	60 μH		48 μH	24 μH	19 μH	12 μH	8.5 μH

Magnetic Properties
Iron Powder Cores

Material	Color Code	Permeability	Temperature Stability	Typical Frequency Range	Optimum Frequency Range
41' HA'	Green	$\mu = 75$	975 ppm/c	10 kHz- 100 kHz	20 kHz- 50 kHz
3' HP'	Gray	$\mu = 35$	370 ppm/c	20 kHz- 2 MHz	50 kHz- 500 kHz
15' GS6'	Rd. & Wh.	$\mu = 25$	190 ppm/c	20 kHz- 5 MHz	500 kHz- 1 MHz
1' C'	Blue	$\mu = 20$	280 ppm/c	40 kHz- 5 MHz	1 MHz- 2 MHz
2' E'	Red	$\mu = 10$	95 ppm/c	200 kHz- 30 MHz	2 MHz- 10 MHz
6' SF'	Yellow	$\mu = 8$	35 ppm/c	2 MHz- 50 MHz	10 MHz- 20 MHz
10' W'	Black	$\mu = 6$	150 ppm/c	4 MHz-100 MHz	20 MHz- 40 MHz
12' Irn-8'	Gr. & Wh.	$\mu = 3$	170 ppm/c	10 MHz-200 MHz	40 MHz- 90 MHz
0' Ph'	Tan	$\mu = 1$	—	50 MHz-300 MHz	90 MHz-150 MHz

Courtesy of Amidon Assoc.

Table 8

Powdered-Iron Toroid Cores — Dimensions

Red E Cores — 500 kHz to 30 MHz (μ = 10)

No.	OD (In)	ID (In)	H (In)
T-200-2	2.00	1.25	0.55
T-94-2	0.94	0.56	0.31
T-80-2	0.80	0.50	0.25
T-68-2	0.68	0.37	0.19
T-50-2	0.50	0.30	0.19
T-37-2	0.37	0.21	0.12
T-25-2	0.25	0.12	0.09
T-12-2	0.125	0.06	0.05

Black W Cores — 30 MHz to 200 MHz (μ = 7)

No.	OD (In)	ID (In)	H (In)
T-50-10	0.50	0.30	0.19
T-37-10	0.37	0.21	0.12
T-25-10	0.25	0.12	0.09
T-12-10	0.125	0.06	0.05

Yellow SF Cores — 10 MHz to 90 MHz (μ = 8)

No.	OD (In)	ID (In)	H (In)
T-94-6	0.94	0.56	0.31
T-80-6	0.80	0.50	0.25
T-68-6	0.68	0.37	0.19
T-50-6	0.50	0.30	0.19
T-26-6	0.25	0.12	0.09
T-12-6	0.125	0.06	0.05

Number of Turns vs. Wire Size and Core Size

Approximate maximum number of turns — single layer wound — enameled wire.

Wire Size	T-200	T-130	T-106	T-94	T-80	T-68	T-50	T-37	T-25	T-12
10	33	20	12	12	10	6	4	1		
12	43	25	16	16	14	9	6	3		
14	54	32	21	21	18	13	8	5	1	
16	69	41	28	28	24	17	13	7	2	
18	88	53	37	37	32	23	18	10	4	1
20	111	67	47	47	41	29	23	14	6	1
22	140	86	60	60	53	38	30	19	9	2
24	177	109	77	77	67	49	39	25	13	4
26	223	137	97	97	85	63	50	33	17	7
28	281	173	123	123	108	80	64	42	23	9
30	355	217	154	154	136	101	81	54	29	13
32	439	272	194	194	171	127	103	68	38	17
34	557	346	247	247	218	162	132	88	49	23
36	683	424	304	304	268	199	162	108	62	30
38	875	544	389	389	344	256	209	140	80	39
40	1103	687	492	492	434	324	264	178	102	51

Actual number of turns may differ from above figures according to winding techniques, especially when using the larger size wires. Chart prepared by Michael J. Gordon, Jr., WB9FHC.

Courtesy of Amidon Assoc.

Table 9

Color Code for Hookup Wire

Wire Color	Type of Circuit
Black	Grounds, grounded elements and returns
Brown	Heaters or filaments, off ground
Red	Power supply B plus
Orange	Screen grids and base 2 of transistors
Yellow	Cathodes and transistor emitters
Green	Control grids, diode plates, and base 1 of transistors
Blue	Plates and transistor collectors
Violet	Power supply, minus leads
Gray	Ac power line leads
White	Bias supply, B or C minus, AGC

Note: Wires with tracers are coded in the same manner as solid-color wires, allowing additional circuit identification over solid-color wiring. The body of the wire is white and the color band spirals around the wire lead. When more than one color band is used, the widest band represents the first color.

Table 10

Ferrite Toroids—A_L Chart (mH per 1000 turns) Enameled Wire

Core Size	63/67-Mix $\mu = 40$	61-Mix $\mu = 125$	43-Mix $\mu = 850$	77 (72) Mix $\mu = 2000$	J (75) Mix $\mu = 5000$
FT-23	7.9	24.8	188.0	396	980
FT-37	19.7	55.3	420.0	884	2196
FT-50	22.0	68.0	523.0	1100	2715
FT-82	22.4	73.3	557.0	1170	NA
FT-114	25.4	79.3	603.0	1270	3170

Number turns = $1000 \sqrt{\text{desired L (mH)} \div A_L \text{ value (above)}}$

Ferrite Magnetic Properties

Property	Unit	63/67-Mix	61-Mix	43-Mix	77 (72) Mix	J (75)-Mix
Initial perm (μ_i)		40	125	850	2000	5000
Maximum perm.		125	450	3000	6000	8000
Saturation flux density @ 10 oer	Gauss	1850	2350	2750	4600	3900
Residual flux density	Gauss	750	1200	1200	1150	1250
Curie temp.	°C	450	350	130	200	140
Vol. resistivity	ohm/cm	1×10^8	1×10^8	1×10^5	1×10^2	5×10^2
Resonant circuit frequency	MHz	15-25	0.2-10	0.01-1	0.001-1	0.001-1
Specific gravity		4.7	4.7	4.5	4.8	4.8
Loss factor	$\frac{1}{\mu_i Q}$	110×10^{-6} @25 MHz	32×10^{-6} @2.5 MHz	120×10^{-6} @1 MHz	4.5×10^{-6} @0.1 MHz	15×10^{-6} @0.1 MHz
Coercive force	Oer	2.40	1.60	0.30	0.22	0.16
Temp. Coef. of initial perm.	%/°C (20-70°C)	0.10	0.15	1.0	0.60	0.90

Ferrite Toroids—Physical Properties

Core Size	OD	ID	Height	A_e	l_e	V_e	A_S	A_W
FT-23	0.230	0.120	0.060	0.00330	0.529	0.00174	0.1264	0.01121
FT-37	0.375	0.187	0.125	0.01175	0.846	0.00994	0.3860	0.02750
FT-50	0.500	0.281	0.188	0.02060	1.190	0.02450	0.7300	0.06200
FT-82	0.825	0.520	0.250	0.03810	2.070	0.07890	1.7000	0.21200
FT-114	1.142	0.750	0.295	0.05810	2.920	0.16950	2.9200	0.43900

OD—Outer diameter (inches)
ID—Inner diameter (inches)
Hgt—Height (inches)
A_W—Total window area (in)^2

A_e—Effective magnetic cross-sectional area (in)^2
l_e—Effective magnetic path length (inches)
V_e—Effective magnetic volume (in)^3
A_S—Surface area exposed for cooling (in)^2

Courtesy of Amidon Assoc.

Integrated Circuits

Replacements for common ICs are readily available. IC part numbers usually contain a few digits that identify the circuit die or function and several other letters and/or digits that identify the production process, manufacturer and package. For example, a '4066 IC contains four SPST independent switches. Harris (CD74HC4066, CD4066B and CD4066BE), National (MM74HC4066, CD4066BC and CD4066BM) and Panasonic (MN74HC4066 and MN4066B) all make similar devices (as do many other manufacturers) with slight differences. Among the numbers listed, "CD" (CMOS Digital), "MM" (MOS Monolithic) and "MN" indicate CMOS parts. "74" indicates a commercial quality product (for applications from 0°C to 70°C), which is pin compatible with the 74/54 TTL families. "HC" means high-speed CMOS family, which is as fast as the LS TTL family. The "B" suffix, as in CD4066B, indicates a buffered output. This is only a small example of the conventions used in IC part numbers. For more information look at databooks from the various manufacturers. Table 30 shows base diagrams for some standard op-amp ICs. Base diagrams for many more common ICs appear in *The ARRL Data Book*.

When choosing ICs that are not exact replacements, there are several operating needs and performance aspects that should be considered. First, the replacement power requirements must be met: Some ICs require 5 V dc, others 12 V and some need both positive and negative supplies. Current requirements vary among the various IC families, so be sure that sufficient current is available from the power supply.

If a replacement IC uses much more current than the device it replaces, a heat sink or blower may be needed to keep it cool.

Next consider how the replacement interacts with its neighboring components. Input capacitance and "fanout" are critical factors in digital circuits. Increased input capacitance may overload the driving circuits. Overload slows circuit operation, which may prevent lines from reaching the "high" condition. Fanout tells how many inputs a device can drive. Fanout should be equal to, or greater than, that required in the circuit. Operating speed and propagation delay are also significant. Choose a replacement IC that operates at or above the circuit clock speed. Some circuits may not function if the propagation delay varies much from the specified part. Look at the "Digital Basics" chapter for details of how these operating characteristics relate to circuit performance.

Analog ICs have similar characteristics. Input and output capacities are often defined as how much current an analog IC can "sink" (accept at an input) or "source" (pass to a load). A replacement should be able to source or sink at least as much current as the device it replaces. Analog speed is sometimes listed as bandwidth (as in discrete-component circuits) or slew rate (common in op amps). Each of these quantities should meet or exceed that of the replaced component.

When necessary, you can add interface circuits or buffer amplifiers that improve the input and output capabilities of replacement ICs, but auxiliary circuits cannot improve speed or bandwidth.

Finding Parts

The explosion of electronic technology has brought mixed blessings for the home builder. While the real cost of parts has decreased over the years, and ICs now perform many complex functions; it may be impossible to get all parts for a project at a local shop.

Table 42 lists mail-order suppliers who can help you get most of the parts you need. Many of them supply catalogs free of charge, while some charge a small fee.

Table 11
Copper Wire Specifications
Bare and Enamel-Coated Wire

Wire Size (AWG)	Diam (Mils)	Area (CM[1])	Enamel Wire Coating Turns/Linear inch[2] Single	Heavy	Triple	Feet per Pound Bare	Ohms per 1000 ft 25° C	Current Carrying Capacity Continuous Duty[3] at 700 CM per Amp[4]	Open air	Conduit or bundles	Diam (mm)	Nearest British SWG No.
1	289.3	83694.49				3.948	0.1239	119.564			7.348	1
2	257.6	66357.76				4.978	0.1563	94.797			6.543	3
3	229.4	52624.36				6.277	0.1971	75.178			5.827	4
4	204.3	41738.49				7.918	0.2485	59.626			5.189	5
5	181.9	33087.61				9.98	0.3134	47.268			4.620	7
6	162.0	26244.00				12.59	0.3952	37.491			4.115	8
7	144.3	20822.49				15.87	0.4981	29.746			3.665	9
8	128.5	16512.25				20.01	0.6281	23.589			3.264	10
9	114.4	13087.36				25.24	0.7925	18.696			2.906	11
10	101.9	10383.61				31.82	0.9987	14.834			2.588	12
11	90.7	8226.49				40.16	1.2610	11.752			2.304	13
12	80.8	6528.64				50.61	1.5880	9.327			2.052	14
13	72.0	5184.00				63.73	2.0010	7.406			1.829	15
14	64.1	4108.81	15.2	14.8	14.5	80.39	2.5240	5.870	32	17	1.628	16
15	57.1	3260.41	17.0	16.6	16.2	101.32	3.1810	4.658			1.450	18
16	50.8	2580.64	19.1	18.6	18.1	128	4.0180	3.687	22	13	1.290	18
17	45.3	2052.09	21.4	20.7	20.2	161	5.0540	2.932			1.151	19
18	40.3	1624.09	23.9	23.2	22.5	203.5	6.3860	2.320	16	10	1.024	20
19	35.9	1288.81	26.8	25.9	25.1	256.4	8.0460	1.841			0.912	21
20	32.0	1024.00	29.9	28.9	27.9	322.7	10.1280	1.463	11	7.5	0.813	22
21	28.5	812.25	33.6	32.4	31.3	406.7	12.7700	1.160			0.724	23
22	25.3	640.09	37.6	36.2	34.7	516.3	16.2000	0.914		5	0.643	24
23	22.6	510.76	42.0	40.3	38.6	646.8	20.3000	0.730			0.574	25
24	20.1	404.01	46.9	45.0	42.9	817.7	25.6700	0.577			0.511	26
25	17.9	320.41	52.6	50.3	47.8	1031	32.3700	0.458			0.455	27
26	15.9	252.81	58.8	56.2	53.2	1307	41.0200	0.361			0.404	29
27	14.2	201.64	65.8	62.5	59.2	1639	51.4400	0.288			0.361	30
28	12.6	158.76	73.5	69.4	65.8	2081	65.3100	0.227			0.320	31
29	11.3	127.69	82.0	76.9	72.5	2587	81.2100	0.182			0.287	33
30	10.0	100.00	91.7	86.2	80.6	3306	103.7100	0.143			0.254	34
31	8.9	79.21	103.1	95.2		4170	130.9000	0.113			0.226	36
32	8.0	64.00	113.6	105.3		5163	162.0000	0.091			0.203	37
33	7.1	50.41	128.2	117.6		6553	205.7000	0.072			0.180	38
34	6.3	39.69	142.9	133.3		8326	261.3000	0.057			0.160	38-39
35	5.6	31.36	161.3	149.3		10537	330.7000	0.045			0.142	39-40
36	5.0	25.00	178.6	166.7		13212	414.8000	0.036			0.127	41
37	4.5	20.25	200.0	181.8		16319	512.1000	0.029			0.114	42
38	4.0	16.00	222.2	204.1		20644	648.2000	0.023			0.102	43
39	3.5	12.25	256.4	232.6		26969	846.6000	0.018			0.089	44
40	3.1	9.61	285.7	263.2		34364	1079.2000	0.014			0.079	
41	2.8	7.84	322.6	294.1		42123	1323.0000	0.011			0.071	
42	2.5	6.25	357.1	333.3		52854	1659.0000	0.009			0.064	
43	2.2	4.84	400.0	370.4		68259	2143.0000	0.007			0.056	
44	2.0	4.00	454.5	400.0		82645	2593.0000	0.006			0.051	
45	1.8	3.10	526.3	465.1		106600	3348.0000	0.004			0.045	
46	1.6	2.46	588.2	512.8		134000	4207.0000	0.004			0.040	

Teflon Coated, Stranded Wire
(As supplied by Belden Wire and Cable.)

Size	Strands[5]	Turns per Linear inch[2] UL Style No. 1180	1213	1371	Size	Strands[5]	Turns per Linear inch[2] UL Style No. 1180	1213	1371	Size	Strands[5]	Turns per Linear inch[2] UL Style No. 1180	1213	1371
16	19 × 29	11.2			22	19 × 34	16.7	20.0	23.8	26	7 × 34		25.6	32.3
18	19 × 30	12.7			22	7 × 30	16.7	20.0	23.8	28	7 × 36		28.6	37.0
20	7 × 28	14.7	17.2		24	19 × 36	18.5	22.7	27.8	30	7 × 38		31.3	41.7
20	19 × 32	14.7	17.2		24	7 × 32		22.7	27.8	32	7 × 40			47.6

[1]A circular mil (CM) is a unit of area equal to that of a one-mil-diameter circle ($\pi/4$ square mils). The CM area of a wire is the square of the mil diameter.
[2]Figures given are approximate only; insulation thickness varies with manufacturer.
[3]Maximum wire temperature of 212° F (100° C) with a maximum ambient temperature of 135° F (57° C).
[4]700 CM per ampere is a satisfactory design figure for small transformers, but values from 500 to 1000 CM are commonly used.
[5]Stranded wire construction is given as "count" × "strand size" (AWG).

If you do much building, a file of their catalogs will be helpful. Occasionally, however, a special project may require unusual parts that are not available through these sources.

Almost any part you need is available—for a price—through commercial channels. Chains of electronics stores supply parts to small manufacturers and repair shops. You can find the closest outlets by looking in a commercial directory, which should be available at your local library. Some such stores will not take orders of less than $25, $50 or $100, while others take small orders with a handling charge. If the parts you need don't make the minimum order, try to interest others in building the same project, or consider selling the extra parts through a *QST* Ham Ad.

When nearby commercial outlets can't supply the part, try contacting the component manufacturer. Return to the library for the manufacturer's phone number or address, and inquire about single-unit component sources. The manufacturer will probably give you the name of their nearest distributor, but sometimes you can get the part directly as an engineering sample.

Ordering by Mail

If you are in a hurry for your parts, send payment as a money order, rather than a personal check. That approach saves about a week that the supplier would wait for your check to clear the bank. Many suppliers provide very quick service by telephone if you order with a credit card. Since there is no written record of the transaction, you may want to gain some experience with a supplier before you order this way.

Table 12
EIA Vacuum-Tube Base Diagrams

Socket connections correspond to the base designations given in the column headed "Base" in the classified tube-data tables. Bottom views are shown throughout. Terminal designations are as follows:

A — Anode	B — Deflecting Plate	IS — Internal Shield	RC — Ray-Control Electrode
B — Beam	F — Filament	K — Cathode	Ref — Reflector
BP — Bayonet Pin	FE — Focus Elect.	NC — No Connection	S — Shell
BS — Base Sleeve	G — Grid	P — Plate (Anode)	TA — Target
C — Ext. Coating	H — Heater	P_1 — Starter-Anode	U — Unit
CL — Collector	IC — Internal Con.	P_{BF} — Beam Plates	● — Gas-Type Tube

Alphabetical subscripts D, P, T and HX indicate, respectively, diode unit, pentode unit, triode unit or hexode unit in multi-unit types. Subscript CT indicates filament or heater tap.

Generally when the No. 1 pin of a metal-type tube, with the exception of all triodes, is shown connected to the shell, the No. 1 pin in the glass (G or GT) equivalent is connected to an internal shield.

*On 12AQ, 12AS and 12CT: index = large lug; ● = pin cut off

Type	Maximum Ratings						Cathode		Capacitances			Base	Typical Operation							
	Plate Dissipation Watts	Plate Voltage	Plate Current mA	DC Grid Current mA	Freq. MHz. Full Ratings	Amplification Factor	Volts	Amperes	C_{in} pF	C_{gp} pF	C_{out} pF		Class of Service	Plate Voltage	Grid Voltage	Plate Current mA	DC Grid Current mA	Approx. Driving Power Watts	P-to-P Load Ohms	Approx. Output Power Watts
5675	5	165	30	8	3000	20	6.3	0.135	2.3	1.3	0.09	Fig. 21	GG·O	120	−8	25	4	—	—	0.05
2C40	6.5	500	25	—	500	36	6.3	0.75	2.1	1.3	0.05	Fig. 11	C·T·O	250	−5	20	0.3	—	—	0.075
5893	8.0	400	40	13	1000	27	6.0	0.33	2.5	1.75	0.07	Fig. 21	C·T	350	−33	35	13	2.4	—	6.5
													C·P	300	−45	30	12	2.0	—	6.5
2C43	12	500	40	—	1250	48	6.3	0.9	2.9	1.7	0.05	Fig. 11	C·T·O	470	—	38[7]	—	—	—	9[2]
811-A	65	1500	175	50	60	160	6.3	4.0	5.9	5.6	0.7	3G	C·T	1500	−70	173	40	7.1	—	200
													C·P	1250	−120	140	45	10.0	—	135
													B·GG	1250	0	27/175	28	12	—	165
													AB1	1250	0	27/175	13	3.0	—	155
812-A	65	1500	175	35	60	29	6.3	4.0	5.4	5.5	0.77	3G	C·T	1500	−120	173	30	6.5	—	190
													C·P	1250	−115	140	35	7.6	—	130
													B[2]	1500	−48	28/310	270[9]	5.0	13.2K	340
3CX100A5[6]	100	1000	125[5]	50	2500	100	6.0	1.05	7.0	2.15	0.035	—	A·GG	800	−20	80	30	6	—	27
	70	600	100[5]										C·P	600	−15	75	40	6	—	18
2C39	100	1000	60	40	500	100	6.3	1.1	6.5	1.95	0.03	—	G1C	600	−35	60	40	5.0	—	20
													C·T·O	900	−40	90	30	—	—	40
													C·P	600	−150	100[5]	50	—	—	—
AX9900/ 5866[6]	135	2500	200	40	150	25	6.3	5.4	5.8	5.5	0.1	Fig. 3	C·T	2500	−200	200	40	16	—	390
													C·P	2000	−225	127	40	16	—	204
													B[2]	2500	−90	80/330	350[4]	14[3]	15.68K	560
572B/T160L	160	2750	275	—	—	170	6.3	4.0	—	—	—	3G	C·T	1650	−70	165	32	6	—	205
													B·GG[2]	2400	−2.0	90/500	—	100	—	600
810	175	2500	300	75	30	36	10	4.5	8.7	4.8	12	2N	C·T	2500	−180	300	60	19	—	575
													C·P	2000	−350	250	70	35	—	380
													GMA	2250	−140	100	2.0	4	—	75
													B[2]	2250	−60	70/450	380[4]	13[3]	11.6K	725
8873	200	2200	250	—	500	160	6.3	3.2	19.5	7.0	0.03	Fig. 87	AB2	2000	—	22/500	98[3]	27[3]	—	505
8875	300	2200	250	—	500	160	6.3	3.2	19.5	7.0	0.03	—	AB2	2000	—	22/500	98[3]	27[3]	—	505
833A	350	3300	500	100	30	35	10	10	12.3	6.3	8.5	Fig. 41	C·T·O	2250	−125	445	85	23	—	780
														3000	−160	335	70	20	—	800
	450[6]	4000[6]			20[6]								C·P	2500	−300	335	75	30	—	635
														3000	−240	335	70	26	—	800,
													B[2]	3000	−70	100/750	400[4]	20[4]	9.5K	1650
8874	400	2200	350	—	500	160	6.3	3.2	19.5	7.0	0.03	—	AB2	2000	—	22/500	98[3]	27[3]	—	505
3-400Z	400	3000	400	—	110	200	5	14.5	7.4	4.1	0.07	Fig. 3	B·GG	3000	0	100/333	120	32	—	655
3-500Z	500	4000	400	—	110	160	5	14.5	7.4	4.1	0.07	Fig. 3	B·GG	3000	—	370	115	30	5K	750
													C·T	3500	−75	300	115	22	—	850
3CX800A7	800	2250	600	60	350	200	13.5	1.5	26	—	6.1	Fig. 87	AB2· GG[7]	2200	−8.2	500	36	16	—	750
3-1000Z	1000	3000	800	—	110	200	7.5	21.3	17	6.9	0.12	Fig. 3	B·GG	3000	0	180/670	300	65	—	1360
3CX1200A7	1200	5000	800	—	110	200	7.5	21.0	20	12	0.2	Fig. 3	AB2· GG	3600	−10	700	230	85	—	1500
8877	1500	4000	1000	—	250	200	5.0	10	42	10	0.1	—	AB2	2500	−8.2	1000	—	57	—	1520

* Cathode resistor in ohms.

[1] KEY TO CLASS-OF-SERVICE ABBREVIATIONS

A1 = Class-A1 AF modulator.
AB1 = Class-AB1 push-pull AF modulator.
AB2 = Class-AB2 push-pull AF modulator.
B = Class-B push-pull AF modulator.
C·M = Frequency multiplier.

C·P = Class-C plate-modulated telephone.
C·T = Class-C telegraph.
C·T·O = Class-C amplifier-osc.
AB2·GG = Grounded-grid class AB2 amp.
B·GG = Grounded-grid class B amp. (single tone)
GG·O = Grounded-grid osc.
GIC = Grid-isolation circuit.

GMA = Grid-modulated amp.
[2] Values are for two tubes in push-pull.
[3] Max. signal value.
[4] Peak AF grid-to-grid volts.
[5] Max. cathode current in mA.
[6] Forced-air cooling required.
[7] Key-down CW.

Table 14 — Tetrode and Pentode Transmitting Tubes

Listed in order of plate dissipation

Type	Plate Dissipation Watts	Plate Voltage	Screen Dissipation Watts	Screen Voltage	Freq. MHz. Full Ratings	Volts	Amperes	Cin pF	Cgp pF	Cout pF	Base	Class of Service [14]	Plate Voltage	Screen Voltage	Suppressor Voltage	Grid Voltage	Plate Current mA	Screen Current mA	Grid Current mA	Approx. Driving Power Watts	P-P Load Ohms	Approx. Output Power Watts
6939[3]	7.5	275	3	200	500	6.3 / 12.6	0.75 / 0.375	6.6	0.15	1.55	Fig. 13	C-T	200	200	—	−20	60	13	2	1.0	—	7.5
												C-P	180	180	—	−20	55	11.5	1.7	1.0	—	6
												C-M	200	190	—	68K[1]	46	10	2.2	0.9	—	—
7551 7558	12	300	2	250	175	12.6 / 6.3	0.38 / 0.8	10	0.15	5.5	9LK	C-T	300	250	—	−55	80	5.1	1.6	1.5	—	10
												C-P	250	250	—	−75	70	3.0	2.3	1.0	—	7.5
5763 6417	13.5	350	2	250	50	6.3 / 12.6	0.75 / 0.375	9.5	0.3	4.5	9K	C-T	350	250	—	−28.5	48.5	6.2	1.6	0.1	—	12
												C-P	300	250	—	−42.5	50	6	2.4	0.15	—	10
												C-M[2]	300	250	—	−75	40	4	1	0.6	—	2.1
												C-M[4]	300	235	—	−100	35	5	1	0.6	—	1.3
2E26 6893	13.5	600	2.5	200	125	6.3 / 12.6	0.8 / 0.4	12.5	0.2	7	7CK	C-T	600	185	—	−45	66	10	3	0.17	—	27
												C-P	500	180	—	−50	54	9	2.5	0.15	—	18
												AB1	500	200	—	−25	9/45	10[7]	0	0	—	15
6360[3]	14	300	2	200	200	6.3 / 12.6	0.82 / 0.41	6.2	0.1	2.6	Fig. 13	C-T	300	200	—	−45	100	3	3	0.2	—	18.5
												C-P	200	100	—	15K[1]	86	3.1	3.3	0.2	—	9.8
												C-M[11]	300	150	—	−100	65	3.5	3.8	0.45	—	4.8
												AB2	300	200	—	−21.5	30/100	1/11.4	64[8]	0.04	6.5K	17.5
6252/ AX9910[3]	20	750	4	300	300	6.3 / 12.6	1.3 / 0.65	6.5	—	2.5	Fig. 7	C-T	600	250	—	−60	140	14	4	2.0	—	—
												C-P	500	250	—	−80	100	12	3	4.0	—	—
												B	500	250	—	−26	25/73	0.7/16	52[8]	—	20K	23.5
1614	25	450	3.5	300	80	6.3	0.9	10	0.4	12.5	7AC	C-T	450	250	—	−45	100	8	2	0.15	—	31
												C-P	375	250	—	−50	93	7	2	0.15	—	24.5
												AB1[6]	530	340	—	−36	60/160	20[7]	—	—	7.2K	50
815[3]	25	500	4	200	125	6.3 / 12.6	1.6 / 0.8	13.3	0.2	8.5	8BY	C-T-O	500	200	—	−45	150	17	2.5	0.13	—	56
												AB2	500	125	—	−15	22/150	32[7]	—	0.36[7]	8K	54
6146 6146A 8032 6883 6159B	25	750	3	250	60	6.3 / 12.6 / 26.5	1.25 / 0.585 / 0.3	13	0.24	8.5	7CK	C-T	500	170	—	−66	135	9	2.5	0.2	—	48
												C-T	750	160	—	−62	120	11	3.1	0.2	—	70
												C-T[12]	400	190	—	−54	150	10.4	2.2	3.0	—	35
												C-P	400	150	—	−87	112	7.8	3.4	0.4	—	32
												C-P	600	150	—	−87	112	7.8	3.4	0.4	—	52
												AB2[6]	600	190	—	−48	28/270	1.2/20	2[7]	0.3	5K	113
												AB2[6]	750	165	—	−46	22/240	0.3/20	2.6[7]	0.4	7.4K	131
												AB1[6]	750	195	—	−50	23/220	1/26	100[8]	—	8K	120
6524[3] 6850	25	600	—	300	100	6.3 / 12.6	1.25 / 0.625	7	0.11	3.4	Fig. 76	C-T	600	200	—	−44	120	8	3.7	0.2	—	56
												C-P	500	200	—	−61	100	7	2.5	0.2	—	40
												AB2	500	200	—	−26	20/116	0.1/10	2.6	0.1	11.1K	40
807 807W 5933 1625	30	750	3.5	300	60	6.3 / 12.6	0.9 / 0.45	12	0.2	7	5AW 5AZ	C-T	750	250	—	−45	100	6	3.5	0.22	—	50
												C-P	600	275	—	−90	100	6.5	4	0.4	—	42.5
												AB1	750	300	—	−35	15/70	3/8	75[8]	—	—	72
												B[10]	750	—	—	0	15/240	—	555[8]	5.3[7]	6.65K	120
2E22	30	750	10	250	—	6.3	1.5	13	0.2	8	5J	C-T-O	750	250	22.5	−60	100	16	6	0.55	—	53
6146B/ 8298A	35	750	3	250	60	6.3	1.125	13	0.22	8.5	7CK	C-T	750	200	—	−77	160	10	2.7	0.3	—	85
												C-P	600	175	—	−92	140	9.5	3.4	0.5	—	62
												AB1	750	200	—	−48	25/125	6.3	—	—	3.6K	61
AX-9903[3] 5894A	40	600	7	250	250	6.3 / 12.6	1.8 / 0.9	6.7	0.08	2.1	Fig. 7	C-T	600	250	—	−80	200	16	2	0.2	—	80
829B[3] 3E29[3]	40	750	7	240	200	6.3 / 12.6	2.25 / 1.125	14.5	0.12	7	7BP	C-T	500	200	—	−45	240	32	12	0.7	—	83
												C-P	425	200	—	−60	212	35	11	0.8	—	63
												B	500	200	—	−18	27/230	—	56[8]	0.39	4.8K	76
3D24	45	2000	10	400	125	6.3	3	6.5	0.2	2.4	Fig. 75	C-T-O	2000	375	—	−300	90	20	10	4.0	—	140
												C-T-O	1500	375	—	−300	90	22	10	4.0	—	105
8117[3]	60	750	7	300	175	6.3 / 12.6	1.8 / 0.9	11.8	3.7	0.09	Fig. 7	AB1	600	250	—	−32.5	60/212	1.9/25	—	—	1410	76
814	65	1500	10	300	30	10	3.25	13.5	0.1	13.5	Fig. 64	C-T	1500	300	—	−90	150	24	10	1.5	—	160
												C-P	1250	300	—	−150	145	20	10	3.2	—	130
4-65A	65	3000	10	600	150	6	3.5	8	0.08	2.1	Fig. 25	C-T-O	1500	250	—	−85	150	40	18	3.2	—	165
												C-T-O	3000	250	—	−100	115	22	10	1.7	—	280
												C-P	1500	250	—	−125	120	40	16	3.5	—	140
												C-P	2500	250	—	−135	110	25	12	2.6	—	230
												AB1	2500	400	—	−85	15/66	3[7]	—	—	—	100
7854[3]	68	1000	8	300	175	6.3 / 12.6	1.8 / 0.9	6.7	2.1	0.09	Fig. 7	C-T	750	260	—	−75	240	12.7	5.5	3.5	—	123
												C-P	600	225	—	−75	200	7.8	5.5	3.5	—	85
4E27/ 8001	75	4000	30	750	75	5	7.5	12	0.06	6.5	7BM	C-T	2000	500	60	−200	150	11	6	1.4	—	230
												C-P	1800	400	60	−130	135	11	8	1.7	—	178
7270 7271	80	1350	—	425	175	6.3 / 13.5	3.1 / 1.25	8	0.4	0.14	Fig. 84	C-T	850	400	—	−100	275	15	8	10	—	135
												AB1	665	400	—	−119	220	15	6	10	—	85
8072	100	2200	8	400	500	13.5	1.3	16	0.13	0.011	Fig. 85	C-T-O	700	200	—	−30	300	10	20	5	—	85

Table 14 continued on next page.

Table 14 (continued)

Type	Plate Dissipation Watts	Plate Voltage	Screen Dissipation Watts	Screen Voltage	Freq. MHz. Full Ratings	Volts	Amperes	Cin pF	Cgp pF	Cout pF	Base	Class of Service[14]	Plate Voltage	Screen Voltage	Suppressor Voltage	Grid Voltage	Plate Current mA	Screen Current mA	Grid Current mA	Approx. Driving Power Watts	P-P Load Ohms	Approx. Output Power Watts
6816[9] 6884	115	1000	4.5	300	400	6.3 / 26.5	2.1 / 0.52	14	0.085	0.015	Fig. 77	C·T·O	900	300	—	−30	170	1	10	3	—	80
												C·P	700	250	—	−50	130	10	10	3	—	45
												AB₁[6]	850	300	—	−15	80/200	0/20	30[8]	0	7K	80
												AB₂[6]	850	300	—	−15	80/335	0/25	46[8]	0.3	3.96K	140
813[13]	125	2500	20	800	30	10	5	16.3	0.25	14	5BA	C·T·O	1250	300	0	−75	180	35	12	1.7	—	170
													2250	400	0	−155	220	40	15	4	—	375
												AB₁	2500	750	0	−95	25/145	27[7]	0	0	—	245
												AB₂[6]	2000	750	0	−90	40/315	1.5/58	230[8]	0.17	16K	455
													2500	750	0	−95	35/360	1.2/55	235[8]	0.35[7]	17K	650
4-125A 4D21 6155	125	3000	20	600	120	5	6.5	10.8	0.07	3.1	5BK	C·T·O	2000	350	—	−100	200	50	12	2.8	—	275
													3000	350	—	−150	167	30	9	2.5	—	375
												AB₂[6]	2500	350	—	−43	93/260	0/6	178[8]	1.0[7]	22K	400
												AB₁[6]	2500	600	—	−96	50/232	0.3/8.5	192[8]	0	20.3K	330
												GG	2000	0	—	0	10/105[17]	30[17]	55[17]	16[17]	10.5K	145
4E27A/ 5-125B	125	4000	20	750	75	5	7.5	10.5	0.08	4.7	7BM	C·	3000	500	60	−200	167	5	6	1.6	—	375
													1000	750	0	−170	160	21	3	0.6	—	115
803	125	2000	30	600	20	10	5	17.5	0.15	29	5J	C·T	2000	500	40	−90	160	45	12	2	—	210
												C·P	1600	400	100	−80	150	45	25	5	—	155
7094	125	2000	20	400	60	6.3	3.2	9.0	0.5	1.8	Fig. 82	C·T	1500	400	—	−100	330	20	5	4	—	340
												C·P	1200	400	—	−130	275	20	5	5	—	240
												AB₁	2000	400	—	−65	30/200	35[7]	60[8]	0	12K	250
4X150A 4X150G[15]	150[9]	2000	12	400	500	6 / 2.5	2.6 / 6.25	15.5 / 27	0.03 / 0.035	4.5 / 4.5	Fig. 75 / —	C·T·O	1250	250	—	−90	200	20	10	0.8	—	195
												C·P	1000	250	—	−105	200	20	15	2	—	140
												AB₂[6]	1250	300	—	−44	475[7]	0/65	100[8]	0.15[7]	5.6K	425
8121	150	2200	8	400	500	13.5	1.3	16	0.13	0.011	Fig. 5	C·T·O	1000	200	—	−30	300	10	30	5	—	165
4-250A 5D22 6156	250[9]	4000	35	600	110	5	14.5	12.7	0.12	4.5	5BK	C·T·O	2500	500	—	−150	300	60	9	1.7	—	575
													3000	500	—	−180	345	60	10	2.6	—	800
												C·P	2500	400	—	−200	200	30	9	2.2	—	375
													3000	400	—	−310	225	30	9	3.2	—	510
												AB₂[6]	2000	300	—	−48	510[7]	0/26	198[8]	5.5[7]	8K	650
												AB₁[6]	2500	600	—	−110	430[7]	0.3/13	180[8]	0	11.4K	625
4X250B	250[9]	2000	12	400	175	6	2.1	18.5	0.04	4.7	Fig. 75	C·T·O	2000	250	—	−90	250	25	27	2.8	—	410
												C·P	1500	250	—	−100	200	25	17	2.1	—	250
												AB₁[6]	2000	350	—	−50	500[7]	30[7]	100[8]	0	8.26K	650
7034/[9] 4X150A	250	2000	12	300	150	6	2.6	16	0.03	4.4	Fig. 75	C·T·O	2000	250	—	−88	250	24	8	2.5	—	370
												C·P	1600	250	—	−118	200	23	5	3	—	230
7035/ 4X150D	250	2000	12	400		26.5	0.58				Fig. 75	AB₂[6]	2000	300	—	−50	100/500	0/36	106[8]	0.2	8.1K	630
												AB₁[6]	2000	300	—	−50	100/470	0/36	100[8]	0	8.76K	580
4CX-300A	300[9]	2000	12	400	500	6	2.75	29.5	0.04	4.8	—	C·T	2000	250	—	−90	250	25	27	2.8	—	410
												C·P	1500	250	—	−100	200	25	17	2.1	—	250
												AB₁[6]	2000	350	—	−50	500[7]	30[7]	100[8]	0	8.26K	650
175A	400	4000	25	600	—	5	14.5	15.1	0.06	9.8	Fig. 86	C·T·C·P	4000	600	0	−200	350	29	6	1.4	—	960
													2500	600	0	−180	350	40	7	1.6	—	600
												AB₁	2500	750	—	−143	100/350	1/35	0	0	—	570
4-400A	400[9]	4000	35	600	110	5	14.5	12.5	0.12	4.7	5BK	C·T·C·P	4000	300	—	−170	270	22.5	10	10	4.0K	720
												GG	2500	0	—	0	80/270[17]	55[17]	100[17]	38[17]	4.0K	325
												AB₁	2500	750	—	−130	95/317	0/14	0	—	—	425
8122	400	2200	8	400	500	13.5	1.3	16	0.13	0.011	Fig. 86	C·T·O	2000	200	—	−30	300	5	30	5	—	300
5-500A	500	4000	35	600	30	10	10.2	19	0.10	12	—	C·T	3000	500	0	−220	432	65	35	12	—	805
												C·T	3100	470	0	−310	260	50	15	6	—	580
												AB₁	3000	750	0	−112	320	26	—	—	—	612
8166/ 4-1000A	1000	6000	75	1000	—	7.5	21	27.2	.24	7.6	—	C·T	3000	500	—	−150	700	146	38	11	—	1430
												C·P	3000	500	—	−200	600	145	36	12	—	1390
												AB₂	4000	500	—	−60	300/1200	0/95	—	11	7K	3000
												GG	3000	0	—	0	100/700[17]	105[17]	170[17]	130[17]	2.5K	1475
4CX1000A	1000	3000	12	400	400	6	12.5	35	.005	12	—	AB₁[6]	2000	325	—	−55	500/2000	−4/60	—	—	2.8K	2160
													2500	325	—	−55	500/2000	−4/60	—	—	3.1K	2920
													3000	325	—	−55	500/1800	−4/60	—	—	3.85K	3360
8295/ 172	1000	3000	30	600	—	6	8.2	38	.09	18	—	C·T	2000	500	35	−175	850	42	10	1.9	—	1155
													2500	500	35	−200	840	40	10	2.1	—	1440
													3000	500	35	−200	820	42	10	2.1	—	1770
												AB₁	2000	500	35	−110	200/800	12/43	110[8]	—	2.65K	1040
													2500	500	35	−110	200/800	11/40	115[8]	—	3.5K	1260
													3000	500	35	−115	220/800	11/39	115[8]	—	4.6K	1590

[1]Grid-resistor.
[2]Doubler to 175 MHz.
[3]Dual tube. Values for both sections, in push-pull. Interelectrode capacitances, however, are for each section.
[4]Tripler to 175 MHz.
[5]Filament limited to intermittent operation.
[6]Values are for two tubes.
[7]Max.-signal value.
[8]Peak grid-to-grid volts.
[9]Forced-air cooling required.
[10]Two tubes triode connected, G_2 to G_1 through 20K Ω. Input to G_2.
[11]Triper to 200 MHz.
[12]Typical Operation at 175 MHz.
[13]± 1.5 volts.

[14]KEY TO CLASS-OF-SERVICE ABBREVIATIONS
AB₁ = Class-AB₁
AB₂ = Class-AB₂
B = Class-B push-pull at modulator.
C·M = Frequency multiplier.
C·P = Class-C plate-modulated telephone.
C·T = Class-C telegraph.
C·T·O = Class-C amplifier-osc.
GG = Grounded-grid (grid and screen connected together).
[15]No Class-B data available.
[16]HK257B 120 MHz, full rating.
[17]Single tone.

Table 15
TV Deflection Tubes

Type	Plate Dissipation Watts	Screen Dissipation Watts	Transconductance Micromhos	Heater (6.3V) Amperes	Cin pF	Cgp pF	Cout pF	Base	Class of Service	Plate Voltage	Screen Voltage	Grid Voltage	Plate Current mA	Screen Current mA	Grid Current mA	Approx. Driving Power Watts	Approx. Output Power Watts
6DQ5	24	3.2	10.5k	2.5	23	0.5	11	8JC									
6DQ6B	18	3.6	7.3k	1.2	15	0.5	7	6AM	C	400	200	−40	100	12	1.5	0.1	25
6FH6	17	3.6	6k	1.2	33	0.4	8	6AM									
6GC6	17.5	4.5	6.6k	1.2	15	0.55	7	8JX									
6GJ5	17.5	3.5	7.1k	1.2	15	0.26	6.5	9NM	C	500	200	−75	180	15	5	0.43	63
									AB$_1$	500	200	−43	85	4			35
6HF5	28	5.5	11.3k	2.25	24	0.56	10	12FB	C	500	140	−85	232	12.5	8	0.76	77
									AB$_1$	500	140	−46	133	4.5			58
6JB6	17.5	3.5	7.1k	1.2	15	0.2	6	9QL	C	500	200	−75	180	13.3	5	0.43	63
									AB$_1$	500	200	−42	85	4.2			35
6JE6C	30	5	10.5k	2.5	24.3		14.5	9QL	C	500	125	−85	222	17	8	0.82	76
									AB$_1$	500	125	−44	110	3.9			47
6JG6A	17	3.5	10k	1.6	22	0.7	9	9QU	C	450	150	−80	202	20	8	0.75	63
									AB$_1$	450	150	−35	98	4.5			38
6JM6	17.5	3.5	7.3k	1.2	16	0.6	7	12FJ	C	500	200	−75	190	13.7	4	0.32	61
									AB$_1$	500	200	−42	85	4.4			37
6JN6	17.5	3.5	7.3k	1.2	16	0.34	7	12FK									
6JS6C	30	5.5		2.25	24	0.7	10	12FY									
6KD6	33	5	14k	2.85	40	0.8	16	12GW	GG	800	0	−11	150			12.5	82
6LB6	30	5	13.4k	2.25	33	0.4	18	12GJ									
6LG6	28	5	11.5k	2	25	0.8	13	12HL									
6LQ6	30	5	9.6k	2.5	22	0.46	11	9QL									
6MH6	38.5	7	14k	2.65	40	1.0	20	12GW									

Note: For AB$_1$ operation, input data is average 2-tone value. Output power is PEP.

Table 16
Semiconductor Diode Specifications

Listed numerically by device

Device	Type	Material	Peak Inverse Voltage, PIV (Volts)	Average Rectified Current Forward (Reverse) I_o (A) (I_R(A))	Peak Surge Current, I_{FSM} 1 sec. @ 25°C (A)	Average Forward Voltage, V_F (Volts)
1N34	Signal	Germanium	60	8.5 m (15.0 μ)		1.0
1N34A	Signal	Germanium	60	5.0 m (30.0 μ)		1.0
1N67A	Signal	Germanium	100	4.0 m (5.0 μ)		1.0
1N191	Signal	Germanium	90	5.0 m		1.0
1N270	Signal	Germanium	80	0.2 (100 μ)		1.0
1N914	Fast Switch	Silicon (Si)	75	75.0 m (25.0 n)	0.5	1.0
1N1184	Rectifier, Fast Recovery (RFR)	Si	100	35 (10 m)		1.7
1N2071	RFR	Si	600	0.75 (10.0 μ)		0.6
1N3666	Signal	Germanium	80	0.2 (25.0 μ)		1.0
1N4001	RFR	Si	50	1.0 (0.03 m)		1.1
1N4002	RFR	Si	100	1.0 (0.03 m)		1.1
1N4003	RFR	Si	200	1.0 (0.03 m)		1.1
1N4004	RFR	Si	400	1.0 (0.03 m)		1.1
1N4005	RFR	Si	600	1.0 (0.03 m)		1.1
1N4006	RFR	Si	800	1.0 (0.03 m)		1.1
1N4007	RFR	Si	1000	1.0 (0.03 m)		1.1
1N4148	Signal	Si	75	10.0 m (25.0 n)		1.0
1N4149	Signal	Si	75	10.0 m (25.0 n)		1.0
1N4152	Fast Switch	Si	40	20.0 m (0.05 μ)		0.8
1N4445	Signal	Si	100	0.1 (50.0 n)		1.0
1N5400	RFR	Si	50	3.0	200	
1N5401	RFR	Si	100	3.0	200	
1N5402	RFR	Si	200	3.0	200	
1N5403	RFR	Si	300	3.0	200	
1N5404	RFR	Si	400	3.0	200	
1N5405	RFR	Si	500	3.0	200	
1N5406	RFR	Si	600	3.0	200	
1N5767	Signal	Si		0.1 (1.0 μ)		1.0
ECG5863	RFR	Si	600	6	150	0.9

Table 17
Voltage—Variable Capacitance Diodes

Listed numerically by device

Device	CT Nominal Capacitance pF ±10% @ $V_R = 4.0$ V $f = 1.0$MHz	Capacitance Ratio 4-60 V Min.	Q @ 4.0 V 50 MHz Min.	Case Style
1N5441A	6.8	2.5	450	
1N5442A	8.2	2.5	450	
1N5443A	10	2.6	400	DO-7
1N5444A	12	2.6	400	
1N5445A	15	2.6	450	
1N5446A	18	2.6	350	
1N5447A	20	2.6	350	
1N5448A	22	2.6	350	DO-7
1N5449A	27	2.6	350	
1N5450A	33	2.6	350	
1N5451A	39	2.6	300	
1N5452A	47	2.6	250	
1N5453A	56	2.6	200	DO-7
1N5454A	68	2.7	175	
1N5455A	82	2.7	175	
1N5456A	100	2.7	175	
1N5461A	6.8	2.7	600	
1N5462A	8.2	2.8	600	
1N5463A	10	2.8	550	DO-7
1N5464A	12	2.8	550	
1N5465A	15	2.8	550	
1N5466A	18	2.8	500	
1N5467A	20	2.9	500	
1N5468A	22	2.9	500	DO-7
1N5469A	27	2.9	500	
1N5470A	33	2.9	500	
1N5471A	39	2.9	450	
1N5472A	47	2.9	400	
1N5473A	56	2.9	300	DO-7
1N5474A	68	2.9	250	
1N5475A	82	2.9	225	
1N5476A	100	2.9	200	
MV2101	6.8	2.5	450	
MV2102	8.2	2.5	450	
MV2103	10	2.0	400	TO-92
MV2104	12	2.5	400	
MV2105	15	2.5	400	
MV2106	18	2.5	350	
MV2107	22	2.5	350	
MV2108	27	2.5	300	TO-92
MV2109	33	2.5	200	
MV2110	39	2.5	150	
MV2111	47	2.5	150	
MV2112	56	2.6	150	
MV2113	68	2.6	150	TO-92
MV2114	82	2.6	100	
MV2115	100	2.6	100	

Table 18
Zener Diodes

Volts	0.25	0.4	0.5	Power (Watts) 1.0	1.5	5.0	10.0	50.0
1.8	1N4614							
2.0	1N4615							
2.2	1N4616							
2.4	1N4617	1N4370,A	1N4370,A 1N5221,B 1N5985,B					
2.5			1N5222B					
2.6	1N702,A							
2.7	1N4618	1N4371,A	1N4371,A 1N5223,B 1N5839, 1N5986					
2.8			1N5224B					
3.0	1N4619	1N4372,A	1N4372 1N5225,B 1N5987					
3.3	1N4620	1N746,A 1N764,A 1N5518	1N746,A 1N5226,B 1N5988	1N3821 1N4728,A	1N5913	1N5333,B		
3.6	1N4621	1N747,A 1N5519	1N747A 1N5227,B 1N5989	1N3822 1N4729,A	1N5914	1N5334,B		
3.9	1N4622	1N748,A 1N5520	1N748A 1N5228,B 1N5844, 1N5990	1N3823 1N4730,A	1N5915	1N5335,B	1N3993A	1N4549,B 1N4557,B
4.1	1N704,A							
4.3	1N4623	1N749,A 1N5521	1N749,A 1N5229,B 1N5845 1N5991	1N3824 1N4731,A	1N5916	1N5336,B	1N3994,A	1N4550,B 1N4558,B
4.7	1N4624	1N750,A 1N5522	1N750A 1N5230,B 1N5846, 1N5992	1N3825 1N4732,A	1N5917	1N5337,B	1N3995,A	1N4551,B 1N4559,B
5.1	1N4625 1N4689	1N751,A 1N5523	1N751,A, 1N5231,B 1N5847 1N5993	1N3826 1N4733	1N5918	1N5338,B	1N3996,A	1N4552,B 1N4560,B
5.6	1N708A 1N4626	1N752,A 1N5524	1N752,A 1N5232,B 1N5848, 1N5994	1N3827 1N4734,A	1N5919	1N5339,B	1N3997,A	1N4553,B 1N4561,B

Table 18 — Zener Diodes — Continued

Volts	0.25	0.4	0.5	Power (Watts) 1.0	1.5	5.0	10.0	50.0
5.8	1N706A	1N762						
6.0			1N5233B 1N5849			1N5340,B		
6.2	1N709,1N4627 MZ605, MZ610 MZ620, MZ640	1N753,A 1N821,3,5,7,9;A	1N753,A 1N5234,B, 1N5850 1N5995	1N3828,A 1N4735,A	1N5920	1N5341,B	1N3998,A	1N4554,B 1N4562,B
6.4	1N4565-84,A							
6.8	1N4099	1N754,A 1N957,B 1N5526	1N754,A 1N757,B 1N5235,B 1N5851 1N5996	1N3016,B 1N3829 1N4736,A	1N3785 1N5921	1N5342,B	1N2970,B 1N3999,A	1N2804B 1N3305B 1N4555, 1N4563
7.5	1N4100	1N755,A 1N958,B 1N5527	1N755A, 1N958,B 1N5236,B 1N5852 1N5997	1N3017,A,B 1N3830 1N4737,A	1N3786 1N5922	1N5343,B	1N2971,B 1N4000,A	1N2805,B 1N3306,B 1N4556, 1N4564
8.0	1N707A							
8.2	1N712A 1N4101	1N756,A 1N959,B 1N5528	1N756,A 1N959,B 1N5237,B 1N5853 1N5998	1N3018,B 1N4738,A	1N3787 1N5923	1N5344,B	1N2972,B	1N2806,B 1N3307,B
8.4		1N3154-57,A	1N3154,A 1N3155-57					
8.5	1N4775-84,A		1N5238,B 1N5854					
8.7	1N4102					1N5345,B		
8.8		1N764						
9.0		1N764A	1N935-9;A,B					
9.1	1N4103	1N757,A 1N960,B 1N5529	1N757,A, 1N960,B 1N5239,B, 1N5855 1N5999	1N3019,B 1N4739,A	1N3788 1N5924	1N5346,B	1N2973,B	1N2807,B 1N3308,B
10.0	1N4104	1N758,A 1N961,B 1N5530,B	1N758,A, 1N961,B 1N5240,B, 1N5856 1N6000	1N3020,B 1N4740,A	1N3789 1N5925	1N5347,B	1N2974,B	1N2808,B 1N3309,A,B
11.0	1N715,A 1N4105	1N962,B 1N5531	1N962,B 1N5241,B 1N5857, 1N6001	1N3021,B 1N4741,A	1N3790 1N5926	1N5348,B	1N2975,B	1N2809,B 1N3310,B
11.7	1N716,A 1N4106		1N941-4;A,B					
12.0		1N759,A 1N963,B 1N5532	1N759,A, 1N963,B, 1N5242,B, 1N5858 1N6002	1N3022,B 1N4742,A	1N3791 1N5927	1N5349,B	1N2976,B	1N2810,B 1N3311,B
13.0	1N4107	1N964,B 1N5533	1N964,B 1N5243,B, 1N5859 1N6003	1N3023,B 1N4743,A	1N3792 1N5928	1N5350,B	1N2977,B	1N2811,B 1N3312,B
14.0	1N4108	1N5534	1N5244B 1N5860			1N5351,B	1N2978,B	1N2812,B 1N3313,B
15.0	1N4109	1N965,B 1N5535	1N965,B 1N5245,B, 1N5861, 1N6004	1N3024,B 1N4744A	1N3793 1N5929	1N5352,B	1N2979,A,B	1N2813,A,B 1N3314,B
16.0	1N4110	1N966,B 1N5536	1N966,B, 1N5246,B 1N5862, 1N6005	1N3025,B 1N4745,A	1N3794 1N5930	1N5353,B	1N2980,B	1N2814,B 1N3315,B
17.0	1N4111	1N5537	1N5247,B 1N5863			1N5354,B	1N2981B	1N2815,B 1N3316,B
18.0	1N4112	1N967,B 1N5538	1N967,B 1N5248,B 1N5864, 1N6006	1N3026,B 1N4746,A	1N3795 1N5931	1N5355,B	1N2982,B	1N2816,B 1N3317,B
19.0	1N4113	1N5539	1N5249,B 1N5865			1N5356,B	1N2983,B	1N2817,B 1N3318,B
20.0	1N4114	1N968,B 1N5540	1N968,B 1N5250,B 1N5866, 1N6007	1N3027,B 1N4747,A	1N3796 1N5932,A,B	1N5357,B	1N2984,B	1N2818,B 1N3319,B
22.0	1N4115	1N959,B 1N5541	1N969,B 1N5241,B 1N5867, 1N6008	1N3028,B 1N4748,A	1N3797 1N5933	1N5358,B	1N2985,B	1N2819,B 1N3320,A,B
24.0	1N4116	1N5542 1N9701B	1N970,B 1N5252,B, 1N586 1N6009	1N3029,B 1N4749,A	1N3798 1N5934	1N5359,B	1N2986,B	1N2820,B 1N3321,B
25.0	1N4117	1N5543	1N5253,B 1N5869			1N5360,B	1N2987B	1N2821,B 1N3322,B
27.0	1N4118	1N971,B	1N971 1N5254,B, 1N5870, 1N6010	1N3030,B 1N4750,A	1N3799 1N5935	1N5361,B	1N2988,B	1N2822B 1N3323,B
28.0	1N4119	1N5544	1N5255,B 1N5871			1N5362,B		
30.0	1N4120	1N972,B 1N5545	1N972,B 1N5256,B, 1N5872, 1N6011	1N3031,B 1N4751,A	1N3800 1N5936	1N5363,B	1N2989,B	1N2823,B 1N3324,B
33.0	1N4121	1N973,B 1N5546	1N973,B 1N5257,B 1N5873 1N6012	1N3032,B 1N4752,A	1N3801 1N5937	1N5364,B	1N2990,A,B	1N2824,B 1N3325,B

Table 18 — Zener Diodes — Continued

Volts	0.25	0.4	0.5	Power (Watts) 1.0	1.5	5.0	10.0	50.0
36.0	1N4122	1N974,B	1N974,B 1N5258,B 1N5874, 1N6013	1N3033,B 1N4753,A	1N3802 1N5938	1N5365,B	1N2991,B	1N2825,B 1N3326,B
39.0	1N4123	1N975,B	1N975,B, 1N5259,B 1N5875, 1N6014	1N3034,B 1N4754,A	1N3803 1N5939	1N5366,B	1N2992,B	1N2826,B 1N3327,B
43.0	1N4124	1N976,B	1N976,B 1N5260,B, 1N5876, 1N6015	1N3035,B 1N4755,A	1N3804 1N5940	1N5367,B	1N2993,A,B	1N2827,B 1N3328,B
45.0							1N2994B	1N2828B 1N3329B
47.0	1N4125	1N977,B	1N977,B, 1N5261,B 1N5877, 1N6016	1N3036,B 1N4756,A	1N3805 1N5941	1N5368,B	1N2996,B	1N2829,B 1N3330,B
50.0								1N2830B 1N3331B
51.0	1N4126	1N978,B	1N978,B, 1N5262,A,B 1N5878, 1N6017	1N3037,B 1N4757,A	1N3806 1N5942	1N5369,B	1N2997,B	1N2831,B 1N3332,B
52.0							1N2998B	1N3333
56.0	1N4127	1N979,B	1N979 1N5263,B 1N6018	1N3038,B 1N4758,A	1N3807 1N5943	1N5370,B	1N2999,B	1N2822,B 1N3334,B
60.0	1N4128		1N5264,A,B			1N5371,B		
62.0	1N4129	1N980,B	1N980 1N5265,A,B 1N6019	1N3039,B 1N4759,A	1N3808 1N5944	1N5372,B	1N3000,B	1N2833,B 1N3335,B
68.0	1N4130	1N981,B	1N981,B 1N5266,A,B 1N6020	1N3040,A,B 1N4760,A	1N3809 1N5945	1N5373,B	1N3001,B	1N2834,B 1N3336,B
75.0	1N4131	1N982,B	1N982 1N5267,A,B 1N6021	1N3041,B 1N4761,A	1N3810 1N5946	1N5374,B	1N3002,B	1N2835,B 1N3337,B
82.0	1N4132	1N983,B	1N983 1N5268,A,B 1N6022	1N3042,B 1N4762,A	1N3811 1N5947	1N5375,B	1N3003,B	1N2836,B 1N3338,B
87.0	1N4133		1N5269,B			1N5376,B		
91.0	1N4134	1N984,B	1N984 1N5270,B 1N6023	1N3043,B 1N4763,A	1N3812 1N5948	1N5377,B	1N3004,B	1N2837,B 1N3339,B
100.0	1N4135	1N985	1N985,B 1N5271,B 1N6024	1N3044,A,B 1N4764,A	1N3813 1N5949	1N5378,B	1N3005,B	1N2838,B 1N3340,B
105.0							1N3006B	1N2839,B 1N3341,B
110.0		1N986	1N986 1N5272,B 1N6025	1N3045,B 1M110ZS10	1N3814 1N5950	1N5379,B	1N3007A,B	1N2840,B 1N3342,B
120.0		1N987	1N987,B 1N5273,B 1N6026	1N3046,B 1M120ZS10	1N3815 1N5951	1N5380,B	1N3008A,B	1N2841,B 1N3343,B
130.0		1N988	1N988,B 1N5274,B 1N6027	1N3047,B 1M130ZS10	1N3816 1N5952	1N5381,B	1N3009,B	1N2842,B 1N3344,B
140.0		1N989	1N5275,B			1N5382B	1N3010B	1N3345B
150.0		1N990	1N989 1N5276,B 1N6028	1N3048,B 1M150ZS10	1N3817 1N5953	1N5383,B	1N3011,B	1N2843,B 1N3346,B
160.0		1N991	1N990 1N5277,B 1N6029	1N3049,B 1M160ZS10	1N3818 1N5954	1N5384,B	1N3012A,B	1N2844,B 1N3347,B
170.0		1N992	1N5278,B	1M170ZS10		1N5385,B		
175.0							1N3013B	1N3348B
180.0			1N991,B 1N5279,B 1N6030	1N3050,A,B 1M180ZS10	1N3819 1N5955	1N5386,B	1N3014,B	1N2845,B 1N3349,B
190.0			1N5280,B			1N5387,B		
200.0			1N992 1N5281,B 1N6031	1N3051,B 1M200ZS10	1N3820 1N5956	1N5388B	1N3015,B	1N2846,B 1N3350,B

Table 19
Metal-Oxide Varistors Transient Suppressors

Listed by voltage

Type No.	Maximum Applied Voltage V ac$_{RMS}$	V ac$_{Peak}$	Maximum Energy (Joules)	Max. Peak Current (Amps)	Max. Power (Watts)	Max. Varistor Voltage (Volts)
V180ZA1	115	163	1.5	500	0.2	285
V180ZA10	115	163	10.0	2000	0.45	290
V130PA10A	130	184	10.0	4000	8.0	350
V130PA20A	130	184	20.0	4000	15.0	350
V130LA1	130	184	1.0	400	0.24	360
V130LA2	130	184	2.0	400	0.24	360
V130LA10A	130	184	10.0	2000	0.5	340
V130LA20A	130	184	20.0	4000	0.85	340
V150PA10A	150	212	10.0	4000	8.0	410
V150PA20A	150	212	20.0	4000	15.0	410
V150LA1	150	212	1.0	400	0.24	420
V150LA2	150	212	2.0	400	0.24	420
V150LA10A	150	212	10.0	2000	0.5	390
V150LA20A	150	212	20.0	4000	0.85	390
V250PA10A	250	354	10.0	4000	4.0	670
V250PA20A	250	354	20.0	4000	7.0	670
V250PA40A	250	354	40.0	4000	13.0	670
V250LA2	250	354	2.0	400	0.28	690
V250LA4	250	354	4.0	400	0.28	690
V250LA15A	250	354	15.0	2000	0.6	640
V250LA20A	250	354	20.0	2000	0.6	640
V250LA40A	250	354	40.0	4000	0.9	640

Courtesy of General Electric Company

Table 20
Japanese Semiconductor Nomenclature

All transistors manufactured in Japan are registered with the Electronic Industries Association of Japan (EIAJ). In addition, the Japan Industrial Standard JIS-C-7012 provides type numbers for transistors and thyristors.

Each transistor type number consists of five elements.

Example:

| $\underset{\text{Figure}}{\underline{\overset{i}{2}}}$ | $\underset{\text{Letter}}{\underline{\overset{ii}{S}}}$ | $\underset{\text{Letter}}{\underline{\overset{iii}{C}}}$ | $\underset{\text{Figure}}{\underline{\overset{iv}{82D}}}$ | $\underset{\text{Letter}}{\underline{\overset{v}{A}}}$ |

i) Kind of device, indicating the number of effective electrical connections minus one.

ii) For a semiconductor registered with the EIAJ, this letter is always an S.

iii) This letter designates polarity and application, as follows:

Letter	Polarity and Application
A	PNP transistor, high frequency
B	PNP transistor, low frequency
C	NPN transistor, high frequency
D	NPN transistor, low frequency
E	P-gate thyristor
G	N-gate thyristor
H	N-base unijunction transistor
J	P-channel FET
K	N-channel FET
M	Bi-directional triode thyristor

iv) These figures designate the order of application for EIAJ registration, starting with 11.

v) This letter indicates the level of improvement. An improved device may be used in place of a previous-generation device, but not necessarily the other way around.

Table 21
General Purpose Transistors

Listed numerically by device

Device	Type	V_{CEO} Max. Collector-Emitter Voltage (Volts)	V_{CBO} Max. Collector-Base Voltage (Volts)	V_{EBO} Max. Emitter-Base Voltage (Volts)	I_c Max. Collector Current (mA)	P_D Max. Device Dissipation Watts	Min. DC Current Gain $I_c = 0.1$ mA h_{FE}	$I_c = 150$ mA h_{FE}	Current-Gain Bandwidth Product f_T* (MHz)	Noise Figure NF Max. (dB)
2N918	NPN	15	30	3.0	50	0.200	20(3 mA)	—	600	6.0
2N2102	NPN	65	120	7.0	1000	1.0	20	40	60	6.0
2N2218	NPN	30	60	5.0	800	0.8	20	40	250	
2N2218A	NPN	40	75	6.0	800	0.8	20	40	250	
2N2219	NPN	30	60	5.0	800	3.0	35	100	250	
2N2219A	NPN	40	75	6.0	800	3.0	35	100	300	4.0
2N2222	NPN	30	60	5.0	800	1.2	35	100	250	
2N2222A	NPN	40	75	6.0	800	1.2	35	100	300	4.0
2N2905	PNP	40	60	5.0	600	0.6	35	—	200	
2N2905A	PNP	60	60	5.0	600	0.6	75	100	200	
2N2907	PNP	40	60	5.0	600	0.400	35	—	200	
2N2907A	PNP	60	60	5.0	600	0.400	75	100	200	
2N3053	NPN	40	60	5.0	700	5.0	—	50	100	
2N3053A	NPN	60	80	5.0	700	5.0	—	50	100	
2N3904	NPN	40	60	6.0	200	0.625	40	—	300	5.0
2N3906	PNP	40	40	5.0	200	1.5	60	—	250	4.0
2N4037	PNP	40	60	7.0	1000	5.0	—	50		
2N4123	NPN	30	40	5.0	200	0.35	—	25(50 mA)	250	6.0
2N4124	NPN	25	30	5.0	200	0.350	120(2 mA)	60(50 mA)	300	5.0
2N4125	PNP	30	30	4.0	200	0.625	50(2 mA)	25(50 mA)	200	5.0
2N4126	PNP	25	25	4.0	200	0.625	120(2 mA)	60(50 mA)	250	4.0
2N4401	NPN	40	60	6.0	600	0.625	20	100	250	
2N4403	PNP	40	40	5.0	600	0.625	30	100	200	
2N5320	NPN	75	100	7.0	2000	10.0	—	30(1 A)		
2N5415	PNP	200	200	4.0	1000	10.0	—	30(50 mA)	15	
MM4003	PNP	250	250	4.0	500	1.0	20(10 mA)	—		
MPSA55	PNP	60	60	4.0	500	0.625	—	50(100 mA)	50	
MPS6547	NPN	25	35	3.0	50	0.625	20(2 mA)	—	600	

*Test conditions: $I_c = 20$ mAdc; $V_{CE} = 20$V; $f = 100$ MHz

Table 22
Low-Noise Transistors

The low-noise devices listed are produced with carefully controlled r_b and f_T to optimize device noise performance. Devices listed in the matrix are classified according to noise figure performance versus frequency.

NF dB	60	100	Frequency MHz 200	450	1000	2000	Polarity
1.5	2N5829	2N5829					PNP
	2N5031	2N5031	MRF904				NPN
2.0	2N4957	2N4957	2N5829				PNP
	2N5032	2N5032	2N5031	MRF904	MRF901		NPN
2.5	2N4958	2N4958	2N4957	2N5829			PNP
	2N5032	2N5032	2N5032	2N5031	MRF901		NPN
					2N6603		NPN
3.0	2N4959	2N4959	2N4958	2N4957	2N5829		PNP
	2N2857	2N2857	2N5032	3N5032	MRF901	MRF902	NPN
					2N6604		NPN
3.5	2N4959	2N4959	2N4959	2N4958	2N4957		PNP
	2N5179	2N5179	2N2857	3N5032	2N5031	MRF901	NPN
4.0	2N4959	2N4959	2N4959	2N4959	2N4958		PNP
	2N5179	2N5179	2N5179	2N2857	2N5031		NPN
4.5	2N4959	2N4959	2N4959	2N4959	2N4959		PNP
	2N5179	2N5179	2N5179	2N2857	2N5032		NPN

Table 23
RF Power Transistors
High Frequency, Low Voltage Amplifier Transistors
Power FETs

The transistors listed in this table are specified for operation in RF power amplifiers and are listed by ascending input power.
Modulation type is given in each application heading.
Courtesy Motorola Semiconductor Prod. Inc.

Device Type	P_{in} Input Power Watts	P_{out} Output Power Watts	G_{PE} Power Gain dB Min	V_{CC} Supply Voltage Volts	Package
1.5-30 MHz SSB Transistors					
MRF476	0.1	3.0 PEP/CW	15	12.5	TO-220
MRF432*†	0.125	12.5 PEP/CW	20	12.5	211-07
MRF433*	0.125	12.5 PEP/CW	20	12.5	211-07
MRF426	0.16	25.0 PEP/CW	22	28.0	211-07
MRF426A	0.16	25.0 PEP/CW	22	28.0	145A-09
2N6367	0.36	9.0 PEP/CW	14	12.5	211-07
MRF427	0.40	25.0 PEP/CW	18	50.0	211-11
MRF427A	0.40	25.0 PEP/CW	18	50.0	145A-10
2N6370	0.62	10.0 PEP/CW	12	28.0	211-07
MRF475	1.2	12.0 PEP/CW	10	13.6	TO-220
2N5070	1.25	25.0 PEP/CW	13	28.0	TO-60
MRF401	1.25	25.0 PEP/CW	13	28.0	145A-09
MRF406	1.25	20.0 PEP/CW	12	12.5	211-07
MRF466	1.25	15.0 PEP/CW	15	28.0	211-09
MRF477	1.25	40.0 PEP/CW	15	12.5	TO-220
MRF486	1.25	40.0 PEP/CW	15	28.0	TO-220
MRF479	1.5	15.0 PEP/CW	10	12.5	TO-220
MRF485	1.5	15.0 PEP/CW	10	28.0	TO-220
2N5941†	2.0	40.0 PEP/CW	13	28.0	211-07
MRF460	2.5	40.0 PEP/CW	12	12.5	211-11
MRF463†	2.53	80.0 PEP/CW	15	28.0	211-08
MRF464	2.53	80.0 PEP/CW	15	28.0	211-09
MRF464A	2.53	80.0 PEP/CW	15	28.0	145A-10
MRF412	3.5	70.0 PEP/CW	13	13.6	211-11
MRF428	7.5	150.0 PEP/CW	13	50.0	211-11
MRF428A†	7.5	150.0 PEP/CW	13	50.0	307-01
MRF429	7.5	150.0 PEP/CW	13	50.0	211-11
MRF421	10.0	100.0 PEP/CW	10	12.5	211-11
MRF422	15.0	150.0 PEP/CW	10	28.0	211-11
MRF435	15.0	150.0 PEP/CW	10	28.0	211-11
MRF448	15.7	250.0 PEP/CW	12	50.0	211-11

Device Type	P_{in} Input Power Watts	P_{out} Output Power Watts	G_{PE} Power Gain dB Min	V_{CC} Supply Voltage Volts	Package
14-30 MHz Amateur Transistors					
MRF8003	0.05	0.5	10	12.5	TO-39
MRF476	0.10	3.0	15	12.5	TO-220
MRF449†	0.3	30.0	10	13.6	211-07
MRF8004	0.35	3.5	10	12.5	TO-39
MRF475	0.4	4.0	10	13.6	TO-220
MRF449A	1.9	30.0	12	13.6	145A-09
MRF453	3.0	60.0	13	12.5	211-11
MRF455	3.0	60.0	13	12.5	211-07
MRF455A	3.0	60.0	13	12.5	145A-09
MRF450	4.0	50.0	11	13.6	211-09
MRF450A	4.0	50.0	11	13.6	145A-09
MRF497	4.0	40.0	10	12.5	TO-220
MRF453A†	4.8	60.0	11	12.5	145A-10
MRF454	5.0	80.0	12	12.5	211-11
MRF454A	5.0	80.0	12	12.5	145A-10
MRF458	5.0	80.0	12	12.5	211-11
MRF458A	5.0	80.0	12	12.5	145A-10
MRF492	5.6	70.0	11	12.5	211-11
MRF492A	5.6	70.0	11	12.5	145A-10
106-175 MHz VHF AM Transistors					
2N3866	0.1	1.0	10	28	TO-39
2N3553	0.25	2.5	10	28	TO-39
2N5641	1.0	7.0	8.4	28	144-05
2N5642	3.0	20	8.2	28	145A-09
MRF314	3.0	30	10	28	211-07
MRF314A	3.0	30	10	28	145A-09
2N5643	6.9	40	7.6	28	145A-09
MRF315	5.7	45	9.0	28	211-07
MRF315A	5.7	45	9.0	28	145A-09
MRF316*	8.0	80	10	28	316-01
MRF317*	12.5	100	9.0	28	316-01

*PNP/NPN complements for Complementary Symmetry Driver. For matched pairs, order MK433.
†Discontinued

*Controlled "Q" transistor

Table 23 (continued)

Device Type	P_{in} Input Power Watts	P_{out} Output Power Watts	G_{PE} Power Gain dB Min	V_{CC} Supply Voltage Volts	Package
2-175 MHz SSB TMOS Power FETs					
MRF138	0.6/1.2	30.0	17/14	28	211-07
MRF140	4.7/3.7	150.0	15/16	28	211-11
MRF148	0.48/0.95	30.0	18/15	50	211-07
MRF150	3.0/23	150.0	17/8	50	211-11
130-175 MHz VHF FM Transistors					
2N4427	0.1	1.0	10	12.0	TO-39
MRF553	0.1	1.5	13.0	12.5	317C-01
MRF604	0.1	1.0	10	12.5	TO-46
MRF607	0.12	1.75	11.5	12.5	TO-39
2N6080	0.25	4.0	12	12.5	145A-09
MRF237*	0.25	4.0	12	12.5	TO-39
MRF215**	0.33	20.0	8.2	12.5	316-01
2N5589	0.44	3.0	8.2	13.6	144B-05
2N6255	0.5	3.0	7.8	12.5	TO-39
MRF260	0.5	5.0	10	12.5	TO-220
MRF212	1.25	10.0	9.0	12.5	145A-09
2N5590	3.0	10.0	5.2	13.6	145A-09
MRF239	3.0	30.0	10.0	13.6	145A-09
MRF261	3.0	10.0	5.2	12.5	TO-220
2N6081	3.5	15.0	6.3	12.5	145A-09
MRF221	3.5	15.0	6.3	12.5	211-07
MRF262	3.5	15.0	6.3	12.5	TO-220
MRF238	3.7	30.0	9.0	13.6	145A-09
MRF240	5.0	40.0	9.0	13.6	145A-09
2N6082	6.0	25.0	6.2	12.5	145A-09
MRF222	6.0	25.0	6.2	12.5	211-01
2N6083	8.1	30.0	5.7	12.5	145A-09
MRF223	8.1	30.0	5.7	12.5	211-07
MRF216**	8.5	40.0	6.7	12.5	316-01
2N5591	9.0	25.0	4.4	13.6	145A-09
MRF264	9.1	30.0	5.2	12.5	TO-220
MRF243**	12.0	60.0	7.0	12.5	316-01
2N6084	14.3	40.0	4.5	12.5	145A-09
MRF224	14.3	40.0	4.5	12.5	211-07
MRF247**	15.0	75.0	7.0	12.5	316-01
MRF245**	18.2	80.0	6.4	12.5	316-01
MRF4070	20.0	70.0	5.0	12.5	316-01

*Grounded emitter TO-39 package   **Controlled "Q" transistor

Device Type	P_{in} Input Power Watts	P_{out} Output Power Watts	G_{PE} Power Gain dB Min	V_{CC} Supply Voltage Volts	Package
220 MHz FM Transistors					
MRF525*	0.001	0.02	13.0	26.0	TO-39
MRF313	0.03	1.0	15.0	28.0	305A-01
MRF313A	0.03	1.0	15.0	28.0	305-01
2N4428	0.075	25.0	10.0	28.0	TO-39
2N3866	0.1	1.0	10.0	28.0	TO-39
MRF208	0.1	10.0	10.0	12.5	145A-09
MRF5174	0.125	2.0	12.0	28.0	244-04
MRF227*	0.13	3.0	13.5	12.5	TO-39
MRF209	0.15	1.0	8.2	12.5	TO-39
2N5160	0.16	1.0	8.0	28.0	TO-39
MRF225	0.18	1.5	9.0	12.5	TO-39
MRF321**	0.62	10.0	12.0	28.0	244-04
MRF226	1.6	13.0	9.0	12.5	145A-09
MRF331	1.6	10.0	8.0	28.0	244-04
MRF323**	2.0	20.0	10.0	28.0	244-04
MRF325**	4.3	30.0	8.5	28.0	316-01
MRF390***	6.8	60.0	9.5#	28.0	744-02
MRF5177	7.5	30.0	6.0	28.0	215-02
MRF5177A	7.5	30.0	6.0	28.0	145A-09
MRF326**	8.0	40.0	9.0	28.0	316-01
MRF209	9.1	25.0	4.4	12.5	145A-09
MRF309	10.0	50.0	7.0	28.0	316-01
2N6439	10.0	60.0	7.8	28.0	316-01
MRF327**	14.9	80.0	7.3	28.0	316-01
MRF329**	20.0	100.0	7.0	28.0	333-03

*Grounded emitter TO-39 package
**Internal impedance matched
***Internal impedance matched push pull transistors
#Typical
†PNP

Device Type	P_{in} Input Power Watts	P_{out} Output Power Watts	G_{PE} Power Gain dB Min	V_{CC} Supply Voltage Volts	Package
407-512 MHz UHF FM Transistors					
MRF581	0.023	0.6	14.0	12.5	317-01
MRF559	0.025	0.5	13.0	12.5	317-01
2N6256	0.05	0.5	10.0	12.5	249-05
MRF626	0.05	0.5	10.0	12.5	305-01
MRF627	0.05	0.5	10.0	12.5	305A-01
MRF628	0.05	0.5	10.0	12.5	249-05
MRF750	0.05	0.5	10.0	7.5	305A-01
MRF515	0.12	0.75	8.0	12.5	TO-39
2N5644	0.20	1.0	7.0	12.5	145A-09
2N3948	0.25	1.0	6.0	13.6	TO-39
2N5944	0.25	2.0	9.0	12.5	244-04
MRF629*	0.32	2.0	8.0	12.5	TO-39
MRF630*	0.33	3.0	9.5	12.5	TO-39
MRF752	0.4	2.5	8.0	7.5	249-05
MRF652	0.5	5.0	10.0	12.5	244-04
2N5945	0.64	4.0	8.0	12.5	244-04
MRF660	2.0	7.0	5.4	12.5	TO-220
MRF754	2.0	8.0	6.0	7.5	249-05
2N5946	2.5	10.0	6.0	12.5	244-04
MRF641**	3.75	15.0	7.8	12.5	316-01
MRF644**	5.9	25.0	6.2	12.5	316-01
MRF646**	13.3	40.0	4.8	12.5	316-01
MRF338**	15.0	80.0	4.3	28.0	333-03
MRF648**	22.0	60.0	4.4	12.5	316-01

*Grounded emitter TO-39 package   **Internal impedance matched

Device Type	P_{in} Input Power Watts	P_{out} Output Power Watts	G_{PE} Power Gain dB Min	V_{CC} Supply Voltage Volts	Package
806-947 MHz UHF FM Transistors					
MRF581	0.06	0.6	10#	12.5	317-01
MRF816	0.075	0.75	10.0	12.5	249.05
MRF559	0.080	0.5	8.0	12.5	317-01
MRF838	0.22	1.0	6.5	12.5	305A-01
MRF838A	0.22	1.0	6.5	12.5	305-01
MRF890	0.25	2.0	9.0	24.0	305-01
MRF817	0.59	2.5	6.2	13.6	244-04
MRF841@	0.7	5.0	8.5	12.5	244-04
MRF870	1.0	3.0	5.0	12.5	305A-01
MRF870A	1.0	3.0	5.0	12.5	305-01
MRF892 @	2.0	14.0	8.5	24.0	319-04
MRF840@	2.5	10.0	6.0	12.5	319-04
MRF842@	5.0	20.0	6.0	12.5	319-04
MRF894@	6.0	30.0	7.0	24.0	319-04
MRF844@	9.0	30.0	5.2	12.5	319-04
MRF846@	15.0	40.0	4.3	12.5	319-04

@ Common base
# Typical

Table 24
VHF and UHF Class-A Transistors

The devices listed below are excellent for class-A linear applications.
The devices are listed according to increasing current-gain bandwidth (f_T).

Device Type	Nominal Test Conditions V_{CE}/I_C Volts/mA	f_T MHz Min.	Noise Figure Max/Freq. MHz	2nd Order IMD	3rd Order IMD	Output Level dBmV	Package
MRF501	6/5	600	4.5*/200				TO-72
MRF502	6/5	800	4.0*/200				TO-72
2N5179	6/5	900	4.5/200				TO-72
BFY90	5/2	1000	5.0/500				TO-72
BFW92	5/2	1000	4.0/500				302A-01
2N6305	5/10	1200	5.5/450				TO-72
BFX89	5/25	1200	6.5/500				TO-72
2N5109	15/50	1200	3.0*/200				TO-39
2N5943	15/50	1200	3.4/200	−50		+50	TO-39
2N6304	5/10	1400	4.5/450				TO-72
MRF511	20/80	1500	7.3*/200	−50	−65	+50	144D-04
MRF517	15/60	2200	7.5/300	−60	−72	+45	TO-39
BFR90	10/14	5000*	2.4*/500				302A-01
BFR91	5/35	5000*	1.9*/500				302A-01
BFR96	10/50	5000*	3.3*/500				302A-01

*Typ.

Table 25
Suggested Small-Signal FETs

Device No.	Type	Max. Diss. (mW)	Max. V_{DS} (volts)	$V_{GS(off)}$ volts	Min. gfs (μS)	Input C (pF)	Max. I_D (mA)*	Upper Freq. (MHz)	Noise Figure (typ.)	Case Type	Base Conn.	Mfgr. (see code)	Applications (general)
2N4416	N-JFET	300	30	−6	4500	4	−15	450	400 MHz 4 dB	TO-72	1	S, M	VHF/UHF/RF amp., mix., osc.
2N5484	N-JFET	310	25	−3	2500	5	30	200	200 MHz 4 dB	TO-92	2	M	VHF/UHF amp., mix., osc.
2N5485	N-JFET	310	25	−4	3500	5	30	400	400 MHz 4 dB	TO-92	2	S	VHF/UHF/RF amp., mix., osc.
3N200	N-Dual-Gate MOSFET	330	20	−6	10,000	4-8.5	50	500	400 MHz 4.5 dB	TO-72	3	R	VHF/UHF/RF amp., mix., osc.
3N202	N-Dual-Gate MOSFET	360	25	−5	8000	6	50	200	200 MHz 4.5 dB	TO-72	3	S	VHF amp., mixer
MPF102	N-JFET	310	25	−8	2000	4.5	20	200		TO-92	2	N, M	HF/VHF amp., mix., osc.
MPF106/ 2N5484	N-JFET	310	25	−6	2500	5	30	400	200 MHz 4 dB	TO-92	2	N, M	HF/VHF/UHF amp., mix., osc.
40673	N-Dual-Gate MOSFET	330	20	−4	12,000	6	50	400	200 MHz 6 dB	TO-72	3	R	HF/VHF/UHF amp., mix., osc.
U300	P-JFET	300	−40	+10	8000	20	−50	—	40n V/$\sqrt{\text{Hz}}$	TO-18	4	S	General-purpose amp.
U304	P-JFET	350	−30	+10		27	−50	—	—	TO-18	4	S	analog switch, chopper
U310	N-JFET	500	30	−6	10,000	2.5	60	450	450 MHz 3.2 dB	TO-52	5	S	common-gate VHF/UHF amp., osc., mix.
U350	N-JFET Quad	300 1W	30 25	−6	9000	5	60	100	100 MHz 7 dB	TO-99	6	S	matched JFET doubly bal. mix.
U431	N-JFET Dual	300	25	−6	10,000	5	30	100	—	TO-99	7	S	matched JFET cascode amp. and bal. mix.

*25°C   M = Motorola.   N = National Semiconductor.   R = RCA.   S = Siliconix Inc.   D = Drain.   S = Source.   G = Gate.

Table 26
Power FETs

Device No.	Type	Max. Diss. (W)	Max. V_{DS} (volts)	Max. I_D (A)	G_{fs} μmhos (typ.)	Input C C_{iss} (pF)	Output C C_{oss} (pF)	Approx. Upper Freq. (MHz)	Case Type	Base Conn. Mfgr.	Applications (general)
DV1202S	N-Chan.	10	50	0.5	100k	14	20	500	.380 SOE	$\frac{1}{S}$	RF pwr. amp., osc.
DV1202W	N-Chan.	10	50	0.5	100k	14	20	500	C-220	$\frac{5}{S}$	RF pwr. amp., osc.
DV1205S	N-Chan.	20	50	1	200k	26	38	500	.380 SOE	$\frac{1}{S}$	RF pwr. amp., osc.
DV1205W	N-Chan.	20	50	1	200k	26	38	500	C-220	$\frac{5}{S}$	RF pwr. amp., osc.
2SK133	N-Chan.	100	120	7	1M	600	350	1	TO-3	$\frac{6}{H}$	AF pwr. amp., switch (complement to 2SJ48)
2SK134	N-Chan.	100	140	7	1M	600	350	1	TO-3	$\frac{6}{H}$	AF pwr. amp., switch (complement to 2SJ49)
2SK135	N-Chan.	100	160	7	1M	600	350	1	TO-3	$\frac{6}{H}$	AF pwr. amp., switch (complement to 2SJ50)
2SJ48	P-Chan.	100	120	7	1M	900	400	1	TO-3	$\frac{6}{H}$	AF pwr. amp., switch (complement to 2SK133)
2SJ49	P-Chan.	100	140	7	1M	900	400	1	TO-3	$\frac{6}{H}$	AF pwr. amp., switch (complement 2SK134)
2SJ50	P-Chan.	100	160	7	1M	900	400	1	TO-3	$\frac{6}{H}$	AF pwr. amp., switch (complement 2SK135)
VMP4	N-Chan.	25	60	2	170,000	32	4.8	200	.380-SOE	$\frac{1}{S}$	VHF pwr. amp., rcvr front end (rf amp., mixer).
VN10KM	N-Chan.	1	60	0.5	100,000	48	16	—	TO-92	$\frac{2}{S}$	High-speed line driver, relay driver, LED stroke driver
VN64GA	N-Chan.	80	60	12.5	150,000	700	325	30	TO-3	$\frac{3}{S}$	Linear amp., power-supply switch, motor control
VN66AF	N-Chan.	15	60	2	150,000	50	50	—	TO-202	$\frac{4}{S}$	High-speed switch, hf linear amp., audio amp. line driver.
VN66AK	N-Chan.	8.3	60	2	250,000	33	6	100	TO-39	$\frac{7}{S}$	RF pwr. amp., high-current analog switching.
VN67AJ	N-Chan.	25	60	2	250,000	33	7	100	TO-3	$\frac{3}{S}$	RF pwr. amp., high-current switching
VN89AA	N-Chan.	25	80	2	250,000	50	10	100	TO-3	$\frac{3}{S}$	High-speed switching, hf linear amps., line drivers.
IRF100	N-Chan.	125	80	16	300,000	900	25	—	TO-3	$\frac{3}{IR}$	High-speed switching, audio amps., motor control, inverters.
IRF101	N-Chan.	125	60	16	300,000	900	25	—	TO-3	$\frac{3}{IR}$	Same as IRF100

*25°C S = M/A-COM   IR = International Rectifier.
(case) H = Hitachi

S = SOURCE   D = DRAIN   G = GATE

(1) (2) (3) (4) (5) (6) (7)

Table 27
General Purpose Silicon Power Transistors

TO-220 CASE POWER TRANSISTORS

NPN	PNP	I_C Max. Collector Current (Amps)	V_{CEO} Max. Collector-Emitter Voltage (Volts)	hFE Min. DC Current Gain	F_T Current-Gain Bandwidth Product (MHz)	Pd Max Device Dissipation (Watts)
D44C1*		4	30	25	50	30
	D45C1*	−4	−30	25	50	30
D44C2*		4	30	100/220	50	30
	D45C2*	−4	−30	40/120	50	30
D44C3*		4	30	40/120	50	30
	D45C3*	−4	−30	40/120	50	30
D44C4*		4	45	25	50	30
	D45C4*	−4	−45	25	50	30
D44C5*		4	45	100/220	50	30
	D45C5*	−4	−45	40/120	50	30
D44C6		4	45	40/120	50	30
	D45C6*	−4	−45	40/120	50	30
D44C7*		4	60	25	50	30
	D45C7*	−4	−60	25	50	30
D44C8*		4	60	100/220	50	30
	D45C8*	−4	−60	40/120	50	30
D44C9*		4	60	40/120	50	30
	D45C9*	−4	−60	40/120	50	30
D44C10*		4	80	25	50	30
	D45C10*	−4	−80	25	50	30
D44C11*		4	80	40/120	50	30
	D45C11*	−4	−80	40/120	50	30
D44C12*		4	80	40/120	50	30
	D45C12*	−4	−80	40/120	50	30
D44H1*		10	30	20	50	50
	D45H1*	−10	−30	20	50	50
D44H2*		10	30	40	50	50
	D45H2*	−10	−30	40	50	50
TIP61*		0.5	40	15	3	15
	TIP62*	0.5	40	15	3	15
TIP61C		0.5	100	15	3	15
MJE2360T		0.5	350	40	10	30
41501		1	225	25	10	40
TIP29*		1	40	15/75	3	30
	TIP30A*	1	40	15/75	3	30
TIP29A*		1	60	15/75	3	30
	TIP30A*	1	60	15/75	3	30

NPN	PNP	I_C Max. Collector Current (Amps)	V_{CEO} Max. Collector-Emitter Voltage (Volts)	hFE Min. DC Current Gain	F_T Current-Gain Bandwidth Product (MHz)	Pd Max Device Dissipation (Watts)
TIP29B		1	80	15/75	3	30
TIP29C*		1	100	15/75	3	30
	TIP30C*	1	100	15/75	3	30
TIP47		1	250	30/150	10	40
TIP48		1	300	30/150	10	40
TIP49		1	350	30/150	10	40
TIP50		1	400	30/150	10	40
	TIP116	2	80	500	25	50
TIP31*		3	40	25	3	40
	TIP32*	3	40	25	3	40
TIP31A*		3	60	25	3	40
	TIP32A*	3	60	25	3	40
TIP31B*		3	80	25	3	40
	TIP32B*	3	80	25	3	40
TIP31C*		3	100	25	3	40
	TIP32C*	3	100	25	3	40
2N6121*		4	45	25/100	2.5	40
	2N6124*	4	45	25/100	2.5	40
2N6122		4	60	25/100	2.5	40
MJE13004		4	300	6/30	4	60
	TIP42	6	40	15/75	3	65
TIP41A		6	60	15/75	3	65
TIP41B		6	80	15/75	3	65
	2N61111	7	30	30/150	4	40
2N6290*		7	50	30/150	4	40
	2N6109*	7	50	30/150	4	40
2N6292*		7	70	30/150	4	40
	2N6107	7	70	30/150	4	40
MJE15030		8	150	20	30	50
MJE3055T*		10	60	20/70	—	75
	MJE2955T*	10	60	20/70	—	75
2N6486		15	40	20/150	5	75
2N6488		15	80	20/150	5	75

*Complementary Pairs.

Table 27 (continued)

TO-204 (TO-3) CASE

NPN	PNP	I_C Max. Collector Current (Amps)	V_{CEO} Max. Collector-Emitter Voltage (Volts)	hFE Min. DC Current Gain	F_T Current-Gain Bandwidth Product (MHz)	Pd Max Device Dissipation (Watts)
MJ12002		2.5	1500	1.11	4	75
2N3902		3.5	325	30/90	—	100
MJ410		5	200	30/90	2.5	100
MJ3029		5	250	30	—	125
MJ411		5	300	30/90	2.5	100
MJ3030		5	325	3.75	—	125
BU208A		5	1500	2.25	7.5	125
2N6307		8	300	15/75	5	125
2N6308		8	350	12/60	5	125
2N6545		8	400	7/35	6	125
MJ12005		8	1500	5	—	100
	2N3789	10	60	15	4	150
2N3715*		10	60	30	4	150
	2N3791*	10	60	30	4	150
2N5877*		10	60	20/100	4	150
	2N5875*	10	60	20/100	4	150
2N3790		10	80	15	4	150
2N3716*		10	80	30	4	150
	2N3792*	10	80	30	4	150
	2N6230	10	120	20/80	1	150
MJ15011*		10	250	20/100	—	200
	MJ15012*	10	250	20/100	—	200
MJ413		10	325	20/80	2.5	125
MJ423		10	325	30/90	2.5	125
MJ10012		10	400	100/2K	—	175
2N3055*		15	60	20/70	2.5	115
	MJ2955*	15	60	20/70	2.5	115
2N3055A		15	60	20/70	0.8	115
2N5881		15	60	20/100	4	160
	2N5880	15	80	20/100	4	160
	MJ15015	15	120	20/70	1	150
MJ150001*		15	140	25/150	2	200
	MJ15002*	15	140	25/150	2	200
2N6249		15	200	10/50	2.5	175
2N6250		15	275	8/50	2.5	175
2N6546		15	300	6/30	6-24	175
2N6251		15	350	6/50	2.5	175
MJ4033*		16	60	1K	—	150
	MJ4030*	16	60	1K	—	150
MJ4034*		16	80	1K	—	150
	MJ4031*	16	60	1K	—	150
2N5269		16	100	25/100	1	150
MJ4035*		16	100	1K	—	150
	MJ4032*	16	100	1K	—	150
2N5630*		16	120	20/80	1	200
	2N6030*	16	120	20/80	1	200
2N3773		16	140	15/60	4	200
2N5631*		16	140	15/60	1	200
	2N6031*	16	140	15/60	1	200
2N5039		20	75	20/100	60	140
2N5303		20	80	15/60	2	200
2N6284*		20	100	750/18K	—	160
	2N6287*	20	100	750/18K	—	160
MJ15003*		20	140	25/150	2	250
	MJ15004*	20	140	25/100	2	250
2N5885*		25	60	—	4	200
	2N5883*	25	60	—	4	200
2N5886*		25	80	20/100	4	200
	2N5884*	25	80	20/100	4	200
MJ15024*		25	250	15/60	5	250
	MJ15025*	25	250	15/60	5	250
2N3771		30	40	—	2	150
2N5301*		30	40	15/60	2	200
	2N4398*	30	40	15/60	2	200
2N5302*		30	60	15/60	2	200
	2N4399*	30	60	15/60	2	200
MJ802*		30	100	25/100	2	200
	MJ4502*	30	100	25/100	2	200
	2N5683‡	50	60	15/60	2	300
2N6274		50	100	30/120	30	250
MJ14002		70	80	15/100	—	300

‡Modified TO-3—60 Mil Pins.   *Complementary Pair

152 Case Power Transistors

NPN	PNP	I_C Max. Collector Current (Amps)	V_{CEO} Max. Collector-Emitter Voltage (Volts)	hFE Min. DC Current Gain	F_T Current-Gain Bandwidth Product (MHz)	Pd Max Device Dissipation (Watts)
MPSU31		0.5	65	10	—	10
MPSU10*		0.5	300	30	60	10
	MPSU60*	0.5	300	30	60	10
MPSU02*		0.8	40	30	150	10
	MPSU52*	0.8	40	30	150	10
MPSU03		1	120	40	100	10
MPSU04		1	180	40	100	10
MPSU01*		2	30	50	50	10
	MPSU51*	2	30	50	50	10
MPSU01A*		2	40	50	50	10
	MPSU51A*	2	40	50	50	10
MPSU05*		2	60	60	50	10
	MPSU55*	2	60	60	50	10
MPSU06*		2	80	60	50	10
	MPSU56*	2	80	60	50	10
MPSU07*		2	100	30	50	10
	MPSU57*	2	100	30	50	10

*Complementary Pairs.

Table 28
Package Information

TO-204 (TO-3)

CASE 221A-01
TO-220AB

CASE 211-07
CASE 211-08
CASE 211-09
CASE 211-11

CASE 303-01
CASE 332A-01

Macro-X
Case 317-01

Macro-T
Case 317A-01

TO-202

CASE 211-10

CASE 305-01
CASE 332-04

SOT-23
CASE 318-02

CASE 22-03
TO-18

TO-237

CASE 215-02

CASE 305A-01

CASE 319-01

CASE 79-02, 31-03
TO-205 (TO-39), TO-5

CASE 144B-05

CASE 244-04

CASE 307-01

CASE 328-02
(μ0.230″ PILL)

CASE 36-03
TO-60

CASE 144D-05

CASE 249-05

NARROW
STRIP

CASE 316-01

CASE 328A-01
(μ0.230″ FLANGE)

CASE 20-03
TO-72

CASE 145A-09

CASE 336-03

CASE 337-02
(μ0 290″ FLANGE)

CASE 029-02
TO-92

CASE 145A-10

Micro-X
Case 358-01

CASE 361A-01

Table 29
Integrated Circuit Operational Amplifiers

Listed numerically by device.

Device	Fabrication Technology	Notes
101A	Bipolar	General purpose
108	Bipolar	
108A	Bipolar	
124	Bipolar	Quad, low power
148	Bipolar	Quad, 741
158	Bipolar	Dual, low power
301	Bipolar	Bandwidth extendable with specific components
324	Bipolar	Quad, single supply applications
347	BIFET	Quad, high-speed
351	BIFET	
353	BIFET	
355	BIFET	
355B	BIFET	
356A	BIFET	
356B	BIFET	
357	BIFET	
357B	BIFET	
358	Bipolar	Dual-single supply applications
411	BIFET	Low offset, low drift
709	Bipolar	
741	Bipolar	
741S	Bipolar	Improved 741 for audio application
1436	Bipolar	High-voltage
1437	Bipolar	Matched, Dual 1709
1439	Bipolar	
1456	Bipolar	Dual 1741
1458	Bipolar	
1458S	Bipolar	Improved 1458 for audio applications
1709	Bipolar	
1741	Bipolar	
1747	Bipolar	Dual 1741
1748	Bipolar	Non-compensated 1741
1776	Bipolar	Micropower, programmable
3140	Bipolar/MOSFET	Strobable output
3403	Bipolar	Quad, low power
3405	Bipolar	Dual op-amp and dual comparator
3458	Bipolar	Dual, low power
3476	Bipolar	
3900	Bipolar	Quad, Norton, single supply
4558	Bipolar	Dual, wideband
4741	Bipolar	Quad 1741
5534	Bipolar	Low noise-can swing 20V p-p across 600Ω
5556	Bipolar	Equivalent to 1456
5558	Bipolar	Dual; equivalent to 1458
34001	BIFET	JFET Input
OP-27A	Bipolar	Ultra-low noise, high speed
OP-37A	Bipolar	
TL-071	BIFET	Low noise
TL-081	BIFET	
TL-084	Bipolar/JFET	Quad; high-performance audio applications

Table 30
IC Op Amp Base Diagrams (Top View — not to scale)

Table 30 (continued)

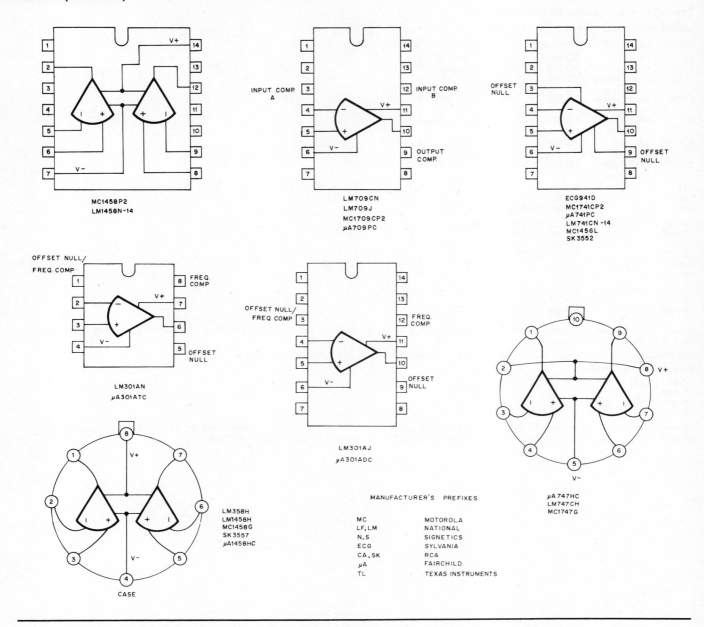

MANUFACTURER'S PREFIXES

MC	MOTOROLA
LF, LM	NATIONAL
N, S	SIGNETICS
ECG	SYLVANIA
CA, SK	RCA
μA	FAIRCHILD
TL	TEXAS INSTRUMENTS

Table 31

Three-Terminal Voltage Regulators

Listed numerically by device

Device	Description	Package	Voltage	Current (Amps)
317	Adj Pos	TO-205	+1.2 to +37	0.5
317	Adj Pos	TO-204,TO-220	+1.2 to +37	1.5
317L	Low Current Adj Pos	TO-205,TO-92	+1.2 to +37	0.1
317M	Med Current Adj Pos	TO-220	+1.2 to +37	0.5
350	High Current Adj Pos	TO-204,TO-220	+1.2 to +33	3.0
337	Adj Neg	TO-205	−1.2 to −37	0.5
337	Adj Neg	TO-204,TO-220	−1.2 to −37	1.5
337M	Med Current Adj Neg	TO-220	−1.2 to −37	0.5
309		TO-205	+5	0.2
309		TO-204	+5	1.0
323		TO-204,TO-220	+5	3.0
140-XX	Fixed Pos	TO-204,TO-220	Note 1	1.0
340-XX		TO-204,TO-220		1.0
78XX		TO-204,TO-220		1.0
78LXX		TO-205,TO-92		0.1
78MXX		TO-220		0.5
78TXX		TO-204		3.0
79XX	Fixed Neg	TO-204,TO-220	Note 1	1.0
79LXX		TO-205,TO-92		0.1
79MXX		TO-220		0.5

Note 1—XX indicates the regulated voltage; this value may be anywhere from 1.2 volts to 35 volts. A 7815 is a positive 15-volt regulator, and a 7924 is a negative 24-volt regulator.

The regulator package may be denoted by an additional suffix, according to the following:

Package	Suffix
TO-204 (TO-3)	K
TO-220	T
TO-205 (TO-39)	H,G
TO-92	P,Z

For example, a 7812K is a positive 12-volt regulator in a TO-204 package. An LM340T-5 is a positive 5-volt regulator in a TO-220 package. In addition, different manufacturers use different prefixes. An LM7805 is equivalent to a μA 7805 or MC7805.

K SUFFIX
METAL TO-204 PACKAGE

BOTTOM VIEW

PINS 1 AND 2 ELECTRICALLY
ISOLATED FROM CASE.
CASE IS THIRD ELEC-
TRICAL CONNECTION.

1 ADJ   2 V_IN
V_OUT

CASE IS
OUTPUT

317
350

1 ADJ   2 V_OUT
V_IN

CASE IS
INPUT

337

1 IN   2 OUT
GND

CASE IS
GROUND

140K-XX
340K-XX
309
7800 SERIES
78T00 SERIES

1 GND   2 OUT
IN

CASE IS
INPUT

7900 SERIES

T SUFFIX
TO-220 PACKAGE

CENTER LEAD IS CONNECTED TO THE HEAT SINK

OUTPUT

ADJUST
OUTPUT
INTPUT

317
350

INPUT

ADJUST
INPUT
OUTPUT

337
337M

GROUND

INPUT
GROUND
OUTPUT

7800 SERIES
78T00 SERIES
78M00 SERIES
140T-XX
340T-XX

INPUT

GROUND
INPUT
OUTPUT

7900 SERIES
79M00 SERIES

H,G SUFFIX
TO-205 PACKAGE

BOTTOM VIEW

ADJ
IN   OUT

CASE IS
OUTPUT

317
317L

OUT
ADJ   IN

CASE IS
INPUT

337

OUT
IN   GND

CASE IS
GROUND

78L00
SERIES

78M00
SERIES

OUT
GND   IN

CASE IS
INPUT

79L00
SERIES

79M00
SERIES

P,Z SUFFIX
TO-92 PACKAGE

ADJUST
OUTPUT
INPUT

317L

OUTPUT
GROUND
INPUT

78L00 SERIES

GROUND
INPUT
OUTPUT

79L00 SERIES

Table 32

Coaxial Cable End Connectors

UHF Plugs — Male†

Construction	Cable RG-		Military No.
UHF-Straight plug	8, 9, 11, 13, 63, 87, 149, 213, 214, 216, 225		PL-259
UHF-Straight plug	59, 62, 71, 140, 210		UG-111

UHF Panel Receptacles — Female†

Construction	Description	Military No.
Panel receptacle (Female contacts)	Standard, mica-filled Phenolic insulation	SO-239
Bulkhead receptacle (female)	Rear mount/pressurized/ copolymer of styrene ins.	UG-266

† Except as noted, all series UHF are non-weatherproof, and have a non-constant impedance.
Freq. range = 0-500 MHz.
Voltage rating: 500 V peak

UHF Adapters

Construction	Description	Military No.
Adapter Polystyrene ins.	Straight/jack-jack	PL-258
Adapter Polystyrene ins.	Bulkhead/jack-jack	UG-363
Adapter Polystyrene ins.	Bulkhead/jack-jack	UG-224
Adapter Polystyrene ins.	Angle/jack-plug	UG-646
Adapter Polystyrene ins.	Angle/plug-jack	M-359A
Adapter Polystyrene ins.	T/jack-plug-jack	M-358

UHF Reducers

Construction	Cable RG-	Military No.
Reducing adapter	55, 58, 141, 142 (except 55A)	UG-175
Reducing adapter	59, 62, 71, 140, 210	UG-176

N Plugs and Jacks

Construction	Cable RG-	Construction Notes	Military No.
N Straight plug	8, 9, 213, 214	Impedance = 50 Ω weatherproof	UG-21
N Straight plug	11, 13, 149, 216	Impedance = 70 Ω weatherproof	UG-94A
N Straight plug	58, 141, 142	Impedance = 50 Ω weatherproof	UG-536
N Straight plug	59, 62, 71, 140, 210	Impedance = 50 Ω weatherproof	UG-603
N Straight jack	8, 9, 87, 213, 214, 225	Impedance = 50 Ω weatherproof	UG-23, B-E
N Straight jack	59, 62, 71, 140, 210	—	UG-602
N Panel jack	8, 9, 87, 213, 214, 225	—	UG-22B, D, E
N Panel jack	58, 141, 142	Impedance = 50 Ω weatherproof	UG-1052
N Panel jack	59, 62, 71, 140, 210	Impedance = 50 Ω weatherproof	UG-593
N Bulkhead jack	8, 9, 87, 213, 214, 225	Impedance = 50 Ω weatherproof	UG-160A, B, D
N Bulkhead jack	58, 141, 142	Impedance = 50 Ω weatherproof	UG-556
N Panel jack		Impedance = 50 Ω	UG-58, A
N Angle female panel jack		Impedance = 50 Ω 1$\frac{1}{16}$" clearance above panel	UG-997A
Bulkhead female		Front mounted, hermetically sealed	M39012/04-0001
Bulkhead female		Front mounted, pressurized	UG-680

N Adapters

Construction	Adapter Ends	Construction Notes	Military No.
Straight	Jack-jack	50 Ω, TFE ins.	UG-29A
Straight	Plug-plug	50 Ω, TFE ins.	UG-57B
Straight	Jack-jack	50 Ω, TFE ins.	UG-29B
Straight	Jack-jack	50 Ω, TFE ins.	UG-29
Straight	Plug-plug	50 Ω, TFE ins.	UG-57A
Angle	Jack-plug	Mitre body	UG-27A
Angle	Jack-plug	Mitre body	UG-27B
Angle	Jack-plug	Mitre body	UG-212A
T	Jack-plug-jack	—	UG-107A
T	Jack-jack-jack	—	UG-28A
T	Jack-plug-jack	—	UG-107B

*NOTE: N connectors with gaskets are weatherproof. RF leakage: −90 dB min @ 3 GHz
Temp. limits: TFE: −67° to 390°F (−55° to 199°C). Insertion loss 0.15 dB max @ 10 GHz
Copolymer of styrene: −67° to 185°F (−55° to 85°C)
Z = 50 or 70 Ω, as noted. Freq. range: 0-11 GHz
Voltage rating: 1500 V p-p. Dielectric withstanding voltage 2500 V$_{RMS}$.
VSWR (MIL-C-39012 cable connectors) 1.3 max 0-11 GHz

Table 32 (continued)

HN Plugs and Jacks†

Construction	Cable	Construction Notes	Military No.
Straight plug	8, 9, 213, 214	—	UG-59A
Straight jack	8, 9, 87, 213, 214, 225	Captivated contact	UG-1214
Straight jack	8, 9, 213, 214	Copolymer of styrene ins.	UG-60A
Panel jack	8, 9, 87, 213, 214, 225	Captivated contact	UG-1215
Panel receptacle	—	Female contact	UG-560
Panel receptacle	—	Female contact	UG-496
Angle adapter	—	Jack-plug/berylium outer contact	UG-212C

†Note: Z = 50 Ω, Freq. range = 0-4 GHz, voltage rating = 1500 V p-p.
Dielectric withstanding voltage = 5000 V$_{RMS}$ VSWR = 1.3
All HN series are weatherproof. Temp. limits: TFE: −67° to 390°F (−55° to 199°C)
Copolymer of styrene: −67° to 185°F (−55° to 85°C)

BNC Plugs and Jacks

Construction	Cable RG-	Construction Notes	Military No.
BNC straight plug	8, 9	—	UG-959
BNC straight plug	59, 62, 71, 140, 210	Rexolite insulation	UG-260,A
BNC panel jack	59, 62, 71, 140, 210	Rexolite insulation	UG-262
BNC panel jack	59, 62, 71, 140, 210	Non-weatherproof Rexolite ins.	UG-262A
BNC panel jack	55, 58, 141, 142, 223, 400	—	UG-291
BNC panel jack	55, 58, 141, 142, 223, 400	Non-weatherproof	UG-291A
BNC bulkhead jack front mount	59, 62, 71, 140, 210	Front mtg/Rexolite ins.	UG-624
BNC bulkhead receptacle	—	Standard	UG-1094A UG-625B UG-625
BNC straight adapter	Plug-plug	—	UG-491A
BNC straight adapter	Plug-plug	Beryl. outer contact	UG-491B
BNC straight adapter	Jack-jack	—	UG-914
BNC straight adapter	Plug-plug	—	UG-491
BNC angle adapter	Jack-plug	—	UG-306
BNC angle adapter	Jack-plug	Berl. outer contact	UG-306A
BNC angle adapter	Jack-plug	Berl. outer contact	UG-306B
BNC panel adapter	Jack-jack	3-56 tapped flange holes	UG-414
BNC panel adapter	Jack-jack	3-56 tapped flange holes	UG-414A
Straight	Plug-plug	—	UG-491A
Straight	Plug-plug	Beryl. outer contact	UG-491B
Straight	Jack-jack	—	UG-914
Straight	Plug-plug	—	UG-491
Angle	Jack-plug	—	UG-306
Angle	Jack-plug	Beryl. outer contact	UG-306A
Angle	Jack-plug	Beryl. outer contact	UG-306B
Panel	Jack-jack	3-56 tapped flange holes	UG-414
Panel	Jack-jack	3-56 tapped flange holes	UG-414A
T	Jack-plug-jack	—	UG-274
T	Jack-plug-jack	Beryl. outer contact	UG-274A
T	Jack-plug-jack	Beryl. outer contact	UG-274B

NOTES: Z = 50 Ω Freq. range: 0-4 GHz w/low reflection; usable to 11 GHz.
Voltage rating: 500 V p-p. Dielectric withstanding voltage 500 V$_{RMS}$.
SWR: 1.3 max 0-4 GHz. RF leakage −55 dB min @ 3 GHz
Insertion loss: 0.2 dB max @ 3 GHz.
Temp. limits: TFE: −67° to 390°F (−55° to 199°C)
Rexolite insulators: −67° to 185°F (−55° to 85°C)

Table 33

Cross-Family Adapters

(adapters described by their own end construction)

Construction	Adapter Ends		Description	Impedance	Military No.
			Rear mounted		
HN to BNC	HN-plug	BNC-jack	Straight	50 Ω	UG-309
N to BNC	N-plug	BNC-jack	Straight	50 Ω	UG-201A
	N-jack	BNC-plug	Straight	50 Ω	UG-349A
	N-plug	BNC-jack	Straight	50 Ω	UG201
	N-jack	BNC-plug	Straight/copolymer of styrene-TFE ins.	50 Ω	UG-349
	N-plug	BNC-plug	Straight	50 Ω	UG-1034
N to UHF	N-plug	UHF-jack	Straight/copolymer/ non-weatherproof/ non-constant impedance	—	UG146
	N-jack	UHF-plug	Straight/copolymer/ non-weatherproof/ non-constant impedance	—	UG-83
	N-plug	UHF-plug	Straight/copolymer of styrene insulation/ non-constant impedance	—	UG-318
	N-jack	UHF-plug	Straight/non-constant impedance	—	UG-83B
UHF to BNC	UHF-plug	BNC-jack	Straight/copolymer of styrene insulation/ non-constant impedance	—	UG-273
	UHF-jack	BNC-plug	Straight/copolymer of styrene insulation	50 Ω	UG-255

Table 34
Miniature Lamp Guide

BULB STYLES

B   G   GTL   RP   S   T   TL

**Bulbs are described by a letter indicating shape and a number that is an approximation of diameter expressed in eighths of an inch. For example S-8 is "S" shape, 8 eighths or 1 inch in diam.

BSC   PFDC   BMN   FSMD   FSCMD   FSCMN
BIDC   BDC   FLANGE BASES
BAYONET BASES

SMD   SMN   SC   SI   WSMN   W   SL   MTP   BP   GMD   SPTHD
SCREW BASES   WEDGE BASES   MISCELLANEOUS BASES

Lamp Base Legend

BDC	Bayonet, dual-contact	FSCMD	Flanged, midget single-contact	SI	Screw, intermediate
BIDC	Bayonet, indexed dual-contact	FSMD	Flanged, submidget	SMD	Screw, midget
BMN	Bayonet, miniature	GMD	Midget grooved	SMN	Screw, miniature
BP	Bipin	MTP	Miniature two-pin	SPTHD	Screw, special thread
BSC	Bayonet, single-contact	PFDC	Prefocused dual contact	W	Wedge
FSCMN	Flanged, single-contact,	SL	Slide (various sizes)	WSMN	Wedge, subminiature
	miniature	SC	Screw, candleabra	WT	Wire terminal

†k = 1000

Type	Bulb	Base	V	A	Life†		Type	Bulb	Base	V	A	Life†
PR2	B-3½	FSCMN	2.38	0.500	15		159	T-3¼	W	6.30	0.150	5K
PR3	B-3½	FSCMN	3.57	0.500	15		161	T-3¼	W	14.00	0.190	4K
PR4	B-3½	FSCMN	2.33	0.270	10		168	T-3¼	W	14.00	0.350	1.5K
PR6	B-3½	FSCMN	2.47	0.300	30		219	G-3½	BMN	6.30	0.250	5K
PR7	B-3½	FSCMN	3.70	0.300	30		222	TL-3	SMN	2.25	0.250	0.5
PR12	B-3½	FSCMN	5.95	0.500	15		239	T-3¼	BMN	6.30	0.360	5K
PR13	B-3½	FSCMN	4.75	0.500	15		240	T-3¼	BMN	6.30	0.360	5K
10	G-3½	MTP	2.50	0.500	3K		259	T-3¼	W	6.30	0.250	5K
12	G-3½	MTP	6.30	0.150	5K		268	T-1¾	FSCMD	2.50	0.350	10K
13	G-3½	SMN	3.70	0.300	15		305	S-8	BSC	28.00	0.510	300
14	G-3½	SMN	2.47	0.300	15		307	S-8	BSC	28.00	0.670	300
19	G-3½	MTP	14.40	0.100	1K		308	S-8	BDC	28.00	0.670	300
27	G-4½	SMN	4.90	0.300	30		313	T-3¼	BMN	28.00	0.170	500
37	T-1¾	WSMN	14.00	0.090	1.5K		323	T-1¾	SPTHD	3.00	0.190	350
40	T-3¼	SMN	6.30	0.150	3K		327	T-1¾	FSCMD	28.00	0.040	4K
43	T-3¼	BMN	2.50	0.500	3K		327AS15	T-1¾	FSCMD	28.00	0.040	4K
44	T-3¼	BMN	6.30	0.250	3K		328	T-1¾	FSCMD	6.00	0.200	1K
45	T-3¼	BMN	3.20	0.350	3K		330	T-1¾	FSCMD	14.00	0.080	1.5K
46	T-3¼	SMN	6.30	0.250	3K		331	T-1¾	FSCMD	1.35	0.060	3K
47	T-3¼	BMN	6.30	0.150	3K		334	T-1¾	GMD	28.00	0.040	4K
48	T-3¼	SMN	2.00	0.060	1K		335	T-1¾	SMD	28.00	0.040	4K
49	T-3¼	BMN	2.00	0.060	1K		336	T-1¾	GMD	14.00	0.080	1.5K
50	G-3½	SMN	7.50	0.220	1K		337	T-1¾	GMD	6.00	0.200	1K
51	G-3½	BMN	7.50	0.220	1K		338	T-1¾	FSCMD	2.70	0.060	6K
52	G-3½	SMN	14.40	0.100	1K		342	T-1¾	SMD	6.00	0.040	10K
53	G-3½	BMN	14.40	0.120	1K		344	T-1¾	FSCMD	10.00	0.014	50K
55	G-4½	BMN	7.00	0.410	500		345	T-1¾	FSCMD	6.00	0.040	10K
57	G-4½	BMN	14.00	0.240	500		346	T-1¾	GMD	18.00	0.040	10K
63	G-6	BSC	7.00	0.630	1K		349	T-1¾	FSCMD	6.30	0.200	5K
73	T-1¾	WSMN	14.00	0.080	15K		370	T-1¾	FSCMD	18.00	0.040	10K
74	T-1¾	WSMN	14.00	0.100	500		373	T-1¾	SMD	14.00	0.080	1.5K
82	G-6	BDC	6.50	1.020	500		375	T-1¾	FSCMD	3.00	0.015	10K
85	T-1¾	WSMN	28.00	0.040	7K		376	T-1¾	FSCMD	28.00	0.060	25K
86	T-1¾	WSMN	6.30	0.200	20K		380	T-1¾	FSCMD	6.30	0.040	20K
88	S-8	BDC	6.80	1.910	300		381	T-1¾	FSCMD	6.30	0.200	20K
93	S-8	BSC	12.80	1.040	700		382	T-1¾	FSCMD	14.00	0.080	15K
112	TL-3	SMN	1.20	0.220	5		385	T-1¾	FSCMD	28.00	0.040	10K
130	G-3½	BMN	6.30	0.150	5K		386	T-1¾	GMD	14.00	0.080	15K
131	G-3½	SMN	1.30	0.100	50		387	T-1¾	FSCMD	28.00	0.040	7K
158	T-3¼	W	14.00	0.240	500		388	T-1¾	GMD	28.00	0.040	7K

Type	Bulb	Base	V	A	Life†
397	T-1¾	GMD	10.00	0.040	5K
398	T-1¾	GMD	6.30	0.200	5K
399	T-1¾	SMD	28.00	0.040	7K
502	G-4½	SMN	5.10	0.150	100
555	T-3¼	W	6.30	0.250	3K
656	T-3¼	W	28.00	0.060	2.5K
680AS15	T-1	WT	5.00	0.060	60K
682AS15	T-1	FSMD	5.00	0.060	60K
683AS15	T-1	WT	5.00	0.060	25K
685AS15	T-1	FSMD	5.00	0.060	25K
715AS15	T-1	WT	5.00	0.115	40K
715AS25	T-1	WT	5.00	0.115	40K
718AS25	T-1	FSMD	5.00	0.115	40K
755	T-3¼	BMN	6.30	0.150	20K
756	T-3¼	BMN	14.00	0.080	15K
757	T-3¼	BMN	28.00	0.080	7.5K
1034	S-8	BIDC	14.00	0.590	5K
1073	S-8	BSC	12.80	1.800	200
1130	S-8	BDC	6.40	2.630	200
1133	RP-11	BSC	6.20	3.910	200
1141	S-8	BSC	12.80	1.440	1K
1143	RP-11	BSC	12.50	1.980	400
1184	RP-11	BDC	5.50	6.250	100
1251	G-6	BSC	28.00	0.230	2K
1445	G-3½	BMN	14.40	0.130	2K
1487	T-3¼	SMN	14.00	0.200	3K
1488	T-3¼	BMN	14.00	0.150	200
1490	T-3¼	BMN	3.20	0.160	3K
1493	S-8	BDC	6.50	2.750	100
1619	S-8	BSC	6.70	1.900	500
1630	S-8	PFDC	6.50	2.750	100
1691	S-8	BSC	28.00	0.610	1K
1705	T-1¾	WT	14.00	0.080	1.5K
1728	T-1¾	WT	1.35	0.060	3K
1730	T-1¾	WT	6.00	0.040	20K
1738	T-1¾	WT	2.70	0.060	6K
1762	T-1¾	WT	28.00	0.040	4K
1764	T-1¾	WT	28.00	0.040	4K
1767	T-1¾	SMD	2.50	0.200	500
1768	T-1¾	SMD	6.00	0.200	1K
1775	T-1¾	SMD	6.30	0.075	1K
1813	T-3¼	BMN	14.40	0.100	1K
1815	T-3¼	BMN	14.00	0.200	3K
1816	T-3¼	BMN	13.00	0.330	1K
1818	T-3¼	BMN	24.00	0.170	250
1819	T-3¼	BMN	28.00	0.040	2.5K
1820	T-3¼	BMN	28.00	0.100	1K
1821	T-3¼	SMN	28.00	0.170	500
1822	T-3¼	BMN	36.00	0.100	1K
1828	T-3¼	BMN	37.50	0.050	3K
1829	T-3¼	BMN	28.00	0.070	1K
1835	T-3¼	BMN	55.00	0.050	5K
1847	T-3¼	BMN	6.30	0.150	5K
1850	T-3¼	BMN	5.00	0.090	1.5K
1864	T-3¼	BMN	28.00	0.170	1.5K
1866	T-3¼	BMN	6.30	0.250	5K
1869	T-1¾	WT	10.00	0.014	50K
1891	T-3¼	BMN	14.00	0.240	500

Type	Bulb	Base	V	A	Life†
1892	T-3¼	BMN	14.40	0.120	1K
1893	T-3¼	BMN	14.00	0.330	7.5K
1895	G-4½	BMN	14.00	0.270	2K
2102	T-1¾	WT	18.00	0.040	10K
2107	T-1¾	WT	10.00	0.040	5K
2158	T-1¾	WT	3.00	0.015	10K
2162	T-1¾	WT	14.00	0.100	10K
2169	T-1¾	WT	2.50	0.350	20K
2180	T-1¾	WT	6.30	0.040	20K
2181	T-1¾	WT	6.30	0.200	20K
2182	T-1¾	WT	14.00	0.080	40K
2187	T-1¾	WT	28.00	0.040	7K
2304	T-1¾	BP	3.00	0.300	1.5K
2307	T-1¾	BP	6.30	0.200	5K
2314	T-1¾	BP	28.00	0.050	1K
2316	T-1¾	BP	18.00	0.040	10K
2324	T-1¾	BP	28.00	0.040	4K
2335	T-1¾	BP	14.00	0.080	15K
2337	T-1¾	BP	6.30	0.200	20K
2342	T-1¾	BP	28.00	0.040	25K
3149	T-1¾	BP	5.00	0.060	5K
6803AS25	T-¾	WT	5.00	0.060	60K
6833AS15	T-¾	WT	5.00	0.060	25K
6838	T-1	WT	28.00	0.024	4K
6839	T-1	FSMD	28.00	0.024	4K
7001	T-1¾	BP	24.00	0.050	2K
7003	T-1¾	BP	24.00	0.050	2K
7153AS15	T-¾	WT	5.00	0.115	40K
7265	T-1	BP	5.00	0.060	5K
7327	T-1¾	BP	28.00	0.040	4K
7328	T-1¾	BP	6.00	0.200	1K
7330	T-1¾	BP	14.00	0.080	1.5K
7344	T-1¾	BP	10.00	0.014	50K
7349	T-1¾	BP	6.30	0.200	5K
7361	T-1¾	BP	5.00	0.060	25K
7362	T-1¾	BP	5.00	0.115	40K
7367	T-1¾	BP	10.00	0.040	5K
7370	T-1¾	BP	18.00	0.040	10K
7371	T-1¾	BP	12.00	0.040	10K
7373	T-1¾	BP	14.00	0.100	10K
7374	T-1¾	BP	28.00	0.040	10K
7375	T-1¾	BP	3.00	0.015	10K
7376	T-1¾	BP	28.00	0.065	10K
7377	T-1¾	BP	6.30	0.075	1K
7380	T-1¾	BP	6.30	0.040	30K
7381	T-1¾	BP	6.30	0.200	20K
7382	T-1¾	BP	14.00	0.080	15K
7387	T-1¾	BP	28.00	0.040	7K
7410	T-1¾	BP	14.00	0.080	15K
7839	T-1	BP	28.00	0.025	4K
7876	T-1¾	BP	28.00	0.060	25K
7931	T-1¾	BP	1.35	0.060	3K
7945	T-1¾	BP	6.00	0.040	20K
7968	T-1¾	BP	2.50	0.200	500
8099	T-1	BP	18.00	0.020	16K
8362	T-1¾	SMD	14.00	0.080	15K
8369	T-1¾	SMD	28.00	0.065	10K

STANDARD LINE-VOLTAGE LAMPS

Type	V	W	Bulb	Base
10C7DC	115-125	10	C-7	BDC
3S6	120, 125	3	S-6	SC
6S6	30, 48, 115, 120, 125, 130, 135, 145, 155	6	S-6	SC
6S6/R	115-125	6	S-6 (red)	SC
6S6/W	115-125	6	S-6 (white)	SC
6T4½	120, 130	6	T-4½	SC
7C7	115-125	7	C-7	SC
7C7/W	115-125	7	C-7 (white)	SC
10C7	115-125	10	C-7	SC
10S6	120	10	S-6	SC
10S6/10	220, 230, 250	10	S-6	SC
6S6DC	30, 120, 125, 145	6	S-6	BDC
10S6/10DC	230, 250	10	S-6	BDC
40S11 N	115-125	40	S-11	SI
120MB	120	3	T-2½	BMN
120MB/6	120	6	T-2½	BMN
120PSB	120	3	T-2	SL
120PS	120	3	T-2	WT
120PS/6	120	6	T-2½	WT

INDICATOR LAMPS

Each has a T-2 bulb and a slide base.

Type	V	A	Life †
6PSB	6.00	0.140	20K
12PSB	12.00	0.170	12K
24PSB	24.00	0.073	10K
28PSB	28.00	0.040	5K
48PSB	48.00	0.050	10K
60PSB	60.00	0.050	7.5K
120PSB	120.00	0.025	7.5K

NEON GLOW LAMPS

Operating circuit voltage 105-125.

Type	Breakdown Voltage AC	DC	Bulb	Base	W	External Resistance†
NE-2	65	90	T-2	WT	1/12	150K
NE-2A	65	90	T-2	WT	1/15	100K
NE-2D	65	90	T-2	FSCMD	1/12	100K
NE-2E	65	90	T-2	WT	1/12	100K
NE-2H	95	135	T-2	WT	1/4	30K
NE-2J	95	135	T-2	FSCMD	1/4	30K
NE-2V	65	90	T-2	WT	1/12	100K
NE-45	65	90	T-4 1/2	SC	1/4	NONE
NE-51	65	90	T-3 1/4	BMN	1/25	220K
NE-51H	95	135	T-3 1/4	BMN	1/7	47K
NE-84	95	135	T-2	SL	1/4	30K
NE-120PSB	95	95	T-2	SL	1/4	NONE

Table 35
Crystal Holders

NOTE: SOLDER SEAL, COLD WELD, AND RESISTANCE WELD SEALING
METHODS ARE COMMONLY AVAILABLE.
NOTE: ALL DIMENSIONS ARE IN INCHES.

Table 36
Properties of Common Thermoplastics

ASTM or UL test	Property	NYLONS (DRY, AS MOLDED) — Type					PHENOLICS — Type of compound						POLYETHYLENE			
		6/6	6	6/12	11	Castable	General purpose	Impact	Non-bleeding	Electrical	Heat resistant	Special purpose*	Low density	Medium density	High density	Ultrahigh molecular weight
	PHYSICAL															
D792	Specific gravity	1.14	1.13	1.06	1.04	1.15-1.17	1.35-1.46	1.36-1.41	1.37-1.38	1.36-1.75	1.41-1.84	1.37-1.75	0.910-0.925	0.926-0.940	0.941-0.965	0.928-0.941
D792	Specific volume (in³/lb)	24.2	24.5	25.9	26.6	23.8							30.4-29.9	29.9-29.4	29.4-28.7	29.4
D570	Water absorption, 24 h. ⅛-in. thk (%)	1.2	1.6	0.25	0.4	0.9	0.6-0.7	0.6-0.9	0.8-0.9	0.05-0.20	0.30-0.35	0.20-0.40	<0.01	<0.01	<0.01	<0.01
	MECHANICAL															
D638	Tensile strength (psi)	12,000	11,800	8,800	8,500	11,000-14,000	6,500-7,000	6,000-7,000	6,000-7,000	5,000-7,000	5,000-6,000	7,000-9,000	600-2,300	1,200-3,500	3,100-5,500	4,000-6,000
D638	Elongation (%)	60	200	150	120	10-50	11-13	12	10	17-25	14	10	90-800	50-600	20-1,000	200-500
D638	Tensile modulus (10^5 psi)	4.2	3.8	2.9	1.8	3.5-4.5							0.14-0.38	0.25-0.55	0.6-1.8	0.20-1.10
D785	Hardness, Rockwell ( )	121 (R)	119 (R)	114 (R)	—	112-120 (R)	70-95 (E)	82 (E)	82 (E)	75-88 (E)	94 (E)	76 (E)	10 (R)	15 (R)	65 (R)	55 (R)
D790	Flexural modulus (10^5 psi)	4.1	3.9	2.9	1.5	—	11-14	12-25	10-12	12-25	11-23	10-19	0.08-0.60	0.60-1.15	1.0-2.0	1.0-1.7
D256	Impact strength, Izod (ft-lb/in of notch)	1.0	0.8	1.0	3.3	0.9	0.30-0.35	0.6-1.05	0.28	0.28-0.45	0.26	0.50	No break	0.5-16	0.5-20	No break
	THERMAL															
C177	Thermal conductivity (Btu-in/hr-ft²-°F)	1.7	1.7	1.5	—	1.7	7.1†	7.9†	—	16.0†	—	8.8†	8.0†	8.0-10.0†	11.0-12.4†	11.0†
D696	Coef of thermal expansion (10^{-5} in./in.-°F)	4.0	4.5	5.0	5.1	5.0	3.95	3.56	4.40	2.60	2.80	3.60	5.6-12.2	7.8-8.9	6.1-7.2	7.8
D648	Deflection temperature (°F) At 264 psi	194	152	194	118	300-425	275-360	270-500	370	310-400	330-380	360-430	90-105	105-120	110-130	118
	At 66 psi	455	365	356	154	400-425							100-121	120-165	140-190	170
UL 94	Flammability rating	V-2	V-2	V-2	—	—	V-1	HB	—	V-0	V-0	HB				
	ELECTRICAL															
D149	Dielectric strength (V/mil) Short time, ⅛ in. thk	600	400	400	425	500-600*	350	350-400	.200	400	170	175	460-700	460-650	450-500	900*
D150	Dielectric constant At 1 kHz	3.9	3.7	4.0	3.3	3.7	5.2-5.3	5.2-5.4	—	4.9-6.5	11.7	7.8	2.25-2.35	2.30-2.35	2.30-2.35	—
D150	Dissipation factor At 1 kHz	0.02	0.02	0.02	0.03	0.02	0.04-0.05	0.04-0.06	—	0.025-0.10	0.15	0.12	0.0002	0.0002	0.0003	0.0002
D257	Volume resistivity (ohm-cm) At 73°F, 50% RH	10^{15}	10^{15}	10^{15}	2×10^{13}	—	10^{11}-10^{12}	10^{11}-10^{12}	10^{12}	10^{11}-10^{13}	10^{12}	10^{11}	10^{15}	10^{15}	10^{15}	10^{18}
D495	Arc resistance (s)	116	—	121	—	—	100	50	—	184	181	—	135-160	200-235	—	—
	OPTICAL															
D542	Refractive index												1.51	1.52	1.54	—
D1003	Transmittance (%)												4-50	4-50	10-50	—

*kV/cm.
*Chemical-resistant compound. †¹¹⁄₆₄-in. thick specimens.
*0.040 in. thick specimen
†(10^{-4} cal-cm/sec-cm²-°C)

ASTM or UL test	POLYPROPYLENE			POLYPHENYLENE SULFIDE[a]						POLYSTYRENE					POLYVINYL CHLORIDE	
	Unmodified resin	Glass reinforced	Impact grade	Glass reinforced				Glass and mineral filled		Polymers		Crystal clear	Copolymers		Rigid	Flexible
				R-3	R-4	R-8	R-9	R-10[b]	R-11	General purpose	Impact modified		Impact modified	10-20% (wt.) Glass reinf*		
D792	0.905	1.05-1.24	0.89-0.91	1.57	1.67	1.8	1.9	1.96-1.98	1.98	1.04-10.9	1.03-1.10	1.08-1.10	1.05-10.8	1.13-1.22	1.30-1.58	1.20-1.70
D792	30.8-30.4	24.5	30.8-30.5	—	—	—	—	—	—	26.0-25.6	28.1-25.2	—	—	—	20.5-19.1	—
D570	0.01-0.03	0.01-0.05	0.01-0.03	—	<0.05	0.03	—	—	—	0.03-0.10	0.05-0.6	0.1	0.1	0.08	0.04-0.4	0.15-0.75
D638	5,000	6,000-14,500	2,800-4,400	15,500	17,500	10,750	11,000	10,000-11,500	11,000	5,000-12,000	1,500-7,000	7,000-7,600	4,800-7,200	10,500-12,500	6,000-7,500	1,500-3,500
D638	10-20	2.0-3.6	350-500	1.1	1.25	0.47	0.5	0.5-0.6	0.6	0.5-2.0	2-60	1.4-1.7	2.0-20.0	1.3-2.0	40-80	200-450
D638	1.6	4.5-9.0	1.0-1.7	—	—	—	—	—	—	4.0-6.0	1.4-5.0	4.4-4.7	2.8-4.2	6.3-10.0	3.5-6.0	—
D785	80-110 (R)	110 (R)	50-85 (R)	—	123 (R)	121 (R)	—	120 (R)	—	65-80	10-90	108	80	101	65-85D (Shore)	50-100A (Shore)
D790	1.7-2.5	3.8-8.5	1.2-1.8	14	17	22	21	18	20	4.0-4.7	1.5-4.6	4.6-4.9	3.2-4.5	5.5-9.8	3.5	—
D256	0.5-2.2	1.0-5.0	1.0-15	1.0	1.1	0.59	0.7	0.6-1.0	0.8	0.2-0.45	0.5-4.0	0.3-0.5	0.5-4.4	1.8-2.6	0.4-20.0	—
C117	2.8†	—	3.0-4.0†	—	—	—	—	—	—	2.4-3.3	1.0-3.0	2.4-3.3	1.0-3.0	—	3.5-5.0†	3.0-4.0†
D696	3.2-5.7	1.6-2.9	3.3-4.7	—	2.0	1.6	1.1	—	—	3.3-4.4	1.9	3.5-3.7	3.5-3.7	2.0-2.2	2.8-5.6	3.9-13.9
D648	125-140 / 200-250	230-300 / 310	120-135 / 160-210	500	500	500	500	500	500	190-220 / 180-230	160-200 / 180-220	235-249	235-249	235-260	140-170 / 135-180	—
UL 94	HB^b	HB^b	HB^b	V-0	V-0/5V	V-0/5V	V-0	V-0/5V	V-0	HB^b	HB^b	HB^b	HB^b	HB^b	—	—
D149	500-660	475	500-650	500	500	500	500	500	500	500-700	300-600	500-700	300-600	—	350-500	300-400
D150	2.2-2.6	2.36	2.3	—	4.0*	4.3*	4.5*	4.8-6.1*	—	2.40-2.65	2.4-4.5	—	—	—	3.0-3.8	4.0-8.0
D150	0.0005-0.0018	0.0017	0.0003	—	0.0014*	0.016*	0.0072*	0.01-0.02*	—	0.0001-0.0003	0.0004-0.0020	—	—	—	0.009-0.017	0.07-0.16
D257	10^{17}	2×10^{18}	10^{18}	—	—	—	—	—	—	10^{17}-10^{19}	10^{16}	—	—	—	$>10^{16}$	10^{11}-10^{15}
D495	160	100	—	—	34	182	180	116-182	—	60-135	20-100	95	95	—	60-80	—
D542	—	—	—	—	—	—	—	—	—	1.60	—	1.59	—	—	—	—
D1003	—	—	—	—	—	—	—	—	—	87-92	35.57	92	—	—	—	—

bV-2, V-1, and V-0 grades are also available.   *At 1.0 MHz

[a] Test specimen molding conditions, 275°F mold temperature.
[b] Representative of a series of various pigmented compounds.

Table 36 (continued)

Polyvinyl Chloride (PVC)

Advantages:
—can be compounded with plasticizers, filters, stabilizers, lubricants and impact modifiers to produce a wide range of physical properties
—can be pigmented to almost any color
—Rigid PVC has good corrosion and stain resistance, thermal & electrical insulation, and weatherability

Disadvantages:
—base resin can be attacked by aromatic solvents, ketones, aldehydes, naphthalenes, and some chloride, acetate, and acrylate esters
—should not be used above 140°

Applications:
—conduit
—conduit boxes
—electrical fittings
—housings
—pipe
—wire and cable insulation

Polystyrene

Advantages:
—low cost
—moderate strength
—electrical properties only slightly affected by temperature and humidity
—sparkling clarity
—impact strength is increased by blending with rubbers, such as polybutadiene

Disadvantages:
—brittle
—low heat resistance

Applications:
—capacitors
—light shields
—knobs

Polyphenylene Sulfide (PPS)

Advantages:
—excellent dimensional stability
—strong
—high-temperature stability
—chemical resistant
—Inherently completely flame retardant
—completely transparent to microwave radiation.

Applications:
R3-R5 have various glass-fiber levels that are suitable for applications demanding high mechanical and impact strength as well as good dielectric properties.
R8 and R10 are suitable for high arc-resistance applications
R9-901 is suitable for encapsulation of electronic devices

Polypropylene

Advantages:
—low density
—good balance of thermal, chemical, and electrical properties
—moderate strength (increases significantly with glass-fiber reinforcement)

Disadvantages:
—Electrical properties affected to varying degrees by temperature (as temperature goes up, dielectric strength increases and volume resistivity decreases.)
—Inherently unstable in presence of oxidative and UV radiation

Applications:
—Automotive battery cases
—blower housings
—fan blades
—fuse housings
—insulators
—lamp housings
—supports for current-carrying electrical components.
—TV yokes

Polyethylene (PE)

Advantages: Low Density PE
—Good toughness
—excellent chemical resistance
—excellent electrical properties
—low coefficient of friction
—near zero moisture absorption
—easy to process
—relatively low heat resistance

Disadvantage
—susceptible to environmental and some chemical stress cracking
—wetting agents (such as detergents) accelerate stress cracking

Advantages: High Density PE
—Same as above, plus increased rigidity and tensile strength

Advantages: Ultra-High Molecular Weight PE
—outstanding abrasion resistance
—low coefficient of friction
—high impact strength
—excellent chemical resistance
—material does not break in impact strength tests using standard notched specimens

Applications:
—bearings
—components requiring maximum abrasion resistance, impact strength, and low coefficent of friction

Phenolic

Advantages:
—low cost
—superior heat resistance
—high heat-deflection temperatures
—good electrical properties
—good flame resistance
—excellent moldability
—excellent dimensional stability
—good water and chemical resistance

Applications:
—commutators and housings for small motors
—heavy duty electrical components
—rotary-switch wafers
—insulating spacers

Nylon

Advantages
—excellent fatigue resistance
—low coefficient of friction
—toughness a function of degree of crystallinity
—resists many fuels and chemicals
—good creep- and cold-flow resistance as compared to less rigid thermoplastics
—resists repeated impacts

Disadvantages:
—all nylons absorb moisture
—nylons that have not been compounded with a UV stabilizer are sensitive to UV light, and thus not suitable for extended outdoor use

Applications
—bearings
—housing and tubing
—rope
—wire coatings
—wire connectors
—wear plates

Table 37
TTL Families
Listed by ascending maximum clock frequency.

TTL Series	Input Pull-up Resistor (kΩ)	Maximum High-level Input Current (μA)	Maximum Low-level Input Current (mA)	Typical Gate Propagation Delay Time (ns)	Maximum Flip-flop Clock Frequency (MHz)
54L/74L[1]	40/8	10/20	−0.18- −0.8	33	3
54/74	4	40	−1.6	10	35
54LS/74LS	18	20	−0.4	9.5	45
54H/74H	2.8	50	−2	6	50
54ALS/74ALS	37	20	−0.1	4	70
54S/74S	2.8	50	−2	3	125
54AS/74AS	10	20	−0.5	1.7	200

[1]Series 54L/74L has two types of standard input.
Courtesy of Texas Instruments Inc.

Table 38
Fractions of an inch with Metric Equivalents

Fractions of an inch	Decimals of an inch	mm
1/64	0.0156	0.397
1/32	0.0313	0.794
3/64	0.0469	1.191
1/16	0.0625	1.588
5/64	0.0781	1.984
3/32	0.0938	2.381
7/64	0.1094	2.778
1/8	0.1250	3.175
9/64	0.1406	3.572
5/32	0.1563	3.969
11/64	0.1719	4.366
3/16	0.1875	4.763
13/64	0.2031	5.159
7/32	0.2188	5.556
15/64	0.2344	5.953
1/4	0.2500	6.350
17/64	0.2656	6.747
9/32	0.2813	7.144
19/64	0.2969	7.541
5/16	0.3125	7.938
21/64	0.3281	8.334
11/32	0.3438	8.731
23/64	0.3594	9.128
3/8	0.3750	9.525
25/64	0.3906	9.922
13/32	0.4063	10.319
27/64	0.4219	10.716
7/16	0.4375	11.113
29/64	0.4531	11.509
15/32	0.4688	11.906
31/64	0.4844	12.303
1/2	0.5000	12.700
33/64	0.5156	13.097
17/32	0.5313	13.494
35/64	0.5469	13.891
9/16	0.5625	14.288
37/64	0.5781	14.684
19/32	0.5938	15.081
39/64	0.6094	15.478
5/8	0.6250	15.875
41/64	0.6406	16.272
21/32	0.6563	16.669
43/64	0.6719	17.066
11/16	0.6875	17.463
45/64	0.7031	17.859
23/32	0.7188	18.256
47/64	0.7344	18.653
3/4	0.7500	19.050
49/64	0.7656	19.447
25/32	0.7813	19.844
51/64	0.7969	20.241
13/16	0.8125	20.638
53/64	0.8281	21.034
27/32	0.8438	21.431
55/64	0.8594	21.828
7/8	0.8750	22.225
57/64	0.8906	22.622
29/32	0.9063	23.019
59/64	0.9219	23.416
15/16	0.9375	23.813
61/64	0.9531	24.209
31/32	0.9688	24.606
63/64	0.9844	25.003
—	1.0000	25.400

Table 39
Aluminum Numbers for Amateur Use

Common Alloy Numbers

Type	Characteristic
2024	Good formability, high strength
5052	Excellent surface finish, excellent corrosion resistance, normally not heat treatable for high strength
6061	Good machinability, good weldability, can be brittle at high tempers
7075	Good formability, high strength

Common Tempers

Type	Characteristics
T0	Special soft condition
T3	Hard
T6	Very hard, possibly brittle
TXXX	Three digit tempers — usually specialized high-strength heat treatments, similar to T6

General Uses

Type	Uses
2024-T3	Chassis boxes, antennas, anything that will be bent or flexed repeatedly
7075-T3	
6061-T6	Mounting plates, welded assemblies or machined parts

Table 40
Voltage-Power Conversion Table

Based on a 50-ohm system

| ──────── Voltage ──────── | | | ──────── Power ──────── | |
RMS	Peak-to-Peak	dBmV	Watts	dBm
0.01 μV	0.0283 μV	-100	2×10^{-18}	-147.0
0.02 μV	0.0566 μV	-93.98	8×10^{-18}	-141.0
0.04 μV	0.113 μV	-87.96	32×10^{-18}	-134.9
0.08 μV	0.226 μV	-81.94	128×10^{-18}	-128.9
0.1 μV	0.283 μV	-80.0	200×10^{-18}	-127.0
0.2 μV	0.566 μV	-73.98	800×10^{-18}	-121.0
0.4 μV	1.131 μV	-67.96	3.2×10^{-15}	-114.9
0.8 μV	2.236 μV	-61.94	12.8×10^{-15}	-108.9
1.0 μV	2.828 μV	-60.0	20.0×10^{-15}	-107.0
2.0 μV	5.657 μV	-53.98	80.0×10^{-15}	-101.0
4.0 μV	11.31 μV	-47.96	320.0×10^{-15}	-94.95
8.0 μV	22.63 μV	-41.94	1.28×10^{-12}	-88.93
10.0 μV	28.28 μV	-40.00	2.0×10^{-12}	-86.99
20.0 μV	56.57 μV	-33.98	8.0×10^{-12}	-80.97
40.0 μV	113.1 μV	-27.96	32.0×10^{-12}	-74.95
80.0 μV	226.3 μV	-21.94	128×10^{-12}	-68.93
100.0 μV	282.8 μV	-20.0	200.0×10^{-12}	-66.99
200.0 μV	565.7 μV	-13.98	800.0×10^{-12}	-60.97
400.0 μV	1.131 mV	-7.959	3.2×10^{-9}	-54.95
800.0 μV	2.263 mV	-1.938	12.8×10^{-9}	-48.93
1.0 mV	2.828 mV	0.0	20.0×10^{-9}	-46.99
2.0 mV	5.657 mV	6.02	80.0×10^{-9}	-40.97
4.0 mV	11.31 mV	12.04	320×10^{-9}	-34.95
8.0 mV	22.63 mV	18.06	1.28 μW	-28.93
10.0 mV	28.28 mV	20.00	2.0 μW	-26.99
20.0 mV	56.57 mV	26.02	8.0 μW	-20.97
40.0 mV	113.1 mV	32.04	32.0 μW	-14.95
80.0 mV	226.3 mV	38.06	128.0 μW	-8.93
100.0 mV	282.8 mV	40.0	200.0 μW	-6.99
200.0 mV	565.7 mV	46.02	800.0 μW	-0.97
223.6 mV	632.4 mV	46.99	1.0 mW	0
400.0 mV	1.131 V	52.04	3.2 mW	5.05
800.0 mV	2.263 V	58.06	12.80 mW	11.07
1.0 V	2.828 V	60.0	20.0 mW	13.01
2.0 V	5.657 V	66.02	80.0 mW	19.03
4.0 V	11.31 V	72.04	320.0 mW	25.05
8.0 V	22.63 V	78.06	1.28 W	31.07
10.0 V	28.28 V	80.0	2.0 W	33.01
20.0 V	56.57 V	86.02	8.0 W	39.03
40.0 V	113.1 V	92.04	32.0 W	45.05
80.0 V	226.3 V	98.06	128.0 W	51.07
100.0 V	282.8 V	100.0	200.0 W	53.01
200.0 V	565.7 V	106.0	800.0 W	59.03
223.6 V	632.4 V	107.0	1000.0 W	60.0
400.0 V	1,131.0 V	112.0	3,200.0 W	65.05
800.0 V	2,263.0 V	118.1	12,800.0 W	71.07
1000.0 V	2,828.0 V	120.0	20,000 W	73.01
2000.0 V	5,657.0 V	126.0	80,000 W	79.03
4000.0 V	11,310.0 V	132.0	320,000 W	85.05
8000.0 V	22,630.0 V	138.1	1.28 MW	91.07
10,000.0 V	28,280.0 V	140.0	2.0 MW	93.01

Voltage, $V_{p-p} = V_{RMS} \times 2 \times \sqrt{2}$

Voltage, dBmV $= 20 \times Log_{10} \left[\dfrac{V_{RMS}}{0.001\ V} \right]$

Power, Watts $= \dfrac{(V_{RMS})^2}{50\Omega}$

Power, dBm $= 10 \times Log_{10} \left[\dfrac{Power\ (watts)}{0.001\ W} \right]$

Table 41
Equivalent Values of Reflection Coefficient, Attenuation, SWR and Return Loss

Reflection Coefficient (%)	Attenuation (dB)	Max. SWR	Return Loss (dB)	Reflection Coefficient (%)	Attenuation (dB)	Max. SWR	Return Loss (dB)	Reflection Coefficient (%)	Attenuation (dB)	Max. SWR	Return Loss (dB)
1.000	0.000434	1.020	40.00	23.652	0.2500	1.620	12.52	58.000	1.7809	3.762	4.73
1.517	0.001000	1.031	36.38	24.000	0.2577	1.632	12.40	60.000	1.9382	4.000	4.44
2.000	0.001738	1.041	33.98	25.000	0.2803	1.667	12.04	60.749	2.0000	4.095	4.33
3.000	0.003910	1.062	30.46	26.000	0.3040	1.703	11.70	63.000	2.1961	4.405	4.01
4.000	0.006954	1.083	27.96	27.000	0.3287	1.740	11.37	66.156	2.5000	4.909	3.59
4.796	0.01000	1.101	26.38	28.000	0.3546	1.778	11.06	66.667	2.5528	5.000	3.52
5.000	0.01087	1.105	26.02	30.000	0.4096	1.857	10.46	70.627	3.0000	5.809	3.02
6.000	0.01566	1.128	24.44	31.623	0.4576	1.925	10.00	70.711	3.0103	5.829	3.01
7.000	0.02133	1.151	23.10	32.977	0.5000	1.984	9.64				
7.576	0.02500	1.164	22.41	33.333	0.5115	2.000	9.54				
8.000	0.02788	1.174	21.94	34.000	0.5335	2.030	9.37				
9.000	0.03532	1.198	20.92	35.000	0.5675	2.077	9.12				
10.000	0.04365	1.222	20.00	36.000	0.6028	2.125	8.87				
10.699	0.05000	1.240	19.41	37.000	0.6394	2.175	8.64				
11.000	0.05287	1.247	19.17	38.000	0.6773	2.226	8.40				
12.000	0.06299	1.273	18.42	39.825	0.7500	2.324	8.00				
13.085	0.07500	1.301	17.66	40.000	0.7572	2.333	7.96				
14.000	0.08597	1.326	17.08	42.000	0.8428	2.448	7.54				
15.000	0.09883	1.353	16.48	42.857	0.8814	2.500	7.36				
15.087	0.10000	1.355	16.43	44.000	0.9345	2.571	7.13				
16.000	0.1126	1.381	15.92	45.351	1.0000	2.660	6.87				
17.783	0.1396	1.433	15.00	48.000	1.1374	2.846	6.38				
18.000	0.1430	1.439	14.89	50.000	1.2494	3.000	6.02				
19.000	0.1597	1.469	14.42	52.000	1.3692	3.167	5.68				
20.000	0.1773	1.500	13.98	54.042	1.5000	3.352	5.35				
22.000	0.2155	1.564	13.15	56.234	1.6509	3.570	5.00				

$$\rho = \frac{SWR - 1}{SWR + 1}$$

where ρ = 0.01 × (reflection coefficient in %)

$$\rho = 10^{\frac{-RL}{20}}$$

where RL = return loss (dB)

$$\rho = \sqrt{1 - (0.1^X)}$$

where X = A/10 and A = attenuation (dB)

$$SWR = \frac{1 + \rho}{1 - \rho}$$

Return loss (dB) = $-8.68589 \ln(\rho)$

where ln is the natural log (log to the base e)

Attenuation (dB) = $-4.34295 \ln(1 - \rho^2)$

where ln is the natural log (log to the base e)

Table 42
ARRL Parts Suppliers List

A,B,I,J,L,P,T,V
A & A Engineering
2521 W LaPalma Ave, Unit K
Anaheim, CA 92801
714-952-2114
*sase

Aluminum tubing & hardware
Alexander Aeroplane Co
PO Box 909
Griffin, GA 30224
800-831-2949
fax 404-229-2329
*free
**$10

A,B,C,G,H,I,J,K,M,R,U,V
All Electronics Corp
15004 Oxnard St
Van Nuys, CA 91411
800-826-5432
*free
**$10

A,C,G,H,I,K,P,R,U,V
Allied Electronics
7410 Pebble Dr
Fort Worth, TX 76118
800-433-5700
**$25

B,I,L,N,R,U
Amidon Associates, Inc
PO Box 956
Torrance, CA 90508
213-763-5770
fax 213-763-2250
*free

F,U, high-voltage parts
Antennas Etc/Unadilla
PO Box 4215
Andover, MA 01810-4215
508-475-7831
fax 508-474-8949
*sase

A,F,G,I,K,P,R,U
Arrow Electronics
Attn: Laura
1860 Smithtown Ave
Ronkonkoma, NY 11779
800-932-7769
fax 516-585-0878
**$25

N,O, WEFAX equipment
Atlantic Surplus Sales
3730 Nautilus Ave
Brooklyn, NY 11224
718-372-0349
*$1

K,M,S
ATV Research, Inc
13th & Broadway
Dakota City, NE 68731
402-987-3771

Avatar Magnetics
see Ronald C. Williams

A,H
Barker & Williamson
10 Canal St
Bristol, PA 19007
215-788-5581

A,B,D,E,G,H,I,J,K,M,N,P,U,V
BCD Electro
PO Box 450207
Garland, TX 75045-0207
214-343-1770
fax 214-343-1854
*$1/year

A,B,D,G,K,L,P,T,U
Circuit Board Specialists
PO Box 951
Pueblo, CO 81002-0951
719-542-4525
*free

A,B,D,E,H,I,L,S,T
Communications Concepts, Inc
508 Millstone Dr
Xenia, OH 45385
513-426-8600
fax 513-429-3811
*free

A,R, tools
Contact East, Inc
335 Willow St
North Andover, MA 01845
508-682-2000
fax 508-688-7829
*free

blowers
Cooltronic
1700 Morse Ave
Ventura, CA 93003
805-642-8521
**$75

I,M,H,U
Peter W. Dahl Co, Inc
5869 Waycross
El Paso, TX 79924
915-715-2300

F,U
Davis RF
PO Box 230
Carlisle, MA 01741
508-369-1738
*$1

A,D,F,H,I,K,L,P,R,T,U
Dick Smith Electronics
PO Box 301
Greenwood, IN 46142
317-888-7265

A,I,J,K,P,U,V
Digi-Key Corporation
701 Brooks Ave S
PO Box 677
Thief River Falls, MN 56701
800-344-4539
*free

A,D,E,F,L,M,T, MMICs
Down East Microwave
RR1, Box 2310
Troy, ME 04987
207-948-3741
fax 207-948-5157
*free

A,C,I,K,L,M,P,R,T,U,V
Edlie Electronics, Inc
2700 Hempstead Tpke
Levittown, NY 11756-1143
516-735-3330
fax 516-731-5125

A,B,C,D,E,F,G,H,I,J,K,L,N,P,R,T,
U,V
Electro Sonic, Inc
1100 Gordon Baker Rd
Willowdale, ON
Canada M2H 3B3

A,C,D,F,G,H,I,J,K,L,M,N,P,R,T,U
Electronic Distributors, Inc
4900 N Elston Ave
Chicago, IL 60630
312-283-4800
*$0.65

B
Elna Ferrite Laboratories, Inc
PO Box 395
Woodstock, NY 12498
914-679-2497

G,H,I,M,N,Q,R
Fair Radio Sales Co, Inc
PO Box 1105
1016 E Eureka St
Lima, OH 45802
419-227-6573
fax 419-227-1313
*free
**$10

T
FAR Circuits
18N640 Field Ct
Dundee, IL 60118
708-426-2431

A,I,K,L,M,O,S
H & R Company
401 E Erie Ave
Philadelphia, PA 19134
215-426-1708
*free
**$25

I,K
Hammond Mfg Co, Inc
1690 Walden Ave
Buffalo, NY 14225

I,K
Hammond Mfg, Ltd
394 Edinburgh Rd, N
Guelph, ON
Canada N1H 1E5

Q
Hi-Manuals
PO Box 802
Council Bluffs, IA 51502
*$2 Catalog req'd

A,B,G,H,I,J,K,L,M,P,U
Hosfelt Electronics
2700 Sunset Blvd
Steubenville, OH 43952
800-524-6464
*free

B,D,G,J,L,N,P,Q,T (8-pole crystal
filters)
Int'l Radio and Computers, Inc
751 S Macedo Blvd
Port St Lucie, FL 34983
407-879-6868
*sase

L,S,V
International Crystal Mfg Co
PO Box 26330
Oklahoma City, OK 73126
405-236-3741

V
JAN Crystals
2341 Crystal Dr
PO Box 06017
Fort Myers, FL 33906-6017
800-526-9825
*free

semiconductors
K2AW's Silicon Alley
175 Friends Ln
Westbury, NY 11590
516-334-7024
*free

C
Kepro Circuit Systems, Inc
630 Axminister Dr
Fenton, MO 63026-2992
800-325-3878
314-343-1630 (local)
fax 314-343-0668
*free
**$15

A,C,D,I,N,P,Q,R,T,U
Lashen Electronics, Inc
21 Broadway
Denville, NJ 07834
201-627-3783
**$15

mixers, signal processing
MA/COM, Anzac Division
80 Cambridge St
Burlington, MA 01803
617-273-3333
*free
**$100

F (aluminum and stainless tubing
and pipe)
Metal and Cable Corp, Inc
PO Box 117
Twinsburg, OH 44087
216-425-8455
**$50

A,K
MFJ Enterprises
PO Box 494
Mississippi State, MS 39762
601-323-5869

A,B,E,H,M
Microwave Components of
Michigan
PO Box 1697
Taylor, MI 48180
313-753-4581 (evenings)
*sase

B,G,H,J,R, high-voltage parts
James Millen Electronics
PO Box 4215BV
Andover, MA 01810-4215
508-975-2711
fax 508-474-8949

A,B,C,F,G,H,I,J,K,M,N,P,R,U
Milo Associates, Inc
4169 Millersville Rd
Indianapolis, IN 46205
317-546-6456
fax 317-547-1729
*free

mixers, signal processing
Mini Circuits Labs
PO Box 350166
Brooklyn, NY 11235-0003
718-934-4500
*free
**$50

A,F,G,H,I,L,M,N,U,V
Modern Radio Laboratories
PO Box 14902-Q
Minneapolis, MN 55414
*$1

F
Moeller Instrument Co
Ivoryton Industrial Park
Main St
Ivoryton, CT 06442
203-767-2104
800-243-9310
**$10

D,E,P
Motorola Semiconductor
Products, Inc
PO Box 20912
Phoenix, AZ 85036

A,B,C,F,G,H,I,J,K,L,P,R,U,V
Mouser Electronics
2401 Hwy 287 N
Mansfield, TX 76063
800-346-6873
*free
**$20

D,P
National Semiconductor Corp
2900 Semiconductor Dr
Santa Clara, CA 95052-8090

A,B,D,F,H,J,K,L,P,T,U,V
Oak Hills Research
20879 Madison
Big Rapids, MI 49307
616-796-0920
*$2

A,B,C,D,F,G,H,I,J,K,L,M,N,P,R,S,
T,U,V
Ocean State Electronics
PO Box 1458
Westerly, RI 02891
800-866-6626
fax 401-596-3590
*free
**$5

B
Palomar Engineers
PO Box 455
Escondido, CA 92033
619-747-3343
*free

A,E,U
Pasternack Enterprises
PO Box 16759
Irvine, CA 92713
714-261-1920
*free

S
PC Electronics
2522 S Paxson Ln
Arcadia, CA 91007
818-447-4565
fax 818-447-0489
*free

B
Philips Components
(Ferroxcube)
5083 Kings Hwy
Saugerties, NY 12477

A,B,D,H,I,K,M,P,R,U
R & D Electronics
1224 Prospect Ave
Cleveland, OH 44115
216-621-1121
*free

A,B,C,D,E,F,G,H,I,J,K,L,N,P,T,U,W
RADIOKIT
PO Box 973
Pelham, NH 03076
603-635-2235
Telex: 887697
*$1

D,E,N
RF Gain, Ltd
116 S Long Beach Rd
Rockville Centre, NY 11570
800-348-5580

A,B,D,E,F,H,N
RF Parts Co
1320-16 Grand Ave
San Marcos, CA 92069
619-744-0700
*free
**$20

V
Sentry Mfg, Co
Crystal Park
Chickasha, OK 73018
405-224-6780
*free

A,F,G,K,U (Mechanical
components and metal)
Small Parts, Inc
PO Box 381966
Miami, FL 33238
305-751-0856
*free
**$12

A,F,J,V
Spectrum International, Inc
PO Box 1084
Concord, MA 01742
508-263-2145
*free

A,M
Star-Tronics
PO Box 683
McMinnville, OR 97128
503-472-9716
**$4

A,B,C,D,E,F,G,H,I,J,K,L,M,N,P,
Q,R,S,U,V,W, high-voltage
parts
Surplus Sales of Nebraska
1315 Jones
Omaha, NE 68102
402-346-4750
fax 402-346-4750

M
Surplus Traders
PO Box 276
Alburg, VT 05440
*$3

K,H
Ten-Tec, Inc
Highway 411, E
Sevierville, TN 37862

I
Toroid Corporation of
Maryland
608 Naylor Mill Rd
Salisbury, MD 21801
301-860-0300
fax 301-860-0302
*free

N,O
Typetronics
PO Box 8873
Fort Lauderdale, FL 33310
*sase

F
US Plastics Corp
1390 Neubrecht Rd
Lima, OH 45801
800-537-9724
*free
**$5

E, mixers, signal processing,
  amps, switches
  Watkins Johnson Co,
    Components Div'n
  3333 Hillview Ave
  Palo Alto, CA 94304
  415-493-4141
  fax 415-493-1027
  *free

I,W
  Ronald C. Williams W9JVF
  (Avatar Magnetics)
  240 Tamara Trail
  Indianapolis, IN 46217

A,D,F,P,S,T,U
  Wyman Research, Inc
  Box 95, RR 1
  Waldron, IN 46182
  317-525-6452

Chart Coding

A—General Suppliers
B—Inductor Cores (Ferrite or
  Iron)
C—Circuit Board Etching
  Supplies
D—RF Power Transistors
E—Microwave Components
F—Antenna Hardware
G—Dials and Knobs
H—Variable Capacitors

I—Transformers
J—IF Filters
K—Project Cases
L—Project Kits
M—Surplus Parts
N—Vacuum Tubes
O—Mechanical Teletype Supplies
P—Integrated Circuits
Q—Equipment Manuals

R—Test Equipment
S—ATV Supplies
T—Etched Circuit Boards
U—Wire
V—Crystals
W—Climbing and Safety
  Equipment

*Catalog Price
**Minimum Order

To the best of our knowledge the suppliers shown are willing to sell small quantities of
components to amateurs by mail. This listing does not necessarily indicate that these firms have
the approval of ARRL.

Chapter 36

Assembling a Station

Although many hams never try to build a major project, such as a transmitter, receiver or amplifier, they do have to assemble the various components (say, for example, transceiver, power supply and antenna) into a working station. There are many benefits to be derived from assembling a safe, comfortable, easy-to-operate collection of radio gear, whether the shack is at home, in the car or portable in a field.

Rather than discuss electronic theory or individual construction projects, this chapter will detail some of the "how tos" of setting up a station for fixed, mobile and portable operation. Such topics as station location, safety, finding adequate power sources, station layout and cable routing are covered, along with some of the practical aspects of antenna erection and maintenance.

Two major themes recur throughout this chapter: Plan ahead, and most shortcuts aren't really, in the long run. The key to a successful installation, whether it's the installation of a mobile rig under the dash of your car or the erection of a 150-foot tower with a large monobander at the top, is proper planning. If you take the time to think the project through to its conclusion, to consider alternatives, to make measurements and rough sketches, your chances of success are much greater than if you start drilling and cutting blindly. You'll avoid 99 percent of such problems as "Oops, that guy wire has to go through the center of this tree," or "Oops, I can't drive my car with the mobile rig installed because I put the rig where my left knee has to go."

Most shortcuts will eventually come back to haunt you, so it's really worth doing a job right the first time. A "bargain" antenna mast for your tower is no bargain if it folds up in a windstorm, sending your antenna crashing to the ground. Not taking the time to weatherproof your outdoor connections is no shortcut if you have to replace a cable after six months because it filled up with water. Running your shack from an overloaded electrical service is no "deal" if the circuit breaker opens and you're off the air every time the refrigerator compressor kicks in. Plan ahead, and

Fig. 1 — W9OBF is quite active from this compact station built into a hideaway desk. A station arranged like this can easily be tucked into the corner of a living room without disrupting the rest of the household.

do the best job you can when putting together your station.

SELECTING A LOCATION

Selecting the right location for your station is the first and perhaps most important step in assembling a safe, comfortable, convenient station. The exact location will depend on the type of home or apartment you have and how much of that space can be devoted to your station. Fortunate amateurs will have a spare room to devote to housing the station; some may even have a separate building for their exclusive use. Most aren't that lucky, however, so usually a spot in the cellar or attic, or a corner of the living room is pressed into service.

Examine the possibilities from several angles. A station should be comfortable; odds are good that you'll be spending a lot of time there over the years. Some unfinished basements are damp and drafty — not an ideal environment for several hours of leisurely hamming. Attics have their

drawbacks, too; they can be stifling during warmer months. If possible, locate your station away from the heavy traffic areas of your home. Operation of your station should not interfere with family life. A night of chasing DX on 80 meters may be exciting to you, but the other members of your household may not share your enthusiasm.

Keep in mind that you must connect your station to the outside world. The location you choose should be convenient to a good power source and an adequate ground. There should be a fairly direct route to the outside for running antenna feed lines, rotator control cables and the like.

Although most homes will not have an "ideal" space meeting all requirements, the right location for you will be obvious after you scout around. The amateurs whose stations are depicted in Figs. 1 through 3 all found the right spot for them. Weigh the tradeoffs and decide which features you can do without and which are necessary for

Fig. 2 — The basement makes a good station location if it is dry. This setup belongs to WB2NPE.

Fig. 3 — Some amateurs, like PP2ZDD, are fortunate enough to have a separate room available for their stations.

your style of operation. If possible, pick an area large enough for future expansion.

SAFETY

Although the RF, ac and dc voltages in most amateur stations pose a potentially grave threat to life and limb, common sense and knowledge of safety practices will help you avoid accidents. Building and operating an Amateur Radio station can be, and is for almost all amateurs, a perfectly safe pastime. However, carelessness can lead to severe injury, or even death. The ideas presented here are only guidelines; it would be impossible to cover all safety precautions. Remember: There is no substitute for common sense.

A fire extinguisher is a must for the well-equipped amateur station. The fire extinguisher should be of the carbon-dioxide type to be effective in electrical fires. Store it in an easy-to-reach spot and check it at recommended intervals.

Family members should know how to turn the power off in your station. They should also know how to apply artificial respiration. Many community groups offer courses on cardiopulmonary resuscitation (CPR).

AC and DC Safety

The primary wiring for your station should be controlled by one master switch, and other members of your household should know how to kill the power in an emergency. All equipment should be connected to a good ground. All wires carrying power around the station should be of the proper size for the current carried and be insulated for the voltage level involved. Bare wire, open-chassis construction and exposed connections are an invitation to accidents. Remember that high-current, low-voltage power sources are just as dangerous as high-voltage, low-current sources. Possibly the most-dangerous voltage source in your station is the 117-V primary supply; it is a hazard often overlooked because it is a part of everyday life. Respect even the lowliest power supply in your station.

Whenever possible, kill the power and unplug equipment before working on it. Discharge capacitors with an insulated screwdriver; don't assume the bleeder resistors are 100 percent reliable. In a transmitter, always short the tube plate cap to ground just to be sure. If you must work on live equipment, keep one hand in your pocket. Avoid bodily contact with any grounded object to prevent your body from becoming the return path from a voltage source to ground. Use insulated tools for adjusting or moving any circuitry. Never work alone. Have someone else present; it could save your life in an emergency.

National Electrical Code

The *National Electrical Code®* is a comprehensive document that details safety requirements for all types of electrical installations. In addition to setting safety standards for house wiring and grounding, the Code also contains a section on Radio and Television Equipment — Article 810. Sections C and D specifically cover Amateur Transmitting and Receiving Stations. Highlights of the section concerning Amateur Radio stations follow. If you are interested in learning more about electrical safety, you may purchase a copy of *The National Electrical Code* or *The National Electrical Code® Handbook,* edited by Peter Schram, from the National Fire Protection Association, Batterymarch Park, Quincy, MA 02269.

Antenna installations are covered in some detail in the Code. It specifies minimum conductor sizes for different length wire antennas. For hard-drawn copper wire, the Code specifies no. 14 for open (unsupported) spans less than 150 feet, and no. 10 for longer spans. Copper-clad steel, bronze or other high-strength conductors may be no. 14 for spans less than 150 feet and no. 12 for longer runs. Lead-in conductors (for open-wire transmission line) should be at least as large as those specified for antennas.

The Code also says that antenna and lead-in conductors attached to buildings

must be firmly mounted at least 3 inches clear of the surface of the building on nonabsorbent insulators. The only exception to this minimum distance is when the lead-in conductors are enclosed in a "permanently and effectively grounded" metallic shield. The exception covers coaxial cable.

According to the Code, lead-in conductors (except those covered by the exception) must enter a building through a rigid, noncombustible, nonabsorbent insulating tube or bushing, through an opening provided for the purpose that provides a clearance of at least 2 inches or through a drilled window pane. All lead-in conductors to transmitting equipment must be arranged so that accidental contact is difficult.

Transmitting stations are required to have a means of draining static charges from the antenna system. An antenna discharge unit (lightning arrester) must be installed on each lead-in conductor (except where the lead-in is protected by a continuous metallic shield that is permanently and effectively grounded, or the antenna is permanently and effectively grounded). An acceptable alternative to lightning arrester installation is a switch that connects the lead-in to ground when the transmitter is not in use.

Grounding conductors are described in detail in the Code. Grounding conductors may be made from copper, aluminum, copper-clad steel, bronze or similar erosion-resistant material. Insulation is not required. The "protective grounding conductor" (main conductor running to the ground rod) must be as large as the antenna lead-in, but not smaller than no. 10. The "operating grounding conductor" (to bond equipment chassis together) must be at least no. 14. Grounding conductors must be adequately supported and arranged so that they are not easily damaged. They must run in as straight a line as practical between the mast or discharge unit and the ground rod. Adequate ground systems are covered later in this chapter.

Some information on safety inside the

station is covered in the Code. All conductors inside the building must be at least 4 inches away from conductors of any lighting or signalling circuit except when they are separated from other conductors by conduit or a nonconducting material. Transmitters must be enclosed in metal cabinets, and the cabinets must be grounded. All metal handles and controls accessible by the operator must be grounded. Access doors must be fitted with interlocks that will disconnect all voltages above 350 when the door is opened.

RF Radiation Safety

Although Amateur Radio is basically a safe activity, in recent years there has been considerable discussion and concern about the possible hazards of electromagnetic radiation (EMR), including both RF energy and power frequency (50-60 Hz) electromagnetic fields. Extensive research on this topic is underway in many countries. This section was prepared by members of the ARRL Committee on the Biological Effects of RF Energy ("Bio Effects" Committee) and coordinated by Wayne Overbeck, N6NB. It summarizes what is now known and offers safety precautions based on the research to date.

All life on earth has adapted to survive in an environment of weak, natural low-frequency electromagnetic fields (in addition to the earth's static geomagnetic field). Natural low-frequency EM fields come from two main sources: the sun, and thunderstorm activity. But in the last 100 years, manmade fields at much higher intensities and with a very different spectral distribution have altered this natural EM background in ways that are not yet fully understood. Much more research is needed to assess the biological effects of EMR.

Both RF and 60-Hz fields are classified as *nonionizing radiation* because the frequency is too low for there to be enough photon energy to ionize atoms. Still, at sufficiently high power densities, EMR poses certain health hazards. It has been known since the early days of radio that RF energy can cause injuries by heating body tissue. In extreme cases, RF-induced heating can cause blindness, sterility and other serious health problems. These heat-related health hazards may be called *thermal effects*. But now there is mounting evidence that even at energy levels too low to cause body heating, EMR has observable biological effects, some of which may be harmful. These are *athermal effects*.

In addition to the ongoing research, much else has been done to address this issue. For example, the American National Standards Institute, among others, has recommended voluntary guidelines to limit human exposure to RF energy. And the ARRL has established the Bio Effects Committee, a committee of concerned medical doctors and scientists, serving voluntarily to monitor scientific research in this field and to recommend safe practices

for radio amateurs.

Thermal Effects of RF Energy

Body tissues that are subjected to very high levels of RF energy may suffer serious heat damage. These effects depend upon the frequency of the energy, the power density of the RF field that strikes the body, and even on factors such as the polarization of the wave.

At frequencies near the body's natural resonant frequency, RF energy is absorbed more efficiently, and maximum heating occurs. In adults, this frequency usually is about 35 MHz if the person is grounded, and about 70 MHz if the person's body is insulated from ground. Also, body parts may be resonant; the adult head, for example, is resonant around 400 MHz, while a baby's smaller head resonates near 700 MHz. Body size thus determines the frequency at which most RF energy is absorbed. As the frequency is increased above resonance, less RF heating generally occurs. However, additional longitudinal resonances occur at about 1 GHz near the body surface.

Nevertheless, thermal effects of RF energy should not be a major concern for most radio amateurs because of the relatively low RF power we normally use and the intermittent nature of most amateur transmissions. Amateurs spend more time listening than transmitting, and many amateur transmissions such as CW and SSB use low-duty-cycle modes. (With FM or RTTY, though, the RF is present continuously at its maximum level during each transmission.) In any event, it is rare for radio amateurs to be subjected to RF fields strong enough to produce thermal effects unless they are fairly close to an energized antenna or unshielded power amplifier. Specific suggestions for avoiding excessive exposure are offered later.

Athermal Effects of EMR

Nonthermal effects of EMR, on the other hand, may be of greater concern to most amateurs because they involve lower-level energy fields. In recent years, there have been many studies of the health effects of EMR, including a number that suggest there may be health hazards of EMR even at levels too low to cause significant heating of body tissue. The research has been of two basic types: epidemiological research, and laboratory research into biological mechanisms by which EMR may affect animals or humans.

Epidemiologists look at the health patterns of large groups of people using statistical methods. A series of epidemiological studies has shown that persons likely to have been exposed to higher levels of EMR than the general population (such as persons living near power lines or employed in electrical and related occupations) have higher than normal rates of certain types of cancers. For example, several studies have found a higher incidence of leukemia

and lymphatic cancer in children living near certain types of power transmission and distribution lines and near transformer substations than in children not living in such areas. These studies have found a risk ratio of about 2, meaning the chance of contracting the disease is doubled. (The bibliography at the end of this chapter lists some of these studies. See Wertheimer and Leeper, 1979, 1982; Savitz et al, 1988).

Parental exposures may also increase the cancer risk of their offspring. Fathers in electronic occupations who are also exposed to electronic solvents have children with an increased risk of brain cancer (Johnson and Spitz, 1989), and children of mothers who slept under electric blankets while pregnant have a 2.5 risk ratio for brain cancer (Savitz et al, 1990).

Adults whose occupations expose them to strong 60-Hz fields (for example, telephone line splicers and electricians) have been found to have about four times the normal rate of brain cancer and male breast cancer (Matanoski et al, 1989). Another study found that microwave workers with 20 years of exposure had about 10 times the normal rate of brain cancer if they were also exposed to soldering fumes or electronic solvents (Thomas et al, 1987). Typically, these chemical factors alone have risk ratios around 2.

Dr. Samuel Milham, a Washington state epidemiologist, conducted a large study of the mortality rates of radio amateurs, and found that they had statistically significant excess mortality from one type of leukemia and lymphatic cancer. Milham suggested that this could result from the tendency of hams to work in electrical occupations or from their hobby.

However, epidemiological research by itself is rarely conclusive. Epidemiology only identifies health patterns in groups—it does not ordinarily determine their cause. And there are often confounding factors: Most of us are exposed to many different environmental hazards that may affect our health in various ways. Moreover, not all studies of persons likely to be exposed to high levels of EMR have yielded the same results.

There has also been considerable laboratory research about the biological effects of EMR in recent years. For example, it has been shown that even fairly low levels of EMR can alter the human body's circadian rhythms, affect the manner in which cancer-fighting T lymphocytes function in the immune system, and alter the nature of the electrical and chemical signals communicated through the cell membrane and between cells, among other things. (For a summary of some of this research, see Adey, 1990.)

Much of this research has focused on low-frequency magnetic fields, or on RF fields that are keyed, pulsed or modulated at a low audio frequency (often below 100 Hz). Several studies suggested that humans and animals can adapt to the

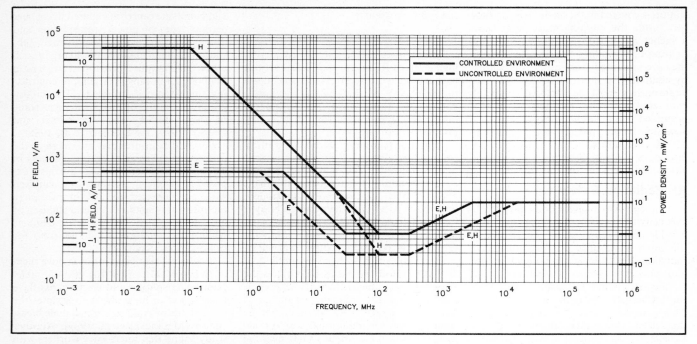

Fig. 4—Proposed 1991 ANSI RF protection guidelines for body exposure of humans.

presence of a steady RF carrier more readily than to an intermittent, keyed or modulated energy source. There is some evidence that while EMR may not directly cause cancer, it may sometimes combine with chemical agents to promote its growth or inhibit the work of the body's immune system.

None of the research to date conclusively proves that low-level EMR causes adverse health effects. Although there has been much debate about the meaning and significance of this research, many medical authorities now urge "prudent avoidance" of unnecessary exposure to moderate or high-level electromagnetic energy until more is known about this subject.

Safe Exposure Levels

How much EM energy is safe? Scientists have devoted a great deal of effort to deciding upon safe RF-exposure limits. This is a very complex problem, involving difficult public health and economic considerations. The recommended safe levels have been revised downward several times in recent years—and not all scientific bodies agree on this question even today. In early 1991, a new American National Standards Institute (ANSI) guideline for recommended EM exposure limits is on the verge of being approved (see bibliography). If the new standard is approved by a committee of the Institute of Electrical and Electronic Engineers (IEEE), it will replace a 1982 ANSI guideline that permitted somewhat higher exposure levels. ANSI-recommended exposure limits before 1982 were higher still.

This new ANSI guideline recommends frequency-dependent and time-dependent

maximum permissible exposure levels. Unlike earlier versions of the standard, the 1991 draft recommends different RF exposure limits in *controlled environments* (that is, where energy levels can be accurately determined and everyone on the premises is aware of the presence of EM fields) and in *uncontrolled environments* (where energy levels are not known or where some persons present may not be aware of the EM fields).

The graph in Fig. 4 depicts the new ANSI standard. It is necessarily a complex graph because the standards differ not only for controlled and uncontrolled environments but also for electric fields (E fields) and magnetic fields (H fields). Basically, the lowest E-field exposure limits occur at frequencies between 30 and 300 MHz. The lowest H-field exposure levels occur at

100-300 MHz. The ANSI standard sets the maximum E-field limits between 30 and 300 MHz at a power density of 1 mW/cm² (61.4 volts per meter) in controlled environments—but at one-fifth that level (0.2 mW/cm² or 27.5 volts per meter) in uncontrolled environments. The H-field limit drops to 1 mW/cm² (0.163 ampere per meter) at 100-300 MHz in controlled environments and 0.2 mW/cm² (0.0728 ampere per meter) in uncontrolled environments. Higher power densities are permitted at frequencies below 30 MHz (below 100 MHz for H fields) and above 300 MHz, based on the concept that the body will not be resonant at those frequencies and will therefore absorb less energy.

In general, the proposed ANSI guideline requires averaging the power level over time periods ranging from 6 to 30 minutes for

Table 3

Typical 60-Hz Magnetic Fields Near Amateur Radio Equipment and AC-Powered Household Appliances

Values are in milligauss.

Item	Field	Distance
Electric blanket	30-90	Surface
Microwave oven	10-100	Surface
	1-10	12″
IBM personal computer	5-10	Atop monitor
	0-1	15″ from screen
Electric drill	500-2000	At handle
Hair dryer	200-2000	At handle
HF transceiver	10-100	Atop cabinet
	1-5	15″ from front
1-kW RF amplifier	80-1000	Atop cabinet
	1-25	15″ from front

(Source: measurements made by members of the ARRL Bio Effects Committee)

power-density calculations, depending on the frequency and other variables. The ANSI exposure limits for uncontrolled environments are lower than those for controlled environments, but to compensate for that the guideline allows exposure levels in those environments to be averaged over much longer time periods (generally 30 minutes). This long averaging time means that an intermittently operating RF source (such as an Amateur Radio transmitter) will show a much lower power density than a continuous-duty station for a given power level and antenna configuration.

Time averaging is based on the concept that the human body can withstand a greater rate of body heating (and thus, a higher level of RF energy) for a short time than for a longer period. However, time averaging may not be appropriate in considerations of nonthermal effects of RF energy.

The ANSI guideline excludes any transmitter with an output below 7 watts because such low-power transmitters would not be able to produce significant whole-body heating. (However, recent studies show that handheld transceivers often produce power densities in excess of the ANSI standard within the head).

There is disagreement within the scientific community about these RF exposure guidelines. The ANSI guideline is still intended primarily to deal with thermal effects, not exposure to energy at lower levels. A growing number of researchers now believe athermal effects should also be taken into consideration. Several European countries and localities in the United States have adopted stricter standards than the proposed ANSI guideline.

Another national body in the United States, the National Council for Radiation Protection and Measurement (NCRP), has also adopted recommended exposure guidelines. NCRP urges a limit of 0.2 mW/cm^2 for nonoccupational exposure in the 30-300 MHz range. The NCRP guideline differs from ANSI in two notable ways: It takes into account the effects of modulation on an RF carrier, and it does not exempt transmitters with outputs below 7 watts.

Low-Frequency Fields

Recently much concern about EMR has focused on low-frequency energy, rather than RF. Amateur Radio equipment can be a significant source of low-frequency magnetic fields, although there are many other sources of this kind of energy in the typical home. Magnetic fields can be measured relatively accurately with inexpensive 60-Hz dosimeters that are made by several manufacturers.

Table 3 shows typical magnetic field intensities of Amateur Radio equipment and various household items. Because these fields dissipate rapidly with distance, "prudent avoidance" would mean staying perhaps 12 to 18 inches away from most

Amateur Radio equipment (and 24 inches from power supplies and 1-kW RF amplifiers) whenever the ac power is turned on. The old custom of leaning over a linear amplifier on a cold winter night to keep warm may not be the best idea!

There are currently no national standards for exposure to low-frequency fields. However, epidemiological evidence suggests that when the general level of 60-Hz fields exceeds 2 milligauss, there is an increased cancer risk in both domestic environments (Savitz et al, 1988) and industrial environments (Matanoski et al, 1989; Davis and Milham, 1990; Garland et al, 1990). Typical home environments (not close to appliances or power lines) are in the range of 0.1-0.5 milligauss.

DETERMINING RF POWER DENSITY

Unfortunately, determining the power density of the RF fields generated by an amateur station is not as simple as measuring low-frequency magnetic fields. Although sophisticated instruments can be used to measure RF power densities quite accurately, they are costly and require frequent recalibration. Most amateurs don't have access to such equipment, and the inexpensive field-strength meters that we do have are not suitable for measuring RF power density. The best we can usually do is to estimate our own RF power density based on measurements made by others or, given sufficient computer programming skills, use computer modeling techniques.

Table 4 shows a sampling of measure-

Table 4
Typical RF Field Strengths near Amateur Radio Antennas

A sampling of values as measured by the Federal Communications Commission and Environmental Protection Agency, 1990.

Antenna Type	Freq, MHz	Power, Watts	E Field, V/m	Location
Dipole in attic	14.15	100	7-100	In home
Discone in attic	146.5	250	10-27	In home
Half sloper	21.15	1000	50	1 m from base
Dipole at 7-13 ft	7.14	120	8-150	1-2 m from earth
Vertical	3.8	800	180	0.5 m from base
5-element Yagi at 60 ft	21.2	1000	10-20	In shack
			14	12 m from base
3-element Yagi at 25 ft	28.5	425	8-12	12 m from base
Inverted V at 22-46 ft	7.23	1400	5-27	Below antenna
Vertical on roof	14.11	140	6-9	In house
			35-100	At antenna tuner
Whip on auto roof	146.5	100	22-75	2 m from antenna
			15-30	In vehicle
			90	Rear seat
5-element Yagi at 20 ft	50.1	500	37-50	10 m from antenna

Table 5
RF Awareness Guidelines

These guidelines were developed by the ARRL Bio Effects Committee, based on the FCC/EPA measurements of Table 4 and other data.

- Although antennas on towers (well away from people) pose no exposure problem, make certain that the RF radiation is confined to the antenna radiating elements themselves. Provide a single, good station ground (earth), and eliminate radiation from transmission lines. Use good coaxial cable, not open wire lines or end-fed antennas that come directly into the transmitter area.
- No person should ever be near any transmitting antenna while it is in use. This is especially true for mobile or ground-mounted vertical antennas. Avoid transmitting with more than 25 watts in a VHF mobile installation unless it is possible to first measure the RF fields inside the vehicle. At the 1-kilowatt level, both HF and VHF directional antennas should be at least 35 feet above inhabited areas. Avoid using indoor and attic-mounted antennas if at all possible.
- Don't operate RF power amplifiers with the covers removed, especially at VHF/UHF.
- In the UHF/SHF region, never look into the open end of an activated length of waveguide or point it toward anyone. Never point a high-gain, narrow-beamwidth antenna (a paraboloid, for instance) toward people. Use caution in aiming an EME (moonbounce) array toward the horizon; EME arrays may deliver an effective radiated power of 250,000 watts or more.
- With handheld transceivers, keep the antenna away from your head and use the lowest power possible to maintain communications. Use a separate microphone and hold the rig as far away from you as possible.
- Don't work on antennas that have RF power applied.
- Don't stand or sit close to a power supply or linear amplifier when the ac power is turned on. Stay at least 24 inches away from power transformers, electrical fans and other sources of high-level 60-Hz magnetic fields.

ments made at Amateur Radio stations by the Federal Communications Commission and the Environmental Protection Agency in 1990. As this table indicates, a good antenna well removed from inhabited areas poses no hazard under any of the various exposure guidelines. However, the FCC/EPA survey also indicates that amateurs must be careful about using indoor or attic-mounted antennas, mobile antennas, low directional arrays, or any other antenna that is close to inhabited areas, especially when moderate to high power is used.

Ideally, before using any antenna that is in close proximity to an inhabited area, you should measure the RF power density. If that is not feasible, the next best option is make the installation as safe as possible by observing the safety suggestions listed in Table 5.

It is also possible, of course, to calculate the probable power density near an antenna using simple equations. However, such calculations have many pitfalls. For one, most of the situations in which the power density would be high enough to be of concern are in the near field—an area roughly bounded by several wavelengths of the antenna. In the near field, ground interactions and other variables produce power densities that cannot be determined by simple arithmetic.

Computer antenna-modeling programs such as *MININEC* or other codes derived from NEC (Numerical Electromagnetics Code) are suitable for estimating RF magnetic and electric fields around amateur antenna systems. And yet, these too have limitations. Ground interactions must be considered in estimating near-field power densities. Also, computer modeling is not sophisticated enough to predict "hot spots" in the near field—places where the field intensity may be far higher than would be expected.

Intensely elevated but localized fields often can be detected by professional measuring instruments. These "hot spots" are often found near wiring in the shack and metal objects such as antenna masts or equipment cabinets. But even with the best instrumentation, these measurements may also be misleading in the near field.

One need not make precise measurements or model the exact antenna system, however, to develop some idea of the relative fields around an antenna. Computer modeling using close approximations of the geometry and power input of the antenna will generally suffice. Those who are familiar with *MININEC* can estimate their power densities by computer modeling, and those with access to professional power-density meters can make useful measurements.

While our primary concern is ordinarily the intensity of the signal radiated by an antenna, we should also remember that there are other potential energy sources to be considered. You can also be exposed to RF radiation directly from a power ampli-

Fig. 5 — Typical LA series MOV protectors are shown at A with various connectors on the leads. A PA series MOV is shown at B as it might be mounted in a service-entrance box.

fier if it is operated without proper shielding. Transmission lines may also radiate a significant amount of energy under some conditions.

SOME FURTHER RF EXPOSURE SUGGESTIONS

Potential exposure situations should be taken seriously. Based on the FCC/EPA measurements and other data, the "RF awareness" guidelines of Table 5 were developed by the ARRL Bio Effects Committee. A longer version of these guidelines appeared in a *QST* article by Ivan Shulman, MD, WC2S (see bibliography).

QST carries information regarding the latest developments for RF safety precautions and regulations at the local and federal levels. You can find additional information about the biological effects of RF radiation in the publications listed in the bibliography.

Lightning Protection

The National Fire Protection Association (NFPA) publishes a booklet called *Lightning Protection Code* (NFPA no. 78-1983) that should be of interest to radio amateurs. Write to the NFPA at the address given in the previous section for information on obtaining a copy. Two paragraphs of particular interest to amateurs are presented below:

"3-26 Antennas. Radio and television masts of metal, located on a protected building, shall be bonded to the lightning protection system with a main size conductor and fittings.

"3-27 Lightning arresters, protectors or antenna discharge units shall be installed on electric and telephone service entrances and on radio and television antenna leadins."

The best protection from lightning is to disconnect all antennas from equipment and disconnect the equipment from the power lines. Ground antenna feed lines to safely bleed off static buildup. Eliminate the possible paths for lightning strokes. Rotator cables and other control cables

from the antenna location should also be disconnected during severe electrical storms.

In some areas, the probability of lightning surges entering homes via the 117/234-V line may be high. Lightning produces both electrical and magnetic fields that vary with distance. These fields can couple into power lines and destroy electronic components. Radio equipment can be protected from these surges through the use of transient-protective devices. The following information originally appeared in a February 1982 *QST* article by Gene Collick, W8LEQ and Ken Stuart, W3VVN.

Protective Devices

The General Electric Home Lightning Protector® is designed to prevent lightning surges (entering through the wiring) from damaging electrical wiring and/or appliances. The protector is a two-pole, three-wire device designed primarily for single-phase 117/234-V grounded-neutral service. It mounts via a ½-inch pipe-thread connection through a knockout in the service-entrance box preferably, or, at the weatherhead or within the meter housing. The purpose of this device is to reduce the amplitude of large transients.

TransZorbs® are silicon devices manufactured by General Semiconductor Industries for transient suppression. They contain a large-area PN junction having integral heat sinks and are capable of handling short-duration, high-power pulses (typically 1500 watts for 1 millisecond and 100,000 watts for 100 nanoseconds). The TransZorb® protects by clamping transient voltages to a safe level, with sub-nanosecond reaction time.

A metal-oxide varistor (MOV) is a bulk semiconductor device whose resistance varies with the magnitude (but not polarity) of the applied voltage. At extremely low currents, a varistor acts like a linear resistor with a resistance that can exceed hundreds of megohms. At higher currents, the voltage-current relation is nonlinear, and at extremely high currents the device acts like a constant resistor with a very small value (typically about 1 ohm). Varistors can respond in low-nanosecond times, with clamping-threshold voltages ranging from 10 to 1500 V, with continuous power from 0.5 to 5 watts and with peak energy of more than 600 joules. MOVs have a capacitance that is a device parameter, and this should be considered for high-frequency applications. GE manufactures devices with wire leads (LA series) and the heat-sink type (PA series). The PA type may be used for service-entrance box and fuse-mounting; use the LA units for coils, solenoids and such within the equipment. See Fig. 5.

Installation

The first protective device you can install is a secondary low-voltage lightning arrester rated at 650 V (a typical device is a GE Thyrite type 9L15BC002). Power should be removed from the feed to the house, and the device should be installed ahead of the service-entrance box by a qualified electrician. The black leads (2) are connected to each hot leg, with the white lead terminated to the meter box (be sure the meter box is directly connected to the service-entrance box). The reason the white lead is terminated to the box rather than the electrical circuit neutral is that the device is being installed to protect against the common-mode (phase-to-case ground) transient.

The second device to be installed is a low-voltage surge arrester such as a GE V130PA20A MOV. These should be connected from each hot leg to case ground. The arrester should be located in a way that provides minimum lead length. These can be installed with an active power feed to the house, but with the main breaker turned off. Connect the MOVs on the load side of the main breaker.

The ac input to the transmitter can be protected by one of two methods. The transmitter may be modified by installing a V130LA10A MOV across the ac input and another one from neutral to case ground. If you do not want to modify the transmitter, a plug-in protector can be purchased or constructed (see Fig. 6). This

device is then plugged into the duplex receptacle feeding the transmitter. This method should be ideal for renters, for portable operation or to provide some protection for those who can't afford an electrician to install the other devices. Receivers, transceivers, TV sets and other electronic equipment should all be protected in a similar fashion. An alternative would be to wire an outlet box or strip with protective devices.

Rotator protection consists of installing a plug-in MOV device in one side of the duplex receptacle that the rotator remote-control unit is plugged into. The rotator control cables should terminate in a grounded metal box. Each control cable conductor should have a GE V56ZA2 MOV connected across it to case ground. If the control cable is not shielded, the same type of protective devices can be installed within the rotator. If shielded cable is used, the devices inside the rotator would not be needed. Check the voltage on the control cable and select a value of MOV rated for a safe operating voltage above the control voltage.

MOVs are available from some of the suppliers listed in Chapter 35. Some may be available from local electrical supply houses. Table 6 lists some transient-protective devices of interest to radio amateurs.

Table 6

Transient-Protective Device Selection Data

General Electric Co., Semiconductor Div., W. Genesee St., Auburn, NY 13021

"Home Lightning Protector"
GE Thyrite 9L15BCB002
"Metal Oxide Varistors"
V130LA10A
V130PA20A
V39ZA6
V56ZA2

The numbers after the V indicate the normal operating voltage (RMS) of the circuit. Voltages at a preset value greater than that will cause the device to conduct heavily, clamping the voltage.

General Semiconductor Industries, P.O. Box 3078, Tempe, AZ 85281

TransZorbs®
1.5KE6.8
1.5KE7.5 to 47
1.5KE51 to 110
1.5KE120 to 150
1.5KE160 to 200
1N6072

Bidirectional, for connection directly across 117-V ac line. The numbers after KE are the approximate breakdown voltage of the device.

Radio Shack

MOVs for 117-V Lines
V130LA1 — Very Light Duty (276-571)
SNR14A130K — Light Duty (276-570)
SNR20A130K — Medium Duty (276-568)

Fig. 7 — An effective station ground bonds the chassis of all equipment together with low-impedance conductors and ties into a good earth ground.

Fig. 6 — Construction of a plug-in protector. Install a V130LA10A MOV across the brass and silver terminals and another across the silver and green terminals.

GROUND

An effective ground system is a must for every amateur station. The mission of the ground system is twofold. First, it reduces the possibility of electrical shock if something in a piece of equipment should fail and the chassis or cabinet becomes "hot." If connected properly, three-wire electrical systems ground the chassis, but the majority of amateur equipment still uses the ungrounded two-wire system. A ground system to prevent shock hazards is generally referred to as "dc ground."

The second job the ground system must perform is to provide a low-impedance path to ground for any stray RF current inside the station. Stray RF can cause equipment to malfunction and contributes to RFI

problems This low-impedance path is usually called "RF ground." In most stations, dc ground and RF ground are provided by the same system.

The first step in building a ground system is to bond together the chassis of all equipment in your station. Ordinary hookup wire will do for a dc ground, but for a good RF ground you need a low-impedance conductor. Copper strap, sold as "flashing copper," is excellent for this application, but it may be hard to find. Braid from coaxial cable is a popular choice; it is readily available, a low-impedance conductor and flexible.

Grounding straps can be run from equipment chassis to equipment chassis, but a more convenient approach is illustrated in Fig. 7. In this installation, a ½-inch-diameter copper water pipe runs the entire length of the operating bench. A thick braid (from discarded RG-8 cable) runs from each piece of equipment to a clamp on the pipe. Copper water pipe is inexpensive and available at most hardware stores and home centers. Alternatively, a strip of flashing copper may be run along the rear of the operating bench.

After the equipment is bonded to a common ground bus, the ground bus must be wired to a good earth ground. This run should be made with a heavy conductor (braid is a good choice again) and should be as short and direct as possible. The earth ground usually takes one of two forms.

In most cases, the best approach is to drive one or more ground rods into the earth at the point where the conductor from the station ground bus leaves the house. The best ground rods to use are those available from an electrical supply house. These rods are 6 to 8 feet long and are made from steel with a heavy copper plating. Do not depend on shorter, thinly plated rods sold by some home electronics suppliers. These rods begin to rust almost immediately after they are driven into the soil, and they become worthless within a short time. Good ground rods, while more expensive initially, offer long-term protection. If your soil is soft and contains few rocks, an acceptable alternative to "genuine" ground rods is ½-inch-diameter copper water pipe. A 6- to 8-foot length of this material offers a good ground, but it may bend while being driven into the earth.

Once the ground rod is installed, clamp the conductor from the station ground bus to it with a clamp that can be tightened securely and will not rust. Copper-plated clamps made especially for this purpose are available from electrical supply houses, but a stainless-steel hose clamp will work too. Alternatively, drill several holes through the pipe and bolt the conductor in place. If a torch is available, solder the connection.

Another popular station ground is the cold water system in the building. To take advantage of this ready-made ground system, run a low-impedance conductor from the station ground bus to a convenient cold water pipe, preferably somewhere near the point where the main water supply enters the house. Avoid hot water pipes; they do not run directly into the earth. The advent of PVC (plastic) plumbing makes it mandatory to inspect the cold water system from your intended ground connection to the main inlet. PVC is an excellent insulator, so any PVC pipe or fittings rule out your cold water system for use as a station ground.

For some installations, especially those located above the first floor, a conventional ground system such as that just described will make a fine dc ground but will not provide the necessary low-impedance path to ground for RF. The length of the conductor between the ground bus and the ulti-

Fig. 8 — Here is an alternative to earth ground if the station is located far from the ground point and RF in the station is a problem. Install at least one ¼-wavelength radial for each band used.

mate ground point becomes a problem. For example, the ground wire may be about ¼ wavelength (or an odd multiple of ¼ wavelength) long on some amateur band. A ¼-wavelength wire acts as an impedance inverter from one end to the other. Since the grounded end is at a very low impedance, the equipment end will be at a high impedance. The likely result is RF hot spots around the station while the transmitter is in operation. In this case, this ground system may be worse than having no ground at all.

An alternative RF ground system is shown in Fig. 8. No attempt is made to ground the station to an earth ground. Instead, the station ground bus is connected to a system of ¼-wavelength radials. Install at least one radial for each band used. Try this system if you have RF in the shack even though your equipment is connected to a conventional ground. Keep in mind, however, that while the radial ground system offers an RF ground, it will not act as a dc ground to protect you from shock hazards.

Ground Noise

Noise in ground systems can affect our sensitive radio equipment. It is usually related to one of three problems:
1) Insufficient ground conductor size
2) Loose ground connections
3) Ground loops

These matters are treated in precise scientific research equipment and certain industrial instruments by attention to certain rules. The ground conductor should be at least as large as the largest conductor in the primary power circuit. Ground conductors should provide a solid connection to both ground and to the equipment being grounded. Liberal use of lockwashers and star washers is highly recommended. A loose ground connection is a tremendous source of noise, particularly in a sensitive receiving system.

Ground loops should be avoided at all costs. A short discussion of what a ground loop is and how to avoid them may lead you down the proper path. A ground loop is formed when more than one ground current is flowing in a single conductor. This

commonly occurs when grounds are "daisy-chained" (series linked). The correct way to ground equipment is to bring all ground conductors out radially from a common point to either a good driven earth ground or a cold-water system.

Ground noise can affect transmitted and received signals. With the low audio levels required to drive amateur transmitters, and the ever-increasing sensitivity of our receivers, correct grounding is critical.

STATION POWER

Amateur Radio stations generally require a 117-V ac power source. The 117-V ac is then converted to the proper ac or dc levels required for the station equipment. Power supply theory is covered in Chapter 6. If your station is located in a room with electrical outlets, you're in luck. If your station is located in the basement, an attic, or another area without a convenient 117-V source, you will have to run a line to your operating position.

Stations with high-power amplifiers should have a 234-V ac power source in addition to the 117-V supply. Some amplifiers may be powered from 117 V, but they require current levels at that voltage that are near, or in excess of, the limits of standard house wiring. For safety, and for the best possible voltage regulation in the equipment, it is advisable to install a separate 234-V line with an appropriate current rating if you use an amplifier.

The usual line running to baseboard outlets is rated at 15 amperes. This may or may not be enough current to power your station. To determine how much current your station requires, check the ratings for each piece of gear. Usually, the manufacturer will specify the required current at 117-V; if the power consumption is rated in watts, divide that rating by 117 V to get amperes. If the total current required for your station is near 15 amperes, you need to think about running another line or upgrading the present one. Keep in mind that other rooms may be powered from the same branch of the electrical system, so the power consumption of any equipment connected to other outlets on the branch must be taken into account. Whenever possible, power your station from a separate, heavy-duty line run directly to the distribution panel.

In modern residential systems, three wires are brought in from the outside to a distribution panel (fuse panel, or circuit-breaker panel). In the three-wire system, the third wire is neutral, which is grounded. The voltage between the other two wires is usually 234, while half of this voltage appears between each wire and neutral. In a three-wire system, the three wires should be brought into the station so that the load can be distributed to keep the line balanced. The voltage across a fixed load on one side of the line will increase as the load current on the other side is increased. The rate of the increase will depend on the resistance of the neutral wire. If the resistance of the neutral wire is low, the increase will be correspondingly small. When the currents in the two circuits are balanced, no current flows in the neutral wire, and the system is operating at maximum efficiency.

If you decide to install a separate heavy-duty 117-V line or a 234-V line, consult the local power company for local requirements. In some areas, this work must be performed by a licensed electrician. You may need a special building permit for the work, and even if you are allowed to do the work yourself, you might have to get a licensed electrician to inspect the job. Your best bet is to go through the system and get the necessary permits and inspections. If something should happen, such as a fire, you might run into insurance or other problems if you didn't follow the required steps, even if the accident had nothing to do with your wiring job.

If you decide to do the job yourself, study the applicable sections of the National Electrical Code and any local building codes. This information should be available from your local building inspector. Books are available at libraries or from outlets selling electrical supplies that will tell you everything you need to know to install separate ac lines for your station. Use only good-quality wire and other materials with ratings as specified in the building codes. If you have any doubts about doing the work yourself, get a licensed electrician to do the installation.

Safety Precautions

All power supplies in an installation should be fed through a single main power-line switch so that all power may be cut off quickly, either before working on the equipment, or in case of an accident. Spring-operated switches or relays are not sufficiently reliable for this important service. Foolproof devices for cutting off all power to the transmitter and other equipment are shown in Fig. 9. The arrangements shown in Figs. 9A and B are similar circuits for two-wire (117-volt) and three-wire (234-volt) systems. S is an enclosed double-throw switch of the sort usually used as the entrance switch in house

installations. J is a non-standard ac outlet and P a shorted plug to fit the outlet. Use of a non-standard outlet is recommended to minimize the chance of inadvertently inserting the shorted plug into a standard outlet. The switch should be located prominently in plain sight, and members of the household should be instructed in its location and use. I is a red lamp located alongside the switch. Its purpose is not so much to serve as a warning that the power is on as it is to help in identifying and quickly locating the switch should it become necessary for someone else to cut the power off in an emergency.

The outlet J should be placed in some corner out of sight where it will not be a temptation for children or others to play with. The shorting plug can be removed to open the power circuit if there are others around who might inadvertently throw the switch while the operator is working on the rig. If the operator takes the plug when the station is not in use, it will prevent unauthorized persons from turning on the power. Of utmost importance is the fact that the outlet J must be placed in the ungrounded side of the line.

The test bench should be fed through the main power switch, or a similar arrangement at the bench, if the bench is located remotely from the transmitter.

Three-Wire 117-V Power Cords

To meet the requirements of state and national codes, electrical tools, appliances and many items of electronic equipment now being manufactured to operate from the 117-volt line must be equipped with a three-conductor power cord. Two of the conductors carry power to the device in the usual fashion, while the third conductor is connected to the case or frame. See Fig. 10.

When plugged into a properly wired mating receptacle, the three-contact polarized plug connects this third conductor to

an earth ground, thereby grounding the chassis or frame of the appliance and preventing the possibility of electrical shock to the user. All commercially manufactured items of electronic test equipment and most ac-operated amateur equipment are being supplied with these three-wire cords. Adapters are available for use where older

Fig. 9 — Reliable arrangements for cutting off all power to the station. S is an enclosed double-pole, double-throw power switch of appropriate ratings. J is a non-standard ac outlet. P is a shorted plug to fit outlet J. I is a red warning lamp. The system at A is for two-wire, 117-V lines; B is for three-wire 234-V systems.

Fig. 10 — Proper wiring for power plugs found in amateur stations. Follow correct wiring procedures to minimize shock hazards. On 117-V plugs, the screw terminal or connection for one prong is brass and the other is plated ("white"). Connect the black wire to the brass prong and the white wire to the white prong. Always use 234-V connectors for 234-V systems; otherwise, you may destroy a piece of equipment by applying too much voltage.

Fig. 11 — Commercially made power strips are available with different numbers of outlets. Some feature built-in fuses or circuit breakers. Three-wire strips are recommended for use in amateur stations.

Fig. 12 — It is possible to make a custom outlet strip for your station. Space the outlets at convenient intervals for your operating position. See text for details.

electrical installations do not have mating receptacles. For proper grounding, the lug of the green wire protruding from the adapter must be attached underneath the screw securing the cover plate of the outlet box where connection is made, and the outlet box itself must be grounded.

Multiple Outlets

Once you have the right line or lines running from the distribution panel to your station, you will need to bring the power to each piece of equipment. All of the accessories, such as keyer, rotator control box and clock, as well as the station transceiver, need a separate outlet. Commercial outlet strips, such as that pictured in Fig. 11, will provide a grounded outlet for each piece of equipment. If the commercially available outlet strips do not suit your setup, you can make your own.

Fig. 12 shows one way to make your own outlet strip. The materials to make this type of strip are available at most hardware stores or home centers. Use wire with sufficient current rating. See Chapter 35 for a table listing the current-carrying ability of different wire sizes. No. 14 wire is rated to handle 17 amperes continuously when bundled in cables, so it is adequate for most installations. The best kind of cable to buy for this job is stranded 14/3 (three conductors, each no. 14) with a rubberized outer jacket. This type of cable is easy to work with and is flexible.

First, measure the length of cable needed to run from your operating position to the station power feed. Include enough extra so that you can run the cable neatly along the floor if necessary. Refer to Fig. 10 to see which color wire goes to which plug terminal. Locate the first outlet box near the first group of equipment. Wire the outlets in parallel, paying close attention to where the various color conductors should go. Wire any additional outlet boxes in parallel with the first. Depending on the amount of equipment you have, you may choose either two- or four-outlet boxes. The individual outlet boxes may be left loose, attached to a strip of wood of the appropriate dimensions, or bolted directly to the operating bench.

STATION LAYOUT

Station layout is largely a matter of personal taste. It will depend to a large extent on the amount of space available, the amount of gear involved and the types of operating activities engaged in. Although no two stations are exactly alike, there are some underlying considerations you should be aware of. These design considerations will help you build a convenient, easy-to-use station around your needs and means.

The Operating Table

The operating table may be an office desk, a kitchen table or a custom-made bench; what you use will depend on the available space and materials on hand. The two most important considerations are the size of the top and the height of the top above the floor. The top of most commercially manufactured desks is about 29 inches above the floor. This is a comfortable height for most adults. If the top is much lower, your knees may not clear the underside, and you will be sitting in an uncomfortable pitched-forward position. If the table top is much higher, you may not be able to reach the equipment, and writing will be awkward.

The dimensions of the top of the operating table are a prime consideration. Although the top need be only deep enough to hold the equipment (a foot or so), a much wider top greatly enhances the comfort and convenience of your operation. Leaving room for a power outlet strip at the back of the table, a ground bus, the equipment and room for writing, the depth of a comfortable operating table grows to at least 36 inches, and preferably more. For an ideal operating table, 42 to 48 inches is about the right depth. See Fig. 13. The length of the top will depend on how much equipment is used.

Fig. 13 — The ideal operating table is about 42 inches deep and as wide as you need to make it to fit your available space. This arrangement leaves plenty of room for equipment and cables, with lots of elbow room for comfort.

Fig. 14 — Two file cabinets and a flush-type door make an effective operating bench.

An office desk makes a good operating table. The top is usually 30 to 36 inches deep by 60 inches wide. The drawers can be put to good use for log books, headphones and the like.

A Homemade Operating Table

An unfinished flush-type door, measuring approximately 30 × 84 inches, makes an acceptable operating bench if the power outlet strip and ground bus are not mounted on the table top. A depth of 30 inches is just enough for the equipment and writing area. The door may be mounted on two 2-drawer file cabinets (see Fig. 14), making an easy bench with drawer space.

A flush door may also be made into an attractive homemade table. Fig. 15 shows construction details for building a simple but sturdy homemade operating table. Side members for supporting the top are made from ordinary 2 × 3 lumber which comes in standard lengths of 8 and 12 feet. Making legs that are good and solid isn't the easiest job in the world, and if the table isn't solid it will be a poor operating desk. You can get around this by using the construction technique shown in Fig. 15A and D. The 2 × 3s are formed into a square or rectangular format, as shown at A. Each joint should be glued and screwed together. Nails will not provide enough sturdiness.

Once the glue holding the 2 × 3s together has completely dried (several hours is sufficient with most types of glue), these assemblies can be drilled and made ready for mounting. If you are planning to cover the top and edges of the door with a plastic laminate, such as Formica, holes should be drilled through the door and countersunk as shown in Fig. 15B. After the holes in the door have been drilled, place the pieces in the final position. Drill through the 2 × 3s at the four bolt locations. After these holes have been drilled, the four bolts should be inserted in the holes, through the 2 × 3s and secured by flat washers and nuts. With the bolts securely in place, fill the gaps between the bolt heads and wood with epoxy cement. See Fig. 15C.

Once the epoxy has hardened (it's a good idea to let it set overnight), the nuts can be removed and the three sections taken apart. If you are planning on having the top

Fig. 15 — A flush door may also be used with a simple frame to make a furniture-quality operating table. (A) 2 × 3 lumber is used to form the side supports. Each joint should be glued and then screwed together. (B) Front, top and side views detailing the method of fastening the side supports to the top. (C) Completely fill the space around the bolt head with epoxy. (D) Table assembly and side covering information. (E) The rear-apron brace should be attached to both side members at the top of the desk.

laminated, now is the time. Most kitchen cabinet shops can do this for you, as they have all of the necessary tools. Pick a color that compliments the rest of the shack!

The table is now ready for assembly. Place the table top on its good surface with the bolts sticking up. Now the side members can be slipped over the bolts and held in place with flat washers, lock washers and nuts. Make sure to tighten the nuts securely.

At this point, the side coverings can be attached to the leg assemblies. Ordinary ¼-inch plywood or Masonite can be used if you plan on painting this portion of the table. An alternative would be to use oak-, walnut-, birch- or teak-veneered plywood. Although this material is a bit more expensive than ordinary plywood, it yields a quality furniture-like appearance. The wood can be stained and coated with clear lacquer to preserve the finish. Another alternative would be to use pieces of wood paneling for the side coverings. In any case, the coverings on the outside of the table should be glued and tacked to the frame. The inner side coverings should be tacked only to the frame so they can be removed and the table taken apart should the need arise. The front face of the side members should be covered with a wide strip of veneer or plastic laminate of the same color used for the top of the table.

A rear-apron brace can be made from a 2 × 4. By painting this brace flat black it will not detract from the appearance of the table even if a small amount of its surface shows. The power outlet strip and ground bus can be attached to the rear-apron brace.

If you have some basic woodworking tools and knowledge, you can construct a larger top for your operating table and mount it on the type of framework just described. The homemade top is fashioned from a single 4 × 8-foot sheet of plywood or particle board. Particle board is less expensive than plywood. Its perfectly smooth, even surface makes a good base for plastic laminates, but it is substantially heavier than plywood and not as strong. Depending on your needs, you may use the entire sheet for your table top, or you may trim it to size. If you make the top at least 42 inches deep, you will have plenty of room for setting up the equipment.

The type of finish you select for your top will depend on the material used. Plastic laminates, while expensive, are attractive and durable; they also make an excellent writing surface and are easy to keep clean. Plywood may be stained and finished with a tough varnish, or it may be painted. If you paint or varnish particle board or plywood, you should use a piece of glass or other hard material as a writing surface.

Stacking Equipment

No matter how large your operating table is, some vertical stacking of equipment is necessary if you are to reach

Fig. 16 — A simple but very strong equipment shelf can be built from ¾-inch plywood. See text for details.

Fig. 17 — Example station layout as seen from the front (A) and the top (B). The equipment is spaced far enough apart that air circulates on all sides of each cabinet. Equipment that is adjusted frequently sits on the table top, while equipment requiring infrequent adjustment is perched on a shelf. All equipment is positioned so that the operator does not have to move the chair to reach anything at the operating position.

everything from your chair. Piling the equipment cabinets one on top of another is not a particularly good idea because most amateur equipment needs air flowing around it for cooling. Construction of a shelf like that shown in Fig. 16 will improve equipment layout in most installations.

The exact shelf dimensions will depend on the size of your operating table and the size of your equipment. This shelf is com-

pletely open both front and back and has no center support; access to equipment and interconnecting cables is excellent. The shelf should be made from strong material, such as ¾-inch plywood. A shelf constructed like that shown in Fig. 16 will support several hundred pounds without bowing in the center. The top, sides and apron braces are all made from ¾-inch plywood. The top and side dimensions can be varied to match your station requirements. Glue and screw all adjoining surfaces for maximum strength. Finish the shelf to match the operating table. If you build it right, you should be able to stand on the shelf without it bending.

Arranging the Equipment

When you have acquired the operating table and shelving for your station, the next task is arranging the equipment in a convenient, orderly manner. The first step is to provide power outlets and a good ground as described in a previous section. Be conservative in estimating the number of power outlets for your installation; radio equipment has a habit of multiplying with time, so plan for the future at the outset.

Fig. 17 illustrates a sample station layout. The rear of the operating table is spaced about 1½ feet from the wall to allow easy access to the rear of the equipment. This installation incorporates two separate operating positions, one for HF and one for VHF. When the operator is seated at the HF operating position, the keyer and transceiver controls are within easy reach. The keyer, keyer paddle and transceiver are the most-often adjusted pieces of equipment in the station. The speaker is positioned right in front of the operator for the best possible reception. Accessory equipment not often adjusted, including the amplifier, antenna switch and rotator control box, is located on the shelf above the transceiver. The SWR/power meter and clock, often consulted but rarely touched, are located where the operator can view them without head movement. All HF-related equipment can be reached without moving the chair.

This layout assumes that the operator is right-handed. The keyer paddle is operated with the right hand, and the keyer speed and transceiver controls are operated with the left hand. This setup allows the operator to write or send with the right hand without having to cross hands to adjust the controls. If the operator is left-handed, some repositioning of equipment is necessary, but the idea is the same. For best results during CW operation, the paddle should be weighted to keep it from "walking" across the table. It should be oriented such that the operator's entire arm from wrist to elbow rests on the table top to prevent fatigue.

Some operators prefer to place the station transceiver on the shelf to leave the table top clear for writing. This arrangement leads to fatigue from having an unsupported arm in the air most of the time. If you rest your elbows on the table top, they will quickly become sore. If you rarely operate for prolonged periods, however, you may not be inconvenienced by having the transceiver on the shelf. The real secret to having a clear table top for logging, etc., is to make the operating table deep enough that your entire arm from elbow to wrist rests on the table with the front panels of

the equipment at your fingertips. This leaves plenty of room for paperwork, even with a microphone and keyer paddle on the table.

The VHF operating position in this station is similar to the HF position. The amplifier and power supply are located on the shelf. The station triband beam and VHF beam are on the same tower, so the rotator control box is located where it can be seen and reached from both operating positions. This operator is active on packet radio on a local VHF repeater, so the computer, printer, terminal node controller and modem are all clustered within easy reach of the VHF transceiver.

This sample layout is intended to give you ideas for designing your own station. Study the photos of station layouts presented here, in other chapters of this Handbook and in *QST*. Visit the shacks of amateur friends to view their ideas. Station layout is always changing as you acquire new gear, dispose of old gear, change operating habits and interests, or become active on different bands. Configure the station to suit your interests, and keep thinking of ways to refine the layout. Figs. 18 through 20 show station arrangements tailored for specific purposes.

INTERCONNECTING YOUR EQUIPMENT

After you've chosen the equipment for your station and arrived at a layout, you'll have to interconnect everything. The complexity of the wiring job depends on the setup; but large or small, HF or VHF, high or low power, every shack needs some cabling between equipment. Commercially manufactured cables with connectors are available for some applications. In most instances, however, there will not be a readily available cable, so you'll have to make your own. Making custom cables is not difficult. Most equipment manuals tell you the pinouts for microphone, key, accessory and control connectors. Many manufacturers include connectors, but they leave the cable construction up to you so you can make up the right lengths for your installation.

You should use good wire, cables and connectors in your shack. Take the time to make good mechanical and electrical connections on your cable ends. Poorly made cables are a source of trouble. Connections may break, requiring maintenance. Improperly assembled transmission-line connectors can cause RFI. More important, cables made from inferior materials or assembled sloppily are a safety hazard. Wire too small for the current load can heat up, presenting a fire hazard. Connections lacking mechanical integrity can work free, possibly shorting a power supply to ground or applying voltage where not expected. Wire with poor or underrated insulation is a shock hazard.

Wherever possible, neatly bundle your wires and cables. There are many ways to do this. Some amateurs use masking tape or

Fig. 18 — This station, owned by K5RC, was designed with contest operation in mind. Note the high-efficiency layout; separate rigs for each band makes for quick band changes. Control switches, keyer and rig are all within easy reach.

Fig. 19 — WA3AXV is interested primarily in VHF work. Each band requires a separate transverter and amplifier. This equipment, all of which is rarely touched once adjusted, is located above the operating table. The transceiver used as a tuneable IF and the accessories are within easy reach.

Fig. 20 — K1JX has an HF operating position and a VHF operating position arranged on a corner table.

cloth adhesive tape. Others use paper labels attached to the cables with string. See Fig. 21. Whatever method you use, proper labeling makes disconnecting, reconnecting or rearranging equipment much easier. Good labels will also help you avoid inadvertently putting voltage where it doesn't belong.

Types of Wire and Cable

The type of wire or cable to use depends on the job at hand. If the wire is to carry

Fig. 21 — Labels on the cables make it much easier to rearrange things in the station. Labeling ideas include masking tape, cardboard labels attached with string and labels attached to fasteners found on plastic bags (such as bread bags).

Fig. 22 — Preparing coaxial cable for use with a connector involves a few easy steps. A — Remove the outer insulation with a sharp knife or wire stripper. If you nick the braid, start over. B — Push the braid accordian-fashion against the outer jacket. C — Spread the shield strands at the point where the outer insulation ends. D — Fish the center conductor through the opening in the braid. Smooth the braid. Now strip the center conductor insulation back far enough for the type of connector you're using and tin both center conductor and shield. Be careful not to use too much solder, making the conductors inflexible. A pair of pliers used as a heat sink will help. The outer jacket removed in step A makes a perfect insulator for the braid if necessary.

any significant current, check the wire table in Chapter 35 for the ratings of different sizes. For safety, always use wire heavy enough for the task. Also, check the insulation rating. Almost any insulation will do for low voltages, but use the right wire for higher voltages; anything you can do to minimize shock hazards around your shack is important for your safety.

Use the right size coaxial cable for connecting transmitters, transceivers, antenna switches, SWR bridges, Transmatches and the like. For example, RG-58/U cable is fine between your transceiver and SWR meter, but it is too small to use between your legal-limit amplifier and Transmatch. Chapter 16 contains information on the characteristics of popular coaxial cables.

Hookup wire may be stranded or solid. Generally, stranded wire is the better choice for most applications because solid wire will break under repeated flexing.

Many interconnections should be made from shielded wire to reduce the chances of RF getting into equipment. RG-174/U subminiature coaxial cable is a good choice for control, audio and some power leads. It is shielded, small and very flexible. Fig. 21 shows how to prepare coaxial cable for attachment to a connector.

Connectors

Connectors found in amateur stations run the gamut from single-conductor ring terminals for use on terminal blocks, to four-conductor microphone connectors, to 50-conductor ribbon cable connectors. Although the number of connectors in existence is mind boggling, most manufacturers of amateur gear use a few standard types. If you are involved in any group activities, such as public service and emergency preparedness work, check to see what kinds of connectors others in the group use. If group members standardize whenever possible, the equipment will be more interchangeable — a definite plus in an emergency.

Audio, Power and Control Connectors

The simplest form of connector is found on terminal blocks. Although it is possible

Fig. 23 — The wires on one side of this terminal block have connectors; the others do not. The connectors make it possible to secure different wire sizes to the strip and also make it much easier to change things around.

(A)

(B)

(C)

Fig. 24 — The plug shown at A is often used to connect equipment to remote power supplies. The multipin connector at B is used for control, signal and power lines. The DIN plug at C offers shielding and is often used for connecting accessories to transceivers.

to strip the insulation from wire and wrap it around the screw, this method leaves something to be desired. Sometimes it is difficult to hold the wire in place when tightening the screw; this is especially troublesome when the wire is large compared to the screw size, which is frequently the case. It's not always easy to get a good connection. Changing the wire on a terminal block can be a headache with the strip-and-wrap method. Also, the conductors in stranded wire tend to separate under compression, making an unsightly mess.

Fortunately, the terminal lugs illustrated in Fig. 23 eliminate these problems. These lugs may be soldered or crimped (with the right tool), or both. A good crimping tool compresses the top and bottom while keeping the sides from expanding, making a secure connection. Terminal lugs are available in different sizes; you'll get the best mechanical and electrical connection if you use the right size for your wire. Lugs are available with or without insulation. The uninsulated kind usually cost less, and you can use heat-shrink tubing after installation on the wire if insulation is necessary. The fully closed ring terminals will hold even if the screw works loose, but they require you to remove the screw completely from the block during installation. The U-shaped spade lugs are easier to install, requiring you only to remove the screw partially, but they may fall off if the screw loosens. The hook type combines the best qualities of the ring and space terminals.

Some common multi-pin connectors are illustrated in Fig. 24. The connector shown in Fig. 24A, often called a "Cinch-Jones plug," is frequently used for cabling between equipment and outboard power supplies. Supplying from two to eight or more conductors, these connectors are keyed to go together only one way. They offer a good electrical and mechanical connection, and the pins are large enough to handle high current. If your cable is too small for the strain relief, build up the outer jacket with a few layers of tape until the strain relief clamps down securely. Properly used, the strain relief will keep your wires from breaking away from the connector because of excessive flexing of the soldered joint or from a sudden tug on the cable.

The plug shown in Fig. 24B is usually called a "molex" connector. This device consists of an insulated outer shell, resembling a honeycomb, which houses many individual male or female "fingers." Each finger is individually soldered or crimped onto a conductor of the cable and then inserted into the shell, locking into place. These connectors are available for different wire sizes and are used on many brands of amateur gear for power and accessory interconnections.

Fig. 24C shows a DIN connector. Commonly available with five, seven or eight pins, these connectors are a European standard that have found favor with amateur equipment manufacturers the world over. They are generally used for accessory connectors.

The connector shown in Fig. 25 is a ¼-inch phone plug, often just called a phone plug. Usually used on amateur equipment for headphones and Morse key lines, phone plugs have two or three circuits. They are available with plastic and metal bodies. Besides offering a shielded connection, the metal-jacketed version is more durable — it won't break when stepped on!

Fig. 25 also shows a 1/8-inch phone plug, often called a miniature phone plug. Used for earphone, external speaker, key and control lines, mini-phone plugs are available in shielded and unshielded forms. An even smaller phone plug, the 1/16-inch, or subminiature, version is not common on amateur gear.

The phono, or RCA, plug illustrated in Fig. 26 is a favorite among amateurs. Phono plugs are found on amateur equipment for everything from amplifier relay control lines, to low-voltage power lines, to low-level RF lines, to antenna lines.

Several styles of phono plugs are available, but the best choice for general use is the shielded type with a screw-on metal body. These plugs are much easier to grip when plugging and unplugging; they are shielded, and more durable.

Microphone connectors seem to change with the wind, and the two most popular types used today are shown in Fig. 27. At one time, microphone connectors used three conductors — one for audio, one for the PTT switch, and one for ground. Today's microphone connectors offer four or eight conductors. In many rigs, the PTT switch does not short to a common ground, but rather closes two contacts independent of ground. Some manufacturers offer a limited amount of frequency control — UP and DOWN — from switches on the mic, while others use a preamplifier in the microphone that derives its power from the rig; hence the move to eight-conductor mic connectors. When hooking up a mic to your rig, consult the manual. You should be aware of the manufacturer's recommended wiring for best results.

Some amateurs own more than one rig but have only one mic. Rather than lopping off the connector at each rig change, you can make adapters with short pieces of cable that route the signals from one mic to the right pins for several rigs. Check your local dealer; you may be surprised at the variety of male and female mic connectors available.

RF Connectors

There are many different types of RF connectors for coaxial cable on the market, but the three most common for amateur use are the UHF, Type N and BNC families. The type of connector used for a specific job depends on the size of the cable, the frequency of operation and the power levels involved.

The UHF connector is found on most HF and some VHF equipment. It is the only connector many hams will ever see on coaxial cable. PL-259 is another name for the UHF male, and the female is also known as the SO-239. These connectors are rated for full legal amateur power at HF. They are poor for UHF work because they do not present a constant impedance, so the UHF label is a misnomer. PL-259 connectors are designed to fit RG-8 and RG-11 size cable (0.405-in OD). Adapters are available for use with RG-58 and RG-59 size cable. UHF connectors are not weatherproof.

Fig. 28 shows how to install the solder type of PL-259 on RG-8 type cable. Proper preparation of the cable end is the key to success. Follow these simple steps. Measure back about ¾-inch from the cable end and slightly score the outer jacket around its circumference. With a sharp knife, cut through the outer jacket, through the braid, and through the dielectric, right down to the center conductor. Be careful

Fig. 25 — The phone-plug family. The ¼-inch type is often used for headphone and key connections on amateur equipment. The three-circuit version is used with stereo headphones. The mini phone plug is commonly used for connecting external speakers to receivers and transceivers. A submini-phone plug is shown in the foreground for comparison. The shielded style with metal barrel is more durable than the plastic style.

Fig. 26 — Phono plugs have countless uses around the shack. They are small and shielded; the type with the metal body is easy to grip. Be careful not to use too much heat when soldering the ground (outer) conductor — you may melt the insulation.

Fig. 27 — The four-pin mic connector is common on modern transmitters and receivers. More elaborate rigs use the eight-pin type. The extra conductors may be used for switches to remotely control the frequency or to power a preamplifier built into the mic case.

not to score the center conductor. Cutting through all outer layers at once keeps the braid from separating. Pull the severed outer jacket, braid and dielectric off the end of the cable as one piece. Inspect the area around the cut, looking for any strands of braid hanging loose, and snip them off. There won't be any if your knife was sharp enough. Next, score the outer jacket about 5/16-in back from the first cut. Cut through the jacket lightly; do not

Fig. 28 — The PL-259, or UHF, connector is almost universal for amateur HF work and is popular for equipment operating in the VHF range. Steps A through E are described in detail in the text.

83-58FCP

1. Strip cable — *don't nick braid, dielectric or conductor*. Slide ferrule, then coupling ring on cable. Flare braid slightly by rotating conductor and dielectric in circular motion.

2. Slide body on dielectric, barb going under braid until flange is against outer jacket. Braid will fan out against body flange.

3. Slide nut over body. Grasp cable with hand and push ferrule over barb until braid is captured between ferrule and body flange. Squeeze crimp tip only of center contact with pliers; alternate-solder tip.

83-1SP (PL-259) PLUG WITH ADAPTERS (UG-176/U OR UG-175/U)

1) Cut end of cable even. Remove vinyl jacket 3/4" — don't nick braid. Slide coupling ring and adapter on cable.

2) Fan braid slightly and fold back over cable.

3) Position adapter to dimension shown. Press braid down over body of adapter and trim to 3/8". Bare 5/8" of conductor. Tin exposed center conductor.

4) Screw the plug assembly on adapter. Solder braid to shell through solder holes. Solder conductor to contact sleeve.

5) Screw coupling ring on plug assembly.

Fig. 29 — Crimp-on connectors and adapters for use with standard PL-259 connectors are popular for connecting to RG-58 and RG-59 type cable. This material courtesy of Amphenol Electronic Components, RF Division, Bunker Ramo Corp.

score the braid. This step takes practice. If you score the braid, start again. Remove the outer jacket.

Tin the exposed braid and center conductor, but apply the solder sparingly and avoid melting the dielectric. Slide the cou-pling ring onto the cable. Screw the connector body onto the cable. If you prepared the cable to the right dimensions, the center conductor will protrude through the center pin, the braid will show through the solder holes, and the body will actually thread onto the outer cable jacket.

Solder the braid through the solder holes. Solder through all four holes; poor connection to the braid is the most common form of PL-259 failure. A good connection between connector and braid is just as important as that between center conductor and connector. Use a large soldering iron for this job. With practice, you'll learn how much heat to use. If you use too little heat, the solder will bead up, not really flowing onto the connector body. If you use too much heat, the dielectric will melt, letting the braid and center conductor touch. Most PL-259s are nickel plated, but there are available slightly more expensive connectors with silver-plated bodies. These are much easier to solder.

Solder the center conductor to the center pin. The solder should flow on the inside, not the outside of the center pin. If you wait until the connector body cools off from soldering the braid, you'll have less trouble with the dielectric melting. Trim the

center conductor to be even with the end of the center pin. Use a small file to round the end, removing any solder that built up on the outer surface of the center pin. Use a sharp knife, very fine sandpaper or steel wool to remove any solder flux from the outer surface of the center pin. Screw the coupling onto the body, and you're finished.

Fig. 29 shows two options available if you want to use RG-58 or RG-59 size cable with PL-259 connectors. The crimp-on connectors manufactured specially for the smaller cable work very well if installed correctly. The alternative method involves using adapters for the smaller cable with standard RG-8 size PL-259s. Prepare the cable as shown. Once the braid is prepared,

screw the adapter into the PL-259 shell and finish the job as you would a PL-259 on RG-8 cable.

The BNC connectors illustrated in Fig. 30 are popular for low power levels at VHF and UHF. They accept RG-58 and RG-59 cable, and are available for cable mounting in both male and female versions. There are several different styles available, so be sure to use the dimensions for the type you have. Follow the installation instructions carefully. If you prepare the cable to the wrong dimensions, the center pin will not seat properly with connectors of the opposite sex. Sharp scissors are a big help for trimming the braid evenly. Properly assembled, BNC connectors are weatherproof.

BNC CONNECTORS

Standard Clamp

1. Cut cable and even. Strip jacket. Fray braid and strip dielectric. *Don't nick braid or center conductor.* Tin center conductor.

2. Taper braid. Slide nut, washer, gasket and clamp over braid. Clamp inner shoulder should fit squarely against end of jacket.

3. With clamp in place, comb out braid, fold back smooth as shown. Trim center conductor.

4. Solder contact on conductor through solder hole. Contact should butt against dielectric. Remover excess solder from outside of contact. Avoid excess heat to prevent swollen dielectric which would interfere with connector body.

5. Push assembly into body. Screw nut into body with wrench until tight. *Don't rotate body on cable to tighten.*

Improved Clamp

Follow 1, 2, 3 and 4 in BNC connectors (standard clamp) except as noted. Strip cable as shown. Slide gasket on cable *with groove facing clamp.* Slide clamp on cable *with sharp edge facing gasket.* Clamp *should* cut gasket to seal properly.

C. C. Clamp

1) Follow steps 1, 2 and 3 as outlined for the standard-clamp BNC connector.

2) Slide on the bushing, rear insulator and contact. The parts must butt securely against each other, as shown.

3) Solder the center conductor to the contact. Remove flux and excess solder.

4) Slide the front insulator over the contact, making sure it butts against the contact shoulder.

5) Insert the prepared cable end into the connector body and tighten the nut. Make sure that the sharp edge of the clamp seats properly in the gasket.

Fig. 30 — BNC connectors are common on VHF and UHF equipment at low power levels. (courtesy Amphenol Electronic Components, RF Division, Bunker Ramo Corp.)

The Type N connector, illustrated in Fig. 31, is a must for high-power VHF and UHF operation. N connectors are available in male and female versions for cable mounting and are designed for RG-8 size cable. Unlike UHF connectors, they are designed to maintain a constant impedance at cable joints. Like BNC connectors, it is important to prepare the cable to the right dimensions. The center pin must be positioned correctly to mate with the center pin of connectors of the opposite sex. Use the right dimensions for the connector style you have. These connectors are weatherproof.

Computer Connectors

Adding computer equipment to your shack introduces you to many potentially confusing connectors. Most of the connections between computers and their peripheral equipment are made with multi-conductor ribbon cable (Fig. 32), with 10 or more individual conductors. Although the computer industry has tried to standardize connectors, there are dozens of types of connectors in use. Some of the common ribbon cable connectors are shown in Fig. 33. Fortunately, these connectors can be divided into three categories, based on how they are attached to ribbon cable: insulation displacement, solder-type and crimp-type.

TYPE N CONNECTORS

Standard Clamp

NUT   WASHER SPREAD   GASKET   CLAMP

FEMALE CONTACT   JACK BODY

MALE CONTACT   PLUG BODY

1) Cut cable and even. Remove 9/16″ of vinyl jacket. When using double-shielded cable remove 5/8″.

2) Comb out copper braid as shown. Cut off dielectric 7/32″ from end. Tin center conductor.

3) Taper braid as shown. Slide nut, washer and gasket over vinyl jacket. Slide clamp over braid with internal shoulder of clamp flush against end of vinyl jacket. When assembling connectors with gland, be sure knife-edge is toward end of cable and groove in gasket is toward the gland.

4) Smooth braid back over clamp and trim. Soft-solder contact to center conductor. Avoid use of excessive heat and solder. See that end of dielectric is clean. Contact must be flush against dielectric. Outside of contact must be free of solder. Female contact is shown; procedure is similar for male contact.

5) Slide body into place carefully so that contact enters hole in insulator (male contact shown). Face of dielectric must be flush against insulator. Slide completed assembly into body by pushing nut. When nut is in place, tighten with wrenches. In connectors with gland, knife edge should cut gasket in half by tightening sufficiently.

Improved Clamp

1) Follow instructions 1 through 4 as detailed in the standard clamp (be sure to use the correct dimensions).

2) Slide the body over the prepared cable end. Make sure the sharp edges of the clamp seat properly in the gasket. Tighten the nut.

C. C. Clamp

1) Follow instructions 1 through 3 as outlined for the standard-clamp Type N connector.

2) Slide on the washer, rear insulator and contact. The parts must butt securely against each other.

3) Solder the center conductor to the contact. Remove flux and excess solder.

4) Slide the front insulator over the contact, making sure it butts against the contact shoulder.

5) Insert the prepared cable end into the connector body and tighten the nut. Make sure the sharp edge of the clamp seats properly in the gasket.

Fig. 31 — Type N connectors are a must for high-power VHF and UHF operation. (courtesy Amphenol Electronic Components, RF Division, Bunker Ramo.)

Fig. 32 — Ribbon cable with various numbers of conductors is used to interconnect computer equipment.

Fig. 33 — Various computer connectors.

Fig. 34 — Insulation displacement type connector (IDC). See text for details.

Fig. 35 — Installation of ribbon cable on an IDC. See text for details.

Insulation Displacement Connectors

An insulation displacement connector (IDC) has three parts: the body, the cover and the strain-relief clamp (Fig. 34). On the body of an IDC there are one or more rows of metal clips — one clip for each conductor in the connector. When ribbon cable is pressed on to the body of the connector, each clip cuts through the insulation around one of the ribbon cable conductors, making contact to that conductor (Fig. 35). The IDC cover applies even pressure during installation of the connector, and clamps the connector in place during use. Some IDCs are also provided with strain-relief clamps so that strain on the cable will not be transferred to the insulation-displacing clips.

To install an IDC, select the appropriate ribbon cable; place it on the back of the connector, making sure each conductor is in the jaws of one of the clips; place the cover on the connector and apply sufficient pressure to seat the cover. Use a vice to apply even pressure across the cover. If the connector has a strain-relief clamp, route the cable through the clamp, as shown in Fig. 36.

IDCs are the easiest ribbon cable connectors to install. If there is an IDC available for your application, use it.

Solder-Type Connectors

Each conductor from the ribbon cable must be soldered to a tap or post in solder-type connectors (Fig. 37). Use a razor or sidecutters to separate the conductors of the ribbon cable by cutting the insulation parallel to and between the conductors. The length of cable that should be separated into individual conductors will depend on the width of the cable and the width of the connector. Assure yourself that each conductor will reach the correct pin on the connector. Once you have separated the conductors, strip and tin each one. Then solder the conductors to the appropriate pins. Use good soldering techniques.

Crimp-Type Connectors

Each conductor in the cable is crimped to a contact; the contacts are inserted into a plastic housing (Fig. 38). The contacts can be either male (plugs) or female (sockets). Preparing ribbon cable for a crimp-type connector is the same as preparing cable for solder-type connectors, except that the stripped conductors should not be tinned. Insert each conductor into a contact and crimp the contact closed around the conductor. Properly crimped contacts should provide secure mechanical and electrical connections. Unfortunately, proper crimping is hard to achieve without the appropriate, expensive crimping tool. Therefore, many amateurs solder wires to crimp type contacts. If you choose to do this, use good soldering technique and be sure not to fill the locking tab(s) on the contact with solder.

Fig. 36 — Completed IDC with ribbon cable, showing proper strain-relief.

Fig. 37 — Solder-type DB-25 connector and prepared ribbon cable.

Fig. 38 — Crimp-type connector with prepared ribbon cable.

Once the contacts are attached to the cable, use a pair of pliers to insert them in the housing. With some connectors you must be sure that the locking tab on the contact will engage the locking slot on the housing. If you insert the contacts backward, the locking tab will prevent complete insertion of the contact.

Computer cabling is often complicated. Time spent on proper selection and installation of connectors will be paid back in time saved on troubleshooting and recabling.

ROUTING ANTENNA CABLES

Once you have interconnected the equipment in your station, the next step is getting transmission lines, rotator cables and control lines outside to the devices at the other end. The exact method you use will depend on the location of your station and the construction of your house. Use the information presented here for ideas for your station.

The run from the shack to the antennas should be as short as possible to minimize feed-line loss and control-cable voltage drop. The most direct route may be to open a window and run the cables outside. Fig. 39 shows a way to do this and still seal your house against the weather (and bugs). Apply a piece of thick foam weatherstripping to the lower sash bottom rail and another to the sill. Adhesive-backed weatherstripping is available in various sizes at hardware stores. For this job, the thicker the better. The foam not only seals the area around the cables, but also protects the cables from being crushed or cut by the window.

On many double-hung windows, meeting rails on the top and bottom sashes no longer meet with the window partially open, so more weatherstripping is needed to seal the gap. You'll also have to devise another way to lock the window. Blocks of wood between the sash and sill will do the trick. Running cables through open windows leaves something to be desired in terms of weatherproofing and security, but

Fig. 40 — A window pane may be replaced with an acrylic sheet and then drilled to pass cables.

it is easy and leaves no permanent scars on the house.

Another popular approach is to replace a glass window pane with material that can be drilled, such as acrylic or aluminum sheet. Fig. 40 shows how to run cables through a window with one glass pane replaced by acrylic sheet. Each piece of coaxial cable from the antennas connects to a double-female bulkhead connector. Bulkhead connectors are similar to double-female barrel connectors except they are longer and the outer body is threaded to accept nuts. UHF and Type N bulkhead connectors are commonly available at electronics part stores. Rotator and other control cables are run through holes in the window just large enough to clear the outer jacket. If additional weatherproofing is needed, run a bead of silicone seal around the cable jacket or use a grommet of the right dimensions. The multiconductor cable runs directly to a terminal strip; from there, another wire runs to the control box. Open-wire line or single conductors may be run safely through the window using ceramic feedthrough insulators. This method offers a neat, weatherproof way to run cables between your station and antennas. The original window pane may be reinstalled at any time, so there are no permanent scars. The only drawback is that you may lose the use of the window.

Fig. 41 shows how to use a dryer vent pipe to bring cables into a house. The vent pipe may be installed in a hole bored through the wall of the house, or it may be mounted in an acrylic or aluminum replacement window pane. The vent pipe hood keeps rain out of the tube, and a bead of caulk around the outside of the tube where it passes through the wall completes weather sealing. A standard three-inch vent pipe will pass more than enough cables for the average amateur station. The vent-pipe approach does not require cables to be broken, and the number of cables may be changed at any time without drilling more holes. For the VHF/UHF operator, it allows a continuous run of hardline from the antenna to the station. It's a good idea

to stuff the pipe with insulation after installing the cables to keep small animals and insects out of the house and heat in.

DOCUMENTING YOUR STATION

An often neglected but very important part of putting together your station is properly documenting your work. Ideally, you should diagram your entire station from the ac power lines to the antenna on paper and keep the information in a special notebook with sections for the various facets of your installation. Having the station well documented is an invaluable aid when tracking down a problem or planning a modification. Rather than having to search your memory for information on what you did a long time ago, you'll have the facts on hand. The best time to prepare your notes is as you're building, so take a few minutes at each step to record your progress.

When documenting your shack, include information such as the type, size and length of the primary wiring, as well as the value of circuit breakers or fuses. Keep track of your cables. Write down the pinouts of the various plugs and connectors joining your equipment, including

Fig. 39 — Many amateurs run their cables through an open double-hung window. The window should be sealed against the weather.

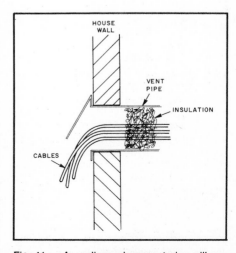

Fig. 41 — An ordinary dryer vent pipe will pass a large number of cables.

microphone cables, keyer wiring and control circuitry. If a piece of equipment has more than one possible hookup configuration (say, for example, high or low impedance for a microphone or 117 or 234 V for a transformer), note which connections you used as well as the ones you didn't. For multiconductor cables, make a list of the colors of the wires and their functions.

Documenting your antenna system is especially important. For towers, make and keep drawings of the entire installation. Include sketches with measurements of such things as the tower base and guy anchors. Write down your guy-wire lengths. If you break your guys into non-resonant lengths with insulators, note the lengths of the individual sections for each set of wires. Knowing what you have in the present installation will make repairing or upgrading the tower much easier in the future.

Make a list of the bolt sizes used for the tower, rotator, mast and antenna(s). List the wrench size required for all hardware. This way, you'll know which wrenches to take along for a specific job. For example, to remove your rotator for repair, you may need a 7/16-in wrench to remove the U-bolts securing the mast and a ½-in wrench for the bolts holding the rotator housing to the mounting plate. If you guess and take the wrong size, you'll have to make additional unnecessary trips up and down the tower. If you bring along all of your tools for a job requiring only one or two wrenches, you'll weigh yourself down and the climb will be harder than necessary.

If your diagram of the mast and antenna(s) includes the size of the mast and the spacing between antennas (if you have more than one on the same mast), you'll be better prepared to add or change antennas in the future. You'll be able to fabricate boom-to-mast clamps on the ground and hoist them up the tower with the confidence that you'll have to do the job only once — the hardware will fit perfectly. By knowing how much mast is sticking out of the top of the tower, you'll know, for example,

whether or not you can replace an antenna that has a self-supporting boom with another requiring a specific number of feet of mast for a boom brace. If you know the distance between antennas, you'll be able to determine if an additional antenna on the mast is feasible. Having the measurements on hand takes the guesswork out of many jobs and saves unnecessary trips up and down the tower to make new measurements every time you want to make a change.

Cables and connectors are worth documenting as well. As you build your antenna system, note the length and type of each piece of feed line, rotator and control cable used. Document the type of connectors used. Be sure to write down the color code used for the rotator cable; if some day you disconnect the control box in the shack and don't have the codes in your notebook, you'll have to climb the tower to find out how they go. If you know the lengths of your cables and the types of connectors used, it will be a great help in troubleshooting. You will be able to prepare test and/or replacement cables before leaving the ground.

Besides documenting the interconnections and hardware around your station, you should also keep track of the performance of your equipment. There are many different performance tests you can make, and what you do will depend on your technical ability and the test equipment on hand. There are, however, some basic tests that almost every amateur can make. Each time you install a new antenna, measure the SWR at different points in the band and make a table or plot a curve. Later, if you suspect a problem, you'll be able to look in your records and compare your SWR with the original performance. You might also want to measure the loss of each piece of feed line before installation. Most feed line degrades with time, so again you'll have a benchmark to compare with if you have a problem later. This measurement is easy; just terminate the feed line with a dummy load, and compare the power

measured at the transmitter end with that measured at the dummy load.

In your shack, you can measure the power output from your transmitter(s) and amplifier(s) on each band. These measurements will be helpful if you later suspect you have a problem, such as your rig going out of alignment. They will also help you see when your tubes start to go soft. For receivers, it may be helpful to turn on the crystal calibrator and note the S-meter reading on various bands. The calibrator output is fairly constant, so future S-meter readings different from the original ones may indicate alignment or other problems. Of course, if you have access to a signal generator you can measure receiver performance for future reference.

As part of your station records, keep a maintenance log showing details of any repairs or modifications to your gear. For modifications, make a copy of the schematic and add in changes on the copy. You can scrape traces from a photocopy with a sharp knife and draw in the new lines and/or components. Also, write down the details and keep a copy of any literature pertaining to it (a magazine article or manufacturer's update note, for example). If you do any before/after testing, note your results.

Keep a list of purchases of station equipment. Include the serial number, price paid, date of purchase, and name and address of the seller. If you purchased the gear new from a dealer, this information should appear on the invoice. These records will come in handy at resale time. It's also advisable to have this information for insurance purposes, should anything happen to your equipment.

Station documentation can be as formal or informal as you like. Some amateurs will keep a file drawer with folders for the various aspects of the station. Others will keep a three-ring notebook separated into several sections. If you keep the documentation simple, you will be more likely to do it, and good records are very helpful.

Assembling Your Antenna System

The antenna system is one area where amateurs have considerable room for experimentation. No two antenna systems are alike, and the shape yours takes will depend on the amount of land available, your resources and your interests. Your antenna system might consist of a multiband dipole, or you might want to chase DX and work contests with monoband beams installed on individual towers. The antenna system is your chance to be creative.

The information presented here explains some of the methods used to put antennas into the air and keep them there. Information on antenna design is covered in Chapter 17, while antenna construction is presented in Chapter 33. The *ARRL Antenna Book* is another good source of information on antenna theory and construction. This section assumes that you have an antenna in mind or assembled and are looking for ideas on how to support it.

SUPPORTING WIRE ANTENNAS

The antenna can be supported at the ends by buildings, trees or anything you may be able to use. Later in this chapter, there is information on putting up poles and masts. A mast may be the real answer to holding up at least one end of the antenna. Many operators fasten one end of the antenna to the house, or to a short pole on the roof, and build a mast far enough away to permit using the desired antenna length. The

spot for the mast can be chosen so the antenna will be in the clear.

You can slope the antenna wire if your two supports aren't the same height. A sloping antenna usually will radiate best in the direction of the downslope. You can take advantage of this effect by deliberately sloping the wire to get a desired "best" direction.

Trees as Antenna Supports

From the beginning of Amateur Radio, trees have been used widely for supporting wire antennas. Trees cost nothing, of course, and will often provide a means of supporting a wire antenna at considerable height. As an antenna support, however, a tree is highly unstable in the presence of wind, unless the tree is a very large one and the antenna is suspended from a point well down on the tree trunk. As a result, the antenna must be constructed much more sturdily than would be necessary with stable supports. Even with rugged construction, it is unlikely that an antenna suspended from a tree, or between trees, will stand up indefinitely.

There are two general methods of securing a pulley to a tree. If the tree can be climbed safely to the desired level, a pulley can be wired to the trunk of the tree, as shown in Fig. 42. If, after passing the halyard through the pulley, both ends of the halyard are simply brought back down to ground along the trunk of the tree, there may be difficulty in bringing the antenna end of the halyard out where it will be clear of branches. To avoid this, one end of the halyard can be tied temporarily to the tree at the pulley level, while the remainder of the halyard is coiled up, and the coil thrown out horizontally from this level, in the direction in which the antenna will run. It may help to have the antenna end of the halyard weighted. Then, after attaching the antenna to the halyard, the other end is untied from the tree, passed through the pulley, and brought to ground along the tree trunk in as straight a line as possible. The halyard need be only long enough to reach the ground after the antenna has been hauled up, since additional rope can be tied

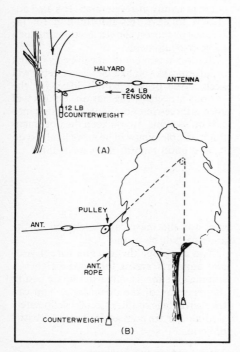

Fig. 42 — Methods of counterweighting to minimize antenna movement. The method at A limits the fall of the counterweight should the antenna break. It also has a 2 to 1 mechanical advantage, as indicated. The method at B has the disadvantage that the point of support in the tree must be higher than the end of the antenna.

to the halyard when it becomes necessary to lower the antenna. The other method consists of passing a line over the tree from ground level, and using this line to haul a pulley up into the tree and hold it there. Several ingenious methods have been used to accomplish this. The simplest method employs a weighted pilot line, such as fishing line or mason's chalk line. Grasping the line about 2 feet from the weight, the weight is swung back and forth, pendulum style, and then heaved with an underhand motion in the direction of the tree top. Several trials may be necessary to determine the optimum size of the weight for the line selected, the distance between the weight and the hand before throwing, and the point in the arc of the swing where the line is released. The weight, however, must be sufficiently large to ensure that it will carry the pilot line back to ground after passing over the tree. Flipping the end of the line up and down so as to put a traveling wave on the line often helps to induce the weight to drop down if the weight is marginal. The higher the tree, the lighter the weight and the pilot line must be. A glove should be worn on the throwing hand, because a line running swiftly through the bare hand can cause a severe burn.

If there is a clear line of sight between ground and a particularly desirable crotch in the tree, it may be possible to hit the crotch eventually after a sufficient number of tries. Otherwise, it is best to try to heave the pilot line completely over the tree, as close to the center line of the tree as possible. If it is necessary to retrieve the line and start over again, let the weighted end drop to the ground and pull the pilot line through the tree. If you pull the weight back through the tree, it may wrap the line around a small limb, making retrieval impossible.

Stretching the line out in a straight line on the ground before throwing may help to keep the line from snarling, but it places extra drag on the line, and the line may snag on obstructions overhanging the line when it is thrown. Another method is to make a stationary reel by driving eight nails, arranged in a circle, through a 1-inch board. After winding the line around the circle formed by the nails, the line should reel off readily when the weighted end of the line is thrown. The board should be tilted at approximately right angles to the path of the throw.

Other devices that have been used successfully to pass a pilot line over a tree are the bow and arrow with heavy thread tied to the arrow, and the short casting rod and spinning reel used by fishermen. Still another method that has been used where sufficient space is available is to fly a kite. After the kite has reached sufficient altitude, simply walk around the tree until the kite string lines up with the center of the tree. Then pay out string until the kite falls to the earth. This method has been used

Fig. 43 — In connecting the halyard to the pilot line, a large knot that might snag in the crotch of a tree should be avoided, as shown.

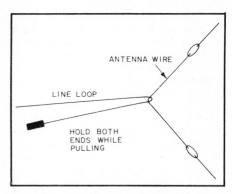

Fig. 44 — A weighted line thrown over the antenna can be used to pull the antenna to one side to avoid overhanging obstructions, such as branches of trees in the path of the antenna, as the antenna is pulled up. When the obstruction has been cleared, the line can be removed by releasing one end.

successfully to pass a line over a patch of woods between two higher supports, which would have been impossible using any other method.

The pilot line can be used to pull successively heavier lines over the tree until one of adequate size to take the strain of the antenna has been reached. This line is then used to haul a pulley up into the tree after the antenna halyard has been threaded through the pulley. The line that holds the pulley must be capable of withstanding considerable chafing where it passes through the crotch, and at points where lower branches may rub against the standing part. For this reason, it may be advisable to use galvanized sash cord or stranded guy wire for raising the pulley.

Especially with larger sizes of line or cable, care must be taken when splicing the pilot line to the heavier line to use a splice that will minimize the chances that the splice cannot be coaxed through the tree crotch. One type of splice is shown in Fig. 43.

The crotch which the line first comes to rest in may not be sufficiently strong to stand up under the tension of the antenna. However, if the line has been passed over, or close to, the center line of the tree, it will usually break through the lighter crotches and finally come to rest in one sufficiently strong lower down on the tree.

Needless to say, any of the suggested

methods should be used with due respect to persons or property in the immediate vicinity. A child's sponge-rubber ball (baseball size) makes a safe weight for heavy thread line or fishing line.

If the antenna wire becomes snagged in lower branches of the tree when the wire is pulled up, or if branches of other trees in the vicinity interfere with raising the antenna, a weighted line thrown over the antenna and slid along to the appropriate point is often helpful in pulling the antenna wire to one side to clear the interference as the antenna is being raised, as shown in Fig. 44.

Wind Compensation

The movement of an antenna suspended

Fig. 45 — The cleat helps you avoid having to untie a knot that may have been weather-hardened.

Fig. 46 — Using a length of 2 × 3 as a support for a horizontal antenna. Lengths up to 20 feet can be used with a single set of guys arranged as shown.

between supports that are not stable in wind can be reduced materially by the use of heavy springs, such as screen-door springs under tension, or by a counter-weight at the end of one halyard, as shown in Fig. 42. The weight, which may be made up of junk-yard metal, window sash weights, or a galvanized pail filled with sand or stone, should be adjusted experimentally for best results under existing conditions. Fig. 45 shows a convenient way of fastening the counterweight to the halyard. It avoids the necessity for untying a knot in the halyard which may have hardened under tension and exposure to the weather.

Man-Made Supports

In practice, a height of 30 to 60 feet is in the optimum region for any band above 7 MHz where the ionosphere plays a part.

You can get by with even less than 30 feet if you have to. However, nearly everyone can put an antenna at least 25 feet or so in the air. This height puts it in the class where, usually, at least one end can be supported by your house. The other end can be held up by another building (if you have permission to use it) far enough away, or by a tree, or if necessary by a pole you put up yourself. The pole doesn't have to be an elaborate structure, especially if it can be erected on top of something. A detached garage makes a good base. It should give you a start of 12 to 15 feet, and generally will have enough roof area to let you put guys on a simple wood pole that can be up to 20 feet tall. It is important to realize that antennas with horizontal polarity should be one-half wavelength or more above ground for best results in long-distance communications.

Anchoring

Wire antennas are not heavy, and even when pulled up tight the strain can easily be supported by a husky screw eye or hook, if it can be sunk 1½ or 2 inches into good solid wood. Screw eyes can be used similarly for anchoring guy wires from light poles up to 20 feet long. Often other anchorages for guy wires offer themselves; use anything that seems solid enough and which gives you the opportunity for wrapping the wire around a couple of times so it won't slip.

A length of 2 × 3 makes a good pole for heights up to 20 feet or so. It isn't heavy, but with three solidly anchored guys it will hold any wire antenna you may use with it. Fig. 46 shows a simple type of construction, using fittings that you can buy at a hardware store. The pulley and halyard make it possible to raise and lower the antenna easily. With the antenna up, only two guys are really necessary, placed 90 to 120 degrees apart back of the antenna, as shown at B and C. The third guy, A, can be part way down the pole so it will be out of the way of the pulley and halyard, and should pull off in about the same direction as the antenna. Its purpose is to hold the

pole up when the antenna is down.

The guys can simply be wrapped around the pole near the top. One is shown in the drawing. To keep them from slipping down they can be run through a screw eye as shown. This avoids putting any strain on the screw eye. Stranded steel wire available in hardware stores (a typical type has four strands of about the same diameter as no. 18 copper) has ample strength for guying a pole of this type. Guy wire also is available from radio supply houses.

Plastic clothesline can be used for the halyard. The plastic kind stands the weather better than ordinary cotton clothesline. If you do use cotton, get the type having a steel core; it has greater strength and lasting qualities. But whatever type you use, be sure to use enough. Remember that you need to be able to reach the free end of the halyard when the antenna is down!

Insulating Guy Wires

Guy wires are like antenna wires — if their length happens to be near resonance at your operating frequency, they can pick up energy from the antenna field and re-radiate it. This may do no harm, but then again it might distort the radiation pattern you hope the antenna will give.

To circumvent this, guy wires are often "broken up" by inserting insulators at strategic points. The idea is to avoid letting any section of guy wire have a length that is near resonance at any operating frequency or harmonic of it. Egg-type insulators are generally used as a safety measure. With these insulators the wires are looped around each other so that if the insulator breaks the guy wire will still hold.

General practice is to put an egg in each guy a foot or so from where it is attached to the pole or mast, and another a foot or so from the point where it is anchored. Whether any more are needed depends on the remaining length. In most cases it is sufficient to insert insulators in such a way that no section of the wire will have a length in feet that can be divided evenly by 16 or 22.

Guy Anchors

Trees or buildings at the right distance from the base of a mast can be used for anchoring guys. However, they don't always "just happen" to be present. In such a case a guy anchor can be sunk into the ground.

A 6-foot length of 1-inch iron pipe driven into the ground at about a 45-degree angle makes a good anchor. It should be driven toward the mast, with 12 to 18 inches protruding from the ground for fastening the wires. Fig. 47 shows the general idea, with a suggested way of fastening the guy so it can't slip off the anchor.

Weather Protection

A wooden mast or pole needs the same protection against weather as the exterior woodwork on a dwelling. New wood

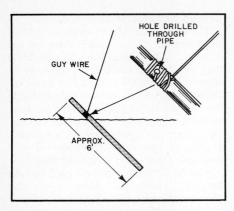

Fig. 47 — Pipe guy anchor. One-inch or 1½-inch iron pipe is satisfactory for a mast such as is shown in Fig. 46.

should be given three coats of a good paint made for outdoor use, with the first coat thinned so it sinks in well. Follow the directions on the paint container.

Masts made from several pieces of lumber should have their individual parts painted separately before assembly. The heads of nails or screws should be sunk into the surface far enough so they can be puttied over. These, too, should be painted — after assembly. Hooks, screw eyes and similar hardware should likewise have a coat of paint to prevent rusting.

Other Types of Masts

Amateur ingenuity has conjured up all sorts of mast and tower designs over the years. It is possible, for example, to make a satisfactory pole, 40 feet or so high, out of lengths of metal down-spouting. Wooden lattice construction has long been a favorite for masts and towers. A number of such designs will be found in *The ARRL Antenna Book*, and new ones keep coming along regularly in *QST*. Then there are TV masts, built up in sections of metal tubing and provided with guy rings and other hardware — readily available and not at all costly. These can be run up to heights as great as 50 feet, with proper guying.

In fact, anything you can put up, and that will stay up, will be satisfactory. Never forget that you can't afford to take any chances with safety. A falling mast can result in accidental injury, or even death, to anyone that happens to be in its path. The taller and heavier the mast, the more necessary it becomes to build in plenty of safety factor — in size of guy wire, type of anchorage, and in the strength and cross section of the materials used in the mast or tower itself.

TOWERS

A mast is fine for supporting one end of a wire antenna, or a small vertical, or even a small VHF/UHF beam, but the right way to support an HF beam or a large VHF/UHF array is with a communications tower designed for this purpose. The infor-

mation in this section is intended to help you choose the right type of tower for your needs, provide information on erecting the tower, and present some ideas on getting the antenna to the top.

Working on towers and antennas is dangerous, and possibly fatal, if you do not know what you are doing. Your tower and antenna can cause serious property damage and personal injury if any part of the installation should fail. Always use the highest quality materials in your system. Follow the manufacturer's specifications, paying close attention to base pier and guying details. Do not overload the tower. If you have any doubts about your ability to work on your tower and antennas safely, contact another amateur with experience in this area or seek professional assistance.

Information on antenna theory appears in Chapter 17. Practical antenna construction projects are presented in Chapter 33. Information on making the cables to connect your antennas, rotator cables and control lines appears earlier in this chapter. *The ARRL Antenna Book* is an excellent source of antenna information, and *QST* regularly features articles on antennas.

TOOLS

Any mechanical job is easier if you have the right tools. Tower work is no exception. In addition to a good assortment of wrenches, screwdrivers and pliers, you will need some specialized tools to work safely and efficiently on a tower. You may already own some of these tools. Others will be purchased or borrowed. Do not start a job until you have assembled all of the necessary tools. Shortcuts or improvised tools can be fatal if you gamble and lose at 50 feet in the air.

Clothing

The clothing you wear when working on towers and antennas should be selected for maximum comfort and safety. Wear clothing that will keep you warm, yet allows complete freedom of movement. Long denim pants and long-sleeve shirts will protect you from scrapes and cuts. Wear work shoes with heavy soles, or better yet steel inserts in the soles, to give your feet the support they need to stand on a narrow tower rung.

Gloves are necessary for both the tower climber and all ground-crew members. Good quality leather gloves will protect hands from damage and keep them warm. They also offer protection and a better grip when you are handling rope.

Ground-crew members should have hard hats to protect them in case something falls from the tower. It is not uncommon for the tower climber to drop tools and hardware. A wrench dropped from 100 feet will bury itself several inches in soft ground; imagine what it might do to an unprotected skull.

Safety Belt and Climbing Accessories

Any amateur with a tower *must* own a

Fig. 48 — A good-quality safety belt is a requirement for working on a tower. The belt should contain a large steel loop for the strap snap. Leather loops at the rear of the belt are handy for holding tools. *(photo by K1WA)*

high-quality safety belt, such as the one shown in Fig. 48. Do not attempt to climb a tower, even a short distance, without a belt. The climbing belt is more than just a safety device for the experienced climber. It is a tool to free up both hands for work. The belt allows the climber to lean back away from the tower to reach bolts or connections. It also provides a solid surface to lean against to exert greater force when hoisting antennas into place.

A climber must trust his life to his safety belt. For this reason, nothing less than a professional-quality, commercially made, tested and approved safety belt is acceptable. Check the equipment suppliers list in Chapter 35 and the ads in *QST* for suppliers of climbing belts and accessories. Check your belt *before each use* for defects. If the belt or lanyard (tower strap) are cracked, frayed or worn in any way, destroy the damaged piece and replace it with a new one. You should never have to wonder if your belt will hold.

Along with your climbing belt, you should seriously consider the purchase of some climbing accessories. A canvas bucket is a great help for carrying tools and hardware up the tower. Two buckets, a large one for carrying tools and a smaller one for hardware, make it easier to find things when needed. A few extra snap hooks like those on the ends of your belt lanyard are useful for attaching tool bags and equipment to the tower at convenient spots. These hooks are better than using rope with knots in many cases because they can be hooked and unhooked with one hand.

Gorilla hooks, shown in Fig. 49, are especially useful for ascending and

Fig. 49 — Gorilla hooks are designed to keep the climber attached to the tower at all times when ascending and descending.

descending the tower. They attach to the belt and are hooked to the tower on alternating rungs as the climber progresses. With these hooks, the climber is secured to the tower at all times. Gorilla hooks were specially designed for amateur climbers by Avatar Magnetics (see Chapter 35 suppliers list).

Rope and Pulley

Every amateur who owns a tower should also own a good quality rope at least twice as long as the tower is tall. The rope is essential for safely erecting towers and installing antennas and cables. For most installations, a good quality ½-inch-diameter manila hemp rope will do the job, although a thicker rope is stronger and easier to handle. Some types of polypropylene rope are acceptable also; check the manufacturer's strength ratings. Nylon rope is not recommended because it tends to stretch and is difficult to fasten knots with.

Check your rope *before each use* for tearing or chafing. Do not attempt to use damaged rope; if it breaks with a tower section or antenna in mid-air, property damage and personal injury are likely results. If your rope should get wet, let it thoroughly air dry before putting it away.

A most-worthwhile purchase is a pulley like the one shown in Fig. 50. Use the right size pulley for your rope. Be sure that the pulley you purchase will not jam or bind as the rope passes through it.

The Gin Pole

The gin pole, shown in Fig. 51, is a handy device for working with tower sections and masts. This gin pole is designed to clamp onto one leg of Rohn No. 25 or

45 tower. The tubing, which is about 12 feet long, has a pulley on one end. A rope is routed through the tubing and over the pulley. When the gin pole is attached to the tower and the tubing extended into place, the rope may be used to haul tower sections or the mast into place. Fig. 52 shows the basic process.

Fig. 51 — A gin pole is a mechanical device that can be clamped to a tower leg to aid in the assembly of sections as well as the installation of the mast. The aluminum tubing extends through the clamp and may be slipped into position before the tubing clamp is tightened. A rope should be routed through the tubing and over the pulley mounted at the top.

Fig. 52 — The assembly of tower sections is made simple when a gin pole is used to lift each one into position. Note that the safety belts of both climbers are fastened below the pole, thereby preventing the strap from slipping over the top section. (*photo by K1WA*)

A gin pole can be expensive for an individual to buy, especially for a one-time tower installation. Often, local radio clubs own a gin pole for use by their members. Stores that sell tower sections to amateurs and commercial customers frequently will rent erection fixtures. If you attempt to make your own gin pole, use materials heavy enough for the job. Provide a means for securely clamping the pole to the tower. There are many cases on record where homemade gin poles have failed, sending tower sections crashing down amidst the ground crew.

When you use a gin pole, make every effort to keep the load as vertical as possible. Although gin poles are strong, you are asking for trouble if you apply too much lateral force.

SELECTING A TOWER

Probably the most important part of any Amateur Radio installation is the antenna system. It determines the effectiveness of the signal transmitted at a particular power level. In terms of dollar investment, the antenna provides double duty; while it can provide gain during transmitting periods (which can also be accomplished by increasing transmitter power), it has the same beneficial effect on received signals. Therefore, a tall support for a gain antenna that can be rotated is very desirable. This is especially true if DX contacts are of prime interest on the 20, 15 and 10-meter bands.

Of the two important features of an antenna system, height and antenna gain, height is usually considered the most important if the antenna is horizontally polarized. The typical amateur installation consists of a three-element triband beam (tribander) for 20, 15 and 10 meters mounted on a tower that may be as low as 25 or 30 feet, or as high as 65 or 70 feet. Some systems use large antennas on much taller towers.

The selection of a tower, its height and the type of antenna and rotator to be used all may seem like a complicated matter, particularly for the newcomer. These four aspects of an antenna system are interrelated, and one should consider the overall system before making any decisions as to a specific component. Perhaps the most important consideration for many amateurs is the effect of the antenna system on the surrounding environment. If plenty of space is available for a tower installation and there is little chance of the antenna irritating neighbors, the amateur is indeed fortunate. This amateur's limitations will be mostly financial. But for most, the size of the backyard, the effect of the system on the family members and neighbors, local ordinances, and the proximity of power lines and poles influence the overall selection of antenna components considerably.

The amateur must consider several practical limitations for installation:

1) A tower should never be installed in

Fig. 50 — A good quality rope and pulley are a must for anyone working on towers and antennas. This pulley is encased in wood so the rope cannot jump out of the pulley wheel and jam.

such a way that it could fall onto a neighbor's property.

2) The antenna must be located in such a position that *it cannot possibly tangle with power lines during normal operation*, or if a disastrous windstorm comes along.

3) Sufficient yard space must be available to position a guyed tower *properly*. The guy anchors should be between 60 and 80 percent of the tower height in distance from the base of the tower.

4) Provisions must' be made to keep neighborhood children from climbing the support.

5) Local ordinances should be checked to determine if any legal restrictions are on record.

Other important considerations are:

6) The total dollar value to be invested.

7) The size and weight of the antenna desired.

8) The overall yearly climate.

9) Ability of the owner to climb a fixed tower.

The selection of a tower support is usually dictated more by circumstances than by desire.

Once a decision has been tentatively made, the next step is to write to the manufacturer (several are listed in Table 7) and request a specification sheet. Meanwhile, lay out any guy anchor points needed to ensure that they will fit on the assigned property. The specification sheet for the tower should give a wind-load capability; an antenna can then be selected that will not overload it. If a tentative decision on the antenna type is made, a note to the antenna manufacturer giving the complete set of details for installation is not a bad idea. Be sure to give complete details of your plans, including all specifications of the antenna system planned. Remember, the manufacturer will not custom design a system directly for your needs, but may offer comments.

It is often very helpful to the novice tower installer to visit other local amateurs who have installed towers. Look over their hardware and ask questions. If possible, have a few local experienced amateurs look over your plans — before you commit yourself. They may be able to offer a great deal of help. If someone in your area is planning to install a tower and antenna system, be sure to offer your assistance. There is no substitute for experience when it comes to tower work, and your experience there may prove invaluable to you later.

The Tower

The most common variety of tower is the guyed tower made of stacked identical sections. The information in Fig. 53 is based on data taken from the Unarco-Rohn catalog. A list of tower manufacturers can be found in Table 7. Rohn calls for a maximum vertical separation between sets of guy wires of 35 feet for this series of tower. At A, the tower is 70 feet high, and there are two sets of evenly spaced guy wires. At B, the tower is 80 feet high, and there are three sets of evenly spaced guy wires. Exceeding the vertical spacing requirements could result in the tower buckling.

This may not seem like a reasonable possibility unless you understand the functioning of the guy wires. The guy wires restrain the tower against the force of the wind and translate the lateral force of the wind into a downward compression that forces the tower down onto the base. Normally, the manufacturers specify the initial tension in the guy wires. This is another force that is translated into the downward compression on the tower. If there are not enough guys and if they are not properly spaced, a heavy gust of wind may turn out to be the "straw that breaks the camel's back." Fig. 53C is an overhead view of a guyed tower. Manufacturers usually call

for equal angular spacing between guys. If it is necessary to deviate from this spacing, you would be well advised to contact the engineering staff of the manufacturer or a civil engineer.

Some types of towers are not normally guyed — these are usually referred to as free-standing or self-supporting towers. The principles involved are the same regardless of the manufacturer's choice of names. The wind blowing against the side of the tower creates an overturning moment that would topple the tower if it were not for the anchoring at the base. Fig. 54 details the action and reaction involved. The tower is restrained by the base. As the wind blows

Table 7
Tower Manufacturers

Aluma Tower
Box 2806
Vero Beach, FL 32960

Hy-Gain Division
Telex Communications, Inc.
9600 Adrich Ave., S.
Minneapolis, MN 55420

Unarco-Rohn
P.O. Box 2000
Peoria, IL 61601

Tri-Ex Tower Corp.
7182 Rasmussen Ave.
Visalia, CA 93277

Universal Manufacturing Company
12357 E. 8 Mile Rd.
Warren, MI 48089

Glenn Martin Engineering
P.O. Box 253
Boonville, MO 65233

US Tower Corp.
8975 West Goshen Ave.
Visalia, CA 93291

Fig. 53 — Diagram depicting proper method of installation of a typical guyed tower.

against one side of the tower, the opposite side is compressed downward much as in the guyed-type setup. Because there are no guys to restrain the top, the side that the wind is blowing against is simultaneously being pulled up (uplift). The force of the wind is creating a moment that tends to pivot about a point in the base of the tower. The base of the guyed tower simply must hold the tower up, but the base of the free-standing tower must simultaneously hold one side of the tower up and the other side down! It should not be surprising that manufacturers often call for a great deal more concrete in the base of free-standing towers than they do in the base of guyed towers.

Fig. 55 shows two variations of another popular type of tower, the crank-up. In regular guyed or free-standing towers, each section is bolted atop the next lower sec-

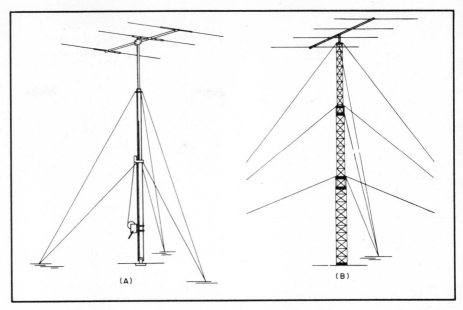

Fig. 55 — Two examples of "crank-up" towers.

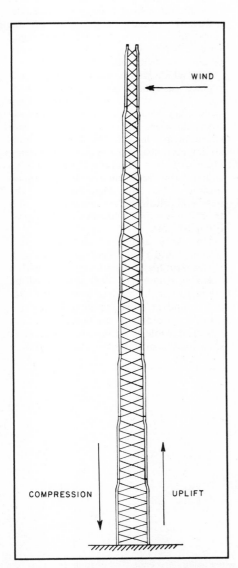

Fig. 54 — Diagram of a typical free-standing (unguyed) tower. Arrows indicate the direction of the forces acting upon the structure. See text for discussion.

tion. The height of the tower is the sum of the heights of the sections (minus any overlap). Not so with the crank-up towers. The outer diameter of each section is smaller than the inner diameter of the next lower section. Instead of bolting together, the sections are attached with a complex set of cables and pulleys. The overall height of the tower is adjusted by using the pulleys and cables to "telescope" the sections together or apart.

Depending on the design, the manufacturer may or may not require guy wires. The primary advantage of the crank-up tower is that the owner must do the antenna work near the ground. A second advantage is that the tower can be kept retracted

Fig. 56 — Fold-over or tilting base. There are several different variations of hinged sections permitting widely different types of installation. Great care should be exercised when raising or lowering a tilting tower.

except during use, which reduces the guying needs (presumably, you would not try to extend the tower and use it during periods of high winds). The disadvantages include mechanical complexity and (usually) cost. It is extremely dangerous to climb on a crank-up tower, even if it is extended only a small amount.

Some towers have another convenience feature — a hinged section that permits the owner to fold over all or a portion of the tower. The primary benefit is in allowing antenna work to be done closer to ground level without the necessity of removing the antenna and lowering it. Fig. 56 shows a hinged base; of course, the hinged section can be designed for portions of the tower other than the base. Also, a hinged feature can be added to a crank-up tower.

Misuse of hinged sections during tower erections is a common problem among radio amateurs. Unfortunately, these episodes often end in accidents. If you do not have a good grasp of the fundamentals of physics, it might be wise to avoid hinged towers (or to consult an expert). It is often far easier (and safer) to erect a regular guyed tower or self-supporting tower with gin pole and climbing belt than it is to try to "walk up" an unwieldy hinged tower.

The Base

Each manufacturer will provide customers with detailed plans for properly constructing the base. Fig. 57 is an example of one such plan. This plan calls for a hole that is $3.5 \times 3.5 \times 6.0$ feet. Steel reinforcement bars are lashed together and placed in the hole. The bars are positioned such that they will be completely embedded in the concrete, yet will not contact any metallic object in the base itself. This is done to minimize the possibility of a direct discharge path for lightning through the

Fig. 57 — Another example of a concrete base (Tri-Ex LM-470).

Fig. 58 — Plans for installing concrete base for Wilson ST-77B. Although the instructions and dimensions will vary from one tower to the next, this is representative of the type of concrete base specified by most manufacturers.

Fig. 59 — Traditional method of securing the end of a guy wire.

base. Should such a discharge occur, the concrete base would likely explode and bring about the collapse of the tower.

A strong wooden form is constructed around the top of the hole. The hole and the wooden form are filled with concrete so that the resultant block will be 4 inches above grade. The anchor bolts are embedded in the concrete before it hardens. Usually it's easier to ensure that the base is level and properly aligned by attaching the mounting base and the first section of the tower to the concrete anchor bolts. Each manufacturer will provide specific detailed instructions for the proper mounting procedure. Fig. 58 provides a slightly different design for a tower base.

The one assumption so far is that you have normal soil. "Normal soil" is a mixture of clay, loam, sand and small rocks. A technical discussion is beyond the scope of this book, but you may want to adopt more conservative design parameters for your base (usually, more concrete) if your soil is sandy, swampy or extremely rocky. If you have any doubts about your soil, contact your local agricultural extension office and ask for a more technical description of your soil. Once you have that information, contact the engineering department of your tower manufacturer or a civil engineer.

Tower Installation

The installation of a tower is not difficult when the proper techniques are known. A guyed tower, in particular, is not hard to erect since each of the individual sections are relatively light in weight and can be handled with only a few helpers and some good-quality rope. A gin pole is a handy device for working with tower sections.

One of the most important aspects of any tower-installation project is the safety of all persons involved. Helpers should always stand clear of the tower base to prevent being hit by a dropped tool or hardware. When two people are climbing the tower, one should climb into position before the

other begins climbing. The same procedure is required for climbing down a tower after the job is completed. The purpose is to have the nonclimbing person stand relatively still so as not to drop any tools or objects on the climbing person, or unintentionally obstruct his movements. When two persons are working on top of a tower, only one should change position (unbelt and move) at a time.

Attaching Guy Wires

In typical Amateur Radio installations a guy wire may experience "pulls" in excess of 1000 pounds. Under such circumstances, you do not merely twist the wires together

and expect them to hold. Fig. 59 depicts the traditional method for fixing the end of a piece of guy wire. A thimble is used to prevent the wire from breaking because of a sharp bend at the point of intersection. Three cable clamps follow to hold the wire securely. As a final backup measure, the individual strands of the free end are unraveled and wrapped around the guy wire. It is a lot of work, but it is necessary to ensure a firm connection.

Fig. 60 shows the use of a device that replaces the clamps and twisted strands of wire. These devices are known as dead ends. They are far more convenient to use than are clamps. You must cut the guy wire to the proper length. The dead end is installed into whatever the guy wire is being attached to (use a thimble, if needed). One side of the dead end is then wrapped around the guy wire. The other side of the dead end follows. The savings in time and trouble more than make up for the slightly higher cost.

Guy wire comes in different sizes, strengths and types. Typically, 3/16-inch EHS (extra high strength) guy wire with a breaking strength of 3990 pounds will be adequate for the moderate tower installation found at most Amateur Radio stations. Some amateurs prefer to use 5/32-in "aircraft cable." Although this cable is somewhat more flexible than 3/16-inch

Fig. 60 — Alternative method for attaching guy wires using dead ends. The dead end on the right is completely assembled (the end of the guy wire was left extending from the grip for illustrative purposes). On the left, one side of the dead end has been partially attached to the guy wire. In front, a thimble for use where a sharp bend might cause the guy wire or dead end to break.

EHS, it is only about 70% as strong. It is recommended that you stay with standard guy wire and that you use nothing smaller than 3/16-inch EHS.

Fig. 61 shows two different methods for attaching guy wires to towers. At A, the guy wire is simply looped around the tower leg and terminated in the usual manner. At B, a "torque bracket" has been added. There probably isn't much difference in performance for wind forces that are tending to push the tower over. If you happen to have more projected area (antennas, feed lines, etc.) on one side of the tower than the other, or a long-boom Yagi at the top, then the force of the wind will cause the tower to tend to twist into the ground. The torque bracket will be far more effective in resisting this twisting motion than will the simpler installation. If you have any doubts about how much twisting a tower

Fig. 61 — Two methods of attaching guy wire to a tower. See text for discussion.

can do, go outside and carefully watch one in a windstorm. The trade-off, of course, is in terms of initial cost.

There are two main types of anchors used for guy wires. Fig. 62A depicts an earth screw. It usually measures 4 to 6 feet long. The screw blade at the bottom typically measures 6 to 8 inches in diameter. Fig. 62B illustrates two people installing the anchor. The shaft is tilted such that it will be in line with the guy wires. Earth screws are suitable for use in "normal" soil where permitted by local building codes.

The alternative to earth screws is the concrete block anchor. Fig. 62C shows the installation of this type of anchor; it is suitable for any soil condition, with the possible exception of a bed of lava rock or coral. Consult the instructions from the manufacturer for the precise method of installation.

Guy wires can receive and reradiate RF energy. Reradiation can, in turn, distort the pattern of a directional array and can sometimes contribute to RFI. These conditions are aggravated when one or more guy wires is resonant at the operating frequency or one of its harmonics. To avoid resonance, the guy wires should be broken up into nonresonant lengths with egg strain insulators. Fig. 63 shows wire lengths that fall within 10 percent of half-wave resonance in the popular HF bands. These lengths should be avoided.

Turnbuckles and associated hardware are used to attach guy wires to anchors and to provide a convenient method of adjusting tension on the guy wires. Fig. 64A shows a turnbuckle of a single guy wire at-

tached to the eye of the anchor. Turnbuckles are usually fitted with either two eyes or one eye, and one jaw. The eyes are the oval ends, while the jaws are U-shaped with a bolt through the tips.

Fig. 64B depicts two turnbuckles attached to the eye of an anchor. The pro-

Fig. 62 — Two standard types of guy anchors. The earth screw shown at A is easy to install and widely available, but it may not be suitable for use with abnormal soil. The concrete anchor is more difficult to install properly, but it is suitable for use with a wide variety of soil conditions and will satisfy most building code requirements.

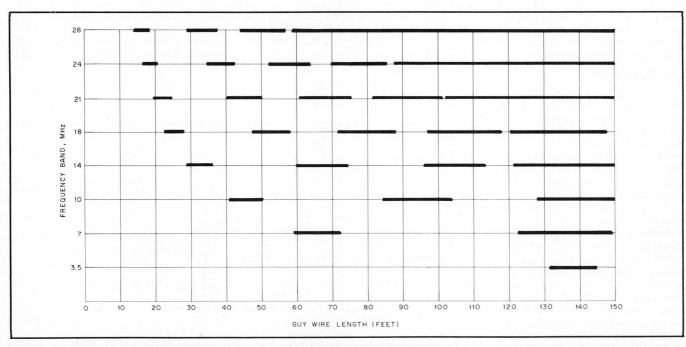

Fig 63—The black bars indicate ungrounded guy wire lengths to avoid for the eight HF amateur bands. This chart is based on resonance within 10% of any frequency in the band. Grounded wires will exhibit resonance at odd multiples of a quarter wavelength. *(by Jerry Hall, K1TD)*

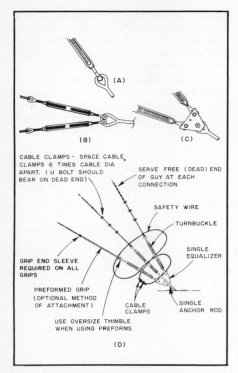

Fig. 64 — Variety of means available for attaching guy wires and turnbuckles to anchors.

Fig. 65 — Z-bracket component pieces.

Fig. 66 — Assembly of the Z bracket.

dure for installation is to remove the bolt from the jaw, pass the jaw over the eye of the anchor and reinstall the bolt through the jaw, through the eye of the anchor, and through the other side of the jaw. For two or more guys attached to one anchor, it is recommended that you install an equalizer plate (Fig. 64C). In addition to providing a convenient point to attach the turnbuckles, the plate will pivot slightly and tend to equalize the tension on the guy wires. Once the installation is complete, a safety wire should be passed through the turnbuckles in a "figure-eight" fashion to prevent the turnbuckle from working loose.

The Tower Shield

A tower can be legally classified as an "attractive nuisance" that could cause injuries. You should take some precautions to ensure that "unauthorized climbers" can't get hurt on your tower. This tower shield, which was originally described by Baker Springfield, W4HYY, and Richard Ely, WA4VHM, in September 1976 *QST*, should eliminate the worry.

Generally, the "attractive nuisance" doctrine applies to your responsibility to trespassers on your property. (The law is much stricter with regard to your responsibility to an uninvited guest.) You should expect your tower to attract children, whether they are already technically trespassing or whether the tower itself lures them onto your property. A tower is dangerous to children, especially because of their inability to appreciate danger. (What child could resist trying to climb a tower once they see one?) Because of this danger,

you have a legal duty to exercise reasonable care to eliminate the danger or otherwise protect children against the perils of the attraction.

The tower shield is composed simply of panels that enclose the tower and make climbing practically impossible. These panels are 5 feet in height and are wide enough to fit snugly between the tower legs and flat against the rungs. A height of 5 feet is sufficient in most every case. The panels are constructed from 18-gauge galvanized sheet metal obtained and cut to proper dimensions from a local sheet-metal shop. A lighter gauge could probably be

used, but the extra physical weight of the heavier gauge is an advantage if no additional means of securing the panels to the tower rungs are used. The three types of metals used for the components of the shield are supposedly rust proof and nonreactive. The panels are galvanized sheet steel, the brackets aluminum, and the screws and nuts are brass. The tower shield consists of three panels, one for each of the three sides, supported by two brackets. These brackets are constructed from 6-inch pieces of thin aluminum angle stock. Two of these pieces are bolted together to form a Z bracket (see Figs. 65, 66 and 67). The

Fig. 67 — Installation of the shield on a tower rung.

Z brackets are bolted together with binding-head brass machine screws.

The panels are laid flat for measuring, marking and drilling. The first measurement is from the top of the upper mounting rung on the tower to the top of the bottom rung. These mounting rungs are selected to position the panel on the tower. This distance from rung to rung is then marked on the panel. Using the same size brass screws and nuts, the top vertical portion of each Z bracket is bolted to the panel. The mounting-screw holes are drilled about 1 inch from the end of the Z brackets so that an offset clearance occurs between the Z-bracket binding-screw holes and the panel-bracket mounting-screw holes. The panel holes are drilled to match the Z-bracket holes.

The panels are held on the tower by their own weight. They are not easy to grasp because they fit snugly between the tower legs. If the need exists for added safety against deliberate removal of the panels, this can be accomplished by means of tie wires. A small hole can be drilled in the panel just above, just below, and in the center of each Z bracket. Run a piece of heavy galvanized wire through the top hole, around the Z bracket, and then back through the hole just below the Z bracket. Twist together the two ends of the wire. One tie wire should be sufficient for each panel, but use two if desired.

The completed panels are rather bulky and difficult to handle. A feature that is useful if the panels have to be removed often for tower climbing or accessibility is a pair of removable handles. The removable handles can be constructed from one threaded rod and eight nuts (see Fig. 68). The two pairs of handle holes were drilled in the panels a few inches below the

top Z bracket and several inches above the bottom Z bracket. For panel placement or removal, the handles are hooked in these holes in the panels. The hook, on the top of the handle, fits into the top hole of each pair of the handle holes. The handle is optional, but for the effort required it certainly makes removal and replacement much safer and easier.

The installed tower shield can be seen in Fig. 69. This relatively simple device could prevent an accident.

ANTENNA INSTALLATION

All antenna installations are different in some respects. Therefore, thorough planning is the most important first step in installing any antenna. At the beginning, before anyone climbs the tower, the whole process should be thought through. The procedure should be discussed to be sure each crew member understands what is to be done. Plan how to work out all bugs. Consider what tools and parts must be assembled and what items must be taken up the tower. Extra trips up and down the tower can be avoided by using forethought.

Getting ready to raise a beam requires planning. Done properly, the actual work of getting the antenna into position can be done quite easily with only one person at the top of the tower. The trick is to let the ground crew do all the work and leave the person on the tower free to guide the antenna into position.

Before the antenna can be hoisted into position, the tower and the area around it must be prepared. The ground crew should clear the area around the base while someone climbs the tower to remove any wire antennas or other objects that might get in the way. The first person to climb the tower should also rig the rope and pulley that will

be used to raise the antenna. The time to prepare the tower is before the antenna leaves the ground, not after it becomes hopelessly entwined with your 80-meter dipole.

Raising the Antenna

If you have a free-standing or crank-up tower, the task of actually getting the antenna from the ground to the tower top is simple. Rig a pulley to the mast as shown in Fig. 70. The pulley should be attached about 2 to 3 feet above the point where the antenna will bolt to the mast. If the antenna is heavy, it is advisable to rig a second pulley, or "snatch block," at the tower base. This arrangement allows the ground crew to use their entire body weight when pulling, rather than just the strength in their arms, making for a smoother and easier installation. The snatch block also keeps the load on the tower vertical, rather than lateral. Although many towers can take some lateral strain, it is better to be safe than sorry.

A properly designed and constructed antenna attaches to the mast at the balance point on the boom. If you rig a sling around the boom as in Fig. 70, you should be able to lift the antenna horizontally from the ground to the tower top. Be sure to rig the rope so that it does not obstruct the boom-to-mast bolt holes. Do not rig the rope so that it will come between the boom-to-mast plate and the mast. Test

Fig. 68 — Removable handle construction.

Fig. 69 — Installed tower shield. Note the holes for using the handles.

Fig. 70 — Installing antennas on free-standing towers is relatively simple. At A, the pulley is rigged to the mast about 3 feet above the antenna mounting point. A snatch block at the tower base is used so the ground crew can pull horizontally, while keeping the strain on the tower in the vertical plane. The Yagi is suspended in a rope sling at the tower base. The ground crew pulls the antenna up (B), and the antenna will remain parallel to the ground if rigged properly. When the antenna reaches the tower top, the tower climber simply bolts it into place (C).

your rigging by lifting the beam a few feet above the ground. If it tilts in any direction, let it back down and rig it again. It should be possible to balance the antenna in the horizontal plane.

When the beam is balanced and safely rigged, the ground crew starts pulling the antenna up the tower. In some installations, it will be possible to bring the antenna to the top of the tower without anyone leaving the ground. In most, however, the tower climber will have to follow the antenna up the tower to keep it from getting caught. When the antenna reaches the tower top, the climber simply has to bolt it into place.

Avoiding Guy Wires

Although the same basic methods of installing a Yagi apply to any tower, guyed towers pose a special problem. Steps must be taken to avoid snagging the antenna on the guy wires. Let's consider, therefore, some ways in which this difficulty can be circumvented. With proper precautions, even large antennas can be pulled to the top of a tower, even if the mast is guyed at several levels.

Sometimes one of the top guys can provide a track to support the antenna as it is

pulled upward. Insulators in the guys, however, may offer obstructions that could cause the beam to get hung up. A better track made with rope is an alternative, provided there is sufficient rope available. One end of the rope is secured outside the guy anchors. The other end is passed over the top of the tower and back down to an anchor near the first anchor. So arranged, the rope forms a narrow V track strung outside the guy wires. Once the V track is secured, the antenna may simply be pulled up the track.

Another method is to tie a rope to the back of the antenna (but within reach of the center). The ground crews then pull the antenna out away from the guys as the antenna is raised. With this method, some crew members are pulling up the antenna to raise it while others are pulling down and out to have the beam clear the guys. Obviously, the opposing crews must be coordinated or they can literally tear the antenna apart. The beam is especially vulnerable when it begins to tip into the horizontal position. If the crew pulling out and down continues to pull against the antenna, the boom can be broken. Another problem with this approach is that the antenna may rotate on the axis of the boom as it is

raised. To prevent such rotation, long lengths of twine may be tied to an element, one piece on each side of the boom. Ground personnel may then use these to stabilize the antenna. Where this is done, provision should be made for untying the twine once the antenna is in place.

A third method is to tie the halyard to the center of the antenna. A crew member, wearing a safety belt, walks the antenna up the tower as the crew on the ground raises it. Because the halyard is tied at the center balance point, the man on the tower can rotate the elements around the guys. A tag line can be tied to the bottom end of the boom so that a man on the ground can help move the antenna around the guys. The tag line must be removed while the antenna is still vertical and you can reach it.

THE PVRC MOUNT

The above methods may not be satisfactory for large arrays on guyed towers. The best way to handle large Yagis is to assemble them on top of the tower. The way to do that is by using the "PVRC mount." Many members of the Potomac Valley Radio Club have used this method successfully to install their large antennas. Simple and ingenious, the idea involves offsetting the boom from the mast to permit the boom to tilt 360° and rotate axially 360°. This permits the entire length of the boom to be brought alongside the tower, allowing the elements to be attached one by one.

See Figs. 71 through 75. The mount itself consists of a short length of pipe of the same (or greater) diameter as the rotating mast, a steel plate and the hardware to hold it all together. The plate is drilled for eight U-bolts: four to attach the plate to the pipe, and four to attach the pipe to the antenna boom-to-mast plate. Additionally, four pinning bolts are used to ensure that the antenna will end up level and parallel to the ground. Two pinning bolts pass through the mast, two through the horizontal pipe. When the horizontal pipe pinning bolts are removed and the U-bolts are loosened, the boom-to-mast plate can be tilted 360°, allowing either half of the boom to come alongside the tower.

After all critical dimensions have been marked, the antenna elements are removed from the boom. Once the rotator and mast have been installed on the tower, a gin pole is used to bring the adapter plate and pipe to the top of the tower. There, the "top crew" unpins the horizontal pipe and tilts the antenna boom-to-mast plate to place it in the vertical plane. The boom is attached to the boom-to-mast plate at the balance

Fig. 72 — Close-up of the PVRC mount. Two of the four locking pins (bolts) may be seen at the midline of the left hand vertical plate. The other two pins are located along the axis of the short pipe section; the head of the right-hand bolt blends in with the U-bolt lock nut to the rear.

point of the assembled antenna. It is important that the boom be rotated axially so the bottom side of the boom is closest to the tower. This will ensure that the antenna elements will be parallel to the side of the tower during installation, allowing the boom to be tilted without the elements striking the tower.

During installation it may be necessary to remove one guy wire temporarily to allow for tilting of the boom. As a safety precaution, a temporary guy should be mounted to the same leg of the tower just low enough so that the antenna will not hit it.

The elements are assembled on the boom starting with those closest to the center of the boom, working out alternately to the farthest director and reflector. This procedure must be followed. If all the elements are put first on one half of the boom, it will be dangerous (if not impossible) to put on the remaining elements. By starting at the middle and working outward the antenna weight will never be so far removed from the balance point that tilting of the boom becomes impossible.

When the last element is attached, the boom is brought parallel to the ground, the horizontal pipe is pinned and the U-bolts tightened. Now, all the antenna elements are positioned vertically. Next, loosen the U-bolts that hold the boom and rotate the boom axially 90°, bringing the elements parallel to the ground. Then tighten the boom U-bolts and double-check all the hardware.

Many long-boom Yagis employ a truss to prevent boom sag. With the type of mount just described the truss must be attached to a pipe that is independent of the rotating mast. A short length of pipe is attached to the boom as close as possible to the balance point. The truss will now move

along with the boom whenever the boom is tilted or twisted.

ROTATOR SYSTEMS

There are not many choices when it comes to antenna rotators for the amateur antenna system. Choosing the right rotator is very important if trouble-free operation is desired. There are basically four grades of rotators available to the amateur. The

Fig. 71 — The PVRC mount, boom-to-mast plate, mast and rotator ready to go. The mast and rotator are installed first.

Fig. 73 — Working at the 70-foot level. A gin pole makes pulling up and mounting the boom to the boom-to-mast plate a safe and easy procedure.

Fig. 74 — Mounting the last element prior to positioning the boom in a horizontal plane.

Fig. 75 — The mast-to-pipe U-bolts are loosened and the boom is turned to a horizontal position. This puts the elements in a vertical plane. Then the pipe U-bolts are tightened and pinning bolts secured. The boom U-bolts are then loosened and the boom turned axially 90°.

lightest-duty rotator is the TV type, typically used to turn TV antennas. These rotators will handle, without much difficulty, a small three-element tribander (20-, 15- and 10-meter) array or a single 15- or 10-meter monoband three-element antenna.

The important consideration with a TV rotator is that it lacks braking or holding capability. High winds will turn the rotator motor via the gear train in a reverse fashion, sometimes resulting in broken gears. The next grade up from the TV class of rotator usually includes a braking arrangement whereby the antenna is held in place when power is not applied to the rotator. Generally speaking, the brake will prevent gear damage on windy days. If adequate precautions are taken, this group of rotators is capable of holding and turning stacked monoband arrays, or up to a five-element 20-meter system. The next step up in strength is more expensive. This class of rotator will turn just about anything the most demanding amateur might want to install.

A description of antenna rotators would not be complete without the mention of the prop-pitch class. This rotator system consists of a surplus aircraft propeller-blade pitch motor coupled to an indicator system as well as a power supply. There are installation problems, however. It has been said that a prop-pitch rotator system, properly installed, is capable of turning a house. This is no doubt true! Perhaps in the same class as the prop-pitch motor but with somewhat less capability is the electric motor of the type used for opening garage doors. These have been used successfully in turning large arrays.

Proper installation of the antenna rotator can provide many years of trouble-free service; sloppy installation can cause problems such as a burned-out motor, slippage, binding and casting breakage. Most rotators are capable of accepting mast sizes of different diameters, and suitable precautions must be taken to shim an undersized mast to ensure dead-center rotation. It is very desirable to mount the rotator inside and as far below the top of the tower as possible. The mast will absorb the torque developed by the antenna during high winds, as well as during starting and stopping. A mast length of 10 feet or more between the rotator and the antenna will add greatly to the longevity of the entire system. Some amateurs have used a long mast from the top to the base of the tower. Installation and service can be accomplished at ground level. Another benefit of mounting the rotator 10 or more feet below the antenna is that any misalignment among the rotator, mast and the top of the tower is less significant. A tube at the top of the tower through which the mast protrudes will almost completely eliminate lateral forces on the rotator casting. All the rotator need do is support the downward weight of the antenna system and turn the array. While the normal weight of the antenna and the mast is usually not more than a couple of hundred pounds, even with a large system, one can ease this strain on the rotator by installing a thrust bearing at the top of the tower. The bearing is then the component that holds all the weight, and the rotator need perform only the rotating task.

A problem often encountered in the amateur installation is that of misalignment between the direction indication of the rotator control box and the heading of the antenna. This is caused by mechanical slippage in the system caused by loose bolts or antenna boom-to-mast hardware. Many texts suggest that the boom be pinned to the mast with a heavy-duty bolt and, likewise, the rotator be pinned to the mast. There is a trade-off here. The amateur might not like to climb the tower and straighten out the assembly after each heavy windstorm. However, if there is sufficient wind to cause slippage in the couplings, the wind could break a casting. The slippage will act as a clutch release, which may prevent serious damage.

Completing the Installation

Once you've completed the tower, mast, antenna and rotator installation, verify that everything works. After you've done this, it is important to put on the finishing touches. Waterproof any coaxial cable connections and control lead connections. Use plenty of electrical tape, some heat-shrink tubing, or putty. Tape the cable along the antenna boom and down the mast. At the tower top, leave a loop large enough that the antenna can turn 360 degrees without binding the coaxial cable. Then secure any cables to the tower leg all the way to the ground. Cables that flap in the wind may be damaged under stress.

Maintenance

It's a good idea to inspect your tower and antenna system several times during the year. Make a checklist and run through it from top to bottom. Look for loose or missing hardware, rust, structural defects and worn cables. Periodically check the tension of your guy wires and adjust them if necessary. Catch problems before they become serious.

Mobile and Portable Stations

A major justification for the existence of Amateur Radio in the USA is to provide a pool of experienced operators in time of national or community need. When the call for emergency communications is voiced by cities, towns, counties, states or the federal government, mobile and portable radio equipment is pressed into service where needed. Aside from the occasional disaster and emergency type of communications, a great deal of pleasure and challenge can reward the amateur when operating portable or mobile under normal conditions.

Most mobile operation is carried out today by means of narrow-band FM and repeaters. The major repeater frequencies are in the 146, 220 and 440-MHz bands. It is expected that this reliable service mode will soon include widespread occupancy of the 1240-MHz band and higher.

Mobile HF-band operation still appeals to numerous amateurs because it eliminates the constrictions imposed by VHF and UHF repeaters, their operators and their normal coverage contours. When operating mobile on SSB or CW with HF transceivers, worldwide contacts are possible for those who enjoy that style of communication.

MOBILE STATIONS

Layout of a mobile station is considerably easier than that of a fixed station. In most vehicles, space is limited so there are only one or two possible spots for locating the equipment. Whenever possible, it should be positioned so that the operator can reach the front-panel controls without compromising the ability to operate the automobile safely. Driving safely is *always* the first priority; operating radio equipment is secondary.

While most mobile operation is done at low power levels, such as 10 watts from a VHF FM transceiver, high-power mobile operation is entirely practical from the 13.6-V dc battery system. There are many VHF power amplifiers on the market today at power levels up to 150 watts that require 13.6-V dc. Also, many HF rigs in the 100-watt-output class will operate directly from the automobile power system. Dynamotors, vibrator packs and dc-to-dc converters are things of the past, making mobile operation much more attractive.

If the amateur transceiver or amplifier requires more than a few amperes at 13.6 volts, it is best to run a heavy cable directly to the automobile battery. Few automobile electrical systems are set up to allow you to safely draw the 20 amperes required for a 150-watt transmitter from the accessory connection on the fuse panel. Consult the wire table in Chapter 35 for the safe size wire for your installation. Keep in mind that the larger the wire, the lower the voltage drop under load; a larger conductor will help you to get the most from your

equipment. Adequately fuse your power cable. Automobile fires are costly and dangerous.

A variety of mobile antennas are available. Chapter 33 of this Handbook contains information on building and using mobile antennas for HF and VHF.

Electrical-Noise Elimination

One of the most significant deterrents to effective signal reception during mobile or portable operation is electrical impulse noise from the automotive ignition system. The problem also arises during the use of gasoline-powered portable ac generators. This form of interference can completely mask a weak signal, thus rendering the station ineffective. Most electrical noise can be eliminated by taking logical steps toward suppressing it. The first step is to clean up the noise source itself, then utilize the receiver's built-in noise-reducing circuit as a last measure to knock down any noise pulses from passing cars, or from other man-made sources.

Spark-Plug Noise

Most vehicles manufactured prior to 1975 were equipped with simple Kettering inductive-discharge ignition systems. A variety of noise-suppression methods were devised for these systems, including resistor spark plugs, clip-on suppressors, resistive high-voltage cable and even complete shielding. Resistive high-voltage cable and resistor plugs provide the greatest noise reduction for the least expense and effort. While almost all vehicles produced after 1960 had resistance cable as standard equipment, such cable develops microscopic cracks in the insulation and segmentation of the conductor after a few years of service. These defects can defeat the suppression ability of the cable before the engine performance degrades noticeably. Two years is a reasonable replacement interval for spark-plug cable. Earlier editions of this *Handbook* described complete shielding methods for inductive-discharge ignitions.

Some late-model automobiles employ sophisticated high-energy electronic ignition systems in an attempt to reduce exhaust pollution and increase fuel mileage. With increased sophistication comes greater sensitivity to modification — solutions to RFI caused by older Kettering systems cannot be uniformly applied to the modern electronic ignitions.

Such fixes may be ineffective at best, and at worst may impair the engine performance. One should thoroughly understand an ignition system before attempting to modify it. One of the significant features of capacitive discharge systems, for example, is extremely rapid voltage rise, which combats misfire caused by fouled spark plugs. Rapid voltage rise depends on a low

Fig. 76 — This may represent the ultimate in portable VHF operation. The aggregate antenna gain represented by this setup could be very effective in time of emergency. This installation was built and operated by N6NB. The antenna shown is effective also for EME work.

Fig. 77 — Field Day is many things to many people, but everyone who participates does so away from commercial power. These gents, members of the Murgas ARC of Wilkes-Barre, Pennsylvania, hoisted a 15-meter beam atop a truck for their 1981 effort. (*photo by Mike Benish, K3SAE*)

RC time constant presented to the output transformer. For this reason, high-voltage suppression cable designed for capacitive-discharge systems is wound with monel wire. It exhibits a distributed resistance of only about 600 ohms per foot, as contrasted with 10 kΩ per foot for carbon-center cable used with inductive-discharge systems. Increasing the RC product by shielding or installing improper spark-plug cable could seriously compromise the capacitive-discharge circuit operation.

Ferrite beads represent a possible means

for RFI reduction in newer vehicles. Both primary and secondary ignition leads are candidates for beads. Install them liberally, then load test the engine for adequate spark energy.

The plane sheet metal surfaces and cylindrical members such as exhaust pipes often exhibit resonance in one of the amateur bands. Such resonances encourage reradiation of spark impulse energy. Bonding these structural members with heavy braid can reduce the level of spark noise inside the vehicle and out. Other types of noise to be described later can also be helped by bonding. Here are the main areas to bond. (1) Engine to frame; (2) air cleaner to engine block; (3) exhaust lines to frame; (4) battery ground terminal to frame; (5) hood to fire wall; (6) steering column to frame; (7) bumpers to frame; and (8) trunk lid to frame.

On the whole, modern automobiles are cleaner from an RFI standpoint than those of 20 years ago. The interference problem, however, at least at VHF and UHF, persists because present-day receivers are about 10 dB more sensitive than their predecessors.

Charging-System Noise

Noise from the vehicular battery-charging circuit can interfere with both transmission and reception of radio signals. The charging system of a modern automobile consists of a belt-driven, three-phase alternator and a solid-state voltage regulator. Solid-state regulators are a great improvement over the electromechanical vibrating contact units of earlier times. Interference from the charging system can affect a receiver in two ways: RF radiation can be picked up by the antenna, and noise can be conducted directly into the circuits via the power cable. "Alternator whine" is a common form of conducted interference. It has the greatest effect on VHF FM communications, because synthesized carrier generators and local oscillators are easily frequency modulated by power supply voltage fluctuations. The alternator ripple is most noticeable when transmitting, because the machine is more heavily loaded in that condition. If the ripple amplitude is great enough, alternator whine will be imparted to all incoming signals by the LO.

Conducted noise can be minimized by connecting the radio power leads directly to the battery, as this is the point in the electrical system having the lowest impedance. If the regulator is adjustable, set the voltage no higher than is necessary to ensure complete battery charging. Radio equipment manufacturers combat voltage variations by internally regulating critical circuits wherever possible.

Both conducted and radiated noise can be suppressed by filtering the alternator leads. Coaxial capacitors (about 0.5 μF) are suitable, but don't connect a capacitor to the field. The field lead can be shielded

Fig. 78 — Automotive noise-cancelling systems. At A, the circuit used in the BC-342 HF receiver. At B, a suggested broad-band noise-cancelling scheme.

or loaded with ferrite beads if necessary. A parallel-tuned LC trap in this lead may be effective against radiated noise. Such a trap in the output lead must be made of no. 10 wire or larger, as some alternators conduct up to 100 amperes. The alternator slip rings should be kept clean to prevent excess arcing. An increase in "hash" noise may indicate that the brushes need to be replaced.

Instrument Noise

Some automotive instruments are capable of creating noise. Among these gauges and senders are the heat- and fuel-level indicators. Ordinarily, the addition of a 0.5-μF coaxial capacitor at the sender element will cure the problem.

Other noise-generating accessories are turn signals, window-opener motors, heating-fan motors and electric windshield-wiper motors. The installation of a 0.25-μF capacitor will usually eliminate their interference.

Corona-Discharge Noise

Some mobile antennas are prone to corona build-up and discharge. Whip antennas that come to a sharp point

will sometimes create this kind of noise. This is why most mobile whips have steel or plastic balls at their tips. But, regardless of the structure of the mobile antenna, corona buildup will frequently occur during or just before a severe electrical storm. The symptoms are a high-pitched "screaming" noise in the mobile receiver, which comes in cycles of one or two minutes' duration, then changes pitch and dies down as it discharges through the front end of the receiver. The condition will repeat itself as soon as the antenna system charges up again. There is no cure for this condition, but it is described here to show that it does not originate within the electrical system of the automobile.

Electronic Noise Reduction

When all electrical noise generated within a vehicle has been eliminated, the mobile operator can be annoyed by RFI from passing vehicles. Some measures can be taken in the receiver to reduce or reject impulse noise. (Noise limiters and noise blankers are discussed in another chapter.) The placement of a noise blanker in the receiver is important. The blanking circuit must be placed ahead of the sharp selectivity; otherwise, the IF filter will stretch the noise pulses, and they cannot be blanked without destroying a major portion of the received intelligence.

The Soviet "woodpecker" over-the-horizon radar has inspired some serious development work on noise blankers that don't degrade receiver dynamic range. Receivers for VHF FM service are generally designed for optimum noise figure at the expense of resistance to overload. Recent advances in RF amplifier design have proven that low noise figure and high dynamic range are not mutually exclusive. A high-performance noise blanker is useless if the front end of the receiver overloads on the noise pulses. A helical resonator at the receiver input affords some protection against noise overload because it restricts the total noise energy delivered to the front end.

Some FM receivers suffer from impulse noise because of inadequate AM rejection. The cure for this ailment is to ensure hard limiting in the IF stages and to use a detector that is inherently insensitive to amplitude variations.

Particularly troublesome vehicular impulse noise can sometimes be cancelled at the receiver input. The technique involves sampling the noise voltage from a separate "noise antenna" and adjusting its phase and amplitude to cancel the noise delivered by the "signal antenna." For this system to be effective, the signal antenna must be positioned to provide the best possible signal-to-noise ratio, and the noise antenna located close to the noise source and effectively shielded from the desired signal.

Fig. 78A shows the noise cancellation circuit used in some models of the BC-342, a WW II receiver. The Faraday shield between L1 and L2 ensures that the coupling is purely magnetic. The coupling between L2 and L3 is purely electrostatic. Adjusting the coil coupling causes the noise to null. The block diagram of Fig. 78B illustrates a more modern broadband approach to noise cancellation. A short wire near the ignition coil couples impulse energy into the active impedance transformer, which is simply an FET source follower stage. The amplitude and phase of the noise are controlled by the attenuator and delay line, respectively. The signal combiner can be a hybrid ferrite transformer at HF or a transmission line multi-coupler at VHF.

PORTABLE STATIONS

Many amateurs experience the joys of portable operation once each year in the annual emergency exercise known as Field Day. Setting up an effective portable station requires organization, planning and some experience. For example, some knowledge of propagation is essential to picking the right band or bands for the intended communications link(s). Portable operation is difficult enough without dragging along excess equipment and antennas that will never be used.

Some problems encountered in portable operation that are not normally experienced in fixed-station operation include finding an appropriate power source and erecting an effective antenna. The equipment used should be as compact and lightweight as possible. A good portable setup is simple. Although you may bring gobs of gear to Field Day and set it up the day before, during a real emergency speed is of the essence. The less equipment to set up, the faster it will be operational.

PORTABLE AC POWER SOURCES

There are two popular sources of ac power for use afield. The first is what is referred to as a dc-to-ac converter, or more commonly, an inverter.

The ac output voltage is a square wave. Therefore, some types of equipment cannot be operated satisfactorily from the inverter. Certain types of motors are among those items that require a sine-wave output. Fig. 79 shows a picture of one style of commercial inverter. Heat sinks are used to cool the switching transistors. It delivers 117 volts of ac at 175 watts continuous power rating. The primary voltage is 6 or 12 dc.

When sine-wave output is required from a portable ac power supply, gasoline-engine alternators are used. They are available with ratings of several kilowatts, or as little as 500 watts. One of the larger units is shown in Fig. 80 where WB9QPI has just completed a maintenance run for the W0OHU/0 Field Day group.

Alternators powered by internal-combustion engines have been used for years to supply 117/234-V ac independent of the commercial mains. Such combinations range from tiny units powered by two-cycle or four-cycle gasoline engines in the low-wattage class to giant multicylinder diesels capable of supplying megawatts of power. Perhaps the most practical power range for most purposes is in the neighborhood of 2 kW. Larger units tend to become too heavy for one person to lift and handle easily while smaller generators lack sufficient power output for many applications. A 2-kW alternator is quite heavy but is capable of supplying power for just about any large power tool. It is roughly the equivalent of having a single 15-A outlet in an ordinary electric service. Of course, it will handle moderate-power amateur equipment with ease.

Maintenance Checklist

Although more complicated maintenance chores should be performed by qualified service personnel, many simple measures which will prolong the life of the alternator can be done at home or afield. Perhaps the best plan is to log the dates the unit was used and the operating time in hours. Also include dates of maintenance and type of service performed. Oil changes, when gasoline was purchased for emergency purposes, and

Fig. 79 — Photograph of a commercial dc-to-ac inverter that operates from 6 to 12 volts dc and delivers 117 volts ac (square wave) at 175 watts.

Fig. 80 — Large gasoline generators of the kilowatt and higher class are excellent for powering several amateur stations from a complex field site. Maintenance, as discussed in the text, is a vital matter to ensure reliable operation. Here, WB9QPI has just finished a maintenance check of the group's Field Day power plant.

Fig. 81 — The numbers indicate the primary maintenance points of a large power generator (see text for details).

Fig. 82 — A simple accessory that provides overload protection for generators that do not have such provisions built in.

Fig. 83 — A simple portable antenna mast may be built from telescoping tubing sections. The mast is assembled and bolted together on the ground, and the antennas attached. The mast is then pushed into the air and guyed in place. If slip-ring guy collars are used, the entire mast may be rotated by hand from ground level. A dipole may be used as part of the guy system.

similar data would fall under this category.

Important points common to all types of generators are indicated for a typical one in Fig. 81. (Consult the manufacturer's manual for additional instructions that might apply to a particular model.) The following checklist relates to the numbers on the drawing.

1) Use the proper grade of fuel. Check the owner's manual to determine whether oil must be mixed with the gasoline. While two-cycle models require an oil-gas mixture, most generators have a four-cycle engine that burns ordinary gasoline with no extra additives. Gasoline for emergency purposes should be stored only in small amounts and rotated on a regular basis. Older stock can be burned in a car (that uses the same grade of gas as the generator) since storing gasoline for any length of time is inadvisable. The more volatile components evaporate, leaving excess amounts of a varnish-like substance that will clog carburetor passages. Also, be sure gasoline containers are of an approved type with a clean interior, free of rust or other foreign matter. Similar considerations apply to the gas tank on the engine itself.

The majority of difficulties with small engines are related to fuel problems in some way. Dirty fuel or water in the gasoline is one source, with carburetor trouble because of the use of old gas being another common cause. Except for minor adjustments recommended in the instruction manual, it is seldom necessary to touch the carburetor controls. Avoid the temptation to make such adjustments in the case of faulty operation. Follow the recommendations in this guide so that more complicated maintenance procedures (such as carburetor overhaul) are not required.

2) Another important factor often neglected in maintenance of alternator engines is oil. While lubrication is one job oil has to perform, there are other considerations as well. The engine oil in the crankcase also collects a large amount of solid combustion products, bits of metal worn away by the moving parts, and any dust or other foreign matter that enters the carburetor intake. For instance, it is especially important to observe the manufacturer's recommendations concerning the length of time the engine may be operated before an oil change is required during the break-in period. If you ever have the opportunity to examine the oil from a new engine, you will note a metallic sheen to it. This is from the excessive amount of metal that is worn away. After the break-in period, much less metal is abraded and the oil doesn't have to be replaced as often.

The oil level should be checked frequently during engine operation. Each time fuel has to be added the oil should be checked also. When storing an alternator, it is also wise to drain the oil and replace it with fresh stock. This is because one of the combustion products is sulfur, which forms sulfuric acid with water dispersed in the oil. The acid then attacks the special metal in the bearing surfaces causing pitting and the need for premature replacement.

Also note the grade and weight of oil recommended by the manufacturer. Unlike their larger counterparts in automobiles, most small engines do not have oil filters, which is another reason required changes are more frequent. Some manufacturers recommend a high-detergent oil that comes in various service grades such as MS and SD. Examine the top or side of the cans in which the oil is sold and see if the letters correspond to those recommended by the engine manufacturer.

3) The carburetor mixes gasoline with air, and the mixture is then burned in the engine. Before entering the carburetor, the air must be filtered so it is free of dust and other foreign matter that might otherwise be drawn into cylinder(s). Particles that do get by the air filter are picked up by the oil. (Oil should be changed more often if the alternator is operated in a dusty location.) Also, it is important to clean the air filter frequently. It contains a foam-like substance that can be cleaned in kerosene and then soaked in fresh motor oil. Squeeze excess oil from the filter before replacing. Also, consult the instruction manual for further recommendations.

4) Once the gas/air mixture enters the cylinder, it is compressed by the piston into a very small volume and ignited by the spark plug. During the rapid burning that then occurs, the expansion caused by the resulting heat forces the piston down and

Fig. 84 — An aluminum extension ladder makes a simple but sturdy portable antenna support. Attach the antenna and feed lines to the top ladder section while it is nested and laying on the ground. Push the ladder vertical, attach the bottom guys and extend the ladder. Attach the top guys. Do not attempt to climb this type of antenna support.

(A)

(B)

Fig. 85 — The portable tower mounting system described by WA7LYI in the text. At A, a truck is "parked" on the homemade base plate to weigh it down. At B, the antennas, mast and rotator are mounted before the tower is pushed up. Do not attempt to climb a temporary tower installation.

delivers the mechanical power to the alternator.

As might be expected, proper operation of the ignition system is an important factor in engine performance. Power for the spark is supplied by a device called a magneto that is normally installed on the front of the engine. The magneto seldom requires servicing and such work should only be done by those qualified to do so. (This is one reason the magneto is often located under a flywheel that is difficult to remove by the inexperienced.)

Faulty spark plugs are the usual cause of ignition problems. Special equipment is required to test a spark plug properly, but an easier solution is to have a new one handy. In fact, keep two spare plugs on hand. Spark plug life can be notoriously short on occasion. However, repeated plug failure is also abnormal; other causes such as a poor gas/air mixture might be the culprit.

Replace the spark plug with a type similar to the one that came with the alternator or a substitute recommended by the manufacturer. Some models have resistor-type plugs, which are desirable for ignition-noise suppression. Resistor plugs are usually indicated by an R prefix. For instance the resistor version of a Champion CJ-8 would be an RC-J8.

5) Little exhaust system maintenance is required. In some forested areas, a spark-arrester type of muffler is required, so be sure your unit is so equipped before operating in such a location. "Quiet hours" may also be imposed in some places during the nighttime hours if generator exhaust noise is too loud.

Two very important safety precautions should be observed with regard to the exhaust system. Never operate an alternator in closed surroundings such as a building. Dangerous gases are emitted from the exhaust. Second, never refuel an engine while it is running or if the exhaust system is still very hot. Unfortunately, this last precaution is disregarded by many, which is extremely foolish. (Experienced service station operators will refuse to refuel an automobile with the motor running, a practice that is often prohibited by law.) Don't become an unnecessary statistic.

6) Most alternators are air-cooled as opposed to the water-cooled radiator system of the automobile. A fan on the front of the engine forces air over the cylinder. Avoid operating the alternator in areas where obstruction to this flow might result (such as in tall grass). Alternators should be operated such that a sufficient amount of air circulation is present for cooling, carburetion and exhaust.

Storage

Proper maintenance of an alternator when it is not being used is just as important as during the time it is in operation. The usual procedure is to run the engine dry of gasoline, drain the crankcase and fill it with fresh oil, and remove the spark plug. Then pour a few tablespoons of oil into the cylinder and turn the engine over a few times with the starter and replace the plug. But never crank the engine with the plug removed and the ignition or start switch in the on or run position. The resulting no-

(A)

(B)

(C)

Fig. 86 — The portable mast and tripod described by WA7LYI in the text. At A, the tripod is clamped to stakes driven into the ground. The rotator is attached to a homemade pipe mount. At B, rocks piled on the rotator mount keep the rotator from twisting and add weight to stabilize the mast. At C, a 10-foot mast is inserted into the tripod/rotator base assembly. Four 432-MHz quagis are mounted at the top.

load high voltage might damage the magneto. It is also a good idea to ground the spark-plug wire to the engine frame with a clip lead in case the switch is accidentally activated.

Moisture is the greatest enemy of an iron product — such as a generator — in storage. The coating of oil helps retard rust formation that might actually weld the two surfaces when the engine is restarted, resulting in premature wear. Consequently, it is important to store the alternator in an area of low humidity.

Although the maintenance procedures outlined may seem like a chore, the long-term benefits include low repair costs and like-new performance. Engines for alternator combinations must be able to handle a variety of loads while maintaining a constant speed in order to keep the output frequency constant. A mechanical governor performs this latter function by metering the fuel supplied to the engine under different load conditions. However, the system cannot function properly with an engine in poor mechanical condition because of lack of proper maintenance.

Grounds

Newer generators are supplied with a three-wire outlet, and the ground connection should go to the plug, as shown in Fig. 82. On older types, the ground would have to be connected separately to the generator frame and then to the common terminal in the junction box. A pipe or rod can then be driven into the ground and a wire connection made to either a clamp supplied with the rod or by means of a C-clamp for larger sizes of pipe. From an ignition-noise-

suppression standpoint, the ground is desirable along with safety considerations when power tools are being used.

The ground connection goes to the green wire in commercially made three-wire conduit. Conduit purchased from an electrical store comes with a color-coded insulation and the colored wires should be connected as shown in Fig. 82. Consult the owner's manual for the generator for further details on power hookup that might apply to your particular model.

PORTABLE ANTENNA CONSIDERATIONS

An effective antenna system is essential to all types of operation. Effective portable antennas, however, are more difficult to devise than their fixed-station counterparts. A portable antenna must be light, compact and easy to assemble. It is also important to remember that the portable antenna may be erected at a variety of sites, not all of which will offer ready-made supports. Strive for the best antenna system possible because operations in the field are often restricted to low power by power supply and equipment considerations. Some antennas suitable for portable operation are described in Chapter 33.

Antenna Supports

While some amateurs have access to a truck or trailer with a portable tower, most are limited to what nature supplies, along with simple push-up masts. If possible, select a portable site as high and clear as possible. Elevation is especially important if your operation involves VHF. Trees, buildings, flagpoles, telephone poles and

the like can be pressed into service to support wire antennas. Usually, drooping dipoles are chosen over horizontal dipoles because they require only one support.

A portable mast up to 30 feet high can be constructed from telescoping tubing sections, as shown in Fig. 83. A mast of this type can be used as a wire-antenna support, or it could support a small triband beam or VHF array. If the guy collars allow the mast to slip, the entire mast may be rotated by hand. Some of the guy wires may be used for wire antennas. The limiting factor in terms of height with a mast of this type is the number of people required to push it into place.

An aluminum extension ladder makes an effective antenna support, as shown in Fig. 84. In this installation, a mast, rotator and beam are attached to the top of the second ladder section with the ladder near the ground. The ladder is then pushed vertical and the lower set of guy wires attached to the guy anchors. When the first set of guy wires is secured, the ladder may be extended and the top guy wires attached to the anchors. Do not attempt to climb a temporarily guyed ladder.

Figs. 85 and 86 illustrate two methods for mounting portable antennas described by Terry Wilkinson, WA7LYI. Although the antennas shown are used for VHF work, the same principles can be applied to small HF beams as well.

In Fig. 85A, a 3-foot section of Rohn 25 tower is welded to a pair of large hinges, which in turn are welded to a steel plate measuring approximately 18 × 30 inches. One of the rear wheels of a pickup truck is "parked" on the plate, ensuring that it will not move. In Fig. 85B, a quad array of antennas for 144 and 220 MHz are mounted on a Rohn 25 top section, complete with rotator and feed lines. The tower is then pushed up into place using the hinges, and guy ropes anchored to stakes driven into the ground complete the installation. This method of portable tower installation offers an exceptionally easy-to-erect, yet sturdy, antenna support. Towers installed in this manner may be 30 or 40 feet high; the limiting factor is the number of "pushers" and "rope pullers" needed to get it into the air. A portable station located in the bed of the pickup truck completes the installation.

The second method of mounting portable beams described by WA7LYI is shown in Fig. 86. This support is intended for use with small or medium sized VHF and UHF arrays. The tripod is available from any dealer selling television antennas; tripods of this type are usually mounted on the roof of a house. Open the tripod to its full size and drive a pipe into the ground at each leg. Use a hose clamp or small U-bolt to anchor each leg to its pipe.

The rotator mount is made from a 6-inch-long section of 1½-inch-diameter pipe welded to the center of an "X" made from two 2-foot-long pieces of concrete reinforcing rod (rebar). The rotator clamps onto the pipe, and the whole assembly is placed in the center of the tripod. Large rocks placed on the rebar hold the rotator in place, and the antennas are mounted on a 10 or 15-foot mast section. This system is easy to make and set up.

Tips for Portable Antennas

Any of the antennas described in Chapter 33 or available from commercial manufacturers may be used for portable operation. Generally, though, big or heavy antennas should be passed over in favor of smaller arrays. The couple of decibels of gain a 5-element, 20-meter beam may have over a 3-element version is insignificant compared to the mechanical considerations. Stick with arrays of reasonable size that are easily assembled.

Wire antennas should be cut to size and tuned prior to their use in the field. Be careful when coiling these antennas for transport, or you may end up with a tangled mess when you need an antenna in a hurry. The coaxial cable should be attached to the center insulator with a connector for speed in assembly. Use RG-58 for the low bands and RG-8X for higher-band antennas. Although these cables exhibit higher loss than standard RG-8, they are far more compact and weigh much less for a given length.

Beam antennas should be assembled and tested before taking them afield. Break the beam into as few pieces as necessary for transportation and mark each joint for speed in reassembly. Hex nuts can be replaced with wing nuts to reduce the number of tools necessary.

BIBLIOGRAPHY

Source material and more extended discussion of topics covered in this chapter can be found in the references given below.

W. R. Adey, "Tissue Interactions with Nonionizing Electromagnetic Fields," *Physiology Review*, 1981; 61:435-514.

W. R. Adey, "Cell Membranes: The Electromagnetic Environment and Cancer Promotion," *Neurochemical Research*, 1988; 13:671-677.

W. R. Adey, "Electromagnetic Fields, Cell Membrane Amplification, and Cancer Promotion," in B. W. Wilson, R. G. Stevens, and L. E. Anderson, *Extremely Low Frequency Electromagnetic Fields: The Question of Cancer* (Columbus, OH: Batelle Press, 1989), pp 211-249.

W. R. Adey, "Electromagnetic Fields and the Essence of Living Systems," Plenary Lecture, 23rd General Assembly, Internat'l Union of Radio Sciences (URSI), Prague, 1990; in J. Bach Andersen, Ed., *Modern Radio Science* (Oxford: Oxford Univ Press), pp 1-36.

Q. Balzano, O. Garay and K. Siwiak, "The Near Field of Dipole Antennas, Part I: Theory," *IEEE Transactions on Vehicular Technology (VT) 30*, p 161, Nov 1981. Also "Part II; Experimental Results," same issue, p 175.

R. F. Cleveland and T. W. Athey, "Specific Absorption Rate (SAR) in Models of the Human Head Exposed to Hand-Held UHF Portable Radios," *Bioelectromagnetics*, 1989; 10:173-186.

R. F. Cleveland, E. D. Mantiply and T. L. West, "Measurements of Environmental Electromagnetic Fields Created by Amateur Radio Stations," presented at the 13th annual meeting of the Bioelectromagnetics Society, Salt Lake City, Utah, Jun 1991.

R. L. Davis and S. Milham, "Altered Immune Status in Aluminum Reduction Plant Workers," *American J Industrial Medicine*, 1990; 131:763-769.

F. C. Garland et al, "Incidence of Leukemia in Occupations with Potential Electromagnetic Field Exposure in United States Navy Personnel," *American J Epidemiology*, 1990; 132:293-303.

A. W. Guy and C. K. Chou, "Thermographic Determination of SAR in Human Models Exposed to UHF Mobile Antenna Fields," Paper F-6, Third Annual Conference, Bioelectromagnetics Society, Washington, DC, Aug 9-12, 1981.

C. C. Johnson and M. R. Spitz, "Childhood Nervous System Tumours: An Assessment of Risk Associated with Paternal Occupations Involving Use, Repair or Manufacture of Electrical and Electronic Equipment," *Internat'l J Epidemiology*, 1989; 18:756-762.

D. L. Lambdin, "An Investigation of Energy Densities in the Vicinity of Vehicles with Mobile Communications Equipment and Near a Hand-Held Walkie Talkie," *EPA Report ORP/EAD 79-2*, Mar, 1979.

D. B. Lyle, P. Schechter, W. R. Adey and R. L. Lundak, "Suppression of T-Lymphocyte Cytotoxicity Following Exposure to Sinusoidally Amplitude Modulated Fields," *Bioelectromagnetics*, 1983; 4:281-292.

G. M. Matanoski et al, "Cancer Incidence in New York Telephone Workers," *Proc Annual Review, Research on Biological Effects of 50/60 Hz Fields*, U.S. Dept of Energy, Office of Energy Storage and Distribution, Portland, OR, 1989.

D. I. McRee, *A Technical Review of the Biological Effects of Non-Ionizing Radiation*, Office of Science and Technology Policy, Washington, DC, 1978.

S. Milham, "Mortality from Leukemia in Workers Exposed to Electromagnetic Fields," *New England J Medicine*, 1982; 307:249.

S. Milham, "Increased Mortality in Amateur Radio Operators due to Lymphatic and Hematopoietic Malignancies," *American J Epidemiology*, 1988; 127:50-54.

W. W. Mumford, "Heat Stress Due to RF Radiation," *Proc IEEE*, 57, 1969, pp 171-178.

S. Preston-Martin et al, "Risk Factors for Gliomas and Meningiomas in Males in Los Angeles County," *Cancer Research*, 1989; 49:6137-6143.

D. A. Savitz et al, "Case-Control Study of Childhood Cancer and Exposure to 60-Hz Magnetic Fields," *American J Epidemiology*, 1988; 128:21-38.

D. A. Savitz et al, "Magnetic Field Exposure from Electric Appliances and Childhood Cancer," *American J Epidemiology*, 1990; 131:763-773.

I. Shulman, "Is Amateur Radio Hazardous to Our Health?" *QST*, Oct 1989, pp 31-34.

R. J. Spiegel, "The Thermal Response of a Human in the Near-Zone of a Resonant Thin-Wire Antenna," *IEEE Transactions on Microwave Theory and Technology (MTT) 30(2)*, pp 177-185, Feb 1982.

B. Springfield and R. Ely, "The Tower

Shield," *QST,* Sep 1976, p 26.

T. L. Thomas et al, "Brain Tumor Mortality Risk among Men with Electrical and Electronic Jobs: A Case-Controlled Study," *J National Cancer Inst,* 1987; 79:223-237.

N. Wertheimer and E. Leeper, "Electrical Wiring Configurations and Childhood Cancer," *American J Epidemiology,* 1979; 109:273-284.

N. Wertheimer and E. Leeper, "Adult Cancer Related to Electrical Wires Near the Home, *Internat'l J Epidemiology,* 1982; 11:345-355.

"Safety Levels with Respect to Human Exposure to Radio Frequency Electromagnetic Fields (300 kHz to 100 GHz)," *ANSI C95.1-1991* (New York: IEEE American National Standards Institute, 1990 draft).

"Biological Effects and Exposure Criteria for Radiofrequency Electromagnetic Fields," *NCRP Report No 86* (Bethesda, MD: National Council on Radiation Protection and Measurements, 1986).

US Congress, Office of Technology Assessment, "Biological Effects of Power Frequency Electric and Magnetic Fields—Background Paper," *OTA-BP-E-53* (Washington, DC: US Government Printing Office), 1989.

Table 8

Equipment Manufacturers List

Codes	Manufacturer
C,D,G,H,P,Q	Advanced Electronic Applications, Inc. Box C2160 Lynnwood, WA 98036 206-775-7373
L,Q	Ameritron 921 Louisville Road Starkville, MS 39759 601-323-9715
J,L,Q	Barker & Williamson 10 Canal Street Bristol, PA 19007 215-788-5581
L	Ehrhorn Technological Operations, Inc. 4975 N 30th Street Colorado Springs, CO 80919 719-260-1191 719-599-3861
G,H,I,P	Hal Communications Corp. Box 365 1201 W Kenyon Road Urbana, IL 61801 217-367-7373
B,E,F,H,I,L,M	Hamtronics, Inc. 65 Moul Road Hilton, NY 14468-9535 716-392-9430
A,B,C,D,E,L,M,Q	ICOM America, Inc. 2380 116th Ave NE Bellevue, WA 98004 206-454-8155 206-454-7619
A,B,C,D,L,M,Q,R	Kenwood USA Corp. Box 22745 Long Beach, CA 90801-5745
G,H,J,P,Q,R	MFJ Enterprises, Inc. Box 494 Mississippi State, MS 39762 800-647-1800 601-323-5869
A,F,J,L,M,P,Q	Ten-Tec, Inc. Highway 411 East Sevierville, TN 37862 615-428-0364
A,B,C,D,L,M	Yaesu USA 17210 Edwards Road Cerritos, CA 90701 213-404-2700 213-404-4884

Product Coding
A —HF Transceivers
B —HF Receivers
C —VHF/UHF Transceivers
D —VHF/UHF Hand-Held Transceivers
E —VHF/UHF Receivers
F —VHF/UHF Transmitters
G —RTTY/AMTOR Equipment
H —Packet Equipment
I —Repeater Equipment
J —Dummy Loads
L —HF Amplifiers
M —VHF/UHF Amplifiers
P —Keyers & CW Keyboards
Q —Antenna Tuners
R —SWR/Power Meters

Chapter 37

Operating Aids

The aids in this chapter are presented for the ready reference of the radio amateur. They were selected to meet two needs: material for daily operation and basic techniques that may be needed in communications emergencies.

The ARRL Operating Manual is the definitive source of information on all phases of on-the-air activity for radio amateurs, and it goes into more detail than we can here. Newcomers and veterans will both profit from the in-depth treatment of everything from DXing to computers in that publication. The *Operating Manual* is available at your local dealer or direct from ARRL HQ.

In addition, two booklets covering operating procedures are available from HQ. *Operating an Amateur Radio Station* covers basic operating skills. It gives an overview of League awards, contests and other operating activities. There you can find a basic explanation of the ARRL Field Organization and a lot more.

The *Public Service Communications Manual* goes into even further detail on ARRL's important public-service program, comprising the Amateur Radio Emergency Service (ARES) and the National Traffic System (NTS). If you are interested in public service, emergency communications or traffic handling, the manual is an excellent introduction to the program.

ALERT FREQUENCY

Local emergency communications leaders should establish a local 2-meter "alert frequency" that is normally quiet. Local hams then monitor the alert frequency whenever they would normally switch off their radios (even at night). When there is an emergency requiring help from amateurs, an "alert transmit station" transmits an appropriate bulletin on the alert frequency. The bulletin should include a check-in frequency so that *responding amateurs do not use the alert frequency*. More trained "alert transmit stations" may then repeat the alert message, on the alert frequency, to cover a larger geographic area when needed.

The alert frequency effectively replaces the radio off switch. It is not the only method of alerting amateurs. It is not a distress frequency. It is not an emergency operating frequency. It is not an emergency check-in frequency. Its only name is "the alert frequency." Amateurs should not transmit on the frequency unless there is a community emergency of sufficient magnitude to disturb any amateurs who may be listening. Personal emergencies are better handled through a repeater—where there can be an immediate response and communication on frequency.

The beauty of this system is that absolutely no hardware modifications or additions are needed and people can participate immediately. The only requirement is the discipline to attend the alert frequency rather than switch radios off. Contact your local Emergency Coordinator (EC) for details of the plan in your area. If you do not know your EC, contact your Section Manager (listed on p 8 of each *QST*), who can direct you to the EC.

DISTRESS CALLING

An amateur who finds himself in a situation where immediate emergency assistance is required (at sea, in a remote location, and so on) would call MAYDAY on whatever frequency seems to offer the best chance of getting a useful answer. MAYDAY is from the French *m'aider* (help me). On CW, use $\overline{SOS}$ to call for help. The distress call should be repeated over and over again for as long as possible until answered. The amateur involved should be prepared to supply the following information to the stations who respond to an $\overline{SOS}$ or MAYDAY:
- The location of the emergency, with enough detail to permit rescuers to locate the site without difficulty.
- The nature of the distress.
- The type of assistance required (medical aid, evacuation, food, clothing, and so on).
- Any other information that might be helpful in locating the emergency area or in sending assistance.

AMATEUR FREQUENCIES

Tables 1 through 4 provide an overview of the amateur bands and their uses. Table 1 graphically depicts FCC subband allocations for US amateurs. Many of these bands are allocated on a shared basis, and there are several bands above 1200 MHz (a complete explanation of rules pertaining to amateur operation appears in *The FCC Rule Book,* published by ARRL). Table 1 is valid for FCC regulated areas of International Telecommunication Union (ITU) Region 2 only (see Fig 1). For FCC regulated areas outside ITU Region 2, see *The FCC Rule Book.*

In addition to the federal regulations,

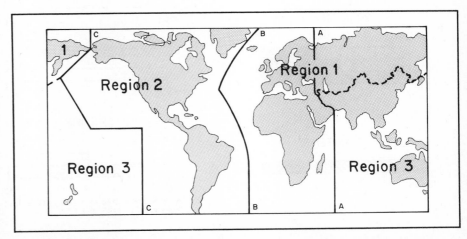

Fig 1—The ITU divides the world into three regions. Geographic details appear in *The FCC Rule Book* and *The ARRL Operating Manual.*

Table 1

US AMATEUR BANDS

Revised Sept 1, 1991

160 METERS

E,A,G

1800   1900   2000   kHz

Amateur stations operating at 1900—2000 kHz must not cause harmful interference to the radiolocation service and are afforded no protection from radiolocation operations.

80 METERS

3675 3725
3525 3850
3775

N,T †
G
A
E

3500   3750   4000   kHz

5167.5 kHz (SSB only): Alaska emergency use only.

40 METERS

7100 7150
7025 7225

N,T †
G *
A *
E *

7000   7150   7300   kHz

* Phone operation is allowed on 7075—7100 kHz in Puerto Rico, US Virgin islands and areas of the Caribbean south of 20 degrees north latitude; and in Hawaii and areas near ITU Region 3, including Alaska.

30 METERS

E,A,G

10,100   10,150   kHz

Maximum power on 30 meters is 200 watts PEP output. Amateurs must avoid interference to the fixed service outside the US.

20 METERS

14,025   14,150   14,225
14,175

G
A
E

14,000   14,150   14,350   kHz

17 METERS

E,A,G

18,068   18,110   18,168   kHz

15 METERS

21,100 21,200
21,025 21,300
21,225

N,T
G
A
E

21,000   21,200   21,450   kHz

12 METERS

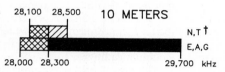

E,A,G

24,890   24,930   24,990   kHz

10 METERS

28,100 28,500

N,T †
E,A,G

28,000 28,300   29,700   kHz

Novices and Technicians are limited to 200 watts PEP output on 10 meters.

6 METERS

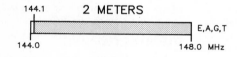

50.1

E,A,G,T

50.0   54.0   MHz

2 METERS

144.1

E,A,G,T

144.0   148.0   MHz

1.25 METERS

222.1   223.91

N
E,A,G,T

222.0   225.0   MHz

Novices are limited to 25 watts PEP output from 222.1 to 223.91 MHz.

70 CENTIMETERS **

E,A,G,T

420.0   450.0   MHz

33 CENTIMETERS **

E,A,G,T

902.0   928.0   MHz

23 CENTIMETERS **

1270   1295

N
E,A,G,T

1240   1300   MHz

Novices are limited to 5 watts PEP output from 1270 to 1295 MHz.

US AMATEUR POWER LIMITS

At all times, transmitter power should be kept down to that necessary to carry out the desired communications. Power is rated in watts PEP output. Unless otherwise stated, the maximum power output is 1500 W. Power for all license classes is limited to 200 W in the 10,100—10,150 kHz band and in all Novice subbands below 28,100 kHz. Novices and Technicians are restricted to 200 W in the 28,100—28,500 kHz subbands. In addition, Novices are restricted to 25 W in the 222.1—223.91 MHz subband and 5 W in the 1270—1295 MHz subband.

Operators with Technician class licenses and above may operate on all bands above 50 MHz. For more detailed information see The FCC Rule Book.

KEY

= CW, RTTY and data

= CW, RTTY, data, MCW, test, phone and image

= CW, phone and image

= CW and SSB

= CW, RTTY, data, phone, and image

= CW only

E = AMATEUR EXTRA
A = ADVANCED
G = GENERAL
T = TECHNICIAN
N = NOVICE

† Only Technician—class licensees who have passed a 5 — WPM code test may use these frequencies.

** Geographical and power restrictions apply to these bands. See The FCC Rule Book for more information about your area.

Above 23 Centimeters:

All licensees except Novices are authorized all modes on the following frequencies:
2300—2310 MHz
2390—2450 MHz
3300—3500 MHz
5650—5925 MHz
10.0—10.5 GHz
24.0—24.25 GHz
47.0—47.2 GHz
75.5—81.0 GHz
119.98—120.2 GHz
142—149 GHz
241—250 GHz
All above 300 GHz

For band plans and sharing arrangements, see *The ARRL Operating Manual.*

Table 2

Voluntary HF Band Plans for Considerate US Operators

The frequencies (in MHz) shown are the result of mutual agreement among amateurs. They are in addition to, and subject to, frequency allocations and subbands defined by FCC regulations.

Band	CW	RTTY	Phone	SSTV†	Fax††	Packet
160 m	1.800-1.840 1.830-1.840 DX	1.800-1.840 1.830-1.840 DX	1.840-2.000 1.840-1.850 DX	1.840-2.000		1.8023†††
80 m		3.605-3.645 3.590 DX	3.750-4.000 3.790-3.800 DX	3.845		3.605-3.645 3.5943†††(Int) 3.6073†††(NA)
40 m		7.080-7.100 7.040 DX		7.171	7.245	7.080-7.100 7.0383†††(Int) 7.0913†††(NA)
30 m		10.140-10.150				10.140-10.150 10.1453†††(Int) 10.1473†††(NA)
20 m	14.0995-14.1005 (b)	14.070-14.0995		14.230	14.245	14.070-14.0995 14.1023†††(Int) 14.1083†††(NA)
17 m	18.068-18.100	18.100-18.110	18.110-18.168			18.1063††† 18.1083†††
15 m	21.000-21.070 21.100-21.1495 21.1505-21.200 21.1495-21.1505 (b)	21.070-21.100	21.200-21.450	21.340	21.345	21.0963††† 21.0983†††
12 m	24.890-24.920	24.920-24.930	24.930-24.990			24.9263††† 24.9283†††
10 m	28.100-28.200 (b)	28.070-28.150	28.300-29.300 29.300-29.510 (satellite downlinks) 29.510-29.700 (repeaters) 29.600 (FM simplex calling)	28.680	28.945	28.1023††† 28.1043†††

Notes

†Establish contact on voice or CW first, then move off frequency to send images. A "gentlemen's agreement" of 20-year standing calls for SSTV operation as close to the calling frequencies as possible. There is an SSTV net on 14.230 Saturdays at 1500Z.

††Always establish voice or CW contact before sending fax. The US Facsimile Net meets Sundays on 14.245 MHz at 2000Z.

†††Automatic message forwarding: Int = Intercontinental; NA = North American

(b) = beacons

amateurs have developed systems of customary frequency usage known as band plans. The plans foster good relations between users of different operating modes (RTTY, data, image and so on) and also allow for allocation differences outside the US. Further, band plans are one way that amateurs police themselves. Our ability to do so directly contributes to our frequency allocations (because we are good "neighbors" for other services) and to our image with governments around the world. It benefits each of us, individually and collectively, to know and abide by the band plans. Table 2 portrays amateur band plans for the MF and HF bands. The VHF band plans are too long to include here (they appear in *The FCC Rule Book*), but Table 3 lists calling frequencies and "activity nights" for the VHF/UHF/EHF bands. Table 4 gives the frequencies and schedule of W1AW code-practice and bulletin transmissions.

ON THE AIR

Operating Standards

Through the years, Amateur Radio has developed specialized operating practices. Some are common courtesy, others save time or help bridge language barriers. Procedural signals (Table 5) must be agreed upon even before a contact begins. Always listen and inquire if the frequency is in use before calling CQ.

Several questions must be answered during each contact: What station have I contacted? How well am I heard? Where is the other station? Who is the operator? Common practice answers them in the first few seconds of communication: Call signs are the first information exchanged, followed quickly by a signal report, station location and the operator's name. Such practices help us all communicate more effectively.

There are other standards as well. Most are associated with one or more operating modes. For example, the RST (Readability/Signal strength/Tone) system of signal reporting (Table 6) is used in all modes except image communications, where the P5 system applies. Nonetheless, some operators use standards or abbreviations inappropriately (such as Q signals on voice modes), where they may hinder rather than aid communication.

CW Operating

Call CQ with a simple "3 × 3" transmission. That is CQ CQ CQ DE KU7G KU7G KU7G. Abbreviations (Table 7) are expeditious on CW. Q signals (see Table 23, in the Emergency Operations section of this chapter) are three-letter abbreviations for many common statements and questions used in radio conversation. General-use Q signals begin with either "QR" or "QS." Q signals developed especially for nets and traffic handling begin with "QN."

Voice Operating

While it may take less effort to speak into a microphone and listen than to operate CW and other modes, it does take some care to quickly and accurately convey exact information. Speak distinctly at all times. Keep your voice level and mike gain constant. If information is to be written, pace your speech accordingly. Keep transmissions brief: A short "3 × 2" CQ is sufficient. Other transmissions should be two minutes or less.

For critical information (or under noisy conditions) spell words with the ITU phonetics (Table 8). ITU phonetics and the pronunciations shown were chosen so that each word sounds completely different from all of the others—regardless of the listener's native language.

Remember that phonetics are used to convey meaning, *not* to aid memory. For example, hams touring ARRL HQ remember our HQ Operators' Club station as: "W1 It's Never Finished" (a memory aid), but on the air it should always be identified as "*WHISkey One INdia NoVEMber FOXtrot.*"

Repeaters

Repeaters extend the operating range of

Table 3
VHF/UHF/EHF Calling Frequencies

Band (MHz)	Calling Frequency
50	50.110 SSB DX
	50.200 SSB US, local
	50.400 AM
	50.700 RTTY
	52.525 National FM simplex frequency
144	144.010 EME
	144.100, 144.110 CW
	144.200 SSB
	146.520 National FM simplex frequency
222	222.100 CW/SSB
	223.500 National FM simplex frequency
432	432.010 EME
	432.100 CW/SSB
	446.000 National FM simplex frequency
902	903.100 CW,SSB
	906.500 National FM simplex frequency
1296	1294.500 National FM simplex frequency
	1296.100 CW/SSB
2304	2304.1
10000	10368

VHF/UHF Activity Nights

Some areas do not have enough VHF/UHF activity to support contacts at all times. This schedule is intended to help VHF/UHF operators make contact. This is only a starting point; check with others in your area to see if local hams have a different schedule.

Band (MHz)	Day	Local Time
50	Sunday	6 PM
144	Monday	7 PM
222	Tuesday	8 PM
432	Wednesday	9 PM
902	Friday	9 PM
1296	Thursday	10 PM

radios at frequencies above 29.51 MHz. Most repeaters are "open" (they may be used by anyone with a valid license), but some are "closed" or private (with access restricted by custom, subaudible tones or use of special codes). You can use an open repeater by simply transmitting and receiving on the appropriate frequencies. Repeater operation has many special techniques. Once you have a suitable radio, either scan until you hear activity or look up local repeaters in *The ARRL Repeater Directory*.

Initiate a contact by simply announcing your presence; for example, "This is K8CH monitoring." Keep transmissions short and pause a few seconds between them. Pauses allow others to join the conversation, and pauses also allow repeater control timers to reset. When the timers are not reset, the repeater may "time out" (go off the air until transmissions cease). One who often times out the repeater is known as a rachet jaw.

Listen for a while to pick up on local customs. For example, "break" is used in some regions to indicate an emergency access, while in other areas it is used to join a conversation in progress (and a double break, "break break," is used for emer-gency situations). The best way to join an ongoing conversation is to transmit your call sign during the pause between transmissions.

Many repeaters have "autopatches" that connect the repeater to the telephone lines. This is a blessing for road-side aid and so on, but requires strict attention to FCC regulations about business use, avoiding telephone charges and third-party traffic.

Repeaters are voluntarily purchased and maintained by other amateurs. Respect the owners' wishes and support their efforts.

Digital Modes

Amateurs are permitted to use RTTY and data modes as specified in FCC Rules and Regulations §§97.305, 97.307 and 97.309. Below 50 MHz, the rules permit ITA2 (Baudot), AMTOR and ASCII codes. (Packet radio uses ASCII.) These codes and their technology are defined in the Digital Communications chapter. When using one of these codes, amateurs may identify in the same code or CW (or voice where that mode is permitted). Other codes are permitted above 50 MHz, but the station must identify in one of these three codes, CW or voice. Common operating frequencies for digital modes are listed in Table 2.

Until the mid 1980s, it was pretty complicated to set up a RTTY station and get it operating. Early "terminal units" (modems) simply detected the incoming "mark" and "space" signals and passed them to a mechanical teleprinter or computer software for interpretation. Mechanical teleprinters are complex machines that make significant noise. Early software and modem connections vary from one computer to the next, and it was often difficult to work out interfaces that connected to "user" ports, game ports or tape-storage connectors.

Thanks to the decreasing costs of microprocessors and support ICs, however, it is now relatively simple to get going. Newer setups have a microprocessor inside the modem that bidirectionally translates the operator's chosen code to and from ASCII, which is then available at a standard EIA-232 port. Hence, you need only a modem, suitable cable, personal computer (with a serial communications port) and an ASCII terminal program to get on the air. In addition, some contemporary modems operate CW, Baudot, AMTOR, ASCII, packet radio, fax and more!

Because digital modes communicate characters, the procedures are very similar to those for CW. All CW abbreviations and Q signals are used.

Most digital operators have a "brag tape." For mechanical teleprinters, this is a perforated tape that describes the station equipment, the operator and so on. It saves a lot of time and typing to send information repeated with each new acquaintance on the air. Most computer-based systems provide for stored messages that serve the same purpose. If you use a brag tape, keep it brief; lengthy brags waste spectrum.

Computer-Based Message Systems (CBMSs), Message-Storage Operations (MSOs), bulletin boards, or mailboxes have appeared on the ham bands. They automatically respond to calls on their operating frequency, if the calling station uses the correct character sequence. Calling stations can write, list and read messages stored in the system. Message handling in this manner is third-party traffic, and the system operator (SYSOP) is required to obey applicable FCC rules concerning station control and message content.

ITA2 (Baudot)

A few character sequences have special meaning (see Table 9). A continuous pattern of alternating Rs and Ys is used for testing. Its bit pattern is a continuous alternation of mark and space; use it sparingly.

AMTOR

AMTOR is a protocol that uses a derivative of ITA2; it reduces data errors. AMTOR has several modes of operation. Character exchanges, acknowledgments and received-data assembly are processed automatically by the modem. The operator simply selects the mode, provides data to transmit and accepts received data.

Mode A is known as Automatic Repeat reQuest (ARQ) and is limited to contacts between two stations. The transmitting station sends a group of three characters. If the group is received correctly, the receiving station acknowledges, and the transmitting station sends another group of three. If the receiving station does not acknowledge, the transmitting station repeats the three characters until acknowledged.

Mode B employs Forward Error Correction (FEC). Data is sent in groups of five characters. Each group is sent, and then repeated once. Collective B-Mode is used to transmit to many stations, as in a CQ, bulletin transmission or net. Selective B-Mode uses FEC but is intended for one or more selected stations.

ASCII

ASCII operation is essentially the same as ITA2 operation, except that ASCII provides a larger character set. Using ASCII, you can send most characters available on a typewriter keyboard plus numerous control characters such as: start of text (STX), end of text (ETX), horizontal (HT) and vertical (VT) tabs, form feed (FF) and end of transmission (EOT).

Packet Radio

Packet radio uses sophisticated routing and error-detection techniques to provide essentially error-free data transfer. The system, its operation, its communications structure, sources of more information and a glossary of packet-radio terms are covered in the Digital Communications chapter.

Packet bulletin-board systems (PBBSs) are a significant aspect of packet-radio operation. One key feature is its "mailbox," with automatic message forwarding. A message placed for a ham who regularly visits a distant PBBS is automatically transmitted through the packet-radio network for delivery at the other PBBS.

Some PBBSs also provide "gateway" service. A gateway PBBS has TNC-radio combinations on two or more serial ports. When in the gateway mode, the PBBS transfers packets, bidirectionally, between the ports. Most gateways transfer between VHF/UHF and one of the HF amateur bands. With the mail-forwarding and gateway features of PBBSs, packet radio offers tremendous potential for automatic amateur message handling.

IMAGE COMMUNICATIONS

Image modes include fast-scan television (FSTV or ATV), slow-scan television (SSTV) and facsimile (fax). Fig 2 illustrates the P5 system used to rate picture quality. Image modes are permitted and used on the

amateur bands as indicated in Tables 1 and 2, respectively. The technical aspects of the modes are covered in the Image Communications chapter. Their operating techniques are treated in *The ARRL Operating Manual*.

WORKING DX

"DX" is an abbreviation for distance. "CQ DX" means slightly different things to amateurs on different bands:

On VHF, CQ DX is a general call used only when the band is open, under favorable "skip" conditons. VHF DX means new states, countries and stations beyond

the customary "line-of-sight" range on most VHF bands.

On HF, CQ DX is a "general call to any foreign station," where "foreign" usually refers to a different continent. CQ DX implies you will answer any DX station that replies. If you won't accept all DX stations, listen and call a station you want.

DX Call Signs

What station do you want? How can you know a station's location before you make contact? You can get some idea from the call sign. Think of each call sign as a prefix that indicates the nation or international

---

Table 4
W1AW Schedule

MTWThFSSn = Days of Week Dy = Daily

W1AW code practice and bulletin transmissions are sent on the following schedule:

ET	Slow Code Practice	MWF: 9AM, 7PM; TThSSn: 4 PM, 10 PM
	Fast Code Practice	MWF: 4 PM, 10 PM; TTh: 9AM; TThSSn: 7PM
	CW Bulletins	Dy: 5 PM, 8 PM, 11 PM; MTWThF: 10 AM
	Teleprinter Bulletins	Dy: 6PM, 9 PM, 12 PM; MTWThF: 11 AM
	Voice Bulletins	Dy: 9:45 PM, 12:45 AM
CT	Slow Code Practice	MWF: 8 AM, 6 PM; TThSSn: 3 PM, 9 PM
	Fast Code Practice	MWF: 3 PM, 9 PM; TTh: 8 AM; TThSSn: 6 PM
	CW Bulletins	Dy: 4 PM, 7 PM, 10 PM; MTWThF: 9 AM
	Teleprinter Bulletins	DY: 5 PM, 8 PM, 11 PM; MTWThF: 10 AM
	Voice Bulletins	Dy: 8:45 PM, 11:45 PM
MT	Slow Code Practice	MWF: 7 AM, 5 PM; TThSSn: 2 PM; 8 PM
	Fast Code Practice	MWF: 2 PM, 8 PM; TTh: 7 AM; TThSSn: 5 PM
	CW Bulletins	Dy: 3 PM, 6 PM, 9 PM; MTWThF: 8 AM
	Teleprinter Bulletins	Dy: 4 PM, 7 PM, 10 PM; MTWThF: 9 AM
	Voice Bulletins	Dy: 7:45 PM, 10:45 PM
PT	Slow Code Practice	MWF: 6 AM, 4 PM; TThSSn: 1 PM; 7 PM
	Fast Code Practice	MWF: 1 PM, 7 PM; TTh: 6 AM; TThSSn: 4 PM
	CW Bulletins	Dy: 2 PM, 5 PM, 8 PM; MTWThF: 7 AM
	Teleprinter Bulletins	Dy: 3 PM, 6 PM, 9 PM; MTWThF: 8 AM
	Voice Bulletins	Dy: 6:45 PM, 9:45 PM

Code practice, Qualifying Run and CW bulletin frequencies: 1.818, 3.5815, 7.0475, 14.0475, 18.0975, 21.0675, 28.0675, 50.08, 147.555 MHz.

Teleprinter bulletin frequencies: 3.625, 7.095, 14.095, 18.1025, 21.095, 28.095 MHz.
Voice bulletin frequencies: 3.99, 7.29, 14.29, 18.160, 21.39, 28.59, 50.19, 147.555 MHz.

Slow code practice is at 5, 7½, 10, 13 and 15 WPM. Fast code practice is at 35, 30, 25, 20, 15, 13 and 10 WPM.

Code practice texts are from *QST*, and the source of each practice is given at the beginning of each practice and at the beginning of alternate speeds. For example, "Text is from February 1991 *QST*, pages 9 and 81" indicates that the main text is from the article on page 9 and the mixed number/letter groups at the end of each speed are from the contest scores on page 81.

On Fridays, UTC, a DX bulletin replaces the regular bulletin transmissions.

On Tuesdays and Saturdays at 2230 UTC, Keplerian Elements for active amateur satellites are sent on the regular teleprinter frequencies.

Some of the slow practice sessions are sent with each line of text from *QST* reversed. For example, "Last October, the ARRL Board of Directors" would be sent as DIRECTORS OF BOARD ARRL THE, OCTOBER LAST.

Teleprinter bulletins are 45.45-baud Baudot, 110-baud ASCII and 100-baud AMTOR, FEC mode.

CW bulletins are sent at 18 WPM.

W1AW is open for visitors Monday through Friday from 11 AM to 11 PM Eastern time and on Saturday and Sunday from 4:30 PM to 11 PM Eastern time. If you desire to operate W1AW, be sure to bring a copy of your license with you. W1AW is available for operation by visitors between 1 and 4 PM Monday through Friday.

In a communications emergency, monitor W1AW for special bulletins as follows: voice on the hour, teleprinter at 15 minutes past the hour, and CW on the half hour.

Table 5
ARRL Procedural Signals (Prosigns)

In general, the CW prosigns are used on all data modes as well, although word abbreviations may be spelled out. That is, "CLEAR" might be used rather than "CL" on radioteletype. Additional radioteletype conventions appear at the end of the table.

Situation	CW	Voice
check for a clear frequency	QRL?	Is the frequency in use?
seek contact with any station	CQ	CQ
after call to a specific named station or to indicate the end of a message	A̅R̅	over, end of message
invite any station to transmit	K	go
invite a specific named station to transmit	K̅N̅	go only
invite receiving station to transmit	BK	back to you
all received correctly	R	received
please stand by	A̅S̅	wait, stand by
end of contact (sent before call sign)	S̅K̅	clear
going off the air	CL	closing station

Additional RTTY prosigns
SK QRZ—Ending contact, but listening on frequency.
SK KN—Ending contact, but listening for one last transmission from the other station.
SK SZ—Signing off and listening on the frequency for any other calls.

Table 6
The RST System

READABILITY
1 — Unreadable.
2 — Barely readable, occasional words distinguishable.
3 — Readable with considerable difficulty.
4 — Readable with practically no difficulty.
5 — Perfectly readable.

SIGNAL STRENGTH
1 — Faint signals, barely perceptible.
2 — Very weak signals.
3 — Weak signals,
4 — Fair signals.
5 — Fairly good signals.
6 — Good signals.
7 — Moderately strong signals.
8 — Strong signals.
9 — Extremely strong signals.

TONE
1 — Sixty-cycle ac or less, very rough and broad.
2 — Very rough ac, very harsh and broad.
3 — Rough ac tone, rectified but not filtered.
4 — Rough note, some trace of filtering.
5 — Filtered rectified ac but strongly ripple-modulated.
6 — Filtered tone, definite trace of ripple modulation.
7 — Near pure tone, trace of ripple modulation.
8 — Near perfect tone, slight trace of modulation.
9 — Perfect tone, no trace of ripple or modulation of any kind.

If the signal has the characteristic steadiness of crystal control, add the letter X to the RST report. If there is a chirp, add the letter C. Similarly for a click, add K. (See FCC Regulations §97.307, Emissions Standards.) The above reporting system is used on both CW and voice; leave out the "tone" report on voice.

Table 7
Some Abbreviations for CW Work

Although abbreviations help to cut down unnecessary transmission, make it a rule not to abbreviate unnecessarily when working an operator of unknown experience.

AA	All after	OC	Old chap
AB	All before	OM	Old man
ABT	About	OP-OPR	Operator
ADR	Address	OT	Old timer; old top
AGN	Again	PBL	Preamble
ANT	Antenna	PSE	Please
BCI	Broadcast interference	PWR	Power
BCL	Broadcast listener	PX	Press
BK	Break; break me; break in	R	Received as transmitted; are
BN	All between; been	RCD	Received
BUG	Semi-automatic key	RCVR (RX)	Receiver
B4	Before	REF	Refer to; referring to; reference
C	Yes	RFI	Radio frequency interference
CFM	Confirm; I confirm	RIG	Station equipment
CK	Check	RPT	Repeat; I repeat; report
CL	I am closing my station; call	RTTY	Radioteletype
CLD-CLG	Called; calling	RX	Receiver
CQ	Calling any station	SASE	Self-addressed, stamped envelope
CUD	Could	SED	Said
CUL	See you later	SIG	Signature; signal
CW	Continuous wave (i.e., radiotelegraph)	SINE	Operator's personal initials or nickname
DLD-DLVD	Delivered	SKED	Schedule
DR	Dear	SRI	Sorry
DX	Distance, foreign countries	SSB	Single sideband
ES	And, &	SVC	Service; prefix to service message
FB	Fine business, excellent	T	Zero
FM	Frequency modulation	TFC	Traffic
GA	Go ahead (or resume sending)	TMW	Tomorrow
GB	Good-by	TNX-TKS	Thanks
GBA	Give better address	TT	That
GE	Good evening	TU	Thank you
GG	Going	TVI	Television interference
GM	Good morning	TX	Transmitter
GN	Good night	TXT	Text
GND	Ground	UR-URS	Your; you're; yours
GUD	Good	VFO	Variable-frequency oscillator
HI	The telegraphic laugh; high	VY	Very
HR	Here, hear	WA	Word after
HV	Have	WB	Word before
HW	How	WD-WDS	Word; words
LID	A poor operator	WKD-WKG	Worked; working
MA, MILS	Milliamperes	WL	Well; will
MSG	Message; prefix to radiogram	WUD	Would
N	No	WX	Weather
NCS	Net control station	XCVR	Transceiver
ND	Nothing doing	XMTR (TX)	Transmitter
NIL	Nothing; I have nothing for you	XTAL	Crystal
NM	No more	XYL (YF)	Wife
NR	Number	YL	Young lady
NW	Now; I resume transmission	73	Best regards
OB	Old boy	88	Love and kisses

Table 8

ITU Recommended Phonetics

A—Alfa (**AL** FAH)
B—Bravo (**BRAH** VOH)
C—Charlie (**CHAR** LEE OR **SHAR** LEE)
D—Delta (**DELL** TAH)
E—Echo (**ECK** OH)
F—Foxtrot (**FOKS** TROT)
G—Golf (GOLF)
H—Hotel (HOH **TELL**)
I—India (**IN** DEE AH)
J—Juliet (**JEW** LEE ETT)
K—Kilo (**KEY** LOH)
L—Lima (**LEE** MAH)
M—Mike (MIKE)
N—November (NO **VEM** BER)
O—Oscar (**OSS** CAH)
P—Papa (PAH **PAH**)
Q—Quebec (KEH **BECK**)
R—Romeo (**ROW** ME OH)
S—Sierra (SEE **AIR** RAH)
T—Tango (**TANG** GO)
U—Uniform (**YOU** NEE FORM or **OO** NEE FORM)
V—Victor (**VIK** TAH)
W—Whiskey (**WISS** KEY)
X—X-Ray (**ECKS** RAY)
Y—Yankee (**YANG** KEY)
Z—Zulu (**ZOO** LOO)

Note: The **Boldfaced** syllables are emphasized. The pronunciations shown in the table were designed for speakers from all international languages. The pronunciations given for "Oscar" and "Victor" may seem awkward to English-speaking people in the US.

Table 9

RTTY Control Sequences (from CCITT Recommendation S.4)

Sequence	Meaning
ZCZC	start of message
NNNN	end of message
CCCC	enable remote reperforator (or other device)
SSSS	enable remote terminal
FFFF	disable remote reperforator
KKKK	ready for test
KLKL	enable remote reader
XXXXX	error signal

---

organization that authorized the license, and a suffix, which uniquely identifies that station among others in the same nation or organization.

Table 11 lists all allocated prefix blocks that may be used for any station—not just Amateur Radio. Prefix characters are allocated in blocks with three-character delimiters. Actual prefix length, however, may vary from one to three alphanumeric characters. Prefixes are generally separated from suffixes by numbers, although a number may be part of the prefix as well. For example, consider A92AZ (A9A-A9Z is allocated to Bahrain): "A9" is the prefix, and "2AZ" is the suffix. AA2Z, however, is in the US: "AA" is the prefix because there is no AA2 block in Table 11 and AAA-ALZ are allocated to the US. (Note that there are no numbers in the US block, so the US cannot use A9 as a prefix.)

Table 11 indicates all possible prefixes,

but some authorities do not use all prefixes for amateur licenses. For example, Canada could use CFA-CKZ, CYA-CZZ, VAA-VGZ, VXA-VYZ and XJA-XOZ, but Canadian amateur stations are typically assigned a VE, VO or VY prefix. Canadian special-event stations, however, have used many other authorized prefixes.

US DX? Certain stations licensed by the FCC are considered DX. Their prefixes even sound a little exotic: KH1, KP4 and KL7. Table 12 lists prefixes for US-licensed areas outside the continental US.

If you become interested in DX operation, get a copy of *The ARRL DXCC Countries List* (available through local dealers and ARRL HQ). The list shows typical amateur prefixes for DXCC countries and many other aids helpful to the DX-oriented amateur.

Ethics

Ethics are important in DX work. Poor or inconsiderate operating can make some DX stations leave the air in disgust. Table 13 presents good operating practices for both W/VE and overseas stations. Read and follow the appropriate guidelines.

LOGGING

FCC has removed logging requirements from the Amateur Radio Service rules, but there are still good reasons to record information about your Amateur Radio activity. A station log is a diary of your Amateur Radio history. Record all contacts; the log should hold all information needed for QSL cards—as discussed below—plus any other desired notes, such as the other operator's name (see Fig 3). The log can also be a strong form of protection should you be accused of intentional interference. It's also helpful in case of RFI complaints or unauthorized use of your call sign. Record address changes, license upgrades and equipment purchases or sales—with serial numbers in case the equipment is lost or stolen—for future reference.

QSL CARDS

A QSL is the final courtesy of a contact, and it is an Amateur Radio tradition. Most amateurs have printed cards, some personalized, some using standard setups provided by printers for the purpose—such as the ARRL member QSL in Fig 4. Whichever form you adopt, be sure your QSL card shows very clearly the correct call of the station contacted, the date and time in UTC, the band on which contact was made and the mode (see Table 14). Most QSL-based awards require at least these essentials, along with your call sign, street address, city, state and country. Some awards require your county as well. Many hams add interesting facts about equipment, antennas, former calls, the signal report and friendly comments.

The time and date are critical QSL information. If you want a return QSL, the other operator must be able to find your

P5 — Excellent

P4 — Good

P3 — Fair

P2 — Poor

P1 — Barely perceptible

Fig 2—ATV picture quality reporting system.

Table 11

Allocation of International Call Signs

Call Sign Series	Allocated to
AAA-ALZ	United States of America
AMA-AOZ	Spain
APA-ASZ	Pakistan
ATA-AWZ	India
AXA-AXZ	Australia
AYA-AZZ	Argentina
A2A-A2Z	Botswana
A3A-A3Z	Tonga
A4A-A4Z	Oman
A5A-A5Z	Bhutan
A6A-A6Z	United Arab Emirates
A7A-A7Z	Qatar
A8A-A8Z	Liberia
A9A-A9Z	Bahrain
BAA-BZZ	China
CAA-CEZ	Chile
CFA-CKZ	Canada
CLA-CMZ	Cuba
CNA-CNZ	Morocco
COA-COZ	Cuba
CPA-CPZ	Bolivia
CQA-CUZ	Portugal
CVA-CXZ	Uruguay
CYA-CZZ	Canada
C2A-C2Z	Nauru
C3A-C3Z	Andorra
C4A-C4Z	Cyprus
C5A-C5Z	Gambia
C6A-C6Z	Bahamas
C7A-C7Z*	World Meteorological Organization
C8A-C9Z	Mozambique
DAA-DRZ	Germany
DSA-DTZ	Republic of Korea
DUA-DZZ	Philippines
D2A-D3Z	Angola
D4A-D4Z	Cape Verde
D5A-D5Z	Liberia
D6A-D6Z	Comoros
D7A-D9Z	Republic of Korea
EAA-EHZ	Spain
EIA-EJZ	Ireland
EKA-EKZ	Union of Soviet Socialist Republics
ELA-ELZ	Liberia
EMA-EOZ	Union of Soviet Socialist Republics
EPA-EQZ	Iran
ERA-ESZ	Union of Soviet Socialist Republics
ETA-ETZ	Ethiopia
EUA-EWZ	Byelorussian Soviet Socialist Republic
EXA-EZZ	Union of Soviet Socialist Republics
E2A-E2Z	Thailand
FAA-FZZ	France
GAA-GZZ	United Kingdom of Great Britain and Northern Ireland
HAA-HAZ	Hungary
HBA-HBZ	Switzerland
HCA-HDZ	Ecuador
HEA-HEZ	Switzerland
HFA-HFZ	Poland
HGA-HGZ	Hungary
HHA-HHZ	Haiti
HIA-HIZ	Dominican Republic
HJA-HKZ	Colombia
HLA-HLZ	Republic of Korea
HMA-HMZ	Democratic People's Republic of Korea
HNA-HNZ	Iraq
HOA-HPZ	Panama
HQA-HRZ	Honduras
HSA-HSZ	Thailand
HTA-HTZ	Nicaragua
HUA-HUZ	El Salvador
HVA-HVZ	Vatican City
HWA-HYZ	France
HZA-HZZ	Saudi Arabia
H2A-H2Z	Cyprus
H3A-H3Z	Panama
H4A-H4Z	Solomon Islands

Call Sign Series	Allocated to
H6A-H7Z	Nicaragua
H8A-H9Z	Panama
IAA-IZZ	Italy
JAA-JSZ	Japan
JTA-JVZ	Mongolia
JWA-JXZ	Norway
JYA-JYZ	Jordan
JZA-JZZ	Indonesia
J2A-J2Z	Djibouti
J3A-J3Z	Grenada
J4A-J4Z	Greece
J5A-J5Z	Guinea-Bissau
J6A-J6Z	Saint Lucia
J7A-J7Z	Dominica
J8A-J8Z	St. Vincent and the Grenadines
KAA-KZZ	United States of America
LAA-LNZ	Norway
LOA-LWZ	Argentina
LXA-LXZ	Luxembourg
LYA-LYZ	Union of Soviet Socialist Republics
LZA-LZZ	Bulgaria
L2A-L9Z	Argentina
MAA-MZZ	United Kingdom of Great Britain and Northern Ireland
NAA-NZZ	United States of America
OAA-OCZ	Peru
ODA-ODZ	Lebanon
OEA-OEZ	Austria
OFA-OJZ	Finland
OKA-OMZ	Czechoslovakia
ONA-OTZ	Belgium
OUA-OZZ	Denmark
PAA-PIZ	Netherlands
PJA-PJZ	Netherlands Antilles
PKA-POZ	Indonesia
PPA-PYZ	Brazil
PZA-PZZ	Suriname
P2A-P2Z	Papua New Guinea
P3A-P3Z	Cyprus
P4A-P4Z	Aruba
P5A-P9Z	Democratic People's Republic of Korea
QAA-QZZ	(Service abbreviations)
RAA-RZZ	Union of Soviet Socialist Republics
SAA-SMZ	Sweden
SNA-SRZ	Poland
SSA-SSM	Egypt
SSN-STZ	Sudan
SUA-SUZ	Egypt
SVA-SZZ	Greece
S2A-S3Z	Bangladesh
S6A-S6Z	Singapore
S7A-S7Z	Seychelles
S9A-S9Z	Sao Tome and Principe
TAA-TCZ	Turkey
TDA-TDZ	Guatemala
TEA-TEZ	Costa Rica
TFA-TFZ	Iceland
TGA-TGZ	Guatemala
THA-THZ	France
TIA-TIZ	Costa Rica
TJA-TJZ	Cameroon
TKA-TKZ	France
TLA-TLZ	Central Africa
TMA-TMZ	France
TNA-TNZ	Congo
TOA-TQZ	France
TRA-TRZ	Gabon
TSA-TSZ	Tunisia
TTA-TTZ	Chad
TUA-TUZ	Ivory Coast
TVA-TXZ	France
TYA-TYZ	Benin
TZA-TZZ	Mali
T2A-T2Z	Tuvalu
T3A-T3Z	Kiribati
T4A-T4Z	Cuba

Call Sign Series	Allocated to
T5A-T5Z	Somalia
T6A-T6Z	Afghanistan
T7A-T7Z	San Marino
UAA-UQZ	Union of Soviet Socialist Republics
URA-UTZ	Ukrainian Soviet Socialist Republic
UUA-UZZ	Union of Soviet Socialist Republics
VAA-VGZ	Canada
VHA-VNZ	Australia
VOA-VOZ	Canada
VPA-VSZ	United Kingdom of Great Britain and Northern Ireland
VTA-VWZ	India
VXA-VYZ	Canada
VZA-VZZ	Australia
V2A-V2Z	Antigua and Barbuda
V3A-V3Z	Belize
V4A-V4Z	St. Christopher and Nevis
V6A-V6Z	Micronesia
V7A-V7Z	Marshall Islands
V8A-V8Z	Brunei
WAA-WZZ	United States of America
XAA-XIZ	Mexico
XJA-XOZ	Canada
XPA-XPZ	Denmark
XQA-XRZ	Chile
XSA-XSZ	China
XTA-XTZ	Burkina Faso
XUA-XUZ	Cambodia
XVA-XVZ	Viet Nam
XWA-XWZ	Laos
XXA-XXZ	Portugal
XYA-XZZ	Myanmar (Burma)
YAA-YAZ	Afghanistan
YBA-YHZ	Indonesia
YIA-YIZ	Iraq
YJA-YJZ	New Hebrides
YKA-YKZ	Syria
YLA-YLZ	Union of Soviet Socialist Republics
YMA-YMZ	Turkey
YNA-YNZ	Nicaragua
YOA-YRZ	Romania
YSA-YSZ	El Salvador
YTA-YUZ	Yugoslavia
YVA-YYZ	Venezuela
YZA-YZZ	Yugoslavia
Y2A-Y9Z	Germany
ZAA-ZAZ	Albania
ZBA-ZJZ	United Kingdom of Great Britain and Northern Ireland
ZKA-ZMZ	New Zealand
ZNA-ZOZ	United Kingdom of Great Britain and Northern Ireland
ZPA-ZPZ	Paraguay
ZQA-ZQZ	United Kingdom of Great Britain and Northern Ireland
ZRA-ZUZ	South Africa
ZVA-ZZZ	Brazil
Z2A-Z2Z	Zimbabwe
2AA-2ZZ	United Kingdom of Great Britain and Northern Ireland
3AA-3AZ	Monaco
3BA-3AZ	Mauritius
3CA-3CZ	Equatorial Guinea
3DA-3DM	Swaziland
3DN-3DZ	Fiji
3EA-3FZ	Panama
3GA-3GZ	Chile
3HA-3UZ	China
3VA-3VZ	Tunisia
3WA-3WZ	Viet Nam
3XA-3XZ	Guinea
3YA-3YZ	Norway
3ZA-3ZZ	Poland
4AA-4CA	Mexico

Call Sign Series	Allocated to
4DA-4IZ	Philippines
4JA-4LZ	Union of Soviet Socialist Republics
4MA-4MZ	Venezuela
4NA-4OZ	Yugoslavia
4PA-4SZ	Sri Lanka
4TA-4TZ	Peru
4UA-4UZ*	United Nations Organization
4VA-4VZ	Haiti
4WA-4WZ	Yemen Arab Republic
4XA-4XZ	Israel
4YA-4YZ*	International Civil Aviation Organization
4ZA-4ZZ	Israel
5AA-5AZ	Libya
5BA-5BZ	Cyprus
5CA-5GZ	Morocco
5HA-5IZ	Tanzania
5JA-5KZ	Colombia
5LA-5MZ	Liberia
5NA-5OZ	Nigeria
5PA-5QZ	Denmark
5RA-5SZ	Madagascar
5TA-5TZ	Mauritania
5UA-5UZ	Niger
5VA-5VZ	Togo
5WA-5WZ	Western Samoa
5XA-5XZ	Uganda
5YA-5ZZ	Kenya
6AA-6BZ	Egypt
6CA-6CZ	Syria
6DA-6JZ	Mexico
6KA-6NZ	Republic of Korea
6OA-6OZ	Somalia
6PA-6SZ	Pakistan
6TA-6UZ	Sudan
6VA-6WZ	Senegal
6XA-6XZ	Madagascar
6YA-6YZ	Jamaica
6ZA-6ZZ	Liberia
7AA-7IZ	Indonesia
7JA-7NZ	Japan
7OA-7OZ	Yemen
7PA-7PZ	Lesotho
7QA-7QZ	Malawi
7RA-7RZ	Algeria
7SA-7SZ	Sweden
7TA-7YZ	Algeria
7ZA-7ZZ	Saudi Arabia
8AA-8IZ	Indonesia
8JA-8NZ	Japan
8OA-8OZ	Botswana
8PA-8PZ	Barbados
8QA-8QZ	Maldives
8RA-8RZ	Guyana
8SA-8SZ	Sweden
8TA-8YZ	India
8ZA-8ZZ	Saudi Arabia
9BA-9DZ	Iran
9EA-9FZ	Ethiopia
9GA-9GZ	Ghana
9HA-9HZ	Malta
9IA-9JZ	Zambia
9KA-9KZ	Kuwait
9LA-9LZ	Sierra Leone
9MA-9MZ	Malaysia
9NA-9NZ	Nepal
9OA-9TZ	Zaire
9UA-9UZ	Burundi
9VA-9VZ	Singapore
9WA-9WZ	Malaysia
9XA-9XZ	Rwanda
9YA-9ZZ	Trinidad and Tobago

Note

The series of call signs with an asterisk indicate the international organization to which they are allocated.

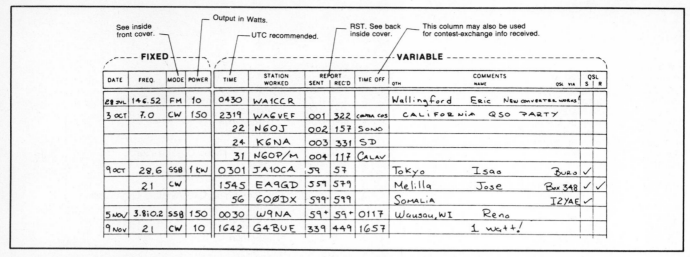

Fig 3—The ARRL Log is adaptable for all types of operating— ragchewing, contesting, DXing. References are to pages in the ARRL log.

Table 12

FCC-Allocated Prefixes for Areas Outside the Continental US

Prefix	Location
AH1, KH1, NH1, WH1	Baker, Howland Is
AH2, KH2, NH2, WH2	Guam
AH3, KH3, NH3, WH3	Johnston I
AH4, KH4, NH4, WH4	Midway I
AH5K, KH5K, NH5K, WH5K	Kingman Reef
AH5, KH5, NH5, WH5 (except K suffix)	Palmyra, Jarvis Is
AH6, KH6, NH6, WH6	Hawaii
AH7, KH7, NH7, WH7	Kure I
AH8, KH8, NH8, WH8	American Samoa
AH9, KH9, NH9, WH9	Wake I
AHØ, KHØ, NHØ, WHØ	Northern Mariana Is
AL7, KL7, NL7, WL7	Alaska
KP1, NP1, WP1	Navassa I
KP2, NP2, WP2	Virgin Is
KP4, NP4, WP4	Puerto Rico
KP5	Desecheo

Fig 4—The ARRL membership QSL card. This example is from Harris Ruben, N2ERN, who designed the card. Your card would reflect your own call sign and address; awards, county and VUCC grid-square are optional. ARRL does not print or sell the cards. Inquire with printers who advertise in the *QST* Ham Ads.

Table 13

DX Operating Code

For W/VE Amateurs

Some amateur DXers have caused considerable confusion and interference in their efforts to work DX stations. The points below, if observed by all W/VE amateurs, will help make DX more enjoyable for all.

1) *Call* DX only after he calls CQ, QRZ? or signs $\overline{SK}$, or voice equivalents thereof. Make your calls short.

2) Do not call a DX station:
   a) On the frequency of the station he is calling until you are sure the QSO is over ($\overline{SK}$).
   b) Because you hear someone else calling him.
   c) When he signs $\overline{KN}$, $\overline{AR}$ or CL.
   d) Exactly on his frequency.
   e) After he calls a directional CQ, unless of course you are in the right direction or area.

3) Keep within frequency band limits. Some DX stations can get away with working outside, but you cannot.

4) Observe calling instructions given by DX stations. Example: 15U means "call 15 kHz *up* from my frequency." 15D means *down*, etc.

5) Give honest reports. Many DX stations *depend* on W/VE reports for adjustment of station and equipment.

6) Keep your signal clean. Key clicks, ripple, feedback or splatter gives you a bad reputation and may get you a citation from FCC.

7) *Listen* and call the station you want. Calling CQ DX is not the best assurance that the rare DX will reply.

8) When there are several W or VE stations waiting, avoid asking DX to "listen for a friend." Also avoid engaging him in a ragchew against his wishes.

For Overseas Amateurs

To all overseas amateur stations:

In their eagerness to work you, many W and VE amateurs resort to practices that cause confusion and QRM. Most of this is good-intentional but ill-advised; some of it is intentional and selfish. The key to the cessation of unethical DX operating practices is in your hands. We believe that your adoption of certain operating habits will increase your enjoyment of Amateur Radio and that of amateurs on this side who are eager to work you. We recommend your adoption of the following principles:

1) Do not answer calls on your own frequency.

2) Answer calls from W/VE stations only when their signals are of good quality.

3) Refuse to answer calls from other stations when you are already in contact with someone, and do not acknowledge calls from amateurs who indicate they wish to be "next."

4) Give *everybody* a break. When many W/VE amateurs are patiently and quietly waiting to work you, avoid complying with requests to "listen for a friend."

5) Tell listeners where to call you by indicating how many kilohertz up (U) or down (D) from your frequency you are listening.

6) Use the ARRL-recommended ending signals, especially $\overline{KN}$ to indicate to impatient listeners the status of the QSO. $\overline{KN}$ means "Go ahead (specific station); all others keep out."

7) Let it be known that you avoid working amateurs who are constant violators of these principles.

The N7BH World Time Finder

You can eliminate errors in local-to-UTC time and date conversion by keeping a two-function clock set to local time and UTC. That solution, however, doesn't help determine the date and time in zones other than local and UTC. The circular slide rule shown here works simultaneously for all time zones. (Within certain limits. Many localities deviate from the system of Time Zones.) The outer scale shows hours in the 24-hour format with plus and minus signs to indicate the gain or loss of a day at midnight. The inner scale is labeled with a letter and longitude to identify each Time Zone, UTC, the International Date Line and abbreviations for Time Zones in the US. For example, 2100T indicates 9 PM Mountain Standard Time or Pacific Daylight Time. (Note that adopting daylight time has the same effect as shifting one time zone to the east, and thus one hour closer to UTC.)

Time Zones

The system of Time Zones is based on a few facts about our planet. Because it takes 24 hours for the earth to rotate 360°, there is one hour of time change for every 15° of longitude (there are 24 Time Zones, each 1 hour different from those adjacent). The Prime Meridian (0° longitude) passes through Greenwich, England, and serves as a location for UTC. The International Date Line is 180° longitude and directly opposite the Prime Meridian. While this all forms a mathematical foundation for the Time Zone system, there are many deviations from a strict longitude/Time Zone correspondence for local convenience. For example, portions of Alaska and Hawaii share the same longitude, yet they are in different Time Zones.

Construction

You can assemble your own World Time Finder by making two photocopies of this page. Cut one copy on the line of the inner circle, and the other on the line of the outer circle. Put each circle between two pieces of clear plastic, or laminate them between sheets of clear Con-Tact® paper (a sticky-backed plastic material sold in many department stores). Punch a hole in the center of each disk and use a 1/8-inch rivet with washers for the center pin.

Use

Operate The World Time Finder by aligning the time zone letter for your area with the current hour. In the example shown, it is 2000 hours (8 PM) at zone U (PST). Zone U is 120° W longitude, or 8 hours earlier than UTC. If the zone-U date is July 1, then the UTC time and date is 0400 (4 AM) on July 2. In Japan (zone I), which is 135° E longitude and 9 hours later than UTC, it would be 1300 (1 PM) on July 2.

Note that this time conversion can be done by traveling either clockwise or counterclockwise around the chart. Going in a counterclockwise direction from zone U to UTC, you pass midnight (in the direction of the arrow pointing to the plus sign) on the outer scale, thus gaining a day. If traveling in a clockwise direction, you pass the International Date Line (with the arrow to plus), again gaining a day. The gain or loss of date is established easily by the + or − signs next to the arrows.

Table 14

Suggested Mode Abbreviations for QSL Cards

Abbreviation	Explanation
CW	Telegraphy
DATA	Telemetry, telecommand and computer communications (includes packet radio)
IMAGE	Facsimile and television
MCW	Tone-modulated telegraphy
PHONE	Speech and other sound
PULSE	Modulated main carrier
RTTY	Direct-printing telegraphy (includes AMTOR)
SS	Spread Spectrum
TEST	Emissions containing no information

Note: For additional information on emission types refer to latest edition of *The FCC Rule Book*.

contact in his or her log, which is usually organized chronologically. It is best to keep a station clock (with calendar) set to UTC, and use it for all logging and time references on the air. (See "The N7BH World Time Finder.")

UTC establishes a uniform time reference, but there is still a problem with how we record dates. It is US convention to write May 4, 1990 as 5/4/90 (M/D/YR). Unfortunately, European convention would write it 4/5/90 (D/M/YR). Either of these conventions could be easily misinterpreted when the day value is 12 or less. Some folks solve the ambiguity by writing the month as a Roman numeral (V/4/90 or 4/V/90 for the date above), and others propose a convention that progresses from most- to least-significant digits (similar to hours:minutes:seconds)—90/5/4 (YR/M/D). Perhaps one of these will become a world standard in the future, but for now it seems best to write out (or abbreviate) the month in all dates, such as May 4 90 or 1 Jan 90.

The ARRL QSL Bureaus

The ARRL maintains both incoming and outgoing QSL bureaus. These bureaus make the exchange of QSL cards between US and DX stations less costly and more convenient. Complete details of the ARRL incoming and outgoing QSL bureaus are available from ARRL HQ for an SASE; request the QSL Bureau reprint.

Receiving DX QSLs

The ARRL Incoming QSL Bureau System is made up of numerous call-area bureaus. Most cards from DX bureaus go directly to the individual call-area bureaus. There, cards are sorted and distributed to amateurs who have claimed their cards.

To claim your cards, send a 5 × 7½ inch SASE to the appropriate bureau (as indicated by your call, not your address). The envelope(s) should have your call sign(s) printed neatly in the upper-left corner to assist the sorter. Some bureaus sell envelopes or postage credits as well as handling SASEs. Such bureaus provide a proper-size envelope and affix appropriate postage upon prepayment of a fee. Inquire with your area bureau for details (send an SASE with your inquiry).

Sending Your DX QSLs

The ARRL Outgoing QSL Bureau System distributes ARRL members' QSL cards to foreign bureaus for a nominal fee. The system should not be used for domestic cards within the 48 contiguous states or for DX stations having US QSL managers. The only address required is the destination call sign. Additional information is available from ARRL HQ.

AWARDS

Awards "chasing" (the pursuit of certificates for various operating accomplish-

---

Table 15
ARRL Operating Awards

Award	Qualification
Rag Chewers Club	A single contact ½ hour or longer
Worked All States (WAS)	QSLs from all 50 US states (see Fig 5)
Worked All Continents (WAC)	QSLs from all six continents
DX Century Club (DXCC)	QSLs from at least 100 foreign countries
VHF/UHF Century Club (VUCC)	QSLs from many "grid squares" (see Fig 6)
Extra Class Certificate	Hold an Amateur Extra Class license
A-1 Operator Club	Recommendation by two A-1 operators
Code Proficiency	One minute of perfect copy from W1AW "qualifying run"
Old Timers Club	Held an Amateur Radio license at least 20 years prior
ARRL Membership	ARRL membership for 25, 40, 50, 60 or 70 years

---

ments) is a popular ham activity. There are hundreds of beautiful certificates and plaques available to hang on your ham shack wall. Table 15 lists some awards available from ARRL (WAC is sponsored by the International Amateur Radio Union). If you live in the US or possessions, Canada or Puerto Rico, you must be a member of ARRL or CRRL (our Canadian sister society) to participate in ARRL awards. In addition, official application forms are required for WAS, DXCC, VUCC and WAC. To obtain these forms, send a business size SASE to Special Requests, ARRL HQ, 225 Main St, Newington, CT 06111.

CONTESTS

Contests are relatively short flurries of competitive radio activity. In general, the object is to contact as many other hams as possible in a given time period. Each contest, however, has some aspect that gives it a particular "flavor." Novice Roundup (30 hours total, over about 10 days) gives Novice and Technician licensees their own "playing field." Field Day gets hams out in the country for emergency preparedness. For an in-depth discussion of contests, operating guidelines and a list of major annual contests, look in *The ARRL Operating Manual*.

MAR
(VE1/VO1)

ME

QUE

1

VT
NH WMA EMA
RI
CT NLI
NNJ
SNJ
MD DE

ENY
WNY 2
EPA 3
WPA
WV VA
NC
SC
NFL
SFL

ONT

MB

MI
8
OH
KY
TN
4
GA
AL
MS

SK

WI
9
IN
IL
MO
AR
LA

ND
MN
Ø IA
NE
KS
OK
5
NTX
STX

AB

MT
WY
CO
NM
WTX

BC

ID
7
UT
AZ

EWA
WWA
OR
NV
6
ORG
SDGO

AK
(KL7)

SV
EB
SCV
SB
LAX
SF
SJV

PR: KP4
VI: KP2 KG4

PAC: KH

ARRL AND CRRL
FIELD ORGANIZATION

Fig 5—A map of North America showing US states, Canadian provinces and ARRL/CRRL Sections. (This Ham Outline Map is published with permission of FM-RTTY Publishing. For ordering information regarding this or other Outline Maps, send an SASE to Jim Labo, KØOST, FM-RTTY Publishing, PO Box 842, Denver, CO 80201-0842.)

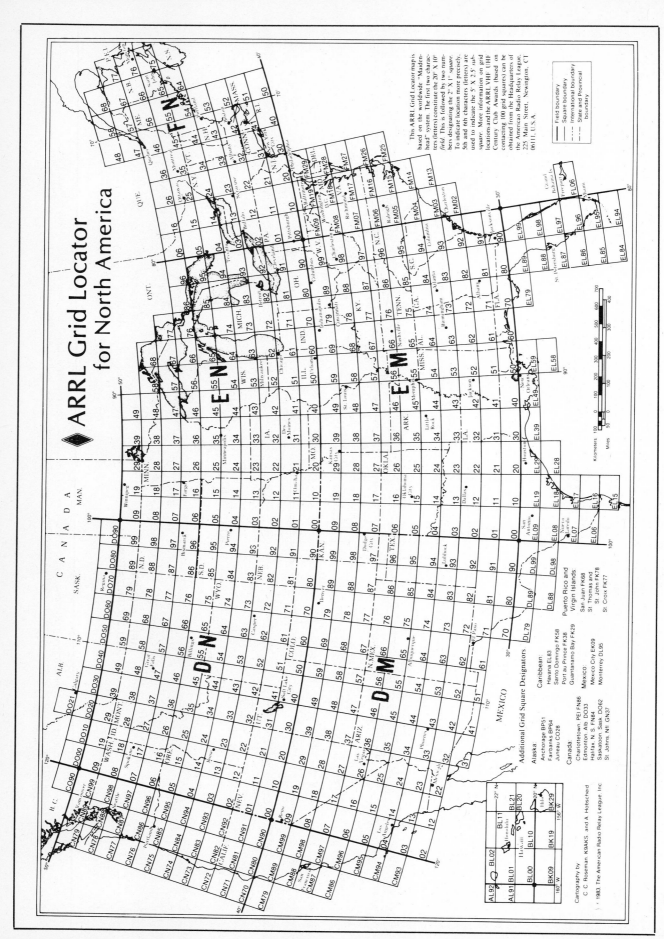

Fig 6—ARRL Grid Locator Map for North America. This and a World Grid Locator Map are available from ARRL.

Emergency Operation

Amateur Radio operators may find themselves the crucial link between their community and served agencies in time of emergency. Each of us should prepare for emergencies by joining ARES/RACES (see ARES/RACES sidebar) and practicing proper emergency communications techniques. Table 16 outlines the principles of emergency communication. Tables 17 and 18 list many items a well-prepared ham should have on hand in case of emergency. The following pages provide a basic reference for emergency operation.

EMERGENCY ACTION

Where to Begin?

The first action is natural—assess the situation. This is the first function of a command post (CP). A CP is any location where someone assesses the situation and calls for help. If commercial communication channels are available, use them. (Your skills as a communicator are valuable even when Amateur Radio is not involved.)

In order for the call for help to be effective, it must reach the dispatcher at an Emergency Operations Center (EOC). An EOC is a facility established to control resources in an emergency. Once given the emergency location and apprised of the situation, the dispatcher can send equipment and additional manpower to help.

The CP and EOC are the essential communications network. Other agencies may join in and command posts may move, expand and multiply to suit the situation (see Fig 7).

If there is no emergency at your location, but one nearby, monitor your local alert frequency (see page 1 of this chapter), or repeater to learn where you can help. If there is no activity on the frequency or repeater, report to your ARES Emergency Coordinator. If there is an official communications emergency, monitor W1AW emergency bulletins as follows: voice on the hour, teleprinter at 15 minutes past the hour and CW on the half hour.

Table 17
Operating Aids for Public Service

ARRL HQ makes available the following free operating aids for public service communications:

Public Service Communications
Manual	FSD-235
ARRL numbered radiograms	FSD-3
Sample emergency plan	FSD-27
ARES registration form	FSD-98
Amateur message form	FSD-218
Emergency Reference information	FSD-255
Field Organization Brochure	FSD-300

This entire Public Service Package can be obtained by sending a large (9 × 12-inch) envelope with First Class postage for 6 ounces.

Table 18
ARES Personal Checklist

The following represents recommendations of equipment and supplies ARES members should consider having available for use during an emergency or public-service activity.

1) ARES Identification Card
2) FCC Amateur Radio License
3) Radio Gear
   a) rig (2 meters)
   b) microphone
   c) headphones
   d) power supply/extra batteries
   e) antennas with mounts
   f) spare fuses
   g) patch cords/adapters (BNC to PL259/RCA phono to PL259)
   h) SWR meter
   i) extra coax
4) Writing Gear
   a) pen/pencil/eraser
   b) clipboard
   c) message forms
   d) logbook
   e) note paper
5) Personal Gear (short duration)
   a) snacks
   b) liquid refreshments
   c) smoking supplies/candy
   d) throat lozenges
   e) personal medicine
   f) aspirin
   g) extra pair of prescription glasses
6) Personal Gear (72-hour duration)
   a) foul-weather gear
   b) three-day supply of drinking water
   c) cooler with three-day supply of food
   d) mess kit with cleaning supplies
   e) first-aid kit
   f) personal medicine
   g) aspirin
   h) throat lozenges
   i) sleeping bag
   j) toilet articles
   k) mechanical alarm clock
   l) flashlight with batteries/lantern
   m) candles
   n) waterproof matches
   o) extra pair of prescription glasses
7) Tool Box (72-hour duration)
   a) screwdrivers
   b) pliers
   c) socket wrenches
   d) electrical tape
   e) 12/120-volt soldering iron
   f) solder
   g) volt-ohm meter
8) Other (72-hour duration)
   a) hatchet/ax
   b) saw
   c) pick
   d) shovel
   e) siphon
   f) jumper cables
   g) 3/8-inch hemp rope
   h) highway flares
   i) extra gasoline and oil

Table 16
Principles of Emergency Communication

1) *Keep the QRM level down:* Remain silent unless called upon. There are only two reasons to check into an emergency net: (1) You have a bona fide emergency; (2) the Net Control Station (NCS) is requesting help that only you can provide.
2) *Monitor established emergency frequencies:* Many areas have established emergency frequencies that should be monitored for possible distress calls.
3) *Avoid spreading rumors:* Transmit only facts, not speculation. Do not repeat messages unless so authorized by the originator, and then only *word for word*.
4) *Authenticate all messages:* Any messages of an official nature should be written and signed.
5) *Strive for efficiency:* You are more effective as part of a team than as a lone individual.
6) *Select the mode and band to suit the need:* Advantages of several modes are listed below.
7) *Use all communications channels intelligently:* The object is to protect lives and property. Use emergency or normal communications channels where available.
8) *Don't broadcast:* Our job is to communicate for, not with, the general public. See §97.113 of *The FCC Rule Book* for details.

Advantages of Various Amateur Modes for Emergency Communications

CW
1) Less QRM in most amateur bands.
2) Privacy of communications (less easily understood by the public).
3) Simpler transmitting equipment.
4) Greater accuracy than voice in record communications.
5) Longer range for a given transmitter power level.

Voice
1) More practical for portable and mobile work.
2) More widespread availability of operators.
3) Faster communication for tactical or "command" purposes.
4) More readily appreciated and understood by the public.
5) Official-to-official and phone-patch communication.

Packet
1) Less QRM in most amateur bands.
2) Privacy of communications (less easily understood by the public).
3) More widespread availability of operators.
4) Greater speed and accuracy of record communication than any other mode.

ARES/RACES

The Amateur Radio Emergency Service (ARES) and the Radio Amateur Civil Emergency Service (RACES) are the umbrella organizations of Amateur Radio public service. ARES is sponsored by ARRL (although ARRL membership is not required for participation) and handles all kinds of public-service activities. RACES is administered by the Federal Emergency Management Agency (FEMA) and operates only for civil preparedness and in times of civil emergency. RACES is activated at the request of a state or federal official.

The ARRL advocates dual membership and cooperative efforts between ARES and RACES whenever possible. RACES rules now make it possible for ARES and RACES to use the same frequencies, so that an ARES group also enrolled as RACES can "switch hats" from ARES to RACES and RACES to ARES as the situation develops. In many areas, however, the two organizations exist separately. Contact local ARRL Leadership Officials to determine the situation in your area.

ARES officials operate under the ARRL Section Manager. Figs A and B show the Section and local ARES structures, respectively.

The Radio Amateur Civil Emergency Service (RACES) comprises certain Amateur Radio operators and stations that are registered with civil defense organizations or licensed as RACES stations by the FCC. RACES frequencies are normally shared with the Amateur Radio Service, but in times of civil emergency and for limited periods of testing and practice RACES operation is limited to the frequencies shown below. During times of official RACES operation, RACES stations may only contact other RACES stations and certain other stations as listed in §97.407(c). Official RACES operation does not allow radio contact with the general amateur population.

Fig A—Section-level ARES structure.

Fig B—Local ARES structure for a country, city or other area of coverage.

Dedicated RACES Operating Frequencies

RACES frequencies are shared with amateurs except in certain emergencies. See *The FCC Rule Book* (§97.407) for details of RACES operation.

kHz	MHz	MHz
1800-1825	10.100-10.150	50.350-50.750
1975-2000	14.047-14.053	52.000-54.000
3500-3550	14.220-14.230	144.50-145.71
3930-3980	14.331-14.350	146.00-148.00
3984-4000	21.047-21.053	222.00-225.00
7079-7125	21.228-21.267	420.00-450.00
7245-7255	28.550-28.750	1240.00-1300.00
	29.237-29.273	2390.00-2450.00
	29.450-29.650	

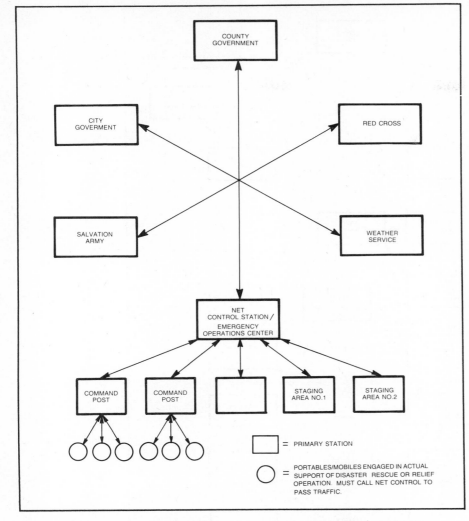

COUNTY
GOVERNMENT

CITY
GOVERMENT

RED CROSS

SALVATION
ARMY

WEATHER
SERVICE

NET
CONTROL STATION /
EMERGENCY
OPERATIONS CENTER

COMMAND
POST

COMMAND
POST

STAGING
AREA NO.1

STAGING
AREA NO.2

☐ = PRIMARY STATION

◯ = PORTABLES/MOBILES ENGAGED IN ACTUAL
SUPPORT OF DISASTER RESCUE OR RELIEF
OPERATION. MUST CALL NET CONTROL TO
PASS TRAFFIC.

Fig 7—The interaction between the EOC/NCS and the command post(s) in a local emergency.

Tactical Communications

Tactical communications are informal ("Who's on first?") messages that make up the bulk of local event operations. The goal is quick communication between the served agencies. Messages are seldom written, and officials of the served agencies can often hear (and speak through) the radio. For speed and clarity, assign tactical call signs to net stations, and use local time in AM/PM format. Tactical call signs reflect a function, location or agency: "Control," "Check Point 1," "Police." Hams must still fulfill FCC identification requirements with their FCC call signs, however.

The Big Picture

When the situation grows, there are a lot of people ready to help. Fig 8 shows the relationship between ARRL HQ, ARES, the National Traffic System, RACES and other amateur facilities. Fig 9 shows a typical local ARES emergency net. As the range of the emergency increases, liaisons to NTS nets and HF ARES nets (Fig 10) may be needed. Formal written message traffic may then become significant.

Experience in major disasters, such as hurricanes and earthquakes, has taught us that health and welfare (called disaster welfare inquiries—DWI—by Red Cross) messages can be a formidable problem. Typically, there is a flood of welfare traffic destined for the disaster area that competes with priority and emergency traffic for the limited local communications channels

available. It seems best to hold welfare traffic for release as facilities in the affected area can handle it—usually a span of several days.

TRAFFIC HANDLING

The National Traffic System (NTS) is an organized effort to handle traffic in accordance with a plan that is easily understood, is basically sound and which uses modern methods of network traffic handling in general acceptance today.

In an emergency situation, traffic flows through the ARES net to served agencies without using the NTS. By the time welfare- and routine-precedence traffic flow begins, experienced traffic handlers should be available for the ARES/NTS interface. Hence, details of the NTS structure, message routing and net schedules are not presented here. You can find those details in the *Public Service Communications Manual*.

NTS message format and procedures, however, have merits when official written traffic must flow through the ARES nets.

Creating a Message

Fig 11 is a reproduction of ARRL form FSD-218(585), which gives information about basic message form, prosigns and precedences.

Fig 12 shows a sample message as it would appear on a simplified form, and identifies the major parts: The preamble provides information for handling (see Table 19), error checking, message tracking and reply routing. On emergency nets, the address will often be only a name and agency or location; the telephone number likely will not apply. ARRL numbered radiograms (Table 20) cover several typical messages. Message checking is explained in Table 21.

Net Etiquette

Tables 22 through 24 deal with net and traffic-handling procedures. Table 22 gives some guidelines for operation in a "directed" net (one that is closely controlled). Table 23 lists the Q signals and special ARRL QN (net) signals. *Do not use the ARRL QN signals on international nets*; some of the signals have different meanings there. Table 24 lists tips for traffic handling by packet radio. Packet radio offers powerful benefits in large-scale emergencies, and it can provide quick, accurate traffic flow in an affected area with less-skilled operators than other modes require.

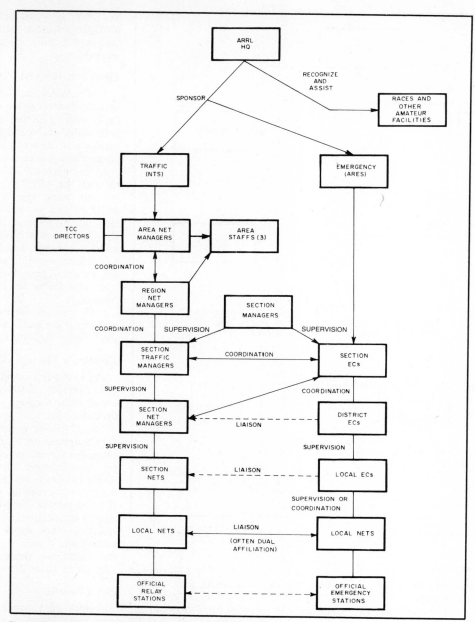

Fig 8—The organization and interaction of ARES and NTS.

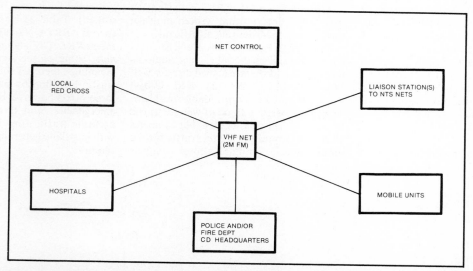

Fig 9—Typical station deployment for local ARES net coverage in an emergency.

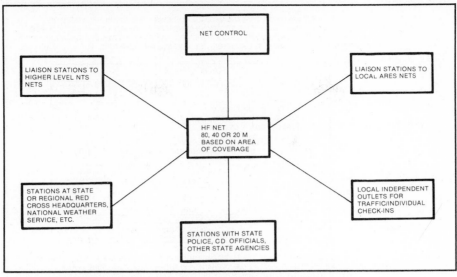

Fig 10—Typical structure of an HF network for emergency communications.

AMATEUR MESSAGE FORM

Every formal radiogram message originated and handled should contain the following component parts in the order given.

I PREAMBLE
a. Number (begin with 1 each month or year)
b. Precedence (R, W, P or EMERGENCY)
c. Handling Instructions (optional, see text)
d. Station of Origin (first amateur handler)
e. Check (number of words/groups in text only)
f. Place of Origin (not necessarily location of station of origin)
g. Time Filed (optional with originating station)
h. Date (must agree with date of time filed)

II ADDRESS (as complete as possible, include zip code and telephone number)

III TEXT (limit to 25 words or less, if possible)

IV SIGNATURE

CW MESSAGE EXAMPLE

I   NR 1 R HXG W1AW 8 Newington CONN 1830Z July 1
     a   b c   d   e   f   g   h

II   DONALD SMITH A̅A̅
     164 EAST SIXTH AVE A̅A̅
     NORTH RIVER CITY MO 00789 A̅A̅
     733 4968 B̅T̅

III HAPPY BIRTHDAY X SEE YOU SOON X LOVE B̅T̅

IV   DIANA A̅R̅

Note that X, when used in the text as punctuation, counts as a word.

CW: The prosign A̅A̅ separates the parts of the address. B̅T̅ separates the address from the text and the text from the signature. A̅R̅ marks end of message; this is followed by B if there is another message to follow, by N if this is the only or last message. It is customary to copy the preamble, parts of the address, text and signature on separate lines.

RTTY: Same as cw procedure above, except (1) use extra space between parts of address, instead of A̅A̅; (2) omit cw procedure sign B̅T̅ to separate text from address and signature, using line spaces instead; (3) add a CFM line under the signature, consisting of all names, numerals and unusual works in the message in the order transmitted.

PHONE: Use *prowords* instead of prosigns, but it is not necessary to name each part of the message as you send it. For example, the above message would be sent on phone as follows: "Number one   routine   HX Golf   W1AW   eight   Newington Connecticut   one eight three zero zulu   July one   Donald Smith   *Figures* one six four East Sixth Avenue   North River City Missouri   zero zero seven eight nine   *Telephone*   seven three three four nine six eight   *Break*   Happy birthday   X-ray   see you soon   X-ray   love *Break*   Diana   *End of Message*   *Over*.   "End of Message" is followed by "More" if there is another message to follow, "No More" if it is the only or last message. Speak clearly using VOX (or pause frequently on push-to-talk) so that the receiving station can get fills. Spell phonetically all difficult or unusual words — *do not* spell out common words. Do not use cw abbreviations or Q-signals in phone traffic handling.

PRECEDENCES

The precedence will follow the message number. For example, on cw 207R or 207 EMERGENCY. On phone, "Two Zero Seven, Routine (or Emergency)."

EMERGENCY — Any message having life and death urgency to any person or group of persons, which is transmitted by Amateur Radio in the absence of regular commercial facilities. This includes official messages of welfare agencies during emergencies requesting supplies, materials or instructions vital to relief of stricken populace in emergency areas. During normal times, it will be *very rare*. On cw, this designation will always be spelled out. When in doubt, *do not* use it.

PRIORITY — Important messages having a specific time limit. Official messages not covered in the Emergency category. Press dispatches and other emergency-related traffic not of the utmost urgency. Notification of death or injury in a disaster area, personal or official. Use the abbreviation P on cw.

WELFARE — A message that is either a) an inquiry as to the health and welfare of an individual in the disaster area or b) an advisory or reply from the disaster area that indicates all is well should carry this precedence, which is abbreviated W on cw. These messages are handled *after* Emergency and Priority traffic but before Routine.

ROUTINE — Most traffic normal times will bear this designation. In disaster situations, traffic labeled Routine (R on cw) should be handled *last*, or not at all when circuits are busy with Emergency, Priority or Welfare traffic.

Handling Instructions (Optional)

HXA — (Followed by number.) Collect landline delivery authorized by addressee within .... miles. (If no number, authorization is unlimited.)
HXB — (Followed by number.) Cancel message if not delivered within .... hours of filing time; service originating station.
HXC — Report date and time of delivery (TOD) to originating station.
HXD — Report to originating station the identity of station from which received, plus date and time. Report identity of station to which relayed, plus date and time, or if delivered report date, time and method of delivery.
HXE — Delivering station get reply from addressee, originate message back.
HXF — (Followed by number.) Hold delivery until .... (date).
HXG — Delivery by mail or landline toll call not required. If toll or other expense involved, cancel message and service originating station.

For further information on traffic handling, consult the *Public Service Communications Manual* or the *ARRL Operating Manual*, both published by ARRL.

FSD-218 (585)   ARRL HQ., 225 Main St., Newington, CT 06111

Fig 11—ARRL form FSD-218(585), available as part of the ARRL Public Service Package.

THIS IS A FORMAL MESSAGE. FORMAL MEANS THAT THE MESSAGE FOLLOWS A PRE-ESTABLISHED FORM OR CONVENTION. A FORMAL MESSAGE CONTAINS ALL THE NECESSARY "RECORDKEEPING" ELEMENTS THAT ARE REQUIRED TO KEEP A HISTORY OF THE MESSAGE AS IT IS SENT THROUGH THE NTS. ALL FORMAL MESSAGES CONSIST OF FOUR PARTS: THE PREAMBLE, THE ADDRESS, THE TEXT AND THE SIGNATURE.

RADIOGRAM

1 PREAMBLE

NUMBER	PRECEDENCE	HX	STN OF ORIGIN	CHECK	PLACE OF ORIGIN	TIME FILED	DATE
3 4 7	R	E	K7ABT	2 5	PHOENIX AZ		DEC 4

2 ADDRESS

TO: ALBERT M COUSINS
337 W 38TH STREET
BRIDGEPORT CT 06645
TELEPHONE NO: 203 334 5678

3 TEXT

DEAR	DAD	ARRIVED	SAFELY	339TH
COMPOSITE	BOMB	GROUP	FLAGSTAFF	DECEMBER
2ND	X	TELL	SHERRY	I M
OK	X	PHONE	6 0 2	3 4 5
9876	SEND	FLAK	JACKET	LOVE

4 SIGNATURE

BILLY 043 89 9078

EACH OF THE ELEMENTS OF THE FORMAL MESSAGE HAS CERTAIN FORMAT REQUIREMENTS WHICH MUST BE MET IN ORDER TO AVOID CONFUSION ON THE AIR AS THE MESSAGE IS SENT, AND ALSO TO ASSURE THAT A SENDER-TO-RECEIVER TRACE CAN ALWAYS BE DONE ON THE MESSAGE.

Fig 12—A sample NTS formal message.

Table 19

Handling Instructions

HXA—(Followed by number.) Collect landline delivery authorized by addressee within _____ miles. (If no number, authorization is unlimited.)

HXB—(Followed by number.) Cancel message if not delivered within _____ hours of filing time; service originating station.

HXC—Report date and time of delivery (TOD) to originating station.

HXD—Report to originating station the identity of station from which received, plus date, time and method of delivery.

HXE—Delivering station get reply from addressee, originate message back.

HXF—(Followed by number.) Hold delivery until _____ (date).

HXG—Delivery by mail or landline toll call not required. If toll or other expense involved, cancel message and service originating station.

An HX prosign (when used) will be inserted in the message preamble before the station of origin, thus: NR 207 R HXA50 W1AW 12 . . . (etc). If more than one HX prosign is used, they can be combined if no numbers are to be inserted; otherwise the HX should be repeated, thus: NR 207 R HXAC W1AW . . . (etc), but: NR 207 R HXA50 HXC W1AW . . . (etc). On phone, use phonetics for the letter or letters following the HX, to insure accuracy.

Table 20
ARRL Numbered Radiograms

The letters ARL are inserted in the preamble in the check and in the text before spelled out numbers, which represent texts from this list. Note that some ARL texts include insertion of numerals. *Example:* NR 1 R W1AW ARL 5 NEWINGTON CONN DEC 25 DONALD R SMITH ĀĀ 164 EAST SIXTH AVE ĀĀ NORTH RIVER CITY MO ĀĀ PHONE 733 3968 B̄T̄ ARL FIFTY ARL SIXTY ONE B̄T̄ DIANA ĀR̄.

Group One—For possible "Relief Emergency" Use

ONE	Everyone safe here. Please don't worry.
TWO	Coming home as soon as possible.
THREE	Am in ____ hospital. Receiving excellent care and recovering fine.
FOUR	Only slight property damage here. Do not be concerned about disaster reports.
FIVE	Am moving to new location. Send no further mail or communication. Will inform you of new address when relocated.
SIX	Will contact you as soon as possible.
SEVEN	Please reply by Amateur Radio through the amateur delivering this message. This is a free public service.
EIGHT	Need additional ____ mobile or portable equipment for immediate emergency use.
NINE	Additional ____ radio operators needed to assist with emergency at this location.
TEN	Please contact ____. Advise to standby and provide further emergency information, instructions or assistance.
ELEVEN	Establish Amateur Radio emergency communications with ____ on ____ MHz.
TWELVE	Anxious to hear from you. No word in some time. Please contact me as soon as possible.
THIRTEEN	Medical emergency situation exists here.
FOURTEEN	Situation here becoming critical. Losses and damage from ____ increasing.
FIFTEEN	Please advise your condition and what help is needed.
SIXTEEN	Property damage very severe in this area.
SEVENTEEN	REACT communications services also available. Establish REACT communications with ____ on channel ____.
EIGHTEEN	Please contact me as soon as possible at ____.
NINETEEN	Request health and welfare report on ____. (State name, address and telephone number.)
TWENTY	Temporarily stranded. Will need some assistance. Please contact me at ____.
TWENTY ONE	Search and Rescue assistance is needed by local authorities here. Advise availability.
TWENTY TWO	Need accurate information on the extent and type of conditions now existing at your location. Please furnish this information and reply without delay.
TWENTY THREE	Report at once the accessibility and best way to reach your location.
TWENTY FOUR	Evacuation of residents from this area urgently needed. Advise plans for help.
TWENTY FIVE	Furnish as soon as possible the weather conditions at your location.
TWENTY SIX	Help and care for evacuation of sick and injured from this location needed at once.

Emergency/priority messages originating from official sources must carry the signature of the originating official.

Group Two—Routine messages

FORTY SIX	Greetings on your birthday and best wishes for many more to come.
FIFTY	Greetings by Amateur Radio.
FIFTY ONE	Greetings by Amateur Radio. This message is sent as a free public service by ham radio operators here at ____. Am having a wonderful time.
FIFTY TWO	Really enjoyed being with you. Looking forward to getting together again.
FIFTY THREE	Received your ____. It's appreciated; many thanks.
FIFTY FOUR	Many thanks for your good wishes.
FIFTY FIVE	Good news is always welcome. Very delighted to hear about yours.
FIFTY SIX	Congratulations on your ____, a most worthy and deserved achievement.
FIFTY SEVEN	Wish we could be together.
FIFTY EIGHT	Have a wonderful time. Let us know when you return.
FIFTY NINE	Congratulations on the new arrival. Hope mother and child are well.
*SIXTY	Wishing you the best of everything on ____.
SIXTY ONE	Wishing you a very merry Christmas and a happy New Year.
*SIXTY TWO	Greetings and best wishes to you for a pleasant ____ holiday season.
SIXTY THREE	Victory or defeat, our best wishes are with you. Hope you win.
SIXTY FOUR	Arrived safely at ____.
SIXTY FIVE	Arriving ____ on ____. Please arrange to meet me there.
SIXTY SIX	DX QSLs are on hand for you at the ____ QSL Bureau. Send ____ self-addressed envelopes.
SIXTY SEVEN	Your message number ____ undeliverable because of ____. Please advise.
SIXTY EIGHT	Sorry to hear you are ill. Best wishes for a speedy recovery.

*Can be used for all holidays.

ARL NUMBERS SHOULD BE SPELLED OUT AT ALL TIMES.

Table 21

Checking Your Message

Traffic handlers don't have to dine out to fight over the check! Even good ops find much confusion when counting up the text of a message. You can eliminate some of this confusion by remembering these basic rules:

1) Punctuation ("X-rays," "Querys") count separately as a word.
2) Mixed letter-number groups (1700Z, for instance) count as one word.
3) Initial or number groups count as one word if sent together, two if sent separately.
4) The signature does not count as part of the text, but any closing lines, such as "Love" or "Best wishes" do.

Here are some examples:
- Charles J McClain—3 words
- W B Stewart—3 words
- St Louis—2 words
- 3 PM—2 words
- SASE—1 word

- ARL FORTY SIX—3 words
- 2N1601—1 word
- Seventy three—2 words
- 73—1 word

Telephone numbers count as 3 words (area code, prefix, number), and ZIP codes count as one. ZIP + 4 codes count as two words. Canadian postal codes count as two words (first three characters, last three characters.)

Although it is improper to change the text of a message, you may change the check. Always do this by following the original check with a slash bar, then the corrected check. On phone, use the words "corrected to."

Book Messages

When sending book traffic, always send the common parts first, followed by the "uncommon" parts. For example:

R N0FQW ARL 8 BETHEL MO SEP 7 B̄T̄

ARL FIFTY ONE BETHEL SHEEP FESTIVAL X LOVE B̄T̄
PHIL AND JANE B̄T̄

NR 107 TONY AND LYN CALHOUN ĀĀ
160 NORTH DOUGLAS ĀĀ SPRINGFIELD IL 62702 B̄T̄

NR 108 JOE WOOD AJ0X ĀĀ
84 MAIN STREET ĀĀ
LAUREL MS 39440 B̄T̄

NR 109 JEAN WILCOX ĀĀ
1243 EDGEWOOD DRIVE ĀĀ
LODI CA 95240 ĀR̄ N

Before sending the book traffic to another operator, announce beforehand that it is book traffic. Say "Follows book traffic." Then use the above format. On CW, a simple HR BUK TFC will do.

Table 22

How to be the Kind of Net Operator the Net Control Station (NCS) Loves

As a net operator, you have a duty to be self-disciplined. A net is only as good as its worst operator. You can be an exemplary net operator by following a few easy guidelines.

1) *Zero beat the NCS.* The NCS doesn't have time to chase all over the band for you. Make sure you're on frequency, and you will never be known at the annual net picnic as "old so-and-so who's always off frequency."

2) *Don't be late.* There's no such thing as "fashionably late" on a net. Liaison stations are on a tight timetable. Don't hold them up by checking in 10 minutes late with three pieces of traffic.

3) *Speak only when spoken to by the NCS.* Unless it is a bona fide emergency situation, you don't need to "help" the NCS unless asked. If you need to contact the NCS, make it brief. Resist the urge to help clear the frequency for the NCS or to "advise" the NCS. The NCS, not you, is boss.

4) Unless otherwise instructed by the NCS, *transmit only* to the NCS. Side comments to another station in the net are out of order.

5) *Stay until you are excused.* If the NCS calls you and you don't respond because you're getting a "cold one" from the fridge, the NCS may assume you've left the net, and net business may be stymied. If you need to leave the net prematurely, contact the NCS and simply ask to be excused (QNX PSE on CW).

6) *Be brief when transmitting to the NCS.* A simple "yes" (C) or "no" (N) will usually suffice. Shaggy dog tales only waste valuable net time.

7) *Know how the net runs.* The NCS doesn't have time to explain procedure to you. After you have been on the net for a while, you should already know these things.

Table 23

Q Signals

Given below are a number of Q signals whose meanings most often need to be expressed with brevity and clarity in amateur work.

(Q abbreviations take the form of questions only when each is sent followed by a question mark.)

QRG Will you tell me my exact frequency (or that of ____)? Your exact frequency (or that of ____) is ____ kHz.

QRH Does my frequency vary? Your frequency varies.

QRI How is the tone of my transmission? The tone of your transmission is ____ (1. Good; 2. Variable; 3. Bad).

QRJ Are you receiving me badly? I cannot receive you. Your signals are too weak.

QRK What is the intelligibility of my signals (or those of ____)? The intelligibility of your signals (or those of ____) is ____ (1. Bad; 2. Poor; 3. Fair; 4. Good; 5. Excellent).

QRL Are you busy? I am busy (or I am busy with ____). Please do not interfere.

QRM Is my transmission being interfered with? Your transmission is being interfered with ____ (1. Nil; 2. Slightly; 3. Moderately; 4. Severely; 5. Extremely.)

QRN Are you troubled by static? I am troubled by static ____ (1-5 as under QRM).

QRO Shall I increase power? Increase power.

QRP Shall I decrease power? Decrease power.

QRQ Shall I send faster? Send faster (____ WPM).

QRS Shall I send more slowly? Send more slowly (____ WPM).

QRT Shall I stop sending? Stop sending.

QRU Have you anything for me? I have nothing for you.

QRV Are you ready? I am ready.

QRW Shall I inform ____ that you are calling on ____ kHz? Please inform ____ that I am calling on ____ kHz.

QRX When will you call me again? I will call you again at ____ hours (on ____ kHz).

QRY What is my turn? Your turn is numbered ____

QRZ Who is calling me? You are being called by ____ (on ____ kHz).

QSA What is the strength of my signals (or those of ____)? The strength of your signals (or those of ____) is ____ (1. Scarcely perceptible; 2. Weak; 3. Fairly good; 4. Good; 5. Very good).

QSB Are my signals fading? Your signals are fading.

QSD Is my keying defective? Your keying is defective.

QSG Shall I send ____ messages at a time? Send ____ messages at a time.

QSK Can you hear me between your signals and if so can I break in on your transmission? I can hear you between my signals; break in on my transmission.

QSL Can you acknowledge receipt? I am acknowledging receipt.

QSM Shall I repeat the last message which I sent you, or some previous message? Repeat the last message which you sent me [or message(s) number(s) ____].

QSN Did you hear me (or ____) on ____ kHz? I did hear you (or ____) on ____ kHz.

QSO Can you communicate with ____ direct or by relay? I can communicate with ____ direct (or by relay through ____).

QSP Will you relay to ____? I will relay to ____

QST General call preceding a message addressed to all amateurs and ARRL members. This is in effect "CQ ARRL."

QSU Shall I send or reply on this frequency (or on ____ kHz)? Send or reply on this frequency (or ____ kHz).

QSV Shall I send a series of Vs on this frequency (or ____ kHz)? Send a series of Vs on this frequency (or on ____ kHz).

QSW Will you send on this frequency (or on ____ kHz)? I am going to send on this frequency (or on ____ kHz).

QSX Will you listen to ____ on ____ kHz? I am listening to ____ on ____ kHz.

QSY Shall I change to transmission on another frequency? Change to transmission on another frequency (or on ____ kHz).

QSZ Shall I send each word or group more than once? Send each word or group twice (or ____ times).

QTA Shall I cancel message number ____? Cancel message number ____

QTB Do you agree with my counting of words? I do not agree with your counting of words. I will repeat the first letter or digit of each word or group.

QTC How many messages have you to send? I have ____ messages for you (or for ____).

QTH What is your location? My location is ____

QTR What is the correct time? The time is ____

ARRL QN Signals

QNA* Answer in prearranged order.

QNB* Act as relay Between ____ and ____.

QNC All net stations Copy.
      I have a message for all net stations.

QND* Net is Directed (controlled by net control station.)

QNE* Entire net stand by.

QNF Net is Free (not controlled).

QNG Taker over as net control station

QNH Your net frequency is High.

QNI Net stations report In.
      I am reporting into the net. (Follow with a list of traffic or QRU.)

QNJ Can you copy me?

QNK* Transmit messages for ____ to ____.

QNL Your net frequency is Low.

QNM* You are QRMing the net. Stand by.

QNN Net control station is ____.
      What station has net control?

QNO Station is leaving the net.

QNP Unable to copy you.
      Unable to copy ____.

QNQ* Move frequency to ____ and wait for ____ to finish handling traffic. Then send him traffic for ____.

QNR* Answer ____ and Receive traffic.

QNS Following Stations are in the net.* (Follow with list.)
     Request list of stations in the net.

QNT I request permission to leave the net for ____ minutes.

QNU* The net has traffic for you. Stand by.

QNV* Establish contact with ____ on this frequency. If successful, move to ____ and send him traffic for ____.

QNW How do I route messages for ____.

QNX You are excused from the net.*
     Request to be excused from the net.

QNY* Shift to another frequency (or to ____ kHz) to clear traffic with ____.

QNZ Zero beat your signal with mine.

*For use only by the Net Control Station.

Notes of Use of QN signals

These QN signals are special ARRL signals for use in amateur CW nets *only*. They are not for use in casual amateur conversation. Other meanings that may be used in other services do not apply. Do not use QN signals on phone nets. *Say it with words.* QN signals need not be followed by a question mark, even though the meaning may be interrogatory.

Table 24

Tips on Handling NTS Traffic By Packet Radio

Listing Messages

* After logging on to your local NTS-supported bulletin board, type the command LT, meaning List Traffic. The BBS will sort and display an index of all NTSXX traffic awaiting delivery.

Receiving Messages

* To take a message off the Bulletin Board for telephone delivery to the third party, or for relay to a NTS Local or Section Net, type the R command, meaning Read Traffic, and the message number. R 188 will cause the BBS to find the BBS message number 188. This RADIOGRAM will look like any other, with preamble, address, text and signature; only some additional packet-related message header information is added. This information includes the routing path of the message for auditing purposes; e.g., to discern any excessive delays in the system.

* After the message is saved to the printer or disk, the message should be KILLED by using the KT command, meaning Kill Traffic, and the message number. In the above case, at the BBS prompt, type KT 188. This prevents the message from being delivered twice. Some of the newer BBS software requires use of K rather than KT.

* At the time the message is killed, many BBS's will automatically send a message back to the station in the FROM field with information on who took the traffic, and when it was taken!

Delivering or Relaying A Message

* A downloaded RADIOGRAM should, of course, be handled expeditiously in the traditional way: telephone delivery, or relay to a phone or cw net.

Sending Messages

* To send a RADIOGRAM, use the ST command, meaning Send Traffic. The BBS will prompt you for the NTS routing (Ø6111 @ NTSCT, for example), the message title which should contain the city in the address of the RADIOGRAM (QTC 1 Dayton), and the text of the message in RADIOGRAM format. The BBS, usually within the hour, will check its outgoing mailpouch, find the NTSCT message and automatically forward it to the next packet station in line to the NTSCT node. Note: Some states have more than one ARRL Section. If you do not know the destination ARRL

Section ("Is San Angelo in the ARRL North, South or West Texas Section?"), then simply use the state designator NTSTX.

* Note: While NTS/packet radio message forwarding is evolving rapidly, there are still some gaps. When uploading an NTS message destined for a distant state, use handling instruction "HXC" to ask the delivering station to report back to you the date and time of delivery.

* Unbundle your messages please: one NTS message per BBS message. Please remember that traffic eventually will have to be broken down to the individual addressee somewhere down the line for ultimate delivery. When you place two or more NTS messages destined for different addressees within one packet message, eventually the routing will require the messages to be broken up by either the BBS SYSOP or the relay station, placing an additional, unreasonable burden on them. Therefore it is good practice for the originator to expend the extra word processing in the first place and create individual messages per city regardless if there are common parts of other messages. This means that book messages are not suitable in packet at this time unless they are going to the same city. Bottom line: Messages should be sent unbundled. (Tnx NI6A for this tip)

We Want You!

Local and Section BBS's need to be checked daily for NTS traffic. SYSOPs and STMs can't do it alone. They need your help to clear NTS RADIOGRAMS every day, seven days a week, for delivery and relay. If you are a traffic handler/packeteer, contact your Section Traffic Manager or Section Manager for information on existing NTS/packet procedures in your Section.

If you are a packeteer, and know nothing of NTS traffic handling, contact ARRL HQ, your Section Manager or Section Traffic Manager for information on how you can put your packet radio gear to use in serving the public in routine times, but especially in times of emergency!

And, if you enjoy phone/CW traffic handling, but aren't on packet yet, discover the incredible speed and accuracy of packet radio traffic handling. You probably already have a small computer and 2-meter rig; all you need is a packet radio "black box" to connect between your 2-meter rig and computer. Cost: about $100. For more information on packet radio, see *Your Gateway to Packet Radio*, published by ARRL.

Chapter 38

Monitoring and Direction Finding

Radio direction finding is almost as old as radio itself. Frequently called RDF, the location of radio transmitters with direction-finding techniques is considered by many to be either an art or a science — or perhaps a bit of both. Although sophisticated and complex equipment pushing the state of the art has been developed for use by governments and commercial enterprises, relatively simple equipment can be built at home to offer the radio amateur an opportunity to RDF.

In many countries of the world, the hunting of hidden transmitters takes on the atmosphere of a sport, as participants wearing jogging togs or track suits dash toward the area where they believe the transmitter is located. The sport is variously known as fox hunting, bunny hunting, ARDF (Amateur Radio direction finding) or simply transmitter hunting. In North America, most hunting of hidden transmitters is conducted from automobiles, although hunts on foot are gaining popularity.

There is a more serious side to RDF, as well. Although not directly related to Amateur Radio, radio navigation is one application of RDF. The locating of downed aircraft is another, and one in which amateurs often lend their skills. Or sometimes a stolen amateur rig will be placed into operation by a person who is not familiar with Amateur Radio, and by being lured into making frequent transmissions, the operator unsuspectingly permits himself to be located by hams using RDF equipment. Jammers of repeaters, traffic nets and other amateur operations can also be located with RDF equipment. Indeed, it has many useful applications.

Volunteer Monitoring

An important aspect of the Communications Amendments Act of 1982, commonly known as Public Law 97-259, is one that authorized the FCC to formally enlist the use of amateur volunteers for monitoring the airwaves and for rules violations. To implement volunteer monitoring, the FCC's Field Operations Bureau has created an Amateur Auxiliary, administered by the League's Section Managers.

The Auxiliary is concerned with both maintenance monitoring and amateur-to-amateur interference. Maintenance monitoring is conducted through an enhanced ARRL Official Observer program, while amateur-to-amateur interference is handled by specifically authorized Local Interference Committees. To locate offenders, such committees must rely in a large part on RDF techniques. Thus, RDF becomes a federally sanctioned activity in Amateur Radio.

DIRECTION-FINDING SYSTEMS

Required for any RDF system are a directive antenna and a device for detecting the radio signal. In Amateur Radio applications the signal detector is usually a receiver; for convenience it will have a meter to indicate signal strength. At very close ranges a simple diode detector and dc microammeter may suffice for the signal detector.

The receiver may be a small portable, a mobile or the regular fixed-station instrument. In government or commercial installations the "receiver" is usually a system of electronics coupled to a cathode-ray tube that indicates azimuth. Antennas used in these systems use electronic beam forming, discussed in a later section. But for amateur use, a standard, unmodified, commercially available receiver works well. Some enterprising amateurs have designed and built their own receivers for RDF work, but their primary goal has usually been portability that is not offered in commercially made equipment. The point is this: If you want to try your hand at RDF, going out to buy a special RDF receiver is *not* one of the considerations.

Antennas for RDF work, on the other hand, are not generally the types used for normal two-way communications. Directivity is a prime requirement, and here the word directivity takes on a somewhat different meaning than is commonly applied to antennas. Normally we associate directivity with gain, and we think of the ideal antenna pattern as one having a long, thin main lobe. Such a pattern may be of value for coarse measurements in RDF work, but precise bearing measurements are not possible. There is always a spread of a few (or perhaps many) degrees on the "nose" of the lobe where a shift of antenna bearing produces no detectable change in signal strength. In RDF measurements, it is desirable to correlate an exact bearing or compass direction with the position of the antenna. To do this accurately, an antenna exhibiting a null in its pattern is used. A null can be very sharp in directivity, to within a half degree or less.

Loop Antennas

A simple antenna for RDF work is a small loop tuned to resonance with a capacitor. Several factors must be considered in the design of an RDF loop. The loop must be small compared with the wavelength. In a single-turn loop, the conductor should be less than 0.08 wavelength long. For 28 MHz, this represents a length of less than 34 inches (diameter of approximately 10 inches). Maximum response from the loop antenna is in the plane of the loop, with nulls exhibited at right angles to that plane.

To obtain the most accurate bearings, the loop must be balanced electrostatically with respect to ground. Otherwise, the loop will exhibit two modes of operation. One is the mode of a true loop, while the other is that of an essentially nondirectional vertical antenna of small dimensions ("antenna effect"). The voltages introduced by the two modes are not in phase and may add or subtract, depending on the direction from which the wave is coming.

The theoretical true loop pattern is illustrated in Fig. 1A. When properly balanced, the loop exhibits two nulls that are 180° apart. Thus, a single null reading with a small loop antenna will not indicate the exact direction toward the transmitter — only the line along which the transmitter lies. Ways to overcome this ambiguity are discussed in later sections.

When the antenna effect is appreciable and the loop is tuned to resonance, the loop may exhibit little directivity, as shown in Fig. 1B. However, by detuning the loop to shift the phasing, a pattern similar to C may be obtained. Although this pattern is not symmetrical, it does exhibit a null. The null, however, may not be as sharp as that obtained with a loop that is well balanced, and may not be at exact right angles to the plane of the loop.

By suitable detuning, the unidirectional pattern of Fig. 1D may be approached. This adjustment is sometimes used in RDF work to obtain a unidirectional bearing, although there is no complete null in the pattern. In most cases, however, the loop is adjusted for the best null.

An electrostatic balance can be obtained by shielding the loop, as shown in Fig. 2. The shield is represented by the broken lines in the drawing, and eliminates the antenna effect. The response of a well-constructed shielded loop is quite close to the ideal pattern of Fig. 1A.

For the low-frequency amateur bands, single-turn loops of convenient physical size for portability are generally unsatisfactory for RDF work. Therefore, multi-turn loops are generally used instead. Such a loop is shown in Fig. 3. This loop may also be shielded, and if the total conductor length remains below 0.08 wavelength, the directional pattern is that of Fig. 1A.

Ferrite Rod Antennas

The development of magnetic core materials has led to the use of loop antennas with such cores. These antennas consist essentially of many turns of wire around a ferrite rod. They are known as loopstick antennas and also as ferrite-rod antennas. Probably the best-known example of this type of antenna is that used in small portable AM broadcast receivers. The advantage of ferrite-rod antennas is their reduced size. For portable work, loopsticks are used almost exclusively for frequencies below 150 MHz.

As implied in the earlier discussion of shielded loops in this chapter, the true loop antenna responds to the magnetic field of the radio wave, and not to the electrical field. The voltage delivered by the loop is proportional to the amount of magnetic flux passing through the coil, and to the number of turns in the coil. The action is much the same as in the secondary winding of a transformer. For a given size of loop, the output voltage can be increased by increasing the flux density, and this is done with a ferrite core of high permeability. A ½-inch-diameter, 7-inch rod of Q2 ferrite ($\mu_i = 125$) is suitable for a loop core from

the broadcast band through 10 MHz. For increased output, the turns may be wound on two rods that are taped together, as shown in Fig. 4. Loopstick antennas for construction are described later in this chapter.

Maximum response of the loopstick antenna is broadside to the axis of the rod as shown in Fig. 5, whereas maximum response of the small loop is in the plane of the loop. Otherwise the performances of the ferrite-rod antenna and of the ordinary loop are similar. The loopstick may also be shielded to eliminate the antenna effect, such as with a U-shaped or C-shaped channel of aluminum or other form of "trough." The length of the shield should equal or slightly exceed the length of the rod.

Sensing Antennas

Because there are two nulls that are 180° apart in the directional pattern of a loop or a loopstick, an ambiguity exists as to which one indicates the true direction of the station being tracked. For example, assume you take a bearing measurement and the result indicates the transmitter is somewhere on a line running approximately east and west from your position. With this single reading, you have no way of know-

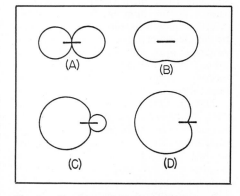

Fig. 1 — Small-loop field patterns with varying amounts of antenna effect — the undesired response of the loop acting merely as a mass of metal connected to the receiver antenna terminals. The heavy lines show the plane of the loop.

ing for sure if the transmitter is east of you or west of you.

If there is more than one receiving station taking bearings on a single transmitter, or if a single receiving station takes bearings from more than one position on the transmitter, the ambiguity may be worked out by a method called triangulation. (Further detail on triangulation is

Fig. 2 — Shielded loop for direction finding. The ends of the shielding turn are not connected, to prevent shielding the loop from magnetic fields. The shield is effective against electric fields.

Fig. 3 — Small loop consisting of several turns of wire. The total conductor length is very much less than a wavelength. Maximum response is in the plane of the loop.

Fig. 4 — A ferrite-rod or loopstick antenna. Turns of wire may be wound on a single rod or, to increase the output from the loop, the core may be two rods taped together, as shown here. The type of core material must be selected for the intended frequency range of the loop. To avoid bulky windings, fine wire such as no. 28 or no. 30 is often used, with larger wire for the leads.

given in a later section.) However, it is sometimes desirable to have a pattern with only one null, so there is no question about

whether the transmitter in the above example would be east or west from your position.

A loop or loopstick antenna may be made to have a single null if a second antenna element is added. The element is called a sensing antenna, because it gives an added sense of direction to the loop pattern. The second element must be omni-directional, such as a short vertical. When the signals from the loop and the vertical element are combined with a 90° phase shift between the two, a cardioid pattern results. The development of the pattern is shown in Fig. 6A.

Fig. 6B shows a circuit for adding a sensing antenna to a loop or loopstick. R1 is an internal adjustment and is used to set the level of the signal from the sensing antenna. For the best null in the composite pattern, the signals from the loop and the sensing antenna must be of equal amplitude, so R1 is adjusted experimentally during setup. In practice, the null of the cardioid is not as sharp as that of the loop, so the usual measurement procedure is to first use the loop alone to obtain a precise bearing reading, and then to add the sensing antenna and take another reading to resolve the ambiguity. (The null of the cardioid is 90° away from the nulls of the loop.) For this reason, provisions are usually made for switching the sensing element in and out of operation.

Phased Arrays

Phased arrays are also used in amateur RDF work. Two general classifications of phased arrays are end-fire and broadside configurations. Depending on the spacing and phasing of the elements, end-fire patterns may exhibit a null off one end of the axis of the two or more elements. At the same time, the response is maximum off the other end of the axis, in the opposite direction from the null. A familiar arrangement is two elements spaced ¼ wavelength apart and fed 90° out of phase. The resultant pattern is a cardioid, with the null in the direction of the leading element. Other arrangements of spacing and phasing for an end-fire array are also suitable for RDF work. One of the best known is the Adcock array, discussed in the next section.

Broadside arrays are inherently bidirectional, which means there are always at least two nulls in the pattern. Ambiguity therefore exists in the true direction of the transmitter, but depending on the application, this may be no handicap. Broadside arrays are seldom used for amateur RDF applications.

Adcock Arrays

One of the most popular types of end-fire phased arrays is the Adcock. This system was invented by F. Adcock and patented in 1919. The array consists of two vertical elements fed 180° apart, and

mounted so the system may be rotated. Element spacing is not critical, and may be in the range from 1/10 to 3/4 wavelength. The two elements must be of identical lengths, but need not be self-resonant. Elements that are shorter than resonant are commonly used. Because neither the element spacing nor the length is critical in terms of wavelengths, an Adcock array may be operated over more than one amateur band.

The radiation pattern of the Adcock is shown in Fig. 7A. The nulls are in directions broadside to the axis of array, and become sharper with greater element spacings. However, with an element spacing greater than ¾ wavelength, the pattern begins to take on additional nulls in the directions off the ends of the array axis. At a spacing of 1 wavelength the pattern is that of Fig. 7B, and the array is unsuitable for RDF applications.

Short vertical monopoles are often used in what is sometimes called the U-Adcock, so named because the elements with their feeders take on the shape of the letter U. In this arrangement the elements are worked against the earth as a ground or counterpoise. If the array is used only for reception, earth losses are of no great consequence. Short, elevated vertical dipoles are also used in what is sometimes called the H-Adcock. The Adcock array is often used at HF for skywave RDF work. In this application, it is not considered a portable system.

The Adcock array, with two nulls in its pattern, has the same ambiguity as the loop and the loopstick. Adding a sensing element to the Adcock array has not met with great success. Difficulties arise from mutual coupling between the array elements and the sensing element, among other things. Because Adcock arrays are

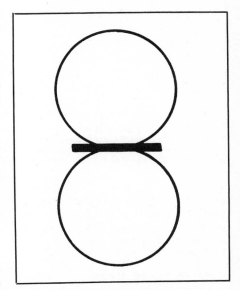

Fig. 5 — Field pattern for a ferrite rod antenna. The dark bar represents the rod on which the loop turns are wound.

Fig. 6 — At A, the directivity pattern of a loop antenna with sensing element. At B is a circuit for combining the signals from the two elements. C1 is adjusted for resonance with T1 at the operating frequency.

Fig. 8 — An early type of goniometer that is still used today in some RDF applications. This device is a special type of RF transformer that permits a movable coil in the center (not shown here) to be rotated and determine directions even though the elements connected at A and B are stationary.

Fig. 9 — This diagram illustrates one technique used in electronic beam forming. By delaying the signal from element A by an amount equal to the propagation delay, the two signals may be summed precisely in phase, even though the signal is not in the broadside direction. Because this time delay is identical for all frequencies, the system is not frequency sensitive.

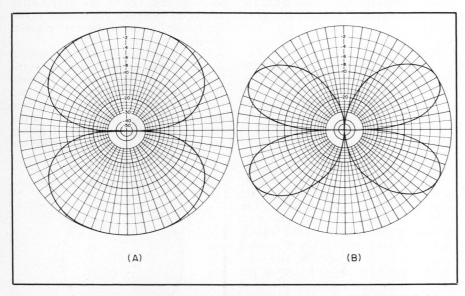

Fig. 7 — At A, the pattern of the Adcock array with an element spacing of ½ wavelength. In these plots the elements are aligned with the vertical axis. As the element spacing is increased beyond ¾ wavelength, additional nulls develop off the ends of the array, and at a spacing of 1 wavelength the pattern at B exists. This pattern is unsuitable for RDF work.

balancing of the antenna for a symmetrical pattern.

Loops are not as useful for skywave RDF work because of random polarization of the received signal. Phased arrays are somewhat less sensitive to propagation effects, probably because they are larger for the same frequency of operation and therefore offer some space diversity. In general, loops and loopsticks are used for mobile and portable operation, while phased arrays are used for fixed-station operation. However, phased arrays are used successfully above 144 MHz for portable and mobile RDF work. Practical examples of both types of antennas are presented later in this chapter.

The Goniometer

Most fixed RDF stations for government and commercial work use antenna arrays of stationary elements, rather than mechanically rotatable arrays. This has been true since the earliest days of radio. The device used in those early days to permit finding directions without moving the elements is called a radiogoniometer, or simply a goniometer. Various types of goniometers are still used today in many

used primarily for fixed-station applications, the ambiguity presents no serious problem. The fixed station with an Adcock is usually one of a group of stations in an RDF network.

Loops vs. Phased Arrays

Although loops can be made smaller than suitable phased arrays for the same frequency of operation, the phased arrays are preferred by some for a variety of reasons. In general, sharper nulls can be obtained with phased arrays, but this is also a function of the care used in constructing and feeding the individual antennas, as well as of the size of the phased array in terms of wavelengths. The primary constructional consideration is the shielding and balancing of the feed line against unwanted signal pickup, and the installations, and offer the amateur many possibilities.

The early style of goniometer is a special form of RF transformer, as shown in Fig. 8. It consists of two fixed coils mounted at right angles to one another. Inside the fixed coils is a movable coil, not shown in Fig. 8 to avoid cluttering the diagram. The pairs of connections marked A and B are connected respectively to two elements in an array, and the output to the detector or receiver is taken from the movable coil. As the inner coil is rotated, its coupling to one fixed coil increases while that to the other decreases. Both the amplitude and the phase of the signal coupled into the pickup winding are altered with rotation in a way that corresponds to actually rotating the array itself. Therefore, the rotation of the inner coil can be calibrated in degrees to correspond to bearing angles from the station location.

In the early days of radio, the type of goniometer just described saw frequent use with fixed Adcock arrays. A refinement of that system employed four Adcock elements, two arrays at right angles to each other. With a goniometer arrangement, RDF measurements could be taken in all compass directions, as opposed to none off the ends of a two-element fixed array. However, resolution of the four-element system was not as good as with a single pair of rotatable elements. To overcome this difficulty, a few systems of eight elements were installed.

Various other types of goniometers have been developed over the years, such as commutator switching to various elements in the array. A later development is the diode switching of capacitors to provide a commutator effect. As mechanical action has gradually been replaced with electronics to "rotate" stationary elements, the word goniometer is used less frequently these days. However, it still appears in many engineering reference texts. The more complex electronic systems of today are often called beam-forming networks.

Electronic Antenna Rotation

With an array of many fixed elements, beam rotation can be performed electronically by sampling and combining signals from various individual elements in the array. Contingent on the total number of elements in the system and their physical arrangement, almost any desired antenna pattern can be formed by summing the sampled signals in appropriate amplitude and phase relationships. Delay networks are used for some of the elements before the summation is performed. In addition, attenuators may be used for some elements to develop patterns such as from an array with binomial current distribution.

One system using these techniques is the Wullenweber antenna, used primarily in government and military installations. The Wullenweber consists of a very large number of elements arranged in a circle, usually outside of (or in front of) a circular reflecting screen. Depending on the installation, the circle may be anywhere from a few hundred feet to more than a quarter of a mile in diameter. Although the Wullenweber is not one that would be constructed by an amateur, some of the techniques it uses may certainly be applied to Amateur Radio.

For the moment, consider just two elements of a Wullenweber antenna, shown as A and B in Fig. 9. Also shown is the wavefront of a radio signal arriving from a distant transmitter. As drawn, the wavefront strikes element A first, and must travel somewhat farther before it strikes element B. There is a finite delay before the wavefront reaches element B.

The propagation delay may be measured by delaying the signal received at element A before summing it with that from element B. If the two signals are combined directly, the amplitude of the resultant signal will be maximum when the delay for element A exactly equals the propagation delay. This results in an in-phase condition at the summation point. Or if one of the signals is inverted and the two are summed, a null will exist when the element-A delay equals the propagation delay; the signals will combine in a 180° out-of-phase relationship. Either way, once the time delay is known, it may be converted to distance. Then the direction from which the wave is arriving may be determined by trigonometry.

By altering the delay in small increments, the peak of the antenna lobe (or the null) can be steered in azimuth. This is true without regard to the frequency of the incoming wave. Thus, the system is not fre-quency sensitive, other than for the frequency range that may be covered satisfactorily by the array elements themselves. Delay lines used in such systems can be lumped-constant networks if the system is used only for receiving. Rolls of coaxial cable of various lengths are used in installations for transmitting. In this case, the lines are considered for the time delay they provide, rather than as simple phasing lines. The difference is that a phasing line is ordinarily designed for a single frequency (or for an amateur band), while a delay line offers essentially the same delay at all frequencies.

By combining signals from other Wullenweber elements appropriately, the broad beamwidth of the pattern from the two elements can be narrowed, and unwanted sidelobes can be suppressed. Then, by electronically switching the delays and attenuations to the various elements, the beam so formed can be rotated around the compass. The package of electronics designed to do this, including delay lines and electronically switched attenuators, is the beam-forming network. However, the Wullenweber system is not restricted to forming a single beam. With an isolation amplifier provided for each element of the array, several beam-forming networks can be operated independently. Imagine having an antenna system that offers a dipole pattern, a rhombic pattern and a Yagi beam pattern, all simultaneously and without frequency sensitivity. One or more may be rotating while another is held in a particular direction. The Wullenweber was designed to fulfill this type of requirement.

One feature of the Wullenweber antenna is that it can operate at 360° around the compass. In many government installations, there is no need for such coverage, as the areas of interest lie in a single azimuth sector. In such cases an in-line array of elements with a backscreen or curtain reflector may be installed broadside to the center of the sector. By using the same techniques as the Wullenweber, the beams formed from this array may be slewed left and right across the sector. The maximum sector width available will depend on the installation, but beyond 70 to 80° the patterns begin to deteriorate to the point that they are unsatisfactory for precise RDF work.

Direction Finding Techniques

Locating a transmitter with RDF techniques is a skill that is acquired only with practice. Familiarity with the antenna being used and especially with its limitations are probably the most important criteria. Of course, knowing the measuring equipment is also a requirement. But in addition to this, one must know how radio signals behave at different frequencies and in different kinds of terrain. Here is where experience becomes the best teacher, although reading about the experiences of others and talking with others who are active in RDF also helps.

GROUND-WAVE RDF

Most amateur RDF activity is conducted with ground-wave signals, where the transmitter is seldom more than a dozen or so miles away. Even if the position of a transmitter has been localized with sky-wave measurements, it is usually not possible to determine the precise transmitter location without taking some ground-wave readings. The considerations for these measurements are discussed in this section. Some of these considerations also apply to sky-wave measurements, but a later section discusses the peculiarities of sky-wave RDF work.

Before setting out to locate a signal source, it is a good idea to note some general information about the signal itself. Is its frequency constant, or does it drift? Drifting means you may have to retune the receiver often during the hunt. Do transmissions occur at rather regular intervals, or are they sporadic? Are transmissions very short in duration, modest in length, or is there a continuous carrier? The most difficult sources to locate are those which transmit at irregular intervals and are on the air for very brief periods, such as a few seconds. Finding these transmitters becomes a real challenge and requires extreme patience. It also requires quick action when the transmitter is on the air, to obtain a null reading in those few seconds. Once you've determined the general signal characteristics, you can begin the search.

Best accuracy in determining a bearing to a signal source is obtained when the propagation path is over homogeneous terrain, and when only the vertically polarized component of the ground wave is present. If a boundary exists such as between land and water, the different conductivities of the two mediums under the ground wave cause bending (refraction) of the wave front. In addition, reflection of RF energy from vertical objects such as mountains or buildings can add to the direct wave and cause RDF errors.

The effects of refraction and reflection are shown in Fig. 10. At A, the signal is actually arriving from a different bearing than the true direction to the transmitter.

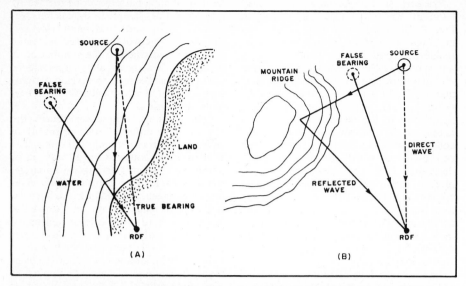

Fig. 10 — RDF errors caused by refraction (A) and reflection (B). At A a false reading is obtained because the signal actually arrives from a direction that is different from that to the source. At B a direct signal from the source combines with a reflected signal from the mountain ridge. The two are averaged at the antenna, giving a false bearing to a point somewhere between the two apparent sources.

This happens because the wave is refracted at the shoreline. Even the most sophisticated of measuring equipment will not indicate the true bearing in this situation, as the equipment can only show the direction from which the signal is arriving. Knowing how radio signals behave at different frequencies and in different kinds of terrain is important in this situation. If the measuring equipment is portable, the experienced RDF enthusiast will probably move to the shoreline to take a measurement with less chance of error. Even so, depending on the direction to the source compared to the direction of the shoreline, a precise reading may still be impossible to obtain.

In Fig. 10B there are two apparent sources for the incoming signal — a direct wave from the source itself, and another wave that is reflected from the mountain ridge. In this case the two waves add at the antenna of the RDF equipment. Without care being used in performing the measurement, the uninitiated observer would obtain a false bearing in a direction somewhere between the directions to the two sources. The experienced RDF enthusiast might notice that the null reading in this situation is not as sharp as it usually is, or perhaps not as deep. But these indications would be subtle, and easy to overlook. Here is where knowing the antenna and the equipment becomes very helpful.

Water towers, tall radio towers and similar objects can also lead to false bearings. The effects of these objects become significant when they are large in terms of a wavelength. In fact, if the direct path to the transmitter is masked by intervening terrain or other radio "clutter," it is possible that a far stronger signal may be received by reflection than from the true direction to the source. Such towers atop hills are prime sources of strong "pinpoint" reflections. Triangulation may even "confirm" that the transmitter is at that high elevation, unless a reading is taken from in the clear, where the true radio path is unmasked by the clutter.

Local objects also tend to distort the field, such as buildings of concrete and steel construction, power lines and the like. It is important that the RDF antenna be in the clear, well away from such surrounding objects. Trees with foliage may also create an adverse effect, especially at VHF and above. If it is not possible to avoid such objects, the best procedure is to take readings at several different positions, and to average the readings for the result.

Triangulation

If two RDF bearing measurements are taken from locations that are separated by a significant distance, the bearing lines may be drawn from those positions as represented on a map. The point where the two lines cross (assuming the two bearings are not the same nor are 180° apart) will indicate a "fix," or the approximate position of the transmitter.

The word "approximate" is used here because there is always some degree of uncertainty in the readings obtained from the measurement. This uncertainty arises from equipment limitations (antenna null width, for example). Propagation effects

Fig. 11 — Bearing sectors from three RDF positions drawn on a map. This method is known as triangulation. Note here that sensing antennas are not required at any of the DF sites; antennas with two null indications 180° apart are quite acceptable.

may increase the degree of uncertainty. In order to obtain a more precise fix, a bearing measurement from yet a third position is helpful. When the positions and bearing lines for all three measurements are placed on a map, the three lines seldom intersect at a single point. Instead, they form a small triangle on the map. The unknown source is presumed to be located inside the triangle. Thus, the name triangulation.

In order to best indicate the probable area of the transmitter location on the map, the bearings from each position should be drawn as a narrow sector instead of as a single line. The sector width should represent the amount of uncertainty. A portion of a map marked in this manner is shown in Fig. 11. Here it becomes evident graphically how the measurement from DF Site 3 has narrowed down the probable area of the transmitter position. The small black section indicates where the transmitter is likely to be found, a significantly smaller quadrangle than that of the sectors from DF Sites 1 and 2 alone.

Several types of maps are suitable for triangulation. Ordinary road maps, however, usually lack sufficient detail, and are not generally satisfactory. Contour maps of the area like that shown in Fig. 11 are preferred for open country. Aeronautical charts are also suitable. City maps and street maps are usually acceptable. Your local city or county engineer can help you find a source for suitable maps, perhaps even through his office.

Closing in on the Fix

In the final phases of locating an unknown source, portable RDF equipment is used to pinpoint the exact location. As the equipment is brought near the transmitter, signals become very strong. Overloading of the front-end circuits of the receiver may lead to confusing and inconsistent readings. One way to combat this problem is to insert an attenuator in the transmission line from the antenna to the receiver. Attenuators are discussed in another chapter of this book.

Even with an attenuator in the line, in the presence of a strong electromagnetic field there may be some energy coupled directly into the receiver circuitry. This effect is noted as an apparent nondirectional characteristic of the antenna. In other words, the received signal strength changes only slightly or perhaps not at all as the RDF antenna is rotated in azimuth. The only cure for this effect is to shield the receiving equipment. Something as simple as placing the receiver in a bread pan or cake pan covered with a piece of copper or aluminum screening, securely fastened at several points, may provide sufficient shielding to eliminate this problem. Of course more elaborate precautions may also be taken.

An alternative to protecting the receiver from overload is to switch to a simple diode detector as you are closing in on the fix. The detector should have a sensitive meter indicator with some kind of sensitivity control, and may be made tuneable in frequency, if desired. It might even include a meter-amplifier circuit to increase its sensitivity. It should, however, be constructed inside a metal enclosure that affords shielding, to avoid unwanted signal pickup in the environment of a strong RF field.

Depending on the nature of the area surrounding the fix, the transmitter may be easy or difficult to locate physically. If the emission is a spurious output from a communications transmitter, a transmitting antenna will probably stand out. On the other hand, a hidden transmitter that is jamming a repeater may be very difficult to find. Sometimes such transmitters are buried in the ground, and the antenna may be a thin wire concealed in the bushes. It may not be spotted by an observer standing right next to it. Sharp eyes and some astute observations are needed here.

A Test or Target Transmitter

Some situations may arise where repeated inconsistent RDF readings simply won't yield a reliable fix. This can happen in mountainous or hilly terrain, or in a canyon, where many signal reflections occur. It also happens in the "concrete jungle" of a metropolitan area where canyons are formed by tall buildings. (In this case it may be advantageous to take a reading from atop one of those buildings.)

A simple aid to locating the source of such a signal is to use a test or target transmitter. This is a second transmitter that is temporarily placed in the general area where the unknown source is thought to be located, and operated on a slightly different frequency. RDF readings from the unknown source may then be compared with readings from the target transmitter to gain a better idea of the unknown location. The target transmitter may even be moved about until the readings coincide, to obtain a reliable fix. Successfully tracking down an unknown transmitter involves detective work — examining all the clues, weighing the evidence and using one's best judgment. For many amateurs, RDF presents an interesting challenge.

SKY-WAVE RDF

Many factors make it difficult to obtain accuracy in sky-wave RDF work. In the previous section, mention was made that the vertical component of the signal is used in taking ground-wave measurements. Because of Faraday rotation during propagation, sky-wave signals are received with random polarization — sometimes the vertical component is strongest, and at other times the horizontal. This necessitates somewhat different techniques for sky-wave work, because the vertical component of the signal should still be the one used for bearing measurements. During periods when the vertical component is weak, the signal will appear to fade. At these times, determining an accurate signal null becomes difficult or impossible.

One important thing to keep in mind with sky-wave measurements is the degree of uncertainty. Accuracy to within 1 or 2°

is the exception rather than the rule. Errors of as much as 3 to 5° are common. An error of 3° at a thousand miles represents a distance of 52 miles. Even with every precaution taken in measurements, don't expect to pinpoint a location to more than a county, a corner of a state or a large metropolitan area. What you *can* expect is to determine where an RDF group should begin making a local search.

Great-Circle Radio Paths

It is generally assumed that a sky-wave signal follows a great-circle path in its travel from a transmitter to a receiver. This is not always the case, however. For example, if the signal is refracted in a tilted layer of the ionosphere, it could arrive from a direction that is several degrees away from the true great-circle bearing. Weather fronts and other meteorological conditions may also result in false readings. Some scientists believe that the earth's magnetic field causes a departure of wave travel from the great-circle path, and propagation conditions during geomagnetic disturbances are known to have this effect.

Another cause of signals arriving off the great-circle path is termed sidescatter. It is possible that, at a given time, the ionosphere does not support great-circle propagation of the signal from the transmitter to the receiver because the frequency is above the MUF for that path. However, at the same time, propagation may be supported from both ends of the path to some mutually accessible point off the great-circle path.

The signal from the source may propagate to that point on the earth's surface and hop in a sideways direction to continue to the receiver. For example, signals from Central Europe have been known to propagate to New England by hopping from an area in the Atlantic Ocean off the northwest coast of Africa, whereas the great-circle path puts the reflection point in the North Atlantic, off the southern coast of Greenland. Readings in error by as much as 50° or more may result from this type of propagation.

Indeed, many factors do combine to make it difficult to obtain accurate sky-wave RDF measurements. The effect may be that the source of the signal seems to wander somewhat over a few minutes of time, or it may be weak and fluttery. At other times, however, there may be no tell-tale signs to indicate that the readings are suspect.

Antennas for Sky-Wave RDF

Loop antennas and loopsticks are generally unsatisfactory for sky-wave RDF because of not only the random polarization shift, but also because the vertical wave angle from which the signal arrives may not be constant. The Adcock or other type of phased vertical array is used most often. Such arrays offer some degree of space diversity over small loops, and

therefore are less subject to fading effects. Greatest accuracy for sky-wave signals is obtained when the vertical angle of arrival is small.

At high arrival angles, even the Adcock array becomes less reliable because its response to high-angle signals falls off. (It will not respond at all to a signal arriving from directly overhead.) Some experimenters have attempted to overcome this difficulty by tilting the array, but little improvement in reliability seems to result. A tilted loop sometimes yields results equivalent to those of a vertical Adcock array for high-angle signals. Signals from high angles often seem to arrive not from a single point, but from a small area in space. This phenomenon is probably associated with scattering of the signal in the ionosphere.

Sky-Wave Triangulation

Triangulation mapping with sky-wave signals is a bit more complex than with ground waves because the paths are great-circle routes. Commonly available world maps are difficult to work with, as the triangulation lines must be curved lines, rather than straight. Depending on the method used to create the map, one showing a country or similar large area may be suitable.

Many U.S. highway maps are usable for triangulation work. Most are some form of conical projection, such as the Lambert conformal conic system. The method of developing such a map is shown in Fig. 12. A cone is made to coincide with the earth's surface along two parallels of latitude, and the axis of the cone coincides with that of the earth. The two latitude lines are called standard parallels, and are chosen for the area to be covered for minimum distortion over the entire projection. The standard parallels are located inside the limits of the projection, as shown. This system of coordinates maintains the accuracy of angular representation, but the distance scale is not constant over the entire projection.

A type of map that can be pressed into service for worldwide areas is an azimuthal-equidistant projection, as shown in Fig. 13. This particular map is prepared for Wichita, Kansas, but they may be obtained for any location. Such maps are available for a nominal fee from Bill Johnston, N5KR, PO Box 370, White Sands, NM 88002. His maps are custom prepared by computer for a specific location.

With an azimuthal-equidistant map, true bearings for great-circle paths are shown as straight lines from the center to all points on the earth. Maps for three or more different RDF sites may be compared to gain an idea of the general geographic area for an unknown source.

A special type of map has been developed that is well suited for sky-wave triangulation. This map is known as a gnomonic projection, one on which *all* great-circle paths are represented by

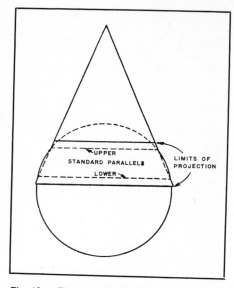

Fig. 12 — The method of obtaining a Lambert conformal conic projection. To make the average distance errors as small as possible, the two standard parallels are chosen for the area to be mapped. Accuracy of angular representations is maintained.

straight lines. To understand how this is possible, see Fig. 14. The drawing shows a transparent sphere with latitude and longitude lines. A small lamp is positioned at the exact center of the sphere and illuminated.

If a large flat card or sheet of paper is touched against the globe at some point as shown in Fig. 14, the surface features will be projected as shadows on that flat surface. This is the gnomonic projection. All meridians and any lines representing great-circle paths will appear as straight lines on the projection. This happens because the lamp is in the plane of each of the great circles, and cannot therefore throw a curved shadow.

Unfortunately, gnomonic charts are not readily available. They are prepared especially for government agencies and military use. Such a projection can be prepared at home if one wants to take the trouble. The work is tedious. Instructions for making a gnomonic projection are given in pages 749 through 758 of R. Keene (see the bibliography at the end of this chapter).

RDF SYSTEM CALIBRATION AND USE

Once an RDF system is initially assembled, it should be "calibrated" or checked out before actually being put into use. Of primary concern is the balance or symmetry of the antenna pattern. A lopsided figure-8 pattern with a loop, for example, is undesirable; the nulls are not 180° apart nor are they at exact right angles to the plane of the loop. If this fact was not known in actual RDF work, measurement accuracy would suffer.

Initial checkout can be performed with a low-powered transmitter at a distance of a few hundred feet. It should be within visual range and must be operating into a vertical antenna. (A quarter-wave vertical or a loaded whip is quite suitable.) The site must be reasonably clear of obstructions, especially steel and concrete or brick buildings, large metal objects, nearby power lines, and so on. If the system operates above 30 MHz, trees and large bushes should also be avoided. An open field makes an excellent site.

The procedure is to "find" the transmitter with the RDF equipment as if its position were not known, and compare the RDF null indication with the visual path to the transmitter. For antennas having more than one null, each null should be checked.

If imbalance is found in the antenna system, there are two options available. One is to correct the imbalance. Toward this end, pay particular attention to the feed line. Using a coaxial feeder for a balanced antenna invites a nonsymmetrical pattern, unless an effective balun is used. A balun is not necessary if the loop is shielded, but a nonsymmetrical pattern can result with misplacement of the break in the shield itself. The builder may also find that the presence of a sensing antenna upsets the balance slightly. Experimenting with its position with respect to the main antenna may lead to correcting the error. You will also note that the position of the null shifts by 90° as the sensing element is switched in and out, and the null is not as deep. This is of little concern, however, as the purpose of the sensing antenna is only to resolve ambiguities. The sensing element should be switched out when accuracy is desired.

The second option is to accept the imbalance of the antenna and use some kind of indicator to show the true directions of the nulls. Small pointers, painted marks on the mast or an optical sighting system might be used. Sometimes the end result of the calibration procedure will be a compromise between these two options, as a perfect electrical balance may be difficult or impossible to attain.

The discussion above is oriented toward calibrating portable RDF systems. The same general suggestions apply if the RDF array is fixed, such as an Adcock. However, it won't be possible to move it to an open field. Instead, the array is calibrated in its intended operating position through the use of a portable or mobile transmitter. Because of nearby obstructions or reflecting objects, the null in the pattern may not appear to indicate the precise direction of the transmitter. Do not confuse this with imbalance in the RDF array. Check for imbalance by rotating the array 180° and comparing readings.

Once the balance is satisfactory, you should make a table of bearing errors noted in different compass directions. These error values should be applied as corrections when actual measurements are made. The

Fig. 13 — Azimuthal map centered on Wichita, Kansas. With such a map for each site in an RDF network, the general geographic area for an unknown source can be obtained by comparison of the maps. *Copyright by Rand McNally & Co., Chicago. Reproduction License no. 394.*

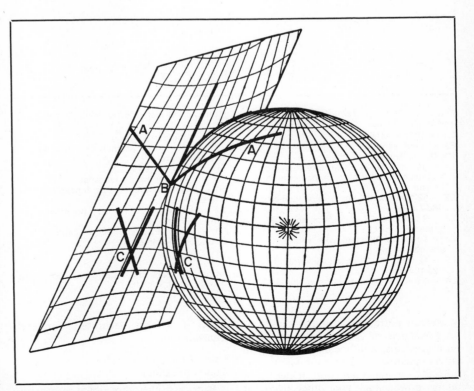

Fig. 14 — Optical means of showing the development of a gnomonic projection. On such a map, all great-circle routes appear as straight lines, and angular measurements with respect to meridians are true.

Fig 15—The linear field-strength meter. The control at the upper left is for C1 and the one to the right for C2. At the lower left is the band switch. The zero-set control for M1 is located directly below the meter.

Fig 16—Inside view of the field-strength meter. At the upper right is C1 and to the left, C2. The dark leads from the circuit board to the front panel are the shielded leads described in the text.

Fig. 17 — Circuit diagram of the linear field-strength meter. All resistors are ¼- or ½-watt composition types.

C1 — 140-pF variable.
C2 — 15-pF variable
D1, D2 — 1N914 or equiv.
L1 — 34 turns no. 24 enam. wire wound on an Amidon* T-68-2 core, tapped 4 turns from ground end.
L2 — 12 turns no. 24 enam. wire wound on T-68-2 core.
L3 — 2 turns no. 24 enam. wire wound at ground end of L2.
L4 — 1 turn no. 26 enam. wire wound at ground end of L5.
L5 — 12 turns no. 26 enam. wire wound on T-25-12 core.
L6 — 1 turn no. 26 enam. wire wound at

ground end of L7.
L7 — 1 turn no. 18 enam. wire wound on T-25-12 core.
M1 — 50 or 100 μA dc.
R2 — 10-kΩ control, linear taper.
S1 — Rotary switch, 3 poles, 5 positions, 3 sections.
S2 — Rotary switch, 1 pole, 4 positions.
S3 — DPST toggle.
U1 — Type 741 op amp. Pin nos. shown are for a 14-pin package.

*Amidon Associates, 12033 Otsego St., North Hollywood, CA 91607

mobile or portable transmitter should be at a distance of 2 or 3 miles for these measurements, and should be in as clear an area as possible during transmissions. The idea is to avoid conduction of the signal along power lines and other overhead wiring from the transmitter to the RDF site. Of course the position of the transmitter must be known accurately for each transmission.

Using RDF Antennas for Communications

Because of their directional characteristics, RDF antennas would seem to be useful for two-way communications. It has not been mentioned earlier that the efficiency of receiving loops is poor. The radiation resistance is very low, and the resistance of wire conductors by comparision is significant. For this reason it is common to use some type of preamplifier with receiving loops. Small receiving loops can often be used to advantage in a fixed station, to null out either a noise source or unwanted signals.

A loop that is small in terms of a wavelength may also be used for transmitting, but a different construction technique is necessary. A thick conductor is needed at HF, several inches in diameter. The reason for this is to decrease the ohmic losses in the loop. Special methods are also required to couple power into a small loop, such as links. A small loop is highly inductive, and the inductance may be canceled by inserting a capacitor in series with the loop itself. The capacitor must be able to withstand the high RF currents that flow during transmissions.

The Adcock antenna and other phased arrays have been used extensively for transmitting. In this application maximum response is off the ends of the Adcock, which is 90° away from the null direction used for RDF work.

A PORTABLE FIELD-STRENGTH METER

Few amateur stations, fixed or mobile, are without need of a field-strength meter. An instrument of this type serves many useful purposes during antenna experiments and adjustments, and may be used for closing in on an RDF fix. When work is to be done from many wavelengths away, a simple wavemeter lacks the necessary sensitivity. Further, its linearity leaves much to be desired.

The field-strength meter described here takes care of these problems. Additionally, it is small, measuring only 4 × 5 × 8 inches. The power supply consists of two 9-volt batteries. Sensitivity can be set for practically any amount desired. However, from a usefulness standpoint, the circuit should not be too sensitive or it will respond to unwanted signals. This unit also has excellent linearity with regard to field strength, which is very helpful in RDF work. (The field strength of a received signal varies directly with the distance from the source, all other things being equal.) The frequency range includes all amateur bands from 3.5 through 148 MHz, with band-switched circuits, thus avoiding the use of plug-in inductors. All in all, it is a quite useful instrument

The unit is pictured in Figs. 15 and 16, and the schematic diagram is shown in Fig. 17. A type 741 op-amp IC is the heart of the unit. The antenna is connected to J1, and a tuned circuit is used ahead of a diode detector. The rectified signal is coupled as dc and amplified in the op amp. Sensitivity of the op amp is controlled by inserting R3 through R6 in the circuit by means of S2.

With the circuit shown, and in its most sensitive setting, M1 will detect a signal from the antenna on the order of 100 μV. Linearity is poor for approximately the first 1/5 range of M1, but then is almost straight-line from there to full-scale deflection. The reason for the poor linearity at the start of the readings is because of nonlinearity of the diodes at the point of first conduction. If gain measurements are being made this is of no real importance, however, as accurate gain measurements can be made in the linear portion of the readings. For RDF measurements, just remember that the indicated strength is not proportional to the distance at the low end of the scale.

The 741 op amp requires both a positive and a negative voltage source. This is obtained by connecting two 9-volt batteries in series and grounding the center. One other feature of the instrument is that it can be used remotely by connecting an external meter at J2. This is handy if one wants to adjust an antenna and observe the results without having to leave the antenna site.

L1, the 80/40 meter coil, is tuned by C1. The coil is wound on a toroid form. For 20, 15 or 10 meters, L2 is switched in parallel with L1 to cover the three bands. L5 and C2 cover approximately 40 to 60 MHz, and L7 and C2 from 130 MHz to approximately 180 MHz. The two VHF coils are also wound on toroid forms.

Construction Notes

The majority of the components may be mounted on an etched circuit board. A shielded lead should be used between pin 4 of the IC and S2. The same is true for the leads from R3 through R6 to the switch. Otherwise, parasitic oscillations may occur in the IC because of its very high gain.

For the unit to cover the 144-MHz band, L6 and L7 should be mounted directly across the appropriate terminals of S1, rather than on a circuit board. The extra lead length adds too much inductance to the circuit. It isn't necessary to use toroid forms for the 50- and 144-MHz coils. They were used in the version described here simply because they were available. Air-wound coils of the appropriate inductance can be substituted.

Calibration

The field-strength meter can be used "as is" for a relative-reading device for RDF work. A linear indicator scale will serve admirably. However, it will be a much more useful instrument for antenna work if it is calibrated in decibels, enabling the user to check relative gain and front-to-back ratios. If one has access to a calibrated signal generator, it can be connected to the field-strength meter and different signal levels can be fed to the device for making a calibration chart. Signal-generator voltage ratios can be converted to decibels by using the equation

$$dB = 20 \log (V1/V2) \qquad \text{(Eq. 1)}$$

where V1/V2 is the ratio of the two voltages, and log is the common logarithm.

Let's assume that M1 is calibrated evenly from 0 to 10. Next, assume we set the signal generator to provide a reading of 1 on M1, and that the generator is feeding a 100-μV signal into the instrument. Now we increase the generator output to 200 μV, giving us a voltage ratio of 2 to 1. Also let's assume M1 reads 5 with the 200-μV input. From the equation above, we find that the voltage ratio of 2 equals 6.02 dB between 1 and 5 on the meter scale. M1 can be calibrated more accurately between 1 and 5 on its scale by adjusting the generator and figuring the ratio. For example, a ratio of 126 μV to 100 μV is 1.26, corresponding to 2.0 dB. By using this method, all of the settings of S2 can be calibrated. In the instrument shown here, the most sensitive setting of S2 with R3, 1 megohm, provides a range of approximately 6 dB for M1. Keep in mind that the meter scale for each setting of S1 must be calibrated similarly for each band. The degree of coupling of the tuned circuits for the different bands will vary, so each band must be calibrated separately.

Another method for calibrating the instrument is using a transmitter and measuring its output power with an RF wattmeter. In this case we are dealing with power rather than voltage ratios, so this equation applies:

$$dB = 10 \log (P1/P2) \qquad \text{(Eq. 2)}$$

where P1/P2 is the power ratio.

With most transmitters the power output can be varied, so calibration of the test instrument is rather easy. Attach a pickup

antenna to the field-strength meter (a short wire a foot or so long will do) and position the device in the transmitter antenna field. Let's assume we set the transmitter output for 10 watts and get a reading on M1. We note the reading and then increase the output to 20 watts, a power ratio of 2. Note the reading on M1 and then use Eq. 2. A power ratio of 2 is 3.01 dB. By using this method the instrument can be calibrated on all bands and ranges.

With the tuned circuits and coupling links specified in Fig. 17, this instrument has an average range on the various bands of 6 dB for the two most sensitive positions of S2, and 15 dB and 30 dB for the next two successive ranges. The 30-dB scale is handy for making front-to-back antenna measurements without having to switch S2.

A SHIELDED LOOP WITH SENSING ANTENNA FOR 28 MHz

Fig. 18 shows the construction and mounting of a simple, shielded, 10-meter loop. The loop is made from an 18-inch length of RG-11/U (solid or foamed dielectric) secured to an aluminum box of any convenient size, with two coaxial cable hoods (Amphenol 83-1HP/U). The outer shield must be broken at the exact center. C1 is a 25-pF variable capacitor, and is connected in parallel with a 33-pF mica padder capacitor, C3. C1 must be tuned to the desired frequency while the loop is connected to the receiver in the same way as it will be used for RDF. C2 is a small differential capacitor used to provide electrical symmetry. The lead-in to the receiver is 67 inches of RG-59/U cable (82 inches if the cable has foamed dielectric).

The loop can be mounted on the roof of the car with a rubber suction cup. The builder might also fabricate some kind of bracket assembly to mount the loop temporarily in the window opening of the automobile, allowing for loop rotation. Reasonably true bearings may be obtained through the windshield when the car is pointed in the direction of the hidden transmitter. More accurate bearings may be obtained with the loop held out the window and the signal coming toward that side of the car.

Sometimes the car broadcast antenna may interfere with accurate bearings. Disconnecting the antenna from the broadcast receiver may eliminate this trouble.

Sensing Antenna

A sensing antenna can be added to the loop to check on which of the two directions indicated by the loop is the correct one. Add a phono jack to the top of the aluminum case shown in Fig. 18. The insulated center terminal of the jack should be connected to the side of the tuning capacitors connected to the center conductor of the RG-59/U coax feed line. The jack then takes a short vertical antenna rod of a diameter to fit the jack, or a piece of

Fig 18 — Sketch showing constructional details of the 28-MHz RDF loop. The outer braid of the coax loop is broken at the center of the loop. The gap is covered with waterproof tape, and the entire assembly is given a coat of acrylic spray.

Fig. 19 — Diagram of a ferrite loop (A). C1 is a dual-section air variable. The circuit at B shows a rod loop contained in an electrostatic shield channel (see text). A low-noise pre-amplifier is shown in Fig. 22.

no. 12 or 14 solid wire may be soldered to the center pin of a phono plug for insertion in the jack. The sensing antenna can be plugged in as needed. Starting with a length of about four times the loop diameter, the length of the sensing antenna should be pruned until the pattern is similar to Fig. 1D.

LOOPSTICK ANTENNA FOR 1.8 MHz

Fig. 19 contains a diagram for a rod loop. The winding (L1) has the appropriate number of turns to permit resonance with C1 at the operating frequency. L1 should be spread over approximately 1/3 of the core center. Litz wire will yield the best Q, but Formvar magnet wire can be used if desired. A layer of 3M Company glass tape (or Mylar tape) is recommended as a covering for the core before adding the wire. Masking tape can be used if nothing else is available.

L2 functions as a coupling link over the exact center of L1. C1 is a dual-section variable, although a differential capacitor might be better toward obtaining optimum balance (not tried). The loop Q can be controlled by means of C2, which is a mica compression trimmer.

Electrostatic shielding of rod loops can be effected by centering the rod in a U-shaped aluminum, brass or copper channel that extends slightly beyond the ends of the rod loop (1 inch is suitable). This idea is shown in Fig. 19B. The open side (top) of the channel can't be closed, as that would constitute a shorted-turn condition and render the antenna useless. This can be proved by shorting across the center of the channel with a screwdriver blade when the loop is tuned to an incoming signal.

A photograph of a shielded rod loop is offered in Fig. 20. It was developed experimentally for 160 meters and uses two 7-inch ferrite rods that were glued end-to-end with epoxy cement. The longer core resulted in improved sensitivity during weak-signal reception.

Obtaining a Cardioid Pattern

Although the bidirectional pattern of loop antennas can be used effectively in tracking transmitters down by means of triangulation, an essentially unidirectional loop response will help to reduce the time spent when doing so. Adding a sensing antenna to the loop is simple to do, and it will provide the desired cardioid response.

Fig. 21 shows how this can be accomplished. The link from the rod loop is connected via coaxial cable to the primary of T1, which is a tuned toroidal transformer with a split secondary winding. C3 is adjusted for peak signal response at the frequency of interest (as is C4), then R1 is adjusted for minimum back response of the loop. It will be necessary to readjust C3 and R1 several times to compensate for the interaction of these controls. The adjustments are repeated until no further null depth can be obtained. Tests show that null depths as great as 40 dB can be obtained with the circuit of Fig. 21 on 75 meters. A near-field weak-signal source was used during the tests.

The greater the null depth the lower the signal output from the system, so plan to include a preamplifier with 25 to 40 dB of gain. Q1 of Fig. 21 will deliver approximately 15 dB of gain. The circuit of Fig. 22 can be used following T2 to obtain an additional 24 dB of gain. In the interest of maintaining a good noise figure, even at 1.8 MHz, Q1 should be a low-noise

Fig. 20 — The shielded ferrite-rod loop for 160 meters. Two rods have been glued end to end (see text).

Fig. 23 — Unidirectional 75-meter RDF using ferrite-core loop with sensing antenna. Adjustable components of the circuit are mounted in the aluminum chassis supported by a short length of tubing.

Fig. 21 — Schematic diagram of a rod-loop antenna with a cardioid response. The sensing antenna, phasing network and a preamplifier are shown also. The secondary of T1 and the primary of T2 are tuned to resonance at the operating frequency of the loop. T68-2 or T68-6 Amidon toroid cores are suitable for both transformers. Amidon also sells the ferrite rods for this type of antenna.

Fig. 22 — Schematic diagram of a two-stage broadband amplifier. T1 and T2 have a 4:1 impedance ratio and are wound on FT-50-61 toroid cores (Amidon) that have a μ_i of 125. They contain 12 turns of no. 24 enam. bifilar wound wire. The capacitors are disc ceramic. This amplifier should be built on double-sided circuit board for best stability.

device. A Siliconix U310 JFET would be ideal in this circuit, but a 2N4416, an MPF102 or a 40673 MOSFET would also be satisfactory.

The sensing antenna can be mounted 6 to 15 inches from the loop. The vertical whip need not be more than 12 to 20 inches long. Some experimenting may be necessary in order to obtain the best results. It will depend also on the operating frequency of the antenna.

A LOOPSTICK FOR 3.5 MHz

Figs. 23 through 25 show an RDF loop suitable for the 3.5-MHz band. It uses a construction technique that has had considerable application in low-frequency marine direction finders. The loop is a coil wound on a ferrite rod from a broadcast-antenna loopstick. Because it is possible to make a coil of high Q with the ferrite core, the sensitivity of such a loop is comparable to a conventional loop that is a foot or so in diameter. The output of the vertical-rod sensing antenna, when properly combined with that of the loop, gives the system the cardioid pattern shown in Fig. 1D.

To make the loop, remove the original winding on the ferrite core and wind a new coil as shown in Fig. 24. Other types of cores than the one specified may be substituted; use the largest coil available and adjust the winding so the circuit resonates in the 75-meter band within the range of C1. The tuning range of the loop may be checked with a dip meter.

The sensing system consists of a 15-inch whip and an adjustable inductance that will resonate the whip as a quarter-wave antenna. It also contains a potentiometer to control the output of the antenna. S1 is used to switch the sensing antenna in and out of the circuit.

The whip, the loopstick, the inductance L1, the capacitor C1, the potentiometer R1

Fig. 24 — Circuit of the 75-meter direction finder.

C1 — 140 pF variable (125-pF ceramic trimmer in parallel with 15-pF ceramic fixed).
L1 — Approx. 140 μH adjustable (Miller No. 4512 or equiv.)
R1 — 1-kΩ carbon potentiometer.
S1 — SPST toggle.

Loopstick — Approx. 15 μH (Miller 705-A, with original winding removed and wound with 20 turns of no. 22 enam.). Link is two turns at center. Winding ends are secured with Scotch electrical tape.

Fig. 25 — Components of the 75-meter RDF are mounted on the top and sides of a Channel-lock type box. In this view R1 is on the left wall at the upper left and C1 is at the lower left. L1, S1 and the output connector are on the right wall. The loopstick and whip mount on the outside.

Fig. 26 — At A is a simple configuration that produces a cardioid pattern. At B is a convenient way of fabricating a sturdy mount for the radiator using BNC connectors.

and the switch S1 are all mounted on a 4 × 5 × 3-inch box chassis as shown in Fig. 25. The loopstick may be mounted and protected inside a piece of ½-inch PVC pipe. A section of ½-inch electrical conduit is attached to the bottom of the chassis box and this supports the instrument.

To produce an output having only one null there must be a 90° phase difference between the outputs of the loop and sensing antennas, and the signal strength from each must be the same. The phase shift is obtained by tuning the sensing antenna slightly off frequency by means of the slug in L1. Since the sensitivity of the whip antenna is greater than that of the loop, its output is reduced by adjusting R1.

Adjustment

To adjust the system, enlist the aid of a friend with a mobile transmitter and find a clear spot where the transmitter and RDF receiver can be separated by several hundred feet. Use as little power as possible at the transmitter. (Remove your own transmitter antenna before trying to make any loop adjustments and remember to leave it off during transmitter hunts.) With the test transmitter operating on the proper frequency, disconnect the sensing antenna with S1, and peak the loopstick using C1, while watching the S meter on the receiver. Once the loopstick is peaked, no further adjustment of C1 will be necessary. Next, connect the sensing antenna and turn R1 to minimum resistance. Then vary the adjustable slug of L1 until a maximum reading of the S meter is again obtained. It may be necessary to turn the unit a bit during this adjustment to obtain a larger reading than with the loopstick alone. The last turn of the slug is quite critical, and some hand-capacitance effect may be noted.

Now turn the instrument so that one side (not an end) of the loopstick is pointed toward the test transmitter. Turn R1 a complete revolution; if the proper side was chosen a definite null should be observed on the S meter for one particular position of R1. If not, turn the RDF 180° and try again. This time leave R1 at the setting that produces the minimum reading. Now adjust L1 very slowly until the S-meter reading is reduced still further. Repeat this several times, first R1, and then L1 until the best minimum is obtained.

Finally, as a check, have the test transmitter move around the RDF and follow it by turning the RDF. If the tuning has been done properly the null will always be broadside to the loopstick. Make a note of the proper side of the RDF for the null, and the job is finished.

A PHASED ARRAY FOR 144-MHz RDF WORK

Although there may be any number of different antennas that will produce a cardioid pattern, the simplest design is depicted in Fig. 26. Two ¼-wavelength vertical elements are spaced one ¼-wavelength apart and are fed 90° out of phase. Each radiator is shown with two radials approximately 5 percent shorter than the radiators.

During the design phase of this project a personal computer was used to predict the impact on the antenna pattern of slight alterations in its size, spacing and phasing of the elements. The results suggest that this system is a little touchy and that the most significant change comes at the null. Very slight alterations in the dimensions caused the notch to become much more shallow and, hence, less usable for RDF. Early difficulties in building a working model bore this out.

This means that if you decide to build this antenna, you will find it advantageous to spend a few minutes to tune it for the deepest null. If it is built using the techniques presented here, this should prove to be a small task that is well worth the extra effort. Tuning is accomplished by adjusting the length of the vertical radiators, the spacing between them and, if necessary, the lengths of the phasing harness that connects them. Tune for the deepest null on your S meter when using a signal source such as a moderately strong repeater. This should be done outside, away from buildings and large metal objects. Initial indoor tuning on this project was tried in the kitchen, which revealed that reflections off the appliances were producing spurious readings. Beware too of distant water towers, radio towers, and large office or apartment buildings. They can reflect the signal and give false indications.

Construction is simple and straightforward. Fig. 26B shows a female BNC connector (Radio Shack 278-105) that has been mounted on a small piece of PC-board material. The BNC connector is held "upside down" and the vertical radiator is soldered to the center solder lug. A 12-in piece of brass tubing provides a snug fit over the solder lug. A second piece of tubing, slightly smaller in diameter, is telescoped inside the first. The outer tubing is crimped slightly at the top after the inner tubing is installed. This provides positive contact between the two tubes. For 146 MHz the length of the radiators is calculated to be about 19 in.

You should be able to find small brass tubing at a hobby store. If none is available

Fig. 27 — The phasing harness for the 144-MHz RDF array. The phasing sections must be measured from the center of the T connector to the point that the vertical radiator emerges from shield portion of the upside-down BNC female. Don't forget to take the length of the connectors into account when constructing the harness. If care is taken and coax with polyethylene dielectric is used, you should not have to prune the phasing line. With this phasing system, the null will be in a direction that runs along the boom, on the side of the ¼-wavelength section.

Fig. 28 — A simple mechanical support for the DF antenna made of PVC pipe and fittings.

in your area, consider brazing rods. This is often available in hardware sections of discount stores. It will probably be necessary to solder a short piece to the top since these come in 18-in sections. Also, tuning will not be quite as convenient. Two 18-inch radials are added to each element by soldering them to the board. Two 36-in pieces of heavy brazing rod were used in this project.

The Phasing Harness

As shown in Fig. 27, a T connector is used with two different lengths of coaxial line to form the phasing harness. This method of feeding the antenna is superior to other simple systems toward obtaining equal current in the two radiators. Un-equal currents tend to reduce the depth of the null in the pattern, all other factors being equal.

With no radials or with two radials perpendicular to the vertical element, it was found that a ¼-wavelength section made of RG-59/U, 75-Ω coax produced a deeper notch than a ¼-wavelength section made of RG-58/U, 50-Ω line. However, with the two radials bent downward somewhat, the RG-58/U section seemed to outperform the RG-59/U. There will probably be enough variation from one antenna to the next that it will be worth your time and effort to try both sections and determine which works best for your antenna. The ½-wavelength section can be made from either RG-58/U or RG-59/U because it should act as a 1-to-1 transformer.

The most important thing about the coax for the harness is that it be of the highest quality (well shielded and with a polyethylene dielectric). The reason for avoiding foam dielectric is that the velocity factor can vary from one roll to the next — some say it varies from one foot to the next in the same roll. Of course, it can be used if you have test equipment available that will allow you to determine its electrical length. Assuming you do not want to or cannot go to that trouble, stay with solid polyethylene-dielectric coax. Avoid coax that is designed for the CB market or the do-it-yourself cable-TV market. (A good choice is Belden 8240 for the RG-58/U or Belden 8241 for the RG-59/U.)

Both RG-58 and RG-59 with polyethylene dielectric have a velocity factor of 0.66. Therefore, for 146 MHz a quarter wavelength of transmission line will be 20.2 in × 0.66 = 13.3 in. A half-wavelength section will be twice this length or 26.7 in. One thing that you must take into account is that the transmission line is the total length of the cable *and the connectors*. Depending on the type of construction and the type of connectors that you choose, the actual length of the coax by itself will vary somewhat. You will have to determine that empirically.

Y connectors that mate with RCA phono plugs are widely available and the phono plugs are easy to work with. Avoid the temptation to substitute these for the T and BNC connectors. Phono plugs and a Y connector were tried. The results with that system were not satisfactory. The performance seemed to change from day to day and the notch was never as deep as it should have been. Although they are more difficult to find, BNC T connectors will provide superior performance and are well worth the extra effort. If you must make substitutions, it would be preferable to use UHF connectors (type PL-259).

Fig. 28 shows a simple support for the antenna. PVC tubing is used throughout. Additionally, you will need a T fitting, two end caps and possibly some cement. (By not cementing the PVC fittings together, you will have the option of disassembly for transportation.) Cut the PVC for the dimensions shown with a saw or a tubing cutter. A tubing cutter is preferred because it produces smooth, straight edges and is less messy. Drill a small hole through the PC board near the female BNC of each element assembly. Measure 20 inches along the boom (horizontal) and mark the two end points. Drill a small hole vertically through the boom at each mark. Use a small nut and bolt to attach the element assembly to the boom.

Tuning

The dimensions given throughout this section are those for approximately 146 MHz. If the signal you will be tracking is above that frequency, then the measurements will probably need to be a bit shorter. If you are to operate below that frequency, then they will need to be a little longer.

Once you have built the antenna to the rough size, the fun begins. You will need a signal source near the frequency that you will be using for your RDF work. Adjust the length of the radiators and the spacing between them for the deepest null on your S meter. Make changes in increments of ¼ in or less. If you must adjust the phasing line, make sure that the ¼-wavelength section is exactly one-half the length of the half-wavelength section. Keep tuning until you have a satisfactorily deep null on your S meter.

AN ADCOCK ANTENNA

While loops are adequate in applications where only the ground wave is present, the question arises of what can be done to improve the performance of an RDF system for sky-wave reception. One type of antenna that has been used successfully for this purpose is the Adcock antenna. There are many possible variations, but the basic configuration is shown in Fig. 29.

The operation of the antenna when a vertically polarized wave is present is very similar to a conventional loop. As can be seen from Fig. 29, currents I1 and I2 will be induced in the vertical members by the passing wave. The output current in the transmission line will be equal to their difference. Consequently, the directional pattern will be identical to the loop with a null broadside to the plane of the elements and with maximum gain occurring in end-fire fashion. The magnitude of the difference current will be proportional to the spacing, d, and the length of the elements. Spacing and length are not critical, but somewhat more gain will occur for larger dimensions than for smaller ones. In an experimental model, the spacing was 21 feet (approximately 0.15 wavelength on 40 meters) and the element length was 12 feet.

Response of the Adcock antenna to a horizontally polarized wave is considerably different from that of a loop. The currents induced in the horizontal members (dotted

Fig. 29 — A simple Adcock antenna and suitable coupler (see text).

arrows in Fig. 29) tend to balance out regardless of the orientation of the antenna. This effect seemed to be borne out in practice, since good nulls were obtained with the experimental model under sky-wave conditions that produced only poor nulls with small loops (both conventional and ferrite-loop models). Generally speaking, the Adcock antenna has very attractive properties with regard to amateur RDF applications. Unfortunately, its portability leaves something to be desired, and it is more suitable to fixed or semi-portable applications. While a metal support for the mast and boom could be used, wood is preferable because of its nonconducting properties. Less distortion of the pattern should result.

Since a balanced feed system is used, a coupler is required to match the unbalanced input of the receiver. It consists of T1 which is an air-wound coil with a two-turn link wrapped around the middle. The combination is then resonated to the operating frequency with C1. C2 and C3 are null-clearing capacitors. A low-power signal source is placed some distance from the Adcock antenna and broadside to it. C2 and C3 are then adjusted until the deepest null is obtained.

The coupler can be placed on the ground below the wiring-harness junction on the boom and connected by means of a short length of 300-ohm twin-lead. A piece of aluminum tubing was used as a mast, but in a practical application it could be replaced with a length of PVC tubing extending to the ground. This would facilitate rotation and would provide a means of at-taching a compass card for obtaining bearings.

Bibliography

Bonaguide, G., "HF DF — A Technique for Volunteer Monitoring," *QST,* March 1984.
Bond, D. S., *Radio Direction Finders,* 1st edition (1944), McGraw-Hill Book Co., New York, NY.
DeMaw, D., "Maverick Trackdown," *QST,* July 1980.
DeMaw, D., "Beat the Noise with a Scoop Loop," *QST,* July 1977.
Dorbuck, T., "Radio Direction-Finding Techniques," *QST,* August 1975.
Jasik, H., *Antenna Engineering Handbook,* 1st edition, McGraw-Hill Book Co., New York, NY.
Keene, R., *Wireless Direction Finding,* 3rd edition (1938), Wireless World, London.
Kraus, J., *Antennas* (1950): McGraw-Hill Book Co., New York, NY.
Kraus, J., *Electromagnetics,* McGraw-Hill Book Co., New York, NY.
McCoy, L., "A Linear Field-Strength Meter," *QST,* January 1973.
O'Dell, P., "Simple Antenna and S-Meter Modification for 2-Meter FM Direction Finding," *QST,* March 1981.
Ramo and Whinnery, *Fields and Waves in Modern Radio,* John Wiley & Sons, New York, NY.
Terman, F., *Radio Engineering,* McGraw-Hill Book Co., New York, NY.

Practical VHF Homing Methods

The most common amateur RDF occurs on the VHF bands and requires mobile or portable installations. Mobility is important when locating sources of deliberate interference, neighborhood electrical noise, or a hidden transmitter for fun. The following material (contributed by Joseph Moell, K0OV) discusses RDF equipment for the popular 2-meter band, but the principles are applicable to other VHF frequencies as well.

Success at mobile RDF requires equipment that is effective and reliable. There are three distinct methods of mobile VHF RDF commonly used by amateurs: directional antennas, switched dual antennas, and Doppler-shift detectors. Each has advantages over the others in certain situations. Many RDF enthusiasts employ more than one method.

DIRECTIONAL ANTENNAS

Mobile FM or multi-mode transceivers can be pressed into RDF service by adding an appropriate directional antenna system. When using directional antennas, the receiver should have a sensitive, easily read S meter. An RF attenuator is needed to keep the S meter usable while "closing in."

Loops

Fractional-wavelength loops are seldom employed above 60 MHz because they have ambiguous bidirectional patterns and low sensitivity compared to other practical VHF antennas. Their usefulness is limited to close-in on-foot "sniffing" where compactness and sharp nulls are assets —and low gain is of no consequence.

Phased Arrays

The small size and simplicity of two-element driven arrays make them a common choice of newcomers at VHF RDF. Antennas such as phased monopoles (see "A Phased Array for 144-MHz RDF Work," earlier in this chapter) and ZL Specials have modest gain in one direction and a null in the opposite direction. The gain is helpful with weak signals, but the broad lobe makes it tricky to take an exact bearing.

As the signal gets stronger, we can use the null for a sharper S-meter indication. Signal reflections and multipath propagation, however, may distort the null or obscure it completely. For best results with this type of RDF set, take bearings from the highest and clearest locations possible.

Parasitic Arrays

Parasitic arrays are the most common RDF antennas in high-competition areas such as southern California. Antennas with significant gain are a necessity because low-power signals are often encountered, and distances of 200 miles or more are covered during some weekend-long events. Typical 2-meter installations feature Yagis or quads with three to five elements, sometimes more. Yagis are commercial or home-made models. Quads are typically home built.

Two types of mechanical construction are popular for mobile VHF quads. "Spreader" quads (Fig 30) use thin wire

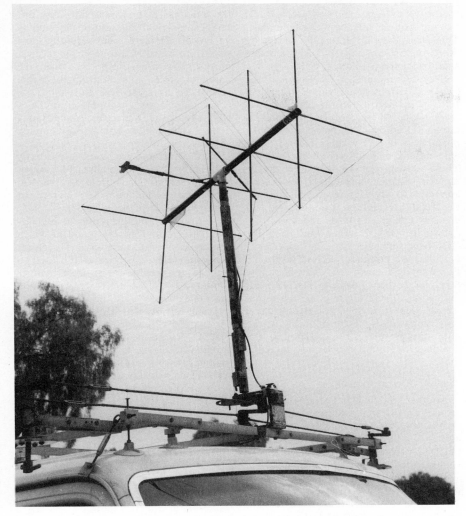

Fig 30—The mobile RDF installation of WB6ADC features a "spreader" quad for 2 meters and a mechanical linkage that permits either the driver or front passenger to rotate the mast by hand. *(WB6UZZ photo)*

Fig 31—KØOV uses this mobile setup for RDF on several bands, with separate antennas for each band that mate with a common lower mast section, pointer, and 360° indicator. Antenna shown is a "spreaderless" quad for 2 meters. *(KØOV photo)*

Fig 32—Elements from two commercial Yagis on one boom form the heart of WA6DLQ's RDF system for 2 meters. A switch box in the vehicle selects from six possible polarization modes. *(KØOV photo)*

strung on wood or fiberglass spreaders. They are lightweight and may be turned rapidly by hand. "Spreaderless" quads (Fig 31) use stiff wire (such as AWG 10) mounted on a plastic-pipe frame. They are more rugged and have a somewhat wider frequency range than models that use spreaders.

A well-designed mobile Yagi or quad installation should include a method to select antenna polarization. Poor results occur when a VHF RDF antenna is cross-polarized to the incoming signal because multipath and scattered signals (which have indeterminate polarization) are enhanced, relative to the cross-polarized direct signal.

The installation of Fig 32 consists of two identical orthogonally polarized Yagis with separate feed lines on a common boom. Inside the vehicle is a switch box that allows the operator to select horizontal, vertical, 45°, 135°, left-hand circular, or right-hand circular polarization. The Yagi outputs are combined in various phase relationships to produce these polarizations.

The installation of Fig 30 features a slip joint at the boom-to-mast junction, with an actuating cord to rotate the boom and change the polarization. Mechanical stops limit the boom rotation to 90°.

Parasitic-Array Performance for RDF

The gain of a parasitic array (typically 8 dB or more) makes it excellent for both weak-signal competitive hunts and for locating low-level interference such as cable-TV leakage. With an appropriate receiver, bearings can be taken on any type of emission, and noise as well. Because only the response peak is used, the null-fill problems and proximity effects associated with loops and phased arrays do not exist with beams.

Multiple directions of arrival can be observed as the antenna is rotated, and the operator can make an educated guess as to which is the direct path. Skilled operators can estimate distance to the transmitter from the rate of signal-strength increase with distance traveled. An RDF beam is useful for transmitting, if necessary, but take care to avoid attenuator damage.

The 3-dB beamwidth of a typical mobile VHF parasitic array is about 80°. This is a great improvement over two-element driven arrays, but it is still difficult to get pinpoint bearing accuracy. Careful meter reading can yield errors of less than 10°. In practice, this is no major hindrance to successful mobile RDF. The mobile user is not as concerned with precise bearings as is a fixed station because mobile bearings are used primarily for general direction to "home in" on the signal. Mobile bearings are continuously updated from new, closer locations.

Rapid variations of incoming signal strength are a problem. The target transmitter may be changing output power; the target antenna may be moving or near reflectors (a well-traveled road or airport). Rapid S-meter movements caused by such conditions make it much more difficult to take accurate bearings. Furthermore, the process is slow because the antenna must be carefully rotated by hand.

SWITCHED ANTENNA RDF UNITS

There are three popular RDF systems that are relatively insensitive to variations in signal level. Two of them switch the receiver input between a pair of vertical antennas (spaced ½ λ or less) at a rapid rate. In use, the indications of the two systems are similar, but the principles are different.

Switched-Pattern Systems

A switched-pattern RDF set (Fig 33) alternately creates two cardioid antenna patterns with lobes to the left and the right. The patterns are generated in much the same way as in the phased arrays described above, with PIN RF diodes selecting the patterns. The combined antenna outputs are fed to a receiver with AM detection. Processing after the detector output determines any phase or amplitude differences between the pattern responses to the signal.

Switched-pattern RDF sets typically use a zero-center meter as an indicator. The meter swings negative when the signal is coming from the user's left, and positive when it is on the right. When the antenna plane is exactly perpendicular to the signal direction, the meter reads zero.

The sharpness of the zero crossing indication makes possible more precise bearings than those obtainable with a quad or Yagi. Meter deflection indicates which way

to turn. For example, a negative (left) reading requires turning the antenna left. This solves the 180° ambiguity caused by the two zero crossings in each complete rotation of the antenna system.

Because it requires AM detection of the switched-pattern signal, this RDF system finds its greatest use in the 120-MHz aircraft band, where AM is the standard mode. Commercial manufacturers make portable RDF sets with switched-pattern antennas and built-in receivers for field use. These sets can usually be adapted to the amateur 2-meter band. Other designs are adaptable to any VHF receiver that covers the frequency of interest and has an AM detector either built in or added.

Switched-pattern units work well for RDF from small aircraft. The two vertical antennas are mounted in fixed positions. For rapid deployment, they may be simply taped inside the windshield. The left-right indication directs the pilot to the signal source. Since street vehicles generally travel only along roads, fixed mounting of the antennas is undesirable. Mount the antennas for ground vehicles on a rotatable mast.

Time-of-Arrival Systems

Another kind of switched-antenna RDF set uses the difference of signal wavefront arrival time at two antennas. Narrow-aperture Time-Difference-of-Arrival (TDOA) technology is used for many sophisticated military RDF systems.

The rudimentary TDOA implementation of Fig 34 is quite effective for amateur use. The signal from transmitter 1 reaches antenna A before antenna B. Conversely, the signal from transmitter 3 reaches antenna B before antenna A. When the plane of the antennas is perpendicular to the signal source (transmitter 2 in the figure), the signal arrives at both antennas simultaneously.

If the receiver input is switched between

the antennas at an audio rate, any difference in arrival time can be detected by an FM discriminator. The resulting short pulses are heard as a tone in the receiver output. The tone disappears when the antennas are equidistant from the signal source, giving an audible null.

Two popular designs for practical TDOA RDF sets are the Double Ducky and Handy Tracker (see bibliography). Both employ short vertical whips working against a ground plane, and are intended primarily for short-range on-foot use. For longer range and mobile mounting, vertical dipoles on a metal boom are preferred for improved performance (Fig 35).

The polarity of the pulses at the discriminator output is a function of which antenna is closer to the source. Therefore, the pulses can be processed and used to drive a zero-center meter in a manner similar to the switched-pattern units described above. "Left" and "right" LED indicators are often used instead of a meter, for simplicity.

RDF operation with a TDOA dual-antenna RDF set is done in the same manner as with a switched-antenna RDF set. The main difference is the requirement for an FM receiver in the TDOA system and an AM receiver in the switched-pattern case. No RF attenuator is needed for close-

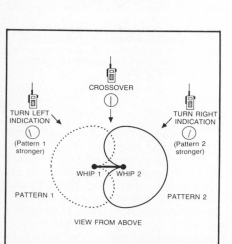

Fig 33—In a switched-pattern RDF set, the responses of two cardioid antenna patterns are summed to drive a zero-center indicator.

Fig 34—A dual-antenna TDOA RDF system has a similar indicator to a switched-pattern unit, but it obtains bearings by determining which of its antennas is closer to the transmitter.

Fig 35—A set of TDOA RDF antennas is light weight, and mounts readily through a sedan window without excessive overhang. *(WB6UZZ photo)*

in work in the TDOA case, nor is a shielded receiver necessary.

Performance Comparison

Both types of dual-antenna RDFs make good on-foot "sniffing" devices and are excellent performers when there are rapid amplitude variations in the incoming signal. They are the units of choice for airborne work. Compared to Yagis and quads, they give good directional performance over a much wider frequency range. They frequently give inaccurate bearings in multipath situations, however, because they cannot resolve signals of nearly equal levels from more than one direction.

It is usually easy to tell when severe multipath propagation is present. Because multipath signals are a combined pattern of peaks and nulls, a multipath signal usually fluctuates in strength along the bearing line. You may have observed this phenomenon with FM-broadcast signals in your auto. If you are receiving a station via multipath and stop at a null, reception improves as you move forward or back ½ λ. Similarly, a multipath signal changes in amplitude and bearing as you move the DF antenna along the bearing path, or perpendicular to it; a direct signal will have constant strength.

The best way to overcome this problem is to take many bearings as you move toward the transmitter. Bearings taken while in motion average out the effects of multipath, making the direct signal more readily discernible. Some switched-antenna sets have a slow-response mode that aids the averaging process.

Switched antenna systems generally do not perform well when the incoming signal is horizontally polarized. In such cases, bearings may be inaccurate or unreadable. TDOA units require a constant-amplitude signal such as FM or CW; they usually cannot yield bearings on noise or pulse signals. Transmitting high power into any switched-antenna system may damage the switching diodes.

Unless an additional method is employed to measure signal strength, it is easy to "overshoot" a hidden transmitter location with a TDOA set. It is not uncommon to see a TDOA fox hunter walk over the top of a concealed transmitter and walk away, following the opposite 180° null, because he had no display of the signal amplitude.

DOPPLER SHIFT DETECTORS

RDF sets using the Doppler principle are popular because they are easy to use. Such systems have an indicator that instantaneously displays the direction of the incoming signal, relative to vehicle heading, on either a circular ring of LEDs or a digitized readout. A ring of four, eight or more antennas picks up the signal. Quarter-wavelength monopoles on a ground plane are popular for vehicle use, but better performance is obtained from ½-λ vertical dipoles in free space, where practical.

Radio signals received on a rapidly moving antenna experience a frequency shift known as Doppler effect, a phenomenon well known to anyone who has heard a moving car with its horn sounding. The horn pitch sounds higher than normal as the car approaches, and lower as the car recedes. Similarly, received radio frequency changes when the transmit or receive antennas move relative to each other. An FM receiver can detect this frequency change.

Fig 36 shows a ¼-λ monopole antenna moving on a circular track around point P, with constant angular velocity. As the antenna approaches the transmitter, the received frequency is shifted higher. The highest instantaneous frequency occurs when the antenna is at point A, because tangential velocity toward the transmitter is maximum at that point. Conversely, the lowest frequency occurs when the antenna reaches point C, where velocity is maximum away from the transmitter.

Fig 37 shows a plot of the component of the tangential velocity that is in the direction of the transmitter as the antenna moves around the circle. Comparing Figs 36 and 37, notice that at B in Fig 37, the tangential velocity is crossing zero from the positive to the negative and the antenna is closest to the transmitter. The Doppler shift and resulting audio output from the receiver discriminator follow the same plot,

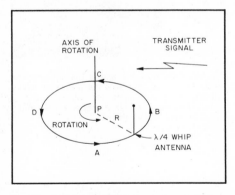

Fig 36—A theoretical Doppler antenna circles around point P, continuously moving toward and away from the source at an audio rate.

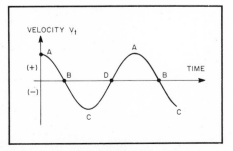

Fig 37—The frequency shift versus time produced by the rotating antenna movement toward and away from the signal source.

so that a negative-slope, zero-crossing detector, synchronized with antenna rotation, senses the incoming signal direction.

The amount of frequency shift from the Doppler effect is proportional to the RF frequency and the tangential antenna velocity. The velocity is a function of the radius of rotation and the angular velocity (rotation rate). The radius of rotation must be less than ¼ λ to avoid errors. To get usable FM deviation (comparable to typical voice modulation) with this radius, the antenna must rotate at approximately 30,000 RPM (500 Hz). This puts the Doppler tone in the audio range for easy processing.

Mechanically rotating a whip antenna at this rate is impractical, but a rapidly rotating antenna can be simulated with a ring of whips, switched to the receiver in succession by RF PIN diodes. A number of commercial Doppler RDF models are available on the amateur market. They must be used with receivers having FM detectors. The DoppleScAnt and Roanoke Doppler (see bibliography) are mobile Doppler RDF sets designed for inexpensive home construction.

Four whips are typical (see Fig 38), but eight or more may be used. A display unit, which detects the phase of the Doppler tone and compares it with antenna rotation, completes the setup. Excellent filtering is required in the control unit to separate the added Doppler tone from other modulation and noise on the signal.

Doppler Advantages and Disadvantages

Ring-antenna Doppler sets are the ultimate in simplicity of use for mobile RDF. There are no moving parts, and no operator effort is needed to point an antenna. Bearings may be taken on very short signal bursts. Power variations in the source signal cause no difficulties, so long as the signal remains above the RDF detection threshold. Doppler systems are excellent for chasing mobile "bunnies," particularly if the hunter is alone.

A Doppler approach does not provide superior performance in all situations, however. If the signal is too weak for detection by the Doppler unit, the hunt advantage goes to teams with beams. Doppler installations are not intended for on-foot "sniffing." The limitations of other switched-antenna RDFs also apply: (1) poor results with horizontally polarized signals, (2) no bearings for microsecond-pulses, suppressed-carrier emissions or noise, (3) no indication of target distance and (4) inadvisability of transmitting through the antenna.

Bearings are displayed to the nearest degree on some commercial Doppler units. This does not guarantee that accuracy, however. A well-designed four-antenna set is typically capable of ±5° accuracy on 2 meters—if the signal is vertically polarized and there is no multipath propagation.

Rapid antenna switching can introduce cross-modulation products when the user is near strong off-channel RF sources. This self-generated interference can temporarily render the system unusable. While not a common problem with mobile Dopplers, it makes the Doppler a poor choice for use in remote RDF installations at fixed sites with high-power VHF transmitters nearby.

MOBILE RDF SYSTEM INSTALLATION

Of the mobile VHF RDF systems discussed above, the Doppler ring system is clearly the simplest from a mechanical installation standpoint. A four-antenna Doppler RDF setup can be readily implemented with magnetic-mount antennas. Alternatively, the four whips can be mounted on a frame that attaches to the vehicle roof with suction cups. The switching circuitry should be installed on the frame, so that only one feed line and one control cable go inside the vehicle (see Fig 38).

A frame also keeps the whips in proper position at all times, with no chance of improperly hooking up the individual antenna lines when the unit is moved between vehicles. It is important that a ground plane is provided, either continuous or with radials as shown, for at least ¼ wavelength around the base of each whip.

Rotating Antenna Arrays

Small rotatable antennas can be turned readily by extending the mast through a window. Installation on each model of vehicle is different, but the mast can usually be held in place with some sort of cup on the arm rest and a plastic tie at the top of the window, as in Fig 35. This technique works best on cars with frames around the windows, which allow the door to open with the antenna in place. Local vehicle codes often limit how far the antenna may

Fig 38—A home-made Doppler RDF set with four vertical antennas on an aluminum chassis. The switching circuitry is inside. Whips are made from 3/32-inch bronze welding rod. *(KØOV photo)*

Fig 39—A window box allows the navigator to turn a mast-mounted antenna with ease while remaining dry and warm. No holes in the vehicle are needed with a properly designed window box. *(KØOV photo)*

protrude beyond the line of the fenders on each side. Large antennas may fit on the passenger side, where greater overhang is usually permissible.

A window box (Fig 39) is an improvement over through-the-window mounts. It provides a solid, easy-turning mount for the mast, and the plastic cover keeps out bad weather. A custom design is necessary for each model of vehicle. Vehicle codes may limit the use of a window box to the passenger side of the vehicle.

For the ultimate in convenience and versatility, cast your fears aside, drill a hole in the center of the roof, and install a waterproof bushing. A roof-hole mount permits the use of large antennas without overhang violations. The driver, front passenger, and even a rear passenger can turn the mast when required. An installation such as that of Fig 31 should include a pointer and 360° indicator (at the bottom of the mast) for precise bearings.

The installation shown in Fig 31 uses a roof-hole bushing made by mating threaded PVC pipe adapters and reducers. When the fitting is not in use for RDF, a PVC pipe cap is a watertight cover for the hole.

BIBLIOGRAPHY

J. Moell and T. Curlee, *Transmitter Hunting —Radio Direction Finding Simplified,* TAB Books, Blue Ridge Summit, PA. (This book contains construction information for the "Roanoke Doppler" RDF project.)

D. Geiser, "Double-Ducky Direction Finder," *QST,* July 1981, pp 11-14.

D. Geiser, "Updating the Double-Ducky Direction Finder," *QST,* May 1982, pp 15-17.

J. Moell, "Build the Handy Tracker," *73 Amateur Radio,* September 1989, pp 58-59 and November 1989, pp 52-53.

T. Rogers, "A DoppleScAnt," *QST,* May 1978, pp 24-28; Feedback: July 1978, p 13.

Chapter 39

Interference

Radio Frequency Interference (RFI): It is a jungle out there! Not a jungle of wildlife and tangled undergrowth, however. It is a jungle of electrical and electronic equipment, each piece of which is a potential source or victim of RFI, or both! Today, a host of new devices are creating an increasingly complex RF environment. Each new gadget brings with it a new set of problems to the residential community.

The Electronic Home

Let's look around a perhaps "not-so-average" home. In the kitchen the blender whirrs and the microwave oven digital timer counts down to the blinking of the Public Service scanner. The wireless intercom emits a mild protest to the electronic activity. In the bathroom a family member is using a hair dryer and a portable radio. Both items are plugged into a ground-fault interrupter outlet.

In a quiet room supplied with mood lighting from an electronically controlled lamp, a color TV set is showing a movie that is delivered by cable. A video cassette recorder (VCR) records another program for later viewing.

One of the older children is in a bedroom doing homework on a microcomputer. Music is coming from the stereo record player in the corner. In the next bedroom a younger family member finds amusement in the video game connected to a portable TV set.

In the hall a pager sits in the battery charger just below a smoke detector. Someone had decided to place a call on the cordless telephone from this secluded spot.

Down in the basement, the water heater has turned on under control of the thermostat. Another thermostat, located upstairs, has called for hot air. The fuel oil gun is running in the furnace (as is the continuous ignition system) — the air is just now hot enough that a sensor starts the circulation blower. Mounted on the wall next to the power distribution box is the doorbell transformer.

Out in the garage the power tools and lawn mower silently wait for someone to use them. The garage door opener waits for a signal to be decoded by the receiver. Outside a loud sound will activate a fixture, turning on an outdoor light. When the family is away, the premises are guarded by an electronic security system. The system has a microwave intrusion detector; alarms are electronically reported over the telephone line.

Every device mentioned in this account has the potential of being either a source or victim of RFI — or both! Many other possibilities exist in the residential environment these days. Even the plumbing and wiring can conduct, radiate or rectify RF emanations from whatever source. And every month some new electronic "whiz bang" finds its way into our homes.

A Technical Problem

Interference is a technical problem. The causes and cures are often straightforward, but they can be mysterious and complicated. Interference side effects have economic and political impact. Experience has shown that nearly all RFI problems experienced with home-entertainment devices result from basic design deficiencies in these devices. The few small components or filters that would prevent RFI are often left out of otherwise well-designed products as manufacturers attempt to reduce costs, and hence to reduce the prices of their products.

Interference is primarily a matter of emanation (sending) and interception (receiving). Unwanted emanations occur by radiation (as from an antenna) or conduction (as along a wire). How and where to treat unwanted emanation or interception will depend on where and how it occurs. If interfering harmonics are generated in a transmitter and are radiated by the station antenna, usually a filter in the feed line will solve the problem. If a TV set lacks immunity to the radio frequency environment, various types of filters can be used to cure the problem.

The source of the energy is not always the cause of interference; the actual cause is sometimes difficult to determine. Interfering harmonics or spurious emissions of an Amateur or CB Radio signal may be generated in the transmitter, in a bad (rectifying) connection in the antenna system, in the affected receiver RF amplifier (preamplifier) or in any poor metallic connection in the vicinity of the transmitter antenna. For that reason, the cause is usually discovered through a process of elimination. Usually, more than one action will be necessary to cure the problem.

The usual procedure for dealing with harmonically related interference calls for filters to be installed at the transmitter and the receiver. That treatment usually solves the problem; if it doesn't, try using direction-finding techniques on a harmonic of the offending signal.

Radio amateurs have traditionally been involved with the analog world — a realm of sine waves and distinct frequencies. Digital equipment can be found in almost every home and ham shack. The digital domain is a realm of square waves.

The frequency spectra of sine and square waves of the same fundamental frequency are quite different, as shown in Fig. 1. The sine wave is ideally represented by a single frequency. In contrast, an ideal square wave consists of a fundamental frequency plus an infinite series of odd harmonics. It is these harmonics that require proper treatment in digital circuits to prevent RF emanations. Treatment, which must be applied to the digital circuit and enclosure, generally consists of proper shielding, filtering and bypassing. The measures that help minimize the possibilities that a digital device will be a source of interference will also protect it from being a victim of interference.

What's Being Done About RFI?

Along with the growth of new appliances in the electronic home come new regulations to deal with accompanying RFI

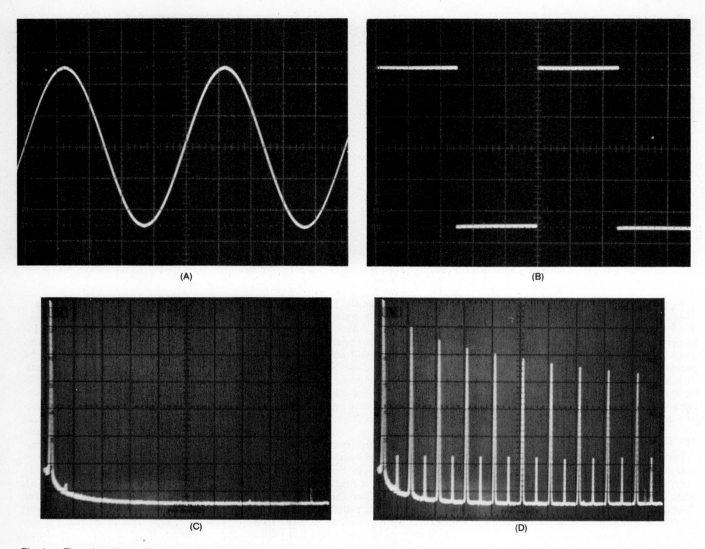

Fig. 1 — Time domain (oscilloscope) displays of a sine wave (A) and a square wave (B). Frequency-domain or spectral (spectrum-analyzer) displays of a sine wave (C) and a square wave (D). Vertical divisions in the spectral displays are 10 dB. With second-harmonic energy down 67 dB, the sine wave can be considered spectrally clean. By contrast, the square wave shows considerable energy in odd-order harmonics.

troubles. FCC rules now deal specifically with such services and devices as CATV, computers, cordless telephones and security devices. Although Public Law 97-259 gives the FCC authority to set standards for home-entertainment devices, the current approach looks toward voluntary compliance in place of legislation. Television sets and Amateur Radio equipment of recent vintage are, for the most part, superior to earlier models. Some VCRs still show a lack of RF immunity.

Cable television (CATV) is regulated by Parts 15 and 76 of the FCC rules. The Commission defines a CATV system as a "nonbroadcast facility" — a plant consisting of cables that carry television programming to subscribers. Cable television offers the amateur service several advantages over conventional reception. Signal levels on the cable are at a higher level than normally received "off air." This effectively eliminates fringe area (weak

signal) reception. In addition, these signals are supplied on a shielded cable, which further reduces the susceptibility to interference.

In the field, however, signals may leak from these ostensibly "closed" systems. When this leakage occurs, harmful interference to over-the-air services can occur. The FCC has specified the maximum allowable leakage from cable systems.

Section 76.613 regulates interference from CATV systems. Paragraph (a) defines harmful interference as "any emission, radiation or induction which endangers the functioning of a radio-navigation service or of other safety services or *seriously degrades, obstructs or repeatedly interrupts a radiocommunication service operating in accordance with this chapter*" (emphasis added). Paragraph (b) says "the operator of a cable television system that causes harmful interference shall promptly take appropriate measures

to eliminate the harmful interference."

Section 76.605(a)(12) spells out the limits for allowable radiation from a CATV system:

Frequencies	Radiation Limit ($\mu V/m$)	Distance (Feet)
Up to and including 54 MHz	15	100
Over 54 up to and including 216 MHz	20	10
Over 216 MHz	15	100

RF emanating from digital devices such as computers, and other incidental radiation devices such as power lines, industrial machines and electrical fences, are regulated in Part 15 of the FCC rules. Communication devices such as cordless telephones, FM wireless microphones and

Form A:

COMPLAINANT'S NAME	CALL	ARRL HQ. CASE NO.
ADDRESS		PHONE NO.
CITY	STATE/PROV.	ZIP/PC
DATE (YEAR/MONTH/DAY)	LOCATION OF RFI (INCLUDING ZIP OR PC)	ARRL SECTION (IF NOT KNOWN, LIST COUNTY)
OWNER'S NAME		PHONE NO.
ADDRESS		
CITY	STATE/PROV.	ZIP/PC

	TYPE (VCR, ETC.)	MANUFACTURER	MODEL NO.	NATURE OF INTERFERENCE
EMANATING EQUIPMENT				
SUSCEPTIBLE EQUIPMENT				

DISTANCE BETWEEN EMANATING & SUSCEPTIBLE EQUIPMENT (FT.) | SEVERITY □ BARELY PERCEPTIBLE □ WEAK □ MODERATE □ STRONG □ OVERWHELMING | COUPLING MECHANISM □ NOT DETERMINED □ CONDUCTED □ RADIATED

COMPLAINT RESOLVED? □ YES □ NO | DESCRIBE TECHNICAL SOLUTION

PROBLEM FIXED BY □ AMATEUR □ REPAIRMAN □ MFGR. OF EMANATING EQUIPMENT □ MFGR. OF SUSCEPTIBLE EQUIPMENT □ OTHER

WHO WAS INFORMED □ UTILITY □ CABLE OPERATOR □ FCC □ EIA □ MFGR. OF EMANATING EQUIP. □ MFGR. OF SUSCEPTIBLE EQUIPMENT □ OTHER

REMARKS

RFI IMMUNITY COMPLAINT REPORT TD 1/84

(A)

Form B:

I-D: Serial_____ State_____

Date:_____

Name of cable company_____

Address_____

Phone Number:_____

Name & Title of Person Contacted:_____

Areas Served by System:_____

Nature of Interference:_____

Method of Observation (List of equipment used):_____

Dates of Contact With:

A. Cable operator_____

B. FCC_____

C. Controller of franchise (town, county, etc.)_____

Steps Taken by Cable Operator:

Does interference still exist?_____

Your name:_____ Callsign:_____

Address:_____

Phone:_____

FCC Involvement (if any):

(For ARRL use only)

NCTA contact:

(B)

Fig. 2 — At A, ARRL RFI immunity complaint report. At B, CATVI Complaint Report Form.

other low-power appliances are also covered in Part 15. These devices may not cause harmful interference to other radio service communications. In addition, specifications for limits on amounts of RF energy emanating from a given device are included. For example, the wireless microphones mentioned earlier in this paragraph may not exceed certain field strengths.

Also, units (such as most 1.7-MHz cordless telephones) that operate under a waiver of the field strength requirements are controlled in another manner: These units must not exceed standards for RF current in the power and telephone lines.

Radiation limits also apply to personal computers manufactured after January 1, 1981. In many cases, labeling, indentification and FCC certification are required for devices covered in Part 15. These requirements help ensure that the device operator understands the nature of the unit, and his or her obligations under the rules. For applicable excerpts of Part 15 or Part 76 of the Commission's rules, contact ARRL Headquarters.

Government regulation is not a panacea, however. We are in a period of shrinking government involvement in the life of the society it governs. Thus, we have seen deregulation on the part of an FCC determined to let marketplace forces resolve their differences. And, with the FCC budget greatly reduced, we are witnessing a Commission less able to enforce the rules. Government rules are a help, but not the sole solution to RFI.

Help is available from other quarters as well. Manufacturers and professional trade associations are aware of the RFI phenomenon. While these organizations are not in positions to dictate policies to members, they can promote the need for responsibility in manufacturing and operations. Associations often publish pamphlets and manuals for their members explaining how they can make products less susceptible to RFI problems. The same associations lobby the government on behalf of their members.

The ARRL, as the principal membership organization of the amateur community, is ready to assist in RFI matters with a three-pronged approach: publications, representation, and local aid through the ARRL Field Organization. ARRL publishes or distributes several books about RFI and radio direction finding. *QST* provides timely information about the evolving RFI picture.

ARRL representation of amateurs includes:
• interaction with industry groups such as the Electronic Industries Association and the National Cable Television Association,
• participation in committees of the American National Standards Institute, Society of Automotive Engineers and others,
• representation to the FCC — and to Congress when appropriate.

Local RFI Aid

Local aid is rendered through two areas of the ARRL Field Organization. Interference inside the amateur bands is handled by the ARRL Amateur Auxiliary/Official Observer (OO) program. In 1982, Public Law 97-259 authorized the FCC to formally enlist amateur volunteers in monitoring the airwaves for rules discrepancies or violations. As a result, the FCC formed an Amateur Auxiliary (similar to those of the Civil Air Patrol and Coast Guard) to be compatible with the amateur organizational structure (ARRL). The ARRL OO program began in 1926 to "help brother

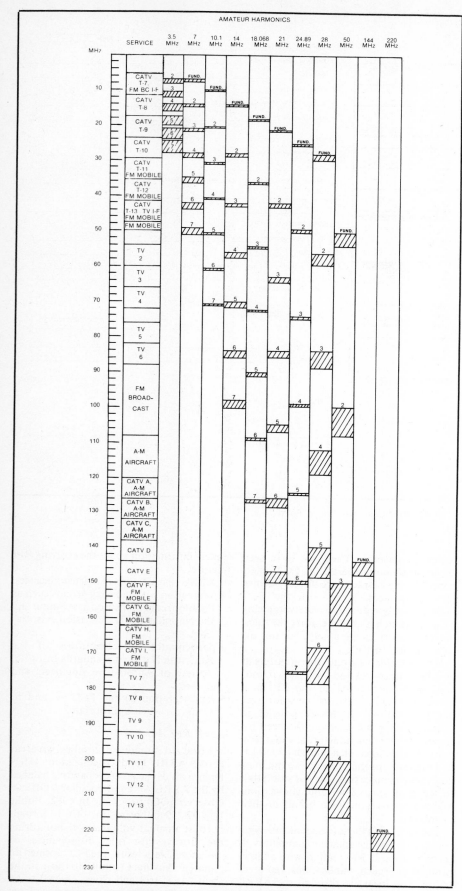

Fig. 3 — Relationships of HF and VHF amateur bands to frequencies used in consumer electronic devices. The CATV channels are used in closed systems, but experience has shown these systems to have poor isolation from outside signals.

amateurs by calling attention to violations of good practice...in the right way...in better operating...and ham enjoyment.'' The Amateur Auxiliary/OO program is administered by the League's Section Managers and OO Coordinators, with support from ARRL HQ. For more information about the Amateur Auxiliary, see ''The Amateur Auxiliary for Volunteer Monitoring,'' in August 1984 *QST*, pp 11-13.

When RFI involves equipment operating outside the amateur bands, help is available from ARRL Assistant Technical Coordinators (ATC) and local RFI committees. The ATC position was created for local RFI support in 1985. ATCs are appointed by ARRL Section Managers as local representatives under the Section Technical Coordinator. It is the ATC's job to assist hams with technical questions or RFI problems, represent the ARRL at technical symposiums in industry, serve on CATV advisory committees and advise municipal governments on technical matters. You can contact your closest ATC through your Section Manager, whose address appears monthly on p 8 of *QST*.

What Can You Do?

Be informed — read, report, experiment and test. As an ARRL member, you have access to publications that contain a wealth of information about RFI. Further, the ARRL stands ready to assist you.

Report — Fig. 2 illustrates the information needed to report RFI cases. Your reports help us spot widespread RFI problems and track down a cure. Similarly, if you experience a problem and find a cure, let your League know about it. The ARRL RFI Task Group needs a complete and accurate picture of the ever-changing RFI scene so it can make appropriate policy recommendations to the ARRL Board of Directors. Send your reports to Box RFI, ARRL HQ, 225 Main St, Newington, CT, 06111. Report forms are available from the same address for an SASE.

Experiment and test — RFI problems and solutions are not always simple. Try the usual; then try the unusual. It is also possible that more than one action will be necessary to cure the problem. This chapter will help you with ideas.

Be cooperative — the first step is to ensure that your station is assembled and operated according to ''good engineering and amateur practice.'' Check your transmitter; try using a low-pass filter. Then, check your own TV set for problems. Put your own house in order before checking on your neighbor's.

When approaching your neighbor, bear in mind that he or she likely knows little of radio or RFI. Proceed accordingly. Explain your interpretation of the situation in simple terms. Then, politely make your recommendations. Neighborhood RFI disputes are settled when a cooperative atmosphere exists.

Be communicative — contact the manufacturer of the offending equipment. Many responsible manufacturers have a policy of supplying filters for eliminating television interference when such cases are brought to their attention. You may persuade a manufacturer to help by writing directly to the manufacturer; send a copy of that letter to the Electronic Industries Association (EIA).[1]

Similarly, if the problem lies with a CATV operator, public utility or other facility, let the responsible party know about it. You will often find assistance in your efforts to track down an RFI source.

If an RFI problem appears to be a violation of FCC rules, and there is no response to your requests for corrective action, contact your nearest FCC district office. See *The FCC Rule Book* published by ARRL, for the address.

Dealing With Interference

Many interference problems are caused by harmonics. Fig. 3 is a chart showing the frequency relationships between broadcast channels and amateur harmonics.

The visible effects of interference vary with the type and intensity of the interference. Blackout, where the picture and sound disappear completely, leaving the screen dark, occurs only when the transmitter and receiver are close together. Strong interference ordinarily causes the picture to be broken up, leaving a jumble of light and dark lines, or turns the picture "negative" — the normally white parts of the picture turn black and the normally black parts turn white.

Cross-hatching — diagonal bars or lines in the picture — often occurs as well, and also represents the most common type of less severe interference. The bars are the result of the beat between the harmonic frequency and the picture carrier frequency. They are broad and relatively few in number if the beat frequency is comparatively low — near the picture carrier — and are numerous and very fine if the beat frequency is very high — toward the upper end of the channel. Typical cross-hatching is shown in Fig. 4A.

Whether or not cross-hatching is visible, an amplitude-modulated transmitter may cause sound bars in the picture. These are shown in Fig. 4B. They result from the variations in the intensity of the interfering signal when modulated. Under most circumstances modulation bars will not occur if the amateur transmitter is frequency- or phase-modulated. With these types of modulation the cross-hatching will wiggle from side to side with the modulation.

[1]Electronic Industries Association, 2001 Eye St., N.W., Washington, DC 20006. Attention: Director of Consumer Affairs.

Except in the more severe cases, there is seldom any effect on the sound reception when interference shows in the picture, unless the frequency is close to the sound carrier. In this event the sound may be interfered with even though the picture is clean.

Reference to Fig. 3 will show whether or not harmonics of the frequency in use will fall in any television channels that can be received in the locality. It should be kept in mind that not only harmonics of the final frequency may interfere, but also harmonics of any frequencies that may be present in mixer or frequency-multiplier stages. In the case of 144-MHz transmitters, frequency-multiplying combinations that require a doubler or tripler stage to operate on a frequency in a low-band VHF channel in use in the locality should be avoided.

Harmonic Suppression

Effective harmonic suppression has three separate phases:
1) Reducing the amplitude of harmonics generated in the transmitter. This is a matter of circuit design and operating conditions.
2) Preventing stray radiation from the transmitter and associated wiring. This requires adequate shielding and filtering of all circuits and leads from which radiation can take place.
3) Preventing harmonics from being fed into the antenna.

It is impossible to build a transmitter that will not generate some harmonics. It is advantageous to reduce harmonic strength through circuit design and choice of operating conditions before attempting to prevent harmonics from being radiated. Harmonic radiation from the transmitter itself or from its associated wiring obviously will cause interference just as readily as radiation from the antenna. Measures taken to prevent harmonics from reaching the antenna will not reduce TVI if the transmitter itself is radiating harmonics. But once it has been found that the transmitter itself is free from harmonic radiation, devices for preventing harmonics from reaching the antenna can be expected to produce results.

Reducing Harmonic Generation

Since reasonably efficient operation of RF power amplifiers always is accompanied by harmonic generation, good judgment calls for operating all frequency-multiplier stages at a very low power level. When the final output frequency is reached, it is desirable to use as few stages as possible in building up to the final output power level and to use devices that require minimum drive power.

Circuit Design and Layout

Harmonic currents of considerable amplitude flow in both the input and output circuits of RF power amplifiers, but they will do relatively little harm if they can

(A)

(B)

Fig. 4 — At A, cross-hatching caused by the beat between the picture carrier and an interfering signal inside the TV channel. At B, sound bars or modulation bars accompanying amplitude modulation of an interfering signal. In this case the interfering carrier is strong enough to destroy the picture, but in mild cases the picture is visible through the horizontal bars. Sound bars may accompany modulation even though the unmodulated carrier gives no visible cross-hatching.

Fig. 5 — A VHF resonant circuit is formed by the tube capacitance and the lead inductances through the tank and blocking capacitors. Regular tank coils are not shown, since they have little effect on such resonances. C1 is the grid tuning capacitor and C2 is the plate tuning capacitor. C3 and C4 are the grid and plate blocking or bypass capacitors, respectively.

be efficiently bypassed to the cathode, emitter or source of the active device. Fig. 5 shows the paths followed by harmonic currents in an amplifier circuit. Because of the high reactance in the tank coil, there is little harmonic current in it, so the harmonic currents simply flow through the tank capacitor, the input or output blocking capacitor and the device interelectrode capacitances. The lengths of the leads forming these paths is of great importance, since the inductance in this circuit will resonate with the interelectrode capacitance in the VHF range. Generally, only the interelectrode capacitance is considered in this respect, because of the relatively large values of capacitance contained in the blocking and tank circuitry. If such a resonance happens to fall near the same frequency as one of the transmitter harmonics, the effect is the same as though a harmonic tank circuit had been deliberately introduced; the harmonic at that frequency would be tremendously increased in amplitude.

Such resonances are unavoidable, but by keeping the path from plate to cathode and from grid to cathode (and between corresponding terminals in solid-state devices) as short as possible, the resonant frequency can usually be raised above 100 MHz in amplifiers of medium power. This places the harmonic energy where it will cause minimal interference.

It is easier to place grid-circuit VHF resonances where they will do no harm when the amplifier is link-coupled to the driver stage, since this generally permits shorter leads and more favorable conditions for bypassing the harmonics than is the case with capacitive coupling. Link coupling also reduces the coupling between the driver and amplifier at harmonic frequencies, thus preventing driver harmonics from being amplified.

The inductance of leads from the tube to the tank capacitor can be reduced not only by shortening but by using flat strap instead of wire conductors. It is also better to use the chassis as the return from the blocking capacitor or tuned circuit to cathode, since the chassis path will have less inductance than almost any other form of connection.

The VHF resonance points in amplifier tank circuits can be found by coupling a dip meter covering the 50-250 MHz range to the grid and plate leads. If a resonance is found in or near a TV channel, methods such as those described above should be used to move it well out of the TV range. The dip meter also should be used to check for VHF resonances in the tank coils, because coils made for 14 MHz and below usually will show such resonances. In making the check, disconnect the coil entirely from the transmitter and move the dip meter coil along it while exploring for a dip in the 54- to 88-MHz band. If a resonance falls in a TV channel that is in use in the locality, changing the number of turns will move it to a less-troublesome frequency.

Operating Conditions

Grid bias and grid current have an important effect on the harmonic content of the RF currents in both the grid and plate circuits. In general, harmonic output increases as the grid bias and grid current are increased, but this is not necessarily true of a particular harmonic. The third and higher harmonics, especially, will go through fluctuations in amplitude as the grid current is increased, and sometimes a high value of grid current will minimize one harmonic as compared with a low value. This characteristic can be used to advantage where a particular harmonic is causing interference; however, operating conditions that minimize one harmonic may greatly increase another.

Suppression Practices

Complete elimination of TVI is often not a simple process. It seldom happens that a single measure such as installing a high-pass filter at the TV set will cure the problem. Rather, a number of methods must be applied simultaneously. The principal factor in any TVI situation is the ratio of TV signal strength to interference level. This includes interference of all types such as ignition noise, random or thermal noise (which isn't really interference but sets the minimum signal that permits snow-free reception), and unwanted signals that fall within the TV channel. A signal-to-interference ratio greater than approximately 35 to 40 dB is required for good picture quality.

In this regard, an area frequently overlooked in TVI difficulties is the TV antenna. A poor antenna with little gain in the direction of the TV station, old and corroded wire, and connections (which can cause the harmonic generation by rectification of a clean signal generated in a nearby amateur transmitter), may result in a TVI situation that is impossible to solve. Generally speaking, if the picture quality on the TV set experiencing the interference is poor to begin with, even sophisticated suppression measures are likely to prove futile. In such cases, the only solution is replacement of the defective TV antenna system components. Corroded and cracked lead-in cables should be replaced, and the antenna terminals cleaned. If the TV antenna shows signs of corrosion and/or deterioration, it should also be replaced. Note: The amateur has no legal or financial responsibility to pay for the replacement of the antenna system — such replacement is the responsibility of the TV owner.

Grounds

Grounding of equipment has long been considered a first step in eliminating interference. While the method is very effective in the MF range and below, for all practical purposes it is useless in suppressing VHF energy. This is because even short lengths of wire have considerable reactance at VHF. For instance suppose a length of wire by itself has an inductance of 1 μH. At 550 kHz, the reactance would be about 3.46 ohms. On the other hand, the same wire would have a reactance of over 300 ohms at 56 MHz, which is in the frequency range of TV channel 2. (Actually, the impedance of a wire becomes a more complicated entity to define at VHF. The delay effects along the wire are similar to those on the surface of an antenna. Consequently, the wire might even appear as an open circuit rather than as a ground as the electrical length approaches a quarter wavelength.)

From a shock-hazard point of view, grounding is important. However, never connect a ground *for any reason* to the chassis of a TV set. This is because many TV sets derive their operating voltages directly from the ac-service line. Although a schematic diagram of a TV set may indicate a power transformer is being used, caution should be exercised to be sure it is actually being employed for this purpose. Often, the only voltage the transformer is supplying is for the TV picture tube filament.

Shielding

Effective shielding is perhaps the single most important measure in preventing or curing any RFI problem. However, unwanted RF energy must be dissipated. The task becomes harder to perform when the spacing between the source of energy and the boundaries of the shield diminish. Consequently, the use of a double shield is one way of reducing residual radiation from the primary shielding surface.

In order to obtain maximum effectiveness of a particular shielding measure, no breaks or points of entry should be permitted. Small holes for ventilation purposes usually do not degrade shielding effectiveness. But even here, a honeycomb type of duct is often employed when maximum isolation is required. (A parallel bundle of small tubing has very high attenuation since each tube by itself acts as a waveguide below cutoff.)

The isolation of a coaxial cable can be degraded considerably unless the ends of the shield are terminated properly. A braid should be soldered so it completely encloses the inner conductor(s) at the connector junction. For instance, the practice of twisting the braid and point soldering it to the base of a connector may result in a 20-dB degradation in isolation. Normally, this effect is not serious if the cable is run through an area where sensitive circuits don't exist. However, the isolation afforded by a filter can be reduced considerably in circuits where such cable breaks occur.

One instance where a shield break causes a serious problem is in the connection between the antenna terminals on a TV set and the tuner. Newer sets have a 75-ohm coaxial input along with a balun for 300-ohm line. However, because many TV sets have direct connections to the ac line, a decoupling network is used. The shielded

Fig. 6 — Steel wool stuffed into a cardboard tube can be used to dissipate RF current on the shield of coaxial cable. Notice that the cable jacket was removed so that the steel wool contacts the shield braid. This tube (about 4 inches × 18 inches) was selected for photographic purposes, but to be effective, the device should be about twice as long.

Fig. 7 — Winding the cable on a ferrite toroid is an effective shield current suppressor in some cases. Reversing the winding as pictured allows more turns with less shunt capacitance. RG-58 will suffice for moderate power applications. The most important property of the cable is complete shielding — avoid "bargain" cable having less than 95-percent braid coverage.

Fig. 8 — A large metallic baffle inhibits waves propagating on the outside of a coaxial cable. For VHF TV channel 2, the smallest effective baffle is a 9-foot-diameter circle, but the required size decreases linearly with frequency.

lead to the tuner is broken and a capacitor is connected in series with the braid. This provides a low-impedance path for RF energy while presenting a high impedance at 60 Hz. Consequently, because of the cable break, high-pass filters at the antenna input terminals are not as effective as those built into the tuner itself.

Coax Shield Chokes

As mentioned previously, VHF currents flowing on the outside of coaxial cables are frequently the cause of RFI. Figs. 6, 7 and 8 show techniques for reducing or eliminating conducted chassis radiation from coaxial cables. The cardboard tube stuffed with steel wool in Fig. 6 works on the absorption principle. The steel wool is very lossy and dissipates the RF energy on the shield. The tube pictured is 18 inches long. A longer tube would be even more effective.

Fig. 7 shows a choke wound on a ferrite toroidal core. Another coax radiation-suppression device is illustrated in Fig. 8. If the plate is at least a half wavelength (at the harmonic frequency to be suppressed) on its smallest dimension, it will provide a very effective barrier. Large pieces of sheet metal are expensive, so the baffle can be made from a sheet of cardboard or Masonite® covered with aluminum foil. The ideal placement of any of these chokes will vary with the standing wave pattern on the coax shield, but in general they should be close to the transmitter. Like all RFI remedies, the effectiveness of these devices varies widely with each interference situation. Therefore, one should not expect miracles. A coax shield choke installed at a TV receiver prevents signals picked up on the coax braid from reaching the tuner.

Capacitors at RF

Capacitors are common elements found in almost any piece of electronic gear. However, some precautions are necessary when they are employed in RFI-preventive devices such as filters and in bypassing applications. In particular, lead inductance may be sufficient to resonate with the capacitor and cause the entire combination to have a high inductive reactance rather than the desired capacitive reactance.

The effect is illustrated in the accompanying photographs. Fig. 9A shows a response curve for a 10-MHz, pi-configuration, low-pass filter. Very large capacitance values were chosen to accomplish the task, and lead inductance made the capacitor series resonant at approximately 15 MHz. As a result, there is a sharp dip in the response curve at 15 MHz and attenuation is poor above that frequency. When a similar filter was designed in a "T" configuration, smaller capacitance values resulted, series resonance was moved well out of the operating range and the response curve at Fig. 9B resulted.

When designing a filter, avoid large capacitance values if possible. If large capacitance values are unavoidable, use

(A)

(B)

Fig. 9 — Capacitor-lead inductance degrades performance of a pi-configuration filter (A) from that available with a "T" configuration at B. See text for details.

Fig. 10 — Additional lead filtering for harmonics or other spurious frequencies in the high VHF TV band (174-216 MHz).
C1 — 0.001-μF disc ceramic.
C2 — 500- or 1000-pF feedthrough bypass (Centralab FT-1000. Above 500 volts, substitute Centralab 858S-500).
RFC — 14 inches no. 26 enam. close-wound on 3/16-inch-dia form or composition resistor body.

low-inductance capacitors or assemble the required large capacitance by parallel connecting several smaller capacitors (this reduces the total lead inductance).

A very desirable capacitor from an RFI point of view is C2 in Fig. 10. Instead of having two or more plates arranged in a

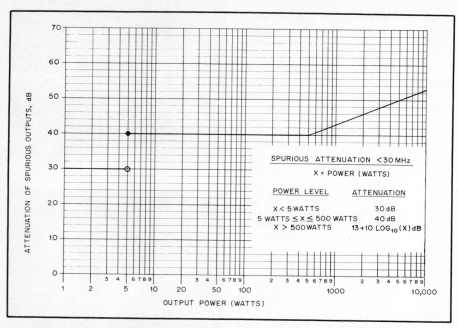

Fig. 11 — The FCC specifies that the spurious signals generated by transmitting equipment must be reduced well below the level of the fundamental. This graph illustrates exactly how far the spurious components must be reduced. This applies to amateur transmitters operating below 30 MHz.

parallel fashion, the conductors are coaxial and are separated by the dielectric. Such feedthrough capacitors are highly recommended for conducting leads in and out of circuits where the radiation of harmonic energy is possible. In addition, the RFC illustrated in Fig. 10 could consist of either a small coil wound over a composition resistor as shown or a ferrite bead on a straight piece of wire.

Decoupling from the AC Line

Direct feedback of RF energy into the ac power service is usually not a problem with modern transmitting equipment. However, currents induced on the antenna feed line may flow in the transmitter chassis and back into the ac line. A rig hot with RF or even the presence of broadcast harmonics while receiving may indicate a problem of this sort. In the case where you are using an antenna that requires a ground (such as an end-fed wire), never use any part of the ac conduits, water systems or other conductors in a building. It is always advisable to have a separate ground system for the antenna itself.

It is also good practice to use an antenna-matching network with no direct connection between the transmitter and antenna feed line. Any matching network that uses mutual-magnetic coupling exclusively will fulfill this requirement. Antenna pattern is another factor to consider; try to choose a type that directs the minimum possible signal into other dwellings. For instance, ground-mounted vertical antennas have considerable low-angle radiation, while a dipole directs energy at angles below the horizontal plane. A ground plane or beam mounted on as high a tower as practical will generally be better from an RFI and TVI standpoint than antennas closer to the ground.

FCC Rules Concerning RFI

§97.307(a) through (e) of the US FCC Rules and Regulations specifies the amateur's responsibility for signal purity:

§97.307 Emission standards.
(a) No amateur station transmission shall occupy more bandwidth than necessary for the information rate and emission type being transmitted, in accordance with good amateur practice.

(b) Emissions resulting from modulation must be confined to the band or segment available to the control operator. Emissions outside the necessary bandwidth must not cause splatter or keyclick interference to operations on adjacent frequencies.

(c) All spurious emissions from a station transmitter must be reduced to the greatest extent practicable. If any spurious emission, including chassis or power line radiation, causes harmful interference to the reception of another radio station, the licensee of the interfering amateur station is required to take steps to eliminate the interference, in accordance with good engineering practice.

(d) The mean power of any spurious emission from a station transmitter or external RF power amplifier transmitting on a frequency below 30 MHz must not exceed 50 mW and must be at least 40 dB below the mean power of the fundamental emission.

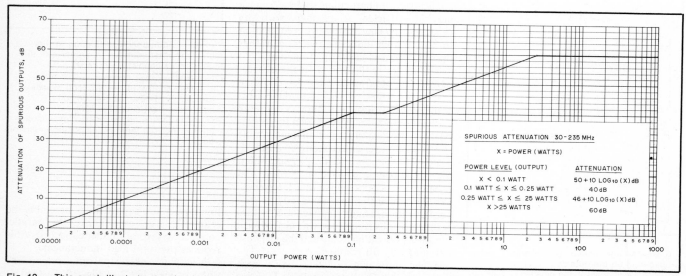

Fig. 12 — This graph illustrates to what level spurious-output energy must be reduced for equipment designed to operate in the 30- to 225-MHz range.

For a transmitter of mean power less than 5 W, the attenuation must be at least 30 dB. A transmitter built before April 15, 1977, or first marketed before January 1, 1978, is exempt from this requirement.

(e) The mean power of any spurious emission from a station transmitter or external RF power amplifier transmitting on a frequency between 30-225 MHz must be at least 60 dB below the mean power of the fundamental. For a transmitter having a mean power of 25 W or less, the mean power of any spurious emission supplied to the antenna transmission line must not exceed 25 μW and must be at least 40 dB below the mean power of the fundamental emission, but need not be reduced below the power of 10 μW. A transmitter built before April 15, 1977, or first marketed before January 1, 1978, is exempt from this requirement.

The numerical limits cited in §97.307 are interpreted graphically in Figs. 11 and 12. Note, however, that paragraph (c) goes beyond absolute limits in defining the amateur's obligation.

Filters and Interference

The judicious use of filters, along with other suppression measures such as shielding, has provided solutions to interference problems in widely varying applications. As a consequence, considerable attention has been given to the subject over the years resulting in some very esoteric designs. Perhaps the most modern approach is to design filters with a digital computer. However, there are a number of other types with component values presented in tabular form. Of these, the most important ones are the so-called Chebyshev and elliptic-function filters. (Butterworth filters are often considered a special case of Chebyshev types with a ripple factor of zero.)

Elliptic-function filters might be considered optimum in the sense that they provide the sharpest rolloff between the passband and stopband. Computed values for a low-pass filter with a 0.1-dB ripple in the passband and a cutoff frequency of 30.6 MHz are shown in Fig. 13. The filter is supposed to provide an attenuation of 35 dB above 40 MHz. An experimental model was built and the response is shown

Fig. 13 — Schematic diagram showing component values of an experimental elliptic-function filter.

in Fig. 14. As can be seen, the filter came close to the design goals. Unfortunately, as with most of the designs in this section, alignment of the more complicated filters requires some sort of sweep-generator setup. This is the only practical way of tweaking a filter to the desired response. While building a sweep setup is not beyond the talents of an advanced experimenter, the lack of one is not an obstacle in the home construction of filters.

AN ABSORPTIVE FILTER

The filter shown in Fig. 15 not only provides rejection by means of a low-pass section, it also includes circuitry that absorbs harmonic energy. A high-pass section consisting of L1, L2, C1 and C2 is terminated in a 50-ohm idler load. This combination absorbs harmonics. The advantages of this technique are that degradation of filter rejection caused by antenna mismatch at the harmonic frequency is not as severe, and the transmitter is terminated in a resistive load at the harmonic.

Construction and Test Techniques

If good performance above 100 MHz is not a necessity, this filter can be built using conventional fixed capacitors. Teflon® -dielectric PC board can be purchased from Microwave Components of Michigan, listed in Chapter 35. Regular fiberglass-insulated board is satisfactory for low power. One such filter has been used with an SSB transceiver running 100 watts PEP output. Although the Q of the fiberglass capacitors will be lower than that of Teflon® -dielectric capacitors, this should not greatly affect the type of filter described here.

Test equipment needed to build this filter at home includes a reasonably accurate dip oscillator, an SWR bridge, a reactance chart or the ARRL L/C/F Calculator, a 50-ohm dummy load and a transmitter.

Once the value of a given capacitor has been calculated, the next step is to determine the capacitance per square inch of the double-clad circuit board you have. This is done by connecting one end of a coil of known inductance to one side of the circuit board, and the other coil lead to the other side of the circuit board. Use a dip meter, coupled lightly to the coil, to determine the resonant frequency of the coil and the circuit-board capacitor. When the frequency is known, the total capacitance can be determined by working the calculator or by looking the capacitance up on a reactance chart. The total capacitance divided by the number of square inches on one side of the circuit board gives the capacitance per square inch. Once this figure is determined, capacitors of almost any value can be laid out with a ruler!

High voltages can be developed across capacitors in a series-tuned circuit, so the copper material should be trimmed back at least 1/8 inch from all edges of a board, except those that will be soldered to

Fig. 14 — Response curve of the filter shown in Fig. 13. Vertical scale represents 10 dB/div, and horizontal scale is 10 MHz/div.

Fig. 15 — Schematic diagram of the absorptive filter. The pc-board used is MIL-P-13949D, FL-GT-062 in, C-2/2-11017, Class 1, Grade A. Polychem Bud Division. Capacitance between copper surfaces is 10-pF per square inch. Values are as follows for a design cutoff frequency of 40 MHz and rejection peak in TV channel 2:

C1 — 52 pF	L2 — 0.52 μH
C2 — 73 pF	L3 — 0.3 μH
C3 — 126 pF	L4 — 0.212 μH
C4 — 15 pF	L5 — 0.55 μH
L1 — 0.125 μH	

ground, to prevent arcing. This should not be accomplished by filing, because the copper filings would become imbedded in the board material and just compound the problem. The capacitor surfaces should be kept smooth, and sharp corners should be avoided.

If the filter box is made of double-clad fiberglass board, both sides should be bonded together with copper stripped from another piece of board. Stripped copper foil may be cleaned with a razor blade before soldering. To remove copper foil from a board, use a straight edge and a sharp scribe to score the thin copper foil. When the copper foil has been cut, use a razor blade to lift a corner. This technique of bonding two pieces of board can also be used to interconnect two capacitors when construction in one plane would require too much area. Stray inductance must be minimized and sufficient clearance must be maintained for arc-over protection.

Capacitors with Teflon® dielectric have been used in filters passing up to 2 kW PEP. One further word of caution: No low-pass filter will be fully effective until the transmitter with which it is used is properly shielded and all leads filtered.

The terminating loads for the high-pass section of the filter can be made from 2-watt, 10-percent-tolerance composition resistors. Almost any dissipation rating can be obtained by suitable series-parallel combinations. A 16-watt, 50-ohm load should handle the harmonic energy of a signal with peak fundamental power of 2 kilowatts. With this load, the harmonic energy will see an SWR of less than 2:1 up to 400 MHz. For low power (<300 watts PEP), a pair of 2-watt, 100-ohm resistors is adequate.

This filter was originally described by Weinrich and Carroll in November 1968 *QST*. The component values given here were calculated by Keith Wilkinson, ZL2BJR.

VHF TVI CAUSES AND CURES

The principal causes of TVI from VHF transmitters are:

1) Interference in channels 2 and 3 from 50 MHz.

2) Fourth harmonic of 50 MHz in channels 11, 12 or 13, depending on the operating frequency.

3) Radiation of unused harmonics of the oscillator or multiplier stages. Examples are 9th harmonic of 6 MHz, and 7th harmonic of 8 MHz in channel 2; 10th harmonic of of 8 MHz in channel 6; 7th harmonic of 25-MHz stages in channel 7; 4th harmonic of 48-MHz stages in channel 9 or 10; and many other combinations. This may include IF pickup, as in the cases of 24-MHz interference in receivers having 21-MHz IF systems, and 48-MHz trouble in 45-MHz IFs.

4) Fundamental blocking effects, including modulation bars, usually found only in the lower channels, from 50-MHz equipment.

5) Image interference in channel 2 from 144 MHz, in receivers having a 45-MHz IF.

6) Sound interference (picture clear in some cases) resulting from RF pickup by the audio circuits of the TV receiver.

There are other possibilities, but nearly all can be corrected completely. The rest can be substantially reduced.

Items 1, 4 and 5 are receiver faults, and no amount of filtering at the transmitter can eliminate them. The only cure is to reduce the amount of 50-MHz energy reaching the receiver, such as by reducing power. In mild cases, increasing the separation between the transmitting and TV antenna systems may reduce or eliminate the problem. Item 6 is also a receiver fault, but it can be alleviated at the transmitter by using FM or CW instead of SSB.

Treatment of the various harmonic troubles, Items 2 and 3, follows the standard methods detailed elsewhere in this Handbook. The prospective builder of new VHF equipment should become familiar with TVI prevention techniques and incorporate them in new construction projects.

Use as high a starting frequency as possible to reduce the number of harmonics that might cause trouble. Select crystal frequencies that do not have harmonics in local TV channels. Example: The 10th harmonic of 8-MHz crystals used for operation in the low part of the 50-MHz band falls in channel 6, but 6-MHz crystals for the same band have no harmonic in that channel.

If TVI is a serious problem, use the lowest transmitter power that will do the job at hand. Keep the power in the multiplier and driver stages at the lowest practical level, and use link coupling in preference to capacitive coupling. Plan for complete shielding and filtering of the RF sections of the transmitter, should these steps become necessary.

Use coaxial line to feed the antenna system, and locate the radiating portion of the antenna as far as possible from TV receivers and their antenna systems.

A complete discussion of the problems and cures for interference is in the ARRL publication, *Radio Frequency Interference*.

FILTERS FOR VHF TRANSMITTERS

High rejection of unwanted frequencies is possible with the tuned-line filters of Fig. 16. Examples are shown for each band from 50 through 450 MHz. Construction is relatively simple, and the cost is low.

Fig. 17 — Interior of the 50-MHz strip-line filter. Inner conductor of aluminum strip is bent into U shape, to fit inside a standard 17-inch chassis.

Fig. 18 — The 144-MHz filter has an inner conductor of ½-inch (5/8-inch OD) copper tubing 10 inches long, grounded to the left end of the case and supported at the right end by the tuning capacitor.

Fig. 19 — A half-wave strip line is used in the 220-MHz filter. It is grounded at both ends and tuned at the center.

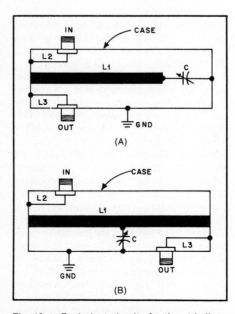

Fig. 16 — Equivalent circuits for the strip-line filters. At A, the circuit for the 6- and 2-meter filters are shown. L2 and L3 are the input and output links. These filters are bilateral, permitting interchanging of the input and output terminals. At B, the representative circuit for the 220- and 432-MHz filters. These filters are also bilateral.

Standard boxes are used for ease of duplication.

The filter of Fig. 17 is selective enough to pass 50-MHz energy and attenuate the seventh harmonic of an 8-MHz oscillator that falls in TV channel 2. With an insertion loss at 50 MHz of about 1 dB, it can provide up to 40 dB of attenuation to energy at 57 MHz in the same line.

The filter uses a folded line in order to keep it within the confines of a standard chassis. The case is a 6 × 17 × 3-inch chassis (Bud AC-433) with a cover plate that fastens in place with self-tapping screws. An aluminum partition down the middle of the assembly is 14 inches long, and the full height of the chassis is 3 inches.

The inner conductor of the line is 32 inches long and 13/16-inch wide, of 1/16-inch brass, copper or aluminum. This was made from two pieces of aluminum spliced together to provide the 32-inch length. Splicing seemed to have no ill effect on the circuit Q. The sides of the "U" are 2-7/8 inches apart, with the partition at the center. The line is supported on ceramic standoffs. These were shimmed with sections of hardwood or Bakelite rod, to give the required 1½-inch height.

The tuning capacitor is a double-spaced variable (Hammarlund HF-30-X) mounted 1½ inches from the right end of the chassis. Input and output coupling loops are of no. 10 or 12 wire, 10 inches long. Spacing from the line is adjusted to about ¼ inch.

The 144-MHz model shown in Fig. 18 is housed in a 2¼ × 2½ × 12-inch Minibox® (Bud CU-2114-A).

One end of the tubing is slotted ¼-inch deep with a hacksaw. This slot takes a brass angle bracket 1½ inches wide, ¼ inch high, with a ½-inch mounting lip. The ¼-inch lip is soldered into the tubing slot, and the bracket is then bolted to the end of the box, so as to be centered on the end plate.

The tuning capacitor (Hammarlund HF-15-X) is mounted 1¼ inches from the other end of the box, in such a position that the inner conductor can be soldered to the two stator bars.

The two coaxial fittings (SO-239) are 11/16 inch in from each side of the box, 3½ inches from the left end. The coupling loops are no. 12 wire, bent so that each is parallel to the center line of the inner conductor, and about 1/8 inch from its surface. Their cold ends are soldered to the brass mounting bracket.

The 220-MHz filter (Fig. 19) uses the same size box as the 144-MHz model. The inner conductor is 1/16-inch brass or copper, 5/8-inch wide, just long enough to fold over at each end for bolting to the box. It is positioned so that there will be a 1/8-inch clearance between it and the rotor plates of the tuning capacitor. The latter is a Hammarlund HF-15-X, mounted slightly off-center in the box, so that its stator plates connect to the exact mid-point of the line. The 5/16-inch mounting hole in the case is 5½ inches from one end. The SO-239 coaxial fittings are 1 inch in from opposite sides of the box, 2 inches from the ends. Their coupling links are no. 14 wire, 1/8 inch from the inner conductor of the line.

The 420-MHz filter is similar in design, using a 1-5/8 × 2 × 10-inch Minibox (Bud CT-2113-A). A half-wave line is used, with the disc tuning at the center. The discs are 1/16-inch brass, 1¼-inch diameter. The fixed one is centered on the inner conductor, the other is mounted on a no. 6 brass lead-screw. This passes through a threaded bushing, which can be taken from the end of a discarded slug-tuned form. An advantage of these is that usually a tension device is included. If there is none, use a lock nut.

Type-N coaxial connectors were used on the 420-MHz model. They are 5/8 inch in from each side of the box, and 1-3/8 inches in from the ends. Their coupling links of no. 14 wire are 1/16 inch from the inner conductor.

Adjustment and Use

If you want the filter to work on both transmitting and receiving, connect the filter between antenna line and SWR in-

Fig. 20 — The proper method of installing a low-pass filter between a transmitter and Transmatch. The transmitter and filter must be well shielded. If a TR switch is used, it should be installed between the transmitter and low-pass filter. TR switches can generate harmonics themselves, so the low-pass filter should follow the TR switch. If the antenna is very well matched to the filter output, the Transmatch can be eliminated. (Any mismatch will degrade filter performance.)

dicator. With this arrangement you need merely adjust the filter for minimum reflected power reading on the SWR bridge. This should be zero, or close to it, if the antenna is well matched. The bridge should be used, as there is no way to adjust the filter properly without it.

When the filter is properly adjusted (with the SWR bridge), you may find that reception can be improved by retuning the filter. Don't do it if you want the filter to work best for the job it was intended to do: The rejection of unwanted energy, transmitting or receiving. If you want to improve reception with the filter in the circuit, work on the receiver input circuit. To get maximum power out of the transmitter and into the line, adjust the transmitter output coupling, not the filter. If the effect of the filter on reception bothers you, connect it in the line from the antenna relay to the transmitter only.

Summary

The methods of harmonic elimination outlined here have been proven beyond doubt to be effective even under highly unfavorable conditions. It must be emphasized once more, however, that the problem must be solved one step at a time, and the procedure must be in logical order. It cannot be done properly without two items of simple equipment: A dip meter and wavemeter covering the TV bands, and a dummy antenna.

To summarize:

1) Take a critical look at the transmitter on the basis of the design considerations outlined under Reducing Harmonic Generation.

2) Check all circuits, particularly those connected with the final amplifier, with the dip meter to determine whether there are any resonances in the TV bands. If so, rearrange the circuits so the resonances are moved out of the critical frequency region.

3) Connect the transmitter to the dummy antenna and check for the presence of harmonics on leads with the wavemeter and around the transmitter enclosure. Seal the weak spots in the shielding and filter the leads until the wavemeter shows no indication at any harmonic frequency.

4) At this stage, check for interference with a TV receiver. If there is interference, determine the cause by the methods described previously and apply the recommended remedies until the interference disappears. More than one remedy may be required.

5) When the transmitter is completely clean on the dummy antenna, connect it to the regular antenna and check for interference on the TV receiver. If the interference is not bad, a Transmatch or matching circuit, installed as shown in Fig. 20, should clear it up. Alternatively, a low-pass filter may be used. If neither the Transmatch nor filter makes any difference in the interference, the evidence is strong that the interference, at least in part, is being caused by receiver overloading because of the strong fundamental-frequency field about the TV antenna and receiver. A Transmatch and/or filter, installed as described above, will invariably make a difference if the interference is caused by transmitter harmonics alone.

6) If there is still interference after installing the Transmatch and/or filter, and the evidence shows that it is probably caused by a harmonic, more attenuation is needed. A more elaborate filter may be necessary. However, it is well at this stage to assume that part of the interference may be caused by receiver overloading. Take steps to alleviate such a condition before trying highly elaborate filters and traps on the transmitter.

Harmonics by Rectification

Even though the transmitter is completely free of harmonic output, it is still possible for interference to occur because of harmonics generated outside the transmitter. These result from rectification of fundamental-frequency currents induced in conductors in the vicinity of the transmitting antenna. Rectification can take place at any point where two conductors are in poor electrical contact, a condition that frequently exists in plumbing, downspouting, BX cables crossing each other, and numerous other places in an ordinary residence. It can also occur at any exposed circuitry in the station that may not be shielded from RF. Poor joints anywhere in

Fig. 21 — The schematic diagram of a 75-ohm Chebyshev filter assembled on PC board is shown at A. At B, the passband response of the 75-ohm filter. Design inductances: 0.157 µH: 12 turns no. 24 wire on T44-0 core. 0.135 µH: 11 turns no. 24 wire on T44-0 core. Turns should be evenly spaced, with approximately ¼ inch between the ends of the winding. If T37-0 cores are used, wind 14 and 12 turns, respectively.

Fig. 22 — Photo showing construction of the 75-ohm unbalanced filter.

the antenna system are especially bad, and rectification may take place in the contacts of antenna-changeover relays. Another rectification problem is caused by overloading the front end of the communications receiver when it is used with a separate antenna. This can result in the radiation of harmonics generated in the first stage of the receiver.

Rectification of this sort will not only cause harmonic interference, but also is frequently responsible for cross-modulation effects. It can be detected to some degree in most locations, but fortunately the harmonics thus generated are not usually of high amplitude. However, they can cause considerable interference in the immediate vicinity in fringe areas, especially when operation is in the 28-MHz band. The amplitude decreases rapidly with the order of the harmonic, the second and third being the worst. It is ordinarily found that even in cases where destructive interference results from 28-MHz operation, the interference is comparatively mild from 14 MHz, and is negligible at still lower frequencies.

Nothing can be done at either the transmitter or receiver when rectification occurs in other objects. The remedy is to find and eliminate the poor contact either by separating the conductors or bonding them together. A crystal wavemeter (tuned to the fundamental frequency) is useful for hunting the source by showing which conductors are carrying RF and, comparatively, how much.

Interference of this kind is frequently intermittent since the rectification efficiency will vary with its susceptibility to vibration, weather and so on. The possibility of corroded contacts in the TV receiving antenna should not be overlooked, especially if it has been up for a year or more.

TV Receiver Deficiencies

When a television receiver is located close to the transmitter, the intense RF signal from the transmitter's fundamental may overload one or more of the receiver circuits to produce spurious responses that cause interference.

If the overload is moderate, the interference is of the same nature as harmonic interference; it is caused by harmonics generated in the early stages of the receiver and, since it occurs only on channels harmonically related to the transmitting frequency, it is difficult to distinguish from harmonics actually radiated by the transmitter. In such cases, additional harmonic suppression at the transmitter will do no good, but any means taken at the receiver to reduce the strength of the amateur signal reaching the first stage will improve performance. With very severe overloading, interference also will occur on channels not harmonically related to the transmitting frequency, so such cases are easily identified.

Intermodulation

Under some circumstances, overloading will result in cross modulation or mixing of the amateur signal with that from a local FM or television station. For example, a 14-MHz signal can mix with a 92-MHz FM station to produce a beat at 78 MHz, the *difference* between the two frequencies (92 − 14 = 78). Since 78 MHz falls in TV channel 5, interference to television reception would occur on that channel. Similarly, a 14-MHz signal could mix with a TV broadcast station operating on channel 6 to produce a beat at 99 MHz, the *sum* of the two frequencies (14 + 85 = 99). Neither of the broadcast channels interfered with is in harmonic relationship to 14 MHz, and *both* signals must be on the air for the interference to occur. Eliminating either at the receiver will eliminate the interference.

There are many combinations of this type, depending on the band in use and the local frequency assignments of FM and TV stations. As noted earlier, the interfering frequency is equal to the amateur fundamental frequency either added to, or subtracted from, the frequency of some local station. Whenever interference occurs in a frequency that is not harmonically related to the amateur transmitter frequency, the possibilities in such frequency combinations should be investigated.

IF Interference

Some TV receivers do not have sufficient selectivity to prevent strong signals in the intermediate-frequency range from forcing their way through the front end and getting into the IF amplifier. The third harmonic of 14 MHz and second harmonic of 21 MHz fall into the television IF, as do some of the local-oscillator frequencies used in a heterodyne type of transmitter or transceiver. If these frequencies are breaking through the TV tuner, a high-pass filter can improve the situation significantly. Even so, the amateur is responsible for keeping his or her radiation in the TV IF region within the limits defined by FCC rules and

Fig. 23 — Schematic and pictorial diagrams of the 300-ohm balanced elliptical high-pass filter with PC-board capacitors. Shaded areas indicate where copper has been removed. Dimensions are given in millimeters for ease of measurement. L2-C2 connects between the points marked x, L4-C4 connects between the points marked y and L6-C6 connects between the points marked z on the pictorial. C1 = 28.0 pF, C3 = 14.0 pF, C5 = 14.8 pF, C7 = 34.2 pF, C2 = 162 pF, C4 = 36.0 pF, and C6 = 46.5 pF. Design inductances: L2 = 0.721 μH: 14 turns no. 26 wire evenly wound on a T44-10 core. L4 = 0.766 μH: 14 turns no. 26 wire bunched as required on a T44-10 core. L6 = 0.855 μH: 15 turns evenly wound on a T44-10 core. These coils should be adjusted for resonance at 14.7, 30.3 and 25.2 MHz.

Fig. 24 — A top view of the 300-ohm elliptic filter using PC-board capacitors is at A. Twin-lead is tack soldered at the left and right ends of the board. At B, bottom view of the filter.

good engineering practice.

A form of IF interference peculiar to 50-MHz operation near the low edge of the band occurs with some receivers having the standard 41-MHz IF, which has the sound carrier at 41.25 MHz and the picture carrier at 45.75 MHz. A 50-MHz signal that forces its way into the IF system of the receiver will beat with the IF picture carrier to give a spurious signal on or near the IF sound carrier, even though the interfering signal is not actually in the normal passband of the IF amplifier.

There is a type of IF interference unique to the 144-MHz band in localities where certain UHF TV channels are in operation. It affects only those TV receivers in which double-conversion type plug-in UHF tuning strips are used. The design of these strips involves a first intermediate frequency that varies with the TV channel to be received and, depending on the particular strip design, this first IF may be in or close to the 144-MHz amateur band. Since there is comparatively little selectivity in the TV signal-frequency circuits ahead of the first IF, a signal from a 144-MHz transmitter will ride into the IF, even when the receiver is at a considerable distance from the transmitter. The channels that can be affected by this type of IF interference are 20-25, 51-58, 82 and 83. If the receiver is not close to the transmitter, a trap of the type shown in Fig. 25 will be effective. However, if the separation is small, the 144-MHz signal will be picked up directly on the receiver circuits. The best solution is to readjust the strip oscillator so that the first IF is moved to a frequency not in the vicinity of the 144-MHz band. This should be done only by a competent technician.

IF interference is easily identified since it occurs on all channels — although sometimes the intensity varies from channel to channel — and the cross-hatch pattern it causes will rotate when the receiver's fine-tuning control is varied. When the interference is caused by a harmonic, overloading or cross modulation, the structure of the interference pattern does not change (its intensity may change) as the fine-tuning control is varied.

High-Pass Filters

In all of these cases the interference can be eliminated if the fundamental signal strength is reduced to a level that the receiver can handle. To accomplish this with signals on bands below 30 MHz, the most satisfactory device is a high-pass filter having a cutoff frequency just below 54 MHz installed at the tuner input terminals of the receiver.

Fig. 21 shows the schematic diagram of a filter designed for use with 75-ohm coaxial cable. Double-sided 1/16-inch FR-4 epoxy-glass PC board is used as a base for the filter components. A section of copper on the top is stripped away on both sides of center to approximate a 75-ohm microstrip line about 3/32-inch wide (see Fig. 21). Both sides of the top copper foil (at the edges) are connected to the ground plane foil underneath.

Slice off the extruded insulation around

Fig. 25 — Parallel-tuned traps for installation in the 300-Ω line to a TV set. Mount the traps in a shielded enclosure with a shield partition as indicated. For 50-MHz use, L1 and L2 are each 9 turns of no. 16 enameled wire close wound on a ½-inch-diameter form (air core). For 144-MHz use, L1 and L2 are each 6 turns of no. 16 enameled wire close wound on a ¼-inch-diameter form (air core). This trap technique can be used to overcome HF fundamental overload as well.

the solder pins on two type-F coaxial connectors (Radio Shack 278-212). Butt the connectors directly against the PC board. Solder the connector shells to the bottom ground plane and the center pins to the micro-strip line. Cut the micro-strip line in four equally spaced places. The capacitors should be mounted across the spaces; inductors can be connected between the capacitor junctions and the ground plane on the top of the board. Use NP0 ceramic or silver mica capacitors. Inductors are wound on toroidal powdered-iron cores; winding details are given in the caption to Fig. 21.

Fig. 23 shows the schematic and pictorial diagrams of a 300-ohm balanced elliptical high-pass filter that uses PC-board capacitors. Use double-sided 1/32 inch FR-4 glass-epoxy PC board. Thicker board will require more area for the desired capacitances. C2, C4 and C6 should be NP0 ceramic or silver-mica capacitors. It is easier to strip away rather than etch copper to form the series of capacitive elements. Mark the edges by cutting with a sharp knife; heating with a hot soldering iron will help lift the strips more easily. Top and bottom views of the filter are shown in Fig. 24.

Neither of the high-pass filters described requires a shielded enclosure. For mounting outside the receiver, some kind of protective housing is desirable, however. These filters were presented in "Practical 75- and 300-Ohm High-Pass Filters," QST, February 1982, pp 30-34, by Ed Wetherhold, W3NQN.

Simple high-pass filters cannot always be applied successfully in the case of 50-MHz transmissions, because they do not have sufficiently sharp cutoff characteristics to give both good attenuation at 50-54 MHz and no attenuation above 54 MHz. A more elaborate design capable of giving the required sharp cutoff has been described (F. Ladd, "50-MHz TVI — Its Causes and Cures," QST June 1954, pp 21-23, 114 and 116, and July 1954, pp 32-33, 124 and 126).

This article also contains other information useful in coping with the TVI problems peculiar to 50-MHz operation.

As an alternative to such a filter, a high-Q wave trap tuned to the transmitting frequency may be used, suffering only the disadvantage that it is quite selective and therefore will protect a receiver from overloading over only a small range of transmitting frequencies in the 50-MHz band. A trap of this type is shown in Fig. 25. These suck-out traps, while absorbing energy at the frequency to which they are tuned, do not affect the receiver operation otherwise. The assembly should be mounted near the input terminals of the TV tuner and its case should be RF grounded to the TV set chassis by means of a small capacitor. The traps should be tuned for minimum TVI at the transmitter operating frequency. An insulated tuning tool should be used for adjustment of the trimmer capacitors, since they are at a hot point and will show considerable body-capacitance effect.

High-pass filters are available commercially at moderate prices. In this connection, it should be understood by all parties concerned that while an amateur is responsible for *harmonic* radiation from his transmitter, it is no part of his responsibility to pay for or install filters, wave traps or other devices that may be required at the receiver to prevent interference caused by his *fundamental* frequency. Proper installation usually requires that the filter be installed at the input terminals of the RF tuner of the TV set and not merely at the external antenna terminals, which may be at a considerable distance from the tuner. The question of cost is one to be settled between the set owner and the organization with which he deals. Don't overlook the possibility that the manufacturer of the TV receiver may supply a high-pass filter free of charge.

If the fundamental signal is getting into the receiver by way of the line cord, a line filter such as those shown in Fig. 26 may help. To be most effective it should be installed inside the receiver chassis at the point where the cord enters, making the ground connections directly to the chassis at this point. It may not be so helpful if placed between the line plug and the wall socket unless the RF is actually picked up on the house wiring rather than on the line cord itself.

Antenna Installation

Usually the transmission line between the TV receiver and the antenna will pick up a great deal more energy from a nearby HF transmitter than the television receiving antenna itself. The currents induced on the TV transmission line in this case are of the parallel type, where the phase of the current is the same in both conductors. The line simply acts like two wires connected together to operate as one. If the receiver antenna input circuit were perfectly balanced it would reject these parallel or

Fig. 26 — A "brute force" ac line filter. C1, C2 and C3 can be any value from 0.001 to 0.01 µF, rated for ac-line service (or 1.4 kV dc). L1 and L2 are each a 2-inch-long winding of no. 18 enameled wire on a ½-inch-diameter form. If it is installed outside the equipment cabinet, enclose the filter to eliminate shock hazard.

common-mode signals and respond only to the true transmission-line (push-pull or differential mode) currents. That is, only signals picked up on the actual antenna would cause a receiver response. However, no receiver is perfect in this respect, and many TV receivers will respond strongly to such common-mode currents. The result is that the signals from a nearby amateur transmitter are much more intense at the first stage in the TV receiver than they would be if the receiver response were confined entirely to energy picked up on the TV antenna alone.

A simple common-mode choke can be formed by winding several turns of TV twin-lead through an FT-114 ferrite core. Best results will be obtained if you use twin-lead with an oval cross-sectional profile.

The situation can also be improved by using coaxial cable or shielded twin-lead. For best results, coax line should terminate in a coaxial fitting on the receiver chassis. A balun can be used between the coax and the 300-ohm balanced input terminals of a receiver having no coaxial connector. The foil of shielded twin-lead should be connected to the chassis near the antenna terminals through a small capacitor (470 pF). RF currents on the outside of the shield can be dealt with effectively by using a shield choke as described earlier in this chapter.

In most TV receiving installations the transmission line is much longer than the antenna itself, and is consequently exposed to more of the harmonic fields from the transmitter. Much of the harmonic pickup, therefore, is on the receiving transmission line when the transmitter and receiver are located close together. Shielded line, plus relocation of either the transmitting or receiving antenna to take advantage of directive effects, often will reduce overloading and harmonic pickup to a level that does not interfere with reception.

UHF Television

Harmonic TVI in the UHF-TV band is far less troublesome than in the VHF band. Harmonics from transmitters operating below 30 MHz are of such high order that they would normally be expected to be

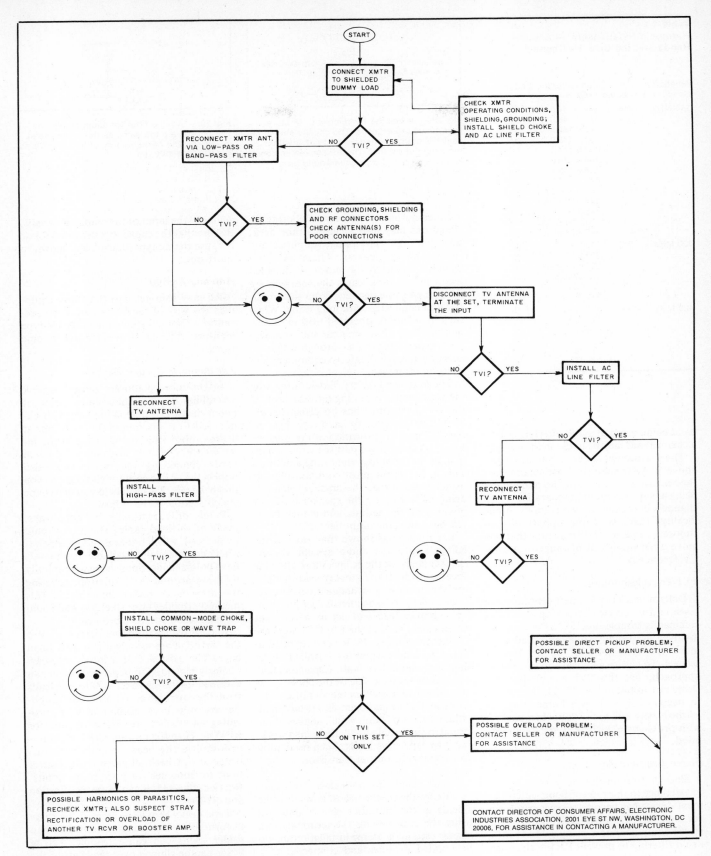

Fig. 27 — TVI troubleshooting flowchart.

weak; in addition, the components, circuit conditions and construction of low-frequency transmitters tend to prevent very strong harmonics from being generated in this region. However, this is not true of amateur VHF transmitters, particularly those working in the 144-MHz and higher bands. Here the problem is similar to that of the low VHF-TV band with respect to transmitters operating below 30 MHz.

There is one highly favorable factor in UHF TV that does not exist in most of the VHF-TV band: If harmonics are radiated, it is possible to move the transmitter frequency sufficiently (within the amateur

Amateur Band	Harmonic	Fundamental Freq. Range	Channel Affected
144 MHz	4th	144.0-144.5	31
		144.5-146.0	32
		146.0-147.5	33
		147.5-148.0	34
	5th	144.0-144.4	55
		144.4-145.6	56
		145.6-146.8	57
		146.8-148.0	58
	6th	144.0-144.33	79
		144.33-145.33	80
		145.33-146.33	81
		146.33-147.33	82
		147.33-148.00	83
220 MHz	3rd	220-220.67	45
		220.67-222.67	46
		222.67-224.67	47
		224.67-225	48
	4th	220-221	82
		221-222.5	83
420 MHz	2nd	420-421	75
		421-424	76
		424-427	77
		427-430	78
		430-433	79
		433-436	80

Fig. 28 — A method for removing RF current from loudspeaker leads. The chokes should be near the output terminals, preferably within the amplifier cabinet. The RF chokes can be 24 turns of no. 18 wire closewound on a pencil.

Fig. 29 — Ac line filter for audio amplifiers. The chokes are the same as those described in Fig. 28. The capacitors must be rated for ac service (or 1.4 kV dc).

band being used) to avoid interfering with a channel that may be in use in the locality.

The harmonics from amateur bands above 50 MHz span the UHF channels as shown in Table 1. Since the assignment plan calls for a minimum separation of six channels between any two stations in one locality, there is ample opportunity to choose a fundamental frequency that will move a harmonic out of range of a local TV frequency.

TVI Troubleshooting

Determination and experimentation are essential for success in tracking down and eliminating troublesome TVI. The variables involved are usually so complicated as to make the task more of an art than a science. To ensure a logical and systematic approach, use the TVI troubleshooting flowchart found in Fig. 27. The best place to begin is in your own home. Lessons learned there will assist you when dealing with problems elsewhere in the neighborhood.

Stereo Interference

Since the introduction of stereo receivers, interference to this type of home-entertainment device has become a severe problem for amateurs. Unfortunately, most of the stereo equipment now being sold has little or no filtering to prevent RF interference. In most cases, corrective measures must be taken at the stereo installation.

Stereo Equipment

Stereo gear can consist of a simple amplifier, with record or tape inputs and speaker outputs. The more elaborate installations may also include a tape deck, turntable, AM/FM tuner, amplifier and two or more speakers. These units are usually connected by means of shielded leads, and in most cases the speakers are positioned some distance from the amplifier and connected with long leads. When such a setup is operated within a few hundred feet of an amateur station, there are two important paths through which RF energy can reach the stereo equipment and cause interference.

The first step is to try to determine how the interference is getting into the unit. If the volume control has no effect on the level of interference, or has a very slight effect, the audio rectification of the amateur signal is taking place past the volume control, or on the output end of the amplifier. This is by far the most common type. It usually means that the amateur signal is being picked up on the speaker leads, or possibly on the ac line, and is then being fed back into the amplifier.

Experience has shown that most of the RF gets into the audio system via the speaker leads, or the ac line, most often the speaker leads. If the speaker leads happen to be resonant near an amateur band in use, there is likely to be an interference problem. The speaker lead will act as a resonant antenna and pick up the RF. One easy cure is illustrated in Fig. 28. RF chokes rated to carry the load current are installed at the amplifier output terminals. Capacitors may be used on the *load* side of the chokes, but should not be placed on the amplifier side. Most solid-state audio amplifiers have high values of loop gain, which makes them prone to supersonic oscillation when working into capacitive loads. Such oscillation can destroy the output transistors in short order.

In particularly stubborn cases, use shielded wire for the speaker leads, grounding the shields at the amplifier chassis and still using the bypasses on the terminals. All chassis used in the stereo installation should be bonded together and connected to a good earth ground if at all possible. It has been found that grounding sometimes eliminates the interference. On the other hand, don't be discouraged if grounding doesn't appear to help.

Fig. 29 shows a method for filtering the ac line at the input of the amplifier chassis. Be sure that the capacitors are rated for ac because the dc types have been known to short out.

Antenna Pickup

RF may also get into the audio equipment by way of the FM antenna, so precautions should be taken here. A TV-type high-pass filter can prove effective in some cases.

Turntables and Tape Decks

In the more elaborate setups, several assemblies may be connected by means of patch cords. It is a good idea when checking for RFI to disconnect the units, one at a time, observing any changes in the interference. Not only disconnect the patch cords connecting the pieces, but also unplug the ac line cord for each item as you make the test. This will help you determine which section is the culprit.

Patch cords are usually, but not always, made of shielded cable. The lines should be shielded, which brings up another point. Many commercially available patch cords have poor shields. Some have wire spirally wrapped around the insulation, covering the main lead, rather than braid. This method provides poor shielding and could be the reason for RFI problems.

Record-player tone-arm connections to the cartridge are usually made with small clips. The existence of a loose clip, particularly if oxidation is present, offers an excellent invitation to RFI. Also, the leads from the cartridge and those to the amplifier are sometimes resonant at VHF, providing an excellent receiving antenna for RF. One cure for unwanted RF pickup is to install ferrite beads, one on each cartridge lead. Check all patch-cord connections for looseness or poor solder joints. Inferior connections can cause rectification and RFI.

Tape decks should be treated the same as turntables. Loose connections and bad solder joints can cause trouble. Ferrite beads can be slipped over the leads to the recording and play-back pickup heads. Bypassing of the tone-arm or pickup-head leads is also effective, but sometimes it is difficult to install capacitors in the small area available. Disc capacitors (0.001 μF) should be used as close to the cartridge or pickup head as possible. Keep the capacitor leads as short as possible.

Preamplifiers

One or more preamplifiers are usually used in a stereo amplifier. The inputs to these stages can be very susceptible to RFI. Fig. 30 illustrates a typical preamplifier circuit. In this case the leads to the bases of the transistors are treated for RFI with ferrite beads by the addition of RFC2 and RFC4. This is a very effective method for stopping RFI when VHF energy is the source of the trouble.

The emitter-base junction of a transistor is a common RFI offender. This junction operates as a forward-biased diode, with the bias set so that a change of base current with signal will produce a linear but amplified change in collector current. Should RF energy reach the junction, the bias could increase, causing nonlinear amplification and distortion as the result. If the RF level is high it can completely block (saturate) a transistor, causing a complete loss of gain. Therefore, it may be necessary to reduce the transmitter power output to pinpoint the particular transistor stage that is affected.

In addition to ferrite beads placed over the base lead, it may be necessary to bypass the base of the transistor to chassis ground, C1 and C2, Fig. 30. A suitable value is 100 pF, and keep the leads short! As a rule, the capacitor value should be as large as possible without degrading the high-frequency response of the amplifier. Values up to 0.001 µF can be used. In severe cases, a series inductor (RFC1 and RFC3) may be required, such as the Ohmite Z-50 or Z-144, or their equivalents (7 and 1.8 µH, respectively). Fig. 30 shows the correct placement for an inductor, bypass capacitor and ferrite bead. Also, it might help to use a ferrite bead in the B+ lead to the preamplifier stages (RFC5 in Fig. 30). Keep in mind that Fig. 30 represents only one preamplifier of a stereo set. Both channels may require treatment.

FM Tuners

Much of the interference to FM tuners is caused by fundamental overloading of the first stage (or stages). The cure is the installation of a high-pass filter, the same type used for TVI. The filter should be installed as close as possible to the antenna input of the tuner. The high-pass filter will attenuate the amateur fundamental signal, thus preventing overloading of the front end.

Shielding

Lack of shielding on the various components in a stereo installation can permit RF to get into the equipment. Many units have no bottom plates, or are installed in plastic cases. One easy method of providing shielding is to use aluminum foil. Make sure the foil doesn't short-circuit the com-

Fig. 30 — Typical circuit of a solid-state preamplifier with RFI preventative measures applied (see text).

ponents, and connect it to chassis ground.

Interference with Medium-Wave Broadcast Reception

Transmitter Defects

Out-of-band radiation is something that must be cured at the amateur transmitter. Parasitic oscillations are a frequently unsuspected source of such radiation, and no transmitter can be considered satisfactory until it has been thoroughly checked for both low- and high-frequency parasitics. Very often, parasitics show up only as transients, causing key clicks in CW transmitters and "splashes" or "burps" on modulation peaks in SSB transmitters. Methods for detecting and eliminating parasitics are discussed in the transmitter chapter.

In CW transmitters the sharp make and break that occurs with unfiltered keying causes transients that, in theory, contain frequency components through the entire radio spectrum. Practically, they are often strong enough in the immediate vicinity of the transmitter to cause serious interference to broadcast reception. Key clicks can be eliminated by proper wave shaping. See Chapter 19.

BCI is frequently made worse by radiation from the power wiring or the RF transmission line. This is because the signal causing the interference is radiated from wiring that is nearer the broadcast receiver than the transmitting antenna. Much depends on the method used to couple the transmitter to the antenna, a subject that is discussed in the chapters on transmission lines and antennas. If at all possible, the antenna itself should be placed some distance from house wiring, telephone and power lines, and similar conductors.

The BC Receiver

Most present-day receivers use solid-state active components rather than tubes. A large number of the receivers in use are battery powered. This is to the amateur's advantage because much of the BC interference an amateur encounters is caused by ac line pickup. In the case where the BC receiver is powered from the ac line, whether using tube or solid-state components, the amount of RF pickup must be reduced or eliminated. A line filter such as is shown in Fig. 26 often will help accomplish this. The values used for the coils and capacitors are in general not critical. The effectiveness of the filter may depend considerably on the ground connection used, and it is advisable to use a short ground lead to a cold-water pipe if at all possible. The line cord from the set should be bunched up to minimize the possibility of pickup on the cord. To get satisfactory operation, it may be necessary to install the filter inside the receiver, so the filter is connected between the line cord and the set wiring.

Cross Modulation

With phone transmitters, there are occasionally cases where the noise is heard whenever the broadcast receiver is tuned to a BC station, but there is no interference when tuned between stations. This is cross modulation, a result of rectification in one of the early stages of the receiver. Receivers that are susceptible to this trouble usually also get a similar type of interference from regular broadcasting if there is a strong local BC station and the receiver is tuned to some other station.

The remedy for cross modulation in the receiver is the same as for images and oscillator-harmonic response — reduce the strength of the amateur signal at the receiver by means of a line filter.

The trouble is not always in the receiver. Cross modulation can occur in any nearby rectifying circuit — such as a poor contact in water or gutter pipes, and other conductors in the strong field of the transmitting antenna. Locating the cause may be difficult, and is best attempted with a battery-powered portable broadcast receiver used as a probe to find the spot where the interference is most intense. When such a spot is located, inspection of the metal structures in the vicinity should indicate the cause. The remedy is to make a good electrical bond between the two conductors having the poor contact.

Handling BCI Cases

Tune the receiver through the broadcast band to see whether the interference tunes like a regular BC station. If so, image or oscillator-harmonic response is the cause. If there is interference only when a BC station is tuned in, but not between stations, the cause is cross modulation. If the interference is heard at all settings of the tuning dial, the trouble is pickup in the audio circuits. In this case, the receiver volume control may or may not affect the strength of the interference, depending on how your signal is being rectified.

Organs

The electronic organ is an RFI problem area. All of the techniques outlined for audio gear hold true in getting rid of RFI in an organ. Two points should be checked — the speaker leads and the ac line. Many organ manufacturers have special service guides for taking care of RFI. However, to get this information you or the organ owner must contact the manufacturer, not the dealer or distributor. Don't accept the statement from a dealer or serviceman that nothing can be done about the interference.

Public Address Systems

The cure for RFI in public address systems is almost the same as that for audio gear. The one thing to watch for is RF on the leads that connect the various stations in a public address system. These leads should be treated the same as speaker leads, and filtering should be done at both ends of the lines. Also, watch for ac-line pickup of RF.

Telephone Interference

Because of a change in FCC rules, subscribers increasingly own their telephone instruments, leasing only the lines from the telephone company. Interference-prevention measures to the instrument are the owner's responsibility. If a fault occurs in the line, the telephone company must make the necessary repairs. Responsible instrument manufacturers should provide necessary modification to minimize RFI.

Telephone interference may be cured by connecting a bypass capacitor (about 0.01 µF) across the microphone unit in the telephone handset. Telephone companies have capacitors for this purpose, but will only service their own instruments. When such a case occurs, get in touch with the repair department of the phone company, giving the particulars. If you have purchased your instrument from the phone company, you will be billed for the service call if the warranty has expired. Section 500-150-100 of the Bell System Practices *Plant Series* gives detailed instructions; for the General Telephone System, refer to General System Practices *Engineering — Plant Series* Section 471-150-200. This section discusses causes and cures of telephone interference from radio signals. It points out that interference can come from corroded connections, unterminated loops and other sources. It correctly points out that the RF can be picked up on the drop wire coming into the house, and also on the wiring within the house, but the RF detection usually occurs inside the telephone instrument. The detection usually takes place at the varistors in the compensation networks, and/or at the receiver noise suppressor and the carbon microphone.

But interference suppression should be handled two ways: Prevent the RF from getting to the phone, and prevent it from being rectified.

A line of filters designed to eliminate telephone RFI generated by Amateur Radio transmitters operating in the 3- to 30-MHz range is available from K-COM. Model RF-1 uses standard, modular telephone connectors, and is intended for use adjacent to an affected telephone. Model RF-2 filters can be installed at any point in the wiring of an affected telephone system (service entrance, protector housing, inside jacks). For more information, contact K-COM, PO Box 82, Randolph, OH 44265.

Additional Information

In response to the many hundreds of thousands of RFI-related complaints it has received in recent years, the FCC has produced a booklet designed to show how to solve common RFI problems before they become serious. Titled *Interference Handbook,* it is available from the Government Printing Office, Washington, DC 20402. The ARRL publication, *Radio Frequency Interference,* covers all aspects of RFI and includes relevant parts of the FCC booklet.

Additional information can be found in the sources listed below.

Consumer Electronics Service Technician Interference Handbook — Audio Rectification (Washington, DC: CES, n.d.)*

Consumer Electronics Service Technician Interference Handbook — Television Interference (Washington, DC: CES, n.d.)*

Nelson, W. R., *Interference Handbook* (Wilton, CT: Radio Publications, 1981).

*Single copies of the interference handbooks for audio rectification and television interference may be obtained by writing to: Director of Consumer Affairs, Consumer Electronics Group, Electronic Industries Association, 2001 Eye St., N.W., Washington, DC 20006.

Printed-Circuit Board Etching Patterns

The following pages contain printed-circuit-board etching patterns for the projects in this book. All patterns are full size and are shown from the foil side. Black areas represent unetched copper. The companion parts layout for each pattern is shown with the project description.

More information on making PC boards may be found in Chapter 24. A list of suppliers of PC board and related materials may be found in Chapter 35.

In the interest of making best use of the space available, the patterns are not arranged in the same order the projects appear in the book. The contents list that follows will help you locate the pattern(s) for your project. In addition, each pattern is clearly labeled with the chapter and figure number of the parts-placement diagram.

Etching Pattern Contents

Project Name	Chapter	Fig. no. of parts-placement guide	Etching Pattern Page
A Digital TR Sequencer for Satellite Work	23	43	17
An IC Voltmeter	25	12	4
A 500-MHz Frequency Counter	25	29, 32,	3
		34	4
A Two-Tone Audio Generator	25	39	4
A Simple Inductance Meter	25	45	3
A Noise Bridge for 160 Through 10 Meters	25	65	4
An AF/RF Signal Injector	26	6	4
Crystal-Controlled Signal Source	26	7	4
A 5-A Switching-Regulator Supply	27	5	5
A 28-V, High-Current Power Supply	27	18	9
A 1.2- to 15-Volt, 5-Ampere Supply	27	23	5
The AA6PZ Power Charger	27	58	7
A Controlled Battery Charger for Emergency Power Supplies	27	61	10
Emergency Gelled-Electrolyte Battery Pack	27	68	7
A 2000-Volt Power Supply	27	72	8
An Audio Amplifier with AGC for Simple Receivers	28	10	5
An Expandable Headphone Mixer	28	13	6
An ATV Monitoring Instrument	28	16	10
A Simple CMOS Iambic Keyer	29	3	6
CW on a Chip	29	7	6
BOB—An EIA-232-D Break-out Box	29	21	12
An LSI Modem for Amateur Radio	29	15	13
The CMOS Super Keyer II	29	11	13
A Cubic Incher for 80, 40 and 30 Meters	30		14
The QRP Three-Bander Transceiver	30	29	14
A Portable QRP CW Transceiver	30	33	15
	30	37	15
A 1500-Watt Linear Amplifier	30	70	14
	30	71	14
TR Time-Delay Generator	31	22	7
Three-Watt Transmitting Converter for 6 Meters	31	38	8
A 2-kW PEP Amplifier for 50 to 54 MHz	31	96	16
A Medium-Power 144-MHz Amplifier	31	106	18
GaAsFET Preamplifier for 70 cm	32	6	16

Project Name	Chapter	Fig. no. of parts-placement guide	Etching Pattern Page
1296-MHz Solid-State Power Amplifiers	32	69	15
A Homemade DTMF Encoder	34	2	16
A Simple DTMF Decoder	34	7	17
Simple and Accurate QRP Directional Wattmeter	34	16	11
A Marker Generator for 100, 50 and 25 kHz	34	60	18

CAUTION:

Thoroughly check the printed pattern before you begin. In case of broken traces, continuity can be restored with a fine-point pen. Any ink bridges can be removed by careful scraping with a sharp, thin knife. Take time to be sure that these potential problems do not exist before you begin—it can save you much time later.

The scraping and drawing techniques described above for knife and pen can also be used to modify or customize patters. If you feel uneasy, practice on a photocopy to sharpen your skill.

Chapter 25, Fig. 29

Chapter 25, Fig. 32

Chapter 25, Fig. 45

Chapter 25, Fig. 34

Chapter 25, Fig. 39

Chapter 25, Fig. 65

Chapter 26, Fig. 6

Chapter 25, Fig. 12

Chapter 26, Fig. 7

Chapter 28, Fig. 10

Chapter 27, Fig. 5

Chapter 27, Fig. 23

Chapter 28, Fig 13

Chapter 29, Fig 3

Chapter 29, Fig. 7

Chapter 31, Fig. 22

Chapter 27, Fig. 68

Chapter 27, Fig. 58

Chapter 27, Fig. 72

Chapter 31, Fig. 38

28 V POWER SUPPLY

Chapter 27, Fig. 18

Chapter 28, Fig. 16 (Top)

Chapter 27, Fig. 61

Chapter 28, Fig. 16 (Bottom)

W7EL QRP WATTMETER - SOLDER SIDE

Chapter 34, Fig 16

Chapter 29, Fig. 21

Chapter 29, Fig 11

Chapter 29, Fig. 15

Chapter 30, Fig 29

Chapter 30, Fig 70

Chapter 30, Fig 71

Chapter 30

Chapter 30, Fig 33

Chapter 30, Fig 37

Chapter 32, Fig 69

Chapter 31, Fig. 96

Chapter 32, Fig. 6

Chapter 34, Fig. 2

Chapter 23, Fig 43

Chapter 34, Fig. 7

Chapter 31, Fig. 106A

Chapter 34, Fig 60

Chapter 31, Fig. 106B

18   Printed-Circuit Board Etching Patterns

Abbreviations List

These abbreviations, revised to conform with contemporary electronics and communications standards, appear in League publications.

a — atto (prefix for 10^{-18})
A — ampere (unit of electrical current)
ac — alternating current
ACC — Affiliated Club Coordinator
ACSSB — Amplitude-compandored single sideband
A/D — analog-to-digital
ADC — analog-to-digital converter
AF — audio frequency
AFC — automatic frequency control
AFSK — audio frequency-shift keying
AGC — automatic gain control
Ah — ampere hour
AIRS — ARRL Interference Reporting System
ALC — automatic level control
AM — amplitude modulation
AMTOR — Amateur Teleprinting Over Radio
ANT — antenna
ARA — Amateur Radio Association
ARC — Amateur Radio Club
ARES — Amateur Radio Emergency Service
ARQ — Automatic repeat request
ARS — Amateur Radio Society (Station)
ASCII — American National Standard Code for Information Interchange
ASSC — Amateur Satellite Service Council
ATC — Assistant Technical Coordinator
ATV — amateur television
AVC — automatic volume control
AWG — American wire gauge
az-el — azimuth-elevation

B — bel; blower
balun — balanced to unbalanced (transformer)
BC — broadcast
BCD — binary-coded decimal
BCI — broadcast interference
Bd — baud (bit/s in single-channel binary data transmission)
BER — bit error rate
BFO — beat-frequency oscillator
bit — binary digit
bit/s — bits per second
BM — Bulletin Manager
BPF — band-pass filter
BPL — Brass Pounders League
BT — battery
BW — bandwidth

c — centi (prefix for 10^{-2})
C — coulomb (quantity of electric charge); capacitor

CAC — Contest Advisory Committee
CATVI — cable-television interference
CB — Citizens Band (radio)
CBMS — computer-based message system
CCTV — closed-circuit television
CCW — coherent CW
ccw — counterclockwise
CD — civil defense
cm — centimeter
CMOS — complementary-symmetry metal-oxide semiconductor
coax — coaxial cable
COR — carrier-operated relay
CP — code proficiency (award)
CPU — central processing unit
CRT — cathode-ray tube
CT — center tap
CTCSS — continuous tone-coded squelch system
cw — clockwise
CW — continuous wave

d — deci (prefix for 10^{-1})
D — diode
da — deca (prefix for 10)
D/A — digital-to-analog
DAC — digital-to-analog converter
dB — decibel (0.1 bel)
dBi — decibels above (or below) isotropic antenna
dBm — decibels above (or below) 1 milliwatt
DBM — doubly balanced mixer
dBV — decibels above/below 1V (in video, relative to 1 V P-P)
dBW — decibels above/below 1 watt
dc — direct current
D-C — direct conversion
DEC — District Emergency Coordinator
deg — degree
DET — detector
DF — direction finding; direction finder
DIP — dual in-line package
DPDT — double-pole double-throw (switch)
DPSK — differential phase-shift keying
DPST — double-pole single-throw (switch)
DS — direct sequence (spread spectrum); display
DSB — double sideband
DTMF — dual-tone multifrequency
DVM — digital voltmeter
DX — long distance; duplex
DXAC — DX Advisory Committee
DXCC — DX Century Club

E — voltage
e — base of natural logarithms (2.71828)
EC — Emergency Coordinator

ECAC — Emergency Communications Advisory Committee
ECL — emitter-coupled logic
EHF — extremely high frequency (30-300 GHz)
EIRP — effective isotropic radiated power
ELF — extremely low frequency
EMC — electromagnetic compatibility
EME — earth-moon-earth (moonbounce)
EMF — electromotive force
EMI — electromagnetic interference
EMP — electromagnetic pulse
EPROM — erasable programmable read-only memory

f — femto (prefix for 10^{-15}); frequency
F — farad (capacitance unit); fuse
fax — facsimile
FD — Field Day
FET — field-effect transistor
FL — filter
FM — frequency modulation
FSK — frequency-shift keying
ft — foot (unit of length)

g — gram (unit of mass)
G — giga (prefix for 10^9)
GaAs — gallium arsenide
GDO — grid- or gate-dip oscillator
GHz — gigahertz
GND — ground

h — hecto (prefix for 10^2)
H — henry (unit of inductance)
HF — high frequency (3-30 MHz)
HFO — high-frequency oscillator
HPF — highest probable frequency; high-pass filter
Hz — hertz (unit of frequency)

I — current, indicating lamp
IC — integrated circuit
ID — identification; inside diameter
IF — intermediate frequency
IMD — intermodulaiton distortion
in. — inch (unit of length)
in./s — inch per second (unit of velocity.
I/O — input/output
IRC — international reply coupon
ITF — Interference Task Force

j — operator for complex notation, as for reactive component of an impedance (+ j inductive; − j capacitive)
J — joule (kg m²/s²) (energy or work unit); jack
JFET — junction field-effect transistor

k — kilo (prefix for 10^3); Boltzmann's constant (1.38×10^{-23} J/K)

K — kelvin (used without degree symbol) (absolute temperature scale); relay
kBd — 1000 bauds
kbit — 1024 bits
kbit/s — 1000 bits per second
kbyte — 1024 bytes
kg — kilogram
kHz — kilohertz
km — kilometer
kV — kilovolt
kW — kilowatt
kΩ — kilohm

l — liter (liquid volume)
L — lambert; inductor
lb — pound (force unit)
LC — inductance-capacitance
LCD — liquid crystal display
LED — light-emitting diode
LF — low frequency (30-300 kHz)
LHC — left-hand circular (polarization)
LO — local oscillator; League Official
LP — log periodic
LS — loudspeaker
LSB — lower sideband
LSI — large-scale integration

m — meter; milli (prefix for 10^{-3})
M — mega (prefix for 10^6); meter
mA — milliampere
mAh — millamperehour
MDS — Multipoint Distribution Service; minimum discernible (or detectable) signal
MF — medium frequency (300-3000 kHz)
mH — millihenry
mho — mho (use siemens)
MHz — megahertz
mi — mile, statute (unit of length)
mi/h — mile per hour
mi/s — mile per second
mic — microphone
min — minute (time)
MIX — mixer
mm — millimeter
MOD — modulator
modem — modulator/demodulator
MOS — metal-oxide semiconductor
MOSFET — metal-oxide semiconductor field-effect transistor
MS — meteor scatter
ms — millisecond
m/s — meters per second
MSI — medium-scale integration
MUF — maximum usable frequency
mV — millivolt
mW — milliwatt
MΩ — megohm

n — nano (prefix for 10^{-9})
NBFM — narrow-band frequency modulation
NC — no connection; normally closed
NCS — net-control station; National Communications System
nF — nanofarad
NF — noise figure
nH — nanohenry
NiCd — nickel cadmium

NM — Net Manager
NMOS — N-channel metal-oxide silicon
NO — normally open
NPN — negative-positive-negative (transistor)
NR — Novice Roundup (contest)
ns — nanosecond
NTS — National Traffic System

OBS — Official Bulletin Station
OD — outside diameter
OES — Official Emergency Station
OO — Official Observer
op amp — operational amplifier
ORS — Official Relay Station
OSC — oscillator (schematic diagram abbrev.)
OTC — Old Timer's Club
OTS — Official Traffic Station
oz — ounce (force unit, 1/16 pound)

p — pico (prefix for 10^{-12})
P — power; plug
PA — power amplifier
PAM — pulse-amplitude modulation
PC — printed circuit
PEP — peak envelope power
PEV — peak envelope voltage
pF — picofarad
pH — picohenry
PIA — Public Information Assistant
PIN — positive-intrinsic-negative (transistor)
PIO — Public Information Officer
PIV — peak inverse voltage
PLL — phase-locked loop
PM — phase modulation
PMOS — P-channel (type) metal-oxide semiconductor
PNP — positive-negative-positive (transistor)
pot — potentiometer
P-P — peak to peak
ppd — postpaid
PRAC — Public Relations Advisory Committee
PROM — programmable read-only memory
PSHR — Public Service Honor Roll
PTO — permeability-tuned oscillator
PTT — push to talk

Q — figure of merit (tuned circuit); transistor
QRP — low power (less than 5-W output)

R — resistor (schematic diagram abbrev.)
RACES — Radio Amateur Civil Emergency Service
RAM — random-access memory
RC — resistance-capacitance
R/C — radio control
RCC — Rag Chewers' Club
RF — radio frequency
RFC — radio-frequency choke
RFI — radio-frequency interference
RHC — right-hand circular (polarization)
RIT — receiver incremental tuning

RLC — resistance-inductance-capacitance
RM — rule making (number assigned to petition)
r/min — revolution per minute
RMS — root mean square
ROM — read-only memory
r/s — revolution per second
RST — readability-strength-tone
RTTY — radioteletype
RX — receiver, receiving

s — second (time)
S — siemens (unit of conductance); switch
SASE — self-addressed stamped envelope
SEC — Section Emergency Coordinator
SET — Simulated Emergency Test
SGL — State Government Liaison
SHF — super-high frequency (3-30 GHz)
SM — Section manager; silver mica (capacitor)
S/N — signal-to-noise (ratio)
SPDT — single-pole double-throw (switch)
SPST — single-pole single-throw (switch)
SS — Sweepstakes; spread spectrum
SSB — single sideband
SSC — Special Service Club
SSI — small-scale integration
SSTV — slow-scan television
STM — Section Traffic Manager
SX — simplex
sync — synchronous, synchronizing
SWL — shortwave listener
SWR — standing-wave ratio

T — tera (prefix for 10^{12}); transformer (schematic diagram abbrev.)
TA — Technical Advisor
TC — Technical Coordinator
TCC — Transcontinental Corps
TD — Technical Department (ARRL HQ)
tfc — traffic
TR — transmit/receive
TTL — transistor-transistor logic
TTY — teletypewriter
TV — television
TVI — television interference
TX — transmitter, transmitting

U — integrated circuit
UHF — ultra-high frequency (300 MHz to 3 GHz)
USB — upper sideband
UTC — Coordinated Universal Time
UV — ultraviolet

V — volt; vacuum tube (schematic diagram abbrev.)
VCO — voltage-controlled oscillator
VCR — video cassette recorder
VDT — video-display terminal
VE — Volunteer Examiner
VEC — Volunteer Examiner Coordinator
VFO — variable-frequency oscillator

VHF — very-high frequency (30-300 MHz)
VLF — very-low frequency (3-30 kHz)
VLSI — very-large-scale integration
VMOS — vertical metal-oxide semiconductor
VOM — volt-ohm meter
VOX — voice operated switch
VR — voltage regulator
VRAC — VHF Repeater Advisory Committee
VSWR — voltage standing-wave ratio
VTVM — vacuum-tube voltmeter
VUAC — VHF/UHF Advisory Committee
VUCC — VHF/UHF Century Club
VXO — variable crystal oscillator

W — watt (kg m^{2}s^{-3}, unit of power)
WAC — Worked All Continents
WARC — World Administrative Radio Conference
WAS — Worked All States
WBFM — wide-band frequency modulation
Wh — watthour
WPM — words per minute
WVDC — working voltage, direct current

X — reactance
XCVR — transceiver
XFMR — transformer
XO — crystal oscillator
XTAL — crystal
XVTR — transverter

Y — crystal (schematic diagram abbrev.)
YIG — yttrium iron garnet

Z — impedance; also see UTC

5BDXCC — Five-Band DXCC
5BWAC — Five-Band WAC
5BWAS — Five-Band WAS
6BWAC — Six-Band WAC

° — degree (plane angle)
°C — degree Celsius (temperature)
°F — degree Fahrenheit (temperature)
α — (alpha) angles; coefficients, attenuation constant, absorption factor, area, common-base forward current-transfer ratio of a bipolar transistor
β — (beta) angles; coefficients, phase constant current gain of common-emitter transistor amplifiers
γ — (gamma) specific gravity, angles, electrical conductivity, propagation constant
Γ — (gamma) complex propagation constant
δ — (delta) increment or decrement, density angles
Δ — (delta) increment or decrement determinant, permittivity
ϵ — (epsilon) dielectric constant, permittivity, electric intensity
ζ — (zeta) coordinates, coefficients
η — (eta) intrinsic impedance, efficiency, surface charge density, hysteresis, coordinate

θ — (theta) angular phase displacement, time constant, reluctance, angles
ι — (iota) unit vector
K — (kappa) susceptibility, coupling coefficient
λ — (lambda) wavelength, attenuation constant
Λ — (lambda) permeance
μ — (mu) permeability, amplification factor, micro (prefix for 10^{-6})
μC — microcomputer
μF — microfarad
μH — microhenry
μP — microprocessor
ξ — (xi) coordinates
π — (pi) 3.14159
ρ — (rho) resistivity, volume charge density, coordinates, reflection coefficient
σ — (sigma) surface charge density, complex propagation constant, electrical conductivity, leakage coefficient, deviation
Σ — (sigma) summation
τ — (tau) time constant, volume resistivity, time-phase displacement, transmission factor, density
ϕ — (phi) magnetic flux, angles
Φ — (phi) summation
χ — (chi) electric susceptibility, angles
ψ — (psi) dielectric flux, phase difference, coordinates, angles
ω — (omega) angular velocity 2πf
Ω — (omega) resistance in ohms, solid angle

Index

[Editor's Note: Except for commonly used phrases and abbreviations, topics are indexed by their noun name. Many topisc are also cross-indexed, especially when noun modifiers appear (such as "voltage amplifier" and "amplifier voltage"). For topics having extended coverage, only the first page of presentation is listed. Numerous terms and abbreviations pertaining to Amateur Radio but not contained in the index may be found in the glossaries indexed herein.]

A

A_L (toroid inductance index): 2-34
Abbreviations, CW: 37-6
Above mean sea level (AMSL): 14-2
Absorption of radio waves: 22-7
AC: 2-4
  In a capacitor: 2-16
  Waveform measurements: 2-12
  Waveforms: 2-4
AC line, decoupling RF from: 39-8
AC line filter: 39-14, 39-16
Access time (memory): 8-25
Accumulator: 8-27
Acoustical field strength (dB): 2-7
Acquisition of signal (AOS): 20-26
ACSSB: 7-9, 18-1, 18-17
Active detectors, product: 18-12
Active filters: 28-4
Active mixers: 12-15, 12-15
Active region (transistor): 4-21
Activity nights (VHF, UHF): 37-4
Adapters, cross family: 35-29
Adcock arrays: 38-3, 38-15
Addressing, computer memory: 8-24
Admittance: 2-38
Advanced TIROS-N (ATN) satellites: 20-25
Advanced Very High Resolution Radiometer (AVHRR imaging): 20-25
Aeronautical charts, direction finding: 38-7
AF:
  Derived AGC: 12-10, 12-29
  Oscillators: 25-20
  Oscillators, wide range: 25-20
  Signal injector: 26-5
  Two-tone generator: 25-21
AFSK: 19-12, 23-29
AGC: 12-10, 12-26, 12-28
  AF derived: 12-10, 12-29
  Applied to IF stages: 12-25
  Audio derived: 28-6
  Failure: 26-15
  IF derived: 12-10
  Range in receivers: 12-6
  RF derived: 12-29
  With audio amplifier: 28-6
Air dielectric capacitors: 26-22
Air-core baluns: 16-9
Aircraft emergency-locator-transmitter (ELT) monitor: 14-13
Aircraft, downed, location by radio: 38-1, 38-18
ALC: 7-8
Alert frequency: 37-1
Alias frequency: 8-20
Alignment: 26-14, 26-15
Alignment of dish antennas: 32-56
Allocations, amateur frequency: 37-1
Alpha cutoff: 4-18
Alpha, of transistors: 4-17
Alternating current (see also AC): 2-4
Alternator: 2-4, 36-37
Aluminum: 4-1
  Finishing: 24-6
  Properties: 35-36
  Tubing, standard sizes (Table): 33-4
Amateur Auxiliary: 38-1, 39-3, 39-4

Amateur bands:
  Relationship with TV channels: 39-16
Amateur beacon stations: 22-12
Amateur frequencies: 37-1
Amateur Radio: 1-1
  Band plans: 37-3
  Equipment manufacturers: 36-42
  Getting started: 1-2
  History: 18-1, 21-14, 23-4
  Power limits: 37-2
Amateur Radio direction finding (ARDF): 38-1
Amateur Radio Emergency Service, ARRL (see also ARES): 37-15, 37-16
Amateur television (see also ATV, FSTV, FMTV and SSTV): 20-1
Ampere: 2-2
Amplification:
  In tunnel diodes: 4-14
Amplification factor: 5-3
Amplifier:
  Transistor instability: 2-42
Amplifiers:
  Audio: 4-32
  Audio, ac line filter: 39-16
  Audio, IC: 4-38
  Audio, transistor: 4-21
  Audio, with AGC: 28-6
  Broadband: 4-23, 11-8, 12-12
  Cascade: 5-5
  Cascode: 4-32, 12-14
  Cathode follower: 5-8
  Cavity: 32-29
  Circuit symptoms and faults: 26-19
  Classes of operation: 3-17, 5-4, 5-5, 5-6, 15-1
  Combined DBM/IF: 12-23
  Common-emitter design example (HF): 15-20
  Cooling: 15-12
  Design, guidelines and examples: 15-15
  Differential, transistor: 4-19
  Direct coupled: 4-22
  Distortion: 26-10
  Driver and output stages: 7-6
  Duty cycle: 15-9
  Efficiency of: 15-1, 15-2
  Failure: 15-20
  Feedback: 15-20
  For 144 MHz, medium power: 15-18
  For 6 meters using the 3CX800A7: 31-31
  For HF, broadband solid state: 15-20
  For HF, high power vacuum tube: 15-15
  Gain: 3-15, 26-9
  Gain control: 7-5
  Grounded grid: 5-8
  Grounded-cathode design example (VHF): 15-18
  Grounded-grid design example (HF): 15-15
  High power, for 222 MHz: 31-54
  IF: 12-26
  IF, small signal: 4-40
  Impedance matching: 15-2
  Input impedance: 11-9
  Instability, at low frequencies: 15-21
  Legal-limit, 1.8 to 30 MHz: 30-41
  Linearity in: 15-1
  Low noise: 12-12
  Medium power, for 144 MHz: 31-39
  MOSFET: 12-14
  Narrow-band: 4-23
  Neutralization: 15-21
  Noise: 26-9
  Operating impedances of: 15-1
  Operational, IC, specifications: 35-23
  Oscillations: 26-10
  Output filtering: 15-8
  Overload: 12-13
  Parallel: 5-5
  Phase inversion (speech): 7-5
  Power: 5-4
  Push-pull: 5-5
  Push-pull, broadband: 4-25
  RF: 12-9, 12-12, 12-13
  RF and IF, FET: 4-32
  RF power: 15-1
  RF power, bibliography: 15-22

  RF power, transistor: 4-23
  RF, small signal: 4-40
  RF, transistor: 4-22
  Sample-and-hold: 8-23
  Solid state v vacuum tube: 15-1
  Speech: 7-4
  Speech, construction: 7-5
  Speech, op amp: 7-4
  Spurious emission limits: 39-8
  Stability: 12-12
  Stabilization: 15-20
  Tank circuits: 15-3
  Transformer-coupled: 5-5
  Transistor: 4-18
  Transistor, feedback: 4-22
  Transistor, FET: 4-33, 4-37
  Triode: 3-14
  Troubleshooting: 26-9
  Tube v solid-state: 11-1
  Vacuum tubes: 5-2
  VHF: 12-13, 12-15
  Video transmitters: 20-3
  Voltage: 5-4, 7-5
  3CX800A7 for 144 MHz: 31-46
  250-watt for 23-cm: 32-29
  1296-MHz Linear: 32-18
  1296-MHz Solid-state power: 32-19
  1500-watt, using 3-500Z tubes: 30-50
  2 kW PEP, for 50 MHz: 31-35
  2 kW PEP, for 144 MHz: 31-51
Amplitude compandored SSB (ACSSB): 7-9, 9-6, 18-1, 18-17
Amplitude modulation (AM): 9-2
Amplitude-shift keying (ASK—see also CW): 9-8
AMRAD (Amateur Radio Research and Development Corp): 21-14
AMSAT: 23-29
  Operating software: 23-30
AMSAT Journal, The: 23-30
AMSAT-NA Technical Journal: 23-26
AMSAT-OSCAR 8: 21-3
AMSAT-OSCAR 10: 23-1, 23-2, 23-3
AMSAT-OSCAR 13: 23-1, 23-2, 23-3
AMSAT-OSCAR 16: 23-29
AMTOR: 9-10, 19-14, 21-6
  APLink: 19-16
  Mailboxes: 19-16
  Mode A: 19-15
  Mode B: 19-15
  Operating: 19-16, 37-4
  References: 19-16
  SITOR SWL operation: 19-16
  TEX/AMTEX/NAVTEX: 19-16
Analog multiplexer: 8-22
Analog switch ICs: 8-22
Analog telephony: 9-5
Analog-to-digital (A/D) converter: 8-20
Analog-to-digital conversion (ADC): 8-19
Analysis, of single-tuned circuits: 3-6
Anchoring:
  Antenna supports: 36-22, 36-23
  Guy anchors: 36-23, 36-23
AND gate: 8-2
Angle:
  Conduction: 5-6
  Modulation: 9-3, 9-6
  Of radiation: 17-2
Angle modulation: 9-3, 9-6
Annie, program for plotting antenna patterns: 17-3
Anode: 5-1
Answer mode (data communications): 19-31
Antenna Book, The ARRL: 23-26
Antenna Controller, Automatic: 23-20
Antenna effect in loop antennas: 38-1
Antennas: 17-1
  Accessories, satellite: 23-18
  Annie, program for plotting patterns: 17-3
  As loads: 16-4
  Assembling: 36-21
  ATV: 20-3
  Bandwidth: 17-2
  Beam tilting (repeaters): 14-3
  Beams, 2- and 3-element: 17-15
  Beams, construction of: 33-4
  Choice of: 17-1
  Circular polarization: 23-5

(Antennas, continued)

Conductor size:.....................17-3
Correcting imbalance:..............38-9
Cross boom construction:...........23-14
Current and voltage distribution:....17-3, 17-7
Delta loops:.......................17-17
Design of helical antennas:........23-44
Diameter vs length:................17-3
Dipoles, bent:.....................17-6
Dipoles, folded:...................16-6
Dipoles, helically wound:..........17-6
Dipoles, trap:.....................17-6
Direction-finding:......See Antennas, RDF
Directivity:.......................17-8
Drooping dipole:...................17-5
Dummy:........25-21, 26-4, 34-24, 34-26
EME:...............................23-44
Feed methods:......................17-4
Ferrite rod:.......................38-2
FMTV:..............................20-10
Folded dipole:.....................16-6
Folded unipole:....................17-12
Gain:.........................17-7, 17-18
Gain vs spacing:...................17-15
Ground plane, for VHF and UHF:....33-32
Half sloper:.......................17-13
Height:............................17-1
Helical, for 432 MHz:..............33-28
Impedance:..............17-1, 17-2, 17-7
Impedance matching:................17-19
Installation:......................36-31
Installation, PVRC mount:.....36-32, 36-32
Insulators:........................33-2
Inverted-V:........................33-9
Isotropic radiator:................14-2
J-beam:............................20-3
J-pole, two-band:.............23-27, 23-29
Length of 1/2 wavelength:..........17-3
Loading-coil dimensions, suggested
   (Table):........................33-17
Long wire:.........................17-7
Loop:..............................38-1
Loop skywire, the:.................33-6
Loop Yagis for 23 cm:..............33-35
Loop, with sensing element for
   28 MHz:.........................38-11
Loops, small, transmitting:........38-10
Loopstick for 1.8 MHz:.............38-12
Loopstick for 3.5 MHz:.............38-13
Maintenance:.......................36-34
Marconi:...........................17-11
Matching:..........................33-16
Matching to transmission lines:.....16-3
Microwave dish alignment:..........32-56
Minooka Special:...................17-12
Mobile whip, approximate values for 8-foot
   (Table):........................33-16
Mobile, 222 MHz, 5/8-wave:.........33-31
Mobile, HF:........................33-16
Mode-L helical array for
   OSCAR 13:.......................23-44
Multiband inverted-V:..............33-9
Noise bridge:......................25-32
Parasitic excitation:..............17-15
Pattern, cardioid:.........38-3, 38-12,
                          38-14, 38-18
Polarization:................17-1, 17-18
Polarization and gain of AO-10 and AO-13
   (Table):........................23-5
Polarization for ATV:..............20-4
Portable:....................33-14, 36-40
Projects:..........................33-1
Quads:.......................17-14, 17-17
Radial networks:...................17-13
Radiation angle of:................17-2
Radiation characteristics:.........17-3
Raising:...........................36-31
Random length, coupling to:........16-10
RDF:.........38-1, 38-8, 38-10, 38-11, 38-12,
             38-13, 38-14, 38-15, 38-16
Repeater:..........................14-3
RF field strengths near:...........36-4
Rod:...............................38-2
Rotation, electronic:..............38-5
Rotator systems:...................36-33
Rotators for satellite work:.......23-13
Routing cables:....................36-20
Satellite:........23-11, 23-12, 23-20, 23-44

Satellite, 70-cm and 2-m
   J-pole:................23-27, 23-29
Sensing:...........................38-2
Stacking of Yagis:.................17-20
Supports:.............36-21, 36-22, 36-23
Top loading:.......................33-18
Trap verticals:....................17-14
Troubleshooting:...................26-13
Tuning adjustments:................17-16
TV, installation:..................39-14
UHF:...............................17-18
Vertical:..........................17-10
Vertical, 1/4-λ for 144, 222 and
   440 MHz:........................33-32
Vertical, 144 MHz, 5/8 wave:.......33-30
Vertical, 5/8-wave for 12 and
   17 meters:......................33-10
Vertical, construction of:.........33-4
Vertical, short:...................17-12
Vertical, VHF 1/4 wave:............33-32
VHF:...............................17-18
Weather satellite:.................20-29
Wire, construction:................33-1
Wire, stressed (Table):............33-2
Wire, supporting:..................36-21
With driven elements:..............17-8
Wullenweber:.......................38-5
X-Beams:...........................33-15
X-beams, dimensions for full-size
   (Table):........................33-15
X-beams, dimensions for minimum-size
   (Table):........................33-15
Yagi:..............................17-14
Yagi, high performance, 144 MHz:...33-25
Yagi, high performance, 222 MHz:...33-28
Yagi, high performance, 432 MHz:...33-21
Yagi, VHF and UHF:.................33-19
Zepp:..............................17-5
Zepp, EDZ for 12 meters:...........33-11
1/2 wavelength:....................17-3
5/8-λ vertical antenna, 12- and 17-meter
   specifications for (Table):.....33-10
30-meter ground-plane, a tree-mounted:33-8
144-MHz Yagi family, specifications for
   (Table):........................33-25
222-MHz Yagi family, specifications for
   (Table):........................33-28
432-MHz Yagi family, specifications for
   (Table):........................33-21
Anticyclone (high-pressure system):....22-17
Antimony:..........................4-1
Antiresonant notch:................14-5
AO-16 (PACSAT):....................23-29
Apparent power:....................2-26
Application Notes:
   M/A-COM AN80-2:.................4-31
   Motorola AN-267:...............11-11
   Motorola AN-271:...............11-11
Arcing:............................26-13
ARES:
   Book messages:..................37-22
   Emergency communication principles:.37-15
   Emergency coordinator:.........37-15
   HF net structure:..............37-19
   Local net structure:...........37-18
   Local structure:...............37-16
   Message checking:..............37-22
   Net operating practices:.......37-22
   NTS interaction:...............37-18
   NTS message format:............37-19
   Packet radio message handling:.37-24
   Personal checklist Table:......37-15
   Q signals:.....................37-23
   Section-level structure:.......37-16
Arithmetic Logic Unit (ALU):.......8-27
Arrays:
   Adcock:...................38-3, 38-15
   Broadside:.....................17-9
   Collinear:................17-8, 17-21
   Combined types:................17-10
   End fire:......................17-9
   Phased:........................38-3
   Phased, for 144 MHz RDF:.......38-14
ARRL:
   Amateur Radio Emergency Service (see
      also ARES):.................37-15
   ARES/NTS interaction:..........37-18
   Assistant Technical Coordinator:...39-4

Board of Directors:................1-4
Educational Activities Department:....1-2
Field Organization:............1-5, 39-4
Field Services Department:.........37-15
Leadership:........................1-4
Membership:........................1-6
Membership services:...............1-5
Numbered radiograms:...............37-21
Official Observer program:.........39-4
Operating awards:..................37-10
Operating awards, Table:...........37-12
Organization Chart:................1-4
Parts suppliers list:..............35-38
Procedural signal (prosign) Table:....37-6
QSL bureaus:.......................37-10
RFI immunity complaint reports:....39-3
RFI Task Group:....................39-4
Section map:.......................37-13
Volunteer Monitoring:..............39-4
ARRL Antenna Book:.................23-26
*ARRL Computer Networking Conference
   Proceedings*:....................23-30
Arsenic:...........................4-1
ASCII:........................19-17, 21-6
   Bauds vs bits per second:......19-19
   Bibliography:..................19-20
   Control characters:............19-18
   Data rates:....................19-18
   Operating:.....................37-5
   RTTY operation:................19-19
   Serial transmission:...........19-18
Assembly language:.................8-34
Assembly, antennas:................36-21
Assistant Technical Coordinator (ATC),
   ARRL:...........................39-4
Astable multivibrator:.............8-8
Astronauts:........................1-4
Asynchronous communications:.......8-17
AT&T mu-law (A/D):.................8-22
Atom:..............................2-1
Attenuation:.......................2-37
   Of twisted wire pairs:.........3-13
Attenuation formula (for filters):....2-41
Attenuator, frequency selective:.....15-20
Attenuator, PIN diode as:..........4-13
Attenuators:.......................12-11
   Direction finding:.............38-7
   Low-power step:................25-37
   Resistive network tables:......25-39
ATV:...............................21-6
   And computers:.................20-1
   And model airplanes:...........20-1
   And NASA:......................20-2
   And Satcom 1R (commercial satel-
      lite):......................20-2
   And STS-9 (space shuttle):.....20-2
   And teleconferencing:..........20-1
   And the Civil Air Patrol:......20-1
   And the National Weather Service:..20-1
   And the space shuttle:.........20-1
   Antenna polarization:..........20-3
   Antennas for:..................20-3
   FM-A5 sound-subcarrier generator:..20-7
   Frequency coordination:........20-2
   Interdigital filter:...........20-4
   Linear amplifiers:.............20-4
   Linearity:.....................20-3
   Monitoring instrument:.........28-8
   Operating:.....................37-5
   Overmodulation:................20-7
   Picture reporting system:......37-10
   Pixel:.........................20-2
   Receivers for:.................20-3
   Receiving preamp and converter:...20-4
   Repeater design books:.........20-4
   Repeaters:.....................20-4
   Sync stretcher:...........20-3, 20-6
   Sync-to-video ratio:...........20-3
   Test chart:....................20-19
   Transmission lines:............20-3
   Transmitters:.............20-3, 20-4
   TVC-1b receiving converter:....20-5
   TXA5 exciter:..................20-6
   Vestigial sideband transmission:....20-4
   Video adjustment:..............20-3
   Video information:.............20-2
   White out:.....................20-3

Audio:.................................7-1
  Amplifier with AGC:...............28-6
  FET power amplifier:..............4-37
  Filters:.....................28-1, 28-3
  Frequencies (AF):.................2-5
  Frequency-shift keying (AFSK):....9-11
  Noise limiters:...................12-32
  Peak filters:.....................13-11
  Phasing networks:.................18-8
  Subcarrier demodulator (FMTV):....20-10
  Transmission, for FSTV:...........20-4
Aurora:..........22-7, 22-12, 22-13, 22-15
Authentication:.........................21-6
Automatic control (repeaters):..........14-1
Automatic level control:................7-8
Automatic Picture Transmission
  (APT):..............................20-26
Autopatches (repeaters):................14-11
Autotransformers:.......................2-32
Auxiliary operation:....................21-3
Average voltage:........................2-12
Average vs peak power:..................18-13
Awards, operating, ARRL, Table:.........37-12
AX.25:.........................19-38, 23-29
Azimuth and elevation of celestial bodies,
  calculator program for determining
  (Table).............................23-47
Azimuth and elevation of celestial bodies,
  computer program for determining
  (Table).............................23-48
Azimuth and elevation of the moon:......23-47
Azimuthal equidistant projection:.......38-8

B

Back EMF:.......................2-17, 2-21
Back pressure (cooling):................15-13
Back resistance:........................4-2
Backplane (computer):...................8-28
Backscatter:..................22-9, 22-12, 22-14
Balance, electrostatic, in loop antennas
  for direction finding:..............38-1
Balanced mixer:.........................4-27
Balanced mixers:.........12-16, 12-17, 12-19,
                12-21, 12-23
Balanced modulators:...............18-3, 18-4
Balanced-emitter transistor (BET):......4-17
Baluns:...............3-12, 11-12, 16-7
  Air-core:.........................16-9
  And Transmatches:.................17-20
  Bazooka:....................14-3, 16-7
  Choke:............................16-9
  Coax shield chokes:...............39-7
  Coil:.............................16-9
  Construction (broadband):.........16-9
  Effective choke (current) (Table):..16-9
  Failures:.........................26-13
  Ferrite core:.....................16-9
  Linear:...........................16-7
  Sleeve:...........................16-7
  Toroidal:.........................16-9
  Voltage:..........................16-8
  W2DU:.............................16-9
Band plans, amateur:....................37-3
Band-pass circuit:
  Resonant cavity:..................14-5
Band-pass filter:...........2-39, 28-1, 28-3
Band-stop filter:.......................2-39
Bands, amateur frequency:...............37-1
Bandswitching:..........................15-17
Bandwidth:...............2-28, 2-41, 9-1
  And rise time, relationships (Table):...7-19
  Assigned frequency band:..........9-1
  ATV:..............................20-3
  Frequency tolerance:..............9-1
  FSTV:.............................20-3
  In linear translators and
    transponders:..................14-20
  In tank circuits:.................15-18
  Necessary:........................9-1
  Necessary bandwidths, examples of CCIR
    (Table).......................9-2
  Occupied:.........................9-1
  Of antennas:......................17-2
  Oscilloscope:.....................25-28
  Required for APT:.................20-29
  Variable, tuning:.................13-9
  Visual display:...................8-31
Bardeen, John:..........................4-16

Barrier voltage, semiconductor junction:...4-2
Base diagrams:
  IC op amps:.......................35-24
  Vacuum tubes:.....................35-7
Base injection (mixers):................4-27
Base-emitter resistance:................4-17
Baseband:...............................9-1
BASIC:.........................8-33, 8-35
BASICODE:...............................8-29
Batteries:
  AA6PZ power charger:..............27-10
  Alkaline:.........................6-35
  Capacity:.........................6-35
  Carbon-zinc:......................6-35
  Controlled charger:...............27-13
  Deep-cycle:.......................6-35
  Discharge planning:...............6-36
  Eliminator for FM portables:......27-8
  Emergency Gelled-Electrolyte:.....27-15
  Gel-cell:.........................6-35
  Lead-acid:........................6-35
  Lithium:..........................6-35
  Mercury:..........................6-35
  Nickel-cadmium:...................6-35
  Overcharging:.....................6-36
  Power:............................6-35
  Primary:..........................6-35
  Rechargeable:.....................6-35
  Recharging:.......................6-36
  Silver-oxide:.....................6-35
  Storage:..........................6-35
  Storage, caring for:..............6-36
Baudot:........................9-10, 19-10
  Code:.............................21-6
  Computer-based terminals:.........19-11
  Speeds and signaling rates:.......19-11
Bauds:..................................8-18
Bazooka baluns:...............14-3, 16-7
Beacons:................................22-11
Beam forming, electronic:...............38-5
Beam power tubes:.......................5-8
Beam tilting (repeater antennas):.......14-3
Beat frequency:.........................2-5
Beat note:..............................2-5
Bell 103 (modem):.......................9-12
Bell 202 (modem):.......................9-12
Bell Labs:..............................4-16
Bell Telephone System (RFI):............39-18
Benchmark program:......................8-27
Bending sheet metal:....................24-5
Bessel, F. W.:..........................9-4
Beta, of transistors:...................4-17
BFO:.......................12-10, 12-29
Bi-phase modulation (BPSK):.............20-29
Bias:..........................5-4, 5-9
  Cathode:..........................3-16
  Distortion:.......................8-19
  Grid:.............................15-11
  Stabilization, diode:.............4-5
  Transistor:.......................15-12
Bibliographies:
  Digital Basics:...................8-36
  Fax:..............................20-32
  Filters:..........................2-43
  FMTV:.............................20-14
  FSTV:.............................20-7
  Modulation, multiplexing and demodula-
    tion:.........................9-13
  Oscilloscopes:....................25-30
  RDF:......................38-16, 38-20
  RF power amplifiers:..............15-22
  RFI:..............................39-18
  Satellites:.......................23-50
  Selected HF propagation:..........22-12
  Selected VHF/UHF propagation:.....22-18
  Spread spectrum:..................21-17
  Transmission lines:...............16-15
  Troubleshooting and repairs:......26-29
  Weather satellites:...............20-32
Bifilar windings:..................3-9, 24-8
Bilateral switch ICs:...................8-22
Binary digital systems:.................8-1
Binary number system:..................8-6
Binary-coded decimal number
  system:...........................8-6
Binary-coded decimal Table:.............8-6
Bipolar keying (digital signaling):.....8-19
Bipolar transistors:.............4-16, 26-24

Bistable multivibrator:.................8-2
Bit:....................................8-1
Bits per second (bits/s):...............8-18
Blankers, noise:........................12-31
Bleeder resistance:.....................6-7
  Minimum load:.....................6-9
Block diagrams:.........................26-7
  Computer fax station:.............20-31
  FMTV station:................20-8, 20-9
  FSTV station:.....................20-2
  Linear translator:................14-19
  RF control-link:..................14-17
  SSTV station:.....................20-16
  Transmitters:.....................11-3
Block receivers, and FMTV:..............20-10
Blower performance, specifications:.....15-13
Boards:
  Perforated construction:..........24-10
  Solderless prototype:.............24-10
Boltzmann's constant:..............4-2, 12-2
Boolean algebra:
  DeMorgan's Theorem:...............8-2
  Identities:.......................8-2
  Theorems Table:...................8-2
  Truth table:......................8-2
Boost converters:.......................6-27
Boron:..................................4-13
Boundaries, and propagation:............38-6
Boundary, semiconductor:................4-1
Bowdoin expedition:...................1-3
Brag tape:..............................37-4
Brattain, Walter H.:....................4-16
Break (voice operating):................37-4
Break-in:...............................19-7
Break-out box:..........................29-25
Breakdown voltage, transistor:..........4-21
Breakdown, insulator:...................2-2
Bridge circuits:........................25-4
  AC:...............................25-9
  Noise bridge for 160 through
    10 meters:....................25-32
  Wheatstone:.......................25-5
Broadband:
  Amplifier design example:.........15-20
  IF responses:.....................12-24
  RF amplifiers:....................12-12
  RF transformers:..................3-8
  Transformers:.....................11-12
  Transistor driver:................11-8
Broadcast reception, interference:......39-17
Broadside arrays:.......................17-9
Broadside phased arrays:................38-3
Brute-force ac line filter:.............39-14
Bubble memory:..........................8-26
Buck converters:........................6-25
Buck-boost converters:..................6-27
Buckshot noise (SSTV):..................20-17
Buffer stages:..........................10-6
Buffer, noninverting logic:.............8-3
Bulletin schedule, W1AW:................37-5
Bunny hunting:..........................38-1
Bureaus, QSL (ARRL):....................37-10
Bus:....................................8-11
  IEEE-488-1978:....................8-28
  Microcomputer:....................8-28
  S-100:............................8-28
Bus master:.............................8-28
Butterworth filter:.....................2-39
Bypassing:..............................3-1
  Voltage regulators:...............6-18
Byte registers:.........................8-8

C

C (computer language):..................8-36
Cable:
  Antenna, routing:.........36-20, 36-20
  Lacing:...........................24-7
  On towers:........................17-13
  Types:............................36-13
  Wiring:...........................24-7
Cable television RFI (CATVI):.....39-3, 39-4
Cable, coaxial:
  In transformers:..................15-8
  Types:............................36-12
Calculating inductance:.................2-17
Call sign:
  DX prefixes:......................37-5

(Call sign, continued)
FCC-allocated prefixes for stations outside
   continental US (Table):............37-10
  Phonetics:...................37-3, 37-7
  Prefix allocation Table:............37-8
Calling frequencies (VHF, UHF, EHF):...37-4
Cameras, TV:.......................7-13
  Optics:...........................7-15
Canadian provinces (map):............37-13
Capacitance:...................2-2, 2-13
  And RFI:..........................39-7
  Design examples:..................15-15
  Formula for calculating:............2-14
  In semiconductors:....4-1, 4-17, 4-18, 4-27
  In tank circuits:..................15-3
  Input:............................5-7
  Interelectrode:................5-7, 15-21
  Output:...........................5-7
  Parasitic inductance:..............39-7
  Tube:............................5-7
  Units:............................2-14
Capacitive reactance:..........2-16, 2-38
Capacitive reactance matching:........15-19
Capacitor input filters:...............6-8
Capacitors:...................2-13, 26-21
  Air dielectric:....................26-22
  Antenna loading:..................33-18
  At RF:............................39-7
  Blocking, ratings:.................15-10
  Ceramic:....................2-14, 26-22
  Characteristic code:................35-2
  Chip:......................15-10, 15-21
  Chip, installation technique:.........32-7
  Cleaning:.........................26-21
  Color code:.......................35-1
  Decoupling digital circuits:..........8-14
  Disc:............................15-10
  Disc ceramic, series resonant
    frequencies:....................35-4
  Doorknob:.........................15-19
  Electrolytic:.................2-14, 26-22
  Energy stored in:..................2-13
  Equivalent circuit of:..............3-1
  Feedthrough:......................39-7
  Fixed-value:......................2-14
  In sample-and-hold amplifiers:.......8-23
  In series and parallel:............2-15
  Mica:...............2-14, 15-10, 26-22
  Mounting in tank circuits:..........15-9
  Neutralization:...................15-22
  Oil-filled:.......................2-14
  Padder:...........................10-5
  Paper:......................2-14, 26-22
  Plastic film:.....................26-22
  Printed circuit:..................39-9
  Ratings:..........................15-9
  Replacement:......................26-22
  Silver mica:......................15-21
  Standard values:..................35-2
  Testing:..........................26-21
  To suppress oscillation in ampli-
    fiers:........................15-21
  Trimmer:..........................10-5
  Using diodes as:..................4-4
  Vacuum-variable:..................15-17
  Variable:.........................2-14
  Voltage as a function of time:......2-15
  Voltage breakdown:................2-14
  Voltage v current phase relationship:...2-16
  Voltage-variable (see also Voltage-variable
    capacitors):...................4-4
Cardioid pattern, antenna:......38-3, 38-12,
                38-14, 38-18
Carrier:...........................9-1
  Unmodulated:......................9-4
Carrier-activated switch (CAS):.......14-5
Carrier-operated relay (COR):.........14-5
Cascade amplifiers:.................5-5
Cascode amplifier:..........4-33, 12-14
Cathode:.....................5-1, 5-2
  Bias:.....................3-16, 5-9
  Follower:.........................5-8
Cathode-ray tube (CRT):.............8-31
Cathode-ray tube (CRT) fax displays:...20-30
CATV:
  Channel chart (RFI):...............39-16
CATVI:.............................39-3
  Complaint reports:................39-3

FCC rules:.........................39-2
Cavity amplifier, 23 cm:.............32-29
CB frequencies (Table):.............18-6
CCIR:
  Rec 405-1 (FMTV emphasis networks):20-12
  Rec 476-2:....................19-1, 19-14
  Rec 476-3:....................19-1, 19-14
  Rec 476-4:....................19-1, 19-14
  Rec 625:.........................19-14
CCITT:............................19-10
  Rec S.4 (Table):..................37-7
CD-ROM (computer storage):..........8-30
Centronics interface Table:...........8-19
Ceramic capacitors:................26-22
Channels, CB (Table):...............18-6
Character displays:.................8-32
  Decoder and driver:...............8-32
  Multiplexing:.....................8-33
Character matrix:...................8-31
Character printers:.................8-33
Characteristic code, capacitors:.......35-2
Characteristic curves:
  Diode:............................4-2
  Hot-Carrier diodes:................4-8
  Hot-Carrier v PN diodes:............4-7
  Junction FET:.....................4-30
  MOSFET:...........................4-30
  Transistor:.......................4-18
  Tunnel diode:.....................4-14
  Voltage-variable capacitors:.........4-9
  Zener diode:......................4-14
Characteristic impedance:............16-1
Charge:
  On a capacitor:...................2-13
  Polarity:.........................2-4
Chassis work:......................24-3
Chebyshev filter:..................2-42
Checklist, ARES:...................37-15
Chemical elements of transistors:.....4-1
Chimneys, vacuum tube:.............15-12
China, People's Republic, weather
  satellites:......................20-24
Chinook wind:......................22-18
Chip capacitors:.............15-10, 15-21
  Installation technique:.............32-7
Chirp spread spectrum:..............21-9
Choke:
  Baluns:...........................16-9
  Coax shield:......................39-7
  Common-mode (RFI):...............39-14
  Input filters:.....................6-9
  Minimum inductance for power
    supplies:......................6-9
  RF, characteristics:...............15-10
  RF, for VHF:.....................31-30
  Swinging:.........................6-9
Choke (current) baluns, effective
  (Table):.........................16-9
Circuit boards, layout:..............15-20
Circuit design (RFI):................39-5
Circuit modeling:...................15-15
Circuits, interface:.................34-4
Circular polarization:...........17-22, 23-5
Circulating current:................15-3
Circulator:.........................14-4
Civil Air Patrol, and ATV:...........20-1
Clamp, diode:........4-4, 4-15, 4-35, 15-12
Clapp oscillator:...................4-26
Class A, AB and C transistor
  amplifier:.......................4-23
Class AB amplifier design examples:...15-15
Classes of amplifier operation:.....3-17, 5-4,
                5-5, 5-6, 15-1
Clipper diodes:....................4-4
Clipping and filtering, speech:.......7-7
Clock speeds (digital):..............8-9
CMOS:
  HCT series:......................8-14
  Logic:...........................8-12
  Subfamilies:.....................8-12
Coaxial cavity filters:..............12-4
Coaxial connectors, soldering:........36-15
Coaxial line:
  Tank inductor:...............15-10, 15-18
  Types:...........................36-12
Coaxial-sleeve balun:...............14-3
Code:
  ASCII:...........................21-6

  Baudot:...........................21-6
  Gold:............................21-12
  Morse (see also CW):...........9-8, 21-6
  Morse, receiving:.................7-9
  National Electrical:...............36-2
  Orthogonality:....................21-11
Code conversion:...................19-20
  Standards:.......................19-20
  Tables:..........................19-22
Code-division multiple access:.......21-8
CODEC IC (mu-law coder/decoder):...8-22
Coefficient of coupling:...2-21, 2-53, 2-54, 3-4
Cohn filters:......................12-3
Coil baluns:.......................16-9
Coils:.............................2-17
  Antenna loading:.................33-16
  HF tank, ratings:.................15-9
  VFOs:............................10-5
  Winding:.........................24-8
Cold front:........................22-17
Collinear arrays:.............17-8, 17-21
Color:.............................7-12
Color codes:
  Capacitors:.......................35-1
  Hookup wire:......................35-5
  Powdered-iron toroids:.............35-4
  Power transformer leads:...........35-3
  Resistors:........................35-1
  Semiconductor diodes:..............35-4
Color perception:..................7-11
Color SSTV:........................20-16
Color TV:....................7-17, 20-2
Colpitts oscillator:.....4-25, 4-26, 4-35, 10-1,
                10-2
Colpitts VFOs:..............10-5, 10-7
Columbia (space shuttle):............1-4
Combinational logic:................8-1
Combiner, hybrid for signal
  generators:......................25-37
Command and data acquisition station
  (CDA—fax):......................20-28
Command post (CP):.................37-15
Common-base amplifier:..............4-19
Common-base level shifter:...........8-15
Common-collector amplifier:..........4-19
Common-emitter amplifier:...........4-19
Common-emitter amplifier design example
  (HF):...........................15-20
Common-gate FET amplifier:..........4-33
Common-mode hum:..................12-8
Common-source FET amplifier:........4-33
Communications:
  Data:............................9-12
  Receivers:.......................12-1
  Satellite:........................23-1
Compact disc audio system:..........8-22
Compandor:.........................9-6
Compandoring, amplitude:........7-9, 18-17
Compensation network:..............15-20
Compiler:..........................8-35
Complementary output:..............8-12
Complex impedance plane:............2-24
Complex numbers:...................2-24
  Addition and subtraction:..........2-24
  Multiplication and division:.........2-25
Complex wave:......................2-5
  And reactance:....................2-26
Component ratings, power supply
  filters:..........................6-10
Components for RF power amplifiers:....15-9
Components, electronic, functions:.....26-20
Components, sources of:
  Advanced Micro Devices:...........29-12
  Advanced Receiver Research:........20-3,
                32-4, 32-45
  AEA:............20-3, 20-23, 20-24
  Alden Electronic and Impulse Recording
    Equipment:......................20-22
  All Electronics:..................34-34
  Amperex:.........................20-6
  Amphenol:........................38-11
  Analog Devices:...................29-10
  Angle Linear:.....................32-39
  Apple:...........................20-31
  Arco:.......................20-5, 20-6
  AT&T:............................8-37
  Atlantic Surplus:.................20-22
  Avantek:.........................32-19

(Components, sources of, continued)

Avatar Magnetics:...........................27-18
BCD Electro:..................................34-34
Belden:.....................14-4, 20-3, 20-29
Bill Johnston, N5KR (maps):..........38-8
Bird:...32-21
Bud:..39-11
California Eastern Laboratories:......32-4,
....................32-6, 32-8, 32-21, 32-54
Calvert Engineering:.....................32-40
Carborundum Co:..........................34-26
Centralab:..............................15-19, 39-7
Chevron Oil Co:...................34-25, 34-27
Circuit Specialists:..........................34-4
Coilcraft:........................20-12, 20-13
Commodore:.................................20-24
Commodore Amiga:.......................20-31
Data Signal, Inc:.............................34-1
Digi-Key:.......................................32-53
Digital Equipment (DEC):................8-37
Digital Research:.............................8-36
Digitran:..34-1
Dow Corning:.................................15-10
Down East Microwave:.......32-18, 32-26
E. F. Johnson:................................34-21
EIMAC:...15-15
Electronic Precepts:........................29-8
FM-RTTY Publishing:.......................37-13
Globar:...15-20
Glynn Electronics:...........................27-16
Gulf Oil Co:...........................34-25, 34-27
Hall-Mark Electronics:.....................34-4
Hammarlund:..................................39-11
Harris:...35-5
Heathkit:...4-14
Hewlett Packard:.......4-32, 8-28, 32-21
Hurst Mfg:......................................20-23
IBM:..8-30
IBM PC:..20-31
Idiom Press:....................................29-6
Instrument Specialties:...................32-34
International Crystal:............32-8, 34-34
J. W. Miller Co:...............................34-17
Jameco Electronics:.....29-10, 34-11, 34-12
JAN Crystals:..................................34-34
Johanson:................32-8, 32-19, 32-30
Julius Jones, W2IHY:.......................29-10
K-COM:...39-18
Kantronics:.....................................20-23
KLM:..20-3
Lea Engineering:............................34-2
Little Giant:....................................32-40
M-Tron Industries:..........................29-13
M/A-COM:......32-19, 32-43, 32-45, 32-56
M/A-COM (FETs):.........4-10, 4-11, 4-31
Macintosh:.....................................20-31
MFJ:..20-23
MHz Electronics:............................32-6
Microwave Components of
....Michigan:.....32-17, 32-21, 32-26, 39-9
Microwave Semiconductor Corp:.....4-32
Mini Circuits Labs (MCL):......20-4, 32-52
Mirage:.................................20-4, 20-7
Mitsubishi:..........................32-2, 32-3
Motorola:........15-20, 20-7, 32-1, 32-53
Mouser:..........29-7, 29-10, 32-20, 32-21
Muirhead:.......................................20-22
Murata:...32-46
National Semiconductor:.......32-53, 35-5
Newark:...23-25
Nippon Electric Co (NEC):......4-32, 32-1,
....32-3
Ocean State Electronics:................23-25
Panasonic:.......................................35-5
PC Electronics:...20-4, 20-5, 20-11, 20-14
Phelps-Dodge:................................20-3
Plessey:...4-32
Proteus Industries:.........................32-40
PX Shack:..20-14
Radio Shack:...................................23-25
Saxton:..20-3
Science Workshop:.........................20-14
Shell Oil Co:..........................34-25, 34-27
Silicon Systems Inc:........................34-4
Siliconix:.............................4-32, 38-12
Solar Power Corp:...........................20-14
Solent Scientific:........20-9, 20-11, 20-14
Solfan:...32-54

Spectrum International:....................20-4
Texaco (Texas Oil Co):..........34-25, 34-27
TONNA:...20-11
TX-RX Systems:................................20-4
W. W. Grainger:..............................15-13
Western Union:...............................20-31
Wood & Douglas:.......20-8, 20-9, 20-14
Xerox:..20-31
Xicor:...8-26
Zenith:...8-30
3M:..38-12
Components, specific:
μA723 (regulator):.........................27-14
ADC7569JN (A/D and D/A
....converter):..................................29-10
Altair 8800 (computer):...................8-28
Am7910:..29-12
Apple II (computer):........................8-28
ATF-10135 (GaAsFET):.......32-22, 32-23,
....32-27
ATF-13135 (GaAsFET):.......32-23, 32-24
AV-415 (transformer):.....................27-18
Belden 8214 (cable):......................20-3
Belden 9913 (cable):............14-4, 20-3,
....20-11, 20-29
Belden 9914 (cable):......................20-3
BFR96:..32-12
BGY41B (amplifier):........................20-6
Bird Model 43:................................32-21
C-2/2-11017 (circuit board):............39-9
CA3019 (diode array):.....................4-39
CA3026 (transistor array):..............4-39
CA3028 (small signal amplifier):....4-40,
....4-42, 4-43
CA3039 (diode array):...........4-42, 4-43
CA3076 (amplifier-limiter):.....4-40, 4-41
CA3189E (FM subsystem IC):..........32-47
CD4049 (IC):....................................8-15
CD4050 (IC):....................................8-15
CEE-22 (connector):.........................8-14
Crystal, surplus:.............................34-32
CT-2113-A (minibox):......................39-11
CU-2114-A (minibox):.....................39-11
D1010-N (amplifier):............20-4, 20-7
Dayton blowers:.............................15-13
Desk-Fax:..20-31
DTMF encoder (Motorola MC14410):..34-1
DTS-423 (keying transistor):...........19-5
DTS-801 (keying transistor):...........19-5
Dummy load (Bird Model
....612):..............................34-24, 34-26
Dummy load (Heath HN-31A):.........34-26
E12-01369-1.5 solar panel:.............4-14
ECG 238 (keying transistor):...........19-5
ECG-5452 (SCR):.............................14-6
EIMAC P/N 154353 (tube socket):...15-12
F9FT (antenna):..............................20-11
Finger stock:..................32-34, 34-34
FL-GT-062 (circuit board):...............39-9
FR-4 (circuit board):.............39-13, 39-14
FT-1000 (capacitor):........................39-7
GAT5 GaAsFET:...............................4-32
GAT6 GaAsFET:...............................4-32
Globar (resistor):............................15-20
HF-15-X (capacitor):.......................39-11
HF-30-X (capacitor):.......................39-11
HFET-2201 GaAsFET:........................4-32
HP-41CV (calculator):....32-7, 32-11, 32-12
HP430C:..32-21
HP431:...32-21
HP477B:..32-21
HP478A:..32-21
HP5082-2835 (hot-carrier diode):....32-15
IBM PC (computer):..........................8-28
Inductor (B&W Miniductor):............34-20
Inductor (trifilar wound):.....34-21, 34-23
Isopole (antenna):..........................20-3
J310 (JFET):....................................32-11
K-550 (fax):....................................20-31
LH0101 (power op amp):.......4-46, 4-48
LM1458N (op amp):........................29-16
LM3011 (small signal amp):............4-40
LM317 (regulator):..........................27-8
LM3820 (receiver IC):..........4-44, 4-45
LM3900 (op amp):..........................27-17
LM723 (regulator):.........................27-14
M67715 (23-cm hybrid):.................32-18
MA-87141-X (Gunnplexer):.............32-44

MAR-6 (MMIC):...................32-52, 32-54
MBM48/70 (antenna):......................20-3
MC10116 (Line receiver IC):...32-53, 32-54
MC13055 (FSK receiver IC):...........32-52
MC1350 (wide band amplifier):...4-40, 4-41
MC1350P (RF amplifier IC):..............30-3
MC1357 (subsystem IC for scanning
....receivers):...................................4-44
MC145152 (synthesizer):................10-15
MC145156 (synthesizer):................10-15
MC1496 (mixer):...................4-42, 4-43
MC1590 (wide band amplifier):...4-40, 4-41
MC1723CP (regulator):...................27-14
MC3359 (subsystem IC for scanning
....receivers):...................................4-44
MC68HC705C8P (microprocessor):...29-7
MGF1100:................................32-1, 32-4
MGF1202 (GaAsFET):......................32-3
MGF1402 (GaAsFET):......................32-3
MHW 710-2 (amplifier):..................20-6
MIL-P-13949D (circuit board):.........39-9
MJ2010 (keying transistor):............19-5
MJE350 (keying transistor):............19-5
MM4003 (keying transistor):...........19-5
MM5369 (timer IC):..........................14-7
Monitoring:......................................19-9
MRF464:..15-20
MRF901:...................32-8, 32-12, 32-13
MRF911:.................................32-8, 32-12
MRF966/967 (GaAsFET):.................32-4
MSA-0185 (MMIC):..........................32-15
MSA-0285 (MMIC):..........................32-15
MSA-0385 (MMIC):..........................32-15
MSA-0685 (MMIC):..........................32-15
MSA-1104 (MMIC):..........................32-15
MSA0204 (MMIC small signal
....amplifier):....................................4-41
MSA0304 (MMIC small signal
....amplifier):....................................4-41
MSC H001 GaAsFET:........................4-32
MV2115 (varicap):..........................20-7
Mylar tape:.....................................38-12
ND751AAM (10-GHz Gunn
....transceiver):.................32-54, 32-54
NE21889 (GaAsFET):.......................32-3
NE25137 (GaAsFET):.......................32-4
NE41137 (GaAsFET):.......................32-4
NE602 (mixer):................................4-43
NE604 (subsystem IC):....................4-43
NEL1306:...32-19
NEL130681-12:................................32-19
NEL1320:...32-19
NEL132081-12:................................32-19
NOVRAM (memory):........................8-26
OE-5 (Oscillator):............................32-8
P432VDG (ATV preamp):..................20-3
PD-FX 12-50H (Hardline):................20-3
Powerstat:......................................32-37
PSF-ATV (filter):..............................20-4
RCS882 (keying transistor):............19-5
RF-1 (filter):....................................39-18
RF-2 (filter):....................................39-18
RG-174 (cable):..............................20-4
RG-213 (cable):..............................20-3
RG-214 (cable):...................20-3, 20-11
RG-58 (cable):.....................20-3, 20-11
RG-59 (cable):................................38-11
RG-8 (cable):.......................20-3, 20-11
Roller inductor:...............................34-18
RS2043 (keying transistor):............19-6
Saxton 8285 (cable):......................20-3
SBL-1 (mixer):.................................20-4
SDT 13305 (keying transistor):........19-5
Silicone grease:..............................15-10
SK-2200 (tube socket):...................15-12
SK-2210 (tube socket):...................15-12
SK-2216 (tube chimney):................15-12
SK-400 (tube socket):.....................15-12
SK-406 (tube chimney):..................15-12
SK-410 (tube socket):.....................15-12
SK-416 (tube socket):.....................15-12
SK-500 (tube socket):.....................15-12
SK-506 (tube chimney):..................15-12
SK-510 (tube socket):.....................15-12
SK-516 (tube chimney):..................15-12
SK-600 (tube socket):.....................15-12
SK-600A (tube socket):...................15-12
SK-602A (tube socket):...................15-12

(Components, specific, continued)

SK-606 (tube chimney):............15-12
SK-610 (tube socket):.............15-12
SK-610A (tube socket):............15-12
SK-611 (tube socket):.............15-12
SK-612 (tube socket):.............15-12
SK-620 (tube socket):.............15-12
SK-620A (tube socket):............15-12
SK-621 (tube socket):.............15-12
SK-626 (tube chimney):............15-12
SK-630 (tube socket):.............15-12
SK-700 (tube socket):.............15-12
SK-710 (tube socket):.............15-12
SK-711A (tube socket):............15-12
SK-712A (tube socket):............15-12
SK-740 (tube socket):.............15-12
SK-760 (tube socket):.............15-12
SK-761 (tube socket):.............15-12
SK-770 (tube socket):.............15-12
SK-800B (tube socket):............15-12
SK-806 (tube chimney):............15-12
SK-810B (tube socket):............15-12
SK-890B (tube socket):............15-12
SK3173 (keying transistor):........19-6
SLOT-10-1-09 (inductor):..........20-12
SLOT-10-1-12 (inductor):..........20-13
SRA-1 (DBM):....................32-52
Stackpole S-5022CD03-0 (switch):....25-37
TA7205 (AF amp):.................4-39
TDA7000 (FM radio IC):...........4-44
Turbine oil (Texaco):.........34-25, 34-27
Turns-counter drive (James Millen):....34-18
U257 JFET:......................4-32
U310 (JFET):.....................38-12
UFM01 (VCO):....................20-8
UT-141 (cable):...................32-7
Variable capacitor:...............34-21
Variac:.........................32-37
Varistor (screen grid protection):.....15-12
VIDIF (video IF):.................20-9
VMP-4 FET:......................4-31
VN67AJ power FET:...............4-35
Xerox 400 (fax):.................20-31
1-42A (water pump):..............32-40
2C39 (tube):.....................32-29
2C782 (blower):..................15-13
2N2222 (transistor):..............29-7
2N3439 (keying transistor):........19-5
2N4918 (transistor):..............27-11
2N5415 (keying transistor):........19-5
2N5416 (keying transistor):........19-5
2N6213 (keying transistor):........19-5
2N6214 (keying transistor):........19-5
2N6246 (keying transistor):........19-6
2N6457 (keying transistor):........19-5
2SC1308K (keying transistor):......19-5
3-1000Z (tube):..................15-12
3-400Z (tube):...................15-12
3-500Z (tube):..............15-12, 30-54
3CX1500 (tube):.................15-12
3CX800A7 (tube):................15-12
3SK97 (GaAsFET):...............32-4
4-1000A (tube):..................15-12
4-250A (tube):...................15-12
4-400A (tube):...................15-12
4C004 (blower):..................15-13
4C005 (blower):..................15-13
4C012 (blower):..................15-13
4C440 (blower):..................15-13
4C443 (blower):..................15-13
4CX1000A (tube):................15-12
4CX1500 (tube):.................15-12
4CX250 (tube):.............15-12, 15-18
4CX250 (vacuum tube):...........20-4
4CX300A (tube):.................15-12
4CX350A (tube):.................15-12
4N28 (optoisolator):..............14-21
5D22 (tube):.....................15-12
15C (flow indicator):..............32-40
19-66-79154-2 (filter):............20-4
50-Ω power resistor (Carborundum
    889SP500K):............34-24, 34-26
70LIN10 (amplifier):..............20-8
83-1HP/U (coaxial hood):..........38-11
850 (doorknob capacitor):.........15-19
858S500 (capacitor):.............39-7
875S (water pump):..............32-40

1250DC50 (converter):............20-9
1488 (IC):.......................8-19
1489 (IC):.......................8-19
7289 (tube):.....................32-29
7289 (vacuum tube):..............20-4
7447 (IC):.......................8-32
7850W (tube):...................15-12
8163 (tube):.....................15-12
8164 (tube):.....................15-12
8166 (tube):.....................15-12
8167 (tube):.....................15-12
8168 (tube):.....................15-12
8321 (tube):.....................15-12
8438 (tube):.....................15-12
8660 (tube):.....................15-12
8874 (tube):.....................15-12
8877 (tube):....15-12, 15-15, 15-16, 30-45
Compound switches:..............4-12
Compression, volume:.............7-6
Computer buses:.................8-28
Computer languages:
    Assembler:...................8-34
    BASIC:......................8-35
    C:...........................8-36
    High-level:...................8-34
    IPS:.........................8-36
    Low-level:...................8-33
    Pascal:......................8-36
Computer memory:
    Addressing:..................8-24
    Design:......................8-24
    First-in, first-out (FIFO):......8-23
    Last-in, first-out (LIFO):......8-24
    Non-volatile RAM (NVRAM):....8-26
    Push-down stack:.............8-23
    Queue:......................8-23
    Random-access (RAM):....8-24, 8-25
    Read-only (ROM):............8-26
    Reading from:...............8-24
    Sequential-access (SAM):.....8-23
    Stack:.......................8-23
    Writing to:..................8-24
*Computer Networking Conference
    Proceedings:*................23-30
Computer operating systems:.......8-36
Computer, MUF predictions on:.....22-11
Computer-based message system
    (CBMS):....................37-4
Computers (also see Digital computers):
    And Fax:....................20-23
    Connectors:..................36-18
    Control of transceivers:.......13-13
    Radiation limits:.............39-3
Condenser:.....................2-2
Conductance:..........2-7, 2-8, 2-38
Conduction angle:...............5-6
Conduction angle (amplifiers):.....15-1
Conduction, electron and hole:.....4-1
Conductivity:................2-3, 4-1
    Ground:.....................17-2
Conductors:
    Size, in antennas:............17-3
    Size in tank inductors:.......15-5
Conjugate match:................16-11
    Pi-network tank, and the:......16-12
    Theorem:....................16-11
Connectors:.............26-20, 36-14
    Audio:......................36-14
    BNC:.......................36-17
    Coaxial:.....................36-15
    Coaxial, specifications:.......35-28
    Computer:...................36-18
    Computer, crimp type:........36-19
    Computer, solder type:.......36-19
    Control circuitry:............36-14
    For Hardline or Heliax:.......14-3
    Insulation displacement:......36-19
    Power:......................36-9
    RF:.........................36-14
    Type N:.....................36-18
    UHF:.................36-15, 36-16
Constant-current source:..........4-28
Constants:
    Boltzmann's:................12-2
Construction:
    Antenna projects:............33-1

Beam antennas:.................33-4
Boards, perforated:..............24-10
    Materials:...................24-2
    Power supply projects:.......27-1
    Techniques:.................3-1
    Ugly or dead-bug:...........24-11
    Vertical antennas:...........33-4
Construction practices:
    Amplifiers:..................15-20
    Heat sinks:..................15-14
    In tank circuits:.............15-9
    Thermal silicone grease:......15-14
Consumer electronic devices:
    Frequencies used in:.........39-4
    Radiation limits:.............39-3
Contests, operating:..............37-12
Continuous Commercial Service
    (CCS):......................15-9
Contour maps, direction finding:....38-7
Control:
    Automatic (repeaters):.......14-1
    Characters (ASCII):..........8-31
    Error:......................21-5
    Key:........................8-30
    Radio:......................21-1
    Remote (repeaters):.........14-9
    Repeater transmitter (COR, CAS):..14-5
    Repeater, flow charts:.......14-9
    Sequences for RTTY:.........37-7
    Troubleshooting:............26-12
    Unit, digital computer:.......8-27
    Wires, on towers:...........17-13
Control links (repeaters):.........14-9
Controller, Automatic Antenna:....23-20
Conversion, double:.........12-1, 12-9
Conversion, single:.........12-1, 12-9
Converters:
    ATV:.......................20-4
    Scan, SSTV:................20-15
    Transmitting, 3 W, for 50 MHz:..31-13
Coolant, oils:..............34-25, 34-27
Cooling:.......................15-13
    Convection:.................15-13
    Semiconductors:.............4-20
    Transistors:.................15-14
    Vacuum tubes:..............15-12
Coordinates:
    Converting between polar and rec-
        tangular:.................2-25
    Polar:......................2-24
    Rectangular:................2-24
Copper tubing in tank inductors:....15-10
Copper wire, table:..............35-6
Copperweld wire:...............33-1
Cordwood modules:.............24-13
Cores:
    A_L values:................2-34
    High permeability:...........3-8
    Iron, inductors:.............2-20
    Material, transformers:.......2-31
    Permeability:...............2-33
    Physical properties:.........2-34
    Types, inductors and transformers:..2-32
Corona:........................2-3
Correlation, spread spectrum:.....21-10
COSMOS (USSR imaging satellite):....20-27
Coulomb:......................2-1
Coulomb's Law:................2-1
Counter:
    Asynchronous:..............8-6
    Divide-by-n:................8-6
    Down:......................8-6
    Frequency:...........11-4, 25-12
    Frequency, 500-MHz:........25-13
    Ring:.......................8-8
    Ripple:.....................8-6
    Ripple-carry:...............8-6
    Up:........................8-6
    Up/down:...................8-6
Coupled circuits and filters:.......2-37
Coupled resonators:.............2-52
Coupling:......................11-8
    Band-pass:..................11-10
    Capacitive divider:...........11-10
    Coefficient:........2-53, 2-54, 3-4
    Directional:.................3-10
    Intentional mismatch:........11-9
    Link:.......................3-5

(Coupling, continued)
Low-Q networks:..................11-9
Magnetic:...............15-8, 34-19
Mutual:.........................2-54
To random-length antennas:........16-10
Transformer:....................11-10
Transmission line to a receiver:......16-10
Transmitter to line:.............16-10
Unwanted:......................14-5
Coupling coefficient:
In matching transformers:..........15-8
Coupling in transmission line trans-
formers:........................15-8
Courtesy tones (repeaters):........14-11
CP/M:..........................8-36
Crest factor:....................2-12
Critical frequency:...........22-3, 22-7
Cross-band ATV repeaters:.........20-4
Cross modulation:...........39-12, 39-17
Cross modulation, mixers:.........12-16
Cross-modulation products:
In electronically switched antennas:..38-19
Crowbar protection circuit:.......4-3, 4-29
CRRL Section map:...............37-13
CRT:...........................8-31
Crystal:
Calibrator:.....................34-32
Case styles:....................35-32
Controlled signal source:.........26-5
Discriminators:..................18-24
Filters:.......................12-27
Microphones:....................7-3
Oscillators (also see Oscillators,
crystal):...........4-25, 4-35, 25-11
Piezoelectric:...................2-54
Quartz:........................2-54
Switching of:..............10-3, 11-2
Cubic feet per minute rating (CFM):....15-13
Cup cores:......................2-32
Current:........................2-2
And electric fields:...............2-3
And tank circuit Q:...............15-5
Density:........................2-3
Distribution, in antennas:........17-3, 17-7
In semiconductor junctions:........4-2
Kirchhoff's First Law:..............2-9
Loop, 20-mA (telephone):..........14-22
On repeater feed lines:...........14-3
Plate:..........................5-2
Regulator diodes:................4-16
Sink:...........................2-4
Source:.........................2-4
Current limiting:
Foldback:......................6-16
In voltage regulators:.............6-15
Current-mode logic:...............8-12
Current transfer ratio (CTR, opto-
isolator):.......................8-15
Cutoff frequency:............2-39, 2-41
Cutoff region (transistor):..........4-21
Cutting holes:...................24-4
Cutting sheet metal:..............24-5
CW (also see Morse code):....9-8, 19-2, 21-6
Abbreviations Table:..............37-6
Backwave:......................19-7
Break-in:.......................19-7
Chirp:.........................19-7
Cutting numbers:................19-4
Filters:........................28-1
Identifier (repeater):.............14-3
Keyer, CMOS Super Keyer II:.......29-6
Keyer, simple CMOS:.............29-1
Keyer, single IC:................29-4
Keyer, W2IHY audio memory
keyer:.......................29-16
Keying:........................19-4
Keying circuits:.................19-7
Keying envelope:.................9-8
Monitoring:.....................19-9
Operating:.....................37-3
Oscillator keying:...............19-7
Power supply regulation:..........19-4
Reception:......................28-1
RF envelope shaping:.............19-5
Timing:........................19-4
Transmitters for:................11-2
Cycle:..........................2-4

D

D flip-flop:......................8-6
D'Arsonval meter:................25-1
Dallas Remote Imaging Group (DRIG):..20-32
Damping resistor:................15-20
Darlington pair:..................4-22
Darlington phototransistor:.........8-15
Data acquisition:.................8-23
Data communications:.............9-12
Data compression (fax):..........20-22
Data interface connections:........19-28
Data link, 2 Mbit/s:.............32-49
Data rate:......................8-18
Date notation:...................37-10
dB:............................2-7
dB (acoustical):..................2-7
dBμV:..........................2-7
dBc:...........................2-7
dBm:...........................2-7
DBM...................12-21, 12-23
Performance Table:.............12-21
DBM/IF amplifier, Combined:......12-23
dBV:...........................2-7
dBW:...........................2-7
DC:............................2-4
Meters:...................25-1, 25-3
To-dc conversion:...............6-23
Dead-bug construction:...........24-11
Decibel (see dB)
Decoder, DTMF, universal:.........34-3
Decoupling capacitors in digital
circuits:........................8-14
Deep-discharge batteries:.........14-10
Deflection, TV:..................7-13
Degenerative feedback:.......4-22, 15-21
Delta loop antennas:.............17-17
Delta match:....................17-19
Demodulation:...................9-1
Demodulator, audio subcarrier
(FMTV):.......................20-10
Demodulators, PLL:..............18-25
DeMorgan's Theorem:.............8-2
Depletion mode (FET):...........4-31
Depletion region (semiconductor):...4-17
Depth of field, optics:...........7-17
Desensitization, receiver:.........14-4
Design formulas:.................3-3
Design Guidelines and Examples:...15-15
Despreading, spread spectrum:.....21-11
Detection:
Error:.......................21-5
Spread spectrum:.............21-11
Detectors:......................12-7
Active:.......................18-12
Diode:...............4-6, 18-9, 18-11
FM:..........................18-23
Infinite impedance:.............18-11
Phase:.......................10-10
Plate:........................18-11
Product:......................18-11
Ratio:........................18-24
Troubleshooting:...............26-15
Deviation:......................18-20
Linearity:.....................18-20
Measurement:.................18-21
Measurement for FMTV video:....20-13
Meter:.......................18-21
Ratio (FM or PM):..............9-3
Device ratings, transmitting:.......15-8
Diac:..........................4-29
Dials:
Eddystone:....................11-4
Electronic:....................11-4
VFO:.........................11-4
Dial tracking:...................26-11
Diameter vs length, antennas:......17-3
Dielectric constant:..............2-13
And breakdown voltages:.........2-13
Dielectric loss:..................3-2
Differential amplifiers:...........4-19
Diffraction:.....................22-18
Digipeater:................14-1, 19-40
Digital:
Basics:.......................8-1
Bibliography:...................8-36
Binary systems:................8-1
Circuit interference:............8-14

Equipment troubleshooting:........26-16
Glossary:.......................8-34
Integrated circuits (IC):...........8-9
Interfacing:....................8-14
Modes (operating):..............37-4
Noise:.........................8-35
Number systems:................8-6
Oscilloscopes:..................25-29
Timers:........................14-7
To-analog (D/A) converter:........8-21
To-analog conversion:............8-19
TR sequencer:..................23-51
Digital and analog interfacing:
Aliasing:......................8-20
Nyquist Sampling Theorem:........8-20
Sampling rate:..................8-20
Sampling resolution:.............8-21
Signal-to-noise ratio Table:........8-21
Digital communications:............19-1
AMTOR:......................19-14
ASCII:........................19-17
Code conversion:................19-20
Glossary:.....................19-45
History:.......................19-1
Packet radio:..................19-26
RTTY:........................19-9
Rules and regulations:............19-1
Digital computer:................8-26
Arithmetic logic unit (ALU):........8-27
Control unit:...................8-27
Display:.......................8-31
Floppy disk:...................8-29
Hard disk:....................8-30
Input device:..................8-26
Interrupt:.....................8-28
Keyboard:.....................8-30
Languages:....................8-34
Monitor:......................8-31
Operating systems:..............8-34
Organization of subsystems:.......8-26
Output device:.................8-27
Peripheral devices:.............8-29
Printer:.......................8-33
Special purpose:...............8-26
Timing:.......................8-27
Digital image enhancement:........20-31
Digital image processing (SSTV):....20-18
Digital pulse:
Duty cycle:....................8-9
Fall time:.....................8-1
Propagation delay:..............8-1
Rise time:.....................8-1
Digitize:.......................8-20
Digitized speech:................21-6
Diode clamp:...................15-12
Diode equations:.................4-2
Diodes:...................4-1, 26-24
As capacitors:..................4-4
As gates:......................4-3
As switches:...................4-3
Clippers and clamps:............4-4
Current regulator:...............4-16
Detectors:.............4-6, 18-9, 18-11
Double base:...................4-29
For crystal switching:...........11-3
Forward-to-reverse resistance ratio of
solid-state (Table):..............18-3
Frequency multipliers:............4-5
Germanium:....................4-2
Gunn:.........................4-9
Hot carrier:....................4-6
Hot-carrier (Schottky), matching:...32-11
In parallel:....................6-6
In series:......................6-6
Light emitting (LED):............4-13
Mixers:..................4-6, 12-15
PIN:..........................4-11
PIN, in RDF systems:.......38-18, 38-19
Protection of:..................6-4
Reference:.................4-3, 4-16
Reverse current:................25-8
Selenium:......................4-2
Silicon:........................4-2
Solar electric:..................4-13
Specifications:............6-4, 35-11
Step recovery:.................4-16
Surge protection:...............6-5
Switching, for antenna rotation:.....38-5

(Diodes, continued)
Switching, series:............................4-3
Thermal protection:........................6-5
Tunnel:....................................4-14
Varactor:..................................4-7
Varicap, specifications:..................35-12
Zener:............................4-15, 6-12
Zener for bias:...........................15-11
Zener, specifications:....................35-12
Dip meters:................................26-4
Dipoles:
Bent:......................................17-6
Drooping:..................................17-5
Folded:....................................16-6
Helically wound:...........................17-6
Trap:......................................17-6
Direct conversion receivers:...............12-8
Hum:.......................................12-8
Microphonics:..............................12-8
Direct current (also see DC):...............2-4
Direct digital synthesizers:..............10-17
Anti-alias filter:........................10-19
Settling time:............................10-21
Frequency resolution and spurious
response:.................................10-19
Lookup table:.............................10-19
Numeric modulation:.......................10-21
Phase accumulator:........................10-18
Quadrature generation:....................10-21
Direct FM:.................................18-18
Direct memory access (DMA):................8-29
Direct sequence spread spectrum
(DS):......................................21-9
Direction finding:.........................38-1
Spread spectrum:..........................21-14
Techniques:................................38-6
Directional coupling:......................3-10
Directivity:
Antennas:..................................17-8
Microphones:...............................7-3
RDF:.......................................38-1
Directors, ARRL Board of:...................1-4
Disaster welfare inquiries (DWI, Red
Cross):...................................37-17
Discriminators:...........................18-24
Crystal:..................................18-24
Dish-antenna alignment:...................32-56
Disk operating system (DOS):...............8-36
Diskette (see Floppy disk)
Display multiplexing:......................8-33
Dissipation:
In transistors:...................4-20, 15-9
In vacuum tubes:...........................15-8
Distortion:...............................26-15
Bias:......................................8-19
Harmonic:..................................5-4
Measurement:..............................26-10
Measurements, interpreting:...............18-15
Distortion in FET mixers:..................4-33
Distress calling:..........................37-1
Dividers:
Programmable:.............................10-11
Programmable, dual modulus:...............10-14
Divisions, ARRL:............................1-4
Documenting station layout:...............36-20
Doorknob capacitor:.......................15-19
Doorknob capacitors:......................15-10
Doppler effect:...........................20-29
Doppler shift direction finders:..........38-19
DoppleScAnt direction finder:.............38-19
Dot-matrix printer:........................8-33
Double-base diode:.........................4-29
Double Ducky direction finder:............38-18
Double-sideband AM (DSB):...................9-5
Double-tuned circuits:......................3-3
Doubly balanced FET mixer:.................4-33
Doubly balanced mixers (see also
DBM):.....................................12-21
Downlink (transponders):..................14-19
Drain (FET):...............................4-29
Drain-load distortion:.....................4-33
Drilling holes:............................24-4
Drills:
Sizes:.....................................24-1
Twist:.....................................24-1
Driven elements, antennas with:............17-8
Driver:
RS-232-C line:.............................8-19

Stages:....................................11-7
Drooping dipole antennas:..................17-5
Drum speed, Fax:...........................20-21
DS (direct sequence spread spectrum):.......21-9
DTMF:
Command, flow chart (repeaters):..........14-13
DTMF (dual-tone, multifrequency):..........21-7
Decoder, simple:...........................34-3
Encoder:...................................34-1
Dual-frequency repeater:...................14-1
Dual-Tone Multi-Frequency signaling (DTMF)
decoders:..................................14-9
Dummy antennas:....25-21, 26-4, 34-24, 34-26
Duplexers:.................................14-5
Duty cycle:
Repeaters:.................................14-2
SSTV transmitter:.........................20-16
Duty cycle (amplifiers):...................15-9
DX:
Ethics:....................................37-7
Operating code Table:.....................37-12
Operating:.................................37-5
Dynamic mutual conductance (FET):..........4-31
Dynamic RAM (DRAM, memory):................8-25
Dynamic range:.............................12-6
In linear translators and trans-
ponders:..................................14-20
Dynamic resistance:.........................4-2

E

Ear, the:...................................7-2
Earth's magnetic field:....................22-7
Eccles-Jordan circuit:......................8-2
Economy power supply:......................6-11
Eddy currents:.............................2-30
Iron-core inductors:.......................2-30
Eddystone dial:............................11-4
Edison effect:..............................2-4
Educational Activities Department
(ARRL):.....................................1-2
Effective radiated power:
EIRP, isotropic reference:..........14-2, 23-7
ERP, dipole reference:.....................14-2
Efficiency:................................2-12
Of amplifiers:.............................15-1
EHF, calling frequencies:..................37-4
EIA-232-D (data interface standard):......19-27
EIA-232-D break-out box:..................29-25
EIA-422-A (data interface standard):......19-28
EIA-423-A (data interface standard):......19-28
EIA-449:..................................19-28
EIA-449 37-pin connector assign-
ments:....................................19-28
EIA-449 9-pin connector assign-
ments:....................................19-29
EIRP:...............................14-2, 23-7
Electric field:.............................2-2
Electric fields and currents:...............2-3
Electrical fundamentals:....................2-1
Electricity:................................2-1
Electrolytic capacitors:...................26-22
Electrolytic paper (fax):.................20-22
Electromagnetic field:......................2-1
Vector:....................................15-4
Electromagnetic radiation, effects on
health:....................................36-3
Electromotive force (EMF):............2-2, 2-3
Electron:...................................2-1
Conduction:................................4-1
Flow:......................................2-4
Free:......................................4-1
Electronic antenna steering:...............38-5
Electronic Industries Association
(EIA):.............................39-5, 39-18
Electronic switching:...............4-3, 4-20
Electronic voltage regulation:.............6-14
Electronically erasable PROM
(EEPROM):..................................8-26
Electrostatic:
Balance in loop antennas:..................38-1
Discharge:................................4-37
Discharge and CMOS:........................8-13
Field:.....................................2-1
Paper (fax):.............................20-22
Potential:.................................2-1
Recorders (fax):.........................20-30
Shield:....................................2-3
Shielding of loopstick antennas:..........38-12

Elevation and azimuth of the moon:....23-47
Elliptic filter:..........................2-42
Elmer:.....................................1-2
EME:...............................22-18, 23-43
Antenna requirements:.....................23-44
Azimuth and elevation of celestial bodies,
calculator program for determining
(Table):..................................23-47
Azimuth and elevation of celestial bodies,
computer program for determining
(Table):..................................23-48
Calculating capabilities:.................23-45
Choosing a band:..........................23-43
Effects of polarization misalign-
ment:.....................................23-44
Libration fading:.........................23-48
Nautical Almanac, the:..................23-46
Net information:..........................23-51
Nonstandard modes:........................23-51
Operating frequencies:....................23-43
Operating techniques:.....................23-49
Operating times:..........................23-50
Path loss:................................23-43
Polarization effects:.....................23-44
Receiver requirements:....................23-45
Scheduling:...............................23-50
Signal reports used on 144 MHz
(Table):..................................23-50
Signal reports used on 432 MHz
(Table):..................................23-50
Sky noise:................................23-43
Transmitter power required for success
(Table):..................................23-45
Transmitter requirements:.................23-45
144-MHz procedure—2-minute sequence
(Table):..................................23-50
432-MHz procedure—2-1/2 minute sequence
(Table):..................................23-50
Emergency:
Book messages:............................37-22
Communication principles:.................37-15
HF net structure:.........................37-19
Local ARES net structure:.................37-18
Local network chart:......................37-17
Message checking:.........................37-22
Message format:...........................37-19
Net operating practices:..................37-22
Operation:................................37-15
Operations Center (EOC):..................37-15
Packet radio message handling:............37-24
Power:....................................14-10
Q signals:................................37-23
Tactical communications:..................37-17
Emergency-locator-transmitter (ELT)
monitor:..................................14-13
EMF:.......................................2-4
Back:...............................2-18, 2-21
Induced:............................2-18, 2-21
Emissions:
Classifications:...........................9-2
Designations:........................9-1, 9-2
Designators (Table):.......................9-2
Standards:................................39-3
Symbols:...................................9-2
Thermionic:................................5-1
Types:.....................................9-1
Types (Table):.............................9-2
Emitter-coupled logic (ECL):...............8-12
Emitter filtering (RFI):..................39-17
Emitter-follower amplifier:................4-19
Emitter injection (mixers):................4-27
Encoder, DTMF:.............................34-1
Encryption:................................21-6
End fire arrays:...........................17-9
Phased:....................................38-3
Unidirectional:...........................17-10
Energy:.............................2-1, 2-11
And power:................................2-11
Distribution, TV:.........................7-19
In tank circuits:.........................15-3
Stored in capacitors:.....................2-13
Stored in inductors:......................2-21
Stored in magnetic fields:................2-17
Engineering Plant Series (telephone
RFI):....................................39-18
EngLan:...................................8-36
Enhanced Graphics Adapter (EGA):.........20-31
Enhancement mode (FET):...................4-31

Equations, network:.................11-10
Equipment:
  Arranging: 36-12
  Assembling: 36-1
  Digital: 29-1
  Documenting:...................36-20
  Fax, home construction:........20-23
  Fax, surplus:............20-21, 20-22
  Grounds:........................36-7
  HF:.............................30-1
  Interconnecting:...............36-13
  Layout:........................36-10
  Lightning protection:...........36-3
  Location:.......................36-1
  Manuals, sources of (Table):....26-2
  Mobile: 36-35
  Operating table:...............36-10
  Portable:......................36-37
  Power:..........................36-8
  Protective devices:.............36-3
  Restoration: 26-28
  Safety:..................36-2, 36-9
  Satellite: 23-29
  Test:.....................25-1, 26-1
  Used: 26-27
  3-wire power cords:.............36-9
Equipotential surface:............2-2
Equivalent logic operations:......8-2
Equivalent series and parallel
  circuits:......................2-25
Erasable PROM (EPROM):...........8-26
Error:
  Control:.......................21-5
  Correction, forward:...........21-6
  Detection:...............8-18, 21-5
Escape sequence:.................8-31
Etching PC boards:...............24-9
Ethics:
  DX:............................37-7
  DX operating code:............37-12
Evaporation inversions:..........22-18
Even parity:.....................8-18
Exciters, for FM:...............18-20
Expansion, volume:...............7-9
Expeditions:......................1-3
Extended ASCII characters:.......8-31
Extended Industry Standard Architecture
  (EISA bus):....................8-28
External devices, interfacing:...8-16
Eye, the:........................7-11

                   F

F stops, lenses:.................7-16
f_a (transistor):..............4-17
f_T (transistor):..............4-17
F2-layer reflections:...........22-13
FAA Air Route Surveillance Radar:...20-12
Facsimile (fax):.............9-7, 20-20
Fading:.........................22-8
  Libration:....................23-48
Fading, direction finding:.......38-7
Failure, transistor:.............4-20
Fall time:.......................8-1
False (digital logic):...........8-2
False bearings, direction finding:..38-6
Fan-out (digital):...............8-10
Fans:...........................15-13
Farad:..........................2-14
Faraday rotation:...............23-44
Faraday rotation, direction finding:...38-7
Fast frequency-shift keying (FFSK):....9-13
Fast Scan Amateur Television (see also ATV,
  FSTV and FMTV):...........9-7, 20-1
Fax:.......................20-1, 20-20
  Amateur 2-way:................20-23
  Amiga Video Terminal (AVT):...20-24
  Analog-to-digital conversion:.20-31
  And computers:................20-23
  APT bandwidth:................20-29
  Bi-phase modulation (BPSK):...20-29
  Bibliography:.................20-32
  Block diagram of computer fax
    station:....................20-31
  Command and data acquisition station
    (CDA):......................20-28
  Computer BBS:.................20-32
  Computer display gray scale:..20-31
  Data compression:............20-22

Deviation, signal (weather satellite):...20-29
Digital controllers:............20-23
Digital image enhancement:......20-31
Display resolution
  (computer):...........20-24, 20-31
Display systems:...............20-29
Doppler effect:................20-29
Drum speed:....................20-21
Equipment, home construction:..20-23
Equipment, surplus:............20-21
Error correction mode (ECM):...20-23
High Resolution Picture Transmission
  (HRPT):..............20-26, 20-27
Image display:.................20-20
Integrated Service Digital Network
  (ISDN):.....................20-22
Machine compatibility:.........20-22
Machine groups:................20-22
Modems:........................20-23
Modulation format:.............20-21
Net (HF):......................20-23
Newsletter:....................20-32
Operating:......................37-5
Organizations:.................20-32
Preamplifiers:.................20-29
Press photos:..................20-20
Printers:......................20-23
Quantized:......................9-8
Run-length encoding:...........20-22
Satellite antennas:............20-29
Satellite table:...............20-26
Satellite tracking:............20-32
Satellite transmissions:.......20-23
Satellites, geostationary:.....20-28
Satellites, polar orbiting:....20-24
Scan-line length:..............20-21
Scanner:.......................20-22
Scanning density:..............20-21
SHF downconverters:............20-29
Standards:.....................20-21
Standards Table:...............20-23
Transmission:..................20-20
Transmission length:...........20-21
Visible and Infrared Spin Scan Radiometer
  (VISSR):....................20-28
Visual Atmospheric Sounder
  (VAS):......................20-28
Weather charts:................20-23
Weather satellite bandwidth:...20-29
Weather satellite spin rate:...20-28
WEFAX:.................20-24, 20-28
FCC:
  CATV radiation limits:........39-3
  Field Operations Bureau:......38-1
  Rules, RFI:..............39-2, 39-8
  Spurious emission limits:.....39-8
FDM (frequency division multiplex-
  ing):........................21-5
FEC (forward error correction):...19-15, 21-6
Federal Communications Commission
  (see FCC)
Federal Emergency Management Agency
  (FEMA): 37-16
Feed methods, antennas:.........17-4
Feedback:..............3-15, 5-6
  In amplifiers:...............15-20
  In grounded-grid amplifiers:.15-15
  To suppress oscillation:.....15-21
Feedback, in transistor amplifiers:...4-22,
                                       4-24
Feng Yun I (Chinese weather
  satellite):..................20-24
Ferrite:
  Beads: 2-33
  Beads and parasitic oscillations:...15-20
  Core baluns:..................16-9
  Magnetic properties:.........2-35
  Transformer matching:........15-8
Ferrite rod antennas:...........38-2
Ferrite toroids:
  A_L:........................2-35
  Permeability:.................2-36
  Physical properties:.........2-35
  Properties, Table:...........35-5
  Size:.........................2-36

Ferromagnetic matching transformers:...15-8
Ferromagnetic transformers and
  inductors:...................2-32
FET mixer:.....................12-16
FET preamplifier:..............12-14
FH (frequency hopping spread
  spectrum):....................21-9
Field:
  Depth of, optics:.............7-17
  Electric:.....................2-2
  Electric, and currents:.......2-3
  Electromagnetic:..............2-1
  Electrostatic:................2-1
  Intensity:....................2-2
  Magnetic:....................2-17
  Magnetic, energy stored in:..2-17
  Organization, ARRL:..........39-4
  Strength:.....................2-2
  Strength meter, portable:....38-10
  Strength, spread spectrum:...21-13
Field-aligned irregularities:..22-14
Field Day:......................1-2
Field-effect transistor (FET):
  Logic families:..............8-12
Field Operations Bureau, FCC:...38-1
Field Organization, ARRL:.......1-5
Field Services Department, ARRL:...37-15
Filament choke:................15-16
Filament hum:...................5-9
Filament voltage:..............15-10
Filter capacitors:.............6-10
  Series connections:..........6-10
Filtering:
  Amplifier output:............15-8
  Negative-lead:...............6-10
  With clipping, speech:.......7-7
Filters:........................18-5
  Absorptive:..................39-9
  AC line:.....................39-16
  Active audio, RC:............28-4
  Applications:................18-6
  Attenuation formula:.........2-41
  Audio:..................28-1, 28-3
  Audio peak:.................13-11
  Audio, op amps as:...........7-10
  Band-pass:..........2-39, 28-1, 28-3
  Band-pass ripple v SWR:......2-51
  Band-pass, for 144 or 220 MHz:...31-29
  Band-stop:...................2-39
  Bandwidth:...................2-41
  BC-Band Energy rejection:....30-16
  Bibliography:................2-43
  Brute-force:.................39-14
  Butterworth:.................2-39
  Butterworth band-pass:.......2-41
  Butterworth high-pass:.......2-40
  Capacitor input:.............6-8
  Chebyshev:..............2-41, 2-42
  Chebyshev (RFI):.............39-12
  Chebyshev, Attenuation table:...2-51
  Chebyshev, high pass:....2-40, 2-52
  Chebyshev, low pass:.........2-52
  Choke:.......................6-10
  Choke input:.................6-9
  Coaxial cavity:..............12-4
  Cohn:........................12-3
  Coupled circuits:............2-37
  Crystal:.....................12-27
  Cutoff frequency:............2-39
  Cutoff frequency formulas:...2-41
  CW:..........................28-1
  Element values:..............2-40
  Elliptic:....................2-42
  Elliptic (RFI):..............39-9
  Emitter (RFI):...............39-17
  FM-bandwidth, available to amateurs
    (Table):...................18-23
  For VHF transmitters:........39-10
  Frequency scaling:......2-39, 2-42
  Helical resonators:.....12-5, 14-4
  High-pass:..............2-39, 39-13
  High-pass low-pass conversion:...2-41
  Impedance scaling:...........2-42
  Loudspeaker lead (RFI):......39-16
  Low-pass:....................2-39
  Mechanical:..................12-27
  Method of generating SSB:....18-4
  Modern:......................2-41

(Filters, continued)

Normalized impedance:............2-39
Notch:..................13-10, 14-4
Output:.........................11-6
Parallel-tuned traps (RFI):........39-14
Passive:..................28-1, 28-3
Power supply:....................6-7
Power supply component ratings:....6-10
RC active audio:................28-4
Receiver:.......................12-3
Rejection, for BC band energy:.....30-16
Response curves:................2-40
RFI:........................39-7, 39-9
RFI, telephone:..................39-18
Scaling formulas:................2-40
Schematics:.....................2-51
SSB:..........................28-3
Strip-line:.....................39-10
Switched capacitor:..............8-23
T configuration:................11-9
Table, Butterworth low-pass:.......2-40
Table, Chebyshev high-
   pass:..................2-48, 2-49
Table, Chebyshev low-
   pass:.............2-44, 2-45, 2-46
Table, Elliptic high-pass:.........2-50
Table, Elliptic low-pass:..........2-47
Table, using:..............2-39, 2-43
Three-element, 1296 MHz:.........32-8
Tuned cavity:..........12-4, 14-4, 14-5
Tuned stubs:....................14-4
4 × 3 × 5 for Mode J
   (satellites):..................23-32
Finger stock:....................32-34
Finishing aluminum:..............24-6
Flag register:...................8-27
Flashover:......................15-11
Flicker:.........................7-12
Flip-flop:........................8-2
   Asynchronous:.................8-4
   Asynchronous inputs:...........8-6
   Clock input:...................8-4
   Direct reset:..................8-6
   Direct set:....................8-6
   Dynamic:.....................8-4
   Edge triggered:................8-4
   Gate input:...................8-4
   Gated:.......................8-4
   Gated R-S:...................8-6
   J-K:.........................8-6
   Level triggered:...............8-4
   Master/slave:.................8-4
   Outputs:.....................8-4
   Race condition:...............8-5
   Static:.......................8-4
   Synchronous:.................8-4
   Toggle (T):...................8-6
   Toggle input:.................8-4
   Unclocked R-S:...............8-4
Floppy disk:.....................8-29
   Double-density (xxDD):.........8-29
   Double-sided (DSxx):..........8-29
   Hard-sectored:................8-29
   Single-density (xxSD):..........8-29
   Single-sided (SSxx):...........8-29
   Soft-sectored:.................8-29
Flow control:....................8-33
Flux density:
   Light, LEDs:..................4-13
Flux, magnetic:..................2-20
Flyback converter:................6-32
Flywheel effect:...........15-3, 15-16
FM:
   PLL:........................10-15
   Transmitter, block diagram:......11-3
FM (also see Modulation, frequency):...18-18
   Broadcasting:..................9-7
   Detectors:...................18-23
   Deviation:...................18-20
   Direct:......................18-18
   Exciters:....................18-20
   Indirect:....................18-19
   Receivers:...................18-21
   Speech processing for:.........18-20
   Transmitters, testing:..........18-20
   Tuners, RFI:..................39-17
FM receiver subsystems:...........4-44
FM-A5 ATV sound-subcarrier generator:.....20-7

FMTV:..........................20-8
   Antennas for:................20-10
   Audio subcarrier demodulator:......20-10
   Bibliography:.................20-14
   Block receivers:..............20-10
   British Amateur Television Club:.....20-14
   Comparison with AM TV:.........20-11
   Equipment sources Table:.........20-14
   FAA Air Route Surveillance Radar:..20-12
   Measurement techniques:........20-13
   Operating Parameters Table:......20-12
   Peak deviation adjustment derivation
      Table:...................20-13
   Receivers for:................20-9
   Station block diagrams:........20-8, 20-9
   Table—Countries Using 525-Line
      Systems:.................20-12
   Test chart:...................20-19
   Test equipment for:...........20-11
   Transmit audio level testing:......20-14
   Transmitters for:..............20-8
   Video deviation testing:........20-13
Foldback current limiting:..........6-16
Folded dipoles:..................16-6
Folded unipoles:.................17-12
Follower, cathode:................5-8
Forced-air cooling:..............15-13
Formants:.......................7-1
Forth:.........................8-36
Forward error correction (FEC):....8-22, 21-6
Forward scatter:.................22-9
Forward wave:...................16-2
Fox hunting:....................38-1
Free-running multivibrator:.........8-8
Frequency:......................2-4
   Alert:.......................37-1
   Amateur allocations:........37-1, 37-2
   Audio:.......................2-5
   Audio, two-tone generator:......25-21
   Beat:........................2-5
   Calling, (VHF, UHF, EHF):......37-1
   CB (Table):..................18-6
   Checking:...................25-12
   Checking, channelized transmit-
      ters:....................18-20
   Classifications:...............2-6
   Coordination (repeater):........14-2
   Coordinator:.................14-2
   Counter, 500 MHz:...........25-13
   Counters:.............11-4, 25-12
   Cutoff:......................2-41
   Dividers:....................25-11
   Division multiplexing (FDM):......21-5
   EME:.......................23-43
   Fundamental:.................2-5
   Harmonic generation:..........3-13
   Hopping:.............21-9, 21-13
   In speech:....................7-2
   Marker generator:.............34-32
   Marker generators:...........25-11
   Measurement:...............25-11
   Meter, absorption:............25-12
   Meters:.....................26-6
   Modulation (also see FM):.....9-3, 18-18
   Multiplication:................11-4
   Of noise in digital circuits:......8-13
   Offsets for repeaters:...........14-5
   Radio:.......................2-5
   Radio control:................21-3
   Relationship, amateur bands and TV
      channels:.................39-16
   Relationships with consumer electronic
      devices:..................39-4
   Resonant (LC):...............15-3
   Response, matching networks:....2-56
   Response, microphones:.........7-2
   Ripple:......................6-7
   Shift keying:..................9-10
   Spacecraft:..................23-1
   Standards:..................25-12
   Tolerance:...................9-1
   Usage in repeaters:............14-1
Frequency multiplier:
   Diodes:......................4-5
   FET push-push doubler:........4-38
   Step-recovery-diode:...........4-16
   Varactor diode:...............4-9

Frequency-Modulated Amateur Television
   (see FMTV):..................20-8
From Spark to Space:..............1-4
Front end:
   Protection of:................12-14
   Receiver:...................12-10
Front-end overload, direction finding:....38-7
FSD-218(585) message format:.......37-19
FSK (frequency-shift keying):.......9-10,
                              19-12, 23-29
FSTV:.....................9-7, 20-1
   Audio transmissions:...........20-4
   Bibliography:.................20-7
   Comparison to FMTV:..........20-11
   Equipment needs:.............20-1
   Operating:...................37-5
   Sound:......................9-7
   Station block diagram:.........20-2
   System elements:.............20-2
   Test chart:...................20-19
   Video frame:.................20-1
Fuji-OSCAR 12:.................23-1
Fuji-OSCAR 20:.................23-2
Full-bridge converter:..............6-32
Full-duplex:
   Signaling:....................8-17
Full-wave:
   Bridge rectifiers:..............6-4
   Center-tap rectifiers:..........6-3
   Voltage doubler:..............6-11
Function key:....................8-31
Fundamental frequency:............2-5
Fuses:....................6-1, 26-21
Fusible-link ROM:................8-26

G

Gain:
   Amplifier:....................3-15
   Antenna:..............17-7, 17-18
   In linear translators and
      transponders:..............14-20
   vs spacing, antennas:..........17-15
Gain bandwidth product (F_T):.....4-18
Gain flatness:...................15-20
Gallium:........................4-1
Gamma match:.............16-6, 17-20
Gaseous regulator tubes:..........6-13
Gate (FET):....................4-29
Gated latch:.....................8-4
Gated noise source:..............25-31
Gates, using diodes as:............4-3
Gateway stations:................23-3
Gauges, metal:..................24-6
General purpose computer:.........8-26
General Purpose Interface Bus
   (GPIB):.....................8-28
General Telephone System (RFI):.....39-18
Generators:
   Ac power:...................36-37
   Ac power, grounds:...........36-40
   Ac power, storage:............36-39
   Audio two-tone:..............25-21
   Constant current:.............4-28
   Frequency, marker:.......25-11, 34-32
   Signal:......................26-5
   Signal, for receiver testing:.....25-35
   Spreading sequence:..........21-11
   TR time delay:...............31-9
Gentlemen's agreement (band
   plans):.....................37-3
Geographic equator:..............22-14
Geomagnetic equator:............22-14
Germanium:.....................4-1
Gin poles:......................36-25
Glossaries:
   Digital terms:................8-34
   Modulation, multiplexing and demodula-
      tion:.....................9-10
   Radio terms:.................3-17
   Satellites:...................23-50
GMS (Japanese weather satellite):....20-28
Gnomonic projection:.............38-8
GOES weather satellites:......20-24, 20-28
Gold code:.....................21-12
GOMS (USSR imaging satellite):....20-28
Goniometers:...................38-4
Government Printing Office:........39-18
Gray-line propagation:............22-8

Great circle radio paths:............38-8
Greenwich hour angle:..............23-46
Grid:
  Bias:...................5-4, 5-9, 15-11
  Current:..........................15-15
  Loading:..........................15-22
Grid Locator map (North America):.....37-14
Ground:...................2-3, 36-7, 39-6
  ac power generators:..............36-40
  Conductivity:......................17-2
  Noise:............................36-8
  Radial systems:...................17-13
  Waves (surface waves):.............22-3
Ground-plane antennas, for VHF and
  UHF:.............................33-32
Ground-wave RDF work:..............38-6
Grounded-cathode amplifier design example
  (tetrode at VHF):..................15-18
Grounded-grid amplifier design
  example:..........................15-15
Grounded-grid amplifiers:..............5-8
Gunn diodes:.......................4-9
Gunn effect:.......................4-9
Gunnplexers:
  High-performance audio system:.....32-45
  10-GHz communications:...........32-43
Guy anchors:......................36-23
Guy wires:.........................36-28
  Avoiding during antenna raising:.....36-32
  Insulating:........................36-23

H

H-Adcock antenna:..................38-3
H_{FB}, h_{fb} (transistor):.............4-17
H_{FE}, h_{fe} (transistor):.............4-17
Half-bridge converter:................6-31
Half-duplex, signaling:................8-17
Half sloper antenna:.................17-13
Half-wave rectifiers:..................6-3
Half-wave voltage doubler:.............6-11
HANDI-HAM System:.................1-3
Handling instructions (message):......37-19,
                           37-20
Handy Tracker direction finder:........38-18
Hang timer:........................14-6
Hard disk:.........................8-30
Hardline:..........................14-3
Hardline, CATV matching trans-
  former:..........................34-23
Harmonic distortion:..................5-4
Harmonic output, VFOs:...............10-8
Harmonics:........................2-5
  By rectification:...................39-11
  Generation:..................3-13, 39-5
  In tank circuits:...................15-5
  Suppression:......................39-5
  Suppression design example:........15-17
  Suppression in Pi networks:.........15-6
Hartley oscillator:...................4-26
Hartley VFOs:......................10-4
Hazards of RF:.....................36-3
HCT-series CMOS devices:............8-14
Headphone mixer:...................28-7
Headphones:.......................7-11
Health concerns about RF:.............36-3
Hearing:..........................7-2
Heat, in transistors:..................4-20
Heat sink:....................15-14, 24-4
  Power supply, size:................6-20
Heater voltage:.....................15-10
Height above average terrain
  (HAAT):.....................14-2, 14-3
Height above mean sea level (AMSL):...14-2
Height of antennas:..................17-1
Heliax:...........................14-3
Helical antenna, quadrifilar (weather
  satellite):........................20-29
Helical resonators:..............12-4, 14-4
  Coupling:.........................12-6
  External loading:..................12-6
  Insertion loss:....................12-6
  Tuning:..........................12-5
Helically wound dipoles:...............17-6
Henrys:..........................2-17
Hertz (Hz):.......................2-5
Heterodyne transmitter:
  Block diagram:....................11-3
Hewlett-Packard Interface Bus (HPIB):...8-28

Hexadecimal number system:.........8-6
High frequency (HF):
  Band plans:......................37-3
  Broadband FET amplifier:...........4-37
  Emergency net structure:...........37-19
  Fax:............................20-20
  Grounded-grid amplifier design
    example:.......................15-15
  Harmonic chart (RFI):..............39-4
  Mixers for:.......................12-16
  Oscilloscope adapter:..............25-31
  Propagation:......................22-1
  Propagation references:............22-12
  Reference Beacons:................22-11
  Safe exposure levels:..............36-4
  SSTV:...........................20-15
  WEFAX:.........................20-28
High Resolution Picture Transmission
  (HRPT):.........................20-27
High-pass filter:...............2-39, 39-13
High-pressure system:................22-16
Hiss (noise):.......................12-31
History:
  Amateur Radio:............1-3, 18-1, 21-14
  Technical developments:............1-4
Hole conduction:....................4-1
Holes:
  Drilling and cutting:...............24-4
  Rectangular:......................24-4
Homing (direction finding):............38-16
Horizon, at VHF:....................14-3
Horsepower:.......................2-11
Hot carrier diodes:..................4-6
Hum:.............................12-8
  Filament:.........................5-9
Hybrid combiner transformer:..........11-13
Hybrid digital meters:................25-5
Hysteresis:........................2-30
  In squelch circuits:................14-6
  In Schmitt trigger:................4-36
  Iron-core inductors:...............2-20
Hz (hertz):........................2-5

I

ICs:
  Analog switch:....................8-22
  Array:...........................4-37
  Audio amplifiers:..................4-38
  Bilateral switch:..................8-22
  CMOS:...........................4-37
  Composition of:...................4-36
  Linear:..........................4-36
  Mixers:......................4-40, 12-17
  Modulators, balanced:..............18-4
  Op amps, base diagrams:...........35-24
  Op amps, specifications:............35-23
  Single-chip CW keyer:.............29-4
  Subsystems:......................4-38
  Synthesizers:.....................10-15
  Troubleshooting:..................26-26
  TTL, specifications:................35-33
  Voltage regulators:................6-17
IDC (insulation displacement
  connector):......................36-19
Identification (ID) timer:..............14-6
Identifier, CW automatic:.............14-7
IEEE 488 bus pin allocations:.........19-29
IEEE 488 parallel interface:..........19-28
IEEE-488-1978 bus (computer):........8-28
IF:
  Amplifiers:.................12-23, 12-26
  Amplifiers, small signal:............4-40
  Choice of frequency:..............12-26
  Derived AGC:.....................12-10
  Filters, receiver:..................12-9
  Interference:......................39-12
  Noise silencers:...................12-32
  Passband tuning:..................13-5
  Port, DBM:.......................12-22
  Responses, wideband:..............12-24
  Selectivity:.......................12-26
  Shift tuning:......................13-5
  Sideband elimination:..............12-26
IGFET:...........................4-31
Image:
  Communications:..........9-7, 20-1, 37-5
  Impedance:......................15-6
  Response:........................12-23

Image generation, mixers:............12-16
Imaginary numbers:.................2-24
IMD in FET mixers:.................4-33
IMD, two-tone test:.................25-40
IMPATT diodes:....................4-11
Impedance:........................2-24
  Amplifier input:...................11-9
  Characteristic:...............16-1, 16-14
  Complex:........................2-24
  Complex notation for:.............2-24
  Image:..........................15-6
  Imaginary component of:...........2-24
  Magnitude of:....................2-24
  Matching (also see Impedance Matching
    and Matching and Trans-
    matches):...................2-31, 33-17
  Matching networks:................2-55
  Modeling in RF power amplifiers:....15-15
  Of antennas:............17-1, 17-2, 17-7
  Of line between ground planes:......15-18
  Of twisted wire pairs:..............3-13
  Ohm's Law:......................2-25
  Parallel circuit:...................2-25
  Ratio:...........................2-31
  Real component of:................2-24
  Series circuit:....................2-25
  Surge:..........................16-1
  Transformation:...................2-29
  Vacuum tube:.....................5-8
  Voltage v current phase relation-
    ship:..........................2-24
  Voltmeter:.......................25-8
Impedance matching:
  Capacitive reactance:..............15-19
  In RF power amplifiers:............15-2
  Testing:.........................15-18
Impulse noise:.....................12-31
Independent sidebands:..............18-13
Indirect FM:.......................18-19
Indium:...........................4-1
Induced EMF:.................2-17, 2-21
Inductance:.......................2-17
  Calculating:......................2-17
  Charts:..........................2-18
  Design examples:.................15-15
  In tank circuits:..................15-3
  Machine-wound coils:..............2-18
  Meter, simple:....................25-23
  Mutual:.....................2-21, 2-54
  Of a flat strip:....................2-20
  Of a straight wire:................2-18
  Of a wire above a ground plane:.....2-19
  Of broadband matching trans-
    formers:.......................15-8
  Parallel:.........................2-20
  Series:..........................2-20
  Variation in toroid inductors:....2-35, 2-36
Inductive link coupling:...............15-19
Inductive reactance:............2-22, 2-38
Inductors:........................26-22
  At VHF:.........................2-18
  Coefficient of coupling:............2-21
  Coupled:........................2-21
  Current as a function of time:.......2-21
  Distributed capacitance of:..........2-18
  Energy storage:...................2-21
  Equivalent circuit of:..............3-3
  Flux density:.....................2-20
  Iron-core, eddy currents:...........2-20
  Iron-core, hysteresis:..............2-20
  Iron-core, permeability of:..........2-20
  Iron-core, saturation of:............2-20
  Laminations in iron-core:...........2-20
  Mounting in tank circuits:...........15-9
  Mutually coupled:.................2-54
  Number of turns:.................2-34
  Parasitic capacitor:...............2-18
  Skin effect:......................2-18
  Voltage v current phase relation-
    ship:..........................2-16
Industry Standard Architecture
  (ISA bus):.......................8-28
Infinite impedance detectors:..........18-11
Information rate (CW):...............9-8
Information transfer rate:.............8-18
Injection:
  Signal:..........................26-17
  Stages:.........................12-20

Injectors, signal:
  AF and RF:....................26-5
Ink-jet printer:....................8-33
Input impedance:....................5-8
Input/Output:
  Handshaking:....................8-18
  Memory-mapped:....................8-28
  Parallel:....................8-18
  Polled:....................8-28
  Program-controlled:....................8-28
  Serial:....................8-19
Insertion loss:....................2-37, 2-38
Insertion loss of resonant circuits:....................12-6
Instability:
  In amplifiers:....................15-21
  In oscillators:....................12-10
Installation:
  Antennas:....................36-31
  Antennas, PVRC mount:....................36-32
  Towers:....................36-28
Insulation displacement connectors:....................36-19
Insulators:
  Antenna:....................33-2
Integrated circuits (IC):
  Digital:....................8-9
  Digital logic families:....................8-10
  Linear:....................4-36
  Part numbers:....................35-5
  Replacement parts:....................35-5
Intentional mismatch:....................4-24, 4-32
Interdigital filters:
  And ATV:....................20-4
Interelectrode capacitance:....................5-7
Interface:
  Buses:....................8-28
  Circuits:....................14-17, 34-4
  Digital:....................8-14, 19-27
  External devices:....................8-16
  High-voltage switching:....................14-10
  Phone-line:....................14-21
  Standard, CCITT:....................8-16
  Standard, Centronics interface
    Table:....................8-19
  Standard, EIA-232-D:....................8-16, 19-27
  Telephone:....................14-11
  Vacuum-tube gear:....................14-10
Interfacing external devices:....................8-16
Interfacing logic families:....................8-14
  CMOS to TTL:....................8-15
  Common-base level shifter:....................8-15
  TTL to CMOS:....................8-14
  Using optocouplers:....................8-15
Interference (also see RFI and TVI):....................39-1
  From magnetically coupled circuits:....................2-54
Interference Handbook:....................39-18
Intermittent Commercial and Amateur Service
  (ICAS):....................15-9
Intermodulation distortion
  (IMD):....................15-12, 39-12
  In repeaters:....................14-4
  Mixers:....................12-16
Intermodulation distortion products (IMD) in
  electronically switched antennas:....................38-19
Intermodulation intercept point,
  mixers:....................12-24
International Amateur Radio Union
  (IARU):....................1-6
International date line:....................37-11
International Sunspot Number (ISN):....................22-5
International Telecommunication Union
  (ITU):....................1-6, 37-1
  Call-sign prefix allocations:....................37-5
  Call-sign prefix allocations Table:....................37-8
  Phonetics:....................37-3, 37-7
Interpreter:....................8-33
Interpreter for Process Structure (IPS):....................8-36
Interrupt (computer):....................8-28
Interrupt-driven I/O:....................8-28
Inverted-V antennas:....................33-9
Inverter (logic):....................8-2
Ion:....................2-4
Ionization:....................22-2
Ionosonde:....................22-3, 22-7
Ionosphere:....................22-2
Ionospheric:
  Layers:....................22-2
  Sounder:....................22-4
  Storms:....................22-7

Waves (sky waves):....................22-3
IPS (interpreter for process structure):....................8-34
Iron core transformers:....................2-29
ISB (independent sideband):....................18-13
ISO 2593 pin allocations for V.35 inter-
  face:....................19-29
Isolation (repeaters):....................14-5
Isolator:....................14-4
Isotropic radiator:....................14-2
ITA2 (Baudot, operating):....................19-10, 21-6, 37-4
ITT Reference Data for Radio
  Engineers:....................15-19

J

J-antennas, for weather satellites:....................20-29
J-beam antenna:....................20-3
J-K flip-flop:....................8-6
j operator (impedance):....................2-24
J-pole antenna:....................23-27, 23-29
Jammers, locating:....................38-1
Japan-OSCAR 20:....................23-2
Joule:....................2-1, 2-2, 2-12
Junction-alloy transistor:....................4-17
Junction barrier voltage:....................4-2
Junction, semiconductor:....................4-1
  Capacitance:....................4-1, 4-17, 4-18, 4-27

K

Kansas City standard (data storage):....................8-29
Kansas City Tracker (satellite tracking
  program):....................23-24
Keplerian elements:....................20-32
Kerchunk filter:....................14-6
Keyboard:....................8-30
Keyclick interference:....................39-8
Keyers:
  CMOS Super Keyer II:....................29-6
  Memory:....................29-6
  Microprocessor-based memory:....................29-6
  Simple CMOS:....................29-1
  Single chip:....................29-4
  W2IHY audio memory keyer:....................29-16
Keying:
  Audio-frequency shift:....................9-12
  Frequency-shift:....................9-12
  Minimum-shift:....................9-13
  On-off (also see CW):....................9-8
  Troubleshooting:....................26-13
Keying envelope, CW:....................9-8
Kilowatt-hour:....................2-12
Kirchhoff's First Law (current):....................2-9
Kirchhoff's Second Law (voltage):....................2-10
KISS mode (packet radio):....................23-29
Klystrons:....................5-10
Knife-edge diffraction:....................22-18

L

L network:....................2-55, 15-17
Lacing cables:....................24-7
Ladder networks:....................2-37, 2-55
Lambert conformal conic projection:....................38-8
Lamps:
  Light-emitting diodes:....................4-13
  Miniature, specifications:....................35-30
Land breezes:....................22-18
Large-scale integration (LSI):....................8-9
Laser printer:....................8-33
Leads, test:....................26-2
Leakage:
  Flux:....................2-30
  Inductance:....................2-30
  Reactance:....................2-30
  RF:....................3-1
Least significant bit (LSB):....................8-6
Least significant digit (LSD):....................8-6
LED:....................4-13
LED displays:....................8-32
Length vs diameter, antennas:....................17-3
Lenses:....................7-15
  F stops:....................7-16
Lenz's law:....................15-3
Letter-quality printer:....................8-33
Leukemia:....................36-3
Libration fading:....................23-48
License, reciprocal:....................1-6
Light, velocity of:....................2-6
Light-emitting diode (LED):....................4-13
Lightning arrestor:....................2-3

Lightning protection:....................36-6
Limiters:....................18-22
  Noise:....................12-31
Line current:....................15-3
Line filters in digital circuits:....................8-14
Line printers:....................8-33
Line-of-sight propagation:....................22-15
Linear:
  Approximations, of nonlinear
    devices:....................3-14
  Baluns:....................16-7
  Transverters for 144 and 220 MHz:....................31-17
  Voltage regulators:....................6-14
Linear field-strength meter:....................38-10
Linear ICs:....................4-36
Linear translator block diagram:....................14-19
Linearity:
  And matching transformers:....................15-8
  ATV:....................20-3
  In amplifiers:....................15-1
  Meter:....................25-8
Link budget:
  Calculations:....................23-6
  Satellites:....................23-6
Link-coupled matching network:....................34-19
Link coupling:....................3-5, 15-19
Linked repeaters:....................14-13
Liquid-crystal display (LCD):....................8-31
Lisp:....................8-36
Lissajous figures:....................25-30
LO port, DBM:....................12-22
LO-19 (LUSAT):....................23-29
Load isolation, VFOs:....................10-6
Load resistance, optimum:....................15-2
Loading, grid:....................15-22
Loading-coil dimensions, suggested
  (Table):....................33-17
Loads:
  Antennas as:....................16-4
  Nonradiating:....................16-10
Local ARES net structure:....................37-18
Local ARES structure:....................37-16
Local emergency network chart:....................37-17
Local Interference Committees:....................38-1
Local oscillator (LO):....................12-10
Logging:....................37-7, 37-11
Logic:
  Buffer, noninverting:....................8-3
  Combinational:....................8-1
  Polarity:....................8-3
  Sequential:....................8-3
Logic buffer:
  Noninverting:....................8-3
Logic families:
  Bipolar:....................8-10
  Comparing:....................8-9
  Emitter-coupled logic (ECL):....................8-12
  Fan-out:....................8-9
  Impedance:....................8-9
  Metal-oxide semiconductor (MOS):....................8-12
  Power consumption:....................8-9
  Speed:....................8-9
  Transistor-transistor logic (TTL):....................8-10
Logic gates:
  AND:....................8-2
  Boolean equivalent:....................8-2
  Exclusive NOR:....................8-3
  Exclusive OR:....................8-3
  NAND:....................8-3
  NOR:....................8-3
  NOT:....................8-2
  OR:....................8-2
  Polarity:....................8-3
  XNOR:....................8-3
  XOR:....................8-3
Logical interfaces:....................8-14
Long-path propagation:....................22-8
Long wire antennas:....................17-7
Loop:
  Antennas:....................38-1
  Current (telephone):....................14-22
  Shielded, with sensing antenna, for
    28 MHz:....................38-11
  V phased arrays for direction finding:....................38-4
Loop skywire, multiband antenna:....................33-6
Loopstick antennas:....................38-2
  For 1.8 MHz:....................38-12
  For 3.5 MHz:....................38-13

Losses:
   Dielectric:..........................3-2
   In transmission lines:..............16-14
Loudspeakers:..........................7-11
Low-frequency fields, and safety:......36-5
Low-frequency instability (amplifiers):...15-21
Low-pass filter:.......................2-39
Lower sideband (LSB):..................9-1
Lowest usable frequency (LUF):.......22-2,
                    22-3, 22-7
LSB:...................................9-3
Luminance, LED:........................4-13

M

Machine cycle:.........................8-27
Machine language (computer):...........8-34
Magnetic:
   Coupling:..................15-8, 34-19
   Field:..............................2-17
   Flux:...............................2-20
   Path:...............................2-31
Magnetic field:
   Loopstick antennas:.................38-2
   Of the Earth:.......................22-7
Magnetic properties, toroid cores:.....35-5
Magnetically coupled circuits:.........2-54
Magnetism:.............................2-1
Magnetizing current:...................2-30
Maidenhead Locator map (North
   America):..........................37-14
Mail-order parts:......................35-6
Manometer (air pressure):..............15-13
Manuals, equipment, sources of
   (Table):...........................26-2
Manufacturers of Amateur Radio
   equipment:.........................36-42
Maps (also see Projections):
   For RDF:.....................38-7, 38-8
   North America (Grid Locators):.....37-14
   North America (with ARRL and CRRL
     Sections):.....................37-13
   US Geological Survey:..............14-1
Marconi antennas:......................17-11
Marine batteries:......................14-10
Mark:..................................8-1
Mark (FSK):............................9-10
Marker generator:......................25-11
   For 100, 50 and 25 kHz:............34-32
Mask ROM:..............................8-26
Master/Slave (M/S) flip-flop:..........8-4
Masts:
   Protection:........................36-23
Matching (also see Impedance matching
   and Transmatches):.................11-8
   Amplifier impedances:..............15-2
   Antenna impedances:................17-19
   Antennas:..........................33-17
   Antennas to transmission lines:....16-4
   Balanced QRP:......................34-21
   Broadband transformers:............15-8
   Circuit modeling:..................15-15
   Circuits for transmission lines:...16-11
   Delta match:.......................17-19
   Gamma match:................16-6, 17-20
   Impedance:.........................2-31
   Intentional mismatch:..............11-9
   L network:..................15-6, 15-17
   Link-coupled network:..............34-19
   Low-Q networks:....................11-9
   Networks:...................2-38, 2-55
   Pi network:.................15-6, 15-16
   Pi-L network:...............15-6, 15-16
   Stub, universal:...................17-19
   T match:...........................16-6
   T network:.........................15-6
   Tank circuits:.....................15-5
   Transformer, broadband, 50 to
     75 ohms:.......................34-23
   Transmatches:..............34-15, 34-17
   Variable-ratio transformer:........11-13
Matching networks:
   Low-pass T:........................11-11
   With transistor amplifiers:........4-23
Matching, impedance in diode detectors
   and mixers:........................4-5
Materials, for project construction:...24-2
Maxim, Hiram Percy:...............1-3, 1-3

Maximally flat response (see Filters,
   Butterworth):......................2-40
Maximum usable frequency (MUF):....22-2,
                  22-3, 22-13
Maxwell's equations:...................15-19
MAYDAY:................................37-1
Measurements:..........................25-1
   AC:................................25-7
   AC waveform:.......................2-12
   DC:................................25-1
   Deviation:.........................18-21
   Distortion:........................26-10
   Distortion, interpreting:..........18-15
   Frequency:.........................25-11
   Inductance meter, simple:..........25-23
   Nonsinusoidal waves:...............25-7
   Power:.............................25-3
   Receiver IMD two-tone test:........25-40
   Receiver noise figure:.............12-3
   Receiver noise floor:..............25-40
   Receiver performance:..............25-39
   Resistance:........................25-3
   RF power:..........................25-9
   RF voltage:........................25-9
   RMS:...............................25-7
   Sine waves:........................25-7
   Spectrum analyzers:................25-41
   SWR:...............................25-10
   Voltage:...........................25-2
Mechanical filters:....................12-27
Medium-scale integration (MSI):........8-9
Membership services, ARRL:.............1-5
Membership, ARRL:......................1-6
Membrane keyboard:.....................8-31
Memory comparison Table:...............8-26
Memory devices:........................8-23
Memory-mapped I/O:.....................8-28
Mesa transistor:.......................4-17
Message:
   Book messages:.....................37-22
   Checking:..........................37-22
   Creating:..........................37-17
   Format:............................37-19
   Net operating practices:...........37-22
   Numbered radiograms:...............37-21
   Packet radio message handling:.....37-24
   Q signals:.........................37-23
Message-storage operation (MSO):.......37-4
Metal gauges:..........................24-6
METEOR (USSR weather satellite):.......20-24
Meteor scatter:.........22-12, 22-13, 22-15
Meteor showers, prominent annual
   (Table):...........................22-15
METEOSAT (European weather
   satellite):........................20-26
Meters:
   AC:................................25-7
   Accuracy:..........................25-1
   D'Arsonval:........................25-1
   DC:.........................25-1, 25-3
   Deviation:.........................18-21
   Dip:...............................26-4
   Field strength, portable:..........38-10
   Frequency:.........................26-6
   Hybrid digital:....................25-5
   Inductance, simple:................25-23
   Internal resistance:...............25-2
   Linearity:.........................25-8
   Moving-vane:.......................25-1
   Multipliers:.......................25-2
   Ohmmeters:.........................25-3
   Rectifier type:....................25-7
   RMS:...............................25-7
   Shunts:............................25-2
   Signal strength:...................12-30
   Sound level:.......................7-2
   SWR:................26-3, 34-6, 34-9
   Thermocouple:......................25-7
   Voltage:....................25-2, 25-3
   Voltmeter impedance:...............25-8
   Voltmeter sensitivity:.............25-2
   Voltmeter, IC:.....................25-5
   Voltmeters, electronic:............25-5
   Voltmeters, electronic, RF probe
     for:...........................25-9
Metric:
   Equivalents:.......................35-36
   Prefixes:..........................2-5

System:................................2-1
Mica capacitors:.......................26-22
Microchannel Architecture (MCA bus):...8-28
Microcircuits (see Integrated circuits)
Microcomputer buses:...................8-28
Microfarad (μF):...................2-14
Microhenry (μH):...................2-17
Microphones:...........................7-2
   Carbon:............................7-3
   Ceramic:...........................7-3
   Crystal:...........................7-3
   Directivity:.......................7-3
   Dynamic:...........................7-4
   Electret:..........................7-4
   Frequency response:................7-2
   High-impedance amplifier:..........4-21
   Impedance:.........................7-3
   Low-impedance amplifier:...........4-21
   Noise cancellation:................7-3
   Output level:......................7-3
   Piezoelectric:.....................7-3
   Types of:..........................7-3
Microphonics in direct-conversion
   receivers:.........................12-8
Microprocessor:........................8-26
   Selection:.........................8-27
Microsats:.....................23-1, 23-2
   Frequencies and modes (Table):.....23-26
   Using the:.........................23-26
Microstrip:
   Construction techniques:...........32-5
   Grounding:.........................32-20
   Parameters:........................32-7
   Silver plating:....................32-35
   Transistor mounting:...............32-8
Microwave:
   Grounding:.........................32-20
   Projects:..........................32-1
   Propagation modes:.................22-13
   Pulse modulation:..................9-4
   Safe exposure levels:..............36-4
   Silver plating:....................32-35
Microwaves, vacuum tubes for:..........5-10
Millihenry (mH):.......................2-17
MINIMUF (computer program):............22-10
Minimum-shift keying (MSK):............9-13
Minooka Special antenna:...............17-12
Minority Carriers:.....................4-20
Mir (Soviet space station):............1-1
Mixers:....................4-40, 12-14
   Active:............................12-15
   Balanced:.......12-16, 12-17, 12-19, 12-21
   Comparisons of types:..............12-21
   Compression:.......................12-16
   Converted from 70-cm transmit-
     ter:...........................11-7
   Cross modulation:..................12-16
   Densing:...........................12-16
   Diode:..........4-6, 12-15, 12-18, 32-14
   Doubly balanced:...........12-21, 12-23
   Doubly balanced mixers, Table
     of:............................12-21
   FET:...............4-33, 4-34, 12-16
   For headphones:....................28-7
   HF:................................12-16
   High level:........................11-6
   IC:.................4-40, 12-17
   Image generation:..................12-16
   IMD distortion:....................12-16
   IMD intercept point:...............12-24
   In VHF synthesizers:...............10-16
   Noise figure:......................12-24
   Performance:.......................12-15
   Selection of:......................12-23
   Terminology:.......................12-24
   Transistor:........................4-27
   Transmitting:......................11-6
   UHF:...............................12-18
   VHF:...............................12-18
MMIC (monolithic microwave integrated
   circuit):..........................32-15
Mobile antennas:.......................33-16
Mobile stations:.......................36-35
   Charging system noise:.............36-36
   Corona discharge:..................36-36
   Electrical noise elimination:......36-36
   Electrical noise reduction:........36-36
   Instrument noise:..................36-36

(Mobile stations, continued)
Spark plug noise:.................36-36
Mode abbreviations for QSL cards:.....37-12
Mode J, filter for:................23-32
Model airplanes, and ATV:............20-1
Modeling:
Amplifier:.....................15-15
Common-emitter amplifier design example
(HF):......................15-20
Grounded-cathode amplifier design example
(tetrode at VHF):..............15-18
Modems:.........................37-4
LSI modem for amateur radio:....29-12
Packet radio:..................19-35
RTTY:........................19-12
Modern filters:...................2-41
Modes:
Spacecraft (Table):.............23-1
Transponder:..................14-19
Modula-2:.......................8-36
Modulated CW:...................9-10
Modulation:
Amplitude:................9-2, 18-1
Angle:....................9-3, 9-6
Bi-phase:....................20-29
Cross:................39-12, 39-17
Format, Fax:..............20-21, 20-22
Frequency:................9-3, 18-18
Frequency, PLL:.............10-15
Image communications:..........9-7
Index:.........................9-3
Multilevel:...................9-13
Phase:...................9-3, 18-18
Pulse:.........................9-4
Spin, satellites:...............23-6
Systems:...................9-1, 9-4
Modulator:........................9-1
Balanced:......................18-3
Balanced diode:................4-7
Balanced IC:...................18-4
Phase:.......................18-19
Reactance:....................18-19
Modules:
Cordwood:.....................24-13
Thick film:...................24-13
Monimatch circuits:...............25-10
Monitor (computer):...............8-31
Monitoring:
ATV:...........................28-8
Volunteer:.....................38-1
Monolithic microwave integrated circuit
(MMIC):.....................32-15
Moon, locating the:..............23-46
Moonbounce (see EME)
Morse code (also see CW):.....9-8, 19-2,
21-6
Abbreviations Table:...........37-6
Backwave:......................19-7
Break-in:......................19-7
Chirp:.........................19-7
CMOS Super Keyer II:...........29-6
Cutting numbers:...............19-4
Keyer, W2IHY audio memory
keyer:......................29-16
Keying and switching:..........19-4
Keying circuits:...............19-7
Monitoring:....................19-9
Oscillator keying:.............19-7
Power supply regulation:.......19-4
Receiving:..................7-9, 9-9
RF envelope shaping:...........19-5
Timing:........................19-4
Tone modulated:............9-9, 9-10
MOSPOWER (FET):.................4-31
Most significant bit (MSB):........8-6
Most significant digit (MSD):......8-6
Mother board:...................8-28
Motor-speed control:..............4-29
Mounting plate, universal:.........33-9
MS DOS:..........................8-37
Mu-law (A/D):...................8-22
MUF (maximum usable frequency):....22-7,
22-10, 22-12, 22-13
Multihop propagation:.............22-3
Multilevel modulation:............9-13
Multimeters:.....................26-2
Multipath distortion (SSTV):......20-15

Multipath propagation (direction
finding):................38-6, 38-17
Multiplexer, analog:..............8-22
Multiplexing:.....................21-5
Frequency division:............21-5
Time division:.................21-5
Multiplication, frequency:........11-4
Multiplier stages:...............12-20
Multipliers, meter:...............25-2
Multivibrator:
Astable:.......................8-8
Bistable:......................8-2
Duty cycle:....................8-9
Free-running:..................8-8
Monostable:....................8-8
One-shot:......................8-8
555 IC:........................8-9
Mutual coupling:.................2-54
Mutual inductance:.......2-21, 2-29, 2-54

N
N-channel MOS (NMOS) logic:........8-12
N-type semiconductor:.............4-1
N7BH World time finder:..........37-11
NASA:
And ATV:.......................20-2
Space shuttle transmissions:...14-11
National Electrical Code:........36-2
National Traffic System (see also
NTS):.......................37-17
Nautical Almanac, the:..........23-46
Near-letter quality (NLQ printers):..8-33
Negation symbol:..................8-4
Negative feedback:...............4-22
Negative-lead filtering:..........6-10
Negative logic:...................8-3
Negative resistance:
In Gunn diodes:................4-11
In tunnel diodes:..............4-14
Net:.............................1-1
Etiquette:....................37-17
Network:
Active:........................3-13
Audio phasing:................18-8
Beam forming:.................38-5
Combinational logic:..........8-1
Compensation:................15-20
Dissipationless:..............2-37
Equations for:...............11-10
Feedback:....................15-21
Integrated voice/data:........8-22
Kirchhoff's First Law (current):...2-9
Kirchhoff's Second Law (voltage):....2-10
Ladder:..................2-37, 2-55
Ladder, effective attenuation
formula:....................2-38
Ladder, insertion loss:.......2-38
Ladder, solving problems:.....2-38
Matching:...........2-38, 2-55, 15-2
Matching, design:.............2-55
Matching, frequency response:.....2-56
Matching, L:..................2-55
Matching, link coupled:........34-19
Modeling:....................15-15
Nonlinear:....................3-13
Norton's Theorem:.............2-11
RF phasing:...................18-8
Synthesis:....................2-39
Thevenin's Theorem:...........2-10
Neutralization:
Amplifiers:...................15-21
Tetrode:.....................15-22
Neutron:.........................2-1
Newton:..........................2-1
Newton-meter (joule):............2-1
Nickel-filled acrylic paint:......8-14
NOAA weather satellites:.........20-24
Node:............................2-9
Noise:
And DTMF decoder ICs:..........14-9
Automotive:.............36-35, 36-36
Blankers:....................12-31
Bridge, for 160 through 10 Meters:..25-32
Bridge to test matching in
amplifiers:.................15-18
Cancellation, microphones:.....7-3
Digital:......................8-35
Elimination, mobile stations:.....36-36

External:.......................12-2
Factor:.........................12-2
Figure:.........................12-2
Gated source:.................25-31
Ground:........................36-8
Impulse:......................12-31
In digital circuits:...........8-13
In oscillators:...............12-10
Limiters:.....................12-31
Power:.........................12-2
Prevention:...................8-35
Reduction:...................12-30
Temperature:..................12-2
VFOs:.........................10-8
Noise figure:...................12-2
Measurements:................12-3
Mixers:......................12-24
Noise floor measurement:........25-40
Noninverting logic buffer:.......8-3
Nonlinear devices, linear approximations
of:..........................3-14
Nonvolatile RAM (NVRAM):........8-26
North Pole, expeditions to the:...1-3
Norton op amp:..................4-46
Norton's Theorem:...............2-11
NOT (digital):...................8-2
Notch filter:...................14-4
Notch filters:..................13-10
NTS:
ARES interaction:.............37-18
Book messages:...............37-22
Message checking:............37-22
Net operating practices:.....37-22
Numbered radiograms:.........37-21
Packet radio message handling:...37-24
Q signals:...................37-23
Null, antenna:.................38-1
Numbered radiograms, ARRL:.....37-21
Numbering system:..............8-6
Numbers:
Complex:......................2-24
Imaginary:....................2-24
Nylon, properties of:.........35-33
Nyquist rate:..................8-20
Nyquist sampling theorem:......8-20

O
Object program:.................8-34
Octal number system:...........8-6
Odd parity:....................8-18
Official Observer program, ARRL:...38-1, 39-3
Ohm:...........................2-7
Ohm's Law:...........2-3, 2-8, 2-9, 2-21
For impedance:...............2-25
For reactance:...............2-22
Ohmmeters:.....................25-3
Oils, heat transfer:......34-24, 34-27
OKEAN (USSR imaging satellite):...20-27
On-off keying (OOK):...........9-8
One-shot multivibrator:........8-8
Op amps:.......................4-44
Applications:................4-46
As audio filters:............7-10
As speech amplifiers:........7-4
IC, base diagrams:...........35-24
IC, specifications:..........35-23
Norton:......................4-46
TTL to CMOS interface:.......8-15
Open-collector output:.........8-10
Operating:
Aids:........................37-1
AMTOR:.......................37-4
ASCII:.......................37-5
ATV:.........................37-5
Awards, ARRL:................37-10
Awards Table (ARRL):.........37-12
CW (Morse code):.............37-3
DX:..........................37-5
EME:.........................23-49
Emergency:...................37-15
Fax:.........................37-5
FSTV:........................37-5
ITA2 (baudot):...............37-4
Nets:........................37-22
Packet radio:................37-5
Repeater:....................37-3
RTTY:........................37-4
SSTV:...................20-15, 37-5

(Operating, continued)

Standards: 37-3
Voice: 37-3
W1AW schedule: 37-5
Operating angles (amplifiers): 15-4
Operating impedances of amplifiers: 15-1
Operating systems (computer): 8-36
Operational amplifiers (see Op amps)
Operators, Boolean algebra: 8-2
Optical fibers (RFI): 8-14
Optical memory: 8-30
Optical shaft encoder: 8-15
Optics, TV cameras: 7-15
Optocoupler: 8-15
Optoisolator: 8-15, 14-21
OR gate: 8-2
Orbit data: 20-32
Orbital tracks: 20-24
Organs and RFI: 39-18
Orthogonality: 21-11
OS/2: 8-37
OSCAR 8: 14-20, 21-3
OSCAR 9: 21-4
OSCAR 10: 23-1, 23-2, 23-3
OSCAR 13: 23-1, 23-2
OSCAR 16: 23-29
OSCAR Mode L: 32-19
OSCAR operating modes (Table): 23-1
OSCAR satellites (also see AMSAT-OSCAR
and Satellites): 1-2, 14-19, 21-3, 21-4, 23-1
Oscillations:
In amplifiers: 15-20
Parasitic: 10-2, 15-20
Oscillator-multiplier transmitters: 11-5
Oscillators: 3-16, 4-26, 12-20
AF: 25-20
Beat-frequency: 12-10, 12-29
Close-in vs far-out phase noise: 10-25
Colpitts: 10-1, 10-2
Crystal: 4-25, 4-35, 10-1, 11-2, 25-11
Crystal controlled signal source: 26-5
Crystal, adjusting frequency of: 10-2
Crystal, FET: 4-34
Crystal, for VHF: 12-20
Crystal, variable frequency: 10-3
Effects of phase noise: 10-25
Hartley: 10-4
Instability: 12-10, 26-11
Local: 12-10
Modified Pierce: 10-2
Noise in: 12-10
Overtone: 10-2
Phase noise: 10-24
Phase noise measurements: 10-27, 10-28
Pierce: 10-1
RF, for circuit alignment: 25-20
Specifying phase noise levels: 10-24
Stability: 26-11
Transistor: 4-26, 11-2
Troubleshooting: 26-10
Tunnel diode: 4-14
VFO, FET: 4-35
Voltage controlled: 10-11
Oscilloscopes: 25-26, 26-4
Alternate mode: 25-27
Bandwidth: 25-28
Chopped mode: 25-27
Digital: 25-29
Dual-trace: 25-27
Frequency response: 25-28
Lissajous figures: 25-30
Narrow bandwidth, HF adapter for: . . . 25-31
Probes: 25-28
Rise time: 25-28
Storage scopes: 25-30
Output filtering: 11-6, 15-8
Output impedance: 5-8
Output power, low: 26-13
Overhead, in asynchronous communi-
cations: 8-17
Overlay transistor: 4-17
Overload: 12-13
Overload, front-end, direction finding: 38-7
Overload, receiver: 14-4
Overtone oscillator: 4-25, 4-35, 10-2

P

P-channel MOS (PMOS) logic: 8-12

P-P voltage: 2-12
P-type semiconductor: 4-1
P5 picture reporting system: 37-10
Packet radio: 19-26
Application layer: 19-26, 19-43
AX.25 level 2 protocol: 19-38
Bibliography: 19-43
Binary baseband coding: 19-37
Channel access: 19-38
Circuit turnaround time: 19-38
Data interface: 19-26
Digipeaters: 19-40
EIA-232-D, V.24 and V.28: 19-27
EIA-422-A, V.11 and X.27: 19-28
EIA-449: 19-28
IEEE 488 parallel interface: 19-28
KA9Q Internet protocol: 19-42
KISS mode: 23-29
Link layer: 19-26, 19-38
Message handling: 37-24
Modem standards: 19-32
Modem testing: 19-35
Modems (amateur radio): 19-35
Modems (general): 19-30
NET/ROM: 19-42
Network layer: 19-26, 19-40
Network protocol: 19-41
Operating: 37-5
Operational modes: 19-28
Physical layer: 19-26
Presentation layer: 19-26, 19-43
ROSE: 19-41
Session layer: 19-26, 19-43
TCP/IP: 19-42
TexNet: 19-42
Transport layer: 19-26, 19-43
V.35: 19-28
Virtual circuit protocol: 19-41
2 Mbits/s data link: 32-65
PACSAT: 23-2, 23-28
Equipment: 23-29
Ground station equipment: 23-9
Ground-station software: 23-30
Protocol suite: 23-30
Software: 23-29
Tuning in: 23-30
PACSAT Beginner's Guide (AMSAT): . . . 23-28,
23-30
Padder capacitors: 10-5
Paper capacitors: 26-22
Parallel:
Amplifiers: 5-5
And series circuit equivalents: 2-25,
11-11, 15-5, 15-19
Circuit impedance: 2-25
Circuit resonance: 2-27
Interface: 8-18
Resonance in low-Q circuits: 2-28
Signaling: 8-16
Parallel input/output (PIO IC): 8-18
Parallel resonant circuits: 15-3
Parallel-tuned traps (RFI): 39-14
Parasitic excitation, antennas: 17-15
Parasitic oscillations: 10-2
VHF and UHF: 15-20
Parity: 8-18, 21-6
Part numbers, IC: 35-5
Parts suppliers list: 35-38
Parts, mail-order: 35-6
Pascal: 8-36
Passband tuning: 13-5
Passive filters: 28-1, 28-3
Passive mixers: 12-15
Path loss, satellites: 23-6
Pattern (see Radiation pattern)
PB program (satellites): 23-30
PC boards:
Etching: 24-9
Fabrication: 24-9
Non-etched: 24-10
Planning and layout: 24-9
Utility: 24-10
PC DOS: 8-37
PCBs, in transformer oils: 34-24, 34-27

Peak:
Envelope power (PEP): 2-13
Envelope voltage (PEV): 2-12
Filters, audio: 13-11
Voltage: 2-12
vs average power: 18-13
Peak inverse voltage (PIV): 4-2
Peak-to-peak voltage: 2-12
Pentodes: 5-7
PEP (peak envelope power): 2-13
Perforated construction boards: 24-10
Perforator (paper tape): 8-29
Period: 2-4
Peripheral devices: 8-29
Permeability:
Core material: 2-33
Cores: 3-8
Iron-core coils: 2-20
Permittivity of free space: 2-1
Persistence, vision: 7-12
PEV: 2-12
PG program (satellites): 23-31
Phase: 2-6
Angle: 2-24
Input v output in transistor
amplifiers: 4-19
Measuring: 2-6
Modulation: 9-3, 18-18
Velocity: 16-1
Phase detectors: 10-10
Phase noise: 10-24
ARRL transmitter measurement: 10-29
Close-in vs far-out: 10-25
Effects of: 10-25
Levels: 10-26
Measurement: 10-27
Measurement procedure: 10-28
Specifying levels: 10-24
Phased arrays: 38-3
V loops for direction finding: 38-4
144-MHz RDF: 38-14
Phasing method of generating SSB: 18-8
Phasing networks:
Audio: 18-8
RF: 18-8
Phenolics, properties: 35-33
Phillips code (abbreviations for Morse
operating): 37-6
Phone-line interfaces: 14-11, 14-21
Phone patch: 14-22
Phonetics (call sign), ITU: 37-3, 37-7
Phosphorous: 4-13
Photocell: 4-13
Photographic drum recorders (fax): 20-29
Photovoltaic conversion: 4-13
Pi networks: 15-6, 15-16
Values table: 15-6
Pi-L networks: 15-6, 15-16, 15-17
Picofarad (pF): 2-14
Picture transmission: 7-12
Picture tubes: 7-17
Pierce oscillators: 4-25, 4-35, 10-1
Modified: 10-2
Piezoelectric crystals: 2-54
Pilot tone: 18-17
PIN diodes: 4-11
In RDF systems: 38-18, 38-19
Pinch off, in FETs: 4-30
Planar transistor: 4-17
Plans, band: 37-3
Plant Series (telephone RFI): 39-18
Plastic film capacitors: 26-22
Plastics, properties: 35-33
Plate: 5-1
Current: 5-2
Detectors: 18-11
Mounting, universal: 33-9
Plate dissipation, vacuum tube: 15-8
Platter (hard disk): 8-30
PLL: 10-10, 10-15
Demodulators: 18-25
Synthesizers: 10-9
PN junction: 4-1
Point-contact diodes: 4-1
Polar coordinates: 2-24
Converting to rectangular: 2-25
Polar keying (digital signaling): 8-19
Polar relay: 8-19

Polarity, logic: 8-3
Polarization, antenna: 17-1, 17-18
 ATV: 20-3
 Circular: 17-22
 Misalignment: 23-44
 Signal, and direction finding: 38-4
Polyethylene, properties: 35-33
Polypropylene, properties: 35-33
Polystyrene, properties: 35-33
Poor Man's Spectrum Analyzer: 20-14
Port:
 IF, DBM: 12-22
 LO, DBM: 12-22
 RF, DBM: 12-22
 Termination, DBM: 12-22
Portable:
 Ac power sources: 36-37
 Antennas: 33-14, 36-38, 36-40
 Field strength meter: 38-10
Portable stations: 36-37
 Ac power sources: 36-37
 Antenna considerations: 36-40
Position indicator, rotators: 23-15
Positive logic: 8-3
Pot cores: 2-32
Potential: 2-1
 Drop: 2-3
 Gradient: 2-2
Powdered-iron toroidal cores, physical
 properties: 2-34
Power: 2-11, 2-13
 Amplifiers: 5-4
 And energy: 2-11
 Apparent: 2-26
 Average: 2-13
 Battery: 6-35
 Consumption in PMOS: 8-12
 Consumption in TTL subfamilies: ... 8-10
 Cords, 3 wire, 117 V: 36-9
 DC input: 15-8
 Dissipated: 15-15
 Dissipated, measurement: 15-14
 Dynamic, digital ICs: 8-9
 Effective radiated (EIRP, isotropic
  reference): 14-2
 Effective radiated (ERP, dipole
  reference): 14-2
 Factor: 2-26
 FCC Regulations: 37-2
 For amateur equipment: 36-8
 In linear translators and
  transponders: 14-20
 Maximum output: 15-8
 Measurement: 25-3
 Output, low: 26-13
 Peak envelope: 2-13
 Peak vs average: 18-13
 Ratings, SSB transmitters: 18-13
 Reactive: 2-24
 RF: 25-9
 Solar electric: 6-38
 Spectral density: 9-12
 Static, digital ICs: 8-9
 Transfer, optimum: 15-2
 Wattless: 2-24
Power line:
 Connections: 6-1
 Fusing: 6-1
 Voltage: 6-1
Power supplies: 6-1, 26-6
 Connector standard: 27-1
 Construction projects: 27-1
 Economy: 6-11
 Filters: 6-7
 For vacuum tube amplifiers: ... 15-10
 Load resistance: 6-7
 Primary circuit: 27-1
 Safety: 27-1
 Solar: 6-38
 Switched-mode: 6-25
 Thermal design: 6-18
 Troubleshooting: 26-8
 5-A switching supply: 27-1
 28-V, high current: 27-3
 2000-V, 1-A: 27-18
 3500-V, 1-A: 27-20
Power transistors: 4-20
Power-to-voltage conversion table: ... 35-37

Pre-emphasis: 9-3
Preamble (message): 37-19
Preamble, spread spectrum: 21-12
Preamplifiers:
 Audio, and RFI: 39-17
 Dual-gate GaAsFET for 28, 50, 144 and
  220 MHz: 31-3
 FET: 12-14
 For satellite work: 23-10
 GaAsFET for 144 and 220 MHz: ... 31-5
 GaAsFET for 432 MHz: 32-1
 Low-noise for 2.3 through 10 GHz: ... 32-22
 MOSFET for 28, 50, 144 and
  220 MHz: 31-1
 Remote switching system: 31-6
 Tower-Mounted, for satellite work: ... 23-15
Precedence (message): 37-19
Prefixes:
 FCC allocated for outside continental
  US: 37-10
 Unit: 2-5
Preselector: 12-9
Primary current: 2-30
Prime meridian: 37-11
Principles of Emergency Communication
 Table: 37-15
Printed-circuit capacitors: 39-9
Printer: 8-33
Priroda (USSR weather satellite): ... 20-27
Probes, oscilloscope: 25-28
Procedural signals (prosign) Table: ... 37-6
Processing, speech: 7-6
 SSB: 7-7
Product detectors: 18-11
 Active: 18-12
Program counter: 8-27
Programmable dividers: 10-11
Programmable ROM: 8-26
Programs:
 For determining az-el of celestial
  bodies: 23-47
 MINIMUF: 22-10
Projections:
 Azimuthal equidistant: 38-8
 Gnomonic: 38-8
 Lambert conformal conic: 38-8
Prolog: 8-36
PROM: 8-26
Propagating bandwidth: 22-3
Propagation: 22-1, 38-8
 Aurora: 22-15
 Backscatter: 22-9, 22-12, 22-14
 Delay: 8-1, 8-9, 8-10, 16-1
 Diffraction: 22-18
 Forward scatter: 22-9
 Gray-line: 22-8
 HF: 22-1
 Line-of-sight: 22-15
 Long-path: 22-8
 Meteor scatter: 22-12, 22-13, 22-15
 Modes in waveguide: 16-3
 Modes, Microwave: 22-13
 Modes, UHF: 22-13
 Modes, VHF: 22-13
 Multihop: 22-3
 Prediction: 22-10
 PROPHET ray trace synopsis, multimode
  parameters—advanced (Table): ... 22-4
 Rain scatter: 22-16
 Reflection from objects: 22-18
 Selected HF references: 22-12
 Selected VHF/UHF bibliography: ... 22-18
 Short-path: 22-8
 Sidescatter: 22-9
 Sporadic-E: 22-2, 22-10, 22-12
 Transequatorial spread-F (TE): ... 22-14
 Tropospheric ducting: 22-16
 Tropospheric enhancement: 22-16
 Tropospheric scatter: ... 22-12, 22-16
 VHF, UHF and microwave (Table): ... 22-13
 VHF, UHF, Microwave: 22-12
 1.8-MHz (160-meter): 22-9
 3.5-MHz (80-meter): 22-10
 7-MHz (40-meter): 22-10
 10-MHz (30-meter): 22-10
 14-MHz (20-meter): 22-10
 18-MHz (17-meter): 22-10

21-MHz (15-meter): 22-10
24-MHz (12-meter): 22-10
28-MHz (10-meter): 22-10
50-54 MHz (6-meter): 22-12
144-148 MHz (2-meter): 22-12
222-225 MHz (135-cm): 22-12
420-450 MHz (70-cm): 22-13
Protection:
 Lightning: 36-6
 Receiver front end: 12-14
Proton: 2-1
Prototype boards, solderless: 24-10
Provinces, Canadian, map: 37-13
Pseudorandom-number generator: 8-8
PSK: 19-30, 23-29
Public address systems, RFI: 39-18
Public Law 97-259: 39-2, 39-3
Public service: 1-3
 Operating aids: 37-15
Pull-up resistor: 8-10
Pulleys: 36-25
Pulse (digital): 8-1
Pulse modulation: 9-4
Pulses:
 Blanking: 7-14
 TV Synchronization: 7-15, 20-2
Push-down stack (memory): 8-23
Push-pull amplifiers: 4-25, 5-5
Push-pull converter: 6-31
Push-pull converter/regulator: 6-24
Push-pull tripler: 11-5
Push-push doubler: 11-5
PVC, properties: 35-33
PVRC mount, antenna installation: ... 36-32

Q

Q (Quality factor): 2-27
 And voltage rise at resonance: ... 2-27
 In coupled circuits: 2-53
 In coupling networks: 11-9
 In transistor amplifiers: 4-23
 Of a tuned circuit: 12-3
 Of inductive links: 15-19
 Of loaded circuits: 2-28
 Section: 16-4, 16-5
 Tank circuits: 15-5, 15-16
 Unloaded: 2-27
Q signals: 37-23
QEX: 1-5, 23-30
QN signals: 37-23
QSL:
 ARRL membership QSL card: ... 37-10, 37-12
 Bureaus, ARRL: 37-10
 Cards: 37-7
 Mode abbreviations: 37-12
QST: 1-5
Quad antennas: 17-14, 17-17
Quadrifilar helical antenna (weather
 satellite): 20-29
Quadrifilar windings: 24-8
Quadriphase shift keying (QPSK): ... 8-18
Quantization (A/D): 8-21
Quartz crystals: 2-54
Quaternary systems: 8-1
Queue (memory): 8-23
QWERTY (keyboard): 8-30

R

R/C (radio control): 21-1
 Frequencies, Amateur Radio: 21-3
 Pulse-code modulation (PCM): ... 21-2
 Pulse-width modulation: 21-2
R-S flip-flop: 8-4
RACES, dedicated operating
 frequencies: 37-16
Radial networks: 17-13
Radiation:
 Angle: 17-2, 22-7
 Characteristics, antennas: 17-3
 Inversion: 22-16
 Limits, CATV: 39-3
 Limits, consumer electronic devices: ... 39-3
 Resistance: 17-1
Radiation pattern:
 Adcock array: 38-4
 Loop antenna with sensing element: ... 38-4
 Loop antennas: 38-4
 Unidirectional: 38-2

Radiator, isotropic:.................14-2
Radio:
    Control:...........................21-1
    Frequencies (also see RF):...........2-5
    Horizon:..........................22-16
    Horizon, VHF:.....................14-3
    Paths, great circle:...............38-8
    Propagation:......................22-1
    Terms, glossary of:...............3-17
    Waves:.............................2-6
    Waves, velocity:...................2-6
Radio Civil Emergency Service (see
    also RACES):.....................37-16
Radio direction finding (RDF):.........38-1
    Antennas for:.....................38-1
    Antennas for sky wave:............38-8
    Antennas, using for communica-
        tions:........................38-10
    Bibliography:..............38-16, 38-20
    Errors:............................38-6
    Ground wave work:.................38-6
    Maps for:..................38-7, 38-8
    Sky wave:..........................38-7
    System calibration and use:.......38-8
    Techniques:.......................38-6
    VHF:.............................38-16
    VHF AM systems:..................38-18
    VHF Doppler shift systems:.......38-19
    VHF DoppleScAnt:.................38-19
    VHF Double Ducky:................38-18
    VHF FM systems:..................38-18
    VHF Handy Tracker:...............38-18
    VHF loop antennas:...............38-16
    VHF mobile installations:........38-20
    VHF parasitic arrays:............38-16
    VHF phased arrays:...............38-16
    VHF Roanoke Doppler:.............38-19
    VHF switched antenna RDF
        systems:.....................38-18
    VHF Time-Difference-of-Arrival (TDOA)
        systems:.....................38-18
Radio Netherlands (BASICODE):.......8-29
Radiogoniometer:.....................38-4
Radiograms:
    (see also traffic, message, NTS):....37-20
    Numbered, ARRL:.................37-21
Radio-wave absorption:...............22-7
Rain scatter:.......................22-16
Raising antennas:...................36-31
    Avoiding guy wires:.............36-32
Random-access memory (RAM):........8-24
Raster scanning:....................8-31
Ratings for transmitting devices:.....15-8
Ratio detectors:...................18-24
Ratio, deviation:....................9-3
Rb (base-emitter resistance):.........4-17
RC active audio filters:.............28-4
RC time constant:...................2-15
Reactance:..........................2-16
    And complex waves:..............2-26
    And impedance:..................2-22
    And tank circuit Q:.............15-5
    Capacitive:................2-16, 2-38
    Capacitive vs frequency:.........2-23
    Chart:..........................2-22
    Diode:..........................4-16
    In parallel:....................2-22
    In RF chokes:..................15-10
    In series:......................2-22
    Inductive:................2-22, 2-38
    Inductive vs frequency:.........2-23
    Matching, series:..............15-19
    Modulators:....................18-19
    Of a terminated transmission line
        section:...................15-18
    Of broadband matching transformers:....15-8
    Stray:.........................15-15
Reactive power:.....................2-24
Read-only memory (ROM):.............8-26
Readability (reporting):............37-6
READY line (handshaking interface):..8-18
Real power:.........................2-26
Receiver:...........................12-1
    AGC:...........................12-10
    AGC range:......................12-6
    Attenuators:...................12-11
    ATV:...........................20-3
    ATV preamp and converter:.......20-4

Band-Imaging CW, for 10 and
    18 MHz:.........................30-1
Bandwidth:..........................12-3
BFO:.......................12-10, 12-29
Broadcast:.........................39-17
Communications, high performance:...30-8
Coupling to:.......................16-10
Desensitization:....................14-4
Detectors:..........................12-7
Direct conversion:..................12-8
Dynamic range:......................12-6
EME:...............................23-45
FM:................................18-21
FM subsystems:......................4-44
FMTV:..............................20-9
For repeaters:......................14-3
Front end:.........................12-10
Front-end protection:..............12-11
Hum:...............................12-8
IF filters:........................12-9
IMD two-tone test:.................25-40
Incremental tuning:................13-3
Local oscillator:..................12-10
Measuring performance:.............25-39
Microphonics:......................12-8
Mixers:............................12-14
Noise figure:......................12-2
Noise figure, measurements:...12-3, 25-40
Noise reduction:...................12-30
Oscillator radiation:..............12-7
Overload (repeaters):..............14-4
Preselector:.......................12-9
Regenerative:......................12-7
RF amplifier:......................12-11
RS-232-C line:......................8-19
S meters:..........................12-30
Satellite:.........................23-8
Selectivity:.......................12-3
Sensitivity:.......................12-1
Signal-to-noise ratio:.............12-3
Single conversion:.................12-9
Singly balanced detector:..........12-8
Step attenuator:...................12-11
Superheterodyne:...................12-9
Superregenerative:.................12-7
Synchrodyne:.......................12-8
TRF (tuned radio frequency):.......12-7
Troubleshooting:...................26-14
Troubleshooting (Table):...........26-8
TV, deficiencies:..................39-12
VHF and UHF:.......................12-1
Receiving DX QSLs (bureaus):.......37-10
Receiving Morse code:..............7-9
Reciprocal license:................1-6
Rectangular coordinates:...........2-24
    Converting to polar:...........2-25
Rectification:.....................5-2
    Harmonics by:..................39-11
Rectifier instruments:.............25-7
Rectifiers:..................4-1, 6-3
    Full-wave bridge:..............6-4
    Full-wave center-tap:..........6-3
    Half-wave:.....................6-3
Red Cross:.........................37-17
Reference diodes:..............4-3, 4-16
References:
    Selected HF propagation:.......22-12
    Selected VHF/UHF propagation:..22-18
Reflected wave:....................16-2
Reflection from objects:...........22-18
Reflection of radio waves:....22-1, 38-6
Reflectometers (SWR):..............25-10
Reflex klystron:...................5-10
Refraction of radio waves:....22-1, 38-6
Refresh (memory):..................8-25
Regenerative receivers:............12-7
Regions, ITU:......................37-1
Register:
    Accumulator:...................8-27
    Byte:..........................8-8
    Flag:..........................8-27
    General purpose:...............8-27
    Program counter:...............8-27
    Shift:.........................8-8
    Special purpose:...............8-27
    Stack pointer:.................8-27
    Word:..........................8-8

Regulation, voltage (Zener):........4-3
Regulator:
    Current, diode:................4-16
    Electronic voltage:............6-14
    High-current:..................6-16
    IC voltage:....................6-17
    Linear:........................6-14
    Specifications (IC):...........6-17
    Switching:.....................6-21
    Tubes, gaseous:................6-13
Relaxation oscillator:.............4-29
Relay drivers:.....................14-17
Relay, PIN diodes as:..............4-12
Relays:............................26-23
Remote control:....................14-9
Remote control, station:...........21-3
Remote preamplifier switching
    system:........................31-6
Repairs, factory:..................26-27
Repeaters:.........................14-1
    Above mean sea level (AMSL):...14-2
    Aircraft emergency-locator-transmitter
        (ELT) monitor:.............14-13
    Antennas:......................14-3
    ATV:...........................20-4
    Audio-control circuits:........14-15
    Autopatches:...................14-11
    Circulator:....................14-4
    Control flow charts:...........14-9
    Courtesy tones:................14-11
    Coverage:......................14-2
    Current on feed lines:.........14-3
    Desensitization:...............14-4
    Duplexers:.....................14-5
    Duty cycle:....................14-2
    Effective radiated power (EIRP, isotropic
        reference):................14-2
    Effective radiated power (ERP, dipole
        reference):................14-2
    Emergency power:...............14-10
    FCC Regulations:...............14-1
    Frequency coordinator:.........14-2
    Frequency offset Table:........14-5
    Hang timer:....................14-6
    Height above average terrain
        (HAAT):.............14-2, 14-3
    Helical resonators:............14-4
    Identification (ID) timer:.....14-6
    Intermodulation distortion (IMD):....14-4
    Isolation:.....................14-5
    Isolator:......................14-4
    Kerchunk filter:...............14-6
    Link polling:..................14-13
    Linked:........................14-13
    Linking controller:............14-19
    Microprocessor control:........14-8
    Notch filter:..................14-4
    Operating:.....................37-3
    Overload (receiver):...........14-4
    Packet radio:..................14-1
    Receivers:.....................14-3
    RF equipment:..................14-3
    Shielding:.....................14-5
    Sites:.........................14-2
    Station-gain calculation:......14-3
    Time-out timer:................14-6
    Transmitter control (COR, CAS):....14-5
    Transmitters:..................14-3
    Tuned cavity:.............14-4, 14-5
    Tuned stubs:...................14-4
US Forest Service communications
    sites:.........................14-2
Replacement parts:.................35-5
Reset state (digital):.............8-2
Resistance:........................2-7
    And tank circuit Q:............15-5
    Back:..........................4-2
    Base-emitter:..................4-17
    Generalized definition of:.....2-11
    Measurements:..................25-3
    Of wires:......................2-8
    Optimum load:..................15-2
    Radiation:.....................17-1
    Skin effect:...................2-8
    Stray:.........................15-15
    Swamping (amplifiers):.........15-21
    Temperature effect:............2-8
    To damp parasitic oscillations:....15-20

Resistivity:................2-3, 2-7
  Of metals:.........................2-8
Resistors:.............2-3, 2-8, 26-20
  At RF:.........................25-21
  Color code:......................35-1
  In parallel:......................2-9
  In series:.......................2-9
  In series-parallel:..............2-10
  Power:........................25-23
  Pull-up:.........................8-10
  Screen bleeder:.................15-12
  Standard values:................35-2
Resolution (A/D):...................8-21
Resonance:.........................2-24
  Curves:.........................2-27
  In power supply components:.......6-10
  Low-Q parallel circuit:..........2-28
  Parallel circuit:................2-27
  Self:...........................2-18
  Series, in RF chokes:...........15-10
  Series circuit:..................2-26
  Voltage rise:...................2-27
Resonant cavity:...................14-4
Resonant frequency:................2-26
Resonant frequency formula (LC):.....15-3
Resonators:
  Coupled:........................2-52
  Helical:........................12-4
  Quarter-wavelength coaxial cavity:..12-4
Response, maximally flat (see Filters,
  Butterworth):..................2-40
Restoration, of equipment:.........26-28
Retransmission of broadcasts:.......14-11
Return loss measurement:...........15-18
Return loss-to-SWR conversion table:...35-38
Reverse current (in a semiconductor
  junction):.......................4-1
RF:................................2-5
  Amplifiers:...........12-9, 12-12, 12-13
  Circuit alignment, oscillators for:.....25-20
  Circuits:.......................2-37
  Clamp, diode:...................4-15
  Connectors, soldering:..........36-15
  Control-link block diagram:......14-17
  Decoupling from ac line:.........39-8
  Derived AGC:...................12-29
  Determining power density:.......36-4
  Energy, thermal effects of:.......36-3
  Leakage:........................3-1
  Phasing networks:...............18-8
  Port, DBM:.....................12-22
  Power amplifiers:..........4-24, 15-1
  Power amplifiers, bibliography:.......15-22
  Power measurements:.............25-9
  Probe for electronic voltmeters:.......25-9
  Resistors at:..................25-21
  Safe exposure levels:...........36-4
  Safety:........................36-3
  Signal injector:...............26-5
  Toroidal devices, checking:.......2-35
  Transformers:...................3-3
  Transformers, broadband:.........3-8
RF amplifiers:
  Small signal:..................4-40
RF choke:
  Filament:......................15-16
  Parasitic oscillation suppressor:.......15-20
  Plate:...............15-16, 15-17
RF transformers:
  Goniometer:....................38-5
RFI:......................26-13, 39-1
  Additional information, sources of:....39-18
  And loudspeakers:..............39-16
  Audio preamplifiers:...........39-17
  Bibliography:..................39-18
  Common-mode choke:...........39-14
  Dealing with:..........39-5, 39-18
  Digital circuits:...............8-35
  Emanation:....................39-1
  FCC rules:...............39-2, 39-8
  Feedthrough capacitors:.........39-7
  Filters:.......................39-9
  FM tuners:.....................39-17
  From CATV systems:..............39-2
  From magnetically coupled circuits:....2-54
  Grounds:.......................39-6
  IF interference:...............39-12
  Immunity complaint reports:.........39-3

Interception:......................39-1
Organs:...........................39-18
Public address systems:............39-18
Public Law 97-259:..........39-2, 39-3
Rejection filter, for BC band
  energy:.......................30-16
  Shielding:..............39-6, 39-17
  Stereo interference:...........39-16
  Strip-line filters:.......39-10, 39-13
  Suppression practices:..........39-6
  Tape decks:....................39-16
  Task Group, ARRL:..............39-4
  Telephone interference:........39-18
  Transmitter defects:...........39-17
  Turntables:....................39-16
  TV antenna installation:........39-14
  TV receiver deficiencies:.......39-12
  TVI troubleshooting flowchart:....39-15
  UHF television:................39-14
  With broadcast reception:.......39-17
Ring counter:.......................8-8
Ripple frequency:...................6-7
Ripple voltage:.....................6-7
Rise time:..........................8-1
  And bandwidth, relationships
  (Table):.......................7-19
RIT (receiver incremental tuning):.......13-3
RL time constant:...................2-21
RMS (root-mean-square):.......2-12, 25-7
  Voltage:.......................2-12
Roanoke Doppler direction finder:....38-19
Rochelle salt:......................7-3
Rod antennas:.......................38-2
ROM (read-only memory):.............8-26
Roof-hole mobile antenna mount
  (VHF):........................38-20
Root-mean-square (RMS):......2-12, 25-7
Ropes:............................36-25
Rotation period of sun:.............22-7
Rotation, antenna, electronic:......38-5
Rotator systems, for antennas:......36-33
Rotators:
  Antenna, satellite:............23-13
  Azimuth:.......................23-13
  Elevation:.....................23-13
  Position indicators:...........23-15
RS-10/11:..........................23-1
RS-232-C:...........................8-19
RST system Table:..................37-6
RTTY:.....................9-10, 19-9
  AFSK demodulators:.............19-13
  AFSK modulators:...............19-13
  ASCII operation:...............19-19
  Audio frequency shift keying
  (AFSK)........................19-12
  Baudot:.......................19-10
  Baudot speeds and signaling
  rates:........................19-12
  Baudot teletypewriters:........19-11
  Computer-based baudot terminals:..19-11
  Control sequence Table:.........37-7
  Diversity reception:...........19-13
  Frequency shift keying (FSK):....19-12
  FSK demodulators:..............19-13
  Modems:.......................19-12
  Operating:.....................37-4
  Rules, safety:.................26-1
Run-length encoding (fax):..........20-22

S

S meters:..........................12-30
S-100 bus (computer):...............8-28
Safe exposure levels to RF:.........36-4
Safety:
  Electrical:...........36-2, 36-6, 36-9
  RF:...........................36-3
  Rules:........................26-1
  Towers:.......................36-24
Sample-and-hold (S/H) amplifiers:.......8-23
Satcom 1R (commercial satellite):......20-2
Satellites (also see Spacecraft)
  AMSAT-OSCAR 8:................21-3
  AMSAT-OSCAR 13:..............23-2
  AMSAT-OSCAR 16:..............23-29
  Antenna accessories:...........23-18
  Antenna, 70-cm and 2-m
  J-pole:.............23-27, 23-29

Antenna Controller for tracking:......23-20
APT format:........................20-26
  Bibliography:..................23-50
  Communications:................23-1
  Communications requirements:......23-3
  Computer BBS:..................20-32
  Equipment suppliers (Table):.......23-10
  Fax transmissions:.............20-23
  Frequencies:...................23-1
  Fuji-OSCAR 12:.................23-2
  Gateway stations:..............23-3
  Geostationary:..........20-24, 20-28
  Ground station antennas:.......23-11
  Ground-station equipment:.......23-7
  History:.......................23-4
  Link budget computations for Mode-B and
  Mode-L transponders (Tables):.....23-6
  Microsat:......................23-2
  Microsat frequencies and modes
  Table):.......................23-26
  Microsats, using the:..........23-26
  Operating modes (Table):.......23-1
  PACSAT:.......................23-2
  Phase III-D:...................23-2
  Phase IV:......................23-2
  Polar orbiting (fax):..........20-24
  Receiving accessories:.........23-18
  Specialty equipment:...........23-11
  Spin modulation:...............23-6
  Station accessories:...........23-13
  Station control:.........23-19, 23-26
  Telemetry:.....................21-5
  Tracking:..............20-32, 23-20
  Transmission losses between Earth and
  Phase-III spacecraft (Table):.......23-6
  Transmitting accessories:.......23-17
  Transponders:.................14-19
  UoSAT-OSCAR:............21-3, 21-4
  UoSAT-OSCAR 9:................21-4
  Weather:.......................20-24
  Weather, Table:................20-26
Saturation:
  In matching transformers:.......15-8
  Of iron-core inductors:.........2-20
  Region (transistor):...........4-21
Scan converters, SSTV:.............20-15
Scanning density, Fax:.............20-21
Scanning, TV:.......................7-13
Schmitt trigger, FET:...............4-38
Schottky TTL integrated circuits:......8-10
Scientific notation:................8-6
Screen supply:.....................5-9
Screen voltage:...................15-11
Secondary current:.................2-30
Section:
  ARES structure:...............37-16
  ARRL and CRRL, map:...........37-13
  Manager:.......................1-5
Section, ARRL Field Organization:......1-5
Sector (diskette):.................8-29
Selectivity:..........2-27, 12-3, 26-14
  At VHF:.......................12-4
  IF:...........................12-26
Self oscillation (amplifiers):.......15-21
Self oscillation in TV booster
  amplifiers:....................38-2
Self-resonance:....................2-18
Semiconductor junctions, current in:.....4-2
Semiconductors:...............4-1, 26-24
  Diode clamp:...................15-12
  Diodes, for antenna rotation:.......38-5
  Junction temperature formula:.......15-15
  Optoisolators:.................14-21
  PIN diodes, in RDF systems:.......38-18, 38-19
  Rectifier ratings:..............6-4
  Substitutions:.................26-26
Sending DX QSLs (bureaus):.........37-10
Sensing antenna:............38-2, 38-3
Sensitivity:.......................26-15
  Receiver:......................12-1
Sequence, direct:..................21-9
Sequential access:.................8-29
Sequential logic:...................8-3
Serial interface:..................8-19
Serial signaling:..................8-16
Series and parallel circuit
  equivalents:...........2-25, 11-11

Series and parallel equivalent
  circuits:................15-5, 15-19
Series circuit impedance:...............2-25
Series circuit resonance:...............2-26
Series diode switching:..................4-3
Series reactance matching:............15-19
Series resonance in RF chokes:.......15-10
Series-section transformers:...........16-5
Set state (digital):......................8-2
Seven-segment display:................8-32
Shadow RAM:.............................8-26
Sheet metal, cutting and bending:......24-5
SHF:
  Downconverters for fax:.............20-29
  Weather satellites:.................20-28
Shield, against climbing towers:......36-30
Shield, electrostatic:....................2-3
Shielded loop antennas:.................38-2
Shielded loopstick antenna:...........38-12
Shielding:.................39-6, 39-7, 39-17
  Digital equipment:....................8-13
  Repeaters:............................14-5
  Transmission lines:...................14-4
Shift register:...........................8-8
Shockley, William:.....................4-16
Short-path propagation:.................22-8
Shot noise:....................12-31, 15-11
Shulman, Ivan A., MD:.................36-3
Shunt diode switching:...................4-3
Shunt feedback:.......................15-21
Shunt, meter:...........................25-1
SI (Systeme International d'Unites):.....2-1
Sideband:................................9-1
  Amplitude compandored:.......7-9, 9-6,
                                18-1, 18-17
  Elimination in IF amplifiers:........12-27
  From angle modulation:...............9-3
  Independent:.........................18-13
  Single:..............................18-1
  Suppression as a function of phase
    error, unwanted (Table):...........18-8
Sidescatter:............................22-9
Sidescatter, direction finding:.........38-8
Siemens:................................2-8
Signal:
  Fading:..............................22-8
  Generators:..........................26-5
  Injection:...........................26-17
  Injectors:............................26-5
  Quality, SSB (Table):................18-4
  Source, crystal controlled:...........26-5
  Strength meters:....................12-30
  To-noise ratio for A/D conversion:....8-21
  Tracers:.............................26-6
  Tracing:.............................26-16
Signal generator, for receiver testing:...25-35
Signal purity:..........................39-8
Signal relay:...........................14-5
Signal report (RST):...................37-6
Signaling:
  ASCII:.....................19-18, 19-19
  Asynchronous:........................8-17
  ATV:.................................21-6
  Baudot:....................19-11, 19-12
  Coding:..............................21-5
  Full-duplex:...................8-17, 19-30
  Half-duplex:...............8-17, 19-29
  Neutral-keyed:.......................8-19
  Parallel:.............................8-16
  Polar-keyed:.........................8-19
  Rate:................................8-18
  RS-232-C:............................8-19
  Serial:...............................8-16
  Simplex:.............................8-17
  Synchronization:.....................8-17
  Synchrony:...........................19-31
  Synchronous:.........................8-17
  Systems:.............................21-5
Silicon:.................................4-1
Silicon controlled rectifier (SCR):......4-28
Silicon diode specifications:............6-4
Silicon diodes, protection of:...........6-4
Silicon-on-sapphire (SOS) logic
  family:..............................8-13
Silicone grease:.......................15-14
Silicone heat-transfer compound:......4-20
Silver plating:........................32-35
  In tank circuits:..............15-5, 15-10
Silver solder:..........................24-6

Simplex, signaling:.....................8-17
Sine wave:..............................15-3
Sine-wave measurements:...............25-7
Sine-wave parameters:.................2-12
Single ended mixers:..................12-18
  FET:......................4-33, 4-34
Single sideband (SSB):
  Full carrier:..........................9-6
  Suppressed carrier:...................9-5
Single-tuned circuits:...................3-5
  Analysis:.............................3-6
Singly balanced detector:..............12-8
Singly balanced mixer (IC):....4-33, 12-16,
                                      12-17
Sirocco (wind):.......................22-18
Ski Trek:...............................1-3
Skin effect:.................2-8, 2-18, 15-5
Skip distances (MF and HF):...........22-7
  Table:...............................22-10
Sky wave:
  RDF:.................................38-7
  RDF, antennas for:...................38-8
  Triangulation:.......................38-8
Sleeve baluns:.........................16-7
Slow-Scan Television (see SSTV):.....20-15
Small-scale integration (SSI):.........8-9
Smoothed sunspot number:.............22-5
Snap diodes:...........................4-16
Snubber network:.......................2-21
Sockets, for integrated circuits:.......4-37
Sockets, vacuum tube:................15-12
Solar:
  Cycles:...............................22-5
  Electric power:.......................6-38
  Flares:...............................22-6
  Flux:......................22-6, 22-13
  Radiation:............................22-6
Solar cell:.............................4-13
Solar-electric diodes:.................4-13
Solar-flux index:......................22-6
Solder:
  Alloys:...............................24-6
  Silver:...............................24-6
Soldering:..............................24-6
  Irons:................................24-1
  Irons, temperature control:...........24-3
  Static-sensitive devices:.............24-3
  Station:..............................24-2
Solderless prototype boards:..........24-10
Solenoidal cores:......................2-32
Solid state:............................4-1
Solid-state CW transmitters:..........11-2
Solid-state relay:......................8-15
Solving ladder-network problems:......2-38
SOS:...................................37-1
                Sound:
  Intensity levels:.....................7-2
  Level meters:........................7-2
  TV:..................................7-17
  Unvoiced:.............................7-1
  Voiced:...............................7-1
  Waves:...............................7-2
Source (FET):.........................4-29
  Impedance:...........................4-31
Source program:.......................8-34
Sources of equipment manuals
  (Table):.............................26-2
Soviet space station Mir:..............1-1
Soviet Union, weather satellites:......20-24
Space:
  Communications:.....................23-1
  OSCAR satellites:....................1-2
  Satellite transponders:..............14-19
  Shuttle:..............................1-4
  Shuttle transmissions:...............14-11
  Soviet Mir station:...................1-1
Space (FSK):..........................9-10
Space shuttle:
  ATV:.................................20-1
Spacecraft:
  Antennas:............................23-5
  Frequencies (Table):.................23-2
  History:..............................23-4
  Microsat:.............................23-2
  Operating modes (Table):.............23-1
  PACSAT:..............................23-2
  Phase III-D:..........................23-2
  Phase IV:.............................23-2

Spacing vs gain, antennas:............17-15
Spark plug noise:.....................36-36
Spatial polarization:..................23-44
SPC Transmatch:.......................34-17
Speaker-lead filters (RFI):............39-16
Speakers:..............................7-11
Special purpose computer:.............8-26
Specifications:
  Antenna, 12- and 17-meter, for the 5-8-λ
    vertical antenna (Table):..........33-10
  Blower performance:.................15-13
  Regulator (IC):......................6-17
  Silicon diodes:......................6-4
  Transmission lines, characteristics of
    commonly used (Table):............16-13
  Tubes, sockets and chimneys:........15-12
  Varistors:...........................35-15
  144-MHz Yagi family (Table):........33-25
  220-MHz Yagi family (Table):........33-28
  432-MHz Yagi family (Table):........33-21
Spectrum analyzer, Poor Man's:.......20-14
Spectrum analyzers:...................25-41
  Applications:........................25-43
  Basics:..............................25-42
  Performance specifications:.........25-42
Spectrum classifications:..............2-6
Spectrum management:.................21-8
Speech:................................7-1
  Amplifiers:...........................7-4
  Clipping and filtering:...............7-7
  Compandoring:.......................7-9
  Digitized:...........................21-6
  Expansion:...........................7-9
  Formants:............................7-1
  Frequency and amplitude considera-
    tions:..............................7-2
  Phase inversion (amplifiers):.........7-5
Speech processing:.....................7-6
  For FM:.............................18-20
  For SSB:.............................7-7
Speed of light:........................2-6
Spin modulation:......................23-6
Split stator tuned input:..............15-19
Sporadic-E:........22-2, 22-10, 22-12, 22-14
Spread spectrum:......................21-7
  Amateur experiments:...............21-14
  Bibliography:.......................21-17
  Chirp:...............................21-9
  Correlation:.........................21-10
  Despreading:........................21-11
  Detection:...........................21-11
  Direct sequence (DS):...............21-9
  Direction finding:...................21-14
  FCC rules:...........................21-14
  Field strength:......................21-13
  Frequency hopping (FH):.............21-9
  Orthogonality:......................21-11
  Preamble:...........................21-12
  Spectrum management:..............21-8
  Spreading sequence generators:.....21-11
  Spreading sequences:...............21-10
  Synchronization:....................21-12
  Time hopping:.......................21-9
Spurious emission limits:..............39-8
Spurious signals:.....................12-13
Squelch relay:.........................14-5
SSB:.........................9-5, 18-1
  Filters:..............................28-3
  Generation:.........................18-7
  Generation, filter method:..........18-4
  Generation, phasing method:.........18-8
  Modes:..............................18-12
  Signal quality (Table):..............18-4
  Single-sideband full-carrier telephony:...9-6
  Transmitter power ratings:..........18-13
  Transmitter testing:................18-13
SSTV:................9-7, 20-1, 20-15
  Buckshot noise:.....................20-17
  Color:..............................20-16
  Digital image processing:...........20-18
  Fax compatibility:..................20-18
  Image processing:...................20-18
  Motion systems:.....................20-18
  Multipath distortion:...............20-15
  Net:.................................20-15
  Operating:...........................37-5
  Pass-band tuning:...................20-15
  Quantized:...........................9-8
  Scan converters:....................20-15

(SSTV, continued)
Standards Table:.....................20-15
Station block diagrams:...............20-16
Station operation:....................20-15
Test chart:.........................20-19
Transmitter duty cycle:...............20-16
Stability:..........................26-15
Amplifiers:.......................15-20
In transistor amplifiers:........4-23, 12-12
In VFOs:.........................10-5
Stacking, of Yagi antennas:...........17-20
Standards:
A/D conversion:.....................8-21
Fax:.............................20-21
Frequency:........................25-12
Operating:........................37-3
Power-supply connectors:..............27-1
Sizes of aluminum tubing (Table):......33-4
SSTV:...........................20-15
Start bit:..........................8-17
State transition tables:.................8-3
States, US, map:.....................37-13
Static RAM (memory):.................8-25
Station accessories:..................34-1
Station-gain calculation:...............14-3
Steel-wool (shield choke):.............39-7
Steering, electronic, antenna:...........38-5
Step attenuator:.....................12-11
Step-recovery diodes:.................4-16
Stereo interference:..................39-16
Stolen radios, recovering:.............38-1
Stop bit:...........................8-17
Stray reactances:....................15-7
Strength (reporting):.................37-6
Strip line:
Plate tank inductor:............15-10, 15-18
Strip-line filters for RFI:.........39-10, 39-13
STROBE line (handshaking interface):.....8-18
STS-9 (space shuttle) ATV:.............20-2
Stub matching, universal:..............17-19
Subbands, amateur:...................37-1
Subsystem IC:.......................4-38
Sun, rotation:.......................22-7
Sunspots:.........................22-5
Super dummy:......................34-24
Superdiode:........................4-27
Superheterodyne receivers:.............12-9
Superregenerative receivers:............12-7
Suppliers:
Parts:..........................35-38
Satellite equipment (Table):..........23-10
Supports, antenna:.............36-21, 36-22
Suppression, harmonics:................39-5
Surge impedance:....................16-1
Surge protection:....................36-3
Surge protection of diodes:.............6-5
Susceptance:.......................2-38
Swamping resistance (amplifiers):........15-21
Swinging chokes:....................6-9
Switched-capacitor filters (SCF):........8-23
Switched-mode power supplies:..........6-25
Basic power-stage circuit topologies:.....6-25
Boost converters:..................6-27
Buck converters:..................6-25
Buck-boost converters:..............6-27
Common switched-mode power supply
topologies, characteristics (Table):.....6-33
Converter conditions, ideal (Table):.....6-30
Converter operation, modes of:......6-29
Efficiency:......................6-25
Feedback and control:..............6-34
Flyback converter:.................6-32
Forward converter, one-switch:.......6-30
Forward converter, two-switch:.......6-30
Full-bridge converter:..............6-32
Half-bridge converter:..............6-31
Isolated power-stage circuit
topologies:.....................6-30
Magnetics:......................6-33
Push-pull converter:...............6-31
Soft-start:.......................6-34
Switches:.......................6-32
Switches:
Compound:......................4-12
Using diodes as:..................4-3
Using transistors as:...............4-21
Switching voltage regulators:...........6-21
Switching, electronic:........4-3, 4-20, 11-3

For antenna rotation:.................38-5
SWR (also see VSWR):
Definition:........................16-2
Indicator:........................34-9
Measurements:....................25-10
Meter:.......................26-3, 34-6
To-return loss conversion table:......35-38
vs band-pass ripple in filters:.......2-51
Symbol rate (ATV):...................8-18
Sync stretcher:.................20-3, 20-6
Sync-to-video ratio (ATV):.............20-3
Synchrodyne receivers:................12-8
Synchronization pulses (ATV):...........20-2
Synchronization, spread spectrum:.....21-12
Synchronous communications:...........8-17
Synchronous demodulation:.............8-23
Syntax:...........................8-35
Synthesizers, frequency:.........10-1, 10-9
Bibliography:.....................10-23
Direct digital (DDS):...............10-17
Hybrid DDS/PLL:..................10-22
ICs:............................10-15
Partial synthesis:.................10-13
PLL:............................10-9
PLL for HF systems:...............10-12
Special receiver design considera-
tions:.........................10-23
Two loop:.......................10-13
UHF:...........................10-17
VHF applications:.................10-14
VHF Mixing:.....................10-16
Sysop:...........................37-4
Systeme International d'Unites:..........2-1

T

T matching section:...................16-6
T networks:.........................15-6
Tables:
American and international interface
standards:......................19-30
ASCII Asynchronous signaling
rates:..........................19-19
ASCII coded character set:...........19-18
Baudot signaling rates and speeds:...19-11
Bell 103/113 modem frequency
scheme:.......................19-33
CCIR Rec 625 service information
signals:........................19-15
Code conversion, ITA1 through 4:....19-23
Conversion from ASCII to Morse and
Baudot:........................19-22
Conversion from Baudot to ASCII and
Morse:.........................19-21
Conversion from Morse to ASCII and
Baudot:........................19-21
Data interface connections:..........19-28
Data transmission signaling rate
standards:......................19-19
EIA-449 37-pin connector:...........19-28
EIA-449 9-pin connector:............19-29
IEEE 488 bus pin allocations:........19-29
Incidental frequency modulation:......10-27
ISO 2593 pin allocations for V.35
interface:.......................19-29
ITA2 and CCIR Rec. 476 (AMTOR)
codes:.........................19-10
Microsat Frequencies and Modes:...23-26
Morse codes for other languages:.....19-3
Morse code character set:............19-2
Morse cut numbers:................19-4
Noise bridge calibration data:........25-35
Pi-network resistive attenuator:........25-39
Power ratio for voltages across 600 ohm
load:..........................28-16
SSB phase noise of an ICOM IC-745
receiver:.......................10-29
Summary of Bell and CCITT modem
characteristics:..................19-34
Synthesizer design trade-offs:........10-9
T-network resistive attenuator:........25-39
Typical maximum phase noise
levels:........................10-26
Tables, operating, for amateur
equipment:......................36-10
Tank circuits:.......................15-3
Efficiency of:....................15-5
Inductor ratings:.................15-10
Matching:.................15-5, 15-16

Output capacitor ratings:............15-9
Q of:.............................15-5
Tape decks, RFI:....................39-16
Target transmitter:...................38-7
Technical developments, history:........1-4
Teflon breakdown voltage:.............15-10
Teflon circuit-board capacitors:.........39-9
Telecommand:..................9-12, 21-3
Telegraphy (see also CW):
Continuous-wave Morse:.............9-8
Receiving Morse:...................9-9
Telemetry:.....................9-12, 21-4
Amateur-satellite:..................21-5
Telephone:
Interference:......................39-18
RFI filters:.......................39-18
Telephone equipment:................28-13
Central office basics:...............28-13
Terminal interface equipment:........28-13
Telephones:........................28-14
Audio:..........................14-21
FCC Part 68 rules:................28-15
Interface:...................14-11, 14-21
Interface specifications Table:........14-21
Phone patches:...................28-15
Remote control via:................14-9
Telephony, analog:...................9-5
Television (see also ATV, FSTV and SSTV):
As computer monitor:...............8-32
FMTV:..........................20-8
Sound:..........................9-7
Waveforms:......................20-2
Television Handbook:...............20-2
Temperature:
And repeater equipment:............14-2
And resistance:...................2-8
And transistor biasing:.............15-12
Control, for soldering irons:..........24-3
Derating for transistors:.............15-9
Effects on cavity amplifiers:........32-29
Effects on duplexers:...............14-5
Effects on local oscillators:..........12-10
Effects on semiconductors:.....4-1, 4-2, 4-16
Effects on vacuum tubes:............15-8
Inversion:.......................22-16
Junction, in transistors:.............15-15
Noise:..........................12-2
Terminal-node controller (TNC):....19-35, 23-29
Test equipment:.................25-1, 26-1
For 24-cm FMTV:..................20-11
Test leads:.........................26-2
Test transmitter:.....................38-7
Tester:
Transistors:......................26-6
Vacuum tubes:....................26-6
Testing:
Capacitors:......................26-21
FM transmitters:..................18-20
Signal tracing:....................26-6
SSB transmitter:..................18-13
Two tone:.......................18-14
Within a stage:...................26-19
Tetrode amplifier design example
(grounded-cathode at VHF):..........15-18
Tetrode and pentode transmitting
tubes:...........................35-9
Tetrode neutralization:...............15-22
Tetrodes:..........................5-7
Thermal:
Design, power supply:..............6-18
Protection of diodes:...............6-5
Thermal sink:......................15-14
Thermionic emission:.................5-1
Thermocouple meters:................25-7
Thevenin's Theorem:.................2-10
Thick film modules:..................24-13
Third-order intercept:................12-24
Threaded code:.....................8-36
Three-state output (digital logic):.......8-11
Thyristors:.........................4-28
Tilting, beam (repeater antennas):.......14-3
Time:
Conversion:......................37-11
Notation:........................37-10
Zones:.....................37-10, 37-11
Time constant:
RC:............................2-15
RL:............................2-21

Time-Difference-of-Arrival (TDOA) direction
 finding systems:.................38-18
Time division multiplexing:............21-5
Time hopping:....................21-9
Time-out timer:..................14-6
Time standard stations:............22-12
TIROS-N (US weather satellite):......20-24
Toggle (T) flip-flop:................8-6
Tolerance, frequency:................9-1
Tone (reporting):..................37-6
Tone, pilot:....................18-17
Tools:
 Care of:.....................24-1
 Recommended:.................24-1
Top loading, antennas:............33-18
Toroidal baluns:..................16-9
Toroidal transformers:........3-9, 11-12
Toroids:.................2-32, 2-34
 A_L values:.................2-34
 Characteristics:...............35-4
 Cores:.....................2-32
 Counting turns:............2-36, 2-37
 Distributed capacitance:........2-36
 How to wind:.................2-36
 Magnetic properties:...........35-5
 Number of turns:..............2-34
 RF core types:...............2-32
 RF, checking inductance:........2-35
 Winding data:................35-4
Totem-pole output:................8-10
Touch Tone (DTMF signaling):......14-9
Touch Tone decoder:..............34-3
Tower-mounted equipment:.....23-15, 23-16
Towers:.....................36-24
 Base for:...................36-27
 Cables and control wires on:......17-13
 Climbing accessories:..........36-24
 Climbing shield:..............36-30
 Guying:....................36-28
 Installation:.................36-28
 Manufacturers:...............36-26
 Safety:....................36-24
 Selecting:..................36-25
TR sequencing:.................23-51
TR time-delay generator:............31-9
Tracers, signal:..................26-6
Tracing signals:..................26-16
Track (diskette):................8-29
Tracking, dial:..................26-11
Tracking, satellite:...............20-32
Traffic:.....................37-17
 Aids from HQ:...............37-15
 ARRL form FSD-218(585):......37-17
 Book messages:..............37-22
 Message checking:............37-22
 Message format:..............37-19
 Net operating practices:.........37-22
 Numbered radiograms:.........37-21
 Packet radio message handling:....37-24
 Q signals:..................37-23
 Welfare:...................37-17
Transadmittance (FET):...........4-31
Transceivers:..................13-1
 Computer control of:...........13-13
 Design:....................13-2
 Features:...................13-3
 Future trends:...............13-12
 QRP for 7 MHz (Optimized QRP
  Transceiver):...............30-37
 QRP for 7 MHz (Ugly Weekender):...30-33
 QRP Portables for 20 and
  30 meters:.................30-26
 QRP Three-Bander for 18, 21 and
  24 MHz:..................30-19
 Troubleshooting:.............26-14
 Troubleshooting (Table):........26-7
Transconductance:................5-3
Transconductance (FET):..........4-31
Transequatorial spread-F (TE)
 propagation:.................22-14
Transformer:
 Oils:.................34-25, 34-27
Transformer-coupled amplifiers:........5-5
Transformer coupling:.............11-10
Transformers:.............2-29, 26-22
 Auto-:.....................2-32
 Balun:....................11-12
 Baluns:...................16-8

Bifilar wound:..................2-33
Broadband:..............2-33, 11-12
Broadband matching:........15-8, 15-20
Broadband RF:..................3-8
Broadcast and TV replacement:.......6-1
Closed core:...................2-29
Construction:..................2-31
Core material:.............2-31, 11-12
Core size:....................2-32
Current equalizing:................6-2
Eddy currents:.................2-30
Efficiency:....................2-30
Equivalent circuit:...............2-30
Ferromagnetic:.................2-32
Flux density formula:.............2-32
Hybrid combiner:...............11-13
Hysteresis:...................2-30
Impedance matching:.............2-31
Impedance ratio:...............2-31
In parallel:.....................6-2
Iron core:....................2-29
Leakage reactance:..............2-30
Magnetic path:.................2-31
Magnetizing current:.............2-30
Matching, broadband, 50 to 75 ohms:..34-23
Matching, variable-ratio:..........11-13
Power:.....................2-30
Power, lead color codes:...........35-3
Power-handling capability:..........6-2
Primary current:................2-30
Primary winding:...............2-29
Rewinding:....................6-2
RF:........................3-3
RF cores:....................2-32
RF, goniometer:................38-5
Saturation:...................11-12
Secondary current:..............2-30
Secondary winding:.............2-29
Series-section:.................16-5
Toroidal:...............3-9, 11-12
Transmission-line:....2-33, 3-11, 15-8, 15-20
Trifilar wound:.................2-33
Turns ratio:...............2-30, 2-31
Types:.....................2-33
Volt-ampere rating:...............6-1
Voltage ratio:..................2-30
Windings, bifilar:................3-9
Windings, twisted pair:............3-9
1/4-wave section:.........16-4, 16-5, 16-6
Transient suppression:..............6-6
Transistor:
 Active region:................4-21
 Alpha:....................4-17
 Alpha cutoff:................4-18
 Amplifiers:............4-19, 12-12
 Amplifiers, differential:..........4-19
 Amplifiers, FET:..............4-37
 Applications:................4-20
 As superdiodes:..............4-27
 As switches:................4-21
 As voltage-variable capacitors:.....4-27
 As Zener diodes:.............4-27
 Audio amplifiers:.............4-21
 Beta:.....................4-17
 Bipolar:...................4-16
 Breakdown voltage:............4-21
 Characteristic curves:...........4-18
 Characteristics of:.............4-17
 Constant-current source:........4-28
 Cutoff region:...............4-21
 Darlington pair:..............4-22
 Diac:.....................4-29
 Dissipation:.................4-20
 Failure causes:...............4-20
 FET:.....................4-29
 FET amplifiers:..............4-33
 FET amplifiers, RF and IF:.......4-32
 FET characteristics:...........4-31
 FET crystal oscillators:.........4-34
 FET mixers:............4-33, 4-33
 FET VFOs:.................4-35
 FET, power:...........4-31, 4-35
 GaAsFET:.................4-31
 Gain bandwidth product (F_T):....4-18
 IGFET:...................4-31
 Inventors of:................4-16
 Junction FET:...............4-29

Junction-alloy:................4-17
Mesa:.....................4-17
Mixers:................4-27, 4-40
MOSFET:..................4-30
Oscillators:..................4-26
Overlay:...................4-17
Planar:....................4-17
Power:....................4-20
RF amplifiers:...........4-22, 4-40
RF power amplifiers:...........4-23
Saturation region:.............4-21
Unijunction:.................4-29
VFO, FET:.................4-36
VMOS FET:................4-31
Transistor amplifier instability:.......2-42
Transistor-transistor logic:
 Circuits:...................8-10
 Decoupling:................8-12
 Inputs:...................8-11
 Interfacing with CMOS:........8-14
 Outputs:..................8-10
 Subfamilies Table:...........8-10
Transistors:
 Amplifier design example (common-
  emitter at HF):.............15-20
 Amplifier stabilization:.........15-20
 Amplifiers, driver circuits:........11-7
 Amplifiers, parasitics:..........11-7
 Amplifiers, v vacuum tubes:......11-1
 And RFI:.................39-17
 Biasing:...................15-12
 Bipolar:..................26-24
 Common-base level shifter:......8-15
 Cooling:..................15-14
 Failure in amplifiers:..........15-20
 FET, replacement considerations:...26-26
 General-purpose power:........35-20
 Japanese nomenclature:........35-15
 JFET:...................26-25
 Junction temperature formula:.....15-15
 Limitations in power amplifiers:....15-1
 Low noise, specifications:........35-16
 Matching:.................11-10
 MOSFET:................26-26
 MOSFET amplifiers:.........12-14
 MOSFET, preamplifiers for 28, 50, 144 and
 220 MHz:................31-1
 Oscillators:.................11-2
 Package information:..........35-22
 Power dissipation (P_D):........15-9
 Power FETs:...............35-19
 Power FETs, specifications:......35-16
 Ratings:..................15-9
 Reactances:...............15-7
 RF power, specifications:........35-16
 Selection rule of thumb:........15-9
 Small-signal FETS, specifications:...35-18
 Specifications:..............35-15
 Tester:...................26-6
 V_{CEO} in RF amplifiers:......15-9
 VHF and UHF class-A, specifica-
  tions:...................35-18
Transition region (semiconductor):......4-17
Translators, linear:...............14-19
Transmatches:..................17-5
 And baluns:................17-20
 Balanced or unbalanced lines:...34-17, 34-17
 Balanced QRP:..............34-21
 Link coupled:...............34-19
Transmission line:
 Plate tank inductor:...........15-18
 Transmission line transformers:....2-33,
                3-11, 15-8, 15-20
Transmission lines:..............17-18
 And circuits:................16-2
 ATV:....................20-3
 Bibliography:...............16-15
 Characteristics:.............16-13
 Characteristics of commonly used
  (Table):.................16-13
 Factors and equations:.........16-2
 Hardline or Heliax:...........14-3
 Impedance-matching circuits:.....16-11
 Loads, nonradiating:..........16-10
 Losses in:.................16-14
 Shielding:.................14-4
 Stubs, 1/4-λ:...............14-4
 Velocity factor:..............16-1

Transmission, pictures:................7-12
Transmitter:.....................11-1
  ALC:.........................7-8
  ATV:.........................20-3
  Basics:.......................11-1
  Block diagrams:................11-3
  Circuits for ATV:...............20-4
  Coupling to transmission lines:......16-10
  CW:..........................11-2
  Defects and RFI:................39-17
  EME:.........................23-45
  EME success, transmitter power required
    for (Table):..................23-45
  Fax:.........................20-20
  FMTV:........................20-8
  Frequency checking:..............18-20
  Gunn diode:....................4-11
  Incremental tuning:..............13-3
  Modified Cubic Incher, 80, 40 or
    30 meters:...................30-17
  Oscillator-multiplier type:.........11-5
  Repeater:.....................14-3
  Satellite:......................23-10
  Solid state:....................11-2
  SSB, and power ratings:...........18-13
  Target:.......................38-7
  Test, for RDF:..................38-7
  Testing FM:....................18-20
  Testing SSB:...................18-13
  Troubleshooting:................26-12
  Troubleshooting (Table):..........26-8[2]
  VHF, filters for:................39-10
Transmitter-distributor (paper tape):....8-29
Transmitting mixers:................11-6
  High level:....................11-6
Transponders:.....................14-19
  Mode Table:...................14-20
Transverters:
  Single board 23-cm:.............32-15
  144 MHz:.....................31-17
  220 MHz:.....................31-17
  1296 to 28 MHz:...............32-5
Trap:...........................17-14
  Dipoles:......................17-6
  Vertical antennas:...............17-14
Traps, tuned (RFI):.................39-14
Traveling wave tubes:................5-10
Trees, as antenna supports:...........36-21
TRF (tuned radio frequency) receivers:...12-7
Triac:...........................4-29
Triangulation:.....................38-6
  Direction finding:...............38-2
  Sky wave:.....................38-8
Trifilar windings:...................24-8
Trimmer capacitors:.................10-5
Trinary systems:....................8-1
Triode amplifiers:..................3-14
Triode transmitting tubes:............35-8
Triodes:.........................5-2
  Characteristic curves:............5-3
Tropospheric:
  Ducting:......................22-16
  Enhancement:..................22-16
  Scatter:...................22-12, 22-16
  Waves:.......................22-3
Troubleshooting:
  Bibliography:...................26-29
  Block diagram level:.............26-7
  Checkout:.....................26-27
  ICs:.........................26-26
  Procedures:...................26-7
  Symptoms and their causes
    (Table):.....................26-7
  Systematic approaches:..........26-16
  TVI:.........................39-16
True (digital logic):.................8-2
TTL subfamilies:...................8-10
  Fan-out Table:.................8-11
  Performance Table:..............8-10
Tubing, aluminum, standard sizes
  (Table):.......................33-4
Tuned cavity:..................14-4, 14-5
Tuned cavity filters:................12-4
Tuned radio frequency (TRF) receiver:...12-7
Tuned stubs:......................14-4
Tunnel diodes:....................4-14
Turns ratio, transformer:.........2-30, 2-31
Turntables, RFI:...................39-16

TV:
  Antenna installation:.............39-14
  Blanking pulses:................7-14
  Booster amplifiers, self oscillation:..38-2
  Cameras:.....................7-13
  Cameras, optics:...............7-15
  Color:.....................7-17, 20-2
  Composite video:...............7-15
  Deflection:....................7-13
  Deflection tubes:...............35-11
  Doorknob capacitors:...........15-10
  Energy distribution:............7-19
  Picture tubes:..................7-17
  Receiver deficiencies:...........39-12
  Scanning:....................7-13
  Sound:....................7-17, 9-7
  Synchronization pulses:.......7-15, 20-2
  Video:.......................20-2
  Video frequencies and bandwidths:...7-18
TVC-1b ATV receiving converter:......20-5
TVI (also see RFI):
  Troubleshooting:...............39-16
  Troubleshooting flowchart:.......39-15
  UHF television:................39-14
  VHF, causes and cures:.........39-10
Twilight zone:.....................22-8
Twin-T oscillator:..................4-26
Twisted pairs, impedance and attenua-
  tion:.........................3-13
Two-tone tests:..............18-14, 25-39
TXA5 ATV exciter:................20-6

U

U-Adcock antenna:.................38-3
Ugly construction:.................24-11
UHF:
  Activity nights:................37-4
  Antennas for:..................17-18
  ATV (see also ATV, FSTV, FMTV and
    SSTV):......................20-1
  Blocking capacitors:.............15-10
  Calling frequencies:.............37-4
  Digital circuits:................8-12
  Dummy antenna:...............34-26
  Filters for RFI:................39-10
  Gallon dummy:.................34-26
  Harmonic chart (RFI):...........39-16
  Mixers for:....................12-18
  Oscillations in amplifiers:........15-20
  Projects:.....................32-1
  Propagation:...................22-13
  Safe exposure levels:...........36-4
  Silver plating:.................32-35
  Tank inductors:................15-10
  Vacuum tubes for:.............5-10
  Yagi antennas:.................33-19
Ultimate Transmatch:..............34-17
Undersampling:...................8-20
Unidirectional radiation pattern:.....38-2
Unijunction transistor:.............4-29
Unipole antennas, folded:..........17-12
Unit prefixes:.....................2-5
Universal asynchronous receiver transmitter
  (UART):......................8-19
Universal synchronous receiver transmitter
  (USRT):......................8-19
Universal synchronous/asynchronous receiver
  transmitter (USART):...........8-19
UNIX:..........................8-37
UoSAT-OSCAR:...................21-3
UoSAT-OSCAR 9:.................21-4
Uplink (transponders):.............14-19
Upper sideband (USB):.............9-1
US Forest Service communications
  sites:........................14-2
US Geological Survey map:.........14-1
US Government Printing Office:......39-18
USB:..........................9-3
Using filter tables:............2-39, 2-43
USSR, weather satellites:..........20-24
UTC:..........................37-11
Utility PC boards:................24-10

V

V.24 interface levels:..............8-19
$V_{(BR)}$ (transistor):...............4-21
$V_{BE(sat)}$ (transistor):..............4-21

Vacuum tubes:................5-1, 26-26
  Amplifier, 3CX800A7, for 144 MHz:..31-46
  Amplifier, high power, for HF:.....15-15
  Amplifiers:....................5-2
  Amplifiers, v solid-state:......11-1, 11-7
  Arcing:.......................15-11
  Base diagrams:................35-7
  Beam power:..................5-8
  Characteristics:................5-3
  Chimneys:....................15-12
  Continuous Commercial Service
    (CCS):......................15-9
  Cooling:......................15-12
  Dissipated power:..............15-15
  Dissipated power measurement:.....15-14
  Driver circuits:................11-7
  Failure in amplifiers:...........15-20
  Filament or heater voltage:.......15-10
  For microwaves:...............5-10
  For UHF:.....................5-10
  Grid bias:.....................15-11
  Grid loading:..................15-22
  Grounded-grid amplifier design
    example:....................15-15
  Impedance match testing:........15-18
  Impedance matching:...........15-16
  Intermittent Commercial and Amateur
    Service (ICAS):..............15-9
  Klystron:.....................5-10
  Matching:....................11-10
  Maximum power output:.........15-8
  Maximum ratings:..............15-9
  Neutralization:................15-21
  Output matching at VHF:........15-7
  Overload effects:..............15-11
  Plate dissipation:..............15-8
  Plate resistance:...............15-16
  Plate RF choke:...............15-17
  Plate voltage:.................15-11
  Reactances:...................15-7
  RFI:.........................39-6
  Screen-grid protection:.........15-11
  Screen-grid voltage:...........15-11
  Specifications, sockets and
    chimneys:...................15-12
  Testers:......................26-6
  Tetrode and pentode transmitting
    tubes:......................35-9
  Tetrode operation:.............15-11
  Traveling wave tubes:..........5-10
  Triode transmitting tubes:.......35-8
  TV deflection tubes:...........35-11
  TV picture tubes:..............7-17
  Vs solid-state amplifiers:.......15-1
  144-MHz amplifier design example:..15-18
Vacuum-variable capacitor:.........15-17
VAR (volt-ampere reactive):........2-24
Varactor diodes:..................4-7
  Frequency multiplying:..........11-5
Variable bandwidth tuning:.........13-9
Varicap:........................4-4
Varicap diodes, specifications:......35-12
Varistors, specifications:..........35-15
VBT (variable-bandwidth tuning):.....13-9
Vector mode (visual display):.......8-32
Velocity factor:..................16-1
Velocity of light:..............2-6, 2-6
Vertical antennas:................17-10
  Construction of:...............33-4
  Radial networks:..............17-13
  Short:.......................17-12
  Trap:........................17-14
  VHF 1/4 wave:................33-32
  5/8-wave for 12 and 17 meters:....33-10
  144 MHz, 5/8 wave:...........33-30
Vertical incidence sounder:.........22-7
Vertical retrace:.................8-31
Very-large-scale integration (VLSI):...8-9
Vestigial sideband transmission (ATV):..20-4
VFO:......................10-4, 11-3
  Assembly:....................10-5
  Backlash:....................11-4
  Buffers for:...................10-7
  Coils:........................10-5
  Colpitts:...................10-5, 10-7
  Dials:.......................11-4
  FET:........................4-35
  Harmonic output:..............10-8

(VFO, continued)
Hartley:................................10-4
In transmitters:.......................11-4
Linear tuning:.........................11-4
Load isolation:........................10-6
Noise:.................................10-8
Planetary drive:.......................11-4
Practical:.............................10-8
Stability considerations:..............10-5
Voltage-variable capacitor-tuned:......4-10
VHF:
Activity nights:.......................37-4
Amplifiers:..................12-13, 12-15
Antennas for:.........................17-18
Antennas, vertical 1/4 wave:..........33-32
Blocking capacitors:..................15-10
Calling frequencies:...................37-4
Crystal oscillators for:..............12-20
Direction finding:....................38-16
Dummy antenna:.......................34-26
Filters for RFI:......................39-10
Frequency chart (RFI):.................39-4
Harmonic chart (RFI):.................39-16
Inductors:.............................2-18
Matching vacuum-tube amplifiers:.......15-7
Mixers for:...........................12-18
Narrow-band FET amplifier:............4-37
Oscillations in amplifiers:...........15-20
Propagation:................22-12, 22-13
Radio equipment:.......................31-1
Radio horizon:.........................14-3
Receiver selectivity at:...............12-4
RF chokes:............................31-30
Roof-hole mobile antenna mount:......38-20
Safe exposure levels:..................36-4
Tank inductors:.......................15-10
Transmitters, block diagrams:..........11-3
Transmitters, filters for:............39-10
Transmitters, oscillator-multiplier
  type:...............................11-5
Transmitting mixer:....................11-6
Weather satellites:...................20-26
Window-box mobile antenna
  mount:..............................38-20
Yagi antennas:........................33-19
Yagi antennas, 144 MHz, high
  performance:........................33-25
Yagi antennas, 222 MHz, high
  performance:........................33-28
Yagi antennas, 432 MHz, high
  performance:........................33-21
144-MHz amplifier design example:....15-18
VHF/UHF propagation bibliography:....22-18
Video:.................................7-11
Composite, TV:.........................7-15
Frequencies and bandwidths:...........7-18
Levels, standard, (Table):.............7-15
Measuring transmitter deviation:.....20-13
Transmitters for:......................20-3
TV:....................................20-2
Video display terminal (VDT):..........8-31
Video Graphics Adapter (VGA):........20-31
Virtual Height of ionosphere:......22-3, 22-7
Visible and Infrared Spin Scan Radiometer
  (VISSR):............................20-28
Vision:................................7-11
Color:..............................7-12[2]
Flicker:...............................7-12
Persistence:...........................7-12
Visual Atmospheric Sounder (VAS):....20-28
VMOS FET:.............................4-31
Voice operated switching (VOX):.......13-11
Voice operating:.......................37-3
Voice packet switching:................8-22
Voice, human:..........................7-1
Voice/data network:....................8-22
Volatile (memory):.....................8-25
Volt:..................................2-2
Volt-ampere reactive (VAR):...........2-24
Voltage:...............................2-2
Amplifiers:.......................5-4, 7-5
And tank circuit Q:...................15-5
Average:..............................2-12
Breakdown, for Teflon:...............15-10
Breakdown, in capacitors:.............2-14
Breakdown, transistor:...............4-21
Distribution, in antennas:.......17-3, 17-7
Doubling:.............................6-11

Drop (also see Potential):.............2-3
Electronic regulation:................6-14
In RF tank circuits:..................15-9
Measurement:..........................25-2
Multiplication:.......................6-11
Peak:.................................2-12
Peak envelope:........................2-12
Peak-to-peak:.........................2-12
Quadrupling:..........................6-12
Reference diodes:................4-3, 4-16
Regulation:...........................6-12
Regulation using diodes:...............4-3
Regulators:............................6-7
RF, measurement:......................25-9
Ripple:................................6-7
RMS:..................................2-12
Transients:............................6-6
Tripling:.............................6-12
Voltage baluns:.......................16-8
Voltage doubler:
Full-wave:............................6-11
Half-wave:............................6-11
Voltage drop:..........................2-3
Forward (semiconductor):...............4-2
Kirchhoff's Second Law:...............2-10
Transistor, when saturated:...........4-21
Voltage regulators:
Adjustable:...........................6-18
Bypassing:............................6-18
Constant-current sources:.............6-18
Current limiting:.....................6-15
Electronic:...........................6-14
High-current:.........................6-16
IC:...................................6-17
Input-output voltage differential:....6-17
Linear:...............................6-14
Package information:..................35-27
Push-pull converter/regulator:........6-24
Safe operating area:..................6-15
Specifications:.......................6-17
Switching:............................6-21
Zener diode:..........................6-12
3-terminal:...........................6-17
3-terminal, specifications:...........35-26
Voltage-to-power conversion table:....35-37
Voltage-variable capacitors (VVC):.....4-4
Bulk resistance:.......................4-8
Q:.....................................4-8
Transistors as:.......................4-27
Voltmeter, FET:.......................4-38
Voltmeters:....................25-2, 25-3
Electronic:...........................25-5
Electronic, RF probe for:.............25-9
Sensitivity:..........................25-2
Volume compression:....................7-6
Volume expansion:......................7-9
Volunteer monitoring:..................38-1
Volunteer Monitoring, ARRL:............39-4
VOX (voice-operated switch):..........13-11
VSWR (also see SWR):
Effect of:............................16-14
VXO (variable crystal oscillator)
  circuits:...........................10-3

W

W1AW:...................................1-5
W1AW schedule:.........................37-5
W2DU balun:...........................16-9
Warm front:...........................22-17
WAS (Worked All States) Award:.........1-2
Water cooling:........................32-29
Water cooling (jacket):...............32-38
Watt:.................................2-11
Watt-hour:............................2-12
Watt-second:..........................2-12
Wattless power:.......................2-24
Wattmeter, peak reading:..............34-9
Wattmeter, QRP:.......................34-6
Wave:
Forward:..............................16-2
Reflected:............................16-2
WAVE (Worked All VE) Award:............1-2
Wave cyclone:.........................22-17
Waveform:
Digitally synthesized:................8-22
TV:...................................20-2
Waveguides:...........................16-3
Coupling to:..........................16-3

Dimensions:...........................16-3
Evolution of:.........................16-3
Modes of propagation:.................16-3
Wavelength formulas:..................16-3
Wavelength formulas for (Table):......16-3
Wavelength:.....................2-5, 2-6
Waves:
Direct:...............................38-6
Reflected:............................38-6
Weather satellites:...................20-24
Antennas:............................20-29
APT format:..........................20-26
Bandwidth:...........................20-29
Bibliography:........................20-32
Computer BBS:........................20-32
COSMOS:..............................20-27
Deviation, signal:...................20-29
Feng Yun 1:..........................20-24
GMS:.................................20-28
GOES:..........................20-24, 20-28
GOMS:................................20-28
Imaging systems:.....................20-29
METEOR:..............................20-24
METEOSAT:............................20-26
NOAA:................................20-24
OKEAN:...............................20-27
Priroda:.............................20-27
Receiving systems:...................20-29
Satcom:...............................20-2
Spin rate:...........................20-28
Table of:............................20-26
TIROS-N:.............................20-24
Tracking:............................20-32
Weather service, and ATV:.............20-1
WEFAX:.........................20-24, 20-28
Welfare traffic:......................37-17
Wheatstone bridge:....................25-5
White out (ATV):......................20-3
Wilkinson divider:....................32-6
Winding coils:........................24-8
Windings:
Bifilar:........................3-9, 24-8
Quadrifilar:.........................24-8
Trifilar:............................24-8
Twisted pair:.........................3-9
Window-box mobile antenna mount
  (VHF):..............................38-20
Wire:................................26-20
Antennas, construction:..............33-1
Copper, table:.......................35-6
Copperweld:..........................33-1
Guy:.................................36-28
Inductance of:.......................2-18
Resistance of:.......................2-8
Stressed antenna (Table):............33-2
Types:...............................36-13
Wrapping:............................24-11
Wire AND:.............................8-10
Wire size in tank inductors:..........15-9
Wirephotos (fax):....................20-20
Wires, guy, insulating:..............36-23
Wiring:...............................24-7
Cables:..............................24-7
Word registers:.......................8-8
Words per minute (WPM):...............9-8
World Administrative Radio Conference
  (WARC):.............................9-1
World Time Finder:....................37-11
WORM (computer storage):.............8-30
Wrapping, wire:......................24-11
Wullenweber antenna:..................38-5
WWV:...........................22-12, 22-13

X

X-Beam antennas:......................33-15
XIT (transmitter incremental tuning):....13-3
XNOR gate:.............................8-2

Y

Yagi antennas:........................17-14
Stacking of:.........................17-20
VHF and UHF:.........................33-19
VHF, high performance:............33-21,
                              33-25, 33-28
Yttrium-iron-garnet (YIG) tuning:......4-10

Z

Z (impedance):........................2-24